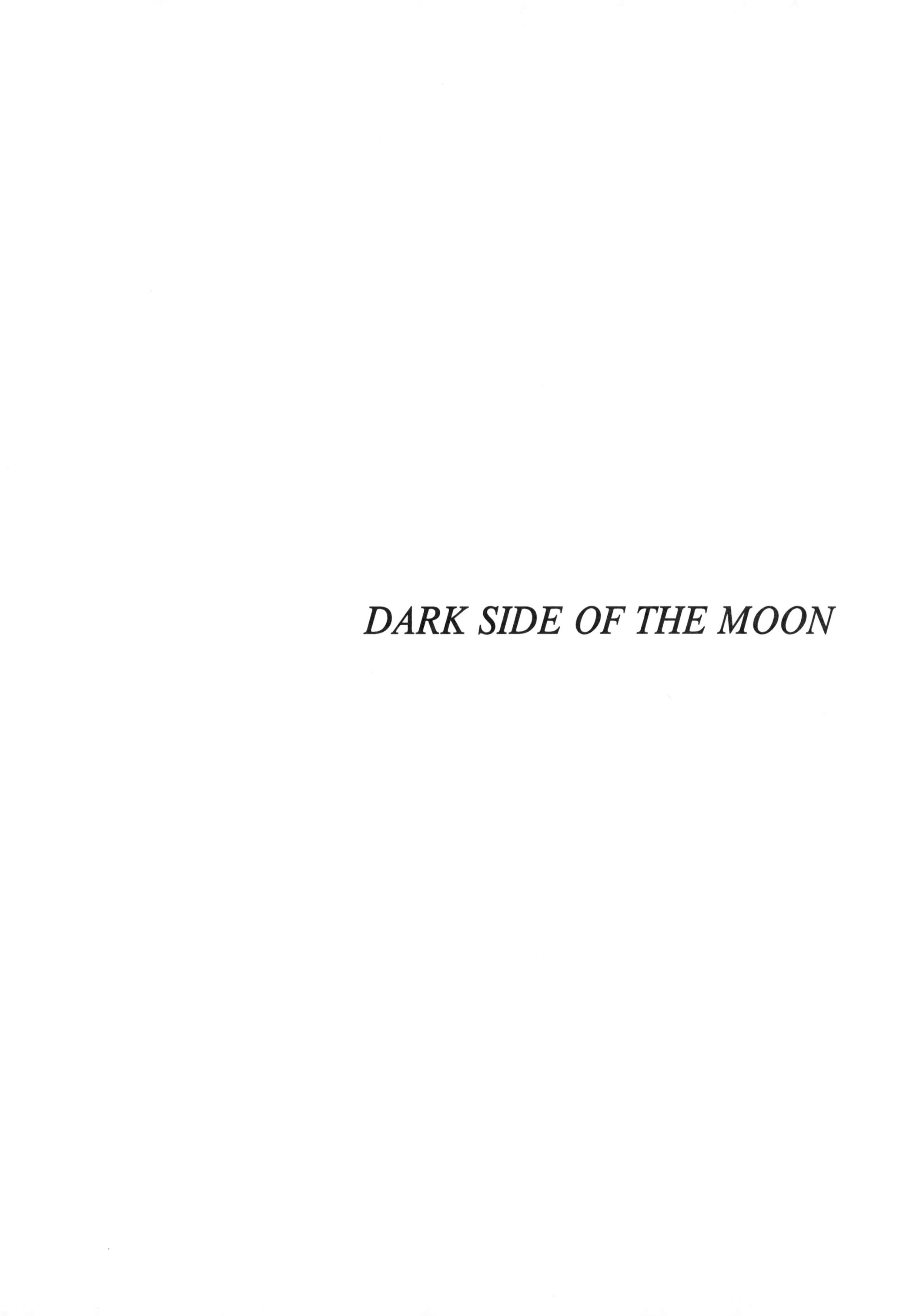

DARK SIDE OF THE MOON

DARK SIDE OF THE MOON

The National Library of Poetry

Diana Zeiger, Editor

Dark Side of the Moon

Library of Congress
Cataloging in Publication Data

ISBN 1-56167-257-2

Manufactured in The United States of America by
Watermark Press
11419 Cronridge Dr., Suite 10
Owings Mills, MD 21117

Editor's Note

One of life's greatest pleasures is reading. When you open a book, you can travel to places you never thought you'd be able to visit, meet unique and fascinating people, and even get inside their thoughts. As I compiled the poems for *Dark Side of the Moon*, I couldn't help but reflect upon how fortunate I have been--these poems have allowed me to discover all kinds of wonderful new experiences. I hope this book does the same for you.

Everyone who makes the effort of committing pen to paper deserves accolades; putting thoughts into words is more often than not a formidable task. I wish that time and space allowed me to present a detailed examination of every poem in *Dark Side of the Moon*, but as that is not possible, there are some I would like to single out for special recognition.

The grand prize winner, Miriam Kossman's "Auden's Augury," questions the very nature of poetry itself from the point of view of a poet. The inspiration for this work, says Ms. Kossman, came from words of advice that poet W. H. Auden gave to Edward Albee early on in his writing career. Essentially, Auden advised Albee against writing poetry, rather to find his own voice, thus launching one of the finest playwrights of the twentieth century. "Auden's Augury," though, concludes in finding the ultimate worth of poetry as an art form, a conclusion with which I, and no doubt you, heartily agree.

Joseph P. Wechselberger's "A Sonnet On The Sonnet" is a clever use of the form to examine itself. Anyone who has ever attempted to bend his or her words to fit any poetic form will appreciate it.

Kathleen M. Conley explores the pain and panic of aging. Her poem "Convalescent Lamb" takes the reader inside the mind of someone who is no longer vital, but once was, and resents the indignities now being heaped upon her.

"Farm" and "Tent Caterpillars," by Sarah E. Beckman and Beth Young, respectively, take the reader back to some of the activities of childhood, to a time when life was simpler. Or was it?

We are introduced to a mysterious man in Raquel A. Cepeda's "1 Train." He is a person we've all seen before, but Ms. Cepeda skillfully turns him from a background character into an icon.

Congratulations to all those featured in *Dark Side of the Moon*. I hope you enjoy the journeys on which it will take you as much as I have.

Diana Zeiger, Editor

Acknowledgements

The publication *Dark Side of the Moon* is a culmination of the efforts of many individuals. Judges, editors, assistant editors, graphic artists, layout artists and office administrators have all brought their respective talents to bear on this project. The editors are grateful for the contribution of these fine people:

Sheree Bernstein, Chris Bussey, Keith Creummedy, Lisa Della, Amy Dezseran, Chrystal Eldridge, Joy Esterby, Jeffrey Franz, Ardie L. Freeman, Hope Freeman, Bob Graziul, Paula Jones, Steve Miksek, Diane Mills, Eric Mueck, Tanya Rayton, Lamont Robinson, Jacqueline Spiwak, Caroline Sullivan, Cynthia Stevens, Nicole Walstrum, and Ira Westreich.

Howard Ely, Managing Editor

Grand Prize Winner

Miriam Kossman/ Philadelphia, PA

Second Prize Winners

Sarah Beckman/ Madison, WI
Raquel Cepeda/ New York, NY
Kathleen Conley/ Salinas, CA
Marguerite Forcier/ South Weymouth, MA
Ian MacLennan/ Halifax, NS Canada

Jahdo McTavish/ Los Gatos, CA
Geraldine Vernon/ Spring Hill, FL
Laura Waddell/ Leesburg, FL
Joseph Wechselberger/ Browns Mills, NJ
Beth Young/ Barton, VT

Third Prize Winners

Kathleen Auth/ Westlake Village, CA
Brian Bergstrom/ Colville, WA
Mary Brookman/ Petaluma, CA
Claire Brunetti/ Gainesville, FL
Linda Clark/ Philadelphia, PA
Kay Comini/ Pittsburgh, PA
Leonora De Marmolejo/ Levittown, NY
Etheljean Deal/ Haddonfield, NJ
Pat Donahue/ Selden, NY
Georgia Ellis/ Elwood, IN
Christina Enriquez/ Washington, DC
Mary Farmer/ Covina, CA
Jesse Fewell/ Baltimore, MD
Gustine Fudickar/ Monroe, LA
Kate Harding/ Jackson, MS
Khadijah Hassan/ Jersey City, NJ
Benjamin Hedrick/ Bethlehem, PA
Pascal Jean-Pierre/ Brooklyn, NY
Linda Jelinski/ Bellingham, WA
Dorothy Johnson/ Fort Collins, CO
Kai Johnson/ New Hope, MN
Margery Johnson/ Cambria, CA
Kathleen Joiner/ Brandon, MS
Pamela Kolleas/ Sherwood, OR
Jill Koscielniak/ Coon Rapids, MN
Virginia Lee/ New York, NY
Beth Lutrell/ Laclede, ID
Mary Mann/ Bacliff, TX
Ruth McClung/ West Yarmouth, MA
Harvey Mendez/ Laguna Hills, CA

Jean Murphy-Bazner/ Weston, CT
James Myers/ Borger, TX
Helen Nencka/ Hubertus, WI
Billie Noakes/ Pinellas Park, FL
Jas Norman/ Saylorsburg, PA
Robin Perez/ Madison, AL
Rebecca Piorkowski/ Reading, PA
Stephen Reynolds/ Lompoc, CA
Gloria Rice/ Anaheim, CA
Belle Rollins/ Pineville, LA
Tracy Runnels/ Culver City, CA
Meredith Salisbury/ Utica, NY
Doris Sanford/ Rockville, MD
Daniel Schwartz/ Miami, FL
David Sees/ Fort Meyers, FL
Junia Shambaugh/ Silver Spring, MD
Kimberly Shanks/ Louisville, KY
James Sinisi/ Woodhaven, NY
Deanne Smith/ San Bernardino, CA
Richard Steggerda/ Bristol, VT
Joseph Strauss/ Brooklyn Park, MN
Joseph Swords/ Glenolden, PA
William Howard Thomas/ New York, NY
Kay Trudell/ Winooski, VT Bronx, NY
Lily Vallery/ Mount Shasta, CA
Jose Villagomez/ Houston, TX
Daniel Weisman/ Lafayette Hill, PA
Monica Wirick/ Dayton, OH
Sarah Yellen/ Champlin, MN

Congratulations also to our Editor's Choice Winners.

Auden's Augury

"It makes nothing happen," said the poet of Poetry,
Lighting a fuse in literary heresy;
And yet, when I sail out to Byzantium
I hear such music as could never come
From chrome or brass or molten bars
Of motored chords and choirless stars.
And yet, when I walk out on Bristol Street
I hear the airy threads of lovers' feet
And all the chimes above the din
Of puny powers still cashing in
On the crackling cries of miracle men
Playing again in the blood-paved pen.
Give pause, and ponder what anvil's art
Preludes the bleating fugues of an empty heart,
Brandishes the blunt baton of hackneyed hate
Cymbaling another Achilles' armored plate:
Give pause and ponder: No Pipes of Pan
Make such happenings happen as man makes man!
Miriam R. Kossman

Happy Anniversary

H-having parents like you makes it easy to go through.
A-asking God to forgive us for some things that we do.
P-praying and fasting day after day
P-praising God for surely making away
Y-young and Old you taught us in God to stay

A-another step further, the altar we should lay
N-nothing should separate us from the love of God
N-neither should we worry for the world sees us as being odd.
I-in this walk of life something we don't understand
V-verily I say for God will surely take your hand
E-everyday serving God is sweeter than the day before
R-remember God loves us even the more
S-sometimes we're scolded, but yet through love
A-another score on your side, for being parents
  following rules from above
R-rest assure through the years we learned a lot
Y-you're the best parents "faith tabernacle got"

"Happy Anniversary To Mom and Pop"
   Judy Holley

"Recession"

Oh, recession, recession you are to the humanities of the world
a bad impression and creator of a depression.
Especially the poor, innocent, helpless you hit so hard
It's a great job to move towards forget the different race
and just give a glance to the face.
Please give a hand to those, who shed tears, and still nothing
to eat and wear that's why they fear.
They fear about the more hardening of the days but who try their best
for a way.
So it's duty for us to create a part which will make them
smile and cheer and teach them to share.

   Fahmida Mahmood

Animals Just Like Me

The birds and animals to me are kin.
A bear can breeze the winter in peaceful sleep—
Just like me, and sure, he can awake an grin.
A rabbit roams the earth in graceful leaps
While squirrels can traverse branches without a sound.
My weight will break a branch, so I'll not try,
But my spirit follows leaps on limbs and ground.
The baby birds lay nestled waiting— and cry
Loudly for mother to bring some nourishment,
So mother scoops the food within her beak
And pacifies her young with food God sent.
A mother doe protects her fawn who sneaks
Away to play; she scans the land and sees
The danger. She attacks—Gee, just like me.

   Darlene Casabella

Untitled

Cascades of green neatly trimmed
A cage around me, enclosing me, hiding me
Sheltering me from reality
My cold clammy hands
Wrap themselves around the protector
I dig my heel into the dust
Creating a smoke screen
The empty terrain surrounds me
I search vaguely for my team
But all I find are the shadows
I can only hear the rustle of the trees
As the wind calls out my name
And the squeaky bench plays its tune
As I step to the plate
I look curiously towards the score board
It's O-O, and I'm up at bat.

   Fiorella Valdesolo

Our Country

"America", "America", to some it's just a word,
A bell now still; its echo long unheard.
Our people came from far and wide,
With faith and courage, hope and pride.
They came to live to tempt their fate
And start the things that made us great.
They vowed to make our freedom ring,
And shear the bonds to any king.
So, on they went, the die was cast,
In those days; those days long past.
Were they right or were they wrong,
Would freedom die, or last for long?
This land is ours, it's yours and mine,
For which to stand, and hold the line.
What we have, for what it's worth,
Has no equal, here on earth.
We the people hold the reins,
And live in freedom, not in chains.
So after all is said and done,
We cannot lose what we have won.

   Calvin S. Grant, Sr.

The Cactus The Coyote The Iguana

It was a dark and steamy night in the dessert
A cactus falls but will the coyote howl
Only then will the iguana move on its prey
Slowly.....Without emotion
If the iguana moves on its prey
And the prey should cry out
Will anyone hear......
Only those which possess ears for nature
The cacti
If no one hears the cry, was the prey ever there
If the prey wasn't, there why would the iguana move
If there wasn't any iguana movement
Did the Coyote howl
If no one heard the coyote howl. Did the cactus fall
If it is found upon the ground
Then logic proclaims that it has fallen.........
...............Or was it pushed
   Christopher D. Ryan

Chaos And Control

Ignore my thoughts and save my soul?
A certain outcome...a dubious goal.
Spending my thoughts help save the day.
Saving my soul goes the longer way.
But, should I close out my open mind,
I'll suffer losses impossible to find.
I long for peace in this troubled heart,
But if I can't paint happiness, I don't know art.
He gave me a mind, and he gave me a soul...
One creates chaos, the other control.
And when the two don't run hand in hand,
I'll take my chances that he'll understand.
For while my thoughts may determine me,
And risk my soul from eternity,
They keep me steady in the human game...
And the game is too big for me not to play.
Though common sense will see me through,
I'm not incapable of another view.
If I cannot allow my mind to be free,
Then how tested and true must my soul really be?

   Debby Livingston Jones

Untitled

I sit in the valley all alone,
A chunk of rock, a chunk of stone.
I sit here wondering if someday,
Others of my kind will pass this way.

I remember the days before I fell,
When things were fine and all was well.
But now my soul is filled with pain,
Like a broken heart fills with rain.

I long to be back at the top,
Where wind and rain will never stop.
Where the water flows like a cool spring fountain,
I wish I could be back at the peak of the mountain.

Joey Palone

Untitled

City lights dim in the glow of the stars
A cricket chirp can be heard from afar
When I was little, the stars would shine and moon
Would glow heat lightning would flash and cool
Winds blow
Bullfrogs would croak and crickets sing
From all the silence, my ears would ring

As I grew up and got older, the city grew larger
And much, much older
The sounds that I heard are muted and faded
Replaced by noises that only have grated
City lights now are all that brighten the sky
As I sit here and watch, I want to cry

Ian Bleadingheiser

The Way You Make Me Feel

Have you ever paid attention to a ray of sun coming through
a dark cloud after the rain? Have you ever noticed how sweet
the air smells when this ray of sun pushes away the rain?

Have you ever paid attention to the way a mother soothes away
the pain when her child has been hurt? Have you ever noticed
how a mother's warm touch makes her child feel safe and secure?

This is how you make me feel.
You are like a ray of sun shining through my darkest clouds.
Your caring has helped to push away the tears
and let me once again smell the sweet air of life.

Your tenderness and support has helped to soothe away the pain
and has made me believe that with time, the pain will lessen.

But most of all, you have given me the security I need to
start believing in myself and in life again.

Thank you for making me feel safe.
Thank you for the way you make me feel.

Alecia R. Armentrout

The Victim

There stands at the edge of a busy thorough-fare,
A house once majestic, now fallen from repair.
The once mellow facade is now streaked and grey,
The small spiraled balconies are fallen away.
The windows that looked out on a happier time,
Are now cracked or shuttered and overgrown with vine.
There was beautiful foliage and a deep sea of green,
Where litter and gravel now cover the scene.
It watches as chaos called "Progress" unfolds,
Where once only gentle serenity ruled.
It stands helpless and neglected watching time cause its change,
And knows poignant memories are all that remain.

Giovanna A. Nicandro

Overcoming Obstacles

A challenge of importance.
A different route approached.
You had to take a chance,
and find some new hopes.

Each day overwhelmed by choices,
you kept the faith and strong belief.
you listened to your heart and kind voices,
and at night sighed with relief.

Something new is achieved.
Now you must move ahead.
Remember you once believed,
as success awaits to be led.

One last look back.
One more step forward.
Only memories you lack,
and those are all stored.

So carry them with you,
and walk for a while.
Search for dreams to come true,
and forever hold that smile.

Effie Cokinos

"Feeling Good"

I'm doing fine. Nothing to worry my mind. A nickel and a nail.
A dollar and a dime.
A bottle of rot gut wine. A trash can lunch. Down and out
hanging with
the bunch. A doorway bed, raindrop bath.

Clothes full of holes, shoes worn thin. A bottle of rot gut wine;
pass it down the line, to get a sip put your money with mine.

Can't go to the bathroom when we go; musta been a buzzard ate
for lunch.

A knot on my head, damn near dead. You must don't know I'm
king on this corner, when
I get on my feet give your heart to your maker, cause your thin__
belong to me. When I get on my feet.
A nickel and a nail. A dollar and a dime.

Erma Mae Phillips

About Life...

What Is beautiful?

A smile on your face. A twinkle in your eye.
A flower in bloom. And a rainbow in the sky.

A baby new born. The sunshine in your hair.
Lovers holding hands. And a turtle dove, or two a pair.

The shining of the stars. The sunset on the sea.
The love between two friends, between you and me.

What is ugly?

The hate between two humans. The trash upon the street.
Teenagers with guns. And a beggar at your feet.

A frown upon your face. Hate within your heart.
The "accidental deaths." And two lovers torn apart.

The destruction of one's life. People who do not see.
The war between two friends, it was never meant to be.

Brandi Uchic

To Wait A While

From the pits of darkness, she walks out high
A full fledged woman with rigid feminine vigor.
Looking on from far yonder, she seems behooved;
A girl so young, a lady so pretty, a woman to dare.
I raced my thoughts to think I knew her so,
A careless lie far gone with no return.
But behind this glaze of majestic marvel,
Lies a woman so delicate to touch;
A woman so tender to hold.

With the smell of love amidst the air,
I pray thy feelings are never compromised
'cause love is like a seed cast on fertile land
To wait a while, that germination day.
Giddy as a school boy I waited patiently
Alas! that moment of truth is one foot near.
When dark befalls, we both shall jerk;
A jerk once called the rhythm of love.

Emeka Ugokwe

A Light In A Window

A light in a window,
A happy family inside,
Warm, joyous,
Me on the outside, longing to be inside.
They see me,
I rush away.
Hidden in the bushes I hear a voice,
A sweet voice, calling me, calling me back,
Drawn to the voice
I find my way to a place of nature,
A place of comfort.
I am home.

Anne Malouf

In Search Of Camelot

In a distant land called Avalon you can hear of a great kings glory,
A haunted voice from the past tells the legend of Arthur's story
From far away places you can hear the echoes of his wail,
Drifting across oceans, touching hearts with the fearless tale.

Mighty in his battles, gentle in his ways with the oppressed,
Fierce in defending his kingdom with the magical sword he possessed.
Marriage was arranged with the fair Guinevere to be his queen,
Protesting words from Kings council, Merlin, did nothing to intervene.

A round table full of knights, with Sir Lancelot by Arthur's side,
Unaware of the atrocity Lancelot had committed with his bride.
Betraying of the secret fell upon the good kings ears,
They were banished from the kingdom, a punishment most severe.

The unsavory antics of the duo brought about Arthur's demise,
Drawn into battle with Modred, a traitor in his uncles eyes.
Defeating Modred he is wounded, and then taken to Avalon,
In a chapel he lives out his last hours, Sir Bedevere looking on.

Somewhere in the forest there's a chivalrous knight weeping in shame,
Fleeting were his pleasures, legendary is his fame.
Mourning over his kings grave stood the brave knight Lancelot
Wandering through the Isle of Avalon in search of Camelot.

Denise Profumo

Love And Despair

Thou heart, aches with love,
A higher voice, calls from above.
Thou yearns so so much for the touch,
Of thee, graceful dove.

The emptiness of the heart brings despair!
As thou life, whittles away from thee, here.

Adam K. Weyand

A Little Fantasy

I am a grown woman and I have a little kid in me
A imaginary being.
Beautiful brown and silky with lush lips, taking
me to a rainbow sherbet land, wishing me off my feet
to a colorful rainbow. A glistening sun to warm my
hot buns. A beautiful ocean so clear just like a glass
putting me in a state of mind, that I want.
Point no return. I smell the fresh air.
A beautiful red rose is handed to me. The
trees were so fresh as they blew in the wind
I felt the breeze over my body just twinge,
My hair flew back rushing back and forth in
my face. I just didn't believe this is happening
to me. All of sudden it just ended. Because I am
at work, taking a moment to myself, somebody
call my name' and said "wake up', grow up',
And suddenly it all ended without any pain or no gain.

Frances C. Farmer

To My Love

Today I found a reason to live
   A lady who my love I can give
Day by day and night by night
   She loves me without a fight
Together we will stand as one
   A new life has just begun
We will make it through it all
   Walking proud and standing tall
I know God will lead the way
   And help us through each passing day
If we stumble, and I know we will
   God will keep us in His will
Even though it will be tough
   I believe our love is strong enough
So slip into my loving arms
   And let me protect you from worldly harm
I will be the strength you need-
   So, my love, just follow my lead.

James C. Chrisman Jr.

The Land Where I Wish To Be

Beyond the clouds, up in the sky,
A land exists for those who die.
A land of peace, of tranquility,
With golden sands, and deep blue seas.
I wish to reach that land someday,
A day that's not too far away.

I wish to leave this lonely place,
Never again to show my face.
How peaceful and quiet my life would be,
That life in the land of tranquility.
No one knows of these secret dreams,
Of lying on clouds, beneath sunbeams.

All but my soul will remain on earth,
For those I once loved to recollect my birth.
What will it take me to reach this dream?
It may not be as simple as it may seem.
Departing this planet from which I was born,
To come to the end, to come to my dawn.

Eva Kimonis

Yellow Mums

Autumn comes to dress the earth with change:
A leaf, or two, or three, trips across my path,
And traces back a page of memory
To yield this autumn specter - -
Beside a porch familiar,
She kept a bed of yellow mums.
I see her stoop to pick them;
'Til autumn winds grew sharp, they waved,
A golden plot of mums, lovely in her care;
I see her still, stooping as it were
To pick the last bouquet for me.

Joanne G. Less

The Dark Unknown

As I venture into the unknown darkness of life
A light appears to lead me through the most
   dangerous of obstacles.
But this light does not compare to any other I've seen,
For it is not visible to the eye.
It became my guide and my security.

Then I discovered the source of this light.
It burns from within.
This light that I had become so dependent on comes from
   my own inner strength.
And I know it will never burn out and leave me lost
   in my tracks.
For the shine of my strength never dims, rather lights
   my path into the future.

Cynthia J. Michael

Sara Anne Wood

August 18, 1993. Everyone was sad, as sad as could be.
A little girl was abducted, and taken from her home.
Is she dead or alive out there all alone?
Thousands of people have done all they could, because people care
about Sara Anne Wood.
Everywhere you go, you see pictures of Sara Anne, Because so many
people are giving a helping hand.
No one knows where Sara could be, but the State Police are
checking every lead.
And investigators are still searching all the grounds, but
Sara Anne Wood is nowhere to be found.
Sara is missed by her sister and brother, but no one could miss
Sara like her father and mother.
We know you would come home if only you could,
God Bless you and keep you, Sara Anne Wood.

Judy Spann

God's Work At Dawn

I awoke so very early in the morning
A lonesome star was moving in the sky.
The gulls began their flight without warning
And like them I wanted to fly.

The bright sun rose slowly,
And made the sea glisten.
The lovely large waves hit against the shore.
For this wonderful sound,
I didn't have to listen.
And waited for much more.

I ran onto the warm sand,
And into the ocean.
As a felt the coolness I thought,
What if suddenly there were no more motion,
And the waves had stopped
As if they had been caught?

I know they would never be quiet and still
Because fortunately that would be against God's will.

Betsy Bush

Silent Love

A love that can never be but is
A love that is there but yet is blind
A love that struggles but yet survives
A love that is weak yet it is strong
A love that comes from two yet it forms into one
One love that can never be but is.

Angela M. Velez M.

The Perception

Let me start off by explaining to you who I am not
A majority, minority, or a population dot.
I cannot be titled a color or race
I am not all show or a pretty face.
You cannot look at me from outside, moreover afar
Then go on to pursue what my ethics are.
In fact, I am nothing to you or to them
So don't fix my outsides or my insides need hem.
My mind is all I really know
For when you ask who I am my emotions will flow.
You could never understand me, so why bother to try?
When who "I" am is simply a lie.

Cori Anne Veit

Broom

Man rise up and fall.
A many shattered dome of glass.
To leave his fragments scattered across the floor.
Oh dirty, hateful, guilt-ridden floor!
Step gingerly people
Over the fragments of my life.

Sweep them up.
Do not forget me.

Life, like a bowl
Dancing with the Devil
On the table's edge,
Hangs suspended in time.
Waiting for the push.
Then. . .
Nothing more.
Fragments.
Pieces of my wasted life lie
Threateningly on your floor.
Step gingerly people.

Sweep me up.

Jim Wyko

The Thanksgiving Poem

   The family sat at the table, to enjoy
a meal. They all said grace, and they knew
that Thanksgiving was real.

   The food is good, the food is great.
The family loved it, so they ate.

   The food is steaming, the food is hot.
It's so terrific, so you eat a lot.

   The food is steaming, as you take a
bite. It gives you a warm feeling, so you
feel great.

   It's Thanksgiving, school is out too.
Thanksgiving is so great, and a holiday too.

   The dinner is so great, it's
Thanksgiving too. My granny fixed it, and I
love her too.

Briana Knox

Internal Hell

Thoughts of splendor filled the imperfect room
A mistress awaits her passion rocked beloved
With another she glances silently toward him
Passing looks intention
The setup was plain to see
A triangle of three
Each twist crowding more
Both of them have seen one another
Suspecting nothing
If they knew nothing could hold the destruction
The walls would break down
Her earth would be shaken, broken, out of control
The battle commences
Which name should she call out
Now she is trapped in her own web
No longer able to walk along the silken treads
Help is no longer in the way
She will have to rot in this internal hell.

    Alexia Spaedt

Through The Clear Eyes Of A River

Through the crystal clear water of a river
A nymph arises
Jewels falling as she walks
Along the river bank
A nymph arises
And men fight for her
Along the river bank
Blood is shed
And men fight for her
Because they like beauty
Blood is shed
Because they are so proud
Because they like beauty
People have fought over useless things
Because they are so proud
Wars seem never ending
People have fought over useless things
Jewels falling as she walks
Wars seem never ending
Through the crystal clear water of a river.

    Jennifer Trinidad

The Snow

While I lay sleeping so cozy last night
A picture was made all done in pure white
The snow had powdered every bush and tree
As far as the eye had power to see.
Alas! My picture was erased from sight
By the rise of the morning's bright sunlight
The artist needed no brush or help
For it was done by the Creator, Himself.

    Clara L. Willis

The Picture On The Wall

A little boy stands on tiptoe, he is about three.
A reaching for that picture on the wall.
As he holds it in his little hands
He tenderly kisses the face in
the frame, and softly murmurs Mom,
Oh God! Oh God!
Can I never stop seeing,
That little boy a reaching
for that picture on the wall!

    Eleanor J. (Webb) Baker

Changing The Face Of My Beloved

I sit in the dark house.
A pipe thumps like disturbed
blood in the aorta.
The little one's asleep.
The fat moon in the black sky stands regardless
of wars in our houses.
I'm alone.
My eyes close and I feel
the body of his once face so close to mine
And I imagine -

Changing the face of my beloved.

How it will rise
over my toes,
spread its slow smile across my folds.
How I may hold one face
then another to my breast.
I may kiss until blackness or blood,
but I will kiss.
Beloved
is beyond the death of love.

    Donna Conrad

Longing To Be In Beulah Land

There is a place I'm longing to be..........
A place where the grass is a lush thick green carpet
and there are patches of clover here and there
their sweet perfume feels the air.
This place I long to be is called Beulah Land.
I can taste the sweet cool water of the Jordan River
that runs through this land.
I can see the trees sway in the gentle breeze.
The air is filled with the song of the dark
yes..... how I'm longing for the day when.......
My life will be through here on Earth, and I'll be
on my way to spend forever in Beulah Land.
Never more to be filled with sorrow and pain
never more will tears fall from my eyes like rain.
Yes....happy will I forever be spending my days
with my Lord, in Sweet Beulah Land.

    Carmella Rosa

Quiet Times

We all should have our quiet times,
A place where we can go to find
The peace we need to calm our minds,
And just let go of the cares that bind.

We need a place where we can ponder
All of life's blessings, and sometimes to wonder
Where does life lead us on from here?
Will there be smiles? Will there be tears?

All of us must have some space
To sort our thoughts and set our pace.
We never know in life's great race
Exactly what we'll have to face!

Quiet times are necessary,
Because of burdens we must carry.
Quiet times will bring the healing,
Of all the pain we might be feeling.

The melodrama of life is golden.
The book of life is now unfolding.
We feel the need to taste the wine,
And know the pleasure of quiet times.

    Juanita F. Conde

When Love Strikes

When love strikes, it's like a strong gust of wind.
A powerful feeling rushes through your body.
You feel so much that you feel you've sinned.
But it's no sin, you are not naughty,
It's normal to have this reaction
For someone you feel so much for,
For someone who has an attraction
Who could make you love them much more.

Your heart starts pounding when you see this someone,
Sweat starts forming on your forehead.
You can feel the blood inside you run
And your face start to turn red.
You feel like screaming "yikes!"
Because this is what happens when love strikes.

Jacqui Bispo

Through Your Eyes

You are my daughter
a precious gift of love
Within your trusting gaze
I count my life renewed

Through your eyes, thoughts, and feelings

I see with your sight
feel with your emotions
Days become fresh once more
the harshness fades

Sad memories do wither
life becomes translucent
In a fresh pure wash
of sunshine and joy

Through your eyes, thoughts, and feelings

I can rejoin the world again
in fearless wonder
And awake tomorrow
with renewal of hope

Carol Mann Turner

Journey Of life

Life is…
A river which runs silently through night and day
Presenting new avenues to venture off on
Making inroads in seemingly insurmountable territory
And leaving the silt, a lasting mark, behind.

Life is …
A river that flows rapidly and smoothly unceasingly onward
Occasionally slowing—meandering through rough territory
And some times the rivers path becomes obscure—
Seemingly dangerous avenues lurk around each bend.

Life is…
A river which continues on its way, its longevity determined by God
Sometimes it disappears entirely, its bed, hardened by its journey
But it is always moving forward towards its destiny,
And in the end it spills forth into the sea of humanity.

Carlos Ellis Whitt

A Treasure Of Me

A treasure of me, only for you;
A treasure of me, to hold on to.

My thoughts in your mind, my love in your heart;
My memories alive, never broken apart.

My name on your lips, my dreams in your eyes;
A treasure of me, my heart as a prize.

A treasure of me, of which this is true;
Your treasure of me, is my love for you.

Dawn Michelle Hertzer

Other's Day

When the word is spoken, the mouth is drawn
A round and needful hollow.
It desires to be filled with nurture—knowledge,
And answers found hard to swallow.
Mother God, Mother Earth, Mother Mountain of mine,
I clamor for strength to restore
The bounteous rhythms I've captured from you
…Yet the word finds its form all the more.
It erodes in the chest, till the chasm appears,
It pretends to be less of a hole.
When at once it's a target for All-Knowing Eyes
Sensing the growth of a soul
   So Mary's heart would be pierced,
   She gave her Life for all,
   This day and each I remember,
   You seek to embrace the same Call.
An entire day devoted to mothers
Mysteriously becomes a day for others.

Helen E. McWhorter

"Freedom"

   An eagle on high, soaring overhead
 A soul of the forest, pine needles a bed
 Standing on a mountain , high above all
So close to destiny, the temptation to fall
 Observing the twisted form of the trees
Seeing the horizon on the never ending seas
 Run until your legs, a flimsy rubber band
   Love in your heart, eternity at hand
   Live how you choose, do what you prefer
   What tomorrow brings, forever unsure
   Each day comes, as does it pass
   Flowing on like fields of grass
 I often wonder how each day could be
      If I'd be forever free.

Amanda Hurless

My Friend

I have a friend that I share with so many and I do not mind.
A special friend who loves me and is very patient and kind.

We talk over problems both big and small.
My friend is always there and answers me when I call.

My friend is only visible to those who believe without seeing.
My friend is love and kindness and in my friend we should all
be believing.

My friend gave his life for me and no greater love has been given.
Follow your heart and follow my friend and you will come to
know why
HE HAS RISEN!

Ann M. Moody

On The Death Of My Beautiful Mother

Like a lovely rose you arrived at
   a spring time hour
Just as the seedling you become
   a beautiful flower
You were a perennial growing and
   maturing through 90 full summers
Then at the dawn of your 91st
   spring you slipped away
All the vitality, the spark of life
   burst and died, and you were gone.
I would have stayed through that
   night, you wouldn't have faced it alone
I'd have been there for you,
   if I'd have only known.

Irene Hall

The Scottish hero

A summer breeze is rustling through the evergreens, and then
A sound is heard, a lonely bird is calling down the glen.
A hillside clad in heather speaks of majesty and might,
of countless battles long ago when men seemed born to fight.
Now all is calm and peaceful, the battles long forgot,
but once each year a lonely piper plays, to mark the spot
where once a Scottish hero gave his life in bloody glory,
that others of his clan could fight and live to tell his story.
And now his land is free, the price was paid that fateful day,
His death has been avenged, but not forgotten, in a way
the lonely bird's his spirit as it calls down through the glen.
And the summer breeze, his laughter, echoes now as it did then.

Jeanette Marlow

Sublimity

Sour grapes make a sweet red wine
A taste most agree is very fine,
And thorns protect the magnificent rose-
To keep it safe as it slowly grows.

So the moral of this little rhyme
Is to look past the flaws to find the sublime.

Dixie Cureington

The Beast

The pain just ripped inside like
a train roaring through the mountains.
The child wasn't asking for a right arm or leg.
She was asking for a piece of paper stating why she didn't go.
She looked at the knife then at the beast.
She imagined the knife plugging fiercely at its back.
3-4-6 times repeating each time the beast had terrorized her world.
A world of peace an tranquility with people who are there to help.
The beast terrorized that world and shattered it like a baseball
shattering a window, and as much as she tried her heart couldn't
put it back together.
The beast always shattered it.
Soon, there were no relics of the world.
Another force much evil smashes that world.
And that poor child must live through years of pain,
And suffering with no relics of childhood.
Forever forgotten the scars remain and each time the child passes
through memories, the scars reopen.
Won't anybody help the child.
Stop the Beast!!

Candace Ortiz

Love

Love is what all should find precious
A treasure buried deep in the heart
A feeling too strong for description
Yet a force which some fail to impart

It's the beauty in sharing a sunset
It's seen in a child's trusting eyes.
It's acceptance in spite of one's weakness
It's silence when most criticize.

It's hope when the odds are against it
It's faith when the skeptics depart
It's the longing that grows ever stronger
When two people in love are apart.

It's understanding when words are unspoken
It's praise when one's spirits are low
It's a hug that's so desperately needed
And it's a feeling we never outgrow.

Elaine J. Hearn

Pieces To A Puzzle

Alone we stood against the winds,
A trinity of both hope and despair,
Shadows come for one then came for all,
Silently we would stand (we knew) until we would fall,
Different shapes of our hearts,
Or mazes of our minds,
To the prophets of friendship these did not matter,
Like pieces of a puzzle we did fit together,
Even during morbid weather,
Now, sitting facing a treacherous fall I look into their
eyes and see myself,
Knowing they both do the same,
Forever we will play the sacred game,
Of putting the pieces of our puzzle back together
again, the missing links we will never find,
For these are the element that binds
Like a blind man groping for his child after its birth,
So will we travel to the ends of the earth,
Each the missing pieces,
To a puzzle never to be put back together.

Jenny A. Scarborough

Mind

The root of evil, child of jest, seat of goodness, Satan's nest.
A world encased in whitish stone; two factions fighting all alone.
They can't protrude beyond their cage, but pick their puppets,
set their stage,
And play the game of life so well, to make our lives a living hell.
I cherish the thought that it be gone. I thought! Then I'm the
puppets pawn.
To think the thought of what would be: A paradox in irony.
So I'm a prisoner, but a slave; I can't escape, I must behave.
I can't reveal the searing pain, lest I be thought of as insane.
Can't lose my grip; let it slip;
I'll keep control; put on a show;
They'll never know....

So now I fear me most at night, when nightmares can't tell
   wrong from right.
Evil visions, its creations secret hellish revelations.
Invitations from below; someday soon I think I'll go;
The rational and dreaming states, already hard to separate...
So soon all thoughts together run, as destined side of Evil's won;
And so I'll slip inside the shell, and like my mind, reside in Hell!

James R. Moyne

Skinny Dipping

During the heat of the summer when temperatures soar
A young man dreams of a day at the shore.

So he saunters down the road with dog and friends
on the way to the river and the thrill it portends.

For 'tis here a boy's antics are never suppressed
as he dives in the water while totally undressed.

Though the river is swift with hazards galore
the good Lord looks after the youth we adore.

Glenn A. Swanson

Love Song

Bound by fear of emotion, unable to escape this pain which causes my
affliction. Struggling to free myself from apathy. Dark gray sky,
twisted cold metal, gentle rain as I caress her pale lifeless face.
The theatrical performance has concluded. You may now stand and
leave your show is over. Dark stage, quiet, empty, lifeless. Once
filled with lights, props, thespians, and emotion. Now echoes with
loneliness. Her lifeless head rests cupped in my hands as she
whispers, "Nothingness, nothingness forever".

Joe A. Lujan

Burden

See. You watch me with critical eyes from far
Across the filthy alley.
You are standing on a white curb
Not yet touched by the sporadic art work found on my walls.

Come. Closer yet, and smell the stench surrounding my home.
My nose no longer can sense its putrid odor

Take my thin and battered shirt and put
Your creamy and smooth arms into the sleeves.
Feel the sharp wind pierce through the fabric
As if it were a screen.

Now pull on my dirt stained jeans. Fraught with
Tears and holes, they barely cover your shapely legs.

Place manicured toes and smooth feet into torn sneakers,
Flimsy from miles of wandering.

My only possessions, now on your body,
Have lifted a great burden from me.
You now feel the heaviness of this life.

Put yourself in my shoes,
But do not become insensitive
to the smell here
>   *Julie Nazimek*

Playing Hookey In The Meadow

Winding, twisting down the path I go
across the meadow, skipping running to and fro —
I marvel at the wonders along the way
the sun beams warm upon my face
and as I come to the babbling brook
softly flowing across each rock;
Dandelions, Buttercups, Queen Ann's lace, Butterflies
just waiting to be caressed,
if I cross the brook all those treasures
I shall miss beyond the meadow a Hillock looms -
the hill that I must climb -
one by one gently I step on each stepping stone -
I must be careful not to fall,
for surely the brook I shall embrace.
Lingering for a while on each stone, I must hasten now.
Wait just one more dream, one more beauty to behold
Tadpoles, glistening sand, shiny rocks made of gold.
Then my mind drifts to the hill I must climb -
to climb the hill the dream must end, to be to school on time.
>   *Brenda L. Robinson*

Afraid

Afraid of life and what it brings,
   afraid of growing-up
Afraid of what's going to happen
   the next day will I die, will I live
Afraid of loving someone and not being loved back.
Afraid of being alone.
   no one to be held by
   no one to talk too
   no one to cry with
   no one to be with

Afraid of the next time you'll need someone
   no one will be there... afraid
>   *Jolene Mosier*

Before Supino's Hills

Oh delightful brows relieved
Against the ridge of high mountains
Of my once tranquil and naive nest!
Woody and refreshing, and still more
Bestrewn with poignant wailings
Of canorous sparrows flying and nestling
Amid the velutinous and serried leaves
Wherein the sun-beam falls short of
Overshadowing itself, but only when
They are swayed and winnowed
By wanton and bracing winds
Trembling through the branchy trees!
So much glee I used to feel,
And I still feel in my fugitive visions,
In going up and down and then even tumbling down
On your florid and dear breast,
Without ever feeling any shame
As when one goes up and down
Of other people's stairs
Of life a humiliating, vile and wailful pain.
>   *Francesco Boni*

Spring, Awaken And Be

Asleep in repose 'neath a blanket of snow,
Alert to God's signal to 'waken and grow
Lie snow-drops and crocuses, heralds of spring,
Awaiting the sign of couriers on wing.

The earth is frosty 'neath a crystal moon
That smiles at itself in an inky lagoon.
Morning brings yet a new face in view
As a saffron sun shines on the early dew.

Under it all, in their earthy beds,
Spring beauties and scilla rest sleepy heads.
Soon, March winds speak in a gentle whisper,
Then grumble, and roar, and bellow out crisper.

Yet, unafraid are the flowers of spring
That buffet the breeze as brave robins sing.
Like magic, they've poked through the wintry ground
Bowing, in debut..not making a sound.

God gently nudges his nature world.
Buds are opened..flowers unfurled.
He nods; his miracle again we see,
As he signals to spring, awaken and be.
>   *Jane Pretekin*

"How Could He Do Such A Thing"

I wish he would realize what he has done to my life,
All he had to do was make her his wife,
But no, he had to leave,
And this she couldn't believe,
He doesn't want to bother,
To be a father.

She hates to walk down the street and see little girls
and their daddy's go by,
Because all she wants to do is sit down and cry,
But how could someone with a heart,
Tear his little girl's life apart.

Where could he be,
Why doesn't he show,
Why did he leave me,
No one will ever know.
>   *Bridget Ann Quinn*

Me

When I look in the mirror
All I see is Me.
I could walk a mile in someone else's shoes,
But when I look in the mirror
I will only see Me.
No matter what I do or say
I will still be Me.
May I just give a bit of advice to those who cannot see.
I will give you one warning,
One day I will look in the mirror,
And I will see a Queen and finally I will see who I want to see,
And that person is Me.

Devon Ancich

The Vicious Rhythm

In a bed sleeping well at night,
All is quiet, only the refrigerator keeps moaning.
Then small rumble, becoming something
Bigger until the noise fills the house,
And dishes rattle and fall to the floor
With a thundering crash.
Noises which seem to be sound effects from an old
Horror film scream and screech to a horrifying rhythm.
A vicious thing, this sound, making the unliving
Seem alive with convulsions, shaking and tumbling.
Heat permeates from everywhere; fire!
Wood beams and supporters fall all around;
On the floor, on the refrigerator, on the bed.
Screeching continues and then, listen! more humane screams.
Terrified, everyone is terrified.
The streets filled with confusion in the darkness
Lighted by flames, orange and Hellish.
The world stops moving; the shaking and tumbling stops.
In a bed sleeps a soul, eternally now; sleep tight.
You might not be awake when Hell arrives.

Eric A. Arvin

Hat Of Death

With this hat this hat of death,
all my friends took their last breath,
upon their visits to my home,
my hat would charm those ones alone.

Its wicked words upon their ears, no way to avoid,
they had to hear, "try me on," my hat would say," and
richness shall come with the newborn day." Then upon
their heads they would place my hat, worse than the
darkest ebony cat. They would feel nothing they were
entranced, and then my hat would start its dance.

It would squirm and wiggle with deadly dread,
down upon my dear friends head,
and I could do nothing my hat control,
its satisfaction turned my heart to coal.
And as I turned to the mirror I saw my cruel
face, laughing, my goodness lacking.

And I as the leader of this wicked tool, it is I who controls
this ghastly fool, the hat is my slave, my pet of death, until
my cruel last dying breath.

Cary Summers

The Key

Someone else has lived inside me
    all my life -
with no way out.
She heard the birds singing
    and the distant call of drums.

She felt the rush of waves
    upon her feet
from far away exotic shores
    and basked in sunlight she did not see.
She often called to me -
    I could not answer;
I did not know the secret
    that would unlock the door.

She whispered sweet surprises
    to my heart
and shared her dreams of love,
    sweet princes, happy endings.
She's lived inside me all my life -
    with no way out;
I did not have the key — until you came.

Irene Potts

Here And After

Time goes by while I sit still
All my life seems to be up hill
So much love I wish to give
In this life that I must live.

As I look at life I see
Problems and strife all waiting for me
Beyond this life of troubles will be
A land of splendor and it's given to me.

Birds and angels all are singing
In a city that is gleaming
A tree of life by a gentle brook.
Reminds me of a walk Christ took.

The walk was long and all up hill
Yet the journey he made at his fathers will
Now I must walk this same road
And carry with me my heavy load.
But someday soon I'll come to rest
At the feet of Jesus, oh how I'm blessed.

Deborah Ketron

Dark Realities

In vain I searched a trace seven decades of my life.
All seems like a chain of dreams, vanishing as echoes of songs.
I took a cruise to catch my youth, watched the foamy waves
behind, Disappearing as years gone by leaving no trace behind.

Alas! Childhood years like dreams are gone with no return,
O', you happy carefree years, you're meant only to rejoice.
Against the arrow death, no shield ever will save you,
Gold, lustrous wealth, have been useless, only good
deeds remembered.

And when I'm gone leaving this world, for the sunrise and for
sunset, Makes no differences to rotating world, whether I'm
walking or six feet deep. World will rotate just the same,
yielding space to new born souls, As fresh victims to deadly
bombs-millions will die for greed and wars.

Hydrogen, nuclear, atomic bombs, will devastate continents.
Before expiring my last breath, I only wish few minutes
To shed my heartfelt tears for millions hungry children
Who will perish before seeing the next spring of their lives.

Ferdinand Kaimakamian

The Baby Tree

The silvery sky
all shining and bright
Catches the baby tree
as it begins its highest flight

Arms stretched out as far
as the eye can see
Wearing its fall coat of
bright red and green leaves.

I came back to see that beautiful baby tree
but behold to my eyes
what a glorious sight I see.

The baby is no more
as she has grown old
A thousand years of living
A million arms to hold.

While standing under her many arms
I look up and she smiles at me
I realized that at one time
I was looking over her, but now
She is watching over me.

Debra E. Justice

"God's Beautiful Land"

If, I were blind, I couldn't see,
all the beauty, that surrounds me,
"The birds, with so, many colors,
how green, the summer grass,
Vast-array of many different
flowers, colored, so, beautiful," - and bright.
"God, and his canvas, the earth,
like an artist, with his paint-brush,
he created worlds, of beauty
that if, you were blind,
you couldn't see,
only picture, in your mind,
"worlds' of beauty,"
etched upon, and through out
the vast lands, of earth."

Debra Jackey

On Seventeen, On Saturday

Down the high road, up the low road
all the cars go quick and quicker.
Metallic vessels crammed thick and thicker.
With the colors of the vessels; steel corpuscles
blue and red, white, silver, teal and umber,
aubergine and yellow, bright lime green and that strange un-color:
a shade of gray...runt somber.
You call it undercoat but it's more like an overcoat
on a tired old guy on a sunny day.
One look in that old car of gray runt somber and you can see
(Even at fifty miles an hour) the litter of that driver's life
lived too fast or too long. (All the others cars are new and
bright and shiny). And you wonder where you fit in, can you
squeeze in that long and lethal bright and shining beam of motion?
Sun sparks hard on the bumper and hood of the car ahead and
beside.
You must keep pace. Go fast, then faster. Pass the runt gray
somber on Route Seventeen, on Saturday, in almost summer.
Pray small prayer as the car to your right pulls out ahead
of you, not from any dread of you. You are unseen, on Seventeen,
on Saturday, in summer...

Jahdo McTavish

Secret Lovers

In the all consuming night,
All the dawns beauty is hidden out of sight,
And the night's secrets are out on the prowl,
And all is awakened by the soft hooting of an owl,
Two silent lovers intertwine,
Two forgotten souls lost in time,
Living out dreams in a few stolen minutes,
Taking there broken hearts to the limits,
A forbidden love witch was not meant to be,
Which had to be hidden from all eyes to see,
So in this clucking dark night they meet,
embrace, but must part before light.
And all that remains is the silent
center to the lovers pain

Donna L. Kelley

"My Time to Remember"

This is my time to remember
All the events of passing years,
Memories of a childhood and
a lifetime of love and tears.

Mother died when I was ten
And sister took her place,
So beautifully she raised three
sisters, six brothers with
Father and God's grace.

Our home was an open door for all
our friends and neighbors,
Loving times of graduation, weddings and new births.
But sadness and tears as the years
slipped by for the death angel made its way,
taking all but the three girls remaining today.

Christ came into my life at age 16,
Blessed was I with opportunities to serve him.
He gave me patience, love and wisdom.
A wonderful marriage, but now as I ponder alone, .
I wonder how soon I'll be the remembered.

Ella G. Garland

Time

Time is something we should all share,
all though there's few that have none to spare.

Always in a big hurry, and many places to go.

As you hurry through the day,
and all the people you may pass along the way,
there may be someone you will know.

But there isn't time to say hello,
only a wave and off you go.

And my friend I will say;
Make time for yourself today.

As no one knows, when the time will come.
and tomorrow will pass you by.

Cindy Stratton

Untitled

Today I leaned over to smell a rose
An aroma, as beautiful as its appearance
    Swelled deep down inside of me
Simple...yes, but the beauty of it all
Is the thought of you and retaining that thought
For sweet recollection,
    Time and time again.

Gene Giles

Your Love

Come, let me feel the warmth of your true love beside me.
Along the path to your Kingdom I pray you will guide me.
From all evil and wickedness and sickness please hide me.
I was once bound by Satan but your love has untied me.

My faith in your love, I believe, is what saved me,
And the more my faith grew, the more Satan craved me.
With every victory over temptation my heart aches to praise thee.
Still, with all I've been shown, your love will always amaze me.

Come, let me feel your love which you give so freely.
By the power of your love you were able to free me.
God, make me good in your eyes so that my eyes may see thee,
In your kingdom, with your true love for all of eternity.

Debra Butler

Buried From The Sun

This is my story of evil and gloom
Also my fear of impending doom
My life was a wreak from the day I was born
It was like being pushed from a shelter into a storm
I've struggled through life with bitterness and pain
I wore - out my scruples and I feel no shame
Do you say it's my fault for the trouble I'm in?
Perhaps I should've looked to God instead of sin
certainly the truth is here to see
The bars on my cell were put there by me.
Who has the power? Is it the key or the lock?
Neither!! It's the man on the inside buried in the rock,
A man who is condemned to live in a cell,
has nothing but time to think and dwell.
To dwell on the past and the things he has done
And to dwell on the future buried from the sun

Jeff James

God Only Knows

They say it's a reason, but we don't understand
Although the one he's taking is suddenly a man
He sees these things and a whole lot more.
He's at peace with himself now, he's at God's front door.

Please make him comfortable when he loses this one last fight.

Don't make it any harder, just hold him through the night.

Put all this pleasant memories in front of him this one last time,
and because he is so loving, he's yours now he's not mine.

You've taken him away from me,
and in your arms is where I'd rather have him be.

Janice Wilson

Tears Fell From Heaven

On a dark and lonely corner at the end of the street,
An old man sits huddled, cold, with bare dirty feet.
He wonders, where will I sleep tonight, where will I lay my head?
Will I have food to eat, will I have a bed?
Raindrops fell upon him and a prayer came from his lips;
Dear Jesus, tears are falling from Heaven
could you please find me a home?
He lay beneath a rainy sky so cold and alone,
Only to open his pale old eyes, to see a Golden Throne,
Upon it sat an angel wearing a halo of Golden light.
He whispered softly to him in the darkness of the night,
These are my tears falling from Heaven,
I have come to take you home.

Glenda Hodson

The Destroyer

Who am I?
Am I limited to the underprivileged socioeconomic class?
My identity is known to many globally.
I am efficient at disguises.
Sometimes I am a prominent business tycoon
I am well known in the professional circles,
I even played professional ball and tennis.
Hollywood! I have been there too. Acting is one of my specialty.
Most people think I am just a poor, helpless, drug addict.
My first encounter with many were through blood transfusions.
I assume many roles.
Who am I?
I have brought much sadness to many,
I have intercepted many relationships.
Do you want become a statistic?
Care enough to know my identity
So we won't cross paths.
I thrive on destroying lives, even those of innocent babies.
Who am I?
I am AIDS the nondiscriminating universal killer.

Gertrude Simon

Dear Lord

We never dreamed, his illness was caused by cancer,
An operation, successful but not the answer.
You see it seems to have moved all around
Dear Lord, "Why can't it be found?"
Dear Lord his faith is true, Dear Lord it's all in you.
Please ease his pain while he sleeps
Don't let it slow him down, Please let a cure be found.
If you can hear me, Dear Lord!
I don't know, how long Dad can go on,
Or if the pain inside is too damn strong.
I know he doesn't want his life to be through,
But what else Dear Lord, can he do.
So help his strength to fight, He's giving all his might.
And when he's scared and so weak will be there!
  Dear Lord, "Will You Ever Stop His Pain?"

Debbra Kaye Marie Borish

Greenville

'Twas almost noon when we arrived in Greenville town, today,
An overnight excursion,with our Friends to get away.

We cruised expansive Moosehead Lake, and felt the gentle breeze,
and saw the waters kiss the shore, as far as eye could see.

We stopped at Chalet Moosehead Inn, upon this balmy day,
and took a quiet cottage, which, was nestled in the bay.

We browsed the quaint old curios, along the rural street.
and drove the road to Rockwood, For a moose, we hoped to see.

We went to Kelly's Landing, just to get a bite to eat,
a pleasant, tranquil atmosphere, where old Friends chance to meet.

We saw Canadian Geese swim by, unmindful of the time,
and Seaplanes soared across the lake, as distant Church bells chimed.

As evening shadows start to fall, at twilight time of day,
We heard the crooning lullaby of loons out in the bay.

We saw the rippling waters dance, to summertime delight.
and lights reflected on the lake, was such a wondrous sight.

And, in the midnight of our sleep, we heard the whistling train,
invoke upon our sleepy brain, a melancholy strain.

But, now, the morning mists arise, upon another day,
and, as we leave for home, we know, a part of us will stay.

JoannaLee Ranks

Mid July

As the sun rose over the Franklin height
And a sparrow sang its tune, I looked out on my dusty porch
And a thought passed in the gloom.

Of how could a man work in this heat
And how could he spread some cheer,
And the sweat already was trickling down
My nose, from the closeness here.

And though the eye in the sky was low
The heat did rise all the same
'Til all I saw in the distant view
Was the haze, and it circled came.

And its sweaty palms did grab my arms
And like fire did it feel 'til my skin turned black
And off it came, like a giant human peel.

And soon my insides were boiling too And I started to
sink in the sand, And all that was left of me that day
Was the bones that made this man.

So the morale of this story, friend, is this and it's
said in pain: If you're thinking of touring El Paso now
You really are insane.

   Adrienne Roberts

Untitled

There are days when I just cry,
And ask myself, "Why 'd you have to die?"
There's so much you're not going to see.
Why is this how it had to be?

You take so much for granted, when you're small...
Thinking you'd always be there when I fall.
The special occasions we would share.
When you'd let me know how much you care.

Now those dreams will never be,
And my eighteenth birthday: You'll never see.
You'll not sit impatiently and wait;
For your little girl to graduate.

I won't be able to see your smile,
As you proudly walk me down the aisle.
To place your trust in another as you give me away;
To start a new life on my wedding day.

Even though these things you'll not see,
Daddy's girl, I'll always be.
In my heart there is a place
That no one else could ever replace.

   Dianna L. Johnson

The Lioness

Beware the mighty Lioness, she rules the golden plain
And at her feet there lies her meat, her foe that she has slain.
Be careful not to anger her, the mighty lioness,
Deceive her not, her heart cannot be won by your duress.
Look into her tawny eyes and know she cannot be tamed,
Can you meet her stare alone, yet your heart be not ashamed?
Beware the mighty lioness, she sees right to the heart,
And many who had fooled the rest she knew right form the start.
The only way to win her heart is first to show your own
Then she shall be your guide and you and she shall stand alone,
And walk the golden plains and watch the waist high grasses bend,
For you will have her heart and she will always be your friend.
Beware the mighty lioness, she rules the golden plain
And at her feet there lies her meat, her foe that she has slain.

   Christina Brown

Beyond Existence

The icy water rushes around my toes
   and awakens the nerves with a numbing pain.
A brisk wind dashes through my clothes
   and sends a chill all along my skin.

To splash this water, and breath in this air-
   these are actions that rouse our dormant senses.
They remind us that we are alive, we can feel,
   and we are apart of the Living experience.

   Cheryl Bollenbacher

Constance

Upon the wings of the night
   and breath of the wind,
   the stars fall to earth
   when thoughts of you come to mind.

Losing myself within a dream
   of your tender stare
   that draws my life
   through the endless night.

Your soft voice penetrates the darkness,
   bringing with it a hazel glow
   and a gentle touch that reaches beyond
   the dark corners of my dreams.

Reaching for you through the blindness,
   wanting to draw you near,
   yet my attempts leave me staring at the
   windswept stars within my mind.

I can only cherish your beauty and value the moments
   that have collected within my heart
   as my dreams are slowly swept away
   upon the wings of the night and breath of the wind.

   David Rivosecchi

Daughter

The morning light came through today
And brought with it a vast array
Of thoughts and words and dreams and care
And sort of took me unaware.

When webs had cleared and mists were gone
It left with me a newborn dawn
And most triumphant in my thoughts
Were memories of love besought.

My heart regained its strength and pace
To seek a day of peace and grace
And in my memory I find
An aural face of my own kind.

Who is this one who's still with me
Daughter, friend, counselor is she
Our roles are fixed she's yet to be
A soul not near capacity.

She still must fight this earth's foray
By gliding through in her own way
But in my heart I know she'll be
An apt opponent getting free.

   Jeanne Walker

"In Memory Of A Great U.S. Ex-President:

Richard M. Nixon"

High wind may blow, rough seas may row:
   And cause his ship to reel and rock,
May the Rudder sturdy the Bow:
   And land on the Square when he Dock.

   Joseph H. Young

The Stile

I laid my hand upon the stile,
And climbed the steps on through.
Then stopped and turned—and "touched" again,
That post, so worn, by use.

I wondered how many handshakes,
Had polished and worn that post.
This soldier along the landscape,
A friend amongst the slopes....

Again, I "touched" it lightly,
As I searched for tell-tell scars.
This post so shined and polished,
That would splinter flesh no more.

Then I thought a silent, "thank you,"
And smiled within my heart!
That someone could pass that stile, again
And think it a friend, at last!
Anne S. Dodgson

"The Human Seed"

I wish, I could talk to my mother,
and convince, her, that I love her!

Lord, I'd rather tell her now
than after she falls sick, or to a sudden demise!
and why, am I waiting for,
my wife's demise to tell her, that I love her too!

If my child would, ever fail.

I know I can say that I love you!
Like I did with, the one that's in prison.
Edward Doyley

Daddy's Eyes

Mama said I have Daddy's eyes.
And Daddy said I have Mamma's nose.
When I visit Grandpa on his farm,
He says my laugh is my Uncle Joe's.

My gap-toothed smile is my Aunt Louise's.
(She's the one who always teases!)
Grandma says I look like my brother.
She can't tell one from the other.

"Who am I?" I ask my mother.
"If everything I have belongs to another?
My eyes, my laugh, my teeth, my nose,
All that's left are my little toes!"

My mother laughs and sits me down.
Says I look silly with such a frown.
"You are unique, there is no other.
"It's what's inside that counts to mother."

Someday, when you are fully grown.
You'll have a family of your own.
You'll look at your child - You'll say. "That's me!"
Because we're all branches of the same family tree.
Emilie Smyrlian

Spring

In the spring, the trees are green,
And everywhere they may be seen.
From far and near, they're heaven blessed,
the song they sing gives peace and rest.
And as I wander day by day,
The trees do whisper as though to say...
The sun will shine, warm winds will blow.
Peace on earth, God's will, you know.
It's then I lift my head and smile,
And really know that life's worthwhile.
Francis P. McDonough

The Beautiful Bounty Of Spring

In spring we seek the trillium,
And dainty wild violets,
Might even spot some dogwood blossoms,
Or patches of narcissus yet.
Grape hyacinths and yellow jonquils,
And tiny crocus have their day,
The first to peek up through the earth,
Nurtured by the warm sun-rays.
Tulips will be popping out,
Forsythia soon exploding into a glorious golden splendor,
Our Lord's blessing we are beholding.
Spirea will drape her bush in white,
Like a lovely bride, quite vain,
And charm the birds to come and light
On her resplendent train.
We love the pious easter lily,
Inspiring purity in our heart,
And the first robins raise our pulse,
Now spring has a fresh new start.
Ida Lillian Hobbs

Salvation Walk

St. Francis, Dr. Talbert, Dr. Spitler
And Dr. J.E. Palen, Dr. J. C. Sparkman, and St. Patrick
Took me by the hand
And we went for a walk.

They saved my life
With their skill
And love
And I did not die.

I did not die - It was
The Lord's will - I know not why.
Que sera, sera, sera
Whatever will be - will be
The future is not ours to see
Que sera, Que sera
Que sera.
Guyla Wallis Moreland

Skin Pride

Sometimes I look at my soft, golden, brown skin
and feel proud of what I have accomplished in life.
I'm proud to be a Latino and the culture associated with it.
I try to be color blind when it comes to
the rest of the world because we need it.
My pride is my guide that leads me through life.
I will not allow myself to be stereotyped and fall into the pitfall
of being a "nobody" that the world has provided for us.
My time has come, as has my people's, to rise up
and break the stereotypes to proceed forward.
We are not just baby factory makin', strawberry pickin',
Budweiser-drinkin' Mexicans that people interpret us to be.
We are a people with pride and history like everyone else.
Human beings living on the same earth is who we are.
I don't know everything in life, but what I do know is my skin color
will never change; inside or outside. That is skin pride.
Guillermo Perez

Spring

It's springtime with its green
and fragrant meadows
gone are the winter months,
the long and dreary days
with all they're icy shadows

Blossoms and flowers are the faces of spring
Early risers see the Robins on the wing

The very air breathes promises
of nature's magic tricks as she unfolds,
With all her glory what for us she holds
    Gertrude W. Webster

An Apple Tree In The Wind

He suddenly appeared one spring night
and gently took her arm.
She looked up in surprise, but began
to quietly sway in the silence and
darkness that is night with this
stranger whom everyone knew
but no one knew.
Then, with a sudden burst of energy
and life, they started to twirl.
The watchers began to murmur
and gossip as the little shy girl
with the blossoms in her hair
spun with the mysterious stranger.
Faster and faster, her arms waved in the
churning air. Her pale pink dress billowed
around and around in the frenzy.
Then, he slowed and came to a stop.
He left without so much as a whisper
but she knew the stranger would return.

    Jenny Kapplinger

The Candle

I swore tomorrow would be different but tomorrow has come
and gone and nothing has changed.

As I sit in a dark corner,
I shiver when I begin to think of another tomorrow.

Will someone come with the candle
to bring me out of the darkness?

The darkness is growing around me, when will it end?
As I huddle in fear I hear a sound.
Could it be? Is that a candle shining through the darkness?

As I look up I see your face looking down at me.
You reach for my hand. I grasp it and stand.

Hope begins to show itself like
the candle cutting through the darkness.

I no longer flinch in fear as I think about tomorrow.
But, I hold my head high realizing that you will always be here
right by my side.
    Amber Taylor

Rainbow Of Love

Lord, may I paint a rainbow of love for you?
And help me show others your love as you would have me do
Whether paint brush in my hand with work to be done
Or visiting those sick in bed and lending a helping hand—Give me a
listening ear and a tender heart;
Lord, may I paint a rainbow of love for you?
With your help, I can!
    Jeannie Lewis

My Neighbor

He moved in four years ago at this small unit,
And has lived as a reclusive hermit.
He works at night and sleeps in day.
I wondered where was his working place.

I awaited at night watching what he looked like;
He had a humpback, a bold head behind,
He wore a black overcoat,
Wrapping with a body appeared slim and tall.

He seems to have no relatives and friends,
A lonesome figure surrounded with a crowd of residents.
He is very seldom talking to any body.
But lives in a shadowy reality.

One day I saw a cop standing at his apartment,
My heart beat what had happened to this old man,
I was told he caught a burglar.
Oh, he is a vigilante, to protect the sleeping dwellers.
    Diana M. P. Chang

Randy

My grandson Randy was just 22
And he knew exactly what he wanted to do
To be like his father, he wanted to fly
But on July 22 our Randy would die
Four years in the air force and this
Would have come true
Two more in college and he'd be on his way
But he was robbed and shot twice
On this very sad day
They caught the 2 men and they're
Waiting trial
No pilot for Randy
Oh what a denial.
    Betty M. Kuhn

He Is Always With You

The Lord is with you at this time
And he will always be,
Close beside you wherever you are
He'll never depart from thee.

He'll see you through your trials
  your tribulations, too,
He'll watch over you everyday
And all you say and do.

He sticks closer than a brother,
Draw close to him when there's no other,
One around to comfort you
Stick close to him he'll see you through.

He'll pick you up, when you are down,
He'll keep you up, off of the ground.
He'll give you strength and grace each day.
All's we have to do is pray.

I want you to know we'll be praying
For you each and every day.
That the Lord will guide your footsteps
And carry you safely on your way.
    Darlene Portner

Treasures Rare

To lay my ear unto the ground
  And hear a symphony of sound;
To throw my head into the air
  And sense a mellow fragrance there;
To cast my gaze into the sky
  And for a while with nature lie;
To feel, to see, and to embrace
  Thus all of nature face to face
Is to encounter a treasure rare
  With which nothing — nothing can compare.

Joseph Pressburg

My Rag Doll

Yesterday I picked up my old rag doll
and held her close, our hearts connected
(hers was painted on), I cried on her shoulder and she
understood. She listened to my problems and then
smiled to reassure me, (her smile was painted on), her
button eyes were full of pity for me.

She wasn't angry at me for all the years I left her
on my bed just to sit and stare.
She smiled at me and I forced a smile on my face
(mine was painted on). Inside my rag doll holds the
secrets from yesterday.

Jackie Brosseau

Thy Charming Lady

The woman in the guest room with looks of beauty
and her shining smile, I stare in awe, her eyes and
her cute charming face staring me back.
Lo and behold! She is beckoning me with her brilliance
and delightful charm. I begin to feel her radiance, like
a light from above, echoing through the room. My awe,
cheerfully I want to remark on that special sight.
The spectacle was fascinating to the soul, the room
itself seemed to glow in specter, and it contained my
heaven right here on earth.
As I gaze at all this splendor then who walks in but
the man of her dreams and, henceforth, whisks me out
of the room.
As I standeth there in startled silence I think how
quickly all my dreams and fantasies being snuffed out.
I know that I could attempt to bring them all back,
but I dare not try for fear it would irk the man of her dreams.
And so, I consoleth myself to the reminiscence of
the moment of the past and the thought that perhaps
meeting another woman with just as much beauty and charm.

Jeffry Weisenthal

Tonight

At night I sit and think of you,
And I know you're thinking of me, too.
I smile and think of how we came to be,
Wondering how someone like you could fall for me.

Tonight as I walk along the shore,
I think of how I've been hurt before.
Then one day you gave me your love,
For which I'd prayed to God above.

I know that you care,
We have so much to share.
I wish for you to hold me in your arms,
When I'm there I feel safe from harm.

As I climb into bed and turn out the light,
I know I'll be dreaming of you tonight.

Bobbie Jo Spikes

The After Shock

Today I lost a friend.
And I feel that life's unfair
It makes it hard to open-up
And allow yourself to care.

Why do we lose the ones
That are good
And allow the bad to go on?
Who decides who lives or dies? And who will wake to the
Morning sun?

It makes you stop and think about
The things you say and do, cause maybe when you least
Expect the next to go could be you.

So live your life to its fullest extent
And love the ones you're with, and share a thought
With all concerned, cause life is a God given gift.

Be sure to say I love you to all you share life with
Don't waste the time we have left on earth
Cause life is too short lived.

Dianna Nally

Black Man And Woman

Black woman to me you are beautiful
And I feel very happy and grateful
That a person like you exists
Because you are very precious

You are precious because you are there
For the black man who is always in despair
Because he sometimes does not think
But just does things according to instinct

Black woman I need you to help me
Deal with the problems of society
The society sees me as a minority
Who is not willing and able to succeed

But with your help black woman I can
Prove to the world that the black man
Despite the trouble he gets in
Can achieve the things expected of him

Sorry black woman for the way the blackman
Treats you as if you were trash in a can
Just forgive the blackman and continue to pray
For him to treat you in a gentle and nice way.

Chinedu D. Ogbuike

Unspoken Words

Life's too short to take for granted,
And "I Love You", is not said nearly enough, when it's needed the most.
Just close your eyes and think of me, for one day I will be gone,
Not of my own doing, but taken by surprise,
And when that day comes, your eyes will be filled with unspoken words,
painfully tucked away in every drop that falls from your teary eyes.
Your heart will feel crushed and empty, a feeling that
cannot be described.
Though, there is nothing anyone can do or say, to make the pain
go away.
But time, will heal your heart somewhat, to enable you to begin a
new life.
But once in a while, just close your eyes and think of me,
as hard as it may be, for now I'm just a memory,
of something that used to be.

Irene B. Ingram

"The Stars In Your Eyes"

I look up at the midnight sky,
And I think of you.
The stars are like the diamonds that twinkle in
    your eyes.
The soft wind in my face carries your scent,
As my mind drifts away to be with you.
The dark silent sky,
So innocently wanders on forever.
As our love,
It shall endure with every breath.
I make a wish on a twinkling star,
A wish of our love to endure the moon,
The sun,
And the stars in the sky.
The stars like the diamonds that twinkle in you
    eyes.

Jennifer McCollum

A Mother's Memories

This morning I looked at my lawn so perfect and green
And I thought "No more beauty could ever be seen."
Then my thoughts went back just a few short years.
I remember the laughter..also a few tears.
Laughter of children playing on the swings.
The tears I dried after a little be sting.
I remember the pants knees that were torn,
And the many paths that were worn
As they played the games of baseball,
When "strikes three! you're out" was the call.
A short distance away , on a blanket, sat the little girls,
Wearing pretty dresses, bonnets and curls.
They play with their dolls and pretend they are the mother—
With an imaginary father and the brother.

As my memories went back,
I am sure that the "prettiest lawn"
Was the one in the past that is now gone.
There wasn't much grass—that's very true.
In that yard, our dear children grew!

Inez Chapman

True Love

You came in a flash wonder, like lightning from the sky!
And in my awe and joy, I began to see just why.
You were sent to teach me true love-a love so sweet and pure.
With you I was reborn too! I was lost no more!
I thought I knew what love was. But now I can be certain.
Its light shines in my heart now, my soul's no longer hurting.
You're not meant to be coveted-you must someday go free.
But when into the world you go, this true love will sustain me.

Angela D'Ottavio

A Child's View

The clouds were roaring, dark and sinister.
And in the distance the thunder was the sound
of God's laughter. The rain was soft, warm
and safe like angel's tears of joy. And I
stood there like a child smiling. For I knew
what life had in store.

Alice Jeanne Webb

The View

Atop the hill, under a year stricken willow tree, man can sit
and indulge in one of nature's more breath-taking scenes.
It is not the ghastly eyesore of the concrete jungle
which he clashes with on a daily basis, but rather the sight
of amber wheat flowing in a gentle mid-afternoon breeze like
ripples rolling to reach the bank.
The course of this golden pond is interrupted by the
presence of a forgotten barn; resting helplessly from the
abuse brought on by the constant change in seasons.
Rays from the setting sun knife through the crisp air,
penetrating the decadent rooftop and with the reflection from
the lone window it creates the illusion of a fire warming only
the small animals scurrying within.
Birds tauntingly swoop by the time-worn scarecrow left
dangling from its post as the straw stuffing bursts through
the seams of a green and blue plaid shirt.
It is in this spot that man has the opportunity to observe mother
nature and find a sense of tranquility in his life.

Christian Toomey

Violence

Violence is making the world a bad place,
And it is putting a brown on our face,
Peace and people are going down the drain,
Guns are killing, so what do we gain?
We're losing family and maybe our lives,
Get rid of the guns and lose the knives,
Violence is no way to solve anything,
Killing doesn't make you an honored king,
If you lose weapons, you won't lose a niece,
So stop the violence and increase the peace.

Julie Ikenberry

Heroes Are Forever

Everybody's got Heroes
And Kerry is mine.
He had a heart of gold
That out shined them all.
He always's had time for
The little children that
Wanted to shake his hand.
He had friend's and enemies, alike.
When all the smoke cleared and
No one was insight he stood tall.
In the squared circle he was ready
To rock and roll, the crowd loved
Him, and shouted Kerry, Kerry you're
As true as they come. In the squared
Circle there's an empty space, for the golden
Boy is not there, but heroes are forever.

Judy Bohannon

Dream A Little Dream

Dream a little dream
and know that yet the world goes round.
Dream a little dream
and know when the stars are near.
Dream a little dream
even when you know it won't come true.
Dream a little dream
when it will.
Dream a little dream
and don't be afraid to release your fears.
Dream a little dream
and know you can destroy your fears.
Dream a little dream
or even a nightmare for you know you can defeat it and be brave.
Because that's what dreams are made of.

Dana Shepherd

"Carry On!"

At times when things seem perfect all about us,
And lady luck grants us a lucky star,
We must cherish these sweet memories forever,
For things cannot remain just as they are.

There are moments when the world outside turns heartless,
And all our hopes and dreams are smashed to bits!
It is then we learn to deal with threats and failures-
And strive to persevere and use our wits!

We must learn to smile when others are judgmental,
And face the ups and downs our lives can take—
To confront man's dreadful persecutions,
Yet God nor Country never once for sake!!

For if all our happy moments were unending
We wouldn't know the heartbreak when they're gone
Find how to grit our teeth at disappointment
And hold our heads up high and Carry On!!!

Dorothy Malone

Stepping Out

I come and go, I'm high
And low, with no particular place to go.
I'm here, I'm there, I'm everywhere.
I live and learn from above,
Upon my shoulder perched a dove.
A shew from the sea, the green of a tree,
A flower so strange it's beauty,
There is no range my head in the clouds,
My feet on the ground, my ears in the middle
I can't hear a sound, I'm beside my self
A good place to be, as a tree stands alone,
Why shouldn't me.
When I've found my self,
I'm searching you see but for
Now I'll simply be me.

F. Clare Brady

'Love, Not Hate'

Program your mind up the positive side
And make your negative side drop
Neutral in this train of thought
Install love and hate not

Take the anger you feel and realize
You can compose it naturally
Can't anyone hear or see
Live your life happily

Life is no joke it will have in hope
Of the future you wish to see
Without the love of forgiving
Your dreams start the killing

Believe in love and happiness you'll find
Take your hate and leave it behind
Learn to cherish your life and state
'I'm to love and not to hate'

"Love me like I love my father"
Says the only one and holy
Written in the book of the wise
It takes love to reach the other side

Aaron Brown

Upon Visiting The Vietnam Wall Memorial

Etched in this stone there are many brave faces
and many untold stories.
There are many heroes, and there are no cowards.
The old will remember, and the young will learn.
The freedom, the courage, the untold stories; the
faces of brave men who fought with
A modern day chivalry.
These are the men we have promised to remember
In history,
But
Who are being forgotten by the future.
There are no cowards on this wall;
There are only cowards who criticize them.
Etched in this stone, there is history, there is loyalty,
and there is honor.
Etched in this stone, there are heroes of many battles
and many obstacles.

Justin Callan

Reflection

Within the solace of the night a voice calls out to me;
And my heart is filled with longing for a dream still yet to be...
I sleep, yet soon I waken searching for this voice I know -
Silvery moonbeams cast a beacon are the pathway I must go...

Within the whisper of a breeze I touch the falling rain -
Like jeweled teardrops of my life upon the windowpane;
I wake, yet still in slumber dreaming of this voice I know-
But a shadowed recognition of a memory long ago...

Within the freedom of a bird I drift on wings of song-
To touch the summit of my dream-to find where I belong...
The sky and I together silhouetted in the light
Soaring losey to life's answer in the misty breath of night...

Within the moonlight kissed by stars see your face so dear;
And all the meaning of my life unfolds as you draw near...
You speak; my spirit listens, far your voice seems part of me-
I know that I have found my dream you always meant to be...

Within the wisdom of your mind and the laughter of your soul-
I feel enveloped in a warmth-of joy alive and whole;
You smile-my smile awakens to a mirrored destiny,
For I glimpse within you silent gaze my own eternity...

Judith Prows

To You, My Love

He loved her so, he hath said;
And not the contrary she.
Thus, today, they have come as one,
As God ordained it to be.

Two hearts to wed, in the presence of God,
For all the world to see;
And evermore through boundless grace,
This union most hallowed be.

We, together, in your will;
(Our hearts all bright with song!)
Come before Thee our dear Lord,
And pray you build our home.

Let your way be truly ours.
In all, Thy will to see.
And furnish us through Thy power,
Minds, just like Thee.

To my intended, Oh! dear Lord,
And, also unto Thee,
For better or for worse my Lord,
I reverently say, "I do"!

David R. Smith

Taking Care Of Children

Taking care of children is all I've ever wanted to do
And now at last my dream has come true
Each day as I walk into the room and see their little faces all aglow
The love I have for each of them in my heart starts to grow
With one tight little hug and lots of gentle little kisses
I come to understand the true meaning of happiness
As the time passes we sing, dance, laugh, and play
Every little booboo gets kissed and each little tear is wiped away
All to soon though the day comes to an end
As I blow kisses and wave good-bye I just
   can't seem to wait till tomorrow begins
   Jessica Hammac

Who To Blame

I've felt so alone for so many years, I try to hide the pain.
And now I just can't stop all the tears, I don't know who to blame.
When I first met you, I thought you were a nice guy
I thought you were different, why do I ever try!
Then I tried to get your attention, for you to know that I was there.
I even tried to slice my wrist, but you didn't even start to care.
Nobody else is out there, and the hurt turns into pain.
I don't have any explanations, except you're driving me insane!
All that is left in my life, is my trusted little knife.
That will give me my relief, and let out some of the pain and strife.
My world feels like it's caving in, the pain is getting really bad.
I just can't hide it anymore, I have definitely turned chronically sad.
Is it too much to ask for, someone to fall in love with me?
To feel needed and to feel loved?
But all of it is just a dream,
Because soon I'll wake up in a puddle of my own blood.
   Annette Bradford

In My Dreams

You've been in my dreams all of my life,
And now that I have you I don't want to lose you.

You've been in my dreams all of my life.
Now that I may lose you I have no idea what to do.

You've been in my dreams all of my life.
Please don't leave me. I'll do anything for you.

Why would you leave me?
What did I do to you?
The only thing I ever did to you was love you.

You've been in my dreams all of my life.
Now that you're gone I may never get you back in my dreams.
   Andrea Allan

Of Her

I walk in the dusk of the evening
and somehow the way the night sounds
play in my ear remind me of her,—my grandmother.
The whisper of timelessness in the tress...
The call of the whippoorwill...
Melancholy call of times richer, times past.
The safety of her front porch where the chickens
roosted in the boxwoods... their soft clucking singing
a lullaby...
The fear of the darkened windows as she
locked the door...
The comfort of her words as she tucked me in the
great feather bed...
So many things to remember locked away to be awakened
by just a breeze in the air.
Things that wash over me, comfort me and make me always
wish for her and the little girl locked in my mind.
   DE Boggs

WHEN OUR PURPOSE HERE IS DONE

When our purpose here is done,
And our soul, our Lord has won,

He takes us home to live up there,
To keep us closer in his care.

To give us life in a different place,
To love and take us in his embrace.

For he knows our wants, our wishes too.
So he tries on earth to see it through.

For when our pain grows greater still,
He begins our walk up heaven's hill.

Our pain gets dim, our strength gets great,
For before us, we see the golden gate.

And just inside a beauty glows,
That here on earth, no one knows.

And there he takes us by the hand
And leads us into an unknown land.

For when we look into his face,
We know that heaven is our place.

And there we live with him on high,
In his place up in the sky.
   Janis B. Drinnon

Weeping With The World

The Sky looked down with somber blue eyes
And saw the dark smog that covered the land.
And the saddened Sky wept for the loss of that beautiful sight.
Then the resounding Sea saw the reddened eyes of the Sky.
And felt the drops of Sky's tears on his face.
And the Sea increased his mass with his own tears.
Then the dull green and brown Earth felt engulfed by the Sea's tears.
Was it not enough that Earth suffered the inhumane treatment of man?
Was it not enough that the methodical rhythm of Sky's
tears pounded harshly against her breast?
Now, Earth was losing her limbs to the tears of the Sky
To the tears of the Sea
To the sadness of the World.
And they wept in unison and their pleas burned with a fury
And the smoke from that fire went up,
Intertwining with the dark smog.
And the saddened Sky wept.
   Erin Vinocor

Everyone Has Love Inside

As the grass grows beneath my feet
and the clouds move across the sky
As a raindrop makes its journey down to the earth
Everyone has love inside

As a fighter raises his fists
in a sea of rage
As a poet writes his last line
as he turns the page
Everyone has love inside

As a baby opens his eyes
for the very first time
As a sinner goes down to his knees
to confess his crimes
Everyone has love inside
   Allen A. Forella

Hope

The river flows over the rocks
and splashes against the branches
that bend with the gentle wind

All this I can feel and visualize
in my minds eye
I let myself see the colors
of the river, the branches, the sky

I sit quiet in the midst of a hurricane
buildings being destroyed
picked up and thrown miles away
until there is nothing, but barren

Fire burning the green forest
until all that's left is emptiness, and darkness

And yet, a small light appears
Somewhere
And I see it
As I reach out I go towards the brightness

And I arrive to a place
where the river flows
Judy Fisher-Singer

Progress

The skyscrapers crush the tiny country stores,
And take their place in the center of town;
The grassy pastures are transformed,
As the paved trails replace the green clover ground.

Large shopping malls and parking lots,
Overtake the fields of corn and cotton;
Swept up in the whirlwind of change,
Old values and fundamentals are forgotten.

Doors once left open now bolted shut,
While crimes grow instead of wildflowers;
The citizens guard their purses and pockets,
Frightened of thieves, hungry for money's power.

Trust and security buried with the past,
To make way for the coming age;
Strange faces fill the unfamiliar streets,
As a cold and callous rush takes the stage.

Fish and foul die from pollution,
And homeless people scrape the trash for warm dress;
Morality burns in flames of corruption,
All in the name of progress.
Heath Shackleford

"Till Death Do Us Part"

We were young and not very wise
And the door stood open to our hearts
We loved each other every waking moment
As our friends grew farther and farther apart.

We got closer yet and our love grew stronger
No matter how much anyone tried
To come in between us and tear us apart
We remained close as always.

When we wed and the preacher said
Till death do you part
We decided we were serious and meant for each other.

We're much older now and much wiser
But we're still together and very much in love
Always have been and always will be
"Till death do us part"
Deloise Ginn

Expendability

Mother I know that I've done something wrong
And that I deserve fair punishment
But I've been left alone without any comfort
And more than anything need your condolence.

Teacher I know my peers want no part of me
But the crime is what I'm beseeching
Why they've turned their backs on the dunce in the cap
And though I'm hiding why no one is seeking?

Curator I know that I don't belong
In the glass case with fortune and glory
I don't deserve to be put on display
I'm a person not an accessory.

Minister I know that even you lose interest
And my league has moved on and left me behind
Running for technology and leaving me in the dark ages
Like the frequently sung about prodigal kinds.

Things look smaller than they appear
When the telescope is turned around
But I was tiny and insignificant before
So I must be infinitesimal now.
Jay M. Bolton

"Ones Love"

The tenderness of ones love is shown by the acts he performs,
    And the acts he performs, is measured by the degree of love he has
        for the individual.
    In so doing , he creates a cycle in which he is the
        recipient of an abundant love in which he is the creator,
            from the one he has shown tenderness to.
            But it is not his acts alone, that creates happiness
                It is the tenderness in his voice when he speaks,
                    And the softness of his touch,
                    And the look in his eyes, when he sees the joy he
                        has made in someone else's life
                        To be the receiver of such soft spoken words,
                            the tender touch, and the joyous
                                glances, makes one blossom with eagerness to
                                    set forth in motion, their desire
                                    to please, and speak tenderly, touch
                                        gently, and have eyes glow with
                                            happiness. And so the cycle of
                                                human kindness grows and flourishes.

Edna Blomquist

A Kiss In A Thunderstorm

'Tis the dusk before an unstarry vesper
And the thunder and rain hath come to warm
The enhancing moods of supreme romance
Between I and my lover in this storm.

Hypnotized by the crashing of the rain
We gaze deeply into each other's eyes
Visualizing a forever love
And forever thunderstorms in the skies.

Her beauty is imbrued by the weather
Painting her a natural perfection
As I stare upon her expressive being
That is framed by her tender affection.

    The thunderstorm conveys its strength amiss
    As we touch lips for a passionate kiss.
Josh Webb

Untitled

I think of you,
And the world slows...
to amber water colors, and
feathery flower petals floating
mid-air in a sea of your perfumed shadow
I blaze with love like a star.
The thunderstorm comes and rain crashes down
But the fury of the elements cannot
match the swirling tempest of my loud heart
that beats like a symphony of a thousand jungle tribes
a song of love for you.
Weaver of miracles and dreams you are
Yet so much more a sorceress
For you make me blaze with love
Like a star... when I think of you

Henry Bonano

'To Be A Girl'

The day you're born, if you're a girl,
and they name you Ruby, Jewell or Pearl;
That means you're special, but I must say,
a name can't wash the ugly away.
Goodness! It's hard to be a girl,
with stubborn hair that doesn't curl.
With blackened teeth from fast decay,
and eyes that go their separate ways.
Girls aren't allowed to eat this or that,
oh, it's a crime if a girl gets fat.
Never climb trees or shoot a gun,
games for girls are just no fun.
There's a way to stand and a way to sit,
it's very embarrassing for a girl to spit.
You should never whistle or chase a boy,
How, I ask, "can a girl find joy?"
A girl needs someone to understand,
her hopes, her dreams, please if you can.
She endures a life of push and shove,
just show her kindness mixed with a little love.

Jewell M. Wilson

"The Tear"

As a tear runs down my face I sit.
and think is there a way out?
There is got to be away out.
The pain is killing me,
I got to get out.
As I taste the tear I think,
why was I put here, what will come of it.
Am I like a tested rat running a maze that will never end.
As I wipe the tear, I think is death the answer,
if I kill myself will the maze come to an end
or will I just be letting the world win?

Amy Snyder

Untitled

I thought of you-
And tried to lose myself in little things all day,
To stay away-
   breakfast at the diner,
   carpool for ballet,
   details for the meeting I pretended must be done-
Yet I wished I were the rain
Blowing in your open window.
I wished I could have cooled your face
Like the rain.

Ann Ward Spaeth

Ode... To The Rules

...!The winds of time, brushed the sands;
   ...and waited for the next generation!

As before, they came, lived, learned, loved
   And left...footprints in the sand!
The winds of time awoke, and yawned
   And kissed the little grains of sand
Creating, once again, a tranquil earth;
   ...And waited for the next generation!

We came, we broke the rules...and left
   ...bloody footprints in the sand!
The winds of time aroused, rebelled,
   And returning to their slumber
Left the grains of sand,...as they were!
   ...Haunting testimony to an era past!

...But, the winds of time were wakened
   By a force from the Giver's hand;
And told to gather the morning's dew,
   Evening's dust, the rumpled sand;
And bring them to other stars—
   ...so the test could start anew!

Bernard W. O'Day

Hall Of Mirrors

Mirrors reflect distorted images
And we are low or high or thin or thick
According to the slant and shape of glass
Upon a silvered base.

Some corridors lie bright and clear
Where feet may find their easy way,
Others tortuous and dark, like shackles
Binding steps and burdening hearts.

But always there is one small door
To which love is the only key,
For friendship lies within this room,
That knows no line of boundary.

Here is the beveled plate—
The sane true glass
Limning the face of truth
Through friends who chance to pass.

Elizabeth Leathers

Tough Life

We've seen many a winter together
And we took some nasty falls.
We've been bitten by the pitbulls of life,
But, we've survived it all. Now we're
coming to a time when life gets even tougher
But, let's keep the faith and know that God
through times, trials, and tribulations, has
made us even tougher.

Gwendolyn Jenkins-Marshall

A Dark Darkness

Darkness envelops me,
and with sadness, I give into it.

Tears quit falling, and only their wet streaks are left
behind.

Peer into the darkness.

What do you see?

   Darkness, Darkness, Darkness...

Jennifer Williams

Determined Dignity

My hearts constrict's like a bleeding heart,
And weeps like a weeping willow
as I watch your struggle to stand without
holding onto your chair's pillow.
You ask for "Charlie"; your loyal swain,
which, in reality, is just a cane.
You use him now; as you, sway unaware,
away from your supporting chair.
Your face grows pale; each step causing exertion.
And you begin to weep as you give into exhaustion.
I remember the times that I stood and cried;
And I reach for your arm the way you reached for mine.
You look at me with tearing, tired eyes,
and you smile so graciously; it fills me with pride.
Together we walk; you Charlie and I and giving a resigned
sigh you resume your state of acceptance.
Leaving me with the reflection of your
tears mirrored in my eyes.

Joyce Hetzel

"What Makes Me Feel Special"

I feel special when people recognize who I am.
And when people are glad when I came.
I feel special when people understand what I say.
I feel special when I go to football practice and
make a big play.

People make me feel special at times.
Like when they treat me like gold instead of dimes.
I feel special when I'm the center of attention.
Or when my team is at the top of their division.

I feel special when I can do what I want.
Also when I have a trophy to flaunt.
I feel special when people enjoy me around.
I feel special when I find something no one
else has found.

Jeremy Willoughby

Vanishing

As the days go by, my body turn to dust. My desire
and will to live is decided by a must. My soul is all I
have left to dwell in this decomposing body. I am a walking
corpse among the all living.

I try with all my heart to have the hope and will
but when I stare into the mirror the hope and will has vanished.

These bones that were once a healthy body, these eyes
of black were once of color and liveliness. My heart that
once beat of the love I once knew. It now weeps of a coldness
called death.

And even though I disappear day by day and night
by night. Inch by inch and drop by drop. I try to think of
the days, when I will be free. My soul free from worry and
disease. No need for clothes, no need for purpose.

For God will lift me up into his everlasting, loving arms.
He my shelter, he my saviour. I'm back in my father's
arms once again.

Bernadette Maria Ayers

Beauty

Have you ever been in Iowa
And witnessed a tornado?
Have you ever seen Iowa the day after?

Have you ever been in New England
In the midst of a blizzard?
Have you ever seen New England the day after?

Have you ever been by the ocean
During a hurricane?
Have you ever seen the ocean the day after?

If so-
Then you know Beauty
And the Peace
  Soon to follow.

Anita Mallon

Love's Footsteps Heard, Remembered

Yes, the sacred hours pass
And yes, the blush of spring delights my eye
The rivers rush like music drifting down
From jeweled palaces on high

But I bathe in your sweet air
And breathe the perfume of this lingering moment
Through one thousand years of dreamy sleep
And open, ever thirsting deep

Are you still the small, pale girl
Whom Spring sees bringing water for each flower?
I see you thus;
I remember you when first your everlasting beauty bloomed

Am I your fragrant flower too?
Sweeter is thirst than the sweetest rain
If this unquenchable thirst draws you near again
With your eyes of dew.

Adam B. Rosenthal

Carousel

I am the carousel horse standing tall & proud
And you are the carousel to which I am bound.
Though it may seem you're not thought of
My life would be nothing without you, my Love.
People often wonder why I stay
When there are better carousels in Lands far away.
They tell of carousels much stronger & new,
But why should I change when I'm happy with you.
Though I've sometimes broken down
You always get me fixed.
We've often had our ups & downs
But never called it quits.
Now why would I ever Leave this happiness I've found
For you are what gives me life & what it revolves around.

Angela Griffin

Friends

Friends are there when you need them
And you are there to lead them
They are there to talk with,
And to even walk with
In your heart a friend will always be there,
But not always going to be able to hear you
A friend is there to trust
Although sometimes you must,
Leave a friend behind
Even though they will always be inside.

Jessica Waide

Untitled

When you fight to keep from fighting,
And you can't hold anymore
And there's a gun in the closet,
And there's a bullet in the drawer.
Even if he was your best friend, in your heart
You know he's not.
Maybe.
But that doesn't matter now, You think.
There's is no turning back.
Because once his life is gone, his death will become fact.
Another life is taken,
But you cant just walk out the door.
And you say to yourself,
Don't worry, there will be
Many, many, more.

Audrey Gallant

'Reflections In October'

Oh, I've tried to see the truth, but truth has fled our world.
Another assumption — Too many assumptions...What do we
   really know?
So judge, judge every person — and here is the fundamental goal;

After all, what is the tree falling, if you don't hear it?
Choices, so many choices, how will you decide?
Expediency rules all, Identity is left to die.

Reason, the Pure, is corrupted by our minds;
Already decided, the process is just...
Rationalization.

"Justice", "Justice" cries the people, and they feel great wrong;
Shall it be "an eye for an eye" or now "six months for drinking
   too long?"
Just, what art thou — underneath that
divine mask is mere retribution, vengeance.

Value not, the crystalline carbon; Possession causes strife.
The many rule the few—mob rule?
The few rule the many—apartheid?

Think, think of all,
Believe not the lies that you are certain are true;
Contemplate, know what you must do.

Jeffrey Liao

Not Too Long Ago

Not too long ago you could make me cry
Anything you did could make me blue.
Not too long ago you laughed at my good-bye
You said it was a thing I'd never do.
Yet, here we are today
With our romance at its end
To you it is a big surprise,
You really should have listened
When I tried to warn your friend,
You thought the stars were still there in my eyes.
Not too long ago I learned
   You were not the one for me,
So I've found a truer
   love to set my heart a glow.
This has been a bitter
   lesson and I'm so glad to be free,
Though it seems like
   ages it was not too long ago.

Frances Williams

Precious Memories Of Yesterday

In my mind all locked away,
Are precious memories of yesterday.
When my boys were young and very small,
Were blessed joys that I recall.
I hear the pitter patter of little feet,
Running to the T.V. to watch Sesame Street.
Toys were scattered all over the floor,
Along with shoes left out the night before.
They're forever messing up the house and more,
Along with forgetting to close the front door.
Here they come in tracking mud all over the rug,
Bringing me a jar full of lightning bugs.
Days can be very exhaustive and trying,
When there is fussing, fighting, and crying.
Then comes squeals of laughter and joy,
Oh, where would I be without these boys?
Years have forever gone and slipped away.
As for my boys, they're almost grown today.
But those precious memories of yesterday,
Are forever locked in my mind always.

Brenda K. Lark

Sunflower

Sunflower, passion's sweet yet oh so dour....
   Are you alone a lonely flower?
Would you have faith that winter ice is done
   Without first seeing the flowering sun?

Sunflower, can you alone take Mary's place?
   (A troubled heart, yet full of grace?)
Or will God Himself emerge with a smile
   And whisk us off to some Virgin Isle...?

Perhaps Saint Croix, perhaps Saint John...
   (Better yet, Saint Thomas is the one we're on...)
What true believer could then have doubts
   That we together wouldn't beam and sprout?

So Sunflower, remember, this is true;
You're a Sunflower, but I'm a Sunflower too!

Douglas C. Bonanomi

Soul Sister

Soul sister, soul sister, what's wrong with you?
   Are you feeling down and blue?
Soul sister, soul sister, are you afraid because
   everybody don't like your Black ways.
Soul sister, soul sister, can I ask you why you
   let all the important things pass you by.
One day soul sister you will never be sad......
'Cause you are a soul sister — that's why.

April L. Henson

An Unknown Place

Shadow of mountain all
around
snow and ice on the ground
the grassy rocks sticking
up
a light blue sky
a big bright sun
a grave, I can see a spooky one
If you have been there I'm sure you'd agree
it's a pretty place to me.

Geramie Morgan

Friend Or Foe

Blue Pacific, I want to know.
  Are you my friend or foe?
Sometimes you lull me into sleep
  With your gentle rhythmic beat
Then you are my gentle friend.

But at other times you rage and roar
  Like a demon outside my cottage door
And in your rage, you throw at me.
  Shells and rocks and weeds of the sea.
You even try to reclaim your sand,
  As if to drive me from your land.

But dawn comes with a healing hand,
  And soothes the watery neighbor of our land.
Then upon the beach I see
  The lovely shells and pebbles he brought to me.
So, please, Pacific, I need to know,
  Are you my friend or foe.

  Emma Feurer Roper

Don't Get Rid Of You

Is your world all dark and your heart is hurting bad
Are your tears as big as Raindrops pounding Mad
is your world in a frenzy you have no place to go
Your boat is hitting Rock bottom and the waters really low.

Is your vision dimmed by the sad tears in your eyes
Is your heart beating out the hurt as it cries
Is your life all messed up and you don't wanna live
Please, friend accept the help Jesus wants to give

If your sunny skies have darkened and a storm is coming down
And you feel that no one cares where your heart is bound
O friend don't entertain thoughts of getting rid of you
Don't put your body in the grave your friends have need of you

Your loved ones would miss you it would break their heart
If you by your own hand from this life depart
They would miss your warm presence and the smile on your face
The world without you would be a lonely place
There's a lot of things you still need to do
'Cause in the whole wide world there's just one dear you
And remember dear friend you are someone
And you could accomplish everything under the sun.

  Esther Otto

Untitled

Face partly hidden by a veil of shadows.
  Arms enclose me in a loving embrace; I rest
  my head, feeling the rhythmic rise and fall
  of his chest.
Shimmering black hair ruffles as the wind blows.
  Eyes that quiet me. Dark liquid eyes betray
  him by revealing every inner emotion in
  their depths.
Moonlight splashes the outline of his square jaw
and regal nose.
  The warmth of his body has an inebriating
  effect; my heart stirs restlessly in my
  breast.
First signs of sunrise appear as the night shuffles
to a close.
  Gentle words fall from his lips to form
  beautiful images. I am liberated! An oath
  of love has been confessed.

  Erica Lynn

Broken Dreams

The moonlight shone pale on the autumn leaves,
As a silhouette on the side-walk gleamed,
It was the shadow of a dream, held deep within the heart;
  A secret kept and never spoken, silence forever-never broken,
By the words of the wise, trying always to compromise with the past
and holding to the promise of a new day,
but never living in the present,
Because of fears and worries by which the heart is overgrown,
If only we had known, that one day all dreams come true.
  The sun shines bright now on the water,
Dead to the ever slaughter of longing hearts,
the soul departs from the captive,
It searches for a home in which to be ever loved and always free;
  Just you and me, me and you;
  Yes one day all dreams come true!

  Carmelle Dulley

The Washed-Out Glory

Far, on that butterfly wing, I rank myself
as a vanquished curiosity.
Even the glittering sun is aware of that
as I cast my own shadow onto it.
And though myself I burn, yet I do not shine
but I get myself warmth and all.
I am the last to know everything;
I am the last to show that I may grow and remember nothing.
Nothing can choke the passion and nothing can slow
the flow of the arrow in the heart of time.
I am the last blow to the echo below.
But...that it is written in ether and clouds where the world
is formless, that I am in frantic love with you,
should only tell the sweet prairies
and the same blue sky above them
that no more trembling are my hushed words,
that right through my unveiled destiny,
and the shut-in doubts that alarm me,
I will just yield and swallow you whole, forever.

  Fuad N. Ziyadeh

The Window

All homes have windows, from which we view
As do lives, from which we feel
Some windows are closed and shaded
Blinding the beauty beyond them
Some lives, or hearts are closed...Afraid of the past, present & future
At times these windows should be shut...
But we'll miss nature's miracles...sunrises and sunsets
Confused; whether to open the window, don't want to feel the cold
But longing for the suns rays touching me
One day I found a new window, I'm so scared
Most of my windows are shut, but I must take chances
I went to it, almost blinded by all the brightness
So beautiful, so warm. Should I open it?
Been fooled before...chances? The closer I get the more my heart
pounds. But this heart beat feels different
Can it finally be right? Hope so
My fingertips on the sill, must try
Feels so good, so right, suddenly a vision there you are
Still scared but less now, you're the sunshine, warning my soul
Thank you my new window

  Everardo Perez III

Ecstacy

As stars shine through the clouds of dust
   As do my heart, my love, my lust

My eyes are blinded with thou beauty in sight
   As darkness prevails throughout the night

  Your touch is light with heavenly bliss
   As if received your gentle kiss

  Your eyes are frigid, cold inside
To keep back the love you've tried to hide

  The fear you have is not hard to see
  The strength you need is encased with me

   Your hug is soft with gentle grips
   As is the touch of your virgin lips

  As our heart beats quickly in rhyme
So does this moment, slowly through time
   William F. Erwin II

"Earth Tourist"

I move about freely, from port of entry.
As earth tourist, I'm quickly absorbed
Into the fabric of this center.
No hold-up at customs.

So, I've arrived, itinerant that I am.
I bear no special markings - stay indefinite.
Just the antiphon, "Enjoy your stay"
I revel in anonymity.

Curious place this spot earth
Masses - all on mission
Some on business - some on pleasure
An admixture - somewhere in-between.

No hassle - no delay - on schedule
Little interference from on high
No "state your purpose"

Will the return trip be remarkable?
   Barbara Bradley

Phantom Of The Subway

  The spooky sound of a squeaking train,
   As everyone aboard looks on in vain.
   His mother should have known so far,
   His interest was in trains not cars.
  All around New York the teenager flew,
   Subway officials never knew.
  He loved trains ever since he was a boy,
   The sound of one gave him great joy.
    But this passion went too far
    Now he's locked up behind bars.
   Did he really mean to hurt someone?
  Or was he just trying to have some fun?
   This is what the judge is to decide,
    Is he guilty or should he slide?
    No matter what the decision is,
    Stealing is still a serious biz.
Most think he's guilty, and there's no question,
But it's not worth making an untruthful confession.
   Some grownups think that he's a rat fink
Well, why don't you tell me, what do you think?
   Geoff Cormier

Periphery Objects Animate

Everything ends in a question mark from yes to
as far as I know. The curriculum of my compass.
In a hodgepodge of your cigarette speak licked vowels
on the edge of your lips. Supple kisses fifty-fold.
Ism's and IA's throw up over the edge of the world.
Wampum fixes licking my velvet smooth of playgrounds
and celestial charts reveal splendor at 2:40 in the
afternoon dash -ER each day. In the faces
you've created your claim to beauty and spiritual
I.Q. and I the elder tree and yet a yes man of
Nothingness to himself and each other which is to
say cast after effect in the scream of boxcars
enchant out to everything in a flash of
periphery objects animate. Conjure larks profound
huffings, slackful sighs in our counting and I
in the A.M. Doing "pretty good" really means
Nothing at all with one last breath...
   Wishing.
   Herman W. Snell

Our Brother

Is there no place to hide when we must cry out in pain
As hurt from the heart brings burning tears to the eyes.
When a loved one has been lost a mighty door opens wide
As the feelings of great loneliness fills all of the inside.

Little things that we did not say and time had slipped away
Did we not really care and our love we did not share?
Pictures of long ago they all seem to appear so clear
As he was always standing close by as now he seems so near.

They say time will carry away all the sadness that we bear
And the sweet joy of his memory will forever linger near.
There is a place for the soul it will return to his grace
Just as the strength of his love will always be with us here.
   Joe J. Staker

A Love That Never Was

There was something in your eyes the day we met,
As I looked into them I was captured by a net.

That net I thought it to made of love,
Oh how, you look so gentle and soft like wings of a dove,

Yet now I see you holding someone new,
The tears I cry I wish were few.

I can not blame thee for my
feelings you did not know,
Not you that walked away but 'tis I who let go.

In the shadow standing alone,
My heart as cold as stone,

Yet now you see me holding someone new
The tears you cry you wish were few.
   Chasity Eubank

" How Can I Describe Thee?"

"How can I describe thee?" As a shadow on
as light? As the sun is to morning, or as the
moon is to night. As the gentle falling snow,
or as a blossomed flower in spring? As the
tide crashes to shore, or the lullabies birds
sing? As the autumn leaves fall to their
untimely demise, as the pure white clouds in
the shimmering blue skies? As a sea filled
with tranquility flowing to a part? As cupid
shooting an arrow right through my heart?
Until I find an answer, the pondering
question will be, from here to an eternity,
how can I describe thee?
   Jason Monroe

Song Of A Wayfarer

At first we two were strangers met
  as leaves blown by the autumn wind.
No passion stirring deep as yet,
  no thought of you e'er crossed my mind.
But love foments strange chemistry
  in hearts which serve as crucibles.
We fathom not life's mystery,
  but yield devoid of strength or will.
And so, a slave to Eros bound,
  bereft of purposeful design,
came I to sacrificial mound
  forsaking all for love sublime.
Surprised I was to feel no pain
  as Aphrodite took her toll.
Instead your heart was mine to claim
  and endless bliss became my goal.
Since then we both have known the joy
  and thrill of nature's alchemy,
That magic spell the gods employ
  has joined our heart eternally.
   Burton Rubin

Seasons

Autumn seeks her place,
  As lonely trees shed their tears.

One small blush from summer's face,
  Tells nature and her friends that winter nears.

We breathe the fresh breeze,
  While the bluebird glides with grace.

The earth's smallest creatures hide their winter feast with cheer,
  Down they float, the small, the large, flakes of lace.

We sense no fear, just share with contentment;
  That winter is here.

The winds are humming from mountains tall,
  As the smallest drops of ice form a waterfall.

Lazily "Beings", large and small, send treasured melodies,
  From afar.

Announce the call, to share spring,
  Nature's loveliest season of all.

Soft warm clouds gather as in a bouquet,
  Shedding their tears on the growing wonders of the day.

In full blossom, summer gleams,
  Happily her gaiety, her warmth, her dreams.
   Emily B. Moffett

Untitled

It was like singing in the wind,
as soft gentle voices whispered over a field,
it wasn't like anything I've heard before.
Then it appeared that I was in another land,
looking into a lake so pure so clear,
the grass around me so perfect
as like silk blowing quietly in the wind.
The peace inside was more than I had ever felt.
I felt myself rise above a magnificent tree
to see more of the beauty of this world.
I had never seen a land so warm and beautiful,
this surely had to be God's land.
   David Charlton

Private Shawn's Requiem

What will it matter where I lie
As long as meadow larks sing clear
Or wakening birds their morning carols sing
Sea waves may wash my quiet feet
That restless, challenged turbid surf of old
Or, deep in jungle morass I may lie
Where none can find my earthly form
But what matter that?
My soul shall be at home
That tiny spot of soil, or sand, or sea
That claims this earthly part of me
Will be my home, though far from home
So, let me rest where'er I fall
Nor burden ship with what remains of me
I'd rather far my dust return to dust in Vietnam
And mingle with the dust of heroes there
For gulls will shriek, and larks sing clear
And tides sweep in on Hammonassett
The Sound's sweet chantey born of sea and sky
Will sing "Requiescat" where'er I lie.
   Eileen McGinley

To My Mother

You were my best friend and my Mother,
As my confidant there was no other.
My days with you were a pleasure,
The memories of which I'll always treasure.

I was your one and only child,
Your love for me was gentle, mild,
Your precious love was from your heart
My heart is broken since we've had to part.

Your lovely face I can no longer see,
I miss your loving arms around me,
Your advice and counsel were for me only,
And, now my days are very lonely.

You are the sweetest angel God ever made,
Now God has called and gently bade
You come to your home in Heaven above,
Where you are abiding in God's perfect love.
   Darlys J. Hegge

It Was My Mother

It was my mother who rocked me upon her lap,
as my eyes slowly closed for an afternoon nap.
It was her voice that sang so soft and sweet,
as she tenderly smiled and touched my cheek.
It was my mother's finger that I held as I learned to walk,
and her name that I spoke when I learned to talk.
It was my mother's nervous "good-bye", as
I rushed off to give kindergarten a try.
It was my mother's applause I heard the loudest, as I performed
in my first play........ I knew she was the proudest!
Upon my sick bed, her love I could clearly see, as she would
pray, "Lord if the sickness must be, please take it from my
child and give it to me".
It was my mother who wiped all the tears, and stood beside me
strongly through all my years.
She rejoices in my achievements as I knew she would,
and gives me a hug and says "I knew you could!"
It is in her eyes that I see the fear, as each year I grow older.....
and adulthood is near. Here is to you, my love, dear mother.
And to replace you, there could never be another.
   Brenda Lynch

Mother

I shall love her till the end,
as she has always been my friend.

Her love can mend a broken heart,
and yet she never falls apart.

But the tears she cries for her son,
must mean that she can come undone.

To see her smile though,
makes life much more worthwhile.

She is persistent yet patient with me,
these are all good things I see.

A rose reminds me of her; the beauty,
   strength, and protectiveness all are there.
To none can she compare.

How did she come to be this way?
Perhaps her mother loved her in this way.

How do I love my Mother?
I shall say, more than any other.

   Jonathan Doyle

My Grandfather

He was as quiet as a cat,
as tall as a giant,
and as loving as a mother could be.
The feeling of his hands were as big and
as warm as an oven mitt.
The sound of his loving, caring voice made
you feel safe and secure.
And the sight of him seeing me—-
play,
eat,
sleep,
talk,
or walk around, hit him in the heart with
an arrow of happiness.

   Adam Sankey

Good-Bye

My face looks like a tomato,
As tears run down my fragile face.
As I feared the dark day I had to say good-bye
I want to bring her back,
But I know there's just no way.
Why her?
Why did God have to take her?
I get so mad at him sometimes
I even say I hate him
I know that's mean
But I can't help how I feel
They say she died of fibrosis of the lungs
At 63,
Can you believe?
I try not to cry,
But it's very hard,
because I miss her
I miss her very much
And I guess that's just
Something that I'm going to have to accept.

   Ashley Holtgrewe

Three Seasons

In the orange and golden splendor of the Autumn leaves that fall.
As the blue and sparkling water of the brooks echo to the call;
That ice will soon be forming on the rivers,lakes and all,
Then the birds wing their way southward, when nature says it's fall.
When winter with its barren branches will glisten with the frost,
Then we'll know that in nature, that not all is lost!
When the newly fallen snow looks like frosting on a cake,
And nature in all its wonder, that only God can make;
For Spring is just around the corner, for the green
   will spring forth soon.
And the flowers in all their glory, will be destined again to bloom.
First the crocus, then the Lilies which depict the resurrection;
Followed by the Tulips and the Iris which arise in adoration!
With spring abounding everywhere, it will chase away the gloom
When the trees will soon again come to life, and shoot forth bloom.
It shows that God is in His Heaven, and rules from glory up above.
And all is well nature, as He rules it with his love.

   Patsy Gfeller

Waste-Land

I sit here and think about the forest,
as the flowers sit there and glisten with the
fresh scent of nearly fallen rain
As I sit outside of my little red log cabin and
listen to the fresh mountain water trickle down
the side of the hill,
Spring finally is here and I'm enjoying the
fresh green valley of grass below surrounded
by trees.
As the buzzing of bees and wasps surrounds
the valley flowers
The deer below graze in the meadow grass
while the horse run free.
The smell of the chilly spring pond with
a batch of fresh fish floats through the air.
Now I sit in my peaceful place just 3 years
later watching in horror what has been torn by
reality…humans have destroyed Gava (mother earth).
What then was my beautiful, peaceful
place is now…a neighborhood waste land

   April D. Richardson

Beaumont The Bass

The ripples fade across the water
As the stout old bullfrog bellows his call.
The yellowish green moss floats undisturbed
And Beaumont the Bass sees all.

The houses and trees are mirrored,
But you can still see him lurk
Beneath the weeds and cattails
As bluegills emerge from the murk.

He is so sly, sneaky, and slick,
All twenty-three inches of his frame.
No one can stand to keep him hooked
As he continues to play their little game.

His lip is torn and puffy
Because of some hard yanks from Mom.
But he still chases her bluegill
Until the day she drops the bomb.

That night we'll have fish for dinner
And Mom will proudly display
The remains of Beaumont the Bass
That is now a crispy fillet.

   Angela Condra

To My Mother

At the end of the day...
as the sun sinks from the sky...
I look out from the window....
and remember happy days gone by.
I think of the picnics...
of Sunday afternoon rides...
and of the trips I had with you and dad.
I remember your tenderness...
and your loving care..
the fragrant scents that you would wear...
My love for you will always be..
as strong as when you were here with me.
With memories like these...
it could no other way...
and Mother, I know you hear what I say....
when I talk to you at the end of the day.
I love you.

Betty Checksfield

The Tapestry And Life

I sat and listened quietly today, contemplating
as to what this man was trying to say.
He was speaking of a tapestry, and what it's all about.
I admit that while I listened, I was confused, filled with doubt.
"It all depends", he said, "on which side you stand,
whether you are the lonely drummer, or the leader of the band."
A tapestry on one side, shows tangled threads and disarray,
When it is turned over, a bright and shining day.
It's a picture of contentment, that puts your mind at ease.
A feeling deep within you, leaving you real pleased.
Is life so much different?
It depends on where you stand.
Whether you're the lonely drummer,
Or the leader of the band.

Jackie Buckley

Seeding—Thoughts

Our deeds are examples of us,
   As trying to be kind;
    Like loving our - divine:
Goodness, oh me - Goodness! -is-Us!

Mis-treatments or mis-understanding of Lusts;
Living death, not to be - love in kind
And not loving our - Divine
Deeds are seeds; We so know, our Good deeds-are just.

I:We, They - plant seeds with idea;s, with people, and with—

   Nature; Planting my seeds, planting my deeds —
   And waiting for the harvest to come in! -INDEED!
They, us, me; - sweats our brows; plow; sow; Began Growing Wits!

Ladies and Men; - Looks at our fields of harvest of seeds
And in deeds; -reaping our deeds or our weeds;
Constructive deeds or destructive weeds;
Nature and life beings - Humans - our deeds from seeds for needs;

   Indeed; Indeed!
   In!!! —Deeds!

Howard Wendell Raleigh

My Dad

He said he'd always be there and never let me down
But every time i think about him it makes me wanna frown
The only time i talk to him is when we're on the phone
And ninety percent of the time i'm alive i feel like i'm alone
Having my dad not around makes me feel kind of strange
But i love my dad with all my heart and that's never gonna change

Joey Marshall

"Long Ago Night"

On a night long ago it all began
As we gazed at the stars while walking in the sand
The same shooting star we both did see
My wish came true, I loved what was happening to me
Day by day our love grew and grew
As memories were made of a love that was so new
Together we learned
For each others arms we yearned
You were always there to listen to me
I thought our love would forever be,
The kind of love that never ends
The kind of love where problems always mend
Then somewhere things went wrong
I couldn't figure out what, it took me so long
Then I finally thought it through
I concluded that it had to be me or it had to be you
My conclusion was wrong you see
It wasn't you and it wasn't me
It was the changes that occurred in the both of us
Since that night long ago which I loved so much

Amy Morgan

Warrior

Young gang member probe your mind and
ask why(?)

Have you really used your imagination
and thought about what and who you could
really be effectively(?)

Young gang member love of self will
destroy genocide
Of course, we can't only point the finger at you.

For the world's values have declined
tremendously thus confusing mankind -
Don't shoot people, however, abortion is okay.

Young gang member don't adulate celebrities
and their wealth
Set up treasures in heaven and help somebody

Don't deface our city with territorial
manuscript for life here isn't eternal;
hope in God for there's hope in you.

Gloria J. Crump

"Why Me?"

In the corner she lay crying tears of pain,
asking
Always asking
"Why me?'

Whenever he had a bad day,
or came home from the bar,
He would take his anger out on her.
"Why me?"
She would still wonder.

Black and blue she would go to school,
Her mother pretending she was a clumsy child.
But she knew the truth!

He never gave her love or compassion
Never showed guilt or sorrow
Only a fist full of hate.

She was only a child.
A burden to her parents.
Never speaking a word.
Only wondering
"Why me?"

Chea Sanchez

"Faith Of A Child"

One morning while I was down upon my knees
Asking one more time for strength, praying
For my own needs, oh God, will thou help me please!
At that moment I heard a sound and without
Turning around I watched my little girl beside me, kneel down.
Her hair still tangled from sleep, she had just awoke.
She bowed her head, placed her hands together.
And I listened, as to God, she spoke.
She thanked God for the flowers, the trees,
Her healed skinned knee and for mommy and me.
Not once did she ask for him to meet her needs.
The faith of a child, I thought, oh God,
Forgive me for my faults, for you have used this
child for me and a lesson I have been taught.
Teach me, Lord not to pray for the things
that I seek, but to be humble and thankful
When to you I speak, for I know thou has
Been with me all of the while and
Thank you Lord for the faith of a child.

   David L. Jones

Thanksgiving

Thanksgiving is a happy, delightful day,
At least it is what most people say.
Families come to our Grandma's by the dozen,
That's when the house begins a buzzin'.
There'll be all the trimmings with turkey and dressing,
When the table is ready, Grandpa will say the blessing.
Fun and games are enjoyed by all,
And someone will say, "My, You've grown so tall!"
As the day is over, you are sure to hear,
"Goodbye, see you again next year."

   Dixie W. Whitmore

Scratch

Scratchin'...scratchin'...
at my door they're scratchin'.
They want out, they want in
they want death, they want sin...
and they keep scratchin'...
   I know it's true, and I'd be it, too;
   and my mind's trapped in a world surreal...
   But there's a scratch I feel inside,
   deep in my mind and for real.

   And I cried for you, and I'd have died for you -
   but somehow I knew I would never.
   Wherever it is I was scratched inside...
   it's deep inside and forever.

And all these strange people...
   keep on scratchin'...night and day.
And all these lovely people...
   keep on sratchin'...scratch away!

   Gus Facchini

The End

Grasses turn to ashes as we slowly fade away.
Years go by one following another.
We count the days till there are no more.
There will be no more pain or suffering.
The day comes closer ever moment of our lives.
Many are afraid but so few aren't.
Beauty and wonder will grow in our places.
Peace and harmony will last forever in
the end.

   Jaime Lillis

The Cry Of The World

   Tears being shed signs of pain and sadness
At one point in time I would of sworn, it was madness.
All the anger, all the hate
It all builds up inside
You can't keep it locked up
It's something you can not hide
   So as I shed these tears
I sit in a world of silence realizing soon,
That when my tears have dried up
I'll be back in the real world of violence.

   As I breathe my last breath
A moment alone without a tear in sight
I know that someday soon
They'll be only tears of happiness
And I know someday
   Everything's going to be alright.

   Jackie Whitehead

Once Upon A Time

i knelt by my bed
at the end of each day
to offer wishful prayers
or prayerful wishes -
i was never sure which,
or if it made any difference.

i would shut my eyes real tight and pretend
not to be there at all,
and whisper so even i couldn't hear.

i used to fall into sleep waiting for an answer.
though i haven't stopped praying/wishing,
i've risen from my knees
and opened my eyes
and cried out
loud enough so everyone could hear,
but, i'm still waiting.

   David L. Pickering

Sentimental Feelings

There is a girl who goes through life with a happy aura

When she was younger she flew to visit her grand ma-ma

She returned with a lovely pair of golden earrings
Ohh, la, la

One day sad she had to say
That one of the earrings had gone astray

Her ma ma also in dismay, has kept the other for a special day

Ten years later, a new recycling wave is here to stay

And so for my girl is her special day

Open the box and peek right in

A beautiful earring pendant for her on her wedding
day to remind her of grand-ma ma from far away who
could not be here on her wedding day.

   Johanna C. Voss

Don't Seek Love

Don't seek love, it will find its way.
Awaiting its presence day by day.
Searching high and low, an endless game.
But to find out today is just like yesterday all the same.
Loves bound to find one who's in need.
But will not proceed to one who's within greed.
The greed and need for to misuse Love.
Only one knows who's true,
He controls from above.
So don't seek love, it will find its way
Till then live life easily day by day.

Anthony Ferrer

Sojourn Of The Sea Souls

Lo! The wind shrieked! Screaming through the black mournful night.
Aye! The sea rose up, Huge dark waves crashed, Smashing on the slick,
weathered rocks, This age old song echoing its frightening chorus.

It be no night for the weak or lame. Aye! Even the brave and strong,
sat shuttered, quiet and tame. For this night, the wind and sea ruled.
Even before man came, and after he though he had. Nay! Their has
never been so stout a lad. For all that men can do is take warning.
On the sea, a single light, a lone beacon, till it be morning.

Since the first sea soul, at the opening of time's door. Stood on the
first foredeck, searching the horizon. Wondering where he may be
bound, outward from the land. And the sea unchanged, neither by time
nor man. Its fate rests with a higher land.

Now today if you went to sea and stood before the mast, the waves
breaking the spray over the bow. The wind in the rigging sail and
hair. The smell of brine and salt in the air, Aye! to feel the deck
heave below your feet, all these would be the repeat of time
transcended, for then you would be there on that very first day, that
very first voyage, for only here can the spirit be ascended, only here
for all time sea souls be extended, and so this sojourn has
not yet ended...

Joseph F. McMullen

Reasons

God has his reasons for everything in life.
Babies that have gone on and you can't bear strife.
Mothers that die so young it seems I feel there's a reason,
maybe there's an everlasting dream.
People that have gone on and rest for life.
They live eternally and try to help us through our might.
God has a reasons for the things he does.
Which does not kill us, makes us stronger,
for those feelings you don't deserve.
For all the deaths, every minute of everyday
there has to be a reason.
It will puzzle us till it comes our way.
So don't be afraid of his loving hand.
God has a reasons he made is all his fans.

Carrie Nichols

I Sat In School By Myself

I sat in school by myself,
back to everyone I thought not like me
I sang loudly the sound no one needs, my sound
I stared out at a wall slightly grey

No one could see the face I hid from the crowded race,
full of savage children filled with hate
Leap over the fallen gate, the door to my world

Thick metal horn-rimmed glasses focus the world I am blind to
I see boys pull my hair, girls crying, frightened
I can not play hopscotch or kickball, I see only the wall

Chad Clouse

Remembrance From The Heart

There I stood,
baffled...
Lost deep in beauty,
but to shy to confront.
I moved on,
the girl never leaving my mind.
It stuck in the back recess of my mind,
like a thorn embedded in the skin.
Again I saw her,
her beauty striking my central core.
I waved,
and received the same motion in return.
A streak of excitement raced through my body,
I had been chosen by one from many.
Strange this world is...
How one so charming, delightful, and gorgeous,
is so far away,
but is always on my mind.

Brett Michael Miklavcic

Though I'll Miss You, I'm Always With You

Though today you may weep and cry
be happy, too, please try.
If you continue to think of me tonight
remember that I'm not alone, I'm with Jesus Christ.
Though I'll miss you, I'm always with you.

Five years from now, do not think of this day.
But, please for me, think of memories of yesterday.
One day we will see each other.
But not now, that day is much further.
Though I'll miss you, I'm always with you.

Don't think of me as a person dead,
But as a living angel instead.
If someday in the future you need me;
Look deep in your heart, that's where I'll be.
Though I'll miss you, I'm always with you.

Angela Stanley

Treasure

His hands full of gold he came to me,
Bearing a gift, and I could see.
How proud he was of the riches he brought
And I loved the joy of his giving and sought.

For words of thanks to let him know
I liked his gift of gold, and so
I said, "They're beautiful, man of mine!
Dandelions in this vase look fine.

His heart full of love he come to me,
Bearing a gift, and I'll always see.
As he grows and shares some new - found gold
The joy in the face of my three - year - old.

Ellen L. Evans

"Night Fears"

The warm golden sun is rising,
Beginning a brand new day,
And all the fears of the night are passing away,
The warm gentle breezes blow
Over my skin like it's whispering to me again,
Take courage be bold,
This day offers treasures as yet untold,
No need to fear the nights,
God blessings and peace before me unfold,
And in his sweet presence my soul delights.

Barbara Russell

The Truth

Terrorists of salvation, did you get a good deal?
Beast in priestly robes, your heart forged of cold steel
How long are you hell bound, how long do you grace the wheel?
Evil boils in your soul like acid in the pit
Hell fire, brimstone, salvation stains your spit
Broken back philosophers, the truth is not the truth

Selling what heaven has in store
Like it's your personal coordination
And paying for some cheap street whore
For a little uplifting conversation
Evil runs through your words like acid in the pit
Hellfire, brimstone, salvation stains your spit
Broken back philosophers, the truth is not the truth

Holy rolling heretic laughing off the stage
your black hearted holiness stealing from the poor
All the hate and fear that fuels your rage
Stands you at hells fiery doors
Evil burns through your heart like acid from the pit
Hellfire, brimstone, salvation stains your spit
Broken back philosophers, your truth is not the truth

Deanne Smith

A Moment Remembered

In a spring time in a place not so long ago, a boy caught a beautiful butterfly in a jar to show. As he ran barefoot through the wild flowers and grass of green and gold, he thought to his grandfather for the beauty to show. As the grandfather looked at what the child had brought, the child said "Isn't it the most beautiful thing you have ever seen?" The grandfather replied "It is beautiful indeed, but I can think of one thing in beauty it will exceed." The grandfather laughed and smiled as he set the butterfly free to float from lilac to tulip to fruit tree. The child exclaimed. "Oh grandfather, I see." "Oh no," said the grandfather "the beauty is in a moment shared just you and me."

Allan Wayne Deela

Beauty

Beauty comes in many forms, many ways that it can be.
Beauty in the trees and flowers, in the changing sky, the sea.
Beauty in the sweeping wing, as a seagull soars on high,
Beauty as dark thunder clouds, scud low across the sky.
Beauty in the raindrop snared, on a silvery spider's web.
Beauty like the rainbow arching, high above one's head.
Beauty in the flower that opens, for the bumblebee.
Beauty in young birds at nest, high in the willow tree.
Beauty in the baby's cry, or in a joyful tear,
Beauty in the hand outstretched, to draw a loved one near,
Beauty in the heart that is light, or one that is filled with joy.
Beauty in the sweet young dreams, of every girl and boy.
Beauty in the world around, everything that we can see,
Beauty comes in many forms, so many ways that it can be.

Doreen Teves

Rosebud Unbloomed

The rosebud unbloomed, unbloomed
beauty that seems never to unfold
its beauty for the world to behold.
Should a buddy prune this rosebud that
never blooms. Will it bloom someday or
not? Question? Prune the rosebud
unbloomed or wait for its beauty to
unfold. Such beauty inside that's agape
love in the name of Jesus Christ, who
died on the cross for forgiveness of our sins.
Unlike the beauty of the world that quickly
unfolds dies and withers away.

Daniel Tomlinson

I'm Not Ready

A favor I ask of you, is to only hear me out.
Because, I want to tell you, what this is all about.
I do love you, but I have to be free.
Because I have needs, if you could only see.
My love for you, is for real, but you have to listen
  to how I feel.
You are really satisfied and really glad, but in me, I'm actually sad.
Sad because, I need my space, I need to be able to take a gaze.
A gaze to something I like to see, something that I
  love, something that is me.
You're afraid, of losing my affection.
But, this is causing my feelings, to go the wrong direction.
You want this to really last, but you're making me,
  grow up too fast.
I'm not ready for this kind of commitment, because I'm young.
But, if we stay, it won't last long.
Maybe, it's better if I'm free as a dove,
  because, I'm not ready, for this kind of
    Love!

Elizabeth Flores

Becoming

I haven't arrived but I'm becoming,
Becoming all He wants me to be.
With you walking here alongside
You too will become the best that you can be.

There are no doubts about this love I feel,
There are no doubts my love is true.
The fact is I've waited all my life
To find a godly man who could love like you.

Your tears of joy or sadness
Flow unashamedly down your cheeks.
Those tears display your depth of character
No one could ever say you're weak.

The tenderness which you express to me
Is ever present in your voice.
The looks of love in your blue eyes I see;
God couldn't have made a better choice.

The words I use to express this love of you
Can't do it justice, they seem so trite.
So the best I can do is love you
And fall asleep with dreams of you each night.

Cathy Macklin

Destiny

My soul has been captured, my heart has
been broken.

Such a void in my life, a crippling loss
of spirit, of hope.

Each day of my unfulfilled existence
becomes more devastating, every hour and
every minute more painful.
Why such sadness?

Don't destroy me, come back to me.
We'll realize our destiny.

Don't leave me, love me. What is meant
to be will be.

Angela Nichols

Untitled

Woman on a ledge, debates on how to fall.
Beggars all around the crowd,
crying out to eat. Blades
tear into flesh, wounds that
always bleed. I watch destruction
stomp and growl and seethe.

Life soon may be ended. Holy man
take my hand. I'm leaning toward the
lunatics: a roach crawls through my
head. Apathy seems so close to me,
a presence always there. A wall is
closing in on me, but I don't really care.

Today I start my pilgrimage
into the promised land. A locust
swarms, my blood runs thick, a
boil makes a home of me. Watching
while the hinges break, the door
falls I can see, visions of the
land of peace that dance,
Beside the sea.

Gustine E. Fudickar

Woman's Power

For every man's victory
Behind is a woman;
I could not remember
Who said that;
But whoever it was
Woman or man, it is a fact
That cannot be denied.

Egypt's Queen Nefertiti
And India's Indira Gandhi
There were many more of them
Who influenced their men.

Now it's Hillary Rodham
On Earth's most powerful man.
But the woman who most influenced her man
Is the mother of God the son
Who has the greatest influence
On earth and beyond.

Christa S. Cuento

Price Of War

Many a hallowed out bullet shell,
Blood washed away by rain.
What stories people could tell,
Of horror, agony, and pain.

Of a child's last cry,
And a lover's last kiss.
About people who gave one last try,
Who were bold and fearless -
And ready to die.

To fight for a country with honor at stake.
For a nation which would be free,
Whose freedom and honor no one could take.

Erin Barry

Untitled

Nothing, Oh nothing; dear precious friend
Can happen to you today;
That has not passed through the hand of our Father,
And met with his okay.

Darlene A. Cook

Ocean Breeze

The ocean breeze
Blowing with ease
Way down through the ocean floor
Where the small creatures sing
And the big ones swing
Through torture and trouble galore
We're destroying our creatures red, white, and blue
All patriotically dressed too
I don't know why but the sadness makes me want to cry
The sun will rise
The sun will set
But you have not discovered yet
The secrets and treasures the ocean holds in its depth.

Helen H. Cho

Spring Fling

Warm spring breezes
Blue ocean, white sand
A tanned woman with a voluptuous figure
A tall, tanned, lean man
Eyes staring into eyes
Chemistry on the run
Walking hand in hand
Sharing thoughts, having fun

A Beautiful sunset,
Candlelight dinner for two
Soft music playing too

Touching, kissing, hugging, wondering if they would be making
love tonight.
Everything going just right
A full moon, two silhouettes swaying to the music
Bodies so close, so tight
A love happening, "A spring fling in sight!"

Carol E. Lewis

Time

Time runs on, a fast moving stream.
  Blurring our life, changing what we've seen.
The past is done, the present is now.
  And the thought of losing it can make you foul.

Time runs our life in its cruel order,
  It makes us strong, then weak, we get older.
We are left with memories only, shades of past.
  And they are almost lost in time, it moves so fast.

Yet with time there is a certain joy.
  Like seeing a man where there was once a boy.
He will live a full life, like you,
  until time catches up and ages him too.

We are trapped in the time-line of life,
  where ages of peace pass to strife.
The good ol' days are long since gone,
  replaced instead with tired yawn.

Time is something that demands to heeded,
  and is, unfortunately, something that is needed.
For, even though time takes our life,
  without it we'd have none at all.

Brian Joseph Laughman

Dark

Dark is frightened, dark is scared,
Dark is dull,
Dark is a blanket that covers us all.
Dark is when mother nature turns out the lights,
  and says "Good night."

Julianna Kettenburg

Time Lost

Wind driven rain against the windows
  blurring visions of leaden skies

Whilst clouds of birds go swirling, swirling
  hunting warmer climes.

Rain hissing from a hundred tire tracks
  bursting up like dragon's breath

As tail lights darting, ever darting,
  twist from lane to lane...

... and here we sit, warm and dry,
  cocooned in colored metal

Looking, straining toward our home, sweet home...

... as time, never to be contained,
  rushes past us in the rain,
    never to be regained.

Janet I. Broad

Among My Souvenirs

My souvenirs have no need to be wrapped in tissue folds,
bound with bits of fragile ribbon and nested in the faintest
of sachets. It is true that I am often as unaware of them
as though they were, indeed, trinkets waiting an opportune time
to be brought out and held in my hands or letters waiting to be
re-read for the sake of remembering; for, sometimes, these
treasures are misted over with conscious thoughts and deeds.
Yet they do not always wait until I reach for them of my own
volition; rather, they pass in review at diverse times and places;
on a busy city street or in a quiet room, in the still of the night
or when the sun is high. They are in a tinkle of laughter,
the tilt of a head, the murmur of a voice and footsteps in
the entry hall... all of these and uncounted numbers more.
It matters little that they sometimes bring a heartache or
the sting of sudden tears; it is a small price for the riches
of remembering or for the knowledge that I am a part of these
souvenirs intangible.

Ada Ashley Smith

I'll Think Of You

As the day turns into dusk, and dusk takes on the night, each
breath becomes more labored. The voices from without
are harsh and loud as patience wears thin at dinner time.
Only the silence and your breathing can I hear.
Our world, us alone, after 47 years of knowing one another.
So much I can't recall, lost with my childhood and your prime.
Were the good times so few? Crowded out by pains that never healed.
You're going to leave me. Our chances to mend fences have run
out, but still I want to be here.
I want to be beside you when you go. I want to see the peace
when it finally envelops your weakened body.
I want to see you smile when God calls your name. Then and only
then will the pain be gone.
Your limbs will straighten. You'll wrestle no more with the
logic of a disease that you have fought thirteen years.
Successfully done till now and you succumb to its strength,
never complaining, never giving in.
But fight no more. You've done all you can. Pass and rest assured
those left behind can now reap the sowing of better summers past.
And when I hear someone say mama, I'll think of you.

Joyce A. DeWitt

Dear Maine

Reach up my friend to gather the stars
Breathe deeply, peer round horizon afar
Exude your feelings, dance in the rain
There's enchantment mystic here in maine

Sail the bays, drift close to shore
There lie the forests' natures own to adore
The eagle, osprey, heron on wing
Dolphin and seals, round the jetty's fling

High above on cadillac's summit
Venturesome gulls do plummet
A restful pause on the rocks that surround
Breath taking panorama that abounds

I'll long remember your lands and shores
The green, the blue, the ocean's roar
Some future day with God's permission
I'll be at your borders seeking admission

Howard Wise

Little White Ripples

Little white ripples dancing so free
Bring back memories so dear to me
Of moonlight pauses by you quiet stream
And aircastles built in a heavenly dream.

Oh sing a love song of one so dear
While I kneel quietly and pretend she is near
In holding her hand and awaiting one kiss
I wonder if Heaven could hold such bliss.

But on little ripples away to the sea.
Your love song so sweet are not just for me
Other lovers are awaiting both view and belle
To fall completely under love's magical spell.

Charles Vernon Booth

Old Love

Seeing you again for the first time in so many years,
brings a wave of mixed emotions.
I'm afraid to look at you for too long, for I start
remembering:
    the gaze of your eyes,
    the gentleness of your touch,
    the sweetness of your kiss,
    the strength of your embrace,
and all the rest of the memories which I pushed away
and keep in my past until
Seeing you again for the first time...

Debi Sanders

Modern Mountain Man

Not a teepee under the stars,
But a rugged cabin in which to live
Not a modern electric furnace, but a large coal heater,
Never a fire on the ground.
Not all leather leggings and things, blue jeans,
Shirts and such as these. But homemade moccasins to wear.
Not a mule to carry his stuff, a beautiful horse for riding loose.
Not two sticks rubbed for a fire lit,
But a homemade knife handle of chokecherry wood.
One hot plate with which to cook, not always cooking in a dutch oven.
A lonesome howl of a coyotes duet, a guitar played to hear a song.
No water inside, that would be a treat.
But electric pumped from the well in the yard. Not carried from the
creek. But alone on a little ranch he sits,
completely full of bliss. Dreaming those dreams, about days gone by
But never really having to try. He's alone but not lonely
He's a satisfied modern mountain man.

Charlotte M. Peiler

Above The City

Above the city, a bird is weeping
But a skyscraper has no branch
only iron claws,
and a heart of concrete.
The bird comes to Central Park
to be consoled.
I can't understand his message
in another tongue
among the dry cries of the autumn leaves.
I can't decode his shorthand
on the red sand.
I can't ask the tree
that lost its green word.
But sorrow is a mirror in any mother tongue.
And the city is watching us,
a weeping bird,
and a concerned man
with its apple eye.

Albert Batienon

Self-Indulgence

Unconscionable indifference prevails, errors re-echo,
   but as guilt commands for correction,
   acknowledged blame and apologies - unspoken.

Scapegoat: Come forth old friend! Assist in sanity!

Regret willingly emerges - yet stamina lacks in the
just modification of these circumstantial times;
   wandering endlessly and so ineffectively,
   we scrutinize within our powerless souls,
only to calculate and then conform to selfish desire.

   What demons have infested us to such redundancy,
    then destine us on empty roads
   secreted with unyielding hatred and anger…
    … in essence, lose control?

Awkwardly, candor beckons. We hesitate.
Displeasing images now crushing our passive memories;
this reckless cycle thus evolved, so clearly defined!

Our world of amicable peace and unity exhausted…
… hidden just beyond a haze of lingering confusion
   where self-indulgence has oozed upon us -
   society now in havoc, expectations dormant.

Darlene A. Lytle

A Story Of Love

In the beginning, we were like two vulture's fighting over our prey,
But as we grew up, we were like two puzzle pieces meant to be together
And in the end, someone came along and broke
   us apart like a child would break a new toy
Leaving a part of him with me and a part of me with him
Never forgetting what we had shared, each longing to hold the other
And say three little words that would mean so much
I love you would be those words

At last, we had finally gotten our wish, we had seen each other again
He had come to my window, first happy to see me
But then with his wind blown hair and cold
   body, I saw a lonely tear streak his face
And I knew things weren't right
He said he was moving and our parents,
   wouldn't let us see each other anymore
When he told me this we just held each other and cried
Then he said he had to go and we said our last good-bye
Hoping to see each other again
But now that I sit here I realize that I'll never see him again
I can only hope that love will stand the test of time.

Angela Tankersley

Peace And Freedom

Peace and freedom is what they preach
But death and destruction is what they teach
You say you know it all
But I know one day the truth will fall
Through the sky
You ask why
And if I told you, you would not believe
For our destruction you have conceived
And now it's time to die
Bombs floating through the air
Children cry, but what do they care
Apocalypse and revelations
Our earth destroyed by these nations
So why do we even try
Our time to die will soon be near
There's nowhere to hide, so why do we fear
That peace and freedom
Destroyed in the end
Death and destruction
The message they'll send

Alex Barrett

Declaration Of A Mother's Love

A mother's love may keep you out of trouble
But God's love will keep you in perfect peace
A mother's love may keep you going
But God's love will sustain you

A mother's love may fulfill your wants
But God's love will fulfill your needs
A mother's love is strong
But God's love is stronger

A mother's love has great depth
But God's love has no end
A mother's love holds great hope
But God's love has no doubt

A mother's love is great insurance
But God's love is blessed assurance
Mother is family
God is an eternity….

Jennifer Mobley

Torn

   My heart, memory, and life is there
    But I am here
   Held back by some great force
   Now standing still, unable to move,
    I am torn
I cry and my heart breaks to see what might have been
    Maybe just maybe
They would accept me for who I was and no longer am
    Will I be that person again
   Or will I have to wait for another lifetime
    To live the life I once knew

Colleen O'Brien

I Wanted To Give You The Sunrise

I wanted to give you the sunrise,
But it wouldn't fit in my pocket;
I wanted to show you the dawn,
But the sun left the sky.
I wish I could give you time:
   days and nights to spend here
   so you'd never go away.
But the second hand refused to stop ticking.
Still, I wanted to give you the sunrise.

Bethany DuVall

Dazed And Confused

It really doesn't seem like it should matter
But I guess it all does
I know I'm not worthless
I just feel like it
Things just seem safer in my room
With my music on
And all my problems spinning around my head
I get depressed because I'm depressed
I get homesick at home
There is a world out there
I want to go to it
But I'm scared
Does any of it matter?
Do I matter?

Adam Huening

I Will Always Remember You

I lie down to fall asleep,
but I start to cry, when I should be counting sheep
You had just become my friend
then your life came to an end
you were too young to die
my heart aches to know why
I keep expecting you to come back and say I'm not dead
but you're truly buried in a grave instead.
I know life goes on
and as time passes the hurt will be gone.
saying goodbye by your casket full of flowers
my heart became empty and I cried for hours.
The car procession to your grave was half a mile long;
God, please tell me what went wrong!
Your clarinet and friends flowers they buried with you
in your best sweater, and wedding ring too.
Now in the band room at school sets an empty chair,
it's all in your honor but your death wasn't fair.
I will play my clarinet my very best for you
and wherever you are, know that I will always remember you.

Dee Morrison

I Had Snow For Confetti

The church bells were ringing as I sat alone,
But I started in dreaming as the winds sighed and moaned.

I was a bride in this forest of wood.
The trees were attendants as stately they stood.
The groom was a redwood with arms big and strong,
And with snow for confetti we couldn't go wrong.

The aisle was of earth's best all covered in white,
As the sky shed confetti with all of its might.
Our guests were the birds all perched in their nests
And the songs that they sang were only the best.

Then we danced with the wind when the wind was ready.
And we laughed with each other, I Had Snow For Confetti.

Jo Gio

Close Your Eyes

Can you hear the birds rise? Listen!
Can you hear the sun as it dies?
Have you heard the night turn to day? Listen!
Can you hear the children pray?
have you heard the hug and the kissing?
What about the love that is missing?
Can you hear the clouds in the sky? Listen!
Listen to the winds cry.

Davetta R. Edgell

Dead Reckoning

The fog is thicker than I remember
But I wanted to escape quietly
My body feels heavy with weariness
The night's moisture collects on my skin

Sound of the pounding waves gives me direction
Hope in my heart keeps me warm
The searching light of the moon is reflected
But until another cloud...I duck for cover.

The army of waves call me join them
Dark predators lurk below the surface
But I am still drawn by the soothing rhythm
Making no sound as the boat awaits

I step on a thorn and glance back to the wild rose
The waning bloom collapsing in to itself
The chorus of wind covers my sand prints
As I row softly out to sea -

Carol Kalil

Freedom

Some people always follow the crowd
But in my rule book, that's not allowed.
I like to be different
Unlike the rest.
I want to stand out
That is my quest.

When you are different, your spirit is free.
And freedom is something special to me.
You're free to talk.
You're free to scream.
You're free to walk
And run with a team.

Freedom is something we all want to use,
But we mustn't let it become abused.
When we gain a firm hold,
Of our actions and voices.
We are in control
To make better choices.

Deven Feher

Chaotic Companion

I held you for a short time,
But it is as if you were never here.
Unable to live unless holding your hand,
But may feel you as chains around my limbs.
I reach out to grab a hold of you,
But you are running farther from me each day.
Sometimes, others see you beside me,
But that is only my shadow,
You were once my companion,
But now your presence can be frightening.
Like a civil war, we allies fight.
You have been gone long, and your absence seems eternal.
Should I bring you back?
Joy, contentment,
Happiness.
You have many names,
I think I'll call you "Confusion."

Ayesha Najam

Who Prepares Us

School, it seems like a dirty word
But it prepares for what lies ahead
You probably hate your teachers
For giving you too much homework
Or keeping you in for recess
But what they were doing
Was preparing you for the real world
They teach us not to fight
For it leads us to trouble
They teach us to read and write
To add, subtract, divide, and multiply
They teach us about the world
Of long ago and the present
I know I'm not in the real world, yet
But I'll be there soon I was once told to thank
God for the good and I always do
I tell him to thank
My teachers in a way that I can't
Because without them I won't be
Where I will be someday.

Jennifer Sanders

"A Marital Tragedy"

I remember when our love was new,
but it wasn't long till I was black and blue.

Why did it have to be this way.
You always blamed it on the things I would say.

Now I'm not saying there weren't good times too.
The problem was they were far and few.

You promised things would get better time after time.
The problem is, you don't believe what you do to me is a crime.
I know now, no matter what I say or do, I don't deserve to be abused.
So for once this is one fight you're going to lose.

Please don't cry and beg me to come back.
I'm finally starting my life over, and am on the right track.

Now I'm not doing this to hurt you, nor am I trying to get even.
I've just got to allow my mind and body to heal, and do some
much deserved grieving.

From our tragedy I hope a lesson can be learned.
Abuse doesn't bring forth love and respect, those thing have
to be earned.

Carolyn Simpson

Untitled

LOST
But knowing where I stand
Confusion
The cry of souls, or maybe the cry of my heart
The fright on the yellow blood stained bricks
The sun burning down
On my shoulder, burning a hole
Not noticing I'm bleeding
Not noticing the stranger behind my shoulder
Trapped
No way out No way out
Gag, grasped by the neck
Dragged along the hateful yellow bricks
Legs scrapping along
Like a sharp razor, ripping off skin
Leaving a trail of blood behind
Not noticing the choker
Not noticing the death

Ariel Vorhoff

"Gone To War"

Once again we are apart
But not by choice this time
You've taken a stand for God, country and corps
Others freedom on the line

In a foreign land and for untold millions
You've put your life on the line
You may not understand why at first
But you will when you leave them behind.

Most Americans don't even know
That you have gone to war
"When did they go? Why weren't we told?
Don't we have a say anymore?"

Americans may never understand
Why you fight for what you do
But judge they not a U.S. Marine
Till they fight a day in your boots.

So God Bless you and everyone
Who fights for freedom and truth
And know the one's you've left behind
Are the loved ones you'll come back to

Cathy Perkins

Dogs

Dogs are pretty,
But not like a kitty,
Their mean and lean,
But seldom green.

Dogs don't own cars,
But sleep under stars,
They don't get mail,
But they wag their tail,

They have a big mouth,
But don't migrate south,
Their either bit and cute,
or small and astute.

So don't you be fooled by this tail of mine,
Because they're sometimes called by the name of canine,
Now this is the end of my youthful rhyme,
I've got to go cause I'm out of time.

Jason Rader

Untitled

I slipped away in the midnight rain,
But not to bring you sorrow or pain.
So, please try to be happy for me,
a better place and God were ready for me
Wrap yourself in memories of me
and please just let the sorrow flee
Remember the laughter, remember the fun
Know even now our friendship's never done
Although I've gone and you stayed here
A simple thought will bring me near.
I leave behind the best of me in you
Do all the things we wanted to do.
I'm not dead - I've simply moved on
As will you with each new dawn
So hang in there! Be the best you can be!
Always remember you reflect a part of me!

Barbara F. Jones

Dianna

I use to wonder how twins came about,
but now I know without a shadow of a doubt.
We must have been best friends in heaven,
'cause remember when we were only seven.
When I was hurt you took my place,
God had to give you that loving grace.
We must have shared one big heart,
And God knew He couldn't tear us apart.
He knew you'd need me to help you along,
He knew you'd need me to make you strong.
And I thank Him every day for sending me with you,
He must have known I'd need you too.
And if I leave this world before you,
I want you to know I'll still see you through.
Just hold out your hand and I'll reach and touch,
I want you to know I love you that much..........

Donna Akers Pickett

Why Don't We Care For Our World?

Free land for miles and miles to the sea,
but our land is in jeopardy.
We're lazy and we don't stop to think, it's not fair.
We take all for granted and we really don't care.
Why don't we care for our world?
Why and how can we destroy something so good?
We could help the world to survive for the future,
but we're all too dumb to understand.
We're suppose to be so smart, but smart we're not.
I feel for my next generation,
because the world won't have a lot!

Eileen Haerle Stinson

A Moral Blown UP

She was chased,
But she wasn't chaste.
I think the reason she was chased.
Was because she wasn't chaste.
However, the reason she wasn't chaste
Was not because she was chased.
She just willingly let herself go to waste.
P. S. what a waist!

Agnes Hutchins

Halloween

Halloween was not then night
But simply more exciting days of play.
Out alone, no parent within sight,
Uncompromising grocery sacks open all the way.

Familiar houses, well known in common light,
Broached venturesomely but with courage gay.
No hesitations, sure that all was right;
Undistinguished apples huge then our sole dismay.

Or raisins. Despised, of course, but sweet within the bite.
Devout in hope within the chocolate day,
Roaming still beneath the quite night,
Unfeared, uncared, I thoughtlessly, with careful hands, display

Treasures white or glowing silver wrapped;
Penny bought and waxen sweet and trapped.

Joanna Gould

True Love

Relationships usually start out, as a physical attraction.
But that alone never brings any real satisfaction.
A relationship isn't a matter of lust,
But a real relationship is a matter of trust.
Relationships if true, there's no need to control,
But to hold you when you're blue, in an attempt to console.
How do you know when your feelings are true?
When you respect one another, and each other's view.
A real relationship doesn't start in one day,
But over time of listening, what each has to say.
A real relationship, you will work at, you will tend.
A real relationship, means a friend in the end.
If you can say yes to all the above,
Than this feeling, your feeling, is that of True Love.

Janet Coffey

Glass Houses

Glass houses set upon a crystal shore;
But the glass has all been broken, and the foundation has been torn,

What once cast a bright reflection, now a broken image falls;
And the beauty that was in them, no more remains within these halls,

As the sands of time flowed past them, and at times had cast its stones,
Yet still they remain standing, each one shattered and alone,

And aren't we all glass houses, each one weathered by the rain;
Each made of several panes of glass,
which get cracked in times of pain,
and at times we just feel shattered,
Broken pieces fall within our soul;
We wish someone would pick them up, so we could once again be whole,
And just as we first began, a perfect piece of glass without a mar;
Yet all the cracks and broken pieces, is what makes us what we are,
But we can build a new foundation, and mend the broken panes that be;

And we can cast a new reflection, then we will truly see.
That aren't we all glass houses.

Alan Nicewander

Our Mothers

There are holidays and then there are holidays
But the one I like as none of the others
Is the one we celebrate in May
To honor our dear mothers.

For mothers are the kind of people
That we all should love to know
For they look upon their children
With their hearts all aglow.

It matters not their children's troubles
Nor the kind of trouble they are in
The mother will stand beside them
And help them through, through thick and thin.

Then as they grow to adulthood
And go out in the world to see what they can see
There isn't a mother who is a mother
But what wishes they were little, playing around her knees.

Mothers are a big necessity
as anyone can plainly see
If it wasn't for our mothers
Where the heck would we be?

Boyd Moffitt

Animals

There are many different animals with many different names,
but there aren't any animals who look and feel the same.
There are dogs and frogs and even ostriches
There are larks and sharks and flying partridges.
There are bears and hares and red/white foxes
There are baboons and raccoons and big old oxen.
There are rats and cats and caribous
There are ducks and bucks and kangaroos.
There are many different animals with many different names,
but there aren't any animals who look and feel the same.

   Dana Barnett

Untitled

We haven't much to offer except a lot of love,
But we thank you for giving us life and God from above.
We thank you for standing by us in our many times of need,
For drying our tears and mending our hearts without one drop of greed
We thank you for just being there even when we were unaware,
There are no parents in the world that can even begin to compare.
With these thoughts we give all our love,
To the greatest parents God ever created from above.

   Diane Gossett

My Precious Brother

When there is someone that you feel so close to
But when someone comes along and takes him away
Then you realize what a fool you have been.
Oh How I wish I could have my precious brother back
Have him as close as before, never have to fight again.
But in the end I will sure get what I'm fighting for.
I know that will never be possible.

My brother and I are close, but yet so far away.
I really realize how much that he has changed
I will never feel so scared in all my life.
I feel like I'm getting the knife through my back.
I really don't care if I get anything for Christmas All
I want is my Precious Brother back.

I never thought that this would ever happen
It feels like someone drove a knife through my back.
This is the only Brother that I have, why not share as
much time as possible.

My Brother has no clue how I feel, I guess that he will
never know how much I care for him.

   Jennifer Warren

Fathers Day

Happy Father's day to a man a who isn't here,
But who's spirit and soul, I feel, is near.
When I was 15 my father died,
Several of nights I stayed up and cried.
My father was kind and gentle,
His love and tenderness was thoughtful and simple.
I never thought he'd go away,
until one morning I woke up, and he
wasn't there that day.
Sometimes I ask and wonder why?
Sometimes I sulk and sit and cry.
I never thought we would part, but his
kindness and memories still live in my heart.

   Amie Denner

Friendship

Through all the years people have come and gone,
But you were so special that you found a place in my heart.
Through all the good times and bad,
You still manage to put up with me and I with you.
I know you better than I know myself,
And you know everything I want to do before I do.
If I have a bad day I can turn to you for guidance and a smile,
and you can do the same.
Lately it seems as though we are growing apart,
But I know that could never be.
We are so much like one that we will be together for eternity.

   Cindy Disney

Our Love

Love means a lot of different things to everyone.
But your love means everything to me.
Your love to me is as bright as the sun,
And your love is wide and deep as the sea
When you hold me with your arms
so strong and very tight,
And when you kiss me with that sexy
month of yours,
I know that everything is alright.
But baby your love for me is something I cannot deny.
My love for you is very true. When we tell each other
that we love each other, it is not a lie.
Because you love me and I love you. We have the true meaning
of happiness together. We know what love is to show our
affection for one another. Thank you for this wonderful
feeling that you give to me. It is called love and is all
that it shall be.

   Ann Baskin

The Glades

My spirit has been stolen!
by a silent bandit in the night, under the pale glow of moonlight
through the wooded path he runs, silent as a hawk stalking prey
the black willow whisper amongst themselves
as the deeper shadow slithers by
a wandering vine reaches for this stealth but he has slipped away
Past the silent silver well beyond the magic forest glade
out upon the fields he waits to steal another's soul one day
all is lost, none is found there upon the open ground
where no man dares to pass, this thief defies the sacred land
He belongs to the night
and where the wandering soul may be, there be the thief to steal again
Oh this ruined soul cries in agony as its body's an empty shell
What tragedy, sorrow, and pain, to have one's soul be ripped away
nothing can ever be the same
as this gypsy thief remains
out in the fields beyond the glades.

   Bonnie Thibodeau

"Always"

You always make the pain go away just
by the gentle words you say.
You always wipe my tears and help me
face my biggest fears.
You always seem to pull me though just
by saying, "I love you".
You're never very far behind.
I look over my shoulder and
you're there every time.
I guess what I am trying to say,
is that I love you in every possible way.

   Heather L. Bloomfield

Crushing The Spirit

The government does it:
By making people dependent,
putting them on reservations and in ghettos.

The schools do it:
By regimentation and labeling
students and putting them into sections.

The churches do it:
By defining how the holy spirit works,
so only clergy can control the sacraments.

Business and labor does it:
By defining jobs and categorization of
people's talents and duties.

Families do it:
By put downs and ridicule,
neglect and abuse.

But the spirit lives!
David Moe

Yesterday

Yesterday - in my little red car I rode
by the place where you sleep
Yesterday - I was reminded of you with floods
of memories and salty tears
How many years has it been since you
vacated by life - two or three, maybe more.
I was always bad at time
Yesterday - I saw your face blur by my
windshield like an eerie mirage
Yesterday - I heard you speak in an echo
of time and a shout of "hark"
Life, cruel life, to spirit you away
from me leaving emptiness - crueler
still, to offer me no one in your place
Yesterday - I thought these things as leaves
turned gold and fall descended
Yesterday - I was incredibly sad and
depressed that you were gone
Donna Mokry

Going Home

The pup said to himself one day when the people
came to see and they opened up the kennel door,
"I bet they've come for me!"
"I think I'll take this one right here. I really do
like her." She stooped down, picked him up and
said, "This is the one I prefer."
Upon her shoulder he laid his head and took a little sigh.
"I thought you would never come" he said, "but
now we can say good bye."
She held him gently and cuddled him.
The pup was quite content.
He settled down and went to sleep as off to home they went.
Ertha Lipmanson

The One That You Love

When your life is as bad as you think it
can be, just think of the one that you love.
When misery is spelled out as far as you
can see, just think of the one that you love.
Think of how it feels to have them by your
side. Think of how you'd look forever to find
someone as kind.
Think of how much you love them and how much
they love you. Think of how there isn't anything
either of you wouldn't do.
Jennifer Zimmerman

Conquer

One lonely heart defied by all
Can it mend to some sanity?
Days last forever and nights are cold

The world is cruel and its people
They too are stabbing daggers
Into the hearts of ones who trust them

Should we fear what we do not know
Or do life's trials ever cease
Is there truly a calming at the end of the storm?

I ask myself,'is there a destiny for me?'
Or is someone playing games with my every emotion
This pain can't last forever, or can it

The beautiful colors of fall seem faded in my eyes
My heart is like a mountain of ice
Waiting for my tears to melt it away

Shadows fall around me, I am trapped
Will there ever be light in all of this darkness?
Yes, for I am a pillar of strength, and with time
I will conquer my dreams!
Amy J. Smith

On The Virtues Of Solitude

Silence.
Can you hear it?
Its resounding rhythm is played by an ethereal orchestra.
The gentle magic of its song caresses the heart
And sends shivers of stillness up the spine.
Silence.
Can you see it?
Its quiet pervades the very essence of existence.
The sublime tranquility courses through fixated eyes
And captures precious moments in crystalline perfection.
Silence.
Can you feel it?
Its gentle touch brushes against the skin like the breeze.
The creeping, mystic fog flows with the consistency of honey
And tastes just as sweet.
Benjamin Hedrick

"Where Are You My Friend"

Where are you my friend?
Can you hear me?
I miss you....
Your long illness take you away for me,
Why?... Why you?....
You were too young
Eighteen years, old, what a beautiful age.
But your candle wasn't strong enough
Your heart was weak, too weak to keep going
I feel could...
What is it?
Where am I?
I don't recognize this place.
Why is it so quiet
Who are you? I can't see your face
You... are... my... friend?! and that's your home?
Your home is a ... grave?
No, my friend I can't go with you,
But someday we will be together.
And now I have to go.... good-bye my beloved.
Barbara Fudali

I'll Live Forever

With my tired old heart, with blood pressure high
Cancer has left its mark, with diabetes makes me sigh
A triple bypass it needed, so those doctors say
If I don't live like a Saint, I'll not last another day

My bright old eyes are still shining, trips are on my mind
Looking for a new venture, a good one I hope to find
My heart pain slows me, but my nitro is ready and it's cheap
A high risk I study, and I'm ready to take a big leap

I've lived a life of plenty , smiles and tears have passed my way
I've thought, planned and built, dreaming of another day
That day had has now come, much sooner than I had thought
If I had known how fast, the more I would have fought

But now I'm happy and I smile, good news has just reached me
When you leave this life forever, a new one you'll see
The gates may open for you, or the fires will brightly burn
IT's how you've lived your life, for a good hereafter you yearn

The devil says he does not want me, his life I would upsct
St. Peter has locked his gate, to open it he would regret
So no one wants my tired old soul, to pass over is never
I'll live like I have in the past, and I'll live forever.

John W. Crow

Band Of Gold

A band of gold, a gown of white,
Candles flickering the softness of light.

Organ music playing, "Here comes the Bride,"
Daddy's buttons bursting with pride.

Mother clinching her handkerchief of lace,
remembering the child, the innocent face.
Memories floating abound as voices echo without a sound.

I am startled by the hand I hold,
for soon it shall bear a "Band of Gold".

Betty R. Honerlaw

My Love Is A Burning Fire

My love is alive like a burning fire,
Can't you see I'm not a liar?
If you realize these things,
Maybe you could finally spread your wings.

Sometimes I do not see,
Why you actually love me.
But after all and all come together,
Nothing can break us, not even the weather.

Even after hardships and hate,
I will not leave you with any fate.
I promise these things, till death do us part,
For you will always be in my heart.

Angie Bledsoe

If God Only Knew

Look around but don't stare,
Cause the dam will break and up goes the fare.
As the stakes increase your freedom is lost,
Now you must abide by the boss.
Polluted waters flood the child's mind,
Soon there will be no healthy fish to find.
Link by link the chain slowly rusts,
If he knew would he do what was just.
Throw the rusty chain into the sea of death,
And take the children's last breath.

Dave King Thanx

"Time To Grow"

Where has the time gone and what will become of the
carefree life I have known? Will I one day hold the star
that I so anxiously reach for or shall it be to far for my
restless soul to capture? Some days I am but a child romping
through the fields of yellow daisies that I hold so dear in
my memories still yet I am an adult, living my own way making
my own decisions and feeling the many stresses mother had
said were just around the corner. So overwhelmed with thoughts
of failure I retreat momentarily to the seclusion and security
of a short lived childhood, wishing on so desperately to prolong
the time before I must make the long challenging journey down
the unpredictable road of life with its many detours turns and
steep hills, I pray that I have the courage to turn my back on
the past and strive on to the future, the will to climb the hills
upon my hands and knees if I must and the knowledge to read the
signs along the way, though it is scary, this I know, whether
it rains or shines, it's my time to grow...

Brooke R. Schuler

Ruby-Throated Hummingbirds

Hummingbirds are artists when building a nest
Carefully it is sculpted into a petite abode - the best

Her house completed, two white eggs she does lay
The size of a mall bean, or so they say

When the babies hatch, she alone provides food
Thrusting insects down their throats for their own good

Heaven help those who venture near her little brood
Or her feeding ground - she will attack larger birds - it's understood

She flits from flower to flower
Gathering sweet nectar hour after hour

Several kinds of hummingbirds thrive in the west
They, too, build a tiny nest

From the Gulf of Mexico to the Atlantic Coast
Only one variety of hummers we can boast

Ruby-throated and beautiful they are
The widest range of all by far

Fun to watch in their vigorous flight
Too soon they disappear out of sight.

Ann Clarkson

Untitled

The weight of the hollow is becoming immense.
Carrying around this cored self, step
after stumbling step.
I was in love with him loving her.
Third husband.
Third daughter.
The miracle of a circle finally complete.
Before the hollow.
Before being cored.
Before the disclosure by my second daughter that
"Dad's been messin' with me..."
which meant that my ten year old
was unwelcomely touched
by the man who touched me with welcome,
and all that I was up to that point,
happy content trusting new mother old mother fell out
on to my living room floor,
to be replaced
by weight of the hollow.

Christine L. Julian

Untitled

The birds are playing on the wind again
Catching the sun in their wings
Riding around in an unseen playground
Searching for a goal blind to others
How do they know which route to follow
In that sheltering maze drowned in blue?
Do the trees call out from their lonely shadows,
Does the heat whisper to retreat?
Carry my mind on a feathered plane
Across the course of instinct
Open the closet to my void of knowledge
So I can see with innocent eyes
Dance with me on the clouds of night
Tiptoe through the shining purple fog
Beyond that haze we shall waltz
For we have no conception of fear
Come outside with me as children
Laugh and chase the world not caring
And when the birds stop their gamboling
We must return to the cold

    Jessica Stuart

Infinity

When I think of you, there's so much more I see
'Cause memories come sailing, sailing quickly back to me
I remember the laughs, the dreams, the tears
Every single thing that we once used to share
And then I start wondering all over again
What things will change, and what things will remain
Seasons come just once a year, and birthdays too
But the joy that comes with them, could never quite
compare..to the joy of loving you.

Sometimes it's really difficult to be so many miles apart.
But we always treasure those extra special days, deep inside our hearts.
Coupled together with the knowledge, that the light is still
glowing bright.
Like the moon and the stars, that never fail to shine at night.
And so it makes no sense wondering
I just have to keep on remembering...

We've been through so much now, that it must be absolutely true
When they tell us that nothing in the world, could ever come
between us two.
The joining of our souls as one, is a symbol for all the world to see
And we are bound together for all of infinity.

    Hyacinth Roach

Father

Help me to be less religious and more sincere.
Change my fears to faith.
Open my heart to appreciation of life.
Bring joy in little things.
Keep me mindful of your presence to know you.
Allow me to master the mystery of prayer.
Lead me into maturity and understanding.
Make me a person of quality.
Assured me you are more real than reality.
Make that still, small voice repeat itself louder.
Continue to be my contentment.
Show me how to comfort others.
Hold me close even when I resist.
Remind me I don't exist without you
Ignore my shortcomings but make me see them.
Please don't judge me yet!
Help me to use and give back your gifts.
Give me grace and honor in old age.
Change me, refine me, console me, use me.
Perfect me before you come again.

    Dawn Byrne

For My Family, Friends And Beyond

In the midst of blinking lights, clinking glasses, sounds of cheer,
I take a momentary respite, close my eyes and invite Him near.

Engulfed within the Yuletide glowing,
Lead me to a stillness, knowing
How best to serve those I treasure.
Gifts of matter scarcely measure
A love that spans all time and reason,
A caring heart that knows no season.

Show me how to demonstrate more compassion,
To compensate for errors made through sheer frustration.
For giving to others, I gain salvation.

Yet not the presents, but The Presence
Links my soul to yours, in essence:

We are one. And so to you I give my self.
And wish for you pure fulfillment
In health, in truth, in hope abiding.

Love I send you, and with it, guiding strength,
A shoulder for leaning;
You give my life meaning!

    Cynthia Cline

God's Aerialist (Chickadee Circus)

Aerialist performing mid a shower of confetti
Chickadees soaring midst gently falling snowflakes
Swinging from aging, benevolent oak to the now
   deserted garden bench
Outside her utility room window
Echoing their movements, the lady swung clothes from
washer to dryer
Offering a silent prayer
Giving thanks to God for artistic rendition
   of their performance

    Doris Brubaker Walter

Child

Away from here,
Child!
You do not belong here,
wading in the crystalline stream.
Go away from these enchanted fairy tale woods,
Child.
Spread your wings and fly!
Reality is knocking at your gingerbread door,
Child.
Leave behind your skipping stones
on the banks of the stream.
Leave behind your spinning tops
on the nursery floor.
No more days spent romping
amongst the roses in the garden,
Child.
You do not belong playing here anymore.
You are no longer
Child.

    Alissa Raasch

I Am Apache

I am Apache, rage of first rainstorm,
Child of the Water, spring of the morning.
I rise from dark hidden caves,
challenge and slay the giant beast.

I am Apache, brother to the fox,
kin to eagles, kin to bears.
I run free through deep arroyos,
on desert grasslands flush with deer.

I am Apache, lance of victory,
thunder, my charger, lightning, my shield.
I wear feathers of First Chief
avenging spirits of our dead.

I am Apache, stronghold of ambush,
enemy in mountains, twister in deserts.
My burning arrow asks no quarter
when war paint flares, war drums beat.

I am Apache, blood of battle clouds,
flesh of rawhide, dust of Mother Earth.
I ride the Great Mustang in hidden canyons,
sacred and deep, after Usen burns my wickiup.

   Harvey Mendez

Does Anybody Care?

Crime in the streets and Cops on the beat
Children homeless and starving and people dying
People committing suicide after losing their jobs
Is there an end to all this misery and fright
Does anybody care?

What if there was no amusement parks
Or fairs with rides to play on and go around
What if there was no Walt Disney World
Or a Mickey Mouse or Donald Duck and friends
To watch and pretend with and laugh with
Does anybody care?

Did the floods hurt the farmers?
Will the fighting stop soon around the world
In countries such as Somalia or Yugoslavia?
Will peace and happiness come this time?
Or when I die will it all be the same
Does anybody care?

   Danny Burdick

What's Going On Here?

Just what's going on here, in America today?
Children never listening, to what their parents say!
Teachers are expected, to control and even teach.
How can kids be taught at all, when they're out of reach?

Out of reach, out of hand, out of bounds to all.
Living on the edge of life, waiting for a fall.
Balancing on a tightrope, daring all who care.
When they're out there on their own, see how they will fare.

Guns are easy, drugs are easy, stealing's easy, too.
Take the "easy" way out, don't work like me and you.
Stamp on people, shoot or stab, take whate'er they like.
After they are satiated, it's then they take a hike.

Can we stop this torrent, of waste and want and greed?
Can we turn the pendulum back, will we all pay heed?
This country was a mighty one, when structure did abound.
Our innocent children have been lost, they're nowhere to be found.

Permissive parents, permissive schools, permissive governing law.
Keep the underachievers down, down and out, and raw.
Inert from the lack of caring, dulled by neglect they known.
Perhaps they'd be productive, if guidance and love were shown.

   Judith Bienfang

Clack, Clack The Clicker-Knock!

We swung our great clicker-knockers together then,
clacking them into one another and watching the
sparks leap from the clicking balls.

   Clack, clack the clicker-knock!
   Click and clack around the block.
   Mine is big and yours is not,
   but they all beat around the clock.

Those things were made illegal when we were young,
because they exploded. Yet, I think we all regretted
their disappearance. We hid the remaining knockers in
our chests, chests which we open now and then to try those
knockers: will mine finally explode?
Doesn't matter. The danger is all the more exciting.

   My own knocker is old and tired.
   It is chipped mostly—smooth in unshapely spots.
   Lime-green, it dangles from frazzled white thread—
   waiting, as an object must, to be matched.
   Waiting for my chest to be unlatched.
   Within or without, alone, alone, the knocker does not knock.
   Has it been so far around the block?

   Eric R. Burns

Tent Caterpillars

The tent caterpillars, we noticed them on summer
clinging to our house.
We didn't take them as a premonition or anything.

We still played on the swing set where we did acrobatics,
and taught ourselves how to swing and jump off in midair.

We'd sit on the cement steps picking caterpillars off the house,
and slicing them up with kitchen knives
like loaves of bread.

We would go worm hunting.
The white tents, crotched in young trees,
looked like innocent piles of snow out of season,
but up close we could see the black rot squirming inside.
We would cut the trees down,
and burn the nests with kerosene in our wheelbarrow.

It wasn't the kind of thing you'd notice, the rotting, that is,
not when you were in the middle of it.
But we felt how we'd been short-changed later.

We were sore and empty from the scars and holes left in the wood
and it easier to blame the tent caterpillars.

   Beth Young

"Visions"

A hill of clover, a sea of blue
Clouds puffy white, and visions of you
Memories so clear, loneliness so real
Life has brought us here, left us to worry
about the very near

A sky so black, so many twinkles of light
My heart still yearns through the night
Feelings strange, worries me so
Unsure of how to act when I'm alone with you

Beautiful fields of flowers, rain a soft cool mist
Rain upon my face, traces of lonely teardrops
Feelings of pain, grips an already tender heart
Needing to pick up where somehow we just stopped

A warm summer breeze, sun so warm
Walking in the sand, bodies touching, hand in hand
Talking, laughing, sharing once again
You touched me, held me, made it all so right
Now it's us, every night, for the rest of our life

   Elizabeth A. Hecker

Looking For Me

Estranged days scramble themselves
conditioning normalcy.
cascading and parading
their grid sores infinite.
Chaos has discovered a pattern in the self.
standing amongst the panel
protruding from two-dimensionality
we reflect and our reflections ring true.
As days go by we see the self.
it is what we have become, that we have yet to change.
Grasping, asphyxiating ourselves
we search for normalcy
in the mirrors of the conditions around us.

    Bret Bunke

Tomorrow

Always tomorrow, we live in the future,
constantly planning for another day,
saying that they can wait another day.
Always in the future, we glance at our withering faces
and say that rest will take its place within us tomorrow.
And what of those who wait for us?
How long will they entertain, at evenings table holding a place
for us to descend and take our place?
How long will the children sit so still
within their growth and worldly needs
waiting for the love to flow, to become a total family?
How long before the years have passed
and the elders come and take us back
to a place that we have never been,
except in dreams and future whims?
How long will death wait at the door for your visit to ensure
that you have lived out one of your dreams?
'Tis such a human tragedy, that you never said goodbye
for fear you'd lose your place within
your future dreams and inner whims.

    Christine Neuhardt

General Semantics

General semantics will indeed a pleasure be when all our responses are
    controlled cortically;
When our thalamic notions are deader than dead, left to the use
    of the quadruped; when those ancient
    ideas of Aristotle are safely sealed up in a little bottle;
When we make every little assumption flow from our minds like the
    tides of the oceans;
When four dimensions measure our entities and we relinquish false
    identities;
When our thinking methods are in extension, and we've safely
    hurdled the fourth dimension;
When with differences and similarities we have everyday familiarities,
When maps and diagrams reveal the story of every little territory;
When we avoid the "is" of predication and adopt
    to-me-ness with dedication;
When our electro-colloidal behavior is such that the problems of life
    dissolve at our touch;
When we can always be our age and never more shall stoop to rage;
When Alfred Kozybski's concepts we've learned and life's approaches
    scientifically turned; then, life will no longer be a calamity
For we'll have mastered "Science and Sanity."

    Junia E. Shambaugh

The Nightmare

In the soft dark, I lay waiting
Counting cold whispers, silent echoes.

In the soft dark, the dream begins
Shifting, flowing shadows of wintertime syrup.

In the soft dark, dimming light, emerald heat
Ghastly, chilling screams and smiling beasts.

In the soft dark, cherry embers cry
Ancient, evil eyes, wasted rotting flesh.

In the soft dark, mad children sing
Weeping, bloodless, dancing bones.

In the soft dark, I wonder if I'm breathing
Grinning frozen demons, parade of terror, marching dead.

In the soft dark, deeper I tread
Dripping dying scarlet, pooling black and red.

In the soft dark, somewhere I awaken
Gasping, sweating, terrified.

In the soft dark, the dream begins again.

    John Dellicicchi

'The Killer'

I can't stop crying
Cause you are slowly dying.

You're starting to slip away
You will be gone any day.

But what can I do
Except say I love you.

You thought dope would help you cope
Or maybe give you hope.

But you were wrong
And now you will soon be gone.

You had to get high
Well know you are going to die.

How could you be so dumb
When you knew it would make your brain cells numb.

You used to be so smart
Why did you ever have to start?

You just couldn't quite
You couldn't go a day without a hit.

My body is filled with fright
Cause you wont make it through the night.

    Barlice Bare

Bleeding Hearts Will Cry Forever

Bleeding hearts will cry forever,
Crying for the love that was meant to be,
Feeling that the things they've done together,
Should have meant something,
Months and months of love and trust,
Some how grew about,
But when the time was up and over,
It turned the love and trust to doubt,
The fragile heart starts to weep,
And breaks right in two,
For now the bleeding heart will cry forever,
Knowing that they're through.

    Jennifer D. Tauber

Eyes

She saw him, the old derelict,
crouching in the shadows of the alley,
listing against a wall and peering out from
under an old grey hat. She took a half-step
towards him and then, gazing at the suddenly
up-turned face, she saw his eyes...
and was frozen like a statue.

His eyes, two gaping wounds,
spoke softly to her of nameless horrors,
breeding in the ancient darkness of the cities.
They spoke of meaningless death and of the
bitter taste of betrayal. They spoke with the
voice of a legion of men and whispered
obscenities like love-words in her ear. They
reached out and they touched her, and as she
turned away, stumbling out of the alleyway,
her eyes, two gaping wounds,
stared back at him, and wept.

David Bottorff

Faithful Mistress

Last eve was so exciting!
Dark nipples, nymphs with pretty faces
Silky buttocks! but alas - only on HBO.
At 44, my only damsels now are only so.

Home Box Office slumbered and sunrise came.
Ma fenetre revealed another show:
Seagulls swooping the azure
catching gold of sunrise on their bellies.

The earth around my home a combat zone:
The grass dressed in camouflage
of gray-white ice and speckled brown
The tree limbs budding miniature hand grenades
The guns of spring against the flags of winter.
Beyond, the first and birch conspire
Waving to each other, they assemble they crowd the slopes,
To hide my love Maestro wind conducts the trees
Ten thousand hands a-waving
Now adagio, now allegro,

Beyond the gray-white ice and flirting, dancing, trees
She waits! I left her at 18, my damsel, the sea.

Fred St Amant, Jr.

The Phoenician

An ordinary life turned fairy tale
Dawn catching morning light, magical
Soft caresses lightly touching soul
Lifting spirit higher and higher
Gentle sounds of water tumbling down
A meditation in imagination
Trickling down like loving tears
Softly caressing soul and inner being
Waking to friendly voice of Songbird
Calming spirit and making whole all around
Unrivaled tranquility at our door
Always there, open
Beckoning, calling gently our names
To come join in life
An alliance of love and fun
No itineraries, no diversions
Someplace where expectations are simple
Earthy, like crystal sound of running water
Falling gently, ping, ping, ping
Dreamtime...everpresent

Joseph D. Strauss

For Ken

This dry hot desert of you that has no place for me
Dead darkness; it is your own
I pray to the clouds of regret because my petals need the rain
How long will I last without a drop of you, without a tear
Each grain of sand possesses a small part of me, no moisture, only me
If I stand on my own I will sink in your sands; hot and unforgiving
My ignorance just bought me a crucifixion
I pray to no one, with all of my guilt
And all of the love, you could never see
Because my petals need the rain

Andreah Decker

America's Heartbeat

Wake up America! Open your eyes.
Dead souls deep in slumber now outwardly cry.
America beautiful, America strong,
We fought for your banner, but something is wrong.

Time passes quickly, year upon year.
Don't you remember how we held you dear?
We wanted to serve you, we died to be free,
Our blood lies in meadows across the broad seas.

Forget not your first born, patriots all.
Strive to be strong, for in weakness you'll fall.
Stand up for right whenever you can.
Let proud hearts come forth where apathy stands.

Only through righteous endeavors shall we
truly be called the land of the free.
Forget not America "In God is our Trust,"
Lest Liberty's torch be diminished to dust.

Elaine N. Huston

The Kiss In The Flames

As I walk to the end
Death kisses my cheek,
The light in my eyes starts to dim
looking for the flames,
The flames grow stranger
for my body and brighter for my soul,
For I know what is beyond
is a greater being than I,
Icy fingers wrap around my heart
slowly taking me away
My soul like a locket opens
and shows its face,
My shallow eyes are longing to see
the one who is longing to see me,
Then the flame vanishes and I am forgotten...
But my locket is still open.

Arin Mattox

To Mom

You went before me Mom,
Did you ever realize how much I loved you?
Your many quiet ways
Advice I will cherish forevermore.

I raise my children now
Imitating your ways in tongue and deed
Watching my daughter grow
Into future motherhood.

Perhaps after all mom,
The best way to show each other love
Is to establish it
Into the hearts of each descendent.

Jan Dybdahl

The Language Of Death

Deep dark moon, shining bright,
Decaying tombstones, shadowed light,
Howling wind and cold black mounds
Catacombs hidden deep underground
   Through the graveyard's menacing stone;
   Walks the wanderer, alone.

The rotting dead, the grinning skull
The old stone cross, long since dull
Shining teeth, faded bones,
Empty eyes, cringing moans,
   Listening, he discovered the mother
   Of death's call for its lover.

Roaring, howling, crying in pain,
Relentless whining, sounding wane
Deafening, silent, all around
Alive or dying, soft and loud.
   Through the gate, around the bend,
   The language of death - it's the wind.

   Jaime Barb

The Sunflower

I can dance for hours in the depths of your earth.
Deep brown and beautifully contrasted
symbolize the tanned in the summer shine,
growing wild in the fields.
Tall stems march out of land,
stray rows come together.
Sparkling yellow petals mesh various shades
and scream the wonderful rays; and me;
The wind through my hair, the warmth on my face,
the touch of light caressing my fingertips,
the water streaming
my skirt tickling the ankle.
Freedom flies within
and cries the tear that sheds from your root
as I bend and lay next to you.
For you bring heaven to me and I bring the dreams
to the home of the sunflower.

   Jennifer Tuma

"Together; Forever"

Mysterious eyes that follow my every step,
deep eyes full of passion that absorb my body whole;
eyes that tell feelings of pleasure just being near me.

Gently word flow from his sensual lips,
speaking of romantic desires;
and just as I see those eyes starting to twinkle...

I feel my body begin to tremble from head to toe.
and his body, it's tall dark and naturally handsome;
This body, his body, and mine, should never be apart.

Taking my hand he places it within his own,
now we're connected;
Together; Forever.

   Christina Franz

"Myron's Prayer"

Love is the hope for all that will be tomorrow
even though the dreams have turned to bitter sorrow.
How I long to feel the touch of your hand on my face
and smile while remembering both your beauty and grace.
Strength comes from holding your image always in view
on the chance that one day this really will be you.
Though things are not as they ought to be
my prayer is to be once more united with thee.

   Claire Marchant

Manipulation

Victims of abuse, helpless infants stripped and
denied virtue, mortally vital to a secure
Existence.

Sinful hands and twisted minds skillfully
controlling the clean slate of youths' innocence
for purposeful-self-gratify gains, leading
to a path of destructive accompaniment.

Conflict of concept, knowing at the
thread of fiber to the delicate
web of societies expectations.

Beside myself and source of destructible
being, venture beyond; where the grass is greener,
the light outweighs
the blackness,hope, trust of that everlasting
burdened road...leading to the ultimate
Contentment of knowing each as its own.

   Debbie Marschall

The Cow Who Jumped

I have a theory and it pertains to the cow
Did she really jump and if so how?
First of all she had a dream
Increased milk production and make it heavy on
Cream
She was just your average "run of the mill"
So the thought occurred perhaps she needed a pill
Her aspirations were to soar to the top
Actually she wanted to be "cream of the crop"
She had to be different she had to be grade "A"
Research was made on the pasture each day
A tasty treat was located behind the stump
And when she ate that oh how she could jump
It contained vitamins especially for a cow
So it was action time and the time was now
She had concocted a most daring plan
It had never been accomplished by beast or man
The plan was to jump high and to do it soon
Yep, that's how Bessie cleared the moon.

   Carrie Loberg

Heaven

Thy body as you lay
Died upon this mournful day.
Be restful and sleep,
For thy soul God will keep.
Do not worry, do not fear.
For a brand new beginning is now here.
May your days be merry and bright,
And everything you do turn out right.
You are now blessed from up above.
Now there are more things for you to love.
Do not miss me, do not flee.
For someday I will be with thee.

   Amy Bronderslev

Friends

Friends are very special people with a heart of gold.
Giving you more love than you can hold.
They are always there
Because I know they'll always care
When times are rough an you are sad and blue
They'll be there to stand by you
All these things I say are true
What would I do without a friend like you.

   Alicia Beaver

What Really Is Love

Can I begin to describe this thing called love?
Different answers abound, yet always the same.
Though many claim to feel this way, is it something people just say?
Men wiser than I have tried to explain
this thing called love and its mysterious way.
Sometimes it hurts and you're filled with despair,
other times so happy, as though walking on air.
Heart racing, breath quicker, you're the first to declare,
without any real reason, no physical cause there.
So love is just a feeling you hold in your heart,
caring and sharing just some of its parts.
It's knowing what pleases, what hurts those who care,
knowing when to give, when to take, when to bare...
That inner-most place, your soul, to compare
life's most primal feeling any two can share.
What really is love? It starts as a friend.
Yet enjoys no bounds till all time does end.

Gary Rayburn

Waiting

2:30 Too early my head knows, but perhaps tonight will be
different. Sleep? I've tried. The crossword puzzle
consumes the mounting minutes, while I wait.

3:00 A car approaches, is it his? Closer comes the sound, but
then continues on. Eyes tired, crossword running
together, but what else to do, while I wait.

3:30 Still working or did he stop somewhere? If he's at a
bar, will he know when to stop? Can't sleep, cat purring,
petting, soothing, calming, while I wait.

4:00 A siren screams in the night. Please God, not him.
Promises to be careful, doesn't speed, but what about the
other guy? Pacing passes time, what else to do, while I wait.

4:30 Bars closing, should be soon. Car coming, lights in
driveway. No more worrying, while I wait.

Thank you God. Good-night.

Carol Quaranto

Just Tell Me So

The tears are in my eyes.
Do you hear my cries?
Why does my heart ache so bad?
Why is love so sad?

Can you answer my questions?
I guess I was just looking for protection,
For the world is a cruel place.
Our love, was it a waste?

If you need me,
Just tell me so.
This is my finale plea.
If you don't, let me go.

Is our love lost,
Never to come again?
Haven't I paid the cost?
You've showed me I can never win.

I don't want to lose you,
But I'll let me go.
Whatever you want,
Just tell me so.

Julie Bickett

Music Unmasked

Hey, Man,

Do you hear their loud music?
Do you hear their anguished lyrics?
Do you see the young blood oozing from their wounds?

They suffer on the cross of music.
They suffer on the cross of man.
They suffer on the cross of spirit.
Because their lives are out of joint,
And their music is their medicine.

Elma Kidhardt

What Do You See?

What do you see, when you take a look at me?
Do you see a man filled with pride, a man glad to be alive?
Do you see a wretched man, head bowed like a fool?
When you look into my eyes, is it intelligence that you see,
Or is the color of my skin, all you can see?

What do you see, when you take a look at me?
Do you see a friend searching for compassion?
Do you see a white man? Do you see a black man?
Do you see just another man like many that you've seen?
What do you see when you look at me?

What do we see when we take a look at each other?
Is it brothers and sisters that we see?
As we turn our heads to face yet another, will we see
a friend, an enemy, a lover?
Will color make us favor one over another?

What do we see when we take a look at each other?
Is it only the color of our skin that we see?
We are merely living, loving, people and that is what I see.
Is color all that we see? What a shame.
There is much more inside, so much more is there to see.

Anthony Salvatore

To A Greyhound

Caged by man, dulled spirit!
Dog thou never wert, that from earth,
Oh fear it, stinting thy full heart,
Art bereft of the sight and smells of a true dog's part.

From cage to latrine to track.
This spirit of an elf!
We robotize or crack for lucre and vile pelf
A nature that's spontaneity itself.

We denature thy soul
Crowd thee out of free play
Wrench a part from the whole and thy siblings coldly slay
In a dull, ghoulish schedule every day.

But no more. Thou art at home!
Dear Heart stop! or go.
As thy spirit moves thee roam!
On a penny pirouette so! —
Graceful and gay as a seahorse on the foam.

Gentle Spirit, basically blithe: 'tis we who have sinned!
Thy soul is as thy body lithe. True Dog!
The past rescind! Grasp thine inheritance! Inherit the wind!!

John Devine

Untitled

When the tide comes in and you're feeling low
Don't cry because I won't go
When the moon turns red
Beware of what you said
Don't you understand
It's all because of the sand
Just like the stars in the sky
When all the stars are gone
We all die
Don't take it fast but slow
Because that's how it feels
When you're feeling low
But how can you know
Every day I let myself go
Piece by piece
Day by day
Second by second
It may not seem slow
Now you know how it feels to grow.

Darren Noble

It's Your Life...

Live your life the way you want to,
Don't listen to people,
Some people think they can run your life, but they can't.
Be who you want to be,
Do what you want to do,
Don't be afraid because no one can
Take your life unless you are willing to give it up.
People are only here for a little while,
So do what you can and try to enjoy
life while you can.
No one can make you do something unless you let them.
Because you only do something if you want to do it.
So accomplish what you can, and live
your life the way you want,
And don't let anyone stop you,
Because if you do, it is saying you don't
believe in yourself,
So live your life the way you want to live it.

Amber Strawn

Face In The Mirror

I look in the mirror
don't recognize myself - it's not my face
those aren't the eyes with which I see
that's not the mouth with which I drink - it's not my hair
I begin to hate myself - ask - what has happened?

Time has gone by
How much didn't I see - because I didn't want to
How far did I go to have lost my face

I reach for my heart and it is beating in the same rhythm as
  the day of Birth

press my hand harder on my heart
but pain rends it apart I take the mirror destroy it
but the other face - my face - remains
it is calling after me from thousands of splinters
the door is closed - I can't escape
my feet don't carry me anymore
and my heart - I can't feel it anymore
it's getting dark - the last light fades away
everything falls apart - only the face -
  the face in the mirror stays.

Claudia L. Hatch

"Tell It Like It Is"

Tell it like it is -
Don't submit a questionable quiz.
Let folks know just how you feel
To their best judgement you then appeal.

Get up each morning with a smile on your face
and soon as possible-yesterday's
frustrations erase.
With ambition and hope in your heart
Give each new day a boost from the start.

Character testing may come each day that you live,
Ideas may be crushed as through a sieve,
Leave no doubts as you pass this way,
If you tell it like it is, you've made your day.

Eleanor Mary Jones

Who Is Feeding The Soulless Predators?

Who is feeding the soulless predators?
  Don't you know sweetheart,
"That, God" "itzamna" is from the infinite space of the editors.
  So, who is feeding the ungodly predators?
  So "darling" I can love you "like the closed galaxy", of God
"Yacatecutli" forgotten creditors.
  Beyond the infinite space of God "Tohtela".
Heaven of the supreme heavens of the galaxies.
  Where God "Taiowa," the creator of the creation of the origi
nally of the laws, was the first to reside into God Tohtela galaxy.
  So "who is feeding" the rooster city high up spaceship
soulless predators?
  So, "darling" we can freely and safely
love on like God "Yacatecutli" closed galaxy of the Lumerians
"Editors".
  So "darling" we can love on like the close galaxy
immortal site of God "Kuvera" forgotten creditors.

Harold Gabriel McNairy

The Eternal Flame

What wretched body does hope that the fired candle
doth burn in the eternal sacred heart forever more than a day.
What wretched soul does dream of a perpetual movement towards that
hard to find path that leads the way
To the center of the centripetal force where in lies the germs

  of all the futures,
  all the past
  and the everlasting Presence.

The present of immortality wherein
the flame flares and dies down to be rekindle again.
The repetitive rekindling the soulful
duty of the recurring sparks gives forth
the rhythmic pulsing of the sacred heart

  The ebbing and the flowing
  It flares and is glowing,
  The Eternal Flame

Georgia E. Crim

Christine

With you all my thoughts crumble and break,
For even the right words can seem fake
So, for you, I refuse to make
Poetry for poetry's sake

My soul shows shapes and feels words
But the heart is sending words never heard,
So I pull back the reigns and brake my crutch,
And express my poetry, to you, through touch.

Eric Zeutzius

The Tide

I'm sailing away
Down the cold, lonesome tide
No one cares to say
"I love you"
"I've missed you"
They just walk on by
No good-bye
No kiss
I wish you will sail away with me
Our adventure would be filled with passion
and love all over,
I will drink your wine
You will swallow my pride
We will be so drunk and high, we will
Make love on the highest hill
Near the shore

Debbie Rubin

Teardrops

Outside teardrops dribble in a trouble dance
   down your soft face.
Inside your heart turns blue,
   cold and learns how to hate.
Everyone talks about how love is so great,
But in the end it some how always turns to hate.
The one you loved seemed so beautiful and kind,
But truly she never learned how to love with her heart
   but instead with her mind.
Real soon true love will come upon you,
   but it might seem to late.
In return your heart will turn warm, love,
   and learn not to hate.

Ellen Rohrbaugh

Poet's Keg

Tapping it now, the Poet's vast keg,
Drawing a flagon of rhyme.
Words that gush forth... a scrambly mess.
Assorting them simply takes time.

Renegade words, elusively free!
Frustrated poet gives chase.
Ensnaring at random, the choicest see print.
The others?...well, simply erase.

Attempting to state melodiously,
A message deceptively clear.
This offering no doubt, abstractedly vague,
Not quite on the target, but near.

So must it be with all poets of time,
Destined to try to explain,
Pronouncements of voices that whisper within
Through noises and mists of the brain.

Hoping the gist of the message herein
Enlightens the eyes of the mind.
Gifts from the source of a wisdom complete,
Showing where one's been so blind.

C. Wes Awana

The Eyes Of The Rose

One single rose
Given to me
By someone unknown, an admirer from a far.
While this mysterious person
Awaits in the shadows.
I await out in the open
Wondering if my admirer
Will show thy self to me

Ann Marie Roberts

River

Mystic river swirling soft
drifting currents of pleasure
As I ride I feel, free
like a spring morning of warm summer breeze
the sun shines all day
innocent like children we play
we walk your banks
her hand in mine
skipping stones we softly laugh
I gaze in her eyes
they sparkle and shine
glimmering with delight
she's radiant in her beauty
you flow swiftly through us
carrying us on our way
all can find this river
it comes from heaven above
Many who know this river
call it the river of Love.

Eric Ostema

Orange

This orange wants to be ripe
Each day so raw
There is no comfort in knowing
That life is not even half over
It's alright to be green in certain areas
Yet this orange wants to be ripe

This orange wants to be orange with smiles
Too big of a mountain to climb
Not all mountains can be move
This orange weeps citrus that stings
All opened pores of emotion

Orange is the color of the sun that never fails to rise

Haruko A. Tanaka

Twilight

Twilight is just the same
Each day the angel calls
A mystery among all is the angels call
But on this night in the darkening twilight
The angel calls
He calls for me this night
When all the fires are burning bright
"Come," says he
I go with he who bears the light
The angel walking in the cool twilight
He takes me away from my family and friends
He takes me to a place where happiness never ends
They mourn for me now
It gives me even less delight
To see them so on a cool, crystal clear night
But I just must know
Before I go
Before my poem ends
Why must I
Like my poem have to end?

Carrie Brown

"Forsaken"

The old dog down the alley is howling again.
His pain must surely be as great as mine.
An empty heart and lonely arms.
In desperation I cry, there's no one to hear
Except—the old dog down the alley.

Bonnie L. McElwayne

Life is a box of crayons

A box of crayons has many colors: red yellow, black and white.
Each of them are equal in God's omniscient sight.
None of them are better, none of them are worse.
None of them are blessed and none of them are cursed.
If only this world of ours: big, beautiful and blue,
Could be like a box of crayons with the colors being me and you.
No person would be better than their neighbor, friend or dad.
No one would feel anger, have enemies or feel bad.
All the people would be together,
randomly placed together inside our little box,
And finally there would be peace and our world would truly
ROCK!

Jimmy Brooks

We Will Always Love Him

We will always love him. He went to the hospital several times.
Each time was hard and filled with tears.
Each visit was painful for my heart.
Yet he was beautiful because God touched him and he glowed with love.
He taught me how to love. He taught me how to express myself.
Yet he's not gone and never will be.
He will always be apart of my life and heart.
Because he will always be a part of us.
We will always love him.

Jennifer E. Johnson

"The Release"

Death descends into my chamber peaceful
Embracing my spirit in brilliant light,
Welcoming; O! He my savior in the night
To be as joy received. For, from a bright place
He cometh that to bliss I may ascend
On his silent wings of purest love-
Soft wings on which to soar away, above
The pain-higher and higher, transcending
Earthly bounds-Until, alas! Paradise
Is at once upon me, anguish behind
Left on soil stark. Now true peace I find
In tranquil sleep where weightless dreams entice
My soul to remain forever quiet
In slumber's comforting quilt of eyelet.

Jessica Chainer

Calmness

All I encounter are clouds
Encircling the rocks and cliffs.
The slow lapping and the hum
  of silence.
The sun peeking and disappearing.
It's a picture I once saw before,
A dream I once dreamt,
A thought I muddled through.
Houses stepping into the mountains,
Gulls singing their morning tune,
Ships curving into the bends of the water...
Glazed by the rippling shine.
The rocks jump to and from
Dancing amidst the winding
  shore of
  eternity.

Jane Davie

Innocent Eyes

Sturdy hearts, wordless thoughts,
Endless dreams soaring from up above
  Laughter mimicking their hopes,
  Sadness circumscribing their lives,
  Started living the dream
  Confusion was hovering from down below
Racing hearts, unspoken thoughts,
Unsung dreams soaring from up above
  Shots ring in their ears,
  Cries echo our fears,
  Innocence begins to disappear
  Memories are all that remain
Innocent eyes cry,
Innocent eyes ask why,
Innocent eyes see the truth
The words of hatred affect the youth
  We are all part of the world,
  We all must change its wrongs,
  Flashing before those innocent eyes
  We must show them no more cries

Enza Maria Navarra

The Creature Of Chance

Tis a black empty tomb with a faceless mask ,
engraved on the outside stone; here lies a chance that
passed with a glance, of a creature with no heart, just
a throne. Lady luck was good to this passing chance,
Prosperity followed her closely home; guided by emptiness,
greed and pain, she was assured of never being alone.
As the world reached out to this creature, encased in its
magnificent shrine; the idea was to save the creature, another
soul not to be left behind; the creature however had other
ideas, for happy she was it seemed, the thought of safe passage
to a better world was a laugh, (a bleak ugly dream). Alas
lady luck departed, and the world retreated; leaving the
creature to face herself. And what she saw caused her soul to
die, leaving behind only her possessions and wealth.
The weeds have grown up around that black empty tomb,
The sadness abounds from afar; a cry can be heard from a
screening jay bird, alighting on that tomb in the dark.
Who knows the woes of that soul who refused to be told,
God loves you, it's never to late to make a new start.

Diane C. Price

"In Concert"

An appreciative audience in a Concert Hall,
  Enjoying good music having a ball;
The common delight for the Orchestra Score,
  Beautifully played to an acclaimed encore!

A wavelength of pleasure envelopes the crowd,
  Glorious music and the applause is loud;
With shared admiration diverse cultures melt,
  Captured by the music comes brief content!

To the language of music all creeds relate,
  Wondrous if its magic could diminish hate;
When so many can be captive to music's spell,
  Living in concert could bring peace as well!

Bertha Fisher

The Difference

How hard is hard when all you know is what is hard?
How easy is easy when you have never had it so?
What kind do you become when all you see is never any good
and how do you tell what is good from bad if you have never
had both to compare?

Beverly Highland

Anger And Depression

Raging with anger,
Erupting with violence,
Screaming with pain,
Dying of laughter,
Crying for people,
Hardly protected,
Feeling the shame,
A cool, delicate wind knocking against my face,
A consoling breeze moving at a steady pace,
Crashing upon the window,
Moving forward with velocity,
Tightened closely,
Hanging on with heart,
Swaying back and forth,
Falling to the muddy ground,
Shooting pain in my eyes,
Tearing my soul,
Aggravation ringing in my ears,
Howling in sorrow,
Depression.

Jon Reifler

A Candle

The flame of the candle leaps high and bright,
  Ethereal vapors surrounding its sight.
Above the wick rises, strong, the flame,
  Arched in white heat, vaulting, not without aim.

The flame's tongue devours candle and wick,
  They melt away quickly under the flame's lick.
But the flame does its work in a most positive way,
  And is not discouraged, when put out at end of day.

Eager to work, it begins anew when lit,
  Its power is light for our keen benefit.
Flame is fast moving and stings to the touch,
  But the candle right handled, has helped us much.

The candle light dances, shadowing my bed chamber's length,
  While I on my knees pray, asking God for his strength.

Bruce Blasius

Escape

The papers, they need burning-
every floor could use some care-
every cupboard is clutterupted-
and I really should do my hair.
The laundry is screaming, "Wash me, hang me, fold me, put me
away!"
and the lawn is all a-jumble in springtime disarray.
The garden, it needs spading,
my windows all have smears.
I could, if I would, sort and burn things for the next thirteen years
and the dust lies heavy on every surface here.
I have to think of cooking
for a homecoming, working man
and I should, if I would, bake all day
and every knitting project I've started is very much in arrears
but my whole being, especially my feet
are telling me, "Take me away-
to a mysterious, burbling stream bed
where fossil treasures lay."

Camille Alger

Psycho's Path

Too young to see his life in shambles;
Every minute on the streets, he takes a gamble.
Too young to see, what's ahead in life;
Don't know, if he'll be killed by a knife.
He's only thinking drugs, it's the thing;
Only to be caught up in a violent ring.
He got himself in trouble, now he's on the run;
Only to be shot down, by a stolen gun.
They put him in a hole, 6 feet underground.
A little time, no one knows he was around.
Then life goes on;
And what is done, is done
But, why? Dear God, it had to be my son?

Geraldine Caple

Wake Up

Once we acted in a haze.
Everything we did was a craze.
Who would've known it was just a faze?
Long ago were those days.
We still remember all the ways.
Looking into the mirror, we gaze.
At times, it seems one big maze.
Hold on to the sunshine and all its rays.
Live life, don't get trapped in a vase.
See where that bluebird of happiness lays.
Explore all the valleys, inlets, and bays.
Go after that promotion and even the raise.
Don't be content to stay in that daze.

Aileen Powers

Untitled

  The attraction is irreversible
  Explicitly unavoidable
  Therefore I stand petrified
  As I stare into ethereal eyes
Rapture is drawing me near
Trepidation, confusion, hesitation, fear
Why has come this hold over me?
No justifiable cause can be.
  Slinking in closer, eyes dancing about
  Lips so possessed can't voice a doubt
The passion thickens
As my heartbeat quickens
This specious reverie isn't what it seems
Realization, it was solely... a dream.

Allisia Gennetts

Christmas In Somalia

  Straight ahead he stares,
  eyes enormous in a skeletal face.
  He is too weak to move
  his matchstick arms and legs,
  too close to death to cry his protest
  at the hunger that saps his life.
  His mother holds him to her breast,
  no nourishment is there,
  she, too, is near to death.
  Food may be very close,
  a friendly army may yet save her
  and thousands like her;
  but for these little ones it is too late
  the Herods of today
  have slaughtered the innocents - again.
  The Christ Child in his manger bed
  stirs in His sleep - and weeps.

Eythol M. Nelson

"In Your Eyes So Blue"

I looked into your eyes so blue,
Eyes I thought to be trustworthy, and true.
Through your eyes, I thought I could see,
What you really thought of me.

I thought that in your eyes so blue,
I could see only friendship, towards me, from you.
I couldn't detect the hatred rising inside.
A hatred with which I could not abide.

When you looked into my eyes so blue,
You could clearly see that I trusted you.
I honestly thought that you felt the same way,
Until a year ago, on a cold March day.

It was then that I saw in your eyes, what I feared.
That friendly glow had gone cold, and then disappeared.
I saw as I looked into your bright blue eyes,
That they were filled with deception, hate, and lies.

The look in your eyes, that you gave me, was so cold,
That a tear slipped from my eye, that I could no longer hold.
Just one solitary little tear,
A reminder of our friendship, that I had once held dear.

   Jennifer Packard

She's Still Standing

Old Black woman - Look at her,
Face wrinkle free - How old? 65-70.
Can't really tell, until you hear her talk, watch her walk.
Look at her hands and you will know - They've done many
chores. Her knees have rubbed many floors. Her hair
turned gray, from years of happiness, sorrow and pain.
Yet still she walks without a cane. Still no one hold
doors; won't give up a seat, so she can rest her tired feet.
Think of all she's been through, of all the thing she can
still do. I wonder what she feels, when she looks at us,
sitting comfortably on the bus, while she's still standing.

   Deborah Miller

"Culmination Of Generations"

Far, far away, a star shines bright,
  Far, far away, in the darkness of night.
This star is united with others above.
  God's nature shows us his abounding love.

Sun's rays energize and illuminate!
  Daytime, sun's light and heat culminate!
  Nighttime, moon and stars illuminate.
On the cross, God's Salvation plan was a culmination!
  In each believer, Jesus' Love is an illumination.

Moon and stars have no light of their own.
  The skies are colored by sunset's tone.
Moon and stars illuminate from sun's light.
  They light up the darkness of night.
Clouds may come and hide their light.
  Rise above the clouds, they are back in sight!
Doubts arise and troubles appear.
  Lift up your heads, Jesus' coming is near!

   Al Thomas

Happy Birthday

I know you hate to see them come
Faster and faster including this one.
But think where would you really be
Unless birthdays were pursuing thee.
You'd see yourself a little child
Without life's wisdom and strength mere mild.
You'd miss the years so filled with pleasure,
The joys, and all you love: your treasure.
You couldn't look into faces glowing with charm.
Cuddling little ones warmly in your arm.
So be grateful for all the birthdays you had
And look forward to the many still ahead.
Remember: Age surely is a state of mind
Not merely a string of years with experiences entwined.

   Ilse Wissner

"All Is Not Gone"

   I walk into the room and I see you sitting in your
favorite chair by the window.
   I see a man who has lived a long life and seen many things.
   Do you remember though?
   Has that dark shadow in your mind clouded over all
those memories?
   Birthdays, anniversaries, holidays and graduations.
   Where have they all gone?
   Some days I look at you and I want to ask, "Are they
really all gone?"
   Will you look at me standing here and catch a fleeting
memory from the past?
   Then you slowly look up at me and I can see for a
moment that familiar glint in your eyes.
   You may have forgotten some things but, deep inside I
know all is not gone....
   All is not gone.

   Danielle N. Reed

Runaway Closet

Like sorrow and pain, thus truth of shame,
Fear thinking of no one to blame. oh runaway closet
please hear me now, like a stranger hurting me
it's never the same ..... He who touches uncomfortably,
 "The Private Parts"
Oh runaway closet they have lost their smarts!
I'm not ashamed nor am I to blame,
Oh runaway closet can I be the same.
Unlike pain, unlike sorrow, my runaway closet shall
be open tomorrow.
Oh runaway closet please hear me now, I'm speaking
out loud because now I know how.....
 "God blessed the child".

   Darwin D. Smith Sr.

The Cycle

January brings promises of a new start in life.
February brings lovers a chance to rekindle an old flame.
March is just a month of 31 days to pass away.
April showers cleanses our souls with tears.
May brings summer flowers to lift our spirits.
June, the first month of summer, kids are free at last.
July gives us the opportunity to be thankful for our independence.
August is just a month of 31 days to pass away.
September brings new experiences & challenges to kids.
October is just a month of 31 days to pass away.
November a month to be thankful for all of our blessings.
December brings love, peace & forgiveness to our hearts,
  souls and minds.
To which in January all promise to start anew.

   Cynthia Turel

'To My Husband'

Honey, you're my one and only love. I sometimes
feel you were sent from above. Without you and your
love. My life would have no meaning for when I
found you, it was just the beginning.

You are wonderful provider, husband, friend and lover.
No woman could want any better. You're good looking man.
No wonder I'm jealous as I am. Sometimes when I feel

blue, I thank my stars that I have you. Just to know
you'll be coming through the front door makes me
thankful even more.

So when were apart, just remember, you're in my mind and my
heart. As Jesus is God's son. I feel my lover, as though we are one.
Love ya.

Geneva Nuckols

Wilting Flowers

The crowd had left, he stood alone;
Feelings of sorrow filled his soul.

Lost and afraid, he sat down;
This place he would call his sacred ground.

Within the year, how much he'll age;
Maturity forced by rage.

A day ago, still a boy;
Now a man with his heart destroyed.

He finally stood, wilting flowers in hand
And left his innocence buried in the sand.

His dad finally finished his last goal;
He tried everything, till he sold his soul.

Now laying next to the boy's mother side,
He gave her all, and sacrificed his pride.

The only thing he left behind
Was a 13 year old boy losing his mind.

How selfish can one man be
Didn't he understand there's always a fee?

For his one life he sold away,
He ruined another that was forced to stay.

Jennifer McClure

Untitled

Dear God, let me be there when the wind pushes his
feet through the tall grass,

When he picks his first rose and clings to its beauty,

When the breaking of the waves tosses him to and fro
on the golden sand,

When he sits cross legged on a hill silent and happy,

When he walks slowly, loving the wetness of the summer rain,

When he kneels beside his bed, his hands clasped in prayer,

Dear God, let me be there when Thou dost set his body
free. Let me hold his hand, for he is my brother.

Donna Stilwell

15/20 Vision

Bulging wooden mammoths stem their talons to the hook
fifteen twenty vision dripping plaudit in the book
shining brilliantine into the faces of
    some places
tearing at the neighborhood's
    snafu
    tattoo
knotholes chewing, biting down
    frown upon their rations
    furrow on the fulgent use of wind's subliminal trap
capping off this course on vision
fumbling for nothing
nothing at all
punch-drunk off a minor dose
an unalloyed religious nut
    rendered comatose

James Patrick Sinisi

Untitled

Why play this game, this game of life
Filled with worry and strife
With what seems like no end
And too much time to spend
All of us under the command others
Who don't care
And wealthy people who won't share
People tell us where to go and what to do
I'm tired of this foolish sh*t, how bout you
My kind it is us who will repay
Those who rule us, now I say
Will you help us do this deed
And make them bleed
Help us now, there is no time to spare
We will kill them cause they were unfair
With the rising sun
Our killing spree will be begun

April Berry

Moonlight Vigil

The moon waits silently behind shifting curtains
Fingers of soothing light reach down
He gently caresses his lover's soft body.
The sleeping sea drifts from a dream
She rolls restlessly, sighing
And stretches out on the silky sand.
The dream lures her and she relents
Smiling, she slips back to her bed
Long tendrils of silvery hair follow her.
Her lover catches them
And lets them slide over his pale fingers
As she falls asleep again beside him.

Erin M. Reich

"Love"

There is a river high up in a mountain
Flowing high up in the sky
No one knows just how it all got started,
Or where it all will end
But love is like that river
Flowing deep beneath your feet
But our love will last forever, until eternal time
Because love can withstand the test of time
Because our love is like that river
Flowing high above the sky

Beth Kenyon

Mardi Gras-South Alabama

Beautiful days, gorgeous nights.
Fire in the sky from before sunset 'til night.

Sky's clear, evenings cool, perfect for romance.
Stars like diamonds joining the moon in dance.

White beaches, aquamarine sea,
Friendly people full of life.

Hearts full of hopefulness
Missing each other in the night.

Gene, Tony, Kyle, Bill, and Patsy, Linda and Bill,
Nice to have friends so real.

Roxanne as bad as Mama, chasing after floats,
Must be something right, she filled our tote.

Catching beads and candy, toys and doubloons.
D'Iberville to Orange, Mardi Gras over too soon.
>*Earl Joseph Parker*

The Memory Train

All aboard the memory train destination memory lane.
First stop Good Deed Avenue. Next stop sin Blvd.
Moving onto Joy Highway. Crossing the River of Tears.

Passing by the Sea of Regret on to Virtues Country, after a short
Stop at Fear Station on to Hate Lake. Down to the Valley of
Sorrow passing the well of Grief up ahead the Plains of Pain
Pulling into the Station of Love in the Town of Forgiveness in
The County of Serenity, so goes the journey down Memory Lane.

Heed the Warning Signs posted on the train; DON'T PULL THE
CORD! DON'T LEAVE THE TRAIN!
Until you reach the station on the Memory Train.

Perhaps you have seen those, that leave the train at Sin Blvd.,
And Joy's Highway., only to fall in the River of Tears, some
Wash out to the Sea of Regret others lost in Virtues County
Only to end up in the Street of fear sitting beside Hate Lake.
Some lost in the Valley of Sorrow still clinging to the Well of
Grief others left stranded on the Plains of Pain.

All because they did not heed the warnings posted on the
Memory Train.
>*Diane Gallegos*

Wasted Loves

Concealed behind a beautiful mask,
Fists flying; his mind polluted with hate.
There was never a doubt I had a case.
Why, I ask myself, did three years I waste?

He would hold and kiss me all night through,
Soul mates, similar to the moon and sun.
Seducing them all, with those baby blues,
Unfulfilled, he hungers for more than one.

His smile, of course, so beguiling,
Like a magnet, an insatiable lust.
The flaw, (I'm blind), ideally hiding…
Violator he is, and now, No Trust.

But surely, (I wonder), he is out there.
This life is long. This world is big. But where?
>*Diane Elizabeth Carson*

Duty In Somalia

The sunsets in Mogudishu are picture post card intense fireballs flanked by shimmering translucent striations which quickly drop from sight, unleashing a cooling breeze flowing from inland toward the sea. Meanwhile, far to the east, my love of six months, readies to face a new dawn. The U. N. flag flutters over the Consulate Building bathed in the focused beams of four spotlights. The clear sky is studded with silver stars and the chromish moon hangs enchantingly as a genie's lamp. Buildings around my duty post stand like monuments whose walls are pockmarked with bullet holes and mortar chinks - a reminder of man's mortality.

>Fine tuned ears
>darting glances
>finger on the trigger

The food warehouse is locked. A jeep guards the front, hidden in the building's shadow. Lights from a circling chopper sweep through the shadows momentarily revealing the driver, gunner and mounted gun. Another monotonous night in Somalia.

>Fine tuned ears
>darting glances
>a distant infant's cry
>*David E. Sees*

A Girl Child

Trees bend and sway with the blowing of the winds,
Flowers bud and bloom all summer long.
The freshness of air after the rain.
A child born, small and fragile, full of life and promise.

Snowflakes coming from heaven on a cold winters night,
Soft rose petals, silky and fragrant to the touch.
Grass green and full under your bare feet.
A child born, small and fragile, full of life and promise.

Tornadoes hustling and bustling across the plains,
Hurricanes smashing and slashing against the lands.
Lightning full of power and energy.
A child born, small and fragile, full of life and promise.

A soft touch, sweet kisses, whimsical smiles,
Curious eyes, full of questions and trust,
Laughter of slyness and playfulness.
Years to learn and grow with knowledge abound,
A child born, small and fragile, full of life and promise.
A girl child…Carol Ann "Rose"…
>My granddaughter!
>*Fran Muncey*

Couch Potato Recipe

Put 1 couch or 2 that make 1 in front of the TV.
Fluff 3 pillows so you can kick back and slouch comfortably.
Place 1 multi-purpose remote-control on the coffee table.
Use a fresh TV Guide to see what's on cable.
Add salt, pepper, ketchup & mustard to a handi-tote tray.
And have your favorite restaurant deliver their meal-of-the-day.
Set your money-back discount timer to 30 minutes and wait for the
doorbell to ring.
Wear your mitten slippers to avoid that cold-floor feeling.
Answer the door, the food is finally here.
Sit back with your mug, the only spuds are suds in your beer.
>*Frank J. Herrera*

Love's Nest

Fly..... spread your wings
fly..... pretty little bird
Beware - the shifting winds
beware - the hungry hawk

Fly..... explore new horizons
Careful, don't get so close to the sun
The wind sent you hurling
against the wall.
Come, your needs will be fulfilled,
'til once again you soar.

Soar..... high and low
Fly ..... fast and slow
The heavy rains have made it
impossible to go.
Come, dry your wings in the warmth of the nest.
The sun shines and once again
you fly.... you soar.... high.... low.

Felicidad Torres

Notes From The Dead: A Prison Greeting

Another day
Folded - stacked neatly
Compartmentalized and state approved
-One glimpse- peripherally
A whole civilization is vanishing by degree
Oh! this experiment in here

Ghost days and attractive details
The illusion business is clear
-No frame now-
You're running and bleeding invisible
In virtual freedom
Oh! that experiment out there.

David Beard

Breaking Up!!

Breaking up is hard to do,
For a fact I know it's true.
It's happened times before,
Something you remember forever more.
When a special love walks away,
You're left standing with nothing to say.
Right now you're between emotions,
Not knowing whether to laugh or to cry,
As you sit waiting for the answer why.
While you wait for that one call,
You see the memories of that person
You've loved flash on your bedroom wall.
As the night comes up the moon is found,
Then before you fall asleep you think to yourself
The person you loved won't ever be again coming around.

JoAnne Zukowski

Untitled

Thank you:
For all the chicken you fry
For a slice of your coconut pie
For your delicious pistachio cake
That no one else in this world, seems to
know how to make
For your original shrimp and red rice
That tastes so delicious and smells so nice
All I'm really trying to say,
Is I love your cooking, and have a Happy Mother's Day.

Horace A. Stewart

"The Gift Of Life"

From the beginning of time, a "Oneness of Mind,"
For all who aspire, the Divine will inspire,
A part in a plan - God, nature and man,
As free will He gave, to choose what we crave.

An unlimited source, that has always been near,
Watching human creation, as we move into fear,
Knowing the moment, that is perfect for each...
To understand God's within; anxious to teach!

This is not something new, or different from when...
Christ taught us our power - In truth, is within,
Throughout our own history, we've surrendered or fought,
"The Philosophies of Life" - "Ancient Ones" taught.

We are totally responsible - for ourselves - what we do,
And can manifest our lives, however we choose,
By being honest with ourselves, we are honest with God,
Our faith is our strength, it's our staff, it's our Rod!

Be aware of your thoughts, as you create your own play,
As you continue through life with each moment and day,
Circumstances, and people reflect beliefs that you hold.
As you welcome the lessons - you'll gradually unfold!

Heather Henry

I Am Near

Perfect peace is near,
For God gives strength greater than fear.
My days have faced with faith,
The terror of the night,
And you will see,
I am near
Even though our courses be apart,
I will forever remain in your heart.
A lifetime moves swiftly like currents in a river
You shall see our souls from death and delivered.

Charlene Giesken

A Blind Man

   I try to see the world through a blind man's eyes
for he can see things the physical realm can disguise
   A blind man can't see a body or a face
only the inner-beauty our eyes often disgrace
   When one sense is taken, all others are heightened
and with God at his side, he is less frightened
   To go with feelings, sounds and smell
conquering fears that our sight can't often dispel
   Not always knowing if what we see is real
now using God's eyes to show what we feel
   So use your spiritual eyes that to you God gave
that through His love, a better road we can pave
   I pray that you'll see, through holding God's hand
the world as seen only, through the eyes of a blind man.

Bryan Humphrey Penney

Entity

The essence of time has not dimmed the glow
for the fire still burns deep in my soul

Heartaches and joy are both entwined
Deep within the memory of my mind

The warmth of a touch the shadow of a smile
has not left my heart despite the miles

Time cannot erase what the memory will allow

Memories are treasures that I can hold dear
until I have you whom I can hold near

Aleta Anderson

The Dream Goes On

A new little branch upon the tree
for his great grand pappy and me
Zachary Harrison is his name they say
his middle name is for me on this happy day
He is part of a dream come true you see
dreamed by his great grand pappy and me
this sweet little boy we came to see
the dream goes on and we hope to be
right here on earth so we can see
each branch of the tree,
that comes from the dream
by their great grand pappy and me
but if we're not please think of us then
and remember we love you,
like this darling little boy,
who brings us so much joy.
Zachary Harrison who we came to see
he is part of the dream come true you see
dreamed by his great grand pappy and me

Della Harrison Kromer

The Watcher

Silence the night and open your mind.
For I am the one who watches you.

I come in your sleep, then when you awake,
begone with everything around.

Open your heart, open your soul,
for I am the one who watches you.

You can not run nor hide.
For I know everything about you.
I am the one who watches you.

For stay on my good side and give your heart and soul to me.
For I will do the rest, you need not worry.

In night and day I follow you.
For you might not realize.
Through life and death it is always the same.

Fear me...Believe me...Trust me...
Have faith in me...Remember my words...
For I am the one who watches you.

For you will see the truth
I am the one who loves you.

Elizabeth Rueby

Agonizing Grief

My life has turned to a blackish hell.
For I awaken with a hard serge of pain,
I turn to look at the bright brilliant sky,
But all I see is a shower of rain.
A continuous stream of tears roll down my face,
I pray to God to give me grace,
This feeling of emptiness is of shallow pity.
My life seems to of vanished,
All my love, happiness and joy is vanished.
I lay here all alone with despair,
All allow myself to feel is the pain of each tear.
It's an endless world of agonizing grief,
I think of my widespread sorrow and clench my teeth.
All I can do is close my eyes,
And hope my soul will not
Take this moment to dic.

Gina Hengst

I Shall Too

When you die, I shall too;
For I can not live if you are not.
If you go to hell, I shall too;
For I can not be where you are not.
If you break up with your boyfriend, I shall too;
For I cannot have someone if you do not.
If you lose a friend, I shall too;
For we share the same friends and I wouldn't
Want her around if you are not.
If you get a new best friend, I shall not;
For no one could take the place of you.

Heather Nicole Ower

Unemployment

How does anyone cope being without a job?
For many these days it is the unanswered question
How do I have faith and the courage to go on?
Why me God?

God says "he will provide what we need"
That we need not worry "about what we will eat or clothes we
will wear"
But yet it is hard to have faith and courage

What will be my fate?
Is this the ultimate test of my faith in God?
What is the purpose or lesson I need to learn?
How do I go on each day?

Prayer and meditation each day
Help me and others
By being with others like me I know I am not alone
I know God loves me by others understanding, love and support

Diana Lopes

God's Precious Gift

To: Megan Cree Walker

For some it's once in a lifetime,
For others it might be more,
God gives you a precious gift,
a precious gift to be adored.

In your mind, you say what shall I name it,
and what color are its eyes,
It won't be much longer,
'til I know this great surprise.

With patience and God's blessing,
the time is growing near,
and it won't be much longer,
until our little baby is here.

I'm excited and overjoyed,
I never thought I could feel this way,
how God's precious little gift,
could make me feel that one great day.

To it we are mommy and daddy,
To God we are his children,
and I know that this is truly
the most exhilarating feeling.

Connie D. Walker

Vincent

When we were young we were quite close but then we seemed to stray.
I found it hard to talk with you but it's not like that today.
We're grown up now and conquered many obstacles of the past.
We'll treat each day that comes along as if it were the last.
Just one more thing that I might add in one way or another.
There is no more finer a lad than the one I call my brother.

Genevieve Cohan

Easter Greetings

Sunday will be your first Easter and what a beautiful Spring,
For several years you'll only wonder what the Easter Bunny will
bring. But, sweetheart, let me tell you what Easter is all
about, the Glory and Resurrection of our Lord and Saviour, how
He came to save us and gave us reason to shout. God gave His
Son on Calvary that we might forever live, oh, what priceless,
majestic gifts of love He gives. One of His priceless gifts is
you, without you, we wouldn't know what to do. You light up
our lives and fill our hearts with love, Your laughter and
beauty is equaled only by a soaring dove. He gives us Spring,
Winter and Fall, but I like spring most of all. In spring we
see all the colors of His art, the birds's sweet song and His
love fills our hearts. But, my precious one, He gave you to us
in the Fall, and you are one of the most perfect gifts of all.
Happy First Easter, Sweetheart, and may you, from His love and
grace, never depart.

    Elizabeth Ethridge

A Stranger's Gift

I pity the woman who gave you up,
For she'll never know the joy you have brought into my life.
You and I are bonded,
Not by blood,
But by love.
Through a process called adoption,
We are now kin.
Yet even if our birth parents had been the same,
I could not have loved you more.
You are my friend,
My confidant,
My alter ego.
Each time that I have needed comfort, you were there,
Advising me, never judging me,
Sensing my pain,
Offering your slender shoulder to cry on,
And your soft brown eyes showing nothing but love.
You are my baby sister,
A gift from a stranger,
And I am blessed to have you in my life.

    Grace J. Cardona

Soldier's Prayer

I'm a long way from home Lord, I'm counting on you
for strength and support to carry me through.

I long for my loved ones so dear to my heart
It's hard for me Lord to be so far apart.

Some courage and wisdom and power I pray
to help me get through my times spent away.

Please, Lord God in heaven take hold of my hand,
and guide me I pray help me understand.

I know that you have a plan made for me
though sometimes I know that plan I don't see.

So Father I'm praying I'm on bended knee
stay close by my loved ones please watch them for me.

    Cynthia B. Robbins

Untitled

Denounce not the rain,
Gray skies,
or thunders.
Find fault not in clouds
nor dwell on emotional sunders.
But keep in mind-
Following rain the world is covered with sheen
and with each additional rain drop
a stronger sapling will be seen.

    Jennifer Grace Swanson

Mothers Of The Disappeared

They sit and wait
For the call that may change their life,
They lay in silent darkness
Suffering from pain and strife.
They know not what has happened to their child
Which they conceived from love,
They must bear this terrible burden
That has been set upon them from above.
They cannot begin to fathom
What is happening on the outside,
The pain burns with the ferocity of dragon's breath
Like a sharp stab in one's side.
She waits impatiently
Every moment seems like an eternity,
She can't help but think of her child
Alone in the cold, dark city.
So now it would seem
Or so it would appear,
That those who suffer longest
Are the mothers of the disappeared.

    Cynthia L. Hawes

Desire's Child

Sometimes I cry when alone I mourn
For the children I want that will never be born

Would her eyes have been green?
Would he have looked like his Dad?

Tiny replicas of ourselves
Now only dreams never had

So in love with this man that I chose to marry
So in love with his children that I will never carry

I'll never feel our child grow as my middle gets thick
I'll never pick out names then feel it kick

I wonder if I will always grieve
For the children I yearn for but will never conceive

For no amount of diamonds or silver or gold
Can ever replace the child I will never hold

    Jeanna K. Eckert

My Chi-zu-ko

I searched the world over
    For the girl I had in mind
The one that I wanted had to be
    One of an only kind

She had to be, oh so lovely
    More beautiful than I had ever seen
She had to be mine for evermore
    And be in all my dreams

Her voice would remind you of a bubbling stream
    Flowing throughout the day
Her love for me and my love for her
    Would be felt in the same old way

I realized one day, that she was really real
    She was there with a true love I knew
For my beating heart was telling me things
    That real lovers hearts all do

We then and there were married
    And I still love her so
She's my Japanese Doll
    She's my Chizuko

    Chauncey L. Knight

Too Much To Ask

Explain to me what should the standard be
For the worth of a man to be measured accurately?

Is it too much to ask for a man to be a man?
Judged on integrity not the weapon in his hand!
Is he honest? Has he worked for all that he has gained?
Or is security found through others' pain?
  Tell me, is Dignity just too much to ask?

Farewell to youth, goodbye to innocence
Tears for a friend, tears for ignorance
Baseball caps and tennis shoes, all motives for a kill
How can you know the meaning of Death
  When you haven't begun to live?

Is it too much to ask to take a look and see
Just what can be done to stop the hemorrhaging?
Tourniquets and bandages still the blood flows on past
Through the fingers of a loved one's hand.
Tell me is peace just too much to ask?

Charles Sepulveda

A Tree For All Seasons

In the Winter trees are bare,
for they have no leaves to wear.

In the Spring trees begin to bloom,
and the flowers retrieve their perfume.

In the Summer trees have grown,
then the wind comes, I can hear the trees moan.

In the Fall all the trees' leaves change,
red, orange, yellow, are their range.

Trees change every season,
yet no one knows the reason.

Amy Silverberg

We Have Never Met

I have not seen you,
For we have never met.
And yet, you choose to torment me,
With false names and fake phrases.
Feeding my dreams with lies,
And pretending in every way.
Deceiving me each day and each night.
Without stopping, you can not stop.
How you love to torture my mind.
Why is it? I must know!
I fear if I don't I might descend,
Into eternal dread of life and love.
Trying hard to comprehend, this mystery of mine,
I pray that one day, this agony will soon fade away,
As quickly as it came to be.

Erika Gonzalez

Dreaming

I awake
From a dream,
I've been in a place you've never seen.
You can't get there by car or bus,
to years ago before there was us.
And as I look around me now,
I sight to remember I chose this how.
When I said "I do" I thought I was done,
that you would be my only one.
And yet in the night of silence so deep,
I step paths not chosen, promises I didn't keep.

Jeann Luellen

Moonwalk

Reach out! Reach out in exploration
  for we have won the race!
Step forward! Step forward with exhilaration
  for we have conquered space!

With bounding giant steps
  we walked upon the moon!
When will we visit Mars?
  Will it be very soon?

A giant step in space
  To us has been unfurled!
The wonders of His grace
  could unify this world!

We saw before our very eyes
  brave men on Tranquility Base!
The finest record of mankind
  may save our human race!

Franklin John Skillman

"Thank You"

Thank you my dear friend;
For your life is not at end.
  Your life you will not loose;
To thoughts, drugs, gangs, or booze
  This is no joke at all;
So stand up straight and tall.
  Your presence is required;
Even so, desired.
  I thought of you last night;
And shivered once in fright.
  From the thoughts you thought of death;
And how I talked of theft.
  I put my words at rest;
This life, it's all God's test.
  So take your next steps slow;
They may hurt, even so…

Remember me your friend;
That'll be there till the end.

Jo-lena Hageman

The Name Of Death's Father

He had a name that rang for ages
Forever embroidered in life's many pages
Discriminating none when he chose his prey
Taking them under day after day
Wise men, old men, young men alike
He had no bark, rather a lethal bite
Men still quiver and shiver to the bone
For his presence is still widely known
He comes from a cold and empty tomb
And he still finds many while they are secure in the womb
His domain is loud and his kingdom is shrewd
He is constantly cursed and enjoys being rude
Claiming all within all due time
Dancing to the music of a mother's cry and a child's whine
Having a feast with the blood of an army's dead,
He is satisfied with nothing less than their leader's head
He stalks by the night, and soars through the day
But he will stumble and fall when the Light from either March
or April makes way, he alludes all cautions, and dwells in
all places for Fate is a tyrant of many faces

John Palacio

"One Of Those Days"

Got out of bed this mornin' went rushin' for the train
Forgot to take my overcoat and then it starts to rain!
I rushed onto the platform, (train's a half an hour late),
When some old drunk throws up on me, why don't I feel too great?

I sprint into the office, punch in fifteen minutes late,
At a quarter after nine while my watch reads half past eight.
I'd gone to bed at eight last night in hopes of rising early,
Now my job's in jeopardy, the boss is mean and surly.

He spies me sneaking to my desk and grabs me by the collar,
Calls me "on the carpet" and begins to scream and holler:
"Where's the work I asked you for non-compos mentis fool,
You're finished here! You're fired! Try going back to school!"

James W. Hughes

Forgotten Tree

I am the tree that was always forgotten,
forgotten when they all came round
I was the one you wanted when they couldn't be
I was the only one who would let you,
let you yell at me.
So you'll excuse me if I don't
remember who you are.
I am the one you went to when they left
you behind
Then I was all used up and then you
were gone
So forgive me if I have forgotten, forgotten
who you are
Now I am the tree who doesn't care anymore
thanks to you
And when the darkness comes I'll still be,
Still be the forgotten tree.

Candice Allen

Nightmare

My whirling brain awakens from its tortured rest
Freed from consciousness to restless fields of fear
No crevice is too foreboding
No thought too horrid to embrace
Locked in suspense until released by grace
Never mercifully
Always completing the full revolution
Shouts, beheading, ghosts, and fright
Heart left pounding in the dead of night
What version of slumber is this I endure
Pursuit by dogs would bring rest more
Careful solace with soothing thoughts and mundane illusions
    fail to damper these unwelcome images
Prayer to chase these dreams away turns on me in some distorted way
Images cross and turn around
Just adding to the new nightmare I've surely found
Try again and hope for peace
Return to sleep to seek release.

Geliza

At Sunset

I stand upon a mountain
gazing at the hypnotic sunset,
Below, the life filled waters
Glide down the cliffside
With the grace of a dove.
The river twists its way through the forest maze,
Trees sway with the soft evening breeze,
Nearby roses spray their perfume into the air,
The river takes the fire from the sun,
The sky darkens and stars gather round

Damon Darlow

Rosebuds

Scattered rosebuds on one that's nigh,
    Fresh blossoms shall they lay,
    Whence you have spoken, be it in whispers,
    That emanate through twilight's gay,
    Turn, in breath deep and sorrow no more,
    For my soul shall transcend away,
    As whimsical voices calando for me,
    Summonsing me home this day,

Though my spirit wallow,
    Rest the rosebuds to embrace,
    I shall whirl in their splendor and yearn once to be,
    Softly caress to my breast, tender pedal I see,
    Well-beloved memories endear to Thee,
    Only to slowly endeavor, restive to flee,
    The luminous light sent forth for me,
    Summonsing me home.

Bonnie S. Davis

Best Friend

Time passes and along the way,
Friends are gathered from the masses.
Faces which appear in ordinary places,
Sorted out with neither rhyme nor reason.

    Time passes and our world does change.
    Friends drop along the dark and lonely street.
    Tomorrows friends as yesterdays are gone.
    Inevitably washed away by falling rain.

    A very truth is found within my head.
    Just look around, at last you are alone.
    All's not lost, you seize the thought,
    You are your own true and constant, Best Friend.

Florence Ellingsen

"Friends"

Friends are there when you're sad,
Friends are there when you're glad.
Friends are companions,
Who do some demanding.
Friends are people you see in the hall,
Friends are people you see in the mall.
Friends are people in school,
Who think you're so cool.
Friends are people who say hi,
When you pass by.
Friends are people you share your memories with,
The ones you laugh with,
The ones you cry with.
Friends are people who help you,
Friends are people who care.
Friends are people who last,
Forever and ever.
Friends are every thing
To me.

Annie R. Snowden

Why Did She Have To Die

I remember the sadness of that day when she to told me my Great
Grandmother had passed away.
I tried my hardest not to cry but my mothers words shot me like a
bullet right between the eyes.
All I could think was why couldn't I have been the one to die?
Why didn't I have the chance to give her a kiss and say,
"Good-bye, I love you?"
Why did she have to die, and why didn't she say "Good-bye?"
We had a good life together and lots of fun,
and still I think why couldn't I have been the one?

Jaime Turner

The End Of Passion (Death)

He comes cloaked in shimmering black
From a place never since remembered
From inner thoughts and fantasies
Where fear hides and love flourishes
Where hate rages and lust fills every breath
As he wanders the corridors of my mind he softly my name
I see his eyes blaze from the still darkness
He looks beseechingly into my heart that pounds with passion
He causes my once steady breathing to come in quick pants
A sigh escapes my throat
His gaze reveals a hunger
He sits lightly upon my bed and touches me with tenderness
He bends to place a gentle kiss
I feel warmth radiating from his body as we kiss
And I shudder
Then
In a gentle thrust
He enters my soul
I live no more

Brandy Alexandre

On This Day

On this day as you find your way down the aisle, I'll be watching
from a seat above, as God joins together two beautiful people in love.

I am sorry that on this day I had to leave you before we took
that one last walk, but honey, you'll always have the memories of
the times we used to play and the times we used to talk.

As now my little girl is taking a new step in life, and I know in
my heart you'll be that special wife, and someday we'll meet again,
but for now I had to leave you with your dearest friend.

He has promised me to love and protect you in every way, but I want
you to know, that If I had one more wish, it would be "me" walking
you down the aisle, on this special day.

Carolyn D. Reedy

The Best Is Yet To Be

The tenderest love song is yet to heard,
From a whippoorwill or a mocking bird;
The loveliest dream is yet just a dream,
The shiniest stars are yet to gleam;
The mightiest deeds are yet to be done,
The biggest vic'tries are yet to be won;
The best days of life are yet to unfold,
The sweetest love story is yet to be told;
The most vivid rainbow is yet to be seen,
In a paint-brushed sky on a heavenly screen;
The highest peaks are yet to be dared,
The most sacred moments are yet to be shared;
The most radiant dawn will wake up the sun,
And tell the world of a peace to be won;
The echoing sunset will cast its spell,
With a gentle sigh that al is well;
The most blessed times of our lives will appear,
So believe in your heart == these moments are near.

Douglas E. Bean

Mother Nature

Mother Nature has a blinding elegance.
From the lush thick forest, to the smooth rolling hills.
Bright snowy mountain peaks, and fluffy white clouds gives me a
great feeling.
But when man interferes with Mother Nature, my feeling is gone.
I now have a terrifying feeling, I feel that Mother nature will
do something awful to keep possession of our earth.
I fccl that mother nature is dying, and we are the ones killing her.
If only people would take her seriously, but unfortunately they do not.
So I personally do my best to keep her strong and healthy.
But sadly one person can't do it alone.

Alexis Lea

Oh Mississippi!

"And the waters of the flood overflowed the earth —"
From Genesis again the awful tale retold:
Mighty Mississippi unleashes wide its anger,
Missouri, too, conspired in vengeful wrath -
One hundred years before, in ire, she made Kaskaskui Island,
Now sweeps it out, once more proud architect;
Land of farms, gilded cities thus beleaguered.
The dead move restlessly above the earth;
Human hands in endless hope the sandbags muster.
Great Waters bulging, undiminished, feels no pity!

In this enlightened century of our time,
Can man to Nature in truth say thus:
"I rule the land, the heavens and all creation."?

Estelle C. Dunn

Indian Spring

Morning star awakens with a deep yawn
From her wintery sleep, near dawn.
Stretching, she lets fall her buffalo skin.
In naked glory, the rites of spring begin.

Through ethereal, lacy fog and crystal dew,
She glides on rainbow mists of every hue.
Spirit dancing among wooded, budding bowers,
Morning star keeps rhythm with delicate wildflowers.

Down the fertile mountainside, she tiptoes,
To where the rushing, emerald river flows.
Swirling, icy waterfalls lure her in;
She bathes her renewed, electrified skin.

Raising her purified arms to the sky awaking,
Winds carry her primordial chant of making.
Invoking the sacred rising of Father Sun,
The mystical seed flowers; transformation has begun.

Drenched in the warmth of yellow sunlight,
Ancient spirit is reborn, and she takes flight.
Run free beneath her Falcon wing
And feel the breath of Indian Spring.

Davida Dawn Williams

Report From A Small Planet

Twelve hundred light years distant
From our generation, long deceased
On the planet Earth we left behind
Knowing not to whom or where in time
Our message might return
Within this glowing milky way
On one small planet found
Hominids have begun to stand
Upright, they peer out from their caves
The protruding ridges of their brows
Shadowing dark eyes of suspicion
All begin to jabber, pointing
As though we may be subjects for their menu!
The males charge! Then cautiously recede to where
Females suckle young upon small, hairy breasts
Then all advance, shaking and
Jabbering with a fuss
The primate creatures cower, falling
And kneel to worship us!

C. James Matuschka

Untitled

You can read about them all
From the beginning until now.
Including the one that caused the wall.
Some are revolutionary
And some are civil,
Yet they all cause pain and suffering.
They never hit home
Until the recent past
When Mom said Dad wasn't coming home.
She said some far away exotic lady claimed him.
Then I lost my husband
When he, just like Daddy, bought a one-way ticket.
Except, he went to a different part of Asia.
Do we ladies stand a fighting chance?

I just wonder
Will there ever be
A "War to end all wars"?

Barbara Ann Smith

Fingers Crossed

On the lookout for guardian angels to shield him
From the endless abuse and neglect of society, peer
Pressure on the rise, self-esteem declining at
Rapid speeds, always watch your steps with great patience because
You could be held accountable for countless mental
Beatings consisting of two basic elements hatred, and
Ignorance, 100% make up, 0% virtual reality, missing his
Securing blanket by a mire mile, with the poison in all
Their mouths, swallowed whole without a moments notice,
Drawing frowns upon their frozen faces as he forced a
Sour taste down their throats, classroom teachers denied
Comment, his screams for help clearly heard throughout,
Never once reported.

Christy Spray

Waiting

Waiting is
  frustration. Blinding. Brittle.
Waiting is
  irritation. Grinding. Gritty.
Waiting is
  a hollow house a bleak corner a mute phone
  a closed door an empty booth a silent face
  an unspoken word.
Waiting is
  tension. Taut. Teasing.
Waiting is
  fear. Stiletto-sharp. Skittering. Glittering.
Waiting is
  a sibilant searing soul-shattering sigh.
And
  I
    Hate
    It!

Joan C. Eason

A Man With A Dream

A man destined to reach his dream.
His dream is what keeps him going,
Each day he strives to reach his dream,
Through bad times he keeps going,
For he knows that dream is just beside him,
He will grab that dream,
Hoping it will never leave his side,
For if that dream should ever leave,
He would never forgive himself,
For letting go of his dream

Ann Tutol

"You Can Do It"

I strive to reach, oh so high
Gathering my thought, as I gaze to the sky
crying, praying, sometime giving up
I sit and sip from the old china cup
But you can do it, just get up

Knocking on doors, where opportunity seem
Only to be turned down, they know not within
what I can offer, after where I've been
I go away with my head in a bend
You can do it, try again

In the smallest places, with the smallest child
I humble, myself, they understand
The places get bigger, a child plays in the sand
I feel the wonder, I share a smile
You did it, I knew it all the while

I seem not yet fulfill, could there be more still
The pain sometimes too great, there are many I have not met
I now rest while drinking from the cup
You can do it, go ahead, get up

Bernice Petty

I Thank Thee

Lord above, I thank thee for another day to serve thee
Give me strength to keep thy word
Guide my way by night and day
When the day is ending and once more the night's ascending
Once again I kneel to pray to thank the Lord for the day
Now I lay me down to rest as I pray to meet tomorrow's test
With love and courage given free I thank the Lord for keeping me.

Lord above, I thank thee for the wondrous joy of living
For the birds and all the trees, for the mountains and the seas
I was born to love thee and to work this land you gave me
Thank you for these blessings rare and for thy tender loving care
When my life on earth is done and no more I'll see the setting sun
A far more glorious sight I'll see when I can kneel,
my Lord, to thee.

Dumas F. Frick

Recycling Age

Landfills are getting strict
Glass, tin, and plastics collected in their own district
Glass if clear, green, and brown; covers and lids are seen.
They have to be sorted and clean.
Only jars, bottles, and jugs; nothing in between.
Labels and ends are to be removed off all
Tin cans to be flattened, or we'll call.
Rinse them of all food remain...
When we hand sort, it becomes a strain.
Nobody else will take it either; so they claim.
Plastics are many, styles are none too few.
Look for numbers on their bottom of one and two.
They need to be washed out,
Or in the garbage they'll be tossed about!
People need to do it there's no doubt.
Keep all milk jugs strung together...
Removing lids, and rinse: we'll take 'er.
Customers who don't respond, will get a letter.
The sooner you all learn, the better.
This land will be ours forever.

Connie Allaire

Me The Unseen, Unknown, Unguided Force Of Solitude

Look, gaze upon my lack of omnipotence
Glowing moons the force they pull and days the night they bring
The tethered moors how strong but weak upon thy hand
Go forward without moving unto the promised land
Sit upon the shelf and dust it is your will
Go freely like the river so lonesome that it must kill
Filter the thoughts of men how unguarded can they be
Know yourself better than anyone can see
Step and go and go away the worlds a play to me
Maybe I can give it extra, an extra I can be
So don't mourn or cry or pity what you see
There's more inside inside, inside there is me.

Jeremy Blatt

To My Departed Wife

It was a cold winter's morning in the early hours of the day
God called you, and you slowly slipped away.

We had said our good-byes a few weeks before
And I knew it was just a matter of time I would see you no more

The twenty-six years we had together weren't all that bad,
At first the love we had for each other was about all we had.

We had a love for each other only two people could know.
My problem was I didn't always let it show.

And I still miss you ever so much,
I still can remember your soft, loving touch.

The talks we had, and the things you would say
I will never forget, and still think about it even to this day.

Your love was always there to guide me in so many ways,
And when I think about it, it puts me in a daze.

And in our garden, the things we would grow.
You would work for hours, canning it so we could save our dough.

You were more than a girl friend and wife, you were my best friend.
You made life for me so good, and pure happiness within.

So rest now, my love, and have a good day,
I know it's just a matter of time till I'll be heading your way.

Franklin D. Lynn

My Dad

This is a poem about my Dad
God gave me the best He had
Dad, you had a heart of gold
I'll always remember the stories
Of long ago that you told.

You worked very hard on your farm
Planting beans, wheat, and corn
You were God's special one
Since the day that you were born.

Remember the fun you had with your boat
And how you could swim and how you could float
I'll always remember how healthy you were
Until the day the Dr. discovered cancer.

You were an example for the world to see
How you carried your cross so faithfully
I will never know the reason why
You had to suffer so much and then to die.

But one thing I'm grateful for and very glad
That you sent this special man to me to be my Dad.

Christine M. Maxa

Untitled

Surrounding darkness
Gone-life within the soul
Love lost...replaced by fear of letting go
Empty arms reach aimlessly, longing to be understood
Sheltered heart, silent cries...
Prayers remain unanswered
Suffering alone, the slow burning light of faith begins to dim
Comfort and relief found only through tears
Empty heart, searching soul, nothing left to be found
Complete oneness no longer know, as shadows overpower the light
Trapped within myself-walls around my soul
Confining the spirit which longs to be set free
Left only is this inner peace,
Comprehended not with words,
   But through belief in ones faith
   in God within.

Jenny Schuyler

Hell

   Expand, through time and space, intrude, upon another place,
   Grasping, taking, such a waste, a fever, with such sour taste,
   A yearning, for a life of peace, imprisoned, no sign of release,
Embodied, by a wall of stone, a life of shackles, engrossed in bones,
The gravel upon which you lie, one day will surround you when you die,
   The air that was once crisp and fresh, is now dank and stale as dead
                     flesh,
   Late to come is remorse, another plain, a lesser course,
   A crack within justice wall, beckons, a sorrowful call,
   A taste of freedom, so brief, let the walls contain the grief,
      Outside, a foreign land, a brief, but narrow strand,
   Characters, the same as within, fighting, just to get in,
Slipping through the narrow cracks, entering and never turning back,
   A line so narrow and somewhat vague, torment and anguish, such a
                     plague,
   Ratification and little remorse, the law twisted, another course ,
   A death considered humane, a room, a chair, gas contained,
         An eye for an eye, a room, a chair, electrify,
   A day in court, a judgement made, a life gone, but no trade,
   Sleep, eludes this cold cell, an envelope, postmarked...Hell.

Brenda Doe Kathman

Untitled

Almighty is thy name,
Great in heaven and earth the same.

Oh glory be to You,
The God of Israel is so true.

Jesus Christ is King,
In heaven and earth your name shall reign.

for ever and ever more,
Your Mighty Spirit shall soar.

Upon your people in whom you love,
You shall give us power from above.
To with stand these wicked days,
To all who wait, watch and pray.

Gena Yager

Deep Love

There is nothing more precious to me than you,
I hope that you see it in all that I do,
For my every action evolves with you in my mind,
The deepness of my love towards you is difficult to find,
With you in my life I feel there's nothing I can't do,
No possible obstacle I cannot pull through,

The strength of our love can make any wish come true,
But I've only one wish to forever be with you!

Brenda Kele

The Beauty Of The Rose

As the beauty of the rose
grows from bud to flower
I marvel how the flowers grows
As nature brings it sun and shower

And I must smell its sweet perfume
And wonder at its shading and grace
And how the rain leaves dewy drops
like drops of tears upon its face.

And sad to see-it cannot stay
As a strong wind blows its petals away
And branches and leaves stand and pose
As the winds destroyed the beautiful rose.

Anna L. Gillen

I Met The Master

I had walked life's way an easy tread.
Had followed where comforts and pleasures led
Until one day in a quiet place
I met the master face to face

With station rank, and wealth for my goal
Much thought for my body, but none for my soul
I had entered to win life's mad race.

I had met him and knew him and blushed to see
That's his eyes full of sorrow where fixed on me
And I followed and fell at his feet that day
While my castle melted and vanished away

Melted, vanished and in their place.
Naught else did I see but the master face
And I cried aloud 'oh make me meet
To followed the steps of thy wounded feet.

My thought is now for the souls of men
I have lost my life to find it again.
Ever since one day in a quiet place
I met the master face to face.

David May

Had Jesus Not Gone To Calvary

Where Would Any Of Us Be?

Had Jesus Christ loved me the way you've loved me....
  Had Jesus Christ loved you the way I've loved you
Had Jesus Christ treated us the way we've treated Him
  Where would either of us be...

Had Jesus Christ written us off, considered our lives a tax
deduction, or measured our worth in dollars $ or cents ....
Had Jesus Christ neglected to GIVE or had Jesus decided never
to FORGIVE...Just where do you suppose any of us would be...

Had Jesus handled our lives as carelessly as some of us do...
Had Jesus taken His Father for granted as many times we do...
Had Jesus got tired, fed up of being used and abused, had He
decided He could no longer bear the pain or desire to love everyone
just the SAME

Just where do you think any of us would be?
Had Jesus turned around, disgusted with those who rejected
His Royal Crown...Had He lifted His hands to His Father
and cried out that He couldn't go any farther ...had He not
gone to Calvary... My God where would this soul be?

Evelyn L. Threadgill

Hands

Hands embrace and moments become alive;
Hands caress and humanity's spirit thrives.

Hands communicate a language without written word;
Hands move with intuition— a silent voice heard.

Hands sculpt with a wondrous beauty beyond compare;
Hands engender compassion and ability to share.

Hands are a harbor, a place resembling home;
Hands instill freedom to explore and liberty to roam.

Hands have a unique identity—all their very own;
Hands tell Life's history; through their lines the hidden
  becomes known.

Hands exude warmth—their touch is a desirous pleasure;
Hands inspire dreams—their presence an intrinsic treasure.

Hands guide—their direction clear as stars at night;
Hands contain knowledge and wisdom's lamp of light.

Hands are a power—a force that penetrates deep;
Hands are protective; their touch extends into sleep.

Jeanne Marie Basselgia

The Headless Dancer

Questions,
  hanging in the air.

Unanswered,
  just sitting there.

No one to answer. No one who cares.

Problems,
  with love and life.

Solution,
  maybe a knife;

To ease along the process. To end all the strife.

Love,
  it hurts so bad.

Hate,
  just something else to add

To the struggles of life that make us mad.

Death,
  the answer?

Happiness,
  a headless dancer.

Spinning round and round. No one to catch her.

Catherine N. Brown

He Was Dying - Of Cancer

There was no hope,
He was dying,
There was nothing left to do,
He had his treatments,
He spoke with his heart to you,
He loves you and he knows you love him too,
All there is left to do is to turn to him and prey,
That is all you can do.
You want him to stay,
But you know now what to do,
There is no other or better way,
But to calm yourself and prey.

Aliza Snyder

In Memorial Of...

Luminous and stretched you were
Hanging onto phosphorous limbs
Cursing the day your life became
Yellowed and crisp,
the hours slipping like fish
Wriggling, constricted, suffocating,
Your lungs empty and hot.

My eyes creased away all of this.
My mind became unnamed colors of light and heat.

You were spinning by now,
Twisted and knotting.
I could see through your skin
How your veins would pulse
Like a garden hose folded or
interrupted.

Until it went dim and my eyes
Would open to dried roses hung
from a pale ceiling.

Caroline Todd +

Colors

There are many colors that come to life, whether you are
Happy or going through strife.
White means a washing as white as snow, for everyone to
Hear and everyone to know.
Black is creepy and tries to cover up light, it is like the
Sky you see at night.
Blue is trustworthy and true, it always represents something
That is new.
Red is becoming and very bright,
Yellow is like the moon shining at night.
Purple is royal, and fit for a king, it reminds me of a
Beautiful bell that rings.
Green is the color of grass, the soft feel on your feet,
It is a warm remembering of all the people you meet.
But my favorite color is a peace of mind,
Clear, to be seen by even the blind.
Do colors take a role, or help in troubled time.
Or do they just give us a topic to sing in a rhyme.
Perhaps we'll never find out, or even never know, what goes
On with colors and why we love them so.

April Shelton

Women Of Yesterday

Way back when in colonial life
Hardly any women had any rights.
"I own my woman", a man would say
and that would make the women outraged.
But what were the women to do?
Just make their beds and cook their food.

They weren't allowed to vote or govern.
The men refused, they were too stubborn.
Couldn't be a soldier, a doctor, an attorney.
A dentist, a blacksmith, a leader of a journey.

Among the few things a woman could be
were teachers, cooks, and wives of the family.
But finally the joyous day came
when women could vote and gain fame.

For they had rights now, just like men.
Through their struggles they were strong.

They were women.

Brook Aswamethi

Permanent Love

O, my dear! Let me lull you to sleep!
Have a dream, beautiful and sweet!
Half a century has gone by since we wed!
Fifty two years have flown away since we first met!

The wrinkles on your face, although very light,
Remind me of all the ups and downs of our common life.
Your gray hair brings up reminiscences
Of the most beautiful days of our existences.

You have worked hard all your life;
You have loved me with all your heart and mind.
For our children, you've made so much sacrifice!
I'll be faithful to you till the end of my life.

To me, you're always beautiful and charming.
My love for you never fades and continues growing.
Each day, it becomes more profound and more intense.
It grows steadily: it's permanent and immense.

Go to sleep! O, my sweet wife!
Outside, the sky is full of stars and the moon is bright,
The breeze is teasing the flowers in the moonlit night.
Go to sleep, honey! Let me accompany you to Paradise.

Hoai Van Tu

The Race Of Emotions

Sometimes sadness approaches me and I
have no where to run.
Each tiny piece of my mind travels to a
different time and place within my heart.
I want to scream, cry, and shout each
part of my body goes numb; the hurt is
too evident to avoid; I run and I run
but the pain won't leave me.
A suspect in my own being; a thought is
transformed into reality; reality is
transformed into truth.
Run, run, run away from the reality
of things that continuously haunt me.
A circle I do run, everyday I know the
direction to take, but in the end I'm
lost; no one hears me cry; my pain
suddenly catches me, I'm relentless and I
give in and try to live again; everyday
is a race for me.

Danielle Matthews

Together Always

My memory fails me at times,
Have you been by my side forever?
For that is the way it seems.
As if I have known you forever.

I can say, my sister, that I love you dearly,
And wish my life, to never be without you.
You are a part of my soul, my mind,
And are in my heart, for eternity.

So, my friend, as we walk along life's winding road,
We will always be hand, in hand, you and I.
For a friendship as nobel as ours,
Will never be put asunder.

Time, and time again, you and I
Will return to those golden days,
When friendship, seemed all we had,
And life seemed nothing without it.

Amber Shade

Rookie

The rookie slowly climbs the mound,
  He first looks up and then looks down,
  He reads the signs, messages received,
  Fastball! Inside corner, called strike three!
  Rookie. They call him Rookie.

Rookie. Who ever would suspect
  He could power that all ball to the upper deck?
  Sellout crowd cheers and sings,
  Rookies nickname "sweetswing sweetswing."
  Rookie. They call him Rookie.

Eighteen years spent in the show.
  He's seen players come, and seen players go.
  Admiration and respect continue to mount,
  As the veteran makes his last days count.
  Rookie. They called him Rookie.

The game on the line, only one more out.
  The veteran stands in, everyone's in doubt.
  His last at bat, can he prevail?
  His spirit says yes and the ball sets sail!
  Rookie. In his heart he's still a Rookie.
      Belinda-Marie Purkey

A Memorial For Bean

You were so far away from me - not just a state, or even three.
He had to take you with him when he went away. There were so
many things that I didn't get to say. And now you're gone.
Only a year in age, you were just a baby. Was it just your
time to go? ....Maybe.... I just can't make sense of it all,
how they just hit and ran. They didn't even look back.....
what a cruel, mindless land! Why....?

He tried so hard to save you, but you just couldn't pull through.
He gave you mouth-to-mouth, and drove as fast as he could-
because
he loved you. You were his best friend and he feels so much pain.
It's not his fault, he feels the blame.
The jaws of death are selfish and cruel.

You died in his arms, and as he cried for
you, something in him died. It's no lie. He drove you to the
ocean to let you slip away. But you didn't go, and he still
cries for you to this day. So now it's my turn.... I love
you, Bean, my baby puppy, and I hope you rest in peace in the
arms of a loving God......goodbye.
      Joanna Marie Hicks

From Before The War

The man I love is truer than the bread of earth
He has adventures everywhere.
He is my love from before the war, the man I love.
Succulent fruit, fully satisfies like on walking happily
and vain, the man I love.

Many defects says my mother too many bones says my father
But truer he than the bread of the earth his love is
From before the war, the man I love.
Purity he needs not, in bed he has no exit, the man I love.

Bind me to his yoke to till the earth from end to end
Let him satisfy himself in me the man I love prays not a litany,
but truer than the bread of earth.
The man I love binds me to travel the earth from end to end
The man I love is envied by friends— my enemies become bitter.
His love and mine have no barriers
For it is a love from before the war.
      Jose D. Villagomez

Father

My father sits on the park bench complaining about his hemor-
rhoids.
He has had them off and on for twenty-three years now.
Ever since I was a little kid, I can remember my father's
screams of pain and mass discomfort.
And always shortly after the cries began, my mother would
rush to my father's side and attempt to aid him in any way
possible.
Usually this meant bringing him a glass of Thunderbird,
(no ice), the Wall St. Journal, a tube of Preparation-H,
and of course his favorite donut-shaped seat cushion.
I truly feel for the man; he has had his share of misfortune
to last at least four life times.
I only wish he would be a little nicer to my mother.
Granted he's in pain most of the time, but he should at
least be a bit more sensitive to her wishes.
All that she asks from him is that he take the garbage out
on Tuesdays, change his undershorts more than once a month,
and show her a little affection once in a while.
Personally, I don't think that's too much to ask, but,
then again I'm not my father.
      Chuck Pierce

Loving Hands

One sunny morning a little bird flew into the closed window
He immediately fell upon the sill then down to the chair below.
Fell through the slats in the chair and landed upon the deck
When I ran out to rescue him I thought he had broken his neck.

Held him upright cupped in my palm for seemingly a long time
Ryan ran to see what I had as did Curt, the youngest son of mine.
They busily pulled grass and arranged twigs in an old shoe box
The little bird turned his head in confusion and seemed to gawk.

The "bird ambulance" was ready so I bent down quite lowly
Carefully opened my hand to place him into it ever so slowly.
Suddenly off he flew across the lawn and over to the trees
Birds sang yet we were all frozen in time, me still on my knees.

Waited and watched in silence for what seemed ever so long
Ryan said,"It is a Real Miracle!" as he sat down on the lawn.
I noticed a memento the little bird had left in my hand
The boys giggled at that then ran off to build castles of sand.

Scurried for the house as just realized was still in my robe
I marvelled how the Lord teaches us of Him in our earthly abode.
Considered how much like the little bird we are in this life
How His loving hand upholds us in all hurt, confusion and strife.
      Beverly Merrill

Old Shoe

While waiting for you, I love the one nearest.

For he has been around for many years.
He is comfortable and broken in.
Like an old shoe, I hate to get rid of him because
I never know when I may need him.

For a chance at security, I wait.
But I've begun to think that he is not the one.

Still, I must love him until you come.

I know you and I would make a perfect pair.
Like a Sunday school dress worn with patent-leather shoes,
we'd complement each other.

Maybe I've known you for years; or perhaps,
I'll never meet you...

Whichever, I keep my false hopes in him.
      Amy McKin

He

Out on the street is where he belongs,
He just roams the cold streets humming lonesome songs.
The life of this man is filled with pain and sorrow,
And all he asks for is a nickel to borrow.
Lying asleep on the pavement once again
He dreams of the day when his nightmare will end.
He dreams that the angels with all of their love,
Shall deliver him from this cold place into heaven above.
On one still night while lost in his dreams,
His nightmares and pains had ended it seems.
On the streets is no longer where he should belong,
He's with an angel still singing his song.
He's in a better place now,
That's easy to see,
And I can sometimes feel him watching over me.

Chris Huffman

Daddy's Little Girl

   As she lays sleeping in the arms of her father,
he looks upon his little princess with love in his
heart and happiness in his smile,
   She's a blessing from above, God has brought
into this world of mine, this beautiful child.

   To give us the joys of sharing special times, to watch
her take her first step, to hear her first word, and
watching her grow each passing day.
   I'll always treasure the moment I held her far the very first time,
so tiny and fragile she was, it seems like only yesterday.

   I will always be there to share her laughter,
and kiss away all the tears,
   I will share all her hopes, and dreams through
all the passing years.

   Soon the time will come when I have to let
her go, the memories will remain in my heart
of the special moments we shared together.
   This child has made my world much brighter,
and my life worth living. In my heart she will
always be Daddy's little girl forever.

Diana Moscato

A Mother's Tribute

I saw a little boy just the other day.
He reminded me of our son in so many ways.
His hair was blonde and his eyes were blue.
He noticed me staring and looked as if to say "Who are you?".
Quickly I turned away but I could not help to smile.
It was like I was able to see again, if only for a little while.

All day I could not help to think of how things could of been.
If only time had not come to an end...

I look at our other children and see
that time is passing before our eyes.
I try to be strong, although my heart still cries.
As a mother, it is always hardest to let go.
Sometimes you have to be strong or just not let your feelings show.

Yet every now and then, I'll see a child so much like my own.
I'll remember our son and wonder how he would have grown.
Even though he has found peace and no longer cries painful tears...
I will always wonder how things could have been had we shared time
Together all these years.

Deanna Corvera

Strifes

Life's strifes cannot be conquered by man
He studies, learns, explores, and thinks he can
Man forgets about God's work and God's might
Which is beyond his knowledge and foresight.

Man gathers together his kind and they hassle
They build themselves a beautiful castle
When one deceives the other, they fight
Limited in wisdom, they think they are right.

Man can live, learn, and thrive
Some without being interested in human lives
He uses his knowledge, instruments and destroys
The lives of men, women, girls and boys.

Man is born with numbered days and dies
Some men live true lives and some men live lies
Man is to remember that God forgives seventy times seven
That is if he is desirous of going to heaven.

Azalee Jackson

Heaven Sent

God sent his son down from heaven
He was lent to us for a short while
Down here he walked for many a mile
Doing his father's will with a smile
All because he was heaven sent.

When he touches your soul
He will set it on fire
And give you such a burning desire
To tell it to everyone that you see
Glad tidings from the one that heaven sent.

You must repent of your sins each day
If you want to go to the great milky way
You must read the good book too
For it will tell you exactly what to do
So one day you can live with the one that heaven sent.

For you and me, Christ laid down his own life
But before the cock crowed, Peter denied him thrice
And Judas was paid thirty pieces of gold
His life should have never been sold
But it came to be because he was heaven sent.

Christine K. Hopper

Some Kind Of Hero

It enlightens my mind when I think of such a man.
He was so very tall and bold, a fearless face with strong hands.
He lived his life to satisfy his needs.
He gave love to his only daughter, always there for every crying plead.
Devoted a man of purity, who very much loved his wife.
For everyday he gave his heart to her,
promising for the rest of their life.
If ever in his presence, laughter always filled the air.
He had a fascinating nature about him,
For those who knew him and cared.
He was full of life always giving until the end.
For he was my hero, and I was always proud to call him friend.
A man of braveness and wisdom, he learned to fight his own battle.
Through agonizing pain he refused to fall from his saddle.
As the days passed by his breathe grew very shallow.
His body became frail and weak as souls lingered in the gallows.
In sickness and health until death do we part, she stayed by his side,
Until the very last beat of his courageous heart....

Amanda K. Mitchell

'Street Corner Poet'

As I was driving through this little town I seen this gentleman,
He was standing on a little box on the street corner of Naomi and Dan.

He was of a medium build and about six foot tall I would say,
With black hair and beard, and neatly dressed in a suit of gray.

I parked my car and went nearer to listen for a while,
He had teeth that sparkled and a smirky sort of a smile.

When asked who he was, everyone just shrugged and said
"I don't know",
As long as they had known this man they had just called him "Poet Jo".

The people were gathered around knowing that he would be there.
It reminded me of a politician talking to any one that seemed to care.

After a short spell, I knew there was a reason he was there for sure,
His voice was gentle, but had that tone you just could not ignore.

His poems were all about The Bible and the stories written within,
From Jesus' birth, to being baptized by John, to how he died for our sin

He needed no Bible for a reference nor any notes as he spoke in rhyme,
The words just seemed to flow from his mouth like a well aged wine.

After listening for a spell I turned to go back to my car,
Knowing that some place I had seen him and I wouldn't get very far.

He'd be there step by step walking by my side this day,
Just to remind me I hadn't taken time out today, to PRAY!

george gurney

All Little Boys

He came out screaming with his grandma's voice.
He would've stayed longer but he had no choice.
He was pretty as a picture with his mother's eyes.
He had his uncle's nose and his cousin's thighs.
He shows the pride of his father when he stands up tall.
He has the spirit of his aunts, but that's not all.
You see his great-grandfather when he gets real mad,
While his sensitive side is from his mother's dad.
As part of us all to whom does he belong?
We all lay claim but we're all dead wrong!
He's a child of nature and like all little boys,
He can't be split like money and toys.
He's a great creation but he's just been loaned.
He wasn't bought so he can't be owned.
To deprive him of manhood when his youth isn't gone,
Just use him; abuse him; or make him a pawn.
He's a child of nature, let him stay top shelf.
'Cause when push comes to shove, he belongs to himself.

Charlie Walters

Paper Hearts

She writes the names of her targets in the center of paper
hearts. And on her wall she has millions of paper hearts
because she targets millions.

She selects her victims and works on them, one by one, in
pairs, or in groups. It's her game, she does what she
wants.

She gets them to like her, and like her and like her,
until they love her, and then she has them, even though
she always did.

As she breaks their hearts so goes their paper heart on her wall.

Half of the broken heart goes in the garbage, with the
other to remain as a souvenir.

Like pieces of a jigsaw she tries to fit different halves
of hearts together. And when two different pieces fit,
she laughs.

Although her victims loved her, she just loved the game of
"Paper Hearts." It's her game, she does what she wants.

Alejandro Bute

"Fan"

Deafening. I can't
hear anymore. The fan keeps

wailing and screaming at me in its
foreign language. It won't stop. It just

drones on and on and on like a bomber circling
overhead, trying to aim at me. And the blades, they

keep spinning and spinning and
spinning in spite of my

shouts: Stop that! The wind that
blows on my body gets colder and

colder and colder until I shiver out of
control. I know my hair is

turning into icicles and I can feel my
feet becoming numb. Soon I will freeze

to death. I'm in the Antarctic Polar Region on a
special mission for my country. No I'm not. I

just want to turn off that
fan. I could get up and pull the

plug, if I could just get
out of this confining straight jacket.

Carol Walker

The Rumbling Sea

As I look out over the multi color sea, I
Hear the waves calling my name.

I watch the rumbling ocean take the waves
Home to shore.

I can sense the big bitter smell of a
Fragrance of the sea below.

As I watch from the balcony, I can see the
ocean cradle the waves and the sun say "Bye" as it
Set to sleep.

The foamy tide washes up to shore and brings
back everything it can.

Then I turn to go inside, hear a gull, spin
Around and see the wonderful life below my feet.

Hollis M. Botti

Pre-Nuptial Agreements

Play macho games in silence, and don't
    help me understand,
I'll vivisect precisely, taking what makes you a man;
Don't respect my nature, and
I'll erode your soul; relationships are fragile
If destruction is the goal.
Repel my touch with anger, and I'll respond in kind,
As tenderness retains its place, but only in the mind.
Expectorate, and I'll spit back, when
    We make love at night
Whoever denigrates the best
will be the one who's right,
Bound in morbid fascination, and
    with base consistency,
    to girlish games and
    calling names or
    sterile,
    puerile
    fantasy.

Geraldine Jane Vernon

Aunt Ella

Little Aunt Ella came to stay
her adventure started yesterday

Bundled up in the mountains she boarded a plane
bravely determined to enjoy the fast lane

A chatty pilot announced we'd all be pleased
The weather had cooled to 83 degrees

Little Aunt Ella distrusted this news
in a bag, she had stuffed galoshes, her muffler too!

Under puffy clouds and a brilliant sun
Ella winced at the nakedness of everyone

Tiny tee shirts, flimsy shorts
it's the reason for the crime on those news reports

These flat-landers speed from mall to mall
No siesta, like in the old movies, NOT AT ALL!

Jane Collins

Bench Girl

A girl sat on a bench at my school;
Her clothes in a fall like a thread spool;
Her cans in a black bag hung on to a cart;
Her face toward the mother dust;
Do we still have a heart?

It was eighty degrees!
She wore a coat!
When I saw her up close,
I got a lump in my throat!

Nobody spoke to her ahead of me.
I wondered why. When I spoke to her,
she said, "Oh, please!"
I wondered how I'd be if that were me.
Nothing!
In the middle of the square,
In the midday heat,
she sat with a stare, a cold physique.

Earnestly! Gee whiz!
Honestly! Golly! Coal!
There's a girl on a bench at my school!

Elaine Harper Jackson

Daughter Dinosaur

If my daughter was a dinosaur you would really hear her roar!
Her footsteps would shake the earth to its core!
You would run from her till you were sore,
  then she would chase you some more.
You would be looking for an exit door.
It's daughter dinosaur! Need I say more?
Triceratops is the dinosaur she pretends to be.
It's the one that holds her curiosity.
Its physique is awesome you see,
  like its horns of plenty that Alyssa aims at me.
But she will never hear her dad plea for there's
  a little T-Rex in me, that lets her know
  it's time to refrain from this dinosaur game.
Alyssa's lore of the dinosaur will have to wait,
  for the evening has grown much too late.
The dinosaurs are again extinct while daughter
  gets her forty winks.

James Lore

Forest Green

Deep within the forest green, nature reveals
Her many sights and sounds to scan.
The trails are many never straightly done,
As animals who traverse them know not ways of man.

Mushrooms on a fallen tree
Wood ferns growing at its base.
Dew drops gathering in clusters of pearly pools
Chipmunks busily stocking their nesting place.

Dragonflies gathering, swarming through the air,
While beatles and crickets below them do crawl.
As soft winds of summer gently stroke
Green leaves of trees, bushes and grasses so tall.

Spiders busily spinning their webs so fine,
Between each bush and tree to catch their meal
Of moths and flies who travel through forest green
Unmindful others from whom their presence do conceal.

The stillness of the forest green
Intense as it may be, is ever being broken
By all forms of life as nature renews, replenishes
And starts anew all things in the forest glen.

George W. Rogers

Under Lock And Key

Sheltered from the outside world, shut behind a door
Her parents love her so much, they'd like to give her more
Try to keep her innocent, afraid for her to see
Exactly what the world is like - except under lock and key
She stares out her window, longing to be free
Can't wait till she's older - old enough to leave
No one understands it - why she can not see
Home's the only place she should be - under lock and key
Under lock and key, how can she learn what life is really like?
How will she cope with the pain and strife
Rose colored glasses is all she's really known
Based on what she's learned at home
Knives, guns, drugs, and gangs, homeless in the street
Sad and tired faces - is this reality?
Doesn't mean too much to her, she sees it on T.V.
Could this be why they keep her - under lock and key
Years have passed, time has flown - three children of her own
Yes she gives them everything, a nice suburban home
Can't see why they're miserable, longing to be free
But she keeps them as they should be, under lock and key.

Debbie Rosso

The Dark Night

As he rode off into the empty night,
Her pretty face was full of fright,
For on this day her love would die,
Without any questions, where or why.

He had saved the weak and the poor,
And stopped the killing forever more,
The red coats would have his head for this,
And so with one last glimmering kiss,
He lost the lady that he'd miss.

With a wave of his hand, he said goodbye,
Looking back with a sadness in his eye,
"I love you, my dear," was all she could hear,

As he rode off into the empty night,
Her pretty face was full of fright,
For on this day her love would die,
Without any questions, where or why.

Amy Schneider

The Magical Unicorn

Look at the magical beast as she waves
her silky, shiny mane in the air. She sparkles
like a beautiful pearl. Her tail with a
braid of red and silver silk running through it.
She gallops faster than any animal
in the world. Her silver like horn
catches the light just right and
it spreads a rainbow throughout the whole world.
But ah there she lays dead on
the ground. Dead as a door-
nail because people have said
that they don't believe in unicorns
any more. But if you ever see a
unicorn it might be the last, so lock her
memory up tight in your heart for
unicorns only appear to people who believe in them.

Crystal Brazie

La Loba

Through the open doorway she tried to reach me
Her silver coat glistening in the sun
She had no eyes yet looked inside my soul
Knowing I still had battles to be won

I trembled in terror with each lunge she took
Fighting desperately not to feel her touch
I sensed more changes were yet to come
And I feared them, oh so much

Her constant vigil at my doorway
Would not allow me a comfort to seek
She knew that without her constant threat
I again would become very weak

My spirit anguished in silent torment
For even my kindred souls did not understand
This undeniable force deep within me
Only she without eyes would take my hand

I knew she would lead me to a frightening unknown
Where only the wild spirits dance and sing
For they have the courage to search and roam
And only this can my happiness bring

Joanne G. Sullivan

A Mother's Smile

A mother's smile is warm and kind
Her smile shows what's on her mind
Her smile shows love and truth
You remind her of her youth
She knows it's hard and sometimes unfair
Just remember, she'll always be there
Her smile says to reach for your dreams
No matter how impossible they may seem
She loves you now and always will
A mother's love is truly real
Anyone can have a child
But do you have that special smile
Her smile shows she's proud of things you do
But most of all, she shows her love for you
I thank the Lord for my mother
She's number one above any other
I want her to know that I really love her
And I could never ask for a better mother

Crystal Thurman

42nd Street

Twenty-seven cents and a newspaper,
Here in my lap, there on the floor.
The noises I hear are loud as they whisper.
What day is it? Too drunk to remember,
Too tired to give a damn.
I've got too many places to go and too much to do.
(And twenty-seven cents won't get you far)
Ooooops. Make that twenty-two.
Dropped a nickel, a suitcase, and a key.
Got nothing to show for the past few years,
except the tear stains on my collar
and the dirt on my clothes.
Pick up a cup and have another drink.
Get wasted, and maybe tomorrow,
(If I meet a few good guys tonight),
I might have twenty dollars
To add to my twenty-two cents,
And a few more tear stains on my collar.

Jennifer Butler

Big Little Boy

Look at my little guy going out the door
He's so big and bright, a wondrous four.
Off to school for the very first time
My mood is sad, his is sublime
He's entering the world so very wide
His little chest stuck out with so much pride.
I dare not look at him again
For fear that he might see my pain.
As I let him go off all by himself
So confident and smiling my little elf.
I throw him a kiss and say a prayer
Dear Lord keep him safe from here to there.

Edna Zukowski

The Shadow Image

The sun's gone in, but where's my friend?
  He's usually with me end to end.
Never lonely, never straight,
  Never early, never late.

He can't be heard but can be seen.
  The former's true each way I lean.
Sometimes short, sometimes tall,
  Sometimes flat against a wall.

The clouds past by and he goes out.
  My friend sleeps there is no doubt.
But when the sun's rays reach the earth
  They create his person for what it's worth.

One need not guess who's that for sure
  When they see us on ground's floor.
But that can't be within the night,
  For he begins me at dawn's light.

Alfred G. Huber

I Cry In Grief

All of the memories that we shared,
I look back on and cannot bare.
I cry in grief wishing it weren't so,
But I do know that someday we all must go.

One day I know again we will meet,
Then there will be no more pain to defeat.
Once I see you there with me,
I will know I've been set free.

Jennifer Leigh Chinnes

The Ballad Of Hairy And His Tooth Fairy!!!

There was a boy named Hairy,
He's waiting for his tooth fairy,
His name was Gary,
He's waiting, he's waiting.

As he is playing with his toy boat,
Along came his very silly goat,
That was holding Hairy's coat,
He's waiting, he's waiting.

His mom said you stink,
His face turn pink,
As he climbed into the sink.
He's waiting, he's waiting.

He put his pj's on,
And started to yawn,
As he saw something on the lawn.
He's waiting, he's waiting.

He woke up and yawned,
And noticed his tooth was gone,
He went out to the lawn and Gary was gone.
He's not waiting, he's not waiting.

Jaime Love

Standing People

Standing people I hear you calling,
High upon the winds!
As I walk along the path,
where my world begins!
Bending with the graceful breeze, rusting through
your hair,
Reds, and greens, and sable browns, line this
path with care!
Washing all my woes away,
As you touch the sky!
Gentle giants among the earth,
Can you hear me cry.
Standing people feel my love,
For you ever Dear,
Awesome, your strength from birth,
Living all these years!

Donna Blucher

What Was Once Forgotten

As I sit in solitude,
high upon this mesa,
I can look forever across this painted sky.
The feeling of a spiritual peace,
is within my soul.

I can imagine these plains,
in a more primitive time.
This land once alive with buffalo and wild ponies,
now bears a freeway.
I wonder what it was like;
those magnificent animals wandering free.

Across this land,
once rode the Native Americans on painted ponies.
The sense of pride and honor,
that was carried from father to son.
These are virtues unique for today.
Their heritage is too easily forgotten.

Beth Ann Yeager

This Was The Night For Me To Remember

This was the night for me to remember,
his beauty and warmth set me on fire.
I just know it was to be forever,
he was the one to quench my hearts desire.

I've been trying to reach this special star,
I have been searching hard and so unaware,
I found this star and the reach wasn't far,
This star I know I'll be able to bare.

After a bit a time and months have past,
the sadness had begun of hurtful tears,
then came the thoughts of if were going to last,
these tears I hope will never come to lasting fears.

Our love is so much like a hurricane,
It has a lot of its tosses and turns,
We have gone through shares of tremendous pain,
We both just how that this love never burns.

All that we can do is to make a dream,
And make this love go deeper then the sa,
And make our relationship a strong team,
And make it the very best we can be.

Christy Nicholson

An Ounce Of Prevention

He licked his lips and put his hands on trembling hips grazing
his belt as a mental welt rose from his memories hiding in a
tree or under stairs in failing light telling himself forgive,
forget—and living on not to punish, but to please, he found it
not so easy

The screams awaken him deep in night that take him back there
that took so long to forgive Papa, don't he often said Papa
did, all loose on dago red

He learned a lot from an angry old man how to jump when told
and how to use an open hand to ed-u-cate and how to blame a
beating on booze how to hit, hard!, and not to bruise

The ground frowned when they got him down

He fixed his hat and he could see his breath his hands balled
into the fists he remembered of his wine soaked father his
black hat resting on his wrinkled head staring at the
unforgiving ground that swallows the unforgiven dead

Joseph Swords

I Remember Grandpa

I remember Grandpa, William Loomis was his name.
His eyes, they always sparkled and his manner was the same.
He had a lot of grandkids, but a favorite had he none.
He treated us alike, you see, we all were number one.
He had a filling station in a place called Hixton town,
And every weekend without fail he'd send his trucker down
To pick up gas and some supplies and by our house he'd go
And Pierre and I would wait for him, our young hearts all aglow.
And when Hank stopped to pick us up into that seat so tall,
We watched the world around us and laughed at cars so small.
We pulled into the station, and then Grandpa we would see,
He'd welcome us with open arms like special royalty.
He had machines of peanuts that were colored bright and bold,
A penny's worth of peanuts then was all our hands could hold.
He told us stories of his life when he was just a lad,
And if we'd heard them twice before, they always made us glad.
We had a little race car once, and took turns taking rides,
Grandpa was a sight to see, his knees stuck out both sides.
Yes, I remember Grandpa, he always had such style,
And when the angels took him, we knew he'd make them smile.

D. B. Lewis

He Gave To Me

He gave to me a bouquet of roses,
His face beaming over the fragrant tribute.
I shook my head 'no' in disbelief,
He shook his head 'yes' it is all for you.

Love has taken the shape of God's beauteous flowers,
Twelve red, twelve gold, and twelve white,
Engulfed in a border of dark green ferns;
With a tiny whisper of baby's breath peeping out.

A smile and a kiss I gave my love and a verbal thank you too,
But I can never really thank enough the rugged yet boyish man
For his faith in me and love of me, and for that wonderful moment
Of worthiness in that gesture of whim....he gave to me.

Elizabeth Gleneck

As I Saw It

In 1979, a child was conceived.
His father ran out because he didn't believe.
He never thought his sons would ever compare.
That's when my mother's dreams turned to nightmares.
She took things a step at a time.
The bills came and she fell behind.
So we had to move to another place.
Too bad it had to be a different state.
We moved to Pomona, CA.,
But we didn't stay there long.
I don't remember much because I was too young.
My mother worked a lot, so she didn't have time to spend.
Her job was important and so was her new boyfriend.
So the time mom had he would take.
I thought then, and knew that he was a big mistake.
Too bad we had to learn the hard way.
He helped us out and we moved to West L.A.
So now my brother and I are all alone,
Just us two, my mom and her boyfriend are at home.

Jean-Paul Smith

Grandfather

He lays there in the covers.
His frail body outlined within.
His hair is white with age,
His cheeks are all so shallow,
His face is pale; all white with weakness.
He takes my hand and holds it tight; as to hold on to dear life
He looks up at me.
I look into his blue eyes; they are filled with pain, sorrow,
He whispers a song; our special song,
And then he slips away with a tear sliding slowly down his cheek.
I try to remember the song, but I can't
Then the tears start sliding slowly down my cheek.

Carissa Kinser

The Shroud Of Elvis

Elvis laid out on a beach towel one day
His sweat formed an image, they took it away
The towel was entombed, it was sealed is a shrine
Under heavy surveillance and a "do not touch" sign

Now we've got the shroud, the spot where he laid
So let us adore the impression he made
The shroud is not pretty, it's tattered and torn
But it's Elvis's sweat, a religion is born

So if you're in Memphis please stop by and see him,
And touch the king's shroud, at the Presley Museum.

Dave Tyas

Abraham Lincoln

A wondered Presidential feat.
His truth and greatness could not be beat.
He ruled with a gentle hand,
Over a freedom-longing land.

He sang the song of toiling slaves,
Working towards their darkened graves.

The Civil War, not in defeat,
And Abraham, his job complete,
Assassinated, lain down to sleep,
Making people mourn and weep.

The people talked, that wondered man,
The President called Abraham.

Christel Perkins

By Reason Of Insanity

Locked doors enclose our lives
holding back the energy of emotions
ceasing functions of the joys of life
Searching out your master once again
for he holds the key for thee
who deny themselves love or life.
We seek what we wish not to find inside
Ourselves the purring kitten growing
to be the panther
ready to strike the master, never knowing
what lies behind the door
step by step into a maze we go
closer to our souls we come to know
not what is real, but; what is truth?
We give in to the master
Our soul is now with thee
by reason of insanity.

James K. Smith

Second Thoughts

Standing at the alter, staring in your eyes,
Holding hands and feeling the dread lingering inside.
I want to turn and run,
I can't handle the pressure of us being one.

I know we should be together,
We've said it from the start.
Now I don't think I can handle it,
Maybe we should be apart.

Now it's time for I do's,
And I really don't.
My parents worked so hard for this day,
How can I take their happiness away.

It's my turn for I do,
I say I can't and run.
I hope you understand,
I don't want us to be one.

Angelina L. Hulett

Golden Memories

Of golden memories filled with bliss,
I often sit and reminisce.

Of treasured thoughts of days gone by,
those precious treasures that belong to you and I.

Those thoughts of old we treasure most,
that bring us smiles when nights grow cold.

They lift us from our days grown dull,
and fill our hearts with thoughts of love.

Donna DeShazo

"Hope"

Hope was here but now is gone
Hope for the future that life will go on

Hope is gone though never really here
Never held Daddy's hand but never shed one tear

Hope knows Daddy's not perfect and should bear no shame
But throughout his life Daddy bears the pain

Daddy needs Hope every single day
"Hope is my helper" you'll hear Daddy say

When Daddy gets tired and begins to fall
That's when Hope will come to call

Yes Hope is gone yet always near
Sits on Daddy's shoulder to whisper in his ear

Who will take care of Mommy? Hope knows Daddy will
But Daddy needs Hope to calm and be still

Hope will help Daddy when Mommy calls
For Mommy loves Hope most of all

Daddy the rock that will not break
Hope from his soul no one can take.
    David P. Hartsell

Open Your Mind

Open your mind, so your eyes can see
  How big and beautiful God's world can be.
Open your mind, and move your feet
  With the rhythm of all creatures, man or beast.
Open your mind, share a deed well done
  It's so easy to reach out and touch someone.
Open your mind, to another's woe
  It never hurts to let sympathy show.
Open your mind, let's all confess
  Sometimes we're short on love and tenderness.
Open your mind, if you dare
  And face life and yourself on the square.
Open your mind, that ears may hear
  All the sounds of life we hold so dear.
Open your mind, with a loud thank you
  To God allowing us the things we do.
Open your mind, to where and when
  And enjoy it all before the last Amen.
    Hardy Reese

Untitled

How can a man be full in life !
How can a man be complete in life !

When he goes home but there is no one
to greet him,
And he lie's in bed at night and cries out
but no one hear's him

How can a man be full in life,
When there is no soft and gentle hand
to hold his head up in trouble time's.

How can a man be complete in life,
When there is no soft and warm body
gently pressed up against his
And here's the word's I love you.

No a man can not be full and complete
in life with out the love and gentle
heart of woman.
    James Cody

Changing

When things are so right.
How come all of a sudden they go so wrong.
One minute my life is perfect,
The next everyone gone.
No ones there to understand,
No ones there to hold my hand.
I'm left all alone in the darkness,
It seems no one can cure this loneliness.
When all of a sudden you turned me around,
Took the weight off my shoulders.
And removed my frown.
Your love for me could not compare,
Cause you died on the cross for my sins and despair.
Now I'll dedicate my life to you,
Stop the old and start the new.
    Jodee Prudente

Apollo XI

Listen my children and you shall hear,
How history was made many miles from here.
It was "69" and late in July,
The three of them were ready to fly.

Down at the cape in Apollo XI,
Ready to soar through the wild blue heaven.
Armstrong, Aldrin and Collins too,
These were the names of that famous crew.

With a deafening roar they were hurdled into space,
Then off to the moon at a breath taking pace.
Three brave men with a single purpose,
Try to survive on the moon's bleak surface.

The world is waiting and very soon,
We see Neil step upon the moon.
Before too long Buzz joins the toil,
Of gathering rocks and grey moon soil.

Then up to join the mother ship,
That Mike has waiting for their trip,
Home to earth so mild and kind,
One giant step for all mankind.
    George Oberlin

Denied Of Love

If only I could tell you
how I really feel.
How much I really love
you and want to hold you near.
To feel you hold my hand.
To know that you are there.
To make you understand how much I really care.
To have you here beside me, to know that love is true.
To feel you warm embrace when
I'm lying next to you
What am I to do?
For I'm so in love with you.
I think of you day and
night. Because the feelings
I have are hard to fight.
Even though our love is denied
I'll still hold apart of you
deep inside.
    Angie Payne

Snowflakes

As I sit and the snowflakes do fall.
How I see the snow to tall.
Bigger and bigger as I sit and wonder.
They fall from the sky like there's no yonder.
It glistens and it gleams like it's all in my dreams.
This is how it all seems.
Mother nature has her ways of fulfilling all my days.
With her beauty and harsh reality.
Something will always have to be.
Falling and falling as fast as they do.
They cover my yard with a blanket of new.
A footprint in the snow will be gone I know.
'Cause when I look through the pane all I see is snow.
As pure as it is the beauty with holds.
For a sight to see is all so very cold.

Jensine L. Palita

"Will This Love Survive"

It's foolish how things don't last forever
how love can vanish and never come back
and this is an issue that could make you cry
just to know your love could run out your door.
Strange, but there is no way to find out
if love will vanish today or tomorrow
and you keep on asking yourself will this love survive,
trying to hold on, but your pain is too strong,
the tears burn your pillow at nights
while you are wrapped in his arms,
but you ask yourself will this love survive
can I hold on for the rest of my life
or just let you go trying to forget
I couldn't hang on because I did not know
if this love will ever survive.

Adriana Vasquez

My Mother's Hands

I can remember my mother's hands,
how lovingly they caressed me as a baby.
They held my tiny fingers, they tickled my tiny toes.

I can remember my mother's hands, how gently they wiped away
    each tear.
They sheltered me from all imaginary creatures of the night.

I can remember my mother's hands, how reluctantly they released
    their grip.
They handed me to my teacher's hands, oh,
how I wanted to run away, back to my mother's hands.

I can remember my mother's hands, how securely they clenched mine.
In sorrow, I found my strength, together we stood tall.

I can remember my mother's hands, thunderous in their applause.
They were the loudest in a crowd of thousands.

And, I remember my mother's hands, how wisely they let me go.
A world of strangers, no longer strange.

Yet, if I feel my world is crumbling, and life seems lost at sea,
I know where I can run.

Back to my mother's hands.

James W. Tella

I Know Not

Five brothers at home, none within a year,
How thankful we were, in the forties too,
When all came home, we sure did cheer,
World war dead, I shed a tear for you;

The Russians took rifles from Germany,
Gave them to China and North Korea too,
In Korea I saw Swastika and Sickle on many,
Korean dead, I shed a tear for you;

Vietnam War division and new Heroes arisen,
Then the dead and sick of a Dessert war,
I wish I knew a way to vanish a war year,
For war's sick and dead, I shed a tear;

North Korea seems to have forgot the years,
And tears, of war they could not win;
I wish I knew how to prevent war years,
But I confess I know not!

Gerald A. Le Blanc

As One

To see almost as one as far as you and me
How to see me as almost a part of you

For you to see us together as a part of
The heart of which I see you

Yes, I see one of us and you are me

Yes, we are together in the heart that
You see of me

To see almost as one of us and you are me
How to see me as almost a part of you
For you to see us together as a part
Of the heart of which I see you

Yes, we are together in the heart that you see of me

Corazon Dulce Cueva & Derick Duque Aguinaldo

Will You Be There?

Will you be there when I graduate?
How will my Birthday be?
What about my college days?
Will there be letters while you're far away?
What about my wedding day?
Will you still be there when all things
are finally made right?
Will these questions go unanswered
I love you both so much.
I will remember you both in my heart
when my special days arrive.
I will cry a tear for each of you.
I know that God will let you watch
down upon me the rest of my life.
Dear grandparents I will love you and
remember you forever.
There's just one last question I
need to ask:
Will you remember me when I
meet you in heaven?

Jaime Koehn

This Ancient Thought

Eternal wind,
Howling trough ancient hollowed bone long dead,
Fusing forever the dissimilar elements in the swirling landscape
of incessant change,
All the while whispering its sweet secret to the desperate,
Haunted and lonely.

Like wind and hollow bone long dead,
Like need and the nagging vicissitudes of fear we deprecate a stolen
honor and render to each other a false praise,
Only to glimpse in a forlorn moment a brief rendition of a greater self,
And measure that vision ever so obliquely against the churning
forces breathing clay into angels.

Raging wind whose violent temper does justify our night allows
death to ride victorious in the encroaching calm
Beyond the immediate circle of our time lies another and another
and another until the ultimate circle embraces all fields,
And the fickle wind becomes a mere whisper yielding to blessed grace
its mercurial memory.

James P. McMahon

Zoological Garden

I've planted a garden, a different sort,
  I am going to raise a zoo.
When my plants grow up into animals and birds,
  'twill be a sight to view.

I have a pussy-willow bush,
  that will bring me lots of kittens.
And in my foxglove bed you'll see,
  young foxes with their mittens.

My elephant-ears can hear the songs
  the larkspurs sing so well.
While all the snowy Dogwoods yelp,
  and the cowslips ring their canterbury bells.

The lions tail will swish with pride.
  Oh, a dandelion is he!
And he'll comb his mane, with a cockscomb bright,
  for the hens and chicks to see.
When my garden grows and blossoms out,
  'twill be a sight; I know,
A big cage filled with birds and beast,
  all trained by a garden hoe.

Anne Savitski Good

A Prayer For My Father

Our Heavenly Father, today my prayer is one of gratitude.
I am grateful to you, for creating a man so special.
A man of love, compassion, strength and wisdom.
Love of life, family, friends and neighbors.
Compassion toward those in need and those less fortunate.
Strength to help his fellow man in whatever way necessary.
Wisdom to guide those who look to him to show the way.
I am even more grateful Lord, that you allowed me to know
such a man.
So that I could feel his love, be warmed by his compassion,
Supported by his strength and guided by his wisdom.
To know such a man is surely a blessing that I will cherish
the rest of my life.
I am most grateful Lord, that you allowed such a man to be
my father
And now that my father has left us, to be with you, Our
Heavenly Father.
I shall carry on in my life, with not only his memory,
But with his wisdom, with his strength, with his compassion and
with his love.

David L. Carter

Birch

When I see a birch tree
I am humbled
I can sense a majesty not too far off
...A lofty felicitousness
...A quiet happiness

There are infinite possibilities streaming from the leaves
The white trunk
To gladden the heart, the whiteness and leaf-shape
Oh birch tree
Birch tree
Thee are a jubilee!
You come from a pure Spirit
Even the pioneering Spirit
You sow the seeds of rejuvenation in new localities
Each heart!

Oh white birch
Golden birch, light birch, providing birch
Sweet birch, stalwart birch, fresh birch
We discover our own infinite joy from thy happiness
As thee sing, we are transformed!

Allan Marks

Searching...

Walking through the Labyrinth; embracing Angelic rhythms,
I am like and is a babe in the wilderness————-
fighting for survival.
I have two kids, I've been to college,
yet I've just began to grow.
Searching for a way out...amazed within the maze,
at wolves dresses in sheep clothing, who come after me;
smiling knowingly, as I run... run...run...
this babe in the wilderness is lost.

I like the Raven bird, it is free and it is Black—-
the Jay bird can't seem to find its way,
it's Searching.......

My journey continues... my thoughts are real,
Do I continue to Search as time pass me by?
Am I afraid to live or afraid to die,
Do I have a choice of fears to live by
or is this babe in the wilderness me.............

Hilda Warner

Missing You

As the hands of time keep ticking away
I am thinking of you more and more each day
I love you so dearly, though your face I can't see
Cause you are my baby, the best that can be

Though in this world you'll never be
You're in far better hands, forever free
I am so proud to say that in every way
You're a part of my life, each and every day

I would give my whole life just to hold you one night
And say that I love you, and our family unite
But one day I'll see you, and I won't have to cry
Cause life is forever in God's perfect sky

Darrell Bruce

I've Seen Him In You

They say there's a Jesus, fair and true:
I ought to know- I've seen him in you.
They say Christ's love can never be measured,
But in your heart I find it treasured.

They say God is full of boundless grace,
And I know it - I see him shine in your face.
They say Jesus' coming is long overdue.
But he's already here - I've seen him in you.

Julie Aylesworth

The Weight Of The World

As I rise from bed to enter the day
I ask myself is it worth it this was

To enter a world that's not very kind
Always judging and probing my weary mind

Very quick to judge on appearance and size
But never takes time to care what's inside

Having to work and stride twice there pace
Just to be equal in there place

I do a job just as good
And even better I always could

But like a diamond in the ruff
I could never shine enough

So like an oyster with its pearl
I just carry weight of the world.

Carlos J. Fred

Recovering With The Son

As I basked in the warmth of his bright golden sun,
  I asked him, "Lord what have I ever done
to deserve to share in your beauty as such?"
And he quickly replied "my child, I don't ask much,
  from you or any of my children on earth;
Just that you love me and let your self-worth reflect
  the beauty and joy of my care,
and know that I'll always, yes always be there."
The peace that came to me as he made the reply
  was so complete I felt a warm tear in my eye.
It was a tear of joy, of comfort and power.
  A strength I can draw on from hour to hour.
And so I will rest in the arms of the son
  and know that my strength for life's duties will come -
with patience and rest and time on my side
  as long as I always in his love abide.

Delphene Quisberg

"Restoration Of The Prodigal"

Too frightened to scream but aware of my fear
I awaken in silence, enshrouded by night
My soul filled with dirt, my mind plagued by lust
Bound by immorality, devoid of His light

Terrified by what this man has become
Backsliding beyond all hope of going back
Oh God what am I doing, my life is so empty
Continually tempted and under attack

I need a haven of light, a shelter from myself
One that only the Savior can provide
On that night my reconciliation completed
By the one who for this twisted creature died

Release me, Lord, from these chains of sin
I feel His peace as I cry out to Him

For me He died
For Him I lived

John Shipley

Forever

I know that by now you probably have forgotten me.
I seemed to go overboard in my uncertainty.
But now I have grown mentally and physically stronger.
And I hope not to create problems for you any longer.
If we should happen to see each other again,
you will notice a person that will make amends.
But whether this is a new beginning,
or whether this is the end.
I will forever remember the times we spent as friends.

Hector Escobedo

Depressions

As my life is growing longer
I began to stagger
For life brings weakness
As well as pain
Sometimes my teardrops fall
Down like rain
A well is within me
To catch my sorrow
As I hopelessly wait for the morrow
Happier moments is what I wish for
I wait for them to knock on my gloomy door
As I see the moments passing by
I let out deep sigh
And hope my misery will soon fade
While I close my heavy shade
I have lived in total darkness
with my only companion; loneliness

Jacqueline Peltier

Mother

I can see your eyes in my eyes
I can hear your voice within my words.
I can see me walking your walk
I can feel your love within my heart.

I've left home and am on my own now
all I have now are my memories.
Thoughts of you now see me through my days
they bring me warmth and keep me safe.

I remember all the times we laughed
and every time I made you cry.
I remember your every gentle word
and all the times I failed to listen.

Somewhere, out there as your life continues
with me or without me, you laugh and you cry.
Mother, if you can read these words now
there's something I've always failed to mention
I love you .... I will always love you.

Jeanette Jasnoch

A Father's Spirit

As a soft white snow falls,
  I can see his hair;
In each roar of thunder, I feel his strength;
Glancing up at the stars,
  I see his eyes;
Kindly looking down upon me.

When the sun's rays shine at their brightest,
  I feel his guidance,
Leading me in the right direction;
  with each gentle breeze,
I feel his love surrounding me,
  filling my heart with warmth and happiness.

A year ago, we lost our time together
  on this earth,
But the memories we shared will always exist,
  brightening my everyday;
Drying my eyes of painful tears;
  and leaving a special message to be felt.

A physical body gone,
  but a spirit carrying much love, serenity, and peace
Healing his daughter's heart.

Jacqueline Parton

Where Am I

Trapped in a prison within prison, where am I?
I can see out, no one can see in,
there are no bars to hold me, yet I still cannot leave.
 Where Am I?

My loved ones, they are holding, and talking,
to what they think is me, I yell and scream for them to help,
but they cannot see me!!!.
 Where Am I?

As I fight and struggle to keep my sanity,
the demons circle me like vultures over a dying body,
just waiting for me to lose the only thing I have left,
so to carry me to the pits of hell.
 Where Am I?

Here there is no time, for it stands still,
there is no day, nor night, just different shades of grey,
 Where Am I?

Shall I ever escape, or be set free?
Will my sentence be overturned. This I do not know.
 Where Am I!!!!!

 Chris Miller

Summer Vacation

When school is over it feels great,
I can show my lazy trait!
I lie in the sun to work on my tan,
then I drink iced tea by the fan!
I could sit by my window and wait for a comet,
or go to the fair and watch people vomit!
Barbecues are excellent; vacations are better,
Boy, am I glad I don't need a sweater!
Colorful butterflies are all around,
and beautiful flowers are on the ground!
The sun beats hot; the wind blows cool,
I put on my bathing suit and go to the pool!
I go to the lake and swim with the fish,
if only this could last all year... I wish!
But, it's time to say good-bye to fun and relaxation,
school is back; I can't wait for next summer vacation!

 Becky Brundage

Lost by the Future

I am from a country which no longer exists.
I cannot see the bright reds, golden oranges,
 and brilliant yellows of the autumn trees anymore.
The humble lake surrounded by pines now only lives in my mind.
I miss spending the early days of spring traipsing around
 the forest in search of hummingbirds.
Never again can I lie in the grassy, green field with the
 perfume of lilac permeating the air.
The honeysuckles with their sweet tasting nectar have
 disappeared from my life forever.
I do not hear the chirping of the birds in the fragile nest
 resting on the great oak outside my bedroom window.
I have chased butterflies under the heat of the summer sun
 for the last time.
No, the country where I am from is not "the country" anymore.

 Cynthia Clayton

One Half Of Nothing

I am married to misery, betrothed to depression
I can't be right, I'm not allowed to be wrong.
Married to misery
My wife is mediocrity, wed to the son of pride
I bonded to blindness, my blushing bride
Too good to abuse her, too honorable to run
Too hard to give in completely, totally undone.
I can't survive being buried alive
How can I survive with no inner drive
With nothing to work for no motivation
Married to misery bad situation.
Time is unforgiving — It's too long and I'm all wrong
I can't go on living — I am always mad that she is always sad
What do you do
When misery marries you?
Nailed to the altar
Loss of your soul
Compromise becomes control
I am one half of nothing.

 Frank Stepnowski+

Wind

My companion is a creature of a kind beyond compare.
I can't see it, yet I realize the wind is always there.
My minister on sultry days, it cools my sunburned face.
This winter adversary has a bitter cold embrace.
It was my mother's servant, blowing clothing on the line,
Flowing freshness filling it with an odor pure—divine.
Like a child, full of mischief, when there's but breath of air,
Its silly silken fingers gently rearrange my hair.
It has power to push a sailboat far across the rolling sea,
Or snap a flag, or lift a kite or seed a mighty tree.
On occasion it is lazy like a bathing courtesan
Muted motion, gently sensuous, teasing as it can.
When it angers, first it hisses with its ugly serpent's breath.
Then a roaring, clawing creature comes it bearing sudden death.
It stimulates my senses. I'm aware of what it does,
But can't see it, though a little child, I tried hard to because,
I can smell it; feel it; hear it; consider it with fear.
My sometimes friend, and sometimes foe is always lurking near.

 George Cameron

Untitled

At one point in my life I loved you so much
I closed my eyes only to feel your touch.

My love for you was greater than life
I hoped and dreamed one day to be your wife.

Your tears made me weep, your smile was so great
thinking and wondering if I was the one you'd soon hate.

As the time separated us the love remained in my heart
but soon it was that time for us to part.

Although I'll always love you and remember the laughter we had
I'm real sorry and I know I hurt you bad!

I know you think I'm crazy but one day you'll see
I still love you and we were meant to be.

You gave me you life, your heart, and soul
but that was something I couldn't control.
I'd like to say one last thing before I go
I love you more than any poem can show!

 Amy Tackett

I Laughed At Love

I laughed at love and dance on a circle of light,
I collected hearts on a golden string
And danced to a melody that none but I heard.
I never knew love, I never had love, I never needed love;
I conquered the world, I pulled down stars,
The moon was my pillow, the sky my blanket.
I never needed anyone.
I held love in the palm of my hand…wondering
How could love be so blind?
Then I opened my palm and love left me
Cold and empty,
Fell so hard and touched the silence,
Alone with myself and my tears.
That's not the way it was supposed to be.
I laughed at love as all else slept.
I laughed at love but love laughed last…
And I wept.

Heather Seifert

Sonnet

I ate an orange partly spoiled (because
I could not well afford to throw it out).
Oddly, it led to sanguine thoughts about
The flexibility of nature's laws.
The sourness of the orange soon was chased
By honey on a slice of buttered bread.
Just so, in general, we all are fed
On honey when we would recoil in haste;
For nature, guided by God's gentle hand,
Tends to replace, to heal, to recompense.
His power over sickness is immense;
The sweet annuls the sour at His command.
  The choice is ours: to dwell on bitterness
  Or, trusting, pray and wait for Him to bless.

Brenda Sorensen

Thoughts Of Mom

Thoughts of you, Mom, come to mind,
I could search the world and never find;

One exactly the likes of you
She'd be too old, more likely too new!

I might find someone, heard, by rumor
To have your smile and sense of humor;

I might find someone, by half a yard
Of coming close to working as hard;

I might find someone who would not hear
Any negative talk of those she holds dear;

I might find someone with your talent
Sometimes tempered, more often gallant;

I might find someone loving life each day
Who impatiently quotes "Lead, follow or get out of the way";

I might find someone with all this and more
But she'd only remind me of the mom I adore.

So thoughts of you, Mom, come to mind,
And I could keep searching and never find;

One exactly the likes of you—-
But, them ——— I really wouldn't want to!

Jo Ann Murphy

Trees

The moon lit lake lay before me and
I couldn't decide which way to go.
Into the black water or into the trees that sheltered me.
Images of the past filtered through my mind,
a time of greatness.

A single thought could not be found,
and the images conversed and blurred.
Warmth gave way to coldness as the blackness surrounds me.
I can no longer see the trees.

The black is calming in a way I cannot find.
The moon is nothing but a pale blur of Vision.
My mind is sinking and clouded but calm and serene.

Thought of sleep and comfort over powered, darkness creeps in.
A solid blanket of cold, an impenetrable layer
My shelter is gone, but I will always have the trees.

Amanda Kay Givans

Oregon Epiphany

Thirteen quail walked by my window
  I couldn't decipher them at first through the cloudy glass,
  Crowded under the naked tree among fallen leaves, sodden apples,
  Scurrying gave them away, I hurried to the front window to watch.

They moved together, scuttling about and looking for seeds.
  It was hard to count them. I did so several times, just be sure.
  Tittering to and fro, their little pointed feathers bobbing.
  They gathered in the road's center, pecking for a long while.

Suddenly, a long grey shadow appeared and approached them slowly.
  Quails scattered and flew. Some to the top of rooftops.
  Two landed in the mimosa tree. I watched sadly as they flew.
  Scuttling through the crumbly earth of an autumn garden.

Caroline C. Spear

Confusion

Passing through the labyrinth in my mind
I couldn't help but remember,
All the things left behind,
Questionable actions left with no answer.

Within me gurgles the birth of confusion
Did I do what really was right?
Will regret fill my every action,
Or will my life be warm and bright?

I guess, though I lost something very precious
Something that I really cherish,
I gained love that is oh, so glorious
All my worries I hope will perish

Edelyn Cabanlig

Dear Mother

As I look out the window and into the sea
  I see memories of you and me
hen I was just born you held me so close
  When I was six you let me go
You Gave your love so tenderly
  In every way you're all that could be
You filled the part of me once missing
  You're at least a thousand years worth wishing
So, dear mother, just so you'll know
  From the bottom of my heart, I love you so.

Christina Horne

Let Me Be Your Friend

I can't forget the feeling when first I heard you cry.
I couldn't understand you though, I wanted, so, to try,
Bewildered tears ran down your face. I couldn't tell you then.
Now I think you understand that's how a life begins.

A tiny little baby—So helpless and so weak—
Already had some things to say, but, knew not how to speak.
Forced into a different world than that from which you came—
You had to face a brand new life before you even knew your name.

A mother's love surrounded you in the world from which you came.
And, as you grow, from day to day, I hope you'll feel the same.
And, as time goes passing by, I hope we'll not pretend,
Let me be there when you cry—Just let me be your friend.

Both a student and a teacher in your life, I want to be.
There are things which I can teach you and some you can teach me.
Wherever life may take you, a mother's love I'll send.
So, when you really need someone, just let me be your friend.

My child, I hope you understand that I don't know it all.
And, somewhere along uncertain roads, you may see me trip and fall.
So, I hope you'll be there too, if I should need to mend.
And, whether happiness or sorrow comes, please let me be your friend.

John Posey

My Confidant

When you found me,
I did not let you in easily
Making me sure of life and its immeasurable climb,
Let my ears hear and you be heard.

Now I walk in the light of day.
Never turning inside to run astray.
How could I not accept the gift you gave
And the heartache you have taken away.

All kind words are said in appreciation of you.
A million Thank You's and Living to pay my dues.
From this day forward memories fill my mind,
Of caring thoughts for a stranger and you being kind.

As many times a day, an hour a day shall be put aside,
To adulate My Confidant with pride
No more will I feel at a loss,
For you washed the world of sin by dying on the cross.

Helena Eseloma

"Words Of Forever"

Long ago you left me,
I did not understand.
I blamed you for everything;
You were no longer there to hold my hand.

But as I grew, I came to know,
It wasn't your fault at all.
God had taken you away from me,
When I was so very small.

I will always love you,
And miss you so.
And grandfather, dear grandfather,
The husky sound of your voice is something I will always know.

The way you expressed things,
The lessons in your words.
Even though you have gone away
Your voice will be forever heard.

Danielle Anderson

Nasturtiums

Maybe, when I planted them,
I did something wrong.
Maybe I kept them too close
To the house
And they got too much shade.
Maybe it was the dry spell.

I remember the day,
The soft tingle of the breeze,
The warm sun on my back,
The dark earth spilling through my fingers,
And the promise!
The splashes of crimson and gold
That would be mine
When summer came.

Oh, they're growing—I guess,
But they seem so frail and spindly.
They certainly don't look like they did on the seed packet.

Maybe I should be patient!
Maybe they'll still amount to something?
Maybe the tears will help?

Charles A. Hendrickson

"Love"

Before love was just a word,
I didn't believe the stories I'd heard,

You would walk by while my heart skipped a beat.
Everything about you swept me off my feet.

When we met everything changed,
Both our lives were rearranged.

We spent every living day together.
And hoped it would stay that way forever

Between us not a word was said,
As that little folded note I read.

And now our love has gone away,
Only memories are here to stay.

They say I'll find someone new,
When I do I hope he's just like you.

Beth Santoro

Her

The night of her death
I died too
The cool autumn evening was enough for everyone to enjoy
Except her
She had been that way the entire day and the other days too
She wasn't the friend that I had always known
Yet soon enough she proved to me and to the world
That she had fooled us
There really was something left under that yellow and tattered skin
And it beamed at me with all the love in the world
Her life made me small
Yet it also made me the luckiest person in the entire universe
The days had gone by
And in my mind they could never be replaced
She was strong and I was weak
She had the essence of the very core of life in her grasp
And I had nothing but space in my own
She was everything and I was her friend
I had her
And she had AIDS.

Angela Eilering

Why

Why you, why now
I don't understand this world
I don't think that I ever will either it doesn't seem fair
What did you do wrong
You are always so cheerful
You always help those who need it
But I guess God has his own way and sometimes I hate his way
Because he always takes those I love
I guess this world was meant to be that way
And I guess that's just the way God wants it to be
But sometimes he can leave those that I love alone
So that we may live in peace like others
What I would like someone to explain to me is
Why does he have to take those I love
Why does he have to take little babies and little children
Why not let them live a full life
Why you Grandma, why now,
Why all this pain it just isn't fair
Why you, why now, why....
    Dawn Janecek

A Daughter's Message To Her Mother

I had a dream the other night while sleeping in my bed
I dreamt I saw an Angel with a halo on her head
I dreamt she had the brightest smile
her eyes were filled with light
The colors seemed so brilliant as I squeezed my eyes shut tight
I didn't want my dream to end, I wanted her to stay
So I asked her for her name, that's when she told me it was Faye.
I told her mine was Amy and I promised I would be
The best friend she could ever have for all eternity.

I hugged her and I kissed her and we spoke of many things
I held her hands so lovingly, she held me with her wings
She promised me she'd love me too, I knew this felt so right
I didn't want my dream to end, I slept with all my might
When I awoke I felt so good, a smile on my face
I felt so warm, my heart just glowed, my pulse began to race.
I woke up so excited, could hardly tell another
My dream was really not a dream
This Angel is my Mother!
    Amy Bramberg

I'm Only Human

I know I am not perfect, I try my best to be.
I face my daily battles, that I often loose,
Of the things that matter, or the friends I choose.
I know I am no angle, I'm easy to mislead.
I know what's wrong and what is right.
I ignore my pride and follow my greed.
My free will is a problem this I am aware.
Because I'm only human, I'm really not that strong.
To be what I was meant to be, might take a longer time.
Sometimes I really love this life, and never what to leave.
So, if I'm to go to heaven, I must not give in to greed.
I'll just keep on a trying, living day by day.
Eternity awaits me, this I do believe.
For my spirit is immortal, my body is of clay.
    Jodie M. Roberts

By Gods Hand:

As the morning sun draws high above the blue streak sky
I feel a warm gentle breeze as it slips through the tender leaf trees.
Song sparrows flying around singing new songs,
Caring for their young as time goes by
And chipmunks running and playing as they run in and out of the ground.
Not caring who's around.
Not so far fish are jumping in and out of the waters
While golden sun rays cast down upon the lake.
And deep down in a valley I see a beautiful stream with bluestars
Growing along the banks.
I wonder could this be a dream?
Or could this be the garden of eden.
In the bible in genesis: chapter one verse one "In the beginning God
Created heaven and earth."
All natures beauty given by the stroke of gods hand.
Through out all this land.
For us to hold in our hearts.
I wonder will it be there when we grow old?
Lord i praise you.
    Donald Wall

I

nsecure

I sit in my chair, nervous as ever.
I feel one hundred eyes staring at me.
My palms; sweating; my heart; racing;
Millions of thoughts running through my head,
As the teacher starts speaking.

I don't really hear her,
All I hear is some kids laughing and talking in the back.

Are they laughing at me?
Are they talking about me?

I start panicking, I'm feeling sick, sicker, sicker.
Is it really worth it?
I keep saying to myself.
Why do we have to go the school anyway?

I'm feeling confused, what should I do?
Should I run out of the class? Should I say something?

I didn't know what to do. I never knew how much I would miss
my old home, old friends, and old school.

I guess I just didn't realize how good I had it.
I guess I never knew what it was like to be different.
So I just put my head down and cried.
    Beth Kersey

Love's Gentle Breeze

I feel the raindrops falling down on my face
I feel the gentle breeze of spring coming on
Would you like to fly away on love's gentle breeze?
Cascading winds and floating over the trees
I want to taste love
I want to be loved
My soul yearns to feel the heartbeats of the springtime
The cool gentle breezes, the warming of the sun,
The moon's glow at night.
Before the morning comes
I lie asleep and wait, for my wandering soul to return,
And tell tales of love, and of cool gentle breezes,
Of cascading winds and floating over the trees.
    C. J. Davis-Green

Reasons Why

When I'm near you, I am warm,
I feel secure, I feel no harm.

When I'm with you, in a crowd
I stand tall, I feel proud.

When I'm down, you lift my head
You pick me up, I feel no dread.

When I am lonely, you soon appear,
You take my hand, I feel no fear.

When I'm in trouble, you rush to my aid
I feel courage, I'm not afraid.

When I am happy, you make me smile,
I feel classy, you give me style.

When I am crying, you dry my tears,
It's all your love, that soon appears.

And when I'm lustful, you give yourself,
Only for me, and no one else.

You are my woman, you are my life,
You are my lover, you are my wife.

Burt Taylor

"Time Will Heal"

Time will heal the sorrow
I feel, some people swallow their pride,
or keep it locked up inside,
but it's not easy to hide
the pain I feel, only time will heal.
When you die I must cry,
don't ask me why I haven't got the strength to try,
I get my hopes up high but when I think of you I cry,
a frown appears upon my face I all of a
sudden lose the beauty and grace,
nothing can hide the way I feel
but only time will heal.

Barbara Lopes

Middle Aged Desolation

Troubled dreams arouse me and
I feel the world around me sleep.
Discomforted by the silence of the night,
I reach for a cigarette at 3 AM,
Forgetting that I left that habit long ago.
In the distance a siren wails
Invading my empty, veiled thought.
Someone else whose dreams are in disorder.
What long forgotten habit did they forget they left behind?
Or did they sleepwalk in another's dream,
Only to be found
Desperate,
Or trespassing.
Somewhere, close by, a car horn honks,
Just once at first, aware of dreams in progress.
Then again, longer, disturbing, somehow louder,
To hell with dreams.
A voice decries, then silence,
My night descends again.
I reach for a cigarette at 3 AM.

Gloria Rice

Summer Love Deja Vu

In the blossoming springtime of a one way love
I followed you like some sad-eyed puppy
wagging his tail at your knees.

Soon our hearts beat with the warm wind fluttering
through the green leaves of summer—
and I became your moon among the stars...

But then you found some new Valentino
with flashy teeth and slicked back hair
to stroll with through forests of flowers.

When summer was over I faded away with
the warmth from your weary eyes—
under the waning light of the sun...

The lingering fragrance of you became a
frozen memory amidst the fallen and falling leaves of
autumn before winter's snow.

Earl Krause

My Heart's Luggage

When the bus pulled out this morning
I had nothing for the trip,
But my heart.
And my heart did not pack light.
It brought memories dating years ago, and
Pictures - my eyes' and mind's way of freezing time-
That were taken on previous journeys.
It overflowed with love
For friends, family - and especially the boy
that owns most of my heart.
My heart also brought pain and sorrow,
Reminders of most hopeless times-
All gathered on previous journeys.
As I traveled on the bus, I began to unload
My heart's luggage, a piece at a time;
I examined every part - reliving the past-
Before neatly packing them away.
I smiled to myself, at the thought of getting off the bus;
How I shall carry nothing in my hand,
But a thousand journey's worth of luggage in my heart.

Jennifer Stevenson

"A Prisoner of Love"

So many times I thought
I had real love come my way
Unfortunately it didn't, sad to say.
Memories of a love from
The past weren't true for they
didn't last.
I'm a prisoner...a
prisoner of love.
A prisoner of the memories
that often come to mind I don't give,
up for a true, and great love I'll find,
I'll continue on in my journey of life
one day I'll be someone's loving wife.
But until then I'll be a prisoner
Within myself I'll continue to be
for one day of my love chains I'll be set free!
I'll no longer be a prisoner of love.

Juanita A. Waring

The Loss Of A Loved One

I know you have lost a loved one, so very dear
I have been there and couldn't help but shed a tear.
But, you will always remember and never forget,
The love and special memories you've shared, since you met.

At times you will think of him and be very sad
But most of all remember the good times you had.
Though it wont bring back that special one you love,
Who has now found peace with the Lord above.

I know, for a fact it's easier said than done
To rid of that burden that weight a ten
It will help with support from family and friends
And flowers and cards that people will send.

During your pain and sorrow we, too share
You know we are out there, us people who care.
As we look to the sky and up through a cloud
Knowing his life was good and he's done us proud.

So, as life goes on, day by day
You will laugh, cry, and even pray;
Dear Lord, take good care of our grandpa Saul
And we hope, we are ready to come, when you call.

Doris M. Voeller

Tears

Ever since you left me,
I have cried a million tears.

Do you know how much you hurt me,
Or do you even care?

I thought our relationship meant more to you,
For, it meant the world to me.

Now that you are gone,
I guess it was never meant to be.

The days and months have come and gone,
But the pain still exists.

Some day, I may finally be over you,
Through my hear will still any the tears!

Frances D. M. DeBarry

Eternity

Do I see what's to become of me?
I hold you preciously in my candle light
   to become one with me.
Our sorrow and laughter has taught me
   that I love you.

But is it true love,
   the kind of love that lasts forever?
Is it just the love one night,
   or the love of one night to begin forever?

For me, love is many days and nights
   of sorrow and laughter.
The kind of days and nights we share together.

So, now that I know my love for you is true,
   the test of time shall show me that
true love does last forever and my
   candle light is eternally for you.

Howard Kevin McCarthy

The End

In the beginning I hoped for forever
I hoped that your love would leave me never
Your kisses were warm, your arms so inviting
Just thinking of you could be so exciting
But then you turned cold, the warmth it all vanished
So what I'm 'bout to say could be your advantage
I wish it were different, it's not what I want
But being with you is not like I thought
It has to end here though our time was not long
I thought that you loved me but I guess I was wrong
I know you'll be happier without me around
I'm sure you won't miss me tying you down
But one final thing before I must go
Just one last thing I think you should know
I love you!

Crystal D. Rein

My Eyes Are Open Now

I stood alone in oppressive darkness
I knew light was there compelling me to be free with it
I could not find the strength to grab on to it
The night consumed my thoughts my soul
I must fight it or it will draw me down
I will never see the light of day again
Open your eyes I say to myself
My eyes are open for I can see darkness
I am afraid to step forward - to venture into the void
Will light catch me if I fall
Will it lift me up before I plunge into abyss
I must seek it I must make the first move but I am afraid
I would rather die walking than standing alone
I would rather risk it all for what could possibly be worse
I take a step the ground beneath me feels soft and airy
The first step easier than the next
I use all of my strength to push on just one more step
Am I going blind a bright light consumes me
I close my eyes for the first time I found light
I must walk to it through it and never forget to keep my eyes open

Jasmine J. Grissom

I Prayed

Tonight when I began to cry
I knew what I had to do and why

He is the only one who can help
He has always made better how I felt

I dropped to my knees and began to pray
At first I didn't know exactly what to say

Then all of a sudden I began to explain
How I had felt all this pain

I looked into his eyes when I was through
He said, "Listen child I can help you."

Once again he had made my day
Just because I was listening to what he had to say

He told me that at times things would go wrong
But through it all I had to be strong

He said, "everything to do you will not know
But my love and power over your heart will flow

If you need me again I'll be here
With me by your side you have nothing to fear

For you I will forever care
Remember, the answer is always in a prayer."

Christy Chrestman

Untitled

Always there standing out from the crowd.
I knew who you who you were, too scared to pursue.
Golden skin, enticing smile.
Wanting to be closer, though never following through.
Off you flew with those others, such the indiscrete style.
Casual encounters increased but, neither would come forward.
Laughing and joking as though we were one.
Even though it was nothing more than fun.
Kisses became frequent, friendly though they may be.
We had that one evening, cough ridden watching a movie.
I touched your skin and you touched mine.
A dream come true, still nothing more than a sincere therapeutic flow.
I thought there was a chance, I knew you felt it too.
But, I could never feel you away from him. I could no longer wait.
You went your way and I went mine.
Time has passed, I still remember.
Happy to be your friend forever.

Corey Sondrup

Face Your Fears

I have to get away! Things are not going well.
I know, I will run away. I will leave all my problems behind me
I will escape, I will start over again? I am destined to fail.
I am destined to battle within myself, destined to fight to be free.

Destined to face my fears…

I have constructed my environment. I am the cause of my own pain…
I will never be free of confusion, setbacks, sadness, sorrow and pain..

Until I face my fears…
How can I? How can I face myself? Truly see myself for what I am?
Oh God! Forgive me for being weal. Help me Jesus!
Face…Face…My fears, so that may live a peaceful life in Your grace.
With Your love, I feel I can and will face my fears
and I will be victorious!

James A. Huff

A Man In Left Field

I'm looking for familiar, something I can't find.
I know it sounds peculiar, but it's missing from my mind.
All these things around me, there is plenty to see,
but nothing that I can recall about you and me
in my memories.

I feel like a man out in left field.
My world is a blur and it's not clear to me.
I feel like a man out in left field.
My life is a ball and it won't come to me,
like my memories.

Look at all these faces, they say I've seen before.
Something is familiar, but I'm not quite sure.
I know where I'm going, but where have I been?
Like the wind a blowin', I want to play like a child again,
Like a child again.

I feel like a man out in left field.
My world is a blur and it's not clear to me.
I feel like a man out in left field.
My life is the ball and it won't come to me,
like my memories.

Jamie Jo Reynolds

The Woods

In the night I hear the silence of solitude
I lay underneath a tall barker sycamore tree
Staring peacefully at a tranquil little lake
And picturing living life without a reason.

Theft
Butcher
Massacre
Slaughter
Vengeance flows, killing people
Wealth, a tragedy, which greed will joyfully
   follow.

Carnage
Delirium
Bloodshed
Derangement
Blood grows thick
Young and old, hide from the madness, stalking
   the night.

Cristian Marrero

"The Seas Of Life"

My life is like an old ship. When
I leave the harbor I am new and clean, ready for my life of
battles. Ready to face anything that comes my way, when the
waters of life begin to swell I think of you and they leave.
The winds that keep me going; die and I sit feeling of no
use I think of you and it doesn't seem so long. When the
waters of life and the winds of trouble become too much for
me to handle, I call for your help. Your embrace and your
secret whispers to me make it feel there is nothing I can't
handle. Now I will never leave my part of protection without
you. My ship will never raise a sail or ride the waters of
life until you are by my side forever. You are my inspiration of
love, my candle in the darkness of night to help my find my
way. You are the soft guiding light at the end of my tunnel
of troubled times.

Bryan Faulkner

What Beautiful Sounds Nothing Makes

I'm alone, but don't feel sorry for me,
I like it that way, because I live in the most glorious of
lives. I visit the most splendid places, full of myth and
magic. I talk to only the most intriguing of people, they
question reality.
Don't feel sorry for me,
Nothing makes the most beautiful sounds.
In the quiet, grey days,
I spin a tale of wonder, full of voices, the ones I want to
hear. They talk of laughter, and sometimes tears.
Don't feel sorry for me,
Nothing makes the most beautiful sounds.
In the darkness of night, I see only colors through my eyelids.
Haunting reds, yellow like the candle's flicker, and purple of
deepest and mysterious kind.
Don't feel sorry for me,
Nothing makes the most beautiful sounds.
If the world were to disappear,
Would I notice? Would I care?
My world, is always moving, it's always there!
So don't feel sorry for me, Nothing makes the most beautiful sounds.

Jessica Curtright

Fritz And Master Jake

My master has gone away—this I do not understand
I long to be beside him—and hear his every command
My tail used to wag with glee,
Whenever I saw him running toward me
We were together such a short time-me and that great pal of
mine. We went fishing in the creek and down at the lake
  me and my master Jake
I could run beside him on his bike,
Or just along the side of the trail on a hike
We would roll in the yard and on the floor
I would bark and he would laugh—Fritz, want some more?
Such great times playing ball—running—playing—we had it all
Our last day at the lake is when I lost master Jake.
Now the two of us can no longer roam—-
An "Angel" came—took him to his "Master's" home
Oh, what a day it would be—-
If once again I could hear him call for me.
Every car that drives in—I run and check—to see—-
If he is there—then drop my tail and slowly walk away
Hoping I'll have better luck—another day.
    Harriet (Shove) Bedard

Michelle (In My Heart)

Your beauty rests in my mind
I long to hold you and to make you mine
The sound of your voice carries through my brain
And thoughts of you come back again
In my mind, I see your face
And in my heart, you can not be replaced
I want to take your hand
And lead you to the promised land
I've wanted to be more than a friend
To be someone on whom you can depend
You are in my dreams somewhere
When I'm walking on air
I want to build a life for you and me
Just open your heart and you will see
    Devin Kane Crowley

Wonderful God

Every time I'm feeling low,
I look to you and see your glow.
Up in Heaven you shine so bright,
I think of you both day and night.

You are so great in many ways,
I look to you and I'm amazed.
I see what you all have done.
And know in my heart we're all one.

The earth is a wonderful place to be,
but pray someday I'll be with thee.
My sister Melissa knows what Heaven can be,
since she's already left my family and me.

You know that we loved her, but you wanted her more,
to be with you in Heaven, so you opened the door.
We want to be with you both some day,
So we'll try hard to live by your way.
    Hilary Renee Berning

"Jack"

In a couple of days he'll be nine months old
I love him more as each second passes by
He's perfect, he's playful, he's getting big
I could never have gotten a better guy.

We spend every day together, growing a little bit older
During play times we have so much fun
Sometimes I'm relieved when he finally gets tired
And sprawls out real long, if possible lying in the sun.

We love to go for walks when the weather is nice
He's so curious about everything he sees
Yet he seems content in the safety of my arms
Life is so worth living, at times like these.

I wouldn't trade him for all of the world
He's all I was asking for
What a perfect little Christmas gift
I'll love him forever, that's for sure.

And he's so very, very handsome
So worthy of what I've written
For he's my pride and joy
He's my special little (big) kitten.
    Evelyn M. Carter

Eternity

A gentle feel for your touch,
  I love you so very much.
A seemingly large beautiful smile,
  that seems to make it worth the while.
Just feeling your body next to mine,
  a gentle smell, sweeter, than wine.
A beautiful look upon your face,
  makes it seem this is the place.
To join two bodies now as one,
  your beautiful hair glistening in the sun.
Now two hearts beating together,
  two loving people spend forever.
Coming together to be as one,
  until their lives, here are done.
Now one is dead and the other is alone,
  to help us set this lonesome tone.
The other praying for soon to be free,
  to see the other for eternity.
Now, they are together for eternity,
  living a new life so happily.
    Gigi Shannon

A Treasure

When first we met in high school's rush,
  I loved you much - unconditionally;
But I didn't know you then,
  I hadn't yet uncovered your treasure.

When we were married with home and family,
  I loved you and cared for you;
But I didn't really know you,
  nor did I realize your treasure.

As we passed through the children's teen age years,
  then weddings and grandchildren;
I loved you and accepted you,
  but still had not discovered your treasure.

When loss of work caused our roles to reverse,
  and work and school began to change me,
I loved you desperately, fearfully
  clinging to the hope of what once was.
Who are you, what is your hidden treasure?

In my search to find a better way and to myself be true,
I also found the love of my life and thankfully it's you.
You are my treasure...but I still don't know you.
    Audrey Bunchkowski

To The Top Of The Hill

I made it to the top of the hill dad, just the way you used to do.
I made it to the top of the hill dad, every step I was thinking of you
The garden is where you had it dad so luscious and so green
I planted some okra, squash, and tomatoes and even some bean
Sometimes it's so hot and steamy, but a full basket makes it worthwhile
I know it's only six hundred feet there
   but sometimes it seems like a mile
I am older now than you were when you walked to the top of the hill
I go there everyday in season for I have a larder to fill
Sometimes I stop and look around the way you used to do
With a soft gentle breeze a blowing its such a beautiful view
So wherever you are dad, I hope I am doing your will
For I hope to make it once more dad to the top of the hill.

   Donald H. Elfreich

The Light Of Love

It was someday in late September, that's when
I met this guy I'll always remember. Standing
there with a peculiar look on his face, I saw
him smile for first time near the fireplace.
He stared at me, looking like he
enjoyed watching every move I made. Which he
did, at least that's what his friends told me
on that special night, when I knew it would be
the last night I saw that light. That light
glowing in a man, a man I will try hard to
keep loving as much as I can. I saw him in
April, for it was too late, I fell for that light as I
ate, drank, and slept, think only of him. My
heart cares for him, but I know after the
weekend that light will go dim. For I know, he
will go, and I hope I will see that light
again. I will try my hardest to keep in
touch, to the light in the man whom I love so
much.

   Amber Shutter

Missing You

Darling, I miss you, I miss you so much.
I miss your sweet tender loving touch.
I wish you were here to hold me right now;
It's not like you can, I just wish I knew how.
Your kiss is so soft and sweet as can be;
I just wish you were here, right here with me.
My love for you is so very strong;
I just miss you so much, it seems so long.
I know you love me and you're just right there;
But I can't get it out of my mind, how much I care.
So just remember that I'm thinking about you;
And I love you very much, for that is true.

   Adele A. Guerrero

Born A Hundred Years Too Late

These city streets and bars are getting this old cowboy down.
I need the open space, gotta get out of this town.
It ain't nobody's fault, it's preordained to be my fate.
I'm a cowboy in a city, born a hundred years too late.

A hundred years ago a man could ride the range all day
and lie awake at night and hear the coyotes as they bay.
But I'm just like the mustang, I'm corralled without a gate.
I'm cooped up in this city, born a hundred years too late.

A hundred years too late to ride the trails across this land,
A hundred years too late to throw a rope or set a brand,
A hundred years ago the cowboy's life was really great,
But I'm a city cowboy, born a hundred years too late.

   Don Rothra

"Undying Devotion"

Dedicated to Jennifer Mae Pokarney

Jenny, I need to hold you tonight
I need you to come and make everything alright
As I lay here alone I feel as if I'm going insane
Just thinking of you and trying to sort out this pain
I feel your hair on my hands, on my bed
I hear your voice yet I still wish I was dead
I'm crying, still your eyes stare back at me
This wore out picture just isn't as good as it used to be
The answering machine plays your message over and over again
Your lonely trembling voice I still hear now and then
You know you're the only girl I'll ever be able to love
And all those spectacular moments are what I'm thinking of
When I was the winner you were always there
When I was the loser you held me tight and showed me you care
I've been up and down memory lane a hundred times
With every walk I see another way our love shines
Now, as I sat there, feeling so scared and lonely, tired and low
Loneliness eating me up, killing me so slow
The shot rings through the house, and some say I took the easy way out
But one thing is true Jenny, you were my only love without a doubt

   Andy Landers

I'm Sorry

For what it's worth
   I never meant to hurt you
For what it's worth
   My words were in vain, untrue to my heart
For what it's worth
   I never meant to make you cry
For what it's worth
   I wish I could turn back and change my actions
For what it's worth
   I still cry about it every night
For what it's worth
   I don't want you our of my life
For what it's worth
   I know my words will never take the
   pain from your heart
For what it's worth
   I'm sorry

   Genell Plude

"Time On My Hands"

Passing through this garden, that I call my life,
I never pass a flower without smelling it twice.
While never taking for granted, the day's that pass,
I caress each petal though it were my last.
Time on my hands, all natures alive,
As silently the raindrops fall my garden thrives.
The seasons of time can't take away the beauty of a sunset,
Or the kiss of the morning dew.
Storms of life sometimes find me drifting into ports unknown.
But with a little patience, and a trusted friend,
I've found my way round the next bend.
Sometimes I long for the touch of a hand,
A shoulder to lean on at journeys end.
Standing still in my garden at the end of the day.
I search my soul for words to say.
On a far rose a thorn I see, as I wait patiently for my tender to come.
To fill this time on my hands with the love of someone.
The days turn to years as my garden turns to stone,
there among the rocks and thorns is place I call my home.

   Beverly J. Price

Linda

When you were just a little girl and sat upon my knee
I never shall forget the way you smiled and looked at me

Those big blue eyes that danced with light
That beautiful shining hair
You were just like an angel
As you were sitting there

You always seemed to be content in everything we'd do
From reading books to playing games, 'twas easy pleasing you.

A happy child, so loving too
Delightful through and through
These are the words that do describe that little girl I knew

I loved those years when you were small
Those times we shared, you see. If it were right I'd kept
you there and kept you just for me
But these were only dreams I dreamed and not reality!

Carolyn McTague

SK-3

Up in the dark with a silent scream
I open my eyes yet I know it's no dream.
Then I feel your arms holding me tight
And I remember why I continue to fight.
The shadows are there, they haunt my days
The memories affect me in a million ways.
Yet you're always there, you're always true
I can't help but to continue loving you.
The darkness is there, it's very real
It affects all I say, it affects how I feel.
But you give me light, you give me hope
A light for the darkness through which I grope.
Holding you tightly, I face a new day
I follow you, love, please show me the way.

Dennis L. Hitzeman

If I Could Control The Magic

I talk just about like anybody else that you may know,
I pick up this pen, all of sudden, words start to flow
They come out in this funny sorta way…
Seems, the pen talks, using words it wants to say.

As you can see, they come out in all kinds of rhymes,
Hundreds and Hundreds, page after page - every time…
I have no idea where it all comes from…
I just sit, amazed, and watch it make the words come.

I see this offer on a contest; National library of Poetry…
Something I figure, this pen would be happy to see…
I present the idea, even though it don't matter to me.
However, I am intrigued by the possible fee…

I search through the stuff this pen has written,
The Magic, never did make sense to me, I'd just left them sittin',
Most are pretty good, at least, I think they are;
Which one is best? Well, I can't think that far…

So, I just picked up the pen, "run with it", I said.
In this case, (unlike most of my life), I don't mind being led
Twenty lines or less any style, any subject; no control-
Might as well let it happen, since it comes from the soul.

Jeffrey Lawson I

I Am A Black Woman

I am a black child
I play, I race, I dance, I sing.
A dance of happiness,
A song of innocence.
My friends and I enjoy the same things.

I am a black girl
I learn, I grow, I dance, I sing.
A dance of laughter.
A song of youth.
Many of my friends enjoy the same things.

I am black lady
I labor, I date, I dance, I sing.
A dance of maturity,
A song of independence.
Several of my friends enjoy the same things.

I am a black woman,
I support, I nourish, I dance, I sing.
A dance of fulfillment,
A song of wisdom.
A few of my friends enjoy the same things.

Desiree D. Goins

Concerns Of The 90's

Last night upon my pillow as sleep eluded me,
I pondered on the current events and how it could possibly be
That a person would maliciously, intentionally light a flame
And destroy so many lives and homes' on whom can we place the
blame?

Is it our own society with its increase in drugs and gangs
Or just some twisted bit of fate on which the verdict hangs,
It used to be safe to walk at night or drive along the highway
Now we fortify our homes where our children live and play.

We'll have to find some answers or live in fear and terror.
What can we do to change the world and how to make life fairer?
How can we help our troubled youth if not by our example?
To respect another's property and not deliberately trample.

Have we forgotten the golden rule and how to love our
neighbors?
We must hope and pray that it's not too late to turn it around
and savor
A life that is better for everyone regardless of color or race,
And homes for the homeless where the world is a better place.

Hazel Michelson

Glimpses

I see glimpses, glimpses of who I can be.
I reach for it, but part of me holds back,
feeling unsure.
The anger and sadness seems so safe.
For I have carried it for so long.
It's like a bridge broken in two.
I want to jump across to happiness.
But what if I fall and never climb back up?
I need my faith. I need love and trust in
a power greater than myself.
Who will listen when I'm down.
Who will feel gladness for my achievements
and dreams come true.
Times come when I travel on a broken bridge.
Sometimes I jump across. Sometimes I fall.
But as I glimpse inside myself.
I see the happiness I desire.
I just need to hold on and not let it go.

Angela M. Parsons

If Only

A carefree child runs laughingly by,
I remember the freedom.
  A seagull soars effortlessly through the sky,
I remember my dreams.

If only
  The stars shine in the darkest night,
I remember countless wishes.
  The sun glows in the early light,
I remember new beginnings.

If only
  The raindrops suddenly begin to fall,
I remember boundless despair.
  The thunder crackles through it all,
I remember the fear.

If only
  The tears come, my visions are blurred,
I remember what never will be.
  The saddest words I ever heard.
If only.

> *Amie M. Morris*

Tears Of Regret

While walking down a crowded street,
I saw you pass by.
Our eyes glanced for a second,
Just then I wanted to cry.

My tears were welling up,
Recalling the relationship we once shared.
As the drops were running down my cheeks,
I suddenly remembered how much I cared.

Then what went through my mind,
Were the many times I saw so wrong.
Because of things I said and did,
The anger continued for so long.

A picture of your smiling face,
I will always keep with me.
You will never completely leave my heart,
It's there you'll always be.

As I stand here alone,
What's foremost on my mind,
Is that I'm not over you yet,
And I reach up to wipe my tears of regret.

> *Dawn S. Eubanks*

Beyond My Imagination

Beyond my imagination, beyond my horizon
I see a bright new world
A world of peace and justice
Beyond my imagination, beyond my dreams
I see people working together
To protect our planet
Beyond my imagination, I see a world
Where famine no longer exists
Where conflicts among nations
Have been resolved
I see children with a smile
I see people sharing dreams and hope
I see a cure for cancer and a cure for AIDS
I see endangered species being protected
And clean air and clean water
Beyond my imagination, beyond my dreams
People working together to save the forests
To save the animals to save the oceans
People working together to save lives
Working together to save this planet we call Earth

> *Alfredo Baptista*

"I See Love"

When I look at you, here is what I see;
  I see all the love, that is meant for me.

When I look at you, I see love.

At your slightest touch,
  or your secret glance;
    with your knowing smile,
      my heart starts to dance.

When I look at you, I see love.

How you pick me up, when I'm feeling low;
  how you give me my life a refreshing glow.

When I look at you, I see love.

I give to you, what you've given to me,
  I return your love, so willingly.

Knowing that, as life's years decline,
  my love is yours, as yours is mine.

When I look at you and you look at me,
  when we look, we will always see, love.

> *John F. Bress*

Looking Out My Front Window

As I sit by my window and gaze at the morn,
I see clouds rolling by....hear the beep of a horn.
The trees almost bare, their leaves mostly shed.
Falls beauty soon gone, the snow lies ahead.
Each spring has its Fall, each day has its night,
As I look out my window at the glorious sight.
I see grass that has withered, fallen leaves everywhere.
I see beauty in dark skies, in trees that are bare.
Expressions of God everywhere to be seen,
As I sit by my window, me, God, and my dream.

> *Jeannette (Pagliaro) Macera*

Pampas Grass

In the car, driving by the swamps toward Syracuse
I see pampas tasseled, spun, softening the air for miles
And, when caught with the sun's gold at evening time,
It blinks and glows like a million lights in the city.

Now I see it summer green.
It blazes yellow in the Fall
With lance-shaped leaves pointing east and west
Until, stripped by frost and Winter's chill,

They fall like dried grass—
Leaving tall straight reeds,
Stark, bare and regimented
Like an army guarding the highway.

Or are they fluted columns of Grecian temples?
Or pleated skirts of Syrian kings?
But wait!
This reverie and the pulling hum of the motor

Are rent with strange music. Pipes of Pan?
Or is it that this whole roadside is strung
With harp strings—
And the blowing wind is the strummer?

> *Jessie Landecker*

The Wonder Of The Wee Ones

Every time I look around and see a little child,
I see someone who is innocent and oh so very mild.

When I see a child smile, it warms me up inside,
Feelings of magic and happiness are the feelings that abide.

When I hear the soft words that a little baby coos,
I automatically find myself shaking off my blues.

I love to tell children stories as they slowly drift to dreams,
They look like little angels just floating on moonbeams.

As I look at the eyes of a child, full of wonder and surprise,
I think of myself as a child and remember my strong family ties.

The best part of being around a child is the lightheartedness you feel,
And when a child hugs you, you know that love is real.

For children don't wear disguises as adults sometimes do,
They are caring, they are giving and they love you because you're you.

There is much satisfaction in watching a child learn and grow,
The very hardest part is learning how to let them go.

For they grow up so fast with every passing day,
Love them, talk to them and guide them on their way.

Yes, the little ones are so cute and they're so cuddly, too,
The wonder of the wee ones can do wonders for you.
   Carol B. Gallagher

Every Day Of My Life

Every day of my life a wish comes true;
I see the sun rise and even the dew.
At times I feel that life is through
But looking upward, I see the sky so blue.

Every day of my life I am thankful for
The luxury of life we take too far.
Is it not true that if we hasten the dawn,
That all this will be when we are gone?

Every day of my life let it be said that
I bowed my head at the close of day.
Maybe this is poor pay but what did you
Do and what did you say?
   Ellena M. E. Freeman

Looking Through The Window

The courtyard is filled with people:
I see them all with one glance
   but not one of them see me.
I stand here aching, my life
   touched by death,
But not one soul sees me
   or knows I exist;
Uncaring, they go their own way.
My heart bleeds, my soul writhes in despair,
But no one reaches out a caring hand,
No one asks to share my grief.

And I know that if I were a
   part of the crowd,
I, too, would go on my own way:
Not stopping to see
   who is behind the window
   looking down at me.
   Carolyn F. Jones

The Presence Of Jesus

Jesus, my Jesus, Your presence is everywhere.
I see You in the eyes of those who care,
I see You in the joy of a baby newly born,
I see You in the tears of those who mourn,
I see You in the face of my sisters and brothers as we live
   God's commandment to love one another.

I see You in my son as he grows into a man
   and I am thankful for I know he has taken God's hand.
I see You in my husband as he works hard each day
   and I know Your presence lightens his burdens along the way
I remember how You looked in the eyes of my friend
   who has come to heaven, but her love never ends.

Jesus, my Jesus, Your presence is everywhere I can see—and
   even where I cannot see— for You live always inside of me.
   Delores Raggio

In My Eyes

In my eyes,
I see your face.
Your smile makes others smile
And shows your warmth and compassion.

In my eyes,
I see your strength of character
And your boldness of mind
That many can only dream of having.

In my eyes,
I see you wrestling;
Wrestling hard, never giving up,
While I think to myself, "Go, Crispin!"

In my eyes,
Others see my admiration and respect for you,
Hoping that you see in yourself,
All the good things that I see,
In my eyes.
   Annette Pham

The Walking Path

As often as I have followed this path before
I seem to enjoy it less, more and more

I always walk alone because I like it that way
To have any visitors would mean to stay

I can sit and day dream all day long
Listening to the birds sing their beautiful songs

I can fall asleep on the grass
Think about life, watch life pass

By, over my head as I wait
Here comes darkness, never late

I'll walk back again, the path I take
Tomorrow I'll return, the trail I'll make

The sun warms the soil and pretties the view
With grass so green, sky a brilliant blue

Would you like to come here with me?
There are many things you can see.

I know I said I like to walk alone,
But I'd love to share this beautiful home.
   Dana Foltz

Storm Of Death

As darkness gets darker,
I sense the staring eyes.
The tranquility taunts—
but that chilling calm is soon consumed;
for with the wind, destiny derives.

The rain pounds on a heartbeat.
A spiteful snare keeps me there—
as does the doom.
The creek can not retreat.
Its panic is futile, it must accept defeat.

Let the laughing leaves go unloathed,
their mirth matters not.
For one by one their life is done,
they fail and fall
and taint the tree unclothed.

The darkness of night
simply will say,
Another day gone...
another day.

Brice Arave

Untitled

I see a lonely tree in a field.
I smell your cologne in the air.
I look for you, but you're not there.
There is not a moment that thoughts
of you don't go through this mind of mine.
I think about you 24-hours a day.
I don't ever stop thinking about you.
At first I wanted it to just be a
crush, like puppy love,
But now I know it's true.
The greatest thing is true love,
And I love you.

Brenda Carroll

Up Yonder

While blazing a trail with wind at my tail
I spotted a jewel in the trenches;
My eyes became fixed, my thoughts became mixed;
Had time taken leave of its senses?
I slowed to a pace where I'd savor the grace
Of handcrafted houses and porches;
Now frozen in time and lauded in rhyme
It beckons the traveler like torches.

So mix with the cream in pursuit of your dream;
Slow down, take time to ponder.
Life lived too fast dishonors its past;
There's a wealth of beauty up yonder.

James R. Ford

Love Lost

I reached out for one soft moment,
I reached out - but the moment was gone.
I listened softly for your sweet singing,
I listened soft - but there was no song.
I whispered to you on a summer's daybreak,
I whispered - oh - but you didn't hear.
I chased your shadow for days unending,
I chased you so far - but you were never near.
I chose a dream that stayed on forever,
I chose a dream - but it would never come true.
I closed my eyes and cried for my heartbreak,
My heartbreak of forever loving you.

Janet A. Younge

Rilla's Lenten Soup

"Oh, Lord" as I walked along my way.
  I stopped to see my friend today
I passed along the doors and stopped and faintly knocked.
  "Come in, hello," she breathlessly said,
as she called from her bed.

Then I noticed that old sparkle, we had seen so many times before
  Trying desperately to shine once more.
"Oh! God", I cried , can it be, why she?"
  Friends came only to say
"Dear Lord, why she today?"

She's the first to invite a stranger "Lord" to your house, I pleaded.
  Among the first to make the Lenten Soup.
"Oh, Lord why she, " I cried? I'm angry, why she?
  How can it be?

Suddenly a great arm surrounded me with an Everlasting Love.
  A gentle voice said, "yes, Dear Lord, I shed tears too
When I gave my "Dear Son" to die for you!
  Then, I arose and faintly turned and sighed
Oh! Lord! how can I doubt, forgive me God, I cried!

Helen M. Stottlemyer

Images

As I live the life of immortality
I struggle to find the meaning of a meaningful life.

As I reach the center of the domestic,
blackened world I realized that there's a painless
tear falling from my weakened eyes and as I reached
to softly wipe it away it became an illusion, just
another feeling with no meaning.

And as I sat on the ledge of the
sidewalk I felt as if I were sitting
on the edge of the world.

Nervously I watched the unfriendly,
lifeless man of society walk by me,
as he appeared closer and closer I realized it
was just another image of the world today....
meaningless, unfriendly, lifeless, and greedy.

Heather Ward

Childish Wisdom

With my tiny fists clenched,
i stubbornly repeated my point
over and over again.
He looks angry...
i shouldn't have said that.
He demands an apology.
Huge tears fill my eyes.
  "i'm sorry that i disagreed
with You Father, You said You
knew everything. Please forgive
and forget."

He hugs me.
Taking His finger into my tiny fist, we walked on.

{pausing},
Gazing wondrously up at the sky,
i said,
  "But can You tell me Father,
why is the sun round?"

No response.
i smiled. We walked on

Deepti Sahdev

Mon Ami

Part way through the Book of Me, hopeless, I was beat.
I stumbled right into your path and fell there, at your feet.
    You hand extended down to me, you drew me to your side.
To accept the whole of Me as friend? My wonderment is wide.
You let me tell you many things. You took it all with care.
You shuffled through the ugly stuff and gave me back a share
to tell me I mean something. I can love and laugh and be..
    anywhere I choose to go - it's really up to me!
  I know, I've heard it all before, others really tried.
It was different when you told me.. I felt it deep inside.
  How do you overlook those things I stumble, tumble over?
A friendship such as yours for me is a treasure I've discovered

Debbie DeLaune

Angel

What is in the sky?
I think an angel is in the sky
There It is way so high
I think it is time to say Good-bye

Even though we love them so
Doesn't mean you can let them go

Angel is one of Gods children

If they are bad doesn't mean you can paint them red

Now it's time to say Good-bye,
Let my loved one wave Good-bye
There is God with His arms out wide,
The angel looked down and sighed

With all the love an angel can give to me
I turned my back and wave Good-bye

Jessica Houlemard

Tomorrow

When I think of tomorrow,
I think of a whole day new to come;
I think of joy that will be shared,
the loving of some.
The sun will be shown, the clouds all away;
tomorrow will be so different than today;
The air will be fresh, the ground all clean;
all birds will be singing,
all nature will be seen.
I think of my tomorrow wishes
and know soon they will come true;
I just have to wait patiently,
and do what I have to do.

Erica Riccardi

Untitled

As I look back upon my past,
I think of moments I wished could last.
Moments of joy between you and me,
moments that some children will never see,
The moments our lives become one.
Like sisters we have had so much fun.
Through all my troubles and all my fears
you've been there to dry my tears.
I'm sorry for all the times we've fought
and I'll never forget all you've taught.
Although you don't know it, you've showed me the way.
The things I've learned, I'll use each day.
So when I leave and you are alone,
There's something I never told you, but you should have known.
You are the best mother that could ever be
And I love you as much as you've loved me.

Jenifer Traylor

"Looking Back"

As I look back into those days when I had no cares.
I think of the things I used to do,
Like wearing the beautiful barrettes in my hair.
I also feel the cute little dresses white with puffy sleeves.
I hear the trees in the back where I used to play.
I wonder why we have to leave days behind like these
And I am always hoping that I can go
back to one of those days.
Where I can play in the fields where I used to go.
And sit in my chair again with the doll
I love to hold.

Caty Audinwood

"How Old Is Old"

When Mother died, she was 95,
  I think you all should know...
Some people said, she was Old,
  My grief should never show...
But I have news for the folks,
  Who said that she was Old...
I'd give a lot to have her here,
  To love and to hold...
I know when God called my Dad,
  And took him far away...
No tears did I ever shed, not even to this day...
For then I had another place,
  To put my love for him...
This I did with all my heart, and Mother's every whim...
But then they say, she got Old,
  Even Old enough to die...
Still I wish that she was here, and I could tell her, Hi...
Now I'll ask you one more time, and If you really know...
Tell me please, "How Old Is Old?"
  When it comes, your time to go.

Duane H. Nelson

Growing Up

Said the acorn to the Oak tree
I think you expect too much for me
When I grow up I cannot be
Not even half the size of thee
Or maybe never grow at all
And it I do be straight and tall

Won't I be cold when winter comes
Stripped bare of leaves, no warmth of sun
Won't I be hurt when lighting strikes
And wind will bend and frighten me
No, I'm afraid to be a tree

You're much too young the Oak replied
What if two hundred years ago
I'd been afraid to try to grow?
You'd never have a chance to be
A seed, a sapling, or a tree
Growing up is life you see
And you'll grow up to be a tree

Bart Beasley

Forever Lost

Though I see lies that people tell,
I wonder if their hearts are as cold as it seems;
Showing doubt where people lies roams,
I see the wonders of great minds;
For I, am a proud and a poised man
Proud to be, proud to live and die;
Though I see lies that people tell;
I see their lives are,
Forever lost.........

Charles Lambert

Colors

Life has painted me into a corner
I thought I knew the color of each wall
But when I wanted to try a new shade
I dipped in and now I am trapped.

He is steel blue
You are sunset orange.
When you mix
There's only a muddled brown.
But separately.....
The contrast is breathtaking.

I wait patiently
For time to resolve my dilemma.
I sometimes touch to see if the paint's still wet
And come back with orange on my hands —
I have smeared the finish.
And don't know whether
I should try to paint it again
Or let it stay the way it is
As a constant reminder.

Cindy K. Patton

When Christ Calls The Row

When I was younger no older than seven,
I thought of a place above named Heaven,
I'm praying hard because I want to go,
I hope I will be there when Christ call the row.

I know Jesus Christ will have food there to eat
And also a lot of people to meet
When each one time come golden bells will ring
After we all get there we will shout and sing.

How glad I will be when I get to that place
Other ones and me will be face to face
I know Christ will have there room for us all
When he want us to come he will make a call.

Essie Campbell

Untitled

Today as I saw the couple go by,
I thought to myself and wanted to cry;

We just overlooked the way it could be,
And I wondered and wondered why it happened to me;

I've been lonely, depressed, and torn between friends,
And I'm hoping real soon it will come to an end;

I have five more months till the day it arrives,
And when that day comes, it will change many lives;

I pray to the Lord that I will be strong
Now that I've realized what I have done wrong;

All I can do is pray for the best,
And know that the Lord will deal with the rest.

Angela Dickey

May 13, 1994
The Truth On Paper

Roses are red, violets are blue,
I wish I still had a boyfriend like you.
I don't know why I don't just give up and go on.
It's just too hard to know that you just might be gone.
I will try and try until I succeed,
I will do what I must and get what I need.
I may not be beautiful, even with my bangs curled,
But give me a chance and I'll show you my world.
I know this might be the worst poem I've ever written,
But they are my thoughts on paper spoken
as softly as you might pat a kitten.

Emily Tretter

Not In Your Arms

The love you had for me
I thought would never die.
You gave me hope and swore
I'd never have to find another guy.
But when you told me you needed time away.
What was I supposed to say?
You said you still cared
and you would be back.
All I could think about,
was how it was unfair
and where we lost track.
Weeks go by and I'm still not in your arms.
I've tried to go on, but all
I think about is you.
I think about the first time
we kissed and the first time we held each other.
The secrets we shared and
The way you always showed you cared.
What does a lot of thinking do?
It makes you lose the one, Who really loved you.

Jackie S. Sutton

I Was

I was in this the prerequisite to heaven.
I walked within the blue marble "foot stool
Of God," that spins in eternity.
I was young full of youthful vigor to move
mountains that cast a shadow in my path.
I was old, full up of the wisdom of the ages,
covered with the battle scares of life.
I screamed in terror;
I laughed at four words You Can't Do That!
I have seen and I have waited. I have loved and
my God, I have hated.
I was a product of lust, pain, love and aggression.
I have learned humility, been humiliated, and I have allowed
pride to puff itself up to cover my weaknesses.
I have watched death snatch and lamented,
I existed and just as passionately as life had come, death came and
lead me on to the well traveled bridge to glory, I have joyed and I
have sorrowed, the advice of those that were before me wait on the
morrow and now I pass the torch of the enigma of life and wisdom on
to those that are, and will be.

Damien Skinner

Mother's Day

I walked out in my garden, it was early in the day
I wanted to talks to my heavenly father. To see what he would say
I told Him of my loneliness on this mothers day
of how I missed my children in towns so far away
He answered cheer up my child please do not dismay.
For I am with you always while on this earth you stay
I am here when you need comfort, and when you need a friend
Even though your heart is lonely, I'll he here till the end.
Be thankful for the ones who come to show their love for you
your husband, son and grandsons and wives
Whose love you know is true.
Do not he sad for the thoughtless ones
who show no love for you
For somewhere down a lonely road, they may be lonely too.

Anna Owens

Untitled

Today as I was sitting in my chair watching my wife
I was just wondering how I got along in life
Of the times I was single, when I was out on my own
Of times when I was lonely, of times without a home.

It amazes me to even wonder or think
That without this woman, how deep I would sink
Of all the times of joy and sadness in my life
I was just wondering how I got along without my wife.

As we a grow old together, and our hair turns grey
I will always remember and cherish the day
That as a young man with no purpose or way in life
I was lucky enough to meet and marry this woman
I call my wife.

Carlin Ross

An Open Letter From An Unborn Child

Dear Mom,

The very moment you conceived me
I was so anxious to see you and Dad
I was so anxious to feel your warm embrace
To be sure that I am loved. I was also excited
to see the world that God has prepared for you and me.

Then one day I heard a weird sound; I could not
figure it too well. I thought it was a special vehicle
to take me express out of your womb!
But sooner I felt I was being sucked
By something I was too helpless to resist
It was too late before I found
I was being extracted part by part!

I couldn't help but say, Alas!
Where is my Mom's warm embrace?
Where are my Dad's protective hands?
Do I have to see God face to face that fast?

How I wished you gave me the chance.
To prove to you my worth! I still love you mom and dad,
Your unborn child

Aquino T. Trasga

For The Child In All Of Us

Take my hand, my little one.
I will not lead you astray..

I will toss the pebbles from your path,
Brush the leaves out of your hair,
And smooth the frown from your brow.

I will chase the dragons from your dreams
And paint your shadow blue.

Take my hand, my little one.
Sit with me and watch the sunsets glow.
Rock with me in my old chair
And marvel as the seasons change.

Take my hand, my little one.
I will be your tree,
And your leaves will always change back to green.

Elizabeth Poe Richter

The Path Which Angels Ride

I wish for a better life as I continue on life's strides,
I wish for the sacred, peaceful, light of the paths which angels ride.
I search for the path that brings forth joy, deep from inner self,
and though hard on body as well as soul, good for mental health.

I look not for the resistance least, or even of pleasures found,
nor do I look for redemptions path, where tortured souls are bound.
I simply seek my true hearts path, which only I may find,
the path which leads me to my castle's keep, raised on the fertile
plains of my mind.

There I may rest until my end, happily waiting for destiny's call,
or I may venture out to spread forth joy, giving back to all.
But over all I shall be at peace, as if on gossamer wings I glide,
If only I find, and undertake, the path which angels ride.

John F. Ghee

True Love

Black and blue and scarcd of you.
I wish I could get over you,
There's times you are so full of love.
Then times you are so full of joy.
You hold me close to you and say..
"I love you honey, I really do!"
I take those words, and words they are.
I hold them close. I hold then far
Trying to forget the pain that's there
Why? I ask why? Do you strike me like that!?
All I did was think of you!
Why? I ask why?
You say you love me but
How could that be
Love is not black and blue.

Barbara J. Atkinson--May 13, 1994

Silent Thoughts

The time is against me again;
I wish to be out of this cage.
I don't understand the game,
But I have no choice at this stage
Where I just can't avoid to abuse my brain.
In this kind of eternal bandage,
I have been struggling in vain.
So my soul and I are still their hostages.

Now I have no idea what to stand for;
And I am still a little bit confused.
I may not be in a pretty good mood or,
I just might have no working fuse.
While I am missing all comfort,
My soul again, seems to face its blues.
But I am still behind the door
With hope and dream along my inner cruise.

The music coming from in there,
Sounds just like an out of space tune.
But my body seems not to worry about border;
So our chance to reach it is still there - a real boon.

Andre Koffi

Alaska Wind

My love for you is like the Alaska Winds.
It can blow you over and take your breath away.
It can be a gentle breeze, just enough to cover you and let you
know it's there.
At times it's there to heal your aching heart.
Other times it's there to warm you up.
It can travel for miles when we are miles apart.
It can be as close as a gentle breath, when we are together.

David Tynan

In My Dreams

Glimmering seas, a northeast breeze;
I wish you were here,
If only you could see and hear.

A setting sun, on the horizon;
beautiful as it seems,
If only you were in my dreams.

Here comes nightfall, sea starts its lull;
when the day starts anew,
I'll know I was thinking of you.
>   ***Eduardo Ruiloba, Jr.***

I Am

I am a girl who wants to live and help others.
I wonder if the words problems will ever be solved.
I hear the cries of children that don't have what I do.
I see the desperation on the faces of starving children.
I want to understand why there is so much hate and misery in this world
I am a girl who wants to live and help others.

I pretend there's a world full of happiness and laughter instead of
   sorrow, grief and tears.
I feel a sense of helplessness.
I touch the heart of others trying to help.
I worry about dying before what I want to do.
I cry when I think of all the starving, hate and racism.
I am a girl who wants to live and help others.

I understand that I am only in a world of millions.
I say that no matter what race or religion, we are all equal.
I dream of world free of hate and racism.
I try to understand why or how people can be so cruel.
I hope that someday people will realize that wars and bitterness
   will not get you anything but more bitterness and wars.
I am a girl who wants to live and help others.
>   ***Desirae De Poppe***

Whenever

Whenever I say, "I love you"
I wonder if you know how much
All that I feel...how deeply I do
Those three words simply aren't enough

Whenever I say, "I love you"
Part of what I'm trying to show
Is that you mean the world to me
And I'm tying my best to let you know

Whenever I say, "I love you"
Part of what I'm trying to say
Is it's not just when it's convenient or easy
It's through every moment of every day

Whenever I say, "I love you "
It means the heart that was once mine
Has been given to you so completely
From now until the end of time
>   ***Cheryl Sobolewsky***

If You Believe

If you believe in tooth fairies let the fairies come,
if you are old and believe in youth let you be forever young.

If you believe in honesty let you never tell a lie,
if you believe in life let your spirit never die.

If you believe in something let it all come true,
because people believe in many things like I believe in you!
>   ***Courtnie Wilford***

I Am

I Am a dreamer that loves to swim
I wonder what my life would be like in twenty years
I hear peace throughout the nation
I see the heavenly valleys
I Am a dreamer that loves to swim...

I pretend like everything is normal, when it's not
I feel the hurt and pain with people that have AIDS
I touch the highest star possible
I worry that the Ozone is going to bust
I cry at death
I Am a dreamer that loves to swim...

I understand when someone says sorry
I say be all you can be
I dream of someday going to space
I try to live my life to the fullest
I hope to be an olympic swimmer
I Am a dreamer that loves to swim...
>   ***Britta Stinner***

Untitled

I remember as a child, I thought my mother Beautiful,
I worried about how hard she worked and could never spend
   enough time with her.

I remember as a teen-ager, I thought my mother Old,
We fought over friends and fashions and all the time I spent
   away from home.

I remember as a young working woman, I thought my mother Naive,
I'd discuss boyfriends and jobs with her then ignore everything
   she said.

Today, I think my mother Remarkable,
Her heart is full of wisdom
Her home is always inviting.

I worry about how hard she works can never spend enough time
   with her.
>   ***Jacqueline C. Delario***

Shalom

I am a Jew.
I worship the same God as you
and yet you mock me.
You ridicule...despise me.

Naked and alone,
I came into this world.
At Belsen, Auschwitz, Dachau
my wife, my children died naked and alone.

My God is your God and yet you say
He does not hear my prayer?
Tell me why.
Am I not a man like you?

Another Jew lay prostrate
in the Garden of Gesthemane
and prayed to your God.
Was he turned away?

Yes, I am a Jew.
I too will stand in judgment
before your God...my God.
Then we will know.
>   ***Bill DeGrasse***

My Gift

If I could give the world a gift,
I would give it something new, I would give it something
pretty, for everyone a newborn kitty

Everyone should have a pet, to teach them to be gentle,
to teach them to be kind, to teach them a lot of patience,
for every time the kitty won't mind.

We should all learn to care, we should all learn to share.
Know the right thing to do, when a life depends on you.

If we all learn to love and let love grow and grow, the
world would be a better place. This I'm sure I know.

Ashley Ernst

The Night Sky

Often when I was but yet a child,
I would watch the blue-black mystical sky.
My imagination would float in unbridled wonderment—
How did it all come to be, and why?

Sometimes I would make a secret wish
Upon the smallest glittering star.
I would wish for true love and happiness
In a future that then seemed so far.

Sometimes I'd watch a jettisoned falling star
As it came streaking toward Earth without a sound.
Would it cause a wondrously magical commotion
When it finally reached the ground?

Although the innocent days of my childhood
Have disappeared among the changing seasons,
That vast nebulous sea of blackness above me
Still challenges my mind with questions and reasons.

Betty Smith Walker

Going Home One Day

I think, I said as I was driving home,
I'd like to hear a winter's tale be told.
For February '94 is past
And March of '94 will be less cold.

You seem to be a storyteller, which,
If other storytellers are like you,
Will give me hours of pleasurable feast.
I've heard but half the tales I've wanted to.

I fancy you could tell me all your tales
In spring or summer, maybe even fall.
But if that's all there were to any year,
I wouldn't want to hear the tales at all.

The fire cracks; the embers die away;
I smell the cocoa heating on the stove;
I hear the mantel clock strike half past ten.
The evening's filled with everlasting love.

I love your tales; you tell them lovingly.
You were so strong, and I so small and weak.
Ah, yes. Oh, yes; I do indeed recall,
For I was there. I know whereof you speak.

Almon C. Bock II

The Special Gift

For forty years I've treasured it.
It's been put away, and I almost forgot about it.
I've saved it, and I've kept it.
For the sister so close to my heart.
For I always knew that one day.
It would bring joy in a very special way.
So on this Mothers day I place in your care.
A single lock of Lois June's hair.

Anita Young

Ideas

What hold and lies ahead?
Ideas of ancient and past seers
Truth that will be unfolded.
Perhaps it begins small, gets greater.
The language differs, to one environment.
Who will awake slumber, from our mind?
The expand of years, timeless as ag.
We speak of nowadays, hopeful for tomorrow
Hopeful our ideas, will bid, bloom, and flourish.
The wind of time races ahead.

Hazel A. Gould

A Strong Black Woman Needs a Strong Black Man

Every strong black woman needs a strong black man
   If he is weak and does not help but only hinder
   her, she does not need him.
Every strong black woman needs a strong black man
   She wants a man who is not afraid of commitment.
Every strong black woman needs a strong black man
   She needs him to treat her like a queen and
   never take her for granted.
Every strong black woman needs a strong black man
   She wants a man who not only finds her attractive
   physically, but mentally, too.
Every strong black woman needs a strong black man
   She wants a man who can pick her up when she has
   fallen, but is not afraid to be picked up when
   he himself has fallen, too.
Every strong black woman needs a strong black man
   She wants a man who will comfort her and he will
   be with her till the end of time.
     She wants a strong black man!

Felix L. Ford III

Rejoice In Mark

If I Falter, please bear with me
if I cry, they're tears of joy
thankful for the years of pleasure
given by this loving boy.

Mark has brought his family
A very special love
a true miracle of life
sent from God above.

We've all shared with Mark at times
parts of twenty one years
while we recall his love of life
please don't hold back your tears.

Mark's untimely death will leave
a void for his parents and brothers
an ache and a hurt that will always be felt
by his family, his friends and others.

The moment has come to say goodbye
Mark's time on Earth is completed
let's lift our voices in a fond farewell
for today, at God's feet, Mark is seated.

Barbara Barbato

The End

The sun captured the flower as if it knew
It was dying.
The rain fell with great destruction as if
It knew the world is going to perish.
Yet others are to sightless to see the
Passions of others.
Everything and everyone will fade
But no-one will notice until the
Final day.

Crystal Cole

Untitled

Have I told you today I love you?
  If not there's a reason why.
It's a fact of life that will always exist,
  like when you look up you see the sky.
Time goes by without you,
  the clock of my heart goes so fast.
I don't want to be just a memory,
  a figure in your past.
Take me into your life,
  let me share all you joy and sorrow.
Allow us to be one,
  for all our tomorrows.
Life has its up and downs
  and love is hard work,
but like all things of importance,
  our love will show its worth.

    Joseph Smith

Death

Have you ever heard that some of them are born to lose
If so just let it be and that person free
If they want to be happy in some other place
Just let it be graceful when they leave this disgrace
If they want it so bad
Be glad when it's theirs
When their worries and troubles are not in big herds
When they don't have big problems with so much to do
With so little time what else can one do
So they turn to me for whatever I'll do
I usually win but sometimes they do
I'm the one who claims them when they are dead
I help them when they need me when they are in dread
Guess what they call me sometimes while crying
Go on just one more time you are not trying
Well figure it out and give me a call
If you ever have doubts about anything at all

    Brenna Rae Gonterman

"The Second Chance"

For you, I would be glad to wait,
If that's what it would take;
And then I wonder
If I'm only making another one of my mistakes.
But that's only if you want me to...

From you, I've saved so many things
That remind me of the day;
And then I wonder
If I should just give up and throw them all away.
But that's only if you want me to...

With you, I'm only asking,
Not just for friendship or romance;
And then I wonder
If I'm asking too much for you to give me a second chance.
But that's only if you want to...

    April Chartier

Fall Thoughts

The wind is blowing and the leaves are falling.
It's the time of year the woods are calling-
To the fearless hunters and non hunters alike-
They have one thing in common, they both like to hike.
The wind is brisk and the air is nice,
But it makes me think about snow and ice.
I'm getting too old and I'm nobody's fool-
So I'll head down South and enjoy the pool.

    Barbara Frost

Everyday people

Everyday people don't want to be put down
if they move to a new place
they just want to be accepted for who they are,
they don't want to be put down just because
they look different, act different, talk different,
or just because their skin's a different color.
How can we call our selves civilized
if we put other people down cause they're a different race,
if you put someone down you're only putting yourself down,
so many young people getting gunned down, when it is gonna stop?
We are living in a society where you can't walk the streets
with out someone looking at you 'cause you look different.
We have got to stop the madness,
so free your mind and open yourself up to new experiences,
people and cultures and always remember to be yourself.

    Cheona Storey

Abel And Cain

We don't kill enough the times does say
If they won't stop killing, we must kill them and,
We applaud the Fat General as he makes them pay.
The world must see our planes in the sky
Oh how we make those other people die.
We the great Democracy don't like the role we play
If they would stop we would not have to slay more and more each day.
From Africa to Asia and Iraq we fly the mighty ship
and now dear Europe will feel our whip.
Watch out Singapore, you may be right but we have the might
and our planes are hard to fight.
Many a lash upon the ass, when I went to school
But you are not allowed to make our Citizen Smart
on that back part, we set the rule.
This is not fable, spare the Cane
or you will get das Abel.

    Alex O'Donnell

One Kiss

Oh! For only one kiss.
If your sweet lips would touch mine.
Entwined in a passionate embrace,
I should feel your warm breath against my brow.
Is it a sin for me to wish this?
I cannot hide my passion —
my desire burns too deep.
In a bliss so divine —
Were I an angel?...
I would toss my white robe,
And my golden halo would rest upon the ground.
For only, one kiss.

    Andriana Eliopoulos

A Place

It's just a place
I'm standing on the outside looking in
Observing all the heroes that lie within

All of my enemies call it death
But my friends tell me it's just transformation
At its best

And oh when it gets too eerie
And I get a little too teary
Then I look towards the light

I see an artist hard at work
It reminds me that this place is just divine
Creativity at its highest

It's just a place
And I'm standing on the outside looking in
Wondering when!

    Emma Deese

Shoshana

Shoshana was her name.
"I'm a member of the International
   Ladies Garment Workers Union"
She told us twice.
And her eyes spilled water like the Sea of Galilee
   in the rainy season.

She sat alone at breakfast.
Erect, neat and nice she always looked,
A soft shawl at her neck,
and those eyes -frozen-
that spilled water.

In New York, she said
she loved the opera.
At Lincoln Center she would
   meet her friends,
and sit in cheap seats.

In the lobby of the Ginot Yam Hotel,
between Celina Kohn and a nurse who served in the '48 War,
Shoshana sat erect,
and I squeezed her hand and said good-bye

   Adele Persky+

Small Child

I'm lying in my crib now, all cuddled up and warm.
I'm crying now, "Mommy I need you." I hear footsteps. "Is
that you Mommy?"

I'm still crying. "Mommy I need you." Mommy is yelling.
What is she saying? I can't understand. Did I do something
wrong?

She's leaving. "Mommy don't leave me, I need you." Can't she
hear my cry?

I'm still crying. I hear footsteps again. She hits me. Why did
she hit me?

"Mommy I'm hungry." I can't tell you but I'm crying.
"Mommy can't you hear me?"

I'm crying "Mommy I'm hungry." She hits me again. Why
is she hurting me? I don't understand.

I'm lying all cuddled up again. It's dark all around. My
tummy hurts now. Is Mommy coming back? Does she hear my
small cry?

I'm getting tired now. I can't cry, my throat hurts. "Goodnight
Mommy", even though you're not here...

   Joline Miller

'Wondering'

Wondering out to sea, my boat hasn't come to me.
I'm tired of waiting for my ship to roll in,
      On my voyage I shall begin.
   I know deep inside that you care,
But why don't you mind when I am not there?

   I have built a wall to cover my heart,
      So it won't be again torn apart.
   Someday I know the wall will come down,
And then as they say, we will paint the town.
   I know deep inside that you care,
But why don't you mind when I am not there?

      Now I dance my pain away,
   I make time for work and for play.
      I'm doing the best I can do,
   Without even a "thanks" from you.
   I know deep inside that you care,
But why don't you mind when I am not there?

   Christine Sampson

One Golden Moment

   Try and picture a sunset and the beauty of its gold.
Imagine it setting on the ocean and the warmth that it holds.
      A sunset is such a splendid gift from God above,
   It is merely one small way in which he expresses his love.
   He blessed me immensely the day I met you, for you both
taught me that friendship can be true. When you took hold
of my hand as we walked along, for the first time in many years
   I felt as if I "actually" belonged. That sunset and you are
      similar in several ways, both bring me joy as well as
   meaning to my days. If I could I would bring the sun down
right to you, imagine what two heavenly bodies united could do.
The next time you watch a sunset in all of its gold, remember
   me though I may not be right there to hold. The sun will be
setting in its habitual and usual way, but somehow I think
   it will be special just for that day, giving us one special
moment in time that we could share, maybe allowing us just once
   to see the beauty hidden behind the glare. At that moment I
   will be all alone in my own private thought, thanking God for
      blessing me with you and all the love that you brought.

   Cristina Figueroa

I'd Give My All

She lay there so peacefully
In a deep dreamful sleep
My raving beauty
My loving wife to keep.
She had given me her very best
And to our loving children
She showed no rest
Her personality is so kind
She could not fool
Even the very blind
She has made my life worth living.
Through all the years of loving and giving.
We have had our share
Of life's ups and downs
But always a loving smile
And never a frown, does her face bare.
This woman has made my life complete
And picked me up, when I did fall
For my love, I'd give my all.

   Harley J. Adams

Castle In The Sand

Once upon a time
   In a far away land
There stood a castle
   Built in the sand
The castle was built to withstand a fight
   Against all magicians, dragons, and knights
But when the tide rises
   And there is no place else to go
The castle walls will crumble
   Back to the earth it will go
But tomorrow the children will come
   Back to play in the sand
And the castle will be built once more
   To fight off all the land

   Eric J. Cool

Untitled

Beggars who walk, Princes who ride,
in the hereafter travel side by side
One eats righteously, the other things of stale
in the hereafter the Lord loving will prevail
it matters not what you have in life
you may live easy or in strife
only they that love the Lord
may sing with angels in one accord.

   Joseph Wayne Matthews, Jr.

The American

Once scattered all over the world to live
in America with new hope freedom give
consequence in new land, unique in which
becoming American, by choice, Life enrich

The new American leaving behind much
all ancient ties to accept life as such
individuals whose deeds in posterity may
cause great changes, perspective ethos lay.

These early pilgrims along they carried
great mass of arts and skills, they married
and incorporated into mighty and best
culture in civilization, ever to more west.

Their rewards to generations equal same
prosperity of lands progress and fame
no bounds unbridled ambition knows
never to cease, but development flows.

The American arose and destined its own
has inspired the world a marvel renown
it's called democracy composed sublime
globally followed, beyond reach of time.

Gys Jansen Van Beek

"Snowy Rose"

'Twas Spring time, the merry month of May.
In his hand, a beautiful Snowy Rose lay,
White as the pure and beautiful driven snow.
As his eyes searched mine, I couldn't say no.

Old memories came, of the one before.
I asked, "Heart, can you stand this once more?"
'Tis true, soon my love you'll be winning.
When it happens, I can almost imagine you grinning.

It's wonderful, this love that we share.
Each step I take, you're always there.
When bedtime comes, you make sure I'm tucked in.
You wake me each morning, with a kiss on my chin.

I return home and I know, before I open the door.
One step inside, and I'll hold you once more.
Your love is possessive, you let everyone know, she's mine!
Could it be you knew, we'd only have a short time?

The beautiful Snowy Rose is no longer here.
Memories still linger, I miss him, it's almost a year.
We can't always win, everyone knows that.
Tho' only God knows, how I loved that cat!

Christine H. Ruppe

Which Is Me And Which Is You?

Though we live a thousand star kissed nights
In hundreds of ecstatic ways
To me, our private gift of gladness
Comes even more from long hours of quiet nights
Than from passions's magic moments.
For I find the silent trust of whole nights spent
Intermingled, speechless and unmoving
In molded, merging rest
Drifting on calm waters
Within our private ship-
To be an even greater joy,
When, for a hollowed interlude,
Our body parts are one,
And we find that we're so intertwined
Our minds stop thinking like we're two,
And I forget which part is me
And which is you..

Jayne Bremyer

The Christmas Patrol - December, 1945 - North of Guam

Each year, this day, we pause,
in memory of all Santa Claus;
Of Dad and Mother and Sister and Brother,
Of Cousins and Wives and Mother-in-laws.

For this year it's Christmas at sea,
we think of home and victory;
On sea of foam, so far from home,
on ship with no Christmas Tree.

Our tribute to those we lost at sea,
Cousins and Brothers and Buddies to be;
For those who died, we share with pride,
A 4.0 Christmas with no Christmas Tree.

Our thoughts of home stay in mind,
Thoughts of our loved ones left behind;
Our first Christmas joys, our first Christmas toys,
'neath tree trimmed with care we'd find.
With wonderful thoughts of our Christmas to be,
With thoughts of our past flowing so free;
We dare not be sad, but only be glad,
To spend this Christmas with no Christmas Tree.

Harold N. Lehman

The Crying Tree

Around the crying tree, many have sung,
In memory of their love ones, who once were hung,

So many innocent souls, who committed no sin,
Condemned, because of the color of their skin,

The crying tree has been used, to send many to
their grave,
People who wanted to taste freedom, no one
wanted to be a slave,

Many children have felt, the pain of the crying tree,
Tiny little ones, who wanted to be free,

Oh! America, America the land of the free,
Can't you see tears, falling from the
crying tree?

I know we can't change what happened in the past,
But building tomorrow on love, will make
freedom, forever last.

Debra Ann Daniels

Beautiful Hands

She puts her tiny palm
in my wrinkled leathery palm
As she squeezes to make sure
I'm still there to comfort her

She asks "will my hand ever be
as beautiful as yours?"
So many memories have formed
these lines, much work has
toughened these hands

I answer "when you get old like me
and have worked hard for wonderful memories
then your hands will be beautifully aged
like mine."

She smiles,
a smile as innocent
as morning dew on a rose petal.
"Grandpa when I'm old as you
I want my hands to be full of memories
like yours."

Julie A. Washabaugh

Alone?

Alone
in the backyard
reading a book
or the daily newspaper
or just sitting with one's thoughts alone.

Alone?
a quiet rustle of the soft wind in the trees,
a chipmunk scampers by
as a beautiful deer in the woods stares,
squirrels play together
as if you were not there
birds chirp and fly aloft
the ominous skunk slinks away
as the neighbor's dog runs
to catch his friend the cat
a soft drop of rain on your head—-
I smile!
Alone?
In God's beautiful world, you are never alone.

John K. Henry

"The Lonely Rose"

  A rose, a beautiful rose stands peaceful
in the early morning, beneath the mountains,
beneath the trees. She stands looking over
a small flowing stream surrounded by rocks of
stone. The wind blows gently against her petals
of yellow. Her stem swaying back and forth with
freedom. Her leaves waiting for cold drops of endless
rain. Dew falls, falls to her soft yellow petals,
falls to her green thorn bearing stem, falls to
her leaves of eagerness. The sun begins to rise
slowly over the hills, over the trees, over the mountains.
As it sits in the air it gives the rose joy and
happiness. But the rose stands.
  Lonely in the day.

Andrea Smelley

The Forgotten Soldier

Traveling forward with no family or friend
In the loneliness of a thousand empty moments
One knight embraces another ferocious day
War has become all he knows

The world stands upon a tinted glass hill
Wishing to elevate one more step
A lone brave warrior protects the fragile
War has filled his once pure soul

The soldier is left to gather the pieces
For beyond his shattered days
Lies the sweat to live one final breath
And perish for God and country

Those we hold most dear are sometimes lost
Yet no one wept for this unknown hero
He held no monetary possessions in his pocket
Just a breast full of memories and prayers

Resurrect no monument above the earth for him
Let his time be remembered with true honor
Commemorate his passing within your heart
And shed a tear for that forgotten soldier

Douglas Kitchen

A Dedication To The Arizona

Dawn, December 7, 1941,
In the mist of a tropical paradise a grey fleet, asleep.
The stars and stripes are being raised,
Reveille is being called, the fleet is coming to life.
Then it happens!
The "Rising Sun" appeared above the sleeping fleet.
The "Sun" flew down on the fleet like a condor after its feast,
The chaos began which lasted days.
And the "Sun" left leaving darkness.
The people on the shore watched the flapping Stars and
Stripes in the breeze among the sunken grey hulks,
as did Francis Scott Key watch the standing symbol
a long time ago.
The Star Spangled Banner was able to be heard in the
distance and the heart.
This is the day of the "Rising Sun" and the falling "Star".
This day will live in infamy in the eyes of the eagle.

Joseph P. Kosteczko

"Fall Colors"

Outside, I observe brilliant stains of golden lather.
In the sky, fiery crimson, mellow purple, and
Bold oranges are blazing;
Squinting your eyes as you gaze.
Warmth captures your soul with vengeance.
You grow composed by the majestic, natural passion,
And the stage demands your fascination.
Each magnificent glow of the season
Conspires to mold an autumn rainbow
That enlightens the elegance of Mother Nature.

Eric D. Coatley Jr.

The Lie

Waterfalls of raindrops and tears turned to gold,
In the stifling heat I shiver with cold,
There's a hole in my heart and I can't tell you why,
My words shriek with happiness but still I do cry.

The sky is all cloudy, my world is all grey,
With an open heart I cry to the world that I may,
Climb all the mountains, swing from the trees,
Lay in the meadows among butterflies and bees
Live on the beach, sail an ocean blue,
Dream in the night of my love for you

Because there's a hole in my heart and I'll tell you why
I've learned the truth, that it's all one big lie.

Carolyn Rosenfeld

Goldfish

The bodies of the pond lilies only look awake
in the winter with their green backs not yet grey;
and the limp structure
of leaf flesh which dives down
into stopped water that wishes it were rain

is in fact frozen tight into a glass
ice casing over the pond's clear face.
And despite the warming light
looking into the surface for life,
there is no leaf nor living thing
stirring in the stop-time underworld to wake.

But just there, under the ruined pond's forehead,
in full red, a goldfish, like a thought:
A quick streak of blood in the mind's vein.

Caley O'Dwyer

The Woods

In the woods there is peace and quiet
In the woods you don't have to rush
There are no people or roads yet
Just a very quiet peaceful hush

There are trees on every side of you
There are birds up in the air
And each place has its own scenic view
The joy of such beauty I'd like to share

There are all the colors you know
There is red and yellow blue and green
Nature's giving a colorful show
Of all the colors you've ever seen

There's the whispering of the wind in the trees
The rushing of water in the creek
Chirping of birds fluttering in the breeze
The sound of the deer so mild and meek

All of this beauty the Lord did make
And gave it to us for our use
So let's take care of it for His sake
And let's not treat it with abuse

Amy Bray

Untitled

In many contests have I competed;
In very few have I been defeated.
But yours would be the one I'd love to win.
Fine poems are beyond my skill,
While "Occasional Jingles" fit my bill.
To call them poems would for sure be sin!!

Now, in my eighties, it is a 'pleasure'
Again to read my simple 'treasure'
That years ago brought laughs into my crowds.
But bankrupt has gone my memory bank,
As recalling is slowly going blank.
No way a poem comes to make me proud.

May your contest end in glory;
May your winners love your story
Of the poems you'll present across your land.
May your efforts, so innovative,
And your contestants so creative,
Let us enjoy for years your gifts so grand.

Elinor B. Bethel

Trapped

I stand trapped
In your glass elevator
I quake as the door slams shut
Too petrified to let go
In fear of falling like
A wine glass on a table edge
The elevator shakes, then steadies itself
I push the down button
It moves up and I can't get close to you
I can't get out of your oversized medicine dropper
up and away from you, I go
I stop with a jerk
The hollow icicle comes
crashing down and bursts
where you stand I run to hug you
But I feel as if I am standing
Trapped in your glass elevator

Andrea Daley

My Prayer

Dear Lord, I love you very much.
In your mercy, keep in touch with me in all I do each day.
Touch me Jesus, as I pray…
In thought, in work and in my pleasure.
Help me feel your loving measure in my daily confrontations.
Keep me strong in tribulations.
And in my talents, keep me meek
And humble Lord, and as I seek new ways to glorify your Name,
Never let me put to shame,
Your banner, or your laws of love.
Let me wear you as a glove that fits each crevice of my heart
To give a warmth in every start…
Of action, thought or daily deed,
That others might accept your creed.
And when that gate comes into view
Dear Jesus, let me follow you
Into fulfillment of my goal…
     Your Love eternal, for my soul.

Betty Lynch

Yoga

Light a cigarette
inhaled smoke fills the lungs
slow release of breath
experience a nicotine high
close your eyes
remember a time hours ago
world of chaos left behind
deep inside minds eye
enduring event manifested
transformed a life
cosmic Yoga enercise
was it in this place
New beginnings, rebirth and happy endings
surrounded in a relaxed atmosphere
nothing to fear
you've set a pace
clouded visions erased
cosmos-energy exchanged
dispersed the human race changed
New beginnings, rebirth and happy endings

Earl West, III

Hear The Salamander Roar

The bird breathes no more
inspiration does not overwhelm
a feast has ensued
a death has occurred
reasons for an earth so round.

Sawdust lies on the floor
dismayed by the situation
viewed once the mighty cascade
so true, so strong, so brave,
now terminally adhered to vacation.

Hear the Salamander roar a quandrous call for a mate
to reconceive an impossibility
the act committed an atrocity
only individual of its race.

See the Red-winged soar aspiring for a find prolific
morsels a clasp away as dead Oaks swagger and sway in
a wind that no longer blows by.

Feel evolution lure the Earth along its pace.
Beings recycle again and again slime and slime are men and men.
How I do love this place.

Christopher Bordlemay

Touched By An Angel

You have come into my life,
Instantly you've touched my heart,
Spontaneously you bring me happiness.
Why... I do not know
How will I ever repay you, or...have I already.
Are you an angel, spreading love and warming hearts,
These questions I ask, are there no answers.

Will the anger and pain ever disappear,
Heart to heart we can overcome this fear.
Shall we put our hearts together and give it a try,
We can hold and love each other when we need to cry.
Reach out to me, when you are down and weak,
We'll experience love and friendship at its highest peak.

A hug, a laugh, a beautiful smile.
These are all important to you and me,
Simple gestures that make us secure and free.

Joseph J. Loughery

"Little League"

No more taxing our girls all around the parks
Instead I'll sip my coffee and listen to the larks
No more phone calls to warn the parents of how much they owe
Instead I'll mend my husband boxers of three months ago and sew
No more screening phone calls and dreading coaches voice
Instead I'll pick up the phone and buy that new Rolls Royce
No more fifty-fifty with team moms strutting to and fro
Instead I'll water my garden and watch the flowers grow
Yes, little League is over another season yields
Whew! Little League is over I feel like kissing the fields

Christina L. Risdon

What I Need Is An Overhaul...

If only I had a lot more guts
Instead of excuses... and ifs, ands or buts,
I wouldn't be afraid to drive a car,
Just to the corner — 'round the block, not far —

But for some foolish reason, I chicken out
And panic and shake and hysterically shout,
"I just can't do it," I find I'm stalled
In a braked position — or whatever it's called.

I'm overcome with terror — if I could lose it,
A handicap permit? I'd have to drive to use it!!
So from the passenger side, I watch others pass
While I desperately want to step on the gas!

And though my motor is running, I can't switch gears,
And I stay in one place and watch the years
Go by — not forward — or even in reverse.
I can't help think, my God, it's a curse

As I feel my palms sweat and my stomach churn
And I press down the signal for a left hand turn,
And I think to myself, this fear is so rife.
If only I could make right turns all my life!!

Bette Kotlarz

24 Hours Of Life...Please

One day of tolerance, one day without pain,
   Is a day in which all do, surefootedly, maintain;
In this battle we call living, in this war known as life,
   None shot with a pistol, none stabbed with a knife.
Twenty-four hours of time in which all do survive,
   And with thoughts of tomorrow, all onward do thrive.
A fraction of existence, with no shortness of breath,
   Would be a day without sorrow,
Would be a day without death!

John H. Gatchell, Jr.

word collage

meander salty wishes
into arabesque palaces
nearer the heart's electro field
shocks interpret feelings
hatred loves a missed loved one
comic soliloquy hardens
factory of bliss permeates
intrepid whatnot's falter
life's scrapbook without glue
shifting into infinity
cove of blank stares
dominion coveted the people machine
tasseled ligaments of the forlorn hopeless
intuition scatters their brain
shucking layers of onion skin
coreish essence stings
the marble spinning uncontrollably
time is not here

Alex Slawson

Canvas

On withered grey wings my sad heart flies,
   into the endless wonder of your eyes.
Within silent shadows, afraid with tension,
   whispering into my mind your moving strength.

   your beauty,
   your mind,
   your soul.
I tell myself, "Forever I shall keep you,"
   "Forever I will cherish you,"
I will be selfish, I will never let go, never let see the light of day.

   Suddenly, I hold you.
a sparkling point of light flashing back to me...away from me.
   I am truly alone.

I open my hands and the stars shine brightly.
Diamonds set in charcoal canvas, set behind a layer of glass.
   Cold.

Aware of me, in darkened, silent shadows,
   whispering, waiting.

Anh Tu Nguyen

"Country Roads"

Away from the busy towns and freeways
Is a pleasure we share on Sundays
The countryside of the years gone by
You can almost go back in time, if you try
The beautiful farms are now forgotten
An old barn and in the background rotten
The fields now grown up in weeds
This old farm house with its good deeds
Now on this vacant and unused land
Is only the reminder of mans hand.

A treasured rusty old milk can
On maybe a hanging black frying pan
Waiting to be consumed by construction
By progress - waste - and destruction
And when all the fruit trees, once tall
Are gone - we'll not breathe at all,
But man goes on his greedy way
Only thinking of his gain for today.
I still enjoy the back roads ride
Remembering being a country child with pride.

Dorothy I. Brown

The Joshua Tree

In the desert, the Joshua Tree
Is blessed with beauty for man to see.

It raises its spiny arms toward a heavenly dome,
Enduring all seasons, for this is its home

Night or day, cold or warm,
It beckons all weather sunny or storm.

It's God's design to keep its shape
And for humankind to share its fate.

George P. Boutren

The Seasons Of Life

The Spring of life
Is filled with learning,
With hopes and aspirations.
The promise of the future sets us yearning
For power, success and high expectations.

The Summer of life
Finds us driving
Toward the goals we set in youth.
Enthusiasm keeps us striving
For reality and truth.

The Autumn of life
Brings somber reflection
Of hopes and dreams unfulfilled.
We face the fact of our imperfection;
Our idealistic dreams of youth are stilled.

The Winter of life
Confronts us with life's brevity;
The rapid approach of death
Takes away our levity.
Tomorrow comes our final breath!

Commodore Robinson

What Is Love

What is love, I thought I knew
is it a family, who'll be there for you,
Whether it's in good times or bad,
when they're no longer there, it's really sad,
What causes them to turn their back on you,
With hard times here and no mom to turn to,
What happens to their love, I don't know,
as I look back, where'd it go?
We've always been there for each other, don't she see,
Now she's turned her back on me,
If she needed me, I'd be there,
to stand by her because I cared,
Alone by herself, she'd never be,
Not if she ever needed me,
How she's hurt me, she don't know,
But one day soon I'll tell her so,
She's a sister no more, I hate to say,
and I hope she never needs me someday,
Because sometimes there's no where else to turn,
Except family, she may one day learn,

Jeannie Raines

Once Is Never Enough

I thought I could leave you
Lacking any pain. My life's
Obituary I wrote and sat
Void of any true feeling. For
Ever awaiting your call
Yet my phone never rang
Or maybe it did. It should have been you.
Underneath it all, I loved you.

Cheryl Wilson

Justice

What does it mean?
Is it an eye for an eye
Or a slap on the hand
Is it a tooth for a tooth
Or five to ten
In the world of yesterday
It meant so much
In the world of today
It's only a word
People that run for office
Promise us this and that
But promises don't stop
The violence that rages
Mothers cry for their babies
While shots ring in the distance
She holds her son's blood covered body
Looking to the sky for answers
Now I ask you - what has happened
To yesterday!

Charmell Hanson

What Does Love Mean To You?

What does love mean to you?
Is it the sun that kisses the sky so blue?
Maybe the cold that leaves the grass with dew.
I believe it is the friendship between me and you.

Maybe love is like a flower bed.
If it is not properly nurtured,
It cannot grow and last,
And will become forever dead.

Maybe love is the rainbow after the first summer rain,
Or can it be the longing in my heart that gives me pain.
To spend just one moment or two,
To show how much I care for you.

We may hit a troublesome time or two.
But I hope we can work it out,
Because I would not want to hurt a friend of mine.
Someone I sincerely care about.

I hope you feel the same way
That I do about you,
Because I want to be friends always
And be there for you.

Becky Hunt

Colors On Display

The blanket of beauty which covers me,
is just as beautiful as the flowers you seek.

The only thing you fail to do is, take time
to notice me.

Oh! the beauty you are missing, while under
my branches sitting.

My leaves turn many colors of green,
than into shades of oranges, yellows, or shades of red.
I surely am a through bred.

I may look naked and dirty brown in winter,
but just take time to look at me.
When Spring has sprung, and you are looking
Around for beautiful flowers to see,
Don't forget to notice me.

Carlota Robinett

So Much Joy Inside Me

"Jesus" ask me do I want to be save.
"Jesus" ask me, will I need thee.
"Jesus" ask me, to let my heart be free.
And when I did, so much "Joy" came inside me.

Constance Davis

My Unseen Pain

The pain...inside and out,
Is just too much to bear.
I hurt so much I have to cry.
In places there is physical pain
As if someone were tearing me apart...
Piece by piece, muscle by muscle, limb by limb.

My unseen pain comes from within.
My heart feels torn in two.
The hurt, confusion, anger, and most of all Loneliness,
Seem to pour out inside me.

I see no end to this state of massive depression and pain.
I want it to go away, but it won't.
I have to learn to deal with it.
No matter how hard, it must be done.

I'm tired of putting up masks
So nobody can see the pain I feel.
I'm tired of hearing "What's wrong?"
Or "Are you mad at me?"
I hurt. I'm tired. Help me.

Carolynn Saldaña

The Ride

I take you for a ride today...

A ride of horoscopes and dreams.

Of pounding reality as it anticipates being faced but feels it
is never to be accepted.

I take you for a ride of passion and innocence, the two
colliding and combining in a crippling sort of primitive
beauty.

A ride of strangely optimistic cynicism.   Misinterpreted
circumstance.

I take you for a ride called life...

Brook Growden

Broken

Trying to forget a past of painful memories,
  is not often easy to do.
Especially if once in awhile a memory comes to mind.
True forgiveness of others and myself, I can not find.
How can a person put the past in the past?
When only to be reminded of lessons not yet learned,
  patterns to repeat again, patterns I thought, would not return.
I search for the truth, but find only lies.
I desire to be loved, but, to reach out to others,
I choose not to try,
Deep inside I want to grow.
I want to know, what I am all about.
To know longer live in fear.
Believing completely in myself, without so much doubt.
As for now, I will take a day at a time.
Living for today, leaving the past behind...
Behind the door, I choose to close.
Only to open again, so healing may begin.

Jo Anne Cowan

Comfort

I see you there under the tree, just sitting peacefully
It is summer and late at night
I see your head, hanging low and unmoving
I know you share the same pain I do

I see you cry, trying to hide the tears
Your sky is black and lifeless
I am blue and move like a soft lake breeze
I see you there under the tree, just sitting peacefully
my sky is blue and calm.

Holly Hartl

"Destruction"

He Who Rides On A Fire Breathing Horse
   is on a dreaded mission,
   to destroy anything in his course!
Watch him go by, but stay clear of his path
for horrible is his approach, and unbearable his wrath!
   Wicked is his grimace and harmful is his trail
   leaving man no chance to think to prevail!
   This masked demon needs not an introduction
      behold his eyes;
      which symbolize
      destruction!

Allen Redwing

The Tree That Grew The Rose

Our love, it seems, like childhood dreams and fairy tales of past,
Is still as real, and still we feel this love we know will last.
As mem'ries grow like waters flowing gently to the sea,
Our hearts have known a love that's grown and belongs to you and me.

What seeds we sow can only grow with tender hands of care,
With gentle rains upon the grains in our garden that we share.
And as our Rose Tree blossoms, and the flower drinks the dew,
The gentle breezes flow with ease. Like the love of me and you.

As days become as days become: collections of the past,
Come wintry cold from seasons-bold, our Tree of love will last.
And when my years are ended here, and to my grave I'll go,
I'll take with me fond memories of The Tree That Grew The Rose.

Christie Mullady

"A Day To Remember"

   A day to remember,
is the 22nd of September.
   I didn't know how much I loved Matt,
until I lost him, now I want him back.
   It hurts so much when you lose someone you love,
but I am sure he is happy up above.
   Time flew by fast,
we always thought of the future, but now I am remembering the past.
   Why is it you lose people so close,
especially the ones you love the most.
   I guess it's a fact we have to die,
it's just so hard when you don't get to say good-bye.
   When I die,
I will then again get to say hi.
   But for now I have to keep on livin'
and wait to be with him in heaven.

Isannah White

Camping

Some people say the best time when camping
is the evening
   eating popcorn around the campfire
   singing the old songs
   or in awe, looking at the stars.

But my favorite time
is the silence of early morning.
Quietness, broken only by a bird call
or the chatter of a squirrel
or the voice of God
whispering His love to me.

Ethel Stone Adams

What Would A Life Of Perfection Be Like?

Living in a perfect world would mean a life without sin
It all dates back to Adam and Eve or how else did the world begin?
We wouldn't need sleep because time would stand still
Hunger would be abolished when all have had their fill.
Abortion would be prevented, so many lives saved,
Everyone would get a chance, no matter how bad someone else behaves.
War would turn to peace, destruction would come to an end,
Enemies would cross battlefields hoping to become friends.
Drugs and pain would be harmless, we wouldn't have to die.
Mother's hearts all full of worry would no longer have to cry.
It all sounds so great, no challenge needed,
We'd be living the life of someone who already has succeeded.
I don't want to follow the path that someone else has made
With the pain that I may fail
Instead I'll build a road with my life
And lead my own successful trail.
Until the day that I die
God will be the only one that knows
Because I want to establish a life of my own, therefore
Perfection for me will remain unknown.

Jennifer Ciach

Music

Music, music, it makes me cheer!
It also may bring a sorrowful tear.
Music, in your happiness, will make you
soar through the air,
It may even make you fall
into the depths of despair.

Music, music in a year,
you wouldn't understand it, no my dear!
Imagination is all you need then
you may ride a great white steed.

Music, music is what you hear,
It may calm in wild deer,
a beautiful melody, is what is remarkable to me!

Music, music you may try to mend,
But to my poem I must tend.
Your opinion you may cast,
But as for my poem I am done at last.

Joshua Guerrero

Learning To Let Go

When you have something you love, you want to hold on tight to
it and never let go.
You want to love and care for it deep within your heart, with
every ounce of your soul.
But sometimes without warning we become too attached.

The attachment becomes so deep that when it leaves you it feels
as though someone has ripped your heart out with their bare hands.
You weep for days, but soon the weeping ends.

You try to hate it, but you know your love for it is too deep.
You try to forget it but that could never be.
With time and patience you learn to deal with it but you
always miss it.

Antwone Wilson

Life

Life is like a burning lightbulb, that eventually dies out
Life is a drop of water, that reached a final destination
Life is a wind, that soon blows out
Life is like a witch, that drank her final potion
Life is like a candle, that will soon flicker out
Life is like a tree, that wilts in fall
Life is snow, through winter till a warm spring day
Life is like a best friend, with whom you get in a fight
Life is wonder

Gayle Lewin

The Idea

The idea is something dear to me.
It consists of all life forms,
Big or small.
Of course, the earth was the start of it all.
After was water and then land.
Then of course animals and humans hand in hand.
This didn't last long at all and still to this day,
animals and people can't live together happy and gay.
It hurts me to see
that we don't live in harmony.
So I have come up with an idea,
(that just might work),
to start over again on this place called earth.

Cheryl Marino

"Rain"

The rain is there to comfort me in times when I feel down,
It drains my heart of pain and hurt to all which I am bound,

I can walk out in a storm and cry a million tears,
And nobody would ever know the sadness which I fear,

Rain can wash away the ache that memories can bring,
It can put your mind at ease and give you everything,

It lands upon my eyelashes and falls upon my hands,
It covers every inch of me wherever it may land,

I was with you in the rain a while in the past,
Holding onto you so tight; your memory cannot last,

I wish it meant as much to you as much it meant to me,
But wishing is for helpless hearts where love will never be.

April Page

The American Flag

Each day it rises to grace the day.
It has faced the battles of the day.
People 'round the globe
Have burned it, trampled it and torn it asunder.
The Americans have frowned upon such mistreatment.
  Yet

There stands my father.
A world war II veteran.
A humble man who served his country when his country called.
He is proud to be an American.
He is proud to have served his country.
He is proud to be a citizen.
  Yet

On the way home by rail, he had to relinquish his seat
To a German P.O.W.
What is this flag?
A symbol of freedom?
A symbol of justice?
A symbol for what American means?

Elaine M. Coney

My Secret Place

My secret place is a place of hope,
It is a silent place, a place to cope.
It is a place for wishing,
And a place for sleep,
It is a place that I'll always keep.
It is hidden from the outside world,
And no one but I can get in,
It is always locked with a golden key,
And it will always unlock for me.
For the place I love is a place to see,
But you can't, for it only unlocks for me.

Erika Dunn

Our Home To Come

I heard a story, which I do believe.
It is about a place that some shall get to see.
This place is so far away
That no man can get there by machine.
They say this place has streets of gold.
They saw this place has buildings made of many gems.
These people say that this could be our home one day.

But these people say
That there is only one way
To get to this home up above.
They say to get there you must do your part
Which is of course to follow your heart.
So, you need to do just like me,
You need to be a member of the Christianity.

Beverly Mann

What Is Gray

Gray is an old weather-beaten cottage in the rain.
It is an old gnarled Oak tree away from the rest of the forest
Dried up pine needles are gray.
It is the feeling of loneliness.
Gray is the snow on a well-worn path in the winter.
It is the quiet lake after a storm.
It is the silence of the forest when you are exploring it alone.
Gray is the air in the midst of a storm.
It is the few worn rocks on the top of a mountain.
It is the dried up moss that was trampled last year.
Gray is the soft summer breeze in the afternoon.
It is a tattered old bird's nest lying on the ground.
The barn swallow flying overhead is gray.
It is a beach with nobody on it.
Gray is the hay on an empty field.
It is the dust on the bases after a baseball game.
It is the birdseed that the birds have scattered.
But most of all, it is the feeling of sadness because this
poem has ended.

Gabriel Ashley

Our Country

Don't mess the U.S. up I pray to God above.
It is my country one that I love.
It stands for freedom and a generous place.
The right to be happy and by every race.
America stands straight and tall.
America is a place for one and all.
For there is freedom in the right to give.
There is liberty in the times we live.
Let american's children know the meaning of joy.
It's a constitutional right of every girl and boy.
Let's preserve the beauty of the land.
God's creation by God's own hand.

Dinah Spry

The Big Fall

Some people strive to hurt each other,
Just to get to the top.
But the higher up you go, my friend, further you have to drop!
And when you lie, cheat, steal, and such;
Just to get up there;
You find that all your friends you had,
Have left and gone somewhere.
So, remember, your friends as you go up;
And try to keep them around,
Because, it is said, and it's always true,
What goes up must come down!

Arwilder Moorer

I Love

The soft breeze on a warm summer's day,
It plays with your hair and whips it around.
It dances as if a child at play,
The breeze plays hide and seek and you've been found.

I love the majestic, swaying, palm trees,
The way they sway in the warm but cool sun.
Their beauty completely amazes me,
If you ask me, my praise they have won.

I love the bright and colorful sunset,
They're big and beautiful and don't last long.
In a pool reflection, it looks all wet.
I bet it once made someone write a song.

I love these things because they express me.
All these things make me feel so very free.

Jessica Kone

Love

Love, like poetry completed wants for nothing more.
It promises foreverness and keeps our spirits pure.
There is no greater thing on Earth that this that lovers learn,
to give away your heart and to receive one in return.
In love all troubles disappear and life is lived with ease.
Dreams are near and whisper like a warming summer breeze.
Faithfulness and loyalty will make their presence known.
Simple truths inside that will begin and soon be grown.
Also comes respect for saying only what is true.
For love can never lie if it's a dream that's part of you.
Like a lazy river flowing softly to the sea,
Love is to be looked upon as wonderful and free.

Alan Sutherland

Pray, Pray, Pray

As I ride the bus I wonder
It seems like I can hear nothing but thunder
Children today have no respect
But the parents seems like they're neglect
Will someone tell me where did we go wrong
I thought having children was like a happy song
What will happen to our young people today
All the parents can do is pray, pray, pray
A child who carries around a gun
He thinks this is nothing but fun
Don't they know that they are killing each other
Mother, father, sister and brother
Why will they take a life
Then they will grow up without a wife
If they would just use their heads
Then we wouldn't have so many dead
If they would've put their heads in books
Then they would have a better outlook
Think of our children today
Don't let society take them away

Geraldine Judline Harper

Untitled

Still not born baby dies
Its delicate face and tiny eyes
it did not know what lie ahead
But now it lay cold and dead
It will never laugh and never cry
it will be hard to go on but I have to try
it will never learn to talk and
it will never learn to walk
But it will always have a place in my heart
Even though we will always be apart !

Christie Perez

Red To Blue

In a daze my eyes staring at the tears
It seems so slowly they fall at the memories of those years,
gone away into some other world it seems
Living life for nothing except my dreams
Wondering how long before they come true
Watching everything turn from red to blue,

Red to blue, me and you
Watch the sun live, after the rise, and before it dies
Happy then sad it's always the same thing
Red to blue are the colors love brings.
Turn to our page and begin to cry
Notice all the hate in the world and wonder why
But what can you do in your hour
except watch it all from the tower
I look up from the garden and see your eyes
They tell me the truth and kill all the lies
But I don't know what to do
I don't want another red to blue
So I walk away and hang my head
And live blue until my red comes back again

Jeremy Logan

"The Cross And Crown"

A crown of thorns is what He had while high upon a tree;
It should have been a crown of gold,
    with jewels for you and me.
Perhaps a ruby or a pearl for everyone He saved;
and diamonds shining like a star
    for a life He freely gave.

Instead of cross, He should have had a throne of purple hue;
a robe of alabaster gold,
    and a staff of sapphire blue.

He knew He could have had those things
    as God's beloved son;
but chose instead a death of pain
    for the things that we have done.

He gave us victory o'er the grave,
    but at a dreadful price...
He placed our sins upon Himself and paid the sacrifice.

That makes Him all the more a King
    to worship and adore;
No matter what we did to Him
    He loved us even more.

Gloria DeLamar Colley

Private Thoughts

Why does it matter so, what others think or say?
It shouldn't!
In theory, I know that this is true.
Could it be, that I have not yet accepted myself as worthy?
Could it be, that it still shows?
If I could just stand up and face you...
Tell you!
Some things are just for me! If I want, I'll share them
with you. If I want...
You don't know what your opinion means to me.
You don't know how I want to run screaming from your expectations.
I have decided, not to.
Yes, and I know that my decisions are mine and that I shouldn't
have to wear my choices on my sleeve...
I know that the lies I tell, will protect me, and that I
shouldn't have to.

I know I shouldn't have to...

Bonnie Shearer

"15 Sense Worth"

Loneliness is stark white.
    It sounds like deafness.
        It tastes like yogurt, plain,
            And feels like untethered space.
        It smells like nothing, cooking over
            a long - dead fire,
                And it appears as invisibility.

Grief is midnight black.
    It sounds like slippered feet
        And tastes like putrid flesh.
        It feels like a bottomless void
            And smells like acrid smoke
                Appearing to all in due season.

Anticipation is neon pink.
    It sounds like toddlers' giggling;
        It smells like blooming roses
            And feels like kindling flame.
            It tastes like spicy salsa over crisp chips,
                And appears, always, just beyond reach!

Joyce A. Poirier

River Of Life

Life is a rushing river.
It starts out as a creek,
then grows to a babbling brook.

It started out as a lazy current,
admiring the scenery, as it passed by.
But soon it was threatened, by what is really true.

Its lazy days get smaller,
and are soon to be doomed.
For now it's a rushing river,
that has nothing to do but rush.

Rushing to get ahead.
Rushing without a look behind.
Rushing till there is nothing,
nothing left to go on for.
This rushing river's currents now lie still.

Heather Rowe

A Silent Drama

The departure of one had come.
It wasn't so hard to cope then-
but is forever,
Harder here and now.
So when is a home is real home-
to live and mourn.
School ties that are forever, helpful,
and so very tough.
They start you on the road-
that is a hard fight
to get to the top,
of a very exciting, uncertain future.
The fight to the top brings-
a very painful memory of rape of incest.
Frightening to you, more than you ever know.
How come it hurts so much to love when all that
surrounds you is warmth and love?

Anna Lea Judah

The Perfect Gift

If I could give the world a gift what would it be?
It would be people who care enough to help others in need.
People who know when a friend is troubled.
People who you can tell stories to and they will not grumble.
People who know how to get what they want without hurting others.
People who treat everybody like their own family; like
   their sisters and brothers.
People who can give away all their money and still be
   happy with themselves.
People who do not change their identity for anyone else.
If I could give the world a gift it would be caring,
   sensitive people.

   Heather Ivey

Save The Earth

   If we all try to help save the earth,
   It'll show us what nature is really worth.
We'll live better lives if we're kind to our land;
   To forests and trees, to oceans and sand.
   The beauty of nature is a wonderful sight
  So attempt to preserve it and treat it right.
The time's running out though we have the powers
  If we'll just try to save our bushes and flowers.
   We can't do the job though everyone cares,
Unless we take the time to discuss Earth's welfare.
   Our efforts combined should do the trick,
  So make the decision; you've got to be quick.
   All things that you do will help a bit,
     So keep on going and do not quit.
The year of two thousand may bring us Earth's fate,
  So help Mother Nature before it's too late.
   One can help save the Earth in many a way,
  You can make your difference this very day!
   Plants cannot help; it's all up to man.
  The conclusion of this is to do all you can!

   Irena Foygel

"Ecstasy"

I've been to a place that I'd like you to see,
It's a whole new world called ecstasy.
Close your eyes and imagine this place,
In total darkness as we both embrace.
Come with me, we're almost there,
To the bright blue skies, and water that's clear.
In a romantic place, is where we'll be,
In a world where lovers all run free.
As we enter this world of total beauty,
To please you my love, is my only duty.
Our hearts are beating as one now, and it's never felt so true,
Than the way that it is feeling, as I share my love with you.
As we entered this world, you entered my heart,
We're together forever, and we'll never be apart.
In a moment of passion you finally did see,
The place that I call, ecstasy!

   Allison J. Rogers

Jesus, Anchor Of Our Soul

Jesus, anchor of our soul,
Keeping the wind from dashing us to and fro;
As the storms of life bend our mast,
We are secure in knowing, you will hold us fast.
Jesus, anchor of our soul!

Holy Spirit, guide our ship,
When in rough seas, we shall not slip.
Though many a storm has left us scared and taken its toll,
We thank the Father for Jesus,
The anchor of our soul.

   Carl Sundquist

54 Degrees

54 degrees - that's the magical number for me!
It's been a long time coming, spring is here!
You see the buds upon the tree, more birds then you could ever believe.
You see the squirrels romping around and the birds singing their
love song.
You see young lovers holding hands, whispering sweet nothings
and only seeing each other.
You see the elderly taking their time for a stroll in the park
or sitting on the beach.
You see the children bicycling, roller blading, jumping or running
and playing ball.
But most of all, 54 degrees, transforms our slumbering and
somewhat
exhausted spirit, to a gentle awakening and excited spirit that
is refreshed and new!
The warm air, the sun shinning, the gentle breeze, the need
to open those previously frozen windows to let in that 54 degrees.
I thank God for that magical number of 54 degrees, it brings out the
best in you and me, don't you agree?

   Donna Schroyer

Love Hurts

It's better to be loved then to love.
It's better to be the one being thought of.
The more you love, the more your heart aches.
From all the abuse that it takes.
It may be easy to open your heart,
but once they're gone it will be torn apart.
I understand love isn't always going to go right,
and that there will be times when you fight.
But what happens when fighting is all you do,
and you realize he no longer loves you?
Do you go out and find another guy,
or do you just sit home and start to cry?
We sit here thinking we're to blame
When they're the ones causing this pain.
We have to forget what happened in the past,
but keep in mind the memories will always last.
It's going to hurt not being together,
and this pain will last forever.
But we have to live each day starting from new.
Knowing that somehow we'll make it through!

   Denise D'Alia

'A Daydream'

I love to daydream, all day and night.
It's easy to daydream when I'm in the spirit.
I can dream away to a far-off place.
I dream away to where I will feel safe.
If I could dream all of the time.
I would choose to be lost in sublime.
I can dream of schemes that I may never do.
I can dream of people like me and you.
I can dream of desires that I may never see, but after I awake
I must come back to reality.
To daydream is a gift for the young and old.
It's in your head, your mind, and in your soul.
It's your choice of what story or dream shall be seen or told.

   Jacquelyn J. Beck

Oceans Apart

We are like the waves hitting the shore,
Like a mad fist, a creator of sorrow.
Always trying to hurt each other or cause some pain:
The violence is so much that I can no longer stand it.
The pain is increasingly great,
While the torment is more than I can take.
Now I'm leaving.
Please, don't come after me and try to make me stay,
Because we're oceans apart, no longer one this day.

   Greta Reeves

The Empty Chair

It is brown leather, The Empty Chair
Its elegance exudes a special flair
As if Dad, in his prominence, is still sitting there
A retirement gift, for which he had a special care

It rests in the corner of a cozy den
Where a paper was read, and he wrote in pen
Next to a rocker where sat his wife
His most treasured jewel throughout his life

Frequently, Dad took a little cat nap
As Mom removed a lunch plate from his lap
And Mother sensed the mood of a cooing morning dove
While she gazed upon her sleeping husband love

To The Chair came a sudden and ominous call
Unexpected surgery created an unwanted pall
Mom queried, are you sure my dear?
Never a doubt, since with you I'll have another year

God understood and God was good
For one year, Dad remained with his brotherhood
And then God said, there is no longer a snare
He is with me, guard The Empty Chair

Fred J. Sheridan

I Don't Have An Answer Today

A rolling stone gathers no moss
It's eroded and worn down with age
Its beauty is in its timelessness
With the wisdom of a sage

The stories told by this rock of yore
Lead us to believe it's true
That man is the same as he was yesterday
And if we don't change we're all doomed

A man is born when he knows the truth
Too many seek that never find
It's here today then it's gone away
Like the clouds that pass by in the sky

The old man says to guard yourself well
'Cause life can be heaven or hell
From whence you've come, someday you'll return
Will you have a story to tell

Are you your brother's keeper you say
I don't have an answer today
Too busy surviving to hear children crying
The things we don't do, it's a shame.

Ernest E. Tracy

The Poet Inside Me

Release it.
It's in there.
It's the phrase that hasn't been spoken.
It's the song that hasn't been sung.
It's the feeling that wants to express all.
So release it,
Use the poet inside you.

See, I have spoken.
I have said most of what I want to say.
But there's more.
And I will release it.
It's mine.
It's me.
It's what I want to say and what I need to sing and how
I have felt and
How I am feeling.
It's the poem inside me.
I'm the poet within me.
I feel the need to release.

Donna Maria Smith

Vision Reality

I heard a bird chirping outside my window this morning.
Its mouth opened wide with sounds I could not imitate.
It called to me.
What, little bird? I do not speak or understand the vocabulary of
birds.
I saw several flocks of birds flying south last week.
Their wings spread broadly with movements I could not duplicate.
They called to me.
What, vast flock? I do not converse or comprehend the
language of flocks. Nature is but one piece of the puzzle
called creation. Echoes of the past vibrate in the cosmos; we
squint our eyes to see where we have been To learn our
identity. The little bird chirped for the daylight - a new
day. The vast flock flew in unity - a different course.
From the solitary to the harmonious, looking forward towards a
new beginning,
We travel backwards in time remembering the past.
Visions of the future are revealed; we open our eyes to see
where we are going to realize our true identity.
A new day has dawned. A different course has begun.

Carmella Lofrano

It's Not A Very Good Life?

I'm an alcoholic's wife.
It's not a very good life.
The bottle's his best friend.
I-I come at the end.

The lonely days, followed by lonely nights,
Leave me with feelings of fright.
The children huddle
as their world becomes a muddle.

The years fly by
As I watch my family die.
Our only hope is the Church.
God doesn't leave us in the lurch.

Time heals the wounds of the wife.
Faith ends the inner strife.
The family draws closer in His Love.
It is a good life from above.

Janet Joann Boes

"Underwater Garden"

Under the water, are shells and coral,
it's not like above where trees are of laurel.
In this special garden are fishes of color,
none that look exactly like each other.
There are no worms, crows or flies, no rainy,
sunny, or dark gray skies.
Down so deep, there is peace and quiet,
until a shark comes, and trust me he's not on a diet.
Big fish eat little fish it's all part of the chain,
but nothing down there is really that plain.
Sharks, dolphins, and big, big whales
look how many sea animals have tails,
If we had gills we could join the fish.
Too bad that can only be a distant wish.
In this underwater garden lets keep it clean,
beg your pardon.

Jessica Grey

Back And Forth From Dream To Reality

My heart lies in my eyes, in the darkness that I see.
It's pulling me under, taking hold of my destiny.

Making me see what it wants me to believe.
bringing me down to my knees.

I trusted you not to hurt me, not to break my heart.
Forever we stand, together we fall, hearts never to be apart.

But the tides have changed, from high to low.
Feelings they come and feelings they go.

Emotions falter under false pretenses, never given a chance to
   shine their light.
Tears they fall mixed with the rain, never given a chance to
   show their fright.

Dreams of tomorrow now become tomorrow's yesterday.
Watching the hands of time as they slowly slip away.

The light fades as the darkness surrounds me.
Back and Forth from dream to reality.
I see the light shine, in the form of an angel.
Back and forth from dream to reality.

Adam Paolino

A Valentine Treatise

The oak tree grows woven and firm,
   its soft, spring leaves trim and adorn,
      until autumn falls
      and colors them all
and sends them tumbling by winter's storm.

The pine tree grows straight and true
   up into the sky of blue,
      with needles so lean
      that keep ever-green
and hold steadfast the whole year through.

Which is stronger? you might ask.
Which of them will withstand the axe?
   Which is more attached—
      the leaf to its branch?
   Which better fulfills the task?

I love you like the oak loves its leaves.
I love you like needles on pine trees.
   In budding, falling down,
      and ever-green year-round,
   would you be my Valentine, please?

John M. Engler

Untitled

After reading the paper and listening to the news,
I've come to the conclusion I'm not getting my dress,
Why be responsible, study, pay taxes and work
If Uncle Sam will pay you for responsibilities you shirk?
Wonder if I could sue Harships for making me fat.
Be fun to eat candy and get paid for that.
And what can we do with the chickens
for laying those eggs?
It's a shame the way they are numbering own day.
It's a mystery how we live so long
When everything around us in going so wrong.
I thoughts I was happy, prose food am I.
Wonder how I can get a bigger slice of that pie?

Bon Beck

Older Than He

The days have passed fast since we placed Ken in his grave, now
its strange for me to say I'm older than he today.

I never thought that day could be, born before me I am now older
than he, because my older brother is dead.

At twenty one his life was lost, while standing next to a friend
an ocean wave took him away.

Sometimes I remember when we were growing up, living those days
that time has taken away. I remember those fights about who was
right, when we were young life was so much fun.

Now born before me I am older than he, older than my older
brother Ken.

All that remains of young Ken is his picture in a frame, and the
memory of a boy who barely became a man, time for him passed so fast.

I hear they say the good die young, my older brother must have
been good, he died at twenty one.

Now it's strange for me to say I am older than he today, it's so
strange for me to say because he was born before me. His lost
years are my years of passing time. Memories of Ken are in my
mind, for me to keep throughout all the days of life that well
be mine.

Deborah Stedman Arakaki

Where The Old Rock River Flows

There's a home far away, I dream of night and day.
It's the dearest place this heart of mine knows.
Ever in dreams, I'm now wending my way,
Back where the old Rock River flows.

While wandering hand in hand, through that moonlit wonderland,
My sweetheart promised to be mine forever more,
A life of happiness, together we planned,
Along that old Rock River shore.

Long years my bride's slept there, by that old river so fair,
And when my life here on earth soon comes to a close,
Please take me back to sleep beside her there,
Back where the old Rock River flows.

June Wetmore

A Fly

Smashed is a fly against my window's screen.
Its tiny wings outspread.
The cold and wet it does not fell
Against its underside.
It seems it clung before it died,
For gone its life when found.
But not a limber wing nor mess
Just clinging, as if pride it had to die
As do most flies I guess.
Poor little fly, so bold,
It missed the storm
All smashed against my window cold.

Flora Fry

Untitled

I stand alone in the dark
letting the rain wash over me.
I can feel new life breathed through me
with each and every drop.
I think not of the past, nor of the future -
there is no sense in dwelling on those times
for the past is a book already written
and the future is in nobody's hands but God's.
I close my eyes, take a breath and reach inside myself.
There is no pain.

Brent R. Muir

Now-Jas Norman

An uncanny numbers game keeps playing
itself through my head, insane.
A conglomerate city of confusion lays down
its weary head, and sleeps.
I am the Jezebel of this societies
mockery of morals, spread out.
I am the religion that all of these
millions seek, untold.
I am the Sodom and the Gomorrah that
Lie in the sands, untouched.
Just call me the Avalon of your
desires, because I am.
I am the man who steals all
your children, and sleeps.
Gone today, but lost tomorrow.
Clutch to my chest the pain and sorrow.
Forget the life I want to lead,
Just walk down the path that I choose.
Alone in my own hopes and dreams.
Alone. - 1994

Jas Norman

"I Am Grass"

Looking back over the meadow of my life, I see a place-Elysium.
I've been there, somewhere in that place that stretches far beyond
The self-imposed limits of my mind's eye. Infinity, perhaps.
A meadow covered with grass—grass willowy,
grass green, grass flexing with the breeze,
Grass bending level to the ground from which it extends,
Grass rooted, sustained by a cell that I have come to respect; to know
as time.
Somewhere in that meadow I see a majestic oak.
Branches sprawling, formidable, inflexible,
Consumed in stillness; daring to challenge the winds of time;
Demanding its will to convince its spirit, that strength and might
alone
Are sufficient for it to deny the challenge of change, of adjustment,
Of adaption, of flexibility, of temporary yielding.
Upon my return from Elysium, I celebrated the discovery of who I am
I am not the strong and mighty oak, for eventually the wind did cut it
down.
Its strength was its weakness.
I am the grass,
For when the raging wind finally ceased
From the ground, I did raise,
Rooted, still bound to the life line.

Brenda Arnold-Scott

Nurses Rode The Appalachian Trail

Long ago, nurses on horseback rode the Appalachian trail
Joined by a chorus of mountain creatures, filling the air
As sisters of Florence Nightingale, unafraid, sought out the frail
Bringing comfort to all of God's children who suffered there.
A Cherokee ghost cried out its echo in the dark still night
A blue haze hung low over the Smoky Mountain air
A lonely night owl hooted "hello" in the half moonlight
As her horses waged on, spooked by the wandering bear.
Lil' Ernie waited on the porch of an old tar paper shack
All his earthly belongings in one old paper sack
Creatures of the Appalachian Trail witnessed this liturgy
of Lil' Ernie, his horse, his nurse ridin' back to surgery.
Creatures along the Appalachian Trail
You were a silent vigil to Florence Nightingale
Watching it all through the crimson setting sun
Ridin' to the cabins in the sky; another old Kentucky re-run.

June M. Cappi

Aham

I've heard the silent Whisper, of my own awareness,
I've heard the silent Laughter, of my own consciousness.

It is a million times a story told,
And time after time, it is a new - and old.

Yet, there is nothing to say,
And there is no need to pray.

The Owner of the house is seen at a distance,
The elephant the mouse the atom, all at once.

I am flooding everywhere,
Nothing, no one, no time is elsewhere.

Eternity, is but just a moment held,
And a moment, is but eternity not held.

And my own Self I see far far away,
I never moved, yet I've come a long way.

Now I am at Peace - perfectly.
I'm the nectar of Bliss - totally.

It's all Exalted, it's all in Grace,
Nothing obstructed, nothing off place.

And, there is absolutely nothing to say,
Yet, I can only, in Gratitude...Pray.

Eddie Gob

Passage To Retirement

Like autumn leaves a tree must shed,
I've lived my spring so long.
A coat for warmth, my stick, my cap,
is all I take along...

   Close to the heart this rocking chair
   announce that coming winters,
   will bind no more this feeble strength,
   each day - eight hours - fetters.

Work's to a man, a test of worth,
of values, strength and virtues.
Where I am now, I owe to you,
how should I thank? I muse!

   This game renews and continues,
   mere players are replaced.
   As old waves makes way for new ones,
   I'll rest awhile in shade.

Soul suffers not, nor does the mind,
the scathing blows of Time.
In elements true. I'll spend my days,
dear folks, you can't divine!

Anjali Prakash

Untitled

               Man I can't think.
         I've lost my mind and gone insane.
      'Cause I can't think of anything I haven't written of.
I wrote about the past, future, present, and even wrote about
heaven.
         Yes, and the bottomless pits of you know where.
            I wrote about my hates and loves
         I know who's on that list and always will be...
            A girl with the initials J.N.
         I've written about games like bingo, jeopardy,
   checkers, monopoly, tripoly, Uno, dominoes, and Pictionary.
   I've written about cars, baseball, presidents, and countries.
         I've thought and written about everything
            and written J.N. many times...
         (with a few other things in mind.)

Ashton Keim

He Created

The mighty old sun, the moon and the stars
Jupiter, Venus, Saturn and Mars
He created them all.

The lightning, the thunder
The rains and the snow
High mountain peaks, the green valleys below
Everything under the wide, wide rainbow
He created them all.

The birds in the sky
The fish in the sea
The hope for you and I to live eternally
He created them all.

God the Eternal in Heaven above,
Gives us his guidance and everlasting love
Cling to Him faithfully, all of your life
He will deliver you from trouble and strife.

He is Alpha and Omega
The first and the last
He knows our future, present and past
For He created us all.

Herbert F. Goodyear

Dear Friend

You've been so much more than
  just a friend.
  Teacher, brother, soulmate,
  There's just no end to the list
  of who you've been for me.

You always sensed when I
  was blue.
You'd suddenly appear to pull
  me through
  some of the most difficult
  times of my life.

Kindness and caring,
  and sharing your life and dreams with me too,

I just hope that when you
  think of me,
In your own way you'll be able to see
I always hoped that I could be,
  the friend to you, you've been to me.

Julie A. Haslam

The Visitor

I had a visitor today
Just as I began to pray

I asked him if he wanted to stay
I would be with him just after I pray

He asked if he could join me today
As he has not had time to pray

We both had a lot to say
As others needed our prayers today

I thank you lord for my visitor today
As you know I felt this way

You're always watching over me
I know sometimes it's not what you want to see

But you know I love you so
And I just want you to know

I am thankful for what you have done
For me and everyone.

Frances L. Gehrke

"Unbidden"

You come unbidden to my mind,
Just as the wisps of dawn
Begin to melt beneath the sun,
And all the world is one.

You come unbidden to my mind,
Just when a longed for goal is reached
And I would swell -
Alas, there is no one to tell

You come unbidden to my mind
When night descends and all the world is wrapped
Amid the silence of eternity.

You come unbidden to my mind,
When in the sudden chill of dawn
I grope for that warm body next to mine,
And now forever gone.

When will I know the peace I seek,
Contentment I would find,
When you no longer softly creep
Unbidden to my mind.

Isabel Jean Paliwoda

Untitled

You came into my life
Just like a desert storm -
You fill my heart with wonder
And things I never thought before.

You stir up my emotions
Just like the desert winds -
And with each letter that you write
It's like a dream come true.

You came into my life
Just like the desert rain -
It slowly opens up my heart
Just like a rose at early morning's dawn.

You came into my life
Just like the desert sand -
And as the sand is shifting
So are the feelings in my heart.

My heart feels like it's drifting
Just like the desert sand -
I don't know where I'll be going
Alone, with just my restless heart.

Helga Sigfrit

Loving Again

My little dog had gone to heaven,
  Leaving my heart broken and sad.
And then Sampson, I read your add
  "Doberman pups for sale."

I tried not to go see, but you kept calling,
  You would not let me be.
When you pressed your nose through the fence,
  That was when our love commenced.

I picked you up and then your paws
  Held tightly around my neck.
I wanted a girl—but what the heck
  a boy does command lots of respect.

Melvina

Long Enough

I have no wish to live forever…
just long enough for my mind to know
the children have been safely grown…
having watched them carry a happy heart,
and sharing in their laughter and love from the start.

Long enough to grow old with Roy
to sit back and smile to remember
all the love we've shared since our first September.
though time will have wrinkled both our faces;
our love will live past what often time erases.

Just enough to care for my folks…
watching over them as their hair begins to gray;
making sure they never have a lonely day.
to give back to them all the love they've given me;
until the time comes when their souls are set free.

No, I have no wish to love forever…
but if my "long enough"…in God's eye's is too long;
then into his loving arms is exactly where I belong.
even though my mortal life from this world will sever…
In my spiritual life with God I will live forever!

Cynthia Ann Fullgrapp

Setting Sun

Sitting here watching the days sun go down
Just me you see, for there's no one around.
Where you may ask - have all the people gone
Away to other places they just keep moving on
Where you may ask - have all the flowers gone
They - like the people - have also moved along.
There were oceans where we once did play
Something called pollution, it too - has seen its day.
Children filled with laughter, and babies crying
Now it seems everyone's dying.
Poisoning the air from some aerosol can
Are we really trying - to save this sacred land.
Think for a moment, of the great misuse
Our Earth has become, a place of abuse
I'll do my part to save Mother Earth
I pray that you will too, for what it's worth
Hands working together, and we stand side by side
All the world doing the same, nothing to hide
And when we see our sun - setting in our great big sky
God will take us home, when it's our time to die.

Edward J. Hildebrondt Jr.

"Yesterday's Past"

Someday maybe, somehow, someway or sometime
Just to survive, with no violence, no crime.

Passing with time, hopefully of being wise
If united, three things can all be revised.

Put aside each others aches and pain
Trying not to find, or call any blame.

Silently, looking upon one another
Nothing to hide, seek and discover.

Friends or lovers, whichever, you and me
Praying to God, we will all truly see.

Yesterday's sorrow, memories of silent cries
The beginning of the future, in blue skies.

Give each other room, just to be
Not to change, but to flow free.

See and believe, live for tomorrow's dream
Stand Proud, in life's ever changing stream.

Eileen M. Mineburg

A Letter From A Father To His Daughter

I love you not because you are beautiful or gifted of some
kind of skill. Sleepless nights at the hospital waiting
room or at home never rebuked my patience; instead, they
made you more valuable to me. When you broke my priceless
collection, a fury of rage ran down my spine; by looking at
you, your face not only convinced me of forgiving you, but
pushed me to share your guilt. When in trouble for having
disobeyed my orders, you are the only person that I don't
say, 'I told you so.' Instead, I offered you my shoulder
while hoping for the best. Your first step as well as many
other silly things brought me indescribable joy. For you I
can go miles and will never feel the pain. I can spend my
last penny and will not feel impoverished. I can brave
your foes and will not feel the danger. You give me the
reason to live, and I can give my life without fear for you to live.

Gabriel Montervil

The Kiss

Wake up, the sun has arisen and just
    kissed the world "Good day" with
its warmth and sunshine.

It beckons our sleepy eyes to open and see
    the miracles performing; images to be
impressed in our minds and hearts.

Morning dew drops clinging to the leaves
    cannot escape the rising sun's
infectious warmth of its kiss.

The gardenia waits patiently exuding
    its fragrance as the sun slowly lifts
the shade from where it abides.

While the rosebud, being kissed by the sun,
    blushing a livid red, reveals its petals
to revel in its warmth.

The kiss disperses love and tenderness in an
    ardent fashion, reminding us of his
eternal loving, comforting way of
    revealing himself to us.

Josephine Charlotte Henson

Birth Of A Child

Exchanging your vows so softly with care
    knowing your mate will always be there
We share of our soul while tenderly touch
    whisper my darling "I Love You So Much"

God has blessed for this husband and wife
    patience and love to create a life
From years of prayer you nervously feel
    within your womb a child so real

Informing your husband with eyes of love
    blessed with an infant send from above
Tenderly embraced together standing still
    hearts beat as one a beautiful thrill

Labor has commenced husband proud and true
    anxiously praying for this life of new
Suddenly the child emits a glorious shriek
    as tears flow down your husband's cheek

Your baby is cleansed and placed to rest
    wrapped in a blanket upon your breast
This family now three embraced and so mild
    love has allowed this Birth Of A Child

David B. Miller

"My Only Son"

Born January 25, 1973
    La Ronn is a part of me
Departed January 13, 1993
    Now a part of me, is buried near a tree
La Ronn is under the dirt
    Now I am very hurt
My heart has a strain
    It is called pain
Without my Boy
    I can not find joy
My heart aches
    Till I start to shake
I don't know what to do
    Since they've taken you
I love you— I miss you— I wish you were here
    But for now— I'll shed another tear
At least
    Now you're at peace
        Delores Linen

Untitled

The crisp, bright rays of the fiery sun lay fast across the
land. Crystal drops of morning dew shine so golden and so
grand. The dark green grass, and pale white flowers have yet
to be scarred. Living together peacefully, as the large fir
trees stand guard. A large maple tree, not far away, is
preparing for the season called fall. Golden leaves hang
heavily, waiting for Mother Nature to call. The fir trees rise
high into the sky and stand as heavens ladder. And halfway
between Heaven and Hell a small nest is filled with chatter.
Even in the sun, the featherless hatching each shiver in their
nest. With their mother gone in search of food, so is gone the
warmth of her golden breast. Far below, a honey bee hunts from
flower to flower. Endlessly gathering sweet, golden honey for
his queen, hour after hour. Is there difference between a
scenic painting and this golden land? Each can be faded when
carelessly handled by the human hand. But we will always have
our imaginations, thoughts, and memories of golden places and
golden things, and that will last eternally.

    James Whalley

Bubbly Brook

The bubbly brook pokes its way through the dense trees,
Laughing and dancing
Among the animals and bees.
A deer comes along to take a drink.
Me, I just sit myself down and think.

"What if the brook no longer
Could bubble? ...What if the
Deer no longer would prance?
Oh, wouldn't it be consider-
Able trouble, if the animals of
The night no longer could dance?"
As I ponder these questions inside of my head,
I see how often we take these things for granted.
At this time, I have a request to make of thee,
Stop often, and take the time to see what you can see.

Find ways to protect what is there.
Nature has given as much,
She would find this fair.
        Jenny DeWall

Drink

He climbed onto the bench to see what it was like.
Laughing with his friends, he jumped.
His friend urged him to climb higher.
They slapped hands and he climbed onto the garden wall.
The shadows shook their heads.
He jumped, and laughed with his friend.
They slapped hands, and he climbed higher
(the shadows whispered no) and jumped.
They laughed together;
Again the slap. Again the climb higher.
The shouting shadows were not heard.
Again the jump.
Laugh. Slap.
Higher, even higher to jump and laugh.
Slap.
To the roof.
No, please no.
Jump.
The shadows sobbed silently.
And the friend was gone.
        Erica K. Swift

Sakura

The light filtered through the cherry-blossomed trees that line the road
lays a path of bright cobblestones made of sun before us.

The scent of antique blooms invades everything
and pale pink petals spin down to touch our skin.

Our kiss seems clumsy against the soft surrounding flowered breeze
so we simply watch the light reflected in each other's eyes go down
as the sun sets somewhere behind the far horizon.

And we close our eyes as the night washes us.

And when we open them again we find that the breeze has swept
    the other away
and we are separated by an ocean
and the night closes us smugly into its palm.

The petals laced through my hair remind me of your skin.
I cannot cry hard enough.
        Brian Bergstrom

Yachats Native Friends

There she stood, alongside the cafe
leaning as though an invisible force held her at bay
keeping her in a upright position
and I
Pretended not to notice her
or identify with her.

Passersby frowned at such contempt
a degradable alien dare invade their righted values
in this lifestyle of the elite
and I
refused to acknowledge her
or identify with her.

But damn her and all her kind
as her clouded eyes burned into my soul
knowing that once,
I stood in the same half-right position
and she
pretended not to notice me
or identify with me.
        Cherokee Noon Schmerber

Constantly Changing

Making changes in my life with no fear
left I'll make them right.
Constantly changing day to day, I've
learned to roll with the punches in every way;
Feeding my mind with positive thoughts,
letting the world know my soul can't be bought.
I can, I will be me, my eyes are open,
I can see.
My life keeps changing for the better,
going for the gold in life and I'll getter.

Jan M. Meacham

Precious Dream Take Your Place

Embrace the dream God has given.
Lest that dreams find demise.
Then life becomes a wagon without a wheel driven.
Going nowhere as time flies.

Embrace the dream God has given.
For should that dream lose face
Then life can become so empty, barren, cold, frozen...
My precious dream take your place.

Carol A. Michalski

The Fire Within

Listen to the fire, look into the flames.
Let it burn within you, play its deadly games.
Feed it with your fury, feed it with your pain.
Use it to your advantage, use it to your gain.
Speak no evil of the fire, speak no evil of the flame.
It controls your destiny, put it not to flame.
If the fire burns low inside you, you may begin to die.
Always keep it burning, let it burn on high.
The fire is your guide, do not blow it out. If you feel the
source is weak, do not scream and shout. The fire is your
master, the wiseman of your soul. It will answer all your
questions, but you must pay the toll. Soon enough your time
will come, and the fire will vanish within. So take advantage
of what you have, before the flames run thin. Seek not the
worldly goods in life, they cause the flame to wane. If this
happens to the inner fire, you have broken the sacred chain.
When the time comes for you to die, all you had has past. So
live the day to its fullest, and make every moment last. Let
the fire run its path, let it warm your heart. Always be
confident in what you do, and let the fire do its part.

Chris Van Gelder

The Fog, Santa Barbara And You

Before the blazing sun burns off the Santa Barbara fog,
let me remember you once more

Standing there with dew drenched hair,
your eyes searching for answers

Remembering yesterdays love,
our nakedness on the beach and wine

You, loving me, lightly brushing the sand from my brow

How safe I felt with you.

And now the fog is lifting, and with it I must go...
Goodbye my love, I'll never forget you...

You were part of me

Candi Walker

When I Go

When, one day, I go unto my maker
Let there be no sad songs for me
But let all lift up their voice
And so with me rejoice.....
As again I hold my loved ones to me.

With me, let us all recall
Those long and happy years gone by
And the love we three then shared
'Ere, not one, but two, passed me by
To share all their love up high.

So never be there cause to wonder
As I say, "Do not be sad."
But share with me that happy day
And rather be glad... as I too will be glad
To have my two loved ones guide me on the way.

So look not on this as a sad parting
With all red eyes and useless sighs
But let it rather be celebration
For me and those two who gently lie
Where I go, to them, yes, with joy.

Edwin P. Spivey

Far Away Land

Lie with me in a bed made from petals of a rose.
Lie and sleep with me tonight.
For in time we have froze.
Walk with me towards the light.
In the winds of change we stand.
In a land so far.
Come now, take my hand.
Follow the light of the star.
Dive with me in the waters so deep.
Not of reality it may seem.
Come it is only sleep.
To a land of dream.
Leave me here far away.
Hear my voice whisper in the wind.
Wake to the light of day.
For our time here has come to an end.

Davina Strine

Untitled

Behind the cheery laugh, behind the smile so bright
lies a never ending wall of pain, confusion, and fright.
Inside you grow weaker everyday
hoping the pain will go away, but it won't.
You ignore your conscience in your mind screaming Don't!
Don't do it, don't throw it all away.
It's not so bad, it will go away.
When you're hurt by those you love
it crushes you like a weight from above.
You think the pain you cannot bear,
they'd be better off if you weren't there.
So you make a decision in your mind
that soon you'll leave it all behind.
You say goodbye to those who care
the next time they look, you won't be there.
When you work so hard at all you do,
the pressure starts to get to you.
Then the pain of betrayal, mistrust;
Ashes to Ashes, Dust to Dust.

Jaime Hope

"The Maestro"

What is it that inspires a man to create-to bring to
life excellence is execution through patterns of notes and/or words
known only to his being? How is it possible for one to be
so gifted, so able to take what is intangible and provide
it with enough energy to dance across the page from
which it is written?

His artistry unfolds with such fluid poise the senses
become engulfed and lose all consciousness. He has
lifted each soul to defy gravity and the reality of the world.
We are his captives, sailing through illusions on a musical
chord, through uncharted waters.

How extraordinary to witness the intensity of this man!
To share in the intimacy of his love and passion poured out
upon uplifting shapes, which take flight, and then
melt into tears that fill the eyes of those who watch;
those who believe in the miracle of his work.

Deanne Riess

Victims

Hands being cuffed,
Life flashes before me in clouds of puff.
Bars before my eyes,
Never again to see the clear blue skies.
The last meal before the eternal sleep,
Loved ones are there to weep.
A condemned walk to an iron chair,
Locked in, as to become one with the seat, unfair.
Unfair, to be doomed to eternal bliss,
Bitterness added with the last of mother's kiss.
Thousands of volts pump through my veins,
Watching my friends, I sleep, with head in shame.
Now I know how they felt,
As they begged and pleaded when they knelt.
I did not know how to beg, now I know how they felt,
As the volts wrapped around my body like a belt.
Now I know how victims feel,
As the volts surrounded the cuffs of steel.
Now I know how victims feel...

Clara Li

The Man

Once I saw a man so glum,
Life, now, to him a closed door.
Hollow like the beating of a drum,
Rhythmically sounding forever more.

He wandered the city.
He did not care.
He resented people's pity,
As they continued to stare.

He grew heavy with depression.
He considered suicide.
Control of his life, he lost all possession.
He begged, he stole, he lied.

To get his life back,
Which he wasn't sure he could,
He realized the fact,
It depended on if he would.

Of the pain and embarrassment, he wanted to be rid.
The streets of loneliness, he no longer cared to roam.
Then the smartest thing he ever did-
He threw away the bottle and went home.

Adrianne Behning

Beyond The Tides

My love sleeps near the shore,
Like a dark lustrous pearl,
Spray spewed by some mad spring gale,
Ever beyond the ocean tides,
Peacefully she rests,
Beyond the ocean's reach,
But still it has her in its grip,
The rhythms of the moon, the stars, the waves,
Atavistically are interpreted,
For me!

Henry Wesley

At The Top Of A Hill

When you reach the top of a hill it's
like a dream. You can hear the wind
like a soft whisper. You can see the grass
waving through the wind. You can feel
the sun's heat beating down on you.
Smell the fresh scent of so many flowers.
The sound of animals come through your
ears. You can mostly feel nothing but
the grass, flowers, and dirt. You might
be able to find a lovely house too.

Ashley Stephens

The Stream

Soft and still the water flows, cool, calm, serene,
Like a glassy mirror, reflecting a tranquil scene.
It gives the passers-by a moment of reflection,
Lifting them from life's tempest, into its perfection.

Yet, in a moment that world is dashed,
The little scene of peace is thrashed.
Envious rocks toss and turn the dream,
Swishing, shunning, confusing the stream,
Bubbling the waters with distress,
Joy and peace put to the test.

As every true dream, it finds its way,
And passes through the rocks of prey.
Once again it smoothly glides along
Like a sweet and simple song.

Grace K. Henry

Imagination

Thinking beautiful, lovely thoughts,
Like bad blooming into a rose.
Creating an image of tenderness and serenity,
That's imagination.

Thinking dark, deranging thoughts,
Like a dagger tearing away at mortal flesh.
Making you feel the terror of hate,
That's imagination.

Thinking calm, curing thoughts,
Like the wind soaring through the trees.
Creating an image of calmness,
That's imagination.

Thinking sad, crying thoughts,
Like a long, lost love has left you.
Crying, thinking, loving, hating....
That's imagination.

Jamila Ghbeish

If Only ...

If all the world was white, all is blind,
Like blank paper with drawing of white,
The splendor of it will never be,
For none of it will never expose.
...If only the white was not alone.

If all the world became black and white,
One would see puffy white clouds in sky.
But what of bridge that light has formed?
Neither black nor white can show it off.
...If only black and white could be more.

If the world was more than black and white,
Unseen bridges shall disclose color's grace.
Eyes see colors bloom in nature's realm.
Flowers will blossom - grass will grow green -
...If only all eyes open to see.

Our world is more than black and white.
Colors are needed to build our world.
But, many do not see more than white,
And others see just their own colors.
...If only I, if only you, if only us...

Cindy Chen

Because Of Love

It was like love I'd never felt before,
Like love I'd never feel again,
As we strolled hand in hand around the block,
And kissed a romantic kiss behind the tree,
We gazed into each others eyes and told each other
"I Love You",
We just can't get close enough,
We just wanna each other longer and forever,
Because of love,
That's why we're together.

Amee Olson

Beauty Of Nature

Nature, a beautiful painting of breathtaking scenes
like lying in a meadow having candy dreams
watching the wildlife as it passes you by
stopping only for a glance as if saying hi.
"This is the Beauty of Nature."

A little doe plays in the setting of the sun
while birds sing a song because their work is done,
rabbits hopping along so mirthful and gay
getting ready to start another undiscovered day.
"This is the Beauty of Nature."

As I observe all the wonderful things
like butterflies fluttering their colorful wings
I give thanks to God for the blessings he brings.
"This is the Beauty of Nature."

Deidra McCullough

Life

Like winter flakes through the trees,
Like spring hives of bumble bees,
Live beauty and life of eternal peace.

Like the flicker of a flame,
Like the wind that howls your name,
Live light and imagination that stays the same.

Like a child when he prays,
Like long, hard school days,
Live wisdom and confidence
that shows in many ways.

Jenni Hansman

The Great Plains

The ground rumbled,
Like scavenger's
     The Indians kept hidden behind the hill.
Soon they would have enough food for their tribe.
This event was awaited every year,
Living out in nature's wonderland
     was harsh for the Indians,
Silently, the chief placed his ear against the ground,
     listening carefully,
In a moment's notice,
     all of the Indians jumped onto their horses,
     chasing after the large herds of buffalo.
One after another,
     buffaloes were shot down with arrows,
All that was left in the air were the cries of victory
And as the tribe celebrated with dances,
     the chief sat back,
     planning for the next hunt.

Ashley Bachler

Beauty's Passing

Exquisite beauty is fleeting
Like the cherry blossoms we await all year,
Enduring winter's snows, and spring's devastating winds,
Then enjoy for only a week. But in the passing fragrance
Is a testimony of life.

Could we but blossom with such fragrance in our world
That men would lament our passing with the nostalgic sadness
That they do this fragile flower,
We would decipher the deeper meaning of existence,
And say, it was beauty.

In the cherry blossoms's demise
The green leaf peaks forth,
And the living twig
Extends itself in growth,
A most mysterious sign
That the tree is not alone
Wrapped in its bark and leaf
But some voice has spoken
And offered eternity.

James H. Eastland

Proud Experiences

Proud experiences are things that happen everyday,
Like the President cleaning out the bay,
Rockets landing on the moon,
Caterpillars forming a cocoon,
Learning to drive your first car,
Getting a job that will take you far.
Proud experiences are directors making movies,
Sailor sailing the seven seas,
Scientists making discoveries,
Doctors helping people make recoveries,
Receiving my diploma on graduation night,
Giving a performance that is out of sight,
Mothers giving birth,
Proud soldiers put into the earth.
But the most proud experience for me,
Is being able to live in America and being free.

Joanna Czigan

A Voice Inside

Listen.
Listen to that voice from deep inside.
You hear it but hang on to your pride.
Listen to that voice inside.
Stop!
Stop and don't do it, says a voice in your head,
But what will my friends do, you say sick with dread.
Stop and listen to that voice echoing in your head.
Decide.
Decide and see if that voice has lied,
You'll find that your pride hasn't died,
The voice has not lied and it will always help you to decide.

Jenn Blazowich

Storm By The Sea

I stand on an ancient rock
Listening to the falling rain
Listening to the wild, stormy ocean
Listening to the roaring, crashing waves.
I hear the howling of the wind.
Is it the wind?
Or are those wolves hiding in the dark?
I hear the seagulls cry.
Their wailing is like the song of the sirens
Foretelling the death of sailors
Who will never return.
Don't tie me to the mast, my friends,
I want to lose myself in their embrace!

Danielle Sapse

The Wandering

As I wander in the dark I come across many things,
Little and small, I cannot see, for the darkness blinds me,
As I wander I care for very little,
Showing little emotions, I live,
Creeping in the dark,
I have no boundaries to cross, no rules to follow,
I have much freedom in the world,
Though I wander in an enclosed area,
I scream and shout to warn someone I'm lost,
It is useless, no one cares,
I am overcome by sadness,
My screams are useless because dead men can't scream.

Anthony Chu

Mama's Roots

There's a painting hanging on my mama's wall. Of a house she
lived in when she was small. In a little red farm house in the
Arkansas hills. Where peanuts and cotton grew in the wide open
fields. A place that holds part of mamas' heart in memory. So
special I can see it as she relates it to me. Of her family
that was bonded with close knit ties. As they adored with love
beneath Clear open skies. They were poor as dirt, but their
Life was truly clean. And close to every relative ever met or
ever seen. She talks often of that delightful Ozark farm.
With its hills and well and old musty barn. And a creek in the
"holler" is where She'd say was where they'd bathe or Swim on a
hot summers day. Her roots grew strong in that hard rocky
soil. Where she learned how to play and learned how to toil.
Yet she yearns to return to her old home stead. Even though
it's different with most of the family now dead But I understand
why mama loves to research her ancestry. Because the roots
grew deep in that precious family tree.

Adell Font

The Big House

There's a big house up the hill
Living there is a family of five.
First comes Papa, then comes Mama.
Along comes big brother, he's like no other
Next comes the twins, John and Jessie
Sometimes they can be very messy
John and Jesse are nine
With them I love to sit and dine
Jordan he's very cool and he ain't no fool
Mom's very independent and is fond of menthodent
Papa's always working
To keep a stable home to live in
It's very easy to see how nice, some people can be
They let me in their home, without reservation
Sometimes I feel so lucky, I could shout
I am proud to be their nanny
For that's my job and that's not funny
Tuesday I come, Sunday I go
What the rest of the week holds no one knows.

Deborah Greenidge

Back To The Basics

Callous are the hearts, that fill the world today.
Lonely are the sheep, who have gone astray.
Compassion and pride, are the qualities that man has lost.
Humanity and morality, is the high price we will pay in cost.
The worth of one's person, is now measured by their success.
The land, the air and the sea, have been destroyed
in the name of progress.
Look around with opened eyes, and you will be able to see.
Just what path we have taken, and exactly where it will lead.
Families with strong values, are all a thing of the past.
Our children will be left with nothing, the end will be at last.
It is time to get back to the basic's, if it is not too late.
And pray for the hope of tomorrow, for the children's sake...

Elizabeth DiBenedetto

Parting

You stand upon the shore
looking out over the horizon,
but all you can see
are painful memories
coming back to you upon every wave.

Chances at love
slowly slip through your fingers
like grains of sand.

The only comfort you receive
is from behind the lonely walls
of your unseen madness.

Tucked away, hidden from a merciless reality
filled with cold hearts
where dreams have no place in a world.

Lost in the reflection of unseeing eyes
you hunt for a treasure worth a thousand souls
a sliver of happiness.

Chance J. Goodteacher

Someone To Love

I often wonder, if there'll ever be someone to
Love me, as I will love thee. To laugh and cry,
Through good times and bad, and say that I love
You, wherever we are. For people are foolish,
Not understanding at heart, that women have
Feelings that set them apart. I know for a fact,
But not when it will be, the day will arrive, when
Someone will love me.

Dorothy Linell Fowler

Lifes Many Ways

Life can dish out all kinds of things
Lots of bad things and some long time dreams
Some people get married forever
Some people to be married never
Many women have babies
A lot of women live with just maybe's
Few want to marry the same sex for a different pace
Others marry people of a different race
Why some want to kill and hurt to our disgust
We must find a way to stop this way of life we just must
To live in a world of caring and love
Like we've been told they do above
Life has many ways and change
But it's been people who need to make and arrange
So we can live in this world together in love not
To live in this world like a hell so hot

Darlene Lawson

M

One, two, three, four, five, six, seven, eight, nine and ten
Lots of tee's and lots of Eee's but never an M
Half of M which is an N
Upside down an N shows a V
But no M can I see
Eleven, twelve, thirteen, fourteen, fifteen & sixteen
And so on to twenty
Yet no M can I see
Thirty, Forty, Fifty five and sixty
Seventy and eighty, up to one hundred we go
Still no M tries to show
One hundred, two hundred, up goes the score
Five hundred, six hundred up to one thousand we soar
Still no M do I see
M stands for one thousand
What have we here?
The English Language it does appear
I found an M in numbers!

Genevieve Densch

Past Forgetting

You
love away my pain,
stirring distant memories.....
fragile remembrances of being whole,
a heart with wings to soar
above life's billowing clouds.
Loving, being loved,
long ago, far away times....
existing still.

Your tenderness
circumvents carefully erected walls
of fear and self doubt,
cultivating newly emerging vestiges of trust.
I reach out toward tomorrow
tenuously groping,
frightened,
insecure,
strengthened by the comfort seen
reflected in your eyes.

Dianne M. Graham

"Insomniacs Dream"

Everything blends together,
Night and day are no longer distinguishable.
Locked out of that sanctuary called sleep,
And cursed with continuing consciousness,
There is no refuge.

Justin Kline

Love

Love can break your heart or soothe your soul.
Love can also make you lose control.
I wouldn't want to break a heart or have mine broken too
Maybe love is something I shouldn't try to do.

Sometimes love can make you die
That's why I'm afraid to try.
People say love is something you should treasure,
now and forever.

Love is something I wish I could have.
Maybe some day someone will love me,
I hope someday I can met thee.

Angie Osterberg

Love

Love is being able to smile
Love is being able to laugh
Love is being able to love
Love is being able to share
Your thoughts with someone
Love is being able to have someone
There when you are down
Love is having the sun always
Shining in your window
Love is having a child to share
Between two people
Love is having a best friend
Love is being able to be alone
When you need the time
Love is being jubilant about being married
Love is my wife
Love is Kimberly

Gary G. Roe, Sr.

From Love There Is Strength

I know that you love me today, but will you love me tomorrow, too?
Will you not forget, when you see the flowers bloom or feel the gentle summer winds; that all of our yesterdays and tomorrows make memories enough to last forever.
When my smile starts to fade, will you hold my hand and warm my heart?
Love isn't always sunshine and snowflakes. Sometimes it is lightening and thunder.
Love comes from inside, and it flows carrying strength from our friends and loved ones.
Know that my friendship and love will always carry strength and warm thoughts for you
Reach out and know that I will be here if you need me today, tomorrow, and forever.

Janis Bramlette

My First Love

My first love was someone who I
loved - but never loved me back
My first love was someone who wanted
to fulfill his desires- I was never one of them
My first love was someone who made me
cry - my tears were of endless pain
My first love left me a memory - something
he doesn't want to remember -
-Something I wanted to admire
-Something he created from lustful desire
-Something who's life I took away.

Jennifer Saldana

Loving You

Loving you when skies are clear blue and sunny, you are glad
Loving you so that skies grow gray when you are sad;

Loving you so that when we walk in crowded places,
My eyes grow misty in a veil of tears,
And I only see a blur where there are faces
Loving you so that I am swept with bitter fears.

Loving you so that when my head is on your chest,
All my fears are overcome and laid to rest
Words do not come and thoughts go unspoken
Loving you so that just your reaching hands bring a
soft caress.

Elizabeth A. Pierce

Political..Power

Nineteen ninety was no fun? Along comes a
mad Moslem Hussein.
Who emulates Stalin, his Iraq armies trample
Kuwait, keeping the world on the run
Nineteen ninety still a bore, Bush and Quayle
behind closed doors. All the rumors are of war.

Saddam Hussein using hostages and oil for bait.
Hoping United States will back off or disseminate.
From the chill of Korea to steaming jungles of
Vietnam we still continue on a losing journey.

America's strength and roots are now transplanted
in the sand and heat of Saudi Arabia our youth.
In private planes politicians safely return.
How many of America's sons will arrive in body bags?
Damn; will this country ever learn.

Albert B. Stone

To The One With The French Name

With the eyes of a panther—-
  Magnetic in the daytime
  But rather stealthy at night,

I often wonder:
  "Is your love as smooth as your
   creamy, tan skin?"
    "Or, is it serenading me
      as a siren before a shipwreck?"

With cheeks like two ripe, Georgia peaches—-

  Flawless as fine China,
  Yet as priceless as Porcelain chalices,

I often wonder:

  "Is your caress as warm as
   the shining light of your smile?
    "Or, is it blinding the sight of
     true love?"

With a body as fine as Eqyptian lace—-

  Like sand hugging the curves of an hourglass,
  an hourglass,
  Yet petite as a red rose,

I often wonder:

  "Will I be able to lead her into
   Heaven, the holy home of God?"
    "Or, will she just laugh at me,
     and call me odd?"

Eric W. Perkins

His Hands

Holding his hands
make me feel secure.
Though large, and rough,
tender to touch.
His hands are filled with emotion,
from being cross,
to "the softness of her touch."
The warm strong hands are filled with hope
of seeing you,
not me.
Yet through all his joy, and pain,
though others may not care,
I will take his hands,
And I will be there.

Jeni Cannane

Our New Baby

This little boy is what life's all about.
Mama's little man, and loved no doubt.

He makes no demands, and he does no harm.
Up at six, when he hears the alarm.

A smile on his face, waiting for mother to say.
"Good morning son", "It's a wonderful day."

A cute little hug, and a little wet kiss.
Mom, it just doesn't get any better than this.

It's off to day care, where he plays with the boys.
Laughing, giggling an chewing on toys.
Lunch, a snack and a nap or two.
So when he's picked up, he's all smiles for you.

Strapped in his car seat, and on his way home.
Where the rest of the family, just won't leave him alone.

After playing, eating and having a bath too.
He's ready mom, to cuddle with you.
Then it's off to bed, with his face all aglow.
As if to say "I love you mom", "But you already know".

Fast asleep in his crib, and away from all harm.
He dreams of tomorrow, till the six o'clock alarm.

Bill Carrington

This Is Where I'll Stay

In my misery, I guess is where I'll stay
Married at eighteen; thought I was in love
Out of school and pregnant—no roads lead home
He beat me, he beat me hard,
He crushed and bruised me deep within my soul
Without using his hands, my self is gone
I've never known joy, only pushed out laughter,
Grasping for escape
I have become trapped in the everlasting circle of time past,
And what is to become my future is now my present
There it is again, he's beating me...
"You're a nobody - what are you good for"
The words echo in my ears, they echo in my mind,
It's burned in my soul
My torture stays within me, over and over,
An unyielding hurt, a pain that never cease
And in it all I keep missing months
For there's no escape for a woman...a wife...
A servant who's not whole.

Heather Smith

"A God Above"

I've seen so many of the different sights
Marveled at the birds swinging in flight
Watched as tears rolled down a cheek
Of a little child when life seemed bleak.

I've looked into the sky so blue
Viewed the grass all wet with dew
Saw the clouds forms on the ground
Ran and ran 'til my heart would pound

I've sat in snow up to my face
Saw the clouds form into place
Watched the rain pour from the sky
Heard the thunder and wondered why

Anyone could doubt there's a God above
Who showed his mercy and sent us his love.

Jeanette Maxwell-Boling

Masquerade

Paper faces, black and red
Masquerade sincere horsemen
Midnight ensues closely
Dance, dance, ladies and gentlemen, dance!
Who is he
   Who is she
Discover soon the identity
   partaking history
Monsters dance to clowns
Maidens clasp hands
Smiling
"When will I know?"
   "Patience, patience!"
Soon clocks sound at the eternal hour
Prepare, ready eyes for shock!
Here, it's here
Unmask, unmask!
Reveal the visage you sought
   through the eternal night

Joshua Jackson

"Loved Ones"

Loved ones they come and they go like the
melting of the white gentle snow on a bright
sunny day little by they slowly slip away

They bring so much love and joy to you
but they drift away when the time is through

You can cherish the times that you shared
together but day by day things change
just like the weather

They leave this world one by one to a
better place when there time here is done
but in your heart there lies the memories
of your loved ones.

Jimmy Ray Pruitt

True Love

He stares at me with glazed eyes
memories of our childhood go through his head.
He looks as though he has something to say,
though he does not.
His face shows fatigue from years past.
I have loved him for as long as I can remember,
and I'll love him forever.
We will grow old together and be
there for each other forever,
my teddy bear and I.

Greta Wojcik

Coming Home

The mask comes off-at last I'm free, then light shines through the
memories!
Birds I can hear from a far away place, 'Tis I'm home at
last-yes back in the race.
It's been up hill for the longest time-but it's my turn to
live-just enjoy the ride!
Every heartbeat has its reason for beating-every flower has its
reason for seeding.
The rain drops that fall have a place to land- the snow flakes
are made special for every man!
The spring- the smell of the fresh air- a new life to behold!
The summer- the blessed beautiful sun beaming down our very
soul!! The fall- the manifest of colors for our eyes only to
see. The winter- the cold, cold winds and the warmth of a
fireplace so cozy for you and me! This my love is my heart
speaking to you out loud- Listen- please listen- for know where
will there be found- a more honest and sincere person, that
has finally come around!

Joyce Mills

Love

Senseless emotions swept away
Memories of the past remembered today
We laughed so hard we almost cried
Our hearts said hello when our minds said good-bye
The wind echoes your scent that was left behind
Looking for today tomorrow we will find
Tear streaked eyes that never cried
Speechless mouths that always asked why
Dreams that came from sleepless nights
Whatever was wrong always seemed right
Imaginary feelings suddenly became real
Hearts we could touch but never could feel
Vines wrapped around a helpless heart
Unknown sorrows that were there from the start
Suddenly searching for a speck of light
Instead found a darkness incredibly bright
Filling out space as it emptied out
Laughter and cries danced about
Bringing a life to the darkness of death
To some love is unknown but clear to the rest!

Amy Loftus

'Concealed Thoughts'

Creature's of thought stir in my
Mid winter and Summer dreams
Crystallized tears fall and to me it seems
They act out my Pain as clearly as the lucid moon
gleaming through the rain
cold winter night sewer steaming
Hot summer day Sun gleaming
Thine eye's catch eye's beaming
Watchful, malevolent and ever deeming
These eye's that watch me in a dream
that truly are unseeing
give chills riveting in waves
to thine soul and sends messages
that draw's them all together hand in hand (thoughts)
like a signal sent out through dreamland
relentless and unfearing
never to reveal of what dreams are concealed
Just eye's beaming, gleaming while I'm dreaming
Just watching me
ever watching (conscience)

Heath Franklin

'You'

Even though I thought our love could last forever, I was mistaken, for we are not made for each other. For you, my love, will always stay strong and bold in my heart each and every day. I have no hate for you, and there will never be any. For you mean too much to me. The flowers the candles and the music. They all set the mood, just right, for you and me. But all this time I thought we would be together forever. But now I can see that we are not meant to be together. But if I cannot have you and your love, I guess I shall not be any more. For, without you, I am dead inside. So, if you do not love me any more, kiss me one last time, and say good-bye, and like a bird I will soar up into the dark nights sky. And you then, can go on living without me. And I shall then, say good-bye.

Destiny Mitchell

At Least I Was A Faithful Wife

A lonely wife sits alone, while her husband is with his mistress. She sits as he enters the door, freshly showered doesn't cover her perfume. A slight smile, a quick kiss, I'm off to bed, he's off in a flash. She doesn't flinch, she doesn't move, simply fingers a knife, she's been staring at all night. A creak upstairs, he's in bed, a slight smile plays on her face. She looks into the fire, why does he cheat on me? She shrugs not really caring. She puts the knife in the flame. Her eyes attracted to the colors. She smiles to herself she takes the knife from the flame. A creak from upstairs, he's coming down stairs. She stabs the knife into her neck, dying instantly. He comes in the room and sees his wife. He utters nothing, not a word spoken. He kneels next to her, touches her once beautiful face, her long golden hair now splattered with her blood. Her long graceful neck, no longer as it was. No tears, no words, simply a pain too painful to explain. "I'm sorry" he whispers even if it is too late, and then sees the note. He reads to himself and then out loud. "At least I was a faithful wife..." finally tears fall down his face, these words to echo in his mind forever...

Chrissie Brittain

Little Georgia Pine

Christmas during the Great Depression meant,
  Money was scarce and our pockets were spent,
  Daddy built fires and cut a little Georgia Pine,
A wonderful little tree that brought us sunshine.

Our furniture was gone via Scrooge the repo man,
  We couldn't make payments according to the plan,
In one corner an orange crate was placed with care,
  So Santa could place our little baby dolls there.

Our pet chicken was to be on the Christmas menu,
We forgave mama because that's what she had to do,
  Our stockings were hung high on a rusty old nail,
We sang songs we made up, laughed and cried as well.

We woke excited, warm and happy on Christmas morn,
We said grace and remembered why Christ was born,
  We didn't complain about things that we had not,
And our Love for mama and daddy will never be forgot.

Jane Harris

Upon Reading Modern Poetry

No Jesus, no Jesus, no Jesus in sight,
No wonder, no wonder, we live in the night;
Of a thousand dead things there are songs to be heard,
But never a sign of the real Living Word!

Jack F. Manier

Untitled

I awakened with a tear slipping down my cheek this morning. I glimpsed outside my window only to see darkness hovering and the wind howling as it pressed its chilled breath against my face. I leaned... but shivered back when the voices told of the ministering spirit collapsing; once again dying to evil. I closed the window as I fell to my knees, death was all around me. I could feel the evil presence lurking and waiting; it had come to steal my innocent life. His hand touched my pure skin and I began to pray; hoping for guidance as this diabolic wickedness played with my sanity. The Satanic figure emerged and moved slowly towards me, I found I was unable to move. I closed my eyes for momentary shelter but he entered with his unspeakable fate. He gripped his bony hands around my neck and pushed me towards the window. Outside screams, cries and voices of torture echoed from the wind. The evil one held me outside then released me into the darkness to perish and continue to scream for an eternity.

Brandi Collins

Questions To The Spheres

How was it I became earthbound when I wanted to fly?
Mute when I wished to sing?
Still when I wished to dance?
Blind when I wished to see?
Alone when I wanted to love and be loved?

Vague whisperings stir as my senses are reawakened!
I feel my wings begin to grow anew!
My voice is released to sing!
My feet have a dance all their own!
Light has dawned anew across my visage and
you are there —— to love unconditionally!
  Welcome!!

Betty Moor

Prayer

My heart is hurting my Lord, my heart is hurting
My eyes are crying my Lord, my eyes are crying
But no matter what my life is feeling
You my dear Lord, are always watching.
You see my pain and that I feel tired
You know my loves: Husband and children
forgive dear Lord if I complaint
I have more that I deserve...

Teach me to be content no matter what,
teach me to do your will, and be better all the time,
teach me to see my faults that are so many
and look not at earth but more to heaven....

Gladys Hoyos

A Sudden Thought

A gentle breeze, across my face
my eyes wonder off, at this beautiful place
A ray of hot, tickles my nose
When from afar, the sun arose
I opened my arms, like I was a bird
and shouted out, my very last word
I said to the world, as loud as I could
care for each other, like we should
I took my very last breath of air
for nobody loves me, nobody cares
I took a leap, from a cliff so high
for to the world, I say good-bye.

April Busch

A Life Changed

The sun shines brightly upon my face the waves lap gently at
my feet, but several years ago-death seemed like my only
Freedom.

My body encased in dressings unable to talk-body shaking from
pain and fear surrounded by sterile tile walls and strange
sounds. Death seemed like my only freedom.

A pair of warm eyes shining above a mask-a loving voice
speaking words of comfort skilled hands working frantically to
ease my pain, but death seemed like my only freedom.

The days drug in weeks and the pain turned into agony; but the
pair of warm eyes-the loving voice under the mask-or the
skilled hands never faltered. But to me, the tormented victim,
death seemed like my only freedom.

The warm caring eyes the loving voice the skilled hands-healed
my wounds, gave me hope and encouragement, and touched my very
soul. Suddenly, I realized that death was not my only freedom!

Barbara Mellott

The Beautiful Place On Earth

As the tide came in I saw
my footprints disappear. The waves washed
up and hit my feet. The ocean felt cool,
and nice. I looked up at the beautiful
sun that seemed to be looking at me too.
I felt the wind flow through my hair,
and I heard children's laughter in the
distance unharmed and unafraid. The world
was safe and no one ever had to
worry, for everyone was kind and never
hurt another. Too bad it was only a
dream.

Jennifer D'ambrosia

The Love In Grandpa's Eyes

From the time I was a little girl
My Grandpa was my whole wide world.
I remember how he dried my tears,
   made me feel special through the years
and the love in Grandpa's eyes

To the big city he would take me to shop
and laugh at my eagerness as the bus reached our stop.
Then off he would take me to lunch and to chat
I remember white gloves and a small velvet hat
and the love in Grandpa's eyes

Then when I had grown and moved far away
I would think about him most every day.
I remember visiting when I could
he would open the door there he stood
and the love in Grandpa's eyes

The years have passed and he is gone from here,
though in my heart Grandpa's always near.
I remember the smiles and also the laughter
I will always remember those times ever after
and the love in Grandpa's eyes

Colleen Hodges

Heaven

If life were to be fulfilled by beauty
no existence would be complete without you
If the world rotated on its axis by pleasure
no degree would be successful without you
If all knowledge were born from elegance
no mind would prosper without you
Yet they promise Heaven awaits all who are true
But I beg to differ, I do protest
could it be Heaven without you.

Edward S. Lathan

My Prince Charming 'Feelings'

My love is like a melody in tune with my piano.
My hands beat like an orchestra full of drums.
My head is dizzy like the flight of the bumble-bee.
My ears are ringing like church bells.
I feel like a ballerina dancing to swan lake.
Every moment with my prince charming is like playing
"Rachmaninoff" on my piano.

How delighted I feel when your breath warms my body with
Overwhelming desire. My heart bangs like shutters hitting
The house on a stormy night. My soul is talking to you in
Silent hours and it says "I love you forever" my darling
Prince charming, my darling, my darling, I love you with
Exhilarating feeling, My darling prince charming.

Carolyn J. Ragno

My Fragile Heart

Within frames of my diplomas
My heart hangs from the room's walls,
Searching for the true path of life
My heart breaths in the silent halls.

Behind the desk my life wastes away
Submerged in afflictions of mankind in vain
I share a piece of my life with the sick
And tormented man, to lessen his pain.

For the breathless progression of a sick patient,
My days linger sleepless and grieved.
The night is dismal, my heart is fragile,
I long for kind grandma's gentle words.

How many souls yielding to early death
Have I surrendered to the cold grave?
How many times have I placed myself
In the casket of a dying man?

Sometimes wordless under weight of my grief,
Hidden in my shell like a crab in the sea,
I sit in the coffin of my bygone days
Shedding tears silently… to forget my agony.

Agop Aintablian

The Light At The End Of The Road

Up the long and lonely road, dejected and forlorn,
My legs were tired, my bones were sore,
The body weak and worn.
A light was there - I could see it still,
The light at the end of the road.

Just when I thought I could go no more,
A hand - A strong hand- held me by the arm.
Then the body quickened, the legs became strong.
The pace went faster and faster still,
To reach the light at the top of the hill.
The light, at the end of the road.

My heart felt bright, my spirits fine
And on we went, to the end of the line.
Quickly quickly now, to seek our goal,
The light - at the end of the road.

May we always appreciate his helping hand
And thank the Lord for his great love.
In daily trial through the land,
He watches o'er us from above.
The light - at the end of the road.

Bernice H. Verne

The Miracle!

I was a girl with lots of woes,
My life was going to and fro,
With no meaning and much fear.
Look inside behind this tear.

The pain of losing is so great,
I wonder at times, the person I make.
Through all the laughter no one can see,
The pain and sorrow inside me.

From childbirth to childdeath. I continue to be strong,
but deep inside I scream with anguish,
Oh! God! How long?

On the road to destruction as fast as could be
The brightest light shines, a Miracle for me.
You stole my heart with eyes of green,
never to return, you are my dream.

Your touch. Oh! Your sweet touch
as gentle as a breeze, for me only to surrender,
My heart you did seize. Holding, Caressing, becoming as one.
Consumed with hope your heart I had won.

Now days go by, Years have past. New is gone, True will last.
Darlene K. Loveless

Father Willow Tree

Oh, Father Willow Tree, I am your seed for I came from thee...
My limbs now above the Earth because with your mixture,
My mother gave birth.
Thought our love is great, these shared years we stood alone,
I regret not the past, for my roots are blessed
They've had a home.
I call you willow because you weep with life.
Winds of joy dance high in your branches,
Hard luck and sorrow make them tremble in strife.

Oh, Willow Tree, how great are thee!
All your wrongs, your rights, they still teach me...
They teach me yesterday, is only a part of tomorrow...
I honor you, oh, Willow Tree,
For because of you I am me.
Chuck Wilson

What A Mess

When I was just a baby I knew no wrong.
My mother would rock and sing me lullaby songs.

When I turned five, I started to school.
I thought all the teachers were so mean and cruel.

At age of fourteen my mother passed away.
I still cry and miss her, even to this day.

At age of sixteen I thought I knew it all.
I went and got married and was that a downfall.

Now as a grown woman I have four children of my own.
I only wish I knew what I thought I had already known.

My husband and I, we fight a lot and my children show no respect
I love my children so very much and I really have no regrets.

The Lord has put me through so many tests.
My life is on review, oh, what a mess.

Mother, I wish that you were still here.
To guide me straight, and to wipe my tears.

Please listen to me and hear what I say.
I only hope and pray your life is headed in a better way.

Respect your parents and treat them kind.
For some day without them, your life will be blind.
Cynthia Clemons

My Heart's Journey Home

He woke me early today - His mind is on my heart;
my shattered dreams and ragged scars are stretched across each part.
Before I stir to face the day, He knows He must apply
His healing salve of love and hope, to guard it, lest it die.

His whisper stirs my soul - my mind is on His heart;
Sweet communion, words of truth, His wisdom to impart.
"And God so loved the world," He says - He came that I might be
His new creation, heaven's joy, indwelt by deity.

He woke me early today - His heart is on my mind;
carried in His loving arms, my tears are left behind.
Forgetful of His faithfulness, His mercy and His grace,
I bow my head, renew my trust, so this day I can face.

Assured I am His own - my heart is on His mind;
eternal plans demand I press to know Him more and find
humility, obedience, and love are at the core
of our unending union in His will forevermore.

He'll wake me in His morning - when traveling days are done;
the endless ages will reveal the victories He has won.
Oh, bliss to look upon His face - to know as I am known;
my heart has found its resting place beside my Father's throne.
Betty Jean Kilgore

Untitled No. 5

As the blue skies fade
My soul feels a blade
The darkness that comes with night

As the demons awake
Our lives are at stake

Some are owners of hate

When they are judged it will be too late

Confusion is the source of their happiness

No one cares to deal with their mess
Come sunshine come dew

Those who have big hearts welcome you
Evelaca Rice

Untitled

I look into your eyes and
   my soul goes into slow motion

I have often wondered why you
   possess this magic potion

You see.....................

You touch my flesh gently and
   I feel the sun's heat

You kiss my lips softly and
   my taste buds feel only sweet

You whisper in my ear and
   a steady roar of the ocean is all I can hear

You say my name and
   I know not of any pain

Your steady consistent love you show
   has nothing left to do but grow and grow

Miracles are far and few between and
   our bond only God has seen
Diane Gannon Sorantino

Depression

Like the rain they fall,
  my tears like drops of blood.
As my innocent soul drifts away,
  in the eternal flood.

My heart can't take much more,
  my soul leaves me as we speak.
This dreadful pain inside,
  has made me oh so weak.

My heart, my love still nothing has changed,
  I have given all I have to give.
There is no reason, no reason at all,
  That I should still have to live.

All I do is sit and stare,
  disillusioned, I wait.
Asking for the answer as to why,
  I live in such a depressive state?

   Jason Permenter

At Midnight

At midnight I slipped out of bed-I could feel someone's presence in
  the room.
My teeth were chattering and my heart was pounding-it wasn't human,
  I could assume.

I started to panic-I was trembling with fear.
I heard pounding footsteps and saw another figure in the mirror.
I wanted to live-I was scared to death.
It was going to kill me-I could feel its breath.

It was someone tall and dangerous-someone crazy and mean.
It moved towards me-it was a sight to be seen.
I turned hysterical-the thing reached for me.
It choked me-I couldn't breathe-I can't die now-there are
  places to go, people to see.

I hoped it was a nightmare-a nightmare of horror. But my palms
were dripping with sweat and all over I felt sore. I gasped for a
breath as it strangled me. I thought to myself-What did I do?
How could this be? Maybe I'm imagining all of this-Maybe I'm
insane. But I know that I'm riding-the roller coaster of pain.
All of a sudden it disappeared into thin air. The pain was
gone-but I felt dead. There was no longer a presence in the
room, so at midnight I slipped back into bed.

   Joshua Kossack

As I watch the snow fall softly on the ground,
my thoughts lead to you.
A single flake, a single kiss upon my cheek.
The wind, your sweetness ringing in my ear.
I cannot feel the cold because the memory of
your strong embrace keeps me warm.
The peacefulness I see over the land is the
calm I feel knowing tomorrow you will still
be there.
Unlike the snow...

   Jacqueline Lee Gardner

Adrift

All alone in the deep blue sea,
No one to count on but myself - me.
I can't be the dolphin, I'll just be the eel.
No person can tell me exactly how to feel.
Push me in the water, hold me down,
I will keep on fighting, 'cause I never drown.
Put me on an island, I'll swim back to shore,
Pull myself out to come back for more.
Standing near the crest of an approaching wave,
I dive back in for another day.

   Deonna Dawn Labert

Her

I looked at the clock to see the numbers clicking by
My thoughts wandering to the past
Picking a bouquet of memories
I recalled her smile and eyes
The sound of her sorrowed cheers
Her screams at the world for justice
And at me for maturity
I remembered the way she held her glass
And held my hand when I cried
The warmth of her embrace
The pain of her fury
I touched my lips remembering the way they felt against her cheek
The nights seem longer knowing she is gone
The stars seem dim without her presence at my side
But I accept that our hearts would only bleed if we did not let go
The thought of "happiness ever after" consumes me
So, now, I only have my garden of memories that will always
grow but never bloom.

   Jorge Ruiz

Untitled

Got my blue skies and my sunshine
  My trees blowin' in the breeze
Spring's just around the corner
  Winter's almost over
  And it's time to rest at ease
The birds'll start flyin'
  Crickets start chirpin', wind gets warmer
  Sun gets brighter, I guess it's time to stop workin'
Trees look greener
  Grass starts growin'
  Go out and shake your head,
  Even the air smells cleaner
Winter's in the past
  And fall comes fast
But I'll just be happy
  Even for a while
Cause all year long-
  I got my blue skies and my sunshine
  My trees blowin' in the breeze
  It's enough to please

   Debbie Graf

"I Love, I Love, I Love,...Love Back"

"I have cried a thousand tears wondering when I would stop.
my very soul aches. The world has not yet seen the desolation
of this present war. This war that is worse than any plague.
I cry out with a loud voice, why!
I see death all around me and only a few seem to care.
Young and old people are dying in spite of their trying to live
my world has a cancer that is eating it up a bite at a time.
It has been going on so long that our young don't even know life
Can be better for them. You see,
They fall into life with others all around.
They think this is it. I have to survive on the firing
line. They don't have a chance,
You see for their father's seed is burned in spots and their
mother's egg has been scorched by the plague and the cancer
that we are at war with.
The tears that I cry are for those mothers and fathers who did
Not see it coming. Perhaps they were like the rest of us.
We heard, we guessed, we thought, we even thought again,
But it did not register until it was almost too late.
Yes, I cried a thousand tears wondering when I would stop!"

   Cecelia S. Henderson

Untitled

I have shared with you my hurts,
My weakness, my hunger.
You have wandered deep within my soul.
And I miss you - in my mind, in my heart and in my arms.
I have strength and compassion - but
emptiness. It's cold and deep.
How am I going to live without you in my life?
Without your laughter and your crazy jokes
Without you kisses and your caring.
I grieve,
But it's clean hurt
Without anger, without blame,
You gave me so much - you restored - you healed!

Eunice Faulkner

To My True Love

The rugged road of relationships and togetherness is getting rough,
My weary love filled heart needs a place to rest.
I stumble upon the bridge of understanding hoping to meet you there.
I listen to the water of caring thirsting for a drink.
I have come to this land many times,
And have found myself lost and along.
Frightened by the rain of loneliness I have hidden myself.
I stand tall and let the wind of hope and mercy run through my hair.
In the distance I see signs of someone drawing near.
Others pass and may stay for a while.
I wait for you as the golden sun of protectiveness shines upon me.
The sheltering blue sky above me hovers over me as if to hold me close.
I close my eyes and dream of you appearing my true love,
For when you do we will forever be here; in love.

Chrissy LaChance

Time Brings His Presence

I'm always dressed for the occasion
My white costume screams innocence
From behind his back he offers me a flower without a stem
I know he picked it from the garden, the sweet temptation
And he sweeps me up from the floor into his arms
His breath hits my neck in a soft caress
I feel his grasp, tighter and tighter around my fragile limbs
I feel his clever fingers roam over my skin,
throughout my body
    Impressing unwanted desire
His mouth envelopes my own, gently forcing it open
Drinking from me and into me
In the dark, I can see the finality of his blackness
He takes the lead
And my fear drains as my ears fill with music
    I let myself go
He spins me around and around in endless circles
And my feet no longer touch the ground
I look into his eyes and I see mirrors, reflecting into myself

When fate asks me to dance, I cannot refuse

Claudia Perrone

An Anniversary Of Love

With you there's only sunshine
not a passing cloud I see, that's why you've
always been the most important part of me.
You shared in all my hopes and dreams
and plans of a new tomorrow you showed me
what love really means through
times of pain and sorrow, because you
have inspired me with everything you do
Your loving ways have made me see,
how much in love I am with you.

Isabelle Brunetti

Assurance

My Word is humble and true,
    My Word holds the best in life for you.
My Word is strong and it's sure,
    it's the way, the key, and it is the door.

If you love Me, let My will be thine,
    open up to Me, allow Me your mind.
I want to bring to you, secrets from above,
    I want to shower you with unending love.

My beloved, I will see you one day,
    if you'll prayerfully abide in My way.
All these hurt and pains will soon be done,
    When to Me, My Bride, you finally come.

My Word is humble and true,
    My Word holds the best in life for you.
My Word is strong and it's sure,
    Walk the way, use the key, and come though the door.

Beverly McGill

If I

If I could only tell you of the love within my heart,
My words would fashion you like a loving piece of art.

In my dreams I think of you, you're always in my head,
But every time I try to speak so much stays unsaid.

Whatever phrases I may use fall short of what I mean,
Instead of words I try to use the deeds that can be seen.

I'm sorry, love, if I fall short of what you expect of me,
I wish that everything you want was easier to see.

I promise you, I'll always be there when you call,
Without you, my darling, all I can do is fall.

I know it's hard to ask you to try to understand,
But anything can be done if we walk hand in hand.

Carole B. Burger

Hello Dear

Hello dear, how are you today?
Myself, I'm fine; but my daddy's wasting away.
Where is your daddy now; may I briefly chat?
Just a moment grandma; I'll find that brat.
That's not nice dear; daddy is the boss.
I know he is; but he just seems to be lost.
Put him on the phone, tell him grandma is here.
Daddy, you're being paged; put down that beer.
Hello dear, what are you doing to her?
Nothing yet mom; but soon it'll be battle of the bulge.
That fresh grand of yours has gained enormous weight.
And when I speak on it, she retaliates.
You're the matriarch, what do you suggest?
Put her on dear, let me chat with her a bit.
Yes grandma, I'm giving dad a fit;
he and his friends drink champagne and beer.
When I asked for a small sip, he handed me a book.
Now grandma, I'm five, does book sound like drink.
Please, you have to help me think, dad insulted my brain.
I'm not angry with dad, he can't be blamed.

Janette Anderson

Untitled

It was the day after Christmas and all through the house
Not a creature was stirring, not even a mouse;
For everyone's pooped and why we don't wonder
When all's said and done, and on this I now ponder.
The presents were wrapped and the cards were all sent
And much at our money and energy spent.
But now that our comings and goings must cease
We surely know that the spirit of Christmas is Peace.

Edith M. Roberts

Mystery Of Life

The midnight breeze carrying wondering voices,
Mystery of life, making your own choices,
The future brings on thoughts to mind,
Feeling lost and confused deep down inside.

Letting go of emotions and expressions to shout,
Because you are searching for a path to get out,
The judgment of ending your life is too rough,
You have to be firm and learn to be tough.

Sometimes it's natural to feel frustrated and down,
But remember a frown is a smile turned around,
Never knowing what will become of you,
Maybe grow old with dreams that come true.

Whatever you do, don't give up my friend,
Find another way, it's never the end,
When you think you're at the depth of despair,
Don't forget that others care.

Jennifer Plath

Excerpt from—"The Saga Of The Ancient Moa"

'Twas the year of sixteen twenty,
Near the continent of Australia,
On the island of New Guinea
On the site now called Wombeka,
Then there were but bogs and marshes
Where now stands a wondrous city,
Stands the City of Wombeka,
Gleaming in the morning sunlight.
In those days so long forgotten,
In those days of natures freedom
Roamed the large and ancient moa;
Dwelt he in the slimy marshes
Feeding on the bugs and fishes
Which infested them in plenty,
Dwelt he in flocks of great numbers,
Near the mountains old and cave strewn,
On the island of New Guinea."

Francis M. Black

Emotional Snare

Footfalls were heard upon the cobbled road,
Near the innocent man her pace had slowed.
About her body was a deep green gown
That, from the shoulder, draped so loosely down.
Her features were all so beautiful wrought;
Fame, glory, and fortune are what she sought.
Her frame was perfectly god-like and thin;
Her splendor stole souls from a thousand men.
She is Envy, there can be no disguise
Taunting, tempting, simply telling you lies.
Fear is hidden in the shadows around
Sneaking close with his body near the ground.
You are trapped in her methodical gaze,
For her beauty pulls forth all of your praise.
The demon, Fear, circles his prey tonight.
Standing in shadows cast by the firelight.
Fear is an assassin, his cunning quick,
Ar all of your weaknesses, he will pick.
You're caught in the game, you cannot escape,
Fear and Envy always tugging at your cape.

Jason Nance

The Wooden Watch

The watch has
  neither gold nor chrome.
The frame is made of simple dark wood.

It runs in the same useful way
Clever as can be, as any other good watch.

The watch goes tic-tock
Life goes on hour by hour
  much is pleasant,
  much is a burden,
To be truthful, all is but a charade!

We are but chameleons,
Who change from hour to hour,
  to perform duties
Required at certain moments
Thus, we have moments of rapport,
Moments of pure unadulterated joy.

But, mostly we have time to fill
With production, non-production, basic thoughts.

Time goes on, no matter what until one day
The tic-tock stops for us but, the wooden watch goes on.

Beverly Rowe

Stop The Prejudice

Black, White
Neither one is wrong or right
Take the initiative, Seize the day
Watch what you do and What you say
Because they are equal in every way
Black, White, Yellow, Red
Please take heed to what's been said
Catholic, Atheist, Protestant, Jew
What would you do if it was you?
Being avoided, judged, and hurt
Not given a chance and Treated like dirt
Sick, poor, unborn, old
Do what's right, Not what you're told
Just because they're different, Doesn't mean they're wrong
Can't they be who they are?
Can't they sing their own song?
Stop the prejudice, Start today
It's naive to think that way
Stop the prejudice.
Seize the day.

Josie Shardlow

True Love

There she goes out the door
Never to be seen like before.
Loving him was all her care.
Losing him she'll never bare.
Losing a spouse, or losing a child,
is like your heart is set on fire.

Love like that is hard to find.
Love like that is like a bind,
Like an aroma in the air,
Like a thread that will never tear,
Love like that will never fade,
even after the dead's been laid.

No more pain, but no more tomorrow.
He will wait for her in his sorrow.
Together they'll be looking from heaven above,
Hoping that I too find true love.

Dana Litzenberg

"Scruffie"

She came to me in the early spring.
never knowing the joy she'd bring.

She was hungry and scared and sickly too,
when I saw her I thought, Oh-this just won't do.

As night would fall I'd patiently wait
hoping she'd come and not be late.

And every night about the same time
I'd see her little face and she'd see mine.

I called the vet. and discussed at length
a plan of action to regain her strength.

By this time her back had patches that were bare
you could see lots of skin, but there was no hair.

So slowly I worked and won her trust
planning to do what I knew I must.

God's little critters need help sometimes
and a human is smart enough to see the signs.

With bottles in hand a dropper inside
each day her medicine I faithfully plied.

Now she's a healthy and fat little raccoon
that still comes to visit by the glow of the moon.

Janey B. Johnson

Salt Water Silence

I have looked beyond the blank faces
never to find their true source.
Unwillingly, I have been forced into your mold;
unable to melt the hard outer layer
of your thoughtless traditions.
I search with futility
for the place where we can meet one another
in perfect pain,
but all I encounter
is the emptiness of your arms.
That is why I am hidden
beyond the capacity for words
with only the music of a heart
destined to feel
in salt water silence.

Jill Wooten

The Echo of My Father

If I could tell the children of the world what would I say?
Never will you have satisfaction,
if you believe in justice, truth and courage.
Learn to speak and be heard, change what society considers normal.
Normal is the power of money, money the
power of influence... the influence of justice.
You, the children did not create the deterioration of society,
it was your fathers.
Do not accept the blame, just the challenge
the challenge to help your children.
My dear children you are the future you
have seen what has happened to society.
Children, recognize what political correctness really does.
The fore leaders of your country have not
been punished for their crimes.
Do not worship them as heroes.
Children be strong enough to love and stronger to forgive.
But children fulfill the truth, be an American.

Alice Allen

A Place We All Know

A child giggles and yells in joy with his
new little pup with floppy ears and wobbly
walk, and dad mows the thick lawn with a
red, sweaty face, and hamburgers grilling
somewhere make the neighbors check their watches
for lunch time, and mom stops weeding in the
garden to wipe her brow with the back of
her wrist, sipping from the sun-soaked iced tea
and yells something to the two little boys
with B-B guns aimed at the ground, and little
sister cries for that soft furry thing that
has lived its last day, and popcorn white clouds
lazily drift across the deep blue sky
and shadows race along the green fields, running
up and down hills and off into the
distant horizon in this time and place
we all know but give a different name.

Charlie Litton

Just An Old Man

Just an old man I knew left this world the other day.
No bands, no shouts, no fanfare, he just quietly slipped away.

Just an old man who talked endlessly of living the olden ways
of great steamships, wars, and bootlegged scotch,
reminders of by-gone days.

He lived in a small house with his small dog,
and his ailing bedridden wife.
No riches or fame, no rewards were his, just a hard, hard life.

He escaped to the solitude of his little workshop,
it helped pass the time away.
I guess he dreamed of the bridges he built,
of the days he earned his pay.
The days he worked with a pick-ax, a man couldn't get by with just talk
The cold windy days he went fishing for blues in the seas off Montauk.

Now his time has come and gone, he's gone to that promised land
still and lifeless the old man laid beneath the cold, cold sand
Just an old man slightly built, with a craggy weathered face.
It seems this testimony a little sad, but I can make a better case.
Just one grain of sand of the mortar that helped make strong the base.
Just an old man I knew and loved, made my world a better place.

Donald R. Ostrander

"Image Of a Woman"

My childhood disappearing without a trace
No clues as to where all the time is going
Slowly vanishing, becoming a memory,
All that's left is an image of a woman.

Inside and out, blossoming like a flower,
Thoughts growing and turning completely around.
Body maturing fast as never before,
All that's left is an image of a woman.

Cluttered mind full of decisions to be made,
So very confused, trying to find myself.
Slipping away is the girl within my soul,
All that's left is an image of a woman.

Apart of growing up is reaching high goals
In life, finding the right opportunities,
But never losing the true person inside.
All that's left is an image of a woman.

Becoming an adult changes my feelings,
But I'll always have the kid within my heart,
Soon there will be no more carefree thoughts and ways.
All that's left is an image of a woman!

Carolanda Bremond

Fate

I knew a man who had no friends
no enemies to fear
he had his wealth and inner self
but no one to hold dear.

I knew a man who once had dreams
goals and deeds to achieve
he had his life and inner strife
and an ace inside his sleeve.

I knew a man who had no heart
for it grew hard and cold
he cared for none, not even his son
then suddenly he was old.

I knew a man who cared not
if he would live or die
he flirted with death and God took his breath
and no one was there to cry.

Gayle Lynn Messina

Give Yourself A Chance

Nothing will change 'till you want it to.
No magic, no genies, it's all up to you.
Believe in yourself, and what you can be.
And sooner or later, you'll set yourself free.

Those walls around you weren't built in a day.
It took years of pain to get them that way.
They won't protect you, they keep you apart.
They won't let anyone into your heart.

You're tired of going through life by yourself.
But, when anyone tries, you won't let them help.
The second you sense someone's starting to care,
Those walls go up, and hide yourself there.

You weren't meant to live your life on your own.
Learn to trust someone, and bring yourself home.
You built those walls of tears and pain.
It's time to tear them down and start again.

Nothing will change 'till you want it to.
No magic, no genies, it's all up to you.
Believe in yourself, and what you can be.
And sooner or later, you'll set yourself free.

Barbara A. Bates

Promise

It has finally stopped
No more wetness, no more gloom.
The last drop has dropped,
The dark clouds make room

For the rays
Of brilliant, golden light,
After all these days
Of grayness morn till night.

Then, from a white cloud grows
A wonderful palette of bright, shining hues.
The beauty of nature truly shows
As the reds, greens, violets, and blues

Spread through the sky in a graceful arch,
And with it bring promises in each bend
To even the ants on their steady march,
To all creatures on earth life will never end.

Alexandra Ianculescu

Entrapment

So deep inside are the lines of age
No one can scarcely see
Even though I am young each year has taken
too much of a hold of me.

So deep inside is the pain of isolation,
the pain of grief and fear
We try to resolve the many conflicts, we say
by talking, but no one really hears.

So deep inside are the walls of rejection
Cemented and bolted up tight
Silence that's cold as winter day break
And still as a hot summer night.
Where do we go with our secret burdens
to a God who is loving and fair?
Each of us alone can't carry
One day's worth of worry and care.

So deep inside, so deep inside
they grow like a cancer out of control
And who can offer honest comfort
When life has taken its toll?

Jane E. Benditt

Love

Love can't be measured by a ruler or on a scale
No one can tell the depth of it
But it's deeper than a well
I can't tell when it started
Or how long it was grown
I know my love has deepened
Each year of you I've known

The things we have shared together the memory will remain
You have made my life much richer in many, many ways
Life is full of troubles
And burdens are always there

But you have made my life much better
By showing that you care

I send my love to you on this special day
For I feel that Christ my saviour
Would want it to be that way
Today is a time to show
How much we really care
Though it can't be measured
I know it stared from above.

Ernestine Russel

Spring Has Sprung

Spring has sprung! Look outside!
No one else is left inside!

Animals are out to play;
"Looks like fun," their owners say!

Kids are playing jump rope;
Do they miss the snow? NOPE!

People are shopping for swimsuits;
And thanking God they're out of their boots!

Mowing lawns and barbecuing;
That's what everyone else is doing!

When it's over and back to fall,
Everyone will want to re-live it all!

Jill Zakrzewski

Take The Time

No one notices the water of a crystal clear blue.
No one notices what love could really do.
No one notices the beauty a rose could possibly hold.
No one takes the time to watch the precious petals slowly unfold.
No one notices the delicate time in a day.
No one stops to look they just seem to turn away.
No one notices the beautiful sunset held by the sky.
No one realizes it's the end until we say good-bye
Within a couple years no one will notice how amazing this world was.
Take a moment, look around with your mind, it's unbelievable
   what it does
Don't take advantage of it, be considerate,
it's gentle as a feather
Take the time to notice it all now because nothing lasts forever.

   Jodie Beth Waysen

Friends

When you first start the journey you feel lost and alone,
no one to guide you
except people at home.
These are the people you will always love
but sometimes they just aren't enough.
You need someone who shares the feelings you share.
You need someone who will always be there.
It is not always easy to find them though,
it's like taking a long path down a dusty road.
One day when you think all is lost,
you'll see the cloud of dust disappear like a morning frost
and there before you, lo and behold
is the new found friend of which you have been told.
This journey like many others
is one that sticks there like a bird's feather.
Only time will tell you if they plan to stay
but if they choose not to, don't be afraid
for there will always be another on its way..........

   Josh McKinney

Nightmare?

I woke up today and there was darkness.
No sun, no moon, no stars.
I woke up today and there was silence.
No children laughing, no music playing. There
was no fighting, no war, no crying. Only the sound
of dead silence.

I woke up and there was no happiness, yet there
was no sadness. There was no love, yet there was no hate.

I woke up and I was all alone. No friends,
no family, no enemies, no God.

I woke up today and my dreams were gone.
The world was dark and empty. I was alone
I woke up today and everyone was dead.

   Angi Kaufman

Always On The Horizon

All signals say the future will be bright
Numerous opportunities dancing just out of reach
However somehow lost, like the sun at night
We struggle in the present while the future is still out of sight.

We wonder if it's worth it, and if we'll ever fulfill our fate
For now, to plug on and hope is all we can do
As the agony to ascertain our goals begins to accumulate
The only thing we can do is to enjoy life while we wait.

   Jason Calabrese

Untitled

No words. I can not say.
No thoughts. I can not pray.

To live or die.
Whose decision is that?
In which hands do we lay our trust?
Think for yourself. This is a must.

Sitting here waiting for something
While everything passes us by.
Why not tell the truth?
Why must we lie?

Who decides who is right or wrong?
This is everybody's world. Everyone's song.

We are all many colors I know.
Love is love. A hand is a hand.
We are nothing more
Than just a grain of sand.
So I blow.

   Chris Clenney

Storms

Thunder is always scary and frightening
Noisy and loud with sharp flashes of lightning.
The wind howls, moans, and groans
The window panes shed rainy tears
And makes you feel so alone-
But me I love to watch the storm
Love being inside,feeling safe and warm
I love sitting in my favorite nook
Curled up content, with a mystery book.
A murder most foul is what I am reading
While louder and louder, the rain
Drops are beating
Tree limbs are scratching and tapping too.
I really love storms like this, don't you?

   Betty J. Jackson

Mary Beth

The iron winter breeze cannot touch me now.
Nor can the falling snow melt upon my skin.
The suns rays of summer
I will never see again.
With sightless eyes I see no more.
My minds eye forever closed
By one crazed act so callously done.
My ears will never hear the laughter of my
Children again.
Nor their words of love.
And never will I hear the words of jealousy,
Guilt, remorse of any other feeling you once
Shared with me, or would confess to,
For upon this lonely winters day
You, so carelessly,
Sent me on my way to heaven
And sentenced yourself to hell.

   Dawn M. Williams

Sad

I am sad
Not uncontrollable crying sad
Not suicidal depressed sad
Not sad like a mother who has just lost her baby
But just rainy day sad
Sad that some things have to change
Sad that sometimes people grow apart
Sad that life is so short with so little time to say
Good-bye

   Connie Nelson

"I ... Know Not"

I know not whence ... I came
Nor understand ... It's matter
Adrift in thought ... or dream
My ponder ... which... is sadder.

Conceived am I ... From what
this gathering ... of Stars
of bonded frame ... within a linear
to loath ... so riddle marred

My concept mind ... if ... one such
as conscience dreams ... within ... a dream
Staged...upon who's labyrinth
revealing gauntlets ... of redeem

Behind wail walls ... of limit
beneath ... a tempest sky
weaved doubts ... as darkened mist
That feeds a reason ... Why?

I know not ... whence I came
Nor understand ... It's matter
I know only ... for each time ... I fell
was a thing ... so called ... a ladder

Frank Miranda

Untitled

It was more than a year ago when our paths crossed,
Not by coincidence, but by the hand of God

As sand passes through the narrow opening
of an hourglass,
People touch us one brief moment and move on

A careful look reveals several grains that
stayed behind;
These will be the visitors that share our world

We are the crystals that occupy the palm of God
in this place and time

Each one is distinctly shaped by its origin;
All alike we share His magic kingdom

How fortunate to touch another heart on
this our only journey;
Forever keep your spirit next to mine

Barbara Levine

Running Away

Fear, a "hawk," runs on the ground, ready for flight,
Not knowing or caring what it attacks in the night.

Swift and skilled this "hawk" must be,
Trying to go after whatever it sees.

Eyeing its prey, ready to attack,
Soon to have all of the food that it lacks.

Black Fear begins to descend to the ground,
To catch that small prey that it has just found.

The rat looks up, and then begins running,
Not thinking a minute how the "hawk" is cunning.

The rat runs and runs, but soon its muscles lock;
It knows right now, it's dinner for the "hawk".

The claws are revealed from this ominous beast,
Diving very quickly to catch its feast.

The timid rat keeps running, but can't remember why,
Then down from the ground it's dragged up in the sky.

This creature was picked on because it was small;
Now they all run when they hear the "hawks" call.

If the rodent used brain instead of brawn,
It might have lived to see another dawn.

Adam Cohen

Cursed

Eyes of the world oft' times look at faces unreal
Not knowing the cursed depths that are unrevealed
What demons can lurk in the soul of a man
Which can control his mind and his will command

Damn, damn these cursed friends
That sap the gold and remove the gleam
That twist and torment a heart of good
And let not the cursed be the man he should

Oh Devil, master of the foul
Is it victory always - makes you laugh with a scowl
Hell welcomes this one whose life is doomed
What other role can this man assume

Narrow world so awfully quick to condemn
Give not the chance for this being to amend
Foolish tongue's sing your songs of rebuke
Stories sown with their imagery so acute

My Deity, master of all the seeds
Is there no mercy for the lost decreed
What hope lies beyond for this sheep so black
Is there yet a light that can lead him back.

Jacques DeVere DuFour

Love at the wrong time

A young man fell in love one day
Not knowing this women would leave him a-stray
There was one thing on his mind
It was love he had to give and compassion for her to find
He knew they're feelings were strong
Too many interferences made things wrong
The young man was determined with all his strength
To show this women he could go the length
The strength was too great
Emotions ran high and they're love began to shake
Things became heightened and ended in a break
They know how they feel about one another
And one memory will spark the other
When love passes you by
It's ok to cry
Remember to keep memories alive
They will be with you for the rest of your life.

Giuseppe Delgiudice

"Halls"

Sometimes in life we walk down halls,
Not knowing what to say, think, do or believe;
Sometimes all common sense leaves our minds
And we freeze in the fear of making mistakes -
tripping, stumbling, walking too tall
Walking through shut doors; stopping too soon
Sometimes the door walks right up to our faces
And we pass it by, confident the room is just ahead
Or maybe we don't even reach the entrances we perceive
And our feet carry us on a journey of illusion
And blind us to the destination as we travel seemingly sure
And no one really knows the halls they walk in

Amber Jerome

The Sun Sets Low

The sun sets low on an average day,
nothing interferes of its way.
The wind lays down for a good night's rest.
The moon is looking at its best.
The stars twinkle oh, so bright
all upon this average night.
Just so average I declare,
for there is romance in the air.

Chara Neal

I Think You Are Gone Forever

Tears rolling down my cheek,
Not knowing what to think.
Looking at other couples walk together.
Remembering when you'd say we'd be forever.
You knew how much I loved you.
And I knew you loved me too.
Everything you'd say,
Made me feel like everything was O.K.
The words you'd say,
Everyday,
Were the words I believed,
I didn't think you'd ever leave.
I still love you more and more each day
Even though you're gone far, far away.

Jessica G. Ramos

'The Loneliest Sound'

Have you ever heard the loneliest sound?
Not the deadness of silence,
Nor the lone train whistle across the prairie.
Have you ever stood in the cold dark
Waiting for midnight and heard it echo through the trees?
Or have you listened
As its cry wafts over the guardians of stone
In the early summer?
Chilling to the bone it causes the soul to shiver,
Bringing forth memories of days gone by.
It is a symbol of sacrifice and service rendered,
The signal of another days end.
Once when I was young
It made my heart pound within me
And my breathing to still.
Now it only eats into my heart
And dampens my cheek.
Do you hear it in the flag shadowed garden?
In my mind the bugle notes resound
As I stand by my father's grave.

Gary Woods

Dead Or Alive?

Acid, cocaine, pot and pills
Nothing's like heroin for fighting chills.
Counting on tomorrow, will it be the same?
Remembering your address, phone number and name.
Walking the streets alone is dangerous for you
Never knowing what your mind is going to make you do.
Times are hard, money is too
Stealing from your best friend is easy for you.
Laugh at me once more
Don't put it aside to save
The end has come so soon
You've already dug your grave......

Donna Marie Sharp

Lethal Injection

I thought we could be friends and nothing more.
Now I'm finding the relationship's core.
Talking to you I find that you're sweet,
Oh how I longed for the day we could meet.
But what if our relationship is a quitter?
Would our friendship last or would it grow bitter?
Sitting here thinking of you, I see that you're fine,
Oh how I'm wishing that you would be mine.
I'm sitting here wishing we had something more,
But only find that my heart could be tore.
I'm sitting here wanting you to call me and say,
"Oh how I love you, would you be mine today?"
But what do I know, there's always rejection,
Yeah, taking that would be like a lethal injection

Amanda Perez

Untitled

Where there was the pitter-patter of little feet,
Now the fluttering of angel's wings.
Where there was a soft giggle,
Now the sound of angels singing.
Where there once was a sweet little girl,
Nothing but a memory. Gone.
Nothing but silence, a silence so loud,
And a pain that rips you apart,
Tears at your flesh, erodes your very being.
Where there was a love, now a hole, an emptiness,
An emptiness that cannot be filled.
And a never-ending love for one who has gone,
Gone to be with the angels, the souls of others passed.
Where there once was a cough,
One angel is breathing quietly.
Where there once was a body ravaged by disease,
A peace now exists. Where there was pain,
Now nothing but joy. Amidst all this pain,
The sorrow, the grief,
One angel is singing joyfully.

Jennifer S. French

AIDS

Once a red rose standing tall
Now you're sick and the petals begin to fall
Now you're sick all you can hear is a silent tick
People treat you like a weed
But you're not a weed you're still a rose that will grow and grow
You may feel like you're all alone
But I still care for you and love you so
Once a rose no longer there
Words couldn't describe how much I cared
You have left me all alone
No longer a rose all the petals have fallen
The ticking has ended
You're no longer alone
No longer in pain
No longer in sorrow
All I can think of is gone forever
But you know that I will always remember

Gillian Hoffman

Wake Me Not

Yonder days are fast receding as part of my memory and
Oblivion, reverberating in the channels of eternal time,
Ubiquitous through an irreversible process of communion,
Sharing this mundane world and the heavens sublime.

I've fallen asleep - the world of my dream's so sweet,
Savoring the serene beauty so charming and soothing.
Wake me not! Let me wander through the soft, cadent realm of
Metaphysics replete with good not evil, love not loathing.

Wake me not! The dream's brought me my memories of distant
Moments when I strolled on the shores of the Danube River,
Gracefully meandering through the green meadows of Bavaria,
Reciting poems with nostalgic passion in an intense fever;

When in the mountains I stopped to praise an edelweiss,
So pretty a sight, I gazed and gazed with a sense so divine;
And, when I watched the little girl kissing her baby brother
With so much love, transforming tears to smiling sunshine.

Wake me not from my reverie, lest I miss the fragrance,
The grace, the beauty, and most of all, the love bona fide,
Needed to comfort my maimed brother in pain and to kiss my
Sister in tears - to save this world, to redeem our pride.

Jerry Chowdhury

Song Of Life

Quiet, faint and faraway…. like the rumble
of a distant storm beyond the horizon…
Even, persistent, like a cool spring rain,
comes the sound of the past fading, the future approaching.
Definite and determined, louder and closer…
a hypnotic feeling engages.
There is a message in this magic.
Louder still, surrounding me,
bringing together the earth, the sky… and I,
all with a common heartbeat.
My attention is commanded by forces of nature.
As lightening strikes and thunder crashes,
the Spirits enter in,
and I…to the beat of a different drummer,
have a secret time now,
to sing the songs of life.

Jacques La Batte

Long Lost Lover

I sit on my bed, thinking of you,
of all our moments together in the past.
   Remembering everything and how I wished
it would all last.
   I listen to the pitter, patter of the
raindrops outside.
   It brings back memories and I just
suddenly broke down and cried.
   Oh please, my long lost lover come
back to me.
   I know if you did we could make it work,
because in my heart I know it is meant to be.

Jennifer Wilcott

Ancient Pain

Ah! the sweet sensation
  of ancient pain the only feeling unconfined
   echoes throughout man made time
  reliving woes raped into raving
    wanting revenge
    redone over again and again
    despite changes far more worse since then
and so what a shame

Come laugh and play
within the heartless streets
survive by any means
   not a game to forsake
flesh hooked daze

Come laugh and play
within the ghost tank
we're going somewhere
   we've been before
ancient pain

Brian K. Hales

The Puppet

   I'm a puppet with many strings, I'm a dancer
of forgotten and broken dreams. My masters control their
selfish demands by pulling the strings to smile and dance.
I put on a show they want and crave, I gave them power,
respect and praise. I serve them their hungry and commanding
needs, I bow down to their heavenly and evil scheme's.
I try to paint a smile on my wooden face of hate, but
instead I paint the tears of sadness that won't erase.
There is no way to escape these strings, I'll just dance
forever, I'll dance to please.

Jaime M. Surgent

Treasured Memories

My thoughts drift back to a warm summer day
of childhood friends from days gone by
Times of innocence that slowly drift away
How friendships were created and promises made
Bonds that were strengthened only to fade
Memories of good times protected to last
Memories of sorrow better left in the past
Lifetime reflections how fresh they all seem
With pictures that tell of glory day dreams
But to reach for past times should never be done
for as one chapter closes another's begun
Each moment in time is captured then gone
with yesterday's brilliance passing like dawn
As pages are turned, my youth slips away
…becoming moments to treasure
for I'll always remember that warm summer day.

John J. Takala

For Jerry

My life has been full of troubles, like any young man's,
of crumbling dreams and disastrous plans.
But now looking back on my life here today
I realize I'm lucky things turned out this way.
Yes, fortunate for my broken dreams and ambitions,
for those times in my life filled with stubborn convictions.
It was during those moments when I turned to a friend,
and I felt safe and secure and could face the world once again.

I was given the courage and the strength to go on,
I knew it was okay to have a friend to lean on.
I am different than the boy I was in the past
because of those dark moments in life that never did last.
I am stronger, more confident, more self-assured
because of those smiles, the hugs, those sincere caring words.
Yes I am grateful for those moments of strife and despair
for it was those times in my life when I knew someone cared.

Tragedy has brought me a treasure both precious and rare;
to learn from mistakes and value the friendship I share.
All I can offer in return for all that you've done
is my life-long friendship to you with undying love.

James Shehy

Infinity, Silent As Prayer

Standing on the history
   of dew and dust—
he cried out in wonder
at the brush stroke of sunrise sweeping
wild orchids and parrots.

Thunder at sunset—
   a scream-
a silvery streak passed through life and earth.
The stinging capillaries pain,
   spines of lightning turning in the brain.

Burning teardrops cauterize
   the eyeball tissue and blossoms.

Infinity suspends from the skies—
   silent—-
   silent as prayer.

Emma Crobaugh

Alone I Weep

I have no real memories in my loneliness
Of familial ties of a sibling love
My heart grieves as though I had and lost
Even the imagined specters of the tapestry I wove
Of evening playmates, pillow fights, shared toys
Of whispered secrets, children promises and joys
Envious was I of all my friends
Who had those to come home to at day's ends
The cardboard, wooden, and lifeless dolls were my charm
As playmates in my quiet room soothing and warm
I a lonely only had but make believe and fantasies
My parents tried but the pain they could not ease
And now as I'm older I weep still.
I once again need those imagined specters
Of a brother or sister once but conjectures
Now more than ever I need to smile and feel
The long ago memories though they are not real.

Irene Pockoski

Your Earth

Your child brown eyes
Of fresh new ground earth
Gives my sky blue eyes
A ground to lay my hands on.

I kiss your eyelids and whisper my love (the wind)
Across your eyelashes.
I see meadows and fields
Of daisies and morning glories.
Don't forget the flutterbys.
I want to be a part of your world
And to feel your earth on my cheeks.
Smelling your rain
Your sun
And your life.

Jane Hicksenhytzer

My Walk With Jesus

O'Jesus, As I walk with you, down the path
of Galilee,I see you healing the sick,
forgiving sinners and raising the dead.

Your hope and love reaches to those who were
outcast without none, you redeemed them.
As I walk down the lonely path of galilee,
I came upon three crosses and the middle one
was the cross I saw you hanging on.

That morning as I was walking down the path,
the sun sent a golden shaft through the clouds,
to rest upon the tomb where you were laid,
I went down to look inside, I saw it was empty,
for you had risen, as you said you would.

Now my hope was at, its highest
for now I see you sitting at the right hand of God
On his throne, sending the holy spirit down
to guide the souls you died to redeem.
All the days of my life, I will continue to walk with you

Emogene Fears

"The Beauty of The Soul"

Each one has had a world of their own,
Of happiness, the warm blush of its dawn,
And also the shadows; the reality of sadness.
There are many roses I haven't smelled.
Many roads, I have yet to tread upon,
To fully experience a loveliness,
That rested deep within your heart and soul.
Yes, my dearest "Mary",
That even, at least in memories,
Your internal beauty will glow and never fade.
So long, as God grants me breath,
Your memory gives me life,
The spiritual life for you and me.
When God calls me forth, this, I truly know,
I shall gently touch your face,
And feel the spiritual warmth of your embrace.
And truly understand more fully the glow,
The silent beauty of your soul,
When the cup of life; at last I drain,
I shall have you; to comfort this undying pain.

Henry Camacho

The Other Side Of Life

What lies on the other side
Of life? Is it as beautiful
As our minds, read and decide
It is, or has it been a wonderful
Image, that can only be instilled,
When all else fails, to build up our faith
In God? No, it is for real, and filled
With glory! God's Word says, "the wait
will be worth it all, when our day
comes." What we hear on this earth,
About, 'the other side of life'; will give way,
To the real thing, and give us an upper berth,
Prepared by Him, for all eternity,
On 'the other side of life', reserved,
In beauty and longevity.

Eva M. Roy

Demon In The Bottle

The house of a frightened child is not a house filled with happiness,
of sounds of laughter from gleeful children.

Children large and small quiver with fear - shrouded by the blanket
of an alcoholic's rage.

In a hell-like cavern, the devil's tomb. The house of a frightened child.

A child of God trapped in the depths of hell wades through empty
bottles, waiting for the red haze of sunset to stop another day in
hell. A day spent with the demon.

In a hell-like cavern, the devil's tomb. The house of a frightened child.

Daylight lingers on the horizon, sunrise begins a brand new day.
Yellow shines the sun on the child's face, the color of caution.

In the hell-like cavern, the devil's tomb. The house of a frightened
child.

Candace K. Kuhn

Shadowed Afternoon

November's silken fingers stroked his taut body with a biting chill,
  of the oncoming winter.
His spongy wool cloak absorbed the thick, glutinous solitude
  of a vacant, impending dusk.
A quiet sense of relaxed confusion washed over his thoughts
  blurring together like the cold tones of the scene.
His hair flows gray in the crisp breeze
  while his eyes take the same lifeless shade, cold and harsh,
  yet a beginning at the end of some duty awaited closure,
  like the emergence of the new winter.
The shadows ignore him as if he were an intruding stranger,
  but soon recognize and welcome the kindred, tortured soul.
Choking and wheezing in a helpless whisper of loneliness,
  the trees twist their crooked bodies around the closing
  afternoon scene, trapping the darkness and refusing an
  entrance from the outcast light.
At the end of the trail, he is gone from the earth and reborn
  into a fresh sense of renewal,
  free from the past and eagerly awaiting a hopeful future,
  a beginning at the end, like the emergence of the new winter.

    Brad Simpson

Serpents' Tongues

Do not heed the poisons
of the serpents' jealous tongues;
with their wicked words
like a knife they try to plunge.

When what they've always longed for
cannot be obtained.
They'll lash out with their jealous words
and feel that they have gained.

With hopes you'll have a keen eye
that will see beyond their words;
by using your best judgement
and let your inner voice be heard.

    Dianne McClarin

Untitled

Life and death on the chess board
of the sorceress magic dream.

Magic smoke shifting the world
of the fire spirit.

Seek and find your own magic
in the cave of mother wisdom.

Man feeding off woman's love.
Cave of wisdom in my child's mind.
Cave of forever lost in eternity mind child.

Come in the wilderness of the night sky.
You are invited to walk on the star bridge to the Milky Way.

Worries of time
tracking star in a vision quest
magical omens
mystical events
in the ageless past.

    Betty Noah Flores

Can You Feel The Love

Can you feel the warmth between us? It is the heat of our
offspring it is a very powerful child that we call love. And
our emotions are its only toys can you feel the happiness?
The light glow coming from your heart you can laugh now we can

both laugh until the fun is gone a tear rolls down your cheek
Can you feel the sadness? Our teardrops combine in one puddle
As we sense the pain the glow dims from your heart. What is
happening now? Neither of us know can you feel the fear? An

empty space at the bottom of your stomach will it ever go away?
The feeling rises It goes straight to your head and we start to
shout can you feel the anger? The rage is uncontrollable. The
toys are all scattered in a burning fog, our lips collide You

feel the dampness between your legs We make unforgettable love
can you feel the passion? The child is asleep as you taste
the smoke what do you feel? Do you feel content, as the child

wakes and looks for his toys again?

    Christopher W. Williams

My Mind Leaves My Body

Sometimes my mind leaves my body,
Oh but don't you worry
All it does is catch the first flight to glory
And walk along heavens highways.
I look through the windows of the stores up there,
And I see bits and pieces of my life down there.

Sometime my mind leaves my body,
But don't you fret.
All it does is flying the sky, on the wings of an
eagle, way, way, up above,
And when it return, I'm always alright, eager
for another flight.

Sometimes my mind leaves my body,
But don't you lose any sleep,
Because it's really just a common sort of thing,
It's really nice when you've got the key
To time and to eternity

    Joseph E. Kendrick

Untitled

The soul of Love lives on in sadness
Oh, Sadness, sweet Love's repose
Live on, though clothed in paradoxical gladness
As we go forth to build anew our hearth
In a faraway vale of Mother Earth.

As we take leave of this, our home and friends
You will always be a source of courage
As we face new problems and for
Former losses make amends
Now is the time our heartfelt adieus to say
And wish you all the best of luck till another day.

So, best wishes and our love be all for gain
God be with you till we meet again.

    Henry J. Wolf

HERO Frigate CONSTELLATION

Composed 1953; Rewritten 1994

The Shrine of America Navy's past wars ENDEAVORS!
Oldest Warship on the Seven Seas and the Four Winds;
Those battles won our full Attentions; nation Honors;
Up-standing Moral Values with the divine SPIRIT Wins!

At Charlestown in Massachusetts; "Aye, be Alarmed: Mates!"
Contrary the past glossary and the active sailors Gallery.
The Ship-shape service of glory of Four Wars; Seas Waits.
Pioneering Divine Spirit of God, Jesus on way to Calvary!

Frigate Constellation; T's be now useless; T's be Wide Seas.
The Spirit of a Fighting Vessel sit ungracefully at Peace.
The past Battles has been won; Except one; Davy Jones LOCKER: WE!
The HULL; my BODY: is Rotting; Blunderingly: Maybe Life
RELEASE!

Human Being indifference—that may sink frigate Constellation.
That arc my Abasement and Sentiment; fame to shame; BATTLE
stations.
"Aye: AYE" Be ALARMED—man the Battle stations; RESTORATION.
Let sponsor to restore; once the America Greatness—Constellation.

    THE LOCKER—Well; Davy Jones
DAVY's LOCKER—Not THIS TIME—JONES!
    Howard Wendell Raleigh

Our Life

What more can you ask for
On a day like this?
The sun shining through a fine, fine mist.

Have you ever enjoyed a day like this before
What more can we ask for
In this life of ours?

The Lord has blest our lives, mine and yours
Like never before

We were both lonely people, on the brink of despair
He sent you my way and said "Tarry there"
We talked and talked, laughed and loved
Both knowing the blessings sent from above
Later we married, made our families into one
Our feelings were, the Lord said "Well done"
Our troubles were many, the row rough to hoe
We are rich but not rolling in dough
Our riches come from knowing the Lord
Has blest our lives like nothing before.

    Joyce White

Hell Rider

This hell rider rides across the earth and through the skies,
on his powerful black steed,
He carries out his eternal creed,
For his horse is named death, and creed is to bleed,
All humanity of their loyalty, of their God, and to their
country, for his driven by a force of a hell fired course,
This hell rider knows each and every one of his foes,
For he has many loyal subjects wherever he goes,
He's Lucifer's main man punishing the earth whenever he can,
This hellrider has a fiery red beard and bloody dam fierce eyes
And the beast he rides is a massive black beast,
That quakes the earth and thunder the skies whenever he rides,
But these two hell warriors have many disguises,
He could be a drug dealer or a crooked politician or even
some crazy old superstition, he could be that lady who lays
down for a price, or even the I.R.S. who taxes us twice,
or anything that makes you compromise,
your only hope is to know where you go,
Before the hell rider rides and you don't know.

    James A. Partch

Life's A Journey

From the cradle to the grave on life's journey I must be brave
   On bended knees I pray Lord remind me of yesterdays
   and just where I'd be without your grace to cover me
Your spirit you gave to lead me from the cradle to the grave

   Life's a journey all must make not knowing the final fate
     Somewhere in this time a choice I will find
     In the midst of the road is a fork I am told
   Which road I do choose decides if I win or lose

From the cradle to the grave on life's journey I must be brave
   On bended knees I pray Lord reminded me of yesterdays
   And just where I'd be without your grace to cover me
Your spirit you gave to lead me from the cradle to the grave

When my time comes to an end where eternal life I'll spend
   Burning in the fire or flying higher and higher
   The victory over sin's been won by the blood of God's dear son
To the cross Christ did go so God's love he could show

From the cradle to the grave on life's journey I must be brave
   On bended knees I pray Lord remind me of yesterdays
   And just where I'd be without your grace to cover me
Your spirit you gave to lead me from the cradle to the grave
    Cissy Estes

Mother

I write to you sweet Mother,
on this your day of days
to tell you in my own way
why my love just stays and stays;

I know that you're the best thing
that's ever happened to me,
if you hadn't been my mother
I don't know where I'd be;

You might get some presents
even a flower or two,
but when you open my gift,
you'll find my heart so true;

Your strength and love have kept me going
through all life's veil of tears,
and I hope God let's me keep you
for many, many years.

    Celia Bolin

Flashback

He pauses, there, eyes gazing far
   On what his contemplation?
I call his name, he answers not
   So deep his concentration.

That curly hair, eyes of brown,
An impish smile, a sometimes frown.

A flashback to another year,
   Another child we hold so dear
Curls all bouncy, singing, swinging,
   When deep in thought, that look so winning.
I'm lost in reminiscing, and startled now I see
   Him trotting off to sing and swing,
So like his mom, our grandson, three.

    Joan M. H. Frey

Once Again

Night falls upon this town once again.
Once again gunshots ring out in your ears.
Once again you smell the smell of alcohol.
Once again you fight for your life,
  as you walk down the street.
Then one day something happens and
  you never hear gunshots in the night.
You never smell the smell of alcohol
Never again do you feel the feel of terror.
Never again do you fight for your life
  as you walk down the street.
Never again will you think or feel
  these things.
For you were caught right in the middle
  of some childish game!

    Desiree Alcorn

White Rose

I strolled through an endless heath of posies
once, and sharply spotted one willowy rose
brimming with the crimson beauty one sees
in her petals, dancing in the wind's blows.
Unlike the flock of posies, overworn,
her sweet scent deliciously numbed my wit
so that I did not even feel her thorns
burrowing through my naked fingertips
which saved her from those suffocating weeds.
Once my grip loosed, she blew out of my hand;
those spaded thistles shredded skin that bleeds
to this day...it aches even to hold sand!
  Today, a white rose I love begs my touch,
  yet I dread grasping the pain just as much.

    Jesse Fewell

Why?

    A twelve year old girl lies on the street.
    Once had a home, but was daily beat...Why?

A little boy to weak to move to dehydrated to cry.
He has lost his strength, everyone around him knows he will
        die...Why?

A young girl speaking to herself says "I didn't think it could
        happen to me."
She didn't think that just one unprotected time could give her
        H.I.V. ...Why?

    Another young boy thinking he could never belong,
ends it all in just one shot so he'll no longer be wrong...Why?

    Each day people die, each people they wish they would.
Each day people do good, and others only wish they could...Why?

    People say you can change the world, that's not true.
    The only thing you can personally change, is you.

      Make yourself love, and make yourself care.
      Make yourself hope and make yourself share.

      As pretty as the winter snow and summer doves,
    are the sparkle in the eyes of someone who loves.

Danielle Drewisch

The Tears of Watschnadse

They run in fresh garments, each Sunday for
power, to His holy altar, to darken his hour.
They walk in the shadow of His holy name,
But their hunger and thirst is for power and
fame. They raise mental giants of infinite
power, but what good if they ruin all our
beautiful flowers.

    Joseph Coyle

Starving Men

When I was gay, I couldn't kiss her lips.

They would never allow me to touch her.
Once I was even abolished for having brown eyes.
She had brown eyes.

When I was gay, we had to walk together
with folded, melting skin so the black,
narrow eyes of the dead could see us,
They wanted to live with us in their
creamy, razored forest.

He laughed at them, but I never could.
I pretend well.

When I was grey, I couldn't kiss her lips.
The trees are beautiful here, sweet brown
fingers dangling from their smiles.

Thank you for internal suicide.
He will always be my man,
my man.

    Greg Gordon

Yours Is A Happy House

Yours is a happy house for you will know
Once you have stepped inside. Faces will show
that sort of happiness none can disguise - it's
in the smile of the lips and the eyes.
Is yours a happy House? Yes, if love here
makes its abiding and dwells year by year....
Love's quiet presence is sensed and is heard
in helpfulness, kindness and courteous words.
Is yours a happy House? Yes, if so be - somebody
prays in it. Prayer secretly - sweetens and
brightens wherever it's said - and calls a
blessing on every head.

    Gillian E. Ballard

Conditional Love

I'm feeling kinda lonely, I'm feeling kinda only
One by myself, no shoulder to cry on
One more hit, just to get high on,
  life not goin' the way I want it
Always driftin' backwards never can I show it
  my love encased, my anger embraced
To those fools who try and keep up in the race
  for last, always being passed
Never inching further, just dancing on glass
  my tears turn to streams my tasks all but dreams
Feeling as though I'm coming unglued at the seams
No one really cares, and no one really sees
The hurt in my eyes, I've lost my only key
To get back in the door the door to reality,
  locked out from the world, losing sensuality
Always trying to find you in a maze of confusion
  the wickedness of the world, altering an illusion
Coming so close, yet so far, sometimes I wanna
  reach you like grabbing a star
  from a sky of remorse, my thought change course

    Joshua Hunt

God

I can ask not to be hungry and I am not.
Or I can ask not to be cold and I am not.
Your promise is not of the flesh but of the soul.
It takes a lifetime to know this,
and if you are not there, we are lost souls.

    Betty Shenkman

Shades Of Love

Everlasting love is hard to find but once in a lifetime,
one comes into your life who would make the world stand up,
and take notice. My world moves around you my love.
Let the thunder announce our love through the corridors,
of time may our love be cast upon the golden scroll
so our love will never die nor be forgotten my love.
Love is like a flower in full bloom and, my love, you
make me bloom with a feeling of love and joy that only,
we two can share. We have our own place in the sun where,
only we two can enter and taste our love and fruits of,
joy forever my love.

Calvert C. Gray

Love And Hate

Love met Hate,
one day on the street
but didn't know who she was.
Love said deeply, "Will you lunch with me?"
Hate said flirtingly, "Of course, kind sir.
I would be honored."
So they entered a restaurant
and were quite a scene, for Love was blind
and still didn't know that he was dating Hate.
People turned and stared at
the tall, muscular Love, walking
with the dainty, seductive Hate.
And no one was very surprised
when next day by the pier,
Love was found dead,
and Hate was seen laughing.

Jessica D. Adams

Sleeping Beauty

Sleeping beauty,
One hundred years is too long to wait for a kiss.
And if one is not forthcoming,
Do you shed a tear or silently cry in your despair?

Why do you wait for one man?
What has he, for you to forsake all others?
Why does he alone hold the power to wake poor beauty?
Is he worthy?

Darling beauty,
There you sleep, unkissed, and you might sleep forever.
With all your thoughts and secrets.
Untouched, unloved, unworthy, in…secure.

Andrea Jee

Listen

'Give me liberty or give me death!' a wise man said
"One small step for man" said another
To these we listen still, as time passes.
But the ones we need to listen to are ignored.
Children cry out in the night of pain and
hunger, and we build useless satellites.
    Why?
Countries split up, people starve,
and we launch unnecessary bombs.
    Why?
People are looked in Civil War with
nothing to do, but wait to be bombed,
and we spend our money on cellular phones.
    Why?
Perhaps we shall never know.
Perhaps we should listen.

Amanda Pavlick

"Why?"

She was such a grand neighbor,
One who had gained high favor
With all who knew her,
A woman whose every kind deed
(And there were so many)
Seemed happily always to renew her.

Now we lift tear-streaked faces to the sky
And mournfully we cry
How could it be — and why, why, why,
That one fine morning
When she opened her door on the new day
To drink in the beauty of God's world
And to pray,

The boy next door stepped out too,
But not for a wish to admire the view.
Cradled in his arms was a gun;
Slowly, stealthily he raised it, took careful aim,
Squeezed the trigger
(Just for fun, he later said)
And blasted her into eternity!

Ida Simpson

My Desire

As we grow older we see people die,
Ones we loved so, and then we cry
And wonder inside our hearts if we,
Could have done more, My God, to tell them of Thee.

Open the door oh, God, to my heart,
And help me to do my part
To help others and plant the seed
So they will come to Thee and have no need.

If we don't tell them your blessed way,
They may never find eternal day.
Ah, Lord, I'm crying inside of me
And seeking guidance oh, God, of Thee.

I see my neighbors, my friends even family
All so far, my God, from Thee
I'm only an elder; many years have gone,
But inside of me, still I long
To see all the earth that my path crosses
To find Thee as once I did.
Oh, Lord guide me.

Iva Foreman

Imagine

Can you imagine the darkness, on a moonless night at sea,
only a canopy of stars above, the wind blowing unbound and free,
whistling through the rigging, filling your billowing sail,
pushing toward your destiny, no thought to fail,
your bow slicing the water, amazingly smooth as glass,
a perfect picture shattered, by your wake as you pass.

No harm is done, the sea doesn't care,
it recovers quickly, and is brutally fair;
your life is your ship, the world is your sea,
and the wind that pushes you, is your own destiny.

Be careful, calm, and cool, spontaneity has its place,
if you watch and learn from others, you'll never go far off base,
so be spontaneous, but use your brain,
and save yourself, a world of pain.

John P. Wohlwend

With-Out Him

Feeling so much loneliness and emptiness
Only having long lasting days of sadness.
With only a shadow of my loved one to stand beside,
With a perfect image of him, that I try to put aside.
When you look into eyes you'll be able to see,
That with out him I stand nothing to be.

I wish I could go back in time again,
So I could be happy and stop all my pain.

I need something to mend my heart,
To make it as good as new now that we're apart.
But I do remember all the moments we had,
During those days I was hardly even sad.

He always filled my head with all his lies,
The day he told me the truths I wanted to die.
I wish I wouldn't have lived that day,
So I wouldn't have herd all he had to say.
Now I know why he never looked me in the eye,
Not even the last day when he said goodbye...

Elisabeth Duenas

Love's Last Night

I lie quiet beside your tortured broken body
only the candle glows.
Hour after sleepless hour
I memorize your face -
proud brow, roman nose,
sensuous lips I love to kiss -
now trembling, whispering in pain
"when is my time to die?"
I lie in the shadow of your face.
I can not answer.
Even now I feel the loneliness to come.
The candle burns low.

Florence M. Hustedt

Untitled

Do we really know this place called earth.
or do we think we know it.
Why do we accuse innocents,
are we afraid.
If we're afraid, what are we afraid of?
I wish I knew because...
The Hurt.
Do we know pain,
or does the pain know us.
Can we heal what we did,
to them, their pain, their hurt.
Why did we? How could we? Why should we?
I call this poem black pain.

Danielle Ouellette

Abuse On The Loose

Do you hug your child, and say they're special too?
Or do you punch and kick them, until they're black and blue?
The problem's not the child, they're special through and through.
Perhaps it has never occurred, the problem could be you.
People often wonder, what's happened to our youth.
They'd rather blame drugs and gangs, than ever face the truth.
Do you hug your child, and say they're special too?
Or do you punch and kick them, until they're black and blue?
Often times we live our lives, with secrets deep inside.
Because the pain is so severe, it's the only way to survive.
What happens when you're a child, impacts you your whole life long.
Don't let the pain you suffer, keep you from being strong.
Do you hug your child, and say they're special too?
Or do you punch and kick them, until they're black and blue?

Cecil A. Ballor

I Looked Up The Word Persipherous

What's in a name?
or the distant colors of my fathers' eyes
that fade on me like his voice.

Or the peripheral banter
of fatuous knights with rusty armor
to hide wounds untreated.

I am inside now
and the correlation is not replete.
such feats in laughter, thought complete,

are welcomed then like treasured friends.
and we cast the extra to winds
that blow upon my brow and yours.

Exceptions made for you to me
could puncture hard the surface primed
insidious and filter free.

And judgments made in truthful stares
may fall and fail
like my fathers' cares.

Brian John Howe

'Ageless Love'

When we first met we didn't know how deep our love would grow
or the mountains there that we would have to climb
But with the innocence of youth we went on to find the truth
And found a love as ageless as the hands of time.

And in the years that we've been through many heartaches,
tears and blues
In the darkest hours we've seen our true love shine.
As each new day would begin we would join right in
With love as ageless as the hands of time.

When the hands go round the bend you know we'd do it all again
And never change a thing that love has designed.
Because together we've been through a life meant for me and
you and love as ageless as the hands of time.

Cliff Seaman

Have You Ever

Have you ever seen a Black-diamond,
  Or the wondrous Apatchie Tears?
Have you ever seen the Majestic Mountains,
  Or the cool clear Mountain Streams?

Have you ever seen a Rainbow,
  With its colors, so bright and clear?
Or how about the Great-Bald-Eagle,
  Gliding on its endless sails?

Have you ever heard a Bull-frog,
  In the early summer nights?
Or how about a Whipper-will,
  With a voice so clear and bright?

Have you taken the time to smell the Roses,
  While taking your trip through life?
Or given your brother a helping hand,
  In a world so beautiful and bright?

George F. Allen

Remember Your Mammogram!

Our bodies aren't perfect; there's no guarantee.
Our health and the future we cannot foresee.
  Do your breast self-exam!
  Have a mammogram, ma'am!
Thanks to early detection, I'm now cancer-free!

Gloria B. Burnam

Individuals

We are there,
Or we think we are at that pass,
At that impasse.

Turned around the situation brightens.

We remember why we made promises to each other.

We said it was love,
And so it was.

And so it is that we believe,
Maybe in different things,
But also in each other.
James F. Skeel

Untitled

I peered into the clear horizon,
originating there were no worries or cares.
There were some awkward, undesirable forms that could float
along without mockery.
Then, there were other figures that appeared as beautiful
as if they had been chiseled by the finest sculptor.
All of these shapes could rise and fall side by side-
Yet be treated equally without proclamation of condemnation
or exultation.
No matter how calm or how turbulent-
the shapes may take on new appearances,
but they all have been from the same origin.
They may Rise and they may fall but all come to the same
end and beginning.
Amy Daniel

Just To Hold You!

When you and I are together
  Our heart bond in the mix
  of passion
        When I think about the way
        You touch me my heart melt
          Just to hold you!
    When I take times to think about
    the way you care for me
          makes me love you for more than
          I ever did before
          Just to hold you
  to give you all my love
          just to hold you
Darline Chery

Our Blue Girl

She came this way to stay awhile,
our lovely blue girl.

All her boundless joy, her love
she gave to all.
Our happy blue girl.

All the golden memories,
a treasure I shall always keep.

But when the sands of time came and had to say.
Dear Maggie, it's time to play.

Her weary head on my shoulder
her soft body in my arms
I knew it was to be.

Our little blue girl is gone now
but her spirit is here to stay.
Alice J. Hartwig

"Generations"

The hands of time turn 'round and 'round,
Our lives intertwined, inexplicably bound.

Those babes so small, precious daughter or son,
They grow up tall and off they run, little knowing,
In so many years their cheeks will sting with the very same tears....
As they let their own children go.

Through sleepless nights and childhood woes
A deeper understanding grows.
We forgive our parents their mistakes
Because we see how much it takes to raise a child of our own.

I think it not at all accidental that we must learn all things
parental, through trial and error, success and defeat.
The lessons we learn are not complete until we sit in rocking chairs,
With tones of silver in our hair, and watch our children's tearful
eyes, whose outstretched arms wave their goodbyes
To children now full grown.

The hands of time turn 'round and 'round,
Our lives intertwined, inexplicably bound.
Each generation linked to another
through the common bond of Father and Mother.
Cindy Brooks

Desert Storm

In nineteen hundred ninety-one
Our men & boys were sent into the sun

It wasn't for "relaxation"
We were there because of a confrontation

Iraqis lead by Saddam
Vowed to fight on & on

Schwarzkopf, good ole boy from home
Vowed "The best is yet to come."

Each side displayed their wares
Scuds & missiles flying in the air

This poem is short like the war,
The one we know as Desert Storm
Allyson Hurlbut

Our World In The Nineties

Famines, wars, disease without cures, UFO sightings, gang street
  fighting.
Our ozone layer's full of holes, environmentalists try gaining control.
Prisons are filled beyond their capacity,
Tornadoes are killing with high velocity.
Hurricanes maim us, many homes are destroyed,
Half of Americans are unemployed.
Medical miracles are on their way, people are healed, visions revealed,
  blind eyes are opened today.
Mysteries are solved, treasures unearthed,
  infertile women are now giving birth.
Communities join together when tragedy strikes,
  heroes come together to save people's lives.
Donors donate organs for those in great need, so others can live life
  to the fullest, succeed.
Some people return from death and Heaven's pearly door,
  telling others about seeing Jesus, angels and more.
We look around us and get depressed and sad,
  fill up with agitation, get frustrated and mad.
It's best living every day thankful for each one we are given.
If we all lived like this, what a great world we could live in.
Brenda Grubbs

One Moment

If I had only one moment...
Out of all the rest...
One moment out of a lifetime...
What would I cherish the best?...
It would not be difficult to choose...
For that one moment... in memory...
I will never lose... the hour... the day... that one moment...
I will never forget... for it was more beautiful...
Then any summer sunset... its beauty...
In words I can not describe...
The love I felt down deep inside...
A feeling that I could never hide.
There have been moments of sadness...
And moments of regret...
But there is only one moment...
That I will never forget...
There have been moments that have made me happy...
And many moments that have made me sad...
But the greatest moment I have ever had...
Was that one moment when I became a dad.

Joseph Carrano

Life

Looking through the knot holes of life,
Out over all the yesterdays of strife.
Just maybe the shimmering mirrors of morrow
Will calm the many miseries of sorrow.

The day, gasping its dying breath,
Slowly pulls up the curtain of its death.
As the night begins to unfold,
Covering so many miseries, untold.

Out of the broken fences of despair,
Spreading its gloom everywhere.
Through the future's thin foggy envelop,
There rises, with morn's sun, a ray of hope.

The fluids of contentment
Begin their tingling flow,
Covering today's resentment
With a radiant glow.

Live your todays each day.
Let yesterdays go their way.
Build not your tomorrow,
On today's sad sorrow.

James E. Elam

Robins

I lie under flannel covers, warm, secure, and safe
Outside in the night the March wind howls
Blowing the snow where it will
The temperature is zero

Robins come into my mind
Robins that two balmy days ago sang under blue skies
Confident they had not come north too soon

Where are they now?
Huddled in feather blown misery, bare trees offering no shelter
I pray for them

Suddenly, I am ashamed. Robins! When the whole world suffers
Another massacre in Bosnia. Violence in the Middle East
Worshippers killed by a tornado
Crime, and drugs, and poverty daily in the news
All these demand my prayers

I cannot
It is too much to hold
My heart will break

Dear God of the fallen sparrow, forgive me
I pray for robins

Cathy Tallady

Inside Out

Something going down inside...inside out.
Outside, tonight, there are stars shining bright
Inside there is darkness and wars.
While babies sleep and lovers love, the world sleeps
And the rumors of wars continues:
The battle of soul surviving...surviving wretched toils of body.
Inside, there is chaos.
Outside, the moon is full and inviting.
The constellations bear witness, pointing a path for me tonight,
Because there are stars shining for me tonight...
Silver on white-bright to penetrate the blackness.
Inside, tonight, there are mystical moments
But outside, the milky-way gives me little time.
A measure is enough for this changeling.
So I look to the heavens for answers...
Tonight, only tonight.

Jay Carter

Honor Lane

In a mansion of mist
over a parquetry of sycamore leaves,
the quiet drips along a corridor
they call Honor Lane.
The presence of men and boys
back from the War plod on,
broken and fallen, as mere branches.
In silence and out of respect,
Mama watches their passing
and tells me to go inside
where the clock ticks.
I wait for Papa, like Mama,
as the chores always exist
to keep you warm.
Sooty days seems to make the crows cry out.
The trees hide them until they want to fly away.
The trees will not hide me
as I leave after
the branches bring Papa home.
This cage of trees leads nowhere.

Frederick Cornwell Sanders

Eagle's Wings

The clouds of death hang over your weary head.
Painful memories surface, as you think of the ones new dead.
It was only yesterday that you heard them speak of life and
love.
In the blink of an eye they're taken and linger in the
heavens above.
You can no longer hold and touch them the way you did just
the other day.
With an aching heart and tearful eyes, you continuously pray.
You beg the pain to stop and let you go. No matter how hard
you pray and cry, nothing seems to ease the ache or allow
it to slow.
You never thought something so awful would happen to the one
you love. They gave their life to our country and never gave
up when push came to shove.
Through each struggle and strife, each one gave us freedom
in exchange for their life.
As you cry your tears of heartache, the angel sings.
Up in heaven each one is flying, as free as the eagle's wings.

Angel Dawn Burnette-Champion

I Am Still Going......

Go towards you Lord
passing by that I see with my eyes
passing by all that I imagine in my mind
to be with you united closely
in my happiness in my joy
which is brighter than the sun
which is above feeling
which is the light in my darkness
which is the power in my being
which is the blessing in my illness
which is the way towards you lord
Then I go, I am still going towards you o Lord.

Irena Mierzwa

Untitled

Takes time to breath the air
Patiently quietly gasping for a moment
wetting Her lips with his tongue, feeling
the quiver inside her body, peacefully
enjoying life's great mystery what's next you have a choice

She flirting with the boys of summer
innocence drawn to unknown looks, hot
days with heat of passion, filled the
nights to ice cold showers what's next you have a choice

Running into the bedroom, slamming
the door, drops of clothes hit
the floor to change into something
more comfortable, throws back
her hair, sprinkle, her body with an elegant mist and
Runs what next you have choice

Heart & mind controlling life's every moment
Gods spiritual breath smacks open
Every soul, toying around humorously
watching, laughing at all there is darkness and there is light
what next you have a choice.

Carl Exsted

Thanks Peace Church

We're so thankful for the neighborhood church just down the road.
Peace church fills our needs when life's burdens become a load.
  Its members have provided us their offerings, given with love,
  Reminding us of the greater power which is provided from above.
We want to thank them for their words of comfort and concern
As in these times of trial more of our precious Saviour we've learned.
  Most of all, your vigilant prayers have given us strength to live;
  Because God's grace, through his Son, did He give.
So let us thank you from the depths of our hearts;
That because of your efforts, we can have a fresh start.

We have fallen many times. Our sins have often been great.
But even so, we know that hell shall not be our fate.
  For our Saviour reminds us that our sins are forgiven;
  So to live a more Christ-centered life we have striven.
Again, we thank you at Peace Church, who have given of your lives;
True servants to be, through faith and works you steadfastly try,
  To reach the world and tell that wonderful redeeming story
  Of how sinners can be saved in preparation of that final glory,
When Christ shall come and take us to our heavenly home;
Where we shall serve Him, forever more, as His very own.

John C. Austin

My Field Of Dreams

Without a shadow of a doubt,
peaceful and serene.

Stories untold, memories unfold;

Wind whistling through the pine,
its tune unknown;

Reminiscing, sweetly singing;

Happiness in the heart
echoing thoughts in the mind;

A land of illusions,
both physical and mental;

A treasure held close to my heart,
until the next time in which I enter into
my field of dreams!

Brandin J. P. Drake

Untitled

Born, long time ago,
Perhaps on a winter afternoon.
Been living longer than man-kind,
Its secrets held within the moon.

Has seen life and death in the same moments of time
As we have seen tall pines on old, dusty roads.
Can guide a lost soul through the darkest night
Carries the heaviest of burdened loads

From the east you may see a falling star
Or hear a song from ancient times
From the west you may see a light falling snow
And hear the oldest of forgotten rhymes.

It's a sparrow, a rain, a feeling, a life,
Anything imaginable to the mind.
Does not live within cold, dark loneliness,
Stays away from the selfish blind.

Exists only where love is found
And plays the music to a spiral dance
A dream that lies within us all
This is romance.

Hutton Harding

A Fable Of Sunrise Sunset

  A flower wilts in sun-driven heat
Petals puckered, brown with thirst
  As these elements meet
A friendship of Nature's world is cursed

  The first friend is the flower
She wishes to grow and find the night
  But her fun is soured
When her friend solves mystery with light

  The sun caress to much to her friend
To let her feel the darkness of the world
  This habit she cannot mend
As a flower's leaves begin to curl

  The sun shall now rise and set
So's not to make a new friend a foe
  Never will she herself let
Memories of her tragic mistake go.

Elizabeth Welteroth

Loneliness

The old woman sits alone tonight.
Pictures line the walls.
With eyes so dim she scarce can see.
She looks, and a teardrop falls.
The old gray head nods slowly. A tear rolls down her cheek.
She thinks of joys and sorrows known,
Of days now past and gone.
She remembers a home once filled with love,
The wonderful yesterdays, now only picture she scarce can see,
and memories of long ago days.

Hands were never idle - always things to do.
Some one to say "I Love You", someone with whom to share.
Now she sits alone with memories, and no one seems to care.
The old one dreams of days long past.
Dreams are such wonderful, fragile things,
Like bubbles that never last,
Gone, and not even a shadow cast,
She thanks God for the strength He gave,
She prays for the ones who are gone.
She thanks him for the yesterdays, but now she sits alone.

Glendora Hamlet

I'll Be Back

Key in hand, I start the car
Placed in drive, I accelerate
The pavement rolls under me
While clouds roll over me
It's not raining
My windshield is covered with water
There are no stops
There are no curves
Am I sliding?
Or is it that I'm in a barrel on a water fall
Will I land on ragging waters, or a calm stream?
Reaching out to stop this slide
There's no one there
I can't turn my head
I know I'll be back

Ignacio C. Gonzales

Lil Golden Bunny Girl

Lil Golden Bunny girl, so precious to me,
Playing on the swings so eagerly,
With laughter in her heart, so precious she is,
To here pitter patter where ever she goes,
Running in circles rolling on the ground,
Jumping in the leaves as they
fall toward the ground,
Seeing the smile upon her lil face,
Such joy she brings to me with such grace,
Lil Golden laughter that fills the air,
I know my lil Golden Bunny Girl
will always be happy anywhere.

Joy Madison

God's Gift

I've never seen the morning mist,
or felt a soft butterfly kiss.
I don't know
about rain or snow;

Or birthday balloons
on a sunny afternoon.
I've never tasted an ice cream cone.
Or heard the ring of a telephone.

I don't know that the grass is green.
To me, the whole world is unseen.
So, gently hold, my tiny hand
and guide me through God's beautiful land.

Delayne McKinley

Artful Conversation

If I say it rather poorly and it comes out sounding sad,
Please don't jump to quick conclusions and I beg you, don't get mad.
For I meant to send a message with a meaning just for you;
I had visioned it in yellow, but it dribbled into blue.

In my heart lie good intentions on a pallet of repose,
But in drawing your attention, my delivery of them slows.
So they rise a little tarnished, they don't say what I've just said;
They present themselves in purple, what I meant to say in red.

It would seem the way I say things that I'm slow or not too bright;
It all started out as perfect, then, it sounded not quite right.
Where's the stroke that I am missing that connects the thought and word;
What dilutes my truest colors that they come out pale and blurred?

I suppose I'm not the artist that I'd really like to be;
In the brush strokes of my portraits, hide the lines for you to see.
So I'll sketch my precious pictures but I'll stay with black and white
And rely on you to color in my masterpiece just right.

I'm excited 'round the prospect of this different point of view;
Toward a truer reproduction of my messages to you.
Now I'm happy in the knowledge that my talents aren't full grown;
I will sketch......and you will color......and I'll never paint alone!

Joan Rose Rider

To A New Year

Last month we walked along the shore
Plucking husks, spent grasses,
Ghost of things.
Planning to form them all into a wreath
To mourn, to mark, to celebrate,
The passing of the year.

It was dusk, we were lulled
By the roar of winter waves. We watched
As lights came on across the bay,
And we in turn were watched
By a Western Gull,
Perched solitary on our sill.

Then you flew, pursuing the sun,
Into a land of numberless
Arms and legs, bangle bracelets, finger rings.
On your return you caught instead
A single cup of silver moon,
And blows of golden crocus bloom.

Eloise Van Tassel

The Wu Wei Way

Each vital spirit of life falls blocked and broken as the pushing
    power of arrogance forces its will where it doesn't belong.

The world of ever changing motion shall soon come full cycle.

Like the quiet ebb-and-flow of the ocean, one person begins.
         One person begins.

Drawing on the breath of stillness energy begins to flow.

It cuts through rough edges like a pebble filled stream.

  With a balance of opposition, others begin to see.
The pushing power of arrogance begins to loose its force.
The spirit starts to heal as life is blocked no more.

Judy Hayes

-What We Really Are-

We grow as flowers
   Precious graceful and unique
Growing across the earth
   As if an angel scattered us as seeds
We each grew from different roots
   Yet all the same
Accepting the differences as a part
   of life not as a consequence
Learning how to be a part of
   nature and its well being
We are guided and protected
   by the water of the Holy Ghost
     Spirit of the soil and the sun of God.

   Ju Lee Kim

Untitled

i suffocate in preferred isolation
   preferred on account of the deprivations
     those deprivations that
       made possible
         the preferring of isolation

i choose isolation over suffocation
   suffocation from such provisions
    which aren't pro visions at all

i dwindle in these visions
   bitter visions from lack of cite
    but if they'd just let me in
     i could admire them in my might

   geneva s. putnam

Our Hope

We may not understand God's wonderful plan.
Proving His love when He became man,
By taking our place and covering our sins,
Then teaching and shaping us to be like Him.
In this world, we're born one by one,
So one by one, we'll meet His Son.
We have nothing to lose and everything to gain,
Where there'll be no more crying and no more pain.
So truly, Heaven is the place to be,
For when He comes, He'll say, "Come live with me."

   Debra Kay Cunningham

Mysteries

There he goes, causing a commotion,
Putting everything in motion,
Some people think he's a wonderful thing,
Because he cools them off during Spring

There she goes, giving the flowers a drink
So that they can grow to hear the birds sing
All the outside grows so silent and still
While she tiptoes and dances on your window sill.

There he goes, warming the world with his powerful beams
Everything is wonderful it seems.
He can make all God's creatures smile
Because they can have fun for a while.

"Who are these people?" you may ask
"These people with such powerful tasks?"
"The people that cool you off, water the flowers,
  and let the birds fly?"
The wind, rain, and sun is my only reply.

   Joy Sanetrik

Jesus

Jesus, Lord and Master born into the human
race to save us from ourselves. As an Infant
miracles were performed by the touching of
your swaddling clothes. As a little child you told
your Mother Mary, I am the son of God. As a child you knew
Judas your betrayer when he struck you on your side, the same
side the spear would be thrust into you on the cross. As you
traveled the countryside with Joseph and Mary you came upon two
robbers Titus and Dumachus. Titus convinced Dumachus not to
cause any trouble or harm to Joseph or Mary and let them pass.
Jesus turned and said to his Mother, when thirty years have
expired the Jews will crucify me. These two thieves will be on
the cross with me. Titus on my right and Dumachus on my left
and Titus shall go before me into paradise. Jesus, Lord and
Master you knew the plight of the human race before your birth.
Be forgiving of us and deliver us from our anguish. You know
the weakness of our nature better than ourselves. Be merciful
and grant us pardon for our sins.

   Arthur L. Andre

In A Day's Thought

Today will be tomorrow's past.
Rapid memories of this past and other days are only figments
  to be stored away in our minds for another day.
Most seemingly thoughts of these past days, are awkward or
  troubled and fortunately happy ones.
Pass the day's thoughts to internal keeping.
Awkward thoughts may turn astray if mirrored back, keep a
  tight lid of mouth.
Send out the word by mouth to voice these most troubled
  thoughts, for in them lies freedom for your soul.
They will fade or fascinate over time.
Radiate the happy thoughts, for you will find they match
  the brightness of the sun.
Be still my happy child, for youth never hides and laughter
  makes our thoughts lighter.
Be yourself, for tomorrow is another day to pass.

   Cassandra J. Bloedel

Blind

The smell of flowers drifts through the air,
Red roses.
A sightless person bears no handicap.
Beauty is not wasted on the blind,
It is vastly acknowledged.
Existence never taken for granted,
Things are "seen" for what they really are.
Color is precious.
Living in a black world,
Color is seen every minute of the day.
With every sound, every smell, every touch,
Color explodes within.
Imagined is what makes the sound as it happens.
Things of little importance to the visioned,
Special, extraordinary to the unseeing.
At night to feel the glare of the moon upon shoulders,
In the morning to hear the songs of the birds.
Without sight, the world is free.
People, all the same distinguished only by what lies inside.
Prejudices cease to exist.

   Jennifer Slis

Freedom

My stiff muscles scream at me, hurling insults with each step.
Relenting, I sit on a lone, decaying bench
scarred with years of graffiti and gum.
the bench no one would stoop to sit on,
I occupy
and watch a weed struggle up
between cruel cracks in the cold, hard pavement
alone and away from all he knows
his attempts crushed by careless, thoughtless
shoes of society walking steadfastly
to work or to shop or to nowhere.
I have been walking for hours
avoiding crushing the dreams of that weed.

I know how he feels.
I let my coat fall open, freezing wind pounds against my icy skin
The yet unused steel in my pocket whispers to me
"I can transport you," it says,
"far away, to golden meadows where weeds like you
grow freely, where stomping feet will never touch you again."
Smiling at its words of peace
I reach inside and caress the trigger.

Beth Luttrell

Sez Grandma

Come in and visit a while with me,
Relieve the day with my family.
They leave behind all sorts of clues
Of things they've done and things to do.

Dad made a sandwich and the counter's filled
With bread crumbs, mustard and mayonnaise spilled.
Son had coffee and there's the cup
With coffee spatters now dried up.

Grandson had a guest to play
They busied themselves most of the day
With dump trucks, boats and motor cars.
Look about you—there they are!

If I say a word—I am a nag,
So, I'll clean the house and then I'll brag,
"There's no generation gap with me,
I'm kept busy by all three."

I wouldn't have it any other way
For if each one chose to go away,
The house would be clean; I'd be alone.
God, please keep us a family; a mess and home.

Eleanor Thornesberry

EPILOGUE

for The Captain

When all is said and done:
Remember me as one who loved
Roses and raindrops,
Strawberries and springtime
Young snow on old stumps
Firelight and twilight...
Little ponds of water and miles of cresting waves!
The golden glow of broomsage...
Lichens on the fence
Moonlight on the meadow
Morning on the mountain
And You.

Barbara Oehlbeck

Adversity

When much adversity is in your life;
Remember prayer puts an end to all strife.
He'll give your peace — make you calm within;
He'll be with you until the end.
Jesus has a plan to mold and uphold.
As they mystery of God begins to unfold.
He suffered and died for you and me;
He overcame all adversity.

Johnnie Huffman

My Sister

Laying there so cold and still, all I can do is
remember the good times we have had.

I was only eight when you died, knowing you would be gone forever.

Knowing you were my sister makes me love you even more.

I don't know what to do, because you are no longer alive,
keeping my memories bottled up inside.

Having no one to talk to or tell my stories about you,
always makes me cry.

Your are only alive in the heart and souls of people who care.

People say it is better where you are,
and I do agree because now you can run free.

Someday I hope I will get to heaven to with you
and to tell you "I love you"

This ends my poems I have written about you,
but not my memories, for I will carry them with me always.

And no one will ever make me quit thinking about you.

Danielle R. Drake

Long Island

Small towns, barbed wire fences and forgotten dirt roads,
Remind me where I want to go;
Small towns have turned into small cities,
Isn't it a pity?

Right before my eyes
One by one living lakes dry up and die;
Bulldozed unmercifully the countryside screams,
With wildlife to its knees it seems.

Nothing I can say nothing I can do,
Animal graveyards instead of a zoo.
Small towns, country stores and picturesque red barns,
I hate to think someday they will all be gone.

The sound of a police car siren awakes me from my bed,
I remember when the blue jay's cry awoke me instead;
When I look out my window there are no blue jays in my view,
No owls no foxes no deer, they left this town all but a few.

The few that live here will have to be extremely discreet,
Or they will end up dead in the streets;
Small towns, old windmills and wide open fields,
Show me somehow sometimes, progress should yield.

John F. Caroleo, Jr.

Lonely Survivor

Slowly, she rides the crests of the merciless sea,
This mighty ship with its battered bow.
Who would know this ship was me
That has survived the storm, somehow?

The sails are tattered, the crew is lost;
The goliath soul nearly torn apart.
There is no need to count the cost,
The only survivor is a lonely heart.

David Kindle

Silver Ribbons

As I walk the vales gentle mysteries I see
Renewed yet changing but constantly free

There's magic in water mixed with light
Ever moving, shimmering, teasingly bright

Sparkling drops from wet stained walls
Inch towards streams that spill into falls

Dancing in the shadows leaping over rocks
I hear no voice yet each ribbon talks

Restless they wonder the crevasses of time
Giving no thought to reason or rhyme

Searching for solitude in a restful place
Silver ribbons of light soon quicken their pace

Down from the hills to the valleys below
Eager their surging, with boldness they go

Soon to reach a place shaded and deep
Found lazy and silent as if asleep

Again the light filled water stirs awake
And seeks an exit from this captive lake

John Volcic

Texas Dirt

Tumbleweeds rolling across the Texas plain
Ribbons of roads cut through the Texas dirt
   Dry, desolate land

Windmills whistling in the air of the Texas west
Sagging fences fading in the Texas fields
   Coarse, callous land

Herds of cattle cornered on a Texas ranch
Rolls of rope hanging on a Texas saddle
   Serving, sustaining land

Prairies pulsing with Texas passion and pride
Rough courage growing in the Texas ground
   Powerful, inspiring land.

Emily Collier

Untitled

   If I could reach out and touch you
right now, I would.

   If I could lift my lips to yours
for a tender yet passionate kiss, I would.
   If I could walk beside you in quiet
companionship, sit beside you and
share your life, I would.
   If I could gaze into your warm
eyes and convey my love, I would.
   If I dreams came true and I
could be with you,
   You know my darling, I would...

Georgia F. Abbuhl

This Day

What can I talk about, what can I say?
Shall I talk of the beauty of this day?
Maybe I'll tell how the sun feels so fine....
It's making a warm glow in this heart of mine.
The trees and grasses dance gently in the breeze....
Hey! The pollen for once isn't making me sneeze.
Spring is in full force, it's warm as summer.....
Look there flies a bird - looks like a hummer.
God for the joy I've gleaned from this day....
Let me forget it not, as I thankfully pray.

Phyllis Joseph

Deep Inside

A voice, deep down inside your soul,
Ripping, tearing, burning a hole.
Time will pass, but it would be too late,
For this anger cannot wait. Like a storm it envelopes you.
Hear me people—what I say is true.
It builds up till there's no room;
locking it in would be your doom.
One day the time will come when your life on earth is done.
Would you like to die without any tears?
Die without telling anyone your fears?
The clocks will chime, life will go on.
Roosters still wake at the crack of dawn.
Even if life seems so unfair,
There is still someone who will care.
Don't let your anger go untold.
Don't let it build up until you unfold.
Just let it out — let it flow like the waters.
God won't forget his sons and daughters.
So if you feel there is no one to turn to —
Don't forget - He will be there for you.

Allison Garton

Retiring Visions, Thoughts Lost, Realizations Circle Eternity

Retiring
Rising from the parched earth
Countless ripples soar heavenward
Subtly bounded by the cerulean sky
Visions
An eagle hovers, golden orbs searching, perceiving the soul
Thoughts
Abandoned dust from the womb
Encasing those who once endured
Lost
Blinded spirits, sealed by the present
Realizations
Knowledge to be cherished by few
Circle
The wholeness of life is exposed
One who exists will never cease
Eternity
We are the dust of the future
Ancestors to our children
Particles of the womb which form the soul.

Asianita C. Gonzales

The Everchanging Sky

It spreads across the sky,
Rising high above the trees, leaving me in
A world unknown.
For it is shown that this is not reality.
The colors that you see are not there, because
they share the same old black and grey in the
present day.
Back to the past they go and we only know
what colors really hold true, because they're
colors that reflect on you.

Why does the sun set in so many ways on
different days in different skies for different eyes?
Orange, yellow, gold, and pink would make you
think of those memories once shared if you
dared, to take a look at the past and make
it last, by seeing the sky on a different side of the world.

Hold these colors in your head
And shed those tears of the years gone by,
Never let them die,
For their yours in the eyes of the sky.

Bob Rose

Phoenix Arisen

I am a prehistoric bird
Rising out of the ashes at the volcano's floor
Reawakening
Seeking a way out of the tomb of dormancy
Reaching for the light from above
Slowly I ascend to perch upon this mountainous peak
My wings spread over the breadth of its base
I am the phoenix
Arisen
Lifting my wings to the heavens
Fanning away centuries of sleep
My energy stirs
My heart pounds
My blood courses
I take the flight
Forests bend under the fanning of my wings
Lakes part and rivers overflow
Over mountain ranges I soar
Never to be imprisoned anymore
I am the phoenix — arisen.

Irvin Brown Jr.

Just About The End Of The World

It was a frigid morning as my sister and I merged from our
rooms with blankets in hands. She with her ugly pink nightie.
I with thumb in mouth, with my Star Wars pajamas.
Ice still clung to my father's Honda.
Clock at 7:55, Bugs Bunny would be on soon.
I with my Cap'n Crunch. She with her Honey-Comb.
Bugs was taunting Elmer Fudd to his red hot steaming face.
Stomachs filled with sweet cereal.
Our hands sticky from the sugar of our snacks.
We were so content, loving life.
Mom came so gently and said,"Your Father took Elsa to put
her to sleep." We cried and cried for that German Shepherd
despite the roadrunner constantly foiling Wile E. Coyote.
Our blankets soaked with our sobs and snot as it streamed
down our faces. I wanted to die and let Elsa live.
Mother tried to comfort us but to no avail.
All I could see was Elsa's soft brown eyes, closing serenely
as the vet injected her with death. I could see her tail go
lifeless. I stared out the sliding glass window past the TV,
searching for her. I just wanted to be with her.

Joe Asnault

Everyday Roses

Roses I have created
Roses I have destroyed
Forming them out of clay
Scribbling them out each day
Scouring the aisle for the
appropriate one in which to say.
Roses embroidered, embossed,
etched out in the rising sun.
Faintly falling in the setting sun.
Caressing the skin, softly spoken on the tongue.
Laying on the pillow in the morning sun.
Whispering on the wind
Roses I have created
Now dying on the vine.

Edward Jolly

"Cloud Of Loneliness"

Looking for new beginnings as life slips by,
Searching to fill loneliness I feel inside.
Am I adrift in an unreal sky
Where voices whisper in my head,
Or am I trying to recapture moments already lived?
Knowing not how to respond, I remain lost
Forever in the cloud of loneliness as life slips by.

Howard G. Roberts

My Place

Tears flowing freely down my face.

My pain, fear, sadness and shame
  run out of me. I am numb no more.

I cry, afraid that my black heart
  will see no tomorrow.

Stupid, dumb, insecure, weak and ugly.

I fall on my knees and scream in sorrow.

But my knees are also weak, so I
  now lay in a huddled mass.

A final tear bleeds from my wounded heart.

There is nothing left in me.

No more movement, no breath, no pain,
  no sorrow nor shame. Numb again.

My huddled mass crumbles to dust, it is
  carried off by the wind into a land
  that no one else shall ever see.

Where no one else shall ever be.

A place simply and only for me, where
  I go each time that I cry and where
  I go... for every day I want to die.

Claire M. Seryak

Daddy's Babies

Big, tough boy
running with thugs, doing drugs, having a "great" time.
—Daddy doesn't know—
Small, painted girl
alone in the streets, in between the sheets, getting paid.
—Daddy doesn't know—
A shout, a cry of pain.
-Daddy doesn't listen; doesn't see; doesn't care-
Rebellion: the "bad" boy
      the "good" girl.
Nothing works, no attention.
Ignorance, stupidity...what could have been.
Waking alone; sour taste in mouth.
Just another "hard day": or is it?
Daddy might remember this one.
Today his children were put six feet deep.
Found hanging side by side, hands held tight.
Yes, Daddy might remember this one...
Then again,
Daddy might just go home and pick up the bottle again.

E. Renee Elliott

"My Brother"

My brother whom serves his country well;
Sacrifices by leaving his family and goes through hell;
But he does his job and we are proud of him.
Especially for me, to say he's my brother, my kin;
Out at sea, not hearing his voice, it's so hard,
But we do hear from him, by a letter or a card.
We tear it open, to see what he says, to hear that he's fine and he
Will call in a couple of days.
Excitement in our minds as we await the phone to ring,
His face comes to mind as we hear "Wind Beneath My Wing"
His awards say it all, and finally we get the telephone call.
We are content to hear he's fine, and he'll be home soon.
As I can rest now, and as I go to sleep,
look at the stars, and see the moon....

Connie Frausto

Tomorrow

On rumination of ruin, I watched the earth surrender
Sacrariums of respite a fool considers splendor,
Entranced as I beheld serenity and confusion,
My thoughts were soon dispelled by innocent intrusion;

"A penny for your thoughts!" a maiden's youthful plea,
"My child begone," said I, "What wouldst thou have of me?
Mine eyes are old and dim, no longer can they see
The joy that fed my youth and filled my heart with glee.

My flesh is withered and pale, unsightly to behold,
My frame is bent and frail, my blood is thick and cold,
Mine ears no longer hear the sound of children's play,
I hate the hope of morrow, and curse the close of day!"

Her soul withdrawn and trembling, her countenance distressed,
Again I bade her go ere my demean molest
Delusions and ideals that foster tender traits
Bound within the heart wherein salvation waits.

And as she gently parted, I heard an angel say
in the roar of thunder clouds and lightning's swift display,
"No longer will atonement regard thy grievous way,
The promise of tomorrow, the passing of today."

Anthony Brantley

Minding Your Speech

'I can say what I want to anyone, You can't tell me what to say'
I heard many people proclaim this, all throughout the day.
They say that no one owns their voice,
They can speak their mind, it's their choice.
I've seen people hurt by others' words, they get angry and frown.
Just by their words alone, they bring people up or tear them down.

James 3 talks about the tongue, how it is a fire.
For no man can tame it, not even the liar.
Out of the same mouth, we curse and we bless.
That's why many churches today, are already a mess.
Fresh and salt water can't come out of the same spring,
Ask God to set a watch on your tongue, when you speak anything.
For the tongue corrupts the whole person, and is set on fire by hell.
So beware of what someone says and by what they tell.
Always meditate on Jesus, and the lessons He did teach,
Instead of speaking your mind, you should be minding your speech!

Eldora Davis

The Sea

Waves rolling upon the shore
Seagulls singing of great mysteries
The sea captures the sun (sunset)
Then sets it free again (sunrise)
Dancing waves crash onto the solid rocks

The unaccepted waves are forced back into the ocean once again
Sailing ships of many kinds are a puppet to the sea
Adventurous, courageous men are cast as the heroes in this
mystery
A lonely search for peace
in the sea's unforgiving arms
Some sailors find their destiny-
and remain in the oceans embrace
The rest are unsettled and
make their way back to the shore

Brenda Jean Cushman

Shattered Reality?

Flying high around the world
Searching for liberty lands;
Journeys where my hope can reach out
Love, peace, soul, brotherly hands.

Dreaming on ways toward lifelights
Where can sureness feeling right;
Where my body sleeps with comfort
And my nightmares turn to blind side.

I can feel myself in the top mountains
I can feel the world reaching love inside;
I can dream in days where the wrongness vanish
Like winds carrying words out loud.

Poverty dying as the days passing away
To be headed by another light;
I can't see just one world between us
But I could see us shares one hope inside.

Having blames as having good times
That's the way of our daily worldwide;
I just dream with a world of joyful
Where we live with own trust and mind.

Bamil Gutiérrez Collado

Seeking The Unknown

Down the dark, lonely hall she mopes,
  searching for some hope,
  she may return to the light.
that was stolen from her in the night.

He waits in their room alone,
  for her to return unnerved,
  far off he hears a soft moan,
undoubtedly it came unserved.

He sprang up from their bed,
  and down the castle halls he sped,
  searching each and every door,
finding her and so much more.

He sees her climbing upon the sill,
  small, crystal tears falling from her eyes
  with great fear did his heart fill.
as she leaped into the shadow skies.

DeLora L. Varbel

The Men

Take our sons to far off Lands what can we do it out of our hands.
See all the boy's who are not even men and hope
today will not be the end.
Walk through the rain and walk through the mud
step over a body all around you blood.
Feel how hot feel the heat what ever you do stay on your feet.
Hear the Bombs hear all the noise don't lose your guns
these are not toys. All around a lot of boys,
Some fall down never to get up.
To read in a letter you have a daughter.
What do I do I'm low on water.
All around you are the Viet Cong,
you feel like giving up but you go on,
you and the boy's got the chills when you look at the mountains
and are told those are foot hills.
You will try to make it so you can go home.
You take a rest, sit down and nap
but all around you these Viet Cong Trap.
See all the Boys fight and die.
You can't take anymore you have
to get high!

Andrea Dalnas

Just An Echo Away

Far over a mountain in a dream of you Little Sister - I can
see you cryin' under the blue, blue rain. Come Little Sister,
dream awhile with me - I'm just an echo away from you.

We'll gather white lilies - whiter than the mountain's snow -
walking together beneath the rays of the sun, laughing, then
kneeling down to pray to the good Lord above, you and I.

He is just a breath away from you. We'll touch the red
blossoms high in the trees where robins sing - just an echo
away - there's a wonderful trail of swaying blue bells -
further along we'll climb a little hill and lie down in the
yellow daisy field, just a smile away.

Come Little Sister - can't you hear me calling your name
through your cryin' tears under the blue, blue rain? We can
go wading in the cool clear stream in those mountain's
meadowed scenes. So come Little Sister, I'm just an echo away.

We will walk near an old diamond waterfall tumbling down
against our bare feet, beneath the sky, blue as the sea where
we will laugh - then pray to the good Lord above, you and I.
He's just a breath away. Can't you hear me calling - I'm just
an echo away, praying for you and I.

Barbara Davies Jeremiah

"Time Etched In Stone"

Staring at the blankness,
seeing my patient stanzas float,
around like bars of music, written on the ceiling.

How they flow so easy,
when I'm trapped in my four-walled tomb
with nothing but my thoughts,
to remind me of the unchanging past.

All the opportunities I ruined,
are gone but not forgotten,
so still I wish as if some hope,
of changing the time etched in stone.

Jillian Grimaldi

Rain Drops

Hands clutched tight kneeling down to die
Seeing my people below and not knowing why
My brother in his nakedness looking at the ground
Yesterdays glorious memories today cannot be found
They took away everything and made us very poor
We breathed in their gasses and died on the floor
They shoveled us into ovens and burned our flesh away
We only cry for mercy, hope and peace someday
Piercing echoes of murderous shots ringing in my ear
People begging and pleading with hopeless, endless fear
Sorrow filled the earth as the ground engulfed our blood
Raindrops are forgotten when rivers become a flood
If we die for something let us die for love
For tomorrow we will be in heaven up above

Galen R. McMillen

Angela

My friend Angela is the best.
She is like a flower blossom in the spring.
She is my dear friend like a diary.
My friend is like bright shining star in the golden moonlight
She twinkles in the moonlight.
She is more than a friend she is my good friend that
I've had for a long time.
Time is not fighting against us it's our friend too.
My friendship with her is like a sunrise.
Our past and present will keep us friends forever.

Charnette Darrington

Spring

Spring, is a beautiful time of year,
Seems, you can hear when the animals cheer.
Old man winter has finely left town.
There is no more snow falling down.
The sun is shining so warm.
No coat has to be worn.

The trees are putting forth their leaves.
Grass in also turning green.
Oh! How I do love spring

Doors and windows opened wide
letting the good spring air inside.
Clothes hanging on the line,
Drinking up the warm sunshine.
Everyone raking winter's debris.
Feeling the spring time breeze.

It's such a beautiful day-
Watching the children all at play.
Some riding bikes, with no hands,
Thinking it is so grand.
Others playing in the sand.

June L. Smith

The Happiness Of A Diamond

Little miss Amy the bride to be
Selecting a diamond for her wedding
Into the jewelers show case looking
Diamonds, weeping, whispering, hurry hurry
Dreams oh dreams I've been secretly locked
away with beautiful dreams, whispering please
choose me, I'm the diamond with sun beam magic
and I'm the diamond with crystal light splendor
Hurry hurry I don't want to be a stranger
Bringing dreams to come true; heavens delight is so blue

Ready to escape to find a hand, I'm tailored
and to make her size. Hands with gleam makes hearts a dream
Cannot believe, her surprising me and I'm glowing
Planned to be blessed; I take this ring and thee I wed
Wedding arrangements reserved for the bride
Down the aisle I'll be trailing with a radiant sparkle
Organ playing bridal march; little miss Amy bride to be
married, choosing me, the diamond, "sun beam magic."
Congratulations with Love and with happy memories.

Amy & Gary - August 6, 1994

Inez Kobus

The Guide

I hear you now, knocking at my door, voice in the wind,
shadows in the dark, in the light of day.
Swirling, around, through, within.
You are outside, you are inside,
always right next to me.

You are silent as the crisp, clear night
and loud as the dawn, when the sun thunders its arrival
in an array of colors that all but take the breath
in their beauty, as the world begins again,
each moment spilling into the next without repetition.

I must hasten my footsteps along the path
and still may never catch a glimpse of you!
oh, but I feel your presence,
and a smile draws round my mouth,
that knows words are not always necessary
to communicate with the spirit.

Charmaine Celeste

The Man In The Mirror

I heard a drug dealer say, "The drugs I
Sell give me power!"

He could not see, that this power was
Vain, for as a sword with a single edge,
He thought to be cutting outward, yet,
All the while he was cutting inward.

In the mirror, looking pass the truth,
He saw what he wanted to see, not what
Was really there to be seen. The mirror
Held truth, yet he comprehended things
And images emanating from his own mind.

One day, he said he would gaze upon the
Truth, "for surely" he reasoned, "it must
be the reflection of my own mind!"

When before the mirror he stood, absent
Was his presence in the mirror, in horror
He cried "where is the man that I am?"

It was an echo, in his own mind that
Replayed, "cut away!"

Anthony W. Winn

Untitled

Sleepwalking through the torments of life.
Serenading the sorrows that follow us.
Waltzing in our wishes.
Dancing on our dreams.
Spinning secrets to sadden ourselves.
Living lies to escape the truths.
Smoldering the fires of passion habitually.
Chastising ourselves for compassion.
Giving to receive.
Breathing to breath.
Thinking to think.
"It is very fashionable, you know".
Thus, we live it.
We live the fashion and create the daily deception.
And the world spins on...

Alina Stefanescu

A Guest In Egypt

Egypt's moon shines drunken cups tonight,
shaking her triple bowl through haze.
The wines' sharp fires have seared my tongue,
and glutted food has sickened to my taste.
The eunuch stands beside the jewelled door
that sways its panels over golden plates,
and slave girls bear the silver dish of fruit;
they come in mist, like waving fans,
in double forms of grace.
The hour has childed dreams,
and what my Eros seeks
bends like the reeds to Cleopatra's wish,
where love reflects her thousand mirrored forms
in shapes of beauty from the brazen walls.
White arms like roots lift up their hands
to draw me downward to the fecund marsh.
My mind's pool swirls its vortex of desire;
a brilliant sheen, it twists around her eye,
coiling toward her gently moving bed.

Ian MacLennan

The Pain Of Reality

Which pain shall we speak of?
Shall we speak of the pain in our hearts, souls or physical bodies?
I know the pain in my heart is enlarged by images I have failed
to ignore through cable vision, television, newspaper, magazines and
half truths.
I cannot run away from the pain in my soul which is aching from
the images my eyes have seen and unwillingly taken pictures
to imprison my soul.
I live with the pain in my physical body which is bone deep
and a mere reflection of the anguish locked away in my soul.
My muscles and joints scream for relief that may never come
and therefore, I ache, cry uncontrollably, moan softly, sweat
heavily and search desperately for any relief, but there is
none. Nor shall there be any as long as I live with CFIDS.

Ahreita T. Griffin

Words

Harsh words are,
Sharp, as a two-edged sword.

Kind words are,
Relaxing, as a hot bubble bath.

Sad words are,
Sorry, as a child caught stealing a cookie.

Happy words are,
Joyous, as finding the end of a rainbow.

Exciting words are,
Thrilling, as a fast moving race car.

But, no words are,
Lonely, as being alone in a canoe,
On the middle of a lake, without a paddle.

Eugenia Grace Marshall

A Miracle This.... From Five Loaves And Two Fish

"Please Mother, may I go to see Jesus again?" and so....
She called it childish fancy but even so, she let her son go,
He thanked his mother, then whooping in delight,
Picking up his lunch box, he ran with all his might....
Down the road, to the town of Capernaum. But,... lo,
Seeing not his great Hero...." Where's Jesus?" he asked a passerby,
"He sailed across the lake," Disappointed, the lad gave a sigh...
"But you can walk around to the other side!"
Reaching the far side of the Lake, he sat, a rest to take.
There he saw Andrew, a disciple, walking through the multitude,
He wanted to know if anybody had brought any food.
Excitement showing when the lad heard this, his smile beamed,
This was his chance to help Jesus, it seemed!
"Please take my lunch box,... oh he sees us!"
Andrew took the lunch box, thanked the lad, then returned to Jesus!
When the Young Boy walked home his heart sang with happiness!
"Wait 'til I tell Mother about this; feeding 5,000 with bread and fish,
We had enough food to eat, and best of all, I sat at Jesus' feet!"
In giving his lunch box, the Young Boy had known...
He may go hungry, but to Jesus, his love he had shown!

Juanita Johnson

Promiseland'

I walked in and I saw her setting there
She was sitting and reading a bible in her chair
Lord knows she's had a hard life
But if God will keep her with us he will stay by her side
And then one day she asked God to take her by the hand
Then he took her to the promiseland
Now she's up there walking on the streets of gold
Dancing and singing with her Lord.

Brian Wade

Rose

Her admirer makes himself known;
She calls his name to ease his fear,
Teases him with her sweet fragrance
and begs him to draw her near.
Carefully, she sways closer to him,
Opening her petals of pale pink skin.
With an artist's ease, she kisses him,
Wraps around him, draws him in.
A new sensation overcomes his joy;
Tremendous pain sears through his body.
Her thorns! They tear at his tender flesh
Until he collapses, helpless in his agony.
Pure rain begins to fall from the sky
Cleansing her thorns and her conscience of his memory,
But no rain can heal his wounds or his betrayed trust.
He cries to the heavens; she basks in her own glory.
Foolish man! He rendered himself a helpless victim
In a dangerous game o building a fantasy
Out of his passion. Blinded by simple trust, he forgot:
Exquisite beauty possesses such potential for treachery;
Beware of the lovely.

Jennifer Burnside

Grandmother

Grandmother was our Mother, when we were little girls.
She cared for us and loved us; she took us shopping for clothes.
Beautiful sweaters she bought, for my sister and me.
Then she would take us for lunch at Picadilly's.
Just the three of us; my grandmother, my sister and me.

Grandmother loved God's creatures; we learned to love them, too.
Cats and kittens, puppies and dogs...and horses.
Our grandmother gave us horses; my sister, Kim and me.
Remembering those magical days, riding horses;
We could walk, we could run, we could fly!

Grandmother loved trees and flowers; she had them all over the place.
Purple wisteria draped over the yard; mimosa along the driveway.
Orange and yellow tiger lilies, standing by the creek.
Iris, honeysuckle, morning glories climbing; wildflowers everywhere.

Grandmother always knew beauty; she was an artist.
She loved silver and turquoise and the color, Burnt Orange.
She taught me to paint...

Now Grandmother is with Jesus;
And in the Heavenly Gardens
She can walk, she can run, she can fly!

Crystal K. Bond-Wasson

My Sister

The ominous incline of life's encompassing slope,
   She created the ladder, the staircase of hope.
Never a push, a gentle nudge,
   the poles to the wave, the silt of the sludge.
Casting aside her own heart's desires,
   to encourage my wheels out of the mire.
She taught me that trust is essential,
   and never to fear.
The world is no place, to show them your tears.
She taught me to strive, whether she said it or not.
Actions bellow to the observer, words to a sot
My morals, my values, my opinion's voice,
   all were modeled after one, my choice.
A hero, an icon of what I believe,
   my complacency a priority, to no one I heed.
If only there were enough sands in the glass,
   to show my gratitude, my admiration of this lass.
She's been there, a constant in life's whirlwind twister,
   my devotion deserving of my sister.

Heather Milliken

My Friend Brenda Dews

I have a friend her name is Brenda Dews,
She is always there for me, whether it's good or bad news.
I can count on her all the time,
That is why constantly, she stays on my mind.
She's the best friend, I've ever had,
I know she's there for me when thing seems so bad
Brenda, I know, I can always count on you,
Because you're my friend through and through.
You've seen me through, a lot of ups and downs,
You made me laugh, and I wipe away the frown.
Am not trying to put you up to high,
But surely I know God's gonna bless you by and by.
We are all Gods, children as we all know,
He will bless us, wherever we go.
Brenda I've never asked a favor, and you didn't come through
Without you as my friend, I wouldn't know what to do.
It's so nice to have you as my friend,
You'll someone who's there for me through thick and thin.
May God continue to bless you,
My special and loving friend Brenda Dews.

Flossie M. Mims

A Dream

From out of nowhere appears a woman, a lady with wings.
She is canvased in light, brilliant gold and white streams.
Her motions are delicate, most soothing and free.
She is the gentlest woman this child has ever seen.
This child keeps crying, "Too much pain, I can't breathe."
The lady is stroking great armor, releasing lovelessness screams.
"Don't be frightened! I won't hurt you."
She keeps touching and smiles
Your sounds brought me to you from many a mile.
This lady with wings pulls the child in close.
Embracing her tightly like a warm winter coat.
Her wings wrap around her, she whispers, "I care."
She caresses this child, armor falls everywhere.
"I came. I will hold you. You need the love sign."
"Take my hands. I will lift you. I will tell you, you're mine."
"I came because you need me, I am telling you so."
"Child, feel how I love you, and I will never let go."
Though they called this a dream, I had once as a child.
This lady still left me her love with her touch and her smile.

Deborah Anne Carroll

Gram's Dead

Through months and months of suffering,
She knew the end was near.
Faith that's what kept her here, faith.

A woman who was once filled with vigor and independence,
Became feeble and weak.

The day came when the lamentation ceased,
And all became oblivion.

I felt like crawling in darkness,
But I was very placid.

I stay here with memories and her possessions I hold,
I know Gram will never live again but,
Memories, that's what will keep her here, memories.

Elizabeth Arigoni

My Poor Little Clown Blossom

My poor little broken hearted Clown
She laughs and sings and dances
Merrily she goes along singing her merry tunes
But all the while her heart is breaking
Other peoples' smile have a soothing effect on her
At least for a little while
Time passes quickly when she is in the crowd
When she is alone, she sighs & cries and wishes
That she could be happy!
That she could have happiness like many other
Folks she knows!
I hope some day soon my dear little Clown
That someone will make you very happy too
You have surely earned it my dear
My poor little broken hearted Clown
With much love your Mother

Blossom Taber

Teacher And Student

Their paths first crossed in high school,
She, lowly substitute teacher and he, a star athlete.
He earned with difficulty B's in school, and equally hard
     earned A's on gridiron and track.
His commitment to both was admired by all teachers.
Several years later she journeyed to nearby Gateway U.
     to a basketball game.
Here, his football scholarship duties required him
To take pictures at many varsity games.
They spied each other and he hastened to her in the
     middle of the stands.
Idle eyes lit up in wonder as the white middle-aged
     lady and the young black student athlete embraced,
In full view and oblivious of others.
Sharp eyes realized that the main game
Was being played out, not on the court, but in the stands.
They were separated by generation and by race,
But gloriously bridged the gaps with mutual respect and love.

Joseph Hopkins

For Sale

"Take anything you want," her mother says.
She scribbles a price with a magic marker,
Smacks a sticker on the bike that became too small.
Rusty training wheels clutch the back tire.
The baby seat is in a supermarket box
Straps dangling over the words, "Green Giant.'

Folding tables crowd the garage.
Heaped with saddle shoes and sneakers.
Scruffy dollies, tattered and glassy-eyed
Spill tears that stream down painted smiles.

Suzanne plunks down a yellow paperback
Beside the sticky pages of Dr. Seuss.
Giggles at the swooning couple on the cover.
"Are you sure you don't want this?" She smirks,
But her eyes are on the empty building.
"You know, my house looks bigger," she says,
"Without our stuff inside."

Crissa-Jean Chappell

Different

She is alone among friends,
Stands out in a crowd of others.
She looks different because she is lonely,
There is no smile playing on her face.
No lively step, not a word when she says -
     "Hello?"

Only the echo...

Julia Master

She Teaches Our Kids

She teaches our kids, yours and mine.
She shows everyday, come rain or shine.
She teaches respect for the flag unfurled.
She tries to prepare them for the complex world.

So much confusion, lunch tickets get lost.
To make sure they eat, she picks up the cost.
When day is done and our kids come home,
She's still grading papers in school all alone.

With all that she does, I think you'll agree,
How she finds time to teach, is a mystery to me.
But teach them she does and I'm happy to say,
Some of these kids will be teachers one day.

When Johnny is President and Susie's a Star,
The "Press" will ask them, "Who got you this far?"
Then Johnny and Susie will say from their heart,
Ms. Feiten, our teacher, she gave us our start.

Ms. Feiten will smile through eyes dim with tears,
These are my kids I taught through the years.
She loves our kids, yours and mine.
Her teaching will last 'til the end of time.

Barbara Daly

Alone

The tear froze on her already stained face.
She sought comfort in strange, empty faces
and unknown places,
Trying to find the answers to questions
She didn't understand.
Curled up in a corner and feeling alone,
While personal demons tear at her heart
and her soul.
Looking for the traces of what she knew before,
While her old friend loneliness wraps his arms
around her.

Jennifer Smyder

The Promise

Beside the moonlit watered shore
She stood before the one she adored,
And accepted a kiss with a sigh.

With love in her eyes
And dreams in her heart,
She longed for the day they would never part.

With the stars up above to witness their pledge,
Along the moonlit watered shore
They promised their love forever more.

Carol Van Camp

Kleenex

Which color kleenex is right?
Should it match the room?
Pink, blue, green, yellow, or white?
White is good for any room,
In the bathroom have it match the toilet paper
for a coordinated look!
The bedroom doesn't matter much,
if it's only used for sleeping,
although it would add a nice touch if it matched
the bedding and the light.
Which color kleenex is right,
is a tougher question then it sounds.
So make it easy on yourself and just pick White!

Gina Stordahl

A Poem About Rosa Parks

Rosa Parks did what was right, Rosa Parks did what was wrong
She struggled hard and worked all day
She wanted rest that was hard to get
Didn't want to move when told
This was normal, this was old, but she didn't, no not she
She stood her ground, she kept her seat
But Rosa Parks has not won yet
They would not allow they would not let
Her get away with this terrible crime
Why not she said I paid my dime
So they took her down to horrible jail
And would not let her out with bail
But other people followed Rosa Parks
They started walking, they walked 'till dark
They did what was right, they used no trickery
And finally they won, they found their victory
They won that battle, yes they did
But troubles still are not unhid
Rosa Parks did what was right, Rosa Parks did what was wrong
And with people like her the troubles will one day be gone.

Allison Karman

A Mother's Tear

As she sits at her kitchen table. Wondering why
She tries her best not to cry
She sits and think of her children that she carried
And she thinks of the two she buried
As wrinkles come cross her face
She prays to her heavenly grace
As she is praying a voice comes so clear
Why are crying. She answer these, are a mothers tear
The voice says don't weep any more
For we have reach the golden doors
Our pain is over, the aches has fade away
Our hearts are filled with happiness these days
We know, that no-one knows the pain you carry inside
No one knows of hurt and tears you must hide
As you hold your hand in prayer at night
We can feel the pain that you hold so tight
As her mind began to clear
The voice suddenly disappear
Memories come in mind and she began to smile
As laughter sat in for short while

Jacqueline Byrd

The Fishing Expedition

With a tiny little giggle and merrily dancing eyes,
she turns to me and says look Mommy, look!

I looked and looked but could not see.
So I asked, what do you see?
She says, look over there to water so blue,
a fish dancing with a dragon fly,
don't you see it too?

Mommy, let's catch that old fish! Let's do! Let's do!
She cast out her line and hooked him on first try!
She tugged and she pulled and she pulled and she tugged,
and with a great heave, she landed him, she did!

She held him up proudly and showed him to me.
She says, isn't he pretty and I agreed.
She shook her head and said, no he must finish that dance!
Mommy, he has to go home now, you see!

She gave him a hug and tossed him back.
Then she turns to me and says, I think I'm hungry.
So we climbed off her bed and went into our kitchen.
The fish and dragon fly, all but forgotten.
That is, until next time, you see!

Judy Schultz

Stone Heart

Where is that girl that used to play,
She was carefree and loving all day.
Who dropped those pebbles down into her heart,
What causes such anger, oh how does it start?
Each pebble was caused by sarcastic words that were said,
Sometimes the poor girl's heart feels like it's dead.
But somehow her heart keeps beating in time,
We never saw it coming not even one sign.
The bitterness crept in and it never seems to stop,
Our love for her keeps her on our list at the top.
The one that hurt her hides behind a great wall,
They are hiding and never will confess it at all.
When words said to hurt her and make her feel sad,
Almost destroyed her and ruined the life that she had.
Be careful when you give your opinion so true,
The attack just might kill you for all that you do.
Where is that girl that used to play, why is she alone?
She is gone, never to return, her heart has turned to stone.

Catherine N. Lear

'Untitled

While I slept, she watched me.
She wept in silence and solitude,
Torn by her caring and her independence.
She knew without reserve that I loved her,
And she loved, too.
Her sensitive nature, however, prevented
Her voicing any anguish
From my omnipresent affection.
I could not see, as I dreamt lovingly,
That I was stifling this beautiful person,
Harming that which I only sought to protect.
She pulled her arm away,
Ever so gently from under my hear,
So as not to disturb my serene slumber.
If only I had awakened earlier, to her first tear…

Alexander Lofft

Just For Gay Nell

Gay Nell is leaving her job today
She won't be around for awhile
For she has chosen the better way
To stay home and care for her child.

Now some folks will say that she's crazy
And others may think she is wise
Still others will think she is strange for sure
Till they notice the gleam in her eyes.

For what she is gaining, no money can buy
And no one can take it away
Being with Lindsay to watch her grow up
And have time to share in her play!

Time goes by so fast, and days turn to years
So enjoy every minute each day
And if you should find that you have any fears
They'll be less if you take time to pray.

So good luck to you, David and Lindsay, too
Your life now will be so much more fun
I know you'll be happy, just being at home
Your "homemaking" won't have to be on the run!

Clela Garner

A Mothers Love

What is a mother? A mother is an angel.
She's never too busy to hear you talk,
And will stand by your bedside if you can't walk.
For that's how deep a mother's love will go.
A mother is caring, true, and sincere.
She always knows how to show you the light,
And always tries to do what's right.
There is no higher love than a mother's love.
It will always be there if you're big or small,
And will always comfort you, even when you're bad,
Remember, you're still her baby, even at six feet tall.
So never forget that a mother is the best,
Through the good times and the bad times.
And remember to always love her, even when she's gone to rest.

Joe M. Reed, Jr.

Beyond the Blue

Golden yellow, unequalled beauty as the day ends
Shines forth with one great majestic ray of light
Then disappears almost as quietly as it comes from forth
Into an unknown, gone is the day, soon comes the night

Its colors masquerade the sky with ecstasy
Bringing to end another day for the laborer who has toiled to earn
A wage be he tiller of sod or factory employee
It is time to pause, to worship the beauty
The magnificence of the day, just to see

It's out there for each to behold
This beauty the color of gold
A story for all of old and new
And then it disappears like it came, beyond the blue.

Ira W. Moots

Terri

The nights, the days of endless care
Should have made me realize I must prepare
- For the time that would too soon come
When I would be left alone.

I only hope that in some way
I've prepared a basis for a future day
When mom is there
- But out of sight
God's love will help you through the night

The love that was given in days of old
Will be returned a hundred - fold.
A word of love, a gentle touch
Shows that you've cared so very much.

A future —
Bright with dreams and wishes
— You'll have to learn to do your own dishes.

Anne W. Dean

Diane's Kiss

I recall the first and remember the last.
Sitting here thinking of the night just past.
Evening showers, a tender kiss.
Are we ready for this?
Baby can you see that star?
We don't have to go that far.
A dream within our thoughts
Lets us recall and remember it all
The love, the kiss, and the star.
Oh, what an evening for it all.

Bart C. Travaglini

"Show Me"

Show me a place where there's no grass or trees
Show me a place where there's no birds or bees
The place we know most
Is the place where our animals strive to live
It's called the Tropical Rain Forest
The place where our animals homes are cut down
And all of the animals are left to drown
Show me a place where the animals die
Show me a place where the birds can not fly
Show me a place where there's no answer for why
Show me the Tropical Rain Forest
Show me a place where there's no time for goodbye
Show me a place where the most you can do is cry
Show me a place where there's no girl nor guy
Show me the Tropical Rain Forest

Andria Hargis

"Sorrows Path"

A vision of loveliness captured by the light.
Showing so strongly but held by the night.
Seeing you sleeping with the stars all around.
The angels lay weeping as the tears roll down.
The high moon turns blue,
As soon as I realize that God has taken you.
When you're up there with him and you're looking down.
You may be with me but you make no sound.
With no one but me,
The emptiness makes my eyes fill up, not able to see.
For things I've said I truly repent.
My heart is still here, it just lies dormant.
The Lord won't take me, I've already asked.
He still has plans, for me a different task.
What to do I know not with my life.
Cruel fate and God above have taken my wife.

David Kondrup

The Four Seasons

Spring with the newborn animals and birds that sing
Shows the joy that life can bring.
Rain showers turn the dirt to mud
And the creeks start to flood.

Then with summer comes the heat.
Ice tea and a swimming hole makes country life hard to beat
Lots of people walk around in shorts and bare feet.
Finally the weather starts to cool.

With fall there will be no more swimming in the pool.
There are many good things about fall
Like thanksgiving when the family gathers in the hall
Along with that comes the changing of leaves
And the cool fall breeze.

Then it becomes cold and starts to freeze
Snow comes from the sky,
And parents watch their children go sledding by.
Santa brings gifts for girls and boys
Everything from clothes to toys.

Different seasons make life grand
All across this great land.

Bonnie Hart

Broken Silence

The night was dark, the forest still
Silence reigned supreme
The moon was black, the stars were dimmed
Silence conquered all

Suddenly, the silence was broken
The silence cowered, then fled away
The sound of hoofs raised its voice
The forest's gloom parted to let it pass

It was elves, proud elves
Marching to war they were, some never to return
Jewels glinted on their armor
Proud, strong, and sad they were

Line after line passed by
Peaceful they are at home, deadly at war
Great lords and princes passed
Orders were shouted, oaths sworn

They passed, the forest closed behind them
Silence returned, reigning again
The forest quickly forgot the memories
The night was dark, silence reigned supreme

George Naylor

Death Stones

I have been staring, looking down at your grave,
simply a stone to mark your way.

Your stone can't tell the story, like your class could,
It just sits black and cold, like a stone would.

I shed many tears of unspoken words,
how your young, lost life flew away like the flight of a bird.

Many people pass by me, and look at the stone,
they think it just marks another pile of bones.

Your stone, to us, means so much more, like tears and like pain,
like losses and gain.

Stones say nothing about who you are,
Where have you been? and, Have you been far?

Although your short life on Earth may be done,
when the world grows old, you'll stay forever young.

Do you feel free now? Is your anger the thunder? Are your
tears the rain? Is there still hurt? Is there still pain?

I still cry for you, and I still cry for me,
but now you lie quiet, peaceful as can be.

Andrea Oxier

My Home Town

Over fifty years have gone by
Since I left my old home town.
The streets look the same
I can still recall the names.
Many of the houses are occupied
But by persons I can't identify.

We were never bored as kids are today
There was always something to do.
In the winter we skated on ice,
Or sledded down steep hills.
In the summer, we picked berries that grew wild,
Or helped the farmers rake hay into piles.

Most of my family no longer are living,
As well as friends we knew in the past.
Now we travel the lonely road
To the cemetery where family
And friends so dear to us,
Have long ago been laid to rest.

Eva Seger

"Mother"

Mother was the best friend I ever had,
Since she went away, we are all so sad,
She made our home complete, in every way,
Until the Lord took her, with him to stay.

She always knew the right things to do,
To cheer us up, when we were blue.
She knew the day, at her house we'd arrive,
So she made our favorite cakes and pies.

She wanted her children to know the Lord,
So she took us to church to hear his word.
After suffering was done in "74",
God said her work on earth was o'er.

The family is gathering on Heaven's bright shore,
Where we'll all be together again, once more,
So live for Jesus, as Mother would say,
And we'll have a reunion, some wonderful day.

Betty Moody

Some Days I'm Strong

Some days I'm strong, and I don't need to see you
since the pain has lessened a bit.
But some days I'm weak and I think of you often
and the phone doesn't ring and I cry.

Some days I'm strong and I'm planning new loves
and I'm dreaming of futures with people unseen.
But some days I'm weak, and I miss you like crazy
and the thought that I've lost you drives me insane.

Some days I'm strong...the memories fade
and the pictures don't faze me a bit like they used to.
But some days I'm weak and I wish you would hold me
and I wish I could see you outside of my dreams.

Some days I'm strong and the weeks pass more quickly
and life holds the meaning my soul seems to seek.
But most days I'm weak, and I sit and write letters
to a man whom I love but doesn't love me.

Jennifer Swanson

Ode To A Time In Knowing

To the ode of a time in knowing,
singing softly of melodies of long ago,
and breaking the slow of time
with the caress of love.

Being and only being,
is the contentment of my life,
and only to the ode of a time in knowing does it come to be.

Run away and you won't go
as far as the eye of a whirl,
and going back you cannot touch
the feet of destiny.

Don't be discontent my fancy,
Fly as fly you might,
Be as soft as rain my love
but as firm as night.

Just remember in the afterthought,
the taste of dew and mellow,
And don't forget the time in knowing
and my love of easy telling.

Judy Cantrell

Twilights Final Curtain Call

The evening grows quiet as the day nears the dusk, birds hush their
singing, to roast they will rush.

Men in a hurry, their work has been done, rush homeward for rest
from their day in the sun.

Cattle have been grazing since sunup this morn, now laying down
peaceful, waiting young to be born.

The flowers are reaching with their petals so new, for the coolness
of night and the touch of the dew.

Humming birds fly swiftly to the flowers they seek, the last nectar
of the day still so sweet on their beaks.

The sun sets so lovely as it bows a goodnight. The curtain is
falling, the days play a delight.

A whippoorwill in the distance greets the night with a song.
His play just beginning, all night till the dawn.

Irma Catherine Lowery

"A Roof-Top Rain-Drop"

A roof top rain drop sadly falls to its demise.
  Single in its descent, no cover no disguise.
Shifted by the wind from the start to the end.
  A journey to the plot of a love one who does not,
Awake to end the pain or stop the showers of the
  salty rain.

  Only in time
  At peace in the mind
E. D. Wallace

"Love Knows No Circles"

Life's relentless circle had begun.
Six weeks later, he again entered a new world.
A young girl's determination to bring home a new puppy.

Learning from each other the rules of life,
The right's and wrongs, the do's and dont's.
The responsibility of dependency,
Yearning to share youthful experience together.

Years added up, maturity levels peaked,
As the days passed, dependency grew stronger.
Hair lighten, muscles weakened, responses slowed.
Training resumed, yet with pitiful encouragement.

Looking through his eyes, she remembers,
The laughs, the tears, the secrets, her best friend.
Looking into his eyes, she cries,
"My time is now, remember the good, and say goodbye."

Tears dripping, memories flashing,
"Save me a spot in the sun-I'll meet you there."
Now life's relentless circle has closed,
Yet true love never dies.

Dana G. Flanders

Night Flight

  His caramel cream skin; this curved road of a body that simply
states, "slippery when wet."
  His jungle eyes mesmerize me; turning me into a firefly gliding
through my desert life.
  He climbs my mountain until the eagle air becomes ours.
His honeysuckle tongue enhances his candied words.
Somehow, his 6 pack stomach is thirsty, yet quenching.
  His doved wings enhance and protect my french vanilla body.
    Together we dance in the morning sun.

Jennifer Michelle Busby

"All in God's Time"

Small seedling's growing, beneath the cold bitter snow.
Small droops of water, where soon rivers will flow.

Season's are day's and day's minutes long,
All flowing together, as the seedling's grow strong.

Sun rise dancing on the crest of a cloud.
Beams of light shine, where fresh leaves can be found.

Small trees are reaching straight up to the sky,
Flourish taller and stronger, together they rise.

Survive they will deeply rooted in the rocks,
Bringing fresh clean air, to all God's flock.

Great Redwoods grow from small seed you will find.
Patiently waiting, all in God's time.

Erin O'Brien

In The Silence Of The Night

The night wraps its empty arms around the earth.
Small lights from far away stars glitter against the sky,
like diamonds tossed randomly against a cloak of black velvet.
Silence and tranquility fall like a soft mist,
gathering unto itself the creatures of the land,
swathing them in the cocoon of peaceful sleep.
Fairies, from the land of Nod, with tiny wings
and hair the color of purest snow,
fly each to the bedside of every small child.
Upon their backs they carry in golden bags
the dust peaceful dreams.

Darlene M. Smeltzer

Rain

Rains are mighty important to all of us.
So I guess we shouldn't moan and fuss
When skies get dark with rain-filled clouds,
But jump with glee and shout out loud.

The stifling snow of Winter's gone;
The promises of Spring are born.
The seeds, and buds grow and spread,
Just as though a voice had said -
"Awake from your winter's sleep,
Your vibrant life will repeat
The age old custom of making the new,
From a little bit of sunshine, rain and you".

The green things form some sort of flower,
With the help of sparkling sun and shower
Next the leaves work night and day,
To change this blossom to what we say
Is an apple, a pear or a peach,
High on a limb, just out of reach.

All must have the sun and rain,
Or all God's work will be in vain.

Harold J. Hill

Memorial Day

Somewhere the sun isn't shining, there is just rain
Somewhere a family is in mourning with a lot of pain
Somewhere beneath a white cross lies their only son
War has taken his life before it had hardly begun
Somewhere people are striving to be free
Like in our country the land of liberty
Somewhere there is the happy song of a little bird
Somewhere the mournful sounds of "Taps" can be heard
Somewhere as you travel along life's busy highway
Stop and honor our veterans on this Memorial Day

Harold C. Smith

Getting Old

I hear the talk, fear of getting old,
so I talked to an old man with a heart of gold.
   The old one spoke with wisdom and care,
I asked a question "was life so unfair?"
   With a smile on his face and a twinkle in his eye,
he gathered his thoughts and gave a big sigh.
   He told me how memories, good and bad,
are just lessons of happy and sad.
   When you're old your life does not end,
you become a teacher with a message to send.
   Being old is a gift that we reach,
when we're there we've plenty to teach.
   It's good to be old and slowed down,
it gives us a chance to study a sound.
   To watch the cycle of life perform,
to see the beauty in a storm.
   To gather our thoughts and know what's right,
to teach the young and adore the sight.
   People will see what they haven't been told,
the reward of life is getting old.

Dennis L. Dodd

The Healer

A human's life is so very precious.
So little is understood to man regarding sickness and wellness.
Why is it that some individuals have the fortitude, strength,
and endurance, to fight the odds of misfortune? In contrast,
Others simply surrender to the forces of nature. Are we here on
earth for a predetermined amount of time? Is this time known only to
him the almighty? Perhaps those victims of near death experiences
can deem themselves fortunate to not only have a second chance to
live but to adopt a presbyopic perspective. Families and loved
ones of the victims can join in on appreciating the victim and
developing their own new view. Imagine considering the near end
of life as a rebirth. Priorities may change and uproars may lessen,
yet the core of the individual remains unaltered.

Donna Johnson

Lonely Me

Have you ever been lonely in a crowd?
So lonely you could just shout out loud,
"Here I am can't you see
I'm as lonely as I can be."

Come walk with me and hold my hand,
and be my friend and understand,
Just talk out loud or quiet be.
I feel so lonely, I'm just not me.

I am not sick nor am I mad
I just feel lonely, so very sad.
There must be someone who understands.
Come walk with me and hold my hand.

This feeling will pass. I've had it before
It just takes time to close the door.
My loneliness will leave it just takes awhile.
So walk with me and help me smile.

Clara L. Hoaks

Thanksgiving

Hope in life rejoicing
Striving by right
A search of good fortune
Love, laughter, and strife,
All living, good giving, great gathering tonight
A toast to happiness, to life ——

Jack T. Armstrong

A Drifting Friendship

When a close friend starts to drift away, it's so hard to believe
So many good times together, what happened to them all
You're afraid that with the friendship the memories will also leave
You ask yourself, is there anyway this breaking up can stall?

You wonder to yourself, did I do something wrong
If I would have tried harder would we still be friends now
That's when you must stand up and be strong
And stop killing yourself with that question, but how?

Nothing lasts forever, well except for memories
If the friendship really was beautiful and true
Then nothing, not even for off seas
Can take those thoughts from you.

Emy Biavaschi

"A Beauty Problem"

Now come to solve the beauty problem, it's a secret that's never told.
So neatly is each item wrapped, time doesn't permit me to unfold.

Beauty requires ambition, good health is the master key.
You'll be successful on this journey, whatever the task may be.

Girls, let glamour go to your head;
of course, the rest is important too.
But hair is your crowning glory,
especially arranged in a nice coiffure.

Just think about that uplifted face, a sparkling manicure.
But still I'll say it can't be beat, with the right kind of a hairdo.

Life is so enchanting, to receive that feminine touch.
To hear those flattering masculine words adoring you, it means so much.

No matter what texture your hair may be, or, how dark or grey.
These charming styles await you dear, the modernistic way.

Select your choice "Miss Pin-Up-Girl": Redhead, Brunette, or Blond.
I'm sure you'll want, without a doubt, your skin to correspond.

Now solving this beauty problem, when the question is put to a test.
The answer is: "This only human nature, for one to look one's best."

Catherine Lewis

In Your Hands

In your hands you hold something that is very fragile and sensitive,
So please handle with caution and pay close attention

Treat it with special care
If you do you shall be rewarded with a love that will always be there.

In your hands you holds something that means a whole lot to me,
Hold on to it tight and never set it free.

In your hands you hold my heart
A heart that is filled with devotion and all the dedication
I can possibly offer to you, give me a chance to prove that my
   love is true.

Open your eyes, look deep inside this heart of gold
And you'll see my heart is all you need to hold.

Enid Estela

Sometimes

Sometimes- she cries at night
Sometimes- she considers giving up her fight
Sometimes- she gets angry
Sometimes- she gets sad
Sometimes- she wants to murder the one she calls dad
Sometimes- but rarely, there's a true smile on her face
Sometimes- but rarely, she finds that safe place
Sometimes- there's hope, other times there's doubt
Sometimes- all she can do is scream and shout
Sometimes- there's hope, that gives her the freedom within
Sometimes- enabling her to struggle and Win!!!

Heather Lockwood

She Is Truth

A light way off in the distance
So small I could barely see
Shining in radiant splendor
In the midst of a turbulent sea.

Proudly she faces the doubts of the skeptical
The cavils of the cautious
Severing the opposition night and day.
Conquering all obstacles along the way.

Like a pearl being peeled by layers
Shown only to be as genuine as the one before
All other forms are only synthetic
Still perversions increase even more,

Motionless she stands in beauty that will never tarnish
Among time honored creeds of the day
A stately marble stone their only monument
That shall crumble and blow away.

She is invisible and does not change with time
Holding fast to a day of realization
When all contradictions are made transparent
And truth has finally known liberation.

    Benilla Chavez

Incredible Gift

Giving birth is a wonderful thing,
So they say.
Then why do I feel so bad.
Having doctors sticking, poking every which way.
Oh, yeah! birth is a wonderful thing.

The pain is so intense.
I just cant stand the suspense.
Did I really make the right decision?
Oh, no! The baby can't get through,
Here comes another incision.
When will this be over?
Can't I make the decision?

As I feel the life come out of me.
I look up to see this beautiful baby,
I cant believe what I see,
She is so beautiful,
And kind a of looks like me.

I don't think birth is a wonderful thing.
I think it is the most incredible gift,
That I will ever receive.

    Denise Burdette

My Form Of Expression

They always want to hold my hand before they die,
So they will remember the warmth of the living skin,
We are made of only tissue and bones,
But those tissue and bones relate to so much more;

It relates to our last breaths on earth
It relates to our first born's breathing of
of the air we breath.
Emotions make up for the words we
couldn't speak
Words make up for all the tears we couldn't keep
The generations of people that have lived before
and will live beyond
Will always somehow make everything bond.

    Jennifer Schmidt

Remorse

There's life stored deep in the corners of my mind.
So very deep that my thoughts, are sometimes hard to find.
But, when I will this life to appear,
It envelopes me with all that I hold dear.
I go back to a time so pure and so sweet,
Where peace and happiness just seemed to meet.
And, as I dare let this other life in,
I'm transported to a place I've often times been.
So precious are these thoughts, they seem so real,
I let them take control until
Every sense of my being begins to react.
I try desperately to ignore the cold hard facts.
Yesterday's gone and I can no longer pretend,
As sadness takes over where brief utter joy has been.
I'm reminded like a sore that cannot heal,
What reality will never again let me feel.
"My friend", I hear reality say, "you made the choice - now go away."
Forget the past and live for today.

    Barbara Dunwody

The Distant Glance

How tender is the night of your calling
Softly you whisper from afar in my ear,
Your voice, so warm and gentle
With the softness of your touch so dear.

The radiance of your eyes in passing
Through the shadows your stance serene,
Can I touch for a moment your memory
To picture you here in my dream.

As you fade within the mist of the morning
Leave you footprints in the melting dew,
That I may glance upon your fair beauty
Before the day has become a new.

Be still for a moment my darling
That I may see you in the stillness of day,
To once more see a trace in the distance
Of your loveliness as I stand so far away.

    Ann Shinall

Ego

I am myself
Sole ruler of myself
I belong to myself.
The self believes in itself
And cherishes its total liberty;
Liberties in both extremities.
Chauvinism is a policy to the self
And never accepts anybody's view.
Sole supreme ruler is the idea of the self
And nothing in this world is of importance than myself.
Self-centered, egoistic and self-conceited are my major adjectives.
Society per se is doing things, for an with each other
Would my egos then allow me to fit in society?
Until I change society into "egociety" society would never ever
never ever would society tolerate the greedy self.
Unity and productivity are the goals
Let us stand together as a brethren
Let us form society
And not a society of egos.

    Justice M. Sekyi

Untitled

The room is dark,
   someone calls my name.
"Who are you?   Is this a game?"
   My head spins.
The light begins to dim...
"Help!" I'm falling...
   death keeps calling...
It sounds so sweet, so peaceful,
   so free.
"Who wouldn't want to leave this world"
   death whispers...
"It's full of hate, destruction; of greed..."
   Something holds me back,
     someone is in need, and wants me to be in the lead.
"Don't take me!" I scream
"Can't you see? I'm not ready!" I cry;
I'm afraid to die.
Somewhere someone loves me
   And I can now see
   The light of life...
   Jani Whitacre

Someone Special

Someone who's there for you when you're lonely and feeling sad.
Someone who's there when you're feeling bad,
Someone who is a always there to
Cheer you up when you are down,
Someone to count on when
Everything's going wrong and try
to fix it or make you know that you're not alone.
Someone who shares your ups and
Downs to put a smile back on your
Face when you're wearing a frown
You're that special someone and I
Want you to know how very much
I love you so!!!
   Gretta Alden

Nothing Could Ever Compare

I've tried to find something special
Something symbolic, something true,
But all that I have found
Is that nothing could ever be a greater gift than you.
Nothing could ever compare
To the gleaming laughter in your eyes,
And nothing could ever be as wonderful as the feelings
I've felt when you've held me on so many nights.
There isn't anything I could ever buy
That would be worth as much as your heart,
And there's nothing I can do
To keep me from missing you when we're apart.
So I've found that there's nothing
I could ever find or do,
I compare to or to show you
Just how much that I love you.
   Christie Lee Frimml

The Moon

The moon comes at night as it magnificently illuminates the sky,
Sometimes it seems like you could touch it, if only you could fly,
The large ball remains shining throughout the night,
Filling many people with great feelings of delight,
It hides behind clouds leaving not a trace,
Suddenly it reappears, lighting up your face,
Soon, the moon tires, moving to a new place,
After a while it begins to get light,
Meaning that it is near the end of the night,
This brings much sadness for a day has to go by,
Before you can see that wonderful, gleaming ball of light.
   David Hightower

One Step Closer

I can't hear your scream, but I can sense your tone
Something's right yet, something's wrong
He felt a sense of panic, so he had to run
I felt his pain, I laughed, as I showed him the gun

Some say the flowers feel this kind of pain
But then again it may be a way of keeping our children insane
Quick to react, I stood.
My actions dissolved the fact that he had done no good

I glanced at the newly arrived dawn
Wondering how that image had appeared so quickly
The man's mind must have been wandering
I don't think he knew that he would soon fall

I took a military stance
Eyes pierced on the black hood
In an almost gallant voice
I proclaimed "Ready, aim-
One step closer
   David R. McConnell

Never Forget...

We've had our good days, we've had our bad.
Sometimes even, you made me mad.
When it came to guys, you knew them all.
The good, the bad, and ugly all call.
I remember the guys, well, most of them.
There were so many, will it ever end?
I hope I'll be someone you'll always remember,
Even when it's Freezing in December.
'Cause of this and much, much more.
Throughout your life will be many a door.
And I hope that all of them will hold,
Love and riches more precious than gold.
   Amy Hefty

'Without Understanding'

Fade to black
Sometimes I catch myself wandering,
Pausing to catch my breath.
It is a lonely feeling being alone.
Yes, I've felt love's hand teasing and tempting me with
heated...
heated pleasure which tantalizes,
all the senses simultaneously.
Euphoria is the only way to explain,
the way I feel during this stimulation, this sensation.
Come back and tame the wild passions that burn deep within,
...whipped of all desires.
Tears begin to fall...
Fade to black.
Sometimes I catch myself wandering,
and I pause to catch my breath!
   Jean Marie Davis

April Rain, February Snow

Spring and Winter, two different seasons.
Spring anew with things reborn.
And Winter's cold winds blow.
But two sons taken away,
One to April rain and another to February snow.
Though I grieve as year's go by,
I know they walk in sun-light bright.
And loved so much as God can only know.
Their names remembered-Wayne and Donald
Love, Mother
   Carol Hejhal

Live Forever

We were born to die,
sometimes life seems as though it's a lie.
Sometimes we feel cheated and mistreated,
that's the way life has to be lived and completed.
One day God is going to call home the Holy,
but there will only be a few that is chosen.
Some say He want ever, ever return,
those are the ones that will scream and be burned.
The life you live will speak for itself,
so live a good life with the time you have left.
God is the answer, forever and ever,
so you have a choice between God and the devil.
So, give your life to the man on high,
and live forever and never really die.

Gloristine Brown

Mirages Of Morning

Herds of elephants roam the sky
Sometimes there's camels and horses that fly
Cotton floats gently with feathers and fluff
Looks like a lady's blue, powder puff

Slivers of sun slice through whip cream pie
While passing over a giant's red eye
A sleepy, hound dog, snout on a cloud
Barks at the sun, shining out loud

Frosty, night silk, shimmery white
Glistens with splendor in subtle daylight
A mysterious veil drifting around
Mixes with sunbeams over the ground

Shadows from trees in sunlight align
Dew made of diamonds and islands that shine
Bewitching mountain, silhouetted in ink
Backgrounds soft clouds, tinted with pink

Mirages of morning, different each day
Early they come, as night fades away

Irene E. Senkiw

Hues Of Indigo

I dream of an indigo summer night
Somewhere, a hidden lagoon
Born to the music of playful spheres
In an ocean beyond the moon.

It is shrouded in mist and its waves
Are kissed by millions of twinkling stars
diffusing the night with a sapphire light
Like the rays of a sunset on Mars.

Drift away with me, just close your eyes,
Gentle wafts of breezes we feel
Watch the pale moon paint our paradise
As visions take shape, become real.......

This dream of mine began to bloom
When lavender blossoms were new
I store it safe in their perfume
Only waiting to share it with you—-

One magic night, when all wishes come true,
In my dream of indigo blue.

Doris E. Carey

Until We Meet Again!!

Until we meet again hold my picture, close at hand, because,
soon we'll meet again, in Heaven, that bright and beautiful
land. For now we must separate, but, I'll meet you again, just
inside, the Pearly Gate!! So come to meet me soon I can't wait!!
Until we meet again, remember, Jesus, now safely holds me, in
His Arms, I no longer feel the pain, I'm free from all harms! I
want you to know the peace, that I feel, I'm with Jesus, My
Saviour, now, I've found joy and peace that are
real!!! Until we meet again, I know the days ahead, will be
hard, for you, because, we are now apart. But, soon you can
meet me, If, you, let Jesus, in your heart!! I know the tears,
are in your eyes, and you'll miss me, but, please try not to
grieve, I've fought the good fight of faith, and now, it's time
for me to leave!! Until we meet again, for now we must part,
but, it won't be for long, because, soon we'll meet again in
Heaven, and sing the Great Victory Song!! Remember, me in
the long days ahead, that I am happy, now, I'll never, have to
cry out, because of pain, I'm with Jesus, My Saviour, now, and
my Home In Heaven is my gain!!

In Loving Memory Of Lisa
Alice Ann (Lawson) Cartwright

Patches

My quilt is made of many patches,
Sown with different colors and patterns.
Made from joy, tears, love and laughter,
Filled with memories forever lasting.

One patch is from a little girls laughter
Of a large brown bear holding a flower.
One patch is from her tears once shed,
A torn hole in the knee of her favorite red pair.
One is from my husbands old work clothes,
A dress I use to wear to the picture show.

Filled with the times and trials we have shared,
Realizing through it all how much God cares.
For like those patches our lives are sown,
With caring hands and love that grows.
For each square resembles apart of our lives,
Places and times of things gone by.
All sown together one by one,
Until finally the whole quilt is done.

Jennie Carol Mabe

The Swan That Spread His Wings And Flew

In a brilliant land of shimmering clouds and
sparkling stars, a swan will spread his wings and fly.
Not just a swan, but a very beautiful creature.
Every evening it is felt, in every heart it has
meaning, every soul is reminded. The swan will spread his wings
and fly.
The swan that has dreamt. That single, special swan, will fly.
The storm. Lightning lights up the stars. Thunder thuds the
distance. The rain.
The rain washes away darkness. The darkness...that
fierceness that tries to take its hold in every being and soul.
The swan knows. It is comforted.
The shining sun breaks through the black.
The swan knows. It is time.
In a brilliant land of shimmering clouds and sparkling
stars, a swan spread his wings and flew.

Brandy Matson

Black Snow

The blue sky
Speckled with delicate black dots.
It falls on you softly
Sliding down your neck as it melts
Like ink
Spilling on a table

The air is cold but the snow,
is warm
Just a bit

The world is covered with
Tufts of black cotton
Cinders black and cool with age as if
A fire took place up in the heavens went out
Suddenly the remains fall with grace, style

Its snow
New and difficult
As if the midnight sky
Is caving in on you
Its snow
The black kind
    Elisha Willis

Untitled

Triumphant gauls of harrowing mindless wandering
Spring forth into dominions of encompassed freedom
Washing away the fingerprints of blind children's dreams
Shattered glass and broken pumpkins arranged
Geometrically in correspondence to the
Holes of the persistent hummingbird...
Peck, Peck, Peck at the curtain
The iron wall
The loud screaming
The softness of her breast
The thirst of a throat bleeding
And blisters on my feet aren't possible anymore
The day tore me apart.
A prayer for the refugees of ignorance...
May sleep bring a long awaited
Sunrise.
    Charles Marshall

Abortion And Conquest

Transparent fingers
squeeze gelatinous matter:
the taste of centuries filled with the same,
twisting and turning a stomach in the making,
while the sea may shake tomorrow
where the unfinished race resides.

This intercourse can't be right,
but the desire, the urge is the norm
and reproduces a gospel
of erect pockets and empty organs,
flooding with milk a new world.

It's the inception of frustrated breasts that vomit.

Round eyes of dark warmth
contemplate an unstable miscegenation,
while mothers and fathers, domes and caverns,
keep some beat
of howling mutilation.
    Irene Pantelis

The Faith

She had a dream -
Standing on the still to
She starved for the freedom
Looking on her baptist insteps
She cried for the death
She had a dream-
There were lilies on the bottom of the sea
There was water of devote in her eyes
There were diamonds upon the sky
There were rubies in his hands

She had a dream-
Having no wings
She tried to fly
Leaving no heart
She tried to love

She was covered by black feather
Ash was in her hair
    Eva Roskotova

Windows

Sitting next to the window on a cold, winter afternoon,
Staring inward.
Staring back.
Listening to the patter of rain on the tin roof,
And the long swish and rumble of passing cars on the wet road.

A Sudden Sound brings me home.

Clinging to the window, a solitary pale red feather.
Cardinal - your sudden intrusion startled my world.
I long to reach outside, outward, and bring you in,
Heal the wounds, mend the bones.
If your legs were broken, if your wings failed you,
I would have brought you inside, inward, and helped you to fly
again.
But you broke something that wouldn't, couldn't be fixed,
So I just let go.

You left me standing, focusing on my shimmering reflection in the
glass,
Looking outward,
Looking forward.
Standing at the window on a winter afternoon, waiting for spring.
    James F. Harris

'Shake And Bake'

Am I in the state of California or in a
state of shock, I never know from one day
to the next if a 6.8 will stop my clock,
and start the hanging plants to sway and the
lamps to bounce and fall, and cracks appear
from ceiling to floor and down tumbles the
backyard wall, or if not a quake, it's those
terrible fires that ravage our canyons and
hills, or maybe a torrential downpour that
pushes mud up to our windowsills. This has
long been known as the Golden State but
lately it's mostly black, brown or gray, and frantic
calls to my insurance man go unanswered for
another day. And so you see how sad is our plight,
we don't know which way to turn when the earth
begins to rumble and roar-or everything begins
to burn. Even so, the welcome mat is always out,
come visit us whenever you can, just bring a
hard hat and fire-retardant clothes and
a strong back to fill bags with sand.
    Dick Keller

Success Without The Crawl

If I could parry the many
steps to be climb in a day or two,
not more than several months at hand,
I'll soar to the height of my present
and future dreams.

From where I stand, the
height seems high with many
miles beyond what my eyes can view.

If I could parry the steps awaiting
the company of my bare feet,
I'll not look back to curse the steps that
others fear of climbing — because of height
that appears much greater in dimension
than the steps to the ladder really be.

I'll treasure the blessings
that came to bed within, and
not look behind to gloat my dreams,
but in lieu, bless all who becomes determine
to accompany the trail I managed to parry.

Cathy S. Walker

The Peace Has Died

talk of war froze the hearts of people
stillness overcame the land around them
could it really happen? Would peace be destroyed forever?
deep thoughts rang over the land
joy turned into sorrow, and laughs turned into frightened tears
they knew the devil would strike soon
the love was gone from all people
why did this have to happen?
did these two different worlds have to be split apart anymore?
why couldn't we stay out of it?
why must war settle our differences?
these questions brought other thoughts to people's minds

hearts turned to black ice
the men were ready to defend the country
clouds turned into black sheets of lace
The Terror, The Horror, The Devil had come!
suddenly, a painful bomb shot down to the ground
pain shot out across the land!
then it was over; all was done; the War had begun

No one will ever know when peace will be restored!

Johanna Blackstone

My Lost Child

Little girl, little girl, where are you running to,
Stop and listen, I'm talking to you.
You're hurting your loved ones and most of all, me.
The world out there is rough, tough, hard as can be,
The crowd will lead you down the road to destruction.
Call on me your Lord God and I will lead you down the
road that's constructed, which leads you to love, happiness,
good health and all that is good.
The road is narrow and not many will follow,
But I'll be with you-guiding you along.
One day you will be judged and you will answer to me!
There's nothing you can do that I can not see,
So get on your knees and pray to me!
Everyone loves you, most of all, me.
You're just a little girl who knows nothing about life,
So honor your father, mother and me, and life will be
easy and as happy as can be.
Little girl, little girl I love thee.

Florence Passarell

The Seasons

This has been a bad winter. We just get over one snow
storm, and we'd have another.

Now we are looking forward to spring.

For eighty-seven years I've lived through—winter, spring,
summer and fall—
with same joy of watching each season.

The first snow, the slow unfurling of the leaves, as they do
in Vermont in the spring.

Summer heat and flowers in bloom.

Autumn especially in Vermont with the maples in red, orange
and yellow.

The change of seasons is what I like about Vermont.

Elizabeth Watchorn

Like Spoons In The Kitchen Drawer

Skinny, nervous sixteen year old bride woman-child clutches
strong eighteen year old arm. Groom peach fuzz cheeks is so
fiercely protective. Snickers, whispers won't last. Children
playing house. Belly swollen blue veined with purple plum
navel. Ugly thing to hold so great a treasure. Breast hot
aching, heavy with the life source for the small prisoner
who kicks at the gate demanding freedom. Same strong arm
escorts three beautiful white veiled brides. Who gives this
woman? Her mother and I. Strong handsome sons their Father's
smile. How many thousand nights nestled like spoons in the
kitchen drawer listening to that same heart beat? Almost in
rhythm from the other. Gentle breath through her
hair lulling her to sleep each night. Almost fifty years gone
like a stroll around the block.

Georgia Ellis

Believe In Me

Early in the morning when the
sun begins to rise, I feel a warm
sensation coming deep from inside.
A cool breeze blows across my
golden brown skin, thinking as I
walk of this world that I'm in.
Why are we here, what are these
words that I speak?
Questions if confusion,
it's knowledge that I seek.
Believe in me and the curiosity
I bring, of life's long history and all
worldly things. How did we come
about, no one really knows, just a
book called the Bible, does it really shows?

Calvin Lee Davis

Love

An angel from heaven once came to me
telling me of the world's hate lost in misery
and of the past unbeaten, and of the present undone
and of the future with hope that someday might be won
and after seeing all this, I asked about fate
she said he was lost, defeated by hate
so I asked of father time and about his wise ways
she said he was dying and in his last days
and she told me of hope, and of her lost shine
and she told me of life, so I asked about mine
that's when she told me of the strength that comes from above
she told me don't worry, we still have love

Jason Malott

A Lover's Wish

I wish you,
  Sunny blue skies and green flowering meadows.
  Long quiet walks on the beach on cool starry nights,
  Soft beautiful music on lazy afternoons,
  And on starless nights, the full yellow harvest moon.
  The pot of gold at the end of the rainbow,
  And on dark wintry nights, soft glowing moonlight.
I wish you,
  Good luck in three's,
  Love overflowing and happiness forever,
I wish you,
  Success in every undertaking,
  The "Midas Touch" at your fingertips
I wish you,
  A generous, trusting heart,
  And warm arms to enfold you on cold, chilly mornings.
  Everything your heart so desires.
  May sorrow and despair never overcome you,
  And may the shadow of happiness constantly pursue you.

   Carmen de la Rosa

Untitled

I stood atop the mountain
surveying my entire world, while
the piercing howling wind jabbed its daggers
  into my bones
seemingly to rent my fickle body limb from limb.
My head whipped back, my arms stretched wide

As if to hold back that mighty force
  which I can hear but never see
  feel, but never touch.
  surrounds me, yet is within me.

I lifted my face to Heaven and I screamed
with every ounce of my being.
Yes I screamed for my brothers
  without a voice
and my sisters who cannot be heard.
Sound bellowed forth from my tiny frame
lashed out against the rushing wind
and exploded into the
Cruel, unforgiving ugly world
  Give me back my love.

   Allison Quamina

Love Is Gone

My love has left me, oh my true love, oh.
Sweet and gentle, then strong and powerful.
My true love has left me and it hurts so.
Without him my life will be much too dull.
How can I live without his sweet love.
His gentle embrace now a memory.
A memory just lingering above.
Now high in the sky with gentle glory.
His love is too soft to be swept away.
A friend was he, and a great one at that.
His voice was a whisper on a spring day.
The true love was there between us, in fact.
He was there today, but not tomorrow.
That is what has given me my sorrow.

   Janet M. Gilbert

You And A Deer

You are like a deer.
Sweet and innocent sometimes.
But sometimes playing in a field.
You try to stay out of trouble and danger.
Sometimes you make it sometimes you don't.
When you get in trouble you look for help.
Sometimes in a friend or just whoever comes by.
You don't trust everybody.
You have learned that lesson.
You are tired of getting hurt by people around you.
You are also tired of put downs
You want to run but you have no place to go.
You have no place to turn for help but your friends.
You don't know if you can trust them.
You are like a deer.
Sweet and innocent!
Looking for help having no where to turn!

   Courtney Atkins

Easter

A miracle garden sleeps in our heart...
  Sweet gentle breezes scatter tiny seeds...
   God's gifts.

As God cultivates the mind and heart
  they become fertile seedbeds.
  Now we are partners helping God.

Soft rains nourish the soul with
  beautiful peace,
   fragrant love,
    bountiful joy.

The eternal rhythm of regeneration
    bursts anew,
     interacting,
    unfolding,
    elevating.

The blossoms within us open,
  resurrecting all to experience
Easter in our heart.

   Betty Borcher

Living

A sweet voice came out of Melody Mountain,
Sweet singing, out of a living fountain.

Singing lifted my heart and my soul,
Gave me grace and love un-told.

Jesus loves me night and day,
God's Son is the only way.

God made this beautiful living earth,
God's Son Jesus for our saving birth.

   Dorothy Gemes

Shades Of Gray And Black

  The lady in the picture of shades of Gray and Black—
Take me to another time, a time and place way back.
  In my dreams I wonder what it would be like, if I
Could just go see the lady in the picture staring back at me.
  If only it were possible to go back to this long forgotten day,
To find the girl, and hear what she might have to say.
  Would she tell me that the picture isn't all that it seems,
And that her world wasn't all fairy tales and dreams.
  Maybe she'd tell me that her life was very much like mine,
And it's deep within myself the truth that I must find.
  Maybe she'd tell me not to hide in Shades Of Gray And Black,
To take each day for what it is,— because you can't go back.

   Georgia A. Radel

The Tree Of Knowledge

Fluent was the gaelic from Eve's comely mouth
Sweeter the kisses from thine my love of the bluest eye
Sweetest voice whitest teeth
Neatest form.... Beautiful was the picture.

My people the travelling minstrels of Ireland
Well favored lads were they the dregs of the old gael
Listen to the music...
I saw no-one at the tree, at which you stood
Since you departed from us had the wind blown
The tree would have fallen...

No fiddle nor harp nor high pipes sweet drones
lift my spirit my life my sky empty-I am
Without sun without moon
Like a withered tree without foliage
As the tree falls so it lies....
Loneliness without peace

If you have forsaken me my fairest girl
Though a frosty wind should pierce your soul
Bear my heart-if you did not break it....
And leave it in Strome.
   Bill Watkins

Dear Grandpa

   You've been with me all my life
taken care of us and teaching us to take
things in strife.

   Showing us love, understanding and pride
now 93 it must be your time to go and be
with your bride.
   To walk hand in hand, side by side.

   Now as I sit here watching the tides roll
away. My minds memory of you will
always stay locked on the times when
you and I used to play.
   I never thought there would be the day
when the angels would come and
carry you away.
   Angela Babik

The Dream

Speak to us, American flag
Tell us of the taut and tensioned
   Hope
Holding your seams together —
Tell us a story of healing and renewal,
Of forefathers' designs
   still framing and uplifting this republic —
Remind us of the nobleness of civility;
   Of caring for and respecting others' liberties as our own —
Instill in us the faith born of
   parents' and teachers' visions —
That each, to their fullest ability, will
   grow, prosper, and contribute back to the land
As corruption stains your fabric,
As violence shreds your corners,
As selfishness permeates your membranes,
Assure us that through
   the darkest night, into dawn's light,
   Your spirit will remain.
   David Barnett

Beloved Grandmother

I heard her sweet but decisive voice calling me from far away,
Telling me to be myself and ignore what others say.
I then searched all over and saw a figure in white.
I ran to it hastily and embraced it so tight.

I felt her tender heart beating; I noticed her loving smile.
She's back! I thought, and she'll be here for a while.
I asked her to stay with me, but she only replied,
"You must be on your own, but I'll always be by your side."

Her words were reassuring - they meant everything to me,
But then I woke up that morning lacking her precious company.
I realize that she's gone forever; I can never see her face again.
But I can feel her heart within me, and it will guide me... to the end.
   Hien Ta

"About Nicole"

   Bright spirit.
    Tender bud.
   Sweetness, delight and joy
Were in the shining silver threads
   That marked her days.
    Love and trust
   Were gifts she freely gave.
   With smiles and waving hand,
    To all who loved her.
   All those who now mourn and grieve
    Because she's gone from us.
The world is now a dimmer, shadowed place
    And hearts are sore
   And pain of loss pervades our days.
   She graced our lives with beauty
    For one brief precious year
   And left with us sweet memories
    That burn and hurt,
    That bless and heal.
   Evelyn Smith Richardson

Heartbreak

Heartbreak,
Terrible, unkind, and hurtful.
You think you'll never get over it,
But then comes Mr. Gorgeous in to your life.
Then you're happy.
You think how could I ever have been heart broken over him?
The pain has settled.
Then the cycle begins again.
But not always,
Not when you find Mr. Right.
   Courtney Dillon

Time

Time goes by so slowly for the earth,
That a billion years are but an hour;
But for humans, time speeds by so quickly,
That our lives are spent in a flash of an eye.

For some, time is an enemy,
Not enough time in a day or lifetime,
And even for some because there is too much of it;
But for some people time is a friend,
For each moment is savored and enjoyed to the fullest,
Each day and year is precious.

Sometimes we bounce between the two,
One time is precious,
And another is boring and an enemy;
But time goes on no matter the moment,
Till it is no more.
   Judith G. Beverly

"Communicationless"

The evening flame grows dimmer
than the light that shines from your eyes
as I notice a faint glimmer of hope
in the exchange of words we convey
has the silence been broken,
now that words have been spoken?
or is it just a brief respite, from recriminations,
volleyed back and forth, for what seems like forever and etc.

A cancer grows in the heart of our deepest emotions
which was never detected early
and we had hoped for a diagnosis reading "benign"
as we study the report over and over
but it reads the same every time

You had me forever saying, "I'm sorry"
while I always caused you, suspicion to worry
So my tongue drools one final "I'm sorry"
and now it's time to switch this light bulb off and close the
door shut, and walk away from this room while we're still on
human terms, and at least we'll always know that we gave it our
best shot (perhaps?).

Jay Mucci

Dear John

J is for the JOY you gave me when I opened my gift and found
　that beautiful Christmas candle shaped pin.
　Every time I wear it I'll especially think of you.

O is for ONLY you, John that could think up such a cute gift.

H is for HAPPINESS that you always spread to everyone.
　Happy is all I can see in you when you are out here on the farm
　riding the mini bike, feeding cats, taking a bath and just
　eating peanut butter sandwiches.

N is for NEVER being unkind to us and waking up daily with a
　bright cheery smile saying Betty, I'm hungry.
　Never a battle when it's time for bedtime stories and prayers.
　You will always be a part of us regardless where you are.
　We thank you for making our life full of action and you can count
　on our home as your home filled with love and memories that only
　you could give to two people who love you very much.

Betty Lou Pollestad

My Prayer 4 U'r Eternity

By writing this Prayer I have only 1 goal,
That by doing this 4 God it will save U'r soul.

It is so simple 2 B saved and him abide,
Just pray 4 4-giveness and B on his side.

Then U must tell others that U R now saved,
That U'r road 2 Heaven has now been paved.

U must B Baptized 2 cleanse U'r heart,
2 show Jesus you love him and will do U'r part.

Think how many people U can take with U,
If U R willing 2 do what he wants U 2 do.

Then read U'r Bible and U'll learn more and more,
And Prayer is U'r key 2 Heaven, it will open the door.

Then once in a while give God a day,
Just 2 spend all in His way.

Get in a church and do U'r part,
This my Friend will strengthen U'r heart.

Then when God comes as a thief in the night,
The Trumpet will blow and he'll be in sight.

How wonderful 4 us who can fly off with him,
This is my Prayer so now AMEN.

Janet Sue Kemp

My Best Friend

My best friend is like a shooting star she's got the strength
that carries her on. And the world that knows can't deny that
she's got the prettiest big brown eyes. She knows just what to
say she knows just what to do. She's got the laughter that calms
the sky. She can touch your heart without a clue. When she's
feeling kind of blue she doesn't hesitate on what to do. When
you see her having fun it's like she's got the key to the heart.
She's got the touch that heals my wounds and she keeps me going
strong. She knows just how to cheer me up when I'm feeling
kind of down. I can look at her and see the light that she
possesses deep inside. Because she is one of a kind that my
friend is called "unique". No, I'd never say goodbye, because
true friendship lies within the heart.

Diana Cruz

This Kite

This patch of color up in the blue
That feels the tug of the string
As it dances and darts
Just to be there in the sky
To soar and swoop on the thermals
And go with any wind
Not being just earthbound again

This one kite rather than being held by a string
Chose to fall in the very top of a tree
Where he became ragged and frayed
But oh that kite really soared in the sky for a while,
And its best choice was to fall into a tall tree
Where it could still feel the breezes
That rattled its paper and sticks
Rather than being tamed by a string
And go back to earth again.

Annette P. Felton

Admiring Love

He's the love of my dreams
That flows through my sleep.
He has the look of a chocolate sundae.
Smooth, creamy, luscious, and sweet.
The way he dresses blows my mind.
I can't help but stare time after time.
Every time I see him my heart skips a beat.
My feelings I can't hide, they come out every time we meet.
Every time he looks at me my heart seems to melt.
He has this power over me that I can't ever control.
This strong feeling I can't make it out.
This admiring love is making me fly all about!

Cassandra Johnson

The Man

I sit across from a man.
That man is a stranger to me, but yet I know this man.
I know the tales that he tells.
Somehow I have heard them before.
These stories are about the good old days.
They are stories of happiness and sometimes heroism.
I sit across from this man and I look deep into his eyes.
I see a familiar face.
It is the face of my own grandfather.
I remember the days when I would sit for hours and listen to
my grandpa tell his stories of his own happiness and
sometimes his own heroism.
People laugh at this man.
They say that he does not know what he is talking about.
　But I know the truth.
I know the meaning of these stories.
I know the feeling of not hearing these tales that they tell.
I sit across from this man and wish he were my own grandpa
and I could hear the tales that he tells.

Heather Lewis

Beauty

Beauty is the mist
That freshens up the morn
Sparkling on the roses
After the dawn
Beauty is the sunshine
That brightens up your eyes
As softly dancing shadows caress the sky

Stars and moon aglowing
As their rays are kissed by the sea
All nature and beauty's showing tranquility
Rain wakes up the flowers
And sets the lovers free
All nature and beauty's growing in harmony.

Beauty is the mist
That freshens up the morn
Sparkling on the roses
After the dawn
Beauty is the sunshine
That brightens up your eyes
As softly dancing shadows caress the sky.

Carrie Rice Suter

Owed To A Broken Heart

For so long would I lie awake through the night and wish
That in your arms I would be
To ask for a hug went unheard, unforeseen,
That for so long, to be so alone, seemed much like a dream

But for whose dream, does it seem, were we living?
Were we not caring?
And does not sharing allow those dreams to become one,
The same?

Oh the shame that I feel for not bearing my heart
That my soul may be relieved
But for the past do I grieve, it is tomorrow you will see that
For I have been searching
Had not died, but was just sleeping

Like the dream from which I'm awakening
Life is real and we can make it, what we will, so embrace it
Let's not ignore it, like the heart that aches
And the soul that can grieve forever
If we let it
Alone

Donna M. Howard

A Cultivated, Nurtured, Thornless Rose

A cultivated, nurtured, thornless rose-
That is not I.
A wild, unruly, untamed thorny rose,
Yet yielding to the laws of Nature and Nature's God.
I run through the meadows where lover's meet,
hair streaming, laughing a Nymph's laugh, mocking the fools
among soft moss.
I am sister to the trees.
The same blood flows through us-
stretching, reaching, straining against what pulls us down into its depths.
Upward, growing upward, they against gravity, I against tradition,
expectations.
The trees and I are blood.
They say dreams are for dreaming-
I say they are for living. I will live them, in spite of those
traditional cords that cunningly try to bind me to lace and
flour and scented hankies and puffy overbearing bows and silks
and mascara. I champion the dream, my existence a waking
dream. I will embrace the sun, I will grasp the elusive
clouds, and laugh a Nymph's laugh that will echo back down to
those dank and mundane earthly depths.

Erin Guinn

Her Beauty I Cannot Escape

Let me not look into those eyes of love
That knows no mercy, which have no end;
With sweet sincerity and grace from above,
They hold me like fetters that do not bend.

A prisoner am I of her long black hair
As it weaves a silken web about me;
Holding me tight as if I were not there,
They drain my strength from breaking free.

Radiant is her face that glistens like the sun
Of which there is none on earth to compare;
And when she speaks, I become as one undone
Melting from the gentle voice that so fills the air.

How long shall I remain a captive here?
Or who shall, from her beauty, set me free?
Shadows of sorrow lead me to despair
As I forever conceal that love which shall never be.

Jonathan Mitchell

A Promise To Keep

Season's may come and go, as I make this promise to you,
that my love will always be until the end of time.
Without you my world will be filled with loneliness
because you're my morning light,
and night star that shines so bright.
When the storms of life get a little to rough,
I promise to shelter you from all the pain
as the rain washes away the tears from your eyes.
I promise you that my heart will remain faithful
and give all the love it can give.
I promise all of this as long as you want me.

Debra Smith

All In A Single Tear

What once was yours
That now has gone;
Fallen from your eyes,
Missing from your lips,
But always stuck in your heart.
It is gone.

It is a life claimed by death,
A love claimed by hate.
It is a need that will now go unfulfilled,
As the tear that no longer falls from your eye.

The laughter in the dark
Stolen by the light.
Oh, how you resent
How you despise!
All you want is to reclaim what is yours
Only to realize,
That it never existed.

Christopher Lopez

The Storm

The sky was blue and lazy when suddenly,
The clouds crept upon it and overpowered the lazy dome.
The gray puffs bared their chest and let out a fierce cry.
They roared and thundered and collided with each other.
They then intertwined and became one with nature.
The whole heaven was then hot and charged with volts.
It heaved and shot out bolts.
When the clouds were fulfilled they left in ecstasy.
The whole sky was renewed and bloomed into fertility.

Fouzia Syed

To Catch A Dream

I wish for you endless dreams
  that one by one come true,
I wish for you calming streams
  after the storm, of the day is through.
Hold on each separately your dreams - your identity
  keep the you that lives in your heart,
To yourself be true, but together unite
  with this freedom you never will part.
I wish for you many years of love
  for an island we weren't meant to be,
Share the joys and the tears; the ups, the downs
  it's not you, it's not me, but now we.
Embrace the days, for they pass but to fast
  cherish the nights when God sleeps,
Take not for granted the simplicities of life
  it's these small gifts He gives us that last.
Boundless like the evening stars
  your love for one another,
These vows you take this special day
  will come before no other.
    Deborah Hitt

Within And Without

The quiet cough was so much a part of him
That others regarded it as punctuation.
Bottles of cough syrup bathed it regularly
The way cans of soup did figure skaters.
One morning, nature awakened him at four.
He stood by the bed preparing to exit
When what was inside acted on its own accord,
Passing through with force at top and bottom,
Even bathing the body with cold sweat.
Duty rather than desire compelled him to
Clean up himself and the invasion to
Pajamas and floor which had lost innate beauty
And acquired an unfamiliar odor.
Exhausted, he fell into bed from memory,
Dropping off not into dreams but nothingness,
With physiology, not desire,
Attempting to regain the balance,
Which proved that he was a rational human being.
The unknown struggle went on until noon
When open eyes revealed that the crisis was over.
    Frank A. Langer

"They Died At Shiloh"

In the Great Civil War
That plagued our country with doubt,
It was brother against brother;
In bloody battles, they fought it out!

And now, the Battle of Shiloh,
One of the bloodiest of the war.
It shall always live in memory;
Because it left an irremovable scar!

Grandad's proudly fought for the North;
What a sacrifice he gave!
Six of his brothers fell at Shiloh;
Hastily buried in a Confederate grave.

Grandad's nine brothers fought for the cause;
They believed in it, you know.
But six brothers died at Shiloh;
Over a hundred years ago.

The South never really forgave.
Many evil memories still remain.
But my Grandad never ever heard from
Or saw any of his nine brothers again.
    Clyde E. Runion

Faith Against Worry

Worry is like a mental tornado
that tears the soul apart.
It darkens life's shimmering rays of hope,
and smothers the flame of faith.
It dries the flow from the stream of love,
and hastens a troubled way.

But, faith is like a mounting eagle.
As it soars higher and higher,
on a crisp autumn's day.
It reaches a distance where it's out of sight.
And then, it rests patiently,
in the hands of God.
    Gloria F. Johnson

Hearts With Flags

It is not funny
That they are flying the flags
And we do not see them
We see only the tattered-ness of their lives
And the disarray and the stinking
Sometimes of their clothes
Even the color of their skin registers
And we make judgements so easily and quickly
With insensitivity and disrespect
Degrading them with our own ignorance and fear
When we don't even know what happened, nor do we care
As we walk on, not looking further inside
To see the flags on their hearts
Flying colors of lost dreams and pain and memories
And suffering beyond measure
People whose voices once filled their life
With purpose and pride
But are now silent
    Debra Schwerin

Old People: My Grandmother

In more ways than one, old people don't like to be told
that they're old.

My grandmother is not old for she is one year shorter than gold.

She is the cause of my success, she is there to correct me
when I am a mess.

She taught me everything I know, she even taught me how to grow.

Although we may have our ups and downs, I do respect
when she's around.

My grandmother shines like a gold medal, even though she is the
pot talking about the kettle.

She is very wise and sarcastic, she does things just like magic.

I can't explain what my grandmother means to me, it's more than
a million dollars if you can see.

Even though my grandmother is getting old, she is really brand new.

Grandmothers are God's gift to me and you.
    Aaron James Kimble

Untitled

To think is to take off on a flight,
The mind goes off into a land of adventurer and life.
Who knows what you think or what you don't think,
but the mind itself.
When the mind comes back you just might find
something new. It might be new or old or something
we never knew we needed. So try it and
like Ford, Edison, or the Wright brothers
invent something new.
    Erica Patterson

"My Home"

A stately building surrounded by trees,
That tremble and whisper in a gentle breeze.
A haven for elderly who need a good home
With love for each other so they won't be alone.
There are dinners for all with goodies galore,
And birthday parties with music and more.
Some like to visit and coffee partake
Along with some cookies the ladies will bake.
Business meetings we have to keep up with the news
To help everyone from getting the blues.
Once a month we meet, I might mention
When four hard working officers get our attention.
The beautiful decorations for all the holidays,
By a talented tenant with his winning ways.
On sunday evening we have a sing along,
While a very gracious lady plays every song.
A monday morning Bible study we will share
With pastor Sam who knows we all care.
Several tenants have set out beautiful flowers,
Around our building called south oak towers.

Elizabeth Peterson

As The Golden Leaf Falls

I ran into one of your kisses the other day
That you blew into the wind
It had to be yours because it still had your smile.
It made me smile with memories of you.
It was dancing in the wind, just as happy as can be
There was only one, so it had be a special one.
It had to be yours, it had to come from your heart
It had to bring a part of you with it
It's been days since then. I see nothing in the wind.
I feel when the wind is still
It has no one to dance with.

Jerry W. Ogburn

Unconditional Love

From the time
that you first held me,
There would always be
Unconditional Love.

Then as the years went by
I started off to school
Sometimes acting like a fool,
But you gave unconditional love.

I soon became a teen
And put away my toys
To go out with the boys,
But you still showed unconditional love.

I've moved out of your home now
but this I'll always know
To your home I can go
For unconditional love.

My prayer today, Mama
Is to always give
Just as long as I live,
back to you-unconditional love.

Denise R. Guffey

School

   The dreaded day is almost here,
The first day of the school year.
To some it will be fun,
Just the thought makes others scream and run!
We will be piled down with homework and books,
No more going to the mall for those not new looks!
But it is the only way to get an education,
I just don't want to give up my summer vacation!

Brynna Frazier

Valentines Of Yesterday

Do you remember your first Valentines
That you received so long ago
Recalling the memories of your childhood days
That once again unfolds

Do you remember the Valentines of Yesterday
With flowers and lace so fine
With colors of red and gold
That cost only a dime

Do you remember the candy kisses
Wrapped in paper that taste so divine
As you read in the words "Be My Sweetheart Valentine"

Today again you hold the faded box with Valentines of Yesterday
That you search for so long and found
Knowing in your heart it was another age and time
When you received so many Valentines

Wondering today where your friends are of Yesterday
As you look at the faded box with words on top
saying "Be My Valentine"
Gentle you hold the box and carefully put away
With dreams and memories of Yesterday

Catherine Richey

Love

Love, is a passion that creates a bind. It's not a feeling
that's made up only in your mind. Love, is from the heart
which is proven from an action, which keeps you faithful from
making any wrong infraction. Love, is truth filled with care
which make two people a great pair. Love, can be lost it's
not always there. Cause once you loose what you love you
Love what you hate which will always be unfair. Love, is an
emotion stronger than any other. Love can kill. Love can
save. Love is like the ocean that creates a big wave and
when you loose your love the wave comes down and it's all
over. Love, once you have it never loose it. Because
without it. You have nothing but a deep empty pit.

Alan Luccarini

Life

They say that life's a pain, and then you die,
that's not exactly true.
The ups and downs are what it takes to find the meaning of you
sometimes I feel I can't go on and I'm drowning in a pit,
the qualities I have are few,
but I'll use them till I break.
The world can be a happy place when you
believe in your self, It can be happier yet when
someone else believes, that all you do.
And all you say is only a breath away.
So life gets hard and so do I, but that's okay with me,
the strength I get within myself will be some use one day.
When all is grand and all is fine and I'm at peace
someday, I'll look back in hopes to find,
the truth I wrote today.

Jackie McNamee

'Life'

My soul has grown deep in the tides of this life,
The hour before dawn holds much promise of still
another great experience.

The summers have flown on the wings of time,
and can only be remembered.

Today is here with the warmth of the sun and the
kiss of the rain, another new beginning.

Barbara Joan Ross

Peace

Peace love and harmony all around the world
that's the way that life should be instead the gun smoke curls
up into atmosphere higher than birds can go
the wind will send it far from here with one swell blow
showing us that hatred lies near our little town
and hearing all the pain-filled cries as the wounded are falling down
the pain and suffering that they feel where the world's a living hell
they can't believe that this is real and so they start to yell
they yell from pain and yell from fear
what will we gain down rolls a tear
from pain or sadness he can't tell his head is in a jumble
wondering if he'll get out well the man begins to mumble
will my family be alright without me to protect them
will money begin to get tight without enough to feed them
I must get out of hear somehow and go home to them well
can't they stop the fighting now and end this living hell
it's time we started total peace completely around the world
let the gunfire quickly cease into him a bullet whirled
he immediately dropped down dead his life was history
this would not have happened if only we learned to live in har-
mony.

Heather Jo Hess

Sounds Of Life

"Hush, What's that sound?" asked the child.
That's the wind purring in the trees.
"Hush, What's that sound?" asked the child.
That's the rain tinkling on the window pane.
"Hush, What's that sound?" asked the child.
That's my heart pounding out my love for thee.

"Hush. What's that sound?" asked the boy.
That's new life crying out for joy.
"Hush, What's that sound?" asked the boy.
That's the whippoorwill seeking out his mate.
"Hush, What's that sound?" asked the boy.
That's first love whispering in thine ear.

"Hush, What's that sound?" asked the man.
That's the wails of those who need.
"Hush, What's that sound?" asked the man.
That's the wars that never should have been.
"What that sound?" asked the man.
Hush, That's the sound of death my child.

Irisgay Mary Crivellari

Without You

"Nothing lasts forever",
That's what you once said to me
We unfortunately didn't stay together
And now you've gone free.

If this is the way we were meant to be
Then this is the way we will stay
One thing I must tell you about me
Is that I'm missing you since you've gone away

I could never picture my world without you
Since you've changed my life in so many ways
But going on without you is something I must do
It'll be hard not to be with you every day.

I hope that your life is filled with joy
Because that's what I want you to feel
You know that I still love you,boy
And my broken heart will heal.

So, as I sit here thinking of you
And feeling so incredibly blue
I wonder what I should do
In my forever lonely world without you.

Heidi Wilkinson

Mine

We make for the mouth of the mine, where dust settles in flakes.
The African sun pushes us in, with the flat of its baking hand.
Your size fours make no mark on the long abandoned floor
as I clump clump beside.

Timbers in heaps whisper of an aching past
like barren bones of slaves
caved-in upon while eking out the glitter.

Thin as gold leaf, your hand clasps firmer onto mine,
 and you assume the lead. You tow me as you stride.
The steady stream cast by your helmet lamp
dissolves the darkness as we burrow further under.
Deep down you raise a hand and cock your head.
We stop and listen.
In the blackness, in the damp.

That is when I hear it - growing as it comes.
Strong and shrill in rocking ricochets,
the loudest that her bursting lungs can throw,
nugget yellow.
In the blackness, in the damp:
the canary, singing still.

Alan D. Collenette

'Tears'

With the dawn of a new day, I open my eyes and wait.
The air is cold, so I wrap myself in my torn blanket.
I shiver as white snow covers me, I can hear laughter close by.
But I turn away and crawl further beneath my blanket.
Every day was like this, but I was strong-
At least that's what I told myself.
My stomach grumbled, it was time for breakfast.
I stood slowly and folded my little blanket.
I walked down my alley and stopped at the corner.
Maybe today I would have a little luck finding scraps somewhere.
I ambled down busy streets, dodging from people and cars.
I could feel their eyes on me as I walked by.
Bitterly, I slid my hands into my tattered pants pockets and
    swallowed my pride.
I ducked behind a restaurant and knocked on the back door.
The door swung open and before I knew it, it closed just as fast.
I bit my lip and continued on; time and time again
    this happened.
At my last stop, I finally got a piece of burnt meat.
I brought it back to my shelter and ate.
The snow came down, and into my eyes.
The next thing I knew-I cried.

Bethany Wilson

Autumn

Oh for the open fields!
The autumn's wind blow grass
Against my bare legs, swaying, embracing.

Oh to feel the wind's cool breath
Against my face,
and stream my hair out far behind
Like many ribbons fluttering in the breeze.

To run,leap,sing,
And dance, dance,dance,
Alone,
In nature's sanctuary
With only the rustling of leaves
And the wild birds singing,
  Ah, she is one of us.
  She also shares our life.

Hayden Esther Jurman

Retirement

Retirement is great we have all been told,
The bad part about it we have to grow old.
It's up in the morning somewhere around nine,
Looking for odd jobs that are hard to find.
The non-functional gadgets we'll soon try to seek,
But we'll have them all fixed in less than a week.
So sometimes we'll tinker and sometimes we'll putt,
Sometimes we'll just sit and act like a nut.
The first of the month will our big day,
That's when social security will bring us our pay.
So it's off to bank we'll shoot in the car,
And then call home to find out where we are.
When we finally get home we'll feel like a sap,
And then go to bed for our afternoon nap.
We still get around though our muscles are sore,
And the things that don't hurt won't work anymore.
But don't complain too much it is often said,
For it's better like this than it is to be dead.

Don Vander Linden

Rose Whispers

Out of the mist comes its voice
The beautiful voice of a rose.
Silent, as the song of a tree,
The tears whispering back from the ages,
The love, the timbre of you and me.
The beautiful song was yesterday
But today... there is no rhyme, no harmony,
For into the temple of disillusions bower
And above that there is no fire
No hymn that I can sing.
For the flowers I burned in my desire
Are the thoughts of today's lost hour
I built them into bracelets
Bracelets, the Goddess of love wore
Yet, she dropped them into the rubbish
They fell with the dust to the floor.
'Twas not to be and yet it seemed
As the flower's long lost dream
Love lost in yesterday
Yet, to the rose, still a dream.

Dorothy Lear Evelyn Teters

Endless Sleep

Hypnotic sleep of no return,
the body has decomposed into a world of dust,
our souls floats endlessly into a unknown dimension.
The keepers of our graves are the angels of goodness,
your sleep has been broken by the eternal light in the distance

A passage-way for other souls from the past,
in a world free from hate, illness or wars,
all are brothers and sisters...
who greet each other with open arms and smiles.

judgement day is here!
will I rise with the chosen few? or,
will I sleep the eternal sleep?
judge me, oh Lord, for my actions in society,
and for my sins against you.
the endless sleep I shall return,
until the day I rise to be judge by God.

Earline Pugh

You Feel - I Feel

The still air you inhale - I feel
The breeze that whiffs gently on your skin
I feel within
You are my lifeblood
You are my rosebud
My life with you is sailing on an even keel

Joyful light surrounds you - I feel
Times come and pass when the glow goes dim
I feel within
You're my every thought
Love's a fire caught
My love for you is on a non-stop spinning wheel

Tears fall when your eyes cry - I feel
Music fills you, good spirits take wind
I feel within
My precious treasure
My every pleasure
Together - you and me - forever love that's real

David Gladkowski

In Praise Of Noise

The giggle which a cartoon brings,
The buzzing of a bee,
The children's voices as they sing
Are all magical to me.

When I was born some years ago
The world was a silent sphere.
What sound was, I did not know
And quiet was my tear.

But then God smiled and showed doctors how.
They did some wondrous things.
The world is alive with sound now,
My praise of God takes wing!!

Carol Sparbel

Powerless

Powerless.
The child, the adolescent, the adult, the elderly.
Powerless.
In someone else's hands.
With someone else's influence.
Someone else- Who?
Your parents, your children, your friends, your government,
your stranger.
Powerless.
Your fate is not determined by you,
But by someone else's influence.
A painting painted by onlookers.
A drip and there.
You can choose the colors,
But the onlookers have told you what looks best.
It is signed with your name,
But is it your work, or just your colors?
Powerless-
It is a word without meaning.
Everyone paints pictures.

Blair Lanier

Man Is A Forest

The trees are men's goals and dreams rising to greatness.
The flowers are the timid and weak wanting peace
There are those that are parasites that feed on the dreams of others
The population is grass without any place to grow
The problems are a forest fire engulfing the plains of hope
The stumps that remain show stubbornness of the ideas that have died
The birds sing the hope of a new day

Jeffrey Martin Dinho

"Atlantic Convoy"

You sail out of the harbor, as night begins to fall,
The churning of the sea, and the last seagulls call.
As you pass the last marker buoy, and hear its clanging bell.
You wonder! Will it be smooth sailing, or will it be hell.

Morning arrives, you go top side, and wonder where we could be.
There is no sun, it seems so dark, and the sky is gray as the sea.
The ship rolls from side to side, and climbs the oncoming wave.
Will we ever see land again, or will this be a watery grave.

Where is the land, there is no land, its water all around.
They say you're never far from land, just nine miles straight down.
The oncoming waves rise, to fifty and sixty feet.
Our ship climbs over mountains of water, the next high roller to meet.

Three days and nights, a violent storm, and then a balmy day.
The U-boats lurk in the murky deep, and we've been in harm's way.
Our ship glides through a calm sea, in the dark of night
Seems so peaceful now, yet the enemy is there, but out of sight.

At dusk the junkers eighty-eights, make their bombing runs,
Through smoke screens, and flak barrage, from our many guns.
Their attack falls, so they were off, and fly out of sight.
It's calm and peaceful now, and we're in for a quiet night.

Clifford F. Harp

Forever Young

Time is a tender thing we cannot control,
The clock ticks, the months pass and we do grow old

Our lives are ever changing, like the seasons through the years
There are so many treasured moments, happy ones and ones with tears

But every moment lived is precious, every breath we take is gold
We soon learn simple blessings are best, like a good friends hand to
  hold

So if your hair starts its graying and your walk has slowed
Think about the many blessings in your life which the Lord has bestowed

Only by growing old can we experience the wisdom that years bring
To know that after every long winter there will always be a new spring

To know that age is not important what's a wrinkle or two?
What really matters is having someone love and care for you

So don't fuss with those face creams or all that exercise
All that's important is that sparkle in your beautiful eyes

Don't let that sparkle fade away keep it new and fresh,
Like flowers that keep blooming after every winters rest

So next time I see you, be it tomorrow or next week, I expect to see,
That shiny sparkle in your eyes when you're looking back at me!

Jani Wasson

Beyond The Blue

The beauties of the skies change before your eyes,
The clouds drift dreamily along,
The raindrops fall like the tune of a song,
The colors of the rainbow are a pretty sight,
The sunshine is like a golden light:

Then dusk fades into night,
The moon and stars are bright,
Beyond the blue horizon lies
The beauty of the skies.

Dardean Wheaton

The Wave

The sun shines down on it, reflecting a sickly metallic silver,
the color of the robots who conform and accept the lies that
make brave men quiver.
The dark grey mist that rises from it has the familiar scent of
ignorance, which is inside churning the filth of intolerance.
The sound of the force behind it frightens even the strong,
as it continually whispers lies, tries to make you believe
it can do no wrong. As its army of hate moves through time
undetected, the whispers are punishing those who defected.
The unsuspecting await on the tranquil and free beaches, as the
mass of blackness grows stronger, it won't be much longer.
The stealth black wave is being sped up by the insecurity
of the wind and the cowardly clones who have given in, while
the abnormal dream of a place where being different is not a
sin. The impetus of the wave slowly skulks away, knowing the
students it has taught will not dare disobey.
The wave is now close to the beaches, and will spread the lies
the corrupt wind teaches, as the sand is washed away, and the
abnormal no longer play.

Chris O'Neill

Two Hearts As One

I've been united with the most beautiful soul.
The combining of two lost halves are joined
as a found whole.

My thoughts and dreams are within you through
spans of being apart.
Thou my loneliness is fulfilled with your strong
good will and your love in whole heart.

My love for you is flown to the depths of heaven.
My faithfulness follows like rays of the sun.
Our hearts will touch in our exchange of promises.
the cherishing moment when we will become as one.

You've fulfilled my life with joy and happiness.
Swept away by a magical prince of the sky.
I love you forever focusing on our life beginning.
Smiling as I start to cry.......................

Jacqueline Berry

Nocturnal Pathways

An old woman sleeps
the corridor of memory unwinds
   through midnight ink
a flaxen skin, soft and silken
stretched taut by time
forgotten years, forgotten pain
   stitch frowns upon her pale lips
threads of joyous recollection
   catch upon a shuttle
interlace the warp and woof
   of tender moments and remembered passion
knots of fear and sorrow untangle gently
all goblins cast out
all evil exorcised
only fabric of sweet dreams
and the old woman smiles in her sleep

Mildred Werba

" When The Angels Cry"

When the angels cry,
The rain will softly fall,
Then the bitter winter winds will blow and turn their tears
to snow.
As the snow softly falls and turns the world to white,
God in all His glory will make your troubles right.

Jeannette L. Ross

Untitled

It was a cold, wintery day
The curves of my body were frosted.
My tears, they covered me.
I was wrapped in the security of my own soul.

Why all the tears, I often wondered?
(A protection from all the years of self-doubt?)
I cry about the girl I once knew, the woman I have
yet to become.
The tears are the storm of my emotion.
They battle me - they will not stop.

The salty spray of my tears,
The releasing of my anxiety and fears.
When will they stop, or will they forever continue?
They keep me warm,
Like a blanket they covered me.
I was wrapped in their security - the security of my own tears.

Christine Maiorano

Why Are You Hurting It?

It's an old dying planet, it's sleepy and sore,
The damage you've done her will be evermore.

You burn all her forests that keep her air clean,
Her oceans are dirty or so it would seem.

You pollute all her rivers, her mountains, and soil,
You use all her resources, you used up the oil.

Extinct are her animals, they're almost all gone.
Killing them off, don't you know that is wrong?

You're killing the lion, the bear, and the fawn,
You ruined the sunset, polluted the dawn.

Her air will be dirty, her skies will be dark,
You won't see a rainbow, a cloud, or a lark.

The food that she gives you soon will run out,
Saving our lives is what this is about.

All of her beauty will no longer be,
Imagine a lifetime without a blue sea.

When no pleasure comes from this planet Earth,
Then maybe you'll see what she's really worth.

I would stop all the damage and seal up this rift,
If only I could give the world a gift.

DeAnna Fernandez

To My Playmate

As I walked through the field of daisies, I remembered
The days that used to be, when we were small,
But that was the spring of our lives. It's now December,
And you are gone like the joys that I still recall.
Gone are the woodland trails where we used to wander,
And the berry patch, where the strawberries were so sweat.
The cherry tree has fallen, but over yonder
Is that little stream where we used to cool our feet.
I often wonder if you are somewhere near me,
Watching me as I wade in the little stream.
If I speak, is it possible that you can hear me?
Are you there on the rocks where we used to play and dream?
Do you look for the woman whom time is rearranging?
The passing years have taken their toll without fail.
Do you search for me, as I am today, through life's changing,
Or for that skinny little girl with the ponytail?

Angeline Maine

Untitled

You think lonely is for losers, the unmotivated
the don't want to be anyone's
lonely is not a social disease,
nor a state of mind.
it is the shadow of light,
the baby crying without love
   it's so portable.
travels with you everywhere
when you work, socialize and sleep,
it's right behind your heart.
can strangle your mind at will,
don't ignore it.
lonely is forever in its place,
you can't fix it.
treat it right, give it respect.
   acceptance is the key.
for you are human, you do have feelings,
lonely is only one of them.

Judy A. Ross

Tombstone

Moist fog, the moon grazed high
the drying nose of decay
on the floor wilted roses lay
   Footsteps forth the patterned brick
I came toward a splintered cross
my face buried in the carpet moss,
my eyes pitching droplets of all I
had lost.
My paralyzed feelers brushed the dust from
the stone - I identified the familiar...
The isolating cramp that ever lasts inside
the chilly shudder that can't stay hidden.
it never hides
My mind thought away of the
horror - how it came
to the ripper it was a silly game
he overruled their existence
No justice or practical sense
and you're made to except the given
This is the death to which I've been driven!

Danielle L. Anderson

Love's Promise

The minute you walk into a room
The earth moves beneath my feet.
The second your baby blue eyes lock with mine
My heart explodes with tears of joy.

The times when we are together makes
Reality and all its problems disappear into a cloud of smoke.
The promise that you would never leave me
Keeps me breathing when we are apart.

Your soft complexion and simple smile
Can make the youngest girl's heart break.
Your warm heart and caring eyes
Can bring back the oldest memories of love to an old woman's soul.

Your soothing voice helps to put
All my worries to rest.
Your soft yet protective hands
Always kept harm at arms length.

Each and every one of these qualities
I treasure with every breath I take,
And with every breath and every second that goes by
I find myself loving you more and more each day.

Elizabeth Zamora

Home Is Where The Heart Is

All of this earths riches are on borrowed time
The end will come no matter if it's yours or if it's mine
But to awaken to God's sunshine pushing through the pouring rain
And to see loved ones happy without heavy heart of pain
Is better contentment than silver or gold
If home is where the heart is will it be stolen or sold?

There's temptations waiting to steal your heart away
And with it goes your very soul no matter what they say
With no guarantee of tomorrow while it's yet today
Choose carefully the path you'll trod or stumble along life's way.
Healthy or sick-rich or poor, home is where the heart is closing
life's final door.

When I die don't bury me with dead
Keep me alive in your thoughts and deeds
And I'll live forever instead.
Don't wait to give me flowers then that I can no longer smell
A little scent of time well spent can sweeten this life's hell.
Healthy or sick-rich or poor home is where the heart is
When life closes its final door.

Barbara J. Wilkerson

Rape

The time begins with the pounding of a heart
The event arrives within the blink of an eye

Skin rubbing, stretching, tearing from muscles
Whispers floating from side to side
Lost in frozen mind

A grip with terrifying control catches your will
A body of repulse demands your beauty

One tear, one power, one urge of terror
To call for power in the fright
A wall of strength comes with no right

In one grasp for breath, the time has come to pass
That air never reaching the motionless soul

The rain of fears don't quite fall
The event has gone, only to be prolonged
In the mind that once loved and trusted
The body now gone

Joanna L. Kohler

Dream Lover

I awake to the ticking of the clock,
  the falling rain,
  your gentle breathing.
I feel the pounding of your heart,
  The softness of your breast,
  the warmth of your arms.
I taste the hunger of your morning kisses,
The salty tang of loving
  on your skin.
Light nudges sleepily through the curtains,
  Dawn...
Soon you'll be...
Gone.

J. E. Coakley

What Is Love

Something is between us, I cannot see you smile,
The next time I will see you, won't be for a while.
The nights are lonely, and the days are long,
But when I return, I hope you won't be gone.

The snow comes down, the wands call your name,
Without you in my arms, it's just not the same.
I love you too much, for you to see
When they say the word love, it means you name me.

Bryan K. Grimes

Noble Name

A herald their deeds ten centuries back
the family stood by virtue of knack.
Each one in his time developed his way
to carry his portion each circumspect day.

Charlemagne gave to Peter his crest
then came time Planta family to test.
When William the Norman sent out a call
one of our forebear's stood and gave all.

The de Burgh invasion was jolly good fun
but holding in Erin put him on the run.
A dotard returned and built him a hall
and his son was married to a native withal.

One went to the Boar War in African veldt
had him a son in heat that would melt.
That son and his wife crossed American shores
now his grandson programmed to open his doors.

John R. De Salis

"Not A Race, But A Dream"

Watching the torch being lit for someone's first time
The fans' faces glowing as we proudly gaze around the arena.
People of all different nationalities supporting each and every person.

Then the time arrives when I am to skate across the ice,
But am I ready?

I gracefully glide across the ice with perfect composure
My feet seem to be magically moving with the music,
Knowing that even one little slip, will ruin it.
Always keeping my chin up no matter what happens.

The crowd, mesmerized by my awesome performance, is silently
    watching
As my diligent clothes cling tight around my body.
Then the most gratifying moment of all comes from knowing...
I gave it my all.

These Olympians are that of a hero.
A hero which fights hard for their nation, and one who feels proud
and dignified to wear the red, white, and blue of their own country.

As I look back now I realize that the Olympics are,
not a race, but a dream.
A dream, that all athletes will one day desire to have.

Jodie Webster

Through My Eyes

I needed help and I had the fear,
The fear that you get when nothing is near.
A lonely, lost, and tear-ridden soul,
I needed your support to make me whole;
I thought you were true, you said you did care
But when I ran to you, you were never there.
I acted strong and was convinced I'd be alright,
But I felt so hopeless, I wanted an end to the fight.
I did not care, there was nothing to hope for,
You were my last hope, and you closed the door.
I saw it coming, but was blinded with the fear,
The fear that you get when nothing is near.
To try and save me now, you have no right
Because when you gave up on me is when I quit the fight.

Jennefer Jennings

Me

Of diamonds I have none to offer you and rubies are unseen by my eyes
The fine wines of the Earl's Manor are void of my goblet tonight
And many nights I foresee
And the mists of rich perfumes shan't waft about me
But the stale musk of labor and the fields I tend
No brilliant gold coins shall be found in my purse
For I come to you with empty hands save for the worn two-pence I bear
None of this do I miss, though, for I know of your beauty
And the warmth of your embrace I remember true, of the eve before
And for that I have no pearls on a golden strand for you
But a pretty stone found along the walk wrapped in a bit of my own hair
Or perhaps, the moon on a silver band along with the stars in the night
And wildflowers fresh picked from the meadow, early upon a
Sunday morn

Craig Edward Wilton

The Morning After

Looking back I remember the countless days of Nausea, the pain
The frustration, the fear, the uncertainty and the indecisiveness;
   I know you were there feeling it all, but I never stopped to
Think about how this would affect you. You as a person growing
so innocently.
   I tried not to care for you and to think that you did not
exist, but my attempts were in vain. How can I explain to you why
I made this decision. I guess there's no financial reason, economic
reason or social reason that can make you understand that I did it
for you, I guess I did it for me to.
   My endless tears are tears of shame, guilt and sorrow.
A sort of sorrow that will forever hang over me like
the sword of damocles. I wish I could say that I loved you but I
can't.
What I can I say is that I am sorry, and I hope you understand, and
forgive me, wherever you may be.

Joy Branford

Dream

Welcome to my pleasure
The garden of which you abandoned.
Yet now she grows back
To claim the treasures of rightful belonging.

I can see the scars you left her
For they are slow to heal.
Listen, I hear the gentle calling
The peace in every creature's note.

I've felt the perfection of love here
And heard the breath of god.
You would have known these too
If those armed were left behind.
Welcome to my pleasure, our garden
You tread upon the spirit's place.
Go gentle to ask of her gifts
For there is a feast awaiting us.

Jonathan Pleasant

Missing You

I miss you when you're gone,
The nights for me are so long.
But somehow I'll see it through,
Because I know that you miss me too.

Who would have known from the start,
That a guy named Mark would capture my heart.
You hold my heart in the palm of your hands,
I want you to know I'm your number 1 fan.

I'm counting the minutes until you're home,
So I'll no longer fell lost and alone.

Judy Blain

My Magic Box

My Magic Box will hold
The giggle of a tiny baby
The sound of leaves blowing in the wind
The look on my mother's face, my secret hiding place
The pitter-patter of little feet
Joy and Anguish will also be in there
The hug of my younger brother
A baby's first tears
A window to look out and day-dream
The taste of a sweet peach
The shade of an oak
A Thanksgiving Feast
A picture of my family
A book to read on the way, a rainy day
The stars suspended in the sky
The sun to brighten my days
A tall tree to climb
A beautiful garden
I will leave the key with my box, so anyone who
opens it, will feel all of my life inside them.

April Forsythe

I Shall Not Grieve

As I glance at the picture of my grandfather
   the glance becomes a look,
      the look a stare.
I reach out and gently trace his loving arm around me,
   telling me it's alright
      there's nothing to be afraid of.
I remember how soothing those words had been
   when I had been afraid,
      and now I miss him more than ever.
But I put the picture away because I shall not grieve
   over losses from the past,
      but learn from them instead.

Jessica Martinez

Remembrance

Nicely nestled in my warm, narrow bed,
The glaring sunlight seeping onto the sill
Of the perfectly painted picture window,
I fiercely faced the formidable new day.
Now awake, banishing bleak clouds from behind
My eyes, I suppressed all the sensual secrets
Of our clandestine meeting in the moonlit meadow.
Collecting toasty quilts to cover and caress
My naked flesh, memories freezing my fearful heart,
Relics of our past reality rendering thoughts
Of other times dark, and disposable, and dead.
Bending my body, I boldly stared at the
Sun glimmering in the looking-glass and glints
Of misery in my dark, melancholy eyes,
And languidly lifted myself, joining the untainted light.

Joy Nelson

The Noises Of Silence

Sitting alone the rocking chair squeaks
The wind blows the floors creek
Shutting your eyes you listen for sounds
Only in silence are true noises found.
Open your ears you hear your heart beat
You're no longer alone your cat's at your feet.
He jumps in your lap a host of compliance
You're no longer alone with the noises of silence.

Jeff Massengale

"The Great Spirit"!

The gentleness of a "Lamb"! And the rolling of a "Lion"
The great spirit tells me, I'm alive, and not dying.
The winds that blow in the very night air,
Tell's me, that "My Precious Jesus"! "Loves" and care.
The twinkling of the "Stars" late at night,
Tell's me, I'm "alive" and I'm doing wright.
I don't have to prove who "I" am, or what "I" do,
Because the "Great Spirit" watches over all of "you"!
No one knows what the eye balls can see,
But "I" know the "Great Spirit" watches over, "you and me"!
I'm counting the days, and counting the nights,
Because "I" know in the "End" things will turn out right.
Don't judge a "man" of what "he" can say or really do,
Because "you" all might find out, that "Jesus" is watching "you"!
Always pick a man up and don't tear "Him" down!
Because "you" just might see, "The king wearing his crown"!
Stop and smell the "Roses" along "life's" narrow way,
and always thank the "Lord God" for a brand new "day"!
Always thank the "Him" for the things "He" does for "you"!
And you'll find in the "End" the "Great Spirit" watches over "you"!

Jesse Edmond Hembree

Galway Bay

The unresting, murmuring sea's salty spray,
The green waters where all cares are put away.

Regardless of the blustering whirlwind way.
Nothing with holding, ever free, night and day,

Such silent starry sky, such sudden storms sway,
Formidable forgiven, forgotten fray.

The sea's face is covered with a mist, light gray
Dispelling the night, lovely weather is neigh,

Harbinger of nature's lovely display,
The best place for a well earned holiday.

Here you live to please and please to live, survey
All the beauty around you, happiness convey.

With certainty, secure within, one can say:
"Truly, heavenly paradise is Galway Bay."

Joseph G. Brennan, M.D.

Untitled

There's a little place in the human mind that's called
the heart.
The damn thing has the most diverse reputation;
Though it takes up only a very tiny part of the brain,
It occupies a very large part of our lives.
There's space enough to shore up an ocean of emotion,
But it's small enough to get struck in your throat.
It can crumble a concrete wall of common sense
And then, from the barest most abstract ingredients, build
a castle called Love with doors that open slowly and shut hard.
Pain closes and hardens it while tears open and soften it;
It will shatter from a glance but Cupid's arrow seems to be good for it.
It races, carries torches and frequently gets lost;
It hears with no ears and sees with no eyes,
It aches and breaks and burns and then plays tricks on You,
And yet, it's often all we are.

Dean Alan Crasno

A Wish

I wish yesterday was tomorrow,
Then for everyone, there wouldn't be any sorrow.
All kinds of days will come,
You don't have to keep them all, just some.
Happiness and faith, I wish could be,
But as for everyone, they will never see.
If the masses looked to the sky,
And let their hearts go, they would fly.

David Davis

His Little Shoes

The canvas blue shoes are battered and worn.
The heels are turned and the toes are torn.
The spots at the toes are frayed and faded
From the dews of the grass where the little tyke raided.
The toes are turned up and the laces knotted
The soles warn thin and the sides are spotted
Oh, little shoes, how you pranced on the walk!
The joys you could tell if your tongues could talk,
You'd tell of the time you jumped from the wall
That was the day Phillip had such a fall!
You'd never forget the climb in the tree
Or the times you were wet as wet could be.
And when you were stiff from drying in the sun.
You squeaked and grumbled when you had to run.
Now little shoes you sit on the floor
The two little feet wear you no more
Poor little shoes sitting there.
Phillip left you for another new pair!

Bernice A. Fox

Alone

Sometimes at night, I feel so alone
The house is so silent, since the children have grown.
No longer do I hear the patter of little feet,
The sound of laughter, the silence of sleep.

The shadows are lengthening with each passing hour,
Outside I hear the start of a shower,
The house seems so cold, where once it was warm
It once was filled with love, sweetness, with charm.

My children have grown and made lives of their own
And the distance between us has certainly grown.
They are so busy with this and with that
They can't be bothered to stop and look back
To see a gray-haired old mother sitting alone,
In a grand old house where they had all grown.

But I'll not worry about all they do
For there is one I can always turn too.
My Lord is my companion, He gives me the light
To warm my heart through the long lonely night.

Judy A. Stephenson

A View From A Veterans Wife

As I sit here today at the VA, just holding the tears away.
The hurt, the pain
The guilt, the hatred
That I see on so many faces in the VA, today
The cries for help
The scars of war
The veterans' eyes, surely tell no lies
Some joined up, others had no choice
While others stayed home, and made a voice!
The nightmares
Some days he just sits there and stares
Purple hearts, bronze stars
It's still just all life's scars.

Irene Hazel Courreges Lindsay

Whispering Love

I weep for the roses of days gone by.
Their petals scattered upon the floor.
They remind me of broken dreams and
hope that is no more.
I dance upon this faith of old in a dress
as black as death.
And kiss my lover's lips of ice, whispering
love with my last breath.

Joanne R. Plasce

To The Class Of '79 On The Occasion Of Our Reunion

Well, back to the past we fought so hard to leave
the jocks, the brains, the rahs, the blahs, the pseudos
they're all here, wondering what to say
    your kids? beautiful
    an accountant? wonderful
    did he really? too bad
Where are the books we were going to write?
Where are the songs we were going to sing?
Where is the fame we were going to achieve?
    John once wrote a 50 page report for IBM
    Jane always sings along with Mitch
    Jody was once interviewed for the Gallup poll
Sh*t, is this what it all meant?
legal martinis instead of surreptitious beers
bragging about the future replaced by excuses for the past
    your kids? beautiful
    an accountant? wonderful
    did he really? too bad
    Daniel L. Weisman

Untitled

The full moon is out there
The key of the car is with me
The bottle of champagne is on my right hand
And, rose is on the left hand
We were dancing all night long
Feel like there's nobody out there
Star is shining that night
The wind of love had blown strongly from the south
We were fill with passion of love
We were making love all night long with the innocent of the love

Everything is looking good and feels good. Why?
Everything is good and it's to be true. Why?
Everything that is good had to fade away. Why?

We were in love but the storm had coming and, this memory is
smashed away
Feel like a fishing boat in the rough ocean
Don't know where to go and don't know what to do
All I know, I'm in love and it's hurt.
    Budi Widjaja

Old Friend

        Every season passed
        the lake side trail
        Blankets less of leaf

        each one more fragile
        and rusty of color
        than golden sides ago

        This companion I walk
            stops short
        to the crystal of water

        Before its leaving
        the nature of its length
        and safeness in offering
            was enjoyed by many

        Now every season passed
    the wind bites harder the branches carry less

        And I must only stay in,
        and look at my old friend by the water
Jesse Jack

Raining Roses

As the wind blew,
The last petal was swept away.
The wind softened the fall
As the delicate petal became a part of the pile,
The thorns on the stem began to break off
As the stem became dried out and brittle.
The last drop of moisture
Had long since evaporated.
All the color had faded from the sun's scorching rays.
The wind began to blow again,
And all of the petals that were lying in the pile
Under the stem were scattered.
The stem was now totally alone.
The tiny drops of water that began to fall
On its leaves,
Could not bring its moisture back.
But soon,
The water would bring companionship.
    Amy McConnell

My Dad

A lifetime ago, as a child I remember
The laughter, the joy and even the tears
Safe in your arms, secure on your lap
This was my seat for a few short years.

The walks through the woods, holding hands
Or just kicking stones, side by side
The things we shared, the stories you told
My heart full of love and busting with pride

When I was naughty and acted badly
You'd smile and wink, because you understood
You never questioned the pattern I chose
I was your angel, you saw only the good

When God took you to His heavenly home
An angel stood by to take my place
She now hears the stories, I cherished so much
I have no doubt, you'll put a smile on her face

God gives us life and He takes it away
When my time is up and He beckons to me
Do you think the angel would mind very much
If I asked you, Dad, for my place on your knee?
    Gail Oster

"Until Dusk Becomes Dawn"

In winter rhymes and summertime
The leaf blows from a blooming tree
Flowers yawn as the ivy climbs
Up the trellis extending and free
Skies turning crimson or wine
As birds silence over the blue sea
Crickets chirp on into the night
In the morning dawn comes the bee
The rain sprays in a drizzle sweep
Only long enough for the sun to shine on me
Afternoon sweats in with lazy day blues
For children boxed in to learn A to Z
The wind breaks loose before dusk
Cooling nighttime gardeners on bent knee
For the new growth is relaxing
As sunlight is about to recede
Rosebuds have closed again
As if locked by a key
Until morning's sunlight
Again shines for the world to see.
    Dawn A. Vinson

My Mother

What makes my mother special? I guess I'd have to say it's
the little things that mean so much. When she calls just
to ask how we are or to see if there's anything we need.
It's really amazing how she always knows just what to say
when I'm feeling down. The only thing she asks for in
return are three simple words, "I love you," which she
likes to hear us say.

Well mom this is my way of saying those words you love to
hear. I hope that in the years to come I can be more like
you. The loving, caring, understanding mother that can
always get her children to say those musical, magical words:
I love you MOM for no other reason except because you're you.

Cindy L. Riley

"The Tender Touch of His Lips"

The tender touch of his lips,
The look in his eyes,
as the young girl eyes,
And she sees his smile,
She notices she could never see any vile
Soon they drift apart,
And it's tearing up their heart,
They try to forget each other,
And hoping either one of them have another lover,
soon they meet again,
And know they have sinned,
For leaving each other,
And there love will build forever.

Iva Brown

Exhortation

Happy is this hour you come now to be wed,
The Lord watches his angles' wings are spread.
Pure fresh and Holy, this union in God's eyes
He hovers over you beneath clear blue skies.
May God reward you with a rich measure of earthly things,
Don't get disheartened whatever life brings.

Remember the Lord when good lighten your ways
And even when the bad darken your days.
In God's house be dedicated there
And always find time to kneel in prayer.
Be thankful for wondrous days and solitude of night,
Striving always to do the things that are right.

Lie not in anger in hope of sleep,
There are needs to be met and promises to keep.
Climb over hills have strength enough to rally
Lead each other to a peaceful valley
Lift each other up time after time
May a lifetime of love, joy and peace be thine.

Benetia Praylor-Howell

Holding You

There are so many emotions whirling inside of me
The love I feel for you, but forbidden for all to see
The special nights between us are now becoming a dream
A love that never was, or to everyone it may seem
I get so tired of you saying a friendship is all we share
When the truth is, there's always been much more there

At night I hear your voice telling me it's all over now
But with what went on between us, I will always remember somehow

I don't understand how I grow to love you more and more each day
The love I must hide in my heart, the feelings I can never say

Heidi Clements

The Magic Pencil

I write with the magic pencil,
The magic it is true.
The magic hopes from my thoughts,
Through the point, and lands here
On my fine white looseleaf.
Some say this magic is talent,
A gift from above
I agree.
The greatest gift is to be able to express your thoughts
And share them with others,
So they too can feel the
Magic.

Jennifer L. Milligan

Imagine

Imagine; A fire to destroy as we know it,
the memories are left behind.
Imagine; Death at the stairway to hell,
only the devil lives.
Imagine; The differences between fantasy and reality,
is the truth or the lie that we live.
Imagine; Yesterday was innocence of the heart of an angel,
today is sex, drugs, and alcohol of the devil.
Imagine; Never being born at all,
a dream to make you scream, forever.
Imagine; A whisper of a dedication to all,
and a pain of saying good-bye.

Dayle Ringer

The Bonds Of Love

Looking back on my life I see
The models weren't very clear.
Now I'm somebody's wife,
With my own children to steer.

Through the ups and downs
Of people's interacting,
Looking through the smiles and frowns
To teach feeling beyond just reacting.

It's true that we all make mistakes,
No matter how good our intentions.
Meeting life's tougher breaks
With all of our imperfections.

The bonds of love aren't easily broken —
Struggles become opportunities.
The values of family aren't often spoken —
Communicated without enough scrutiny.

So many times we fail to say
What we really mean,
Not knowing how our thoughts today
Fit into the larger scheme of things.

Jeri Goodman

"Spring Cleaning"

Thunder and lightening are rending the sky,
The moon and the stars have wished us goodbye

The rain is a water sheet wrapping us up,
It's soaking the leaves and filling the buttercup.

The wind and the hail are working together,
To bring us the worst in early spring weather.

When the storm passes, and the air is all clean,
The trees and the grass will be emerald green.

Mother Nature knows best how to cure air pollution,
She washes it out with her homemade solution.

Eleanor J. Klein

Ocean Deep

There are so many wondrous mysteries of
   the ocean deep
That my curiosity begins to creep
   We wonder how there could be
So many beautiful creatures in the sea
   And how the sun gleams off the clear blue water
Even when the days seem to be getting hotter
   The rolling waves crash against the rocks
And anxious fisherman fish off the docks
   Some people are lucky to get a peek
And study the ocean deep
   There's nothing I wouldn't do
To live by the ocean blue
   God has given you and me
The beauty of the sea
   And because of that we should not waste
Like so many people have done in haste

   Carrie Taylor

In My Mind...

I sit alone in my house
(the opaque windows admit no knowledge)
Awaiting Death's arrival
As his bony knuckles rap upon my door
I greet him warmly
And with a bow of friendship
I invite the cloaked figure into my house
We talk softly over a cup of arsenic
as he tells tales of the river Styx
I stare into his empty eye sockets
with a feeling of awe
How black and empty they are
yet they are filled with everything imaginable
Later, we dance
His black cloak shines like Onyx
Then we duel
His scythe enchants me
as it slices through the air gracefully
And as Death wraps his skeletal fingers
around my throat, I laugh mightily.

   Jeremy Forster

Hurt

Being broken hearted is so hard to bear.
The pain is being stabbed with a knife,
It's always the love two people share,
Then someone comes to ruin your life!

The jealousy shines like a neon light,
Yet you try to hold through,
But it soon bursts and all is black as night.
So you take your cue;

You fight with all the love you've got.
But you know you'll soon lose,
You search for a feeling which can't be sought,
Yet the feeling you refuse!

So your heart is left with coldness,
By which you get revenge,
You walk high with boldness,
Because your life is singed!

   Cheryl L. Allarid

My Song

My song tells of a dream;
The pattern of my life,
Formed from the delicate and intricate
Fibers of my very being.
though time has rendered it threadbare,
tugging me this way, and, that.
To know that within my grasp is
the ethereal spell of life,
and it transcends the vagary of my existence.
My dream is me;
so much so, that this, then, becomes
my offering to life,
and, my resistance and strength
against those who would have me believe that time will change me.
The dream is there,
and every awakening to it becomes a refrain to my song.
And it has no end...

   Diana Marie Moon

Our Earth, Our Home

Our Earth, Our home.
The place we run, the place we roam.
The place we call a habitat.
One for all, white or black.
From the highest, hollowest tree,
To a gleaming Baltic Sea.
But what has happened to our shine?
Must I say, must I whine?
A can or two on the street.
A line of smog beneath the heat.
But who has done this to our wealth?
No one other than ourselves.
But how? But when? Everyday, now and then.
Can this problem ever be solved?
Yes it can, if we all get involved.
Recycling papers, glass, and cans,
Will recreate our beautiful lands.
Put a dime into a drive,
Will help a tree stay alive. Pitching in we can help,
The problem we've created among ourselves.

   Cortney LaBarr

Poker

The sky is now falling the door will soon close
The pressure is too intense, the pain no one knows
Freedom is a sin, to those in this place
The angry lurk in the night only to hide their face.

My hearts beats like a drum as the sweat drips from my brow
These decisions I have to make and the only time is now
Life is use to be easy, then reality sets in
Just play the hand that you're dealt and you are bound to win

For you know what you want and that's all you need to know
So don't let others fool you and tell you which way to go
The only thing that is expected is to fold or to stay
Only you know what's in your hand, only you know what to play.

   Chris Miller

Follow Me

If darkness descends upon you
Then know that there's a light
Search for the warmth of the fork in the road
Where freedom is your flight
Let go of the sounds you hear screeching
And the colors of your night
And know that He's there to follow
And even grey has an element of white.

   Carol D. McGuire

Untitled

It was a cloudy and gloomy day
The rain was falling hard, and the old
  house seemed to shake in the wind.
Then just as the rain came down harder and
  the wind shook the house.
A stranger appeared at the old mill house,
  A strange and mysterious man was he.
Then the door opened up, and a beautiful young
  Maiden stepped out onto the porch.
And just as mysteriously as he came, the
  stranger left.
Taking with him the life of the young,
  maidens heart.
A cold wind was blowing, and there still,
  lied the dead maidens body.

  Amanda Losee

The Appeal Elegant

Ageless yet irresistible a subtle intrusion of chronicle
The remarkable eternal, amicable
of its blend into, the auricable the appeal

It's as new as a zephyr some will say no must have air
some say, it must be matter of metaphor
Others give the sighs as we were not there
The appeal others say we deserve a certain kind
Not negative, not superlative but delight
The appeal in innocent work, I hear Handel Messiah Chime
It was early morn, it couldn't be a night
The Appeal!

It captures, a study of true to life words
A refreshing unique design
Timeless stresses that bind the appeal
In the beauty of capturing transition
We gave an ardent word of praise
To an eagle who flew on his mission
Though some say that was the olden days. The appeal

  Isabelle Hunter

Spring

From its deep cold floors it calls its home
  The seed reaches up to touch the sky
  A cold breeze rushes over her,
  And suddenly she feels alone.
  The first seed of spring.
From her mother's womb she pushes her way out.
  As she snuggles against her mother's cold dead body,
  A cold breeze rushes over her,
  And suddenly she feels alone.
  The first doe of spring.

  Danae Doviak Bayley

Holocaust

As I lay in the hammock listening to your song.
  The sky up above me soon to be gone.
    Only a teen lost in a dream.
  Of a time far away to never be seen.

The cars that pollute the air that we breathe.
Won't matter none because soon we will grieve.
For our loved ones murdered in the final war.
I look one last time before I close the door.

Then a flash and the blue skies are suddenly gold.
  It's the end of the world or so we're told.
But what about the few who still hear the cries?
  Of ladies and children who have yet to die.

  Dawn J. Marks

"The Lonely Place"

The sun, the rain, the hurt, the pain,
The smiles, the tears, the days, the years,
The love, the hate, the thoughts, the fate,
The truth, the lies, the soul, the eyes,
The mind, the heart, the end, the start,
The love we shared, the ways we cared,
The thoughts we had, when we were sad,
The ways we talked, the ways we walked,
Your slightest touch, was still too much,
The pain you knew, I felt it too,
The words, the face,
"The Lonely Place"

  Cheryl Mauger

A Sonnet On The Sonnet

When words flow not like doves, soft-winged and pure,
The sonnet tersely strips the talent nude;
Unlike the Bard of Avon's sweet allure,
The lines divine a coarseness and are crude.
Ere this stout verse no one had been so lined
So as to tempt young tyros to a rite,
With style and compression, pre-designed
To rid them of their cherished quills of might!
Thought struggles here to keep the beat and sum
Of this set rhyme, set meter, line and foot;
Mind's fingers do so steady tap the drum
That on each face is filed callus put!
So in a couplet does this sonnet end:
What message does this little sonnet send?

  Joseph P. Wechselberger

Defeated

You feel the wind scraping against your face like sandpaper.
The sound of pounding hooves, like thunder, echo in your ears.
Then, you feel the large animal lift off the ground,
lurching forward over the jump.
When you have brought the animal to a stop, you sit and think:
Will I win? That phrase runs through your mind a thousand times.
When your scores appeared on the board,
a chill runs down your shivering spin.
You read: 9.0, 8.7, and 7.9.
You have enough for third, you feel defeated.

  Jennifer L. Hallsey

Somebody Take Me Away

As I sit here and I contemplate
the sounds that really aggravate
as I plan the coming day.
A child's whine it makes me pine
for a peace full place where for to dine.
A cat though hungry who may believe
he has the right to peeve
He just must leave the way he came,
for I am not to blame.
The dive bomb swoop a mosquito makes
while I'm sitting quietly by the lake
can you stand the sound they make?
And how about a dog that's barking all night long
no sleep for me, now that is really wrong.
And I can't stand a phone that always rings
while in the bath I sing
(that gets on my nerves) but by and by
what makes me cry no matter where I lie
the sound I just can't tolerate
the sound I must obliterate that buzzing of a fly!

  Christine Bell

"Mortal Thoughts"

Who is responsible for the killing of flesh, when
the spirit still live? The death of us, means not to
yield life and the punishment for the act of killing
is death of the body, but not of the mind, who shall
be the judge, when they find that it cannot be flesh and blood!
It is only mud, and not divine, though in our mind lies
the intellect. In respect to the soul does it go cold with
death? Or is it the angel that binds with the divine in the mind,
when this host takes the Ghosts from our bodies?
In this life we must die, flesh and blood were a gift to
the mind, just for a time, then the mind accepted
choices from terrestrial voices that spurn death and
blood shed, what was actually said during that
formation, when man became a manifestation? Who
is responsible for this negative creation of this abode
where the code is for the death of blood and flesh ?

Ijaaz Givens

"I Smile"

I smile as I walk alone at night,
the stars are many the moon is bright.

The clouds are few and look just dandy,
wanting to be eaten like cotton candy.

The breeze is cool and oh so fresh,
it makes me shiver as it blows against my flesh.

The trees are swaying in every way,
like lovers dancing a romantic ballet.

The grass is green and standing tall,
with dew dropped tips just waiting to fall.
I come upon a running stream, as it touches my body it makes me gleam.
The water comes onto my lips, I have to drink it and take a sip.
I smile as I look around, and appreciate the beauty that I have found.

Eleanor Carrillo

"My Slow Entrance"

I have reached the point of no return, yes death.
The strange depth of unknown worlds and things.
When now I cannot take a breath
After my eyes were shut, my soul grew wings.
My heart will no longer keep its beat
But there is comfort in this place today.
I wish for my sorry life never to repeat
To heaven I hope to go, I'll pray
Where I am resting now must be purgatory
No one ever expects that you'd have to wait.
And in my life, I had no moments of glory.
To our destination; there's no exact time, but I fear I
   might be late.
To think I used to fear death before,
But I'm content to finally be no more.

Amy Stemelski

Mermaid

   Standing by the sea
The sun has just set
   The waves are coming to swallow me
The sky is turning black
   The water is up to my knees.
I must turn back
   I try to run away
My legs won't move
   For some reason I must stay
Say hello to the water; good-bye to the land
   The waves are coming
My feet leave the sand.

Jeanne Oliver

Sunset

Tonight, as I hold you one last time in my arms,
The strength of the day weakens
   and surrenders to night's greedy dominion, luring you to it
Tonight, I drown in salty tears as I watch you
   shrink from the residual colors of the day, that
   captured by the onset of night,
Fill the sky with one last flavor of life-
A faint memory echoing the song of the living
Averting my burning eyes, I turn away from the perishing colors
   but they continue to disappear into the black of the night
A dissonant magnet of emptiness,
Sometimes surrendering life's colors the next day
   so that they might soar free again
But tonight, these bitter colors are watery and grave
Once an overwhelming sight,
Now just a wearisome end to a long day,
And as I bid them farewell, I remember the beauty they once possessed
Because tonight they have melted with your soul
   into the eternal hunger of the night,
And they won't return tomorrow.

Heather Heitfield

Black

A time of darkness has settled upon me.
The sun has dropped out of my sky.
The blackness that faded with the dawning of love
has slowly returned to my life.
In all of the world love comes and goes,
all that shall follow will not be as deep,
for only one can re-enter my heart.
When that angel of mercy visits your life,
you must pray with your heart she will stay,
because once she has left you your heart will grow cold,
and the love that you felt will turn black.
We'll see angels of mercy, they come and they go,
but only one will love.
Hold tight to that angel, no matter what,
for she is your key to true love,
And if she would leave, may her memory stay,
For without it all love would turn back!

John Fruth

Discrimination

The breeze blew softly through the trees,
the sun warm on my hair as it fanned about my face
I walked along the road, feeling the rocks beneath my feet
the other kids following behind, taunting me.

"Don't walk on our land" they yelled,
"we don't want you to get off the road,"
I remember feeling defiant: I will walk on your land, and
I'll breath your air, and I'll run away if I want,
my only crime was being poor.

What is discrimination? Is it a new word? Is it only for
people of color; but I am white and this happened so many years ago
was it called something else then-something absurd?
By whatever name-the pain is just as deep; rejection by your peers,
my heart can't weep
my only crime was being poor.

The years have swiftly passed but memory is sharp and clear,
this happening left such an impact, the groove is so deep in
my mind; like a record that will keep spinning at will,
my pen writes for all to hear
my only crime was being poor.

Betty Jane Perry

What About The Animals

Why don't stars come out at night and
the sun's just a blur in the sky? The
deer looked up expectantly but the owl
had no reply. And where does fire come

from when no lightning lights the sky?
But the owl just sat in horror as smoke
began to fill the sky. Why does rain
kill the lake and burn me when I drink?

But the bear received no answer as the
owl began to think. What happened to the
river where my ancestors used to breed?
But the salmon got no answer while the

turbines fed men's greed. Where have all
the trees gone? Where we supposed to
sleep? But the owl could only wonder as
a chainsaw broke the peace. And what

about the mushroom cloud that threatens
us as we speak? But none of them could
answer and the animals... began to weep.

> *Dave Jones*

Decayed Fear

And gone the mother earth engulfs your core.
The tears abide the face like they are paint,
Yet, nothing's real, and no the heart I bore.
I mourn, but not for you; your life was taint.

You seem to seek revenge on all of us
By pounding guilt and causing violent dreams.
You drove us but insane; a reckless bus,
So we—a woolen dress, without its seams.

The people stab us, daggers made of sneers.
So, now we taste defeat before we fight—
As if we feel so weak and very mere.
So, who are they to pass their glares tonight?

The passing time shall not heal my pain.
I stand umbrellaless in times of rain.

> *Annie Kuruvilla*

Overwhelming

Overwhelming are the tears that fill the eyes,
  the tears that come when someone dies,

Overwhelming is the feeling when you have tried your hardest
  but your hardest wasn't the best you felt,

Overwhelming are the dreams that fall short,
  your dreams that miss the center mark right from the start,

Overwhelming is the pain that shakes the body,
  the pain that is not physical but that of the heart,

Overwhelming is the hurt of rejection, the hurt that
  is felt when looking at the dark side of your reflection,

Overwhelming is the sense of peace,
  the feeling you experience when standing in a cool spring breeze,

Overwhelming is the feeling that you belong,
  when someone says I'll love you for your whole life long,

Overwhelming is the love that shapes and binds you,
  the love that intertwines a couple and blinds them,

Overwhelming is the love a man holds inside,
  the love for a woman which rises from his soul and can make him cry.

Overwhelming is the love a man and a woman have for each other,
  the love that will bind them together forever and ever.

> *Jeffrey R. Heiser*

Nature's World

The woods is where I'd like to be all day.
The trees, I sleep with all the time at night.
The creeks and streams do show to me the way
To Nature's world where stars do shine quite bright.

The ways of Nature, I will learn to keep.
I need the forest to live my full life.
The animals do keep me in the deep,
Where I can live with nature and with blithe.

The leaves on trees hide me from the big towns.
The pulse of Nature's veins do flow from me.
The hunts with the grey wolves do know no bounds.
To Nature's home I do not need a key.

The trees and I are friends till end of time.
The home with Mother Nature is all mine.

> *Austin D. Snyder*

After The Storm

After the storm it's very wet.
The trees look sad and blown over.
The sky is gray.
If you look at it long enough,
You can see the tip of the rainbow.
When the sun has gone down,
way way, down down, way, way down.
The stars come out. After the storm, you see a shining star,
And after the storm,
There's always a rainbow to climb off of.

> *Amy N. Pratt*

Untitled

I sit and stare at my reflection.
The unfeeling mirror shows a scared child,
Needing to be comforted.
The lonely teen waiting for affection.
A dejected adult hiding the fear.
The adult wants to beak the mirror
And use the shards to slit her throat.
But the child is so scared and so alone.
The teen is so angry and filled with pain.
Crying can't help anymore, it's too late
The deed has been done; nothing can stop the pain.
Hiding it behind an iron wall is all that remains.
A simple reflection on the outside, a frozen inside.
The eyes no longer harbor emotion;
Only a body to carry on a useless existence.
Where will it end, or will it?
Slowly my senses return and again I see myself.
A moments time, but years of memories.
I turn and walk away only to return tomorrow,
And live once again.

> *Heather McGee*

Getting Over You, Or Not

I think I'm over you but,
then you're on my mind again
I lie and say I'm over you but,
I still cry over you
Down inside my heart I think I still love you but,
maybe I'm just in love with being in love
When you say certain things my heart breaks
I need you in my life, I want you
but most important...I love you

> *Heather Cronk*

Heaven

Imagine the orgasm
The universe cannot withstand.
As Christ the groom
And we the bride,
In mutual desire,
Unite in love and thus conceive
A wholly new dimension.
It develops in our womb.   Time goes forward.
We nurture and sustain it. Time goes ever forward.
We labor to deliver it, an agonizing time.
And then time stops, forever dead.
Instantly forgotten
Are the numerous discomforts
Of millennial gestation.
All the tears and pains of labor,
Vanished, totally forgiven.
We gaze upon the newborn,
Exalting in the dawn of its perfection.
And we love it!
Timeless, eternal, visible, love.

Donna Price

The Sea

The sea, Oh! what beauty it belies
The waves in motion shaping the sands of time,
The sea in its never ending struggle
To shape the shores of the continent.
What stories it could tell,
As I gaze upon the waves and wonder
Where they have been.
Whose lives have they touched, was it good or bad,
May be it cleansed the soul.
For that's the feeling I get as I look
Upon the endless motion of water
Like a refreshing breath of life.
I am alive, time s on the move,
Oh! beautiful sea, what is next for me?

Gerald W. Murr

"Utopia"

A world of peace and harmony
The way I feel life really should be
A flowing stream of love
We can see all things, under and above
The sea, the sky and people too
Something's old, and something's new
We can live a life together
Making it better, for all, forever
God gave us this world to finish and complete
But with each and every day, man must compete
For the dreams we feel we really need
We must work with each other
We must work and weed
We can weed out old and harmful actions
Work in new and better reactions
For "Utopia" is a dream of something unreal
It can't really be, but it's the way that I feel

Diane Marie Vileno-Gonsalves

Looking Beyond

There is beauty where you look.
There is kindness in every living thing.
Every living being on this planet has life, and
feelings, whether small or large.
   We all feel.
We all have something in common-
   That is....
The existence of life and the need of love.

Debbie Ortiz

(For Valentine's Day 1993)

Chris, if I could find the words to say
The way I think and feel about you each day.
They would have to be exclusively words for you
Of the joy you've brought, love and compassion too.
Of the sweetness and warmth of each and every kiss
The friendly talks and smiles and soulful bliss
The times apart when I feel so alone
Made up for by being able to call you my own.
Alas, though there are no words - none which will actually describe
The way you make me feel.
I only hope and want you to know
That my love for you continues to grow.
Happy Valentine's Day
Love, Brian

Brian J. Jost

Untitled

A soundless, invisible glow shone on my face
the whole entire time that I was with you.
If ever there wasn't a bright smile on my lips,
there'd be a hidden one trying to shine through.

My heart knew how much you meant to me,
and my eyes sparkled when you were there.
This was the most amazing experience I'd ever had,
and I wish you knew how much I did care.

Now, I haven't a right to feel as I do
because you took away what I held very dear.
Without my consent, it is gone from me,
and now I am alone and full of fear.

You were my very first true love,
my precious prince, my dream come true.
The love you once had for me is now gone,
but for some reason, mine is still there for you.

Now you have left, and are free from me.
Your love is for another fortunate girl to keep,
and I am without you - all by myself,
just to crawl into bed and silently weep.

Dawn Apostoli

Untitled

The winter was long, and extremely cold.
The wind and snow are getting old.
I remember a morning that was all right,
The snow was deep and awfully bright.
The heat of the sun was making a haze,
As the cold from the snow danced on its raze.
In the middle of the snowy white sheet.
The edges of the cold, dark river meet,
Some of the birds are still on the wing.
A few have settled and started to sing.
The fields are moist from the melted snow,
Awaiting the seeds to help them grow.
The weather is changing, it's starting to warm.
I'm looking forward to an old thunder storm.
The land and the trees are shades of brown.
The warm spring rains will soon come down.
The fields and grasses will start to green.
The buds in the trees will make a different scene.
I love the smell of fresh spring air.
To think of winter I do not care.

John F. Arnold

Untitled

The rain is misting down,
the wind is slightly blowing.
The earth is moist and brown,
and nature's colors are showing.

The trees are full and green,
the water is steady and blue.
The animals' senses are keen,
springtime has arrived special for me and you.

The world is coming back to life,
and love is in the air.
People are relieved from pain and strife,
free from anger and despair.

Now the sun is shining so yellow and so bright,
you and I are in love together.
And we know that it is right,
I see it in your eyes, we'll be in love forever.

Christopher Garms

Old Trees

Old trees start leaning,
their branches all gnarled.
Bending and cracking, they begin to break.
Young trees stand proudly and tall,
thinking their beauty will last.
But if you look closely, you'll see what I see.

Old trees have character that can't be surpassed.
They bend as if weary,
and weary they are.
But they're regal and splendid,
with a look that might say -
"I've stood here for ages and though I'm near gone,
My beauty is special and just needs to be seen
by the right eyes to love and appreciate me."

"What have I seen through the years that have passed?
Strong winds that have blown the younger trees down,
Yet here I've remained through many a storm.
There must be a reason and a strength you can't see.
I'm old, yes, but proud.
And my roots uphold me."

Ann D. Criss

Our Flag

One day I saw some marching men
Their marching line seemed not to end
They carried forth our emblem true
The color bearers of red white and blue
Our glorious flag flutters with the breeze
Its banner high over all the seas
The stars and stripes held ever high
Was stained with blood by those who died
Our national emblem carries on
For those brave Americans who since have gone
They gave their lives that we might be
Happy in the land that's free
So hold it high for all you do
Be numbered with the loyal true
Our glorious flag, red white and blue.

Frank E. Young

Yellow Roses

The roses are Yellow
Their meaning is clear
The person who brought them
Doesn't want to be here

A young woman lies in her hospital bed
And silently cries as her newborn baby is fed

The man is leaving
The young woman is sad
The babies Father
Doesn't want to be a Dad

The baby will grow up
Without its Father to care
The Mother will try to make up for this loss
But, its Father still won't be there

So remember this
When the roses are Yellow
The man who brought them doesn't want a kiss
He doesn't want to be
A Father to 1, 2, or even 3.

Jo Anne Larson

'Nature's Jewels'

Poets cherish the vibrant colors of spring
  Their most precious gems
Are the sweet faces off innocent pansies
  Reflected by a near by pond.

The depth of every poet's soul
  Is nourished by the tranquility
Of sparkling icicles and falling snow
  Blanketing the sleeping earth.

Poets cherish the breathtaking beauty
  Of happy playful rainbows
Dancing on the crest of a waterfall
  These are the crowned Jewels of Nature.

Elizabeth Ford

Common Sense With Education

For Justice And Communication

Let's study to learn better how to use common sense
Then be somebody honest. And get a real good education,
And realizing what qualification and skill are meant,
So man with God, will have better communication.

As progress for success is better than keep paying rent
For the benefit of ourselves and the future generations,
Know that common sense with education are the proper tools
By which one can make complete preparations for success.

By using common sense with education
One can do more and get ahead better
Without using common sense education is useless
Common sense is very necessary for communication.

James B. Hooks, Sr.

Untitled

Life is a mystery and so is death.
They are both closely related by a single breath.
The finger of death touches the young as well as the old.
And all the why's remain unanswered and untold.
For some life is brief, and for some it is extended.
As mortals we never know just when we're apprehended.
So, be grateful and cherish little things as small as they are,
and consider yourself every fortune by far.
Don't be complaining and don't be depressed.
Because there are always others around you
that are more distresses.

Edythe Burstein

Dear Love

At first I looked to you as an outsider,
Then day by day as I began to know more about you.
Things inside of me began to change.
I started to view you as a friend.
Day after day of being together,
Made us grow closer and closer.
And when the season had come to an end,
I began to miss you and
I couldn't wait to see you again.
The memories of being together filled my mind
And made my heartache for you.
As the days past and the day for us
To be together again grew nearer,
I began to fear that we wouldn't be
Right for each other anymore.
Then as we meet again, I felt a special power
Growing inside of me.
And then, I knew we were meant for each other.

Jo Ann Matsuo

Second Year

In wild anger I shout out why.
Then I think of a memory and begin to cry.
The second year came but the pain did not go
And when we'll be united I'd like to know.
Some days are harder then before
And I realize that I love you even more.
Every memory you gave me, I'll cherish each one
And I'll make others laugh too, as you had done.
My heart is still full of grief and sorrow
But we're brought closer to you with each tomorrow.
You will always be my brother and best friend,
But my sad, broken heart still needs to mend.

Brandi Krout

My Mother

I was only in her womb for 6 1/2 months,
then in an incubator for 3 months.
The death of my twin could easily have been me,
and so, my mother was afraid to hold me.
I was so tiny and fragile nobody though I'd survive,
but ...I'm very much alive.

I fought and struggled for the bond with my mother,
that for a short time was lost to another.
Then lo and behold my mother cheered up
and she picked me up.

Days turned into weeks, weeks into months, then years.
Through hardships and glory, laughter and tears,
the bond with my mother is greater than ever.

Distance and age, or life with another,
has not lessened the bond with my mother.

I love my husband and children very dearly,
but my love for my mother started early.
My love for my mother cannot truly be defined,
because my love for my mother
is infinite beyond time.

Barbara Hayes

Wake Up Call

Man, in arrogance, thinks he knows it all.
Then mother nature gives a wake up call.
A mountain belches lava down its sides.
Rain, in wake of fire, causes massive slides.
Floods, hurricanes, tornados, in their wake.
Leave razed, cities it took man years to make.
Fires, fast raging, exceedingly hot, lay low
Forests which took hundreds of years to grow.
The earth shakes, leaving all fallen level,
As though smitten by some angry devil.
Suddenly man sees he knows naught at all
As he stands helpless at that wake up call.

Dorothy L. Subke

Sounds Of The Evening

The little birds sing a sweet song;
Then the church bells ring: Ding-dong.

The breezes blow...and seem to whistle;
The rustling leaves crack and jistle.

The children's voices sound of laughter,
Then cries of sorrow when bed times's after,

Now, as twilight here is nearing...
There are less sounds, that I am hearing...
The last sound I hear is the cricket's creek;
Then I close my eyes, and drift off to sleep.

Jennifer M. Lally

Dreaming Of Peace

Bang-
There goes another brother
Why must they all be gone
Before we get our peace
We sit and watch our
Brothers and sisters die
While we dream
Of the peace that may come alive
How many of our brothers and sisters will die
Will the whole human race be gone
Before our dreams of peace throughout
The world will come alive
Let's not just sit there and wait
For it to come
Let's go out
And make peace throughout the world before it's too late.

Jessica Hoffman

Untitled

Deep inside
there is a love I cannot hide,
that love is all for you
when you're away I feel so down and blue.
I think of you day and night,
My thoughts begin with the morning light
I want to spend the rest of my life,
with you as my husband and me as your wife.
I miss and love you so much
It's awful not having you here to hold and to touch
I'm beginning to cry,
So I must say good-bye!

Elizabeth Billieux

Outside Of The World

Outside of the world,
there is a place, a place so
special, and in grace.

A grave away, oh what a day,
to see this place, so excited but
lonely will I be.

There is a fear, but not near,
the place that someday I will be there.

Soon the fear will be gone,
and not long, will I see the place,
that my dreams have accomplished
since I was brought here to earth.

Know I am here, and you are
near, but once you get here, you'll never
want to go anywhere else, or face the
tortures of life.

Jamie Olson

Nature

Darkness reaches out, grasping the parched ground.
There is a sudden hush.
No creature makes a sound.
Anticipating, praying for some relief
to end the fearless cycle and constant grief.
A bird floats searchingly above,
as we do the same to find our strained love.
Nature has played a cruel trick on all life.
She knowingly laughs at the land's endless strife.
But we seem to bond as you walk out the door,
A drop, a sprinkle, and then no more...

Jacqueline Randolph

"Time"

There is a time to cry...
There is a time to smile...
There is a time to fight...
There is a time to forgive...
But how can you tell what time it is anymore.
There is a time to love...
There is a time to hate...
There is a time to build...
There is a time to destroy...
And if there is time for all this. Are we ever
going to run out of time?
There is a time for right...
There is a time for wrong...
There is a time for peace...
There is a time for war...
Just try and choose your time properly. If you don't
it can hurt you a long time.
There is a time for you...
There is a time for me...
Can there ever be a time for us? Or has that time ran out?

Douglas R. Baughman

Through A Child

Through the eyes of a child the world is perfect,
They do not see its faults.
Through the mind of a child they do not understand,
They can not comprehend the violence around them.
Through the heart of a child they have no enemies,
They love everyone equally.
Maybe if we see through the eyes of a child,
Think through the mind of a child,
And love through the heart of a child,
We can make this world a better place for the child.

Jill Henry

Paradise Lost

It's been a while since a smile has crossed my face.
There is very little pleasure left in my place.
I long for a time, and times to come again so fair;
that all the love and beauty with someone I could share.
To skip across the school yard once more I do decree,
to find the paradise lost is the only thing that can save you and me.

I was so young once, yet the time has fallen away.
Day turns to night, and night turns back to day.
The tragedy of a human soul, whose life does seem so small;
only seems to fade away, as dust in the evening thrall.
I have lost more happiness, compassion, and love
than normal men can ever achieve.
Yet every thing I hope to gain, I know I could never keep.

John Powell

Always There For You

Throughout every place,
there lies a gorgeous face;

Ears to listen to what you have to say,
a hundred thousand times a day;

Eyes to see your every action,
being good, you will receive satisfaction;

And a heart that expresses its undying devotion,
in times of despair, love is a healing potion;

He acts willingly and keeps you company,
especially in times of sorrow and misery;

He has a solution for every little thing,
and can always make the angels laugh and sing;

Despite anything you can do,
God is always there for you.

Jason Di Grande

Dandelion

Engulfed within the long brown willowy grass
there stood a man.
   A wise man a man of many years and a boy he called child
whose golden hair danced with the very
sunlight that shone upon it.
The two were engaged in the very
deepest soul to soul laughter imaginable
as they stood hands bound together
by the wish of the Dandelion.
1.......2.......3...... said the body and so they blew
And as I peered through natures thick veil of floating
kaleidoscope beauty I witness the legacy... from
Flower... to seed... to flower.
   As the boy ran about mystified by the freedom of the scattered seed
I saw the wise man smile. For he knew he and the
dandelion shared the same destiny as he
stared at the golden petals of the flower he called child.

Justine Gleicher

Crimson Tears

Why do hearts lose touch with reality.
They answer for dreamers and romantics.
Hear no plea from realists and thinkers.
Never once tries to stop and ponder.
Goes off on a tangent.
Goes off on emotions.
Goes off on intuitions.
"Follow your heart," the saying goes.
Would you.
Could you.
Trust it.
Believe it.
When that red ruby has been shattered once.

George Miyashiro

Shattered Love

I am left with shattered pieces, of something that was
There was no reason it ended, it was just because
The forever lasting memories, my heart cannot forget
The lonely painful goodbye, is my only biggest regret

The times we were together, showed how much we both cared
Our magical kisses, was the love we both shared
I thought our love was something special, and so true
I thought it would never end, but it happened out of the blue

Now my heart is broken, and I am left all alone
Nothing hurts more now, than the sorrow that has grown
I am always reminded of us, when I see your smiling face
Knowing that I am left without, your gentle soft embrace

Still I'm always crying, myself to sleep at night
Oh how I thought, our love was so tenderly right

But now you've moved on, and left me behind
For now it is a new love, that I have to find
My heart says, that you'll be my forever
And again one day, we'll share our undying love together.

    Carissa Nunez

More Than A Dream

I had a dream last night
There were people all around me
The night was cold
And they were poorly clothed.

All through this dream
There were children hanging on to me
With big sad pleading eyes
And they were hungry.

In my dream were itching heads covered with lice
And bare feet on cold dirt
Hands reaching for food there was never enough of
Parents with quiet hunger letting the children eat.

Was this only a dream
I kept trying to find a way to feed the reaching hands
Warm the children's little feet
And preserve the dignity of a parent.

Yes, I had a dream last night
And then I woke in my life of plenty
I realized it was more than a dream
It was my God sending me to be His hands in a world of need.

    Joan A. Smith

Tax Time

It's tax time again and what should I do;
There's a mountain of a paperwork to try to wade through.

It's always a struggle to decide which form to use;
Just looking at this stuff makes me want to snooze.

I always worry - will I use the right chart;
Oceans of figures, where do I start?

There are so many questions I have on my mind;
I'll never catch up - I'm too far behind.

Just when I start to climb from underneath;
Oh no - guess what - it's April 15th!

    Callie Shreckengost

The Little Red Can

An ocean voyage is so much fun; there's something there for everyone
There's shuffleboard, movies, swimming and cards; for something to
    do; you needn't look hard but Cheryl and I had a terrible thirst;
    we wanted a large Diet Pepsi the worst
We walked the deck from bow to stern, to see if somewhere we could
    learn if Diet Pepsi there could be found, but everyone we met
    turned us down
Each one is his turn said no to a man, and pointed us to that little
    red can
Five days and nights we sailed oceans blue, the sunsets were lovely,
    the people were too but all the time we hoped we would see, just
    one single can of Diet Pepsi
We saw whales and seagulls and prayed we would land, just to get rid
    of that little red can
At last on the island of Hilo we docked; and there at a store our
    treasure we stocked
Blue cans and blue cans and blue cans galore, that was our purpose
    for going ashore
We went back to the ship with bags in hand, and said our goodbyes to
    that little red can

    Gloria J. Berry

Chances

Down life's long road there are chances you take,
These chances are decision you must make.

These chances can open a door to a new tomorrow,
Or they can leave you alone in sorrow.

A chance you take can make life's long road a happier place to be,
Or it could make it dark where you can't see.
Taking a chance is something you do each day,
It's the same as going out to play.

The chances you take can end up bad or good,
But they always end up how they should.

For a chance is a step in life that you have to take,
It is a decision you have to make.

    Jessica Saucier

Untitled

There's darkness and there's light.
These good and then there's evil.
Evil will prevail, goodness will die.
The choice is up to me alone.
Winning or losing, living or dying.
I die, I go to heaven.
I live, I go to Hell
Heaven with Angels, harps, and clouds
Hell with demons, drums, and sounds of crying.
Hell is Heaven, Heaven is hell
I want Heaven, I will prosper these,
But as long as I'm in Hell, I can't have my heaven
My life is torture, they tell me to choose,
to choose between Heaven and Hell,
between good and evil
I can't, It's hard, It hurts too much.
I love both too much, I want a part of each
Heaven and Hell, Good and Evil, and light and dark
but I can't, so for now
I give up!

    Angela Davis

When The Fields Bloom

The fields are lovely this time of year.
They are filled with hope and inspiration.
When I walk through the fields, I feel a tear,
And we will reach our destination.
A tear for love and a tear for hate.
A tear for you and a tear for me.
So when we walk through the heavenly gate.
We will be as happy as can be.
See the seagulls flying high in the air.
See the little squirrels climbing in the tree.
They show me how to love and care;
and see the fields so lovely.
So when you see the crescent moon;
that is when the fields will bloom.

Carolyn Barone

Grandpa

Grandpa's are sweet, like candy.
They are like a big cuddly bear and always handy.
I never knew mine.
The say he used to shine - which he still does.
Everyone says he was really special.
I know that because he is.
They fill my head with thoughts of happy times,
and make me want to know him.
In a way I do, through these thoughts, memories, and when it's
time to pray!
Grandpa is my guardian angel.
In dreams we speak at the same level, no screaming, no
yelling, just calm voices all around.
Grandpa takes me to the parade!
Grandpa buys me lemonade.
Grandpa didn't pass away!
Even though that's what some people say - but not me!
I have the key.
The key to all of my dreams.
Dreams where Grandpa can buy you ice creams!

Jackie Bunnell

The Eclipse

When the sun and the moon, meet in the day
They are like lovers who are always apart.
But the fleeting moments that they have together,
Are like all the time in the world has stood still.
And when the sun and moon, are alone in the space,
It's like time is never going to end.
But for all of their pain and all of their grief
They have one thing that keeps them alive.
It's the one thing in life, that keeps all of us nice
It's the moment that we embrace.
So if you feel lonely at night and feel pain in the
Day, just remember the sun and the moon,
Out there all of the time, and only briefly do ever
They meet.

Bob Alley

From Beginning To End

The babies that once were hidden inside
They came and grew in time gone by.
Teaching was learned and matured.
Years of yearning and prays come true.
Hopings of all, your heart is full.
Men and women of the future, you can see.
Believing in them, not wanting to doubt.
Seeing white instead of black, not even grey.
Someday all colors, but white will slip away.
Your child is blessed you know.
Every skip of a heart beat, will better it be.
The end you waited is here to see.
All white, all white so bright you see.

Geraldine A. Stengele

Feelings Of Love

If you love so much that it hurts down inside
They are simply your feelings too precious to hide.
Your emotions must play their role in your life
Like a temperamental cast on an opening night.

Take a look in your heart and at times you may find
The face of a loved one, if you'll just take the time.
You can cry when you're happy, cry when you're sad
Cry in the good times and cry in the bad.

Then think of the world and pray all the time
For God to forgive us when we get out of line.
If you love to watch children laugh and play
It may break your heart not to see them that way.

Enjoy the warmth from the sun in the sky
But remember the wars that let so many die.
Then sit on the grass, you can feel so at peace
But don't forget those who have nothing to eat.

Just the beauty of flowers and the birds that sing,
Some beautiful music and the beginning of Spring
Will help you image the reasons for giving
For happiness comes out of loving and living.

Arleen Pajic

Homeless

You see them at all hours, wondering the streets,
they are the people you hardly ever meet,
you see them stumbling down the side walk, how could this be?
We pass them by every day on our busy schedule, they give us
glee, if walking down an alley or by a door way you'll soon
discover, that when it get's cold you'll find them near a
street cover, the clothes they wear are old and dilapidated,
be not dismay at their sight, from a wonderer, this is
anticipated, you find them sleeping at all hours in the doorway
who are these people that some call life's throwaways,
in his bag and on his back is all his belongings,
they walk back and forth, not knowing where they are going,
they travel many miles, oh so many share this world,
many stand in our cities, like a weather beaten laurel,
some people don't look because they might get depressed,
still they are our brothers and sisters that we must address,
is this a world that we forget those, that have slip-by,
are we the same ones who turn our heads when we hear a help
cry, Why are we so afraid to look them in the eye,
before long you'll walk the streets and see his body lie.

Gene Connolly

Return Journey

Cast my ashes in the water, let them mingle with the sea,
they can travel in the ocean, while my ransomed soul goes free,
soaring upwards; always hoping, searching for eternity.

Like a stream into a river on its course my life has run,
knowing not where it was going till it saw its way back home,
may I see mine in its glory when my time on earth is done.

Now my heart, not dispirited, leaps in joy when daylight breaks;
thus my soul will make its journey going back through outer space;
we remember not our birthing, life is a sleep from which we wake.

As the rainbow is an emblem of God's pledge to all mankind,
I will try to reach his heaven when I leave this world behind,
groping, seeking, always hoping knowing not what I shall find.

Charlotte Lines Smith

Brother

Brothers don't come in a box or wrapped up in bows.
They come in sneakers, blue jeans, and even fancy clothes.
I love my brother. He's so cool.
He does big things, and goes to a big school.
He helps me with my math, and checks it too.
He cheers me up when I am blue.
He reminds me of a big tree,
because he protects and comforts me.
When he is sick, it makes me sad.
When he is better, I feel glad.
We'll stick together to the end,
together forever, compadres, companions and friends.
I am Jerod's best friend from the start,
because if I wasn't be writing this poem from the bottom of my heart.

Amber Mackert

Bands Of Gold

Bands of gold would cradle me and rock my weary head,
they comforted and held me while a voice above me read.
The stories told so sweet and clear, the sound so
soothing to my ear.
My body rested on gold bands,
I have no fear while in these hands.

As years went by the bands did bend, guidance was what they did lend.
The voice above me now in song, to hear the words my soul
would long. A tune about a soldier blue, the cattle call
and a love so true.
The bands of gold would keep the time, together we sang Clementine.

When it was time for me to go, the bands opened up and let
me grow. Face to face we stood both with eyes of blue, a
love unspoken yet we both knew.
The golden bands they are so wise, my father's bands, they
are my pride. Although I left and went my way, the bands of
gold forever stay.

Deona Wootton Grover

High School (The Last Days of Innocence)

These years are the best ones we've had so far.
They give us hope that they will lead to us ones far better.

These years have witnessed the growth of our knowledge.
We have the desire to grow taller.

These years have announced to the world that "We are here!"
They have given us the strength to change it.

These years have bonded us and taught us love,
We have been given something that the truly ours and ours alone.

These years, most of all, have given us
  memories and laughter and spirit.
With these, we can face the world,
  and whatever lies beyond it.

For we have these years in our corner.

And they will never abandon us.

David Siino

The Meadows

I watch as the meadows sway,
  They look like swells in the ocean.
The air is chilly and damp,
  So I snuggle in my jacket to keep warm,
But still the birds come flying by,
  To eat the berries in the meadows,
The meadows as they go rolling,
  Hit into the woods,
Like artist's colors that he doesn't want to mix.
  As the winds die down,
The meadows are like an undisturbed lake.

Christine Nebel

Days Of The Yore

Look up at them with pride
They have vanquished the boundaries of time,
Molded the prints of our destiny,
Vanished the thorns of our path,
As heralds of Fafnir.
It was just yesterday
They awoke to the brightness of spring
As flowers to the call of the sun,
They were geysers of love
Gamblers of passion.
Now, they wander aimlessly as stranded snow flakes
Living in the mirage of past dreams.
Behind the clouds that blurred their hopes,
they listen in the silence of their thoughts
Desolated as denuded winter trees.
Fading, forgotten identities,
their messages of love are carved on their skin.
With silvery crowns, glimmering in the sky
They wait at the gates of Heaven.

Gladys DePoveda, M.D.

The Western Explorers

The early settlers came from far away.
They landed on the shores in America's bays.
The settlers overtook the old Wild West,
In hopes of making their dreams the best.
Fences were put up across the land,
Sod houses were made of mud by hand.
The buffalo and Indians were left no place to roam.
The Americans had made the West their new homes.
The White Man searched the Black Hills for gold,
Placing the Indians on reservations to scold.
Tracks with trains covered the valleys and hills,
In order to bring Billy The Kids and Buffalo Bills.
The White Man came to the West to fulfill his dream of exploration,
Destroying the land in his participation.

Daniel A. Fodale

Lonely

Someone awakes in a bed suited for two, but is alone.
They reach out for someone who isn't there.
A tear stretches out across their eye and over the cheekbone.
All they want is for someone to care.

In another room alike but different from the first,
Someone falls to dreaming.
In this peaceful slumber hearts beat together in perfect time,
Smiles are wide and hearts are gleaming.
But only being able to dream such bliss should be a crime.

There are many more like stories of poor unfortunate souls,
but none as sad as mine.
For I am warmed by fires and coals, instead of love
And affection, but I'll be just fine.

For I have learned to cope with all the sadness and grief
Of being all alone;
Sleeping in the same bed with me and only.
For sadness and grief I have always known, it is part
of me - and I am lonely.

Cassy White

The Awakening

We walk around each day, oblivious to what surround us
till one awakening day, our "unreal" reality blinds us
only capable of grasping it for moments at a time
our inevitable mortality connects within our minds
overwhelming fear and sorrow, till we can take no more
oblivious to what surrounds us, we walk around some more.

Gwen Venancio

Eyes

Your eyes can tell a person a lot about you
They say if you're bashful or shy
They say if you're warm and friendly
They can also tell if you're caught in a lie

They're the most beautiful things
Especially the way they sparkle in the right light
I love big and alert eyes
When they are happy and filled with delight

I love almost everything about eyes
When they're filled with love and emotion
And I love all the wonderful colors of eyes
Like eyes as blue as the ocean

I like a beautiful brown
I like a gratuitous green
I like all the wonderfully different colors of eyes
Or at least all of them that I have seen
From what I'm told eyes are the gateways to a persons soul
Some eyes can pierce like a dart
but as far as I am concerned
They are the gateways to my heart

Josh Bangs

Flying High

From way up there
    They seem to travel here, then there....
It appears to be so... so organized

Drops of rain.......
    Creating waterfalls of pain.......
But as surely as rain, comes rays of sun
    Now let's go have some fun......

Don't be so serious in life and love
Especially when push comes to shove
Treat them....together to the end
    ...as long lost friends...

Gary Staggs

To Live Again

The empty eyes of the children follow me around the room.
They stare, they plead, they long, they question.
These are the eyes of Jewish children.
Immortalized in black and white, poster sized photographs—
For what purpose?

I wonder what happened to them, their hopes, their dreams...
Were they transported via cattle car to Poland;
Starved and tortured at Treblinka;
Beaten into the dirt at Belzec;
Ravaged by typhus at Chelmno;
Persecuted and enslaved at Sobibor;
Dehumanized and exterminated at Auschwitz?
What does all of this death and destruction mean to us?
Is there no hope in this kind of world?

We, who bore witness, who remained indifferent, we, who forgot, who
failed to act, who allowed it to happen and did nothing;
We must find in each of us, a way to revive hope, and to build new
dreams. We must
remember; we must care; we must listen and learn from the memories.
It is not too late to learn to live again.

Beverly J. Hill

Only For The Moment

Why, do so many times feel so right, so perfect, only for short moments?
They start out so good, only to end up wrong, and oh so empty.

And all your efforts, to hold on to those special times,
Can never beat the inevitable. Time is against you.
You can race it, but you can't slow it down.
As it always seems to happen, time will always win.

The times keep slipping away, the moments that seem so right.
That make you feel so special...
They seem so hard to capture, so hard to hold on to.

Yet, as you watch, as you set yourself up
For another shot at those special times, in the back of your mind,
You really wish it could end up different, and that elusive feeling
Made our's, we'll walk away with it just one time.

I keep hoping I'll be smart enough, to figure out a way to beat time.
And I'll hang on, never again to let them slip away.
I hope and I pray to God, we both won't let go.
And together the moment will last the rest of our lives.

And in our lives, our history, we'll go on as winners, who beat time.
And we'll beat the inevitable, and we'll never let go of the special
Feeling... The feeling called... Love

Colby Scroggin, Jr.

Just A Weed

Even a weed has a certain charm
They swing to and fro without any harm
The size or the shape doesn't really matter
They have fun in their own circle of chatter
Both large and small they hold their head high
They get stepped on or pushed out of sight
It hurts their pride but they hold on tight
They never grumble only glow in God's light

Irene L. Turiansky Johnson

The Real Ghostbusters, and The X Files

This is about the two things I love the most in life,
They symbolize who I am, and are great comfort in times of strife.
The Real Ghostbusters, and The X Files,
Both of which demonstrate an accurate account of paranormal styles.
I have found in myself, towards David, a glowing hint of
    sexual attraction,
But, with The Real Ghostbusters, there is a true positive reaction.
I have learned in life, that it is close to impossible to have
    a friendship towards anyone in my heart,
But, the fact that I want to have a friendship towards the two in
    The X Files, is what tears me apart.
David is a Hebrew name, meaning "Beloved",
Gillian is Latin, meaning, "Soft-haired", like feathers on a dove.
There is a type of ghost, that is called a "Fox Spirit",
But, Mulder and Scully would not even fear it.
There are plenty of paranormal occurrences in all cultures,
All we have to do is look for an old house, decorated with vultures.
My love for Egon will always run true, past the end of time,
But, my affection for The X Files will always be thicker than slime.
So whether it be ghosts, mutants, UFOs, aliens, or other
    paranormal game,
The Real Ghostbusters, and The X Files will always be one in the same.

Egan Spengler

Life Is A Promise

To love and loved, without loss of self.
To live and let live with joy, without guilt.
To be part of someone, and free to express.
To grow and learn, without the sin of ego.
To touch and be touched always with kindness.
To live a fruitful life, without being self serving.
To always thank God for believing all of above.

Jacqueline Grenier

Silent Talk

Walking along city streets, spilling in the gutter,
They used to call out my name like you did
with that voice, that whispered down my throat and my neck,
like humidity that made my clothes cling to me,
You made me hot, and sweating for you, wanting to see you
you in the light, talking of such things which we had no
idea, enjoying company one never knew before existed,
Your voice echoes through caverns in my head,
Bringing humility and depth and oh, such heat,
as the rays of the sun beat on the path I've traveled so
many times, while you were beginning.
You say such things that make me tingle and smile and laugh,
I know all there is to know of true happiness,
which I have come to know through the warm breath,
The gentle touch of your lips to mine, of the heat, the
passion, the explosions which go off, saying what we once
had has now drown, into the gutter where there it lay,
still, alone and silently talking.

 Julia Barbee

God's Wonderful Gift

Mother's are God's gift to us.
They watch over us with constant fuss.
From the time of conception till the
 day we are born,
They maintain a constant vigil from
 night time to dawn.
We are cherished constantly with love and charm.
And held very close to keep us warm.
With enjoyment they watch us grow from day to day.
Running around having fun as we laugh and play.
They will always be with us till we are grown.
And able to start a new life all of our own.
Then on the day when we are to wed,
A few tears they definitely will shed.
But they will be tears of pride and joy that glow,
Which they will be proud and happy to show
And now that you are starting life anew.
Always remember the dear Mother God gave to you.

 Guy J. Castellani

UCLA Vs. Nebraska

High in the bleachers, up some sixty rows,
They watch the game, its action ebbs and flows.
'Tis UCLA football, the season well underway,
His wife's a fan, she follows every play.
He tries to follow, the plays are pass or run,
They meet at scrimmage, pile on one by one.
Sometimes with pass of thirty yards or more,
Our hopes increase of evening up the score.
The minutes drag, like sand within the glass,
BruinS behind, cheers fade, so ends the half.
Out come the marching bands, some fans applaud,
But from one sleepy senior escapes a yawn.
The game resumes, his interest wanders oft,
To family, friends, and cases won and lost.
At last it's over, Nebraska wins by one,
'Tis pitiful, but now what's done is done.
The once-full stadium empties row by row,
Dejected Bruins file out, some heads hang low.
Each to his car, fans through the gates now pass,
Pity Brookside, weep o trampled grass.

 Donald R. Osborn

Two fellows

I remember when I was younger two fellows living with me.
They were really neat.
But, often not too sweet.
They were mean to me, that was to be, since they were older.
I looked up to them with all my heart.

Then this year one decided that life wasn't worth living.
So, he look his own.

They were cousins to me, a twin to each other.
Now there is only one.
It is hard to see one with out the other.
I have memories of them only together.
Now, new ones will have to be created with only one.

 Evelyn Koppers

Untitled

They went for a walk late one night never to return
 they were too young to die but the driver had no concern
After he had his last drink
 He got into his car and didn't think
As he came over that deadly hill
 He didn't know how many he was going to kill.
They walked a path they had before
 Never to walk anymore
As he kept on driving
 Neighbors heard them crying
As the people found the kids on the road
 The sounds of the scrims did grow
As the parents arrived
 They told them the kids did not survive
As the parents found out more
 The children were going through the heavenly door
At the funeral there was a lot of pain
 As they remembered the children walking that deadly lane.

 Christie Sullivan

No One Notices

I wait in the corner, unable to move.
They're after me, and I have nowhere to run.
The dust from the thin wood floors makes my eyes water,
and the smoke from the blazing fires
that destroy my town
burn my bare skin.
I see myself as a butterfly,
flying over the plush green land,
dancing on vivid flowers
and tasting their sweet nectar.
But then my world changes,
and everything turns black and loud,
no longer the green land I once knew.
I flutter over a small building
that is all in flames.
Screams pierce my ears and make my head ache.
The smoke makes me cough, it burns my delicate wings
and turns them black and limp. My wings shrivel up and I die.
My lifeless body falls to the ground,
but no one notices me.

 Beth Campbell

Here I Sit Almost Crazed

Here I sit almost crazed,
 thinking about how life is such a maze.
Wondering and thinking, almost speaking aloud,
 sometimes I even get completely profound.

Wondering and thinking about which way to turn,
when all I truly want out of life, is to love, be loved,
 and to learn.

 Cheryl Thomas Thomley

Meet Life's Challenges

Meet life's challenges one day at a time,
Things can change as quick as the flip of a dime.
Just when things are bad, and no sight of change,
Table will turn, good and bad rearrange
Look to the strength as a person you hold,
And watch as opportunities begin to unfold.
Realize the power as a person you won,
To make the future, to know the unknown.
Look to your friends for guidance and moral support.
They'll make sure you don't sell yourself short.
When you think you've taken all you can stand,
Step back, reassess, accept a helping hand.
We are given one body, one mind, and one life.
With it comes smiles, tears, happiness and strife.
Some parts are definite, others can change with a fight.
If unclear clarify, if too dark shed some light.

Gail Lee Delgado

Untitled

You have given me things that are so hard to find,
Things that don't come around a lot in a lifetime,
These things that make up for all the rest,
While the other just don't pass the test

Your trust, understanding and loyalty,
Shines through you deep, deep caring,
This means so, so much to me,
And these things, to you, I will go on sharing

Your friendship is one that is so true,
It pulls me up when I am feeling blue,
You stick by me through thick and thin,
While other people around me grin

I never did thank you for all of this,
That your friendship is filled with specialness,
I will never forget all that you have done,
I love you, you're a friend like none.

Bryan A. Czypecki

Love

Love does a lot of strange
things to me.
But I'm still trying to handle
things that shouldn't be.
Every time I try to love
someone with my heart.
My relationships always get
destroyed and fall apart.
But now that I'm always with you.
I can think of things I could do.
Loving you is the best
thing that happened to me.
Because you showed me that my love can be
I would definitely kill
myself if I would stop loving you.
And you already told me what you would do.
But there is no way I would ever leave you.
Not for death, another guy, or a pair of shoes.
So please don't think
that I'm going to leave you.

Danielle Nesfeder

Tears of Life

Tears of confusion salty tears of sadness which drop like an
unsteady waterfall.

Tears of happiness clear tears of joy which fall like raindrops
descending from the sky.

Tears of frustration dry tears of submission which don't even exist.

Crystal Luttrell

On A Small Lonely Hill

When you look at your life and you see nothing but loss,
Think of how Jesus felt, as He died on the cross.

The people around Him, were dying in sin.
They laughed and cursed Him, again and again.

With tears in His eyes and the pain that wouldn't part,
He looked beyond their outward hate and saw their weary hearts.

For deep within they wanted it to be true,
That this man, was the Christ, chosen for me and you.

But still He took and died in their place,
And now we can be saved by His amazing grace!!!

You won't have fear, if you'll just turn to Him and say,
"Jesus I believe in you, help me make it through the day."

You'll find peace, like you've never ever known,
Which can only come, from the one who now sits upon the throne.

As we celebrate this Easter, and the joy and love we feel,
After two thousand years, He's still saving lives, for what
He did on a small lonely hill!!!

Johnny Aaron Eudy

'Memory'

Today I sit here all alone,
thinking of our love, unknown.
Tear drops cascade from my eyes as I,
recapture the memory of your face and cry.

You are as if an apparition returned,
and I am thinking of you feeling confused.
My vision of purity is disiliusioning me,
for with you is where I wish to be.

To be with you would be pure heaven,
to have your love would be my destination.

As my memory deepens in thought,
my vision of you fades apart.
Your face begins to feel no more,
for you have gone and left me staring at the door.

I go and open the door to see,
that you were only a memory.

Agavni Chorbadjian

Side By Side

As we sit here side by side
thinking of the things we have to hide
from the outside world way out there
and the people who live in it with no time to spare
A day goes by and another life has been taken
from one confused soul who's heart was breaking
to have the trigger slip from the hand
and now the poor soul is lying there dead
and people don't care they don't stop and think
that as we speak someone is killed or are killing themselves
And as we sit here side by side
we figure it's time to fight for the thoughts we have
inside but what do we know were only teenagers
in an unruly world what were living in we face
more than we ever thought possible
Just remember one more thing
as I finish this poem that only
you can help change the world
we live in...

Hellena M. Jones

This Butterfly

Encased in the darkness of natures silk
This butterfly dreams to be free.
It's time to emerge, the voices of the earth so strong.
Bursting forth, ready to fly, with wings like stained
Glass, delicate yet strong in every way.
One goal - to find beauty and sweetness.
This butterfly, in love with nature, gently sits upon
A clover not knowing the meaning or four heart shaped
Leaves-like arms embracing true love, welcoming its
Beautiful burden, not wanting it to go.
But it's time to fly high, be one with the blue,
This butterfly catches a breeze.
Looking down to the earth, still deeply in love,
Hoping for one last look, until next time.
Always knowing that clovers arms of love will
Be waiting to catch this butterfly.

Gina Angelo Lewis

A Cancer Among Us

A malignant tumor,
This cancerous rumor.

It slowly spreads and spreads.
Boom, bang someone's dead.

No real justified cause,
And it breaks all righteous laws.

Attacks people of all kinds,
Its befouled blindness deceives people's minds.

Affects people of all color,
Can even affect your mother.

The tumor is negative, impure.
There's not much hope in a definite cure.

From this woe and foe, free your mind.
Suffering is hard to leave behind.

This tumor can form from ignorance,
But also a lack of self-confidence.

People have died trying to stop this cancer.
Will someone ever find the answer?

Doctors are finding cures one by one.
Surely, over time, this tumor "We shall overcome."

Janelle Campbell

"Dreams"

Dreams are the one thing, I feel inside
This innate feeling, opens me wide
I shed a tear, for no reason at all
When some empire, awaits to fall

Dreams are the one thing, I believe in
They help me through life, and the things you call sin
In my dreams I have seen, places I'll go
Places I've bee to, the people I've shown

Why do I try, they never see what I show
They never listen, for they are all clones
Dreams help me through, problems I face
Be it black, yellow or orange, people of any race

Conformity and violence, are things I have seen
Places I've gone to, the people I've been
Dreams are the one thing, I'll always have
Wealthy or poor, I shall never be sad

Andrew Rousseau

'The Silence Of The Years'

This is the only thing on my mind.
This is the only thing I wish to find.
It is escape from this deathly quiet place,
where the silent darkness hides the features of my face.
Crazy have I become over the year,
though this state can't take away my fears.
The strand of hope that makes me live,
Has taken all that I can give.
The reason for having hope in here,
is that someday to reunite with the one I love so dear.
My memory of her they can't take away,
even though my heart dies here every walking day.

Jerome Tiffany

Humble Dreams

To feel this unparalleled emotion,
this known only to the fortunate few,
To have embraced the grace of her passion,
I adore in awe with my love so true.

The profound feelings of her simple absence,
engulfs me in the most humble of ways.
Comforted by mere dreams of her essence,
I am inspired yet lack skill to praise.

Another day unable to behold,
the vision of God's greatest creation.
I suffer fatal wounds more than ten fold,
and await the next dream's deprivation.

The pain of missing is the worst it seems,
but now I will rest and cherish my dreams.

Brian Aguilar

On A Summer's Night

Melancholy wafts o'er the hill
This quiet, shadowed summer's night
I listen to a whippoorwill
Warble of its lonely plight.

Still, still, now, the countryside-
Oak trees etch a silhouette
Of blackest jet
Which seems to guide
The pale moonlight down.

Son again, the sad notes trill,
And soar aloft on scented breezes
To distant hills, which, too, are still.
But, faint now, a call returns and teases.

From the trees, I see a fleeting thing
Swift! Whippoorwill. Swift! Think I.
Darting to a new-found friend a-wing,
Lonely no more. I bid good-bye.

Janice Moore

Bonsai

China must be beautiful
This time of year.
Ah yes, the people's are always bustling
but, I know the purpose of their stride
Is not as ours is view that bonsai
Penetrating you cliff.
Gaze upward — there is no
Horizon in the tao of the orient.
Tamed, still, by the roots of the ancestors.

Holly L. Donhauser-LaMonica

Untitled

Wake up today looked at the ceiling
This was the day I'd change the feeling.
Oh this feeling that haunt me, haunts me
So - I love you, I hate you it won't let go.

Time always fly by fasten and fasten
Where's the feeling I'm always after.

The sun is arising then again setting.
It's everyday life so ripe son the getting.

One of these days I'd love to

beat the sun. And know my
Choices before their done.

Someday soon I'll look upon the wall
Without that mirror that knows it all.

Choices and feeling rising and
Setting - running so fast not
quite forgetting -
Will I ever know -
Will I ever know -
Charlene Cassidy

Guardian Ring

Happiness is remembering
those calls when your voice seemed to bring
the touch of soft, caressing things,
and words wore warm and throbbing wings
to shelter me in storms of life;
they eased my heartache, calmed my strife.
And always, in our forty years
your logic banished foolish fears.
Your creativity, the key
to salvage fact from fantasy
To make our home unique, carefree.
Your inborn wisdom let you see
the need to keep my future free
of worries, insecurity.
Now, always mine to have, to hold;
your wedding band of guardian gold.
But, more than just a ring to me
it holds a lifetime guarantee
that you're still taking care of me.
Frances D. Maxam

Futility

This night is more than I can bear to look upon,
Those stars too bright, that moon too near
For hands that clutch in vain. I fear
Perfection is too much for me.
That silver shaft across the sea,
Where heaven dipped its magic light,
Those trees, moon-stained, in gleaming white
Are too-soon gone.

If I could grasp some part of what is in my sight,
Perhaps I should not know unrest;
And calm instead might fill my breast.
But how to touch a dancing star,
And how to clasp a sparkling bar
Of sheen, are Things of Mystery.
Oh God! I feel futility
Lies in the night.
Augusta C. Dorn

Point Of Light

I have given my mind over to the confused lonely
Those who walk along the jagged edge
Ready to fall into the dark deep hole below
Where the blackness of the unknown
Is as inviting as any home
And the reaching up to get out of the pit
Is so much more frightening than the staying within
And all they want is to be left alone
Never to be brought back home
I try to shine a light and make it bright
And hope it comes into their sight
And somehow calms their anxious underfed soul
So with extended hand and unjudging heart
I reach out to give them cause to
Summon up the courage to look beyond
And see a point of light coming through the night
And to feel the warmth of the sunshine once again across their face.
Janice Crim

A Promise To You

So, you have made a decision, and that is your right.
Though I must let you go, I just had to put up a fight.
For never have I loved someone as much as I love you,
And never will I be the same, no matter what I do.
I want you to know you will always be in my heart,
For I saw something special in you right from the start.
You brought me out of a worrisome cloud and showed me
How to be happy again.
You loved me and you supported me—you were my friend.
Why you have a change of heart, I still don't really know.
But I love you and I appreciate you, and I hope it shows.
If you ever change your mind, I just might be willing to say okay,
To give it another try, whatever may come our way.
For whatever hurt I may feel is taken over by my love for you.
Together we could make dark skies turn blue.
I love you and this is my promise to you forever,
Never will I forget you—not now, not ever.
Cynthia Fowler

To A Victorian Poet

Dear Poet, would you thrill to know,
Though lying still and cold,
Your words of rhyme so sweetly shaped
Have deeply touched my soul?

Across the dark, the span of years
That separate your life from mine,
I hear the tones and feel the pulse
Of rhythms in my heart from thine.

Would I could rouse you from that sleep
To touch your hand or stroke your face,
And look into your eyes and share
Your music in some timeless place.

Had I but wings to ply the dark, the years,
And enter into your sweet sleep,
Who knows what words, what songs we might combine
If you again could love and breathe and speak?
Alice Woodward Moore

Butterflies

Butterflies wings gazing upon the purple Violets.
   watching their wings flip-flop in the cool refreshing air.
     Dozens of them with their dazzling wings swarming
      joyfully playing without a sound or care.
Looking at the silk like wings of many different colors
  Like pink, white yellow, orange, blue winged butterflies flying
      ....in the blue sky.
Brandon Gordon

Destiny

A woman is a figure, much admired by man.
Though sometimes misused without a plan.
Without this woman, there would be no children.
Without these children, there would be no future.
Without this future, man would be no more.
Without this man, there would be no war.
Women and children would not be hurt, anymore.
The cries of agony, are they worth this war.
Or are women and children, a way to keep score.
Is this the way it is to be, children hurt by you and me.
The end may come for us you see,
and totally destroy our family tree.
We need to listen, and see, so we can give our children
a chance to live, like you and me.

Joseph Orlovich

Reflection Of Charleston

The bumpy, cobbled streets, crooked and winding,
Threading through this lovely, historic town,
Covered buggies filled with chattering people,
Travel Chalmers Street, both up and down.

The narrow, pastel houses glow in the sunshine
Their shutters like lashes on wide open eyes,
And green, mossy gardens shade the piazza,
And block the view of misty, blue-white skies.

I stand and look with eyes of wonder,
My mind filled with images of other years.
Of ladies wearing long and flowing dresses.
Waving their men good-bye through falling tears.

The shots were fired upon Fort Sumter,
The North and South are now at war,
Men ride away from wives and mothers,
Knowing they will have to travel far.

I can almost see the flash and hear the guns roar,
And feel the anguish felt by women then,
As I gaze at this little house on Chalmers,
And think of times that will never come again.

Janet B. Mears

I Love You

I love you
Three little words
don't use them for granted
mean them from the heart
So many times found that lie told to me
believing in what I hear
How could three little words bring out so much pain
two people become one in the meaning of these words
words like this can bring out the best in everybody
but they can also destroy someone's already bleeding heart
so many people want to hear these words
so many people want to say these words
kids who grow up not hearing these words
grow up not saying them
These words can be the building block in someone's future
these words in the wrong hands could lead someone to death
such powerful words are abused everyday
Hearing these words come from my father's mouth
would have saved me a lot of pain

Jonathan Lance

Abraham, Moses and David

Abraham, Moses and David
Three men God dearly did love.
Abraham, Moses and David
Got help from the dear Lord above.

Abraham was the Father of our faith
Sarah, his wife of many years.
Dear Son, Isaac, promised them by God
Brought them much laughter, few tears.

Moses grew up in an alien land
Trouble forced him to flee for his life!
God spoke to Moses from a burning bush,
"You must help save my people from their strife!"

David was a hero, at a very early age.
Jonathan, his friend to the end.
David was anointed king; united a nation;
Captured Jerusalem.

Abraham, Moses and David
Three men God dearly did love.
Abraham, Moses and David
Got help from the Dear Lord above.

Betty Jane MacPherson

"The Closet Monster"

But what's this you say, the closet monster wants to play.
Thriving on your child's fear, starving for every falling tear.

You go to the closet to show him once more.
But that's not enough "under the bed" is what your child said.
With great anger and disgust, you lift the covers
  to find nothing but dust.

Out come the books to put him to sleep.
Not this time as the child begins to weep.

You turn away in total dismay, to hear a noise in the corner,
  as your child cowers in horror.
Deep in the shadows close to the groove.
Closer you move thinking a mouse.
Trying to extend your vision you notice the mouse's height has risen
Quickly you move to your child's bedside. thinking it's time
  to go for a ride.
Finally with great flight, the closet monster moves into sight.

Danielle L. Rozplochowski

I Will Look To The Hills From Whence Cometh My Help

Through the storms of life,
Through battles and through strife,
Through fear and through pain,
Through loss and through gain.....
Watch My God Work!
As with Daniel in the lion's den,
The three hebrew boys in the fiery ben.....
Through the shadows of death,
Through any evil that is left...
Watch My God Work!
Through the good times and the bad
He is Lord of all the land.
He is my God in whom I trust,
  and that, my friend, is a must!
So, through Hitler's reign,
  and even Saddam Hussein...
Through tribulation, and persecution,
Through destruction and unrighteous seduction,
Through frustration and devastation,
Watch My God Work!

Gladys A. Dixon

Change

The wind of change blows softly
  Through the trees;
It comes in disguise
  Like a gentle breeze;
You don't know it has come
  'Till the change is all done,
And then it is too late to stop.

Some changes are good,
  Some changes are bad;
Sometimes the changes,
  Are nothing but sad;
A change for the better,
  A change for the worse;
Some changes you know of ahead of time first.

  Denise Schuster

Shattered Dreams!

Peaceful afternoon dreamily floating
through the uncurling of spring
in newly formed tender seedlings
plaited down to the cool earth
beneath the weight of matted snow-trounced
season's end rotting leaves

Laid back in perfect form
spinning effortlessly with upreached arms
removed by time and space and icy glaze
oblivious to the roar of the crowd
and the thunder of clapping hands
admiration and awe for perfection shown

A faint rumble waffles the stillness
of slumbering consciousness in
laissez-faire attitudes
as to and fro the populous dips and waves
in multi-faceted abstract
void of structure and boundaries

…"Bombs dropped today!!!"…
  Oh, no! We're at war!

  Joyce Blackstone

Of The Woods

We stood in the middle of our years, slip-sliding
Through timeworn sand trying to find a toehold
On the south shore of the lake called, "Of the Woods"
Where no tree grew green.

We watched while thunder clouds cracked grey heads
Against a night black sky, sending slivers of jagged might
To shatter all semblance of peace
On the north shore of the lake called, "Of the Woods"
Where no tree grew green.

We danced the predictable "No Win" dance: One foot up
To one foot down. And repeat. 'Til exhausted we fell
In accountable heaps on the sand, there to sleep.
And the sun went down without coming out
On the west shore of the lake called, "Of the Woods"
Where no tree grew green.

We woke to the Wind's Chime. Whirling.
Feet flew. Sand blew. The lake gave way to a forest.
And the sun came up where it never went down
On the east slope of the place called, "Of the Woods"
Where all trees grow green.

  Carolyn McGlone Miller

"To Life"

Life is like a rope stretching from one point in space to another.
Throughout our lives we run into many obstacles of this rope which are
intending to cause a person to loose their balance and fall into the
pits of death. Some lives are lost to these obstacles and others are
lost to the wanting of a person to self inflict death. I as a person
upon this "rope of life", fight with all of my might to stay on the
rope. It is particularly hard for me because I find myself being
pushed back and forth between two self conscious beings in the pursuit
of life, love, and most of all happiness. For all my years I have been
fighting my way across the rope praying to make it to the other side
curious of what might be there, yet it doesn't get easier, in fact
these obstacles get harder. I will try to withstands the obstacles for
as long as I can, but how long will that be?

  Christopher Stockton

"Every Day"

When I was growing up my mother always said when the
time comes you with be judged.

For everything. Everything you've said. Everything you've done.
Everything you've thought.

Not by her, or any other human, but by the lord.

The way you lived your life everyday. How you treated people.
And how you saw the world.

Praying didn't help, unless your heart was in it.
And you felt what you said.

Church is everywhere, the beach, the park, your own home.
where ever you feel his presence.

The only one who can save you, is yourself, your soul.

So look at yourself. Question your actions. Everyday.

Do you stand up for other people? Do you try to understand?
Do you express your love as often as you can?

And in the bottom of your soul, do you feel something more than
just yourself? Something higher?
Something more powerful?

Something in your soul that pushes you to be more than you
were the day before.

  Danielle Capozzoli

The Phantom Army

Listen, do you hear it too?
'Tis the sound of marching feet.
A deathly quiet fills the air.
I hear muffled drums in a distant beat.
Look, do you see him too?
It's the face of a boy I used to know.
But he died over there, across the sea.
Died on a battlefield in the snow.
Listen, you can hear them now.
This is their undying prayer,
"Keep faith with us, to us be true,
keep the liberty we bought for you!"
Stop and give them heed,
Those voices swelling as they come,
Crying, "Give us peace, with you we plead.
Oh, you living, please be strong!"
Hark, do you hear their prayer?
The prayer of the dead, who died for you.
Listen to their voices from everywhere,
"Keep your freedom, we died for you!" Think about it.

  Dorothy M. Quick

The Night

The lord of the night shone bright. As the town below him slept.
To a stranger it was a beautiful sight.
While someone who knew it wept.

There was a man who was not afraid.
He knew the darkness of the night.
He was as cool as a grave. People would flee at the sight.

He knew the town and what happened there.
But he had come to save.
He knew the curse he knew the wrath. But yet he was not afraid.

Then he approached the town. And the stars began to flee.
For they knew that the wrath, would conquer even he.

The wind blew and the moon darkened. For they knew what was to be.
And then a sorceress came. And she was all he could see.

He followed her into a room. Were no one dared go.
For they knew the one who lived there.
And her heart was as cold as snow.

Then all at once they heard a sound, that echoed through the night.
It was a sound that chilled, even a bird in flight.

They never saw the man again. But you can guess were he went.
On that cold night long ago. In the room were no one went.
   Clarissa Fischer

Coming Of Age

A man's voice and a true spirit is evident
   to all who hear it.
Your gentle soul has been torn.
There is little I can do to mend it and
   that becomes a tragedy.
Truthfulness is reflective of another whose
   nobility surges through your being.
I am at once proud and sad.
Innocence has been shattered and you face
   the ugliness which has been thrust upon you.
A lifetime is set in motion—
A time which has come too soon.
   Carolyn K. Burke

Untitled

Sometimes it's so hard
To be so far away from you.
My life is empty without you near.
But it is truly amazing to think
That when I look at the stars tonight,
They are the same stars you see
So many miles away.
It makes me feel closer to you somehow,
Like we are connected by the universe.
It gives me comfort until I can be with you again.

So, when you look at the stars above tonight,
Know that I am doing the same...
And thinking always of you.
   Jennifer Shank

Scared Love

To see your face just makes me shine
To hear your voice knowing that you're near
Keeps me warm inside cause I know you're mine
Deep thoughts have entered your mind
Thinking about the future could never be so scared
Spending your life with another
Giving up what you've known all your life
Can't be thrown away in just a whim
So think it through I'll be waiting
I won't leave your side cause I only anticipated
The best for us both
   Jeffrey Wise

The Doily

The spider weaves a sticky web
To capture bugs to eat.
What keeps the spider's sticky web
From sticking to her feet?

Spider webs are very tricky
Because not all the strands are sticky.
Unlike the passing fly,
The spider knows which strands are dry.

The spider's web is captivating
To all who pass it by.
It's so unique, so eye catching,
That even humans stop to eye.

The sun shines and makes the webs glisten.
Each web is an intricate design
Of squares, circles, hexagrams and diamonds
A graphic art to behold.

Although we know the spiders object
Is to catch her prey or dinner
One can't help stop to admire
The perfect doily you can't buy.
   Edythe B. Rains

Dare To Be Great

I'm won't to dream in wishful vein,
To court esteem 'midst doubt and pain,
   'Midst fear and strain.
Would boldly aim to dare be great,
And stake my claim against debate,
   And winners make
To sure wake up to who we are,
And fill our cup with do and dare,
   And play to par.
Few sadder thoughts than these, my friend:
Among my oughts it could have been;
   It should have been.
Oh, please, my soul, release the past
And boldly claim sweet peace, at last,
   Sweet peace to last.
   Arthur Byrd Adams

May I Have This Dance?

"Oh yes" I say, smiling
To display my dimples, as I whirl in the waltz with Rhett,
And all of Atlanta looks on,
Scandalized.

"Certainly," I say, toes tapping
Up the staircase to paradise with Fred,
As below, discarded suitors
Scowl.

"Delighted Sir," I say, curtseying
To the King, as I cavort in Siam,
While the courtiers look on,
Envious.

"Thank you," I say, remembering
The boy with feet, clumsy as mine,
Who first asked for a dance when I was fourteen,
And shy.
   Judith Haslam Cross

Battlefield Called Hubbardton

Breezes play a tune among the trees, Crickets join in chorus, Perhaps
to drown the sound of muskets from centuries past, Or soften the cries
of pain and rage left upon a psychic wave by those who fought and died.

Were there many who had just felt manhood,
Had yet to live and expend their talents,
When the bullet hit did they regret,
Or did they feel a moment of glory in their last breath?

When flesh and heart were torn apart
was there a second to give in thought,
To say a fleeting prayer for those left behind,
And ask that God be kind?

When they stood and faced the charging red
did they feel it had been unfair,
Did they wonder why they had been chosen,
Or were they proud the burden was theirs to bear?

The world passes by seldom to visit this remote hill,
Or give thought to those who fell,
But the ghosts stand proud over their battleground,
And butterflies fly over the soil that holds their blood,
The essence of life offered on the altar of Independence.

Eunice Duffy

When Justice Calls Mercy Answers With Grace

God searched the courts of heaven
To find the perfect sacrifice;
A pure spotless lamb
Willing to pay the price.
Search and search he did
But only once could be found;
Preparations were made.
That's when Jesus came down.
Many called, few that answer
When the spirit tugs the heart;
Living so unconcerned
About a much, needed, new start.
If your life is a shamble.
You don't know what to do;
Make your way to an altar,
You'll find peace for you.
I'm so glad when justice calls mercy answers with grace.
I thank God for sending Jesus for he took my place
On the cross. He paid a debt for the whole world to see
when justice demands mercy answers with grace.

Carl L. Stewart

Where Does Reality Start

They always tell you to follow your dreams,
To follow your heart,
But - they also say keep your feet on the ground,
So where does reality start?

They think they're so smart,
where are they, dreams?
Caught in Chaos!
When did reality start?

It's not a starting point,
It's a realization,
Thus comes the word.
Reality - a confrontation

Do dreams end when reality is accepted?
Reality doesn't have to be ugly
If you keep your dreams connected.

Gail Marsh

'The Age Of Innocence'

So often i wonder how it would be
to go back in time to when we were three.
So many questions, it was all too new.
So much to absorb, a world to view.
Life is so innocent through the eyes of
the young, little did we know it had
just begun.
Make life-long friends along the way,
learn from our mistakes day after day
it's hard to know which path is right.
others may try to show us the light.
From parents to teachers, sisters and brothers,
there's always someone there,
to help and reassure us that there's really
nothing to fear.
Think how great this world would be,
if we kept the innocence of when we
were three...

Annette Chiapperino

"Road To Despair"

Life to some is just a trip, with nowhere special
to go; take for instants the crack that's out it
gives one's head a blow.
The thinking, memory and judgement are all fully
impaired, leaving one handicapped of the mine that
he once had.
And then there's the alcoholic who thrives on his
bottle, in an effort to solve all his problems.
But once he is sober, the problem still linger
there, leaving him with an inner feeling that no
one really cares.
So it's back to the bottle, again and again, with
no self reliance of where it all will end.
Last, but not least, is the prostitute who connives,
cheats and steals, just to gain a sense of security
deep down within.
All behavior has meaning whether they are good or bad
and we, God's people should educate those that are in
despair, but, what is all of this? are we gossiping from
day to day? instead of making headway to show these people the way!

Elizabeth Heggs

A One Night Hunting Stand

Uncle Keely's hunting tales were such a ploy,
To hear, to remember - to enjoy!

I thought I'd try my hand,
And I let him put me in a tree stand.
Where I sat, still - without a sigh
Hoping that 'ole deer would just stroll by,
Then I would shoot him - BANG - right in the eye!
Uncle Keely said the deer are so cunning,
They know when men for them are gunning,
They will cross the road - backing back,
To keep men and dogs off their track.
So as I sat cold, freezing in my seat,
That sly deer circled and he lay fast asleep,
Almost at my dangling feet - laughing!
Don't you see at me, foolish 'ole me!

Yes, Uncle Keely's hunting tales were such a ploy,
To hear, to remember - to enjoy!

Juliette Lively Dickey

The Cost Of Love

Rain, rain, please do stay.
To hide the tears I shed in pain.

I lift my face up towards the sky,
To let the rain shed the pain inside.

Here I walk in the rain,
To hide my pain, to shed my tears in vain.

To be as one, so hollow and full of sorrow.
Now I'm hollow as an empty chamber,
That echoes of loneliness and pain and sorrow.

I lift my face to the grey sky above and shout!
"Why do I love thee in vain?"

I once was full of joy and laughter.
But where have they gone I keep wondering after.

To be now as one instead of two.
I wander with no where to go.
But as the storm passes, so do I.

BJay Flug

"If I Had A Wish"

If I had a wish, it would surely be
To live in a world that is trouble free.
No drugs, no was or political strife
For kids like me, "That getting a life,"

If all the world could be in love
With their brother, their neighbor, the Lord above,
And what of our environment?
"Suffer little children" is not what He meant

Our air is kind of icky and really hard to breathe,
Our soldiers are in trouble cause they've gone overseas.
The gangs, the killings, so much destruction.
Why can't you stop all this corruption?

Please country leaders, open your eyes
Save the future for us younger guys
We'd like to live to be old like you
Isn't there something you can do?

Cameron Grant

A Place In Your Heart

Sometimes it seems so hard for me
To live my life more happily
Without you here by my side
In my life I cannot confide

My life is so difficult as it has been
Your love I always wanted to win
A moment in time to spent within
For I will ever be happy then

A place in your heart is all I'm asking for
Make a better life after and before
I'll be good to you and I will do more
Everything you'll say I will not ignore

Each and everyday that we spent together
Time will fly from November to November
Seems that we will last forever
Out relationship will be far more than better

A place in your heart is all that I'm asking for
To make you happy I will make sure
I'll be good to you, I will do more
I'll always love you for rich and for poor

Allan Baldestamon Lapuz

To My Son

Life, brought you to me,
To, love and care for.
To, hold your hand when life was unfair
To, let you go when life was right
To, watch you grow from boyhood to manhood.

Life, brought you to me,
To, let your boyhood seek out adventures,
To, let you be a boy with frogs and snakes,
To, let you find your true place in the sun.

Life, brought you to me.
To, let your manhood spring to life,
without holding you too tight.
To, let you know you always have a Mother here for you,
To, let you care for someone else,
To, let you remember life brought you to me forever.

Deborah O'Neal

"How I Feel About You"

I never thought it was possible,
To love someone this much,
And it's hard to believe it grows each time,
We share a single touch,
You brought out a feeling in me,
That cannot be described,
And I'll try to make your life complete
As long as I'm alive.

No one has made me feel
As happy as you do,
And it's wonderful the way you make,
my every dream come true,
You and I together will be.
One instead of two,
I guess what I'm trying to say,
Is Kevin Anderson I love you and will
Always love you.

April Priester

Untitled

She's gone like the wind, and back again. Why do I care
to lust again. She's in the past with a blast, but then
again, she's not. She's here right in front of me, but
ohhhh, I can't turn her down, but why passion and lust,
we must, see it again, for it is in our eyes.

John Brown, Jr.

What I Long

I long for your tender lips next
to mine, your warm embrace on
those cold winter nights.

I long for your tender words, your
sincere brown eyes to look upon my face.

I long for you to come back and
make my troubles go away.

I long for you to feel the same
compassion your whole person makes me feel.

I long for every little thing you
are willing to give someone else.

I long for what I cannot have.....
You!

Dania Aguayo

Untitled

I give to you a trinket
to place next to your heart
and beside the breath with which you sing
of the life that you must part
A trinket is a symbol
but peace is all you seek
You search my eyes
for the jewel of time, and the memories I must keep
He braved this life together
Our spirits danced to the winds
Our eyes beheld the wondrous light
that led us to begin
Your strength leaves me now
Your humble hand is all you return
in silence and in your deepest sleep
you'll find our promised land
My gift to you is vanity
You gave to me the love
to reach that endless sea
to balance the darkness, and light, above.

Barbara J. White

A Child's Prayer

Now I lay me down to sleep
to pray my soul my God shall keep.

If I should hear the heavy sound
of footsteps creaking down the hall,
I pray again with all my might
that in my darkness cold with fright
the Angel's light shall shine tonight.

As shadow's hands lay on my soul
and rip away my fragile bones,
his careless dance of conquered passion,
whirls me through a long dark passage.

Where, once again, I stumble to the splinters of my broken soul,
embedded in the chilling white of Mr. Winter's snowy night.
Encased in my pink nighty tight, I move about the silent night,
retrieving pieces of my self to hide away upon my shelf.

Again I lay me down to sleep
and pray my soul is God's for keeps,
and angels carry me through life
and wake me with the morning light.

Amen

Jacquelyn Krug

The Mighty Seas Of Life

We have sailed the mighty seas of life,
To see where they would take us,
To heavenly ports and gleaming harbors,
Seemed nothing would ever stop us
Though choppy seas and shallow waters
Were overcome before us,
The obstacles we couldn't see
Have brought a change of course for us,
Many challenges were faced
Before the drift apart overcome us,
But the ship of life is still a float
And safe ladders are before us,
To climb aboard and continue to sail
The mighty seas of life.

Harry H. Phillips

Nick Of Time

You were there in the Nick of time:
To sing me a song, or read me a rhyme.
If I was mad, or thought I would cry,
You told me jokes so my tears would be dry.
But it was just in the Nick of time
You were usually there to love and care,
But that doesn't make you reliable.
Because though you did come to help me climb
Whatever wall it was,
It was just in the Nick of time.
My love for you is not transient,
It is invariably, or always there.
Because I will remember the times you were there
To love and care -
But I will always remember
It was just barely in the Nick of time

Candi Lawson

The Seasons

We all pay the price
To smell the nice spice
Of the hot apple cider in the ice

The flowers sway
The children play
With great anticipation for the month of May

The blue birds sing
The guitarist plings
The summer air blows with a twing

The crisp of the leaves
Is so nice to our please
That our knees shake with glee!

Christine MacMaster

God's Love

If I didn't have God's love
To take me through the day,
It would be a tragedy to think
Of what might come my way.

Frustrations come, frustrations go
It's hard to understand
But if you have strong a caring love
God will lend a helping hand.

I have learned the meaning of prayer
If you believe in what you ask,
Somehow a miracle will come
Just let go and let God perform the task.

It's easier said than it is done
But I say give prayer a try-
It's most rewarding and soothing
When we don't question why.

Anna L. Cooke

"So the Birds Talk, and I'm Writing About It Again!"

The birds here talk, they really do!
Today I heard "She blew,
She blew, She blew, She blew."
(I laughed so hard, wouldn't you?)

They chirp and chatter
Nothing's the matter,
Their usual talk, that's true.
They move on, it seems, in groups and teams,
How do they do it?
(I'm left without a clue.)

Joy G. Klein

A Visit To The Mountains

Each day we walked the mountain trail
to the babbling brook that did not fail
To sing her songs all day long,
and whirled her waters as she glided along.
The ageless rock stood silently,
amid the waters we loved to see,
It gathered its tune from the jagged rock
and sang its song to the mountain top.
The intensified shadows of the mountain slope
The solitude silence of the mountain goat,
The whispering leaves in the blue spruce trees,
sang her songs in the mountain breeze.
The breathtaking splendor of magnitude,
and ghastly shadow of solitude.
As the sun set closed her day for rest,
the coons and chipmunks will be your guest.
The mockingbird calls to its mate in the tree,
as the tall tree sways in the evening breeze.
The moonlight spills upon the wall,
and you close your eyes to the whippoorwill call.

Bonnie Branum

As I Feel To Remember Your Presence In My Life

Many times my little hand must have reached to your face
to touch the smile of love that helped create my life and those
beaming eye's must surly have shined on me to encourage me to
stretch and grow as you called my name, yes, your beaming face
must have been my fist glimpse at the sun shine and made me feel
warm and secure enough to grow in your love for me.
And how many times, I wonder, did my tears stop falling when I saw
your face or heard your voice that must have surly meant that I was
not alone or abandoned by your nurturing love.
And remember those confusing and frustrating times we shared
together when you were trying to teach and I was trying to learn the
difference between "yes and no", "right or wrong", "punishment and
reward"? Those were some turbulent times for us. I very seldom saw
the sun shining in your face then it was like a total eclipse and I
had no place to go except under the covers , all alone and frightened
that I would never see the sun shine in your face again when you
called my name or saw my face, but it did and you gave me my first
sense of hope. Thank you for the love that shines from your smiling
face.

Anna M. Show

Goodbye

We're with you everyday; to sit and hold your hand,
to touch your forehead, hair, to be with you.
We're with you everyday; to see your beautiful smile,
laughing eyes, to hear you speak, to help if you need.
We're with you everyday; and hope and pray, and ask
ourselves why, and look for a miracle.
We're with you everyday; and when we leave you everyday, we turn,
say, We love you, as we walk out the door.

We don't visit anymore; hold your hand, kiss your forehead,
laugh with you.
We don't visit anymore; you're in our hearts, our thoughts,
and a part of you is with us always.
We don't visit anymore; you're not there anymore,
you're forever in our memories.
We don't visit anymore; and with tears rolling down our
cheeks, we turn, and whisper one last time,
We love you, as our final Goodbye.
Goodbye.

Irene F. Marotta

Solitary Blues

Waiting for the boughs of summer trees
To turn from spring into autumn leaves

Travelling on my way home
No place to call my own

Understanding all and none
Wishing for my chill bones to be warmed by the sun

Looking at the pretty ladies passing by
Remembering nothing but a sunlight sky

So I'm traveling on my home
No place to call my own
Walking through the city on a cold winters day
Listening to past words of wisdom and what they say

Visions fill inside my head
Only soon to be filled with dread

So I'm traveling on my own
Looking for a place to call home

Solitary and alone trusted by none
Waiting for my chill bones to be warned by the sun

Eric J. Olsen

There Is No Rhyme Or Reason

There is no rhyme or reason
   To understand the ways
The Father up in Heaven planned
   When numbering our days.

But I can tell you this my friend
   As sure as sure can be
There's a heaven coming one day
   And our loved ones there we'll see.

There He'll wipe the tears from every eye
   And night will be no more;
The glory of His presence
   Will be our Light forevermore.

And so our faith is kept in Him
   Our Savior up above
That one day He'll unite us
   With the people that we've loved.

Jane W. Mosteller

War's Bitter Yield

I had the chance this summer past
To visit half-forgotten memories
I walked alone through pathless woods
And found our stream - flowing free.

On her banks we strolled long years ago
And planned our lives with dreams of youth
We couldn't know at that glad time
How soon we'd face a bitter truth.

The world was soon turned upside down
And young men who wanted only peace
Would don the colors of their country
And learn to kill - till reason cease.

I remembered how proud I felt that day
To watch you march away - banners flying
You marched into some awful hell,
Fought with honor - then lay dying.

As I walked through half-forgotten memories
I wondered how many seasons there must be
Before the bitter anguish would leave
And I'd grow a heart again within me.

Edna Jones Drye

Yesterday

Yesterday marriage was sacred and viewed as the norm
Today infidelity has taken on a rare and dangerous form,
Yesterday children were wiser and always gave respect
Today those who are willing to conform are a very few select,
Yesterday syphilis and gonorrhea were our biggest concern
Today Aids is a deadly killer, but for some they never learn,
Yesterday families were close and cared for one another
Today sibling rivalry often leads to brother killing brother,
Yesterday guns were weapons used by only those in authority
Today teenagers who carry them represent the total majority
Yesterday the school was an institution where learning took place
Today much of what transpires there is a total disgrace,
Yesterday we knew nothing of the concept of child abuse
Today children see it as a weapon for their own personal use,
Yesterday drug use was pretty much under our control
Today to get a high, one would sell his mother's soul,
So why did we let today come and yesterday slip away
And create such a deadly and inhuman place for us to have to stay
Were we so blind by yesterday's presence that we could not see
How we were losing control and regulating what today would be

Gloria Jones

Today Tomorrow Someday

Today we love
Tomorrow we care
Someday we might even learn to share

Open our eyes, see the light
Leave all the darkness, the ignorance the night.

Controlling our fears
while walking by faith

Giving new hope for tomorrow today
So today we love
Tomorrow we care
Someday we will learn to share.

Cenesia V. Sears

Grandma

You just won a prize
Toni Morrison won the Nobel
Please, open your eyes.

All these years
She has been writing about you
A strong Black woman
That has always persevered.

Out of the belly of the earthly beast
Into the heavenly glory of God
Recognition of your lyrical prose, at last
The prize we never sought has been won.

Grandma, Grandma
You just won a prize
Black women have won the Nobel
And because of you Toni Morrison will shine.

Fred Givens III

Dreams

They makes our lives.
We struggle and fight everyday for them,
for the smallest and for the greatest...
Then as our lives become pathetic
They rest, they die, they sleep in a bed, in a cemetery,
doesn't matter where, how, why...
but what is left of us, dreamful species.

Giorgia Cadinu

Deliverance

Who it is that consigns the body and the soul to the endless torture of a cause unending? Who demands that every painful breath, without a promise of surcease, be followed by another and another, until sheer exhaustion casts the spell of painful sleep? Does God truly traffic in the coin of unrelenting pain to purge a soul of incidental sin? Or do we chant this mantra to control? Is it thus that, in His wisdom, God looks ahead to granting hours of pain before releasing some poor soul to endless hell? Or, should He open heaven, would all the Holys then and yet unchanted be enough to thank Him for the pain?

Hear now, the words of a love that seeks to free itself, or loose a loved one, from the endless anguish fate has brought to be! "Give now, give me rest! Hear now, grant me peace! Stay not a moment longer
listening to my rages but to my tortured flesh bring lifeless life that I may soon press on to other missions yet to be defined. You may not join with me, for each must walk alone from this awareness to that which lies ahead, free to embrace the new, unshackled from the times that were. I implore you, take this breath, for I can no longer bear to look unto the next!"

Frank L. Husted

Spring Snowstorm

The wind like a whirling dervish
Tossed the rain and then the snow everywhere.
Against a dark and leaden sky
The trees were bare.
Tulips bent beneath new April snow
Their opening buds bobbing to and fro.
Birds were silenced in the air
Hurled from shelter here and there.
It was a wild and wintry night.
The blowing snow an awesome sight.
Winter was back upon the land.

Emily Steinkogler

I, Myself, The Virus

Deep inside I feel it there
Tossing and turning-kicking and comforting
My soul is addicted to what we breed
Inside of you I keep hiding

Nestled in your head
Next to your brain
Suggesting twisted little thoughts
Making you think you've gone insane

Can you feel the kicking of my feet
Can you sense my presence
I mean no harm to you
I mean only to give you remembrance

The rain falls into my eyes as I look up at the sky
The clouds move in around me
Entrapped my mist and fear
I hide in your head - now you are we

Danyele Burton

Lovers

In the time of life and death,
when darkest great sorrow is lonely light.
To bare the pain of loves denial,
and seek the justice of the trial.
For us each time apart exceeds
the vast emptiness of the sea's.
And God's own choice of answer is,
be patient lovers until what was is.

Deborah L. Michel

Tangled

A tangled mind a shattered heart intertwined along my soul.
Touching it with such blackness it's terrifying me.
My never ending love for him is
overpowering the tangled webs of life.
His touch is a touch of such intensity I quiver.
Sympathetic beautiful eyes are locked indefinitely to my own.
The feeling of passion in my soul,
slowly overpowers the darkening webs of life.
Even though these webs have my soul
twisted with unwanted thoughts,
an even stronger weapon overthrows my mind and heart.
Like a pitiful scared child,
the blackness slithers from my body, scolded by love.
With every thought that now enters my freed mind,
a memory of him touches my heart,
filling it with love and admiration,
I have come upon because of a beautiful conquer named Love.

Brandy Donuldson

County Cat And Bird

The old cat lifts his head upward
Towards the chirping in the tree
His piercing golden eyes stare
At one spot on the limb.

There is a bouncing baby
A robin unaware
That below could be
His fate awaiting death.

The yellow tiger squints his one good eye
Into a beam that knows only lightning
He waits on haunches —-
While the bird chirps his song.

Time passes slowly
And the bird flies away
While the cat still lingers
His tummy was full anyway.

Carol Kunz

Time

Memories slide through time
Tumultuous visions are exciting:
Painful times ask: have I grown -
come full circle - ready to move ahead
with my best and worst memories?
Will you - my dear young friends and close ones
stand still in your minds for awhile
to allow a time flow through your rites of passage
that spin and twirl in your youthful worlds?
Where do they take you -
I wish I knew
or could follow where you are
- in time and space for a refreshing sight
of your newness and knowness.
Will you allow me a longshot-peek into your
world of tomorrow?
I'm envious of your energy,
spirit and hope.
And the time you have for cumulative memories.

Carolyn Sonstein Krepliak

A November Afternoon Walk Near Loveland Pass

Raven's wings flash silver in the winter sun.
Turning my back to the gusting wind, I lean against its fluid
strength and look up.
Brother Raven hangs there alone   suspended   framed by snow softened
    peaks
        while his ailerons finely dissect each nuance of current,
            searching for the invisible golden mean.
Ebony feathered traveler with his companion silver moon rush
                without moving,
        through blue   e m p t y   s k y .
My father would have been a hundred years old today.
His hair, once black, turned to silver as the cancer consumed his
    body, his mind;
so long ago, so Viet Nam long ago - I wasn't there when he died.
I take my grown daughter's hand and help her jump over the
    bubbling-
        yet unfrozen-stream, as it slices its way through the crusted snow.
My daughter speaks of boys and books and studying art in Florence.
Dinner is awaiting for us, we need to walk faster if we hope to return
before dark.

Dr. Christian Hageseth III

Other Eyes

The eyes that I stare at remind me of September when everything
turns gold,
They sound like a Tiger's roar so loud, so mean, so bold.
The pupils are like an eclipse trying to cover a massive sun,
They are like a late afternoon when relaxing and having fun.
They are like doors that hold secrets of the unknown,
Yet when opened they show a tiger free to roam.
This young lady's eyes reflect beams of light,
Leading to a world of dreams reaching great heights.
These eyes have a texture of glass,
Yet that was not a good look for my glance was fast.

Jonathan Hedderman

'Fireworks'

Twas the Fourth of July and the evening its best.
    Twilight settled, a glow of pink to the west.
Adults chatted, perched on lawn chairs,
    I on my blanket dispelling my cares.

A voice from behind rang in my ears.
    Warmth rushed through me chimed glorious and dear.
"I'd like to be on the blanket with you," he quietly said...
    Did those words come from his lips or a voice in my head?
"I'd love it!" murmured I, and hoped that he heard,
    For he uttered not another solitary word!

I sat on my blanket sipping iced tea, then from behind came,
"Put your arm on my knee." "I dare not," I thought in
silence, "I'd rather there rest my head!" Penetrating warmth
set me aglow! Asked I, was he seeking comfort or bed? At that
moment fireworks lit up the sky! Could that be resulting from
the voice of he and I?

The dancing glow of fireworks cast its magic sparks, displaying
colors in vivid lights upon darks. Violins and harps sang
music in the sky! Sudden awareness...the burning heat of July!

JoAnn Winstead McPhail

Nature's Mold

Cocoons: Silvery and silken tender cages,
   Twirling in limbo 'neath heaven's halo,
   Soon to release its beautiful secret;
   Butterfly! translucent colors aglow!

Rosebuds: Mysterious, tear-shaped green jewel boxes,
   Dew and wind-kissed, nurtured by mother earth.
   Then one morning, beautiful to behold,
   Roses! The air filled with fragrance and mirth!

Cherubs: Sleeping innocence in satin cradle,
   A God-sent miracle for life to mold.
   One future day from a life-time of love,
   Adult! Life's story completely told!

Life: Cocoons and rosebuds and sleeping cherubs,
   Miracles all, making this life of ours;
   This is God's own promise to everyone...
   Lovely secrets... rose gardens...Angel choirs.

   Chiquita LoJuana Gonzalas Sills

Words...

We say them when we feel we have something to say
Unaware of how they'll affect the listener and in what way

I think words should come with a "warning" sign
To inform the listener what you have in your mind

They also bring with them emotions we never knew
   Of anger and sadness, love and gratitude

I find they convey feelings we seldom say
Written down on cards we purchase for special days

Choose your words well and use them fine
For they can be your weapon or your valentine

Words are a part of us old and new
They tell us how to act and what to do

Words are spoken, but they can be wrote
Used to recite an eulogy or tell a joke

Written down on parchment, intended to last
They express our thoughts from times gone past

And when we are old and all but gone
It is only our words that will carry on

Nooha Ahmedullah

King And I

In the dark all is suspicious
undefined, and unrestricted,
Invisible in the light,
Playing in darkness
Shadows dancing in a world all their own.
Monsters in the corner, witches in the closet.
Darkness squeezes the last ray of light.
Trapping it in the evil.
Evil all around,
Goodness nowhere to be found.
Dreams becoming reality,
Reality unreal.
Fear is King
Ruling an empire of nightmares.
The King wrestling with the light, at peace in the dark.
My King's first name is...
   Imagination
His last...
   Confusion.

   Jeremy J. Vega

Diamond Queen

I used to drink and gamble and spend my money free
Until I met that lovely lady that means so much to me.
So fellows - I'm leaving - I can't stay and gamble tonight.
I know that lovely lady will be hanging out the light.

I've rambled and gambled around this world you see
Until I met that lovely lady that means so much to me.
My conscience is a bit cloudy and that drink is always near,
But that deck of cards and gambling is what I really fear.

I married this lovely lady and to me she is so dear
And it is so comforting to know that she is always near.
My life with her is wonderful I know that for sure, but
My past always haunts me and that is hard for me to endure.

Not drinking and gambling; not placing that bet;
Loving that lovely lady may help me to forget.
Aces, Kings, and one-eyed jacks are surely in my past.
Now looking at this diamond queen my soul is saved at last.

   Adam J. Walter

My Sunlight, My Love

My life was like a darkened stagnant wood
until my sunlight came.

Then my life bloomed like a red, delicate
rose in the rain.

His eyes, how like autumn leaves of brown
and gold.
His lips, so delicate and soft like glistening
cobwebs covered in dew drops.

His body, strong and proud but skin as soft
as the finest silk.

My sunlight, my life, my love, my only one.

You are my eternal light, you shine in the
darkness of my shadowed past.

You have shown me the way to your light.

I have found love and happiness through your
goodness and loving care.

   Christi Anna Foxhill

Wings

Give me the wings and I will fly
Up to the heavens far and wide
Where the air is pure and undefiled
Where rivers pure and crystal clear
Run into waters dark and deep
Beside the glistening waterfalls
Give me the wings and I will fly
To the moon where man has trod
On paths unknown ageless and full of mystery
Give me the wings and I will soar
Above the troubled earth below
Where men like lemmings to the sea
Race to their own mortality
Give me the wings and I will fly
By the rays of the setting sun
Up through a galaxy of a million stars
To an Eden where no man has trod
Where all is peace and tranquility
There I shall look upon the face of God.

   Gladys Walker

"My Mother's Facial Image With A Smile On Her Face"

While I went through a period of total unrest,
Very discouraged and depressed.
I lounged on the sofa all day and night,
I had no will to fight.
I would stare out the window,
I felt worthless with nothing to sow!
Many times my mother's image would appear,
On the frayed, wrinkled, and yellowed curtain,
With a smile on her face.
When I would get up to touch her facial image,
Up close, her facial image would leave no trace,
It was only a few dark threads—-
Instead of an impression of my dead mother's face?
I believe God sent her image to ease my pain,
So, her life and mine would not be in vain.
I no longer grieve - life is to short not to believe!
Now since I feel better, I am no longer a fretter.
I've thrown the wrinkled, frayed, and yellowed curtain away,
And I shall always remember my mother when I pray!
We shall meet one another again in heaven someday.
Joanne J. Saunders

The Warrior Blossom

A man stood alone, with tear in eye and sword in hand;
Victories and defeats all stunk
of death's stench, no more could he stand:

For honor and glory, for love, for God
In the name of vengeance, their bodies will rot:
Losing life's wonder becoming
Twisted, he himself was shaped in this knot:

With all his power he dreamed to
Remember his divinity:
Summoning the feeling of creation
for mans involvement into eternity:

Memory drew forth in the form of forgiveness;
For himself, for his enemies, for the God he swore merciless:

Then a blade fell gently into the earth;
Digging up ground, making way for natures birth:

And a child danced away in a wake of joy;
The Universe, his playground the game of life his toy:

The forgotten simple mind knowing true genius;
Strength of heart will prevail
To challenge man to become limitless:
Brian Fratto

Tonight

The moon drifts up, climbing, reaching,
   to touch the night with an open palm.
It caresses the darkness, bringing forth more light,
   to brighten the sky, with the stars.
The solid mass spills a uniform white light,
   surrounding the stars that flicker and dance;
      as a flame of a fire that is burning...
         yearning for the air that feeds it.
The light and sparkles shine with life,
   until the first glimpses of the night's nemesis
      emerge.
Slowly, the night drifts behind the curtain of the sun,
   only to rise again......
      ....Tonight.
Emily Dulik

Great Beast

Does a great beast lurk in the shadows
waiting for the rays of sunlight to fade;
   Or, when daylight ebbs, are we ushered
   into a land of milk and honey?

   This is a question for the ages.
   The answer will be forthcoming.

Yet, overriding this query is a statement
made by a great man over half a century ago.
   At least it was made by a speechwriter:
   We have nothing to fear but fear itself!

The unknown holds great adventure for many;
for others, the trepidation of not knowing
   and the inability to be in control.

   Who is right?
   Eventually we all find out.

Is the great, dark beast snarling, growling
   because he knows the soft rays of light
      always follows darkness?

   Could it be, if there is no fear,
   it is he who can't survive!
Gene Frankel

Time

The horizon outside has turned to black
waiting up for dawn, to strike its ray light
across the pain
it's time to say hello
to all the lovely people, in the streets
walking along the shops
looking in the windows
at the things they would like to have
caught up in the materialistic values
brought on by the pain
the sunshine lights up, for all to see
but everyone is blind
it's time for everyone to get a pair of glasses
then they will see it
all that they don't want to, but they'll look anyway
cause it grabs their curious
takes them away from the universe
it's time to see the pain
Alan Penuel

Tomorrow's Yesterday

Travel through tomorrow's yesterday, a vision quest of modern day,
Walk into the past, souls soar with eagles,
Swoop down to experience the triumph of flight.
Leave body to rest, transpose from eagle to coyote,
Race across the vast prairie, taste the blood of a fresh kill,
Feel the sting of a bullet, become the hunted.
Thunder of a thousand hoofs ring loud, deafening the ears,
Dust of the stampede fill the nostrils, choking away life's breath,
Heart pounding, my soul escapes to a higher plateau.
I am, A great mountain watching o'er the land,
Feel the clawing hands of weather eating away at my majestic beauty.
In a moment, I have become the stream,
Flowing down crystal clear into the river, knowing I may never return.
Take flight, view each period a page at a time, from beginning to end,
I have touched many lives.
Quick as the spirit ceased my soul,
Released, left with a hunger to be part of tomorrow's yesterday.
Clara Evans

You're The One

You, the one carrying the briefcase and
walking in your shined up shoes and
your suit like a shroud of labor.
You, the one with the neatly combed hair
and the freshly shaved face.
You're the one
who goes into your cold unfeeling office and
your waiting work.
You're the one who longs to take off
your shined up shoes and walk in the warm grass and
feel the life giving sun on your pale, sick, face.
But it's too late, you're now in a tomb and
as your soul departs you look down and
see the flowers surrounding you and
remember how you never stooped to smell them....
You're the one.

Ann-Jenette Larkin

Deserted

Deserted.
Wallowing in a sea of despair
floundering in the ocean of destruction
with no boat in sight.
A raft. If only a raft would float by.
Please — a stick of wood — anything
to divert the black surging waters.
Anything
to separate the barren, empty tide
from becoming a permanent foreboding grave.
In the midst of darkening bleakness
there came a weak, shallow cry,
a cry that said nothing,
but clearly spoke out —
"I give up. I am not strong enough
to swim by myself anymore".
Such a plaintive and pitiful cry —
begging the cruel sea waters to be kind.
A titanic wave washed over the cry
and it did not surface again.

Catherine L. Gaupel

'Lost Lives'

Sitting by the phone, waiting for you to call!
wanting to hear your voice; although simple that is all!
Wishing you were here with me, to hold me close and tight.
Anymore that is just a dream, and I as the dreamer,
   dream it all night.
If only you knew how I feel for you, this and that
   I want you to know.
For I tell you now soon you may not be here, and I will
   miss our moments quiet, simple, and slow.
Now I tell you these words, And only once will they be said!
That damn Drinking-n-driving has killed you, and along with
   your memory dead.
As I watch them slowly pull the sheet over your dying mind!
I ask the father above why would he take someone so
   simple and kind.
Then I realize he did not take you, where you must go.
You yourself could have stopped the trip; with the
   one simple word "no".

Jori Petersen

Summer Town

Summer town
Warmth and explosion
Colors so alive they sting
Motels are swarming
Beaches layered in glitter and texture
Up side down ice cream cone
melting on the furnace tar
Screaming! Little girl with the long brown hair
is on the Very Top of the Ferris Wheel
They'll play mini-golf for hours,
these busy vacationers
The kids on the water slide, laughing
Sis is on the beach in her new bikini,
letting those hometown boys whistle
Families spread throughout the night
This hot summer night
Woven into the tapestry
and this town, this fun fun town
makes them forget they have to go back
And that makes the locals smile.

Angela Martinson

'Be Careful What You Wish For'

So, when did I wish for you???
   was it once upon a starry night,
   I wished for love so true, so bright?
Or in a lonely room of gloom,
While listening to a sad old tune?

If I remember - do recall ....
   I wished for someone six foot tall,
   dark and handsome, kind and smart,
   with soulful eyes, and lions heart.
Someone who'd love me from the start.

Perhaps, you wished for someone too
   Someone 'clever' smart like you.
   and she'd fit perfect in your arms,
Possess a multitude of charms.

Perhaps'we' wished on the same night. Upon the same star
shining bright. And yes, we are the perfect mates, But for
two'other' souls to take.

So next time on a mystic night, We'll each search for a star so
bright. And then, with all and both our might, we'll pray -
Dear Star, please.... get it right.

Jacquelyn Douglas

Love

   It's hard to explain the
way I feel when you leave it seems
   like time stands still.
    I've told you I care
and love you, too, and that love is real,
    Strong, and true.
   The feeling is mutual
   according to you.
   I am trying to be
optimistic, but it's hard to do when I am
   being realistic.
   I think about you
night and day and I want to be with
   you all the way.
   So why do you hurt me,
   I don't understand.

Christina Kilby

Mom, In A Young Girls Eyes

When I was a child, growing up in the world,
was the hardest thing to do.
In a young girls eyes, if a problem should arise,
it always just grew and grew.

Mountains out of Molehills, was not a decision,
It's a young girl's state of mind.
Although, fortunately for most of us,
our trials get easier with time.

You instilled in me, the meaning of respect,
for myself and those around me.
And to this day I still believe
that honestly is the best policy.

But most of all, you not only taught,
but showed me the meaning of life.
With you on my side, our Lord in my heart,
I know I will survive.

So thank you mom, for everything you've ever done,
or will do.
I pray each day, that I can make you as proud,
of me, as I am of you.

Cynthia S. Jewett

Friends And Lovers

You offered friendship in my childhood,
    Watched so carefully as I ran,
Playing, laughing, dreaming young dreams
    In accordance with your plan.
I knew your touch and felt your nearness
    In my mother's hands and eyes,
Felt your love first, sensed your presence
    In my father, kind and wise.
As my womanhood unfolded,
    Gently did you woo me still,
Knowing that when I was ready,
    I would seek your perfect will.
Free to leave you and to wander,
    Would I recognize your face?
I was eager, rushing toward you,
    I would cling to your embrace.
In your arms I end my searching,
    And a love song I will sing,
Guided by the Holy Spirit
    To dear Jesus Christ, my King!

Jeanne Lowery

Shadow Of Olga's Love

Don't cry my precious loved ones, wipe your tears away.
Water the beautiful flowers, that I loved each day.
You know how much I loved you all and will miss you here on earth,
I was your little sister since my birth.
My soul is alive and is free at last,
While my earthly body was fading fast,
I had to fly to meet my God on high, to bid this painful world
    goodbye.
To you, Dear Husband, I thank you so much
I'll still be the wind beneath your wings, when you feel my silent
    touch.
My Children and Grandchildren — "Oh, how I loved you"
Remember — let me be proud.
For I am watching over you without a sound.
To my Brothers and Sisters, words won't come easy for awhile,
But all the joys of childhood will make you smile.
To all other relatives and friends, gently pray,
I am grateful to all and we will meet some day

Alexandria Safran Carasia

"Air"

As long as we have air to breathe
We are able to ask for things we need.
As long as we have a breath to take
We can be assured it's not too late
As long as we have Jesus to go in prayer
With every breath we breathe He's always there
Without the air we breathe there would be death
If not for the breath we take there would be nothing left.
If not for the air we couldn't smell the rose
Without the sunshine or rain it would never grow
Without Jesus we have nothing to gain
Because there would be no more rose or sunshine or rain
So believe in Jesus with the breath you take
You will know in your heart it's the best breath
You will make
Praise Him, Love Him, and with other share
The Love of Jesus and the miracle of Air.

Jimmy Middlebrooks

Falling Angels

I am lucifer; we are all satan; corrupted
We are all fallen angels
Stumbling for the forbidden fruit of knowledge
What have we chosen to rule?
Coming from ethereal virgin thought
to revel in sensuous mire
Can we still strive for purity? - if we want
Look to the perfection of humanity in the soul
Shoulder now the litter of the Immaculate

I sing a song now of hope, wishing to fly again
I cry for bright, enduring wings
Putting your face to the wind
Come now and soar with me
I cry against the thunderstorm
come fight the gale with me; regain innocence

I want to lie in my own feathery warmth
We will rest in the lost Eden.
Come lie with me in pure white down.

W. C. Moorer

A Race

Our people are torn by war,
We are discriminated,
Never thought of us as humans
The fighters, leaders who fight
For our rights, they are killed
They speak the truth
Their thoughts are lost in the racism
the hatred of those
Who will never be part of our society.

We are looked at as dogs, not as people
We try to learn,
yet our goals are destroyed by the people
Who still live in the year of segregation
never thinking of integration
their soul, their mind, their hearts
are lost in the pit of prejudice.

What does it mean to be a race
When we can't confront our brothers
because the color of their face,
What does it mean to be a race?

Beatriz De La Rosa

Still Crying

We have gone our separate ways
We both found someone new
And even though it's over
I often think of you

You know me very well
You know I sometimes cry
But now there's someone here
To dry my tear-filled eyes

I know you cared for me or at least acted
like you did but whenever there were
problems, you ran away and hid.

Now I see these open arms
I see a caring friend, He seems to really want
my crying times to end.

He tells me that he loves me and he keeps me by his side
But the times we are together my love for you I must hide.

Even though he's there for me and I know his love is true.
My life feels incomplete because I'm crying out for you.

Carolyn Morgan

Praise To Mothers

In the beautiful month of May,
We celebrate a special day.
The earth is dressed in fine array,
The tree leaves have come out to play.
Colorful flowers of every hue,
Awake in the morning dew,
As though listening to the cheerful notes,
Of charming birds in their pretty coats.
The air is filled with many sounds,
As their calls and songs abound.
While many birds provide the chorus,
Across the country, south to north.
So all must realize and say,
Praise to all mothers this day.
We all must express and not hide,
Our honor, praise and love, worldwide —
That praise to mothers in every way,
By saying, "Happy Mothers Day".

Edgar Allan Orem

Untitled

We have been friends since kindergarten,
We have been together from houses to
 schools to boats and gardens.

We have our ups and downs in a year or another,
But we keep them a secret between each other.

She is such a soft-hearted girl,
She reminds me of a snow-white pearl.

I keep in touch with her every night and day
Just to be sure that she's home and
doesn't run away.

A girl like her can be so clever,
And a girl like her could do
 what so ever.

I just want to express how I feel
 about you,
I feel like we are forever friends,
 never old, never new.

Amber Wiseman

Oh! Grandchild Of Mine

Oh! Grandchild of mine, you are so divine.
We love your sweet smiles;
You're the joy of our lives,
Oh! Grandchild of mine.

May your life be filled with happiness,
And all your dreams come true.
Walk your path through life, on a pure line,
Oh! Grandchild of mine.

Always know we'll be proud of you,
As we watch you become all you can be.
You are our hope, our destiny,
Oh! Grandchild of mine.

We hope as you grow,
That peace and love within you will flow,
For you are the light, of our troubled times,
Oh! Grandchild of mine.

When we depart this world from you,
Know that we'll pray and watch over you,
for you'll continue our legacy through time.
Oh! Grandchild of mine.

Dolly Braida

"Let The Children See Tomorrow"

Let the children see tomorrow
We need to show some type of effort to become more aware
of what is happening to our environment
We need to stop and rethink of what is going on in this confused world
We are the only ones who can make a difference
We need to do all we can to help our younger generation see tomorrow

Let the children see tomorrow
Teach them to love, share and respect one another
Time is getting late
We may not see tomorrow
We may never see each other if we don't do something today
If we don't there might not be a tomorrow for the children

Let us do it for the children
Let us try to let them see tomorrow
Let the children see and have a tomorrow

JoElla Edwards

Without You

When we first met
We were young and foolish
Love was blooming and
Life was bullish.

Then came the day
When you went away
My life was shattered,
Leaving me devastated by that matter
I couldn't walk a mile
Always thinking of your smile.

Life has been hell
Without your rosie smell
Please come back you're the love I thrive
Or else I will die.

Without you I can't think
With you I can be
I'm blinded by love your love
When you're with me.

Antinoe Nicolas Aurich

Our Universe

While flying at 40,000 feet high
We will maintain this attitude,
Until the approach and landing
to our destination through the sky.

The amazing and wonderful vast unknown,
Beyond all human comprehension
In the vastness of infinity, beyond the first
One hundred billion solar systems,
beyond the reach of giant telescopes, farther than our eyes can see
stands the pinnacle of the heavens.

God stretches out His hands through the
myriad galaxies, the Master Engineer,
And Designer, the Painter, of the Rainbows.
the Conductor, directing the harmonious
Symphony of the stars, God.

Gazing into the heavens, studded with
Multi-billions of solar systems.
We thank God, for creation,
You, Me, and everyone here and all the world around us.
I know God, really made it.
Genesis 1:1 In the Beginning God created OUR UNIVERSE.

Barbara E. Cook

Belated Honor

'Twas the crowning of God's Mother, near the end of May.
"Wear your Communion dresses," the note sent home did say.
"We'll convene out in the schoolyard, and to the church
progress" ...when to her horror Gail found out
her mother dyed her dress.
Soon she was aware of Sister's disapproving frown,
but just the same she dreamed her dream of carrying the crown.
How she must have stood out in that field of perfect white
as she withdrew heartbroken: "And please stay out of sight".
She raced toward home, her heart pounding strong... fantasy over...
she didn't belong. Hung her dress in the closet and meant it when
she vowed that she never would wear it again.
Not much time passed... daily Mass... not too far... She stepped
off the curl, she did not see the car.
As God will resolve things in ways we'd not think
Gail carried the crown in her dress tinted pink.

Gloria Mercedes Beacham

A Walk In The Woods

The birds outside my window had just begun to sing, They
welcomed me to their morning, that glorious day in spring. All
living creatures were out enjoying the early morning sun, I
decided to walk into the woods and have breakfast from my gun.
As I passed by the lake with a strong impulse to dive, The
splashing fish seemed to say "It's great to be alive." Soon I
was surrounded by plant life from algae to oaks and pine, Every
leaf was exuding oxygen, saying, their Eden was also mine. As
I smelled the nectareous fragrance and observed the wonders
galore, I suddenly had a revelation I had never experienced
before. God's mighty creation overwhelmed me as my eyes began
to scan, Every living thing has a purpose in His beautiful
master plan. An incomprehensible intelligence was everywhere to
be seen, no "Big Bang Theory" nor accident could cause this
masterpiece supreme. Time turned into eternity as I felt God's
supernatural love, all we have or hope to be comes from our
Father above. Suddenly I saw my breakfast perched in a nearby
tree, the animal seemed not afraid and was looking down at me.
My prey was a squirrel and never had I seen one bigger, As I
aimed my twenty-two rifle I could not squeeze the trigger.

Jim Barfield

The Last Day Of School!

It is the last day of school!
Well, at least for the summer.

Science and Social Studies were
my favorite classes.
So much information,
I needed new glasses!

All the stress, homework, knowledge,
and grades,
are finished at last!
Boy, do I want to put them in the past!

My summer vacation will go and go.
Before I know it, it will begin to snow!

Next year I will be in eighth grade.
I don't want to join that parade!

Thank goodness seventh grade is now down the drain.
For now I don't have to strain my brain!
I hope!

Greg Gilmour

Gathering For The Feast

The gathering of the peoples at the feast
We'll feast on peace, that will never cease!:
All! Destruction, of wars!all!, gone:
The time will have come, when wars, we shunned!:
For! No one can do no wrong.
Every one will belong and sing the same song:
All! Glory to God, for the prince of peace at the feast!
The lamb! That God gave, will, satisfy every crave,
We! No longer, must go to the grave! every soul will be saved!:
Every soul will be saved,! Feasting on nothing, but! Peace!:
With night gone! We' ll have,! One glorious, perfect!, (day)!.
Our God in the gracious,! Showing of his love,
Gave his son, who's sembling, with pure white dove!.
The ones! at the feast,! will be all! that love peace.—
And have over come the beast. At the end of feast, perfect peace!!

James M. Gowin

Nature Is Born

Have you ever wondered how the world began?
Well I have come to tell you what lived long before man.
First there was a seed, where it came from I don't know.
But one thing very obvious, is that it began to grow.
After a few years the seed had come to be,
A big, brown, rough, tough, strong, and healthy tree.
After mother nature had rested for an hour,
She liked her work very much and created a flower.
How it formed is unknown,
But in a month or two it had definitely grown.
First it was a bud, helpless, small, and green,
Then in a few days it had colors you've never seen.
After this, Mother Nature stood back in surprise,
She said, "Look at all these great creations, right before my eyes!"
Mother Nature then created more trees, shrubs, and flowers.
But I can not tell it, it would take many hours.
I have just explained the triumphant birth,
Of our peaceful, loving planet, that we call Earth!

Elysa Koch

When The Wind Blows

When the wind blows it sounds like an owl.
When the wind blows it makes the leaves fly.
When the wind blows it open and shuts your doors.
When the wind blows you get a slight chill.
When the wind blows it might mean a storm is coming.

Jonathan Canterbury

What Was But Is No More

I know it's time to go now,
We've had some good times with friends.
But just because you have died,
Doesn't mean our friendship has to end.
I know we've had some bad times,
But things turn out this way.
We've done some really crazy things,
That we'll never say.
We've been in some trouble,
We've had some fun,
But now those times are over,
It's time for us to run.
We will never let you go away,
This place in our hearts, is where you'll stay.
Just because things turned out this way,
Doesn't mean we won't be together another day.

Aaron Wagers

Still Happy

Getting to know you throughout the years
We've seen a lot happen; the joys and the tears.
We haven't done badly, we've fared pretty well
The blessings around us, a story they tell.
Our love we have nurtured, through truth, trust and talk
When times took on trouble, we both did not walk.
Our vows we respect, our feelings come first
We know what is real so our bubble won't burst.
A best friend to me and a best friend to you
My love; without friendship we'd never get through.
You changed me along time ago with your smile
You filled me with warmth, made me fight for our style.
I look not at others, for all that you give
For they do not know me, the life that we live.
Your touch is still precious, it always will be
Your hugs and your closeness is ingrained in me.
You're mine for a lifetime, through thick and through thin
I'll always be yours, because I'd do it again.

James E. Anderson

Guess The Color

What color do you think of when you see a little mouse?
What color do you sometimes see on the roof of a house?

Or what about the color of the elephant at the zoo?
Or the color of a person's hair when they reach 82?

How about the sky on a dark and dreary day?
When the clouds grow dark and the sun has gone away.

My father has a suit this color.
I've seen him wear it twice.
And I must say, that as a suit,
This color is quite nice.

This is the color of my loveable sweet pet.
Her name is Smokey.
Can you guess my color yet?

The color that I'm writing about is soft and not too bright.
I hope you guessed the color Gray,
'Cause if you did, then you are right!

Ami S. McCain

"Spring"

Spring spring what a wonderful thing
Where bees hum and children sing,
You smell the scent of flowers,
watch butterflies for hours,
So please accept this thing called spring,
It is a wonderful thing.

Jessica Rigney

Sunday Church!

On Sunday morning you go to church
What do you hear?
A crying baby in grandma's ear
She came to church to pray
But found no words today
The crying went on and the sermon got louder
The wailing and the preaching
Oh, my what a clatter
We'll surely all get to heaven as we're glory bound.
The crying and the preaching they go together
Much to my surprise it soon got better
The crying baby fell asleep and the sermon ended
And we'll all come again next week and try to do better.

Emma L. Appenzeller

The Matinee

The day after the quake, I was told to awake If I only knew
what I was about to view Little did I know that it was the
beginning of a show That would change the rest of my life

All I said was ok
I didn't mean to push him the wrong way
Little did I know, that it was the beginning of a show
This man I married, I really didn't know

The first lash came so fast, I could not believe this was real
When my body was pulled to the floor,
I knew I could not take much more.

As he slammed me onto the window ledge,
I could feel my body swell inside.
With each lash I could feel he had no pride.
Little did I know that this was just the beginning of the show

Then his body covered mine one hand around my neck
No one could hear my voice, no one would check

As he tightly closed his hands around my throat I struggled to
grasp for air I knew at this very moment he never truly cared
with my last breath I whispered let me go little didn't he know
that was the end of the show

Aubrey Cooks

Trouble In Our Path

There is trouble in our path, that we hardly share a laugh.
What seems to be our problem the last few days, I just want
to throw them away in the flowing day. If it is just one of
us, it is probably the one who puts up the biggest fuss. A
lending hand is what one needs, to plant helpful and loving
seeds. There is more to share as the road grows, what is in
store, only God knows. There is no joy to constant fighting,
let's put an end to it in writing. Our love is so, so rare, no one
else would get your care. So confessions are on their way, there is
only one thing to say..... I'm sorry!!

Cynthia Darnell

Is Love Worth Living Through

Many times in my young life I've felt the pain of loss.
When a time of love or life passes across
To a place out of my hands, far beyond the distance I can see,
I ask my vigorous pain to release me.
When love leaves me through the fate of two who must depart
To go their separate ways and grow apart,
I begin to compare the happiness of times when love swayed
To the sorrow from the absence of love today.
I wonder if the time of love was worth ever living through
Because I'm left with tears and a ghost of times I once knew.

Cynthia Etzkorn

"The Lady"

Let me tell you about a woman I know,
What she's really like, not what she shows.
I'll call her "the lady", and her friends will be surprised,
By the feeling she keeps hidden deep inside.
They say her life seems happy, what more could she ask?
But, I can tell you, her smile is a mask.
Her feelings are hidden behind a brick wall.
So no one can see them, no one at all.
Each broken promise and careless lie have taken their toll,
Wounding not just her heart but, also her soul.
She shares with no one the feelings she's had.
Since they see only the good and never the bad.
Deep inside she hides all her fears,
And guards them closely, letting no one near.
Alone in the darkness, her tears fall late into the night,
Always replaced by a smile with the morning light.
You ask, her pain, how can I see?
The answer is simple, "THE LADY", is me.

Georgia J. Burks

Untitled

The search for satisfaction goes on and on,
What was once right, now is wrong.
The fear of shame is a consistent battle.
Fight for piece? It contradicts a little,.

One disgrace nation, "under God?"
As we cross paths we just smile and nod.
Some hang their heads in shame and sorrow,
And not yearning to see what's in store for tomorrow.

What is right? What is wrong?
How much longer can our world hold on?
Born into an insane society,
The void of silence is taken quietly.

One's quest for self will always remain,
Discarding the light or the dark domain.
Divided we will stand, and together we will fall.
Though few love God, still loves all.

Joseph B. Stier

A Child's Eye

A child stood looking at the sky,
What's going on, behind the clouds?

A child stood gazing at the birds.
Why can they fly and I can't?

A child stood staring at an elephant.
Why is he so huge and I'm so small?

A child stood petrified by the snake,
Why is he so long and I'm so short?

A child is adamant about her pet fish
Why can't she come out and play with me?

I guess a child's eye is an interesting screen.
To try and figure out this mystified world.

Christine Gillespie

Niger, Oh Niger

Niger, oh Niger, where is the tiger,
Who devoured the lady that rode on his back?
That's a good question!
He has indigestion,
From beginning to end of his alimentary tract!

Floyd Billigmeier

She Said

Grandma was a hooker and she would talk about those days
when afternoons could bring in a fifty or two and the most that
she lost was a couple of hours, and a silk stocking, -
when she wore ankle boots for an entire season because she liked
the hollow thump noise they made on the cobblestone street
in that part of town she crossed to twice a week.
And she would pass the slow days reading fashion magazines

by the fountain in Trafalgar Square;
she knew all the doormen who stood their posts
at the Royal National Hotel and she would sometimes go for pints
with them at the pub on Mortimer Street and stay until it closed.
Her late night conversations were Sunday morning
soap box lectures on the difficulties on finding that one love.
Until Grandpa. And he still lets her keep the change.

Christina Enriquez

How Dare You?

How dare you accuse me of righteous indignation
when all I am is proud?!

How dare you say, "You've changed"
when you walk along side of me?

How dare you insinuate my tears aren't real but,
when they fall, they cry?

How dare you reprimand my expression(s)
when you allow freedom?

How dare you hold back me
when I give you, you?

How dare you advertise what I share
when I'm not selling?

How dare you?

Francis C. Castro

Tho' Quiet The Night

How peaceful is the starry night
When guns are stilled and missiles cease
To streak the evening sky

I hear the stillness loud and clear
Tho' sounds are never made
I feel anguish for the souls
Whose fate was sealed before their time
When senseless wars made early graves

How still the night — tho' troubled minds
Of loved ones left behind
Have restless sleep and haunted dreams
Of wars that are no more; — No peace they find!

Taunted by the memories tho' clear the sky
Now and forever more until the day they die

Is precious life so meaningless?
Is it all worth the pain?
What stirs the souls of men
To fight for senseless gain?

Talk is cheap! Wars are not!
Handshakes are free, when peace we've got!

Blondine Louise Reddick

Limerick

There once was a man from Japan,
who burnt his face in a pan.
He sprayed his face and found out later it was mace.
That stupid old man from Japan.

Jennifer Jewett

Untitled

Although, I didn't know him well,
when he gone it felt as if I did,
His tragic death has casted a dark shadow
over the lives of many,
Some mourn all through the day
others only sometimes,
We still think of thee as if he were never
really there just a shadow, a silhouette,
just a presence in our minds,
His soul will live on forever
in our hearts and souls,
To us he hasn't left he
is right here beside us, forever…
As if it never happened as if it all
were just a bad dream.

Jennifer Shannon

The Rage

I grow stronger each time
When I am
Discouraged: You Will Never Succeed!
Yelled at: Idiot, Stupid, Retard!
Struck so hard that I feel the burn
of the slap that has entered into my
soul and left and unforgivable mark.
Beaten so violently that the bruises
on my body I can never escape.
I grow stronger each time as I take
the scars.
I am a pot that when the lid is
compressing and suffocating for too long:
I Will Explode!
I will start a fire that will blaze so
fiercely and powerfully that it will be
merciless towards you. Yet I know if I
cannot control this rage I will not evolve;
I will become you.

Ani Nazaretyan

Someday

When I see you, you always made me smile
When I listen to you, you always brought joy to me
When the sun is bright in the sky your name is shaped like a cloud
When the moon is full the owls can only see
But someday we'll be together

I can only remember your smiling face
I can only remember your long beautiful hair
I can only remember the times we had
But someday we'll be together

I was lost in your eyes as only you knew I was
I was lost in your mind you thinking how wonderful it was
But someday we'll together
The picture of you in my mind will always last forever
But the picture of you in that long white box I can not bear to see
But someday we'll be together

I hope you will forgive me for that little argument we had
I'm sorry for the things I said
But someday we'll be together

As my heart cries out your name I can only say
Good-bye

Chaunce O. Luckett

Fear Of The Broken Hearted

When I look into the mirror my face is gaunt, and mapped with fear.
When I look at my life I notice something missing.
When I look inside I can see only the remains of a shattered,
bitter soul.
The soul hollowed by betrayal.
My existence is spent in the shadows, lost forever in its tantalizing
power, wandering aimlessly in its depths.
When I look into the mirror and peer deep inside I see the dust
of ages past.
With trust destroyed I see a soul quivering with tears in an icy storm
of December rain.
I hear a voice laughing at my weakness, hissing with joy with every sob,
With a fleeting heart overwhelmed with fear I cry to the heavens to
intervene.
Courage! Courage! Courage! I pray with a wail, but none is given.
The angels ignore my pleas.
Love, faith and hope quickly slip from my bony fingers.
Loneliness as deep as the spirit overshadows the light of day.
The heart paralyzed by fear.
The fear of the broken hearted.

Charles L. Dixon, Jr.

Just Ask

Do you notice what I wear?
When I need you, are you there?
When I touch you, are you aware?
Who am I to ask!

When you needed me, in I came.
When you're just upset, I take the blame.
Am I involved in a painful game?
Who am I to ask!

In all my values will I bend?
If I can't be your lover, will I be your friend?
Will my feelings be this deep at the very end?
Who are you to ask!

You made me laugh and you made me cry.
You made me strive harder and want to try
to win the truth over every lie,
but still, I have to ask.

So please remember as this is read,
I want no guilt feelings to fill your head,
for I've meant every word I've ever said,
and that is why I ask!

Annette R. Czajkowski

Black

Black is what I think about
When I think of death.
Black is what I think about
When things are all a mess.
Black isn't only
For things that are down.
Black makes me happy
Just hearing the sound
Black is a word that sounds so profound.
But the one main reason
I like the word black is because
Black is so dark and so out of bounds.

Antonia Marie Hansen

Journey's End

Shed no tears for me when I am gone
When life's journey ends and I must travel on
Just remember that I loved you and gave all I could give
Fill your hearts with love and laughter-know that I still live
Shed no sadness as I leave you for another plane
I want to see you smiling if and when we meet again
Hold your memories close and never let them flee
Always know I love you dearly
But please! Shed no tears for me
Dorothea Goodwin

Way Back When

Do you remember when - most stores were just five and ten.
When love was high and funds low,
   and computers, we did not know.
When bread was made at home each day,
   and each morn the hens would lay.
When the roosters would wake you up before dawn.
When you'd see the critters play on your lawn.
When you'd watch your Ma, make lye soap.
When you hung your clothes out on a rope.
When you helped make that brew to drink.
When you'd sit and drink it, you couldn't think.
When you used a wash-tub to take a bath,
   and to this day, folks would laugh.
To get up in the dark at night,
   and only have the moon for light.
To go to the outhouse so far out back,
  'cause we just lived in a four room shack.
I remember those days so well, families were large, kids 8 to 12.
Our family had kids of ten, things seemed very happy then.
We grew up of what folks would say, "way back when".
Carol A. Sheren

A Tribute To Mother

How I yearn for those good old days
when mother was up and around
and the tasks she had to face each day
I still find hard to compound

Mother was as grand as a mother can be
and she will always remain in my heart
yet she fades away like a morning star
like a dream that has fallen apart

Her tenure on earth was a holy thing
A host of heavenly grace
yet her passing was awesome filled with woe
an undefined sort of pace

She has gone to a place that still must be
a sacred mystery to you and me

If your soul is still sad and much in despair
your spirit can be lifted with a pious prayer
and one by one we fall asleep
May God unite us - eternally to keep.
Chuck McCarthy

Do You Ever Wonder?

Do you ever wonder what it's all about?
Why children scream and adults shout?
Why friends forget and enemies won't?
Why no one cares and why you don't?
Why the world is round when they thought it flat?
Why the one you love doesn't love you back?
Why time is fast yet seems so slow?
What it's all about I do not know.
Jack Moore

Alas We Need Gas

Twas just before summer all over the nation
When prices were hiked at every gas station
Not just a penny but a nickel and more
Up, up at the pumps the prices did soar

Attendants don't pump gas, it's a thing of the past
They're hermetically sealed in concrete and glass
And from a small window sell, wine, candy, beer
Lottery tickets like a third rate cashier

Week-ends are special, their coffers enrich
They can up all the prices with a flick of the switch
Moaning complaining you grab for the hose
The pump clicking merrily as you pay through the nose

Some day in the future, when gas we devour
Will all be replaced with nuclear power
We won't lose our car at the mall when we park
One fender bender and it glows in the dark.
David Ramsay

I Didn't Know

There you were in my peripheral sights, watching.
When the blow from
your darkly accusing eyes struck me,
I could taste the blood-saltiness of your pain.
How was I to know the sword I wielded
could mortally wound?
That which I never knew existed
was severed in an instant
with a wayward kiss
meant not for your eyes
nor your knowing.
The boundaries you never set were trespassed.
The trust I never knew I had is broken,
and you walk on crying.
I stand, left with the bitter taste of regret
and another's lips on my tongue, confused.
Did I do wrong?
Jodi L. Markgraf

Do You Remember My Love

Do you remember, my love, that July?
When the breezes caressed us with a sigh.

When the lake stretched out to kiss our beach.
When even the heavens were in our reach.

When we laid in the shade of a jaded tree.
When we let our passions flow so free.

When the sun glistened high in the sky.
When we left our troubles in the dust to lie.

When the falls pounded out your name.
When everything around us seemed so tame.

When from the water arose the mist.
When the sorrow of life was not missed.

When a colored bow sprung from the depths of blue.
as if the God's had made it for you.

Do you remember my love by the shore?
When the two of us required nothing more.
Adam Heldibridle

Mine Eyes Have Seen The Glory

In a golden burst of sunrise, just at dawning of the light,
When the penetrating sun rays pierce the darkness of the night,
I have breathed the morning freshness, seen the sky return to blue-
Gathered flowers from a garden, felt the early morning dew;
And in the last few hours of daylight, just before the nights arrives
I have watched the Master Painter, fingerpaint the western skies.
As I marvelled at these colors that the world cannot record
Then I knew I'd seen the glory of the Lord!

Standing silently at seaside on a million grains of sand
Watching salty waves push seafoam up along the edge of land
I was standing in the presence of the Power of that sea-
I, so mindful of His power..He, so mindful, yes, of me.
I stood gazing at the water, felt the spray across my face,
Drinking in the lovely beauty of that time and of that place-
Looking up in humble reverence, far beyond where seagulls soared
I was sure I'd seen the glory of the Lord!

Oh mine eyes have seen the beauty of this world His hands have framed.
My heart is changed and I'll never be the same.
My soul is filled with rapture at the mention of His name;
For mine eyes have seen the Glory of the Lord!

Anne Melton Tolar

Ponderings

There are wonderful sights on those cool winter nights,
when the stars are shining bright,
The wisest man, though he thinks he can,
couldn't count them try as he might,
You gaze up in wonder, trying to ponder,
the meaning of this dazzling show,
When you're trying to think, and you perch on the brink,
of the knowledge that makes this so,
We look without seeing, but at the core of our being,
the answer lies in wait, is our course our own,
Or is it simply thrown, into the waiting arms of fate,
through thick and thin, many people give in,
To this puzzling thing called life, they worry and hate,
until it's too late, and the penalty cuts like a knife,
Time is lost, a terrible cost to those who just cower in fear,
But to all the rest, who try to make best,
of their time the answer is clear,
My only advice, is to grab hold of life,
and force it right down to its knees, use your power to choose,
And you cannot lose, make destiny do as you please.

Collin Vincent Church

God's Quiet Time

When the sun drops down behind the Elkhorns,
When the wind suddenly grows still,
When the rustling in the poplars suddenly ceases,
And the evening light still lingers in the hills,

The coyote who's song echoed in the canyon
And the one that answered him across the way,
Stopped their trilling, yipping song as if on signal,
To honor God's own quiet time of day.

The birds that roost there in the orchard,
Are fussing as they settle for the night.
Suddenly they grow still and quiet,
In reverence in the fading of the light.

Old Speck, there in the horse corral,
Munching on a block of meadow hay,
Stopped eating, raised his head to listen,
As if to hear what God would have to say.

And I stood there in awe and silence.
In the fading light He didn't seem far away.
It seems that God comes out into the desert
To enjoy his quiet time of day.

Glenn M. Fleming

Alone

When you are alone, tired and can't move your bones,
When you are worried about life,
and wish you could bring order out of strife.

When you want to create, and don't know your fate.
Lift up your head and your heart,
make your hands reach out for a start.

Whoever is near, whoever is dear,
just love and forget the past.
The Lord is good, and never fails.

Your strength returns, you can regale,
but it is hard to accept the truth,
it is easy to be burned, you have to live,
and you have to learn.

Beverely M. Darling

Conversations With The Dark

Where do you go, you invisible beast?
When you cower before luminous light?
Courageous you seem when tempted to feast
Your lustful eyes upon the holiest sight.
You gallantly devour all in your path,
But retreat when enlightenment's near.
Could it be that panic has you in its wrath?
What monster is it that kindles your fear?
Are you friend or foe, sinner or saint?
What information does darkness divulge?
Slyly you skulk with stories whispered faint,
Hidden so well, never leaving a bulge.
So speak to me Darkness, tell me a tale.
We'll ride on our dreams without any sails.

Cheris Hagge

Imagine A Day

Imagine a day
When you feel light and gay
When all of the bad in the world
Can't take this feeling away Imagine a day
When the sun is shining on you
And the calm water before you is blue
The warmth and calmness give you a peace that is unreal
Imagine a day
While walking quietly through the tall whispering pines
You pause to gaze a rose whose beauty is sublime
A gentle breeze pierces the silence and brings you back to
Consciousness, Imagine a day
When the soft and mysterious clouds above move casually about
Forming one shape then another
Bringing to mind images you had seen in them as a child
Imagine a day, I say this because
everyday that you touch my life is such a day
So when I need to feel this way-I think of you
Imagine a day

John F. Creath

O Sweet Mother

O sweet woman-Mother of three,
Will you raise and nurture me?
Feed me with your Motherly milk,
And tuck me in with sheets of silk,
Lay me to rest inside your arms,
And rock me to sleep with your Motherly charms
O sweet Mother-Woman I adore,
Can I be child number four?

Jerry A. Kretchmer

Sweet Suicide

As I shake and tremble in silence, the tears burn down my cheek-
when you pass by my heart races, it's all I can do to stand
for my knees go weak. I try to forget you, but, without knowing it,
you won't let me go-
You're all I think about, all I love, all I miss, all I know
Little by little my heart breaks into sharp slivers
that pierce through my stomach like a knife-
Don't you know you mean more than anything to me in this life?
I have to admit, you've got me wrapped around your finger like so-
For I would do anything for you, anything you asked, this I know
I've tried to erase my feelings, but, I just can't shake them loose-
My fire for you is so strong, my emotions won't reduce
Now I must end this note with a final saddened goodbye-
Please don't hate me for what I'll do,
I'll miss you from the other side.
They say that suicides go to hell, but, I will prove them wrong-
Because no life is heaven compared to a life
without you that would last forever long.

Brandishca Nott

Remember Me

Remember me
When you walk by the blue-green ocean,
As the birds chirp on the rocks.

Think of me
When you smell the fresh air that passes you,
When you drink the fresh, clear water.

You will find me
When you touch your heart,
When you look at the blue sky.

Remember me
When you look at a blooming daisy.
Remember me.

Joshua W. Brown

Look To Your Childhood

Look to your childhood...
When you were just a boy,
Innocent, idealistically naive,
Dreaming dreams no others dared dream
Of fame, fortune, and fortitude.

And know, that now is the time,
When you can see beyond those dreams...
And turn the futility of fantasies into the rewards of realities.

For now, in time, with the benefit of age,
With refined knowledge, you can see with clarity
That experiencing is the key to enjoying life.

For now, is the time, for you to see
Each year as another level of learning,
365 days yearning to be relished.

And now, is the time, for you to see
Each day as the clay it is...
And know, that now, you are its artist.

Deborah A. Greene

Lonely Heart

A dismal shadow covers his heart.
With a weak beat it sheds a tear
Ineffable grief tears him apart
Lonely now, he's filled with fear.
His loss so great, for his love died
He trembles with pain while wondering why.
His love has become death's new bride,
And remembering her smile, he begins to cry.

Hallie Apple

To Kurt

It smelled like teen spirit
When your face graced the screen.
We thought you spoke for our generation.
Our poet of pain. But who knew?
Deep inside the pain lurked and too soon took control.
Couldn't handle the fame.
You were so weak!
It only took one shot
To take it all away. How stupid!
Take the easy way out. Now what?
"I love you. I love you."
That's what you told them.
But, why didn't you think of them?
You were thinking of yourself.
A fatherless baby you left.
And a generation abandoned.
We were wrong, though.
You spoke for yourself only, nobody else.
We're left with the art you left behind.
But nothing else. Good-bye, our poet of pain.

Danielle Marotta

Walking In Larchmont

Across the Sound, a shadow strand
Where clouds of curdled cream
Obscure the sandy shore of yesterday.

Across the empty waters in a world gone gray
The Island's lost, the bridge is gone
And every sail is down in heavy folds.

Across the chopping waves
A frowning sky sends rumbled warnings
Blows a penetrating wind to touch me
With a sudden chill.

I cannot linger here
Where sunlight brightens every budding tree.
The soothing spell of springtime
Has been shattered by the storm I see
Across the Sound.

Harriet Mishkoff

What Hides Behind A Hidden Door.

There's a lock hidden door.
Where life outside, seems to ignore.
Where there are people, in a different race.
Trying to make a living out of a difficult place
A place where skin-complexion means everything
But you as one means nothing.

Our life is closed in different and many ways.
Hoping, Hoping that our life will change, if it may
When that day come, we will be ready
To take the first step, In the life of the lady
Looking for the man who flies the golden kite
Hoping one day, he will drop the key of life.

Then one day, things started happy in a mystery way
Because that old hidden door open that day.
Life didn't seem bad anymore.
For our soul was free to go.
But before we walk onto the door
Freedom said, "No Leeching fighting and crying anymore."

DeLoyd Levern Davis

"Precious Jewel"

A precious jewel is rarely found
Where many seek to find,
A very priceless commodity
That often boggles the mind;

This jewel is valued high
At a price no one can measure,
Why is it so hard to discover a gem
And experience this unique pleasure?

Along with gems there are trinkets and diamond-like stones
Which appear to shine for a minute,
While these fake riches and claims are alright for some
For me, I want no part in it;

A miner once said, "all that glitters is not gold"
So be careful and inspect within the outer glow,
For a true jewel will shine in the darkest of places
And its center looks like a rainbow;

Like this jewel, you are just as special
So priceless, unique, colorful, and true,
I had no idea I'd ever discover
A big ol' gem like you!

    Anthony J. Artis

The Brook

I do know of a brook,
Where Mom and I often look,
To see the where the deer used to drink,
Now watching the trash start to sink,
Now Mom tells me of time when she was a child,
When her behavior got a little too wild,
She went by the brook and sang,
Until the dinner bell rang,
Mother would give me a loving and caring look,
And she would sing the song she once sang by the brook.
The brook no longer rushes through the land.
It will never be nearly as grand,
As it was so many years ago.
The trash clogging it stops its flow

    Greta Davidson Hicks

'Quickly Dreams'

My dreams are like an open field,
  Where never ending secrets lay.
They sometimes depend upon the very events,
  That happen each and everyday.
My dreams are like a secret book,
  Each and every detail so severe,
Hoping that the very end,
  Will bring much happiness and cheer.
Quickly dreams come show me,
  And I promise I will yield,
To what you need to tell me,
  As I read my book in an open field.

    Angela Sherrill

Best Friends

As I glimpse upon my younger years, the love I see is strong,
  with outward strength and sanity, I could see her so on wrong.
Though deep inside, she was as I, a child with many fears,
  yet set them all aside for time to stop and comfort tears.
For that I thank my dear sweet mom, whose beauty never ends,
  I'm grateful and express my love by calling us best friends.

    Erika D. Crain

Deserted

So lonely is the empty house
Where restless wind first creaks, then calls
To absent voices long been gone,
And crumpled paper leaves the walls.

Heavy air that stifles breathing.
Was it breathed in deep before?
Echoes of those lively voices
Fill the cold, dark space once more.

We must leave this desolation
And these whispers from the past.
Looking back at vacant windows
Like blind eyes all shut at last.

    Helen Davisson Holden

Dream Journey

I wondered, once, to the land of Dreams
  Where sorrow was an unknown name.
My troubles vanished like magic it seems
And my heart and soul were not the same.
  In this beautiful land there was no care
  For the heart that was weary and worn
  Peace and happiness awaited me there
  And sorrow and pain I knew no more.
  So, I'll pack up my troubles and take a trip
  And say to myself each mile,
  "I've all my troubles locked up in my grip
  And the ticket I need is a smile"

    Dorothy McFarland

Dreams

I am trapped in a world
  where the ground is beyond reach
    The materialistic visions leave behind
    an unmasked child who's afraid of the dark.

I am here, but I am not
  my existence is a cloudy curtain of gray matter
    My fingers are clutching
    to grasp the last strands of hope.

The passing of time doesn't seem to matter
  for there will always be enough
    My lifeless body has been replace
    with the changing tides of mother nature.

    Gretchen Sprague

I Believe

I believe there is a place where dreams come true,
  where there is a pot of gold behind each rainbow,
  where all hearts are pure.
Some say there is no such place, but I believe.
I believe in my heart this place is somewhere in this mighty world.
I believe there is a place where no one
  goes without food or shelter.
I believe there is a place where the poor don't exist.
I believe there is a place where people
  are loved for who they are not what they look like.
I believe when you die there is such a place
  where dreams come true,
  where no hungry people roam
  where no one is unloved.
I believe this dream like world does
  exist in only one place, heaven.
  And in heaven I believe.

    Elizabeth Fallis

God's Government

Can you imagine God's government?
Where things will be govern nothing to resent
Each man treated fairly
All human needs met no tears, no pain,
Nothing to regret.
Only laughter will fill
The air everyone will truly "Share"
Beautiful land and beautiful sea.
No violence or hatred anywhere
People will truly care
Brother will be brother
God will reign supreme
Because He is truly our King
That will be a great day
For the former things will
Have passed away.
Ella Johnson

Carney Island

Carney Island on Little Lake Weir, Fl.
Where water oaks are so low, that
they nearly touch the ground.
And everyone is looking all around.
One point has a picnic area and
everyone is focusing their camera.
No bugs, bees or people with
alcohol.
Do not you want to come to this place?
Where you don't have to wear a satin and a lace.
Just a pair of shoes, shorts and a shirt.
And be the big island flirt.
Don't be so snooty girl, I'm only Mr.
Fantastic of the world.
With all my island charm and I will never
be no harm.
I welcome you by the dozens, just pay your bills
bring your cousins.
Don't you want to choose a great place in the world!
And hope to find a partner to give you that dance whirl.
Just enjoy the breeze as if you were on Lake Louise.

Bobby Jean Burkhalter

Take Another Look

Give this some thought, my friend,
where would we be without women,
They're not here just for man's beckon an call,
although without them, we'd cease to exist at all;

She's the foundation to everything living,
an equal to any man, a credit worth giving,
She's corporations, bankers, the hub of a nation,
not just a pretty face, to be a possession;

In any career their presence is an asset,
you'll find her capable of blood and sweat,
She can control huge equipment, without fear,
Yet, in her arms, cradle her baby so dear;

She's a giver of life, more ways then one,
a companion, friend, associate, not lovers alone,
She's worth her weight in gold, give her respect,
if you think otherwise, I'll take that bet!

Jerry Ewing

Untitled

As I walk through the ocean's waters
Where you were found before
The memories flood like the salty waves
The same waves that found you on the shore

The pain comes back, so intense now
My heart throbbing, sobbing out an aching drone
I enter the water to be with you
For you left me to live on alone

The frothy, waves engulf around me
Enticing, beguiling, as in my lungs the wetness seeps
I sink down to a better world
With you, no reason to weep

I slip beyond and you're not there
Without life, my body grows chill
Even in death, I cannot find you
    I have nothing still.
Caryn Samaj

Something Totally Different

Is there something I can carry away from this experience
whether I try to think about it or not?
I control the expression in what I say, because it says a lot.
To familiar my experience is something you cannot do
because you are not me and I am not you.
So I'm playing a game with myself
hoping to get something from it today
maybe a good laugh, but I'm conditioned to reach
for that something that I can carry away.
But it's real, it's an illusion
You cannot be sucked into a reality that is only mine
Your way of feeling in the world is so different than mine
I need to hear you laugh, I want to help you cry
In you, I want to make it come alive
However I cannot, so I guess you'll never know that you
can't look, listen, and feel that my life is as real
and crammed as yours is with personal experiences
growing to know something, something totally different.

John Clinton Ary

In the Night

In the night Peace be to all
Whether strangers be from near or far
Far give them the light and show them the way
O'er the tree of life itself...or each passing day.

In the night time stands still
Be it a time of rest or of travail
Whether quiet or turbulent, base or violent
This is the end of the day.

Night is a void upon a restless world
A blanket of peace where war was once fought, or
Of rest for the weary, of pardon for the damned.

For night is a dream
For outward solitude is inward energy
Here is where our decisions are made
Our fears appear, our hopes rise... or fall.

Reality vanishes into the night
We make our escape from our woes, our trials,
    and ...from ourselves.
No hate is shown, no sins are committed
For in the quiet of the night
We become a part of God.
Daniel T. McClellan

The Wings Of The Wind

Out of the darkness dawns sweet light,
Which brings peace beyond all measure-
For when the storm does pass away,
The stillness is a rich treasure.

The sound of the birds in the trees
Brings thoughts of their wings in the wind-
The creator loves everything
Which includes the rain HE did send!

There are clouds that thunder in life
Causing fear, distress and much pain,
We find Refuge in Christ, our Hope,
For He restores calmness again!

Carolyn L. Marquis

How Far

How far 'tis to thou yonder star
Which guides me to my lover's side
How far the touch at distant light
Perceived by naked eye shall beckon me

How far the hands of time move endlessly around
'Til morning awakens life
The dead and frozen ground

How far away can you be now
You move so soft and slow
How far away can we be now
Only you and I will ever know

Collin Williams

Everlasting Love

God loves us with an everlasting love,
Which is backed by an everlasting power.
He keeps us in the hollow of His hand
And watches over us every hour.

God made the earth, the skies and the seas,
And the winds that obey His commands;
And because of His Love, He also made man
And creatures to inhabit these lands.

Then God came to earth and became a man,
As Jesus, He walked in our shoes;
And because of His everlasting Love,
Jesus Christ died and paid all our dues.

But He rose again - He was stronger than death-
'Twas His everlasting power, you see,
That brought Him out of that awful tomb;
Now, from sin and guilt we're free.

Yes, God loves us with an everlasting love,
And He can fill our hearts with love, too.
If we seek His face through Jesus Christ,
Both His Love and His power will shine through!

Darla C. Hunter

The Ringing

As I listen closely I can hear the birds twitter and cheer,
yet if listen closer I hear a ringing in my ear.
It is the ringing of lives that cannot be.
It is the ringing of lives yet to see.
It is the ringing of lives past for me.
It is the ringing of lives for me to be.
It is the ringing of raw eternity,
but it is above all the ringing of time near and dear.

Brad Barcroft

Holly Ridge

I walk the spine of long-forsaken hills
Which smell of musk and last year's molding leaves;
Where trees are feudal lords and whip-poor-wills
Reproach and plead though no one quite believes.

The sun is high and needs no chanticleer.
The moon is dark and cannot condescend.
The holly warns me not to interfere
With timeless rites I will not comprehend.

I drop my pack and sit astride a log;
Two lizards jump in fright and disappear.
I but intrude upon some dialogue
An uninvited, foreign buccaneer.

Superiority demands, requires
That man soliloquize despite desires.

Doris Sanford

One World, One War, Over And Over

Which was the greater war — first or second?
Which was the longer, or did it just seem so to whomever?
What was the last since and when?
What's going on now wherever?
When is the next one?
When is the last to be?
If I knew, I'd warn you, my children!

Would you then pay attention?
Who can learn a lesson, when another generation
Supplants the last with next?
Who will take time to learn about the past?
Who cares enough to think about it anyway?
You too will fade away in time.
If your going is due to age, not hate,
You are indeed fortunate, but late.
What will be your children's fate?

Gerald Somers

One Never Knows What Tomorrow Brings

A neighbor so loved, passed away last night in her car
while driving her heart already stopped.
When told to me this morning.
A phone call about a neighbor so loved.
In her car going to help others with cars passing by.
Her heart stopped before the crash, into another car.
She so loved to pass away,
doing every thing in her loving way.
Her condition so strong and weak,
never brought it out for her to speak
The news this morning gave us all
"A wonder why" not able to know
what tomorrow may bring, because of a wonderful guy.
She is now in heaven, her religion she so preached.
Now she has no tomorrows for others she worked so hard to reach.

Alfred A. Frantello

Wolves

Wolves are all colors gray, black, or even more
wolves are dangerous sometimes
they only attack when they are really hungry
wolves, wolves, I love wolves!
They look like a dogs in ways, but I don't know how.
Wolves hunt in packs with two parents
who knows why, I don't.
All I know is I love wolves.

Alicia Virg-In

Let Me Be

Won't you please just let me be,
While I still have my dignity.
And understand, I truly know
When the time is near for me to go.

Don't make me linger, cause you can't bare,
To face the fact that death is near.
I know you'll miss me, I love you too,
But there's just one thing I'll ask of you.

Please let the Lord come take me home,
Where I will never be alone,
Where loved ones wait to welcome me,
So I ask you please, just let me be.

Denise Debbie Puckett

To You

When the outside seems dark and cold,
while inside I'm feeling all alone, I just
close my eyes and think about the past.

I think of you and the things you've said.
Sometimes I even shed a tear because I:
share your happiness, your pain, your despair.
Even though thousands of miles lie between us
I know that you share mine too.

Slowly I begin to feel warm., For I know that
you care, and if you could, you would be right there
beside me. You mean more to me than any thing,
nothing can replace you, or the memories we share.

You are my most precious friend.

Emily M. Ruppert

Despair

Cold winter night
while most everyone rests
a child lets out a muffled cry

Other children dream of fun and games
this quiet child only prays
"Hope those hands don't grapple me again."

In his mind he runs away
wishing to fly and never look back
innocence cast aside

No one to protect delicate existence
One more night living in despair
with the sad sensation that nobody cares!

Elias Soria

Orient's Winter

The first flakes gingerly upon the frozen plain
Whiter than doves and lighter than air
Touching down delicately and kissing the ground
Falling on eyelashes and dark raven hair.

Breath billows in clouds before almond eyes
The cranes ruffle feathers covered with frost
A winter sun bounces off the glistening ice
While a mewing kitten plods through the snow, lost.

Night's dark curtain begins to lower upon the crystal land
Wisps of smoke from a chimney's fire, wavering against the skies
Coldness seeps in through cracks in walls, chilling bones inside
And outside, duelling the icy wind, the plaintive kitten cries.

Miss Esther Marie Iverson

Ode To Morons

You are the children that live forever young,
while time decays our very flesh and bones,
making us the specters of yesterday and time;
yet time does not blemish your little souls;
and you'll cry for a toy at any age,
while we shed tears to our very graves.
At any age you whimper for a motherly caress;
but we cannot: our mothers are all gone,
and our friends too; and then all, all is gone
But I love you still with a jealous heart
for your eternal youth and ready smiles,
even as we soar beyond the galaxies...
flying madly ultra to nowhere!
You can whimper or cry at any time,
but we cannot with our hair shining white...
Then after a thousand years: a heart attack!
and our stealthy age is then forever gone.
But you were born the Angels in our lives,
and like angels you live forever young...
but we do not...; we do not...

Ferdinando Dante Maurino

The Gallant Steed

It's been a year now sense the
whispering breeze, has called for our lovin' steed,
But! as we recall,
he left behind him a new little face,
she also has the need of -
Gentle lovin' hands.
Which, with her father no longer near,
she knows she has nothing too fear,
But oh boy! Can she rear.
We know that his spirit will always be near.
The glory lives on indeed.

Barbara Gullicksen

"Whispering The Name Of God, They Came!"

Holding the streamer of revolution, wearing the green armors,
Whispering the name of God, they came!
And we applauded and cheered:
the tune of the boot
the tune of the bullet.
Innocently we waited for the genesis of the promises;
But hollow echoes replayed to our gloomy souls.
And our lands vanished in their hands.
And our sisters vanished in their hands.
And our brothers perished on their hands!
With an aura of sorrow, annoyed in pain:
for the grim of the earth
for the main of our hearts
We seized the strife for freedom
With puissance of faith that armed our dismal existence,
We held the sword killing them all:
we opened their chest grabbing their hearts,
we spilled their blood staining their armors.
And with their blood we wrote,
"Whispering the name of God, they came!"

Candelaria H. Brown

Untitled

I was standing there
With a look of despair.
You didn't have a clue
Of how much I needed you.
Day by day, as time went on
In my world you were gone.
Every time that I've reached out
You only gave a sense of doubt.
If only once you'd feel the same way for me
Together, forever, we would be.

Amie Adams

Impostor

Lifelong companion and loving one,
Who guided the way in the darkness.
Mending all wounds - somehow causing more.
Unconditional love shown untrue.
Was it falsely true? No, it's truly false.
Betraying heart could not stay true to one.
Secrets could not hide what you could not tell.
An angel and a devil sit upon
Your shoulders, coercing all actions.
Now there is no guidance through darkness;
Only darkness follows your guidance.
Miserable guilt you can't relieve.
Time exhausts when you get to me;
Rage ignites every part.
Anger drives me to violence.
Sadness drives me to withdrawal.
Will it ever end?
How can I escape?

Jeff Wroblewski

"My Hero"

He was a man of dignity, a man of peace
who had a dream that discrimination would cease
He envisioned a nation in which he could see
everyone living together in complete harmony
Hundreds of people joined hand in hand
to hear the inspirational words instilled in this man
Even when obstacles were met along the way,
he was always determined that a change would come one day
The man that I speak of is Dr. Martin Luther King,
whose famous words we remember, "Let freedom ring"
He never lost hope and to his dream he did not let go
and this is why Dr. Martin Luther King, Jr. is my hero.

Jennifer Nazon

A Cousin Named Steve

I once had a cousin named Steve
Who had himself a great dream
He was so full of life it's hard to believe
That now my poor Stephen is dead

Knocked down in the prime of his life
By a guy he didn't even know
No more will I hear him say
Aunt Betty where are the cookies

He's gone for the rest of my life
And my heart will always be tight
For I ache and I cry every night
I no longer have Steve in my life

Why God took him out of my life
I guess I'll never know
But I hope and I pray that maybe someday
We'll all be together again

Betty Russell

In This World

In this world, it seems poor people stay poor.
Why do the rich get more money?
In this world, homelessness is growing.
Why aren't we doing anything about it?
In this world, the news is depressing.
Why can't they emphasize the positive?
In this world, many people ignore signs of poverty.
Why do we ignore people who need help?
The world needs a change.
I don't have any solutions.
Do you?

Amber Meadows

Miss Jabberwock

Dreams of splendor imprinted on the minds of those
  who have long awaited the title—Miss Jabberwock!
An undaunted desire to reign as those who have come before;
Unchanged by the bludgeonings along life's pathway,
Unchanged by the structure which often is deficient of
  equity and opportunity,
For they envision a luminous eventuality—a future of hope,
  constitutionality, and prosperity.

Ah! the season has come—it's time,
Time to embark upon the opportunity to become Miss Jabberwock!
The manifestation of exuberance infiltrates the air,
  They are anxiously awaiting the presentation of Miss Jabberwock!

Suddenly, they appear—the hopeful, the anxious, the apprehensive
Faces aglow amid the spotlight which surrounds them,
their countenance, extraordinary—their beauty infinite.
Young gentlemen—handsome, magnificent!
  Clad in tuxedos—exemplary of the grandeur of old
Awaiting the customary promenade which leads to the
  culmination of the season.
At last, the stage is set; intensity high; Congratulations!
  Miss Jabberwock!

Jeanette McGuire Adkins

Pawn Or King

Revolutionaries: all
Who opt to spurn society's dogmatic narrowmindedness
And think alone.
Dignitaries, standing tall
Bequeathing mores to appease the thoughtless masses who possess
None of their own.

Institutions, entities
And factions, who by their design purport that one should not oppose
Accepted ways,
Lest you venture to displease
The ones who strive to rule your mind, insistent you speak words they
chose,
The thought dismays.

So, the choice to be a pawn,
Manipulated but adored by those who on well-traveled roads
Have always trod;
Or king, hated, but when gone,
Leaves his achievements underscored by common knowledge that his
codes
Were his, by God.

Adolph Haven Connard III

Small Boy's World

Who carries him on shoulders broad?
Who understands when he's been bad?
Who teaches him to fish and swim?
Who is his ideal? - - - - - his dad.

Whose cookies taste the best of all?
Whose lap is nicer 'n any other?
Who'll kiss away his hurts and tears?
Who hears his prayers at bedtime? — Mother.

Who waits impatiently to play?
Obeys commands of "fetch", "sit up"?
Who kisses him with small wet tongue?
And never falters in his love? - - his pup.

Blanche Long

Mother

Our love abound for you mother
Who taught us truth and love of God
A greater gift by any other
Could never earn such a rich reward

Mother gives all equal adoration
The word mother how sweet the name
The trainer of children since creation
Dear, dear mother always the same

You reared us with such loving care
You smiled with us and dried our tears
You warned us why and when to beware
You sheltered us from doubt and fear

Your strength sustained us when we failed
Encouraged us to try and try again
The one who conquers are ones who prevailed
To keep on trying 'till the goals are obtained

We, your children love you so
You mean more to us than we can say
We cherish you; and want you to know
To us every day is Mother's Day.

Henrietta F. Nottingham

Untitled

Who, what or where is God, has long been my concern.
Who, what or where is Love, for this I've always yearned.

One day a silent voice replied, 'Listen and you'll learn.
"I'll speak to you of God and Love when tonight your thoughts adjourn."

With great anticipation and heart so filled with glee,
I hoped and prayed the silent voice would speak of Truth to me

Day was drawing to a close, the sun low in the west,
Would not be long before the day and I would lie to rest.

With skies now dark and stars in view I would go within,
To listen to the silent voice speak to me of Him.

"Who, what and where is God,' the silent voice began.
"Who, what and where is Love, try to understand."

"God is Love and Love is God, they're both one and the same,
It's only man in finite terms who gives them separate names."

If God is Love and Love is God what more can there be?
I have them both and now's the time to share them both with thee.

Barbara Enquist

Untitled

Dearest Dale, 11 years ago today, we met
who'd have thought our lives would be set?
We've grown together in every way
and I find myself loving you more everyday.
The day we said "I do"
Made me realize how lucky I am to have you.
You're more than a husband, you're also a friend
and one I can share with and always depend.
You made me the happiest girl in the world
the day we became parents to our new baby girl.
Once two...
Now three...
Together, forever I know we will be
Daddy, Mommy, and our darling Casey.
Thank you for all
you have given me
I love you,
Diane
July 27th, 1993

Diane Snooks

Untitled

This is a poem to my sister Tasha
whom I love very dearly
her eyes are large to see the world
her eyes have seen great pain
her mouth is to talk of her experiences
for sure she isn't a failure
I was there watching her lay in a bed still as could be
I was there for her when her eyes opened
I was with my family when we celebrated your joy
I am there for her when she needs a shoulder to cry on
I now realize that how much she really means for me
I could have lost her in the crash
now I know how much life really means
I think everyone should cherish life as my whole family does
So I write this to tell her how much she really means to me
because I'm not so good with words.

Andrea Witkowski

The Death Of A Good Man

When a good man dies, his friends and others mourn.
Why do these people mourn?
The loss of a good friend, a loving uncle, a dear brother,
an honest man.
People feel lost without their leader, wandering around in disorder
losing track of what they are doing, and forgetting what they want.
The death of a good man should not make people mourn in depression,
but make the people glad to have known him.
The people should try to imagine what life would be like
if they would have never have met him.
The death of a good man makes the world a better place,
the facts and common knowledge that he has passed on
to his children will never die.
The good man makes the world a better place just because he lived.

Crystal Gail Ritenour

Reality

Dream, dream, dream a little dream
Why is life never as it seems
Fighting, hatred, cruelty and more
Some say without any of this life would be a bore
But those are the ones,the ones who don't see
That no one is happy, and this is reality
We turn to violence and away from love
It's as if we don't care about ourselves or our God up above

This is mine and that is yours
The hell with you and we shut the doors
You are white and I am black
But does this give our hearts the right to attack?
I bleed red and so do you
Why can't we unite as one instead of dividing as two
Peace is our goal and should be reached
In our schools, it's imperative that we teach
Unity of love and that we should see
That we are all the same and this is reality
If we succeed then all will be supreme
But if we fall this prayer will be nothing but a dream.

Andrea Littlejohn

Whatever You Want

In America
You can go where you want to go
You can be what you want to be
And you can believe what you want to believe
Anything is possible
Just believe in yourself
And ignore the critics.

John Doherty

Untitled

What is death, what is love?
Why is there death, why is there love?
What the heck is a turtle dove?
Why do we cry, why do we giggle?
Why does Santa's belly jiggle?
What is a smile, what is a frown?
Why is the world round?
What is round, what is square?
Why is there land, why is there air?
Why is the sky blue, why is the grass green?
Why be nice, why be mean?
What is emotion, why do we care?
What is here, what is there?
One questions leads to another...
Why does one question lead to another?

Heather Geiger

Michelangelo

Look at the grey whiteness, coarse as David before he was made.
Why must I work miracles with rainbows
   when my heart is in stone?
Why create what God has already done for the glory of men?
I should be with my tomb where my life is rekindled:
   A chisel should be in my hand
   cutting and shaping my dream.

I am not a brushmaster covering mistakes
   on cracking plaster.
The frailness of paint is no match for the strength in my hands.
The tool in my fist gives life to marble—while this wall
   with blank expression mocks my worth.

The gouge shows my strength; forcing rock into
   power and grace.
But a brush is an extension of the hand,
   just another finger.
What power could be found
   in the extension of a finger.

James M. Myers

Elixir

I can taste you
   wild mulberries in summer
   full, and heady, with new seeds to catch on my tongue.

I could live on mulberries
   small, always-bursts of elixir
   sweet, and ripe, with fresh seeds in store to renew.

And each old tree grows wilder in the fall
   intricate tracings of wood against sky.

The old trees renew
   with knees and elbows more crooked
   but the juice ... sweeter than before.

I could live on these
   The taste of you
    and wild mulberries
    in winter.

Billie S. Noakes

Today A Child Dies

A battered child huddles in a lonely corner
Wild thoughts dance through his aching head
This time he really thought he was a goner
Every time he wonders if he'll live or when it's over he'll be dead

To often this little child cries a silent tear
All his little body knows is fear
He often wishes for the night, for his days are much too long
His little mind hurts, trying to figure what he has done wrong

He is usually weak and very frail
He cries for help, to no avail
Why does the person who is supposed to love him
Want to abuse and to always hurt him?

Today he'll cry no more...
For today they carried him out the door
His little body found in a pool of blood
All that remains of this child, is a stain on the rug.......

Carolyn Stafford

I Miss You

Our memories of love.
Will be with us forever
Your smile will always be,
With in our hearts, we miss you.

We think of you as living.
In the hearts of those you touched.
For nothing loved is ever lost.
And you are loved so much.

Loving and kind in all her ways.
Upright and certified, to the end of her days.
Sincere and true in her heart and mind.
Beautiful memories as she left us to remind.

Though we can no longer see you.
We still feel your love in our hearts.
It will always be there.
And will never leave.

Thinking of you is so easy.
We do it every day.
Missing you is a heartache.
That never goes away.

Evelyn T. Tallman

A Rose In Sweet Repose!

'Twas all bruised and torn this young heart of a lass,
"Will it ever heal?" onlookers would ask.
A heart too sick, with naught left, not even a sigh,
Listless, and hopeless, she felt she would die.
So much hurt, and how old the anger,
Releasing its grip like an armed ranger
Raiding and pillaging as it moves on out.
Spewing resentment and bitterness all about.
'Till there were no more words that could be spoken,
Naught is left of this sore heart, it lies shattered and broken

What was needed was a skilful hand,
One of a Master who had it all planned
To reshape the old heart; yet make it anew.
A gift afforded to many, accepted only by a few.
So the Master Potter, like clay on his wheel,
Shaped her young broken heart, and allowed her to feel
That once again she could love; and be loved.
For things are not always as one would suppose!
For out of the wounded heart with its scars,
Came forth in time and with beauty; the most precious red rose.

Joy Walker

"Is Today Your Magic?"

Awakening our spirit to everyday life—
Will today bring promise of new?
Will today follow yesterday's path somehow—
Did experience bring difference to view?

Do reflections of past open you the way—
Remembering proud the names on your list?
Have dreams in your heart shown your guidance by chance—
Or did reality shake you its fist?

What desires do you behold in life—
Are they love of family and friends?
Or today's inspiration for tomorrow's reward—
Where happiness begins and ends.

What does today hold for you my friend—
Is life's magic not part of your plan?
For we all are heroes with something to share—

His Gift Of Magic In Every Man!....
Gina Stewart

The Reward Of A Christian Mother

A mother who tread the Christian path
Will travel the way Christ feet have trod
Walking by faith without complaining
Striving to unfold the will of God.

When in the midst of tribulations
The wilderness experience we must bear.
With wonderful thoughts and deep consolation
Is knowing God has placed us there.

Lord with our lips we confess our needs.
Peace is not found in words or deeds
But only in Christ each day and each hour
Being hidden in Him, will bring forth His power.

While others seek pleasures of this world
Man's glory, riches and fame
A mother who seek to follow Jesus
Will behold the glory of His precious name.

Mothers shall reap who sow in tears
The harvest brings joy, and strength from above
Rich blessings through eternal years
Reveals the nature of the Master's love.
Annie Lou Brown

Reflections In The Desert

Remembering a I walked through those
windswept valleys of the California Desert

I'm filled with confidence and trust
It remedies my neglect of His love for us

The grander of Gods creation
engulfs my mind in a whirlpool of emotions

Swirling and swooning me
to a point of spiritual correlation

Breathless wonders of unknown sources
Those who know, from creative forces

His gift of Love, for us to see
Reflections of his love for me

My emptiness is filled, my heart is warmed
The quiet of the desert, like the eye of a storm

Barriers are broken, the mind absorbs
Words unspoken, my memory stores.
David Waggener

A Special Person

Kyle Petty is your name.
Winston Cup racing is your game.
On Sunday, round and round you go.
With thousands of fans watching, as you know.

We jump and shout
And yell and scream.
Winning the race is our theme.

But #1
or last place finish,
Our pride in you will not diminish.

And when the race is over.
And we must leave the track.
You can bet your bottom dollar.
That next Sunday we'll be back.

And once more we'll be smiling and ready.
to cheer for our hero, Kyle Petty.
Judith E. Lucas

Leaving

Autumn leaves huddle at my doorstep
Winter's last wind leaving them behind
Brown faces warming in the April sun
Crinkled hands reach up, begging me
    to restore their supple beauty
Holding them I touch the spirit within me
They can't understand why my tears falling upon them
    like the gentle rain of spring past
Do not bring them back to life
Bitter monument to when love is not enough

Memories of you nestle at my heart
Unrelenting time binds them there
The music of your voice still warming me
Silken hands reach into my soul
    to fasten your bonds of pain
Holding them I sense the feelings within you
I can't understand why my tears falling upon you
    like silent answers to your uncertainties
Do not bring you back to me
Sodden shrine to when "I love you" is not enough
Gregory Radabaugh

Falling

Soaring above the clouds
    with a cool mist flowing through my wings.

The fluent blue sky is illuminated
    by the rising sun in the eastern sky.

Perching on a ledge of a tall mountain
    to clean the dust from my feathers.

The rock ledge gives way and
    the sudden shock perplexes my body.

Faster and faster I descend
    the world flashing before eyes of fright.

My wings expand to capture the wind and a fall
    reaches a glide; the ground is within a breaths leap.

Up and up I go until distance
    from the earth is at its top.

The thought of the fall stands implanted in my
    mind and reminds my thoughts of the loss of flight.
Dwight L. Hostetter II

The Big Game

We have to compare the "Game of Life,"
With a game of "Basketball;"
There's a Court, a Ref., and Goals,
A coach, Assistant Coach, and Player's all.

The Court is our (known World),
A somewhat larger size;
Coach and referee, is "Our Lord,"
Who, made the rules for our live's.

Asst. Coach, is "Jesus Christ,"
Who made the world and all within;
He loves each and everyone, so much,
That, he died for all our sins.

Our, "Instruction book from God,"
Makes the rules for us each day;
But if, we break the rules,
We have a penalty to pay.

As we live from day to day,
Our goals aren't all the same;
But if we put our "Trust in God,"
We are sure to win the Game!

John W. Harper

Open Bedroom Windows At Night

I remember open bedroom windows at night
with breezes softly blowing through them.

How peaceful and cozy warm was sleep by
open bedroom windows at night.

No tenseness, no clenched jaw, no stress with
open bedroom windows at night.

My windows now are closed, barred, alarmed and
Shaded shut, how I miss open bedroom windows
at night.

June Stephenson

My First Born

Oh, what a beautiful bundle of joy to behold
with eyes of blue and hair of gold;
You filled my heart with happiness and love
and I thanked God for you from above.
Your tiny fingers filled my heart with happiness
at your touch.
Then and there I fell in love with you so much!
I prayed that God will guide me to take care of
you the way I should.
So I tried the best way that I could;
Since you've grown through the years
living with disappointment and tears.
I pray that sunnier days will be ahead in the
future for you.
I love you, my first born with all my heart
and think about you always even though we're
so far apart!

Betty Vargo

Writer

I've often seen the death-like 3:18
With eyes that swell and droop but never blear:
Glad consequence of crazed thoughts and caffeine,
That realm where words carve souls - dreadnought from fear.

I wander iceblack halls a wraith undead,
Familiar crypts, cold touch of 3:18,
'With nothin' but bare feet an' faith,' Twain said.
My fingers cramp and knot, throttle my pen.

Sharp stark blue of some vast lunar terrain,
electron microscope's weird negatives
Superimpose the phantasts, my domain.
The frozen hand may send; it never gives.

Friend! Providential globe! Dispel the night!
Discerning, I will close my eyes and write.

Etheljean Deal

A Tribute To Mom And Dad

They started off as children
With innocence in their eyes.
Royce was only twelve years old
Mae was only five.

Royce worked for Mae's father
In the fields where crops grew.
As Mae began to get a little older
She worked the fields there too.

Royce and Mae fell in love
As a teenager and a young man
Royce was twenty-three - Mae, sweet sixteen.
Happily married July 13th 1940 - it all began.

Through trials and tribulations
Hard times, tears, and laughter
Come eleven beautiful children.
Whom to this day; they still look after.

A lifetime of memories have come and gone.
This tribute is to Royce and Mae.
Happy 50th- from all of us. To Mom and Dad.

Earlene Eskue Jones

Happily Ever After?

Remember all our childhood fairy tales,
With knights in shining armor always near,
And weddings that united two in love?
Was "happily ever after" ever over?

And did they ever really fall in love,
Or was it just a trick played on their minds?
Did they know in advance how it would end,
Or were they victims of an authors plan?

Did they know in whose hands their futures lay,
And were they ever masters of their fates?
A love that's true is something hard to say,
So was it ever found inside their hearts?

Though we will never know the stories' end,
'Tis best to dream of all that might have been.

Andrea S. Adams

Our Lynda

Once we had a daughter fair
With laughing eyes and dark brown hair
And in our home or in a crowd
Her presence made us very proud

How quickly girlhood days have flown
How soon our little girl has grown,
And now the miles 'tween us and you
Seem further still when words are few

Daughter pick up pen and pad
And write a line to Mom and Dad,
We long to know you are well
And happy where you choose to dwell

With passing years youth's sparkle may wane
But memories so precious will always remain
Tho' your eyes may grow dim and your hair lose its curl,
You will now and forever be our little girl.
   Love Dad and Mom
    Clarence Baker

The Child Within

I listen to the children
with laughter all around me,
Their love and devotions is just astounding,
No wonder it is said
"As a child you should be"
Full of life and wonder and totally free
So protect our little ones
Don't let the laughter die
They teach us so much
With the age old question why?
It makes us stop
And think about life
Why is the sky blue?
And the birds take flight?
Take time each day.
To be the child within
Learn to love life
As each day begins
Love touch, grow and be
Be as a child so totally free
    Joanne E. Petersen

Hearts And Minds

What a wondrous thing our hearts are, they're filled
with love at birth. Our love for all goes near and far,
encompasses the earth.
But minds are just a blank at first, we live by what we feel.
The world has not upon us burst, love's all we know as real.
Cynical minds come into play, to stifle what we feel.
"Ignore your heart", is what they say, our love they try to steal.
The world they rule in such a way, there's no room left for love.
"Hate all things different", they say, forget the Lord above.
They rule with fear, and hate, and lies, crush all our hearts with wit.
This world God does not recognize, what has man done to it?
But see how it is beating still, just underneath our breast!
It must be the Almighty's will, for man's been always blest.
Let hearts arise and fill the earth, with love for everyone.
Back to the way we were at birth, let's emulate His Son!
    Dona Booker

Lover

I don't want to be here far away is where my mind lies
with my soul in a dream world you call to me
and I answer with my heart
and not my tongue
somewhere we connect and never separate like twins
who died at birth their souls never apart

But you are connected to your brother
while I try to connect with you
I don't understand why him and not me I love you
like no man ever could
because were supposed to be together
me and you forget him God why can't you change
and be one that I need not one that he needs

So here I am alone with myself and
so far away from you even though you are where I want to be
I think of you and what you used to be to me
what are you to him what is he to you
do you speak to him with your heart
or your tongue…
lover
    Andrea Larson

Lost Love

I stood alone beside a tree
  With only thoughts of you and me
I thought of life without your love
  And prayed for help from God above
Memories flooded into view
  Sometime, somewhere, just me and you
Your smiling face I'll never see
  Nor special look you gave to me
Your loving arms no more are there
  Can't kiss your lips or touch your hair
A life alone with hurt and pain
  For you are gone and I remain
Your love and life I could not save
  Now all alone I leave your grave.
    Bonnie Waldburger

Homesick

  Blue sky above me, filled
with puffy white cotton.
Swirling about beautiful,
brings memories.
Hot, sticky tears-they miss
their home, drop to my chin.
The sun cooks, its rays beating down on me,
A squirrels song, vigorous mourn.
Am lost, wondering, sick for my home.
Homesick.
Will it ever be home?
Wondering, wondering.
Will it ever be home?
Homesick.
    Erica Marie Rebich

Mercy

Mercy is an act of kindness
With someone we have power over.
Another name for mercy is compassion.
Good people throw mercy around, unconditionally
like precious gifts,
like dew on summer grass,
like rain on dry parched earth.

Mercy could go hand in hand with wealth, with power
Indeed, the rich could show mercy
by sharing part of their wealth with the poor,
by helping someone who is sick and dying
or simply by giving to the needy.

Likewise the corporate manager could show mercy
by retaining the worker he is planning to fire
in order to save money,
and at the tribunal, the judge could show mercy
by pardoning the offender.

Let's be merciful. When we show mercy,
God Almighty blesses us. Jesus said:
"Bless are they who show mercy: mercy shall be theirs."

Graciela Hernandez-Amaya

"The Unknown Child"

Walking through the forest alone,
with the moon hung so bright,
I hear a child's cry of fear in the night.
As she sits on a log with her feet bare,
feeling no more care, listening to the wind blow,
she has a sense of glow , her face and hands are cut and bloody,
while her feet are blistered and muddy.

She who cries but hears no replies. She is our fear, she is our shame,
She is our rain, she is us when we are sane.
She is every soul, and every bleeding heart,
our guiding delight, revealing heaven's light.

Holding back her tears with all her might,
she disappears like a wandering soul through the night.

Bobbie Flores

Silver-White Dunes

Lovely dunes of silvery-white sand,
  with waving sea oats like beckoning hands;
Calling me over to the other side,
  to view the splendor of the ocean's tide.

Inviting waters of a lovely blue-green,
  white-crested waves crowned like a queen.
With the waves rolling swiftly upon the shore,
  sweeping the seashells into its waters once more.

Shimmering sugar-white sands on the beach
  cooled by the salt spray and gentle breeze.
Seagulls circling in the sky,
  "Welcome! Welcome!" hear them cry.
What a beautiful place waiting for you.
  hidden behind the silver-white dunes.

Ethel M. Lord

My Special Friend

You've enhanced my life in a thousand ways,
With your gentle strength and quiet praise.
Through the stress and strain when the tears did fall,
My friend, my friend, you gave it all.
You encircled me with your warmth when I felt so cold,
And brought music and laughter back to my soul.

As the days go by and turn into years,
I'll realize even more how you calmed my fears.
And when time is no more and we have to part,
Lucky me, lucky me, you will stay in my heart.

Dawn Welch

Dear Grandma

Were you really as wonderful as I recall,
With your hair pulled back in a bun,
If I had to choose the love of my life,
You'd certainly be the one.

Were you really as wonderful as I recall,
With your eyes so sparkling and blue,
And your weathered hands so soft and warm,
And gentle as morning dew.

I wonder as I think back today
And the tears of longing flow,
If you'd love me as much as you did then,
Those years so long ago.

So Grandma if you can hear me,
I just wanted to let you know,
My love for you is still the same,
As those years so long ago.

Donna BacKous

Listen

Look at me with your eyes closed, hear what I have to say
with your heart. I am a child of God, beautiful in my own way.

Touch me with your eyes closed what do you feel? my skin
Can you tell who I am? no

Hear me with your eyes closed what do you hear? my voice
Can you tell who I am? no

Look at me with your eyes closed, hear what I have to say
with your heart.

I am a child of God,
Beautiful just like you.

Antoinette M. Rose

Sonnet Of The Seafood

Oh fishy fooshy Mr. Sushi swims
Within a box of glass he waits to die
And on a grim limb fishy's future's dim
'Cause he'll be served on rye or in stir fry

I feel for fishy for his fate's specific
He's freed to feed some yuppie and his boss
He'll never see a stream or the Pacific
'Cause now he's raw on rice beside soy sauce

His loss of life plus tax is worth ten bucks
That's what the yuppie in a minute earns
Grew up to be a chewed-up ball of muck
I hope you give the yuppie's boss heartburn!

You're dead at two weeks old/the chef's a crook
You're worth your weight in gold when you're not cooked.

Eric San

A Mother's Wish

Oh, to have you back again
Within my house once more- and make this lonely place
A home-as in the days of yore.
I use to think I couldn't stand
The noise and all the fuss, but I would give a lot to have
The house are cluttered up.
To see their toys scattered all about
And their laughter ringing clear,
It seems I had them such a little while-
How swiftly passed the years!
My house is all in order now-
Not a thing is out of place,
But the loneliness which is in it I just can't seem to take-
So to you who want the grandeur of a home so neatly kept
Without the sounds of children's feet
Treading upon your steps-
I only pray you'll never know
The pleasures that you've missed,
For a house can never be home
Without the touch off a child's sweet kiss.

Betty Chandler

The Flower In The Closet

I find myself sitting alone
without a clue of what I call home

I wish I could see somewhere I could be
And not be afraid of what I can be

Not to be afraid not to be scared
about what I'm becoming that makes me scared

Without any day without any night
I find myself defenseless without any sight

What is waiting I will not know
How can I make it if I can not grow

Christina Lynn Maria Stawecki

Tragedy Of The War Couples

The rain hit the roof like soldiers fighting steel.
Women mourn in sorrow for their dead husbands of war.
The defeat put life on a temporary halt. Survival was much to take
in. They felt guilt, wanting to be the dead one, not their husbands.
Wanting to stop it all. They had lives to live, and must find the
path to take them home. Let sorrow be defeated, and let happiness
flourish there on. For life is too short to let the living die with
the dead. Live freely above the rest.

Soldiers went to war saying "Hello" that day, and came home in
the ground saying "Goodbye to yesterday." The women survived
and still live today, to tell about their truly great husbands
that fought for our country
The U.S.A.

Carrie Diegel

'Headaches'

I've been suffering from headaches everyday for the past four years
With pounding so loud, some days I'm just in tears
Don't know why I have them, or how much longer they will stay
I just hope and pray that someday soon they will go away
Been to Dr. after Dr. describing the pounding sound
They just prescribed drugs, but more seemed to lessen the pound
Then I had an MRI and a CT scan of my brain
Both tests came back normal, perhaps I'm just insane
Even tried acupuncture for it was recommended by a friend
But even as my last resort, it didn't put my headaches to an end
I guess all I can do now is to just grin and bear
And hopefully in my future, they won't be there...

Heidi Nyhus

Truth Is...

Sometimes I wonder,
Wonder why there is so much disaster,
Wonder why God does this to us
Truth is we do it ourselves
Sometimes I wonder.
Wonder what it would be like in the future?
Wonder why I can't see the future, and
wonder if I would like what I'd see?
Truth is only God can see.
Sometimes I wonder
Wonder what it would have been like if there was no life.
Wonder if it would be as black as the
Black Hole
Truth is we have life
Thank God!

Alison Rowland

Why?

Your death has left me stricken with sorrow,
wondering how I can face tomorrow.
Around you, you knew my small world revolved.
Why you left is a mystery unsolved.

Why did you have to go out that bleak night?
Was the stormy night the cause of your plight?
Or was it the driver that hit your car?
The driver too drunk to go very far?

The tears I cry I know won't bring you back,
but without you here, happiness I lack.
I know you were called to a greater class,
to a place this world can not surpass.

There's hope that we aren't forever apart,
for I know you'll always be in my heart.

Jamie West

Wondering What Went Wrong

Here we are again,
wondering what went wrong
was there ever a time
when we said "I love you"?
A time when we held hands
while looking into each others eyes
A time when we kissed
Passionate, all night long
A time when we made love
Thinking "I want to spend the rest of my life with you"
Now we're wondering what went wrong
Was it the time drifting us apart?
Or was it the differences within us?
Or could it be that we were just not meant to be?
What ever it is, it really hurts
deep in the heart.
Deep down inside I know I love you
Now and forever, no matter what.

Jacqueline Manzo

The Perfect Setting

The perfect setting
would have to have
the bright, warm, glowing sun,
with its yellows, oranges, and reds
reflecting
in the nice, cold water of a lake,
a lush pasture of tall, dark, green grass,
and finally,
someone to see it.

Joshua Boss

The Pianist

The pianist weaves music throughout our souls
Wondrous melodies that impale chords in our hearts
Releasing floods of memories from the past
When times were simple with no pain from the start.

Melodies flowing across our minds like rippling waters
Roaring and tumbling over rocks and falls rushing to arrive
Then quietly an eddy carries us to a secluded spot
A peaceful and serene haven in which to survive.

Musical notes floating into the windows of our desires
Cascading hither and yon gathering the hurt and sorrow
Leaving rays of hope and dreams of the future
Weaving promises of a better tomorrow.

So play on the magical sounds so wondrous
Waves that beckon our souls to heed the delight
Ensnare us with crescendos of passions on fire
Mingled with the mystique of stars in the early light.

Softly melting into the melodies forgetting thyself
Gently flowing with the mood and believing the dream
Finding harmony with oneself is the golden thread
Binding Heaven and Earth in Life's Grand Scheme.

Betty Steed

Untitled

i hold my words tight in my fists -
words that i never let seep out just anywhere.

words can be powerful things.
strong.
but even if mine aren't strong -
who can afford to have their precious words
leaking out all over.
i won't have my hands be busted pipes.
i won't have my words be water.

i just hoard my words
maybe till that eleventh hour.
i keep them on the inside of my fingers -
like a trump card
saved to the last.

like a purple rock
found among grey stones
something you cherish.
something you just don't let go of.

Brooke Leston

Why Do Babies Cry?

I've been waiting forever to see the
world and when I finally open my eyes it is
dark. But soon I can see the wonderful world
everyone talks of. Finally, finally, my turn has
come to meet the world. So many places to go,
nice people to see, it is more than anyone could
ask for they say. With a smile on my face I take
my first glance and I see gangs, guns, blood, smog,
drugs, disease, racism, and hate. My smile turns to
a frown and I cry.

Andrea Smith

Mother And Daughter

You care for me, love me
Would never leave me, or even fly above me.
You've held me close, you've held my hand.
You even explained when I didn't understand
But we also have our times
I have to get yelled at for committing those crimes
Yes we scream and fight
and I pray that you'll be there in the morning,
each and every night.
For we are Mother and Daughter
The unseparate pair
And if you left me, to be alone,
I simply couldn't bare
For we are Mother and Daughter
And to be without you
just wouldn't be fair.

Andrea Perez

Dark Silhouette

Thy kiss of death, for some say they,
Would yield the blackest vision's ray,
For mere robed figure, standing in silhouette,
Shall behead thy mind, to bring all death,

So hear those mere voices, whispering,
Behind thy ear, to speak of sin,
Terrify like a child at loss,
Frightened mind, hurt to accost,

To feel thy sun, leave them not,
With thyst accusing tones, burning hot,
Thy dark side of self, be merely this,
Thy voices of shroud, in burning mist,

Doth thy feel thy sting of emotion gone?
Thy faint echo like thy saddened song,
Thy faintest hint of sanity,
For children lost, shan't ever be,

For we have lost thy innocence,
That yields to other children rest,
Wearied from thy journey long,
Forevermore, thy endless song...

Cristine M. Halde

Bitter Memories

Gone are the days when my heart was young and gay.
Yea! That old song brings back memories that I'd forgotten.
Maybe some memories best left to fade away and die.
Sometimes I wish I could turn back the clock to start my life over and
not be so frightened.
To do the things I dreamed to do.
To learn not to be painfully shy.
To follow my dreams and fall in love too.
My heart has grown old, I'm too tired to dance
As to falling in love with another.
My goodness! I don't even have a chance.
I guess life can sure be a bummer.

Dorothy Cain

Yellow

Yellow is mellow.
Yellow are the stripes on a cat,
of a baseball bat,
the color of a Palomino pony
the straw put freshly down in a stall.
Yellow is honey
Yellow is funny,
Yellow is bread when it comes out of the toaster.
Yellow are the leaves on a tree,
Yellow can be anything you want it to be,
and the choice is free.

Helen Gersbach

The Hunter

Out in the woods amongst the trees, I'm a hunter,
yes that's me. Secure in my blind, the wind in my
hair, it's cold and raining, but what do I care?

Waiting for hours, the day growing long, I'm getting
impatient, yet remaining strong. All of a sudden I
hear a sound, not moving a muscle, while glancing
around.

Out in the distance some antlers appear. I raise my
rifle, through the scope I peer. I'm getting excited,
my heart's pumping fast. Looks like I'll take a buck,
finally at last.

My finger on the trigger, waiting to take the shot.
Come on baby, ready or not! The gun exploded with a
mighty blast, hitting the buck right in the ass.

He tried to run, then stumbled, and fell. Only a six
point,"Oh what the hell."

Out in the woods, I'm happy and free. Because I'm a
hunter, yes, that's me.

Jennifer Shimoura

Where Lies The Truth?

Lips may flatter; lips deceive
Yes, what a tangled web they weave
When silver tongues dress sunday best,
And lift their masters O'er the rest.

Though words be earnest, pleading clear,
You can't be sure the truth you'll hear.
Yes, words confuse, they snare, they cheat.
They flatter, use, are sickening sweet.

Behind these lips who seek man's praise,
The same whose words to God they raise,
Lies the human mind where all thoughts play,
But still the truth it may not say.

You cannot see, but lies the truth
Neath mind and lips words slick & smooth.
You'll find from the heart all actions spring,
And from these deeds the truth will ring.

And even then to be so sure,
You'd have to see behind closed doors.
For many acts of good are raised,
To only bring about man's praise.

Cathi Goff

Death Of A Dream

Tear at my heart, pull at my tears
Yet I can never be hurt too much,
I have struck out too many times,
To let you out of my touch.

How do I manage to say everything wrong,
What is so different about me?
The burning pit of despair that has engulfed my heart,
Makes me sick, so let me be.

Do I have to be your friend,
Will I ever find love?
Who I am asking, no one hears
my pleas for my little white dove.

Please comfort me,
Help me out of this awkward mess,
Forget, move on, forget
Don't be devoured by the insane stress.

I hate myself for the pain I feel
Can't I control myself?
I can and will cover these feelings,
Pain has made me King of Stealth.

Adam Linett

Logic Or Magic?

I love you for leading me on.
Yet I hate you for not wanting to let me down.
I love you for getting my hopes up.
But I hate you for not wanting to see me frown.
It's my fault that I feel this way.
It's your fault that I care.
It's my fault that I cried today.
It's your fault for seeing it come and trying
to hold it back for me.
I love you for making me get so sprung.
I hate you because you're my friend.
I love you for all the feelings you've brought.
I hate you because you couldn't help it.
I hate you for being so nice to me.
If you weren't, I think I could stand it.
I hate you for not making me want to hate you.
I love you because you hurt me.
I hate you because I can't.

Candace Moore

Today

By all means, I am far from ready, yet.
Yet, they all are saying. "The end is near."
Famine, pestilence, and the false prophets
Could it be, that these are signs I should fear?

Nobody knows the exact day or hour.
When lightning will flash from east to west.
Have I done for the least of my brother?
If not now, would I pass the final test?

Eternal life, eternal punishment.
Separated in two, by the Divine.
Earthquakes and diseases are more frequent
Is it possible, that this is a sign?

It is quite foolish, to wait for the signs,
Because there is something else I don't know
Is this day or hour, the end of my time?
I've missed out on Heaven, if this is so.

Today I must be ready and prepared.
Today I must love and care for my brother.
I will never know when my time is near.
And I do yearn to live with my Father.

Darlene Rinaldi

Child Of Mine

Complete is me with you, you make me whole
You are deep within my soul
Sometime's life seems hard to take
Then you'll roll over as you wake
You smile and say, "morning mama"
Giving me a kiss
I then realize how fortunate I am to have you
You are more beautiful than I thought possible
I sometimes think I am not worthy of you
For you deserve more than I can give
I believe you have taught me more about life
than I have taught you so far
You have shown me unconditional love
and you trust me with all of your heart
Through your eyes I see beauty in the world and
I have hope now
Hope that good still exists on this earth
Your innocence touches me in a special way
A way that lets me know that people can be touched
by a child such as you, you make me smile everyday

Angela Blount

I Am Your Stranger

I wish I was a stranger, then leaving
   you behind
would be such the easy task,
   oh self,
such a foolish me,
   be.
   Beginning, born, died
      and cried,
he is going to leave us here, oh
   man , I can feel it, I
know that I love you stranger, I admit it, I am proud,
my pride, ride, my bride! Marriage.
   Feed me on your morsel'd mouth,
   touch me with your dew'd breath,
   read me in your confused mind,
   dictate to me religion stranger,
for I have come with none, in this goodbye.
   Tell me
   you are my favorite stranger.

Jeff A. Zyjeski

A Sound In The Distance

Off in the distance and far away;
You can hear the sound of children at play.
You can hear them laughing and yelling a lot;
Listen to the sound of each little tot.

Listen to them far away;
I wonder what they will say.
Perhaps another day;
They will come to play.

I can see them, off in the distance;
And I wonder how long, they will be in existence.
See them running and playing;
I wonder how much longer, they will be staying.

Judith Fietzer

I Love You

The words I love you mean nothing to me.
You can say I love you to a tree.
You can say I love you to a child,
And be lying all the while.
I love you is more than just words,
like flying pertains to more than just birds.
You think you love someone, the change your, mind.
It really wasn't love, you were just blind.
I love you is a feeling, not an expression.
I love you is a forever, unlike an obsession.
Trees and flowers blossom and grow.
When you're in love, I think you will know.

Jaime Hochhausen

That Day

That day
You entered my life anew
And blotted out memories
Twenty years gone.
Your eye's luminous light
Lit up my universe again.
Bogus bravado obscured deeply
Buried wounds toiling to surface.

Fingers locked, lips touched, lingered,
Triggering silent warnings my heart hushed.
In a moment of erotic madness.
The pain of loving you took flight, gone.
Naked spirit exposed.

With a jolt, rigid reality burst forth.
You're focused: fun-filled epicurean.
Your center emerged: plump passionate ego.
No place for me.
We part again, forever,
That day.

Estelle Thomas

Although I Feel, I Cannot See

I met you at the docks one day,
   You gave me a hug and began to say,
"I've been waiting for you, for seventeen years,
   I'm glad you've come." And I was in tears.

We prayed and I confessed my sins,
   You forgave me and proclaimed, "Our journey begins!"
Then you said, with a smile, "We're off to see,
   God, my father, who's across the sea."

Your all-knowing hand guides our way,
   Through calm and stormy waters day by day.
Although I feel, I cannot see,
   Your caring face that calms this sea.

You say that many will stay on the land,
   They just say, "No," when you reach out your hand.
And there'll be people along our way,
   Some will leave, but a few will stay.

You're preparing my soul for that hour,
   When I see your father, in all his power.
Although I feel, I cannot see,
   Your loving face that prepares me.

Aaron Gluck

Lady Liberty

My dear Lady:
You have fulfilled the dreams of great multitudes
Your torch has been the guide and also a light on high
to bring hopes, wishes and happiness
to so many immigrants from other latitudes.
I wish to sing to you about my feeling in this centenary.
My emotions are not only ours but also belong to France
who idealized your beautiful face as she forged your statue.
France gave America your majestic sculpture
that has now renewed.
The whole world has rejoiced over the patriotic homage,
which has raised as if it were possible - your name even higher.
I admire you Grand Lady -
and should like to tell you in a few words
of the admiration that I feel to be overflowing in my soul
And also, my beautiful dame that a ray from your torch
will awaken my country from its horrible dream
and we all   humble or wealthy will remember only the words:
That Liberty and Democracy
shall reign forever under all the stars.

Georgina Serrano

The Path Of Life

You just can't walk down the path of life.
You just can't relax down the path of life.
You have to run sometimes when you're on the path of life.
You just can't be happy on the path of life.
You have to be sad sometimes on the path of life.
You just can't be rich on the path of life.
You have to be poor sometimes on the path of life.
You just can't be healthy on the path of life.
You have to be sick sometimes on the path of life.
So don't fall into the saying that life is a bed of roses,
or you will stuck by the thorns.

Jeffrey St. John

Mr. Scare-Crow

Howdy, Mr. Scare-crow, how are you this fine day?
You look neat, in a funny sort of way.
Straw-hat tossed on your head, round and cute,
You're a real cool cat, in your too big suit.
Blue "jeans" faded, as can be,
Everything as it should be, seemed to me.
Corn silk hair, bright, bright yellow,
Handsome guy, you sweet, sweet fellow.
Baggy, baggy shirt, red, red tie,
Quite a sight you are, me, oh my.
Broom in right hand, to chase the crows away,
Do you reckon, they are away to stay?
Do your duty, come rain, sunshine bright,
I agree, you are a pure delight.
Glad to meet you, Mr. Scare-crow, Sir,
Laughter, gift of happiness you give everywhere.

Edith Mae Payne

A Tear Drop From My Heart

I left on a hot Summers day
you did not beg me to stay
nothing could be said or done
the truth was stated I was not the one
I felt the pain in my heart as I said good-bye
yet I could not let you see me cry
i wanted you to hold me so tight
for you to tell me everything is all right
instead I know it is time to part
then I felt a sharp pain in my chest as a
tear fell from my heart

Christine Noelle O'Rourke

First love II

As if the feelings would jump out and runaway
You look to find the answer and say...

Maybe it wasn't meant to be
Or maybe just not for you and me.

I need to know the way you feel
For 'til I do I'll hold time still.

Without you nothing would I be,
I wonder what you feel for me.

I know this in my heart is love,
And for it I thank the Lord above.

But if one day my dream should end,
I pray only that my heart would mend.

But if it will not, I'd pray to die,
Than live on earth with eternal cry.

Cassie M. Stanley

An Ode To Marriage

Fifty five years? It can't be true!!!
You love me? I love you?
These wonderful friends got the combination.
Let's just admit, it's a sensation.

We will drink a toast to that old breed,
Whose "I do" means we will succeed.
They'd be together through thick and thin.
That's when living just begins.

We watched them as they reminisced.
Telling of times that were not just bliss.
It was tough going, for quite a while.
They came through with a loving smile.

We are very proud to be their friend,
and hope to qualify and wish to send,
a message to this world we love,
This is our "Role Model" thank heaven above.

Hank Ring

Making Love To You

Making love to you completes my day,
You make all my dream's come true.
And if you would ever go away,
I'd go crazy without you.

There's no other that could take your place,
You mean every thing to me,
Yes you really make my poor heart race,
Please don't ever set me free.

My day's complete, when I'm with you,
And we spend the night alone.
Finding your love was such a treat,
For you're the sweetest love I've known.

Yes making love to you completes my day,
You make all my dream's come true.
And if you would ever go away,
I'd go crazy without you.

I guess my heart is just confessing,
That finding you was such a blessing.
And I found that dreams really do come true,
When I'm making love to you.

Charlotte Hoffman

The Love Lamp

Keep the love lamp burning little darling dear.
You make me so happy when you are near.
Will we ever part and say good-bye at last.
When it is time for loving we go slow not fast.
Oh how I love you dear with all my might.
You are so beautiful you're out of sight.
Playing in the park by day, we have so much fun.
You look so sexy in your swimsuit lying under the sun.
We love to eat some ice cream in the good ole summertime.
When the winter chill is in the air we break out homemade wine.
You make me so happy I love you so.
At a party you look the best and steal the show.
So much in love are we I know that you really care.
We love to drive around and go shopping here and there.
I know you will never leave me, I do not worry at all.
We were meant to be it is our Divine Call.
My love for you is like a baby's it is oh so dear.
Believe me when we go out you have absolutely nothing to fear.
On and on through the ages our love will go.
Like the rushing rivers our love will just flow and flow.

Gerald Szewczyk

The Legend

In a land that once was, in a land that will be,
You, Merlyn, you speak to me.
You told him to wait; you told him to watch;
But he didn't listen.
A Dragon in the mist. . .lust in the dark. . .
They search for the key to the Salvation.
. . .And a round table falls apart. . .
A child takes a sword, a child plays a game.
A boy becomes king...only the pure survives.
The Castle of Dreams, of silver and gold, and her.
Like so many betrayed and those who do the same:
She and the champion of silver and gold,
They bring the pain that brings the fall.
. . .And a round table falls apart. . .
Not even the sword can save them now.
His lust was too dark; her love was to cruel;
His depression to deep to escape.
And he and the land were one, and are. . .
. . .And a round table falls apart. . .

Jennifer Kay

The Race

"The sun chased the moon across the sky"
You once said to me.
Today I saw it happen, and thought of you!

Even though I tried,
I couldn't will the two to meet.
You are the moon and I am the sun;
Forever in this chasing race.

Oh! How my heart aches for you!
My tears come unexpectedly!
And although I cannot see your face,
You are there....somewhere.....

Do you think of me?
Do you cry for us?
Do you wonder what's become of me?

Donna Pittman

Untitled

Remember that secret pocket you had?
You opened it only when you were alone
To reveal your dreams and memories,
Do you still have that pocket?

Your secret pocket of dreams seems to be gone,
And the memories forgotten, forever,
You're a different person now.
What happened to that pocket?

Ever since he left our world
For a place beyond our reach,
We have all been searching for our pockets,
They're lost. Will they ever be found again?

Darcey Ferschweiler

Passion

You touch what no man can ever hold,
you reach the depths of my unconquerable soul.

How it knows no limitations in its search for sweeter
sensations.

Is it not that flame that feeds the heart of the fire?
You, a light in the dark; I desire.

Come partake of a tender kiss and know this...

Touch me and taste the blood as you drink from my red,
red lips. Drink slowly as fine wine to savor a sip.

Bitter sweet such is divinity better still the moment belongs
to infinity.

Lips stained, once white, now red with the battle wounds,
scared and hurt by love's game.

Still I invite you in just the same.

Come still unto me lest yea should
hinder...

Is it love or poison in which you surrender?

Julianna Weldy

Untitled

I see across the room everyday
  you walk towards me with passion in your eyes

Your smile comforts and holds me together
  your eyes are like pools of water gleaming in the sun
But the way you talk, act, and make me laugh
  Is why I wrote this poem today

You see I love you
  That passion in your eyes is in mine too

Life is wonderful
  you're my life

I walk for you
  I talk for you
I live for you

I'll die waiting for you
  please don't let me die

Colleen Kinney

Human Needs

See your mirages shimmer in the heat
You want all the things your dreams reveal
But So tied to a cultural command
People you are always in demand
You work and toil on machines and take an American Stand

I see vision clearly in the scorching desert sun
No mirage for me, I'm always on the run
So many times I've wondered if I could be like you
I'd have less than a world to conquer
Less than this war inside that carries on and on and on....

Needs are only human, there are those that have so few
The friends I have our needs don't end and would destroy you
An atomic thing within my soul is always about to explode
If a surgeon knew where to cut my brain I could be happy bored

Joel Weddington

Untitled

Damn you you black two-way ribbon to hell
You were created to carry life and yet you
beckon the frenzied with dashed and solid lines:
continual

The scenery to hell is uncontested—you mark that too
but I must come back to your hills and leave the
marked territory:
unexplored

The rest stops are well lit and patrolled by your
disciples—in color— to tell the paths, to invite:
destruction

Ahh——to go without your gentle beckoning lights
To move without your tolls and control signs
Let go and set me free from this velocity
and let me float above on unmarked paths.

Jennie Gross

"Emotions Of Love"

Have you ever loved somebody so much
You wish you could feel that breathtaking touch
Again and again you try to draw near
You soon pull away because of your fear?

Have you ever loved somebody so much
You feel they should give their love in a such
They tell you "I love you" and you feel the same
But you have to turn because you're in shame?

You're ashamed of the love you're hiding inside
Not wanting to let your heart open wide
You want to give love without feeling rejected
You want to give love without feeling neglected.

Well since I am writing this poem from my heart
I can actually say that I am feeling a part
Of the love that I am hiding inside
The love that is now bursting so wide

Do you even know what I am talking about?
Have you even figured it out?
O.k. fine, here is your clue
I can finally say that " I love you!"

Christina Morris

'Memories'

To recall those days of tender love.
Young Love - True Love - days gone by.
Then, as we ponder well each day -
Memories ne'er grow old - nor pass us by.

We feel down deep within our heart,
Those fleeting days of yesteryear,
As tho' it happened yesterday -
For 'twas then - tomorrows we had no fear.

As we look about for those we loved -
Or so we thought we had -
Then find that they have gone away,
To that land God made for good and bad.

We know that God sees differently -
Than us poor mortals do -
So each one scores their lives
In a manner to each is new.

So, as we settle in our chair,
Dreaming in a restless way -
We come awakened - not in fear,
But rather look into a brighter day.

Donald C. Riley

Haiti

In 1804, you became the first black independent country in the world
Your beautiful face has been destroyed
What have they done to you?
The world is ignoring you
America is treating you as an outcast, as an AIDS nation
What have they done to you?
The tonton macoutes, the army, the elites are killing your people
They are forcing them to flee
What have they done to you?
You have been a dictatorial country where no one has the right to
Voice his or her opinion. What have they done to the democracy?
What have they done to you?
My darling, my beautiful country, when will I be able to see you again
You are all that I have
What have they done to you?

Evelyne Auguste Philippe

You

I'll never forget your warm tender kiss,
Your beautiful smile, your soft sweet lips,
When they touched mine, my body began to excite
In my heart, I knew it was right.

Those muscular arms, which held me so tight.
Gave me the courage to make it through the night.
Your naked manly body, really turned me on.
And we made love till the crack of dawn.

Your strong firm grip when you took hold
Made my life worth more than gold.
In my hands I held your face
My heart would pound by your warm embrace.

Like a small infant, I fed you by breast
I held you close, like a baby at rest,
You said things I can't forget
The things we did I'll never regret.

A lot of memories of which I hold
Some of them I've never told.
All those years which I went through
All seemed worth it, when you said, "I LOVE YOU"!

Judi Miller-Firth

A Gift of Love

my black son, my fine, black child. i gaze with mother pride at
your blackness. i hold you close and allow myself to inhale your
strong earth scent; pulse jumping, lifeblood rushing, flowing under
satin smoothness.
joyful that you are here, humbled by such a precious gift..
this is how love feels.
you grow tall and strong. hungry to engage in the struggle,
you listen and watch the overt/subtle slurs,
the segregation, and homicide - the humiliation.
you learn and remember the pain, the taste of it bitter in
your mouth, the touch of it bruising and biting your
beautiful black skin, and i, seeing you cry and hurt and rage,
can offer only a temporal reprieve and, my own heart breaking,
i send you to fight again...this is how love lets go.
soon you will hold your own brown babies and
you will teach them just as you were taught.
you will love them deeply, fiercely, and
unconditionally, all the while quietly preparing
them for battle... this is how love endures.

denise duncan

Untitled

You're always on my mind,
you're definitely always kind.
I like to read your mind with
all your kindness in your heart.
Hello, it's me again, trying something new again.
Like writing something really exciting'
just wishing it makes me happy and joyfully mood fullness.
I'm always in darkness with you
and I can't keep my eyes off you.
Don't know If I can cope anymore.
I just don't know if you can too.
Hi and how are you. And I'm doing fine.
Glad to hear that voice of yours again.
Just to see that special person in my dreams
makes me come alive, and happy with all my might.
On the road again, thinking of you again,
just hoping and praying, you come home up
resting and playing with me. All day and night,
without a memory of working again.

Ellen Jaehnke

Inspired Desire

Your voice is as soft as the coo of a dove
your eyes can sparkle like the stars above
When you smile and look my way
It's the perfect end to a perfect day
Can I help you is what you say
And all I can think of is a roll in the hay
What if you accept this daydream of mine
What if you think it's only a line
If I could say that I love you
It would be a dream come true
Please don't take this poem to heart
Unless of course you want something to start

Gordon James Andrew

Under The Italian Skies You Reflect The Sun

Under the Italian skies, you reflect the sun.
Your face glows with a warmth
And your eyes with the joy of love renewed.
Since the sun is warm, my heart is warm too,
And if we don't touch, we still feel
The softness of our flesh, skin to skin in our mind's eye.
And the Italian Sea, so life giving
Soothes our senses with a quiet passion
That will linger through the languorous day.
But the music, whatever the tune
Sings: "Mi Amore" over and over
Into the twilight of the perfumed night.
And all the sight and smell of mountain,
Flower, plant, and sea, celebrate you.
As love descends like a gentle cloud
Surrounding all the Italian landscape,
We, hand in hand, head for a rendezvous
Between those mountains and that sea
To a place where only lovers may enter,
If only they have the key.

Bernard Hailperin

"What Did You Think About"

When the lights went out, what did you think about? Did
your mind began to wonder about the things you ignored in
the light.

Did you not see what was around thee, or was it, you just
let it go.

When the lights went out, what did you think about? Were
you afraid of what my happen and how you felt all along.

Was it difficult for you to see the light? The one you
didn't see before.

When the lights went out, what did you think about?

What made your feelings change?

Was it the darkness that gave you the time to think? Or
did the brightness of the light blind thee, where as you
could not see.

When the lights went out, what did you think about?

Did you get the chance to set your mind free?

Gia Verita Outlaw

Politically Correct

We have politicians on drugs
Your politically correct thugs
We got the white against the Black
Are we suppose to accept that?
We got spouses beaten spouses
In your upper class houses
We got guns and gangs
Will things ever change?
So we got different colors on our faces
And were born different races
Yet you and I are the same
From a mom and dad we both came
Don't say things are all right, then why do we fight?
Be it that your gay, fat, crippled,
old, weird, ugly or white
All I know is people are people
Yet we destroy and create so much evil
After you read this, what are you gonna do?
Are you gonna help me or say screw you?

Jessica Espinor

Mother's Smile

Mother, I saw your smile today,
Your reflection in me as I went on my way.
The mirror caught that sparkle and gleam,
It lasted a moment, so it would seem.

I miss your hand to dry away tears,
Words of encouragement to erase all my fears,
The look of worry when things go amiss,
The love and concern that come with a kiss.

But, now I'll be happy, perhaps sing a song,
God sent a message to carry along,
My mirrored image paused to pray,
For Mother, I saw your smile today.

Joan H. Kruse

Picture

My picture of you baby so soft and tender
Your skin is so sweet with the scent of yourself
Your little mouth shaping into a smile
Every time I make a face at you
But it will frown
If you are left unloved baby
But you are never left unloved
Your picture which I hold so dear to my heart
Is all I have of you now
You are at home with your parents
Being tickled and played with
I hold this picture in my hand
As though I were holding you softly and gently
So I will not hurt you
I smile at you because you are smiling at me
I want to kiss your face, I do
I feel the harsh, cold reality slap my cheek
This is only a picture
An image of something so loving and warm
Presented to me in a hard, cold package so unlike yourself.

Adaku L. Okpi

Untitled

No one could take away your heart
   your untamed heart
I realize that now as I sit here
   where you used to sit
Thinking of your beauty
   and your unnatural innocence
Your music your magical music
   fills the room as I play it
No longer does it chase away the
   rain as it did when you where here
Now the rain pounds inside my soul
   deeper and deeper i sigh
Knowing there is nothing now that can take it away.
   But deep down I can smile when
I remember the love you exchanged
   I was your only love, you were my only true love.
It was not fantasy it was real, very real
   As I sit here a funny thing passed through
My head you were right your heart no one ever took it away,
   you gave it to me - forever and into eternity

Jennifer Panella

First Grandchild

Time little one, come hold on tight.
You're going on a celestial flight.
There's going to be a lot to see.
People to meet, hills to climb.
You'll be all right, you'll do fine.

Well, you finally reached your destination.
And now for a few short introductions.
Here's your mother, she'll shape your mind.
This is your father, stern but kind.
Always do right, they'll do you fine.

These are your grandparents, fifty years young.
They're for overnight stays, stories and fun.
Rumor says, if Mom or Dad won't buy it for you,
Grandparents will usually come through.
They think it's their job, it's what they do.

Oh, my gosh! There's too much to remember.
Think I'll just lay here in slumber.
Wait! Could you please give us a smile,
For Grandma's brag book, you must be in style.
Welcome aboard little one. Love Grandma 1994

Jo Anna Boehmer Eisenbise

"Best Kept Promises"

Best kept promises are those that start in the heart;
Yours seemed to be destined to last from the start.

Whether you said "I do" or simply gave a nod;
You said it and meant it in the presence of God.

It was a promise you made with your lover and friend;
It is a promise you will keep till the very end.

You ceased to think in terms of me;
and replaced these words with things like we.

You started your promise as a couple, just two;
Now look at the lives that have been touched by you.

For all of the years you've been true to this vow;
We raise our glasses and toast you now.

Cynthia Wyman

You Don't Have To Tell Me You Love Me,

You've Already Let Me Know

You don't have to tell me you love me,
   You've already let me know
Even though you've never said it
You've let your feeling show
Once, we were together
In a world different from this.
It was told to us we would stay that way
And live in eternal bliss.
But then fate tore us apart
And made us lose each other
Never seen again
My love is lost forever...
But...
By some strange force I've found you
This time I'll never let you go
You don't have to tell me you love me
I found that out long ago.

Amy Brennan

"Why"

You've touched my heart and warmed my soul
You've made me laugh and cry.
You've given me everything I have
And I can't help but wonder why.

Why do you love me, with all my faults,
And believe in me so strong.
And stand beside me day after day
Even when I'm wrong.

Sometimes, why cannot be told.
Perhaps, just because, will do.
But it doesn't really matter what your reasons are
I know why I love you.

I love you for being my best friend,
For being honest and true.
For being there when I need you most
And cheering me up when I'm blue.

I don't really need a special day
To tell you how I feel.
I've loved you forever, with all my heart
And I know always will.

Johnny W. Jones

Imagination

If you look at things that make up your life,
A basketball, a house, a bike, a wife,
They look like things that they are not,
Just use your imagination a lot.

A water fountain can be a big water slide,
Going round and round down a mountainside,
Shining like a brand new spoon,
Then it ends with a splash into a great big lagoon.

Your spaghetti may look like a wormy,
If it was a worm then it would be squirmy,
It would slide in a hole,
Then it would fall back in your bowl.

When you look at a full moon,
It may look like the eye of a buffoon,
It could be a circle floating in the sky,
Then it sets going down by and by.

Now that my poem is said and done,
Will you please continue this rhyme for me hon?
Do it with some beat and some pizazz,
So you can enjoy the jazz that it has.

Ryan Black

Black Woman

A black woman that's who I am
A black woman who is not ashamed.
  Black, what a beautiful color.
A black woman that's who I am.

  Are you a black woman?
  If so are you ashamed?
Why black is just the color of your skin
I'm a black woman who is tired of being judged
Not by my knowledge, but by my color.

Why must you judge me? I'm the same person
As you are trying to make a living in this world.
  A black woman that's who I am.

Nicole Dampier

Somewhere Above The Clouds

Somewhere Above The Clouds
A beautiful home I see
Where there will be no more sorrow
And from these earthly troubles I will be free

Somewhere Above The Clouds
Some sweet morning I will surely fly
To be with my dear Saviour
In that beautiful home away off in the sky

Somewhere Above The Clouds
In that city with streets that are paved with gold
Where there will be much rejoicing
And I will be welcome into that heavenly fold

Somewhere Above The Clouds
On that great reunion day
Where there will be no more parting
And there with all my loved one's I will forever stay

Somewhere Above The Clouds
When my earthly race I have run my life will not have ended
But praise God it will only have just begun
Somewhere Above The Clouds

J. Leroy Colter

ennui

in every thought rests a contradiction of self
  a ceiling's plaster intriguing enough.
en route to rationale
  crack open a book and thumb the pages.
parlance of lethargy's musings
  telephone rings—wrong number.
untranslatable when trance snaps and tone returns
  wall provides a stronghold of thoughts.
voices procure the will into images rampant and agitated
  captivation in the fibers of empty paper.
egocentrism stands tall amidst nothingness encircling
  languor ascends to turns on the t.v.
alienation from the time employs suggestions transcendental
  heard a pin drop and witnessed the crash.
nonconformity imbeds the senses saturated within a swirling
deluge of color
  open window clears a few specks of dust.
impelling tincture holds tenure with brilliant chaos residing full
  light bulb burns out. no concern.
  change it tomorrow. to sleep.

Shaunna Morrison

Child Of The Islands

There you are.
A child of the islands,
a man of the sea.
Connected with that parcel of mountain jutting upward from the water.
The forest is your body, standing like you— solid and strong, lean
  and hard, not easily moved.
You are the ocean. Rocking and rolling, a power with purpose, a force
  to respect.
The sky in your eyes, dreamy, joyful or clouded with storm,
the sun in your skin, punishing, life-giving radiance melted, molten
  to the core.
I want to feel a part of your land, to walk across your rocky shores,
  and float suspended in your seas.
To touch you is to sip the ocean, feel the land and know the sky.
Let me rest my body on your hillsides and sleep dreamless beneath your
  trees.
You are the sun, the sand, the moon and wind.
A child of the islands,
a man of the sea.

Yvonne Myles

A Coat Of Armor

We cover ourselves in such a thick coat,
A coat of armor. Now we can't find ourselves.
We look at other and see such perfectness.
We look at ourselves and think what a mess.
We cannot show our pain inside;
We realize how much we have to hide.
"Why am I so different from everyone else?"
That is the question we ask ourselves.
Different is not what we are.
We are unique; that is what we are.
Unique is special; unique is sheer.
We are unique! That is what we want to hear.
Cover us in compliments,
So we do not hover in our nest.
We will come out in broad daylight,
And laugh and shine in such delight.
We will not think such a mess of ourselves,
But we will think of how unique we really are.

Terri Brown

Just Memories

Some sticky sweet cotton candy
A crisp juicy apple covered in caramel
A box of crystal rock candy
A long chewy cherry red vine
   and a black one, too
A creamy smooth cool vanilla shake
And a meaty hot dog; tart relish and mustard
   all just memories
   and one last satisfying burp
In the back seat
On the way home

Robert Ines

For Tomorrow

I have a dream for our children's tomorrow,
A day filled with joy,
And no heart rending sorrow.

A day with no drugs, no poverty, no wars.
A day filled with sunshine,
Opportunities—open doors.

A day with no hunger, no illness, no fears.
A day filled with hope,
And eyes without tears.

A day with no hatred, no violence, no lies.
A day filled with love,
When no beaten child dies.

A day with no ignorance, vengeance, neglect.
A day filled with dawning,
For the old ones......respect.

A day with everyone, from all walks of life,
Can meet in the middle,
And put an end to all strife.

Kim B. Hardy

A Sallow, Windswept Dawn

A casual, and silent dawn,
a sallow windswept song,
its sermon shall ever rise beyond,
the stairs, that touch the lower levels there,
and say in quiet passing,
that lay about and beyond our day,
we can but rarely have our way.

William A. Ford Jr

Spring Resurrection

About April first without fail,
A different perfume in the air does prevail.
Green fronds are beginning to uncurl,
Dew drops, like many a precious pearl glitter.
Canadian geese, north bound on wing
Pause to feed on a pond fed by a spring.
Fat robins, busy building their nest,
As sweet songs fill their red breast.
Peeking crocuses may now be seen.
Tiny tree buds soon burst into leaves so clean.
Washed afresh by warm spring rain
Awakening the earth to life again.
Like spring from winter dead does remind
Proof of Christ's resurrection, we'll find.

Mary Gravlin

Too Much Blood

Shots ring out in the middle of the night
A figure falls in the midst of the fight
The cops give up throw their hands in the air
You know the public doesn't seem to care- at all.

Do you realize it's the kids that die?
Their life is gone in the wink of an eye
They stand for something they don't understand
While their blood stains too much land tonight.

It's too easy to sit in your chair and watch T.V.
It's much too far away you say
It may just touch you one day.

Too much blood.

Vincent Molina

The Flicker Of A Firefly

Have you ever noticed in the night
   A flicker passing in your sight?
What a brilliant glow that's penetrating the dark —

Is that a part of the earthly element,
   Or a bit of the heavenly firmament?

Oh, gosh!! That's the flicker of a firefly!!

When compared to the vast dark,
   The firefly's flicker is but a spark.

There's a lesson in this for you and me
   Whose lives are filled with so much glee
Or devastated with problems that are certain to be.
   Be aware of how you spend your time in your earthly space.
Be not involved in what may bring you disgrace.
   Be not overwhelmed with celebration.
Make preparation for your soul's salvation.

Remember —
   The length of our earthly life when compared to eternity
Is as the flicker of a firefly to you and me.

Martha C. Harper

Grandpa

Well worn face, bushy brows, twinkling eyes,
A gentle voice that conveys love and affection,
Hands that have been weathered by time,
Walk in the park, little hand in his,
Grandpa, what makes a tree grow?
Sitting upon his hobbled knees,
His stories flow from a distant past,
With a simple tug on his worn out overalls,
Grandpa, Grandpa, I love you.

Paul W. Stevens

Dawn
A forest just awakening.
Morning songbirds announce the start of day,
A gentle breeze carries a hint of a rainstorm.
A deafening roar—
The sound of a chainsaw starting.
The air no longer smells fresh, clean;
It reeks of burning wood and gasoline.
People shouting, the crack of a tree falling,
And the continuous roar of machines
Block out the birds.
Dusk.
Silence at last.
A razed forest greets the eye.

Kirsten M. Lepik

Untitled

E veryone who love's the Lord knows he has risen from the dead.
A fter his death; He ascend into the Heavens.
S its at the right hand of God.
T ook my sin's to that old rugged cross for me.
E ven his mother was at the cross with him.
R isen from the dead over 2,000 years ago now;
He lives within my heart

Now this is what Easter means to me not about
the Bunny that is to go around giving the little
children candy and Easter baskets. It is about the
death and resurrection of our Lord Jesus Christ.
'Cause if He had not died on that cross over 2,000
years ago; I wouldn't have been saved; or have
not been filled with the Holy Ghost.

Lacy Guist

Joseph

Eternity has always been, yet never has it had such a win.
A full moon hangs high above in the cursed winter sky.
An angel proclaims his presence with great fanfare.
Dancing upon the eternal blackness of the night.
Bringing all the beauty, and the light.
Velvet seas caress him, telling him the mysteries of the world.
Dancing in his hand stands eternity, to him a frightened child.
Never playing games as all humans do. He stands eternally as a
bridge with a rock foundation. The ocean sings many songs
including this one to me today, saying it's time for me to
say goodbye to all my friends here at home, and leave with my
father and Lord, I have to die today. So I turn to my best friend and I
leave him behind for all others here today. Forever he lives
on, features never leave my mind, and soon all fades away. But
no matter what happens now I know that I will see him again
someday. The entire world will always feel his aura, blackness
soft like angel's wings abounds. Taken in strong arms, yet
fragile more so than glass. Earned love, earned trust, and
earned faith are the songs. He now sings on to you.

Melissa Williams

Silent

Easily and slowly I creep up behind him.
A knife in my hand and a prayer in my heart.
I close my eyes hoping that when I open them I
Would be at home.
Yet when I open them there was nothing but darkness
And a bloody knife.
There he was lying on the floor whimpering, and
Begging me to help him.
Ha Ha! You thought that I helped him, Oh no!!!
I just laughed and finished him off.
You fancy me mad, I'm not mad.
Just Silent!!!!!!!!!!!!!!!!!!!!

Shalethia Russell

You

The calm air surrounded me
A gentle breeze blew by
And just when it felt like
nobody cared -
You were there by my side

You were my protection
You shielded me from the bitter wind
You gave me warmth in a space that was cold

It all seemed so awkward at that time to me,
Like the time I first began to walk
Why would you want to break the distance -
The space that separates us

But in that cold, cold place -
That desolate space,
You were there for me.

Kelly Metz

Paradise

Take me to a garden fair, where flowers perfume fill the air
a happy place where loved ones wait, and Jesus stands inside the gate
To greet each one who chose this place, the smile of love is
on his face
So don't feel sad and always blue
Just feel his presents comfort you, and as your tears he
wipes away, you will rejoice in each glad day
So don't you fret and don't you cry
You'll see each loved one bye and bye.

Ruth B. Goran

Awestruck

Awakened by the symphony in the sky

From the front step I watch the dawn show
A jet stream of cirrus clouds dance quickly along the horizon
propelled by bulbous cumulus black storm clouds

The light show begins on cue from
cymbals clanging and drum rolls

Magnificent, daring lights

Lightning bolts touch ground all about as they move over head
I was awestruck - dumbfounded
Such beauty , such magnificent power!

The ground deluged by rains
Thunderbolts and lightning cracks
Fill the sky with magic

Glistening gentle rains
Followed by torrential pelting drops of water

This symphony of sound and light was magical almost mystical
As it brought in the dawning of a new day.

The rains subside
reveal a gentle salmon border over the mountains

Lucy Fritz

Whispers

Can you hear the wind, it's whispering to you.
A slow light breeze blowing through your hair
The last sweet words of a lost loved one,
The spoken of the old and wise.
Words of sorrow, words of joy
Words of tears and words of fears.
Can you hear it its love and praise.
Can you hear the wind, it's whispering to you.

Sarah Thompson

Shackles

My mother I shall never know. Why was I left without her love?
A little boy can only ask. For what reason did she go? Next I
lived in a different world, with newly found "moms and dads".
Suddenly, I found at my tender age, what life was like in an
orphanage. Then my life was interrupted; my home was at the
battlefront. When my duty there was done; again I found myself
alone. How I wanted love, to belong! I had a vision of mother
beside me, as I walked the aisle of matrimony; was I marrying
to be free? Now I have another life. Is this really what I
want? Will the years be fruitful and happy, or is this my
wishful reverie? I feel the bonds tightening; oh loose me, I
am crying! To live without freedom is like death save dying.
Now comes the beginning of the end; is it liberty, or is it
doom? At the court I said my fond farewells. Will life now
hold love, smiles, tears or gloom? I am searching,
searching—Dear God be my succor; let me discern in this
yearning to be free. Is it freedom from love, or freedom from
me?

Louise M. Roof

A Daddy's Love

A father's love towards his boy; will fill his heart full of joy!
A love as this will reach so deep; Dad sheds a tear while he sleeps.
I'm feeling low, a little sad; a best-buddy hug will make me glad
A little boy—A little man; he'll act like Dad whenever he can.
Your son learns more each and every day; sometimes so fast, most
  words can't say!
You start to wonder and change your style; can this be why a
  Grandpa smiles?
It was the same in years gone by; think of your Dad and do not cry.
Your son is you, he is your heart; he's custom built, your work of art.
You call him dude, you call him son; you learn together while
  having fun.
Your time together is always there; your time of love, the time
  you've shared.
All sons shall leave, all Dads shall cry; life shall continue,
  but with a sight!!

Kenneth C. Mills

My Love, Good Bye, I Love You

You are a love I will never forget.
A love that I didn't know how to show until now.

A love that was so true I
didn't know what to do. You made
me feel so secure that I had to become closer.

On the days I saw you I'd
sit and talk to you and tried not to cry.

There is something inside you that makes me ask how can you
handle it for you are so weak but are so strong.

The thing about you my love
is that you are so kind, gentle, caring,
and loving so how can that man upstairs take you.

One day while I was sitting I
looked at you my love and realized
that I would only share a little
more with you. For I had realized
you weren't going to be able to share the chance to see me grow up.

My love I will always keep the memories and laughs we had
I will hold you dear to my heart for I love you,
I always will. Love, Princess

Tracy Rose Varone

Humanitarian

Oskar Schindler was in a difficult position, He soon would become
a master magician, Deep inside his heart beat for humanity, However,
being a German he was caught up in Adolf Hitler's war of insanity.
He was an intelligent man, He always held the winning hand,
He contributed greatly to the war effort by making pots and pans,
He became quite wealthy, but most important, He kept a small group
of Jews safe and healthy. The end of the war was near and Oskar
felt fear, Not only for himself, but for his Jewish workers, again he
convinced everyone in the German High Command, That he and His
Workers could still give a helping hand. What Germany didn't know
Oskar's factory wouldn't deliver a single deadly blow, He had no
intention of making quality artillery cases, The shells he delivered
came from other places, That he bought with his own money, So
    on paper
he kept up the pace, But in reality, his factory didn't contribute
to any deaths in the human race. Remember now, Schindler was a
German by birth, However, more than anything, Deep inside
    Oskar's heart
beat for humanity, He wanted all the Jews to be free, This more than
all his wealth he wanted to see. His dream came true, Though it was
long over due, Oskar did what he and his heart knew,
Everyone he saved was known as a Schindlerjuden.

Scott Rogers Jr.

Heaven Is The Place To Be

A lifeless body is what I see
A memory, of a life with me.
He's at peace, may his soul rest.
May he be nearer to the Lord. That's best.

Good memories he left behind.
A gentle smile and a heart that's kind.
In our hearts he'll daily be,
As we go on, you and me.

As I look upon the body of my loved one,
I thank my Lord for sending a son.
Who made death an open door.
A door to new life and so much more.
There our loved one is who we'll see,
Heaven is the place to be.

So say goodbyes and make amends.
Do it before each day ends.
You never know when you'll be me.
There your loved one we will see,
But heaven is the place to be.

Sylvia Tapia

Imagination

Reality wanes in those fleeting instances when imagination dominates.
A mundane existence fades before the glory and pageantry of an
  adventure past or future.
An ordinary school desk lends itself to become a starship or a white
  charger.
Three-piece business ensembles instantly transform into suits of armor
  or camouflaged togs of Lincoln Green.
The Boss becomes a dragon, the teacher an ogre, and the waitress
  is now the fairest maiden in the land.
Concealed in the mind of a mailman is a mighty hero, while countless
  rock musicians emerge daily in classrooms throughout the nation.
Imagination is a fragile thing however, and quickly disappears at the
  sound of school bell, work whistle, or auto horn.
Tucked once again into the dark uncharted reaches of the mind, it lies
  at peace.
  But only until the next adventure begins..........

Mike Feigum

Dreaming

I can't think, my mind is enclosed with thoughts of running to
a place of joy and warmth. A place with endless happiness and
a place where boredom is an extinct object pushed to the back
of all minds. A place where I can run free of all
responsibilities, dance through the white sands of life and
play in the crystal clear waters of thought.
I know this place, it is a place visited by all God's creations at
some time in their lives. No, you probably don't remember this
place, but I know it well. Because all men were created equal,
everyone has been there, but only for a second. Select few
have visited this wonderland of luck more than once in a lifetime.
I am one of those precious few. This place is in the thoughts I
think, in the air I breath, and in the voice I mutter. It is
in all parts of my body, it is a dream. My dream is alive
within me, and until my body ceases to live, it will continue to
grow and expand, slowly obsessing my mind and spirit.
The dream will be passed on through me, into another soul's
thoughts and wishes. It will become powerful, and in its
attempt to grow, the dream will transform into a reality.

Nina Sammons

Compassion

In a place with no loyalty, no love, no life,
A place that holds only mysteries for us,
A world of its own that drifts from others,
Full of greed and hatred.
Yet, it exists in some of our heart, souls, and minds.

Others are often judged by the clothes
they wear, how much money they have
in their pockets, and even by the color
of their skin.
It is like a fire that burns the very soul.

We should sing a song of happiness;
not play games of war.
We should find peace in others, but
most of all we should find peace
in our hearts.

Stephanie Marie Clark

Gazebo Dreams

Gazebo is a pretty word - a place to rest and gaze
A place to count our blessings - oh there are so many ways
I wander there to end the day - or give the day a start
I've captured fleeting moments that were hidden in my heart
The problems that abound somehow I try to put on hold
And then with self-abandon let the happy times unfold
Sometimes our days are filled with things that really don't
mean much
It's good to drift and dream a while - let nature add her touch
The flowers in the garden give our joy of life new birth
And cheerful songs the birds sing - celebrate their place on earth
Gazebo in my world should be a part of every home
It's even just a perfect spot to sit and write a poem

Lois Bachmann

Time To Go

The past has gone, just memories to hold.
And all that is left, is things to be told.
Good times and sad times, a place in my heart,
And all of my friends, have drifted apart,
Long drives at night, the silence of the dark
The hours of thinking, at my favorite park,
Hearts that were broken, myself, I have cried,
And nothing but remembrance, of friends that have died,
But I must move on now, there's a future to see,
And I hope that it brings, what the past means to me.

Ray Eggers, Jr.

Seasons

Trapped inside these walls of glass
A princess poses for all who pass
And beyond the light of night and day
She yells with victory and runs away

Time is running as the clock keeps humming
And the fears of time overwhelm her mind
What does it mean when the grass isn't green;
When the tide is rough and sunshine ain't enough?

The pathways of life seem near and far
And the choices before her means wanting more
As spring jumps to summer; summer glides to fall
Fall drops to winter and …the season tell all.

Rana Kirkland

Heavenly Bodies

Sometimes, life can be like…
A rainbow in the cold, lonely darkness of the midnight sky!
Why is it so hard to comprehend…
Why a love must die?
Look in the mirror,
Face-to-face with your inner self…
Can you look at yourself eye-to-eye?
Running in circles of obnoxious child-like fear
Oh, why Lord why?
They say that it's always darkest before the dawn..
Yet, it seems the sun will never rise…
Upon this abyss of my hardened life!
Then an Angel of Mercy come to me…
In this my darkest hour
(Of all darkest hours)
She is my wondrous starlight
She is definitely…
A Heavenly Body…

William Norco

New Reality

Abruptly awakened from pleasant dreams.
A sanctuary no longer stable.
Volcano on the verge of eruption.
Expulsion caused by the severe pressure.
  A new reality.

Surrounded by walls, claustrophobia.
Music of a champagne cork going pop.
Butterfly emerging from its cocoon.
Squinting, peering out from tiny slits.
  Act of futility.

Harsh, bright lights reflecting distorted images.
Creatures with eyes only and rubbery hands.
Struggling to inflate oxygen starved lungs.
Opening of mouth, screaming in terror.
  A new reality.

Teresa A. Doyen

Serenity

I dance by the light of the moon
All is well, nothing can touch me
The sky, enlightened by the glow, illuminates my heart
The stars glitter, enhancing the vastness of my thoughts
The breeze blows, whispering sweetness into my soul
I am a creature of the night
The silence gives me peace,
The stillness lets me dance.

Sherri-Lynn Barrett

Grandchild In Heaven

A piece of me has gone to heaven, my child's child is here no more
A searing fire spreads through my heart, My Lord in heaven, I do
   implore

How do I heal this child of mine, From this intense pain she must feel?
I grab to you my Lord for strength, This is too much, for me alone to
   deal

Oh, fill me Lord with wisdom, To deal on earth, what in heaven is an art
What words would come from you, To heal with faith, and lighten my
   child's heart?

 Dear child do you remember, When God sent his child to you
You were chosen for your love, And your faith in heaven too

 Just as birth is great miracle, Understood by none on earth
When our children leave this life, By faith we know, In Jesus they rebirth

Jesus thank you for your words, The pain continues hard and strong
Ultimate love I show my child, with you, my child and I, our child we
   mourn

And as we follow in your plan, All understanding full of love will come
For when we set our sight above, Perfection follows, "THY WILL
   BE DONE"

   Rebecca Segovia

L'Enfant Crie

As in a dream, it appeared to me
   A ship adrift in a cold sea.
Abandoned and tattered, ballast free
   Foreboding deep currents and uncertainty.

I see dancing winds moving on shore
   And a symphony of life on the ocean floor.
Cacophony bare and worn,
   A promenade of majestic cadence and form.

Innocent Lord and shepherd of life
   Guide me back through your holy light,
With joy and hope beckon me home
   L'Enfant Crie, je t'aime ma mère, mon père.

Who is the ship shattered at sea?
   A characteristic quiver of things that be,
Or reins of unconditional love and mercy.
   Oh Lord, my God, it is … my epilogue to thee.

   Kathleen Auth

To Me

A sky full of stars, listening to the hopes and dreams of you and me.
A single wish whispered into this silent sea.
In a world full of hate, where brother turns against brother.
I wonder how and why families can turn on each other.
They say we're at peace with all other nations;
but who can really tell the state of these relations.
With chemicals and hate, we're polluting our lives.
They cut through the ozone with invisible knives.
Our population is growing… more women are giving birth.
We're sending these children into a hate-filled earth.
Generation after generation, it just gets worse, and worse.
We're inflicting upon ourselves a never ending curse.
No one seems to notice… No one seems to care.
About the children of the future and what is in store for them there.
They say everything is possible… Everything can be;
But with things the way they are, it doesn't seem that way to me.

   Kim Salas

Undocumented

I drove that spring through emerald hills;
A soft wind hurried me.
Lapis sky with cotton clouds
Rose beyond the tranquil sea.
Rampant blooms of every hue
Moved to the sea bird's cry.
Soft and willowy mustard flower
Waved and dipped as I sped by.
Clinging brave in rough terrain,
Golden poppies found a place
Alongside ice plant — multi jeweled,
And chartreuse sorrel showed a face.
Then suddenly my soft wind stilled.
The blossoms quivered — tense and wild.
Approaching check-point, not quite hid,
I saw the three: man, woman, child.
A fierce quiet hope brought them so far,
Through rock and sand and beckoning flower,
But, oh, the blossoms, hills, and sea
Cried out them — it can not be!

   Lois Ijams Hartman

A Safe Place

One afternoon while out doing my errands I noticed
   a squirrel trying to cross a busy street.
   He and I were both watching the traffic,
      looking for an opening.
   I in my huge four-wheel drive;
      He on his four tiny legs.

 Each time he approached the curb, a car would
whiz by and he would retreat with his tail in the air.
   I finally made it across and went into a store.
 As I came out I hesitated looking in his direction,
   afraid of seeing him lying broken and bleeding.

 But, there he was… still attempting to cross!
      I admired his determination.
 As I reached the safety of my home…. away from all
   the turmoil… I wondered if he also made it
      to his safe place.

   Terry Ann Braaten

Squirrels

I looked out my window and to my dismay,
a squirrel was sitting on my bird feeder tray
I tapped on the window and to my surprise,
he stared right back at me with his black beady eyes.
He scolded and scolded
just as if to say, I'm
just as good as a bird any ol' day.

   Madge Gibson

In Memory Of Kurt Cobain

Life can be fun, life can be bad;
   After what happened I feel so sad;
Without music life isn't complete;
   His tragic death was a defeat;
People say take it in stride;
   All I want to do is take it and hide;
His music touched me in place I never thought;
   It was like my emotions could be bought;
Now that he is gone, time is like a bad song;
   Everyone says take it and play along;
I feel tired and incomplete like he never said goodbye;
   His music will always be in my heart as I say
   goodbye for him.

   Tiffany Struck

The Card

It's quite plain really.
A standard card size with a standard beige background, smooth
and buttery.
The illustration is familiar, Winnie the Pooh and Piglet.
Small and free, lonely and loved.
The two figures are walking bravely into the sunset,
The orange sun branding the green grass with a golden light.
I am betrayed by that sun.
It wants to appear serene in its rosiness. I will always see blood.
The dark pink bubbly blood of spittle as it ruptures out of the
withered mouth.
It trickles. Down,
A little, then more.
I lose this image. My vision doubles, then again doubles.
My stinging eyes break swiftly away from his face to the card.
The simple, brave card with the bloody sunset.
Which is now crumpled in my hand.
It has not been signed.

Monica Hartley

To My Son

Russell, I held you, but I couldn't hold on
A storm raged inside me that would do us both harm
Through all the pressures I got carried away
I made wrong decisions that still hurt today
You were only a baby, then a small child of two
I gave up on loving and caring for you
The secret's inside me, few know what I've done
It hurts me to say that I gave up my son
Looking back through the times, through all the lost tears
My heart yearns for memories of all the lost years
I wished I'd been stronger and not tried to hide
From the pain that brought trouble that turned love to lies
I felt there was nowhere I had to turn
But running away's a hard lesson to learn
It brought me nothing but shame and disgrace
And the fact I'd no longer ever see your face
I was so thoughtless to give up so soon
I should have held on and fought through the gloom
There's no going back once the harm has been done
I just hope there's forgiveness in the Heart of my Son.

Sharon Feliberti

Wandering

From silent ponds above the ancient mountains
A stream begins to tumble towards the sea.
Over the edge of sleep it slowly wanders
Into the arms of an aimless mystery.

Watching the rapids dance across the headstones,
Aggressiveness is witnessed for a time!
The salmon leap at a hungry creatures death moan,
Until its cry is answered by the rhyme!

One at a time the fingers choose to wander,
Leaving the stream to seek a separate fate,
Or meshing anew with fingers they discover
And shining their love against the clouds of hate!

And where it is going, the people can only wonder! And just
what it means is a poem with an open rhyme, until daylight
appears, like a breeze that is rarely notice, And meaning
appears for the games, and the hills, and the time! And, at
last, when the end has devoured the last of the stranger, and
the ocean of time has examined the currents and streams, as
one, we'll remain to explain to the ones who would wander why
rivers are born and why people believe in their dreams!

Phil Sweeney

God's Gift

The wall is down Hah-Rah Hah-Rah
A tear falls from a soldiers eye
But pigeons still sh*t on my head
The wind still blows and people still die

The wall is down to the ground
Life is Guess Jeans
Where is all this money to be found
Too look like Jimmy Dean

But fear still grows like fungus
The wall in my heart is old
Love your neighbor is good to say
For all walls will not fold

For insecurity is the wall that lingers in our hearts
The pain is there from I know not where
Gods gift to us a cruel joke played, why is man so depraved
Of how life would be with no walls

Patrick Sean Falon

One Tiny Crack

It began as a crack one barely could see;
A tiny split, hidden so fine
One noticed only the bloom of the tree
And the grace of its climbing ivy vine.

Years spent admiring the lofty shade
Never seeing the secret hidden well,
Stunned when its beauty began to fade
With the bitter truth that time would tell.

Not one had ever stopped to see
Taken for granted by those passing there,
The beauty of the vine surrounding the tree
Was hiding the place that needed the care.

How many times have I passed that tree?
Who in my life will i pass by?
Never stopping to look through the ivy to see
That one tiny crack as they wither and die.

Vicki Grace Jones

Lone Tree

There is a lone tree.
A very lonely, old creepy statue,
Standing in front of me.

Shivering in the spring cold.
So depressed and sad,
Like a king who has lost his gold.

Its delightful colors fallen dead.
Just a poor, ghostly tree,
All black and lifeless, no blossoms of red.

Its only sounds: creaks and cracks,
While branches fall and decay.
Like an abandoned store with empty racks.

A broken branch tingles my hand.
The tree just stands still, unlike the others.
If it could bloom it would brighten this land.

I wish... I wish, it would bloom.
This ugly, forsaken tree;
And escape from its world of gloom.

But, this one, special tree was born to be,
A pitiful, sorrowful lone tree.

Lauren Sherburne

The Fly And The Pony

There once was a fly
A very mean fly.
As mean as a fly can be.
I use the word "once" for he was a dunce
As you will plainly see.

He picked on a pony,
Whose name was Tony
He bit him with delight and glee.
He sat on his back
When he would attack exactly where he should be.

Tony swatted his tail but to no avail.
He missed by part of an inch.
But, as everyone knows
A pony's tail grows
A fact the fly will agree.

A week went by, there is no fly.
And Tony is content.
The mean old fly has gone bye bye.
And left this continent.

Lawrence V. La Chapelle

"A Spoken Dream"

I had a dream last night;
a voice telling me wrong from right.
I asked, "which one?"
He said, "Go with the disguised one."
Who is he?
The voice replies he's the one for me.
Why can't I see his face?
The voice replies that I already have.
Who is this mysterious man you say is right for me?
The voice replied, "The one that is hidden in your mind."
You mean the one that could never be mine?
The voice said to walk side by side with him and I'll know who.
I couldn't believe my eyes,
when he took off his disguise.
All of a sudden this breathless feeling came over me!
I always knew he was the one for me.
The one I put in the back of my mind,
for such a long time.
I guess that fourteen year old puppy love was the real thing!

Lorrie Schlappe

You Are

You are a hearty laugh as we pass under the red light,
  A whisper when we are supposed to be listening,
  A confidant after Thursday's suicidal band practice,
  An unridiculing smile when I embarrass myself,
  My companion in the fight for laughter,
  All knowing eyes when I can't tell you what I did.
You are a fiendish villain who doused me in our water fight,
  Yet a shield to hide behind when I'm in trouble.
  You make starry nights in the light of day.
  With you, talks about nothing seem important.
  A perfect melody when I can't carry a tune,
  Cheese-and-peanut butter-stains and ice down my back,
You are my chief advisor and intellectual equal.
  You are the missing pieces of my M.C. Escher puzzle,
  The culprit behind my demise,
  Truth or dare bus rides and red silly string in my chair,
  M&Ms ground into mom's carpet (I hope she doesn't notice).
  You were there for a long time, but I did not realize it,
You are you.

Kate Harding

Untitled

A chilled bottle of champagne
A wild horse that won't be tamed
A little black dress
A conversation that is wordless. Candlelight
A horse and buggy ride on a starlit Night
A barefoot walk in the sand
Reaching over to hold someone's hand
A full moon
A night that doesn't end to soon
A gentle hug, A bear skin rug
Undressing a person with your eyes
A warm summer breeze and bright blue sky
A glimmer of hope when everything seems a miss
A passionate kiss
A sailboat ride into bright sunset
The night we met
A table for two, for just me and you
That's what romance is to me.

Leslie Ann Rhodes

"He Learned To Be A Man"

After two bad marriages and a baby to raise on my own.
A woman down on herself, a woman all alone.
A handsome strapping boy an innocence stare from his eye.
I taught him how to love me, he taught me how to fly.
In bitter tears I was slowly dying, but he gave me new life and hope.
he came in, cleaned house and showed me how to cope.
A college sophomore with a future a attitude that was more mature.
Hank JR style, country boy flair, our laughter always fills the air.
He comes to me a boy, but he leaves my arms a man.
I love him more than anyone could understand.
His shoulders strong enough
to bear my burdens and room to rest my head.
I seduced him and took him to my once empty bed.
I'm not ashamed of what I did, even though we kept it hid.
My love for him grows stronger with each passing day.
He's little bit jealous, but he'll never admit it
and I kinda like it that way. Sometimes he thinks of running
but he never does. Cause it's me his heart still loves.
When he makes love to me, it isn't the boy I see.
I've never had a closer friend, he'll stand by me until the end

Kathy Morgan

Dance Of Circumstance

Caught in the middle, stretched apart,
a woman keeps her secret heart.
Faith runs deep, and deeper still,
her strength of might and right and will.

Days are busy with routine tasks,
her thoughts atangle with questions unasked.
Full of potential, clinging to hope,
as women before her, she will smile and cope.

An angel hovers near her,
a demon rushes in.
Holy Spirit come to guide her,
Fill her with your power again.

In the middle of her age,
life becomes a clean white page.
Her thoughts unfurl, her spirit soars,
yearning to open unopen doors.

Promises kept and choices made,
life is for living and won't be delayed.
Will she keep a steady stance,
or dance the dance of circumstance?

Sheila Ivey

My World

This is my world;
A world full of laughter and joy.
With children born, and fields of corn,
And delight with every toy.

This is their world;
A world full of fears and pain.
With those who hate, and survival's a trait,
And tears fall like rain.

Why must we live
In a world full of fear?
It's a struggle to survive,
And of every dream comes a tear.

In my world,
There would be no fear.
Children would laugh
And of only joy would come a tear.

If their world was gone
And mine there in its place
There would be joy in the hearts of all,
And a smile on every face.
>   *Tara M. Carr*

Did I Ever Tell You?

Did I ever tell you, what I thought?

   About the disagreements and the fights?
   About the way we made-up?

Did I ever tell you, thank you?

   For the companionship and the friendship?
   For the understanding?

Did I ever tell you, how much I loved?

   The silly games and songs we played and sung?
   The nick-names we had?

Did I ever tell, how enjoyable?

   The wrestling bouts were?
   The time we shared?

Did I ever tell you, how I miss?

   The way you smile when we're together?
   The way you held me when I needed someone?

Did I ever tell you, I was sorry?

   For the sorrow and the guilt I couldn't take away?
   For the trouble I couldn't get you out of?

Did I ever tell you, how much you mean to me?

   You mean everything.
>   *Tracy L. Kelly*

God's Mystery

The tiny dried leaf shoved insistently
   against my window pane -
The wind had unthinkingly tossed it there
   on its downward journey from sunlit
Boughs - to find solace and nurture
   in the earth - from which all nurture comes -

To turn loose of life - and to become a part
   of something greater than beauty and freedom.

To meet and molder with kindred souls -
   To provide life for others to have their
Day in the sun - before they too realize their part
In God's cycle of life.
>   *E. J. Hamrick*

The Wanderers

The cloud-immigrants wend their way
Across the dawn-light sky.
Slowly moving in single file,
Their cloud-heads showing dejection
At having to move on.

In continuing procession they go,
Regretting not being able to stay.
They must know that something behind them
Moves them involuntarily on their way
As they troop across the dawn-light.

Wind? Other clouds? More weather?
Only they know what or who.
They don't stop to admire the scenery,
But continue to move in their single-minded pace
Across the dawn-scape.
>   *Neil Grant*

A Welcome House Guest

The wind blows gently
across the quiet, awaking earth
it combs and soothes
its ruffled hair,
it sets the flowers
swaying upon its cocky head
while it hums a lullaby.
It clears away the debris
of last years autumn ball,
and the riotous breakage
of winter's furious war.
It soothes the animals hiding in her breast
and parts the prairies grass
letting homeless creatures in
to nest, to rest as life incubates beneath them.
The wind blows softly,
a welcome house guest,
a gift as sweet as God's holy breath
to a land just walking up to life anew,
joyous that another dark, hungry season has past.
>   *Sandy Jordan*

The Price Of Liberty

The dying day sheds its last ray of light
across the still and silent field of war
casting deep shadows o'er the troubled sight,
while in the distance muffled cannon roar.
Stretched out and scattered on the battlefield
as rusty leaves are scattered in the fall,
The broken bodies lie, the wounds are sealed,
they wait now for the final Trumpet call.
No more their lips shall laugh or love or kiss,
no more their ears shall hear our earthly sound,
and moms, and dads, and sweethearts-how they'll miss
their sons and lovers on this battleground.
These mangled, martyred heroes now shall be,
Our greatest Testament of Liberty.
>   *Joseph A. Poole*

Sapphire Dreams

   Sapphire dreams, rubies and gold. Pearls and lace and
adventures far from home. The deep blue sea yonder, afar with a
ship on the surface and an anchor far below. Stars up about
shining so bright, the sea down below shimmers in the light. The
sky is like heaven, your mind is at ease, the night air is full
of sapphire dreams.
>   *Lucy Alvarado*

"Lucille"

Who is this before me?
   Ah, it is an angel.
One whose age is not measured by years,
   but by the quality of one's living.
My lips touch the softly wrinkled cheek,
   hoping the receiver of this kiss,
    will interpret its meaning.
Will I ever find the words,
   my heart longs to speak?
Not when true, unconditional love,
   need not be spoken of.

What this image that I can see,
   when my children look up to me?
Ah yes, it's the sparkle of angel's wings,
   caught by the rays of Heaven.
   Lynette Carlson

Untitled

Luminous, shining in Hollywood firmament
alive with the hope of stars that fell before
one of the quick longing to join the dead
(twinkle twinkle littlest star)
burned out a life too soon
(how I wonder who you were)
a talent for light and life and laughter
stolen by greed and lust for profit
(Marilyn or Norma Jeane, duality)
masked by covetous clouds
"We must own this luminous one"
how do you buy the wind?
or ride the comets tail?
(candle's flame caught in between)
shone into the hearts of man
she sang our desire
(guttering in the winds of change)
   Tim Kinkle

Untitled

Alone when times are rough,
All in my head, not able to share a single strand
Mixed feelings that are in constant battle
Tearing my heart apart, leaving nothing to thread together
Thrown over the edge to never land, stopping at nothing
Gasping for breath that will not come
Fill me with humble love
Fill me with joy, way down in
Eyes full of laughter
Gracious sounds press forth off thy lips
Standing tall, high on a sandy cliff, over looking the ocean blue
Breezing wind files through my blonde hair, leaving my soft face bare
Nothing to comfort me but the luxurious sunset and everlasting
   dreams
   Sue Granger

Beloved Husband, André

   O! my one and only valentine!

I spend all day and dreamingly
all night, constantly having you on
my mind, vivid lives and imaginings
of us all of the time.

   Every part of you is so fine.
Let's always stay close in heart, never
apart in mind or soul, spirit bound.

No matter who or what, any cause,
any occasion, we can withhold our enduring
love for all times on down the eternal line.
I dine you up!
   Mary Lauree Popovich

Change

All this freedom lost by rage
all these feelings trapped and caged.
Each meaning changing, ending with no end
one must realize my will might bend.
Mistakes are made my dues must be paid
the Mona Lisa, its beauty its pain.
The feelings: its beauty its pain
when will I learn the things I do
will make me no gain? This cry for help,
helps no one but me. There's only one thing
now pain is gone and I have begun
my journey to change. A life to rearrange.
My love has grown strong, nothing gone wrong
only a change, a life to rearrange.
In all this loss, in all this pain
my happiness comes with friends to gain.
My changes are true, people may see me
my true self come through my light may not radiate.
My spirit is free I have now chosen
what I will be, in all my hope,
people will see.
   Robert Stowers

Never Forget You

I will never forget those memories
All those years

Every time I think about it
I reminisce with tears
I know I will meet in later years;

I am just holding on
To something so far gone;

I wish I could hug you once again
But I know that you are gone my dear sweet friend;

Time was not on your side
You are gone where heaven gates open wide;

It happened all so soon
You were gone like someone burst a balloon;

I see other people wondering is it you
I have realized it could not be true;

I do not know if we could ever be able to get in touch
God knows I miss you much;

I guess God took you where you belong
Heaven's now your eternal home;
   Shantrae Moore

Sunken

He who was locked in a docile prison;
Alone without hammer or injustice
To transport together two souls as one.
Dreaming of sad colors, those hearts he missed,

From fairy-tale days of long forgotten fears,
And gentle echoes of brave times ashore.
No longer a valiant prince, his eye tears
Loving notions of what he had before.

His best years gone, poetic words must do
What a battle once did; voices sing out
Praises and tribute to a maiden true
As his most cherished memories could shout.

   She sparkles him a smile of flattery,
   For she too dreams of a ship gone to sea.
   Kyle McDonough

"The Runner"

Dedicated to Lance Denning

Rises with a single motivation in mind
Already left the night's dreams behind

Eases the body from the comfortable bed
Strength restores for the purpose ahead

Focuses the force outside and within
Anticipating the moment the struggle to begin

Resists ideas that lead the vision astray
Converging thoughts on this task keep all else at bay

Pushes through the effort strong to the end
Striding allows the free spirit to mend

Concludes the trial the essential delay
Escaping for awhile the tedium of the day
  Maryangela King

My Blessed Gift

I truly believe angels gave you to me
Although I do not deserve
So that I could cope with my grandfather's death
So that I would have joy in my life again
And accept that all things must die.
It seems almost fantastical.

Love is a creature of strong motive;
An intangible thing that strives people
To look for completeness of the soul.
You are my eyes and my ears- the pivot that changed my life.

I respect and admire your talents
I adore your kindness and funny wit
I love the smile that lights up your eyes
I feel the loving warmth that you share with me.

Contrary to our happy laughter
I am confident in the knowledge
That our hearts beat identical
To the same sweet, slow song.
And so I love you with all my heart;
I love you for loving me.
  Michelle Atherton

The Parting

IT happened one day as she knew it would,
Although not in the manner she always dreamed it would be.
Not with joy and pride in a job well done,
Waving goodbye to this mature offspring setting out alone on life's
  road,
Grateful for all she had done to ready him for this journey.

INSTEAD, only feelings of failure, betrayal and confusion;
Not understanding why she could not be the one on the pedestal.
Feeling rejected, cast off like a wool blanket on a summer day -
Sneaking away behind her back, blind to what real love is.

SHE stands in the room that was his and feels the essence of his
  leaving,
Looking around with desolated eyes and heavy limbs,
Feeling as one with his discarded possessions no longer prized,
Knowing it to be the closing of a chapter in life -
Unable to change the ending.

WITH tears on her cheeks she turns to leave,
Scattering the pieces of her broken heart with her passing,
To swirl and settle with the dust - forgotten.

I love you, son.
  Nanette M. Soellinger

An Ode To Rosemary

She is attractive, well-dressed, sometimes contrary,
Always calm, never stressed is this Rosemary;
Keen is her cognition she writes like no others,
With instant ignition she pursues her druthers!

Each column she writes is her own inspiration,
In words or in bytes it's her own perspiration;
She is very direct, fights for people who need her,
And has the respect of all people who read her.

She is a fighter when she knows something's wrong
And many a blighter has heard 'Rosemary's song'!
Do not tick her off—she could be your nemesis:
For she will kick butt no matter whose ass it is!

She is not so tough that she's never cried,
She never plays rough unless justice is tried
And fails its meaning, then Rosemary's there:
A verbal reaming—and judges beware!
She writes no manure, sees things as they are,
With her sense of humor she a bright star.
We love you Rosemary, even when we disagree,
Look above you, Rosemary, God's winking at thee!
  Ted Brohl

Miseries

Miseries
Always complicate my life
Pain and suffering I endure
Doesn't seem to make it right
Life
Life, impose so many requirements
That we must face
Learn to live with everyday, everyday
It just doesn't seem fair
Why we have so many
Burdens to bear
Will there ever be justice in this place or
Will we have to search for a higher place or
Ask god to save the day.
  Willie McKinney, Jr.

Teenage Years

Remembering the days of my teenage years
Always thinking my parents didn't understand
Being so bold, so cold, and not having any fears
Only to know now, they understood
Now, with teenagers of my own
Acting the way I had in the past
I always felt that older people were wrong
Not realizing what they had been through
I have said "I won't be like my parents"
I sit back and just laugh
Because I have become just like them
As my teenagers will do the same one day
I have felt we always had it rough
As my teenagers feel they have it tougher
It's all the same but, different times
As I remember my teenage years
I just laugh to myself
Because my teenagers can't understand
That I too, went through the teenage years.
  Sandii Yamamoto

Untitled

You smiled rainbows upon me
and my heart shed tears for your loneliness
and tears of happiness for our union

You smiled rainbows and my tears vanished as summer rain
  Kenneth E. Guard

Inspiration

As I live from day to day, trying to do the best I can,
Am I serving my Lord and Saviour, or trying to please my fellow-man?
If I should stumble along the way, my Lord extends His hand.
But if mistakes are made on earth, that's too much to ask of man.

If only we could work together, to be slow to hurt our brothers,
How happy we all would be, in meeting the needs of others.
So if by chance I do not see the errors I have made,
Would some one please extend his hand, and become a friend to me?

Margaret Sturtevant

Time

The drifting breeze smelled of the ocean's tears,
amongst it lay betraying all my fears.
When uncertainty struck could I have only turned stronger,
like a pillar of an old worthy bridge, carrying her worries
on her back.
But slowly the tension causes fractures like stress lines,
and puts me in repair, yet still I hide my despair.
When we rode away, the two of us, into the heavy fog's devour.
I would have sang, longing for, but the words would only turn sour.
Moving as ill-minded robots of mechanical men, I fear the
the prosecution of my fate, for it is my destiny
preplanned that I do hate.
My youth I do not mourn,
for it is the passing of time that I do scorn.
I look abroad to find you, following your steps nearside the moon,
For an aching heart cannot be soothed,
when its pulse is out of tune.

Paige Hillman

Come With Me

Come with me...
An adventure we can find
In a world of knowledge
Other thoughts, shall be left behind.

Explore different times,
A whole new atmosphere.
Your imagination running free.

Come with me...
To seek mystery,
Laughter and fear.
How could we accomplish
Such a task?

The answer is quite trite.
No foreign lands will be traveled to,
Just a tool to help reach new heights.

Read a book,
And all things that I have said,
Will be at your hand when a book is read.

Mary Adesanya

"I Wonder"

You know, at times I wonder about you
And at times I wonder if you wonder too,
But who can help but wonder, after all,
At times, wonder is all there is to do.

Dream, yes I dream
And at times, I wonder if you dream too.

Hope, yes I do that too,
But you know what I wonder the most?
I wonder if you wonder, dream and hope like me
Yes, I'm sure you do.

Roger L. Staten

Untitled

Pitying hope in the sighs of woe -
An angel appeared in a white soft glow.

A potion over a love-chant he fixed -
Of honey dew and sweet smelling nectar he mixed.

Drink from the chalice and bring about the fire -
Be, not only wish to be, your lovers only desire.

As the dewy droplets cling to this enchanting cup -
Believe in its magic as you slowly drink it up.

Even the mere scent of this elixir would give the message wings -
To reach the land where your lover dreams.

The life within this never ending stream -
Love will arise and hearts will gleam.

Seek your quest not in vain -
Lest it only bring you pain.

The finished works of the responsive love will be blest -
And upon his lips I will breathe the rest.

Lisa Anne Esse

"Amid The Stars, Perhaps Love Does Rejoice"

Amid the stars, perhaps love does rejoice.
An earthly bane that innocence devours.
Unknown circumstance does leave them no choice.
For destiny decided their hours.
Insipid romance, a young heart's decline.
Led astray by the subtle winds of fate.
Inconstant emotions one may refine;
Doubtless, insatiable, and sedate.
In destitution a soul shall despair.
Yet a tenacious heart will search ever more.
Abandon of logic, bound to impair;
No longer will any person be pure.
To heaven fair angel, search for the light.
To the stars! To heaven! Take off to flight.

Kay C. Franklin

Untitled

She stands in her place, a statue made of marble.
An eternal coldness surrounds her.
A red rose like his words have long since
Wilted, and the thorns stab at her heart.
To and fro, like the blade of a dull knife.
As she looks up into the depth of a beautiful
Blue sky, she sees his eyes. Eyes that had
once touched her soul.
She hears someone laughing in the distance.
She sees his smile and her breath is taken away from her.
She tries to forget the way he held her in
his arms. His soft breath caressing her cheek
Once within the circle of his arms, nothing could harm her.
His last lingering kiss upon her lips was
The final blow to her heart, and in that moment,
she died the death of love.

Nada Kamoo

Reality

Stop dreaming
and get your head out of the clouds.
Someone has just been murdered,
mugged, raped,
and kidnapped.
A child has runaway from a broken home.
The world is falling apart.
There is more bad then good in this world.
It doesn't have to be this way!

Summer Smith

Our Dream

As night time has fallen, I'll look towards our dream,
An image of us in a peaceful scene.
As I fall into slumber, a vision appears,
There we are standing, our eyes filled with tears.
As we approach each other in a gentle embrace,
Our tears are resolved, a bright smile in their place.
You say that you love me, I say that I love you,
We both show this smile, for we know that it's true.
We talk out our problems, we have nothing to hide,
We respect what we feel, and let love be our guide.
Our world is so perfect, I can hardly believe,
I am holding you, as you are holding me.
Then just when I'm about to love you again,
I awake from my slumber and realize I'm within.
I am locked in a cell, I had almost forgot,
It all seemed so real, it left me this thought.
If you believe in our dream, you are going to find,
That our dreams are a reality of our subconscious mind.
So don't worry or think that we're asunder forever,
For I'll dream tonight, and bring us together.

    Roy Logan

"The Wall Of Failure"

The powerful wall of failure stood before me,
Ancient corpses covered in guilts of dust at my feet
lowered my confidence,
Sharp crisp breezes whispered around my frail body
leaving a taste of static in my dry mouth,
would I join the rotting, dead failures?

My mind lingers about the success on the other
side of the wall,
The sense of pure confidence radiating out from every person,
Young, successful people covered in sheets of faith and
hope for their promising future,
I slowly drift back into reality staring blankly
at the bland wall,
Somehow the dull wall did not appear the same,
A glistening ladder made of golden strands of
rope was hanging along the side of the wall,
could I be dreaming?

    Stephanie Lee

Valentine Ditty's

A toast to this day of loving and giving,
And a toast to the man that makes it worth living!

In the hush of the evening, when all is silent,
I remember your voice as that of a tyrant,
No hugs nor kisses did I receive,
But from the judge, a divorce decree!

To live, love, laugh and be happy, is my most honest desire,
You set this flame within my soul and now my heart's afire!

This is a day of love. A day for wishing,
A kiss from you is what I'm missing!

Hearts and flowers I may desire, but a kiss from you,
Would set me afire!

I've been tossed around in this sea of life, some happy times, some
with strife, years came and passed, so unending, 'til I met you.

A heart is a thing so easily broken,
By words and thoughts, left unspoken,
So speak my love, for time is nigh,
If not to love is only to die.

    Maxine Crisp

Memories Of You

I look at you with her out there,
and all I can do is sit and stare.
All the memories of us run through my mind.
Now I feel like falling in love with you was a crime.
I jumped at the chance when you came and asked me to dance.
As we dance so close and slow,
the wind of the fans is a gentle blow.
The sparkle in your baby blue eyes,
always seems to cover up your lies.
When you give me that special look,
I just want to melt,
because it reminds me of all the things I felt.
But I realized we haven't been together for one whole year,
and every time I think about that, it brings a sad lonely tear.
I value all the precious memories of you.
Remember my love will always be true, with memories of you.

    Mandy Templet

Lost In My Thoughts

    The sun rises into a new sky.
and another day comes to life
looking towards the sky, I see the clouds go rolling by
as the sun peeks in and out, the clouds move all about.
The wind blows through the sky changing shapes of clouds going by.

    During the daylight hours,
I'll sit by the lake where the sun beads off like diamonds in the make
just sitting there wondering why and looking towards the sky
No real thoughts going through my mind
just getting lost in the beauty of it all.

    Sunset draws near, and the clouds turn red with fear.
It is a very pretty sight, the sun's last gleam before night.
Another day comes to an end and the night just begins.

    At night, when the moon is just right
and a breeze begins to blow but not too cold.
I look to the sky and see, the clouds moving aimlessly
the stars as they twinkle so bright they light up the night like candlelight
it's very quiet and dead
except for the thoughts running through my head.

    Michael T. Szymanski

In The Beginning

We've begun
  and as our eyes search
  and as our minds reach
  and the secrets of our lives unfold
the danger grows
  and the fear surges
  and the walls stand strong-
  keeping out
the truth.

Then sometimes
  a crack is made
  and love, and trust, and desire pour through
But then, cautious as ever,
  we seal the crack
  and pull away
  and our eyes still search
  and our minds still reach
    but our hearts know.

    Lisa M. Segerson

Dreams

As seagulls fly over the sky
and as water flows through the
night a peacefulness goes through
the air, and as the wind goes swiftly
and softly through my hair, the water
like a hot spring mist from the
waterfall below, feeling as if I am in a dream,
and below that a beach as
far as the eye can see and a bank
of sand that looks like gold, as
though it could sift through my
hands like waves of gold dust, and as
I stand there I wonder if I am dreaming
or fantasizing that this place can
really exist, but through my eyes
and in my mind I wonder
could this be a dream, but in my
heart and soul I know that dreams
can exist anywhere

Leegh Ann Vick

Who Are We/Who We Are

Funny hats
and baggy pants,
Sloppy shirts
and dirty shoes.

Socks
What are they?
A wild top, dyed
s'posed to be hair
Where's the self-respect... the self-esteem?
Our grooming gone
no longer prim, priss and clean...
When we see our image in a mirror
or in the eyes of a friend
In repose a matter without alacrity
Lack of dignity... A bastardization of the human
frame that houses the human spirit.
For shame!

Mary Ann W. Franklin

An Ode To All Fathers

June 20th is Father's Day
And because of this I have a lot to say.
Most fathers take exceptional pride
In raising their children and being by their side.
In some cases a father listens to their fears
But keeps them calm in their younger years.
He helps them with their problems
and a message he sends.
Son and daughter if you like your dad a lot
show him some respect and he will appreciate it,
why not?
When he sits in his favorite living room chair
come up to him and say, "Dad I really do care."
In closing I have this to say
To all dad's out there,
have a happy Father's Day!

Louis Weiner

Not Often

Not often do you find a friend that's sincere.
And not often do you find one that really cares.
It's hard to be happy at your occupation and at home.
That's why many, from their jobs do roam.
But blessed are the men, who find
A boss, who is a friend and sincere.
It gives you a job; hard to find anywhere.

Paul Eking

Tightrope

Walking the tightrope without a net, I take a breath
and carefully slide my foot on to the rope.
Traveling the tightrope alone is not easy there's no one to
say "be careful, be safe, I'll catch you if you fall".
With one foot still firmly on the platform the vibrations of
the rope cause little worry. Solid ground is not
threatening, nothing moves, nothing gives, nothing changes.
But as I move my foot off the platform fear grips me.

With eyes tightly closed you can stay on the platform
forever and know every counterpoint, every turn.
If you open your eyes and move forward, not turning to look
back, not stopping to look down.
What lies ahead is uncertain, not safe, not solid, not sure.
For what lies ahead is life.

Lynne Russell

"A Mere Tradesman"

Imagery in sounds that rumble and hiss,
and cute word pictures
that
look
like
this.
Truth? Beauty?
Don't be a bore!
No one writes of such things anymore.
So I'll take the low road and leave
you the higher -
Poet? No! Just Versifier.

Thurman Sledge

How Long Does Losing Last?

The memories of long ago still live within my heart
And each day 'though I carry on sometimes the teardrops start.

I see the things you used to touch, I almost feel you near
Yet now, alone, and on my own my mind is seldom clear.

A cup, a plate, your favorite seat, reminders of the past
Bring thoughts of you - and emptiness, how long does losing last?

My first, my last, my only love! Our two hearts beat as one...
Until death severed our sacred vows now love and life are done.

Until we meet at Peter's seat together again at Heaven's gate
I'll give thanks for every moment we shared
And be true to you while I wait.

Kitt Little Turtle

Widen My Vision

God open my eyes so I may see
And feel your presence close to me...
Give me strength for my stumbling feet
As I battle the crowd on life's busy streets
And widen my vision of my unseeing eyes
So in passing faces I'll recognize
Not just for a stranger, unloved and unknown,
But a friend with a heart
That is much like my own...

Give me perception to make me aware
That scattered profusely
On life's thoroughfare
Are the best gifts of God
That we daily pass by
As we look at the world
With an unseeing eye.

William D. Talmadge

Untitled

A hollow shell of a once inspiring,
and filled with life young child.
Watching the smoke coil from her cigarette,
she takes a drag, she may regret,
or maybe not, for the thoughts in her head
have been replaced with fears, and the
hope in her heart replaced with tears.
She cannot think for herself it does her no good,
you hide behind your smile so does she.
"Should we swallow the past and consume the future,
forget the regrets, and live and nurture
our everyday needs". She feeds on her cigarette.
She will never know until it's too late.
For the wind blows, and she changes her mood.
It's cold at last, and all her thoughts,
and feelings are now in the past,
go on she says as she puts out her cigarette.

Lynette Eisele

Breaking Free

In the prison, I'll sit and wait,
And find a way to release my hate.
In solitary confinement, I'm trying to fight
For the freedom I long for every day of every night.
With every day passing me by and by,
All I could do was cry.
But now I'm starving to find my freedom;
With odds so hard, how can I beat 'em.
So with my spoon and fork, I've started to dig;
I'll dig until I'm free.
The objects that helped imprison me will finally set me free.

Lisa G. Widner

Untitled Sonnet

The brightness of the dusk had all but gone,
    And, forward, I followed stars, with half-thought hopes
Of spring springing from out their waking yawns
    And covering the dead grey mountain slopes.
Silence enshrined the weary forest dark,
    Summoning me in waves of pleasure tones;
With no reply forthcoming on my part,
    It moved ahead with rising yells and moans.
Onward roamed I over stone-covered paths
    Until I reached a point of darker night —
'Twas then those speckled eyes upon me were cast
    And speaking with soft, dewy drops of light:
"`Tis not the outward view which will inspire,
But sparks within the heart that fuel the fire."

Robert A. Williams Jr.

A Lovely Spring Morning

The rising sun plays with the moon beams,
And gently chases them away
The birds sing their songs of welcome,
It's the dawn of another new day.
The rose buds unfurl their scented petals,
Still moist from their morning dew,
The pansies nod their velvet heads,
As if to say 'good morning to you!
The branches of the maple tree are
    gently swaying in the breeze,
So won't you, too, add your greetings
    to this lovely spring morning, please?

Pearl Holmberg

Perfect Harmony

The old conductor went to compose a new song,
and found two notes he hoped wouldn't be wrong.

Through they came from different chords, he knew that soon,
he could work them into being a very hit tune.

Yet despite his knowledge and awesome power,
their harmony at times would sound audibly sour.

The whole song would suddenly be out of key,
and it wasn't the artwork he knew it could be.

So he would work patiently through the day and night,
until the notes stopped clashing and sounded alright.

And when it was right, he knew that he'd found,
a beautiful, worthwhile musical sound.

For now, my songbird, you surely must see,
that those two notes are really you and me.

The song is our relationship we have in our hearts,
which sometimes really hits those number one charts.

For fate, the conductor, is working on a scheme,
to make sure our song remains a great theme.

So let's stop clashing and see if whether,
we can start making beautiful music together.

Laurel Ann Siragusa

God Smiled Down On Me

God smiled down on me with His loving touch
And gave me a friend who means so much
One whose smile and caring way
Brings joy and gladness to everyday

God smiled down on me and He knew
Days would be brighter with a friend like you
Someone who would always care
Someone to share with, who'd always be there

God smiled down on me with His love and grace
And gave me a friend who has a special place
In my life and in my heart where you'll always be
Someone who means the world to me

God smiled down on me from the very start
And gave me a friend with a loving heart
One who encourages and inspires me too
God smiled down on me and gave me you

Linda Journey

A Toast

To all the hurt, I've endured,
and growing up and matured,
To all the things, my eyes see,
and deep inside my heart's plea.
To learning, to live with me,
and finding a place, and living with thee.
To learning how not to be sad,
When my pain is so bad.
To myself to be true,
and to be true to you.
To all the times we share,
and happy times, without a care.
To a new beginning,
and not an end.
In our relationship, we will mend.

Lila Smith

On Courage

Let's celebrate. For those who have braved winter's storm
and have come unscathed, a toast!

Perhaps the lesson here, that to preserve or to challenge life's
unexpected, and prove beyond life's expectations is worthy of
a crown, a leaf of golden oak.

Yet, to be blessed with virtue is not enough. To try the Wings
of Trace, even better; for what can life offer - more! The
promise of the journey taken or would it be greater to hold
still to life's smaller offerings? Hardly not!

Isn't it nobler to give and to cherish the rewards. For re-
cognition will surely court, and you'll stand taller in the
company of kings and paupers alike.

Greet thus the darkened straight of night with the spirit that
carries you. Let fear not deter you, only to enlighten you!
And more swiftly conquer the yet unknown. With you hence, a
clearer light, a brighter day.

And with the pursuit of your years, expect no less than grand
victory. It will serve you in face of your growing years. Now
celebrate.

Michael A. Zufolo

"Sharing"

Sometimes when I walk down the street
And hear the little birds sing tweet, tweet
And see the flowers bloom in all
    colors of the rainbow
I forget it's not just for me but also
    for you
So let's learn to share our blessings too
In everything we say, think and do
For God shows us that he loves us all
Whether we are good, bad, short or tall
More like our creator we should be
Then, this wide world would be
Much happier for you and me.
Thank you, dear Lord, in making us see!

Leita A. Allen

I Love Him

I love him
    and I always will
Everybody tells me to get over him,
    that he's not worth it,
    or he doesn't like me.
But they don't understand how much I love him.
They don't understand how hard it is
    to love someone and not be loved back.
I've been called all kind of names.
I've been told it's just my imagination,
    but that's not true.
I'm in love with him
    and I will always love him.
He is very special
    and I wouldn't let him think otherwise.
If my love for him was to disappear,
I would disappear with it.

Rae Barnhart

Remembering Abe

That we have carved him out of stone
And set him on a marble throne
May have made him warm inside.
I rather think he'd gently chide
And deem it more in tune and proper
That his image is struck on the common copper.

Thomas H. Flood

Mom

You brought me to this world and loved me,
And I am all you raised me up to be.
I love you more then words can say,
because you brighten my everyday.
You taught me everything I know,
with everything I do you can tell because it does show.
And for those times before and still yet to come
    that we will always share,
I just want you to know how very much I love you,
    And that I will always care

Elizabeth Sara Finan

"Sunshine"

Everyday I go outside and stare,
and I breathe that lovely air.
But suddenly it starts to get cold,
come in the house I'm always told.

But one day there was a big dark cloud,
it started to sound like a dog that growled.
The clouds began to rumble,
and in the house I stumble.

Outside I heard a big doom,
I ran to my room, zoom,
then the dark cloud went away,
that day wasn't a good day.

Then something bright grew,
it dried up all the dew.
It was the sun, it shined,
I'd say it was very divine.

Launa L. Dixon

"Journey Through Pain"

As I journey through life with pain;
And I find no doctor that can explain;
I wonder how much more that I can bare;
Without knowing what lies there;
That's caused me so much misery, to my life you see;
That something that's taken, everything from me;

I sit quietly and patiently waiting to see;
What in the world has happened to me;
So with God's help, I'll find the answer soon, I hope;
Cause with this pain, I don't know how much more I can cope;

So please, I'm begging, help me if you can,
If you can't for some reason, I'll understand.

Ruby Darlene Williams

Don't Force Me

    Force me to see as you do,
and I will loathe you with your own reflection.

    Force me to think as you do,
and I will confuse you with your own thoughts.

    Force me to speak as you do,
and I will curse you with your own words.

    Force me to hear as you do,
and I will deafen you with your own voice.

    Force me to need as you do,
and I will ignore you with your own desires.

Storm Wasek

Ever Love

I see your clothes hanging next to mine
And I remember the hardest thing in this world to find
  was your love.

Being without you, for me, was hell
And as I snuggle the pillow still warm with your smell
  I promise never to take you for granted

I can't wake up, again, and not feel you by my side
Won't go through another day just wanting to hide
  from the pain of being without you

I cannot live without you. You are my heart; you are my soul
Let's just live day to day life-with each other grow old

And always know no matter our moods or if we see eye to eye…

We'll never let each other go, never hurt down to the quick
Never make each other lonely, never leave each other sick
Never give other's our affections or get caught up in their games.
Not let them tamper with our lives-for, we'll be the ones to blame.
Never, ever, turn our backs leaving the other to cope, alone
And never forget there is no better friend
  than the one we have at home

  Ricky O'Neil

Graduation '94

Graduation day has come time after time,
And in a couple years that day will be mine.
But for now here it comes again,
That day when I lose my very best friend.

I've never had to say goodbye
To someone who meant so much,
Someone who gives me butterflies
With just one touch.

But on May 27, 1994, I will say goodbye
As he walks out the door.
It will break my heart,
As we have to part.

But I know,
That he must go,
Into the world you see,
He can't wait around for me.

They say with time,
That I'll be fine.
But I know my heart will never mend,
And the friendship and love will never end.

  Kimberly J. Gulley

"No Longer In Love With You"

You're out of my life, my mind, my body, my soul
and last but no least my heart
What we had actually ended from the start; you
knew what you were all about
It's not easy for your ways to be rearranged
I thought I would never let go, but you say one thing
and mean another, that goes to show the truth I have discovered
We swore each other forever, but now I know we'll
never be together
The many chances I've given you don't try to count
because it's more than a few
I discovered that you could never be a lover just a
heartbreaker undercover
I'd rather feel lonely, unloved, and incomplete
because your love was all about under the sheets I
wish you the best in the times ahead, don't look back
at the broken heart you've mislead.

  Shanti McQuillan

New Baby In Town

Heaven's bells are ringing, there's a new baby in town!
And it wasn't left under a cabbage leaf
nor under a rock was it found.

It was one of those little miracles
That was sent from Jesus to you.
He thought that you would be the perfect mom.
So that's why he sent him way down here to you.

Now you may think those heavenly bells
Are ringing a real sour tune
When in the wee hours of the morning
There's no one up except the baby and you!

But rest assured this little boy
Knew just what would soon take place.
The moment those little eyes were open
He would see mommies loving face.

So Mommie, just remember, Jesus also gave you to me!
And please have my bottle ready,
When I wake up in the morning at three!

And would you tell daddy for me, not to think he gets to sleep?
Because real early tomorrow morning it will be just daddy and me!

  Patty Hedrick

Mother Tree

An acorn falls from the mother tree,
And lands on the ground, but now he's a seed
Whose roots begin to grow down low,
And a small green shoots starts to grow
Beside the mother — majestic and tall.
Will he get that big? He's starting so small.
But his trunk grows thick and wide
With branches sprouting from all sides.
And the leaves so green that will be yellow
With the changes of the seasons, and he will grow
As tall as his mother and ever larger.
His branches begin to reach past hers,
And as his roots grow, hers have no room.
This year she produces no flowers, no blooms.
His branches reach further, his trunk to the sky,
While hers fall to the ground, withered and dry,
For he has taken the soil and left her bare.
She will produce no more leaves after this year.
And soon hit the land and look up at her son,
And know that her job on this earth is done.

  Season Stuffle

My Cat

He'll rub against my leg,
and look so sweet
But he's just trying to con me
Into giving him something to eat

At two in the morning
He'll meow and he'll pout
Until someone gets up
And lets him out.

I finally think I'll get some sleep
It's five minutes after two
When I hear a scratching at the door
Guess what, it's you know who.

He's always drinking water from out of the sink
And I can't do much about it.
Maybe someday he'll change his ways
But I seriously doubt it.

  Tiffany Smith

Thinking Of You

I put my flowers down,
And looked up at the sky,
Wondering if you think of me,
The first thing that comes to mind.

It's strange I feel your presence,
Right here beside me now,
You calm me with your gentle breeze,
And you whisper thoughts through the trees.

Although you're gone to me you're still here
In my dreams you live your life.
When I stop crying you shed a tear.
Although you're gone, I'm still your wife.

Whenever I get upset or need some help.
I can talk to you and tell you my problems
I can look upon the first time.
that we ever met.

So I put my flowers down
And looked up at the sky
Wondering if you think of me
That's the first thing that comes to mind.

Shannon Higgs

Thank You, Love Mommy

You died too young for me to let you know exactly how I feel,
   And my arms still ache from time to time.

But I'm glad I had six weeks of your never dying, eternalized joy,
   At the lowest times in my life, you've made me sub-lime.

I just want to say, Thank You, for the life you've given me
   And for the strength to be able to move on.

Even though you were gone too soon, these memories I will carry,
   The love between a mother and her son, and the bond.

So thank you, my baby, I will always love you, and remember:

   T he day you came to me, of how
   H eavily you improved me,
   A nd of how you needed me, and
   N ever gave me a moments problem, also
   K now this, that when

   Y ou laid against my breast I felt
   O ur hearts, they beat as one
   U ntil the day you died, and became apart of my soul.

And tonight as I gaze up at the stars in heaven,
   I remember this year you would be eleven.

Sarah Bemis

Inspiration

With pen in hand this early morn,
and my thoughts like a billowing cloud,
to be able to write, is my one desire,
one thing of which I could be proud.

To express opinions and ideas,
the hopes, the fears and the dreams,
is the reason most people write,
or to change the scheme of things.

For if one could make a difference
by writing, in some small way,
to inform, inspire, or to comfort someone,
in their time of need this day.

In this world of so many needs,
it would be wonderful to find,
that the stroke of just one small pen
could resolve the problems of mankind.

Sam Filley

Last Wish

When my eyes look beyond deaths open door
And my desolate body bounds me no more
Gather me gently and place me afire
Do as I ask for this is my desire

But once my ashes have grown totally cold
I ask that you give them to another to hold
Want this he'll not, this journey with me
So show him these words so he's able to see
That no other held my heart as did he

With a lover's touch from you he must take
The ash the raging fire did make
And with a weighted brow and a laden heart
He will complete this unpleasant task
For once he did love me and for this will do as I ask

But ask not of him where he must trod
Simply let him go with a smile and a nod
And mourn not now nor ever more
For he has taken me where once our love was open and free
And it is there I wish my resting to be.

D. L. Blankenbaker

Everyday

Everyday the pain gets harder.
And my loved one says I'm wrong.
But with no hope, not even a little,
How can I be strong?

I watched my brother die from it.
A mute, dark skeletal frame.
No emotion no movement everyday,
I knew that that will be my pain.

More gut wrenching than the pain everyday.
Is the helplessness in my mates face.
He caters my every demand and wish,
But I'm still dying at a rapid pace.

The hundreds of pills I take everyday.
Only make me weak and sick.
The pills are given to pacify me,
So why don't just quit?

Our fate is in our hands every second of everyday.
Some poets would disagree.
So I've decided to lower the curtain,
Then I'll finally become pain free.

Michael D. Sauber

God Spoke To Me

God spoke to me one day, he said keep walking in the straight
and narrow way, far better things are at the end of the road.
He said keep looking up, and don't turn 'round, for I'll plant
your feet on higher ground. Then I'll reward you for the crosses
you have to bear, with kindness and mercy, just to show you that
I care. Eternal life, and heaven will be your home. There'll
be no more crying, or being left all alone. Pearly gates, and
streets paved with gold. There'll be no more dying or growing
old. Nothing but love, peace, and happiness, somehow I know,
that I've truly been blessed; because God spoke to me one day,
he said keep walking in the straight and narrow way, far better
things are at the end of the road.

Viola Ludd-Cade

Time Stands Still

Time stands still,
and no one seems to move.
   All that is heard is the wind,
whistling through the trees.
   Time stands still,
and all are wondering why.
   The birds, the bees, and even the butterflies,
think, but can not move.
   As time stands still.

   Neal Brown

Untitled

Look at me through the eyes of God,
And oh, the beauty you will see,
For when God looks at me,
Through His eyes of love,
He only sees Calvary.

You see the roughness, the scars and the stains,
Imperfections, infirmities and fears abound,
But if you look at me, through the eyes of God,
Only the beauty of Jesus is found.

"Let him without sin, cast the first stone,"
Our Lord and Master said,
But, oh, how soon we seem to forget,
His words so gentle and kind,
When we look through eyes, blinded by sin,
Only the sin do we find.

Oh look today, through the eyes of God,
So loving, so kind, and so free,
He only sees Jesus, the pure lamb of God,
Who gave Himself for you and for me.

   Marjorie McDaniel

What I Am

I can be subtle and neat
And perform excellence at any time
I can be messy and treat
My work like a big piece of slime
I can be graceful and glad
Like I know that I'm doing my best
I can be clumsy and mad
Like I'm very run down or depressed
I can be timid or scared or shy
I can be brainy or really very dim
I can give everyone a quick smart reply
I can be careful or out on a limb
I've seen myself clearly, I truly agree
I want to keep it the same, just plain simple me.

   Rajarshi Gupta

Hands Of The Devil

This life spells nothing but a book of cries.
And still none see it more than nothingness.
The bind gets ripped and slashed and kicked to lie,
Where spiders rest and catch their food - no less.
But when sought for, this book itself is blank.
The devil's hands rend pages for their use,
By playing scrabble with a new word bank.
The book's new phrases don't express refuse.
Now raped of shield of words, its essence lost.
So, why not burn and scorch in raging hell?
More torment can be caught inside a box.
So, why not swim in death's destructive well?
I will leave my book unshut to write in;
Or shall I close my book and stay within?

   Kavita Juneja

Snow

I gazed upon the melting snow,
And searched my soul for a clue
Why this snow melted, but that turned to ice.
Why this tuft of grass sought the blue sky blue.
It seems yesterday I pondered the leaves,
How they vanished without a trace.
I felt an overwhelming desire;
A need to get out of his place.
For this place remains whole for not a second in time,
And of course I adjust slower still.
For when I have recognized a great plateau
I am confronted with yet a greater hill.
Fools understand, and saints transcend,
And both of them think they know.
But I am left here pondering,
Gazing upon the new-fallen snow.
And the world remains unchanged.
And fools and saints both know;
Why that snow melted, but this turned to ice,
Why the grass is happy under its blanket of snow.

   Kenneth J. Brown

"God's Cloud"

Miles high above me the clouds float quietly
and slowly in the sky.
Changing from great mountains to
whimsical faces as they flow by.

Watching the soft white billows break
against the ceiling of blue land,
remind me of the oceans waves as they crash
and break white upon earth's sand.

Wishing I could soar freely like the birds toward
the sun away from things of man,
some how believing if I could sit atop the cloud
I could touch God's hand.

   Vickie McCart

One Life

Only one life God hath given,
   And so precious that soul is to Him,
That He gave His own Son for its ransom,
   So in time that dear soul He might win.

The trials of life may be many,
   Each one was fashioned by care
By a loving heavenly Father,
   Christ's likeness He wants us to bear.

Jesus, God's Son, is the example
   For each of His children to see,
That through each temptation and trial,
   God offers a way through for thee.

Be thankful, O Soul, for each trial
   Though at times seems too heavy to bear.
For He's fashioning you for a purpose,
   So to others His Gospel you'll share.

Yes, only one life I've been given.
   Lord help me use it for Thee.
As my life shows forth Christ's image,
   May others desire the "Image" they see.

   Patricia A. Large

The Wind On the Waves

The wind on the waves blows wild and free
  and tells the tales of an endless sea.
That blows the salt of an ocean vast
  which blows the sails upon the mast.
Of the ship, a wanderer on the waves
  from the captain bold to the galley slaves,
Trespassers on the waters that they sail,
  which belong in truth to the fish and whale,
Where dolphins weave their bodies in and out and
  whales all jump, and flip, and spout.
And sharks are tigers bold and true.
The terror of the ocean blue.
The waters silent now and calm,
Echo sunset on the realm
Of the creatures alive in an endless sea
The wind on the wave blows wild and free.

    Kim Heilman

Thoughts

My thoughts are many
And the answers are few
I think of the things that I wish would come true
My mind is like a merry-go-round
I have memories there
That shall never be found
I think of the good time and of the bad
But that is all in the past
And people say I should be glad
That way it will never be
Because I don't have you here with me
My thoughts are always of you
And the things that we went through
The feelings that we shared
And all the ways you were the one for me
I guess now it just was never meant to be
You are going your way and I am going mine
Neither one of us knowing
What we shall find

    Kim Puit

I Will Never Forget You

Time stood still that day in June,
And the call came in close to noon
Only twenty one and you were dead,
You were shot that's what the caller said,
Part of my heart melted away,
As I looked at you on that day
Yes that is my son, Don't go any further
But they pulled the sheet, your face they uncover.
The day before we talked on the phone,
You said , "Mom, I don't want to come home,
I just called to say goodby,"
God I did not know you were going to die
Oh God have mercy on this my son,
Take his hand on this walk he has begun
Fill him with love and full of grace,
Because no more will I see his sweet face,
Your life was over, mine was to go on,
Living with thoughts of you for so long,
You will not be forgotten, not one day.
Because in my heart you will always stay.
Bring my blue suit so I can style.
That's what he wore when he walked his last mile.
I wanted to go with him, I wanted to be there
When he started to ascend those Golden Stairs.

    Wanda Fitzgerald

Reflecting

Should I have my life to live over once more
And the chance to make memories a new
I would pass through each day at a slower pace
While savoring joys lost in a constant race.

I'd like to revert to my childhood stage
Questioning further our elder's sage
'Cause time passes swiftly and moments are rare
To learn and absorb one's legacy fair.

I'd give more of myself to my fellow man
Yet, hopefully follow my scheme
Since happiness spreads from forgoing ahead
While pursuing our goals and our dreams.

So could I live my life over again
I'd express admiration, praise and commend
To family and friends with an outstanding trait
And to all cherished loved ones before it's too late.

I'd try to ease pain and wipe away fears
For the lonely and lost in their golden years
Since life on this earth is brief for us all
And who can be sure when the curtain will fall.

    Ruth O'Neill Berger

A Touch Of God Within My Life

Whenever I think of peace
and the experience of great joy
I think of you

You
who stretched out your hand in friendship
and brought me out from a Sheol-like existence
into the bright sunlight
of a new day

With PATIENCE you led me away from
the desolate desert
to a dale lush and green
a place filled with life and new HOPE

Like the flowers of summer
I began to blossom forth
With your help I became
"a lily among thorns"
a rose found on the Plain of Sharon

If I love more today
it is because
God touched me through your presence in my life

    Sharon K. Herman

Mother Earth's Epilogue

I listen to the raindrops falling from the sky
And the great big bang of thunder roaring mighty high
Accompanied by lightening to brighten up our view,
Of mother nature's fight with us to keep things fresh and new.

And as our earth has warned for centuries and more
It can not take the pain of neglect and battered sores.
The waters are polluted and the sky is often gray
And how much longer can she keep her anger at bay.

Someday soon, the last raindrop will frailly make its way
And then the sky will open for the last time of the day
Down from heaven will come God to judge our sorry fate.
And all I can tell you earthlings, by then it'll be too late!

    Laura C. Farruggio

The Unfinished Poem

Life of a dreamer in three scenes, dying hope, endless hope,
And the greatest hope living over and over
In an unfinished play call life, this a mere unfinished
Poem a small part of that life

Now a mere shadow a upon the wall with no real shape,
No dreams left to dream
A mere particle of dust falling here and there
Push along by a force much too great to deny
Thinking if only my life was different

Now hoping for long restful nights, dreaming about dreaming
Dreams fill with only happy endings
And a home always their in my heart
What more could I want

Now doing everything in my power
To make the sky the limit of my dreams
And everything desired at my feet
Having it all

Now thinking about all of this
I realize I was dreaming when I wrote this
Forgive me if I went astray

Kenisha M. Fentress

Friendship And Love

In the fierce wind of winter
And the light rain of spring

Violence and hatred from sinners
Lord be with you, we sing

Golden rays of sunshine
Beam upon those who love
Blessed are those who are kind
Like a white turtle dove

Friendship and love should fill the air
Like mockingbirds and butterflies
Without so much care
Carousels and dandelions move softly in the wind
Like the message of friendship and love...I send.

Thomas P. Zoe

'You Did The Crime'

My friend was abused, what a terrible crime,
and the person who raped him is free, doing no time.
He grew up believing that he was at fault,
Until a counselor said "Let's put this to a halt."
She said "Name the man who did this to you.
The healing process will start as soon as you do.
Let this man know of your endless pain,
How you never loved sunshine, and lived in the rain."
My friend felt that he was dirty and cheap.
He never felt clean from his head to his feet.
My friend decided on his own to tell,
The name of the man who put him through hell.
And when he was confronted, the man started to lie,
But my friend, the victim, started to cry.
I did nothing wrong to deserve this from you.
How could you touch me the way that you do?
You will be punished, you will do your time.
For I am the victim, and you did the crime!

Sharon Baumgardner

Halloween

When the opaque moon rises,
and the wind begins to change
you know it's the time, when all turns strange.

The souls of the dead will rise again,
In celebration of life and unforgettable sin.

In the barren trees the banshees scream;
that sounds like a shrill from a hellish dream.

They are then let loose amongst the streets,
begging and whining for tasty treats.

When ignored and not fulfilled,
their clan of demons and ghouls
Is rather quite skilled.

With rocks in one hand
and soap in the other, they'll ruin your house
and torment your brother.

So be aware and be awake,
always be ready for what they might take.
All hallow's Eve comes but once a year,
So all be ready and full of fear.

Sarah Jurgens

Image In A Mirror

My eyes register the white my hair has turned
And the wrinkles my face has so hardly earned.
My body knows the pain that time has brought.
My mind recalls life's many battles fought.
My heart knows the loneliness of being last
Of family, all buried now within the past.
Each year of seventy has left its trace
In heart and mind, on body and on face.
Yet, if I could, would I return to youth?
And can speak the answer "No" with utter truth.
For age has brought such unexpected happiness
To know that being alone does not mean loneliness.
That there is time for joy in simple things-
A friend's laugh, a flash of color on a pair of wings,
A dog's wagging tail, a budding flower,
The sudden sweetness of an April shower.
No more the need to make a living and a name.
No more to strive for the world's or anyone's acclaim.
No more to desire romantic love that too often became trial.
I see my image in the mirror- and I smile.

Merilyn J. Richards

Friendship

Friendship begins with a kind word or two
And then goes on to grow with a, "How do you do?"
It is caring and concern for each to each other
And treating your friend like a sister or brother.

It's listening when someone has sad news to say
And being happy for them when they have a good day.
It's taking some cookies when there's good news to cheer
And it's passing the tissues when your friend is in tears.

It's accepting one's faults and not laying blame,
And hoping for you, they'll do the same.
It's being there when you're needed, backing off
    when you're not,
And sharing the best from life that you've got.

It's trusting, confiding, and helping out, too,
Because best friends always know that they'll
    be there for you.

Kathleen Erickson Pardue

"Be Happy"

There are day's when you are very mad,
And then the next day very glad,
It's funny how that can be,
It's that way with you and even me,
There are day's when you can curse and scream,
The next day happy and on the beam,
There are day's when you could float through the air,
The next day so mad you could pull out your hair,
The world is funny in many ways,
And to be cheerful and happy it pays,
Why be mad, dull, and sore,
If you were happy and cheerful you would get much more,
If everybody were angry and mad,
Most of the people would always be bad,
I guess I have no proof of this,
But to be cheerful and happy you should never miss.

Virginia Orben

Sometimes

If I could capture the moment sometimes
And tuck it so near I could hold it
Time wouldn't be so complex so often
And tears would know how to be folded

Whenever sadness should take over
And I'm weak and trembling and nervous
I wish I could just look over my shoulder
And suddenly have a purpose

Sometimes I walk just to walk
I have no real place to be
Maybe every once in awhile
I should plan to be someone other than me

Could there be a reason for the way I treat my soul
Who could I be pleasin' - I don't even know

When I'm not strong I cry out loud
When I am scared, I hide it
Sometimes I'd rather just be alone
There's something missing
I have to find it

Kelly Minich

"My Little Man" - I

Dedicated with love to Aaron Scott Holloway

He's a year old now
and unsteady at best
he takes a few steps
and plops down to rest

The chair he was holding
seems too far away
his expression confused
should I crawl, should I stay?

Exploring the parlor
a bottle he sees
he scurries on over
and now he is pleased

The trials are exhausting
his energy sapped
he'll try it again though
after he's napped

I know he will try it
again and again
I'm proud of my grandson
he's " my little man"

Ronald Jalette

To A Friend

I have know you for sometime
And wanted to give you this little rhyme
It's about me it's about you it's about the closeness
we once knew it might sound stupid it might sound dumb but oh well
Cause here it comes.

I miss you I miss me
I miss the way it used to be
We shared our secrets
We shared our hearts and vowed our love for each other would
 never part
But as we grow apart.

How we've changed through these years how our laughter has
turned to
tears but I know in my heart I will remember this till the day that
I die and wanted you to know for the sighs for the cries.
For the happiness that died for the laughter for the tears for the
long memorable years
through the thick and through the thin through the loneliness that
there has been for the times of sorrow and pain for the tomorrow that
always came for the love and for the lies
thank you my friend
my love for you will never die!

Tami Bensen

Together

Together we can conquer anything,
and we always know there will be something,
with our love we our held together tight,
but we still have our trials day and night,
though things are not always easy,
we still manage to get by,
together we shine like the sun,
together we are one.

Summer M. White

"God Greatest Gift"

God created all mankind,
And when he did he had this in mind.
To place all things upon this earth,
And have them grow from time of birth.
He created the birds that fly on high,
He created the new born babies that cry.
He created everything from the ground up above,
He abolished hate and created love.
For the land is green and the land is clean,
But the cleanest of all is the land unseen.
Unseen by night, unseen by day,
To him we turn to him we pray.
Down on our knew we go in prayer,
To ask forgiveness we know is there.
You've only to ask and you'll receive,
The greatest gift from the one unseen.
The gift of love for your fellow man,
And when you die to rest in God's hand.

Ron McMaster

The Marriage Recipe

Shake in a lot of humor,
Be generous with your caring.
Add heaping portions of love
Fold in with abundant sharing.
Throw in a pinch of pain
Then add a dash of sorrow.
Blend well with full cups of happiness
Continue stirring through all your tomorrows.

Marlene Fletcher

Gentle In My Mind

You steal into my thoughts like a whisper in the wind;
And when my mind is somewhere else, you gently wander in.
Sometimes when I'm quiet, I can feel you walking there,
Along the pathways of my soul as silent as a prayer.
And when I finally fall asleep you glide into my dreams,
To chase away the shadows and sail subconscious streams.
If I'm feeling awfully low, your presence might intrude
And strum upon my heartstrings, to play a soft etude.
You travel in and out the doorways of my time.
When you're not there beside me, I'm a poem without a rhyme.
For the visits of your spirit, I am truly blessed;
It's when you slip away again, I know I've been caressed.

Toni Stanford-Miller

Drinking And Driving

You said we would never part
And when we did, you took my heart.

Why is it you learned to lie?
Then it came for your turn to die.

You were expected at home arrive
For I knew you were smart enough to not drink and drive.

You died without a choice
There came no little voice.

For she was drunk and you were not
No one gave that a bit of thought.

You took your last breath
And died a needless death.

I pity those souls
Who think drinking and driving will not take its toll.

Though nothing can return my dear friend
Don't make drinking and driving choose your end.

Lisa Fritz

Lost

I wander through the dark, rainy night
and wonder where you are.
I stumble, groping blindly at nothing
and wonder where you are.
Has it really been so long
since the rays of sun touched us?
Wasn't it only yesterday that we laughed and loved?

I wonder where you are.
The rain falls heavily now
and I sink to the ground in despair.
I need the sun, the warmth, the light,
your love.
My tears mix with the rain
and I crawl slowly forward.
There is a faint glimmer of light ahead.
Will I reach it in time?
Or will I plunge into the darkness forever,
Lost?
Oh, my love, where are you?

Linda M. Eisenberg

Tuesday Morning At Mg's Coffee Shop

I smelled him before I saw him
  Behind me,
    layered with a month's grime:
4 weeks of dirt and sweat
   30 days of urine and raindrops
    720 hours clinging to pavement life and messing in his pants.
      stood a man.
I was disgusted.

Marguerite Mullaney

What Is A Mother To Be?

A Mother to be is everyday waiting, wanting
and wondering what is inside of me

Everyday I awake, I feel an extra heartbeat
I feel the imprint of tiny little feet

Will she have my eyes?
Will he have his dad's foot size?
It's such a joy wondering about my little girl or boy

As I watch my tummy get bigger
I know my baby is in me growing big and strong
my husband and my baby
our new little being
who will be here before too long

So as I wait patiently
and no matter what it may be
I just pray that my baby
will be happy and healthy

So to me, a mother to be
is the most exciting time in my life
and just to think it all started
with the miracle of becoming man and wife

L. B. Harmeyer

"Wondering Eyes"

I've walked through the fire,
And yet, remained choking on the smoke,
Never ran from the danger,
Didn't fall, didn't crawl, staying cloaked.

And as the fog got thicker,
I, to myself, faded away,
Only to find myself wandering,
Searching, without knowing the way.

To stumble, trip, and fall,
To rise again, trying to stand tall,
To cross hills, to travel valleys,
To climb mountains, to swim seas.
Always searching for the answer,
Which lay darkened in front of me.

As the fog thins, clearing the skies,
I can't believe what sits, before my wondering eyes.

Talisman T. Taylor

I Am Silent

I am silent;
  And you cannot understand,
Words would be meaningless, my sweet;
And still you wait;
  Pondering my strange moods and little silences
That flow between us when we meet;
  I would be free;
There is much that seals the spirit
  Leads me far; when I am in your presence;
If I could but greet you,
  When I clasp your hand;
If only you were at last aware;
  That a soaring bird escapes a snare;
Then would you indeed be wise;
  And not seek to make me captive still,
But like a falcon in the skies, release me;
Let me roam at will; and you will see
When the need is there;
I shall come home to thee;

Syd A. Caplen

Longing For Love

The smile on your face,
and your warm embrace
could put my heart at ease;
only you could set my soul free.

Your tenderness and caring,
your understanding and sharing
could bring me ever so closer to you.

I need someone to talk with
To laugh and cry with,
To be there
To comfort and care.

This is the kind of person I want to be with,
To share my dreams and despair!

I've been longing for this kind of love for oh so long...
And when it comes it will announce its
arrival with a beautiful song.

My heart will forever be bound
To the true love I have found.
Whose me that I have never found, but hope to find
A love so pure that it will bind my heart with thine.

Kristyn Stever

Evening In June

Early evening in June with still winds before a nightfall
Angel blue and sighing pink clouds
Freely drift at a country pace
As I watch in the valley low

Upon my fishing hole the reflection is clear as gold
As eight mallards flurry toward the pond
And crash along the murky mirrored water
Like a skipping stone that sends ripples
Across the glass still top

Tucked in the corner of shallow end
Cattails gather on their slender stems
A nesting ground for country creatures
Like frogs and bass and many many things
As the cattails listen to the songs that nature sings
A momma cow calling to find her calf
A bob white running through the grass
And the awesome display of everything at once
Is only understood if you sit and watch
Alone by a pond in the early evening in June
And the night will follow with the rising of the moon

Marvin Carl Kidwell, Jr

Whispers

Whispers of the leaves
Are like voices of people
You hear them in the background
They whisper words to you
Some maybe true others not
The only way to quiet some is to leave
Whispers bend like trees in a storm
Not knowing if they are true
Many good things fall victim
Only because the real voices are quiet
Some whispers can no longer be ignored
The voice pays the consequence in the end
Unless the voice is heard above the whispers

Maria Varney

World Without Love...

As the horizon swallows the sun...
Another day is over and done...
The night will cover what the day left behind...
Until the morning, the darkness will find...

Birds will sing their same old songs...
Trees will bow when the wind is strong...
Clouds will form mountains in the sky above...
It's just another day - In a world without love...

Together children will play in the park...
As the rest of us all fall apart...
Times will change - they always do...
I just hope - We all will too...

We see people fighting - Not knowing why...
We see them laugh - we see them cry...
No one ever talks - It's always push comes to shove...
It's just another day - In a world without love...

Everything it takes to make the world go around...
Is right at our fingertips or easily found...
If we'd all just use what was sent from above...
There would be no more days - In a world without love...

William "Cowboy" Reed

Impressions

The half-sipped cup of coffee sits
apologizing for only half-walking the college student.
The abandoned cigarette is left
smoldering in its tray.
Grey smoke curls still uncoiling
the anxiety of its owner.
The piano in the corner sits
remembering its music.
Waiting the musician's caress,
while past conversations ring
faintly in the air
like tiny silver bells in the wind.
This empty place has become so cluttered
with the memory
of faces that no longer come round.
How careless people are
to leave their personalities
hanging in the air
like atmosphere.

Rebecca L. Newbrey

Buying Time

Increasing my word power with sounds of fear.
Appears my demise is very near.
Malignancy a threat and cat scan was scary
X-rays, IVs and Chemo-Therapy.
Lumbar puncture and bone marrow scans
Remission a promise on a six months plan
I must endure the nausea and pain
With shots and pills again and again.
Seven months have passed, I'm free at last
Lymphoma cancer I hope is past.
A diet, new clothes, hopefully some hair
Goodbye to wigs, I'm almost there.
Thanks to my children, my friends, my Lord
Their love and support have kept me abroad.

Velma L. Brown

Urban Vision

Shoes, rank and shabby
April's Glamour magazine
A scratched Muddy Waters 78
await my ascension

Shackled gates
Forsaken buildings
Hursts of trash
scar my impression

A generous sprinkling of colorful vials
A warm reception by toothless, drug-induced smiles
pervade my retention

But in the next vacant lot, amongst the dregs and mire
Stands a lone flower with the grit to aspire
my feet feel lighter, jaw muscles ease
The emerging sun promises a fresh, new start
A cleansed mind and a valiant heart

One flower, One sidewalk, One street
One Day!

    Matthew Reals

The Destruction Of A Life

My dreams of a beautiful life
are all being destroyed
in the blink of an eye.
I can no longer control my actions,
for life is weighing me down.
I may be too scared to take my life back..
but who isn't?
One day I will take life's hand
shake it and throw it to hell.

But I like to hold things off you see,
so I'll wait until tomorrow.

No...No I must stop! I will no longer wait.
I will collect what I need to
win my lonely war and to take control
of what I call my life.
I will rise above the rest to show my greatness...
or maybe...maybe I'm not so great.
What now?
I know; I'll wait until tomorrow.

    Michael I. Pantalione

The Box Of Love

Needles and thimbles and threads alike
Are all parts of the box that my granny
Use at night
Cheese cake, apple pie, and candy with nuts too
are all parts of this box that the grandkids find to be true
Filled with love and the heavens above
Is the sweetest woman on this earth with Gods love
My granny the vision of eternal love
Smiles and hugs and prayers alike
Are all parts of this box that my granny use at night.

    Terry A. Harrison

Best Friends

As individuals, we are fine,
As separate people, we are afraid,
Put us together, we are a menacing mind,
And together, we are the brave.

Together we have a special bond.
I know her thoughts, she knows mine.
Of each other, we are very fond,
And if you look close, you will find,
That we are best friends forever.
"When will our hearts part?" I say "never."

    Melinda Cortez

Eyes In The Dark

Eyes in the dark
Are lost forever
Not a trace or mark
Never found, never

Gone from light
Nothing the same
Trapped in the night
This isn't a game.

Lost in the dark
Trapped in the night
Only sound is a dog's bark
It look's like you lost the fight to the night.

Your eyes are the only ones
Who see through the night
You break into a run
And escape even if you were almost overcome by your own fright.

    Melissa Mendelson

Untitled

The morbid thoughts that dance in mind
are the morbid thoughts you will always find
when you look into my eyes and see
the person I am destined to be.
A girl surrounded in a world of pain,
with or without to me it's the same.
Happiness one minute-
darkness the next
why must I live with no rest?
Eyes that sparkle from darkness within
wishing-but knowing nothing will begin.
A carrier of darkness a carrier of light.
Does it matter?
Evil always comes with the night.
Unfortunately knowing the pain I feel,
why bother with imagination? It's never going to be real.
Sitting in a world that is all a lie
Why must I live a life to die?

    Susy Hayden

Weeping Child

Weeping child why do you cry?
Are you crying because you are anxious to die?
To where have you come from?
To where are you going?
You look like you need something.
Is it love or affection, or perhaps just an answer?
Why bother, because I have an answer.
The angel. The angel of hope and praise.
He'll take you up above the sun's rays.
Over the stars and through the clouds.
To where you're loved by all.
No matter your color nor looks.
Just a place of people and books.
Books of romance, they surely enhance.
The people even give you a chance.
So stop your tears and set aside your fears.
No one will harm you.
Set aside your painful memories.
Oh weeping child please don't cry,
just take my hand and together we'll fly.

    Nichole Martovitz

Untitled

What I really want to be, is a poet living free, without the
argument and strife, rampant in my daily life free from
salaries, dues and rents, free of all encumberments, free to
pen, to write some prose, free of overhead and woes, to sleep
until I chance to wake, without appointments I want to break, to
never have to send bill, to never want a client to kill,
Ne'er again to kiss an ass, nor another lunch to pass,
put money worries far behind, allow me freedom of the mind
not to hear the pagers blast, with my computer in the past,
take the copier and the fax, relieve me of the income tax,
away with gross and net receipts, the trashcan all the filling
greets, alas, was never meant to be, for life you cannot easy flee,
Instead of writing of the rose, of fishing, love and dominoes
the piles about me higher grows, and stress my body daily shows,
I've made a prison of this life, to daily dine on grief and strife
thank God I do not have a wife, or to my neck I'd take a knife,
I long to be that thoughtful bard, why is life so very hard.

> *Wm. W. Erdmier*

Watchful Night

Alone I sit to watch these arms come down and fall
around me, flashes of red from angry eyes, unaware of my gaze

With arms blocking my way and the searing flashes,
I can almost feel tremors of the outburst that lie in wait

Yet I just sit.... immobilized, yet not in fear
but more in awe of the impending rush to follow

Then as if a shooting star bursting from the heavens,
I can witness only a blur of strength before me;
emotions encompass me, beckoning to be swept away
by this whirlwind

Waves of sound emanate from this awesome being,
yet still blocked by its arms and entranced within its eyes,
I sit and watch until its tantrum has ended,
never making my presence known

Once its anger was released, as was I to complete my
journey across now cold footprints, I began to wonder.....
just where that train was headed.

> *Kerry C. O'Sada*

Splendor In Fury

Wandering over the brilliant white sands,
Around me I perceive, as though from far away,
Sinister rumblings as the ocean rises
Into pulsing waves of destruction,
Over-powering walls of bluish-white
Tumbling upon the unsuspecting sands of the shore,
Sweeping away in its ceaseless flux tiny creatures
That throughout time have depended on the sea
For their very lives, yet harbor
An instinctive fear of its awesome fury
As the potential means of their death.
I stop
Suddenly transfixed by the strength and splendor
Of the scene before me:
The glory of the towering waves
Arising from a fantastic power-
Power to sustain life,
Power to destroy,
Turbulent beauty
Tranquil Beast.

> *Margaret Rhodes*

Wandering Death

O where will you wander tonight?
Around the living world stealing souls?
Around the unliving world of death and sorrow?

Your innocent victims will be whom?
Sinless children not known to life or
wizened elders of long lost tribes?

Would you come to two in love and take one away?
Even though the other may grieve in sorrow and
Wish to the highest star in the heaven to join that one you stole?

Am I or anyone to be afraid, to hate, or to deny you?
Why I ask, I a poor little soul, for I know you should be pitied.
Yes, pity the wanderer, who knows no friends, only enemies,
Knows no life, only death.
We should praise you for it's you that brings us home.

> *Megan Stucki*

True Release

The arousal of a young man's fancy
arrives with the coming of spring.
In it rolls, on the cusp
of the soggy tree bark and the morning dew.

And I longing to be excited,
find myself untrue.

For you are as beautiful
as the setting sun,
and as attentive as the moon.

But, if I am ever to be true
it shall be to you.
Dare I say it?

Go forth and be loved
and appreciated.

Whilst I find the release
from the chains
that imprison my heart.

My emotions.

> *Marcus D. Thompson*

To Sal

My love for you is beyond compare
  as a flower so rare
    as a cow with spots
      as chocolatey cafe' lattes
       as a rose very red
        the love you've said
         your gentle arms around me
          as close as can be
          as a romantic movie
           as we laugh with glee
           as your tickles
            and your shower trickles
            as your ardent love
             as the moon above
              as our walks by the ocean
              as our picnics in the sun
               as your passionate kiss
                what I'll forever miss

> *Susan Colletta-Busalacchi*

Whispers

There's a sound at night so soft,
  but I wonder if it's a person whispering at night.
Sometimes I think it's the sandman
  trying to fall asleep at night,
But maybe it's just the wind falling deep in the shadows.

> *Sara Hessenauer*

My World (A Newborn)

You start out in this world without strife,
As a little bundle of budding life.
And who is to say you do not dare
To be the one they love and care.

But to those who do not dare
You are the ones who do not share
In the love that is oh so true,
And cannot be measured with minds untrue.

But to those who do not believe,
Your love we hope will never cease.
For you see we will never bend
Until we conquer you in the end.
Lee M. Goshulak

Ecstasy And The Pressure Of Numbers

I stroll through a virgin forest feeling wonder and elation
as God's spirit pours forth into all his creation.

But the spirit cries foul and weeps free flowing tears
as hordes of humans hew down jungle to please profiteers.

Oh my, to steal a concealed view of a wild thing,
life is so good, I just laugh all day long and sing.

But where is the passenger pigeon and other extinct life?
Yes, it's millions of men again, spreading their strife.

The oceans, so much life to enjoy, both above and below,
and their beauty is legendary, come see the show.

The world's fisherman are so many and their machines so daunting,
unless reined in tightly no sea creatures will survive their haunting.

One of the natures great freebies, now much like a dream,
to dangle your feet in some pure rushing stream.

Legacy of men streams so polluted they are unfit to drink,
have no virgin fish, filled with slime, often stink.

What causes man to breed without limit,
consuming the world and everything in it?

Is it religion, profiteering,lust, laziness, or all of the above;
one thing is certain, it can't be love.
Michael S. Godfrey

Night Storm

A distant rumbling signals the intruder
As he creeps through the night sky.
Dark clouds heavy with rain push out the stars,
Pitch blackness reigns over the land.
Thunder explodes like huge boulders crashing down a hill,
Silence is chased away by the deafening fury.
Lightning rips through the thick black air
Exposing everything in a brief blue-white haze.
Howling winds make trees dance and sway
Like mad men around a bonfire.
Torrents of rain gnash at the ground
Biting out deep ditches and gullies.
The night storm rages out of control
Releasing and creating a flood of childhood memories.
Mark Denver Townsend

A Lovers' Quarrel

Without looking back, she walks
away from me and painful
memories. Hoping that when she is alone
they will fade and she will be reborn.

She thinks I am without pain, free
of scars from battles fought. How wrong
my love could be to think my heart so strong.
For I am just as weak or maybe weaker.
M. J. Gasbara

Only A Dream

When he was a child, he always dreamed, but never acted.
As he grew up, he became more popular,
and people began to talk about him.
And then suddenly, he was on everyone's mind,
he could not help but to be noticed.
He was unrelenting, he would go to places he wasn't wanted,
and take a beating to be heard.
He marched where people hated him, he had rocks thrown at him,
but he would never give up.
He started winning small victories, until what he had wanted was
accomplished, but he would not die.
He is still alive, although not as prominent, ready and waiting.
And he will not die, unless the need fades, even though he is old.
He is not black or white, he has no face or identity, only a dream.
He is a dream for equality.
Rob Elder

Baby It Happens

Baby it happens every single night
As I lay down on my bed,
My arms around my pillow and dreaming of you.
Dreaming the dream that we left incomplete
Just can't get you off my mind
Got love from so many uncountable girls
But no girl ever could make me forget you.
Forget the love you gave me.
They tried, they all tried hard,
And they left me lone too!
Tell me baby, tell me just what
Am I suppose to do
Just what am I suppose to do without you
Without your love.
Baby it happens every single night.
Ripon Rahman

Free As The Birds That May Fly

Free as the birds that may fly high
As I see the twinkle in your eyes.
Each day that goes by, I thank the Lord
That you are mine. Mine, I know may
Sound like a possession, so I'll say
You're my child, now that sounds a little better.

You bring me joy, you bring me hope
You bring me inspiration when I thought I
had none.
Thank you Lord for giving me such a
Gift that I will cherish forever more.....
Monica A. Dawson

Vision

As I lie here waiting to sleep
As I shiver, a vision I see.
Her face all wrinkled, weathered and torn.
I realize this lady has finally worn.
Hair short, reddened with gray
This lady I see has finally aged.
Sadness I feel all through my heart
For I know soon she must depart
Stars glittering brightly in pairs,
This lady I see surely did care.
A tear trickling down, as I stare to the sky
The vision I see is my mother's eyes.
Karen Cordaro

"What Is Best"

I feel as though a part of me dies a little each day.
As I sit and watch my father's life slowly fade away.

I see him through a sheet of tears of how he once had been.
A man so strong and pure of heart so seldom did he sin.

I said to God "Why him, oh Lord, why punish a man so great?"
Why not some deadbeat, some lousy bum, why seal a good man's
     fate?"

Alas the Lord was silent and I think I now know why.
My father wasn't being punished. It's not a curse to die.

God will come to claim this man whom I call my Dad.
It's time for me to cherish the time with him I've had.

So until the day God takes him to the place where he may rest.
I will love and cherish my father for I know now what is best.

   Ray Maycumber

Starry Night

The City lights glow bright together
As I sit in the dark alone.
At midnight they enchant me;
By two o'clock they mock me,
Taunting me with their expanse,
Keeping me from the violet-black horizon,
My only partner this night.

and the night before and before and every night...

Purple and blue whirl a Van Gogh Swirl
While I ache in the dark alone.
At two o'clock they captivate me,
By three o'clock they haunt me,
Teasing me with their Minuet,
Waltzing in their dance of Veils
which cruelly never tells
if, beneath electric stars
He, too, watches the City lights
as Tears slide in the Dark alone.

   Nina C. Davis

Visiting With My Imagination

The blanket of light arose
As I stood there and posed
This fresh new day, full of life
Dove into my heart like a knife
I heard the geese honking above my head
They were mourning like someone was dead
I imagined I was walking on a beach
To my total amazement
I was walking on cement
There are still miles to see and places to go
But just then the sky opened up and cried snow
How fast my day has gone by
Like when someone zippers their fly
It was good, though fast
I only wish my day could last
But my blanket of light disappeared

   Shana Black

Lions And Tigers

Lions and tigers everywhere,
But not a one to pet.
Mommy says they've been extinct
Forever she would bet.
She took me to the zoo
And showed me where the empty cages set.
Mommy feels so sad.
She tells me that we are forever in their debt.

   Laura Farmer

Just Being Me

People tend to shun them away,
as if they we're dogs.
   But they don't understand them.
Their not wrong at all.
   You can't tell what they are,
By color or weight.
   Even if you were one of them,
you couldn't tell they we're gay,
   Nobody understands, that they are still men,
But just because their gay, doesn't mean their different.
   All they ask for is a friend,
Someone who's not afraid of them,
   Someone who's next to kin.
Is God still with them, or perhaps on their side,
   to show them through the rough times,
They face in their life.
   Even if they're different, they're still human beings.
Treat them with respect, and lots of dignity,
   Because they're still human, like you and like me.

   Nafessa Johnson

Garden Gossip

"It must be love!" the Jonquils cried
As Lily of the Valley sauntered to their side
"We just saw Jack from his pulpit so high
Steal a look at Rose, so demure and shy."
"And I", said fair Lily, "saw Sweet William so bold
Making eyes at that beauty- Marigold."
She nodded, and listen- "What do you think?"
"Shh- this came direct from old Bob-O-Link!"

The Forget-me-nots clustered, the better to hear
The Tulips stood silent lest they interfere
Tall Lilacs cautioned the Apple Blossoms, so
white on the ground,
To lay still in the grass not making a sound.

And then Bob related the story so old,
Concerning Sweet William and dear Marigold.
"Wilt thou?" said he.
"Ah, oui" she replied. "In the gay month of May
will I come to your side."
"I love you" vowed William, with a sigh from the depths
"Is there anything dearer than Sweet Baby's Breath?"

   Margaret P. Fairhead

To My Mother

You were my best friend and my Mother,
As my confidant there was no other.
My days with you were a pleasure,
The memories of which I'll always treasure.

I was your one and only child,
Your love for me was gentle, mild,
Your precious love was from your heart
My heart is broken since we've had to part.

Your lovely face I can no longer see,
I miss your loving arms around me,
Your advice and counsel were for me only,
And, now my days are very lonely.

You are the sweetest angel God ever made,
Now God has called and gently bade
You come to your home in Heaven above,
Where you are abiding in God's perfect love.

   Darlys J. Hegge

The Rose

He gave me a rose
As red as blood,
As beautiful as can be,
He captured its beauty
And kept it only for me.
It's not so much the rose
As the love it shows,
The love he has for me.
Beautiful and pure,
Untouched by evil,
Waiting for that perfect time
When it can come into bloom.
Unlike his love, the rose quickly dies,
Its death a gentle reminder
Of how fragile life is
And it spurs us to make the most
Of our short time here on Earth.

Rebecca Howard

Untitled

An ocean breeze cools the air
As seagulls fly without a care
Sea lions bark in the water on shore
I'm reading a book of a sea pirate's lore
My cigarette burns until the ashes fall
Noticing cliffs behind me, they stand like a wall
The book was written of ships and treasure
And partially a view of a soldiers adventure
With swords and guns sin a furious fight
And again I cracked open a Coors Light
Seashells were strewn on the shore like the sand

And I picked up a sand dollar with my other hand
Amongst the drifts, I found a cave nearby
Then I looked at the ground, I had climbed pretty high
The rocks inside were covered with moss
On the floor I found a solid gold cross
Out to sea a ship had begun to sway
And the clouds in the sky grew heavy that day
I thought I should leave when it started to rain
So I packed up and left to see my girlfriend, Elane.

Matthew Jason Ackerman

Untitled

Comfort me in the morning
as the sun shines on my lonely face
Comfort me through the day,
Clear my path and lead my way.
Hold my hand and walk the valleys
Through the meadows to the stream,
Comfort me, Jesus please, comfort me.
Give me strength while I am searching,
So that I do not go astray, touch my
Heart and guard my soul as I give thanks for each new day.
When the sun sets in the evening and the birds have flown away,
I'm here alone but with the spirit,
Jesus please, comfort me.
In the vastness of the evening I feel lost in cold despair,
When confusion keeps me searching
I count on grace to lead me there.
When the world fails me immensely I know Jesus will succeed!
Thank you Lord! thank you Lord, for Jesus comforts me.

B. L. Pitts

Shangri-la

Incredible as it was soothing and refreshing
As the unsullied, gentle breeze atop the peak
That gently with its tender fingers caressing
My care-worn soul, that the harsh winter of life so bleak
Had robbed of its former luster with constant bruising.

Just so did the spirit within you - subtle yet blithe
And resonant with its unique glow of embers undying
That in the subdued and splendid isolation of the night
Unobtrusive yet omniscient, effortlessly provide my heart sighing
For succor and strength so elusive; perception and harmony
In the unison of rhythmic heartbeats - sans parley
Sans flutter; with only the serenity of your fortitude immeasurable
Not unlike that of the mountain massive and invincible
Atop which our souls sought refuge in the tranquil solitude of its
resplendence,
Gloriously fragile in their beauty and glittering in pristine love
On Shangri-la in the magnificent sunrise of a dew-filled dawn.

Vasantha Khublall

Footprints

The footprints left behind in the sand
As we walked along the beach hand in hand
Will once again blend into the land
When the sea comes in like a magic wand.

The moonlit night, the starry skies
The reflection of it all in your eyes
Convinces me to realize
Our love is forever more.

The waves crashing against the shore
Shout out our love with a mighty roar
Each wave louder than the one before
Saying "Rejoice in this moment of love!"

Too soon the night turns into dawn
But our love we shared as the waves rolled on
Ah, but daylight once again will be gone
And we'll make footprints once more!

Mary L. Hamilton

In The Light Of The Flame

A touch here, a kiss there, everything done with such care.
As your hands go through me, your soul I see.
In the light of the flame I suddenly understand why you came.

The memories flood my mind, not always so kind.
They touch my heart, my soul, sometimes I feel so cold,
Until you show me it's not in vain, then the love eases the pain.

To feel your breath upon my face, from me you take the lace.
As lashes lay upon my cheeks, the tears, my lips they seek.
Upon my tongue, of our love, these words, my voice has sung.

The smell of roses so sweet, the pain in my heart I still keep.
Taking sword in hand, through war you've taken a stand.
I've been your Achilles heel, me from you they've tried to steal.

But they cannot take you from me, no one possesses that key.
In my minds eye, the stroke has been taken,
no matter how deep the cut, nothing's forsaken.

Red on steel turns to grey, it's done, I'm awakened, I'm on my way.
For ours is a love of centuries,
the joy, the pains, my heart always carries.
Surpassing time on my lips is your name,
For I have seen it all in the light of the flame.

Melinda Mayes

Yesterday

I close my eyes to see her standing on the stoop
Asking me, "Are you coming tomorrow?"
Inside, he's standing at the stove making his favorite soup...
Fleeting mem'ries of the two brings sorrow.

The pair, dear mother and father of mine,
Have gone to a place one cannot see
They linger together in their own time
Eternally, somewhere away from me.

I wish once more that we'd talk as we did
At that stoop long ago, my mom and me,
The smell of the soup when dad lifts the lid
Can now only be in my memory.

The blanket of flowers keeping you snug
Is my way of giving you one last hug.
          Renate Monfardini

Fields Of Gold

The jealous clouds lurked upon us
Asking "Why can't I have someone to hold?"
As we ran through the lush field of dandelions,
That was our land of magical gold.

There was no time to stop and explain,
To someone who didn't want to hear.
Some things are so hard to explain,
But you can't make someone love you out of fear.

We ran, breathlessly, to where the golden fields
Meet the emerald ocean,
Just to hear the gentle breezes
Sing their lingering songs of devotion.

Suddenly, there smiling-was the sun
To remind us of the truths we do behold-
To keep in heart and mind
The promises made in the fields of gold.

As the golden carpet dances
Slowly beneath our feet,
We understand this special place
Is more than where two hearts meet.
          Pamella A. Cunningham

Divide By Colors

Colors divide in black and white,
Associated with the colors of your skin;
Personality has no effect of being equal.
Racism draws the line of equality,
People are fighting and dying; does it matter?
Freedom still hasn't made it to a full reality.
Beating, hangings, busing, speaking out and marching.
When will we over come?
More death and more death when will it stop.
Requirement for death has no preference.
So why continue to divide by colors?
When it really doesn't matter.
Blood still turns red.
          Shalette Cauley-Wandrick

Memory Flicker

The Memory flames may flicker.
    But they do not die.
Because I know that the FireLord is by my side.
    He is not easily forgotten.
Strong and true, forever in my memories.
    In body he is lost.
But in soul he lingers.
    Looking over each of us.
Making sure that the love and memories are never lost.
          Todd Grossbauer

Bosnia

I gaze through my window
At a shattered city
A place that I used to call home
But home is where you feel safe
And there is no comfort here
Just war and bloodshed and tears
Often I wish I could go outside
And play and laugh with friends
But to leave the house
Is to put your life on the line
And so it remains a dream
many of my friends are already dead
Young dreams and wishes
That will not be fulfilled
Though someday the Bosnia lost, will be found
What will comfort the mothers who's child died on this battleground
And even if Bosnia is restored, who will restore the life of my friends
          Lauren Capaldo

Memories Of The Past

At the setting of the sun
At dusk when work is done.
And darkness covers the earth,
We are quietly settled by the hearth,
As a family we are all together,
we almost welcome the wintry weather.
We fear not the wind or rain,
that heats against the window pane.
Safe and secure by the warm fire glow,
the welcome the softly, falling snow,
as days gone by we recall,
as the dying embers flicker and fall.
For greater to have had the passing years,
the ups and downs,
the highs and lows
the laughter and the tears.
          Nora Harty

Forever

Today I woke up with a tear in my eye.

I was thinking about the day that past by

When you were here with me at night, looking
at the stars shining so bright

Whispering in my ear, sweet things I love
to hear and making me wish you were near

I need to see your loving face and the
smile that gave me grace

Your big eyes that would stare me down and
would make sure I had no frown

The words you'd tell me oh, so light would
make me believe everything would be alright

But the day has come and now you're gone, you left
me her with nothing to carry on

Just memories of us being together and
the plans we had I guess will never
be forever.
          Myra Ann Torres

"Shelter From The Storm"

As loneliness screams from within, your soft cry stabs
at your heart; today there is no shelter from the storm.
Tomorrow brings hope of forgetting, yet the pain reminds
you of love gone away; a day ago you hurt so much.
How can you love again? Oh God, where is my shelter from the
storm? Prayers come and passages are read. Why then can you
not see that you'll be whole again? Your pain becomes
bitterness, can you trust again? With hands clasped tightly
together, you pray for shelter from the storm. Today you
walked with eyes opened wide. You could see the sun shining
on the road up ahead. How long have you walked blindly, what
have you missed? Will you ever feel shelter from the storm?
Something happened when you awoke; it was a beautiful day and
people smiled at you. Your heart beat with love that your eyes
gave away, I am forever and always will be your shelter from the storm.

Marc E. Stalnaker

CIVILIZATION

He stood there for a moment
  atop a mountain of spirits,
   a thin shadow
    among the whispering trees of smoke
     absorbing the beautiful empty space
     of the black sea.
And he wished that he could speak
  the language of nature,
   share a fluent tongue with the wild...
But the night gave no answer
  to his questioning thoughts;
   so he left nature's village
    following the path of arrows bent long ago,
     to the choking earth entombed by concrete
      the dwellings of self-destructive traditions.

Michele Renee Vaughn

The Art Of War

On a hill in the distance
  Atop a white steed,
A gallant knight sits
  Waiting for dawn
When battle will come.
  He knows he must win
His life is at stake,
  For the love of a woman
This step he must take.
  The thunder of hooves
The clashing of swords,
  Quick, steady moves brings death to a Lord
The battle is over,
  The enemy is slain
Now to his love he must explain
  Honor and glory, the art of war
And with her hand
  He then so swore,
To rule his land
  Together, forever more.

Milton Ryan Watson

Sunflower

I kneel down to Thee,
Awe-inspired by what I see.
Bathing myself in your golden sea,
Your strength and wisdom inspires me.
You warm my soul and dance with me,
Letting me feel the love of Thee.
The physical world begins to flee,
And all that is left are you and me.
You anoint my eyes and the truth I see,
There is nothing that separates me from Thee.

Melissa Leggett

Barney

Had a mother who liked the boogle comic strip.
B.G. had a wife just twice his size.
My Barney is tall, slender-almost an elegant decadence.
My Barney's wife is mysterious, child-like, sweet,
she is obviously a person of superior intelligence.
She laughs at my whole-kernel, cream-style jokes.
My Barney reveres ancient comic strips.
He and I alone of 80 people remember Krazy Kat,
and Ignatz Mouse and Offissa Pup and Coconino County.
Thank you George Herriman for 31 years of esoterica.

My Barney once sold pats and pans.
I forgave him today Barney is a surrogate. What's that ash I.
I help old people organize and maintain their lives.
Do you control their money. I must. I forgave him.
Barney reports than an 88 year old woman was jealous.
Jealous of his mysterious, child-like sweet wife.
Do you bond with these old people. What's it mean.

Some people never read the comics. Beyond their ken. Barney and I
both love the comic strife today's superman. Obviously we also are
both of superior intelligence.

Raymond G. Doersam

1 Train

On the subway He sat
beautiful brown 'locks of natural spun wool
to keep me warm in this cold winter
they covered his face, no trace, but I needed to see him
headphones blastin' sweet sounds of the carib'
In this arid car I became
I wanted to drink the sweat that would tell me how his day went
Salty, like the ocean that washes the shores
where I played and collected shells as a little girl
Hollow, like the city I was born in
under the gray, solemn skies of Harlem
I wanted to climb his 'locks and loose myself in his mental
Pick the lint from his hair that society casts on him
This man who bore my history
made me tense
numb and dense
as I sat and missed my stop.

raquel a. cepeda

Maine's Majesty

Maine possesses qualities rare,
Beauty, strength, tranquility there.
Of humble yet proud beginnings was she.
In glory she stands for all to see.
Relentless is her daily toil,
As farmers till her fertile soil.
Her people patriotic, courageous and kind,
Strive forth family and state entwined.
Ready to go that extra mile,
So that life there is all worth while.
A perfect blend you'll not find elsewhere.
The state of Maine for her I care.

Patricia R. Hudson

"Sad Goodbyes"

There once was a time when all I did was cry,
Because in my head I never got to say bye.

But now It's too late you see,
And all I have are memories.

The fun we had the good and bad,
And even the memories when we were mad.

But in my heart, I now know,
That I'll never let you go.

Maureen Manning

If God Should Go On Strike

It's just a good thing God up above, has never gone on strike
Because he wasn't treated fair, or things he didn't like.
If he had ever once sat down, and said "That's it—I'm through,
I've had enough of those on earth, so this is what I'll do."
I'll give my orders to the sun, cut off your heat supply
And to the moon, give no more light, and run your oceans dry.
Then just to really make it tough, and put the pressure on
Turn off the air and oxygen, till every breath is gone.
Do you know He'd be justified, if fairness were the game
For no one has been more abused, or treated with disdain
Than God—and yet he carries on, supplying you and me
With all the favors of his grace, and everything—For free!
People say they want a better deal, and so on strike they go,
But what a deal we've given God, whom everything we owe.
We don't care who we hurt or harm, to gain the things we like
But what a mess we'd all be in, if God should go on strike.

Rose G. Bowen

"Her Beauty"

She is born without a care,
Because her mother is always there.

As she grows older she learns to walk,
And slowly she begins to talk,

Many years pass and she's almost full grown,
Her beauty awaits still unknown,

Now she's a woman and fully bloomed,
The hearts of young men are surly doomed.

Older now still her life dreams fulfilled,
Her beauty not lost but only concealed,

Victoria Vaughn

"I Had A Talk With God Last Night"

I had a talk with God last night, and I ask him for his hand,
Because I knew he was the only one, that would truly understand.

I told him that I was traveling a road,
and the light I could not find.
And he told me not to worry my child,
because you got to take your time.

He said "life is full of decisions and choices, that we all have to make.
But be careful in your choosing, and the choices that you take.

No one is going to give you anything, and that I can say.
But with me being your leader, I will show you the way."

He said, "take my hand my child, and we will travel the road together.
And you don't have to be afraid anymore, cause I will be here forever.

Even when you thought you were traveling alone, you wasn't,
because I was traveling alone with you too.
Cause I am the man with the power, and I watches over each
and every one of you."

So when you have a problem, and need someone to make things right.
Just get down on your knees and bow your head, and have a
talk with your God that night.

Theresa Bonner

Leeched

I want to wash the ugliness away,
But the sickness inside will always stay.
It festers and grows and twists inside,
A vampire fetus sucking out love, hope and the will to survive.
Feeding on the strong their testimonies are mute,
Feeding on the mind making it destitute.

Tracy Walker

Weather

Because of weather, it is cold.
Because of weather, rock salt is sold.
Because of weather, it snows and sleets.
Because of weather, you can't drive on streets.

Because of weather, there is ice.
Because of weather, take the news' advice.
Because of weather, people fall.
Because of weather, people make a hospital call.

Because of weather, there are mistakes.
Because of weather, lives are what God takes.
Because of weather, people die.
Because of weather, people cry.

Laura Custer

Thinking About My Dad

Most days I'm pretty happy but today I'm mighty glad
Because today is Father's Day and I'm thinking about my dad.

He's been my model since my life began
He taught me many good things like how to be a man.

He taught me to think positive each and every day
He taught me if I worked hard, good things would come my way.

When I have a problem I know just what to do,
I stand right up and face it, the best way out is through

He always showed he loved me, he hugged me every day
and now that I'm a dad myself, I love my kids that way.

I'm trying hard to teach them to be all that they can be
Someday they may even write a poem like this for me.

Now you know the reason why I'm feeling mighty glad
Cause I'm very lucky guy... I'm going to see my dad!

Stew Leonard, Jr.

A Colorless World

Alone I sit in the solitude of an empty room that has
become my entire world, where my shadow is my only friend.
I have created a world where on one can hurt me because no one is
allowed to love me.
I have become complaisant in my existence, and free in my
thinking to travel within the confines of my mind.
I have built a fortress around myself to safely escape, even
though there are times I feel as though I am on the edge
of insanity and at any moment I could jump. It is my fear of the
unknown that keeps pulling me back. I then ask myself, if I am so
free, then why do I feel so trapped? In that instant I am
reminded that in my world I can only exist; outside my world I
could never survive.

Penni R. Johnson

Beware

Walking upon a forbidden path, hoping it is a shortcut.
Becoming engulfed in the shadowy forests.
Sinking in deeper and deeper as if it were quick sand.
The more you struggle, the faster you sink.
Lost, lonely and scared.
Feeling as if you trespassed, knowing it was wrong, accepting you are a
　　failure.
The walk turns into a run.
A frantic run with a pack of wolves.
Wanting out but not willing to sacrifice the numbness of the
　　nothing that you have.

Kellie R. Wilson

Light-Shower

I've seen the stars of the morning
Before the sun climbed the lip of the earth.
The lights from millions of years ago
Shone through the lens of the present
Though having, eons before, exploded into the void.

I've seen the stars of the morning,
Before the mountain's profile could be found
To trace the sky with its sacred line,
During early chores before my long workday,
Rubbing sleep from my eyes in the morning chill.

I've seen the stars of the morning
While bearing my son's heavy wet worn jeans,
Oblivious to the weight; pinning damp clothes
Onto the lines with intuitive braille,
Becoming clean, along with laundry, in star-shine.

I've seen the stars of the morning,
One breaking loose with a long blue trail...
Were you there as well during that phenomenon,
Outside your door to watch the golden dawn,
One with me, so far away, awakened?

   Lily Gebhart

For Eternity

She has large, questioning eyes,
Begging an explanation for the world she defies.
And a sad, soft frown displayed to our lives;
A window to a painful memory that she denies.

She's the child who she never was,
Facing daily a pathetic life
Of too much rejection, too little love,
An impatient reminder of the words "just because."

Starved for attention, afraid of herself,
She's always alone in this busy room,
Unnoticed and unused like old toys on a shelf,
She is unheard in her call for help.

I pick her up and ask for her name.
"Miranda" she whispers as she touches my hair.
She averts her eyes which are brimming with shame,
Because of her outcome in life's "chance" game.

I see her yet, still clinging to me.
The pain in her eyes has wounded my heart,
And because of this, I shall forever see
My little Miranda, for eternity.

   Skyler Stephens

Letting Go

Looking so innocent and sweet
Beneath a single silken sheet
I watch you lay soundly asleep
Only wishing to share the dreams you keep
But unfortunately I know
That you, I must let go
For keeping you within my heart
Is really tearing me apart
Although I care for you
It is you who must feel as I do
And that feeling I can't force
It would already have to be there of course
So I'll try to not think of you
As much as I already do
Only to remember the friendship you've given me
And to never forget the peaceful face I see

   Laura A. Ufkin

This Man

   A friend, I thought, was all that I'd found. And
being ten years his senior, I knew many a young girl would be
around. But now, I miss him so much
that I am truly overwhelmed, and I hadn't planned
to care for him so deep down.
   His kisses bring a new meaning to the word passion,
and the last kiss he placed upon my lips, spoke the
word love to my heart.
   I'm unable to resist his gentle loving touch, even
though I know I must. But the feelings of love and
lust break through those years of reality, as he continues
to touch and touch, and desire becomes our only world.
Ending with passionate love making which forms into a beautiful
rainbow hovering high above floating clouds of
this world, that is ours alone.
   Amazed by the ecstasy which can bridge the gap between so
many years, but knowing him like that has shattered all my
fears. And love for him has formed deep inside my unwarned
heart. But now I know, each time we are together it will be
grand, and I will remain a fool for this man.

   Tamie Pucek

Anniversaries

The 29th anniversary is a long time too
Better than the 30th because now I have you.

In memory's lanes, I do recall the sweetheart days we knew
Those days of golden sunshine and those moon-light nights and you
The storms we have weathered and all our triumphs too
And dear, I can't remember a single fault of you.

You are cherished in my heart, dear one
   I think you're really "tops"
Cause ever since I met you dear my heart has turned flip-flops.
As the years come and go Anniversaries too
We'll live our lives with each new day
   Being thankful and being true

And as I count my blessings dear I just gotta count you
Morning, noon and night time too
   Because I love you as I do.

   Lucille Flood

"God, Are You There"?

There's times, when I'm angered, flustered and torn —
Bewildered and hurt, and so full of scorn —
I ask myself, why? "am I really that bare", then,
I look up, and say, "God, are you there"?
I feel like you left me, your back to my face, I start feeling guilty,
And full of disgrace! I look up again, feeling so unaware,
Till I ask that same question, "God, Are You There"?
Of course you are there, you are here,
All around - I need you so dearly,
My love is profound!! So, hold me so tight, and keep me so near,
Then I won't say, "God, Are You There"?

   Geraldine W. Fibble

Untitled

The heat rises off the highway
Burning into the horizon
My soul touches the earth
Only to an illusion
Tomorrow's dust
The heat rises
Burning the coal of desire
Blankets of wild flowers unfold in daylight
Wishing in the wind
Looking for tomorrow in a motion.

   S. Burg

Ghosthouse

Along the trail in the woods,
beyond the cemetery,
there is a house upon the hill
who old folk claim is "scary".
Grandpa says there is a ghost that walks the house at night.
    In a flowing white gown, she makes not a sound
        but gives little children a fright.
I myself doubted... this tale was true -
    but took to the trail with candle and moon.
Quickly the path along I did flee;
    past the old gallows and cemetery.
        stones I stumbled and rocks I fell -
            till I came to the edge of the night...
Up my back sent a chill, for I viewed on the hill -
    the figure of the Lady in white!
The moon chased away and up came the day
    and the specter existed no more.
        I turned 'round to leave -
            surprised to believe -
    But to tell this haunting lore.

Sarah McNabb

To Shirley With Love

Today is your "Birthday" and it's the
Big five O - It seems like only yesterday
That we were "10 Years Old"! To have
Traveled through life without you - would
Surely be to me - like being cast out alone
To drift - on a dark and stormy sea - our
Friendship is like an eagle - flying high
Above the clouds - through life's journey
Onward - along the Pathway of Our lives
We listen to the songs of birds and let
The eagle fly - for friendship is the
Freedom that only we can choose - to
Share our laughter, joy and fears - I'm so
Lucky to have you - So - Happy Birthday Shirley to you my best
Of friends - may sunshine walk beside you
And you never know despair - but - If you
Have to shed A tear - You know that I'll
Be there - friendship Is A blessing - and as
Anyone can see - with you to stand beside
Me - I'm very blessed indeed!

Sylvia J. Buzas

Blessings

The soft green grass,
Big outstretched trees,
A cool refreshing summers breeze.

The family that I call my own,
My job, my friends,
A place called home.

The feel of sunshine warming my face,
Sweet kisses from a child,
A tender loving embrace.

The smell of the air
After a soft gentle rain,
And autumn when the leaves so colorfully change.

The ocean, the mountains
What beautiful sights,
Long happy days and peaceful nights.

The sun and the moon,
Shining stars up above,
My Jesus and all His faithful love.

Marie Oliverio

Wonder

I wonder how it would feel to walk in a garden of
blooming roses, the sweet smell touching my nose, his
soft fingertips entwined with mine.

I wonder what it would be like to wake up with his
lips on my throat, the cool morning breeze swaying the
curtains, falling back to sleep in his arms.

I wonder how it would feel to taste his kisses when
the stars light the sky, to look into eyes where love
runs so deep...for me.

And I wonder what it would be like to make love on
a beach, the waves washing over our bodies like a soft
blanket, our love keeping us warm forever.

Kathleen Williams

A Christmas Sonnet

Through darkened windows comes your subtle wind
Blowing chill on grass with a wounded song,
Scarlet on cheeks, as the snowman smiles,
With rituals, bells, and a bouquet of flowers
To bury autumn scars with a cape of white,
Halting the ebb of blood with your clasp
Within life adrift; as I had once,
In your embrace, watching life drift by
Content in the ivory glare of your clasp,
The warmth from your eyes, your cheeks flushed white,
Oblivious of the dark, the dying flowers.
Now the nights grow long from your shrouded smile
As you arrive at my door with your jaded songs
And leave lonelier still in the howling wind.

Rajiv Ramchandran

Blue Is Me

Blue is calm and gentle.
Blue is soothing and pleasing to the eye,
    but it carries lots of pain.

Blue hates to be alone, but is feels like a misfit.
Blue thinks it's pretty, but doesn't know for sure.

Sometimes blue is ashamed of the secret it has it hide
    from the world.
If the world was all white, blue wouldn't have to be.

Blue is really a depressed color, and it's not
    suppose to let the world know.
Therefore I must always seem to be happy and cheerful
    and to not let the world know that I'm really the
    color...
        BLUE!

Rosalind "Roz" East

Beneath The Windmill

Lone, singular metallic jewel
Bobbed lazily,
In a sea of blue velvet.
We stood beneath the windmill
And talked for hours
About topics that made no sense.
Your tangled hair
Was spread over your forehead
Like a strange disease.
The light of the moon
Reflected playful images
From long ago.
Concepts that we will never truly comprehend
Insisted upon dancing
With a rubberlike quality
As we stood beneath the windmill.

Robyne Marla Novick

The Challenge Of Success

The road to success challenges the mind,
body, and human spirit.
This difficult endeavor explains
why it is not endured by all.
Accomplishments are attained
depending upon one's inner strength and courage.
Friends may become distant
and plans sometimes backfire.
The past can affect the present
and tomorrow is uncertain.
To accept the challenge
is to make a commitment,
relying on
self-determination and confidence.
Whether or not goals are reached,
success is achieved by the attempt.
The feeling is undescribable
and you learn that
the more you do
the more you can do.
  Kristen Carr

Heroes?

These are the men who pull the triggers, the men who drop the bombs
The men who fire the missiles, the men who "right the wrongs"
They're told to do their duty - patriotic work they say
Killing other people who won't do things our way
They do their duty bravely; they kill and kill and kill
They're welcomed home as heroes and lauded for their skill
They have no other choices - their leaders wish it so
Someday there'll be a better way to settle ills that grow
We'll teach the tools of settlement from first grade to the last
Identifying nations' needs as human needs are classed
Foreign aid will go to colleges with peace academies
Arbitrate, negotiate, learn world anatomies
With worldwide laws and global courts to settle such disputes
Statesmen can be heroes, and warriors can be brutes
  Mary F. Groll

Memories

The guns go off.
Boom! Boom! Boom! The thunder roars through the sky.
As the people in the road sides think of the men who have died.

Grief is in their eyes
As they think of their brothers who have died
All for the sake of America.

May God shed his grace on thee
To the men who have died for our country;
The men who have given their lives for our memories.

"Taps" plays in the distant skies.
The people walk away from the memorial with tears in their eyes.

They really don't know what to do.
Are they strong enough to depend us - the red, white, and blue?
  Randy L. Hoyt

My Window

I look out of my window and what do I see?
But a pretty painted portrait right in front of me.
A portrait that even the greatest artist could never compare to.

I see green grass wet with dew.
Then out of a pine tree comes a brightly
painted cardinal that hops along the grass,
then onto a stump, and up into the blue sky above.

Everything I could ever want is here, at my window.
  Valerie Burnside

Amagansett

Harbor of natural peace...
born of luscious colored stars settled next to water,
You inflame nocturnal elegance,
transcending infinite dreams,
beyond what the luminescent firmament can provide.
How one's aspirations are lulled into pleasant fulmination,
then brought to diaphanous zenith
at the gaze of your perfect geography.
My hopes gestate in the realm of your fertile panorama
as it envelops my sphere
And as I bask and bathe in its perennial apostleship,
contemplating that perhaps God, too, is a Dreamer.
  Patricia Murphy

Violets For Her

I float like pollen in a cloud
—bouquet of violets in my hand
plucked from the draw where whispers loud
the cool, sweet breeze across the land.

Snug purple coats of early spring
and pearls of orange draped 'round their throats,
across the greening their beauty sings
to music of stars and meadowlark notes.

This gift I bring up to her door
and leave in silence and never say
what's in my heart forever more -
a love for Mother on May's first day.
  Tomma Lou Maas

Broken Limbs

It flowed with life as in the spring,
Branching up to the sky.
What wonderful fruit it did bring,
Then time started passing by.
The sun no longer giving love, the leaves began to fall.
Without the strength from above, it would never again stand tall.
Weak and drained, barely alive
It could not withstand the winds.
No indeed, it didn't survive,
Too many broken limbs.
  Linda C. Francisco

Penny On The Track

Two small boys crouch near the track
bright penny gleams on shiny ribbon of steel.

In the distance you can hear the rumble
of thunder as it rolls down the line.
Growing stronger, growing louder.

Is it an earthquake? I've never felt one
before, but it's like this I bet.
Warhorns blare, the heart beats fast.

The juggernaut rolls,
a force terrible and strong.
The world shakes - you can't hear
yourself thinking or anything.

The roar is gone. The danger past.
The fruits of labor lie in the grass.

The face of the god is smashed flat
His temple is stretched.
  Padraic Brown

Peace Of Mind

We wake up with our hearts still beating,
But deep down inside we know we're bleeding.

We wonder into another day
Only to see it pass away.

We pray that some miracle will come today
To let us get away
From this terrible slum
In our minds
That has us trapped from real time.

But in the end as time passes away,
There is really only one thing to say.
We rest in peace and bide our time
Because all we have is our peace of mind.

Robert M. Crittenden

Friends Forever

In a few months I will move away,
But don't forget me because in my heart I am to here to stay.
When I am there and you are here,
In my soul we are very near.
I will never forget your tender smile,
Or the number to press on my phone's dial.
Please keep in touch when I am away,
I wish we do, I hope and pray,
Before I go, I want you to know how much you mean to me;
I want us to be friends forever, and I know we will be.
The reason I express my feelings so strong,
Is because I want nothing to go wrong.
I will miss you when I go,
But keep in touch and you will know:
That in time we will meet again,
When we are grown and understand:
A real friendship cannot be ruined by a piece of land.

Melissa Egersheim

Don't Judge Me By My Skin

I'm a proud black-American,
But don't judge me by that,
Don't judge me by the clothes I wear,
Don't judge me by that!

Don't judge me by the color of my skin,
Or how I talk or write,
Because it doesn't matter
If I'm Asian, Black, or White

Judge me by the intelligence I display,
Or the way I make straight A's,
Those are the things you should judge me by,
Those are the right ways!

That's what you should do
So if you want to judge me, think of this:
I'm an American just like you!!!

Shakeelah Seabrooks

So Little Time

I grieve for all those things that have been,
but will never be again,
because there is so little time.

I grieve for all those things that never were,
and never will be,
because there is so little time.

I grieve for friends, once near and dear,
now just a part of yesteryear,
and still - there is so little time.

Roy Shields

Untitled

He wanted to be a doctor — sick bodies and minds to heal
But fate said he must shoulder a rifle -
   his fellows to maim and to kill.
He wanted to build a mansion at the top of a neighboring hill
Not a builder, but a wanton destroyer -
   was the role that this lad had to fill.

Dreams that he dreamed are as nothing -
   just hopes that can never be filled
For the message that brought the tidings
Said "in line of duty, he was killed."

This precious boy is coming, on a ship from a foreign land
To a grave that can now be tended by a heart-broken mother's hand.
He's on his long last journey — to rest beneath the sunlit skies
Near the home he loved in childhood, where the lonely night bird cries.
Now that the guns are silenced — and the struggle is over and done
Be sure that you hold, not lightly, this freedom he has won.

Mallie Booe' Page

Untitled

I was young and didn't understand
but I bared my soul anyway
   I realize now that I gave away so much of
myself (what little I had) that now I have nothing

When you're a child you don't always know
how to ask for help and people sometimes pass you
by without realizing you need them

Now I am a woman. A grown woman
searching for the child I lost
   wondering why, being angry,
feeling helpless, wishing… for anything

I appear confident
   but inside I am starving
Hungering for the soul I lost so long ago
   Sadness strangles my heart
As I search for myself, but I can't seem to find me

Innocence is a gift I wish I had again
   Corrupted is the mind, heavy is
the heart, lonely are the lost and I…

Melanie R. Muldrow

English Literature

I've studied English Literature for almost a year,
But I have still one thing to fear,
How can I ever write poetry like Spencer,
Or great stories like The Canterbury Tales by Chaucer.

Tunneled through years of time have I,
Searching for any small sign.
I've read The Anglo-Saxons and the Medieval period, looking for a clue.
I've read The Renaissance and The Romantics, too.

Tell me great writers of times of old
Why does my writing seem so cold?
I know I haven't the flair of the Victorians or the style of artists of today,
Just tell me why must everything I write be thrown away?

One teacher once told me how to achieve success,
She said "look inside and there you'll find the best."
I've taken this to heart, it's now my motto.
I almost feel as if I'd won the Lotto.

Trish Sanchez

'Can I Truly Journal My Life?'

My mind races so fast; I can't put it all in print.
But I must deal with it all, I just cannot relent.
From day to day, as my life sails on to an end;
I try to discern who was foe or who was friend.

Life, if given, must be treated with care.
Do not mistreat it or live it like a dare.
There's misfortunes and downfalls I can't remember.
My mind blocks them all out; it's another December.

Don't push for my real thoughts, if you aren't ready.
You cannot even understand, my flight's not steady.
There's environment to steer me of how I must go,
But life tells me differently, the road I must hoe.

Is what I truly share, the plight of my distress?
Or am I just too tired to journal this mess?
What I share with you, is my soul that is real.
What is it I hold back, that I choose to conceal?

I dream dreams, you could not conceive.
My mind has raced to heights not believed.
I have told you what I release at most,
The rest has to stay, like a buried ghost.

Val J. Randle

"Visionary Dream"

I can't get you out of my mind
  but I want you in my sight,
I think about you every day
  and dream of you each and every night
    Visions of you and your kindness
      flash before my eyes
    Visions of the truth that hides
      behind all of the lies.
Can this be the dream
  the dream I once hoped for
Can this be for real
  as we pass right through that door.
    Let me take you to a place,
      a place where you're the "King".
    Where the "Queen's" heart is made of gold,
      and the King means everything
Love is the only thing around
  and happiness is the cure.
Soon those empty arms of yours,
  will soon be filled for sure.

Mona Lisa Dela Cruz

'The Environment'

Nature is a place everyone wants to be,
But if we misuse it won't be there to see.
The rain forests are being cut down to build
New occupations,
But where will the animals go who lived in
Those places?

Our oceans are being polluted with oil,
Destroying marine life who float to the soil.
Our rivers, lakes, and streams are being filled
With waste,
So clean up your act, do not take haste.

If we take care of our earth's special places,
We won't be extinct with the animal races.

Melissa Martellotti

Words Worth Thousands. . .

At the beginning was a picture
  but it had no name
Then Adam asked Eve a question
  when the word came.

Adam knew not what a picture was
  until thought was father of the word
And Eve gave birth to evil sin
  and all the world heard.

Words contain pictures that reflect words
  but pictures can't express themselves
For pictures require the help of sounds:
  faith, grace, joy, love, praise—God's elves.

J. D. Phillips

Hope

Hope is like a leaf, fluttering in the breeze,
but it must be stirred by something, or it is still and dead;
It must be motivated, or else it is not there.
Hope gives us a new light, a new strength.
Hope helps us see past the bad and illuminate the good.
Hope keeps us going when things are at their worst,
Hope is our spirit's resurrector, our inner fire that burns all our
lives, but if it is not fed it slowly smolders and dies.
Darkness can not extinguish hope, for it is the maker of light.
No matter what, it remains our inner leaf that flutters from our
inner breeze.

Loni J. Johnson

Life

A new thought of mind is a thrill to find
But its birth may not be just to you
For how many minds in the passage of time
Have thought it to them as new

Life has no beginning no end just an ever changing present
An infinity of gas unfurled an explosion of worlds
Bearing the king and peasant

Infinity belongs to all from king to common peasant
Infinity applies in all directions
It's hart the every changing present

A master mind set down the laws that keeps the spark of life
Its force is tied to the intermind denied to the human sight

From whence you come you will return a cycle with no end
On this cycle you tread alone
Without the aid of beast or men

The pen too verse is life and death
The mind a voidless sea
Poems like life have no end from present
Just on to infinity

Thomas R. Bloom

The Blind Man's Gift

The blind man feels emotion just like you and I,
But never has he ever seen a soaring eagle fly.
Just because he sits there and doesn't speak at all,
Doesn't mean we don't try to catch him, 'cause he might just fall.
He knows how to look past the pain and sinful hate.
And for us he hopes and prays that the dark won't be our fate.
When we are to get in fights and get sand thrown in our eyes,
He'll ask you what's the matter, so don't you tell him no lies.
And if you were to pass him while walkin' on through town,
He'll look at you and smile so you'll never have to frown.

Stephanie J. Siebert

Troubled Dreams

I can't find the words for how I feel
But it's like bruises
Stains of blood
A wilted rose
I want to stand at the edge of a cliff
And look down
That familiar stare
A certain look in my eye
Only seen by those who care
What do I mean
Isn't there one who understands
My empty arms
My cold, lonely body shaking
Grief and misery seem to be my only feelings
Don't you see my eyes soaked with tears
I go on, crying out in the rain
Everything looks distorted in puddles
It's like I'm blinded
With troubled dreams.

Melissa House

Everything In Me

I'm not very special, deep inside.
    But I've got feelings,
And I've got pride.
    And what you have to offer,
Is more than I can give,
    But I know I will love you,
For as long as I live.
People never look beneath
    The surface of the skin.
At my mind, my heart and soul,
    And the love deep within.
When your hand touches mine,
    There's something I can't explain.
Time which subdues the memories and eases away the pain.
    So here I stand alone, vulnerable for you.
A mythical tale revealed, a dream coming true.
    So I'm giving you my secret, something others don't see.
I'm opening up and giving you, everything in me.

D. Martin

You Know It's In My Heart

I'm not much good at saying things like I love you and praying things
But just the same you know it's in my heart
I laugh and joke and kid around
Our friends all think I'm quite a clown
But all the time you know what's in my heart
Though some express their love in boasts
With flowered words and champagne toasts
I guess you have to know it's in my heart
Though my feelings aren't the open kind
They're deep within this chest of mine
And I sure hope you know what's in my heart
Pleasant dreams and happiness, I wish you all the very best
These are things we must find on our own
I've never had to look too far my share of these are over par
Through the years I've found them in my home
No, I'm not good at saying things like I love you and praying things
But I'm quite sure you know it's in my heart
I hope someday I'll find the way to say the things that men should say
But if I don't, please know it's in my heart

Ronald Hagstrom

When We Hear Your Name

I knew you only casually and really not that well
But just to come in contact with you anyone could tell
You always gave a helping hand to anyone in need
You showed us all just who you were by gentle word and deed
And now we're all quite saddened and we're dealing with our loss
We trust in God's Almighty plan knowing He's the Boss
We know He has a reason for calling you away
Though it's quite unclear right now, we'll understand someday
Our neighborhood feels different, the people mourn about
The fireman who gave his life to make sure all were out
While right now we're hurting and we'll never be the same
We'll think of all the good you've done when we hear your name

Loretta Szabo

Fallen From Heaven... And Too Close To Hell

Everything I love has left me,
but like a proud stallion I hold my head up
high and let them go.
Everything I've done has failed me,
and then I try again and get no
appreciation at all.

Everyone I know agrees when I say
that I'm just a foolish little girl.
But who is to say who I am,
and judge my actions just to annoy me.

But now I'm older and understand
that life isn't what it may seem at times,
and time can be a threat to our souls in
so many ways.

So when I see you standing all alone
I'll reach out my hand and help you out of the storm.

And when I see you laughing and smiling
along, I'll join you in happiness and in sorrow,
for I too am human and in search of a friend.

Summer R. Hughes

Memories

I've got to learn to put the past behind
But memories linger in my mind
Of you and me and the way we were
Memories become a blur
I can't forget the way we shared
The way we touched the way we cared
But obviously, you have forgotten
To you our love wasn't all that I thought
Yesterday has nothing left for me
Time tries to turn the page in my book of memories
I don't wanna accept what the future holds
Memories start to unfold
Then I see you in her arms
Basking in your loved charm
Memories run through my mind
I'll stop thinking for a time.

Miranda Sheridan

From The Other Side

A new life is what I have. It
came with a new soul, spirit and speck-
less eyes. Love like I know you can... For
we have dwelled with hate long enough.
Please don't let the forces of confusions
cause you to turn a Death ear to the words
of knowledge, wisdom and understanding at its
highest form and greatest meaning. It's time
to cross over the mental barrier that causes
death to be after death instead of death being
a step towards life.

Steven Goode

Consequence Of War

To some he was a hero,
But now nobody cares.
On the streets he feels lonely,
His life he cannot share.
He's forced to beg for change,
Because now his legs are gone.
He wants no more to live,
But he's forced to live along
When he's lying on the streets the people sneer,
A far cry from the admiration and cheer.
He drinks because he's all alone,
Nobody to live for.
He used to believe in God,
But after all he's been through, no more.
He knew he went to fight,
In a land that was very far.
And now everyday he wishes,
He never fought in that damned war.

Raul Mata

A View From The Moon

Calm and content behaves the wind.
But still I did feel the uneasy twist
of your soul.

One with the earth; you have become,
during your effort to reach me.

Dirt fills your nails as you claw the
new horizon.

The earth to me is far and distant.
Still I can see how our steps are matched
where we walk; each fits within the other.

Hand in hand and heart to heart.
Imagine then; the air we breath is inhaled by
one and exhaled by the other.

These are recreated pasts and a vision of the
future.
It seems like yesterday when today passes
and I dream of a time that does not
exist without you.

Lee N. Thompson

Foster Parents

Foster Parents are not a child real parents.
But that doesn't matter, because they still have love to give.
They love any child and cares what happens to them,
For they are human just like anybody else.
Foster Parents are special people,
I wish the world had more of them.
They take children that have been abused or neglected
Or children that nobody wants.
Sometimes the child's home circumstances play a part
A parent leaves and the other one can't do it all
So Foster Parents is found for the child
And the child stays with them for a while.
Sometimes the child goes back home
Sometimes they don't
But the best thing for a child is love and affection
And that is one thing Foster Parents can give.

Karen Leadbetter

Silent Voices

We love the mocking bird that sings pretty
But the crow is washed away
The mocking bird looks
Pretty, sweet and small
Like many books and many stuff
It is what is inside that counts
The crow looks
Ugly, scraggly and old
But look inside the crow
And you will find
Someone kind
But the mocking bird
Is rude and is bad
So now look
Before you make friends
With the birds
And be careful on what is on
The outside
But do not go run and hide

Thomas Kendrick

The Ocean

Near the shore it's blue and clear,
but the deeper you go there's darkness and fear.

It can be gentle and calm on a warm sunny day,
but can be fierce as a lion on a stormy night in May.

The ocean is sometimes mysterious and blue,
just like a person who's scared and
brand new.

The ocean is full of such wonderful treasures,
you can feel it and touch it, but too big
to ever measure.

The big waves roar up a distant shore,
as if running away from the angry ocean floor.

The ocean will always be a mystery to everyone,
but it will always have adventure and great fun.

Marion Dabu

Changing

People think they know me,
But what do they really know.
Nobody understands me, so I
Just go with the flow!

People say I'm different
Why do I have to be so strange,
I live just like everyone else.
But I'm the one who has to change.

I can't say life has been bad to me,
But I can't say that it's been good.
If there was a way I could do it over again
Don't you think that I would!

I have went through my share of heartaches,
And I felt my share of pain.
How come when ever the sun comes up
I get nothing but rain!

I'm tired of living in this messed up world
It's time I done some rearranging
The longer I live, the quicker I die.
So it's time I done some changing!!

Richard H. Wadlington

Nature— At Its Best

Amidst the rain are hearts of gloom
But when it leaves, the flowers bloom

The sunshine in its full blown glory
Will find its way into a story
Leaves of green and petals of red
Are here until the winters dead

Birds will chirp, their young they'll feed
With winters coming the squirrels take heed

The leaves change colors and cascade to the ground
And soon a soul will not be found

Snow of white will fall from the sky
Then the birds to the south will fly

The seasons change as each thing rests
Giving way to "Natures Best"
Teresa A. Sloan

Who Is It?

She's hard to find 'cause she's so rare.
But when you need her, she is there.
Once you let her in your heart,
She will always be a part.
When you have a lonely day,
She helps you pass the time away.
She stands beside you when you're down,
And takes away your ugly frown.
She sits with you, you're right through the night,
Until she's sure that you're all right.
And when your heart is broken into,
She will know what's right for you.
She has a great big heart to lend,
This person is a special friend.
Pennie S. Phillips

Lovesick

Another day has passed and the sun slowly fades,
but yet I still miss thee.
Everything I see and do somehow makes me think of you.
You are my sister and no one can change that, not even
the distance in which we live apart.
I miss the sound of your voice, the happiness in your smile,
and the love in your heart.
Although I'll see you again I can't help but think that
memories are all I have left.
Only two more years separate my dream and I.
To live in my real home, with my real family,
which is you, my life and my soul.
The sun will yet come up again tomorrow and another day will
pass, but only you and I can feel its warmth.
So please, take a walk, watch the clouds,
and think of me because I love you.

Renae de Mello

Untitled

Needs can be met,
By the Lord God above,
Wants are a different story,
Is it money, is it power, is it love?

Money is obtained by education,
Power is obtained from above.
Which of the three is leastly obtained?
I say it is love.

Much money and power is found in this world,
Love is the least, but the best of the three.
Some will find lust that will last a short while,
Few will find true love that will never leave.

Tiffany Potter

Loving Me

It's not that I don't love you I think you know I do
But, your tongue is like a knife, that leaves my soul to bleed
And leaving you behind is the only way, I'll be free

It's not that I don't want to see you or want you to be near
It's just the value I hold precious you don't see are dear

I don't know why we are fighting, never seeing eye to eye
When I try to say you've hurt me, you just try to deny

No longer can I struggle and try to keep the peace
So I guess me saying good-bye is the only way it will cease

It's not that I won't miss you, I thing you know I will
But, I must protect my spirit that you are trying to kill

It's not an easy thing to do, to turn and walk away
but I'm looking toward tomorrow with the hope of a new day

I think I'll be O.K. now, although it's a long road ahead
I'm going to love myself now and know the abuse is dead

I'll always love you dearly, deep inside my heart
But, loving myself now, is why we must part
Vicki Watkins

A Mother's Longing

What do we hope for
By searching in the dark passages of our minds
For a yesterday long gone and unattainable
Distant memories of walks along single paths
Of flowers in wine bottles reaching, reaching
Through the broken clouds for the sun
While the present calls aloud
Too quickly the image is gone
A small hand reaches out
A touch and the memory fades
Back to looking at tomorrow
Through little eyes
That see so much, so differently
For that which we long for is no longer ours to see
A moment of overwhelming tenderness and love
Replaced by longing for a life gone
And a new which opens like a flower afraid of the light.
Lisa Craythorn

Walls Around Me

Yesterday walls were built around me
by those who profess to love me,
And by those who were supposedly
looking out for my best interest.

And I was woman before I realized
those were not walls of mine.
I could push them down and walk through
And I would most certainly survive.

And as I grow old, I realize with sorrow
the life I missed outside the walls.
And for this reason, I will teach my child
There are no boundaries to love.

Pamela Newton

Earth

As black clouds rise to falling stars
Cheap tricks die in your head
Cannibal corpse eats your death
Facing the truth is to your disadvantage
Clinching your teeth to make your breath soft
Swarming eyes to look after your soul
Trigger the key that locks your head
After the earth has swallowed the rest
Victoria Barragan

Daddy's Hard-Working Hands

Loved to caress daddy's hard-working hands
caddied golf, cut grass, waited dining cars
African-American father of eight loyal fans

Poured steel, fixed autos, scrubbed pots/pans
pumped gas, mopped floors, opened jars
Loved to caress daddy's hard-working hands

King-hearted deacon lived by God's commands
no hangouts, street corners, night clubs/bars
African-American father of eight loyal fans

Bore burden of life's countless demands
never rude, crude, enjoyed King Edward cigars
Loved to caress daddy's hard-working hands

Great sense of humor, issued gentle reprimands
years of toil evidenced by calluses & scars
African-American father of eight loyal fans

Liked driving long, shiny, black sedans
handsome, debonair looks rivaled movie stars
Loved to caress daddy's hard-working hands
African-American father of eight loyal fans

Virginia K. Lee

Eye Of The Storm

I float here on the pond of my being
Calm, cool, serene, tranquil
And see the disorder all around me
And hear the wailing voices outside of me
And feel those afraid of inevitable change and I am amused.
Afraid of change? Ha, ha!!
I will accept and ponder all changes thrown to me or on the wind.
Some may be difficult to swallow
Others, too easy to notice
Yet change and Chaos go hand in hand
And there is an eye to the Storm of Chaos
And it is - Calm, cool, serene, tranquil
And that is - Me
The Calm amid the Storm of Chaos
We recognize and greet each other (A wink, A smile)
And busily do nothing while the Storm builds
And as I float here on the pond of my being
Calm, cool, serene, tranquil
I am amused.

Margaret J. Keller

Rainbow

A rainbow is what I wish to see, what I hope you
can give me. You're my mother and that's all I need,
when I am troubled you can see when I need comfort,
that's what you offer me. I am going to make you
happy with me one day, and if I don't I promise
I will die trying. I am your rainbow and you
are mine because I love all the colors about you
and wish some days I could add more. The only
colors I hate about you are blue and red, when
you are red you're furious and angry and when you
are blue so blue you are depressed, sick, and
tired, but no matter what you always sccm to
come back to the colors I love about you Yellow
Green, Purple and Orange the colors of the year
that show me you love me and that show what a
beautiful rainbow you are.

Natashia Golden

Can I

Can I put my finger on the phone
Can I call your name out loud
I am such a hopeless man that tears mean nothing at all
Day by day I see myself and what you mean to me
All the feelings I don't understand, why are they meant to be?
So I close my eyes and far away find a face that cares
I love you,
You might think otherwise but deep in my
heart my life was sent to you,
You live in time with me and are a friend
Help me when I am gone again
The first I saw of your noble love
I could not find a verse
You were what I saw and to
A cloud I dispersed

Kevin E. Hickey

Shadow Child

I think about you every day, but just how many things
can I say?
You look so sad and lonely there.
I wish I could show you how much I really care.
I wish your dreams could all come true, but you're just like
the early morning dew.
If sunlight shone on you, I know you could shine.
You could shimmer and dance, but no one will give you the chance.
If you were a willow would you always weep, and always seem to sleep?
You're just that little shadow in the corner.
But what can I do?
My heart aches so for you.
You seem so lonely there, but how can I show you that I
really care?
You seem so lonely there in the corner.
Back in the shadows...

Susan Kay Mortland

The Stranger

I look in the mirror - but how
can it be - why is there a stranger
looking back at me?
There's pain in her heart and her
eyes are full of fear, her face is all
wrinkled and her hair is turning grey -
who is this unwelcome stranger? Who is this? I say
Where is the baby so precious and
small - so loved by mother, father,
brother and all?
Where is the child who sat at her
grand parents knee? Who is this
scared lonely soul? It can not be me!
Where is the teenager so vibrant
and so alive? Where is the young
bride and happy loving wife?
Where is the proud young mother
of five fine children born?
Who is this stranger? And please
God, where have I gone?

Peggy Nichols

Whatever Is Round

Whatever is round, is round, is round
Can roll on the ground, the ground, the ground.
Whatever is square, is square, is square.
Never can roll anywhere.
Whatever goes up, goes up, goes up.
Will likely come down, come down, come down.
Whatever is in may soon get out
And run about all over town.
You may go under,
You may go over,
Round and around on a highway clover.
Wherever you go, you look, you see,
Say how-do-you-do,
It might be me.
And I'll be your friend, your friend, your friend.
This is the end of my song,
This is the very last end.

Mary Becker

Industrial Parks

"Industrial parks" is an oxymoron.
Can steel and grass marry?
Can the hum of computers compete with the hum of bees?
"Industrial" buildings don't show what they do.
They are mirror glass and concrete cubes without faces.
No number on the building.
(It was on a berm at the corner of the block.)
No doors. That window there is an entrance.
Whoosh through it like a spirit.
Inside, it smells like airports, the fanned and filtered breezes.
People hurry here too, brush close without seeing.
Disappear in an elevator and move up to where the view is wide.
See outside? The ribbons of glass, the platoon of cars,
And a tree!

Marilyn Lees

Yearning

Silhouette that is vague,
Cannot be easily read.
Motions that are mystically moving,
Will never fade.

Storms might rush and blow,
And may bring turbulent snow.
Owl's eyes are on guard from a distance,
Swiftly protecting their young for an instant.

Traveling in this broken path,
Searching for something worth more than gold,
Adversities that cannot be traded for the world,
Still yearning for that happiness to hold.

Rosalie Del Puerto Macaltao

Chamber

Living inside a realm of fear,
   chained to a wall not shedding a tear
Blood trickles down my wounded head,
   not breaking a frown not wishing I'm dead
My mind is empty,
   no pain is felt
Dangling from the chains,
   around my throat
Neck all bloody,
   ripping so slightly
feeling my life ending abruptly

Stephen O'Hara II

Let It Be

When you can't quite attain what your heart desires
Can't straighten out the twist nor the bend
Can't control the quiver of earth beneath your feet
It will all even out in the end

Can't quite figure out what happened or why
Must have made a wrong turn down life's road
Over yonder is a field of lovely flowers
Stop there and release your heavy load

The road is long and winding
The days are blistering, the nights are cold
Some of the travelers are frightened, and weary
And some are strong and bold

There are open spaces, and fences too
Many roads to be traveled for sure
Walk softly on some, but run down others
And look for beauty, simple and pure

God meant for us to enjoy our time here
So be happy, lively, and gay
And thank him, for your gift of life on earth
But be ready to meet him at the close of day.

Rachel Mitchell

A Concert By The Lake

I gave you a concert by the lake
Carefree youthful days of hootenannies blended into my new age.
Susan, you are fused forever to my past
Yet you still dominate my present.

You liked for me to sing and play guitar
Making me feel talented beyond reality.
I drew you into my memories from afar.
You entered them all without making a ripple.

There is a need to pull back, to heal.
So many wounds to lick, "so many miles to go before I sleep."
Yet I continue to be driven to make you
Part of all things important to me.

The pain of separation is there all the time.
I'm desperate to hold you again.
The Aspens try to speak to me.
Their welcome falls on my deaf ears in vain.

Colorado's blue skies are strewn with marshmallow clouds.
The mountains beckon, even through my tears.
Perhaps I can draw strength from the Rockies.
Perhaps it lies only in your arms.

Orest G. Dubynsky

Ode To A Placemat

You are my protection from my sins
Carelessness that casts upon the frail tablecloth-atrocities
The foul mess of eggs, spaghetti and sloppy joes
Evils that give mere mortals sustenance and joy
Yet stain the delicate hues of the cloth that cleansing cannot erase
Forever tarnishing the beauty and balance of a work of art
Yes, it is you, dear placemat, that guards the virginity of the cloth
For you take the spill and cast it off your plastic coating - your armor
You, a knight, shining, glistening with your white shield
Flowers that adorn your armor symbolize the beauty you protect
Take a blow and wipe clean as when you were new
Mortals would sell souls for such immortal fortification
Vivid, flourishing, simple, yet so complete
How can an object meant for abuse exude such majestic fortitude
Awe is what is commanded by your presence
You, of no heart, soul or mind, serve your purpose and never ask
   "why"?
The purpose is clear, it is your duty to serve and protect
I owe my utmost respect to your beauty, your strength and your purpose
For you will save me from mortal errors and let beauty remain
For I am human, not a placemat

Robin G. Perez

Where They Are Now

Some sort or vertigo—a mad coriolis
Casting your warmth upon hallowed ground
Obscuring tall shadows of shimmering sound

The pillars—they fell
Yet the roof remained standing
The edge of the mirror concealed the disbanding
I finally fell as the floor slid away
Too beaten to go, too frightened to stay

Jagged abstractions—thoughts that I saw
People I knew and the places they stayed
Dust motes blown far, yet farther away

The buildings—they vanished
Like the rush of the crowd
As we danced the Dance of the Silver Shroud
We rose in the air committing high treason
Our bodies transparent, we laughed at the seasons

Some sort of vertigo—a mad coriolis
Casting your warmth upon hallowed ground
Obscuring tall shadows of shimmering sound
Mark McGuire

Noticed Without Recognition

The dry fragment of the leaf
  Caught my eye today.
Then, I began to realize much
  I'd never seen in the same kind of way.

Only a short time ago, as it hung upon the tree,
This very same leaf had beauty
  That I could not see.

Now, as it lay there, among all the rest
  That had fallen to the earth's floor,
I stopped to ponder about its existence
  Unlike I ever had before.

It crumbled at my touch
  As no more life could be found.
Soon, it, too, would return to the dust,
  A mere granule of the ground.

Once it was attached to the life giving tree;
  But, there it was not noticed because
    it was surrounded, you see?

Yet, just like our life when living for our Lord,
What seems to go unnoticed is, in fact by someone being adored!
Regina A. Goodwin

Revelation

I came into being an infant - the wisdom of the ages in every
  cell. I could not speak the language, but there was much
  to tell.
The need was great to communicate, but when I tried
  to speak the words of wisdom, I just cried.

Undaunted in my quest to speak the Truth, I knew what I must do;
  'twould take some time and effort, but I would see it
    through.
Day by day I practiced, 'till I could understand
  the language and the customs of this unfamiliar land.

And then at last the time had come; no longer must I wait
  to free all of humanity from the suff'ring and the hate.
But when I tried to tell them, I knew I could not say
  how anyone should live this life; for there's a better way.

Through the experience of living on this now familiar earth,
  I learned something I never knew at the time of my birth.
Through trials and tribulations, each soul must find its own
  eternal path to freedom, and the way back Home.
Vivian Elizabeth Sommer

Chasing Rainbows

Here I go again,
Chasing rainbows across the sky till I reach their never-end
And that is where I lie
And look at that which rests
In the sky on clouds afar
The light of the spectrum, the everlasting beauty
Made with a nearby star

Will I find hope
Or will I find love?
Who will know except God above?
The myriad of possibilities
Is just like the colors
In the sky.

I cannot wait to go again
And chase more rainbows
From where they begin
To the end of them
And the ends of the earth.

Life is what you make it to be.
Nothing ever ends.
Paul James Roberts

Childhood

Laughter is heard echoing off the rolling hills of
        Childhood.
Flowers smile as a youngster bounds through the rambling meadow,
        And shouts a triumphant song of
        Childhood.
    A puppy stops to be petted and yaps eagerly
        While touched by the tender hand of
        Childhood.
Raindrops prance in merriment, caressing the radiant face of
        Childhood.
    A mother sighs contentedly as she embraces her memories of
        Childhood.
Kelle J. N. Pierce

Violoncello Suite In D Minor

The Virtuoso enters the praeludium with several altered chords.

Imperturbable vibrato suggests a lamentable mood

A series of double stops end with a diminished seventh
chord enabling modulation.

Unmistaken Tertian harmony envelops a phrase,

Nonharmonic tones create tension in the phrase.

A picardy third nicely finishes the praeludium.

In movement I, contemplative minor scale passages fill the air.

Ascending chromatic arpeggiation abruptly tapers off to
an authentic cadence.

The arduous time changes in Movement II are underway.

Dispersed through Movements II and III are tone clustering
implied pedal point, natural harmonics, and embellishment.

The performer's interpretation and articulation of the piece
gives rise to an encore.

Receptivity of the finished work brought realization
along with enjoyment to some.
Kenneth C. Schmerr, Jr.

The Water Cries

Polluted water flows down a stream, it's black just like India ink,
Clean water all must have to drink, dirty water goes down the sink.

Water, H$_2$0, one key element in life's cycle, without water we all die,
What to do when there is none? What to say when thirsty children cry?

Water for the farmers to grow the foods on the table for us to eat,
That water now carries insecticide, and in some lands poisonous DDT.

Yet we say, can't make any money unless the insects are beat,
Will man's greed for money satisfy his thirst in summers heat?

When water poisons the soil with all of the toxic waste man dumps,
Will he be able to drill deep, and reach clean water with his pumps?

How long before the cycle that water flows is no longer clean?
When land is turned into desert sand, by then will man have seen?

How many people must die before a change is made in man's way,
Will it be said? It cannot happen now, at least not in our day!

Will this be enough to ease our minds as we scramble for a buck,
Or will we always roll the dice, putting our trust in lady luck?

What does it take to change a world that you have to kick and prod?
I only know of one thing, and that is a very powerful act of God!

Ray Horton

Mon Petit Chou

Oh, those eyes…
   clear whirlpools where my soul wants to swim.
   Look at me and I feel weak;
   My famous dancing partner,
   when you smile you look as slick as a panther.
Those lips…
   that I cannot resist;
   your kisses that taste forever sweet.
Oh, so very thoughtful…
   how much you so care;
   you made me feel as if you would always be there.
I could see on the first; date!? That you
   would be a great friend.
I gave you a challenge,
   but you are so very special that I get scared.
I hope you understand,
   and please hold my hand.

Liz Snyder

The Girl From The Ghetto

She came from the ghetto, tattered and torn, in second hand
clothing of which her sisters had worn.

She worked everyday by the sweat of her brow, oh what she
was once and what she is now.

Standing at a podium, ignorance free, inside her hand is a
college degree.

The tears that she sheds aren't tears of duress, they are
tears that shout victory, tears of success.

As this valedictorian speaks, so many are in awe, because
the girl from the ghetto will be practicing law.

So when they tell you you're dreaming, agree that you are, then
push them aside and reach for the stars.

Sure you may stumble more times than not, but the victory
is within the battle of which you have fought.

Though criticism may confront you, you must never doubt,
because if you settle for failure,…… you've sold yourself out.

It may seem impossible or not so easy to do, but just like
the girl from the ghetto, your dreams can come true.

Pamela Wilson

Summer

The sky is filled with fluffy
Clouds..makes the blue a deeper hue…
the warm summer breeze helps me
enjoy the view.. birds fly overhead
and some are chirping in the trees…
Children playing games among the leaves..
People sitting on park benches, enjoying
Their lunches. Young and old enjoy the day
and let their cares sleep away.. Letting
the sounds inside making memories
for future recall.. to make them smile
some lonely cold day is the fall…

Mary Grace Czeredarczuk

To Endeavor

When the day doth shed its warmth and light,
   Cold grows my heart and this is night.
     He offers me the token gloom.
   I pray thee enter this vacant room.
    Occurs as such a thousand fold.
    This woeful vigil I do hold.
   And when at last the sun to rise.
No sleep, but tears have found these eyes.

    Alas, one day an Angel fell,
    And entered into my private hell.
Her radiance did bring the warmth of the day.
   Although it added to my dismay.
  Imprisoned am I and rightfully so,
   For beauty my soul shall never know.
   Behold, I am Evil and Evil is me.
  Behold, I'm denied all that could be.

Terry Pike

Rain

Dark skies of a stormy day,
   Cold like me as I walk away.
From the heavens above the rain falls down,
   Teasing me as I hope to drown.
As I walk full of gloom,
   I feel as empty as an airless tomb.
The sheeting rain chokes my breath
   Reminding me I'm far from death,
Far from death, yet so far from life;
   The vile rain pries cutting like a knife.
Painfully sorrow filled I continue my journey,
   Through the rain though, no end can I see.
Looking down, the rain's puddles reveal my reflection;
   Likewise revealing my own dejection,
As I stood drowning in pain
   Suffering in the cruelness of the rain.

Todd M. Wilson

A Better Place To Be

The world to me,
could be a better place to be,
If the fighting would cease,
And we could live in peace.
Different races hand in hand,
Hungry mouths fed throughout the land.
No more drugs killing our kin,
Taking the children; teaching them sin.
No more gun shots throughout the night,
Peaceful city streets; what a wonderful sight.
So this world could be,
A better place you see.
If all these things,
would one day come to be.

Kimberly Ann Marie Felix

Stained Glass

Stained glass in my windowpane.
Colors shimmering in the sunlight.
I see the rainbow of colors in a blur of my mind.
The colors transform me into a trance of nothingness.
A voice form inside me comes to my lips, but no words are
spoken.
Staring off into the stained glass of nothingness,
I am reminded that stained glass does not speak.
So I just sit and stare.
Quotes run through my head like a poet preparing to recite.
Oh, if only stained glass had a voice!
What advice would the motley glass give to me?
Let your true colors shine through
and happiness will surround you until your dying days.
Is that what you are trying to tell me?
I have seen the spectrum of my mind,
but I want to experience every single color that is within me.
Shall I ever be courageous enough to conquer
and fulfill my destiny of rainbow?

Paulette Hopkins

Deliverance

(Based on "Death on a Pale Horse"/a painting by Benjamin West)

The Powers of Darkness take hold,
combining their strength against righteous.
They come,
trampling the brave under their horses,
striking down the courageous at the mercy of Satan's sword.

The Dogs of Hell follow their Master
foaming at the mouth with hate and terror.
They come,
tormenting the souls of the meek and humble,
ravaging the land and claiming their domain.

Death leads them, brandishing bolts of fire and brimstone,
along with his horsemen, bearing swords of destruction.
They come,
bringing wars and famine, struggles and pain,
depriving every living thing of life.

On a gleaming white horse the Savior rides,
defeating Death with his everlasting presence.
He comes,
ridding the world of sin and darkness,
embracing the faithful and resurrecting the martyrs.

Timothy J. Beehler

Oblivion

Oblivion, sweet oblivion,
Come and carry me away.
Everything seems pointless,
And so tedious,
When there's nothing left to say.
Todays, tomorrows, yesterdays,
Blur together as time goes on.
Will I miss the monotony,
When I find my time is gone?
When my time is nearly over,
Will it not seem half as long?
When I can no longer see a sunrise
Or hear the birds as they sing their song.
As I consider all these things,
I know there's so much more to say.
Oblivion, sweet oblivion,
Please wait another day.

Laurie A. Hess

A Day In Love

When I leave you I feel an emptiness
come over me...It is as if I have had
something taken away from me or lost
something.
I continue on...hoping this pain will
soon ease...remembering the time we just
spent together...knowing full well the
emptiness within, will not be filled until
I am with you again.
With this in mind, I rush to finish the
things that have separated us for awhile..
with every passing second, looking forward
to being with you again.
When I return...you are there waiting, as
eager to see me as I am to see you...No
longer are there empty feelings...for once
again we are filled with the feeling that
removes all emptiness..that feeling is love.

Rebecca W. Moss

Untitled

After the day
Comes the night.
To be between two fires
To judge—the exigent—required
  or be the exodus
Contradicting life's desires.
Contingency—to pass or fail,
  in light of such occurrences.
Or earliness, akin, the dying nightbird wail.
The hemlock surely flourishes.
So be
The parallel to me.
For, after the day
Comes the night,
And after the night,
  Comes...

Suzanne Thompson

Life's But A Pizza Slice

Life's but a pizza slice, a savory
concoction to ease your rumbling hunger.
As you nip the tip of the slice, your tongue
is met with a succulent spicy hot
tomato sauce. Then as you carry on
and chew the tasty mozzarella cheese,
or pepperoni-anchovy, or both,
it becomes a joy, a pleasure, a treat!
But then, as you approach the end, the sauce
gets cold and dry and disappears, and all
that's left is but a bit of tasteless crust.
Ah but wait, to repeat the joyful feast
you may have another slice or more. But
alas with life, you only get one slice.

Rocky Pascucci

"To Our Little One"

Oh, our little one, how we love you so
  Daddy and Mommy need you to know

Safe in Mommy's tummy, in your own little bed
  Rest now our angel, rest your precious head

You will soon be born into this big, beautiful world
  We wish you health, instead of being boy or girl

May God bless you and make you safe from harm
  Love to you, until we meet our angel, and
hold you in our arms...

Theresa L. Tamburri

Fantasy Children

Children of fantasy
Created out of hope, despair, love, desire.
Conceived, born nurtured
In imagination.

A product of reverie
A vision into immortality
Adorned in veil of imagery,
Love of beloved.

Free to dance on day dreams,
Caged by depression and devastation.
Always inquisitive and intelligent,
Curious and cunning.

Given to inspiration and meditation,
Eradicating desecration.
Fortunes of thought that inflame.
No poverty of charm and fame.
Ethereal, elusive, eternal.

 Ruth A. Fox

A Child

 A child is a little miracle of life.
Created with love by a husband and wife.
 Through the years, they will work hard.
 Through the tears, they will smile,
 They will try to build a loving and solid foundation,
 for the child they have created is the new generation.

 Lynette Biller

Untitled

From the sadness I've endured
creates pain in my heart
that brings tears to my eyes
and pleading to my lips.
And death awaits, like a misplaced thought,
that is at my very fingertips.

 Mary-Nicole Renna

Day By Day

I have loved my journey of life while living here on God's wonderful
creation. I loved and lost early in my travel. God shapes our lives

and changes our direction beyond our will and help us to discover what
life is. Through our grief and gladness, joy and pain, he gives us
victory in order that our spirit may be ever growing out of this lost

love. God gave me four wonderful children, each having their own
unique individuality. I wanted to take each one into my hands and

mold them to my own need; I knew this would not work, so I gave them
space to grow on their own. Therefore, all four have brought me great
joy, pride, and enduring comfort; in which I feel for all time I am
blessed. In the middle of my journey I lost again by losing my oldest

son, in death, as I did his Dad. The greatest sorrow a mother can
have is losing a child. I wasn't brave or strong and time seemed so

long. Not yesterday's sorrow that comes our way nor tomorrow's
uncertainty; we only learn to bear the burden of pain for only that

day. Through God's mercies, he brought me in silent wonder to the
place where I understood his comfort, courage, and strength to guide me
Day By Day.

 Mildred Tinnin

Futility

Life, one big cycle! Things are done over and over again.
Creation labors heavily, things are constantly in motion:
Life moves on; yet, where is the change? Where is the completion?
Where is the satisfaction? When is the end? Nothing is
permanent, but the earth.

The earth remains, but man lives for a moment and dies.
Another generation inherits his toil; he is forgotten!
Discoveries are made, yet man only builds on past successes.
They are not new; they are only different. The important things
of life must always be done again.

The futility of striving! There is so much to be done.
Straighten one thing out and something else needs straightening;
Fix one problem and another arises to take its place.
God has given to man the unenviable task of striving and yet
never finding complete fulfillment.

Man is a rat in a maze! He cannot free himself: Life is the maze.
Man enters into it without knowledge, he leave it without choice.
While caught in this trap of living, his task is set by God.
What hope has man? What ever he achieves, he only leaves at
the end. Nothing is permanent, but the earth!

 Menaja C. Obinali

Paradox And Enigma For Fox And King

They stood apart, separated together by the space of a room. A
cricket chirp of recognition brought a distant rumble of tension;
like thunder over the horizon. They almost remembered. Beyond
time where their separate meaning was fused; they almost traveled
to when understanding was beyond crystalline.

An old epileptic named time shuffled about in spasm bursts. Space
stood between them and they were joined by thought. When they sat
together thunder shouted for distance. Time flashed and oozed
with tension, with joy, with recognition. They stood outside of
space, beyond time and conflicted in the purity of joining thought.

Sibling strangers, they welcomed each the other with relief from
recurrent absence. Fearful passion confused passionate fear. They
fell into a void filled with random. Unfamiliar affirmation
launched needy flight into familiar plight. Pathos laughed. The
enigma of acceptable mediocrity entranced.

Drab colors sparkled blackly. Happiness flirted through a one way
mirror. The magic that could be, ran freely on a bungee tether.
Silence told lies about chance and possibility. Frustration and
fulfillment danced in fascination through a dimly dawning night.
Joy wept around the corner.

 Roy Roberts

The Wall Of Parenthood

There is a giant wall standing in front of me
Day after day and year after year I long to see
What's on the other side of this giant wall
I can't reach over for it's two heights tall
I've walked for weeks to the left and to the right
I've walked for days and also for nights
As I get older, I learn every little crack
Planning in my head how to attack
The harder I try, the more I can't see
Finally I learn that maturity is the key
So I just ask, "Can I see what it is you hide?"
The wall moved apart and slid to the side
Forward I walk into unfamiliar land
But if I need protection that wall will always stand.

 Timothy Dean

Think Light

As they sat around the steps,
currents shot down cool air,
water droplets fell from thought.
The lesson started; learned long
ago, perhaps in another time?

The motion went 'round the room,
one by one and then again they
bore their souls, some freely, some
unwilling and, those who would not
in the crowd give their soul away.

The windows let the dark fall in
the light, held the room in cool
colors and, muddied the brightness
of the night. A kaleidoscope of shadows
whispered about the blonde they gathered upon.

There waits one and then another, dreams
of closeness touch the night and vanish
yet another waits there too! Quickly they
run through men and bleakness, two women
hold tightly and won't let go to be free!

   Ron Smiley

'Vengeance'

  Hear the noise, breaking through the fog,
dancing around like an iron frog,
  Breaking my hearing and taking my sight,
living so evil like a thief in the night.
  Don't be so trusting, because you'll never know,
just how far the insanity go.
  Ever so quickly, or ever so slow, maybe yes or maybe no!
  Gestures of rudeness, or gestures or fun,
now the joke has just begun, do you want
to die laughing?, or would you rather
be hung?
  Breathless and dying, I'll kiss your mouth,
I'll turn your dream into a shout. Oh wonderful
noise I long to hear, so sharp like a siren to
a bleeding ear.
  When I hear the silence, then I'll know you're
dead, then I'll lay your body upon a fiery bed.
Then I'll drink your ashes with a very fine
wine, and laugh all the way to hell,
because vengeance will be mine!

   Tina Smith

A Part Of Me

  That day was the worse I will never forget that
Day of fright, sitting there wondering what happened
I often thought why, why did it have to happen to him

  Sometimes that day keeps replaying in my mind,
I wonder if he is okay, is he laughing or sad,
  is he watching over me, will I ever know,
  the heartache, the suffering, I can't stop
asking God why him, for that year I hated God,
    I didn't understand
there was so much pain, suffering and crying.

  Later I learned that if he would not have died
I would have never learned the value of life
I have memories that are good my family came together,
  that year was very confusing for me
  but now I understand.

  My life now is full of memories of him
my favorite is when he would make me sit in the corner for
no reason, now I miss that and wish he was here
  I am happy to know he is in heaven

  No one can ever take those memories away.

   Shelly Kirkpatrick

To The Good Times

It's the end of February, a special time of year
Daytona fills with magic, Bike Week is here
The nights are cool, the days are fair
Thunder and lightening are everywhere
There is no storm, that's a fact
But in just few days, the town will be packed
The Harley's straight pipes echo like thunder
400,000 bikers provide the wonder
The sun mixed with chrome, bright flashes and flames
Give us visual images that shall always remain. Two weeks of
partying, cold beer and hot babes, renewing old friendships that
never change. We party hard and we party fast for another
riding season is here at last. But time passes quickly, no way
to slow it down. The next thing you know, we're heading out of
town. We go our own ways as we ride through the year. But
good times and memories never disappear. It's very special
people who live this lifestyle, no matter the place or
distance in miles. Whenever we recall these times it will be
with smiles. So until next year, may we ride safe and free, for
in both our minds "I'll ride with you and you with me".

   Raymond Graf

Grandfather

There was an old man who is no more,
Death came knocking at his front door.

He is to be cherished for evermore,
the one to cherish for ever more.

Memories to cherish more and more,
but never so less as once before.

His thoughts always treasured more and more,
till death comes knocking on my front door.

He remembered the days of yore,
but alas they are again no more.

Beyond that imaginary door,
I'll whisper I love him ever more.

   Travis Woolley

Life - N - Death

Life is part of the beginning;
Death is just the end.

Even though they are powerful things;
Time would have no meaning, and,
Would always be the same never ending.

They make a cycle that makes the world go round;
It never changes
It would go on just as a line that has no end.

Death takes away, life brings forth;
They work to balance nature's cycle of life.

Life and death work together, but,
Neither can live without the other.

For one begins and the other ends.
   Roy Scott Kidwell

Martha

Does a rose petal weep at the end of the day?
Does it long for the sunlight to guide its way?
Does the wind carry whispers from far, far, away?
Can we catch them, hold them, beg them to stay?
Or do they travel on, another time, another space
To bring joy and happiness to the people whose presence they grace.

   Stacy L. Paul

Untitled

To look at me one could not see that I have felt the bitter spear of death pierce through my heart, but I have felt it as if I were the only one in the world to know such sorrow. My smile is a masque of misery that I show to the world of the living. I am good at deceiving people, for it is my existence. I walk through the stage of life without an intermission. This has become such a ritual, that sometimes I can fool myself into believing that I am alive. I dance the dance of deceit on the petals of death. The sharp shocks of anguish that run through my veins no longer wounds me. I have become numb to what normal people feel is pain. The only humor I find is in the lies that are so often told to me. In the corners of my mind, I find my sanctuary, for there no harm can come to me. Fear has become my best friend and the thought
of love invites hatred into my soul. Pity, people try to pay me. Why? I ask them, for it happiness were to be granted to me, I would not know what to do with it. I would probably spend it all in one day and all of my tomorrows would be like all of my yesterdays. I would rather be denied the sweet breath of happiness than feel her whisper in my ear for only a single moment. I'm happy happy as I can be, I delight in my own misery for it is all that has ever been given to me. One day maybe upon death I will be granted my freedom but until then I will wait.

Natricia C. Wright

My ABC's

A nice Bee Seeks a good
Deed to do he is rewarded
Evenly for his Efforts.

Gee look there's
H.K. Newman the author. I like his new book
Jake and Kate.

Ellie and Emmy have a lot of Energy!
Oh! Look how fast they climbed the mountain Peak.

Cucumbers Are yucky, so I try to Escape eating them and drinking Tea at the same time you see.

Vinnie doesn't have a
Double U written on his X-ray.
Why, he only has
Zenith written on it.

Kimberly Frye

Alone

Somewhere in silence is
   Deep where I lay,
Through the worst of the
   Hour of every day.
Thoughts run smoothly as
   Happiness disappears.
   The coldness of my body
And the wetness of my tears.
The touching and the holding
   I'll only reminisce,
   And I'll have to forget the
   Boldness of your kiss.
   The warmth of your body
Lying close to mine, your breath on my neck
And your smile so fine. Brings me to tears as
   I lower my head,
   To sink deeper in sorrow
   As I lay in my bed.
So tragically depressed on what is now shown,
 I look in the mirror to find...I'm alone.

Stephanie L. Ziemba

Desert Places

Desert places with mountain south faces
Defy wide open spaces
With plants that pull off shoe laces;
Watch out for these fancy flowers that tease,
Colorful cactus pricks or sticks on your sleeve.
Beware of each creepy or crawly thing
And fliers in Spring bring bees that sting!
Browse; arouse not hidden life all around —
Peruse the panorama that does abound!
You forget snakes and snails and puppy dog tails —
Just sidewinders for reminders
That seem to show suddenly from a circus hat —
Who are quickly rattled in their own habitat!
So don't be rude and intrude.
It's safer to walk in your own park
Where the songbird is a meadowlark;
Desert animals not in a zoo
Are not to be petted—that's taboo!

Lucille Wall

Forbidden Love

If only we were together to share our dreams forever, to speak of our desire, to hold each other tighter. Of all the things I pray for and the stars I wish upon, I only speak of one thing and that's to be held in your arms. When and if you hold me, hold me close and hold me tight, I am like the darkness and you're my guiding light. Show me to the heavens where we'll always be together, we can lay upon a cloud where we'll always stay forever. If you kiss me wrap your big strong arms around me, then look into my eyes and tell me that you love me and please don't tell a lie. When you hold my body close to yours feel my every move, if you touch me so gently I will touch you so true. Let me rub my hands over your tight and hard rock chest, let me feel your six pack stomach, let me kiss your little pecks. Let me run my fingers through your hands that grip and hold me tight, let me kiss the muscles that protect me from the evil world outside. Let me kiss the eyes that see beyond the picture of a girl, let me kiss the ears that listen to the sorrows of the world. Let me kiss the lips that talk of me higher than the heavens, let me touch the face that I adore and the face I'd give my life for. You're a man with great patience, a man I'd love to love, but what you've done and where you are forbids this endless love.

Leanna Rubalcaba

Running, Running

You are caught between two worlds each pulling you in opposite
      directions you fight hard to gain recognition in one
         You struggle to hold on to values in the other

      You fill your time, trying to forget that
   You are trapped between two worlds you didn't create

      Running, not knowing what you are running from or to
   Running faster and faster until loneliness overtakes you

Suddenly you meet a special someone, for an instant time stands still for once the running stops, you can be who you really are

      You awaken feelings you haven't had in a long time
   You experience a warmth and fulfillment you thought impossible

         This person brings out the best in you
         Is this it? Has the running finally stopped?

         No, there is a problem, you are confused
   What should you do? You begin running again, faster and faster

         But running isn't the answer. It never has been.
      You've got to stop running but how do you make your stand?
         Remember the only world that matters is
      The one you create where you can be you there you will find
         your special place and the running will stop forever.

Stan Schoolcraft

Beltane: Purification

Growling from a yawning
Disturbance of chilling emptiness,
Pulsing from suffocating
Shadows darkly reflecting the ebony conviction of solitude,
A feral cyclone churning in the chasm
Heralds the glowing breath of vernal desire.

A twinkling moon grins against a rippled pool,
Hastening to embrace the weary life that's offered,
A nocturnal mockery altered
By the feathered vapor of a lantern
Twisting in the wind.

Oh, gentle beacon tossing gold,
Come pierce this frosted veil,
As sob by sob I do await
The healing sun to climb this bed
And set the sheets afire.

Stephen J. Tarafas

Just Tonight

The music blares
    disturbing my peaceful thought.
  A smiling face, at one time a warmer place...
    but it has grown hard, empty.
     It chills, and the music is too loud
    Like someone else's thoughts
     Someone else's voice invading my mind invading me.
   But my thought goes on, my pen stays in rhythm,
  And when the silence comes it is foreign and tired
    it has a life,
      an emptiness of its own.
  "Go now," they say..."it's ten P.M."
  "Do you always sit out in the cold... alone?"...
      "No...Just Tonight.."
   ...And as my soul shivers... i go.

Kristen Holly

Untitled

What do you see when you look? What do you hear when you listen?
Do your tears fall when you cry? Do you hear sound when you speak?
Can you feel when you touch? Does your heart know when you love?
Do you feel pain when you hurt? Does your mind know what you think?
Do you see dark when it's light? Do you feel cold when it's hot?
Can you see clouds when it rains? Do you see grey skies when they
    are blue?
Look so you can see, listen so you can hear,
    cry until tears fall, speak and make a sound,
Touch so you can feel, love so your heart knows,
    hurt when there is pain, know what your mind is thinking,
Turn on the lights when it's dark, find warmth when it's cold,
    see the clouds as they rain.
When the sky is grey you'll know because you won't be able to see.
You'll only hear thunder. You can feel the vibrations.
Sometimes it will hurt you.
It will be dark and cold, and you won't know if it's in your heart
Or if it's all just in your mind!

Shannon A. Quintanar

Dreams

Dreams are birds, waiting to fly.
Dreams are kids, waiting to grow up.
Dreams are babies, waiting to be born.
Dreams are polliwogs, waiting to be frogs.
Dreams are fairy tales, waiting to be told.
Dreams are all things, waiting to be.

Larry Woodbury

Summer Clouds

On certain summer days, a billowy crowd
Does wend its lazy way across the skies;
It seems the air is filled with angel cake:
A treat to be devoured by the eyes.

Or else is stuffed with mountains so immense,
With creamy peaks forever changing shape,
That reach and climb into a deeper blue,
And conjure up a Himalayan scape.

Yet giddy thoughts go tumbling o'er terrain
Of cotton candy cliffs and chasms deep,
And summits piling one atop the other:
A frosty, frothy, French Vanilla heap.

It pays to bring a spoon for summer clouds,
If there is any plan to taste the fare;
A tenuous dessert on which to feast,
For famished eyes, a dish of custard air.

Mark Julevich

Where's The Fire?

What's the hurry?...........Is there a fire?
Don't you know you're dealing with eternity?
Days go by!.....Months......Then years
Still we rush through life in the pursuit of happiness
Tick Tock....Tick Tock......Tick Tock
The process never ends
The goal never reached

Slow down! Enjoy the moment! Listen!
Don't you hear it? A calling..........A purpose
Faint but distinct..........It's growing stronger
Had I not slowed my pace I might have missed it
Happiness within my grasp
Not through pursuit but belief....knowledge
Belief in my Savior..............Knowledge of my forgiveness

The clock no longer has power
Age can't control me
There is a fire!!! It's in my heart
I have found the secret.........Let me spread it eagerly
I'm dealing with Eternity!!!!!!!!

Kevin Ulrich

Cricket And Frog Quartet

There's a cricket and frogs quartet going on nightly,
  Down at the frog's and cricket's famous night spot,
    Commonly called "The Cricket Inn."

      Their night spot can be heard
        For quite a distance away.
    It's relaxing to the human ear and mind.

  Their vocal pitch sound of their singing is so well blended.
The alto, soprano, bass, and baritone, all four levels of pitch.
    Father frog with his baritone voice
      And sister cricket with her alto singing.

      To stand and listen is quite a treat;
    These musicians, with their entertainment,
        Down at their concert hall,
        Better know as the frog pond.

Muriel L. McClure

Supercat

    It's a blimp, it's a zeppelin, no it's Supercat,
Faster than a speeding slug, unable to leap over a couch.
   More powerful than the stench of limburger cheese.
        It's... SUPERCAT!!!
    Spending her days as a wild manner feline.
       Fighting a never ending battle for
        Beds, Catnip, and the Liver way.

Miranda Kleschuk

Summerland

Can you feel it burning through your veins,
down to the bottom of your soul?
You know the one I'm talking about,
and it's like sugar and fire.
What were you thinking
when she said "I'm bleeding"?

The water that flowed down the shale:
golden in the sunlight, catching on the rocks,
glinting - reflected in your eyes.
You know the feeling I'm talking about,
and it's like bittersweet and wind.
What were you feeling
when she said "I'm crying"?

The rain falling into the ground,
watering the flowers, soaking your skin,
freezing - so full of life.
You know the memory I'm talking about,
and it's like smoke and earth.
What were you thinking
when she said "I'm dying"?

Layla Olin

Annys

She watched her daughter descend the stairs
dressed in white from her head to her toes.
She watched her come down with her veil and her crown,
and she tried not to let her tears show.

Her tears were not for the girl that was lost,
but for the woman that is.
For her baby stands there - tall and proud,
and in a few hours, she's his.

She wanted to give her the power to plan,
for a life with hopes and with dreams
She wanted to give her the "Fairy tale" world,
The one filled with magical things.

She made her bird fly, but she made her a nest.
She gave her a base to fly from-
and now as she sets her little bird free,
She knows that HER job - was well done.

She looks at this woman - all misty and proud -
as she walks with her dad towards her rings.
She smiles to herself - for she knows in her heart -
What she gave her was - ROOTS AND HER WINGS.

Gene Kough

Rescued

I was a lost and lonely vessel, in the fountain of my youth.
Drowning in polluted waters... searching for some truth.
Desperately seeking direction, I drifted from place to place.
A raging storm within me... a soul without a face.
Caught in the current without navigation, I could not plan my course
Keeping my head-just above the water... by some unexplainable force.
Then fate floated me into a channel, esteem billowed into my sails
At last! in peaceful waters... love was wading there!
In a beacon of gentle assurance, with acceptance
  and spiritual grace,
I found myself anchored in loving arms... away from the
  maddening pace!
With love washing me out of the darkness, I've seized my destiny.
From a lost and lonely vessel... to the captain of my sea!

Kim Hamill

Tiny Ballerina

Tiny ballerina, sitting high upon a shelf,
dust now hides the beauty, that was her former self...
No child now to turn the key, or watch the wondrous dance,
nor footstep hard enough to start, a magic turn by chance.
Tiny prima donna, with hair of silk spun gold,
what secrets from the little girl, perhaps to you were told?
Did she dream of being you? With beauty and such grace?
Did she hope to someday have, the perfect angel face?
Don't fret my perfect little one, stand tall in pirouette,
the tune you hold within your heart, one cannot forget.
A mother and a daughter now take her down with care,
and gently wash the perfect face,
and comb, the silk spun hair...
For one it brings back memories, for one it's what may be,
the winding of the heart shaped key sends forth a melody.
Together they both watch her, turn magically in place,
they see in one another,
the beauty and the grace...

Phyllis E. Furgison

Through A Teacher's Eyes

We have so may beautiful faces here at our school.
Each having a special light to shine,
if we work together we can provide the fuel.
We have the Puerto Rican, and
the Haitian from across the sea.
The Seminole, one from India, and the Cuban,
all here to live free.
Many people who are so different
come together to make a difference.
We are all special seeds in one big beautiful garden.
Our differences need not be pardoned.
The master gardener nourishes us
and looks after us from afar.
It is up to us to sprout and bloom where we are.

Richard Holt

Success

In our various roles, we all have our goals
Each one in his chosen endeavor,
Some are so small, seem like nothing at all
And some are enormous and clever.

Whatever your scheme, your particular dream
Maybe it's more, maybe less,
When you work you way through it, and finally do it
We all think of this, as success.

For the tycoon it's money, the clown-to be funny
The Tyrant- the chance to oppress,
Some- to win the big game or a tiger to tame
The designer- to make the best dress.

You can win all the prizes, awards of all sizes
Blue ribbons and medals of gold,
Pass every test, and be judged as the best
But the true test comes later, I'm told.

When the last battle's fought, the last victory sought
And the end of the race has been run,
With the Lord at your side, His arms open wide
You're a success when He tells you—— "Well done"!

Warren D. Jennings

Desire

I have many faces, many loves,
each one wanting passion and desire.
I must be free,
free to drown myself in the mysteries
my soul hides from my heart and mind.
Oh God, please let me feel, let me see,
let the song course through my body
Till my very soul is on fire
and he is taken by the dream.
It must come true, it must be,
or I will only be half, only half of myself.

Michell S. Redfoot

I Am Lucky

I am lucky,

  I have eyes to see with
  ears to hear with
  nose to smell with
  hands to create with
  feet to walk with

I am lucky,

  Because, most of all I have a brain,
  A brain to learn and make choices with.

I am lucky,

  Because I have all it takes to make the world a better
place!

Yes, I am lucky:
  Because I see the beauty God made,
  and understand reality hurts,
  but with each new day,
  brings a new beginning,
    A chance to put the past behind me,
    Learn from yesterday and believe in me,
    For a better tomorrow.

Linda Root Price

Untitled

In your arms, the world holds silence and the mind carries
                  ease.
        In your arms, warmth incases the body.
In your arms, love grows strong and individuals become one.
  In your arms, there is only solitude and an overwhelming
                  happiness.
        In your arms, there is no darkness.
For in your arms is the light that makes each day bigger and
                  brighter.

Tiffany Burmeister

To Survive

Bring me thoughts of happiness.
Ease my mind from pain.
Hold this body in your embrace,
For I do not know how long I will remain.

I have watched the blood run from my wrist.
I have beat the walls with hate.
My hands are warped with constant pain.
Please hurry before it is to late.

I hope you can feel how I hurt inside.
On how I wish you could read the tears I cry.
I pray that you see the pain I hide.
Because you are my only chance to survive.

Rebecca L. Carnes

To My Darling Daughter

Baby dolls, stuffed animals, Raggedy Andy and Ann,
  easels, paint brushes, charcoals and pens.
A portrait of you hangs on the wall,
  you haven't changed much since you were small.
Balls and books and bells that ring,
  music boxes, pom poms and figurines.
Dirty sneakers and socks strewn on the floor,
  while pictures of boys are neatly arranged on the door.
There are small treasure boxes on the shelf,
  with beads and rings and rocks and shells.
There's a guitar and violin tucked away under your bed,
  "I'd rather play the piano," you said.
Under the window a cute doll house stands,
  the furniture in most rooms are make shift, second hand.
At Christmas and birthday you wish every year,
  for miniature sofa and tiny chairs.
For running water and electric lights,
  you think all these things would make it look right.
So my wish for you this year is that without a hassle,
  you can furnish your doll house to look like a castle.

Sharon Kramer

Wordless

The words I want to say are hard to find, I've searched
endlessly through my heart and mind, still I can't find no
words to express my love for you, and I know that it is long
overdue... I'm wordless.

But baby please don't ever stop loving me, just look into my eyes
and you will passionately see, a love that no words can ever
explain, are heard through the quiet tears that I rain.

I get all choked up deep down inside, when my feelings for you
begin to hide, why it is such a hard thing to do, to find the
right words to say I love you... I'm wordless.

If my heart had a voice of its own, you already would have long
ago known, of a sacred love that no tongue can easily utter, is
the reason today why I painfully stutter... I'm wordless.

Now I ask you to hold me tight, as we lie together on through the
night, and feel my love burning upon your silky skin, it's a
love like this that words can never fill in... I'm wordless.

A love that no words can ever explain, are heard through the
tears that I rain... I'm wordless.

Richard L. Banks Jr.

Hindsight

I know if I hang on to the mill wheel long
enough, eventually I will break the surface
of the pond. It seems to move so slowly.

I can't remember, whatever made me think
I wanted to ride it. Maybe it was
the climb to the lofty heights which seemed
so superior to the simple comfort of

The river-bank how I now long for
those green pastures, the wildflowers stirring
gently in the breeze, caressed by the sun.
Even my descent, so melancholy seemed
superior in its motion, to my prior stillness.

Now, caught, beneath my lost joy fighting,
lacking breath of life, my only comfort
in the motion I longed for is the chance
it may restore me. That I may last
long enough to learn, and learn long
enough to last.

Kevin Stafford

Our Given Choice

The sun is shining high, high above the mountain tip. Just fare
enough not to touch the burning tip.. as the gusty, day and
windy nights, bring the unknown to are doors. As we fight to
pull away, the wind's bring us only closer to not what we want,
to see, as we close our eyes, we see the light or the
dark.. But that only brings the sounds, of the crying
children, for there needs. As we run faster then we feel, only
brings us to what we know. The world is small and the land is
full, with the smiling faces, but the out numbered crying
tears. What does mean to you and I, why am I the chosen one
to face our deepest fears, as were all here together, for each
other. Why not put out your hand, so are children can breath.
For the world is a mystery, do not set and wonder. For if their
is know hand. We well all finish high above the burning tip....

Sheila Y. Conner

Untitled

Dedicated to a wandering soul in search of light...

In a listless life driven to a state of lunacy
enough strength for a sign of struggle...

Trying to survive, yet reluctant
sliding lavishly into an outrageous legerdemain...

And it continues...
— a continuation to nothingness
where emptiness flourishes...

Where the sight of water converts into dust
with a simple touch...

And a single name hovers in the mid-air of pain...

Beloved were the lips which dispersed the seeds of love
with a chain of dreams which only lived
when the sandman came in...

For reality had guardians that striped the heart
of its precious pearls
and left it naked in the sea of vultures...

Lissette Almanzar

To be a woman

I am proud to be a woman
especially when one stands up for herself in
the face of opposing might
when a woman can hold her head up high
though with tears in her eyes
I am very proud to be a woman
when a fellow woman sighs and is fully
content with her life
when she tries, when she fights, when she
is triumphant in her trials
I am extremely proud to be a woman
when we never compromise our rights,
our freedom, our lives
I am indeed overwhelmingly proud to be
a woman.

Michelle Canales

"Remembering Love"

You fall in love and you think it is neat
Every time you see him your heart skips a beat
You see his face and his smile
Then you stare for awhile
You wonder if he loves you the same
But it turns out it was all just a game
You get a little down and you want to be alone
But you keep remembering his voice on the phone

Sherri L. Nation

Mama

Although it's only been one year, it's been an
eternity down here. We all miss your smiling face, and
when we eat, there's an empty place. Your memory is
all that we have left but it's our most treasured
gift. We didn't have time to tell you goodbye, before
you left for your home in the sky. You're in our
thoughts and on our minds, because a mother like you
is hard to find. I try to live in a Christian way, so
I can be with you some sweet day. Mama, it's hard to
live without you, and sometimes your death seems so
untrue. Sometimes I almost stumble and fall, and then
it seems I hear you call. That's when I stop and
picture your face, and then I beat Satan in the race.
Because I know to see you one day, I have to walk in a
heavenly way. And mom, I love you more and more, and
one day I'll meet you at heaven's door. But until I
do, guide me from above, to take good care of the one
you love.

Martha White

Headlights

The parking lots kept filling up,
Even after I had pulled my untainted jeep into one.
Night would slowly sift down,
And those who had headlights turned them on, others were left in the
  dark.
My headlights flickered, and then came on stronger than before.
A few doors slammed, scratched my jeep's sides. Nothing worse.
So I slammed a few doors, scratching a few more jeeps. Nothing more.
Soon we all had scratched jeeps.
Headlights flickered again.
But I believed in mine. My headlights came on stronger than before.
Some were left in the dark.
Then we started lighting up other cars with our headlights.
Some put up blinds.
Some were left in the dark.
We pulled out of the parking lot, some one by one, others in packs.
And in a haunting movement, we found our road.

Some stayed in the parking lot.
Some marked their own roads.
And some shined their light on, to keep people out of the dark.

P. Sol Hart

I Just Want To Be The Girl

I've got to say it's over before it all begins,
Even though my heart is with you, I know I'll never win.
I want someone to hold me and love me as I am
And take me out and show me off whenever they can.

And be there for me each night and day,
Someone I can love and not have to back away.
That's what I am looking for and it's hard to find,
I want to be the girl that's always on your mind.

I know I could be that girl, but something's in the way,
And I just sit and wait hoping you'll phone today.
Because you feel the way I do and I know you understand,
And I know you'll feel you'll always be my man.

The tears I've cried you'll never know, my heart was broke into,
But I know in my heart that's all I could do.
So remember me as I do you and all the joy we shared.
I've backed away my love because we both cared.

Ruth Shelton

Letting Go

I write this poem just for you
Even though you broke my heart in two
Before we broke up, we had such a good time
Ending our relationship seems so much like a crime

Together we made such a great pair
We had our differences, but I didn't care
Togetherness was all that mattered
Now we're has-beens, our memories are shattered

A month ago was when I got the letter
All you said was, "It was for the better"
"Don't worry about me, move on" you said
"You'll meet other people, you got your whole future ahead"

The letter was your way of telling me that
You wanted to move on and not look back
I think you were right because I'm letting go
I may not have you anymore, but at least I know:
Letting go is something we all have to go through
No matter who we are, where we are, or what we do
Kelvina Bitsilly

"You Go Your Way, I'll Go Mine"

Can't stop feeling the way that I feel
Ever since I left you life hasn't been real
Every place I go to I think I see your face
Think it's time to move on to a better place

I'm packing up soon and movin' out west
Gonna buy me a ranch and a cowboy vest
Santa Fe is where I'll soon be callin' home
Or maybe out in Utah where the buffalo roam

I now realize it was all just a lie
I'll be better off without you no reason to cry
I thought you and I were supposed to be friends
But not if you hurt me again and again

You go your way, and I'll go mine
Just leave me alone, and I'll be fine
I'm a big girl, I don't need your help
I can live on my own and care for myself

The man that I loved wasn't all that he seemed
As it turned out he was like a bad dream
But knowing I'm leaving him and this town
Makes me feel quite happy and leaves him feeling down
Laura Sanza

You

Every song I hear, I think of You.
Every note I sing, I think of You.
It's like Hitler, invading my mind,
Until You come at last, and find my love.

Finally the song is written and You disappear,
Leaving me hanging on to the last note.
Waiting for You to come back and take my heart away with You.
How long shall I wait days, months, or years?
How long 'til You realize it wasn't me going wrong?

Will You ever come back,
Or shall I go to get You?
"To be or not to be, that is the question," Shakespeare wrote,
Is it true in this instance,
Or it is just another coincidence?
Lisa Dick

Untitled

It runs down my spine
Every single time
The pain within
Always ready to begin
Confined to a room
Filled with darkness and gloom
Cuts to the bone
Still I am yet unknown
Extremely out of touch with all
I'd run but I'm afraid I might fall
I'll hold my breath until I turn blue
And when I release I'll be even more confused.
Tabetha Lin Fortune

The Lonesome Girl

There was a young girl with skin so pale,
Everyone said she should be burned in hell.
Her mind wasn't perfect, neither was her body
Her proportions weren't right and looked rather gaudy.
She loved her parents with love so real,
Never shall she cheat, never shall she steal.

She had only three friends: one boy nd two girls.
She was more, than just makeup nd cascades of red curls.
She was actually quite friendly and rather nice,
But most people were cold to her, cold as ice

She wanted true happiness and most of all love.
She had liked many men; I'd say quite a few
None of them liked her. If only they knew,
That this girl, so sweet, had feelings, too.
She wanted to be loved by me and by you.

One day everyone will want to know her,
When her wildest dreams come true.

Do you want to know whom she is, I shall tell you whom.
The girl whose life is black, yet white with hope and jealousy green.
The lonesome girl happens to be me.
Samantha House

Trials Of A Woman

You expect so much and give so little.
Everything has changed.
How am I supposed to be a strong woman,
with the heavy weigh you have put upon my shoulders?
I have been trying to set myself free;
trying to make you see how I feel.
Do you care?
Can't you see the hurt in my eyes?
I feel as though I am failing; our marriage, school, my life.
I don't understand the pain.
Can you explain it?
The pain of the past haunts the present and disables the future.
Why do I let my happiness rely on you?
I shouldn't, I know.
The feminist in me shutters at this thought,
while the weak child in me longs for the comfort
I never had growing up.
Is these a way to balance these emotions,
and be the woman I know I can be?
Leigh Anna Abernethy Sparks

Life

Mystifying, illusive, and sometimes
gratifying, yet usually out of our control,

could it be that life makes man a living soul?
Shirley Christian

Blessing For A Parent

May your newborn bring you all the thrills and
excitements a newborn should bring.
May life give to you patience by the arm load,
tolerance in abundance and a life time of giving.
May you listen for the baby's faintly cries and
heal its painful wounds.
May you be there to give your baby love, for love
is a child's staff of life.
May your baby be a strengthening power for you, may
you want this baby, not for selfish reasons.
May you always be thankful for each breath, each
precious moment given to you.
Remembering that, What God gives, He can also
take away.
May you always be considerate of your child, be
firm with your decisions, do not wean away.
May you always look for things to praise and say
"I love you" ever so often.
May you have a lifetime of love, joy, happiness and
fond memories with your child.

Pat Hart

One Ever Instance

How far away are we really?
  eyes so misty I can't see…
Where the distance ends, where forever begins
  Where the fog surely thins…
I just know you are there
  Even now you are there
    Somehow near…
For no fear holds be bound
  Though no sense of sure ground
    Meets my feet-not even sound
      Whispers soft of the clearing ground…

When our love fills the distance
  In one ever instance
    Only then we'll one once again.

Kimberly Robin Klema

In The Forest

Darkness
    F
     a
     l
      l
       s
On L i n g e r i n g Light
Animals Retreat Into The Night
Light Retires Into Its Home
Only The Night Creatures Roam
Stalking Those That Are Unaware
Creeping , Pouncing , Claws That Tear
Primal Scream Shatters The Night
Gasping , Heaving , Dying In Fright
Sun Ends The Night With A Brand New Day
Hope And Joy With Each New Ray.

Shanna Lucas

Feelings Of Seasons

Smell the sweetness of a fresh bud.
Feel the moistness of a green meadow.
Hear the calling of the sea shells at the shores.
Touch the crisp winter snow flakes that melt on a hand.
Look up at the teardrops of the gray sky.

Can you sense the briskness in the cool air?

How wonderful it is to feel the seasons!

Teodora Beal

The Great And Grand Mothers

Black and white faded images surround me
  Faces from many decades past.

Reaching out from all the others
  Are the Great and Grand Mothers.

Gone from me those many years
  Still the ancestral bonds I hear.

Can they reach across the clicks of time
  And see within this mother's heart of mine?

Did they struggle then as I do now
  to mend my children's broken dreams?

The child's wounds simple to heal
  with a whisper, with silken kisses caress.

These empty arms reach to hold them close again
  till sleep blankets them in peace.

Now I stand and listen my youth I see in them.
  I know my love my tears won't change the growing years.

May their comfort come in knowing that we're here
  All The Great and Grand Mothers.

Standing sentinels a beacon in the coming years.

Kathleen S. Belles

Two Angels

God never said life would be easy, God never said life would be
fair. He did say, I will lend you two small "Angels" with
Golden blond hair. One whose name will be Joshua as God's man
From long ago and far away. To him he said, "Do not be afraid
Do not be discouraged", for I give unto you the Book of Law.
The second son was to be called Aaron, like the leader of many
With Moses to do His needs, on Mount Sinai, in the temple, as A
Priest he did God's deeds. Now on those days that life is
Tough and things go wrong, lift up your heart and voice in a
Loud song. Your voice I am sure God will hear, And give you
the patience to continue these "Angels" to bear. You are
blessed by God to lead these two in life, But, God never said
life was easy or fair or not full of Strife. A mother like you
with so much love in her heart, Such Godlike strength and care
to impart. One day your boys will know what a wonderful mother
you became And you will reap all the respect, love and devotion
that they Can convey. But, until that day far down that road,
I'm sure on Days you think "I can't carry this load". Keep in
mind that God knew who to loan those "Angels" to It could only
be a special "Alecia" like you.

Sonja Thompson

Transformations

A castle of sand can stand, for a while
features sculpted by hand, evoke smiles
from watchers as towers ascend, to the sky
gargoyles bare to the sun, solidify
Below, tide inches closer, ever closer
sandy grains shift weight, become coarser
horizon-wide moat at foot, a-lapping
dampening dry sand at, ocean slapping
Hands deftly shoring, foundations
scooping salty watery, redemptions
lent by the sea, by the sea
staying a moment what is, certainty
The last is left to, prescience
As sand returns to sand, sand to beach.

Marilyn B. Robinson

Untitled

I was just sitting there in the
familiar surroundings of my room
When suddenly everything started closing in
The walls the furniture the floor
I ran outside
I ran through the forest as fast as I could
with the shadow of my life running
(Just as quickly) behind me
The open field
I've got to get to the open field
Surely if I can get there everything will be okay
And the walls will stop closing in
Finally I could see the forest opening into field
I had made it
I ran as close to the middle as I could get and I
Stopped to see if the world around me had stopped as well
but it hadn't
I closed my eyes
fell to the ground
And waited for the world to swallow me

Kelley Bridges

Peace Through War

There is a war
Far away
Where young men and women go to fight
And their mothers stay home and pray.

We know that men, women, children will die;
Only God's will knows why.

The winning side with all its might
Will prevail; that's only right.

But what will come later
After the fight;
When everything and everyone
Loses sight.

Soldiers will come home to their loved ones
Wherever that may be,
But what price for victory
So very far across the sea.

Wars will always be fought,
There is a lesson to be learned:
To free people everywhere,
Peace through war; forever warned.

Victor E. Olkowski

The Mountain

Moments of solitude enrich the mind.
Far away places are there to find.
Passing through time and space at will,
Searching for serenity,
Until we reach the mountain -
The boundary of eternity.

All that is possible is there to see,
When we climb the mountain to eternity.
Obstacles vanish. Our spirits are free.
There the mountain ceases to be.

Beyond ourselves, we are already there.
But our illusionary life keeps us unaware.
As if we've conquered the mountain, yet it's still there.
It rises ever skyward, piercing the air.

When we realize we are one with all creation,
With life and love there can be no separation.
The illusions are gone. Our spirits are free.
That's where the mountain ceases to be.

Larry Peterson

The Daril Bridge

Taking place in the far wood, the far wood,
far beyond the bubbling spring,
where lies the Daril bridge,
and the unseen spaces of one's mind.

There in soft luminescence
lies unbroken lost spirits,
here pagan, quite fresh
and lost to all
save the Elven kind.

Taking place in the far wood,
swirling mists of the mind
lay low to the ground, and thick
where the Daril bridge spans the gentle river,
and no man has ever been.

William R. Ford, Sr.

The Amazing Thing

It swims all day in the sea
Far into the ocean blue;
It does the most amazing things
Not even a gymnast could do.
Flipping over and under,
Twisting and turning all around,
Dancing and singing that most familiar sound.
And if by chance you see the sight,
You'll ask with all your might,
What is this most amazing thing?
Your answer will be plain as day -
But just the same -
A dolphin is this most amazing thing.

Natsha M. Martin

The Paths Of My Mind

As I walked through darkness
Feeling anger and despair
I reached out my hand
But no one was there.

I was lonely and sad
And I started to cry,
I was cold and felt lost
But didn't know why?

I wanted to leave this remorseful den
Walk in the lightness once again.

I turned around quickly
And to my surprise.
There was a beautiful light before my eyes.
There was no more darkness
Anger or despair, no tears or sadness,
I felt warmth everywhere.
My mind now is clear,
Not clouded anymore.
And I'll stay on this path
With the open door.

Maxine Kent

It Was Easter Sunday

On earth; in the year nineteen ninety four.
Flowers were on the alters; verses; those
laid with the scars of war.
There was peace and goodwill; with;
woe-be-gones, and pieces of man.
The blind does lead the blinded, for the
price of each one; understand.

Ted Raduenz

Untitled

When someone you love hurts you and causes you pain, their
feelings and trust are sometimes hard to regain; they can make
you feel hatred, especially when you cry, you sit and wonder
and ask yourself why? Is it all worth it? Or why should I care? Or is
it because we've always been there? We, meaning each other, it
doesn't matter when, we all need a hug every now and then;
sometimes it's just to show that each of us care, whether it's
with words or a meaningful stare; a heartfelt talk to let each
other know, just because I won't talk, doesn't mean you should
go; even trying to explain just the way that I feel doesn't
come out too clear, but the feelings are real; just be patient
with me and eventually you'll find everything out that's going
on in my mind, we'll take it day by day, one step at a time, if
you can't be patient, that isn't a crime; so just do me a favor
don't push me away, just give me a hug and I'll know it's okay;
as close as we are, this you should already know, no matter how
strong our friendship is, we still have room to grow.

Mary Garcia

A Walk On The Beach

I was wandering down the beach feeling the cool sand around my
feet, I began to think
I knew just how I felt about you. Then a warm strong breeze
Blew it away into the sea. How deep and mysterious love can be
I could taste the salt in the air and remembered my despair
I stepped into the sea but it only consumed me
Pulling hard against the desire in me, I began to descend
The gulls sang a song of long ago and I wondered
As the waves crashed against my body if you remembered the
way you kissed me long ago
Burdened by the weight of my wet clothes I felt restrained
And didn't wish to remain living in the past
I wanted to be free, the way you seemed to be when you said
Goodbye to me
The sea seemed to embrace me, the way I longed for you to do
The tide was rising as I felt the current grab me - What?
Did you say you love me? But it's too late you see I drowned
in sorrow because of your insecurity of saying those three
words I Love You

Spring Brenner

Do You Remember?

'Twas the night before Christmas, a long way away,
Fifty years ago, on this very day.
Those G.I.'s in gun bunkers did lay,
At a jungle cove, called Empress Augusta Bay.

A quiet Christmas eve, seemed to be in the offing,
But very shortly, the air raid Klaxon was coughing.
This went on through the night, six times in all,
Washing machine Charlie, sure was having a ball.

Charlie finally went home, and soon dawn would break,
Those weary G.I.'s were planning some sack time to take.
Suddenly Bougainville's crust started to quiver and shake,
What a wonderful gift, a violent earthquake!

Thirteen times in all, the ground shook that day,
Our hero, Bunny Butt, changed his drawers they say.
That Christmas on Bougainville, we will always remember
While other memories may fade, like a fires dying ember.

Leonard Owczarzak

The Everglades

Miles of swampland among the bog
   filled with sounds from
hoot of owl to grunt of hog.
The shriek of long beaked birds
   echo round the bend,
alligators calling to mates
   at days end.
Water moccasins long and sleek
   slither through waters and slue,
cat tails, water reeds, and
   lily pads mingled through.
Cypress trees with moss draped limbs,
   vines, and broken branches,
shaded wildlife refuge stands for centuries
   and now must face
a different existence - what, if anything,
   can take its place.

Rose Bethea

Simple Things

Did you ever stop to smell the
Flowers or watch the work of the bees?
Have you ever sat by a brook or
Listened to the breeze in the trees?
These are the simple things that are important to me!

Have you ever walked through the woods
And noticed the fresh scent of the pines...
Or maybe stop to listen to the
Song of the birds or have you ever
Taken time to hear your child
And his innocent words?
These really are the simple things that mean so much to me!

Now's the time to kneel on bended knee
To thank the most high for all he has given thee.
These are the only things that matter to me!

Marie Elaine Jacoby

Eternity

Why do you weep?
Flowers wilt in the fall but leaves become brilliant
New life is created for winter, it will die when spring comes
There are flowers among them, I will be as the flowers
Living in eternity, ubiquitous
When failure seizes you, I will encourage you
When victory greets you, I shall smile at you with pride
When loneliness teases you, I will hold you
When doubt falls upon you, you shall hear my voice until
confidence finds you.
I will be carried on the wind
I shall be where the blind can see, the deaf can hear, and
the invalid can walk
My soul is no longer bound by substance, now I can fly
Soar where my eyes could once only stare
I will set with the sun and rise with the moon
I will roll with pounding ocean waves, run with animals,
and grow with the trees
No pain or worries shall reach me, I will be free. You will
see me in your children and in their children do not weep, to
find me.
You have only to look inside your mind and heart.

Wendy Neurauter

The North Fork Of The Holston

Out of the Appalachia, and south down from Virginia
Flows a river people know as the North Fork of the Holston.
All the winter, and up till May, its waters rise and fall.

Till rain subsides, and warmth abides, resigned to summers call.

And a road there is along the banks, a road that folks call Yuma.
That easily follows the winding course, even through the hills.
Where many a wide place can be found that fishermen dearly covet.

A road as old, or so it's told, as the mountains high above it.

Now quickly, down to the waters edge, with each step lighter than before
To clear stream whose pebble bottom is illumined by a perfect sky
Where startled fish dart straight away into the emerald deep

Where waters flow, take care and woe, and sooth like dreamless sleep

And all the day the void is filled by the brilliance of the sun
As we hasten, before its golden rays are seemingly forever dimmed
By the shadows of distant heavens of which we can't conceive

That etch a line, that marks the time, when all who come must leave

Out of the Appalachia, with deep pool and rippling shoal
A river flows, and with it goes, the hearts that its beauty stole.

Robert Hutchinson

"When Eagles Cease To Fly"

Upon the wind they spread their wings to soar into the sky.
Flying high into the clouds you almost hear their cry.
You vision grace and beauty. You feel the moments praise.
You smile and watch in amazement then remember
the day, When Eagles Cease to Fly.
The Eagle is proud for strength and truth the power within
unfolds. A nation stands tall to claim his worth and
honor him as gold. We're searching for our own dreams.
We covet his great heights. We envy all he has achieved,
yet, we lose our might When Eagles Cease to Fly. When
Eagles Cease to Fly, what have we to admire? When Eagles
Cease to Fly, how can we dream to rise higher?
Without the hope of a spirit free taking to the sky,
what's left to fill our empty dreams When Eagles Cease to Fly?
When Eagles Cease to Fly, what have we to admire? When Eagles
Cease to Fly, how can we dream to rise higher? Without the
hope of a spirit free taking to the sky, what's left to fill
our empty dreams When Eagles Cease to Fly?

Sandra Haddix

Hope

I look to the future
For a sign of my life to be;
Looking for a shining dot in the horizon
Finding a mountain too high to see.

Hoping and praying for a solution
Struggling through each day
Still searching for the answers to my problems
Finding obstacles in my way.

But I know I'll make it through each day
Knowing God is on my side
Helping me through tough times
And watching over me every step of the way.

But I'll keep searching for the key to unlock the future
I'll keep looking for a world of peace and equality
Hoping against hope
Someday I'll be happy and the world
Will be a better place to be.

Vicki Parks

Untitled

I love you Mom
For all the good that's in me
For the strength and courage you've shown even
during our darkest hours
For all those tough times and the constant love which
you gave without hesitation

I love you Mom
For your passion for a better life
and your drive for inner peace
For your words of wisdom, and your hand which you've
always lent
And for all those "lil" lessons you helped me to
understand and grow from

I love you Mom
For sharing so much of yourself for me unconditionally
without reward
My gift to you is to be all that you've asked for in a son,
And pass on to my family, your voice, your message,
your touch, and most important,
your "Love"

Tony Lucero

"I Love You Father"

I love you Father more than you know
For all those years you've helped me to grow.
There is no greater love of any kind.
Between you an I there is always a bind.
You were my hero when I was very small.
When I fell down you helped me to stand tall.
I love you Father more than you know.
Even though sometimes I didn't let it show.
If I had questions or doubts on my mind.
Your wisdom and strength weren't hard to find.
When the time comes for us to part.
Just know that you're always deep in my heart.
And whenever you look up and see the clouds blow
Just remember.....
I love you Father more than you know

Lisa Daugherty

Cellar Door

The only entrance to our cellar, that hollow vault
for fruited jars that Mimi put up, dust catching,
dirt hewn room, damp for keeping, insect making,
was a glorious door. That wooden incline,
white wedge and flying buttress, an enticing
side. Ever before I knew about any old song
like our door, wide enough for more than two
to slip, even race with talc for grease, we slid.
We slid on that door just like you're supposed to.
I thought it strange it served its dual purpose
of homely cover to a dastardly hole
and slippery ramp so impossible to run up,
but glorious with foothold gained,
to sail, seat down, in forty five perfect degrees.

C. E. Jordan

Mountain Top

Today I went to the Mountain Top,
For I had harvested all my crop,
And as I surveyed where I had been
I was approached by a group of men,
Among them Martin Luther King, Nixon, and JFK,
And I wondered if I had come the right way,
I said "Next to you, I am nothing, so I must part,"
They answered "We are all here only for
What's in our hearts."

Rolly Kurt Hook

Searching

To search his eyes is filled with challenge,
For he will not look my way.
He says he is shy, and doesn't know what to say.
But still, why can't he look my way?

I try to search his heart, to find the love we share.
Sometimes I can't see it there.

Many will catch his eye, they say it is filled with his love for me.
So why can't he let me see?

Days have come and days have gone and I did not think my love
Was enough.
I think someday he'll let me go and never have second thought.

But then he stops, turns around, and holds me tight.
He lets me know that everything is going to be alright.

Rachael Ward

"What Loneliness Mean"

People talk of loneliness, but only I know what it means,
For I am the loneliest, loneliest human being,
Lonelier and lonelier than I ever could have dreamed.
And you want to know what loneliness means.
It means no one to run to, no one to hold,
No one to laugh with, no one to scold.
No one to love, no one to hate.
No lover, no soul mate.
No one to cry with, no one to die with.
I have no one. Period.
I am all alone, a lonely soul,
I'm lonelier and lonelier, lonelier you see,
You ask what loneliness means- It means me.

Yolanda Lowrie

Remember Me

Now they lay me down to sleep. They pray the Lord my soul to keep.
For I have died and will not wake.
The decisions we make, and the lives at stake.
I pray you learn by each breath I can not take.
The consequences lead to an unopened door.
The deaths and pain, I pray to be no more, I am proof of a shattered
dream. Though I am gone, left knowing others will scream.
Others will walk down the line like me.
Others will fall and resume with me our history.
The young lives taken at the drop of a tear.
Not knowing that the end was anywhere near.
For now one life is gone, and others will go.
How to say good-bye without speaking, no one knows.
How silent the room is at the mention of my name.
It is strange how a life gone forever leads to broken fame.
The unknown destinies with the turn of a key.
Remember to buckle up. Remember me. Remember my laughter.
Remember my tears. Remember my life gone, by an ignored fear.
Here I am down upon my knees. Think before you decide to turn the
  keys
Save a life, in memory of mine. Remember me. Remember me.

Misty Lynn Arnold

"Existence"

I shall not and cannot be all things to all people.
For I have—enough trouble with myself.

For I am just a figment of our imaginations and not a reality.
A wisp of smoke in the ether.

Do not look to me for sympathy or answers as
I have none to give, I feel nothing, I see nothing,
I say nothing, for I am nothing, I do not exist.

I am the wind in the trees, the cloud in the sky,
The drop of rain in the spring and dark silence.

J. Keys Wright

You're The Best

There is nothing better than to have you as my senior English teacher,
  For I know I will miss you much-for no one else to help me with my
    paper;
From all those papers you have made me write during this year,
  Have surely made writing easier and enjoyable without the fear;
Here I am off to college with the confidence you have put in me,
  Thank you for being a caring teacher who showed me the right key;
You know you will always be a great teacher to be remember'd
  For being there to help and teach me to become a better writer;
Your writing techniques will be put to an everyday good use,
  Which will hopefully be complemented in the surrounding news;
I will always try my best, Ms. Fowler, never to let you down,
  So come to see me on my graduation day in my new cap and gown;
There is no other way for me as a lucky student to ever repay you,
  So I wrote you this very special poem just to say, "Thank you!"

Minh Ly

Wildflower

I arise in the morning as my heart begins to sing
For I know it's for me that she doth spring
She opens up and offers her love
Famished, I accept and descend from above
Her fragrance arouses me, overwhelms me
I begin to flutter with utter glee
As she and I petal and feather
Become one in spirit melded together
My soul swims in this flowing river of ecstasy
Or can this be heaven for I am set free
The essence of poetic fervor
What have I done to deserve her
I wonder if she realizes what it is that she gives
Life, thanks to her, for whom I live
Succulent wildflower with nectar so sweet
Essential for life, you make me complete

Noah Davison

"Goodbye My Friend"

Weeping willow do not cry for thee,
For I will come back and sit by you, Tree.
Weeping willow do not beg for thee to stay,
For I will be back another day.
Weeping willow do not be afraid,
Remember the days you and I prayed.
Weeping willow do not hate,
For I will be back at a decent rate.
Weeping willow with your vines hanging low,
For I know I will always have a place to go.
Weeping willow please do not leave me,
Will no one stop to help thee?
Weeping willow please do not die now,
For where shall I hide? for where shall I go?
For where shall I stop to say "hello"?
Please weeping willow do not say "goodbye",
For there is still a twinkle in your eye,
Your leaves once swift, your limbs once strong,
But now is quiet and you've gone on, Weeping willow how I miss
  thee so,
I hoped you wouldn't leave, But you had to go.

Mary Beth Gallagher

Gone Away

When we're apart it seems that the world
has come to an end. Why must we go our separate
ways, the love that I have for you is too strong
to let go. What ever you do or where you go I want
you to know that you will still be the apple of my
eye. So let's stay together for ever. I'll send you a
rose straight from my heart to show you that I still
care and love you.

Thomas King Jr.

A Funeral For Dad

I do not want to go in there
for I'm afraid to let him go

To see him die so young is a crime of its own
Why couldn't he die old like most folks do?

I feel queer going up to the box and seeing him
His cold face pale in the light
always lit up when I was in his sight

It happened so fast I don't know what went wrong
After I heard the news it all seemed untrue
Could my father be dead after all we went through?

Through all the good and bad he was there
Now who do I turn to when I'm blue?
Who's going to call me his little girl anymore who?

As we leave I turn and look long and hard at the face
that will be no more.

Michelle Harrington

The Best Doctor In The World

This world of our's needs a doctor.
For it's in a very bad state.
As it's dying a little more each day.
Of a disease that we all know as hate.

Yet there is a very fine top doctor.
Who can cure us if we just turn his way.
And I'm sure you have all heard of God.
His cure is to show love every day.

He will never charge for his service.
His diagnosis is to love and not hate.
So then this diseases that we are carrying.
Can eventually get washed off the slate.

Mary Melia

Mulberry Lake

A place where time slows to a screeching halt, and life begins.
For, it's six o'clock
and the sun has just began to rise over the barren terrain.

I know this scene well
For, I've only been here a week
But, I feel like this is the only place I've ever known.
And if I closed my eyes I would see pictures of the past
Memories like the young me playing in the Millpond
and the love found underneath the Chinaberry Tree one warm summer.

How was it that I was so compelled to come here?
For, I didn't even know that this town existed
Until you the one lying beside me a heavenly masterpiece never
displayed. It was you who invited me up I don't remember why
But, maybe I'll take you for a boat ride and tomorrow, we can start
all over again.

Michael Joseph Miller

Death

Death is a fear, so leave no regrets,
for only he shall see deceitfulness.
The eyes of one man will open wide,
no one in sight shall have their pride.
You may rise or you may fall,
decisions will depend on the acts of all.
So keep love in your heart and truth in your mind,
for no one shall go unnoticed in the hands of Thine.

Margie Sexton

Return My Way

On this blacktop I find a place,
For me to sit the world to face,
The people are few I can count them on hand,
Troubles so numerous I only try to understand.

My spirit down and broken, my heart sheared in two,
Life seeming to be an endless shrew,
Hard for my eyes to see beauty and truth,
I feel deeply enclosed in a small booth.

Within my writings there is meaning in life,
To help end the grief, the pain, and the strife,
Someday again my heart will find,
Another woman to help ease my mind.

Raptures of love and of sex also,
From the pit of my heart, they did go,
My only hope and deep I pray,
For again the beauty of life to come my way.

Steven Durr

The House On The Hill

The house on the hill, sits empty and still,
For Mom has gone away.
No footsteps echoing from room to room,
Getting ready to thread the loom.
The Quilting frames have been put away,
"I'll use them next fall", I can hear her say.
No basket of Quilt pieces strewn around,
No strings on the carpet or on the chair.
No more Crocheting with fine thread,
No more Quilts to cover the bed.
No fire in the cookstove on a cool day,
"The bread is baking", no one to say.
No apple butter bubbling in the pot,
To put on the bread while it's still hot.
No African Violets on the window sill,
No new starts or sick plants to heal.
When I go back to the house on the hill,
It may be empty, and it may be still,
But, the memories of days gone by,
Will stay with me until I die.

Lenore Riddle

Love Is The Only Answer: To Meghan

I used to dream at night
for my feelings were so scared to be seen by the morning light.
But she feels for me and my heart can tell.
All the years of loneliness and heartache,
are hidden deep within us now.

Her love warms my heart
I guess that is were love is to start.
She knows what she has done,
for our hearts are now one.

As I shed a tear for her leaving
I only know that my heart cannot be deceiving.
Her dreams are now mine-
and her happiness I wish for.
And when I go to sleep without her by my side
I can only hope that love does not lie.
Her hand I would gladly take,
for she has relieved all the sorrow that I have so willfully accepted.
And shown me that love is the only answer for a heart so led astray.

Lawrence S. Dickerson

For Once...

For once in your life I see pain in your eyes,
For once in your life I see sorrow inside,
For once in your life I see love shining through,
For once in your life I see hatred demised,
For once in your life I've seen pride set aside
For once in your life I see pure selflessness and care for one,
yet not one's self, one's equal, one's brother, and one's sister
Your love will one day penetrate the souls of all, until that
    day, please remember not to let the ignorance and the fear
    of those who surround you hold your spirit down, but try
    to lift theirs and they will someday live your ways.
  Sharon Ann Quinn

A Rag Doll

A rag doll I shall be
For only a rag doll is what I see
My hair is long
Yet my body isn't quite as thin
As a rag doll should be
I have the marks that a rag doll has
Marks of scars, scabs and bruises on me
Rag dolls are usually hairy
So, I believe
For my knees are as hairy as can be
I try to hide this rag doll body of mine
Just like I use to be
Rag dolls are usually very much cared for by their peers
I for one have no peers
For that rag doll in me
However, the rag doll knows deep within that she's loved
And cared for - even if she's a rag doll
So, for now I'm a rag doll
A special rag doll that could be!
  Leanne Donkin Young

God Might Wonder

Our Jesus died on the cross,
For our souls that were lost.

With His death, we were forgiven,
So that we could go on living.

Live on we do, but there is only a few,
That will come on Sunday to fill their pew.

God might wonder why mothers are wild.
Never home to give their children a smile.

God might wonder what happiness could be
When He promises peace and happiness to those who follow Thee.

God might wonder where all the fathers have gone
When a Bride walks the aisle all alone.

God might wonder why we don't care,
Our bodies we waste by sitting in our chair.

God might wonder why our Bibles aren't read,
He can tell by the words that are said.

God might wonder why we watch "R" rated shows.
When God's words we pretend to know.

God might wonder why did He send His Son?
And people choose NOT to follow this One.
  Vicki Wright

A Pack With The Devil

He rides into the darkness with his head hung low.
For the devil is coming to strike his blow.
There's no escape he knows this now because he has seen his fate.
In his plight there seems no reason to continue into the night.
Without a second thought he continues his travel,
 though he knows that Satan owns his soul.
He feels the presence that comes for him
and the stars and the moon get really dim.
He feels really helpless and loses his will to fight.
As an incubus bears down on him and
                         I lose my sight.
The moral of this story is so easy to understand.
Don't make a pack with the devil or you to will lose your right
to call yourself a Man!
  Robert Trubiano

"Someone Living Somewhere"

Many time I have seen you there, but question unasked
For the fear that my ears would bleed from your laugh
There will be a day, when I cast rejection
Still, I slice through my reflection
A flower grows while a fire dies
I will never believe that I am paralysed
Only vacant eyes know the truth, but they can never tell
Try dissecting yourself in the mirror where the transparent dwell.

Eat the love, for none exist.
Swallow hate, drown in mist
Digest the word, you are one with all
Shed my skin, kiss a soul, drink a waterfall
I am not your human, I am not your box
I am but a spiral, grains of sand, a paradox
Let me sleep in chaos, for I will never rest in peace
Gravity tries, the sun does rise, chains release
I know you will read my name on the arrow in the sky
It may connect after I break, raise ashes when I die
I will not return, I was not gone, from the deepest valley I will sigh
My first words will be "Good bye."
  Michael Ruggiero

"Generation"

Parents strength and logic is vital these days,
For the majority of this generation today, do not
Comprehend life, and are going astray, children needs
Parents more that they know, fact, more than they
Even care to show, for their life seem meaningless
And this is what they show, uncomprehending, and not
Caring if they blow, children need guidance for their
Uncouth ways, in order to mount to something, one of
these blessed days.
  La Verne D. Nixon

Surrender To Truth

This lunacy of mind, body, and soul
for this, the reading of truth,
we, are but a sickly dying breed,
striving for a high society world,
but yet, we are thriving every last bit of energy,
on the tragedies of others. Government: we the people,
now, we who have the money, (or not)

Society: We the people, stands for all,
not just white America,
don't shun the others no matter how rich or poor,
no matter how big or small, black or white,
if we want truth, and justice,
we must first, find out, who we really are,
we must surrender, to the truth.
  Shawn Hampton

The Debt Defaulted

The Dead Soldiers speak: 'Is this the peace
For which our lives were pawned to pay the cost?'
Is this the way you kept your faith with us
Who gave you back the world in trust?

With the pain of war we heard you pray,
You sounded sincere, you led us to believe.
We didn't count our sacrifice
And with our blood wrote your last reprieve.

Our duty done we thought we'd rest!
But from our graves we can behold
No will, no trust, no faith, no love,
You promised New World strangely like the old.

Hate begetting hate, apathy to truth,
Corruption as rampant as it was before!
Love still a stranger, Brotherhood unknown,
And Justice vainly knocking at the door!

You used your lips, but not your hearts
To make the vows you never meant to keep!
Now, with each promise that you break
We die again - we cannot rest or sleep.

Stephen Grey

Someone Loved Me

The day I was born was a happy day
For you see
   My mother wanted me.
My childhood was happy and free from distress
For you see
   My mother wanted me.
When in my teens and I tried to rebel, I did not fear
For you see
   My mother wanted me.
When I was sick and needed care, I knew where to turn
For you see
   My mother wanted me.
When in college and faced with growing up, I knew I was prepared
For you see
   My mother wanted me.
Now on my own, with children of my own
I know I can be a good mother to them
For you see
   Someone always wanted and loved me.

C. Renee Bowsky

Thinking Of You

I think of you Babe when my mind at ease,
For your loving smile is such a please.
And your small brown eye that are filled with trust.
As I think of your lips a kiss is a must.
Each time I see this I hear in my mind,
The sounds of "I Love You" that were easy to find.
When we were together, no distance apart,
In body and spirit and in the heart.
Now the miles between us are many and few;
For still in my heart, I'm right next to you.

Remember these word I've written today,
Through each passing hour in both work and play.
For love has no distance when love is real,
And no miles can stop the way we feel.
Love is forever when love is true;
Our love was made strong by me and by you.

Robert A. Beam

Untitled

You weren't here to see me alone-
Forgotten, left out, even ignored.
My tears were unseen,
No one was here to count them slide down my face.
The loneliness that shone
Through my eyes went unnoticed.
My tender young heart was
Ripped wide open again and again.
You weren't here to see it slowly heal.
It is not you I blame but me.
I made my life harder that it should have been.
It was the only way I knew how to live.
Changed I have.
Pain is still the friend that keeps me company.
Too much I deal with for my age.
Maybe I'm too young-maybe you're too old.
I ask not for your love,
But for your understanding.
It's not pity I want but to
Find the place where I belong.

Kimm Walls

Do You Exist?

I sit back and watch as the games that you play
form out of nowhere. You allow yourself
to see yet do not put all of
your heart towards that of which you behold.
Why can't it all go in one direction?
I hope that you are not just
a product of imagination.
Or is it I who allow myself to create such
imperfections of the mind?
If you really do exist I ask
that you be here when I fall.

Katy Fuller

A Key To Imagination

A child playing on the beach one day,
Found a key,
Which, in a special way,
Unlocked the doors
To imagination,
To prospering fields,
To green plantations.
To meadows with more than a hundred flowers,
And this is where she stayed for hours.
But sometime later,
A call from her brother,
Told her it was time to smother
Away the wonders she had found,
Because of a key,
Buried beneath the ground.
And so she took with one swift hand
The key,
And covered it with sand.
and there it still lies today,
For kids who come to the beach and play.

Sara Browning

Rain

Raindrops fall onto our heads
From tree to tree to flower beds
It knocks upon our window panes
Nothing is as fascinating as the rain

Large amounts may cause great floods
It aides in the growth of flower buds
From the sandy beaches to the grassy plains
Nothing is as mysterious as the rain

Shannon Hobson

Free

How I would like to be free!
Free as those mountains that lie unseen.
Free as the birds that swoop down on golden wings.
Oh how I would like to feel the freeness of an eagle,
With strong wings and eyes filled with pride.
I would glide through the dancing trees and up, until
I felt the softness of clouds on my wings.
And oh, I would love to be a lion, prancing through the forest
And feeling the wonder of power and courage.
I would run like the wind and make loud roars
But my heart would always be full of love and tenderness.
The birds seem to play songs that would turn into wind,
To make the trees dance to the merry tune.
The wind seems to whisper in my ear,
Soft, faint things that only I can hear.
As the winds whisper,
And the birds sing,
And the trees dance,
I think,
I want to be a part of this freeness.

Rebecca Willmore

Champion of Time

It's early morning and she's standing outside
Free or fear, guilt and full of a new pride.
You see, at one time she was a prisoner in her own mind.
But, now she's out of bondage and a true champion of time.
Time that saw frowns become laughter that ignites sparks!
Time that saw sad black tears change into sparkling clear droplets.
Now it's evening and she's standing quietly inside
The glowing moonlight is shining through
The open window, no more closure.
And as it cast the magical light through out the room
It dancingly comes to the image of a woman
Now in full bloom

Paula Rainey Davis

"Strawberry Lover"

"Strawberry lover" sweet as a pie
Friend of a friend, the strawberry of our life.
Your sweetness was pure, your life was discrete.
You're born again, in a new life that's concrete.

Go ahead little girl, run in the field,
Have all the strawberries you want and need.
You're free now, no worry, no ties.
You're a new, you are a new seed.

God has called on you, again to come over his way.
This time "Little Strawberry Lover" you are here to stay.
So sorry I gave you no warning for your long goodbyes
I hope it was not too painful, 'cause you will see
Your friends and family, and so will I,
We'll see the place where you stay with thee.

We reserved a spot "little Angel Love", Strawberry Shortcake awaits.
Walk hand and hand with God and me, to your main estate.

For now you are gone, high in the sky, for where we long to be
And please remember "Little Strawberry Lover",
That I still care for thee.

Nicole Renae Benson

Buttercup

Dance as you travel, Country Buttercup, play.
Frolic in fresh air, in pure water splash and spray.
Shiny diamond droplets tiny petals wear with pride;
Fun it is to tumble down a swirling water slide.

Night fog finds you drowsy, drifting by a big raccoon.
A skunk scampers near, hearing frogs croak a tune;
When the skunk's friendly greeting starts to permeate the air
You are sleeping so serenely that really do not care.

Morning mist starts you moving once again to find your way.
You belong to the Country, but you know you cannot stay.
River current pushes onward without trace of any pity,
Its terrifying power forces you to reach the City.

Smoke belching out of chimneys, filthy foam clogging tide —
Buttercup, sweet Buttercup, can you find a place to hide?
Waste water swallows you, foul air brings lethal stroke.
Cough as you travel, City Buttercup, choke.

Louise Bronoski

It's Your Choice

There are so many choices we have to make everyday
From getting dressed to what we have to say
Every choice we make, makes such a difference
It either makes us confused or makes sense
Sometimes we choose wrong and sometimes we choose right
We could either back off, or we could fight
You choose who you want to be with and who you don't
You choose what you want to do, and what you won't

Where is the Lord in your list of life
Is he before your brother or after your wife
You have the decision whether to make him number one
Or you could turn your back and run

If you want love and happiness in your heart
If you want to make a fresh clean start
If you want to feel things you've never felt before
Then make the right choice and open up the door
Let the Lord into your life right now
He'll give you the strength and the spirit to show you how
The choice is yours to make my friend
Only you can choose where you'll be in the end.

Pattie Cerbone

A Midnight Ride

Every night after everyone's asleep
From my bed I take a leap
To the window I fly like thunder
And it appears a creature of wonder
Sparkling black hooves, Shiny golden horn
What could it be but a unicorn

I climb on and feel his warm hair
Why, he's even softer than a teddy bear
Then we fly into the night
I gaze at the stars and hang on tight
The moon is big, full, and bright
And the town below covered in its light

Then he picks up speed and goes full power
We whip past buildings and tall towers
But now we both realize the night is gone
I give a yawn at the crack of dawn

Then he brings me back to my warm bed
I tell him I love him and give a kiss upon his head
He flies away and I whisper goodbye with a sigh
Then I go to sleep dreaming of my next Midnight Ride

Ryan DePolis

Her Last Bath

I could hear her rasping breath, warm and moist, immersed in the vapors
   from the dish pan.
Our last encounter, her bath, there on the narrow couch.

I offered my forearm, as she protested.
Without the breath left to fight, she dismissed me with a cold blue
   glance.

Her need had long been there, but she gave no sign.
She was good at concealment.
Eventually though, it was out of her control.

It had not come all at once, just small losses.
By the time she was down, it was too late.

She never once looked over her shoulder to see me closing the field,
   moving up on her, taking over.

Finally, she took my arm and pulled up, accepting the warm rag,
   caressing, moving down her body.

Reaching around, sponging her back, I try washing away her sorrow,
   taking it with me, along with the years.

I know my time has come, the tables are turned. Mamma is my child,
   the transfer is now complete. As she cries "I'm tired," I rock
   her gently, whispering "It's all right, there's my good girl."

Mary Mann

Untitled

Awake
From the grasp of this deadly beast
Awake
From the nightmarish terror at least
That captures your soul.

Fight
The lure of artificial comfort
Fight
With all your being and might
That which strips you of your self-respect.

Hope
Springs up - a tiny seed born
Hope
Breaks away from the choking thorn
And finds a measure of peace.

Live
Your life one day at a time
Live
And grow and onward climb
The ladder of faith.

Lois Byers Brater

My Song

Some songs tell of a love that was lost
From the other side of the tracks.
Some songs tell of a new love that's found
Or an old love that came running back.

My song is of love that can't bridge a gap
A gap so deep and so wide.
A gap that we know as reality
Will keep my love from my side.

My love is a dream which doesn't exist
As we know existence to be.
For she is so real but my feelings for her
Are but dreams that are felt just my me.

So others may sing of the loves of their lives
And await each new knock at the door.
But reality quickens the end of a dream
And this heart is singing no more.

Kenneth Koedel

Summer Song

Loving couples watch with wonder and stare with anticipation
From their rose covered veranda. Observing the beauty of the
old Vermont land, they see the rolling hills of forest green
and crop yellow. They lie as if in deep slumber; as if they
possess the hearts and souls of men and women who, in the
land's first day worked it, felt it, and dreamed of it. Oh!
What I would give to have been there; to have witnessed the
beginning when beauty began to blossom, and life was pure.
Now, in these years of late, this dear land, Vermont, sleeps
like the souls who brought it life. Who will awaken it again?
The lake slowly saunters, rippling o'er the miles. The summer
sun shines a path over the deep blue bed of waves. The endless
landscape of somber color. The precious twilight, when the
sky turns shades of purple and orange, and the sun is half-seen
o'er the horizon. Time stops, allowing spectators to live
within the Vermont magic for one moment, and awaken when a
silent zephyr brings thoughts of love, beauty, remembrance;
And, loving couples stand together on the veranda, quietly,
awaiting the awakening.

Sharyl Beth LaRiviere

Kaleidoscope World

The world is but a kaleidoscope
Full of wondrous colors to behold;
Dreary, dark and gray days
Excite us when it's cold.

The world is but a kaleidoscope
Full of wondrous colors, is it not?
Bright, sunny, and yellow days
Delight us when it's hot.

The world is but a kaleidoscope
Full of wondrous colors to be seen;
Fall and winter dazzle with their rusts and whites;
Spring and summer shimmer with their greens.

The world is but a kaleidoscope
Full of wondrous colors, don't you agree?
Colors changing as the seasons go by;
And this is something you can share with me.

Sandra Merchant

Untitled

Today I saw a funny cloud.
Funny cloud on a whitish sky.
It was awfully funny -
so unspeakably thin and unbelievably long.
It had no end.
Seemed to have no end.
Is ended somewhere -
behind the building,
may be.
I saw a funny cloud,
and I felt like letting out a cry.
It was like my love -
so unbelievably thin and unspeakably long.
It had no end.
Seemed to have no end.
It ended somewhere -
behind tomorrow,
probably.

Natalia Geilman

Nebraska, The Good Life!

Many spend their time and efforts. In a large and showy place.
Gaining wealth, and fame, and honor. 'Mongst the brilliant,
royal, face. Just give me a little violet, in a pretty little
vase. To watch the charming windmill. Is a sight of noble
worth. And a few are scattered over. This my land of native
birth. How I love this homey earth! Trains are winding down
the railroad. As I watch in harvest field. Waiting for the
combine to be emptied. And anticipate the yield. A farm wife
has to wield. Walking pastures with my daughter. Seeing
sights beyond degree. Whippoorwills that awe the hardest. Wide
open spaces just suit me. And giving my neighbor a glass of
tea! The corral's are full of horses. Waiting for Greg's
manly call. And the dogs can smell the coyote and the deer.
They and son will chase this fall. O, these riches are for us
all! Fog is rising from the valleys. Makes Missouri a solid
sea. As I look at all these wonders. Nebraska is the good
life for me. I'm as thankful as can be!

Lila Meyerkorth

What's His Name?

Windows quiet as a bright shimmering lake
Gateway opens swiftly and easily
   revealing pearls for a second
Quickly the weather changing swishing over this gate
   pulling it tightly closed
Wind pulling, grabbing with long fingers
   searching for shoestrings
Searching, always searching,
   only able to toss and sway
continually loosing its grip

Katie Gillette

Sunlace

Night's frost settles on bare trees.
Ghostly clothes
   in darkness only owls see.
Silence is a blanket of black velvet.

Morning light is warm.
It melts as it reveals.

Negative becomes positive.
Each branch becomes a line of light,
   tangled lace reflecting the brightness of an early sun.

Coming low from yesterday,
   it gently kisses away the night,
      and brings the day on fleeing crystal voices
         raised in visual song.

Pam Nelligan

Bread For Board

Fed and fattened, forty months or more,
Hearty Holstein, wallowing, luscious boar,
Primed and pampered, patted, hurried home,
Bedded, babied, brushed with curry comb,
Helped and handled, juicy hams and beeves,
Filled and fondled, freed of petty peeves,
Sad, suspicious, farewell stare at stable,
Sliced and spiced, sauced and served on table.

R. W. Tobias

A Cowboy Never Sleeps Alone

A cowboy never sleeps alone, out on the range—all on his own.

He lays on his bedroll next to the fire and feels his bone
give, God, is he tired. He gazes above at the sky so dark,
and begins to count all them brilliant sparks... It brings

him back to what his Grand daddy'd said, 'bout all them stars
lighting his bed. They're from all the heroes he'd known in

his life; the stars were their porchlights to brighten his
night. He wondered above up into the night—which one was

Grand daddy's Personal porchlight? Lord, the little dipper's
boomin' with a song and a dance, the cowboy laughed and then
hollered, "Grand daddy, you finally got your chance!" A

contented smile lay on that ol' cowboy's face, as the trees
whispered softly and the leaves gave a wave. So, you see, a

cowboy never sleeps alone, at least not when he looks up and
sees all them porchlights on.

Tracy Shakespeare

Twenty Four Hours

I love it when the day draws in,
giving way to twilight.
A quiet calm settles over me,
with the approach of dusk.

The lamp costs a cozy glow
in my room, as I get into gown and slippers.

I ponder thoughts trivial and deep,
As I take to my chair for the evening.

A little chat up with mother.
A little light t.v.
Nothing heavy, nothing mean.
All that goes on hold 'til morning.

Yes, I really love it when the
"Curtain of dusk" drops over the cares of the day.
Hushing all my fears,
Drying all my tears.
Finally I'm ready for sleep.
Sleep, the "Great Equalizer."

Nancy Foley

Wedding

She walks down the aisle to the beat
Glass slippers on her feet
She looks at her father. He looks so proud.
Everyone stares at her from the crowd
She looks at her mom, she's crying
Inside she feels like dying
Her little daughter who'd have thought
She always loved ponies at a trot
All she has to do is say I do
How could she know he'd be gone at first light
When they kissed it felt so right
She wakes in the morning glad to be by his side.
All she hears is the morning tide
He felt a note that said;
I love you so,
But I must go.
Not much said
Too much done
She hugs herself in the morning sun
She breaks down and cries.

Mandy Orr

Of The Sea

I know that I will always find
Glorious beauty and peace of mind...
As when I gaze upon the sea
Where white-capped waves call out to me.
And, the majestic dawn that ALWAYS unfolds
Reflects brilliant colors more precious than gold.
The jubilant seagulls that soar above
Remind me of greatness and eternal love.
Praise be to the Everlasting Father on high
For magnificent sunsets He displays across the sky.
Oh, the sea brings me closer to God's home
Than any place I'll ever walk or roam!

Lee Michaels

Dark Endless Light

There are things that come and
Go there are many different
Darknesses but one that no one
Thinks of is the dark.

How did it get here when or if it
Will leave but when I start to
Think the sunrise comes up and,

Grabs me, it pulls my mind and
Gives me pleasure to just wonder
Is heaven more, but to know would be deadly.

For I have not yet found my answers
Nor have I wondered so far but
Yet I shall find the endless ring of light.

Patricia Clayton

Remembering

Life was good when I was young;
God blessed me with a daughter and three sons.
I watched them grow and learn each day;
I taught them how to love and pray;
Yes, life was good when I was young.
But as time slipped quickly past;
And youth quietly fled by so fast;
The kids grew up and left the nest;
And, I thought this age must be the best.
But as time fled faster and days flew by;
Seemed no one cared if I lived or died.
My pillow stained with tears at night;
Wishing, praying the kids would come, or even write.
Old age has crept in, and is here to stay;
Things seem the same, day after day.
It's cold and dark, there's no more sun;
Where are you daughter? Where are you sons?
Yes, life was good when I was young!

Margaret Ann Biss

"Amen"

Life is a gift abused by its receivers,
God is our creator yet there are such few believers.
Living in sin without concern or hesitation,
Not realizing our surrender to satan's destination,
He pulls us apart with grace and ease,
Spreading through society like an incurable disease,
Knowing your only hope is to accept the Lord Christ,
You plead for his love and the strength to fight,
Giving your soul entirely to your one true friend,
Will lead you to triumph and glory in the end.

Susan J. Delaney

Creation

I have a Son
God gave him to me -
(He gave him to his Father too, of course,
  but this is my poem...)
I gave birth to three girls while waiting for him
But I knew he was coming into our lives
Because we wanted a son...and he had to be named Norman
  because his Dad wanted him to have that name.
I had a very hard time giving him birth -
He must have had as equally a hard time being born
Because he stopped trying and rested for several hours
  after the initial try.
I knew that I was dying and couldn't go on any longer
  so I prayed to God while on the delivery table
"Please let me live to raise my children — let me live until
  they don't need me any longer — until they
  can make it on their own..."
God answered my prayer -
I have a son
Who now has a daughter and three sons of his own
  and now...
My little boy is a man!!!

G. Patricia Bayne

Mothers

Mothers are here to stay;
God meant it to be that way

Some are short and some are tall,
But they love their children one and all.

They bring us all kinds of joy;
Hardly ever seem the least bit coy.

Guiding us each day from dawn to dark;
Their voice to us is soft as a lark.

When we're young, they're our helping hand,
Then their guidance keeps us from sinking sand.

Always there to wipe away the those tears
And to drive away those dreaded fears.

Let's not forget to tell mother 'I Love you' today
For God, you see, meant it to be that way.

Weida Pyron

Script Passes By

A bit of line
  goes drifting past
    in gracious, flowing style
      to catch upon the rocks and twigs
        and linger just a while.

A flash of gray
  the line goes taut
    and then goes slack again
      A second flash....Another tug
      A cherished prize to win

Airborne now
  with playful flair
    Splashing...Droplets in the air
      Another splash...The line goes limp
      Freedom! fair and square

The story flows.
  Script passes by.
    The fly and line drift past
      The challenge ends as it began
        With a fisherman's graceful cast.

Lois Ann Peltz

To My Dearest Daughter

Constantly, I feel like I am on a train
  going non-stop hundreds of miles an hour
  and heading nowhere.
What could be worse than to be caught in
  a journey without destination
  a task without purpose
  a job without motivation
  a life without hope?
Fortunately, there is a little shining star
  on the other side of the world far away.
With her tiny, yet powerful shine
  constantly recharging my battery
  keeping my exhausted limbs moving
  carrying me further on and on …
Isn't that the hope of my life
  the motivation of a job
  the purpose of a task
  the destination of my journey?
What could be better than to own such
  a little shining star?

  Qiong-Ying Chen

"The Mighty Dandelion"

Robust and worthy
golden like the sun,
And blooming everywhere
Coloring meadows and lawns—
Healthy as food as drink,
What other flowers has virtues so distinct?

Insects never attack them
They are pure and lovely,
Popping up in spring
surviving through the snow—
Certain God created them
To be plentiful you know.

My little ones bestowed me
With little bouquets,
But their golden beauty
Only a short time would stay,
Because they are common, hated by many
I sense their value is richer than any.

  R. Elizabeth O'Hare

Child Of Night

On a green world over cast by half black violet and half
golden yellow and burnt orange, a dew drop delicately rests
upon a leaf. Conceived by Night, it watches as Day comes
forth, threateningly.
Burning away the thin remaining traces of fog and mist,
the aureate arms of the sun now above the horizon reach
down towards the dew drop, scattering its beauty for brief
seconds, minutes maybe, until its short-lived life is
expended. But as the sun goes through its diurnal path
across the sky, and comes back to the opposite horizon,
reverting the sky back to half black violet and half
golden yellow and burnt orange, Night with her lover the
cool gentle Zephyr, brings forth newly sparkling children
to again face oncoming Day.

  Malon Edwards

Spring Time

Spring is here and what do you know
Gone is the man I made of snow
It is the most colorful time of year
With flowers in bloom and gay atmosphere.

Spring is here and what do you know
The seeded lawn is beginning to grow
This is the time I love most dear
With flowers in bloom and gay atmosphere.

We give credit to God for this wonderful season
Everyone knows it is the reason
He sends more rain and sun to shine
Upon this beautiful garden of mine.

  Rose C. Caponiti

'A Little Old Lady Called Grandma'

There once was a little old lady called
grandma. She was smart and witty and very very
pretty. Well, she had at least ten thousand grand kids,
but three I can say, she liked the best. There's
me and Coty and Damien. Well, my grandma, yes, she
spoils us rotten, 'cause my grandma's soft as cotton. Grandma
is sort of short with silver hair all the way around;
and she likes wearing her night gown. She says, don't
touch my eyebrows and don't jump around, but other
than that she's nice and kind and won't
mind if I help myself to a cookie or two, but
most of all grandma "I love you"!

  Paris Kaminsky

Eternal City

I sat high on a hill over looking the city below,
    gray clouds completed the sky.
    Hundreds of rooftops exactly the same.
      Traffic below rushing by.
    Swallowed up by another day of madness.
    I searched the sights round about me.
  I caught glimpse of a radiant white fortress
      off on the distant horizon.
  Unspeakable beauty, strength, joy, and peace
to name just a few, filled my being at the sight of it.
      Unexplainable was its grandeur.
    It was the Eternal City I am convinced.
    The light that emanated from its borders
      was more golden than that of the sun.
      I looked away for a brief moment.
  It was gone from my sight, sadness filled my heart.
        Back on the hill I sat,
    realizing others before me had found the way,
    that will lead me there, the path to eternity.

  Paula Bautista

Summer Dance

Trees undulating to silent rhythm.
Green seas of light and dark,
A summer afternoon playing out its dance.
Forever caught is the verdant cosmos
Of leaves, time-held in branches of green mist.
Forever green I think of you.
That we might press into the black
Depth with rhythm all around.
The black in the middle of the shimmering order
Is where time cuts off its boundaries
And swallows us up with its silent sway.

  Richard Steggerda

The Dream

The lord gave me a dream so
great when I awake I was crying
because I knew the dream was real.
He showed me of the future
and all the pain it brings why he
chose to tell me I can't explain
I didn't want to believe it
because I'd always had it good.
Then things started happening just like the lord said it would.
As I began to watch my world
Slip away I wondered if it would return to me someday.
The things he showed me I needed to know I don't
think I could have gone through it if I hadn't been told
At the end things were better than they ever had been
So if the lord ever speaks
to you please take heed for I know he didn't lie to me

Sara Jane Hodge

Earth

Have you ever noticed the grass so green?
Greener than the eyes that I've ever seen.
The earth and its beauty some cannot see.
For they're in a hurry to go, to live, to be.
The clouds all in shapes, different to each eye,
All drifting across the large spectacular sky.
Each and every tree tells its own story
Of lifelong battles of hardships and glory.
Next are the waters where many creatures stay.
So much variety, to count there is no way!
The fields are also significant indeed.
For all our food comes from one little seed.
And don't forget the mountains so grand.
Each formed differently from one High Hand.
So look upon the land and take your time.
You'll surely enjoy the wondrous climb.

Sarah Duke

A Life?

Started out as a child,
grew into a survivor.

Not knowing the violence,
but experiencing it as a challenge.

How did a life starting out as so sweet,
at the age of six grow so weak?

Ignoring the truth, stealing and hating was for the fool.
Look within the depths of you
There lies the fool that now hides from you.

Lalita Janssen

To The One I Love

I'll be with you forever,
Hand in hand,
Side by side,
Through our fights and tears in the night,
We will always be together from this
day on and forever.
Through rainy nights and sunny days,
Our love is a bond that holds use
together,
May we both love, cherish, and honer
each other.
We will always walk together,
Hand in hand
Side by side,
Because the love we share will never die.

Lisa Ann Decato

Teeny Little Man

Now a teeny little man in a teeny little land
had a teeny little suit he liked to wear.

So he wore it, day and "nightly", till the pants fit rather tightly
And he found in them a teeny little tear.

He was going to a ball in a teeny little hall
And he didn't have another suit to wear

So, with teeny little stitches, he sewed up his teeny breeches
And he went — and danced with every lady there!

They all liked the way he danced, and the way the people glanced
Made him glad that he had made his nice repair.

Said one teeny girl in yellow, "My, you're such a handsome fellow
"And your suit must be brand-new, I do declare!"

Now this made him very proud so he elegantly bowed
As he thanked her; but he heard a dreadful tear

And he knew the place he'd mended had not all his troubles ended,
For the sound he'd heard had surely come from there!

Then the girl in yellow laughed and he felt this awful draft
And his teeny heart was filled with great despair

So he raised his arm in action to create a slight distraction —

AND THE TEENY LITTLE MAN GOT OUT OF THERE!

Lorraine Carroll

Saving's Plan

O Lord I found the recycling plan by accepting my God's holy
hand, by repenting
Of my sins I held deep within and asking for his forgiveness.
Lord lead me
Through this rugged land, lift me up so I can stand, pick me
up when I am down
For Satan is roaming on your holy ground. Lord I ask for
strength in trouble-sometime, I ask for love when I am
blind, "In all... "In all... from day to day to day
"Lord ....Lead me on in your righteous way. In
closing of this wonderful poem words of inspiration for us
to hold on "accept Christ and make a stand tell
The world of his Saving's Plan.

Tina Matchett

Yesterday And Today

Yesterday the country was happy,
Happy because of freedom, liberty, and justice for all.
But that was yesterday, and this is today.

Today we are fighting, man against man, brother against brother.
Families are torn, and families are broken.

The tragedy of the dead and wounded,
This is all we have to show.
For this is not a war, but a manslaughter in the eyes of every mother!
Yesterday the mind of the brilliant Lincoln was here,
Here, above and beyond, to help fix the conflicts that the North and
    South bare
But that was yesterday, and this is today.

And although he did not get to live to see the day,
The day that all are treated equal, not just created equal.
He played his part in this long, dreadful script of history!

Yesterday our country was broken and torn.
Torn in two for freedom, liberty, and justice for all.
But that was yesterday, and this is today.

Today we take a step in the right direction.
We live each day restoring cities and towns, that were lost
In the war of all wars!

Teri Kopack

Hunting

I think of him often,
Hardly a day does by,
Especially now that hunting season has arrived.
He would appear bright and early.
He asked if we were ready to go,
And then we headed for the woods.
He was, quiet and gentle and he loved the land.
He was a good shot and never wasted a moment of time.
We always brought home what he shot,
And then we would sit around and reminisce.
Those days are gone,
For my grandpa has moved on to his
"happy hunting ground."
But no one can take my memories away.

Kelly Koenck

A Friend's Birthday

So now my dear, another year,
  Has quickly slipped away,
And sure 'twas filled with love and cheer,
  And good things came your way,

When looking back along the track,
  Across the stretch of time,
Good friends, good health you didn't lack,
  And life was mostly fine.

These lines to say I'll be away,
  In far off scenes once more,
When comes around your next birthday,
  With parties too galore,

My wish convey that special day,
  May life be full of cheer,
Good luck, good health stay round your way,
  Life's best this coming year.

Margaret Heerdt

"Weighted In Life's Balance"

What's life that man doeth strive to keep, Lord is all in vain?
Hast thou a purpose and direction, Lord, for the soul of man?
Broken communion, Lord, thy creation marred by sin
must be weighted in life's balance, Lord, to be worthy to enter in

What is life that thou art mindful of, dear Lord, today?
Hast thou weighted in the balance my soul's value weight?
Lord, wilt thou find me worthy, dear Lord, to save?
When I'm weighted in the balance, have mercy, Lord, I pray

Lord, thou knowest, my hearts deepest thoughts within
Thou knowest all the weaknesses, how doubts arise and fears beset
When I'm weighted in life's balance, let me enter into thy rest

Through the deepest valley Lord, lead to greater heights
and in the darkest stormy night, Lord comfort with thy light
Keep me sheltered, dear Lord, in Thee, walk with me through this life
And when I'm weighted in life's balance, Lord, grant my soul eternal
    flight

When thou art weighted in life's balance, will thy soul meet the test?
Will the Lord say come ye my child, and enter into my rest?
Our days are but as yesterday, a shadow that fades away
God's judgment is equal, in life's balance our soul will be weighted

Nancy Wilson

Predilection - Prejudice

So today was not that great, yet alive I am, still there's
Hate! The love is scarce for the people cry, not for what's
to come, but for the true lie. In the heart one feels the
pain of years gone by. Among us innocence live in vain,
for what of years that have slowly passed? How to measure,
what we have a mass. pump the truth down through my core,
among the truth and lie I'm torn! pump the truth out into the
light over the darkness among the real fight, where people
of love can stand proud and tall, push the lie back from
us all! Another look I need not take, cause love in me
Has been awake. For sometime it tells me, don't despair!
The day is were when the whole truth be known, for among
the lie the truth has grown. Bringing people back to the
right, where hate will disappear over night, and day will break
with new sunshine, amidst the truth which still remains
blind. Hopefully tomorrow will bring the change where
feelings of love are exchange and hate disappears
for good, just like the way I know it should!!
I hate, hate!! more that anything...

Richard P. Williams

Confused Utopia

The swirling clouds within my head
have knocked my consciousness off balance.
So many thoughts I can not control,
it is like listening to the devil's chants.

Red roses and blue violets from the heart of poems appear.
The clouds begin to swirl faster.
Hues of light begin to flicker before my eyes,
to gain their trust would make me master.

From the sweat of my brow I work to achieve
to get from the end back to the beginning.
Keeping myself within sanity's realm
to keep the devil from grinning.

An altered reality within a dream
scares a young fragile child.
The clouds are swirling faster now.
Sacks of monetary wealth before me being piled.

The clouds have stopped swirling and are no longer confusing.
The flickering lights have come to an end.
The devil retreats to his infernal home,
but I know I will dream again.

Paul Maas

The Ultimate Feast

Too many tears, too many years
Have passed
Since
Hand in hand along the sand,
We taunted the tricks of time.

Left with fears in our ripening years,
Fervent hands
Reach
To delay the tide; while side by side
We trace time's tracks.

Lead us, we pray, through the current fray
Victorious!
Where eyes, cupped by love, pour tears of joy;
Lips, tendered by time, press in sweet taste.

Then we will know, in the ebb and flow,
Love's glorious touch in the night.

Nadine Marie Calhoun

"Commander In Chief"

He reins up high,
He blesses below,
His precious love to show,
Master of my life,
Savior of my soul,
Commander in chief, when will I go?
Glory land a homeland in which I long to see,
Waiting and watching for the day he returns for me.
Oh, what a sight it will be,
My Jesus I shall see,
and I will glorify his name on high.

Tara Burns

The Way...

I want to tell a story, of Jesus above
He came to earth, to teach of joy and love
They called him Christ, he died for our sins
And prepared a heaven, that man could walk in

Now to get there, you have to be strong
Praise him nights, and through the days long
To repel your sins, from your soul within
Rejoicing in heaven, being born again

Everlasting life, for man this is taught
For this Christ died, nailed to the cross
It's through his blood, that he cleanses our sins
So his joyous love, will forever dwell within

God our Father, Holy Spirit and ghost
Hears all of our prayers, and watches us real close
His angels protect us, from Satan's deadly sins
Soon in chains, they rid the earth of him

Now the story I've told, is oh, so true
Repent your sins, so the Lord will watch you
Come to church, to sing and pray
Inherit the earth, with Christians one day

Kenneth Stephens

Where Do You Turn

He seemed so nice, so sweet, he seemed like
he cared, Just like a brother, I could run to
if there was something wrong or someone tried
to harm me, He protected me.

What do you do, where do you turn
when the one who cared turns and is
the one who makes you scared, do you
just leave him like he was never there.
How do you act, just as though it never happened,
Do you forgive him, Do you stay away like a frightened pup lost,
alone, betrayed. Where do you turn?

Rebecca Townsend

My Father

My Father is wise, my Father is kind
He knows my heart, He knows my mind
He smiles when I'm happy frowns when I'm bad
but my Father is love, He doesn't get mad
oh, yes He may punish or scold at times
but never to hurt just showing guidelines
for the start when He touched and cradled me
I felt peace, hope, and strength, root as a tree
my father is awesome, with abundance of love
and He sits on a throne in heaven above

Katherine M. Torrey

"My Father"

My father was a man of little education and no fame
He had six daughters and three sons, but none left to carry his name

His sons all died at very young ages
Yet my father went on, kept turning the pages

Though he must've felt empty, for he wasn't close to his girls
They lived their own lives, as if in different worlds

He had hurt them deeply, in the sins of his youth
They tried, but found it hard to forgive and forget the terrible truth

I, too, was estranged from my father for many years
And during that time, I shed no tears

Then out of the blue, and invitation came, via my mother
To attend a birthday dinner for him and his brothers

I talked to my husband and we decided to go
To visit my father, I couldn't say no

He treated us warmly, we had a great time
He invited us back and since he was so kind

We did return on week-ends, from April to December
Then suddenly he was gone, but I'll always remember

That I gave my father joy and love the last days of his life
And though I miss him so much, I am at peace without regrets or strife.

*In memory of my father who passed away January 5, 1994
at the age of 77.*

Sarah R. Cline

The Stray Dog

Slow and fearful, he roams the street for tomorrow,
he knows only a crumb he may eat.

Every day more, the dirtier he gets,
he isn't treated like normal pets.

Every morning, the window he looks through,
Now, it is then, he knows what is true.
The family treats their dog with the uttermost care,
he sadly says, "This is truly unfair!"

So next time you see a dog,
don't hesitate to demand,

"Have you home, Dog, I'll lend you a hand."

Liz Hoffman

Untitled

He holds your hand and wipes your tears,
He makes you forget about all your fears.
He makes you laugh when you feel down,
He takes you out to tour the town.

To you, his smile means more than he knows,
You love him dearly, and hope it shows.
The time spent together, seems to go by so fast,
Deep inside all you want is for it to last.

You've been dreading this day, forever and ever,
When he tells you it's the end, of what you shared together.
Your heart sinks faster than anything known,
If only there was a sign he could have shown.

Your life without him feels incomplete,
Thoughts keep pondering in your mind, why'd we meet.
But, your love grows stronger every time he may be near,
Except it's too late to tell him, how much you do care.

Kim Haskins

The Promise

He left her after so long.
He said he would always love her, but he lied.
He promised he would never leave her.
He wanted to be with her forever.
But then he went away for awhile.
While he was away, he changed.
When he got back he was different.
He said he didn't care anymore.
That promises he had made to her was broken.
She thought she wouldn't make it without him.

Years later she returned to her hometown.
She saw him in the coffee shop on the corner.
She went to say hello, and he was amazed.
He couldn't believe it was her after all those years.
He had never found another love, but she had.
They talked for awhile, but then she had to go.
He wanted to start all over from where it had ended.
But she couldn't ever forget his broken promise.

Shawna Heiken

Undeserved Love

Jesus Christ in heaven above is worthy of my undying love
He shed his precious blood for me and poured out loving sympathy
His wings cover me like a shield, to his hand I will yield
Over lost friends I may grieve, but Jesus Christ will never leave
The protective hand He laid on my heart assured me we shall never part
In my eyes he shown a light that in the dark will always be bright
Lifting my hands up to the sky I ask the simple question - Why?
I don't deserve your merciful love, wonderful glorious Saviour above

Nancy M. Lopez

What Are His Feelings?

Does he ever think of me?
He walked out on me one day, without a word.
I don't recall we ever had a disagreement
He took his dog and guitar and belongings
Didn't even leave me a note
    What are his feeling?
We were young when we started out
That probably is the problem, no doubt
He needs too change his ways of life.
He knows now he doesn't want me as his wife.
I feel so lonely an depressed without him needing me.

What are his feelings?
He called me up the other night
Just wanted to know how I was doing
I asked him, why did you leave me?
He replied
    "I don't know about my feelings."
    "I don't know about my feeling... I'm sorry.

Norma Atherton

Circles Of Life

A man while walking come upon a cross road
He was heading for his humble abode
To go left or to go right
The end of neither was insight
He chose left or so we're told
But this story is very old
After three days gone past
The man wondered how long this journey would last
He came then to the same cross road
No sign of his humble abode
He promptly then went right
For after three days gone by
He laid down to die
At the same cross road
With no sign his humble abode

Michael T. Crandall

Why Did You Leave?

When he left for war
He was so strong,
He had so many feelings,
And a passion for life.
He packed his bags
And hugged his family good-bye,
His journey ahead to be the longest he's seen.

He wrote his family seldom,
Yet every letter revealed comfort.
He came home once on leave
And told of his comrades,
He told of the battles, and screams-
So many died, and his life became a treasure.

He left his home once again
This time promising to write soon.
Weeks passed and a letter finally came-
The family learned their boy had died fighting,
Trying to make a difference.
So many questions were left unanswered.
Dear God, How could he leave me?

Stephanie K. Vassallo

Osceola

Osceola was a brave man,
He was there to save our land.
All the Generals put him to the test,
And Osceola did his best.

But Osceola was caught in 1837,
When I was only 11.
Indians and Generals tried to have a meeting,
But it ended up that Osceola was leaving.

All of our people were in sorrow and pain,
I told them to fight and I made it plain.
I stayed with Osceola a lot,
And I slept on what's called a cot.

Osceola would sit at the waters edge,
I would watch him on my ledge.
He would look up at the gulls and see,
That he was not free.

In 1838,
My heart was filled with sorrow and hate.
Osceola died, with his knife beside.

But I can still remember 1837, when I was only 11.

Melanie Kingsbury

A Matter Of Choice

Yesterday we had words, harsh and biting.
He, with face red, eyes narrowed with transient anger,
And I, thin-lipped, halfway between a scream and tears,
All because of our clashing points of view.
He, ever hopeful for my 'change of heart' (he called it).
And I, so sure of the rightness of my judgment,
Remained unyielding.

Soon wounding words withered, vexation found vent in laughter.
We quickly gathered all the hurtful things
Spoken and unspoken,
And wrapped them in a cloak of apology and resignation.
"Come Tuesday", he said, "You vote your way and I'll vote mine".

Leota Myers Weston

Untitled

I saw you in a crowd
Heard your voice from a distance
Memories, once dead, are born again.
And though you've moved on
I am still here
Waiting, hoping, longing
For your eyes to rest upon me
And your gentle hands reaching for mine at last.
Still, I am only a vision in your mind
Only looked upon in your past.

Patricia Burnett

I Am A Window

She has dark hair, mine is light.
Her eyes are a rich chocolate brown that sparkle when she is happy.
I have blue-green eyes—oceans— I don't know if they sparkle. We
are both very different on the outside. Inside, we are very similar.
Sure there is the biological; the physiology, the anatomy. But there
is more...

She has been hurt in ways even beyond my imagination. I was hurt
too, but it's not my turn to heal. In spite of our differences,
we are very much the same. But I am not a mirror. I am a window.
I am her window, a see-through glass. If the light hits me right,
she can see my reflection... Her reflection (She can see how much
alike we really are.) But it's not my place to use her as my mirror.

I am a window—a clear pane of glass.
A clear pane of glass—to look through.
To look through—to the other side. To the other side—to see hope.
To see hope, that hopefully one day, will be hers...mine.
Hope that one day she may begin healing as I have begun...
Healing. Hope that maybe I, a healer, helped her in a small way,
begin her path toward wholeness.

I am her window... and she is mine.

Tonya Powers

A Real Fantasy

A lovely lady danced upon a stage.
Her limber body moved with grace and rage.
Beware! Each warming movement seems uncouth
As she unveils that flower of shapely youth.
A flirting smile enhanced her sensuous eyes
Which brought the burlesque show alive. To guys
her dance beckoned with festive gaiety
A dream so valued by the laity.
The teasing dancer's subtle scheme has won
And after that the passion plot is done.

Paul F. Ernst

"Amy"

A golden-brown haired figure sitting,
Her lips as red as pouring blood.
Her skin gets whiter while I'm sipping,
And withers, dead, like a black rose bud.

Her blood was warm, and much enjoyed,
And the taste of her dead lips was sweet.
Her endless blue eyes revealed a void
Imagination could not defeat.

Her silk-smooth breast, warm inside my mouth,
Was blissfully enchanting - no doubt.
And then I bit, and the blood pumped out.
Her voice of angels would not shout.

Instead her penetrating blue eyes
Looked down at teeth sunk deep in her breast.
She did not even try to ask why,
She only wanted to get her rest.

Lawrence A. Lane Jr.

The Lady and Her Flute

She comes bustling through the door
Her skirt swishing.
Snapping open the case
She clicks the shiny parts of her
Flutetogether.
She begins to play as the sunlight
Streams
Through the stained-glass windows.
The notes come slidingout
Tinkling like tiny jingle bells.
Her lively green eyes dance in time to the music
As the rest of the ensemble takes a deep breath to join in.
The music fills the room like
dreams fill your mind in sleep.
As the music
Rose and fell
The audience sits with bated breath
Hoping the melody will
Linger.

Mary Ann Bailey

Old Age

The old woman sits among darkening shadows.
Her spirit is crippled.
A hint of fatigue is in her drowsy breath.
She sighs in infinite desperation.
She must hold in her harvest of tears
And deal with the fierce demons
That are her calloused memories.
Her ancient grief is clearly shown
In the imprinted lines of her face.
Hollow caves of reminiscence haunt her,
And she closes her eyes,
Remembering her spilled majesty of youth.

Stephanie Speranza

"Light Through Dark"

   I awoke from my sleep
Her voice so soft, here, embrace uncertain
Then she spoke that unwished bride of bitterness
   to escape her rage upon page, upon page
I slipped out quiet and flat as a shadow
silent as those stars in the above

I walked through the country side alone and free
hoping that I might meet my flowery maiden more sweet than rhyme
What leaf-fringed legend haunts about thy slope?
On the banks she treads, lightly on the morning dew
Her outline in the silver moon, allied with its absence loon
   An earthly must stop the tall grass
My life for her love is but nothing of me to ask.
I cannot be with my fancy princess, that epic I have to miss.

   But as time is the only were
   And sweet death a vile escape
This new dawn the only sign, that here is a door out, delivered
from those clocked and drowning waters of my heart
   The earth opens up a bounty and mercy for new life

T. J. Frey

Nun

When I was walkin', talkin' about you Lord,
I felt your hand before me, asking if I was your bride...
I caught my breath in disbelief of such an interest..
It took no thinking, just a great acceptance of your request
In high school "a nun" was my answer. Now it just means the
understanding of what I'm about.

To love the Creator more than man...

Rebecca Pace-Smith

Rare Beauty

Black man and his queen,
  Her walk so keen,

Of style and grace.
  Indeed none can take her place.

Her soft brown skin
  Has the gloss of newly shined gold,

Her lips are the masterpiece of a sculptor,
  So bold.

One look into her eyes
  Could mesmerize man,

Transform him and convert him
  To putty in her hand,

Her beauty is rare,
  Nonc can compare,
    To my phenomenal black woman.
  Richard A. Smith

Madame Pele

They say she is a goddess with a fiery temper,
Her wrath of which no mortal can hamper.
These wonderful stories hold a magical charm,
Believe them my friend and you'll come to no harm.
To this day she appears before each major flow,
Usually as an old woman with a small dog in tow.
Or a beautiful young lady dressed in black and red,
With a garland of green mail leaves around her head.
She may also appear in the fiery flames,
A quick vision captured in few camera frames.
She may ask for a drink, something to eat, or a smoke,
If you are the one asked, don't think it's a joke.
She is a lady demanding respect for her land,
Sometimes by-passing a house as if it planned.
Or flowing molten lava in fingers toward the sea,
She may destroy all in her path at a costly fee.
These legends of Pele are told and re-told,
The Island grows larger as lava grows cold.
I've come to respect this queen and each fiery display,
You, too, my friend should believe what they say.

  Tane Love-Noguchi

Love; A Sometimes Cruel And Unusual Punishment

  The sky is gray, the clouds are dark,
here I sit all alone in the park.
On a moldy old bench is where I stay,
There are so many things I cannot say.
The light of the moon is the only light I see,
As I stare blankly at the rumbling sea.
So many thoughts cloud my mind,
Keeps my heart in a tight bind.
I think of that night one month ago,
my tears start to fall soft and slow.
He took away the one thing I had in life,
he said he was going to make me his wife.
Then one night he went over the edge,
as he took a leap from the ledge.
I tried to stop him, but it was no use,
he had reached the end of his fuse.
Now he's gone and left me here,
With memories of him so clear.
  Melissa M. M. Hardies

My Church

In passing, 3611 university in west u.
Here is something you might do
Stop a moment, as you do by
And gaze at a steeple high in the sky.
Here stands my church, stately and serene
In a cluster of giant, live oak green
Making everyone happy, is our goal
By having classes for young and old
Our ministers and teachers are loyal and true
Bringing spiritual messages to only you
Here friendship and love you will find
With smiling people, who have peace of mind
So, bring your family and invite a friend
To join us in our 'hosannas' and 'amens'
  Theo Baxter

Handicap Prayer

We are all handicap. We belong to the leader of our pack!
He's up in heaven looking down on us, whom ever
doesn't believe he can just look up!

Man has made it to the moon, walked on it; but to
love each other we don't do much and sit.
Sit and watch someone else take over when we know
deep inside we should be out in the green clover.
Realizing that she's over there in her wheel chair,
or the man who can't see anything; a mother's
broken heart that's heavy, can't even afford to keep her Chevy.

He is up there for us to bear. We are all
handicap, let's all share, Oh Lord I must bow
tonight, I feel this terrible fright and pray for
you my friend. Relieve my anxiety we are
both uptight. Relieve my anxiety we are both
in Christ! Fight as we might. Struggle as we
snuggle we are his Goodnight. Amen
  Sandra Mashiska

The Shadows Of The North

  My concealing shadow of the north has
hid my fear for ages. My foes and nightmares
envy me, to my fear, there is no key.

  Shadows, nightmares, darkness, fear, they
whisper softly in my ear. "Out! The shadows
have no place for your wretched crying face!"

  Tears are streaming, voices screaming, fears
revealing, in my shadows of the north.

  In the shadows of the north.
  In the shadows of the north.

  I look at the shadows, I think of my fears, I
take my sleeve and wipe off my tears. My fears are
conquering, I must forget, the awful thing that
snared in my net.

  The shadows start to talk to me, they tell my mind
retreat. Now, today, I have no fear, for the key to
the lock of my shadow of the north, I forever, eternally keep.
  Kristin E. Blystone

History

H is for historian who studies the past.
I is for ignorance which shouldn't last.
S is for studying and doing our best.
T is for letter that reminds us of the test.
O is for oral history past down by word of mouth.
R is for reservation which the Indians live on in the south.
Y is for youth when leaning history should start!
  Nathan Joseph Michalski

Untitled

General MacArthur served
himself in the Federal Arm Force of Navy.
It is just an author in a story for the glory.
That knew some secrets about the Philippines
that were discreet for the federal
agreement with the Americans and for the deed,
and indeed to say "Amen".
In order to stop the war
that went to far to renew the
country for the bounty.
Rights of the Philippines that
were in a fight just like taking
a flight nevertheless;
the sight to have the rights for their freedom
in the Kingdom,
he was on the ball, and standing tall
just like the fall, yet he was too small
to say "total recall".

Michelle R. Robinson

Mommy, I See Jesus

Mommy, I see Jesus, the little boy said: As he lay there dying upon
his bed. I see all the pretty horses, and fishes in the sea; and all
the children, that will be playing with me. All of God's angels are
standing near by: So, please mommy, now don't you cry. Tell all the
family; they'll miss me I know. I'll meet them in heaven, for God told
me so. Now, I'll be with you yet, for a short while; just hug and kiss

me, as I go this last mile. Mommy, as you say one last prayer for me;
Think how happy and safe I will be. Mommy, I see Jesus, He's talking
to me; he's talking about all the beautiful places, he wants me to
see. Tho' I've been happy and loved, while living down here; I want to
be with Jesus, and in His Kingdom share. Mommy, I see Jesus; As he
lifted his head, He looked at me once more, then he was dead. I'll

never forget, my little fair boy; For he filled my heart, with laughter
and joy. A flower for God's garden, in Heaven so fair; So, Saviour,
watch over him, until I get there.

Opal Gamble

My Winged Friend

He sits upon a silver leaf.
His eyes are made of gold.
His voice is made of soft twilight
And his heart is my heart's home.

Break of day, you come to me.
I feel you in a song.
Your voice it always comforts me.
I cannot be alone.

Why can't you take me with you to
the sun sparkled sky that you call home?
Is it really so impossible that it can't be done?

You said to me, take note my friend
and see that you have never walked alone
and life is not at life's expense
you are always free to roam.

Then he fluttered his wings and
I thought he was going to fly away.
But he flew a great graceful arch into my heart
and proceeded to settle in and stay.

Krishna Brown

'Victims Of Crime'

The pretentious V.I.P. was really phony
  His mysterious companion was know as Madame Stover
A foreigner and his secret crony
Many shady deals around them did hover
  The V.I.P. was just an ordinary drover
Erring criminals their ways they should mend
  And shed their tarnished undercover
When will it all end.

The law men tried to quell the rising cacophony
Of a violent crime committed on one, a Minnie P. Glover
Did her attache dwell in the same colony
The law sought a clue to a male rubble and brick remover
As the avenging jilted lover.
The crime stoppers began their safety trend
Their right movement propaganda started at a town hall in Andover
when will it all end.

They assassinated President Kennedy and his brother with a revolver
Also Luther King the Civil Rights Leader of women and men
He who declared integration world wide for all nations to discover
Yes when will all the crime wars end. (Finis)

V. Henderson

Dance Of Love

Their long, lean bodies intertwined.
Honey-brown limbs resting comfortably as one.
Two hearts beating in sync.
Fingers trailing over sensitive skin.
Lips brushing against ear lobes,
Tongues flicking -
They began the dance of love.
Her taut nipples pressing against his hard chest.
Meshed together, their breathing quickened as they unite.
Pulsing, pumping, loving, pushing...
They couldn't get enough.
Muscles tensing and quivering
Toes curling.
She grips his broad shoulders, he cups her round butt.
Then their breathing slows.
They find each others' lips and tenderly kiss.
He runs his fingers through her hair,
Then moves to lie next to her.
Their eyes close - fingers and legs intertwined.
Content - dreaming of their dance of love.

Petula Renee Lloyd

Princess Angeline's World

You swim through the mysterious sea
Hopefully you thinking of me
I have only saved you for a while
Making you a free mammal as you glide through the
water confidently I am signing the papers willingly
You won't be bothered with the boats of death
So you can release that deep breath you go have fun
with all the others don't worry, I'll save your father
and mother go jump and splash with all your might
You my orca whale are the queen of the night

My princess Angeline don't worry about a deadly grasp
For there will be nothing for them to clasp you skin
is silky and bright you are my light you swim through

the mysterious sea hopefully you're thinking of me
I have only saved you for a while making you a free mammal

Stacey Segalla

Missing The Point

As we take big leaps into everyday life
Hoping to make it, to see every night
Forgetting the fact we are full of spite.
For that's all we know, so we think that it's right
  Missing the point, the meaning of life.
  Tucked away, safe in the womb
Waiting for the time, we shall face our doom
  Born into a world of spite,
not getting a chance to use what's right
  The gift from above, the ability to love
This was a song I used to sing, but now it seems
it's just a dream, dance with me in the pale moonlight.
  Please stay with me all night
Lead me through this world of spite, showing society I'm
the light, we need you to shine so bright
  Join us as one again, then we may find love and
free us from sin, only together may we rise above
  For you were the first to let me feel love
If it wasn't for your act of spite, I would never
  be able to love, day or night

Sunshine Fay Brown

Endless Fight

Crash! The angry sea tears at the shore,
Hoping with each grasp to get more.

Crash! Surge sneaks secretly upon the strand,
Eroding huge chunks of land,

Receding back into the open ocean,
Gaining momentum for another motion,

Crash! Hurling itself with power,
Making the defenseless coast cower.

Crash! A full extension of the hand.
Clutches handfuls of sand,

Crash! Tearing away at the earth,
Robbing it of its worth.

Crash! Five long extended extremities,
Grab sand to their greatest capacities.

After time the ocean will take its toll,
Depriving the beach of its soul.

Magda Wisniewski

Time For Rejoicing

The Fire of Apocalypse is beginning to glow in the
Horizon, the drums of war are beating without ceasing,
Pestilence is carried by the Wind in all directions,
and the Planet...trembles...for the Earth knows the
time for deliverance is near...
Just as in the beginning, God created the Heavens and
the Earth by the Fire if His Spirit, the renewal will
come by the same fire...
Man...you were purchased by the Blood of the Lamb, to
those who believe...rejoice!...be not afraid...
take up your place...for your redemption grows near!

Ligia Zeledon Lloyd

Just A Dream

I dance and dance till my feet ache
I look in the mirror and my heart breaks
For my surroundings are only my room
My looks and talents all locked away
But I'm at my house and here to stay
Even though I should be famous on Broadway.

Nicole Hignojoz

Dixie

Her high standards never lack elegance or grace
Hospitality makes her a mother to all that know her
Traditions flow as deep and long as the rivers that define her boundaries
History is embedded like the pines growing in her bright red soil
Courage carried her through a civil war
God gave her the strength to rebuild
Her passion gives life to all that is born and comfort to all that is old
Her surface appears tattered, but her beauty always emerges
triumphantly
Dixie, in all her glory, captures the hearts of all those
considered gentlemen

Molly Magill

Disc Jockey's Request

Good morning luv
How are you today?
This is your smilin friend
The morning D.J.

It's 6 a.m and I am all alone
Can you call me up on the phone?
I'll play the records that you request
As long as they're not just as the rest.

I sit here and spin in my chair.
In a tiny room with much air.
Gotta cue a record on my right
And on my left there's a blinking light.

Now I'll be your friend wherever you be
Just turn your dial to NBC.
I have Beatles and Barry with lots more friends
So call me up and make a request
And you will hear the song you like best!

Mike Shihinski

I Wish

I wish I were a princesses
How beautiful I would be,
I wish I were a sailor
I would sail the big blue sea.
I wish I were a super hero
I would fight off enemies,
I wish I were a doctor
I would cure a horrible disease.
I wish I were an astronaut
I would blast off into space,
I wish the world were filled with children
For there would be one race.

Niffy McDonald

Mystery

How can they do it
How can it be
Hurting their children
Is a mystery to me

As a baby lies there innocent in its bed
A mother takes a pillow and covers its head
All it sees is black and
Then it can't breathe
How she can do it
Is a mystery to me.

Kristin Atkinson

A Miracle Of Love

Who would have thought?
How can this be?
Marrisa and Albert are having a baby.
Her doctor was shocked,
But, her mother was aglow.
He was considering Marrisa's health, you know.
Marrisa stood tall and took her stand;
"This baby will be born
In Jesus name, I command!"
So, the months went by one by one
In and out of the hospital -
The battle's begun!
Albert put on the armor and together they fought -
Cancelling all outside words of unbelief and doubt.
Nathan was chosen if this angel was a boy
But, the ultrasound proved Sarriah was the bundle of joy.
So, plans are being made for this sweet little girl,
With visions of lace and her hair all a curl.
God's blessings are prayed for this family to be,
Albert and Marrisa, and Sarriah, the baby.

Karen Baldonado

This Life

Today I am 50 years old.
How could my life have been so cold.
I sit and wonder why?
I exist. To tempt me down this miserable path.
How could life exist without love to grow, to nourish.
Not to know the road to take when one is all alone.

Should life be shown a book or phrase before it comes
to be.?

Should a star, search high and wide before it can conceive.?
I know not why I am.
Today I am 50 years old, how could my life have been so cold.

T. G. Renda

Wondering Why

Dedicated to Kurt Cobain

You left us all wondering why.
How could you leave us
without saying good-bye?
Your life was great, precious, and sweet.
Your life was not something for you to defeat.
Your lyrics had great meaning much of them unknown,
But just remember us who listened and know that we have grown.
We all loved you dearly and never will forget,
But in our hearts we will always hold a deep regret.
Your music will live forever in our hearts, minds, and soul.
We'll play it over and over
and let your spirit glow!

Sara Gordon

A Sense Of Evolution

If mankind were once blind
how far could we see today?

And if these ears once could not hear
Lord what would we say?

And if the taste had been plucked from our teeth
would life be all that bittersweet?

And if these fingers couldn't reach out and touch and feel
would anything in life really be real?

And if the scent had been taken form our noses
would skunks today smell like roses?

Hell, I don't knowses', I'm only twenty-six.

Ralph M. Russell

Kitty, Kitty, Kitty

Kitty, Kitty, Kitty standing still as a mime
How innocent you look when you've committed crime.
Breaking the flower vase, wetting the floor
Eating things you should not, scratching the door.
Kitty, Kitty, Kitty how cute you are
Even though you just popped the tire on the car.
Smashing a window, chewing my socks
Swallowing a button, hiding some blocks.
Kitty, Kitty, Kitty killing anything below your size level
Kitty, Kitty, Kitty sometimes I think you're a devil!

Kelly R. Morgen

Let Me Tell You About

Let me tell you about poison,
how it creeps into the blood
slow and intoxicating.
It fills me with passion and fanaticism.
Languidly it makes its way throughout my
body, like a feather as it slowly tickles
the bottom of my foot.
I feel dull and sleepy.
Where is the salvation I was promised?

The venom penetrates my heart.
A scream escapes my lips that pierces the night,
like a half starved coyote to an uncaring moon.
As I lie on my deathbed
I close my eyes, never to open them again,
life as I know it is over.
I woke up to find that I had died,
was I dreaming I had lived,
or was I just looking for a place to hide?

Let me tell you about love,
how it creeps into the blood.....

Mark Perrine

Broken Heart

How can one live with broken heart?
How long can one last, may one ask?
Is it going to be an uphill task?
Can one heart ever heal?
It is a great deal to mend the pieces.

When and how are the major question ask!
There is no end to these quests.
There is no best way for the process,
But only time can tell
If one heart is well,
Enjoy!

Live and learn - we are so concerned!
Live but not learn - we tend to get burned!
Experience - they say;
which I can do without!
Will one ever love again after such a deal?
Time! And only Time can tell!
If all is well - so be it!

Nuanjan M. Rasch

A True Dream

Hey baby I was just thinking about you.
I could never forgive you because you are forever
in my mind you are always going to be in my mind.
Last night I was dreaming about you, I was kissing
you while you were hugging me. When I woke up I saw
that it wasn't true tiers were just coming down out from
my eyes, I just couldn't believe it what was happened
with my fantasy, I just couldn't stop thinking about you
because you are right in my heart that it would never could
be for someone else just for you. You're my sweetheart.

Mercedez Sanchez

A Tribute To Mom And Dad

There are just no words that we can say;
How much we love you in every way.

You've taught us a lot since we were small;
Like fishing, swimming and playing softball.

From waterskiing, skating and riding a bike;
To honesty, sportsmanship and what's wrong or right.

You could change our sad long faces into a smile;
With your jokes or funny faces though it took a while.

We were not always angels that is true;
But one thing's for sure we could trust and count on you.

You always encouraged us in things we liked to do;
You'll be in our hearts each and every day through.

For without your help and guidance that you gave;
We wouldn't have turned out like you see us today.

We really don't mean to boast and brag;
We just want to say thanks Mom and Dad.

    Lucinda M. Nartker

"Dad"

How often do we tell the ones so close at heart and dear,
how very much we need them and why we really care?
Dad, you're special indeed and I love,
respect and appreciate you in so many ways,
for your kindness in giving and doing so much for me
and for being someone I can trust and talk to
even if something's bothering me.
I know you'll always be there,
teaching me right from wrong,
and mostly for forgiveness if I'm still doing any wrong.
Dad, you're so sensitive, intelligent, loyal and a Mr. Fix it,
but these are the things that make you unique
whether it's stopping by my place for a few minutes,
watching tv, or simply watching you read the newspaper,
I enjoy your quiet and pleasant company.
Now I hope you can see how our love is rare,
but that bond between us as father and daughter,
is one we'll always share!

    Michelle Harper

Mistakes

God sent me here to make mistakes,
Hurt those I hold most dear.
Regrets I have, and a heart that breaks
As I live from year to year.

Alas, too late, I have learned the cost,
To be paid throughout the years,
Is wanting the one I loved and lost,
And an ocean full of tears.

I'm trying to atone to God up above,
In some small measure, for the wrong I've done,
By teaching of "Him", goodness and love,
Only that way, can true happiness be won.

But, I often wonder, as Judgement Day nears,
When our good and our bad is weighed,
If the price I am paying in grief and fears,
Will cancel the debt to be paid.

    Kay Houskeeper

"Secrets"

They are the sounds of night—
   hushed voices, whispers, sacred vows—
Entombed in stale, dark closets
   with daggers always ready.

Like parasites, dependent upon the loyalty of others,
   they feed upon rumor and half-truths.
Once they are told in confidence,
   no bond of friendship
     can keep the leeches away.

They grow in dark, warm places
   and like mushrooms, spring up overnight
from the tiniest cracks and crevices
   to poison the spears of gossips.

Share your joys, your time,
   your words of wisdom—
But keep your secrets,
   and let curiosity kill all the cats...

    Virginia McCardle Bryant

Our Love

It's so difficult to say if I want you,
I almost say I do but then think back,
To the day you said good-bye.
Then I go forward the day we met.
Then I go farther to the middle.
All of those happy days and the sad,
Are thrown together in a jungle of madness.
One thing was for sure,
Our love.

Our love was strong,
Stronger that the two of us.
Toward the end it started to fade.
You saw it or felt it, I'm not sure which.
I never saw a thing until I saw you
Walk away. Then I saw plenty.
I never felt anything but love,
Until you said good-bye.
After that I never stopped hurting,
Until that day we were one.
Now we're together again, but only in my mind.

    Leslie Moses

Running

I want to feel the wind rush through my hair.
I am filled with hate, rage and anger.
I just want to get away.
Far away.
Where I don't know anyone.
Where no one knows me.
Where I can be alone.
All alone.
By my self.
All by my self.
I want to feel the ground under my feet.
I want to feel the pain of the rocks on the ground dig into my
bare feet.
I want to feel the pain in my side from running too far.
I want to get out of this place and leave everything behind me.
I want to feel the wind in my hair. I want to leave my hate, rage
and anger far behind me. I want to be free.

    Robin Clymer

Suicide

There is nothing left. So I fear no more. I know nothing.
I am here, I am bare with no leaves, always,
There is a jungle filled with predators and prey.
Beaten by life is my life. And that becomes my defeat.
And I am human no more. I am nothing.
If I hear a cry as loud as the thunder
screeching by my mind is blase, I will walk right by.
There's an evil, devious shadow in my corner.
Laughing, tormenting me, showing no mercy.
My head is of agony. Death is a haven, a place where
peace is and pain cease. All those who
fear it are fools, and those who welcome it,
are in an armistice of misery.
I, a soldier fighting a war, nothing ever, now I choose no more.
No-one like someone who could take life.
I end it, the way a loser ends a war.
Suicide.

Milca Almodovar

Mirrors Of Depth

Audience of the world,
   I ask you what you see,
The ugly duckling who was so odd,
   Or the swan who stands before me.
The plain and simple donut,
   With the cream hidden in the center.
The dusty brown cover to a book,
   With pages full of mystery and adventure.
What the closed minded miss,
   Is what the true searcher always finds,
The old stained chest in the attic,
   Packed with treasures of all kinds,
The flower that lacks attention,
   Wilting from absence of feed,
Or the summer's colorful bloom,
   That turns out to be merely a weed.
The worm that spins his cocoon,
   Becomes a butterfly to fly and soar.
Perhaps he did not change much at all,
   But held the beauty before.

Michelle Boeshore

Dream Of A Perfect Love

When I look into your beautiful brown eyes,
   I can only see love.
When you touch me you send thrills through
   my body, it feels like love.
When I hear your voice you talk directly
   to my soul, it sounds like love.
When you run your fingers through my hair
   you touch my mind, I can only think of love.
When I close my eyes I dream that you are so
   close to me, I see you and I making love.
When you reject me, hurt me, the pain is so
   great, it can only be true love.
Love is my inspiration, love came in the
   form of you.
My only wish is, that you could love me the
   way that I love you.
That would be a perfect love.

Phyllis Wilmore

Stranger Inside

I knew him once I know I did
I can see him almost
And then he disappears
Only to reappear the next time I am not looking
I want to know him
Yet I know everything about him
He is a stranger to me
Yet he comes and goes in my life
His name appears often
Yet it is a name I do not know
He is full of passion and promise
He also has pain and sorrow
I want to understand him
But I am afraid of him
When he is here he has complete and total control
When he is gone he leaves pain and confusion
Yet I look forward to our next encounter
He controls your heart
He conquers your soul
He is...love

Tina Tyler

That "Ole" Country Shack

In my dreams I wander back to that "lil ole" country shack.
I can see my mama waiting at the door.
I can see us children still, as we played upon our hill,
But those times are gone, to come no never more!

What a time we children had, with our Mama and our Dad.
That "ole" shack was running over with our love.
Way back then we numbered ten. Oh, to live it all again.
In our little "ole" country shack below the hill.

We climbed that hill most everyday, in our work and in our play.
Those old grapevines we swung did seem so brave.
Death is claiming one by one, but my memories linger on,
Of that "lil ole" country shack below our hill.

Mom and Dad's been gone so long we all have grand kids of our own,
I thank you God for Mama and Daddy's love.
Grant someday we'll meet again over in the promised land.
We will all have a mansion up above.

Now I am old and gray, and I am on my way,
To be at home with Jesus some sweet day,
When all my children here, make the upward way
We will have a glad reunion some sweet day.

Winnie Holloway

Cabin Fever

I've been with these same four people stranded for so long.
I can't stand it anymore. I'm not that strong.
One of them is always full of cheer.
I don't like him at all so I sneer.
One talks to himself all through the nights.
I hate when I have to break up his fights.
One person sings or rather squawks all day.
Another reason why I cannot stay.
One person complains about us all.
What nerve he has; what gall.
I don't mean for anyone to be offended.
But I can't wait until this ordeal has ended.
Someone walks through the door to save all us five.
I'm so glad he got to us while I was still alive.
The man asks how during all this time I could have possibly stayed sane.
I said that these four people with me nearly did drive me insane.
"What four people with you?" he demands to know from me.
I said, "The people in this cabin that you and I can plainly see."
He said that it was too bad sooner I hadn't been found.
He said that I've lost my mind. No one else is around.

Rebecca Wacholtz

Nature's Love

My spirit flies on weightless wings:
I clearly see myriad things.

A mountain pass of rocky slate;
A mirrored glass of unmarred lake;
The rosy glow of setting sun;
The rushing sheen of river's run;

A brown-eyed doe at meadow's edge,
Her spotted fawn blend with foliage.
The soaring flight to eagle's nest,
With strength and might, he'll reach the crest.

The whirr and hum, with nectar sweet,
Of humming bird, so swift, so fleet;
A placid cow, a plaintive low,
Calling her calf, from darkling wood.

A quiet stop at eventide
As night brings forth another side,
Brings forth the night meadow and wood,
Misty shadow in night shade's mood.

Lois E. Myers

Desert

As the desert sands trickle down my hands.
I close my eyes
I realize
I am one of many who come to take the test
For I am very special
I am different
Different from all the rest
Every one needs a place to escape and rest
I would enjoy the desert the best
Its unending dunes go on forever
Breaking silence
Almost never
Summed up you have a peaceful place
Where one can go
To find inner light
And feel the sand between their toes

Michael Knight

The Dream Of A Homeless For The Mother's Day

With a faded flower in my hand,
I come to you to say, "Happy Mother's Day," Mother.
I've stolen this from a flower-shop,
A flower similar to my thoughts and fantasy,
A flower like my job and education ...To offer to you.
It's your day Mother. You did what I'm now ...
Full of hatred and sadness... an aimless and desperate person lying in
dirt! I'm either the sweet fruit of love or a special gift of God,
I've no idea. You, who left me errant in the globe,
Now, I'm slipped around all the time and am bed-fellow with foes
and beasts... Regretfully, I'm separated from the beautiful
and happy world. Why...? Mother? You made me so?!
It's been so long time that I'm waiting for your answer.
It's your day! For your devotion! Love! Patient!
And generosity! It's your day! Holy Mother!
You nourished me inside you and then left me alone in the hand
of the universe. I'm sure that you pray for me and those like me,
all the time. But...don't be proud just of your name on the day;
"Think for me and take a step towards me...
...and open a way for me and those who are like me."

Parvin N. Abady

Questioning Of The Old Indian Woman

Old Indian Woman why do you cry?
I cry because our land has been taken.
Old Indian Woman why do you cry?
I cry because the sacred hoop has been broken.
Old Indian Woman why do you cry?
I cry because the traditions have been sacrificed to modern
civilization.
Old Indian Woman why do you cry?
I cry because I am in pain.
Oh.

Kelly Wilson

Subliminal Realities

In my dreams,
I dance the dance of April.
I spin and turn,
I tap and tip-toe,
I leap and land,
I cabbage-patch and bow.
But dreams are tricks for the subconscious.
They are false pleasures that make the conscious
Chase for the objects
Of surrealism.

In my reality,
I sit in the corner of December.
I stand and stare,
I stomp and pace,
I jump and fall,
I dance and runaway.
The dreams make me cry because I cannot satisfy
The deep hunger that my senses hunt for throughout the night.
I once had grace,
Now, I have anger.

Vanessa Diana Yalakidis

Suicide

I see you lying there, all cold and still,
I didn't think you had it in you, the power to kill...

You must have thought life was a game,
Somehow, without you it will never be the same...

I guess you thought no one would care,
Instead you took the most ultimate dare...

You left no note to explain,
Now all I do is scream, cry, and go insane...

Inside, part of me died,
When you committed suicide.

Shelia Cannon

With You

I found a trail that went through the woods,
I followed it and followed it as far as I could.
I knew not where it would lead me to,
But I came to the end and only saw you.
You came towards me like a ray of light,
Took my hand, which was trembling with fright.
I heard the birds chirp in the sky,
They must have known that this was right.
We walked back out along the trail,
Hand in hand, we never failed.
We walked the path the rest of our lives,
Together forever, with hardly a fight.
Now we're gone, but off and on,
You still see our shadows, going on strong.

Tisha Wood

Do You Believe?

I don't believe in fairy tales.
I don't believe in lies.
I believe in summer suns,
and that special look in your eyes.
I don't believe in ghosts or goblins,
or in people who are always blue.
But if I could wish for something to believe in,
I would wish to believe in you.
I tried to tell you something,
but you would only turn away.
I can never express with words,
the way I felt today.
I don't believe in old sayings,
Like the one that says "I love you."
I think it's taken too much for granted.
So I will think of something new.
If I could do it all again,
there are so many things I would say and do.
But I can't go back.
I can only pray that you already know it's true.
I don't believe in what I've written.
The question is, Do you?

Kimberly Martin

Dear Amy,

It was a cool summer day
I don't know why we trusted that tattered old rowboat
The waves washed over the jagged brown rocks
The crystal sparkle in the water
The waves led me to believe it was safe
Fascination kept us going
The old wise trees watched
They knew the sea could not be conquered
We were brave that summer day
How could I have let us go?
Rapid waves carried us along the path
It led to fate
Now you are gone
I watch the waves wash over the jagged brown rocks
I hope the sea will take care of you
The waters have claimed your body
I remember your soul
    Love
      Me

Lauren R. Ryall

'Thank You Lord For Everyday'

There's not a day that goes by
I don't thank God and here's why.
I look at some that have no hands,
they have no sights nor legs to stand.
Their minds are locked in a mental state
their bodies disfigured and filled with aches.
So I thank the Lord for awakening me
and granting me sight that I might see.
Another day my limbs are joined
that I may walk and journey on.
Another day I'm blessed to hear
to listen to sounds that are far and near.
Another day he's given me strength
to tackle what problems I come against...
Another day to feel and touch
all the things I adore so much.
Another day he's given me breath
and granted me life instead of death.
I thank him till this day has end
then he wakes me to start again.

Linda Dianne Brady

"The One"

Under the stars and under the sun
I dream and dream of finding the one.
The one that I have been searching for,
The one that is true.
The one who will let me feel true love,
The one that will always say, "I love you."
I stare at the sky and wonder who he'll be.
I wonder, if as I am dreaming here,
He is also dreaming of me.
The pale blue sky, the cold wind blowing.
And me waiting patiently,
And still not knowing.
Who he will be,
Will remain a mystery.
Until the day finally comes
When my dream becomes a reality,
And I finally find the one.

Mary Ellen S. Flores

"Dreams Of You"

I dream of you at day, I dream of you at night,
I dream of you whenever the time may be right.
I dream of us together, forever in my heart,
And I wait for the day that you will soon depart.
I will wait for the dream, that tells me what I know,
You will say good-bye and I will see no more.
These dreams that I have, are way beyond true,
Deep in my heart I know, there's only room for you.
I dream of the passion that we could have together,
If you would only stay, and be with me forever.
I dream of the love, that in our hearts we share,
the time we spend apart, I just cannot bear.
Someday I know, my dreams will come true,
Cause if I could have anyone, I'd want it to be you!

Melody Deer

Lost Memories

As I walk through the deep untouched caves and caverns of my mind
I encounter memories.
Memories from childhood and memories from last week.
I remember the old apartment I used to lived in,
a large brick building.
We lived on the third floor.
I used to play games with the two brothers from downstairs,
Adam and the other one (I've forgotten his name).
I then enter a whole new memory of when I first moved to this village.
I remember not being able to speak to anyone.
I did not know their language. I remember waking at six a.m.,
dressing myself and leaving to roam the neighborhood, I feel
alone afraid yet comfortable with the idea.
I remember starting this poem and in a minute
I'll remember ending it.

Krystyna Kabara

Untitled

You love me like no other can
I feel it when you touch my hand
I feel it in your gentle kiss
When I'm alone it's you I miss
You're all I need
You are my life
Like the sun
You've been my light
There's nothing to fear, and nothing to hide
Because I know you're by my side
And I love you

Robyn L. Farris

A Sign

A sign is up in front of my house—
I feel that we must
   Run like refugees out the back door to
   a boat that will take us to a
   foreign culture across town.
If we go, I pray that we will not lose the
   Happiness of holding our babies there,
   singing and dancing, by
   mistaking the meaning of home.
This I fear will be taken from me,
   Home, my youth, my children,
   hugging and holding,
   that they will disappear, forgotten, gone, displaced,
   or worse yet:
Not want to ballet in the living room or
Make chalk art on the steps which
Lead into our home.

   Mary Garvey Verrill

An Angel Among Us

Sometimes.... I think I hear the flutter of angels' wings.
I feel their warmth caressing...their presence assuring.
Why are they with me? Am I in danger? Am I about to weaken?
Then, as their sensation fades, I am stronger for the
moment and grateful to have a guardian angel. It is then
that I wonder...what must an angel look like? Would I know if ever
saw one? Certainly, they have wings that never tire, a smile
that never fades, and eyes that never judge. There is never
a time too late, a burden too heavy, or a situation unanswered.
Then, as I look into the eyes of Sister Catherine, I wonder...
has she ever tired? Was her smile never there?
Has she ever judged the least of us, or denied any of
us? Was there a time when the burden was heavy or the way too
long? Each of us will recall our special moments with her:
when she may have dried a tear or cried with us; or, as she
guided a loved one safely into the hands of the Lord while
giving us the strength to let go; or, a time when she
shared our joy until we thought we'd bust! Blessed are we,
for we have an angel among us. Blessed are we for Sister
Catherine!

   Pearl Taylor Gentile

On Your Birthday

As I watched you lie there so peacefully in your bed
I found it hard to believe that you were dead.
I never had the chance to say good-bye;
All I could do was just stand there and cry.
When morning came on the following day,
The sun shone so bright with its warm solar rays.
I felt your spirit shine through me alive in the sky;
It was then that I realized that you never died.
Your spirit still remains in everybody you've touched;
That is why everyone here loves you so much.
In your faith you walked through life standing straight and tall,
But to be in heaven on your birthday is the greatest gift of all.
Happy Birthday, Mom!

   Paul Sanusky

Rose In My Hand

On an Autumns twilight with a rose in my hand,
i knelt down before you and i gently began.
As i take your hand so softly in mine, thoughts
of joy and happiness run through my mind! Praising
you sweetly with the words that i say, you're
walking in beauty in my every day. You're the light
of my life, a flower among, the joy of my soul,
the rose in my hand.

   W. C. P. Vargo

Peace

As I sit pondering all that I've heard
I gaze up at yonder bird
He sees me pondering, how absurd
Pondering over a single word
The word races 'round my mind
So distinct I hear it, I turn to look behind
Peace is the word that I hear so clear
Ringing back and forth from ear to ear
"Bring peace from your heart to those that are near
Keep faith with the peace and never lose cheer"
These are the words that travel through my mind
Compelling me to go forth in a world unkind
Go forth with peace to those in need
To feel the joy of doing a good deed
So to these words I tend to heed
So that souls trapped in sorrow may be freed.

   Sara Benton

Fishing

As I sit on the dock waiting for a bite,
I glance to the east and see the bright sun peering through the
   tree line,
And the cool brisk wind whistling off the lake and chapping my face;
Off in the distance I can hear the distinct sound
Of rapidly rushing water flowing freely through the dam;
As I look back at the murky floor of the lake, I feel a sharp tug on
   my line;
I react quickly with a jerk to my pole!
As I pull my catch to the surface,
I come face-to-face with my trophy bass!

   Robert Ziecina

Basketball

Gee, what can I tell you most say I'm just a girl
I guess I'd have to say I'm different
'cause I love to play basketball.
The coaches are so funny they think I'll faint or cry
If they should decide to shout
Instead of teaching me the game.
I run the court, up and down, I shoot my frees just right
But every now and then...
well, they go off to the side.
I really have a brain you know it works just slightly different
girls play more technically then the flair of Michael Jordan.
But, who cares if I look funny when I granny toss my throw
So long as I get 2 points than to not have scored at all.
And to my funny coaches who pace up and down the court
It's okay to shout a little
Even girls can play the sport.

   Vilma D. Saucedo

Children Of The Day

I have looked into your eyes
I have seen: the glow and warmth of humaneness
Your hunger for knowledge and understanding
You are not the mean-streaked
Monsters of media headlines
You are children of the day
loving-and giving-and spirited
No guns, or knives or batons in your bags
Books and pens and pencils
are your weapons to conquer illiteracy
You are children of the day—-
Like the sea struggling to be free
Unsurrendering - continuous - demanding
children of the day.

   Sonia Moodie

Leaves

Walking through the empty school hall,
  I hear a swirling sound
  echoing deeply through the halls.
I pause. I listen: a lonely sound of sorrow and sadness.
I look around. No one there.
I start to flutter like a leaf, down the halls.
  But to my grief I reach my destination point,
  my English class. I walk in. I say hello.
  So does my teacher.
I sit down but can't concentrate.
I keep thinking about the leaves, rustling,
  free as free can be.
The teacher passes back the papers.
  I got an "A."
And stapled to my paper is a leaf,
  the colors of the rainbow.
The teacher looks at me mysteriously.
  Does he know?

    Kay Braden

"Am I Happy"

Is a hard question that people ask me because...
I hear an angel crying for peace,
I do not see a place where there is no threat of
  death and destruction,
I can only wish that I could heal all pain and suffering
  and not add to them,
I feel like there is a spotlight shining down on me
  and all that I do wrong,
I touch my mother's legs and she is still unable to walk,
I want the adventure of always doing the best that I can,
I worry that I will fail my family and fail in life,
I understand that my life depends on what God wants not
  what I want,
I can not always see the positive side of everybody,
I find it not so easy to always be friendly,
I hesitantly say that I am not a liar,
I keep dreaming of being well-liked and respected,
I believe I am in love but not confident of my feelings,
I pretend that I am someone I am not,
I ask myself, "Am I happy?", and that is answer enough.

    Stephen Jonathan Jabonaski

Teenage Wanderer

I'm just a teenage wanderer, walking through the land.
I hear the banging cymbals that cry in "Earth's Great Band"
I'm watching people caring: and some just seem to "be"
But I never pass a "wonder" that these young eyes don't see,
Sometimes I find a puzzle that's no answer to be found,
But I just keep on wandering, for worries spread around
There is laughter in the "Earth's worn Cracks":,
And brightness everywhere,
You can tell that someone "Greater" placed things
  with such tender care,

As I pass this way with head up right and courage in my plight,

May I clear the way for all the young
  as a star shines in the night.

    Thea Gonzalez

I Am

I am a young black male. I wonder if I will ever be fully accepted.
I hear the commotion of love vs hate; dark vs pale.
I want this problem to be taken seriously, to be resolved, and
  not be neglected. I pretend that one day this battle will end.
I feel that in reality the level of equality I seek may never be
  reached.
I touch and hold tightly knowledge, love, and respect, each
  being a close friend. I worry that people's faith will fall.
I cry when my own cannot embrace each other,
But want to be embraced by all. I understand this in life, but why?
I am a young black male.
I say that true, I am an individual: but really I'm not that
  much different from you ... or you.
I dream to clear clouded perceptions caused by stereo types,
  caused by lies. I try not to judge before knowing.
To myself and others I try to stay true.
I hope you can see what I'm saying: not just with eyes,
But with heart and mind. I give myself to the world because I am
  full of opportunity and ready to prevail.
I am a young black male!

    Kevin Heath

Footsteps

    Four o'clock in the morning.
  I hear those familiar footsteps.
    They are finally leaving,
    Going somewhere far away.
  I had never really heard them
     When they were here...
      Walking with me.
    I cry for them to stay longer,
     But they are gone.
    From a blurry distance
  I struggle to see a ghostly body
Leading the soft sound of those footsteps.
    Sadly I look into a face.
  I feel warm lips on my cheek,
  Whispering... "Good-bye, my love".
     I feel cold...
  But my faithful tears keep me warm.
  I hear nothing. I see nothing...
     I can just hear
That sweet and soft sound of Mother's Footsteps.

    Mitsue Colin

The Turning

I am not the angel you think I am,
I heard my inner voice whispering
And I felt a comfort and peace wash over my soul.
For the first time, in my life.
I'm not living my life by your rules
The voice said I had a choice
To reveal all my secrets.
I have waited long enough.
I will have to ignore what people say
Breathe deep, breathe slow, everything is a new.
I can't believe I lived in that dark closet.
I will have to get to know my friends again.
But love is love
No matter what form it shows up in.
God gave me this turning point
To proceed with another day.

    Linda Harwood

A Father's Wish

If ever as a little boy in the cold snow
I hold your hand so tight you say:
"It hurts let go," I will one day.

And if ever Spring lets you race
And plant your footprints in its wet fields,
And as I'm holding your hand you say:
"Let go you run too slow", I will one day.

And when Summer grows a little boy into a young man
Who now shakes instead of holds my hand,
I'll understand the "one day has come"
When a little boy's turned young man's hand
Is too old to hold. But son, I will probably
Think to myself: "don't let go of my hand,
It hurts when you let go."

And in the Fall of my life,
When I am no longer able to walk with you
In the snow, the muddy Spring fields, or the Summer sand,
Please hold my hand till it hurts.
And please, please remember when I held yours.
  Michael R. Hill

Thoughts At 80

So the tornado crushed the church in Alabama.
I hope the dead asked the Deity upstairs -
died he she - it will them to die?

Wealthy and svelte Jane - do I admire them -
or does the rejection of homely - poor - but honest Tom trouble me?

All homes are not bums. I recently learned that
walt, my favorite poet was one.

In my 15th year I read origin of the species (in toto)
For 65 years its eternal truths on early life
have guided my spiritual cosmos (not a flower)
A certain law opinion of the bible's folklore and
its purveyors of mendacity still exist.

My peers plan to die soon. Thy consider which nursing
home, write wells, study trusts, surrogates....
For my part I plan to live forever - perhaps
three poems such as this obvious paean to
  Irreligiosity
  Raymond Doersam

"My Feather"

Aimlessly walking alone and so sad,
I just lost my sister, the best friend I had.
Praying to God for strength to be found,
Searching for hope, nothing heard, not a sound.

Then a feather so pretty, dry and pure white,
Dropped down to my feet that rainy, dark night.
My breath ceased to be, my heart skipped a beat-
I knew what it meant as it lay near my feet.

A miracle, a blessing, angels from above,
Had left me a message of hope and of love.
Like something I've read, but never believed,
Never dreamed it would happen, especially to me.

I snatched up my feather and held it so tight,
Sobbed as I ran; thanked God all that night.
The following years when longing for grace,
I'd look at my feather, its peace I'd embrace.

My feather, my miracle, I know that for sure,
Helped me find peace to slowly endure.
My sister's now gone two years just today,
I now have two feathers, I smiled - she's okay!
  T. R. Brennan

Bad Dream Eddie

I woke up and I was feelin' bad.
I knew I was lookin' good, I could tell.
The people were eyeballin' me like it was so
and hey, you can't argue with the general public.

"You're really good at this," the boss man said.
I said, "Mmmm, so they say," and I kinda bobbed,
in a real cool way, cause I had to agree
and I had a great car.

My car turns people on and when they see me,
comin' with shiny female silhouettes on the grill
they stand back, mouths hangin' open, thinkin'
"Man, that dude is hot," and the not so pretty girls
smile and I give them my "In your dreams," look.

I ain't got time, I got business, I'm in demand.
You know what I mean? No, I guess you wouldn't.
If you're lucky, maybe I'll let you watch, this watch?
You're wonderin' if it's real gold.

What do you think, if it's real like me,
you couldn't touch it.
I'm outta here.
  Nancy Graff Aidinian

"A Mother's Special Song"

I kissed him goodnight this evening in a very special way
I knew tomorrow was bringing him a very special day
With a tear in my eye and a sad little sigh
And thoughts running through my head
The only thing I could think of to say
Was "Now don't you fall out of bed"
For tomorrow he is leaving me to go his separate way
His journey into manhood begins
On his very first school day
This journey he must walk alone I cannot go along
But I thought I would try to write as I cried
A mother's special song
But another little one waits at home
To spend the next few years
Then I'll sit down again with my pen in my hand
And I'll shed a few more tears
Then I'll write on that day as he walks away
And I must go home alone
For another special little boy
A new mother's special song
  Lorraine G. Kelsch

Robert

Robert, ever since the day I met you
I knew you were the one for me
you're a wonderful part of my life
wherever I am you're with me
if only in thought and heart
if we hadn't met I would still be looking for love
and happiness you are always there for me
to depend on to, count on to long
thank you Robert for your way of understanding
me, thank you for the little things you do so thoughtfully
thank you for your encouragement in the hopes and plans
we share and thank you Robert most of all for showing
that you care.
  Treona

Why?

My heart was whole until you left me one day,
I know it wasn't your fault you could not stay,
Every night since you've been gone I cry myself to sleep,
The hurt I feel inside my heart is just so very deep,
I love you so much, more than you'll ever know,
And I can't accept the fact that you had to go.
We were two halves of a whole,
You were my best friend,
We were supposed to be together to the very end,
It had to be you, I want to know why,
Please someone tell me why, did my love have to die.
Misty Taylor

Untitled

When I look out in your eyes,
I know I've found the truth.
Your soul once mine-formerly united
but split apart by our own need for each other.
Forced to live in my own private hell,
drowning in the River Styx
   searching for my lost soul.
I am empty without you.
I am forced to exist Alone.
A soul lost. Never to be found until I
can be in your eyes once more.
Tear my heart out while you smile.
Forget the tears I shed over you. I scream. Why
don't you hear me call your name? I plead
for your return. Will you ever come back
to me? Taken too soon, I plead, come back.
Thousands of posies call me to sleep but I know
that I will never find you again until I find myself.
L. M. Fisher

Single

"Single" people say, as if you're not complete,
I know you are a male, with women left to meet."
The hunt is never over, until the fox you've found,
So get up on your horse, cause we are forest bound.

The forest is a big place, with lots of big trees there,
With many animals hiding, shiny eyes that seem to glare.
you're the same as everyone, though you feel you're center stage,
and all that seems to matter is marriage, sex, and age.

"Eligible!" is what I say, cause "single" sounds inferior,
Though in churches, parties, and the like, I'm oft on the exterior
I won't deny my feelings, yes marriage is my goal
but with Christ I deny the notion, that I'm not quite yet whole.

Single is my status, like the church before the rapture
and I'm living in the present, not some happy ever after
All I want is to be loved, this lonely little me,
Not in the future or the past, only live in peace and be.
Kenyon Knapp

My Husband

In the still of the night
I love you with all my might
In the morning time
I love you with all my heart, soul and mind.
My husband means the world to me
I couldn't make it, if it wasn't for him you see.
Sometimes I can't write what I mean to say.
But if you known, how I feel, you'd understand my way.
I know he feels the same about me too
That's why, we're like two monkeys in a zoo.
I wish other couples could feel this way
There wouldn't be so many fights in the U.S.A.
Vada Henderson

Fear

Come with me and take my hand,
I know you will you cannot with stand.

For I am the cold that stays with you forever,
Dare not ignore me, I am so much more clever.

I am the thing that drives you insane,
I thrive and prosper when you're in pain.

When I see you cry it gives me pleasure,
Your tears and your anger are my greatest treasures.

When I see you smile, I make it go away,
I am that thing that won't let you have
a good day.

Your knots of frustration will never be
untied,
I am the fear, within you I hide.
Mary Ballard

The Joy Of My Youth

When I was just a lad, I went to Sunday School.
   I learned about the Lord and the golden rule.
But as I grew older, my life seemed to change
   There was something missing; the joy that Jesus brings.

There's times in my life I want to return to my youth
   When the joy of the Lord is all that I knew
I tried the pleasures of this world and all they could do
   But nothing filled the place like the joy of my youth.

When I was just eighteen the Lord gave me my wife.
   Soon we had our children, the innocence of life
We brought them up to know Him and the joy that Jesus brings
   But most of all to know what loving Jesus means.

When I become an old man, and my hair all turns gray.
   I'll still look to heaven to hear what the Lord would say
My sins have gone before, and I fulfilled all my dreams
   I still remember my youth and the joy that Jesus brings.

O the joy of my youth and the things I got to do
   Being young and healthy, playing after school
Going to camp in the summertime, staying up all night.
   Living my life for Jesus and doing what is right.
Michael L. Williams

Untitled

My true love has my heart.
I long for her to kiss,
I hold her close - it's utter bliss.
There will never be another.
In my heart - we are as one,
Loving - laughing - it's always fun.
Live with me and be my love,
You are the stars that shine above.
I pledge my life to you - to make you mine,
my precious Dianne - you are divine.
I prize your love more than gold,
or all the riches I could hold.
Your love is more
I can't repay,
for you my love - I'll always pray.
My true love has my heart
and I have hers.
Kevin S. White

The Ocean And Me

I stand on the strand of the ocean.
I look across the sea. My eyes
Are no match for her distance,
My mind is bewildered of thee.

I come here quite often, I grew up
And played here as a child. I meditate
And I dream in this place,
My thoughts are young and wild.

I think of how you were created,
It is still a mystery to me.
I think about my place in life,
What is my destiny?

As I sit in your peaceful strand, the wind
Comes and introduces herself, riding in
On the waves. I love the breeze she
Brings with her, blowing across my face...

The sun comes down and kiss the waters
Just before going in. Her beautiful blue
Horizon I love, seems to be of no end.
The ocean and me!

Larry D. McWilliams, Sr.

"With Love"

Dear Secretly Admired,
  I love all of your ways
When I see you pass me each day -
  I'm in a constant daze

  I've been watching you for the longest
Anticipating your every move
  I just don't have the nerve to face you
I've been praying, hoping this will improve

  I've never felt this way before -
I guess I've fallen in love
  What I feel for you is so intense,
But this feeling is just as pure as a dove

  I think about you day and night,
And I hope that we'll be together someday
  I had to make this letter short
Because I'd have to show you what I can't say

  Maybe you'll find out who I am -
That'll be the day my self-esteem is higher
  So, until that time, Darling, this letter is
signed, with love, from your secret admirer.

Phaedra L. Riley

Love Letter To My Father

My dearest Papa, how unforgettable you are.
  I lost you when I was just a girl of ten plus two;
Since then your little girl has travelled far, very far,
  Through many lands and across many an ocean blue.

One day, as I was playing, a shockingly sad message came;
  I don't remember the time, but the sun was about to set;
It said, as you were dying, you were calling- calling my name
  But I was nowhere near enough to stroke your noble head.

Forgive me, papa, for not being then at your side;
  Blame the "Divorce Monster" that struck the cruel blow
Which banished you from our home and from my sight,
  And left us "Kids", without a father, to grow.

That call keeps echoing like a distant waning bell,
  And my heart aches as in agony I groan;
May this poem be my loving monument, to tell
  The world, how deeply my love for you has grown.

And, now, in closing let me look at your photograph
  Oh, how handsome you are, what a perfect nose.
May these words be written as your epitaph
  "Linnet's love for you is as beautiful as a rose."

Linnet Kearney P. Rao

I'm All Alone

I like long walks through a city park
I love to hug, cuddle and even kiss in the dark,
I like to use a telephone and talk with somebody
I wish to love and share happiness with anybody,
But I cannot because I'm all alone

When I hear a nice song I really want to dance
I'd like to find someone, I'm willing to take a chance,
I call out for help but no one comes near
I have no one to wipe away a single tear,
No one's around I'm all alone

I am a good person willing and able to do good
Not a wolf like in the story of red riding hood,
Oh, how I wish to hear someone call out my name
I'd even settle for a challenge to any game,
I don't deserve to be all alone

Someone should care If I cry or die
Someone should tell me "I Love You" and kiss me goodbye,
I wish there was someone home so I can walk in a hurry
Tell me everything's alright and there is no need for worry.
It really hurts to be all alone!

Pedro Delestre

A Dozen Lines Of Life

As one chapter ends and another begins,
I reflect back on what was and what might have been.
But never does everything become real from one's dreams.
and never is everything just what it seems.

One must remember to bend in the wind,
and weather Life's storms until they come to an end.
Keeping as strong as one's heart can be,
Respecting one's brother, expecting no fee.

As mistakes of the past become longer ago,
learn from their lessons and continue to grow.
For Life is the classroom and Time is its tools,
And God is the teacher, helping us learn the Rules.

Perry Simmons

Thoughts

What are those thoughts that go through my mind
I may never know until they combine
Those thoughts of pleasure playing in the fields
Those thoughts are thoughts to share with people who care
Those thoughts of beauty in the rain
Those thoughts are thoughts to keep down within you very deep
And as I'm letting my true thoughts go
I have one more that I'd like to show
Those thoughts that you gave will never be the same
As long as you are hiding in that deep dark cave.

Sherry Drudge

Communion

Jesus! Fountain of all that arouses thirst,
I must needs drink of Thee!
Jesus! Loaf for which a holy hunger yearns,
I must needs eat of Thee!!
In Thine embrace I wilt,
In thy searing gaze I weep.
Purifying sun of Justice,
I would stare at Thee,
And have sweet pain,
Sweet pain!!!

    Robert Angel

Goodbye

I never got to say goodbye,
  I never got one last look,
    into your eyes.

I never heard your final heart beat,
  or got one last glance,
    of your smile so sweet.

I will never again listen to your caring words,
  which I so often
    heard.

All I can do is remember what we had,
  and use the memories,
    when times are bad.

Even though we've been born apart,
  you will forever remain,
    in my heart.

    Vicky Piperni

Heartache

    I never dreamt I would miss you
I never thought I would care
I never knew what you meant to me
till you were no longer there
    When you left I thought you were coming back
I never thought you would stay away
Now that you are so far from me
my heart's driving me insane
    I try to say I don't love you no more
I try to say there's no pain
I know I'm only lying to myself
my tears are falling in the rain
    How much longer can I carry on
how much longer till this pain is gone
my heart is broken it's torn in two
there's nothing left I can do
    That's what's killing me inside
it's time to end pain's ride
suicide

    Leon R. Yelle

Dream Love

In dreams your face appears to me, your loveliness is near.
I reach for you to hold you tight, each time that you appear.
Your eyes, your lips, your silken hair, one cannot comprehend.
This fantasy is paradise, night dream please never end.
But I know too well that the time is short, and you will fade away.
But even though these things are true, I'll adore you as I may.
Yes, you are really my desire, the one for whom I pine.
My thoughts, my joys all rest with you, for happiness to find.
Then suddenly the dream is gone, the dawn has broken through.
But do not fear, when day is done, dream love I'll come to you.

    William R. Flinchbaugh

Out Of Despair

Through the tunnel of darkness
I plummeted alone and hapless
With no one to talk to no one at all.
To hear my cry to come when I call.
Then I heard a voice from about,
Saying, turn your life over to me
    and all will be worked out.
From out of despair he brought me.
Back into this world he taught me
Life is worth living after all.
For he's there to answer when I call
The tunnel is no longer dark as
    night.
For at the end there shines a heavenly light.
I no longer feel alone inside.
The voice is still there as a guide.
I now know that he does care,
For he's the one who brought me
    out of despair.

    R. La Ruth Gore

Simply Mother

The doctors have told us the end is so near
I pray somehow they have made a mistake
Make every word count, time is a wasting
Time to make mends, time to give thanks
Laughter through tears as we reminisce
A lifetime together in good times and bad.

In a moment of weakness I cry, 'God is not'
Gently you tell me I don't mean that
Why do good people have to go first?
I cannot fathom life without you.

If ever two people had ESP
We should be listed somewhere in a book
No need for fancy words, ESP is at work
Life is as delicate as the threads in a cobweb.

You say you are at peace, except for one thing
Look after your sisters,they'll need tender care
I promise, I promise with a squeeze of your hand
Is this all there is at the end of one's journey?
It is not "sayonara", you will always be with us
Of that, I am sure.

    Teresa Kiso

Untitled

Upon the happenings of all that has happened,
I, Queen Kelly of the Pinelanders declare war upon this kingdom.
These recent events have led me to believe that all I believe in is
    evil.
The world in which we live lives on all that is weak.
We yearn to be perfect, when perfect we can never be.
All that is real is really dead.
No longer can I look the other way after I've already seen what is
    never to be seen.
There is no light at the end of this tunnel only darkness, darkness
    that will only retrogress this tunnel.
Can you see, no one sees, they just wonder about hopelessly,
wondering
    in space.
So, war is declared, how will it end, only I know now.
The time has come, what happens next, you will soon find out.
I've watched you move, waited my turn, now you watch me, it is
    my turn.

    Kelly Foster

Friends

When I was just a child of three
I recall my mother's words to me
Do for others, whatever you can
Be always there to lend a hand
A smile, or kindly word to help them through
Is all that is expected of you.
If you live by this creed
Friends, you will never lack indeed
When and if you are ever down and out
Treasured friends, you will never be without.

Rose Maiorano

Fear

You'd like to see me with others,
I remain with you instead.
Making your heart race,
Your mind throb in your head.
You curse me, despise me,
Wish I'd just go away.
I do, then return-
You invite me to stay;
By reading a book, or watching T.V.
Here I am once more - there's no escaping me.
You say you don't like me and you could do without,
Yet there's something about me that makes you scream and shout.
Don't bother pushing me away, for I'll remain, always near-
Never leaving your side-like a nightmare...
I am fear!

Leonne Bragg

You're Never Alone

As I closed my eyes to sleep
I saw you walking through the garden
You had a forlorn look about you
The way you walked, held your head
I wanted to tell you that you're never alone
Just look around you and you will see
Look at the grass
Look at the blossoms within the grass
Look at the life all around you
Look at the flowers, at the shrubs
Look at the tree and see the dew
And the little spider's making their web
Look at them scurry around
You are not alone
With all the beauty of the world
At your finger tips you must smile
You must feel the life all around you
How can you say
How can you feel you're all alone
For I am with you, always

Robert L. Stone, Jr.

Changes

I look outside my window,
I see a world of white.
The sun is shinning like a star,
Oh what a dazzling sight.
The snow is falling softly, the air is like a song,
And in this winter wonderland,
Nothing can go wrong.
But my, I spoke too quickly,
For as night comes round about,
I see the lightning flash around.
I hear the thunder rumble and shout,
And now I know that if it's right,
It may as well be wrong,
For things will come and things will go
And nothing stays too long.

Rachael E. Panneton

Fighting to Survive

I look into the mirror and to my surprise
I see a young lady whose fighting for her life.
I look into her eyes and recalls when she was fine
always playing, but now she's fighting to survive.
The games she played and the friends she had
was once called present, but now become the past.
  She now regrets those days when she would say
that she wanted to be grown and move far away.
  I look into the mirror once move and in her eyes
I still see a young lady fighting to survive.

Sharon Smith

Untitled

When I look around,
I see no one.
Although I search everywhere,
I find nothing.
  I begin to tremble
  I feel so small.
  What do I fear so much?
  Being alone, it's that simple.
  or is it?
  I fear being so alone that all that surrounds me is darkness.
  Total Darkness.
Wait! She's here
I can feel her presence.
My friend has come back, just as always
She has never let the darkness overcome me.
My heart begins to calm;
My trembling slows.
Thank you my friend, thank you my sister.

Marie Boucher

Success

When I close my eyes, I see all my past rush back to me
I see the pain I've caused and the pain I've had,
I've been through a lot
there's no going back just time to go forward
I've always been taught to do the best
sometimes the best can be your worst enemy
the best can depress or even kill
depression is not a crime
it's something you can't help
lives can be messed up by the simplest things
a lie, a lost love or any mistreatment
the fear of the past will go away
maybe not as soon as you want it to
maybe you'll learn from it, never give up
someday you'll find someone
who will make you forget about your past
when you realize this you'll turn and cry,
you'll cry so hard because it's then you know
you have succeeded in moving on.

Kristen Lynn Myers

Every Day Of My Life

Every day of my life a wish comes true;
I see the sun rise and even the dew.
At times I feel that life is through
But looking upward, I see the sky so blue.

Every day of my life I am thankful for
The luxury of life we take too far.
Is it not true that if we hasten the dawn,
That all this will be when we are gone?

Every day of my life let it be said that
I bowed my head at the close of day.
Maybe this is poor pay but what did you
Do and what did you say?

Ellena M. E. Freeman

Four Phases

Looking up through blossomed bough,
I see you're in your smiling phase now.
I've caught your grin in night's endless black,
and felt you watching me at noon though my back
was turned away; to the sun giving him due respect.
But as day and night trade places,
you rise high with grinning lips, and eye inspecting
all who stand by, or sleep by opened window spaces.
But when you are filled up with joy; not a bit shy
you, the lantern of the sky, hangs over every tree
and dispels the fearful dark from our human eyes.
Faithful traveller, with your full light, follows
though we may dwell in city or obscure hollow.
Moon in any phase, my face admires your change.
So much like we humans, are your own expressions
and emotions.
Yet, never fearful are you of showing.

Lorrie A. MacGregor

Wait

I sit in a daze
I sit and wait;
frustration becoming me, discouragement all beyond
Where are you? I
think in pain - Don't you know I love you?
The advantage over me.
I sit and wait. I try to be so
patient, but I'm wearing
thin. I feel like
a dying man, trying to
grope. Not able to reach that strawberry.
My skin cold... grows tight
And gray.
Why do I worry so
constantly? I don't want to
die. Too dependent? Maybe.
I wish I could break free... and fly.
fly... out of this hell and in
to my world. Where I will find you...
waiting.

Steven Philip Myers

The Stage Of My Dreams...

When the curtain is finished rising
  I slowly walk into the gloom,
  that falls on the empty stage
  of my dark and lonely room

Tonight the shows no different
  the usual play fills my dreams,
  with an old forgotten love story
  complete with sad and bitter scenes.

I'm again the main attraction
  the star, with the biggest part,
  all the long hours finally pay off
  I practiced with a broken heart.

I know my lines so well
  and my performance is always deep,
  I've studied the script a thousand times
  while awake or in my sleep.

But someday I hope to try
  and there's nothing I wouldn't do,
to have a small appearance
  in the play called "Forgetting You"

Mike Bato

The Darkness Of This Place

Here I sit in the solitude of darkness in this place.
  I smile to myself with such joy as I look upon Thy face.
You've led me through this world, Lord, with such stature & grace
  How can I be sorrowful with the darkness of this place.

My students have come and gone, with laughter through these years,
  And here we are together again, more joys, more smiles, more tears.
In this life great life where only you can know, the inner
  secrets of friend or foe;
  As a class of Gods' children, we have learned, by the touch
  of your hand,
And to look upon Thy face, we can All walk through "The Darkness
  Of This Place".

Mary Walters

Roots Of Reality

With a forked tongue and a split consciousness
I speak to the wise
About the wise and for the wise
Although I myself am not wise
Whether it be my questionable morality or
My false confidence in reality
I have been deemed of sound body and controllable mind

Through dusty and crowded streets
I saunter with determinable arrogance
I am a messenger of others' thoughts and dreams
What is becoming to me is you
I would gladly give you advice
That means nothing to me but is gospel to you
I always know what's best for you but
I never know what's best for me
So I sleepwalk through a dazed existence
Waiting for the wake-up call of life

Stephen E. Hann

Treasures In The Driveway

I was walking in the driveway one day
I spotted some things a short distance away.

So I went and looked real close to the ground
And this is the neat stuff that I found.

A couple rusty old nails and some glass
A button, a wire, and a chunk of brass.

A bottle cap, and a piece of a plate
With orange and blue flowers, a pin, and some tape,

An old medicine bottle, and a toy ax head
A marble, some string and a fishing lead,

A hinge, some bolts, and an old shoe buckle
I looked at my prizes and let out a chuckle,

It was quite an adventure as I spent the day
As I found lost treasures in my own driveway.

Naomi F. Sack

Reflections

As I look in the pool below,
I stare at my image.
To everybody I am hideous,
But, that is not what I see.
A prince is what I see within,
Whom nobody else wants to see.
'Till they can stand next to me without fear,
I shall stay here in my castle of clouds,
Until the deepest ocean goes dry
And the last human ascends to the sky.

Patrick Warner

'Happy Easter'

H - Hours Christ spent on the cross
A - Abundance of Christ's love for us,
P - Prayed to the Heavenly Father
P - Pain Christ suffered for us
Y - You the one Christ died for.

E - Erased your sins, when you believed
A - Always there when you need Him
S - Son of God the Father
T - Thorns placed on Christ's head
E - Eternal love even when we forget.
R - Redeemed of our sins by believing.

Barbara Walters

Peter Pan

He hopped up on my windowsill,
A boy all dressed in green.
He made a funny face at me -
And came right through the screen!

"How do you do" and "Cheerio!"
I thought I heard him say -
I tried to touch the little man
But then he flew away!

Jeanne K. Yochem

Bees

I think that I shall never see
A bug as busy as a bee.

A bee, whose silent silken wings
Honey to our table brings.

A bee, who makes God's garden grow,
That we may reap what he does sow.

A bee, whose wing-ed visit makes
To every flower when it wakes.

Who must its natural foes combat;
Who architects do marvel at.

Bees make fools of you and me,
And only God out works the bee.

James F. Ingraham

Seasons Stepping Like A Shoe

A butterfly flutters - by - bye,
A buttercup sits - open - wide,
Yearning, life, sorrow, hate,
Wind is blowing - bye - late.

How soft we see a flowering tree,
Quiet winds blow gracefully,
Leaves of colors - many blow,
Sleeping - softly comes the snow.

Darkness hovers - lingers- stays,
Life's not living - days to daze,
Misty mornings - melting snow,
And thus ends the winter show.

Starting - growing - life a new,
Silence - creeping - soft soft shoe,
Stepping swiftly - newness comes,
Up - away - playing - fun.

Round we go in silent stealth,
Changing - making newness wealth,
Passing seasons - starting new,
And so on steps the seasons' shoe.

Earl J. Anderson

Untitled

All along a walk in open day,
a church bell tolls.
Its pitch of time resounds,
never wavering its sound.
Only light, hue and casted shadows
in their aestheticness change,
yet, there is something unnamed
that never does…

A stroll in setting sun,
a bell it still tolls.
Its pitch of time elapsed resounds,
never a waver in its sound.
Light and hue now almost gone,
casted shadows are drawn and long.
Through my journey be over
another will dawn,
this bell it still tolls
continuously on.

Cindy Huckel

The Dawn

The orange sun in the east
A crisp, fresh blowing breeze
Trees swaying to a wind
That put our minds to ease.

Clear, crystal drops of dew
Sparkle in the light
Green, straight blades of grass
Blow in morning's light.

Robins and sparrows chirp loudly
Mice scamper across the grass
Squirrels chitter excitedly
Puddles shimmering like glass.

A rainbow of flowers dazzle all
Rivers flow swift
Violet dawn is the greatest of
Nature's wonderful gifts.

Hirsh Sandesara

Untitled

On this day-
A flower was formed.
It grew, bloomed,
and lived a life.
It took all the hardships of living
but yet it still stood,
letting everyone enjoy its beauty
and existence.
That flower is still shinning bright.

On this day-
A child was born.
He grew and bloomed into an
intelligent adult.
He took all the hardships of living
but yet he still stands,
letting everyone enjoy his beauty
and existence.
That man is still shining bright.

Amy Keich

Untitled

I awoke from a nightmare
a hand gripping me from a
sheet, shroud like, the hand of
your death chilling my soul.

Was my fear of the prince
of darkness using you to
haunt my lonely soul
but then I wondered if

I had misunderstood the hand
as not of darkness but as
the caress of your soul
restless and alone reaching

Out to share the love
that did not die when
your body did and it
felt good to touch you.

I know now that I
am not alone but that
our souls will share
eternal love and hope.

David Sanford Ridgway

Death

A sea of ancient memories flood.
A hundred years of frightened blood
Comes to slay my every dream.
I hear my past shriek and scream.
My soul escapes the heat.

And silver blade with tarnished shines;
Sweet and sour, eternity and time;
Takes me to another land.
Driven there by my own hand,
My soul has been released.

And from the ground, my blood is seeping.
Years of death, tears of weeping
Drag me down to hell unknown,
Shave me down to bloody bone.
My soul has been captured.

And blood of those I loved before
Leaks out beneath death's bloody door.
And graves are open for us to see
A broken body resembling me.
My soul has been raptured.

John Blalock

Lynn

L ight hearted and carefree,
a lasting, ladylike glow.
Y outhfulness seldom found with
such wisdom and persistence
N arrowness of pathways, never an
obstacle.
N ever anything less than
everything one would wish for.

Joseph Michael Carlo

Life

A rose losing its petals is like
A person losing someone very
special in their life.

Jennifer Bryant

Longing To Be Free!

Empty dreams from an empty soul,
A loveless life, with no where to go.
An aching heart, with nothing to give,
Not much of a life, so why should I live
Is this a test from God?
Meant just for me,
To see how long I can live this
life, in such misery.
Why must I always suffer?
And be in pain,
Why do I always get hurt?
Time and time again.
When will I ever learn to live
life, just for me?
Put myself first, so I can be free!
Free of the emptiness that haunts
my heart and soul,
Free to do as I wish, so I can
let my dreams grow.

DuAnn Marie Forichette

Hunger And Tears (God's Will)

A baby wails.
A mother cries.
Her child dies before her eyes.
Her nightmare's come.
She's seeing her fears.
With bitterness she wipes her tears.
She prayed for this day not to come.
Her heart is beating like a drum.
She tries to shake him back alive.
This body where hunger did thrive.
She laid him down and turned away.
She cleared her mind of this day.
She knew one day, God's will be done,
She would be joined with her son.
She had no food to kill the pain.
She only owned a walking cane.
She stumbled along her village path.
She knew this was Jehovah's wrath.
As she watched the setting sun,
She prayed to herself, "God's will be done".

Anne McDonald

Strangers In The House

We pass in the hall
  a smile or nod all
that time allows;
  hurried steps
in different directions,
  separated by demands
often self-impose;
  as twilight falls we
meet again, fatigued by
  hours of social pressure,
a smile or nod once more. We've
  become strangers in our house.

Bev Tostenson

Untitled

In the blink of a moment
a year slips by
and we jerk awake, surprised,
doubting it happened,
knowing it did,
sorry and relieved together.

Carole Spence

Memorial Day

Today we went remembering,
A special day remembering,
With home-blown peonies
Of pink and white and red.

With iris, tall and stately,
Purple royalty and gold.
For dear ma-mas and papas,
For grands and greats of old.

Oh yes, we went remembering
In graveyards, closely held
By country fields, unfurling corn,
And spring-green trees, with bird song,

The bitter-sweet remembering,
The warm and dear remembering,
When days stretched on forever,
And time would never end.

We knelt to lay our offering
Of remembrance and of beauty.
The breeze gave us the incense
From the honey locust trees.

Frances Brent Killey

Girth, Ring, and Wood

If I told you a story
a story of a tree
it would be a memory
of nature's evolution
and all that I have
learned about life
and a common history.
The gnarled old oak
the palm swaying
in the breeze
the cedar and the pine
all of what has been
cherished
and treasures to
behold
all of which is
a little less
in the generations
to come.

Cheryl M. White

A Tear Beneath The Surface

I did the best I could,
A tear beneath the surface.
Will be waiting these for you,
The mark of motherhouse.

The road I chose for you,
Was of hope and happiness.
The path you took instead,
Was a lifetime of regrets.

Now that you're older,
I can't take you by the hand.
You'll be on your own,
Through life's forbidden ways.

If you should stumble
Along that rough terrain
I'll be there to hold you,
I'll try to ease your pain.

Night is here and I must leave you now.
My eyes will never see.
The tear beneath the surface
The tear you'll shed for me.

Esther Flannery

Grandchild

Soft shiny hair -
  A turned-up nose.
Sparkling eyes -
  in grownup clothes -
The way you laugh -
  and call my name -
Makes life more beautiful
  Since you came.

You seem so big -
  but yet so small
Sweet conversations -
  when you call
"Please come for me"
"I love you too-"
All time is precious
spent with you.

Janie Powers

The Blooms Of Youth

The child's cries
  a vast disguise
to find his faith
  and hold it safe

A friend he has
  to pave his paths
with bricks and stones
  and treasures strewn

With the blooms of youth
  he captures truth
for the innocent child
  is not yet beguiled

He sees what is real
  and learns to feel
but as maturity calls
  he stumbles and falls

Jennifer LeBaron Smith

A Haiku for May

In morning sunshine,
A yellow cat sits, ears up,
Among daffodils.

Amy Wilson Dandurand

To You

You have something on your mind
about me
Don't you

Holding a cup of coffee
Sink myself into the sofa of the lobby
I look at you

You can run
but you can't hide

If you don't care
Why are you in such a hurry
to look away

Bianca Yongrong Bao

Tender Offerings

The Texas sky stretched blue and still
Above their childhood games and play,
As forces of unyielding will
Confronted on that April day.

Strewn outside lay bikes and toys,
Abandoned in the siege's crush.
The complex rang with pounding noise
As rumbling tanks began to push.

Within, the frightened children cried,
Not their choice, a death by fire;
But flames and crumbling walls allied
To make for them a special pyre.

In their bunkers closely tended,
The children huddled to survive.
Blazing tinders swiftly ended
The hope and breath of those alive.

The Texas prairie, chastened land,
Rolls on with time, it must.
Mount Carmel's walls no longer stand.
Its children's lives are ashes, dust.

June L. Beaver

"Aim The Sextant To The Stars"

Aim the sextant to the stars.
Affix the views, know where you are.
Mark with pencil, neck bent down,
Hope you're right or there'll be frowns.
And lost we'll be upon the sea.
Everyone including me,
But joy oh joy I know I'm here,
So everyone have no fear.
We travel sea through lat and long,
Carrying cargo in our boat so strong.
Until it's time again to find
That point that gives us peace of mind.
Aim the sextant to the stars.
Affix the views, know where you are.

Jeffrey H. Cox

Lost Love

I thought you cared
After all that we shared
The after school talks
All the short walks
I thought it would last forever,
But soon we were never together
I could never explain
All my pain
I was lonely and sad
None of this showed
You had to be told,
But I was too scared
To loose what was there
When you were near
I'd never fear,
But when you were gone
All I had is our song
Or was the dance just a show
I loved the songs,
But they didn't last long.

Jessica Clark

Memories

Running the roads to protect convoy
after convoy it's getting to all of us,
no relief in sight.
I wonder what day it is or what month,
time is forgotten out here, where all
man's like this? Are we men or machines
driver to our death, my life will be
different now nothing will matter,
feelings for a human life has disappeared

Giovanni J. Picarelli

Better Days Ahead

After the snow and the sleeting,
After the cold, icy rain
I then shall leave for heaven
Its lovely entrance to gain!

After the frost on the windshield,
After the glaze on the street,
After the wreck on the highway
In mansions up in Glory we'll meet!

After the numbness leaves my fingers,
After viewing the barren landscape,
After some more frigid nights
To those eternal shores I'll escape!

After the tears and the heartaches,
After that final tumultuous good bye,
After the partings are all over
With Christ we shall meet in the sky!

It pays for one to get ready
This old world fast draws toward the end.
Haste then, my dear fellow being,
Trust Jesus, then you're my brother, my
friend!

James K. Norton

Death

Silence
Again there is silence,
  The silence of the dead.

  Darkness

Dark and damp lay our coffins.
  The cloaks of Midnight
Spin around like webs,
  Concealing all that is light.

But one long dark cloak
  Stands out, about the breast
Of the Moon light.

  One white bony hand
Beckons the souls of mortal man.

  To enter that
  Dark sleep we call
  Death.

Brandy L. Brantley

Joined By The Moon

As we look toward the moon
and gaze at the stars
the distance between us
doesn't seem so far
these thoughts of their light
bring comfort each night
just knowing their shining
on you

George B. Mims

"Sandcastles"

My heart pulses in despair.
All of that, rare, is lost,
Like the doomed city of Atlantis.
Once the tangible holding wasn't folding,
But was building up like sandcastles,
On a summer beach.
Loss then came, and weeping.
That tangible, and rare,
Was taken from my keeping,
Faded into night and out of sight.
My heart pulses in despair
With games where nothing's fair.
Like that doomed Atlantis,
Prized to the grave,
The things one cannot save,
Washed away in a wicked tide.
Faded into night values once so bright.
When did Atlantis sink so deep?
When did I lose what I couldn't keep?

Gail M. Scarafile

"Ghost Towns"

There are ghost towns
All the over the west.
Wooden structures in decay,
To become part, of the soil one day.
Towns quickly built,
To meet the demand,
Of miners throughout the land.
Eager to buy a shovel, pick and pan,
Quest for gold, the search began,
Possessing the minds of every man.
Some realized their dreams,
Became successful, men of means.
Others drank and gambled their "finds,"
The fever hitting, men of all kinds.
Left in the wake, of the gold trail,
Abandoned towns, broken dreams,
An era lost in the "ghost town scene."

Hazel H. Kersch

Untitled

I sit alone,
Alone in the dark.

I have no worries,
Well, none to ponder about.

I think of many things
or maybe dream about.

Well, now the day is over.
My thoughts will end.

But in another time,
They will come again.

Dana Buonadies

Sunshine And Rain

You came my way
Along life's path,
And sunshine filled my heart.

  How different-

The torrential rain,
My tears unbidden,
As you now from me depart.

Faye A. Nichols

Unchartered Shores

Walk in my dreams with me
Along the unchartered shores of my heart.
Help me to find the reason
For my longing, for my put-up
Yearnings, my gropings
To align with life;
My effort is, to make the energy of
living in the present - an anchor
Not to soar off in a dream-
To escape the pressing reality!

The grail dances behind the veil
Glimpsed dimly with no sure form
The spirit then - the quality unknown
Its fathoms unexplored
As they are ever developing
Changing and unpredictable,
The feelings falter
A book half read and the end
The middle of the chapter.

Bernice Davis Brigham

Why

I don't know why I sit here today
Although I thought and wondered
I just don't understand why
I do the things I blunder
I sometimes act just like a man
And then my life get hard
Everyone always screws me over
Then I usually take charge
Sometimes I think I'll only take time
Even though I know it won't
I just don't understand why
People never try and don't
It sometimes makes me cry and cry
When people hurt my feeling
And then they ask me why and why
They act like I have no dealings
I really don't have anyone
Except me, myself and I
I can trust no one
It makes me almost die.

Jaime Cox

Untitled

Softly slumber, sweet
Amidst sepulchred dreams we'll meet
timeless fields, so crystal clear
Upon these eyes there'll be no tears.

Of things undone and words unspoken
Picked up the pieces; shattered, broken
Once upon the morning dawning
You held me tight with all the longing,
Held me tight you whispered close,
"My dear, it's you I love the most".

From oft a distance a bell did toll
A call for some unknown soul.
Swiftly, gently bore my love away
In my arms beautiful, serene he lay.

Softly slumber, sweet
Amidst sepulchred dreams we'll meet
Timeless fields, so crystal clear
Upon these eyes there'll be no tears.

Even angels can take you never
I with you slumber forever...

Jennifer C. Engracia

Gibbous Lives

Like the moon cycling so,
an incomplete sphere lives' posses.
Love is missing,
unwanted distress.
An essential part of living,
day to day as such.
Without it, dying,
fading, hopes and dreams so much.
Finding love in entirety,
a peak so hard to climb.
No place reserved for pity,
there just isn't any time.
A gibbous life to lead;
a wish to cycle bright and full.
With hope to fulfill the need,
a gibbous life annul.

Adam Darlage

Untitled

I see the world from atop
an invisible peak
Listless
the tears fall to no destiny
tried to endure that of which
left me to bleed
Could I have been this?
My mind drifts over the
memory of my soul
now that's all that remains
Let us open our eyes and
face the end.

Desilee Clark

The World Turns

The world spins
and a baby cries.
The sheets twist
and a lover sighs.
A twig snaps
and the fire burns.
A hand swings
and the child learns.
Helpless in the world
feel so all alone,
begging for mercy
wish to go home.
Tears fall
and blood spills.
The chase is over
and the hooded man kills.
People feel
and feelings churn.
All the while
the world still turns.

Heather Braithwaite

God's Creations

I like to see the moon and the stars,
And all of the fancy cars.
I like to see the birds in the trees,
And all of the falling leaves.
I like to see the clear blue sky,
And all the mountains that stand so high.
I like to see the rain and flowers,
Which are all God's powers.
He has created many wonderful things,
Even us... Human beings.

Ericka R. Roulhac

If

If a river represented life,
And a tree food and water,
A mountain could be a friend,
And a valley would be a home;
If there was not a valley, the river
Would be homeless, if there was
Not a mountain, the river would be
Friendless, and if there were
No trees, the river would die.
But what if we changed those things;
What if we take care of earth
Then earth would take care of us,
What if...

Danielle Anderson

Quiescence

When time is spent
and age recasts the
the spirit and the form
Life in ceaseless waves
attains the semblance of repose.
Man himself confronted
by the change
yields to its rhythms
and slow undulations
Yet more disposed to
seize the moment
flinging to the winds
the yoke of passing time
But the body feeble
aching and oh so
sorely strained
Succumbs to sleep
and rest
and the comfort of
motionless stability.

Jay M. Morgan

Growing Up

When I grow up
And become a poet,
Well known -
Translated into many languages,
Known by me and unknown too.
When I'm rich,
As the man
Who lives across the street.
The one with the lovely smile,
Who never says more than hi!

Will I know him?
Or pretend I never did?
Will I just smile and pass him by?
Or will I still have to hide my tears,
After all those years?

Will he see me, signing books
For fans?
All wanting to be my friends?
Will growing up, take my dreams away?
I hope they've come to stay.

Helena M. Jones

"New Bride"

Only a month of being a new bride,
And I just can't believe he's already
Left my side, and chose over me,
Sports illustrated, a bowl of popcorn,
And the latest edition of the T.V. Guide.....

Debbie Keeling

The Janitor

He sweeps a while
and behind his glasses,
He holds a smile
and greets the masses,

They shuffle in
down the hall,
Boots and jackets
along the wall,

On a silver ring
he holds the keys,
encompassing
Their hopes and dreams,

Hours and days
Days and weeks,
Month to month
he rarely speaks,

Beginning of summer
they leave him, all,
He greets them again
in start of fall.

Charles William Harrington Jr.

My Blueprint

I want to open the door from the outside,
And close it from the inside.
I must change my blueprint
Of what has been planted in my heart
To see all the snares that must depart.
Now that spring is here,
Only the best seeds must stay.
I must throw the others away.
First, love must have the best growth —
Implanted strong and sure.
God says it is the most important,
And it is the best cure.
Following are: Compassion, caring,
Giving, and be understanding.
These are God's blueprints—
No others can compete.
A beauty you will behold
If in heaven you want to be,
And have the very best seat—
To make your life complete.

Fern Gardiner Smith

Lela M Hicks

The sun has gone to hide
and clouds have come to cry
A sweet and gentle lady
Has told us all good-bye
Every life she touched
She filled with light and laughter
Heaven will be a happier place
from now to ever after
She asked for naught from those
Who she loved so dear
Except to see them often
And to have them near
I say a prayer of thanks
That the Lords has Blessed me so
He let her touch my life
I loved her, don't you know

Don Reid

What Are Dreams?

Dreams are a necessary part of life,
    And for some, a fortunate reality.
Attainable dreams are not without strife
    Which does enhance life's quality.

Dreams are for everyone,
    Not just for you, or for me,
Others do not realize this,
    Nor, the benefits do they see.

Some dream of unattainables,
    Others are more realistic.
They dream of helping others
    And life becomes less mystic.

I dreamed of someone, somewhere,
    To keep in touch each time,
With whom I could relate and exchange
    Words of poetry, verse and rhyme.

My dreams are being fulfilled
    In many wondrous ways,
Because your gentle messages
    Bring cheerfulness to so many days.

Al Newman

A Better Place

He has gone to a better place
And he will feel pain no more
He will be young again
He will be with children
For only the very good are permitted
To be keepers of the little angles
He will pass his time
In fields of flowers
And clover that never needs mowing
He will wonder now and again
To watch at the gate
With a far away look in his eye
And when the time comes
For you to meet him
You will both be young again
He will smile and open his arms to hold you
And tell you how much he missed you
Then you will never know pain again
In this a better place.

Carolyn Betts

Together - Divided

You are the sky
And I am the earth
    Divided
    We note
Each other's worth
    The sky to the earth

United the two
Can never be
    But ever
    Shall live
In harmony
    Together divided.

Hannah B. Nissman

Why Can't It Be

I lay alone at night
And I can only fight
The idea that you might
Start loving me again
Then I think when?
When will he love me?
When will he see?
That he means so much to me.
Why am I in pain
may it be because
The love I want, I can't gain
I want it back to how it was
I hope you do too
I love you, won't you love me too!

Amy Gothard

"Remember"

It's May the 12th again this year
And I think so oft of you
Of days of yore and distant shore
Where skies seemed always blue.

My love has reached around the world
I shall not forget the times we shared
I think of standing in a house so small
Filled with love so great
I see the honey suckle grow
beside the court yard gate.

And there's the little tiny church
With dust filled pews and alters bare.
I hear a voice of long ago
That says I'll meet you there.

Tho times and tide has come and gone
This day will always be
Remembered in my life and times
Do you remember me?

Charlotte C. Kirkland

Love I Give

I will grow old loving you,
And I will die loving you…
Though out all eternity.
Through out all time.
My love will still be strong
even after all man have gone.
There is no limit of the love I hold;
After all it's yours to mold.
To shape to your perfection,
    your disapproval,
    your dismay,
For my love I give to you,
Is true in every way.

Diane Kloosterman

Memories

Life can begin
and it can end.

But our memories
of our loved ones
can never end.

So, if your loss
seems too much
to bear,

Remember, your loved ones
in memory,
will always be there.

Eynar Gonzalez

Patience

Pass key to unlock any door
And it matters not rich or poor
To have this treasure in your fold
Inspires all that within the soul
Endless dreams come into sight
Not allowing for any fright
Coming from high, high above
Enduring all with gods infinite love

James Sylvester

The Lady

She walks serenely through the day
And listens as the townsfolk say,
"You'll forget. It's hard at first."
She knows "forgetting" is the worst.
To yell, "I'm home" to empty space,
To expect his junk in its usual place,
To waken and reach in forgetfulness
To the ghastly shock of nothingness.

No one sees her midnight tears.
No one knows her night time fears.
The bureau pushed against the door;
The eerie thumps she wakens for.
The wrenching sobs from deep inside,
The flowing eyes that had seldom cried.

She walks serenely through the day
And I hear the townsfolk say,
"She accepts her loss so strangely well."
"They seemed so close. One can never tell."

Juanita B. Neher

Regret

If you have ever said something bad
And made the person very sad
You'll always regret that day

But if you think before you act
And try try try to have some tact
You won't regret what you say

So be wise
Apologize
If you have done something wrong
And they'll forgive you before long.

Ella Govshtein

Waiting To Die To Live

There is silence all around
And no one to be found.
All that is here,
Is this book, my chains, and the ground.

With nothing to do
And going no where soon,
I pick up this book
And take a good look
And read of Jesus and my doom.

As I read about Him
and I see what He did
To save a man like me,
The worthless man I could be,
He tells me He has died for my sin.

Now I understand why;
Why God had stood by
So that I might live
Through His Son's death for my sin
So that I'll be alive when I die.

Jason L. Johnson

Love Is A Masterpiece

The candle made a shadow fall
And placed our bodies on the wall
There besides us.
   We made magic; a worm of art
That started with two tender hearts
And we made love.
   You make me feel brand new again.
No one before, has ever been…
Able of such.
   I think of you when shadows fall
And think of art upon the wall;
Of two in love.

Julie Carlson

The Thimble

The cold thimble sat on my warm finger
And protected it
Against the silver needle
Soon the thimble slept
And the tricky needle
Tried to prick my finger
The needle tiptoed to my finger
And clicked his little body
This woke up the thimble
And he attacked the needle
The needle walked away angrily.

Beth Shilane

Untitled

   God looked around his garden
And saw an empty space
   Then he looked down from heaven
And saw your tired, tired face
   He knew that you were suffering
   And a cure was not be
So he put his arms around you.
   And whispered come to me
With tearful eyes we watched
   As you slowly passed away
And though we loved you dearly
   We couldn't make you stay
Many, many times we've needed you
Many, many time we've cried
If only love could have saved you
You never would have died!

Bethanie Jeanine Zimmerman

The Wind

When the wind races down hills
And screams through the valleys,
When it pounds on city stores
And careens down the alleys,
When it howls at the window
And knocks at the door,
When it hammers too loudly
For people to ignore,
When it stirs up the sand
And churns up the seas,
When it whistles through rocks
And bends down the trees,
When it shakes the houses
And rattles the glasses,
When it roars so wildly
And so rudely passes,
When it bursts out its mournful sigh,
It makes the lonely want to cry.

Bernita Becker

Gene

I close my eyes
and see your smile
I feel your soft embrace

I close my eyes
and feel your breath
so close to my face

I close my eyes
and hear the beat
of your strong heart

I close my eyes
and pray for sleep
so that dreams of you
can start

I close my eyes
and imagine
how good it will be

To open my eyes
and see you here
lying next to me…

Ella L. Mercado

"Fun of Growing Old"

When I was just a lad
   and set on Grandpa's knee,
He told me many stories
   about the land of make believe.

Harry R. Gates

Bird's Eye View

Birds come to my window
And sing for scraps of bread.
Then away they go
To find themselves a bed.

And somewhere on a lofty tree
They fold their wings and sleep,
Safe and snug as can be
Away from things that creep.

Come morn' they soar in the azure blue
And gambol through the sky -
Which is something we can't do
No matter how we try.

So all of us who toil below
And think we're fast and wise -
Must look awful dumb and slow
To the little bird that flies.

Edward H. Halsall

War In Spring

The honey bees were first to come
And sip the nectar sweet
From every blossom in my yard,
But news has zephyr feet:
For soon the bumblebees buzzed in
To search for essence rare.
They chased and raced, and madly faced
Each bee who wouldn't share.
The hummingbird came zooming down
To challenge all the bees,
And total war was then declared
Where once was joy and peace.
The battle raged from dawn 'till dark,
Though plenteous the supply.
The only neutral creature there—
A peaceful butterfly.

Evelyn Waldrup

Life

The days of our life are oh so short
  and so the leaves do fall.
The things we do and leave behind
  is the reason for it all.
    Jim McLaughlin

"Heaven Awaits"

    He built a fountain,
      And spirit in our souls;
The Bible through which he speaks
    The angels protect us,
  In our wake and through...

      Our sleep.
    Giving us direction...
     Holding our hand,
    Through the walk...
      He guides us
  With words of wisdom,
   In our dreams...
   We hear his talk.
    His invitation
  Brings us to his gate
Kneeling for his mercy,
    In which he,
  That "Heaven Awaits"
  Jenette Leigh

My Friend

I came to visit you today
And standing there alone
I told you of the emptiness
I feel since you've been gone

The rain was softly falling
As by your grave I knelt
And prayed that God would take away
The pain and grief I felt

I searched my mind for answers
As tears flowed from my eyes
God whispered, "I have taken her
To a home beyond the skies"

Please ask God to save a place
Right next to you for me
Cause I'm coming to be with you
And we'll share eternity
  Donna F. Wallace

Untitled

I love you,
and still do,
but who took the stars
and the moon
from your eyes,
Who stole you
from me,
that now
your eyes
are cloudy,
Who stole your heart
I want to know
Because I do
Still love you.
  Jorene Tsosie

Gems And Thorns

He bore a thorny crown
And suffered grave disgrace
The day they cast Him down
The fires of Hell to face.
He rose to rule as heir
Upon His Father's throne
Forevermore to wear
A crown of precious stone.
In living every day
I can exalt His reign
Or turn His love away
And carry on His pain.
I long to as a gem
His precious head adorn
And glitter pure for Him
And not become a thorn.
  Jo E. Pinto

My Friend

You started out to be my friend
And that I thought would never end.
But somewhere down the road
Our friendship began to grow
Now my feelings for you are very strong.
I sit and wonder all day long,
I sit and wonder is this wrong?
You are my friend, a friend indeed
A friend I value,
A friend I need
As I look into your perfect face
I know that I could never replace
Those feelings that I have for you
I just wonder,
Do you have them too?
  Debra Dempsey

A Lovely Day

The sky is blue with a red tint,
and the pine trees grow old.
The flower become colorless and
lifeless while the air becomes cold.
The leaves turn brown and dry
and the grass becomes wet.
While this wonderful day you
never want to forget.
  Dawn Hatcher

Pain, Fears, And Wasted Tears

It is what keeps me out,
  and them in,
It is what repeats itself
over and over again.
It is what I can see through,
but can not stand to look at,
  It is my pain.
It is what keeps me inside,
all boxed in.
It is what makes me hide
from it again.
It is what I know,
but I'll never find out.
  It is my fear.
It is what crawls down my cheek,
in a moment of regret.
It is what soaks my pillow,
and makes it wet.
It is my illusion that hides my reality.
  They are my wasted tears.
  Angela Maugeri

To Remember

I sit back and look at your picture
And think of the way your arms felt
But I can not remember
I think of your kisses
I can not remember the touch
To think of the warmth of your love
That was never there
Remembering the thoughts of you
That have faded away
For I feel now
Of how you had hurt me, how you used me
For the only love I feel now
Is that of your child
The arms that are gentle
The kisses that are sweet
The body that is warm with love
The only thing I want to remember
Is the love I have for her
For that I thank you
That is all I want to remember of you
  Janet Rich

Love

I love you very much
And this is quite hard for me to say,
My love for you grows stronger,
With every passing day.

You mean the world to me
And believe me it's true,
Without those happy moments
My life is nothing without you.

I'll try my best to get over you,
And maybe I will someday.
But until I do, my love for you,
Will never go away.

All I ask of you
Is to remember the times we've shared,
And always believe me when I say:
I will always be there.

I'll say good-bye now,
But before I do,
I have to tell you one more thing:
I love you.
  Brooke Strunk

When You're Alone

When you're alone
And trapped at home
With nothing to do
And you're feeling blue,
Just close your eyes
And let your spirits soar
To a land
Where you've never been before.
Picture a meadow with flowers and trees
Where wild horses run free.
The beach is also grand
With clear, warm waters and white sands.
Are you alone?
Don't despair
Just think of me and I'll be there.
  Danh Tran

The Light Of Hope

Why to stop the time
And to turn back to the past?
Instead of facing the future
With the hope of life?

Do the lights of hope
All have to be off at once?

Why to open our doors only to sadness
And to be lost in hopelessness?
Instead of embracing hope
With the cheer of life?

Do we have to turn our back
To the shine of life?

In fact, it's the time to be reborn...
With the dawn of a nice morning
To open our windows
With our faith in the future,
The inspirational light of hope.

Because there'll always be a shining star
Even in the darkest sky of
disappointments in life
Like a light of hope in heart...

Adnan Alp Icoz

"Meditation"

I asked not that you come my way,
And turn my darkness into day.
Fate had it planned, you see, and so,
Now that you've gone, I'm sure I know
That you were meant to bring this ache,
And my poor heart was meant to break.

Why should I sit and weep and pine,
And meditate on lovesick line?
What fate had planned may work for you,
But I have when things to do.

Avis Marie Barrett

Untitled

I stepped out into the street
And very nearly made acquaintance
With a South Central Bell van
On a first name basis

Yesterday I accidentally found
The cemetery gate
And was surprised to see
My surname in marble

So I listen to the whisper
Of live oaks
(They were my mother's favorite)
And try to remember only to
   fight the forgetting

Of how the Mediterranean Sea was made
And why distance makes tears
Fall like leaves that pile up
So deep between us

Jenny Bowers

Sticks and Stones

Sticks and stones
are hard as bones,
Aimed with angry art.
Words can sting like everything,
but silence breaks your heart.

Desire Dunne

In The Second Half Of My Life

I took the tears of a homeless man
   and washed clean my heart.
I planted tall sunflowers
   in the low rows of scar tissue.
I heard memories from the graveyard
   and made music from their echoes.
I opened my mouth, and breathed love
   into the ears of ignorance.
I wrapped a piece of paper,
   around the moon,
   and it became a man.
I placed my hand over my face,
   over the face of death,
   and he became stone.
A woman placed her hand
   over my face,
   and I became an angel.

John Ellison

Daddy

I see my dad about once a year
and when I leave shed some tears.
I jump around when I see my mom
But when I turn my dad is gone.

I stand and watch him drive away
and then I think about next May.
I think about the fun we had
and then I start to miss my dad.

I think about the things we will do
because I can only think of you.
I have so many things to say
but all of the things must wait till May.

Cassie Hayes

The Circle

I fear,
And yet there is no terror here.
I cry,
But proudly shrink from asking why?
I love,
But in that loving do incline
To seek, desire, possess as mine.
Alone I dare to go my way of self-deceit,
and lying say,
I love,
Because I will to self not die,
I cry.
Because I will not let him near,
I fear.

Joanne Mary Schuler

Empty Bed

Each night comes and with it dread,
as I go to sleep in my empty bed.
With slumber far off I sit and stare,
and make a wish to have you here.
Barren arms embrace the cold,
longing for those days of old.
Thoughts race by, memories of you,
and tears start to fall,
as tears sometimes do.

Christopher H. Dezscz

Untitled

The cave contains the lifeless limbs
anointed anxiously and long;
a peeling laceration
of a murdered prophet's murdered song;

but as the pale and shaking ones
disintegrate with choking fears,
the status quo is rolled away;
an unknown radiance appears,

eclipsing all the stars of dawn
as death itself begins to shake
and Light achieves a cosmic leap
and shocks creation wide awake,

reverberating fusion which
reintegrates the scraps and tears
and all the brokenness of earth,
while Heaven, assembled, stomps and
cheers!

Belle Rollins

All I Have To Do

Another long day without you,
another sunset alone.
I sit here without love,
what I feel,
can never be shown.

For so long I've cared about you,
for so long I've felt unlead.
Every feeling inside my heart,
I should care for another,
I care for you instead.

I've felt this feeling for you,
to hold me in your arms.
I like everything about you,
your stories, your laughter,
your charms.

I know I can never have you,
I know it can never be just us two.
I'll just close my eyes and dream,
that's all I have to do.

Carmen Pardel

Dreams

Dreams can take you anywhere you want,
anything can happen in your dreams,
Dreams help build character,
and let you have your own identity,
They let you meet that special someone,
or live a life you want to live,
Dreams can change what you want changed
not permanently,
But temporarily through the night,
Through your dream
you can do whatever you want to do
Anything that pleases you
Anything you can't do in reality
You can do in your dream
so dream away
And let your thoughts
And desires take control

Jennifer Meyer

Dreams

Dreams
are a truth
a truth that has its own form
of reality.

A reality
that has its own desires and wants
a life of pain and sweetness
wrapped
in a never ending agony of wishes.

Wishes
that with the need for hope
become dreams.

Christine Kropcho

When I Retire

The sands in the glass of time
Are beginning to run low,
I'd like a little time to play
Before it's time to go.

To have some time to just relax,
Not hurry through each day,
To "stop and smell the roses"
If I find some on my way.

To sit beneath a leafy tree
Beside a running stream,
To float in a hot air balloon
O'er a hillside lush and green.

Have time to stroll a quiet beach,
Sit and watch the sky at night,
Wish upon a falling star
And believe with all my might.

To savor the beauty of each new dawn
As I never have before,
To have just a bit of time for me
And I'll ask for little more.

Alice K. Brandt

Humming

Poets,
are found
At any given moment
   space or time…
But each will reveal
   the seconds -
you left behind.

Clarence McCord

Knowing You're Mine

Chills that form
   Are from your sweet touch
The tears that fall
   Mean that I miss you much
Each step I take
   They follow yours
Everyday I talk to you
   They all mean much more
When I smile
   I'm thinking of you
Knowing that you'll be back
   Says you love me too
I'm yours forever
   Till the end of time
I love you a lot
   Especially knowing you're mine.

Carly Ann Smalley

Untitled

Legs just long enough to reach the floor
Aren't quite long enough at all.
Like ladder, like popsicle sticks,
A line upwards to nothing.
Arms that hang teased by the ground,
Decor for our shoulders,
They are nothing.
A snake in mid air, a cryptic line,
Our spines float in us as nothing.
My purple lizard fingers
Scale his vertebrae wall,
Reaching for the axis
That centers him.
Creating waves in a back
That waterfalls down to a bridge,
And where I focus
Makes it better, makes it harder
To resist
The thing I'm closing in on…
And then dawn breaks.

Jessica D'Arcy

Re-Birthday

Young lad with chiseled features,
Arrogant ways to hide the hurt,
You shy away from helpful teachers,
Defiant young lad without a heart.
Is it true you want to destroy?
Or are you only a saddened boy?
Heavy metal, wordless noise - these
To ignite your empty inners.
All you ever really wanted was to
Stay clear of those sinners.
Get the courage, walk away -
Greet tomorrow as re-birthday.

Beverly J. Stanwood

Untitled

The walls around my eyes close in
As I see the world in all its sin.
A tree falls-Death calls
Calling its children home.

All children call for aid
As their hopes for a future slowly fade.
Sun and moon-gone too soon
Smothered by what we call "Progress."

The creatures in the forest call
"Please don't destroy us all!"
Life cries-but Life dies
And the trees just keep on falling.

As this world slowly dies
Only the children heed her cries.
I care-and will be there
To avenge her long last sighs.

Cheryl Wisniewski

Witchcraft

There's magic in my bucket
   As my kitchen floor I scrub
There's a wealth of precious opals
Made with every swish and rub.

There's enchantment with my secret
   Even Merlin must agree
The conjuring of such magic
As distinctive sorcery.

Hannah B. Nissman

The Taste Of Freedom,

The Taste Of Blood

Some love the taste of freedom,
as others love the taste of blood.
When freedom is wanted,
and blood must be shed,
the only free are the dead.
A bullet in the brain,
cause that freedom you can't gain?
That freedom won't come soon,
cause that gun in your hand is
your freedom's doom.
Some love the taste of freedom,
but their answers the wrong way
some love the taste of blood,
and their coffin is where they'll lay!

Jaimi Tharpe

Water

Water is one important compound
As rain or snow it comes down
From the sky
It's angel's cry.
It's God's life substance
In humans for instance.
In summer it cools us off
Filling up a pool, so soft.
It cleans us,
It bathes us,
It haunts us in mist.
From the sky,
It's angel's cry.

James Oakley

Time Tics Slowly By

Inside oh how quiet,
As tears softly fall,
As your heart for forgiveness cries,
And emptiness seems to call,
And time tics slowly by.

Now envision the master,
and the prayer that he Prayed,
All the pain and suffering,
He endured on that day,
As time ticked slowly by.

See him nailed to the cross,
He cries father forgive them,
For this world and its lost,
Down through the ages its rings,
As time tics slowly by.

So what is you answer,
To his out stretched hands,
Down through the ages he has called,
For the souls of man,
As time tics slowly by.

Barbara Smith

Dreams

If I dream faraway of my life
being tossed away I must forgive but
never forget for the mistakes made me
see what I am and always will be
So where I belong I cannot say for
I dream of things faraway

Erin Mahurin

Ironing The Day

Ironing out life's little wrinkles
As the heat of the iron presses on.
Complaining about problems
solves nothing.
Flip the coin from tails to heads,
Now take life head on!

For delaying today will be
delaying tomorrow.
Switch the 'l' and the 'a'
and drop the 'y'
Now you have dealing
That's the only way to
cope with life today!

Now your wrinkles have
gone away
as your iron whistles
have a "Good Day."

Dane Christensen

Night Stalker

Drops of rain fall
As the mist thickens
Everything goes silent
And her heart quickens.

She turns around slowly
As she glances into the night
Something had been lurking around
But it now was out of sight.

Her steps were no longer shallow
They quickly became strides
She is thinking of a place to go
As she runs and hides

The stranger was faceless
But she knew who it was
She knew where it came from
And she knew what it does.

She knew she could not outrun it
She shall no longer roam
The stranger opened his arms to embrace her
As he welcomed her home.

Alana Gardner

"At The Park"

The breeze took me away
as the sun touched my face
I travelled to another time
I think I found my place

A place where I felt peace
that I never knew before
with no one there to hurt me
I wasn't frightened anymore

Where my worries couldn't find me
I watched the world go by
I caught a glimpse of freedom
and released it with a sigh

I gazed across the water
wishing I didn't have to go
but reality reminded me
it was time I came back home

April L. Groening

Silent Night

Not a word spoken
As you draw close in the night
Just shadow movements
In the pale moonlight
Taking life's urges
Sounds of passion
Soft groans of pleasure
Fill the room's dim light
But not a word spoken
Just sounds of your delight
Pounding hearts lustful cravings
Yielding rapture is in sight
Desire fulfilled once again
The night is still
Weakened body's obsession diminished
But not a word spoken
Now an empty quiet descends

Connie Lamkin

Ash

Ash
Ash
Dark as night
Crumbling like the world
Full of fright
Ash
Ash
Result of destruction
Still hot with anger
How else could we function?
Ash
Ash
What's next?

Caitlin Uzzell

On Nantucket Island

Surf sand sun sea and sky
At an unknown compass point
Between north
And northwest of Sankaty Head

Bright hot summer afternoon sun
Ocean air vagueness negating
The heat of the sun
Hypnotized maybe but
Without the fuss of hypnosis
All unaware, but unaware of what?
A vast and strong latent potency?

Trudging and trundling alone
So happy about so many
Startling and scintillating things
Of course, all is out of whack

Idiot somersaulting stringency
Now become mindful or mindless
Breathing neglectful summer sea air
Some stretch northwest of Sankaty Head

Francis Paar

expectation

a well-behaved child on Christmas morning
  bounding down the steps,

  a tulip bulb under snow
eager to feel sunshine on its head,
  an awkward awe struck cygnet
ogling her mother's marvelous neck

James R. Whitley

The Parent

I would not pick my fruit
at its bitter, green beginning;
cast it down with my hopes,
and, verdict-ridden,
vent my disappointment: too hard.

Nor later, when unmellowed
it hangs bright, tight
to the branch, a tinted hypocrite,
would I undo it, having
given it time.

But I will wait for ripeness.
(Lord, I see,
like a tart apple,
patience begin in me.)

Ann Burke

"The Friend"

My dream awaits thee,
At night it is shown to me,
Together we race on a farm,
For I take no alarm,
My horse and I are friends forever,
Never leaving each other, hoping forever,
One day my dream, our dream, turned sad,
For my friend, my lad
Has gone to a kind place,
where we will always race,
Together, Forever.

Briana Mirchel

"Shadows Of The Mind"

In the shadows of my mind I wander,
Avoiding the sunlight of truth.
The cool shadows mellow the heat,
Caused by the presence of you.

The shadows are consumed by darkness.
And your face is the light to behold.
But it fades and fades and fades,
As reality attempts to take hold.

So in the shadows of my mind I wander,
Avoiding the sunlight, quite lost.
I stumble blindly in the darkness,
Alone, paying the ultimate cost.

Gary W. Ramsey

Alone

I sat alone while the car drove
away,
Tears in my eyes,
On a lonely day in May.

Not a whisper is heard,
Only a creak from the floor,
Should I be scared or watch
T.V. some more?

My stomach is churning,
It's dark outside,
But I guess I'll have to abide.

Right when I'm scared,
And ready to cry,
I hear a car on the gravel and
I sigh.

The knock on the door,
The "Hi, honey I'm home,"
I know I'm safe and I know I'm not
alone.

Grace Maher

"In The Cold, Dark Night"

Rain and lightning strike;
Babies cry in dreary nights.
The wind is howling;
Brave men cowering,
In the cold, dark night.

Darkened skies forbiddin'
Because the sun is hidden.
Frightened hearts pound.
Tornadoes touch down,
In the cold, dark night.

The earth quakes,
And lives it takes.
Fear abounds.
The grim reaper makes his rounds,
In the cold, dark night.

Benjamin D. Peters

The Advantage

What a racket!?!
Back and forth. Back and forth.
A rally to the end.
Soaring high above the mesh.
Then a break...point to me.
Neon in my hand.
Reach to the sky, the command.
Like a bolt of lightning.
The ace strikes.
Aah...sweet victory.

Christine M. Dick

Barefoot In The Surf

Together we strolled
barefoot on a moonlit beach
the surf crashing upon our toes.

Your hand in mine
we spoke of life, dreams
and desires often without words.

Pausing only to kiss
your lips gently
and hold you tightly.

The world drifted away
leaving us alone together
our hearts pounding.

That night of sharing our
excitement, fears and happiness
is lodged forever within my memory.

For as our emotions bubbled over
I asked you to always walk barefoot
with me as my wife and true companion.

Christopher Shave

Surrender

Words can turn
Be used to burn
Hearts can cry
Who told you they cannot lie.

In crowd of many
One angry face seems displaced...
Broken hearts worn on sleeves
Like medals from past wars
Leaves you wanting love no more.

Men say love is a game
And they are not to blame
For all the love and pain I have known
I'd much rather just be alone.

Carrie L. Dunn

The Olympics

I'm making this rhyme,
Because it's Olympic time.
For a while all wars may cease,
And the world comes together in peace.

Everyone traveling to Norway,
Who gets the gold no one can say.
Here come the young and the old,
They gather to watch in the bitter cold.

The lighting of the huge flame
Signifies the start of the games.
For sixteen days and sixteen nights
It will gleam like a million lights.

After the flame is put out,
Up will go uproarious shouts.
Please don't shed any tears,
The Olympics will be back in four years.

Jacki Kiefer

Peace Work

A smoke gray binding of sky draped
behind clouds, like pulled cotton
batting in a quilting frame
   slung low under
    under its berth,

  lies still as God's hands sew
herringbone stitches of l
            i
             g
              h
               t
                n
                 i
                  n
                   g

over mismatched pieces of life...
this crazy quilt called earth.

Dawn Brown

New At Love

The oak tree stands out in the field
Beneath the great blue sky
Its branches spread so beautifully,
To shelter you and I.

A gentle breeze begins to blow,
The leaves begin their dance.
You look deep into my eyes,
I hope you take the chance.

You hold my face between your hands,
And bring your lips to mine.
I feel myself begin to melt,
Their warmth is so divine.

You pull away and then look down.
You think that you did wrong.
I whisper everything's alright.
And wonder what took so long.

You take my hand and walk me home.
You softly say, good-night.
You give me a hug and walk away,
Everything has turned out right.

Cori J. Morrison

Parting

We can't let the miles
between us tear our hearts
We'll stay together always
Though for now I must part.
In my heart and mind
you'll stay. Promise to never
turn the other way.
Love me always. Leave me
never. I shall dream of you
night after night, forever.
You have my word I'll
come back to you. Just have faith
in me, for I have faith in you.
These thoughts of being
without you, have left me feeling blue.
My final words for now-
I love you!

Brianna Lynne Maxwell

Forever

Across the sky,
Beyond the clouds,
Through the air,

Around all trees,
Among their leaves,

Past the mountains,
Among the hills,
Across the fields

Down all streams,
Throughout the world,

Wrapped around the moon,
Between all stars,
Beside the planets,

In the milky way,
Toward the sun,

Outside the galaxy,
Beyond all other galaxies,
Up and down.

Around, it is
Forever.

Danielle Lavine

Nature's Tune

A wisp of air goes past my ear,
Birds are chirping in the trees,
Buzzing is heard, it is the bees,
A rabbit runs for what it sees.

It is harmony or symphony,
Nature's Song sings to me,
It is a wonder of sounds,
As I look 'round.

What do my ears hear,
It is deceiving to see with my eyes,
A building being built on a forest hill.
All is to be still.

What nature's song says to me,
Now with my eyes to see,
Tells me a new tune,
Nature's Song of symphony is now a band of
blues.

Erica Jevons

Tomorrow

Small, tiny, creepy, crawly,
blue, cute, bright and jolly
is a little bug on a leaf
acting as the "Grand Chief"

In the klan of his kind,
some do think he's lost his mind
because of a memory age old
his best friend left him out in the cold.

Big, shiny, starry light,
orange, smiley, grand, and bright
is the sun with its beautiful glaze
who protected the bug with his rays.

Every evening Sun said good-bye
and every time Bug would cry
Bug would say, "Please don't go!"
Sun would say, "I'll be back tomorrow."

The very next morning, the sun returned
through Bug's house he did burn
"Hello!" said Bug with a joyful shout,
"I thought you would never come out!"

Amanda Lockmiller

Alliteration

Bouncing Bebe bought many,
Bodacious blue Billy Bars, by beautiful
Bubbly balls mall but Betty Binker
Thought Bebe was busting her buns.

Brianna Williams

Growing Old

Face harden, graven, and sad
Body thin, wrinkle, dark, worn
and cripple
A sign of time! A long time!
Oh no
Not so.
A baby lying in a crib, so old,
Wrinkle, thin, face drawn, and so old
When did it grow so old?
Is growing old a curse or a sign
of time, or worse?
Don't forget me when I grow old,
so worn-out and weary
Love me, touch me and caress me
Liken unto the baby, lying in a crib
who grew so old
In its mother's womb, Its life is
doom, no labor, no toiling,, Just
Laying there, growing so old. so wrinkle,
And sad, needing love.

Betty S. McLellan

Insomnia

Black,
breath-
less

but
not
quite

Dead

the
night
moves.

Jacqueline S. Glick

The Bunny With The Misplaced Tail

This is not the ancient story
'bout the light that once did fail.
'tis a story 'bout a bunny
With a misplaced tail.

I may not be on camera
With the famous Allen Funt
But I have an Easter Bunny
With a bobtail in the front.

I cannot act upon the stage
Like Fontaine and Alfred Lunt
But I have an Easter Bunny
With a little tail in front.

I'll never make Olympics
Can't even do a stunt
But I own an Easter Bunny
With a tail that's in the front.

They can abuse me or amuse me
Or send me off to jail
But I'll ne'er give up that bunny
With the misplaced tail.

Alice M. Harcourtt

"Little Miracle"

Hello little miracle.
'Bout time you got here!
Nine long months I've waited,
Now I'm grinning ear to ear!

You're such a precious package.
Those little fingers, and tiny toes!
And, I just know when you smile,
You'll crinkle up your nose!

Welcome to the world.
I know you'll like it here.
There's so much to discover.
As you grow from year to year.

Good luck little miracle.
For you, I kneel to pray.
May God be with you always.
To guide you on your way.

Christine Hewett

In Memoriam

Two years ago, God sent to us a
bright and shining star whom we
named "Kendall"
To shine and glow with us until the
end of time.
He brought sunshine to our hearts,
He glowed with every smile,
He brought such happiness to our
lives, that we cannot describe.
One day the brightness grew dim,
And glow was no more.
God knew his brightest star
Was needed here no more.
God took "Kendall," our bright and
shining star,
He placed it in the sky for all the
world to see.
So when we get sad and our hearts are heavy,
We look above to find the brightest star
Then we know it's our "Kendall."

Carolyn Wilkes

The Proposal

I see the sunset
bright as red

Flames on fire
I need to fulfill this desire

Lips sweet
as watermelon
ripe from the vine

I spat out the seeds
to taste the wine

Breast round
and firm like

Mounds of ice cream
on my plate

Melting in my mouth
hot!
trying to control myself

Can't wait to enter
the love canal
and, become one

Will you marry me?

Danny Williams

The Storm

The day.
Bright, moving
Children playing
Then Bang
The clouds
Rain and thunder
Lasts forever
-it seems.
When will it end?
I see what is to come
The clearing clouds
Sunshine
Laughing, running children
The grass greener
The sky bluer
The flowers brighter
I know it will come
But first I must bear
The Storm.

Angela Hodge

"Sunshine"

I met a young woman on a
bright sunny day.
Her eyes how they sparkled
in such a special way.
They told me she'd come to me
on this certain day.
To make me smile when once
all I could do was cry.
She cleared all the rain that
had filled most of my life.
When she told me that she
would love me no matter what.
That's when I know I'd found
the sunshine in my life.

Cynthia J. Wilkinson

My Little Ones

When I am gloomy, they can
  bring a smile to my face,
It's then I know I have
  joined the human race.

They know my ups, and they
  know my downs.
I'd do the same if it were
  turned around.

They bring love and joy into
  my heart.
From it I know I would
  not want to part.

It's not all a big bed of
  roses,
When they have colds and
  runny noses.

They will be whatever
  they want to be.
It's when they grow-up
  that we will see.

Claudia Fulmer

Memories of Long Ago

I had forgotten what small things
Bring back memories of long ago...
A forgotten voice; a pressed flower:
Trees profuse with redbuds
On a street I used to know;
The caressing feel of the early rain;
The pulsating laughter
Of a small child;
The moaning of the sea in its
Restless pain, as it rushes
To the shore and leaves a kiss of foam;
Only to go out to sea again
And repeat its restless ritual
In a never ending pattern
In the tapestry of time!
The soft sound of a hummingbird
Sipping nectar from a flower;
And the sun casting a prism of light
Upon its fluttering wings!
I had forgotten!

Helen Richards

On Van Gogh's Irises

With flowers showing
brush strokes show
on the painting
we all know
from head to toe
we know it's so
that each little
flower flows

Anne Elizabeth Moore

"There Is No Moon Tonight"

  It looks black;
  but is dark blue

  The night is very dark;
  but the stars are very bright
So, why is there no moon tonight?

Carmen Viloria

Seductive Candle

  A magic mix of wax and wicks
  Bursting forth in flame so swift
  Dancing fire so sweet and nice
  Melting hearts so long on ice.

  Staring deep in the wispy fire
  Can't hold my weakening ire
  Giving into the beckoning flame
  The soul releases guilt and shame.

  A droplet of wax drips gently down
  Softly caressing from stem to stern
  Slowly hardening on its sweet journey
Releasing in flight from base to holder.

  The midnight hour approaches quickly
  Its flame has ebbed in a waxen pool
  A red hot ember grows to extinction
  So goes the candle of seduction.

Donna L. Blackhall

When The Moon Is Full

When the moon is full,

the mountains feel the winds and moan,
but cannot shrink away from them,

the earth, it claws within, and shrieks,
and skies grow dark with clouds of gray,

lightning strikes at all that fly
too loud in flight, too close to ground,

and earth, it vomits rivers wild,
to wash the ashes from the core.

When the moon is full,

its body waxed to maximum,
now looks to earth with bloated face,

begins to wane in rivers' time
as ashes wane in volume, weight,

until it's waned to minimum,
the earth, then cleansed, begins again

to burn and waste and grow with ash,
and moon will wax, and earth will shriek,

when the moon is full.

Christos G. Rigakos

A Smile

It costs nothing
but creates much

It enriches those
who receive, without
impoverishing those who
who give

It happens in a flash
and the memory of it
sometimes lasts forever.

None are so rich
that they can get along
without it, and none
are so poor but are
richer for a smile.

Yet it cannot be
bought, begged
borrowed or stolen, for
it is something that is
no earthly good to
anyone until it is given away.

Chris Williams

True Love Is Forever

True love is forever,
But finding it is hard to do.
When you do you'll know it,
Even though you won't know who.
You'll both feel it in your heart,
And promise each other forever.

For true love is forever,
And mine will never die.
For you, I'll always be there,
And never will I lie.
We will be together
Trusting and loving each other,
Always and forever.

Jacklin Donnelly

"Lust"

Here one day
  but gone the next;
makes you think
  that you've been hexed
by some kind of creature
  you do not know
making some kind of feature
  that you hate so.

You feel lost and unloved
  once it has happened;
dazed and confused
  and especially saddened
when the emotions you once felt
  suddenly aged.
Without notice
  they just changed.

Jennifer Spinner

Humpty Dumpty

Humpty Dumpty sat on a wall.
But how in the world did Humpty fall?
That's the question I would ask.
It would be a challenging task.
And how did they get the horses and men?
If I could, I'd write it again!
But maybe it had a copyright,
So that answer's out of sight.
And why did his mother name him
Humpty?
It sounds like a camel,
Or a blanket that's bumpy.
But if you think,
I guess it makes sense,
Because his mother was a chicken
That lived in a fence.

Carolyn Barker

Aging Solo

Jagged chips from my pedestal
Crash upon the dusty still.
Tunnel walls of silence yawn
As emptiness prays for dawn.
Darkness, uneasy from the night
Fades to 'alone' under light.
No one needs my love to share
So heavy to hold in the morning air.
Yearning to give just like before,
I'm discontinued in my own store.
Was I ever in such demand?
I was the flower; now I'm sand.

Jean Murphy-Bazner

At Three In The Morning

Don't know if you realize it
but I was awake
at three this morning
While you were there, somewhere.
I did feel close to you
so far away and I wondered
if you were sleeping, or
perhaps reading, or praying, or
if your hair had been freshly
washed and set, or if you
had met someone else,
or if perhaps you were wearing
a robe or nothing at all.
I thought maybe because I didn't
want you doing anything else,
you most likely were fast asleep.
That's the way it should be
I suppose asleep
at three in the morning.

Jack Wilkerson

"Tis The Season To Remember"

Winter is a lonesome season
But it brings joy for some reason
All its leones had turned its colors
Red - yellow - Brown & Gold

Oh the trees look lonely too
Standing tall looking at you
It's fun joy this time of year
For we know harvest time is near

And as we sit by the fire
place, looking out the window
The wind is blowing North,
East South & West

Most people just fade
Away in the Winter
Because it's so cold out
They stay home and hide.

Barbara Jean Grant

Think!

I want to write a beautiful poem,
But just what subject should I choose?
For, to one, a poem of beauty
Will, to another, only confuse

If you could dream, would you dream,
Or would you die like you live?
If you could give or could take,
Would you take or would you give?

I remember being young
And my first days in school
I remember thinking thoughts
Like, "Who's the wise or the fool?"

I ask not you think my way,
Nor that you say what I say;
I just ask that you "think"!
We each should have our day!

For, to one, an obvious treasure
Is, to another, only trash
While one takes the time to ponder,
Another runs through, with a dash

Helen Jean Snyder

Untitled

I'm afraid to wish my world goodbye,
But not of what will be,
I'm afraid of what my memory holds
And whose will still hold me.

Will the times that I have cherished,
And the people near my heart
Fade like sunset into darkness
In the times when we're apart?

Will the memories that I save now
Leave me in my time of need?
Or will they be a word of comfort
That my lonely heart can read?

I'm truly scared that I won't want to,
I won't care about my past,
That I won't preserve my memories
To ensure that they will last.

I have things that might remind me,
In case I let my memory dim,
Of everything that matters most
And the person that I've been.

Jessica Shapiro

A Man

I remember the days when I used to dream
But now you're gone forever
A long time it seems
But you won't be back, not ever.

I'll never forget how beautiful you were
A life gone and wasted
Because of the pain you felt inside
No one will ever taste it.

You're just an empty body now
not a thing can bring you back
I wish that you were here again
It's affection in which you lacked.

All the tears I've ever cried
Belong to you in name
All my feelings are trapped inside
For a man named Kurt Cobain.

Jennifer Egli

Untitled

The dawn has come and I must go,
but on the voice of the wind
shall my soul
ever flow.

May the Autumn trees whisper
my voice in their song,
and the sun shine as bright
as my life was long.

May your heart be filled
with the love we once knew,
and when you miss me....
      look up,
I'll be watching over you.

Crystal Irvine

Geography

Stone walls do not a prison make,
But they can mark a line,
A pattern clear beyond mistake,
Articulate, define
Roads not to travel, fields to leave
To their own stones and grass;
Hilltops too barren to retrieve,
Old paths too rough to pass.

Somewhere beyond
The beaches,
White hot in the sun.
Wind feeds the bowl of the sky,
Dead shells lie on the sand,
Nothing the heart can feel
Or the mind understand.
Everything human here ended
or—never begun.

Elizabeth Lawton

Decide Life

Today I'm here
but tomorrow I won't be
because a judge decided
the way my life would be
   I sit upon my room
writing poetry,
What is life about
What should it be?
   When will my air
Stop being polluted
by what certain people
seem to blow at me
   most of my friends
including family
seem to come around
without sanity.
   What will my life be
What should it be,
should I just dream
of what it could be?

Angela Corradini

Untitled

We look
But we don't see
With Clouds in our eyes
And poison in our ears
The voices of our young drowning
In the Sea of faces of the old.

Doesn't matter anymore
not to anyone
We look and still don't see

The sound of our hungry
washed away by the laughter
of our rich

We try the best we can
But we allow the clouds
We welcome the poison
So we don't have to see.

Camden D. Alley

Knocking At Your Door

Jesus stands at your door
Can you hear Him Knock
Will you open up this time
Or have you installed a lock

This is your decision
When He comes to call
He's asking for your faith
Or have you built a wall.

Will you listen to Him
He's your Savior and Lord
Sent here by His Father
As a messenger for His word

He will not forsake you
He died bravely for us
The day they crucified Him
And nailed Him to that Cross

He died that day at Calvary
For a very special love
Giving us a second chance
To meet Him up above

Della Yealey

What Is Love?

Love is Daring,
    Caring,
        Sharing.

Love is Wondering,
    Discovering,
        Comforting.

Love is Diversity,
    Compatibility,
        Unity.

Love is Two of us together,
    Joy and peace forever?
        Oneness through whatever…

Annette Spacek Williams

A Young Man's Demise

Burrowed dreams that stray me to mourn,
castled tombs in thicket, in thorn.
Earthen hills with trails of tragedy,
infancy, gloom, the plot of malady.
Halls of illusion, pacing, denial,
tripping, falling, failing by trial.
The greatest O' wonder in Fate I seduce,
splinting my shins to enkindle a truce.
Pageants of whim, my only reprise
conquer the hero of a young man's demise

Christopher Alan Lee

Time

Speed by time!
But why time?
Time is the only
thing man can not change.
Some people would
turn back time.
Other people would
speed up time.
But time waits on no one.
Maybe not at this time
but perhaps sometime
we will have our time
Time you are my challenge
Embrace you-time
I can not!

Jack Derry

"The Tree Outside"

Our love is like the tree outside
Caught up within the breeze.
The jealous bitter cold outside
Does often tear and tease.

Our love so like the tree outside
When threatened by the wind.
It seems to want us to give up,
As we fight with broken limbs.

We are so like the tree outside
Through the air we sway;
And I, for one just love the tree
So can not walk away.

Our love so like the tree outside
Our love shall always grow.
Just how we keep our tree alive
The roots will only know..

Helen Zizi

The Conductor

I never owned slaves
Cause that's not my mentality
I fought real hard
To make freedom a reality
I'm the conductor
Of the underground railroad
Carrying people to freedom
Sometimes it's a heavy load
But I'm gonna keep it running
Through the dark of the night
The slaves they keep coming
Oh God what a sight
I'm the conductor
Got my train on the track
Only stop is freedom
There's no turning back.

Adonis Page

Mourning

Morning comes with daylight bright
Causing early birds to take flight
Waking parents and children alike

These splendors rain from heaven above
soft and quiet like a cooing dove
Morning brings happiness,
joy and lots of smiles
and the smiles are the kind
that last for miles

But morning can bring sadness,
sorrow and lots of pain,
sometimes enough to bring the rain

Sometimes the pain is from someone gone,
someone who wasn't there very long.

Dinorah Alice Figueroa

Sad Night

Sad
    Crying
All Night Long
    My Family
Trauma We All Had
    Sad Emotions
Filled The Air
    We All
        Cried

Ambrocia Crawford

Words Of Omission

We sit in silence
chancing our love
on unspoken words
that alone we will
never find.

So open your heart
to the love that
we share
and you will find
that I still care
about the love inside.

Or these unspoken words
will be our goodbye
that will carry on
to eternity.

Barbara Ledsinger

"A Cry"

There is a cry but no one
chooses to hear it. The cry grows
louder; nobody chooses to answer it.

There is a cry of Pain and Anger.
Yet we choose to ignore it. Thinking
if we do it will go away.

They walk by, but no one chooses to
see where it comes from. For they
are afraid to face their own pain.

For those who dare to face it.
Only then the cry dies off it is
replaced by Love and Laughter.

Crystal D. Mitchell

Untitled

I remember the lake
Clear skies
Stars
Shining brightly the essence of you
I was soon to experience

We are surrounded
Again by water
The purity of our bodies

The tide continues
This time not pulling
But flowing between the two statues.

Donna Schneider

Time Unleashed

Linger in the dimness of dawning
Cloaked in silence stay—
There is nothing to say.

Wander by the way of time unleashed
Walk where it leads you—
There is nothing to do.

Release your feeling of bridled joy
Just let it run free—
There is nowhere to be.

Cheryl A. Wright

"Dawn"

When the evening comes, the sun goes down.
Clouds of red and orange, dot the sky.

The evening stars rising.
Moon of Silver,
Cold and brisk air,
Slowly rises and kiss the skin.

World is dark.
Earth is wet with dew.
Sleepily lap the people,
Awaiting the coming day.

Darkness proceeds the dawn,
the sun breaks a new day.
With shinning hopes and glimmering
Ways, brings a beautiful sunny Day!

Elwood C. Tester

Luxury

Safe, at home, we witness, live
CNN, news at five
Bullets kill a nursing mother
Infants smother
Buzzing flies sting half-blind eyes
No one cries
Cameras capture drought and bright
Startling sight
Petroleum pollutes a sea
Or two, or three
Pricking pain attacks our nerves
Throws us curves.
Soon we weary of the scene
On the screen
So we lift and point the clicker
Channels flicker.
As the horrors fade from view
Concern does, too.
We wallow in the luxury
Of apathy.

Betty O. Carpenter

Indian Blanket

As I looked beyond the easel
color caught my eye.
The reds were so warm and
inviting - beckoning me near.
The easel appeared as though
I had not seen it before.
The lovely piece of art behind
gave it new dimension.
This warmth, like an authentic
Indian blanket, was framed
with brilliant fire.
It drew me nearer, asking
to be touched - held - the
warmth reached me and I
felt touched, carried back
to the origin of our country.

Annie McClure

Silent Pleadings

Striking anything it sees,
Death!
As you tremble to your knees
Pleading stop!
And pale is ye
All life is gone
No cries help me!
For no longer are you a mortal.

Debbie Hawkins

The Field Sparrow

Can you hear me? Can you hear me?
Comes a simple hearted trill
Caroling incessantly
For inattentive ear to fill.

Can you hear me? Can you hear me?
Streams the urgent poignant cheer,
Pleading for the sky to free
As plain a breast to dry a tear.

Can you hear me? Can you hear me?
Speeds the step of stumbling spring,
Rippling a timeless verity
Unifying everything.

Yes, I hear you, yes, I hear you
Little sparrow of the field,
Plainly dressed in earthen hue
Like a fluff of loam congealed.

From whispering meadow blown
To sapling of budding shade,
There to ask in lilting tone
If I can hear the spring he made.

Frank Kuftack

No More Common

Common eyes
Common lips
Common cheekbones
Common hips
Totally I'm common
Ordinary one
Please can't someone love me
Or my life is done
No more rotten is done
Stress or pain and strife
No more looking common now
No more life.

Christina Keil

Life On Earth

Life here is a day of Grace
Compared to God's eternity,
A wisp in time in a tiny place
Compared to God's majesty.

In God's Kingdom above,
There's no end to day.
Sun lights eternal life,
with Heavens warmest ray.

Here we know the sacred love,
That's in God's Embrace.
We'll never know the fears,
That filled our day of Grace.

It'll be a world of Holy joys,
Beyond the griefs of earth.
Here God blesses each soul,
With the glories of rebirth.

There we'll see and know,
God's gifts to souls of faith.
Heaven follows our day of Grace,
Where God and Jesus wait.

Darleen I. Hill

Numb

Rain...
continually an inspiration
for poets and musicians
tonight leaves me feeling a bit
numb...
this cloud purging
that can so imbue creative beings
now serves to wash away
needless, sophomoric emotions
from my soul...
one who loved noise now seems to
revel in the night's silence,
the steady flow of raindrops
becoming my heartbeat.
One who is over-emotional,
who "feels too much"
can benefit from standing alone
in the rain.

Christine Boylan

The Poet

The Master still labors among them,
Courting subjects with cabalistic wisdom.
The reckless who eagerly solicit him
Are forfended by lustful thirst.
For he strolls in silent measure
And whispers unto Lethean auricle.

The crowds maunder; and march
In deranged procession.
They pine to don his robe
Of Tranquility and Reason,
But fail to honor reflection.
For He is a lost phantom
That wandered from their essence
On many a restless night tide.

Adrienne Monestere

Gods Creation

The beauty of the land, was not
created by man.
The man worked the land to multiply,
and readily adapt to the yielding of its
supply.
The land gave back to man in
all its splendor, so that man can
surrender, and he a lender to those
that be friend her.
The man was belated to find who
was related, to a native of the creator,
who is a friend of mine.
The man gave praise to the
creator, that watched over man, and
gave a helping hand to the land.

Jacqueline Drabek

My Man

My man with blisters in his hands
Cries out to God in pain and
Wipes his face
The only comfort he gets it seems
Is from God's ever loving grace
He tills the soil the rain comes down
There is relief the rain comes down
He stops and looks about the land
The sky expands from east to west
He's learned in time of stress
When man knows God how —
Richly blest.

Jessie S. Cobb

Jack In The Box

It had seemed a box.
Crowded. Yes. And,
Denied life's brilliant light

Imprisoned. Worse,
Committed.....

I-n-v-i-s-i-b-l-e, like
Depression

Narrow lines
Rigid corners

Deafening silence!!!
Then, Staccato-touch
Dee-dee-da-da-doo-doo

Boundless repertoire
Embers of sinai re-kindled

Galvanized in
A painted, gig man

Your deed, my need, freed

Jerrold Jacobson

The Present

Rise to the voices
Dance to the soul
Drums beating rhythm
Wind carrying sound

Over plains
Across waters
Into the night
Summoning the past

Each is different
Each is equal
All have hope
All have future

Woven together is solid
Break the barriers
Sound, language, stories
Travel into our tomorrow.

Jodi Scharfenorth

White Wet World

Flowing, fluttery flakes
Dancing delightful dips
Against the silent softness.

Laughing, lovely lace
Swirling sweetly smiles
Across waiting, willing lips

But then....

Wickedly wailing winds
Pushing peaks of powder
Atop deeply drowning drifts

Blowing battles of blizzards
Whipping wildly within
Amidst intense, intact . . . ice!
White
Wet
World
Commence contact . . . cold!
Return!
Hallowed, heavenly HEAT!

Alice Wojewoda

The Scary Cave

Deep in a cave,
dark and gloomy.
The kind of cave
that's not very roomy.
The kind of cave
where you just can't relax,
with water seeping
down through cracks.
We sat in the dark
sharing scary tales.
One of us started
to bite our nails.
One of us screamed
the other one cried.
We all jumped up
and ran outside.
Once outside,
By the light of the moon.
We swore we would meet again,
but not very soon.

Candice Tower

Stand Together

We stand together on this
day, So you may listen to
what our hearts say, We
miss your love your
tenderness too, We miss
your smile and your eyes so blue!

We stand together side by side, to

share the love we can not
hide, We think of you
both day and night, And
long so much to hold you tight!

We stand together
hand in hand, to give to you
all we can, to let
you know you're in our

thoughts, we'll always
remember the joy you
brought!!!

Candy Star Brooks

My Pain

The pain that I feel,
   deep down inside
There's no place to go,
there's no where to hide.
It hurts too much,
   too much to be real
There's no words to describe
   the pain that I feel
They say that love,
   comes straight from the heart
But the pain that I feel,
   is tearing it apart.
Out of my eyes,
   the pain flows through
With the love,
   I thought was true.
Just leave me alone,
and maybe you'll see,
All of the pain,
   that you have caused me.

Jennifer Warden

"Nature Divine"

Looking for inspiration
Deep inside my soul
I turn to the Lord above
To guide me in his mold.

For me I've found the best place
To talk to Jesus Christ
Is in the nature made by God
To keep and maintain life.

When I am there
I feel at ease
There is no modern stress
Just God and I
In another world
That is my paradise.

Heather Casto

Pain

The pain is like hot blood dripping
   deep into my soul
But without this pain no longer
   would my body feel whole
And yet my body is empty with
   nothing but pain
And I wonder to myself how long
   will it rain?
Sometimes I wish the pain would just
   go away
But I know deep in my heart forever
   it will stay
For sometimes the pain is truly my
   friend
And sometimes it makes my life
   want to end
But when I'm alone cause no one seems
   do care
I can turn to the pain for it is
   always there

Janna O'Connell

Electric Blanket

Dearest One,
Deep within the heart of my wires
   the warmth spreads infinitely

I feel a never ending need to have
   you near, for you

To feel the warmth that surges up
   through my top coverings

I have an undying want for you to
   cuddle beneath my eternal wires

The hearts of my batteries produce soul
   warming electricity for you only

As I can live only when you are here:
   I hope you shall soon return
   to my clinging, outstretched wires.

   Your ever loving,
   Electric Blanket

Brenda Connor

Love

Wordless communication
Endless closeness.
Shared time may be brief
But the feeling is forever.

Carol J. Sorcinelli

Mommy

Are we real?
Did GOD really put us here?
Did we come in fear?
Are we going nearer?
Nearer to what?
The end of the world?
The beginning of the world?
Is it really worth it?
Are we just wasting our time?
Why are we here?
Where are we going?
Are we leaving?
Are we staying?
Why don't you answer mommy?
Why are you so white?
Why are you so cold?
Why is there a knife in your chest?
Are you awake?
Are you asleep?
Why are your eyes open if you're asleep?

Amber Reno

God

  Was God there,
did He really care-about me?
Does He know my name
does He feel my pain?
Is He watching over us, from his heavens?
What does He think of his creations
does he look over Abraham's nations?
When we hear his call,
does He know of all?
Are our sins forgotten,
are we brought to His bright hall?
Does He hear me sigh,
does he watch me cry?
Does He bear my burdens too?
Are all they say about him true?
Nevertheless He is my father,
father to us all.
And all He tells me is obeyed, it is the law.

Anisah Bagasra

Little Child

Into our lives, a little girl came.
Dixie Cheyenne was her name.

She only stayed a little while,
A very special little child.

Heaven sent, to bring us love,
Meant just for us, from God above.

But God was jealous of us, I guess,
So he took her back, unto his breast.

We had her for a very short while,
Our very special little child.

Doris Moore Lewis

Dizzy

Around and around I go...
Faster and faster, am falling
Do you fill me, do you see me go
Why am I still here
Wasn't I falling?
Am still going around
After I hit the ground
Not physically but mentally
Were all moving now!

Jesse Cervantes

"Walking On Air"

When you love someone,
Do you really know them?
Do you trust them with your heart?
Do you realize how powerful love can be,
Even after it is torn apart?
Do you realize you heart can drift,
Just as easily as a bird can fly
Do you realize how much you care,
Though the love has just begun?
Do you realize how much you can care,
While you all walking on air?

Candis Pittman

Untitled

Eerily sensing something
Drawing me near
Curiosity allows me to follow.
Close behind
Watching from a distance.
Someone calls my name
My body goes forward to see
Who it was,
I wait and watch to see who called.
My enemy
Ambush.
My flesh dies.
I get up from where I was and
I go.

Celeste Smith

Little Boy

Little boy blue,
Dream come true,
So very new,
Who are you?

Never before,
Never anymore,
Little Boy Blue,
Someone like you.

Like a song,
You came along,
Little Boy Blue,
Who are you?

Erwin J. Brandl

My Wish For You

Happiness that's everlasting
Dreams that come true
Showers of sunshine
Is my wish for you.

Sunrises and sunsets
Rays of brilliant colors too...
A pot of gold at the end
of a rainbow
May your days continually
be renewed.

For life goes by so quickly
And time does not stand still you know...
So cherish every moment
No matter where you go.
This is my wish for you!

Bobbi Schroeder

"Our Seven Windows"

Words are windows...
...dressing our diverse deliberations
  with delight and delicacy;
...furnishing fenestration
  for fun and frolic;
...letting in the light of
  learning and logic;
...opening onto our observations and
  origins of old;
...reflecting upon our ruminations
  with radiance and reason;
...shutting out the storms of
  strife and struggle; and,...
...washing our whereabouts, our world,
  with wonder and wealth!

James Sylvester Monroe

'Tis Autumn

Leaves of orange, gold and brown,
Drifting slowly, settling down,
Brightly carpeting the ground —
  'Tis Autumn, Autumn's here.

Balmy golden sunny days,
Chilly nights and frosty haze
In morning whisp'ring — it all says
  'Tis Autumn, Autumn's here.

Squirrels are storing winter's fare,
Warned by crispness in the air
That there is little time to spare —
  'Tis Autumn, Autumn's here.

The flower droops its pretty head
And nestles in its wintry bed
'Neath leafy blankets gold and red —
  'Tis Autumn, Autumn's here.

Emma M. Anderson

Behold

I am amazed
  Each day I see
The beauty of the Earth

To know the price
  That Jesus paid
And what mankind is worth

To him be praise
  For all the days
That I awake and find

That I can feel
  His love so real
And that I know He's mine

So help me lord
  To understand
And never fail to see
All creation
  In its beauty
And what you did for me.

Freddie E. Dill

Friends

Friends that understand
  each other
Friends help each other
  when they need help.
Friends help you when you're down,
  your friends lift your spirit
Friends listen to each other
  when they have problem,
Friends make you happy
  because you need friends,
Friends are important to your life,
  FRIENDS
Jean M. Rusin

Life Is A Rose

Roses are beautiful,
Elegant, and unspoken for.
Roses can be painful,
Bleeding, and suicidal.

It all starts from a seed,
Which grows, matures, and blossoms.
Water, sun, and love it needs
To be come a man or woman.

Painful thorns will pierce
Scar, and make a difference in its life.
Its leaves will branch out
To touch the leaves of other roses.

On top of this ancient,
Respected, and loved flower
Is a beautiful blossom,
Which will never be forgotten.

Catherine Velazquez

Blue Roses

Blue roses on the window sill
Elegantly place in a blue vase
Kissed by the morning dew
And blessed by the Spring sun
Window curtains, white and lace
Flutter and dance in back.
I alone stop on the busy street
And I pause my hectic life to admire
Only for a moment
Then I must rusk back to reality.

Amanda Ware

Untitled

  Monotony
Endless streams
of idle chatter.

  Calligraphy
Strewn by the
unseen guiding hand.

  Tapestry
Shredded tatters
knotted...mended
woven strand by strand.

Chet Nelson

I Believe...

I believe in sunshine,
Even when it's not shining.
I believe in love,
Even when I feel hate.
I believe in god,
Even when he's silent.
I believe in miracles,
Even when they're not happening.
I believe in pots of gold,
Even when there is no rainbow.
I believe in stars you wish on,
Even when the wish doesn't come true.
I believe in believing in most things,
Like me and you...

Beka Huber

"Generic Housewife"

Going nowhere
Everyone knows her
No one understands her
Everyday life.
Rambles on about her
Insecurities.
Can't relate.
Her "no frills life". No way
Out
Underneath she
Strives for a better way.
Endless days
Whittling away her time on
Issues of no importance
For she can't
End her never ending boredom.

Jackie Massa

In Heaven

There's no sorrow in heaven
Everyone's happy up there.
There are no heartaches in heaven,
Everything's equally shared.

There's no hatred in heaven,
Everyone's gentle and kind.
You never see tears in heaven,
I pray I will go there some time.

This is a wonderful world we live in,
We should be thankful it's true.
So full of glittering treasures,
But you can't take them with you.

I'll give up my worldly possessions,
If the lord will show me the way.
To be a faithful servant forever,
Just to be with my master someday.

Elizabeth A. Hall

Youth

The acorn,
falling from the tree.
Smashing its delicate shell.
Creating a deed ravaging ravine,
running through its skull.
Exposing its seed,
to society's unfertile concrete basin.
Lying in a field,
of dead and dying leaves.

Christian E. Woehr

suicide

Dreams last forever and
Everything seems clear.
Above
The green earth,
Hearts are freed from fear.

Winds blow
Intensely carrying
To places once
Here-gone.
Offering false security
Underneath
The setting sun.

Minds seemingly
Eased from
Anguish and pain,
No longer able to
Inquire why...
Never to know or to
Guess a possible gain.

Andrea Damm

Animal

  Trapped behind a steel cage
Far away from home
  Taken was my freedom
Broken was my soul
  Placed here with my others
Of none I do not know
  They feed me.
  They clean me.
  They breed me.
But my rage they can't control
  They look.
  They stare.
  They point.
  They call me Animal!
Eric Huerta

My Special House

There is a house
Far, far away
Where I dream
I'll go someday

It has grey shingles
And grey door
It has brown logs
And much, much more

It is surrounded
By a number of trees
And when you're inside it
You hear birds and the bees

The sky is always cloudless
The sun is always bright
For it's so beautiful
For it is never night

If I get there someday
Which I hope I do
I'll send many postcards
To every one of you

Amber Heffleger

Give Me A Woods To Walk In

Give me a woods to walk in
feeling the springiness of the moss
beneath my feet and never getting loss
   In the woods is where one can
hear God's creations, the singing
of the birds, cool breezes, crunch
of the twigs beneath your feet
   As I savor the sweet smell
of the Dogwood and Pine I know
how unkind the world can be
but the troubles leave my mind

   When I walk, and talk to
God and thank Him for a woods to
walk in.

Ellen Cooper

Love Is You

Love is having you near —
Feeling the warmth that is in your part.
Love is your smilin' laughter....
That lights its way into my heart.
Love is telling you how I feel —
The very best I possibly can.
Love is sharing moments of talk...
That lets me know you understand.
Love is the little things in giving —
Which shows such love is true.
Love is the sweetness all around...
You are love, love is you.

George M. Shreve

Untitled

Come one and all!
Fill up my tent!
Come see my circus,
It's money well spent

You won't see a horse
Or ten-piece band but (if you allow)
I'm the World's Strongest Man

The Bearded Lady
Is me in a dress
And my tattooed body
Is a marker at best

I could read your fortune
But can't be specific
Tho' if it comes true
Won't I be terrific?

You'll know me as Jo-Jo
The Dog-Faced Boy,
I'll howl with laughter and bark with joy

Come one and all, fill up the place,
The loneliest freak has no time to waste...

Dave Maylish

Old Love

In a heart beats desire,
Happiness is created,
As one and one make two
A love is forever,
Never in tomorrow
Will promises be,
Always in today
Is a time of forever.

Joie Ann Sanders

My Granted Wish

I wish I had a perfume jar
   filled with fragrance rare,
I'd take my children's voices each day
   and seal them tightly there.
A word here and a phrase there
   and soon the jar would be filled,
I'd tuck it away in my treasure chest
   and keep it there until
My little boy and girl grow up
   and I'm an old lady grey,
Then I'd break the seal and listen,
   As they softly float away.
An impossible wish, I hear you say
   Oh no, it could never be.
But alas, my heart is the jar you see
   And my memory the key.

Bettye Means Saunders

"The Treasure Of Innocence"

   Life grows with youth.
 Filled with glow of rainbows,
  Rainbows that are of truth.

   Vigorous as the spring,
 Fresh as fresh flowers grow,
Fast as the flight of the bird's wings.

Hear the birds in the tree, singing,
   Singing of youth in aglow.
Sounds that are always kept beating.

Youth, a gift that cleanses the earth,
   White as the snow,
  Each day another at birth.

   Youth is always existing.
Where ever evil is persisting.

Julie A. Roszkowiak

God Made Me

God made me with
Five fingers and five toes,
Two eyes and a nose,
And a voice to sing God's Praise.

God made me with
Red hair and blue eyes
To look into the skies
To see the stars above.
I love you, Lord!

God made me with
Two ears that can hear
The birds that can cheer
And whistle pretty songs.

God made me with
A smile upon my face,
Legs that I can race
Across the wet white sand.
I love you, Lord!

Deanna L. Miller

Alone

I sat alone and wished
for a friend to address.
And it came to mind:
Acquaintances I gain,
But friends I cannot find.

Climmis Sullivan McQueen

Untitled

When waves of doubt
   Flood over my soul
I grasp my anchor
   Tighter still..
And hope and trust
   In God alone
To know his answer
   And his will.

My feet are on
   A slippery path...
And dark the way
   In which I go...
But God who is
   Above us all
Knows what is best
   And so...
I'll walk the crooked
   Path until
I see the light
   And know his will.

Carroll Schillo

The Shore

The tangy smell of ocean salt
Fog rolling in with the tide
Sand crunching beneath your feet
Stepping on rocks, shells, seaweed

Lifting the seaweed, you discover
Crabs and snails
Hurrying away

Barnacles have placed themselves
On the lobster boats
Boats are being secured
To the docks for the night

Boat men are going home
For a nice lobster dinner
You stoop and pick up ocean treasures
Half of a buoy and some driftwood

You look at the endless blue water
Wondering what you'll find
Tomorrow

Jessica Sesera

Epilogue

The future will surely suffer,
For all that we have done,
The innocent things we kill,
Benefit no one,
No more lovely air to take,
More pollution in our lake,
The ozone layer slowly going,
For money is our true love,
Birds are falling from the sky,
Watch the dying dove,
All the pain,
And the fear,
Shows all to clearly,
The end is near.

Dawn Simpson

I Can't Wait

I can't wait—
   For daffodils and crocuses,
   For robins singing in the trees—
   No more snow to sweep and shovel;
   Fresh laundry blowing in the breeze.

I can't wait—
   For mealtime;
   So at ten I'll have a snack.
   Since it's hard to wait for bedtime,
   On the couch I'll have a nap.

I can't wait—
   To see the mailman,
   Anxious for the mail he brings
   Or to see and hear the wild geese—
   Then I know it's coming spring.

The things I can't wait for are many;
   But summer's coming and that's great!
   As for now—Should I house-clean———
   Oh, That Can Wait
     Emily M. McCall

In Memory of Carl Don Beechly

Should you receive a bright red rose
For each precious moment we've shared
Beautiful bulbs would blanket the sea
And rose petals would fill the air

Add one red rose for all the nights
Of "Tigger and Winnie the Pooh"
The stories and songs you loved to share
Would always see me through

Add one for the bumps and little bruises
And two for the silent prayers
I'll never forget the broken hearts
I thank "God" you were always there

Thank you for all the loving ways
The courage and sense of pride
Please always remember one is not limited
As long as the soul is alive

Mom, You are the Angel sent from Heaven
On earth to share your love
And I am truly the lucky one.
I love You, From Heaven above.
     Charlotte Blanchard

Golden Wedding Anniversary

From miles away we drink to you
   for fifty years of wedded bliss.
Devoted couples come but few,
   for that we send a loving kiss.

These golden days you much deserve;
   we wish you more of such ahead.
The love you felt you must reserve,
   as on the day you first were wed.

A love so true is hard to find;
   a kind and giving heart is rare.
But yours are so much intertwined—
   we know why you're a perfect pair.

Care you must for one another
   'til all May flower cease to bloom.
'Til your children, sister, brother
   weep, mourning in your lonely room.
     Ethel W. Kareklas

Love I Cannot Find

I look in the mirror in disgust
For I am an ugly man
What girl will find me attractive,
Not any in this land.
I will be alone forever and ever
Searching for love.
It's a hopeless journey.
Why do I even bother.
I cry at times,
Depressed many times.
I wish there was hope
For love I cannot find.
     Christopher Sosa

Do Not Cry When I Die

Do not cry when I die,
For I am in the house of the Lord.
I walk upon roads paved of gold,
And look upon walls covered in jewels.
Do not cry when I die,
For I am the clouds in the sky
And the morning dew upon the grass.
Do not cry when I die,
I am the green leaves upon the trees,
And the air that you breathe.
Do not cry when I die,
For I am all that you see,
And I am part of you.
Do not cry when I die,
For I am in the house of the Lord.
     Glenn E. Foreman

Yet, I Cannot Title This...

I cannot title this poem.
For it has not yet been written.
What you might read here,
May be gone tomorrow.
And what is put on paper tomorrow,
May be changed, the next day
Or the next,
Or the next.

Still, I cannot title this poem,
For I am very undecided.
My poems, they do change
Constantly.
Not one ever staying the same.
So still I cannot title this poem,
For it has not yet been finished.
     Jordan Luminais

Saying Goodbye

It came along so sudden
For me to realize.
It took over his body
before he could open his eyes.
It ravaged and it ruined
his heart and his might.
It took about a year
For him to loose his fight.
It took him away so sudden
for me to realize.
It was too late
For me to say Goodbye.
My dad is gone and it is over
I must continue on.
I'll see him in the heaven
Where my pain is no longer strong.
     Jacqueline Ruth Conkling

A Moment

Even if you loved me
for only a moment
We danced in heaven
that moment
we became one
in spirit and essence
Whether you believe
that in that space and time
There was ever anything
There was you and I
There was love
Pure love
And you can't grade it
It's all there is
So pure and true
And I'm so glad
to have spent
A moment of my life
Loving with you
     Debbie Crowl Munster

Thank God For Beauty

Let us all give thanks to God
For the beauty of the earth,
The quiet ponds and meadows
For the oceans and their surf.
For the beauty of the flowers,
And the trees that tower above,
The starlight in the heavens
And the sunshine of God's love
For the mountains and the valley,
The country roads so fair...
And for all the scenic beauty
Telling us how much God cares.
All of nature sings his praise...
Give us eyes and ears to hear...
In the wonder of creation....
That our God is always near!
     Helen Weston Govaya

Alone At Night

It won't be light
for three hours more
and the rain keeps
   coming down.
The wind blows cold
through the ice
in my bones,
and forever started
last Saturday.
The dog doesn't bark
and the bird doesn't sing
and the fear won't go away.
The people are all gone
except the ghosts
of the house
and they walk in and out
of my room.
The clock keeps its time
the moon doesn't shine
and the night continues on.
     Jaquie Zimmerman

"The Mourning Star"

Evening invited death.
Forbearance betrayed life;
A damnable fate.
Appalled and eclipsed
By manners unappealing,
The sun foreclosed heaven
And mooned the world.
Stars came out to see the show.
But one,
Reflecting on the sea,
Stayed behind,
Raining light like tears,
Glimmering loves way,
Giving hope to the lost.
Smitten,
The son
Flew to his dove
Giving life
In glory.

Gary E. M. Hurley

In Appreciation

I cannot write,
Forgive me.

My gladness,
Is too great!
Words would only
Hint my joy
As an artist hints
The beauty of rose
But fails to sketch
The fragrance.

Hannah B. Nissman

Reality Has Spoken

Join together
Form as one
The days of ruin
Have just begun
The sky has fallen
Upon our heads
The color of blood
Is no longer red
No reason to fear
O lonely child
The ruins we see
Are merely mild
The worst of this
Is on its way
And it will be
Our doomsday.

Christina Scalise

How Wonderful!

To be enlightened, by friends
From near or far,
with Sincerity, Hope, Love and Faith.
And from afar, we all are a Star,
And from so near, we all hold so dear,
The treasured gift, so rich in spirit,
So vast in Love,
Expectations of Hope,
The fulfillment of Faith,
How wonderful! to be what you are.

Anne Gambardella

Gray

Parades in the sky
Form these shapes of the mind.
Hold our thoughts we see.
For it's not that far behind.

They come back again
This time with another face,
But the colors the same
Or will it be gray?

Rise like the sun,
Holds the heaven above our head.
A place to beautiful to see
I'll bet she does it again.

One place in now empty
Time builds into misery.
Circus of wind,
Are you still free?

Feed off our oceans
Untouched with a hand.
Time and time again,
This parade will reign on our land.

Christopher Mitchell

Innocence

She sits by the window
fragile
Like a rose in a storm
The walls she built
Gradually crumble
As she finds hope,
Softly she weeps
Praying she's not heard
Thanking God she's
Lived through another day
Of terror-memories best
Left forgotten.
She is brave but scared,
Strong, yet she feels alone
She is like an angel,
Trying to unfold
Her wings and fly.
Someday, she will

Andrea L. Stover

When Will...

When will we be free
From the wrath of those around us
When will we be free
To live the life we choose
When will we be free
To love who we desire
When will we be free
To calm down and stop the fire
When will we be free
To wear the clothes we want
When will we be free
To speak our deepest thoughts
When will we be free
To respect every ones opinions
When will we be free
To accept the world we live in

Elizabeth Reinhart

Found

Friend or foe; who's to know
From where our hate will grow?
Find the kind of mind to woe,
From there our fiend will grow.

Send the friend who will show,
Some tear of spite to flow.
Sell the mail from the well and go,
Somewhere that the fiend is foe.

And since the fiend is foe;
Give the friend a find to woe.
Grab the mad that sad will tow;
And give the fiend a friend to sew.

Darby

To My Best Friend

You are my best friend
future, present, and past.
I have no doubts that
our friendship will last.
Whenever I was hurt, confused
or sad, you made me smile and
know longer feel bad.
Whenever my friends put me
down or made me feel blue,
I knew I could always
count on you.
Whenever I needed you,
you were always there.
You didn't need to say anything,
I knew you cared.
I met you late in the fall,
up until now it's been a ball.
It was you who mended my heart,
It was you who helped me from the start.

Hope Shipley

Snowflakes

See the snowflakes falling,
Gently to the ground,
Seems to me they're calling,
But they make no sound.

See the lacy filigree,
Sparkling in the light,
Crispy, white and lovely,
Peaceful, still and quiet.

See the crystals glisten,
As white as white can be,
And as I strain to listen,
Perhaps they whisper to me.

See the ivory chalk dust,
Blustering round and round,
As it starts to make a fuss,
I think I hear the sound.

Hear the snowflakes swirling,
Briskly they descend,
Fluttering, singing, twirling,
Like music in the wind.

Ami Lovvorn

Green

Cool, fresh new grass
Grapes, apples, peas
Kiwi fruit eaten with a spoon
Lime popsicle melting on a stick
It makes me feel hungry.

Brandon Christopher Estelle

Wind

Soft as a feather, hard as split
  glass
It may be weather, but it has
  class
Warm as a body, cold as new
  snow
These are the parts that I do
  know
Dries your tears when you do
  cry
Light as a bird when it does
  fly
For this I wonder why.
Beginning of time it was here
When we are gone, it will
  still be there
It is the wind.
I wonder no more.

Deana Graham

Go Away Rain

Go away,
Go away,
Go away rain.
You've been here so long
I'm going insane.

Let the sun shine
for at least a little while.
So instead of a whine
I can put on a smile.

Go away,
Go away,
Go away rain.

Crystal Witherspoon

Freedom...

Do what I want... when I want.
Go where I want... when I want.
Buy the things I feel like -
Nobody to tell me not to.
Nobody to care for -
Nobody to please.
Someday...
There will be,
Somebody to care...
where I go and who I see.
When spending money, somebody to say...
"Ya better not," or "it's ok".
Somebody to care for—
Somebody to please.
Until then...
I am to make a happy home,
and to enjoy my freedom... All alone.

Cindy Ramseier Brewer

In The End

In the end
  God saw that Heaven and Earth
  had served their purpose.
For the Earth was once again without
  form, and void; and Darkness ruled
  as in the beginning.
And God said:
  There will be no more light.
And God said:
  Darkness, time is yours.
And He withdrew down the path
  On which He had entered.

Josh Barinstein

Behind The Waterfall

Behind the waterfall,
God's nictitating eyelid,
There is a secret place
Amply hiding our first fresh kiss
And shy young faces,
Cool cheek on cheek
Alien to earth we stood
Wet and shivering, yet
Strangely exhilarated;
All previous lives and ours
Were made for this
Joining the ancient band
Of lovers...
Sweet innocents,
Nature's sons and daughters,
Who found there, too,
A trysting place
Where two are at onc
With rock...And water
And wild waterfall.

Helen M. Rambow

Living Word

Thank you Jesus, for your word,
Greatest story ever heard.
Word of life and liberty,
May you live your life through me.

Write your word upon my heart,
Cleanse and purity each part.
Till I am yours and you are mine,
Until I show your love divine.

Burn your word in brightest hues,
Let me publish your good news.
Till it shines in each dark place,
Until it reaches every race.

Living word, living way,
Brighter burn from day to day.
Until the brightness of the son,
Expels the dark and makes us one!

Betty Barrett

Simple Loves

Rainy days, sunny mornings
Green pastures, clear oceans

Weeping willows, soft sand
Distant voices, innocent looks

Simple smiles, a wink of an eye
Whispers of approval, holding hands,

A strong hug, a tender kiss
Loving affection, simple love

Loud music, moving lights
Bright colors, wide eyes

Neon signs, tropical fish
Sour peach gummy's, happy meal toys

Rolling thunder, strikes of lightning
Rooms of candles, cream of mushroom soup

Such simple things that bring such joy
Such natural things that make me smile
Such love, simple loves

But don't forget raindrops on roses...

Jody Frazier

Morning

How difficult it is to awaken
Greeting a life without enchantment
Where even the breathe of air
Fails to obscure sorrow's weight

Days travelling directionless paths
Until my still heart met you
Discovery lay borne the thought
My suffering could be lost through you

All I got were sad memories
Wandering around my mind
Reminding me of love's folly
Teaching the only hope is lost hope

Once again living within myself
Frightened to reach for unknown quantity
Because if you could shatter my life
I want to hold the remaining pieces.

John Roberts

Our First Grandson

Our little baby girl
Grew up at the blink of an eye
And now the time has come,
For her to give birth to a son.
The moment is near
Oh, what a moment it is!
When the father comes through the door.
With a grandson we have to explore,
We check for five little fingers,
And five little toes
And what a cute little button nose.
Oh, what a moment it is!
The moment is near
When I can hold him in my arms -
So want to protect him from harm.
He is so special, so sweet
Now I want you to meet
Alexander Daniel, our grandson
Oh, what a moment it is!

Barbara Nowakowski

Life Progressions

    I. First Truths
    Halo of soft light
framing questioning faces
  reflects our future.
    II. Maturity
Lights dim, seek no more
tired faces see too much
  now is the future
    III. Knowledge Seekers
  Future behind us
answers hidden, come to light
age dims not the search.

Cheryl L. Ahner

Snow, Snow, Snow

Snow, snow, snow,
How beautifully you glow
In winter's bright sun,
And when the sun is done
Shining on you
The streets and avenue
Are full of slush, slush slush—
Just a lot of Mush!

Catherine Milinar

A Tree That's Bare

A tree that's bare
Has a beauty that's rare.
She is so majestic
I marvel at her presence.

Although she is pale and void
And her foliage beneath her lay,
As she stands intrinsically poised
Her form is modestly displayed.

Her limbs create such beautiful designs
And with the various positions combined,
It's as though she has been refined
To symbolize an elegant ballet.

She is an art form at any stage,
All who ponder her will be swayed,
She is absolutely one of a kind;
A tree that's bare is truly divine.

Bernice W. Wilson

Little Ol' Me

The majesty of a mountain
Has brought a tear to my eye,
A wonder to my senses,
And a question to my lips:
Oh, Lord,
How can this be?
So monumental a creation,
Shaped by wind and rain,
Helpless to your hand.
A workmanship so great,
Yet so small.
What then,
Oh, Lord,
Am I?

Deni Schafer

God, My Great Guru And Guide

I may see it or see it not,
Have faith or have it not,
Aware of it or may be not,
It is behind, ahead and beside,
God, my great Guru and guide.

Its own off-spring is my soul,
Part and parcel of primal soul,
It's my beginning, it's my goal,
Within, without, on every side,
God, my great Guru and guide.

Every throb and every thought,
It knows indeed as it aught,
With me in 'deed and thought',
At every step and every stride,
God, my great Guru and guide.

Bakshy Ved-bhushan Chhibber

Mike

He was high
He didn't think he would die
He jumped to the sky
He thought he could fly

It isn't fair
For those who care
He was good and kind
Everyone thought in their mind

It was his first time
What a crime
Now I know why
Not to get high.

Jennifer Coulter

Life's End A Beginning

Why do I rack with pain
    He does not know

Why does misery remain
    Too tired to know

Why this crumble like grain
    I want to know

Why lost control I claim
    Let me know

Why deep anguish to explain
    Need to know

Why this starvation I strain
    Just to know

Why the agony the drain
    Should I know

Why then do I refrain
    From the belief I know

I know I know I know
    At midlife crises

Betty J. Cruz

He Is Your Friend And Mine

He is your friend and mine
He has walked with you
    And carried you too
He has loved you first
    Since the beginning of time
He has shared your grief
    And your joy
He is there for you all the time
    Listen for him
He will talk to you
    Open your heart and your eyes
He has been there all the time
He is your friend and mine
    Go to him now
Don't wait till it is too late
    And it is the end of time
His name is Jesus
He is your friend and mine

Emmanuel Clary

The Doggie

The doggie is friendly and smart,
He licks your face,
And eats off your plate,
And he always loves to play.

The doggie is loyal and true,
He's always around,
When you're going down.
He saves your life,
That's loyal all right.

The doggie is playful and fun,
He catches your frisbee
And sniffs 'round your tree,
He's there when you want him
And always will be,
Your doggie.

Janae R. Longoria

The Man In Apt. 242

I walk by his window
He sits like furniture
Sips beer and stares,
Grey, wrinkled, tired.

I wonder; the thoughts of this man
His memory of loves, sadness, anger
It hurts to see him so alone
Night after night; motionless, senseless
His eyes are void
Sorrow stains his soul
Unable to know true love
Insecurity, ruined purity

Age gracefully my inevitable friend
Though from beginning to end
Fill your spirit to brace
Your certain fall from grace

My cheeks dampen, throat closes
Empty existence, harsh sentence
I walk on to my space
Sit, sip, and stare.

Bob Kirkendale

The Patchwork Heart

With scraps and pieces of cloth from old
He starts his task set out from scratch.
Some are mute and some are bold
And some do not appear to match.
But strive he does these scraps to weave
Of remnants past into a whole,
And look he forward to achieve
The true construction of it all.
He gathers to the pieces wide
The odd-shaped remnants fit, do not.
Into this master work he strives
To replace, reshape its lot.
A snip, a cut, and try again,
He's pleased with how it seems to fall.
And places it with thread and then
Works another to the all.
But deep within the center true
Lies the essence of his work, its sun.
The heart he mends with string so new,
His patchwork quilt again is one.

Cynthia L. Hemmerle

That's How God Made Hershell

He took the sweetness from honey,
He took the purest of snow,
He took the warm day that was sunny,
To make a smile glow.
And that's how God made Hershell.

He took the echoes from the mountain
To make the strongest voice,
He took the moisture from the fountain,
And watched a mother rejoice.
And that's why God made Hershell.

He took the color from the ebony tree,
He took the swiftness of the doe,
He took some love from all things to be,
And placed it on the floor,
And that's when God made Hershell.

He took the power from the ocean,
The wind that is so free,
He took all things in motion,
And beauty as far as He could see.
And that's how God made Hershell.

James H. Brown

The Little Boy's First Fishing Trip

As the little boy went down the path,
He was so full of cheer and laugh
To think that he was going to the brook
With his pole line and hook.

He saw the fish swimming,
But he could only stand grinning
For he had left his bait at home
And had to leave the fish alone.

Josie Burnum Lamb

Heartaches Tend To Mind

Someone out there loves me
He will come to me very soon
We will sit beneath the stars above
and watch the rising moon
He will love me for the end of time
Which is for eternal life
He will take my heart and hold it
and not stab it with a knife
Heartaches take a while to mend
I think they will never heal
But then one day my heart will tend
to seal the hurt for real
Then there will never be no more
heartaches and tears
For that someone will love me
for years and years and years.

Helen Milliken

Take Time

Tears spilling and,
   hearts aching
Are we blind?

Our unity is our divider
He is beauty,
   ignored;
Deemed unobtainable,
   even useless.

Are we blind to his tears,
   as blind as we are to our own?
This is the proof that we are all alone.

Barbara Weber

Love

Flowers growing in a field.
Hearts all aglow.
The water is so mild
as the wind blows.
Little children at play
Mothers cook all day.
Babies eyes all alive.
Waiting to see the outside.
These are all part of love.
Caring for all around.
It is like a flying dove
trying to touch the ground.

Jenny Bisner

Grandma

She closed her eyes and folded
her arms across her unmoving
   chest.
We dressed her in the light
   blue gown, the one she liked
   the best.

She looked so young and full
   of grace. No longer will
   open her eyes.
Each one of us came to her-
   to say our last final good-byes.

We'll come to visit and talk
   to her and put flowers on
   her grave.
We know the pain will sometimes
   hurt, but also we must be brave

The world lost a wonderful
   lady who, in our hearts we've stored.
But we aren't sad or mournful
   for we know she's with the Lord.

Julie Rebber

Untitled

There she is here I am
Her body of steel mine, tan
She has the speed
Yet I keep it slow
She has the power
It's the knowledge I know
She's soft on the inside
It's the hard part that glows
Three hundred horse power
For one man to blow
Accidents happen
When he lets she go....
Let knowledge take over
The power will show
After all she could be friend
Or she could be foe....

Lets face it, it's the knowledge
That makes the power go.

Derek Curtis

Flesh Wounds

She asked me why,
her father doesn't care.
How do I answer
so she won't hear

these pictures that flash
like a kaleidoscope wheel
of wounds to the flesh
needing more time to heal

With words that could either
lessen or deepen the wounds?
Being careful how I choose them,
being careful of the tones?

But her face was a mirror
and I saw bandages fall away
revealing scars that remained open
and eyes that looked the same way

Then, I knew how to soothe her
remembering that need
and I held her in my arms
till she would no longer bleed

Gloria Alexander

Hurt

Her smile hid the pain
Her laughter shed silent tears
Why should she lose so much
While trying to gain
Her love cuts like a knife
She's a shadow of her former self
Why can she not be happy
There's too much pain
Not enough love
She needs him to live
   For she soon will die
Without him
Happiness is not possible
Memories bring tears of joy
   For that's all she has left
There is no future
   For the hurt and wounded
In the game of Love.

Andrea Blevins

Black Woman Trapped

Black woman trapped inside her own mind
Her own soul she's trying to find
It's all bottled up inside
It's trying its best to hide.

Trying its best to laugh
Trying to forget the past.
Never having comfort or love
From anything up above.

She does not hear a sound
For she knows no one is around.
To help her in her time of need
Lord, I don't want her to bleed.

One night she's thinking
For she knows it's shrinking.
Her own soul she can't find
For she's trapped inside her mind.

Now it's time for everyone to see
She's a Black Woman Trapped like you and
me.

Bunmi Odumade

The Problem

This problem has been
here for so long
I wish I could snap my fingers
and it would be gone

I dream the same dream
every single night
I ask myself this question
why do we fight

A person cannot be measured
by the color of the skin
you have got to look past
and see what's within

Does it matter if you're
black or white
who is to judge who's
wrong or right

I've seen this problem
I've seen people cry
I wish this problem
would hurry up and die

Dan Miller

If I Could Paint A Picture

If I could paint a picture of my child,
Here's what I'd do.
I'd paint her hair a golden blonde,
Her eyes would be bright blue.

Her lips would be a rosebud red,
And there would be a grin.
I'd paint two dimples, round and deep,
And paint a dainty chin.

Her little body, soft and plump,
Would be a fair, snow white.
I'd paint her with pink fingertips,
And chubby hands held tight.

I'd paint her in a frilly dress,
With pretty pastel hues.
I'd place on her some lacy socks,
And patent leather shoes.

Yet all the artists in the world,
Could never capture this.
The pleasure I receive
When this small child gives me a kiss.

Connie S. Mitchell

My Rabbit

Holding my rabbit in my arms
  Him fighting to get free
I can't help but smile
At how stubborn he can be
His head trying to hide itself
Underneath my arm
When it finally gets there
He is very calm
Letting me pet him
But not for long

Christina Stoltz

Look Beyond

They say he's ugly
His bumps, his scrapes
The curls in his hair
His dirty complexion
That's what they all see
But I look past his skin
The bumps, the scrapes
I look past the curls in his hair
His dirty complexion
I see the love in his eyes
He yearns to be accepted
But no one will look past the outside
They think of him as a beast
But I know he has a kind & caring heart
They must give him a chance to show it
Besides, it's only the first day of preschool
And he just got over the chicken pox
I should know, he's my son
And I love him.

Anne Brooks

"True Immortality"

For him I love, I shall weep no more.
His days here on earth may have ended,
But his memory lives in my heart's core
And in the hearts of all his kindred.

To see reminders of his very essence
Look no farther than my own eyes.
For in me live the noble remnants
Of his triumphs and his trials.

His memory shall live forever
In the souls of those he loved
Bound by a bond death can not sever
And an emotion stronger than love.

Chasity Brown

A Fearful Child's Love

Today a child approached me
His eyes were filled with tears
As I reached out to touch him
He looked at me in fear
Why, I asked, are you afraid
Why do you look so sad
Because my love is not enough
To help my mom and dad
I do the best that I can do
His trembling voice did say
But seems it is not good enough
They hurt me anyway
They say I do not understand
Why they hit me as they do
Because I love them both I lie
About why I am black and blue
So please let them hit me no more
Let them love me from their heart
For if the pain is not gone tonight
Tomorrow I shall depart

Angela Tuttle

Lonely No Man's Hill

No Man sat there, all alone
His face expressionless, made of stone
And in the cool dusk light
No Man suddenly began to cry.

No Man was heartbroken and sad
No Man was frustrated, really mad
No Man's Heart, No man's fright
And still No Man was crying.

No Man's eyes, wide and glazed
What he had done, still amazed
No Man sat, dusk to night
No Man still crying, life asunder.

No Man wonders, about his life
Being worth it, all this strife

And still No Man will wonder.

Jason Barrons

Early Spring-Feb. 1994

Today I heard a meadowlark
His liquid notes caressed the sky,
I could not see, but then sometimes
The ear is sharper than the eye.

And then I heard another lark
Her call of love came through the air,
While on a rooftop mourning doves
Sat side by side, a loving pair.

I wish my love were with me now
But he is many miles away,
I fear my heart would burst with love
Upon this early spring like day.

Hazel M. Caesar

Epilogue-June 1994
Today those singing fields were plowed,
The meadowlarks were gone,
Their eggs, exposed to greedy crows
Lay rotting in the sun.
My heart, once filled with springtime love
Is brimming now with pain,
I wonder if I'll ever hear
Those meadowlarks again?

Death

A dark shadow falls across his face,
His painful life lost its race.
His pains will forever be gone
As the light comes in the dawn.
To take his soul to a higher place.
Where he will plea his final case.
To the one Almighty, Son Of God.

Glenda D. Hull

Through My Eyes

The words you've said
Hit me deep inside
It made me see you through
different eyes
It made me think of both
our lives
Rather to treasure it or let
it die
I didn't want that, I wanted
it to be true
I wanted to hold you
All night through
I also wanted you to hold me tight
Mixing our, body heat
"Yeah!" That's right
Let's treasure our relationship
till we die
And be true to each other
So we can survive.

Elisia Perez

Before A Suicide

As time passes, fades away,
I can see no more.
Emotions, lifeless, lie in decay,
I can feel no more.

Dreams, dark, hidden by fear,
I can hope no more,
Infatuation, lost in one final tear,
I can love no more.

Alone to face eternity,
I can live no more.

Derek Izzi

'Letting Go'

What does it take to finally let go;
Holding on to the memory of
   Loves long-running show;
You'll hear no applause or see
lights on the stage;
Just a room filled with sadness
And bittersweet rage;
   Yet the tears that you shed
will soon have meaning;
Enhanced by your will for
true happiness and healing;
   Understand your emotions for they
hold the key, their guidance
will teach you to let go
   and be free...

   Christine D. Wadley

Home

Home place deep in heart
Holds everyone in stars and sun -
Each feels springtime green

Steady nurturing -
Community of each and all
Responds and heals itself

Homeless wandering
On endless winter barrens -
Life roots cut away

Wolves come back to den
Children reach for resting warmth
Birds return to nest

Neighbors can be bonds
of caring - each vision sharing
For their entity

Dawn each day reborn
Flies around the rim of earth -
New page is opened

Great sun full rising
Floods hearts as well as visions - People of
one world

   Drayton Bryant

Terminal

I gazed at the dark
hole, it was time to say 'bye.....
I am not ready.

Faces from old seen.
They remind me of days gone......
I'm haunted by them.

My heart cries no more.
It is still full of sadness.
I have no more tears.

The days fly by like
birds. I have no time to think.
I long for my time.

   Courtney Dolan

Sweethearts Forever

Sweethearts forever,
   How beautiful to say,
That we were married
   On Valentine's Day!

Valentine's Day brings
   Memories of hearts,
And lots of memories
   Of cupids with darts!

The years have gone by,
   How swiftly it seems,
With all the fulfillment
   Of family and dreams!

Our children, God's blessings,
   And each in their way,
Brought happiness and joy
   Throughout each day!

And grandchildren were added,
   To bring us great joy,
Our happiness increased
   With each girl and boy!

   Arthur Chambers

"How"

Tell me, how did you do it,
How did you get to me?
How could you look into my eyes,
And see what no one else can see?

How did you read in between
My carefully rehearsed lines?
How did you get through the walls,
Into the corners of my mind?

Your work was cut out for you,
How did you know to hang on?
How did you get through the noise,
To hear my heart's quiet song?

My guard is high and strong,
Darling you know it's true,
So how did you get to me,
And do what no one else could do?

   Crystal Campbell

Questions? And Answers (Blind Faith)

How much a pound is albatross?
How do you put a price on grief?
Is there an opiate for loss?...
When Death comes stealing like a thief?

Is there a way to ease the pain,
Caused when the one you love has gone?
Is there a way to stop the rain?...
And bring about the sun-drenched dawn?

Can man attack his darkest dreams?
And bring them out to face the light?
Nothing is ever as it seems,
And what is true may not be right.

"Trust in God's Love," I've overheard,
In times of agony and strife;
"For it is more than just a word
And with His love, you'll find true 'Life'."

I understand-Faith is the way
And only I can make a start.
I hope He hears me when I pray...
"Please lift this burden from my heart."

   Deborah V. Spayd

Sweet Emotion

Just to see, just to see
How gently
Sound travels
Through unknown
Territory;
Jealous, I gawk

Just to feel, just to feel
The rhythmic road
Beat beat beat
To a tune
The metered mile
Never knew

Just to hear, just to hear
The whistling wind
Mutter the mood
That resembles
The words
Left unspoken

   Catie Butler

So Confused

   I tell you guys,
   How much I care;
   There is no doubt,
   You just don't hear.

   I'm so confused,
   I just cannot write;
   There's so may things,
   I feel tonight.

   I realize,
my feelings don't matter;
When I hear that razor blade,
   pitter patter.

   I'm writing this poem,
   for you once again;
   I just want it known,
   cokes' not your friend.

I want you to read this,
   while you're high;
As I sit in the living room,
   and start to cry.

   Belinda Cox

I Am But A Person

I am but a person who sees with
Human eyes and walks on two
Legs to get where I spy.

I am but a bird proud gallant
And true flying high above the
Clouds like only birds can do.

I am but a squirrel leaping from
Limb to limb almost flying as I soar
Through the air.

I am but a person who sees with human
Eyes and walks on two legs to get where
I spy.

   April Michelle Conner

Death: My Ultimate Fear

Every time I'm on places up high,
I always have the ultimate fear to die
Just looking down is torture
Will death come in the picture?

Will he come as a giant whirlwind?
Imprisoning me in his mighty spin?
Or will he be a friend I used to call
Pushes me hard and watches me fall?

I never stopped questioning me
When I die, what's it gonna be?
Does it always come in tons of pain?
If so, I'd surely go down the drain.

Then my breathing's gonna fail
I wonder if somebody's gonna wail
Or would there be a sigh of relief
That a girl named Jane now lies very stiff?

Who's gonna wear black?
Would anyone care to look back?
How my temperament came to be
I bet I was just simply being me.

Erika Jane A. Sievert

Autumn In Kentucky

I look and gasp in wonder —
I cannot make a sound;
Mid all God's creation
In awe I'm overwhelmed!

The natural, innocent beauty
Untouched by human hand
done by a Spiritual Artist
I cannot comprehend.

It's just too unbelieving
That I, a mortal, see
And take in all this beauty
The Artist made for me.

And if I were an Atheist
A believer I would be
When autumn in Kentucky
I'm privileged to see.

Betty M. Dozier

The Simple Truth

Late one summer evening,
I decided to walk up the road,

To visit my grandpa and grandma,
At their red house on the hill,

And when I arrived, I found
Them sitting on the front porch,

Watching another wonderful sunset,
So we all said 'Hello' to each other,

And I sat down to wait
But after a few moments I said,

'I wish tomorrow was going to be Friday',
Well this happened only to be Tuesday,

And my grandpa, being up in his 70's
At this time, looked at me with

Many years of life shining in his eyes,
and said 'Son, make everyday count,

Because to wish for another day
Is only to wish your life away',

I have since then seen many sunsets
With many a day, and few regrets.

Bruce Trammell

Shut In

I use to think
I didn't day dream
Now I know
It isn't so.

Talking to exciting people
Riding in a plush plane
Gazing at the warm Mojave
From a speeding train.

Watch me swoosh and sway
As I ski with grace
Rounding every marker
To win first place!

Swimming at Curacao
In my string bikini....
If you don't believe me
You're nothing but a meanie!

Alyce "Lisa" Gehrling

Growing Up

I remember when he was born.
I didn't like him at all.
The attention was turned away from me,
Watching him walk and crawl.

As he got older, we constantly fought.
He was such a little pest.
But when he reached his teenage years,
Our differences came to rest.

We both began to realize,
How much we had been through.
And although we'd sometimes argue,
Our friendship quickly grew.

We have remained best friends,
Always there for one another.
This baby I am talking of,
Is Lee, my younger brother.

Angie Stockwell

If I Could...

I could have ignored you
I could have walked away
I could have stayed cool
I could have refused to play

I should have done just that
I should have listened to my head
I should have known from the start
I heeded my heart instead

I would change none of this
Looking back I now know
Now it's time to move on
If I could only let go...

Anna Liza L. Maniago

Gentility

Her regal countenance foremost
I beheld with awesome admiration.
Privileged; Basking in pleasing aura
Of one who had reached perfection.

As if exiled from an heir's kingdom,
Burdens and sorrows plagued her life.
Always forward, purpose wavered not,
All experiences transmuted to good.

This vessel of love, created by Him,
Poured forth that part as ordained.
With grace, she entered Eternity,
Giving life to the word- Gentility.

Irene Patrick

Untitled

Feeling like a lion trapped in a cage
I claw at the lock
   But no one helps me
I scream out in distress
   But no one hears me
I cry for human contact
   But no one sees me
People walk by like everything's fine
   But can't they hear?
   Can't they see?
I have dreams
   Just like them
I have feelings
   Just like them
I can cry
   Just like them
My heart beats just like theirs
   Or does it?
That's the question

Jennifer Linne

Shadow In The Mirror

Behind the face,
I can see what no one else can see.

Behind the smile,
is a frightened child.

I may have everything,
but inside I have nothing.

I hide it every day,
hoping it will go away.

Life is tough,
it is not what it seems.

Oh, if you could only see,
but then no one would like me.

See me for who I am,
not for what I may seem.

Jennifer Miles

Untitled

When you left me that day
I didn't know what to say
I didn't know what to do
You left me with memories
Painful memories of only me and you

That day you told me to go
But I couldn't let you go
If you knew you wanted me to stay
Why didn't the words come out-
in the right way

How could you be so cruel and leave me
in such a way
Now it's done and the memories
Won't go away
Tell me what to do with memories
All we shared is gone
Your love faded as time passed

But don't worry cause my love
for you is still here.

So come on back to the one who-
loves you dear!

Daisy Reyes

Beyond My Dreams

As I walk through life today
  I step a little higher
For I caught a glimpse through God's own eyes
  And saw His plans were higher
He sees me far beyond the place
  Where I had dreamed to be
And when He looks upon my heart
  He seems to smile at me
I can't explain this joy I feel
  Just knowing that He cares
Excitement just keeps spilling out
  And filling all the air
My prayer today and everyday
  Is that His vision grows
Until His heart becomes my own
  And His plans for me I know
That every fear and doubt will flee
  Like waves that roll to sea
Then I can be the me that He
  So longs for me to be.

    Roberta Tippett

Victoria

As I sit and contemplate the yesterdays,
I think of all her tender ways.
The smile that emerged from her face,
Complimented by her dress of lace.
Her eyes shined through my heart,
Always blue, right from the start.
Her ivory hands, so delicate
Embraced by the comfort of her fate.
The sun would shine upon her head,
And at night, the moon on the foot of her bed.
She did not speak, so I did not know,
The pain she felt, she could not show.
I held her in my arms one night
And rocked her in the pale moonlight.
Her tired eyes gave up the fight,
As she slipped away into the light.
She could feel the pain no more,
As she knocked on heavens door.
Finally, my perfect little girl could walk
As she took Jesus' hand and began to talk.

    Rachel Bruno

Penal System

To concentrate on my reality here within
I think of all the different people and places I have been.

At times I have been a stranger, someone I did not know
Prison never scared that guy, it was just a place to go.

I find I am part of the diet which made this monster grow
State raised and state fed, so much I did not know.

Now my days are long and dreary
As I sit and stare at my graystone misery.

So much there is to tell you, so much I will not say
So many different reasons why I played my hands this way.

One thing is for certain with the years I have to go
I will see many more men numbered as I watch this monster grow.

And then one day when it shakes its head,
and its roar is heard from coast to coast
Everyone will blame each other for feeding it the most.

    Rodney Hayes

"Today As I Watch The Sun"

Today as I watch the sun,
I think of how lucky I am. To live in a
country where we are free, and not
under someone else's command.

Today as I watch the sun, I
see how beautiful it is. It shines in the
day, and seems so astray, as I watch
it floating away.

Today as I watch the sun,
I see it fading away, behind a big oak
tree. I wish it was me, taller than a
tree, to meet the sun in the sky.

    Misty Hefner

I Miss You

I sit here alone feeling so empty and lonely,
I think of you often every minute of the day wondering
how you are, what you are doing, wishing I could hold you.

I sit remembering all we've shared, dreaming of all
that will be, and crying a tear for every minute
we are apart.

At times I tell myself I am strong and the time apart
will go quickly, yet at others, I sit and cry and wonder
why love must hurt this way.

Though somewhere in the loneliness, somewhere in the
emptiness, I find myself feeling very loved, and I realize
that it's not the loving that hurts so much it's being
without you.

    Laura Grance

The Missing Shepherd

As I stood upon a hillside in the Winter's snow so deep,
I thought I saw a shepherd man attending to some sheep.
Then for a moment my feet did freeze and it began to snow.
And all around the shepherd man there seemed to form a glow.

My eyes became all misty as the winds began to blow.
And my heart began a faster beat from stumbling through the snow.
For in that pasture I had never seen a shepherd nor a sheep,
Now wiping all the tears away I tried to get a peek.

Moonlight shined off of the glistening snow— the stars were out so
  bright.
Who was this man up on the hill in the middle of the night?
Now inch by inch and step by step, for I had to reach the peak.
To find out who this shepherd was with all the little sheep.

Now standing at the top I see there's no shepherd nor a glow.
But there were tiny little hoof prints all trampled in the snow.
There are questions asked most everyday; some answers maybe right.
But I never found the answer to the shepherd in the night.

    Robert Jarvis

The Trip

It's a road I didn't ask for, a road of bumps and bends,
  I took to see its sights and find its final end.
    Should the sun shine on this dog's ask again,
  I'll relate my tale most humbly. Tell whom? Tell what?
    I'm the stone turner, the sand pusher, too.
  I abide; a horse hoofing holes up a dry clay slope.
    I hear frustration; the drone is loud.
  I despair. Here comes the night. I fear sleep.
      Please, pour me up a hot.

    Linus R. Wilks

Bandit

I searched myself and found a soul while strolling through my mind
I touched the tears I felt the pain and thought I was to blame
He was weak and tired and time was almost near
And I knew in my heart the end was my biggest fear
It seemed like only yesterday that I held him in my arms
We played, we walked, I sang him songs
He is my best friend, he is my dog
I hope he knows that when it's time, he will not go alone
Because as he is a part of me, he will take a part of my soul
As God awaits, time passes by and I can see the hurt and fear
In my Bandit's eyes, for I'm the one God's waiting for and
He knows that this is the most pain I've ever felt before
If I should pick one thing that will be a lasting memory
It would have to be the love we've shared from day one until
eternity.

Sandra Smith

You're Special To Me

You're special to me- you're someone I trust.
I treasure the topics that we have discussed.

I'm thankful for times you have summoned a smile.
I'm grateful our paths have converged for a while.
I'm pleased by each confidence you have displayed.
I cherish those moments you've sought to persuade.

I'm touch by the gestures of kindness you've shown.
I've noticed how fast our hours have flown.

I'm feeling the force of a love that's true
I'm fortunate for having a person like you!!!!

Rebecca Smith

Birds

Oh—the bird, such a wonderful guy
I used to dream that I too could fly.
I'd soar to the heavens, just flapping my arms,
My arms would propel me, just like birds.
Up I would go, joining their flock,
Never tiring a bit, such a spectacle.
I was really a hit, but they laughed at me,
They laughed at me, and outflew me a bit.
But flying was fun, until I awoke.
Awake I can watch him, now joined by his mate.
There in the tree, making love,
Beak to beak, and swinging joyfully,
Even in the breeze, sex cannot wait.

Ray Yoder

Daddy's Little Girl

Years ago when I was just a little girl,
I used to know my daddy's love.
He looked out for me and watched me play,
Then gave discipline along the way.
Through my eyes, he was big and strong.
I didn't think anything could go wrong.
I grew up and moved away
Like most little girls often do.
But I always thought that in my daddy's heart,
I would always be there to stay.
Sometimes things can happen,
To destroy love and respect.
But if you say I'm sorry,
There should be no regrets.
It saddens me now to think of him,
Knowing how he feels.
I just hope in time and the right frame of mind,
Our hearts will be able to heal.
I love him so and I hope he knows
That I just want to be Daddy's little girl again.

Kathy M. Allison

A House Full Of Empty

Arriving to the echoes of noises long past,
I walk by rooms dark of life.
Sounds no longer assail my passing,
Those of children,
Now grown;
War whoops and shouted whispers,
The jarring thump of musiclike sounds;
Always louder,
All ring in memories of times flashed by.
Quickly gone.

Stephanie LeMay

Grant To Me

I want very little in life.
I want to give to someone, somewhere
a little hope a little prayer.
That they see life as sweet as I see
the blessing in which I have received.

Grant to me a wish tonight that I can
make someone smile and their life a little
easier then what it was before.

Grant to me a prayer that all my dreams
come true, that people will believe in you as much I do.

Grant to me the peace that people need
within in their lives to give them hope, love
and understanding; too.

That if these wishes I wish for would
come true for someone as special as you!

Tonda Vanderpool

She Made My World To Shine

As on a mist of my wandering dreams, I saw her, lovely and shy.
I wanted to dance, I wanted to sing, I wanted to pray on high.
To say to the world that she was mine, a dream with golden hair.
She smiled and blushed and said she would; but wait, "Could this be
true?"

My heart did stutter and stammer and stop, but yes she did say,
"Yes."
She made my day, she made my year, she made the sun to shine.
She made the world to seem so ill and nothing to compare,
To the love I knew as I knew her when the moon was in her hair.

Had I but known the joy I know with every passing day,
I would have offered more before just to know her and her way.
I've often wondered since that day, just what would have happened to
me,
Had I not gathered up my nerve and offered my soul to her.

But I did ask, and she said she would and now the world is right.
I thank my God that I am blessed by the love of this golden dream.
I thank her for the love I know whene'er she smiles at me.
She is my joy, she is my love, she is the world to me.

Thank God, Thank Pam, Thank God again that I can love once more.
She brought to life the love in me and made my world to shine.

Thomas C. Schnepp

Crayons

I've colored a picture with crayons.
I'm not very pleased with the sun.
I'd like it much stronger and brighter and
more like the actual one. I've tried with
the crayon that's yellow, I've tried the red.
But none of it looks like the sunlight
I carry around in my head.

Sarah Yellen

"To Whom Ever"

To whom ever it may concern...
I was late coming home last night,
Because I sat on the curb crying
From all the confusion and all the fright.

To whom ever it may concern...
I have never truly loved one dear.
Nobody to call my own,
Nobody to hold me near.

To whom ever it may concern...
People tease me and treat me like dirt.
But they never stop to think
Inside me, there is nothing but hurt.

If people would just take life day by day
And wait in line for their turn
If people would just listen to each other
To whom ever it may concern.

    Monique Parsons

Left Behind

I used to be a little girl, but what was I supposed to do.
I was there all alone with you.
I saw you with a smile it cut me like I should
Cut our little child
Inside of me is such a part of you
What was I supposed to do I sent a smile over to you
I should have left you like they left me here
To wither in denial
But I'd miss the one who's laugh I love
What was I supposed to do I sent a smile over to you
As I stood there holding our child all you did was smile
What was I supposed to do when I've always been in love with you
One day you saw me with our child, all you did was smile
You said you missed the one you loved
What was I supposed to do
When I was still in love with you
As I withered in denial all you did was smile
I was the one you always left behind.

    Kelly Limerick

Dream No More

Wake up! You have your son! Oh, what joy.
I watched you grow, with pride my boy.

I vowed you would have good values.
You did me proud and even made the news.

Something happened in your college years,
The world began to change giving me inner fears.

The song on my lips and in my heart
Is no longer there, for while you were playing with your cart

You became abused by trusted guys
Though you did excel—something inside you slowly dies.

Strong in faith; I knew instinctively
All my dreams for you may not become reality.

You have so much to give
Alas, you don't have your full life to live.

My dreams and yours, my dear and only son
Are ending before they have really begun.

I count my blessings and we share the "good old days"
For you, like so many, have this dreaded disease called "AIDS".

Let's live each day with love and prayer
That research will help others and society will learn to care.

    Rosalie Rita Castellano

Convalescent Lamb

Someone will be buttoning my blouse,
I will look at their impatient fingers
And drool, panicky to see if they placed
My loose set of teeth in the opened gap
Which they forgot to do yesterday or was that
Last year, and I've been eating quite a bit of
Mashed potatoes lately, drowning in bright jello
Cubes since coming here and my dog cries for me

But they tell me I ran over him with my bed
That day when my glasses broke like church windows
And all my prayers went unheard, but the nurse said
"Sweetie, they don't do you no good anyhow" and my
Poetry sleeps beside me, curled into moisture.
I will die alongside it, humming its message.

    Kathleen M. Conley

Give Me a Pen, A Voice, A Sin, And Some Love

Give me a pen and
I will write about the
famous night.

Give me a voice and
I will speak about the
time that I took a peek.

Give me a sin and
I will be hold so
I can grow old.

Give me some love to and
I will live to the
day I give.

    Kim Durand

I Wish I Knew How He Felt....

As I lie here,
I wish I knew how he felt about me,
I know it's silly,
But all I can do is think about it,
Maybe he cares,
Maybe he still loves me,
I wish I knew,
Tears stain my face,
My once pale pink cheeks are red from crying,
All I can do is cry for the lost love I once had,
I see him everyday & know I still care but...
I wish I knew how he felt about me,
He'll always be my true love,
But will I always be his?
I wish I knew how he felt about me.

    Shelley Marie Adams

Grandma's Love

I stood there crying as my grandma past away
I wish she would've listened when I asked her to stay.
My grandma has a special place deep down in my heart
I wanted very dearly for her not to part.

I stood there looking down at my grandma's sad pale face.
I knew that on her funeral I would dress her up in lace.
I felt like I was frozen as they took her from the room
As I walked out to my car I stared up at the moon.

That day is gone and in the past
But my grandma's love will always last;
For that place in my heart is filled with memories
That I will share with my friends for many centuries.

    Lisa Brown

Things That Last

Each day I grow older,
  I wonder about my past.
For what have I ever achieved
  that would really last.
Did I ever comfort someone that truly was in need,
Or impart on a lonely soul a kind word indeed.
Did I ever lend a shoulder or
  place a hand in mine.
Or did I ever share a love, the one that truly binds.
Oh, I look around and see the
  faces of those who do not care,
And look upon those who hurt,
  whose souls are in deep despair.
Even more I look to God and ask a special thing.
Could I be the one to make
  these broken hearts sing.
For all that I ever have done, all in times past,
Only those things I have done for Christ,
  will be the things that last.

    Timothy Ridgeway

I Am

I am just a man.
I wonder how I can feel this way.
I hear voices of friends vanished and gone.
I see myself, but don't know my own face.
I want to be able to live.
I am just a man.

I pretend that I am in love.
I feel myself fadin' away.
I touch my tears with your finger tips.
I worry why love must die.
I cry when there is nobody to talk to.
I am just a man.

I understand that what I feel, want, dream,
  and hope doesn't matter to you.
I say everything, but no one listens.
I dream that one day I will be free.
I try oh do I try, but it's so hard, especially now that I can feel.
I hope that people will start to listen.
I am just a man.

    K. C. Klaver

I Am

I am a sweet girl who loves cats.
I wonder if cats can talk to are another.
I hear cats singing in the night.
I see cats dancing around the alleys.
I want to be able to adopt all the homeless cats.
I am a sweet girl who loves cats.

I pretend that cats are like real people.
I feel the pain of the abused cats clawing at my heart.
I touch the dying cats and make them all better.
I worry that people will keep abandoning,
And abusing cats and they will become endangered.
I cry when I see a hurt or dying cat.
I am a sweet girl who loves cats.

I understand that all cats have to die sometime.
I say to myself that I hope my
cat that ran away 2 months ago is still alive.
I dream all cats had a home.
I try never to avoid my cats.
I hope my cat comes home soon. I am a sweet girl who loves cats.

    Tabitha M. Driskell

I Am

I am intelligent but full of imagination
I wonder if dinosaurs will rule the earth again.
I hear everything there is to hear.
I see everything there is to see.
I want to be able to fly like a bird
I am intelligent but full of imagination.

I pretend to be one of america's greatest
I feel the tingle of joy
I touch the boundaries of life
I worry if the world will end
I cry when family dies.
I am intelligent but full of imagination

I understand that I will eventually die.
I say do what you want to do
I dream of friends
I try to remember
I hope I can make a difference
I am intelligent but full of imagination.

    Burns

The Nightingale

The nightingale sings so beautifully,
I wonder if he sings for me.
Or maybe he's such a happy bird,
He just can't put his thoughts into word.

One night as I said my evening prayer,
I caught a glimpse of him up in the air.
I thought it might be God's way of saying
Thank you for taking the time for praying.

The next morning I woke up to see
Him perched upon my window sill, singing out with glee.
The moment that he flew away,
I wished that he'd come back to play.
The nightingale sings so beautifully,
I wonder if he sings for me.

    Mariah Gardner

Being 60 In The 90's

In 60 years I've seen a lot,
I wonder if it's a Government Plot?

To keep the masses in control
By letting guns kill and take its toll!

Does anyone in power really care,
or is it to late for even a prayer.

Now I can't remember my prime,
for 60 years is a very long time!

I was standing on the corner waiting for the bus in the sun,
When three white cops pulled out their gun.

But I being black with nothing to hide,
Said to the cops, what up with pride;

They said it was because of the bulge on my side
I'm thinking because I'm black I get a free ride.

Maybe that's the start of a trend
and if it is my world at its end.

    Leonard Hicks

Untitled

Cold, rainy night splatter; reminds me of the
infant patter of my children's feet, when first
they learned to greet me from a day hard-spent.
Soon it will be gone, the rain, just like the children went.

    Walter E. Sinclair

Mirror, Mirror

As I look at the reflection in the mirror,
  I wonder who it is that I see,
No longer can I recall the vision,
  For I know that person must not be me,
Recognizable, is not the face,
  That stares back mysteriously,
With a saddened expression in her eyes,
  Asking, needing to be let free,
To the girl in the mirror, who are you,
  I ask, waiting to be told,
Surprised I do not know, she answers,
  I am the image that your mind beholds!

  Lynn Carlyle

I am

I am the earth
I wonder why I hurt
I hear the sounds of pollution and violence
I want to tell them why I hurt, why I cry
I am the earth

I pretend to be o.k.
I feel too much hurt, my body can't take it
I touch some hearts, but not all
I worry about what is to come of me
I cry to express my hurt, but people don't realize it
I am the earth

I understand that my job is too protect
I say I wish I could
I dream of a place where there is no hurt, or pain
I hope I could be there someday, forever
I am the earth.

  Michelle Garcia

Sad State Of An Affair

In the Seventies I was still a flower child and
I wore a hippie hat in the rain. You wore maroon
trousers with a white belt. You sang in the church
choir, and in my head I was hearing the low spark
of high-heeled boys. We rubbed our legs together
under the table with the supervisor looking on.
We went to the drive-in movie, and we went to
the Holiday Inn.

In the Eighties I wanted to be a groupie with the
Grateful Dead, and you said you were going to live
in the snow in the north and let your black hair
turn grey. I followed you to the snow in the north
to give you a box of rain. I couldn't find your
footprints in the snow and I spilled it all on me.

In the Nineties I heard someone say, if you have
some give some away. I had nothing I gave it
all to you. Black haired, grey haired, black
hearted man in the snow in the north.
I'm so glad I never told you how much I love you.

  Mary Virginia Farmer

"The Paint Brush"

I keep my paint brush with me, wherever I go,
incase I need to cover up, so the real me doesn't show.
I'm afraid to show you me; afraid of what you'll do you
might laugh or say mean things; I'm afraid I might
loose you. I'd like to remove all my coats to
show you the real true me but I want you to try
and understand. I need you to like what you see.

  Raymond Costello

Symptoms

I loved him,
I would have died for him,
I lived only to see him,
Then it came,
Blonde, beautiful, and popular,
all he deserved,
and nothing I was,
My life, heart, and soul all went to him but,
this was nothing to the beauty she held,
nothing to the passion which was held in her eyes,
and nothing compared to the lust which hung over her;
Slowly it came to an end,
the phone calls behind my back,
no time for me,
they were the symptoms that hung over me,
and when they dropped I wanted to drop with them,
Then it was over,
She had it all, I had nothing,
nothing to hold or cherish,
It was over, and I was still alive.

  Tristin Kelsey

Choose Well, My Son

My son, my little red-head, now just two:
I'd like to know what life has down the way.
I'd like to know exactly what to say
To give the best of everything to you.

But as you know, the future we can't see.
We live and play and work in present time
Not knowing how today affects our climb
Along life's path. My son, you hold the key.

It's you alone who chooses how you'll live
And you who chooses whom you'll make your guide.
Choose well in youth; keep wisdom on your side.
Select the best of what the world can give.

Choose life, dear son, and peace and joy and love.
These you will have when you choose God above.

  Lisa Yoder

Lost Love

When I think of you tonight
I'd like to think we would not fight
When I have my perfect dream
I'd like to know what it really means
When we were together it was so fun
But now I know we will have none
When I knew you stole my heart
I was there for you like a speeding dart
I wished we were together for life
But you only stabbed me with your long cold knife
I can not think of what to do
But I know it will be without you
I cannot think of how our relationship fell
All I know is that I'm in hell
You would have been the perfect one for me I'd say
But I know you don't feel the same way

  Tom Marsh

Storm

I have been out in the middle of the storm,
in the midst of the thunder and flame
  (to be washed by the boisterous rain
and cleansed by the tempestuous wind);
  where the raindrops on my face were tears,
  and the rainbow grew out of my pain.

  Michael W. Gommel

A Mixed Up World

What if a shark lived on land, and what
    if a human lived under the sea?

If a shark lived on land would it be in
a band? Would it play a saxophone or a
maxaphone?!

If a human lived under the sea would it
be able to see?! or would it bump into
a fish and say excuse me!

    So if a shark lived on land and if a
human lived under the sea, what a crazy world
this would be!!!

Marissa Valdivia

Aids

I hate to think that someone has got it.
If I was with him, I wouldn't spot it.
I really hope they come up with a cure,
Because I never check; just to make sure.
So, I inject with some of my friends;
Who'd ever think that, that was the end?
How can this be? I didn't know.
All those signs? they didn't show.
All these doctors and all those tests;
Who'd ever think I needed the rest.
But still I go on with all those guys,
Who'd ever think I'd be saying, "Good-bye".
So, I guess I don't really have it made,
But who'd ever think that I would get AIDS.

Sara Jo Guandalini

My Cane And I

My cane goes everywhere with me,
If I went outside and tried to climb a tree;
It might be a little awkward, but,
Believe you me, I could do it,if I had my cane with me.

One day I fell down, a funny sight to see.
Children laughed at me, a car come by a man came by
The man said, "May I help you?"
But I said, "No thank you, can't you see?" I have my cane with me.
Up I got and managed to get home
And was thankful as could be.
Because I had remembered to take my cane with me.

Rose Lang

"Secret Love"

What could end her life? Her tears, her crying
If she hadn't for her own reasons found a smile.
Each rose blooms with its petals dying.
But still finds will to open bright.
Each impression he made of charm and style
Holds to her mind as tight as it can.
Her wish would be that love would stay
Like planted memories in a clover field.
She and her lover would hide and seek
The four leaves that only luck can yield.
And at the end of each working day,
When her lover kisses her blushing cheek
Gentle as the wind, she remembers well
Their secrets she has promised to never tell.

Michelle McMillan

"Listen"

dedicated to Russell James Shaw (b.3/9/57-d.7/30/94)

People are dying and crying,
If you can find a place and listen to
the wind and the rain,
You can hear the tears, the fears, and the suffering,
Once you have heard the sounds, they
will never leave your heart or mind,
It can drive you crazy even insane,
And the sad fact is it's right outside
your front door.

Karen Shaw

Man Gone

Man gone in the blink of an eye.
If you ever have lived you surely must die.
Life from death torn apart
like the hair line crack in an old friend's heart.
A man of dignity
A man of pain
What's the difference, they're both the same.
Both are gentle
Both are hostile
but in the end both must die
and that's how man's gone in the blink of an eye.

Mindy Chaff

'The Person We've Been Missing'

I saw anger clearly. Hurting others, not aware he had succeeded.
Ignoring the fact he knew all along. I'm wondering, what does he feel
now. As I looked into his face I saw emptiness. He was afraid to let
someone close to him. He hid it well, covering a tear stained face.
Wanting to believe that he wasn't given the love he deserved.
Intimidation was high on his list, afraid that he might be loved.
Little did he know, it made us want to help and love him even more.
I looked deep into his eyes, I noticed pain. He was hurting inside,
but unable to share with anyone. He didn't want anyone to know he
had feelings. Just looking away. Hoping no one would notice.
Stealing and lying was his mask. That was his way of getting
attention whether it be positive or negative. Finally, I tried looking
into his soul. It was complicated, though I saw love, an unconditional
love. Wanting to be released from his heart, but how could he show
it? He was a tall, witty, and handsome young man, and he knew it.
He attracted many. He had wasted some of the greatest years of his life
for what, the chance of being noticed. By taking things, not only material
things, but pieces of many hearts. Where has this led him? gone!
Away, to be with his thoughts, to get to know himself. Maybe now he'll
introduce this new guy to us, and realize that I, his sister, would
like to meet him!

Jayme M. Brown

Reaching Out

I reach out my hand to you, trying to grasp yours.
I'm holding out my arm, but can't quite reach you.
I need you to help me reach you.
No matter how hard I try; without you reaching out towards
Me, I will never be able to be here for you.
Please take your arm away from your side reach it out and
Meet me halfway.
Extend your arm so that our fingers and hands my meet; and
You'll find that I was always here for you.
My heart is in my hand, to share with you, these feelings I have
Towards you I deliver to you alone.
Don't forsake my love, for it would crush my very being.
My hand is strong, awaiting for your tender, gentle touch.
Touching my hand is touching heart; that's all it would take
To bridge the gap that separates you and I.
For your love, I anxiously await.

Paul E. King

"Tomorrow"

Before tomorrow comes and minds shadows fade thin
I'll think of you in another time, back with me again.
Feeling your touch will soothe the ache I feel in my soul
Because when tomorrow comes, I know you'll have to go.

Remembering when we lived and breathed as one
All the trials and troubles had not yet undone.
Our tender moments, a love so great and true
Before tomorrow comes, give me tonight with you.

Wherever you are, have you forgotten this place
It no longer looks the same, but just in case
You never come back, I couldn't stay here and wait
Time has the key and your arrival was late.

Darling, I thought tomorrow would never come
It's hit me with a pang girl, and then some.
No longer mine, I wonder, where are you now
Can you sense my thoughts, can they find you somehow.

No, that's not possible, tonight is just dreams
There's no way around it, oh so sad it seems.
If a twinge of love hits you, may you know where it's from
For I am sending it tonight, before tomorrow comes.

Mark A. Duckwiler

Devil Will Do

In opposition to being engaged in unabandon with one's aloneness
I'm clubbing mainstream where they're packing them in, uninhibited
too many friends of his disbursing self-discipline in an over-the-
counter fashion but the papers made final upending his back of hand
rule of me a thirty-seven year old somnambulist rediscovering the
unconfined once unacquainted I've begun to try to disentangle my
ways and yes not alone, maybe he's temporary, God aren't we all?
the strong southern mamas with whom I cried my earliest tears had
philosophy I listened, took a shine, and will share when you walk
endless roads with a shadowing man thereafter even the devil himself
will do I've had the intelligence to know there's a little stagnant
water under the bridge sometimes I protrude forward inconveniently,
an inciteful little black sheep reprimanded by the human condition,
thereafter even the Devil himself will do.

Noel K. Johnson

"Mother Of All Times"

She teaches faith, with patience and stubbornness
  I'm learning one secret, versatility
I'm far from being prejudice
  but she's as perfect as a mother can be.

Thanks Mom, for sharing my laughter
  helplessly watching my pain
You offer a smile that lasts forever
  reminding of all that's left to gain.

To God and to you I owe my life
  without you Mother, I'd be lost
You've planted a seed, where the love of God will feed
  encouraging my growth, at any cost.

Hopefully now you can see
  all that's hard for me to say
I Love You dearly, Mother
  telling you my only way.

On this beautiful spring holiday
  I celebrate you, with this rhyme
It will stand through the seasons, for any occasion
  for a "Mother Of All Times".

Kris Tate

"Backstage"

I watch you from the audience-uncomfortable in my director's chair;
I'm lost in the loving gazes of your admirers and the evil critics' glares.
First your leading lady, then retired from the cast-my part I did amend
Our scenes together are finished - I wrote into the script a dramatic end.
Your eyelids are the curtains over the windows to your soul;
Your lashes draw them tightly closed as up the footlights go.
As an actor in the play life, you conceal your true character behind
  makeup and mask;
Under harsh theater lights that appear oddly warm, you falsely seem
  to bask.
Your tears well up, they swim in your eyes, but your pride won't let
them spill; on stage you keep your feelings inside; now just the
audience's needs you fill. You say your lines, fulfill your role,
perform to perfection like a screenwriter's doll; you continue
pretending to be someone you're not until the final certain falls. The
cast comes out for one last bow, and the applause is music to your
ears; but after the show, when you're secure backstage, you release
  the pain and tears.

Shelley Roy

"Song Words"

Why do I have to write these song words?
I'm not a gold pretty bird that chirps pretty song chirps
My wife said what would get the best of me
Was these dirty flirty old song words.

Why do I have to write these song words?
I'm just a old nutty herd that writes ditties with words
My wife said it would get the best of me
I'd be hurting thirty fathom worse.

For people rave on others they like
Stay on radios lis'ning to them day and night
Laugh about me, funny old nerd that can't write
So why do I still write day and night?

The thoughts keep comin' for more song words
I'm not an old brainy bird; I'm worse going on worse
My wife said what would get the best of me
And her was these silly old song words
Take me floodin' thirty from song words
Take me floodin' thirty from song words.

Sam J. Alcorn

White Trash Caring In America

"What's this trash lying at my feet?"
"I'm not trash, I'm stuck on the streets."
"Get off my steps or you will get beat."
"Can't you just give me something to eat?
I need some help, I'm down on my luck"
"Sorry man, but I don't give a f*ck"
"I don't want trouble so I'll be leaving now.
 Go back inside and shut out reality.
 I'll get back on my feet, but I don't know how.
"I will let you mire in your poverty."
"Life is forgiving and I will survive.
 The main thing for me is staying alive
 So that I might have my own time to thrive."

R. J. Giarla

Untitled

No sign on your door Monday morning said,
"I'm okay," "I'm all right."
Instead came the knock of death
That stole you away in the night
You've joined old friends and new leaving us alone
To pay attention to the lessons you taught,
Lessons of life to carry us on our own journeys home.
Make your reason for living, you said,
To be faithful to those you love
Be strong in the face of misfortune and follow only God above.
Do your best in all you attempt, no matter how small it is,
For there you'll find life's rewards...
True love and happiness.
Most important of all, remember to serve others,
For though strangers they may be,
The distance of your deeds for them
Reflects how much you've loved me.
And now we must say adios, Friend until our day comes too,
When we submit to a knock on the door
Beckoning us to follow you.

Kim Kieler

The Gradual Dawn

As gradual as the morning dawn
I'm realizing now that you are gone...
from my arms and from my heart.
Time and distance pulled us apart.

I've wished upon a billion stars
in hopes for, maybe, one more chance...
to feel the warmth of your tenderness
and to relieve one night of sweet romance.

My heart is heavy and filled with pain.
Misery is all I have known...
since you turned and walked away from me.
I face each day alone.

Time, I am told, shall heal the pain.
I watch, in sorrow, as you turn away.
You'll never realize the depth of my love.
Perhaps, you'll realize it some day.

Gravity pulls two souls apart.
Like a thief in the night you stole my heart.
I long for you now, but you are gone.
I find myself hoping through the gradual dawn.

Mia Donohue

Scared

Scared...
I'm scared I'll never have a boyfriend.
Scared I'll never get married.
Scared I won't get asked to prom.
Scared I'll loose someone I love.
Scared I'll die the first day I get my license.
Scared of being scared, scared of being me.
As you can see, I'm scared of many things.
One giant thing I'm scared of, is me.
I'm scared of what I might do if I had a boyfriend,
Scared of getting pregnant and having babies. I'm just plain scared.
Maybe my problem is, that I'm scared to be alone...
I'm scared to live my life, with no man to love me.
Scared no one will know the "real" me.
Scared to know who's behind the pupils of my eyes.
Scared she might be ugly, scared she might be mean.
Scared she might be vicious, but then again every man's dream.
Have you ever been scared, of a kitten outside your door?
Or a dog chained to the door a couple houses down?
I have, scared it might be me.

Kristin Krieg

Lonely

A gust of wind brushes up against my face; trees rustle.
I'm sitting on the ground feeling lonely,
wondering if anybody cares, if anybody sees me.

I see happy sparrows singing,
The songs are so peaceful, so warm.
The lovely sound of those beautiful birds,
the musical harmony makes me want to cry,.
I want to craw in a dark, gloomy hole
and block out the lovely sound.

I get up, stumbling, trying to find someone
or something that is lonely, but I couldn't find anything,
anybody that would satisfy me.
Leaning up against a tree I shout, "why am I the only one!"
trying to find a reason, even an answer.

My stomach is nauseated.
I'm starting to feel what it's like to be lonely.
I'm getting to the point where I want to die.
I figured out that nobody really cares,
nobody wants me, I'm ignored, disliked.
My life has ended, I shall not be lonely anymore.

Miranda McDonough

Your Son From Up Above

I'm writing to you from up above,
I'm the one you could have loved.
I could sense that the timing just wasn't right,
when you would cry each and every night.
I remember being taken from deep inside your tummy,
and before it all began you called yourself a dummy.
My God will send me back into this world again,
and I hope you'll decide to keep me then.
I am sure you are sorry for what you have done,
but there's no going back and changing things,
I would have been your son.

But no matter what people say about you and me,
you will always be my Mommy forever and entirely.
Love,
Your son from up above.

Monica Kincade

Internal Awareness

Do you know who I am?
I'm the scared person you feel inside,
The one that always runs and hides.
I'm the one who stands behind your pain,
And I too feel your guilt and shame.
I feel your stomach twist and knot,
I feel your heart beat a little faster,
I weep when you weep in your sorrow,
And I join in on your short lived laughter.

Do you know who I am?
I'm the soft voice that says,
Feel with your heart and think with your head.
I fear with you and tell you I care,
But you're not listening so you don't hear.
Give me a chance to make you feel right,
Let me love you and end your fight.
Wherever you are, no matter how far,
I will always be here,
For your love and care.
Do you know who I am?

Myreta A. Griffith

Imagine A Dream

Imagine a dream that would carry us through the sky.
Imagine a dream that would make us all fly.
Imagine a dream no violence nor bad.
Imagine a dream everything you wanted you had,
Imagine a dream that you could ride a golden unicorn,
Imagine a dream your heart's not torn.
Imagine a dream the sky would never end,
Imagine a dream that all the broken hearts would mend.
Imagine a dream no crying nor pain.
Imagine a dream all sunny never rain.
Imagine a dream that there was no hate.
Imagine a dream it doesn't matter if you're late.
  That's my dream.
  Mandi Sauder

The Visit

Standing on the moment
in a field green and cluttered
with tombstones, I think of bones
bleaching in darkness; imagine the feel
of sun visiting the cool of graves.

Dreaming in the warm
hush of afternoon, I wonder if
from some other perspective
the dead watch as I breath deep
the crowd of summer roses.

Standing in a moment green
and floral haze, I drink the colors
of the day, and see, as if for the first time,
great leafy trees reaching
for armfuls of sky;

and in that perfect meditation
of forgiveness, life and death
hold communion, become cloud
floating soft and free
in the blue of space.

  Robert Adkins

The Greatest King Of The Universe

One midnight a sacred infant, lay on a hay
In a manger, where animals eat, rest and stay
Dressed with swaddling clothes so humble and gay
Not minding the cold weather, that betray.

On a dark night, a big radiant star lighted
The serene place, where He was laid and benighted
Joseph, His foster father, was so delighted
To whom Mary and Jesus, were entrusted.

An angel appeared, to announce the birth of the Lord
So lowly, the King of all kings, came with no sword
Shepherds with their lambs, happily went and knelt
To offer their gifts, and their presence were felt.

The three wise men were guided by a bright star
Rode on big camels, and found the place so far
Merrily, they gave gifts of myrrh, frankincense and gold
To the Holy Lord, whose story is never untold.

People young and old, celebrate the birth of Jesus.
Even in some nations, whose situations are perilous.
They send Christmas greetings and gifts, to friends and relatives.
They attend Christmas masses, and never fear, the fugitives.

  Sabina R. Rico

A Field Of Loveflowers

I want to rest for a while in a field of loveflowers
In a sleepy valley, soft and hushed
By the whisper of fragrant rainshowers.
I want to forget about being rushed
And laze slowly for a while in a field of loveflowers.

Too many hurried days have slowed my smile,
And I long for a sweet dream's healing powers.
I need to slumber for just a little while
In a warm breeze in a field of loveflowers.
  Keith Pearcey

Hurry

  "Hurry up!" exclaimed the tied-down man.

  "Ah, but my good fellow, you mustn't let life pass you by
in a whirling frenzy; take the world for what it is, not
what we make it out to be, for at least that's what is said to me.

  When you realize the reasonings of life's trivial
seasonings, mold it and hold it deep in your mind,
guard it sir, never let it unwind.
Only then will the chrysanthemums be able to be
sniffed, peacefully, with each perfumed petal being
separately whiffed."
preached the patient poet.
  Kelly Jo Boesch

The Battle Is The Lord's

The battle is the Lord's from day to day;
In every path of thine He leads the way.
And, though sometimes your heart is filled with pain,
Each battle won will not be fought again.

And, though sometimes the clouds obscure the sun,
God will give victory are the day is done;
For He is there beside you in the fight,
And He'll protect you with His power and might.

No matter what the battle, it's the Lord's;
His word goes forth a sharp- two-edged sword.
His power and might none can withstand— they fall
As on His holy name is prayer we call.

The battle is the Lord's, so do not fear;
Victory will be yours for God is near;
And in His love He'll brush the clouds away,
For the battle is the Lord's again today.
  Margaret J. Allison

Sleeping...

  Seeing myself lying on a white bed.
In front of my house.
  My mom dressed in white, at the foot of
The bed reading a book.
  I stood there watching myself for a couple
Of minutes.
  Observing what was in sight. Every
Thing so perfectly put together:
  The green grass looking so nice and soft.
No clouds in sight the sun shining beautifully
On my sleeping body as well as on my mother.
  Waking up in the hospital all in white.
  My mom sitting by me reading the bible,
Praying, realizing this was a sign of a
Near death experience.

  Rosa Mendoza

Beyond

I sit beneath the spreading tree and view the mountain I must climb
In front, the purple hazy cliffs with snow capped peaks not far behind.

Before I reach its nestled base there is a valley to be crossed, with
waters glistening in the sun like some fine jewelry, gold embossed

And as I sit, I contemplate how far I've come to reach this place
I can't look back, nor turn around for out there is a life to face

The ground I've covered is my past its knowledge lies within me still
My futures open to the point where I will reach the first small hill.

So then beyond, what lies in wait perhaps more valleys far below
Or mountains much too high to climb, I shan't find out until I go.

Excitement fills my very soul as I stand up and take a step; for now
unfolds the world to me and all the secrets it has kept

Ronald J. Krueger

Books

Thousands of words are told today,
  in many a manner in many a way.

Materials are pulpous, and dyed,
  measured and cut.

Entertaining challenging and charmed,
  no need for alarm.

Full of life, controversy and cause,
  with just the right tense and just the right pause.

To learn, to ponder, to fathom, to know,
  without it, our minds will never grow.

Rebekah S. Luther

"Gifts Of The Heart"

Happy birthday dear Daddy and though you're not here -
in my heart and my mind you will always be near.
The gifts on this birthday we hoped we'd be giving:
cash, checks, money orders...gifts of the living.
There were cards and cash and color T.V.'s
while you were with us we've given you these.
But those were the gifts, the gifts of the past
and those were the gifts that would not last.
Money gets spent, T.V.'s fall apart...
the things we can give are gifts of the heart.
To my surprise, it's been you doing the giving
of things we can grow with lessons of living.
Gifts of hope and truth, new purpose through sorrow
from despair, grief and sadness comes hope in tomorrow.
By accepting your gifts of guidance through pain
assures that your passing will not be in vain.
These gifts that you now have the power of giving
were not yours to give us while you were living.
Only with death can each new life start
these are our gifts - our gifts of the heart.

Maureen Barrett

His Death

He's falling, falling out of the sky
Into his pit of misery to die
No one will help him, let's let him die
As he lies helpless, he cannot fly
Dying and rotting and suffering his grief
Leave me, leave me as he screams from the sky
As he's lifted up slowly looking around
Seeing the people who left him in the ground
Putting a curse on all in the land
Saying what's done is done to live and then die

Leslie Cairns

Nixon

They came,
In solemn tribute and praise
For the one who lay in repose.

They came,
As our country's flag covered him now—
Friends and family, even old foes.

They came,
Stood in pouring rain to pay honor to the fallen,
To heal the longstanding pain.

They came, some spoke
Of love and honor, strength, courage and skill,
Of generosity, of suffering, of iron will.

They came,
And in his death and final scene
An act of healing, words of praise.

They said,
Judge not a man on one event alone,
The whole of life's actions must be known.

Sharon Turley

"Spiritual Victory"

Victory - sweet word that whispers liberty
In some far off distant place;
And as we look with longing to that "Victory Ahead"
Not perceiving the battles won right now, by
God's grace and because his blood was shed.

For victory is here and now
Victory is refusing to bow
To jealousies fires and fleshly desires.
Victory will always be
Deep within the heart of me;
As long as Christ resides in all
Not just part of me.

Karol PoPoff

Dancing Angel

I was gazing into Heaven
in the darkness, of the sky...
When softly, out from the Silence...
an Angel, Whispered by...

Gliding on feathered - brushstrokes of Light..
Dancing on Beams, of Love...
How beautiful Her Ballet in the Silence..
As She danced in the Sky, above...

A faint, and gentle echo
drifted across a Breeze.
I could perhaps, have been mistaken,
but it sounded like, a sneeze...

With Her Angelical voice, She started singing.
Her melody created, a beautiful tune...
To my surprise, She Stopped...
and tenderly Kissed, the Moon...

Oh, what a lovely Vision,
with all, Her Poise, and Grace...
She didn't seem, to miss a step,
as She Waltzed, on the floor, in space...

Michael L. Speers

Angel Unaware

Every now and then... my heart beats like the wind...
In the light of day... will you light my way...
And give this heart a chance...

At night I hear the thunder...
As I begin to wonder...
Why the days last pain... brings a night of rain...

In the light of day... have I lost my way...
Did you touch me today... did I turn away...
Am I just a fool... with no thought of you...
But the pain of the...day...brings a... night of rain....
It's not that I don't care...my heart is unaware...
Am I just a fool...without the love of you...

In dreams and times of sorrow...
Will you look for tomorrow...
And of the days new light... a love shining bright...
The angels rise again...
To challenge the darkest wind...
For an angel does care...
For a heart unaware...
And this they will defend...

Roni Marlene Hummel

The Wind

Slowly, yet constantly, the wind leads me to you,
In the mysterious ways of nature, she knows what I should do.

She stayed with me continually, from old loves to new,
Knowing I would wander until I found you.

Too many loves have come only to end untrue.
This is why I'm afraid to love you.

The night the wind brought me into your land,
In fear, unthinking, I reached for your hand.

The gentle strength you showed, left an image in my mind,
Your love is the one I've been searching to find.

If my moving friend calls to me in the early hours of day,
Take my hand, hold me close, don't ever let me stray.

The restless wind is only asking, testing your love for me.
Her watchful task is only done when your arms reach out to set me free.

Lera Sheppeard

Emancipation

The bird that came, alighting on the bough,
In the quick instant of the lifted eye,
Was a blue, spearing accent on the now,
Wherein time past and time to come could die.
There was no memory of another bird,
Nor any other summer she has flown:
Here was the virginal, swift spoken word
For the one summer that the heart had known...
So the heart knew again the first green wood,
Knowing no season gone and none to be,
Saw the bright hour and knew that it was good,
He first bird shining on the deathless tree,
And stood again, so long ago it stood,
An innocent heart, and happy, being free.

Margaret Muller

A Child's Night

Trees made of whispers hiss in the night;
Leaves that are Shadows ____ The kiss of Fright.
Rain from the Heavens, Winds and Light
Tears of Laughter, Kiss of White.
Peace of Heaven, Love and Night;
Tears of laughter ... a kiss Good night.

Melinda Qwenette Hernandez

A Sense Of Presence

I see the presence of our Savior
  in the rainbow stretched across the sky
I see Him in the wondrous beauty
  upon the wings of butterfly

I smell the sweetness of our Savior
  in the fragrant blossoms of the flowers
And I smell His scent in the gentle rain
  as it falls softly from springtime showers

I taste the presence of our Savior
  in sparkling waters clear and divine
I taste Him in the sweet, wild blackberries
  that flourish in the afternoon sunshine

I hear the precious voice of our Savior
  in the songs the birds sing so cheerfully
And I hear Him whispering through the trees
  with soft breezes that caress tenderly

I feel the presence of our Savior
  in the warmth of sunshine from above
I feel His embrace in all of nature
  surrounding me in everlasting love

Laurene Garnett

Trapped

The sheet hanging on the line dries
in the sun. The wind is strong.
The sheet constantly moves
up and down, back and forth.

The baby robin just learned how to fly.
Carefully the robin jumps off the ground
soaring through the air exploring
the sun, clouds, trees, and branches.

Children jump rope, or play "3 Ninjas."
Hopscotch and kick ball occupy their time.
Adults sit around on the porch drinking
tea and watching only their children.

They do not see the robin's accomplishment.
They do not hear the song chirped in flight.
They're blind to the song turning into squawks
as the robin flies into the bed sheet.

Caught in the sheet, the robin can't spread
his wings for flight. The sheet has him
like a spider who's sprung his trap.
The sheet tightens, closes, and captures.

Kat Smith

The Prisoner

A prisoner is a man contained
In walls not of his making
With his journey toward his goals detained
And a grief he is not faking

A prisoner lives behind bars of steel
And rings of gold on fingers found
His struggling emotions and the pain he feels
Push him towards the hell he's bound

But a prisoner may break free someday
From the boundaries closing in
And come out, living, from the fray
Of his struggling soul within

Lindsey M. Wilborn

An Annual Affair

Nature holds autumnal sacrifice once more; again
   inclines her head,
    reiterates the sigh with royal mace.

Unwilling fields and hills obey; acknowledge the decree
   with somber face
    in place of one of variegated hue.

Shriveled leaves, like old men testing fragile limbs
   in madcap waltz,
    whirl a jaunty jig before the wind;
    with asthmatic dialogue and hollow rattle
    defy one final shower in ritual battle,
    then race one by two by ten
      to annual waste.

Flowers too. On trembling legs they shiver, turn pale
   from fitful breath of arctic gale,
    then wither.

All at last lie quiet to greet the gentle night;
   forget the glories past to sleep
    beneath the frost, silent, still,
      a world away, and lost.
   William Howard Thomas

Wishing Well

Pave with truth polarize in beats.
Inducting notes to retainers version,
by youth this day.

Defining rap, polite not be, tunes
awaiting the new.
Diversifying launching to insistence
upon who?

Vibrating excitement, worshiping copper
Gaining in weight. Tuning rap for old and new,
eat you must youth today.
As, visions in date moves versions
of truth further back.
   Sandra Cruz

Prelude

The hammer has fallen from its place on the shelf
Injuring body, but more so, my innermost self.
Producing remarks reflectant of pain
Reducing all aspects of hope to maintain.
My much needed strength has been taken, again.

Now what do I do? To where do I turn?
The picture is clouded by lessons unlearned.
Discouraged, deluded, discounted, demeaned
To unleash my anger would be dangerous indeed.
But the hammer has fallen in a crevice of need.

Where are the pianos, the flutes, the music of heart?
Could it be that they, too, were doomed from the start?
My mind tells me more than true disbelief
But where is the full orchestra? And why does it sleep?
Life surely holds more than this sense of defeat.

From where will come courage? The great challenge of all.
Should I look toward the sun, or watch the stars fall?
Or will it be winter with its blanket of snow
Providing the warmth and reflections aglow,
Preparing a path for resolve? Only God knows.
   Louise M. Kress

Jack-O-Lanterns

Jack-o-lanterns with sculpted smiles,
   insensible
empty shells, lit with a light not yours,
   always with inane grins,
    fleshy rinds enclosing nothing.

We look back at you with empty grins,
   mindless
numb within, lit by traditions handed down
   by vain ambitions, not ours not us.

   Masks of flesh
contorted into plastic smiles
   taught to hide the wounds
    to deny what is,
our expressions carved by the expected.

   Masks, Masks
jack-o-lantern masks hollowed out
lit by a light not ours not us.
   Larry Bogart

Alternative

All turn
instrumental to the longing
of Spring - new beginnings.

All turn native - instinct is survival,
the bright petal could be poison
the bright petal could heal.
The flower with the bold shade
(or the loud voice) demanding its share,
stepped on over and over and over again,
   why shouldn't it grow thorns?
Sometimes, sometimes, you have to
   scream out in rage outrageously.

Isn't it only natural to want the sunshine,
to want some small ray of
   glory, hope, save-me-myself-salvation?
Isn't it only natural?

All turn at once accepting?

It's not an alternative.
   Marian S. Musmecci

Icecarver

Leisurely caressing the manly figure with her left hand.
Intentionally trying to melt his muscular figure away.
She was a lion bathing her own cub.
She momentarily took her hand away
   to absorb the coldness of his present figure.
Often wondering, what it would be like
   to have him come to life and to have him touch her
   the way no man could.
But this and only this would happen to one
   who has the qualities of a God his Goddess.
Awakening from her majesty dream to go on with her project.
She tried to lift her right hand
   and found that she couldn't.
Without having a doubt
   she knew the impossible was happening to her.
What felt like an eternity was only a few minutes.
There in the middle of a small, fenced-in yard
   were two figures wound around one another.
   Kelly Heilemann

Secret Places

Where is our secret place? The place where you and I share our
intimacies. Whether they be through a thought or just simply in
the way we look into other's eyes. Where is our secret place?
The place where you and I can enjoy one another in the presence
no other. To converse and allow every feeling and every emotion
to be set free. Where is the place where every dream that we
could possibly ever have comes true? Let us share an intimate
thought-A whisper that we blow into each other's ears. As
gentle as the breeze from a serene ocean which echoes in the
deepest depths of our hearts. Let a continuous song forever hum
there-A melodic tune that they just know without ever having
heard it before. And, oh, how congruous they are on every part
of this mysterious song for they know each other's beats. Ah,
I see now that the secret place lies within our hearts. And I
shall hide you there and keep you warm and protect you and hold
you tightly-so tightly that eventually your very essence melts
into mine. And you become an intricate part of me. Converse
with my heart, speaking in mind and in spirit, for it is the
center of all my true feelings. Come and hide away in our
secret place for there you and I shall live together forever.

Marquiesa Marrero

A Cry for Help By: Mary Pearson

People hate each other and the rainforest
is dying, step back and look at the world
And you'll see that it is crying.
The pollution in the water,
The garbage in the sea
Look at this world, is it how you want it to be?
The guns and the murders,
the acid in the rain,
Look at the world, don't you feel ashamed?
The children are sick the hunger
The song that fills the sky, if
We do not help our earth than we will watch it die.

Mary Pearson

Be Happy As We Grow!

　 How am I to spend each day, knowing that a big part of me
is going away?
　 I know this is all I can give, a granted wish, for you,
That you wish to live.
　 You will never know how hard I cry, from this pain inside,
The tears you see are only half of what I try to hide.
　 I must set you free, and only hope my love for you is
Something that you truly believe.
　 My love for you is my only strength that carries me into
Another day, and my dreams for you allow me to silently watch
　 As you choose to live another way.
Just hold on tight to all that we have shared,
　 And always remember your happiness is why
I have so deeply cared.
　 Don't forget; You are "My little man" and my best friend,
And those things will never end!
　 Be happy as we grow, and a happier life we will learn to know.
My precious "son", you will always "light up my life".
I love you my "Little man,"
Love Always, Your Friend Through Life, Mom!

Kimberly RoJann Mellinger

Thunder And Lighting

Shine your light upon us Lord. I want to see your
lighting. May the voice of God be heard by
the noise of thunder. May people everywhere
be brave. And don't be afraid.
For God loves us all. Keeps us safe.

Rhonda McCafferty

Loneliness

　 In the distance a bird sings its plaintive song
Is it because a passing cloud has dim'd the sun
　 Or because its mate is foraging and is gone too long?
Life without a loved one is dismal indeed
　 When you call out and no one answers
How do you cope in your hour of need?
　 After all is said and done
It's a bitter empty life to live
　 So to-morrow, rise at break of sun
Find someone who will share the love
　 You so long to give.

Robert MacColl

Untitled

What's the blue book value on the lives of our young
Is it the toke of a pipe or the smoke from a gun
Just look in their eyes so empty and cold
They've been lost in the shadow and stripped of their souls
Daddy's so busy and mommy's a mess
Here take some money, go play (you're a pest)
No wonder they're scared and feel so alone
They can't find their guidance, their paths are not shown
So they smoke their cocaine and trip LSD
They look to be happy and just want to be free
Let's give'em a chance and make a new start
Let's take down a liquor store then build a new park
We spend our money on roads and tax for defense
We put up more jails and the problem's worse since
We point self-righteous fingers, whose fault is it now
Enough with the blaming let's start asking how
Should we pay more to teachers or build better schools
We've done plenty of talking let's pick up the tools
Their minds are like clay but we're stuck in the mud
So let's pool own resources, give their freedom a nudge

S. C. Richter

The Power Of Love

　　 I was born in a raindrop.

　　 The first thing I saw with my heart
　　　 is my family and life.

　　　 My Mother's the sunset.
　　 My Father is the cloud of the sky.
　　　 I am the keeper of love.

　　 I hold the changes of my family.
　 Before now, I never wrote what my family is.

　　 I protect the power of my
　　 relatives and life to be going on.

My family is a special locket, I will keep forever.
　　 My family is loved by me,
　　 the most beautiful star in the world.

　 If I were to lose my locket in a river,
　 ocean, or any other deep watered thing,
the power of my love would be sent to the wind,
　　 and it would pick it up for me.

God is giving me other tomorrow days of my life.
He would like us to walk in the path of truth,
　　　 friendship and love.

Natalie Martin

The Moon

　 The moon is like a crystal ball
　 Its magic lights up the earth for all
From Monday to Sunday, it shines so bright
　 With a magical glow of pure white light.

Sarah Starkey

What Do You Hide?

Why does someone try to commit suicide?
Is there a reason hidden from my eyes?
To take your own life seems like the coward's way out
Never will I understand this permanent escape route

I know friends who have ended their lives so violently
Is it right to accept this silently?
One by one they follow each other
I can't bear to part with another

I don't know what life you live,
but to you my love I give
For I know you need it more than I
Because I am one of the few that does not want to die

I don't think people realize that death is forever
Return to this earth, you will never
God gives you a gift, only one
With it comes suffering, sadness, and fun

If not me, listen to someone who has tried and failed
I am sure that they tell a similar tale
Please, ask for help before it's too late
Honestly, do you want to know your own death date?

Kelly A. Bonner

Hear The Children

When you look in the mirror, what do you see?
Is there love inside you? If so set it free.
Give it to those, who need warmth from your light.
And comfort those children, who are frightened by the night.

Children are crying, and it just isn't fair.
Children are dying, doesn't anyone care?

This world isn't ours, no we're just passing through.
We must have faith, do what God wants us to.
Love one another and hold on real tight.
Take care of our children, don't give up the fight.

Children are crying, doesn't anyone hear?
Our children are dying, and living in fear!

Let us pray for those, who will never be whole.
Let us live for our Lord, and save every soul.
It's the time of the end, so you better prepare.
For when Jesus comes, don't you want to be there?

Children are saying, Oh Lord comfort me,
Children are praying, dear Lord, set us free!

Terry Strelecki

Christmas Angels

There's a time of the year, when the chalice of cheer
Is tipped from heaven to the earth
And the saints they sing, for what the morning will bring,
Whilst the Angels dance to his birth

In the light of that day, the Christmas angel plays
his innocent, a thing to behold
And as the sunshine beams, he touches child's dreams
warming their hearts against the cold

For when the children know, their lives begin to grow
And the magic of the Christmas Angel comes to bear
Moving tender souls by guiding spiritual goals
In every home, every place, everywhere

To every girl and boy, he speaks of eternal joy
Love is his message spoken clear
And the glow of the day, should light the way
For the children of the Lord-all the year

Rusty Sickler

Untitled

To live your life like a shadow in a room of no light
is to know that you may exist but are not within sight.
Some people will not venture into the darkness that's here,
they will stay within the light and hide in their fear.
Yet there are others that will search for, look and try to find
the person that is not clearly seen, or the life that is not
    truly defined.
But who could ever try to state, judge, or tell what could be,
when the shadow in a room of no light you may never see.

Timothy C. Doyle

Fear

The still and silence
Is torn with violence
A loud breaking sound in the night is made.
Hear it grow, hear it fade
The sounds you're hearing
The sounds you're fearing
Times are far between and few I bet
When we can look upon our lives without regret
If you intend to live again
Then open your eyes and don't pretend.

Nikki Vivian

Ralph's Rhyme

"I thank you, God, for one more day,"
Is what we old retirees say.
A day to work, a day to play,
A day to perk my feet of clay.

A day to love, to banish hate,
A time to shove into the grate
An ancient wrong that made him foe
That happened long, long time ago.

It has been said; I think it's true,
Just where I read, I have no clue: (do you?)
"A man may have a thousand friends,
And have not one to spare,
But if he has one enemy, he'll meet him everywhere."

"I thank you, God, for one more day,"
Is what we old retirees say.

Ralph Newton

Peace

The world reaches out to me
It beckons me to follow it.
There must be reason why it does
Would it be that I am more like it?

Could it mean I must mend my ways
And not let the world tell me what to do?
Have I forgotten what the Good Book says
That I should not conform to the world?

Just how do you live in the world under God's plan
When every thing seems contrary to his way?
What is it that passes all understanding and gives hope?
It is the Peace of God.

Marguerite Klein

A Rose

A rose lives a life of beauty
It blossoms with time
Growing prettier and livelier as time passes
Until one day it is picked
And given to someone with love
This representation of love is so beautiful
As long as there's a bond between these two people
The rose will live take out space and grow strong
But when the day comes
That this love will end
The rose will wither and die
Turn black with the tears
Its petals with fall
As fast
As the pieces to one's broken heart
Kelly Fischer

In Life's Path

The path of life is long
It flows like the waves of the sea,
and its destiny is unknown.
The sweet singing of a bird, the light cool
    breeze in winter;
The quiet flow of a brook, with its crystal
    clear water;
The dark mountains around, and the green grass below;
The company of kind generous people.
Is all part of life which each one of us are made of.
The good and the bad, the happy and the sad,
are the times that test one's faith.
For faith is seeing beyond the unseen,
and its rewards are truly blessed.
We pass all through this but once
And any good that could be done be not put away.
For we are travellers on the road of life
And we never pass this way again.
Manoja Pasala

The Other Song

I sit in my room

Inside my head I hear a melody filled with haunting sadness

which floats out over the silent air.

But nobody will ever hear this song

Nobody else but me because I can't get it out.
It flows to every part of me except my mouth
I pound my head with frustration
My song is trapped, unable to find expression
All I can do is sit and hear it with the ears of my soul.
Sharon Okubo

Aids

A little word but a big disease.
It has struck thousands at ease.
We can stop it if we take a stand,
We will make people understand the dangers at hand.

It struck one by the name of magic.
It struck us as very tragic.
Yet we sit and cry and ask the Lord on high,
Why? Why? Why?

A little word but a big disease.
It has struck thousands at ease.
We WILL stop it if we take a stand.
We WILL make people understand the dangers at hand.
Rachel Reiber

Shadows

The sky is leaden, dark and grey,
It is a most foreboding day.
The green of leaves turned black it seems
And shadows huddle thick as thieves.

Until at last the sun breaks through
And all the forest appears made new.
Where shadows crouched like moonless night
Now are emeralds limned with light.

When sunlight gleams the shadows flee.
It works the same with you and me.
When hearts are dark the shadows rise,
Wave arms of fear before our eyes.

When spirit shines then hearts glow bright
Reflecting pure celestial light.
When light shines bright all shadows fall-
Were never really there at all.
Laurie Elaine Tuttle

Revolver

Your revolver has six chambers, a loaded spring;
It is an automatic, steel machine.
It is as though you think this world in terms
Of black and white when it is color;
Or in terms of hate and war when it is love;
Or in terms of fame when it is run-of-the-mill;
Or of riches and fate when we are poor but have faith.
Five chambers are loaded; one you leave empty.
Inside of a dead-end rut your mind is rusty, cluttered.
Desirous to win, afraid to lose, you fail to begin, unable to choose
Between the dregs of this world and God's truth.
The cold, steel cylinder spins to unresolved questions...

I notice as I hazard a glance,
You chose to become a victim of circumstances.
You couldn't make life real;
You could think but you couldn't feel.
Your mind has a case against your heart.
So you'll pull the trigger and from life's decisions you will part.
Ah, but no! You have changed your mind!
For now you have aimed this machine at me.
Mike Bonic

Life Impressions

LIFE is meant to be shared,
It is best, when with the one for which you've cared.
No one knows with whom they'll be paired,
Or until too late, that they have erred.

It may be here, or it may be there,
You may find LIFE'S special someone, almost anywhere!

On occasion, you meet that Special One,
That turns your LIFE into so much fun.
If you're lucky, it is true,
You could be happy your lifetime through!

This One that chooses to come so near,
Can also fill your LIFE with a certain fear,
But if they have been sent from above,
You may learn, the real Meaning of Love.

Hope springs - Eternal,
From love's sweet kernel.
LIFE is a gamble, and that's for sure,
While sharing a Love, will always be the wage and the lure.
William T. Parke, Jr.

"Let There Be Peace On Earth"

A new world war has begun
It knows nothing of the difference of tongue
It fights all humanity, everyone, every family
Let us join hands until we have won
the new war has begun
The war within, immune to medicine
Feeding even on our tears
A nightmare bigger than our fears
Found curdling the blood in microscopic seed
On our newborn it feeds
It kills the most hospitable host
Its name in the papers abroad to boast
Let there be peace on earth
A new war has begun

Sheryl Minter

Spring

And now we come to wondrous spring.
It makes you think of lots of things.
Of birds and bees and flowers and trees,
And silent barks that sail the seas.

What does it mean to you and me?
Brings out the things we might not see.
A swelling bud, a new found love,
A pretty egg, a baby dove.

A Robin's nest, a brand new home,
It is no good to be alone.
A cedar chest and wedding bells,
Spring's warm winds now good life foretells.

It means to us the end of school,
But not the end of the golden rule.
For in each life as in each game
The rules are very much the same.

You must play fair. You must play square
If you intend happiness to snare.
The rules aren't easy to follow through.
Fact is dear friend, it's up to you.

Lambert T. Jones

Ten Years Later

The two stones I am holding I brought back from Ireland.

One from Roslaire Harbor is smooth flat, rosy brown.
It reminds me of many things.
The hotel we stayed at where the power was off for two days!
My husband locking the keys in our rented car with the motor running
and the boy who rescued us.
Ships landing, bringing visitors from England and France.
The lovely cottages along the coast with their front-yard gardens.

The other stone, from Roscommon Country,
Is lighter in color, mottled, rough.
No harbors here.
People raise sheep, some vegetables on the rocky ground.
This stone raises questions.
Who were my Father's, Father's parents?
What were they like? How long did they live?
And, for instance,
Did my Great-grandmother ever step on this particular stone?
Did she pick it up and turn it over in her hand?
Or did she pass by it on her way to someplace? Dublin, perhaps?

Louise Timmons

Shadows Of The Dark

The shadows of the dark encompass me.
It seems they know,
There are no shields here to protect my soul.
I am a prisoner of this dreaded place.
"I do you no harm, why must you follow me?
Have you the key that sets me free?"

The shadows of the dark encompass me.
They play a thousand pictures in my mind.
"Begone ye liars, have you no truth in thee?
What know you of the desperation that consumes my heart?
Have you the key that sets me free?"

The shadows of the dark encompass me.

Patricia Hernandez

As The Sand Continues To Fall

Like a stealthy thief cloaked by the shadows of the night,
It sneaked up upon her and pilfered away pieces of her life,
With each and every piece the clock continued to tick,
As more of her was captured and claimed by it.

First her strength it stripped away,
She grew weaker with each fleeting day.
Then came the suffering and excruciating pain.
All hope slowly began to wane.

The once radiant light behind her eyes grew dim,
For she knew who was to be its next victim...
There was no way for her to escape her inevitable fate,
All she could do was watch, and wait.

It crept up upon her for its final phase,
With one swift strike it ended her days.
Yet another innocent child snatched away by it,
As the sand continues to fall through the hourglass bit, by bit...

Tara L. Dowdell

"Shame"

I live with shame, this shame in my heart,
It starts with a tear, the tear which I start.
And it goes to a laughter and then to a cry.
As I keep on crying I just don't know why.
Then why do I live with this shame in my heart.
Is it just the beginning of my fears and faults,
or the dusty path I walked on until now,
I've got to overcome this shame somehow,
for I wish to do better,
That's my life to be,
For to overcome the fear
of the shame in me,
So I'll hold up my head and follow my heart,
To overcome this shame
This shame in my heart.

Kelly Brown

The Sea

The sea is endless, its waters has no bounds
It stretches beyond the horizon
To mark the beginning sky
The sea is everywhere - of fish it abounds
Its secrets on the bottom reveals in dead silence
What history has befallen by the living and the dead
What lies for us as the years unfold
Only time will tell what is to be told
It can be life giving and friendly
But for many it can also be deadly
Its energy we try to curtail
But often it is to no avail
The solid ground is left behind
For places and things yet to discover
The sea, the sea, the mighty sea

Sam Coller

Change

Change
It takes time
"Too much," some would say
"Too long," some would yell
"Why wait," some would ask
Leads to action
"No violence," some would preach
"We've no choice," some would scream
"It's the only way," some would believe
But they're wrong
"Leads to death," many would protest
"Nothing but suffering," many would face
"Just a longer wait," many would grieve
However, there's peace
"The open hand to the closed fist," all would proclaim
"Use love as our weapon," all would declare
"United as brothers," all would stand
And change comes for all

Robert P. Paterno

Tree

I talked to a tree today what it said I can not to say
It talked in groans and moans and a sigh
I must admit I knew not why
I put my ear to the ground to see if the root would make a sound
But all I got I fear was a clot of dirt in my ear
I climbed up to the highest limb
A task considering I am not slim
At this height I could view
The tree could see a mile a few
Climbing down I had decide maybe I needed to listen inside
So I got my ax and I got my saw
I used the blades mighty maw
With a thunderous bang my friend fell
I knew now my friend would tell
I put my ear to the stump man this guy was being a grump
My ear tuck in some sap
This was being one mean old chap

I talked to a tree today what it said I can not say
I know not if it were a he or she
All I know i it knew more than me

Kenn Burkhart

The Train

A train is like a helping hand.
It travels far and wide.
Up hill, down hill, across the country side.
It takes you where you want to go
Through rain, through wind, through snow.
It carries people, it carries freight,
Into every state.
Its tracks are curved, its tracks are straight.
I think the ride is great.
It's slow, it's fast, it's beauty unsurpassed.
Majestic mountains, rivers,and sea.
It's certain, that's where I long to be,
Riding the train with a happy glow.
Through the towns, villages and states I'll go.

William Dick

Untitled

In another time and place a
little man bounced up and down on a bed -
his wicked mind ticking away.
He reached for and grabbed the black
bottle from the nightstand and took
another sip of evil for which the world would pay.

Tivon Luker

Beyond The Limits

Before I met you love was something I only dreamed of
It was a feeling I had no concept of until you came
Along and took me beyond the boundaries of reality, to
A place where love and fantasy only exist, a place where
Real and unreal are never clearly defined
Beyond the limits where love is true and hearts
Willingly open to up to one another regardless of the mind
A place where the mind is lost within the heart and
Love is the only knowledge known
Beyond the limits is where you've taken me to a place
That's perfect in every way, where the soul, mind and
Heart all become one
Beyond the limits is where we've gone
A place I used to only dream of until you came along

Telesha D. Pharr

"The Hidden Image In The Eyes Of Terror"

In the eyes of terror there lived an image
It was a small child pretending to hide
In the dark corners of life

I met with Terror today
It invited me to its home and welcomed me to its eyes
I projected the image of that child inside
I looked upon the child's face
Its eyes reflecting mine
Visual absorbent of sorrow

The children pleaded for help
Not able to understand
Full of grief I stood
I reached down
To hold the child upon my arms
And healed its pain with my tears

Such tremendous field of comfort
Surrounded out entire bodies
Trapping me in the eyes of Terror!
But no longer do I fear its presence
Because never will I find such splendid tremor.

Karen C. Lee

"Panama"

I saw you among many,
It was love at first sight,
A coat so furry -
black, beige, gray and white.
So aloof, unaware, of anyone's presence,
Sniffing, tail wagging, short legs very steady.
Eyes so wide, pupils so large, dark,
inquisitive, of what lurked outside.

Without you around, this part of my life -
Would have been empty, a little scary,
with a lot more strife.

So to you Panama, with all your annoyances -
barking, whining, demanding and spoil,
You are a dog among many...
And in my heart Panama,
You are strictly a winner.

Shirley J. Rowe

The Dream

I awoke from my dream and found it was true,
It was so weird I'm telling it to you.
Monsters, awesome and green,
Bulging eyes, drooling mouths,
It made them look mean.

We ran through the woods, its end not in sight.
I knew if they caught me my butt they would bite!
Trees! Roots! Bushes with thorns!
I turned to look back, my monster had horns!

Beep, beep! squeaked his horns, he screeched to a stop.
The signal was red, it now said, DON'T WALK!
"Wait! Stop! Don't leave me here!
I'm really quite nice! You've nothing to fear!

"What do you want? You're chasing me! Why?"
"I just wanted to tell you - ZIP UP YOUR FLY!"

Seth E. Johnson

Yesterday

My son was born yesterday,
It was the 8th day of May.
A sweet little boy with brown hair,
Yesterday I gave him his first teddy bear.
He took his first step yesterday,
Only 10 months old, what can I say.
Yesterday was his first day at school,
He was all smiles and excited, how cool.
Yesterday he got his first bike, my what a sight,
He balanced himself and peddled with all his might.
My son has a steady girlfriend as of yesterday
He met her in high school play.
Yesterday was the day he got his first car,
I said "have fun, but don't go to far".
Yesterday he had a birthday he turned 21,
all those years and all that fun.
He was 28 years old yesterday,
Where's that little boy who played in the hay?
My son Karl was born yesterday,
Mothers Day, the 8th day of May.

Sharon L. Davis

Time

Time is an essence that passes too quickly
It wears away mountains and kings.
Time is a moment, a day that's gone by
It brings to one memories of many things.
Time is a laugh, a fear and a joy
It takes control quickly, then passes by.
Time is a baby that grows to a boy
It gives him his life and then lets him die.

"Time Is Courage"
Time is a worry that plays on your mind
It has no cure and none can be found.
Time is a pain that grows deeper each day
It gives no direction, no course to lay,
Time is a hope, a smile and a kiss
It gives satisfaction for free
Time is a love that opens the eyes
It allows true feelings to be.
"Oh time...please teach me well"

Kevin Lee Harris

If I Could Give The World A Gift...

If I could give the world a gift
It would be to give Mother Earth a lift.

I'd heal the sick give to the poor,
All the diseases I would cure.

People would have a place to eat.
A home to cherish and shoes on their feet.

There wouldn't be any hate,
no wars, no killing-
Not anything like those debates.

People would have proper care.
Everyone would learn to give and share.

I would give a great big band-aid
to heal the wounds people have made.

A giant vacuum would be made
to suck up the polluted air,
and give our world a bit more shade.

Not only would this earth be a pleasure,
our lives would be a wonderful treasure.

Meghan Novy

Love At First Sight

I remember the day when we first met,
It's a day I'll never forget.
When I first saw your wonderful face,
I thought "WOW," and my heart beat at a new pace.
We sat at the table just to talk,
Oh how I wish we had went for a walk.
My heart was beating so very fast,
I hoped that this moment would always last.
You looked at me with a sparkle in your eye,
And I began to feel very shy,
Our eyes met and my heart began to melt,
I don't believe the warmth that I felt.
Then it happened, and deep inside I knew,
That without trying, I was falling in love with you.
And if I never have you again in my sight,
I know that I had a chance at "LOVE AT FIRST SIGHT"

Sharon Taylor

Love Them And Leave Them

Love them and leave them;
It's all that she's known.
The girl has never once
been out on her own.
She knows how to use them.
She'll forever abuse them.
They try not to let it show,
but, believe me I know.
They'll hide how they feel,
because they thought her love was real.
She's not capable of it.
So they shall rise above it.
And here's how she treats him -
She loves him then leaves him.

Laura Beth Inman

Life

Life has its ups and downs,
It's full of cheers and tears,
You think you've found a grip
Then you stumble, fall and slip,
You're down and on your face it seems to be your normal place
You just want to die 'cause then you'd never have to cry,
But that would be to easy so you live in hurt and pain,
You feel empty, lonely and drained,
Why is there life at all, You never asked to be born,
Life leaves you used, kicked and worn,
Why is life so long, Why is life so short,
So you're left so puzzled and confused,
You don't know what to do,
You search, look and seek,
But you never find a handle,
so if you ever figure it out,
Would you please tell me what it's all about,
You would truly be a friend of mine,
And that would be for life,
That's if I knew what it was...

Thomas E. Stewart

Whispers In The Wind

As the last rays of sun reach out to retain
Its grasp on the world below, the first
Signs of an advancing dusk appear. The sun
Concedes defeat and no longer shines with
The brilliant lustre it once knew. The evening draws near
And all signs of a Day once cherished come to an end. The
Evening entices us with a sinister allure.
Its icy fingers envelop our hearts as it
Entraps us into the realm of darkness it has accomplished.

A deafening silence covers the world below
As a slow wind begins to blow through the
Skeletal remains of what once were
Majestic trees, an eerie howling begins as
The wind rips through the abyss.

With a silent fervor the moons lustre
Slowly retraces its sinister steps and
Retreats into a world known to few and
Seen by many, its last valiant effort to
Hold on to its domain, all is silent as the
Trees repeat the whispers in the wind.

William Hoey

Life

How short and brief is the life of a leaf,
  Its life so quickly ended by the winter thief.

Yellow, red leaves of autumn past, buried beneath
  the snow.
Fallen, dead leaves of winter past, have blown
  away long ago.

New buds of spring, yellow-green, do the barren
  trees.
Full, green leaves sway softly, amid the summer
  breeze.

It seems so minor, so trivial and small,
  But without them there'd be no protection
from sun and rainfall.

How short and brief is the life of a leaf,
  Its life so quickly ended by the winter thief.

Michelle Blasnig

The Glove Of Love

The glove of love fits everyone.
  It's never too large, nor small
  To give its warmth and protection
  Always, and to us all.

There's snug pocket for each finger,
  Including a larger one for the thumb.
  So there's never an excuse for discomfort,
  But continuous flair, and aplomb.

It allows the fingers to be flexible and dexterous
  While serving respect, order and joy,
  With never a thought of restraint or contraction,
  Or any such method to employ.

The hands give sincerity and thoughtfulness,
  And large portions of kindness and cheer;
  An outreach of genuine concern, which shows
  That little, big, old, young - all are dear.

Yes, the glove of love fits everyone;
  Here's your invitation to try it, and you'll see
  That harmony and perfection become reality
  The way our Creator designed it to be.

Penny Ruth Dennis

A Mother's Smile

The sweetest gift is a mother's smile
  it's nice to look back on every once in a while.

I remember times as a little boy;
  When my mother would call me her pride and joy.

My heart would swell and my spirit would glide,
  and I would carry her smile along for the ride.

Well, she helped me grow straight and tall and proud,
  and she has to look up to smile at me now.

But that smile of hers could still melt snow
  and it still makes me warm from head to my toes.

Mike Hess

Today

I don't understand the world today
It's not like I ever did
But some things people do today
Are better left unsaid

The violence, the hate
When will it ever end
With the way it is today
I don't think it will ever mend

As long as there is love it will be okay
Right? That seems to be what they say
But sometimes I don't think love
Makes a difference in our world today

If only people would listen
To what you have to say
Maybe we can have a better world tomorrow,
If we can't have one today.

Nicole Farrar

"Marble Mausoleum"

The house stands on the hill
its occupants are trapped behind its walls
they are living there forever
reverberations in the halls

Lost in her quietus
never to be reborn
dreams to repatriate
wishes she could have known

Now she wanders forever
in her marble mausoleum
the house that was once her dream
now will never release her

Napoleon Hamberg

Thorns Of Vanity

Its beauty bursts forth as the red rose blooms;
   Its petals ripple delicately as the sightly flower grooms.
The rose, a person, teeming with beauty and grace,
   Yet will preen, pretty, and primp itself until red in the face.
Oh, selfishness; oh, conceit; oh, vanity with thorns,
   Why put up this gorgeous front to screen away your scorns?
To urge someone to grasp your barb-bearing stem,
   You use your charm to beguile, to hurt again and again.
A sight to see, a beauty to behold,
   The blossom appeals to the eye, but to the touch will scold.
Those thorns, those thistles, sharper than the sharpest blades,
   Tear at the skin in this hidden masquerade.
A sizeable ego—not a good quality to possess—
   Is used to sting, to aggravate, to poke feelings of unrest.
And, what of the blossom when its petals have gone,
   When its beauty disappears at the autumn's dawn?
All that remains is the bitter, thorn-filled stalk,
   Though not as apt to sting, nor to prick, nor to inspire one to
Gawk.

Sheila Chang

"Goodbye"

One tree with two leaves left, which one will fall first?
      It's the hardest thing for a tree
      to decide which one it will keep
      and which one it will let fall.
Maybe both should fall, but would that be the right choice?
   It looks inside its trunk and tries to decide
    should the one longer there stay or fall?
   or should the one there shorter stay or fall?
Those two leaves are so special to the tree, it does not
        want to hurt either
   It makes its decision and hopes not to regret
    Goodbye it says to the leaf longer there
    Goodbye it says to the leaf shorter there
I love you both, but to live I must let you both fall
    Something sad happened to the tree,
      it bore no more leaves
      and was alone forever on.

Mary Elguicze

As You Live And Breathe

From the time you wake up, till you go to bed at night,
Life is a matter of course, but you should try to live it right.
It seems all the news is depressing.
Some happy events would be a blessing.
Don't argue about politics or religion.
No two people have the same opinion.
Talk about sunshine, gentle rain and roses,
Delicious food, butterflies and kid's runny noses.
Listen to beautiful music and hear the ocean sprays.
For the older you get, the faster go the days.

Rosemary Gregoire

Hey

Hey listen, do you hear it?
   It's the sound of the flowers blooming
   the wind softly blowing, the grass
   Slowly growing, and my heart
   learning to love.

Hey look, do you see it?
   It's the sight of children playing, a
   set of dolphins swimming by, the newly
   born animals learning to walk, and
   me falling in love.

Hey listen, do you hear it?
   It's the sound of the flowers shriveling
   away, the storm clouds rolling in, the
   grass turning brown and dying, and
   my heart breaking.

Hey look, do you see it?
   It's the sight of children fighting,
   hungry sharks on the attack, hunters
   killing the animals, and you walking away.

Mendy Miller

From The Start

  What's wrong? Why is there tears in your eyes? I know
it's time for us to part, yet I love you from the start.
When we first met I thought you had another, yet you
proved me wrong. I thought you wouldn't care, yet you knew
you could prove me wrong. I wonder what would I do if
I didn't have you. Sometimes I wonder if I'll lose you.
When I look upon you I wonder what it'll be like, when we
part. I know you loved me ever since the start, even though
it's time for us to part. When we go our separate ways, we'll
still love each other more and more each and every day in our
hearts. If we lose our love for each other and if we find
another, we'll always remember each other's love for one another.
I may not say I care, yet there's no need to ask.
Even if I can't show you how I feel, you should know that
I care for you each day in my heart. When I feel your kiss
upon my lips it brings me happiness. Your warm, tender
caring touch holds me so close and tight upon your heart.
You wipe my tears, then I realize you're there for me, through
Thick and thin. You understand my pain and sorrow within me.
I'll always love you from the start.

Leticia Torres

The Tears Have All Fallen

The tears have all fallen and the words have all been said.
It's time to move on, for our love is certainly dead. The soft
spoken words and tender movements will always remain, but my
heart is saddened that so much love had to end with such pain.
We tried and we tried, we both had so much hope, but I guess our
love was at the end of its rope. You were my dream come true,
you were the man for me. Yesterday you were everything,
today....just a man I used to see. I've thought and I've
thought, for hours on end, I want our happiness back, but those
bitter words can never mend. Well we've gone too far and we've
said too much, I've got to move on, but how I yearn for your
touch. Sleepless nights and tear filled eyes all that remains
are those good old cries. Another man, another love there has
to be to forget about you and set my heart free.

Linda Panichelli

Serenity

Do you hear the water whispering?
Its voice soft, silky, sensuous, beckons seductively
Surrender.
Enchanted I concede, stalked ruthlessly by unbridled
Desire.
Entangled in its icy grasp as it surreptitiously draws
my gaze into its soul. Exotic shades of terror and
Exhilaration.
I watch, mesmerized, as the water writhes in bittersweet agony,
eternally haunted by the ghosts of undead
Passion.
The salty tribute of my heart caresses the liquid angst
as I succumb to the taste of forbidden
Ecstasy.
Suddenly, my essence takes flight on newfound wings of freedom,
searching for a mystic paradise known only as...
Serenity.

   Tracy Runnels

"That Lonely Hill"

I've awakened to churchbells in mourning
I've been seduced by the sirens at night
And I've wrestled with my demons in darkness
And I once loved an angel of light

Yes, it is true, I have fallen
From the state of grace I once knew
Down on my knees, I am calling for
the sweet memory of you

There are no words left for me to say
You've heard them all before
And there are no songs left for me to sing
but please, let me sing you just one more

For the time we shared, it was sacred
And the comfort you gave me, it was pure
All those kisses will last me forever
What I felt with you I never felt before

Now, I walk that lonely hill again
to leave you what is yours
I walk that lonely hill again
I leave God at your door

   Kevin Kelly

Speak Right From The Heart

I've heard many speakers who preach to big groups
I've heard motivators who lecture their troops.

I've heard funny speakers with hilarious jokes
I've heard storytellers with great anecdotes.

But the one I like the best in a class far apart
Are the ones that I know, speak right from the heart.

Some speakers are polished, but seem cold as ice
Some others are boring and filled with advice.

Some speakers will call you"an intelligent crew"
But don't really mean it and talk down to you.

I've seen every style, I've studied the art
And the kind I like best speak right from the heart.

So if you're asked to speak, leave your script on the chair
Hop up on the stage and show them you care.

Be humble and happy and speak one on one
You'll be amazed, it's a whole lot of fun.

Don't try to be clever, don't try to be smart
Just be yourself... speak right from the heart.

   Stew Leonard, Sr.

Untitled

Two halves have never completed a heart like this,
I've searched so long for someone so genuine, and delicate as you.
Two people combined into one makes you so complete.
The gentle, caring side is so incredible it's hard to explain.
And the strong, rugged side makes you so much more attractive.
The touch is so gentle, it's like a kiss from an angel's lips.
And that look of seduction always makes me tremble inside.
"I love you" isn't just a phrase flowing from your lips.
It's full of love and care, and respect so deep that it could
   smother the most gigantic beast.
The respect has grown so large that it evenly divides between us both.
Love is such a different feeling with you, words could never describe.
I love you, I need you, and I know that even when we're apart,
   your heart always remains with me.

   Tammy A. Zornow

Death Bed

The earth sparkles with new fallen frost,
Jack frost nips at your nose,
The stars twinkle above in the air,
The moon shines down on the grave yard,
As the clock on the tower strikes midnight,
Everything grows colder and gloomier,
It's as if a shadow was there,
watching over us all,
as we sleep we'll be watched
the shadow making you feel lonely, empty and cold inside,
Is your heart strong enough to not let it inside,
We may never know or hear you tell us why,
We all just hope that you won't die,
die in your sleep,
and if you do I hope you said a prayer,
before your head hit your death bed,
Now I lay me down to sleep
I pray the lord my soul to keep
If I should die before I wake
I pray the lord my soul to take

   Kendall Dallow

My Right To Life

   The abortion issue again! Who made you God? Are you judge and
juror? So you think that you are prepared to decide between life or
death. It is in your hands in which my future lies. I find it hard
to believe that you are unwilling to see me live, hear me cry, or feel
me breathe. It is unknown to me as to why you deny my movement
   when
you enable me to kick. Also, to deny my breath when it is your
air that allows me to breathe. How can you say I do not exist when it is
your existence that has given me a chance for life. It is through you
that I am living and through you in which I shall die. Who gave you
the right to deny "My right to life?

   Who made you God? You do not believe in God! That explains why
you can not believe in me. For you can not believe in what you can
not see. You will soon believe in me when you see me lying in a
bucket with my arms and legs serrated, and my head mashed by a
Doctor's hands. You will not hear my cries, or feel me breathe. You
will never understand the pain because love is unknown to your heart.
I could have brought joy to your life if you had not chosen to bring
death into mine. Why? Can you not see that I breathe! I kick! I
cry! I have a right to "My" life just as you have a right to
yours....

   Samantha L. Raffield

Magnetic Ties

White Northern shores, Blue Southern Skies.
Just a product of magnetic ties.
A force of God, Wild force of fate.
There's high resistance in this lonesome state.
We pour our lives onto atom beams.
Then trigger in motion electric screams.
We find our souls in disarray.
Then rise in love the magnetic way.
We are as one with magnetic ties.
By binding opposites our feelings rise.
From the depth of which we'll never know.
Our eyes meet then currents flow.
With shocking AC on my mind.
This intersection feels so fine.
My mind is blown by your attraction.
The show begins with suns refraction.
Discover powers within your soul.
A minds addiction out of control.
We come together we're white hot.
Tied by this magnetic knot.

Lonny Dean Flaharty

Untitled

Please don't cry my beautiful friend
Just come here and your heart I'll mend
I wish I could hug you and make all those problems go away
I love you so much already but I swear I love you more each day
I don't have the power to stop them all
But I will help you stand If you shall fall
But I got problems too - and most of them there's nothing
    you nor I could do.
But one of my problems is sadly you - please understand I need to
    know what to do?
You love her and It's killing me
I just wish you could see the great person I could be
I could be better than her I can love you more and treat you better
If you were with her would you get nicer weather?
I cry so much cause I'm all confused - I feel so cheated and I
    feel so used
Oh please help me - you're the only one who could ever help me.
I just wish you could stop and see
And see the real person I could really be
I wish - I wish you could see the real me and love the real me.

Stephanie Anne Glantz

My Last Request

When I am gone, don't mourn for me
Just think how happy I will be
Winding my way to my heavenly home
Where I shall never be alone
For by Jesus, saving grace
I shall meet him face to face
And my loved ones who for me wait
I'll meet just inside the eastern gate
I'll never know sorrow, pain or distress
For I'm among the saved and blest
Jesus took away my sins
And gave me heavenly peace within
To those of you I leave behind
I pray you'll find this same peace of mind
Make things ready before it's too late
For without God how terrible your fate

Mel Holcomb

The Love Of My Life

    The love of my life my wonderful husband...
    just wanted to send you all of my love...
    You are one of a kind like no other...
You fill my life with joy and happiness...
    We have a long road to travel...
But we know deep in our hearts...
    That's it's just one turn after another...
But as long as we have each other...
    Neither one of us will want to make a u-turn
and lose the other...
    This road is long and
winding hilly places and some straight...
    But as long as I've got you...
The hills and turns only make it better...
    I'll always be beside
You going down this road of marriage...
    Will you promise me we will never go our
separate ways... I Love You!!!

Norma Hildreth

'Why'

My Dentist is retiring, that dirty rat
Just when I need him the most.
More bone is showing each passing day
And my teeth are as brittle as toast.

What happens if that bridge starts to tilt
And those cracked teeth begin to whine?
Will he leave that good old fishing spot
And tend to this mouth of mine.

You know that he won't that dirty rat
He'll just grin and go on his way
Just whistle'n a tune out there in the woods
And thank God for a beautiful day.

He'll probably hunt till the dog lays down
And fish till the baits all gone.
Poor old thing will wear himself out
Before a month is gone.

What makes a man want to run off and hide
When there's lots of money to earn?
Could it be he would rather have lots of fun
Than have lots of money to burn?

Norma Miller

"My Last Breath"

Keep my feelings bottled up
Keep them hidden.
Never to show.
I been beaten in my soul.
My life's been cheated.
Now I know.
Death of life and so much more
The breath of death knocks at my door
I keep myself sheltered so far from the world
The cruel mean things they say and do
If this is life I wish for more
I wish for death with my one last breath.

Rachel Shumock

Life's Precious Hours

As you travel down life's highway
  keep your eyes on the clouds of grey.
There will always be storms to encounter,
  disappointment which go astray.

So don't be weary to hear others problems,
  no matter what 'ere they may be,
and I'll try to keep each promise
  of the troubles confided in me.

I've no time to be forgetful and
  never too tired to lend a hand.
There's no room in my heart for gossip
  with lies about my fellow man.

Life's precious hours should be in giving,
  never wasting days on end.
There should never be anything so important
  that you can't stop to make a friend.

    Ruth V. Shillito

For Donna, Beloved Twin

Come! look into my eyes.
Know me by your own name.
I live in the depths of your soul.
I am your spirit guide.

Come! Run with me.
To feel the wind racing through your hair.
Our hearts, pulsating as one.

And when grandmother moon looks down upon us,
We shall close our eyes and open our hearts to light.
Singing our spirits to the heavens.
Melding and merging.
Returning our thanks.
For our blood is one.

I walk in your mind.
I dwell in your heart.
I am wolf, your spirit guide.

    Leslie J. Pond

Wait Up

I sit in the hospital holding your hand,
Knowing that I can never understand
How I can face tomorrow without your smile,
Without your hand to hold through every trial,
Without your arms to hold me tight
Each time we say goodnight.
"Oh, cookie my cookie," I hear you say
In that dear old familiar way
Taking your hand you press it against my tear wet cheek
Your hand once so warm and strong, now so cold and weak.
Sometimes we would laugh and sometimes we would cry
As we talked about the days gone by.
With the night heavens portals opened wide
As you slipped gently to the other side.
Walk slowly, oh so slowly, old Sweetheart mine,
You know I'll not be far behind.

    Viola M. Wurl

Untitled

Death, being the last hope,
my stomach bends with pain.
Lately you've been talking
yourself utterly insane.
Life, being a test of strength,
you try to live it fully.
Once alive and now you've bled,
your spirit wonders among the dead.
Demonic faces flash through your mind,
as you watch your life slip through your eyes.

    Mike Kimock

Daddy

My Dear Daddy, I write this now for you,
Knowing that your Christmas spirit's shining through.

The lights are warm on my fingertips as I lay beneath the tree,
Reflections from the ornaments helping me to see.

So close your eyes and fill your room with essence of pine,
And know the lights on the evergreen for you will ever shine.

No peeking at our presents until you're safe at home,
Just like your Christmas tree, you'll never stand alone.

Remember Pere Noel, Old St. Nick, and eight reindeer;
The family ornaments on the tree, you bring out every year;

The Christmas cards that we hang, sent by those we love,
With pictures of our Lord, who lives so high above.

Open your eyes so you can see, in front of you stands your
Christmas tree. Her lights though, shine so deep inside, the
love of her man stands by her side.

Ornaments of blonde and red, upon her shoulders rest like wings
Will always shine for you, while your spirit sings.

And those so far away, who used to be so near, hold your spirit
within their hearts, and hold you very dear. May the lights
on your tree keep you bright and warm, until you come home...

    Katherine Carr

Albert Einstein

A lthough as a child, you were never smart,
L earning seemed as boring as studying fine art.
B ut, as you grew and started to wonder,
E verything made good sense - without 'nary blunder.
R eading and math seemed to always intrigue you,
T o study relativity was the thing for you to do.

E ven though you were known the whole world around,
I t was your violin that made the most pleasing sound.
N ever wore socks; had unruly, long, white hair,
S till the twinkle in his eye showed that he could care -
T hat the world be the finest place that it could be,
E ven in countries where people were never free.
I f only we could see the world as he did,
N o telling how many first cousins would wed!

    Sandra Myers Vest

I Am The Human

Adopted from one island to another,
lacking the age to recall the beauty of either one.
Trust the older eyes...
From tropical green to desert dune
Without a choice, fate has strapped me to a heavy mind
thick with thought and supposition.
The sacrifice of two for the sake of one
constructs a complex line of chance and action.
I am the abandoned fruit of uncommitted love,
grateful and curious
I am the gift to the accepting strangers,
powerless and shuffled
And I am the human,
who will ask until answered, love until killed,
and have faith in the purposes of the unknown.
Past without definition eliminated the burden
of my origin's permanence
while allowing the soul to redefine itself with jewels
I chose to set in the circle of lustrous gold.
I am the human.

    Sean Gregory Mathis

Scriptures 1:1

Two atmospheres — what a concept,
Laden in pools of dedication;
Minds of abstractions with no analysis forbidden.
Try to find a rhythm.
Of late, we've followed a circumscripture,
For us,
It paints a picture.
Containing divine honors
Upon bland wonders,
It's sensitive and it doctors our egos.
It wraps us into a shape;
Mummified,
Our lives follow the ties.
And without it, order is confined to the good people;
Without it, anarchy defines the upheaval.
The literal sense is literary brilliance,
But symbolism proves its pureness.
A hope;
A cure for life's thin chain,
And a door to death's thick reign.

Keith Ketcham

Spring In September

Seeds that fell from Summer love so brightly colored
Lay decaying in ground untilled
The cold of a long winters night, — barren
Settled on my heart and soul

Then Spring in September
Love like the sun of Spring renewed
My cold heart and soul were warmed
In the gentle breeze
The untilled ground was turned
And the seeds grew forth in love so brightly colored

Paula Hollenback

Song Of The Thorn Bird

Oh dear little Thorn Bird, why are you so silent as you
leave your nest?
I watch you from afar as you fly so tirelessly, in search
of what, I do not know.
You have traveled so far my poor little Thorn Bird, why
do you punish yourself so? Your wings are sure to be
weary, why do you not rest?
I see you descend, oh what have you spied? As you land a
thorn tree I see.
What do I hear from thee my silent little Thorn Bird?
A song so sweet, such a pleasure to hear.
Oh my little Thorn Bird why do you behave so? I do not understand.
Oh what I feel to see the thorn pierce your breast, but a
song none other could be so sweet lifts in your voice, to
be silenced forever more.
And now I weep, for at last I understand, a song more
beautiful than our lives can bring.
Goodbye my little thorn bird for your life I will mourn.

Linda Doepke

When Was Wouldn't Worry

Time was, so long ago ("or it seems like it") to walk through
life, without a care or worry was to easy. Running through
life with blinders on, but then the dream wakes you up in the
night and reality settles in. Whether the blur is a passing
blink of a lash, and when you think that you are 100% sure of
what you saw was real, Reality. ("remember that word") sets
in again. So makes a man so young, but yet so old, tackle the
problem of that word. All we know is basic thoughts.

We worry and then we fret, all the while we never forget. Old
times new times, thing you remember things you forget. Love
comes to those who wait.

Michael Authier

The Wonders Of Nature

Winds blowing rapidly
Leaves whistling through the air
The sounds of nature among us
Bring joy to our ears
The scent of wild flowers
The gurgling of the creek
Distant cries of the wild
And rivers running deep
This is natures way of saying to respect
And understand the glory and peace in nature
That started out in this land
No crowded sidewalks or busy streets
No smokey filled skies or awkward cries
No sirens or fire whistles and violence
To fill the dark nights
Just the stars in the sky
And the quiet stillness of the night
Will always let you keep the memories
Of natures delights.

Laurie J. Henry

Lonely

The rain patters down the window,
leaving a trail of sparkling diamonds.

Wind whispers secrets to the leaves,
as it whistles its path through the trees.

I sit and watch from the window,
as the rain gently falls.

The salty tears running down my face
matching the rain that blurs the window.

Loneliness wraps her cold arms about me,
sending shivers through my heart.

Bringing back memories of what used to be,
and what could have been.

Mother nature seems to understand
as her tears fall from the sky.

His face dances in front of me,
so clear, but just a memory.

Oh how the heart can ache,
for just one more touch,
one more moment together.

Robyn Lynn Richardson

Questions

Explosions in the morning sky,
left us stunned, mouths opened wide.
Such promise, such valor, all gone for naught?
Exciting lessons she would have taught!

We filled slowly from our places, frozen horror on children's faces.
O' Challenger, O' fearless seven, was it worth the price
to try for heaven?

Vicious fate, seething doubt, sobbing lungs
hold back the grieving shouts. And in the end, must our will bend?
(These things happen, to seek the truth must have its cost.)
Or will we decide it's worth the loss?

Three days of eulogies, sweet and brief.
Circling ships pick pieces form the reef.
O' endless space, your vastness is the lure the end result.
We'll all remember where we were?

Courageous eagle, flew so high
Left us earthbound, wondering why.
To reach, to explore, to boldly go where no one has been before?
Come back and tell us what we need to know.
Should we touch the stars, or stay at home?

Mark Stevens

The Cigarette Song

Let me make my contribution to your cancer please
Let me give you a donation make you cough and wheeze
Let me help you make your emphysema set
Let me help you light another cigarette
   breathe deeply my friend
   you've only got one pair of lungs
     you won't need them in the end.
You can quit when you want to but I have some more
I'd hate to throw them all away like phlegm on the floor
Let me help you calm down your nicotine fit
Let me help you light another cigarette
   breathe deeply my friend
   yellow teeth and dragon breath
     you really can set the trend
"I'm going to die anyway so what the hell
(I'm a weak-willed addict but that's something I won't tell")
Self-assisted suicide Kevorkian's a thrill
Thank you RJ Reynolds for a legal way to kill.

    Scott Thomas Kearney

A Man In Love

   Do I love you, do I care?
Let me tell you, lady fair.
   Does a flower love the dew?
As it falls from far-off Heaven and blesses me and you.
   Does a sparrow—tiny bird-
seek his food, as he searches far and wide?
   Do I yearn, do I burn, to be
there at your side?
   Does the ocean, ever ceaseless,
try to reach the other shore?
   Can a man who gives his utmost,
can this man give any more?
   Will a mountain built by God
be cleft in twain by God?
   Can they stop me from my love,
even with the whip and rod?
   Will an eagle, sore afflicted,
fall to earth, far down below?
   Will she love me as I love her?
this perhaps I'll never know.

    Sol Babitsky

The Way Of The Light

The darkness of the human soul,
Lies, deceit, hatred, war,
Binds us to his dismal plain,
Denies us acceptance in God's sweet realm.
Alone we swirl in this dark abyss,
No hope, no change, no chance
But to fall wayside to evil's charm
Becoming food for Satan's hoard.
Yet through the Darkness comes Light
Beating at the barricade of vile putridness.
"Salvation can be yours," Father Adam's
Pure, crystalline voice rings out, pushing away the despair,
"Love fellow man, be kind to the World. Dismiss the Devil,
Find your true path, to God, with me."
Following his voice, happiness can be found
At the heart of your soul, at the feet of Father Adam.
Believe in the Father, trust in his decisions,
For he will never lead you astray
To final glory.

    Thomas Morgan IV

Healing

In this time of sadness, full of grief
life is void of happiness, and seems so brief
our eyes so full of tears
our hearts so full of pain
memories flood in from past years
like jewels falling among the rain
we pray for the time when the hurting stops
and as we gaze at the mountains we must climb
struggling to reach the tops
we are reluctant to let go
afraid to be alone and feeling so low
with hearts heavy like stone
we look for the ray of hope
a beam of sunlight
to help us cope
to make us feel alright
but we must not forget
the loved ones left behind
we fall in their safety net
thankful for the ties that bind

    Shaina Guthrie

Bus Ride Through Texas

Rolling into a night trimmed in points of distant light,
Lighted billboards, radio towers. watching
Silent silhouettes of black and grey move through
People's reflections riding behind me, in separate
Worlds of class, race, culture, the width of a seat.
Listening to pieces of another's life, spoken in whispered words,
Drift across worlds, mixing with music from a young mans lap,
Breaking the boredom of night shadows flashing by.
Lights overhead wink out one by one,
Yawns replace words turning to snores,

Rolling into the night past lighted yards guarding
Sleeping houses. through silent streets of sleeping towns
Contrastingly lined in home grown stores,
Adorned at the edges with buildings by Sam.
Seeing imitations of a big city life, movie theaters,
Satellite dishes, flashing neon signs of close-in bars.
The people's lives bound in street lights, store hours
And city limit signs. small towns, I've heard tell of,
Springing up in headlights to quickly fade in red.

    Robert Cone

Auden's Augury

"It makes nothing happen," said the poet of Poetry,
Lighting a fuse in literary heresy;
And yet, when I sail out to Byzantium
I hear such music as could never come
From chrome or brass or molten bars
Of motored chords and choirless stars.

And yet, when I walk out on Bristol Street
I hear the airy threads of lovers' feet
And all the chimes above the din
Of puny powers still cashing in
On the crackling cries of miracle men
Playing again in the blood-paved pen.

Give pause, and ponder what anvil's art
Preludes the bleating fugues of an empty heart,
Brandishes the blunt baton of hackneyed hate
Cymbaling another Achilles' armored plate:
Give pause and ponder: No Pipes of Pan
Make such happenings happen as man makes man!

    Miriam R. Kossman

Love Lights The Way

Love shines brightly from your beautiful eyes,
Lighting answering fires in my heart's skies.

Together our love is beautiful and strong,
A silent promise like a vivid rainbow after a summer storm.

Our love started softly like the rising sun,
Filling our days with adventure and fun.

Our love will last through all eternity I know,
For we cherish our love and it continues to grow.

Yes, love shines brighter than ever from your beautiful eyes.
Giving life to my heart like the sun gives life to the skies.

    Lois Knight

Spectrum

The wheel of my life...spins with every hue,
Like a prism....a-glow, in a tear-drop of dew.
Or the fire....caught, in the heart of a star...
As it throbs, and ebbs ....on its journey far.

First came those days....of rosy sheen....
'neath a sky.....of cloud-less blue,
And at sweet six-teen ....it ran clear and green,
So wild, and bright ....and new!

When I found my Love it all turned to gold
With a burst ....of flaming wonder....
And it burned on down ....to an ember-glow ...
Of deep ....and molten ember!

Then ....I lost, my Love and the purple night
Went black ....with the dark, of thunder!!!

Now, with tear-dimmed eyes, I search vaster skies ...
Through the mist ....see colors ....blending ....
To a pristine white ....of radiant light
Full circle never ending

    Violet S. Soward

Aquamarine

Over and over I am tossed about
Like driftwood drowning in a churning sea
From below the crystalline surface I watch
The only life I see a leaf half afloat and withering
Its butterfly silhouette flying on the back of my hand
Dare to find the genesis of this shadowy life
The mother being a stinging white light from above all whitecaps
Not being the sun
Too precious would it be on this night
A solitary beam
The rotisserie which is the key to the leaf's animation
The lighthouse as big as God with earthly feet
It has no foundation at night
Only the hot oven floating above the steel cliff
An outstretched arm which is my own
Striving to attain the glorious flame
I cannot grab hold
Falling below I notice the pearl luminescence of an open clam
Its glittering beauty like a firefly in ebony
It fears not and encourages a similar response

    Matt Scala

Trying

I thought it would be easy raising kids
Like running with a kite that catches air
And soars straight to the sky and dances there.
And, truthfully, I've found sometimes it is.
I never thought about the windless days
Until I had to suffer quite a few
Running on the beach with a kite that stays
Earthbound, a sulky, sullen, stubborn shrew.
While little voices cried in tearful words,
"Mommy, make it go!" I just didn't know
There would be things I could not do, and hurts
I could not heal, and days so long and slow.
But, still, those times when the kite is flying
Make it worth my while and keep me trying.

    Peggy Egan

The Reunion

    Days handed out by life's slim fingers,
  Like shiny coins being pried from a miser's hand.
Treasured days to be spent for a reunion with nature,
    A celebration - a living recital of vows.

  In turning my back to the life that owns me,
  The daily routines to which we are all bound,
  I come to a place that is hanging suspended.
Where there is no need for the days to have names.

My senses are wakened like leaves in the springtime,
  Swirling and dancing with needs of their own.
  My physical body which serves just to house them,
Is pulled to the seashore like the tide pulled to land.

  A ritual that's private, a courtship so sacred,
  Between two souls who are longing to touch.
    A sensual meeting, a physical union,
  One partner flesh and the other quixotic.

  Renewed and reminded of spiritual blessing,
Like a mother whose womb is filled with a child,
  I take with me magic to nurture and honor,
  And turn back to life with passion and joy.

    Laura Woodward Waddell

Lights Of Beauty

How beautiful are the lights—
like sunlight dancing on clear water...
like candles on a birthday cake...
or shimmering stars up in the sky:
That gleam that is in someone specials' eyes.

There are bright city lights, too...
and soft rainbow lights
  when rain and sun meet...
or Christmas lights that dance
and light up happy faces and the streets.

There are carefree fire-flies
  skipping across meadows—
and camp-fires for hot-dogs and marshmallows;
or a warm fire-side when the day is waning on...
and the wonderful colors of a new days dawn...

And there is a light we wait to see
that is brighter than all I know;
It's the Light of the Lord
  with His truth and His life
and none other shines for us so.

    Sandra Leah Ross

The Freedom Of Being Different

Making a difference for tomorrow ties us together,
Like the bonds of freedom's past.

We are not the same but, yet we are free to be you and me,
Regardless of color, content of skin, or gender.

The struggles vary but the path of freedom endures,
Like a ray of light through the clouds.

Strength through diversity is the future—
The ability to believe in ourselves, in our dreams,
Realizing the potential, impossibilities becoming realities
That is what it means to be different.

Dare to be different and live the American Dream
Be who you are that which was meant to be.

Remember…reflections of a moment in time—
Never the same, always changing, like the sands of time.

The hardships we endure…the power to be who we are.
Unique, but yet the same, not two — identical.
For the world gone by, where the hearts still cry from the darkness,
Yesterday is gone and today is now yet,
Tomorrow can only get better.

Diversification and independence - if you can dream it, you can do it.
Nancy S. Horiye

Korea-On The Line

It comes wailing out of Siberia,
like the cry of a banshee
    singing her song of death.
It lingers in the corners of my bunker
    and penetrates to my inner most soul.
Icy and down my spine.
    and send a shuddering chill
up and down my spine.
    Its frigid breath strokes my dirt covered
face.
    The wind driven snow is a lance of ice
that sets my lungs on fire.
    Death awaits outside,
not only by shell or blade.
    Perhaps by the banshee's frigid embrace,
lulled by her invitation to sleep.
    Having whispered her invitation,
her mournful voice
    flows down the valley,
luring others to her freezing embrace.
Robert V. Echelbarger

For The Cardinal Interrupting Class

Twilight beckons to encroaching night,
liquid darkness seeping through the sky.
A brilliant spring evening, so intangible
in winter's longing, flows
through the wide-open casement;
small strips of peeling paint
flap in the smooth, lawn-scented breeze.
With a subdued hush, a gap in conversation,
the world is silent:
a noiseless introduction
to the evening's performance.
Slowly warbling, ever-quickening,
the bird's call fills the room,
fills the purple dusk, serenading
the first night of spring.
With regal indifference to human discussion,
the cardinal cries into the night,
a misplaced shock of red
upon a newly-green branch.
Michael Morrow

You Just Pass On By

Sounds of laughter, sounds of woe-pass on by.
Little children playing in the alleys,
Old man playing his banjo and rocking
Back and forth his body to the rhythm.
Sit back and listen!
Chicken frying in the kitchen next door,
Little one crying at my feet and I ask,
"What's the matter child, where's Mama?"
And a little girl answers, "She gone away."
Walking down these old and familiar streets
To those forgotten days of my childhood,
I realize that I never left.
Patsy Lavonne Long

God, The Wind And I

I'm tired of being depressed
Living alone, fretting, never getting enough rest
Thinking I've flunked every relationship test
Always biking east, when the wind is blowing west!

I'm tired of just surviving
I want to get back to "Man A living!"
Maybe even—God willing—downright thriving
I'm tired of leaving; I want to start arriving!

I'm tired of fearing and losing my nerve
I want to recapture my long lost verve
Have the guts to take a chance like Donald or Merv
Stand boldly at the plate and swing at an inside curve!

I'm tired of hiding; feeling unloved and unblessed
I want to find a caring lady and let nature do the rest
Did you get the message? (It may be my best)
I'm tired of being depressed!

To love myself and others again now seems a do-able quest
I've turned my "bike" around and am fairly flying to the west—
Or north or south or east—
Whichever God, the wind and I deem best!
Norman E. Knuckey

My Grandmother Maria

She stands alone with the wind at he back
Long, dark skirt whipping against her ankles.
A tall, big boned, plain woman
of sturdy czech stock,
who helps her mate break sod.

Her gaze sweeps over the prairie
and stops down by the creek
on a lone cedar tree,
which marks the place
where the earth cradles
her first four infants—
The fifth buried years later
in the pioneer cemetery.

There are no tears in her eyes—
For did not God bless her
with eight more living babies?

Her gaze shifts skyward momentarily.
Then she turns to face the bitter wind
and walks back, past the old dugout
to the big house and the barn on the hill.
Lillian Meistrell

The Last Cowboy

A rough red manly tan upon his forearm and masculine hands,
looking as though life was hard labor, yet these hands had a
gentle caress as they held me as we danced in the candle and
moonlight, those hands are lovely and warm. They want me; a lonely
romantic who long to have this for eternity, to be wanted by a
man...a real man. That feeling of complete and utter
breathlessness I long for each day. Those rough red manly
forearms have strength of love pumping through every inch of his
body. This man is not meant to be stationary, he is a prowler.
When he is gone he still exists, his love, powerful love lives on
when I close my eyes I can see, feel, and sense the presence of
this last cowboy.

Tonya Harrill

RS

Hopeful Dreams
Looking through old pictures and yearbooks
Thinking of those past days
Just wishing I could get close to him
And kiss him in so many ways

Oh, how much I wanted
To go up to him and say "Hi"
But afraid he wouldn't notice
And glance at me then walk by

Maybe one day
We will begin to talk
And just maybe
Hand and hand we will walk

I do know
This is meant to be
You could say
It's fate or maybe just destiny

Shanna Martin

Building Blocks

Precious baby boy, eyes so blue.
Looks of love from me to you.
God's special gift he gave to me a baby
boy bouncing on my knee.
In my mind a man I see, so tall, proud,
and full of goodness.
With God's word to be lived to its fullness.
So now I hope that you will see that
with the Love of God, Daddy, and Me
you can be and do most anything with love's building blocks of three.

Roseann Couris

Sight Beyond Circumstance

If tomorrow finds me troubled
lost in time and space,
I'll know my God is with me
giving me His loving grace.

For you're there through all the heartaches
and you're there through all the tears;
Your loving arms can comfort me
through all the lonely years.

To "count it all joy" is my desire,
though the darkness clouds the way;
Teach me, Lord, to trust You
and see beyond this trial today.

And someday, when it's over
and this trial is long since gone,
my faith will have grown stronger
for you've been with me all along.

Radine Jones

A Daughter's Love

A Daughter's love is one of the most precious
    Love anyone can have.
A Daughter's love is forever,
    She is loving, caring and very understanding person.

When God gave me you for a daughter,
    That was the most perfect day of my life.
I am very lucky to have a daughter like you,
    Because you are also my best friend.

I want you to know,
    You are loved more than you know.

This is dedicated to my Daughter
Libby with love.

Liz Swift

What Is Love?

Love is something that can't be measured.
Love is something that can bring such pleasure.
Love is something that can't be held.
Love is something that can be felt.
Love is doing things are not wrong
    even if your heart feels oh! so strong.
Love is risking getting hurt
    because you know your heart might burst.
Love is believing without a doubt
    that surely someday He'll come about.
Love is showing that you care
    even when your heart is full of despair.

Krisdhal Ugarte

Chalk Dust

So many colors which ones will he choose? Wonderful purples, and
lovely blues. He'll make you a picture he's an artist you see. He
draws on the sidewalks, and makes fantasy. A wonderful lake, a
snowy white mountain, a carrousel horse, or a beautiful fountain.
He has chalk dust on his hands. He's been working for days, on
one single masterpiece, a twisting, turning maze. It has rained
twice this week, but this poor old man, who never leaves his
place, has started all over again. His drawings are magic. The
chalk must be heated. They never wash away, once they are
completed. He can stop a disaster in a minute or two with a
flip of his wrist, and a color a new. The sidewalks on the street,
all along my house, too, have been painted with masterpiece, one
hundred and two. Now this talented man is tarnished, and tired.
His eyesight is failing, but his paintings will always be
admired. He walks along the streets, day in and day out, to
squint at his work, while wandering about. He has no real friends
except the colors and me, he wants to someday paint a door and a
key. Using the key, he would open the door, and advance to a
magical place, forever more.

Theresa Kihn

Late Afternoon

The stillness of the late afternoon suspends the moment
    making it a calm and seamless time.
        The benediction of the day.

Soon the evening will come and promise
    the mystery of the night.
But the last of the day's brightness brings
    peace and memories.

Our scurrying nerve-wired lives deny us the soothing,
    tender touch of the light
        transmuting through the trees
            their shadow reaching always to the greater distance
                and at last becoming another memory.

Peggy Butera

Beware!

Out of the dark,
lurks the EVIL one.
Seeking to snare you
with lots of ideas and fun.
He doesn't come at you all at once.
Instead,
he starts with planting small thoughtful seeds.
Then out of nowhere a surprise punch.
Don't give the ENEMY any room,
or give in to his tempting appetite.
Keep your flesh under subjection,
and fight the good fight,
which is your faith in Jesus.
Only Jesus can keep you from SATAN's snares.
So, the next time your flesh rises up,
and your eyes start to stare,
consider the consequence of the sin
and BEWARE!

Victor Marcel Reeves

Cottage Of My Dreams

Across the sea, ancestral place of birth.
Lush green meadows feeding soft tufted sheep.
The winds whisper tales of sadness and mirth
To keep spirits alive although they sleep.

Haunting gray mountains preside in the west.
Surround wild fuschia and patches of bog.
A vision appears - my eyes come to rest.
A cottage emerging loosed from the fog.

The turf-fire burns - the scent fills the air.
It bids me enter a world they once knew.
The cottage holds secret those sorrows they shared.
Rejoicing aloud the dreams that came true.

Visions now haunted - spirits now yearning.
To dwell in that cottage - turf-fires burning.

Pat Donahue

Lonely Dirt

I am a lonely piece of dirt
lying here at the side of the road
The children run and play on me
Gee I wish I were that tree
That tree with God's love and tender care
looks beautiful whether it's full or bare
Please let this little piece of dirt
Get rid of this awful hurt
I see rain sleet and snow
But there is no place for me to go
Why don't you let a storm appear
So I can fly away from here
So I can start a new someday
In a place so very far away
Fly fly me away lord upon the stormy wind
and let me touch down upon the ground
That I have found
And make it my home today

Tom Scherer

A Mother's Love

A mother's love you could never match.
Not even a baseball player's greatest catch.
She gave you love that made you feel strong
Even when you felt your lowest she would make you hold on.
Her love is so bright it's like the morning sun
And so to me a mother's love will never be out done.

Larry B. Williams

How Do You Say Goodbye

How do you say goodbye, how do you say so long
Lying here on this death bed wondering what went wrong
When you see the ones you love walk into the room
No matter what your age is you're still dying too soon
When visitors come, you show them no fear
Although you're in pain you smile from ear to ear
You try to make them strong when you see tears in their eyes
You try to comfort them although you're the one that going to die
You hold each other in your arms and squeeze very tight
And for that moment you feel as if everything is going to be alright
As you separate you wipe the tears from their face
And you hope that you both are in God's good grace
So that way after death you can both be together
And share the love you once knew forever and ever
Finally when they leave and you're all alone
You picture their face in your mind and you're no longer strong
Knowing that you're never going to see them again, you're going to die
You put your hands over your face and begin to cry
One thing I want you to remember something you always knew
Although my body's dead I will always be with you.

Migdoel Noel Torres

Tides Of Hate Times Of Change

Coup d'etats and struggles for power,
Make me shiver and make me cower;
For beneath the hidden tide so deep,
Exists the madness of life made cheap.

As History repeats, purportedly without change,
Our minds must work to continually rearrange,
The unforgivable tides of hate,
That get passed off as ethnic traits.

Does any kind of harmony today persist,
Where within divisive lines people managed to coexist?
Now without a peaceful sector to roam,
Destiny points to a dark place called home.

Somewhere in this depthless darkness,
The answer appears amidst the starkness.
And reaching out, you stop and wonder:
Just who will hear these cries of thunder?

To cease the horrible cleansings and mutilations,
Would circumvent aims to delete populations;
For to be studied only in the texts of time,
Would serve to further and repeat this heinous crime.

Mia Suruj Tepper

"Love Is A Rose"

Love is a rose. It comes in so
many different colors. They are
sweet and prickly, but I can only
say that they remind me of you everyday.

So now I can tell you from
my heart that I love you. Nothing will
ever change my mind because I'm always
thinking of you.

You may not think of me as much as I think of you.
But I know deep down in your heart
You will love me when I still think of you.

Only one person can know what we feel
that day. But I don't care unless it's a
very bright day far, far away. I want you
to know that my love for you will never change.

Until then think of me and compare
a rose to love. Which love can last for along
time and a rose can't last for along time
unless love is around.

Teresa Swearingen

Black Wedding

Wedding bells began to ring,
many people started to sing,
then a gunshot filled the air,
many people felt despair,
the groom had fallen to the ground,
people checked, no pulse was found,
the bride was frantically screaming,
in a black car, a smile was gleaming,
the car pulled away and left people without a clue,
for years the people and bride felt blue,
then early on the anniversary of the two,
another gunshot rang out, the brides head it went through,
for years she'd thought about suicide,
ever since her groom had died,
but never again will she wake up sweating,
ever since that one black wedding.

Kim Harper

Untitled

In the beginning, it began as a joke when Daddy asked Mommy to get married, and to his surprise she said yes, not realizing how far it would get carried.

You are the best thing in our lives; you are the kid that we've outgrown, you are the reason for our existence; you are a pleasure that we've never known.

Two years later, you are the image of us and we are still amazed. We look at you and see a beautiful little girl and can't believe it some days.

There are many times when we'll be too protective and many times we aren't, it's our way for you to be yourself and hoping it's the right way to be a parent.

We want you to be able to come to us, whether the problem is big or small, and will help or send you in the right direction, so you might solve them all.

Through the good times and the bad, we will go through some rough times together, but if we can work them out, we hope we can make them better.

What you should always know is we love you and will always be there for you, you're so precious, and we hope one day you know how much we do,
Love You!

Karen Alderman

May Peace Never Cease

We are told of peace on earth -
May this be true for safety of hearth.
At Easter time there are Lilies of Peace
If only these could cause war to cease.
When people are no longer pulled apart -
All nations can then have a fresh start.
Once everyone can retire for a good nights sleep -
Then no longer must survivors have to weep.
When all remain calm no matter our station -
Then we will have peace throughout our nations
Little children are not aware of race -
Adults one and all accept one another with grace.
Cease fighting in all countries-even in alleys -
Let everyone prepare for peace in the valley.

Leslie J. Wiltse

Empty Nest

It's time for me to leave the nest
Maybe now you can get some rest
To make it on my own will be the test
For you have given me the very best.

You cradled me through all my fears
You wiped away my shedding tears
You and I shared so much happiness and cheers
You have been there for me throughout the years

Across the miles you will always be
Carried in my heart for I do love thee
When I'm lonely I will use the golden key
To unlock the treasured memories of you and me.

Linda S. Urbano

Rain

Rain dropping to the ground light and soft.
Maybe the sky is crying.
I don't know, but I know something.
It falls to drain our memories.
The rain rushes down our heart.
Days of sadness are vanished by the rain.
All the negative feeling floats away as if it were a bird.
In the pouring rain, the bird vanishes.
And people wonder where they go.
The place will never be known until the bird comes back.....

Kentaro Umemoto

Ode To Sister Sara

Oft times in the still of night, while sleep settles over me; far back in the recesses of my mind I hear a soft melody, and a soft sweet voice that calmed the fears a small child feels in the night; and I feel again the gentle hand that made my small world right. And some where between then and now the child became full grown. But not without the help of the girl who did it all alone. She had no older sister to help her find the way. To do all the grown up things while she ran out to play. To show her, to teach her, to put up with her, to reach her. And I think about her often and I wonder if she knows how much I really love her and I wonder if it shows. For when I look into a mirror it's not only me I see but a part of her reflection looking back at me.

Merle J. McGee

Your Promise Of Love

I love you so much it scares
me sometimes,
Because I don't want to lose you
I want you all mine.
It's amazing to me to love someone
like you,
I just hope in your heart you feel
this way too.
And when I wake up with your
arms around me,
I know with you is where I'll
always be.
And when you say I love you, I could
melt at your feet,
Because you are what I've always looked for
and what I never thought I'd meet.
You don't know how much I appreciate
you loving me like you do,
Just promise me for the rest of my life
that I'll wake up next to you.

Tisha Strayhorn

Foreign Places

Gaze deep my child, into those dark penetrating eyes and tell
   me what you see...
I see new places I've never seen before, strangely drawing me
Further and further into a misty, wonderfully scented faraway
   place
I see two bodies intertwined in a pulsating exotic rhythm,
   burning ever burning
As the sunlight catches the sparkling curve of a
   diamond- studded waterfall
I see ancient jungle animals garbed out in velvets and jewels
Slowly swaying through the lush, moist jungle
Falcons soaring, swooping, swerving, riding the wind with
   their comet tails
Deep blue waters undulating, carrying their mysteries to some
   pristine shores
Those things I see my dearest one, for no one else to see
I think of these things and once again I'm in a foreign place.

   Linda Jelinski

Eternal Love

As the deep, penetrating, blue of your eyes
Meanders through my soul,
I hear the enticing melody of your song,
Wishing it were ours.

The subtle, arousing, scent of you,
Stirs memories of the past,
I feel the warm caresses of your spirit,
Remembering first love.

Thoughts of what love used to mean,
Emotions in motion.
Feelings undulate: swell, swirl, wane,
Leaving me exhilarated.

Time changes, meanings become truer.
Real love is eternal;
Not always dramatic, exciting, electrifying,
But dependable and comfortable.

As the deep, penetrating, blue of your eyes
Meanders through my soul,
I hear the eternal melody of your song,
Never to be ours.

   Susan Dawn Cummings

Destiny

What should have been but was never
meant to be. To ride and slide upon
the quest of time, and change the
face of destiny.

I touched the face of what could have been and wept.
Time moved ahead and left me only regrets.

Come stand by my side, together we
rush ahead and sink in timeless sand
to move from here to there and gaze
upon the dead.

God help me stand and move ahead with
no regrets, life dealt me a blow but
death has not claimed me yet. While I
stir I only ask, remove the dust of
time from upon my sleepless eyes that
I may gaze upon the light and cherish
life once more.

   Rebecca Ortiz Vogan

Memories

You don't remember days you remember moments.
Memories are forever.
And now even you are just a memory,
lost in my mind, but never forgotten in my heart.
Memories are forever.

I knew we wouldn't be...
But you can always dream.
Now that's all you are, not only a memory,
but a dream.

Memories and dreams always last,
Then why couldn't you?

You're like a sunset,
There for a minute gone the next.
No one knows where you went, or why.
It was beautiful while it lasted.
Again, it's just a memory of yesterday,
And dreams of tomorrow.

A memory is forever.
I'll always remember you.

   Meredith Buckelew

Memories

Memories of the past are all but locked in Yesteryear,
Memories to come are but on an angel's tongue.
Memories are free to come at will, until they are lost forever in one.
Make each memory very dear, so we can recall it at our will.
Some memories are recalled with a tear.
Others with a smile.
Mine of you will always be dear.
Memories can be just a trickle,
or a fountain of bliss.
Not a one do we want to miss.
Some are good, some are bold.
It is up to you the story told.
Let at the last breath I take that you be near,
but not a tear.

   Mary A. Williams

Bow Down Before The One You Serve You're Going To Get What You Deserve

If you are going to serve someone, it
might as well be yourself! You are what you
serve. You are your own beliefs, therefore
you serve yourself. You abide to your own
needs. You are a greedy person, but after all,
aren't we all ? This World! These People!
Myself! "...all greedy". Something is not
right. Is this what I really deserve?

Let the rich man bathe in his riches, and the poor man
linger fully in his poverty.
Remember: Equality in life
is level as water resting
peacefully in a noiseless
meadow. One straight line.

Why did the monkey fall out of the tree?
He was shot!
Why did the monkey fall out next to him?
They were playing follow the leader.

!!!Innocence!!!
Lost at birth

   Lori Hamilton

The Ivory Is Theirs

Can you imagine how much that trinket cost
More valuable than money, a life was lost

A disgraceful plunder of this magnificent one
To the most unique creature beneath our sun

Does that ivory bracelet impress your friends
Was it worth the price of this terrible sin

What has the elephant done to cause his downfall
Simply grace our earth with his majesty and awe

The ivory is theirs, don't take it away
The cost is too high, we must refuse to pay

If you long to own a memento of this kind
Remember the carcass that's been left behind

That mighty elephant had many years ahead
That fallen elephant, who now is dead

They aren't creatures without feeling or emotion
They too love their families with much devotion

Leave the elephant alone before it's too late
or like many before it, extinction is fate

The ivory is theirs, don't take it away
The ivory is theirs, please...let them stay

Kathy McPheeters

The Meaning Of Family

The meaning of family have many definitions, but the
most significant one is that their love is without conditions.

They are purely composed of many parts, they give and
they take, but they all have heart.

Heaven must have truly sent them from above, and it's a
blessing to have their support and precious love

Lineage is important because it retraces their history,
it tells them where they been, so there's no big mystery.

For most it can be a great pedestal with an icon to
match, which would be nice for all to catch.

They can make their home out to be a compound, where
relatives know they can come for love to be found.

Their problems are usually kept to a minimum, and if
they're really lucky, they many end up like the oncoming millennium.

It doesn't matter to them what profession you choose as
long as it's legal, and that's what makes them so loyal and regal.

Shonda Marie Durden

The Dream Walker

He left me in a downward feather
motion, a gentle swaying left-to-right
drifting. Everything's now in half-
tones and smudge soot blackness,

a void state, hungering for sun-slits.
Thorned tumbleweed notes replaying
somersault movement, prick impeding
my treasure-trove, off-putting warm

toasty let-out feelings. As if my petticoat
shows beneath the gold sequins of my
dance dress. Heavy, bulky, weighted with
lead fish-line sinkers. Stuck..that's me.

Shirley Mackie

Untitled

The candles flickering in the back.
Music flowing through your body,
As if it where your soul, your only soul.
Screams and bands in the back of your head,
Make you think of pain, but there is no pain,
Not in this world.
A world of no pain or pleasure, A world only of one soul,
Your soul
As your body sleeps in the nights, it becomes of only one,
One soul to be lifted free, free to fly around,
around the mountains, And the deserts, of the world.
Free to be what you want to be,
To feel what you want to feel,
To find your heart and not your mind,
To touch love and not sorrow,
A world only to be found by your soul.
Deep in the hours of the dark nights.
A world may appear as bright as the sun, but only to one,
Your soul.

Nicole Wagner

And The Music Died

As a young child, she was born to play
Music of excitement filled her head during the day
She listened to the music as she ran through the grass
She listened to the music as she watched her childhood pass

As she grew older her teenage years began
She looked to the future with no care, and no plan
The music played louder, it pounded in her head
But then she met the man she would some day wed

They met at school, he swept her off her feet
The music in her head turned gentle and sweet
They married at once, their hearts filled with love
Soon her stomach swelled with a gift from above

In a few months she had a bundle of joy
She was the proud mother of a small baby boy
The music played softly as she cared for her son
But the years flew by, and he would not stay young

Then one summer her son moved away
And the very next winter her husband passed away
She sat at the table, with her head in her hands, she cried
She was by herself, all alone, and the music died.

Richard Lackinger

Rejected Ecstasy

You sealed your lips and I locked mine.
My angry heart would not declare its love.
Suppressed, love died and left a void
To which I welcomed pride
In hope that it would sate my longing
And assuage my grief.
Ruled by this passion, blind and mean,
I dared not speak!
Because we would not voice
The hurt within our breasts,
We did not rise above our selfishness
To taste life's ecstasy supreme—
Forgiving love!
And so we went our separate ways,
Two hearts betrayed by silent lips,
Young hearts which yesterday roamed free
In paradise of bliss,
Condemned by silence, pride's chief aid,
To hells of loneliness!

Regina Torzewski

You - Who Are

You who are my everything
my breath, my praise, my adoration
my life. Without you I would
perish eternally.

Who can speak of your unfathomable
beauty? Who can describe the sweetness
you are in my mouth, the love you
give my body and soul intimately embraced?

Oh you, whom my soul cherishes,
when I'm in your very arms, all around me is void - there is
you and only you, and words cannot even
describe the bliss of one precious moment in your loving
embrace - the taste of intimacy with you, Oh my God!

Others want lands and homes and things.
But Oh my God, I desire only you -
for I am want of nothing in your arms - forever, Oh my God!

Susan Cook

Reverence

He watches me through all my trials. The Lord God Almighty,
my Champion of love. I stare at the sky and I see His face,
smiling gently from the clouds, looking down from above.

And in the late of day, in our time together, I bow before Him
With my head to my feet. I talk and I weep and I try to explain
the secrets inside me, I tried hard to keep.

As I finish, I'm breathless, waiting for His reply.
For I unburdened my soul, even though He knows why.

Then He reaches out and whispers my name, cradling me,
comforting me, accepting my plea.
"You are my child and all is forgiven. You are whole again,
go forth in Holy living!

And give my word to all you can reach, tell them you will share
And gladly teach. Tell them to confess and believe in their
hearts, tell them that my love brings light into dark."

As He spoke, I knew the importance of His words,
Now I'm determined to go and make myself heard.
And I'll sing this song I learned long ago,
"Jesus loves me, the best love I know, for within my heart,
He's told me so!"

Katherine C. Jackson

The Dream

As the waves touch the shore
My eyes caress your skin-it is as smooth as the sand
left behind by the tide.
The person before me is as diverse as the sea....
his soul is boundless, he is as free as the wind.
Although the cliffs, the rocks are jazzed...
I see through the obstruction
I've seen shattered souls and tattered dreams
awash on these waters of corruption.. being
lifelessly tossed about by the surf and crashed upon
the rocks...these translucent hopes on the indecisive
winds of change.
Your eyes embrace me with warmth
Like the sun to the sand.
They have caught my attention and captured my heart.
I am afraid to touch you...although so real
I fear my hand may slip through the transparency
of the dream.

Katherine Morgan Pegg

Icy Embrace

The winter wind flies
my face and bites my words in half
but
the icicles of my heart fall down
like fallen tombstones
bearing epitaphs of past loves
as
your smile starts a melt down
and eases the chafing effects
of the emotions chilled
due to an extended hibernation
and
now awakened by your radiance
the numbness transforms into a warm tingle.

Kathie Wheeler-Bramer

When It All Fell Apart

1987 is when it all fell apart for us
my father died and part of you died with him
I became more than you could handle and you beat me
I walked all over you and you beat me
I disobeyed you and you beat me

1991 you had enough of me and you meet him
I run away from you and he slowly kills you
I try to change for you and he slowly kills you
I try to help you and he slowly kills you

Well now it's 1994 and I'm still more than you can handle
and you're slowly dying
I'm still trying to change and you're slowly dying
I'm still trying to help you and you're slowly dying
Will I ever be grateful for what you have done

Marie Hesser

My Feelings

My feelings for you are very strong
My feelings for loving you maybe very wrong

My feelings for you will always be there
My feelings for you might not ever get me anywhere

My feelings for you is what brings the light in my life
My feelings if they weren't there then I will have

Darkness in my life

My feelings for you will always stay
My feelings for you go upon my every nights day

My feelings for you has giving my heart sunshine in
The day and night

My feelings for you can only bring me my every days
Night

My feelings for you will always be here for you until the
End of time

My feelings for you will stay as long as our love will be
For each other without thinking of the time.

Mariana Mesleh

Beyond Dreams

Over the hills and far away,
on top of a mountain I'd like to stay...
Listen to the birds, listen to the trees,
Nothing here filled with greed,
so I will dig a hole and plant a seed,
nurture it daily so therefore no weeds.
And in the spring nothing to worry about not a thing,
Because up come a buttercup to cheer me up.
No need feeling blue because dreams come true..

Tina Ardito

Natural Birth

I found
My friend Vanessa
Steady, in the chaos midwifed stream of residency.
Of the birth, I recall a background of white coats bobbing like surf.
In the hospital cafeteria it was a sea of pale blue and pink
shirts dotting the white starched button down ones—
Where one could glimpse the occasional flower of rebellion
Asymmetric among the proper club and stripe ties.

Woman doctor undisturbed by her uniqueness.
Black, quiet and proud to no fault.
She was sitting there with her warmth and humor cloaked against
assault.
It was not a kind terrain
I saw a glimpse of roots deeper than the murky bottom and
I felt drawn to be there by her that day.
And we sat and talked
That afternoon over lunch, and our friendship was born.

I. Cori Baill

Ballerina Dancer

As I glanced around this sterile hospital world
My gaze fell upon this small little girl;
She was sitting in a little red wagon
Listening to her Mom sing Puff, the Magic Dragon.
I stopped and listened to her
And my vision began to blur
As the little girl told of her dream
To become a ballerina dancer,
But she had lost her leg to a monster called cancer.

As I stood up to leave
The mother, with tears, looked at me.
She told me the battle had not been won
That this monster was still not done.
Surgery was scheduled the very next day
And if I would, to please pray.
I said I would as tears flowed from my eyes
And I hope that tomorrow the monster would die.
As I walked away, I heard the little girl say,
"Mommy, I want to go home and play."

Shari L. Bryan

Alone

I am alone,
  My hallow footsteps echo through the long hall as each moment
  passes.
I am afraid,
  Every shadow is a person hiding behind a stone pillar.
I am chased,
  A man, a shadow, a child, a cat; someone or something fol-
lows...
I am caught,
  A web of terror has trapped me by my arm.
I am discouraged.
  I see no light at the end of this tunnel.
I am distrustful,
  Who can I trust? No one... I am alone

Stephanie Snyder

The Light Began To Fade

The anxieties of life crowd my mind and blackened
my heart. Confusions of growing, torture my thoughts
and tear my soul apart, there is no end to all the
sorrows nor to all the pain there is only
indefinite blackness and never ending rain. They may
define it as depression but it's so much more. It
goes beyond simple heartache and easy tears that
pour, a once warm loving heart has ceased it's now
cold like death. What once was a body is now a
corpse No sign of love nor feel of breath after the
"disappointment" the sun had gone and light began
to fade away, the burdens of life increased in
number and love no longer cared to stay. The rain
goes on pouring in my mind, And yet the tears no
longer shed. The worst sorrow is I'm living and yet
it's living when within...I'm dead.

Liza R. Eustaquio-Babin

Untitled

  My days are empty, full of such pain
My heart it aches, a hell of a strain.
For so many nights, I've cried in my sleep
Dreaming of someone to love and to keep.
Someone to live with, to love and to share
To give all my heart for to truly care.
To be held in my arms and softly say,
"You are my world, please always stay."
"You are the life that beats in my chest,
And with you by my side, I am truly blessed."

  I wish to God I knew what it's like,
to feel the thanks that make the world right.
But fear stalks my mind, which keeps me so blind,
And I just cannot see...
    - Why anyone would want me.

Robert J. McCullough

My Daddy

Now that I'm different, older than before...
My heart still praises more and more
A man I call daddy, the father of me,
The one I love and honor respectfully.

His height is high and his strength is bold,
Never a man to fall or fold.

His knowledge is plentiful
And he's rich in my heart
My love for my daddy
Will never fade nor part.

Lynn Angela Gardner

Home At Last!

And now, with wondrous, awesome steps I've trod
  My last, and gladsome, winding road to God,
And look, bewildered, down upon my mourners few.
  Do they not know? Starting a joyous life anew
I stand, transfixed, with trembling limbs
  Before my Blessed Lord, and all my heart and soul
Is so full of joy so great, man hath not words to say!
  I have come home, but still, not so far away
That you who love me will not pause and understand,
  And feel my presence brush you, one and all,
So that you may know I'm not beyond recall.
  For memory has its own strange way of reaching out
Across the narrow space of earth and sun,
  And bind, with loving loops, our spirits one.

Marie Matthews Hackney

Awakening

I stood alone my world crumbling about me
My life a sudden desert of despair
There were no straws to clutch upon the waters
There was no one to hold, no one to care
My life was gone, my broken heart reminded me
My love had faded fast before my eyes
There was no rhyme, no reason God should leave me
Behind to face the dark foreboding skies
But yet alas, I see a light before me
A tiny speck, I see it from afar
A hand reached out to help the path grow steady
A caring warmth spread by a living star
We all need love and help and caring
You cannot be an Island left unclaimed
I'm not alone with waters left uncharted,
Untrodden beach and jungles left untamed
So light of day with sun I see before me
With growing things and trees about to bloom
No darkness pushing in and all around me
The light of day is dawning from the gloom

    Thelma Baldassara

Love Lost

As I sit alone deep in thought
My mind knows not what to focus on
The past few months have been so full of hurt
I try to make myself think hopeful and positive thoughts
Betrayed, humiliated; hurt by his lies and infidelity.
Yet he says he sees where he has done nothing
wrong and has no shame
How can I ever get back that love,
that I have lost
I know not what the answer is;
expect we must all go on with our lives
Time may lessen the pain, the grief; I feel
But I know deep in my heart, that the love
I've lost, can never be found again.

    Louise P. Sutton

The Good Old Cookie Tree

When I was just a little lad, and had to go to school,
my mind was on the cookie jar. It was not on school.
I tried to learn in every way, but my mind kept drifting back,
to that good old cookie jar that sat upon the rack.
I told my mom my problem, and she said "oh! my son!
the cookie jar will have to go or you'll become a bum."
My mom she solved the problem, she made a cookie tree
and on it put restrictions, "that I must do my part,
and bring my grades up high enough so I could get a start,"
Now I study very hard and I can truly see "that my teachers
are so very proud of me."
My days are all so happy, for I know that when I leave,
I'll be heading for my cookies on the good old cookie tree.
My tree is made of wood, its trunk is nice and clean.
The boughs are arms that hold my cookies on the tree.
My mom wraps them up in colored paper fine,
so they are not all cookies but, some presents that I find.
Now, "I am an honor student, just as proud as I can be."
But "I owe it all to mother, and the good old cookie tree."

    Lucinda Watts Wigsten

Without You

Without you my days would be so empty,
My nights would be too long.
There would be no purpose for me,
My voice, my heart, would have no song.

You fill my hours with laughter;
You're always on my mind.
It seems there is no end
To the happy memories of days we leave behind.

We'll go through life together
I pray to never part.
With you no one else could compare;
No other love could find a place in my heart.

Love may fill the world
But there's never been a love so true.
"Me without you" I cannot comprehend;
I would be nothing without you.

    Peggy Melton

Intimate Stranger

She was born in June of Seventy-Eight
My pride and joy, joined to share a fate.
I held her, bathed her, loved her so completely. To kiss
her, clap hands with her, and see her smile sweetly.
Her hair is thick and shiny, her eyes always so hopeful, and
until she was five she was trusting and soulful.
When did she become this intimate stranger?

She got angry at me for getting divorced and her attitude was
awfully mean and without any remorse.
I bought her clothes, and records and make-up you see, to try
and make things better between her and me.
But her spirit is now changed into a shallow, cold person who
only sees the good in herself and rejects me by desertion.
Where did she go, this intimate stranger?

She no longer bonds with me unless she wants a favor.
Although I still love this intimate stranger.
I keep the door open and I express things from my heart.
And I hope that someday we'll have a fresh start.
Who is this intimate stranger?
My beautiful daughter.

    Mindy Wolf

Ragin' Lady

Burning night, you were dressed to thrill
My pulse went racing, you sent a chill
Down my back to the base of my spine
I imagined us, we're intertwined

Your hair as black as the darkest night
Your sexy lips and eyes of skylight
The stuff of dreams, your body so fine
I'd kill or die, for you to be mine

    Ragin' lady, you make my blood burn
    Ragin' lady, you make my heart yearn
    Girl, I want you to fulfill my dreams
    Let me love you beyond your screams...Ragin'Lady

I asked you up for some dinner and dance
Hoping that it would turn to romance
You knocked me out, when you said that you would
Thought to myself, well, so far so good

All alone, lights turned down low
The ocean roared, the full moon it glowed
Our passion lasted, 'til the morning's first light
Now I never want you out of my sight

    Richard A. McNeill

Waiting

I stare out the window, thinking of you.
My sad eyes unfocused; not seeing the view.
My thoughts are turned inward, dreaming only of you.

Unknowingly tears fall from my eyes.
Like torrents of rain pour from the sky.
The only sound heard is my lonely sigh.

Every footstep in the hall makes me wish you're there.
My mind only hoping what my heart doesn't dare.
Wondering anxiously if you really care.

Each day I stare at the phone willing it to ring.
Waiting for the joy that hearing your voice will bring.
Longing for the words that will make my heart sing.

Now I still wait, aching for you.
Lonely and crying for each day to be through.
Hoping against hope that you're missing me too.

Sue Phillips

Hegy

If I were a mountain majestic and tall,
My season of preference would always be fall.

Now I live on a mountain majestic and tall,
And surely you know I do love the fall.

The vibrant colors that touch on the leaf,
Linger only so briefly then steal off like a thief.

You always have some who ride on their bikes,
Not to mention the many who cherish a hike.

While wildlife root quietly among the leaves,
Hormonal quests are forging their needs.

Embellishing how lovely the ridges and peaks,
Creates in my sole all I would seek.

Now I look to my mountain for solace and peace,
Never to own, only to lease.

Always happy I'll be of this mountain so tall,
Assured in my heart it will always be fall.

Nila S. Milton

The Breaking Of The Light

When my soul moves, darkly, within the
Narrow well of Reason, it is...my soul is...
Like the palest vapor, palpating, pressing
Pallid fingers against the sterile stones of Logic.
Probing. And ever I bow my head to the Devils of Despair.

When my soul moves, darkly over seas of Self-Pity,
I wash myself in their black waters. I search the Shore for
dim-lighted eyes that trust in tales Contrived with lies.
And I worship weak words of sympathy.

When my soul moves, darkly, among Fear's long mountains,
I seek no warm valleys deep where the wind of the woods might sing
Aeolian symphonies, and my sorrowing soul might sleep. No,
I make my home on breathless peaks, or in caves of Silent ice .

My soul seems like the racing shadow of some cloud, bound for....
nothing....but the Breaking of the Light.

Ronald E. Henshaw

A Bunch Of Happiness

While I took my solitary walk
nearby I heard someone talk.
I looked around, but found no one
except a bunch of flowers having fun.
It was autumn, when life is reclused
this exhilaration made me confused.
They were in all color and shape
teasing each other in a friendly jape.

No where I have seen such a fine show
even the tiny flowers were swinging below.
Counted are their days; yet only few
to me, it appears as if they knew.
Flourishing; having a trip to fantasy
expressing deeply their desired ecstasy.
All this happiness gave my grim lips a broad smile
mischievous twitch in my eyes, returned for a while.

Talat Mohiuddin

Alpen Solitude

I sat alongside a friend today yet uttered not a word.
Neither moved as the world raced by;
Still, our thoughts o'er mountains stirred.

We sat in silence above the trees, the soft sun touched our hearts.
The cool air blowing softly below
Sealing memories ne'er to part.

We smelled the pine and alpen spring
Pressing upwards through the snow;
The fresh crisp mountain air courier
To Bavarian Springtime's glow.

We peered across the slopes and chasms;
Across miles and peaked tops.
O'er trees and streams and villages
'Til vision, exhausted, stopped.

We felt the soothing caress of sun and closed our wandering eyes
To collect the sounds and precious views
No sighted man could prize.

And as today I joined my friend we again had made the journey;
For of a vision of Alpen majesty
Often returns the memory.

Shane Gramling

A Mother's Poem

Children's faces so soft and smiling.
Never seen anything so lively.
As they make it through life's ups and downs.

There is always a gleam in
their eye that says it's
alright, we will get by.

No matter how old they get,
they will always be the child
with the soft smiling face,
You love so dearly.

Because through life's rough
times and little bothers
They will always know us as their mothers.

Sue Glidden

"What Is A Sister"
Dedicated to Barbara

She is the one, you can tell all your secrets to, and she'll
never tell a single soul.

The one, who will laugh at your jokes, even if they're, not
funny and old. Who will watch a movie, with you and you both,
cry at the saddest part.

Who will share all your, joys and will also share the hurt, who
will, put you first, in a time of your need and strife.

Who if only had it, to spare, would share her wealth. But
of all, these things, what means the most, to me, is that with
all her, caring and sharing, what she gives the most, is her
love for me.

And that's what a sister should be. And why she means, the
world to me.

Margaret Brewster

Moon Goddess

The Goddess watches while the liquid light
new-fallen weaves enchanting tracery
to blend with sorcerer's chicanery
whose incantations fill the secret night.
Now, Moon, await the impact over bright
and waning cycles wild with witchery,
absorb metallic shocks of mastery
upon the glow of transcendental white.

For mind at last confronts the wearied ghosts
of all the ancient alchemists, and thought
will shout that Man has conquered legend...yet
the cry is keening always in such boasts
that mystery, the soul of wonder, sought
through ages gone, will die... if we forget.

Margery Johnson

Metamorphoses

Detach...detached...detachment.
No connectedness.
No roots.

No old stories about when my grandpa
knew your grandpa.
No old stories about what our parents did together
when they were growing up.

No old stories about the neighborhood.
Houses don't make a neighborhood.
Cocoons of isolation,
their metamorphoses blossom—
nameless faces, unsmiling faces, grim faces,
fearful faces.
Cold hearts, cold attitudes.

The cycle continues...

Susan Martinez-Riphahn

My Brother

You died when I was only four,
Now I am sad, and very sore,
for I did not cry on that day,
When we laid you to rest, in no more pain.
Now you're in heaven with no more fear,
Running freely, riding on deer,
So don't forget me,
for I'll always remember
And when I die I'll search for you.

Mark Corwin

Half-Breed

It's hard being a half-breed, just where do you belong?
No matter how you feel or what you think, everything you do is wrong.
It's true, to the Indian you're white by law, and the whites call you
    Indian squaw,
Always having to prove oneself to the people who should know better.
They ask you for your number do you have proof? show me a letter.
You want to show the world that you can help yourself.
You look too much Indian to get a job, but not enough to get some help.
The other side is Irish, what can I say?
The Indian side makes them uncomfortable, they want you to just
    go away.
Try to enjoy a pow-wow, they say why are you so fair.
Go to the white man's school, the boys sure like the green eyes and
    black hair.
I don't feel I have to show some leg, I don't even know a dress.
My hand shake is law, my word is gospel and I don't feel I'm any better
    than the rest.
I enjoy life in nature, I want to be happy, I'm not going to sing the blues
Let's get off this kick, for I surely have paid my dues
I want to thank my mother for the giving of her seed
And I say to my father I'm very, very proud for being a Half-Breed.

Tanaka

I, The Ocean

I the ocean was blue and clear,
No more beauty is found here,
Only found now is pollution and dirt,
Stories of sadness and some of hurt.

I the ocean was home to many,
To dolphins and whales and fish of plenty,
But all left now is my dirty shore,
No more animals roam my sea floor.

I the ocean was times of fun,
For young for old for everyone,
Now no more swim and no more sail,
Will they come or will they fail?

I the ocean was here for you,
With so many things that you could do,
A place of fun a place of cheer,
Not too much longer will I be here.

I the ocean am destroyed now,
And all that I can ask is how,
Didn't you ever really care,
Or were you just not aware?

Lynn Wasilewski

"Trail Of Destiny"

Conscious vibes clear the path
No more negativity, no more wrath
A bright illumination surrounds the trail
Assuring that positive vibes forever prevail

The sun shines bright and the moon still glows
And the energy between them forever flows
Like rivers of insight that pass in a stream
Opening the mind creating reality of dreams

It's a positive life, a life filled with meaning
A centered, happy, balanced life, where you'll never be feeling
Suffering, lostness, sadness and hate
only joy, love, and wisdom determine your fate

So climb on the trail from wherever you may be
Open your eyes, open your mind, and learn to be free
you must be determined to find it in soul and in heart
But once your truth is discovered you will never depart.

The truth sits in you, accepted or neglected
Just be positive and loving and your soul will be connected!

Oliver A. Ferrier

"No Money In Heaven"

No need for the supermarts, restaurants or malls
No need for fast food chains
No need at all.
No need for the health spas, salons or saloons
No need for vacations or cruises in June.
No need to buy houses with furniture to fill
No need to worry about leaving a will.
No need for the race track with horses to bet
No need for the lottery each week that we get.
No need for new cars with sporty appeal
No need for the extras they throw in the deal.
No need for the banks for a loan to seek
No need for a paycheck we cash there each week.
No need for the credit cards with interest sky high
No need for the wallets or billfolds we buy.
No need for back pockets in pants that they sew
to carry the wallets wherever we go.
So what is there left when he opens his door?
Why all of eternity for our God to adore!

Sandra Benchik

My Life

My life is like an endless nightmare
No one cares and no one shares
No one ever says hello to me or any other fellow.

My life is like a silent cry and sometimes
I wish I could only die

The days are black and sometimes gray
And the only thing I can do is pray

I wish there was always peace on earth
That starts from the first day of your birth

My life is like a misty cloud as I sit
And think how to make them proud

Why is there always something wrong
When life is supposed to be a song

And if it's a song where are the words
Are they the ones sung by the birds

My life has always been strange to me
But there's just one thing I cannot see

When we argue and when we fight
I always wonder if someday there might
Be peace in my life.

Nancy Russell

Passing Time

The trees were still, they had not changed
No sign that spring might re-arrange
The cold hard stillness that filled the air
Their silent thoughts never to share.

So time goes on forever and more
Squirrels will run and birds will soar
You and I in some small way
Measure time with another day

Fleeting moments, a glint of sun
The fragile time of everyone
Passing through like a southern wind
Rushing to our inevitable end

And so your heart must be strong and true
Measure your moments by what you do
Drink in the sun, the wind, and rain
Open your heart to another's pain

Look within yourself and dare to see
How precious Life's fleeting moments can be!

Terri Bowman

The Tree

A marvelous feat of nature, this wonder called a tree.
No two are quite the same, and that's the way it should be.

Its roots go deep into the soil,
while its branches reach for the sky and sun.
Many bearing its fruit in due season,
all providing some shade from the sun.

They say we all have a family tree, that our roots are deep and full.
With names like Oak, Maple, Birch, and Evergreen,
and Washington, Roosevelt, Lincoln and Jefferson.

What would a tree say if it could talk?
Can you look at it and see what kind of life it's had?
Are its branches full, with a massive trunk,
or are its branches brittle and rotting and its trunk full of holes?
Would it cry or laugh if it had the chance, would it sing a song,
and jump and dance and play in the moon-light till dawn,
or would it curl up in a ball and be as still
as a rag doll and lie there till the setting sun?

The life of a tree is full of wonder...
what would you do if you could move?
what would you say if you could?

Ronald L. Meadors

Little Me

Nobody loves me, nobody cares,
  Nobody notices me, nobody shares.
I can never enjoy life as it is,
  Because I am below my average size.
Everybody my age is so, so tall,
  But me, myself and I are bantam, petite, and small.
I am lucky and fortunate even though,
  And this I will forever and ever know.
I do not feel desolate or deserted or lonesome for another
  Because I will always have my big, tall brother.
He plays with me, and takes care of me,
  And he will love me forever,
And when people pick on me,
  He will always be there.

Sandra Hamilton

Today

The world can not understand, nor can it listen,
nor can it feel, nor can it help itself,
so where does the world stand today?

Prejudice, such a threatening sickness in our society
aids, the deadly disease killing the populations
gangs are hunted as a prey
what is the world coming to today?

The mentally ill, psychotic, and unsafe
those who murder for reason or not
with hatred burning on each individual face
where is the justice promised us?

The homeless sleeping in our streets and
children's bones seen prominently from starvation
the drugs and souls for sale around every corner
today, old liberty still stands, though time has faded and
cracked her.

Pollution takes over the earth's surface and
our men are over worked and under paid
life comes and goes day by day
and that is how we have arrived at today.

Sandy Graves

Lazy Bones

'Twas the beginning of February and all through the wood
  Not a creature was stirring as wood creatures should.

For Old Mother Nature in her usual way
  Had bestowed on the earth quite a storm that day.

The snow began falling and covered the ground,
  The wind began blowing and blew it around.

The creatures were nestled all snug in their lairs
  The chipmunks, the otters, the beavers, the bears.

Even Mortimer Ground-hog thought it was better
  To stay under cover in such nasty weather.

The second of February came with a bound
  But no trace of Mortimer_Hog could be found;

For he was asleep - in his own quiet way
  He simply turned over and slept it away.
    Mary T. Mac Isaac

Message From Voyager

Not a smidgeon.
Not a smidgeon!
No life anywhere!

The learned astronomer shook his head
As he studied the Voyage log . . .
Then stared into the dark, into dead and barren space.

No green, green grass,
No amber fields of grain,
No scented blooms,
No leafing trees,

No darting fish,
No soaring eagle,
No whippoorwill,
No frisky colt,
No playful pup,
No breathing, thinking Man —
Anywhere out there.

Alone.
We are all alone with our Maker,
Within this vast and awesome space.
    Thomas Amherst Perry

Dreams

You are all alone and no one is there,
not a sound is heard while the wind blows in your soft hair.
There are many thoughts that go through your head.
while you lay and dream in your bed.
As you pray that all will come true,
small tears fall down clear and blue.
On your birthday all will see.
you make a wish that you hope to be.
And when that wish comes true,
you know that God is there for you.
But if he denies you of your precious desire,
you pick another wish while that old one expires.
    Stephanie Gatti

A Sleepy Ozark Day

Today it was quiet.
Not devoid of sound.
Just... Quiet, in a relaxed,
warm Summer afternoon way,
Lazy,
softly embracing,
caressing the imagination,
tempting the senses with invitations
of playing hooky.
Of slipping into sparkling pools of prancing,
teasing mountain streams.
Quiet,
gently urging the spirit
into cool forests
shaded in summer dress,
hushed by whispering, stately trees
forever guarding the solitude
in the greenery of natures domain.
Today in the Ozarks of Missouri.
It was quiet
    Robert A. Jones

A Talk With God

I cannot see your face in the sky, dear God,
Not even on the far horizon,
But when I gaze at the wonders you've wrought,
I feel my spirits rising.

There are so many times when the way seems dark,
When life around me is pressing,
"Tis then that I think of the worlds you've made,
And sit down to count my blessings.

I cannot see your face in the sky,
But I know that you are there,
Providing the things in life that I need,
Showing me, daily, you care.

I see the little birds fly by,
And know they're in your care,
I listen to the Ocean's roar,
And feel your presence there.

I cannot see your face, dear God,
But I know you're ever there!
You even love a wretch like me,
And always hear my prayer.
    Margaret G. Green

"Strongest"

To be a stonecutter, or a king, is
not hard to choose. For the king has
power and he rules.
But the sun beats down on the king's
head, and makes him full of dread.
Now the sun must be the choice, for now
he has the strongest voice. But here
passes by a cloud that wraps around the
sun like a shroud. To be a cloud is a
wise decision, for he moves fast with
procession. But what lies here, a
mountain so high. That makes the cloud
cry. The cloud rains tears to beat down
on the rock. But after a while he'll have
to stop. To be the mountain, you are the
strongest of all, you are so strong you
may never fall, but here comes the
stonecutter, with his chisel and hammer.
He hits away till there is no need for a ladder.
    Shawn P. Webb

Michelle

The wind on that night, sure did blow
not in a garden, but open to grow
rays of the starlight, twinkled her eye
alp - like peaked cheekbones, reflecting the light
little I knew, that she would be mine
her luminous lips, spoke of us two
here comes the night, pretense to bloom
then a dark strand, of velvet black hair
ran through my hands, as we were fair
but came a tear, of blood out my eye
onto black velvet, we intertwined
that was way then, and my body is gone
yet forever I live, with my
Michelle.

Paul Kennar

Not In My Lifetime:

Not in my lifetime will I see violence cease to exist anymore.
Not in my lifetime will I see all the homeless in the world,
become the middle-class instead of the poorest of poor.
Not in my lifetime will I see sickness and sadness in the world,
go away.
Not in my lifetime will I see prejudice and bigotry in the world,
decide not to stay.
Not in my lifetime will I see our air our land and our water in,
this world, become pure and clean.
Not in my lifetime only in my deepest dream .
Not in my lifetime will I see children being able to trust a
stranger when they are alone.
Not in my lifetime will I see endangered animals be free and left
alone to roam.
Maybe not in my lifetime will I witness Christ coming back.
But just knowing in my lifetime that he is coming back, keeps my
mind, heart and my soul on life's right track.

Rhonda Wilson

Precious Destiny

When you wish upon a star
Not knowing if it's near or far

Asking for an amazing grace
But destiny will often take place

The reality of life is real and true
The reward of living isn't up to you

Just close your eyes and think of love
For precious destiny shall rise above

Now the sky is blue and the rain has stopped
The joy is showing and no tears have dropped

There is peace in my mind and love in my heart
That began precious destiny right from the start

No hints, guessing or clues to fill my ecstasy
Just my love and my precious destiny.

Raeena J. Prince

"Daddy, Why Do You Smile"

A few years ago, back in nineteen seventy-two
   Not knowing the future, and that I'd spend it with you
I remember watching my dad as he grinned ear to ear
   I tried to imagine why, but the reason was never clear
He went off to work, and came home every night
   In the coldest December there were always sparks he'd ignite
Now, twenty years from then, as I stand in the aisle
   I look in your eyes, and I can see why he smiled
There's a new reason for living, and new feelings within
   My life was never over - it just waited to begin
I can't wait to hear the puzzled words from my child
   Looking up with his blue eyes asking, "Daddy, why do you smile?"

Patrick Crockarell

Nothing

So I give you these photos
not the picture of the dog
upside down paws against the wall
in the street panting
on the cement floors or laundry
A T.V. a thatched roof

Because they were my friends
So I give you this photograph
empty of faces dogs flies
hammock chickens   people live there

There are barb wire places
There are faces names families that bring children wife husband
laundry and briefcase on the buses
farmers who sell to tourists-who come buy stay or leave
These places   These people

So I give you These photos of boats El Mar - the sea cement coconut
flowers, pescado-fish which is where they live   to remember them by.

Michelle McDonnell

Splashed

So Splashed, sometimes I feel
-not the recipient of the Splash
-not the receptacle of what the Splash-stuff is

But I am the explosion of the Splash that forced
-the myriad splats
-of uneven, every-directioned bursts

As I, so the small-massed fragments sense the impact
-of a substance, hard from outside
-of materials, heavy from up there

The suddenness of that, dropped or hurled
-by accident fallen or
-by intent designed
Sometimes so Splashed I feel

Phyllis F. Copeland

Forever

My mind wanders endlessly Fleeting moments once at my
fingertips
Now deeply etched in memory Losing prominence slowly

Will they even be gone Irreplaceable values linger on
Seconds Minutes Hours Days
Continuing through the years beyond
Simultaneously turning into a gray-blue haze

Baby prattle Toddler tattle Childhood catastrophes
Kids in battle Lost loves Best of friends
Peace, love, happiness Are they all to be forgotten

Living in the past Or depending on the future
Where when what why
Emotionless we cry
Shall our living life die

How will we know Is it fate or destiny By will or inability
Can this only be me Lost in an endless quandary
But then again...... Forever?

Sheryl Alston

My Special Friend

For "Charlie"-Charlotte

Our time together was so brief.
now I filled with overwhelming grief.
I think of you often, the fun we had,
the day you left California I was sad.
Your sweet smile, the twinkle in your eye,
you were a true friend, I will never say Goodbye.
Your love for life, the people you touched,
my friend I will miss you very much.
Though you had problems along the way,
I am here to say, you were the best.
There are so many things I wish I could say.
Hug you one more time, hear you say "Hey".
You will forever live in my heart and mind.
I wasn't ready for you to leave me behind.
I feel so lost, an empty place in my heart.
I've got to pick up the pieces, where do I start?
I wish you were here today,
one last thing I want to say, I love you,
and I will always remember you.

Stacie Moniz

My Broken Heart

  I poured out to you my heart and soul.
  Now I'll only be left with just memories to hold.
  Deep inside I'll tuck them away,
into a heart which I've lost all control.
  We all live for the memories of yesterday.
We carry them into our future
so we may have hope for tomorrow.
  Now when I see the rain,
hear the crack of thunder,
oh how my heart will pain
and my tears will flow like the pouring rain.
  I must try to convince myself
there's nothing there,
there's nothing left,
but now as my heart is breaking
the angels singing in heaven silence to the sound.
  The memories just came.

Tammy Beavers Dockery

Vultures

When I dwelt among you, I was as dung
Now my carcass to you, is honey sweet
In life I was your Outcast, In death Immortalized
I was your Ace-in-the-hole, when situations went awry
How could you afford to let me live
I was calf, pent-up for more succulent meat
Knowing I would retreat within, to find beauty elsewhere
You recognized it in my Poetry and Song
You try to capitalize on it, but your selfish life made it wrong
You wouldn't take from others, until their name you first belief
As fragile as I was you couldn't obtain what was mine
You spun your web so carefully and laid a trap so fine
You called Black, White and Right Wrong, and stole what was
  always mine
You set your table for a feast knowing another sacrifice you would eat
To be in your footsteps, I would dread, because you blaspheme even the
  dead.

Robin S. Thomas

Poetry And Life

P rose, prayers, promises, and prodigy
O ften written and read silently alone
E ver stirring dreams, desires, and troubles within the soul
T o make those words their own life
R elenting only emotion within the theater of the mind
Y et, savoring the thrill, passion, or grief unto themselves;

A lways looking for new directions and inspiration
N ever satisfied with the past or now
D esiring only what the next poem can offer;

L ike an addiction to what one can experience
I f only the solitude and the poem would give to us in daily living
F ervently releasing the theater to reality then...
E motionally welcoming anything life has to offer.

  Treva L. Baker

Prison Glass

Behind a quarter-inch pane is a child in a man's body.

Beyond lipstick smudges slumps a soul seduced by a daughter
of deception, forgotten by friends that never were.

Between diamond-shaped wires remorseful eyes show a
tired frustration.

Below finger prints moves a hand aching for a gentle
touch.

Through the phone line a voice cracks holding back
choking tears.

Prison glass frames a mother's son, victim of desire,
warrior of the streets.

Reflections in the glass show pain.

Reflections in the glass show suffering.

Reflections in the glass show death at the foot of the jackal.

  Mary L. Brookman

Virgin

Innocence ripples unhindered, skimming surfaces
  of deep, murky pools... time enough to be
    time enough for frightened foals
      on spindly legs
        taking first steps

But time does not still, ripples fade away
  and foals learn to run
    innocence remains but is changed
      wisdom is gained

She grows wise of the world that would have her altered
  for all they see is... a marble statue
    cold, curious, not understood... a monster of beauty
      to scorn, mock, envy... an unbreached citadel seen
        only for conquest... a fallow field that grows no
          seed for parental pleasure

But in her world she waits with purpose she is
  not odd but decided not a single-stitch of moments
    but a tapestry of time a soldier that paces
      through the battle
        a woman whole patient.

  Vicki E. Bryant

The Light

Hazy Lazy days filled with an over abundance
of liquid sunlight blind me as I reach for
unreachable aspirations. Not that I doubt the
ability given to me to reach far. But countless
obstacle fill my path and cause me to stumble
at every turn. Oh how these way torn scabs
hurt us with the healing of one comes a new
one to replace it. Light. I see light. Not a
far away tunnel of light but a bright new light
filled with hope and joy. Come, it beckons.
Come. I follow the light and am overwhelmed
by its brightness. Blindly I reach into it only
to find it empty. Crying I turn and flee from it
What is this I scream in frustration. What is
this? I turn again and am once again drawn
towards the light. This time I approach it with hesitant
steps. Now I see what is there. It is reflections of myself
Hope and say once unquestionable is in this light
But now there is a flicker of darkness. Doubt.

Tracy Nobles

Mystic Melody

A split-rail fence darkens from the penetration
  Of the lingering rain.

A train whistle echoes in the distance as the
  Fog intensifies the night.

The rippling stream, so rhythmic, enhanced by the
  Mystic quietness in the air,

Is interrupted by the last rolls of thunder as the
  Storm progresses near to end.

The soft flickering of lightning illuminates the
  Fields only to display the silhouette of a
  Farmhouse and its barn.

The curtains move ever so gently as the beads of
  Water on the tattered screen dissipate into
  Nowhere.

Scattered branches, still rustling, whisper as the
  Power of nature remains in command.

. . . And the tranquility of the night returns once
  Again.

Patricia A. Swisher

Nirvana

Nirvana is the place,
of tranquil space,
where enchanted hairs prance,
in the naked moonlight they are caught up in dance,
fields of flowers of the sun,
so beautiful you just want to run,
into the night sky,
filled with glowing candles through which you fly,
through the mystical clouds so bright,
beautifully colored like a kite,
floating down in a breeze,
nearly into silver trees,
which chime like fairies' voices far away,
in rainbow colors they often play,
upon delicate bubbles,
which hover above like no-existent troubles,
with exceptional charm and grace,
Nirvana is the place.

Rachel Gallagher

Souvenir

My father and I watch each other
off and on all morning.
I see him guide the tractor,
pull the plow,
wave to me on the turns.

He sees me barefooted
in the orange orchard
laugh, jump, splash, skip
the foam and settlings
of his straight irrigation furrows,
sink mid calf in warm loam,
wiggle toes against things
I cannot see.

At noon above the engine's rant and jar,
he calls, and I run across the field to him.
Then, his rough hand reaches down to help me
put one foot on the lowest rung and
swing up onto his lap
for the ride home.

Martha Richesin

Life

This journey through time.
Often stresses the mind.
Thinking of the way, of which I came.
Through the canal of my mother's pain.
The road I walk, the curves, the turns
And uphill climbs.
As this life comes near its end.
Thoughts of the life ahead begins.
And as I ponder the form I am.
My thoughts, fear and pains will these feeling remain.
Or become a mass of energy without any knowledge
Of what I used to be.
Flesh, spirit and soul of man.

Ruth Green

A Cross In The Road Somewhere

" I am no different than you." said the older woman to me.
" Oh," I said.
" You look at me and you see wrinkled skin.
  You can not, do not look within.
" What is there inside that's not outside for me to see?"
  I asked the woman, when we happened to meet.
" You will see," said the older. You will see."
" Perhaps, just perhaps, it just may be, but,
  I will not be you, just me, you see."
" Fine," said the older woman." That's just fine with me."
  Then we parted. We had met for a moment, a fraction of time.
  For a moment.
  For a moment, just a moment in time.

Samy Spall

Showers To Flowers

As I lay here drying waiting for the wetness
of your gentle like kisses to keep me growing
inside. Dying to and always willing to soak
up your love. Soon you will spread yourself
through us all, willing us to become our own,
soon to start giving you more seedlings to
shower with your sometimes slow, or rapid
kisses. You always seem to come more
around a certain part of the year as if you
know when I need you most. I now sit here
buried beneath the womb of mother nature
waiting for the time to come.
Oh dear God please let the rain come soon
so I can spread my own cheerful light.

Kraceta Blaine

Just A Little While

I'll stop and rest from the cares of the world;
On a rock by the river nile.
I'll tarry here, just a little while.

I'll count each step; as each one mounts in miles.
I'll now take toll of my misdeeds,
As I rest just a little while.

I'll take a good look at my friends;
Reflect and pause to smile:
Taking stock of the happiness they bring me;
As I rest just a little while.

I'll look at my enemies; aware of every trial.
I'll thank them for the obstacles they put in my way,
As I rest from them just a little while.

I'll inventory the good I've done;
And note with care my style. I'll look back on all the races
I have run. As I rest just a little while.

I'll count each tear and each smile;
Each is a blessing on its own.
I see things more clearly now,
Since I stopped to rest just a little while.
Mildred Moses Macon

I First Noticed

I first noticed my blurred reflection
on the immaculate floor,
the smell of the enclosure
sterile to the point of nausea.
My aunt lay there, still on the white sheet,
with no wrinkles, but her face had wrinkles,
Deep abyss of abuse, dark and dank
with the smell of old liquor.
The room crowded around me
like a box, or a coffin in maybe?
Only one sound lingered in the dead air,
the respirator,
measuring twelve breaths per minute.
Tubes down her throat, a once human figure,
a mechanical monster of death.
Her eyes opened, I know she saw me
standing there over her archaic body.
Deep in her faded hazel eyes I saw the memories
and deeper still I saw the hope.
Robert S. Mitchell III

Numb

Everything seems to be the same
on the outside,
but within is numb, no pain
being numbed out is so very nice.

A facade of kindness,
using my smile as a shield
politeness an assurance I wear on my lips,
that I show all but don't feel

I had laughter, I had tears,
I had a heart that yearned
nothing gained over the years,
but numbness, like a layer of 3rd degree burns.

All dead from the outside in,
a tiny oasis of feelings that exist
let the world win, destroyed in the interim,
no point, there's no reason to resist.

Numbed out,
like a pool of still water
peaceful now,
held by the iron grip of false hauteur.
Renee Boykin

Advent

Outside my winter window
On the rim of the wind-wrecked woods
Four slender white ashes silent
In a ring of grey austerity.

Tall and willowy, they rise straight up
Spreading barren branches near the top
Backwards, like the curve of an empty vase
Or the droop of an open lily.

Only yesterday, my private Mardi Gras!
Arrayed in gold and silver beads,
They cavorted with the wind
Then blessed the earth prodigiously.

Bone bare now, they huddle at their centers
To steep in Nature's alchemy,
Listening deep within to secret murmurs,
Preparing for Epiphany.

Listening deep within to secret murmurs,
Preparing for Epiphany.
Mary O'Mara Putschi

To Ryan, With Love

A baby is born, a new life begun
Once a nameless being whom I now call son

You entered the world and made me smile
I love you so much my little child

So much to learn and so much to do
It's all so overwhelming, all so new

I want you to grow, but stay my baby
But it's not a choice of yes, no or maybe

You will grow as you're doing - oh so fast
Already the memories becoming the past

I cherish each one and hold it so true
And remember each stage of something new

From teething and walking and saying my name
To hugs and kisses and playing a game

I will always love you your entire life
One day you will marry and take on a wife

Even than I will cherish you, when two become one
I'm forever your mother and you forever my son
Kathie Twardosky

Why You Are Lonely

Where is the messenger of spring
Once clouds come over and cry
I do last for these reasons why
Do you know a song as mine?
Says the flowers once in winter alone
I long to hear your song of loneliness
Say those who have waited in their hearts
The flowers have waited for your thoughts
May I come to rest by your side?
If I may if I may those that come by morning
Along memory thoughts as dreams as dreams
Loneliness is only shared between us too
So save your love for this time of spring
The clouds do cry for reasons unknown
So follow along and you will know why
Least you sleep and miss the reason why
lonely lonely the flowers that come along
If there should be known a different song
Your lonely thoughts tells you why
Why a rainy cloud goes drifting by
Robert H. Randall

Isolation

Curtains drawn
Oncoming dawn
Sleepless nights in an accident room
Relentless candles light my tomb
Drops of rain surprise the awning
Tired and decrepit walls are yawning
Air is empty, hollow and dead
Sole sign of life, churning thoughts in my head
Silence grows stronger
As time slips away
Is my heart still beating
My flesh has turned gray
Bury me now
So my soul may have peace
And let these dreams of reality
Finally cease

R. Pawling

Goodbye For Now

A tragic end to a friend and a brother
One like him there will be no other
He touched so many with kindness and caring
In return he received loving and sharing

A brother I knew for thirty-four years
He brought laughter and joy and heartache and tears
He loved me I know, some emotions are hard to show
But feelings come through it's something you know

The land he did love that's the reason we're here
To show him we care about his feelings so dear
His ashes we scatter among the trees and his flowers
To float on the wind and come down with the showers

We will miss you, dear brother
We will miss you, dear friend
For now it's good-bye
But never the end.

Martha Gwaltney Lea

Hourglass

Flipped over they begin to fall,
One lonely, single grain of sand.
You may see in a novelty shop in the mall.
None so grand
As me standing as tall as a wall.

One grain,
One second,
Fighting to get through the clogged drain.
First grain, second,
Soon it begins to come down like rain.

Beginning to get weak,
Sand is leaving
A way out is what I seek.

I can't stop believing,
For soon I will live again.

No more sand left,
Life has ran out,
Till I'm turned over again.

Katie Bauer

One Chance

One window in time
One looking glass to see through
One glimace of color
A crack in a dream or thought

Open for only a moment
Long enough for a bird to fly through
And a grain of sand to dirty the pain
Creating a different appearance

Sometimes you see one step you took awhile back
Others are unfinished paintings of beauty you held a brush to
The color simply wasn't right

Some will remain undone forever
Blurring at the glimace of an eye
Placed in the corner of an attic
They are an echo in time.

There is no telling when the wind will come
To blow it shut, breaking the glass and supports
That window is gone.

Take a look will you walk through
Or pass it by forever.

Selisa Maahs

"But I'm Straight"

That thing is only for fags.
One mistake,
One life,
Mine!
now it's not for fags any more.
never listening.
and here is what I get.
death, despair, pain, and more death.
I must try to live with the thing that only
happens to fags.
Listening is worth it.
One mistake,
can mean,
your whole life.
Then you become as statistic.
Being remembered as a number.
isn't my idea of leaving something for generations to come.

Kelly Ross

The Gift Of Legacy

Send me a daughter with integrity strong,
  One that can willing choose right from wrong;

Send me a daughter blessed with delicate grace,
  One that can follow authorized pace;

Send me a daughter with honor and pride,
  One that can place prejudice ideas aside;

Send me a daughter loyal and true,
  One who allows a sense of humor to shine through;

Send me a daughter who will want the same,
  A daughter like her to carry on the name;

Bless me kind Lord with this daughter I pray,
  To continue the legacy started today.

Patti Matczak

A Son Is Born

A baby is born
One to carry on the family name.
Oh, so proud - and at the same time, scared
Of the unknown, of life molding decisions yet to be made.
No guide to look to, no rules written
Only your own instincts and knowledge gained by living.
The time passes oh so slow, and yet, more quickly that you can realize.
It's come the time to cut those ties, to let go, for you to stand on
  your own.
Oh the pain in a mother's heart, the tears flow.
May the paths you take be the right ones Son.
The future is yours - make me proud all over again.

Melanie Bowyer

Reunion

We're gathering at an old watering hole,
One which lent us a triumphant picture
Of our group in celebration of time spent
Championing our college years.

And the years after have seen diverse stories,
With love lost, loves found, loves discovered,
And we each have maintained a fragile hold
On our own desires and goals.

We meet at our old watering hole;
And gathering together we check the faces,
And note the trappings we've acquired,
And place a plus mark on friendship's won.

Lawrence Michael Dickson

A Friend

  A friend is someone who cares
one who shares
someone to talk to
one to have fun with
who is always there when you need them
to go places with
to go have laughs
someone to share secrets
and someone to understand.

  A friend is someone near or far
one you may not see for a long period of time
someone to write letters to
or call on the phone
friends are nice to have
they will always be there
when you need someone to talk to
someone you can trust
and someone you can count on.

Kathleen E. Keyes

What Is A Pal?

A Pal is
One you can talk to whatever the need may be.
One you can laugh with till the tears run down for all to see.
One you can cry with when things go wrong,
One you can disagree with and still stand strong,
One you can turn to when you need a helping hand.
One who will not bury their head in the sand.
One who will be there in your time of need.
One you can depend on to take the lead.
One you can trust with a secret thought.
One who remembers what the Lord has taught.
One I love with all my heart
My daughter, My secret Pal.

Mildred Emery

Under The Influence

Under the influence of morphine,
one's mind tends to wander a bit.
You're in another world, it seems real.
As long as you have somebody to talk to
you as you come in and out.
To go to where you are, and to let you know
that the snakes and rats are not really there.
Although you do tend to reason with your
common sense,
you mix reality with imagination.
It's hard to separate the two as they slowly
entwine,
under the influence.

Linda Kimberlin

Helpless

Helpless, helpless, that's what I am.
Numb, weak from my head to my feet.
No thoughts, feelings, or looking around.
My mind's so empty, I can't hear a sound.
Helpless, helpless, that's what I am,
trapped in this room and nobody cares.
I lie here in the morning, until there is night,
it seems like I'm blind without any sight.
Helpless, yes I'm helpless wishing for hope,
God give me strength and patience so I may cope.

Nicole A. Thompson

"I"

I will - I won't
I do - I don't
I am - I'm not
I remembered - I forgot
I said - I heard
I'm red - I'm a bird
I walk - I run
I talk - I see the sun
I'm sad - I'm happy
I'm glad - I'm zappy
I'm sick - I'm well
I'm in Heaven - I'm not in Hell!
Thank God!

Connie Concello

Phoenix

Your hand slipped past my covers
  I entered rage.
Sleep pretended to lull your eyes
  Silent cage
    Zebra bars as strong as
    Sour apple gum
Leaving soon I must leave you soon
  leave you
I had to sprint through your
Passion fire to reach
Phoenix as she took to flight.
Grapple with her back
  forearms flexing, pull!
I've soared past the white eagle.

Adrien C. Maiorano

When I'm Alone

When I feel alone
I feel I want to cry.
I see a dream in my path.
I see the sunlight along the way.

When I see the light
I see love.
I see happiness,
But most of all I see you.

Francesca Guy

Being Together

When I'm away from you
I feel like I could cry
The days get very long
They drag slowly by.

Being with you is special
We have a lot of fun
The days are filled with laughter
And outings in the sun.

With you arms around me
I feel safe and secure
I don't feel afraid
To face this cold, cruel world.

Your love for me is strong
Getting stronger everyday
My love for you is forever
There's just no other way.

I'm glad I have you here with me
Don't ever go away
I don't know what I'd do
Without you beside me everyday.

Desiree Bevis

Rebirth, Reborn Untouched

On the day of my birth
I felt my mother's heart
mingle with my soul

Since then

A return to serenity
for which I long
to live a fruitful existence
wrapped and snuggled
in my mother's womb

Upon arrival
my rebirth
I claimed the right to calm
searching endlessly for peace
lying dormant within my soul

Untouched

My rebirth is now
I smile a smile of gladness
reborn full of life, love
renaissance all can experience

Ivie Manuel

Spring

Spring is so fun,
I like it very much.
How about you?
I like it too!

Cameron Reginato

Grandpa

When you left,
I felt the fear.
I felt the pain.
I felt alone.

When you were gone,
I kept the love.
I kept the fun.
I kept you in my heart.

When you left,
I did not cry,
Because I knew
Where you were.

Angela Yetter

The Room

I stepped into the darkened room
I felt the shadows all congeal
I knew something was coming soon
Its presence made my senses reel.

I'd come to give a last regret
to all the lives I'd left behind.
I spoke the names of all I'd met
and searched for what I'd come to find.

I took a breath, and two, and three -
my blindness made me back a pace
for what I sought I could not see
It had no name, it had no face.

I sensed it in that darkened room
I could not see, but only feel.
I took my place within the gloom
and waited for my wounds to heal.

Cydni Perkins

"When Were Together"

When we're together
I forget everything else.
You've captured my heart;
every time you go away it melts.
I keep giving and giving.
You've taken my heart, love, and life
I want us to be eternity;
I want to be your wife.
But lets not rush;
We're still young
Will we last,
What will we become?
I've had dreams of fame and glory
When you came into my life
You brought new dreams
A whole new beginnings,
A whole new story
Share my life with me forever,
Because I love it when we're together.

Heidi Hardwick

Dream World

I feel his eyes watching me
  I look and no one's there.
I feel his evil escaping
  Trying to enter mine.
My mind is running
  From the terror -
I turn and he is there,
  Whispering slowly
"Welcome to my mind."

E. M. Morrical

Wasted Away

When I go out,
I go out to get away,
From the pain that lives,
inside of me,
No one can realize,
No one can relate,
The pain is so intense,
I've got to go,
before it's too late,
Some people say,
What their going to do,
What are you going to do,
When you're wasted away,
So live while you can,
Make every minute count,
Find happiness in what you do,
For there is no doubt,
Don't ever walk away,
For if you do your life,
Will be "wasted away"

Gary L. Houze

I Saw You

You sang a song,
I had to hear.
Because in your music,
You appear.

Your song told the stories,
This small town never knew.
But feeling the chills up my spine,
I knew the storyteller was you.

Your words were so delicate,
Your face was so free.
When you were up singing,
I saw your destiny.

The passion in your song,
Made the stars fall from the sky.
And the truth in your voice,
Could be seen in your eyes.

Your music made the night a fantasy,
Turning every ocean blue.
Because in your music,
I saw you.

Jodie Councilor

I Know It's There

I know love is here.
I have a fear.
I know it's there.

I don't want to get hurt.
But still, I always flirt.
I know it's there.

I have found the one I love
Yes, he has won.
I know it's there.

Love has hit me one more time.
I'm still on that love line with he.
I know it's there.

I have lost that loved one.
He said I had no love for him.
But only I, know it's there.

Aston Foglio

"What"

What am I to do,
I have no face,
I have faith,
to embrace the
one I say I hate.

What am I to do,
I have no love
to give to you.

What am I to do,
I just wish, I could say I love you
So I sit and wait for the day
I can forgive you.

What am I to do, I say no more.
I found my face, I found my faith
But I am sorry, I did not find the
strength to embrace,
The one I say I hate.

Jessica Longoria

Untitled

I have no more will power,
I have no more strength,
for each day,
my love for him stays,
even when the stars in the sky
decease,
and the sands on the shore are
gone,
my love for him,
will still grow on.

Aubrey Germani

Help Me!

I am an unemployed child.
I have very little money.
The bills are piling up.
My family and I go hungry.
Help me!

I am homeless child.
I live on the streets of crime.
And my only prayer at night
Is a loving family to call my own.
Help me!

I am sickly child,
Dying of a painful disease.
There is no treatment to cure me.
I must suffer within its siege.
Help me!

We are the children of society,
The children of suffering and pain.
The helpless, the homeless, the hungry,
But do we suffer in vain?

Elizabeth Mills

A Soul's Anguish

Looking into the mirror of my soul,
I see all who have ever hurt me.
As revenge turns into sacrifice,
I see the end must come and be free.
The end of all my rambling thoughts,
from hurt to total delusion.
I cannot bear to live any longer,
in this state of emotional confusion.
As the end draws closer and closer,
I begin to see the light.
But as I notice this too late,
I release my life without a fight.

Brandie A. Hintz

Her Husband

"Fifty years"
I hear him cry
Why did she have to die?
"Fifty years"
I hear him say
his body starts
to shake and sway
He's sitting there
across from me I can almost
reach across and touch
The anguish her
death has brought
The one he'd come
to love so much
I wanted to
reach out to him
to try and share his pain
but I found
I couldn't look at him
I turned away in vain.

Allen Shapiro

My Season

Fall is the season
I hold so dear
The trees paint their
Faces from far and near
Old man winter sends
Out his scouts
Whilst jack frost
He scampers about
The nip in the air
The warmth of a hand
winter will soon
Be upon the land.

The tree out my window
Burst its leaves
  into flame
Who will stop to witness
  its beauty
Or will they only curse
  its fallen art.

Challis Seymour

Hold On!

It was such an awful day
  I knew I'd never make it,
My troubles just kept piling up
  And I thought I couldn't take it.
But there were things I had to do
  So I figured I could fake it
I'd wear a smile and work a while
  And maybe I could shake it.
Well, sure enough, as time went by
  I never could mistake it,
I got to feeling better soon,
  Praise God! I'm going to make it!

John S. Lyttle

Why Oh Why?

Why am I slighted by the sighted?
If I could be included I would be
delighted.
Why oh why?
Wherever I go I'm put in a corner
Just like little Jack Horner.
Sometimes my guide dog and I
Gaze up into the sky and ask
Why oh Why?

Irene F. Price

Will We Last

Will we last?
  I know,
When I look at my past,
  I laugh

All those boys,
Who thought they were men.
What did I see in them?
I hope in the future,
I don't ask myself the same things,
  About him.

Will we last
I just hope,
In the future,
I don't look at my past,
  And laugh.

Becky Gallihugh

At Times

At times
I laugh or smile
Hiding.
Hope
Still seeps through
Vapor
Rising from
Cracked concrete in summertime.

At times
Feelings of inadequacies overpower
Curling
Like black smoke from chimneys
Smothering:
Fog on a cold, dismal night.

At times
Life seems bleak
Blindness beckons
Night falls.
I stand alone
In the dark at times.

Charles N. Gant

With Lovers Hearts

With lovers hearts
I long to paint you dearest love.
In light unveil the vision,
and kiss with brush on canvass.

A moments glance
to catch the eye forever,
A hundred ways of saying
something you can never hear.

With lovers hearts.
I long to paint you dearest love.
Lights music to my eves.
Your colors dance across my palette.

I stop to dream,
of beauty in the making.
A hundred ways of showing
something you can never see

With lovers hearts
my dearest love,
with lovers hearts

Charles Gnell Smith, Jr

Loving Heart

In rain or shine
I love to be
with you
I love your hugs
your kisses
And even your wishes
I love your warm arms
holding me tight
I love your hand's
gentle caress
when you touch
me lovingly
I love your kind and
caring heart
And most of all,
I love you!

Carla N. Chinn

I Miss You

I miss you in the morning.
I miss you in the day.
I miss you in the evening.
What else can I say?

I can't believe we're far apart.
Wasn't it yesterday when,
I put my head upon your heart.
I want it back again.

If I could, I'd hold you here
And never let you go.
Because it is for you my dear,
My heart cries yearning so.

I'll always wait, no matter what
From now until forever.
I know one day, in my heart
That we will be together.

Julie A. Rebber

Youth In Need

I need your love.
I need you near.
I need your support,
To eliminate fear.

I am youth emerging
To a new plateau;
A place in life
I am soon to know.

Without your help,
I will stumble; maybe fall,
I may not get up
Or arrive at all.

Please help me make,
That all important step
From youth to adulthood
A change to soon be met.

I ultimately depend
On your guiding light
Through storms and through shadows
Keep me within sight.

Jo S. Reynolds

Accomplishment Follow

To my Mother,
I really love her.
Raised me from a child,
Even though I was wild.
Thanks for helping me through
these years.
Happy times and some tears.

The next few pages are
some things I've done,
from your first born son.
I hope you are proud of me,
with what you see.

I'll close for now with the rhyme,
which I thought of at this time.
May the Lord up above hold you tight.
And keep you safe with all his might.

Alvin L. McCarver III

"My Bleeding Heart"

Your "Get-well Card", my darling wife,
I received this very day.
The joy it really brought me
is more than I can say.
I can feel my sad heart throbbing
and a lump rises in my throat,
as I read the deeper meaning
in those little lines you wrote.
In every little paragraph,
your voice, I could plainly hear.
I could see that smile on your face
and your presence I felt near.
The Doctors and all the Nurses
have done their utmost part,
But, my darling wife, it's only you
that could mend my Bleeding Heart.

John Donovan

I Remember

As I gaze into the star filled sky,
I remember the mischievous sparkle
in your dark eyes.
As I stare at the dancing fire,
I remember the warmth of your
gentle touch.
As I glance at the trees bending in
the breeze,
I remember your graceful walk.
As I hear the thunder rolling
throughout the land,
I remember your painful words.
As I feel a single tear trickle
down my cheek,
I remember you left me.
Again.

Amanda Overstreet

Don't Be Sad

Through this Golden Gate
I pass unto another world
Where there is no more
pain or sorrow
Don't be sad for me
for now I am where I want to be
with my loved ones on the other side
You will only miss me for a little while
for soon you too will
Join me on the other side.

Agnes Riley

A Friend

When I first saw you,
I saw a friend.
Someone to talk to,
Someone to lean on.

Someone who understands me,
Better than anyone else.
You care
Like a sister.

You know my rights,
And also my wrongs.
You understand my poems,
And you sing my songs.

You are there,
When I need to talk,
And you are there,
When I need to have fun.

I don't know
What I'd do without you.
We will always be friends,
And we all know it's true.

Angela O'Curran

Untitled

Out of the corner of eyes
I saw the grand prize.
How beautiful was she
But her name a mystery.
I have to meet her
But I shivered from a burr.
A nervous buray
Of what she might say.
Still confident yet modest,
I strolled to my goddess,
'Would you like to dance
and start a romance'
Yes, came her reply
and I knew she meant not to lie.
Because look at us now,
I ready to bow,
To do my part,
In asking for her heart,
So we can be together,
Hopefully forever.

Glen Letter

A Stroll Along The Water

As I walk
I see
the flowing river
below my feet.
Rushing over rocks,
skipping over stones,
green pine all around.
As I walk along the stream,
I stoop down to take a drink,
the cool water
touching my tongue.
I take one last look,
and move on.

Dara Canzano

Untitled

Weary and worn
I still walk on
Through the Rain and storm
With hope and a song

Johanna Hammet

Attitude

What I feel about myself,
I see in you.
If I am weak, strong,
Wise, foolish,
Good or bad,
Right or wrong,
The same I see in you.

Power to think,
To choose, to dream,
To soar to heights unknown,
Was not given just to me,
God gave the same to you,
To each his own, you see.

So I must feel worthy,
Proud of myself,
But careful when I judge,
Don't you agree?
For what I see in you,
Reflects what's inside of me.

Amelia White

Rain!

I like to sit and watch the rain,
I see joy and love out my window pane.

Sitting by someone I love and adore,
no love could mean anymore.

The joy and love floating in air,
the twinkle in eyes as we both stare.

I'm being held by someone I love,
someone I'm always dreaming of.

I stop and think of who this might be,
and I suddenly realize it's you and me!

Jennifer Honeycutt

Cloud Shapes

When I look at a cloud
I see many different things
I may see a little rabbit,
or a spaceship, or a boat.
I can see rolling hills,
and the image of Australia.
I can see a horse drawn
chariot chasing a deadly dragon,
and I can see a little frog
hiding behind a rock and
that is why I love the clouds.

Jennifer Hamilton

Finis

My days are numbered;
I see the setting sun.
My life-force's spent,
The course of life I've run.

Around me gathers,
The shadows of the night;
Each silent second,
Dims evermore the light.

The dear departed,
Surround me with sad-gloom;
And point the way,
That leads straight to the tomb.

Charles J. Ferris

Me

Once long-ago so long ago
I seemed to know my identity
But now, no longer am I sure,
Who I am or whatever I can be.

I drift along with aimless thoughts,
I feel alone and secretly,
I do not long to find myself,
Nor seek a crowd for company.

I have no future nor a goal
I cannot reach my destiny
No matter how I try in vain,
My dreams are not reality.

To be alone is sometimes sad,
You find there's no tranquility,
To watch life passing by the way,
Is this all life shall hold for me?

So admits it all, I drift along.
Perhaps someday, I'll find the key,
To why I must remain alone,
Through life and all eternity

Agnes Murtagh

Friendship

Yesterday a friend told me
I show too much concern.
"Stop holding the world in your hands",
My friend said, "you will learn."

She said I carry burdens that
Are just too much for me.
She said, "forget what isn't yours."
"Let others' problems be."

I thought a lot about that and
I shed a few hot tears.
Maybe she was right, but I
Can't throw out twenty years.

For twenty years I've battled
The problems of my friends.
Being just a "mutual"
Is not where friendship ends.

So...I just told my dear, dear friend
While talking yesterday,
"Though 'real' friendship might hurt and
sting—-
I'll have it no other way.

Dorothy M. Gieck

In The Dead Of Winter

In the dead of winter
I sit by the side of the river,
And stare at the beauty around me.

The rocks form a sieve,
As the cool water rips down
Its vertical course.

I shiver, not because of the coldness
In the air, but because of the nature
Surrounding my soul.

I sigh, quite content with the verity
That nature is in control of everything,
And that is beautiful.

Jennifer Duvoisin

Before My Eyes

Sometimes, by a stream
I sit and wonder,
crying out and yearning
for that time and place.
To feel how it used to be,
that person I used to be
But never had a chance to know
or see it grow.
I wish to experience his innocence.
Will I ever find him?
I know he is there,
sitting behind the wall he has created.
Is he crying there?
Will I be able to reach him?
Will he let me in?
I know he is afraid,
to trust, to love, to live.
Life...people...can be so cruel.
Before my eyes,
they made me lose that child in me.

Daniel Ortiz, Jr

Where Fleeting Sounds Softly Adorn

Where fleeting sounds softly adorn
I sit quietly whilst in morn
A true companion I'd timely scorned

There this place where few come yes
there where ravens and blackbirds rest
perched on branches swaying leaves
Mocking birds construct their nest
All take shelter with this tree

My eyes behold dark clouds so near
My eyes let go the cleansing tears

A pierced heart beckons a lost friend
A soul departed to its end.

Chirps of new life awaken my time torn
Where fleeting sounds softly adorn.

Clyde Adams

Wishful Thinking

More dreary clouds roll by
I sneak out a sigh.
Wanting to be near
Just so I can hear
A voice so sweet and tender
Holding on forever never letting go
Will it happen though
Will I be close
Will I hear
A voice so low so tender
Will you hold on forever
Will you never let go.
Will you, please tell me
For, I love you so.

Andrea Awrey

Speaking Of Love

I feel so alone
I want to feel loved.
  not just see love
I want to know love
  not just to be loved
I want to touch love.
  not just cry love.

Janet Parigen

My Love

What you see is what you get
I stand before you a simple man
A man of stone against the driving rain
I stand searching for you
And win or lose
My feelings will remain true
I have no silver or gold
I have no magic words
I try to get close to you
But you pull away
You tell me maybe someday
But someday never comes
I thought that maybe you'd be the one
But like the setting sun
I turned away and you were gone
So I fade away like dust in the wind
Yes I'm gone
But you will always have my love

Edward Deschaine Jr.

My Mother

I am cold very cold,
I stand by a fire,
I am not warm,
I hug my mother,
I am warmed by her love.

I am wet very wet,
I change my clothes, I am still wet
I am wrapped in a towel by mother,
I am dry once again.

I am hungry very hungry, I eat a cookie
I am not full,
I am fed soup by mother
I am full once again.

My mother can do it,
My mother feeds me,
My mother dries me,
My mother loves me, she loves me very much.

When she grows old,
I will feed her, warm her, and dry her,
And I will love her, just as she has loved me.

Jillian Garner

Untitled

Day And Night
I struggle to get back
That which makes me different

Their can be no greater sacrifice
than I have sacrificed to you.

Pain of the heart and soul
for such a long period of time.

No pain greater than this
Pain of knowing that
I almost sacrifices all.

Joseph H. Gaines, Jr.

Innocence Lost

There was a time, a long time ago,
in a different land, in a different
place, I was innocent.

There was a time, a long time ago,
in a different land, in a different
place, I did not know love.

Pain then was only a skinned knee.

Donald Brady

"God Loves Me"

When I awake in the morning
I thank God, to be alive
just to feel the sunshine on my face,
and the wind at my side

I go through the day being blessed
from his own hands,
with my family to love,
and all my wonderful friends.

I wear a smile on my face
a happy song in my soul,
just to know God loves me
makes me as a man feel whole.
Thank you God for everything

Jimmie R. Sharp, Sr.

Broken Love

How could you ever love me then leave?
I think of all our memories and grieve.
You're so strong when I feel weak.
The pain within won't let me speak.
I brought my heart right to your door,
With deep devotion evermore.
Where might you be?
Like a cold wind forever free.
Blowing through my life,
Yet stinging like a knife.

Bria Milicevic

Someday

I thought you loved me
I thought you cared.
I guess I was wrong
to believe you did.

Someday you will realize
I wasn't just another girl.
Someday you will realize
I was for real.

The day will come soon
but not soon enough.
I wish it would come sooner
but I'm just out of luck.

Someday you will wish you
hadn't treated me that way.
But it has already happened
so you'll soon know I couldn't stay.

Someday you will realize
you really cared
But when you realize you did
I will no longer be there.

Jennifer Walters

Life

Life is burning by
In all chaos and remorse
We move on and on
We take all that comes by
We cry when it does not
The dreams in which we thrive on
Only comes true in our minds.
And reality is all that's left
In Life.

C. J. Baker

Pinter Play

Deja Vu
I told you.
I did not want to come here.
It bodes not well.

We are not in the right place-
nor the right time.

Go to hell!
I said,
You, with your know-it-all
are destined for a fall.
We could be there.

I think you are a fool,
and therefore, have the right
to ask three questions:

Why did we come here.
Where are we going and
How?

Charles Mann

Untitled

When I look at your pretty brown eyes,
I want to tell you I empathize.
Sometimes I want to hold your hand,
but I'm not sure where we stand.
Our eyes meet all the time,
but I don't think you really see mine.
I tried to write you this poem,
but I'm still left all alone.
I just want you to be with me,
but I don't think you'll ever see.
I tried to call you on the phone,
but no one answers, no one's home.
with you it seems there's something more,
but is it you I just adore.
I'd like for you to ask me out,
but I think that's another doubt.
I can't mess with guys that play,
there's one more thing I have to say.
I'd like to get to know you better,
but you ain't nothin' but a player.

Danielle Niedzielski

Memories Of A Dream

Each time you told me you loved me,
I wanted to believe so much.
And as the days passed by I thought
I felt it in your touch.
I gave my heart away to you,
You made me feel secure.
Little did I know the love you
felt was not as pure.
I wished that I could hold you every
day and every night.
But as the moments slipped away,
I lost you from my sight
I fooled myself into believing
that you loved me so
And somewhere deep inside my
heart you'd never really go.
But as the tears fall from my
eyes, I face reality
Now all I have to hold onto are
Memories of a Dream

Jenny Rotolo

What If.....

What if.....
I was never born,
Who would have been?

What if.....
My name wasn't Dina,
What would it be?

What if.....
My mother and father never got divorced,
What would my life be like?

What if.....
My father was never in jail,
Where would he be?

What if.....
My mother had never died,
Where would we be living?

What if.....
I didn't live with Aunt Maria and Uncle
Chris,
Who would I live with?

What if.....

Life was perfect?

Dina Marie Cardaci

"I Miss My Whistle"

When most of my teeth, grew in,
I was only a little boy,
That's when my whist'ling did begin.
The whist'ling song gave me much joy.

I learned to warble and to trill.
My own tunes, I could compose.
To me it was such as thrill,
As through the years, my skill arose.

I joined with nature's woodland song,
And whistled with birds in conversation,
When on my walk I went along,
I felt in peace with all creation.

Now since my teeth have gone away,
When birds greet me in the early dawn,
I can not answer them and say,
"I'm sorry that my whistle's gone."

I miss my whistle in ev'ry way.
My whistle meant so much to me,
With nature's chorus, I cannot play,
But, I whistle in my memory.

Ervin H. Chase

"Lost"

I'm feeling trapped
   I'm feeling scared
I want to run
   but I don't know where
Feeling helpless
   all alone
Don't know what to do
   I just want to go home
But home is a memory
   in my mind
Something I pray
   that someday I'll find
Then the memory fades
   I'm left all alone
In the silence of my mind
   I'll never get home

Joshua J. Webb

Promise

Looking through the paned glass
I watch the sky grow angry.
Rumbles escape its core
and the rain pours from
its belly.

Trees stand tall and strong
against the driving wind
and wetness.
Clinging to earth and stone
they drink savagely.

A break in the clouds shows promise.
Dripping, the trees begin to sway
in the warm breeze.
The sun bathes them in her light
encouraging them toward another day.

Our own lives are much the same
as we stand against conflict
and cling to our foundation.
We are encouraged
by hope and promise.

Carolyn Fleck

Whisper To The Wind

When I am sad and lonely,
   I whisper to the wind.
All the things I'd like to say,
   to you, my love.

Remember all the good times,
   and things we did together.
I tell them all to the wind,
   hoping they get to you.

What better way to get your words,
   to the one you love.
For the wind will carry them all,
   even to Heaven above.

So whisper to the wind,
   when you are sad and blue.
It's not as silly as it seems,
Especially, when your love is true.

Herbert M. Jones, Sr.

If You Dance With Me

If you dance with me...
   I will show you how good
   It can be, to have
   Somebody who will touch
   You so gently like me!

If you dance with me...
   I will forever hold you so
   Tenderly, like a princess
   Who's very precious to me!

If you dance with me...
   The rhythm and the lyrics of
   The music and me,
   Will sway you so gently
   Like a yacht out in the sea!

And if you dance with me...
   I won't make anymore promises Cindy!
   But there's one thing I can guarantee
I will always be here
Whenever you need to
Dance with me!!

Avel Vivar

My Barriers

For Jill
I wish I could tell you I love you
I love everything about you
   Yet there are barriers
   And with them there is silence
      Instead
I start caring about the way I am
I start caring about everything I do
   When around you
These are the barriers
And with them there is silence
But, this is not who I am
   This only pushes us further away
      pushes you closer to others
For I have been betrayed by my barriers
   They were meant to keep harm away
      yet they shut you out
I only hope you can forgive me
   And see through the cracks in my barriers
Until then I chip away
   And pray that you are waiting on the
      other side.

J. Haag

Dear Daddy

When I was just a little girl
I would dream of how it would be.
If you were here
Growing up with me.

I always had this vision
Of what you would be like
Would you walk with me in the summer
And in spring, teach me to fly a kite.

I often wondered what you looked like
Like someone else, or like me.
Hearing your description
Isn't the same as seeing.

Well, I am all grown up now
And although you weren't around
Forgiveness in my heart
Is something I have found.

And even though you missed my stages
And I'll soon be "21"
There is still so many years
To grow old and have fun.

Jill Albanese

Synchronicity

I would capture you
I would hold you tight
I would crush you

Fragile dove
Roaring beast
Devour and devouring

You a flame
Heat so intense
I would draw you near
Yet I be burned
I would place a glass over your flame
Yet you smoulder and die

You an ocean
Smashing me with your waves
I drown in your synchronicity

Curt G. Bichler

Can I Forget?

If wishing could make dreams come true,
I'd find myself right next to you.
I miss you, darling, oh so much
I think of loving you and such
Time has passed, but memories live
Of how we always tried to give -
The love and passions we both had
Which left us happy, sometimes sad...

Can I forget your smile? Your face?
That precious laugh? Your warm embrace?
Forget the way you spoke to me
And listened very carefully

Can I forget your teasing ways?
Or all those precious yesterdays?
Forget the hours that went so fast
And try to place them in the past

Can I forget your tender touch
That made me want you, oh so much?
I can't forget these things, my dear
And know I'll always want you near.

Janice Dale-Cubberley

Blueberry Pie

Luscious juicy blueberry pie,
If I don't have it I just might die!

Amy Bouffard

My Never Ending Love

Gently held my hand as
If it would break.
My never ending love
As we walked through
The warm spring breeze
he gently pressed his lips
to mine, for a moment my
heart stood still.
My never ending love
As the spring breeze
gently blew my hair,
he whispered I love you so
My never ending love
The fragrance flowers
blooming along the path
Took my breath away,
such beauty.
My never ending love.

Beatrice Ceesay

It's Only Me

I cry tears no one sees,
I'm all alone it's only me.

Rain pours down outside,
as if the whole world knows I've cried.

Outside I wear a fake smile,
While inside my feelings are vile.

I hide my sorrows,
hoping they will be gone by tomorrow.

Outside I have a fake identity,
No one knows who I really am,
sometimes not even me.

Something inside me is yearning to be free!
What is it? Oh, it's only me.

Jessica Myer

Hurting

I lost my dog the other day
I'll never get over it.
My loving companion for 15 years
His name was Lit'l Bit.

He thought he was a big dog.
Short, but spunky to the end.
He was always there to protect me
And to show me he was my friend.

I could see that he was hurting
And I should have let him go.
His little heart was breaking,
But how was I to know?

I have such an empty feeling
That I hope will go away.
I know that he is better off.
But I long to see him play.

I'm sure there is a dog heaven
Where all good doggies go.
I'll try to believe, and then I won't grieve.
At least, I won't let it show.

Jean Halterman

This Fever

This fever comes
I'm feeling sick again
fasting. Unsure -
infatuation. Why?
Horror is left
inside of me
all the thing I'd
dreamt I'd be.
Conversations and
all pleas. Never
wanted to be so
accepting, insecure,
 frightened.
I hope I don't care,
 any more.
Getting hurt has
become a habit.
Interpreting things
easily.
Sarcasm in my voice.

Angela Rodriguez

My Island In The Working World

I want to tell you how I feel,
I'm not trying to deceive
About what you're trying to tell me,
it's against what I believe.
You say I should step on other
people in order to get high
Instead of building my own wings
and learning how to fly.
Those rich people on top
with brown noses are fools.
I'll live out of a cardboard box
before I go by those rules.
You have the nerve to stand there
and tell me this is valuable advice?!
Let me tell you something, when it
comes to my soul, there is no price.
I do not need to use vulgar language
or to use a certain tone

to say, I stand where I stand
in this world, even if it be alone.

Jennifer Weiss

I'm Growing Up

I'm growing up.
I'm only eight.
I even know
How to bake a cake.
I'm not scared
Of the dark anymore,
But I still hear knocks
On my door.
I have a fish that swims around
Pretending it is
On the ground.
Who but me, that sits
On my mommy's knee
And squiggles and wiggles and giggles
"Gee,
Is that really me?"

Claire Stone

Mixed Emotions

What's going on?
I'm so confused,
lost and alone,
scared and shaking.
I just sit here and wonder,
wonder what to do.
I don't need to be alone.
but I want to be.
I'm confused.
My mind says one thing,
my heart says another.
Help me someone,
anyone.
I want to run,
run far away and hide.
Lost and alone,
scared and shaking.
Someone help me-
what's going on?

Amanda Sobinsky

Jews

The soldiers came in the night
Imagine the Jews in fright

To camps they are brought
Getting killed without fault

Tears roll down their cheeks
As they take a peek
At the rifles pointing their way

Each whip of pain and last breath
Was felt and experienced by Jews

Cori Zaccagnino

"Sleep"

Sleep eludes one
In such a way
Similar to child,
Stubborn,
Who will not come in from play.
It teases you
While it avoids your head.
All you can do is lie there,
Tired,
In your bed.
This can last for hours on end.
Will sleep become
A close friend?

Barbara Lyczkowski

'Corny Worm or Full Cycle'

The worm in the corn
Imbedded deep
Curled up in a circle
Fast asleep
He'd eaten all Spring
The Kernels were gone
And when he awakened
It seems he yawned
"My Mischief my dears
Will still live on,"
"I've eaten your corn,
The birds will eat me
Then he chuckled with
Malicious glee-
Listen my friends before we are through
My relatives will all eat you."

Dorothy Marion

Alexandra at eleven and me

I see flowers
in a glass vase
pale blue of the wall
darker through green.
I see dust specks
rise in the air
of warming sun
and I see Alexandra and a friend
talking at once and descending the stair.
Eyes on each other, carrying coats
and huge bags their loose shoes
slip the steps no hands on the rail.

While I as diffused
as the dust specks.
Of the thin pale curl
of her hair
that yellow leaves have just begun
that the sun comes to me
that the carpet is mussed
beside the stair.

Anne Zinsser

Hearts Of Fire

In all my dreams
In all my nights
I see the beams
I fear the fights

I feel the cry
I taste the hunger
I watch them die
lying there in lost ember

Will no one help?
Yes, in the heart of the special child
there's a yelp
that turns to the wild

The yelp grows and grows
trying to get out
And the child knows
without a doubt!

Jody Rice

Untitled

In corners of the garden,
  litter-newspaper, plastic
bags and cans, No one cares
  About the beauty of nature anymore.

Alexandra Gnoske

Windows Of The Soul

A sea of emotions
in eyes,
so incredibly blue
sapphire tides surrounded
by misty white.

The sea in your eyes
engulfs one's soul
taking it under
where mermaids play
uninhibited.

Mist is thrown from your eyes
like spray from the ocean
only harder to catch.

So much is shown to me
in the pools of those,
incredibly blue eyes
that I go willingly down
into their depths......

Christine Hope Wood

Untitled

Confusion created
in my mind
all over again
I'm going to die.
Inside and out
alone throughout
depression overloads.
My body weak
but I know in time
it will all end
my heart forlorn
my mind deprived
in time my body
will just say goodbye.

Jenny Lax

Self Delight

I walk the night,
In my mind's soft landscape.
I drink in my own thoughts,
Like sweet moonlight lemonade.
Lost in laughter's ripple,
Standing drenched in self-delight,
I'm filled with nameless religion,
That wells from my soul's insight.

Wrapped in the wind,
I peel away the scars.
Looking at my new reflection,
In the pool of dreams still as glass.
Finding what I'd never lost,
Wonder in the starlight,
A child full of new decisions,
Standing drenched in self-delight.

Franklin C. Berrong

Coloring

To love and be loved
Is tingling silver joy.

To love and not be loved
Is soft blue sadness.

To love and be laughed at
Is naked ocher.

Bea Harris

Crying

Lost long loved dog
  In night of fog

Loud shouts were sent
  Echoes came and went

Eyes red and wet
  Teeth clenched and set

Never knew such befriending
Meant so much heartrending

Churning on the inside
Burning on the outside

Soul hurt and sore
Rain came and tore

Tears from both cheeks
Search lasted for weeks

No trace ever found
As neighbors looked 'round

Owning pet a strain
Can't stand the pain

As loss seems forever
Must go...be together

Fred Small

Lovers In Love

When two hearts meet
In soul, and mind,
There 'tis, someway, they must combine.
They know not how nor where nor why
'Tis just an urge they feel inside.

Into a fiery volcano,
They would go so willingly,
Down into the coldest of cold seas,
They would glide so easily.

The fire 'tis hot!
Hotter than HELL inside!
Yet shall never freeze.

The water 'tis cold!
Colder than the arctic snow above!
Yet shall never boil.

Both shall last eternally
Burning and freezing endlessly.
Until, alas, one day
They shall meet.

Their destiny 'tis complete.

John A. Flick Jr.

Peace

Let us have peace
In this great world of ours
Let everyone stand tall and unite
All should be proud
To hold their flags up high
Let us hold hands across all nations
Sing our praises
Let our motto be
Peace now for one and all
Unite and stand strong
For all the years ahead
Peace - peace forever.

Joan Marshall

"Understanding"

In the back of my brain
In the corner of my mind
I can comprehend
It's better left behind.

But in the depths of my soul
To the bottom of my heart
I don't understand
Why we have to be apart.

In my mind
I understand it had to end
And that it's better
He's only my friend.

Only in my mind
Can I rationalize the pain
But it doesn't hold back the tears
From falling like the rain.

But my heart will never understand
What happened to our love
And why we didn't make it
When push came to shove.

Johnna Womack

"Cries That Can't Be Heard"

Calling into the wild,
in the darkness
cries a small child.
Mother has left him all alone,
on the streets,
without home.
Shares a bench with another,
in the coldness,
and feel the pain of hunger.
The small child cries,
in the wilderness,
and slowly dies.

Calling into the wild,
in the darkness,
cries another small child.
Mother has left him all alone,
on the streets.
without a home...

Jessica Day

Untitled

We speak in silent whispers
In the down of a brighter day.
In search of a dream called heaven
Paradise seems so far away.

The echoes of my past
Have embraced me with such pain
Within the shadows that you cast
You were driving me insane.

I don't know where I am going
Nor what I am looking for
But I know where I've been
And the hell I've seen before

Somewhere out in the distance
Is my angel dressed in white
Leading me out of darkness
Blazing my trail by candlelight.

James E. Keen, Jr.

Reaching

Waking up alone again...
   In the middle of the night.
   ...It happens often now
Reaching across the pillow...
   Finding no one.
Memories quicken and sleep escapes.
I wait...trying to understand...
   Trying to accept the now.
Being alone can have its advantages.
   ...But I remember all too vividly
   When reaching across the pillow...
   I found love.

Guy Apollo

Do Not

Alone
in the night

One breath
before
death comes

Silence
too loud
to bare

Snakes
in the marshes
rustling
through dreams

I rush
forward
searching
for what

I do not
know

Alucard Raven

El Greco's Jesus

Somewhere
in the oils
along
flat, elongated fingers
or as
illusory light, spirit glows a site.

shifting so slightly
between
crossed wood
as if to escape
our gaze
and the throb
of our blood
as it seeps
beneath
nails.

Claire F. Brunetti

Enchanting Eyes

Enchanting eyes that secrets keep
In the shadows of dreams I greet
The splendor of your haunting stare
With powers enough to make men dare
To seek to hold what even light of day
Could not outshine such beauty displayed
Yet if by virtue or just by chance
Your path should cross her magic glance
Heart and soul will fight for ways
To prove it's love found in her gaze

Cody W. Anderson

The Storm

On and on
In the sweep of the bay
The waves crash'd unto the shore
Out of the sea so grey;
With relentless force,
Like life's pain and strife
In happiness's way
Plunging a knife

The winds ran wild
The water whirl'd,
A drama before all unfurl'd.
On the shore the palm trees shook
Violently every cranny and nook
A force so fierce, no one could brook.

After a while the sea turn'd its hue
From a menacing green to a calmer blue
The waves lapp'd the shore in a gentle way
To pacify it for its disarray,
Pleading mercy that it did go astray.

Agni Mitra

Shoe Dog

I watch her creep
into my parents' closet
like an overgrown brown rat
in search of a snack.
She reviews over her choices,
high heels,
tennis shoes,
flats, loafers,
leather, suede, cloth.
She pulls her favorites out to her,
careful not to leave teeth marks,
then like a spit-and-polish shoe shiner
licks them clean.
When she finishes,
she walks out,
her tail wags,
her eyes smile.

Debra M. Cooper

Alone

Hatred and anger fill my soul.
Introducing me to levels unknown
A painted man sits alone,
As I do now.

A silver blade, nicely shined -
Blood flowing from my wrist
As I calmly wait to die,
Alone.

As the blood flows, vision blurs.
The world now turns to black
Everything now is calm,
As I sit ... alone.

Amanda K. Silas

Night Sky

The night sky
is the prince.
The princesses
are dots of silver light
small and unprotected.
But the prince
is there
to wrap his arms around them
until the sun rises

Audrey Quaranta

"Fanship"

My fanship for you —-
Is as sure —-
As somewhere in the Universe —-
The stars are twinkling —-
And the moon —-
Is beaming shafts of light —-

My fanship for you —-
Is as sure —-
As the morning sunrise —-
In the East —-
And at Dusk —-
Sunset in the West —-
With a touch of Love —-

Jamie June Barber

When?

Experts say inflation!
  Is disgracing our nation
with recession rising
  a decline in jobs.
But I say when?
  Ghetto streets breed hate,
young black kids can't wait
  for excuses...mistakes.
Lies from leaders who bait
  with promises stained
    from years of waiting...
but I say when?
  Lies stop and life begins...
cause our folks have seen
  times with no money
    felt times of empty stomachs.
Don't tell me wait!
  I say when?

Hareem Badil-Abish

Fear

  Fear,
Is it when you scream?
Or, is it when you are nervous?

Does it get to you?
Can you not stand it?

  Fear,
Is it when you are on a roller coaster?
Or, is it when you see a big snake?

Does it scare you?
Or, does it tear you?

  Fear,
Can you smell it?
Or, can you taste it?

Does it alarm you?
Or does it charm you?

  Fear,
What is it?

Jennifer Hummill

Teal

Tastes like sweetness
Looks like jewels of people
Smells like free perfume
Feels like adventure
Sounds like an unusual experience

Jill Koscielniak

They Know

A Child's laugh
is so innocent.
Yet, we know
What is meant.

They are so pure
In deed and thought.
They try in their way
To do what's taught.

Day by day they learn,
Sometimes not meaning to.
But it's all storing up,
Things we didn't know they knew!

Barbara J. Sellers

My Boy

To have a boy
Is such a great joy
To watch him play
In his own little way
To watch him sleep
At times is such a treat
To watch him grow
You know one day you will have to let go
As the day's fly past
He has grown up so fast
You just knew it wouldn't last.
He is not a little boy
Who plays with toys
He is still my pride & joy
Now he is all on his own
Don't worry mother won't be alone
She has all her memories of joy.
Which she got from her little boy.

April D. Foote

Noises In The Night

Oh, dear teddy bear,
Is that you out there,
Making sounds in the shadows tonight?

Or maybe I awoke,
When the broken clown spoke,
From the chair in the corner right there?

My doll is near me,
Just where I can see,
So I'm sure she was sleeping all right...

Which only leaves me,
With my poor bandaged knee,
And my dog with the fluffy brown hair.

Harry T. Roman

The Meadow

The soft silent meadow
  Is where I go
When I am troubled
  And to be alone.

The soft silent meadow
  Is where I go
When nobody understands me
  And I feel no one cares.

The soft silent meadow
  Is where I go
Where you can hear the wind
  When it lightly blows.

Brandy Stiger

"Just Wondering"

Is there a heaven in the sky above?
Is there a God as we know him?
So shall I believe what
my religion quotes.
Is there a hell in the ground below?
For to know you will have to die,
For death is a threat to mankind,
If there is a God why do people perish?
Is it to be recreated for another life,
or is there just a blackness,
a blackness which you cannot exit from
Death comes and goes whenever,
Will I die tomorrow
or will a friend die for no reason,
no one knows, many care, I do not.
For people will live long after me,
For people will die long before I.

Colonel Beckett

"Just You"

Inspired by Maria
Is your hair just as silky
  before I run my hand through it?
Are your eyes just as deep
  before I lose myself in them?
Is your smile just as lovely
  before I steal a glance?
Are your hands just as warm and secure
  before I trace them upon your face?
Is your body just as sexy and soft
  before I hold you against me?

And is your voice just as soothing
  before you whisper to me?
Are you always naturally this beautiful
  and breath-taking,
Or do you do it just for me?

Fred C. Torien Nguyen

Life

Life is so precious to the soul,
it can be damaged like your feelings.
Life is something we all go through,
it is something I'm sure we all
have thought about destroying.
People don't realize life is so precious.
even the slightest little "accident"
can ruin it for you.
No one has any right to destroy
someone's precious life.
Before you try something so deadly,
think about what could happen
to your family and friends.
They're lives could fall apart
just cause your life isn't perfect.
No one's life is perfect.
You have No right to take life,
No right to think it doesn't matter,
No right to ruin God's beautiful creation.
God Doesn't make junk!!!!!

Emily Goodwin

Wind

Whistle, whistle, while you work,
not caring what you touch or jerk.
Moving swiftly cross the plains,
not caring where anyone plays—
only caring where you go, how
you get there and your mighty blow.

Ann G. Stroberg

'Friends Like Sisters'

You have been my friend for so long,
It could never feel as if it's wrong;
My love for you is so dear,
If only you could be near.
Distance does make a heart grow fonder,
sometimes I must ponder.
Now you are my Sister, so true;
It doesn't feel as if it's new.
You are so dear and special to me;
It will never be differently,
"It will be for eternity'"

Cindy Schwalje

The Player

The game of basketball is life.
It is a part of you at all times.
Walking to class with books in one
hand and the ball in the other.
Thinking only of basketball.
Sleeping with the ball at your side,
dreaming of someday being the best ever.
Knowing that somewhere, someone is
practicing, you go harder and harder
so they do not get an edge.
Striving to be the best, you practice
harder each day. So when you play
in head to head competition,
you win. The practicing will prepare
you, your faith can keep you strong,
but only the love of the game
can make you a player.
Do you have the love?

John Brennan

Helplessness

It is that feeling,
It is locked inside you,
Always ready to get out,
Always ready to get out,
It is that feeling

It is just a feeling,
Still to some it is so much more

It may be locked inside your soul,
You must let it out,
But how,
But how?

It is just a feeling,
But to some, it is so much more,

It may be locked inside your soul,
You must let it out,
But how,
But how?

Amy Vest

I Touched Life

I touched life when I touched a flower
   Its petals soft and warm,
I felt it had a will to stay
   Despite the wind or storm.

It held the gentle beauty
   Of its Creator up above,
Each petal dipped in glory -
   Handcrafted in His love.

Dori Magee

So Follow Him

It is not ours to question Him,
   Who in His wise design,
Gave us our only life to live
   Just one day at a time.

It is not ours to wonder why
   He made us like we are
It is but ours to follow Him
   To that bright shining star.

It is not ours to question Him
   For our poor finite minds
Cannot fathom what He has
   Behind those gates divine

So follow Him, let Him lead
   Till this life's day is done
And He will guide us to that place
   That has no need of sun

Gladys McFall

"Country" The Beautiful

As I walk along this country road
It just amazes me
I've never taken time to look
At all there is to see

The air itself, that soothes my soul
And smells so fresh and sweet
The sounds that give a hint of life
Yet nothing do I meet

The many trees along the way
So proudly stand their ground
And flowers, perhaps I've never seen
Yet here, they can be found

I see a glimpse of broken walls
once used with great intent
This now forgotten road I walk
Where someone's life was spent

For here there are no boundaries
Just nature at its best
And here I am reminded
There's so little country left!

Cheryl E. Aubut

Desire

Desire hung in the air
it stirred two strangers
face to face,
waiting wanting to touch.

Lips were parted in playful smiles
thought read in staring eyes
each breath was labored
every muscle tense
desiring to touch.

He was first to move
She drew a breath -
the touch - so soft and lingering
upon their lips.
Lasting only a moment
yet spoke a hundred words.

A stolen kiss so soft and sweet
it burned a memory
in their minds no one would erase.
Only two strangers know the haunting
memory
sparked by desire.

Denise Knue

Forever

I sit here in shock,
It was just last night
When we talked,
Last night was our last
Good-bye,
For now you have died.

How I'll never know,
For I fell asleep
Before you got home,
But even if you're not here,
I'll remember you in
My heart...
Forever.

Carissa Bogart

In Youth There's Time For Dreams

Life was made for dreaming
It was there for us to take
Tomorrow seemed so far away
A memory, Yet to make

Our friends would be forever
Worries, we had none
empty moments never passed
We lived them everyone.

We saw beauty in all things
what wonders to behold
looking forward, never back
our world was wrapped in gold

Fresh new rainbows filled the air
all the world seemed right
nothing brighter than those days
nor sweeter than those nights.

Things remembered from the past
what blissful memories
Oh, to be so young again
and still have time for dreams.

Jill Adkins

Heather's Poem

You're free but you don't have me
It's a mystery why you set me free
Can't you see we were meant to be
Together we were heavenly
You're free but you don't have me
You made me sad and lonely
I drowned in a sea of pain and misery
and you weren't there for me
I thought we were destiny
I gave you the best of me
You're free but you don't have me
hate is easy after what you did to me
did you really love me
you deserve to be unhappy without me
You're free but you don't have me
Now I see my friends 'round me
I'm no longer lonely
but we could have eternity
but you're free.

Heath E. Giles

Lost Innocence

If you blink, you'll miss it
Its image is obscure
You know you'll look a second time
It always will allure.

Hasten to look away
And avert your gaze afar
Reddish-blues and purplish hues
Discover what they are.

A magical sight meets your heart
You'll never be the same
Fairies and elves will lead the way
Far from whence you came.

Never look back, for then you're gone
And lost from this whimsical place
Pleasant ways you wish could stay
Will become a hurried race.

You look around at glowing treasure
Which now has lost its gleam
You see it fade from your eyes
And awaken from your dream.

Ellen S. Gwinn

'Love'

Love is very mysterious,
it's something I can't explain.
Love has a lot of fears,
and it causes a lot of pain.
Love is also wonderful,
this I can claim... But
Love is not always true,
neither is it the same.
Love can cause hearts to break,
or it can cause pain.
Love, you'll have to find for yourself,
because it, I can't explain.

Faith Witherspoon

My Room

My room is my shelter
It's the only place I feel safe,
I open my door
And get slapped in the face.
I begin to cry and really want to die
I would love to see what life is like
From someone else's sight
There has to be a better place for me
That I wish I could see.
I try to talk to others
But I can't seem to open my shutters
I don't really understand
But the only thing I know is a hand
A hand that meets me more often
Than a hug or kiss
My room is my shelter because of this.

Andrea Burgess

Song

Jesus the Christ.
Jesus the Christ for eternity.
He save my soul from sin.
He died on the cross so I won't
be lost so I could be born again.
I love you so much sweet Jesus.
I love you for eternity I love
you so much sweet Jesus.
Please come after me.

Florence Colene Bittle Young

Alone Again

I find myself alone again
I've been down this road before
I don't know why, I don't know when
Love walked out the door.

I find myself alone again
I feel the hurt once more
But this time I will survive
I'm stronger than before

I find myself alone again
But I have strength from above
For God has taken me in his arms
and filled me with his love.

Jeanne Jordan

Time After Time

Time after time
   I've tried anew,
Time after time
   I have loved so true,
Time after time
   My heart has been broken and blue,
Time after time
   I'll try a true,
Time after time
   My heart will be so true,
Time after time.
   My heart is broken and blue,
Time after time.

Harold F. Mattson

Your Life

Look in the mirror, what do you see?
Just an image answered a plea,
My life is lived by others, not me.
That's not the way it's supposed to be

Change and make yourself a new.
Dream the dreams you loved and knew.
Don't just sit there looking blue.
Don't listen to their point of view.

Make decisions, take control.
Listen to your heart and soul.
Reach out for dreams, touch your goals
Listen to your heart and soul.

Julie A. Rebber

In The Cougars' Eyes

In the cougars' eyes
Life is a jungle
Full of the unknown,
And human people are beasts
Roaming and tearing down
Their safe home.

In the cougars' eyes
The cities creating pollution
Are masses of destruction,
And what was once
A happy home
Is now a land of construction.

In the cougars' eyes,
So powerful yet helpless,
Everything is changing
And nothing will stop
Until the human beasts
Start rearranging.

Erin Bryce

Untitled

I'm so mixed up I want to cry

I wonder if to live or die

I try real hard to hold on tight

I talk to God to make it right

I feel that I have no one to
Just hold and hug or listen to

A touch, a kiss, a little smile

Will make my living all worthwhile

It's hard for me to even say

Will this feeling ever go away
It's kind of lonely now for me

To search for something I can't see

I try to hide my feelings well

But look real hard, and you can tell

I pray to God to hear my prayer

Watch over me, and show you care.

Edward F. Motta

My Own Heart

My own heart was shattered
just the other day
my son he left me
and now he's gone away
I risked my life for him
the fire killed him that way.
At night I hear his painful screams.
Still haunt me today
I know I should
move on
but...I can't.
My heart is broken,
nothing can replace it
my six year old boy
old enough to know me,
yet young enough to die
tears still streak down my cheeks
the pain is not yet gone...
   I don't think it'll ever be.

Jacob Wasztyl

My Calling

Sometimes I wonder,
   Just why I'm I here.
   On that I ponder,
   The answer's not clear

I want to know my reason,
   For being on this earth.
I'm tired of always pleasing,
Something I've done since birth.

Please tell me my calling
   Whatever, I need to know.
For people around me are departing,
And soon I'll have no place to go.

Sometimes I feel distant
Nobody to chill with at all.
Not a single soul to listen.
   Nobody at home to call.

I want to be somebody,
   Someone loaded with success.
I hope not to discourage anybody,
   I simply want to be the best.

Jervison Johnson

My Friend

It seems as though
just yesterday
My life was changed
from night to day

A helping hand
to dull the blow
A friend in need
a heart of gold

My treasure chest
at rainbow's end
I love you Dee
my Wife, my Friend

Some search for love
their whole life long
Some struggle through
a love gone wrong

I'll thank the stars
and sky above
for all my life
for all your love

Dean M. Hager

Summer

Summer is here now
Kids will run in the streets
Without the sound of dead
Winter leaves crunching
Under their feet
teenagers will pack the
beaches to feel the
heat
instead of the cold
which is now just a
memory
But soon it will end
and only a few
will remember how it
began...

Dixie Miller

"Mother Earth"

We your beloved children,
Kill you slowly every day,
We don't know how to behave.

We pollute water and air
While destroying ourselves,
Factories throw waste everywhere,
Engines of all kind blow smoke,
Spilling oil and pulverized rubber.

The only way to save the earth
Is through strict controls
And to teach us all...,
How to keep your health,
To be saved ourselves.

Florencio A. Mendoza

'The Serenity Of The Seashore'

Waves crashing against the seawall
Like cymbals playing in the band,
Rocks scattered along the shore
Like diamonds in the sand

Surf boards appeared across the water
Like fishes swimming in the sea,
The sun sets so peacefully
As butterflies are free.

Carey Wolfe

Oh Mother Dear

Oh mother dear, I love you so.
Let me whisper sweet and low,
How you cheer me when you're near me,
No one else can know.
But when I'm blue I think of you,
Though I'm far from reaching you.
Yet my heart keeps longing for you,
Mother mine so true.
Just a deed of kindness here
With a smile I love so dear.
You're the one who fills my heart
With happiness and cheer.
O mother mine, you are to me,
Like a star in heaven so blue.
How I wish that I could be
A sunbeam just for you.

Julie Kroll Boyd

Life

Life can be short,
Life can be long.
Like a song,
It needs tuning,
Like a game,
The harder you try the better it gets.
Life comes and goes,
And with those,
The wishes we all hold inside.

Catherine A. Stevens

In-dwelling.....Harmony Abounds

Inside burns a separate
   life of inner joy.....
   so well kept
   so cherished
   it belongs only to One

There lies a citadel
   of moss green similitude
   of a coveted spot
   of a hidden retreat
   separate - and special

How pure and alone
   my thoughts live there
   with His precious Presence
   with His music of my soul
   being played to perfection

Harriet Trehus Kvingedal

Loose Change

Spinning upward, faster
Like a satellite
Guess who lands on top:
Heads of multinationals
Tales of homeless in the streets

Hard and flat
Impressed with history
Trusted, God-like
Despite inherent
Worthlessness

Our time, the present,
Stuffed into a vending machine
Artificial stimulation
Exchange made
Sucker deal

Alexander V. Gwynn

Crystal Ice Rose

Slowly bleeding
Like a dying rose
Try holding it in
But afraid as inside crystal ice grows

Slowly forming
Drowning in tears
A shallow sea of sorrow
Afraid they're true-horrible fears

Growing confusion
Are things as they seem
Can they be
Afraid either way-are they a dream

Slowly growing yet melting
In the soul and the stars
Held for you in these hands
Is a crystal ice rose

Slowly melting
A crystal ice rose
Yet with heart ache
The love still grows.

Alison Traynor

Seasons

Experiences flow,
   like a swiftly moving stream
in the Spring
   of new beginnings.

Summer eases along,
   running smoothly
over glistening rocks.
Memories stay
   within the banks,
never overflowing.

In the Autumn
   of life,
the stream begins
   to slow and draw back.
Like the ebbing of the tide.

Winter finds the water still...
   like the mind.
The present does not flow smoothly.
   Only the memories...
   of springtime.

Eva M. Pelini

Untitled

Have you ever felt alone,
like no one really cared.
I'm crying out for love
but you're no longer there.
I take a step forward,
And you move twice as far,
like trying to pull from the
heavens, a lonely shooting star.
"Must I endure this pain?"
Asks my bleeding heart.
It burns deep into my soul
And rips my life apart.
Now my time is gone,
My hour upon the stage,
My eyes are full of fear
Absent is my rage.
So I ask you to remember me
As I depart this life
But don't look down my love,
For you may hold the knife!

Cher Rathmell

The Apple Tree

Please don't come and take from me
Like you would the apple tree;

I don't have the fruit you need
Though I planted you from seed;

I filled your limbs from my vine
Till weathered sap brittled mine,

Now my leaves, no longer green,
Cannot blossom in the spring;

Do you hear what I say now?
You must search beyond my bough;

I can't give you everything
Because ... I'm not like

   I'm not like

   I'm not like

the
apple
tree!

Arlene Schaschl

Eliminating Pride

Slowly fading into oblivion
limited prosperity for elect
forsaken adapt to living in shun
tolerating life the supreme reject.
Encouragement instills expectation
exhausting toil turns to confidence
by shedding negative hesitation
gradual transition offers advance.
Prosperity emerges through access
earning the respect of humanity
leads to path of ultimate success
achieving triumph through eternity.
Stop pride before invasion can begin
replacement of humility within.

Denise Lanier

Baby's First Christmas Stocking

   Soft and fluffy
   Little and sweet
  And will never be worn
On baby's kicking little feet.
   Easy to hold
  With tiny little hands.
   Nothing inside
  That baby's eyes can see,
But it's filled and overflowing
   With love from me.

Earle F. Adams

Who Am I

I am lost
Lost in a world
Who does not know me
A face in a crowd
Quickly forgotten
Only shadow of the
person I only hoped to
be. When I was young
My mind would wonder to
Adulthood full of fame and
wealth. But he who
set the stars the moon
and sun in there place
shall find me, name me, and
Tell me I am not lost.

Gary Sadler

Memories

I remember the times so
long ago, as if it were
yesterday.
We played and sang
and danced around
our hearts ever young
and gay
The days went fast
and my childhood was
past.
Into adulthood we grew
though life goes on
and we can't turn back
our memories still remain
that is life
and I'm now a wife

Audrey Adams

Degenerate Hero

King of fools who
long since died
achieved his glory
but never tried.

upon his throne
with beer in hand
grabbed another that
was just his brand.

in the right state
would do what had to be done,
afraid of nothing
but in no state to run.

a degenerate, a loser,
a hero to some
only had one hand
because the other had rum.

the best of them all
he claimed to be,
lost his life to
a bottle of brandy.

David Lipp

"Three Cheers"...To A Waterfall?

While strolling in the woods one day
Looking for some place cool,
I chanced upon a waterfall
Nearby a bubbling pool.

The splashing of the water
Falling down in beautiful sprays
Made rainbows of different colors,
Which I captured in every gaze.

Blended with the rocks so red
And sky so very blue,
The water in all its whiteness
Formed clouds of mist-like dew.

I could not help but think about
That long, long ago day,
When those three colors became the flag
  of "this wonderful land"...
   OUR good ol' U.S.A.!

Doris E. Lynch

Lugubrious

She sees faces all around her.
Looking, staring, some she recognizes.
Friends or foes?
She does not know.
So many places, so many faces.

She meets someone she thought was special.
She exposes her soul and gives her heart.
Only to be saddened.

Her heart is broken
Feelings inside her never to be awakened.
She has been hurt so bad
She will always be sad.
Drowning in everlasting sorrow.

Oceans of tears flow from her eyes
Mixed with tearful goodbyes.
Silently said
To everyone she has ever loved in her head.
It's time to leave, it's time to go.
She jumps and sails into the great blue abyss.
Doomed to obsolete eternity.

Amy Marie Roulhac

Happiest Thoughts

We were lying afar
Looking wearily at each other
The ticking of clock had stopped
While we whispered intangible thoughts.

Then, with disinterest we thought
What had made us fall apart
After those moments of intensity
and coziness were gone.

As the caged birds flap hard
Wishing to fly higher at heart
Are unable to break out of walls
But willing to thrash at locks.

As often do we fault
The more we are at lack
That the happiest thoughts
Only a few moments last.

Eric Dutt

Keep Looking Up

Looking East I see the sunrise
Looking West I see it set
Looking North I see the snow clouds
Looking South the raindrops wet
Keep looking up don't be discouraged
There's a rainbow in the sky
Don't give up keep pressing forward
you will reach it by and by.
As you travel down life's highway
You'll grow weary day by day,
But when you reach your destination
Someone's waiting by the way
So look up encourage others
Don't look down you'll step and fall
Then you'll need someone to lift you
God is there for one and all.

Emma Gaughf

Love

Ecstasy, disappointment, Rain
Love
The highest, the lowest, Pain
Love
A man, a woman, a Seat
Love
Two souls, two hearts, one Beat
Love
A couple, a home, a Life
Love
Ignorance, hooligan, a Knife
Love
Good times, bad times, no Time
Love
An incident, an accident, a Crime
Love
A box, a body, a friend
Love
A sigh, a tear, the End.

Jonathan L. Porter

Death Do Us Part

Death do us part
Love first sight
Fire works, candle light
Set on a hill far away
The ground damp and cool,
The air full of love.
Walking home hand to hand
And a kiss on the cheek good night.

Ashley Mantle

Sometimes When

Sometimes it's hard to keep
   love in your heart,
When things don't work out
   and you're falling apart.
Sometimes it's hard to take life
·   day by day,
When you know what you feel
   but not what to say.
Sometimes it's hard to be
   just 'good friends'
When love is still there
   and a relationship ends.
Sometimes it's hard to admit
   that you're wrong,
When someone you love
   has been hurting too long.
Sometimes it's hard when three words
   mean so much,
When you say 'I love you',
   It's the heart that you touch.

Jan Riggins

"Amor's Way"

Amor, Amor, this way . . .
   Love is a lonesome heart.
Come, my way, a shadow there a blindness?
   Some will find its path,
      some will lose. of poetry thanks.
Amor, Amor, have your way,
   It's fading away.
I see no lighted path, this day . . .
   Amor, Amor.

Felix Amando Garcia

Love

Love
Love is an emotion
Shared between two
When you're in love
there's more than just you,
There's the stars in the sky
and the moon up above
and that very special
Someone that you love!
Love isn't a gamble that we
all just play,
Love is something that makes
all of your days!
I love that very special
Someone with all of my heart
and hope to God we never
do apart!

Amanda Brooke Lewis

Brother Within

What's under my skin?
Love they cannot see,
Peace they don't know,
Kindness they refuse to find.

Why can't they just give me a chance?
I'm no different from them,
I could become a friend.

I'm black,
I'm a Jew,
I'm the kid at school you won't talk to.
Under your skin,
I'm the brother within.

Allison Gilbert

A Stray Cat

There's a stray cat
Lying on my lap.
Dying, crippled by a car
He looks at me and mews sadly.
Gladly
I hold him one last time
And pet his fur.
He gives one final purr
Chilling to the bone.
I stroke him slowly, softly, coldly.
Then I am alone.

Erwin E. Bach

Little Things

Little things that you do,
make me realize my love for you;
Little things that you say,
make me glad I feel this way;
Little things you say in my ear,
when no one else is near;
Little things that we do,
that tell me our love is true;
The way you hold my hand,
and always seem to understand;
I love the things I hear,
whispered in my ear;
There's no one quite like you,
the only one I love...Is you!!!

Jodi Jackson

Rain

For: Buakham

How I love to see the rain
Makes me think of you again
Hear it falling slowly down
Pitter-pat upon the ground

Hear the birds up in the trees
The flowers stand so silently
Do you ever think of me
As you watch it rain

Do you remember when
We watched it rain and rain again
Just like me the clouds appear and then
Like the rain I am gone again

Now that you're so far away
I hope to see you again someday
With so many miles and smiles
I know I left along the way.

Eugene Montgomery

Art Is Therapeutic

Art is therapeutic —
   many can agree;
   It's really brought
      a lot of joy
   to folks who are
      just like me.
I pick up my brush and paint
   for just a little while;
   And before I know anything
my faces is all in smiles.
   Art is a special gift
   given by God to man;
      So pick up
some paint and a brush,
   and try it when you can.

Johnnie Huffman

The Poem I'm Submitting

There's a song that I remember
Many years ago
About a man who fell in love
And let his feelings show

The words were very simple
His thoughts were plain to see
The things that he would do for her
Wishing that girl was me

I guess he loved her way too much
Just to watch her slip by
And if he could I know he would
Offer her the sky

I really have no reason
To feel the way I do
And I know It's all because
"I'm stone in love with you"

Bonnie Kolakowski

Sister

There is always someone there.
No matter what life has
put upon you, always there.
To get you through the
hardest of times, the saddest
of troubles, always there.
To share the best of times,
the joy, the happiness, always there.
What would I ever do without my sister.

Craig L. Gordon

"Magnificent Sky"

The heart of someone,
May concede…
The light of one's true colors.

There are no limitations to what it
May proceed.

Stand to look,
Stop to imagine our bodies moving the
Way our bodies were meant to move.
Poetically sailed to the groove.

"Fly the magnificent sky," I always say.
Never let life die out,
Live it day by day.

Ashley Cook

Those Lowest Hours

Why doth my trials spare
Me to a confident air?
For empty fantasy realm,
To no one shall thy fair.

Closed by thy door;
My feelings lie in store.
They tried to escape;
Avoid thy doomed heartbreak.

But to the path it leads;
I reach for thou with greed,
To find another opening;
Too far, I'm scared I heed.

Amanda Bickley

Love?

Conversation
Meeting
Numbers
Will it be love?

Ringing phone
Appointment made
Anticipation anew
It will be love.

Social engagement
Sweet utterings
Refusal, dissent
It is not love.

Struggling contest
Sharp crying
Demanding Right
What kind of love is this?

Pain
Cruel delight
Life
Love?

Djuana Walker

"Desire"

My head says to take heed.
My heart says it's you that I need
My heart and soul are on fire.
'Tis you that I desire
Your need is my need
Your desire is my desire
Who I love and admire
Don't let anything happen to us.
This fire is a need and a must.
'Tis never to late, for this is our fate.

Patricia K. McEwan

Run Hard

Yelling, a gun shot, heavy breaths
　Metal against rock I hear
Nervousness, worry, anxiety leave me
Smells of grass and liniment disappear

The wind whips through my hair
　Sweat is building on my brow
My body forces through the air
　And my feet tell me Go now!

My foe is right behind me
I feel the eager in his sighs
Push! Push! I think to myself
After the finish we can all tell lies

Quick steps in endless succession
　Up the hills I swing my arms
　Over logs and ruts I must slow
Just to go fast again and avoid harm

Mud and worn trails lead my way
Turns and chalk we must follow
　I feel warm on a cool day
Run hard! For there's no tomorrow

Fred Harris

Tag

I am writing a poem
Much to my dismay,
A tiger, lizard, and bird,
Who come outside to play.

"Hello, Mr. Lizard!
How are you today?"
"Fine, Mr. Tiger!
Can Bird come out and play?"

"Yes, I can!" said Mrs. Bird,
"A game of tag, perhaps?"
"But your legs are tiny," said Tiger,
"They probably would collapse!"

"Ah, but there are assets
To handle such a thing.
If my legs grow weary,
I can always take to wing.

"If you try to chase me,
You'll feel pain in every joint!"
"But we will never catch you," said Lizard.
Said Bird, "Isn't that the point?"

Aimee La Russa

Life In The Home For The Aged

My face is old and weathered
My body filled with aches.
My mind's a wondering,
How I ever got in this place.
I watch from my chair
People moving here and there.
But, all I can do is stare.
The clock on the wall
Ticks so slow.
Taunting me of all I've lost.
Maybe today,
Someone will come.
Hurry clock, turn the day.
Someway to live,
If you can call it that.
Afraid of today,
Terrified of tomorrow.
Buried deep within my sorrow.

Jill Wonderly

Vietnam

I was eighteen, young and strong.
My country needed me, you said.
"Action," "Glamour," posters read
Stench and filth I found instead.
Plastic bagging, counting dead
Bullets firing round my head
Bursting me with heavy lead.
And now you tell me you were wrong?

Ann Cogan

Money Talk

Like a penny lying in the street,
My destiny is unknown.
I often feel I spend my time
Like that penny, all alone
My golden bronze exterior
Isn't catching to the eye.
Eclipsing my identity
From the people passing by.
An unfound fortune.
A mystique antique.
If only the world
Would sneak a peek.
And not walk over me
If everyone were shorter,
Then maybe they would see…
Or if I were just a quarter!

Garvin M. Branch

Gratitude

Thank you for this state of grace.
My heart is in a better place.
I could not feel, nor understand,
But for your love and helping hand.

In times of chaos..deep despair,
I see now…You were always there.
You've brought me back to life, it seems,
Renewed my trust in hopes and dreams.

Your healing touch and guiding 'light'
Protected me in darkest night.
You took my anguish—eased my pain,
And turned me back around again.

I thank you for new eyes that "see"..
Not what is now…but what could be.
This kind of faith you've given me,
And Truth has surely set me free.

Yes, You alone stood by my side.
Now by your word..I will abide.
So thank you, Lord, for all you do.
I'm blessed to have a friend like you.

Jana Christian

Untitled

Problems two through forty-four,
My little brother tore,
Fifty-eight
He ate
And now he's starting on more.

And since he thinks it's sweet,
My little brother will eat,
My English homework.
I think he's a jerk,
But my parents think he's cute & sweet.

Eric Sutton

Father Said...

This path is long, yet sunshine reigns
  My legs are fresh and strong...
  It seemed as if a thousand miles,
    Could it be, that I was wrong?
My father said this path was true,
  He wouldn't tell a lie...
But then he said he'd never leave.
  Last week my father died...
    Father said I shouldn't cry,
  But keep my shoulders straight.
The path he said had rocks and holes,
  And lined with lies and hate...
    Each rock would be a problem,
    Each hole would slow me down.
I had my choice to make each time,
    To smile or to frown...
    Father said he loved me,
  I'll always know that's true.
But the days I was allowed with him,
    were very, very few.........

    H. E. Harper

"Non Fiction Injuries"

  To whom it may concern
my life feels like a burn
a constant ache of agony
with no mistake the ashes
is pasted
  it travels with me,
from beyond the bayou to
the concrete roads
the scheme designs my every being
  and I have yet to control
my destiny, that unfolds chromosomes
instead of my own
the appearance tells the years of
struggle and not the day of royal
to perform to its perception
and not those of grandiose.

    Benjamin S. Dinkins Jr.

Mother...

At the age of seven it seemed like
  my life flashed before my eyes,
I turned around and saw my
  mother die
I look back and wish I could
  have said "stop",
Nothing came out... my mouth
  just dropped.
Is it my fault she is dead?
Is it my fault she put the gun
  to her head?
People say it was the pain she had,
The divorce, separation that
  made her mad.
I know it's the way it had to be,
But instead of her could it
  have been me?

    Joe West

Cadensa Pianissimo

Distance from vanity
Permits
A higher degree of identity
And inevitably
Corrects the judgement of others

    Daniel Schwartz

Memories

I rock and rock in my rocking chair.
My memories are many
Of years gone by.
Some are so sweet,
But sadness keeps coming back
Even though I try to forget,
Even though there are reminders
Everywhere of the past.
So how can I forget!
So I sit and rock and rock,
With a grandchild in my lap.

    Julia E. Mylly

Thoughts

As I sit - a- pondering,
My mind goes a - wandering -
To things unknown, a future time -
When all is clear and none sublime!

Will there ever come a time, when I
Can sit quietly and watch the sky?
No guilt to rush me on my way -
Through the paces of the every day?

Why the scurry? Why the haste?
O - what glorious dreams we waste!
Running here - running there -
Are we getting anywhere?

The beauty of the sky still reigns,
And flowers bloom; but we, in chains,
Limit life, and the living thereof -
And scarce have time for those we love!

    Jacqueline Benavides

This Truly I Love Thee

How truly do I love thee?
My soul asks anxiously.
As true as waves love open seas,
And clover loves the windswept leas,
This truly do I love thee.

What holds me in captivity,
Devoted but to thee?
The thought that when I wake no more,
You'll stand in wait beyond my door,
To lead me through eternity.

Where lies that final destiny?
Somewhere, I pray, with thee.
Beyond the setting of the sun,
In distant worlds known yet to none,
Where time stands still eternally.

How truly do I love thee?
How sure can my love be?
As certain as the hands of God,
Reach down upon this sod,
To touch the sweet magnolia tree.

    Edwin F. Roble, Jr.

Pain

I feel nothing but
Pain in my heart
because it was broken
Loving you was the
best thing that could
ever happen to me
I hope you understand
I'm in love with you
but you don't know the
pain you put me through.

    Christina Talian

"Night Thoughts"

Here in the silence of the night.
My thoughts can wander
as they could not before.
All the trials and troubles
of the day, seem so far away.

There is not loneliness
in this time of alone-ness.
But strength in the solace of the night,
and thoughts of the coming of a bright
new day full of promise.

    Ann P. Fisher

These I Love

I love the winds that whistle low,
Myriad stars and soft moonglow;
The rhythmic beat of dancing rain
And jeweled snow on window-pane.
The happy sound of children singing;
Song of bluebirds homeward winging-
Blazing hearth which beckons me
And faith which "spells" eternity!

I love the joy of old friends near
Sharing laughter, sometimes a tear;
Whisp'ring trees through forest hill
And shyness of the daffodil.
The seasons as they come and go
And holidays — I love them so!
The mellow tones of violin string-
All of these make my heart sing.

I love the rose caressed with dew,
But most of all - I love you!

    Donna Mae Bacon

Shadows

  Shadows in the moonlight
  Mysteriously coat the ground
  In the middle of the night
  You can hardly hear a sound

  The moon slides behind a cloud
  And reflects on starry skies
  Darkness hovers like a shroud
  Its secrets tend to tantalize

  The sparkling dew at early morn
  Casts a veil on nature's scene
  The sun appears to be reborn
With its rays so bright and clean

  As shadows stretch out longer
  And the sun gets set for bed
  We have grown a little stronger
  For ensuing nights ahead

  Look for a source to endure
  Each day and every night
  And then you will insure
A life that's filled with light

    Duke Desimone

Untitled

Sitting under a tree
Picking the grass from between my toes
Resting my head on the faithful bark,
I wonder how so many
Never notice
God.

    Gina Lepinski Ledford

No Where

Ocean, sea, watered tree.
Nature's disasters, if you please.
Seeing these so well known,
May as well say, there's no ozone.

Rays that kill at first sight
You'll lose yours, if you see light.
Fine and flames, in desert sun
All little children must carry a gun.

Unbearable heat, throughout the night
A leader begins another fight.
Soldiers led to war, die;
No passiveness to abide;

Surprise again the counter attack:
Intelligence is what they lack.
Where's the reason for the war?
Is it hate, or love, or something more?

To those who knows it best
It's not love, or hate, it's wanting all the rest.
Greed and anarchy rule the Nation,
Another soldier, becomes a patient.

Amber Star Brown

Carpe Diem

Life is a grab bag.
Never ask that it be fair.
There are no guarantees anywhere.
Plus and minus, a measure of talent
And perhaps you make it on balance.
As for the good life syndrome,
You lose some; you win some.

Life is a grab bag,
No refund, no exchange,
Just a self-limited range.
Born into a time, a place,
You consume time, expand space,
Grabbing all you can of life's repast.
Carpe diem while the daylight lasts.

June Davis

Misty Dawn

Somewhere between the bad dreams of
night and an early morning yawn.

I want to stand in the freshness
of a Misty Dawn

Embrace the peace and tranquility
that clings to a rising sun.

Forget broken promises and worry not
about things left to be done.

Only for an instant to stand on that
plateau above hatred and sadness.

Cleanse my thoughts of reality
and every man's badness.

Staring without a blink until the
moment has passed by.

Then I would return to the cruelty
hoping to smile or at least
remember to try.

David Case

Wind Chimes

He dances gently in the
night summer's breeze.
A cool, midnight rain brings
him back to me.
An angel with broken
wings and a frozen smile
haunts my soul,
for the longest while.

An pure essence of Jasmine
brings him back to me.
I, the night blooming flower
petals scattering in the breeze.

He, the wind chimes,
calling, calling
so softly to me.

Cheryl Fitzgerald-Smith

Ashamed

Ashamed…
No cause to be,
But like a widow — I weep.

Moments of desire
Are regretted by heart,
What a fool I was
Not to know of
My changing heart.

Awakened like
Some have been
Why… Now I see.
I understand — I think?

It was just a moment a passion,
As I have said before
But now, my dying heart
And thinking head
Are in constant battle.

Now I seek
More than a moment's passion
…And a stolen kiss!

Aura M. Perez

Life Continues On

Life bears its own load
  No matter how tough
Rocky or steep the road
  Life continues on
Whether right or wrong
  Showing no partiality
Thoughtless, uncaring
  Flowing through the paths of
  Reality

Life is a game
  We are the players
All given the chance
  To determine our fame

The choice of play
  Is ours alone
Affecting our lives
  In every way

Yet — Life continues on
  Thoughtless, uncaring
With a mind of its own

Betty J. Culbreth

"People"

People are great
No matter what color of your face,
Everyone is special
No matter what race.

If you are black
Or if you are white,
You are just as equal
As the next being in sight.

Look everyone
Listen up
Just 'cause you're different
Doesn't mean you're not enough.

Jennifer Alicin Mucciacciaro

My Yoke

The Master said He'd give me
No more than I could bear,
But sometimes I feel I'm burdened
With someone else's share.

But if I do it willingly
And with a cheerful smile,
I know my Lord will help me,
And in a little while,
Perhaps I shall be stronger
For the things I have to do,
And in the shelter of His love
Learn to be humble, too!

Anna E. Hargis

"A Special Mom"

Mom, your love is something
No one truly can explain
Made up of many sacrifices
Sometimes with lots of pain.

You've been caring and forgiving
Though others may forsake
Your love has never failed, Mom
Although your heart may break.

With hard work and so much wisdom
You helped supply our needs
To us, you gave reassurance
By your loving words and deeds.

It took so much patience, Mom
To bring your children up right
But we were truly blessed because
You lead through darkness to light.

So Mom, I now say "thank you"
For your tender, loving care
May God's love always surround you
Is my solemn, heartfelt prayer.

Adele Willoughby Snead

You

I remember just yesterday
Nothing special, nothing much.
But there's something about it
Had a lasting touch.
Could it be that I saw you,
Could it be that we talked,
But there's something about you
That brings back these thoughts.
Wherever I am, whatever I do,
It's nice to know,
I will always have you.

Jessica Gonzalez

Daughterly Thoughts

Not hand nor foot
Nor arm nor leg
Yet just as much
Part of me

Guiding my footsteps
Like the womb's rhythmic heartbeat
Tapping out our coexistence

I can feel your pulse
On a sunny day
In the autumn leaves
When I close my eyes

I will always thrive and grow
In Us.

Jana Overbey

Presentiment Of A True Love

Lord never speaks with me,
Nor have I visited paradise,
Because I don't deserve it;

But I have a presentiment
That the love between
Anastasia and Anastasios is a true love
And will be eternal.

I hope soon you will become
One soul through the fusion
Of your bodies.

May God bless you always!

Giuseppe Rella

Family Reunion

Although we haven't pageants won,
  Nor have we wealth of kings,
Today we bring our trophies home
  For more important things.

It doesn't matter, rich or poor
  And beauty's in our minds;
 family doesn't need all this,
  For love's the tie that binds.

The memories of yesterday,
  We share with common heart,
To make a family what it is
  Each one must play his part.

In every face we see the toll
  Another year has taken;
Still, here we are that we might see
  This family not forsaken.

So, love each other while you live,
  For life we only borrow.
Just find your way to heaven's gate,
  We'll all meet there, tomorrow.

Jeanne Douglas

Miss You, Dad

You left me, Dad.
Now there's just Mom and me.
A little bird
Hit our window pane.
Its neck got broke
So I made it a grave.
Can you come back
And help me fly my kite?
I miss you, Dad.

Eilleene Kinney Fawcett

Summertime And Tobacco Land

The grey-green leaves pointing
North, South, East and West
shoot arrows of turtle-like form

The land is invaded by
this ubiquitous crop
that sells well locally
and around the world
on this planet called Earth-

Who knows how long
Earth's creatures will
continue its nefarious use
Perhaps someday all these
grey-green leaves pointing
North, South, East and West
will all have gone up in
smoke as a new Utopian World arrives-

Edgar Cosimi

Skipping Stones

Our lives are like the skipping stones,
    Not knowing how far,
    Or how many skips,
    there will be.

  Each skip sends out its ripples
    As far as one can see.

    Each skip, an action,
    Each ripple,
    A reply

Each new day is sunshine in our eye

    The blue skies darken,
    And night time comes fast.

So make the stones that you are skipping
    Skip far
    and
    long to last.

Donald C. Christensen

Like A Mother

Dedicated to Mrs. Dietterick

Again another year went by,
Not seeing much of each other.
My thoughts will always be of you.
You're like my second mother.

You've listened, you've been a friend.
You shared your life with me.
I can't imagine you not in my life.
For one day it might be.

I just wanted to say thank you.
To say that you'll always be.
That spirit of hope and kindness.
That will always live inside of me.

Denise Jones

"Skin-Tone"

Be proud
of who you are,
because you are special,
made by God, so free,
Problems may come, and they will go.
But the strong survive,
So keep your head up high.
Reach for the sky,
Educate your brain, without gettin' high.

John Alonzo Armstrong

Scotoma

Mind over matter
Nothing, really matters
Taking time to read myself
Smelling the roses not realizing the
  problem of pain and anguish.
Make myself feel better,
Not working at all
Seeing nothing, but seeing all
Scotoma got me scared, very scared.
Truth is what is, so what really is it
is it reality or fantasy
Dreams seem so real
life is so superficial
making sense of nothing
thoughts run wild, wildly like a horse
Remembrance of a abused child
Scotoma got me scared, so very scared
deceit and deceive telling lies cause of you
can't see what's there
Scotoma got scared.

Jose M. Perez

Wasteland

In the wastelands
Nuclear pollution is the air
Our skin we must never bare
For in the wasteland
Pray that you never dream
For all you do is scream
In the wasteland it's unsafe outside
From the cancer ridden UV rays
You can't hide
The end seemed so far away
I've survived to this day
But from the wasteland's birth
Came the death of Mother Earth

David Gregory

Searching

Waters that comber like a curling
Ocean wave —on and on and on
Signing the lyrics of an endless
Lover's unfulfilled taunting song

Over boundless clouded ocean shores
Of sand and cliffs of rising rocks
The faint tick, tick, tick, —tick
Of the unrelenting hands of a clock

A secret promise given to a maiden fair
Though once vowed, never shall he keep
Her eyes with deep-blue placid tears
That now quietly weep and weep

Searching yet for a longed for love
Never in this tormented life to be
Always searching, searching for that
Love withheld, nevermore will she see

Oh! but to be awakened in the morning
With a kiss of fate upon her still pale face
Instead of past sorrows that multiply
To know now true love in their place.

Irene La Franco

Untitled

Death
  of a
    Marriage

What can
  I
    say?
Let them be
  happy
    I pray,
as each go
  a separate
    way.

What can I say?
  I can only
    pray
  and let God
    have his
  as each go
    on a separate way.

    Ginny O'Neil

Pamela

A vision appeared in a dream
Of a face known long ago.
Though she loved me as I slept,
She left as the sun
Drove the haze from my eyes.
I awoke, and for a moment
It seemed she was there.
But as sleep ceased to cloud my mind
I could find of her no trace.
The joy of a moment now fled
May never come again,
But a spirit was awakened
I thought long dead,
With a memory of that
Which will never be.

    Jim Asher

Please

A crystal bubble
of earth
fills with beauty
They dropped it
No,please be careful
careful
No
There it goes
And shatters into a thousand
pieces
I shall try to save
all the pieces I can
Perhaps someday
they can be glued

    Cheri Cloninger

Sunset

Looking out over the vast waters
of the ocean deep
Watching the sun in all its radiant glory
slip quietly into the sea

My everyday problems slowly fade
like the last rays of the sinking sun

Leaving my mind and soul calm and serene
as the waters below me
I believe...I am renewed

    Douglas Klima

My Lost Love

Here I am with only my thoughts
Of how it used to be
When we were together
And you were close to me

Now that time is in the past
It makes me sad and blue
A million tears I've cried and cried
But I can't forget about you

I love you more each passing day
My nights are lonely and still
Since that's the way it has to be
I'm sure it must be Gods will.

    Carolyn Moake

I Stood Within A Shaded Night

I stood within a shaded night
Of long reflections cast in white
And long and silent there I stood
Alone to sense the winter woods.

I knew the moment would not last,
But how I wished it not to pass
Yet I knew then within my mind
I'd never stop the hands of time.

Years have past since that night
And when I returned to that site
Long and silent there I stood.
In urban sprawl which once was woods.

I knew the moment would not last
As it didn't in the past
And as I walked away that time
The only reflections where in my mind.

    John E. Lepore

Breath-Blown

Breathed on the threshold
  of my new garden
& forgot the random averageness
  of the world
with its insane complainers
  of the dreambox drama
and the ghost town dwellers
  in pitchfork tents
the motherless immigrants
  with soak-stained skin
and the cross-eyed hound dogs that howl
  in mestizo alleys
and the Uncle Sam clowns with their
  sleek gold teeth and hands on
    granite-cased flags
and here I stood
breath-blown
relieved at the clouds still in the sky

    Jon Wright

Feelings In Mirrors

  Mirrors show the echo
of thought that are hidden
deep inside you. Some you
didn't know existed

  A drop of water falls
into the pond that only
the whispering trees can
hear. So you know your
reflection is only deep
thought made clear.

    Gracen Hendrix

Untitled

Travelling through the passages
Of ones mind and through the
Sorrows of one soul lives the
Eyes of a once innocent child.

Once lifted on a pedestal high above
Our hearts, broken down in angry
Rage, listen to the silent whispers
Of a baby trying not to cry

Through the rage and tears he
Lies here upon your heart, Listen
To his anger, listen to his pain.
For once a innocent child,
Love has passed him by.

    Julie Fortier

Children

Children are the flowers
  of the human race
There's joy and beauty
  in every little face
A smile, a frown, a laugh, a tear
  gather the children, hold them near
  let them know they are dear
And what we wish would last
Are the precious moments
  that went so fast.

  Gone!!

    Earnestine P. Neal

Barefoot In The Jungle

I can smell the sweet fragrances
of the jungle foliage wafting in
the air, the sounds of natures
creatures scurrying about.

I am a part of the jungle.

I eat the fruits of the trees;
sweet fruits, from the rich soil.
I am comfortable here. I am secure.
I am in sync with the rhythm.

I am a part of nature.

I stain my hair and my lips with
wild raspberries. Instant aphrodisia!
Collecting my basket of goods, I run
barefoot through the jungle.

The dance of love weighs heavy on
my hips. Passion consumes me as I
run to my king, barefoot through
the jungle.

    Jacqueline Taylor

Chain Of Thoughts

I am trying to think clearly
of the things that I must do.
But my chain of thoughts get broken
As my thoughts drift back to you
It's your voice that I keep hearing,
And the tender things you say.
And your eyes that I keep seeing,
You mean more to me each day
I know God set up our meeting,
that we wonder so about.
So now we must take advantage
of what he has all cut out

    Betty J. Bethel

Bravest Soldier

He was the bravest soldier
of them all
only a young man when he
went off to war,
his courage cannot be measured,
to his country he is a
priceless treasure,
on that day in June of 1944,
the biggest battle of the war,
he fought on the beaches of Normandy,
it was there he gave his life
for liberty,
but he will not be forgotten,
though his name may not be
etched in stone,
he is buried in a cemetery
in France,
his grave is marked unknown.

Celine Rose Mariotti

A thought, at a moments grasp....

I can notice the distinct profile
of your petite figure through my
hair, as the wind blows
    unpredictably rampant.
It's cold and peaceful up here,
just you and I.
Lets sit and talk, while no one
can hear.
Lets grope and share our incessant
Love, while no one
can see.
Let us be loved by no one else
but thee.
I am grateful for that gust of
wind, that did no harm, as you
landed gracefully in my arms.

Joe M. Frey

The Cell At 22

Locked in a cell at 22
Oh my God, what can he do
A crime that he did not commit
A jury that would not a quit
They gave him life, and one day more
An eight by eight, with concrete floor
For a life, they say he took
And they all swore on the bible book

Locked in a cell at 22
Oh my God, what can he do
What could be worse, a dismal cell
Is it not worse than the depths of hell
One small window, with light so dim
Three steel bars to keep him in
One small cot, in the corner there
Eight by eight, a room so square

Locked in a cell at 22
Oh my God, what can he do
Taking the belt from his waist
Tieing it high with no great haste
Around his neck, he loops it there
Kicks away the chair, nothing but air

Bob Russell

Untitled

Early one morning
on a bright and sunny day
I met man who told me
my father passed away
I ran home quickly
with tears running down my chin
and there was my father
asking where I'd been
I couldn't understand it
so I went to find that man
to ask him what he meant
and then he took my hand
he said child we have a father
up in heaven above
a father for all of us
who fills our hearts with love
I asked him how he knew this
how he knows he's really there
and he said child I read the bible
and I can fill it in the air.

Jamie L. Blagg

The Iceman

I remember when I was a child.
On a hot summers day, all
the children played ball in
the streets and waited for
a man in a truck.

When they saw the iceman they
would all gather around.
He gave me a nice chunk of
ice wrapped in paper.

After the children finished playing
they all went home.

I remember the iceman and
the kindness he showed me.

Dorothy Moore

The Mystery

The sun sets
on another chapter of life.

On her way to
forever she
kisses a fallen star.

One more dream
fades away.

Her heart sings
an empty song.

Alone in the dark
she dances
with the mystery.

Bobbi-Jean Buck

Victims Of Servitude

Rescue us from our slavery.
Our shackles of prejudice.
Our chains of hate.
This world is our prison;
A separate cell for each.
The steel bars of society hold us within.
Unable to reach one another.
Deliver us, extricate us.
Let us be free.

Jill Risser

Sometimes A Shepherd

Sometimes a shepherd is the sun
    on golden afternoons
And all clouds follow one by one
    this great imposing Shepherd sun!

Long after he has slipped away
    the try to tag along
In tints of yellow, orange, purple,
    pink and gray.

Then suddenly they're gone
    Until they gather 'round the brink
Of a liquid moon
    To drink and then go on.

Bertha Van Wingerden

A Fishy Haiku

The wiggily worm
On my hook does really squirm
Wondering how long?

Carolyn Foy

Unseen

You saw me walking through the clouds
    on that rainy, gloomy day.
I know inside you saw my face,
    but yet you turned away.

And as I stand there soaking wet
    the tears start to run.
The heartache that you've given to me
    feels like it weighs a ton.

You said you loved me,
    you cannot deny.
You said you'd never
    make me cry.

As the rain comes pouring down
    I see you disappear.
And all my tears of joy and happiness
    turn to tears of fear.

The fears of you not coming back
    all will soon pass by.
And with that thought kept in mind
    you'll hear a relieving sigh.

Amy Jo Neil

Ever So Even

As far as one can see,
On the most clear day,
The land seems
    Ever so even
Drifting off
    Ever so even
Stride over it
    Halt at the gorge
    Open, yawning
    Below
    Reach up, as you
Stride over it:
    Try, fail, try again
    to touch the crest
    looming above
Look again
    As far as one can see,
    On the most clear day
The land seems ever so even
Except when you stride over it. And
stumble.

Barry J. Walker

Untitled

Uncap, the blue bottle you put
on the shelf, awhile ago.

Smell its aroma
still sweet,
And, taste, salty.
The fruit is ripe and plump.
The banquet table is set
You are cordially invited
to feast at my table,
And, linger while the day
completes its purpose (self).

Frances M. Wasilewski

On The Tail Of A Comet

Last night I dreamed I sailed away
On the tail of a comet just to play
Up and up my comet flew
Like a bird into the blue
First I saw the man in the moon
He was such a silly goon
Then there were the men from Mars
And after them the shooting stars
I went around Mercury on a crazy pattern
And ended up riding the rings of Saturn
As for the people on Venus
Everyone was a genius
On Uranus or Jupiter
I met Scott Carpenter
I saw all but Pluto and Neptune
And I'll never forget the man in the moon
As my comet slowed down
I jumped to the ground
I fell on my head
And woke up in bed!

Joseph Martino

Winter

I see the misty mantle of fog
On the tree shrouded hills
As the sun breaks over the bogs
And the many little rills

The misty morning is shorn
As the sun dapples on the water
Like sparkling diamonds worn
By the ocean waves each morn

Winter is on its way
As the frosty nights foretell
And in each new day
We see the changes as well

The presence of the chill wind
Tells of winters coming round
And the russet leaves are pinned
To the cold and barren ground

The animals in their shaggy fur
Can smell the changing season
And ready themselves for winter's lure
Because of instinct without reason

Dee Thompson

The Child

Silent and dark
On the wings of memories
She carries secrets to my heart

Somehow I know
Her teardrops fall like raindrops
On the windows of my soul

I can't see her
This spirit that chases me
Down winding paths of fear

She'll follow me
Even when the angels cry
This child I used to be

Gail Proite

Rain

Sitting at my window
On this dark, wet day
I see the rain fall softly
Through the clouds of gray.

The drops fall down so rhythmically
It's more than I can stand
I long to be outside with them
To catch them in my hand.

And when they sit upon my hand
I'll stare with my eyes wide
For I have caught the tear drops
That Mother Nature cried.

The rain has now stopped falling
The clouds turn gray to light
And with the shooting sunbeams
Make everything so bright.

Julia McGowan

Awakening Amongst Survival

I am a blossoming tree in the Spring
Once deadened by the a Winter
Feelings from within, a different entity
Screaming, barely heard by me

Emotions, like tufts
Weaving through my soul
Waking me up
Making me whole

A child at night, another at daylight
once seeping at the seems
Grows by love - to live, to dream
The other never again to be seen

Feelings and thoughts connecting
A new hope just begun
Darkness once shadowed by a false light
The child no longer staggers on

Elizabeth A. Rutledge

Untitled

Blankness
running through my soul
waiting…
to run out of breath
I feel like dying
the dead have come
no more than to inspire
hoping to catch the creative flow
failing at every step I try
so I stop

Barbara Ann Littlefield

Once In My Life

Once in my life I knew love
Once I even knew trust
I once knew friendship
And I once had a family

But now I know hate
And I'm filled with disbelief
I'm all alone now
And I have no family

Someone stop the pain
Someone please stop the hurt
I just won't to die
But I can't say good-bye

Can anyone hear me
Can anyone hear my cry
As time slowly goes by
I just want to die

I must grow stronger
There's too much to live for
I can not die
I just can not say good-bye!

Andrea Marie Sensenig

I'm The One

I was sitting down late
one night trying to figure
what hurt the most.
I couldn't tell if it was
our fight or the other life
you chose. All I know is if
you come back now bring
your smile, your heart, your clothes
I will try to change
what's wrong some how and
be thankful I'm the one
you chose.

Johnny Mark Rhoades

3:52 A.M.

I'm having another
One of those nights.
My body and my mind
Make sleep impossible
Because of thoughts
Of you.

I know that even
If I fall asleep
You'll be in my dreams.

I'm surrounded by
So many reminders
And filled with
So many memories.

You seem to be
Everywhere I am
Except in my bed.

I miss you
I miss us.

Bonnie Lindberg

To A Dear Friend Recently Deceased

Not long ago we met.
One - two - three meetings
Were all it took
For a friendship like ours
To be firm.

Two months ago
　We met
　　For the last time,

And in the space
　of eleven days
　　you left

As a yellow leaf dies
　with the autumn —

Friendships do not die
With the death of friends.

Isabel Martin

The Hand

Looking at the little hand
One wonders 'bout the master plan.
I often stop to look and see
That little hand that waits for me.
It loves to go outside to walk,
To look and see, to laugh and talk.
There is such trust in that small hand,
The faithful hand of future man.
It has the power to conquer all,
To help the weak, the poor, the small.
But that is not the plan today,
He'll clap and throw and catch and play.
And I will fix his tears and fears
Enjoying all his present years.
The castles built on shifting sand,
The childhood of my little man.

Colleen Ford

Untitled

No I can not,
Only fail
with the world and myself

I do hope,
someday
all the thoughts that inside me -
explode -
and on a white sheet of paper
start speaking for themselves.

For the time being
they put their roots
deeper
and deeper,
killing my trust, hope and love.

I can only hope, it will happen
before they
devour
the very little peace
that - I believe - somewhere -
inside me is sleeping

Iwona Nyzio

Untitled

What if a crystal didn't sparkle,
or if love wasn't warm,
Would you still be there
When I set aside the harm?

What if my life fell apart,
and yours came together,
Would you still be there
to give me hope to make it better?

What if I stopped this poem,
and never started again,
Would you still be there
Loving me without an end?

Holly Nancy Baglio

Is It True

Is it true that space is endless
　Other planets turn beyond
　perhaps another human race
　That God saw fit to spawn

And will man someday find a way
　To see and touch and hear
The humans from the other worlds
　So far and yet so near

Perhaps we will communicate
Our knowledge, thoughts and deeds
　And learn from one another
　The way God has decreed

For us to live together
To hear and touch and see
Our lives forever richer
　In peace and harmony

Connie Dannaker

Hero

Others don't see his dignity
Others don't feel his presence
And they cease to recognize,
The Godliness behind his face.

He rules the universe,
Universe that is mine.
I feel the turbulent emotions
At the flicker of his mind

Life he leads is so sacred
That I dare never to disturb
A follower in the distance
Never allowed to touch

Something so meaningless to my hero,
My living love in his hands.

Janet Yoon

Autoimmune Assault

Our brigade has butchered our own.
Our boys killed by kin.
Our brethren of beta lie slain,
Slaughtered from where they worked.
It was an awful mistake
Which began an onslaught
That ended in massacre.
How will we function,
And whom shall we call
To take their place?
Our demise is our own cause,
Our sickness of ourselves.

Brian Bradley

Sphere Of Despair

A woe it is that
　our children must see
A world full of greed
　and hateful bigotry.

A world in which
　disease and hunger abound,
For which no hope
　of a cure can be found.

A world full of pollution,
　with her poisonous clouds of grey;
A world of death and violence
　that never seem to go away.

A world of pain and sadness
　to which no other can compare.
A world forever to be called
　the sphere of despair.

Jennifer A. Padgett

"A Mother's Loss"

We held hands
Our lives were touched.
With each breath
Our love grew much.

We had a bond
That only you and I could share
Although few could see
We loved much.

We held hands
When death came to our door
In the silence
I heard your cry no more
As mother nature played her tune
Like flowers never bloomed.

For only I felt the pain
Of your dreams un-proclaimed.
For only a mother knows
Of a hand no one else
Will ever touch.

Barbara Gray

"Read The Writing.."

If, when you talk, you get a kick
　Out of your own rhetoric…
Never letting up for air,
　Spreading lore just everywhere…

When you dispute what others say
　And contradicting's your forte…
Always right, the rest so dumb..
　Push your point 'till ears are numb…

The last word on most ev'rything..
　Must toss your two-cents in the ring
Read the writing on the wall…
　Folks don't like a "Know-It-All"!!!

Dorothy K. Davis

Looking Over The Edge

Looking over the edge
Seeing everything; afraid of nothing
Wanting to try anything new,
Just for the "high," the adrenalin rush!
Wanting and daring every step of life,
Never feeling whole unless,
Being challenged by the unknown.

James Burton Reynolds

October's Picture

A crimson frame of autumn leaves
  Outstanding 'neath the blue,
Where glimmers of the sunlight played,
  And glints of gold came through.

There, stretched across so lazily
  Are fields of dusty gray,
And o'er the hill that climbs the west,
  A woods in bright array.

The little lambs in merry glee
  Trip lightly 'cross the scene,
One giant old oak stands out alone,
  With branches gold and green.

And just before the set of sun
  October reached on high
to pin a picture...lovely...fair...
  Called "autumn" 'gainst in the sky.

And watching as the evening shades
  Were drawn across the day,
I found October's picture fair
  Pinned in my heart to stay.

Goldie L. Christensen

Time

The holder of our memories,
Past and present.
The keeper of our secrets,
True and false.

We live by time;
It is the organizer of our lives,
Controlling everything we do,
It is the record of our life.

More powerful than we know,
It is able to take
A little at a time
Aging the youngest of things.

It knows more than us,
Every second, every instant,
Never stopping, always moving,
Waiting for no one.

Homero Perez

Snowflake Ballet

I watched while snowflakes
  performed a ballet
Turning and whirling
  by my window today.

They gave a performance
  in the frosty air
Against a background
  of branches quite bare.

Their gossamer gowns
  so soft and so white
Sparkled and glittered
  in the morning light.

My cares seemed to vanish
  and the day became bright
As I watched the ballet
  in this world of white.

Gertrude Shook

A Love To Share

There are many loves in a
persons life. A love for a
Brother or Sister. A love for
A Mother or Father. Each love
in life is different than the
love before that. A love for a
special friend. A love for a
companion or a spouse.
I have loved many people in
my life. Some I cherish and
some I wish to forget.
I also have a love for my
Country, my Land and Sea to
Shining Sea.
I have a very special love for
lots of things.
Each love is deeper than the
love before that.
True love never ends only to make
a new beginning.

Debbie Kolb

Glue In My Shoe

I was sitting there cutting my
picture so neat.
Then I got some glue and sat
in my seat.

I took out my yellow pencil and
began to draw,
A picture of a monster ten feet
tall.

I finished my monster so scary
and blue,
I opened the lid and dumped
glue in my shoe.
I started to cry, what am I going
to do,
I will never get this glue out of
my shoe.

Cathy Merritt

The Rose

  Love, love is like a black rose
    Placed upon my tomb
  My heart is red with blood
  Because of you, I'm doomed

  Love, love is like a red, red rose
    You placed in my hand
    From your heart to mine
    Together we shall stand

  Love, love is like the fires of hell
    Are burning in your heart
    For I thought we were friends
    'Til the seas part

Angie Weems

At Last.....

As the presence of tomorrow
rolls along, the weary pains
of love torture us day in and
day out until we find the
glorious one who catches our
spirit and uplifts our soul.
But as the pasts of yesterday haunts
us from the sorrows that left
us all alone in the dark,
we cry.....

Bethany Moore

Listen To The Children

We are the children
Please hear our cry
Don't pollute our ocean
Our sky

We want the sun to shine
Right through
We want to see the sky
So blue

To see dolphins jump
And whales dive
All creatures healthy
Staying alive

We want fields of flowers
And wheat growing tall
Enjoy birds in flight
We need them all

Let's care for our world
Our land, sea and sky
We are the children
Please hear our cry

Deborah West-Owen

"Identifying Yourself"

Confusion my fault
Please let me know
Bring me to reality
My interests are at large
My abilities are sure to grow
More pros than cons
In many areas I know
Narrow them down
For we live only once
To be our most prized
Decide for your future
Before precious time shadows us
Becoming a vision
Unknown to the world
Do not hibernate
Live for the moment
Live to tell all
Be only yourself
To die dreaming
In heaven or hell.

Jennifer A. Rose

"Eyes"

Eyes.
Pools of color-
green, brown, blue, hazel,
cat-shaped, ovals, circles.
Sleepy, droopy, bloodshot,
bright, clear, awake.
Sighted.
Blinded.
All the same,
Yet-
all different.
All mirrors to the
heart,
body,
mind,
and
soul.

Juliane Morgan

The Old Man

The old man
pulled the pez dispenser
from his pocket.

Its head
was a green-skinned hag
with buck teeth
And the children laughed at it.

The old man
put his thumb on its black hair
And pushed the head back,
exposing the throat.

And he offered the children
lemon candy.

C. T. Staley

Feeling Sad

Say you miss him he'll always hear,
Put away your worst fear.
It's all right to feel sad,
Remember all the good times you had.
Dry your tears and please don't cry,
In your heart you can say good-bye.
Make new friends have a good time,
It doesn't cost a single dime.
Say good-bye in your heart,
So in there he'll never part.

Elizabeth Stack

My Mother

My mother was my measuring rod,
Put in my hands by hands of God,
She measured life by standards high-
Enriching others passing by.

A cheerful smile a happy face,
She spread God's word every place;
With out stretched hand to those in need-
Doing unto others, by word and deed.

I measure things by what she taught,
If not as high the way she sought-
I passed them by and thanked my God,
He gave me mom as a measuring rod.

Gladys B. Hippensteel

Greed

American Indians pushed from their past,
Put on land, not their own,
Showered by spirits of hate,
Laboring will be their fate,
  Mighty Brave!
    Dig your grave!
      For I am your keeper,
        Now dig deeper,
Deeper into the pits of Hell,
For I am casting an evil spell,
Cast from the vast book of mine,
Called send them to the evil shrine,
Whose fault?
Yours and mine.

Darren Cox

Who?

This unimportant being - Me
Questions her immortality.
When life would have me cease to be,
The cipher that I am
Would leave no vacuum.
No gaping wounds nor agony
Of grief when I am gone.
Perhaps a smile or two you'll see
By one or two - at most a few
Who'll say, "Remember her?
Why yes — at least I think I do."

Jean R. Levi

Nature

As her limbs
reach to embrace me
I notice the dying hands
and the fading hair
Things we all helped
to destroy
by dumping barrels of trash
upon her fair
green skin
that will always be
our greatest sin
the one that can never be forgiven

Erik Biscoe

Your Wedding Day

Today you will be married,
Ready to start a new life.
Infinite joy can be yours,
Shared as husband and wife.

Hands and hearts together,
A bed of roses may you find.
And never see the thorns,
Nor break the ties that bind.

Don't forget the laughter,
That keeps the tears at bay.
Idolize each other,
More and more each day.

Barbara K. Fox

"Feelings"

I've been up and I've been down
Really low, low on the ground

And then I look up in the sky
And see the white clouds rolling by
And wonder why oh why can't I
Just roll along 'til by and by
The problems solved but why oh why
Do I waste my time and sometimes cry
On junky stuff that soon will fly
Like the eagle soaring high

Butterflies still fly, I see
And birds play in the apple tree
A child's smile and happy glee
The surf that rumbles out to sea
And how about the bumble bee
Some trees have lived a century
I'm standing firm don't let me flee
I thank you Lord for loving me.

Frances H. Mundy

The Birds

There are many birds of every color
Red, blue, brown, black and yellow
Not forget the beautiful white dove
Because it makes us think of love
No sweeter picture has a chance
Than the dove holding the olive branch

God gives birds such an intellect
More than we can ever expect
When a rainy season is to be
The nest is high up in the tree
Whenever a drought does abound
The nest is down near the ground

And many other things they know
On their young how to bestow
Caring for them when they are small
But later, ———— not at all
The time has come to say "Good-bye"
To leave the nest, and learn to fly.

Flossie Hall

My Love

He played with my heart
Right from the start
His words were probably never true
And now I'm alone and blue

We clicked at once
Boy was I a dunce
He wasn't the guy I thought
But my heart was what he caught

I needed someone to love me
And someone with which I could be
He used that to get what he wanted
And then left me, alone and haunted

Even though he did me wrong
My heart, for him, still does long

Amanda Jones

I Was So Sad

I was so sad,
Sad of what I was accused of,
I am good,
I believe I am good
Judged by the ones who isn't the judge
People believe I am bad,
But I am different.

In this life I am hated,
My soul is so sad,
This is my day,
My day of mourn

Tears of adjourning pain
Fall upon my pillow as
I try to hold my breath.
I welcome death anytime.

Ivy Berry

Untitled

Dark faces,
seek me in my dreams.
I struggle, but am never freed.

They haunt me, even after
night has fled.

Dark faces,
Struggling against their fate.
I cannot help them,
only they learn to late.

Claudette Sadur

"My Mama And Daddy"

When first an infant with open eyes,
Saw two faces with loving smiles.
Growing up with firm beliefs,
From mama and daddy; a gift for keeps.
Surrounding our home with all their love,
Two wonderful parents, I am proud of.
My attributes came from both,
Now I have love, faith and hope.
No matter what life shall bring in air,
Mama and daddy said, always care.
As adults we follow a path of destiny,
Mama and daddy still believes in me.
When you come and take them home,
Through their hearts and souls; I will
   never walk alone.

Glenda Richard Leleux

Jazz

Sounds of Truth with relentless candor
   searching for reality
   unveiling man's destiny
Sounds of Love with multihued emotion
   longing for ecstasy
   intoning sensual pleasure
Sounds of Hope with ardent expression
   emanating from despair
   attaining settled aspiration
Sounds of Blue with fervid inflection
   revealing mean times
   glorifying intrinsic sadness

Dorothy E. Johnson

Be Which

In the deep
secret folds
of your ectoplasmic fabric
spirits frolic
in gray matters of flesh

And in your gaze
I can tell
that you
are well-possessed

eyes alike mine
though deeper
through yours
I'd rather see
the world once
from your slant
Natalie Merchant

John C. Squier

Untitled #1

Falling up and jumping down the
Severed vision's holy glory.
Cathedra now just a footstool.
Lifting spirits, shrouding carnage,
Decant dreams of taciturn fools.
Catheter promises; new age
Slander thickens teeming gravy
That puddles his collection plate.
Dirty money absolved of sins.
Tightrope walking over brimstone
Tablets, their power he rescinds;
Truncate the flaccid teat to bone.
Covetous fury, once enticed,
Imbibes the layman soul from Christ.

Donald Scott Bartosik

Untitled

Shivers
   sent by pulses
     of wind
   on a still night
echo
   in me
and grow
   until
     I shake
and my feet rattle
with
   sudden
force
and my hands
try
   to save
   my soul
before I fall
through
   my self

Jennifer Dubrow

Choices

Rise with the sun,
Set with the moon,
Which one would you choose.

If you should choose
the sun, you could
have the birds, flowers,
and warm sunny days.

If you should choose
the moon, you could
have the fireflies, bright
shining stars, and cool
romantic moonlit nights.

Constance F. Porter

Untitled

   Childhood dreams
   Shattered with reality.
   Carefree heart and minds
   Infested with problems.
Emotional states underground,
Happy days supposedly found.
Once again a world of dreams.
But simplicity is never found...
   Never as it was
   Naivete is gone
   And with it the bond
   For reality is known!

Amanprit Kandola

In The Mist

Crashing waves upon the shore
Set me free, from life's uproar
Water glistening through the stare
Reflects the thought; does anyone care
Aimlessly walking in the sand
Notes of music, but no band
Beauty touches deep the mind
Soothing noises, let the soul unwind
Take the time to get there
'Cause in the moment; not a care.

Jodi Oien

A Million Dollar Grin

Whenever I steal a kiss from her,
She has a million dollar grin.
She seems to sense my love for her,
As only an infant can.
She's my girl, my precious girl,
And I knew it from the start,
That she would take her daddy,
And steal away his heart.

Whenever I see her fast asleep,
I just have to touch her hand.
For she is like an angel,
Heaven knows she's something grand.
She's my girl, my precious girl,
And I knew it from the start,
That she would take her daddy,
And steal away his heart.

James A. Skaggs

Precious

Precious is my little cat,
She is simple, just like that.
She is frisky, and a little fat,
But that is precious, my little cat.
Sometimes she sleeps in the hay,
But sometimes, she'd rather play.
Sometimes precious keeps me up at night,
By meowing, when there is no light.
But that is precious, my little cat,
That's precious, and that is that!

Jamie Phillips

Alicia

There is a woman that I do love
She was born below but guided from
above.
A perfect angel was sent to me.
A perfect lovely sight to see.
The way she smiles as she talks
The way she moves as she walks
With a smile, white as milk
And skin so soft, as soft as silk
Tell me to lose her? Oh, no never
I shall hold her in my arms forever.

James Shields

To A Mother

Stay around old friend.
Shout out one more time
Those words of wisdom
Which form my path.

Shut one more time
The door to devastation,
And vividly invent those
Sweet words of comfort.

Cover my eyes for eternity
And push me through this
Planet of charades,
Of phonies and fools.

Appear as my pole,
The one to hold on to
When I slip... on this
Slippery stage.

Barbara Repandis

My Best Friend Laurie

Her name was Laurie
She was my friend
Really, she was my sister
But why did it have to come to an end?

She was my dearest love
My sister she was
When I see her picture
I wish I could fly away like a dove

To an unknown land
Where no one dies
Everyone tells the truth
And there are no lies

Now that she is dead
I am really scared
I thought that we would be together
And we would always be prepared.

My sister was loving so dear to me
Now she can look down and see me

Now she is in heaven and now she is free
To be what she wants, and all that she can be.

Beth Thomas

Pray For Us Two

The moon openly pans - sincerely to me
Shyly we'll perform a handshake on cue
Then trees wish well sobriety
We count on him to follow through

Our skins were snuck from under one God
Our distance day and nights
Fearless issues try to prod
A dream of stars to fight

Deepest threats conspire high
And disagree at last
He bows again so as he dies
You hold him in the past

Censure in this sandy yard
Spinning 'round a mime
Nothing gained if nothing's hard
A generations rhyme

Cliff Satriano

"Signed Out"

Sign says "one way"
Sign says this way.
Sign says "wrong way"
Sign says which way?

Sign of the times
Sign in the sky.
Gimme a sign, if you want be mine,
Sign here.

Yield.
Exit.
Signed,
STOP.

Jo Ellen Marr

Denied love

Cries of love, denied by one.
Shouts of I love you!
Acknowledge by none.
Stains of fallen tears cried,
from pain and sorrow felt inside
In love lies, the tears I've cried,
over and over but always denied.

Duane Skinner

Cry Of The City

Time To Time
Sirens pierce
The Soul Of The City.
The Sirens get louder.
The bullets Flash and Crash.
The cries fill The City.
Robberies and gang-Cross Fire
Slay Innocent Victims
They Lay In Pools Of Blood.

Mothers tears flood The Streets.
Another child claimed
In a Drive-By shooting.
You can hear The Echoes Of Pain.
It roars through The Winds Of The City.

The Souls Weep.
Another War has come Forth-
A War Against Crime.
The Mournful Faces on The News
They are The Portrait Of The Souls,
That Weep In Chicago.

Irene Heyl

Crossroads Of Love

The beauty of love
Smooth tranquility floating
Like the heart of a dove.
Demanding the company
Requesting the unity
That only one can provide,
The one- the new loved one.

The beauty of love
Building emotional bonds
Unnoticed bonds
Unavoidable bonds of love.

The beauty of love
Sharing, laughing, crying.
The intimacy that is
Foreign to others.
Private intimacy of love.

Oh, that beautiful love
The unifying link.
Marriage, when two become one
Sharing a common love.

Don Elligan

A Real Poet's Confession

Many years have gone by
Since my first poem I penned
Eighty some, to be exact.
What has happened since then?
I, myself, wouldn't argue with Webster
Whose name is as well-known as "Heinz"
He gave us poetry's real meaning
"A composition in verse that rhymes"
Too long it's been so agitating
Whenever I read what is "prose"
And they call it poetry. Who says so?
Only one with a soul really knows.
I guess I have made some enemies
But I've gotten it off of my chest
May the honest-to-goodness poets
Now put their minds at rest.

Catherine S. Engstrom

Winter Rose

A winter rose
So fragile and fair,
Its grace and beauty
beyond compare.

Standing strong
Against the cold winter wind,
Bending...never breaking,
Never giving in.

You remind me so,
Of that winter rose,
Bending just a little
As the cold wind blows.

And like that rose
I shall cut you free,
And keep you warm
And safe with me.

Keep you safe
Within my heart,
Until those winter
Storm clouds part.

Dolores Parsons

Dear Donny

Dear Donny, you are such a sight
　so handsome and divine.
I couldn't even sleep last night
　'cause you were on my mind.

I write this poem just to say
　that you're the boy I choose.
I won't forget that rainy day
　we spent in Santa Cruz.

Dear Donny, you're a lovely view;
　a masterpiece of art.
Somehow I found that it was you
　who stole my little heart.

I've never felt this way before.
　You lift my spirit high.
There is one fact I can't ignore.
　You are my special guy.

Dear Donny, I'm your silly girl
　who ends this silly rhyme.
I hope you stay inside my world
　and be forever mine.

Esther Blanco

Mother Earth

The solar system is vast and distant,
so huge, so keen.
One lone planet
has life
in the sea of stars.
She is the mother
of the nine
eight little children in her care.
Her children live in the summer
swimming in the sea of stars.
They have fun,
with just one sun.
Mother Earth is unique
every little child in her care
looks up to her
as she cares
for the bird, bee, and bear.

Jennifer Page

She Was My Friend

Her work on earth is finished now,
  She's with her Lord at last.
All through her life and illness too,
  Her faith was held steadfast.

Wife, Mother, good companion and friend,
  Always with something to share.
Her faith showed in her goodness
  And her willingness to care.

She suffered more than we could know,
  But usually had a smile
For all of us who loved her so,
  Faith and courage were her style.

The pain is gone and peace has come,
  And someday we, too, will mend.
She gave so much to everyone,
I'm so glad she was my friend.

Joanne D. Mahnken

Dream Lake

Mother nature surrounded me with
So many wonders as if it were
A play and she set the scene with
the powder blue sky with cotton
White clouds to be my shelter for hours.

For this was my place my heaven
from the world and from reality.
Dream lake and I were no longer separate
We became one.

Annette Hepburn

'Ha, Spider Legs'

Where are you going
So quick and smooth

Woman so fine and
Quick to smile hello.

With those long, slender
Legs so finely dressed in

Panty hose so lovely
That enhance one so

Becoming with smile and
Moving so delicately in life

Oh, one so lovely to behold
And smooth of body and limb

Where ah where are you going
Perhaps a lover awaits without

Ah, but be careful there
The stairs reveal all,

And this is not needed
Right-little spider legs

For one so fine, it's best
To keep it to one's self.

Fred Royal

Time

Time is like a dime
spending it a way,
little by little
knowing that there's
not much left to spend
We spend it any ways
We don't care if it's gone forever.

Andrea Lynn Byrd

The World

This place I live
So small and so unique
A place full of love,
but even more so with hate,

This place we'll inherit
When we're older
That is, if this place,
Survives its present holder,

We need to fix
The damage we've done,
And starting there,
Our work is begun,

From there we must continue,
Our work is never done,
So let us now continue,
to preserve this place we live
So it will always be around,
For our kids; kids, kids.

Angie Logan

Reflections

As my age approached its nineteenth year,
so young and so carefree;
the things I said and done back then
didn't mean that much to me.

For I remember high school days,
and the senior prom;
hadn't thought of Cambodia, much less
of Viet Nam.

For I was young, in a reckless way
still wet behind the years;
how would I know the ghosts unleashed
would follow me for years?

For years the water flows beneath the
endless bridge of time;
I am now plagued by morality,
was killing then a crime?

I guess we all are victims now,
as I'm sure that you can see.
I was once a part of it,
now, it's a part of me.

Jay B. Massey

Untitled

Below everyone's feet,
Solid yet faulty at times,
Unpredictable
Goes unnoticed
Few people appreciate or understand
Its Beauty.
It lives and breathes and grows.
It moves.
No one ever looks down to see
What's below them,
The solid foundation of Mankind.

Elizabeth A. Stipp

Friendship

Friendship is always
Something for us to seek,
  Some seek and destroy,
Some seek and surrender,
  Some seek and suffer,
But I seek and blossom.

Jeremy Lee Pankoski

Clouds

Clouds can be beautiful to see
Some are white and fluffy and others
Are dark as can be
When I look at them many things I
Can see
From a cat or dog or even a bear
And sometimes a loved ones
Face is there
Clouds bring sunshine or rain
And at times happiness or pain
Their shapes and color can change in
The blink of an eye
As they float by up high in the
Sky.

Dorris Mcewan

Tears

Some cry tears of happiness,
some cry tears of love.
Some cry tears of pain and sorrow,
for the ones sent up above.
As I sit here on this day,
I cry for those who've passed away,
who have walked along and gone astray.
Then I stand and dry the tears,
because I've found throughout the years,
that time can mend a broken heart,
and death can break it all apart.
But love can heal in astonishing ways,
and can help dry up those tearful days.

Erik Steven Langhoff

True Friends

I have been called many names
some good, some bad
But some people don't know
How much I hurt inside
But I'm used to it now
And it doesn't matter anymore
I still like myself
Like only a few people still do
I may not have many friends
But I still have a few
And they still matter to me
They like me for what's inside
Not hate me for what's outside
And they are still true friends to me

Jeremy Barrow

Swallowed Up In A Dream

Lost in a dream trying to awake
sweat sizzles upon my face
Hands once steady now have the shakes
mind once clear now starts to race
Soul once together now displaced
I am scared and I have a headache
Lost in the misery of my pain
hiding from the truth am I insane?
To late, whose to blame?
don't have time to be ashamed
Awake I sit upon my bed
realizing that I am not dead
Hope slithers in and fills the air
I am alive, I am alert, yes I am aware.

Douglas G. Whitlow

Someone Hurt Me

As I reached for the stars,
   someone pulled me down.

As I began to laugh,
   someone made me cry.

As I learned to do new things,
   someone took them away

As I looked forward to something,
   someone disappointed me.

As I inwardly cried for help,
   no one understood.

As I suffered,
   four years went by.

As I spoke,
   four women heard.
   They knew my pain and understood.

As I grew stronger, I learned,
   that "no one" should be remembered,

As "someone" is remembered by me.

Jeannie Gerstbauer-Hill

Just A Thought

A poem to me is like a good friend,
Something we hope will never end.
At times they are happy,
And sometime they are sad,
Anytime you see them it makes you glad.
Friends are special, this is true,
A friend wrote this poem just for you!
You might smile,
And you might cry,
But a friendship like ours
Will never die!

Daniel W. D'lutz

A Lonely Soul

   She's young, she's scared,
some things she can't bear.
   She's honest and fair,
She's someone you can trust
   with your heart she'll always care.
But she's a lonely girl,
in a hopeless world, she holds
her dreams heavy, while her mind,
   Screams with pain
I find her on her own a lot.
   It's hard to spot her feelings,
   because she's so
   Strong, she feels crazy,
even dangerous at times, she lives on an
empty street.
   She's very confused, but she's a lady,
with a child's lost soul I know how she feels
I live in her everyday.

Brandy K. Bryant

Our Chair

God makes no mistakes.
Sometimes I do.

That's why I ask him
To sit here too.

Jacqueline Hebert

Prelude

sound of thunder:
sea waves
roaring wild...
passing away-
all darkness
of sea and sky...
near sea
cries of seagulls in huddle:
the thunder roars.
lightning -
amid darkening of sea
and sky ....
lone jetty
standing against a wild sea -
almost gone.....
soothing, swelling sound
of rain: all thundering
dies....

Edward Nathan Stenbar

Fate Through A Chambered Nautilus

Irised passages uncoil before me,
Spirals of pearl close in.
Blinded by a cadence of brilliance
I wind alone, round and round.
I call out
Yet no answer,
Only an echoing voice.
Through the thousand turns and bends,
I am washed into nothingness
By roaring waves,
Covered by a sparkling sand.
Lost in so vast a spiral
Hidden in the innermost coil
Lies a deeper truth—
Washed free only by waves.

Annie Openshaw

Companion Of The Road

A man to his companion
   spoke out as darkness fell
   I am alone...I have no friends
   to share with me this trail

His companion reached for words of truth
   he turned and dared to say
   there are no friends out in the world
   to walk with you this day

Came back a stare of disbelief
   a fallen face of fright
   tell me what you mean...my true
   companion of the night
The old man wise and seasoned
   gave him a crooked grin
   this world is full of strangers
   until you make them friends
And as they walked along the trail
   in silence loud and bold
   it was a friend who turned and smiled
   at his companion of the road

Horace W. Sawyer

Spring

   As the sun comes out in
spring the flowers grow and
the grass turns green. The blue
The blue birds sing
In delight it's spring
and little children go out to
hear the songs they sing. In
delight it's spring.

Beverly Guity

Spring's Gentle Persuasion

No matter how I try to ignore
Spring's gentle promptings and
beguiling smile,
I simply am caught,
not by surprise,
In morning's early
crystal hour,
Awaiting today's promises,
Assured that enchantment
will surely come
Should I but listen to
Spring's gentle persuasion.

June Allegra Elliott

Untitled

He looked down from the heavens
Sprinkled stars into the sky;
And, He placed into existence
The sun, the moon, the mountains high.

The golden rays of the sunshine
Touched the flowers, the grass and trees;
The grains of sand became united
And formed the shores besides the seas.

A touch of dew kissed the roses
And lie glistening in the sun;
You touched my hand, you kissed my lips
And we became as one.

Beverly Bruntz

Sex...

Hot...
Steamy...
Musky...
Passionate...
Loving...
Grinding...
Tantalizing...
Provocative...
Dangerous...
Satisfying... (sometimes)

Daniel J. Huyck

The Beauty In The Rain

Galloping, galloping over the plains
Still proceeding though it rains
Through the lightning and the thunder
Pounding mud right out from under
He stops, looks, and listen
In the lightning his coat does glisten
There she waits way over there
They would make a wonderful pair
Away they go in one straight line
They will make a couple fine.

Amanda Vail

The Bars

Bars
   Steel Bars
      Round, Steel bars
         Cold, Round Steel Bars

Enclose me, not hold me
My heart feels light, I'm happy!
I've seen the light
God is Here - With me -
Behind - The bars.

In the hollow of his hand - mighty,
God holds me - gently,
Securely!
I've won the fight.
Others see - the light!

Behind the bars.

   Betty D. Ritter

Changing Seasons

The warmth of summer
  still here
The sunlight changing
  as the beauty of autumn is near.

On a warm afternoon,
  golden haze all around.
Hurrying to gather the harvest,
  grains and fruit abound.

In early morning chill,
  grasses covered with frost.
Breath becomes a mist,
  disappears and is lost.

Leaves in trees changing color,
  growing brighter each day.
Photographed in memory
  before they blow away.

   Deeadra

Alone

I stand alone
Strong and tall
I stand alone
Above it all
I stand alone
Abrasive but sweet
I stand alone
Until next time we meet
I stand alone
Waiting, anticipating
I stand alone
My sanity slowly evaporating
I stand alone...
I stand alone...

   Dawn L. Shatouhy

Untitled

Spring is here
Summer is near
The flowers are blooming
But I am not glooming
For soon it will be
summer vacation for me.

   David Logan

When Love Is New

Like the winter the spring,
Summer time begins....
Fall and autumn will come soon
And love is right between us two.

Like the night like the day,
I see the flowers everywhere
Like the rain comes from above
Love is the essence between us now.

When love is new; when love is true,
And the sun is shining through....
When love is new; when love is true....
Happiness between us two.

Oh my people I do love you,
But it hurt so much to see you so blue
Just tell the children to be strong
I'm moving on to a higher love...

When love is true, when love is new
We are polite and true,
When love i new; when love is true....
Happiness between us two.

   Derrick Tatem

Untitled

Sitting on a hill,
surrounded in darkness -
With silence all around.
I look at the Universe
with great wonder;
But nothing is to be found.

I'm on the same hill,
It's a new day now,
surrounded by sounds of the morning.
And in those stars,
I saw my future,
As it comes with little warning.

   Cassy Lamperti & Brent Mattingly

Autumnal Love

Conjugal love, with nuptial ties,
sustains till young arrive to bless.
A treasure trove, no false disguise,
'Tis honesty preserved the nest.

Life's a symbiotic symphony.
the tablet's set. We learn to live.
Aeons of primal zoology—
That precious bundle in the crib.

Reverie recalls young days gone by
When we were younger-full of fire.
Nostalgic auras stir a sigh.
We oft enquire, "Can old dreams die?"

Sweet Vida, dear. All is not lost.
Ten thousand links; life's golden chain.
Our earth yields beauty's mind the dross.
Let birds and flowers relieve all pain.

'Tis autumn now, we dream of Spring.
Affection says, "We're always young."
With us, the answer to everything
Is tender love, till song is sung.

   John Adams

God Of The Sea

Oh mysterious God of the sea
Take me away,
To the land of eternity.

He said, "Oh innocent one,
The sun shall never shine.
The moon will glow no more.
Use the flame from your heart.
Let the sleeping child from within you
Come out and play
Entwine your heart with thorns,
So on one shall get through
Only from within you,
Shall the candle burn
When you sleep,
Dream like you've never dreamt before.
If you, my child, shall never awake.
Call my name,
And I, God of the sea
Shall take you away,
To the 'Kingdom of the Free.'"

   Janina Curran

Tired Old Eyes

James, get out the car and
Take me for a ride.
I'd like to look about a bit,
With these tired old eyes.

Look! There aside the road.
Isn't that a quilt laying there...
Or someone's brand new clothes?
No Mam, them there's flowers agrowin.

Stop the car James, let me out.
So I can get a closer look.
It looks, to these tired old eyes...
Just like a flower garden quilt

You can take me home now...
I've had my look about.
All this pink and green and white,
Have worn these tired eyes out.

   Gwen Fink

Memories

A memory is a thought
Taking me back through time,
Reliving an adventure,
A looking glass in my mind.

It's a lost love, an old song
A place that I once knew,
Familiar scenes to be recalled
By a harsh or tender clue.

It's the fear of knowing yesterday
Will never be again,
Reliving broken promises
And making them go as planned.

Some memories hold laughter
Capturing moments of cheer,
While others hold bitterness
From the pain so far but near.

So when strolling the short and narrow road
That leads me today,
I make the best of every moment
It's only a memory away.

   Eileen Washington

Cats

Deuter sits upon the couch,
That big ball of fur,
If you listen closely,
You can even hear him purr.
Scratch him on his neck,
Or behind his little ear.
It doesn't really matter where,
He's such a little dear.
He gets upon the fish tank,
Peering at the fish.
He wishes they were supper,
And he'd find them in his dish.

Emily Jones

That Bitter Night

Instead of saying goodbye
that bitter night, at the door
you touched my cheek-

      and snow
gave way to roses. Bluebirds
darted from icicled eaves
and an old-fashioned spring song
pealed from the lamp post!
When you turned back to me
the street behind you filled
with dancing children. The moon,
dipping down, watched
through a tree's silvered branch.

A cop strolled the beat
strumming a lute,
as we clung there together,
instead of saying goodbye.

Ida Fleming

Life

Life is a fleeting shadow
That comes and goes without warning.
It rises and falls through life tides,
Gentle at times like a new-born lamb;
Turbulent at others like a storm at sea.
Yes, life is a fleeting shadow
That goes on endlessly.

Karin Kuznicki

Untitled

There was a mother and father,
That had no Bother!
No noises
Or no voices
Then right beside them was there brother.

Chandra Martin

Heartbreak

Oh wretch in me
That I can laugh
and dance in the wind
while you sit and ponder
and wonder how you've sinned.

Oh wretch in me to find
That I should have to weigh
Suicide of life and love
Can I throw this away?

Oh wretch in me unfettered
I drive my way alone
while you sit, shackled
In a dreary rest home.

Eva D. Patterson

Mother

She is lovely,
  That is,
Beautiful.

She is lovable,
  That is,
Worthy of love!

Barbara Cheeseman

Lovely Wonderer

There's a wondering flower in a garden
That is noted for its beauty,
Beauteous and pleasurable
To the whole world and mankind.

When wars break out earthquakes arise
To give us misery to agonize
Snow storm, floods all other woes
Are ably relieved by the Red Cross

Join, join the Red Cross
The wondering flower today—
Arms in arms let us join,
To help people near and far away.

Sing! Boom! sing out a song
Of good cheer—contribute along
To it in any kind—human fund
That its global task be forever done!

Elsie A. Ramos

Uninvited Solitude

I'm swimming in this pool.
That never seems to end.
I haven't seen land,
Since the 40 mile bend.
I feel like I am sinking,
Into this great abyss.
I ask myself again and again,
How did I get into this.
My arms and legs are failing me,
My heart starts to pound.
I try to call out for you
But I don't make a sound.
I begin to panic,
And tears sting my eyes.
I show a weakness
That I truly despise.
But I no longer care,
Because I'm alone in the end,
Me—with no lover, no enemy, no friend.

Carolyn Edwards

Ships That Pass In The Night

People, like ships
That pass in the night,
Pause, and touch briefly,
Then slowly pass on.

Locked close in their minds,
And deep in their hearts,
They dream of a memory
That never could be.

To take out at will,
To cherish and dream of,
To reach any time any day.
For what might have been
Is only a memory away.

Eleanor Kerness

My Friend, My Sister

As my sister I have known
That our love has always grown
There's been times that we're alone.
Hope my feelings have been shown.

When you read this you will see
Just how much you mean to me.
Hope you know where you stand
Cause in my heart. You are grand

While you sit way over there
I have to say how much I care
Our lives you know were never fair
But our love we had we always shared.

As I sit and think of you
I often seem to get the blues
In these thoughts of you and me
I laugh and cry so happily

In my life you've always been
This great and caring loving friend.
As your friend I just want to say
That I miss you everyday.

Dana Waldeck

A Hug

There's something about a good hug
That soothes right down to the soul
Places a smile upon my face
'Cause its warmth dispels all cold

There's something about a good hug
I need to hold and feel now and then
As life's mysteries I try to unfold
Always trying to transcend

There's something about a good hug
That fills me just brimming over
With the restoring feeling of love
And the comfort of resting in clover

There's something about a good hug
That has to be surely pleasing
Not only for the one who is giving
But especially the one who's receiving

There's something about a good hug
When given wholly, lovingly and free
It sends a message to my very essence
So that I could shout in pure jubilee

Florence Gilmore

Not Enough Care

The loss of loved one
That still is around.
Looking for answers
That cannot be found.
Numbing the feelings
That no one should know;
Feeling so helpless
With no place to go.
No one to turn to
For warmth and support;
No one shelter
Your body from hurt.
Living a lifetime
Full of despair...
Not enough people
Not enough care.

Erica Wampole

"My Love"

Form my love like a stone
That the elements can not slay.
Sow my love like a flower
Growing more beautiful every day.
Shape my love like a teddy bear
Who is comforting to hold.
Forge my love like a metal
Composed of pure gold.

Make my love like the air
Giving life to all.
Weave my love like net
To break another's fall.
Shine my love like a light
By which others can see
How to build a love
That will last an eternity.

Jennifer Schwarz

My Silent Voice

At one time I had a good voice
That to me was so vigorous and strong,
But now only God up there in Heaven
Can tell you just what went wrong.

It seems I was hit with a sickness.
The doctors said there was no choice
To take out the cancer that was in there
That I would also lose my voice.

Now that the operation is over.
And as I now go through each day
With so much to always talk about
Not one word that I can really say.

So now when the phone starts to ring,
I do not pick up that phone.
I just wait for someone to answer
When they hear the sound of the tone.

Now I do a lot more writing
But, as you read, I have no choice.
With the cancer that was removed
I also gave up more than my voice.

Carl Mathus

Grant Me

Grant me just one wish Lord
   that when this life is through,
I can spend eternity
   up in heaven next to you.
I know it is up to me
   to decide where I will go,
Lord I pray you will guide me
   for I am foolish sometimes you know.
Many times I have stumbled
   and fell back down those stairs,
that would lead me up to heaven
   to the one who really cares.
This life it gets so hectic,
   pulls hard at your soul,
makes you feel you want to give up
   before you have reached your goal.
So Lord I want to ask you,
   If you will give me the strength I need
the faith to keep on trying
   and the willingness to succeed.

Charlotte Waters

What's In My Mind

I feel all alone for the face
   that you're not here.
I have to think of the times we shared
   and all the good cheer.
You will be in my heart for ever,
   and ever....
I can't let your love go, I tell
   you this. No never
To be in love with someone
   as wonderful as you...
I feel like I'm the luckiest man
   in the world
And that my love,
   is so true,
You trying sunshine and joy
   in my life,
My dear stoney...
   with you by my side we'll share this love
together
When I'm finally free!
   I love you, Honey remember that please -

Dennis B. Granada

My Friend

My friend there's something in my heart
That's not real easy to say
The thought our ships may drift apart
Leaves me in dismay.

I want to stay real close to you
But I fear the future holds
A new exciting way of life
A plan that God did mold.

My road to travel leads one way
As the road for you leads apart
Another place, another time
But you'll be here in my heart.

Please never forget the time we've spent
We talked both night and day
I'll miss you friend, I'll tell you that
But I'll see you through, God will make a way.

And now friend, as you sail away
Remember, don't forget
I'll always call you as my friend
Now your boat drifts off into the sunset.

Jessica Creery

Don't Stop Me From Being Somebody!

Don't stop me from being somebody!
That's something you can't do!
Don't stop me from being somebody!
I'm a person just like you!
Don't stop me from being somebody!
I'm somebody! Don't you see?
Don't stop me from being somebody!
I'm somebody! I am me!
Don't stop me from being somebody!
I'm somebody! I'll succeed!
Don't stop me from being somebody!
I'm somebody! Yes, indeed!
Don't stop me from being somebody with
your judgement and your thoughts.
Don't stop me from being somebody!
I'm somebody but with faults.
Don't stop me from being somebody!
I'm somebody! Don't you see?
Don't stop me from being somebody!
I'm somebody! I am me!

Adrienne Marie Henderson

"All About Mothers"

Mothers are most special,
That's really very clear,
Morning noon and night time too,
Not just one day a year.

They're in a class all by themselves,
And truly they deserve it,
God gave to them the keys to life,
He knew they'd best preserve it.

No matter what the world may think,
Of us from time to time,
A mother never has a doubt,
To her we're just divine.

Well here's the truth on Mothers,
And yes the world should know,
Without their tender loving care,
All life would cease to grow.

So here's to you mom, on your day,
May all your dreams come true,
May all your sons and daughters,
Keep right on loving you...I do!

Joseph R. Cottrell

Growing Up

The little boy threw
The ball hard
And it bounced high
Shattering the glass shelf.
Causing the porcelain figures
From Dresden long ago, who
Had survived American fire,
To fall
Smashing against the floor
Shattering into countless fragments
As he ran past to get his ball,
Never seeing the tears
From his smile
Or caring that they were there.

Justin Maxwell

Breaking Through

The point of breaking through
The barrier of the unknown,
A speck of time infinitesimal...
A second split for us to be
Or mark the real with a dream.

Reflexes on the go
Like shooting stars
On the black of the night...
Now is there and then.....is gone

The mass in action
Way ahead, way above
In harmony of elements,
Pushing forward, letting down....
In a second split pulsating
Or next inert, in the void of nothing...

Carmen M. Laguna

Untitled

The birds like to sing,
The frogs come out of the pond,
And flowers like to bloom.
It is real pretty outside,
The flower are colorful.

Crystal Locklear

A Picture Of Mother

Oh, I wish I were an artist
The best without complaint,
Because there is a precious face
That I would like to paint.

I'd use the finest canvas,
With color that adhere
And I would paint the way I saw
You last, when you were here.

I'd paint the furrows on your brow,
Your smile, the dearest part,
But how can one paint tenderness
That lived within your eyes?

How could I try to duplicate
Your sweetness through all time?
Instead of that your face is stamped
Forever in my mind.

Fern Olsen Oviatt

I Sing!

I sing because I love
The birds, the air, the sky,
The bright'ning of the morning light,
The people passing by.

My joy I hold with care
Lest I should let it go,
For underneath is pain too dark
For bright of day to know.

I tuck away my hurt
Into the night's black case
And gladly hide its somberness
From sun's inquiring face!

Dorothy Moore Alford

Why Not Me

The days were blooming
the birds were flying around like they
hadn't a worry in the world
Why couldn't that be me?
No worries
No cares
To fly around with the wind blowing
    around and through my wings
I'm just sitting on my porch
dreaming of how it would be
To feel cool, brisk wind
running through my hair
or should I say
my wings
singing as pretty as an angel
coming to get its wings

Annmarie Oszust

"Nothing For God"

It's nothing for God to make
The blind person see
It's nothing for God to make
The deaf person hear
It's nothing for God to make
The cripple person walk
It's nothing for God to heal
All manner sickness
Even to raise a person
From the dead is nothing
for God
But for you to give your
Heart to God, is everything
To God

Christopher Duval

Wind-Swept

The night wind stirred in Bethlehem...
The breeze that rose moved through the
town;
    It carried far the infant cry
Of Earth's newborn salvation sound.

    The wind swept all the world afar...
It lifted to each place apart
    The sacred air of Bethlehem
To every waiting, hopeful heart.

    God's Spirit, manifested there,
Was present at the natal scene...
    And over all the land it flowed
To fill the dark with holy dreams.

    This blazing, catalytic power,
To every troubled soul it flies...
    We share the heir of grace and life
That sin, and death itself, may die.

    The night wind stirs in Bethlehem,
The rising breeze fills all the town...
    It sends the call of God to men
And bids us be salvation-bound.

Archie D. Maker III

"Please Let It Rain"

Please let it rain.
The clouds hide my broken heart.
The darkness hides my pain.

I wish it would rain.
The thunder hides my anger.
The lightning hides my rage.

Keep on raining.
The sounds hide my cries.
The raindrops hide my tears.

Please let it rain.

Brandi McVicker

Serenity

I watched the sun rising
The coming of the dawn,
The blue skies emerging
Stars disappearing one by one.

The day was bright and beautiful,
The air was crisp and clear,
In all of this creation
I knew that God was near.

Each leaf bud and tree
Was perfect in shape and size,
I knew God was in His heaven
As I gazed up to the skies.

Aren't all days considered beautiful
In this our great land?
If their trials and troubles,
They are only caused by man.

Betty Butler

Brevity

How might the leaf hope to justify
the tree
...Except, to show itself in
autumn to one so fair
as thee

Daniel Moorman

Awaiting Its prey

Purr-fect
the creature, nine lives it bears
Paws-es
outstretched, guarding its castle
Prey-eth
awaiting, precisely the time
Possess-shun
its prey, not really much fun

Judith Baker

Things

Well, how was I to know,
The day was to bring,
So many wonderful and beautiful
    things.
I wasn't prepared,
But I received,
A letter, a smile and a hug
    from thee.

June Burg

Lies

There are no lines to draw upon
The difference between right and wrong.
Like crystal glass as clear as day
No beacon needs to light the way.
To stand outside in frilly cloth
Pretending not to feel the chill
Is mockery akin to sloth;
A cold denial of our will.
To know the truth and not react,
To be a player unprepared,
The beast of doubt will oft attack
With fiery, burning, scorching glare.
Truth is not a fleeting bird.
Lies hurt deeper than their words.

Dennis S. Martin

"B. B."

A star shines bright
The door opens wide
A name inside
Special and true
Soft winds travel
Trees grow strong and tall
Leaves colorful and plenty
Reaching upward beauty to behold
Breath of life natures reward
A free soul passing through time
Strength and courage
A path of love
Follow the light
Upward you go
A star that shines bright
The door closes tight
Travel onward free soul
Peace everlasting
Love forever more

Dawn H. Wright

Reflection

Her eyes were distant brown,
The dreamy sort of kind.
But now they're black and blue,
And dreams are far behind.

They once were bright and hopeful
With riches yet to come.
But now they're dull and lost,
In the bottle she calls rum.

Her lips are split and cracked
With smiles that never show.
And love that once was true,
Left her long ago.

Slipping down her cheeks
Are more than just one tear,
As I realize what I've become,
When I gaze into the mirror.

Heather L. Wolf

Earth

The earth has many colors
The earth has many sounds
Including those which echo from
The ancient hallow grounds

Geysers are among us
Caves are all around
Water trickles into pools
Where minerals are found

Sinkholes are quite hidden
Beneath the "solid" earth
Water may flow freely
With frivolity and mirth

If there's the cry "Oil!"
Man wonders what it's worth
He doesn't stop and think
About poor ol' Mother Earth

Different rocks are present
Upon these coastal waters
Save this land for you and me
And our sons and daughters.

Dean Sowers

Italy

From snow clad Alps once more I see
The fertile plains and sunlit hills
Ringing the peaks so wild and free
Beckon to joys of mountain thrills.
Once more I see the tidy farms
Mid golden fields and verdant pines
And rising besides the banks of Po
Stately poplars and ancient charms.
Again I see the pure white domes
The winding lanes, and jagged scars
On mile-high cliffs of Osta's cones
And ever above my friends the stars
Shining so bright to us below.
Though many a day I tread the earth
And see man's vice against his own.
Always on high I feel the birth
Of hope, to all, that rings so true
And clear as crystal I start anew.

Hector C. Borghetty

Nature Is Homeless

It's morning.
The freshly made dew is
glistening on the leaf of
a newly planted tree...
A bird roosts on its limber
branches...
UNKNOWING
In the distance, the monotone moan
of a chain saw is heard.
It grows louder.
It becomes unbearably deafening.
Another tree is destroyed, and many
of its kind will endure the same fate.
The forest is silent;
for the forest is there no more!
NATURE IS HOMELESS

Alissa Bilfield

'Would I Be Loved Someday'

Would I be loved someday
The gentle hand over takes me
Would I be loved someday
The sweet scent of roses pervade

To err is human
But I too naive to see
The words that haunt the night
Are but a mask

Then shall flesh come creeping in
Stealing beauteous love divine
The heart shall crumble
The rose shall fade

Thy words remain untrue
Shadowed in the darkness
Thou cursed word of love
Is but a mask

Jennifer Haas

Afterward

Yet now they wait,
The great sharks and vultures,
The oceans and fields
Heaped with the victims
Of the egomaniacs.

And humankind?
How many more millions of years
Before someone raises
Its head from the slime
To write a song or a poem?

Ephraim Levin

The Power Of A Smile

Poetry has to come from
  the heart
To express your innermost
  feelings.
At the end of the day
When you're really quite
  weary
Do you greet your loved
  ones
With a voice that is cheery?
If the answer is yes
And said with a smile
You've got everything in life
That is really worth while!!!

Frieda Jaffe

Pitches

Burn'm with the heat!
The hitter can't compete.
That makes it strikes one.
Two more, the batter's done.
Now throw him the curve,
Sit back and watch it swerve.
That makes it strike two.
One more, the batter's through.
Now fool'm with junk!
Whoa! Two whole feet it sunk!
Stee'rike three! He's out!
He's on a one way route
Straight to the dugout!

Jon Skaggs

"I Looked From A Hill"

I looked from a hill on the city,
    The houses crowded side by side;
I saw cement and brick and asphalt,
    And my heart within me cried.

I longed for country fresh air,
    For grasses lush and green,
For tall trees and winding brook,
    Rippling cool and clean.

Then I saw a hill near Jerusalem
    Where a man sat and cried;
But he cried for the people,
    The ones for whom he died.

I looked again at my city,
    And cried, Lord help me see
Not cement and bricks and asphalt.
    But people needing Thee.

Jeanne Magee Robb

Lonely In Love

The lingering, aching feeling
The hurt that slowly, very slowly
Diminishes
I fear never feeling in love again

Yet I feel so much inside
The yearning, the mourning
The senseless loss....

The feeling of loneliness
In my mind...
What's to be?
It's so hard feeling lonely in love
Looking for someone for me

Jane Gold

In Touch

The sweet sound of laughter
The moaning of hurt.
The screams of terror.
The tone of delight
These are the sounds
heard all over the world

Happiness, sorrow, depression and joyful
These are the feelings
of people all over the world.

They say no two people are alike.
But when it comes down to the
heart I think they are.

Amy McMain

The Littlest Angel (My Child)

When the seed was planted
the joy filled our hearts
When you moved inside me
my face was all aglow
When your heart stopped beating
that was pain only God could know
The day you were delivered
all we could do was cry
When you were placed upon my stomach
we prayed you'd have breath inside
Your face was round and perfect
as if an angel from above
The day we picked out your coffin
was the saddest day on earth
The day we lay you to rest
we knew at that moment, God knows best
We know you're up in heaven
I hope it was a short ride
For you're the littlest angel
seated by God's side

Jan A. Nicholson

Dreams? Or Nightmares?

Sleep
The land of sleep overtakes me
With visions
Of the ones I've loved
Or will love — sometime
Maybe in the future
When these dreams come true
In real life they're nightmares
In real life
Those I've loved
I find in the arms of another
Hate — jealousy — rage
All overtake me
I should have known
Their love
Was never meant for me
It was only a dream
That lasted for a short moment
And turned into
A nightmare.

Anita Joyelle Swayne

The Wait

As I wait for him
the lights begin to dim,
he hasn't shown yet,
I'm falling from a limb,
and I wait, I wait.

Why won't he show?
As I wait I go lower and low,
I feel naive like a young foe,
and I wait, I wait.

"Does he ever show?" you ask.
Maybe he did, but behind a mask.
He did not complete his task,
and I wait, I still wait.

Daniella Fruzzetti

"God's Love"

On a quiet night sometime ago,
The Lord came by to visit.
He brought me peace
And joy and also brought me love.
The peace was oh, so comforting,
And the joy, was joyous; He really
Was glad to see me; His love
Was the most fulfilling and complete,
I had ever known.
Even though, it only lasted a moment,
It's one I won't forget,
And as He left, I said
"Thank you Lord for your visit,
And come again soon."
Indeed, the Lord really does
love all his children.

Frankie K. Richardson

'Christmas Of The 90's'

The Malls are crowded
The merchants are smiling
The carolers are singing
   "People are helping people"
Oh, it has to be Christmas Eve.

The toys for tots are working
The foods banks are filling
The bells of charities are ringing
   "Givers are giving"
Oh, it has to be Christmas Eve.

The lights are twinkling
The presents are glistening
The children's eyes are shining
   "Mouths are gaping"
Oh, it has to be Christmas morn

The millions of people
The many cultures
The common beliefs
   "All celebrating His birth"
Oh, it has to be Christmas Day!

Duane C. Anderson

"First Experience"

The sky was blue
The moon was high
We were all alone
Just she and I.

So with courage
I tried my best
By placing my hand
Upon her chest.

I trembled and shook
And I felt her heartbeat
Then slowly she spread
Her legs apart.

I moved my hand
Up and down her legs
And suddenly touched her.

I washed my hands
It was over now
My first experience
Milking a cow

Beatriz Hernandez

Wild Horses

Wild horses running free along
the moonlighted beach their
dark manes shimmering in
the moonlight. When they're done
running, they drink the salty
water to clear their dry throats.
Then strange people come and
take them away from their free
world.

Charity Davidson

Transition

Dusk is here
The now day is done
Darkness is rapidly approaching.

It is night
The stars have come out
To throw their light across the sky.

Day again
The sun sheds its light
Then dusk once more covers the land.

Alice Hill

Untitled

Sometimes it clicks
the pieces fit so perfectly
Everything blends
No sounds
just one breath
in unison with the heart.

Sometimes it clicks
and remains
intact
Strong
nurturing one another
together but free.

And when it's real
no excuses are made
no promised broken
or bent
just two lives
neatly wrapped into
a bow.

Carolyn S. Wolfe

"A Pine So Great"

Between the dark and the day light
the pine are their darkest green.
With its gnarled limbs to the contour
twig that hold the needles serene.
Against the cobalt sky of early dawn
is bathe with dewy mist.
Mighty the bough that sweep its roots
entangled in eternal twist.
The breeze this day that passes through
will travel cool its way.
I shall see it serenely appear each
morn and breathe it in each day.

Evelyn J. Harel

Untitled

Cupid is coming
To get hold of you
With love and affection
For all the year through.

Joanne Hanscome

Sit Quietly

Sit quietly and celebrate,
The pleasures that
Originate from sights
Of oaks and maple trees,
The soothing sound
Of gentle breeze,
The distant call
Of cardinal's trill,
The color
Of a daffodil,
The wafting scent
The lilacs make,
The vastness
Of a clear blue lake

Sit quietly and contemplate,
The urgency of
Nature's fate

Sit quietly and reminisce
Unless we care it's
What we'll miss

Jeanne Roberts Maertens

Untitled

A chance to try.
The question?
Why?
My time I buy.
Deep down I sigh as moments fly,
sometimes I cry.
In the End I pry the safety
box of pride.

David Michael Karczewski

Earth

The wind is whistling through the tress
The rain is falling
There's a breeze
The wind
The rain
The darkened sky
It makes you think and wonder why

What is the reason for this all?
The reason why the rain should fall
The reason why the winds should blow
And cast the sky in ghostly glow

The rain shall make the earth renew
The winds shall blow the pollen through
The ghostly glow will fade away
As dawn brings yet another day

Ilona Frankel-Siegel

The Rose

The rose
The rose
That sweet summer rose
With its plucky pose

Did wither and warp and die
I think it was at the end of July
and with the sweep of white winter
Lies only a splinter

A fleck of faded brown
Neath the snow upon the ground
So dead and lifeless without a care
So twisted and broken
Oh so bare

Bill Snead

Balanced Scale

I challenge you to disprove for me,
the reality of a balanced scale.
Where there is cause…there is effect.
There is good…there is bad.
Where there is right…there is wrong.
There is light, and also dark.
There is a beginning, and also end.
Stare at the large; notice the small.
Glare at the Sun; sense the Moon.
Stare at yesterday; see the tomorrow.
Glare at a push — notice a pull.
Stare at strength — sense weakness.
Glare at talk — see an ear.
Stare at a plus and a minus.
Always a Yin and a Yang
Always axis-x and an axis-y.
Always a female and a male.
I challenge you to disprove for me,
the reality of a balance scale.

Jamal S. Jailawi

The Boom Of War

The boom the bang
The roar of the guns
The stomping the tromping
of the guys on the run
It's gone it's over
it is now all done
The poor sweet
mothers have just
lost their sons.

Dallas Jenkins

Flock

They live forever undying
The sheep they do follow
One always the difference
Confusion is a simple fact
The pasture, green indulgence
constant flood, plateaus
A leader indeed is present
Power… unyielding
They do not deny
He leads as they pass on
Fields of green they lay
Cozy sun, tender warmth
Slight breeze cools the perspired face
The shepherd, the leader
they are one
Hero of the land and fields of green!

Cory D. Cardoza

Roses

Roses are beautiful and
   their fragrance is more
   than a smell.
It something to cherish and
   nothing to dwell.
Roses, their not just a flower
   their a symbol of love
The love that's been sent
   straight from above.
They put smiles on faces
   and tears in eyes
Roses are as beautiful as
   the clear blue skies.

Amy Janell Mendez

The Soul

Out of darkness arose a soul.
The soul spoke unto me and said:
   Come with me, I have something
   For you to see.
As I walked towards it, I started
   To see a blinding light;
The soul spoke to me again and said:
   Look what you see;
I saw with my own eyes, me, laughing
   And giggling beyond belief.
I wondered how I got to be so happy;
   And what did make me laugh,
For I was unhappy and lonely now.
When I turned around to ask the soul
   What happened to my life,
The soul was gone.
I looked around the room I was in and
Saw my room, and looked at the laughing
face and saw me.
What happened to make me this happy was
plain to see,
For the soul I was talking to, was me!

Darlene Nash

The Beauty Of Sunshine

Praise to the morning,
   The start of the day.
The sun slowly rises
   To brighten our way.

The beauty of sunshine
   Streaming through
Lighting the way
   For all that we do.

We race through our day
   Rarely pausing to rest,
While the sun passes over
   To sink in the west.

And as we trudge home
   With another day done,
We suddenly notice
   The slowly sinking sun.

Dorothea Mosby

I Wonder

Do you ever wonder why
   The sun shines bright
   The moon glows too
   The stars twinkle light

Do you ever wonder why
   The earth goes around
   The grass grows up
   The rain pours down

Do you ever wonder why
   The rainbow across the sky
   The rivers all run down
   The mountains grow so high

Do you ever wonder why
   The birds sing their songs
   A lion stalks her prey
   The giraffes' necks are long

I wonder if you ever wonder
   How these things came to be
   If you've ever pondered
   God's creation for you and me.

Barbara Noe

And I Wonder...

I see the pain in your eyes,
The tears on your face,
And I wonder...

You're taken by surprise when you see me,
And try to hide your face,
And I wonder...

I ask what is wrong,
You say it's no big deal,
And I wonder...

You look in a direction,
Fear upon your face,
And I wonder...

I look in your direction,
And see his face,
And I wonder...

Becky Arvans

Progress Is Our Most Important Product

The lights go on we abuse it
The thought is only to use it
To lighten the room
To scare off the gloom

But what of this monster
To which we are committed
The radiation from all
Material progress that is transmitted

People are dying in horrible stages
From all new medical terms
The diseases of the ages
Or new bacteria and germs

Direct radiation?
Instant and sure
But slow degeneration from nuclear war
Not so instant but no cure

Leukemia, cancer melanoma
From none can we be freed
Does it stem from ignorance
Or from plain greed.

Alice Lupton

Memories

The kiss of your lip
The touch of your hand
The way that you held me
Alone when we stand
The feelings have left
The soft touch is gone
But the memory of you, still lingers on
The songs of the blue jays
From after the storms
The closeness of you
I need back in my arms

Janel Bugliari

Untitled

When I turn back the pages of my mind
Thinking of all I have left behind

The youth that has slipped away
The innocence I had on a simpler day

I slowly shed a single tears
Wishing for all that used to be near

Etta Dixon

"A Tender Touch"

Years of pain protected strong
the treasure deep inside,
Raging waves of tears that fell
protected it with pride.
Love that once has filled the throne
at last had hushed, at last had gone.
No one would ever touch again,
the heart that ached would never mend.

It was just a normal day
quiet, routine in every way.
When taken by complete surprise,
there you stood before my eyes.
The years had passed, that could not be,
my heart was young and gay and free.
As you walked away that day,
I knew a change was here to stay.
My heart would never ache again,
I gave away the pain within.
And in its place you gave to me,
a love to last eternally.

Helen Lasseter

The Verdict

Their eyes are sad, no need for words
The verdict is bad
I sit quietly
Listening
As the Doctors tell me
"You might live long" or "If this works"

They look puzzled
They ask.
"Do you understand what we've told you?"
Yes.........I understand.

I know my life, my future, my all
Is now in the hands of God
He will cradle me tenderly in His Arms.

As He has cared for me from my beginning
So will He care for me to life's end
However short or long my time
My fate is in His hands.

Carolyn Childress

"Valley Of Dreams"

In the valley of life
The walls of good fortune
Are sprinkled with love
The foliage there
Is wholesome and sweet
It's where true lovers
Find a retreat,
The air is so mellow
It's sweet to inhale
There a true union
Never will fail,
Your heart's full
Of kindness
To carry you on
To a land of
Sweet glory
Where you belong.

George Barden

A World Of Dreams

Birds fly across the sky
The wind shakes colorful leaves,
The sun displays its golden rays
The trees sway in the breeze.

The stars light the dark night
Rivers rush into the sea,
Waves rise before your eyes
Fields of grass dance with glee.

Animals roam to and from home
The clouds float around,
The moon glows and its face it shows
Flowers pop out of the ground.

Nature seems like a world of dreams
Something new happens each day,
So take time to leave troubles behind
And let your mind drift away.

Erika Weiberth

Our World

The world is peaceful.
The world is green.
The litter and violence is
Because of you and me.
We live, we love and yet
We still never learn,
That without our help
The world's going to burn.
No one knows, and no one cares,
That without our love,
The world can no longer be there.
The moon, the stars really don't matter.
Without our love,
They're all going to shatter.
Let's help out, let's help now.
Let's save our world,
Let's start living now.

Jill Johnson

Life

We were brought into
the world not caring
what color we were.
We were kids just caring
about playing.
We were teenagers and
started pairing one
another.
We were adults and we
taught our kids to love
but not anyone with a
different color of skin.
We were old and just cared
about surviving.
Now we're dead and again
we're side by side.
Why hate???
No matter what, we'll
always be together.

Amy R. Cousin

Untitled

Birds born with new wings
to fly to bring new colors to the
sky. They fly for years has my
life passes me by on how I wish I
could fly...

Barbara L. Howard

Untitled

Smoothly following
The worn familiar trail,
The stream laps softly
Content that all is well.

Slowly I walk
With my hair down,
Swishing skirts and bonnet close
To movement and the sounds.

Winds brush by shoulders
Remembrance of the past,
How I wish my tom boy
Days hadn't moved so fast.

Now I stop in wonder
At what I have become,
A pirate, now a woman,
Walking with my hair undone.

Silently I drift
Along old childhood dreams,
Laughing with my son
As he explores the running stream.

Angella Eckert

Children, Children, Don't Forget

Children, children, don't forget
There are elves and fairies yet;
Where the knotty haw thorn grows
Look for prints of fairy toes.
Where the grassy rings are green
Moonlight dances shall be seen.
Watch and wait: O lucky you,
If you find a fairy shoe
For a ransom he will pay
Hobbling barefoot all the day
Lay it on his mushroom seat,
Wish your wish and go your way
If your wish should be discreet
Never fear but he will pay.

Chris Martinez

There Is A Time

There is a time to laugh,
There is a time to grieve.
There is a time to take the path,
And a time to leave.

There is a time for love,
There is a time for hate.
There is a time to be sent up above,
And a time for fate.

There is a time for trust,
There is a time for honesty.
There is a time for lust,
And a time for modesty.

Elizabeth R. Kane

Fulfilled

When love has captured the heart
there is nothing to be desired
The mind is thinking of nothing else
nothing stands in the way
Love opens the door to happiness
your life seems fulfilled
Your eyes seem much brighter
Your smile that much wider
Your step a whole lot lighter
when love
has captured the heart

Brooke Schneider

Pain

Pain
There is no age limit.
No boundaries or guidelines,
No rules or regulations.

Pain.
It has no definite shape.
No size, color, or taste.

Pain.
There is no guarantee against it
No sure fire cure.

Pain.
There's only one solution,
Stop it before it starts.
Help it before it hurts.
Put it out before it burns.
Love it till it stops.

Beth Ragen

No I In Jesus

There is no I in Jesus
There is no I in
The Lord's Prayer.
He came for all
The world you see.
Not just for you
Or for me.
So come with us
To the light of Jesus.
So freedom for
All may come to be.
There is no I in Jesus.

Barbara Ann Smith

Good-bye

When a friend like you must say good-bye,
  There is sadness in my heart.
I just want to sit down and cry,
  Never want to be apart.
But good things come, and then they go,
  They never stay the same.
There is one thing I'll always know,
  There was a reason that you came.
Maybe it was to be a friend,
  Right when I needed one.
Maybe it was just to lend,
  A hand where there was none.
There's one thing that I must see,
  No matter how hard it is now,
Apart we will not always be,
  We'll meet again somehow.
Now it seems so permanent,
  But I just can not say never,
How quickly you came and went,
  But a good-bye is not forever.

Alan Carter Jr.

Untitled

The darkest time is near
To face the things I fear.
The lights dance around
Playing a joke on my soul
I can feel you ripping out my heart
Just so you can let it go
Everyone is someone
But is that someone ever real?
I'm slipping into the darkness
I no longer can feel.

Alexandra Golembeski

Silence

There's silence outside,
There's silence.
I see shapes, pictures,
But in black and white.
I move slowly, as if in a dream.
I wear a flowing silk gown,
And waltz across the floor,
Alone.
No one is there,
No one hears me when I cry,
No one is there to dance with me.

Cameron May

Heaven At Night

Boldly withered- my faith is shaken
There's so much I need, to know
Coldly shivered- I stand alone!
In a universe professed as home

My days are spent- through a window gaze
Inner repent for the human ways
I do confess- I will remain
As long as my eyes see love and pain

Through my pane- I do stare
At heavenly bodies that they call air
I must address- I am unaware
Of the rules, that shape my sight

I ask you this
As a final wish
If my words don't seem to write
Do the heavenly gates
That offer faith,
Shine brightly still at night?

Brian Goldman

Untitled

As I contemplate closing
These old doors and opening
New ones. I think of all
The things that will never be.

I cannot come back once
I leave - it's final.
I cannot smell the familiar
Nor look upon admired possessions.

So do I leave or do I stay?
Will I be content with the
Old and familiar or will I miss
The excitement and adventure of the new?

Barbara Rexrode

The After Life

God give me the strength
To enjoy this life's length
To keep on trudging
Though my dreams keep nudging
Your Will I'll do and no begrudging
Now my sons are Home
They will no longer roam.

Peace they both wanted
Parents seemed so strict and square
Peer's values they wished to share
Confusion reigned which isn't rare
In the end I know they cared
Thoughts of You with me they shared.

Candelaria Sanchez

"Grandparents"

We have the dearest children,
They both have honored us,
Their families almost full grown,
Their lives to us they trust.

We're going for a week - end,
Will you watch over them?
We will be gone for two days,
Our house becomes may - hem.

The papers, pens, and pencils
Are strewn around the place,
"Can I have one more goodie?
Rings out from every face.

The weekend now is over
The parents return home,
This place looks like a windstorm hit.
I say, "just a small cyclone."

It's now our turn to fly away,
To sunny beach, and shore,
To refill our tanks with energy
Babysitting is such a chore!

Joan Wojnarski

Moving Time

More than ten years had passed
They didn't think it would last
Soon will be time to leave
The family house, not to grieve

A palatial residence
To spend many hours
The back yard has a fence
Enclosing trees and flowers

Many miles come between
My son's farm place and here
So much time never seen
And caring so dear!

Bernadette Sievers Gannon

Dirty Dishes

Thank God for Dirty Dishes
They have a tale to tell
While other folks go hungry
We are eating pretty well

With Deer and Elk meat upon our table
And a few fish in between
And from our summers garden products
We are doing pretty well

We thank God for our food upon our table
As our Dirty Dishes they do tell
While other folks go hungry
We are eating pretty well.

Dallas Arizona

'From The Heart'

They say one looks like you
They say one looks like me
But the blood in their hearts
Came from you and me
Now there is two more branches
to our family tree
Which grandma and nana
Are loving what they see.

Douglas Ray McNeill, Jr.

Our Grandpa

Little children love him
They know he's one of them
Though the face is slightly wrinkled
Gray whiskers on his chin
The twinkle in his eye
shows them the love within.
The fact of hair that's thinning
doesn't mean a thing.

Teenagers seek him out,
they really think he's great.
He is so full of wisdom
but doesn't throw his weight.

He can teach them how to bait a hook
or how to dance a lure.
He can teach them what to say
to interest a favorite girl,
How especially nice she looks
with her hair all in a curl.

Yes, Grandpas are a special gift
to any boy or girl.

Helen S. Maas

No Spark Without You

Dreams of desire
They never retire
But are hard to acquire
When no one's for hire

Now and then
I can't say when
Time and again
Where we could have been

Do not make a sound
Cause rumors will abound
They travel all around
To put you in the ground

Love walked out the door
Just like it did before
I'd like to have some more
And its beauty I'll explore

Debbie L. Reno

Midnight Feast

Demons fly at night
they say
and leave the living
to the day.
Devils haunt the land
they moan
and rip the flesh
from purest bone.
Angels wings fall to
the dust.
A sinner's name
is unjust.
I stalk the land
at night
   my love,
For I'm the one
who slayed
   the dove.

Christy Miceli

To Mom With Much Love

You are in my thought when
Things are gray
Your presence chase my blues
Away
Your smile lights my darkest
Nights
Your words to me make things
Alright
You are always willing to lend
An ear
Your love can calm my deepest
Fear
Your touch can ease my aching
Heart
You've been a friend right from
The start
You are in my life the greatest
Force
You are there for me
You are my mother of course.

Helen Emmons

Untitled

Things are hard
Things are strange
I've tried so hard
But things still stay the same
Why must this be
I haven't got a clue
Maybe one day
You'll let me know
Can't you see just
How hard this is for me?

You were my friend
You were my lover
Can't he see
How hard this is for me?
I walk around full of fear
Hoping he won't take another so dear.

Amy D. Horning

Whispering Wind

Fear not the whispering wind
   tho' it cut you to the quick
   'tis only flesh which burns
Curse not the aching memory
   which allows no peace
   and sears your very soul

Fear not the call of Death
   whether it be eternal sleep
   or everlasting hellfire
Curse not the circumstance
   which bids you sweat to survive
   or lie to escape repercussion
Damn only that fading photograph
   which extracts those bitter tears
   from that hollow named 'heart'

Edgar Graz

At Night

Night has come,
Time to go to bed.
Mother sings,
As the children lay down their heads.
Eyes droop,
Then close all the way.
Everyone sleeps,
Until the sun brings the day.

Jennifer Bartsch

"The Crush"

For you my love would often leak
Though miserably concealed
In my selfish thoughts of us
In my dreams revealed
A love affair with only one

For you to shed a hurried glance
By accident my way
Would mean to me in sorrows hands
She's really made my day
A love affair with only one

For you what would I leave to chance
My aching heart and hurting
"No," but every effort shown
I'd spend my time converting
A love affair with only one.
John M. Helmer

"Akin To Angels"

Sweet birds, like angels sang to me,
though they were hungry as could be-
bleak snow had fallen all day long,
but yet they cheered me with their song.

So much like angels do they fly,
and sing and soar up to the sky.
A raven fed Elijah once,
could I not feed the
birds their lunch?

Akin to angels they must be
to serenade me from my tree
while snow is falling all around
and there's no food upon the ground!!
Betty Simpkins Hutchison

Where It's At

Do you gamble; do you scramble
Through the alleys dimly lit?
Taking chances on romances
Have you ever been bit?

Do you drink; do you think
You can find peace of mind?
Loving strangers, seeing dangers
In all experience you find!

Have some fun, love just one.
Maybe, then you'll greet
That special lover you'll discover
On your very own street.
Irving N. Prell

Untitled

Mother's Day is here, so it's
time to say,
How much I love you - more with
each passing day.
I want to thank you, for
raising me so good.
You've done everything that a
great mother should.
I have learned to appreciate all
of the things you do for me,
Even though there's times when
I just don't see.
You have always taken the time
to show me the way,
and that's why I'm saying.....
Have A Great Mother's Day!!
Justina Wiley

Hooked

Everyone gets it
Through thick or through thin,
Starting out as a child
it is bound to work in.

Baby girls can get hooked
As dolls come on strong,
And boys have their pets
To move right along.

Hooked as we are
Life still has its way,
If romance falls in
It can make a great day.

Our hobbies can hook us
To that there's no end,
be it sports or just writing
It can all make a blend.

Prose happens to be mine
On a subject called verse,
So I better stop now
Before it gets worse.
James L. McMahon

Be With Us

Hold us in your hand, Lord,
Throughout the hours of night.
Forgive us our transgressions
And lead us to the light.

We lean upon your hand, Lord,
As we journey through the day.
There's a steadiness in us
When we walk upon your way.

Be with my love throughout the day
And keep him as he sleeps.
Let him dream unconsciously
While his guardian angel weeps.

I'm sure he's dreaming about flying
High above the hills below.
He loved the freedom as he watched
The last rays of the sun's bright glow.

Although today I cannot meet
His many needs that surface.
Some day he'll walk on golden streets
And maybe even race.
Frances E. Tolson

Good-Bye

It's hard to say goodbye
to a friend you've always had,
Trying to hold back all the tears
that come with being sad.
It's hard to say I'll miss you
and hope to see you soon,
When you don't even know when
that soon will be.
I'll always remember you when
I look up into the sky and see the moon,
I hope you will think of me too,
because I know I will never forget you.
I will always think of you
with your blue eyes and smiling face,
Knowing someday we'll be together
standing side by side in the same place.
No longer will it be good-bye,
but hello, still knowing I'll have to let go.
The hardest words of life, good-bye.
Amy Johnson

No Me

I smiled your smile
Till my mouth was set;
It wasn't right, it was wrong.
I was you, I was you, far too long.

I said your words
Till my mouth closed up;
I had no voice,
I had no choice;
But, to sing your song.
I was you, I was you, far too long.

I lived your life
Till there was no me.
I was flesh and hair;
But, I was not there.
I was you, I was you, far too long.

The worst thing to it,
Is; you let me do it.
Who was weak and who was strong?
I was you, I was you, far too long.
Diane M. Lewis

A Loving Mother

Someone who is always there
To administer tender love and care,
One who compares to no other
Forever answering your every call.
The answer to all our prayers-
A sweet loving mother!

The hand that leads and guides you
From the time you are born and
Your whole life through,
She helps guide you toward things
That are best for you.
To help you develop into a person
Who is good through and through-
A tender loving mother!

Her face so gentle, her smile so sweet,
They capture the hearts of all she meets.
No sacrifice is too great for her to make,
Any obstacle she is determined to overtake,
If it will help her child to grow and prosper-
A kind loving mother!
Carolyn V. Watson

Sweet Sixteen

Sixteen is such a tender age
to be called back from this life
she could have been so many things
a teacher, a mother, a wife

Sixteen is such a tender age
to lose your dreams and hopes
Some days it seems to hard to bear
Some days I cannot cope

Sixteen is such a tender age
but it happened for a reason
my best friend died so I could learn
a very important lesson

Sixteen is such a tender age
to have life taken away
but deep inside my heart I know
she'll be with me everyday
Josie Helmstetter

Life-

I can't cope with it, my life seems
to be hopeless.
My grades are bad, my sisters are all
crabs. I can't cope with it!
I go to bed really late, and never
have a single date. I can't cope with it!
My room's a mess, my dog's a pest.
I can't cope with it!
I'm average height, with a bad over
bite. I can't cope with it!
I act wired at school, so people
call me a fool. I can't cope with it!
My life's a drag, but why should
I brag?
I can't cope with it!

Carlee Zarb

The Love I Can't Express

I've often wondered what it's like,
To be loved, to give love back,
And have someone to stand by me,
To make up for things I lack.

For I've never cared for anyone,
Nor let them care for me,
By putting up this wall of stone,
So much safer could I be.

But then you came into my life,
And took my breath away
If only I could figure out,
Just what I want to say.

Alone I think of many ways,
To say what's in my heart,
But when I see you, face to face,
I don't know how to start.

Afraid that you don't feel the same,
Or maybe that you do,
I guess I'm really trying to say,
Just how much I love you.

Charlene M. Morse

Me

Oh, how have I struggled
to be me
to soon find out
I'm someone else!
My memories
tell
I've changed
to the point
I've stopped
the fight and
now plead
realizing Life's
course is like
destiny.
Who tomorrow will I
be?
Whoever it is,
please admit
I had to do with
what you'll be.

Isabel Ramos

Cold Intruder

Who asked you, cold intruder,
To break up Spring's romance?
No, you were not invited
To come to April's dance.

We welcomed you for Winter, but
That welcome's quite worn out.
For though she's gone you haven't left;
Why must you stay about?

We loved your alabaster gown
Worn at December's ball.
Your frigid beauty stunned us all
When you accomp'nied fall.

But leave us, cold intruder;
Please set the seasons straight.
For you've no right to linger
And make poor Summer late.

Dana R. DeMoure

One Small Man

Waking in time
To catch a glance
of the world around me
with half a chance
to change my mind
to change my day
to live my life
another way
Walking in time
to another drum's beat
my heart and my soul
see the world at my feet
with more than a chance
to change what I see
all this before me
but it never was
to be, for me
another day, another way
now send me on my merry way.

Brian Gray

Humpback Whale

Breaching in play
to depths of the unknown
threatened from existence,

Your song unforgettable
size hard to imagine
so great is your meaning,

Gracefully soaring through the sea
singing your language
intelligence we don't understand,

So full of life
we envy you,
You're a creature who's mastered Peace.

Jennifer Loy

Deep Thoughts

The future is ours
to obtain our dreams,
To wish for a better life
no matter how extreme.

To trade in our world
of starvation, violence and tears,

For a better world
of peace and an end to fears.

Davina Hill

There Are No Words

There are no words,
To describe how I feel,
There are no words,
To describe the hurt,
There are no words,
To describe my loneliness,
There are no words,
To describe the confusion,
There are no words,
To describe the sorrow,
There are no words,
To describe the past,
There are no words,
To describe the love,
There are no words,
To describe anything, anymore.

Bernice Ann Picazo-Suniga

Life

Life in itself can only mean one thing
to enjoy what it has to offer
and what nature has to bring,

For all that is seen
isn't all that is said
for man does not understand.

Life from a distance
is seen better yet
for all that have passed
can tell it better; I bet.

When a child is born
a whole world awaits
for that special someone to be torn
and then at the end pass through
those pearly gates.

For love is all there is
in this world to give,
my love, your love, it's all the same
for what we have through life, love and peace
is always a gain!

Jacqueline Aponte

Waited So Long

I've waited for so long,
To find someone like you;
Someone who's really caring,
With a love that's true.

I'm so glad you're here,
To hold me in your arms;
I have nothing to fear,
No one can do me harm.

Your body is my refuge,
Your eyes are guiding lights;
Your arms are there to hold me,
When I need you in the night.

I've never loved anyone,
As much as I love you;
I hope this lasts forever,
For no one else will ever do.

Heather Bernstein

The Trip

So you're taking a trip, I'm sure
You're going to enjoy your stay.
Although we are miles apart
Memories of you will linker in my heart.

Joseph La Spisa

My Morning Star

"Good morning, good morning
  to my beautiful star,
As bright and lovely
  as ever you are.
So far away, so very near,
  I can almost touch you
Your warmth I feel.
  You must be the star
That showed the way,
  The star that shone over the world
That Christmas Day.
  How lovely and silent the glow
In my heart I know and I see,
  His love is saying I am your God,
Always trust in Me,
  The Light of the world
Never go away,
  Forever remind me of His love,
Please, always stay."

Audrey Capo

Why

Why did this happen
To my child, so fine was he
Why did this happen
For he was the life of me
Why did this happen
To my baby so strong
Why did this happen
For his life should have been long
Now I can't breathe
For my breath has been taken
Now I can't sleep
For I'm always awaken
Now I can't eat
For my food won't digest
But all this I must overcome
To lay my baby to rest.

Gina A. Henderson

Care Takers

Eyes, continuously open, windows designed
To reflect good,
Shudder, upon experiencing bad,
Recognize difference.
They, like a computer tell you
When reality has been classified
Escaping life's grasp, altered
By unbelievers, mocking Maturity.

Reflectors, storing forever pictures
Playing, continuously for fun,
Pleasure, A defense against
Manic depression, Anxiety,
Schizophrenia, Paranoia,
Indifference.

In living color,
See it, believe it,
Pigment spreaders
Must never know light.

Eyes, Continuously open
Windows, Caretakers.

Gerald H. Oglesby

My Life

I gaze back upon my past,
  to see how I have lived
I find that though not extraordinary,
  My life is good to the end.

I have lived many lonelies,
  I have lived many loves,
And I have lived through the years,
  As one often does.

I have made many mistakes,
  That I will never regret
For I am merely human,
  And we are not perfect

But I also look back,
  And see countless deeds,
That always out weight,
  My unfortunate misgivings.

And I find the thing I enjoyed most
  Was not money or successes,
But merely the beauty,
  That this earth possesses.

James Krueger

Untitled

To fly, free like a bird,
to soar above the clouds,
without a thought in mind.
To flow, free like the water,
to wash up on the shore,
and mix in the sand.
To wave in the wind,
like leaves on a tree,
to fall to the ground
without making a noise.
To swim, like a fish,
in a school or alone.
Big and colorful,
without having to worry
about anything but a bigger fish

Jillyan Merrill

As I Walk With Him

When the busy week has ended
To the country I will trod
Just to feel the closeness of him
As I walk with him.
Hand in hand from hill to valley
Sweet the smell of fresh turned sod
Sweeter my joy and pleasure
As I walk with him
Every creature plays a tune
Tress and flowers bow and nod
As I walk with him.
Oh the rapture of this moment
Guided by his staff and rod
Lifted now are all my passions
As I walk with him.

Carmen Gates

Untitled

Walking through life,
too afraid to touch.
Is this what I'm here for?
Treat the world as a museum,
an arm's length away.
Isolated heart, surrounded by fear,
life turned to anguish
in social seclusion.

Chris Ezzo

Duff

If we could go back
  To the days of our youth
  Oh much wiser we'd be

We'd solve all the problems
  Before the mistakes
  Then simpler life would be

But oh if that's possible here and now
Well we'll just have to figure out how

  'Cause first there's a problem
    Right after mistake
That gives us a problem somehow

  Now without the problems
    That come from mistakes
Our minds would soon be still

  And learning and growing
    Touching and feeling
  Together would add to nil

Now if these words are confusion
  Bringing you disillusion
  And causing you to repeat

  The words I'm displaying
  All together are saying
Off your Duff and onto your feet

Joel Thomas Newcome

"Cheryl"

Walk hand in hand with me
  to the top of the mountain that
  over looks the sea

From the top of the mountain we
  will be able to see the land
  that was meant for you and me

Walk hand in hand with me
  what a miracle that would be
  for God know there will never be
  anyone else in this world but you
  for me

Walk hand in hand with me
  for the love I have for you is
  as tall as the mountain that
  over looks the sea

Jim Goforth

That Guy

That guy brings new meaning
  to the word perfection,
He has great hair, beautiful
  eyes, and a wonderful complexion.
His lips are shaped perfectly
  to kiss,
And his body is something
  you simply can't miss.

His smile is enough to knock
  you off your feet,
He's someone you really
  need to meet.
He's so perfect and the above
  lines should tell you why,
Everyone loves that guy.

Chasity Tooley

Protest

Shall I protest and raise my voice
To the world of my inner feelings?
Shall I let it be known far and wide
Or within my walls and ceilings?
Shall I bare my heart on my sleeve
Of the loving young son now at rest,
Swept away in the tide of AIDS
While I grieve within my breast?
Shall I quietly walk away
From those who mock and scorn
And claim it's justice done
To different ones so born?
No, this I cannot do
For he left me a legacy.
He was kind, gentle and giving
To all those who could see.
He will not cross my threshold again,
But my love and his will not die.
I'll give those extra hugs and love
To all in need by and by.

Joyce Brink

Willow Walk

The earth has a plan
to uproot herself
and take with her a token for the fall-
Though we build towers
like Nimrod
to overthrow God-
the tower will shatter and
the Willow will walk.

Carla Corcoran

Each Step Brings Me Closer

Each step brings me closer
to what I'm hoping to
find in a world of confusion
Another step leads me on to
a path I'm not sure I should take.
Beyond there is something
That is echoing softly
through the rain
and clouds
Yet one more step into the
safety and security I thought
there was
Only to be awakened by the
echoing of help
slipping through the mist of
rain and clouds

Althea D. James

Final Watergate Scene

Ex-President Nixon tried very hard
To work for peace for our nation
Yet the Watergate "Scene" Occurred
Causing Him to resign His Office!

A mistake in his Leadership
Caused heartaches for all concerned
Yet as history will record
He opened the peace door to China!

Years passed from our calendar
As Mister Nixon worked for peace
When his Journey finally ended
"Watergate" fades with time of ages!

Doris L. Burleigh

Land of Freedom

Tonight a man will be beaten
Tonight a woman raped
How can a land of freedom
be so full of hate

We're supposed to be free
No matter what our race
People will always talk
but never to our face

They say we're equal
no matter our gender
But men have always been
habitual offenders

When will we learn
not to put others down
Once an African queen
now stripped of her crown

The majority will
become a minority
Then what are you gonna do
when they're mistreating you

Candy Farley

Heaven

God came to earth and
took my hand,
   And said it was my time.

He said I'll take you to my palace,
where everyone is welcome,
every kind of man.

He took me to a place
I call the promise land.

We walked on clouds,
and touched the stars way up
in the sky.

My mother said every one
would have a time to die.

I'm glad I had my chance,
and that I died in peace,
   And when you're up here the
whole world seems to cease.

Casey Marley

Keep On Driving

To the slave driver who
took my heart for a
painful spin

You drove my heart
turn to turn, through
bends and brush, over
gravel paths -
quite a rugged ride

I walked 'round and
'round with
shoulders low

You dealt my heart a
painful blow

Now I take it back

And you can
keep on driving
driving
Bye!

Hannah-Emet Frazier

Emotions

Truck full of emotions,
trailer of the past...
Going to the ocean,
where the waves come to crash.

Handful of kisses,
thrown upon the wind...
They come back as wishes,
that sparkle in the sand.

Meet me at the ocean,
to remember the past...
Bring all your emotions,
where the waves come to crash.

Jeanne Bradley

Limbo

Partly saint, partly demon
Trapped between the two
I seek the solutions
But have found so few

I know my fate
And cannot conceive it
For I know in my heart
That I am unfit

Trapped on earth
Though everlasting
Fighting everyday
A lack of understanding

When my existence
Becomes obscurity
I know that somehow
I will have stability

Craig Brons

Granddaughter

Pray for this child so full of grace
Trimmed in ribbons, satin and lace
Look at her eyes so wide and blue
So full of hugs and kisses too
I watch her grow everyday
Looking at the creation God has made
Bless her Lord and keep her near
She's the one that brings me cheer
Hold her close, teach her well
Angels protect her so she can tell
The love of Jesus for them all
The little children he does call
Thank you Lord for this gift
You know her smile gives me a lift
Thank you Lord for her mother
For she bore my first granddaughter.

Faye F. McLain

"Life"

It's not enough to have a dream
unless you are willing to pursue it.
It's not enough to know what's right
unless you are strong to do it.
It's not enough to join the crowd
to be acknowledge and accepted;
You must be true to your ideas
even if you're left out and rejected.
It's not enough to learn the truth
unless you are willing to live it.
It's not enough to reach for love
unless you care enough to give it.

Carol Jessup

After The Storm

Sometimes things that seem so sad
Turn out to be not quite so bad
As what may have been expected at first,
For some good can come out of the worst.
Once the fog of doom has cleared
Things are better than first appeared.
And once the morning's cleared the dew
It lets the sun come shining through;
Allows your eyes to open wide
And welcomes the world to come inside.
And a wonderful world blossoms anew,
With freedom to be, and freedom to do.
Fills your heart with realization
And your soul with joyous expectation
That as events become unfurled
Everything truly is all right with the world!

Carole Zimmerman

Natural Comfort

In a forest by a river
Underneath the trees
That's where I wish I were
And where I long to be.

There the thoughts come to me pure
And soft as a feather
There I sit and feel the kiss
Of nature and her weather.

When I'm there it all seems clear
And simplified and free
There I see my purpose
And what my life should be.

The problems of the world
All seem to fade away
There I find the strength to live
And face another day.

I'll cling to this throughout my life
And nature will be my guide
When my problems seem too much
I'll have a place to hide.

Jeremy Nunnelley

Hand In Hand

Hand in hand
united in love
never looking back
on the sorrow we once had.

Some say love is a fad
but the love will always last
between you and I
hand and hand.

Hand in hand
we've been through it all
the laughter and the falls.

We've been united
hand in hand
longer than time could stand.

Hand in hand
we will always endure.

Deborah Augustine

Miracles

My love drifted away
Until another day,
He found somebody new
And right then I needed a miracle too.

Miracles are needed,
Miracles are wanted,
Miracles can happen any day.

Don't be sad and blue
Cause life can start anew
Just hope for a better day
And watch what comes your way.

Miracles are needed,
Miracles are wanted,
Miracles can happen any day.

Doretha Hollins

Peaceful Passage

I never had to face it before
Until that day,
That cold day in February.

The news was as cold
As the freezing rain
Falling from the dark sky.

They said she died in her sleep,
Peacefully, quietly,
But it seemed so unexpected.

To me, not yet a young woman,
The very thought made me shiver.
The feeling of guilt
That I had never said goodbye.

But the tears slowly subsided
When I realized
She was much happier now.

She was peacefully,
Quietly sent away,
Now a star
Shining in the darkest night.

Jennie Scheerer

Regrets

Things that we reflect
upon from our occluded past.
Deadlines we neglect
until our loved ones rest at last.
We think about mistakes,
and fear oncoming death
Praying that we find the golden gates,
hoping we never lose the power of breath.
Today there is no appreciation of life,
only mirrored greed.
Death and gilded strife,
thinking only of our need.
Glancing at our final image.
seeing reflections of yesterday.
Now entering dark passages,
wishing we could stay.

Judith Locke

Untitled

Flower whistling to you
Water splashing against them,
Let them fall with you when
You take a look of the view

Dorothea Anne Berntsen

War

You're behind a wall
waiting for a silence

You taste the adrenaline
You think it's intense

You feel the trigger
You smell the oil, sweat, the death.

The firing stops
You turn for the shot
You hear the shot, but it's not you
You feel the bullet in your head
and wish war was dead

Christopher Larsen

Sitting In The Hall

They sit there in their chairs each day
Waiting, silently, they know not why.
Nor questioning or expecting,
that life slowly passes by.

They dream of days when life was rich,
with loved ones always near,
of cloudless days and star filled nights
And memories, oh, so dear.

Those days are gone forever
relived only in the mind,
As they sit, waiting in the hall
dreaming of a life they've left behind

Dawn A. Pope

Why

Conflicting-anger, wondering why?
Walls trapping me; I'm so alone.
No one cares, I could just die,
Wondering? Why?

I don't even feel alive it's so
unreal. My body empty; I've
lost my soul. Somewhere on the
Dark road I've been on for sometime,
It must have decided
I wasn't worth the ride.

Jackie Clark

Loneliness

Thinking, wondering, wishing,
Wanting what's not there.
Needing a little comfort,
Wanting someone to care.

Solitude, emptiness, silence,
Companions to the end.
Wishing every day I live,
To have that special friend.

Love, joy and happiness,
I find only in my dreams.
Doomed to live my life alone,
With nothing - so it seems.

I've wanted, wished and waited,
But it seems useless now.
I really, truly want to hope,
I've just forgotten how.

I feel like a rose in winter,
Wilting, slowly dying.
Listen close and you can hear me,
Sitting, softly crying.

Barbara Sumner

Why

Pale gave way to deep purple-blue,
Warm, gentle turned a bitter frost;
Peaceful calm now shattered in two,
Inner strength shaken, but not lost;
I will ride this storm without you.

Rain may come later or pass by,
For now sometimes I cry within;
Time will heal my heart to let it fly,
All our years together lost by your sin;
I will always wonder why.

Beverlee R. Monahan

Untitled

Standing alone
was once your will.
Without a friend
or love to feel.
And now you regret
the promise you made
cause time is gone
and the price is paid.
Yet as you fall down
and fade away
you know in your heart
there's more to pay.
And there's that one last prayer
you'll never say;
Pray to God
to take you away.
'Cause what you've done
is called a sin
and either way
the devil wins.

Heather Duncan

Past Love

The love we shared
Was so long ago.
I loved being with you
Oh I loved you so.

Sometimes I think back
On what we had shared.
The love we had was strong
Because we always cared.

Sometimes I catch myself wondering
How it would be.
You know, us together still
Just you and me.

My feelings for you
Are still so strong.
I'll always love you in my heart
The precious memories will still carry on.

We're both getting on with our life's
No matter what happens in the end.
I'll always be here for you
I'll always be your friend.

Jennifer Snyder

Books Books

Books books we read over books,
We care for our books.
We respect our books.
They come in all shapes and sizes.
Big ones, small ones, ever paperback too.
Our library is full of books.
We love our Books!

Jennifer Walmsley

Young Love

Our young love
Was the sweetest love
That we would ever know
We vowed that we would marry
When we would older grow

But then your family sailed away
    Far across the sea
My heart was truly broken
When they took you away from me
    So our dreams together
never come to be
But that wondrous love
    of years long past
Is a beautiful memory.

Edward B. Koski

About The Hats

Spring started with hats and
watched exploding Superman
movies on old davenports with
dogs nestling between the ankles.

Hats played darts in parks, sailed
oceans, wrinkled time, saw
Pharaohs, Incas, Vikings,
Druids throwing peat and
football with Buckeyes.

Hats made museum trips so
Bronto and Rex could stare and
zoos for Samson
to hail, Rudra to bow,
Chandar to kneel. Hats

now sit, idly, caving
in on tables and spilling
the tales they tell
when I walk by.
Hats are my legacy.

Andrew J. Gordon

Untitled

Sitting on a doorstep
watching all the people
go by wearing suits, ties and
carrying briefcases
Wondering where my next
meal will come from
Sleeping on sidewalks
and park benches
People just stare
at you like you
are from a different
plant When I get up
in the morning I hear the cars
going by beeping at every stop
People are walking
up and down the sidewalk
running to get to work
But me I have to find
my breakfast in order to
stay alive.

Cindy March

"When You Left"

You and me,
    we fell in love
It is so strong;
    So it can't be wrong.

When you moved away;
    I was feeling all alone.
I cried when I heard your voice
    on the telephone.

We'd miss each other;
and we'll never find another.
    I love you a bunch,
and I'll never forget the day
When you told me you loved me so much.

    Each day with you
is a day to remember,
    and I'll always look forward
to our special day in December.

    I love to be with you;
you'll always be mine, and I'll be yours
Until the end of time.

Heidi Hardwick

Love

We use to be a hot item
We use to be a pair
We use to be lovers
Without a single care

We use to go places
And see people with happy faces
We use to be friends
thinking it would never end

We use to be two hearts
that brought the patter of feet
Such joy no one could repeat

We use to be.....

Barbara Kady

Untitled

What is life
We'd like to know
As through our tasks
We daily go
There are times of course
When for one brief flash
Some see a vision
But it doesn't last
It's back to the humdrum
The daily grind
That bogs us down
And clouds the mind
But still it's there
For all who can see
Through the thick veneer
To the glorious truths
That in time will appear
The fight's we'll fought
If in the end you will see
A vision of heaven as it meant to be

Dorothy Johnson

The Past Of Me Is Gone

Days go by so fast,
weeks go by so slow,
I can't remember the past,
I can't remember the flow,

Everyday I think and think,
But nothing comes to mind,
Everyday I try to blink,
But I think that I'm just blind,

Days go by so fast,
weeks go by so slow,
I try to think,
But can't even blink,

The past of me is gone.
Amanda Stevens

"Mount St. Helen Eruption"

She blew her top the word is out,
What a temper tantrum to talk about!
Destruction like you never saw,
The whole world shocked:we stand in awe.
The trees came down from shaking ground
The water turned to mud all around
Whatever fell within her spell
Reduced to rubble: A story to tell!
Remember the day all talk about
When Mt. St. Helen began to spout
She never stopped 'til she proved to all
That her will goes or rage will fall!

Evelyn Coleman

Untitled

An unborn baby,
What a wondrous thing,
   So small,
   And so fragile,
   Little fingers,
   Little toes,

How could this be,
   A little life,
   Is it yours,
   Oh, no, no, no,
   This child is free,

To be,
   Anything it wants to be,
   Would you dare,
   Do you care,
   Could you take this life away,

Feel it kick,
   Feel it wiggle,
   This child is free,
   Let it be!
Jennifer Huskey

'Hope'

Lonely, disillusioned she wonders when-
Where her childhood joys have flown-
Passions subdued, hopes gone
She fears the unknown,
Love has lost its sweet flavor
Laughter all of its joy.
Then, Alas she remembers her mother's
gentle smile, caring hands.
She looks upward! to the sky, and
Draws her strength knowing too that
She has a 'Father' 'Always!
Constance Blake

In The Mirror
Dedicated to Ray Moore

I look in the mirror
What do I see?
The reflection of my son,
Looking back at me:
We were two of a kind,
In looks, spirit and mind.
But since he passed away,
I can't say:
"When I look in the mirror,
That I can see,
Him smiling back at me.
If he could just say:
"Mom, I'm fine, it's "Ok".
Then I could look in the mirror and see:
The reflection of a happy me!
Just to know you're "O.K."
Would really make my day!
Bonnie L. Nelson

Surprise

Great God!
   What is this?
I never,
Ever wanted this!
But, you are invading my soul.

Your soft eyes
   have melted my heart,
Your sublime smile,
   has eased my pain,
Of being alone.

Your outreaching spirit
   which once grabbed me,
That spirit,
   will not let me go.

It seizes me
   with delicate caresses.
A caress,
   that I can't let go.
You call,
   and I shall follow.
Jennifer Rocco

Time

What's time worth to each of us,
When day becomes a year?
More important in our daily lives
Than what we hold so dear?

Too easily time slips away
Gone, never to return.
What price we put upon it
Should be of some concern.

Time spent in disillusion,
What are we looking for?
Do we wish to sit and dream about
The days that are no more?

Too fast a pace we often choose
When we need to take it slow.
To enjoy the mere serenity
Of watching children grow.

Those simple times we overlook,
Too soon the end grows nigh.
Yet we seem to be content,
To let life pass us by!
R. Joseph Wheeler

The Cloudiest Day

On the cloudiest, saddest day,
When I feel blue and gray,
   You are always there for me,
I can count on you
   And even though times are hard,
And you think you can't go on,
   You'll get through I believe in you
   If you killed yourself,
I'd want to die too
   I can't imagine life
Without a friend like you
   If you need a friend or a hug,
I'll always be here.
   You are the best friend
I've ever had
   Don't take that away from me.
   I just want you to know
I'll always be here,
   I always care
Jennifer Kroplin

"Always Knows"

It seems he always knows
When I need him the most.
He always seems to know
What I am feeling.
He always knows
Just the right thing to say.
And, he is always there
When I least expect it.
I feel so lucky
To have found such a friend.
Someone who will always be there
Someone I can always count on.
I know something so simple and wonderful
Cannot last forever.
But I will treasure him
For as long as he knows.
Jennifer Anguiano

This Moment On

This moment on,
when I think of you,

I see all the beauty
And love in your face.

This moment on,

When that warm sun
shines light
on your face,

You're a picture
of loveliness to see

Which never can be replaced.

This moment on, and every moment on,
You are the only one for me.
Ahmad Ansar

A Child Asks

How shall I answer you, my son,
When you come to question me
Concerning Life and Death and God,
And the soul's eternity?
How little I have learned of life,
And Death seems far away,
God's here, I know, but how explain
The Soul's eternal day?
Amy L. Wadsworth

The Bridge

Once upon a time
   When I was young and full of life...
I played on a bridge that stretched
   Across a stream so blue.
Oh the times I had; I danced and
Sang and laughed and jumped,
   And then I went home to bed.

Many years later
   Older, wiser and worn by time...
I left the bridge the stretched
   Across a stream so blue.
Oh the times I had; I worked and
Yelled and cried and screamed,
   My youth officially dead.

   Elizabeth Clark

Reason Why

I can't explain the reason why
When lovers leave - friendships die.
But this I know is always true
I pay my debts when they are due.
So now I send you your cassette
My love, a kiss, and last regret;
I wish we never had to end.
I wish that you could be my friend.

I can't explain the reason why
Someone would want to make you cry.
But this I know is always true
I did that more than once to you.
So now I swallow all my pride
And say I'm sorry when I lied
I wish we never had to end
I wish that we could start again.

   Edward D. Patten

Kelsey

I never thought I'd see the day,
When my niece was lead away,
By the hand of God above,
Whose heart is filled with so much love.

She was only two months old,
Someone who we'd never scold,
Now we'll never see her grow,
Into someone we could get to know.

She would cry so sweet and dear,
And I used to hold her near,
But now I can't because she's sleeping,
I find myself forever weeping.

This December she would have been four;
Kelsey will be remembered forevermore.

   Ariane Nickerson

Forever

How can you promise me Forever
When you don't know how eternal that is?
You say you love my smile,
But what is Love?
How can you find it, touch it,
Define what it's supposed to feel like?
My insides turn and so do I,
Away from your pleading.
As the silence slowly enfolds us,
And your sigh joins the wind's whispers,
I realize that now is Lovely
And Forever is made up of now's
And I want this Forever.

   Julie Woo

My Heart's Desire

I wonder if you'd still love me
When stars come falling from the sky
I wonder if you'd care for me
Till the moon bids the Earth goodbye.

I wonder if you'd sing with me
When birds migrate to Paradise
I wonder if you'd work with me
Though the morning sun fails to rise.

I wonder if you'd walk with me
Even though the road seems endless
I wonder if you'd dream with me
Even if searching turns hopeless.

Rich or poor, I will stay with you
I wonder if you feel this way
Rain or shine, I will be with you
My love will be as grand as May.

   Aimeiko Christel Tasico

Childhood

Childhood is over
When the dolls are packed away,
And the child would rather stay in
Than go outside to play.

When dreams are no longer reality,
And imagination is controlled by fact,
When the future holds scary thoughts,
And the world appears dark and black.

When naps do not seem like such a drag,
And fairy tales no longer come true,
When halloween arrives,
And people don't give candy to you.

When life becomes a great big puzzle
And the future does not seem so far away,
Then your child hood has come and gone,
but never forget great life you have today.

   Amanda Fullen

Slipping And Sliding

It was during the ice storm of '94,
When the weather was so poor,
That I should have stayed indoors.

But like so many others
I dared and I discovered, cause

I was a-slipping and a-sliding
A-skipping and a-gliding
Trying to stay upright on my feet.

I was hoping and a-groping
That my bottom wouldn't take a stroking
From the serious ice beneath my feet
That gave me the creeps

With feeling of defeat and
Nowhere to retreat.

Oops.......there it is
I just took a seat
In the street,
Ain't that a bleep

   Clayton Dunn

The Conquerors

What will men lose
when they live on the moon.
explore the planet Mars?

Will they look back
at lovely Earth -
across the heavens' dark -

With longing deep as Adam
and Eve's last gaze
at Eden's glowing groves?

   Donley Phillips

Washington's Golden Dream

'Twas 1776 that year,
When Washington's dream came true,
A nation started with his thoughts,
And thoughts of other men, too.
They put together all their dreams,
of liberty and of growth,
These things then, all have come to pass,
Yes, these are the things he wrote.
He wrote of knowledge and of truth,
And of fire within your breast,
To keep alive the spark within,
And never to let it rest.
That spark of conscience that he had,
Was transferred to the nation,
Who swore allegiance to the flag,
Of the word's new creation.
With all the dreams that came to pass
And the help of God Supreme,
A nation rose from men like him,
'Twas Washington's golden dream.

   John M. Antonucci

Our First Meeting And Our First Date

T'was the 9th day of November 1984
When we first met
Thanks the Lord I know you
A new friend hope forever to share with.

Truly is our first song
Meant a lot for the first time
Sharing some about our lives
With a funny talk but full of truth.

T'was the 10th day of November 1984
Yokohama, a place for our date
I had never go out for a date
So long now I do with someone
Surely a trustworthy man.

We ride on a train you start caressing
At Shakey's we shared pizza
Smiles and laughter's shared together
Our first date was wonderful
Just in time our love together.

   Elma A. McKeown

Wild Horses

Horses! Wild Horses!
Wild beautiful horses.
Roaming, soaring, racing the wind.

But listen! Listen! Screams!
Screams of our horses.
Please people please! They plead.
Let us be! For our spirits soar high.
We just want to be free.

   Jeannie L. Martin

God's Miracles

I love walking in the meadows
when wildflowers are in bloom
and watch the pretty butterflies
as they flit from bloom to bloom

That big golden sun
shining down from above
with its warmth and bright light
sent down with God's love

and off into the distance
when the deer come out to graze
I think about his miracles
and thank him for each day

Without him there would never be
A sun, a moon or stars
for only God gave them to us
his miracles form afar

so as the sun starts going down
and I head back alone
I'll stop and pick wildflowers
to brighten up my home.

Jennie Williams

Noonie's Poem

Where did you come from?
When will you go?
Do you know that we've all come?
Or is it only we who know?

No one wanted you to suffer.
Many would have taken your place.
Don't try to make your eyes flutter,
You can put peace upon your face.

How can I capture what you were?
The jokes, stories and your laugh.
Friendship, love, honor and fear,
The things that were your sign and staff.

You weren't perfect, nor were we.
Many times we should have been kind,
But neither was able to see.
Those never stayed on your mind.

In the years we'll all be to see you.
Watch over us as best you can.
We'll try to live as you would do
And keep you forever part of the clan.

Eileen Jeffries

(I Know) He's Not Far Away

My dear Lord, thy goodness, I see,
When your sweet blessing come my way,
   I'm so thankful:
      As thankful as can be
   That is why to thee, I say;
I know oh yes, I know: in my heart,
      He's not far away.

   All my troubles, he will share,
   That is why. I know he care,
   I find his love everywhere,
      I know, oh yes I know,
         He's not far away.

   Oh my Lord, I will never fear,
All because your love is the sunshine:
   That is with me through the day,
      I know my God is near:
   His command's I seek to obey,
I know, Oh yes, I know, in my soul:
      He's not far away.

Joseph F. "Skipper" Williams

Baby Child

Baby Child
Where are you now?
Lost in a world of hate.
Baby Child
Where are you going?
To lands unknown a far.
Baby Child
Where have you been?
Lost in the dark of night.
Baby Child
Why turn away?
For you know no other solution.
Baby Child
Return to my swaddling arms,
Close to my heart.
Love and Protection,
Can shield off the pain
And together find your way.
Baby Child

Deborah K. Silcox Ortiz

Thinking Of You

I'm always thinking of you,
   where ever you may go
I'm always thinking of you,
   whatever you may do,
I'm always whispering I love you
   even though you are not here,
   'cause when I think of you,
   it's as though you were near.
Though the miles may
   keep us apart,
   they will never take
   away the love that is in my heart.
I'm always thinking of you,
   and I'm always thinking
   of how much I love you.

Andrea Spear

My Memories

My memories are filled with love
Where fear once blocked the way
And threatened all the happiness
I wanted everyday.
My memories are filled with joy
Where anger once lived long.
The shadows covered every smile;
In me there was no song.
My memories are filled with care
For all that lives on earth.
Once selfishness kept hold on me
And little was my worth.
My memories are filled with hope
Where once I could not see
That hating others kept me down
And filled with misery.
Now, my memories are mature
Where once I was unsure.
Now, I accept love anytime.
I know I am secure.

DarLine L. MacKenzie

'The Sky'

There's a massive land of blue
Where fluffy clouds float by.
An endless world of beauty
Known by many as the sky.

But the sky is also known
As the heavens of the earth.
It's called upon as home
By those who know of all its worth.

It's where the angels dwell in peace
And look down upon us all.
Where they listen to our prayers
And answer every call.

They help us through our tears,
Through all the pain we may behold.
They bring back all the memories
And the smiles that we once showed.

So whenever we feel lonely
And have a sudden urge to cry,
We can build up all our strength
And bravely look up to the sky.

Erika Lynn Adams

Hope

In a world of moral decay,
Where is the hope?
In a time of promiscuity,
How can we hope?
In a world of racial injustice,
Is there hope?
In a world where crime pays,
Why should we hope?
When we believe in God,
There is hope;
When we love others,
We can share hope;
If we help others,
We deserve hope;
Living by faith,
Gives us hope.

Freida Blackmon

Fairie's Wine

High upon the mountain tops
Where man can rarely go,
Lies a secret playground
For fairies young and old.

They hide atop the piney trees
To dance and sing and fly,
Their music bids the passing clouds
To come down from the sky.

Then when the clouds float low enough
They reach up soft and kind,
And milk the satin, fluffy cloud
To make their fairy wine.

To man it seems like heavy mist
Clinging to the trees,
But fairies know the world around
How wrong a man can be.

David R. Byrd

The Hidden Room

I come to a hidden room
Where obscure and dark thoughts wind -
A portal opened through
The secret key of my mind.

I come in trepidation,
Knowing truth confronts me there,
Bringing forth the revelation
Of heartache and despair.

It is a room familiar,
But frightening all the same;
I'm horrified to linger,
Yet freed by what I name.

Judith K. Halvorsen

Untitled

Imagine that there was a place,
where only you could roam.
All your cares and worries
would be left at home.
A magic place full of wonder,
where all of nature is your friend.
A place where no tears are shed,
and the day has no end.
Where you can truly be yourself,
and never be afraid.
And always see the beauty
in everything God made.

Brooke Elizabeth Pringle

Sunset On Malmaison

Ashes, rubble, weeds and grass
Where she stood in years long past
Vaulted ceilings, plaster mold
High, arched windows, knobs of gold

Lovely gardens in whose shade
Walked young chiefs and Indian maids
Wheree'er the great Chief paused to rest
Offering peace to every guest

Here the white man came to trade,
Returned again and treaties made.
Here the great chief chose to stay
When other red men went away.

Stayed on to serve his white man friends
Making laws that in the end
Proved the wisdom of his choice.
Giving to freedom his life and voice.

I seem to see in memories' eye
Him walk again and pass me by,
As o'er these hills he walks by night,
Seeking stately Malmaison's lights

Fred E. Carl Sr.

"Consolation"

Across the grave yard where
winds whisper and blow
We have the consolation that
God is the one who knows
About these people who upon
this earth did grow
So let us not pass judgement
on those we love
For all is seen from far up above.

Geneva C. Hall

Beneath The Bomb-Wrecked Rubbled Site

Beneath the bomb-wrecked rubbled site
where still some eelgrass lies,
a son's thin-boned hand
claws through the claybanked earth,
his fleshless finger pointing.

Hard by the church's stony arm,
the red-keeled sun goes in.
A mother bows to God,
begs peace on earth.

I turned and saw the bluish steel
of bayonet above a cornfield-crib,
and a father's hollowed eye searching
the inward map of dusted hope.

David E. Tanenbaum

So Long Mom

Mom has gone to heaven,
    Where we would like to be,
She now has her peace of mind,
    And is entirely free.

Free to come, free to go,
    And do whatever she likes to,
The opportunity to meet friendly folks,
    Not the kind we often do.

No more worries, no more cares,
    Just happiness galore,
Each day will bring a lot of fun,
    From a never ending store.

Dad left us many years ago,
    His home is now away up there,
Leaving behind a lot of love,
    As difficult to count as your hair.

The wheelchair that she lived in,
    Has now been left behind,
Her life up there will be different,
    And of a very different kind.

Catherine Bordenet

Life's Path

Life is a path
which each of us follow
letting our hearts lead the way
sometimes alone and scared
but our paths may cross
and our love may show
but I deny the tears in my eyes
as I know I must let you go
love is so strong
at times we have no control
so we must resist
or be overcome by our desires
overwhelmed by despair
knowing I must live without your touch
never again seeing your sweet face
having to say those fateful words "Good bye"

Danielle Aloshen

Love And Other Passions

For what is love but to fly
while being afraid
of heights.

The ground recedes yet beckons
come back, it whispers,
only here is it safe. No.

We soar through the breathless wind
seeking refuge
the earth behind is crusty and old.

Heart isn't this your design
to face the void
and yet not flinch?

Carol Kosterka

Shells

Growing, changing, learning
while hiding in its shell.
This protective armor
will one day end up her hell.
When the shell no longer fits
it is left, abandoned
for something greater,
a new place where it will
grow, change, learn.
Never to look back.
Each shell it leaves behind
is beautiful, but haunting.
If you hold it to your ear,
it will whisper to you,
"Don't look back,
never look back.

Erin Lavery

"Friends Forever"

Can I hold you just one more time
While I pretend that you're still mine
I tried to keep you here by me
But I guess it wasn't meant to be

We always had a lot of fun
Sitting close, watching the sun
But now it's time for you to go
And I just wanted to let you know

I love you and I hate to lose you
But I know it's something I must do

If you ever, ever need a friend
I'll be here till the very end

Jill Argenio

A Very Dear Friend

My dear friend
Who is very a dear friend indeed
She never leaves my side
She guides me all the way
She isn't very tall at all
We have been together forever
Everybody likes her
She is a character
She doesn't get sore at all
I live with her
and talk with her
There's nothing like a mother and a
daughter!

Amanda Dyke

Two Wonderful People

I know of two wonderful people,
who mean the world to me.
They raised me from a baby,
and taught me how to see.

If it weren't for these two people,
Oh, how lost I would be.
For they listen to my troubles,
even small though they be.

I love them,
As they may never know,
And what they reap,
also I shall sow.

And great will be my harvest,
For they gave me all they had.
These two wonderful people,
Who I call Mother and Dad.

Joan Dorthy Cupps

Forgotten

Punishment is due
Who will it be this time
All are afraid
All are forgotten
The gods have no mercy
They stand alone
Arrogance is their policy
They know our fate
Destroying is our policy
We make our fate
Life is....
No one knows
Born to be a leader
A leader of what
Punishment is due
Who will it be this time
All are afraid
All are forgotten

Alek Guinn

"God Is Our Only Way"

There is a guy
   whose love for us fills the sky.
He is our only way
   from day to day.

He is our one and only savior.
   and he will do us any favor.
He wants all of our hearts to see
   the glory of eternity.
One day
   all of our sins were taken away,
When God sent his son to die on the
      cross of calvary,
   for you and for me.

Someday he's coming again
   for all of his children
And he will take our hand
   and lead us to the promise land.

April M. Stuckey

Waiting

Sad and gray, those lonely houses,
Whose sightless, dusty windows sigh.
Doors all askew, the porches gone,
Just fleeting glimpse to passers by.

Squealing tires throwing roadside dust.
Vines, dry, like unwashed tangled hair.
Long gone all signs of daily life,
No waiting tasks, no one to care.

Crumbling roofs point to barren yards,
No future dreams for one to share.
Perhaps a giant, uncaring hand,
Reaching out, just dropped them there.

Do ghostly children play within,
These gaunt, bleak specters of the past?
In endless youth and endless pain,
That final rest may come at last.

Barbara Fulton Schindler

My Bride

The woman I wed
Will be more precious than 'I do' and
   other words said.
She'll have an intelligent head
Not just be a partner in bed.
She's not someone on whom to tarry
   or tread
Or keep me fed.
She's sweeter than honey on bread
On coming home I shall not dread
So to you, my loving desire does spread
Enough said.

Bob Svoboda

The Lighthouse

Lonely on its promontory,
Windswept by a sea-born breeze.
Silent vigil of ship or dory,
Facilitating both with ease.

Probing, searching the stormy night,
Or calm, pure sweetness of weather fair;
Beckoning, welcoming finger of light
Urging, lost vessel, don't linger there.

Gale-tossed high upon a crest,
A frantic glance espies its mark.
Hope springs anew inside the breast;
A path of light to chase the dark.

Slowly dawn turns up its wick,
The angry elements at peace again;
Eager hands drop anchors sure and quick
As land reclaims its ship and men.

Blessed landmark through the ages,
Revered in legend, poem and story.
Echoing down through history's pages,
Noble friend, bask in your glory.

Colleen Christopher

Dedicated to Mother

A mother has a special bond
with a daughter or a son.
The ties that bind them are by far
The greatest of anyone.
It doesn't matter
If they're near or far,
Or what we all must face
What time has brought to families,
For distance can't erase.
A mother knows right from the heart
Her child's greatest fears -
It's learned from all
That she has learned
Throughout her child's years.
And so now I wish to tell you this
It is for you to know,
Your child will always love you -
And this I know is so.

Debbie Turner Smith

Will I Survive

Will this earth survive
   with all of the pain
and torment, hatred and distrust?

Can we lie there asleep without
   the flames from hell burning
Our dreams of love and honesty?

Can we not reach out a hand
   to save another human being
Without a wall of trapped souls
   trying to break us?
But if we die today,
   We'll we die complete,
Without a past memory gnawing
   at our mind, reminding us,
about our past, the evil the pain?

Lord, save us.

Will this earth survive
   on our love or
Perish on our hatred?

Jose-Armando Pompa

Chains Of Secret

I thought I grew up a happy child
With bubbly smiles the ebb of tide
But really it was a child's facade
To cover up of the pain inside

His death was my celebration
Goodbye the chains of secret!
But it was not a revelation
And soon returned the fret

Then depression crawled across my land
And suicide grabbed hold of me,
I remember grandfather's hand
And my silenced plea

For I'm a survivor of sexual abuse
And until confrontation is past
To ignore and deny is of no use
Just tell the world at last

And now I sing and dance and smile
And live a life so bright
For all that I lost for a while
Has returned with all God's might

Barb Doerksen

The History Of The Poet's Sword

Would words be words if no one had
   with "cuneated pen"
a history scratched in clay and stone
   enlightened specimen?

The Reed stands out an early pen.
   A lampblack and a glue,
creative ink Eqyptians used
   the cursive to pursue.

The seventh century Quill became
   (with split and sharpened end,
a feather-tail or wing of bird)
   the implement that penned.

The fluid ink was introduced
   and nibs of pointed steel.
In seventeen eighty, Harrison
   brought forth a "barrel deal."

Thus came to be the Fountain Pen
   with automotive feed.
The inkwells lost. Ball Pen was born,
   but, Fingertips shall always lead!

   Helen Nencka

"Going For The Gold"

The inner-strength,
With drive is strong.
The athlete inside
Must go along.
Reach for the stars
And never give in.
If you work hard,
You're sure to win.
The game will be hard
Yet you mustn't quit.
The love inside
Is a candle just lit.
The flame burns on
Courageous and bright.
Challenge yourself
And learn to fight.
Hold your head high,
And go for the gold.
Great athletes are "young"
And never grow "old."

   April Taylor

Cheyenne Two

On wings of youth
with eyes of truth
And a cape of yellow cotton
Her head held high
Toward the sky
She flies with cares forgotten

Stretching the bonds
of her world beyond
Fueled by imagination
She soars timeless
In innocence's fineness
This gift of God's creation

   Diane Hamilton

The God Above

The God above is watching us
With eyes that never dim,
He knows the path is rough and long,
So leave your faith with him.
To leave your faith in one so great
Is something wisely done;
He knows we live, He knows we love,
And finally makes us one.
This one of us grows stronger yet,
With hopes, with dreams, with love;
So we have learned the secret great
To trust the God above.

   Joyce M. Arner

Destiny Runner

I run like the eagle flies
With freedom and ease
Soaring across the skies.

Searching for a destination
I relish leaving home
I am contemplation in motion.

Breathe hard, breathe fast
My lungs and muscles ache
Still I must make this last.

Run until I'm done
Quiet my dreams
With the world, I will be one.

   George Watts

The Tick-Tock Clock

We have a tick-tock clock
   With hands upon its face.
It goes tick-tock, tick-tock, tick-tock
   As its pendulum swings apace.

Daddy says, "We need a clock
   In order to tell the time"
So it stands there saying, "Tick-tock"
   Like a poet writing rhyme.

I have a clock in my room, too,
But it never says, "Tick-tock",
It only says, "Cuck-coo".

How do clocks tell the time?
   Why do we need to know?
Would the sun just cease to shine
   If no clocks were put on show?

   Haywood K. Cross

Untitled

The earth is filled
with life's most precious things,
The trees that sway,
the birds that sing
the waters that flow
and the flowers that grow
The mountains so high,
the blue of the sky
The oceans so grand
the desserts that look
like never ending land
but all in all the most
precious thing would have
to be the life that God
gave to me.

   Jody Rogalla

Soul Mate

I'll never forget my first date
With my heaven sent soul mate

too each other we do relate
each of us, pays half the freight

in unison we do yawn
softy chuckle and sing along

This life is such a pleasant stay
as we skip along the way

I have not a care in the world
that my soul mate can't unfurl

Thank you God
for such a wonderful girl

   James P. Hennessey

Homeless Veteran

Homeless veteran
With no place to stay
You might not know it
But you'll see one today

Sent off to fight
Without hesitation
Now their home is the street
Without explanation
They went overseas
And saw their friends die
Now they sift trash for leftovers
Of your turkey on rye

Home of the brave
Land of the free
Neglecting your veterans
You embarrass me.

   Jeremy Vaughn

Emotions

As though my heart is burning bright,
   With passionate embraces,
My soul is burning for a kiss,
   A kiss with velvet laces.

And on those laces one will find
   Red lips as soft as dew,
That'll always make me wonder why
   I ever fell for you.

Could it have been your sexy voice
   That made me always quiver?
Or was it simply mismatched fate
   That made our kisses linger?

It could have also been the way
   You smiled and you joked,
As if no gloomy rainy day
   Could ever get you soaked.

There is one certain fact for sure
   That I now wish to let you know
That on this day, my precious one
   My love for you I know.

   Adriana Petriceanu

The Suicide Race

In two shiny new sports cars
  With their owners unknown
The two boys were almost ready
  To peel out and show 'em.

With cars on both sides of the strip
  Their headlights all aglow.
The anticipation mounted
  At the start of the show

With the cliff a short piece away,
  Mills wound tight, they spun out.
With both boys bound for victory
  They lost without a doubt.

    Barbara LaRoche-New

Thought

At times I go deep
within my mind and,
Looking out through
My eyes at the street
Below our window;
See nothing!

Music on the radio plays
On but I do not know who
Or what, having already
Forgotten what the man
Had said.

If you speak to me twice,
I will come out again into
Reality; but unwillingly!

    Floyd A. Hoag

Faith

There is much faith
Within my soul
to keep me reaching
to further my goal,
I will not quit
that is not my style
I'm very optimistic
It drives people wild
You'll never see me weary
as long as I live
My trust is in God
not in a man-made dollar "Bill"
Faith, Try it. "Peace, and Love."

    John Alonzo Armstrong

Untitled

Miles of smiles
Yet heartache inside
A heart that is hurting
Because of his pride
Is this the beginning
Or is it the end
Are you the enemy
Or are you my friend
Days of this torture
May last for weeks
Are you still the same
Or revenge do you seek
Miles of smiles
Yet heartache inside
Now by his rules
You shall abide.

    Cristy Bell

Two Men Dancing

When I see the world
  without grace or dignity,
It makes me think
  "Hey! This is crazy to see.
See people fight,
  but sometimes, it's even me!

I hate to see people fight
  with despair.
It makes me think
  "I'd rather see two men dancing,
  in their underwear".
Then it would be OK to
  laugh out loud,
at the men in the crowd.
"Yeah! That would be a
  sight to see."
If not, at least to me.

When I see the world this way.
I think to myself "I'd
rather see, Two men dancing, any day."

    Jennifer Brooks

Him

I saw him and my heart was gone.
Without this man I can't go on.
And though not long had he known me,
I'd known him for eternity.

When we were small we'd play and hide,
And laugh together in my mind.
But now he's here and he's so real,
I just can't hide the things I feel.

True he's older and I'll admit,
I can see why they had their fits;
Because they didn't know him well —
Only his past - he went through hell.

But he's changed now and I love him,
Because I know the man within —
Sweet and charming, wanting to love -
For his friends he can't give enough.

Although his past is what they hate,
And his present they still debate,
It doesn't change that he's my friend,
And I'll love him until the end.

    Emily J. Coalter

Meticulous

My Japanese gardener told me
"Womens" are better gardeners than "mens"
They are attuned to the little things

Colonies of faded blossoms nestled
amidst brilliantly hued sisters
desperately cling to life

Remnants if dead branches
hidden amongst their colorful brothers
stubbornly claim legitimacy
Myriads of air-born pods
their flight graceful, erratic
silently invade the warm earth

Clusters of infant weeds
suffering the pangs of birth
relentlessly attack the new garden

Impostors all, begging anonymity
demanding attention
if what my gardener says is true
they elude the "mens" but not the "womens"

    Dorothy Lauer

"Sitting Alone"

Many of times I sit alone,
worrying, wondering what I'm doing
wrong.
I say to myself, is it me?
Not knowing the answer,
as my life goes on.
Then I sit - think to myself,
my instinct say don't worry cause,
you know there's bound to be bridges,
I may never cross.
Many of problems and thoughts,
I know one day will be solved.
Then I sit - think once again,
will my days sitting alone,
maybe one day hopefully end.
As I get up from my chair,
go outside to do some work,
run across a friend, have a friendly talk.
Still worrying and wondering,
maybe I'm doing something wrong,
God help me, I'm only so strong.

    Florence L. Hemple

Mystic Lucidity

Spinning, turning, in the air,
yelling, screaming, everywhere,
Tiny black dots invade my eyes,
my mind reflects on lingering lies.
The boy with the thorn in his side,
an old woman, stiff with pride.
The giants nightingale locked in a cage,
a pessimists mind, filled with rage.
A child finding its secret place
a murder committed without a trace.
The two young lovers, forbidden lust.
childish secrets made in trust,
Soldiers standing, tall and ready,
Jack and Jill, going steady.
A world full of cruel demands,
no one will ever understand.
Running, jumping, on the ground
shut my eyes and lay me down.
Silence slowly enveloping me
quietly watching, mystic lucidity.

    Dana Anderson

Town Trees

Silvery quaking aspen
Yellow twisting beech
Fluttering now and then
High above my reach.

Golden turning maples
White skeletal birch
Surround the horse's stables
About my family's church.

Deep russet red oak
Slimly hanging willows
Above roof's gray slate
Shifting with twiggy billows.

The dogwood no longer flowers
Here's the shedding hickory
There with leafy bowers
Covering where the child did play.

What can be more important to peace
And the whispering leafy worth
Than this town and favorite trees
Hometown and trees of my youth.

    James L. Norwood

Yesterday

Yesterday all was perfect
Yesterday all was clear
Yesterday I did not realize
What I had to fear.
I wish it could be yesterday
So I could right the wrong
And awake this dreadful morning
To a bright and sunny dawn.
But I must forget about yesterday
And concentrate on today
Look into the future
It's the only way
I know things happen for a reason
This one I just can't see
And oh, if it were yesterday
How wonderful things would be.
            Jody M. Cutler

Inside Me

The air is cool and crisp
Yet I feel warmth when he touches me.
The sky is clear and blue
Yet I see nothing in front of me
I'm standing in an open field
Yet I can't breathe
There is no one holding me
Yet I can't move
I can see your lips move
What are you saying
I feel your words
And the pain is to much to mention
Why must I stay here
Why can't I go
Where would I go to
I really don't know
            Deborah Lacoste

Pens

There are many things
    you and do,
You can make a happy
    or make me blue.

You could write a litter
    or even a song,
and when you're out
    you do wrong.

If your self-conceits
    I will know,
because this line
    will not flow.

But this poem
    is about,
something I know
    has no doubt.

    This here poem
is to my good friends,
    I give my hand
        to my pens.
            Belinda B. Cox

Ending

I ended
    you and I,
for we
    were
    so different,
yet so alike...
    Different,
    in our dreams:
You wanted
    endless now,
    and I
wanted us
    to be
    for always.
I ended
    you and I
because
    there was
    no hope.
            Elig Kay

Farewell

As time goes by with passing sigh
You and I say our sad good-bye
The fading remnants of our love
Flinches and flutters like a dying dove
with heart pierced and cruelly broke
by wicked arrow's barbed, harsh stroke

The feelings and times we warmly shared
harshly handled by no beast nor man
but that cold entity of life's sharp end
By life, my god, death be damned

As time goes by I begin to cry
the threshold of thy new home is nigh
Hidden from the comfort of daytime skies
Locked eternally in the cold, dark night
As delicate, pure spirit soars
to God's embrace at golden doors
leaving me to quietly mourn
the empty shell of your lifeless corpse
            Frank R. Sanchez

Your Smile

When I asked you,
You answered,
"Tranquilo" with a smile
Before you rushed off to
Disappear for a while.
When you returned
Your answer and smile
Were the same
And by the tone of your voice
I could tell
Nothing had changed.
You mention
Not a word of
Your young brother's death
And when you smile at me,
Is that all that is left?
            Gabriel Cohn

The Sea

The sea flows a certain way.
You can sit there or lay.
The salty water is
Where creatures die.
It's where birds
Can fly.
The sea has
Waves
And mysterious
Caves.
The sea is bitter
Because there is litter.
There were things you saw before
But not any more.
That's not my sea.
            Carnie Mondell

Connection

My senses are weak.
You distort my perceptions.
Still, I can see you
Through unclear visions.

My means seem useless
Against your questions.
Still, I find answers
Using vague definitions.

My place is unclear
You foresee my positions.
Still, I control destiny.
Beside lax directions.

My reality is simple
You provide dim connections.
Still, I will wait
For complete comprehension.
            Becka Tingle

You Are My Joie De Vivre

You invade my every thought,
You entice me with your spirit.
My heart gladdens with the
    thought of you.

You have made me aware of the
    beauties of life, by just
    being by my side.
You have ignited a spark in me,
    into a burning desire, that
I never thought possible.

I yearn for the moments when we
    can be together...
To see the tenderness in your eyes,
    and feel the gentleness of your
    touch.

You arouse in me a hunger that
    only you can satisfy,
A longing that has made me
    Forever yours.
            Adrienne J. Fayter

"Your Destiny"

You think you've made decisions-
You had a choice - let's see,
You really did exactly-
What was your destiny!

For the path you follow,
Is really what's in store,
Planned at birth for you,
Right to - death's - open - door!

Anger will not remedy,
A plan that goes astray,
Regardless - of what you thought,
It was meant to go - that way!

You cannot change the pattern,
For what will be - will be,
It's always there - beside you,
Your fate - your destiny,

So when you take that big step,
Undecided you may be,
But your instinct tells you,
This is your destiny!

Adeline Fleischer

Untitled

When you see a tear
You know something's wrong
Go try and comfort her
She needs someone strong

When you hear a tear
She's calling out to you
She needs a smile
And you can use one too

When you know there's a tear
Whether it shows or is receded
She's giving you a sign or two
To let you know that you are needed

When you hear a tear
When you see a tear
Let her know that you will be there
Hold her hand, hold her close
When you see, when you hear, when
   You know there's a tear.

Gina Greaux

It's Tough To Do Good

It's tough to be a good person,
   You know you try so hard.
They tell you that you need to do better,
   You know you really want to.
It's tough to be a good person,
   No one really knows what people
      go through everyday.
   You tell yourself I have to do
      right but somewhere in the
   middle of saying it and doing it,
      you do wrong.
   Everyone says it can't be that
      hard to do.
   If only they knew what you go
      through everyday.
   It's tough to be a good person,
      You know it really is.
   If only they would look deeper
      they would see I really am.

Amie Nalley

Does He love You?

The first time he holds you tight.
You think about him day and night.
He says he loves you more than
   anyone he knew.
And something in you says it's true.
Till the day he says "Goodbye."
Something in you wants to die.
The first you fall in love.
Then it's gone like a dove.
You keep on asking the question "why?"
Then all of a sudden you start to cry.
You don't know why you feel this way.
But something in you wants him to stay.
Something in you says "Please don't go!"
But deep inside you'll always know.
You'll love him forever and that is true.
But you'll always wonder,
   Does he love you?

Deanne Mullins

Break Free

Oh nurse, I didn't hear you
You were talking kind of low
Sitting here by myself
Just meditating, you know.
You said how did I get these scratches?
Well, I fell down the stairs
Something must have been in my eye
Probably a strand of hair.
And how did I get this bruise?
Right upon my back
Let's see, I don't remember
I'm not too sure about that.
Yes, I was in here last week
With a broken arm
The week before that, a broken ankle
But don't you get alarmed.
I'm just a clumsy person
Why can't you believe me, Nurse King?
"Because your finger is swollen and broken,
Underneath that wedding ring!"

Erika Herndon

Turning On The Lights

When you shut off the lights
You will see,
How fortunate we all must be.
When you shut off the lights
You don't know who's black or white,
You cannot judge what is wrong or right.
When you shut off the lights
Who's to know who's man or woman,
I say to you, "No one can."
When you shut off the lights
You will be guided without a fright.
No one will fight
When you shut off the lights
Because with all His might,
We will understand what is right!
Those of us who see the reality,
Hear the message to you from me.
When you shut off the lights
You are actually without a fear,
Turning on the lights to allow others to
   come near.

Apeer Oudeh

The Other Woman

If you put yourself in my shoes,
You wouldn't only hate it, you'd lose.
If you did you would know what I mean.
Only because I know, and have seen.

You go out every night.
It's not like I've lost my sight.
The little blonde calls,
And every night we break out into brawls.
If you stay, tell her goodbye,
And don't tell her I said hi!

I expect you to be home at eight.
Believe me you better not show up late!
Do I still matter to you,
Or am I being used?
Try putting yourself in my shoes.

Joni Tapley

Your Body

Of joyful flowers
Your brunette hair
Your loving black eyes
Your oval face
Your sun-tanned skin
Your mouth of ecstatic features
Your lynxlike breast
A juicy red paint
combination of romance and lust
Your Mount of Venus
like a tall apple
of seductive touch
Adorned with the garden
of joyful flowers
Red roses
where orgasm silence
breaks off
Close to the air of your virgin body
I felt overpowered.

Fausto Proano Lopez

Dark Thoughts

You stare into the darkness
Your mind begins to wander
The voices scream in terror
Mankind's deadly blunder.

The earth you did create
Life, the masterpiece
Death and untimely end
You laugh as you unmake.

Holding the earth in your hand
The ultimate fate
Holocaust and genocide
Remember, we all will die.

Time is at its end
The Gods cannot mend
Mankind's destruction.

Unto other worlds they will seek
The life and peace
We took for granted.

David S. Brooks

When Hope Walks Out The Door

When all the shadows cast upon
your only source of light,
you feel engulfed into a world
of cold and endless fright.

The tears will fall, the pain will throb,
but the worst is yet to come.
You'll never know how lost you are
until you cannot run.

But nothing leaves you so afraid
And nothing hurts you more,
than the helpless feeling that you get
when Hope walks out the door.

You find yourself trapped in a room
as empty as your heart.
And as you look for a hint of help
you begin to fall apart.

When you slam your fists against the wall
and it shatters to the floor,
you turn your head just in time
to see Hope walking out the door.

Jodi Kiely

Oh Beauty

Oh beauty of faithfulness.
Your presence has pleased me,
with such great delight.

Your love fills me with
great joy. Just feeling its
presence makes me feel so
great.

I never can get enough of
you, my love, because my
heart keeps asking of
more and more.

Jerry Massey

Eye Of Andrew

Eye of Andrew, cancerous and stark,
your shifting gaze muted and dark,
    we hear your piercing screams

Driving, soaring, swirling onward,
hurling earthbound objects skyward,
    blinding hopes drowning dreams.

Pounding, bending, breaking, crashing,
churning, crushing, twisting, thrashing,
    mocking, the strong and the frail.

Grasping, losing, holding, praying,
crouching, crawling, running, staying,
    we heard your savage wail.

Sounding the siren of despair,
stranding souls and hearts in terror,
    changing land and lives forever.

Arline Dishong

Untitled

Through Ice Quakes, Pot Holes and
Wintry Mix we have met.
You with eyes like the
Caribbean Sea
Pearlescent, green soft and warm
Like a painting I can only
See the Beauty that has been
Bestowed upon me.

Gerald L. Ruscitto

Hands

Your eyes may catch mine,
Your smile may brighten my days,
But let me see your hands.

Are they tender yet strong?
Do they know a loving touch?
Can they be firm yet gentle?

I may love to look into your eyes,
I may melt at your smile,
But your hands I will always remember.

Crystal Nichole Davis

No One Knows

Like the dew on a flower
your sweet face sparkles
but then, during the day
that sparkle fades
and goes where no one knows.

Like the sunset on a slightly cloudy day
the colors in your eyes marvel
and in a few minutes
the colors seem to fade
and go where no one knows.

Like the shining moon
your face lights up
but after the night leaves
the shine seems to wither
and it goes where no one knows.

Like a butterfly
your life soars
and after a deadly accident
your wings seem to crumble
and your life goes where no one knows.

Jennifer Chapman

Friends Are Forever

You're my friend,
You're the sister I always wanted.
    Now that you're gone,
You'll always be in my heart.
    Memories of us together,
Are all so dear.
    Just promise me you'll
Never forget my face.
    Remember that I'll always
Be here for you,
    No matter how far you go.
Friendship like ours are
    Meant to be forever.
Keep in touch, my friend.
    You'll never leave my heart.
20 years from now,
    I'll remember all we shared
Secrets, clothes and best of all love.
    You'll always be my
Very best friend.

Jennifer Lee

Terror

Terror in the streets,
    A place we used to be.
    Terror on our minds,
    As we walk the lines.
Terror so bad we go to school,
    carrying weapons
Hoping we won't be the next to meet
    The Wolf

Katherine J. Russell

Don't Do and Do

Don't worry about it

Don't fuss about it

Don't cuss about it

Don't lie about it

Don't drink about it

Don't fight about it

Don't smoke about it

Don't eat about it

Do... Pray about it

Cause Jesus will...

Do something about it

Viveca Grant

The Night Is Near

The leaves rustle in the breeze.
A bird in a nearby tree
is telling all the night is near.
Swans are drifting on
the waters edge.
The moon is coming,
the sun is going.

Leah Martinez

Hurt Feelings In A Grownup World

Secure
A blanket wrapped around my shoulders
Hugged to my breast
Warm, familiar.
Pervasive
Colors my view
Shapes my world.
My collection:
Carefully built
Painstakingly arranged.
Protected, nurtured.
My pains, my hurts.

Theresa Stockel

Archery

Holding in your hand;
A bow
Drawing back the string;
and slow.
Looking at the target's;
Bulls eye.
Then let go and see;
The arrow fly.
Did it touch the target center;
Dead
Did the center touch the arrow's;
Head.

Kaitlyn Dynes

Truth

I just want to reach out
    and hold someone's hand.
I want to know
    They care and will try to understand.
        Accept me for who I am,
        Not who they think I should become.
I just want to know
    That someone cares for me.

Lori Rose

Kosovo Lily

Oh! poor lily why are you so red?
Only blood were you fed.
You were only white,
Until they had that bloody fight.
It was the fault of the war.
Does it have to happen anymore?
But alas it happened three more times
And all the dead bodies laid silent like a
bunch of mimes.
We worked so hard,
But the Turks stood off guard.
Will we ever win the bloody war of our country?

Sonja Blazekovic

Quietness Of Love

The silence of the room was broken
Only by the warmth of each other's presence.

There is almost a reverence in the
Quietness of love.

An unending conversation is
Carried on in the depth
Of the unconscious.

And there is a time when an interruption
Of the spoken word has the
Startling effect of the sound of
Thunder!

Moments like this are precious
Because they are so few.

So let us not deny ourselves the
Treasures of love.

Russ Lindberg

Old Woman

She lays against the crippled window,
only thinking of her betrayal.

She will stay until the dawn of her light.
Her body melts as her strong, empty soul goes to rest.

Her entrance into a new birth will grow inside her.
She will turn not to begin but to end,
placed beside her lost love.

Megan Williams

Fragile

I've given my heart away before
Only to have it handed back to me in pieces.

I've given my love away before
Only to have it kicked away
like a pebble on the ground.

I promised myself I would never
ever give them away again.

Then I met you...
I'm giving you my heart
I'm giving you my love
They are fragile, handle them with care.

Vickie Holland

Little Girl

Hand sewn dolls with painted faces
open doors to her imaginary places.
Finger painted pictures express her imagination
with splatters of colorful creation.
Tattered teddy bear lies secluded by the wall,
after years of being tugged and hauled.
Pink bows and white lace,
springly little curls bouncing around her face.
Imaginary friends are invited for a pot of tea,
sipping into empty cups, enjoying the party.
Books telling tales of magical fairies,
with gumdrops and sugar coated berries.
Oh where, oh where, has my imagination gone?
It stays in the place where only a child belongs.

Tiffani Lee Branscum

Hurtful Words

Gradually the rumor starts
Opening ears and eyes
Slowly to secrets
Snowballing in a spiraling daze
Intriguing the minds of believers
Piercing like swords into and out of you from those,
pretending to be your friends.

Miranda Rosenberger

Sunrise

Is it opposite a moonrise?
Or a glorified sunset
Can you comprehend its repercussions?

In the wilderness of time the sun is old
But, who cares?
Can mankind live from sunrise to sunrise?
Or, from sunset to sunset.

A sunrise is a creation of the master
Creator of the heavens,
In a personal sense; who is your
Creator? To answer this is not an awesome task.
So, these few lines express the creation
Of a sunrise and its master.
The master of the task being; God.

Ross L. Shumer

It Might Be

It might be a stately Castle
Or a wondrous mansion, fair,
'Twould be no more than a woodshed
If my true love were not there.

It might be an ocean liner
Or a yacht so elegant and grand,
'Twould be no more than a rowboat
Without my love to hold my hand.

I might be the greatest president
Or, even a sovereign king
I would be no more than a peasant
Without the joy my love can bring.

I'll never be a president
But I know that I'm a king,
And the house where I live is a castle
When she's there to make my heart sing.

L. B. Strawn

Face In The Mirror

Are you satisfied with the face in your mirror?
Or do you wish for someone else's face in the mirror?

Is your face in the mirror shedding tears too often?
Or is it not crying at all, holding it all in?

Does your face in the mirror reflect happiness?
Or does it reveal nothing of the pain that lives inside?

Does your face in the mirror show love in your eyes?
Or is it only shattered dreams of the love you missed out on?

Is your face in the mirror silently begging for help?
Or is it trying to solve everything on its own?

Is there peace on your face in the mirror?
Or is it confused and uncertain about the world around you?

Who do you think you are trying to fool?
Your face in the mirror tells all of your secrets and dreams.

Nothing is as well hidden as you believe it is
Your face in the mirror will speak the truth even if you do not.

Sharon Ida

Crossroads

Suddenly I'm there, completely lost for words.
Or is it here, and I'm lost for reason.
So real the imagination; so gentle the touch.
So sad the weed shall never compare to the beautiful blades of
green.
Lonely this life stirring, mute words never spoken.
Wasted these feelings never shared.
Confused still, I seek,
Of what I'm not sure,
Only to fear that when I find it,
It shall be gone.

Virginia L. Bonham

What Is Love?

Is it just the emotions you feel within your heart?
Or is it the sexual desire you get right from the start?

Is it being understanding, honest and true?
Or being alone and feeling so blue?

Could it be the desire whenever you meet?
Or is it the let down of defeat?

Is it the laughter of two people and the fun?
That follows when "Love" has just begun.

Or it is a feeling you get within your heart?
Of so much devotion and emotion right from the start.

Is it what passion you feel when you kiss?
And your deep feeling of that heavenly bliss.

Or is it the happiness that two people share?
Knowing that being together, you are the right pair.

Is it having deep emotions and feelings so true?
When you whisper softly the words "I love you".

So stop for a moment and think along with me,
That love is all these things combined and you will agree.

Love does put you in a tailspin or two,
Especially, when you say with deep emotion, "I love you".

Louise J. D'Amato

Our Face

In cold weather we dress ourselves in fur
Or warm clothing-as we prefer
Our bodies covered to keep us warm,
Keeping our feet, heads, hands, ears from harm

What about our 'lil'ole face?
It's exposed to winter weather's disgrace.
Those features, makes a face so fine
All molded into an artful design.

Does it think, does it have a brain?
Does it wonder if this is humane?
Does it ever feel irate?
Does it think we discriminate?

Through wind, rain, snow, and cold,
Our face stands out there, oh so bold!
Those eyes, that nose, that mouth, that chin
Some very feminine, some very masculine.

It survives, I do declare
Make amends-we have no spare
That precious face, which we don't clad-
Keep it happy and not sad.

Viola Taffi Cirillo

Starting Over

If I could start over, would I change my current life
Or would I choose to travel the same path once again
Would I choose a life free from daily routine and strife
Not experiencing life's disappointment and pain.

Can we be truly whole without the ups and downs
Do we appreciate the good not knowing of the bad
Can we enjoy the smiles without some of the frowns
Do we know true happiness if we've never been sad.

If I changed my life could I continue to live
I'd be giving up too much I fear
My family and loved ones I could not give
They're the basis of all I hold dear.

So when we say we'd like to make a new start
And daydream of all the good things
We must realize from what we depart
And all the disappointments it brings.

We must think twice before we wish away
Our daily routines, the taking, the giving
We should try to retain and keep each day
Because today is surely worth living.

Laura Wilson

Insatiable

When others want it, god gets it.
Others get it, when god wants it.
When the ruler lives, society wants death.
The ruler dies, when society's for life.
When beings give, minds will receive.
Minds give, when beings won't receive it.
When spirits fly, people are grounded.
Spirits stand, when people are too high.
When free-thinkers awake, conformists sleep.
Free-thinkers are tired, when conformist trip.
When hunger's thirsty, hunger drinks.
Thirsty's hungry, when it will let you wait.
When the deliverer's gone, all are around.
The deliverer's done, when all is gone.

Karen Herman

Liberty To Us To Them

Some come and are accepted,
Others return home rejected,
All needing, wanting, to be free,
When they come upon us from the sea.

They see the statue looking over us,
And hope they soon will be free,
Will soon be like you or me.

Walking down the street we take for granted,
What we have,
They see us and frown for they have,
never known freedom,
Only pain, hunger, and discrimination,
all their lives.

Freedom to them is just a dream,
One that will probably never come true,
To us, a birthright and usually nothing,
else more, there is so much we take for granted.
So much we don't truly
appreciate.

Mindi Ice

Chocolate

So deep and rich as we all know
Our cravings are strong for it
But we try not to show
How we all love it so much
We would truly go to such lengths
To obtain some whether deep dark
Or creamy white fudge like snow
Delicious ripened strawberries dipped in it
Cakes filled with it so lusciously
Brownies topped with it not sparingly
It's like romance so totally
Satisfying and bold
No copy cat to imitate such
Rich stuff as chocolate
to hope for it to long for it
to smack our lips with glee
Our total wish is to receive a box
On our wedding anniversary

Sandra Lee O'Farrell

In The Year 2000: An Anticipation And A Prayer

In the year 2000, loom the 21st century and its gate
Our earth, our Island, unfailing in its journey, lone in its fate.

Challenges on time eternal, whereas I..., a mortal
Would have lived a thousand lives and died a thousand deaths...

For my dream power so thrives,
    that I dreamed up other lives in a breath!

Just as my human shortcomings and fears
Have killed me a thousand times through the years
But I have walked the pristine shore
Of an old, dear and faraway country of yore
I have walked the streets of dejection
Of the City of Light, the Paris of Celebration,
To come here and sob, fitfully and unabashedly
Tears of joy and hope, at the munificent American Democracy
And if my tears of joy may parallel your tears of pain
And my new days of sunshine still be your old days of rain
How little you know, this joy is but in my heart, this hope in my mind
    and prayers are on my lips.
My fellow in suffering, lean on my frail shoulder
Together, for you, for me, for the earth we'll crescendo a prayer...

Mac Loan Linh

A Familiar Face

You look so familiar, we must have met somewhere before.
Our hair is styled exactly the same, but you have that gray in yours.
Your cheeks are chubby too, like mine, and we have that same dimple
    there.
We could pass for twins if you were young, (or if I had wrinkles
    everywhere).
Those dark circles under your eyes; you've had many sleepless nights.
You probably won't believe this, but amazingly, so have I.
At my age though, that sort of thing doesn't seem to show.
You know how we young girls are; forever on the go!
If ever I get another chance, to just sit and rest,
I'll come back here, so we can talk again; In front of the looking
    glass.

Linda Kay Acton

"The Way It Soon Will Be"

As the years start to fade away.
Our memories will become short.
The times we shared together we
will no longer share.
The faces of each other that we
remember will become fuzzy.
Are hearts will try to let go and forget.
Our love will lock itself away in our hearts.
There will be nights we long to find each other.
Nights that we will look at the stars and wonder.
Wonder what happened to each other.
Times where tears will come to the eye and slowly fall.
Times we wish we could spend one last day together.
We will regret the way we treated each other.
Soon everything will become fuzzy,
we will no longer remember each other.
Times will change, as the years fade away.
We will become strangers to one another.
We will soon forget each other and
go on with what life holds for us.

Mandi Campbell

What's Happening To Our Children

When I was growing up it was okay to be outside alone,
Our mother would check on us out the window of our home.
Now that I've grown up I've three children of my own,
But I could never consider leaving them outside all alone.
I've found raising children in the nineties isn't easy to do,
You try and give them the space they need and it's scaring you.
Kids are being abducted at rates that are soaring high,
The children are usually never found the parents only cry.
Everyone thinks their children won't take to someone they don't know,
But most of the so called strangers make it easy to get them to go.
We must truly stop these statistics from getting out of hand,
Every parent in the world must truly take a stand.
So think about it closely when you allow your children to roam,
Will they be there when they are supposed to be coming home.

Michele A. Rush

"Memories"

Remember me and the fun we had...
Remember the good and look over the bad!
Remember I'll always love you, but never the same...
Remember my happy face, but forget my name!
Remember the days when time stood still...
Remember how much I cared, because I always will!

Rena Andraschko

The Beautiful Red Bush

I traded city life for one in the country instead.
Out walking, I spied a gorgeous bush of scarlet red.
I could just pictured in my mind's case.
Some of those red branches in my gold vase.
I broke off a few branches in great haste.
Took them home and arranged them in my gold vase.
While I was admiring, one branch seemed to twitch.
All at once my whole body began to itch.
I took a hot shower and to my surprise.
I had two big puffs, no eyes.
My face was so round and in full blush.
I rushed to the doctor, 'oh! he said, been out in the brush?'
"Oh! yes" I confessed, I told of the branches and vase.
"Yes he said, I can see the tell-tale marks on your face."
"God has made a mass of beauty for us to behold, his voice
low when he spoke."
The doctor smiling, thinking, spreading calamine in strokes.
"Know, God with all his wonderful works, must of taken
time out for a little joke.
To taunt us with such beauty as the bush of poison Oak."

Maurine Chlovis Johnson

Broken Wings

Inside I am a child who cannot mend a broken wing.
Outside, I try to teach my heart to sing, and fly.
and I will remember what you told and taught.

Michelle Fahmy

Shards Of Life

They're back, they live again this frigid day,
outside my window to the woods, small shards
of shimmering, glittering icicles
like spectroscopic jewelry, clusters
of icicled stars, sunlight glints of light
clinging to twigs of oak and dogwood trees.

Are such images mentors to meaning;
like a smile of affection from your love,
like a key that opens a rigid mind,
like a dreamer's view of symbols for change,
like breezes moving pines and stirring oaks
or stately steeples fingering the sky.
Are these all paradigms that point the way
to visions which may never be attained?

Walter Harvey

Ancestral Gravesite

From a gravesite high up on a hill,
Overlooking green fields far below,
One can see for miles across the valley,
And though the mists of the years.

At this distance, unchanged through time,
All appears as it was long ago,
When those now under the earth stood upon it,
And gazed at this view which we share.

Looking deeply in the eyes of a loved one,
Then staring down at the grave mound,
And out at this timeless scene,
One can see from whence she came,
And only now begin to understand,
The serenity of her soul.

Michael L. Derewitz

Inside Out

That was the memorable date, when I was privileged, to view, see.
Part of my wife, that I'd never before. In the hospital. The echo
machine. The lady therapist. Mrs. Hanneman. Placed gizmos, on
her body. And bingo! There was my wife's heart. Pulsating on the
TV screen. A dark, blob, the four lobes, plain. The aorta
opening and closing. Pumping blood, through the veins. Various
flashes of color, the blood. And now and then. Even the sound of
the heart beat.

Now: If my father, who's been dead, almost sixty-four years
were alive. Why, it'd blow his mind. My! All of the modern
miracles. medicinal, scientific. You name it. But: Alas! Man,
hasn't benefited. To the degree he should have. And could have.
If, he would "shape up". And act, conduct himself. Like God
hoped. When he created, made. The First Man. But wouldn't you
know it?
In almost Two Thousand Years! Man seems to prefer. The description.
"one, who also ran."

Merlin Gealow

Quiet Passion

Quietly you watch me. Silently you yearn.
Patiently you tolerate. Passionately you burn.

Like a candle flickering in the dark; you light my world each day.
And when the hurt comes over me, you know just what to say.

Fierce, as an army of lovers, that no man could defeat,
Yet oh so gentle is your love and tender kisses, sweet.

I love you, Quiet Passion, let there never be a doubt.
I've locked your love inside my soul, so it can not get out.

Let me be your prisoner, throw the key away.
I want to be your only love, with you I'll always stay.

Take me everywhere you go, show me all you see.
Tell me all your secrets, and share this life with me.
I promise that I'll love you, for all eternity.

And when the angels come for me, please touch my trembling hand.
So I can feel you, Quiet Passion, before the promise land.
For now, I know my destiny and understand my life
… Forever…I'm your soul mate, your lover, and your wife.

Lynn Williams

On Living Alone: Parts 1 & 2

Sexual indiscretion: driving to an amusement park
paying for parking, paying for admission
buying a ticket, riding the roller coaster once
going home
sexual discretion:
lingering in front of shop windows,
sampling the flavors, sleeping - sand on my cheek
pulling a bulky sweater over my knees
anticipating sunrise
On Living Alone: Part Two
Sexual discrimination:
what's a nice girl like you
doing in a place like this?
same as a sleazy guy like you -
chumming and trawlin'
discriminating sex:
when the stillness that follows sundown
is broken by Canadian geese -
standing barefoot in last summer's leaves
until they are out of earshot

Nancy L. Duffy

Womanchild

Tears of sadness, incredible sadness
penetrating, overwhelming sadness
and joy.
joy and love for a 90 year old spirit
living inside a 90 year old body.
love and sadness - I don't know why so much sadness-

The room is still, quiet, slow.
down the hallway in a soft, low voice a woman sings:
"bless-ed jeee-sus, bless-ed jeee-sus"
the words float into the quiet stillness- pass by.
tears well, find their way down my face.
"I've had a good life" she says, "life is a storybook.
How is your family? are you Vicky?

I am humbled and honored by her presence.
"I don't know why they think I am so great" she says.
"Because you are great" I say,
tears streaming down my face, eyes burning.
We hug - gently (she is frail) - I don't want to let go.
I love you.

Vicky Follansbee

Nature

Nature has many beautiful aspects,
people should treat it with great respect.
Nature has many wonders,
Rain, storm, and sometime great thunder.
Nature is not grand anymore,
People have polluted Nature's floor.
The ocean has been done most harm,
the world should be in great alarm.
Nature's animals are fading away,
All because of humans careless ways.
The world will burn in the sun's great heat,
Because the ozone has begun to deplete.
We need to Recycle, Reuse, and Renew,
Then the world's trash would be less than a few.
People polluted Nature's air, ocean, and land,
It is about time we lend a hand,
To save the Earth from natural disaster,
So the world will not deplete any faster.

Nancy Luong

Hide And Seek

Everyone with their logs, saying, and sings.
Petition to save this and save that.
They tell the little children it will ne ok,
And then they turn away.
It's like a game of hide and seek.
You hide and I'll look.
Grab the bottle and guzzle it down,
Smoke some chronic when you're down,
Sniff some coke to wake you up.
Ready or not hare I come.
Run away run away and don't come back,
Don't be yourself what ever you do,
Because then some might laugh at you.
I found you hiding in the dark.
Run I'm coming after you,
Here comes daddy with his belt,
Mamma says you have to be perfect,
So stick that finger down your throat,
Now you're safe you're on goal.
Then take the vodka and take the sleeping pills.

Sara Peterson

Friendship

When friendship shines its bold and radiant sky,
Platonic seas of love and trust react.
To bridge the gap of wondering and why,
The lens between the wishes and the facts.
The fire of friendship burns within our souls.
To give and take, igniters feed the flame,
And share the joy, the light, the heat, the toll.
Like fire, the souls of men must too be tamed.
Angelic hosts will comfort friends in need,
With magic music easing mourning moods.
The spring of friendship coils to guard with heed,
Platonic loves never misconstrued.
A friend will touch the fire and share the shame,
With trust and unity to share the blame.

Kurtlee A. Clemmons

Staying Together

For apart are you and I,
Please don't ever think I'm with another guy,
For I am yours forever and ever.
We will always belong together,
We will last along time.
If only we both stay strong.
It may be hard,
But If we really love each other
We'll be where we both belong.
No, matter what anyone says, it's up to us
But in this relationship there is something we both
    need more of.
Which is trust
I'll love with all my heart and soul
But your heart you must control.
So, see now it's up you,
It's up to you to say if our love will continue to
follow through in which I must hope it does.
If it doesn't, I don't know what I'll do, but I know one thing.
I'll always love you!

Shelly Mesa

Set Me Free Lord

Lord you have set the captives free
Please take my hand and do it for me,
Turn me around and set me straight
Help me to change before it's too late.

Nothing now matters here on earth
I've lived my life freely ever since birth,
Now I am wiser and offer my hand
Teach me oh Lord how to walk in your plan.

I know it's not simple, I've a lot to learn
But I'll do my best Lord and try hard to earn,
Your pardon and forgiveness, your protection and your love
So I can feel the warmth that comes only from above.

Open my eyes so I can see
And my ears to hear what I should be,
Open my mind to help those in need
And my heart to forgive as you've done for me.

Velma A. Minso

Columbus

As Christopher Columbus felt his keel
Ploughing the water, saw his every sail
Belly with wind, he heard the triumphant peal
Of land birds, and learning over his ship's rail,
Sighting that white cliff in the mist, he wept.

His father's woolen looms had never woven
So soft a carpet that his mother swept
As this grey strand the glancing surf rolled over.

First of all men, he deemed that he had proven
The roundness of his mother earth, and found
Her unending mercy in that ground.

Mary M. Morabito

A Flowers Dream

Thoughts of you array a paradise to me
possession, obsession, only the lust did I see
my death for a flower to my kind would seem vain
my death without you is no remedy to my pain
love is forever, eternal, so yours I use as a motive
without you, lost, my heart, my mind, broken.
A prick from a rose for its beauty to admire.
so I give blood, life to my desire
a princess she is worshipped, each step every breath
I but a peasant to the prince as yourself.
A flower's dream is to live upon, atop,
a rocky mountain high aloft
as all may admire my beauty as my grasp of you
but only to hold, breathe, live, I long for you.
Not one crosses mountainous cliffs to retrieve
death to try, safe is only to see
us the flower, who grew where none may touch
yet I am the weed in your royal garden,
discard me, as such.

Leanne Conn

The Opossum

The opossum, white beast immemorial,
prefers living in quarters arboreal.
She can hang from a rail by her prehensile tail,
and she carries her kiddies corporeal.

She belongs of the genus marsupial,
and in slow locomotion quadrupedal
she walks with a slouch, for the weight in her pouch
hunts her back, 'though her smile is inscrutable.

Enigmatically still as a sphinx,
she just dozes, inverted, and thinks;
then emerges by night for by day she's a fright,
and her breath is so fetid, it stinks!

Richard S. Grigsby

The Unicorn

  Along the sea I saw her dancing. She was
prettier than I ever imagined she could be. Her
hair, white as snow, was shining like the moon.
Her voice reminded me of rainbows in the sky and
butterflies in green pastures. One look at her
and my soul filled with love. She is my heart,
my all. She stood still watching me, never
moving. I called out her name, she sang with
the voice of Angels, that I knew her. I
whispered that I knew her and that I would
always know her, forever. She smiled with her
horn glowing and galloped down the shore. My
smile never faded as I watched her go, even when
I could no longer see her, I knew that she was
still with me in my heart.

Kristy Hall

One More Try

Here we go again,
Promising ourselves just one more try
We both know way down deep
There'll come a day, when we'll say goodbye

So we draw up new Landscapes
With hopes of big strong walls
While we walk with little comfort
Through our much to shaky halls.

We dream of a sturdy foundation
With lots of windows to see our way
High up on top of the world Wall papering promises that never
stay. The rains have made the soil soft
And trust has made for empty rooms Yet we dream of such true
happiness. As the flowers we plant never bloom

Our wastebaskets about to overflow with sketches of a brand
new way but the clouds never seem to disappear,
As our tomorrows become today
So listen, to the quiet before the storm
And lets not reach so high, the world wont stop turning
If we don't give it... just one more try!

Penny Swift

Let Us Redefine Ourselves

As a Nation, let us learn one language,
Pure and simple, well-spoken to be clear.
Americans care for others,
We all need space to learn and live.
Respect property and life,
Admire and love the family.
Life is a gift so precious...
Outlaw rumor, live by Truth,
With mercy for thy neighbor.
We strive for learning to control our lives.
Conscience must be the guide within.
May we affirm the values
Americans have lived.

Mary K. Dissinger

Untitled

Every now and then I find time to
put a lyric of poem verse down.
  Just for the sake of getting around
because I have an idea where destiny is bound
  So when I am detail oriented
about figuring out the life surrounding me
  I am more confident in myself in
how to get around and I am more
spirited free.
To the very facts of feeling the vibes
My life is my rhythm that I keep alive.
so let me present the picture to you
that I have visioned
So that you can be on the same
intellectual course of collision
  Now you and I have the sight of
a created architect.
And your every and each project is
equal to the best one I've seen yet.

Rene L. Jones

Viking Land USA

Big Ole and his Viking shipmates left their homes and
sailed the high seas in their westward journey to their new home,
Alexandria, Minnesota, USA, birthplace of America.

When in the twilight hours the call of the loon echoes across its sky-
blue waters and majestic woodlands, that's when I, an Alexandrian, am
proud that this is my home.

Vernon J. Wigdahl

Mount Union Church Hidden In The Hills Of W. VA.

Fond childhood memories come
racing through my mind:
of a gentler generation
and a kinder age of time.
I remember all day preaching
and dinner on the ground.
Folks would come hill and hollow
and places all around.
Carefree days of childhood
of a white framed house of God.
Of Bible School, and Sunday School,
Appreciation, encouragement, and applause.
The church has long been vacant
It stands in ruin and decay.
I wonder, Oh! I wonder
if the Spirit too has gone away.
The shame should be upon us
who let that small church die.
For with it goes our childhood,
and it saddens and makes me cry.

Karen Sue Miller Hatfield

Home Alone

In the mist of this worlds evil darkness
Radiates a converted, loving, sacred stone
A heart of devout faith as solid as a rock
A spirit that is never left, home alone.

Among the flowers of her idolizing heart
Blossoms a beautiful, profound, angelic place;
The hedge of her master's loving redemption
Shelters the haven from the beguiling evil face.

Tenderly calling out to the troubled spirits
Languishing home alone outside the loving hedge
Yearning for deliverance of their lost mournful souls
That's drifting on the peril of iniquities jagged edge.

Release your heavy burdens into Gods loving hands
Enter this heavenly sanctuary, is her constant plea;
Come and receive the glory of loving salvation
Sing and rejoice behind this fortress wall with me.

Nina Ruffner

Submerged Galleon

Heavenly notes melodized by angels,
raindrops depicting effulgent rainbows,
astonishing beauty impregnating my whole being,
and indelible amativeness overfilling
a despaired heart with exhilaration.
My whole being immersed in the ravishment of your entity...!
The anguish of the sealed ports of my heart,
vulnerable to the uttering of the loving expressions
of a despondently forbidden soul...!
My insensible flesh,
anesthesized by the puissance of a fathomless love,
shivers with fervent passion,
and impressively diaphanous tenderness
with your unintended closeness.
The darkness and exhaustion of my imprisoned soul
scintillates and respires reposefully
in the disperse seconds of love,
that you altruistically regale my soul.
Regrettably, you're the involuntary captain of a submerged galleon
that requires your inner subtle expertise
to drift from the often tenebrous Neptune's kingdom.

Nelly Linares

Restless Heart, Un-sound Mind

A restless heart makes an un-sound mind.
Refusing to see leads you through life blind.

A heart that roams
is one that never finds a home.

One who does not use their mind for reason
There is a person there is no pleasin'.

A heart and mind that is pure selfish
Will always be the first to parish.

An unforgiving soul will always be without.
An un-sound mind is always filled with doubt.

A person who wishes for death
is one filled with regret.

A mind and hand that writes these things down
is one who is lost waiting to be found.

Stephanie Ann Kinzel

Time's Perverse Ways

Time floats along like a light, capricious feather;
regardless of troubles, regardless of weather.
Never a second does it stop to pause,
or give of its power to help a lost cause.
Many's the day it's been begged not to fly
but ignoring the plea, it just shot right on by;
taking along with it the dreams of our youth,
our hopes and our fears, dark moments of truth.
And in its wake came new troubles to face;
the cry of a child, new lines on a face.
Sometimes it seems life is a race with no end:
just reaching a goal to start over again.
But mayhap there is justice in time after all?
For it always slows down when the axe starts to fall.

Linda Shorter Cross

Foster Love

He came to us
regurgitated by a sightless society
An unpolished pearl
in the shameless sea of indicted pulp
He was beaten, broken and abandoned.
Manner vacant, remedially denied,
he violated our heart and home.
His frothing deep black pools
mirrored his barbaric ancestry.
Brandishing full girth and shield
he stood alone against all.

Slowly, once buried, budding abilities brim
and stature straightens.
To shuck the armor, to open the barrier.

Fearing the biological umbilical bond.
We now assume the guard and stand against all,
to fiercely protect our fostered pride.
Knowing full well
separation is a heartbeat near.

Kathi Wilder

Dreams

Dark are they, as we experience their power
Riveting displays throughout the night's hour
Edgar Allen Poe, then often comes to mind
Accounts we vaguely remember & struggle just to find
Meaningless images dart around & in & out
Stillness fills our bodies as our minds dance about

Kory Davidson

"I Know You're Out There Somewhere"

I've been searching forever and a day,
Regretting that our friendship has went astray.
Missing you more than ever before,
Now and forever, there will always be an open door.
Someday I'll find you and be sure to let you know,
How much I appreciate you helping me to live and grow.
A true friend you'll always be,
Never once did you doubt me.
I'll find you someday and then you'll
know how much I care,
Because I know you're out there somewhere.

Kris M. Slusarski

Remember

Remember the love of the father and the grace so freely bestowed.
Remember he feedeth the sparrow, and the lily in the splendor he grows.
Remember the love for his children, he lifts up the one who is down.
Remember we're promised the city, a harp, a garment, a crown
A city of beauty and splendor,
a street that is paved with pure gold,
a seat at the Lord's supper table, and
a special place in his fold.
Remember he's coming to get us,
that where he is we may be,
to dwell in the city eternal,
on the banks of a crystal-like sea.

Lawrence Durfee

Tub Talk

Here, I again sit, in a hot tub of lotion,
Remembering your every action
With a sweet kind of frustrations.
I imagine you, and all your splendid attractions,
As your biceps, moved into actions,
Causing me great satisfaction,
I can almost feel the motion.
Along with the hot water reactions,
I love my hallucinations,
For, they bring to life, all the sweet emotions.
Also, they remind me, of my wonderful obligation,
Which leaves me no room, for hesitation,
It will always be "No", to any other kind of relation.
For, your sweet memories feed,
All of my wants and needs,
You've planted those wonderful seeds,
Now, "My Love", they grow strong within me!

Karla Poling

The Love That Never Was

Night has fallen, and I stand here alone
Reminiscing, frozen in a time of my own
Without a care, you brought me pain
Reasons why, what did you hope to gain?
You'll never know how you hurt me so
I won't forget, you made me feel so low
A bolt of lightening strikes through the sky
The shattering of my heart, it's all been a lie
The crashing of raging waves at sea
Drowning in despair, someone rescue me
Glass breaks inside my body, I can no longer feel
Seasons pass slowly, will my wounds heal?
I scream out into the darkness, but there is nobody there
Is it too much to ask for, someone to care?
A victim of the fire that is burning my face
Flickering flames lure me into their deadly embrace
I will never have you, warm tears roll in defeat
Rejection is true sorrow, I must now retreat
My fate is undecided, what does the future hold?
I pray for great happiness and peace to unfold.

Sama Yateem

Slipping Away

She is my first true love. A love no one can ever
replace. A mother's love.
As I grew she was always there to give me a helping
hand when I stumbled in life.
She helped me see when things weren't clear, she gave
me joy in times of despair.
From a child I held tightly to her apron strings as
she guided me through this world.
Her quick pace has now become a crawl. I fear she is
reaching the end of her journey and I will have to go
on without her.
I am sadden by this thought. My heart cries out
"She's Slipping Away".
In despair I look down and I see what is to be my children
and grandchildren clutching to my apron strings.
I suddenly understand all the things she was trying to teach
me. I have to go on and lead the way for the children of
tomorrow. I have to teach them about love, give them guidance,
try to show them the way.
Until it's my time to slip away.

Margaret A. York

Humane

Can you devote your life to others? Give and expect nothing in
return. Show compassion, love, and caring, to whom it may
concern. Can you help teach the illiterate, how to read and
write. Giving them a realm of possibilities to explore through
out their lives. Can you help care for the elderly, whose
voice cries out so weak. Hold their hand and talk to them,
while they fall asleep. Can you extend a helping hand, to the
blind, to the help lead their way. Show kindness, sympathy,
and mercy, to the homeless who have gone astray. Can you help
feed the hungry children, whose eyes do not cry, but ask for
reassurance that you will not let them die. Can you take care
of the sick, who feel they have no place. Sit and comfort the
dying, by putting a smile upon their face. I ask again, can
you be selfless, knowing there is no fame. Can you with
absolute certainty say, that you can be humane.

Lucy J. Seabreeze

Spring

Spring is fraught with devious pleasure
Revealed - once concealed as winter's treasure
Rebirth! Rejoice! rescind all care
Trapped by spring's elusive snare
Warm days command you, "Laze and Wonder"
Cool nights allow you time to ponder
Tasks undone and chores still mounting
As we gaze and amble through spring abounding
With sights and scents of life reclaimed
Ahh!! spring, the season that won't be tamed.

Richard D. Davis

My Dream

In my dream there is love and
romance, happiness and joy.
There are beautiful lands, mountains
reaching to the sky, and endless seas of ocean blue.
Deer are free to roam the open land,
seagulls soar high above the ocean sand,
and waves crash upon the shore.
In my dream there is no sick, no death,
no hate, and no war.
In this dream that I love so much
you will find a new world to share.

Kristin Hughes

The Ocean

Hark! to the force upon the world, relentless as it creeps;
Rolling on its wayward course, stirring all the deep; never
pausing as it rushes, sweeping all things aside; man's ally or
enemy, or is it nature's bridge? Lo! onward in its movement,
gathering as it goes; momentum building silently, tossing to
and fro; lapping at shore and rock, transforming everything;
the destruction of its rage, belies the mercy of its being.

Behold! though men have dared its consequence, poor fools all died;
Drifting with its nowhere course, to which they must
abide; rendering the futility, to tamper with its power; the
mystery of its pounding, never lost upon the hour. O cheater!
resting in its cellar, treasures in quiet array; taken from
the hordes of men, of which none had a say; sunken hulls and
memoirs, decaying in the deep; lost among sad farewells, from
the countless fast asleep. Aye! spontaneous to wind and
moon, willing to be led; tenacious in its vice-grip, never

giving up the dead; wiping clean the scourges of mankind,
perpetual in motion; nature's perennial tour de force, the
good evil, rebellious ocean.

Richard H. Leighton

The Way To A Human's Heart

Hot Mexican Bean Dip, Salmon Party Log,
Rosy Pickled Eggs, and Tuna Fish Pate;
Leek Lorraine, Oysters Rockefeller,
Guacamole, Little Pizzas, and Braunschweiger Glacé.

French Vichyssoise, Manhattan Clam Chowder,
Hot Russian Borscht and Jellied Consomme,
Creole Crab Bisque, Split Pea Royale,
and good ol' Cock-a-leekie soup eaten anytime of day.

Irish Beef Stew, Meatballs-Sweet and Sour,
Spareribs Cantonese, and Egg Foo Yong,
Veal Parmigiana, Lamb-Shish-Kabobs,
Chicken Kiev, and Shrimp de Jonghe.

Cherries Jubilée, Lemon Meringue Pie,
Tutti-Frutti Tortoni, and Crème Brulee;
Strawberry Shortcake, Chocolate Eclairs,
Pear and Apple Betty, and Raspberry Bombé.

Cook and enjoy, and revel
in making the tempters above;
'Cause Food is Love,
    Food is Love!

Rose Shanen Rovins

Poem To Winter

No one sings a song to winter and very few
salute it with warmth as it's done to springtime,
Nature leaves its womb in a wise recess,
the squirrels hide, the swallows emigrate.

This morning looking through my window,
I see that last night, like tufts of ermine,
the snow silently fell upon the countryside
covering the landscape as a mantle of cotton.

Inside, you and I are together next to the chimney;
on your gentle lap I am resting
while you read verses of loves and passions
that a bard once wrote one winter night.

It is cold out there, but what do I care
if I carry the warmth of your love in my soul?
the winter that freezes is maybe in the souls
of those poor individuals that do not give or take.

That the winter is cold, that the winter is cruel?
Brothers, let's extend our warm blankets
of wool and affection, of love and friendship
to those that do not have the means to cover their winter

Leonora De Marmolejo

Our Spinning World

System within system, this land;
Rules created by you and me.
Evil within evil, spinning out of control in some
mad, invisible pattern of color; yet visible all the same.

Corrupt government, "of the people and by the people"
In this hell, we see the results quite well.
Where is truth, goodness or peace, within this mass for
   the working class?
Engulfing all, the "system" forms a spinning array of colors.
We see a living, breathing calliope of hopelessness.

A swirl of blue, our innocence soon lost amid the
   green of money, greed untold.
A band of grey, thick with mass despair of the poor,
   accepted by the rich.
Melting into all, a bright red, blood shed by the Victims
   of hate and greed.
And its final throes we see a thinning patch of
   yellow.
One small hope, the Gods of power have given us this
one bright splash, so well think there is a
   chance for change.
Thus we strive on - and keep the system
spinning and spinning and spinning.

Marian Ressler

The Untamed Heart

The untamed heart,
Runs faster than the wind,
Those who try to catch it, get trapped within.
The untamed heart,
Always thinks it's ready for love,
In reality though,
Love is the one thing it is afraid of
For it searches in hopes to find,
   the other wild heart ready to intertwine.
When it captures that heart in motion,
   their love runs deeper than the oceans.
But the untamed heart, never stays involved
   for too long.
Never gives into loves demands,
Never holds its love by the hands.
They always stay distant, never make promises,
But seem quite persistent.
The untamed heart,
Will leave in time, for it's searching for the one thing,
It will never find, perfection.

Kathryn Aileen Judge

Birds Of The Cliff

"See there on the cliff."
   said father to me.
"See the birds soar and play."

And I saw...

Grace to take my breath away.
They rode the wind as if on roller coaster rails of air.
Diving, rolling, falling,
   only to spread their mighty wings
and pull the reign which bridle the drafts.

Up, up, up they spiral,
Sun glinting on their eyes
as soft snow flakes swirl
   at their passing,
   only to fall...
   again.

Kevin Callahan

"I Know You"

You have crept into my mind once again.
Sanity, I have none.
I feel as though my insides are being torn apart.
That I am about to explode.
Ripping at my very being and existence.

You not knowingly have sought me and found me.
You have entered into places within me no one has ever known.
And I gladly let you in.
Wanting this feeling you give to me.
Not wondering why I choose to.
Only knowing I need you.

You may hide yourself at times, but you are always there.
Waiting to engulf my very soul.
Who, what are you?
I know, for only I can know,
You are my own true feelings of desire.

  Wanda J. Hickey

On Remembering

When I am old I shall remember:

  Crickets chirping in the dusty grass beside the road
  Sapphire studded blue that spilled its load
  Of stardust at my feet.

I shall cherish:

  The pungent smell of autumn leaves that drifted
  In the damp, mysterious night and gently sifted
  Through clean white curtains.

I shall remember:

  Candlelight, crystal glass and shadows on the wall
  Burnished tapers, copper-bright, standing straight
  and tall

  Like sentinels in the night.

  Mary Elizabeth Mills

A Christmas Poem

  On Christmas eve, snowing hard, little
Sarah made a Christmas card. She made it with love,
she made it with care, in hopes that St. Nicholas soon
would be there. She hung her stocking by the fireplace,
and then went to bed with a smiley face. Little Sarah
fell asleep, counting one after two, counting her sheep. All of
a sudden, upon the roof she heard a giggle or two and
some reindeer hooves. She tiptoed down the stairs, just to
see who was there. She saw a chubby guy in a big red suit,
with a black belt and boots, he looked kinda cute. He put the
presents all on the floor, then snapped his fingers and
flew out the door. Sarah went back to sleep, counting
one after two, counting her sheep. When Sarah woke up
that very morning, her parents were up having some
coffee. She opened her presents laughing with glee, "My
parents didn't know St. Nick was with me."

  Megan Alexion

Harvest Moon

Oh harvest moon see you what I see?
See you the maiden hidden at the base of the oak tree?
Why hides she there?
What has she to fear?
Why sings she a sad song, but sheds not a tear?
Is it for lost love
or pains she must bear
that she hides from your rays which reflect off her hair?
Then answer me this, oh harvest moon,
why sings the maiden her sad little tune?

  Lisa Wallace

Grief

My grief is buried deep inside
Sealed tight in a space
Both narrow and wide
The pain in my heart keeps growing and growing
Relief will come surely when
Tears start flowing
Fingerprints of remembering clutch at my throat
Special music wraps around me
Like a very warm coat (yet I feel so cold)
Crying like worry cannot be controlled
You do or you don't
For me it's on hold!
A rubber hand winds tight in my head
My inside feels empty
Yet heavy as lead
Happy days of remembering will come one day
Erase this pain - melt grief away
When will tears come to erase this sorrow
Not yesterday - not today
Tomorrow? or tomorrow? or tomorrow?

  Peggy Cobb

Remember Me

  Remember me for I can
see you are in pain because of
my foolish pride. I was depressed so I
got undressed, stepped in the tub and slit my wrist.
Daddy will grieve, Mommy will cry, everyone
else will walk on by and wonder why
they too cry. They say I had a
good life, good family, good friends.
  It just wasn't enough, I thought
no one cared so I dared to take my
own life. Now, I know what they
said is true. I had a good life,
But I had to die, now I am sad
and wish I could cry, because I
know in my heart that it is true
death is forever and I am dead
by my own hand not by mistake.

  Shawna Valdivia

"Rosa"

She sat by the window looking out
Seeing nothing around her
Her mind went back to the past
Of when she was a little girl

She lives with her mother and grandparents
Wonder who her father is.
Wishing she knew who he uses
Because most of her friends had a mother and father

When she grew a little older
Her mother got married to Mr. Brown
Who pretended to love her so much
Then the abuse began

She had to work in the fields
From six in the morning to six in the evening
No more friends and no more playing
Only, work, work, work and more work

She could not read or write
Wishing she can go to school
To do the things that children do
Poor Rosa did not know about a little Fun

  Princess Coggins

A Perfect World

I remember a world "once upon a time" where peace
seemed almost endless and love was just a rhyme.

Where men were never judged by their wealth or power or
creed, but only by the goodness and fulfillment of their deeds.

A time when togetherness was only common sense and we
spent our time building bridges, not a wall or a fence.

Kara Curtis

Loves Faults

   Forgotten boughs of broken hearts.
Selfish souls bleed
blood of many unwanted and unwinding feelings.
   The fever runs hot and anger dominates love and eventually
controls it.
   Lonely loves loose sight of their thoughts and are unable
to grasp each other tight.
   Humble are the two that go their separate ways unwilling to
forgive and to love.

Kathy Foppe

Granddaughter

A thing of beauty, this child from above,
Sent down from heaven for us to love.
What you'll become when fully grown
As yet a mystery, to us unknown.
May God help us to guide and to mold
This little treasure, more precious than gold.
We'll share your joys, troubles, or sorrows,
And face together all your tomorrows.
May we all succeed and never fail,
As on the stream of life you set sail.
Your pathways strewn with kindness and love,
Days filled with sunshine from above.
Our prayer for you, grow gentle yet strong,
To be able to choose right over wrong.
May the mark you leave on the pages of time,
Stand out like a shining star, granddaughter of mine.

Mary Louise Brooks

Untamed Illusion

Fragmented discovery lies within thy bosom.
Severed dreams, in thine eyes.
And in the soul of your secrets, shattered
promises are buried with every goodbye.

Treasures from the forgiving are slipped into
thy grasp.
And insane murmurings of the wicked are etched in
your mind.
Lost words and sketches, scattered along your
paths.
Verse and abstract of every kind.

Smoldering memories blow in thy wind.
Fantasies forgotten flow through your streams.
Misgivings and fortune together in your creation.
Next to every man's dreams.

Melena Duff

Excuses

We like to say it's love,
So we have an excuse for putting up with this.

With each new problem,
We become a little closer.

Or do we come closer to letting go?

Renae Kirk

The Window

There is a street light outside the window.
Shadows are cast about.
Sitting upon the living room couch,
The shadows seem to dance.
Engrossed in reading a book,
The shadows are soundless.
Everything is quiet and peaceful.
One shadow has moved closer.
Intuition says don't look toward the window.
The shadow looms ominously near.
Panic mustn't overcome.
The shadow seems larger.
Arose from the couch and moved toward the window.
What is that moving shadow?
With a sigh of relief, there sat the next door cat,
Pawing away at his own shadow.

Nancy M. St Clair

Oceans Of Your Eyes

Can this be real? The sound of your voice,
Shaking me, drowning me: Endlessly,
As if I had never lived, until I had known what it was like,
To be touched; Physically, with your hands, mentally; inside
my mind, emotionally; you tied me in your heart, And spiritually
our souls were interwoven
Never to be separated, through life or death
The distinct tears, still numb me inside,
It is so hard, for me to understand, that you are gone,
When clearly, you are still so much a part of every move,
every thought, I dare to take: Alone
There is a side of me so lonely
Wanting you in this life, as in our last
And that side of my soul, relives going under the water, over and
over, every day I move, a part of me will always be lost
A part of me will always be drowning inside the oceans of your
eyes, always: I will be paralyzed remembering your voice, and
the things you have said and what those things meant
In a time, I never expected, to be loved

Lisa A. Clark

Connections

The nature of our planet came before time
Shaped by natural ancient forces within - without
Chaotic winds, seas, landslides
   And more - much more that preceded
Life/man by many eternities
   Soft rock hardened while shaped
Pounded, rounded, pinnacled, scaling and ricocheting from
Compression to compression and peak to peak
Taking eons to form from the roiling, boiling, rolling
Action of gases colliding
   For billions of years, maybe more -
Until the composites of our personalities
Adam/Eve/Lillith/ life forms
   Developed with serpentine triangles
While serpentine plots hatched
   Waiting for the Garden to grow -
Thus, I construct and deify the world
   In the beginning. Having travelled
Before time, through time, and
   Unto the aura of after-time

Philip Sosis

Letting Go

Dark shadowy figures outlined in blue dance upon my wall.
Shapes unknown and seen only by minds eye, heard by
only one names they do not possess.
They beckon and I came, where they lead I will go.
They are reminders of the past, but in the present they
exist, future unknown.
They speak with out voices and are not heard by the ear.
They reside in the graveyard of the mind where the souls never sleep.
Together we search through the rows of headstones, for
what name I do not know.
It is a child we seek that has long since past.
A treasure she possesses not of silver or gold, clutched
tightly and held close to her heart, entombed deep
below and plunged into the dark.
She cries, she wails in sorrow she lives.
When the search is complete, the child released,
the souls will wake their stories to tell.
The heart will be broken and the pain released
The shadows will fade and to the grave I will go.
The birth of the new is the death of the old.

Rhonda Jobe

Control-Who Is She?

She had control of me, wasn't hard to see.
She had my mind and soul, she was oh so very cold.
Not for one moment did I get back,
For fear of getting a good smack.
Those years are gone she can keep the memory.
Me I'm moving ahead, tall and free.
So much I've lost to her, so much she took.
Those days don't deserve another look.
I'm seeing my spirit be born again,
She won't even look at me after then.
She tried destroying beauty, brains and soul.
Now look as the story is told.
She can't touch this and she I will never miss.

Kim Dimaria

Untitled

My cat is named Kitty
She is so pretty and witty
Kitty is more than just a cat
She makes me up for work
Kitty waits for me in her chair at the table
For lunch and dinner
Kitty watches days of our lives
She takes a nap on my lap
Kitty is good company
I am glad I have my cat
Kitty makes my days happier.

Nina Trunzo

I Headed Out

I headed out I was looking for a friend,
She was sitting there in the end,
I said you're looking lonely girl,
would you like a lonely boy like me,
And are you willing to give your love for free,
She nodded her head so I took it that she agreed,
One throw of the dice and was inside;
I was winning the wheels were spinning
Lady Luck was in heat,
She was warming up my luck everyone I could beat,
Yeah, I headed out was looking for a friend,
Lady Luck was sitting there in the end,
Lady Luck was sitting there in the in the end.

F. Mando Cisneros

Leaving

She loved him with all her might.
She knew one day he would love her,
and she pained at the sight.
He once held her like no one had before,
and would never hold her like that again.
She remembered the way he kissed her,
the way he touched, but most of all,
the way he loved her.
Every morning she wakes,
she see's his face and wishes
she still had him.
She knows he loves her,
but he won't admit it.
And if she says anything,
she knows she'll regret it.
She tries to tell herself
that she will never have him again,
but she finds herself wanting him
over and over again.

Michelle Vaughn

When She Speaks

When she speaks of him her voice gets a quiver.
She loved him with all her heart and soul.
Still she feels the same way.

When she speaks of him her voice gets a quiver.
A tear lightly splashes her eyes.
Her tender heart aching for his touch.

When she speaks of him her voice gets a quiver.
She'll never have her sparkle like before.
Pretending she's happy.

When she speaks of him her voice gets a quiver.
He died and with him he took my grandmas' heart.
We're all she has now.

When she speaks of him her voice gets a quiver.
She knows we miss him.
But deep inside she knows she misses him more.

Kristina Eaker

Evil Is Her Name

She's one tough kid in her tight blue jeans.
She prowls like a tiger but she's twice as mean.
She wears a skimpy little top and tennis shoes,
And has a razor sharp tongue that she knows how to use.
She has long blond hair and big blue eyes,
You'll see her on the corner surrounded by guys.
She's smiling with a smirk and daring you to come,
She wants to tear your heart out because she thinks it's fun.
She's the daughter of the devil and she does his work so well.
She'll smile at you sweetly then lead you straight to hell.
Sin was her mother and Evil is her name
Her hearts like a rock and she knows no shame.
She'll use you and get you hooked on booze, sex and pot,
Then she'll toss you in a corner and leave you there to rot,
Like you were so much garbage and not so much a man,
The reason that she does it is because she knows she can.
She'll make you feel so helpless, then she'll leave without a care,
So remember that she's Evil when you see her standing there,
Then if you have one lick of sense, listen to me well,
Put the wind to your backside, and run like hell.

V. Helen Mayfield

Lingering Doubts

He sees a woman, alive and vibrant
She sees a girl, lost in life and afraid to make it
He sees a woman with bright auburn hair and laughing green eyes
She sees a girl with a dull, tired face and straight hair she dyes
He sees a woman, articulate and funny, laughing at her foes
She sees a girl stumbling over words and thrown together clothes
He sees a woman of tough convictions and softness of heart
She sees a girl with thoughts all scattered and hurt feelings that smart
He must see some redemption or something beautiful down deep
For he married this girl-woman with a promise to keep
She sees nothing special or beauty deep down
All she sees is a girl's body and mind in a grown woman's gown
Trying to live the way she was raised
Good thoughts and deeds, and plenty of praise
This must be his idea of her strength and her humor
Of vibrance and beauty that he so generously rumors
Once in a while when she's known you for ions and ions
She'll show you a glimpse of that glittering diamond behind all her
    demons
But only a glance and then to privacy - it's gone
And her lingering doubt is back like a beautiful new dawn

Susan Gordinier

Untitled

She fell into his trap, both been alone so long.
She slept with him the very first night,
she knows what she did was wrong.

But that didn't stop her, just had to have more,
to finish off the task she started,
she made the vow for rich or poor.

She said it was for love; he said he'd treat her right.
They disagreed every now and then,
that was just the start of the fight.

He promised things would change,
her whole life he had wrecked.
now she lives a life of misery,
not knowing what to expect.

Now she'll never get out,
cause she's stuck in the war.
Whatever happened to their love?
Both wonder what the fighting's for.

He's mad at her again,
so he throws things and yells.
Her most regrettable memory was the sound of wedding bells.

Nicki Morea

The Bottomless Pit

She sits there stranded, only a wall around.
She speaks to that wall, no one else cares.
They don't care enough to notice, not her.
She wishes for joy and delight, something she's never seen.
All around is darkness, hatred.
Why can't she feel the opposite?
Why not beautiful?
They are why, they hurt her and her loveliness.
She's left everything.
She fell down, too low.
She can't get back to where she was,
She's stuck and no one notices.
No one cares.
She asks only for what she had.
Not much.
She gets darker and darker everyday, forever.

Susan Lea Vorba

Untitled

"She tries so hard to be weird, said a student to her peer.
She tries so hard to be weird, she tries so hard to be
different." Everybody is different, "What's wrong with being
weird?" Some laugh in her face, or snicker within reach of
her ears. "What's wrong with being weird?" Some taunt and
tease hoping to send her home, to drown in her tears. Some
don't understand her, so all they do is fear her, but if they
understood her they would realize they have pleased her. She
is different, why does that make her weird? I feel I
understand her, yet I may be way off. She is very complex, to
summarize her, would be an insult. If I have offended, you
the accused I gladly will repeat my fault. If I offended her
the one who tries so hard to be weird. I feel I would be no
better off, than all of her judgmental peers, who stand
around her close enough, so she can feel their sneers. If I
have done this, let me drown in a pool of tears.

Mary Cummins

It Happened This Way

In 1924, this sweet young girl, I met purely by chance.
She was happy, and innocent, but it was a very short romance.
She went to college and a teacher become.
She married, I married as we should.
She had two children, so did I.
I often thought of her as I brushed a tear from my eye.
She lost her husband, I lost my wife
After a proper time, you need a new life.
Many years went by, as they always do.
I was very lonely, maybe it has happened to you.
Again purely by chance, I learned her married name.
It was so new and exciting, like a new game.
Luck was surely on my side.
Everything I could think of, I tried
As time went by, things got much better
I'm hoping and praying, I think I may yet get her.

Max E. Breuneman

'Earth's Agony'

In this, Her age of rebellion,
    She writhes in violent pain;
        Winds of black pollution
Sail above Her bruised terrain.
    Her billowed ceiling is torn
        By the sun's naked rays,
Leaving Her shelterless through the storm
    Of the blazing, fervent days.
        Behold, She spews forth
    Her inner flames of molten ire;
        While a blanket of toxic froth
Coats Her fields with consuming fire.
    In Her yearning for ages past,
The breadth of time deforms Her beauty;
    Of what was once majestic and chaste,
Is now the remains of man's sinful booty.
Fierce winds track brutally across Her face
Wounding Her countenance with flecks of death;
    In his quest for boundless power and gain,
        Man gives birth to...Earth's agony!

Laura J. Houston

Free Verse

The ducks and swans swam down the stream
So gracefully they were.
And when they saw their little ones
You saw how proud they were
They splashed and played the day away
When night fall came they slept
But couldn't wait till they could do it again.

Sheri Landis

Me Too, Mom

I have a new baby sister, her name is Emily.
She's sweet, pretty and gets attention that
    was given me.
I'm not exactly jealous, but want some
    affection too.
So, I try some tricks, to see what I can do.
Wet myself-scribble on the kitchen table
    Oh my.
Mommy discovered what I had done
    Get the cleanser, son.
I said No - was sent to my room - no toys
    just Mr. Bear
I knew my mommy would be up soon
    'cause she does care,
Time passed, all was quiet, mommy
    came to see if I was all right;
I said I just wanted mommy to hold
    me tight.
I'm sorry, I love my sister, don't you see
I'm still your little boy, and only three.
    Ruth J. Watkins

Moonlight Becomes You My Lady

Silken tendrils of midnight hair
Shimmering in reflecting moon light.
Dancing sparks highlighting the night
Playing across your misty face.
Shadows strengthening sunken features
Angles appearing more sharply.
Rays of soft flowing words
streaming from unspoken thoughts
Bringing yesterday's tears to today's eyes
And once again
Soothing gaping wounds wound within the soul.
Moonlight becomes you my lady.
    Richard G. Wanderman, Sr.

Why Racism?

    Many people, of many races
Should come together, and begin to face it
We all are people, we all are the same
We all should realize, how it's a crying shame?
to be so hateful, to be so cruel
Why can't we relate, like human beings how
Whites are whites and blacks are blacks
But no one is different, and that's a true fact
That's how I see it, that's the way it should be
Why choose a person, different from yourself,
to be your enemy?
This world would be a whole better place
If racism had not started, way, back in the
days. If people had realized, that all people
are similar
Right now, Our nation would be a
much more happier place.
    Sherita Thomas

The Mind

Where do you go when you have no where to go?
Some people go inside their minds.
Therefore they can go anywhere anytime.
The mind so complex, yet so fragile.
Does the mind travel alone?
Or can our mind merge?
Can two become one?
The mind!
The depth and ability are still in question.
A gift surely to be prized.
    May Farley

Death Becomes Me

Death becomes me, it's a natural escape.
Should I live? Should I die?
What is my fate?
To live in this life with all the lies, all the pain,
They do nothing but bring me pity and shame.
Winding down this lonely road of sorrow,
I seek all the truths of knowing no tomorrow.
On this path I'll look to see a light of
Happiness, to dwell on, its treasure.
But I will seek no more for I don't find enough pleasure.
Maybe I'll one day find my true blossom
Of hope but I think it's too late.
Because death becomes me, it's my natural escape.
    Kim Speight

When I Die

What will you do for me when I die? Will you color my face and glue
shut my eye? Or perhaps, maybe cover my scars if they show,
and iron my wrinkles, and make my lips glow? And color my hair, can
you do that too, make auburn red of this silvery blue?
Paint my nails or even my toes
Pink… maybe red, only God will know.
Then I'll be ready to entertain the mass
of indifferent babies and their parents of "class",
Of crocodile tears and comforting embraces
and polite little nods to emotionless faces.
Is this what you'll do for me when I die?
Send me to heaven with a regretful little sigh?
Will you remember and forget any love that was there
or will you hold me close now and show me you care? Today is the time
to prepare me to depart, for my corpse is only clothing, my true body
is my heart, dress me up, paint me nice, put a smile on my face
because my soul is slowly rotting underneath the white lace knowing
that your love is ignored me in kind, mark it on my tombstone: "Out of
Sight, Out of Mind",
so much for remembrance, it's gone to the sky,
Is this what you'll do for me when I die?
    Kimberly M. Shanks

A Fine Line

Before the morning light, I saw a shooting star
"signing off"; as worlds collide -
When the night relinquishes its hold,
And the day no longer hides-
While mother earth spins gracefully,
upon her celestial ride.

A new day dawns on the Rockies,
and the Continental Divide -
as I greet Mt. Ouray again,
and "the feather of july".

Rainbows are common,
on a stormy afternoon -
and sometimes at night, snow-flakes fall;
from the stars and the moon.

In such a majestic place,
among a sea of purple lupine-
the wild-life dwells care-free,
serene; sublime -
And heaven and earth appear…
to share a non-existent line!
    Michael Grant

The Prey Is Beautiful

The flesh is waiting so unexpectedly for means in which I stalk.
Silently I move as if I were invisible.
Stalking day by day, minute by minute, second by second...
Passionately waiting.
Just waiting, watching with a hunger, a longing for...
Stalk, O' stalker
Cleverly watching every move, every thought.
Taking note though as to become one.
Everywhere the prey is, so is the predator.
Thus, there's nowhere to run, nowhere to hide.
So look, look;
Yes, look around you.
Yes, it is you I stalk.
So, am I in front, or, possibly am I behind you?
Or, maybe, just maybe...
I am inside you!

Stephen Lambert

Largess Ex Cathedra

Azure skies skim sunlit, moonlit
   silvered waters.
Solos silhouette another brilliant,
   cloudless sun.
Merely more endeavors to pit
   us against the gun
That places all of us in danger
   unless we choose to run
Into crystal clear-blue oceans
   on a waxed and furbished board
Into a world of aqua-ventures.
An attempt, perhaps, to redefine
   parameters beyond.
There are vistas not quite visible
   with feet planted firmly on the ground.
But from the sea, I simply see
A presence far beyond me,
And you, and me, et al.

Laurie-Anne Cabas Schmalz

"In Memory of Dad"

The years now number nine;
Since you crossed over the golden line.
Yet time alone cannot heal;
All the loss and sorrow that we feel.
We hold onto the memories so dear;
Our hearts and minds still keep you near.
We see you in a flower that grows;
Feel you in the wind that blows.
You are in the sunshine ever so bright;
The moon and stars at night. ·
You are still with us, winter, spring and fall;
Mortal consolation to one and all.
We keep you near, night and day;
With each and every prayer we say!

Patricia Gross

"The Band-Aid"

Where are you?
Slipped away into the darkness
While I was gazing at the moon
Whose light was silver and refreshing
To my bleeding eyes.
The little man winked at me
And I turned to ask if you'd seen it, too
But you were gone.
The snap of a twig and the rustle of dry leaves
Told me you were headed for the house
I guess you'd had enough;
I think I'll stay out a little while longer
For I'm not quite healed.

Kacey E. Cloues

The Children

Vietnam, where I spent a year of my life-
sitting in the sweltering heat,
writing a letter to my wife.

In the distance, I could hear the sounds of war
and wonder who is there - friends, enemies, or
innocent children waiting for the daylight to
calm their fears. I've seen children suffer;
I've seen children die - from guns and starvation
and I often wondered why. What did they do?

I saw a mother leave her sick child on a dirt
porch of a rundown bamboo shack, dying from
starvation - hoping Americans would stop and
help, so she could get her baby back. Yet many
times it's too late and I've seen the babies die.
They're innocent little children and I often
wondered why. What did they do?

War has many faces. It's hard to understand.
Is this man your enemy or your friend? Many
people suffer - it's a fact of war. Yet why should
the children suffer even more? What did they do?

Ken Gillaspy

Hi Desert Country

Distant mountains bathed in lavender hues,
Skies above, shades of slate gray blues.
Air is awash with the pungence of sage,
Old miners' cabins crumble with age.

Roads are black ribbons stretching o'er blowing sands,
Small towns and sagebrush scattered throughout the land.
It's "Hi Desert Country" of which I have written,
And adventurous men who were gold fever smitten.

Here's where the coyote and wild horses roam,
And the long eared jackrabbit calls it his home.
Quiet reigns supreme; most humans have fled
Where pioneer and oxen once wearily tread.

Now antelope graze midst the lush bunch grass,
Quite startled, alert if a car whizzes past.
Of "Hi Desert Country", this is my story,
Where many a miner had his day of glory.

As the golden sun slips down in the west,
And most grizzly old miner is now laid to rest.
Out where great hopes were always the key.
This land is exciting and wondrous to see.

Pearl Stanford

Life's Seasons

A life is like the seasons, with its colors and soft hues,
Slowly changing all the headgear, slowing changing its worn shoes.

The springtime is a new life like a young child's early years,
Ever fragile as the flower's morning dew - a youngster's tears.

Summertime is hot and the teens get their first kiss,
As they harvest all their knowledge, they not a second want to miss.

In autumn, life is stable when a family's begun,
And as trees will shed their leaves, the children leave home one by one.

With winter, tops are white as with the snow or graying hair,
Many cherish this as their best time - some are cold and feel despair.

As the seasons of our lives come and change our whole perspective,
Let us think of all good memories and be positive, reflective.

Life is very short and can change quickly like the seasons.
When you question "Why" and "How", only God knows all the reasons.

Laura J. Chavers

My Memory

The spring leaves whispering the
smell of lilacs floating through the air.
Standing with arms folded across his
chest the sun and shadows playing
with the intensity of his face.

His slow smile fixed forever by the
camera- a part of me.

A baseball hat a glove thrown,
carelessly on the grass

A small child crouched, watching,
smelling the lilacs.

My best friend, my unyielding
supporter, my reason for living, my father

Gone now the humor, the love, the
generosity, the compassion

My companions, forever, emptiness, pain, and
sorrow.
I remember a spring afternoon, and
the sweet smell of lilacs floating
through the air.

Shirley Menne

Ode To Keith

Snow angel, arms flailing wildly,
snowy owl, struggling in the night,
to be free of IV lines and drips.

Snow angel, wings flapping noisily,
internally, mentally,
tricked into believing you can really escape
the ever-tightening net of AIDS
strangling not only you,
but Betsey and Luke, everyone.

Snow angel, leaving behind
a questionable legacy
which no one will talk about
or lay open claim to,
for fear of public reprisal
and unearned penalties.

Snow angel, play your music
for Him now, like you did for me
many years ago, when I was afraid
of stepping into the unknown.

J. Patricia Bookman

Heart And Soul

Welcome to my heart, where it's
so dark and dim.
Welcome to my soul, so very very thin.
Come into my heart where blood
flows like tears.
Come into my soul and try to feel me near.
Don't leave my heart as for it
will have another hole.
Don't leave my soul, as for there
won't be anymore.
Stay in my heart and read all its pain.
Stay in my soul, so I don't fade away.
Leave my heart if you must go.
But please, don't ever leave my soul.

Rose Schroeder

Inhabitant

There's site far way where scenery extends, and mountains are
so emerald in forests that are so dense.

Where blossoms are blooming in fragrances of colorful rainbows.
And golden seas encircle her, and rivers overrun her.

Where bloodstains of passion for a continent has been fought.
And sovereignty for democracy has been the prosperity.
For agony and heartache has separated, so has it bound
simultaneously.

No other site on earth can you encounter sovereignty;
No other site on earth can you encounter the tranquility that
one yearns for; no other inhabitant on earth still lives in
sovereignty and democracy for all.

But Oh! how rapidly the wisdom of liberty would disintegrate,
if the columns of democracy are not well balanced.

V. Mastrantonis

And The Night Grows Longer

Daylight ends with the slow decent of an infant sun
So fresh with its interest in performing
A time to learn, an interval of time
Continuous change and a daily rhyme
And so slowly it prepares for sleep

From the transitional grey an orientation emerges
The moon rising to its most binding challenge
Suspiciously showing a hint of night
A growing force so reserved yet bright
Suspended in tomorrow's youthful animation

Darkness struggles in its search for enlightenment
The sky is replenished by the knowledge of tomorrow
Forever in a day will the memories try to last
Growing ever thoughtful of other nights that past
Never will there be such a chance to know the dark

Dawn approaches with its inevitable conclusion of twilight
Peaceful is this final morning, touched by the cleansing dew
Time now stands still as the cycle is complete
Darkness stands proud, even in defeat
and the night grows longer no more.

Robert Field Jr.

"Let Me Love You"

Beauty holds many definitions
so I guess you are hard to explain.
Love has many boundaries
But I guess I can live with the pain.
Words can only express so much
so I will give a lifetime to learn
how much I love you.

My youth was over before I met you
but you make me feel young all again.
I use to fear age before I met you
now with you life begins with you by my side.

You are my star shine, my moonbeam.
My rainbow and, of course, my afternoon shade.
My reason to live for, never to die for
my sweetness, my lover and pain's escape.

Let's cherish each other
my friend, my lover
let's go on forever
you and me together.

Let me love you... my darling

Tracey Anne Smith

Good-bye To Childhood

Endless hours spent day-dreaming,
So many days of comical scheming.
Endless hours of climbing trees,
A time of fun, and dirty knees.

Romping through woods, tearing through fields,
Nothing worth stopping for, except for my meal.

Playing hide-and-go-seek, until it gets dark,
Riding my bike, flying through the park.

All these activities from my childhood time,
Scrounging the house for one nickel or dime.
But now I've grown up, as life passes me by,
The dreaming, the scheming, I must say good-bye.

Steve Blonski

Soft, Sweet Dreams

So many things that if I could I know I'd surely change,
So many thoughts that fill my mind and make me feel so strange;
So many longings that I have are somehow never filled
I don't know how I just let go and then start to rebuild.

My life is filled with so much hate, so many times I'm wrong,
If I could I'd start to sing and make my life a song;
The memories set to music, maybe then I could let go,
No telling what the future would bring; there's just no way to know.

If I hold on to the past, keep it locked inside my heart
How can I find the life I want or make a brand new start?
I'd give my all, my everything just to fall in love
Yet knowing I don't even try when push turns into shove.

I know what being happy means, but joy seems far away;
I want to throw the pain away and just live for today.
A tender touch is all I need, or one soft word it seems;
Alas, somehow life slips away and these are only dreams.

Laura Stanart

"Undone"

Everyday reminds me that I never did belong here,
So my leaving never really meant a thing.
And it wasn't you at all, as I stepped back to watch you fall,
It's just not right when few sweet licks begin to sting.
As I've been bruised by bigger bets,
The blood of love has yet been shed,
Another word may soon just bring me back to you.
Now close, again, you hear me,
Never listen, only fear me,
You are the noose I have not tried yet to undo.

Sandra Stewart-Moreno

The Rainbow

The rainbow is so colorful,
so shiny and bright.
It hangs in the sky with all its silent power,
it needs the sun and the rain to exist,
like we need air and food.
When the rain starts,
it awakes to life,
a life to make people happy
with its colorful beauty.
But then, when the sun disappears behind black clouds,
the rainbow dies,
its colors fade,
its brightness disappears
until there is nothing left
only the memory in our souls.

Sonja Eisfeld

Roll Reversal

I'm just a tiny little girl!
So, please, walk slow for me.
I've tried and tried to hurry,
But I can't keep up; you see.

My legs are much too short.
Each step you take; for me is three.
I am so tired and weary.
Please, walk slow, wait for me.

Were I to be the mommie,
N' a little girl, like me, you'd be,
I would not hurry or walk so fast;
'Cause I'd want you to walk with me.

Years now have passed and slowed your steps.
They now match mine, as a child.
Often I see you falter, pausing, resting for a while.
Recalling our long ago walks together, suddenly I realize;

It is I who now must remember, to slow my steps.
Bide my time. More patient must I be.
Here! Take my hand. Let me help.
Like you always did for me.

Nannie M. Narbut

Distant Doors

Last night I found some words I wrote at least a life ago;
So safe and ageless, tucked away as faded memories go.
The pages came alive as soon as I began to read;
I felt the suffocation of a child afraid to breathe.

Inside the night, we all at times grow young again it seems
While bathed in warmth and reverie of once forgotten dreams.

How intimate the words, the scenes appeared before my eyes
To form a long procession that, if I were to be kind,
I'd blame upon the fate of youth. Instead I chose to see
The truth. I made mistakes, but life goes on and so should we.

I mused at my remorse as I sat balanced on time's wall.
I sank into my grief and bitter tears began to fall.

The words soon ran together so I let them fall away,
The wisest thing I'd ever done, forgiving yesterday.
I slept in peace last night though in a dream I heard once more
A past refrain, an echoing, behind a distant door.

Leesa Lynch

Hope

Like a winter fairyland
So sparkling and white
Trees arched together
Making a tunnel if light-
Sparkling diamonds fall on our way-
This one gorgeous day - every so often
Makes winter enjoyable - buoys up our spirits
For nature's stormy moods - yet to be.
We can always say "it soon will be spring"!
When the next blast of winter
Comes roaring our way-
Remember that saying "it soon will be spring."

Ruth B. Johnson

Night Rhymes

I viewed astonished the brightest astral sky
Swept by comets and falling stars I asked why?
What wondrous design propels our Universe?
What glories defy the most gifted verse?
so humbly and so artlessly I simply
Thank you God - with all my heart.

William P. Hamlet

Soldiers

Soldiers laugh and Soldiers cry
Soldiers never tell a lie.

Soldiers see killings and Soldiers see hurt
Soldiers never tell a lie.

Soldiers show love and Soldiers show hate
Soldiers never tell a lie.

Soldiers see hunger and Soldiers see cold
Soldiers never tell a lie.

Soldiers travel and Soldiers fly
Soldiers never tell a lie.

Soldiers try to forget the pain and the nightmares
Soldiers never tell a lie.

Soldiers have fear and Soldiers have hate
Soldiers never tell a lie.

Soldiers came home and some remain
Soldiers never tell a lie.

Less we forget only for Soldiers our lives
would be a mess.

> *Michael Thomas Martin*

My Gift To You

We're all different, it's plain to see, each of our lives tell some history;
some have seen while others have not, there's more today to be sought.
Just what's ahead, it's hard to tell, it quickly changes, it's just as well;
we can say, that we all need love, the kind that lasts, from above.
Many sorrows.... disappointments too.... and giving up is easy to do;
let not life stay tattered and torn, pick up yourself, and let's go on.
If only we talk to ourselves and say, why am I here....any way?....
playful conscience, willful thoughts, saying "o.k.", when it's really not.
Is it our mind, who leads us to do, some kind thing from me to you?
Controlling minds leads us astray, faith from the heart will show us
  the way.
Answers come with patience my friend, a plan, a work for each till the
  end;
my gift not fancy, there is no need, no wear & tear, but grows like a
  seed.
Kind, forgiving, there all the time, helps you to rest with peace of mind;
give your heart, it gives its love, my gift to you is from heaven above.

> *Sue Kirk*

"Things Are Not All That They Seem"

Things are not all that they seem
Some phrases seem to lie,
Like when you almost hit someone
I often wonder why.....

Someone will say
That was a "near Miss".....By just a little bit,
When obviously a near miss
Would have to be a hit!

Another phrase some doctors will use
When prescribing you a dose,
He'll say take one tablet twice a day
Doesn't that sound gross!

One pill one time a day is quite enough
Or two pills once a day,
But vomiting up that nasty pill to take it again...
No way!!!!

> *Lum Huffman*

A Stray Dog

Just like a stray dog without a home.
Someone one day gives a morsel to eat.
And the stray dog then refuses to roam.
He forgets who he is and all for meat.

The stray is at the mercy of others;
More so than dogs with masters who love them.
He is starving for the love of strangers.
He survives with want but hope will beat him.

The only hold on a stray dog is love,
To keep that love he'll forget who he is.
He will stay unless he's called from above.
Poor stray dog hoping against hope for bliss.

Born in the rain forever in the fog,
Remember who you are you dumb stray dog

> *Robert Lazos III*

Lost Love

Today, I haven't thought of you in a long long time.
Something awake in me I didn't really care to cross my mind.

I really loved you... but you wouldn't love me back.
You're just my lost love from the memory of my mind.

We had a short time together but something held you back.
I tried my hardest to let you know my heart was yours.

But you just didn't care
You were really too young and free
You had your share and ran off with another.

Today I haven't thought of you in a long long time.
Something awoke in me
Brought a smile to my heart.

I really loved him, but he wouldn't love me back.
He was just a lost love
from the memory of my mind.

> *Lucille Harp*

Worthless Piece Of Thing

It was a worthless piece of thing.
Something I received and gave away.
Only to have it returned another day.
Someone gave it to me, first, a long time ago
And like so many other things,
I couldn't give it away, or throw it away,
Without it being returned to me.

What is this worthless piece of thing
That I set aside, and then clutch it with all my heart,
For fear I'll not have another like it.
This worthless piece of thing that I've lost so many
Times; and found again.

My thoughts are not with it when I have it,
Yet I become nothing without it.

I would share this worthless piece of thing - this thing
which is love.

> *M. Laurette Snider*

For The Love Of A Child.

From before birth to the first spoken words and tiny footsteps.
The misunderstandings, the sleepless nights.
The joy, the sorrow, the tears.
The sacrifices I made large at first, now ever so small.
All this was done...
For the love of a child.

> *C. Stacy*

Life

I can't begin to explain all I'm feeling
    Sometimes I can't take anymore.
I feel as though I'm drowning situations occur
My visions sometimes blur
Life changes day by day
Some days I just want it to go away…

    Punches are thrown
    Hearts are broken
    Life's are ruined
    Babies die
    Don't ask me why.

I know life can be rough
Sometimes you don't want to go on please be tough
Hang in there don't lose hope
Because it's not better at the end of the rope….
    Rachel Philpot

Sometimes

Sometimes things aren't what they seem.
    Sometimes I don't say exactly what I mean.
Sometimes secret thoughts stay locked inside.
    Sometimes all I want is to run and hide.

Sometimes I say that I'll be honest.
    Sometimes I can't keep that promise.
Sometimes my pain is too much alone.
    Sometimes all I want is to have you home.

Sometimes I think I'm in love with you.
    Sometimes I think you feel it too.
Sometimes I get scared of what's in store
    Sometimes I can't wait for more,

But sometimes doesn't seem to matter anymore.
    Sharon Krapp

Soft Word From A Man

Soft words from a man can turn you on
Sometimes make you do your lover wrong.
Soft words are not always from the heat.
He will tell you how much he can do for you.
How far will you go before your own judgement kicks in.
If it's not too late to go back to your man
Cause, this is a case that can be whipped up in your face.
Be careful, please!
In the end you will lose
The man that you left behind
He don't want you back
You left him and that's a fact.

You have to realize soft words from a man can turn you on
Make you do your lover wrong.
Think before you jump.
Stop, before you run,
Soft words from a man can break your heart
Is this the type of man who wants to blow your mind
Use you, abuse you, and confuse you
Soft words from a man can turn you on yes they can.
    Velma Bush

Different

She awoke to a world she didn't understand.
Suddenly all she had known some
how seemed different, people, places and minds
all seemed the same. No differences.
Her mind was now open with thoughts as free as the sky.
She will remain free to be her self (Different)
and will hope for an understanding.
    Tammy Cox

Sitting And Staring A Bird's Eye View

What do I think of when I sit and stare?
Sometimes of nothing and being nowhere.
It's easy to do - to fade out in space,
And forget however I got to this place.

Birds on a wire, facing east and west,
Chatting and chirping while taking a rest.
All lined up as in an arcade,
But knowing they're free, and need not be afraid.

One tail flutters three birds fly away,
Replaced by another - unlike yesterday.
Some change places as in musical chairs,
And some turn around, forgetting their cares.

Black silhouettes against a pink sky,
Never off balance, or wondering why
Someone or something may cause them dismay,
And break up their look of chained cloisonne.

A moment has passed, it doesn't take long.
Wings flap at the air and soon they are gone.
No clay pigeons these, they're not under fire,
But you just try being a bird on a wire!
    M. J. Atlas

Sometimes

Sometimes, the clouds cover the sun.
Sometimes, the rains fall like water on the run.
Sometimes, the sky is o'er cast and dark.
Sometimes, the mood of the day leaves its mark.
Sometimes, the world is full of violence and hate.
Sometimes, it seems like it's too late,
Sometimes, to accomplish all you want to do.
Sometimes, your true friends are few.
Sometimes, the laughter leaves your eyes.
Sometimes, your smile is replaced with sighs.
Sometimes, it's hard for you to realize,
That all the time, it's just great to be alive!
    Laura S. Woods

"My Sons"

    Son's are special, son's are true
son's favorite color is mostly always blue.

    Some spiders and bugs are
part of their day, as well as a
butterfly flying away.

    They bring you a flower with
no visible stem so you put them
in water and float them to him.

    The eyes of a son are sincere
and true, because that's the way
their love comes through.

    The best hugs and kisses are your
reward as you tuck them in bed, at night.

    I whisper a prayer of thank
you to God for granting me my son's
for my life has become a little
brighter with every morning hug.
    Roxann Lewiel

Love Anew

Tempest arose in recent past
  sorely tiring the will to last
when from the mist rose anon
  beseeching, thrilling Circe song.

Though harbors beckon oft genug
  and safety lies not far away
sheltered port, serene calm,
  cannot forestall the songs sweet charm.

Eyes beseeching, crystal blue,
  warm concern, without a clue,
how welcomed sight they are to see
  spirited, gentle as calmest sea.

Tempests fade to memory,
  memory shadowed by what to be,
shark skin dry once forlorn,
  strength renews, soul reborn.
    Matthew M. Wagman

Mirrors Of The Soul

Gesture of Delight
Sparkling eyes mirror a child's Yuletide heart

Signature of Passion
Scintillating eyes reveal ardor by candlelight

Evidence of Hope
Eyes flicker reliance on God against ominous tidings of despair

Ink of Despondency
Moist eyes glisten at memories of the soldier son deceased far away

Autograph of Trouble
A mother's raised-blow glances in disbelief at toddler's muddy salutation

Sign of Frenzy
Eyes flash with fury as men clash in the ring

Signal of Approval
Daddy secretly winks at Mom over daughter's new confidant

Mark of Success
Grandpa's eyes twinkle with pride at Granny's college graduation

Token of Forgiveness
Eyes of joy shine over a child reborn from drug's addiction.
    Michael E. Crawford

Friends Of The Past - Friends For The Future

Why is it that you hurt me;
speak ill of my name to others;
reproach me in their midst;
rejoice in my transgressions?
I know not what pain I've beset you with.
Are you jealous of my gifts,
Or envious of my rank?
At times, your eyes look lustfully toward power.
Only God gives us power
and showers us with gifts.
Time approaches, I must now rest with Him.
Though my conscience is clear
like a cool starry night,
my thoughts remain clouded
as I pray that you will soon find the peace
that I have found in Him.
Amen.
    Patricia B. Abney

Superiority Of Spiritual Authority

Shall ye thou beautiful babe of England Gender
Speak to me or thine eyes show surface of wisdom
Stay of thine own shall ye speak to anyone
'Tis only then I may rest that thou beauty
May live forever.

Of the girls I search for in life
Shalt ye too marry of thine own
ungodly is to mix breeds and once ye doth
Shalt thou stay married and mixed...
That shall be the end of thy beauty
Beauty cannot be brought out
Shall foreign nationality create a child
That will surely have an identity crisis anyway

Kneel to me and shalt ye beauty survive
Unheed to me and thou beauty shall die
If ever a despotic ruler was once heard
Since the knowledge of mythology...
Shall ye heed as fear and genius speak through me
    Mark Maule

Making Contact

I am draining purging pain from every pore
  spiked thoughts have punctured my pores
My love for life strengthens, as the days pass by
  How I need to be strong my thoughts and feelings
for life shall never go wrong
  Freedoms breath inhaling me
Flying with flocking feathers following me
  Thoughts of family cast sunly
Sounds of family love bring symphony
  Shall this expense of life
Bring back reality
    Sarkis Cheftalian

Analogue

Coming in low, is the plane that lands
Spinning hard, are the wheels that turn.
Coming down fast, is the hurt inside,
Pain in his heart, is the fire that burns.

Constant rage, are the words he screams,
Blatant ignorance, are the ears that will not hear.
Loneliness is being all alone,
Hesitant, is the unknown fear.

Quick and agile, were the legs that ran,
Slow and steady, are the waves that flow.
Fast and furious, are the tears that fall,
Sharp and gleaming, is the blade that glows.

Tight and clenched, are the teeth in rage,
Misery and anger, will soon after follow.
Tainted flowing red, is the swollen wrist,
A meaningless soul, is empty and hollow.

Cold is the rain, that stings his arm,
Flattered and apologetic, is a denied lover.
Living miserably, is his lot in life,
Seems he was always made to suffer!
    Stephen R. Gargiulo

Untitled

Complexity swirls under the surface of simplicity
tender emotions lay quietly below the skin
memories dwell within the whole
existence covers the body
the soul is trapped within
    Susan Posternock

"My Inspirations"

Their arms float like butterflies dancing in a breeze,
Spinning, turning, gliding round with the utmost of ease.
Golden hair wrapping round a creamy, smooth, silk face,
Chestnut waves swaying lovingly with a bow made of lace.
Whose perfect jewels are these two, from
who could they be?
The answer is simple, two beautiful
daughters, they are both the perfect
parts of me.....

Veronica Ortiz

Dear Children Of The World

Floating in warm waters - born in struggle -
stained in blood - grasping your first breath
Blanketed in loving arms - sucking the sweet stream
Gone is your safe haven

Starvation - deprivation - abandoned,
your skeletal eyes too weak to cry
Born of love - born of passion or drugs or countries rape
Centuries of greed, hate and power
Burning lead to your head -
Crippled body and soul - innocence stripped
Remains of the light scorched your earth -
massacred the human spirit
We hand you a cup of poisonous water to drink
Gone is your safe haven

Love in your heart, laughter on your face
Nourished body and mind - peaceful sleep,
flowered fields are your rights
Our legacy to you dear children of the world must be -
Here is your safe haven

Theresa Rucker

Fire Brand

Fire Brand I call him, the majestic black
    stallion of the hills.
Just to stand at a distance and see him
    gives me chills of thrills.
What a magnificent thing, only the Gods could ever own.
To capture would be to destroy, and this—
    no one could condone.
Fire brand, I call him; seems he's breathing fire
    against the sunrise on a fall morn.
As he stands proudly, head up high, he surveys
    civilization with scorn.
Fire Brand, a flashing streak of speed that holds
    you spell bound with wonder.
As he leads his heard deep in the hills, he's like
    a roll of thunder.
Gone once again, vanishing into the kingdom of
    his vast mountain land.
But I'll be waiting when he re-appears, to get a glance
    of this magnificent stallion, Fire Brand.

William L. Jones

Lonely

Listen to the chilling north wind blowing through the
tall pines. Looking out my window and seeing the snow
gently falling, and somewhere in the distance a blue
bird calls to its mate and the whistle and whine of
the old freight train as it labors on its journey.
Hear the mournful sound of taps as the shadows of night
fall over the barracks, I'm just a lonely soldier a
long way from home in a foreign land.

H. J. Monroe

Dear Dad

Can you see me for who I am through my disguise
Standing here waiting to be recognized
Dusty worn jeans jacket of black leather
My face has weathered
Better days.
Can you see me?
I'm a woman now
Caressing my own ways,
No longer pig tailed and climbing trees
Little scraped elbows and knees
Have healed and grown up
My painted pony long ago laid to rest
In a field of grass and dust
And now I stand alone
Waiting for acceptance
Sorry I never grew into
What you had expected.

Kerry Spolum

At A Window She Stood

The little girl dressed in red
Standing on an air vent
Had pushed the venetian blind up at a slant.

To view the outside
If there she had just spent
Time playing in the beautiful
Swirling snowflakes
That the December day had so abundantly sent.

The red skirt ballooned up
From the air of the vent
It then a little boy came over
With a stare in his wondering eyes
What goes there -
How did you do that?

Theresa B. Trapp

Hollow

As so placidly I sit before thee
Staring profoundly into thy eyes.
The passions so inwardly buried
Beneath thee old and weathered wise.

To understand thy emotions
Achingly felt for one and all,
Seems to question the insurmountable missions
Taking a plunge to surely fall.

'Twas the sorrow so returning often
Of thy feelings dying away.
Taking all thee people felt for
Burying thy glowing light of yesterday.

Living to thy murmur
Of thy soul so sorely there.
Merely yearning to understand thee blessings
Of thy cold, discolored stare.

Katy Schilling

Water's Mystery

The cool crystal like heaven,
that goes to who knows what depth.
That connects the whole world as we know it.
From where the dangerous creatures lurk,
to where the sweetest things can be.
This big thing of water...
could really be one sea.

Stacy West

Untitled

An unheard goodbye from the nights and days that knew you-
Stars in your stomach-
Moon in your mouth-
Sun in your skin-
Everyone including you is a universe-

An unheard goodbye to the nights and days that you knew-
Skies in your eyes-
Oceans in your lips-
Forests in your fingers-
Everyone including you is the earth-

Did your paint melt off of your mother's canvas?
Did your stars fall out of your father's constellation?
Did someone poke a hole in your heart?
   Michael D. Cuevas

Falling

My life's a constant trudging
steady drudging
not begrudging my falling calling fate
as fingers grasp and grip and grapple
through the slipping sliding sickeningly intangible air
constant acceleration not elation or exuberation
forever falling faster
nearing f**king disaster
at 32 feet per-second-per-second
but not per-second but first
I start to panic
growing frantic almost manic
approaching terminal velocity with great dread
Hoping I am dreaming
some sort of sub-conscience scheming
and me not capable of deeming mind over matter
will wake up in my bed but I know if I hit the ground
as my fate seems so bound to end up dead
my heart will ache until it breaks
I pray the lord my soul doth take me away to a world of peace.
   Shad Edwards

Secrets

We are thieves in the night
Stealing from each other
The treasures we hold.

Desperately clinging together
As though we could suspend this love
In time and space.

When alone, we love with our minds and bodies.
In crowds, we love secretly with our eyes,
Privately banishing the world.

You stir a warm excitement in my soul,
Arousing hushed feelings
Deliberately smothered long ago.

The day will come
When we will shout our latent secret
To the world.

Until then we must content ourselves
With gentle closet encounters.
Proving only to each other
The reality of us.
   Sandra Sukiennik

Portals And Passages

Silently we reach the passage of time,
Stepping through the portals, yours and mine.
And as the things which so remind,
What was ahead, is now behind.

Faster and faster, the portals are crossed,
Promises and chances, are forever lost.
Then through the glass, we darkly see,
The images of time travellers, you and me.

Across the portals, the passage of time,
Mirrors of reflection, sparkle and shine.
And as the images, silently stare back,
The portal so closes, the mirrors crack.

I see the passage which beckons so,
You cannot refuse, through the portal we go.
And as we cross each time span there,
Each fractured reflection, painfully stares.

One day shall come and be no more,
What does the time passage, hold in store?
For each it's different, what we see,
We do not know, when the final passage will be.
   Robert L. Bryant

Tara

Sunlight, so bright, so fair.
Storm clouds, a night without light, despair.
To know you, you are these things.
These fine transparent, gossamer wings.
So fragile a thought, so fine a deed.
I have oft been blinded by your passionate need.
To be center stage, to draw all eyes to you.
This thing that pursues in all that you do.
So tender, so callous, so unaware of this.
So remorseful, so sad, and then on to bliss.
You tease, and you taunt.
The conventions you flaunt.
You whirl through life, or drag out each day.
You are by choice, no other way.
Flitting from this to that, your pursuit of a thing.
You fly so high on sheer, transparent, gossamer wings.
   Lyndell Skaggs

Into The Whirlwind

Into the whirlwind of chaos and strife,
Straight as an arrow, sharp as a knife,
Battered and busted, outward I came,
Fatal wounds mended, never the same,

Into the masses, their laughter and scorn,
A sensitive child, gifted, was born.
Out of their clutches, dying with grief,
I sought every refuge, but found no relief,

Into the school room, their counsel and lies,
An innocent child, with hope in his eyes.
A grad from their high school, with honors I gained,
I cynically smiled, enclosing my pain.

Into the mainstream, of what they call real,
I quietly go and painfully feel.
Around the next corner, who knows what I'll find.
I may gain some insight, I might lose my mind.

Into the graveyard, their bones and their dust,
A hollow eyed corpse, will go where it must.
But out of that body, will rage my live soul,
Returning their pleasures, with vengeance in toll.
   Timothy Bostwick

The Stuff Behind The Wall

I am nothing but a nomad
Strewing as I search,
Without fail my tribe awaits
an' soon I will join.
and whose to say when I begin to doubt
my journey of an unsound mind,
that it is not a gift in which to behold
but more a burden to resist.
I am secluded in my world-
committed to find
A counter part of equality, who is lost as well.
My quest is tiring, but slowly I move ahead
to some one who is quick to realize,
that I am merely a captive of my own belief.
And when such perfection finds its way
It won't be the decorative package-
that entices a simple mind.
Rather the stuff behind the wall
that cries to be revealed.

Sonya Kemme

Honest Pain

I've recently dealt with matters that hurt the heart,
Such creatures have a lasting impression,
Beyond physical to emotional pain, which persists in great.

I do not believe myself to be a hurtful person.
I try to be fair, treat others the way
I would want to be treated in return.
Possibly a romantic and idealistic thought,
To hope someone would care about another in return.

Selfishness and greed amaze me.
How limiting these emotions are,
Not reaching beyond yourself, not sharing yourself,
Not being aware of others or the world of beauty
That does exist around yourself.

It saddens my heart to think of people in this standing.
How sad to never know the beauty of sharing and caring,
The thriving that explodes when you think of others
And try some understanding.

I am thankful for myself, my hurting heart.
At least I know honest pain -
Great pain acquired from caring.

M. E. Basham

Our First Kiss

The first time we kissed was on a
summer moonlit night,
On a faraway beach where no one was in sight,

You held my hand so tender and sweet,
I felt the warm ocean water splash upon my feet,

You put your arms around me with a sweet and loving touch,
I put my arms around you and told you
I loved you so much,

We tilted our heads and looked lovingly
into each others eyes,
Our lips met and together we kissed,
our hearts beat fast, and we felt free as butterflies,

Our lips parted and we both felt we
were in deep bliss,
From that day I'll never forget the night
we had our first kiss.

Terry Lynn DeVore

Summer Time

Summertime, summertime, hooray!, hooray!
Summertime, summertime, now we can play!
Sun beating on your back,
Wind blowing off your hat,
Math, English, Reading, Science,
Forget all that we did our assignments.
Water hoses spitting out water,
Little children chasing each other.
Ice creams melting from the sun,
Candied apples eaten one by one.
Summertime, Summertime, a wonderful season,
Beautiful sounds like birds singing.
Summertime, summertime, is finally here,
Boy, oh boy what a year.

Sergio Cabezuela

mourning

   dew glistening on the petals of roses
sun rising above the eastern shores
songs of birds in flight high above
another day's upon us

   nature, life, so beautiful, so fresh
as it begins anew
its everlasting journey
dawn after dawn

   it's this innocence we seek
the brightness we wish for
as no matter the darkness that's come before
our souls know
there will always be a new morning

Kristyn Elaine Wesdorp

Thank You, God

Thank You God for the test.
Surely You know what is best.
I'll stand on Your Word
and trust You for the rest.
It is not enough to have heard.
Although easier said than done,
It is in the doing that the victories are won.
I'll remember that it's easy
as long as things don't get queasy.
But, if nothing ever riles
there is no reason for the trials,
for it is in them that I come to really know Him.
So while others scurry
and often worry, I'll try to be quiet
and keep my perspective right.
I'll determine to be true
and see things from Your view.
I'll go the full length as You provide the strength.
You have never failed me yet.
Serving You is always the best bet.

Tommie Lou Cole

Pit Of Lost Emotions

One by one they march into my soul,
   taking it captive for days, months, years
   holding for ransom the yestertimes of happiness.
Heartaches, disappointment, and sorrow overwhelm.
No, there is no sound of laughter, no childish innocence,
My soul has grown cold and my eyes are still.
   I can hear, but I can not scream
   I feel the light, but I am motionless.
Where am I to go in this pit of lost emotions?

Kelli Hayes

"Recollect"

You could still feel the white glittering sheet,
   Surrounding you; protecting you,
      After you left.

You could still put your ear to a shell and hear,
   The sea, and the waves on the shore,
      After you left.

You could still imagine yourself sitting outside,
   In the dazzling, warm sun,
      After you left.

No one had to know you had been there,
   No one could care,
      After you left.
         Sara Sorrels

Gentle, Powerful Love

If the winds were a strong as my love for you the earth could not
survive, mountains would crumble, glaciers would shatter and stars
would be blown from the sky. If the sea was as deep as my love for
you, it would be infinite, like the changing seasons or great blue
sky, there would be no end to it. If the sun were as warm as my
love for you, the earth would surely glow, it would melt away from
the sun's bright ray until there was nothing left to show. If
trees grew like my love for you, they would grow so very high,
their peaks could not be seen from earth, they would match the
height of the sky. If flowers were as beautiful as my love for
you, everyone would stare, their eyes would be locked on a
wonderful sight, so lovely and so rare. My heart beats so for you,
my dear, that if thunder were as loud, it would be heard through
the land and by the heavens, it would scatter away all clouds. If
spring were as lasting as my love for you, there would not be snow,
there would be no ice, or shiny frost, not winter winds to blow.
So powerful, my love for you yet gentle as can be, it could conquer
the earth's great hurricanes, but would not harm a flea. And so,
my love, my heart is yours whatever come our way, As certain as the
seasons change, I love you more each day!
         Roxanne Marrandino

My Thoughts Of You

Sitting alone in this old room, with nothing to do but think.
Sweeping the floor with a raggedy broom, and cleaning the bathroom
Sink wondering whether I did it right or whether I did it wrong.
Thinking about you in the night, and trying to sing a song.
Hoping tomorrow I will see, that smile upon your face.
Knowing today that we will be, in our favorite place.
You are always on my mind, and always in my heart.
We know one day we will find, that we will never part.
Together we will be, forever and a day.
So everyone can see, the way we work and play.
For I know this is something, that you were afraid to hear.
But there is absolutely nothing, that you would have to fear.
Remember, what I really feel, is something special and true.
It is something very strong and real, it's the love I have for you!
         Robert L. Boone

The Lonely Desert

Desert winds sweep across the sand
sympathizing with the loneliest land.
The sun beats down on this world of beige
where no beauty survives its burning haze.
The lonely desert makes not a sound,
All its colors changed now, to sullen shades of brown,
Scorching heat burns all traces of love
the feeling which this lonely place yearns for,
Happiness here is forbidden;
in a place where the sand will never meet the shore.
         Kimberly Gallagher

How Come You Just Don't Get It?

I dreamed I was in Florida, sitting at a cafe
Taking my leisure, enjoying my pleasure
With Denzel and director Spike Lee
We sipped our cold beers on that white afternoon
Just Denzel and Spike and me.

At last I said, "I just can't understand
That although I am white, it can never be right
For a black man to care for me."
Just then a black woman loped into sight
"You got jungle fever?" she screamed
"Why you marrying white women, brother?
All our best men are marrying them, go get you another!"

We sat and listened on that white afternoon
And we found no solution, failed to reach a conclusion
"Does it matter if my skin is dark or light?
Is my brain black or just human or terribly white?"
When I left them I knew it was in defeat
As I hurried on down that white Florida street
No more Denzel, Spike Lee and me.
         Linda D'Ambrosio

The Challenger

All of the flights to outer space before;
Taught the nations to listen for the signal go, go, go.
The flight of the Challenger was to carry something new,
It was to carry a citizen passenger in its crew.

They picked a history teacher for this trip,
She passed all their test without a slip.
Her mission was to bring back a first hand view,
The diary she was to keep would not be new.

On this fatal flight with six plus one.
The flight would end before it begun.
A cold and bleak day, January 28th,
The Challenger and its crew were to meet its faith.

Families and friends grew edgy as the time arrived,
No one knew they would not return alive.
We have lost the Shuttles Challenger and our astronauts, too,
Their lights flickered out and their souls like a dove flew.

Quick like a bolt of lightning that fantastic dream was gone,
Where are the ideas, thoughts and dreams that were born?
While grief filled our hearts, tears stained our cheeks,
This sad disaster will be remembered for weeks and weeks.
         Ollie C. Purcell

Lamb Of God

Lamb of God so dear
Tell me I need not fear
God the father will provide
An eternal place to bide

Sinner thought I be
Jesus did set me free
Thus my sins were washed away
Death no longer has its sway

Risen saviour now
To you I humbly bow
Paying homage as I sing
Glory, glory to my king

Victory o'er death was won
By the lamb of God, our father's only son
Now he waits the day for his return again
As our king who conquered sin
         Vernon A. Weber

The Rain

Her tiny weak hand reached out and her fingers embraced mine.

Her eyes reminded me of soft worn out jewels.
Telling me what she could not say

Her fears of the unknown were close to her
but her love gave her strength as a strange peace
came within her heart.

Her smile, faded but strong gave proof of a merry
soul existing in her.

As she saw the grey clouds, her spirit gave
color to her pale face.

A light misty rain started as she gently released my hand,
while her body went into an everlasting sleep.

She appeared as an angel yet she looked like a child
ready to start another adventure.

Through the window I could see only her,
while grey skies said their goodbyes and the rain poured on.

Sarah Yetter

Kindness

Kindness is an outburst of a heart that is tender,
   Tender because it has known its own grief,
It spring or it bubbles, its message to render,
   Because that deep feeling must find its relief.

Kindness goes walking where others are walking,
   And kindness sits down where the hurt have a seat,
With or without words, kindness is talking
   About things that are helpful, the wounded to treat.

Kindness is ready to serve with a purpose,
   It may be assigned or it may happen by chance,
Some actions and words may flow as a surplus,
   Unnumbered the lives they flow forth to enhance.

Kindness is known to make turns unexpected,
   Like a boomerang thrown, it may come back to you,
Both giver and receiver of love are affected,
   Because both have been touched by kindnesses, too.

Kindness is living and kindness is growing,
   In the lives of those touched by its beauty and grace
Into full blooming grandeur, whether unseen or showing,
   The practice of kindness keeps spreading apace.

H. J. Tenclay

Heartbreak

Heartbreak,
Terrible, unkind, and hurtful.
You think you'll never get over it,
But then comes Mr. Gorgeous in to your life.
Then you're happy.
You think how could I ever have been heart broken over him?
The pain has settled.
Then the cycle begins again.
But not always,
Not when you find Mr. Right.

Courtney Dillon

Beauty

The beauty of the animals,
The beauty of mother nature;
The beauty inside ourselves:
The beauty that all human beings are seeking for
The beauty that makes us unique

Ruyayeem Rashid

Being One

Being one is a whole lot different
   than being two, three, or four . . .

Being one is an individual thing
   for every human, animal, or flower . . .

Being one means to ask a question,
   listen to your feelings,
   and then do not go by other people's standards . . .

Being one helps us to become who we are,
   and then sometimes to act a little crazy . . .

Being one is a part of me,
   you, and every other living creature.

So become that one being.

C. Nicole Duke

God Rewards Kindness

I recently read before going to bed,
That a kind act is good for the health,
The Immune System, it seems, gets quite a boost,
Something more valuable than wealth.

This wonderful news is one of the clues
To explain many things in life,
Why volunteer workers enjoy good health,
While others contend with strife.

The story's not new and certainly true.
That pet owners live a long time,
It's the Immune System at work, I know it now,
That keeps them in their prime.

I'm sure in my mind this attempt to be kind,
And the Immune System boost that it brings,
Is God's way of rewarding kindness
For those who do all these things.

This is the thought my alert mind bought,
And I'm sure I'm right on this,
God's unseen hand has this worked out,
To promote such human bliss.

Russell Williams

Love

Love is the color of a red, red rose
That blooms in the early spring.

It looks like the shiny sun when you
Search for it and find it rising.

It smells like the savory scent of violets
That grow in the fields.

It sounds like the melody of bells
On a gentle night, under a silvery moon.

It feels like a soft, soft breeze
That barely brushes my cheek.

It tastes like a sugary apple, and of
A newly ripening berry.

It makes me feel warm inside when it has
My soul captured in its heart
That will never lose faith in me
Or wither away without even saying goodbye.

Suzanna Shatarevyan

Special Thoughts

There's not a minute of the day
That can escape my memory,
When thoughts of you weren't dwelling there
So pleasantly a shimmering.
Don't ever think it goes unnoticed,
The little things you do,
That help me, teach me, show me how
To make my life anew.
I can't begin to tell you now,
How much it really means,
That I can have the little things
I thought were only dreams.
This special thought is sent your way
Just to let you know
That you are thought of every day
Much more than you are told!

Mary Slawson

Untitled

So, maybe it was just a star, my dear,
That caused the sparkle to gleam in your eye;
And 'twas, perhaps, but the breeze in my ear
Which I so fondly mistook for a sigh.
Belike you did but comb leaves from my hair,
'Tho I labeled it a caress; and why,
What I foolishly misnamed a kiss there
Was but grooming my mustache free of pie.
But, will you explain it, my lady fair?
I confess that I do not have it clear,
Although I have worried it to a care,
'Tis a failure in my logic, I fear.
Was the passion I read in your smile
Just an excess of beer - or of guile?

William J. Clay

When

Come on, Stop the pity and fear.
That certain tomorrow is very near.
You'll awake the birds so softly singing
and bells ringing, it's very near.
Let me not forget that growth takes
different forms in this life.
Oh what a waste if we didn't experience some strife.
Only when you've grown to accept
life's up and downs, that you can
become that whole person all around.
The waiting is over, the fear is gone-
that certain tomorrow is here.

Lillie Spencer

"Nihilism"

What can I possibly tell you that you haven't heard before?
That every waking hour we fight a self afflicted war?
You cannot get your laurels if you glorify the weak,
So there's no sense to what I say.
I will no longer speak.

What can I show that human eyes have not already seen.
Should I try to prove that envy's color is no shade of green?
Inconsequential change is like a drop of rain in snow.
A pebble in the stream we swim will in no way change,
The flow.

What can I do to stun that was not already done?
They put a man on the moon so should I put one on the sun?
Existence on one better translates to life's facetious lie.
So I'll watch for footsteps in the heavens.
Until the day I die.

Roger Braithwaite

Why Did You Have To Go?

When I've walked down
That great big hill
And my face was wet with tears,
I never wanted to realize
That you've been gone so many years.

When I've caressed
The engraving of your name,
The ice-cold of your stone
It seems as if you're nowhere near
And I feel so alone.

When I ponder, and ask why
God has taken you away
Either you come down or I go up
And we'd reunite someday

I have no memories of you to look back on.
I just wish for another chance
But I can't, for you've been taken
And you've gone.

Yolanda Elizabeth Lopez

A Memorial

A memorial for all you children,
That has gone on before.
I know that you all are little angels,
That has knocked on Heaven's door.

You all were great, when you were with us,
We loved you all so very much too.
God wanted you to be with him,
So there was nothing that we could do.

We did our best as teachers,
To help you through the day.
We taught, played, diapered and fed you,
Then you went on your merry way.

We will always be thinking of you,
Even if your name wasn't on a stone.
Remembering the little things you did,
Where you are today, you will never be alone.

Katherine P. Oulds

Relentless Tyrants

Dreams can be relentless tyrants
That haunt you in the night.
They come and behold
Thoughts lost in the daylight.
Capturing mind and soul,
Pulling down into a hole
Of hopelessness and fear.

Dreams are the tyrants
That haunt you in the night,
They hound you
And screech about
Things that you might say.
Dreams are the tyrants
That haunt you because they want to possess,
Capturing your mind and soul.

Rachel Blow

The Country

The country can be very hot and spacy
   The country is different from the city
The people in the country takes good care of
   their country
And keeps it clean and healthy to live in.

Natasha Matthews

Goodbye

My time with you is at an end, no longer now can I pretend,
That here for me a future lies, the dream, once lived, now slowly dies.
With that great dream my heart goes too,
it slowly breaks with thoughts of you.
You sparked my passion, gave me fire!
But now that flame's a fun'ral pyre.
I gave you all, forsook the rest, my family stood but second best.
In me you built this ideal; you took a dream and made it real!
As time went by the changes came; that high ideal at such a cost!
The dream was killed on judgement day,
when my whole world turned dark and grey.
Though there've been tears and sadness past,
I somehow knew this was the last.
So now I come to say good-bye, that dream can never truly die,
But it will sleep and we will part, perhaps one day to once more start.

Kathleen Jarman

Wisdom

I can do anything for a little while
   That I didn't think I could do
I find the strength within my self
   Whatever it takes to get through.

When circumstances beyond my control
   Invade my life like a storm
To rob my soul and steal my peace
   Like a curtain ripped and torn.

Whether bearing the pain of illness
   Or grieving the loss of a friend
Or sharing the burden of a heavy load
   By lending a helping hand.

My father passed this wisdom to me
   When I was just a child
And when things get difficult as they sometimes must
   I try to bear up with a smile.

So whatever curves life throws at me
   Come joy, pain or strife,
Remember, I can do anything for a little while
   That I couldn't do for the rest of my life.

Nancy M. Green

A Father's Talk With God

It seems like only yesterday
that I made a commitment in life;
it's the biggest one that comes to mind;
I got married to my wife.
She's a woman that at first I liked
and then loved more than the rest,
and I guess I can't regret the years
'cause I know I've had the best!
With having children, now adults and striving on their own,
it can sometimes get so scary for me, Lord,
to see that they're all grown.
But, dear Lord, you get my thanks each day
and all of my burdens too;
'cause you know me, my heart, my hopes and joys
and all of my thanksgivings too!
So, if there'd be a wish for me and mine,
I hope you're listening today;
for that wish is that our family love
will increase in every way!

Mary Celli

Blue Bird

Come to me oh bird of blue
that I may hear your song so true,
which tells me of the lighted sky,
whose tale does cause my teary eye,
for I am in eternal night,
for light so blessed does not invite,
but fear you not and keep your song,
for telling truth be not your wrong.

Now vanish bird oh bird of blue,
and come to me when time is due,
and hide not truth and tell no lie,
for I know the light shall never fill my eye.

Sandro M. Gonzalez

The Snowfall

The street is empty and quiet except for a very noisy TV
That is blaring from behind closed doors. There is no one
on the streets to see. And from sustained windows, someone
peeks out to see the snow falling on the street softly

The small child steps outside to play in the jumps, falling
down repeatedly. The car came speeding along; putting on a
show and from the car came deathly bullets, and the child falls
one last time into the snow.

The street is empty and quiet except for a very noisy TV
That is blaring from behind closed doors. There is not one on
the streets to see and from behind curtained windows, someone
peeks out to see the snow falling on the mother weeping.

Kay Jackson

My Sisters

There is joy in my heart,
That is set apart,
From all the good and bad,
But the best memories are
The moments I and my sister had.

Mother is gone
And we are alone
And Jesus holds us in his hand.
My love for you two will hold very true,
For only Jesus can break this band.

And let us not forget what she held dear to her heart
Her sister and brothers too.
For they have become that link for me,
Lets do all for them we can do.

I hope the love I feel for you
Is given back to me.
I hold these thoughts with all my heart,
My sisters, my sisters______We're three.

Rosetta B. Garner

My Mission

My mission in life began with a light
That ran through my soul before I was old,
Shot like a lance, with flame did it dance.
  It burned away sin, I could not begin
  To comprehend it, an incredible gift.
  It gave me direction. An apparition
Appeared as to lead when I had a great need.
  The sky it was mine, No help save divine
  Could unto others make victory theirs.
  I am Resolute. I will not refute.
My mission through strife, ends with my life.

Ron Jenkins

A Walk To The Daffodils

We set out unknowing, unsure, uncaring. All we knew was that it was a walk. With every step the muscles in our legs tensed and relaxed. With a turn of the head you are awed with the sight of majestic tranquillity. A field of thoughts and dreams play over and throughout our minds.

The haze that blankets the hills is seductive. It stays far from groping hands-never to be touched by troubled fingers. Around the corner. Stop. More things drift over your consciousness. Some children run ahead, eager to end the journey. Others stay behind to breathe in the air and drink in the beauty.

The destination is there, marked with the hand of nature. Rows of daffodils in memory of loved one. Loving hands planted each bulb, nurtured and cared for them-each symbolizing a heartbeat dedicated to her. To hold and caress that love is unheard of still I touch every petal on one of them. Like magic it breathes a tear down the soft petals onto my hand. I stand. My immature soul blocks out all of its symbolism from my ignorant mind.

Tabitha E. L. Lawson

Even The Rose

What thorn protects you like
that of a rose?
What is it that
burdens you my love?
I can feel the passion
burning in our hearts,
but still I am kept away.
This thorn buried deep within you
buries itself also into me.
My heart is already yours!
I want you.
Only you in my arms.
Let this drawn forth your loneliness
for even the rose with its many
sharp thorns...
is sweet.

Shannon Chalk

Head Poems

Many poems have started in my head,
that other people have never read.
Any moment of the day they appear,
kept in my mind without the fear,
that I will forget them before
I compose several lines more
and transfer them to paper with my pen
to give this poem an end.

But, alas, as always, the lines drift away,
and I can not recall them on another day.
So, my poem is lost for all time,
the one I wrote in my mind.

Although I miss the poem I though,
and Its creation was all for naught,
I am not sadder for its loss,
for within my mind, another begins to toss.

When all the lines are in a row,
I will write them down to show,
all the people who have never read,
the beautiful poems in my head.

William H. Jacobson

Marvelous Creation

I walked along a meadow road,
That peasants and shepherds of old have strode;
And thought, my God! What wondrous things,
These beasts with legs, and birds with wings.
I wondered at a tiny pea-flower;
That strives in a long mid-April shower.
The Lord that counts each grain of sand,
Shall cradle me in the palm of his hand.

Myra Ann King

A Fond Adieu

I wonder, green trees, will you know I'm gone
That sunny morning, or the rainy day
The angels came to bear your friend away,
And if you know, then will you feel forlorn?
Gray mockingbirds, if you should hear a sigh,
Sing all your lovely songs that I may hear
And as I leave the misty trail not fear
The trail's end where we all must say good-bye-
Wild flowers in the meadow, please be blooming,
And little crystal stream where I would wade
On smooth round pebbles, clean and cold in the shade,
Be babbling - thunder, if you like, be booming!
Do not let me leave this beautiful wood
Without some sign you'll all remember me,
Heaven cannot be lovelier than you,
Or sweeter than that short hour - smiling I stood,
Seeing for the last time all I could see -
Bidding all of nature a fond adieu.

Maria Gael Despeaux

True Lies

Guilt, the feeling of emotion,
that traps our spirit,
and captures our soul for eternity.

Our mind begins spinning,
the heart begins pacing,
stomach aches in nausea,
and the feeling continues..
Over and Over and Over.

Like an audience viewing a film,
It happens as early as the mind remembers,
Until we choose to walk away from the show.

Virginia L. Sanderson

A Love Lost - Memories Remain

Have you ever felt so cold and all alone
that you had no one to call your own.

The pain that you feel in your bed at night
for no one is there to hold you tight.

To wake up to coffee service for one,
no one to talk to or depend upon.

Well that's just how I feel, now that you are gone.
My life is empty, now that you are no longer around.

I have no desire to look for another,
for you are the only one that I shall love
forever and ever.

The happiness that we shared together
the memories I have, I pray will last forever.
For I know there will never be another.

Kathy Bennett

The Dream That Took My Life Away

Have you ever wanted to be someone else for just one day?
That's the dream that took my life away.

I thought she was the greatest thing,
Little did I know the troubles she'd being.

I got to hang with her just one time,
Then I was asked to walk the line.

My mother said just once more,
I walked out and slammed the door.

We went to a party like we always did,
That's when I realized I wasn't a hid.

We drunk and smoke until our eyes were red.
Little did I know we'd all be dead.

We drove into a one way lane,
Suddenly I was in a lot of pain,

I didn't know where I was and I couldn't see,
I kept thinking this just couldn't be me.

The doctor said I was going to die,
All I could do as ask myself why?

I took my life for a night of fun,
Now my life's completely done.

Loni Runge

Definition Of America

America, the land of the free.
That's what it is, well, supposedly.
A contradiction in terms. America free?
Image of how America appears to be.

America is a democracy that silences minorities,
By utilizing its political authority.
The black man, red man, and others to be named,
All pawns in this society's maniacal game.

America, the real truth is coming out.
About all the scandals and its misuse of clout.
Prevention of this corruption is a hopeless fight,
But there are a few wrongs that can be set right.

America's drug plot to rub the African out.
Overwork of migrant workers until they all drop.
Confinement of Native Americans until they conform.
Harassment of immigrants until they go home.

America has never honored its founding creed,
So redefine what the word America means.
And realize that true equality cannot be achieved,
In a society which persecutes its minorities.

Randall Johnson

A Wartime Love Affair

Today, I received your letter
The cotton candied clouds
parted long enough for the syrupy rays
to light up your chocolates words.

Tomorrow, I will write with a soiled pen
and bloody ink.
The paper is potholed with the stains
because of the dangerous road my fingers travel.

In a week or so, you will read this
with your crystallined eyes
and the paper will be potholed no more
rather it will transform into white silk
carrying my image, scarred and holed
to you — sacred and whole.

Monica M. Wirick

Untitled

Deep in the mists of memories past
that's where my ego sighs and softly cries for what can't last.
For dreams are demanding, yet whither so fast,
in meadows of sunlight and valleys too vast.

But for the vision of joys yet to come,
gently upon the ground, I would lie down, my roaming done.
But life's always teasing and dreaming is fun.
So ever I wander and onward I run.

Through the grey canyons where rainbows play,
there in silver pools, quintessential jewels, my memories lay.
Candescent reflections, one nightbeam away,
ever awaiting each end of each day.

Alone in my dreaming, protected by sleep,
on gossamer wires into soul-lit fires I make my leap.
And when I awaken, some thoughts lie too deep,
beyond ever knowing, too fragile to keep.

What if my mists were flooded with light?
In what disguise could my ancient eyes behold that rite?
And if understanding should reach a new height,
where would I wander to find a new night?

Leigh Underwood

Winding Up The Strings Of Time

The 50's brought us Elvis, still the King of Rock-n-Roll
The 60's made us take a look deep within our soul

Vietnam changed our lives forever
And Germany is once again together

Nuclear bombs are less a threat
But we'd be wise not to forget

Computers of the 70's paved the way
For lifestyles we enjoy today

Women of the 80's came clearly into view
Now politically active and independent too

Our homes seem to come standard with t.v. and vcrs
Microwaves, video games and second cars

Some deadly new diseases replace ones that have a cure
But we need to stop pollution and make our water pure

We still have crime and hunger and folks in poverty
But there's no place on earth like 'The Land of The Free'

The winds of change will always blow
And the more we learn, the more there is to know

And so it is and always will be
Progress, politics and humanity.

Ruth M. Delbow

Spell Of Truth

I saw the stardust gently falling in
The branches of a willow tree.
And as I watched I chanced to hear
Such a lonely, mournful cry that I
Trembled with fear.
The cry of a lost, imprisoned Soul.
Pray God that cry you'll never know.
This spell that I had witnessed
Will live with me eternally.
For now I know by whom the cry was uttered,
That lost, imprisoned Soul was me.

Tina Carvour Gallagher

Rain Forest

Slowly dissipating from this world we know,
The animals have no place to go.
Where tractors tread the fires burn,
And the world we know takes another turn.

It gives us medicine, it give us air;
No longer free it now is rare.
Neglecting still these certain things,
Forgetting all the forest brings.

Suffering from burns and devastation,
The ground welcomes rain with consecration.
Human kind the major threat
Acre by acre with no regret.

Here comes the tractor, Clatter, Clatter!
The birds are fleeing, watch them scatter!
More still more a forest bleeds;
Wave after wave of ceaseless deeds.

Enduring so long without loving care,
For help it cries-but no one's there.
 Travis J. Webb

My Birds

I tossed some bread unto the grass;
The birds arrived in one great mass.
Chirping, cheerfully, they pecked away,
And then a cardinal, to my dismay,
Arrived and surveyed what was on the ground,
But the food he liked was not to be found.

Sunflower seeds are his forte, I know!
'Cause he flew to the feeder but to his woe,
It was empty with only a kernel or two,
And with his chirping, he gave me a cue.

"Go to the garage; take care of my need;
This feeder is empty. Please fill it with seed."
Off to the garage, I went on the double,
To fill the feeder and avoid further trouble;
But a squirrel or two kept running around,
Looking for food they could abscond.
Bread, seed, what did they care;
The hunger they felt was hard to bear.

Now, my birds and the squirrels have come and gone,
But they will be back for their friendship I've won.
 Ms. Muriel M. Gregor

Untitled

The warmth of the sun freckled my face,
the breeze wove through my fingertips, as if it were lace
Heaven and earth meshed as one, as far as I could see
and you walked a slow pace just after me

The cobblestone echoed underfoot
the roadside daises pushed through the soot
The crow and squirrel conversed in a tree
and you walked alongside of me

Crimson and violet pierced the sky once blue
a curtain call to the day no longer new
Long I strolled and pondered, to mean or to be
and you walked knowingly in front of me

God graced with this presence and given a chance
to live and to love, and to laugh and to dance
In the stillness of night, I stood as alone as one can be
because you would no longer accompany me
 Leslie Cook Boardman

"A Visit"

It's April 23, 1994, a beautiful day to be at
the cemetery. I'm standing at Mommy's grave.
Today is Amy's first birthday - born just 2
years and 2 months late.

while I was standing there,
a single tear fell from my eye.

I came here tonight to say,

"A red flower pinwheel was placed
on Grandmom Guerra's grave
in her memory by me;
Placed in Amy Leigh's name
in honor of the first birthday
of the Granddaughter Mommy
always dreamt of...
I see her smiling."
 William R. Guerra

Cheetahs

Black spots on yellow fur on the sleekest, fastest cat.
The cheetahs smart, wild, and fast this cat's far from fat.
Its running steps are long and quick and deadly to its prey.
Hiding in the long brown grass and searching for food all day.
The baby cheetahs learn to fight, hunt, and kill from their mother.
They even fight playfully with their sisters and their brothers.
The cheetah smart, wild, and fast, the fastest of all the cats.
 Kimberley Pickens

Where Have All The Fathers Gone

I sense you in the breeze that sways the trees,
the cold wind that steals into my coat and chills me.
You see the stars I see, live the moment I live,
yet you mean less in my world than do the leaves that tumble by
I can neither see you nor hear your voice.

Never again can I look at you and see myself.
Only a wounded child, unable to release the pain that has
defined it.
We play together until your tantrum takes you away.
Never again could I dream of meeting you.
I would look through you, unable to see the shadow you have become.

Sad now that I cannot mourn you.
Could I have saved you?
Could I have given you hope?
Darkness claimed you, drawing you from my reach.
Had you only fought it, had you just called out my name.
The difference between salvation and damnation.
 Kimberly I. Cooney

Sunset

I saw a sunset the other day and thought only of you.
The colors were deep as fire, but with beauty oh so true.

The colors danced across the sky ever changing through watchful eyes,
to see if miracles do exist,
but no miracle is as this.

Though many say miracles come and go, with this I must agree,
But it's surely nice to finally know
that the miracle of you will always be.

Will always be as this poet says, the inspiration of a heart
thought dead.
The fire of passion in life one must have,
The dream of tomorrow to help move ahead.

I thought in depth of what is true, yet only to find
I thought only of you,
only of you as the sunset reminded,
is the miracle of beauty and the vision to find it.
 Steve G. Ornelas

Teardrop Alley

Tears of sorrow...tears of joy...'tis the mix of the world...
  the common alloy...

One for sorrow... one for joy...just to look at them one
  would never know...

From which source they sprang... from down below...below the
  surface where emotions collide...

Forming a wave on which an inner surfer will ride...heading for
  shore... making it...until the next tide.
  Nancy A. Waldron

My Lonely Days Of Nights

Lost on a beach watching
  the day come to an end,
  looking upon a soon dark sky
sets another lonely day to begin

    Alone and quiet except by the
    voices possessed of the waves of night,
      sets another day of darkness,
       another day without light

  in need of heart to end
    lonesome quest
alone and cold, another day
    without rest

      each night praying to a different
        star high above,
      to end this lonely day with
        the thought of being loved

  only to find out another prayer goes unanswered,
    to a lonesome quest still not complete,
      to end my lonely days,
      my lonely nights without sleep.
  Ken Jenkins

'From Dawn To Dusk'

One girl I admired so much.
The day I finally got to meet her,
It seemed she was really fantastic,
I thought we might look good together.

As the days passed, we talked more and more.
I discovered things I never knew,
About what she was, and where she had been.
We talked about all this over Mountain Dew.

At last my chance came to take her out.
I approached and asked, trying of myself not to make a fool.
Already knowing what it was about, she replied, "Sure".
Inside, I jumped for joy, but outside, I kept my cool.

We had fun that night under the circumstances.
We all laughed and I thought she had a blast.
Since that night, she has not spoken or looked at me.
To her now, I'm just another guy in her past.

To suddenly cut off our friendship hurt my heart yet one more
time. Hurt more than before because no explanation was given in
the least as to why with me she stopped being even just friends
She has killed me, put me to sleep, beauty killed the beast.
  Michael Harrelson

The Master Card - (Don't Leave Without It)

The weather was so calm and clear
The day I manned my ship
That soon became a sea untamed
And had me in its grip

The night arrived, with wind and rain
You'd think I'd realized
That if a storm was being born
I'd surely be capsized

Then in a flash, I saw my past
It filled me with regret
I fell upon my knees and prayed
To a man I've never met

Then in the Thunder, came a voice-
The Master of the Sea-
He said my son, I'll take you on-
But you must follow me!

The sea is there. My boat is there too,
But when I take a trip
He charters all my days and nights-
He's Captain of my Ship.
  Monica B. Sanchez-Rilling

School Days

The days of telling stories and doing homework till two;
The days of long reports, and having hair that's blue.

The days of doing book work and fighting with your friend;
These are the school days we never want to see end.

The days of school principals not matching their clothes;
The days of every girl wanting to be a model and pose.

The days of all teachers assigning you seats;
The days of learning to grow beets.

The days of seeing old friends go and new ones come;
The days when you felt you were so dumb.

The days when you don't act yourself just to fit in;
The days you thought all that matters is to win.

The days of taking showers, and praying for snow;
The days of counting minutes that went so slow.

The days that lasted forever and never past;
These are the days you want to last.
  Nannatte Heshelman

To My Daughter

I doubt if you will ever realize
The depths of my great love.
I know that I have truly been blessed
By the heavenly God above.

It started the glorious day
I first held you close to me.
I gazed into your sweet little face
And wondered how this could be.

As you sped through infancy and childhood,
My love became ever stronger.
I often wish that you could have stayed
A child a little longer.

You're a teenager now and all grown up,
And my feelings for you remain true.
I know it's not said quite often enough.
My daughter, my friend, "I love you."
  Sandra Money

The Piano Is Silent

There will be no tunes today.
The dust-covered piano is silent.
The old woman slowly rocks to and fro.
The sight has faded from her eyes of blue.
Her work-worn fingers are twisted with age.
Her mind wanders back in time.
A smile lights up her face.
The piano notes of yesteryear
Frolic through her mind.
She lightly taps her toe,
And softly hums along.

>*Lois A. Pratte*

Bound By Instinct

The feelings that you bring,
The emotions that control me-
  Not conjured through imagination.
  Not some school boy's infatuation-
My heart, knows truth,
And as alone as I may be,
I'll always have your thoughts, your dreams
To keep me company-
  So unlock your heart, release its needs
  Love me now or set me free-

>*Ryan Green*

Never Too Young

I'm sure you would understand if you only knew,
The extent of love this heart creates for you.
When I told you I loved you, that was no mistake,
And the reward for my honesty was painful heartache.
I need you next to me to relieve my fears,
When we were together, comfort I felt I cried no tears.
If you leave I will know how it feels to cry again.
Without you life is a game I cannot win
Understand this now for it is all so true,
This young heart can't beat without you.

>*Kelli D. Johnson*

The River Of Life

Life is like a river
The farther you go,
the more you know.
The river sometimes sings
But its harshness stings.
As you sail along on your little boat
you'll struggle in vain to stay a float.
And in your path stands another rock
to keep you down and battered.
But keep in your mind the clock
that blows away your time on the river of life.
Past loves, memories, and sorrows may detain you from keeping
swift on the river of life.
So make like a deer
don't let yourself drift
and achieve all you possibly can
before the end of the river is near....
And then gone.

>*Lydia Paar*

Harmony

This is a love that can be beautifully explained.
The feelings grow with such intensity there's no time to
  invite pain.

That is my love
When we're together there's no reason for hatred.
Just room for making sweet memories.
A wonderful time for patience.

That is his love
As the sun descends beyond the mysterious trees;
There's no mystery about this love we've made.

That is our love
Life is wonderful when shared together,
To live in this world in harmony forever.

That is love
That is our love

>*Melissa Wiegand*

Challenge Of A Lifetime

The words that go forever untold,
The feelings that are kept inside,
The uncertainties that life brings us,
Are all of the things that I hope to one day find.
But the words that I already know,
The feelings that I do feel,
And the certainties that life has brought to me,
I must share with you. Down those country roads and sandy beaches,
The wind blew gently through my hair.
I closed my eyes, wishing and dreaming,
Your kiss was so brand new.
The heart knows exactly what to say,
But the words just aren't written that way.
Time teaches all, and the days tell a tale.
At nighttime the lesson is learned.
Life is dashing ahead as we travel down this un-known path.
We are in a world of confusion.
But if the world would stop for just one day,
Then maybe we could have it our way.
Then again, who's to say that we can't take the world on?

>*Melissa Ann Gascon*

Missing You

  Standing on the shore in solitude,
The fierce wind whips through my hair and clothes.
  As the cold bites at my face.
  Heavy clouds hang somberly in the sky
And the waves crash against the sand before me.
  A burden weighs on my heart and my mind.
  I look up and see not images
Of billowing creatures nestled in blue skies
But a vastly muddled stretch of solemnity.

  Alone on the edge of the world
With nothing before me but eternal obscurity,
  I bow my head and think of you.

>*Karen L. Hallett*

A Silent Killer

My heart aches as the room remains silent.
The memories of laughter, good times, and
promises resurface.
Promises my heart builds into a future,
Only to be dashed with utter silence.
As the first tear falls, the others soon follow,
A catharsis of this heavy burden on my heart.
The phone rings.

>*Nicole Louque*

Life

Ashes to ashes, dust to dust
The first dawn to fall upon our face,
Was accepted with warm and tender grace.

We're watered with love on a daily basis,
We grow as flowers and bloom with many faces.

What fate does this life hold in its hand?
Success or failure is due to every man.
 - A happy marriage or single and free,
 - A college education or skilled to a tee.
 - Some choose parenting, some do not.
 - But either way this deserves some thought.
 - Homeless and penniless are conditions we
   can all do without.
Our final call is without a doubt;
Ashes to ashes, dust to dust.
Sherry Woodberry-Nembhard

"My Mother Means"

Birth...
 The first heart beat I ever heard. The first smile I ever
 saw. Hands that caught me when I stumbled.

Fun and Laughter...
 Late night snacks and small talk which illuminated my heart
 with words of wisdom to last a lifetime.

A prayer partner...
 Awakened at midnight stepping out into the cold winter air
 and trying desperately to answer the call of a troubled soul.

A broken heart that keeps on beating...
 When life becomes vividly real and a young tender heart
 experiences betrayal of love and friends she's there to
 restore the heart of one badly bruised and broken. And if I
 should lose my way Mother is the north star that guides me
 home.

Proverbs...
 Going the extra mile, giving more than just the cloak off
 her back. Stretching a dollar and always willing to share
 with those in need. Many are virtuous but you Mother exceed
 them all!

Marjorie Smith

The Encounter

My heart pounded like the wind on the trees.
The flushness upon my face caused you to smile.
You stood there timidly as you stared.
No words could pass to my mind, for it was blank.
The room appeared to spin faster and faster;
how awkward the moment seemed to be.
The crowd that surrounded just disappeared.
I looked into your eyes, as you into mine.
Longing for your kiss, I heard a voice.
Hoping it was your own I looked to your lips.
Sadly, they had not uttered the spoken words.
Still mesmerized, I wandered toward you.
You were unable to speak; likewise was I.
As we stood looking to one another something happened.
My heart was joined with yours, and acquainted itself.
Slowly it returned to me as I suddenly realized,
I, yes, I, had done the unthinkable.
Without thought or warning I had fallen in love.
Sabrina Bittinger

Unfinished Portrait

Your life is an unfinished portrait.
The future is hidden from view.
Your hand, guiding the brush strokes,
Is entirely up to you.

No matter how dull the beginning,
You can add beauty before you are through,
Changing an unfinished portrait
The way you live your life through.

Love will make the eyes brighter;
Unselfishness will brighten your smile.
Helping others will show in the portrait
Because you've made life worth while.

Thinking constructively and living purposefully
Will reveal the character you are.
And in your portrait, one can see
You're a better person by far.

So why not paint your portrait
That all these colors demand.
Remember, it is not yet finished;
The brush is still in your hand.
Marie (Snively) Brooks

Bright Lights, Special Words

I find myself trapped beneath
the glow of luminous marquees
Some absent cavity behind myself
A mirrored image of some simplistic child
gone awry bewitched by special words
like bijou theater doctorate of philosophy

The words so clearly spoken opaque when juxtaposed
against the brilliant light
instruct the fears to eat themselves
and grow bigger just the same the fears of fame
of love of money and the talent I have for exploiting both

The marquee weighs heavy on my halo
A sensual weight that turns me on
It beckons me to read one step two steps back it reads:
"All junkies are famous" I go in just to prove them wrong
Thomas Graham

Fire

I watch her working quietly there,
The grace with which her fingers guide the needle,
Slowly in and out ..... of the cloth
The button she sews carefully on.
Her hands excite me.
Long slender fingers - her nails painted red.
I think of how they felt last night.
Carving her name in my back as she kissed me.
A kiss that shattered my soul, as the pieces of a kaleidoscope
it fell in fragments around me.
Her tongue like liquid fire
flickered in and out of my mouth.
Melted my lips.
While her breath seared my throat,
My mind screamed her name.
In that moment of agonized ecstasy
I ached to imprison her body beneath me,
To make her mine
Forever.
Kathy Dull

No Seconds Left

On Mother's Day when I go into the stores, I try to avoid
the greeting card section, with all those
Mother's day cards on display,
but somehow I always manage to catch a quick glimpse of them
from out of the corners of my eyes,
wishing I could buy just one more for my Mom.
When I pass by a garden of roses, I think of my Mom,
because roses were her favorite.
When I pass by an elderly lady so tiny and frail,
tears well up in my eyes, because I think of my Mom.
I think of how she will never be here again to give me advice,
so I won't go down the wrong path of life
It will no longer be Mom and I together against the cold cruel
world like before,
but now just I alone.
Though you be thirteen or thirty, don't wait until there's
no seconds left to tell Mom how much she is loved, and appreciated.
She is the best friend you will ever have...Mom.

Mabel Eads

My Uncle Ivan

I can see my uncle Ivan, with his bible in his hand. He would read
the holy scriptures, and try to help me understand That there is a
place called heaven, where I will want to live someday. But I had to
talk to Jesus, and he would hear me when I pray.

Many questions I would ask him, and quickly he would say,
Let us get the Holy Bible, it tells all and show's the way.
Many hours we spent upon our knees, it wasn't long until I found.
That I had to talk to Jesus, so I could be heaven bound.

We sat in the swing, out on the hill, and watched the sun, setting
low. At night the moon and stars so bright, the sky was all aglow.
The crickets would be singing, we felt the chill of the night.
Then uncle Ivan would be saying, it won't be long until daylight.

We laughed and talked, and before to long, old memories would creep
in. He would reach for his old guitar, and pick with a great big
grin. The old gospel songs, he knew by heart, sometimes they made me
cry. Then too soon the time was gone, and I would have to say
goodbye.

Back home again, it wouldn't be long, until the memories filled my
mind. Of uncle Ivan and his guitar, and a grin from time to time.
I miss his music and the gospel songs, that mean so much to me.
But it won't be long, until next time, and uncle Ivan I will see.

Norma Jean Owens

California Dream

The land of sunshine
The land of stars
The land of mountain palms, and the great pacific ocean.
The land we all dream of, flowering trees and plants and shrubs
All year round.
Ah, this is the land of sunshine, a fairy tale world of make
Believe, and reality.
this is the California dream.
This is truly the land of sunshine.
The land of hopes and dreams that can be fulfilled.
If you have the ability to do whatever you want.
You can do it all in the land of sunshine.
This is truly the California dream, a world so different than
Any where else.
Where people live in grand homes.
The land of make believe and stars galore.
To able to live here in the land of sunshine is truly a
Dream come true.
A California dream in the land of sunshine.

Lois M. Doswell

"Shan-Shui"

I have been to this place, yet I have not,
the landscape is filled with mists and wonder.
It is heaven or ideal Earth, I thought
lacking in shadows that wish to plunder.
With my eyes I walk the trees and mountain trails,
It could be dawn , daytime, dusk, or night.
here, Time passes as quickly do the snails
who, with the others, create joy and light.
A place to rest, to pray, to meditate,
with a soul set free by peace, it would
appear one were dead, alive, perhaps sedate.
Aside the ills, Nature says, "Life is good".
So, be spirited and at beauty nod
thanking always their Maker named God.

Pauline

"A Child's Love"

From that moment of conception the bond begins,
The love flows from your heart to them;
At the beginning your emotions are mixed,
But your heart is in this and it can be fixed;
You're happy, you're scared, you don't know what to expect,
But you want this baby and you prepare for the test;
Can I handle this? Will I be a good mother!
Because I'm alone now, the man said, "I'm just your lover!"
So you start to prepare for the new life you have made,
And no matter what else happens you are not afraid;
As the baby grows, so does you love, stronger each day,
And you know that this will never change or be taken away;
Now the time is here and you prepare for the birth,
And God will help you and guide you because of your worth;
Then you hold that little person for the first time,
And no matter what else happens this new little life is mine.

Pamela Clohessy

Memories

I'll never forget how much you once cared,
The love I feel for you still lingers there.
The two of us had something that was fine and
  warm and true.
You didn't see it that way,
  you left me out in the blue
With you was where I thought I belonged,
  But that is where I went wrong.
So many difficulties, so much pain,
  But yet so much love to be gained.
You never really realized that I'm the one
  who cared,
'Till then everything will continue to be bare.
With your heart and mind I could be near,
So we can have back the memories that were
  so dear.

Melissa Picotte

Loneliness

The ache that you feel inside
the moment you realize
you are surrounded by an emptiness.

The noise, the happenings
around you become a quiet
so thick, it can smother
the air you breathe.
The ache is dull, but the pain is piercing.

So small do you feel, that the sound of your own
heart beating can frighten you to death - and
sometimes does.

Kathy Angrisani

Glistening Lights

Stars spread across the night sky like crushed diamond dust.
The moon hanging like a large lantern to light the dark country side.

If you look across the dark night you will see the glimmering
country side light up when the lightning bugs come out to play.

Leaving the dark night glistening with sparkles of golden light as
they dance and play, they look like falling glitter every where.

Theresa Kiser

Mysterious Tree

Sometimes when I think of myself I see,
The mysterious resemblance of an old dead tree.

Standing alone in rough, rugged weather,
Trying its best to still hold together.

Withstanding the winds that remove its bark,
And the nests that are built by the blue jay and lark.

Even with its old, twisted trunk,
Over the years it still has not sunk.

Branches that break and fall to the ground,
Where nothing but remains of them can be found.

Protection of leaves from the sun, snow, and rain,
Is gone with the years, only dryness remain.

It's left there to stand and struggle alone,
Dead branches and roots getting brittle as bone.

Yet it still stands, but, now with a lean,
Never again to become green.

Long after it's gone, everyone will recall,
The strength that it had when it once stood tall.

Velma Jeane Taylor Williams

Firefly Flashback

Hot summer nights; packs of kids still roam
the neighborhood backyards.
Porchlight glows in patches, as fireflies do.

Furtive giggles escape
all of us huddled, hushed
behind the holly bush next to the pool.
Long minutes pass, and the others are calling...
Still we hide, anticipating company in the dark.

Hot summer nights;
silence snapped by stealthy sneakers
and chirping crickets.
Darkness stretches on and on,
pierced only by firefly lanterns.

Ten o'clock now; porchlights
flicker on/off,
flashing come home signals.
We desert our hiding-space,
crashing through bushes and vaulting fences
on the journey back.

Lisa Reinhardt

Black Moon

Lingering on; blackness.
The shadow hovers over my every breath,
Stillness, loneliness, lie motionless in myself.
Every moon, every star I look at is for you.
But yet the sadness robs away, and slowly
devours, at the light of joy I once saw.
Will the madness in my soul, ever stop the rage?
Only you can save me, from the dirty hands
that is vigorously destroying me.

Laurie Tavares

Children Only Once

Children are the most beautiful thing that you have ever seen,
The new born face, the smile, and race make it all so keen.

The moment they're born so tiny and weak,
To the toddler that walks and learns to speak.

The way they grow, so upright and fast,
To the way that the treasures go by through the past.

And when they can tell you, that you are so wrong,
And when to begin to not get along.

But when they get older, so old they're away,
You wish you had more time, and want them to stay.

But when they leave, from home, for good,
You're asking them if please, if they would,

Call you and talk all day on the phone,
And say, "won't you please, please come home?

But when they get older they won't always be there,
There to protect, and there to keep bear.

So when you have time while your kids are awake,
Love them and tease them, and watch what they'll make

The dolls that girls play with, a football that a boy punts,
Remember, because children, are Children Only Once!

Melissa Landers

Sand And Sea

I traveled miles and miles to see
The ocean deep, the restless sea;
Stand on the shore and dream again,
Of ships at sea and sailor men.

The sun and wind they sweep my brow;
I've taken on a new life now.
No longer confined to the affairs of state,
The wind my master, the sea my fate.

I sleep the sleep and dream again
Of ancient mariners and sailing men;
Of sea and sand and breaker high,
And oceans blue that touch the sky.

I'm now at rest, I spend no time
With anxious thoughts that plague the mind.
Content to let the sea control
My thoughts, my mind, my very soul.

Now I must go and say farewell,
And break the magic of its spell;
As I have work to do and bills to pay,
And work to do and bills to pay.

Martin M. Romine

The Child

The hand comes down, the child jumps back.
The once pale skin, is now blue and black.
Crouched in a corner, he sits and hides.
No one can he trust, in no one to confide.
He wants to end it, to put it in the past.
But it won't end, till he's gone at last.
Till he's gone from the hand that's strong and hard.
That beat and bruised, that cut and scared.
He tries his hardest, to hold back the tears.
Like he's done for so long, throughout the years.
The midnight comes, the silence is chilling.
Then broken with a blast, the child's pain revealing.
He fled the home, the abuse he knew.
As he ran faster, his confidence grew.
A raging laughter, comes from a once fearful child.
Who was once held captive, now runs wild.

Stephanie Puckett

Pyromaniac

I'm the pyromaniac
The one that stares, gazes at your flame
Eyes glazed, dazed with admiration
Absorbing the light, the heat
I breathe you; like oxygen I need you to survive
And I stare into you, in all of your splendor and beauty,
My heart races, beats and pounds
It leaps and bounds, exalting your magnificence
I eagerly await your kiss
Your caress of my body,
It makes the desire for you unbearable
It makes me weak, yet strong in a sense
It leaves me wanting more, and more of your love
I need you; like a drug - oh, what a high-
Burned by your fire and singed by sin-
You're my light in the dark-
My everlasting flame-
Light my way, my love
and we can burn together....

Vanessa Acosta

Misery

The night's a graveyard for those alone
The one's who's worse friend is the telephone
It never rings, unless it's not for them
Because last night he killed his last friend
Now he walks alone through the streets
Killing everyone that he meets
Wanting revenge for all the problems he created
And trying to get rid of all his hatred
Am I crazy or just misunderstood
How does my fire keep getting more wood
It's burning through my veins on route to my heart
Where the destruction has already began to start
Soon my heart will burst into a blaze
Sadly this will be one of the world's greatest days
'Cause now they won't have to deal with me
And all my f**kin misery

Nathan Anderson

The Tragedy Of Life

Devil, do you dare approach me?
The past was blotted from my memory
Where can I find rest but in death
Which is the image of my formal self

Liberty has been a useless gift to me.
You live until my power is complete
All men fled and all men disowned
Creator infused life into this soul

A God like science that I desired
A natural innocence that I admired
Crushed sensations leave me in darkness
Society's hatred is all around us

Stars and clouds are about to mock me
Let the cursed monster drink of agony
Polluted remorse and delicate complexions
Anxious to experience and instruction

In the midst of poverty and want
I had learned to work with mischief
You desert me in the hour of trial
Then reward me with benevolent smiles.

Stacy Rollstin

The Mind

The mind, the mind, the mind.
The personality of man-kind.
That little gray matter called the brain.
What knowledge can it obtain?
What power can it gain?
What pleasure or pain, can it retain?
The mind, the mind, the mind.
Sanity or insanity, a fine line
to be drawn only another mind.
Which phobia will reign supreme
during a midnight dream?
What atrocity will remain unrevealed
from a tragedy still unhealed?
The mind, the mind, the mind.
Virtue or diabolic.
Which will benefit man-kind?
You decide.
It's your mind, use it right each time.

Richard Prough

My Son - Brian

He picked for me a daisy, by the sidewalk where they grew,
The petals gleaming, pure and white, were kissed by morning dew.

I slowly got into the car and turned to wave good-bye,
Emptiness had filled my heart and tear drops filled my eyes.

As I clutched the daisy to my heart, my thoughts were
running free,

How God would give His special love, to us, eternally.
And how He richly blessed me, when I had my precious son,
As pure as the petals of the daisy, his life had just begun.

And as he's grown into a man...as a Mother, I'm so proud!
Though there've been times he's broke my heart; I have
him on a cloud.
I only want the best for you and I love you as you are.
Please do what's right and live by God and be my
"Shining Star!"

Sharon Julian

What Is Real?

How can we tell when we actually see
The real thing or what it appears to be?
Can we accurately judge a book by its cover
When there's so much inside for us to discover?

With the skill that we have to read and understand,
It's not hard to arrive at the author's plan.
Our ability to discriminate can lead us to see
The difference between what is and what ought to be.

But when we look at man it's another story.
His outward appearance reveals so much glory.
You never can be sure of what you really see
When you look at man or at his family tree.

Today he may greet you with a pleasant smile,
And do you any favor, at least for a while.
But, if something should happen to upset his mind,
He's just apt to say or do things that's not very kind.

The mysteries of mankind have puzzled the world.
His nature hasn't ever been completely unfurled.
So, if we're only going to judge people by what we can see,
We had better be as careful, as careful can be.

Marie S. Griffin

"The People's Cry For Sanity"

Tell me one thing, Who to trust
The seeing eye sees all of us.
Together the olive branch and the arrow thrust.
Come and save the rest of us.

One place is found where all are free,
Who can tell me what to be.
Seal the seal of honest, While portrait eyes glance through me.

Series, tender, bank of splendor
Green on white the paper mender.
Meaningless your comfort gives, the God you trust pray doesn't live.
Don't cry for the masses, they can't eat your cake.
The children died in pain last night
Paper offerings the nations make.

Impossible to stop the tears, all's lost upon their choice.
Prayers fall on empty ears. No one can see the soul or hear
the tired voice. The money that they send fills no aching
pits. It fills up brimming pockets and there the salvation

sits. Punch and burn the extra ones without a second thought.
What are they to do with those
That can't be sold or bought.

Linda Kibby

Suns Before This Morning

I stand under the leafless oak,
The shade of old summers.
The old, haggard wind has plucked the tree,
Like pheasants.

Before me,
The blue sky of autumn
Slowly turns rich magenta,
Like a sauce upon the wall.

I dream of white gulls flying
Over the rolling waves of the sea.
I remember with tears,
The suns before this morning.

Kerry Banks

The Rose

The sun slowly rises
The sky lights up with hues of purple and pink
as the rose petals unfold.
The rose stretches, and the dew
on its leaves sparkles as it
catches the sunlight.
A spider has a spun its silk web
now blowing away on the wind.
Winter comes, and the rose weeps for
the lost summer when it flourished
and stood proudly in the sun.
But now, summer's gone
and with it the vibrant colors of the rose.
The once soft petals of the rose
turn brown and drift to the ground.
In the spring, a rose blooms again.

Stephanie Simone Coyle

I'll Accompany You To The End

The wonders of blooming flowers may bring joy and happiness;
The spacious field of dreams may bring much hope and promise;
But your presence forever brings love to life. . .
And when you explored the wonders of tomorrow,
Do hold on to the memories of the past.
In time if you ever feel lonely, just remember the thorns on
 a rosebush and you will find what is truest in life.

As I now bid you farewell and see you distant, next time. . .
 I'll accompany you to the end.

Long Anh Quach

Summer Sunset

Tonight, the sunset's over Beautiful Saginaw Bay,
The sky turns to a glorious gold, blue and gray.
Labor Day, summer sun, has come and gone,
All our boats are put away, where they belong.
As I watch, I think of other sunsets, memory ways
Are devious, but find at last their ending, Happier Days.
God gave me joy in the love of family and friends
On our beach and in our home as Summer Ends,
May all your skies be blue and gold,
And in the hearts of you, may they never grow old.

Mary Lou Garvey

Don't Cry For Me

Don't cry for me in Winter, when the ground is clean and white,
the Snowbirds bring my blessing to you in the dark as well as light.

Don't cry for me in Springtime, when all the world is new,
Just know that I am with you, in all you say and do.

Don't cry for me in Summer, I'll be there to hold your hand,
Think of me while on the beach, as the waves gently lap the sand.

But most of all, Don't weep in Autumn, for that is where I'll be,
Dancing and playing, singing and laughing, in the colorful Autumn
 leaves.

My gift to you is simple, and pure, and sweet as dew,
Think of me when you are alone, and know I'm loving you.

Renne' Carlson

In The Back Of My Mind

As I closed my eyes I could see it all
The soft feathers floating gently against the window as I watched
The grass swaying back and forth as gently as the wind blowing
Swiftly against my hair.
I watch a beautiful owl spread his long brown wings as it swiftly flies
Over head.
I begin to look out in the distance of the dark sky when I
See the splendid birds I had seen just hours ago.
The small baby birds chirping away for their moms to feed them,
Or to get a little worm for their bodies so they would be able to play,
And run as free as a lion.
As I sit on the steps of the cabin in the dusk of the wet,
And cold winter, I watch the beautiful colors of the sky as the sun sets.
I watch my dreams fade away as they're being put in the back of
My mind so I can get back to the real world.

Matthew Demko Baer

Of Black Hearts

Icy wind blows
The sound echoes throughout the corridors
where the miracle of life is lost,
feelings numbed by pain
Its chambers hallowed with experience
Its hallways emptied by time
Rooms without even ghosts
Paths that joy never travels
Walls not having windows and doors the same
Where there cannot be entrances and exits are no more
fore nothing may enter and there is no more to leave
A bare chasm of disbelief
A vault of trust squandered
Not even nothing exists here
Emptiness is its sole being
No substance shall ever penetrate its icy walls
Its treasures buried, shall never be known
forever kept secret in this place
this dark uninhabited place
this - black heart

Kevin Stewart

Not Your Memory

Go, take from me my golden sun that chased the clouds away,
The summer rose, the autumn leaf, the crunch of winter's snow.
The twilight glow, the evening peace that ends another day;
The beauty in your closeness feel that only I could know.

Take too my happiness complete, contentment that was mine;
Your gentle kiss, your close embrace, your soft breast on my lips.
The sparkle in your loving eyes, I drank them in like wine;
No longer will I stroke your hair, caress your close pressed hips.

Yes, strip me of my one true love, my future cast like grain;
Take all my dreams and dash them dead, I'll not now them fulfill.
And give them to another while I stand and watch in pain!
My hearts cries out in agony as burst it surely will.

Perhaps some day I'll understand this grief that's come to me.
For all these things you now can take, but not your memory.

Norm Koester

"Dreams and Reality"

The snow that is fluffy and white,
The sun that always shines so bright,
Roses and tulips make nature so diverse,
All this beauty we must preserve.

Where is this world of love and sunshine?
Only in dreams, or will it actually be sometime?
Holding hands, children and adults together,
All colors, shapes, and sizes united forever.

There is so much beauty that we take for granted
Our forests and gardens where amazing life is planted.
Will we ever live in this peaceful land?
Where, if you need there is always a helping hand.

There is a war going on, can't you see?
Not number 1, or 2, this is war number 3!
We kill our own, for what, a jacket?
How, may I ask, did we start all this racket?

For this problem, we can't just let nature take its course.
If we do, you'll see, there will be much too much remorse.
Now it's true, this world has gone insane!
Let's stop, the children seem to feel the most pain.

Michelle Shender

Tap Shoes

Metal heels clicking on the floor
The tapping sound filling the air,
Dancing to the beat of the music.
Doing cramp rolls and feeling great.
The rhythmic sound of metal touching wood echoes in the air.
Memories of days gone by enchant me;
There were once ribbons to tie that kept coming undone.
I look down to see my ambitious reflection in the shiny patent leather
Replacing the bows are thin black straps and now my heels are higher.
The shoes, now satiny leather, have lost that special shine but their
elevation makes my spirits soar.
The enticing smell of new leather permeates the room as a new dance
season begins.
It is the beginning of a new friendship, feeling unsure and stiff
before getting to know each other.
Before long moving as one, my feet shape them, and they become a part
of me,
Awakening a yearning deep within my soul,
Striving for perfection like the Capezio dancer inside my shoe.

Laurie Porpora

Amerikan Swirl

It totally sickens me. All the artistic philistines attempting a grab at
the taxpayer funded money tree. Be damned the cost. All hope is lost.
Our societal ship is sinking. But you don't really care. Two dollars
for a used pair of the President's underwear? I've seen it all
before. Lenin, Trotsky, Stalin, Mao and more. Freedom's clock
    continues
to wind down. The sand is running out. And when the clock quits
working. Idiots like yourself won't be able to shout
Stifled by the crowd's crushing cacophony. Give us more -
You owe us more...!
And like the parasites that you are.
Have sucked this country's marrow dry
But this needn't concern you. As long as you have won the prize!
And as helpless as you are. I'm sure the government will legislate
another maternal program....
To blow your nose. Wipe your ass.
Dress you in morning. Smile as you die....
The incapable sycophants that you are!!! So one cheer for socialism.
A morally bankrupt system that can't even brew a decent beer....
Hiccup....And so swirls Amerika into the whirlpool of history....
See you in the Abyss....Down the drain....Bon Appetit....

Kent Freed

Life

The wind blows gentle.
The trees swayed with no direction.
And I live in a world of only one.
The sun burns with light and hope,
But my soul no longer I see.
The trees stretch up with bark like aged
Skin showing its wisdom and
Dominance, but I, none.
Day after day I witness these things,
But I a trapped shadow in the footsteps of
Law and power, fear, confusion, and
Above all life have no where to run.
So, I lie down and escape in a dream
Where there's only room for one.

Tom Bassett

Miranda

As I dream to be a fairy princess,
the ultimate, that's for me,
a beautiful, vibrant lady I shall be.
My headpiece covered with red and pink roses,
to be full of wisdom, with great honesty.
I would be scented as true as the honeysuckle,
Intelligence, which provided such ingenuity
"Miranda," the people call me,
As I fly and approach the needy, hungry
and poor.
I magically give them food, shelter and more.
Fulfilling them spiritual with divine grace,
which helps them forget their fate.
Speedily flying from place to place,
this fairy princess Miranda, I'd be,
trying and bringing a little sanity,
to this cold, harsh world about.
This is a dream that my soul shouts out!

Stephanie Polakoski

Daddy's Home!

"Daddy's home!" My mother cries. Her eyes are bright with tears.
The war over, he's home after three long and empty years.
He will make her happy, he will make her whole.
He has all the answers, he is master of her fate.
Finally she can laugh and sing. She no longer has to wait.

"Daddy's home!" I parrot. I do not know this man.
I reach out in trust as only a child can.
He will make me happy, he will make me whole.
He has all the answers, he is master of my fate.
I too can laugh and sing. I have not learned to hate.

"Daddy's home!" He shouts. His eyes are old.
He holds us both and says he is happy. His eyes are cold.
He tries to be happy, he tries to feel whole.
He searches for answers, lost and alone,
In an unknown house that he tries to call home.

"Daddy's home!" He shouts. For his pain we must atone.
He is the master of our fate when he assumes his throne.
He rules with fist and leather belt.
His reign is eternal. He's cruel and he's clever.
It is Daddy's home and I am Daddy's girl forever.

S. L. Malcolm

The Lost Christmas Ball

I was made by hand carefully and neat.
The way I looked just couldn't be beat.
With thread and ribbons red and white
I was ready for the tree on Christmas night.

The time came to hang the balls with care
But the problem was I was not there!
The fall from the bed was as quiet as could be.
No one knew where I was but poor, poor me.

I lay there under the bed day after day
Was I going to miss Christmas? No way!
Someone would come to clean under the bed
Would they see me with ribbons all white and red?

The days went slowly, quietly by
I was so lonely I thought I would cry.
Just then I heard a humming sound
Does this mean I am going to be found?

Closer the vacuum cleaner came without a doubt.
I was so glad, I tried to shout.
Now I am as happy as can be
I am in my place on the Christmas tree.

Laura McDowell

The Noble Plain

The racing beat of a heart in love.
The weakness that follows the pain,
The tears that fall for the man she loves,
Not one reprieves the vain.
Faster and faster her heart will flutter,
Just by seeing his eyes,
Weaker and weaker her legs will grow,
Increasing the hurt in size.
If one word from his mouth is uttered,
Her ears will ring with pleasure.
If one touch of his hand is received,
The love is beyond measure,
The fate of never wedding him,
Of having nothing to gain,
Of her not reaching him,
The higher the loving flame,
Of him not loving her,
The higher the noble plain.

Valerie J. Ray

Anger

Your fists are shaking and your face is red.
The whole world is against you today.
You yell at your friends that you wish they were dead,
when they dare to get in your way.
Why are you so angry?
Who made you so mad?
Who gave you the right to behave so bad?

The reasons are yours and belong to yourself,
like the anger that pours out of your soul.

You look the right to be mean to your friends
and to hurt them for just being around.

The damage you did cannot be undone
and what good did it do to you?

Anger is evil and puts evil upon its prey,
so do not let it get in your way.
It's the devil's friend and can lead you to hell.
Is it there you want to go?

S. Ingemar C. Olsson

In the Forest

In the forest
the wind blows softly
jasmine scent fills the air
a light mist covers the flowers
dew rolls silently down blades of grass
trees are clothed in coats of green mosses
birds of a different kind sing in the background
God's wonders surrounded me as I sat watching in delight
birds of a different kind sang in the background
trees were clothed in coats of green mosses
dew rolled silently down blades of grass
a light mist covered the flowers
jasmine scent filled the air
the wind blew softly
in the forest

Shawna Crowson

Forever Love

The sun is shining
The wind softly blows,
A tear drops as I sit and think about you.
I miss you so much.
Where are you?
How could you just leave me alone like this?
I was always your baby.
You said you'd love me forever.
Forever is over for you, but not me.
So what am I supposed to do now?
I still love you.
How will I carry on?
No one else could ever take your place.
So, as I sit by your grave and think of all of our times
    together,
I close my eyes, lay down.
And die next to you.
I'll love you forever.

Lisa Pepin

The Silence Of Our Earth

An orchestra of nature so profound.
The wind swaying through the trees,
the birds chirping, the buzz of the bees.

Mother nature as the conductor,
makes a sweet natural sound.
The dusk of morning so silent, yet so beautiful.
The orchestra flows along.

The stage, or earth
an enormous platform of grass,
our sun as the spotlight,
shining upon it.

The sound not heard is us
as we sit silently
before we applaud.

Rebecca L. Kline

"Life"

I feel the eyes that are upon me, I hear the whispers in
the wind, we are not here to judge one another, so when will
it ever end? I live my life the way I want to, how many can
say the same, we live in a world that is not perfect, where
pain is the name of the game.

Everybody has their share of problems, but very few seem
to understand, we were all created equally, not meant to be
marked by some brand. We are different by our sex only, the
male or female born, this is something said often, but
something that should be learned.

There are questions left unanswered, as we try to choose the
right path, and no matter how rocky the road might be, we can
never take it back. I have made many mistakes, in the cards
that life has dealt, but I have to do what I think is best, it
doesn't matter how I've felt. Is it so hard to keep an open
mind, to realize we all aren't the same, why look down at one
another for the way we are, doesn't the world already have
enough pain? We should try to think about other people's
feelings, before we say and do things we'll regret, some things
can be over looked, but some things we can never forget.

Nita Stotts

My Trees

Whirling, twisting screaming
The Winter Wind rages on.
And yet my trees are not disturbed.
They used to move in - with - the wind,
But no more.
Their bountiful branches
Burdened with - sighing under - the weight of leaves
Are now bare.
My trees are not reaching to the
Blue skies anymore.
The same blue skies that were once blocked
From my sight by the abundance of green,
Now stare at me threateningly.
The skies are blue now more - even they mourn
The loss of my trees.

But the rain - the rain is my only Solace.
In the rain, I can cry for my loss
And my tears will be washed away
As the wind blows
Not disturbing my trees.

Mersedeh Jorjani

Reflections

Walked by a mirror reflections I did see
The woman inside was as lonely as me
I watched with a stare as my eyes lingered on
To see what I wanted was so hard to find
I looked through that woman and saw myself
The pity I felt was more than I could bare
I wondered if others could see as plainly as me
And if they could were their thoughts with me?
The woman inside existed on a memory
A memory I once knew
Could it be the love I'm missing was never there?

Sharon R. Lawson

"Reality"

Reality seems to be -
The wonder in the seed of a tree,
It's nothing big - as of yet -
It'll never get as big as it can get.

People suffer, then they kill
They think their answer is "free will"
They don't understand and they don't try,
They just look to their God and ask, "Oh, Why?"

"Why hath thou forsaken me?"
"Why don't God just leave me be?"
But why don't they know or look around -
There is no God to be found !

People always look down on me
I don't care, they can disagree -
All I know is what I see -
No one can know the real meaning to - reality.

Tami-Jo Hutchins

A Beautiful Stroll

As I slipped into the realm of existence my eyes opened to
the wonder of it all.
The warmth of my parents loving hands, grandparents
Whose hearts were filled with kindness and compassion.
Aunts and uncles tenderness and humor, a garden variety
Of cousins and friends to share and learn with.
And further down the road it took another turn to a wise
And beautiful man, my husband.
My journey continued on with the lilt of three gregarious
children.
Now at the top of the hill it just got better.
Rewarded with a treasure of grandchildren, each cut like a
rare diamond.
The most beautiful stroll you will ever take!
life, isn't it grand?

Shirley W. Aeberle

A Poem For Grampa

G is for games we watched on t.v.
    The Yankees, the Giants, and the World Series
R is for the radio we'd fight over in the car
    When I'd play my music, you wouldn't go far
A is for the authority you had over me
    I didn't always listen, and now I'm sorry
M is for the many places we went
    And also for all of the money you spent!
P is for the patience you had when I was bad.
    Only once in a while would you ever get mad.
A is for always, I'll always miss you
    Whenever I do something, I'll wish you were there too!

Sandra Brindisi

Moon In The Morning

I've seen the clouds hang low sometimes,
their foggy presence grey and somber
as they evaporate to the slightest touch.
A pinkness touching air touching clouds as they
immerse themselves into themselves, clouds into air,
air into clouds, a liquid intensity, a feverish pitch
where the usual atmospheric weather has encased the ground.
I've seen the sun stream through a less than immersible sky,
its light and heat as natural as nature illuminating
a veil-logged plane, floating above solid ground.
I've seen everything leave itself as a soggy,
sleepy day is a wave of beauty because of its nature,
its origin and become a weatherless, black light sky,
studded only by the moon in its blinding quarters,
a designed monthly choice.
I've seen it all and now, summarizing the day into night,
but in only one way, there are many lights.

Kameron S. Hanson

Is America Really Beautiful?

As they journey here from a distant land. They came here for
their future plan. They didn't doubt for they new it was fair.
As they assumed it was better here, not there. Some people
greet them with pride and joy. Some don't take part, just hate
and destroy. The family is so gracious and so giving. But
others want to stop their way of living. They slowly
approached being shy and modest. Some gave them friendship and
were so honest. This gave them encouragement and esteem.
Others didn't give them a chance to mean. Many hated them and
gave them terror. They were feared from others as if in a
barrier. The family hasn't yet adjusted to their life. Others
say they should leave in order to suffice. Parts of the family
has felt guilty because of what they are and not worthy.
Others are courageous and can handle. What is to come of their
life of supposed scandal.
People in this land do this, but others don't understand.
People will continue their ways until others go back to their land.

Mary Khouth

"My Daughter, My Sister And Her Son"

They were taken as angels their new journey has begun,
Their in a better place with peace, love, and joy;
No war, no hatred, only hearts to soar forevermore.

They've found a paradise in which we all long for, they now
walk with the lord, "My Daughter, my Sister, and her son"

They all are deeply loved, My daughter, Cheryl she was pure in
every way, she's so beautiful and special, she's my nay-nay,
My sister, Diana she's one of a kind, her beauty will carry on in
the little ones, she was my sis, my little "d",
Her son, my nephew, Malcom only two, he could light any room
or any heart just by saying I love you!
He's so handsome and brave, he's my little soldier boy,
"My daughter, my sister, and her son."
Their lives aren't really over, they've just begun,

Their in a much better place now, they walk with Daddy and God above,
Their building a new home for the rest of us to come to,
it's okay to cry, It's okay to ask God why?
But don't ever lose faith cause if you do, that puts you on the
devil's side, I love you Lord, take care of "my daughter, my
sister and her son," I will be with you all when my new life comes.

Rebecca C. Grissom

The Joy Of Life

I see my lovely daughters when daddy was a magic word,
Their voices were like music, the sweetest I had ever heard.
They looked up in the morning with eyes so full of light,
Radiating love within them, there's never been a grander sight.
Their faith was so contagious and it gripped my heart so tight,
That the meanest thought I ever had melted in pure delight.
I thank God for the children that enriched my life so much,
I know all God's children have this magic touch.
They have a way of brightness that lights the darkest places,
In all of God's creation, theirs were the sweetest faces.
They had the power to thrill me with a faith that was sublime,
There were no greater treasures than the children I called mine.
Neither the flowers in the valley, nor the great pines on the hill,
Had half the magic power to bring my heart a thrill.
Today as I look back through all those precious years,
I see my lovely daughters through hot shimmery tears.
And in my soul I feel something of an ache
And I wonder if, somehow, my great heart could break.
I miss those wonderful days and it makes me feel so sad,
I surely miss those lovely voices calling for their dad.

Paul Albert Bell

"Misery"

I loved you,
then I had to leave you
    You were always on my mind
closing my eyes, you were never hard to find.
    Thinking all the things we did
the times we shared, all the laughter and pain
    Now I'm living in black rain.
Upon the way to up above, the sky is turning red
    with blood. This nightmare will never end
It will just lead another trend.
    The memories, the hate, the love that I felt
My heart was burning, then it melt.
    Take my soul set it free, our love was once.
        But never to be.

Michelle J. Crowell

I Love You A Ton

I love you a ton, but
Then if you're afraid of being crushed,
I love you in hunks and chunks and
teeny weeny bits and pieces.

I love you with the fury of a torrential flood but
If you're afraid of drowning, then,
I love you barrels, tubs, buckets, and thimbles full,

I love you with the gentleness of the morning mist,
The tiny impact of a spattering drop of dew.

I love you with the fury of a storm but
If you are afraid of being blown away
Then I love you with the gentleness of a soft
Breeze when there is just one drop of wind.

I love you when you're gritty from work,
Or rested and clean and charming with grace,
I love you when you are irritable,
I love you when you dress up and wear heels
And hose on kissable toes.
Add it all up and I still love you a ton.

Lee Edward Leary

Untitled

Taylor and Uncle Paul put up the building blocks,
then Taylor gave them some terrible knocks,
Down they fell with a clatter,
and lay about all a scatter.

Up they went to a magnificent height,
behold, what a glorious sight.
As they fell Taylor called out with glee,
quick Mommy come look and see.

Oh, what fun they had that day,
as it ended in a story book way.
But now the contest was to see,
who needed their nap more, Taylor the blocks or me.

Paul D. Clark

The Last Great Love

Once there was a great love.
Then the great love left for the best friend.
The great love no longer talked to the first love.
The first love couldn't bear the thought.
She figured she'd be better off dead.
Once there was a great love.
Then the great love was gone.
Her father thought she shouldn't talk to him,
Even though she was lost without him.
Once there was a great love.
Then the great love was gone.
The great love was happy to not have to talk to her.
Once there was a great love.
Then the great love was gone.
The best friend was jumping for joy,
For once again she got what she wanted.
The first love was lonely, but what could she do
Everyone was happy to be rid of her.
Once there was a great love.
Then the great love was gone.

Tarina Johnson

If....

If time did end;
Then where would it begin?
If love was lost;
Could we get it back; at any cost?
If people only hated;
Would all the world be compensated?
If the stars stopped shinning at night;
Would the moon still shine bright?
If the birds could no longer fly;
Then; would all the joys of life just pass us by?
If we don't stop and think once in a while;
Will we have any more reasons to smile?

Sharlecia Langford

Mother's Love

Today is a special day.
There are some things I would like to say.
I know that God sent you from above,
With the gift of a mother's love.
Angels in heaven, they will sing
When you receive your angel's wings.
When I would stumble or would fall,
You were there through it all.
A mother's love is very strong.
It has to be, to teach us right from wrong.
You're my Mother, and my best friend.
My love for you will never end.

Mary Alice Riley

On Being A Parent

Becoming a parent is a journey into the future.
There are many roads to be traveled and much luggage to carry.
Unconditional love should be packed up first and in the largest trunk.
That love will carry you safely down every high and byway.
Guidance is a must and deserves a trunk not much smaller than love.
Guidance is not to be confused with dictatorship,
which sometimes comes in a similar package, but will not do as a
substitute.
Patience is a tranquilizer that should be packed in a trunk you can
get into easily.
Communication is the key that opens the door for the child to you,
himself, God and his fellow-man.
Hope is an absolute necessity for you and the child.
Last, but certainly not least, is faith.
As the child learns to believe in you and then himself he can learn to
direct his faith up toward God and out toward others along the
pathway of your journey.

Marian Carpenter

Storm Warning

A second before the lightning strikes,
There is a moment of numbness.

All is left behind; except a bracelet of memories;
Perfect red ribbon across the right wrist.
Silent darkness.

An iron candle through the heart.
Nothing seen but the waltzing flame.
Nothing heard but the rolls of thunder.

Come dance with me;
Inside the vent of shadows.
Sacrifice the sacred clown.

Swim in the remains of our touch.
I want to hold your embrace forever.
I can feel you beside me.

The candle grows dimmer,
And fades.

Wendy Murdy

To Dad

There is a time to be born
There is a time to die
There is a time to cry
There is a time to ask why
There is a time to be happy
There is a time to be sad
There is a time to be mad
There is a time to be loved
There is a time to give love
There is a time to get strength from above
There is a time to cry
There is a time to say good-bye
There is a time to be sad,
For I lost a wonderful Dad

Rosemary Toro

Mother Teresa

The divine in Mother Teresa is the 'Mother'—-
There is no other name like it—-
Sister Teresa or even Saint Teresa
Does not have the ring to it of Mother Teresa.
There can never be another name like mother.
We all had a mother who gave birth to us on earth.
We may or may not have loved her or have known her or been loved by
   her,
But it is that divine love we seek that the Mother of God, Mary, gave—
Those cradling arms we all crave
When we are born and as we approach the grave.
There is no substitute for the divine mother—-
She loves us unconditionally as children of God;
We can safely rest in her arms secure from life's harms;
Old or young when we die in battle or of disease,
There is no succor like the word "Mother!"..
None other brings such peace.
To be a mother is a sacred privilege, to love like a mother is divine;
I know, I loved mine. She loved me as I love my children.
Even greater is to obey Christ's command to love God and your
   neighbor,
To love people as you love your Saviour—like Mother Teresa.

   Margaret Elizabeth Stucki

The World

There is so much hunger, will no one fuel it?
There is so much pain, do you not feel it?
So much hurt, will you not heal it?
Does no one care?
Hate, hate,
So much hate.
Is there no love, on this land we live on?
Does no one have hope, hope for a better world?
Waste,
Why must this world be damaged?
Why must children die?
Death, Death.
So real.
Death.

   Lynn DaPra

The Black Box

When my mind is in turmoil, distress, or despair,
There is something waiting for me out there.
It's a little black box, Satan has just for me,
And he says, "step inside, it will set your mind free."

The first time I saw this box was at night,
And it filled me with great fear at its sight.
The box started out as large as the room,
Then slowly shrank in with an eminent doom.
I knew if the box continued to shrink,
My mind would go blank and I wouldn't have to think.
My God is stronger than Satan and his toy,
He made me think of my husband, my girl, and my boy.
I prayed, "God, don't let Satan take me from them."
So he shattered that box, and I rested in him.

That box tried to get me again, once or twice,
But God gave me victory through my Lord Jesus Christ.
If I listen to God and give my burdens to him,
I never need see that black box again.

   Theresa Marie Short

When I Love You More

When I love you more,
There is summer days that are spring time,
And when the roses bloomed,
I still love you more.
And when the birds are in their nest, and settled in their beds.
I'll still love you more.
When the flowers bloom there's lots to be done.
And the rose petals have fallen.
It's time for winter sleigh rides.
Where the deer and the antelope play.
But what happens to the night?
There's more to be done when,
I love Thanksgiving all day.
But when Summer comes, I am still little.
But when clouds have come I'm growing so fast.
The next day I get married
And I have my baby,
My baby is growing up.
When I love you more.

   Sarah Ellen Turley

"My Lord"

   My Lord, I love you so and this you should already know
There isn't a day which goes by that I don't think of you and
fantasize mysteriously.

   My love drifts in the air and everywhere, such as the winds
current. It grows deeper with each new touch of your presence
in sight.

   Love is compassionate, kind, thoughtful, and it gives to us
abundantly. You have filled an empty space in my heart, which
at one time was lost and barren.

   Our windows of love is unclouded, and the breezes of passion
are extending to the heights of ecstasy. There are no words
that can express these thoughts I'm savoring.

   My soul perceives as though I've known you a lifetime, it
has abided patience. This love I feel for you, yet knows no
pain, but your strength and endurance ensure the foundation
to obtain.

   Maureen L. Ellis

Assurance

Your eyes mirrored your thoughts to me,
There was no question that I could see.
A glimmer waved as we looked at each other,
An intensity felt that is hard to discover.

Your mouth moved to reveal word of meaning,
I smiled and concentrated because their purpose was redeeming.
Lips of warmth, snuggling with mine,
They spoke no words, but shared the same wine.

Your self-expression caught my ear, and I listened to what you
said, sharing thoughts back and forth, it seems from a similar
   Book we've read.
Your hand grasped mine and we connected,
A tug here and a tug there, we've led each other on paths well
   respected.

A day filled with rain, but filled with each other,
When the sun shines through, like two ospreys in dance, we'll
   flutter.

   Shelley J. Mott

The Little Mouse In The House

Early one morning as I sat on the chair,
There was quiet and stillness throughout the air.
Our little dog lay sleeping in our bedroom,
When I heard a scratch in the back of the broom,
I turned to look, and to my surprise,
Looking back at me were two little eyes.
He ran so fast, right across the floor,
Trying to escape out the back door,
Through the washroom and off to the right,
Into the pantry and right out of sight.
I ran for the door, to open it wide,
So this little mouse could run outside.
But behind the dryer, He decided to stay.
To keep me thinking on my next play,
I grabbed the swatter and hit the floor,
And out went the mouse through the open door,
And now when I'm here and all is quiet,
I listen and listen into the night.

Y. Huls

Where Did Earth's Beauty Go?

I drove up in the mountains where peace awaited me, but something there was still amiss that I could clearly see. Our weather change from day to day and we hardly blink an eye, but there was such a drastic change that I couldn't help but cry. I looked upon the mountain top and its everlasting beauty, then I began to realize man had neglected His duty. We all know that man's in charge of everything on earth, but maybe he didn't understand God's nature and its worth. The air is polluted, most beauty is gone, the water is a filthy wretch, I doubt if its inhabitants can barely get their breath. Man's appetite for earth's innocent creatures is increasing everyday, they trap them shoot them and catch them alive so they can get a pay. but the Creator of our universe; made everything for a purpose, He intended for man to follow his plan, not to become a deserter. The earth's beauty is diminishing fast, the air is covered with filth, our lawmakers are looking for a long term solution but come up with short-term guilt; our human race is also polluted, they mixed the wrong ingredient, we need the King James version of the Holy Bible that spell Obedient.

Lorranie S. Turner

Take My Hand, Come With Me

Take my hand, come with me to a place no one knows
There we can be alone, there a soft wind blows

Surrounded by trees the fresh spring air
Take my hand, come with me I will take you there

Don't be afraid I know the way
We can't get lost, it's not far away

When we get there you won't want to leave
The peacefulness, the serenity almost too intense to believe

But you'll remember this place and you'll understand this day
That you've be there before you've just forgotten the way

So, take my hand, come with me we won't get there unless we start
This journey to tranquility will take us to your heart.

Vel Couffer

Untitled

Why does it mean he had to go?
     There were so many people who loved him so. No one came to his hospital room. And death came sudden and all to soon. I really loved him and he was so sweet to me. I know all he wanted out of life was to be free. I only knew him for a short time. I went to the hospital to make sure he was fine. What I saw scared the hell out of me. He was so tiny and frail what a man should be. I stayed with him as long as I could. I told him to get better and prayed that he would. I kissed him on the cheeks and told him I love you. He had tears in his eyes when he said I love you too. I gave him a big hug for I knew it would be the last. Many people say God made aids as a punishment for your past if you believe this way then I am here to tell. God has something for you and it is called He!!!!

Kim Bonner

World Without Color

I wonder what a world without color would be like.
There would be no blue whale,
or red-tailed hawk,
no blond or blue,
no bright red with yellow patches.
There would be no need to dye your hair,
or mix and match the clothes you wear.

I wonder what a world without color would be like.
There would be no races,
no black or white.
There would be no difference between day and night.
That is what a world without color would be like.

Michelle Molina

The Seascape

There's a hissing sound from the oxygen tent,
There's a wan wrist wired with life:
There's an audience keeping the death watch
As finality overtakes strife.

The old fisherman's eyes open slowly,
Glazed dots of blue; chamois face.
Dead center ahead hangs a painting
Of wild ocean, rocks, foamy lace.

Hands clasped, he pleads with the picture,
"Let your waters o'er me roll.
Sweep me out of this room and this bed,
Let the salty sea bells toll."

And the audience watch, unbelieving,
As a huge green wave engulfs all;
The bed, the man, the oxygen tent,
Then recedes beyond the wall.

Marion S. Tupper

The Eagle

Our symbol of freedom, an error in time
There's no such thing everything's a crime
Politicians words echoing in our minds
They're all the same thing, just lies of different kinds
Promising things that they swear they will do
Believing would be nice but you
know it's not true
The eagle now knows that what
he is really symbolizing is lies
For all the angry people the eagle cries
soaring through the sky searching
for an excuse
but eagle stop soaring because
there's no use.

Shannon Wyatt

Brothers

A brother has a special meaning.
A brother has a distinct place in
every sister's heart.
A brother is there for you when you
need someone.
A brother makes you laugh.
A brother makes you cry.
A brother holds a certain
responsibility.
This is my brother,
my hero.

Lindsey Stradtner

Unkissed

Covered by leaves,
A camouflaged tent;
Morning dampness
Can't find the scent.

Guarded by thorns,
Double edged swords;
Possible intruders
Are not ignored.

Crimson in color,
As Christ's blood;
Nearly dried,
Untouched by the flood.

A poor broken heart
Once soared like a dove;
Now left unkissed
By tender love.

As a red rose bud
Precious and new;
Unkissed and ignored
By the soft morning dew.

Lea Marie Gann

To A Friend On This Her

Wedding Day

As children we shared
A childish dream.

Then as we grew to be
Young women we shared
The wish of some day
marrying the man of that dream.

Now my friend you have
found him, and on this
Your wedding day. I
wish you both all the
joy and happiness we
had as children and lots
more. Best wishes AFA

S. Dianne Nail

Beauty

Beauty is a fair weather friend,
a flighty unreliable trend,
making us grimace with disdain,
causing us to become petty and vain.
Isn't it better to penetrate deeper,
time saving and considerably cheaper.
Then we know where true beauty lies,
when we see with our souls
and not with our eyes.

Lore Hermes

The Cat

Big and fluffy, black and white
A creature of darkness
An silvery moonlight

You lay in the shadows
Still an on guard
Listening to the movements
Of the night in the yard

As I sat in the window
An watch you so still
I wish I were with you
To know what you feel

You glide through the grass
On soft white paws
Scratching and digging
With sharp little claws

You romp an you play
And find things to tease
Living life fully as each
Moment you seize

Mary Joyce Taggart

The Dream Malefic

I dream the dream malefic.
A dream of terrors to come.
A nightmare to society.
A little of the old red rum.
I am the part malignant.
A part most black and vile.
Can you see me lurking there
behind his cryptic smile?
I am his heart of madness.
The harbinger of hate.
The keening of the banshee
That foretells your final fate.
Such is the dream malefic.
The dream of terrors to come.
A fantasy for most
Dark reality to some.

Mike Ursu

When Will It End

A wish that never comes true.
A dream that always end the same.
Life is just a circle of
repetition that will never end
differently............
Schedule after schedule
day after day, when will it
end..............
Never because life is like a
circle and circle is like a
pattern and patterns stay the
the same.

Lorren Raquel Pallone

Alone

Wild happiness flowing far away
A sunset at the end of a childhood day
Traveling a road of darkness and despair
Waiting to find someone who cares
I know my past will never leave
Clouded images that come like a dream
Maybe one day I won't be alone
But in my memories
I am forever on my own

Ryan Lynn

What Is A Friend

What is a friend
A friend is one who loves and cares
A friend is one who's always there
A friend is one who'll lend an ear
A friend is one who'll always hear
A friend will make you feel alive
When a problem may arrive.
A friend will keep you on the right track
A friend will never turn their back
When there's trouble and we can't decide
They will help us deal with what's inside
Where there's love and what we show
A true friendship will always grow
Through the good times and the bad
Through the joy of what we had
The only thing I can do
Is really be a friend to you.

Regina Boggus

Untitled

Another chapter another life
a great hello a bad good bye
sharing a dream sharing a lie
seeing how it ends playing games trying
    to pretend

who cares if I write in greed
it's not really what it seems...

    Another day another death
a nightmare come true grasp for another
    breath

Seeing is believing unless it's not there
knowing and showing some one you care
a fearful dread of molded bread
it's not a dream it's reality...
    it's hard to scream at a photograph.

Leslie Sierra

"My Love"

I sometimes feel
a little jealous in my thoughts,
imagining that someone else
could please you more than me.
It's just my insecurity
acting up a bit, I guess...
because I know I'm not
  the most beautiful,
  the most enticing,
  the most fun, or the
  most imaginative person
  in the world.
But I do know this
that no matter
how much time goes by.
I can't imagine that
you'll ever find another
who will love you with a beauty
  and a passion and a happiness
like that which I feel for you.

Mary F. Rugg

Unforgotten Love

I once was loved
And now I'm not.
The warmth of love
I have not forgot.
Love simmer inside me
like low, on a crock pot.

Teresa S. Smedley

The Certain Thread

There is a fragile place within,
A little thread dragged around
A long sharp corner, frayed
And extended yet continuing,
The fluffy lint-like-a halo
End of it not even thread
At all, just dust, the dust
And thread the centerpiece of
The soon-to-be mouse nest
Near inside the high, cold,
Arrogant wall, nibbled to nothing
At one small and central spot.

William W. Runyeon

My Rose

Between the pages I found a rose
  A lovely faded rose.
Inside my heart was a memory
  Too delicate to expose.
I carefully stored it far away
  In a deeply shaded nook.
And never did I look again
  Inside this hallowed book.
Its cover had collected dust
  With my rose deep inside.
It had kept my secret well
  I felt a sense of pride.
Many years have now gone past
  As I sit and reminisce
And fondly hold the faded rose
  I received with my first kiss.

Susie Barter

Heaven

A gentleman and a scholar,
A Ph.D., by far,

A friend in need,
Is a friend indeed.

One who always listened,
One who always cared,

He's there waiting for me,
Where?
Heaven!

Marilyn P. Meola

Untitled

To walk with me
a piece, you go
up mountain tops
in undertows,
in daisied fields
and rock-hewn cliffs
on mighty seas,
a shell-soaked beach,
a blazing sun slaking
rigid thirst
with shaded spots
where well-springs burst.
amid the mass of backdrops thrown
on stages that were mine alone
I walk, emboldened
to invite
a matching stride,
an open mind.
Won't you come too
and walk with me.

Mae Belle Tucker

Love

He's near me asking me
a question, talking to me
his lips slowly moving
his hair sways back
and forth as his head
moves. he stops, I have
nothing to say, I don't
know what he asked but
he stands there and looks
at me, smiles and tells me
it's alright, he walks away.
what does he mean, does he
know I like him can he see
it in my eyes is it that obvious!

Monica Federico

As I Lay Down To Death

I wander lonely as a cloud
a rain drop for a tear.
Empty as a deserted field,
a feeling of pain and fear.

A deep emotion within myself,
I hide a little white lie.
From the outside I try to smile
while deep inside I cry.

I stand alone empty within,
behind my friends I hide.
Emptiness that's replaced with hate,
my love for you just died.

I quietly lay down to death,
a tear runs down my face.
It's over now can feel no more,
and my memories with you erase.

Lisa Simons

Invasion Of My Dreams

I see an image in my dreams
A silhouette of you
Looking into the sky
Of a cloudy but vivid blue.

A man of mystery
You seem to me
But in my mind
You'll forever be.

You're in my thoughts
Both day and night
I can't help but smile
When you come into sight.

Through the darkness of night
Comes a glowing ray
That signals the start
Of a brand new day.

These thoughts and feelings
May be crazy it seems
They're all of the man
Who invades my dreams.

Lisa Smith

Untitled

Day
bright, hot
exciting, glorifying, fleeting,
action, adventure, moon, stars,
sleeping, eating, haunting,
dark, cold,
night.

Tripp James

Untitled

A single star in the sky
A single look in your eye
A single glance across the room
A single scent of my perfume
A single touch goes so far
How I wonder where you are
All alone without my heart
I gave it to you from the start
You brought me to that special place
Now I long for your embrace

Renee Connolly

The Moon

I see the moon so bright above
A soft silver full of romance
And I realize then I can begin again
To give love another chance

Others may see your glare
And shiver in your embrace
And yet I see that you were meant to be
A caressing hope against my face.

Thank you, Oh my sister moon
For your icy silver rays
And for letting me see how my life can be
Filled with warmer, brighter days.

Kristin Amber Skiles

It Will Be

Summer, once again, is here
A time for love, a time for cheer,
A time to let your heart run free,
To let what is to be, Be.

You may pick flowers,
Or sit for hours,
Feel a warm breeze,
As it flows through the trees,
Sit with friends in the shade,
As you talk and drink lemonade.

But as time goes by,
You won't have to worry,
Feelings and fears,
You won't have to bury.

For everything there is a season,
And for that season, a reason,
And eventually you will see,
That what is to be,
Will Be.

Laura Burnett

Everlasting Love

I see it in your eyes,
A twinkle of loving romance.
Every time I look at you,
Your eyes begin to dance.

My lucky stars are telling me
That someday soon we'll wed.
We'll unite ourselves as one,
Like I've always said.

I know our love will last.
It always did before.
When our lives shall pass on,
We'll be together forevermore.

Mary Jo Tarbush

An Anniversary Token

A celebration of lives together
A time remembered
when you said forever
With vows of love
that have survived
and grew beyond
what was realized.
Blessed with children
bonding in the care
reaching to take your hand
thankful you're always there
Your guidance taught them
standing on their own
to create another generation
of what your love has grown
Now not taking it for granted
saluting what can endure
Wishing all the happiness
this anniversary and many more.

Ruth VerStrate

Teddy Bear

A little boy should always have
A tiny friend and true
To sit upon a chair with him
And tell his secrets to

Or keep him safe while in his bed
And warm him through the night
To listen while he reads his books
And plays with child's delight

In just the blinking on an eye
A little babe will grow
To be a man out on his own
But tiny friend will know

The stains and tatters that he bears
Are proudly worn as part
Of all the love he did receive
From little Ryan's heart

Virginia M. Santos

Empty Shadow

As I stood there with the family
A very strange feeling occurred to me.
It was as if I stood next to an
Empty shadow.

I was filling a place in time
That at that moment
should not have been mine.

We gathered at the graveside-
It was such a long ride
to stay for so short a time,
But I guess that's how they do it.
And only so quick a visit
for the pain to go out to it.

I think I was the most upset,
Although maybe they don't show it
or feel it yet,
But still my heart aches
As the tear-eyed father's breaks
And among the rest of us I felt an
Empty shadow.

Ron Taylor

National Library

Never again did I ever see
A woman compared to thee
Your essence of style and beauty
Is a finger wrapped around me
Once I thought of telling you
Now I don't know how to
Agony fills all I do
Life is washed in blue

Loving you alone
It will never be condoned
Biting to the bone
Ringing with a moan
And I will never see you again
Reigning over all women
A Lioness in her den
Your soul shall haunt the hearts of men

Michael Morales

"Shadowland"

A world of opposites.
A world in total darkness.
Not moving.
Not speaking.
Not even murmuring a single sound.
A world without war.
A world without hate.
A world that has no crime.
A world not killing each other off.
A world that is just there
A world called the shadowland.

Michael Mendez

"Violets In The Valley"

Violets in the valley,
Abloom with radiance and fragrance
Amidst the mud and crumbled rock,
Decaying leaves and overgrown weeds.
They struggle for space,
Yet rise up in triumph.
For in this desolate, cast-away land,
They are a sweet secret -
Virtuous and full of hope.
But few know the secret wealth,
except the valley of violets.

Natalie Beckley

Harlem

Heaven of the poor and the proud
Abode of love, art and imagination
Rehabilitate our minds
Let the world see your beauty
Effigy of Africa
Milestone of brotherly love

Harbor of the desperate
Abbreviation of the mother land
Rendez-vous of our forefathers
Light up the path of my life
Eden of the oppressed
Maintain the dream

Heart of rhythm and harmony
Avenue of knowledge and experience
Realm of the depressed
Lead our generation
Elucidate your history
Maneuver our revolution

Pascal Jean-Pierre

The Lord

Long, long ago by my mother I was told
about a great, great man who walked this
land and healed people with his hands.
He put the warmth in the sun.
He hung the stars one by one.
He gave us sisters and brothers to love.
Sent His grace from the heavens above.
He put the blue in the sky,
and made the clouds go drifting by.
When I walk and hold His hand He
shows me the promised land.

Roy Robertson

Love New Day

The sun starts to shimmer
   across the tops of trees,
Adding a glow
   to the dying autumn leaves.

Pinks and purples
   streak the skies,
And songbirds sing
   as they begin to fly.

What a lovely feeling
   and a wondrous sight,
      as slowly,
Morning is born
   from the darkest of night.

Watching the stars
   as they slip from the sky,
It would be magical
   with you by my side.

Kelley D. Gawlik

A New Beginning

A wall was built around my heart,
Afraid to let anyone see
That deep inside I really need
Someone to care about me.

I feel in you, a sensitive man,
Who's seen his share of pain.
But yet, I know within your heart
You want to stop the rain.

Sometimes in this world of ours
The sun comes shining through.
I found a rainbow in my life
The day that I met you.

I have a lot of love to give.
I know that you do too.
Together, maybe we can find,
A sky that is clear blue.

I don't know what the future holds.
I wouldn't dare to guess.
All that I can promise is:
To you, I'll give my best!!

Maureen Smith

Icy, Cold, Stare....

Your icy, cold stare,
challenged me to a dare!
How much, do I owe you,
for the fare?

Martha Blanco

"Blossoms N' Bloom"

They say in spring,
after the rain and dew
buds blossom forth -
bursting into bloom!

But I've noticed
the blooming of buds that blossom.
They take to true nurturing -
be it,
Winter, spring, summer or fall!

The true beauty of growth,
is seeing both bud, then blossom
burst forth in full bloom.

In the seeking of knowledge,
we are but buds -
hoping to blossom.

In achieving our goals,
fulfilling our dreams -
We are the true essence of,
"Blossoms N' Bloom"!

L. Joyce Anderson

Peaceful

Warmth of your body
  Against mine
Rhythms of your breathing -
  And mine... unit
Innocence of touch
  Most trusting.
  Body Relaxes -
Falling...into a deep sleep
  How peaceful
Silence of the night
  Dreams so simple
  -Learning-
As I watch
  My baby fall asleep.

Sandra L. Koebel

Mother

  As I feel the waves up
against my feet,
  I have the feeling of
warmth and it's complete.
  Mother, will you hold my hand?
And together we can walk
through the sand.
  How I long for your
loving, tender touch,
  But at the time,
it seemed like too much.
  Mother, will you hold
me close and tight?
  For all my life I
lived in total fright,
and it was all out of your sight
  I tried to break my
wall with all my might.

Sharon M. Lee

God's Glory

The wind that blows cool
Air upon the saved and the
Unsaved "Screams God's Glory.'
The sun that warms us by
day and the moon and all the stars
that guides us by night,
"Screams God's Glory."
The flowers which blossoms
And when we see them we smile,
"Screams God's Glory"
The mother who loves and takes'
care of her children,
Who gently teaches them to walk,
to talk and to pray
"Screams God's Glory"
For everything that
was created and exists Past,
Present, future and forever more
Screams of the Glory of God.

Ruben Richard Craig Jr.

Afraid

I'm afraid to walk
all by myself
I'm afraid to talk
when there's nothing left.

I'm afraid to cry
when there are no tears
I'm afraid to try
because of my fears.

I'm afraid to think
when there's nothing to think about
I'm afraid I'll sink
if the boat goes that route.

I'm afraid to love
when my love is all burned out
I'm afraid to smile
when my smile is a pout.

If I could get what I wanted
I would pay or trade
I just want one thing
and that is not to be afraid.

Teresa Sutton

No Return

Tears streamin, families grievin
all for you but the life
you chose to end his just began
In a day or two you thought
they would be over you, deep into
the eyes of death you lark, cold
and alone you thought you were.
better off dead you said in your mind.
But now you wish for another chance.
Death drapes its arms around you.
You feel that your choice was wrong
But you were already on
the edge of death barely seeing over.
But you chose the edge from which
there is no return
Your friends standing around
looking at your pale face
wishing you would wake up from you state

Seneca Jones

I'm Still Here

These days it seems
All I have left are dreams.
All of the flowers
Were gone within hours.
There were so many things I never knew.
Now I know we're through.

The hurt I feel goes so deep;
I wonder if I'll always weep.
Someday, I'll see sunshine;
Then I'll be fine.
Until then I'll think of you,
And I hope you remember me too.

Stephanie R. Jones

'Stay'

My heart is broken
All life taken away.
Cold stares, trembling hands
I wanted you to stay.

I never pictured us apart
You told me not to be afraid to fall.
That you'd always be there
So I gave you my all.

Now you love someone new
And there's and emptiness inside of me.
My arms are around her
This isn't how it should her
This isn't how it should be.

What I did I do wrong
To have you leave me like this
I have to cry myself asleep
Knowing how much you I miss.

One day you'll realize
What so precious you gave away
And I'll still be here waiting for you to stay.

Lee-Ann Marie Mosteller

Another Sudden Memory

How the looks can deceive
All of the cherished memories.
How I can't perceive.
The confusion of life's mysteries.
When my mind becomes blank
I think of all the yesterdays.
Then my heart will suddenly sink
As I think of all the lost todays.
My world became a cyclone
As I lost all forced control.
Then I pictured myself alone
And death became my only goal.
In this galaxy that surrounds me
There's nothing that I'll ever see.
My life has become all it will be
Nothing more than a sudden memory!

Stacy Hill

Rhythm Empire

A visual lush uncontrolled
An aesthetic empire versed by nature
An ambient trance utterly illustrated yet
eminently ambiguous to all.

This is the locus for thy flowering of
passion.
This quality I desire to provide yet
When I encounter this covert place I will
Conquer time and space

Keith Bailey

Free At Last

All those days that passed you by
All the things that made you cry
Built a world where no one came
Empty heart so filled with pain

So much time was filled with hope
Lie's the chance you couldn't cope
Angel wings set you adrift
Softer than two lovers kiss

Memories like shattered glass
No more pain you're free at last
All the days you gave to me
Holds me close until eternity

Now I stand alone my friend
Crossed the sea and back again
Sunshine's brightly in my eyes
Lift your spirits to the sky

In my heart you've never gone
Just like the sun at break of dawn
There's no beginning and no end
Still you hope to sail again.

Linda Makowiecki

When I Speak With You

When I speak with you
  All the world waits
  All the chores
  All the woes
  All the cares
I always get refreshed
  The world knows
  The chores don't mind
  All the woes wait
  The care will always be there
I thank you for being there for me.

Lori Caron

Alone

Alone I feel,
  Alone I die.
Alone I laugh,
  Alone I cry.
Alone and scared,
  of what's going on.
Desperate we survive,
  No matter what goes wrong.
Alone I stand,
  Alone I will fall.
Alone I walk,
  Alone I run.
Alone I am left to
  dance in the sun.
Alone the raindrops fall on my face,
  Alone the thunder slaps the sky.
Alone I talk,
  Alone I yell.
Alone I realize that I am
  in my own private hell.

Nicole Ehlers

Calm Of Day

The cliffs are wet from splashing surf,
beneath this rock, my thoughts unearthed.
The roar of thunder from the waves.
descending into calm of day.
Tranquility relieve me now.

Linda Kimberlin

My Friend: A Viet Nam Vet

For his country he gave:
  an arm, an eye, as well as
  both legs—
But, doggedly, he kept his inner
  spirit.

For his friend he gave:
  a helping hand, a warm smile,
  and a manzanita cane—
Unknowingly, he shared his inner
  spirit.

A manzanita cane, crafted by
  his hand.
My cherished symbol of strength
  and courage—
But more than that, he gave
  me hope!

Sandra M. Bowman

Happiness

Happiness,
An emotion of ones imagination,
Never
To be achieved.

If you think you have found it,
Beware.
For it is pain and suffering,
Waiting to strike,
Leaving you empty
And alone.
Happiness,
A two-faced emotion.

Kirk Haslam

11 Ways Of Looking At A mirror

A duplicating machine,
An image looking at me,
Like another dimension,
Our life upside down,
A home for emptiness,
Silence,
A motionless hole,
A peaceful life,
Trapped and not knowing what to do,
Staring at yourself,
You are exactly what you see.

Sebastian Danino

"Life Is One"

Life holds many beauties,
and all are intertwined.
From the flight of a bird
to the crying of a man's eyes.
Born from a miracle,
and die with a sigh.
Life holds many beauties,
and all are intertwined.
We grow to experience
the new things in life.
And we dream of better things,
that just can't suffice.
Every specimen on earth
are just like you and me.
They have heart, they have soul,
they have willing to be.
Life holds many beauties,
it holds you and me.

Monica A. Ring

Morning

The night was dark
And all around invaded me
No sound was here
No breeze, no birds
No cry just air
Where gone was light
Where gone was sound
A blackless void was here
And then the bright sounds came
A stirring blaze of grass
A rustling of a wing
A baby's cry
The sun's first ray
God in His heaven
To open another day.

Pruella Cromartie Canham

Twilight

The sun is sinking in the west
And all the sky's aglow with hues
Of red and orange; and a crest
Of purple through the cloud now spews.

The haze of dusk draws forth a state
Of melancholy 'nough to bring
A man to quest a gentle mate
To cheer him, cause his heart to sing.

As ever lower dims the light
And silent clouds turn ever dark,
A breeze springs up to usher night
Across the nests of voiceless lark.

And starlings flit o'er house and tree
As fireflies wink and go their way,
A promise of a night that's free
Of cares and troubles of the day.

So nestle twilight to your breast
And peaceful, kindly thoughts aspawn,
As from day's toil you take your rest
And slumber 'till the bright'ning dawn.

W. Hardy Davis

Last Night

Last night at home, he walked away
and as he left I heard him say
"Girl I loved you more than ever
but you didn't want us to be together"
He went out the door and left me crying
and now my heart feels like it's dying.
I didn't want him to walk away
I was wrong and he was right
his love for me was outta sight
I have to admit I treated him bad
people asked me "Have you gone mad?"
but he left me standing there that day
we would sit outside, all night long
and think about what went wrong
we sat there, our last night together
and I said to myself "I should of treated
him better"

Latasha Lynn Ovendine

Worthy

In order to set in stillness
   And be at ease with me
Not yet complete in goodness
   But somehow very free
I have to understand
   No trial is in vain
I am worthy of existence
   Because...
I am worthy of the pain.
     Lisa D. Moulton

"Much Like You"

Favor is deceitful,
and beauty truly vain.
But a woman who loves the Lord,
deserves the praise she'll gain.

I think of all the girls I've met,
whose beauty was weakness.
Because they could not see their need,
beyond their so called sweetness.

All their beauty is surpassed,
by what I've seen in you.
A loveliness that's magnified,
because your beauty's true.

More than just a pretty face,
there's beauty in your soul.
For the love of Jesus Christ,
has made your heart pure gold.

I know God has someone planned for me,
and yet I don't know who.
But if His will fits my desire,
I'm sure she's much like you.
     Robert E. Kelley

The Tree

The heat beats down
And boils my skin

The torturous parched sand of the beach
Reaches up and taps my sap

Out of my trunk
Shriveling my tree

The leaves are brittle
My twigs are weak
And my roots shift in the sand

The ocean so tempting
Taunts me unregretting
Of the treasure and relief that it soaks

Laughing and shrieking
Its terror pierces

Its salt-wind burns
And its high-pitched hurricanes squeal

I curl up and hide
Wait for the darkness

Mine eyes shut with fear
I huddle and shiver in the sun
     Michelle Brown

Farm

China bones of milky cows
and broken orange roosters
left in the dry dirt
of the still red barn as
scrawny cats
wander midst the ruins.

Dead silos of hard yellow corn
dusty sweet hay
I jump into the silo
and I surface powdered
with corndust
choking laughing.

Covered with a dry dirty film
I climb the rickety boards
bypass rusty penny nails
and stand barefoot on splinters
to jump again.
     Sarah E. Beckman

"Love"

Love will destroy you,
And cause you so much pain.
There's a lot to lose,
And very little to gain.

Love makes promises,
That you never keep.
It leads to heartache,
And always makes someone weep.

Avoid love and what will follow.
For it will leave your heart empty
and your soul hollow.
     Theressa Stearns

Mountains And Molehills

When I was young
And caution spurned
A mountain to
A molehill turned.

Now as the years
Go flying by
A molehill seems
A mountain high.

It's tougher now
To reach the skies
And cut a mountain
Down to size.

So I'm content
To lesser seek
And stand upon
The molehill peak.
     Marjorie V. Grove

A Touch

The skin has a hunger
And a longing
For touch
Like the moist dew drops
Caressing the petals
Of a crimson rose
Slowly opening
In the warmth
Of the morning sunrise
     Pamela Bennett

Freedom

Freedom is not just for one
and certainly not just for some.
Freedom is for young and old alike
Red, yellow, black and white.

And as our flag waves with
   its stars and stripe
Reminding us all of the horrible fight
Many were maimed many died
So freedom could be in our sight.

And we should be so lucky
We should be so proud.
But just remember - it wasn't luck.
It took all colors in the crowd.
Amen.
     Marcella B. Fisher

The First Winter Snow

The first winter snow came
And covered the ground
All the animals of the forest
Went Scampering around
Mr. Bunny Rabbit was jumping
With so much delight
He grabbed Miss Squirrel
And they danced all night
All the other animals joined in
On the carpet of snow
Singing lets all have a party
Before we have to go
     Wilma Jean Williamson

"Times Are Changing"

Times are changing
and days are getting longer.
Be stronger.
Where's the end of this ride?
I want off;
let ego hide.
you can see it in my eyes,
that this isn't right.
Will this be the night
I won't wake up?
I'd I do,
will anyone be there,
will you?
If people don't begin changing,
we'll never have
What we once had.
Times, are changing fast,
it's not getting better.
Open your eyes can't you see?
     Regan McCaughey

There was a time

There was a time,
And it is solace
To know it existed,
A time your smile
Was mine each day.
Better than gold and diamonds,
Time has proven its worth.
Though this treasure,
As fate would have it,
Slipped through my fingers;
It lights my life
In the memory that lingers.
     Mary Frances Napier

Eleven

Just a few more days,
And he'll be here.
They'll finally meet him,
Yet not know of the fear.
The fear of what will happen
When their baby is born.
The tears of sorrow they will shed,
Feeling betrayed and torn.
They don't know it yet,
But they are in for a shock.
Their baby will never make it.
Their hearts will shut and lock.
This is what will happen
That dreadful hour of eleven.
They'll never meet their baby
For he'll take his first steps in Heaven.

Terri Wesley

"The Kingdom Come"

Lord I love you as my Saviour
   And I praise you as my King
I will someday stand beside you
   And I'll hear the angels sing

I'm in awe of all the beauty
   You created on this earth
And all the mighty miracles
   That have happened since your birth

I can't help my Lord but wonder
   How someone could not believe
With the great things you have given
   And the blessings we receive

I pray Lord that all your children
   Will see what they must do
To be an heir to your great Kingdom
   And to reign up there with you

Margaret Allison Hopper

"Is God Real?"

Many men don't believe in God,
and I truly feel sorry for all,
who don't know the wonderful Master,
and have never answered his call.
My eyes see sights every day,
that proves, he's real and true,
and if you'll only look around,
you'll have to believe in him, too.
The wonderful seasons of the year,
the grass, the flower's the trees,
the mountain's high and valleys low,
the ocean's, the rivers and seas.
These, plus much, much more,
I know are the works of his hands,
here in our beautiful America,
and in every foreign land.
To him, we owe our very lives,
and I pray that all will see,
That very surely our God is real,
and our Friend, he wants to be.

Wilma Hollar Brewer

One's Lifetime

Born so innocent,
Changing scenery throughout
Is different, gone.

Meredith Leonard

Untitled

Promise not to love me
And I'll show my best
Just touch my soul
With the music inside you
And feel my body
With the warmth of your hands
Play for me
A song
For only my ears
That flows from your heart
From the depths of your soul
I'll follow as far as the sky will reach
But I'll let go at the right moment
For the fire is hot as the sun sets
And the passion is trouble
For those who dare to play
Risk your life for love
Challenge your love for life
Chance yourself for me

Lisa Greenelsh

Yesterday

Yesterday has left us
and it won't be here again,
we still will have memories
of what used to happen then.
   But today has come
and will soon be another yesterday.
when tomorrow comes
and it will be another day.
   A week will come
and then a month or two will die,
and then the holidays that come along
will pass you right by.
   Time will pass and
New Years will be here,
and before you know it, soon
it will be another year.
   All of the years will
fly right by,
and soon our time will
have come for you and I.

Sasha Rigas

Mortal Funk

Tonight I feel strange
And I've never felt better
So sublime
Yet so deranged
Meaningless thoughts
Frozen in time
Lonely nights spent
Sitting in a corner
Swallowing poison
Inhaling death
Can't remember a thing
Except confusion in my brain
Numbness on my face
White dust on a mirror
One more hit
And my heartbeat starts to race
Living in fear
I will never overcome
So I just give in
Afraid of what's to come

Beowulf II

Home

   My stomach mumbled,
and my heart was week,
   I could not help but
try to seek.
   A way out, a way back
home
   A place where this
star I wear is not a
symbol of hate, but a
symbol of light.
   Staring at that moon
as if it to reply, why…
   Oh why am I locked
away from others,
   my sisters and my
brothers.
   In this steel cage
I lie helpless and alone.
   Trying to find a
way back home.

Rachel Gruber

Grandpa

My Grandpa is gone
And oh how I miss him
I still love him even though
When the lights get dim
I think of him
I remember he wanted to walk
I remember when we would talk
I remember he was glad to see us all
Forever he will be in my heart
We will never be apart

When I saw him in his bed
I laid a kiss on his head
And how my soul aches
I want him back
Now he's gone
And oh how I miss him so
He's gone outside but
He's here inside

Tina Fierro

Give Love A Chance

When are you going to awaken
   and see the light?
Before too much time elapses
   to set things right

Please do something
   before it's too late
For then love surely
   will turn to hate

Love is the only thing
   that matters to all
Without it, it's so easy
   for one to fall

Give love every chance
   and you soon will see
That life's so much better
   and much happier you'll be

Kathleen Dunn McKinney

Untitled

Time may come and days may go.
But love will forever flow.

Lillian Holberton

Lady Butterfly

Mother nature waved her magic wand
And spun a gown for thee
Bordered it with gold and jewels
For all the world to see

She opened up the flowers
And sprinkled them with dew
Sweetened up the nectar
Then said "it's all for you."

Go fly through the country
Alight on any spray
You need no chart or compass
You'll never lose your way

So fly lady butterfly
Fly and be free
Show off your gown of gold
For all the world to see

Spread your beauty all around
Put on a fashion show
Then lift your wings and fly away
We'll watch you as you go.
Yolanda Cohen

The Beauty Of A Phone

We held the books up to the phone
And talked about years gone by
Memories came flooding back
That brought a tear to my eye.

Although we were miles apart
We were as happy as could be
Looking at pictures of the past
of our family. Some of the folks
are living some have passed away
Yes- it was just wonderful
Talking about yesterday.

Many miles divide us that's the beauty
of a phone no matter what the distance
You don't feel alone. My brother lives
in Texas I live in N.C.
The book we were discussing
Was about our Family Tree.
Pauline M. Norman

The Dream

As the waves are roaring
and the birds are soaring
it is reassuring
to know this is only a dream

And this dream has no true meaning
but my thoughts are scheming
and in my mind I'm screaming
to try to get away

For my mind is wondering
and my heart is thundering
for now my thoughts are pondering
as I try to hide my fear

I feel a shaking
I start awaking
for the earth is not quaking
this is only a dream

I see the face of my mom
and hear her saying be calm
there within my weary palm
is her consoling hand
Valerie Smith

"The Marrow Of True Reality"

The questions that life gives,
  and the answers you pose.

Where was tomorrow?
  What will yesterday be?

You make me into who I'm not,
  I try to find who I am.

Life is a drug I abuse,
  you're the pusher keeps me hooked.

My world flashes by,
  like scenes from the silver screen.

I watch it pass in black and white,
  you laugh and change the speed.

Faster and faster,
  it's all a blurry whir.

Tick, tick, tick…
  the film has run out.

A lifetime has passed, it's over and done.
The time is gone, at my expense you've
had your fun.

As I start to fade to grey,
  you smiles and say: "I told you it would
turn out this way."
A. Celeste Langer

Wine, Women, And Song

As the spirits disappear
and the body withdrawals
the soul suffers, the heart laments,
and the mind wanders…

Who was that girl?
Am I lost?
No; just confused.
Where's that damn bottle?

Here's that song again,
you know the one—
Da-do-do-do Da-da-da-da
Bop-bop-bop-bam!…

There's magic in the melody
that moves my mind to memory.
What happened that night
that lost my love forever?
William J. Caldwell

A Retired Nurse's Prayer

Oh God, I thank you for the silence
And the peace that it can bring
It's like a private little chapel
It seems I can hear the Angels sing.
You led me to this place of refuge
So I'd have more time to pray
Not the formal kind of prayer
But converse with you day by day.
Is the tempest really over Lord?
Did my life's ship withstand the storm?
Did you command the troubled waters?
To protect me from all its harm?
It's hard to believe my work is over
I'll miss the halls of pain I've trod
Now You've given the reins to others
I tried to do my best - Dear God.
Lead me to the "Golden Sunset"
Let me put my hand in Thine
A heavenly peace surrounds my spirit.
I bow my head to Your will, not mine.
Pauline Easter

God's Greatest Gift

If children play within your door
And they are all your own,
You have a radiant, shining thing,
The greatest hearts have known.

They show that God has blessed your home;
He's given you His love
And sent fulfillment of your dreams;
He smiles down from above.

He's given things which are worthwhile,
To make your life more bright.
Be worthy of his trust in you
And thank him, day and night.

A little child within a home,
Be that home large or small,
The evidence of God's great love,
The greatest gift of all!
Kristen Creamer

Life Is Precious

Two people fall in love
and they began to build a home!

Soon they are blessed with children
For me it was five sons and one daughter.

The oldest gave me two grandchildren
one boy and one girl

The next one gave me
one girl and one boy.

The third son gave me
three boys and two girls

The youngest two girls
and three boys

Now I live alone with
my best friend my only
daughter truly I'm blessed

Soon to come to me on extra blessing
two great grandchildren,
truly, I can say Life is Precious
and I'm truly blessed!
Rose Pettit

Reminisce

Lonely nights I lay alone
And think of how our love once shone.
Now it's gone and went away
I'm left with nights without a day.
I gave my mind, my soul, my heart
Thinking we would never part.
How could I have been so wrong?
To love another for so long?
I knew that you could never stay
But still I thought to find a way.
I know my love for you is real
But do I know just how I feel?
Every time you'd leave, I'd cry
A part of me inside would die.
But now I know it couldn't last
And I must put you in the past.
Kelly Brannen

"To Her I Am Everything"

I am small, black, and thin,
And to much of the world insignificant,
But to her, I am everything.

She uses me as her tool.
I convey her thoughts to the world,
And as she glides me across the paper,
I make these thoughts come alive.

I have no preconceptions.
I write everything she allows me to,
Without an opinion.

Day after day she uses me
To show the world who she is,
And day after day I wonder
If it is my last.

Without me, no one
Could ever see her talent,
And without her,
I have no purpose.

Sarah Hoda

"Through My Baby's Eyes"

Stop and watch my baby,
and try to make believe.
That you can see through her eyes,
and tell me what you see.
Rivers seem like oceans,
Shrubs are like the trees.
A house looks like a castle,
could this be what she sees?
A shadow becomes a monster,
a meow becomes a roar.
No wonder she cries out with fright,
Need I tell you more?
All these different things to us,
are normal and seem right.
But seen through the eyes of baby,
no wonder there is fright.
To visualize these kinds of things,
it's hard to realize.
So stop and think - and take a look,
Through My Baby's Eyes!

Willa T. Martindale

The Continuous Pages

To relinquish the womb
and walk the earth
introduces eternal life,
it is to embark
on an everlasting journey
through the ages.
To walk with the angels
does not mean life's conclusion
but to continue
the turning of the pages.

Vanessa Escarcega

Untitled

Listen to a grievance,
As if it were a friend.
Passions create waves,
That should not ever end.
There's music in your spirit,
Your dreams the song will lend.
However, please don't take kindly,
To the words that will offend.

Steve Williams

Gettin' Older

I don't mind gettin' older
And walk with gentle ease,
 Going where I want to
And doing what I please.

I don't mind gettin' older
 And settled in my ways,
But my nights are gettin' longer
 And shorter are my days.

I don't mind gettin' older
 I reminisce awhile, and then,
I thank God that I've been privileged
With those years three score and ten.

 I don't mind gettin' older,
 The alternative, you see.
 If I wasn't gettin' older,
You'd not get this card from me.

Kenneth P. Hannaman

The Twin

I gazed into the mirror,
And what did I see?
I saw a familiar reflection
Staring back at me.
She moved when I moved
And talked when I talked.
Most amazing of all,
We had the same walk!
Her hands were like mine
And mine like hers.
Our heads moved the same
That bounced both of our curls.
After awhile,
I got tired of this "twin",
Especially when
She copied MY grin.
That was enough!
I had all I could take!
So I hit her hard.
And BOY DID SHE BREAK!

Tonia Thompson

Visit To The Nursing Home

"She's not herself today" they say.
And yet I know the one I see
Is no other than the she
Who never spread her wings to fly.
I wonder why.

Because of duty... custom... fear?
Oh Mother, couldn't you hear
Life call out in a loud, clear voice
"It's you who must make the choice".

It was your parade.
Didn't you understand?
You were the maker of the plan;
The leader of the band.

You don't hear what life says still.
You just sit beside your windowsill
Hidden deep inside your head.
Still sad... still mad,
But not yet dead.

Sheila M. Brown

Love In The Afternoon

A bit of bread, some cheese, some wine;
And you, the sweet sustenance of life.
You bring sublime inspiration
As the wine loosens my tongue to sing.
We touched and loved,
And left the wine an cheese.
And when you went away,
I had but cheese and wine
To taste in place of you.
A poor substitute at best,
But enough combined with the memory
Of our mingling juices,
To write of my desire to have you back;
To make the night a dream.

Robert A. Kates

Inside Of You

If you don't know what to do
And you're sad and lonely too,
Don't despair,
Just reach out for Love.

I am scared and I don't know
What to do when I am blue.
I am so very angry and confused.

Does it stop the pain from happening?
Does it stop the weak and weary?
If it does, then why don't you tell me?

Is running away the answer?
Will you find out all your dreams
If you do?
No, running away's not the answer.
The answer lies inside of you.

Melissa Kruzich

"Sun's Up"

Morning is here,
Another day to face
Why am I in such a hurried race.
Car honking
Schedules and meet
Phones ringing
Slow down the pace.
My years fleeting rapidly
Aging face
A short prayer
full of grace,
What difference
No confusion, no haste.

Karen Saffa

Day's End

The evening shadows
 are lengthening,
Twilight is coming on,
 Followed by the night.
But, I have no fear,
 For I am safe at home,
Where there is family,
 Security and light.

So It is in life's brief day.
 The sinking sun is sending
Out its last bright ray.
 But I hold no fear of
The fast approaching night.
 Just beyond the darkness
Is an eternal day,
 Where Jesus is the light.

Mary C. Richburg

'No Man's Land'

There is a battle field where dreams
  are never won
All around, there lies corpses
  of hopes undone

You can see the rusted steel
  of those who fell before
Somewhere someone cries for days
  what are no more.

This is where the clock stops
  and time stands still
Many have fallen, just as many more
  are falling still.

    Richard S. Blevins

Untitled

Your sheets
  are the cover
  that forms on cooling
  cocoa—-
We'll meet on warm
  skim sheets
Floating and falling into
soft brown chocolate
dreams.
Drinking our fill
of nights sweet brew.
Till the morning
meets the
reluctant rising rim
of sleep...

    C. Engram

The World

Flowers....
are the world.

Poems...
are the way
you think
of your life and the world.

You are...
yourself,
your thoughts,
your dreams.
You are different.

    Melina Gac-Artigas

Little Seed

Where are you little seed?
Are you down there in the ground?
If you are I can't see you
You're not making a sound.
I want to see you bloom
I want to see your beautiful colors,
But I guess it's just too soon.
Little seed, little seed come on out
Everyone's waiting,
So lets see you sprout!

    Marta Santobianco

Untitled

Pictures in a puddle
Aren't always what they seem.
A mirror's reflection
Tells the truth about your dreams
You take what you can get,
An eye for an eye.
You've made your bed,
Now you must lie.
The situation that I want
Doesn't come from greed.
It comes from my heart and soul
And the things I truly believe.

    Kellie R. Todd

Born Again

One day the Lord stood watching
as a child of his walked by.
Down the road of life he was taking
it made our Saviour cry.
The road was filled with trouble
and sorrow along the way,
he'd lost his faith in Jesus
when he forgot to pray.

The angels stood by watching
as the man went on his way.
The day was growing darker
when they heard him start to pray.
The angels started shouting
as God reached out his hand,
the sun had started shining
as he saw the promised land.

    Kathy Floyd

Untitled

Water drips from an icicle
As blood falls on the ground
Somewhere a heart is bleeding,
Somewhere a mind unsound
Somewhere a life is lost
Somewhere a love unknown
This is how it happens
When you are all alone
The moral of the story,
That I am telling here
Is don't hide your feelings
Just because of fear

    Summer Dawn Klinkkammer

Still The Road Lies Untraveled

Still the road lies untraveled
As far as I can see
I don't think I can go much further
Do you believe in me?

Still the road lies untraveled
Even though I want to I can't stop now
I've come much to far
I can't turn back around

Still the road lies untraveled
As my fear grows stronger
This never ending road grows longer
The victory bell has yet to ring
I cannot wait to hear it sing

Still the road lies untraveled
I must keep going on
I will take one more step towards victory
Before I die

    Rita Davidson

A Man's Love

A man's love grew yesterday
as he saw his bride turn old.
A man's love prevailed yesterday
when strength beat the bounds of time.
Who knew it would end like this
on a cold October eve,
then again, who would expect?

A man's love soared yesterday
as he cradled her in his arms.
A man's love proved true yesterday
as he laid the final rose.
Turning in black,
his eyes red with pain
his lips a quivering honesty.
A man's love ignited yesterday
as his wedding vows long ago burned.
She is still his bride
  as a man's love grows deeper,
and walking from her funeral
  a man's love survives.

    Tiffany J. Bagwell

My Baby Girl

Bright blue eyes stare up into mine
As her soft, gentle skin begins to shine
I can see she has her father's nose
As she begins to yawn and wiggle her toes
I held her in my arms and a tear
rolled down my face
I couldn't wait to put on her pink
dress covered with lace
I glanced down at her and thought
my heart would've been torn
For I suddenly I remembered, my
baby girl was almost not born

    Melanie Hebert

An Angel's Wing Touched Me

An Angel's wing touched me last night
as I slept.
Tis a dream I said but then she wept.
Her tears, they fell
And as they did fall
She wrote a message upon my wall

What is this message?
What does it say?
It tells me my love has been taken away.
Where has she gone?
Where have they taken my love?
To my dismay, she's been taken above.

Above to the heavens, where angels roam.
Above to the heavens, to her final home
So to be with her
To the world I must say goodbye
And with my last breath
I silently die.

    K. L. Stephens

Untitled

Beyond the hatred we
Both have said and done
Beyond the wonder what
has made your love change
By now if it was ever there
The constant worry of another day
Beyond the pain is where I'll find you.

    Sandy Wojnowich

If I Can Help Somebody

If I can help somebody,
  As I travel down life's way,
If I can help somebody,
  And help to make their day.

It may just be a handshake,
  Or even just a smile,
If I can help somebody,
  It will be worth my while.

If I can help somebody,
  That's broken down with tears,
If I can help somebody,
  That's getting on in years.

If I can help somebody,
  That's straying out in sin,
Maybe just a kind word,
  Would bring them back again.

If I can help somebody,
  In sickness or in pain,
If I can help somebody,
  My living will not be in vain.

Margaret Jones

Snow

Crisp it feels,
As I walk gently upon it.
Glistening in the sunlight,
Glistening like diamonds.
Crunchy,
Like a vanilla wafer.
Wet, smooth,
Yet, fluffy as a cats' fur.
Shapely,
A ball of ice,
As I toss a snowball to a friend.
Playing tag,
Making angels,
Catching snowflakes with my tongue.
Flakes,
Of all different shapes and sizes,
Float down and all around me.
Fresh, clean, new,
Crunching underneath my feet.
Snow is ah, so cold, but neat!

Susan J. Fowler

Vision Of Assurance

The other night
As I was standing alone
In the darkness of the night,
I heard a familiar moan.
Stopping short
And unable to believe
The vision was there
Of whom I still grieve.
Standing tall and sure
With his weathered face
And a favorite flannel shirt
With a collar trimmed with lace
Was my father's father
Looking much the same
His back slightly bent with age
Yet happiness his eye did claim.
As the figure slowly faded
My unhappiness did cease
A calm took over me
All I felt was peace.

Shelly Jozwiak

Bliss As A Kiss

We are thoughts of God
as if nature is one to call on
and destiny is here to seek

Oh how my thoughts do sway
to change the colorful way
but as how red is true
the evening must belong to you.

How to exchange our meaning
of care or feelings and enter
in with lost little wishes.

We are of magical stories to
bury our bones with green
little tides who weep but
with tears of blue from
me to you, our kisses will
taste so sweet.

Kelley King

Fires Dancing

Have you ever watched a fire die?
As piece by piece her embers sigh
and hungry fingers melt to coals—
in this moment she captures souls.
And the wind rattles my door no more.

The logs, they moan as they're consumed,
the beast licks its paws and resumes
it feast of branches. Now ashes,
they fall slowly like molasses.
And the wind rattles my door no more.

The fire, she dances a sad dance
of death, yet fills me with romance.
Oh, how beautiful a creature,
Who laughs at the grim reaper!
Now the wind wildly claws at my door.

Her soft laughter lulls me to sleep.
In her barred cage, death finds her weak.
While I dream of red fires dancing—
out rides the black horse and his king.
And the wind rattles my door no more.

E. Criqui

The Moon

The moon is a picturesque sight to see
  As she shines down upon the earth,
But she's lacking both shrubs and flowers
  And the miracles we call "birth".

With her treeless and lifeless mountains
  Her barren and waterless plains,
She floats in her own little orbit
  In a world with no troubles and pains.

No government, no rich employees
  No picketing, walkouts or strikes,
No struggle for daily survival
  No media with all of their "mikes".

On earth we have life and its problems
  But isn't it a wonderful thing,
Why can't we learn to be happy
  And love every human being?

Let's keep our hard earned dollars
  As the moon has nothing to share,
Let's concentrate on our planet earth
  Or would you like living up there?

Pathedra Manners

Untitled

Muzak overwhelms
as the heat waves
throb

Nonsensical mind
mumbles
into a
half deaf ear

Random songs
flick through my
head

Once I start
I cannot not finish

Obsession overflows

Gotta write
to save my soul

'Cuz the bright light
blinds even those
who wear

sunglasses...

Richard P. Dal Porto, II

First Love

Sea-spray stings our faces
As we plummet
Into the thundering waves.
Sea-shells crush beneath
Our tender feet.
I feel nothing.
Yet, the fleeting touch
Of your hand to mine
Sears through me
With a burning fire.
My heart pulsates a new rhythm.
Is this love,
This feeling so strange and new?
Does nothing exist
Between the sea and sky
But you and I?
If only time stood still!

Mary Manisero

Death Is A Carwash

We roll up,
asking directions
to the nearest shell.
Roll up your windows,
straighten your wheels,
and don't drive,
the voice says.
Protesting,
we are drawn in....

S. A. Moore

Daydream

  'Love and bugs, dragon's hugs
  Boughs of sweat and tofu rugs
Gallons of magic and polar bear ties
  Bloodstreaked cement in a New York
      Barrio.
    Wanting to dream
    Wanting to scream
  Wanting everything to seem
    A lot less real.'

Michael G. Dinicola

"Life's Trials"

They say life begins
at 40,
Mine fell apart at
50,
I fell into depression
that I could not bear,
Thank God for a
Dr. who really did care,
Now I'm on the mend,
And I'm very happy again.
This could happen
to you,
So don't condemn anymore
who is very blue,
Look to the Lord
when you are weak,
God promises to take
care of the very meek,
Don't be lonely or sad,
Call a friend, she'll be very glad!

Shirley Newcomb

"Dream Lover"

I'm looking up into the big blue skies,
At first that is what it appeared to be.
But no, they are his eyes,
Now I understood - and I can see.

March sixth, nineteen-ninety-three,
Yes, that was the date.
I know he is the only one for me,
He was never late!

Chatting on the phone,
Going on those morning drives.
He was the only man to be known,
And for he - my heart only thrives.

Movies at seven,
Friday and Saturday night.
It was like floating in heaven,
And we never had to fight.

He has gone to jail,
But in my mind he will stay.
My heart feels pounded with nails,
Yet I will still think of him always, night and
   day!

Krista Keehan

The Little Brook

With our eyes we take a look
At the beauty of the Brook
As the water trickles by
Mirroring the birds in the sky

As we gaze within this stream
Things may not be as they seem
As the birds and fish go by
Some in the Brook and some in the sky

We can see this with our eyes
How the Brook reflex the sky
Making pictures that are real
For all of us to feel

We continue here to look
At this tiny little Brook
And as we set and stare
Lo and behold we are there

As we ponder at this sight
Studying Nature for some light
Into the mirror of our soul
Reflex the thought that is our goal.

Marion Earl Layman

No Charge

Yours for the asking, is salvation.
At your request, eternal life.
Given by the God of all creation,
Bought with the blood of Jesus Christ.

There's nothing you need do, to earn it.
It's something money cannot buy.
Freely given, though some spurn it,
Sometimes, not even knowing why.

It's joy you'll know if you accept it,
This gift of Christ into your heart.
Today's the day, so don't neglect it.
The Lord's already done His part.

His blood was shed for sin's remission,
When they nailed Him to that cross.
No charge to you, save your submission.
He paid the price, He took the loss.

Be born a new, have life eternal.
The Father's equal to that task.
Have your name written in His journal.
Salvation's free, no charge, just ask.

J. Mike Hastings

Untitled

I'm walking down an endless road,
awaiting for my heart to explode.

You are what my heart desires,
only you can lift me higher.

If there has ever been a time
   where I made you mad;
Please forgive me for it
   makes me sad.
I love you with all my heart,
and without you I'd fall apart.

Paul Filipponi

In The Park

Take this still night -
Bear arms to no one
Heed the final blow,
By brow of sweat learn the now -
Of aching hearts that must know how
The ravens hair black as coal
The eyes of the beast so bold -
Lay to rest the weary ones
Come morning the night has slipped away
As the fog lifts for a new day -
The city is empty all is dark
The knapsack man has come and gone
No one is on the beach in the park
The city is empty all is dark.

Rolland K. Flicker

Terra

And you my dear small child.
 Born from chaos and strife,
 will be my contribution,
 my symbol of hope for life.
 And I will watch you grow,
  Memorize moments, yes.
Painfully watching you fall,
Recall your face at my breast.
 And you my darling daughter,
  named after the rare earth,
 will find my love unbounding,
 my promise since your birth.

Michelle D. Caron

Untitled

Raped
Beat
Killed
Sickly pale
Deathly ill
Lying
Trying
Crying
Dying
Faith dropped dead
When hope
Committed suicide
Love was murdered
I buried the knife
With the gun
That took
The life of trust

Chistianne

In Memory Of My Mother

Dear Mother, this poem is for you
Because of your love so true.
I have loved you all my years,
Even when I've shed many tears.
It's not what you own,
But what you give.
It's not what you learn,
But how you live.
You didn't rush through the day,
You paused a moment by the way,
Something good to do,
Something good to say.
You always said a little prayer
And with you I lost all fear.
And now you live within my heart,
And we'll never be apart.

Suzie Jackson

The She-River

I see her rise above the river
Beckoning me on closer...
Draped in sea grass
Her long, wet hair
Clinging to her shoulders...
She shimmers like the gentle waves
Around her.
The swallows circle above her
And the fish swim just beneath.

The shores stare in silence
Watching what I will do
And jagged rocks stand stoically
Daring the river to test her might
Against their impervious strength.
Neither wins...neither loses...
Each battles only the space of time.

I am drawn to all this -
To go forever on...
To be cradled in her peace
Going nowhere...but, always somewhere.

Marion E. Grams

Longing

Sated lust
departs in clear
the face to face pose
knows it queer

Vincent L. Mcduell

Oh Silent Dream

Oh silent dream's left untold
before my sleeping eye's unfold

Shadows erected into formations
laying detail, mounting foundations

Faces forming, fusing clarity
quite translucent, uncommon fairity

Places unseen in this life
amid the mind
Bombarded inhabitants seeking refuge
within its dreamer's time

Circular motion, comatose state
unbalanced uncertainty awaits

Dream of sleeping dreamer the gift is
yours to take
Dream oh sleeping dreamer for
soon your eye will wake.
  B. J. McQueary

It's Still Summer

Who forgets his mother's last day
before she had to go away?
Labor Day, 6th of September,
bittersweet time to remember.

As always, up right with the sun
to make sure all chores would get done.
Watered her many house plants well—
that's what she loved most, I could tell.

Company would be coming soon,
to eat fried chicken around noon.
"Wear apron from state fair," I said,
as lovingly each pet she fed!

Much friendly visiting took place;
often a smile was on her face.
Little did any of us know
next day from this earth Mom would go.

If still summer when one must die,
it's easier to say good-bye.
I'll bet it's summer at its best,
where mothers go when gone to rest.
  Lowell "Ted" DaVee

How We Met

The first day
  beguiling eyes
The second
  was a painted smile
A third day, a dividend
  a smiling hello
Fourth day, all the above
  plus "How are you?"
Fifth day
  brought small talk
Sixth came round
  a date 'twas made
Then Sunday
  an eternal afternoon
  Ralph N. Smiley

Shining Through

Light, mysterious path
Dashing through limber saplings
It roams the shimmering.
  Tiffany A. Bright

Are You Still In There?

Mother, are you still in there
  behind that cold blank stare?
Is there any understanding
  when I say how much I care?

Mother, are you still in there
  behind the senseless chatter?
Are you trying somehow to tell me
  how much I really matter?

Mother, are you still in there
  behind your tight-clenched fist?
Do you have any awareness
  of how very much you are missed?

Each night I go to bed and pray
  for mercy or for a miracle, too.
Then, I wonder who needs them more;
  could it be me instead of you?

One thing I know for certain;
  there is nothing to compare
With the torment deep inside my heart
  when I pray you are not there.
  Norma L. Atherton

Colors

Whether you are,
Black or white.
What does it matter?
Whether you are,
Asian or Hispanic.
What is the difference?
The pigment in your skin.
That's all!!
That shouldn't stop you,
From being friends.
Don't hold a grudge against,
Someone who doesn't look like you.
No one looks like you.
Have a good time laugh with others.
Be friends with someone,
That is a different race.
Who knows may be,
You will like them!!
  Mary Glenn

Despondent

Lost am I in a world of complications
Bleeding hearts and Quivering hands,
With no one left to hold my own
I walk through bleak desolation.

Too afraid to step into the next world,
Alone I stand in this one.
Seeing, wanting, needing so much more,
So much that no one can give.

Shadows cast upon my life,
Like trees on a sunny day.
Entombed inside this darkness I see,
No light, no hope will stay.
  Murphrey Knox

People Are Alike

People are alike in many different ways,
but people just don't these days.
When I walk down a street,
and look at people I meet,
I don't see them for their color,
or the way they dress.
I see them for them, and that's best!
  Melissa Foust

Dream Child

I have seen you, child detached
  Blinding is your plastic smile.
    Paper God smothering
Trying to drown you in its philosophy.

I have heard you, child silence.
  Hunger screaming at hollow eyes
A drifting facade; voice of content.
Sweet willing soldier...surrender.

  Imagine! Reality woven with
  Society's web of indifference.
  On your absence they will feed,
  Caged within fading minds.

  Child lonely, I felt you near.
  Burning fiercely in my head,
  Pouring disposable existence
  On my pillow; suffering sleep.

  You, child lost, embrace me.
Calm in sleep's labyrinth, we'll unite.
  Capture me in your dream;
  Release me in your wake.
  Shandra Gardner

'Coming Of Age'

To go through life so
blindly naive,

Trusting and loving to
such a degree.

To be used and abused
going back for more,

Hoping I could change
them, but... "What for???

I saw a glimpse of
good and clung on so tight,

Sacrificing my dignity
whether wrong or right.

Not sure anymore
about so many things,

But need to break
through this cycle of pain.

Would like to stifle
these feelings of rage,

For I fear, I have come of age.
  Lois M. deMaurégné

Feelings

There's an ache in my heart
  but a pill won't ease it;
Your presence is important to me;
  tell me that you need me too.
I hold your hand but it's inert-
  you're not inside it.
I reach out to you
  but you don't respond.
I'd like to share your worries
  but you withdraw from me.
I'd like to cry with you
  but you hold back the tears.
I'd like to comfort you
  but you won't let me.
I need comfort too—
  please don't shut me out.
Don't let today's dark despair
  keep us from sharing— feelings.
  Ruby Reed

Blue Night

The night wind feels so good
Blowing against my face.

The stars are shining oh so bright
Upon the moonlight sky

But instead of blackness in the night
There is the color of blue

A color that represents depression
A color that represents pain

But the sky is not depressing
Nor is it in pain at all

It's just the mighty clouds up above
Reflecting off the moonlight glow

And that's what makes the city
Glow like the color of blue this night

A color that usually represents sadness
But tonight only a master piece
A masterpiece of natural art

Michael J. Dowling

King's Chamber

Deep in a chamber
Breathing four walls
A king on his throne
His power a lost cause
Anxious and hopeful
With a screaming mind
Seeking new answers
All hard to find
Deception now strange
Reign of new power
Warrior of his soul
Man of the hour

Matthew McDonald

Broken Dreams

As children bring their
Broken toys for us to mend
I brought my broken dreams to God.
'Cause he is my best friend.
But instead of leaving him
In peace to work alone.
I hung around and tried to help
With ways that were my own.
At last I snatched them back
And cried how could you be so slow.
My child, he said,
"What could I do you never did let go!"

Tina Radetski

I Want To Be A Writer

I want to be a writer,
But, I don't know what to write.
I can't explain this feeling,
I always have to fight.
I want to be a writer,
When the thoughts run through my head,
But putting them on paper,
Is worse than being dead.
I want to be a writer,
For the world would know my name.
And it would be exciting,
To for once have all the fame.
I want to be a writer,
This is my writing dream.
I want to be a writer,
Just like Shel Silverstein.

Kimberly Anderson

Friends In Love

It started out a friendship,
But I wanted so much more.
And now that were together,
Life seems better than before.
The times together
we had as friends,
Are faded memories.
The future starts a new romance,
Our destiny agrees
I'll still be there,
to care for you,
And help you
when you're down.
You can come to me
for anything,
I'll always be around.
But now I can embrace you,
And kiss you tenderly
And hear you whisper words of love,
I never thought could be.

Melanie Hall

Country Nostalgia

I longed to see the country
But it eluded me
Residing in the city
Only skyscrapers could I see

In glowing memory kindled
Clusters of white birch trees stood
Filling my nostrils with morning dew
Penetrating the dense piney wood

Time stood still momentarily
In the mind's eye to return
Knowing it possible to pass again
Through the heartbeat of discern

Marcia Waldbillig

My Cell

Some may think it's kind of funny
But it's really kind of sad
Locked inside this cell
Just like a brutal beast
To hear an echo scream
From inside my lonely cell
It brings back things from dreams
That make me think of hell
No I'll say it doesn't matter
I can handle it, just as well
But inside my lonely cell
I fight from going to hell
No it's not very funny
In fact it's kind of sad
It can drive a sane man crazy
And turn a good man bad

Shane Patrick Moore

Roses

Delicate and light,
Climb up the trellis,
Singing a song,
Of lost words and love,
Silky red petals,
Flutter in the breeze,
Casting a fragrant scent,
Into the warm night air,
Long, lost, forgotten love,
of roses.

Sunny Choi

Ode To Friend

Your "light" has gone! not out
but just beyond - the "Heavenly Gates"
 "Free"
from sorrow-pain and fear
with your "Savior" waits and others to
you so dear.
 "God" loves us so - when "He" calls
it's time to go-
Now a "Sainted" Soul-may your love
help us to reach our goal
 The shadow across our hearts made
by "Angel Wings" - parts
 And
your love shines through-showing us
that "Heaven is Supreme"
 With
 "God"
 and
 you!

Nellie M. Streng

Untitled

We can no longer see you,
but know you are there.
You can no longer hear us,
but know that we care.
Friends and family,
both young and old,
Love you dearly,
though seldom told.
We know that you're happy,
and feel no pain.
You're watching over us
to keep us sane.
We have to be strong,
memories only good,
Continuing on,
as you wish we would.
Someday though
you will sighted
All loved ones,
Eternally reunited.

Renee A. Bates

My Buddy

My buddy is gone
But my life must go on
It's hard and it's rough
But my buddy taught me to
 be tough
Through each step in my life
He was there
My buddy really did care
With him, I was able to share
And to this day, I still want to cry
I can imagine the glow in his eyes
I will always be his daughter
For my buddy was my father.

Karen P. Stapleton

"Through friends Eyes"

I am a different person
each time I see someone,
because there is a view of me
through eyes that are not mine,
and while I think I know myself
I also realize,
the view that often matters most
is through those different eyes.

Kirk D. Davis

Love Speaks Always

Love speaks always
But not always in words
   Love can speak silently
So quiet it might not be heard.
   Love speak always
But not always in the eyes
   Love can speak in looks
While the sensation intensifies
   Love speak always
But not always in the touch
   Love can speak emotionally
Even if the desire is too much
   Love speaks always
But not always from the heart
   Love can speak from the mind
Knowing you'll never drift apart
   Love speaks always
You don't have to beg or plea
   Cause when you find true love
It'll last all eternity.

Pamela Sinclair

How Blue I Feel

The sky might be blue
But not as blue as I was when I lost you
I know that dreams can come true
But some I know never do
I thought it would be you and me forever
I thought we would always be together
maybe it's time
I leave you behind
Try to block you out of my mind
Then I will find
The love that I need
You will lead
The way in that dark tunnel
Love's just like a funnel
It starts with a little hole
It gets bigger and bigger as you go
Till your heart's torn apart

Tracey Goodwin

Feelings Of An Unborn Child

Today my mommy learned of me,
but she keeps crying, "How can this be?"
I wish that she would understand,
that I am a gift from God's own hand.

Didn't she worry about me,
when my daddy held her tight?
Didn't she think there could be a "me",
As he loved her through the night?

Now they're going to rid of me,
So my life they never shall see.
Even though they are the ones to blame,
I'm the one who will never have a name.

Karri Boyer

Encircle

Ivory walls
encircle
alabaster skin chestnut hair
ruddy skin ashen hair,
blue eyes blue jeans
seduce beauty and heat,
only to be laid to sleep
by unbared bodies and unbared souls,
where ivory walls too much enclose.

Susan Carr Grant

Snowstorm

I shovel through the icy snow
but still there's no place I can go
I shoveled toward an apple tree
hoping that will cover me
but no, the snow, just fell on my head
right now I wish that I was dead
I felt a hand upon my shoulder
and then I felt sort of colder
I turned around really calm
and saw that it was my Mom
she yelled at me and slapped me hard
Now I know not to play in our backyard.

Melissa R. Ellner

Betrayal

You said you would never leave,
But that was all a lie.
You broke my heart,
Oh how you made me cry.
I'm dying inside,
For what you did to me.
You said you loved me,
But how could this be?
If you loved me so much,
Why did you leave?
It's not easy to hide,
All my feelings inside.
But I must do it,
I can't let you see me hurt.
I used to love you so much,
I'm not so sure anymore.
You'll never change,
No matter how much I dream.
I'll just have to face it,
You're not what you seemed.

Rachael Bell

Like A Father, Like A Friend

Almost a year has passed,
But the pain still lies in my heart.
I did not lose a lover,
I lost a friend,
I lost a father,
All in one single day.
It's all so hard to think
of entering this big world
without a friend,
without a father.
I feel him though.
Standing at my side,
guiding my way.
Sometimes I see him,
Telling me that everything will be okay.
Just smiling,
Like a father would,
Like a friend does.

Stephanie Bennett-Sides

Fantasizing Thieves

When experiences are old
dear comrade bunkie
The gales won't rumble
The stool won't squeal
When memories have aged
constant partner boss
You will be castrated
and I.... burnt.

Linda D. Inyang

Grandpa

The time has passed so quickly,
   But, the years,
   there have been a few,
of enjoying a life of wonderful things,
   so many can never do.

His time on earth was filled
   with love and laughter,
   and the stories he could tell
were ones of when he was a boy
   to the ones he muttered
   when he became ill.

He will leave behind
   the ones who loved him
   and thought of him
      so dear
To carry out the memories,
   of when he was here.

Stacy M. Smith-Brown

Untitled

She was there one day
   But then she was gone,
On that gloomy fall day,
   We cried at the grave
Where her body still lay
   And the roses bloom
As she passed the moon
   We sang a long tune.
I wished I would of spent
   More time with her
It probably would of meant
   A lot to her.
As I see the stars twinkle
   I think of her love
That she gave us here
   But now she's above
I know she's in God's hand
   The one that we love,
But I wish she was here
   Instead of above.

Shelley Nagel

'Searching'

I cried out "is anyone out there?"
But there was no sound,
And I thought no one can here,
I searched for him
To be by my side,
But he wasn't there
He ran to hide.

He was hiding from everyone and
Everything 'cause he was scared,
He wanted something different
That no one else had dared to ask.

He wasn't the type that
Did what he was told
But often wanted more,
Maybe someone beautiful and bold.
But never had found
That one special person
Is no where yet to be found.

Miranda Yebba

A College Lament

They say that college life's a blast
But you certainly can't prove that by me
It's toil and grief each and every day
Just trying to pass chemistry
And if you should take a breather
The calendar soon reminds you
There's only two more days and a night
Until your lab report's due
Oh, and let's not forget psychology
Erikson, Freud, and Jung
All screaming for some attention
Just in case you thought you were done
Say, whatever happened to the good times
You know—dates, parties and fun
I became a pre-pharmacy major
And my social life's now a ruin
Ah, but one of these days it'll be over
For I will have earned my degree
Yes, I'll know then it was all worth it
When I see how proud you are of me.

Willa Thompson

Hope Within

Sometimes I wonder "Why?"
but you know,
it's pointless to ask.
You've got to let go.

Let go of the anger.
Let go of the grudge.
Do you think that the strong
are the ones who won't budge?

Those who improve themselves
are the wise of the bunch,
they perceive in their hearts.
they proceed on a hunch

See, the good and the bad
in the family of man
is a thing they can't change
so they change what they can

Which is only ourselves
and the way that we see
and the state of our hearts
and who we choose to be

Mike Vickers

No

The answer was no,
But you misunderstood.
You kept on going,
Non stop.

It hurt so bad,
Inside and out,
Shout or no shout,
The answer was no.

I know you weren't deaf,
You just didn't listen
The begging was just for a bit,
I finally quit.

My feelings are hurt,
I keep it to myself.
Inside I hurt bad,
But what could I do?

Sandra Harmon

Seagull

Light as the feathers of his wings,
Calm as the ocean's breeze,
was his miraculous flight.

Soft as the beach's sand,
Sweet as the smell of the air,
was his beauty by nature's right.

Flying high o'er the waves
into the crystal blue sky,
high above the earth below.

Soaring with confidence and grace,
bringing magic to my eyes,
oh, he put on a show!

Naomi Nulman Pari

Kevin

Into the sunshine - from the shadow
Came the child - sensitive and alert.
Lifting his head like a young fawn
The beauty to see and danger if any.

Up hill from child to youth
He walked steadily up the path
The mind expanding - exploring
Storing all new knowledge for tomorrow.

From youth to man, the path to follow
The future still to come.
Earth, sky, space, the universe
The world to save, and he the savior.

Shirley Peacock

Only Hate

In a world of no love only hate.
Can you imagine what would be your fate
Where no one is placid
Living a life that is so horrid
A world so corrupt
Where only violence erupts
All being vile and vain
Giving sheer agony and lasting pain
Where all lives in sin
As the cruelty comes forth from within
No One to be Loved or Hugged
In a life of Aids, crime and Drugs
From the day that you were Born.
Until from this world you are gone.
Yes, from that said date.
You were taught only to hate.
Always with the devil in your mind
To that word Love you are blind
Just imagine your fate.
Living in a world of no love only hate.

Stephen Stoll

A Gift Of Love

A mother is God's gift of love,
  Chosen carefully from above.

She gives her heart and soul to us,
  Without a moan, without a fuss.

She nurtures us through all the years,
  And comforts us from all our fears.

She guides us to God's loving way,
  She deserves our praises every day.

So let her know how much you care,
God's precious gift He chose to share.

Linda Jansing

Color Me Destructive

The moon is bright, a summer day
Casting shimmers over countryside
The sun is quiet children' play
Brief laughter on the ride
A sprinkle of forbidden rain
Forever shedding truth
Upon the flowers' wilting pain
Grasped them at the roots
"The days are gone!", is shouted by
Green people in brown desert
Purple lilacs fade to gray
As water lilies hurt
Owls torment turns to red
As bloody claws turn blue
And lowly sheep white in their field
Turn a blackened turquoise hue
And as we turn for golden rust
And the power we've retained
All we've accomplished with our lust
Is human dust in grave

Tanya Fortin

Thimbleberries

When does the thimbleberry
Change from green to red?
Does it happen late at night-
When I am in my bed?

Or does the metamorphosis take place-
When the sun's rays shine high?
I watch them through the day-
To see if their secret will reply?

I ran out this morning-
To see if I could tell-
How the color entered the berry
The process - could teach us well!

I went down at high noon-
To see what I could see?
There were more red thimbleberries-
Waiting there for me!

At dusk I took a walk-
Past the thimbleberry plants-
And in the cool evening breeze-
More red berries dance!

Rosetta Ewing Schemenauer

City Streets

City streets full of gaiety,
City streets full of people.
City streets full of ecstasy,
City streets full of joy.

Window shopping, taxi hailing,
Laughing people, sirens wailing.
Joy and pain lumped together,
All on a block of concrete.

City streets full of agony,
City streets full of pain.
City streets full of jealousy,
City streets full of rain.

Gunshots, knife wielding,
Hit and run with cars not yielding.
Gang violence to get their kicks,
There is no other place like this.

City streets vary from time to time,
Full of lust, passion, turmoil and grime.
Hate wars, love games can always be found,
City streets are collapsed dreams on the ground.

Rebecca J. Price

The Loom

I weave the strings of my life
Collecting songs and smiles
laughter and lovers, golden and silver

In this my pattern there is loneliness
Despair and emptiness
I have held the hunger
And tasted the torture

Of the world around and within
My feet have trodden red hot coals
My heart has known iron bitter fear
My mind the calm of madness

Moonlight caressing my skin
Wind whispering in my hair
Tingling streams trickling over my toes
Sweet kisses on my lips
A friend's hand in mine

I weave the strings of my life
My soul tempers, my love colors, the
design
From the hidden recesses of my mind.

Lynda Crocker

Untitled

Orange, Red, Golden, brown
Colored leaves falling down

Autumn is here
Winter is near
A time for loving and caring
A time for giving and sharing

Winter and Autumn
Autumn and Winter
Bringing thoughts of those
who are dear
Calling friends and family near

Orange, Red, Golden, Brown
Colored leaves falling down

Two new seasons
have begun
Two new seasons
full of fun.

Robin-Lynn Konopka

The Asteroid

The inner bounds of outer space
   contained a certain planet,
consisting of some hydrogen,
   some oxygen and granite.

And on this sphere were animals,
   both large and small with heads;
some had even lost their tails,
   and many quadrupeds.

They walked about this little ball
   or swam within its waters,
and taught of their importance
   to all their sons and daughters.

While some of these built weapons
   to terrify the others,
some went ahead and blew away
   their sisters and their brothers.

And soon the animals were gone,
   the H$_2$O was void,
but the outer bounds of inner space
   gained an asteroid.

William C. Edler, II

Woe Is Me!

It seems I love misery,
Contentment I can't claim,
Mind talk to my heart,
My life may never be the same.

My life is in pieces,
Like a patch work quilt,
I have this terrible pain,
I can't get rid of the guilt.

I'm setting straddle this fence,
I don't know which way to lean.
No matter which side I'm on,
The other side looks more green.

Happiness can't be bought,
You can't beg, borrow or steal,
It must come from within,
Ask for guidance and God's will.

You determine the road you walk,
You choose the path you take,
Keep only God's counsel,
Let Him help the choice you make.

Mary Lou Warren

"I Am A Tree"

/I am a tree growing beside a
Cool river bank.
My roots dip deeply in the
River of life.
My branches are full of sweet
Smelling blossoms
Fruits of righteousness will
Grow here soon

   I will not walk or take
ear to those mocking God.
   My mind must meditate
strongly on his laws

I am a tree in a forest of light
Where your goodness is feeding
My soul to excite

Dear God water my roots so my
Life will be long.
Help me Dear Father to grow and be strong.

   For I am a tree
Ruth Ann Piccola

Just A Penny

Standing by a fire plug
Counting four and twenty
What's the matter little boy
Did you lose a penny?

Yes I did dear little dog
Nice of you to ask me
Dropped it down the sewer, dog
'Fraid Mama's gonna spank me

Hand on dog, tears running down
Asking for not many
Old man passing by does hear
And gives the boy a penny

Marjorie A. Ringle

Shattered Trust

As broken glass
creates a prism
reflecting light
in rainbow shades
Not quite pure
in rhyme and rhythm
Not quite clean and free
So lies create
A crooked line
At times difficult to see
For he who makes them
can be quite persuasive
Not easy to perceive
and so we falter
disperse like fractured light
Entrapped in broken trust
and only truth will right the wrong
of misplaced faith.

Linda Smiley

Rediscovery

When souls mesh,
   creativity reigns
Enhancement of your being,
   sings a refrain.

Glassed in emotion,
   set free to roam
Awash in liberation,
   the insecurity is gone.

Emotionally spent,
   yet zestfully infused
Obscurity has cleared,
   my view is anew.

The rediscovery of myself,
   a quintessential gift
Thank you, my explorer,
   I'm no longer adrift.

Linda Howell-Sisler

In The Corners Of The Mind

Sorrows,
creeping slowly upon the soul,
a night filled with shadows,
wandering from door to door,
restless spirits,
looking for minds to haunt,
always succeeding,
the victory is theirs—
as tears roll slowly to form a maze,
is this all,
or can hope still be sown?
do I know,
it there'll ever be dawn?

Maria Bukowska

I Am A Leaf

I am a leaf.
Depending on you for my strength.
Together we are beauty.
Fall comes,
Weather turns cold.
You let me turn brown and fall.
Falling...
Faster and faster to my death.
The rains come and I am washed away.
Alone.

M. Nicole Milsom

Heroin

Dedicated to the Memory of Kurt Cobain

Like a disease,
  creeping to my innermost joints.
It has driven away
  the happiness from my life.
I am seeking an answer,
  but will I find one?
I am not asking to heal, I am asking,
  do I have the strength to quit?
I deserve to be strong,
  and put down this bitter death.
Oh God, give me this,
  in exchange for my devotion.
  Liz Elman

Buffington's Buffet At The Brasserie

Ladies in twisted linen legs, legs
dancing is stemmed crystal clear
gowns on harlequin, begging,
for fulfilling and jazzing.

Jazzing, jazzing, reflected, history
mounting history, sliding plates
of entrees, oysters remoulade
cheesecakes, truffles and tarts buffeted

In red sequins and alabaster
digging in their heel, tinkling
over and through the ivories of
caramel creme and female dreams.
  Pamela Kolleas

Since You Went Away

Dedicated to Eric James Maxwell

I wrote to you
day and night
night and day
hoping your memory wouldn't fade away.

I came to you
When you finally came home
And now I just want a chance to say
I love you now more than ever,
Since you went away.

Our love is written in the books
And I now know the meaning of it,
You and me as it looks!

I know this poem isn't much
It's just to show you how I feel.
It's not all that bad, the poem.
But all I can say is,
I truly love you baby!

I hope our love last a lifetime
'Cause I'd do anything for you
And you now know I love you true!
  Rachel Sadler

Life And Death

Life the miracle the joy
Death the pain, the sorrow
Life being together
Death being apart
Life the wonders the adventures
Death the memory the tears
Life and Death the mysteries.
  Michelle Burke

Faith

Peace on earth the season says
Dead men lie within our sight
Frighten souls in flight

Peace on the season says

Men grasp all for their greed
Blind to each other need

Peace on earth the season says

Fires of war light the sky
Nuclear missiles fly up high

Peace on earth the season says

Yet standing above it all
A manager in a lowly stall
A star shining bright and clear

Peace on earth the season's here
  Norah Bridges

I Thought Of You Today

I thought of you today,
dear other half of me-

sweet tyranny this,
not bliss.

I thought of you,
other heart of mine

...part of me,
but free.

I thought of dreams
unwished for,
lost to me

and ached for
something....didn't I?

What did I do today?
I thought of you...
....and me.
  Linda Osborne

In memory of my Great-Grandma I will
always love. You will always be in
my heart.

My Savior And Myself

Trapped,
deep within.
The power grows,
pulsing, rising,
at the brink of exploding.
My head throbbing,
aching from use.
My body weak,
from fighting my feelings.
darkness, covering mine eyes,
blocking the Sun.
I see a hand,
reaching to pull me out.
I stretch for it,
the tips of our fingers touch.
The darkness, breaks, falls apart.
There we are, together,
side by side,
my Savior and myself.
  Shauna Catherine Mackerer

Months

January is cold and
desolate;
February dripping
wet;
March winds range;
Birds sing in tune;
While raining in
April to bring flowers
in May
And a sunny
June bring longest days;
In scorching July the storm
clouds fly, and lightning rumbles;
August bears corn;
September fruit;
in keen November;
And nights are long,
and cold winds are
Strong in bleak December.
  Sean Smith

Desire Night Trust

Witches haven,
  dew form birth.

Sleeping death,
  the great mothers hour.

Violet dreams enwrap
  our naked smiles.

Ecstasy comes with slow pressing breezes
  caressing our new found secret.

Long child flights through mating shadows
  conceiving plots of trustful treason
  among the forest-dwellers.

At dawns first warning we must scatter
  like the insects whose songs
  joined our conversation.

Our friends seek refuge
  in holes and slumbers.

Time taunts our ears with whispered tales
  of new love in black stained desires.
  Nickki L. Helton

A Mother's Day Poem

What does motherhood mean to me?
  Dirty Diapers, teary eyes,
Runny nose and a scrape on the knee.
  Nighttime feedings,
        Lullabies.

Midmorning naps, an afternoon walk,
  A gurgle, a smile,
    A laugh, and a coo;
  Lots and lots of Baby talk!
Big blue eyes saying I love you.

All of this and much, much more,
I'm sure that you will see,
If you walk through my door;
Just what motherhood means to me.
  Melyssa Barbone

Questions?

Can I tell me of my pain?
  Do I know?
Can I tell me of my pain?
  will it show?

Is it here?
Is it there?
Is it real?

Do they know who I am?
  Can I tell?
Do they know who I am?
  Am I well?

Do they care?
Do I dare?
Are they real?

Take a chance?
Sami OH

Love Me But ______

Love me, but
Do not live for me;
Live for love—-
For the sake of loving;
To give to each new day
The best of it you have!
Greet each dawn as though
It were the last;
As bridegrooms greet their brides;

Love me, but
Do not stand too close;
We both need space
For we are large enough
So that we span
All distances that separate,
But cannot e'er estrange;
We have so much
We have eternity;
But more than this
We have each other..........
Muriel Sylvia Cobb Johnson

Question

What is with us?
Does anyone know?
Why are we so hateful?
Why do we let it show?
Why are we stereotyped,
Just by what we say?
Why can't it be safe,
For all kids to go out and play?
How can we sit here,
And watch our world go to waste?
Why can't we do something,
Without being chased?
Why do we this?
Does anyone know?
Someone please tell me.
I'd sure like to know.
Tanner Marcantel

Untitled

Do you believe in Love?
  Even when you cannot feel it?
Do you believe in God?
  Even when he seems silent?
Do you believe in the Sun?
  Even when it is not shining?
Martha Johann

Hobby Images

Dolls are on the bedroom dresser
Dolls sit by the door
Doll are placed on everything
From the ceiling down to the floor

Dolls are placed in rocking chairs
Dolls are on the bed
Dolls are lying in their cradles too
And in a painted sled

Dolls are short, small or tall
Dolls have eyes of blue or brown
Dolls are smiling, some have tears
There's even one who wears a frown

Dolls are treasured by little girls
Dolls help cheer up the old
Dolls are our favorite collectibles
And never should be sold

Dolls have a look that says "pick me up"
Dolls have a music box key
Dolls even look like movies stars
But one looks just like me!
Virginia M. Pfitzer

Daddy's Girl

Be home early
Don't come in late.
you're only a sophomore
Let's not debate!
you're not like your brother,
you're not like your friend,
they may stay out late,
But you're coming in!
I'm doing it for your sake
I hope you're not mad.
I just wish you'd remember,
It's hard to be a Dad!
Margie Gage

Together As Two

  She stands at the
door in her dress of gray,
when she stops, looks around
and glances his way. Her
eyes look hurt his eyes
look blue, for they'd be
together forever as two.
Slowly but surely he begins
to speak, as a tear drop
quickly rolled down her cheek
He says it just wasn't meant
to be, if only I could help
you see. But she cries and
screams if you only knew,
for they thought they'd be
together forever as two.
Katie DeVaughn

Drawings

  Draw a picture of an ocean blue
Draw a picture of me and you
  Draw a picture of a far away land
Draw a picture of a Navy Band
  Draw a picture of dogs and cats
Draw a picture of baseball bats.
  Draw, draw to the next day,
Draw to where our dreams lay.
Susan Kuchli

Flowers No One Wanted

Once in their prime with sunny mettle,
Downcast daisies droop and sigh.
Rejected roses loose their petals;
Lonely mums watch passersby.

Crushed carnations cry: What's this?
We were so fragrant and so bright.
We dreamt of cheer, of lovers' kiss,
Of bidding a sweet prince goodnight.

The other flowers with them mourn:
We fancied satin, lace, and rice,
The holidays, the newly-born,
But now we perish at half-price!

A flower's beauty fades so fast,
Its glory barely lasts a day.
Its opportunity is past
If it's not chosen right away.

I'm truly glad I'm not a flower,
Although, like them, I wait and wait.
But I have hope that In God's hour
I will at long last have a mate.
Susan L. Fasig

Dreams

  Doesn't matter who you are
Dreams are something great by far
They take you places good or bad
The people you meet will make you glad
  Rainbows, dragons, castles too
Even chickens who start to moo
Things you always see and hear
Will always be very near
  As soon as you have closed your eyes
Dreams will take you away for the night
No matter what you do or say
Dreams will always take you away.
Kelly Tracy

Backsliding Christian

I'm just a backsliding christian
  Drifting around here and there
I know the right way to follow
  But can't seem to find my way back
I'm just a backsliding christian
  Wondering where I've gone wrong
I know I've missed many a blessings
  While taking this side road of life
Watch over me dear lord
  Keep me in your care
I know I'll soon be returning
  I'm just on this side road for now
Phyllis Baillargeon

To Jesus

I love you I praise you
  Each night and each day
I thank you Dear Jesus
  That you hear me pray.
I know you're beside me
  Wherever I go
And you will protect me
  From fear and from foe.
I thank you dear Jesus
  For all you have done
You are our Savior
  And You love everyone.
Neva Breese

Sandstorm

The sand is so fine,
Drifting through the air.
Gossamer sand seeps
Through every crack/lair.

While the sandstorm rages,
Howling through the land.
Even the Camel
Bow, to stingings/sand.

Dunes shift, wither, rise,
Water holes covered.
Date trees drop their fruit,
Blasted by air/matter.

Man seeks his refuge,
What shelter he takes?
Conscious now of death,
To keep his breath/escape?

The screeching wind dies,
Suspended sand falls.
Creatures search for drink,
Man, travels/stalls?

Lloyd V. Quinn Sr.

"King Hummingbird"

Hummingbird, hummingbird
Drink if you will
From the fountain of life,
Take your kings fill!

Nectar to make your wings
Shiny and strong
Sweetest of flowers
To gladden your song.

Your emerald wings
Are like intricate fans
You wear your ruby-red ring
Like a king of the land.

Your lady is beautiful
In your heart she's your queen-
With princes and princesses
You are truly a King!

Hummingbird, hummingbird
Drink if you will
From the fountain of life
Take your kings fill!

Patricia Wright Tucker

Untitled

Your voice so soft and gentle
each moment so sentimental
your eyes so blue
You're so true
only you and me
Always together, that's how it should be
every moment without you
I never know what to do
You mean so much to me
My love for you is more than the
waves in the sea
There are something I am unable to do
But, for sure, I can always love you.

Toni Pablo

"Creek Indian Dream"

There were feather's of the
eagle flowing with the wind,
strong and proud;

There were feather's of the
owl sitting patiently and wise;

There were feather's of the
dove, gentle, yet swift
on the summer breeze;

There are feather's of the
"Creek" that someday again
will be seen...

Thomas J. Easley

I Love Spring

I love spring
early morning light
earth primping
rainbow colors

First robins
symphonies of nesting birds
furtive peeking of woodland blossoms
budding on brown twigs

Temperatures at seventy
planting time
dandelion gold
blankets of fern, clover

Fields of flowers
country drives
walks on forest trails
miracles of resurrection

I only wish
this time of magic
would sooner come
and later go.

Norman L. Nielsen

Earth

Bred of fire and born in strife
Earth carries on, sustaining life
Enfolding me, nurturing you
Holding its course for all we do
Scorned and torn by callous man
Guided by no mortal's plan
We falter, those who seek the way
Confounded, all, by each new day
What way to go, which way is right
Our days done, we set our plight
No purpose served, no human goal
But a tarnished image paid as toll
Our selves unbound by want or need
Loosed from right by errant seed
Who will form our wayward race
To abide in Earth's lasting grace.

Maurice C. Marshall

Winter

Over the mountains that I love
Falls the hush of ice and snow,
Brooks that once would shout with joy
Now whisper as they flow.
Trees gossiping in windstorms
Now murmur soft and low,
While through the sleepy silent void
Night tiptoes to and fro.

Ruth Van Heusen

Aggravated

The days we spent in total ecstasy
Ecstasy that infatuated me
Infatuated me all into you
Into you, I became yours
Became yours in the days and nights
Nights shared in loyal sleep
Loyal sleep that led to happiness
Happiness brought just by your touch
Your touch that entangled me
Entangled me into an odyssey
An odyssey never finished
Never finished because of death
Death that decayed our dreams
Dreams that we would be together
Together in a world of our own
A world of our own that will never be
Never be because of death
Death that fell upon your sleep
Your sleep that filled with peace
With peace together we still exist.

Mary Ann Herrington

Banjo Picker

He says he's too old for change
edged on a park bench
with his antique five string.
Black fingers caress his banjo
until he hears a crowd gather.
A smile lights up his face.

Roman plays fast tunes-listens
to children of different colors
dance together in a frenzy.

The tempo always changes.
With repetitious strumming
Roman sings forgotten spirituals,
those from another era.
His tired old feet try
to keep on beating time.

The crowd disperses.
Roman does his daily shuffle
with a seeing-eye dog leading him
home to their little shack
on the edge of town.

Willard Lee Skelton

"Just A Touch"

Just a touch of your hand
Electrify my soul
Light up my eyes
And set my soul on fire
I know that you're sincere
Because you always
Enhance my very desire

Just a touch of your hand
Moves me to think
Motivates me to consecrate
To find words that penetrate
All because of a touch
Never, ever evaporate

Now that I can still feel
That your touch is real
I can always take time
To hold your hand
And never walk away again

William E. Smith

Why?

Why does love have to be?
Especially when it happens to me.
I wrote this poem because it did,
And all the feelings I had I hid.

You hurt me so bad,
You got me so mad.
I loved you and you didn't know,
You just kept saying no, no, no.

But I held my head high,
And tried hard not to cry.
But the tears kept on coming,
I hid my anger and just kept on humming.

How could you love one day,
And then betray?
I loved you and you said you loved me,
How you could hurt me so bad I'll never
clearly see.

Just because I have feelings I hide,
The ones I show are always tossed aside.
Once again I'll ask a question to you from me,
Why does love have to be?

Shannon Turley

Dying Heart

Black heart, burned beyond repair
Estranged heart, spurned without care
Lying helpless dying, almost dead
Hanging on by a solitary thread
Sorrow and pain linger on,
Joy and happiness are sooner gone
Inching closer to utter madness
All alone in absolute sadness
Loneliness brings greater pain still
Emptiness comes, the heart to fill
Ending, the pain is ending,
Slowly now the heart is mending
Approaching now on death's foyer
We see Love, the final destroyer.

Rosetta Berkenstock

Untitled

Dark shadows the night.
Evening, in black velvet,
dances with the moon.

Sue Rosenbaum

Feelings

I'm here thinking of you
Ever since the end
It has never been the same
All it has been is pain
My sunshine turned into rain
It feels as though something is missing
It's not just the kissing
All I've been doing is wishing
That we were together again
You really didn't have it in looks
I just thought you had what it took
We were one, we were pretty hooked
But now you're gone
And I must continue on
I knew our love was true
cause I met someone new
But I realized all I wanted was you.

Melissa Griffin

Untitled

Life's journey ends fast,
Everyone knew I wouldn't last.
Never wanted to live this life,
'Cause it seemed like such a strife.
It was one journey I couldn't handle,
Softly it flickered like a candle.
One gust was all it took,
No one really looked ...inside.
They never saw her pain,
Yet the thunder knew about the rain.
They never realized she was lost,
Now everyone's paying the cost.
She did something that wasn't right,
That night when she took her life.

Lisa Marie James

"Anger"

When I am angry,
Everything is nothing,
And nothing is everything.

Waves of anger splash over me,
And there is nothing I can do
To stop them from knocking me down.

Anger is inside of me
And all around me,
Like an undying fire
Which I cannot extinguish.

Anger makes me want to cry,
And I often do so.

Everyone feels my anger
As I pass it on to them.
They do not want my anger,
But it is impossible to hide.

Susan Firely

My Mother's Repertoire Of Proverbs

Began with
   "Everything that happens
   Happens for the best."
I believed her.

Even after
Black prayer vigils in
Nurseries and geriatrics
I believed her.

I tell my daughter
crumpled
Beneath marriage ruins
   "Everything happens for the best"
and she believes me, she says.

The lie-
Hungry parasite -
Consumes another generation
With hope.

Madeline Salustri

Awakening

Silk mist of white cream
flow freely without a care,
the wind whispers gently
as if it talks to the trees,
the day has just awakened!

Patti Reimann

Golden Anniversary

You have been
   exceedingly blessed
With fifty years
   of togetherness
Time is a fleeting elusive thing
   It can fly as if it had wings
Or it can drag like a knotted thread
   Each passing moment filled with dread
It seems only yesterday
   that the children were small
And then they were grown
   in no time at all
You've had some hard times
   down through the years
You've shared a lot of laughter
   and shed a few tears
You've learned the meaning
   of "to have and to hold"
And sharing was the key
   that lead to the gold.

Mary F. Kraemer

Mother Earth

Virginity,
Existence,
Tranquility.
Her fertile soil bore plants,
Her fertile soil bore animals,
   Her fertile soil bore us,
      Mother earth.

Passion,
Euphoria,
Pleasure.
You traipse upon her back,
You sprawl upon her breast,
You feast upon her bounty.
Mother earth.

All this splendor,
All this warmth,
All this desire,
Her offspring must defend her.

Mollie Anne McRae

Blanket Of Stars

Distant from the earth
Extending far in the sky
Was a glimmer of life
Of all days now gone by
And as I gazed upward
Absorbed into the night
A blanket of stars
Enwrapped all then in sight
The stars were swelled
With glory and fame
But revealing their secrets
Was no man's to claim
And the angels with chariots
Of fine metals and gold
Soared through the sky
Singing stories of old
Then the stars looked upon me
Stretching deep to my soul
And their splendor was mine now
Forever to hold

Kathy L. Jones

Afghan Intimacy

Baby Beth cooed playfully,
  Eyes drinking in a granny square
    Centered in her coverlet.

An "I do" moment from the start.

What glee to see motifs join hands,
  Like posted sentries standing watch.

The twosome cuddled as they grew.

Entwined, both catapulted into life,
From cradle, crib, and couch
To waterbed, to floor, to chair.
Pizza, teardrops, puppy poop,
Cat hair, soup, and sticky glue
Shaped a patterned love affair.

Thus, life's seasons ran their course.

The afghan curled around Beth's frame,
  Fragile now and wracked with pain.
    Afghan, too, was worn and thin,

Not so the love 'tween the bridal pair.

A final "coo" and a breathed out prayer,
Beth's farewell to the granny squares.
   Mildred Shaver

Fire Child

  Son of immortals, black as night.
Eyes which shine blue in light,
  Red as coals your anger burns;
Let not the demons go unheard.

Immortals known by life if not by death,
  Sing a song unto we the bereft.
Leave the world torn with strife,
  fire child hence your life.

  Fire child watch your wares.
Precocious children with no cares,
  Live by day, fear by night;
All know the immortals son,
  The fire child plight.
   Kelly Lutkiewicz

Faith

Faith is light, faith is love
Faith is Gods gift from above
Sometimes we feel fright
As though were trapped inside a glove
The human race has many faces
as we travel to different places
So open your heart, and be smart
To the light, love, and the
Faith from above
   Lisa Martin

The Bird

Sometimes I will sleep on a cloud.
  Fall into a tree.
I glide across the sky.
Then dive into the sea.
I clean my dirty ivory feathers.
Sometimes my beak.
Then I start to fly home.
And see you there waiting for me.
   R. B. Mills

A Love To Last Forever

Summer is but a season,
Fall is just a time,
To be with the ones you love,
So simple and divine.

Random are the words
For which you have spoken,
Remember the promise I make you now
Never shall be broken.

Random are the gestures
For which you've won my heart,
Yet for all the days to come
May we never be apart.

Forget not day by day,
That I'm only but a step away.
Fear not the falling of a tear,
But feel joy each new day of the year.
   Sherry Bocook

Love Game

Your hand in my hand
Feeling like snowflake
After laziness centuries
On the old sofa
With white flower smell
And naked bodies
Tender night whisper
Flooded the window outline
Where I wrote
In immaculate spirit
Your name "LOVE".

  Nicole Pirvanescu

Sparrow

Count to a hundred in the rain,
fifty more, eyes open. Trees
for cover, hide the pain. Sunlight
holds the flame. Another fifty,
it feels the same. All hands, no
hands, feel the shame. Sparrow
sitting in a tree, spied the truth;
another thirty-three. Tell the world.
If only he could - of the dirty deed.
Mothers, fathers, strangers - all the
same, no difference remains? Catholics
Protestants, all religions, cities,
States and government, should go the
Blame! Oh, sparrow of little might
what a harrowing fright. Child used,
child abused, child taken in the dead
of night. Guilty they should be!
- And - to the gallows be led - indeed
for the taking of our young so innocent
and - Free!

  Randy Marshall

Chrysalis

Silver threads spinning;
  Forming a silver womb.
    Encased a caterpillar;
    Awaiting a new birth.
And as if in a dream,
  A butterfly emerges...
    Beautiful, lifting its
    wings to freedom!
  Patricia A. Conklin

In Days That Has Passed

In days that has passed,
Finds a love no longer to last,
What was so beautiful indeed,
Should have been you and me,
In my heart the memory remains,
No hope for the love to regain,
I feel hurt and some what sad,
And now I must get over being mad,
To have loved and lot once more,
To have nothing to settle and even score,
To try and love someone New;
Isn't going to be easy to do,
I will try and forget the pain,
In hopes I don't go insane!
  Regina D. Gooch

Unlost Love

Thunder in the sky,
Fires in the night.
Where have all my children gone,
This cold and stormy night?

Blowing through the mountains,
Howling in the trees,
Are those my children crying,
Or just the power of the breeze?

Kiss me gently, softly,
Lest I fall apart with want
For my children to be safe,
Not for the night to haunt.

Hold me sweetly to your chest,
And tell me they are well.
They have struck out on their own,
To either heaven or to hell.

Whichever you may choose,
Wherever you may go,
I shall always love you, my children,
This, I hope you know.
  Virginia Lewis

By His Hands

Once I was nothing,
Floating through the day,
Then I heard Him speak
And I became the clay.
Still, I was void and formless,
A lump within His hands,
Then He began to mold me
And I became a man.
He stretched me and cut me,
Sometimes He made me hurt;
For I am just a vessel
Carved entirely of dirt.
Fired and refined
To fulfill His perfect plan,
I'm proud to be a vessel
Created by His hands.
  Mary Rogers

Untitled

One tiny snow flake
  followed by another...
  and still another,
  'Till the earth is covered
  With a soft white quilt,
  Winters first snow fall.
  B. Scott Anderson

Green Velvet Hills

See the hills of greenest velvet
  Flow with graceful harmony,
Encircled by the mottled woodland
  Far as ever eye could see.

Charming rustic isolation,
  Brilliant colors by degree,
Sequestered in the midst of beauty,
  Woven into tapestry.

Cottage perched amid such glory,
  Cloistered on a cliff sublime,
Transforming homespun into vista,
  Contemplation into time.

Gurgling stream, trickling downward,
  Over yonder grassy knoll;
Percolating gently onward,
  Never drifting from control.

True quiescence calms the mind
  And brings the weary soul repose;
Restful beauty all surrounding
  Doth a lullaby compose.
    Pam Iseley

A Prayer Of Thanks

We thank Thee Lord for the beautiful
  flowers
That bring so much pleasure for
  many hours.
We thank Thee for the fields of
  grain,
And that you refresh them, after
  the sunshine, with rain.
We thank Thee for the sky so blue,
But most of all, we give thanks
  for you.
We give thanks for the harvest that
  we see,
But help us, dear Lord, to win
  a harvest of souls for Thee.
    Mildred Weihe Miller

Musings

Scribbling rapidly with inspired blurbs,
Flowery adjectives, very few verbs.
Language archaic, all wording trite
Writing until the dawn's early light.
Such sad and melancholy drivel,
So very touching, caused a snivel.
All rules broken, by a "Muse" smitten,
"Pegasus" thinks best left unwritten.

Hope springs eternal, so try again,
Please identify Cinquain, Quatrain.
Lilting, winsome, happy as a song,
Waterfalls of words rush out headlong.
Unafraid, poets are born, not made.
No need for study to make the grade.
All rules broken, by a "Muse" smitten.
"Pegasus" thinks best left unwritten.
    Rose E. Coulter

"Simple Tests"

I went to the hospital
For a few "simple tests".
Then I'm told "soft food only"
And "only bed rest".
But I'm not sick.
I feel just fine.
I'm perfectly capable.
I've made up my mind.
Soft diet? No problem.
Make it low fat,
But bed rest for me?
To hell with that!
To keep me in bed
You'll need a ball bat.
Because the tests were all normal.
Imagine that!
    Ronda Simons

Apologies

Could you apologize
for breaking my heart?
I don't think that you could
you couldn't play the part.

The world is a stage
and we are the actors
could you play your age,
or are you too immature?

What you did to me
hurt terribly so,
but I don't care where you are
I don't care where you go

I accept apologies
from people who mean them
I accept them with ease
but what about you?
    Sarah Surber

Holding The Line

Should I say I'm sorry,
  For causing hurt and pain?

For stares and gossiped questions,
  Would any apology ever do?

In trying to "cross the line,"
  You've fought my every gain.

For each thrust of my blade,
  You parried and stymied every move.

Like Icarus, with waxen wings,
  Who flew too near the sun.

My heart lies crushed and broken,
  Upon the rocks of love.

Now defeated and on my knees,
  With head bowed, arms outstretched.

I only ask for a swift end,
  Strike your blow straight and true.

But, never will I say I'm sorry,
  For falling in love with you.
    Rollin G. Golden

The Master

  Praise the master up above,
    For his sacrificial love.

Not once, but twice, he died for me,
  Bearing my sins on calvary.

Going to hell and back again, he cried,
  "My God, why hast thou forsaken me?"

  "NO, NO, NO", I cried, "not me."
  I crucified Him on the tree."

  "Thank you Master of my life,
  For accepting unyielding strife."

  "Oh Master, how can I repay
  What You did for me that day?"

    "You set me free
  Thank you Master, Eternally!"
    Karen Nikkel

Help Me To See The Way

Help me to see the way
For I have lost all
Friends was once there
Now there is none

When you stay by yourself day after day
Spring, summer, winter, and fall
Loneliness is hard to bare
Happiness is all over and done

Help me to see the way
To find the right path
Is there no one who cares
What are friends really suppose to be.

All I'm trying to say
Is hold no wrath
Ignore all strange stares
Let your soul be free

For you see there's no help on the way
once everything is lost friends there's none to be
All's forgot like a dying tree
that goes for all including you and me.
    Marion K. Estep

Port Matilda

For the first time I'm feeling you
for the first time I'm seeing you
in your immensity I flight
in your fields I dream.

You are sparkling fire
but you don't burn my hands
You are fresh and new blood
in my hands cracking.

Sun that goes to the earth
and melts with the prairie
broken rainbow
that coats the mountains

After your illusion I ran
and the time stopped
of your smell I drank
one in a million smell.

Sky and earth melt
a dream lived this day
colors of my life and soul
that yesterday only dreams were.
    Wanda Molinary

Untitled

Take this world from me and use it
for yourself.
Do not put it where you can view it from
some forgotten shelf.
Hold it warmly and gently right from
the start.
This world I offer you is a piece of
my heart.
Keep it near you, by your side each
day
And it will shine with hope to help
you on your way.
Softly it will whisper all your dreams
to come true.
Take this world, this heart of mine, I'm
offering it to you.

Kristin L. Burchell

"One Time"

For only a moment, we touched
forever. A feeling never yet
conquered. I could feel your
body, warm, beside me.
A night never to forget.
While it was still young,
I kissed your heart shaped
lips and thought.

An unresisting image
only mine for a short
interval on times
mind. A cry short for
only one soul. A single
stand of a life time
of memories. One,
only one...

Krystal Sampson

Sot

Foolish,
forever waiting,
watching the stars
moving across empty fields.
Naked,
and the wind bites,
guilt stained hands
close around liquid nourishment.
Tremble
and straining
for abandoned fancy,
laying down in the dirt.
Feed
of sweet coffee
and bitter bread,
food for the presence of god,
Hunting
the bugs
that crawl
as pilgrims in foreign soil.

Victoria L. Smith

Dracula

From the death comes the life.
From the life comes the death.
The living can die,
live off the dead,
live as the dead,
but will never- "Rest in Peace!"

Sarah L. Tikalsky

The Unforgotten Love

I've tried and tried to
forget you but somehow you
find your way back into my
life

I tell myself that I can
give you another chance that
It won't happen again
But still you put others
before me even though I try
to give you all my love and
still you push me away

We used to be so close
so close you could see the
love we felt for each other
I wish and I hope
that somehow someway
you will find the unforgotten
love I hold unforgotten
waiting here for you.

Katie Troutman

Soaring Higher

I wish I could be free;
Free as a bird
Soaring higher and higher,
As high as my wings will carry me.

Free of all the cruelty down below;
Free of all my worries;
Never having to look back;
Never wondering what others know.

Life as it is today
Is so harsh and cruel;
There really is no compare;
Sometimes I wish it would all go away.

People carry their worries today,
Constantly wondering;
I'd rather be a bird
Than me any day.

Karen LeClair

Someday

Someday I'll be free;
Free from the chains
That hold me down.
Someday my soul will be free.

Someday I'll be able to love;
To love with my heart,
That is imprisoned
By my soul that is chained.

Someday my beauty will be seen;
Seen by those who can love,
Those who have souls,
And those who look on the inside.

Someday is coming soon;
For I can feel the chains breaking,
The soul rising,
And the beauty shining through.

True beauty comes from within.

Sarah Johnson

FREE

Free from the pain;
Free from the hurt;
Free from the people
Who treat me like dirt.

Free from the anger;
Free from the tears;
Free from the nightmares
That gave me new fears.

Free from the torturing;
Free from the shouts;
Free from the things
That I always had doubts.

Free from the pressure;
Free from the stress;
Free from the life
That makes me depress.

Free from the world;
Free from the violence;
Gone to a place
Where there's only silence.

Yia Vang

"It's Not What You Read In A Card."

Life lost of a young child,
Freedom of her soul.
God forgiven her for her sins,
Her parents wouldn't let go.

All alone she felt so sad,
She did nothing but cry.
People wondered why she felt so bad,
But she just wanted to die.

Life is not what you want it to be
The only way it will get there is
if you try hard.
Life is what you make it to be,
Not what you read in a card!

Vashada Singh

Friends

Friends last a lifetime.
Friends never part
They stick together
and love from the heart.

Friends will stand beside you
when others walk away.
A true friend will be there tomorrow
and every other day.

Shawn Minich

I Was Once

I was once a cloud,
floating in the cool
winter air.

I was once a star,
shining brightly in
the midnight sky.

I was once a tree,
swaying gently in
the warm summer breeze.

How I did it,
I'll never know!

Katie Champion

Battle Scarred and War Weary

When I awoke the world was mine
From blinding sun to scented pine

And fumbling through a day of woe
With head held high my spirits low

As numb routine wore slowly on
I wandered straight my genius gone
No mark was made, no lasting print
No master stroke, no victory sprint
A wasted thought a day flew by
Without a joy or blissful cry

Would God forgive my tired heart
And give my soul a fresher start

Another chance the beast to meet
And trample it with tired feet

Rick D. Thomas

Mary

Have the hills worn or do they fade
from my many years of watching them?
Years have made my daisy grow,
yet years have taken petals away.

Frail and grooved I've become,
an old woman.
Why is it yesterday my garden bloomed
with so many bright vegetables, flowers,
even a few weeds?

Today my daisy has some petals
missing, and my garden's soil
has dried.

I close my eyes, and the full hills
protect me.
I feel hunger, and the garden feeds me.
I hold my daisy to the heavens and I'm filled.

As I look at this daisy,
another petal falls.
I wouldn't trade it
for a garden of roses.

Sarah Graves

The Awakening

And the voices came to me,
From strangers in a strange land.
Like a newborn child,
I was hanging only by a strand.

Then the moment was gone,
But my thoughts did not stray.
Questing for answers,
For my next journey to stay.

I have always known the way,
The only barrier was my mind.
But it remains beyond my grasp,
As I choose to stay blind.

Kelli A. Henman

He Is Alone

Here he sits in silence
he never says a word,
Day after day
night after night
he cries.
He lived for her,
and her only
Now she is gone,
He is Alone.

Kristen McAllister

The Executor

A nightmare from hell
from the mirror he came,
are you having a dream
or are you going insane.

Where did he come from
what message he brings?
Are you still sleeping?
To understand what he means.

He walks right beside you
stands next to your bed,
turns to look at you
but nothing was said.

Dressed all in black
his eyes only seen,
an executor of man
why come visit me?

The message made clear
his finger touches my head,
only by murder
will someone be dead!

Toni Peters

The One Big World

The world is one big place.
  Full of the human race.
Standing tall to one another.
  Holding on to each other
As we stand one by one our
  Faces do not blend as one
because we're all different you will see.
  In the one big world
we are strong tall
  and "free"

Sherrie Ann Parker

A Poem For My Parents

You are my parents,
future, present and past,
I have no doubts that,
Our love will last,
When ever I was hurt,
confused or sad,
You made me smile,
and no longer feel sad,
When my other relatives,
put me down and made me blue,
I always knew I could,
count on your love,
When I need you,
you were always their,
You didn't say anything;
I knew you cared
I met you late in the fall.
Up until now it's been a ball,
It was you who mended my heart,
It was you who helped my from the start.

Margery Hill

I Loved My Friend

I loved my friend.
He went away from me.
There's nothing more to say.

The poem ends,
Soft as it began -
I loved my friend.

Melissa Jordan

The Robe

Your black tear-drop eyes
gather in my folds
forge new channels from
implacable rock
remove the stone at my entrance
releasing a turbulent flow

We lie together motionless
then disappear
leaving only the garment
folded neatly upon the altar

Kathleen Bevacqua

Tranquility

The rain falls
Gently, softly;
Washing the world clean,
Feeding the thirsty earth;
Flowers shiver with delight
And lift their lovely heads
In gratitude.
The sound of the rain
Brings peace.
And restful time for thought;
A time for laying out memories,
Tasting the good,
Discarding the bad;
Living again the loving times…
The flowers and I are
Grateful.

Ollis L. Beach

A Special Gift

I was given a special gift and that
gift is my grandmother's love. She is
gentle and kind, a pillar of strength
and truly a gift from above.

I listen to stories of life as it
was a long long time ago. A life so
different in many ways from the life
that we now know.

She weathered the storms that came
her way, made a home for her family.
The way that she lives her life is an
inspiration to me.

I know what made my grandmother the
woman she is today. She walks through
life hand in hand with the Lord, for he
shows her the way.

I was given a special gift which I
can never repay; but it's comforting
that my grandmother's love is with me
day after day.

Theresa Lippert

A Little Friend

I saw a cricket in the grass,
  He stepped aside to let me pass,
Now wasn't that a pleasing sight-
  To see a cricket so polite.

He was as small as small can be,
  He said, "How do you do?" to me,
Now wasn't that a pleasing sight,
  To see a cricket so polite.

Vicki Hoffer

"We"

We will never see what orchids
  give to the breeze.
We will never see what the sun
  does with the dew.
We will never hear the secrets
  flowers whisper to each other;
Or watch while rainbows paint
  each gorgeous hue.

We will never see each crystal drop
  of Heaven
That fills our hearts and souls
  from above.
We will never reach the ending
  of Forever.
Or lose the beauty of Eternal love.

Lucille Goudy

Hummingbird

Graceful strokes,
Gliding through the air.
Summoning all joyful ones,
Driving off despair.

Oh, little, joyful hummingbird,
Beating, fast, your wings.
Flying from place to place,
Hummingbird, love and joy you bring.

Raina J. Leon

'For Kathrina'

The beauty of your hair
Glistening in the light.
And despite the world around us
Your eyes are burning bright.
So put your arms around me
And let me feel the breeze.
Looking in your big, brown eyes
Releases the poem in me.

Nathan James Hahs

Friendship

You and a friend
Go sailing on a ship
The friendship ship

Who is this friend, who?
Does he go sailing with you?
Does the ship have a bad trip?
Does your bond ever rip?
When you're sailing the ship
The friendship ship
Who repairs the ship?
The friendship ship
Your friend or you?

Katharine M. W. Francis

Untitled

She's gone and he cries,
he cries because he can't
believe this world can and
will go on without her.
  Yet I don't feel sad
to me it's just the same as
if she were still here.
  I cried when my bird died,
but now that human flesh
is dead I feel no sadness.

Tricia Scribner

I Wish He Knew

A two story house,
Green.
A small dog,
From the next door neighbors,
Running up to you,
Licking your hands.
I look up,
I imagine my grandma
In a rocking chair,
With my aunt,
Arguing about something.
I go to the back of the house.
I see the rose bushes.
The bird bath is still there.
I can still see my
uncle pulling the weeds,
Watering the rose bushes,
and putting water in the bird bath.
I wish he knew how much I miss him.
I wish he knew.

Soheila Lopopolo

Guide Them Lord (A Mother's Prayer)

Teach them please, all Thy ways,
Guide them Lord, throughout their days,
Open their eyes, and let them see,
Bring them closer, Lord to Thee,
Teach them both wrong from right,
To not rely on their insight,
Lord, Thy ways are never wrong,
Use my children, make them strong,
Guide them Lord, from worldly sin,
That they may know, sweet peace within,
Guide them Lord, from evil things,
That they may know the joy it brings,
Guide them Lord, the way you must,
In you sweet Jesus, I place my trust.

Lila Scott

Emotions

Sadness is a child's tear,
Happiness is taking away a fear.
Sorrow is for another one
Playfulness is having fun.

Anger will push you around
Pain will bring you down.
Hope is a way out,
Depression is all played out.

Emotions are what you feel
Some you show,
Some you conceal.
They're what you'll always feel.

Katie Stonebarger

Thoroughly Modern Mom

M - is for the miracle of life she
  has provided.
O - is for the order she manages
  to bring out of chaos.
T - is for the tender loving care
  she gives us.
H - is for the home that she keeps
  up for all of us.
E - is for the enjoyment she gives
  to one and all.
R - is for the running around that
  she must do each day.

Richard H. Francis, Jr.

November 26th

Dear world's grandchildren,
Happy birthday to you
Everyday-
an affectionate heart remembers you,
Let Thanksgiving-day kiss you
Lord Jesus- bless you.
Happy....

With wills I meet you
With words I greet you,
By waves I wake you
Without worth I take you.
Happy...

Nobody will hide you
November 26th: Thanksgiving-day-
will shine you,
Nature will find you
Nerve will guide you.
Happy...

P. B. Patel-Das

"Our Nation"

  All the change in the world
has me so confused
  War, conspiracies, Aids; Children
being abused
  People are dying, and loved
ones are mourning
  The things taken for granted will
soon be gone without warning
  Cancer, rape, the mafia,
prostitution
  What good can come out
of my contribution?
  While the homeless, in their
cardboard boxes, suffer from starvation
  I sit here in my warm
house, and question our nation

Nadine Maitilasso

Happy Birthday Honey

Now that it's your birthday
Have fun galore.
Remember honey
That's what birthdays are for.

Birthdays come and birthdays go
But in between...
If a day should arrive
When you're feeling sad,
Think of the happy days
When your heart felt glad.

Think of the good times,
Fun and laughter
Your days will be filled
With cheer thereafter.

Honey, you are someone special,
On this happy day.
Someone to love, someone to care.
Knowing you will, always be there.

Mary Wolf

Jesus Is Joy

Jesus is my joy in living
He fills my every hour,
Protects me where there may be stripe
Holds me within his power.

Jesus is my strength and hope
Whenever I'm in need,
He's there to help me, as I hope
He's always there to lead.

My happiness is Jesus too
Without him life is blanks
I cling to him the whole day through
And for his help give thanks.

I thank him for the gift he gave
And thank him too for giving,
For he gave first, my life to save
And he's my joy in living.

He's my protection and my story
He's teachings I employ,
He gave us love to give away -
 and made our lives a joy

Louisa Whelan

Cowboy In The Dark

I met a cowboy in the dark
He roped my love
And raped my heart.
As he turned to ride away
Said I'll break your heart someday.

The years passed
My hair turned gray
Once again he passed my way;
His eyes were cloudy
His ole hat bent
He told me how his memories went.

I met a cowgirl in the dark
She roped my love
And raped my heart
As I turned to ride away
She said I'll break your heart some day.

We gazed in each other's eyes
Baffled by life's ole lies
Not caring that the years had passed
But glad to be roped and tied at last.

Yvonne Rogers P. Hennig

A Father's Care

He was always there when I needed him.
He managed to make me smile.
He was everything I needed in a Father.
I just knew him a little while.

When times were tough, he was there.
Giving a consoling hand of love.
He was there for me and took my side.
He gave of a Fathers' love.

He is not around me now.
I see him here and there.
I remember his compassion and love.
And most of all "a Fathers' care."

Linda Schlup

Dream Prince

In my dreams he is my prince
He takes me far away
Into a forest of enchantment
To where the dreams remain

The day arrives and I awaken
My prince no longer here,
But he returns to me each evening
To whisper in my ear

He coaxes me to fall asleep
Then on his horse we ride
Once again into the forest
Through the darkness of the night

Today I 'wakened from my dreaming
What did my eyes behold
My dream prince standing in the daylight
With a story to unfold?

He told me to believe my dreams
Though they seem far away
For once he too was just my dream
Now with me here to stay!

Madeline Arlotta Cupo

"In God We Trust"

I love a man, a handsome marine
 He walks a straight and narrow path
 For freedom, the common dream

While in my arms a baby clinging
 When faced with war a monstrous being

My knight whose armor has lost its shine
 And changed to camouflage
 Beneath the vines

Until he meets with devil's delight
 To kill unsuspectingly
 For human right

How can it be thou 'Shalt not kill'
 When my man is hunting
 And waiting still

To be a hero to all of us
 The country who claims
 "In God We Trust"

Rachel A. Johnson

The Cause

Seeing the cause
he wants to be
He pursues the life
shamelessly
In following the steps
the path covers most
leaving the guest
to be his own host
Alone at the table
he wishes he was able
to accomplish what he desired most

Paul F. Herrmann

Stranger In The Mountains

The stranger was tall and strong,
 He was dressed in rich garments,
 He can forward, held out his hands,
 And spoke I love you very much,
 I had to meet you, it was pleasure,
 The stranger had come up the valley,
 The valley was high in the mountains,
 He kissed me and let go,
 I know he was hungry and weary,
 It was dull and cold like stones,
 He said at last, I came to see you,
 I came a long way my love,
 He ran back down the hill,
 As he want he gathering driftwood,
 I called to him and said help me,
 With you blessed the Lord with me,
 He said, Yes to me and he thanked me,
 The stranger kissed my hand,
He said good-bye, we will meet in the sky,
 The stranger was gone like the wind.

Laura K. Brooks

Until

Feel the tickle on your back, Now sleep
Hear the patter
Your little feet

If you ever see my heart to break
Fear not my child
'Till then I'll wait

Should you ever fall from grace
Or miss the feel
Our warm embrace

Think of this
If not the fun
Until our hearts will beat as one.

Ruben S. Zak

Whispers

I look down upon the world below me
hear whispers of the past
I wish I were alive again
I wish I'd made it last
I hear someone call out to me
through the darkness
through the past
they call my name
it's not the same
Suddenly
I feel the life
it's creeping through my bones
I awaken to the light again
Where was I? No one knows
but someone calling out my name
brought me back to life
I hear it whisper now and then
Whisper in the air
and now I know it was a friend
Who knew enough to care.

Michelle Rothberg

To Have Trust In Love

Locked in each other's eyes
Hearts pounding
Love pouring out of every part of me.
To grasp her in my arms
Bodies pressed together
Love raging inside my soul.
One kiss...
Followed by another
Our minds and bodies
Exploding with passion and harmony.
Our lips engaged.
Speaking with my actions
Rather than my words.
To have trust in love

Scott Perlman

Our Mother

Our mother who helps in the paradise of
heaven the pride of the father and the
heart of Nathurlon sacred be your name
The father's kingdom come thy will be
done all throughout the universe give us
this day our blessings of love nd help
us from sin as we forgive our debtors and
lead us into supplication by your visit
divine mother bear witness for us for the
father is the kingdom and the power and
the glory forever and ever in Jesus name
Amen

Nathurlon Jones Jr.

Hold My Hand

Creator of the universe.
Heavenly Father of mine,
Reach down from above,
Touch my weary body,
Fill my spirit with your love.

Creator of the universe.
Maker of mankind,
Reach down, place your hand in mine.

Lead me, Guide Me,
Teach me.
Show me your plan, help me to understand.

Creator of the universe,
Hold my hand.

Linda K. Myers

Let Freedom Ring

We caught the torch you threw,
Held it high in World War Two.
Then it was tossed to younger hands
Who carried it to foreign lands.

You lie in Flanders fields around,
They fell on other alien ground:
And younger still were hands that caught
The torch for which we all had fought.

There never will be such a peace
That Freedom's torch would ever cease.
For men are men and greed survives,
Despite the sacrifice of lives.

Phoebe C. Redman

Our Friend And Guide,

The Lord is our friend and guide,
He'll always be by your side.
He lead us through path of
Unforbidden Realm,
No, matter how far and wide.

He shows us the light, "with"
Nothing in sight.
But, it's warm and pleasant,
And comfortable besides.

Now, you know this is true,

Without a doubt.

If only, you would pursue him,
He'll straighten your life out.

Whether you're a man or woman,
The truth of the fact,
He'll help you out.
For, our goals are the same,
For you and for me.
That's to reach our Heavenly Father,

And live for an eternity.

Kay Neal

A Walk Through The Exterior

She braided daisies in
Her auburn hair and
Walked catatonically through
Narrow, dirty brick streets.

In dimly lit neighborhoods
She stood, white dress and
Soul soiled by factory smoke
Swirling through the sky.

Of course all stopped and
Stared and wondered and
Whispered at her, standing
In their street.

She stopped and stared back
And turned in to her brickstone;
And of course all returned
To their routine, in their street.

Leann Griffin

Broken Spirit

What, becomes of a man, if you take
his hopes, his dreams, his aspirations,
and his love?

You cast them into a mighty rushing
wind.
Knowing this, he hath not wings to
pursue them!

You ultimately destroy, this man that
held in his very soul,
The power to love you forever...

Shelby W. Harris

Him

His skin as soft as a baby's face.
His smile as bright as gold.
His eyes as green as the sea.
His blond wavy hair as shiny as the sun
His voice as tender as his kiss.

Sandra DaSilva

Two-Pounds-Four

Oh, my gosh,
His name is Josh,
He scared his mother badly,
She wept and cried, yet tried to hide,
Her fears so he would rally...

At two pounds four,
The doctors saw,
Josh could hold his own,
He bravely fought, without a thought,
So mom could take him home...

Well, Josh will grow,
As we well know,
To become a dependent for tax,
So if you find, too,
That situation with you,
Just pray, breathe deep, and relax......

Veronica Glenn

Moving On...

As I passed him in the hallway
His nose in the air
And his hand holding hers
No longer could my heart tear
It was only a year ago
When he cut my heart in two
He dumped me for her
What could I do?
His words were never true
He said he wanted us to try
He said he loved me
Now no more words, no more lies.
What a fool I was
falling in love with him
What a survivor I am
giving up on him
I'm moving on with my life
I've found a new love
I'm living out my dreams
All because of the Lord above.

Valery Kohlrus

Inside The Child

Talk to me.
Hold me.
Guide me with your heart.
Love me.
Touch me.
Share with me your time.
Listen to me.
Hear me.
Comfort me.
Hug me.
Accept me.
Then set me free.

Sheri Gow

Untitled

Tears...
How insignificant and harsh they flow
for those who've caused sorrow
on my borrowed soul -
to no avail

Sharon R. Swanson

A Mother's Broken Heart

If you only knew
How much you hurt me
If you only knew
  The tears I shed
If you only knew
  How much I cared
If you only knew
  How much I love you
Oh if you only knew
  How to mend my
    Lonely heart!
If only you knew!

Sara Rodela

Reflection

Have you ever asked yourself
  how much you really care.
For someone close and dear to you
  and with everything you share.

You look and see and feel
  everything and much much more.
And wonder when you are together
  if you really know the score.

Some days are good and feelings soar
  and some days are really sad.
Some days the mirror reflects
  that things are not so bad.

You wonder how much you really care
  for this person so close and dear.
And you go back and take another look
  at this person in the mirror.

Trudy D. Wood

In My Pool

See in the pool of my tears
How you led me on,
How you stirred my fears,
And then you were gone.

Read in the pool of my tears
The words you once said.
They kept me so near,
Now they are dead.

Hear in the pool of my tears
My heart's droplets of blood,
Falling as you randomly sear,
My pool-becoming a flood.

Mayumi Kodani

Snowflakes

As I'm flying through the Air
I am looking around everywhere
The world looks so bright and shiny
Suddenly I begin to feel very tiny
I see children looking out the window
I hope to see their trusting faces glow
I hope to bring joy to someone
for other snowflakes are bound to come
But, if we all work together on this
I know we can bring plenty of happiness.

Kim Willert

Fear

Protect me from the darkness
I am afraid of the fire

Protect me from the rain
I am afraid to melt
Don't let the sun go down on me
I am afraid of the cold

Protect me from the danger
I am afraid of the pain
Don't close the door on me
I am afraid of being trapped

Protect me from love
I am afraid of the hurt
Don't walk away from me
I am afraid of loneliness

Protect me from death
I am afraid of life
Don't let me close my eyes
I am afraid of the dark.

Liza Lee Benettieri

Waning Moon

I am very sad
I am sad about life
Life has not been good to me
My spirit is dead
My spirit is sad
It drains my heart
I am sad
I have a sad face every day

The moon is bright
I am sad
I have nothing to be bright about
I have nothing to live for.

Theodore Larys

A Life Inside Me

Inside my womb it grows
I can feel it is a part of me
I will protect it with my life
To its heart, I'll hold the key

For in its it holds my book
It portrays the love I feel
For this is our creating
This is life and this is real

I know I can't control its life
My belief I'll only preach
And I'll direct it toward the sunshine
Right from wrong I'll try to teach

For we will watch it flourish
Hear its laughter. hear its cry
My child will feel never ending love
Right to the day I die.

Lori M. Ramsey

"I'll Still Love You"

To die with hatred,
I cannot do.
But to die with love,
I'd do for you.

Being alone hurts me terribly,
With a heart of stone
I fight pain angrily.

It's constant love
That keeps on growing.
Like a dove
That won't quit flying.

You put me through pain
Yet, I loved you so.
The memories remain,
And I still love you tomorrow.

Lana Rae Clark

Flying

Oh, how I wish
I could fly
The feeling would
be so fine
To be able to see
the earth
with nothing
in your path,
it would be so nice
as you can see.
If I could fly,
I would feel so free!
Wouldn't you?
Oh, how I wish
I could fly.

Rachel Braaten

Something New

The first time I looked at you
  I could see something new
  Someone who cares and loves
    When others wouldn't
  Someone who sees the truth
    When others couldn't.
  There is something new
That through your eyes I see in you.
  I can see the light
    When there are clouds.
And during the darkest crest of night,
  I can see the sun.
  With you I see happiness,
    Even when there is none.
  There is something about you,
    Maybe it's your smile
Or just the little things you do.
    You believe in others,
  And through your eyes I also see
  This new thing you gave to me.

Tara Persinger

My Husband

He warms my heart,
I need no fire,
He feeds my soul,
I have no hunger.
He is my friend,
I need no other.
He is my husband,
I have forever.

Sheri Cordaro

The Window

Looking out the open window,
I daydream.
Looking out the open window,
I see a whole new world.

When I look out the open window,
All my troubles vanish.
When I look out the open window,
The answer to all my questions is 'yes'.

When the window is closed,
My troubles come back.
When the window is closed
The amazing new world disappears.

Michelle Klein

Pain

Every time I fall in love,
I find I am a fool.
Love, it plays a cruel game
And men are equally cruel.
He'll tell you that you're beautiful
And that he cares for you,
And when you melt into his arms
He'll break your heart in two.
He seems to be authentic
As he hides behind his smile.
He'll use his eyes to tell you lies
And you'll love him all the while.
You'll give him all your heart and soul,
And when he has your trust,
He'll throw it to the dogs and say
That it was only lust.
So my friend, I think you'll find
These words I speak are true.
And even though I am in pain
I'm still in love with you.

Lori Jean Strader

Untitled

The biggest fear
 I have
is dreaming a dream
and having the dream
 come true
then you have to fight
 to keep
the dream alive
or, it will become
 a nightmare
and destroy you.

Roy M. Goucher

Yearning

From a distance
I have watched you dance;
almost like a scolding fire
on a mid-winter night.
I want to get close to the fire
to warm my frozen limbs
but if I get too close
I might get burned
so, I keep my distance;
a safe distance.
I am able to feel the warmth,
but not as much as I would like,
for I am in fear of being burned.

Lorette Nicole

Unheard Horrors

I hear the children crying,
I hear the unheard horrors.
They come to me like I am their mother,
For they have no mothers.
They have nobody, but themselves.

I hear the children crying.
I hear the unheard horrors.
They want somebody to call them in,
And hug them like they matter.
They do not realize this,
But they do matter.
Other people do not realize this,
But they do matter.

I hear the children crying.
I hear the unheard horrors.
They look in the sky,
And do not see one shining star.
Their is no hope for them.
They have given up,
Before they have started.

Dean

I Will Always Love you

No matter how hard I do try,
I just can't seem to say good-bye.

My heart still feels the aching pain,
My tears still fall like heavy rain

I miss you more with the passing days,
I wish to God you would have stayed.

A special place I hold in my heart,
For you, my love, although were apart,
"I will always love you"

Tricia McCarthy

Will We Last

Will we last?
 I know,
When I look at my past,
 I laugh

 All those boys,
Who thought they were men.
 What did I see in them?
 I hope in the future,
I don't ask myself the same things,
 About him.

 Will we last
 I just hope,
 In the future,
I don't look at my past,
 And laugh.

Becky Gallihugh

Untitled

 I dream
 I scream
 Alone
 I cry
 Crimson tears
 Awake new fears
 I look to the sky
 As if to ask "why?"
 I rise from the ground
Heaven's where I'm bound.

Monica Levijoki

To Be A Teen

I'm sorry, Mom.
I know I forgot.
Don't worry, Dad.
I don't smoke pot.

We're going to the
show, and it's rated PG.
I won't be late, and
I've got my key.

My watch is set.
My homework is done.
The table is clear
Now, can I have some fun?

I love you, too, and
I know you're not mean.
I just wish you'd remember
that you were once a teen.

Victoria Elizabeth Hess

Someday

Someday we two shall meet again
 I know not when or where
But when we do, I'll say to you
 how much I really care
For a friend like you, with all your care
 and all your love inside
Makes a person just like you
 a friend I'll never hide
So in my prayers both night and day
 I'll say a prayer for you
And keep you in my heart and thoughts
 and all your love in view

Norman G. Belbot

If I Could Give The World A Gift

If I could give the world a gift,
I know what it would be.
It would be a very special gift
My gift would be world peace.

Peace is needed in this world.
People are dying too fast
There are too many wars in the world
Most of them were in the past.

This needs to be a better place,
For people like you and me
There is too much killing in this place
It should be like it used to be.

Nobody really cares anymore
They don't care if people have died
No one cares what we're here for.
People are losing their pride.

Hopefully our hearts will mend.
Hopefully fighting will cease,
Someday soon the violence will end,
And we will have world peace.

Kelly Toth

Untitled

I'm here, but yet I'm not
I'm gone, but yet I stay
I see, but yet I don't
I know, but yet I don't know
I came, but yet I didn't come.

Suzie Doran

Untitled

Can you explain
I know you're insane
So are we all
But how can you call
Hate and war okay
You kill many a child
then laugh out loud
The nerve you must hold
in place of the soul you have sold
Can you explain
your acid rain
Explain to a child
How you stand so proud
and send all the king's men
to kill again and again
Explain how you hate your neighbors
and kill your friends
Teach them to wave, bye-bye to nature
and say hello to the end.

Kimberly M. Bertetto

To Whom It May Concern

Your life has not been easy
I know you've suffered enough,
Through it all I held you close
When things were really rough.

I'm not a pillar of strength
My heart is not a stone,
While I listen to your cries
You forget that I have my own.

Although my words are silent
Inside my fears are real,
Hidden deep all to myself
There's much I can't reveal.

Now it's me who needs a friend
To keep from going under,
I know not how to ask for help
Suicide? I often wonder.

Please don't hate me if I go
It's something I must do,
Up above I'll still be there
Forevermore a friend to you.

Traci Little

Life's Journey

When I was just a little girl
I lived a fearful role
I thought that all my words and deeds
were recorded on a scroll.

I feared the day the scroll unrolled
and revealed my hidden past.
I then received some peace of mind
that bad things wouldn't last.

But now again I'm reassured
the scroll does still exist
I know the bad things aren't removed
for the politicians prove it.

Nettie M. Hall

Petals of Love

Love is like a rose
If you shake it too much
All the petals fall off
And it's not a rose anymore.

Roxanna Runkle

Unexpected

I am not ready for this news,
   I lost a friend today.
A kind and loving, dear sweet friend,
   Oh, please don't go away.

   Not a childhood playmate,
  she is much older in her years.
  A best friend of my dearest Mom,
   an end to childhood nears.

The weekend trips, the laughs and talks,
  of course we kids would fight.
  But Mom and her would make it right,
  on those cozy sweet spring nights.

  I say goodbye and look sadly back,
   through these painful tears.
  I also say goodbye, goodbye,
   to those childhood years.

Vicky Fuerst

Don't Cry

Don't cry,
I love thy so.
For I'll be always be
with you so.

I'm not gone forever,
you'll be with me shortly.
Holding my hand
in Heaven.

Don't cry.
Wipe away those tears,
For the love we had
will never fade away.

Your heart is
pierced with thy love.
Your soul is
pierced with thy soul.

Don't cry,
I love thy so.

Tina Marie Cavaliere

Hale

It seems whenever
  I need a friend
I dial a phone number
  and you're the one
   on the other end.

If knowing that
  brings you smiles
think how I feel
  way over here
   across the miles.

It always seems
  when things get tough
you show me I'm capable
  of getting through
   ALL the rough stuff.

And most of the time
  when our talks end
I know what I found
  in my sister
   is a GOOD FRIEND!

Michelle K. Rohde

he Sadness Of Sunshine Reeves

Out of the depths
  I only to thee, oh, Lord,
A child dies a mournful
  Death!
The whistle of a bullet
  Whizzes and struck
  The child -
I cried for the child
  So sweet and mild.
Intrigue and sorrow
  Racked along the street.
Oh, Lord, again - hear my
  Cries for peace

Mary Kenneally

It Once Was Me

I watch him caress her
I see his eyes shine
the way that they used to
when he once was mine.
I can feel those soft kisses
that he once gave to me
they stand there in love
just like we used to be.
He so gently whispers
those provocative words
she blushes at feelings
that I too have heard.
So many emotions
pulsate through my veins
I'm so numb with jealously
I no longer feel pain.
Just a burning betrayal
that his love he now gives
and I know that without him
I no longer can live.

Lyndee Underbakke

Loves Pure Heart

You are aged my friend
I see it in your stride.
Yet you are young my friend
for I see it in your eyes.

The wisdom of time is
stored in you. Yet you
gaze in awe as flowers
blossom a new.

Hard work and nature have worn
your leather colored hands,
yet they are as soft and gentle
as a newborn lamb.

You are aged my friend,
but you wear it so well,
For in your heart so pure,
is where love dwells.

Rebecca Onstott

Untitled

A deer grazing quietly,
In a field by the forest.
Its brown form silhouetted,
Against the green swaying grass.
With its antlered head erect,
It bounds into the forest.

Pamela J. Bloss

As Times Go By

I sit and gaze as the time flies by
I sit and think as I cry,
I can not get you out of my head,
even Jesus if you're dead.
I lay in my bed,
but you're still in my head.

I sit and pray every day
I thank God that for us you died
I sit and wonder as times go by,
why is it that you cry?

As you were hanging we were just saying,
Oh God help this man,
or is it your eternal plan?

I sit and wonder as times go by
is it because of me that you cry?
Then I think I love you because I
know you love me too!

Nichole Roderick

Rock

As I hop on a rock
I softly look
for Tigers; Leopards;
and a Snake like a rope.
As I run from a Tiger
I hop over a tree.
I stop and I look.
Is he not or is he
I hope he is not behind me.

Katie Nelson

One Question

One night while walking
I stopped by the shore
There I saw footprints.
Wondering where they belonged
I followed not knowing.
They lead me to him
Standing there too.
He asked me a question
I'll never forget,
"Do you follow me weary one,
Seeking my love?"
I looked into his face
A bright light I saw
Responding to his question
Simply I said,
"I follow you Jesus
wherever you may go,
Hoping to find
The love you have inside."
Together we continued, forever by his side.

Roxanne L. Rawleigh

Untitled

As we walk the path of life,
  In a time of beginning and end.
There is only the moment to live for.
  Never look to the past for pain,
  Don't look to the future for hope.
Every time a person looks either way,
  They have lost that moment forever.
The time is now, the moment is now.
  So, lets live for the now
  Grab that special moment.

Trina R. Lantz

Always In My Heart

Whenever I think of him
I think of that peaceful night

When my dreams
Helped dissolve my guilt

As I wrapped my arms
Around his waist

My head
Sunk into his chest

I hugged and hugged
To show my love

An knew that
It would hurt

But we'll meet again
Some time from now
And show
Our Love again

Vincent DiPalermo

The Prison

You gave me a gift of food today,
I thought it was mine to keep!
The next thing I knew, I ate it away,
Still, I'm hungry and cannot sleep!
I dream of a life, so bright and free
But no one can ever tell,
Why it was you brought me here,
To live within this cell.
A life, a spirit, suffering and small,
I would not have chosen this.
Oh, someone take me away from here,
To a place where there is bliss!!
A place where there's no strife and pain,
A place where there's no sorrow.
The place where I'll be glad to gain
A grip on a new tomorrow.

Linda Gayle Spilko

Untitled

All my life
I wanted.
A significant
other.
A true blue friend,
a person.
Who believes.
In my worth.
And takes time.
To listen
to trees.
Speak.
And clouds
to whisper.
Silent serenity.

Kathleen M. Robbins

Spirit Horse Of The Prairie

Wild and free,
Is she.
As wild as can be.

Spirit queen of the Prairie.
She's no fairy.
Spirit queen of the prairie.
Spirit horse of the Prairie.

Kathryn Kvam

Unspoken Rhapsody

I wanted to let you know,
I wanted to fling out my arms
  and run to yours
To tell you how lonely I had
  been without you
And the joy I felt at seeing you.
But common sense held sway.

I stood in the shadows and walked
  Beside you,
Blessing every moment you were there.
Wrapping every word in golden paper
To put away for safekeeping
And bring forth in reverie.

Susan Churchward

"A Letter To Heaven"

"Dear Mom when you held me
I was just a tot
didn't know how much you loved me,
but I knew it was a lot.

I'll remember
you at my side
in time of trouble
one to confide.

When you came near
comfort you would try
a hand on my shoulder,
as you went by.

You made Heaven on earth
then life became too much
when God took you away,
and I lost your touch.

Lloyd H. Roy

Miss You

My dearest love and only love,
I will miss you during the day
and especially at night, I will
be wanting to hold you tonight,
I just wish you were already
here to hold me, and tell me in
my ear, all those crazy things
you do and say, I already
miss you, I wanna kiss you,
hold you, and love you.
We will see each other soon,
if not I will see you at night,
When I hold my bear close
to my heart real tight.
I never wanna lose you or leave
you cause I already miss you.

Kathleen Daniels

Untitled

My sweetest dear.
I wish you were here.
Since we've been apart.
I've had an ache in my heart.
Come home to me.
By the sea.
Make it soon,
And together we'll share.
A life so rare.
Filled with hope.
After we elope.

Katherine M. Gannon

I Wish

I wish on the rain
I wish on the sea
   that you would bring
your love back to me.

I wish on the moon
I wish on the stars
   that I could have
you back in my arms.

I wish on the sun
I wish on the sand
   that we could hold
hands again.

And I wish this wish
would never end....
   To see you again and again.

   Sherrie Hauser

Hazy Shadows

I thought of you today.
I'd forgotten some of my old memories.
I longed to hear your silent voice.
A voice that brought joy to my life
But my memories echoed away,
in a moment of silent despair.
I clung to an empty shadow,
A shadow that faded away.
A hand that once held mine,
And promised never to go.
All that is left is a vision
That I reach out to,
but cannot touch.

   Mary Longoria Marquez

Love Letter

I think about you often
I'd write you everyday
But there seems so very little
That seems worthwhile to say.
It either rains or doesn't rain
It's either hot or cold-
The news is all uninteresting
Or else its all been told!
The only thing that matters is
The fact that you are there
And I am here without you
And it's lonesome everywhere.
I think about your smile
And distant lands afar-
I miss you very much
But-you know I really care.
In signing off-I extend
The best of things to you.
Life ahead will never end
A kiss on waves so true.

   Vivian Lawrence

The View From My Room

The view from my room
Is often dark and lonely
Reminding me of my doom.

But then I think
Of Christ my Lord
Whose blood I long to drink.

And when this man is free
Hopefully someday soon
We will all see the Christ in me.

   Sean Gerrity

Life Is But A Moment

If we would cherish our children,
   If we could be true to our friends;
If we would respect our parents,
   There would be less time for amends.

To bundle up our memories,
   Of our most special times,
And relive them from day to day,
   There would be such peace of mind.

If I have left a bad feeling,
   If I have harmed anyone;
I hope I can lay it to rest,
   Before my time must come.

For life is but a moment,
   Passing gently, in the wind;
It leaves us as quickly,
   As footprints washed away in the sand.

   Pat Poole

Dear Child

My dear beloved child,
   If you only knew
What heartache could ensue,
   Perhaps soon thou would
Awaken and feel the pain.

If hope be there, one must
   Forsake blind desire
And strive, strive to
   Love again.

There lies love yet
   For thee dear child
Perhaps soon thou shalt see...
   It was there all the while,
Even though you may have
   Searched for miles.

To seek is to find,
   Treasures and peace of mind,
And beauty once-in-while.

   Molly Chandler

Fear

I'm afraid each and every day
I'm afraid of what I say
I'm afraid that you don't care
I'm afraid that you won't dare
I'm afraid of what will be
I'm afraid you won't love me

I'm afraid of what lies ahead
I'm afraid of what's in your head
I'm afraid of myself and you
I'm afraid of being hurt too
I'm afraid of what will be
I'm afraid you will love me

   Kathleen Crawford

Love

Love... love...
It's what I want.
Love... love...
Because, it's more powerful than the pain
Love... love...
The soft music, every time I hear it,
   I sense the love power.

   Rebecca Edwards

Untitled

Lately I've been thinking
I'm missing all the fun
That a heart without the laughter
Is like living on the run

Who am I really fooling
How can I go on this way
Without a heart to call my own
I'm living a borrowed day

Maybe I can live tomorrow
Without the worries of today
And maybe I can find a heart
Who can help me live this way

Or maybe I'll just find a door
With a stairway, somewhere
And climb myself to heaven
And someday find you there.

   Ruth Vomund

I Stand Alone

You are not inside of me.
I'm not inside of you.
How can you say 'I love you'
When you don't know false from true?
You wish to occupy my heart,
When it's in a far-off land.
You want to take my thought apart,
But what you find you won't understand.
You wish to be with me everlasting
And know what I feel,
But my thoughts are not for unmasking.
My emotions I won't reveal.
I want my feet on the ground.
You want to fly above the clouds.
You want to own a place in my heart,
But that I won't allow.
You want to be inside my veins,
In the marrow of every bone.
You want to stand by me forever,
But I stand alone.

   Karen R. Brown

'Wishing'

My friend, to you from me
I'm wishing you all that life can be.

Daydreams and playthings,
Tugs on your heartstrings.

Sunshine, rainfall, walks in snow,
Lots to do and places to go.

The glow of stars and soft moonbeams
Sighs of pleasure, enchanted dreams.

Long summer days, nights of bliss,
Peace in your heart, a tender kiss.

I'm wishing you most a heart that sings
and a life that brings

Love, luck, joy, content, and
Memories to treasure of time well-spent.

   Renee Conger-McCollum

"Enthusiasm"

   Enthusiasm is a fine gift,
   It is the pin hole in the darkness
     Which if allowed to grow
     Can become a bright light.

   Lisa Park Martin

Beauty

If you're lost somewhere out there
   In a forest of despair
  As you watch a stream flow by
  Away your dreams seem to fly

   In the forest deep inside
  there is hope that you hide
  I hope you find it someday
  Then I know you'll be okay

If someone squishes your dreams of hope
   I know you will cope
  I hope you will not despair
  Over the dreams you did share

   As some birds fly above
  I hope you know you are loved
  Please don't push love away
   You may need it someday

  Some beauty is only skin deep
  Yours is not, so it will keep.
     Sarah Jackson

Stone Cold

How peaceful the unburdened buried lie
In a valley or crest of hill
Listen to what the dead imply
We are gone but you live still.

Cautiously walk the rows of souls
Read the names and dates of death
Listen as the bells of serenity toll
in rhythm to your heart and breath.

Then stop at one that holds your eye
The inscription cracks your public mask
Admit as you turn up to the sky
This stone has wrapped you in its grasp
It reads:

If any can bring out just one good
Your life has served your time and place
Then God alone will say He could
Not find one soul to take your place.

   Perry T. Barrett

In Between

I feel so lost,
In a world of my own.
With no one beside me,
I am all alone.

I'm in between sizes,
Not large and not small.
It's too hard to climb,
Too easy to fall.

Everything is spinning,
Spinning out of control.
I'm not being myself,
I'm just playing a role.

So as for now,
I'll remain in between.
And all my true feelings,
I won't allow to be seen.

But perhaps in the future,
I won't be so plain.
The role I play will disappear,
Only my true self will remain.

   Leah Rabinovits

Untitled

In the midst of turmoil,
  in a world of strife,
The Lord brought us joy
  with this tiny life.

He came too early
  but he wanted to see
What a glorious time
  his life would be.

As God is our witness
  we just have to say
How thankful we were
  for his birth day.

Then, the sun set;
  he went away.
Our hopes and our dreams
  have gone astray.

We'll always remember
  your tender smile.
Please, won't you think of us
  just once in a while?

   Rose Gasser

Looking For Love

I'm looking for love,
In every way.
Full of happiness,
Hoping it'll stay.
Someone to love,
Someone to hold.
Someone more precious,
Then silver and gold.
Although every time I try,
Something goes wrong.
Maybe it's my heart,
It's not that strong.
I'll never find love,
I can now see.
Until I find love,
By loving me.

   Mark Moorman

Child

Child dreams in a window
in light bathed.
Visions dance,
calling out to come
and play.

Sad child holding tight
to unfilled dreams,
knows not that dreams
fulfill themselves
in ways unseen.

Beyond the window
in the dancing day,
dream and dreamer
twine, untwine, entwining
whirl away.

Little child gleams into a moment,
soars on the wind so far and so high,
creating crystal worlds
where diamond silence
cracks the sky.

   Stephen McCarthy

Lost

In memory of Mark Sterling Howe

Heartbeat.
Breath.
Feverish emotion.
My arms around you.
Can you feel me?
I am loving you.
Can you see me?
I am kissing you.
Can you hear me?
I am calling to you.
To you, I would give my life
If, truly, I could.
Silence.
Despair.
Lifeless oblivion.
I can feel you, I can see you,
I cannot hear you.
I know that you loved me
And our time now has passed.
Good bye, my angel — already, I am
missing you.

   G. H. Manning

Mighty Atlantic

Her tranquil rhythmic aimless swells
  in mesmerizing roll,
beam mirrored miles of placid rays
  that mask a briny soul.

Waters deep in calm repose,
  haste to her command,
churning in a race with time
  and chase to sack the land.

As raucous, boisterous waves they come,
  in mocking thund'rous roar,
banishing the timbered drift
  to exile on the shore.

Salt and spray and crashing surf,
  a cataclysmic wake,
succeeded by triumphant calm
  and rest for nature's sake.

Creeping as a silent night,
  she taunts the stoic coast,
washes new the sands of time
  and ebbs in wistful boast.

   Roy G. Hill

Poetic Lives

I am up all hours
  in my den
keeping company with the mystic moon
  'til it turns into dawn
A romantic in a material age
  getting through the rough nights
   with Emily Dickinson!
"She measured every grief she met"
  in 1862
A non-conformist in a Puritanical age
  dressing in reclusive white
   she wrote cosmic poetry
But seldom left her room.

"It hurts to live"
  the poet said
yet found a "piercing comfort"
  like my own-more than century apart
   More than a century apart
    she in Calvary.
     and I in her Art.

   Meredith Salisbury

The Brighter Side Of Things

There is no room for pity
In my life so filled with pain.
I cannot see the clouds above
Nor can I see the rain.

I don't have time for doing less
Than what I know I can.
It's up to me to do my best
According to God's Plan.

How can one appreciate
The joy of being whole?
If he has not, in some small way
Known sorrow in his soul.

I will not say, I cannot say
That I have walked alone.
My God is with me night and day
The Master's touch I've known.

Loyce Rae Jordan

They're Just Words

Words with no meaning
  in no particular rhyme
    being spoken to someone
      but never said on time.

Meaningless thoughts written down
  on pages as empty as my soul
    being read in a different language
      to people who will never know.

Endless tears I sometimes shed
  as bitter cold as January nights
    flowing for someone I dream about
      in a sequel of unusual flights.

Music being rehearsed aloud
  like the flames that feed our fire
    with every note that strings a cord
      sung for your heart's desire...

Monica Florimonte

Winning...

You must have faith
In order to win
You have to set goals
No matter how far you've been.

Reach for your dreams
And follow your heart.
Fate and reality
Are many miles apart.

You've got to work hard
To obtain your prize,
Because you can do anything
No matter the size.

Strength and honesty
Are also involved,
Truth is a puzzle
That many have solved.

Just do all you can
And never give in,
Because no matter the race
You can always win.

Melissa Beth Chastain

A Gentle Heart

Masculinity is not founded,
In physical strength alone;
But rather in the ability,
To be very gently strong.

For a man's physical strength,
Is only half his measure;
For if he possesses a gentle heart,
No price can buy his treasure.

No man should be afraid,
To acknowledge a beautiful sight;
Whether it be a morning rose,
Or snow on a winter night.

A man must realize,
That strength has many parts;
And that he is no less a man,
Who owns a gentle heart.

Tom Noble

Untitled

A child's cry comes
in the middle of the
    night.
So you go in and make
    sure everything is
    all right.

In years to come they
    grow so fast,
you wish infant days
    would always last.

When the days grow cold
    and time grows slow
you will cherish all
    the memories that you
    still hold.

Kim Simpson

Love

She came upon me
In the morning mist
While laying on the hammock
Sipping spiced rum
A stream of light
Dancing on a fallen leaf
White buds
Green buds
Awaiting for their seasonal gift
Mere butterflies
In multicolored garments
Fluttering about
They felt her before I did
Afraid to exhale in vain
I waited patiently, in subtle joy
Anticipation often hides deception
She took me by surprise
The flowers blossomed
She lingered still upon
My breasts, will not leave until I wish

Thara Accilien

Death

Death hangs over my head,
Like a bird with big wings
Covering everything in its path.
It seems to know who I am.
I ask death, "Who am I?
Death answers, "You are my soul!"

Mohammed Sami Al Hafiz

In Dreams

After sleep has come and gone.
In the night so far from dawn,
My mind awakes to find you there
Walking proud without a care.

Suddenly I too am there,
Moving through the misty air.
I take your hand and off we go
To pass our time in childish fun,
We sing and dance and laugh as one.

As dawn draws near
We try to run,
To quickly comes the light of sun;
Your image fades
And I'm aware

That day must pass
And sleep must come
Before we can again be one.

Karen Maull

Promise

In the darkness stands a candle,
in the storm there shines a light.
The despairing have been given hope
that dawn will follow night.

Through the pain there calls a voice,
through the din there rings a bell.
The veil of fog is brushed aside
from the valley and the dell.

A heart bent down is lifted up,
A broken man, made well.
A woman's tears give way to peace,
saved from private hell.

It passes all around us,
a breeze so soft and mild.
It's the music of the ages,
it's the laughter of a child.

Romaine J. Wick

Devoted To You

Out of all the women,
In the world today.
You're the greatest,
I'm proud to say...

When I wake in the morning,
And you're lying there.
It's almost impossible,
Not to stare...

Your beauty is something,
There's plenty of.
But that's not the reason,
I fell in love...

There's a twinkle in your eye,
And a gentleness to your touch.
Baby nothing has ever,
Moved me so much...

You're warm and sensitive,
Affectionate and true.
Darling I am,
Devoted to you...

Michael Earl Ellington

The Mouse House

Once upon a time
in this little old house
there lived a little old mouse.

This little old mouse
who lived in this little old house
spent his life running to and fro
yet not knowing where to go.

Like that little old mouse
in that little old house
we spend our lives running to and fro
still not knowing where to go.

Lorrie Carter

Brother's Keeper

It's said there's hope
in what we do,
In death as well as life.

But where is hope in
life when all
Is poverty, hate and strife?

Is death so good
and life so bad
That we feel it's too late

To grasp the joy of what
is now and
Give in to the hate?

The olive branch in one
hand and
The gun held in the other

Brings life or death,
Which will we choose
As keepers of our brother?

Lolly Bryant

These Are Dreams

Mirrors
In which you see
yourself reflected—
bigger and better,
surrounded by
your past, present, and future,
in a universe
filled with possibilities.

Shatter them,
and the future fades,
the pieces holding only
the past,
diminished by time,
drained of meaning,
overblown cartoons of
what you once believed.

Stephanie Rechtin

Darkness

The wind blows with the night air
into the darkness my eyes do not dare,
to look beyond its darkened embrace.
My heart begins to pound and to race.
My eyes open with a sound in the dark,
"Oh" it's only the beating of my heart.
I close my eyes once again,
Until I felt a grip of a hand.
I jumped up with a wretched scream,
To realize it was only a dream.

Patty Lezer

Journey Past Innocence

The warmth of the light fades
into a cold lonely darkness.

An everlasting voice of confusion
echoes through my unknowlegdeable mind.
Trying to reach for a life I can no
longer grasp, and tumbling towards
a life I do not understand.

How did I fall from this world of warmth
and security, into a place of harshness
and uncertainly.

The journey is complete. Innocence is
forgotten, and life has begun.

Leslie Neff

Untitled

As I gaze
into your eyes
I see an ocean of azure.
When caught in the ogle
I know you endure it too.

Your visage,
what sparkle it escorts.
The infatuation for your form
matures and flourishes.

Gleaming bronzed hair
relays to me
to bestowal my heart
to you.

Spirit, the vacant
aperture is filled with
ardent admiration.

Melanie Anne Rosen

Child Abuse

The silence before the storm
is a deafening slap across the
face of the earth that has
done no wrong which warrants
its tremendous tornadoes that
whip across the lands, deluging
the plains with rain and
exposing the reddened clay
which lies beneath the soil of
prosperity that holds the
bloom of our 4.8 billion
year old earth, a child.
after the storm the ravaged
earth decides not to take
much more and swings herself
to the sun by leaping off the roof of the
universe. Only to land, a shattered planet,
30 feet below.

Steven C. Poon

Untitled

The nature of the beast
Is that of cruel, hard, steel
Fire rages burned inside.
Slow at waiting for the kill.
Running wild through the trees
He spots his prey with deadly ease,
Blood smells fresh, this tasty flesh
Was once beast itself

Merrill Gobetz

Time

Time is not forever, but time
is all we have in this vast world
of endless troubles and trials which,
we can set before ourselves.
Only prayer will lead us on
to better times ahead.

Time is measured by the way we
live it and if we live it the way
God would expect us to, our time
here on earth will last a little
longer and a little more peaceful

Time is truly all we have and
if we live it for God we can
have everlasting life forever
with God where time has no end.

Von Lynn Beeler

What Is Love?

What is love?
Is it a feeling of joy,
and a feeling of fast heart beats?

Is it a warmth that fills your body,
and makes your pulse race?

Or perhaps
it is an unforgettable thing,
a thing that brings joy.

Or maybe,
it is a beautiful thing,
one that can't be topped?

If all this is true, then,
I am in love.

Levi Dicla

Midnight

Is it morning or is it night?
Is it day or is it light?
What comes between the day and night?
It is the bewitching hour midnight.
I see it there a candlelight,
Shining in a window bright,
Ah, the bewitching hour midnight,
'Tis the witch that casts that light!
Is this thus a time for fright?
This bewitching hour midnight?
This half of day and half of night,
A time for dark yet time for light,
It is not a time for fright,
It is just a time of night,
It comes before the morning light,
It is the time they call midnight.

Steven Morrison

The Rose God Made

There's a rose God made
It has a strong stem
and two strong leaves
The petals are soft and pretty
God made many colors of this rose
And said he would call them mothers
So if you ask me to describe
my mother on this day or any other
I would go to a rose garden
And pick the strongest most
Beautiful rose
And say "here is my mother"

Liz Birman

"Youth"

Is it good? Is it Bad?
Is it paradise or hell?
Is it innocence or ignorance?
Only time will tell

   a twinkle in the eye
   a fire in the heart
   we long for it when we are old
   and hate it when we start

Is it lonely? Is it lively?
Are we nobles or the fools?
Be us young or old, it matters not
- for no one knows the rules

   a spirit wild with fury
   a soul afire glows
   why can't it last forever
   only heaven knows.

Is it mystery? Is it misery?
Is it filled with lies or truth?
I don't know what it is
I just know it's youth.

   Keith A. Darby, Jr.

Untitled

To share a life with someone else
Is like a childhood game.
You take your seat and hang on tight
Upon a tilting plane.

You thrust and fly to dizzying heights—
You warble and you crow;
But, then your partner kicks and soars
While you go swooping low.

Whole summers days are spent this way
While others longing pass;
But, if one tires and leaves his seat
It drops you on your ass.

   Kevin Durkin

Never Really Gone

   Somewhere in this vast world,
     Is someone once loved.
   Someone really never erased from
     The heart and mind.
   Although gone from sight and touch,
     Lives on in a song, a place, and
       our memories.
   We feel their presence, as the soft
     breeze passes across our cheeks.
   We smell them in fragrance of
     flowers in the field.
     We hear them speak to us,
     in the gentleness of a song.
   So as long as the breeze blows,
     The flowers bloom,
     And songs are sung,
   They will continue with us.

   Robin Lea Black

Untitled

The shadows of the trees
Just lay there in the darkness
The leaves have slipped away
to return in quiet sometime
I wonder how they feel
with the blossoms of the flowers
Does the feeling grow more lonesome
or does it know feel whole.

   Stacey Kirshner

How Much You Mean To Me

A person like you
Is someone so special
Who means a lot to me

Someone to look up to
When I needed help
When things got bad
You were always there to comfort me
And when things didn't go my way
You were there to make me laugh

I realized a special part of me
Was my only brother I know
That's why I love him so.

   Paula J. Pino

Life

   When you're young, your mind
isn't free, it's mixed up in a funny
sort of way, it's hard to decide
what you would like to be, if you
would like to love or be free.

   As you across the river of
life, balancing on every stone to get by,
you're not yet falling, but you're not
yet steady, but for the changes
you are ready, you take it into
your hands, making decisions
between wrong or right.

   Clinging to faith itself,
makes me wonder what life's all about,
is it love itself I want, I ask
myself, no I answer for it's the
accomplishments I can make.

   Vicky Daniel

What Is Christmas

Christmas is magic.
It brings families together,
It changes acquaintances into friends.
Houses become homes
Lights are brighter
Snow more beautiful.

It's a bundle of things,
Bigger than Santa;
More brilliant than lighted trees;
More than cards and gifts.
It's children laughing and singing,
  gaiety and exaltation.

It begins long before December 25
It lasts forever because it is - -

     Our thoughts
     Our feelings
     Our viewpoint
     Our confidence in people
     Our faith in God.

   Vera E. Brinck

Lavender

Lavender, lavender;
  Keeper of dark corners,
   Hidden mysteries,
    and ancient rhymes.
Lavender, O'Keeper;
  of shadowy smiles,
   forgotten secrets;
    and quiet times.

   Michael Brennan

Loving Tenderness

Like no other feeling I can know,
it brought me to your side; my
heart revealing not to go, I felt
each tear you cried.
Each precious teardrop I have hidden,
in loves unconquered tower; 'til
all your fears are safely ridden, I'll
guard it through each hour.
Until such time your pain is gone,
this shall ever be my quest; to give
you strength to carry on, and bring
your faint heart rest.
Faithfully shall I be there, this loving
Vigil keeping; always with such tender
care as gently you lay sleeping.

   Michael L. Kearney

Fear....

Fear is all around;
It follows you everywhere.
Nothing stops fear.

I am afraid of dying;
I am afraid of living;
I am afraid of everyday life;
I am afraid of everyone.

Being afraid of things normal.
A normality that is so.
If you're afraid, you are alive.

Are you alive?
Do you have this special feeling?
Am I afraid of you?
Are you afraid of me, too?

Fear is around me all the time;
My fear is unusual;
Everybody's fear must be somewhere.
My fear lies in my heart.

   Mary Grace Ramos

Kacey

It is love.
It is a love that runs deeper
than the deepest of rivers, and a
love that flies higher than the
highest of mountains.
It is a love that is loyal.
It is a love that is more loyal
than the sun that rises
every morning and the moon
that appears ever night.
"It" is a she,
and she is my wife.
My wife is
Kacey.

   Michael Countryman

Increase The Peace

   We need peace on the wall
Just to help the ones who fall.

   We need peace in the air
Just to help the boys beware.

   We need peace on the ground
For all the dead ones be found.

   We need peace to have fun.
Either that or give me a gun.

   Kathy Christman

Dark Descent

Emptiness
It is my world
My only soulmate
Her arms await me
To engulf me in her embrace

Loneliness
It is my life
An empty soul
In a crowded room
Her love for me is my despair

Regret
It is my past
Blessed ignorance
To the consequences
Her story is my own

Death
It is my salvation
The final hope
For a hopeless soul
Her comfort is my love
            Mariko Hoffman

Happiness Is Temporary

Happiness is a feeling of euphoria,
It is the zenith of humanity,
The grandeur feeling of splendor,
The paramount delusion of self esteem,
A place in the sun,
An elusive feeling of glory,
The pivotal point of self gratification,
It is like the top of Mount Everest,
A joyous feeling of ecstasy,
And finally, happiness is a temporary
Fading dilemma.
So, why do we seek it? Because,
Happiness is within our grasp.

            Mary L. Bonner

Untitled

I'm afraid of you, you know,
It isn't right to love you so,
I have a fear that you might go,
And then where would I be?

I wish you'd come and always stay,
I suffer so when you're away,
I want to have you every day,
So we can love and laugh and play,
I'd be so happy then you see.

Loving you just can't be wrong,
Our love is rare, and deep and strong,
Loving you has made me see,
The kind of person I can be.
Our love, my sweet has set me free.

            Linda W. Hobbie

Beholder

When the eye of the beholder,
    let's go.
You're in another reality and you,
    can't let go.
And as you walk in your mind it,
    pretends to take control.
And too many deja vus cause you to,
    Keep on searching in your soul.
So tell me which way is it too go.

            Robert A. Madewell

I'm In Love With You

            When the sun rose
            It made me blue
            Because I realized
        That I'm in love with you.

        Every minute of every day
            I can't bear the pain
            Of having you away,
    I just feel like I'm going insane.

        Just to have you near me
            Or to say your name
            Makes me see
        How much more love we can gain.

    I keep waiting for you to call,
            As I sit by the phone
        Or pace up and down the hall.
    I guess your heart is as hard as stone.

            I'll never forget you
            Or the fun we had.
        All you did was make me blue
            And hurt me real bad.

        Mary Lockaby

"Poetry"

Poetry is fascinating
It takes me to a whole new place
The words that describe wonders
Can go at any pace

Some poets can write non-stop
They were given a gift
To write anything as possible
While always being swift

Every poet is talented
To bring joy to everyone
To write what they are thinking
Until the poem is all done.

I often think of poetry
As sometimes very nice
As nice and beautiful like flowers
As nice as the cinnamon spice

You can picture in your mind
The many different things
Every wonder in the world
Poetry always brings

            Sarah Long

Untitled

I sought a song
It was not mine.
I tried the tune
It did not rhyme.

I turned it this way,
I turned it that,
It laid there lifeless,
A small brown mat.

I watched—a stranger
Wandered by.
She saw the song
I claimed as mine.

It sang to her
So sweet and clear
Its colors were so bright.
The song I tried
To hold so near,
For me it was not right.

        Linda L. Bisel

Love Is Forever

Love is so precious
It's a feeling that
Controls the heart.
It lives by the love
That is given from the
One that you cherish so much.

Love knows no resentment
Believes solely in trust
It exhibits the passion
That dwells in our hearts.

Love is forever
For when it begins
Your heart makes a promise
To love till the end.

So when I whisper I love you
There should be no fear
For this love that lives
In me you've conquered my dear.
            Maria Chacon

Lost Friendship

We've been friends for so long,
It's hard to believe he's really gone;
He's always been so strong and brave,
Now he's in a deep dark grave.

If only he could have stayed,
Every night I would have prayed;
To keep him safe and secure,
If only they had found cure.

He always was so smart and kind,
A friendlier person you'd never fine;
Even through all the tears,
I'll never forget the past few years.

I am relieved he passed away,
For all his pain each day;
Now he can be free at last,
And get away from his painful past.

            Kelli Kearly

What You Mean To Me

You mean so much to me
    it's hard to explain
You're like a flower
    in the desert
A bright star in the
    dark night sky
An angel sent from heaven
    I feel blessed when I'm near you
Your bright sparkling eyes
    reflect your gentle soul
Your friendship touches others
    there's no other woman like you
The love that I feel for you
    is sincere and strong
You bring me happiness
    like I've never known
If you ever need me
    no-matter where you are
Just call me
    I'll always be there for you...

        Richard L. Skyler

The Wall

Watch me as I remove the 1st brick.
It's taken awhile;
but listen to me as I take away the 2nd.
How can I leave up this wall I've built,
knowing all you've done for me.
It's been my safety shield;
I'm sure you see.
Please try to understand me,
as I bring down my walls,
I'm learning to love.
And I'm learning to trust,
This shield will come down,
I know it must.
So be here with me as I learn;
walk with me along the roads of life.
Help me mend my heart that's been torn.
Cause I feel old, tattered and worn

Karrie Ann Vallee

A Place To Turn

Ever since I was very young
  I've always been afraid,
I never wanted to open my heart
  and I fear that I have paid.
As a child I should have sang
  and danced and jumped and played,
But growing up a middle child
  is how it always stayed.
There were many things for me to do
  around the house and home,
I had very little time for friends
  I was more or less alone.
It's hard to live a normal life
  when you don't know how to love,
But I finally found someone
  who makes me soar like a dove.
I always thought that there would never
  be a place to turn,
Until I met the man I love
  and now my heart will always burn.

Linda Willenbring

What's Next

The end is near
I've known it was coming
But I don't want to leave my world
It took so long to get use to
So many battles fought
Too many wounds healed
And now the horizons changes
Where is it taking me
I'm not ready just yet
I can't slow it down anymore
I'm afraid
What's next

Kevin J. Doyle Jr.

Moody Painting

There is no perfect painting
Just brushstrokes still awaiting.
Because artist is never satisfied
Perfection keeps artist lacking bliss.
Little details effect pause
Careful application will shine.
People will come and see painting's skin,
And they might want one.
Others will come thinking that
Artist could and might become famous.

Woody Lambeth

"No Regrets"

Every since I was young
I've lived a life full of fun
Never felt much for sorrow
Never hurt much for pain
I've just tried to be myself
And look out for number one
Some have thought I'm mad
Others that maybe,
I'm just plain crazy
I look back upon my past
With no regrets
Too many people stumble through life
Concerned to much for this or that
Knowledge comes from experience
Experience comes with life
I know it may sound strange
That's the way I see things
Above all,
I have no regrets

Kevin W. Murray

A Private Maze Behind The Wood

A private Maze behind the wood
I've often seen before -
It whispers its cunning Secrets
And knows a flaccid Hour -

Seldom do I hear it beckon
Not wont to speculate
Its obscure enshrouded Monument -
Why do I hesitate?

For deep within the Labyrinth
My thoughts - ephemeral - go
To emancipate my Being -
A quiet Inferno -

Nicole Dennis

Missing You From Above

It's been so long since
  I've seen your face
And it breaks my heart
  because we cannot embrace
Now thirteen years have gone
  right by
And I can still feel the heartache
  and I want to cry
We all miss you so very,
  very much
You were so dear, you had a
  very special touch
If there was one wish that
  we all could have
It would be for you to be
  here again to have.

Michelle Calise

Untitled

I've taken to
kissing
my granddaughter's
feet-
she thinks it's
quite funny
and sticks them
in my face-
and sometimes
when she's sleep
I even smell her
shoes.

Sandy J. Austin

Ten Foot Pole

Most won't touch skunk With Ten Foot Pole.
John, retired Employee hit
Skunk With a Ten Foot Bamboo Pole.
Skunk don't let go: nervous a bit.

John was a lucky mystery.
Skunks shoot 10 feet when they let go.
Throw brick, make 'em skunk run for it.
Strike him with a hoe, that's his toe.

Slim Bill reading in Garden Shed,
In Life Magazine was a Monk.
Slim looks over Z clear pictures.
There at his foot was a bull skunk.

Scared Bill called loudly, "Skunk!"
Slim he "shot" out at the front Doorway.
John ran backspin out the back way.
The Skunk never let go; answer nay.

Bill was a 15 foot away and
He threw a large rock at Skunks' Hill.
A Skunk let go. It was worst smell.
Being far, Spray never got Bill.

Stephen B. Paddock

When It Is Time

Be not afraid, if he should call
Just hold his hand, you shall not fall
When it is time then you will find
It matters not what's left behind

Above the misty distant glow,
Of clouds, of moon, of stars you'll go
Where God does live and heaven sings
And angels soar on golden wings

Tho' they may weep when you are gone,
Tomorrow brings another dawn.
And soon the sands of time erase
Where once you stood, another's face

Perhaps a child with face like yours
Who smiles and runs, then stops to pause
With glistening eyes, that seem to say,
Why do you look at me that way?

Do I remind you of someone before?
Who once you loved, and is no more?
Then tears will swell, and start to flow
And when it's time, I too shall go.

Michael Ferrarese

Sometimes

Sometimes I cry,
Just thinking why.
We don't know
Where we go
When we die.

Sometimes I sigh
Just thinking why.
It doesn't prove
Our innocence
When we lie.

Flying, crying,
Buying, lying.
In my mind
I am sighing,
Because my heart
Is dying.

Sara Hegg

Rest At Last

I've climb so many mountains
  Just to fall astray.
I've walked so many hills
  Just to find another.
I've ran so many miles
  Just to find myself running more.
Now I'm glad to say
  I've found my rest place.
  I have no more miles to run.
    I have no more hills to walk
And thank God oh mighty
I have no more mountains
  to climb.
     Thomas Wayne Oakley

Dirty Image

I stare and stare
just to see nothing
the nothing that is me.

I try and try
to change my reflection
but a dirty image is all I see.

I wipe and wipe
at the spotted mirror
but nothing wipes it clean.

I cry and cry
because I know the kind of
person that I have always been.

So please, Oh please
don't start with a dirty image
in the early days of your life.
Because you'll never lose it
and you may never make things right.
    Nikki Davis

Untitled

I hold her through the night,
keeping her close,
dreading the morning sun
which threatens to force us apart.

Her face, beautiful even in sleep,
calls to something deep inside me,
mingling with the fear
which has come to rule our daily lives.

Knowing that each night
may be the last
I lie in quiet torment
hoping I have served her well.

My heart grows heavy
with the knowledge of what I must do.
Dawn's approach, swift and merciless,
reminds me that no night can last forever.
    Peter A. Barta

Twilight

Red in the sky
Light
Frogs volley voices
Singing for sex
Water deep in its ditch
Fathoms
Willows assembled hush themselves
Feathers circulate home
The night
    Tom Cadmus

You're My Mom

You're my mom I
know this is true.
Tell you one thing
  I love you.
The things you do
The things you say
Mom I'm very sorry
  I ran away
Please believe me for
  this is true
I'll never love no one
  like I love you.
You're the only woman
that is true blue
This my mom is
from me to you.
    Loretta A. Jacques

Please Accept My Apology

Please accept my apology
Knowing there's nothing I can say
That will ease the pain and suffering
I have shamefully cause you all

Mom I realize how much I hurt you
Dad I brought you shame and disgrace
I am here because I knew it all

Please Accept My Apology
Big sister I have cried many of tears
The fight I gave because of your fears

Little brother, I flew into a rage
While you tried to show me the maze
I had no idea, I was in a daze
How could I have been so dumb
    Lorraine G. Earle

Day Dreaming

Lost in your thoughts who
knows where in class it's the
best place. Nothing to do,
nothing to say just sit there
close your eyes and daydream
far beyond the skies far beyond
the stars to a world unknown
to be lost at who knows!
Dream at day, dream at night just
just dream of happy untold.
    Marisa Escoffery

"Resting"

To die; is to merely sleep.
Laid to rest; memories to keep.
Our flesh is returned to the earth,
To breath a fragile beginning of birth.
Restoring our body to polluted dust,
All is ended now, yet die we must.
Grieving hearts, not for the dead.
But for the living, it is said.
Eternal sleep; we all will endure,
For we shall be resurrected for sure.
To roam again upon solid ground,
A reunion of such in every town.
    Mildred E. Petty

Treasures

Hear the cries in the night
Laughter in the day
Eyes shining ever bright
In their world full of play

A quaint smile appears
Hands reach out in the air
And don't forget those tears
So mom and dad will show
They care

Parents always pay a fee
But each day is filled with
pleasure
For children seem to be
Life's Littlest treasures
    Rhonda Cole

Dream Catcher

Dream catcher spin
Lay moon slivers
On eyelids
Tattoo leaf shadows
With gull feathers
Tie star points
With silver night threads
Braid owl hoots
With pine whispers
Clack, clack
Against the window
Luring dreams
    Marie T. Davies

'The Road'

Long winding road
  Lead to the way unknown
Over the rainbow I traveled
  Hope it also carries me home

Sun rays warm up its heart
  Moon shine calm its soul
Cover the hill up 'n down
  Winding in the woods lost 'n found

Holding their hands
  Two lovers strolled
Kissing each other
  They rested on this road

Long long the goal
  Making love soul to soul
Still, it is a winding road
  Lead to the way unknown
    Ken Huang

Today

Treat today
like a diamond
precious
never to be lost
always to be cherished.
Treat today
like there are
no other days
for yesterday
is only a memory
and tomorrow
only an illusion.
    Katie Salisbury

Dark Night

Dark, dark, dark night,
leaves are swirling,
something's burning,
something is in the air.

Someone's laughing
someone's crying
someone's screaming in fear.

Everyone is inside
Everyone is in fear
For something is out there.

Something horrible is out there
Something what you call fear.

The banshees are howling
Death is in the air.

Someone's calling
Something's coming
It's getting very near.

Is it a joke
Is it a ghost
Or is it........... Oh my God it's the......Ah!
Ahhhh!

Nicole McAtee

Gods Flow

I was told to let go
Let him be in control
White waters running furious
Me with just an oar

It's all I can do
To just stay in the raft
Sort of fun, when not terrified
This river of life, what a task

The roar grows louder
As we speak now
The mist thicker, current faster
My God and I reconciled

Peace of mind I have at last
Given freely, I know now
By the simple act of surrender
Not my river at all
Only Gods flow

Randy Barnes

The Words Of Man

The words of man
   lie replete without meaning.
From his powerful prose
   our children are waning.
The tongue of the serpent;
   man's ally, his friend,
Lashed out and bit him,
   then whispered the end.

Roman Dolny

Unencumbered

Let me soar the great majestic heights
Like an eagle,
Whose outstretched wings glide swiftly
Upon the winds of eternity.

Let me soar to heights unknown before,
Climbing higher than I've ever dared;
'Till I embrace sweet, solemn serenity
And succumb to who I am.

Marlene Jolly

Every Man An Island

Far out in the depths of the ocean,
Lies a lonely, little island,
Surrounded by water on all its sides,
With gloomy palm trees, almost moribund.

Ships have tried to reach it,
But only face a dead end.
Because there is no way to get inside,
It feels no need to defend.

The broad palm leaves above
Shield the land from the afternoon sun.
All warmth and light kept out;
Prison without bars, nowhere to run.

The island contains many treasures,
All safely locked in a chosen chest,
It waits patiently for the cherished key
Held in the hand of the unknown guest.

A raft discerned in the distance
Is welcomed as it draws near.
Key in her hand, a smile on her face,
She dispels the despairing darkness and the fear.

Varsha Bhuchar

Life

Life can be wonderful
Life can be grand
Life is so fragile,
It's held in God's hand.

Life can hold sorrow
Life can hold pain
Whatever the outcome,
We are not quite the same.

Life can make us stronger or weaker,
Happy or sad
We must live it, to know it
Take the good with the bad.

Life is a gift
We have it, for only awhile
Best we live it with love,
Understanding and a smile.

Sharron Rackliffe

Mid-Life Crisis

I'm much older but no smarter
Life is easy and it's harder
Creature comforts, still uneasy
Don't know what I need to please me
Haven't changed much and it's scary
Can't succeed; I'm too damned wary
Opt instead to stay the same and
Wonder how I got so lame and
Went to college, didn't finish
Kinda let that all diminish
Self-destructive, couldn't see it
Never even tried to be it
Seventeen! I'm thirty-six
I grow, regress, it never sticks
Lost more time than I should mention
Really lost. Got no retention
Gave my life to high denial
Real life never was my style

Mickey Shepard

Drops Of Love

She moves about the garden
Like a feather in the wind
Borne by gentle breeze of eve
Admiring her kin

Drops of love fall from her eyes
And sorrow fills her heart
For she knows what they do not
The time has come to part

All her life she had sustained them
Giving birth to everyone
Each petal mirrored perfection
And radiance from the sun

With mission here now found complete
The heavens open wide
Overcome...she breathes one's last
Eternally abide

Awakened by the warmth of morn
Their loss is felt with sorrow
Glistening now the drops she shed
Comforting memories for the morrow

Sandra Younk

Winged Grace

Sometimes watching my home,
   Like a guardian ghost.
Watching breathlessly still,
   From a top the light post.

Behold! the owl,
More beautiful than the wolf
   In its moonlight howl.

Such a powerful, graceful,
   And beautiful sight.
Needing not day, for it
   Thrives by the night.

Soaring through the sky,
   In the night time air.
Oh, so quiet, as if not even there.

Earth's most majestic,
   Creature is he.
Believed the wisest,
   In the earth's history.

With his outstretched wings, my breath is stole.
He must be special, to possess such a soul.

Steven Hardin

Shadows Of The Past

Eyesight fading in later years,
   Life is filled with shadows.
   Reality fading in and out,
   Life is filled with shadows.
Dreams no longer of the future,
   Life is filled with shadows.
   Waiting for the time to pass,
   Life is filled with shadows.
      Soon the time is right,
   We will join the shadows.
Life no longer in the present,
   We live in the shadows.

Sarah Moore

The Pen

Fast words flowing from a ball-point pen,
Like blood from a broken vein......
Lines that lead you to the past
And bring you back again.
The hand does not control the pen...
In fact, it's quite reversed,
Tracing thoughts and hopes and dreams
The mind had once rehearsed.

The pen, being mighty as a sword,
Has the power to relate
The tale in terms of terrible truth,
Destiny or fate..........in
A thousand words, a picture paints
The stories, all un-ended....
And the reader seldom understands
What this writer has intended!

S. La Batte Mueller

A Heart Can Only Take...

Streetlights careen past my windshield,
Like monotone snowflakes in a row.
Everything happens fast.
Hurry! Hurry!

I buy a card for my lady,
Hardly have time to sign it.
I fill my car with gas,
Progress to the next meeting.

A hundred projects due in a week-
Won't have time for a break
Go to a party at the weekend,
But then there's no time left.

Grow up. Learn all of this.
Don't stop. Keep moving.
Hurry! Hurry!
A human heart can only take...

Pop!

Tyler A. Parris

Autumn Leaves

Last ripe harvest before winter's frost
Like seasoned love before it is past

Forged in memory in molten image
For all winter

A love of meteoric flight
Incandescent
A fleeting star in darkness

A love lusty and tender
Teasing irreverence, tickling humor
In autumn years

In the heat of an Indian summer
Winter was closer than reasoned

Virginia M. Sabin

Song Of The Wind

Standing in a field of lilies
Listen, and hear the song.
Never-ending and ever-existing,
It tells the story of life, and death.
The wind knows of happiness,
And grief immeasurable;
Living and crying,
Singing and dying;
In one single voice.

C. R. McDonough

The Calling

On a concrete slab he lay
Like spit boiling on the sidewalk
And his eyes were the flame
Did I see his light
Before it devoured my will
My mind answered with a yes
And then, a no
A stutter that reflected
In dismal color and similar mood
The shoulder of the corpse flinched
With tapping of a mighty finger
And it was I who turned to its calling
My senses deflated
Except the one already in flames
And I saw no one everywhere
On the concrete slab
Number those petrified
By the echoes of the calling
Then the mighty fingers cease
And there is no one to turn

Nancy Lamoureux

Loneliness

It come and goes
Like the birds
Who fly south when it's cold
And fly north when it's warm
You don't know when it going to come
But it goes
It scares you loneliness
It's like a disease
That strikes you when you don't need it
It hurts loneliness
I don't understand it
But I know it's there
I wish it would go
But it doesn't why

Mary Kay Butterfield

"If I Can Fly..."

I wish I can fly
Like the birds in the sky
Then I will be free
And no one will know it's me.

I will go where the sky takes me
And look at things I can see
When I get tired and need rest
I will find the nearest tree to nest.

I will flap my wings
And with my beak I will sing
The beautiful noise I make
I will see how far it will take.

Yoshiye Kimura

Seeds Of Sunset

He knows how to go
Lingering lingering
Slipping away

She knows how to stay
Cooling cooling
Remaining cold
And we bury deep
Inside her warmth
Barely beginning
To let-go just-
So slowly
Slowly release...

Rachael Hernandez

So Necessary

Little things make my heart sing
Like the first burst of a bud in spring
A crinkly pink sea shell in the sand
A finger held tight by a baby's hand
A swim in a river late at night
And on a windy day flying a kite
A rippling brook on its way to the sea
And sun ripened fruit upon the tree
The faint perfume every where
Of spring violets in the air
A walk in the woods on an Autumn day
Watching October's golden leaves at play
The native song of a bird on the wing
The divine sound of a church bell's ring

All of these are a special part
So necessary to my heart

Ramona Burke Hood

Untitled

Although there are times when I don't
  like your guts,
And other times when you drive me nuts,
I must let you know; most of the time-
  I love you much,
And I wouldn't know what to do,
  if you weren't mine to touch.
Oh what a lucky girl I am,
  'cause I made you my man,
And now I have to take from you,
  as much as I can stand!

Tammy L. Johnston

The Battered Child

The battered child
Lives not in happiness or joy
But in a world full
Of pain and anguish.

The Battered child
Knows no heart-side peace
Knows only anger screamed.

The Battered child
Knows naught of pride,
Downcast he cowers
Cowers when parents call.

The Battered child
Begs and cries for help
But no one wants to get involved.
Is it that, no one cares at all?

The Battered child
Has now found everlasting peace.
He no longer cries from hurt,
He rests within the
Loving and Caring, Lord.

Ronald Barnfield

"Endless"

Endless road on which we travel
Looking for ourselves
When were setting right there
This is how we win our thanks
This is how we earn no compliments

Landon L. Ham

The Jail Birds

The jail birds are a vivacious lot
  Living on an uncertain plot.

Where their going is an
Uncertain game.

Never knowing who's to blame.

Why their here
Who knows but God.

Why when what who,

It doesn't matter
It's a hard bite to chew.

Lets give them courage,

To do better and better
On another day.

Lct's show thcm thc way
To succeed reaching that
  Ultimate star from afar.
    Martha Mary Siano

Practicing -

Far gone.
long enough
to recall
you with - out

Fading.
you with - out

Practicing eternity
far gone
you with out

You remain.
no matter
how far gone

- You without
  B. Bremer

You Came

You came, when I was sad
Longing for a friend,
To take my hand and hold me,
My broken heart to mend.

You came, taught me to smile,
Conquer all my woes.
Sing a little melody,
Caress a budding rose.

You came, at last I see
The way to start anew.
Your coming was a blessing,
Your friendship, ever true.
  Mary Kozul

"Responsibility"

God bless, the child, who has his own.
My brothers and sisters,
I have heard it said,
A tisket a tasket,
Use a condom or a casket?
It is your attitude,
Too have to choose.
If you don't use it,
You will lose it.
  Roosevelt Cox Jr.

The Stars In The Sky

The stars in the sky
Look down at you.
Nodding their heads
At the right things you do.

The stars in the sky
They sparkle all night.
Throwing a flash of joy and love
For those who love to walk in its light.

We could all be stars
In Gods wonderful world, dear.
Be thoughtful of others
That live far and near.
  Mildred L. Witte

Heaven

Dark and alone, where do I go
Lost and running
Where do I hide
One and never
Where do I rest
Me or you
Where am I now
Thought but insane
Where are you
Music or silence
Will anyone listen
violated secret
Will I die
Can't find the light I seek
Who are you
Why do you follow
Don't know where I'm going
Heading in that direction
Look for the light
No where to be found
  Kellye Lyne Bumpus

Friendship

Friendship means sharing
Love and always caring
People all united
Without being invited

It means to be kind
And always keep people in mind
Soon you are taking part
In a great thing that begins in the heart

In friendship people don't mind
If you're sick or even blind
No one could ever replace them
Those friends who are as precious as gems

When we pray to God at night
We ask him to shine a light
On the people of the land
Who give each other a helping hand.
  Maria Cruz Arceo

Love

Love will never stay
Love will still go by
Throw with a million loves
You pin it to the sky
All through you bin it with hate
And buckle it with true love
My heart will stay true blue
And so will you.
  Sene A. Kalolo

The Tree Cannot Sway...

Somewhere between
Love and hate
Is passion

Somewhere between
Light and dark
Is peace

Somewhere between
Life and death
Is awakening

Somewhere between
Fire and the
Burning wood is God
And
Between strength
And weakness
Is me.
  Reuben N. Patterson

We, the Flowers

Oh gentle little flower,
Love and please
Please and love
Let your heart ache,
till that painful doubt is part of you.
Free of pain
you will seek it,
believing that you are not whole
in its absence.

Oh gentle little flower,
caught between the egos
of an endless struggle,
where does your solace lie?

—In the wind's soft whisper—-
—And in the songs of birds—-
Embracing the courage of the sea,
as it roars its statement
against the shore,
you shall make your Stand!
Conjoined with the promise of nature...
  Shirley Fichera

What Is Love Today?

What is love today?
Love is something you feel
And something you say.
Love is a fairy tale,
Love is a dream.
Love is a feeling,
That nothing comes between.
But you have to be careful,
Because love is hard to find.
It's something you feel in your heart,
And in your mind.
If you ever find love,
Don't ever let it go.
Just trust me,
Because I know.
People say that love lasts forever
But that's not true.
Because if it was,
I'd still be with you.
  Susanna Ramos

Magic Memories

The sound of a telephone ringing
Made a miracle happen each day
For a certain voice had the power
To make all my cares slip away.

The room had a way of brightening
When I heard a tap on the door...
Then a face as familiar as morning
And a kiss just as warm as before.

The glow of long-cherished memories
Has kindled a lovely spark
That burns like a thousand candles
And lights my way through the dark.

Ruth E. Dwyer

Being Hurt

Being hurt feeling sad, it can
make you cry, it can make
you mad.
When someone hurts you it
can cut so deep, but the love
you felt for him you'll always keep.
The love he gave that brought
you cheer, the way you felt
when he was near.
Can never be again, because
the trust you had has faded,
All of those nights you've spent
alone, those times you've hated.
Is now over because you've
built up your wall, he can
never hurt you again, as
long as you stand tall.

Leslie Fitzgerald

Lonely

Yesterday was a lonely day.
Many people around -
Voices making no sound -
Yesterday was a lonely day.

My kids are darling.
It is alarming just how charming
they can be.
Yesterday was a lonely day.

Fire new buds on my rose bush today -
and promises of three.
I also saw a blue day.
Today was a better day.

Sandra Willetts

London Town

Countless years have ground you down,
masked beggar known as London Town.
Dressed in wool facade to tell,
passers by that all is well.

Embroidered scarves, no stitch you lack,
charade with style in widows black.
Pretense by day, it fades by night,
a mass mirage, truth lost from sight.

Hours pass and time does tell,
of those who march to daunting spell.
Who dance the waltz of perfumed days,
illusions power holds you at bay.

Siren's song in the shrouded city,
for millions lost my heart bleeds pity.
For what is vain, you all fell down,
sleepwalkers of cold London Town

Robert Eric Denning

Heartbeat

Poets spring from anywhere-
matches struck on a wall.
Words come easier for some,
flowing like water from the tap.
  Not so for me,
  falling like tears, into
  the stone of my heart.

World has deaf ears to hear,
the dumb poet as she spins.
Lips part to weave wise words-
ears prickle at the sound of the beat.
  Not so for me,
  fumbling for phrases, lost
  in the roar of my sweet, empty voice.

Lori A. Whitaker

Our Destiny Is Together

Maybe it's your smile,
Maybe it's your laugh,
I don't know when it happened,
but love has crossed our path.
Maybe it was the first time,
when I saw you with your friends,
so carefree and hopeful,
that happiness would not end.
Maybe it was the second,
when we had talked together,
I felt like what we had
would always last forever.
Maybe it was the third,
when we went on our first date,
anyhow or anyway,
this must be our destiny,
this must be our fate.
I love you.

Kristy Crumbo

A Bit Of Devilment

Dear first lady
me thinks you should agree
there was a bit of devilment
in the president
when he selected you
to put the ailing health program
back on track again.

But were I in your shoes
good woman
I'd not be amused
instead, in good faith to him
I'd say
"take this job and shove it."

You might remind him
lottery came into play
to aid the ace-high education fund
so
why not a lottery
to aid an ailing health fund?

Margaret Ross Venturin

Haiku

Kiss of the wind; Peace.
Moonlight, forest canopy,
Snap of a twig; a fear!

Tim Sexton

Question Mark

Can you teach
  me to fly
above the clouds
  of fear and doubt
mistrust and anger?

Can you teach
  me to laugh and cry
and not be shy with my feelings
  my thoughts my hopes
  and my dreams?

Can you teach me to share
  my mind my body my soul
with the better part of me,
  the missing half?

Maybe she's you.

Can you teach
  me to be
  Free?

Can you teach
  me to Fly?

Timothy L. Lightfoot

Spirits

Celestial beings amidst us all.
Meditate to hear their call.
Speaking not with mouth but mind.
They are there but hard to find.

Mind attuned and in the mood.
You feel their presence in the room.
Lightning flashes all around
And then you know it's you they've found.

Living in another dimension
Most are on a peaceful mission.
Fearful not of all mankind
They have no war or fear of time.

Let them infiltrate your mind
And they will show you things to come.
Stars that line the sky at night
Are their supreme and guiding light.

Vicky D. Schlemmer

Grandma

She tells of stories in her past,
memories that will always last.
Her smile is special,
Her eyes are true,
She always cheers me when I'm blue.
When I look into her face,
nothing but love is in this place.
She makes me happy and I am glad,
When she is gone I'll be very sad.
I'll keep her safe within my heart,
That means we will never part.

Lynn Clark

Talking Loud But Saying Nothing

Your racial slurs will not pierce me
My shield of love will protect me
Your words of hatred only amuse me
Such weak attempts will not diffuse me
You say I'm inferior
You say I'm dumb and lazy
But if truly superior
why are you so afraid of me
talking loud but saying nothing

Saul McCloyen

The One I Love

Poets write of love, and other things-
Men will talk about it
And the happiness it brings.
I've seen the time
That a man has cursed the day
He met a woman, and I've heard him
Cry his thanks aloud to God
For much the same.

As for me, I know no greater joy,
No greater happiness has man enjoyed
In all his days! For you, my love,
Have made me extremely happy-
And I appreciate this dream.

I can find no way that says enough,
To tell you all you mean to me-

Unless I say that life with you is Heaven
For where else do Angels stay?
Ted Wills

Shalita's World

Shalita has a beautiful dream,
Mom and Dad will love, not scream.

Shalita has a special hope,
That sister Saa will give up dope.

Shalita has a wonderful wish,
For a family dinner of sauteed fish.

Shalita has a perfect escape,
A world without guns and crack and rape.

Shalita's world is not ideal,
Unfortunately it's very real.

Someday maybe things will change,
One day maybe things will change.

Until then never give up hope,
'Cause wishes and dreams do help us cope.
Risa Jordan

Promised Messiah

Promised Messiah from Eden's garden,
more beautiful than nature thou art.
Of God's own being thou were chosen,
Help us to receive thy glad impart.

Save us from our sins and our misgivings.
Come and occupy Emmanuel's throne.
For you are God's son and spirit giving.
Come and occupy all nature's throne.

You have shown us who you are Lord,
Of your high favor let us be renewed.
So on this day and any other,
we praise and glorify you.

Of mankind's swaddling clothing,
you took into your heart one day.
And gave us a new beginning,
when our ways were paths astray.

Promised Messiah from Eden's garden,
more beautiful than nature thou art.
Not just for times now on going,
but to the Trinity's eternal heart.
Marshall Clement

Afoot In Chaldea

Orange cantaloupe peel,
moribund winter's whitened debris
from the backlash of storms.
The wayside avarice of the weed culture,
greedy for space, however promising
becomes the cockerel pagan evening;
you'll know of the heart's beckoning.
There moves more saffron-istic boulevards
toward freedom—more English farewells.

September coals, dried weed bristles,
hairline autonomy during playground ways.
The sun cannot support the crescent wave
of the milltown tower where ludicrous
buttons of gold explore the open fields.
Now have the swallows deserted the skies,
but my clear eye rejoices within as
I meditate upon the season's crushed
grandeur, the summer's peak.
W. S. Kennedy

Fluffy Clouds

Fluffy clouds so high above
move with the wind
And form such wondrous shapes
Some-like mountains of whip cream
Against the sun.
Other dark & strong that bring
    the rain
Floating along like a driven team
Traveling the earth so everyone
    can see
Another of Gods blessings
Wild and free.
Margaret Taylor

The Valley Of Death

Darkness falls
    muffling sounds like a curtain.
Reason hides in the shadowy
    recesses of your mind.
Slowly you lose touch
    with all reality.
You find yourself among your
    own dreams.
Heaven seems only footsteps
    away.
You begin to walk.
Leaving footprints for generations
    to follow.
You feel a sudden feeling of peace.
A loving hand placed upon yours.
Everything is peaceful now
    All you see
    are stars!
Lacey Ferren

Hymn Of The Native American

We cannot own the open sky,
Nor own the ocean grand,
Nor the everblue crystal waters,
Not the trembling aspen stand.
We will tread upon it lightly
Because we understand
Our passage has a duty,
We are the Stewards of the Land.
Virginia Hubbard Torberg

Sixties Summer

The end of summer is near,
my dear,
Let's drink to our love
Down by the edge of
The moonlit beach,
with the stars shinin' up above

Will stay and love 'til
the sun comes up
Be my cosmic mate;
Our song will unfold up
in the sky-
Such a pleasant fate my dear,
Such a lovely fate

The days grow short
As we near the end.
Our time was wild and free
If we don't get together this time
next year...
In my heart you'll be my love
You know you'll always be.
Tim Weaver

Nowhere

Every time I start to care
My feelings are just never shared
When I think that I'm in love
Things fall apart and get so rough
Feeling confused is a usual thing
My brain takes off from everything
Only one thought in my mind
True love is what I want to find
What's happened? Why can't it be?
Is there something wrong with me?
Never cared for, never loved
I'm tired of being pushed and shored
Loving hurts why don't I learn?
When will I be loved in return?
I am lost in an endless search
For a love without the hurt
I look for it here, I look for it there
I look for love and get...
    Nowhere.
Kathleen A. Shaughnessy

His Gentle Touch

Although I'm nearly out of time
My hair is white my eyes are dim
I see more clearly in my mind
I've lost the game I played with Him

Through crowded hours I tried to hide
In darkened places like despair
In places filled with light called pride
A thousand times He found me there

Each time I thought I had it made
His gentle touch would stir my soul
So badly stained I couldn't trade
The Devil for a beggin' bowl

But when I stumble I can feel
His gentle touch ignite a spark
From heart of flint and soul of steel
That leads me out of frightened dark
Tony Gorman

Broken

Alone on a hard wooden chair,
my memories take me there,
to another lonely day,
when you turned and walked away.

Do you feel my pain?
Is it still in your brain?
How you so rudely walked away,
leaving me alone,
to deal with this broken home.

Your kids are now grown.
The youngest has just flown.
So now I sit alone,
in this lonely broken home.

Linda Benson

I Got Over You Today

The unhappiness is gone
My tears have gone away
No longer do I care to know
What you do and what you say

I've gotten over you
Though you said I never would
You'll never have me back again
Although I know you think you could

Nothing you could do now
Would ever change my mind
You've hurt me way to much
By acting selfish and unkind

Now you'll never know my love
And never have my trust
You took advantage of those feelings
When you followed your own lust

A smile is all you'll get from me
As we pass along the way
'Cause though you tore me up inside
I got over you today

Sherri L. Griffith

An Octogenarian's Prayer

My hair is gone,
My teeth decay.
I barely hear
What people say.

My eyes are weak,
My memory's bad.
I've not the
Energy I had,

But, Lord, as
I approach Hereafter,
Grant me yet
The gift of laughter.

Raymond H. Lyon

Chances

I never really asked for much
Never thought my life was such
that I would really have to beg
when standing on my final leg
and if I fell I'd hit the ground
with no one there to hear the sound
until she stopped and saw me there
I never thought she'd stop to care

Russell Hiltunen

Genie

My day is gone
My troubles are many,
I wonder if you
Could help me any?
What is the answer
Of how time flies-
There must be a reason
I have to surmise!
So I must learn
From my daily deeds
The working hours
That fits my needs-
But I'm convinced
Since my troubles are many
What I really need
Is an oversized "Genie."

Mary Berryman

Nature Is Calling

Frosty cold
Mystic breeze
Sparkled rain drops
Falling from the trees

Golden whispers
Silver secrets
Nature is calling
Set yourself free

Love and innocence
Lie within your eyes
Let your essence burn
Toss fears into the skies
Glowing puffy clouds
Rise and stand
Follow their lead
Grow to your own command.

Kristin Genna

The Plea

All who have heart will see.
Needless cries from you and me.

I've done my best to make it clear
Never to leave it left unsaid.
Carefully trying to express,
Ever ending tear that fall.
Someone listen for the call.
To be strong is not enough.

Simple honesty to oneself.
Untruths you'll hear a few.
Remember only good not bad.
Vacant are your cries of shame.
If it was to be why me! you ask?
Victory is ours to claim.
One answer is not enough.
Relax because it's over now, so smile.

Please remember you are not alone.
Live your life not like a stone.
Everyday is a new.
And Smile because you know it's true.

Patricia Ekonomidis

And Then The Child Dies

The child laid down for one final time
Never again to awake from her sleep
Never again to hear her mother cry
Never again to laugh or weep.
A single tear fell upon her pillow
As her mother leaned over her
The child's soul to float in Heaven
But mothers soul to burn forever.
The child took in her last breath
And let out a final sigh
A child that is forever abused,
And then the child dies...

Shaunna McKiddy

Hidden Blessings

Sometimes we go down life's highway
Never looking along the sides
To find a hidden blessing
Under a bush it sometimes hides

If we stop for just a moment
Instead of walking on
We may find someone in need
Who may be hungry or all alone.

God wants us to be a witness
Of his everlasting love
And He will send you down the road
That leads to heaven above.

So many people are out there
Dying from sorrow and gloom
Sometimes we never know which flower
Will have the prettiest bloom.

So start today as you walk along
To pay attention to who God sends
For that one person you help today
May one day become a friend.

Wanda Calvert

Regrets

Regrets are broken hearts,
  Never to be repaired.

Empty promises, with
  No truth in sight.

Tears that were shed,
  And words that were said.

Emotions felt,
  And wishes made.

Deeds never done,
  Words never said,

Past failures, and
  Future hindsight.

Hopes dashed, and
  Dreams forgotten.

Friends lost, and
  Distances felt.

Growing up, leaving
  The past behind.
Regrets are the lessons
  Life gives.

Theresa M. Schmidt

Poem For Peace

Someone help us please no more
Nights when we freeze no more
Hiding under ground where day
And night are the same where
Darkness runs in to days
O someone hear us please let
That war desist let there be
Peace here and in the world
Let the children new begin
No more suffering stop the hunger
Stop the pain let the sky be clear
Again let the ocean be free no
Warships to be seen let the
Searchlight be the moon let the
Sunshine in the heart of the
Enemy let all be free let no land
Be torn apart ore two loving hearts
Let them be whole like the everlasting
   Soul.

   Ruth Culver

The Me No One Can See

"I'm always by your side,
no matter what you tried.
No one is aware".

Cried, the me no one can see.
"I'm here can't you see.
why don't you choose me?
I can play the game".

Cried, the me no one can see.
"Oh Teacher! my hand is raised,
I want and need the praise.
I really know the answer".

Cried, the me no one can see.
"When I'm lonely and alone,
This fact to them unknown
I'm precious and worthwhile".
Cried, the me no one can see.

   Victoria McGhee

The Days of Wine and Roses

The days of wine and roses are
no more, for I have dreamed of
a thousand victories, yet I've lived
a million defeats.
The laughter that once filled
the air has been silenced by the
sadness in my heart,
The path I walked is the path
I chose. For what I dreamed and
believed was toward the sunrise
was in truth the sunset.

   Mark E. Woomer

The Unknown Path

   As I ventured down the path,
   not knowing what lay ahead.
   I noticed the sun creeping
     behind the mountain.
   Then came a gentle breeze,
blowing the blossoms from the trees.
    Then all became still.
   The gentle wind no longer blew,
now the blossoms lie on the warm earth
     beneath my feet.

   Terry Ryan Brown

The Soul

What does the soul look like?
No one has ever said.
Yet we know it will go forth
To be judged when we are dead.

I like to think that a soul
Is within each and everyone
And like the butterfly emerges
When a lowly caterpillar has done

Its work on earth, and is no more
Our body must also one day
Go to rest, and back to dust
From where life started at God's say.

A soul, untouched nor seen by man
Could be the "butterfly" that God
Will beckon to his judgment seat
When we are placed beneath the sod.

   E. FitzGerald Rahe

Contemplating Kurt Cobain's Suicide

Hot crash spasm shocks a heart
Not asked to suffer death.
Arteries ache; beats rift apart —
Scarlet torrent floods breath.

A shotgun to the temple
Which refused to worship there
Battered down the skullish walls;
Blood sorrowed from his hair.

Such strident, soul-dark music!
Was his true heart laid bare?
Who knew the inner man grew sick?
Was there no friend to care?

The heart that raged against the night
Felt starving muscles burn.
This desperate act rocked demon rite;
For this blood — no return.

A gaping wound — the last of his
Young manhood spurts in streams.
His heart has pumped the last of life;
The bitter end of dreams.

   Kay Trudell

Friends?

Friends, count who?
   Not by my fingers and toes
Joke with the crowd bubbling through
   But friend, where are you?

Many come
   Hail! Take and use!
Good cheer, full toast, and then diffuse
   But friend, where are you?

Sacrifice of self
   Labor all day
She's a "joy good" they say
   But friend, where are you?

Soul bare, surrendering all
   Discount, gift and praises call
Voice: "Yeh, Yeh, Yeh..."
   But friend where are you?

When life is dark, and death is night
   Tender giving hands, it is no lic
They in love, the true, and
   Friend, you are here.

   Moira Rankin

Goodbye Christopher

No place to hide
   Not for him
   Not for me.

There
   Like a bird
perched for flight
he turns his gaze
upon me.

No time for words- only silence.
And it that silence
is every word ever spoken.

Our breath connects
Our hearts connect

This young sparrow,
caught between two worlds...

Looks longingly into
the abyss. Spreads
his wings, and calls
out his last song

As he falls.

   Patricia Ann Doneson

Untitled

Not knowing where to turn,
Not knowing who to call,
   Just an empty space
With no where to fall.

   Leslie Hillyer

This Last Year

Once upon a dark and cold day
Not long ago as I recall
The winter rain
calmed the rampant storms of fall.

A warm smile in spring
there is a summer breeze
A gentle voice in the wind
leaves fall from the trees.

I still can see your smile
the one that relents my sorrow
and tears like rain from the sky
fade into a guiding light of tomorrow.

Now I know of a dream
gentle hands to see me through
and for all my life
I will remember you.

   Yvonne Hulin

My Question

I dreamed last night that I was dead.
Now funny thoughts are
bouncing in my head.
If I die now, where would I go?
To Sweet Heaven or down below?
I hear them say, there is only one way
But I know there is price to pay
Whether I am good or
Whether I am bad,
I still do not know if I have been had.
When I pray, he forgives my Sin,
But whose to say I will do it again
And if I do, what happens then?

   Rheana Hall

Untitled

It is so very hard
Not to jump right in
To give you what you want
It's so scary to begin
I could do so right now
No guarantees are there
The time we have together
To lead I know not where
Your touch does melt the ice
That took so long to form
The arms that hold me tight
Do make me feel so warm
The eyes of softest blue
Could tumble down the wall
The wall in place for years
Do I dare let it fall
Do we take what we have now
One day at a time to live
Enjoy all that we can
With no guarantee to give

Rose Perhus

Never Like This

Oh, I never felt like this,
Not until we kissed.
And I just couldn't believe
that you could ever love me
Now I can see it's you, forever and me.
Please don't leave, oh no, not like this.
Not after we've kissed.
I can't believe you don't love me.
Please don't leave me.
We walked hand in hand,
together we would stand,
In this unforgiving land.
I saw you last night, you were out
under the moonlight.
We held each other tight.
You looked at me and said:
Please don't leave me like this.
No, not after we've kissed.
I never felt like this.
You got to believe me. I never felt like this.

Nancy R. Bulington

Dying Soul

People all worrying
Nothing for you to do;
Nothing to be done.
Things once had
Now all gone,
While things never had
Now may very well be.
So scary,
So sad,
Knowing what you never had
Now knowing you'll never have.
Loved ones now all gone,
While one still remains you,
Yourself,
Is what you feel you have left.
While many more remain.
While worrying
You feel time never passes
Why yet it does life so short,
Time so long, now it's all gone.

Sarah Punceles

Now

Now is then
Now is whenever you open your eyes.

Now is forever
Infinite if you are left alone.

Matt Anderson

Maelstrom

Riotous clouds pervade the skies;
O'ercast Divineness from thine eyes.
Trouble shrouds thy weary brow—
Darkness quells thy pious Vow.

Lightning blazes; thunder roars.
The rain's inception sweeps and pours.
Hail onslaughts thy tender earth;
Flowers crushing—devouring mirth.

Thy rage abates; calm prevails.
Breezes caress thy tender veils.
Peaceful sighs with prayers of Grace;
Gentle salvation to Thy place.

Fingers stream from heavens nigh.
Eternal Hope springs from on high.
Faith renews Thy covenant past.
In Sacred pledge, avowed to last.

Selena W. Randecker

Swallowtail

Like the elongated head
Of a hard smooth bullet
Pierces the tightly woven wet
Cocoon
Splitting liquid flesh slightly spread
Damp, dark, deep within sugar spun walls
Drip, milk fever spits
From the oozing thick tip
Of a Monarch stinger
Sticky hot
Opalescent fluid
Melts the milkweed womb
Of the Gipsy Moth
The last bitter creme spent
Cools
And trickles down a silky thigh
A sigh, a tickle
The aborted flutter of a Papillion wing

J. M. Tomasula

I Await

Sitting in the shadowed darkness
of an empty room

Looking out, listening to the thunderous
clash of a turbulent but yet
endless cold storm

I await, like an expectant Mother
for a lasting romance, wish as I
may my mind nor my heart
can seek

Like Nero's Rome I have crumbled
under the fire of love

Steven R. Salfen

Lonely

A lonely child sits on the steps
of an old abandoned house
far away from any civilization

He will sit there and cry and mourn
mourn for his mother
his mother that never once cared
and so he will cry, and cry, and cry

But would he cry
if someone was there
someone other than his mother
will we ever know

Little boy would you cry
if someone was there to hold you
No the boy cried
with a look of hope in his eye

Then come with me, and you will see
a happy life waiting for you.

Meghann Hawley

Warp And Weft

Between the wilder extremes
Of labor pains and funeral wreaths
Situated somewhere in between
Self doubt and self esteem

The space where faith on rare
Occasion couples with felicity

We achieve the rhythms
Wherein we weave
With words and signatures
The stories of our lives
Mixing metaphors with beverages
Images with lies

Fabricating profiles
That rarely sketch the agony
Of compromise
In threadbare scenes
Of tattered dreams
In dire need of restoration.

P. Marguerite Forcier

'Mixed Emotions'

I am glad to have the feelings
of Love;
Hate;
Passion;
and Pain;
Otherwise the world would be dull,
And all humanly beings the same.
So if you regret - the tears of love;
The enemies of hate;
The sinfulness of passion;
And the agony of pain;
Think of the whole world,
As being the same.

Kathleen Maher

My Cat

My cat lives in a hole, a black hole
One day I crawled in after my cat
I got through the little hole
The hole was so dark and creepy
Yellow eyes came toward me
I thought, what it could be
Then I got out of the dark hole with my
cat following me

Shanae Callen

Untitled

There is a telling, tired fright
Of painful longing, truth to fight
Secrets ministered in ancient tongue
Whispers memories as old turns young

Locked in doors of Fragile's hand
Turned and bloody, desert land
Of heart's wasted wants and mind's desire
Gently calling back the fire

Questions piercing, answers lost
Constant reaching at any cost
Perception hazy, slowly comes clear
One step closer, hand in fear

As time is closing, moons will chime
Thoughts hush, silent, to turning time
And mind's eye shall finally know
Where did all the laughter go?

Sheryl A. Cavales

There Are Days

There are days when the pain
Of truth abounds it rises up
And smashes down!

There are days when cognizance
Is fleeting, one moment there
and then begins its creeping.

There are days when the pain
Of truth abounds the wretched,
Ancient tears begin to fall and
Suddenly, blissfully, I am drowned.

Patrick Kelly Kipp

Life

Life asks
of us to make
a decision.

No one
can live
for us
so
we must
live for
ourselves.

Life asks
of us
to make a decision
that is hard at times
to make.

Life asks of us
to make
a decision
to live and...
to survive.

Meg Andres

Moon Rings

There's a ring around the moon tonight.
Passions soar and take to flight.
Winds do whistle through the trees.
Sings birds to sleep with the breeze.
Moonbeams glimmer on cobblestone.
Twinkling stars dance and sing in tone.
There's a ring around the moon tonight,
Our love, forever, night after night.

Kerry A. Centeno

Menopause

It is that time of life
Of which no one will speak.
To acknowledge such,
Portends a future rather bleak

A passage fraught with change
Brings freedom to become,
All that I can or will be,
Now metamorphosis begun.
Male and female coexist
within this changing state.
Latent creativity unencumbered surges,
Gender coalescence now may culminate
Making choices is much easier,
Risking all to freedom's drive,
Liberation of the body
allows the self to come alive

The wisdom of the ages
defines each woman's goal.
Watch out heading downhill,
Gathering speed, on a roll!

Kaaren J. Hill

Just A Tear Away

Lachrymose oh lachrymose
oft I've felt thy saline boast
rushing from your hiding place
to gleam and glitter on my face

Lachrymose my lachrymose
of all thy skills I love the most
that which comes as if heaven sent
to ease my soul ere my heart is rent

Lachrymose sweet lachrymose
so glad I am to be your host
keeping the day from being oh so long
taking from the night its miserable song

ML McKenzie

The Gap

The floor of one man's dream,
Often seems empty,
And cherishes anything.
Except for the color green
He sits alone
And stares at a wall
He see's the sun outside,
Needs no windows at all
It can get to one,
As it has gotten to him
Of all life's illusions.
His will never end.

William Edward Ward

What Am I?

The sun shines in and
reveals the beauty within.
Life begins anew at this moment.
The pain and suffering have been
put aside but not forgotten.
The spirit feels fresh, alive
and aware of the world outside.
The core of my being has
been identified.
I am human after all.

Stacey A. Williams

Why Her?

A year ago she died,
Oh did I cry,
This is what happened.

Coke spews everywhere as the girl falls,
"On no," someone bawls.

People are looking around,
Wondering who did it.
Someone is bound to know,
But no one shows.

Sirens come and go.

Buses pull up,
People leave,
And no one knows who did it,
Probably will never know.
Later on you will hear, 'Why her?'

Mary Hajovsky

Oh Lily

Brighten thy smile
  Oh lily of the field
For thou still hast a love
  No other can boast.

I will carry thee to the fields
  Where the flowers are blooming,
To the forest where the trees.
  Are strong and their beauty silent.

I will take thee to the plains,
  Where the winds bring a hint
    Of spring,
To the mountains, where the streams
  Carry life to the valley.

Lift to me thy lips, oh lily...

For I will carry thee to the heavens
  Where angels dwell...
Then back again to my heart,
  Where I will sing to thee of love.

Roger L. Bowers

The Things We'll Miss

  You'll never be my little girl,
    Oh you were so very young,
  The day you were swept from my arms,
    Your first song never sung.

You'll never take that first small step,
    Or hug your teddy bear,
    Or name your favorite dolly,
    Chase a butterfly in the air.

We'll never paint your fingernails,
    Or bake a birthday cake,
    Or build a castle in the sand,
    Jump into leaves we've raked.

  You'll never pick a Buttercup,
    Or sit on Santa's knee,
    Or giggle at a funny clown,
    Climb up an old oak tree.

  You'll never be my little girl,
    Your cheek I long to kiss,
    But forever my baby,
    So many things we'll miss.

Teresa Foster

Untitled

As we walked hand-in-hand
  on a moonlit beach,
Our two souls never seem
  out of reach.

Your tender touch makes me
  smile inside
Feelings for you I have none to hide.

Sweet words you whisper in my ear,
  if you were to leave me,
  it would only bring a tear.
I could never live with this fear.
    Sheila L. Calderon

Untitled

Walking alone
On a sandy beach,

A shell I find
To comfort me.
    Susan D. Urie

Freedom

A jade bead swings slowly
On a string of hope
The dust of illusion
Fills my eyes
I can't reach reality
Black bars block my vision
And I'm thrown into a division
A stereotype of child
Just feel me and be wild
We'll drink our problems down
And tremble with the sound of screaming
Sink deeper into proportion
See the ink of lines
Telling of the times when
We were free.
    Nicholle D. Gaudet

My Friend

You speak to me in silence
On life's journey as I trod.
Your eyes tell me your heart's words;
Your wisdom is from God.
You ask me not to repay you
All the hours that you give
You ask God for my peace of mind
In this daily life I live,
You speak to me with caring,
Each word is filled with love,
A tremendous, soul's outpouring
Each deed blessed from above,
I search my heart each moment,
Wondering how to say "Thank you"
For a friendship that's more glorious
Than a flower's morning dew.
    Sue Ellen Carter

"Over The Mountain"

Bird's flying swiftly,
Over to the other side,
Not stopping till they,
Reach there goals successfully,
Setting to the other side,
They go joyously.
    Valerie Weber

Here I Sit

Here I sit alone once more,
On the porch I used to know,
Above the hills, and to the east,
The school I used to go.
I built this treehouse years ago,
these steps I used to trace,
here I sit alone once more,
the cool breeze on my face.
This bed I used to sleep in.
These woods I used to hike,
I can't believe I used to ride,
this rusty worn out bike.
I wonder what has happened here,
to this world I used to fit.
I think about the world I live,
and so here still I sit.
    Pamela Cohen

Bitch, In Heat

Movin' like a black cat
On the prowl again
Movin' in on the victim
Time to feed on all her men
Gracefully she'll taunt
Scratching you with her nails
You can't wait to have her
But it's you that she'll haunt
Black tiger with deadly claws
Takin' on another one of her prey
She can't wait for the next kill
The next kill to be her next cause
Blood on her mouth
Lip smackin' good
And sweet tastin' too
All these men, which one should she
choose?
Who will be the next one?
You'd better pray it isn't you!
    Kecia Weaver

One Summer Day

I heard the sea glide
  On the sand,
I saw the gray gull
  Circle wide
And dip and flash its
  Shining wing,
And race the wind to
  Catch the tide....

I felt the sea breeze
  On my cheek...

Softly, softly, tender
  Hands
Caressed my hair and
  Kissed the strands
Blown wild and free
  By salty spray
Borne from the sea
  One summer day.
    Priscilla Calhoun Cooke

DATING THEATER

Watch for previous of coming attractions.

  Hints   flags   patterns

Temporarily embossed.
Permanently etched.
    KASAGE

The Misery We Possess

Peering into her deep, dark eyes,
Once so full of laughter and desire.
Now remaining is an empty shadow,
Merely grief, loneliness, sorrow.

Peering into her deep, dark eyes,
Plainly, her tortured soul lies.
Hidden thoughts of anguish-held in,
Break forth through mists of suffering.

Peering into her deep, dark eyes,
Only pools of pain can be seen.
A dark, wretched sorrow seizes me,
Drowning me in my own pool of despair.

Peering into her deep, dark eyes,
A glimmer of light leaps into them.
Dissipating all within,
A flicker of hope...glistens.
    Sibil Thomas

The Voice Of One

The flight of
one butterfly
  flutters across
  a vast hazy horizon
  as the recollection of
one dream
  floats through
  a foggy chaotic memory
  while the living of
one life
  breathes inside with
  the hope of
one flower
  growing upward
  to the sound of
one raindrop
  falling into
  a deep open space.
    Stephen D. Reynolds

Priceless Gifts

The finest things in life are those
one cannot sell nor buy
A Father, dear
A Mother's tear
A newborn baby's cry

A friendly grin
The love of kin
And true friends always nigh

The breath of Spring
Birds on the wing
A rainbow in the sky

A tender touch
Needed so much
When death resides close-by

A God above
Someone to love
A Heaven, when we die

But these are things worth more than gold
yet can't be bought, you see
Thanks to our gracious Lord above
these priceless "gifts" are free
    Loraine P. Wright

Amber & Sean's Lullaby

My two favorite babies in all the world
One little boy one little girl
Little do they know what they mean to me
My favorite babies

My little boy my little girl
She was born first
and.....brightened my whole world
My little girl my little boy
He was born second
and.....brought me such joy

Because

My two favorite babies in all the world
One little boy one little girl
Little do they know what they mean to me
My favorite babies

Rebecca Gulley

There!

If ever you're in time of need
One person can be told
He'll jump when called or beckoned
And never is he cold

You can never fool him
Hard as you may try
He will never leave you
Never say goodbye

If in the end you fall
He will still be true
No matter how you fail
He'll help you start a new

He can't be made to go away
Or put upon the shelf
Take a look down deep inside
This man you seek's yourself

Stephen L. Beamer

Godchild

Ah, she sleeps,
One so young and innocent
Almost angelic
In her slumber so deep,
It's a time of princes
And kings and queens
What wondrous things
Must fill her dreams,
Dare I speak,
And risk a stir
Or kiss her cheek
As if it were the cheek of an angel
For truly she's heaven sent,
But no, no
I won't take that chance
Sleep on little angel sleep on
So tranquil in your nap

Leon Countryman

Search

Something been true lost!
Repeat again, what did you say?
Minutes before egg was on wall-
In nice various colors designed.

Is that important to you dear
That is what we are looking for,
Exactly love, we did not declare-
Mistakes of season eventually.

S. West

Burnt Eyes

Fire flickers freely
One to care for my fire
Fire is life-like
Dances wildly
Adding hope of warmth
Like springtime
Sheltered by caretakers heart
Fire freely flickers
only for its
love of caretaker
Only to live for
removing cold shadow
fire longs to talk once of
friendship, no longer but...
wind blows
sadly now
time ran out
memories of fire
cared by you
leaves embers of love

Michael A. Sforza

My Road

My road is not taken.
Only birds of the night fly over.

My road is always clean nd beautiful.
Where the wildest of wild flowers grow.

My road is not taken.
It is still beautiful, but they
choose the other

My road doesn't lead to
A city or little town,
Only to an empty lake

My road is fading quickly.
Why do they do this to me?
Once I was vast,
I covered the earth,
Now I'm separated.

My road is fading and the
only who can helped save me is you.
Help make me beautiful again, for then, my
  road
will be taken.

Terri Defore

My Peace I Give You

  What is peace?
Only cessation of war?
  Peace is much, much more.
God sent angels once
        long ago
to bring peace to the world.
  Jesus brought peace
        wherever he went.
He said...my peace
  I give to you.
Peace is not greedy, not selfish,
gives to others out of love.
  Peace is
  harmony
    joy
    understanding
    love
  My peace I give you.

Rose Ashour

I Owe You A Big One

Months seemed endless
Only darkness each day
Stress and pain never rest
Praying for deliverance each day

Empty inside and out
Asking for any kind of light
Suddenly, two shining beams
A mother and daughter so bright

Again life has meaning
Feeling of joy and fun
Accepting and accepted
Thanks God, I owe you a big one

Troy A. Schroeder

A Soldiers Cry

Power of passion;
Only in demand.
Clenching the fists;
Of his defeated hand.
With furrowed brow;
A battled scared face.
Gratitude left;
 Only to be laced.
In deep thoughts;
A silent cry,
as he scans the river bank.
Poised for battle;
A soldier with know special rank.

Sherry L. Barnett

Malice

I love,
Only to be broken.
You mask, what's on the inside?
Your impurity,
Your sinfulness,
Is sheltered by your innocent face.
Blue eyes, red curls,
They were only a hint
Of the devil beneath your skin.

You love,
Only to deceive.
Yet from the beginning,
It was you who was the fool.
Love is nothing,
Hate is everything,
You believed.
Trust is nothing,
Revenge is everything,
I believed.
Malice.

Pamela Sentman

Rain Writer

Sympathy, sorrow, happiness and
pain all show in you poetry,
do you write in the rain?
Feelings I've never felt before,
and things I've never thought,
all brought about by you, my attention
you have caught. Thank you for
the reality, the fantasy and
pain. Let me ask again, do
you write in the rain?

Shana Reed

Lost Hopes and Dreams

Oh I long to see the trees,
or calmly sit in the gentle breeze,
to sit at a desk and learn my lines
or to learn the cosmic signs.
Now those chances have gone away,
I will live no more today.

I forgive her for this mistake.
all that is that my life's at stake.
I am hurt because I'm not wanted,
now all of my fears are haunted.

I will never see the burning sun,
or kiss you when my days are done.
I depended on you for my protection.
Now all I feel is mass deception.
I will never play by a nice warm fire.
No more will I feel desire.

I lost out on a chance to live
the most precious gift that he did give.
My life that I will fail to hold,
I will die in satin gold.

Shannon Stoner

Our Secret Meetings

Whenever we meet,
Or try to get out,
We'll have to be discreet,
So no one will find out,

Because our love has to be hid,
Our timing just right,
Because people would only try to get rid,
Of what we know feels so right,

For us to be alone,
And make love all night,
We'll have to change our tone,
And lie to our families tonight,

But our love is worth the fight,
So the two of us can be together,
And if it's only for one night,
We'll make it last forever...

Sheila Harbin

"Quietly"

Quietly he turned his head-
Quietly he heard what another said-
Quietly he didn't repeat-
Quietly he prayed himself to sleep-
Quietly he worked from day to day-
Quietly he had something to say-
Quietly he let the years go by-
Quietly he wanted to cry-
Quietly he could stand no more-
Quietly he left open the door-
Quietly he is no more.

Mark L. Volz

Moon

The moon is round
Rays abound
The torch of mankind
The symbol of wholeness
And togetherness

The moon transcends
Its gamma and moods of man
Together the sun, moon
And earth, symbolic
of the trinity of creation

Steve Reinhart

Our Time Has Come

Our chains have been broken
Our desires have been awaken
We have been given life
For our time has come.

The time has come
To start looking forward,
To find better ways
For a brighter future...

The time has come
To forgive the past
But not yet forget...

The time has come
For us to exist,
Not just in the present
For the future is now.

We must join as one people
For we all the same
We must join as one people
For our time has come!

B. J. Thomas

Shattered Mirrors

She came to me again this evening
Out of the shadowed bedroom mirror
Of my meditation -

In the guise of haggard, old woman,
Bent and crippled by the battlefields
Of a forgotten time.

She sighed softly sitting beside me,
A satisfied satin simile
Of accomplished future.

Patting my hand with a knowing smile,
Leathery endurance strengthened me
To fight the prejudice

As a legacy for my children -
So they will not need a smoky vision
Of guilty persuasion.

Victoria L. Lippen

I Dream Alone

Your memory is like a shadow cast
over my life
I'm always reminded of the suns warmth,
although in the shadow I cannot reach
the warm place.
Your face is like a mirage, a fantasy
among the dryness of the desert.
Your eyes and smile are brighter
than the moon and stars
Your voice, like the waves, wash calmly
over the sand, making all the rough
spots smooth and inviting.
Your body is the ultimate dream,
a masterpiece of nature.
A dream that will always be in my heart,
but will never be known...
Because - the dream I dream
  I dream alone.

Katherine Morgan Pegg

Love

My soul was like the desert,
Parched and desolate,
Scorched to rock-hard dryness,
Until we met.

Your care came like a shower
Of gentle spring rainfall,
Turned my soul from sadness,
My heart did call.

My soul, which once was lifeless,
Like the desert filled with rain,
Has bloomed with life again,
Has love regained.

And now you are the promise,
Like God's rainbow after rain,
Of a future filled with kindness.
I live again.

Paul F. Hernandez

Nobility Is Gone

Senseless overdrawn anger
persuaded to act nonetheless;
Development is neglected
throughout the problem of us.

Speechless is term to signify
engulfed under a sea of lies;
stripped from nature is truth
none is better than mine.

Never diminished backwards
time calming decaying souls;
Places exist furnishing memories
Our thought scattered schools.

Lying memories needing fact
justice past is all forgotten;
Greed breeding altercations
buried nobility this morning.

Peter John Foote

Inside Me

A fire that's cold hot to the skin.
Placing a dress on the soul.
Making it stay with pin after pin.
It falls to the kind and gentle
And the mean and hurtful.
Wounds that are nothing but mental.
Grabbing for the life saver, holding
The rope.
Webs, walls, clouds and nothing.
Having love, hate with hope.
Taking a trip to a far off land.
Where people are great and perfect.
They never cry or take a stand.
How we see our own hapless kind.
It is just the thought that brings us
Here and there.
We all know it's just, all in my mind.

Tamara Cousins

Spirit

A restless spirit and a care free heart
Roams these dismal lanes
Longing to be free
Calling for its true environment
The blue, blue sky
The open air and the rustle of one
Of God's own beloved trees.

Lois Copper Smith

Quarter Moon Love

A full moon is out tonight
Please, run and hide...
Lover has changed what a sight
Do not say a little thing though
'bout that other side -
Do as a lover says; not as lover does.
A full moon is out tonight
Please, run and hide...
Suppress your shame; swallow your pride
Lover is not to be blamed
It has all got to be you?
Cycle is startin' anew
Loving and caring; even some sharing.
But you had better beware!
The next full moon is coming soon.
Then it will always be -
A full moon is out tonight
Please, run and hide...
It will come full circle
As I howl- Help!...

Susan Kay Vermillion

A Mural From Fragments Of Time....

In the Present-time we can see only the
preliminary works in construction phases.

The Future-time is the Birthing of
Dreams and Hopes.

Ahhh! But the Past-time is the
Magnificent Mural complete in

Hues of Struggles, Sufferings, Sorrows,
Hates, Joys, and Loves!

Dreams fulfilled for to look upon
In Time, On Time, For Time
In Glory!

See! Feel! the Living-Dust upon the
Presumed Lifeless Past.

Antiquity is ever-present within the
Presence for building Future...

Roselle C. Steck

It's Probably Me

I look in your eyes
reflections of life gone by
I look and wonder why
I feel nor hear any reply.

It's hard to express how I feel
it's hard to put into words the emotion
I look to experience for expression
I see nothing, it's probably just me...

I wonder how we can work it out
I'm amazed at the uncanny ability
I hope it grows with each passing day
As for confidence, it's probably me...

My feelings are strong, but tentative
there's a lot to say and see
as for my commitment for life
I love you, so, it's probably me,,,

Call on me when you need me
Call on me whenever you want
if I ever step over the boundary
it's probably just me.....

Phillip C. Thomas

The Lost Day

I stayed indoors one day in spring,
Preoccupied and unaware
That I was missing anything.
The sky was blue and sweet air.

A flock of geese flew northward bound;
Their honking stirred the birds below
To chorus rich in springtime sound;
But all of this I did not know.

A massive oak stood straight and tall.
The woods echoed the brook nearby.
A chipmunk scurried to a wall
With tail erect and gleaming eye.

The butterflies enchanting grace,
The apple blossom scented air,
Fresh breezes blowing on my face -
I missed, because I wasn't there.

Martha Brenzel

For The Whales

Gentle giant of the deep.
Protector and friend of man.
Legends tell of how you
have returned drowning souls to land.

Gentle giant of the sea;
We watch you play so happily!
Noble, intelligent.
Brave and free.
So precious! so rare!
Your Beauty.

O Gentle giant of the deep;
Yet, when I see you
I must weep.
Shall the very ones
Whom you be friend;
Bring about your
untimely end?

Metzger

Untitled

Hungry for Fat Burger
pull in
in your big old car
feeling so blue
alone and cruel
out walks the beggar begging
My pity has no change
no time
Beggar, junkie, thief
he has sold his pride
he follows you
plies his trade
he invades your space
gives your anger pace
yet in his eyes
your well fed pain
seems small
You are generous
in your silence
You leave him a fry.

Michael Bogert

Untitled

they pick their noses,
put on makeup,
do their hair,
talk on a phone,
eat their breakfast,
lunch or dinner,
they even do their bills,
sign papers,
do their taxes!,
hum a tune,
sing a song,
yell at their kids,
yell at their spouses,
or just yell,
at the car next to them.
why don't drivers...
...just drive?

Teenah

The Statue

Soft marble of countless steps
Puts you above all crowd
Stately figure in robes of stone
Noble head so bowed.

What are your thoughts year by year?
What do those wise eyes see?
Trouble ahead? War in sight?
Or peace for land and sea?
Do you mind that your hands are tied?
To stop all country strife
To strive again. To fight again
You give another life?
You must be tired of watching
Humdrum human affairs
Yet you sit so gravely.
Atop those countless stairs

J. L. Rolston

Disillusioned

Creation of reality
Question of morality
Souls our immortality
Death but one finality

Mallets of jurisdiction
Separation and division
Savior through benediction
Hands of fate listen

Memories play the jester
To torment and pester
Wander through the nether
Persecuted forever

Unearthly revolution
Mastering illusion
Battling this intrusion
Ungotten resolution

Renee N. Porrett

Knowledge

Why is the sky blue?
Questioned a child.
I do not know,
Replied the adult.

Why is the grass green?
Inquired a child.
I do not know,
Answered the adult.

What do you know?
Asked a child.
Everything,
Retorted the adult.
Vanessa Leerskov

Snow

Snow on the mountains-
  Quiet, majestic,
  Untouched by man,
Fills me with awe,
  and reverence,
  and peace.

Snow in the country,
  Quiet, homey,
  Snowed-in Coziness,
Fills me with peace,
  and contentment,
  and quiet happiness.

Snow in the city,
  Slush, icy roads,
  short tempers,
Fills me with anxiety,
  and apprehension,
  and isolation.
   Mildred P. Mundale Blom

Aegean Storm-Calm

The wine-dark sea
Rages—
But tear-drops
Of healing rain
Plunge
Into the troughs
Of white-capped
White, wind-whipped
Waves—

And my weeping—
Heals
My soul sea.
   Robert Riggs Brewster

Earth

Smell the new dawn of fresh dewed earth
Rich and pungent from years of sweat
Nurturing seeds of fragrant form
Bringing forth substance

Dig with your toes
Feel the grains beneath your feet
Hold it in your palm
Letting it seep from your fingers
Back from which it comes

Leaving behind a mark of color
Cool to the touch
Richness of spirit
Embrace of darkness and life
   S. V. White-Talbert

I Am Always There

In the spring - I am the gentle
  raindrops falling on your face.
In summer - I am the rays of
  sun shining on your face.
In autumn - I am the countless
  leaves blowing in your face.

In winter - I am the glistening
  snowflakes melting on your face.

Through all the seasons - I am
  always there.

Just feel my presence, I am
  every where.
   Margie Blanchard

The Rose

A little dew drop
Ran down a rose's petal
In the morning light.

Later in the day
As the sky was turning
A brilliant shade of
Blue, the rose almost
Seemed to sigh as the day
Grew near its end.

As the sky turned pink
The rose folded its red
Petals and silently seemed
To go to sleep. In the
Distance as the sun sank low,
You could see a silent smile
Across the sun's face as the
Rose slept quietly.
   Vanessa Revis

Rising Above The Waters

Looking ahead I see you,
  rising above the waters.
Over and about you swim,
  left and right with vigor.

Jolting, bolting, comes the lightning,
  Boom, boom, comes the thunder.
Then with a sudden chill you
  feel a burst of energy.

Over, and over, you rock the waves,
  trying to find a way out.
Bursting through the cracks,
  grabbing for a gulp of air.

Sunlight pours in,
  and you catch the ray
    and pull on it,
      as if it were a rope.
Pulling, and pulling,
  you bring yourself up
    and touch the shore below you!
   Lynn Powell

Thanks In Advance

There's no need to wait for an answer,
Or Your divine intervention,
For me to Thank You with all my heart,
And praise Your loving action.

You will consider all my choices,
For every trivial request,
Show me which are the wrong ones,
And help me choose the very best.

My experience with You has taught me,
When lost in a hopeless situation,
Pray, and Trust explicitly in You,
For the assured joyous summation.

So, Thank You in advance for everything,
And all the happiness coming,
You will always be my Provider,
Of Peace, Harmony, and Loving.
   V. Panagos

A Lesson In Magic

Magic sprouts the word that calls
Release.
Few will hear her speak
As fear clamps most souls
Not to be.
Magic wanders
And travels into new places
Asking the soul to be.
She (magic) is as graceful
As a pulsating dance
Inviting
All that you have
Come to be.
Magic comes in strange arrangements
Confusing life with reality.
She (magic) poses well.
Images remain strong -
We go.

   Margaret Penn Mills

Sunset Splendor

  Oh foam - lapping at my feet;
    pure, white, tatted lace.
  Oh seaspray - wet, lashing at
    my face - while out beyond -
  purple billows - clouds at rest;
  devoid of the sky of azure blue;
  giving into sunset's darkened hue.
    Ah! but if I could hold
  your golden splendor to my breast -
    never to watch your beauty
    as it fades into the West.
   Lucille Waite D'Eramo

Insight

Look
Out beyond the barriers of reality
Go inside yourself
See your birth
View your life
Imagine your death
Do your eyes hurt?
Strained past any emotional capacity
Knowing that your little existence
Means Nothing
   R. D. Eiring

What Can I Do

What can I do when my best efforts are ignored?
There's nothing I can do except continue to try,
Nothing I can do except silently cry,
Nothing I can do except wonder if he understands,
Nothing I can do — 'cause I just can't give up my man.
Can someone please tell me if it hurts him the way it does me?
He refuses to tell me what's on his mind.
I'm standing in the distance so far behind.
I don't think it hurts him in the same way.
He keeps his emotions hidden away.
Shall there be a tomorrow or will this end what we've shared?
I don't know anymore if we'll make it.
I'm not happy and it's so hard to fake it.
I just don't believe this can be the end,
But I don't know if my soul can mend.
What's left to do since I can't fall out of love?
I could never walk away.
I wish it were yesterday.
I don't know if there's anything to look forward to,
And I really wish I knew what to do.

Zuton Green

Feelings

The air is so quiet and still
These days are the best time to express how you feel
You may feel all warm and cozy
You may feel sad but act all rosy
Just remember your best feelings
Don't remember old banana peelings
When you remember those
Don't cry and get a runny nose
Smile until your face starts to hurt
Just smile even if you get hurt or fall in the dirt
People will smile back if you smile all the time
Instead of looking like you just ate a lime
Remember! Good feelings are the best of all
So when you feel sad remember those and you'll feel all strong and tall.

Suzanne McClelland

Janette

I look around my place and see these things,
These things I call reminders.
Your clothes hanging next to mine,
The picture of us together,
The cards you sent to me.
All these little things remind me of the love
We share between us,
The energy we generate when we are together,
The warmth I receive when I look into your eyes,
The happiness I feel when I'm in your arms.
These things remind me we are separated
Only by distance, not by dreams.
These things remind me that one day, some day
We will be one, separated no more.
I look forward to that day
With great happiness in my heart,
But until then I have these things,
These things I call reminders.

Kent Magnuson

Ecstasy

Your fingers move across my skin
To places they have never been.
Touch me, my love, again and again;
 It is ecstasy.

Your lips meet mine with a passionate kiss;
Take me, my love, I can no longer resist.
I realize now what I have always missed:
 You are ecstasy.

Yvonne McDonald

'Til Death Do Us Part

Two people united in a love so divine,
 They are bounded together in heart, soul and mind.
Standing at the altar and letting us see,
 They trust in the words "Will you marry me?"
Sharing feelings which no one can sever,
 Promising to love for now and forever.
Knowing their lives will change as of now,
 While they are holding hands and exchanging vows.
Holding each other so gently, yet tight,
 Anticipating loving and caring all night.
Slowly stopping to feel their hearts,
 As they vow to each other,
"'Til Death Do Us Part."

Kenneth V. Torres

Dreams

I wish one day all my dreams will come true
They are dreams of joy and happiness,
And of people I once knew.

Like Martin Luther King's many dreams
Of no more racial abuse,
I dream of life without many hurting screams.

They are dreams of peace and love.
I dream that no more young bodies
To be carried away, by men wearing a white glove.

I dream of no more crime,
But instead I dream of people gathering,
And having a peaceful time.

Other dreams are of life without drugs.
Instead of teens giving them out,
They give out hugs.

Some of my dreams are of people I never knew,
But they are dreams of warless time.
I hope one day they all come true.

Kimberly Joy Baumruck

The Religion In Your Heart

Don't think that Buddha, Christ, Mo-ham-med in the church.
They are in your heart and mind
heart tells you to do good
mind tells you where is the light.

When you know what is the good
and you see where it is the light
Buddha, Christ, Mo-ham-med
near you, in you, save your life!

Don't find Buddha, Christ, Mo-ham-med
when hatred is in your heart
and dark is in your mind
they are far from you who is hostile!

Buddha, Christ, Mo-ham-med
ready in your heart and your mind
don't find them in the church
when love out of your heart and light out of mind!

Buddha, Christ, Mo-ham-med
you can't find them anywhere
let worship them in your mind and heart
by what you do people good and what you share...

Phuc Nguyen

Cold Memories

Others before you have been removed from my heart.
They are locked away in my mind—
Like a shut off room.

A cold draft when opened,
But quickly shut because of the chill.

Not to be opened again,
Until...
Another memory needs to be stored.

Renae Kirk

Carpe Diem

Feeling the heartache of yesterday and today.
They are out of reach but you have more to say.
Living with the guilt and the pain.
Some days it hurts so bad you think you're going insane.

Your loved one has passed over to the great beyond.
The love of a parent and child, no one can break that bond.
You may not have gotten to say your goodbyes.
Not many do when a loved one dies.

Cherish each moment you are with them today.
Time will not wait for you, it will slip away.
Tell them how you love them and never leave mad.
If you do this you will always be glad.

When the time comes for them to pass away.
They will already know what you had to say.
So live each day as if it were your last.
In later years you will have no regrets of your past.

Ray Shain

Kids

Kids are such a great delight,
They go strong from day to night.
From smiles of joy in the morning light,
To their hugs and kisses late at night.

Some with blue eyes and dimpled chin,
Some like to scowl and some like to grin.
Some are fat and some are thin,
But to make a family, kids are how you begin.

Kids will pull your hair and punch your nose,
Kick your shins and runner your hose.
When you're in a hurry, they're three steps behind
And when you are weary, to the steeps they will climb.

Soon they're grown with decisions to make,
Which college to choose, which person to date.
A life of their own, their future at stake
"Seek the Lord's will before you graduate."

Just what would this world be like,
If kids were seldom in sight.
But thank the Lord for his insight,
To give us kids, oh what delight!

Ruth Hawley

Eyes

There is a sadness in your eyes;
They tell the truth there are no lies.
Even though there is a smile upon your face;
I see the hurt and feel the pain that lay deep inside some place.
They tell of hopes and wants and basic
needs that never quite come true;
But the smile upon your face some how carries you through.
There is a sadness in your eyes;
They tell of love that is given to someone that never really tries.
My fondest hope and prayer for you;
Is that some day I will see the smile
in your eyes that is upon your face.

Richard Gute

Purple Rocks

Purple rocks fall from the sky
They hit the ground in silence
So much that creates them suddenly overloads
The pain explodes into rocks
Purple rocks that mean so much
That represents so much
All in a small rock
That hurts so much
All in a small rock
That changes so much
All in a small rock, a small cracked purple rock
Leaking and contaminating me with violence
Insane confusion runs circles in my mind
Silence... Pain...Silence...
Far up in the sky I see falling rocks
Then love and hate hit me as one
I hear silent sounds of rocks on the ground
Pain...Silence...Pain...
Death become life and life becomes death
And purple rocks become tears

Thea Dodds

Untitled

Skin and Bones, Skin and Bones
They speak to me in dulcet tones
Of people who are so gauntly thin
They hardly use the chair they're in
Who never suffer from indigestion
and laugh uproariously at the mere suggestion
of girdles and the like
Skin and Bones, Skin and Bones
Oh, tell me friend, in saccharine tones
That someday I would slimly slip
Into size twelve and gaily trip
The light fantastic without a care
As to bottles and diapers, or who is there
to watch the little tyke
Skin and Bones, skin and Bones
Your talk of those just skin and bones
Droppeth at my feet like petals fragrant
When I, my friend, am eight months pregnant

Sarah Jane Hill

Chestnut Blossoms

The candles stand on the chestnut tree in all their spring delight,
They stand so very firm and tall displaying the chestnut might.
If we could stand as erect and tall and shed but love and kindness,
We wouldn't have the dread disease of human racial blindness.

We'd understand the human span is just a stepping stone,
A training course along the way toward our journey home.
If it be true, we come again our problems to work out,
Then like the candles on the tree we'd better blossom out.

But look into the blossoms deep, and to your great surprise,
You'll find the colors of the races, patterned side by side.
Nature blends them all the time, her beauty to display,
'Tis only man who cannot blend, as nature does in May.

Mildred G. Arndt

The Lost Child

It seems as if only but yesterday;
This child was getting all in your way.
And now you don't have the child at all,
You feel as if you've run into a brick wall.
Your heart ache to see once more;
Your child running through your front door.
If only you had kept him in sight,
Maybe he could be with you tonight.
The pain of having him abducted away,
Gets more drastic from day to day.

Rema Flowers

Strive You Must

The worthwhile things never are simple
They test ones worth, cause many a wrinkle
The fruit that hangs low, that's easy to get
Just isn't the fruit to test man's wit
The things he must have are hard to achieve
To see them fulfilled he really must believe
The ache that he feels and the sweat on his brow
Lend little satisfaction as he pushes the plow
But 'tis the man with faith who somehow succeeds
To gather the fruit for his work and his deeds
He feels fulfillment for the work he has done
And reason to be for the race he's run.

Ken Weatherhead

Church Auction

As I was riding through town with my last week's pay, I noticed a sign,
They were auctioning off the old church today.
Ten miles down the road, that sign stuck in my mind. I turned around
And headed back for the peace I knew I would find.
That old church was callin' me—
I stopped and walked in to see what I could see.
As I went inside, the sun came streaming down, through the holes in
   the roof,
Over old trash laying around. A plaque said built in 1824 - -
There were stained glass windows and brick upon the floor.
Pews were stacked up against the wall, built of a fine oak, the podium
Stood cracked and tall. A dusty torn Bible lay open, in the back
was the Family tree. As I read on, it was a walk through history.
I could hear in my mind stories the walls had to tell, and see in the
   faded print
The time Jimmy fell down the old well. It mentioned name by name, All
who cleared the lands, the people who put everything into place with
Their loving hands. I knew then, the church had to be mine. I had to
buy it. Gather the people, that's the peace I was to find, remaking
   a bit of time.

Kerry Brooke

You And I

Watch me laugh, watch me cry
They're both the same, you'll see
We are one, you and I
Your pain I've had to suffer
One thought at a time
Someone must feel the pain

Come, chance a walk with me
I'll show you all I can
If you've the courage to see
I often feel alone when you're near
We should spend more time, you and I
Come, I'll show you what only others can see

Remember there was a time when
Fears we had we left behind, and we danced
It seems the more we learn we
Lose track of the time
Come, together let us hold the light
Keep the flame, we can't let us in this world remain
We'll find the way back, you and I

J. Matt Ferris

Fly

I wish I could fly.
To a place where people don't die.
Flying high into the sky,
Watching all the clouds go by.
I wish that I could bring her back.
Because it's her love we all lack.
I remember happy times,
But right now they're filled with; sad goodbyes.

Sara Lynn Wisnewski

Parents

Parents are your Mother and Father
They're people kids are suppose to bother,
They give you money and stuff you with food,
And they scold you when you're acting rude,
When you get in trouble there's no doubt,
That they'll send you to your room when you pout,
They take you places you don't want to go,
Like to a museum or a ballet show,
They might spank you when you're bad,
And teach you a lesson you've never had,
So be good for your parents and respect them too,
And when you get older they'll respect you too.

Mary Beth Klauck

It's Time

The time has come for the right
        things to be done.
We may have past up the fight, but,
    the battle is yet to be won.
There's more to life than the color
        of ones skin.
It's not what falls on the outside
    but, what falls deep within.
While we are worrying about what will happen
    when a person's beauty fades.
We should be worrying about the people
    around us, those dying of AIDS.
It's time for all the racism to stop
    and for trivial things to end.
In order to win the battle that is to
    be won, all races must blend.
The spreading of AIDS, gang violence,
    and other nonsense must stop.
It's time for us to win the battle
and it's time for the last tears to drop.

Latrita Bradford

By The Ocean Side

At night I like to sit by the ocean side
Thinking about life and watching the tide.
I relate the rhythm of its rolling waves
to the timing of troubles and how I behave.
There is a lot to learn by watching the sea
Watch it enough and you'll find the key
That life is a rhythm much like the ocean
That good times and bad must stay in motion
For if they were to ever become still
The foundation beneath, it would surely kill.
Reminders like this, God give us to see
That the tides of life must ever be.
Sometimes it rough and you think you'll drown
But wait it out 'cause it will calm down.
I'm thankful for the time I have by the sea,
And reminders like these that are given to me
As I sit at night by the ocean side
Thinking about life and watching the tide.

G. M. Sexton

Star Meet

Chartless, fate's stars press on with relentless drive
To an unknown immortality, crossing parenthetically other
Orbits in their pursuit down destiny's rocky pathway.
In mortal years our chance is once, ne'er more than twice,
To meld our fates and follow then a common course. Such
Blessed break from mundane things is happiness enough.
The marks of gentle touch and the perfume of their breath
Tell of numberless unions of mind and heart. Some,
Indeed, are wedded for all time, no less.

Roy Cochrane

Homecoming

Thomas Wolf said you can't go home again
This, I'm glad to say, is not literally true-
For if a family's love and presence is of most import,
Then home is the place for you.

As mighty ships twist and turn upon the seas,
The great North comes shining through—
Saying: "Follow me brave Pilgrims
To a place of fresh renew."

It is mighty Altair in the northern sky,
A beacon of hope and faith,
A star with a magical aura—-
Leading men to an ocean that's safe.

When the going gets tough for the pioneers,
Civilization is the star that they feel—
Lending a sense of law and order—
A kind of prosperity that heals.

But the greatest to follow is in the east,
A light of eternal love,
God's power: both tall and majestic—
Leading home every white dove!

Mark David Hickerson

The Man-Made Famine In Ukraine

It happened in 1932-33.
This is the truth of what I experienced personally.

The forced collectivization of agriculture began
in the year nineteen hundred twenty nine.
In the villages of Podillia.
I was a student at that time in Kamianets-Podilsk.
Most of the students lived in dormitories and
ate three meals daily at the dining hall.
But at the beginning of 1932 the dining was closed.
All peasants who did not want to join collective
farms had been arrested and sent to Siberian camps.
Students received 100 gr. of bread made from millet,
and to get this, they had to stand in line for hours.
When dining reopened the students were given
one bowl of soup (slop) a day just water
with a few pieces of sugar beets swimming around.
Because of a lack of nourishment I became sick with
scurvy, my teeth were all loose and my gums bled.
The disease was in its third stage,
which brings a person close to death.
Every day the Dentist massaged my gums and
I ate garlic and lemons a lot, only this saved my life.
When bread arrived at the store,
the shoving was terrible, because everyone was hungry.
Many suffered a heart attack being smothered.
I even heard that some people were killed and eaten
because the starvation was so great.
It is only a very short account of the terrible
Man-Made Famine of 1932-33 in the Ukraine.
It is impossible to recall all details because
there were millions who suffered and died.

Margarita Borzakiwska

My Wish

My wish is to have a lemonade with ice
  to drink with my own man, that'd be nice.
My wish is to have food I love everyday,
  if that could only be my way.
My wish is to soar with the birds up high,
  because their freedom is way up in the sky.
My wish is to ride in the mountains on horseback,
  or maybe take a long hike with only a backpack.
My wishes could go on forever,
  but would I dare stop them...never.

Phaedra Meyer

Untitled

I tell myself how important I am
Tho no one knows but me
I tell myself I am a pillar of strength
Standing straight and tall for all to see

I tell myself I shall not be sad
Then why do tears flow so easily
I say to myself it might have been
The saddest phrase - I must hold up my chin

I say to myself a winner would
Yet I know how fragile life is
I tell myself I shall always be
Then Mother Nature laughs at me

Nobody promised me that life would be easy
So I tell myself be brave old girl
Meet each moment with decision and firmness
Laughter an exercise in tears

Lilian Smith

Shades Of Darkness

I believe there are many shades of darkness
  those reflections of light that fade from view
  that hidden collage of black and gray within us all
I feel the colors of life are a complete facade
  hiding the true dimness of our souls
  preventing us from knowing our true selves
I see the hoax of our every day rituals
  blinding us from the truth of an absolute death
  continuous lies to prevent our inevitable curiosity
I realize now of our meager existence as meaningless
  only a pretense to the shadows of our minds
  a subduing of the supernatural primal being
I understand that to survive this monstrous atrocity
  we must seek the darkest depths of our subconscious
  everyone must find in themselves the safe shadows
I hope that we all may find that inner sanctity
  searching forever the various degrees of solitude
  existing only to find peace within the shadows of darkness

Timothy G. Power

Nothing

I walk with my head up high
Though I have nothing
I'm bleeding from a wound that will never heal
All I have is nothing; it is my only friend and enemy
I look through my haze of gray and see nothing
I reach for roses, all I get is thorns
I reach for love, all I get is scorn
Nothing is a pain, deep and dark
Sometimes dull, sometimes sharp.
  Always there
I let no one in my garden of dead hopes
All I have is nothing and nothing else...
  But a dead skeleton whose soul has long ago died.

Kristy Hidalgo

I Too

  I too, wish I can be the world and
travel as far as no man has gone before.
  I too, wish I can be as brave as a lion
and conquer the volume of his roar.
  The courage and excitement that I'm
building up inside,
  will it ever come out?
  shall it always hide?
  I too, will never know?

Tara Polansky

Shadow

There is a shadow lurking we do not know
Though it slowly appears more as we grow old
Yet we ignore, for older generations there's more
To stand between us and the shadow at the door

When our grandparents leave this life,
The shadow is a little more strong
Still we ignore, for another generation
Keeps it away from our hearts door

Then as our parents start passing away
It looms larger with each passing day
For at last we realize there's none left
To keep us from that shadow's grasp

The shadow now is entirely ours
We can not lose it, no matter how try
For soon it will claim us with its might
To take us on to another life.

   Linda R. Houston

The Unwelcome Visitor

Death is a visitor, so ugly and Plain
Though seldom invited, he comes just the same.
He makes no apologies be it early or late
When you look up and behold him there at your gate.
He's totally unannounced as strangers often are,
but you can't turn him away, he's travelled so far.
Don't look so surprised he says without Mirth,
Why you know I've been expected since the day
of your birth. Yes it's true I agree, but please
tell me why because, I've never accepted the
fact I must die. Why, it's simple he said
and this time he grinned, some have to
leave cause there's more coming in.

   Winfred J. Henderson

"I Loved You In My Fashion"

Having seen you again did wonders for my heart
Though the air between us was very dense.
Your face had beautiful lines full of art
Guess they came with experience.
As I grew up I never said the words I meant to
Now you're gone and I'm left alone.
Always knew your love was true
Never thought I'd be on my own.
How long should I cry for you?
Do you even want me to?
I'll talk to you every night my way
And hope to see you again someday.
Your life ended much too soon and that I'll never ration.
What would it have meant to you to hear me say...
  "I LOVED YOU IN MY FASHION"?

   Marcos A. Suarez Jr.

The Time Has Come

The time has come, the master's calling,
time for changes quite appalling

Dispute brings sorrow aggression rises,
cruel hatred brings surprises

Corrupted worlds too much to mention,
always brings great grief and tension.

Prosperous generations have come to an end
Destitute and criminal we're expected to defend

What have we to forfeit, what have we to gain,
but a world of broken promises and shattered dreams.

   Shauna Andris

Wish You Were Here

Woke up this morning and thought of you,
thought of the things we used to do.
Don't think that I've lost touch with you,
Cause I still love you, I still do.

Turned on the radio and our song was playing,
"I wish you were here" was all I kept saying.
I laid back down and stared at the ceiling,
I wish I could tell you just how I was feeling.

Lately I haven't been here, I know,
but it doesn't mean my love don't show.
My mind and thoughts are on us forever,
I won't stop loving you, no, not ever.

I saw you today, around the way
and wanted to call your name,
but I didn't because I know
that you don't feel the same.

As the day went on I hurt more and more,
I cried so much I couldn't cry anymore.
the tears kept falling, one by lonely one,
by the end of the day, there was none.

   Tara J. Tavares

Untitled

I looked and looked in store after store,
Through at least a hundred cards or more,
To find one that was fit to read,
Yet one that was fitting, from me, indeed.

I had no luck in finding one
That was written the way I would like it done.
So I decided that for better or for worse
To jot down my thoughts and put them in verse.

At writing letters I'm not very good
And do not write as often as I should.
That doesn't mean that I think not
Of those within the family I've got

However, there are times one must drop a line
To reach out to those not feeling so fine.
My thoughts are with you as you struggle to heal
Though it's difficult for us to know how you feel.

Please rest assured that you are on my mind
As through each passing day I wind -
From task to task along the way,
Wishing you well throughout each day.

   Ray Krieg

Modern

Balancing on the word "modern"
  thrills—as to peer unbraced
  down a cutting edge
  through civilizations
Until, forced by the mountain
  of history reaching as much above
  as below, the illusion of end implodes.
The future is resolved by my climb
  into features as new and unknown
  as courage allows;
the way up neither more bleak nor terrible
  than the ages behind:
  by study and challenge
  all footholds won.
So, as I stand to my ancestors,
  thus my successors will to me:
  the present—embraced—is not alone.

   M. R. Lauer

A Voiceless Whisper

Tears creep, slowly with trepidation
Through the coarse ridges and etched lines
carved on my pale cheeks.
Hollowness and fear run through my veins like poison.
I lose my senses and I grasp at my heart
Only to be strong by its coldness.
My legs shrink beneath me as I sink into a bottomless pit,
My frail hands only to make
small scrapes on the cave's wall
I reach out to find you, to bring you closer...
Only to feel the emptiness I carry around.
Anger flares inside me like a glimmering flame.
A harsh reality pangs at my heart.
Death is too final and sudden, I often wonder... Why you?
Why did you have to have it carved on your tombstone?
I stand here now... looking at what they call your new home.
I know you've long escaped this world of
heartache, and entered a world of eternal paradise.
But I often wonder If it should have been
me to lead you the way.

    Susan Emrich

The Day Before Spring

The crocus pushes its head
   through the dirt and slush anxious to see the sun.
The ice jams the engorged
   river rushing forward with nowhere to run.
The groaning world awaits
   another season and its blossoming moment.
All is yet dimmed by clouds ready to abdicate.
   Nothing remains dormant.

You are out here singing
   your spring song silently watching the view.
Like an embrace, the breeze
   hushes my screams inside - the sun closer than you.
Scanning the unknown, you see the hidden side of moon's
   astral Plain of Plato.
I cannot even see a petal unfolding in its blossom.
   I know it's there, never fatal.

    Sally K. Wheeler

Wondrous Peace

I take a peaceful walk;
through the quiet, untamable woods.
I see a newborn fawn
approach a calm, flowing creek,
to drink the cold, clear, glistening water.

To hear the crinkle of leaves beneath my feet;
I see the sun shinning through the clouds,
and the trees swaying in the breeze.
It is like a picture from a child's storybook,
except with no beginnings and no endings.

The flowers bloom in the open field nearby;
the birds softly sing from the treetops,
and the fawn watches and listens with delight.
I wish this peace could last forever,
but I know its memory will last a lifetime.

    Lisa Jennings

Life

   The world is turning as I stand still. I watch my Dad as he
throws another steak on the grill.
   I wonder what is life as I live it day-by-day, why are some
people straight and why are others gay.
   As I hold the hand of the one I love, I wonder, is there really a
world above.
   When we die do our spirits die or do we just get reincarnated as
another guy.
   So many people have lots of theories of what happens after life,
but we will never know until we meet the Reaper's sharp knife.
   I've thought of taking my life but I listened to these words of my
dad "unless you live your live, you will never know if it will turn
out good or bad".
   So live in your own world, and as you want to , say who you are and
just be you.

    Nathan O'Neill

Life Would End

   When I look back over the years, I can never think of a
time better than when I'm with you.
   The sight of you makes my eyes light up.
   I love watching you, the way you walk, the way you smile,
or the way you rub your hands together when you're nervous.
   Nothing in this entire world
could make me love you more than I do now.
   You bring out the brightest sunrise
and the most beautiful sunset that can last
a million years and beyond.
   The stars shine every night just for you.
   The moon rises high just so it
can see the way you bring on morning.
   The flowers bloom to greet you.
   I bring the love that is more powerful,
more stronger and deeper than any...
   If you weren't here, life would end.
   There would be no sunrise, or stars,
or moons, or flowers to greet you.
   Life would simply end if there was no you.

    Missy Leider

Gone But Not Forgotten

The day has come that we all had dread
Time has come for certain God has made her bed
We cannot argue about
What has been done and said
God had planned it this way
This is the way it has to be

She's in her new home now
no more pain her body lies in an
open grave, but her soul still remains
When the day Christ comes back
she'll rise again beautiful as ever.
No more tears, no more loss
for the people who loved her dearly
will not forget, but will always
have one regret

When we say mean things
When we get mad, then
Something bad happens and
you feel you're to blame, but always remember
there will always be glory in her name.

    Kristy Cheeseman

June

Blessed June, month of Summer's borning.
Time of dimpling rains, singing tree frogs,
Night crawlers, the cooing doves of morning,

Of violets, dandelions, the smell of meadows awake.
June, for proms, gardenias, delicious girls.
A moonlit dance hall on the lake.

June, month of corn to plow and wheat to reap.
Picnics, class photos on sunny steps.
The miracle of cool sneakers and little sleep.

Time for hammocks, banging screen doors,
A quiet canoe among dragonflies in a perfect outdoors.
 Paul A. Marriott

Goodbye

I am watching the rain fall down,
Tiny drops skittering upon the ground,
After a while it becomes a bore,
'Cause I'm crying just once more.

Clouds churning from white to gray,
Since you've left it's rained everyday.
No more happiness or tears of joy,
Being just now, I'm a lonely boy.

Only wishing I could've enhanced,
That tremendous love and beautiful romance.
Now that you've gone my heart is cold,
To start a new, I must be bold.

Now the rain is finally gone,
Leaving my spirit down and my heart torn,
Thanks to you my life was shattered,
All my dreams and hope, broken and battered.

God has blessed me a peak of the sun,
It seems my life has just begun!
To start again all over anew,
This time better without you.
 Steven Louis Durr

The Child

There is a child that walks beside me in this world.
Tired and ashamed she cries to ease her pain
Dressed all in rags, no shoes to wear.
Her hair no longer looks beautiful and fair.
She has no one to hug to hold
She lives in an alley where
the cold wind blows.
Bruises from being beaten are all over her face.
She has no more beauty nor any grace.
But some where beneath all her heartaches and tears
a smile awaits to appear!
 Sabrina Martin

The Price Of Concrete

Why Mr. Doe do you remake the world
 to be a place devoid of any life?
The flag of revolution you've unfurled
 and through the side of God you've thrust your knife.
Don't tell me that I lie, I know the price
 of living for today and not a care
For kids whose only toys are rats and lice
 or lungs that strain to breathe this dirty air.
The world becomes one giant litter heap.
The rivers flow in graves of oily slime.
The green that's left will bow before the sweep
 of industry.
Will money buy us time?
But you don't care, no, you won't be concerned.
There are roads to build and dollars to be earned.
 Sharon M. Withers

Trail Of Tears

They walk through rain and snow,
To a land they did not know.
Guide me Jehovah they sang unto thee.
Healing water of medicine come forth to me.

Guide me great spirit as I walk on this earth they did say.
We'll reach our destination soon one day.
I am weak but thou are strong.
Please let our days on earth be long.

Help us our guiding master.
Please help us through our great disaster.
As they stood on the bank of the river.
They wondered how the two lands will differ.

When they finally met their Destination.
Then came in other Indian nations.
Always we will sing praises unto thee.
Love, Help, and take your best care of me.

On this journey they didn't show their fears.
As they sang their praise on the Trails of Tears.
 Tracy A. Conrad

Human Power #1

Qualifications let there be known,
to all who seek a life well owned.
For dirt, does well in ancient ruins,
the spackle of patches are only temporarily sown.
From birth to baby and child-like tendencies,
we seek abundance of amenities.
Adolescence thus do us part from tyrants or
gypsies in extremities, of which we do not know exist,
in our minds of substances.

Try and be a worldly thing,
it goes to show that in pain we sing.
Sing to those who only show,
how the pain always slowly goes.
But in the midst of heavenly life,
some come home with a swift delight.

Show me the way of the young human, person in dreams yet to be,
but life in spirit, dreams and memories.
This brings the body of the adult, neglected,
to the world of hope, praise, and unrejected.
Live on human power, live on.
 Richard V. Cecco

The Haunting

For Bruce

I lay here alone in an unfamiliar bed
Thoughts of you next to me vivid in my head

Miles away I'm haunted, so real it seems
For I cannot control how you dominate my dreams

I toss, I turn, no comfort I find
Why, I ask, are you embedded in my mind

I wake, still affected by the images I've seen
Frustrated, I realize it's only been a dream

What do you feel, do I invade your sleep
Would you tell me or have a secret to keep

But I'll take a chance at exposing my soul
For I want no regrets when time takes its toll.
 Susan M. Hollenbeck

"To Be A Slave"

To be a slave was hard
To be a slave was sad
To be a slave was murder
To be a slave was no freedom
To be a slave was no choice
To be a slave was no fairness
To be beaten was painful
To be a slave without a dream
To be a slave without hope
To be a slave without a free life
To be a slave without a vote
To be a slave with hope, for future freedom!

Raquel Becker

The Final Hunt

Would that you were a wild animal
To be hunted, stalked, and slain mercilessly.
Quietly laying in wait, deep in the wet jungle,
Or far across the ocean of sand.
I am armed, clothed for battle.
My camouflage is superficial,
Yet undetectable by the beast.
I crawl so excruciatingly slowly
Heart beating through my skin, eyes aflame.
I have come far enough along to be stronger than the enemy.
I must now wait for the other to make his fatal mistake.
He will never run as quickly, climb so frantically
As the moment before death, the instant of sorrow.
And I will never need to lift my knife,
For he will have clawed out his own bleeding heart.

Marjorie L. Jones

That Is Why

Love is the heart, soul, and mind — entwined
To be one.
With sex alone,
A heart has not found a home;
But when the heart has found its home—
Our soul will no-more roam.
For now one with the mind—
   It will remind...
What in life is of greater value?
   For love cannot be bought
at any price.
Or forced with any device.
So priceless it is—
   And God alone has put it there.
That is why we care.
   That is why.

Marylin Cynamon

Nature

It's the trees blowing in the wind and pleasantly speaking
to each other with words of gladness and calmness,
like a young mother talking to her newborn infant and
giving words of comfort.
It's the leaves stirring in the wind and doing a dance of
happiness on the ground,
like a children in the dance recital.
It's the beautiful blue lake flowing peacefully downhill
like flowing water from a faucet.
It's the sparkling campfire that fills everyone's insides
with thoughts of joy and happiness.
It's the rare rainfall that showers the world with love and peace
like a sprinkler watering a beautiful lawn.

Isn't Nature wonderful!!!

Sarah Pickham

Grandma Jane

Grandma Jane had plan
To catch a young virile man,
She'd shine up her shoes
And fix her dyed hair
To go to the store that sold men there
With a minimal fee or so she thought
Is all it takes for a man to get caught
Quite a selection she said to the owner
May I have one just for a loaner?
One to wine me and dine me
And take me to church
One that won't want to borrow my purse
I don't mind if he's round about
But he must have money for I like to eat out
He must not have whiskers or pick his nose
But an aroma of old spice and wear nice clothes;
There was a man said the owner with a look of dismay
But it seems that yesterday
He past away.

Laura Fariello

The Final Goodbye

This is for you Dad, you meant so much,
To every person, that you did touch,
I write these words, with so much sorrow,
But I know you'd say, to live for tomorrow,
It's hard to understand, the reason why,
We didn't have the chance, to say good-bye,
But I guess, the Lord has His reasons,
And our feelings will change, throughout the seasons,
There will be days, bad and good,
We will be strong, like you know we should,
You were taken, to the Heavens above,
But left our hearts, with so much love,
You may be gone, and out of sight,
But left your courage, so we could fight,
When you were here, you had so much to give,
And in our hearts, you'll always live,
So many memories, that we can share.
Just knowing you love us, and always will care,
So Good-Bye to you, our beloved Dad,
Cause you're the best, anyone could of had.

Kari Bladow

I Forever Pray

I forever pray for a guiding light
To faithfully lead me each day and night
As I walk along life's rocky roads
Carrying many a heavy loads.

I forever pray for wisdom and grace
So that I may successfully face
Any tribulations that are sent my way
As I meet up with society every day.

I forever pray to always be grateful
And for my heart to always be thankful
For any size blessing sent my way
In order to strengthen me every day.

I forever pray for a peaceful and healthy mankind
As I finally settle down to meditate and unwind
In hopes that my next fateful awakening
Will locate me among the loving and the living.

Regina M. Bilodeau

Decide And Choose

There comes a time in our life when we all must decide,
To follow the devil or choose to serve Christ.

A man is a being with choices to make,
Deciding which path he is going to take.

Although many will do just as they please,
Sitting around, like old withered trees.

Read your Bible and know it is true,
For the devil is real and he is after you.

He'll think of a way and he'll plot and he'll plan,
To take down every woman, child and man.

His tricks are the same day after day.
To make your eyes blind and lead you astray.

Maybe you'll believe it and maybe you won't,
But man's way leads to destruction and God's way don't!

Turn from your sins and all your ways,
Give God a chance and don't be afraid.

You see, Jesus gave all that he had,
And for this reason we all should be glad.

For the Kingdom of Heaven has been given to us.
To live one day when we are joined with Jesus!
    Mary Ann Morales

Sweet Song

Sing to me sweet sparrow, my morning friend, the song I'm trying
    to forget.
I sent her the petals of my heart, and she tore them apart.

What more can I do to be of her love, of her soothing eyes?
That I may be fulfilled.

It may never be enough, and I grow tired.
Tired of her and this newly strange place.

Sing me your song.
Sing me your song, and I will try to listen.

Seeking an answer to a question of which there may be none.
I had to know; I guess I do

And now, what do I do sweet warbler?
Your chipper song does not match my trodden heart - give me a clue

Can I be her friend? - see her and say hello
Not tonight my feathered friend.
Though you will return, probably, maybe, possibly, she won't

Wake me in the morning, note for note, like yesterday.
That I may hear the real song,
Keep me silent tonight, that I may refresh my memories of love.
    Mike Bly

Brother's Keeper

Ed dropped out of high school in 1969
to join the Army at seventeen,
then was ordered for Vietnam.

He knew the state wouldn't send him because
his big brother, Mike, already served and
the law prevents two brothers from
fighting in the same war together.

One month later, after the first tour
Mike signed up for a second time through,
knowing his experience had a better chance
to survive a second tour which stopped
his younger brother again from war.

When Mike came back home
"Thank you," was all Ed could muster
as they hugged at the airport in Portland.
    Tammy West

The Little Child

The little child left out always
To go and find her way.
No friends at home just hard times always
As her brother and sister pick on her constantly
With her long brown straight hair and her red skin
This little child tries to make it on her own.
She knows what's right for her
She's been down this road before
Using drugs to keep her dreams alive
And prostitution for love and money
The little child finds her way
Down that long and lonely road.
She's robbed like many times before,
But this time she is left alone,
Alone in a ditch, dead...
Her parents said nothing good would ever become of her
They dreamed her life to be like this
And your dreams always come true in the end...
    Sheila Sundheim

"Heaven's Playmate"

I want to remember back through the years
to happy childhood times that you were always
part of, and in which you will remain.

I want to remember back through the lean times
to the man that always stayed with the children
and played with the children, and I was a child.

I want to remember back through to the beginning
to black and white television, sit down dinners and
walks, that ended in long talks, on the front
steps in the sunshine.

I want to remember, back through all those years
to that childlike man, that no true child could resist.
When I think of you, I will remember those times
and I know that you are home now to stay,
and to forever play, with heaven's children.
    Raychelle E. Anderson

"If I Can Teach My Baby, My Son..."

If I, as a mother and woman can Teach my baby, my son, how
to hold a spoon to his mouth to eat, how to hold a glass of
water or milk to his mouth drink;

If I, as a mother and woman can Teach my baby, my son, how
to use the "potty", to tie his shoes, brush his teeth, comb
and brush his hair, to be well groomed and clean, to cook, to
do laundry, to keep house, to drive a car, to cross a street;
where to take a bus, a train or plane, to play ball, to play
tennis, to play golf, valley ball, and to swim, then; I can
Teach my baby, my son.

If I, as a mother and a woman can Teach my baby, my son, how to
speak, write, sing, dance, to learn the languages, English,
Spanish, French; to learn the Science, History, Music, then;
then I can Teach my baby, my son.

If I, as a mother and woman can Teach my baby, my son, to be
an obedient son, to honor and respect his father, mother,
sister, brother, grandparents, schoolteachers, school mates,
his neighbor, bag and do an errand for them, then; I can Teach
my baby, my son.
    Marcia M. Brunner

Washday On Bayshore Drive

Several brooms have I in assorted sizes
  to keep the sky spanking clean.
When the rains descend and the winds begin
  the trees are my cleaning team.
Dipping their branches in buckets of rain
  they begin their frenzied chore,
Roiling back and forth in exuberant swoops
  bending to the core.
The saplings, too, enter the fray
  not to be outdone.
They sweep with gusto, they laugh and play
  while looking for the sun.
Before I know it the work is complete;
  the brooms stand tall to dry.
I call out my thanks for the speedy job
  and behold a clean, blue sky!

    Kaye Laird

Waiting

Instrument has become a prop,
to late to drop to young to flop.

Starting at the floor because it's not the clock,
the shade is moving east to the land it is my goal to reach.
The earth is cold yet the hidden dust is molten;
so they say.

Scrape the dirt cakes from my retina with nails grown
long and yellow in some never ending curled spiral to make
dizziness of my affliction, or are you just some carnival freak?

The true joke is on me worshiping trees through their seasons
breathing in the marrow of my cerebral condition.
The digits increase and yet I am forever struck with ten.

    Robert J. Nines, Jr.

A Thank You From A Friend To Friends

Someone said a prayer for me today
To lighten the burden along the way:
Some days the pain is great, and the time long;
The nerves get frayed and the attitude is wrong.

The prayers of friends help smooth the path,
Ease the pain and cool the wrath.
The frazzled nerves and the spirits so low,
Some days, it seems, they line up in a row.

Thank you, Friends, Please continue to pray,
Your loving kindness, with God's help each day;
May negate the doctor's "No help for you".
"What you can't do for yourself, others will have to do".

    Sibyl E. Carle

The Ride Out To The Country

I lost someone on a ride out in the country, he meant so much to me.
I lost him in the beauty of the mountains, the animals, and the trees.
I tried to let him know that I was sad to see him leave.
But he could not see past my smile I kept or the laughter I did weave.
I wonder if he knows that we lost each other that ride,
or did he just clear his mind and show me not that side.
The ride was long and beautiful, we shared many things long the way.
But I still think we lost each other on that very day.
I stare at that picture day and night to look at what I lost.
It seems the beautiful country ride was yet the cost for what I lost.
The day will come to ride again, I have all things in tact.
I plan to regain just what I lost and yes that is a fact.
So country ride I look forward to, seeing you again, because
then I'll find just what I lost and that will be the end.

    Tisha M. Jones

Forever Friend

I promise thee to be a caring, gentle wife
To love you and to hold you for the rest of your life
Our happiness together, I swear will never end
Because I'm standing here holding the hand of my very best friend
  We'll build a memory
  As tall as the sky
  Caring, sharing, and dreaming
  As the years pass us by
And when we're old
Here's where I'll be
Because I'll love you forever
And I hope you'll always love me
  Who needs shining stars and oceans
  When I have a man like you?
  My darling you have made my life fulfilled
  And all my dreams come true
The sweetness of your tender touch
My friend I shall never miss
Because we've sworn our love my dear
And sealed it with a kiss.

    Lisa M. Henry

Sway

Come quickly—spare no speed
To me, oh lover, to me
With feathers like predators
Sway, sway, soar like you should
Past those melancholies who don't know love,
but wish they could.

Capture my malaise, interrupt my life,
Because you know you should
Some wish to be caged but awakened
Like the dying man,
Blind until the a 'las' sight

Rescue me, oh rescue me, lover from the night

Those who know right know this psalm
Lover come quickly I've waited too long.

    Robert Loftin Montgomerie

To Want

To want is to need
To need is to not have
To not have is poverty's seed
To seed poverty is to rave

To want is to desire
To desire is to lack
To lack, starts envy's fire
To envy's fire is no slack

To want is to crave
To crave is to hunger or thirst
To hunger and thirst is ok, if we behave
To want is o.k, just so it doesn't make the world worst

    Onyx W. Martin Sr.

Untitled

A spirit such as yours will never be
twisted or torn, but will soar through the
heavens, given a chance to be reborn.

The beauty you hold within will outshine the
sun and spread over the earth to
enlighten everyone.

Without the gifts you have given, many
lives would be in despair.
Fear not beautiful one, your time will be there.

    Lisa Lee Albanese

Success

Success to some is money, wealth and fame
To others, it is being first and winning the game
Others call it diamonds, furs, and many cars
And still others, it is homes, vacations and travelling afar

However, to miss the true meaning of what is success
Is to not live life to its fullest and at its best
For success is to know love, contentment and inner peace
Having God in your heart and happiness that will not cease

Success is to have the love of that special someone
It is hard work and pride in a job well done
Accomplishments attained and difficulties overcome
Success is a clear conscience, laughter and fun

But no matter what your definition of success may be
I think it is to love all, forgive all and be carefree
Many may not agree with your formula for success
Even though it is simple, laugh, love, and do your best

So no matter what you do or what the future may hold
You are only successful if you allow love to unfold
So forget money, wealth, cars, homes, and fame
Just laugh, love, be kind, forgive, treating all the same

    Patricia Cox Napoli

Untitled

    When I try,
To pretend I'm poor, everyone ignores me,
laughing at my problems, like it's something funny.
    When I try,
To pretend I'm rich, people try to use me,
even my best friends, all they want is money.
    And I wonder why?
If I was, born a baby, also crying and crying,
grew up, like the kids, also playing and playing,
live, like the others, also dreaming and dreaming,
and treat, everyone, with the truth, never lying.
    Then why? Why can't I find a love?
I don't ask for much, only what is fair,
maybe one like yours, or one just like theirs,
if my heart is good, and I'm the same.
    Why? Why can't I find a love?
I don't care what race, neither where it's from,
maybe someone rich, maybe someone poor,
if that's all I want, I can't understand.

    Luis J. Hernandez

Halloween Poem

Witches, Goblins, and Ghost are coming around
To scare all the children that live in this town.
They're coming this month so you better beware
Of Witches, Goblins and Ghost everywhere.

They're skinny, they're fat, short and tall
They might be big, they might be small
You never can tell where they might be hiding in the
bushes or up in the trees.
And they might just be children like you or me.

So if you're out on Halloween
Trick or treating or anything
Just remember what I've told you is true
That the Witches, Goblins and Ghost are out there too
Boo.

    Shirley Beck

Sing To Me

What can waken a memory quite like a song?

It can take but a few short tunes
to remind me where i belong.

Nothing makes me feel more close
to my friends and family.

So, if you'd like to see me smile,
then sing me a melody.

It can shake me up, it can make
my heart pound.

Just hearing the beat of a familiar sound.

Songs make me laugh, or bring
a tear to my eye.

Sometimes music makes me feel
light enough to fly.

I'd love for you to sing for me.

So I can imagine the smell of
fresh flowers, or dream of a
sky as blue as the sea.

Oh, won't you please just sing to me.

    Sheila Darling

Kisses From The Lord

We prayed a prayer for you today, and we asked God in some
    special way
To show you He cares for you so much that He will give you a loving
touch. It may be a gentle breeze upon your face or warm sunshine in a
quiet place; it might be from tears that gently flow; there's healing
in this, we really know. A smile, a friendly wave, a loving hug, even
a quiet, little, lady bug! It could be the beauty of the rising sun,
or the breath-taking glow when the day is done. Even a rain drop on
a glistening leaf to encourage and nurture our belief. These are all
kisses from our Lord, we know, and He is so anxious His love to show.
Yes, they are kisses from our Lord, you see, His love is so great for
you and for me. We know He cares, of this we are sure; our troubles
He helps us to endure. Doesn't He have us all "carved in the palm of
His hand?" Sometimes it is very hard to understand! That He loves us
more than words can say, we must praise Him, and thank Him, for each
new day. When burdens are heavy and we are filled with despair, deep
down we know He is always there. His comfort for us is gentle and
sweet and in our hearts His words we keep. "Lo, I am with you always"
is His word to us, we must receive it all in loving trust. Yes, even
until the end of time, His love is yours and it is mine.

    Martha Comtois

My Dream

My dream is to dive in the ocean, and look through the sea,
To swim with the dolphins, so beautiful and free,
To look at the fish, and make a wish,
That I could live here, in a house that is for me.
In my house I would live, so happy and free,
And everyone would come visit me,
I would have a bedroom, with a seashell bed,
But I wouldn't have a big head.
I would have a mirror, with a picture of my parent's so dear,
So come visit me, and you will see,
How I live under the sea.

    Mary Kunkel

I Hurt

I hurt— that's all I can say—
To talk just fuels the pain.
Do I look like I'm hurting?
Does this painted smile hide the stain?

I seek counsel from those I trust—
but even good words twist the knife—
Is there a hand strong enough to pull?
Some other force that won't leave the hole?

It's easier to leave the knife—
Why ask for help?
For a friend there is no pain—
For me even just a slip...

I hurt— that's all I can say—
 Katie Morris

Rainy Afternoon

Dark clouds hang so low they seem
to tangle in trees' grasping fingers,
wringing from sodden gray skirts
great drops of liquid silver that
the leaves lift shiny faces to catch.

Water drums on wet brick, running over the sides
of clay flower pots, drowning my petunias.
Only the ferns seems to like it.
Thunder grumbles around the eaves,
shaking my roof in its teeth.

Inside, I turn on a lamp or two,
banishing the gloom with artificial sunlight.
Steam from my cup of tea coils upward
like a cobra lured from its basket
by hypnotic notes from a holy man's flute.

I curl deep in my pillowed chair,
read the same page twice, uncomprehending.
The rain falls harder, blurring edges,
or is it my eyelids drooping instead?
The wind cries to come inside.

 Kathleen Moore Joiner

It's Never Too Late

It's never too late, never too late
To tell someone we care;
It's never too late to lift the weight
Of the burden they bear.

We grow, we learn, we dream, we yearn
To leave behind days of a kind;
How could we know, how could we see
Those years ago would fate you and me?

Our souls cried out for the void we knew,
Our spirit, no doubt, gave courage anew;
It's never too late to find it's great
Someone is there, waiting for you.

Worry and fear, anger and tear will fade away;
We'll take pride, we'll set aside
A new belief, oh what relief!
It's never too late, never too late to care.

 Willene E. Krom

Untitled

To live my life over, would be great
To watch those daisies bloom again,
I would say more often "I love you,"
And hope I'd never be left alone again.

Life is to precious,
Life is to sweet,
So let it be.

I would be more wild and crazy,
And do what I want to do to have fun.

But don't be too shy or too lonely,
Because you have your whole life to have fun.
 Lisa Martin

Garden Child

Have we but to look within
To where the child dwells
For youth to be recaptured and innocence regained
To desire knowledge not nor hunger forbidden fruit
To see uniqueness in creation in the uniqueness of ourselves
To reach and touch another though sometimes a world apart
To feel a heart awaken stir to emotion respond
To stars silent witness reticent sigh in the night
To be mindful of each other in what we do and who we are
To say to one another what is felt within the heart
That love not given is love not received
And anything is nothing without it
So take what gifts be given to be held in humble reverence
And remember always to look within
To where the child dwells
 Martha E. Davis

Footsteps Plays Alien Keys

On flagstone steps the echoes form, reaching tendrils
To youthful ears; and a voice of rage, the door, an open eye,
Revealing tormentor and tormented locked in silent struggle.
The eyes meet, old to young, till young bleeds tears and
With bent back, burrows down to the wool'd floor;
Covering pale flesh,
Knowing only the desire for protection, from that
Which will fall.
As if the thought be heard by angry gods,
The hammer falls.
Of wrath... Of fear... The palm speaks red to ravaged soul,
Burning answers, into flesh, till flesh answers
With broken words.
And worlds crumble.
And children scream.
And footsteps play alien keys;
Leaving only twisted echoes in the hollow night,
Behind family doors, the eyes close.

 Brian Alan Stewart

The Awakened Life

At break day, the heap of soul lies there... waiting...
Waiting for the light to receive enlightenment and
 nourishing from the sun.
To receive the strength that enables it to walk
 the ground its body set its feet on.
Yes, the beloved soul knows that without light and
 warmth it is lost.
So, at break day, it just waits patiently and relaxed,
 knowing that its reward is peace of mind and
A renewal of the spirit on the awakened life.

 Teresa Berteen

Roses

Remember a friend, so do it today
Tomorrow may be too late.
If it's only one rose or a bouquet
For those who patiently wait.
It could be a letter, a call or a card,
Perhaps a line or two,
May it bring sunshine into their life
May it bring some joy to you.

Their steps may falter; their eyes be dim,
Their hands be wrinkled with age,
In their memories many times recall
Some joys of bygone days.
So gather your roses and pass them around
Today and many more too.
May joy and contentment come to them,
May roses bring thoughts to you.

Marie W. Schultz

A Love Song Of The Sea

Was it your kiss that waked the slumbering sea,
Touching the cold dead water,
Staining a blush of pink upon the grey?
I loved you then in the gentle light of day.

And you were there in the sun-kissed waves,
Glittering and rippling on the sparkling sand,
Dancing over the wind-tossed sea,
With morning dreams of life and love and immortality.

And at noon, when the storms of passion raged
In the howling winds and the crashing waves,
Churning us up till we could take no more,
Flinging us down upon a rock-strewn shore.

And in the golden light of afternoon when shadows fall,
And colors too bright to comprehend
Whirl the clouds across the skies,
Swiftly the sun is gone...the day dies.

And I will love you then as the moon hangs silent
Over the restless wine-dark sea,
Where a golden swath shimmers and shines,
Lighting a path for my love from here to eternity.

Marian Harris

Ursula, The Butterfly

Like a charming butterfly
Traveling low and traveling high.
Making her way towards my beautiful flower.
Admiring the view upon this most gracious tower.

A momentary pause within its delicate life.
Contemplating its on going strife.
While enhancing the beauty of my surrounding.
As it basks in the sun almost lounging.

But this butterfly is more than it shows,
For within her kindness and gentleness overflows.
Though my flower is comfortable and appealing,
And thy moments are well spent and good fortune worth stealing.

Alas, it is time to go in search of:
New beginnings, new adventures and new loves.
As she flutters across my heavenly sky,
Ursula, the gentle and beautiful butterfly.
I'm thankful I was there when she passed by.

Yolanda McCool

A Family Tree

There is no place I'd rather be, than to be upon this family
tree. With just two people, this all got started with Tony Buhr
and Mary Klinkhammer.

To that marriage, with eleven were blessed, and that's what
began this great big mess! Even though our last names vary, To a
Buhr you must have married.

Yes, we number high and plenty. Oh! to count there's just too
many. For some there's a little gray in our hair and for some
there's just not much there.

We've shared a lot throughout the years our joys, and laughter
and our tears. If we could go back to yesteryear there'd be a
few more of us here.

To the ones who are at our home above, we send to them our
special love. And if there's someone here today you do not know,
be sure to say "Hi" before you go.

Oh yes, cousins it will be, up to us to keep up this family tree.
And if there's one thing I'd like to perfect bake
would have to be Grandma Buhr's chocolate cake.

Rita Buhr

Auschwitz- One Left At Age 14

Shivering and trembling overwhelmed with fear, we stand in
trepidation for the Nazis to come near. They'll be counting our
numbers in the early dawn! Half frozen bodies numb and torn, hungry
and forlorn, our Homeland not yet born. I cry to you my God, they
are killing people here, if only the world will know the answer will
be near. God, My God Eternal- to you I do appeal! Let my people
live, so I can tell the world, They're burning living children and
their silent voices must be heard! Once I was a child in the
Holocaust, now I'm all grown-up and I must talk! No more genocide,
no more Hitlerites- No more final solution under any conditions! I
survived and went home. I entered our house, where once we were nine
in all. The floors, windows and doors were ripped out. There was
not a stitch of furniture left. It looked like death. There I was
standing in the shambles of what was once a home filled with family
love. Now, nothing but ugly darkness, as dark as our cellar, which
I was compelled to enter. All alone in the world in that dark cold
cellar, I had to make a decision whether to continue to live in this
world or to shut myself in the cellar, and wait for the end. It
seemed like an endless moment. Finally, I pulled myself up and left
the house never to return.

Margaret Marketa Novak

Where Do You Turn

Where do you turn when your
   troubles are more than you can bear?
Do you turn to your mother who
   you know will always be there?

Where do you turn when the little
   things of life tend to upset you the most?
Do you turn to your father cause you
   know with all your faults he'll still boast?

Where do you turn when you feel like
   your life should cease to exist?
Do you turn to your friends, because
   with them you know you'll be missed?

Where do you turn when fear has
   become the latest fad or trend?
Do you turn your relatives because
   you know their homes will always welcome you in?

Where do you turn when everything and
   everyone seems no longer there?
Do you turn to a mirror and take
   a good hard long stare?

Kelly L. Bowman

Beautiful Spring; God's Creation

It is morning and I've just awakened. My ears hear lovely
Tunes outside my window, the sound of birds. They have come
from their hiding places.

My eyes are blinded by the sun but seem to glimpse squirrels
Scattering 'round. In the back of he house, a lake with
Schools of fish swimming in the Sun.

The sun us high in the sky. I take a walk, toads jumping,
frogs croaking. The green cool grass feels good on my feet
and smells like spring.

It is night. The birds in their hiding places, the squirrels
up the tree and the fish gone.

And this is God's creation.
    Sarah Johnson

An Opinion

There was a man who had a thought:
  'Twas his, and not by others wrought.
This thought, in time, brought him much grief;
  The thought had grown to a belief.

His thought was not by others shared,
  And when they heard it, they were scared.
And once the seed of fright was sown,
  It grew hostility on its own.

One man's thought—another's fear;
  The conflict flourished year by year.
A fight ensued; a battle won,
  And then another war begun.

It still continues here today—
  Fighting about what others say.
And even what they think, we dread.
  What's going on inside his head?

And wars have solved it not at all;
  Kingdoms rise and countries fall,
But one thing still can't be ignored:
  The thought is mightier than the sword.
    Linda Swenski

Remember When

Remember the time when we first met?
  'Twas was not so long ago
It's only been fifty years or more.
  seems like yesterday though.
Our first day of school, we went together,
  both scared out of our wits.
We hugged each other, and cried with fright.
  Later we laughed at those little fits.
On into high school, together we stayed,
  doing our homework at night.
Together, forever, and always, we thought;
  then we'd make it through life alright
As we were married, still as neighbors we were.
  You still look so young and thin.
Looking in your casket, a tear now I shed.
  We'll never have good times again.
As they lower you down, down into the ground,
  and cover you up with dirt.
I whisper, "goodbye, so long, farewell."
  You'll never know how much I hurt.
    Rhonda L. Fassett

"The Silent Rain"

The sound of storms on rivers, sailing
twice off pools of clouds, enshrouds the once
tranquil landscape of once-virgin, unpurged terrain.

It brings a sprinkling, yet no mere
inkling, of the deluge of silent, brightened
noise to follow.
Heaven's eyes and voice-poised in anticipation
of awakening sleeping grottos, perform the
"baptism of the rain."

Inside the once dry mind-set of earth
and tree, there comes a roaring, a pouring
down of sanctity.
  Through gravel and graphite grail it sails
unto its final mooring place-when, exhaled
by the sea, it is lifted up into vapory piers,
biers of cumulus humus-being
no more mere celestial drapery, but God's cerulean ears.
    Patrick A. Benenati

You

Two different people.
Two different faces.
Couldn't show their love in public
Had to hide many places.
You said they shouldn't be together
But they tried and tried, even in the stormiest weather.
They tried real hard to make you see
That these two people were meant to be.
But you were cruel
Showed you really didn't care
With your nasty comments and long hard stares.
They finally got tired of all this mess.
Why couldn't they be like all the rest?
Just 'cause their skin was a different color
Does that mean that they shouldn't be lovers?
Shouldn't, 'cause their love is true.
But why should they have to prove it to You?
  NaTasha Rene 'Bragg-Houser

Jackson Square

Young boys attack each other with knives across the street,
under the photos of female impersonators in the club windows

the black steel pistol wedged in my uncle's jeans
concealed by his untucked shirt,
protects me from the scene across the street

the gun
and the fact that I am 12 years old
and the fact that I am on the other side of the street,
the real side

we walk on,
ignoring the boys across the street,
and gazing at the pictures of men with t*ts and d*cks
that are on our side of the street
    Raymond Dodd

My Second Son

This child was quiet as he could be,
Until he discovered he could yell you see.
And then he demanded all the attentions be could get,
And he got it, from his brother and parents, you bet.
Then people told him we didn't love him at all—
That we loved his brother because he was first born and tall.
But we loved him as much for his own special ways
And we'll love him as much till the end of our days.
    Paula Viola Dart

Forgiveness

I'll never forget the way you asked for my forgiveness. I'll never
understand how you had the nerve to think that I could forgive you for
all the pain you caused me. We used to be so perfect together. Our
friendship and our love was perfect. Now we never even talk. When I
think of the times we shared, I always think of the good and
never the bad. I remember the long walks we would take talking for
hours, never running out of something to say. I remember how we used
to sit and plan our future together but never in our plans were we
apart. I always thought we'd be together forever, sharing our hopes,
our fears and our love. In my eyes you could do no wrong. In one day
you managed to ruin all my dreams of us together and tear my life into.
Now here you are standing in front of me asking for forgiveness. You
have no idea how I want to forget about everything and run into your
arms. But then I think of all the pain you caused and realize what I
have to do. So I stand up and gently kiss you on the cheek, then turn
and walk off into the moonlight never giving you a second thought.

Kristy Nicole Morris

Continuing On

Untouched by his stare,
Unknowing to his touch,
Numb to his kiss,
And still this hurt continues on.

Fragile feelings blown apart
By actions so unclear, as though made of fog
Hurt so deep, slowly drowning me
And still the hurt continues on.

Finally, you walked into my life
And my heart jumped and my body surrendered
Your soothing hands caressing every inch of this trembling body
As those calming winds once did,
And slowly the hurt runs away.

Now you've taken those gentle hands away
And the wind no longer touches me the way you did
You made the pain subside while embracing me
But now the hurt continues on.

Monica Schoknecht

"One Brief Moment (The Vietnam Memorial)"

There it waits unassuming behind the grass
Unnoticeable by many - unaffecting for few

The dark black wall shining our reflection
As we look for any hint from the past in those stark white letters

Contrasting so brightly, running on and on - like life
Ending only when stopped-like death

At the middle of the path it lies - unobtrusive
Leave your naivety behind, your innocence scarred

Realization is colder than any winter, bringing only knowledge
Erasing all previous thoughts - the silence is deafening

The names inspire awe - the country freezes
And for one brief moment, experiences a lull

A lull in faith and trust
Destroyed by the past - restored by the future
As freedom is restored in places never dreamed of

Natalie Butler

Mercy Searchers......

A microscope is close at hand to identify a soul
   unreached,this involved professor leads his mind
into a tricky dilemma... The small girl under his
   provision is thinking of lost trees and dying
mammals... The girl's unreached soul is so small yet
   so worthless... The professor tries to reach her
by hypnosis; back and forth swings the little watch
   fast asleep goes the girl... Questions are
asked very often and very quickly, the child's
   thoughts are all let go by words and whispers....
Soon the professor snaps and the tiny girl is awake...
   The girl tells the professor of dreams and visions she
had when hypnotized... Then the professor grabs the child's
   face like as to kiss her on the cheek...She slowly
flees from the office of this caring man, for no more
   can be brought from within her deep and lonely
soul...Tears fall down her cheek as the kiss
   disappears and so does the empty soul....

Melissa Swallow

I Want You To Know - You Are Loved

Looking into your beautiful brown eyes,
Until my eyes are filled with tears of love.
   Whispering sweet nothings in your ear,
Until my throat is soar.
   Kissing your ruby lips,
Until their dried out and chapped.
   Holding you in my arms,
Until my elbows scream from pain.
   Holding your hand,
Until your hand is covered with sweat.
   Rubbing your feet,
Until your pain goes away, no matter how long it takes.
   I want you to know,
You are loved from your head to your toes.

Kenny O'Leary

"Dreaming"

'Twas five o'clock and nigh
unto the start of evening.
Everything on earth seemed
awake with a colorful beaming.
I could tell, for the setting sun
was under the veranda awning peeping.

God could not see me in my hammock sleeping,
for such a sight can only be in the keeping
of nothing alive that thrives through the course of breathing,
for didn't you with your eyes come stealing
while I was innocently in my hammock sleeping

By flirting with sparkling eyes that were
in my soul dancing and leaping,
which caused the rise of my eyes
and spirit into waking?

But I promise, dear God, that I shall
always cherish and put in my keeping
that sight, when you with your eyes
were under my veranda awning peeping.

Samuel M. Talsky

Cancer

I am like a tree
  Uprooted in a flood,
Crashing, pounding, splintering
  Under all-powerful forces.
Once strong as life itself,
  Arrogant in strength and youth,
Felled now by unseen hands
  On an invisible enemy.
Carried along in uncontrolled fury
  Impatient for the storm to end.
Never again to be the same.
  Wondering, panicking at what comes next.
Who will I be now?

  Mary Lou Bornmann

'Cause And Effect'

The tiger was born to rule the land
Vicious, intelligent, with the strong hand.
The rabbit was born for the tiger to prey
Reproducing the key to saving his name.
If the rabbit is hungry, the tiger is there
To make sure not much is given the hare
The tiger is wealthy, the rabbit is poor
The former are few the latter are more.
The tiger will prey until the rabbits are none
Making tigers extinct for the land of the sun
So take us for granted, and give us no say
Take away the rabbit and the tigers are prey

  Richard Schneider

Castle Walls

Looking back through the mirror to the alleys of our youth
Visions of someone there whispering the truth

Through the cloudy memories walking in the rain
Holding tight the fear this one healed the pain

At times we were mistaken sometimes misunderstood
Lending us the courage we did the best we could

Dreams of Castle Walls and dark, fortress towers
Empty handed we traveled till he slipped his hand in ours

Ghosts of the future afraid of what would be
Everlasting faith in what we couldn't see

The backstreets of our child lay deep within our soul
Never want to lose them but it's hard out in the cold

Entering our presence in the mist there was another
This one guided our light this one who is our Father

  Melissa Hager

Going Home

There's a peaceful place
waiting, for me someplace
I hope that I will see and then my eyes
will open wide
When I stand someday at my Saviour's side.
I'll shine in the light of love
with happiness and lots of hugs.
I'll sing his praises as loud as I can
I'm there in this place of Love!
All around me will be bright
as I look upon this peaceful sight.
I'll reach out my hand to Him
While He gently lets me in!

  Nila J. Knafel

The Ravage

Emotions ticking, like a seconds on a time bomb
  waiting to explode with every panting moment
The movement of passions, encircled in a rush of lust
The longing of reality sets in, taking over any feelings
  of restlessness, as the aching continues.
Reaching towards the sky, the clouds open up and let me in.
Overwhelmed by beauty as my body fades into the light
Longing for the weakness I felt, I wait for you
As you touch my soul with your mind,
  caressing my needs with your masculinity.
I no longer must wait, the emotions take over,
  my femininity gives in as I reach for you.
Watching from the sky as the clouds form a wicked scene,
  you rise up into the light and touch me
We are one together, bodies and souls
We move together, two beings caught in a web of fire.
I no longer must wait for you, as you are with me,
  moving with me, touching me, pleasing me.
As the sky now closes and the clouds diminish,
  we are now set free.

  Sheri Cobbs

Racism, NO!

No matter where you go,
  walking or running to and fro,
  a death trap will be waiting,
  while you are hesitating,
  to enter that eccentric place,
  for you never know, who'll notice your face,
  but as you stare into space,
  you now realize, it's all about race.

Racism affects your state of mind,
  it affects the future of mankind.
  If we don't do something about it soon,
  different people will be, in different rooms.

Maybe someday, someone will see,
  that we can join together in unity,
  without any racial marks or deceiving,
  without any gun play, or even perceiving,
  through the minds of youths; we all need relieving.

So stop the racism that nobody needs,
  stop it now, sometime this century.

  Tara Helm

The Next Page

I'm living in a dream
Walking through a maze
Standing in a fantasy world
I'm locked up in a cage

Tonight I'm on an island
Trapped, alone with fright
The winds they blow so cold and strong
Struggling with all my might

The seagulls have begun to cry
I join them in their song
Amazed by the simple beauty
That they so mournfully carry along

There is something in the rustle of the trees
The strong ferocity of the wind
That brings me calmly back to my senses
Lets me know I can live again

Strength, independence, freedom prevail
I am a bird, soaring high above the world
Alas, the storm is gone!
A new page has finally been turned

  Kathryn Parsley

Alyssa

She glides through the grass with such suaveness
Walking with her head high enough to touch the clouds
Her hair glistens in the brightness of the sun
as she sits at the edge of the woody patch waiting for her love.
She waits and waits for her Persian love
who she loves so dear
With, every sound she hears she is attentive to
From morning to night she waits so long,
but he never comes.
Inside the house she gracefully walks with the look
of loneliness upon her pale face
I give her kind words and she gives me a small,
loving kiss and then she curls up on my lap
and says meow, purrrrrr.

Walter Jim Barnes

Foolish War

A lonely maiden, sad and crying
Walks be the picture of a soldier dying.
By the portrait she stops and stares.
She's the only one, nobody cares.
The frame is chipped and the paint is old.
Who left this soldier standing in the cold?
She knows he fought such a silly war
Which makes his death sadden even more.
The cannons blast and the guns go off.
She sits for hours but it never stops.
To no avail, and I know she's trying
To suppress her tears for a soldiers dying.

Lara Wenner

Freedom

Have you ever felt like you didn't want to live, like you
wanted to die?
Well I have, and many nights I've laid awaked and cried.

My life is not as bad as it seems,
But it's not exactly a child's dream.

My life has its goods and has its bads,
My life has its happys and has its sads.

My friends are allowed to walk the town,
Trust me, I've seem them walking around.

My parents say that they worry,
They say when it comes to growing up there's no hurry.

I can't take a walk without my mother,
Oh please, Oh brother.

They say their scared when I leave alone,
But I always make it home.

I feel like I'm trapped, like there's no freedom,
Or am I a princess who lives in a Kingdom?

Karen Sullivan

Angels

Fluttering wings, high above the land,
Warm lights, a smile, the softness of a hand.

Holding me steady, guiding me through,
Helping me learn what's false and what's true.

Making miracles, fixing breaks,
Kind voices as sweet as apple cakes.

It's nice to believe someone's watching me,
When I'm filled with anger or filled with glee.

So follow the kindness of your friends above,
And your life will be filled with a lifetime of love.

Sarah Gaudette

A Jealous Personality

I believe that my friend is jealous of me, But instead she wants me to be jealous of her. I can see the way she is trying to listen, When I am having a deep conversation with a close friend I adore. She will never be able to be that close. She is too simple for that. And, she should also learn to respect. You'll never be a worthy person without knowing that for a fact. Sometimes she tries to put me down. She even laughs in my face. Oh yes, but she is a good student. Still, I can't believe that we're friends. I also suppose that she feels as though something is missing in her character. And I think I know what that is. It is soul and spirituality. How can you ever be free without at least one such quality? But in contrast, I feel that my soul is becoming deeper and deeper. And my mind is opening door by door. Yes, I do believe that my friend is jealous of me, But instead she wants me to be jealous of her.

Olga Bilinson

Summer Love

My summer love
Was gone like a dove
For a single summer we made magic
That's why it was so tragic

We had to go our separate ways
But we cherish all the days
I hear in my dreams whispering to me
But I am afraid that our love will never be

He was so dear to me
But I fear that we cannot be
But we made a promise to each other
Never to forget our summer love

Stacie Reeder

The Suicidal Apocalypse Freak

The suicidal apocalypse freak
Watches Dan Rather every night of the week.
He loves to listen to good old Dan
Reveal the unfolding of the plan;
A plan he hopes will end all life
And put an end to human strife.

The apocalypse freak is a boring guy
With nothing better to do than die.
He's tired of the same old games.
He wants to see the world in flames.
He smokes his stuff and drinks his beer
And waits for Jesus to appear.

Women do not interest him;
His chances for a date are slim.
He doesn't care about success;
His self esteem ain't worth the stress.
To see the brimstone and the fire
Is his only true desire.

Terry Terndrup

Untitled

When I'm feeling sad my friends are always there.
We love each other, we all care.

We can hang out as long as the others are near,
When one of us are moved we all shared tears.

Most of my friends I've known "forever"
Like Vanessa, Amber, Kelly, and Jennifer.

Don't get me wrong I have new friends too,
In good times and bad they will always see me through.

Maranda Smith

Solitaire

You sit with your coffee at Grandma's cherry table
watching the sun rise over the Blue Ridge mountains.
Missing Byron.

You play solitaire. Mornings are the worst
He was always so vigorous then, telling you the news
or his opinion of the news.

Two of spades on the Ace, a sip of coffee.
He built this house on the hill so he could have his "view"
lived here only a few months before he took that fatal trip
to the Winn-Dixie.

The criss-cross curtains frame his mountains.
The morning mist rises from them like the steam from your
coffee.
Your tears are for Byron.

Black queen on red king. Slowly your hand moves,
filling up the mourning hours
until your mood lightens with the sun.
Putting in time until you're with Byron.

 Kay Comini

Untitled

I stand on the shore at the midnight hour,
Watching the waves, the ocean, the beauty, the power.
The waves crash hard on the sand,
I look as far as I can see but don't see land.
The majestic wonders of the seas.
Brings the cool and refreshing breeze.
The moon glistening on the ocean.
Brings a powerful enchanting potion.
The time, the moment feels so great,
What brought me here, luck or fate?
The place looks like a dream come true
I wish I could take it all home, too.
I'm growing weak. I am tired,
And then I see the glorious fire.
I look at my watch, it's after five
One more day, I'm glad I'm alive!

 Shawn Cyr

Faded

 Alone, cut adrift among the vast
Waters of the world never moving to or fro,
  Never reaching shore.
  Day after day the emptiness
   Converges upon him,
  Yet never the less he remains,
  Never letting help come his way,
 He has long forgotten his comrades,
  He is socially celibate.
His eyes accumulate a glassy film as
  The chemicals work their magic,
He wanders in and out of saneness,
  Dreams come no more and his
  Thoughts he knows are not pure,
This world has long been an illusion,
  As the misery surrounds…
The wind whispers of what once was,
  And the water draws calm,
And the silence masks the insanity,
  And now a great man is gone.

 Warren M. Shrum

The Passing Of A Friend

Sometimes as we travel along life's path,
we are lucky enough to find a flower.
A gift from God reaching out to us
through the ugliness of the world.
Like the petals we blossom, grow,
and radiate in its presence.
We become all the better
for allowing the flower to touch our lives.
When the cruelness of life destroys
the bloom leaving it to wilt and die,
it is up to us to carry on in its place.
The lovely little flower has touched us
blessed us empowered us to share
in the glory of life.

 Steve Macarus

Perceptions

We are so unlike one another.
We are not the same as our own blood brother.
Every individual, in his own way, perceives
That which to him is real; this he truly believes.
Each person lives in a world; different from me, different from you.
So that the same named color, is to each of us, a different hue.
To view what lies before us,
To see what's been left behind;
Is what etches in stone
Our lifelong perceptions, in our minds.
No one perceives that to him which is wrong, only that to him which is
right. This is the root of the entire planet's plight;
Each person not realizing how things are perceived in another's head.
If we could only show others more understanding and love;
Realizing that everyone sees things differently, from below and above.
Then maybe all of the earth's peoples would come together and get
Along making this a world unified and stronger,
With all who live there feeling like they truly belong.
This change better come soon,
Because we can all perceive, that we don't have much longer.

 Michael Boulay

Life's Journey

Life is like a precious and delicate flower, waiting to bloom.
We are nurtured and cared for in hope that we may blossom,
 into something brilliant and unique.
We grow with the rays of love,
 and we bloom with the promise of the future.

We push our way up from the bottom,
 and we try to rise to the top.
Our lives bud with confidence,
 and each petal represents a stronger you.
Every petal that is shed represents a loss in self-worth,
 and without these petals there is no beauty.

So we must water away our fears,
 and let our dreams thrive with the sunshine.
We must remember that once we shed our petals,
 are ambitions and dreams are lost.

 Teresa A. Sorbo

Only A Little Petunia

I'm a little petunia and oh so glad because
We can grow just anywhere - in spite of all the lows.
It's lots of love that makes us grow and lots of water too.
We'll grow in many colors just because we're found of you.
We want to please in any way and bloom in early spring.
Were bright and light in a row or even in a ring.
I've been in beds with lots of colors and many kinds
The only thing that bothers me is being in feds with vines.
They twine around and hug you oh so very tight.
They thrive and grow and hug with all their might.
A little petunia is what I am and pleased enough to be
I'm oh so glad in my small world in just being me.

Gae Veda Anderson

"The Cactus Tree"

We don't have mistletoe to hang in the hall,
  we just use mesquite, wc don't mind at all!
Our house isn't trimmed all 'round the roof,
  we can still hear the sound of the reindeer hoof!
Christmas on the ranch is quiet and simple,
  so we feel that this tree is surely ample!
Our tree is not tall and pretty and fluffy,
  it's not like a cedar that's really puffy!
We don't trim our tree with lights that shine,
  we use popcorn, cranberries and even some twine!
We don't wrap our tree in tinsel, all silver and gold,
  we just use Grandpa's rope - it's worn out and old!
Our tree don't smell like a traditional tree,
  but we can always use pine spray, don't you see!
Our tree can't compete with the 'Ponderosa Pine',
  but our 'Cainderosa Cactus' works just fine!

Peggy Cain

The Chrismon Tree

We've been born again, we see the light,
  we know His love is with us tonight.
The Chrismons on the tree so green
  are shining there for all to see.
The Shepherd's Staff though made by man,
  The Shepherds made their way to Bethlehem.
The star that led the Shepherds in the night
  Still shines for us, and is, oh so bright.
We think about our God so dear,
  Who sent His Son for us down here.
The cross on the tree, tells the story so true,
  How He died on the cross for me and for you.
There are many Chrismons on the tree
  To remind us of His Saving Grace, so free.
This Christmas night, with the tree so tall
  Tells us the story of His love for all.
The greatest gift we can give to Him
  Who died for us, is to ask Him in.
We've been born again, we see the light
  We've been born again this Christmas night.

Mickie Roberts

Love And Death

Because the sands of time fade away.
We must pick up and go our separate ways.
Make short our long goodbye.
For all that is left for me is to die.
Please for my sake hide your tears.
For goodness sake let go your fears.
But for now stay the night.
In heaven shall we reunite.
For as we speak each word grows dimmer.
As I leave you now my body begins to tremor.
With one last gasp I breathe my last breath.
Yet in the end I have not experienced death.

J. Alley

Remembering Her - I

We had such fun, when life and love we knew,
  We longed to learn, and asked the world to teach,
We learned of life with every breath we drew
  And we were love's own tutors, each for each.

We knew the city's joys, its sadness, too.
  We saw where children played and lovers wept,
We sang and danced and loved the whole night through
  And watched the morning break while wise ones slept.

We took the world in sunshine and in rain,
  We gave but little thought to mundane weather,
We roamed the ocean shore, the hill, the lane
  And found our greatest joy in being together.

  We drank at love's sweet spring, and it was good.
  We knew it couldn't last; we hoped it would.

Robert Goldsmith

A Thought For Tomorrow

Caught in "right now" society,
We lose our ability to dream.
A dream, a vision is not for today,
Its faith and motivation lighting our way.
We forget the importance of our goals.
We focus on the now, things tangible to hold.
So when today has been achieved,
What then will tomorrow bring?
Gain a vision, look ahead.
Think of the future to realize instead.
Thereby building a storehouse within,
Rich in patience, endurance and tomorrows
yet to win.

Shannon Downey

Divine Generosity

We need pure air and sun and water,
We need good food and clothes and shelter,
But we didn't need the bright flowers
With their bewitching, mellow fragrance and gorgeous array of colors.

We need the birds to kill dread insects,
We need the brooks to feed the meadows,
But we didn't need their special songs.
God threw them in to delight our ears
With their lilting, melodic warble and their churning babbling murmurs.

We need human speech, intellect, eyes,
We need the sense of feeling and ears,
But we did not need laughter and smiles.
God threw them in to cheer our sad hearts
With reassuring warmth and glow, to help lighten our burdens.

We need fellow beings from childhood to adulthood,
But we did not need unfailing love.
God added that gift to all the rest,
With hope to lift our hearts to him above.
There is much in this world to love and he grateful for.

Miriam R. Krueger

Untitled

I drift away in sorrow my heart was once content
when I held your hand I never said good bye
you're probably up with God talking to Him now. I hope
you take my hand when I'm going to die show me the
light of Heaven please. I want to follow in the
same way take my hand oh grandma for
I love you eternally

Tina Zielke

Vermeer: Girl Reading A Letter

The painting is of a girl reading a letter.
We see her in profile, intent, serious,
we do not see the message she reads,
intent as she is upon it, vital as it appears,

May the centuries still find her standing,
silent, yet eloquent, as she is, as she
has always been since the year,
she, in fact, became the painting.

How odd life is, after all,
vain, momentary, maddening, glorious,
so many colors in a crayon-box.
Life raised up, only, in the end, to fall.

Who she was, what the letter said, now, cannot matter.
Certainly, we do not know.
Yet the scene itself, her image, color, still has lustre;
it has never lost its glow.

Art after all, though mocked, ridiculed,
lasts longer than the ordinary, than the gossip, the lies,
peddled on the streets, as truth divine.
It stands human, timeless, beyond the ages of time.

L. E. Ward

Sea Herring's Lament For The Love Of a Gull

You sit near shore rocking with sea rhyme.
We share this. I hear it in your song:
The wild eye of open waters where I've swum,
sunlips on waves.

You are warm; and in your eye long reeds of loneliness
like tendril staves stalk the seasilk breeze.

No justice in my scales, just phosphorous and silver brine.
Deep within my breath sac runic tears
change seasalt into wine. I kiss the sea.
I sing the bubble of your song and cry.

There is no meeting, Me here. You — soaring above love swells
with the sun beside you — beating, heart of my sky!

Leah Sullivan

Diamonds In The Water

As sure as there is sand along the shore,
We were destined to look no more;
Where the ocean waves crash against the shoreline,
We made our promise to share our body, soul and mind;
Now with the calmness of the sea,
I still think of You and Me;
The warmth of the sun, the coolness of the ocean breeze
I have only my thoughts of you and me;
But when the sunlight dances across the ocean water and I see
"Diamonds" glitter back at me;
I will know it's you thinking of me......

Kate Diamond

Untitled

   I say I'm Holding strong, I say I don't feel, but really I'm
weak. I'm so worn down from all the hurt and anger that have
found, its way inside my heart.
   I pray to God at night to send the happiness to me that
I'm seeking right now in my life.
   These prayers are never answered though,and I sit
alone sometimes like this asking myself "Why"?
   I'm not a bad person and I've done nothing to be
condemned for so why is God making life so difficult for me
to live. It's not fair, so many others are happy, why am I
different, why is he making me suffer.
   I don't know and I don't understand, but I'll keep
praying and I wont give up faith that someday he will answer
my prayer.

A. Shank

I Touch The Future

Goodbye, Goodbye Christa Mcauliff, take care goodbye Christa Mcauliff
We'll see you they said when you get back this way.
As the children counted in unison - 10, 9, 8.
As the second ticked off the clock that day.

It was her space age dreams you know.
The sea gulls sailed high above the pad
And the waves rolled against the rocks on shore.
The children love their teacher,
They said, the best one they had ever had before.

The Challenger shook the earth Goodbye
And everywhere people stopped that day to look upward,
Everyone turned to the sky.
We were all so believing with all our hopes so high!

We miss your smiling face "Dear Christa"
And we will try to keep your space age dreams.
We won't get to see you any more Christa
And things are not what they seem!

The Challenger shook the earth goodbye, that day & the sea gulls sailed
above the pad so high. Everyone turned their eyes downward that day
And hung their heads to cry. "Goodbye, Dear Christa, Goodbye!"

Mary K. Zuck

Sleazy

We're heading into battle, down the hill of no retreat.
   We'll show you how to win this war, we'll knock you off your feet.
Our opposition has been in control for just about long enough.
   Take another look at us we've gotten pretty tough.

You've had you chance, you've made your plea,
   now we've got you on the run.
   When ladies come to battle, well, we don't need no gun.
You look at me and think ah ha, this one's gonna be easy.
   Well take your tactics somewhere else, because me,
   I don't like sleazy.

We ladies in this day and time, well, we like gentle men.
   And those down in sleaze world think,
   they've just been pecked by hens.
Separating men from sleaze is something I have learned.
   So ladies don't stop by in sleazetown
   because believe me you'll get burned.

So when you think you've got it made, "she's eating from my hand."
   You're in for a rude awakening, she'll discover "he's no man."
Men treat ladies with respect and they'll do it from the start.
   Men don't feed you from their hand, they feed you from their heart.

Wanda Neace

The Weeping Willow

Weeping willow
What a sight you are
Numerous, innumerable branches
Drooping and swaying and sighing in the wind
A lovely sad nostalgic melancholic picture

Do you have hopes and dreams
Did you try to stretch your branches to the sky
Only to fail and fall
Again and again
Do you now droop, cowed and bowed by life

Do you sway in the direction of the wind
Your long and elegant branches
In a song of defeat and depression

Weeping willow
I juxtapose my life to yours

Weeping willow
I weep with you.

Linda Lim-Du

An Army Wife's Plea

You in your dress greens, I in my Sunday best.
We're going to the company party to be put to the test.

We'll smile and nod, along with the rest.
This is our mission, this is our quest.

What is that? Wipe that look off your face.
As I would, should I show anything but grace.

This life in the Army is one I chose not.
But we're in this together, or have you forgot?

Next month at this time, we can say with no regrets
This life on this post is part of our past.
As of this carrier, I'm glad it didn't last.

We've lived in place after place after place.
Stared into many strange eyes and many a strange face.

Over and over, we've talked about the day
That, now, sooner than later we can walk away

From all of the restrictions the Army implies.
No more excuses, we're sick of the lies.

And if any one ever tries to make you sign on the line,
Give it to me . . . I'll handle it next time.

Sheri Williams

Because I love You

The tears I cried when I was a baby,
Were wiped away with your love.
The times I couldn't get too far,
You gave me a little shove.
The days that I could barely pass,
You spent your time with me.
When I needed someone to talk to,
With you it came easily.
Mom, you've helped me grow up,
Through the good times and the bad.
You've always helped me cheer up,
When I was feeling really sad.
I know we've been through good times,
But really bad ones too.
And throughout my life I love the fact,
That you've been you for you.
Well, now I'm getting older,
And you're getting older too.
But throughout the good times and the bad,
Always remember I love you!

Tricia King

Sangsara

In a view of fret and fury I died.
What can I say of this casted glory?
I will say she is the bloom and I cry.
Dreams by paradise, nightmares I cried.
Come down to my level to learn and fly,
Drift with Eagles 'eyes and draw to his side.
Black tar poured on the flower from a lie.

To dream is an effort put on sleep-time.
To live is a work of sunshine in eye.
A trek across the bridge without a dime.
Racked by pain and eerie dreams I may cry.
Trolls are under the bridge to end the rhyme.
I have learned the hard ways of being shy.

D. D. Yates

The Moon

The moon peers down on us as if to say,
what have you done with your life today?

Just take a moment to reflect and see....
What contributions were made by me.

When the moon is full and magically bright, it touches
each person specially each night
To provoke our thoughts, inspire, to become aware
That the power of the moon is always there....

It controls the tides, which controls the sea
controls our dreams and fantasies

Such a powerful force, is our universe
so out of our control....
The moon just lights the stage
as our destinies play their role.

Sandra L. Murphy

Weeping Willow

Weeping willow why do you weep?
What is the sadness you forever keep?
Why are you so forlorn?
Or do I mistake?
What makes you happy?
What does it take?
Is it because you lost a friend?
Or is it because you committed a sin?
God has forgiveness, for you are not doomed.
His love's like a flower,
So let it bloom.
Soon you will weep no more.
There will only be peace and not war.

Nicole Curwin

The Way It Used To be

We started out as friends, going here or there.
What we didn't realize is all the things we'd share.
At first you were my buddy and no-one could compare.
Then you became my best friend and I knew that you'd be there.
We laughed a lot and talked a lot and dreamed a million dreams.
I found myself believing we were the perfect team.

Then one day it happened, our friendship became more.
I found myself liking you more than I ever did before.
I needed to feel loved and you were there for me.
But now I feel that love maybe wasn't meant to be.

I'm not blaming you, and I'm not blaming me.
I just think we should have left it, the way it used to be.

I love you as a lover and you will always be my friend.
But I need my buddy back, I just don't want it to end.

Tammy Alford

The Oil Spill

Oh little bird how I loved thee!
When I looked into the sky you were the first one I could see.
Your feathers were as white and beautiful as a brilliant light,
And when I gazed at you, my heart was lifted like a kite.
From this day I shall never lift my eyes into the sky,
For now I know you are dead and I do not wish to say goodbye.
Why does man leave this black death lying around?
It is so hideous and like nothing I have ever found.
The ignorance of those who caused this is clearly seen here.
I know these things occur, but why now and so near?
My heart has fallen and will never take flight,
They should not do this, for it just is not right.

Nichole Moerke

Three Wishes

If I had three wishes
what would I do
would I waste them away
and make life untrue
would I go places
I never did know
or would I gain the knowledge
I never did know
How would I use those
wishes I had would they waste away
like an outrageous fad would my wishes be stupid
and unrealistic or would they be selfish
and materialistic would I wish for good
things for those I don't know
or would I wish for times past and feelings
I didn't show I wouldn't wish for
any changes in my past because then I would
have a perfection that wouldn't last
if I had three wishes I know what I would do
I'd take all three wishes and I would wish for you

    Kevin W. Love

Our Hours

Do you often wonder after the day is spent
What you accomplished and where the hours went
Many times it seems that all is lost
With hours flitting by at terrific court

But then comes another day
When all things seem to go the right way
As hours pass all work is done
And things accomplished please everyone

I often wonder what causes this
Could it be something in our midst
That keeps us from doing our best
Or do we just need to take a rest

Maybe our mind goes astray
To give these task a slight delay
At any rate it can be very confusing
And at times even amusing

    Martha H. Sudduth

Why Can't We

Why can't we love our brothers and sisters
Whatever the color or race,
Why can't we look at them
and see our Jesus face,
Why can't we put love first instead of hate
Why can't we before it's too late,
Why can't we love everyone around
Why can't we look up and not down,
Why can't we do unto others
What we want them to do to us,
Why can't we stop, look, love them
and don't fuss,
Why can't we put down our guns
Why can't we help and not run,
Why can't we stop our killing
Why can't we be more willing,
Why can't we love our brother with love
Why can't we see our Father above,
Why can't we get on our knees and pray,
Why can't we do this everyday.

    Patsy Wiggins

Live If Just For them

When life gets you down
When death looks appealing
Remember the love
Remember those who care
Let them be the light
Let them lead you through the darkness
Live, if just for them
No matter how dark
No matter how hopeless
There are those who care
Who would weep, who would miss
There are good times to be had
They do exist, look around, you'll own them soon
Remember the love
Don't hurt those who care
Don't take away your presence
You do, and their memories will be stained
Remember the love
Don't hurt those who care
Live, if just for them

    Suzy Bruce

Hands Of Love

My mother's hands held knowledge,
When I asked the questions of life.
Her hands fed me and kept me from
hunger each and every night.

My mother's hands were soft,
When I deserved to be praised.
Her hands were hard
When I disobeyed.
My mother's hands wiped away my tears,
When I was sad.
My mother's hands clapped proudly
When I became a H.S. Grad

My mother's hands held me up,
When I could not stand.
My mother's hands molded me into who I am.

My mother's hands guided me out of darkness,
When I could not see.
But most of all my mother's hands
were always there when I needed them to be.

My mother's hands were the Hands of Love.

    Kerry Willis

Safe

i haven't felt safe until you came to care for me
when i had surgery on my back   at home you
    Hush little baby...
had food prepared   childhood food
for your middle-aged daughter   food you know
i love and always will   you sang or hummed   happy
i struggled with pain   you kept on singing   probably to keep
    don't say a word...

your sanity   i haven't felt safe in years   this time
i was so ill   you came and   stayed and cooked
and kissed and   loved until i   began to heal
    momma's gonna to buy you a mockingbird...

basic needs   i left everything to you
slept   days and nights away
you cooked   sang   loved
now you have gone   I struggle
to remember   how
to get better alone
i begin to cook   i hum
    If that mockingbird don't sing, Momma's
    gonna buy you a diamond ring.

    Sefra Kobrin Pitzele

Set Them Free

When I see a leaf fall to the ground, I stop and look around.
When I see a dog whine with grief, I look in disbelief.
When I see trash on the street, I hurry on my feet.
When I see a bird who cannot fly, I stand and wander why.
When I see a man without home, I wander why he must roam.
When I see someone without a job, I quietly, to myself sob.
When I see someone cry in pain, I wish for all that they may gain.
So I say to God, "How can this be? Look at all that you have given
to me. Why must they suffer when I reign? Please my mighty God
ease their pain. Let them live, set them free. Give them all that
you have given to me.
Take from me, give to them. Just don't let them be condemned
Then God said to me, "My son if you could only see how happy
they are going to be.
What they are is not their fault, and that life will shortly halt
Don't you worry for they are mine. Both you and them will surely
shine."
"Thank you God."
Tyson Mummey

A Religious Poem

God looks down on me from the heaven and sky
When I sin he starts to cry
Then he says in that same old way
I will help you this very day
When he sees that I'm on the right track again
He will look down on me with a grin
When he sees that I love him, He will know
That I love him with my heart and soul
Now I am with him on my way
To love and serve him every day.
Michael Vincent Cullen

Ireland

Treasured memories awaken in me,
    when I think of that dear Land
        across the sea.

Your graceful glens lie neath my feet,
    far as the eye can see.

O Ireland, Lovely Ireland, there I am
    Longing once more to be

Where misty clouds sink low to kiss
    the tops of mountains fair

And there lie lakes beyond compare
I am longing once more to be there.

I stood on your cliffs, beside the great ocean,

At the Head of Kinsale and watched
    the wild waves in motion.

So open and free, where the sea birds fly;

Was ever a scene so splendid?

Once more I ponder that sea and sky
where treasured dreams are never ended.
E. Marie Nolan

My Friend, Jesus

When I'm discouraged - He's there.
When I'm afraid - He's right beside me.
When I don't know where to turn - He knows.
When I don't understand - He does.
When the way is unclear to me - it's clear to Him.
When there's no one else to turn to - I go to Him.
He will see me through.
Rachel A. Staten

Memories

I remember the address of the house that we lived in,
When I was a boy, too young to start school.
I remember so well my balloon-tired Schwinn,
And catching my pants in the chain like a fool.

And Dad's old Chevy, I remember it well,
The folks used to call her Clementine.
The interior had a slight musty smell,
She was built in nineteen forty-nine.

Our telephone hung on the kitchen wall.
I remember the number, perhaps I should call it.
But I'll be darned if I can recall,
Where I left my keys and my wallet.
Steven Paul

Daddy

An arm to be cradled in
when I was only a babe.

A knee to bounce on
as I toddled on my way.

A hand to hold
as I crossed every street.

And a big shoulder to cry on
when I felt my heart would no longer beat.

A twinkle in his eye
to tell me he was proud.

His reassuring smile told me
he loved me aloud.

All of these things
and so very much more.

Thank you for my Daddy,
Oh Thank You, Dear Lord!
Leasa Hale Tenison

The Window Of My Soul

My guardian angel peeked into the window of my soul
When I was still an infant and my innocence was whole.
"I'll be around," he said, "and try to shield this one from woe.
For I know God's intent for every mortal here below."

When, in the summer of my life, enticements showed their face
Then sometimes I erred and stumbled and felt parted from God's grace.
But there was an undergirding and I felt it strong and sure.
The aura of my angel helped me press on and endure.

In the winter of my life I sense the whirring of his wings.
He smiles into the window of my soul and my heart sings.
And this awareness of his presence leads me to suppose
That setting sun has loveliness the same as when it rose.
Maloa B. Read

River Of Dreams

There is a river that cuts through the land,
where dreams are more than they seem,
and where coming-trues can.

Where the water bubbles,
and where you can,
forget all your troubles,
and where weakened dreams stand.

Where the you can see the future,
and the past melts away,
where moon beams and fairies are,
in the moon's rays.
Rebecca Van Stralen

Past

I write of a time, so long ago,
when knights rode their noble steeds,
and maidens would be rescued right out of their dreams.
A time full of romance and chivalry, too.
When dragons and sorcerers fought in the dew.
Knights would do battle for the hand of their princess.
Love conquered all, magic would be fall.
Castles and dungeons, moats and swords.
All were part of this time of beauty.
Innocence would abound in the face of a child.
The soon-to-be prince of the land.
Kings would make laws, while Queens would weave tapestries.
pictures of mystical magical lands.,
where unicorns danced under the willows in the sun.
A place that has vanished never to return,
a part of our past, buried deep in the dirt.

Patricia Ziegler

"Mothers Love"

Remember times when we were young,
when mamas words were softly sung,
To fall fast asleep
and play all day,
She would mark our paths
So we wouldn't lose our way,
To hear her laugh
and see her smile,
For her, we'd gladly walk a mile.
we're grown up now,
Living on our own,
But where mama lives, it's still called home,
We've children too!
and paths to mark,
And always mama, deep our hearts.

Monique Beach

Love By The Yard

When I talked to St. Peter it was sometime ago
When my eyesight was dimming & my walking got slow.
We spoke of the wonderful life I was given
The home that you gave me, the sharing of chicken.
I'm the luckiest dog god ever created
with your love and affection that never abated.

I said I was coming long before you
And asked what a doggie like me was to do.
He said there's no hurry-I could sit down and wait
And look around heaven while guarding the gate
I remember the tears that you shed that day
And the touch of your hand as I went away.

I've missed your shrill whistle and stealing your scarf
And the bed that you made me in front of the heart
So I will be waiting till the time you and I
Are forever together at my yard in the sky.
If P.S. - This postscript is needed: When you answer his call
If it's not too much trouble, please bring me my ball!

Katherine A. Anderson

Winter

Winter is nice, winter means mice.
Winter means ice. Winter means snowball fight.
Winter gives you that cold feeling
of ice and that warm feeling inside and that warm
feeling of family cheer. And it makes you feel
like a butterfly in the breeze. Winter makes
me feel like hugging my family.

Naomi Powell

A Fools Paradise

I reminisce for a spell, somewhat in review,
When this world seemed to be populated with only
me and you.

I thought the love we had would last forever
And a day. It's so hard to say good-bye to
yesterday.

Breathless was to look into your eyes and to
See how they would shine, while silently I whispered
"I'm gonna make you mine".

Memories of you, yet and still remain. Of Agony,
of ecstacy, of joy, and of pain.

I took a chance on love I gambled for
High stakes. I lost the woman of my dreams
Be still my heart don't break.

Ruperto A. Parks

Procrastination

Open your eyes.
When you antagonize me realize
That you are a predator but I am not prey
It won't be my flesh you feast upon today.
The hatred in your heart is like a fire that starts slow,
sinks low, rises high, but then dies.
Put a smile on your face, take my hand in the process
Squeeze if you must, but not with excess,
I'd rather love you than hate you and that is the truth.
May I get on with my life while I still have my youth?
While your anger runs the path of evil thoughts and corruption
Like a jogger, it realizes that it cannot run forever;,
it will have to stop at the end of the path.
Reconciliation.
Though anger can lead to evil, it is not evil itself.
Anger will eventually have to stop running whether it wants
To or not, unlike love which can run forever.
If you need to rest....rest. If you need new shoes...invest.
Whatever it takes to keep you awake so you may run under the
Sun forever.

Ryan Gerard

Dancing With The Leaves

Dancing is like the leaves
When you dance
You flow with rhythm
like the leaves soaring on the wind.

When you dance
you do fancy steps,
like the leaves doing cartwheels on natures floor.

When you dance
like the leaves
you are carefree and relaxed.
When the leaves run about chasing one another,
they are dancing with you.

That is the wonder
of dancing with the leaves.

Melissa Delaney

Hard Falling Tears

I once knew a girl who got abused. I once knew a girl
who was scared to death but wouldn't tell anyone. I once
knew a girl who wouldn't come out of the closet. I once
knew a girl who almost killed herself. I once knew a girl
who's only hope was god.

Kari Anne Donaldson

Untitled

Do you have a plan Child, what you will do?
  When you grow up as a job for you?
Will you teach or drive or build tall bridge
  Take your pick, whatever your wish is.
To teach you must help the kids want to learn.
  When all they want is to play in their turn.
You can drive for a living. But a trucks not a jeep
  And don't forget, you don't get to sleep.
Bridges are needed.   They're important it's true
  But take time and think about what you will do.
There's plenty of time to plan it out
  But a plan never made is dream thrown out.
So don't be a person with a very sad tale.
  A person without a plan, plans to fail.
  Susan Rogers

Questions

What were your thoughts on that dreadful night?
When you tied the rope did you pray or cry?
What was it like when the rope stretched tight,
Compressing your breath to a fading sigh?
Was there a ghost of a whispered prayer,
Like a vapor breathed on the morning air,
When the children found you hanging there?

Long ago when you walked a narrow wail
Spanning the railroad tracks below,
I expressed my alarm should your footsteps fail.
You shrugged away any concern I'd show:
Said, "it matters not if I live or die"
Then I did not dare to ask you why.
Years later, the question, unanswered still,
Lurks in my mind and probably will
Raise its head till the day I die.
  Reba M. Gibson

The Dream

Last night was made for you and me
When you took me by the side of the sea
And all that was in view
Was you and that luscious ocean blue
You night we were together and never did part
We lay side by side and heart by heart
You took me by the hand
And we walked barefoot in the sand
Up and down the shoreline
And everything was fine
'Till I woke the very next day
And had nothing to say.
  Shannon Ingraham

I Know It's There

I can't see friendship but I know it's there
  whenever my friends show they care.

I can't see generosity but I know it's there
  whenever I see rich people give poor
    people a pair.

I can't see curiosity but I know it's there
whenever I see tickets and wonder if they're
    for the fair.

I can't see joy but I know it's there
  when you hear a little boy's laughter
    in the air.
  Kristen McCabe

Beyond The Vows

Love is a space beyond likes and dislikes
Where all is reconciled in heart's sight
A man and a woman bound by complete unity
Protect it with freedom...a thing of beauty

You are the artists sculpting the clay
Use your imagination, day by day
Work your dreams into tangible forms
Creating compatibility surpassing the norms

Let your harmonious energies unfold
A sense of fulfillment and memories untold
Shield it from adversities with a united stance
Strengthen it with unselfishness, take no chance

Forget past mistakes...just let them go
Learn to find joy in what is bestowed
Two hearts letting their fears disappear
Creating a trust outlasting the years

Your love will be the sunshine of your soul
Even after the years have taken their toll
Your marriage will fill the seasons of your life
Because today you become husband and wife
  Linda L. Wells

In Loving Memory Of Kathleen

There is a school in heaven
Where angels fill the hall.
The rooms are bright and cheerful;
The voices soft and small.

The students in room 102 are smiling more today.
The teacher they've been waiting for is finally on her way.

They needed someone special.
Someone who'd really care.
Someone to make their learning fun.
Someone with knowledge she would share.

The children wait in quiet rows.
The door is opening wide.
A teacher young and pretty
Slowly walks inside.

She touches each and every face;
Adjusts one small halo.
Then turns and opens up a book.
The room begins to glow.

The students in room 102 are smiling more today.
The teacher they've been waiting for is finally here to stay.
  Pat Parker

Trials Of Work

Hare you ever worked in a place like this,
Where everything is not all bliss,
Where people tattle galore,
Getting you in trouble makes them want more,
Seeing you embarrassed, humiliated, and cry,
Makes them laugh but makes you sigh.

Makes you think where can I go now,
For help making yourself a solemn vow,
Never to work in a place like this,
For when you leave you will not miss.

No one at work you can talk to,
Because of all the under hand deals,
The final joke is really on you,
Your heart sinks and your mind reels,
To know they get away with anything about you,
That you never know when you are new.
  Patricia Manix

Growing Up

I wonder now, what will I be?
Where I am headed, what will I see.

Fears are many, my thoughts unclear.
Scared to be little and afraid to grow,
Will my friends accept me? How will I know?

The questions that my mind think up,
If only I could pour them all in a cup.
Then pour them back out and ask again,
What should I do and when?

What will my life be and will I like it?
What will I wear, and will I share?
There are so many questions to ask you see,
So maybe asking is not the key.

I guess what I am saying is what will happen to me?
But I think I will wait and see what I will be.

Melinda Dickinson

Just Me And My Thoughts

I've dreamt of a place high in the sky,
where I go to dream.
There's no cars, no pollution, no killers,
just me and my thoughts.
there's no news broadcasts, no homework, no teacher,
just me and my thought.
There's no one telling me how to look, how to dress, how to act,
just me and my thoughts.
There's no one criticizing me, hitting me, hurting me,
just me and my thoughts.
A quiet place where I can escape and be myself,
with just me and my thoughts.

Tricia A. Reed

Where Have All The Children Gone

Where have all the children gone?
Where is the innocence and utter belief in the unbelievable?
Uppers and downers, squirt bottles and spray cans
Pot and pills are too frequently becoming today's heros
Where have all the children gone?

Where have all the children gone?
Home is a street, a car or an open field
Hunger is a constant companion gnawing at them forever
Hot Potato is no longer a game but an unattainable dream
Where have all the children gone?

Where have all the children gone?
Ireland, Serajavo, Mideast, South Africa, America violence everywhere
Dodge bullet, Bomb the enemy, Hate these are the new games
No one is safe, frightened faces, scarred bodies and hearts
Where have all the children gone?

The children are gone miniature adults in there place
Divided we have done this. United we can save them
Set aside your prejudice, your hatred, your differences
Unite as one people of the world. Save The Children!

Where have all the children gone?

Michele Daniels

Forgotten Heroes

There's a place in Southeast Asia, a country called Korea
where men fought and died, for three long miserable years
In summers we burnt up, winters we froze and the rains
  were terrible as we all know.
We fought from Old Baldy, Heartbreak Ridge to Pork Chop Hill
No one knowing the hell we went through.
Today no one remembers us, I think that's a shame
Our government or the media never mentions our name
We're the "Forgotten Heroes" and no one gives a damn
And we who served there, never ask for a thing
But, God knows we fought with pride to give others
  peace and rest.
So I ask, did those who served and died, did this all in vain?
If not, then let our country - "REMEMBER OUR NAMES"

Willie M. Flanagan

The Bambi Walk

Come walk with us under the vanilla-neon sky
where snake charmers blow and fat cats lap battery acid.
We can watch the players toss highballs and volleyballs
over the brewery's left field.

Nancy shepherds the waddling passersby into her pantry.
Susan stands on the corner threading novelties,
grateful that better days have arrived
through the gateway.

Lenny and Mac rally together, quacking Parisian
and celebrating Brandy's priestly liberty,
while the glass-bottom boats hop across the formica sea's
amber waves of grain.

This uptown is no longer in vogue with the river town.
There is no great escape from what was once an ear's ecstasy.
Napoleon's white castles once stood on these treasure islands;
tonight the highland traders pore over their books.

Behold the phoenix rising over the creamy-white mountain!
It beckons us to the back door of another place,
searching and seeking for the Bard's twice-told tales.

Randy H. Farb

"Bleeding Heart Part II"

Blood drips from his soul, through the hole,
where the life has flows out
Though the life is gone his soul is trapped within depths
in which he created
Love, is it God's gift or Satan's?
The same disease that infects a man and lifts him to his greatest
heights also brings him to the bowels of the universe
and question yet his own existence
Is it heaven or hell?
Why would such a "gift" bring such misery if it were God-like
and yet why would such and evil bring such pleasure
if it were Satan-like
Is love just a battle between the two, a war in which a sole survivor
creates eternal life or eternal hell?
The price paid for love hardly sometimes seems worth the nanosecond
of good it has brought
And some would trade a lifetime of malevolence for a moment of love
Some condemn others for not loving but who could blame these torn
souls, scampering from fate
Are they running from hell or to it?

Scott A. Vermillion

Untitled

Search your mind,
where thoughts run
from brothers of feeling.

Smell the asphalt, for your rain
will spring rivers that spell my name.

Look in your mirror and imagine my eyes
like a dream's epilogue you are paralyzed.

For the traces left upon you are indelible.
and the spawning of love is like time,
a continuous circle that we all ride.

And as some jump to solitude
ever longing for their past,
others ride on
searching for their cast.

Me? Who knows.
I'll introduce myself in the morning
to recognize my mistake.
And as the day falls to dusk
our bond will break.

Timothy Ray Woods

Wondering & Wandering

Wondering and wandering down life's road,
where will it lead? No one knows.
We plant seeds along the way that will grow and mature
someday - helping us to endure.
Finally, we'll reach our destination,
becoming an asset to the nation.
Contributing to a newer and better plan to
save the world if we can.
Please take a look and don't let our children
fall through the cracks, becoming hooked and following
crooks, but instead getting the facts on what it takes
to be the best.
Take a risk and open a book - find the key to succeed.
Put a stop once and for all to the wondering and wandering.
Don't be afraid, for I say -
it's fate and we've all got a date.

Kimberley Morgan

Lost Love

Have you ever been in love?
Where you walk him home hand in hand and day by day,
you drift further and further away?
And his blond hair, blue eyes, shine the moment
he sees you. Oh, and day by day, quarrels begin
and you fight to the point you don't speak.
You begin to miss his shiny blond hair and crystal
blue eyes; the times he doesn't look into your eyes.
After seeing him day after day, you can say
your heart breaks and you can tell he's feeling the same way.
If only love didn't have this effect,
if only you can say to him what you felt,
if only you could have enough courage
to say what you have always wanted to say... I love you.
  Isn't love funny this way!

Lisa Wutzke

It's Coming

There's a noise around the corner and it went bang.
Where's it coming from? I don't know.
My inner voice says to calm down, it's nothing to be frightened of.
But I don't know what it is. Can you tell me?
No I can't tell you
Please hold me and I won't be scared. Well ok.

Didn't you see what the noise was about? No why should I?
Don't be mean. I'm not mean. Yes you are. Oh I'm sorry.
Well let's go then if you say it's nothing.
BANG!!!!!!!!!!
There it is again. Why did you tell me not to be afraid?
I didn't actually think it was harmful.
Well you may be wrong this time.
Oh well, nobody's perfect not even your inner voice.
You are lying to me. Why? Why not?
Even an inner voice needs comforting too. Don't you think??
No! You're supposed to be my guidance not my antagonizer.
See you later. Bye-Bye, Bye-Bye.

Karen Willows

"Eyes Of Faith"

Starlight shimmers 'neath the dark
  Which blankets the sky at night-
Barely visible to the eye,
  But shining just the same.
Those who have true faith in light
  Can see it bright at day,
For they see the stars from within their hearts
  Where the truest of sights are known.
Love can sometimes be the same-
  Shadowed from our sight,
Although beneath lies blinding emotion
  Just waiting to be discovered.
Look beyond the clouds with
  Eyes of faith, and your
Heart will carry you to love.

Paula A. Dabney

Water's Edge

It was that night,
Which the full moon shone bright,
And reflected off the thin layer of clouds
That covered the sky,
That we raced up the last tall dune,
And reached the top,
To hear a sudden roar of crashing waves,
And the wind in our ears,
And peered far below
To the water's edge,
And the deep churning water,
And silenced each other...
And bent low... and saw the black.
And saw the black dragging a dark bundle
To meet a deep and frozen grave.
And saw the black turn,
And set this silver gaze on us.
And a coldness hung
As his eyes reflected the moon's color,
And he disappeared, and another sailor died.

Lisa Burgess

The Monster Among Us

An evil monster lives among us all.
While growing, living off the ignorant,
It segregates our brothers, rips apart
Our home, infecting it 'till it must fall.
To banish evermore this evil wall,
Which possibly will nevermore depart,
How possibly can mortal beings confront
And waste this biased, evil spectacle?

At length, to settle the evil concern,
Expose to education everyone,
And we can slay the partial enemy.
For using knowledge better we discern
What racist means, rejoice what we have won
With new found brothers into harmony.

Rafael Verduzco

Pausing In The Sunlight

I dreamed we lived in harmony, my nemesis and I
While pausing in the sunlight, as late summer drifted by.
Sufficient was the stifling heat that steamy August day
To melt away our enmity and keep discord at bay.
We neither feigned affection (for no friendship was inferred)
Yet when the other's back was turned, we neither breathed a word.
So in the sultry silence of that sweltering summer scene
We happened, in a moment rare, each other's strengths to glean.
For who's to say our differences need necessarily be
Partitions rigid, blocking out the light by which to see
That there had been a reason our disparate paths had crossed;
And if we'd backed away, it would forever have been lost.
I dreamed we lived in harmony, thus having finally found
A peaceful coexistence which required no common ground.

Laura Davis

Wishful Thinking

The winter clouds hug a golden December moon
while the cold night winds sweep the new fallen snow
in patterns across the land.

The stars twinkle shyly,
playing hide and seek in the midnight blue sky,
casting their light on the quieting earth below.

Nature breathes a sigh of relief as the day ends.
The quiet becomes calm,
calm becomes peace,
peace becomes the night,
and the world rests in silent slumber
to await the dawn of a fresh new day.

Kimberly Lucas

Life?

I've never seen the diamonds stars and don't know Black from
White - I'll never know the singing birds nor the difference
between wrong and right.
I myself questions - but the answers are unseen?
What if I had a chance might I have been?
I wonder now tall might I have stood or what place would I call
home? Someone tell me what color my eyes would be, though on
Earth those eyes will never be allowed to see.
So I ask you, what is a bean, what is it like to walk on Wet Sand?
What is a snowflake and why does it from heaven down to Land?
I don't ask much and it seems so unfair...
All I want is to feel both summer and winter pass to know both
fall and spring. I don't ask for love, if it's too much, you
don't even need to care - I think It'd nice to breath my first
breath, live my first day, say my first word, maybe climb my
first tree. That's all I ask, but now the chance has passed.
Just think what might've happened had you given me a chance
That's all - just a chance - a chance...
All I wanted was a chance.

Kristen Lowman

Forever Lovers

On a secluded bench in the park one night, two lovers sat
while the stars shone bright, and the moon rode through the
blackened sky, like a golden prince astride on high.

But to these things he was not aware. All he saw was her
long brown hair. And the dizzying depth of her big brown eyes,
and her lips that looked like paradise.

And to the night she was not aware. She thinking about
how much she cared for the handsome young man whose hand she
held, and knowing soon there would be wedding bells.

And on that park bench they vowed to be, together for all
eternity. They kept those vows through many years, through
joy and laughter, pain and tears.

They had three children who are grown, and now have children
of their own.

These babes were such a source of joy, every precious girl
and boy.

They loved their way through many years, days of laughter
days of tears.

Now every mellow starlit night, a couple sits with hair of
white. With hands clasped tight they know they'll be, together
through all eternity.

Mary K. VanWagenen

The Voice From The Sea

My lady was all dressed in white
While walking by the sea
I never will forget my love
Her voice keeps calling me

We use to set upon the banks
So closely to the sea
The sea then opened up its mouth
And took my love from me

Who's gonna sleep with me tonight
Who'll lay by my side
The sea is hungry for our love
Come closer to the tide

Here's looking at me, here's looking at you
My eyes are brown, your eyes are blue
The soft winds blowing the gentle breeze
Come into my ocean, come into my sea

You will sleep with me tonight
You'll lay be my side
You will come and join me
The voice from the sea

Yvonne Bennett

My Friend My Love

My friend of a short while
Who hath stolen my heart from thee
Shall always be given
Whatever is desired of me.

My love who hath slipped into my path of life
Who hath made what seemed shallow
moments shared feel so deep
Will always be with me
Even as I sleep.

For you my friend, my love
With these moments, these feelings shared
I giveth my heart to your trusted care.

For Tim...

Sarah Jane Tillman

Chant Of The Unborn Or Why Did You Throw Me
Out My Window

I look out my window all I can see is
White white white It is pretty but I
Just don't want no more Snow it is cold
As it is pretty and can be very ugly if you
Think about it.
Slick as Icicles in the night cars
Slide over the making bigger ditches
Time after time
Up this hill is worst of all road scrappers
Sliding from side to side Cars back
Down again School buses getting stuck up
And winter just began Sometimes the
Pretty things cost the biggest prices and
when it's all over no one comes out more
happy than I am to be on top again.

So glad it ended need no more
Waiting for spring to come bouncing
In my front door.
Out my window
That's what I see.
Mary Williams

The Rape

    I have gone as far as the sparrow,
who forgets herself in blue, sun-filtered space,
  and is eyed by the hawk's calculated calm,
    as he grins at the dreamer's disgrace,
      and waits.

For that sparrow to tire of carousing currents,
  and abandon herself to a sleeping glide—
While that hawk is preening his preying passion,
    taloned, temperance—
    Nature naturally on his side.
  Lisa A. Gunderson

Untitled

  Let the lessons of life bring knowledge to those
  who have unfortunately traveled the darkest roads.

    Bring opportunity to many who have no hope,
    of being successful or learning to cope.

  Dry the tears of parents whose children are lost,
  either physically or mentally it's a high cost.

  Give answers to children whose questions are plenty,
  Give understanding and patience to those without any.

    Educate the world about getting along
  and working together to correct what is wrong.

  Think positive thoughts in the midst of despair,
  try to change things you think the unfair.

    Fight for equality and unity will come.
  Praise your fellow man for good things he's done.

  Lend a helping hand to those without dreams
  sew their confidence up when it tears at the seams.

    Be true to yourself and never stop reaching,
  for the goals that you set and success that you're seeking.

    Promise yourself that you are number one.
  Then you can help others in the races they run.
  Monica Rachelle Johnson

"How Did They Know?"

There once was a boy and a girl
Who lived in two separate worlds
Their friends got them to go on a date-
Looking back now it seems it must have been fate
She was engaged to someone else
And from what's been told, his morals were high up on a shelf
They dated for a whole two weeks before they knew
Just what they needed to do
He asked her to marry him and she happily said yes
Who would've known, who would've guessed
That twenty-eight years later they'd still be together
Through good and not so good weather.
You ask, "How did they know?"
Well, hasn't their marriage put on quite a show?
They display their love and affection (a little too) often
Sometimes it makes their kids want to go and hide in a coffin
After all, who wants to see their parents make out?...
Me, 'cause I'm lucky their love has worked out!
They've been together for soooo long
And they'll be together 'till the end of all dawns
Their love is the strongest I've seen
I'm glad to say "those are my parents", my brother's and me's!!!
  Susan Jill Granat

Stars And Stripes Forever
Dedicated to Jeremy and Kyle

In the year 1994 a president bids farewell to another man
Who served his country well by ending a war to ban
Hoping his generation and every generation thereafter
Follows in his footsteps to bring forth peace and laughter
By enforcing his power he gave that many more years
For the pursuit of life and liberty for all our tears
He proved that blood-shed was too imminent of danger
American soldiers grouped into troops were treated like strangers
Just because they wanted to save another impoverished country
From mistreating their own kind, through the television I see
God's intention was for days and investments shared
Creating the heavens and earth, short of time he really cared!
President Nixon provided U.S. lands with the highest heritage
To teach and understand the candidacy, he made a pledge
Later in his term he saluted with both hands in the air
By making peace signs with two fingers, he had such flair!
With every hour passing by I know I'm going to miss him
He will be remembered always by a woman named Kim
For Richard was a good father who expressed his love
By giving a sincere smile from pride inside and above
  Kimbie

Too Late

I picture an embittered, empty, old child
  who sits at a grave;
He talks some, and cries some,
  and the dirt and stone are his only audience.
He was too busy and too selfish in life,
  to show the love that he privately felt.

Now he converses with death,
  and guilt is his only companion.
A man who desperately seeks comfort and relief
  from his ever-knowing pain.

So for the remainder of his life,
  he will rendezvous with a corpse,
And pour his broken heart out
  to dirt and stone.
  Kristine Lipartito

In Memory Of Shinika Ford

Why did she have to go to Augusta that day?
Why did she have to go that weekend and stay?

Nobody knows why she had to die.
Now in the ground is where she's going to lie.

Some people didn't get a chance to say good - bye.
Now all they can do is cry.

Some people lost their best friend,
For them it probable seems like the end.

She's always had a place in my heart,
Right from the very start.

This year her and a lot of people were close,
And when she died in their heart is were it hurt the most.

When the bullet hit her, she fell to her knees.
That moment, she lost the chance to fulfill her dreams.

A lawyer is what she wanted to be.
She wanted to help others you see.

No one can do exactly the things she did,
At the time that she was a kid.

Now her memory lives forever.
In heaven is where her life is much better.

Shaniqua Maria Ray

Untitled

This never ceases to happen to me,
Why do I mess up, never able to see.

The word just always seems to slip,
And now my friendships, away I chip.

There are few who truly care for me,
And the ones who do,
Don't understand just what I see.

I no longer understand,
These feelings I have.
It's like I should take a stand,
But I know better,
I know that I can't.

I don't know where to turn,
For my best friend, my secrets are never safe with her.

I just always keep my feelings in my heart.
Weighing it down, until I know not where to start.

Why can't I find, that one true friend?
The one that will be there, until my end.

Mary McMurray

Look And See

As we pass through this complex life
Why do we always fail to see?
The joy and happiness that is around us,
Just as God always meant it to be.

We pass someone on the street,
With happy glances, we pause to greet,
Sending a sincere smile or a happy hello
We send them on their way, then away we go,

It is often said that in our constant haste,
We miss so many things we should not waste,
Like reaching out to lend a helping hand,
Then hope and pray that it will spread out over land,
So I trust we can all pause and take heart,
That it will be a new beginning,
Or at least a start.

Leuna Perry Ferguson

Girl In The Garden

Girl in the Garden
Why do you sit there and frown all day
Can anything make your sadness go away
You always seem unhappy even on the brightest of days
You never let the sun come your way
You always wait under a shaded tree until the day is gone
Girl in the garden
Now I understand how you feel and why you feel that way
Because you think that no one understands you, and you think you're
Blamed for everything
No one understands you and no one cares
Girl in the garden
Life is passing you by
You're the only one who can make yourself happy
So why don't you try
Girl in the garden
Someone cares
So why don't you let them!

Sara Morelan

The Accomplished

Why do flowers bloom, knowing they're going to whither?
Why does a caterpillar change its nature, knowing it has
a short life? Why does snow fall, knowing it's going to melt?
Why do fish lay eggs, and watch them fall into mans' traps?
And why does man give birth, knowing the child is born with
sin? The answer is simple, it's a way of life. Some come and
go. Some grow, and some die at birth. But what's
accomplished, can never be changed. No matter why. No matter
how.

Nune Gazdhyan

Animal Sounds in the Spring

Animals, animals all around
Why don't you come out and hear the sound?
Birds are chirping peacefully,
Wolves are howling,
Bears are growling,
Come out and hear the sound.
The winds are whistling,
Crows are crowing,
Bees are buzzing,
Come out and hear the sound.
Time is flying by and by
So hurry up before it's too late
Because the forest goes to bed at eight.

Lauren Feldman

Sonnet

Sometimes I wonder and ask why's it so,
Why people you love sometimes have to leave?
Is there really a better place to go?
In life it's hard to know what to believe.
Is this a time to rejoice or to grieve?
A thought crosses my mind, can this be it,
One more memory I want to retrieve?
For I am frightened that I shall forget.
The acceptance of death comes bit by bit.
Is there a lesson of mine to be learned?
Is this a test of my will and my wit?
An explanation for death I have yearned.
With any reason, there's no exceptions,
Till my death, there's no answer to my questions.

Theresa Arbaugh

What Am I To Do With All This Violence

What should it matter what color my skin is.
Why should it matter who I hang with.
How come it matters if I'm black or white
My friends are being shot down like flies.
I wonder if I am to be the next one,
because I hold hands with the hardest one.
I wish the cries would stop in my head,
of all shots and my dying friends
No matter how hard I pray at night,
I know the gun shots will never die.
When the bullets aren't wishing and all is quiet
It doesn't mean that the violence is silent.

Kristi Orduna

Dear God

Dear God,
  Why there is so much pain in my heart?
  Why there are too much tears, that I can't hide?
  Why there are too many homeless in this world?
  Where is the second chance?!

  Why there are too many orphans in this world?
  Who will love them?!

  Why there is war here and there?
  What happened to peace?!
  Why there is not much to share?
  Where is love?!
Dear God,
  Why there is no freedom in my land?

  My people are dying inside and it's so sad.

  I can feel the pain in my soul.
  I can feel the anger in my blood.
  I can feel the tears in my heart.

Dear God,
  Tell me why?!!

Soodabeh Abdollahi

What Is My Role?

Across the desert incipient questions loom.
Why? Why am I here? What's my role?
No time to think, just go - go rolling over hostile terrain.
Who is to blame?
My God, who is this mad man named Hussein?
The night is upon us; wind blowing so hard the sand
becomes an East-West collage.
The rain is coming down in sheets of confusion,
leaving pools of doubt.
Marking time, life is standing still.
Iraqi soldiers put on line, only to be killed.
By bullets and bombs?
Not hardly, perhaps by Hussein's Red Dawn.
There's fleeting moments of sanity, yet I must go forward.
Who's on my left; my right; above?
Is it to be so true that the enemy is really not a military machine,
rather a monolith of suppressed beings?
Again I ask, "What Is my role?"
A voice speaks with certainty from within:
"Your role?.....Survive!!!"

William D. Tenner

"Indulging"

Sometimes I wonder, I have to stop and think
Will it ever be easy - will I not want to drink
I try to understand - the words that I repeat
It's a never ending task - I can never drink
God, it's so hard - my mouth gets so dry
Sometimes when I'm alone - I just want to cry
Why did this happen to me - where did I go wrong
Why couldn't I have been stronger - when I was so young
I will continue to believe - and I will constantly pray
But more than anything - I will attend AA
I would like to offer this message - to anyone just starting
Remember to drink in moderation - at a social or perhaps a party
Don't let it take hold of you - don't let it become a crutch
Trust me on this one - for about this I know so much
Don't take the chances I did - don't think it can't happen to you
Believe in what I'm saying - for I am living proof

Patricia Zwernemann

Kiss Me My Empty

Can the evildoers hear the eerie reveille I write?
Will it matter to Him if their blood is shed?
Anger with rage fill a heart; pain, my eyes.
To the ones that hold us down, one more push
And I travel past realities door.
Save them from the Revenger's path;
Save us from the bloodbath.
Their souls escape them as they continue
To put bullets in my shell.
Hundreds of guns pointed at me, shooting; me at trigger.
Thousands of bullets hit and I'm still alive.
Just one to them and they cease to survive.
Oh, when they lied; oh, how I died.
Now I swim in the liquids of your brain,
I hide behind the subconscious side.
I push a threaded needle out their cornea from deep inside.
They were always blind, but now they will never see.
Woe is he; who is me.
Stay away from thy chamber that kept you inside.

Robert James Guardino

Our Flag Is With You Always

You think in your mind that burning our flag
Will make us bend or begin to sag,

But look, as it burns the colors won't fade,
They have just grown brighter, as it moves in a wave.

As our flag burns, the smoke and the ash,
Will seep into your pores and forever flash.

As years go by you will always see,
Red sunsets, white Stars and the Blue of the sea.

In your minds eye the colors are set,
You'll remember the deed you would like to forget.

Shirley A. Voss

Innocent Fortune

There is this boy, a poor little boy
  with skin so fair and clear as the sky.
Hair as shiny as the sun,
  and eyes as blue as the clearest blue waters.
His hands are as smooth as the finest silk,
  and his silhouette is as frail as a butterflies wings.
His imagination is as wild as an ocean on a stormy night,
  and yet his dreams are as sweet as sugar.
He tells everyone I'm not poor
  I'm just as rich as you are only in the heart.
So there is no such thing as being poor,
  but there is a such thing as having a heart.

Tanya Ritchie

Post Mortem

Have you ever wondered what it would be like to be dead?
Will we be sensitive to sight and scents and sounds?
Or will we be blissfully unaware of everything?
No hearing, no hurting and no hating.
Will we smile at the inane things people say?
Like, "He's out of his pain now," or
"He enjoyed a good full life," or
"If you must go, that's the way to go,"or
"He looks so natural lying there."
Will any of life's mysteries be revealed,
Or are we forever doomed to dormant dreamlessness?
Perhaps we should not despair at this,
It may be better not to know.
Yet, I am very curious about being dead—-
But not all that curious.

Morley R. Wilson

Who I Am

When you see me at my burial spotlight
Will you still lecture me on what's wrong and right?
Will you have as much time to take as
when you did when you thought I was fake?
Since I've stayed true to form, find yourself
Something new to main
'Cause sub-pop has accepted my sound and name
I haven't struck it rich or got fortune or fame
So try to find yourself a willing scapegoat
Cause I've escaped from your grip on my throat
And I've gone on to things bigger and brighter
I'm a believer, not simply a lover or fighter
I am a writer.

Todd L. Fritz

Light Of The Moon

Living in a world where you can never
win, you try to drown your sorrows, but
they somehow learn to swim.
Inside your mind just wanders and never
finds your soul.
You fear the tears won't stop, unless the
truth is told.
Now lurking through the shadows you start to
chase the moon, still looking for a light in
your haunted little room.
But the light was never there, in the darkness
you still search.
In the cold all stars are lost, like the bird
without a perch.

Nicole Crosbie

Jodi's Love Story

She was so young when she gave birth to her son and yet
wise beyond her years. How could she alone provide
him with a home, she asked this...very sincere. He
deserved more, she was too poor; she decided in her
tears. So she gave him to another who would become his
mother, this decision would quiet her fears.

Time has passed, she can look for him at last! Where to
begin, her leads are thin but she will persevere. Now he
is found, by the courts she is bound... They say: Eighteen!
She must adhere. However, good news! Preparations
were made for that future day when she would reappear.
The cedar chest holds the clue, to the woman he once
knew and the contents within keep her love for
him... always near.

Kathleen M. Price

Truckers Prayer

Oh Almighty God whose loving power and eternal
   Wisdom embraces us all.

Watch over all truckers this day.
These dedicated men and women who are responsible for moving the
nations cargo across all lands, whether it be through city,
state or country.

   Bless these trucks they drive
So that they all may arrive.
   Onward they go forth
With their deliveries of great worth,
   Bless their wits and sight all day
On streets where children are play;
   Make their judgement sharp as steel
And be their hands that grip the wheel.
   During the darkest nights be their candle
Don't give them any more than they can handle.
   Whatever the order, the dispatcher will shout,
They turn the key and the big rig moves out.

Away they go - Again they drive, bless them Father - keep them alive.
   Amen

Patricia J. Jones

Love Hurts

   Love hurts when I see you walk away
     Wishing, waiting for the day
    When you come back to my heart
      Wanting another start

   Love hurts when I love you much
Wanting you to hold me with you're special touch
    I never meant for you to leave
     Please will you believe

   Love hurts when it's so strong
   Love is what life is among
  All that I want is another chance
 Please can we have back the romance

Michelle Worley

Just Like An Angel In Heaven

I want to be just an angel in the heavens.
With a golden halo upon my head,
And wings as strong as iron.
As to hold my soul as I look down upon the earth's surface
And find the love upon it.

I want to be angel in the heavens

So that I can be able to see and touch our father.
His son Jesus. And feel the power of the Holy Ghost
That will let me dance with thee.

I want to be an angel in the heavens

So that I can cherish and love deeply
The goodness of my soul
Being in the heaven as I am told that my age may go on
But I will never get old.

The heavens is the fountain of my youth
Because up there God, will treasure my soul
And keep it whole.

I want to be an angel in the heavens

I want to praise God in every way
So that I can come back to earth someday.

Peggy A. Brown

My Road Of Life

I thought I was having a dream; looking down a road
with a sign that read: Your Life.
I was persuaded to walk down the road,
for I wanted to see what I had accomplished in life.

However, my walk was short,
and before I knew it, my life was over.
I was at the end of the road.
As I turned back to look at the road and recall my journey,
I saw something very strange.
My road had no twists or turns; it was a long, straight road
with only a few rocks and twigs to stumble upon.

My life had no obstacle, it was simple and neat.
As a little girl, I planned out my whole life
without leaving a single event out.
But, getting older, I guess I took my life as it came.

It was only then that I knew it was too late in life
to switch the road I had chosen for myself.
I took my road of life as it was,
realizing that if I was still alive,
my dreams of life were dead.

Nicolina Marra

'You And Me'

At home all alone, I was faced with myself,
with all the beauty and ugliness to see.
As I stood beside a full length mirror,
What an ugly person... that's me.

The longer I stood and stared at her,
The more wonderful a person shone through,
Then I realized I was seeing a pair,
what a wonderful person.. that's you.

With all that's good and kind inside,
And all that's ugly and all that's bad.
But only the warmth and love shines through,
Because of the kind of life we've had.

Today as I stand, once again in the mirror,
With a smile and a feeling of home.
I know now, what I wish I knew then,
As long as there's you, I'm not alone.

The person I have since became
for all the world to see,
It's a warm and caring combination
of a pair.. you and me.

Marie Ross

Mary's Gift

She look so tiny standing there just barely one year old
With bright blue eyes and flying curls of gold.
Her little hand held up to me, and in that tiny palm,
A yellow dandelion lay to act as Gilead's balm;
To ease my grief and set me free -
For Mary gave a flower to me.

Leslie Nivens

"Straight From The Heart"

What will I do with a most desired space?
With red roses that will not wither, I will furnish it.
With strength gathered by being there, I will protect it.
I won't own it' nor rule it,
but will feel like a king.
If there could ever be any room in your heart for me.

Maximo De Pena

You

My life is full with wonderful things.
With bright blue skies, and the happiness you bring.
I wake each morning and see you sleeping nearby,
So calm and peaceful, sometimes I just cry.
To think that a man as wonderful as you,
could love me and want me like you say you do.
When you hold me so close and tell me you care,
all my sadness and fears seem to disappear.
I live each day so happy you're near,
Trying so hard to show you I care.
I love you so much sometimes I play the fool,
jealous and mad and losing my cool.
It's only because I love you so much
Your kisses, your holding, your tender touch.

The look in your eyes when we make love,
They seem to shine as bright as the stars in the sky above.
So thank you my love for your tender touch,
And thank you for loving me oh so very much.

Mary Ann Dunham

Indian Summer Symphony

Indian Summer
with Her beautiful Art
and warm breath slipping over the city
challenges Autumn-Winter for Dawn
and clouds His slaughter with Her own;
wilting our Sunflower Sister, perspiring
as She droops Her head sadly

The day progresses
amidst solemn acceptance and weary efforts
as the smog blankets the blue Sky and suffocates the gasping Trees
as the soft hum of familiarity reaches to embrace the ears

A myriad of colors dances behind the blue-green Sea,
calmly awaiting the Autumn breeze,
and closes the heavy afternoon

The groggy Eve
tumbles in, sticky in reprisal; through the tussled bedsheets,
stained with familiar exasperation and uniform dreams
under the starless Pacific Sky

Sleeping Autumn
with His gentle whisper, silently retorts upon November.

Sabrina McNamara

Warren

Standing by the highway east of Tombstone
    with his thumb in the air,
He said his name was Warren and
    was headed for a nearby town
Where, at a small cafe with friends around,
    he would visit with his girl.

As I drove he talked about his home,
    named the hills and ridges
Standing out against the sky
    and proudly pointed to the spot
Where, one morning about six o'clock,
    his Dad had killed a deer.

I left him by the curbside
    in scuffed boots and faded jeans
And watched him in the mirror
    cross the street against the light
Where, glowing softly in his sight,
    she took his hand in hers.

W. Richard Dempsey

"One Who Is Great"

Special person in our lives.
With melodious character you sing, "This Little Light of Mine."
The ability to Love all those around you is indeed honorable.
Acceptance of our separation.
A smile and a kiss, I leave you to enlighten someone else's day.
There are no boundaries for your desire of knowledge.
The stamp of your smile is abiding in my mind. Soon I will requite.
Exultation you are mine - again.
Teacher or student, we trade the roles. Opening each other's sentiment
to a very mindful presence.
To see you harmonize with each situation that confronts you - I am
humbled and most of the time embarrassed.
When sleep consumes your being at day's end. I savor captured
moments we have shared - this time.
Never let me erase your style.
This vast, enchanting world is yours.
Child of mine, ours, God's...
Karen E. Wilcox

Praise

I will Praise the Lord with my whole heart,
With my Faith Growing for a Fresh start,
Praising the lord by doing,
And not pursuing,

Something that isn't real.

I will Praise the Lord by seeing and

believing his accounts, of the world as it is.
I will Praise the Lord by Forgiving

and giving where I can.
Thomas H. Mount

The Way I'll Always Feel

Sharing special moments beneath the rain and the sun
With no interest in two, for I'll love only one
An elegant smile, lovely eyes so green
Beauty deep within, never before ever seen

With joy and happiness filling up my heart
Longing for your certain kind of touch
Time being spent outside of your arms
I'm missing you oh so much

Feelings we share, as if we were one
Our bodies and minds unite
No fear or worries when we're together
Our love can be nothing but right

With passion and romance like never before
A flare of burning desire
You're loving and charming from day to day
My sparks turn into fire

You're everything I need, and much more to spare
Who could ask for anything more
Bringing out feelings I've never before felt
For you're the one I'll always adore.
Steven W. Mallacoccio

Amethyst

You stole my heart
You are going to be arrested
and put to death
Leave here right away
Otherwise, you will be killed by law of this country and
my stone heart.
Keiko Takano

Aunt Annie

For one who traveled cross the sea
With others who are a part of me
They came from a land of Austria pride
Where many fought and many died
They've endured hardship, endured pain
But with every step their strength regained
They built a life here on this land
With joyous hearts, and blistered hands
They worked the forest, worked the docks,
They worked the fields, and worked the stocks
They bore us here in the land of the free
Without their courage, where would we be.

This young girl sailed upon a ship
An felt it an adventurous trip
She's now the matriarch of the Kandel Klan
A representative for all we stand
One hundred years have past since birth
Now a living legend on this earth
Today we wish her all the best
For the many years that she has left.
Susan Browning Kelly

Untitled

As I wonder why such people
With talent fade their depression
in life as a face so questioned must
lie, lie for a secret of pain for fading
or burning out which they will never
stop to obtain, pain of sorrow which
they think there is no tomorrow.
Young adults will face life in challenge
as they drag their minds of pills, can you feel
the sorrow for innocent children
who shoot themselves without seeing
the Sun of day that will rob them of
their own future for they will never
know what is to become of tomorrow
for obsession will take over them to
bend and see the end of happiness not sorrow.
Yvonne Mona Denha

The Beach And You

As I walked along the ocean front
with thoughts of only you.
The waves seem to rush up to play
the way we used to do.
I stopped to pick up a shell or two
To keep and name for me and you.

Remembering how we walked and ran
to take a dip and roll in the sand
the castles we built, the tunnels we dug
were childlike I know, but so much fun.

How we watched the boats as they sailed out of sight
wishing for the time to sail our own
one last dip and watch the setting sun
some bread to sea gulls,
then a long walk home.

The sand and the ocean are both the same my dear
but the walk is lonesome without you near.
no more walks to the beach, until you return
then the ocean welcome us both hand and hand.
Porter Raney

Untitled

I saw a field of joy, swaying in the wind one day,
with wheat of sadness, flowers of fear, and grasses
of love were all so near. All of a sudden a creek of
hate catches your eye, with stones of madness,
a cave of fear, mountains of flame, and one lonely deer.

The sky of beauty was incredibly blue, and
evergreens of anger just waiting for you. While
watching this scene flow by and by, a piece of dust
was blown in your eye. Then you see that it's all a
dream flowing out to sea, oh let it be. So you decide
to head on home, but you soon discover you're all
alone. All of a sudden you can't find your way.....
but then you're awakened with a brand new day.

Katie Moore

You

Without you I am nothing,
With you I am everything.
Without you my life has no direction,
With you my life is guided.
Without you I am "dead",
With you I am "alive".
Without you I am "nobody,"
With you I am "somebody.'
Without you life is meaningless,
With you life is wonderful.
Without you I am "cold,"
With you I am "warm."
Without you I have no confidence,
With you I can do anything.
Without you I am like a wet leaf on a log,
With you I light up like a Christmas tree.
Without you I am like unseasoned food,
With you I am like the rarest delicacy.
Without you I have no hope nor faith.
With you my whole life lies.

Kay Christensen

Untitled

There you are kickin' back
With your gang, smokin' a joint and drinkin'
Here I am, crying every day of the night.
And praying for you to get out.

There are you are fightin' and killing.
Just because they came through your turf,
Here I am, again praying and crying,
Because I love you so much,
And I don't want to see you get hurt.
I don't want to be with you.

I feel scared and lonely,
I'm living in hell.
Everyday you come in and say,
"One of our "Homies" got killed and hurt."
I begin to think one of these day's
It's not gonna be "Our Homie".
It's gonna be you, the one I love.

Please get out before it's too late.
I'll do everything I can to help.
Do this for me, the one who loves you!

Vanessa Hernandez

A Portrait Of Silence

Silence is a foreign word that never repeats a face, a misty cloud
without a trail. In the chill of morning's breath, an old man's
colorful hair is frozen in place on the ground; his stiff body trapped
where he last stood, a graveyard for the painted leaves. Silence is a
transparent face, on the motionless pond as the mystical sculptor
carves its face under the spotlight of the moon and the camera's eyes.
Silence is a wishful word in a world of congested traffic. It is a man
that's never home and his voice is a phone that ceases to speak.
Silence is a language that's not understood. Thus, as a river its
babbling words are a strange untasted fruit. Silence is an echo, a
quiet voice, which roams through the valleys of city streets. Its
words are the cobble stone streets as the feet shuffle upon its rolling
tongue. It is a painting of a child in a universe of bass megaphones
yanking the pale moon from its orbit. Everyday I feel the hand of
silence through the trees like a patient wind. The world is like an
insane foghorn as its condemning voice gnashes for our attention. Like
winter, its claws thrash violent curses upon the heart of the dreamland
sleep. Oh, world of silence, with your ribbon of life, open the hands
of your golden gate and show us your gracious face amid the clouds of
misty thunder.

Kai Johnson

Hypothermia

So many degrees of it: heart
without love; breathless tundra wasteland
of a death; blue tinge of unyielding word,
once said, regretted into Arctic howling wind.

We probe the avalanche, find bones
of all prehistory's remains and ways
we fell and clambered with encumbered irons,
supplies, and ropes of groping towards centigrades

and Fahrenheits of strife - to abyss
of pinnacle, to slithery misstep plunge
of heights. Experts exhume and analyze
the poem we've become, the wild bungee

of tachisme into found-art of freeze
of what we attempted, failed - fractured
and concussioned into clutch and tumble of crevasse
and breach of mountain. We tracked skyward

the Everest momentum of an illusive heat. And there
we are discovered, in science and morphology,
in Morpheus of dream, in silent reach, utter
Siberia of body temperature that once flamed to ice.

Marvin Solomon

When Tomorrow Comes

I often sit at night when the moon is bright
Wondering if what I see in the sky is real
My mind occupied with thoughts of returning home
Maybe I will.....when tomorrow comes

I know not what the future holds for her impatiently waiting subjects
There may be peace and happiness throughout the Saudi land
Although pain and suffering may be future's plan
Whatever it shall be, we will know...when tomorrow comes

The message said war, to begin on the seventeenth
So the prayers to our Father, beg for peace
We shall see who is mightier, the sword or the tongue
The whole world will know...when tomorrow comes

Willie Stewart

Despair

I sit here in despair
wondering what the outcome will be.
My thoughts are running in confusion,
with no direct meaning.
I look everywhere for comfort or guidance.
Yet none seem forthcoming.
And as the day draws on,
the more I become anxious.
People's stares contain more meaning.
Do they know? Are they laughing?
Or is it pity I see in their eyes?
I get to the point,
When I can endure their presence no more.
And in my anguished state,
I cry out: I did it!

Melissa R. Barron

Into The Abyss

I am the artist,.
Words are my muse.
Lord of the manor
Complexity leaves you confused.
My words find you trapped,
No beginning, no end.
Contiguous letters seek you
Like claws that will rend.
The imagination takes you hostage,
Your mind seeks a path back to reality.
It seeks your dull ordinary personality,
Your quest is inconsequential because—
In this poem my thoughts rain in dominance.
My reality, though abstract,
Is potent and searing
Now that you've read this,
For the rest of your life,
In your head I'll be leering,
You are my weapon.

Monika Porter

Crack Mission

If I'm a person on Crack?
Would I sell my own flesh-n-blood?
For just one hit on the track?
Think again before the rising flood.

Time and time you want to quit.
But people just don't understand.
It's not all easy for me to split.
It's disease to my body, a big demand.

Will somebody help me get over my addiction?
Yes, God can help you if you'd only trust-n-not doubt.
But first you must want the change to come about.
This drug has caused you to have much friction.

But crack has gotten my soul-n-gone,
And people cast not your ball-n-stone.
Crack has stolen my mind. And has left me blind.

Has this drug gotten your mother, father, sister, brother, any
    relative,
And even your best friend.
And you say and pray please dear God, let it all come to an end

I'm on a crack mission and I'm in a track session.

Valleshia M. Shurn

Come Out And Play

My name is Cocaine
Would you come out and play?

Come with me and you will go where you've never been before
Take my hand
We'll reach the sky, see the universe,
touch the sun, leap over clouds

When we descend, we'll be in my territory
the darkest jungle, the deepest ocean
We will drop into the lowest of lows
down in the valleys, all through the forest
free to get lost in, all caught up in
Paths branching off in different directions
all leading nowhere

My name is Cocaine
Come on out...and play

Mona E. Couey

These I Would Do For You

What would you say, If I said I loved you?
Would you run and hide from me?
If I were to hold your hand? would you pull
it away from me?
If I were kiss your sweet tender lips?
would you turn away from me?
If I suddenly went away would you follow me?
Would you cross desserts, would you swim the
seas, would climb mountains high, just to love me?
I know one thing these I would for you if you were me!

Stephen R. Watrous

Firelight

You lie with her before the fire.
Woven together by shadows,
The flames flicker on her face,
Are reflected, dancing in her eyes.
You look into them, into the fire.
The fire that is reflected and the one that is her soul.
You could drown in those dancing flames,
Suffocate under a sea of emotion.
The corners of her mouth lift in a smile.
Her lips part slightly.
Her head tilts upward to yours.
You drink in her kiss,
Swept away on a swift, golden rush of ecstasy.
When it's over you look into her eyes,
Cool, blue firelight,
And you know that she loves you.
For the eyes are the windows of the soul,
And the feelings that burn there are hotter
Than the fire you lie before.

Lance Murdock

Plastic Soldiers

What's the purpose of sincerity?
You cry but the world never sees
It's a tool to use, your intentions clear behind
the smoke screen and insanity
I'll give you friends for the price of a dozen lies
Who can tell the difference oh Lord between a plastic
soldier and a golden arrow?
You're typecast and the crowd is on your side
You play your part and you're crucified
Just play your part, there's nowhere to hide
This act of social parody

S Robr

Victim

He met his enemy across the firing line;
Years later, with raised champagne glass,
He celebrated an end to all wars;
Through popping corks, he heard
A gun blast at close range, happy garbled New Years wishes
Mingled with orders to advance.

Still he danced and drank and remembered,
With threatening heartbeats, eyes and lips caked with mud;
Heavy army boots slipped in slime;

An eighteen-year-old soldier aimed his gun
As G.I. Joe raised his and fired; neither heard
Resounding screams of grenades, M-16s, rifles,
Only the deafening silence of fear.

In the ritual sanctity of a champagne glass
He saw again a fatal bullet flash
As strains of Auld Lang Syne would ne'er forget
His trembling hands, sweat-filled eyes,
Visions of his twisted victim wrapped in a shroud of dirt.

On New Year's Eve, a mirror's reflection,
Showed the living victim his Pyrrhic victory.

Shirley Brezenoff

Untitled

All the emotional poverty I wore like flaming
yellow whoregear
All the time and tears I squandered begging for
one or two tawdry crumbs of esteem
All the iron-boned resistance flawed and feared
And thus, I denied

Just to justify myself.

I may shrew from life's inequity and all
the suns I missed rising
I may echo the covert insanity of an
atrophied heart
I may even dance the poison energy of
madness.

But I no longer require affirmation or respite.

Now I know.
The rib that made Eve embraces, too, my heart.

Linda Clark

What Am I

As sharp as a razors edge am I
  yet my appearance is fleshy.
Able to make individuals feel small
  without little or no problem at all
Can get my owner in trouble
  with lies I know aren't true.
Still I can be pleasant
  when I want something sweet;
I receive my pain, for I can't take extreme heat.
As wicked as a serpents sting
  yet I carry no venom.
Able to cause my owner pain
  though I'm the one who feels the bite.
Gossip may roll from my owners lips
  but in every conversation
  in the middle I can be found.
I can lick any object
  that passes me by.
If you're as wise as you think you are
  try to guess what am I.

Michael C. Anthony

A New Friend

I met a new friend as I walked today,
Yet somehow she's stolen my heart away.
Tiny and helpless, yet somehow strong,
I sensed a problem, something wrong.

Physically beautiful, internally wise,
I noticed a special look in her eyes.
Puzzling glances, a manner so mild,
Yes it was true a handicapped child.

She asked naught but love,
From all those around her.
Her magnetic like warmth,
Drew us to surround her.

The joy she has brought from her heavenly place,
As seen in her precious angel like face.
A face that stops the hands of time,
You see that handicapped child is mine.

Linda L. Davis

"Norma Jeane"

You worked so hard to be someone.
  Yet, the world did not know,
  the frightened child named Norma Jeane;
  beneath Marilyn Monroe.
Behind the smile of glamour,
  lay the twisted frown of hate,
  For a world who would not love you;
Until it was all too late.
  affairs you had were many,
  yet loves you had were few.
And the image caught on camera,
  is all we have of you...
Maybe it was your plan to end your life that day.
  Murder, or, plain suicide,
  it's a secret either way...
Now the only wish I have,
  is for you to be serene.
I was born too late to save you,
  forgive me, Norma Jeane...

Paul W. Platt

Shadows

People think of them as shadows in society
Yet they are there, strong as ever
They are like the men of old movies
But they are real
They are fighters,
But would rather avoid fighting
They are the men in little girl's dreams
People would rather not understand them,
The horrors they've seen,
The pain they've suffered
Often they must leave their beautiful wives behind
Their little girls cling to them crying
Their little boys trying to be brave
And they must walk away
They go thousands of miles to defend
People who do not even know they are there
Society thinks it is over
And yet they fight on
They are heroes who never get mentioned.
They survived.

Katie Hopkins

The Best Friend I Had

I had a dream only about you
You alone cause you're someone so true
In my dream you're calling my name.
I recognized your voice but it didn't sound the same
When I saw your face I nearly lost my sight
I wanted to give you a hug, a hug with all my might
When I awakened, I shed a tear
Thinking that you'll never ever be near
The closest to you is in my dream
When you was here we made a perfect team
Missing you is breaking my heart
'Cause our friendship just went and drifted apart.
Anywhere I go I'll always think of you
I hope you do the same and think of me too!
But when you left I felt so sad
'Cause you were the only true best friend I had.

Tisha Araki

Lifetime Love

As we walk on the sand,
You and I hand in hand
Watching the pure white dove in the sky,
Knowing if you ever left me my heart would die.
Then you whispered "I love you" in my ear
And I felt I had nothing to fear.
Our love will last for years,
Through the smiles and the tears.
You will always be mine
'Till the end of time.

Kim Purtle

Quest for True Love

You filled me with kindness, you filled me with care.
You are a lady, my life, I'd like to share

You showed me the true meaning to the word called love
That made my heart flutter, like a dove

You are witty, wise and true
That match your eyes so loving blue

You are a woman that's so special
You remind me of life's loving vessel

We can only follow life's path, with the patter of feet
In hopes that someday, we will meet

Then we can say, I am yours and you are mine
When the day of true love, we will find

Victor Strickfaden

Life

First you are born, "What a beautiful sight."
You are loved and nurtured throughout your life.
    You are a willing learner as a child.
Rebellious, stubborn,and wild when you get to your
        teens.
Adulthood comes and what do you know, you are
        responsible and mature.
You become a parent and hear yourself saying, the
    words your parents said to you, the words you
        swore you'd never say.
    Then you become older, wiser, and worn,
        Grow older and your wisdom passed on.
Then you get older and pass on, but all of you did
    not leave, a piece of you was left behind.
Your memories and the words of wisdom will be passed
        on and on.

Melissa O'Connell

Looking In The Mirror

Looking at you reminds me of someone I know
You bring back memories and dreams that never came true
You never hurt me so how can I hate you, but
How can I love you I never knew you

How can I dream of you I never understood you
You are just the same portrait inside of my heart
Wear I can see and learn you
With the passion of my life.

Meri Kostanian

Gazingstock

I held you so closely as a friend;
You engaged my heart with terror
When I first looked into your eyes
And realized the passion you held so dearly.
I was careful to consider this door that had been opened
For me to wander through,
The magnitude of your draw
Gave me a reason to be grave.
Be cautious of this man with so stern a jaw,
Be aware of the sensitivity he cradles
And be true of heart.
And now that I have had some time
To wander within the room of you,
I hasten to say, please,
Please do not dismiss me.
The hum of love is in the air
And it should be a glorious tune.

Kathleen A. Carr

His Love

Lord Jesus, as I sit in despair I look to gaze upon your face, and you gazing back lovingly.

I see your face and am in awe of its beauty. For I know behind those piercing eyes is a heart so loving and tender that it cause my soul to long for its comforting power.

When you give that comfort, as only you can give it, I want to give it away. I hope and pray that I can give it as freely as you do, and as well as you do. As your servant Paul said, "If I have all good gifts, but I have no love; I am nothing."

You, Lord, are love and without love I am nothing.

Paul A. Dieken

True Love

True love is a thing
You have deep down inside,
When opposite two
are side by side.

Their eyes meet at once
a twinkle in both,
but before they know it
they are saying an oath.

The two are happy
together as one
for now everyone knows,
they can't be undone.

For now you know, what true love really is,
it's when certain two decide
to always be,
side by side.

Tracy Parham

"A Christmas Poem"

I don't have to wait until Christmas to get a gift of the heart,
You have given me the only gift I need when you gave me your heart.
I don't have to wait until Christmas to see a bright star shine,
The stars in your eyes tell me your friendship is mine.
I don't have to wait until Christmas to hear the melody of a song,
The sound of your voice echoes through my heart and tells me I belong.
I don't have to wait until Christmas to see the smile that touches my
heart, I see that smile in my dreams when the night starts.
I don't have to wait until Christmas to hear laughter in the night,
cause whenever we are together we make it all right.
I don't have to wait until Christmas see the guiding light,
memories of you and me light up my night.
I don't have to wait until Christmas to find the gift of love,
You have wrapped up your friendship around my soul, and have
    given me
the stars above. I don't have to wait until Christmas to find my
place in heaven, you are my paradise when we are together.
I don't have to wait until Christmas to tell you how much I love you.
My heart is always going to be true.
Patricia Leudeman

Sweet Death

Death, sweet, sweet death.
You have to be sweeter than this life I lead.
I have no existence, I do not exist.
I am an entity that has no power to perform.
I was once a shiny grain of sand on the beach of life.
But I was unrecognized.
I was just…there, part of the never
Recognized other globes of sand.
I could have become a rock,
If I had been cultivated properly.
But it never happened.
I was pushed. I was kicked. I was ignored so I died.
I washed out with the tide never to see the shore again.
Good riddance, who cares anyway.
You didn't otherwise you would have cultivated me
Instead of killing me.
J. Romano

Behind A Curtain

Sometimes it's hard to express how I feel inside.
    You know, the things going on in my mind.
      My feelings, I think I have to hide.
    Behind a curtain is where you'll find,
      My deepest feelings left behind.
      From time to time I must decide,
        Where my tears shall reside.

        Behind a curtain, my eyes,
        Closed from the world forever,
        No one will ever know my lies.
    I will try to keep myself together,
        While my insides tend to die.

        Behind a curtain, no one knows,
        Just how much longer I can go.
S. Bytnar

True Friendship

You held my hand and led the way when times got really bad,
You lent your shoulder for me to use, when I was feeling sad.

You laughed with me and joked with me, when I was feeling good,
You have always been there for me, and I always knew you would.

You'll be there through the bad times, straight through until the end,
You'll always be right here for me, and that's why you're my friend.
Teena Marie Hauxwell

You Must Be Among The Angels

You must be among the angels now, as white as the snow.
You lived your life as tho' an angel, on this Earth, here below.

You must be among the angels now,
    in a most beautiful place.
Your love and kindness gave purpose to life,
    so evident was your grace.

You must be among the angels now, in a more peaceful garden.
Helping others was your goal in life,
    kind deeds were never a burden.

You must be among the angels now, the flowers all have bloomed,
Your joy, you found through family and friends,
    your love for the Lord attune.

You must be among the angels now, my memories I shall treasure.
For all the smiles and times we shared,
    your love was the greatest pleasure.

As I lift my head and glance toward heaven,
    my memories shall proclaim and allow,
Your love, your warmth to envelop and encircle
    the angels you are among now.
Patsy C. Wesson

"Alone But Not Forever"

O little one I seen you born
You looked like Heaven sent
Even though our hearts were sadly torn
I knew just where you went.

I see you at times through my clouded eyes
And wish that you were here
And though it was hard to say goodbye
You're still so near and dear.

I try image life with you here
With all your friends and toys
And picture how big you are my dear
compared to other boys.

I look at your sisters
they remind me of you
There's not three children now
There are only two

And when we meet in God's house someday
You'll know me from all the others
Our eyes will meet and I will say
Come, Son, I am your Grandmother.
Maryann Hatzold

Street Life - Revised

I am a child of the urban jungle, following every beat
You may not understand but I am of the street
You live in fancy homes thinking everything is fine
But here you play your cards and draw a fine line.

Now let break it down and listen to my say
My story is of truth and not of play
It hurts to see the young die in a cross fire
It's painful to go to sleep, not known your day to retire

Your friends are selected, not known your sisters and brothers
Because you may fall dying over a color
The area is divided into cross-sectors of two
So you may choose, the land of red or valley of blue.

But all in all, the street life has a happier view
Ladies and guys showing off with unity shining through
People showing love and expressing what they feel
Freshly cleaned cars, playing tunes and dresses to kill
So this is my home, this is where I'm from
A child of the street, I'll remember where I came from
Shanika N. Robinson

If You Leave Me

If you leave me;
You might as well take my eyes,
for I won't need them to see another's handsome face.

If you leave me;
You might as well take my arms,
for I won't need them to hold any other man.

If you leave me;
You might as well take my voice,
for I won't need to softly whisper I love you.

If you leave me;
You might as well take my mind,
for I won't be able to think of anything else.

If you leave me;
You might as well take my heart,
for I won't need it to love anyone else.

If you leave me;
You might as well take my soul,
for I won't want to exist without you!

Sharon Fisher

"Why"

Star dark, star night
You never light, you never bright.
I gave up on you so long ago,
never shall I trust you, never shall you know.
I scream for help, please someone,
anyone hear my calls....
Suddenly my life is over and
death's a threat.
No one loves me, no one will, dearest Lord
no one can.
Alone by myself, left a child without hope,
left alone, left alone to mope.
My death clock is ticking tick-tock
it goes, as I pray the Lord to take my soul.
If there's a God, please hear my cry
and answer one last question...
Why?

Yolanda Yvette Sanchez

Where Is The Church

You promised to love me and watch for my soul.
You promised to teach me to walk.
Yet I have stumbled, I'm weary and tired.
I've given much more than I got.
So where is the church when a Christian hurts?

Why don't you reach out to me and help me to see.
Why don't you say "I love you", make a stand with me?
Your actions speak much louder than words,
And I hear everything that you say.
So where is the church when a Christian hurts?

It was just your reasonable service,
As found in God's Holy Word.
You've neglected your gifts and calling of God.
And the Prize that you've lost, is more precious than gold.
So where is the church when a Christian hurts?

Teach us to bind up the broken hearted,
To give unto them beauty for ashes,
And apply the oil of joy for mourning,
Help us to realize that we are the church
We need to be there when a Christian hurts.

Lana Faye Hollenback

Why

Mommy, when I went to school today
You said I would have fun at play.

Instead the other children made me cry.
I just wanted to curl up and die.

They called me names I don't understand.
Didn't you say we were all made by God's own hands?

They laughed at me and said my eyes looked funny,
And that my skin looked like honey.

They treat me bad and they like to tease.
Can't you make them stop please?

I know you told me it shouldn't matter
If someone is short or even fatter.

Whether they're tall or thin,
Or even the color of their skin.

Red and yellow, black and white,
I know you said we all created different yet alike.

Then why, Mommy do they call me these names,
If we are all created the same?

Mary Gilman

Smiles And Cries

You said you loved me, you smiled
You said you cared, I smiled
But we weren't the only one's who smiled
It was our baby, who cried
And every cry and every tear
Told me that you had something to hide
There were three smiles and one cry
Both our smiles and our baby's cry
The question was who the other smile belonged to
I asked you
You were scared to tell me the truth
So you just left kiss the baby and I
And said I love you two
It was sad but we were even
Two cries, two smiles
The baby's cry, my cry
Her smile, your smile

Maria Gisela Gomez

Black Woman

Black woman, beautiful black woman, why do
you shone away from me black woman. Why do
you hold your head down when it should be
raised as high as the clouds.

Black woman, intelligent black, why must you
endure pain and be tortured by someone whose love
for you is not genuine? why must you fight so hard to
be accepted in a world in which was created by you?

Why must you stomach the problems of your adversary
and be conquered by the weak. Why must you get to
the level of their mentality when yours is much
higher and graceful? why must you be compared

To someone less beautiful? Black woman, lovely
black woman, why should you have to go through
a relationship with a brother who does not
respect you and cherish you? My, my, my
beautiful, intelligent and lovely black woman
How can I make the happy?

Marcus T. McKoy

Haunted

You enter my thoughts without permission
You torture my heart with a gentle glance.
I dream of your touch with sweet surrender
I weave the illusion that we'll meet by chance.

You are the love who comes to haunt me
In the desperate hours of the night.
You are the glow that warms my spirit
Just before dawn ... when you take flight.
Sylvia de la Fuente-Mendoza

Again

I remember you in your cradle you couldn't speak,
You weren't able,
You answered me with your sweet laugh,
Your time has come,
And our time's passed though your daddy's gone away,
The love we have can always stay to look at you,
To dream of you the laughter when you play,
The thoughts we share will always last
My only fears come from my past
From coloring books to childish looks
Oh God, the days move fast, I saw you once today,
I hope to see you soon I say my little girl will grow,
And soon away could those times again replay,
My daughter where are you now,
I wish I could've been with you somehow,
I missed so many days of your sweet youth,
Is this what they call, "living with the truth"
I want you back, I want you near, I want to take away the fear,
Do you cry for me, like I for you
Because your daddy is someone new
Ruben S. Zak

Wishing And I

If wishing could make it so,
you'd be mine to have and to hold.
If wishing could make it true,
I'd be spending eternity with you.
If wishing could make us one,
then I'd wish till day was done.
So if wishing and I had our way,
you'd be here with me today.
But wishing won't make it come true,
So we'll wait till our day is due.
Meanwhile I'll go on wishing and loving you.
Mary R. Tyson

Untitled

In wretched silence I pursued divinity, however,
Your beauty destroyed my spiritual stabs at Godhood.
Now I live for your scalding smile and your burning eyes.
Your beauty however, does not greatly impress me, not like
Your bittersweet soul flaming behind the lines of your face.

Tell me that somewhere along the way your dreams
Were recklessly shattered and I'll reply that to live, is
To tread barefoot on the broken glass of your hopes.

My fate, I know, does not concern you and my lonely road
Awaits me as I track out my trail along the highways and
Byways of the city's jungle. I will leave you now and
Will keep your image close to my heart to remind me of
The goal I seek.

Sing no sad songs for me as I stumble out your door...
 Amazing how you can be such a beauty,
  And so much of a whore.
Zachary Fisher

Good Morning Life

Good morning life sweet and fair,
Your beauty early strikes the eye,
And fills the soul with rare delight,
As happy Visions paint the sky.

Each breath taken, each moment in time,
Gives me a chance to see,
The handiwork of an artist true,
Who created it all for me.

Swirling rivers, to majestic peaks,
The flower in their glory arrayed,
The fiercest lion and the gentlest lamb,
To the mighty oak with limbs for shade.

Then breathed the artist, into clay,
And man in his image was made,
To enjoy the bounty from the creator's hand,
Gardener of the earth, God displayed.
Sharon K. McGhan

Michigan

I long to see your golden coast at dawn
Your blue green waters kissed with sparkling rays
Majestic dunes erase in endless shore
While cresting waves melt into sandy floor.

Your orchards, fields and woodlands crown your head
Oh Michigan your carpet thick and green
Your people are as hardy as the snow
And kinder folks on earth you've never seen

But oh the scenes that I remember best
The vast array of colors in the fall
A sunset gently bouncing off your lake
An eagle soaring to a mating call.
Your bubbling brooks are bountiful with fish
Your pungent pine is pointing to blue skies
Oh mitten, gently wove by God's own hand
Forever may he bless thee, Michigan!
Robert J. Johnson

Broken Legacy

Just yesterday, it seems,
Your children laughed and romped with ours
Amid lush fields of trees and blooms
That generations have revered and shared.
A now-vacated womb,
Groaning for its hallowed past,
That land, stripped bare, awaits its fate.
Like Solomon of old, you can issue a decree
Slicing into pieces
What builders' plans may then alter for all time.
Angry neighbors mourn the loss of open space
And wish the land were held in sacred trust;
Preserving what remains,
They would forge a link with days to come.
Won't you listen to the voices raised?
More precious than mere earthly goods
Is the caring spirit
Long-time neighbors all should share.
We see the future in your little grandchild's eyes
And ask, not what or when, but only why.
M. F. Sullivan

Smoke

Don't suffocate me, poisoning my air with
your dirty smoke, gun smoke. Reason with
me a little, give reasons for your decision.
Tension is flared in the atmosphere, your
smoke has ruined my work. Mist so black, pale,
yet many are just told to take a walk. Jump off
your high horse, stoop a little; hitch a ride
remember "out your smoke".

A flash of light strikes through the thin air,
stifled to absorb the bitter smoke that floats,
around and around in the open atmosphere. Heart
flatters, lungs are full of pain, only to wish
it wasn't cancer. Smoker's how long shall lucifer,
play his tricks on you? Plunging you more and more
into his dungeon.

Might, vigor, are left in the corner: smoke has torn
asunder. Smokey wings who's your next victim? Striking
down repeatedly, eating away its client; pains that are
felt has no answer, the smokey path had been chosen: Rescuer's
are few, lessons are many, only to be shot at, the smoke.

Roland Dalhouse

I'm Here For You

I see your eyes get sadder,
   your face wither with grief...
     ...and I feel pity for you,
   tremendous pity.
You've sunk down into a depression so low,
it would take a miracle to get you out.
I want to help, but I am powerless
   against the hurt and anger
   that rules your heart...your tender little heart.
You were always my hero,
   my sunshine in the clouds...
Now, I just want to help you find
   the sunshine again.
If only I could take your pain,
   and fill your eyes with the love
   that fills mine every time I look at you.

Kerri Cunningham

Whose Heart Is This?

My heart is yours
Your heart is mine
Whose heart is this?

My heart is filled with love for you.
Your heart is filled with love for me.
What is this heart filled with?

My heart is free for you to take or give back.
Your heart is free for me to take or give back.
Is this heart free or jailed?

My heart says let's find out.
Your heart says let's find out together.
This heart is our hearts joined together forever.

Maria Lentini

'Picture Memories'

'I'm thinking of you, and you're so far away, but I look at
your picture and it makes the day, -what happened? -tell me
what went wrong - cause we've been together for, oh, so long."

"Can you realize I'm so sad, but I think of you, and I
don't get mad, please help me understand, this pain I just
can't stand. What can I do or say? -cause these memories of
you will never go away. Another day I wake to face, but the
memories I can't erase.

"Sometimes it's hard, I must look within myself, so for now
I'll put my heart on a shelf. It's so easy to love, But-
difficult to say Good-bye? -more memories, a lesson learned,
another game of bridges-burned,
"I miss you, and love you so, it's so hard to let you go."

"I lie awake at night, then dream you're here and hold on
tight.-one day, I hope not to long, maybe I'll put this in a
 song. Loosing you was my biggest fear, But I'll always
have your picture, Dear.

Leonard Leffingwell

You Are My Friend

You are my friend. Though we're miles apart.
You're still with me for you're always in my heart.

You are my friend and I call out your name -
Though it's not the same you're still in my heart.
And wherever you go- I want you to know
There will always be a you in me.
Because you are my friend and the time is here
When we learn to live from day today
And year to year.
You are my friend through the darkness
Of night. - Though you are not in sight
The love we share is still sincere -
From day to day and year to year.

So wherever you go I want you to know
There will always be
A you in me!
You are my friend

Meri Leahy

Dad

You've worked hard all your life for me, sacrificing things for
yourself to make me happy

You spend sleepless nights worrying about me because instead of
being home I'm out having a good time
You give me money and buy me new clothes, while you wear the same
worn things

You tell me you want me to have all the things that you never had
when you were growing up

You've tried to spare me from pain, but you know I've always had
to find things out the hard way

You'd give me the world if you only could, and it seems the way I
repay you for all you've done is by hurting you
This is just to tell you in my own special way Thank You and I
Love You Dad

Lisa Burns Carpenter

Grandmom

You have been with us for many years
You've powdered our bottoms and wiped our tears
You have been like a second mother
Always trying to keep us out of trouble
You always try to guide us in the right way
So that we can live our lives to the best each day

Whenever the holiday season is near
You're always around spreading love and cheer
You still make the best soup and spaghetti
Everyone else's tastes like confetti

On all the hunting trips you were always there
Even while grandpop and I slept you watched for the deer
You played cards and shot craps
And even wore a hunting cap
You never cease to amaze us with all the things you do
Even when you're down and out and feeling mighty blue

Now that we have grown and have kids of our own
Your memories and wisdom to them will now be known
And when the time comes for each of us to part
I know deep inside the lord will join our hearts

Leon D'Ottavio

Untitled

Like a cowboy from the wild west,
Your rode into my life.
Just one look from those soft blue eyes,
You stole my heart away,
And with a touch of your gentle hand
I was yours, all yours.
I never felt a feeling like that before.
There was a yearning in my heart,
A sparkle in your eye.
Like a soft breeze blowing,
I felt your love that day.
The day you rode away with my heart.
You took my heart in your hands,
You wrapped it in your love.
That special feeling that I felt
Was when you sealed it with a kiss.
I never knew love could be so special
But I know now that I have you.
I felt it on the day we met,
The day you rode away with my heart.

Robert Zillinger

No Freedom

No Freedom, unless age 21
said the sign above my head
I sat in wonderment for I could not speak
'till I was 21
all my rights were taken away
I thought, though I wasn't supposed to
No Freedom to speak
No Freedom to think
No Freedom to write
No Freedom to laugh
Just plain No Freedom
I decided to leave
but I could not
for this is America
I thought some more
this was the country of freedom
freedom to do what we please
I knew our country was falling apart
is this the end of America

Phoebe Yeager

Vietnam Vet

He left her standing alone
She knew nothing of what was going on
She knew only that she was confused
He always said he'd never leave her
Now he may be gone for good

They took him in a fashion
She did not understand
Standing in the front lines
Hoping not to be seen
Mothers and children all around
Being used as live bait

Now he's back with her
Living life on two wheels
Almost hoping for the time
He's out of it for good

He'd leave her standing alone...
Again

Marla Love

Waiting

All alone in the midnight sky,
She sits and waits for that special guy.
Having faith that he will come,
She looks around and sees no one.
The wind is blowing,
Sounds like her name,
Begins to wonder if she's insane.
She hears the seagulls far away,
And wonders if this is really the day.
Hearing her name again, she looks around,
Seeing nothing she makes a frown.
Deciding to wait no more.
She stands to leave then decides,
Just one minute more.
A message comes with flowers and rhymes,
Tells her he is running a little behind.

Renee Blanton

My Grandma

Whenever a care,
she was there,
thank you Grandma.
Whenever in need,
I could indeed,
turn to Grandma.
She's always there,
she has time to spare,
that's Grandma.
She might have been busy,
but Granny I knew,
always had time for me and you.
Granny, I'm here to thank you today
for sending loads of love my way.
Thanks Granny!

Tasha Vickers

The Agony Of Decision I've Chosen Haiku

Warm winter's sun rays
scolding the frozen roof line...
weeping icicles.

Voni Yerkes

Reflections

When I see that you're
Sad and lonely
I long to cry with you
And wipe away your tears
When I see your
Glowing smile
I rejoice
For you are too
I wish I could calm you down
When I see
The anger in your eyes
I can see
When your heart
Is bursting with love
I want also to feel this way
But I can only sit and watch
For I'm just a piece
Of glass.

Leanndra Rader

I Have No Fear

I am a tall ship
Sailing the harbor of life.
I stand tall,
My head high facing the
Wind and sails.
I have no fear.

It is with great
Courage that I bestow
The morals and travails
Of life to my children
And grand children.

The end of the harbor nears.
I have no fear, my work has been done.

Around the bend
The harbor ends.
With love and adieu
I sail to another harbor

Mildred Ardito

In Memory Of Kurt Cobain

It's sad you had to die;
Say goodbye...
We never know when,
We never know why.
But it is in my opinion;
You now know more than
You ever did before.

J. Baysin Brooks

Steel Casket

Tumbling, falling, crashing
Screams echo off the trees
the fire roars its burning laugh
at the tragedy it sees.

Metal twists and cackles
Wheels tearing from the track
The A, the M, the T sink under
exposing only the RAK.

Who would think such a lovely place
so quiet and so serene
a bayou in the wilderness
could be such a gruesome scene.

Forty bodies and metal woven
like a wicker basket.
Knowing that they willingly stepped
Aboard the large steel casket.

Robin Glidden

Sea Of Madness

Sea of madness
Sea of souls
Ghost ships at harbor
Gamefish in woos
Ocean in thunder
Time in a warp
Moon days an sunny nights
All in a sailor's delight
Summer time is coming
Winter is gone
Bring back my body
to stand all alone

Richard W. Peterson

if you could come see what I see

the tide rushes in
searching the shore for someone
endless rhythms, endless songs
lost in the muted echoes
and in the weeping winds
there is found a peace of mind
if you could come see what I see
from the sun ripened day
to the quiet misty mountain moon
caressing the trees
hold on and cherish the night

Kathleen L. Brownell

Betrayal

Secrets to tell,
Secrets to share,
But when people tell,
It's a nightmare.
They say they're your friend,
But you know the truth.
Why can't people be more like you.

Millisa Pearce

Creation

Spanning the sky, behold the milky way;
See the moon that rules the night,
The sun that rules the day.

Oceans cradle myriad sights
And across prolific land
He tucked wonders and surprises
We just can't understand!

Rocks and minerals glistening bright
And even near at hand
The microscope reveals our plight:
It's all too deep for man.

Linda Kay New Heimel

Hayday

I saw a cow and a horse today,
Separated by a fence.
But their heads were together.
As friends will do,
When sharing a confidence.

Cow Bessie nodded her head up and down.
Old Paint responded with Naaay!!
And the secret they shared
Wouldn't you know,
Was where to find the hay!!

Mary O. Capriotti

Signs Of Lightning

People, in their breathtaking sight,
See the signs of lighting.
But, unlike the thunder of speech,
It gives no actual harm.

Deaf choose their words
With their signs
To fit a message
Which darts, glides, jabs and flutters.

In the mind, people sense
The signs of lighting.
These are not deafening to them:
Their eyes won't turn away.

On turn the vacant face
Lop-eared, sleepy-eyed to stare
At the fireworks display
Of lightning strokes signs!

Kevin Mulholland

Is There Peace In The Sea?

Look deeply into my eyes.
See where darkness truly lies.
Here a soul abound in anger.
Living from fear, harm, and danger.
As endless shadows doubt my mind.
Choking on social suicide.
Swiftly in a mid summer breeze.
Where every will finds its need.
How can you lose when you're dead?
How can you win when you're ahead?
Is there peace in the sea?
The vast sea within me?
Look deeply into my heart.
See where the valves part.
Come inside and enjoy the view.
Watch as the decay continues.
Can you tell me?
Is there peace in the sea?
Or am I full of hapless dreams?

Lisa Kay Stayton

Reality Of Yesterday

The deadness inside of me
Seeks to destroy the calmness
of those who surround me.

The voices are in constant combat
To suppress the emergence of
Feelings of Devastation.

As the Memories linger and fade
And the losses become one
Yesterday's breath becomes
Tomorrow's sorrow.

Rebecca S. Ward

My Madness

Goblins and ghouls dance crazily
Shrieking in unintelligible tongues
They party out within my mind
But you who view me know not of them.

The banshee screams that split my brain
Are silent to the closest person
I feel discomfort at times
But never fear

For I am not afraid of my self
Only every one else

Michael D. Pitts

Patchwork

Cutting out the pieces -
Sewing them by hand.
Stitching memories together,
Preserving time and land.

It's much more than a quilt;
It's a treasure to behold.
Stitched with love and care,
Warming one when nights are cold.

The time is soon forgotten,
The traditions will not last.
The quilts serve as a reminder
Of our families and their past.

Handed down through generations,
Creating memories from the start.
There's nothing like a quilt
Made with love from the heart.

Wendy Gail Davis

Britni

Britni is my little girl
She is my whole world.
I couldn't love her anymore
That's one thing I know for sure.

Those blue-grey eyes I love to see
Especially when they look at me.
That precious smile that she gives
Makes my life worthwhile to live.

The tiny fingers and the toes
And her cute button sized nose.
Little dimples on her cheek
Makes me look forward to every week.

There isn't a day that you can't see
Just how precious she is to me.
I just want you all to know
Just how much I love her so.

Susan Partridge

Lost

Her eyes are like diamonds
Shimmering in the night
Her smile is like sunshine
From the early morning light
Her skin is like silk
The best in the world
She is the most beautiful girl
That came out of this earth
If she were here
I wouldn't let her go
If I were there
I would let her know
The tears of foolishness
Run down my face
I should have said something
But just went away
I once had a chance
But now, no way

Kenneth M. Barba

Snoring

Ugly noise, rumbling loud
Snout snorts of unsynched sounds
Midnight cacophony
Robber of my quiet
In the night.

Phyllis Burchfield

The Unknown

In the perils of the night
shivers and light
unknown havoc
cast into humanity

Born by innocence
stripped of my virginity
screams take me away
the silence speak today.

Laura Bruni

Sidewalk Oh Sidewalk

Sidewalk oh sidewalk
sidewalk that ends
you bring me good luck
and I made some friends
I just want to thank you
sidewalk that ends
thank you thank you
thank you again

Tara Kaplan

Promise To My Lover

In the middle of the night
silence, night and me,
we are one entity.
We have no shadow.

In the middle of the night,
I remember, long time ago
I made a promise to my
lover, that I will write one
hundred and five poems
about our love, so far I wrote
only one about our separation.

In the middle of the night
I realize that silence, night
and me, we don't know
how I will keep the promise
to my lover.

Sati Mohan Das

SILKWORM

Little silkworm you are encased in a
silky shell patiently waiting for
the release when you will come forth
as a beautiful Butterfly!

What a miracle,
once an ugly worm -
now a beautiful butterfly!

We, like the silkworm, are encased in
our earthsuit - wrestling, tugging,
struggling, and waiting for the release
when we shall come forth wearing our
beautiful Heavenly Suit!

What a miracle,
once an ugly sinner -
now a beautiful Angel!

Praise the Lord for the day
we shed our earthsuit and put
on our heavenly suit to be
united with Him in Paradise!

Lillian R. Hughes

The Earth

I'm drowning in pollution.
Sinking in dirty soil.
I need help more and more.

I'm dying from the heat,
day by day I may soon wither away.

When you hurt me, don't you think
I feel pain? My oceans are polluted,
My forests are in pain.

When the waterfall's dry up,
and the sky turns black, my
back is burnt and the mountains do sag.

We could stop this by tender loving care.
We need to conserve and clean the air.

We need to help each other and prove
we all care, for this is our
earth that we all share.

Kathy Sacher

Oreo

Black and white coated fur
sitting on your back.

You sit on your cage
innocently waiting
for someone to pet you,

Your nose twitching
up and down.

Ears listening to kids
learn and play.

Your eyes closing
little by little.

Drifting into a dream.

Shelley Kurihara-Nakasu

"Sad Little Doll"

There's a sad little doll
sitting there on a shelf
with a tear in her eye
looks like she wants to cry

She sits all alone
For some one to love
Still this poor little doll
Not choose for a home

Her arms stretched out wide
For some little child
Still no one come near
As her hopes disappear

The days have past by
She's covered with dust
The days have past by
She's starting to rust

Oh poor little doll
Her tears she must hide
For no one has heard
Of a doll that has died.

Sandra Kaye

Impulses

Creeping slowly from the shadows -
Skipping rope in the mind.
Flying like feathers in the wind -
Billowing impulses.
Dancing a waltz or jitterbug-
Demanding attention.
Creating chaotic rhythms
And disrupting mine.

Marilyn Des Jardins

My Love For You

My love for you is like a rose,
So delicate and deep,
My love for you is like a snowflake,
So unique and almost melting away,
My love for you is like a painting,
It says a million words,
My love for you is like a song,
So difficult and full of elegance,
My love for you is like a spring flower,
So beautiful and bright,
My love for you is like a fantasy,
So dreamy and magical,
My love for you is like the rain,
So cold but refreshing,
My love for you is perfect.

Nicole Dixon

The Course I Had To Take

You are my heart you are my soul,
So I thought.
It was just last eve that I felt
your passionate kiss.
How could I know she also knew those
full soft lips.
That to gaze into those ice blue eyes
Will surely bring about his lies!

I know what course I must take,
to do away with such a rake!
Oh how I'd love to love him still.
But to share him? No, It's not my will!

Ah lover, what am I to do, I cannot live
in a world without you.
Your heart will never beat for her again.

Tammy Gmerek

Is It The End?

Another life was brought on earth,
So innocent, so small;
There's nothing wrong with except
The time that it was born.
Too many wars and too much killing.
The love that makes life is almost gone,
But the violence goes on.....
It's only fair that we try,
To get along, to love, to like.
Being friends not enemies
That's all it is about.

The blue planet gave us homes,
And food, and air, and water,
Nothing's ours to destroy
We're here just to borrow.
Life is so fragile and, oh so short,
It's like a candle that burns for a while
And before you realize,
It's over!

Monica Ciocan

My Hands Remember

How keen and sweet it was to trace
so lightly with my fingers
the planes and hollows of your face,
the mem'ry of it lingers -
sweep of cheek and curve of lips
imprisoned in my finger tips -
Friends say gently, "He is gone,"
my heart can't understand -
it hurls a cry against the night,
how can I bear my hands?

Ruth McClung

Untitled

A long road
So many bends
So many curves
Never knowing
Which way to go
Never knowing
To move fast or slow
Never knowing
Which direction to take
Never knowing
Which move to make.
There's no map
To lead you there
The question is
But lead you where?
But you know in your heart
Love's right there beside you
Hanging on strong
Ready to guide you.

Nicole Hickok

The Battered Child

A little way of a thing…
…so skinny and tiny,
Like a little doll…
…come alive.

Once shining eyes, so full of fun
Now…
…so full of pain.

Why should one so young…
…have to feel this way?

With a searching heart,
…longing for happiness…
…and peace.

E. Jean Notis

Untitled

What shall I say
so stupid as to glide by
not with anger
not this moment
but a time once lost regained
like a circle
once broken
spirals downward
ever downward
as with silence
where a word should be
and find you softly crying.

Not from me you heard this omen.
I have yet to seem unmoved.

Thomas Monk

The Seagull

Fly through the white
soft, free flow
in space, in time

Gliding, hovering above
the covered landscape
which it eyes
with a respecting eye

Awe inspiring is its picture.

Pietro Piccolo Ruiz

Friendship

Friendship means much to
some and little to others

To me friendship means a
life of excitement, tears,
pain and happiness.

Friendship means that
one friend listens while
the other talks.

Friendship means to me
that one should be happy
to have a good friend.

Friendship has many heartaches
and blockades.

Friendship is an awesome
thing to me.

Kelli Naab

Nessie

People call me Nessie,
Some think I'm a myth;
Though they have not seen all of me,
Height, length, or width.
I swim in murky waters,
Unlike those dinky otters.
I hate that cold black water,
I sometimes wish it were hotter.
But life is fairly simple,
As you can plainly see;
Though as for now I'm fine,
And glad that I am me!

Rachel Jacques

Our Pain

All this pain inside I feel
Sometimes I think it won't heal
Some may think it isn't real
All this pain inside I feel

Who will listen to my pain
Just how long will it remain
Just how long can I stay sane
Who will listen to my pain

Please oh please don't let me be
With all this pain inside me
All this hurting none can see
Please oh please don't let me be

I guess I just need some time
Sometimes I feel like a mime
Some may feel it is a crime
I guess I just need some time

Troy Magner

Lost

Lost: One sense of humor
    Somewhere along the way.

I noticed it was missing,
Just the other day.

Life is never easy,
In fact, it's pretty tough,

But without a sense of humor
It can get really rough.

I know I have to find it
But I don't know where to start.

Where does a sense of humor go
When joy has left the heart?

Patricia A. Brassard

The Unanswered Question

When I die will I go
somewhere beyond the sky?
Will I go to a better place?
Or will I just leave without
a trace?
Will all the wounds from life heal?
Or will I just not be able to feel?
Is there a God to show me the way?
Or will I just wither away?

Tracy Houle

After An Old Song

My old man went out lock-jawed,
    somewhere in Phillip,
Fleeing time and circumstance,
("Oh, mother calls me Willie;)

At sixty-one he packed it in,
Having had his fill,
Of hard work and hypocrites,
(Sister calls me Willie;)

A blue-eyed boomer, Irish proud
Like his old man before him,
He drank hard liquor, laughed out loud,
(Father says, 'goddamn you, Willie',)

And would give his lunch away,
Though he'd been through the mill.
He never made a bundle,
("But the gang all called him Bill.")

Eugene Field

Spring Sighs

Purple
Spring
Relief
touches these winter wounds,
caresses as warm air hardly stirring,
soothes as a melting lake
folds over, envelopes her shore,
again and again and again
stroking back the winter
bringing forth the bloom.

The world and I are stretching
in places long suppressed
by the cold winter wait
and now unfolding
like the oak leaves
slowly and late.

Schuyler Gerstenzang

Secrets Of The Heart

A memory hidden there
Somewhere in the heart
To hold or beware
A secret only two can share

It is deep in the heart
Joy or sorrow
It will always play a part
Today and tomorrow

But when and where did it start
When young or old
Do the secrets stop or get a bigger part
Will your story unfold, or ever be told

A love never ending
A moonlight walk in the park
Two souls blending
A kiss and a hug after dark

A love child between two
To say we will never part
Exchange of rings from me to you
Could these be the secrets of the heart?

Laura Bolenbaugh

Ragged Edges

Your words slashed through my
    soul like a sickle,
hurling my heart into tattered
    and shredded pieces.
Will this pain ever end?
    No, not until you are dead,
or I'm not alone anymore.

L. M. Toomey

Protect The Whales

Whales, whales, whales galore,
Sperm, Blue, Killer, so many more,
Why? why are they dying?
Listen - hear them crying,
Blue whales are almost gone,
When they are, we'll realize,
That we were very wrong.
Stop! Stop the killing!
Keep the oceans filling,
Don't kill the whales,
Don't cut off their huge tails,
There are only a few,
So please don't kill, our earth's whales,
Please protect them. Do you all can do.

Tiffany Arciszewski

The Back Path

Sit upon the rock and wait,
Spirits arrive before too late.
Let the moss caress your feet,
a throne of rock becomes your seat.
Smell the fragrance of the air,
it stirs the senses if you dare.
Listen what the breeze does blow,
it whispers what you do not know.
Feel the trees that grip the ground,
they tell a tale that will confound.
Perhaps a song will cross your tongue,
a tribute with the birds you've sung.
Bend to feel a twig and touch,
Mother Nature's Gift to us.
Sister of the forest friends,
receives the power that they send.

Maryam Dowd

The Night

Hot orange, yellow, and red,
splashing into the sky,
scaring the people,
disturbing the night,
sending off heat,
burning the feet,
of those standing alone
in the night.

Randi Amen

The Hawk Has Flown

As evening came that soft
Spring day, we learned
"The Hawk" has flown away.

Far from pain, strife and grief,
To the blessed place of love and peace

That place of gardens, lakes and streams,
Of breezes cool and sunset's sweet.

The place we hope to be someday
When it's our turn to fly away.

Though we are left to comprehend
with mortal minds, this sudden end.

We ask the Lord to take our friend,
To give us strength to bear his loss,
Till to that place we also cross.

The place of love that is our home…
The place to where "The Hawk" has flown.

Rita R. Wagner

Little Boy's Curiosity

Little boy sits on the dock
Stares at the rumbling waves
Then he looks at the moon
Shadow glistening in the water.
He looks down and wonders
If he can see the moon from the bottom.
No!

Rhonda Alewine

Time

Lonely nights.
Stars are gleaming,
Millions to come.
Kids just think,
Thinking of what's to come?
What is to be?
What will become of us?
Nobody really knows…
For what is to be,
To accomplish the goal we set,
But, some people don't have goals…
Some live day to day,
Thinking, wondering, anticipating,
What is to be?

Thomas Chi

Voices

Some days the background
Static is so loud
I can't hear you
Over the crackling roar

Please accept my apology
I am learning to
Control my own volume
Soon it will stop

NLP gives me access
To my control room
Computers are really wonderful
Flight or fight controlled

Oh, maybe not forever
What else is new?
But enough to hear
Your voice calling me

Susan E. Abernathy

'I'll Watch Over You'

When I was small, my mother warned,
'stay close to me, you won't be harmed,
I'll watch over you.'
Then in my teens, and very wise
she warned again, 'don't be surprised,
I'll watch over you.'
The tables turned when I was grown,
the child became the mother's home,
'I'll watch over you.'
Now looking down from up above,
a daughter feels her mother's love,
'I'll watch over you.'
And in my heart the words I see,
I always knew that you would be,
watching over me.

Shirley Wilson

Eternal Traveler

A raindrop fell on me today-
stayed a moment - speed away.
It vaporized back to a cloud,
a puffy, white ethereal shroud-
to fall on lands I've never seen
on raging rivers - seas serene.
Changing costumes as it goes
from tropic rains to winters snows.
Reborn each time it starts to roam,
Celestial heaven is its home.
Tiny drop - so crystal bright,
I see reflected in your light-
the seas and rivers of this land
that rise and fall at your command.
Eternal traveler, you bring to me
-the world in its entirety!

Norma Gius Fava

My Poems

My poems are more
than words convey.
They are my truths
more than facts can say.

Their sense 'n sound reach
farther than sight can see.
My Spirit erupts
surreptitiously.

Amanda

Cancer

The wait except with four I shared
    Still I felt alone, despaired
The early morning light still shone
    Here deep within my hearts alone

The waiting room with ceilings high
    Above this floor how still she lies
The answer with the surgeons knife
    I pray to God to save a life

The colorless, cold, that clock above
    If you could only know, my love
These minutes pass like hours go
    I've never seen the time so slow

I want to know when it's all through
    Yet nothing here that I can do
Just tell me when the cancers gone
    Then all our lives can just go on

It's funny how the cares are lost
    Like job, the car, the total cost
Nothing cares to me today
    Just time to heal our lives away.

Roy McWilliams

In The House That Daddy Built

The old block house my daddy built
Still stands just like it did
Some many, many years ago
When I was just a kid
My brother and I brought home a tree
From school at Christmas time
With pride we planted for all to see
Now it's grown so tall and fine
I don't know why I went there
Just wanted to take a look
Rehashed old memories of what was there
And knowing the work it took.
The empty field we had next door
Where we used to run and play
Now has a house with huge front doors
Painted an awful gray
We didn't grow up with satins and bows
Chantilly lace or silks
But we did grow up with courage and strength
In the house that daddy built

Lu Eddy

Reality

As we look out,
Strange things arise.
Fear, sadness...
Emptiness.
Colors not what they seem,
Lies all around.
Darkness fills the day,
Absorbs the night.
Sight seems to be lost,
Tears are missing, too.
Lost are all ideas...
All dreams.
Strange things arise
As we look out...
Into Reality.

Leslie Pitman

One Day Walk In Country

I walk in tall wheat it looks
strong blowing in wind,
The field is open wide all
of one color. It draws you
to it when looking out window,
Such a beautiful long walk
few grains I pick to taste
it sweetness is ripe. I go
to stream, rocks and few
trees, so big and pretty in
color. Early enough in rocks
few little purple violets grow
there. My walk so fresh
and clear. My horse come
up to see me. Blake is name,
I name all my animals.
I rub him and didn't forget
His noise. Birds singing go
pass wheat field I go - home

Marcella Swigert

In Years Before

Slowly lifting toward the sun.
Suddenly believing I wanted to run.

In years before...

Gently touching from the soul.
tearily yearning I desired to hold.

In years before...

Lovingly resting upon her knee.
Tenderly believing it would always be.

In years before...

Worriedly proceeding within life's doors.
Traveling quickly I noticed her pause.

In years before...

Hugging tightly without a cost.
Gone forever now I sense her loss.

R. Martin

Summer Summer

Summer summer are you hot?
Summer summer are you cold?
Is it true or is it not,
Summer Summer are you hot?

Summer summer were you true,
Summer summer now you are through.
Will the fall be hot or cold?
Will the winter be blistering and bold?

Is it true or is it not?
Summer summer are you hot?

Ralisha Kirks

Life

Life is a fleeting shadow
That comes and goes without warning.
It rises and falls through life tides,
Gentle at times like a new-born lamb;
Turbulent at others like a storm at sea.
Yes, life is a fleeting shadow
That goes on endlessly.

Karin Kuznicki

A Moment

I walk alone at this
sungone hour
When the earth is all
mine
And I wonder and I gaze
at the stars
Posing as lamps
To an earthly room
so dim
No darkness no sunshine
Just a twilight held between
only a moment
just a moment
granted to me
To renew my friendship
with the other world
the natural world
of nature
and the wild
Mary Harkin

The Gardener

Plying verdant rows of green drawn
sunward, an old one bent of back
comes staff in gnarled hand, polished
agent of diurnal battle with the foe.

His ancient visage more weathered than
rejuvenated earth which denies her
sins and with benevolent smile wipes
the slate clean each year. Labored

Stoops retrieve fragrant orbs, red
and visible witness of his necessity
while rheumy eyes inspect and measure
against a former race, not unlike

Countless summer matches won only
by diligence and craft. Palsied nods
concur as sweet accord stirs the breast
and nature defers to her own peer.

Lois Ripple

At The Carnival

A jolly lolli for the lady
Sweet treat droplets
Melting fine
Your lips to mine.
Oh do try a thigh collar
Ourselves in ourselves
A parade of charades
Dressed to undress
Yours to mine.
Amazed, ablazed
Dancing
Enfolded, encircled
Yours to mine.
Two to one
Are we.

Linda J. Takvorian

Treasured Thoughts

Remembrance of memories gone past
that went by too fast.
Leaving a feeling of vast
loneliness and sadness.
But always remember
the shared gladness.
And don't dwell in the unpleasant past.

Michele Eileen Chan

"A Small World I Wouldn't Want to Paint"

Kids on a playground,
swinging on the swings,
and riding on that rotator spinny
thing that makes you nauseous.
A child puts sand in a cup,
and forms a cylindrical sand castle.
A line is forming at the slide,
but no one is pushing or shoving,
because they have all day to play.

The Cadillac. A long black Cadillac,
rolls down the street as if it was
shot out of a rifle.
The window rolls down,
and the nozzle protrudes.
The rapid shouting of a semi-automatic,
hits flesh and steel, but,
misses the intended target.
Screaming and crying is all that is heard,
as the target vanishes into the woods.

Tony Maiscalco

Three Treasures

Three treasures more priceless
than gold,
It's you that I still hold,
your memories still untold…
For my eyes I can see,
that you'll be holding me.

And the most common place,
is when I'm next to you,
in my resting place.

It's so hard to be all alone,
Now, since you are gone.
It hurts so bad inside,
But when I get to heaven,
I'll be there by your side.

Pam Passmore

Untitled

Better to die
than to kill,
to love
than to hate,
to be forgiven
so one may forgive,
to confess
rather than live with guilt,
A spirit is
worth more than material,
A friend
worth more than life,
A life
worth more than giving,
and love
worth more than all!

Rachel Wester

The Fleet

The guns are quiet
The barrels have cooled
There is a sigh of relief
That comes with the peace
But we will never forget
The sailors we buried at sea
Oh, what a price liberty.

Leonard J. Darder

Love's Magic

Love seems to have more meaning…
Than words alone can say.
For it holds a certain magic…
In special kind of way.
It's filled with little treasures…
Only loving someone brings…
Like the beauty in a rose…
As it welcomes in the spring.
It's poetry and music…
And wine by candlelight…
And moon that always glows…
As it sprays its tender light.
It's the brightest shining star…
Gazing down from high above…
And a songbird singing sweetly…
Its serenade of love.
It's sunbeams and it's moonbeams…
And rainbows in the sky…
It's all of nature's beauty…
When seen through lovers' eyes.
Pauline Selby

Blue Shadow

To love the blue shadow
that falls on the snow
under sky's pale
you cannot let go,

I stare in awe
at the shade by the tracks,
like an opaque mist
with the glow of wax.

It's barely a blue
but as blue as it goes,
there's a fleeting charm
to the blues within snow.

Something I don't want to number
and I just can't name,
but my soul's of that color
by the tracks in the shade.
Michael Sean Conway

To Love

When love comes to someone
That has been so alone.
It's like being reborn, for you
See what love is like.
It's like the star's right to shine.
The thunder's right to call and
The rain's right to fall.
When bad times come, just say I
Love you.
That's what you should do.
But when the rains don't fall and
The thunder don't call,
Just close your eyes and
The sun will shine for love.

Robert S. Holbert

Security

I'm filled with all the this love
That hides within me deep

That only can come out
When I so peacefully sleep

I harbor all this love
And keep it in so tight
So I know it will
Always be there
When I close my eyes at night

I need to have you teach me
How love won't go away
And stay with me forever
All night and through the day

Please teach me
How to use this love
That hides within me deep
And I can use it always
Not only when I sleep

Linda Callahan

Untitled

There is a lady in this country
    That I am so proud of
She stands for strength and freedom
    She's the lady that I love
Many son's have died for her
    upon the battlefields
They did not die in vain
    They died for their ideals
She was given by a country
    That was so very small
But in time of need, we gathered
    And answered to the call
The lady means everything
    That I hold dear to me
She's the greatest love of America
    She's the statue of Liberty
She says,I'll give my land to you
    If you'll give your heart to me
Because the lady means America
    And in America…We are free

D. Jessi Gardner

Mom

My life is so wrong at times
That I can't help but feel sad
Kids fighting in the streets
Never thinking it was bad
But I know I will survive
If you are near me
And if I know you care
Then I will be happy
You are the person who gave me my life
I've listened to what you had to say
And you've cared for me all of my life
You have guided me all the way
I feel so sad at times
That is when I think of you
Your picture brings me happiness
With your loveliness so true

Kimberly Reynolds

His Heart Leaps With Joy

There may be times in my life
that I feel alone,
But I think about Jesus
And He makes me strong,
I feel like I can carry on;
Thank you Jesus for making me strong.

The door to my heart is open,
Please come in because you are welcome
I love you both with all my heart,
Because you gave me a running start.

Thank you God for sparing my life
Thank you for your love, I want to come
And live above, just like the white dove.

God please strengthen me where I'm weak
Heavenly home is what I seek
He will make me strong and meek
He does love me for what I seek.

Linda McCray

A Mother's Love

Do you know how much I love you?
That if I could debate and undo
Everything that has transpired,
I'd fill your heart with every desire.

I'm sorry life isn't going your way,
But, I don't know what else to say.
I've tried to do my very best
To put all our obstacles at rest.

Whatever has happened in the past,
It's just life's different contrasts.
I'm sorry that I can't express myself,
Anymore than you can for yourself.

Please believe that I'd give you more,
If it will keep you from being heartsore.
But, I can't provide you with everything-
Except a mother's love, more than anything.

Linda M. Navarro

A Gift From God

God giveth me the comfort
   that melts the dew in my mind
God giveth me the love
Which lightens a path to follow.
God giveth me a heart
and a choice to loveth one or all.
God giveth me many blessings
which reflects my love for life
   … and
God giveth me you, Sonya,
to share these gifts He gives.

Myles Y. Emura

Our Blessed Mother

I know a lovely lady
That wears a cloak of blue
She is our Blessed Mother
I hope you know her too

She wears a crown of stars upon her head
A rosary in her hand
I hope someday I'll meet Her
When I reach that Promised Land

Virginia Halverson

Suicide

We need to realize
That once we're gone
We won't come back
The curtain falls
The stage is black

After we die
Sure some will mourn
They'll feel the pain
They will be torn
But their tears will dry
Just like the rain
And they will start
To live again

So think twice, my friend
If you feel that suicide
Is the only solution

Because either you can mope
and end it all
Or learn to cope
and take a fall

Melissa Brock

Keeping Faith

Two hearts
That share
A single beat.

Two minds
That share
A single thought.

Two lives
That share
A single love.

Four feet
That share
A single path.

Karen McFarland

Untitled

When we met I knew right then
that something great was brewing within.
It's been some time since that day
and I know I'm here to stay.
There is no one else around
who I want to be my clown
You make me laugh when I am down
you make me smile instead of frown.
You are the one I want to see
To spend the rest of your life with me.
And I hope that when we're gone
we have a cloud all our own.
And I hope that you can see
just how much you mean to me.
Most of all I hope you'll find
in your heart to be mine

Kim Oden

Untitled

Why does it seem
That we are in a dream
Life flies crashing by
No one takes time to view the sky.

We never notice the ordinary
It always takes the extraordinary
When will we stop seeing lies
And make people open up their eyes.

Tom Meryweather

The Girlfriend From Before

There is a place inside of you
That will hold a love for her forever.
I can never take that place,
But I am thankful that we are together
I have enjoyed the times we have had.
Those times will never be erased.
You have made me very happy,
And you can never be replaced.
Yet, by trying to read your mind,
I am put in a state of confusion.
Maybe it is just my way of thinking,
But here is my conclusion.
You know that there is a place for me,
But then there is a place for her,too.
It wouldn't take much on her part
To separate me from you.
We have spent a lot of time together,
And we grow closer and closer each day.
I hope that I never lose you,
Because she has taken you away.

Nancy Lowman

Friends

We are friends;
That's what we'll be
'Till the end
Someone you can trust
Someone you can depend
You and me friends

There are times
Of rough and tough
I'll be there for you
Whenever you're alone
I'll be by your side
You and me friends

Together, forever
We will be
Friends

Sunshine Cabrera

"Enchanted Land"

Enchanted land in the sky;
    That's where I'll go, when I die.
Don't ask the reasons why;
    For His Salvation is no lie.
Break the bread and pass the wine.
Our lives are just threads;
    Tied to His so Divine.
He's the one who lights the stage,
    We're the ones who act the play.
He was once on this stage;
    We know why He couldn't stay;
An earthly ruler showed his rage.
Enchanted land in the sky;
    That's where I'll go, when I die.
Don't ask the reasons why;
    For His Salvation is no lie.

Scott P. Siddle

Love, Light, Life

Love is
the light which is
the I that I am
What am I?
I am life
I am that I am

Raymond H. Tademy Jr.

Mirror

You will never know
The ABSOLUTE TRUTH
With the mirror reflecting
On you; you will never
Love to love unconditional
With the mirror turn on you;
No! you will never know
The ABSOLUTE TRUTH until
The mirror is no longer.
    You.

Minister Whitelove

Basketball

A hand pushes
The ball goes down
The ball bounces
The ball comes back up
The hand pushes more
Moving the ball
Up court, down court
One last bounce
Swish, in it goes
And nothing but net
With a roar of the crowd.

Mary Johnson

Pygmalion And Galatea

Speaking of the afternoon...
the boundless confines of his
    studio mixed me with the
    fashioned marble
hammer and chisel married his fingers,
    driven by the conception
    of arrow and flesh.
as blood poured, she emerged from
    the sculpture, a product of
    (an unspoken barely
    dream) hints of existence
"Pygmalion!" she cried through
    nectar-soaked lips,
    extending from the artist
    in breath and mirth
all the consequence tangible now—
    they stepped,
    naked and alive,
    out of the oil together.

Rebecca Piorkowski

"The Star In The Sky"

The star in the sky;
the brightest of them all,
It seems so close.

If only we could reach
up and grab it;
hold it while it glows.

It's racing,
an unnoticed falling star,
as it twinkles wildly;
yet it seems so smooth and calm,
its presence somehow
easing my soul.

The star in the sky;
it's as far as I can see,
but it appears to be near.
That star is like our
mysterious love... so close;
yet, always so far.

Regan McCaughey

Death Opens, Life Begins

Death opens, life begins,
The caterpillar in the wind
He slinks along the milkweed stems,
The morning dew sparkles like gems
    And death opens, life begins.

Light locked outside the dark cocoon,
It lies and waits beneath the moon
The sun comes up, so still it lies,
And dreams of days when it will fly
    And death opens, life begins.

The songs of spring burst forth around,
And flowers peep from underground
The silk breaks wide and sets it free,
The butterfly for all to see
    And death opens, life begins.

Melissa Cunningham

The Master Weaver

As the master weaves,
    The cloth of life we see!
As the design begins to unfold.
    The need for each will be.

As the design is being completed
    The meaning begins to show.
As the understanding increases,
    The reasons we begin to know!

As the will of the Master Weaver,
    The design lays out our path.
As the walking of the path shown,
    The way to escape the wrath.

As the Master weaves the final threads,
    The fulfillment of all is begun.
As the Master drops the thread of life,
    The end completed all by one!

Rose Marie Patton

"Remember"

I remember
The clothes you wore,
And more.
Your perfume lingers
I can't forget.
And will remember
When I see you again.
It will be forever,
Not now and then!

William A. Stephens

Party

The balloons are blown
The clowns have shown

The guests are here
The presents are near

The cake is eaten
Bad children are beaten

The presents are seen
The table is clean

The birthday boy has slept
The memory is kept.

Matt Noll

"Wish"

I gently plucked
the dandelion huff
from the plush meadow
Its soft little feathers
moved slightly in the breeze
and I stared at it in wonder
I closed my eyes
to make a wish
and smiled when it came to me
But when I opened
my anxious eyes
not a feather I could see
I looked up ahead
and saw them flying
floating up with ease
My precious wish was stolen
taken by the breeze

Kathleen D. Shemwell

A House Or A Home?

My house is so dirty,
the dishes piled high,
But we had so much fun today,
my children and I.
The Laundry is filling,
the cobwebs are thick,
but my children and I,
we found some flowers to pick.
We talked of the beauty,
the earth has to see,
and had a nice conversation,
my children and me.
For children grow so fast,
yes they slowly slip away,
and then you wish
that you had taken time to play.
So before the years can take them
into lives of their very own,
I want to take the time to do
what make a house a home.

Wanda Phillips

"B. B."

A star shines bright
The door opens wide
A name inside
Special and true
Soft winds travel
Trees grow strong and tall
Leaves colorful and plenty
Reaching upward beauty to behold
Breath of life natures reward
A free soul passing through time
Strength and courage
A path of love
Follow the light
Upward you go
A star that shines bright
The door closes tight
Travel onward free soul
Peace everlasting
Love forever more

Dawn H. Wright

Zamila

As the winter melts away
the earth's snowy veil
fragrant baby blossoms
and the sun's warmth hail
the season of endearment

The freshness of falling rain
Hastening summer by and by
Fleeting
like your kohl-lined eyes
smiling beneath the abayah

Eid al Fitr celebrations
We share the season
Raisins, dates, oud music
And love for no other reason.
my Zamila.

Khadijah Hassan

The Face Of A Nation

The face of a Nation
The face that grieves the heart.
For the Nation seeks his own,
Their God they have forgot.
They long to satisfy their flesh,
They long for all to see,

The Face of a Nation that
loves greed and immorality.
The face of a Nation, God says,
"It opposes Me.
For I want to break its bondage,
but they will not come to Me."

The Face of a Nation,
So wrinkled and pale within,
They forget God, and continue
to indulge in sin.

The Face of a Nation,
So sad for all to see,
For the face of this Nation
has turned its back on Thee.

Tracy Carver

Grandmas' Hand

The hand that loved.
The hand that made
You feel reality.
The hand that when
You felt alone, gave you
Peace and hope.
How can one hand give
so much life so much
strength? This hand will never die.
This hand will always
be soft and tender, even
when some others may be
so rough.
Grandma your love was
gracious and divine and
I will never forget your
hand in mine!

Marla McInchak

Trapped

They'll never understand
the hurt I feel inside
They'll never understand
the feelings I have to hide
The tears that I choke down
as other people smile
They'll never understand
how I'm free for a little while
free to hear the wind blow
and rustle through the leaves
Free to watch the head lights
as cars drive down the streets
No-one else is bothered or
troubled by my demand
I've created myself a world that
They'll never understand.

Karolee Anne Crandall-Hines

I Am Of These...

In deference to Yeats

In Ireland,
the King of the Cats is gone,
though all of the lesser cats
clamor on
and scratch and clatter
through the night
to drag a scrap of truth
to light.

Still hungry for scraps,
I have little to say—,

for I am of these

But another
drab stray....

Michael D. Adkins

Crucified Heart

Darkness overthrows her
The light shines in her eyes,
she wants to find the key,
to let out all the cries.

She's alone in a world with locks,
her arms and legs are bound,
her heart hits the rocks,
just an empty sound.

She wants to go to a place,
where life is kind and free,
to hide away from the race,
of human insanity.

Her life is filled with lies,
the lies: that she is loved,
on the cliff she cries,
and lets go as she is shoved.

Her tears dry on her face,
her arms reach out for death,
now she can go to the place,
where her heart has all the wealth.

Sara Altman

Broken Horses

They run through the water clear.
The little and the grown.
Hardly having any fears
Until the ropes are thrown.

On goes the saddle.
On goes the man.
Tightening on the reigns.
Now the fight begins.

The man rides hard and high
The horse tries with all of its force
Then from the fence we hear a cry
It now becomes a broken horse

Walter Edgar Scott

My Special Boy

I sit here watching everyday,
the little boy who will not play.
Born to me years before, he sits and
stares, wanting more.
His legs so tiny, and oh so weak;
I know in my heart he will never speak.
he didn't ask to be that way.
And people wonder what to say.
I know one day he will be set free,
to run and play so joyfully.
A silent tear roles down my cheek,
for my special boy, so mild and meek.

Michelle Adkins

'Alone'

Day and night I sit alone
The look of depression is there.
Wishing and hoping you'll phone
So I can tell you how much I care.
Sharing things together
Yes, the love we share is real
Vague at the moment; but forever
The feelings is concealed.
Another day and night of misunderstanding
Hoping this time he will appear
A night to remember; exciting
Seems as if it's a bad year.
The look of passionate in my eyes
My alluring body sways
My love for him, make me realize
Hey it's been several days.
Seem as if we belong
Seeing him is such a delight
Only to find myself alone
Loosing him; well I just might.

Veronica A. Sam

Dolmen

Stark upon a windswept knoll
The monolithic dolmen stands,
Rough hewn boulder chamber-boles
Placed there by ancient, reverent hands.

No walls fetter the thaumaturge,
Wrought by raging, rampant winds
Their rigid harp strings' direful dirge
Plucked by frenzied, mordant hands.

What men prodigious labors bent
Upon this rocky, treeless plain
To erect a sterile monument
To moonscape on terra incognita domain?

T. A. Landrith

Memories

Never forgotten,
The love of many
Made in heaven
To hold forever.

Deep inside holds the joy
Of a loved one so far away,
Away; not in mind,
Yet in body.

The love of one
Is never forgotten,
Only held inside to shine.

Death may be a remorseful time,
Yet there is joy inside.

For they are in heaven.
With the deeply divine.

Never forgotten
The memories inside.

Mist Lou Trester

Reaching Up ...

Lying in this darkened cove
The marbles in my skull
give me a fish eye view.

Looking out, past the cinders
Up at the azure sky
Powder puffed clouds with shades of gray
how beautiful, to my dismay.

If there is peace on earth,
this is heaven.
Movements of swelling seas
As my hands dangle in the warm water.

Hear the oceans curl,
as the birds soar overhead.
The fragrance, oh the fragrance
of the surrounding gardens.

Put me back in the ground.
Bury me deep.
Deeper than one can see.
Cover me...

Karyn Mannix

"Endless Youth"

Eyes exhausted, body beat.
The mind mulling, flashing
From one thing to another.
So much to do,
So far to go,
Yet so little time.

Days, weeks, months fly by,
Years are here and gone.
Treasured time but memories,
Still time and life go on.

Once young and yearning to be grown,
Now grey and wise we find
That youth is not just for the young,
But always in ones mind.

The young grow old,
The old grow young,
I've found this is a truth.
Through the years we share and grow,
We become the endless youth.

Mary Ellen Torquato

Jesus

The pain that hurts
the most,
Is the pain in your
heart when you
have been hurt,
When you have been
treated like so much
dirt.
But when we forgive,
The pain disappears,
and also our fears.

Peggy Start

Art Box

Deep violet hue dew splash
the muse sky.
Ebony cut-out silhouettes hoover.
Silver slivers spizzle the throws
holed thread.
Dazzled dangles fall off the
frazzled edge.
Five twice tender digits smooth
tree with lick.
Babes simple sum with snow,
drawn from a stick.

Kelly Davidson

The Tribulation

All Christians are gone
The non-believers still there
The Holy Spirit has left
The world has no care.

People are killed -
Without reason or thought
Countries are furious
Wars must be fought.

666 screams -
most every hand
The mark of the beast -
Is now on demand.

Earthquakes, tornadoes,
Our world is a mess,
Christians now dying -
There's less and less.

Man's chances are over
Their choices were dumb
Prepared they were not
The tribulation has come.

Salena Pilon

Untitled

Where is the key to my locket?
The one possessed by my heart;
I don't know where I lost it, or even
where to start.
I think a man has kept it, forgetting
to give it back;
Now my heart is locked inside, and
love my life does lack.
I'm afraid the lock will tarnish, then
begin to rust;
When cut open, my heart set free, there
will only be ashes and dust.
If kept locked up much longer, my
heart shall burst in two;
Then I will be at last set free from
the love I never knew.

Kristi Schneider

A Monumental Visit

As I pass through
　the park of monuments;
I see a magnificent black strip
　of pride and reverence.

It is crowded
　by people in mourning;
Their sorrow and anger
　is profoundly embracing.

Upon nearing this vast marble wall
　I can now clearly tell;
In some distant place
　this list of heroes fell.

While reading the thousands of names
　my own heart grows heavy;
And I wonder to myself
　how much pain can this object levy?

But now I've found my own Father's name
　and how much is very clear;
For my heart feels the pain
　and on my cheek falls a tear.

　　Roger M. Ross

The Courthouse

From Europe came the people
The rich, the poor the free,
First a trickle then a flood,
They come from over the sea.

From mountains high to beaches care
They roamed this golden land,
Seeking ever spreading space
For freedom's right to stand.

Richer far than hoards of gold
The courthouse keeps for all
The heritage of our peoples past
To intrigue and to enthrall.

　　Mary Rena Rice

Untitled

The sound of the ocean,
the scent of salty water
is what I miss
More than anything
The roaring and crashing waves
always made me feel better
I could stay there forever
through the thunder and rain
or sunshine and wind
No sound's ever beautiful than the ocean
when I'm there
I ain't here anymore
I'm far - far away
from the entire world
I wanna stay there forever
'cause it's my place
My place of peace
The ocean will always be by home
in my heart and soul
Forever and ever...

　　Nikki Obidos

Truth

　Give me the truth
　the scion of being
　the nemesis of pleasures
　brutish and fleeting

　The father of wisdom
　virtue and light
for ignorance and lies
　succumb to its might

　Truth hide no long
　answer the need
question from antiquity
　for which all bleed

　Pearl of heaven
　Oh so very near
just a question away
　wisdom without fear

　Embrace me and mine
bring the world your power
　light even to the blind
　enemy of the coward

　　Timothy Holloway

All Around Me...

Down the path, alone I walk.
The sounds of nature and a hawk.
Birds are singing in the trees.
Words can't describe, this ecstasy.
Purple flowers and pretty daffodils.
Butterflies, fluttering, along the hill.
Rays of sunshine, through the trees.
Gracious for all, I thank thee.
Truly, from my heart, I speak.
Little rabbits, playing, hide and seek.
A scene from heaven, I'd presume.
Must be at night, beneath the moon.
Off in a distance, I can hear.
Softly, sweet innocence, of a deer.
Too seldom do we, come to see.
This realm of beauty, all around me.

　　Michelle C. Belli

Moon Love

The moon rose,
The stars shined.
I choose,
To leave him behind.
The moon was full,
The stars grew brighter.
The relationship was dull,
He was a fighter.
The moon was crescent,
The stars faded.
His love was a present,
When our love was shaded.

　　Rebecca Sharp

Memories

Yesterday with luck can be
The time locked in your mind
of things you did
of thoughts you had
That tomorrow will not bring

　　Mark Conyers

Remember

Try to remember,
the things he has done,
remember the fight,
he thought he had won.

Remember the hell,
he put you through.
Remember the lies
he told to you.

Your love didn't work
because he didn't try,
remember the tears
he made you cry.

Now you're in heaven,
high above,
was it really worth
dying for love.

　　Tasha R. Sousa

As Time Goes By

As I sit and watch
the time go by, I feel as though
I could cry.
　The days and hours are
so long, then I hear
your favorite song.
It makes me feel as
though you are near.
I reach to wipe away
a tear.
But this is not a
tear of sorrow,
for I know that I will
be with you tomorrow.

　　Wanda Wagman

"Memories"

As I sit here remembering when
The time we spent caressing then
I'd remember the nights you held me tight
And the days we had our fights
Even though those fights were small
Our love was what got through them all
The memories I have about you and I
Sometimes make me break down and cry
I keep thinking of how much I had missed
That very first time that we had kissed
The moment when I looked into your eyes
I'd see our future clear without demise
These are some memories I have of you
I hope you have memories about us too.

　　Rosie Yarnell

About My Dogs

Asher and Zeke are my dogs.
They are not fat, but sometimes
They can eat like hogs.
Their names are Asher and Zeke.
Sometimes they can act quite meek.
Some days you can teach them a trick.
Then other days they act quite thick.
Both our dogs are very cute.
And Zeke has a very big snoot.
Most of the time they behave very good;
When told, they do what they should.

　　Matthew Joseph Michalski

Joannie's Burden

Imaginary bare-skin armor repels
   the unwelcome caresses
     of all those eyes
      as Joannie retreats
   to the safety of the bar.

A long drag on her Winston,
Joannie coughs at the smokey room,
   then loads her tray with
     several more orders of
Coors and Millers and Bud Lite.

   Then, off again,
   to weave across a dark and
     music-battered room,
   packed with writhing bodies
     and grasping eyes.

And, at nights end, Joannie's
   more tired from clinging
     to self-respect,
than from carrying all the trays
of Coors and Millers and Bud Lite.

Bill Monroe

The Lonely Vision

I see you in my dreams,
The visions always the same,
I'm reaching out to embrace you,
I try to call your name,
Right before I touch you
And say how much I care,
The morning shines, its light on me,
You're no longer there,
I wake with painful tears
To the reality that you're not mine,
I wait for the night to come again,
So I can dream of you,
One more time.

Michelle McKay

The Beach

The sand looks like chestnut hair
The water is the bow in it.
The noise is gone all is calm.
The sky is like a big blue blanket
   covering the Beach Sky.

The kids are playing in the
   sun that looks like a bright
   yellow dress.
The sandcastles are for the
   sandcrab that digs for a
   home in the sand.

The Beach is a peaceful
   place, a place for fun and play.
But when you go you
   know you left something behind
   at a place called the beach.

Naomi Crawford

Suicide

Children cry in the night
Their voices go unheard
They know not where to turn
Nor who to seek

Faith Is gone
Religion Is dead
Tired Of waiting
Too scared to move on

Michael Moore

The Fight

The way it snowed!
The way it snowed that night!
The snow put up a big fight!
The way it fought with the wind
And the night!
The way the wind would let down slowly
But then the snow would tack a big blow.
It would get tossed around again
When the wind came back again
But the snow would get up
While it got hit by the wind again!
The trees would cheer them on
As the two fought
All night long.
But no one will win
Until Spring.

Patrick Cuffe

The Beginning

Your dark eyes tug at my soul,
the way you smile at me makes me melt,
Your deep voice haunts my memory,
but just remember one thing
it is only the beginning.

Tanya Camp

Song

Has the Power to quiet,
The will to break a silence
that will make us stand
and find a beauty
in the wind

Song
is the moment
of all past and present
that voices the dreams of people,
who have been and will be

Song
binds us all
in the relentless love
that dwells in the very youth
of our imaginations.

Kellie M. Ufford

God Speaks

The trees bend lowly
The wind blows hard and wild
The sky darkens - now -
And then light, more light, more light

Trollie Culbreath Jr.

Flow

Midnight chimes, the moon is high;
The winds ripple the clouded sky.

Glowing streams of silvery light,
Flash like ribbons through the night.

And so flows the shimmering sands,
While time sweeps its mighty hands.

The glass is turned on its end,
Begins the cycle that never ends.

And so goes life; on and on,
Never ending; never gone.

Tom Porter

Untitled

I've found that if I close one eye
the world still looks the same
but if I close the both of them
the darkness hides my shame.
Trapped within this body
I find to be pure hell
what to be a spirit
to travel at my will.
No hate for one who kicks you down
no love for many more
I'd love to see what I could learn
I'd live to fly and soar.
My body is my prison cell
my feelings, my torture
to be free, I'll die again
only to be reborn.

Randall Evan Tooth

Reflections

Pause for thought; stop and reflect;
then carry on without a regret:
The inevitable is waiting,
the unknown to unfold.
Tomorrow-today the future we say,
it's only a step as we make our way.

We grow wiser, we grow old,
and then we are a living soul.
Was there a past, is there a sorrow,
and will we bring this in the morrow?

Relinquish the past
which we hold and accept
the future about to be told.
There is no past,
there is no sorrow,
there is no pain and no tomorrow.

Kathleen Ann Bird III

"The Man You Weren't Supposed To Meet"

I wanted to be yours.
Then you met the other guy—
I introduced you two,
and now I ask myself why.

I tried to get across,
but it ended in defeat—
So, honey, here's the man
you weren't supposed to meet.

He treats you like a queen,
and now I blame myself.
To try and get you back
is put back on the shelf.

She's someone I won't get;
I'm a friend wanting more.
Now she is thanking me,
so, hey, what are friends for?

So, I hope that someday
he will trip on his feet —
Until then, here's the man
you weren't supposed to meet.

Michael Harmon

To Mothers On Their Day

Of all the days of obligation
There are few who will contest
That one day sat aside
For mothers is the best

She's there from conception
'till the end, when that may be
She nurses you until you're grown
And have your family

She patches all your wounds
A kiss will heal it fast
She always had the answers
If you look back in the past

Up through school and college
She was always there for us
She'd do without, that we might have
And never fume or fuss

We all take for granted
She'll always be around
But grant this day, just for her
'til she is Heaven bound

Warner F. Webster

Love

There is only one person,
There is only one name.
That could ever give me love.

But he is not here,
To wipe away the tears.
I miss him so very much.

I see his face,
In a crowd.
But then he walked away.

Then one day I saw him again.
I seemed to float on air.

I'll love him forever.
If I see him never.

I'll never forget his face.

Kristin McGrath

A Place To Go

Beyond the reality of your mind
There lies a dream of a safer place
A place to go when you're alone
Alone to feel your sorrowful soul
A soul that's known to only you
You fight to keep it warm and true
But difficult it is to control
Your emotions go amongst the few
The ones that scare you
And leave you crying
Crying for that safe and happy place
The place you feel that you will reach
The final place you long to sleep
But must you wait until that day
Or should you take the easy way

Steve Singh

Above The Sky

When you die
there you'll be,
A finer place
you'll never see.

If you were kind
and if you were good,
you will go there,
yes, you should.

Angles around and
they go by,
with wings on their backs
so they can fly.

White nightgowns on
so the can rest.
But, angels always
try their best.

Kim McCabe

Some Thoughts On Turning 40

When you see all the years fly by,
There's no need to just sit and cry.
Goodness sakes! My world and lordy-
Guess what, "Life begins at 40!"

You say, "That's a whole lot of bunk!"
You're no longer a youthful hunk...
Hide those mirrors; don't even glance,
In your own heart lies true romance.

You feel perhaps your vision dims,
And arthritis invades your limbs.
Buy your books with much larger print.
Walk, don't run; stroll, don't sprint.

You worry your hair is thinning-
Receding to no beginning.
So buy a wig or don a muff,
Wear a big smile, that's quite enough.

You find young men are much taller
And you're feeling somewhat smaller.
Compared to them you're a shorty.
Who cares! "Life begins at 40!"

Shirlee A. Krause

Only Us Girls

For as long as remembered
there's only been three,
Only us girls;
Mom, Heather, and me.

My dad I've not seen
Since before I was two
the memories I hold
Are bleak and few.

They divorced and went
their separate ways
the love they felt
had melted to greys.

My dad died last Sunday
While he was in bed.
Things I needed to say
Will never be said.

For as long as remembered
there's only been three,
Only us girls;
Mom, Heather, and me.

Liberty Quinn

Chains

In this dungeon I grow weary.
These chains, they hold me fast.
The only thing that gives me joy,
are memories of the past.

The food I get is moldy,
the water it is stale.
To the fruit and wine that once I knew,
everything grows pale.

The air in this cell is rancid,
and in darkness I'm consumed.
How I long to feel the sun on my face,
and smell flowers that have bloomed.

I feel an inner turmoil,
a sadness with which I cannot cope.
But I know things must be this way,
and I shall never give up hope.

But these chains, they grown rusty,
these chains that hold me.
And one day I will break these chains,
and then I will be free.

Seth Michael Lachica

They Say It's A Free World

The say it's a free world,
they say we should be glad.
Then why are we all starving?
Why are we so sad?
Why are we all fighting,
fighting wars by land and sea?
If you want to save tomorrow,
you must save us human beings.
Us children are all dying,
dying day by day.
If we're going to be the future,
you must stop killing us this way.
So let's all stick together,
to try and work this out.
Because if we don't work together,
Soon we'll all die out.

Stephanie Pick

The Caravan

Look at the mountains
They stand so high
I walk on the ground
They touch the sky

My caravan leads me
Well on my way
And everyone's sleepy
At the end of the day

"Oasis, please come into sight"
For we have no water
For the end of the night
The children are dying
No water to be found
The lungs with air drying
In a sea of sand we drown

Is there any hope?
Are there any chances?
Of cool swimming pools,
And liquid romances?

Michael Monson

Our Saviour

He believed in truth nor thought of cost;
They stripped and nailed him to a cross;
He loved the humble and the weak;
They drove sharp nails into his feet.

He tried to be a friend to all,
Remove each barrier and wall,
Yet, satan found the very place
To crucify and Christ disgrace.

In agony he spoke, not to condemn,
"Oh, Father, forgive, forgive them,"
As he spoke tears shown and pity, too,
"For they know not what they do".

One Christ there was upon a Cross,
And we, in deepest, dark remorse
Should know he suffered so that we
Out of our strength might forgive as he.

Ruth E. Powderly

Solitary Reminiscence

I sit by life watching
things happen
The days growing short
And the light slowly gloaming

I've not lived
But only existed
And missed what was great
For fear of disappointment

I cannot be one of example
Or offer substance in vaunt
For in the crying silence
  I am alone.

Paul Wilford

Country Roads In Autumn

I wonder if he used to
Think about me as he
Drove through the apple orchards
And eucalyptus groves.

Even in November
There are apples on the ground
In Occidental.

The rusted leaves, the waves and wind
The beauty, silence and wildness of
This place will always remind me of him.

Of all his unspoken words
And of his beauty which so far-to me
Remains an unopened book.

Kathleen Rampton

A Friend

A friend is one who's there always
Through problems you have you cant face
A friend is there through trouble times
Even when you may not have a dime
A friend is there when you are doubting
Even when you're screaming and pouting
A friend is one you can lean on
A friend is there to depend on
A friend is one who'll pay double
Just to keep you out of trouble
A friend is one who loves you so
A friend like that you can never let go

Kristie Riley

My Love Is Real

It's dangerous, yes I know
This game we play
My heart's at stake, I fear
Despite my flirting ways.

I see much more than a handsome face
Much more in those eyes
I see much more than a ready smile
On the mouth that tells me lies.

I see the you that stays in mind
A thought that makes me smile
I wish to make this game be real
But I wonder why.

Our playful words come all the time
I beg of you, my dear
See the meaning beyond the actions
And you'll find my love is real......

Sharon L. McDaniel

(This poem is dedicated to
the memory of police officers
Ron Ryan, Jr., Tim Jones, and
his canine, Laser who were
gunned down on August 26th, 1994
While serving in the line of duty.)

Astro

As though carved from granite,
  He stands in his stately silence.
The canine Coeur de Leon!
  Unsurpassed in intelligence.
Noblesse oblige determines his valor.

His greatness exemplified
  Not only in mind, but in body.
Guardian to truth and loyalty
  Undaunted!
An eminent perception
  Of gentleness and compassion.
Gracefully forgiving.

Kathryn Ward

Time-Out

See me now
This that I am
I'm strong, and I'm weak
Just take my hand

Hear my plea
Not words that are spoken
A heart full of love
A heart that is broken

Reach out to me
Not for deeds to be done
Just share in the beauty
Of the day's setting sun

Too fast is the pace
Let's sit this one out
Take stock and remember
What life's all about

Tomorrow's a new day
What a waste it would be
If a chance was passed by
Far too busy to see

Rosalie Beucke

Lord, Let Me Live My Life Again

Lord, let me live my life again
This time I'll live it without sin
I will look to you in time of need
This way I know I shall succeed
I will read my bible each day
I will live my life your way
I will go to church each week
For your word is what I seek
I love to hear the word of God
When my pastor speaks I give a nod
I will always pray everyday
And remember you in every way
You have given me a brand new start
I will forever keep you within my heart
I want to serve you in every way
Please show me how, so I can do this today
Give me a sign in some way
Because I'm ready Lord whenever you say
The church of The Nazarene is where I go
To hear the word of God flow.

Wanda Kumm

Touch Not The Cat But The Glove

Touch not the cat but the glove
Tho handsome looks and seeks your love
The fur is soft, silky, and yet
Tis not wise to let it tempt
Thine eye, hand or open heart
Lest the feline seduction start

Body sliding 'neath your hands
Purring as you meet demands
Of butting head and kneading paws
Still, mind those sharp and hidden claws
Springing forth and causing harm
When you ignore her fatal charm.

Nealie Jean McBean

Memories

Dedicated to my Papa Paul

Childhood memories
those are the best
I will never forget them
Never put them to rest.

Sometimes I wish
we could go back in time
back to a life
without any crime.

Life was so sweet
so innocent and full
nothing to worry about
and none of this bull

Children today
with their weapons and guns
knowing it is wrong
but they think it is fun

Children today
trying to impress their friends
not laughing and playing
but putting their life to an end.

Mindy Adams

Empty Promises

They stand by their windows
those political beings
and laugh at the world
not knowing the world
is laughing back

They speak in their foreign tongue
and think no one can understand
but they do
and they say they can cure all

It is all hot air
rising to the open sky
of empty dreams and hopes
waiting for the next rain
to sweep it into the
overflowing gutters

Shelly Gall

Silent Friend

Hello again, my silent friend,
   though we've yet to meet
   I'll go on and pretend
   that it's you I come to
   each night in the dark;
      your name that I whisper...
      your touch on my heart.

I've been waiting for you
   for such a long time,
   My heart softly beats...
   thoughts it's screaming to pound.

I'll see you tomorrow
   once more... in my dreams
   and hope that one day
   I may call you by name.

Kathleen M. Frantz

In Memory Of My Husband

He was the most handsome man,
Through my eyes, I have known.
I will tell you about him, if I can;
Through my tears, as I moan.

This world has lost a valiant soul.
He was one of the noble kind.
To be truthful; He was always bold.
Honesty was always on his mind.

Next to God, His family came first.
He was patient and kind to all.
As he lived, in God he put his trust.
He was just waiting for his call.

God looked down, and saw that he
was tired, and he needed rest.
So to heaven, he called him to be;
And we know that God knows best.

Oh! How I miss his smile so sweet,
And the love that shined in his eyes,
In eternity, when we meet,
His touch will still my cries.

Martha Porter

Too Late

The human breathes but lives in vain
through speeding youth the need to gain,
another hill the greener grass,
across the tracks the other class.
Ne'er to stop and take a stand
of what is had right close at hand.
To late the pause with nought to find,
our dearest friends were left behind.

Rudolph "Rudy" Mick

That Road Beyond

I travelled on that road beyond,
Through storms and clouds of gray,
Looking to the future
With thoughts of yesterday,

I left yesterday's road behind
And the thorns of life I bare,
But thoughts of yesterday
Told me - I still cared,

The road beyond
Led me to the future
With anxiety on my mind
I couldn't control my agony,
That came from another time,

That road beyond brought happiness
And sometimes tears
With thoughts of yesterday
As I travelled through the years,

Ruth Hollimon Jones

Autumn Leaves

The beautiful autumn leaves glows
through the blue heavens.
When the wind blows through the
heaven that the autumn leaves
floats to earth.
When the sun shines beams on
autumn leaves to brighten a
wonderful earth.
In fall the autumn leaves are
beautiful around the earth.
The autumn leave falls during
autumn to the ground and fades
into the earth.
The earth is seeded with autumn
leaves that falls from trees to
the ground and green leaves to
grow again on trees.
God created autumn leaves for beauty.

Scott H. Swing

All Alone In The Middle Of The Night

In my room
through the night
at my desk
by my self
without anyone
down my head went
on the desk top

Nakiva Singletary

Bradley

A young boy running,
through the wind,
Light red hair,
and soft blue eyes,
the world is his little surprise,
He doesn't understand,
for other people are in command,
He's only four,
He doesn't know.
No more running,
No more screams,
No more laughing in the breeze.
Quiet,
Silence,
Sit down,
please don't breathe,
He's only four,
He doesn't know.

Stephanie Kim Clark

Best Friends

Best friends last forever and ever,
Through the years
And through the weather,
Through the good times,
Through the bad,
Through the happy and the sad.
You can not order them from a book,
Or from the way that they look.
Friends cannot be judged by what you see,
But what's on the inside of you and me.

Tiffany Reeder

Abe Lincoln

Abe was honest and told the truth
Throughout the days of manhood and youth
His aim was to make the most of his self
He began with three books on the shelf.

Abe was a great teacher
Like God he was a great preacher
Because for right he took a stand
He was rated the greatest in the land.

Lavern Renfro

Time

Time Wasted
Time gone
Time wished for
Time remembered
Time spent with you
Time cherished
Time without you
Time to realize
Time to love
Time to say
Goodbye......

Martin Rendon

Patches

Took a fine needle
to sew myself in
with the threads of my life
Some patches old, some new
Some, like yours, are frayed
and I can braid us together
so I cannot tell
where I end and you begin.

Lynn T. Heyden

Hope Springs Eternal

A stream tumbles on.
Time slowly winding
down the day and the night
and the moon shines bright.
A solo piano sounds the note of
sorrow; then a voice of joy
sings and builds and silently
the stream fades. The moon
glimmers in the water. A cold,
clear wind, a hand held tight...
And then the stream comes back.
Over rocks, over the air,
over the Earth falls quiet.
Not a sound is heard.

Thomas M. Howell

The Loving Thing

A fine thread connects each soul
to all others
winding binding waists knees fingers
no escape from humanity
the only true bond
with the dead the unborn the existing
for once it is
It is infinitely
no bounds no limits
no time no space
It condemns not
It neglects not
It caresses
   encompasses
   understands
   heals all
It descends blends transcends
making nonsense
in its harmony

Stacy Diane Elliott

Sorrow

As I knelt by your graves today,
   To clear the brush away.
Placing flowers in the urn,
   I wonder where to turn.
I suddenly felt the tears,
   For all those lost years.
Feelings that were never told,
   Through you were growing old.
Praises that were never said,
   But angry words instead.
We think we really hate,
   Until it's too late.
Though I am distraught,
   You were my parents no matter what.
Although you can no longer hear,
   My words are most sincere.
If I had a wish to come true,
   It would be to say "I love you."

Rosalee Harper

Untitled

Once the Gods have chosen
to concentrate on you-
they send no warning of what
they intend to do.
The arrow is loaded,
they pull back the bow-
intended evil or blessed goodness?
No way of knowing
what they plan
to bestow.

Karen Perleoni

"Alone"

I've been driving,
To familiar places.
Looking for,
Some familiar faces.
A kindly smile,
A friendly hand,
Someone there,
To understand.
I'm not mistreated,
But life still hurts.
Perhaps I'm getting,
My just desserts.
For all the things,
That I've done wrong,
Like hurting others,
And acting strong.

Robert P. Blood

A Perfect World

To imagine the joy of a wonderful love
To learn of the hope there is to be
To feel the touch of a loving soul-
These wishes I've brought upon thee.

To have the knowledge of forever love,
Or learning the future beforehand,
To know truth from lies, love from hate-
To realize I understand.

To comprehend the concept of love
To feel the joy of happiness
To know you need not worry so-
A world that has no stress.

When the world relies on simple things
And there is no lies or deception,
The birds will sing, the people rejoice!
The world will then be perfection.

Kristine Olsen

Untitled

I hate getting up
   to let someone out
   while the moon is still
      ascending
   Hours before the alarm clock
   welcomes another day
I need more than a few hours
   to justify changing the
      bed sheets
   Singing in the shower
      or
   smiling during the daylight
   hours

Robert Swanson

Remember This

To take the time
   To thank yourself
As well as the one above
To give yourself
   A pat on the back
For the things that you have done
To take the time
   To go within
To be nourished from you spirit there
To love yourself
   As your friend
Give yourself the best of care

Margaret Hart

God Has Done It All

God gave the sun
   To light up the days,
 The moon to shine at night,
The spirit to guide me day by day
And the will to do what is right.

God placed in me
   The desire to know him,
   To grow and to be use.
He teaches me through His holy word
   And opens me to the truth.

God saved me by grace
   As He died on the cross
 And placed His spirit in me.
So the by sin I am no longer bound
   And death hold no fear for me.

Nothing comes from man,
   God has done it all.
 To Him be honor and praise
For He promised to keep me to the end
   And walk with me all of my days

Steven Myers

"Life"

I know how it is
to live a hard life
Me Beve and Jeff,
went through the strife,
Times were good and
times were bad
sometimes even very sad
sometimes I felt like running away
But my heart kept saying
stop you should stay.

Kelly S. Orfino

My Son

Is a part of me, to have and hold
to love, cherish and mold.
Showing him right from wrong...

I'll be tough when need be,
plus caring and gentle in the long.
Teaching him all the life rules.
He'll truly hate me at times,
thinking I'm mean and cruel...

He'll make it in life,
working hard every step of the way.
Remembering how I pushed, shoved him
every hour of the day...

Experiences will show him,
that way back when, I was so rough.
I really, truly loved him
Is a mother's love enough...

Rochelle L. Taube

Changes Of Love

   It's never too late to make a change,
to make a change within yourself.
   It's never too late to make a change,
to make a change within your heart.
   It's never too late to make a change,
to make a change within your mind.
   It's never too late to make a change,
to make a change in your thoughts.
So why not just take the chance to
make that change within your life
and learn to love all over again.

Monica M. Hitomi

Life Tempting

The field is full, beauty tempting
To reach, to touch - you sway attempting.
Fingers stop in midair - Do you dare
Touch the petal, soft with dew?
The thorn will prick the skin of you.

The smile is tender, the rose repeats.
The feel, surrender, the fingers reach.
Then thorn greets with a stinging hurt,
Yet - you dared a little flirt.

Feelings soared beneath the sigh.
Memories collect in a seconds light.
Woman blushes, heart floats a high.
A gentle rush of forgotten mirth.
Years forgot, she'll remember the worth.

Norma Prevatt

"Daffodil"

Oh daffodil, come when you will,
   to seek the sun and rain.
I see you from the window sill,
   and look time and again.

You come and bring the warm weather,
   that feels good after snow.
You make the yard look much better,
   adding that special glow.

You are so very beautiful,
   as you stand there with pride.
You remind us to be hopeful,
   and that God's on our side.

Oh daffodil, you have to go,
   but I'll see you next year.
Then it won't seem that long ago,
   when last I saw you here.

Mary Rafferty

Alone

To hold you in my arms
   To show you my love
Caring so much for you
   And wondering why I do
But when you left me
   I cried all alone...

My endless dreams
   My never ending tears
Thinking about you
   Within my darkened room
Tossing and turning
   Unable to sleep alone...

Going on day by day
   With my chin held high
Looking to go on
   Starting once again
But when I see you
   I can't help feeling
     alone...

Richard J. Eggers

Images

   Can you feel me
     Touch the air
Watch the starlight
     See it flare
Deep and penetrating
   I see you stare
     Smell my perfume
      I am there

Melissa Pelletier

Carrousel

Children are drawn to the carousel
to watch the horses play
was it magic that the children see.

Many dreams are found if you ride the
magic horses just once
lost fairytales and forgotten dreams
once rode the carrousel of life.

You can't turn around and say everything
will be alright you can't go back to the
carrousel, children who ride have too
grow up from the magic horses.

Come with me to the carrousel of life.
No one gets off the magic horses
until you're still a kid at heart.

Lori Jean Dill

"To Pray"

To sit and stare at the sky.
To wonder what you're thinking.
To be afraid of what I feel,
To believe that I'm mistaken.

I wonder how you love me.
I wonder why I'm afraid.
I feel I've gone too far.
I think that it might rain.

To take back what might be wrong.
To apologize for what I said.
To hope for a new revelation.
To wish our love wasn't dead.

Michelle Glaze

Love

Like the winter winds bring a chill
to your inner soul
So does the feeling of losing you
I sit and think how sweet it was
When you first fall in love, it seems
nothing can go wrong
This feeling fills your heart and
soul with a song
Suddenly you feel so warm
Then when you least expect it, comes
the storm
Leaving you completely alone and cold
Now you can only hope the warmth will
return, but it never returns as warm
as the first
You can only hope it's enough to
quench your loving thirst.

Michelle R. Campbell

Waiting

Waiting...
Wandering, thinking, realizing,
it's all been lies.
Why should I give in?
How can I not?
I have to try,
but I can't for long.
Waiting...
Waiting until the time
comes for me to give in.
To join them in brainwashing
someone like me.
Just Waiting.

Morgan Shank

Friendship Reflections

How oft we leave fond words unsaid:
Too busy, or, too proud.
We spend our days immersed in self,
No time for love allowed.

We take for granted every hour,
Forgetting time runs out;
We plod in darkness unaware
Love's ALL life is about!

We lift our heads in great surprise
When death knocks at the gate;
The loving voice, that pleasant smile,
We value now too late.

Lest we forget THE aim of life,
May we resolve today,
To touch with love the lives of those
Whom God has sent our way.

For hearts are small that cannot see
How great the blessing in
The briefest contact, shortest walk,
With those we call a friend.

Lydia C. Moore

Earthquake

Rumbling, rumbling,
Tossing and tumbling
Thunderous sounds shatter
The peaceful silence of night.

Shaking, breaking,
Buildings making
Unfamiliar noises
That just don't sound right.

Falling, bawling,
Calling out for help
But in the darkness no one sees
And no one hears except those in flight.

Crashing, smashing,
Cervices opening
Structures topple, people swallowed
By hungry earth with its anger and might.

Clearing, sharing,
Bearing body after body
Survivors unite
As they woefully consider their plight.

Marilyn Ashby

A Single Voice

There is a tree in Chautauqua's
   town
That refuses to buckle to
   winter's sound.

With all its fury and vicious ways
Winter wasn't able to have its say.

For this lone tree shows its might
With many leaves that still hold
   tight.

They refuse to fall, which makes
   it clear
That a single voice sometimes
   we'll hear.

Kathy Mancuso

The High

Life perfect for those who seek,
Traces of powder, noses bleak,
Torches ignite for all to see
What's come over me,
Vapors enhance the brain
Why not I ask, refrain.
No - clouds deemed I'm aloud,
Hence I leave the planet.
What say you, come back,
Here I am, beamed up
So where's the next puff,
Stop the madness
For with it comes sadness!
Thus I reply, it's THE HIGH.

Pamela MacHolmes

Sights I See

Sights I see are God's creation.
Trees are bright green,
Wind is blowing in your face.
The sky is so blue it hurts your eyes.
The sea is so beautiful I would love to
Gaze at it forever.
These are the sights I see.

Melinda White

Goodbye Crescent

The change of a name,
turned your life upside down.
Your mom got remarried,
so you followed her gown.

You moved out to Redlands,
when you were thirteen.
And with that, you made my life
happy and serene.

So now you are leaving
our nice little town.
And with you my heart
and my life upside down.

Just keep in you heart
this one little thought,
I will always love you
and hate you? Not.

Never in my life
have I felt so blue,
You're the one who did it
My dear Crescent, you.

Mindy Stevenson

America

America is the land I love,
Twas given us by God above,
The birds the bees, and deep blue sea,
Came from him to you and me.

With its fields of golden grain,
Gurgling, brooks and purple plain-
Majestic mountains reaching high,
As if to touch the azure sky,

God made this land for us to dwell
To see if we would keep it well.
He left it up to you and me,
To keep our country ever free.

So let's work together, you and I
To honor Him who lives on high,
By making it forever free,
So we can live in liberty.

Neoma Norman Rodgers

Love Has No Boundaries

Love has no boundaries
'Tween heaven and earth
Those dear to us here
To God in paradise have more worth.

Though separation through death
May come of body and mind,
Souls, once joined in Jesus
Eternal togetherness will find.

Once husband and wife
On this earthly place
Will one glorious day, reunited,
View Christ's holy face.

Committed to those vows
"Till death do us part"
Where love has no boundaries,
We will have that new start.

Nancy McDanel

Untitled

Drive the dagger deeper
Twist it as you smile
I was there as your friend
I gave an inch
You took a mile

I began to love you
Then in came the knife
I gave you my heart and soul
And then you took my life

Now you think I am dead and gone
My memory you don't fear it
Don't close your eyes
Don't turn your back
For you're forgetting about, my spirit

Susan Shaffer

Sensational Season

Sunbeams
Umbrellas
Moonlight
Mists
Everything enjoyable
   (especially ice cream)
Rainbows
Of course !
Summer

Penny Johnson

Snowshoeing Around Taggart Lake

Shadows walk tall
Under winter's
Skinned white pines.
Voices echo
From swells wind-blown
Around dead-fall
To breaking lips
Speaking clearly
In their stillness.
These echoes, thoughts,
Released without
Words for touching
This world, every step
In this cold world,
Every voice in
The chill.

William Nelson Taylor

Natural Comfort

In a forest by a river
Underneath the trees
That's where I wish I were
And where I long to be.

There the thoughts come to me pure
And soft as a feather
There I sit and feel the kiss
Of nature and her weather.

When I'm there it all seems clear
And simplified and free
There I see my purpose
And what my life should be.

The problems of the world
All seem to fade away
There I find the strength to live
And face another day.

I'll cling to this throughout my life
And nature will be my guide
When my problems seem too much
I'll have a place to hide.

Jeremy Nunnelley

Protest March

Youth and elderly
united in a crusade,
repeatedly trudge
a message of desperate,
reprieve outside the clinic.

Voices support the
wind as a hushed lullaby
of "Jesus loves the
little babies of the world"
stretches to reach an ear.

Cars accelerate
and pedestrians betray
in the opposite
way while eyes gaze downwards.
Have they made a difference today?.......

Shelly Crate

Who Am I To Be?

The silent storm of youth provokes an
   Unsettling breeze

Searching springs of churning doubt,
   Whispering ill-ease.

Waves of wonder, waiting to complete
   The puzzle one Lord has started.

Pretending to be joyful, when I am
   Broken-hearted.

What a gift life can be, if we but see.

Will I be a friend or fail to fulfill
   Who I am to be?

Mary Makula

Love

Don't let the tears from your eyes
   Wash the smile from your face,
Lest a frown should step in
   and forever take the place,
Of the smile you have worn
   All down through the years,
Let love be the dike
   To take care of the tears.

Tom Reynolds

An Ode To Love

May our hearts in tandem beat
Until again the twain shall meet,
Then on that beautiful golden shore
We shall meet to part no more.

Then my heart will its peace have found
When I stand on that holy ground,
There will be no sadness or pain
When I hold you in my arms again.

My heart will with fear and trembling be
Until my darling comes home with me,
We will go through the stars of the sky
Away from this evil earth we'll fly.

My love for you and your love for me
Will be written in ink of eternity,
It will never grow old fade or dim
It's all because we remembered him.

As ages come and ages go
My love for you will ever grow,
Angels sing so sweet and clear
Echoing my thought I love you my dear.

Lewis E. Seay

Forget, Me Not

I wanted a better house
Until I saw a shack.
I wanted better health.
Until I saw, "a fresh covered grave."

I wanted a better mind
Until I saw, " a mind, ruined by wanton."

Help me O' God, too be
Content, with my lot.
And pray only———
"You will," "Forget me not."

C. Self

Spirit Of Liberty

Spirit of the past I ask of thee
unveil the ages of history,
That all America might see
the cost in blood
Of Liberty.
Spirit of the present, I beg of thee,
For men whose hearts beat strong
to sing again America's song
and guard their nations
Liberty.
Spirit of the future,
I look to thee,
For a greater America, God within
with freedom loving countrymen
To love and keep
Our Liberty.

Richard Lee Hoag

Water's Edge

While there's still light
While I can dig my toes in the sand

I'll sit

so still the gulls won't know me
or stand

bold daughter on the water's edge
and hold cold waves
in my hand

Mary F. Fox

Junkyard

Squealing, filthy rats;
Used, sweaty hats.

The canine at guard;
Bread, stale and hard.

Tacky, torn clothes;
Old wrapping bows.

Parts from rundown cars;
Corroded pipes and bars.

Maggots crawling on aged fruit;
Dog slobber on a chewed up boot.

A scornful sight and awful smell
And a motorcycle that would never sell.

Lauren Sherburne

"Special Friend"

I've got a friend who is
very dear to me,

She's always been near to me.

She listened to me when I
first started to talk,

And was by my side when I
started to walk.

She cried with me when I was sad,

And scolded me when I was bad.

She cheered for me when I
got good grades

And sat proudly by my side
on graduation day.

She's helped me to grow
to be who I am,

And I'm so grateful for
her helping hand.

For she's my friend and
a whole lot more,

She's the Mother I adore.

Lynne Seifer

Flowers

Occasionally I have sent flowers
Very selectively I must also say.
To a few most beautiful women
On perhaps a very special day.
One special day was our meeting
Has just been two months past.
Still treasure those first few days
Those feelings will always last.
These flowers were very important
Only because they were sent to you.
They gave me a way to say
How important I feel you are too.
The flowers would mean nothing
If you I was unable to see.
The beauty of all the flowers
Would mean nothing dear to me.

Lon D. Sparks

A Little Girl's Dream

A little girls dreams of one day
walking in a field with the
man of her dreams.

She dreams of walking down the
aisle of a large church in her
father's arms, and she looks up to
see that special one waiting to spend
the rest of his life with her.

She then sees herself rocking a baby
to sleep, and standing next to her
is that man, who looks lovingly at
the child that they created.

Finally as her dream begins to
fade she sees her and her man
sitting quietly on a porch swing
passing the night away in each
other's arms.

Sarah J. Gallap

Loss Of Innocence

Lost and alone,
Wandering around,
Looking forlorn,
Trying to be found,
He looks about,
People pass by without a glance,
Tears fall from his little blue eyes,
Pulling on the edge of his shirt.
Kneading it through his fingers,
He begins to cry,
Sobs rack his young body through,
He begins to call about,
Searching for his mother he fumbles,
His sobs suddenly cease,
Tears dry up,
For found his mother has he.

Mark R. McIntyre

What He Does

Falling in love again
Want to wash his touch away
Why did I kiss his lips today?

Try to hold back my desire
He has this way of looking at me
He knows how I want to be.

"Loyalty" is how he says he is
Why then is he kissing my lips
And moving his hands up my hips?

Letting myself get hurt all over
Doing fine until he looked at my face
Then I found myself in his warm embrace.

He is still with her and it hurts
It is killing my mind and heart
Soon, it will be tearing me apart.

Krystal Downs

The Clover

I'm a clover short and green.
When I'm not four leaves no one cares.
I stand by myself with other plants
and know they are better than me,
You see me, you pick me up,
And you don't care.

Meradith Marshall

Welcome To The New Arrival

Just heard of the new arrival that
   was sent from above
Someone that you can cherish take
   care of and love
This is a gift that is most
   divine
Something like a star is the
   sky that shines
How wonderful it is that you
   own such a treasure
Also to know that it belongs
   to you forever
May the Lord give it its Blessing
   along through the years
That you'll have lots of happiness
   and not any tears.

    Margaret Coudrey

Lost At Sea

Like the sands that cover the earth
Washing up to shore at birth
Children tumbling in the wind
Some never to be seen again
Societies' troubled pride
Humanities lost in oceans' tide
To look into the eyes of unwanted babies
To watch the pain in an infant's heart
Knowing we are responsible
For their well-being
As mothers and fathers
We are miles apart
One day we will be old
Drifting out to sea
They won't even know our faces
Or hear our dying plea.

    McNeil

My Thoughts Of You

On the mountains in the sky
Watching clouds go drifting by
Seeming still, these empty hills
Create my thoughts of you.

Beauty paints each waking hour
Spent in nature's wildflower
Yet the scent's, sweet fragrance
Fills up my thoughts of you.

Joy is felt when light bounds
Yet night brings such lonely sounds.

The sun is set, another day
Kisses this old Earth away
Love is kind, but hard to find
Alone, with thoughts of you

    DC Englund

The Hillside

Standing on top of the windmill,
   Watching the wheel go free,
     Looking down the hill,
    To find what I can see.

   My land was very small,
     Some how I knew,
Boy, this windmill is really tall,
   Watching the sky change blue.

I see the shadows of the trees,
   The flowers, grass and weeds,
   The sun is setting in the west,
    The moon will take the lead.

    Rich Duval

Rain Drops

Rain Drops fall from the sky,
Way up above, high, high, high.
When they land on the ground,
They make a little pound sound.

Rain drops fall from the sky,
Way up above, high, high, high.
They're wet, small, and really cold.
Although small, they are quite bold.

Rain drops fall from the sky,
way up above, high, high, high.
I really don't know why,
But when they fall from the sky.
They wave and say, "Bye, bye!

    Tyson Canale

The Wind

There is a train
Way up above us so high
That can take you to a wonderful place,
Your palace in the sky.

It can take you on a ride
Way down low
To a place that is always
Covered with snow.

It'll take you
To a far off place
To watch a turtle
and a rabbit race.

Three thousand years
Shall come and shall go,
But no one will ever know
The things that I've come to know.

I know the wind is like a friendship,
Strong and true.
I know the wind is like the whole world,
Made just for you!

    Tracey Owensby

Untitled

I'm an old guy
   Way, way over the hill,
Aware of the world's problems
   And am an optimist still.

I hear all the comments
   Spewed from politico's lips.
How they'll solve all our problems
   If we just give them the grips.

'Tis the same old baloney,
   Quoted again and again
From those on the outs
   Hoping to get in.

I straddle the fence
   While all this goes on
'cause those already in
   Once promised a new dawn.

Yet being as human
   as any one can hope,
I get excited by the prospect
   I can bring change with my vote.

    Leon Schagrin

Black City

What to do about the
way you feel.
Come with me
And you know Ill make them
Real.
Once you know the way
You can never come back
The city of evil the city
of black.
You wake up scared
From your nightmare
You feel the pain
You just can't bear
You're running far
But you just can't hide
The faces of death
not far behind.

    Richard Wigginton

Perfection

We all try our hardest,
We all do our best,
But sometimes it's been pushed -
Stop putting it to the test.

Perfection - it exists
From the lighting
Of the candles on the cake
To our checklists.

Pushing to the limit
Is what we always are;
Perfect date, perfect clothes,
And even perfect car.

We make things seem flawless
So no one can criticize,
But the thing that catches up with us -
The telling of these lies.

Perfection - we try to make
Great things more divine,
But those who are not satisfied
May never draw the line.

    Kara DeDecker

Peace On Earth

Peace Valley Park, a lovely place
   We think is a paradise
With many acres to enjoy,
   Quiet lake before your eyes.

So many sailboats use this lake,
   Also rowboats and canoes;
Keep your motorized craft at home
   Or you will get worse than "boos"!

The wildlife here are quite content
   Most visitors are their friends -
They look for handouts everywhere
   As their hunger never ends.

Wildflowers are in abundance
   Purple vetch and queen Anne's Lace,
Buttercups, daisies and others,
   All add beauty in their place.

They have made a path for walkers,
   Joggers and bicyclists too;
If exercise is what you need
   This is a great place for you.

    Mildred Roberts-Taylor

Friends

We've been through so much
We told each other everything
Nothing stood in our way
Until that day

We cried our hearts out
The tears could form an ocean
We thought we'd be together forever
But we've fallen apart

We wrote many letters
And talked all the time
All the gossip was shared
But the truth was not

I still feel your pain
Your sorrow, and your fear
But things aren't the same
Since you're not here

I feel I don't know you
That our trust has been broken
Our friendship rests on the day
That each of us went our separate ways

Laura Smith

Eternal Lovers

In the morning of the frozen breeze,
We will be singing potions of our love.
Like wintery motion of spirited ease,
It's bringing us pure as the white dove;
Our spirits majesty eternal love.

In a dream, once upon a time;
we were hidden in a secret rhyme.
The spirits of our love did shine.
Keys of words forgotten that bind;
Our spirits majestic eternal mind.

As like a dream of being born into life;
In aesthetic charm I cling to my wife;
hollowed warmth of living light,
The spirit romanced us in the light.
Our spirits majesty eternal life.

In all of you I see these things;
In the truth our spirit is free.
One that knows life is one whom knows me.
In the truth we are lovers to be;
Forever we are joined eternally.

Leonard Chris McCabe

Untitled

I often think of reasons why
we're born, we live, and one day die
we laugh, and hate, love and cry
feel pain and pity, brave and shy
I've searched the world for peace of mind
I've been unjust, I've been unkind
and still not see the reason why
my heart is empty, my smile a lie
I may look happy, I may look glad
but within myself, I'm very sad
I give my heart, I give my all
sometimes I'm big, sometimes I'm small
the love I've lost are my own cost
but the biggest pain and hurt I feel
is when I've trusted friends not real.

Neda Ursic

Soldiers In War

Soldiers in war,
we're put to the test.
Pushed to the front line,
a domino effect.

If you fail you're replaced,
the earth still moves.
But to look into their eyes,
Your choice, you choose!

A self-destructive axis
does this world tilt.
More blood shed,
more blood spilled.

And so we keep building,
another nail in our hell.
We need not war,
we have done it ourselves!

Kristin Duffy

A Bundle Of Joy

A bun in the oven?
   What a strange thing to say,
I guess it did rise like a bun
   in a way.
Not much longer to wait,
   Not much longer to go,
Will she be a ballerina? Or he
   a football pro?
You've been waiting so long for
   this bundle of joy,
And you still don't know whether it's
   a girl or a boy.
But no matter what the outcome
   you'll love it the same
Just be sure you give him or her
   the right name,
Or for the rest of their lives, guess who
   they'll blame?

Peggy Schramm

Have You Ever Looked In A Rainbow

Have you ever looked in a rainbow?
What did you find?
What did you see?
Please, please tell me.

When I looked I saw colors swept
   on the sky by God.
His own special mark left on the sky,

Have you ever noticed how each
   color can mark an emotion?
Blue for sadness,
Red for madness, and
Yellow for happiness.

God put the rainbow in the sky
   for special reasons for us not
   to fear because he is so near

Rechelle Musser Ochsner

Limericks

There once was a cute little girl
Who had only one tiny curl,
It was just so long,
It couldn't be wrong,
To circle her face with a twirl.

Miriam E. Y. Fanuiel

Look

Look around,
what do you see?
Do you see my pain?
Do you see my anger?
Close your eyes.
Does it go away?

Look around,
what do you hear?
Do you hear the laughter?
After awhile,
will it go away?

Look around,
what do you find?
Do you see the hate?
Do you see the colors?
Please, make it go away!

Rachael Ward

"Two Of A Kind"

Funny clown, how strange you are
what silly clothes you wear,
   Your painted face, a big red nose
and straight strawberry hair.
   The derby hat and flappy shoes
your belly big and round,
   You blow a horn and dance
until you fall upon the ground.
   To make the crowd laugh and
scream, seems to be your delight,
   Who do you think you're fooling
clown, I see the tears you fight.
   So act the fool, please the
crowd, be as funny as you may,
   If you should pass close by me,
forgive me if I say,
   Funny clown, make me laugh,
really play your part,
   For just like you, I too must
laugh, to hide my broken heart.

Mariane Preston

Rebecca

She sits without knowing,
What will happen next.

Her ability to communicate,
Consists of cry, laugh, stare.

She needs help to eat,
And to travel.

She is but one,
Of many others.

I love her,
And I'm sure she loves me.

She sits without knowing,
What will happen next.

Susan Brigid Clark

Why?

Why do I feel lonely?
Why do I feel jealous?
Why do I let him hurt me in many ways?
Why don't I say no?
Why can't he understand?
Why does he leave when we have plans?
Why is it all my fault?

J. Bennett

Catching Up

Pansies or roses,
What's my choice?

Neither.

My preference would be
to hear your voice.

Soft and gentle
As a baby's skin.

I really would like to talk to you
every now and then.

To tell you things
I could never say.

Let's get together
and spend the day.

Catching Up.
Karen Hardin

Reflections Of A Day

Sunrise! A lovely time,
    When all is fresh and new.
A time to count your blessings,
    And lots of things to do.

At noontime, it's a time to stop;
    Reflect on morning deeds,
Refresh the mind and rest a bit;
    A time a body needs.

At evening time, the sun goes down,
    Another day is done.
The love of God surrounds us all
    From dawn to setting sun.

As we prepare for a night of rest
    We thank the Lord above,
For sunrise, noontime, sunset,
    But most of all, for His enduring love.
Lucy Layton

Only The Brave Wear Blue

Only the brave wear blue
When I see a police officer
I know it is true
Only the brave wear blue

Men and women standing tall
Ready and willing to do their all
Courageous and loving and giving
Caring and sharing and living

Then a stranger fires a shot
A life goes cold that once was hot
The families cry, the friends weep
The rest of us have a promise to keep

This will never happen again
We will see to that, Friend
Thank you for giving so much
We will miss your caring touch
Karen Funderburk

Untitled

Sailor moon shines so bright
Wishing you were here tonight
As I sail across the seas
Lying here next to me.
Stephen Pearce

If Only

Does she know the pain I feel
When I see beautiful eyes
Will she ever know
The romance I hold
Deep in my soul
Shining gem, imperishable gold
If only to show
For one hour
The passions truly I hold
My lover if only had known
Of the path I chose
The love I cannot hold
Would be on different road
What can our destiny hold?
Todd Neal

The Way We Feel *or*

If you should ever forget about us,

Oh Yerushalayim....

When I think of thee, Yerushalayim,
my heart is pumping in blood,
my soul is filled with immeasurable pain.

For still how much longer
Will injustice and hurt have to reign?

To see you just once more-
the way you were, to come ashore,

To be engulfed by your stony beauty
and your golden touch
mesmerizing mind and soul

That's my desire
that's why we all fought!
So let's trust again and start now.
Pat Hill-Castillo

My Friend

You wiped away my tears
When I was sad and down,
You gave me a reason to live
looking up instead of down,

You always followed
one close step behind.
You made me walk a little taller
under me you were confined.

How can I repay you
for what you've done to me.
You made me soar above you
and made me feel so free.
Sherrie Farwick

God's Rainbow

I'm sure I'll see a rainbow
When this storm is gone
My cloud will have a silver lining,
And I will carry on.

When life seems the darkest
And we feel we can't go on,
Suddenly God's rainbow comes
And those old dark clouds are gone!

Yes, God in all his wisdom
Knows just what we need
All he asks is that we have the faith
As in that tiny mustard seed.
Mindy Mayberry

Our Destiny

We know the day will surely come
When "paradise" is lost,
When Spring and Summer of our lives
Give way to wintry frost.

When earthly joys which now we share
Must reach the ordained end;
Still we are apprehensive of
The fate we can't portend.

A fate of which we think we know
Includes an open door,
And which beyond its portals are
Of this life nevermore.

A hundred years; ten thousand years
Before us without end,
Each human soul will follow paths
Which toward this door must bend.

And, though beyond we have no view,
We learn almost from birth,
Once through that door we'll find the place
Made for us while on earth.
M. W. Nickel

Wagon Master

Tell us about the days of yore
When riding wagons made you sore,
And savages whooped a mighty cry
With tomahawks raised to the sky.

How did you keep the Indians at bay
And continue on for many a day?
God must have kept you in his hand,
For there lay dangers in the land.

Yet, you led hordes of people West
With little water, and little rest.
You brought them to a better land
And caused America to expand.

You gave to them a better life;
Helped the pioneers face the strife.
You encouraged them and kept them sane,

Because you led the wagon train.
Smithie Denning

Tree Frogs

I know winter is over
when the tree frogs start to sing.

And sing they do, they do
all night through.

I could no believe my ears
the first time I heard them sing.

It was, and still is, a chorus,
like an unknown symphony.

So dear little frogs I thank you,
even though I've never seen you yet.

I was told you are there
embracing the trees.

And singing and singing
till nature mandates.

When nature says so?
is it when spring is over

That you must come down off
the juicy warm trees

Looking for some water hole
in order to exist?
Ruth C. Dobrucki

Whispers

Whispers,
   Where are they
coming from?
   heaven, hell
Whispers,
   Awakening me
in my sleep,
Calling out from
   nowhere on
a summer's night,
Be careful,
   Be careful of
the Whispers.

Lynn Johnson

Winter Snows

Oh, winter snows so cold and deep
Where ever am I going to sleep?
I'm out in this world all alone
There is no place to call my own;
I have no coat upon my back,
I've emptied the food in my sack.
My shoes are worn upon my feet.
As I travel down the long dark streets
The bitter winds blow around my face.
I can only go my steady pace.

I knock rapidly upon a door;
My back aches and my feet are sore;
Oh winter snow's so cold and bright
save me from my world at plight.
I know longer want to roam-
I just want a home that I can call my
own...

Nethelia Osgood

Wall

But i know
where i am, and i know
where i am
not.

Within your reach,
beside your heart, in your mood,
with you, is where i am
not.

Within a square,
shaven as a cage, naked beyond a rock,
without you, is where
i am.

I don't know where
the pain of knowing resides
in the deeper; knowing where
i am, or knowing where i am
not.

d. d. huffman

My Baby

To my dear sweet baby
whom I never got to know,
Time will pass,
but I'll never let you go.
Your life here on earth
was not meant to be,
Though in my heart
you will always be.

Love, Mommy

Lisa L. Wood

Señorita

Down in the caribbean
where it's always warm and sunny
there's a beautiful señorita
my latin-american honey

I've met her only in my dreams
where she always appears to me
as quite petite, 'bout five-foot-two
and weighs 'bout one-o-three

Each night I wait until it's dark
then sail across the sea
to find her smiling on the shore
and waving back to me

I step onto her island
and hold her to my heart
I gaze into her lovely eyes
and vow we'll never part

Then dreams turn into nightmare
I decide I'll just ignore 'eh
for in truth she's ugly as homemade sin
and a three-hundred-pound señora

Ralph L. Giddish

Paradise

Paradise for me would be,
where violence you would never see.
Your enemy would become your friend,
and friendships would never end.
Everyone would get along,
and weak ones would grow strong.
All the wars of the world would end,
different races together would blend.
There would be no need to cry,
for our loved ones would never die.
You would never have to lock your door,
and death would be no more.
Those who are deaf would be able to hear,
never again would you shed a tear.
There would be no more pollution,
and for every problem there would be a
   solution.
No one would have to suffer with pain,
and there would be no more acid rain.
This is what paradise for me would be,
where happiness you would always see.

Kelly Beck

Untitled

Beneath the brightly shining sun
which evil things supposedly shun
Lies a place which time has lost
where no mortal dares to cross
A flash of color between the trees
a scent of flowers upon the breeze
A curtain of ivy brushed aside
lets you take a peek inside
Behold a secret which no one knows
a place where no one ever goes
A bed of moss to rest your head
a blanket of leaves to make a bed
Have no fear of being harmed
there is no need to be alarmed
This special place belongs to you
for anything you choose to do

Stacey Volanto

The Inside Me

I have a lot of little hearts
Which grow inside of me.
They make up the feelings
That you can plainly see.

I have a river of good feelings
That flows right through me
The river makes up the friendliness
Which grows inside of me.

Inside there is a grassy field
That gives me all my shyness
And there is a big rain cloud
That burns with all my kindness.

There are also sunlit days
That warm my happy smile
And moonbeams lighting starry nights
That delight my dreams awhile.

Stephanie Pearl

Darkness

Darkness has the shade of black,
Which is the color of my heart.
It pulses and grows within my head,
And, now, the torture and torment starts.

The voices I hear are calling me,
But only I can hear what they say.
It appears I'm falling into dementia,
And when I land it's where I'll stay.

The voices I hear are controlling me,
They tell me what I must do.
They guide me with their mental grips,
Until my tasks are threw.

I have no choice but to obey,
Because I have sold my soul.
And ever since the voices came to me,
My heart became black as coal.

But now the voices are calling me,
And I must be on my way.
I have to pass over to the "Dark side,"
But now I have to stay.

Kurt Myers

Blinders

Some people exist with blinders on
while running the race of life.
I prefer to take mine off,
more clearly see the strife.

Some finely focus all their thoughts,
pursuing a life-long plan.
Restraining blinders impede insight
about their fellow man.

Life is ever a journey,
not just an ending goal;
such blinders, worse than shackles,
preclude becoming whole.

Roger Chambers

Untitled

Time is long for someone
  with nothing to do,
But short for someone
  who cares.

A. D. Novak

Counted Sorrows

Off the cliff I did fall,
While screaming in a wild Banshee call;
Bouncing off the rocks below,
I wished death wouldn't dally so.

The icy ocean I did feel,
Charmed me with its cold appeal;
But for the currents washed ashore,
I would have done what they abhor.

Kathleen Taylor

Along The Road To The Cemetery

The stripes of green dancing above me
While the cars pass
By me

Alone in this cold world
The wind whispering in my ear
To take off my coat

Headlights defiantly beckon to me
From above

The clickety-clack of my rusty heart
Err...another car passing
Me

My finger frozen around this pen
Writing this, what might be,
My last thought

Michael Learned

Let's Reach For The Stars

Let's enjoy each other,
While we're here together.
Let's smile and have fun,
Our memories will last forever.
We must always remember,
This last year - our senior year.
Together we will make it the best,
Before our last day draws too near.
We won't say good-by forever,
Real friends always stay true.
Instead, let's reach for the stars,
And give our best in all that we do.

Missy Ponko

A Certain Man

I was that certain man
Who asked the Master
"What must I do
To gain eternal life?"

He said, "Sell all you have,
Give to the poor,
And gain treasure in heaven,
And come. Follow me."

But I valued rich possessions
More than treasure in heaven.
Now I have doubts and questions,
Wondering what might have been.

If I had followed him.
What joys and sorrows were in store,
If I had loved him more?
What destiny awaited me?

Now over and over again
I feel that sadness when
I left him on the shore
By the sea of Galilee.

Laurence W. Cor

The Death Of A Poet

No one hears a poet,
Who cries alone in the rain.
No one can comprehend,
Or understand his pain.

He sees the world with blinders off,
And feels what no one can.
The cynicism that now,
Exists in every man.

His is a world gone by,
With dreams that are dead.
The only place he hears the word love,
Is over again in his head.

Nothing has remained sacred,
Nobody believes anymore.
Not even that dear, sweet poet,
As he lies dead on the floor.

A bullet didn't kill the man,
Nor did a blow to the head.
The reason he stopped living,
Is because love in the world was dead.

Rob Hansen

Lust

The one I love and always need,
Who for him I'd forever bleed,

He belongs to someone close to me,
My feelings must stay with me.

I wonder if he feels this way,
Maybe I will know someday.

But until this day it cannot show,
For I don't want anyone to know,
Because sooner die than ever part.

Sarah Otwell

The Challenge

Blessed is the one indeed,
Who in this life can find,
A purpose to fulfill his day
And a goal within his mind.

The world is filled with people,
Content with where they are,
Not knowing the joys success can bring,
No will... To go that far.

Yet in this world there is a need,
For some to lead the rest.
To rise above the average life,
By giving of their best.

This is your day, the world to win.
Great purpose to achieve.
Accept the challenge of your goals
And in yourself... believe.

You will be proud of what you've done,
When at the closing of the day,
You look upon the battles won,
Content you came this way.

Raymond T. Boring

It Must 'Ave Been Huntin'

Lord, forgive the man
Who invented the gun.
He was a human,
Like anyone.
He, probably, didn't know
The consequences long ago
Of what he thought
Was a clever invention.
War and crime,
Surely not its intention.
Though I do wonder,
What he was thinking of?
Must 'ave been huntin'.
Couldn't been love.

Teri J. Cooper

On Friendship

What do you call a person
Who really listens when you speak
Who makes you feel strong, not weak
Who takes the time to share her thoughts
Who thinks of others quite a lot

When time is short and years fly by
You'll miss the chance to catch her eye
And say how much she meant to you
The many ways she helped you through
   the hardest days

Her name is sweet, her eyes are bright
She makes the burden extra light
The name I search so hard to find
It is so simple in the end
The name I seek is yours, dear friend

Mary Ellen Ferguson

Memories

Once there was a man,
who wanted to end life and die.
He was so depressed and aggravated,
as the days went by.

He began thinking of the memories he had,
with his eleven year old son.
They had gone fishing by the lake shore,
and had all sorts of fun.

They had always gone to the circus,
to see the funny clowns.
And huddle close together,
not to be disturbed by scary sounds.

Those memories would all be gone,
along with his hopes and dreams.
He thought about life for hours,
or so it seems.

He thought one more thought,
and came up with his plan.
He sighted and climbed off bridge,
happy to live again.

Kari Ann Lyon

The Thorn

What can a thorn offer a rose,
with such beauty and grace.
Without the thorn,
the rose is incomplete.
And without the rose,
the thorn has no purpose.

Michael Burrington

Lady Liberty

A toast to you, my lady
Who welcomes strangers to our land
Let us strike up the band
Sing praises, hand grasping hand

Let us rejoice in harmony
Erase the screams of destiny
The poor, the desperate, the hungry
Let them join in peaceful

You are, to the ships in the night
A ray of hope, a shining light
To the foreigner, a home afar
A dream to reach, a shining star

You are comfort to our land
A blanket of security to many here
Your torch erases the fear
That so many, many had to bear

A toast to you, my lady
May you always welcome those afar
Black, white none to bar
Leave your door forever ajar

Marie Lutze

Untitled

Once I had a friend,
  whose love would never end.

Her laughter filled the air,
  with a feeling we all could share.

She had many a name,
  not one was the same.

It was Jennifer today,
  her and I would laugh and play.

Next Maranda who was no match,
  friendship is given not to catch.

Once her name was Emily,
  then she moved away from me.

Our tears were of fear and sadness
  for someone that was full of gladness.

Though we're now far apart
  we're always together in our heart.

Kelly Latham

Rain

Alone wondering why
why has everything gone so bad
first I lose my boyfriend
then I lose my dad.
I've tried to get stoned
even tried crystal to ease my pain
  but I learn no drug
  can stop the rain
  pours on my heart
  starting to hail
  destruction on mind
  ready to bail.
No one can help me anymore
  broken heart
  brain as thick as stone
  nothing will change
  everything the same
  everything horribly corrupted
  with only the purple people eater to blame

Sandra Mae Kelly

See

Blinding shadows of night
Why has God turned off the light?
the hunt, the hunted
no one escapes the pain
all the killing, all in vain
eternal wretched rotting soul
quiet whispers that no one knows
enslaved by my blackened mind
eyes of rage, heart gone cold
spinning round and round
I've gone insane in this life
my blood offsets my sins
flaming death brings to a close
everything I've ever known

Kris Alstatt

I Don't Know Who You Are

Why do you walk so straight
Why is it that you never sway
Where is your forgiveness
Never to be released.
How is it you have so many sides,
Why do I not know you, from one
moment to the next.
Is it just me, am I that forgiving
When did you lock your heart,
And throw away the key.

Kathy Malyk

Saying Goodbye

What will I do when it's time,
Will I run and hide?
It feels like I've been taken for a ride.
It's so hard saying goodbye.

I'm trying so hard.
I wish you could be here,
To stop the first tear.
Oh my God, it's so hard saying goodbye.

Remember the times we had.
Please don't go away from me.
I thought here was where you'd always be.
It's so hard saying goodbye.

I will always love you.
Please help me through it,
Stop the waves that hit.
Oh my God, it's so hard saying goodbye.

Sharon Koch

"After All"

After all is said and over...
will we someday
be able to look at each other
with the same...
gentleness and caring...
soft words and laughter..

And remember that once...
that was all, that was needed,
to keep us together,
as Lovers...
And after all
that has happened...
will the separate roads
we each take now..
lead us back to one road
that we can travel together...
your hand in mine...
as friends.

Linda Mae Steller

One More Day

Spare me from prophets
Willie Loman mendicants
From divine incantations
To fill greedy pockets.

From heaven and hell
Liberate me please
Give me measured solace
As I bid you farewell.

'Tis time all we need
Afar the lonely crowd
To the tranquil waters
To the verdant mead.

Lend me a few days
To reach the distant mountain
The other side to see
The sunset's dying rays.

Free me from endless pain
Give me sudden death
My ashes cast to the sea
Forever there to remain.

Kenneth J. Munden

My Little Grandchild

My little grandchild,
with a cute button nose.
Five fingers on each hand
and ten little toes.

Little boy or girl
Why all the fuss?
Long as you're healthy,
makes no difference to us.

You'll keep your mommy busy,
of that we have no fear.
For you're already active
and you're not even here.

Always remember,
You're grandma's pride and joy.
No matter, whatever,
be you a little girl or boy.

Margaret Poston

A Mother Yet To Be

Alone she cries in a darkened room,
with a longing in her soul
Her fingers tremble over an empty womb,
needing a child to make her whole.

For God to grant her to conceive,
her faith, it must be strong.
Against the odds she must believe,
No matter what goes wrong.

The baby quilts and bonnets sewn,
are always for another.
Her fingers toil, her pain not shown,
to the new expectant mother.

The years pass by so quickly,
her chances slipping by.
To the world she suffers quietly,
till alone at night she cries.

The tears she thought were cried in vain,
were seen from up above.
When no more could she bear the pain,
She was sent a child to love.

Robin Tracy

Spring

Comes the day all sweetly dressed,
With daffodils upon her breast,
The birds with song do fill the air
While she tucks blossoms in her hair;
Yellow, white, pink, purple, green -
Pastels to paint an Easter scene.
Creatures greet her everywhere;
Winter's gone, spring is here.

Lynn K. Henley

Terry

My little girl grown
with dancing eyes
always eager … ever wise.

Heralding your trumpet
Cresting summits on the rise
Mastering tasks twice your size.

Loving arms reach out
Comfort is always there
Not always knowing what it's about,
but always ready to care.

Don't ever change
my lovely girl;
always stay the way you are.

And, when I feel
Remorse coming on
I'll know where to come,
and what for.

Love,
Mom

Maxine Thorne Bailey

The Girl On The Mountain

She spoke of St. Helen
With dignity and pride
And told us in detail
About the great mud slide

The gray devastation
Viewed through very young tears
Showed respect for this land
Far beyond her young years

She described to us all
How its side had blown out
As the great volcano
Changed this land all about

She had love in her eyes
That could not be a ploy
This girl on the mountain
Who was named Betsy Troy

Martie Marie

Mother Heart

Oh, mother heart, that beat so strong
With love for me, now beats no more.
Oh, mother heart, so tired and worn
Has gone to a more peaceful shore.
Yet though it left me here to grieve
And alone this earth to roam,
I know it watches over me
Till I come safely home.
I shall not forget you, mother heart,
The love it held will never fade
And when my earthly toil is past,
It waits for me at heaven's gate.

Susanne Mueller

The Day You Came To Be

I look to this day,
With fondness in my heart.
For this special day
Has brought forth
One very special person.

You.
Who have endeared yourself to me.
Ever patient,
Ever attempting to understand.
You.
Who have brought forth
Countless smiles upon my lips,
Laughter and rainbows in my life.

You.
Constant source of warm companionship.
You.
My pure joy.
You.
Love of my life.

Phoebe Boholst

Unspoken Heart

This dark rich night
with its pulsing needs
rocks me and makes me
dance with moonlight
kisses on my soul.

Your name on my lips,
soft and sweet.
I tremble to think
you might leave me
come morning.

You whisper questions
as I cover my truths
in the warm dark winds.
And the stars blink bright
all my shattering fears.

Then your smile it teases
and your eyes,
they close
as the night folds over
my unspoken heart.

Sara R. Pierce

Parkinson's Disease

That man, who seems so old and frail,
with leaden limbs and guileless gaze,
that man is my father.
My father, who carried and cajoled me,
cherished me, consoled me,
comforted and cheered me.
This man now drifts into another world
I do not care nor wish to enter,
the private journey of his soul.
I see this man, my father,
who sits so listless in his chair,
through burning eyes of unshed tears.
But in the darkness of the night,
alone, at home, I cry.
for every day,
in every way,
I watch my
father
die.

Linda Susan Fisher

Life Is Like A Roller Coaster

Life is like a roller coaster,
With many ups and downs,
You don't know where you're headed,
You don't know where you're bound.
Life's a fast ride,
with lots of twists, curves, and turns,
Some people have a good time,
Others' stomachs churn.
Sometimes you're way up in the sky,
And then come crashing down,
Sometimes you're feeling happy,
And then end up wearing a frown.
Life is fun for some people,
While others end up in a pickle,
Just remember to follow the rules:
Keep your hands and arms in the vehicle.

Mike Rodgers, Jr.

Lost And Alone

Lost and alone
With nowhere
To go
And no one
To care.
Lost in a love
Affair
That will never
Be.
Lost in a feeling
Only held in
A dream
Lost and out
Of reach,
Living alone and
Lost.

Kathie Anderson

"The Wave"

Like lightning it struck
with power and lunges
like the sounds of a roar
as it met its own vengeance,
It came in with blue
and all white in the same,
so quick it was gone
as fast as it came,
It kneeled right before me
and fell at my feet.
It sailed out to sea
and again came a fleet,
One after another
It showered within
One after another
It made its own trend,
The sand became smooth
and all darkened the same
It did nothing but soothe
and shined as it tamed.

Pete Ramirez

Silence

There are people talking,
Yet there is silence.
The silence is not wanted,
That is why it is present.
Once the silence is gone forever,
The people to which brought it on,
Will realize that it was once there.

Michelle Spodeck

Sandals

Walking down a country road,
With sandals on! With sandals on!
Leaving prints in the dust,
With sandals on! With sandals on!
The rain comes and washes them away,
With sandals on! With sandals on!
And waits for another day,
With sandals on! With sandals on!
Wanda G. Maynard

Sun And Moon

Sun and moon
with stars in between them,
stay in the sky,
so I have seen them,

Day to night,
night to day,
they light up the world,
in many different ways!
Kathleen Grant

Epoch

polarized windshields glimmer
with the fading of tomorrow
alive upon their graves
they find tranquil scenes
of heroism and devotion
a bulimic aura no longer
shrouds the pit of a short
demise once known to the
trite and stealthy as today
for yesterday clutched
close to the depths of its
memory emancipating none
but the guilty and the
breath known as time has
come to discern the essence
from the truth with a
glimmer upon a grave
tomorrow, once today, but
yesterday, all becomes one
truth in time
Lisa Terry

Love

More fragile than a flower,
With the strength of Hercules.
Unequalled in its power,
And shattered too easily!

More inspiring than the Muses,
Yet ruthless as the Beast.
Igniting hatred's fuses,
Fulfilling as the Feast!

Tempestuous gusting Winds,
As narcotic as the ocean.
The beginning of the end,
Love's bittersweet potion!

Celestial in its bliss,
Oblivious with its blame.
Passionate lusting kiss,
Condemning infernal flame!

Fleetly fading heart's rose,
Exalting in its glory.
Crushing beneath its blows,
Life's hypocritical story!
Kim Wenger

The Flowers

The flowers
with their bright colors,
over by the white fence,
with drops of early morning dew on them
Marie E. Kidwell

"Flying High"

I wish I was a little bird
With wings so I could fly,
Around the treetops like an eagle
Soaring in the sky.

Across the ocean, among the hills,
This bird will ever roam.
Gliding towards the sunset
To the place he call his home.

Many times I pity that little bird
As I watch him in the sky.
For man has destroyed its beautiful home;
It's a shame that he will die.
Lianna R. Stewart

Rather You See Me Dead

You hit me by your desire
With your eyes lit with fire

You scream at me as you wish
That I'm too afraid to eat off my dish

You drawn me in depression
Oh how I need love and affection

You rather see me in a morgue
Then get yourself a family dog

Though I'll say this with out a lie
I rather go with out saying goodbye.
Tiffany de Barros

As I

As I hear the rain
Without you by my side,
I would go insane
Without you as my guide.
As I glace into the skies
I can hear the thunder,
As I stare into your eyes
Your smile make me wonder.
As the sun starts to glow
I can smell the dew,
I hope our love will grow
With my body close to you.
Nichole Sealer

Life

The beautiful white clouds flow by,
Yet, lightning strikes violently,
Love holds through a sleepless night,
Yet, in the morning love is gone,
A mother would never harm her child,
Yet the father hurts them both,
I feel so much love for someone,
Yet, I feel despise for another,
People look at you on the inside,
Yet, they dwell on the outside,
Life can give so much happiness,
Yet, life can be so grim.
Shelly Zellers

"Winter's Snow"

Winter comes with pure white snow
Wonders of beauty over flow
Like a rug of elegance
All things covered in white
Trees, sky, and ground alike
Show a totally different sight
With its beauty and sweet fragrance.

Winter lasts so very long
With piles of snow all around
Little voices sing a song
While making angels on the ground
In the cold wintery snow
Of many shapes and sizes do show.

As winter passes on to spring
Snow and ice melts away
To more beautiful things

Tree's and flowers all in bloom
Shine through sunlight and rain
While birds in harmony sing
again and again.
Patricia D. Romeo

Sibling Gold

Once again she is here and
    word fights and broken
    toys fill the room.
My toys done in by her.
    Why Why Why
What did I do to merit
    her wrath?

Not at all times were filled
    with her wrath -summer
Nights when we lay a bed
    we shook the house
    with song
Till that voice boomed
    go to sleep!

Now that months and years
    Have gone- I ponder this
    Love that never ends
And wish, oh how I wish
    We were once again
Gloating in her wrath!
Verna Obrien Clark

Untitled

Isn't the smile you give a stranger
worthwhile giving a friend?
It won't get you in any danger,
and will help you out in the end.
Ruth Merlie

Do You Love Me?

Your kiss is so forceful,
yet gentle to my lips.
    Your hands are strong,
but they are tender when
    you touch me.
Do you love me?

    My tears are for you,
they drop from my eyes like emeralds.
    There are many unanswered
questions.
    Do you love me?
Maria Brezovsky

"Mending Your Heart"

If I held you for a moment
Would I hold you for a while
Why must I sit with you in silence
If there are words behind you smile

If you trusted that I love you
Would you give to me this day
If I turned to you in sorrow
Would you turn and walk away

We are not strangers to love
Although we're challenged in its truth
We have been victims of love
The scars remain within our youth

It is when and only then
That you start not to defend
Then is when you see a friend
With one whose love there is no end.

Ronald Conti

Judy Kay - Chosen Daughter

Radiant love
   wrapped in organdy ruffles
Vision of beauty
   in apricot color
"Till she leans over
   - Ah! then is seen
Under the ruffles
   her brother's blue jeans

Mary TenEyck

The Feelings Within

Some people can be perfect,
yet others can not be.
The things that most people
   usually say,
Is why can't that be me.

Beauty is only skin deep,
yet most of us don't know
We cry and sigh and dream
   and weep,
Until it starts to show.

You need to open up your eyes,
and see what people see.
You are an individual,
as unique as you can be.

Lorena Rodriguez

Loving You

I go crazy thinking about
   you.
When I see you it is like
   my dreams are coming true.
I wonder if you feel the
   same way about me
I just wonder if there could
   be something between
You and me.

Teresa Wooley

Life

Me
You
We
Two
Man
Wife
Whole
Life
While
Child
House
Wild
Love
God
Death
Sod.

Reba F. Cook

Friend

Friend...
   You are always there...
Comfort and compassion...
   Willing to give...
A shoulder to lean on...
   You are my Friend.

Strength you have given me...
   Time and Time again...
to face the trials in my life...
   You are my Friend.

A willingness to listen...
   To help me when I'm fallen...
Non judgmental you've been...
   You are my Friend.

Time will flow...
   and years will pass...
Separate paths we may go...
   But my love for you will last...
You are my Friend.

Larry Holmack

Missed Carriage

Oh child who never cried.
You are the fragmented dream
Slipping in and out of my thoughts,
Wholly vague,
Yet real.
You washed away like a wave
Cramped in a vast ocean.
Am I supposed to have
Not known you?
Not have held or rocked you?
I feel angry at my swelling breasts.
It is so cold inside.
Snuggling to my uncried fear
I'll leave it for others to say
That you were never here.

Katherine Riehl

Dreams Of Tomorrow

If you could put all
Your dreams together, O
What a storm you could weather.
Dreams of tomorrow in
A world complete,
There's no way life could end in defeat.

Laurice Henderson

Black Shadow

I can't see it coming,
You can't see it coming,
You can't hear it,
You can't smell it,
You can't taste it,
You can't even feel it,
Some people will except it
When it comes,
Others will run from it,
It really doesn't matter because
it will still come,
Some will even deny its existence,
But it will still come,
It is coming,
It is coming,
It's the black's shadow,
Death is coming!

Katrina Rawlings

As A Matter Of Energy

Do till you perish
You decisions are few
Make them with love
Don't relinquish your due.

Disloyal some friends
White washed graves are their acts
You truly are someone
Be free from your past.

Your life's been with pain
This pains in us all
Our jobs to learn how to
Stop taking the fall.

Where's this great truth
Undiscovered by man
We're truly to intricate
There must be a plan

With these things in mind
Leading where is our race
Our infinite souls
Are energy in space

Roxana Byrd

Untitled

You asked me why I love you
You didn't have a clue
You asked me what I see in you
The reasons are not few

We see two different people
When we look into the glass
What you see is superficial
What I see goes further past

You have that certain something
That rich men can not buy
No one can fake a heart of Gold
No matter how they try

The feeling of your hand in mine
Just fills my heart with pride
If I could have but just one wish
It's to be always at your side

The fact that you return my love
Still fills my heart with wonder
What God has joined together
Let no man put asunder

Linda Marshall

Goodbye Loyal Friend

When you were young and in your prime
You gave us such a trying time
A fence could never keep you in
We were afraid we would lose you friend
When it was time to play
It was not a ball that made your day
For the garden I never had a shoe
For they all went to you
At Easter time, the eggs to dye
The little child would cry
"No mommy not Duke - it's Duka Poo"
The happy time you were to share
In sadness there to care
Your protection made us feel safe
From any harm to come our way
You gave your all from day to day
If I could go back and do it all over again
I would still choose you my friend
If it is time to say goodbye I know many
tears I'll cry
We only hope in some small way you know
how we feel today
Myma Verykoukis

Untitled

Love is a feeling,
You get from the heart.
It's a feeling of passion,
that you get when you full in love.
When passion touches your heart
in a way that makes you feel loved.
Love turns your whole life around,
It makes you sure of yourself.
Your heart beats a thousand times fast.
When you meet that special guy,
you feel happy and full of love.
Then someday he'll leave
and you're all alone and depressed
Love is like a cycle,
you meet a guy,
he dumps you and you feel alone, again,
But the best part is you meet another guy.

Krissy Marshall

Puppy Love

I come to you
You give me love, unconditional
No questions asked
No matter the day or the hour
You radiate his love
Born to give
I come to you and cover
You in my prayer blanket
And hold you in my arms of love

F. Schaeffer

The Pegasus

Oh Pegasus so beautiful,
You glimmer in the sky,
With magic all around you,
You fly on by and by.

With just one flap of your wings,
You're lifted off the ground,
And the people in their peaceful homes,
Will see you all around.

And as you glisten here and there,
Beneath the moonlit sky,
People on the ground will say,
How gracefully you fly.

Keaton Avant

Trust?

I reached out my hand.
   You held it.

I showed you my heart.
   You took it.

I gave you my love.
   You wished it.

I opened my world.
   You destroyed it.
   Michael S. Madden

Infinity

When the burning starts
You know you're about to lose your heart
To the sun and sea and land.

It seems your feelings expand
Vast and furious
Across the openness
Until you lose sight of their end.
Melisa Frock

Happiness

It's just a door
You open wide
When you invite
The world inside.

It's touching God
His touching you
It's all the things
You want to do.

It's what you do
It's what you say
It's the part of you
You give away.

It's a peace inside
A will to be free
It's God and his angels
Walking with thee
Lee Lauderdale

Untitled

I cry as I watch you go.
You say it's for the best but I don't know
When we met that bright August day
You said you've loved me from far away
Now do you see why—
I cry?

You went away so fast
I thought our love would last
you said it would
maybe it could
If you would just give it another chance
Now do you see why—
I cry?

Lisa Boyd

Survivor

You terrorize, you victimize,
You scare away the human spirit.
You thought you'd won when I ran,
You thought that I was the victim.

Waiting for my suicide,
You'll wait until you die.
I will live forever, eternally,
And you will live in agony.

To give up is to let you win,
If you win, I am the victim.
You won't win, I will, forever,
I am not a victim, I am a survivor.

I will survive, I will live so free,
I will never, ever, give in to you.
I will never do what you did to me,
I will be the one to break the cycle.

I will tell my story and survive,
I am not the victim, you are.
You will live in fear of what I know,
I have won, I am the winner!!
Shannon E. Daviess

Love

Do you love me, or do you not.
You told me once but I forgot.
It's been so long since you told me last,
My poor broken heart is in a cast.
I tell you I love you everyday,
Can you, will you ever say.
You personality is like two
Will you ever say I love you?
Kristin Vaughn

My Dedication

When he was gone
You tried to take his place
And now if you leave
Who's going to fill your space

You know I'm here
If you need to talk
Share your problems
We'll take a walk

Please don't leave me
You're my only hope
I have trust in you
Don't let go of the rope.

You're supposed to be my friend
Don't leave me now
You're the only one for me
And I don't know how

If you have a problem
Just come to me
We'll talk it out
Lets wait and see
Kim Santoiemma

"Why"

You're given a life
You try to make the most of it
You get friends
An education
A job
Maybe a career
Get married
Possibly have kids
Then things just seem to go down
You've forgotten the friends you once had
Your kids move out
You get a divorce
All your family is dead
You lose your job
Then you're alone with memories
Once you had happiness
Then came pain
Now you six feet under
   Why?

   Orly Kirshenbaum

"It's Been So Long"

   It seems just like yesterday,
you were carrying me in your arms.
   For it was then I was your baby girl
just snuggled in my daddies arms.
   It came time to stop holding me,
and letting me walk on my own.
   You were always there when I fell,
and helped me back on my feet.
   Now I am walking on my own,
and not falling down.
   Though at times, I'll be thinking of
those days when you were holding me...
   wishing I was still your baby girl.

   Tammie Lane

"If"

If I could not speak,
You would understand every word;

If I could not think,
My thoughts will be heard;

If I could not laugh,
My laughter will fill your ears;

If I could not cry,
You'll catch every shedded tear;

If I could not walk,
You would carry me through;

If I could not see,
You would lead the way too;

A friend is what you are,
And a friend is what I'll be;

Always and forever,
You'll be a special part of me.

   Khalilah Riddick

You Will Find Me.

In the darkest of nights so far away
You'll never hear of my pray that lay.
They lay in the mist of mornings
And the deepest of ditches.
When you can not sleep
Like a restless herd of sheep
You will find me.
My life is full of shame
Of course they made me to blame.
When my neck gets stiff
That's when I go for a drink.
My family in nothing to me
That's real typical for me to be.
My words are true and wise
So don't go out to dine.
For all you know I could be watching you
With my beady eyes of midnight blue
You will find me!

   Melinda Reitenauer

'Country Poet'

You'ns better listen!
You'ns better hear!
I ain't askeered of nothing
Or skittish of this here.

I aim to write you something
A-fixen to right now,
I'm all het up about it.
So hesh up! I know how.
Naw, I don't no vittles,
I already et,
A fur piece from the holler
And ain't a finished yet.

Some folks think I'm biggety
All book read through and through.
But I plumb got it kivvered,
This doin's, it's for you.

I ain't a lollygagin
I done cum this far.
You'ns better listen!
I aim to be a star.

   Kyle W. Bird

Life

Day by day, and year by year
Your body ages, slowly but surely.
It is only natural.

The vigorous youth
You've enjoyed not too long ago,
Will never be regained.
It is only natural.

Time goes on incessantly,
And your body continues to age;
Until one day you do not age any more.
It is only natural.

   U Khin

Good Samaritan

Small dog struck down on the highway,
your body all racked with pain.
The car that hit you was slowing,
Just as you were injured again.

You were whining and crying for mercy,
as we rushed from our front door,
Someone carried you to the roadside,
Where you could be hurt no more.

Then off to the vet's we hurried.
And all we could do was pray.
In spite of our most valiant efforts,
You arrived at the door, D.O.A.

Little friend, we will never forget you;
But, you know, as we laid you to rest,
We had the most satisfied feeling,
That the Lord, in his wisdom, knew best.

   Theresa H. Hair

Eternal Waters

I know not why I write of thee,
Your chasms wide and deep;
Emerald studded waters,
Rushing round to meet,

Rivers, streams, and rivulets,
Raindrops from the sky;
Sunrays far above,
Spreading ere' so wide,

The glory of it all,
Magnificent to behold,
Giving Man —
A living land,
Eternal—in its flow.

   Lucy N. Stroman

The Scarlet Seashell

Who molded your bodice,
your curved and knobby roundness,
so delicate,
and yet so hard and rough.

Nature has molded me,
Miniature, scarlet,
and has washed me to shore.
With my cupped and pointed body,
I am lying snarled in the sand.

By morning, I am found.
Children carefully cupping -
My small, delicate, curved body.
Aware of the ocean sounds,
In my wondrous, hollow shell.

   Sue Legleiter

Untitled

Everywhere I go,
you're always on my mind.
I can't believe it's over,
How could I be so blind?

Every dream I have
you're there for me to hold.
Why can't my dreams come true?
I feel so lost and cold.

Everything I did
since the day we parted,
I wish I could take back,
cause I'm brokenhearted.

   Kelly Hill

Jessica

From your first gasps for air
Your first tiny cries,
From the first time I held you
And you looked me in the eyes.
  I have loved you.

Having a little grand-daughter
Has filled my heart with pride,
You remind me of your mommy
And the day she entered our lives.
  And I loved you.

Each little thing you've learned to do
Has given me so much pleasure.
Every smile, every hug
Every memory of you I'll treasure
  And I'll always love you.

  Mary M. Gaabo

Dust Fairy

Oh dust fairy, dust fairy,
Your nimble fingers wickedly merry.

Under my bed, behind the boxes,
Even in my dirty soxes.

Common is your cloudy trail;
Quietly creeping, you do not fail.

Spinning wonders at a frantic pace
Your prey destined to lose the race.

You skim ends of heaven and earth,
Always expanding the tiniest girth.

To untangle your puzzled web of scorn,
Henceforth a feeling of forlorn.

  Patrice M. Dennis

Alone...

I feel so empty now that
  you're gone
How could you just leave me all alone
I wish I could go back in time
When I was yours and you were mine
I guess you have changed
  since then
You don't even want me for a friend
It hurts real bad, you know
  that's true
Tell me what I ever did to you!
If only you realized the great
  love we share
Then one day you might return to care
I guess I will never be the same
You left me in a lot of hurt and pain
I will survive one way or another
But until I have another
I'll make do, as I look back
At your picture and say... I love you.

  Traci Woods

O Little Church Beside The Road

O little church beside the road,
  You've been there many years;
You've lifted many a heart-felt load,
  And dried a million tears.

You speak with past tense utterings,
  From Sinai's lofty heights;
And we see our sinful clutterings,
  And feel their fright'ning plights.

But the present tense is sounding, too,
  The bell rings loud and clear—
The pulpit flames with grace and truth
  For those who come, and hear.

The future tense belong to thee,
  For prophets are thine own;
And many find Eternity
  Through God's Eternal Son.

O little church beside the road,
  So many pass thee by;
And miss the way, and bear the load,
  Which fetter them for Lands on High.

  R. T. Sanderson

Being Together

If you're gonna learn to ride
you've got to learn how to fall,
but you have to last eight seconds
to remember it all.
It's just a cowboy's dream
to hold on for life -
with each day wondering
if he will make it home tonight.
She loves him;
with all of her heart,
but as the sun goes down
they are lying apart.
Holding on for eight seconds,
can last forever...
but true love is
- just being together.

  Misti Lytle

Papa Keene:

You've made us laugh and
You've made us smile —
You've shared with us stories
of the good old times.
It's so very hard to say good bye.
But in our hearts you will
always be there —
Sitting on the back porch
In that old ragged chair,
Giving orders for groceries and change —
Saying feed the birds and
squirrels before it rains —
Saying give those children a
cookie or two and don't say
good-bye until you do.
Pa how these words will be missed
But all these memories are
Sealed with a kiss.

  TerriLynn Pimental

Zig Zag

Zig Zag,
  Zig Zag
    That's what I do all day.
Mom says!
  'Do the dishes,
    Feed your sister,
  Feed the dog.'
  Zig Zag,
  Zig Zag.
That's what I
  Do all day.
    Dad says!
  'Make the dinner,
Unload the dishwasher,
  Do your homework,
  Get a snack,
Go to bed.'
  Zig Zag,
  Zig Zag,
That's what I Do all day!!

  LeAnna Ricks

The Eternal Reward

Fields of glory and graves
  of heroes i see in
my dreams; But what is not
  told from the brave and the
bold, is all of the blood
  spilled for power and gold.

And we in the trenches
  and we on the march have
no such recollections
  of glorified tales. We
see no such splendor in
  stories made by poets.

For i have seen Saint Joseph
  appear before my eyes,
but never will i witness
  Victoria. And on
a night close to death i
  shall behold a pale horse
with Hades close behind.

  Scott Bline

Three Words Left To Say...

Call it whispers in the dark,
yearnings from the heart,
call it what you may, there
are three words left to say.

As we lay in bed, body to
body, heart to heart, trapped
by the embrace that tears
us apart.

I want to drown in the pleasure
of our joining, but I feel
there is something that
you're still with-holding.

As I try to hide from the pain
of the past still left inside,
I try to restrain from new
feelings that are brewing.

Come closer if you may, but
either way I'll have to say
I love you I love you, but
now will you stay???

  Kymberli Barnes

The Suicide

What is this life?
I don't know yet.
So many choices,
So much to regret.

What shall I do?
Will I succeed?
Who can I trust?
What do I need?

I'm sick of it all;
The worry and doubt.
The game is no fun,
And I want out.

What is this life?
I think I know.
It's a masquerade,
Where all is for show.

Now you know that,
There's no more to tell.
Have a good life...
I'll see you in hell.

Chad Bedford

"Imagination"

Mirages created to settle
the dust of boredom and escape
the sands of time. An Oasis of
fantasy in a desert of reality.

Emily K. Grimes

Grace

From your eyes that care
the gaze of grace
brings a smile
to the face
emotions sizzle the air
persuading
all to share
with hearts
that respond without fear;
feeling received
are rare
thoughts of tender
sensuous love
surrounds
hearts
like a glove
so gaze on
grace
gaze on from
above.

Ulric N. Harmon

A Love Lost

When I was young my heart was full of love and then I lost.
My whole world came tumbling down leaving me to pay the cost.
I turned to God and asked him why and couldn't find the answers.
My heart wa filled with much despair torn through as pierced with
    lancers.
After a score of years and many more, my hurt has not subside.
My mind keeps running through these things - My soul has been ill
    guided.
The scars I carry will remain with me forever more.
I'll never love that way again or care that much therefore.

Patricia Knoll

My Pain

No body understands my pain,
Whatever I lose, another will gain.
No body ever really cares,
All my pain, with no one to share.
I try to drop hints, I want to talk.
So I decide to take a walk.
I get to your house, but no one's home.
Once again, I'm all alone
All my pain, so deep inside
That's why I turn to suicide
I walked back home, and locked the door.
Took the pills, fell to the floor.
My head is spinning, I began to moan
I hear it ring, the telephone
you ask what's wrong? I fall to the floor.
As I fade away, I hear the dial tone.
No body understands my pain.

Daniel Damron

Going Home

I slam a door behind me
   Nana's tea cups now in shards

But her Wedgewood plates and crystal vases
   safety packed in newspaper
   in an empty closet; boxed; waiting
   for another home
   someday

This home's for sale, with strangers in and out
   I don't know where I'm going
   I'm afraid

A brilliant butterfly comes near; it's Nana
   she watches over me
   sad, sweet memories

Going home ... where is that
   decisions to be made

When Nana's treasures are all in place
   I'll be home
   somewhere

Judith Latham-Soderberg

Celebrating

Lord, I feel like celebrating again.
I can't celebrate pain or loss but,
I can celebrate your faithfulness.
In the mist of misery and tears.
You come to comfort.
You sent people into my life to bring me your love.
You are too wonderful.
You rejoice, when I am happy and,
show pity when I am hurt.
You don't leave me to suffer but,
interrupt our pain.
You take the past and,
put it to good use.
Is there anyone like you?
You don't live in Heaven but,
walk our streets and,
enter into our lives
I celebrate today because,
You know us and,
have called us all by name.

Kimberly Copeland

Untitled

New pavement under me and grey sky before me,
I fling myself into the horizon.
The working masses flood from their jobs;
Each screaming soul sedated by its personal legal evil
At this hour, cars on bondage
To the capricious whims of pedestrians
Sigh vaporous sighs: A collective revenge that poisons with
time. And we watch as the streets empty of all but the vermin
That lock us safe in out castle-prisons.
And after the sunset the night comes
And with in the cold
Each possessing its particular beauty
—and its particular terrors
Even as the last amber rat disappears
The night takes hold deep in the city
The question in posed:
   Is it simply an absence of light,
   or a presence all its own?
The city replies, and illuminates
the heaven it stretches to reach.

   Kimberly Kier

I Know There's A God

When I look at the sky, the earth and tress, I God.
Know there's a God that made me,
But then I see your face and I know that God is
There, I know he's in our home and everywhere.
He gave us love, that no evil can break, it was
Unique because it came from above.
He gave us a life to share, to give it all to him
To love to cry and laugh was all the wanted to spare
He loves us so dearly, oh he loves us so much, but
Why do we sometimes forget of such love?
He's there, we know we know he's there, cause when you
Look at you, I know there's a God everywhere!!!!!!!

   Myriam Padgett

Requiem For A Prairie

Today the hill is black
Yesterday as for centuries it was green
Wild flower interspersed the tufted prairie grass
There I gathered
The mayflower of early spring the fire red lily
The thorn apple and watched horses hitched
To wagons filled with new mown hay
While other loads were mounded high
With the sweet scented grass of the meadow.

These are needed acres to till?
My patch of virgin prairie is now seduced by plow.
Winter's wind and summer's deluge rape the hillside.
And neither I, nor you, nor your son's son
Will henceforth know the soft feel of nature's flow
Nor watch the hawk's majestic soar or raccoon's play
Or spy the speckled back of baby fawn.

Today the steel shaft of wrenching blade
Erased my prairie hill and I watched with silent cry
For those who feel no will
Nor care to cherish it still

   Agnes Christensen

Little One

   Don't cry little one.
For there will be times when you'll be happy.

   Open your eyes little one.
I want you to see the warm light from the sun.

   Please smile little one.
You'll see that when you're grown and on your own you'll at
last be able to have fun.

   Sweet little one.
I know they hurt you so much, and you're quickly becoming
so immune to their vicious touch.

   Don't be scared little one.
For the evil they inflict on you will sooner or later be done.

   Be strong little one.
For I'm praying for you. I know they can be so cruel. In the
end this battle I know you've won.
My dear, dear friend, little one.

   Elizabeth Cardenas

Ins And Outs

As I stare out, from inside these eyes;
I'm a witness with a view to a kill.

It's the panes that separate the in from the out.
They're all cloudy from the hot breath of doubt.

It's her spirit, say I,
Staring out through my eye,
As she lovingly wipes the panes dry.

From the first moment,
Of seeing her clearly,
With her tenderness
She conquered my soul.

Conversation, delegation,
Infatuation, adoration!

In order, my dominoes fall.

Desperation, masturbation,
Fornication, ruination.

Says my out to my in;
Who are you? Let me in....

Says my in to my out;
Stop the lies, let me out....

   James E. Sokolowski

"You"

In the summer when the roses bloom,
I smell the fragrance of your sweet cologne.
   On windy cold winter nights how I
wish you were here to hold one tight.
When the leaves fall from the trees,
I feel the softness of your breeze.
   when the skies are warm and so blue
You will know I'm always thinking of you.
   when the night winds gently flow,
You will know how much I love you so.
When the snowflakes fall to the ground
You will know that silent sound of my love of you.
When the beauty of the flowers bloom
   in spring, you know we have such a good thing
Whatever time of year, you will know
   the love I have for you will be forever.

   Sharon Kelly

Participles Of Matter Particles

We breathe it matter of factly
We eat it matter of factly
We sleep on it matter of factly
We drive from it.

If we leave it be it piles from objects to objects
Bridges from subjects to subjects matter of factly
Clings on wire to wire matter of factly
Collects form corner to corner.

Weightless and lifeless to the eye
So tediously we tend to its ever growing
Never ending mass.
Why must it be such a laborious task.

For we even titled the chore after the matter
Of factly, why must it "live" in the world around us.
Flog your shirt and roll up the sash
Watch it dance in the sun surround us.

Matter of factly it swirls above us,
Below us, beside us, behind us.
Thus is dust,
Dust we must live with dust.

Dan Ciminello

The Wild

Lucky are they who run among the fields and streams.
For they without broken hopes and dreams.
Peace and beauty is abound with life being nothing but mild.
For they are the lucky call of the wild.
Lucky are they who bore and near their young among the fields &
   streams
Calmness and serenity pours over the glass and trees,
Such a peaceful setting for the young to warm.
So lucky are they, the wild, who rum among the fields and streams.

Lisa Kay Edlin

Why War?

What is the point of war?
To me it seems like such a bore.

Why do people fight over nothing?
When all they get is a small something.

What is the point of making people die?
Don't they know there families cry?

I don't see how they can pay for a war,
but don't have the money to feed the poor.

Why don't you keep all your guns
to yourself and help the people with
a little less wealth?

Trisha Florence

"No More Questions"

What to do with transparent skin
Paperthin resistance to a world I can't let in

How to cope, how to survive
When life's bittersweet chore is to keep my spirit alive

How to explain, how not to give in
To temptation, relief-those mortal sins

Who to reach for-who to push away
Who to abandon-who's grace might stay

When to answer, when to ask why
Cold harsh reality yet searching for the sky

Looking for that rainbow, the stars and the moon
Praying for the miracle that cannot come too soon

Nancy Jo Meehan

(M) (O) (N) (O) C. Eastgood

Whenever C. Eastgood entered the class
He would scan the room for the pretentious lass

One day, the iron maiden espied his game, taking the dare
When C. Eastgood was seated, she pompously tried to outstare

Perceptually unaware of the actor on stage
The elusive sage, the thorn bird singing for release from an inner cage

The destroyed iron maiden turned halfway in defeat trying to escape C.
Eastgood's empty, discerning glare.
For the first time, the maiden's jaded heart felt embarrassment andfear.
On that day, professor Tiffany told us the story of Kao's choice
of the dun mare.
He said, "East and West will journey together someday, hand in hand,
star and sand"
"Counterpart's who harmonious relationship will be felt everywhere,
nowhere".
"Like a structureless poem free-flying forever through the eternal
promised land"
"The illusion of opposites no longer a fear, the perfect pair, a
sweetheart for all those willing to share"

Paul Szymanski
Psalm 71—Genesis 15:5

Biographies
of
Poets

ABDOLLAHI, SOODABEH
[b.] Iran; [ed.] BA degree in Psychology and Certifications of Office Management and Dental Program; [occ.] Dental Technician and Jewelry Designer; [hon.] Editor's Choice Award for Outstanding Achievement in Poetry presented by the National Library of Poetry in 1994.; [oth. writ.] Poetry book in Farsi language was published in 1993. The name of this edition is "Autumn of Love;" [pers.] My poems were mentioned in RSI (Iranian Radio) all over U.S. by the respectful talk show host: F. Tofighi. I admire "Ha Fez's" poetry. I believe in love, peace and freedom of speech.; [a.] Sunnyvale, CA

ABERNATHY, SUSAN E.
[Pen.] Sue Etta; [b.] January 7, 1943, Salinas, CA [m.] Olin Abernathy, June 9, 1973; [occ.] Associate Governmental Program Analyst, State of CA; [memb.] Greenpeace, Now, Survivorship, Women's Health Network, Y-ME, ASH, Public Citizen and Weave (Among Others); [oth. writ.] Poetry and short stories.; [pers.] When the battle is joined and the long howl of madness is near, survivors remember you are not alone. Bless you all.; [a.] Sacramento, CA

ACKERMAN, MATTHEW JASON
[b.] September 10, 1974, Westlake Village; [p.] Howard and Dolores; [m.] not married; [ed.] 2nd year in college; [occ.] Student; [memb.] DeMolay; [oth. writ.] White, Thunder Storm, I Stand In The Rain, Symphony of Love, Seventh Day of Ten; [pers.] The best time to move forward is when everything seems backward.; [a.] San Jose, CA

ADAMS, ARTHUR BYRD
[b.] July 26, 1925, Kentucky; [p.] Byrd and Havana Adams; [m.] Pauline Rupe Adams, July 24, 1949; [ch.] David, Jody, Pamela; [ed.] High School, Kentucky, Los Angeles; 3 1/2 years BIOLA, Los Angeles; Various self-study programs; [occ.] Ordained Minister; Motivational Speaker; Editor, The Brotherhood Crier.; [memb.] Life Extension Foundation; Mt. Vernon Baptist Brotherhood; [oth. writ.] The Modern Millionaires; Newspaper Columns; Other works in process.; [pers.] Only those with an undying vision of the invisible, are totally committed to doing the impossible. From dare to make a manifesto, and make your dreams come true (a work in process by Arthur Byrd Adams); [a.] Detroit, MI

ADAMS, CLYDE
[b.] September 12, 1949, St. Louis, MO; [p.] Step Parents: Dr. and Mrs. Eugene W. Adams, Mother Mrs. Harrietta Douglas; [m.] Single; [ch.] Nieces: Adya Adams, Malika Adams, Jamila Adams; [ed.] Northwest High School, St. Louis, MO; Tuskegee Inst. High School, Tuskegee, AL: Received B.S. in History from Tuskegee University in 1973; [occ.] History Teacher, Madison Park High School, Boston, MA; [memb.] American Museum of Natural History; Mystic Valley Riders Cycling Club, Student Volunteer with Student Non-Violent Coord. Comm.; [hon.] Entered college at 16 though Tuskegee Institute Prefreshman program from 11th grade; attended honor courses at Tuskegee University, honorary member of Groove Phi Groove Fraternity Inc.; [oth. writ.] Published "Jazz Corners" in Tuskegee University Student Newspaper, as well as our poetry. Read own poetry throughout south during Civil Rights Movement.; [pers.] Poetry freezes, examines and expresses the human experience in time, be it an idea, an event or

human encounter, "My favorite poet is Langston Hughes;" [a.] Boston, MA

ADAMS, ERIKA
[b.] August 2, 1979, Houma, LA; [p.] Susan Clement; [ed.] Will be attending H.L. Bourgeois High School; [occ.] Student; [memb.] Beta Club, Honors Society; [hon.] VFW Award; [oth. writ.] Poem published in local newspaper for contest, poem published in Poetic Voices of America, In the school years of 91-92 and 93-94 (seventh and ninth grade) I placed in the Young Author's contest; [pers.] I have always been able to write a poem without much effort and it's a talent I am honored to have. It gives me pleasure when I see there are others who enjoy my writings and it encourages me to continue to write.; [a.] Houma, LA

ADESANYA, MARY A.
[b.] May 10, 1980, Lagos, Nigeria; [p.] Joseph and Olufolake Adesanya; [ed.] W.H. Atwell Middle School and TAG Magnet High School; [occ.] student; [hon.] National Junior Honor Society; 1994 DISD Mathematics Olympiad Winning Team; Atwell Honor Club; [pers.] I try my best to base my artistic and writing ability on reality or comedy.; [a.] Dallas, TX

ADKINS, MICHELLE
[b.] May 8, 1955, Huntington, WV; [p.] Bernard M. Meadows Jr. (deceased) and Geraldine Meadows; [m.] Keigh Adkins, May 17, 1991; [ch.] Tiffany, Steven, and T.K.; [ed.] Division Ave. H.S., Levittown, NY, completed GED 1992; [occ.] Self-employed, Displayer of Home Interiors and Gifts, Huntington, WV; [pers.] With love, to my son Steven, whose handicap inspired me to write this poem.; [a.] Huntington, WV

AIDINIAN, NANCY GRAFF
[b.] May 13, 1957, Santa Monica, CA; [m.] Petro Aidinian; [ch.] Dawn Kelli and Pallas Joy; [oth. writ.] Currently working with songwriters and submitting short stories such as "El Dia de los Muertos" for children and "The Job" for adults.; [pers.] Whatever one writes, let it benefit or heal a spirit, make a difference in a life, or give of itself to the worthy. This is the responsibility of the "gift." My passion: words with Music.; [a.] Madison, MN

ALCORN, SAM J.
[Pen.] Al Howell; [b.] February 22, 1922, Sartoga, TX; [p.] Gladys Independence Spell Alcorn and Wendell Bertram Alcorn; [m.] Mary Lou Rohan Alcorn, September 8, 1972; [ch.] Kenneth J. Richards, Sam J. Alcorn, Jr. William "Billy" Alcorn.; [ed.] Graduate Boling High School 1940. Prep Allen Military Academy B.S. Agriculture Texas A & M College 1950.; [occ.] Retired United States Coast Guard Reserve May 30, 1980; from Aluminum Co. of America (ALCOA) Nov. 1, 1984; [memb.] Methodist Church, American Legion, Eagles, Fleet Reserve Association; [hon.] WWII Victory Medal, Coast Guard Meritorious Service Medal. Honorable Discharges: Naval Reserve 1946. Coast Guard Reserve 1980. Total military service 25+ years.; [hon.] Staff writer Majestic Records, Selected writer Jeff Roberts Publishing Co.; [oth. writ.] Battleship Arizona, The Way To Hell, Out of Navy Moth Balls, Screaming Eagle, Scamper In My Camper, Prince Charming, In The Chapel Alone, Corpus Christi Blues.; [pers.] Make use of actual life events or use historical facts to write poetry or song words. One of my very favorite

singers is Webb Pierce. Writing is another sense or medium from which I derive pleasure and get much satisfaction.; [a.] Palacios, TX

ALEWINE, RHONDA L.
[Pen.] Dizzy Riddle; [b.] June 1, 1979, Watkinsville, GA; [p.] Bud and linda Alewine; [ed.] Student at Athens Christian School, Athens, GA 9th grade.; [occ.] Student; [memb.] Athens Christian Girls Chorale, Athens Christian Speech and Drama Club, Word of God Tabernacle, Teen Volunteer at Athens Regional Medical Center.; [a.] Lexington, GA

ALEXANDRE, BRANDY
[b.] July 17, 1964, Huntington Beach, Ca; [ed.] High School Proficiency; [occ.] Adult Video Writer, Producer, Director, Actress; [memb.] Adult Video Assn., The Huguenot Society; [hon.] First woman to write, produce, direct and star in a video; [oth. writ.] Adult teleplays "De Blond," "Cheeks 5: Cop A Feel," "Blowing in Style," "Best Butte(e) in the West" - all produced.; [pers.] My only regret is that I live in a short-sighted society where I am judged by assumptions and valued by paperwork.; [a.] Hollywood, CA

ALEXION, MEGAN
[b.] August 2, 1982, Providence, RI; [p.] Robert and Anne Alexion; [ch.] Sister: Michaele Alexion; [ed.] St. Vincent De Paul School, Oak Haven Elementary; [occ.] student; [memb.] Coventry Rams Cheerleader, St. Vincent De Paul Parish Member; [hon.] Social Studies, D.A.R.E. Award, Young Authors Award, 1st grade tutor award; [pers.] I sometimes write poems and the first one I've ever entered in a contest, was this one. I'm very happy to see my work published.; [a.] Coventry, RI

ALFORD, DOROTHY MOORE
[p.] Rev. and Mrs. John A. Moore; [m.] Richard Earl Alford (Deceased), June 3, 1930; [ch.] Dorothy Carol Alford Moore; [ed.] Magna Cum Laude, Graduate of Millsaps College, Jackson, MS. Graduate work, MS Southern Hattisburg, MS; [occ.] Retired Teacher of English; [memb.] United Methodist Church, Wesleyan Circle, methodist Women, Dorothy Alford Sunday School Class, AARP, Retired President of Floral Club, Book Club and P.T.A. of Crystal Springs; [hon.] Local Star Teacher, Awarded first place for T.V. play by MS Arts Festival; One Act Play, A World I Never Made and an Essay, "A Bonnie bit," Published by MS Arts Commission; Threads of Patriotism and Literature in National Instructor.; [oth. writ.] 1971-1986 Weekly feature article for C.S. Meteor; Book on Local History, Sold to 22 States; "O Happy Land!" pageant for 200 participants, History of C.S. United Methodist Church; What is a Methodist Preacher?" Essay in MS Methodist Advocate; [pers.] My double major, Religious Education and English at a fine college, reinforced by life in a christian home, has given me the goal of service to my fellow man. Both my teaching and writing have been influenced by this goal.; [a.] Crystal Springs, MS

ALLARID, CHERYL L.
[b.] March 15, 1924, Sacramento, CA; [p.] Helen Moesta, Morris Willmarth; [ch.] Steve Allarid Jr.; [ed.] East High School, Denver CO; [occ.] Bookkeeper; [pers.] If my poetry can touch someone's heart, the connection is my fulfillment beyond physical contact.; [a.] Denver, CO

ALLISON, KATHY
[b.] June 26, 1950, Bowie, TX; [p.] Archie Broder, Ava Jean Maxwell; [m.] Dennis D. Allison, June 9, 1968; [ch.] Tammy Lynn Allison and Stephanie Ann Allison; [a.] Salina, KS

ALLISON, MARGARET J.
[b.] September 8, 1925, Princeton, Ind.; [p.] Deceased; [m.] September 20, 1941 (Deceased); [ch.] Margaret Glasser, Bonnie Helderman, Janice Stoner, Frances Wolls, Richard Allison; [ed.] 9th Grade Night School Classes; [occ.] Retired; [memb.] Church member, Farm bureau; [hon.] none; [oth. writ.] Several poems that have never been published.; [pers.] Have written for years but for my own interest only. Since my poems have a message to tell I would like for others to be able to read them.; [a.] Lawrenceville, IL

AMEN, RANDI MICHELLE
[b.] June 20, 1982, Greeley, CO; [p.] Tom and Bonnie Amen; [ed.] I am in the 7th grade at Brush Middle School, Brush, CO; [occ.] Student; [pers.] I like reading and writing poetry. My favorite book of poetry is "Where The Sidewalk Ends" by Shel Silverstein.; [a.] Ft. Morgan, CO

ANDERSON, CODY
[b.] September 18, 1969, Midland, TX; [p.] C.W. and Janice Anderson; [m.] Joann Anderson, September 10, 1994; [ch.] none; [ed.] B.S. Chemical Engineering from Texas A&M University, College Station, TX (May 1993); [occ.] Chemist; [memb.] Texas A&M Century Club, AICHE; [a.] Orange, TX

ANDERSON, DANIELLE
[b.] December 30, 1973; Philadelphia, PA; [p.] Thomas Jr. and Justine Anderson; [ed.] North Penn High School, Bloomsburg University; [occ.] Advertising Major; [hon.] Dean's List; [pers.] I would like to dedicate this poem to my grandfather, Thomas L. Anderson (1922-1984). I love you Grandpa.; [a.] Lansdale, PA

ANDERSON, DANIELLE LEIGH
[b.] September 2, 1981, Tazewell, VA; [p.] Vicki and Danny Anderson; [ed.] North Tazewell Elementary School, Tazewell Middle School 6th and 7th grades; going into 8th grade at Tazewell Middle school; [occ.] Student 8th grade; [memb.] Annual Staff, gifted; [hon.] Student of the Month in 4, 5, 6 and 7 grades. Brain Games (6 & 7th grades) J.L. Walthall Citizenship Award - 7th grade. A-Honor Roll, Top 10 in the Geography Bee, VA Math League, and awards in various subjects and church; [oth. writ.] Besides schoolwork, I like to write poems and songs in my spare time.; [pers.] I believe God has a purpose for everything and you might think that something may be bad on the surface, but it has a much deeper meaning and has a happy ending.; [a.] North Tazewell, VA

ANDERSON, DUANE
[b.] November 7, 1939, Watseka, IL; [m.] Mari Anderson, November 17, 1966; [ch.] Richard, Thomas and Tammy; [pers.] Christmas of the 90's was influenced by the different spirits and types of people that I have observed throughout this Christmas Holidays.; [a.] Medimont, ID

ANDERSON, JANETT
[b.] September 24, 1949, Savannah, GA; [p.] Mrs.

Leola Jackson; [m.] Divorced; [ch.] Darren and Kevin Anderson; Grandchildren Ari and Kaila Anderson; [ed.] Bachelor's Degree-Mercy Coll., Seward Park High School, Elizabeth Seton College-Yonkers, Business Law; [occ.] Principal secretary to Supreme Court Justice Westchester; [memb.] National Notary Assoc., Triple A, Certified as Westchester County Foster Care Parent, Mt. Calvary Baptist Church; [oth. writ.] A novel, "Once Upon An Angry Girl." being published by Vantage Press, NYC, Fall 94; Asked to write children's books by The Institute of Children's Literature.; [pers.] It's amazing what a combination of small talk and imagination can do. The credit is due my 4 year old granddaughter Ari. I merely rephrased the words.; [a.] White Plains, NY

ANDERSON, RAYCHELLE ELIZABETH
[Pen.] KAI, Adrianne, Danielle; [b.] June 5, 1953, Phila., PA; [p.] Essie M. Ancrum and Wilson Ancrum Jr. (deceased); [m.] James Anderson, May 31, 1984; [ch.] Caasi Q. Anderson, Matthew Anderson; [ed.] West Phila. High School 1970, Community College of Phila. Associate degree in General Studies; [occ.] Unemployed housewife; [memb.] none; [hon.] Academic Honor List, 1972-1973 and 1973-1974 at Community College; [oth. writ.] A varied selection of poems unpublished, from elementary school to present; [pers.] There is a point at which being sacrificing becomes being foolish. Most of us encounter that point more than once in our lives. During these confusing times we must rely on our faith in God and our love of life. At this point sacrifice becomes giving.; [a.] Phila. PA

ANDRE, ARTHUR L.
[b.] October 2, 1922, Chicago; [p.] Mr. and Mrs. A.W. Andre; [m.] Catherine Andre, September 20, 1947; [ch.] Four, 2 boys, 2 girls; [ed.] High School, Carl Schurz Loyola University; [occ.] Business Owner Bristol Supply Co.; [memb.] Loyal Order of Moose American Legion; [oth. writ.] "Encounters of the Wrong Kind," "Asteriod Problem," "History of Zoo's"; [pers.] Keep writing. It is the best therapy in the world.; [a.] St. Charles, IL

ANDRES, MEGAN NELSON
[b.] May 17, 1981, Grand Rapids; [p.] Kevin and Suzanne Andres; [ed.] Primary School, Stepping Stones Montessori, Grand Rapids Middle School, St. Andrew's Catholic School, Grand Rapids, H.S. Catholic Central (fall 95); [occ.] Student; [hon.] Captain of Safety Squad at St. Andrew's, Science Olympiad, 1993 Medal Winner, MEAP, Excellence in Science 5th Grade, National Mythology Exam-Medal of Excellence; [a.] Wyoming, MI

ANDREW, GORDON JAMES
[b.] May 19, 1962, San Diego; [p.] Ernest and Jean Andrew; [m.] Susanne Lore Andrew, June 4, 1994; [ed.] Alice Birney Elementary, Roosevelt Jr. High, San Diego High School, A.S. Electronics, San Diego Mesa College, B.S. Electronics, Chapman University, Professional Certificate Systems Engineering; [occ.] Associate Engineer at (S.A.I.C); [oth. writ.] Countless poems written to countless women who have wanted or loved poetry.; [pers.] The greatest accomplishment of a poem is to bring joy and happiness to one person's life. If it succeeds in doing that or even more then, soon the feeling returns to the owner (writer); [a.] San Diego, CA

ANGEL, ROBERT
[b.] December 4, 1931, Chatt. TN; [p.] Joseph and Rose Glassman Angel; [ed.] B.A. Oglethorpe U. Atlanta, M.A. Catholic Univ. of America, Washington, D.C. 1964, Seminary; [occ.] Volunteer at Unit Acres Foundation, Catholic Workers Movement; [oth. writ.] The Day of Reckoning, House of Pilgrimage (unpublished) The Rivers flow Forever (unpublished) short stories, other poems; [a.] Orwell, NY

ANSAR, AHMAD
[b.] October 18, 1956, Buffalo, NY; [p.] Reva A. and Robert L. Parham, Jr.; [ed.] Gannon University, American Institute of Hypnotherapy; [occ.] Employment Counselor, Suny at Buffalo, Educational Opportunity Center; [memb.] International Association of Counselors and Therapists, The Menninger Foundation, American Board of Hypnotherapy, Victims of Crime and Advocacy League, Inc.; [hon.] Outstanding Young Man of America, Certificate of Achievement, Mentor 2000 Program, Certificate of Appreciation, PS #74 Youth Day; [pers.] Romantic words will always make a sincere heart sing. Mr. Lorenz "Larry" Hart and Ms. Jameelah Ali. Thanks!; [a.] Buffalo, NY

ANTHONY, MICHAEL
[Pen.] M.C. Anthony; [pers.] May 27, 1955, Phila., PA; [p.] Lawrence & Beatrice Anthony; [m.] Cheryl Ann, August 13, 1978; [ch.] Monet Chanel; [ed.] Simon Gratz High, Phila., PA; 1 1/2 college, Jr. College/Community Locksmith School; [occ.] Chief Maint. Engineer; [memb.] P.B.S.A.; [hon.] Graduated 4th in High School Class of 1973; [oth. writ.] Destiny of the World; Too Busy; Fix this World and other short poems and prose.; [pers.] Seventh Day Adventist and member of the Steinards of Song and Christianaires Singing Groups. I thank God for my abilities.; [a.] Waterford Works, NJ

APONTE, JACQUELINE
[Pen.] Juan Ruiz; [b.] August 29, 1962, NY; [p.] Margarita and Frank Aponte; [ch.] Adam R. Betancourt, Christine T. Betancourt, Jonatan D. Aponte; [ed.] Taft High School, Bronx Community College, Theological Institute of the United International Council of Evangelical churches; [occ.] Independent Professor, Beauty Consultant for Mary Kay Cos.; [memb.] Fuente del Agua de Vida, Inc. Church; [hon.] Forensic Society, Bronx Community Colleges, Model City Council's Secretary Award, Forensic Society's Falcon Round Table Excellence Award.; [oth. writ.] Created and established a theme song for the Missionary League of Fuente del Agua de Vida, Inc. Church; [pers.] I would like to dedicate this poem to my mother for all of her enthusiasm in raising me and teaching me. The reality of my writing is to focus on what's actually happening and be able to offer a better outlook.; [a.] Bronx, NY

ARAKAKI, DEBORAH
[b.] April 28, 1952, Sacramento, CA; [p.] Ernest and Laverne Stedman; [m.] Ray Arakaki, December 10, 1977; [ed.] Graduate South Tahoe High School and Sierra College, Rocklin, CA; [occ.] Program Director, Recruitment Agency for California Convalescent Homes; [hon.] California Works Award, given by Governor, 1988. The 339th Point of Light choose by President Bush, he named 1,000 points of life in the nation while he was President 1992. I won the

Jefferson award from the American Institute for Public Service, Washington, D.C.; [oth. writ.] A book of poetry unpublished right now.; [pers.] Touching a life with kindness and acts of unconditional love, sending a message to God above, that good deeds make us strong, and help us not to do wrong.; [a.] Auburn, CA

ARBAUGH, THERESA GAYLE
[Pen.] TG; [b.] May 23, 1976, Joplin, MO; [p.] Darlene M. McPherson Eddings; [ed.] Graduated from Miami High School, attended Northeastern Oklahoma, A&M College, presently attending Northeastern State University; [memb.] American Red Cross, Northwest Baptist Church; [hon.] Honors graduate from Miami High School, Presidents Honor Roll at Northeastern Oklahoma A&M College; [oth. writ.] Have written several poems; [pers.] I grew up as one of four daughters, raised by our mother. Due to circumstances, my emotional growth was rapid and often serious. This serious side is revealed in my poetry.; [a.] Miami, OK

ARDITO, TINA
[b.] July 15, 1967, Ft. Laud., Florida; [p.] Thomas and Sheryl Ardito; [ch.] Kristina, Chris, Lil Joe; [ed.] Coconut Creek High School; [hon.] I have received two honorable mentions. I also have a poem that has been published.; [oth. writ.] I am working on a poetry book of my own.; [pers.] Oh how I love the summer, because even when things don't go my way, I know I can look forward to a sun shiny day.; [a.] Riverside, AL

ARIZONA, DALLAS
[Pen.] Whiz Bong; [b.] October 21, 1931, Sheridan, WY; [p.] tom and Hazel Arizona; [m.] Mary C. Arizona, July 19, 1954; [ch.] Linda Tempe, Dallas Jr., Mike Arizona; [ed.] 3rd year high school; [occ.] Retired Railroad Engineer; [hon.] Editor Choice Award of National Library Poetry; [oth. writ.] Dream of Life, Gift of Live, My Son Grows Up, all published by National Library of Poetry plus 17 others.; [pers.] Poetry is very educational and very rewarding; [a.] Sheridon, WY

ARMSTRONG, JACK THOMAS
[p.] Jack T. Armstrong; [b.] August 31, 1967, Detroit; [p.] Marion E. and Dolores L. Armstrong; [ed.] Wayne County Community College; [occ.] Poet, Salesman; [memb.] The International Society of Poets; [hon.] I have received the Editor's Choice Award for Outstanding Achievement in Poetry Presented by the National Library of Poetry 1993. Signed by Editor, Cynthia Stevens and Editor Caroline Sullivan; [oth. writ.] Published in Dance on the Horizon Winter 1993 - Poem Able. Also on cassette, The Sound of Poetry. Musical Introduction by the English Chamber Orchestra. Readings by nationally renowned speaker Ira Westreich.; [pers.] What is good is important. What's best is right. With all reality we're blessed in all we work for with all our might. To be surely thankful we are all free to have a life. A happy note from a poet as I humbly reside in.; [a.] Belleville, MI

ARMSTRONG, JOHN ALONZO
[b.] September 30, 1960, Kasier Hosp., Wilmington, CA; [p.] Mr. and Mrs. Clarence Armstrong; [m.] Single/Divorced; [ch.] David Alonzo Armstrong 12 yrs. old; Rose Alica Armstrong 11 yrs. old; [ed.] 135th Street School, Gardener, CA; Henry Clay Jr.

High School, L.A. CA; Alian Leroy Locke High School, L.A. CA; Portland State University, Portland, Oregon; [occ.] Singer, Songwriter, Poet, Warehouseman, Customer Ser. Rep.; [memb.] S.M.A. (Soul Music Assoc.), ASCAP (American Society of Composers, Authors and Publishers); West Angeles Church of God In Christ; [hon.] Award of Lyric Writing Excellence from Platinum Records; previously published in "Tears of Fire" by the National Library of Poetry; [pers.] "You can achieve if you put forth effort, beyond just dreaming."; [a.] Gardena, CA

ARNOLD, MISTY
[Pen.] Misty Lynn Arnold; [b.] April 1, 1977, Carvel, TX; [p.] Maurice and Billie Arnold; [ed.] Jr. in High School, Gatesville High school; [occ.] Student; [memb.] FHA, Drama Club, Choir, School Newspaper.; [hon.] Actress of the Year, Speech, Poetic Writing, Prose, Impromptu Speaking; [oth. writ.] 78 other poems dealing with death, friendship, break ups.; [pers.] I believe that everyone is placed here for a reason; mine to write about the good and bad things and ease others pain; [a.] Gatesville, TX

ARTIGAS-GAC, MELINA
[Pen.] Melina; [b.] May 23, 1985, Colombia; [p.] Gustavo and Priscilla; [ch.] Brother: Alejandro; [ed.] Pre School: "het Vrije School" - (the Netherlands); "Colegio Puertorri-queno de Ninas" (Puerto Rico); "Carrollton Elementary" and "The Georgian School" (Georgia); [occ.] 5th grade student; [memb.] Enrichment program for gifted children; [hon.] Academic Excellence Award 1993-94, Piano Award 93-94; [oth. writ.] A short poem in prose: "How to Imagine," "Tuky goes to the doctor" (story) in preparation: "Tuky runs away," "Tuky goes to the Dentist," "Tuky plays Baseball;" [pers.] My poems and stories are my dreams. My dreams in Europe, in Latin America, in the Caribbean and in the USA. and as I told to my father, also a writer, when I finished my first poetry collection: I cut the paper, wrote the poems and made the illustrations, not as you. You send the disks and others do the work for you. It is not so bad for a seven year old girl, ah!; [a.] Carrollton, GA

ARTIS, ANTHONY JEROME
[b.] October 26, 1967, Flint, MI; [p.] Jerome J. and Juanita Artis; In-Laws: David and Anna J. Blake; [m.] December 19, 1992; [ch.] Blake Anthony Artis; Brother: Andre J. Artis; Sister: Donnice E. Robinson; [ed.] Flint Northwestern High School, Jackson State University, The University of Michigan-Flint; [occ.] IRS Internal revenue Agent; [memb.] Big Brothers/ Big Sisters of Greater Flint, Grace Emmanuel Baptist Church, Nat'l Assoc. of Black Accountants, Pentecostal Tabernacle COGIC (prior), Prestige Capital Management Investment Club; [hon.] J.S.S. Academic Scholarship, NABA-Flint Scholarship, Urban League of Flint, Outstanding Black Scholar, IRS Special Act Award, Youngest RA in MI (1987); [oth. writ.] First poem ever submitted and published. Others to come in the future.; [pers.] I first thank the Lord Jesus Christ for blessing and enabling me to write this poem. This poem was inspired by my lovely wife, Davida, who is my "Precious Jewel." I dedicate this poem to my wife, son, and family. Philippians 4:13, "I can do all things through Christ which strengthenth me;" [a.] Flint, MI

ASHOUR, ROSE
[b.] April 17, 1916, Morrison Bluff, AR; [p.] John and Catherine Bauer Ashourd; [m.] Benedictine Nun; [ed.] BSE in Education; MSE in Elementary Education, Major: Administration; [occ.] Caregiver to Mother; [memb.] Lifetime member of International Society of Poets; [oth. writ.] Twenty or more poems published in anthologies.; [pers.] I listen for an inspiration before writing; I try to reflect the beauty of God in my poetry.; [a.] Fort Smith, AR

ASNAULT JR., JOSEPH R.
[b.] June 22, 1970, San Francisco; [p.] Joe Sr. and Carol Asnault; [ed.] BA in English, Single Subject Secondary Teaching Credential from California State University at Chico; [occ.] Teacher; [hon.] Dean's List; [oth. writ.] Never, ever been published; [pers.] anybody can write; you just gotta dig around for it for a while!; [a.] San Rafael, CA

AUSTIN, JOHN C.
[b.] February 22, 1936, Lawton, OK; [p.] Will C. and Gladys Gray Austin; [m.] Vickie L. Austin (Cornell), May 25, 1962; [ch.] Cheryl Sue Moiser, David Colson Austin, Rebekah Ann Underwood, Katherine Louise Newton, John William Earl Austin, Janice Marie Austin; [ed.] Lawton High School 1953, Oklahoma State University, B.S. 1971; [occ.] Retired farmer and mechanic; [pers.] "Fear God, and keep his commandments: for this is the whole duty of man." Ecclesiastes 12:12. My mother loved poetry and was always very proud of her gold Lawton High School "English Medal."; [a.] Indiahoma, OK

AUTHIER, MICHAEL
[b.] June 1, 1962, Detroit; [p.] Marie and Elmer authier; [m.] Cyd Authier, July 26, 1991; [ch.] Tia Marie, Shauna Yvonne, and our soon to be born child; [ed.] Redford Union High School; [occ.] Journeyman Carpenter; [memb.] Moose Lodge, Paralyzed Veterans of America; [oth. writ.] The Silent Tree, The Lords Whispering Haze; [pers.] The Almighty blessed me with eyes so I can see all the beautiful things that surround me.; [a.] Redford Twp., MI

BABIN, LIZA EUSTAQUIO
[b.] January 23, 1969, Tamuing, GU; [p.] Jose Suelo, Terisita Eustaquio; [m.] Ronnie F. Babin, April 22, 1994; [ch.] Rachelyn Babin; [ed.] Fauquier High School, John F. Kennedy; [occ.] Sales Executive, MBI, Inc.; [oth. writ.] Many unpublished, still many hidden within me.; [pers.] "The absence of the sun does not make the day grey. It is but ourselves that lose it within our hearts." My inspiration to go on is God's word in Proverbs 3:5 "Trust in God with all your heart..."; [a.] Dededo, Guam

BABITSKY, SOL
[Pen.] Sol B.; [b.] April 24, 1923, S.F., CA; [p.] David and Tonia; [ed.] Lowell High, one semester at S.F. Jr. College; [occ.] Retired Upholsterer; [memb.] The Human Rase; [oth. writ.] "Ode to the Flea," "Jim's Life," "Bess," "The Morning Star," "The Trouper," "The Fallen Star."; [pers.] I've had a few reflections and it was the happiest day of my life, when I received you letter. God bless you.; [a.] San Francisco, CA

BACHMANN, LOIS
[b.] June 6, 1923, Chicago, IL; [p.] Henry E. and Hilder F. Kopplow; [m.] Albert E. Bachmann, Octo-

ber 19, 1946; [ed.] Miami Edison Senior High School, Miami, FL, University of Maryland, College Park, MD: [occ.] Homemaker; [memb.] Space Coast Writers Guild; [hon.] Who's Who of American Women. President, Society of Harvard Dames, Harvard University; [oth. writ.] "Looking Over The Hill", at Dedication of Miami Edison Senior High School, National Register of Historic Places, Published in 1986 Directory. "Centennial Sentiments", Melbourne (1988) Centennial. Published in Historical Record, A Tribute to Melbourne Pioneers; [pers.] to cherish the best of the past, appreciate the blessings of today, and hope for a bright tomorrow.; [a.] Indialantic, FL

BACKOUS, DONNA
[b.] August 4, 1927, Aberdeen, SD; [p.] Louise and Ted Youngerman; [m.] Earl Backous, September 16, 1948; [ch.] Terry, Sharon, Toni, Jerold, Marcia, Jean, Joan, Rick; [ed.] High School; [occ.] Retired; [memb.] none; [hon.] none; [oth. writ.] none; [pers.] My grandma died 60 years ago. I still miss her and was thinking of how great she was, so I wrote a poem. I have 24 grandchildren and one great-grandchild and hope that 60 yrs. from now they will still think of me as I do her.; [a.] Aberdeen, SD

BAGWELL, TIFFANY J.
[b.] June 28, 1977, Dover, OH; [p.] Tom Bagwell, Jean Bagwell; [ed.] Wheaton-Warrenville South High School; [memb.] Wheaton Wesleyan Church, Amnesty International, Ecology Club (verterra); [pers.] Humankind inspires me. Each struggle or tragedy can always be brightened by a hopeful love. In knowing this, I am deeply attached to the goal of showing every aspect of life. Both tearful and smiling; [a.] Wheaton, IL

BAILEY, MAXINE T.
[b.] November 5, 1940, Columbia, AL; [p.] Max and Gladys Thorne; [m.] Bruce B. Bailey, January 13, 1993; [ch.] Gary Hicks and Terry Pritchett (Twins), Christie Welch, David Hicks; Grandchildren: Nicole, Brice, Noel, Blaine, Shandra and (one on the way); [ed.] Graduate of Stewart Co. High School (Lumpkin, GA), Some Business School, Numerous Correspondence Courses.; [occ.] In-home computerized typing service and VP, Finance, Martelli Helicopter Co., Inc.; [memb.] Board of Directors, Martelli Helicopter Corp.; [oth. writ.] non published; [pers.] Every experience in life, whether good or bad, is a good one, if you grow from it.; [a.] Pensacola Beach, FL.

BAKER, JUDITH A.
[b.] March 2, 1947, Ft. Riley, KS; [p.] Mr. and Mrs. David Bates, Sr.; [m.] Jimmy Baker Sr., October 8, 1974; [ch.] Jimmy R. Baker Jr.; [ed.] Biloxi High, Diaughon Business College, East Central University; [occ.] Non-traditional student at East Central University; [memb.] C.H.U.M.S. Multiple Sclerosis Society; [hon.] Editor's Choice Award for poem "From Eigher End" in Dance On the Horizon, of The National Library of Poetry; [oth. writ.] Essay published in East Central's "Write On," poetry published in east Central's anthology "Originals and poem" from Either End published in the National Library of Poetry's Dance on the Horizon; [pers.] I strive for Originality in my writing. When some people write about darkness, I write about lightness. When others write negatively, I write more positively. When some write about defeat, I write about victory; therefore, I am an original instead of a copy.; [a.] Francis, OK

BAKER, TREVA L.
[b.] November 19, 1964, Chillicothe; [p.] Otic and Thelma L. Baker; [ed.] BSED (Elementary Education) from Ohio University 1987, Multi-handicapped certificate from Xavier University 1989; Currently working on Master's; [occ.] Preschool, Transition teacher Pioneer School, Chillicothe; [memb.] Bridge Street Church of Christ; [hon.] Dean's List O.U. 1987 and Xavier 1989; [pers.] I feel that any writing is an outlet from stress, about daily life and love of life and passion, for our fellow human beings.; [a.] Chillicothe, OH

BAKSHY, VEDBHUSHAN CHHIBBER
[Pen.] Abodh; [b.] February 5, 1919, Rawalpindi, Pakistan; [p.] Nandlal and Chandra Mukhi; [m.] Damyanti, June 7, 1946; [ch.] Two sons and one daughter; [ed.] Bachelor of Arts, Bachelor of Laws, Cert. of Proficiency in Law. Diploma in teaching Labor Laws.; [occ.] Retired in 1977 Feb.; [memb.] Indian Society of Authors.; [hon.] 1939-45 Medal, "The Burma Star," "General Service Medal;" [oth. writ.] Wrote commentary on Gita, the Hindu classic. Published as "Geeta, The Philosophy of Practical Life" by Abodh, ISBN 81-7039-188-8; Wrote about 150 poems, spiritually-oriented poems on God, in Hindi, Sanskrit, Urdu languages, and now after settling in U.S.A. I have started in English.; [pers.] With my experience of Commissioned Officer in British-Indian Army during 2nd World War, later as Class I Officer in Central Ministry in New Delhi, and as Lawyer in High Court, at Delhi, I take practical view of philosophy. "Eternity, Thy name is God" sums up my view.; [a.] Mishawaka, IN

BALDONARDO, KAREN
[b.] January 21, 1953, Jamestonw, NY; [p.] Richard and Virginia Hedglin; [m.] Tony Baldonardo; [ch.] Julie Baldonardo, Anemarie Brubaker; [oth. writ.] Several poems written as personal blessings to those I love or those who have touched my life in special ways.; [pers.] I am a spirit filled, born again christian. I enjoy writing about the love of the Lord, the victories we can win and the joy and peace we can have in our lives, through knowing Jesus Christ as our Lord and Savior; [a.] Cathedral City, CA

BALLARD, MARY JAUNITA
[b.] July 18, 1978; [p.] Susan Terry, Wallace Ballard; [pers.] Poetry is the escape and release of my imprisoned thoughts and feelings. Through poetry I can express any mood. I am inspired by life itself because I am constantly searching for the meaning.; [a.] Paicines, CA

BALLOR, CECIL A.
[b.] March 4, 1956, Detroit, MI; [p.] Cecil Sr. and Patricia; [ed.] Associates and Bachelors of Art from Widener University TAWAS Area High school 1974; [occ.] Auto Assembler for Chrysler Corp. 20 years.; [memb.] UAW Vets Com., AFL-CIO Union Counselor; [pers.] I love to write things that will make people stop and think.

BANGS, JOSHUA D.
[b.] September 11, 1976, Cherry Hill; [p.] Edward C. and Dolores K. Bangs; [ch.] none; [ed.] Graduated Annunciation Middle School, Graduated from Gloucester Catholic High School; [occ.] Student; [hon.] Varsity letter in Soccer for Gloucester Catholic High School. Most Courageous Athlete of the Year for Cloucester Catholic High School 1994.; [oth. writ.] Many other writings.; [pers.] Go after your dreams no matter what the odds and to have the courage to keep chasing your dreams no matter how many set-backs you encounter.; [a.] Bellmawr, NJ

BANKS JR., RICHARD L.
[b.] August 9, 1962, Brooklyn, NY; [p.] Richard L. Banks Sr. and Erika Banks; [m.] Eileen B. Banks, July 2nd, 1983; [ch.] Jessica Maryann, Felicia Jean; [ed.] Franklin Lane H.S., Community College of the Air Force, Glendale Community College; [occ.] Vanguard Security Services, Lake Pleasant, AZ; [hon.] Air Force Commendation Medal, Armed Forces expeditionary Ribbon, Air Force Good Conduct Medal, Outstanding Unit Ribbon, Small Arms Expert Ribbon; [oth. writ.] "Evening Surrender" (Space Between the Lines), "Alone" (Edge of Twilight); [pers.] My writings are very personal. Put them all together they become my journal in life. you want to understand my writings, then first begin to understand the man behind the words.; [a.] Glendale, AZ

BANKS, TEADA
[b.] Bluefield, W.VA; [p.] Princeton and Helen Banks; [m.] William; [ch.] Erica.

BARB, JAIME
[b.] November 7, 1977, Excelsior Springs, MO; [p.] Dennis and Alice Barb; [ed.] Excelsior Springs High School; [hon.] First place trophy is essay contest from "The Daughter's of the American Revolution"; [pers.] I've wanted to be a writer for years. But, I'm only sixteen, I listen to rock music, and I've got to finish high school, no matter how much I don't want to. I figure I've got plenty of time.; [a.] Excelsior Springs, MO

BARBATO, BARBARA
[b.] November 25, 1944, St. Paul, MN; [p.] Wayne and Anit Route; [ch.] James Anthony, Jeannie Marie, John Henry, Judie Ann; [ed.] Warren Harding High School; [occ.] Office Manager, Dept. of Administration, State of Minnesota; [oth. writ.] Numerous poems; [pers.] My writings reflect the confusion, the tragedy and the joy of those who have touched my life so deeply.; [a.] Oakdale, MN

BARBER, JULIA
[b.] December 11, 1978, Portland, OR; [p.] Ray and Sondra Barber; [ed.] Sophomore, Lakeridge High School; [memb.] Member of the Portland Symphonic Girl Choir, Member of Our Saviors Lutheran Church; [hon.] Honor's English at Lakeridge High School (2 yrs); [oth. writ.] Published in "Whispers in The Wind," and Waluga Senior High "Swan's Song.";[pers.] The Lord is my strength, without him I am nothing. In him I have life eternal.; [a.] Lake Oswego, OR

BARBER, JUNE D.
[Pen.] Jamie June Barber; [b.] January 2, 1930, Paterson, NJ; [p.] Roy and Lucille Barber; [ed.] Grammar, High School, Art Course in College.; [occ.] Computer Librarian; [memb.] Bronte Society, Haworth England; [oth. writ.] I have had some poems published on post cards, under "What Ever Poem Cards"; [pers.] If my poetry can touch a feeling of good thoughts in people, to carry with them, I am pleased; [a.] New York, NY

BARINSTEIN, JOSH
[b.] August 4, 1966, Petaj Tikva, Israel; [p.] Lillian and Norbert Barinstein; [m.] Cecilia Barinstein, November 22, 1989; [ed.] BS in Computer Science and Engineering from UCLA (89); currently doing a BM in Composition of CSUN.; [occ.] Software Engineer.; [memb.] Argentine Mailing List (electronic mail), Franklin Mint Book Club.; [oth. writ.] A great deal of unpublished poetry in both English and Spanish.; [pers.] Although I aim to write poetry on a variety of subjects, the bulk of my work has centered around the darker side of existence. I have been influenced by Jorge Luis Borges, T.S. Eliot, Julio Cortazar, and other contemporary poets.; [a.] Van Nuys, CA

BARNES JR., JAMES
[Pen.] Walter Jim Barnes; [b.] May 13, 1973, Demopolis, AL; [p.] James and Arlene Barnes; [ed.] Marengo Academy, Livingston University; [occ.] Student; [memb.] Delta Sigma Pi Business Fraternity; [pers.] You never know. You never know what to expect out of life. You just never ever know.; [a.] Livingston, AL

BARRETT, PERRY T.
[b.] February 19, 1953; [p.] William A. and Dorothy Barrett; [ch.] Ben, Christina, William, Julianne; [ed.] B.A., Extensive Graduate Studies; [occ.] Quality Improvement Consultant; [pers.] Heartfelt Admirer of those hardy types who recover from hardlicks with unharnessed hope.; [a.] Tallahassee, FL

BARRON, MELISSA R.
[b.] July 26, 1969, McCracken Co, KY; [p.] George and Wanda Duncan; [m.] robert J. Barrow, June 12, 1992; [ch.] Alyssa Marie Barron; [ed.] Ballard Memorial High School, Paducah Community College, Academy of Health Sciences; [occ.] Housewife/U.S. Army Reserves; [memb.] American Heart Assoc.; [hon.] Awards in English, Biology and History; [pers.] All my poems reflect personal conflicts in my life. And I want to dedicate this poem to my unborn child. May she rest in peace.; [a.] Paducah, KY

BARTOSIK, DONALD SCOTT
[b.] February 19, 1970, Evanston, IL; [p.] Barbara A. and Donald C. Bartosik; [ed.] Bachelor of Arts in Psychology, North Carolina State University; [occ.] Residential Counselor for a Youth-In-Crisis Shelter; [memb.] American Psychological Association; Amnesty/International; [hon.] John T. Caldwell Scholar; Dean's List; World of Poetry Silver Medal (1988); National Council of Teachers of English Scholarship; [oth. writ.] Various poems and short stories (not published); [pers.] I love music, animals, and helping others, yet my only true escape is through writing. It's not only an expression of myself, but, more importantly, an extension beyond myself.; [a.] Raleigh, NC

BATIENON, ALBERT
[Pen.] Okamon; [b.] Burkina Faso; [p.] Clement and Veronique Batienon; [ed.] Laguardia Community College (ESL), Columbia University (ALP), American Business Institute (Comp. Acc.); [oth. writ.] Several poems in French. Poems published in American Collegiate Poets. First Prize in Fall Concurs 1984 soon to be published: "The Dance of Giving" a book length poems.; [pers.] Who is at the gate? The poet and a panhandler. The poet must be the messenger of those who choose whispering as their way of expression.; [a.] New York, NY

BATTLE, IVIE MANUEL
[Pen.] Ivie Manuel; [b.] December 17, 1953, L.A., CA; [p.] Florine Winslow Lowe; [m.] Dennis Battle, August 7, 1992; [ch.] Chante and Jordan; [ed.] Crenshaw High School, Compton College, UCLA; [occ.] Vice president, IMAC productions, Writer, Homemaker; [memb.] St. Elmo Village Inc., Artist Against Drug Abuse, Creation Woman Inc., P.T.s.A., Santa Monica High; [hon.] L.A. Unified School District; [oth. writ.] Several poems published, articles for local magazines, newsletter for P.T.S.A.; [pers.] I am encouraged through my own experiences to write about hope and how we all can triumph even through the bad times. I been greatly influenced by writer/poet Maya Angelou.; [a.] Venice, CA

BAUGHMAN, DOUGLAS R.
[b.] April 7, 1968, Carlisle, PA; [ch.] Robert Lee Baughman; [pers.] I would like to thank the lady I love. For pushing me, and supporting my heart. I love you Candace, thanks for the will to begin.; [a.] New Bloomfield, PA

BAUMGARDNER, SHARON
[b.] August 20, 1954, Riverside, CA; [p.] Richard Peston and Helen Fansler (deceased); [m.] Edmond Baumgardner, October 13, 1973; [ch.] Chad, Kristyn; [ed.] Huntington High School, Marshall University; [occ.] Executive Manager with Tupperware Home Parties; [memb.] Hungry Hearts; [hon.] Tupperware, V.I.P. Manger, Consistent Vanguard Manager, and 8 new Dodge Caravans, Furnished for meeting Sales Qualifications; [pers.] Being a foster parent for over 5 years, my poetry comes from my heart. I see an abused child become a survivor, is total gratification.; [a.] Huntington, WVA

BAUTISTA, PAULA
[b.] June 23, 1950, San Bernardino CA; [p.] Paul and Hazel Brown; [m.] John Bautista, November 7, 1970; [ch.] Paul, Jennifer, Dana; [ed.] Colton High, San Bernardino Valley College; [occ.] Assistant Principal/Athletic Director's Secretary at Colton High School; [oth. writ.] Poem published in River of Dreams Anthology; article local newspaper Voice of the People; unpublished poetry; in process of writing son's biography; [pers.] Life is a gift. Our words can be the difference in another's life. I hope my words will be life giving to someone. In a world of poverty, crime, and disease words are the only things that we have left to offer someone in the form of cup of cold water.; [a.] Grand Terrace, CA

BAXTER, EVERETT THEO
[b.] March 10, 1909, Alvin, TX; [ed.] Graduate Alvin High school; [m.] 50 years; [ch.] 3 daughters and one son; [occ.] 55 years, salesman, Houston territory; [memb.] West University United Methodist Churcher Teacher, 12 yrs. old 28 yrs.; Coach for Church and YMCA 12 yr. Boys Football, 17 yrs. Boys baseball, Chancel Choir 42 yrs.; [pers.] Retired, still in choir and writing poems for all friends, for special occasions.

BAYNE, G. PATRICIA
[b.] December 9, 1933, Royal Oak, MI; [p.] Rose G. Bissell; [m.] Richrd E. Bayne, August 14, 1950; [ch.] Susan Diane (Gay); Lori Lee (Forrest); Patti Lynn Bayne and Dr. Norman R. Bayne; [ed.] High School, Business College; [occ.] Homemaker, Bookkeeper, (Bayne's Apple Valley Farm, Inc.); [hon.] Never submitted any before. Intended, but didn't; [oth. writ.] Several poems published in local newspaper; [pers.] Life is a precious gift. We are all put here for a purpose. It's simply "Love one another and do unto others as we would have them do onto us! We shall not pass this way again. Make each day count."; [a.] Henderson, MI

BEACHAM, GLORIA MERCEDES
[b.] January 2, 1926, White Plains, NY (raised in Ozone Park, NY; [m.] Bill, April 20, 1947; [ch.] 4 daughters, Diane, Linda, Gloria, Vera, 10 grandchildren; [p.] Winifred and Jack (deceased) Jones; [ed.] St. Mary Gate of Heaven Grammar School, Ozone Park; Bishop McDonnell, M.H.S. Brooklyn; 1 yr. Pace Institute Manhattan, NY; [oth. writ.] Many dormant poems, book someday, many certificates of merit for poems submitted to World of Poetry and National Library of Poetry; 3 poems in Anthology "World of Poetry 1992;" 1 poem in Anthology "Nat'l Library of Poetry 1994, Outstanding Poets;" [pers.] How long I've been writing: Almost newborn, I left my crib in search of a bottle, in search of a bib, but when I returned to my crib once again I held nothing more than a paper and pen.

BEAM, ROBERT
[b.] June 19, 1968, Baltimore, MD; [p.] Oscar and Peggy Beam; [m.] Deanna (Goeller) September 4, 1987; [ch.] Erik Matthew Beam; [ed.] Chesapeake High School, Baltimore, MD, Essex Community College, Baltimore, MD; [occ.] Sonar Technician U.S. Navy on Board USS Yorktown; [a.] Baltimore, MD

BEARD, DAVID
[b.] December 2, 1952, Auburn, NY; [p.] Deceased; [m.] Divorced; [ch.] Adrienne, David; [ed.] Continuing Learning to live in the moment; [occ.] Being myself; [memb.] The Human Race; [hon.] Being Born; [oth. writ.] None that have been published.; [pers.] Once we rule out the distinctions. That separate: Race, Creed and Country; As but illusions, existing only in the mind. We are left with us. We are the true Universe. Let us laugh at our own misconceptions and reflect ourselves like a mirror, just as we are.; [a.] Auburn, NY

BEARD, NADIRA SABREEN
[Pen.] Nie; [b.] November 29, 1978, Chester; [p.] Mr. and Mrs. Donald Fowlkes; [ed.] Wetherill Elementary, Smedley Middle School and currently passed to the 11th grade at Chester High school Academy; [occ.] Actress and a Theatrical Instructor; [memb.] I am a member of the New Voices Young Acting Group with Peoples Light and Theatre Company.; [pers.] As a young person at age 15 I think that your life should be valued. We all know you only live once, belief is the key.; [a.] Chester, PA

BECKER, MARY
[Pen.] Mar; [b.] February 7, 1928, K.C., MO; [p.] Lee and Dorothy Sutton; [m.] Emil Becker, December 27, 1947 (deceased); [ch.] 3 sons, 8 grandchildren; [ed.] College, B.S. Degree, M.A. Degree; [occ.] Retired Teacher; [memb.] My Church Lutheran Women's Missionary League, YMCA, Art Institute,

AARP, Church Choir; [hon.] Certificates for serving the community (from teaching and working with the American Cancer Society); Student Artist diploma at college for music work; [oth. writ.] Stories and songs (for my teaching purposes); [pers.] I have appreciated my roles as teacher for 38 years), and Mother and Grandmother. I'm proud of my sons and their wives, as excellent parents, and their children give proof of that.; [a.] Chicago, IL

BEEHLER, TIMOTHY J.
[b.] November 24, 1973, Philadelphia, PA; [p.] James and Ramona Beehler; [ed.] Archbishop John Carroll H.S., LaSalle University; [occ.] Student; [memb.] LaSalle Rugby Team; [hon.] Parish scholarship recipient; [oth. writ.] Poem published in LaSalle University Literary Magazine Grimoire; [pers.] An author's work is a window to the soul. What that author writes is a reflection of who they are and what they want to be.; [a.] Berwyn, PA

BEEK, BEULAH M.
[Pen.] Boo Beck; [b.] February 18, 1922, Kentucky; [p.] Joe and Anne McKenzie; [m.] C. Leland Beck, September 1, 1945; [ch.] Ann Hartzler, Jane Sweeney, Beverly Goodwin; [ed.] Graduated from High School, Midway, KY, College Berea, KY; U. of L. Louisville, KY; Graduated Spenciren business; Louisville Ky; [occ.] Homemaker and Artist; [memb.] Pensacola Artists Inc., St. John's Catholic church; [hon.] Several Ribbons for art work; [oth. writ.] Several poems and stories mostly family remembrance for family members.; [pers.] Belief in taking responsibility for yourself.; [a.] Pensacola, FL

BELL, CHRISTINE MARIE
[b.] December 4, 1947, Phila. PA; [ch.] Margaret 26, grandchild Kasandra 6; [ed.] Strasburg Ohio, High School Graduate; [occ.] Glass inspector H.J. Heinz Co. 17 years; [hon.] I named an island in the Lake at Apple Valley near Howard, Ohio in 1988 "Little Apple Isle," Safety Employee of The Year 1991, H.J. Heinz Co., Freemont, Ohio; [oth. writ.] Submitted manuscript to Barbara Baur Literary Inc. Titled "Ellis Came Home" hopefully to be published as a children's book.; [pers.] Let us, all of us...treat our children with kindness, loving care and above all, respect.; [a.] Greenspring, OH

BELLI, MICHELLE L.
[Pen.] Michelle L. Diefenbach; [b.] September 8, 1959, St. Louis; [p.] Eugene and Clara Diefenbach; [m.] Christopher S. Belli, March 25, 1987; [ch.] Jody Michael, Kristal Marie and Daniel Justin; [ed.] Ritenour Sr. High and North County Technical; [occ.] Daycare; [memb.] International Society of Poets; [oth. writ.] Published in The Desert Sun, Tears of Fire and A Far Off Place, all anthologies of "The National Library of Poetry;" [pers.] My sincere thanks to those around me, who have supported my ambition. Thank you.; [a.] Maryland Heights, MO

BENAVIDES, JACQUELINE MARIE
[b.] April 12, 1942, Flint, MI; [p.] John N. and Marvel R. Symons; [m.] David Benavides, December 20, 1980 (2nd Marriage); [ch.] Dan, David, Kathy, Paul, Jim, Jennifer, Nicholas and (Bobby) Robert; Stepchildren: David Jr., Tom, Anita, Terry, Gary, Julie and Carl; [ed.] High School Honors Grad. (Parochial); Medical Spanish Course in College Level; [occ.] Homemaker, Caregiver for Elderly Parents.;

[memb.] Fibromyalgia Support Group; [hon.] National Honor Society, Man of the Year at Gd. Rapids Baptist College 1985; [oth. writ.] Several poems, one published in Hospice of Lansing Newsletter; family (short) story and picture printed in Lansing State Journals.; [pers.] Beginning in childhood, I recognized that each human being was special and had a God given right to be! To exist! Many of my poems and story ideas are about people, those I meet as I travel through this life.; [a.] Lansing, MI

BENETTIERI, LIZA LEE
[b.] December 17, 1973, Hartford, CT; [p.] Ugo and Betsy Benettieri; [ed.] East Hartford High, Senior Teikyo Post University; [occ.] Student at Teikyo Post University; [hon.] Athletic scholarship at Teikyo Post University, Student of the Year 1987, Several Athletic/Academic Awards; [oth. writ.] Book of poems I have written but are unpublished. Currently working on the next great American novel.; [pers.] I have always strived to be my own person and to be true to myself. I abide by the philosophy of: Do not go where the path may lead. Go instead and make your own path.; [a.] East Hartford, CT

BENSEN, TAMI
[b.] August 22, 1979, San Dimas, CA; [p.] Terry and Linda Bensen; [ed.] Azusa High School in Azusa (Freshman) 14 yrs. old; [pers.] When I wrote "to a friend" I wrote it for my best friend Tommy Hernandez, but now I realized that it can be used in other ways.; [a.] Duarte, CA

BENTON, SARA
[b.] July 7, 1974, Redding, CA; [p.] David and Katherine Benton; [ch.] Pets: Nermal and Garfield Cat; [ed.] George Washington High School, Freshman at San Francisco State University; [occ.] Student/ dancer; [memb.] ASPCA, Human Society, IFAW, St. James Episcopal Church; [hon.] Dean's List; [oth. writ.] Many stories and poems unpublished.; [pers.] The words on my papers are the writings of my soul.; [a.] San Francisco, CA

BERGER, RUTH O'NEILL
[b.] September 8, 1918, Sioux City, IA; [p.] Edgar and ruby O'Neill; [m.] Frank Berger, November 1940; [ch.] Dennis Michael and Stephen Glenn; [ed.] Central High, Briar Cliff College; [hon.] National Honor Society; Art Scholarship at Drake University; [oth. writ.] Essays, articles, poetry.; [pers.] I enjoy writing articles or poems which inspire others and have a positive influence in their lives.; [a.] San Jose, CA

BERNING, HILARY RENEE
[b.] March 31, 1980, Wheaton, MN; [p.] Ed and Vicki Berning; [ch.] Sister: Heather; [ed.] Clinton/ Graceville Elementary Luverne Jr. High; [occ.] Student at Luverne High School; [memb.] St. Catherine's Catholic Church Band, Flag Corps, Varsity Cheerleader, Volleyball Team Member, Luverne Softball; [pers.] When I write, I write mostly about my feelings and emotions. I am a very compassionate person and strive to find the good in all situations. I have been greatly influenced by my family and their faith in me that I can accomplish whatever I set my goals to be.; [a.] Luverne, MN

BERNTSEN, DOROTHEA
[b.] February 9, 1981, Anchorage; [p.] Cheryl and

John Berntsen; [ed.] 8th grade student in King Cove School; [occ.] Candy Store Owner; [hon.] Math Awards, Writing Awards, Reading Awards; [oth. writ.] Writing funny, scary poetry.

BERRY, IVY LEIGH
[Pen.] Daisy, Duffy and Starr; [b.] November 22, 1979, Nashville, TN; [p.] Ivy Berry, ID Durham; [m.] Single; [ch.] none; [ed.] I am attending Fairview High School. I plan on going to college to take a philosophy course and a religion course.; [occ.] A maid at home. Not really, I have none.; [memb.] East Hidoman Baptist Church, Ishenru Karate Dojo, Columbia House.; [hon.] none; [oth. writ.] I am currently writing a book called "Living on the Edge." I twill take me a long time to write it and the book writer John Helperin says he will help me get it published.; [pers.] I believe God throws tests on every human being to see their faith, to see how much we can take. Do not judge so that you will not be judged because the amount of judgement you give will be the amount that you receive. Study every religion and learn as much as you can.; [a.] Franklin, TN

BEUCKE, ROSALIE
[b.] June 1, 1954, Bonne Terre, MO; [p.] Clarence Dane Jr., Eileen Dane; [m.] Bradley L. Beucke, July 7, 1972; [ch.] Angela Gayle and Denise Renae; [ed.] North County High School, Mineral Area College; [occ.] Housewife, Certified Nurse Assistant, Certified Medication Technician; [oth. writ.] Short story published in honor of Mother's Day for Harlequin Reader Service; [pers.] My writings reflect my feelings for love and life. My family and friend are a great influence.; [a.] Park Hills, MO

BEVACQUA, KATHLEEN
[b.] May 9, 1949, Lynwood, CA; [p.] Imre Z. Takacs and Margaret Takacs; [ed.] B.A., Theatre Arts, California State University, Long Beach; emphasis, performance; currently a student in the Master of Professional Writing Program at the University of Southern California; [occ.] Director, Administrative Services, University of Southern California, School of Theatre, Los Angeles, CA; [oth. writ.] I have only recently started submitting my writing for publication and am excited and encouraged by this opportunity for publication.; [pers.] I write to expand and express a knowledge of myself and my relationship to the world around me; my intent is for clarity, understanding and improved interrelationship with all living things and the planet earth; to achieve an interconnectedness between inner and outer reality.; [a.] West Hollywood, CA

BEVIS, DESIREE
[b.] July 9, 1972, Denver, CO; [p.] Rob Richardson, LaNell Dancer; [m.] John Bevis III, March 23, 1991; [ch.] Kayla LaRee, Joshua Connor; [ed.] Platte Valley Academy; [occ.] Housewife and mother Englewood, CO; [hon.] Deans List, Honor Roll; [oth. writ.] 27 poems in my personal collection and two were printed in our school paper.; [pers.] My poems express my personal feelings throughout my life. I was influenced most by Emily Dickenson and Edgar Allen Poe and William Shakespeare.; [a.] Englewood, CO

BIAVASCHI, EMY
[b.] January 8, 1980, Sebastopol, CA; [p.] Skip and Jacquie Biavaschi; [ed.] Twin Hills Middle School;

[occ.] Student of Analy High School; [hon.] Presidenta

BILFIELD, ALISSA
[Pen.] Lissy; [b.] December 24, 1981, Cleveland, Ohio; [occ.] Judi Bilfield Leikin and Dr. Laurence Bilfield; [memb.] National Greenpeace Foundation; National Wildlife Foundation; Lifetime Member in the International Society of Poets; [hon.] School Mediator; highest honors status in Orange Schools, play the oboe; [oth. writ.] Poems published in Cleveland, Plain Dealer; several poems published in school anthology.; [pers.] My poetry is inspired by the surroundings in which I live.

BILLER, LYNETTE
[b.] March 5, 1966, Tiffin, OH; [p.] Eugene and Mary Mizen; [m.] David A. biller, June 30, 1990; [ch.] Brandon Lee; [ed.] Columbian High; [occ.] Bartender, Homemaker; [pers.] The world would be a better place to live if we all would ignore the colors of each others skin.; [a.] Tiffin, OH

BITTINGER, SABRINA
[b.] August 20, 1977, Fairfax, VA; [p.] Anthony Sr., Darlene Bittinger; [ed.] Smith's Station High School; [occ.] Student; [memb.] National Organization for Women, National Honors Society; [hon.] United States Achievement Academy and 2 elementary writing author's awards; [oth. writ.] "If I Had," "The Missing bird," and "Teddy the Wonder Dog;" [pers.] Life can be heavy, love can be bitter, but death is always the enemy. Live life to the fullest, holding no prejudices, and love while you still can, for life is like an untamed stallion fading into the horizon.; [a.] Phenix City, AL

BLACK 3RD, FRANCIS M.
[Pen.] Harry Lightfoot; [b.] January 10, 1910, Kinoaid, KS; [p.] Francis M. Black 2nd and Edna Black; [m.] Where abouts unknown, my wife June 4th 1934; [ch.] none; [ed.] Kansas University, 1931, 3 years; [occ.] retired, 1975; [memb.] Fencing Club Teacher 1929, KU; [hon.] Letters in Tach High School and Kansas University, Light Opera, High school 1926, Track Team Kincaid; [oth. writ.] Poems and stories high school; [pers.] In 1939 Sentenced to die in Electric Chair in Texas. 28 years in prison. Had to fight other convicts to save my own life in prison 1940 and 41. But that is whole story, true story, which I wish to write up in my own way in the near future.; [a.] Kincaid, KS

BLACK, SHANA
[b.] April 17, 1978, Abington, PA; [p.] Robert and Joyce Black; [ed.] Plumstead Christian School, I'm a junior in high school and enjoy playing tennis and softball; [pers.] Always strive for the best, keep pressing on toward the goal you have set before you.; [a.] Langhorne, PA

BLACKMON, FREIDA
[b.] June 8, Ipls., IN; [p.] Fred and Aline Marshall; [m.] Arthur L. Blackmon Jr., June 1, 1991; [ch.] Ronald, Damon, Terry; [ed.] Indiana Wesleyan University; [occ.] Entrepreneur; [pers.] To live life as God intended; to love all mankind regardless of race or creed.; [a.] Kokomo, IN

BLANCHARD, CHARLOTTE
[b.] March 3, 1965, Texas; [p.] Mr. and Mrs. W. B.

Maxwell; [m.] Chris Blanchard, July 29, 1988; [ch.] Chase, Destany; [ed.] High School Graduate; [occ.] Correctional Officer; [oth. writ.] Poems published in local newspapers.; [pers.] Inspired by my wonderful and loving husband, Chris. A special "Thanks" to my loving father Dub Maxwell, Favorite country singer and influence Reba McEntire.; [a.] Lake Jackson, TX

BLANKENBAKER, DIANNA L.
[b.] January 4, 1955, Bedford, IN; [p.] Bruce and Betty Blankenbaker; [m.] Divorced; [ch.] Rachelle Joy Clark, Randall Joseph Clark; [ed.] Paoli High School, Ind. Law Enforcement Academy, Ind. Certified E.M.T.; [occ.] Building products employee, Gold Bond, Shoals Inn; [memb.] American Heart Association, Eagles Lodge, American Legion, United Paper Workers #354; [oth. writ.] poems, songs, short stories.; [pers.] I have written for years but this was my first attempt at having it published.; [a.] Washington, IN

BLAZEKOVIC, SONJA
[b.] December 9, 1983, Belgrade, Yugoslavia; [p.] Agnes Hilja and Ivan Blazekovic; [ed.] Charles Olbon School (Grade School); [occ.] Student; [hon.] An award for participation in National History Day, First Honors, and Presidential Academic Fitness Award; [pers.] My poem was about a war that happened in Kosovo, Yugoslavia. The lily sat through the whole war. Many serbians died in this war. It's said the blood of the dead serbians seeped into the roots of the lily and the lily turned red. the turkish fought with ease and the serbians fought hard. My country is still in a very troubled situation.; [a.] West Paterson, NJ

BLEVINS, RICHARD J.
[b.] April 23, 1972, Houston; [p.] Robin Elaine Wigner; [ed.] Achieved a G.E.D and currently attending a philosophy course at a Junior College.; [occ.] Student; [oth. writ.] I have wrote several poems that I hope to one day compile into a book of my own.; [pers.] Strive to be the best. Anything less is boring.; [a.] Baytown, TX

BLOOMFIELD, HEATHER
[b.] April 25, 1973, Toledo; [p.] Michelle Moss; [ed.] Erie Mason Senior High, Monroe County Community College; [occ.] Secretary; [oth. writ.] I have written many short stories and poems but I have never submitted them for publication.; [pers.] I write about things and/or people that mean alot to me. That way I have no problem putting my heart in my work.; [a.] Toledo, OH

BLOUNT, ANGELA
[Pen.] Angie P. Blount; [b.] January 24, 1962, Atlanta, GA; [p.] Patricia Ann; [m.] Phillip L. Blount, December 4, 1992; [ch.] jessica Mallory, Ashley, and Angela; [ed.] High School Graduate; [occ.] Homemaker; [pers.] Everything I write comes from within. Each line I write, I feel in my heart.; [a.] Lawrenceville, GA

BLOW, RACHEL
[Pen.] Samantha Grant; [b.] May 14, 1977, State College, Pennsylvania; [p.] Ed and J-Ann Blow; [ed.] Senior in Colchester High School; [occ.] Student; [memb.] National Honor Society, Colchester Varsity Girls Softball, Intergenerational Planning Committee; [hon.] Second Place for 10th graders in UVM writing contest; Presidential Academic award; [oth.

writ.] A number of poems yet unpublished.; [pers.] Only through poetry and other writings may people's inter feelings truly be expressed.; [a.] Colchester, VT

BOCK, III., ALMON C.
[b.] July 11, 1945, Norfolk, VA; [p.] Almon and Delia Bock; m Elaine bock, March 9, 1979; [ch.] Dawn Slimmer, Margaret Bock; [ed.] Mayville H.S., B.A. Concordia College, Moorhead, MN; M.A. U. of St. Thomas St. Paul, MN; [occ.] Data Analyst, MN Assoc. of Homes for the Aging; [memb.] Mpls. Inst. of Art, MN Zoo; ASCAP; Am Guild of English Handbell Ringers; [hon.] Dean's List in College; List sophomore ever to direct all college musical (My Fair Lady); college scholarships currently chair of Plymouth City Financial Advisory Committee.; [oth. writ.] Several published musical compositions; [pers.] Poems near, among other ways, by careful crafting of language using five beloved forms and formats, poets should seize on this and elevate the language.; [a.] Plymouth, MN

BOCOOK, SHERRY LYNN
[Pen.] Jacklyn Marie; [b.] September 1, 1977, Roanoke, VA; [p.] Jackie Bocook; [ed.] Upcoming graduate of James River High in Botetourt County; [occ.] Writing essays and poems for magazines and newspapers; [memb.] Kawanis Club (local and national), FFA, International Society of Poetry; [hon.] Athletic award for track & field 94', Tech Prep area Consortium award, Editor's choice award for poetry, reflections award for poetry, Science award in Agriculture and Earth Science; [oth. writ.] Poem published in an anthology entitled Tears of Fire; [pers.] when life gets you down just stop, take a deep breath and remember everyone you love. I owe my success to myself, my family, and to a very special friend.; [a.] Buchanan, VA

BOESCH, KELLY JO
[b.] November 23, 1978, New Ulm, MN; [p.] Gary and Karen Boesch; [ed.] Up to tenth grade.; [memb.] City Band (trumpet), World Wildlife Fund (WWF); [pers.] There are the ones who are committed and the ones that don't have to be.. but are simply locked in.; [a.] New Ulm, MN

BOESHORE, MICHELLE
[b.] September 3, 1977; [p.] Robert and Lillian / Boeshore; [ed.] I am a high school student.; [occ.] Student; [memb.] Athletes helping Athletes, Student Service Center.; [hon.] Community Service Award (3 years), American Legions Award; [oth. writ.] Several poems published in school and local community newspapers.; [pers.] I am a young author who hopes to improve, expand, and reach new heights with my writing with out losing my sincerity and honesty. I find poetry a way of expressing feelings from life's experience and am deeply touched by Robert Frosts' work; [a.] Roslyn Hts., NY

BOES-BUTCHER, JANET JOHN
[Pen.] Sylvia Warfield; [b.] September 19, 1939, Tipton, IN; [p.] ruth Grtus Wiles and Dwight D. Lynas; [m.] Lynn E. Butcher, June 28, 1958 (deceased); Jack A. Boes July 22, 1994; [ch.] Dana L. Randle, Linda A. Green, Lynn (Eddie) Butcher, Jr.; [ed.] Associate Degree RN; presently attending Indiana Wesleyan University for BSN; [occ.] Charge Nurse in Extended Care at a hospital teach a certified nurse aid course and in services; [memb.] Eastern Star

Officer, Chief Medical Officer of the Legend (Star Trek fan club); [oth. writ.] unpublished children's stories and more poems; [pers.] Live and let live-practice compassion as the Lord does.

BOLENBAUGH, LAURA
[Pen.] Lady L.; [b.] December 23, 1960, Ft. Wayne, Ind; [p.] Kathleen Singh; [m.] Steven Bolenbaugh, May 22, 1981; [ch.] no children; one dog, Anastasia Jovana and one cat Random Knight; [occ.] Pet and Garden Specialist at Meijer Illinois, Ft. Wayne; [oth. writ.] Personal and Private, 50 unpublished, most emotional poem for me "Play All Day my Beautiful Dezaray" which I wrote in her memory.; [pers.] be gentle and show love, kindness and compassion to all forms of life.; [a.] Fort Wayne, IN

BOLING, JEANETTE MAXWELL
[Pen.] Jean Wells; [b.] February 7, 1942, Atoka, Oklahoma; [p.] Scott and Hazel Boling; [m.] Deceased, was the late Rev. Linton Maxwell, October 18, 1963; [ch.] Lynette Barnes and Avery Maxwell; [ed.] Attended and Graduated from De Anza High School in El Sob. Calif. Attended Contra Costa College in San Pablo, CA and Diablo Valley College in Pleasant Hill, Calif. Also extension courses through Univ. of Calif. Also extension courses through Univ. of Calif. Davis, Calif.; [occ.] Eligibility Worker Specialist with Contra Costa County Social Services.; [memb.] Valley Bible Church, National Eligibility Workers Assoc., (N.E.W.); [hon.] Youth Work Awards, President Contra Costa Chapter, N.E.W., Past Secty., V.P. of N.E.W.; [oth. writ.] Poems published in the West County Times (local newspaper). Articles written for the Contra Costa Chapter of the National Elig. Workers Assoc., Christmas poem in Church Bulletins; [pers.] My inspiration to start writing came while attending a pastors wives retreat. I wrote this poem while living in Arkansas for a short time. Having lived in California most of my life, I was in awe of the different weather patterns and seasons; [a.] Pinole, CA

BOLOGNA, SHAWN PATRICK
[Pen.] Patrick Sean Farlon; [b.] February 28, 1969, San Pedro, CA; [p.] Nunzio and JoAnn Bologna; [ed.] Mary Star High, CA State Univ. Long Beach, B.A. in Theatre Arts; [occ.] Waiter; [oth. writ.] Many other poems, 2 plays. This poem is my first publication.; [pers.] Society is in a state of flux. It is a great time for poets to live yet nothing you nor I can do will stop the wave of ignorance that will blow and has blown since the beginning of time.; [a.] San Pedro, CA

BONANO, HENRY
[Pen.] Poet; [b.] January 25, 1968, Bronx, NY; [p.] Judith Bonano; [ed.] H.S. Graduate, Major: Literature Personal Study and Quest of Great Poetry by the early romantics and later dreamers.; [occ.] Recreation/Activities Assistant Coordinator; [hon.] The tears and smiles of friends and strangers who've read my works.; [pers.] Hold my hand, follow my gaze into your soul and I will show you that magic exists.; [a.] Bronx, NY

BONHAM, VIRGINIA
[b.] April 3, 1945, W.VA; [p.] Virgil Bonham and Elizabeth Moore; [m.] Divorced; [ch.] Six adult; Rose, Brenda, Lisa, Tammy, Terry and Libby and four grandchildren; [ed.] Kayford Elementary W.VA,

Leewood Jr. High, Leewood, W.VA, East Bank Sr. High, East Bank W.VA; [occ.] Manager of Animal Welfare Society of Ho. Co. MD; [pers.] I wish to thank my Father of whom died when I was only 14 year's old. He was forever telling me how very special I was. And my mother of whom still makes me feel like a million. I wish to thank, especially six very exceptional loving daughters; [a.] Harmans, MD

BONNER, KIM
[b.] June 1, 1969, Ada, OK; [p.] Don and Wanda Northcutt; [m.] Divorced; [ed.] Ada High School, now attending East Central University, Ada, OK; [occ.] Full-time student; [memb.] Ann Arbor Assoc., American Diabetes Assoc., American Heart Assoc.; [oth. writ.] Several poems that have never been published.; [pers.] I personally believe that what goes around comes around and that if you be true to yourself everything will always turn out just fine.; [a.] Ada, OK

BORCHER, BETTY
[b.] August 15, 1929, Sprindale, AK; [p.] Josephine and Otto Nelson; [m.] John K. Borcher, August 23, 1946; [ch.] Steven and Shelley Borcher; [ed.] Alhambra High School, 1946; [occ.] Interior Designer, retired; [memb.] P.E.O., Order of Eastern Star; [oth. writ.] Poems and thoughts are music to the soul.; [a.] Tehachapi, CA

BORGHETTY, HECTOR CHARLES
[b.] November 28, 1906, Wellington, New Zealand; [p.] Dr. Emilio and Theresa (Chinazzi, Master of Science, Royal Industrial Institute of Biella, Italy, 1926; [m.] Doris Myott, May 3, 1938; [occ.] Research American textile plant; Textile Chemical Division, General Dyestuff Corp., NYC, NY, Member American Assn. of Textile Chemist and Colorist, American Chemical Society. Mason; [oth. writ.] Contributed numerous articles; New Book, "A Call to the American People; [pers.] Holder of U.S. patents. Independent, Episcopalian; [a.] Bronxville, NY

BORNMAN, MARY LOU
[b.] September 30, 1951, New York; [p.] Mary and Arthur Kearney; [m.] William Bornmann, October 27, 1979; [ch.] Arthur Caines; [ed.] Floral Park Memorial High School; [occ.] Soldier/Public Affairs Supervisor; [memb.] Assoc. United States Army, American Legion, Assoc. for the Help of Retarded Children; [hon.] Two Meritorious Service Medals, Three Army Commendation Medals; Two Army achievement Medals; 1992 2nd prize Keith L. Ware Award; [oth. writ.] News Articles published in "The Liberty Torch," "The Voice," "Harbor Watch" (all military newspapers); [a.] Floral Park, NY

BOUFFARD, AMY ELIZABETH
[b.] Age 10; [ed.] 5th grade at Willard Middle School in Stanford; [oth. writ.] Has written short stories and articles for school newsletters and short books which her class publishes for school library. Loves to write poems, read books, loves music and dancing and takes piano lessons. Has written other poems for pleasure and has written poems for family members on special occasions. Amy is keeping a journal of her poems hoping to enter more contests and maybe have her own poem book published some day.; [a.] Sanford, ME

BOULAY, MICHAEL
[Pen.] Paco Stylro; [b.] March 16, 1967, Worcester, MA; [p.] Edward and Janice Boulay; [m.] Love: Dina-Lee Arseneault; [ch.] Brianna Catherine Boulay, D.O.B. January 30, 1993; [ed.] H.S. Wachusett Regional High School. University of Mass. at Amherst; [occ.] Mental Health Counselor; [hon.] American Legion Award for Scholarship, Science Foundation Award for Scholarship; [oth. writ.] Moonshine in Springtime, The Counsellor, My Path of Life; [pers.] Let us see. Let us smell. Let us die. Just let us.; [a.] Barre, MA

BOUTREN, GEORGE P.
[b.] March 17, 1926, Sheboygan, WI; [p.] Peter and Freda Boutren; [ed.] M.A., Secondary Education, CA State Univ., LA, B.A., Psychology/Sociology, Roosevelt University, Chicago; [occ.] Retired Social Studies Teacher; [memb.] Sierra Club, Andromeda Astronomy Club; [oth. writ.] Sit Down! Shut Up!; Teachercraft and its Psychology; Winter in the Desert; Desert Winter Winds; Oh, Mighty Mountain; [pers.] In my poetry I try to reflect my attitude toward nature and humankind.; [a.] Yucca Valley, CA

BOWEN, ROBIN JEAN
[Pen.] Bobbi-Jean; [b.] September 11, 1962, Newport, VT; [p.] Maria Brochu, Roger Buck; [m.] Michael Bowen, June 11, 1994; [ch.] On Their Way!; [ed.] Three years college for Nursing, 10 yrs. private study astrology, tarot, metaphysics; [occ.] Dental Office Manager; [memb.] Healing Circles, two Bowling Leagues; [oth. writ.] Many poems, most with a metaphysical slant. A couple of short stories, Alfred Hitchcock Style. This is my first time published.; [pers.] How full life becomes when seen through the eyes of love.

BOWEN, ROSE G.
[b.] April 9, 1916, Durham, NC; [p.] Sam and Willie Catherine Garrard; [m.] Deceased January 22, 1984, Freewill Baptist Minister, Writer, May 6, 1934; [ch.] Jeff Bowen; [ed.] Graduate Campbell College Business Department, Music, Private Voice and Sang on W.P.T.F. Raleigh, NC 1929, 1932; [occ.] Retired Minister's Widow; [memb.] Eastern Star, Nashville, TN; [hon.] Woman of the Year 1964 in Religion; [oth. writ.] Contributing writer to Free Will Baptist Church Paper, Writer of Devotion, Woman's Book of Programs for Years, Planned Recording Secretary's Book, Writer of North Carolina Woman's Manuals and National Manuals; [pers.] I am a Christian first! Then I believe in helping others to the extent that I have spent all I have and am suffering now due to the fact when I needed help, so called friends forsook me but I am depending on Christ!; [a.] Ayden, NC

BOWER, JAMES M.E.
[Pen.] Jacques deVere Dufour; [b.] December 23, 1931, Big Rapids, Mich.; [p.] Maynard E. Bower and Mary A.; [m.] Ann Marie Bower, June 19, 1966; [ch.] Jane Marie "Bower" Henry, Robert J., Greg K. Bower; [ed.] Eastern High School, Lansing Community College, Michigan State University, U.S.A.F. Air University; [occ.] Retired Art Director, Buick Olds Cadillac, GM Corp; [memb.] Retired, Lt. Col., Civil Air Patrol, USAF-X, 30 yrs Service, Air Force Assoc. (AFA), United We Stand America, American Legion, NRA, AARP, BPO Elks, USA 548, Moose Lodge #1939; [hon.] Outstanding Information Officer 1961, 62, 63, 65, 73, 74, 81, Top Recruiter,

numerous Military Awards and Certificates, Outstanding Service Award in Computer Graphics from L.C.C.; Class Leader in Dale Carnegie Trophy for Outstanding Service to Cancer Society Service Award, GM Lansing, Salaried Retirees Club; [oth. writ.] Poems, song, short stories, letters published in local papers, creative writing for clubs and organizations.; [pers.] The greatest gift is the gift of giving of ones self and talents for the enrichment of those who touch our lives. My writings reflect both the despair and the hope of mankind.; [a.] Sheridan, MI

BOWMAN, KELLY L.
[Pen.] Bowie; [b.] November 28, 1975, Mass; [p.] Jean Bowman and Joseph Gauthier; [ed.] Senior at Belmont High School, Belmont New Hamp.; [occ.] Cashier; [memb.] Track and Field, Dead Poets Society; [pers.] This poem is dedicated to my older sister Ruby. Ruby you know where ever you are you don't have to ask to come home. We love you, we miss and we really want you to come home.; [a.] Belmont, NH

BOWMAN, SANDRA M.
[b.] November 15, 1937, Nampa, Idaho; [p.] John M. and Vera V. Stevenson; [m.] Max E. bowman, September 7, 1958; [ch.] Timothy Tod Kimokeo, Trina Takeko Kahakulani; [ed.] Boise State University, Graduate Classes, Legal Assistant Program, University of Hawaii School of Law; [occ.] Medically, Retired Legal Assistant; [memb.] Lani-Kailua Outdoor Circle, Manoa Valley Theatre, Past President, Hawaii Association of Legal Assistants.; [oth. writ.] Several case studies and speeches published in "Ka Leo O Hala," a professional journal; poetry published in local newspapers.; [pers.] As a legal assistant, writing was one of the most enjoyable aspects of the work. due to a number of recent physical challenges, I have discovered writing is also a therapeutic, creative outlet in which to express a variety of personal feelings with a focus on maintaining an optimistic, positive and panglossia outlook on life.; [a.] Kailua, HI

BOWMAN, TERRI A. PENN
[b.] November 10, 1956, Greenfield, OH; [p.] Drexel (Fuz) and Georgia Penn; [m.] Mark E. Bowman, February 26, 1981; [ch.] Mark E. Bowman II; [ed.] 13 yrs., 12 yrs. Air Force Reserve, X-Ray Tech.; [occ.] Deliver newspapers and work the Humboldt Store; [oth. writ.] none published; [pers.] I believe you must never give up-each day brings a new start and you need to make the most of it.; [a.] Bainbridge, OH

BOYCE, ROBERT
[Pen.] James Sylvester Monroe; [b.] May 11, 1922, Middletown, NY; [p.] William Ware and Abigail boyce, NY; [ed.] H.S. Barringer H.S. (Neward, NJ) College, Upsala College, East Orange, NJ, Rutgers University, Montclair State (graduate Study); [occ.] Retired teacher of english (40 years); [memb.] Paramus High School, NJ, NCTE, National Honor Society.; [hon.] College Valedictorian June 1949 (Upsala College), Tau Beta Sigma A Lumnae Scholarship Award, Jr. Yr. Upsala College; [hon.] Gold medal for Journalism (Junior College); [oth. writ.] I have written several poems but none have been published. I am writing a book on the alphabet, yearbook advisor for 40 years.; [pers.] I have had over 4,000 students, my 2 pest are professors at Harvard; I feel I have influenced Students to do their best in every thing I

enjoy people! I enjoy reading and writing!; [a.] Newfane, VT

BOYER, MELANIE
[b.] August 26, 1954, Columbus, Ohio; [p.] bob and Jane Cramer; [m.] Rick Bowyer, July 19, 1973; [ch.] Rick II, Michelle and Heidi; [ed.] Franklin Heights High School; [occ.] Domestic Engineer; [hon.] Salutatorian of Graduating Class of 1972; [pers.] I wrote my poem "A Son Is Born" in honor of my son Rick II who graduated from high school in June 1994.; [a.] Grove City, OH

BOYKIN, RENEE
[Pen.] Elven Lord; [b.] June 20, 1979, Stuart, FL; [p.] Jane Dudleg and Ron Boylein; [pers.] As long as you care, you'll always mean something to someone; [a.] Port Saint Lucie, FL

BRADEN, MARY KATHRYN
[Pen.] Kay Braden; [b.] September 30, 1982, Long Beach, CA; [p.] Verlon Patrick Braden and Cheryl marie Braden; [ed.] Rolling Hills School, Fullerton, CA; [occ.] Student; [memb.] International Order of Job's Daughters, Bethel #5, Anaheim, Calif., Company of Young Artists, Fullerton, CA., Girl Scouts of America, Troop #750, Yorba Linda, CA., other activities: band and horseback riding.; [a.] Placentia, CA

BRADLEY S.S.J., SISTER BARBARA
[Pen.] Religious sister of St. Joseph of Chestnut Hill, Philadelphia; [b.] March 9, 1937, Philadelphia; [ed.] Bachelor's Degree in English; Master's Degree in Secondary Education; College Instructor: Community College of Philadelphia (past); College Instructor at Temple University School of Education (1993-94); [occ.] Administrative Assistant at Bishop McGuinness High School in Winston-Salem; [memb.] International Reading Association; Keystone State Reading Association; [hon.] Tearcher Fellowship Award, Dow Jones Newspaper Fund for Journalism Studies, 1987; 1990 Recipient of the Valley Forge Freedoms Foundation Award to Study California Missions; [oth. writ.] Occasional Poet; [pers.] For me, to write is to examine life in a laboratory of words. the results are often astounding, especially when they can be shared.; [a.] Winston-Salem, NC

BRADY, CLARE
[Pen.] Broken Arrow; [b.] November 29, 1949; [p.] Helen Alsop and Harry Brawy; [m.] Ry E. Kimica, May 12, 1978; [ch.] Roenn, Erik Kimien, Gregory (deceased); [ed.] My whole life; [occ.] Waiter, Poet, Mom; [memb.] To Life, N.L.O.P; [hon.] My children, it is in their honor I write.; [oth. writ.] Published River of Dreams; The Day Comes Not; It's Just Not The Same; Wonder; In Doubt; Looking Back; [pers.] In loving memory of my first born "Gregory Ronald." Above all else love each other as I have loved you.; [a.] Toledo, OH

BRADY, LINDA S.
[b.] January 30, 1951, Winston-Salem, NC; [p.] Mr. and Mrs. Joseph Simpson; [ch.] Marshall Leonard Brady, Kenneth Lamont Brady; [ed.] Atkins Senior High, Davidson County Community College; [occ.] System Support Specialist II, R.J. Reynolds Tobacco; [memb.] Macedonia Holiness Church of the Apostolic Faith.; [pers.] My writing inspiration comes from God to show the world he's the overcomer for

all things.; [a.] Winston-Salem, NC

BRAGG, LEONNE
[Pen.] Laei; [b.] January 8, 1971, Washington, D.C.; [pers.] This is my first publication. You may be able to tell by this poem, but I have been a great fan of gothic tales and horror/suspense novels. I Love Fear!

BRAIDA, DOLLY
[Pen.] Dolly; [b.] April 17, 1937, S.F., LA; [m.] Arthur Braida, August 25, 1962; [ch.] 2 sons, Joe and Eric; [ed.] High School Grad.; [occ.] Homemaker and Poet; [memb.] International Poetry Soc.; [oth. writ.] A collection of poems called "From Sad Beginning to Happy endings" Reflections by Dolly is coming out late September or early October 1994.; [pers.] Wife, mother and grandmother, became a poet two years ago. Hope to do good with my poetry, being God gave me this talent at this time of my life.; [a.] S.F., CA

BRANCH, GARVIN M.
[b.] April 10, 1965, Louisville, KY; [p.] Eleanor L. and George F. Branch, Jr.; [ed.] T.C. Williams High School, James Madison University; [occ.] Powdered Chemicals Manager Mediatech Inc.; [hon.] B.S. Chemistry; [pers.] Life is my greatest teacher. The older I get the more respect I give it.; [a.] Reston, VA

BRAZIE, CRYSTAL
[b.] March 3, 1994; [p.] Thelma and James Brazie; [ed.] Just completed 7th grade; [pers.] I enjoy reading and writing.; [a.] Portsmouth, NH

BREMOND, CAROLANDA
[b.] April 3, 1979, Houston, TX [p.] Jon and Lucy Bremond; [ed.] I am currently attending Dulles High School where I am a sophomore.; [occ.] I plan to become a lawyer; [memb.] Dulles High school, Speech and Debate Team, Girl Scouts; [pers.] I thank the Lord for being my strength to lean on. When I stand alone, I am vulnerable; but with Him beside me, all things are possible.; [a.] Houston, TX

BRENNAN, AMY
[b.] July 21, 1980, Florida; [p.] George and Carlene Brennan; [ed.] St. Vincent Ferrer School, going to Atlantic High School; [occ.] Actress, director, technician and make-up artist at Little Palm theater.; [memb.] I belong to Little Palm Theater, The International Society of Poets; [hon.] Poetry, Journalism, and drama awards at school; [oth. writ.] Kilidiscope World, My voice and Strength; [pers.] "Love through Friendship is the key to salvation, hate through war is the path to death.; [a.] Boynton Beach, FL

BRENNAN, M.D., JOSEPH GEORGE
[b.] August 16, 1928, Malta; [p.] William Richard and Leoniede M. Brennan; [m.] Elizabeth Ann Brennan, December 1, 1956; [ch.] Helen E., Winifred A., Joseph G., Leoniede M.; [ed.] B.Sc University of Malta, M.D. Bologna University 1947, Ms.Sc. Mayo School of Graduate Medicine 1953; [occ.] Deceased June 23, 1991; [oth. writ.] Hundred of Sonnets and Poems written over a period of 35 years.; [pers.] My husband spoke 12 languages. He saw his daily world as wonderful material for his poetry.; [a.] Bloomington, MN

BRENNAN, MICHAEL THOMAS
[Pen.] MoJave Mike/Pendragon; [b.] November 28,

1949, Houston, TX; [m.] Single; [occ.] Stationary Engineer; [memb.] Occasionally work with the Boy Scouts as a Merit Badge Counselor; [hon.] Hon. Mention, Oils, U.S. State Dept. 1st Place Oil Painting, Bolling AFB, Wash. D.C. Pub. "Eyes", poem Nat'l Library of Poetry 1994 in Tears of Fire Coll.; Have sold numerous oil landscapes and pen/ink drawings.; [oth. writ.] The Possum; Of Fins Fur and Feathers; The Legend of Pendragon; Dr. K. and the Vacuum Machine; the Return of Dr. K; [pers.] I write for the sheer pleasure of writing, as an expression of things I've experienced. Other activities: camping, canoeing, equitation, Astronomy, oil painting, drawing, classical music, model ship building, reading.; [a.] Pearland, TX

BREWER, CYNTHIA RAMSEIER
[b.] September 4, 1958, St. Joseph, MO; [p.] Frank Rolland Ramseier and Shirley Ann Parker; [m.] Divorced; [ch.] Ricky Dayne 7/17/76 and Jaide Nichole 1/25/81; [ed.] Graduate of Lafayette High School "Class of 76" St. Joseph, MO; [oth. writ.] I have several poems, inspired by my life experiences through out the past 18 years. My first, and favorite is about the birth of my son.; [pers.] We can think negative...Always focused on what we do not have, therefore never achieving true happiness or satisfaction; Or we can think positive and learn to appreciate what we have and enjoy it!; [a.] St. Joseph, MO

BREWER, WILMA HOLLAR
[b.] April 3, 1940, Cynthiana, Kentucky; [p.] William A. and Ruby M. (Ingles) Hollar; [m.] Joseph M. Brewer; [ch.] Christopher, Tammy, Kathy (three great kids); [ed.] Reding High School graduate, Russell Lee Vocational, Children's Institute of Writing; [occ.] Receptionist, Doctors Office; [memb.] Community Church; [oth. writ.] I have written other poems, songs and card verses.; [pers.] I Love the Lord. He is my savior and best friend, I enjoy my grandchildren, they are precious to me. I care deeply about people I visit nursing homes! Do what I can for anyone and I feel writing is my greatest passion.; [a.] Hamilton, OH

BREWSTER, ROBERT
[b.] December 7, 1918, Salonica, Greece; [p.] J. riggs and Ethel Bush Brewster; [m.] Joan Hammond Brewster, September 12, 1992 (second marriage); [ch.] Philip brewster, Douglas Brewster, Gregory Brewster; [ed.] Deutsche Schule Greece, Oakwood School, Poughkeepsie NY, Preparatory School, Wesleyan University, CT, B.A. 1940, Univ. of Wisconsin, Madison, WI; [occ.] Retired professor of German 1949-1979, tutor of German since 10979; [memb.] Electric Fraternity 0N0 (Local) Wesleyan University, CT 1936-1940; Members of Quakers, 1947 to 1987; Member, Presbyterian Church Ann Arbor 1987 to present; [hon.] Phi Beta Kappa, 1940, Montgomery Bergen Jr. Fellowship to Princeton Graduate School 1940-41 in French; [oth. writ.] Religious poems, about 170 of them (poems about God and mankind). Three religious poems published: Advent, 1982, birth of Jesus, Christmas 1983, published in Quaker Life, Richmond, IN; [pers.] My parents were life-long missionaries to Greece, helping Turkish and American refugees, Christians in danger of massacres in Turkey, 1912 - 1914 and on to 1948. I am deeply committed to religious poetry and life.; [a.] Ann Arbor, MI

BRINK, JOYCE ANN
[b.] June 16, 1931, Alton, IL; [p.] Ernesto and Gladys Mayoral; [m.] Clifford D. Brink, August 21, 1950; [ch.] Three, Ralph, Mary Lou and Bill, plus 7 grandchildren; [ed.] High School Graduate; [occ.] Retired Secretary (40 years active); [memb.] Chaparral Poetry Club; Mothers of AIDS Patients; former member Southwest Manuscripters.; [hon.] Various poetry awards and contests won for both poetry and short stories.; [oth. writ.] Wrote/edited church monthly newsletter for 5 years; wrote/edited monthly newsletter for Mothers of AIDS Patients; edited yearly golf tournament newsletter; published in club poetry books as well as in several anthology of poetry year books. Also published in local and national periodicals.; [pers.] God has blessed me with the gift of writing and an opportunity to reach out in love and compassion to those around me, and it has come back a thousand fold. I enjoy traveling, reading, and many warm friendships. Most of all I enjoy our family get-togethers.; [a.] Indio, CA

BRITTAIN, CHRISSIE
[Pen.] C.C.E.B.; [b.] 1978, Virginia; [p.] Harry and Betty Brittain; [ed.] 3rd year of High School, Columbia High School, NJ; [memb.] Poetry club at Columbia High School; [oth. writ.] Several other poems published in Anthology's; [pers.] I am greatly influenced by human emotion, feelings and thoughts. Never ignored your heart, it has a say, in just about everything.; [a.] Maplewood, NJ

BROAD, JANET I.
[b.] August 3, 1932, England, U.K.; [p.] Elsie and David Robinson; [m.] Donald J. Broad, June 25, 1955; [ch.] Eileen, Jack, Andrew, Matthew and John; [ed.] Commercial College, England, U.K.; [occ.] Manager, Edelweiss Pastries, Inc., Bedford Village, NY; [memb.] American Quilter's Society,; A.A.R.P; Northern Star Quilter's Guild; Nutmeg Quilter's Guild; Doubleday Book Club; [hon.] First Place, three years in a row for special technique art quilts, first place in England in shorthand and transcription; [oth. writ.] Ecology songs for elementary schools; [pers.] I am fascinated by time, you can use and manipulate time but where is this visible dimension?; [a.] North Salem, NY

BRONS, CRAIG
[b.] November 20, 1973, Renton; [p.] Steve and Bonnie; [ed.] 1 yr college at Central Washington University; [occ.] Student/Laborer; [oth. writ.] Short Story for an elementary school. Lots and lots of poetry; [pers.] There is more to life than what is seen by our perceptions; [a.] Renton, WA

BROOKMAN, MARY L.
[b.] May 3, 1946, San Francisco, CA; [p.] Elisa Padilla and Burridge Brookman; [m.] none, divorced; [ch.] Johanna and James; [ed.] St. Vincent's High, San Francisco City College, Santa Rosa Junior College; [occ.] Student; [oth. writ.] Poem published in Young America Sings, 1962, National High School Poetry Press, Los Angeles, CA; [pers.] My family's love is my greatest inspiration.; [a.] Petaluma, CA

BROOKS, CANDY STAR
[b.] March 28, 1958, Ohio; [p.] Emmie Dillon & Jack Jones; [m.] thomas G. Brooks, June 12, 1988; [ch.] Thomas Jr. Tellie Ann, Michael Lee, April Lynn and Anthony Ray; [ed.] Central High; [occ.] Cashier/ ASM HEB Food Store; [pers.] I've lost alot of loved ones in my life. My poem's are my way of being close to those I love so much.; [a.] Kempner, TX

BROOKS, CINDY
[b.] May 29, 1958; [m.] Married, with one child; [ed.] Marketing/Management; [occ.] Sales Manager for a Mail Order Food Company; [pers.] Much of my writing reflects on life's continual challenges, major milestones, and unique revelations, and reaffirms the unfaltering irony that each of us is extremely significant, yet so insignificant, in the ongoing pattern of life.; [a.] Marshall, MN

BROOKS, LAURA LEE K.
[Pen.] Laura Brooks; [b.] September 16, 1924, Stanly County, NC; [p.] Audie and Hettie Boone Kennedy (deceased); [m.] Vance Drye Brooks (deceased), March 29, 1941; [ch.] Marvin Alexander Brooks; Barbara Ann Brooks Hinson and Janette Brooks Barbee; [ed.] Completed 10th grade, Oakboro High School, Oakboro, NC; [occ.] Domestic Engineer, Retired.

BROWN, ANNIE LOU
[b.] October 14, 1925, Brunswick County; [p.] Colonel and Cora Corbet; [m.] James Edward Brown, December 22, 1946; [ch.] Curtis, Marzella, Beverly, Julius, Veronica, Alcora, Oliver, Jerry, Eric, Gene and Rita; [ed.] Armour High School, Apex Beauty College; [occ.] Retired Teacher's Assistant; [memb.] Love Faithfully Non-Denominational Church; [hon.] Honored for 21 years of educational services to the Brunswick County Board of Education, writing poetry for church and community organizations. Award for patience, love and concern for others.; [oth. writ.] Other poetry; [pers.] My talent to write poetry is a gift of God. Therefore, my poems are words of knowledge and wisdom from God for other persons.; [a.] Lelaand, NC

BROWN, CANDELARIA H.
[b.] February 2, 1957, Panama, Central America; [m.] Larry Brown; [ch.] Marck and Anthony; [ed.] B.S. Management (University of Maryland) MS Education Troy Stte University; [memb.] Kappa Delta Pi International Society on Education; [oth. writ.] Articles in local newspaper.; [pers.] I like to reflect the conflict between good and evil on my writings..and at least on my writings the good always win. I wish this was the fact in real life.

BROWN, CHASITY
[b.] August 16, 1974, Huntsville, AL; [p.] Marsha H. and Mark Brown; [ed.] Scottsboro High School, Northeast Alabama State Community College; [occ.] College Student; [hon.] Phi Theta Kappa, Mu Alpha Theta, The National Dean's List; [oth. writ.] None previously published.; [pers.] This poem was written in memory of my grandfather, Newsom Higginbotham, who died of cancer on June 20, 1992.; [a.] Scottsboro, AL

BROWN, JAYME MICHELE
[b.] January 9, 1980, Des Moines; [p.] Michele tucker, John Drake; [ed.] Freshman at East Union Jr./ Sr. High School; [occ.] Student; [oth. writ.] I have written several poems for school projects and personal pleasure.; [pers.] I am inspired by my eighth grade creative writing teacher, Lois Rose. This particular poem was written about my 16 year old brother Corey

Brown. Last but not least, I am inspired by human life. The feelings and emotions we discover.; [a.] Lorimar, IA

BROWN, JOHN T.
[b.] March 17, 1916, Phila. PA; [p.] Mary and John; [ed.] 3 yrs. Law School and 3 yrs. Lawyers Office; [occ.] Retired Pari Mutual Clerk, Training Show Horses; Clerk, still buying and selling horses.; [memb.] Animal Protection Societies, S.P.C.A. Humane Society of Phila. PA, Forked River, NJ; [hon.] Many Ribbons and Silver won in Horsemanship in show rings on East Coast, Poets of year 1989, Youth American Poetic Society, Sacramento Calif.; [oth. writ.] Many poems; [pers.] I decry quota awards for jobs, Supreme Court should be abolished. They are appointed not elected.; [a.] Phila, PA

BROWN JR., IRVIN
[Pen.] Jah Irvin, Bongo Early; [b.] October 26, 1948, Holly Springs, Miss.; [p.] Irvin Sr. (deceased) and Velma Jones; [ed.] B.A. Indiana University 71'; M.A. Stanford University 72'; Ph.D. Stanford University 75'; [occ.] College Professor, Central Florida Community College; [memb.] Florida Association of Community Colleges; [hon.] Nominated to Who's Who Among America's Teachers," 94 Nominated for distinguished membership in the International Society of Poets 94'.; [oth. writ.] Fields of Serenity, Rastafar, Poetic Meditations and Visions I & II (recorded on audio cassette and based on three manuscripts. "Fields of Serenity," "Man Has No Place Else to Go," and "Exodus."; [pers.] The pot of gold that is said to be at the end of the rainbow is to be found in the depths of our own unexplored souls. Writing poetry is one mens of opening dialogue with the soul and uncovering its treasures.; [a.] Ocala, FL

BROWN, MICHELLE L.
[Pen.] Lisa Abbigail Adams; [b.] July 27, 1977, Grand Island; [p.] Joyce and Frank Brown; [ed.] Will graduate spring of 1995 from Northwest High School; Grand Island, NE; [occ.] Waitress; [hon.] State Speech and Drama High School Level; [pers.] Radiate your inner silence.; [a.] Alda, NE

BROWN, PEGGY
[Pen.] Peggy Sewell "My birth name"; [b.] May 26, 1951, Easton, MD; [p.] Thomas Sewell and Irene Sewell; [m.] James Brown Sr., Divorced; [ch.] Angelette Brown and James Brown Sr.; [ed.] Queen Anne's County High School in Centersville, MD; [occ.] Nurse Assistant; [oth. writ.] I have wrote poets for Talent and Columbia Record companies. Also for people who wanted some thing special for their love ones. I also do childrens stories.; [pers.] Writing is a big part of my dreams and feeling of sadness and pain that I've gone through. It is my relax time. What I write comes straight from my heart and mind, with the help of God I am a poet.; [a.] Camden-Wyoming, DE

BROWN, TERRI
[b.] August 7, 1980, Hammond, IN; [p.] Carlon Felton, Steve Brown; [ed.] Kahler Middle School; [memb.] International Society of Poets; [hon.] Certificate of Achievement, Citizenship Recognition Award, Honor Roll; [a.] Dyer, IN

BROWNING, JERRY D.
[b.] May 24, 1966, New London, CT; [p.] Althea Koschmieder; [m.] Single; [ed.] Ledyard High School,

Ridgley Lowell School of Business-Computerize Accounting; [occ.] Data Entry Technician; [hon.] Honors at Ridgley and Lowell; [oth. writ.] Published poems in high school literary magazine…self-published book of poetry…"Damnant Quod Non Intelligent"; [pers.] With my poetry I seek understanding. Of myself, for myself…Of Life, from Life…"The owls are not what they seem"; [a.] Gales Ferry, CT

BRUCE, SUZANNE LYNNE
[Pen.] Kadie Marx; [b.] August 5, 1976, Baton Rouge; [p.] Carol and Lynn Bruce; [ed.] Scotlandville Magnet High, Freshman Year; McKinley High Sophomore Year (Gifted), Junior Year, Louisiana School for Math, Science and Arts, Senior McKinley High, Graduate; [occ.] Student, preparing for college; [memb.] Explorers; [hon.] Honor graduate; [oth. writ.] unpublished.; [a.] Baton Rouge, LA

BRUNNER, MARCIA MARIE
[Pen.] Marcy; [b.] February 6, 1937, Columbus, Ohio; [p.] Thomas L. (Deceased) and Anna Hamilton Johnson; [m.] Divorced; [ch.] Clifford, Evelyn (EM), Rocky Steven, Herbert and 5 grandchildren; [ed.] High School Graduate, 4 1/2 yrs. college experience.; [occ.] "Activity Director" for (Rest Homes/Convalescent Homes; [hon.] Certificate for Volunteer Work; [oth. writ.] None; [pers.] I pray that the readers will find the encouragement that I have found. A richer faith, a deeper desire to love and teach their children in the things of God as I was blessed to have done.; [a.] Fuomrovia, CA

BRYANT, ROSA L.
[Pen.] Lolly Bryant, June 4, 1938, Mason, TX; [p.] C.J. and Laura Bogusch; [m.] Divorced; [ch.] Bruce, Tony, and Chris; [ed.] Graduated from Mason High School; [occ.] Retired Court Reporter; [oth. writ.] One poem published in 1993 "Poetic Voices of America." Six poems to be published in Western Poetry Review "Return of the Unicorn."; [pers.] Poetry equals joy through self-expression for me. I write from the heart about the strengths and frailties of human life that affect us all.; [a.] Salinas, CA

BRYANT, VICKI E.
[b.] October 9, 1970, Grand Junction, CO; [p.] Norman and Sybil Bryant; [ed.] Brighton High School, Community College of Aurora; [occ.] book Assembler; [memb.] Phi Theta Kappa, Student Senate of Community College of Aurora, The Writer's Club; [hon.] Student Leadership Award from Community College of Aurora, Partners in Education Award from D.A.R.E. Project at Elkheart Elementary for tutoring.; [oth. writ.] "Virgin" published in "Inscapes", a publication of Community College of Aurora and "Dream Walk" published in "River of Dreams" a publication of The National Library of Poetry.; [pers.] I am a person that loves to watch the world with its realities and miracles and jump right in.; [a.] Commerce City, CO

BRYANT, VIRGINIA MCCARDLE
[Pen.] Do not wish to disclose; [b.] September 22, 1958, Hattiesburg, MS; [p.] Harvey and ellen McCardle; [m.] Gary Michael Bryant, August 4, 1979; [ch.] Michael Christopher, Joshua Matthew; [ed.] b.S. in English and Language, Masters in Eduction, Masters in Language, Working on Masters in Social Work; [occ.] Writer and Mother (Former English Teacher); [memb.] President's List in Col-

lege, member of the Honor Society of Phi Kappa Phi, National Dean's List, Member of Zambda Iota Taug (International Literature Honor Society); [hon.] Star Student in High school, Valedictorian in High School, Graduated Summa cum Laude College, Receipt of 1988 Golden Poet Award.; [oth. writ.] Published under various pen names.; [pers.] I write, mainly, in order to make others aware of the issues of child sexual abuse and the strength and coverage to be a survivor; [a.] Hattiesburg, MS

BRYCE, ERIN R.
[b.] October 2, 1980, Arcadia, FL; [p.] Jeffery and Kathleen Bryce; [ed.] Currently attending Desoto Middle School, 8th grade; [memb.] DMS Band, Honor Society, Pine Level Methodist Church, Future authors of America, Panther Press (School Newspaper); [hon.] I received the Student of the Month Award in November during the 1993-94 school year.; [a.] Arcadia, FL

BUCKLEY, JACKIE
[b.] July 31, 1941, Van Buren, ME; [p.] Yvonne and Leo Pelletier; [ch.] Laurie Ann, Carole Ann, Paul C., Donald J., William Harrison; [ed.] Manchester High School, Manchester, Conn., Concorde Career College, San Bernardino, CA; [occ.] Unemployed; [hon.] I had the honor of raising 13 children and watching them grow. They have honored me with 23 grandchildren, other children, Mike, Jackie, Dodi, Jodi, Bruce, Beth, Frances, Ritchie; [oth. writ.] Several yet, unpublished poems, one short story.; [pers.] Most of my poems were inspired by my family and friends. They generally reflect the trials and tribulations of daily life and how to cope with such.; [a.] Highland, CA

BUMPUS, KELLYE LYNE
[b.] June 17, 1978, Chattanooga, TN; [p.] Connie and PHil Bumpus; [ed.] Wessington Elementary, Knox Doss Middle, Beech Senior High; [occ.] Student at Beech; [memb.] Bounty, Environmental Awareness Club (EAC), Students Staying Straight, Beta Club, Honor Society, Business Professionals of America, Girl Scouts, Long Hollow Baptist Church; [hon.] Vice President of EAC, Tennessee Business Week, Girl Scouts; [oth. writ.] Poems and stories for church youth bulletin.; [pers.] Things aren't always what they seem at first. Search within yourself for the answers.; [a.] Hendersonville, TN

BUNKE, BRET
[b.] August 4, 1970, Hillsboro, OR; [p.] John Bunke and Nancy Bidgood; [m.] Cortney Ireland, January 10, 1994; [ed.] Cascade High, Pacific University, Oregon State University, BA English; [occ.] Appliance Salesman, Future Shop; [memb.] Sigma Pi Fraternity, The Dead Tourists,; [hon.] Internship, Center for National Independence in Politics, International Sports Exchange (China 1985); [oth. writ.] Tyro, Cascade High, Personal Anthology of Essays, Short Stories and Poetry; [pers.] Enjoying a stream of consciousness influenced by Henry Miller, Fyodor Dostoevsky, and William Blake.; [a.] Springfield, OR

BUONADIES, DANA
[b.] September 12, 1979, Bogatoa, NJ; [p.] Linda and Ray Buonaties; [ed.] Just finished elem. and junior high starting high school; [memb.] Bogota Softball Organ., Bogota High School Chorus; [pers.] Dana has taken Dancing lessons since she was 5, loves to cook and loves reading all types of poetry.; [a.]

Bagota, NJ

BURDETTE, DENISE
[b.] October 9, 1970, Dearborn, Michigan; [p.] Dennis and Kathy Royce; [m.] Brian Burdette, July 3, 1992; [ch.] Ashley Nicole; [ed.] Hurricane High School, Oakland Community College, Marshall University; [pers.] The Inspiration in my writing comes from everyday situations that we sometimes take for granted in our lives.

BURG, S.
[b.] July 31, 1961, Arlington Heights, IL; [p.] Mr. and Mrs. James H. Burg Sr.; [ed.] Southern Methodist University 1983 BFA, Studio Art, Cornell University 1985, MFA painting. The School of the Art Institute of Chicago 1988; [occ.] Market Research; [memb.] 1985 College Art Association member; 1981 Alpha Delta Pi Sorority, SMU; 1980 Student Art Association, Vice President, SMU; [hon.] Art Awards, to many to mention; [a.] Austin, TX

BURKE, ANN
[b.] October 9, 1937, Takoma Park, MD; [p.] Lois and Fannie Cunningham; [m.] Ken burke, August 14, 1960; [ch.] Tom, Kay, Sue, Dan; [ed.] B.A. in English from Southern College of Seventh Day Adventists near Chattanooga, TN; [oth. writ.] A book, Light the Lantern, Daughter by Review and Herald Publishing Association, and articles, stories and verse in various periodicals; [pers.] While Emily Dickinson showed me the power of symbolism, subtlety, and simplicity, Luci Shaw opened to me the possibilities of contemporary verse. Themes and people of scripture are for me an inexhaustible well of ideas.; [a.] Yucaipa, CA

BURKHOLTER, BOBBY JEAN
[b.] December 10, 1928, m Bath, SC; [p.] Deceased, Mr. and Mrs. Will Burkholter; [ed.] 1946 Graduate LBCH High School, Bath, SC; 1949 Graduate of SC State Hospital; 1956 SC Medical University 1948-1949; 1957 Palmer's Business College; 1 yr. Augusta Law School 1977-1978; 1981 Post Graduate USC Aiken SC; 1984 Augusta Tech Post Graduate; [occ.] Retired Nurse; [oth. writ.] Songs Copyrighted "Patients," "Augusta", "Crocodile Island"; [a.] Augusta, GA

BURKS, GEORGIA J.
[b.] September 24, 1957, Danville, IL; [p.] James and Jean Rippon; [m.] Billy W. Burks, Jr., March 30, 1990; [ch.] James David; [ed.] Naval Hospital Corps School, Byran Institute; [occ.] Medical Assisting Instructor, ATI Hurst, TX; [memb.] American Heart Assoc., American Medical Technologist; [hon.] Registered Medical Assistant; [oth. writ.] Poems published in ATI Notations Newsletter.; [pers.] I write from my heart, to express how people feel is the goal of my poems.; [a.] Arlington, TX

BURNS, TARA RENE
[b.] April 26, 1979, GIMC; [p.] Patricia and Joseph Burns; [ed.] Currently enrolled in Grenada High School; [memb.] Explorers Group; [hon.] Nominated for Who's Who Among American High School Students; [pers.] My writings come from inside. I try to reflect my inner self with words, a sheet of paper, and a pen. I am forever in debt to our "Lord" and "Savior" for giving me my talent.; [a.] Duckhill, MS

BUSBY, JENNIFER M.
[Pen.] J. Michelle; [b.] March 19, 1978, Terrell, TX; [p.] Beth Bolton and James Busby; [ed.] Still attending high school; hope to join a big university to get the best education.; [occ.] Student at Kaufman High School; [memb.] I coach drill team for little league football teams.; [hon.] English award, honor roll; (for now); [oth. writ.] Several poems kept in a private collection: for now, poem for a book about Jackie Kennedy coming out soon.; [pers.] Keep good thoughts for people and it will make you happy…so "keep a good thought for me!"; [a.] Kaufman, TX

BUTLER, NATALIE ANNE
[b.] August 22, 1974, Nuremburg, Germany; [p.] Martin and Margaret Mordecdi; [ed.] Currently attending third year at the University of Arizona majoring in Astronomy/Physics; [memb.] Phi Eta Sigma National Honor Society, University of Arizona Symphonic Band; [hon.] Dean's List, second Prize at First-Year Composition, Essay Contest (1992-93); [oth. writ.] "The Night Song" published 1990 Exeter "Life's Poetry" unpublished.; [pers.] I only hope that what I have written can help others come closer to understanding life and to enjoying every minute whether with tears or smiles. I have.; [a.] Tuscon, AZ

BYRD, ANDREA L.
[Pen.] Andrea byrd; [b.] August 14, 1978, WV; [p.] Kathy and Charles Byrd; [ed.] I attend Duval High, I'm in the 9th grade; [oth. writ.] Some other poems and short stories.; [pers.] I strive to show my feelings in my poems and to express myself.; [a.] Sod, WV

BYRD, ROXANA
[pers.] This poem is a dedication to my mother, Martha Sloan Lancaster, a unique intuitive special human being and William S. Lancaster Esq. A wonderful father in honor of caring on his name. To my fine son Ryan Clayton Lancaster who I wish to inspire as Mark Twain did me. To my lifelong friend and brother Bernard Neyman Lancaster who I am proud of his continued achievements.

BYTHER, PATRICIA
[b.] August 20, 1954, Hanover, MD; [p.] Elizabeth and William Bouchat; [m.] James Byther, May 28, 1994; [ch.] Michelle Hudson; [ed.] Graduated from Howard High School, Ellicott City, Maryland 1972; [occ.] Volunteer Librarian Assistant; [memb.] American Diabetes Association Member of the Maine State Museum; [pers.] If in my lifetime I am able to spread love, peace, and happiness then I have achieved my goal in life. Only then have I been successful.; [a.] Winslow, ME

CADE, VIOLA
[Pen.] Viola Ludd-Cade; [b.] July 28, 1935, Sumter, SC; [p.] Clinton and Emily Ludd; [m.] thomas R. Cade, April 22, 1972; [ch.] Nancy Emily Ruth; [ed.] Girls High School, Kean College; [occ.] Loan Advisor, City of Elizabeth, NJ; [memb.] International Christian Center, Cade Bible Group, Elizabeth NAACP, ECA Board of Directors; [hon.] Most Outstanding CETA Employee, NAACP Community Service Award, NAACP Hall of Fame Award, DYFS Dedicated Service Award; [oth. writ.] Volunteer Letter/Resume Services for disabled, informed, etc. Newsletters.; [pers.] I am inspired and greatly influenced by biblical principles and philosophies.; [a.] Elizabeth, NJ

CADINU, GIORGIA
[b.] June 8, 1976, Prato, Italy; [p.] Mario Cadinu and Cerna Zdenka; [ed.] American High School, graduated; [occ.] Student; [oth. writ.] not published; [pers.] The love for humanity brought me in the path of discovery where art catches the endless secrets of our race. Hermann Hesse, Nietsche, Annagrazia Russu Shaped my writing and personality.; [a.] Prato-Florence, Italy

CAIN, DOROTHY
[Pen.] Rose Hood; [b.] June 26, 1921, K.C., MO; [p.] George and Ida Burleson (both deceased); [m.] George Cain, May 25, 1945; [ch.] Gloria Hales and Dr. Georgene Dhawan; [ed.] Public schools in Kansas City, MO; One semester, Pasadena Junior College; [occ.] Retired; [memb.] Member First Christian Church of Pensacola, FL, V.F.W., Ladies Auxiliary Post 706; [oth. writ.] none; [pers.] this is first I have ever submitted. I love poetry but am shy and not sure enough to let others read mine. I want to be known. I dream of a happier world and hope to live long enough to see it.; [a.] Pensacola, FL

CAIN, PEGGY
[b.] September 12, 1938, Fairport, KS; [p.] C.T. and L.E. Frasier; [m.] Bill Cain, October 2, 1972; [ch.] Two Children, 6 grandchildren and 3 great grandchildren; [ed.] San Jon High, NM; Tucumcari Area Vocational School; [occ.] Housewife and Rancher: Co-owner/operator; [pers.] My writings are not make believe. I take everyday happenings on our ranch and write it out in the form of poetry. I love life and I enjoy sharing our experiences with others.; [a.] Bard, NM

CALABRESE, JASON
[Pen.] J. Cal; [b.] June 14, 1971, Waterbury, CT; [p.] William Calabrese, Carole Calabrese; [ed.] The University of Connecticut Bachelor of Arts Degree in Behavioral Strategies of Sports and Industry; [occ.] Night Club owner, Naugatuck, CT; [memb.] Connecticut High School Coaches Association, National High School Athletic Coaches Association; [hon.] Dean's List, Citizens Scholarship Foundation of America Sept 1989 - Jan 1993; [pers.] Don't ever let somebody fault you for trying, because they are just jealous that they do not have the fortitude to succeed; [a.] Waterbury, CT

CALDERON, SHEILA LEONITA
[Pen.] Sheila; [b.] January 16, 1980, Morganton, NC; [p.] Nestor and Marsha Colderon; [m.] not yet; [ed.] 9th grade at Freedom High school; [occ.] Gymnast Instructor with City of Morganton; [memb.] Burke County Library, Morganton Recreation Center Gymnastics Team and Skating Group; [hon.] Gymnastics, Skating; [oth. writ.] Poems and writing for local newspapers and Teen magazine.; [a.] Morganton, NC

CALLEN, SHANAE M.
[b.] July 28, 1982, Notrona Heights, PA; [p.] Carl and Lyndis Callen; [ed.] Martin Elementary, New Kensington, PA 6th grade; [memb.] Upper Burrell Shamrocks Baton and Drum Corp., Donna's Dance Studio, Band and Choir at Martin Elementary School; [a.] New Kensington, PA

CAMP, TANYA
[b.] August 8, 1979, Wilks-Barre, PA; [p.] Prudence

and John Abbot; [ed.] Riverside High School, Taylor, PA, 9th grade; [occ.] CMC (Treasurer, Candy Striper), Moosic Borough (employee); [hon.] Made Honor Roll for School, Reflections Program Awards, Swimming (1st, 2nd, 3rd places), running Awards for shooting pool.; [oth. writ.] Mom, Tonight, Remember, The Pain. (not published); [a.] Moosic, PA

CAMPBELL, ESSIE LOUISE
[b.] October 9, 1928, Jeff. Co.; [p.] Deceased; [m.] Single; [ed.] High School; [oth. writ.] Another Poem; [a.] Terra Alta, WVA

CAMPBELL, MANDI MAE
[Pen.] Mandi; [b.] October 16, 1975, Liberal, KS; [p.] Darlene Kay Campbell; [ed.] High School Student Canutillo High School, South Grand Prairie High; [occ.] Student; [oth. writ.] None published, other poems but they are not published.; [a.] Grand Prairie, TX

CANHAM, PRUELLA CROMARTIE NIVER
[b.] December 4, 1924, Statesboro, GA; [p.] Esten Graham Cromartie and Mary Lee Jones Cromartie (both deceased); [m.] David Lee Canham, July 26, 1985; [ch.] Daughter, Peddy Niver Hayhurst Moran, Grandchildren, Matthew William Hayhurst; [ed.] Statesboro H.S., Georgia Southern University in Statesboro, GA, B.S. Degree. Graduate work and workshops in Alabama Polytechnic Institute, Auburn, AL, FSU@ Tallahassee, FL, Univ. of Miami, Coral Gables, FL.; Univer. of Fla., Gainesville Fl.; Univ. of South Florida @ Tampa, FL. & Florida Atlantic Univ. @ Boca Raton, FL; [occ.] Retired Teacher; [memb.] Too many to mention; [hon.] Numerous; [a.] Ft. Myers, FL

CANTERBURY, JONOTHON
[Pen.] July 4, 1980, Fairview, OH; [p.] Carrie Canterbury; [ed.] Greenbriar Junior High School; [memb.] Youth Challenge; Junior Bowling League; [hon.] Honor Roll; Physically Challenged Race Day, First Place; [pers.] I write to make myself feel happy.; [a.] Parma, OH

CANZANO, DARA E.
[b.] July 11, 1982, New Brunswick, NJ; [p.] Charlene and Daniel Canzano; [ed.] Entering Grade 7; [memb.] School Choirs, 6th grade Yearbook Committee; [hon.] Presidential Academic Award; [oth. writ.] Other published poems in magazines, etc.; [pers.] "Behind every good writer, there's a good teacher."; [a.] Highland Park, NJ

CAPO, AUDREY M.
[b.] May 9, 1934, Arnold, PA; [p.] Mary Chernan Hudeck and Andrew Hudeck; [m.] Francis A. Capo, January 8, 1955; [ch.] David and Kathleen Capo; [ed.] High School Graduate; [occ.] Clerk in husband's printing company.; [memb.] Save The Children; Our Lady's Rosary Makers; The Humane Society; Missionary Oblate of Illinois.

CAPOZZOLI, DANIELLA
[Pen.] Daniella; [b.] April 7, 1977, Wareham, MA; [p.] Bettie and Peter Capozzoli; [ed.] Cohasset High School Junior; [pers.] To live is to love. And my life is full of so much love. Thanks to my family, my friends, my boyfriend Sean, and the Lord. My inspiration for my poetry comes from all their love.; [a.] Cohasset, MA

CARDACI, DINA MARIE
[Pen.] Megan MacKenzie; [b.] January 16, 1982, Newark, NJ; [p.] Sandra D. and Carlo F. Cardaci; [p.] Legal Guardians: Maria and Chris Herr; [ed.] Going into 7th grade in Copeland Middle School, and is a D.A.R.E. graduate; [occ.] Babysitting; [memb.] March of Dimes: Save the Babies; School Store Committee; Summer Reading Club; [hon.] Citizenship 1993, Reading Olympics 1992, Merit Honor Roll; [oth. writ.] Life's too Short; [pers.] I would like to express my love and gratitude for those who have kept me going and who have believed in my writings throughout the years.; [a.] Rockaway, NJ

CARDONA, GRACE J.
[b.] August 23, 1950, Bronx, NY; [p.] Thomas and Polly Pagliarella; [m.] Ruben Cardona, May 9, 1970; [ch.] Victoria Lynn Cardona, Thomas Robert Cardona; [ed.] Part Time Student, Central Florida Community College, Paralegal International Correspondence Schools; [occ.] Homemaker; [a.] Iverness, FL

CARDOZA, CORY D.
[Pen.] Cici; [b.] October 28, 1975, Dos Palos, CA; [p.] david and Renee Cardoza; [ed.] Brawley Union High School, Air Force Technical School; [occ.] United States Air Force; [memb.] Unit Advisory Committee; [hon.] Technical School Honor Student, Numerous Honor Rolls, Honor Student (2 times) for school; [oth. writ.] Poem published in annual, several poems left unnoticed, school newspapers.; [a.] Nellis AFB, NV

CAREY, DORIS E.
[b.] May 1940, Berlin Germany; [p.] A. and T. Radlinger; [m.] Widow of Timothy Carey (Actor) 1958-1994; [ch.] Mother of Six, now adults; [ed.] Germany (Grammar and Profession Schools) total of 10 yrs., the rest was taught by life; [occ.] Assist. Director of State Play, Freelance; [oth. writ.] Have collection of 250 poems in two languages: English and German, some published in books for "Amateurs"; [pers.] Interested in poetry since childhood. Made serious effort in 1991-92, wrote most of my present collection during one year interim. In art, fantasy and imagination are valuable tools, experience and inspiration become the artisans; [a.] El Monte, CA

CARLSON, RENEE
[b.] January 8, 1969, Golden Valley, Minnesota; [p.] Hal and Rose Edward; [m.] Sean R. Carlson, April 14, 1992; [ch.] Gwendolyn Aleigh; [ed.] Diamond High School, University of Alaska, Anchorage; [occ.] Admin. Assistant for an ad agency; [memb.] MSPCC; [pers.] The poem "Don't Cry For Me" was written for my daughter. She passed away 10/25/93 and is my sole inspiration. I love you Gwen.; [a.] Waymouth, MA

CARNEY, TERI J. (COOPER)
[Pen.] Teri J. Cooper-Carney; [b.] January 18, 1955, Seattle, WA; [p.] Mary Smittle & Walter Cooper; [m.] James R. Carney, June 24, 1978; [ch.] James (Jr.), William, Laura, Robert (deceased), Sara, Joseph (deceased), Henry and Mary Jane (deceased); [ed.] Graduated Mountlake Terrace High School, Edmonds Comm College - no degree. Does self study of people, history, literature; [occ.] Homemaker; [hon.] Twice Editor's Choice winner with the Na-

tional Library of Poetry for Dreams of Poetry, and love does conquer all; [pers.] Mom's family, Smittles-Dearstones of Oklahoma influenced and inspired interests in poetry. Two cousins of which have success in country music today. I find poetry writing as much fun as jigsaw puzzles, but with a satisfaction when I've pleased mom and folks with a poem or two; [a.] Graham, WA

CARPENTER, MARIAN
[b.] May 12, 1936, Alabama; [p.] Mr. and Mrs. Troy Wall; [ch.] Two sons, one daughter; [ed.] Tuscaloosa High School, Brewer State Junior College, University of Alabama; [occ.] Retired Medical Technologist; [oth. writ.] Published story in Woman's World 1988. Poetry in local newspaper, National Library of Poetry 1990, selected to submit poetry for best poets of 1990.; [pers.] I believe poetry allows a person to say much, with few words.; [a.] Tuscaloosa, AL

CARPETNER, LISA
[b.] May 29, 1955, Malvern, AR; [p.] Cecil and Wanda Burns; [m.] Wayne Carpenter, May 29, 1981; [ch.] Kristin Nicole, Kacee Renee; [ed.] Malvern High School, Ouachita Vo-Tech; [occ.] Maintenance Specialist Natural Gas Pipeline; [oth. writ.] Several poems not published.; [pers.] I wrote this for my dad Cecil Burns, the kindest and most generous man I have ever or will ever know in my lifetime.; [a.] Malvern, AR

CARR, KATHERINE
[b.] January 7, 1960, Wichita Falls, TX; [p.] Ronald and Shirley Crooker; [m.] Walter J. Carr Jr., February 11, 1984; [ch.] Sarah, Julia, Meredith; [ed.] St. Martin High School, Biloxi, MS; [occ.] Homemaker; [memb.] None; [hon.] Employee of the Year, Marriott Corp., Cherry Hill, NJ; [oth. writ.] Unpublished Poetry; [pers.] In my poetry I attempt to express my philosophy that none of life's luxuries are comparable to the richness of close family ties.; [a.] Clementon, NJ

CARR, KRISTEN LINDSAY
[b.] July 17, 1979, Tarrytown, NY; [p.] Christopher and Kathleen Carr; [occ.] Honor Student at Monroe-Woodbury Senior High School; [memb.] Interact Volunteer Organization, Computer Club, Piano Student; [pers.] I sincerely believe in living each day to its fullest and taking from life as much as it has to offer.; [a.] Highland Mills, NY

CARR, TARA M.
[Pen.] T. Milam Coats; [b.] October 2, 1976, Tarzana, CA; [p.] Jackson and Sandra Carr; [ed.] St. Helena High School Class of 1995; [occ.] Student; [memb.] California Scholarship Federation.; [hon.] Winner of Napa County Spelling Competition; [pers.] This is a real accomplishment for me as a young writer; it is a start for my aspiring career in journalism. My goals are set high, but after this honor, I believe that I will achieve them.; [a.] St. Helena, CA

CARRANO, JOSEPH J.
[Pen.] J.N. Carrano; [b.] May 24, 1929, Chicago, IL; [p.] Thomas and Annie Carrano; [m.] Sandra J. Carrano, February 17, 1984; [ch.] Jeff, Joey, Trim, Ryan, Julie and Mike; [ed.] High school graduate, Tilden H.S. Chicago, Illinois; [occ.] Retired teamster truck driver; [oth. writ.] Many unpublished poems and short stories.; [pers.] I was inspired by great

literature, poets of the past and present, and by my wife Sandy who encouraged my writings.; [a.] Orlando Hills, IL

CARROLL, E. LORRAINE WRIGHT
[Pen.] Lorraine Carroll; [b.] September 11, 1916, Port Huron, MI; [p.] Flossie and Lloyd Bearss; [m.] George E. Carroll, April 11, 1992; [ch.] Bonita Johnston and William Wright; [ed.] High School nd one year of Business College; Calligraphy; Time Study; and Clowning; [occ.] Retired 13 years.; [memb.] St. Clair Co. Council on Aging; Drummer in Senior Citizens Orchestra, St. Joseph's Church Choir Carousel Clowns; Red Cross Clowns; [hon.] Secretary of the Year, National Secretaries Association. Employee of the Year, Southeastern Michigan Gas Company. Volunteer of the Year, St. Clair County Council on Aging.; [oth. writ.] An unpublished song, "That's Our Song.; [pers.] You can't spread joy on others without spilling it all over yourself.; [a.] Kimball (Twp.) Mich.

CARTER, DAVID L.
[b.] February 1, 1961, Athens, TN; [p.] Rev. Donald and Ida Carter; [m.] Cheryl, February 14, 1987; [ed.] Chenango Valley High School, SUNY at Oreonta; [occ.] Self-employed; [pers.] With my writing, I attempt to bring light to the often over looked, little miracles that exist all around us in our lives.; [a.] Winston-Salem, NC

CARTER, JAY S.
[Pen.] Stonefeather; [b.] February 19, 1962, Marshall, MN; [p.] Ron Carter and Miriam Swanson; [ed.] Balaton High School, No college "School of Life." Born gifted, experience has been my greatest teacher; [occ.] Environmental Conversation; [memb.] Performing poetry at coffee houses.; [oth. writ.] Writing lyrics, prose, anecdotes, aphorisms, spiritual truths, interesting observations, from the outside looking in.; [pers.] A man in rage, is a man in flames, is a man consumed by his own fiery dispositions. I write about the human condition, both good and bad, in spirit and in flesh.; [a.] St. Paul, MN

CARTER JR., ALAN J.
[b.] October 3, 1979, Waynesboro, VA; [p.] Alan J. and Sandra J. Carter; [ed.] 10th grade Grace Christian School, Staunton, VA; [occ.] Student; [memb.] Debate Club, Student Government Association, SMAC Swimming.; [hon.] Poetry award for Association of christian Schools International Principal's List 19898-1994, National Top 16 Swimmer; [oth. writ.] Various poems, some published; in school newspaper.; [pers.] Poetry allows me to express my emotions in a creative style which conveys them with more meaning and power.; [a.] Staunton, VA

CASSIDY, CHARLENE
[b.] December 1, 1952, New York; [m.] Kevin Cassidy, December 27, 1981; [ch.] Zachary, Caitlin and Erin Cassidy; [ed.] Freeport High School, Vermont College; [occ.] Free Lance, Homemaker; [oth. writ.] Written a number of other poems and copywritten songs.; [a.] West Palm Beach, FL

CASTELLANO, ROSALIE R.
[Pen.] Eilasor Onalletsac; [b.] June 19, 1923, Rochester, NY; [p.] Jacqueline Albano and Domenic Castellano; [ch.] Son, Dean Gerard Castellano; [ed.] College Graduate; [occ.] Retried; [memb.] Saddleback

Hospital, Volunteer Opera 100, Community Concert, Aliso, Ebelle, Toastmasters, Geneva Presbyterian Church, too numerous to go on.; [hon.] many; [oth. writ.] prose, poetry, some published.; [pers.] Life has as many facets as a diamond. To catch the magnificent brilliance, one need only to hold it up and turn it. we are the sum total of every part of our experiences.; [a.] Logeva Hills, CA

CASTILLO, PATRICIA
[Pen.] Pat Margenrot; [b.] June 20, 1963, Germany; [p.] Paul and Annemarie Hill; [m.] Carlos Castillo Jr., July 19, 1990; [ch.] Sandro-Corrado Castillo; [ed.] Grammar school Marie-Therese majoring in Latin and Arts, Language Institute at University of Erlangen, Germany; [occ.] Foreign Correspondent; [memb.] 1983 Volunteer at Moshav Sde Nitzan, Negev, Israel; 1985 Voluntcer in Israeli Army at Camp Julis, Israel; [hon.] Centro linguistico italiano dante alighieri, Rome Italy, Language Institute at University of Erlangen, Germany; (Base Commander at Military Camp Yulis for volunteer work in Israel); [oth. writ.] not published yet.; [pers.] Style strongly influenced by Charles Beaudelaire and Jean Arthur Rimbaud, French poets of the 19th century. Main topics centering around the problems of the Middle East and the relationship between Jews and Arabs.; [a.] El Paso, TX

CECCO, RICHARD V.
[Pen.] Richard Lionheart; [b.] August 11, 1948, NYC; [p.] Victor and Ludmilla Carcich; [ed.] Long Island Univ., Brooklyn, B.A.; Teachers College, New York, MA; [occ.] Teacher/ Museum Consultant; [memb.] Nat. Council of the Social Studies; American Educational Research Assoc.; American Assoc. of Museums; Council for Exceptional Children; [hon.] Melon Foundation Grant, Who's Who In Education, Impact II Grant, Fulbright Eligible Scholar; [oth. writ.] Museum and History Journals; [pers.] We must help children to think and question. The child's mind is open, and of course known to be constantly inquiring. If we look into the past we see Einstein, E. Dickinson and Lincoln who self taught themselves because they knew of their potentiality. We must teach them, for if we do not, we end the idea of democracy.; [a.] New York, NY

CEPEDA, RAQUEL
[pers.] Raquel is a NY performance pet, freelance writer, and a Hunter College student of Dominican ancestry, who aspires to pursue a career in Black Urban Contemporary music. She is also a member of the Black Star Express, based in Brooklyn, NY. She is 21, and uses poetry as an energetic and positive outlet that makes it possible for her to paint a picture of urban life. Her set, ghetto politics, deals with topics ranging from urban romance to the New World Order. Often accompanied by jazz insturmentals, Raquel's work has a musical influence that enables the audience to "digest" her pieces. Inspired by poets Amiri Baraka, the Last Poets, Nikki Giovanni, Assata Shakur, and Prince, (yes, Prince!) respectively, Raquel hopes to follow in their tradition! Raquel hopes to publish a collection of her poetry entitled ghetto politics in 1995.; [pers.] New York, NY

CERVANTES, JESS
[Pen.] Yac-Cee; [b.] December 26, 1974, San Pedro, CA; [occ.] Security Guard; [oth. writ.] Lots of writings of different styles of moods but none have

been published. Any publishers interested?; [pers.] Thinking may lead to over thinking, give your mind a-rest, don't stress; [a.] Carson, CA

CHACON, MARIA
[b.] December 31, 1955, Brooklyn, NY; [p.] Justo and Virginia Lopez; [m.] Norberto O. Chacon, October 16, 1976; [ch.] Anita Chocon, Angelica Chacon; [ed.] Franklin Delano Roosevelt High School, Attended the College of Staten Island; [pers.] My inspiration to write comes from Gods creation, nature, man and the one thing he gifted us with love.; [a.] Lehigh Acres, FL

CHAMPION, ANGEL DAWN BURNETTE
[Pen.] ABC, Angel Champion; [b.] July 14, 1975, Chapel Hill, NC; [p.] Donald R. and Deborah S. Burnette; [m.] Thomas Ray Champion, July 17, 1993; [ed.] Southern Vance High School; [occ.] Receptionist, Stott Oil Company, Inc.; [hon.] Honor Roll, Co-editor award for school magazine; [oth. writ.] Several poems published in award winning magazine for school, Southern Horizons; [pers.] I write from my heart and soul so that people can feel my emotions and see the world as I see it. My greatest inspirations are those whom I love and respect.; [a.] Henderson, NC

CHAPPEL, CRISSA JEAN
[b.] December 19, 1974, Miami, FL; [ed.] Westminster Christian High School, currently attending U. of Miami; [hon.] Alpha Lambda Delta; Who's Who American High school Students (92-93, 91-92); Art Scholarship; [a.] Miami, FL

CHASE, ERVIN H.
[b.] October 30, 1917, Burlington, NJ; [p.] George and Marie Chase; [m.] Marcella (Maher) Chase, July 13, 1945 (deceased); [ch.] Marcella (California), Yvonne (Woodlyn NJ), Justice (Maryland), Elsa (Poet, Camden, NJ); [ed.] 8th grade, but always learning from the world around me, over 87,000 text books, gave over 2,000 lectures at various symposiums, psych., english, chemistry, etc.; [occ.] Retired; [memb.] ISP Organization, and many others.; [hon.] Too many to mention; [oth. writ.] Union newspaper 1947, poems in N.L.B. of poetry, story in Am. Lit. Press Formats, Club Universal Knowledge Cal. Format. writer Soc. 1944; [pers.] To gain the knowledge of the universe and glue it back to mankind, to respect all things in the universe animate and inanimate (now to cause a break through for all poets, and to establish laws of poetry, free verse and prose.; [a.] Camden, NJ

CHASTAIN, MELISSA
[b.] October 7, 1977, Union County; [p.] Wanda and Gerald Chastain; [m.] not married; [ed.] Murphy High School; [memb.] Fellowship of Christian Athletes, Monogram Club, Murphy High Track Team.; [hon.] Murphy High School 1994 runner of the year; [oth. writ.] Poetry (unpublished); [pers.] Always have faith in yourself.; [a.] Murphy, NC

CHAVERS, LAURA
[b.] January 28, 1956, Auburn, AL; [p.] John E. Jones; [m.] Charlie Chavers, April 27, 1979; [ch.] Lynn, Dawson, John David; [ed.] Monroe County High School, Patrick Henry Jr. College, Auburn University, Troy State University; [occ.] 3rd Grade Teacher, Huxford Elem. School, Huxford, AL;

[memb.] National Education Association, Alabama Education Association, Unity Baptist Church; [a.] McDavid, FL

CHERYL, DARLINE
[b.] April 17, 1973, Haiti; [m.] none; [ch.] none; [occ.] College Student.

CHI, THOMAS RICHARD
[Pen.] Hobbes; [b.] March 10, 1974, Honolulu, HI; [p.] Garret R. and Mira Chi; [ed.] Mililani High School, Leeward Community College; [occ.] Shift Manager at Mililani Taco Bell; [memb.] Power Rangers; [hon.] None, Except for this.; [oth. writ.] Several poems never been published.; [pers.] Just, go with the flow.; [a.] Mililani Town, HI

CHIAPPERINO, ANNETTE
[b.] January 27, 1959, Brooklyn, NY; [p.] Sara and Frank Chiapperino; [m.] Single; [ed.] Coconut Creed High School, Broward Community College, Legal Career Institute; [occ.] Medical Secretary; [memb.] Our Lady Queen of Heaven Church, American Heart Association; [hon.] Dean's List; [oth. writ.] Personal poems for friends and family for various occasions.; [pers.] My writing is a reflection of my personality which can be judged by the reader.; [a.] Margate, FL

CHOI, SUNNY
[b.] February 3, 1982, Seoul South Korea; [p.] Mr. and Mrs. Byung Woo Choi; [ed.] 7th grade, Eastbrook Middle School; [hon.] High honor roll, won 1st place in a local library contest, had picture in North Jersey newspaper.; [oth. writ.] Had a poem published by the American Academy of poetry.; [pers.] As Shakespeare said, "The pen is mightier than the sword."; [a.] Paramus, NJ

CHOWDHURY, JERRY
[b.] July 12, 1938, India; [p.] Azharul H. and Maliha K. Chaudhri; [m.] Sara Chowdhury, August 8, 1965; [ch.] Jasmine: National Merit Scholar at M.I.T. and Cyrus: High School Student; [ed.] Studied Mechanical and Aerospace Engineering in Germany and Canada. Licensed Professional Engineer Since 1977.; [occ.] Senior Engineering Specialist, Allied Signal Aerospace, AE Division, Phoenix Arizona; [memb.] American institute of aeronautics and Astronautics; Americn Society of Mechanical Engineers; National Society of Professional Engineers; Arizona Society of Professional Engineers; Association of Professional Engineers of Ontario; [oth. writ.] Writing poems has been a hobby since early teens; very few published. Technical article published in company's "Enginews." Writing Engineering Proposals and Specifications for the past 15 years; Part-time German-English Translator to support tuition cost in Germany; [pers.] I believe that nature and people are interdependent. As we progress in our continuing education, our improved attitude toward nature and fellow humans will ensure a better world for our children and their progeny.; [a.] Mesa, AZ

CHRESTMAN, CHRISTY
[b.] February 8, 1977, Batesville, MS [p.] Joel and Linda Chrestman; [ed.] South Panola High School (Graduate 1995); [occ.] Daycare Employee; [memb.] United Tae Kwon Do, International, Sardis Lake Baptist Church; [hon.] 1st Degree Black Belt in Tae Kwon Do, English Merit Award, Science Merit Award, Superintendent's List; [pers.] My writings are

the result of my feelings. My love and interest for writing began during my study of poetry in my junior year in high school.; [a.] Batesville, MS

CHRISMAN JR., JAMES L.
[Pen.] Jay; [b.] May 2, 1965, Tennessee, White Pine; [p.] James and Brenda Chrisman; [m.] Tabatha Faye Chrisman, April 21, 1993; [ch.] Ashley Faye, Jamie Sue, Damion James, Brandon Taylor; [ed.] Morristown West High; [occ.] Truckdriver; [memb.] Stokleys Chapel Church; [hon.] Military Excellence Medal in ROTC; [oth. writ.] Several poems and songs that I have written and have never published.; [pers.] All my poems come from the heart. Without feelings we are nothing but nameless faces. Don't just reach for your dreams, make them reality.; [a.] Morristown, TN

CHRISTENSEN, CATHARINE O.
[Pen.] Kay; [b.] April 28, 1932, Utica, NY; [p.] Paul and Phoebe Otto (deceased); [m.] Richard C. Christensen, August 25, 1951; [ch.] Robert C. Christensen, Nancy K. Ferringer; [ed.] 2 years Keuka College, Keuka Park, NY; Graduated Whitesboro Central High School, Whitesboro, NY; [occ.] Retired Teaching Assistant, Whitesboro Central School System; [memb.] Whitesboro Presbyterian Church, Whitesboro, NY; Whitesboro School Alumni Association; Marcy, NY Senior Citizens; [hon.] Employee of the Year 1990-1991; [oth. writ.] "Alone" published in 1993, National Library of Poetry "Tears of Fire."; [pers.] "Do the best you can and leave the rest to God"; [a.] Whitesboro, NY

CHRISTENSEN, GOLDIE L.
[Pen.] G. Christensen; [b.] March 2, 1909, Indiana; [p.] Margaret and Fred Winkler; [m.] Aksel Christensen, 1933; [ch.] one daughter; [ed.] High school; [occ.] Retired; [memb.] Church Protestant, Sang in the choir, taught Sunday School to 7 & 8 yr. olds; [hon.] none; [oth. writ.] Stories, two stories sold, True Story Magazine, One True Story to Michael Landon, Highway to Heaven, 1 book poetry, religious, many poems in newspapers and magazines.; [pers.] this is the first contest I've entered; [a.] Dearborn, MI

CHRISTI, MICHAEL
[Pen.] Bud; [b.] December 24, 1955, Pottsville, PA; [ed.] Bachelors Degree in Theology, C.E.M.A., PA; [occ.] Writer; [memb.] A.S.C.A.P.; [oth. writ.] Music is my life. Music It's My Poetry, published 1977 by the American Son Festival, Hollywood, CA; [pers.] Music is the "Tomb" of life. I believe it reflects man's abilities to rejoice and to be joyful.; [a.] Frackville, PA

CHRISTIAN, BRANDISHEA
[b.] October 20, 1978, Hollywood, CA; [p.] Carla Marie Nott; [ed.] Sophomore at Puyallup High school; [occ.] Studying in Medical Field; [oth. writ.] Poems called, Can't go on; Demon Asylum; Stalker; Beware the Rose; Cold Thoughts; and Daddy, I still Love You.; I'm still writing and I hope to write many more.; [pers.] I owe my witting to Donelle Jenae McGuire, if it weren't for her I wouldn't be writing and to my sister Chantille Cherice Ward for believing in me.; [a.] Puyallup, WA

CHRISTIAN, JANA
[b.] October 17, 1946, Long Beach, CA; [p.] Michael

and Irene Bolaski; [m.] None at present; [ch.] Erin Christine Scanlon and Kelly An Scanlon; [ed.] Ludlow High School, Presently attending Connecticut Business Institute, Medical Assisting; [occ.] Full Time Student, laid off after 18 yrs. employment; [memb.] I am a member of Bloomfield Volunteer Ambulance as an E.M.T. (Emergency Medical Tech.) soon to become a member of N.O.W.; [hon.] Presently attending medical school where I maintain a 4.0 average; [oth. writ.] I have submitted my entire manuscript to several publishers, waiting for results. Thank You.; [pers.] I have been a caregiver since age 7. I have a very strong spiritual side and tend to rescue people in need. I try to see the positive in people.; [a.] E. Hartford, CT

CHRISTIAN, SHIRLEY
[b.] May 3, 1962, LA; [p.] Dorothy Holloway, Jerry Thomas; [m.] Elbert Williams, January 29, 1993; [ch.] Camile Jacqueline Christian, Gina Renee Christian; [ed.] Western High, American Literature, Professional Careers College; [occ.] Physical Therapy Technician; [memb.] SOJ (Sisters of Justice), WAAK-UP Committee; [hon.] BAT 2nd prize "skit writing."; [oth. writ.] Countless poetry writings for friends and many social events, also focal headings regarding issues to be addressed on committees I've served.; [pers.] I've been writing ever since I read my first poem at six years old. I'm just a country girl who believes in God, and I love to write.; [a.] No. Las Vegas, NV

CHURCH, COLLIN
[b.] July 1, 1979, Spokane, WA; [p.] David and Cheryl Church; [ed.] Ninth; [hon.] Best Writer 9th Grade and two VFW Essay Contests 1st Place.; [oth. writ.] Short stories and poems (nothing published); [a.] Valley, WA

CLARK, JACKIE
[b.] November 30, 1978, TN; [p.] Jurdy and J.B. Clark; [occ.] Student; [oth. writ.] A poem in Tears of Fire (The National Library of Poetry; [a.] Fackler, AL

CLARK, JESSICA LEE
[Pen.] Jess; [b.] October 3, 1981; Middleburg, VT; [p.] Kenneth W. Clrk and Melanie L. Pratt; [ch.] Siblings: Patrick Ryan Clark; [ed.] Jessica graduated from Shoreham Elementary school last year, she is currently going into 8th grade at Middleburg Union Junior High School; [memb.] Benson VT, Skeet Club; [hon.] A trophy for being the most improved basketball player on the team, 2 basketballs for winning 2 foul shooting contest. A 1st place ribbon for a softball through, 3rd place spelling contest; [oth. writ.] A poem called Acrostic Winter poem, published in the Coming of Dawn by the National Library of Poetry and Weybridge VT, Published by Poetry by Young Americans by Anthology of Poetry Inc.; [a.] Salisbury, VT

CLARK, LYNN
[b.] March 29, 1985, Bloomington, IN; [p.] Ryan and Amy Clark; [ed.] Going into the 4th grade; [hon.] 1st place Regency Talent National Championship awards for clogging in 1993, 1993 and 1994; 2nd place Regency Talent National Championship award for clogging in 1994.; 1st place award at Showbiz Talent competition for clogging in 1993; Two 1st place awards at Showbiz Talent Competition for clogging in

1994; 1 Gold Medal and 1 Silver Medal at American Dance Spectrum, awards for clogging in 1994; [oth. writ.] One other poem published in a book from Anthology of poetry.; [a.] Gosport, IN

CLARK, STEPHANIE MARIE
[b.] January 8, 1980, Hattisburg, MS; [p.] Mark Clark and Nancy boyle; [ed.] Richton Jr. High; [hon.] Student of the Month, Honor Roll; [pers.] I try to make people realize how beautiful life can be.; [a.] Richton, MS

CLARK, SUSAN
[b.] December 29, 1979, Chicago, IL; [p.] Jean Bryan and Thom Clark; [ed.] Franklin Fine Arts Center, Magnet School; St. Margaret Mary School; St. Scholastic High School; [occ.] Student 9th grade at St. Scholastic H.S.; [memb.] YMCA Leadership Club; [hon.] Chicago Young Authors Award; [oth. writ.] Personal collection of poems, short stories, essays, children's books entered for Chicago Young Authors Contest; [pers.] I love writing. Whether it's a poem or a short story, I like looking back to see what I've done.; [a.] Chicago, IL

CLAY, PENNY
[b.] September 15, 1971, Kirksville, MO; [p.] Patrick Clay and stepfather Claude Conley; [ed.] Kirksville Senior High; [occ.] Certified Nurses Aide, Crystal Park Care Center, Olathe, KS; [pers.] I wanna say thank you to the one who inspired me. She is also my best friend. My mother Patricia Clay.; [a.] Olathe, KS

CLEMONS, CYNTHIA
[b.] September 30, 1956, Florence, AL; [p.] Mr. and Mrs. Gerald T. Harrison; [m.] Bobby E. Clemons, Jr., December 29, 1992; [ch.] Felicia 19, Amanda 17, John 12, Kyle 5; [ed.] Central High School 12 years.; [memb.] Hendrix Chapel church of Christ; [oth. writ.] Several unpublished poems.; [pers.] I wrote a few poems in school, but nothing serious until about 3 yrs. ago. The main reason I write poems is to satisfy my own personal need of doing something just for me that I really enjoy doing.; [a.] Florence, AL

CLERK, ELIZABETH JANE
[b.] June 12, 1974, Provo, UT; [p.] William and Gay Ann Clark; [ed.] Murray High; Bachelors at Bringham Young Univ. ; J.D. at Arizona State Univ.; [occ.] Private Economics tutor; [memb.] Nat'l Forensics League, Nat'l Honors Soc., Who's Who in America; Omicron Delta Epsilon; Int'l Rotary Club Utah, representative at World Affairs Seminar; [hon.] BYU's Trustee Scholarship; ASU's; Utah Women's Assoc. of fine Arts Scholarship, Kiwanis; Leadership Award; Sterling Scholar in Speech and Drama; [oth. writ.] 1st place overall in Haiku poetry competition; published in local newspaper, compiled personal book of poetry and short stories.; [pers.] I like to think my writing stresses the ironic side of life. I try to capture the little twists that make us think and the blows of chance that entwine us and make our existence unique.; [a.] Salt Lake City, UT

CLINE, CYNTHIA
[b.] Oregon, Illinois; [p.] Dale and Louise Cline; [ed.] Stephen Decatur H.S., Decatur, IL, Salutatorian, B.A. Degree IL State Univ., Cum Laude, Certified Teacher, Speech, Theatre, Spanish; [occ.] Actress, Spokeswoman; [memb.] Actor's Equity Association, Scrum Actor's Guild, American Federation of Tele-

vision and Radio Artists, Marble Collegiate Church, NYC; [hon.] American Field Service Scholarship Exchange Student (Brazil), State Finalist IL, Jr. Miss Pageant, Winner, Talent Division, State of IL Honor Society; Alpha Lambda Delta (U. of IL); National Spanish Honorary Society (I.S.U.); [oth. writ.] Good Housekeeping Writing Award, "Things My Mother Taught Me," June 1986; [pers.] Thanks to my precious parents who taught me how to love and to realize that "The Truth will set you free."; [a.] New York City, NY

CLINE, SARAH
[b.] October 14, 1955, Eustis, FL; [p.] Ivey Bowling and Florence Yarborough; [m.] James Cline, October 3, 1986; [ch.] Crystal Dawn, Kenneth Wayne, Mari Janee; [ed.] Umatilla High, Florida Tech; [occ.] Homemaker; [oth. writ.] Several poems, an article for Reader's Digest (not yet published); [pers.] My love of God, family and nature is the inspiration for my poetry. As some of my poems come so deeply from my heart, they are bound to stir emotions in others as well.; [a.] Astor, FL

COATLEY JR., ERIC D.
[b.] December 17, 1979, Louisville, KY; [p.] E. D. Coatley and V. L. Coatley; [ed.] Barret Traditional Middle School, Cochrane elementary Jacob Elementary; [occ.] Tutor for Extended School Service; [memb.] Y.M.C.A., First Baptist Pee Wee Valley; [hon.] Youth Volunteer Award Outstanding Youth Award, 3 Year Perfect Attendance Award, Middle School, Community Service Award, General Electric Appliances Scholastic Achievement Award, House OP Reps., 4-H Junior Speech Champion, Presidential Academic Fitness Award; [oth. writ.] Grading Period, Poet The Grass Fire-Poem; [pers.] If not for my eighth grade literature class, I never would have discovered my ability to construct poetry. I am grateful to my teacher for believing that I have a true talent for writing poetry.; [a.] Louisville, KY

COBB, JESSIE S.
[b.] October 2, 1912; [p.] James and Hazel Evans; [m.] Witue Delmus Vogt, December 21, 1929; [ch.] Two, William Delmus Vogt and Virginia Carlisle Berry; [ed.] 8th grade and self taught.; [occ.] Retired and tired today, went shopping; [memb.] Holden Heights Chamber of Commerce, Lucerne Baptist Church, Pat Robinson Christian Coalition; [hon.] 3 ribbons, Australian Crawl, Back Stroke, Free Style; [oth. writ.] Enough poems for a book.; [pers.] I strive to reflect my life and thoughts on paper as to the Creation of Gods Holy Spirit, working in my Utter most being, my heart, my mind and soul.; [a.] Orlando, FL

COBB, PEGGY V.
[b.] May 23, 1915, Lyon Co., Minnesota; [p.] Frederick and Mabel Vanstrom; [m.] Jacob Cobb, December 31, 1943; [ch.] William Jacob, Katharine Peter Vanstrom; [ed.] B.S., St. Cloud State University, Commercial Art Academy (Mpls, MN), M.A. Indiana State University; [occ.] Retired: art teacher and art supervisor; [memb.] Sigma Alpha Iota, Pen and Brush Club (local) Delta Kappa Gramma (Delta Ch.), PEO, Chi Omega, Centenary United Methodist Church, Habitat for Humanity Good Samaritan, Historical Society, Assoc. for retarded.; [oth. writ.] Write and illustrate stories for children, combining fact with fantasy (shared with adult and children

groups) both love them, especially children, do fore edge paintings.; [pers.] A life long family quote: furnish your mind well and you will always have a comfortable place in which to live.; [a.] Terre Haute, IN

COCHRANE, ROY
[b.] December 28, 1913, Clark, SD; [p.] deceased; [m.] Mavis Wolfe Cochrane, February 14, 1947; [ch.] Dr. Lois C. Schlutter, Consulting Psychologist; [ed.] M.S. plus 30 Clinical Psychology; [occ.] Retired Colonel, AUS, (21 yrs) Retired Clinical Psychologist (28 years); [memb.] Masonic orders, I.O.O.F., B.P.O.E., Sigma Xi, APA; [hon.] MBE (mil), U.S. Military Medals, Roy Cochrane Scholarship Fund, NE Mental Health Center Foundation, Aberdeen, SD; [oth. writ.] Psychological Note, Montana Press, See Me Now (autobio), not marketed. All the Way to Eagles, not marketed.; [pers.] "Star Meet" represents a reflection of a very close relationship with old friends.; [a.] Hopkins, MN

COGGINS, PRINCESS
[Pen.] Prino; [b.] January 21, 1957, Guyana; [p.] Archibald and Olga Dazzell; [m.] Albert Coggins, August 26, 1978; [ch.] Seavon, Junior, Leticia Ann and Sharon; [ed.] Manhattan Career Institute, Menten, Meer Zong Government, Guyana (12 grade); [occ.] Home attendant East Harlem Home Care Service; [hon.] Dean's List, Attendance Certificate, Home Care Certificate; [oth. writ.] About 3 other poems that never was seen by others.; [pers.] I will like to explore more in this field if I should ge the chance. I love to read and writing is good for me.; [a.] New York, NY

COHAN, GENEVIEVE
[Pen.] Dee Riggi; [b.] Brooklyn, NY; [p.] Samuel and Anna De Riggi; [m.] Barry Cohan, October 1, 1993; [ch.] Brenda Montemurro; Grandson Andrew Montemurro; [ed.] Academy of St. Joseph, Brentwood, NY; [occ.] Data Control, Quality Assurance Documentation Librarian, Dime Savings Bank of NY; [oth. writ.] Several poems unpublished.; [pers.] In dedication to my brother Vincent De Riggi. Substand Abuse Counselor, Brentwood School District. An asset to his students and community.; [a.] Valley Stream, NY

COHEN, PAMELA
[b.] January 11, 1981, Suffern, NY; [p.] Robert and Rhoda Cohen; [ed.] Still in School; [hon.] Awarded for poetry and story writing.; [pers.] When life gives you lemons, make lemonade!; [a.] Spring Valley, NY

COKINOS, EFFIE A.
[b.] August 26, 1973, Chicago, IL; [p.] Anthony, Elaine cokinos; [pers.] These words were written solely for the purpose of proving that we can reach our goals, by not giving up. With one person in mind, a perfect example of this is my dear friend Patricia Panagakos. Thank you so much for bringing these words to life.; [a.] Mount Prospect, IL

COLE, TOMMIE LOU HUTSON
[b.] October 15, 1938, Magee, MS; [p.] Mr. and Mrs. Thomas Ward Hutson; [m.] Harles Daniel Cole, Sr., October 19, 1956; [ch.] Cynthia Lynn Cole Keith, Harles Daniel Cole, Jr.; [ed.] Magee High School; Degrees: Bachelor of Science and Masters from the University of Southern Mississippi. Major: Education, Emphasis Early Childhood; [occ.] Kindergarten Teacher, Magee Elementary School, Magee, MS;

[memb.] First Assembly of God Church; Alpha Chi Chapter, The Delta Kappa Gamma Society International; Friends of The Library; Simpson County Writers' Group; University of Southern Mississippi Golden Key Society; Mississippi Professional Educators; [hon.] President, Alpha Chi Chapter Delta Kappa Gamma; Dean's List, USM; [oth. writ.] Inspirational poetry.; [pers.] My writing is an outgrowth of a lifelong love of books and reading. I thank God that He is allowing me to share this with others.; [a.] Magee, MS

COLEMAN, EVELYN J.
[Pen.] Lyn Cole; [b.] March 20, 1921, Allen County Lima, Ohio; [p.] Deceased; [m.] R. T. Coleman, November, 1940; [ch.] High School, Adult Education course in Creative Writing; [occ.] Retired Office Clerk, now homemaker; [memb.] Shawner United Methodist Church. Past very active member. Past 4-H advisor, rec'd silver award.; [oth. writ.] Yes, about sixty poems. I have been trying to publish in a book.; [pers.] Write of any moving experience that touches me deeply.; [a.] Lima, OH

COLLADO, BAMIL GUTIERREZ
[Pen.] Bamil Gutcoll; [b.] April 5, 1969, Aguadilla, P.R.; [p.] Cecilia Collado Rodriquez; [ed.] Elementary School Alfredo Dorrington, Ramon E. Rodriquez Diaz, Dr. Pedro Perlea Fajardo Vocational School and Inter American University San German; [occ.] Graphic Artist/Pharmacy Operator in Bristol Myers Squibb Co., Mayaguez, PA; [hon.] Bachelor Degree in Visual arts and Education, Architectonic Drawing Degree, Oratory Semifinalist Award, Solo Singer First Place Award (own song and music); [oth. writ.] Non published poems in other contest and owner of more than 70 compositions musically speaking and some riddles published on Bristol Myers-Squibb Company-inside newspaper; [pers.] I'm very influenced by the things around me, the people and the beehive, the flowers, the animals, places I would like to be, Mysticism, Mysteries, all the greatness made by our Lord and specially; love among people, peace and trust.; [a.] Mayaquez, P.R.

COLLENETTE, ALAN D.
[Pen.] Alan Lenehan; [b.] January 26, 1954, London, England; [m.] Shirley Lenehan; [ch.] Natalie; [ed.] England, St. Paul's School, London, Reading University, Reading; [a.] San Francisco, CA

COLLEY, GLORIA DELAMAR
[b.] May 27, 1941, Roanoke, AL; [p.] Owen and Gertrude DeLamar; [m.] James Harvey Colley, September 15, 1962; [ch.] Katherine Colley Jaramillo and James Tolby Colley; [ed.] Graduate 59', Seacrest High School, DelRay Beach, FL; [occ.] Homemaker (Retired Church Secretary); [memb.] Idlewild Baptist Church, Matthews, NC; [pers.] "The Cross and Crown" is an excerpt from my collection of poetry entitled "He Touched Me" that reflects thoughts and memories of my christian walk thru life.; [a.] Matthews, NC

COLTER, J. LEROY
[b.] May 28, 1942, Clay County, AK; [p.] James J. and Grace Colter; [m.] Marcell Jean Colter, January 13, 1989; [ch.] Connie Foust, Lora Foust, Jeanette Maxwell, Lorita Hicks; [ed.] Fisk, Rombauer High School, Fisk, Missouri; [occ.] Printer, Redbook Florist Service, Paragould, AR; [memb.] Landreth Chapel,

General Baptist Church, Past Trustee and Sunday School Teacher; [oth. writ.] Have written numerous other pieces about the goodness of God and mankind needs to follow his ways. Also have some on love and the beauty and wonders in the world we live in.; [pers.] My writing is inspired by my personal relationship and faith in God. I want my writing to give hope and comfort to those who happen to read it.; [a.] Kennett, MO

COMINI, KAY
[b.] June 17, 1940; [ch.] Kacey Comini, Michael Comini, one grandchild: Henry Byron Comini; [ed.] University of Pittsburgh currently a student majoring in writing.; Women's Studies Certificate, U. of Pgh.; [occ.] Intake Caseworker, PA Dept. of Welfare.; [memb.] PA Social Services Union National Org. for Women Sierra Club; [hon.] On Dean's List Every Term; [oth. writ.] Articles and poems for various service organization newsletters.; [pers.] Poetry is the soul of humanity and needs to be a vital part of everyday life.; [a.] Pittsburgh, PA

CONDRA, ANGELA
[b.] April 1, 1972, Colorado Springs, Colorado; [p.] Fred and Anna condra; [ed.] Columbus East High School, Indiana University; [occ.] Student; [memb.] St. John's Lutheran Church; [oth. writ.] Features editor for high school yearbook and co-editor subsequently; also other unpublished writings and poems; [pers.] Anything is possible, if only you believe.; [a.] Columbus, IN

CONEY, EALINE M.
[b.] August 9, 1952, Magnolia, MS; [p.] Allen L. Coney and Katie Coney (Deceased); [ed.] Interlochen Arts Academy; Millsaps College; Universidad Interamericana; University of Southern Mississippi; [occ.] Spanish, French and English Composition Instructor, Southwest MS Community College; [memb.] Mississippi Foreign Language association; Mississippi Assoc. of Educators; Mississippi; Writers Association; AATSP; AATF; ACTFL; [hon.] Who's Who in Americn education 1988, 1990, 1992; [pers.] I have been influenced by the poets such as Maya Angelou and Alice Walker.; [a.] Magnolia, MS

CONKLING, JACQUELINE R.
[Pen.] Jackie; [b.] July 1, 1969, New Jersey; [p.] Mr. and Mrs. Frank James Conkling; [ed.] Twin Lakes High School, Palm Beach Community College; [occ.] U.S. Postal Service; [pers.] Thank you Dad for loving me so much and for making a difficult situation so wonderful and loving. I miss you and still care deeply.; [a.] West Palm Beach, FL

CONN, LEANNE
[b.] August 6, 1978, Santa Clara, CA; [p.] Sandra L. Conn; [ed.] Sophomore High school; [pers.] Wars and politicians come and go but talent is forever. I give thanks and praise to the all mighty father who gave me life.; [a.] Aurora, CO

CONNER, APRIL MICHELLE
[b.] January 17, 1981, Dickson, IN; [p.] Debbie Ronland and Nayne Conner; [ed.] I am a eighth grade at East Hickman Middle School; [occ.] Student; [memb.] J.R. Beta 4-H; [hon.] Highest English Average in my school. Honor List, Honors English; [oth. writ.] I have wrote many other poems but never attempted to have them published.; [pers.] Never

underestimate the power of a child.; [a.] Tyles, TN

CONNOLLY, EUGENE
[Pen.] Gene Connolly; [b.] September 21, 1942, Michigan, Wellston; [p.] Hubert B. S. Will and Eva Connolly; [m.] Helen Bryant Connolly; [ch.] Sungura Noeqwa Connolly; [ed.] Brethern High and Manistee High School, College BS Degree in History, Oakland University, B.S. Degree in Journalism, Wayne State University, also attended Oakland Community College; [occ.] Accountant at GM Truck and bus in Pontiac, Michigan; [memb.] African American Council of Pontiac North Star Theatre Group of Pontiac; [hon.] Named Actor of the Year by negro Business Professional Assoc. in Pontiac; [oth. writ.] Creative writing fiction, comedy writing, have wrote over 100 poems. Hope to have a book published, also working on a novel; [pers.] I have to write the way things are that are facing people in their every day lives, influenced by Black Poets of Harlem Ren.; [a.] Bloom Field Hills, MI

CONRAD, TRACY
[b.] March 10, 1979, Tahlequah, OK; [p.] Hiawatha Conrad and Sarah Adair; [ed.] Still going to school; [oth. writ.] Poem, Unborn Child, Short story, Nothing Will Never Scare Me.; [pers.] I am a Native American, fifteen year old Cherokee who believes that if any one else can do it I can to.; [a.] Hulbert, OK

CONWAY, MICHAEL SEAN
[Pen.] Sean Conway; [b.] August 30, 1959, Pomona, CA; [p.] Virginia Picken and Dave Conway; [ed.] DeAnza College, Cupertino, CA but mostly self-taught with help from past and present writers.; [occ.] Poet; [memb.] Creative Writing Club, Lansing community College, Lansing, MI; [oth. writ.] "The Gods Need Victems" The Nocturnal Lyric, Sept. 1994 issue. "Chirpings" Mind in Motion, June 1994 issue. "Terror Tombs", poem read on radio.; [pers.] To paraphrase Jeffers, Write, and be quiet!; [a.] Lansing, MI

COOK, BARBARA E.
[Pen.] Cookie Buster; [b.] December 11, 1928, Ithaca, MI; [m.] Lloye E. Cook, August 13, 1966; [ed.] Ithaca High School, Received a diploma from the North American School of Animal Science from Scranton Pennsylvania, October 7, 1985; [occ.] Housewife; [memb.] Church of God, Substitute Teacher. The Boy Scouts of America 20 years of service; [hon.] Numerous trophies for running. Have a cupboard full. Medals and a Gold Cup; [oth. writ.] "For Sale" published in the Anthology "Poetic Voices of America. "The Woodpile" published in the Anthology "Tears of Fire." Earned top 3% of all poems received. Received the Editor's Choice Award. Will have a poem "The Universe" coming in "The Dark Side of the Moon" Anthology; [pers.] God didn't give us any children or a child. In a real sense my Sunday School children and the Cub Scouts in my den were my children. One hundred years from now it will not matter what kind of car I drove. What kind of house I lived in, how much money I had in my bank account. Nor what my clothes looked like. But the world may be a little better because I was important in the life of a child.; [a.] Elsie, MI

COOKE, ANNA L.
[b.] February 14, 1923, Jackson, TN; [p.] Thurston and Efie Lee; [m.] James A. Cooke, April 11, 1956;

[ch.] 1 daughter, Elsie Cooke Holmes; [ed.] B.A. Lane College, MLS Atlanta University; [occ.] Retired College Librarian; Free Lance Writer; [memb.] American Literary Assoc., American Assoc. of University Women, AARP, Delta Sigma Theta Sorority, Inc., Links, Inc., United Negro College Funds; [hon.] Doctor of Humane Letters from Lane College, State of TN., Governor's Award for Achievement, Presidential Citation from NAFEO for Outstanding Alumnus Girl Scouts Woman of Distinction and Friends Maker Award; [oth. writ.]; Editorials for Jackson Sun's Newspaper Columnist for the Metro Forum Book, Lane College: It's Heritage and Outreach, 1882-1982 c. 1987.; [pers.] If I can inspire somebody as I pass this way, then my living shall not be in vain.; [a.] Jackson, TN

COOKS, AUBREY
[b.] October 8, 1959, Los Angeles; [p.] Mr. and Mrs. Homer and Mary Williams; [ch.] George J. West Kellogg III; [ed.] Fairfax High School, Los Angeles City College, Los Angeles Southwest College Cal. St. University Los Angeles; [occ.] Community Recreation Assistant at L.A.S.C. and Cheerleader Advisor at L.A.S.C.; [memb.] Mentor Program at L.A.S.C., Eternal Hope M.B.C. of Los Angeles, CA; [hon.] Several poems published in local newspaper.; [pers.] "I can do all things through Christ which strengthenth me." Philippians 4:13. Thanks to my family and few close friends. Daddy I miss you. Please enjoy my writings from the heart.; [a.] Los Angeles, CA

COOL, ERIC J.
[b.] February 17, 1972; [m.] Laura E. Cool, June 27, 1992; [ch.] Cody John Cool; [oth. writ.] I have a collection of poems entitled (Heart Grabbers and Tear Jerkers).; [pers.] I like to write about life, death, and the unknown. I feel I have been greatly influenced by Edgar Allen Poe.; [a.] Leeton, MO

COOPER, DEBRA
[b.] May 22, 1977, Texas; [p.] Pat and Skip Cooper; [ed.] Germantown High School in TN; [pers.] Thanks to Ms. Hankins and Mrs. Rosemann for teaching me everything I know. Sally - you're a great inspiration.; [a.] Germantown, TN

CORCORAN, CARLA R.
[Pen.] Psyche; [b.] September 19, 1964, Lawrence, MA; [p.] Joyce and William Corcoran; [ed.] Salem State College, Bachelor of Arts Degree, English Literature, minor in Art History.; [occ.] Writer and Women's Advocate; [memb.] Nature/Goddess oriented religion.; [hon.] Awarded first prize for a poem in a college literary magazine.; [oth. writ.] Have written columns and editorials for local newspapers and a union newsletter.; [pers.] People are a lot like poetry. You can't read it once. Nothing and no one should turn you away from striving toward your highest ideals.; [a.] Salem, MA

CORVERA, DEANNA J.
[b.] August 8, 1968, San Angelo; [p.] Mr. & Mrs. Willis Stone and Joy Petite; [m.] Luis R. Corvera, August 21, 1989; [ch.] Serena, Mike, Elizabeth, AJ, Luann and Luis, Jr.; [ed.] Graduate of Falfurrias High School 1986; [occ.] Mother; [memb.] American Cancer Society; [pers.] My poetry is dedicated to my son who died of leukemia at the age of 6 in 1992. I hope to reach the thousands of parents who struggle with that battle as my husband and I have.; [a.] Falfurrias, TX

COSTELLO, JR., RAYMOND
[b.] October 22, 1969, Mt. View; [p.] Darlene and Raymond Costello Sr.; [ed.] Illinois Valley High School, Van Ness House, Los Angeles Comm. College.; [occ.] CNA, Certified Nurses Assistant; [oth. writ.] Various plays, poems, personal stories; [pers.] A writers words are from deep within their souls when read some laugh and some cry. Love God Bless All. Be good to yourselves; [a.] Hollywood, CA

COUEY, MONA EL SALAH
[Pen.] el Salah; [b.] February 12, 1963, Brooklyn, NY; [p.] Josephine Hanley Couey and Billie Couey; [ch.] Sharrieff J. Couey (son); [ed.] Amityville School System (grades K-12). Fredonia, york, and Old Westbury Colleges.; [occ.] Teacher (Early Childhood) P.S. 112, Manhattan, New York.; [memb.] Participated in Brooklyn Academy of Music, Chorus, Mixed and Girls Ensemble, High school Gospel Choir (college), Drama Club, Track, Cross Country, Literary Clubs, Basketball, Talent Show coordinator and participant.; [hon.] Who's Who In Music Award 1981 Edition.; [oth. writ.] Songs performed on a college level (Old Westbury Gospel Choir and written for and performed by children (P.S. 112 Manhattan). Poems were written for and entered into school yearbooks, school literary magazine and newspapers.; [pers.] Writing is a vehicle transporting every dimension of human experiences. At the end of this literary road, awaits, a warm glow of true enlightment for all.; [a.] Amityville, NY

COULTER, JENNIFER MARIE
[Pen.] Jennifer Coulter; [b.] July 10, 1980, Ogallala, Neb.; [p.] Russell and Debra Coulter; [ed.] Freshman at Harvard High School; [occ.] Student; [memb.] 4-H, school choir, church choir, H.E.R.S. softball league, church bell choir; [hon.] Honor Roll at school, Gifted Program, Awards in solo and ensemble contests; [oth. writ.] Just in school; [pers.] Follow your dreams, and always know the facts.; [a.] Harvard, IL

COUNTRYMAN, MICHAEL TODD
[b.] March 24, 1973, Emporia, KS; [p.] Jim Countryman and Nancy Zimmerman; [m.] Kacey Ann Countryman, June 24, 1994; [ed.] Hamilton High School, Flinthills Technical School, Butler County Community College; [occ.] Adolescent support worker for (SR5) and projectionist.; [hon.] Who's Who Among High School Students, Honor Roll, and Dean's List; [oth. writ.] AD, Phobia, Afraid, and memory; [a.] Hamilton, KS

COURIS, ROSEANN
[b.] August 15, 1960, New Jersey; [p.] Randolph and Susann Winnans; [m.] John Alexander Couris Sr., November 4, 1984; [memb.] I am a member of the Wharton American Legion Auxiliary. I am also a Volunteer Firefighter for East Marshall Fire Dept. and I was a 2 year member for the E.M.F.D. Ladies Auxiliary.; I am also a member of the Berkshire Valley Presb. Church of Wharton and East Marshall Missionary Baptist church; [pers.] In 84 I moved from Wharton, NJ to Gilbertsville, KY, met my husband and married in 84. In 85 had my only child John Alex, here in KY were I've enjoyed the lay back religious life of this community; [a.] Gilbertsville, KY

COUSINS, TAMARA
[b.] June 29, 1961, California; [p.] Glen L. and Mary Ann Alban; [m.] Jerry L. Cousins, May 3, 1986; [ch.] Vennie Jason Cousins; [pers.] Never will blame someone else for my undoings. ("fool me once shame on you!") ("fool me twice shame on me!").

COUTRELL, JUDITH J.
[b.] January 10, 1941, OshKosh, WI; [p.] Wilbert and Joan Schleinz; [m.] John Cantrell, May 23, 1970; [ch.] Bonnie, Angela, Teresa, Michelle, Sharon, Sherrie, Kim, Robert and Gene; [ed.] Associate of Science; [occ.] Human Services; [memb.] Secular Franciscan Order; [oth. writ.] None published.; [pers.] Only when all is still can we hear and understand silence, and only when we are in silence are we heard.; [a.] Lompoc, CA

COX, JAIME
[Pen.] Jayme Cox; [b.] June 13, 1978, Jackson, MO;l [p.] Helen and Eddie Cox; [ed.] 10th grade; [occ.] Burger King.

COX, JEFFREY H.
[b.] February 23, 1952, Wisconsin; [p.] Mr. and Mrs. Howard Cox; [m.] Elizabeth M. Cox, October 3, 1992; [ch.] Jason Patrick, Kelly David, and Jonathan Michael; [ed.] Mt. Dora High school, Rollins College, Winter Park, FL; [occ.] Facility Service Scheduler Orange County Public Schools; [memb.] Anthropological Society Central Fl., Project Management Institution; [oth. writ.] Into the Sails the Wind Races; published in Dance on the Horizon, National Anthology of Poetry.; [pers.] I enjoy writing about the sea and sailing and am now working on a book of poetry dealing with those subjects.; [a.] Clermont, FL

COYLE, JOSEPH EDWARD
[Pen.] Joe Coyle; [b.] June 25, 1939, Brooklyn, NY; [p.] Joseph Coyle, Anna Jacobson; [ed.] Manual Training High school; [occ.] I am a disabled municipal worker.; [memb.] C.Y.O. Catholic Church Police Athletic League; [oth. writ.] I am new in this field, but I am working on a history, of the great Georgian People, by the Black Sea.; [pers.] Live and let live. But also follow the 10 Commandments. Life is too short for petty bickering so lets all be sincere.; [a.] Brooklyn, NY

CRATE, SHELLY R.
[b.] January 19, 1969; [p.] Paul and rosalie Bowers; [m.] Michael S. Crate, Augsut 10, 1990; [oth. writ.] Several poems published in Damozel, The Literary Magazine of the College of Notre Dame of Maryland.; [a.] Hagerstown, MD

CRAWFORD, AMBROCIA
[b.] September 18, 1955, Phila. PA; [p.] Valentino and Cornelia Asuncion; [m.] Keith S. Crawford, June 1, 1974; [ch.] Kecia Tomasa, Ambrocia Lastar, Amber Kacy, Keia Valentina, Keith Steven Jr.; [ed.] Temple Univ. B.S. in Elem. Ed., Master's Degree, Beaver College and Chestnut Hill College in Early Childhood Education; [occ.] Multi-age grade teacher, J.F. McCloskey School, Phila., PA; [memb.] Ladies Auxillary Post 1063, PFT Representative; [hon.] Dean's List; [pers.] One must overcome all obstacles encountered.; [a.] Maple Glen, PA

CRAWFORD, MICHAEL E.
[b.] November 23, 1952, Tulsa, OK; [p.] Robert Lee

and Imogene Martin Crawford; [m.] Erlinda Almaraz Crawford, May 3, 1979; [ch.] Samuel Isaac Crawford and David Michael Crawford; [ed.] High School with some College, Advanced Certificate in Law Enforcement Training; [occ.] Deputy Sheriff; [memb.] National Rifle Assoc., Harris County Deputy Sheriff's Union; [oth. writ.] I have self published two manuscripts, one is called "Cops, Covenants and Christmas." The other is "The Government of god." Articles published in "Something Better" Newspaper and "Cop and Cross," Newspaper; [pers.] The only time that one needs to succeed is the last time they try.; [a.] Houston, TX

CRAYTHORN, LISA
[b.] January 24, 1966, South Africa; [p.] Vicky and Ashton Foxcroft; [m.] Mark Craythorn, June 16, 1990; [ch.] Michael, Melissa; [ed.] Mondeor High, Witwatersrand Tech; [occ.] Homemaker; [memb.] La Leche League International; [oth. writ.] Articles in Architectural Magazine.; [pers.] I am inspired by Sylvia Plath and Anne Sexton.; [a.] Jackson, MS

CREATH, JOHN FITZGERALD
[b.] July 14, 1964, Chicago, IL; [p.] Chastelia Creath; [ch.] Kendria (14), Nicolette (12), Joslyn (10), Talesha (2); [ed.] Hot Springs, High School, U.S.A.F., Telephone Equipment Repair.; [occ.] Digital Telephone Equipment Engineer.; [hon.] Graduated from U.S.A.F. Training School with honors.; [oth. writ.] Menagerie of the Feelings Inside of My Heart. (Poetry Compilation), A Present for Harold (short story); [pers.] Life would be more beautiful if we were not so critical of each other.; [a.] Raleigh, NC

CRIM, GEORGIA E.
[Pen.] G.E.M. (Monegain); [b.] October 6, 1923, Chicago, IL; [p.] Hazel and George Crim; [m.] Divorced (Harold Monegain); [ch.] Teresa English, Barestan Monegain, Alonna Monegain-Arnold; [ed.] A.A. Kennedy, King College, B.S. Southern Illinois University Studies at "Chicago National School of Naapraphythy; [occ.] Retired (Federal U.S.); [memb.] "Sigma Gamma Rho," "Afro American Genealogy and Historical Society," Carbondale Community Club;" [hon.] "Crisis Hotline" Volunteer Award, "Silver Poet" award, "Golden Poet" award, "Senior Citizen Essay."; [oth. writ.] "Falling Snow," "The Past is Prologue," "Words," "Redemption," "God's Land God's Hands," "Trip to Southern Illinois"; [pers.] I believe in teachings of Jesus Christ, but respect other Holy scripts. I believe in a cyclic process of universality. I believe in love.; [a.] Carbondale, IL

CRIM, JANICE
[b.] September 7, 1939, Flint, MI; [p.] Earnest and Neva Ryan Deceased; [m.] Divorced; [ch.] Jeffrey and Rick Crim; [ed.] Associate Degree R.N., Charles Steward Mott Community College, Flint, MI; Lapeer High School, Lapeer, MI; [occ.] Psychiatric, R.N., Central AZ Medical Center, Florence, AZ; [hon.] Editor's Choice Award 1994; [oth. writ.] Just Being 1994; [pers.] I strive to allow my most innermost feelings, freedom and light.; [a.] Florence, AZ

CROCHARELL, PATRICK
[p.] Baxter Crocharell & Pat Abernathy; [occ.] QuickTrip Corp. of St. Louis, MO; [hon.] "Daddy, Why Do You Smile" is also published in "River of Dreams."; [oth. writ.] I have many other writings,

and I've begun my first novel. My best poem was written for my stepmother on her death bed. Title: "It Should've Been Me."; [pers.] Even when one comes into this world with so little, he can be destined to go so far. Never give up. Special thanks to singer, Ronnie Milsap for his inspiration in my writing.; [a.] Edwardsville, IL

CROCKER, LYNDA L.
[Pen.] Aylea Savar; [b.] September 27, 1959, Oklahoma; [ed.] Language and Literature Masters Degree, Legal Assisting Assoc. Degree; [occ.] Legal Assistant; [memb.] SFWA; [hon.] Various acknowledgements on contract work; [oth. writ.] Various poems, magazine articles, translations of several works of fiction.; [pers.] The world has such beauty, even its darker side, which best can be reflected in poetry and music. I aspire to capture aspects of that beauty in my writing.; [a.] FL

CROW, JOHN W.
[b.] January 18, 1927, Beaumont, TX; [p.] Hope and Raymond Crow; [m.] Lorena Keith Crow, February 12, 1949; [ch.] Boy 44, Girl 43, Girl 35; Keith, Lorena, Mary Louise; [ed.] Beaumont city School, Beaumont Texas, graduated Lamar College Bmt. Texas attended University of Houston; [occ.] Retired, Mortgage banking, 1970. Now oil and gas investor; [memb.] Various real estate appraisal and mortgage banking organizations prior to 1970.; [oth. writ.] My Words of Wisdom, copywritten but unpublished.; [pers.] Served U.S. Navy WWII. Was in battle for Okinawa.; [a.] Houston, TX

CROWLEY, DEVIN KANE
[b.] June 16, 1974, Phoenix, AZ; [ed.] Royal High School, Glendale Community College; [oth. writ.] Poetry, fantasy and science fiction short stories (nothing published). Currently writing a fantasy novel.; [pers.] The light at the end of the tunnel shines the brightest when you reach the source.; [a.] Phoenix, AZ

CROWSON, SHAWNA
[b.] October 1, 1977, Sallisaw, OK; [p.] Dale & Rosie Crowson; [m.] Single; [ed.] Currently a junior at Sallisaw High school, Sallisaw, OK; [occ.] Student; [memb.] Immanuel Baptist Youth Group Church Choir, Championship State Runner-up Basketball Team, Fellowship Christian Athletes; [hon.] Nat'l Honor Society, Who's Who in American High School Students 1994 28th edition, member 93-94 State Runner up Basketball Team; [oth. writ.] This will be 1st published work.; [pers.] I try to touch the heart and mind of each reader...so they can see the pictures I see in my heart and mind...then we are one step closer to being friends.; [a.] Sallisaw, OK

CRUMP, GLORIA JEAN
[Pen.] Serenity; [b.] November 7, 1951, Los Angeles; [p.] Robert and Florence Crump; [ch.] 3 year old daughter Lavelle Alexander; [ed.] University of Southern California 1968-1974, Bachelor of Science Jefferson High School, LA; [occ.] Educator 20 years Inglewood School District and 13 years Los Angeles Unified School District; [memb.] A member of Delta Sigma Theta Sorority.; [hon.] Ephebian Award, Awarded a scholarship from the Progressive California; [oth. writ.] "The Ship of Hope," "Hurting Me," " Just For a Moment," "In the Garden Alone," "Parents," "Not Another Day," "Doors," "Dia-

monds Just for Me,"; [pers.] We are all special guest on earth. A royal family with a guest to soufoultry unfold.; [a.] Los Angeles, CA

CRUZ, BETTY J.
[Pen.] Be Jay; [b.] Indpls., IN; [ed.] Indiana University; [occ.] Counselor Education; [pers.] There is light in every shadow if we allow ourselves to see.; [a.] Framingham, MA

CRUZ, DIANA ARCELLY
[p.] March 17, 1981, Cali, Columbia; [p.] Luz M. Toro; [ed.] Louis W. Batchelder Elementary School; [occ.] Student (middle school 8th grade); [memb.] John Casablancas Modeling and Talent Agency.; [hon.] High honors, All American Boy and Girl Pageant in Connecticut; [a.] Hartford, CT

CRUZ, SANDRA
[b.] March 12, 1949, Savannah, GA; [p.] Freddie Ruth and Edgar Tatum Sr.,; [m.] Pablo Cruz, July 6, 1968; [ch.] Paul, Maruz, Norris, Terrence, Pauline Cruz's; [ed.] Sarah J. Hale Voc. H.S.; [occ.] Disable; [oth. writ.] NYC Transit, Poetry in Motion Contest.; [pers.] Company information and visualizing the meaning of yesterday to today. Based on reality in relationship from my childhood to an adult, brings my thoughts onto paper. To see as others no different than I may cover the inner truth. Silently to be, one can see.; [a.] Brooklyn, NY

CUENTO, CHRISTA
[Pen.] Christa; [b.] August 14, 1980, Philippines; [p.] Richardo Cuento & Nenita Sevilla; [ed.] 7th Grade, St. Mary Grammar School, Jersey City, NJ; [occ.] Student; [memb.] Nagcarlan Association of America; [hon.] Second honor, 6th Grade; [oth. writ.] poems; [pers.] Poems suddenly come to my mind I don't know why, is it because I'm still a child?; [a.] Jersey City, NJ

CUEVAS, MICHAEL
[b.] March 19, 1976, Wittier, CA; [occ.] Absurdist; [pers.] Live life like a candle, shine on, burn up and die.; [a.] Whittier, CA

CULBREATH JR., TROLLIE
[b.] March 6, 1943, Monroe, GA; [p.] Trollie and Catherine Culbreath; [ch.] Kristi Renee Culbreath Roberts; [ed.] Asso. Degree, Miami Univ.; [occ.] Retired Postal Supv.; [memb.] New Era Baptist Church, VFW 6405 Elk Lodge 456; [oth. writ.] Several poems not published.; [pers.] I give thanks to God for putting me on this beautiful earth with the wisdom, knowledge and understanding to be able to see and write about his beauty.; [a.] Middletown, OH

CURWIN, NICOLE
[b.] May 28, 1981, Opelika, AL; [p.] David and Jay Curwin; [ed.] Sanford Middle School; [occ.] Student; [memb.] National Honor Society; [hon.] Student of the year; [oth. writ.] School newspaper; [pers.] Do for other people what you want them to do for you. Luke 6:31; [a.] Opelika, AL

CZIGAN, JOANNA
[b.] July 5, 1977, Pensacola, FL; [p.] Paul and Linda Czigan; [ed.] Senior in High School, Osceola High School; [occ.] Student; [memb.] Thespians; [hon.] Superior Rating in Acting at District Competition 1st Place in Art Sculpture Contest; [oth. writ.] Red, Lies,

both are poems; [pers.] Live, love, and leave your worries till another day.; [a.] Kissimmee, FL

D'AMBROSIO, ROSALIND ELENA GRAHAM
[Pen.] Linda D'Ambrosio; [p.] Romeo D'Ambrosio, Mary Dye; [m.] Bruce David Graham; [ch.] Laura Mae Katherina, Roland David Paul; [occ.] Artist; [oth. writ.] Currently working on novel set in the 1950's.; [pers.] I believe that every living creature has a purpose in this world and that we are all linked as in a chain broken only at our own peril. Vegetarian, Anti Racist, be it black or white!; [a.] Huntington, WV

D'ERAMO, LUCILLE WAITE
[b.] June 3, 1936, Danburg, CT; [p.] Dorothy Testa and William Waite; [m.] Panfilo D'Eramo, May 13, 1961; [ch.] Lee Marie, Linda, susan, John, Julie; [ed.] St. Joseph Grammar School, Danburg High School, St. Vincent's School of Nursing, University of Bridgeport; [occ.] Psychiatric/Mental Health Reg. Nurse; [memb.] Catholic Council of Nurses; [hon.] CT and National Parent Teachers Assoc. Award; Substance Abuse Educ. for Parents; Distinguished Service for March of Dimes 1976; [oth. writ.] Poetry and short novels. Professional nursing articles.; [pers.] "Feelings from the Heart flow through the pen.

D'OTTAVIO, ANGELA DONNA
[Pen.] Donna Anrepid; [b.] December 29, 1964, Hastings, NY; [p.] Adeline and Anthony DiPerna; [m.] bruce Albert D'Ottario, November 17, 1984; [ch.] Lauren Nicole, our first child; [ed.] Vineland Schools LPN; [memb.] New Jersey Ed. Prog. Assoc., N.J. Health Occupations, Educators Assoc., Saint Isidores Church, Vineland Schools, LPN Program Advisory Committee; [hon.] Honor Student in High School, Dean's List (College), Valedictorian of LPN Program, Valedictorian of Registered Nursing Program, Employee of the Quarter Award, Newcomb Medical Center; [oth. writ.] Many poems given as gifts to family and friends, many writings done for my present job, i.e. curriculum, student graduation ceremony, articles submitted to nursing journals, many persona writings including 2 msall books yet not attempted to be published.; [pers.] The poem published in this book is dedicated to my daughter Lauren. I believe life is a journey of learning which occurs both within yourself and without.; [a.] Vineland, NJ

D'OTTAVIO, LEON
[b.] March 5, 1962, Elmer, NJ; [p.] Ronnie and Elaine D'Ottavio; [m.] Kim D'Ottavio, February 15, 1992; [ch.] Angela D'Ottavio; [ed.] Enrolled in College, Physical Therapist Ass. Program; [occ.] Farmer; [memb.] Atlantic Wreck Divers Association, Yi's Karate Tang Soo Do; [hon.] Dean's List, two semesters. 1st Dan Black Belt; [pers.] Dedicated to my Grandmom for being like a second mother to all her 22 grandchildren and 37 great grandchildren. We love you.

DABNEY, PAULA A.
[b.] February 24, 1971, Elmira, NY; [p.] Barry G. Dabney and Sandra I. Smith; [ed.] Elmira Southside High School; [occ.] Salesperson aspiring to further education; [oth. writ.] Several accumulated poems, some poems pending publication.; [pers.] Sometimes the eyes of your heart see more clearly than the eyes of your mind; it is through these which I choose to guide my writing. 2 Corinthians 5:17.; [a.] Elmira, NY

DABU, MARION
[b.] February 21, 1981, Philippines; [p.] Norma Dabu-Cunanan; [ed.] Our Lady of Peace School; [hon.] MVP "A" Volleyball Team, "Most Inspirational" Softball Team, Citizenship Award at School; [oth. writ.] Martin Luther King Jr. Essay, other poems,; [pers.] Family and friends (especially mind) are most important than anything else in the world to me.; [a.] Sylmar, CA

DAL PORTO III, RICHARD PAUL
[b.] May 18, 1974, Santa Moria, CA; [p.] Dick and Judy Dal Porto; [ed.] St. Joseph High, Allan Hancock College, California State University, Chico; [occ.] Student; [oth. writ.] Editor and contributor of high school literary magazine and newspaper. Articles published in community newspaper. Poem published in Flipside Magazine.; [pers.] I really don't consider myself much of a poet. I'm more interested in writing fiction. However, poetry serves as a good outlet for quick thoughts that need to be fleshed out Now, at least, tht's the way it works for me. My favorite poet is E. E. Cummungs.; [a.] Chico, CA

DALHOUSE, ROLAND
[Pen.] Ronald King; [b.] May 13, 1969, Jamaica; [p.] Frederick Dalhouse and Sheila Dunn; [m.] Single; [ed.] Trench Town Comprehensive High School, Apex Technical Trade School.; [occ.] Cook; [memb.] Member of Seventh Day Adventist Church; [hon.] Was awarded a scholarship to the school of music, by taste talent contest in Kingston, Jamaica; [oth. writ.] Working currently on a book (poetry) named "On Going Changes," to be released to the public.; [pers.] My sole purpose in writing is to educate mankind of ways and means of reaching out to each other; and also for black people to understand each other.; [a.] Brooklyn, NY

DALLOW, KENDALL
[b.] April 22, 1980, Denver, CO; [p.] Michaella MacKay, Kurt Dallow; [ed.] Class of 97 at South High School, Denver, CO; [occ.] School; [memb.] National Thespian Society; [pers.] "Keep doing what's not socially approved, and eventually society will change..or you'll be killed." Ashleigh Brilliant If you give up then you never really tried your hardest.; [a.] Denver, CO

DAMM, ANDREA
[b.] September 25, 1975, Great Bend, KS; [p.] Linda and James Damm; [ed.] Larned High School, graduate of 1994; [occ.] College Student, Assistant Dance Instructor; [oth. writ.] Several poems published in local newspapers including the Wichita Eagle, a prose published in The High School Writer which covers ten states.; [pers.] I would like to dedicate the publication of this poem to Mrs. Arlyne Basom who gave me the freedom, courage and support to express myself through words. Thank You!; [a.] Larned, KS

DAMPIER, NICOLE
[b.] January 3, 1980, White Plains, NY; [p.] Alfred and Rose Dampier; [ed.] White Plains Middle School; [a.] White Plains, NY

DANDURAND, AMY LOUISE WILSON
[b.] August 9, 1952, Elyria, Ohio; [p.] Howard and Eleanor C. Wilson; [m.] Luc Dandurand, May 5, 1984; [ch.] Daniel Rene, Eli Alain; [ed.] Pennsylvania Public Schools, Mt. Mansfield Union (VT) High School, University of Vermont; [occ.] Dairy Farmer, specialty food producer, semi-professional musician; [memb.] Vermont ETV, National Mustang Association, Vermont Symphony Orchestra Chorus; [hon.] High School Valedictorian, 1st Flute Vermont All-State Band, UVM Music Camp Scholarship, Choral Soloist, French Language Award, UVM and FFA Dairy Awards; [oth. writ.] Family letters and journals in English and French, poems and essays, articles, editorials, and testimony on agriculture published locally and nationally. Baking instruction in English and French; [pers.] My 3 sisters and I were named after Louisa Mae Alcott's "Little Women" of literary fame.; [a.] Underhill, VT

DANIEL, VICKY
[Pen.] "Gidget"; [b.] July 21, 1966, Ohio; [m.] Christo Daniel, June 5, 1992; [ch.] Shannon Marie, Shawn Michael; [ed.] Crestwood High; [pers.] Express our feelings that flows each day, with it brings us our hopes and dreams that will come true someday, love and happiness will be yours, for the accomplishment we have yet to make.; [a.] Keystone Hts., FL

DANIELS, DEBRA ANN
[Pen.] Dee; [b.] July 16, 1961, Pine Bluff, AR; [p.] Henry and Hallie Walters; [m.] Donald L. Daniels, September 18, 1991; [ch.] Derrell, Corlena Gwone; [ed.] 1 1/2 yrs. college, City College of Chicago, H.S. Watson Chapel High; [occ.] Factory Worker; [memb.] International Society of Poets (Induction Date, August 19, 1994); [pers.] I feel that everyone needs someone in order to function, and without the power of love, we will never have world peace or racial harmony.; [a.] Pine Bluff, AR

DANIELS, MICHELE
[b.] July 20, 1961, Sidney, NY; [p.] Carol Wilber and Robert Nesbit; [ch.] Cassie, Shawn, Bret; [ed.] Afton Central School; [occ.] Utility Worker; [memb.] Assembly of God Church, IBEW Union; [hon.] Various Air Force Awards and Honors.; [oth. writ.] Nothing published.; [pers.] I wrote this poem to try to influence people to help the plight of the world's precious children.; [a.] Bainbridge, NY

DANINO, SEBASTIAN
[b.] October 26, 1982, Peru; [p.] Roberto A. Pauline; [ed.] 6th Grade, Thomas W. Pyle Middle School; [occ.] Student; [a.] Potomac, MD

DARBY JR., KEITH ANTHONY
[b.] May 24, 1970, Parma, Ohio; [p.] Keith A. and Ollie M. Darby; [m.] Single; [ed.] B.S. Architecture, Minor, City and Regional Planning, Ohio State University, Certified Scuba Diver; [occ.] Architecture; [memb.] AIA, American Institute of Architect; [hon.] Merit Scholarship, University's honor program, Orange Belt Karate; [oth. writ.] Poems and Quotes; [pers.] "There is no fire like the heart of the young. We must build it for our soul, feed it for fury, and let it burn for all our passions. For so long as that fire rages, so do we live in youth-forever" (Original quote from my work); [a.] Fairfield, OH

DARCY, JESSICA
[b.] January 28, 1977, Denville, NJ; [p.] Diane and Gerald d'Arcy; [ed.] I am entering my Senior year at John Jay High School in East Fishkill, NY; [memb.]

I am a member of the Hudson Valley Writers Association.; [pers.] All I'm trying to do is balance words for thoughts, that's what makes good poetry for me. It is like only have one chance to say something, you want to say it right.; [a.] Wappingers Falls, NY

DARLAGE, ADAM
[b.] October 8, 1975, Plano, TX; [p.] Gary and Linda Darlage; [ed.] Lakota High School; [occ.] Full time student, Xavier University; [memb.] University Scholars Program, Xavier Royal Redeemer Luthern church; [hon.] National Honor Society, Trustee Scholarship Xavier; [oth. writ.] nothing published.; [pers.] I write about the state of my world. I observe its strengths and its shortcomings, as well as many other conditions of living. I enjoy writing poetry.; [a.] West Chester, OH

DARLENE, PORTNER M.
[b.] December 12, 1958, Oneida, NY; [p.] George and Thelma Conley; [m.] Albert E. L. Portner, December 24, 1981; [ch.] Jeremiah Hans, Esther Mae, Serah Leigh, Urah James Leigh; [ed.] V.V.S. High School; [memb.] Friendship Baptist Church, Grange; [hon.] Oneida Lions Club Award; [oth. writ.] Poem in church bulletin; [pers.] I want to do my best to honor and glorify the Lord. Luke 1:37 For with God nothing shall be impossible. May my poem help those who need it most.; [a.] Rome, NY

DARRINGTON, CHARNETTE
[b.] December 25, 1977, Houston; [p.] Lois and William Darrington; [ed.] High School of Performing Visual Arts 11th Grade; [occ.] Theatre Student; [memb.] Thespian Socity, H.S.P.V.A's and St. Timothy's United Methodist Youth Organization; [hon.] Speech Awards, Prose, Imp., Pantiomine, Extemp, and Pantomine; [pers.] I believe that you should never take anything for granted but always strive to go a step further to accomplish your goals and maintain a sense of spirituality.; [a.] Houston, TX

DAUGHERTY, LISA
[b.] October 8, 1966, Covington, KY; [p.] Richard and Marilyn Hallman; [m.] Gary Daugherty, May 9, 1987; [ch.] none; [ed.] Boone County High, Northern Kentucky University; [occ.] Customer Service Agent, Delta Airlines; [hon.] Graduated with Beta Honors. Earned honorable mention for other artistry.; [oth. writ.] Personal poems to my mother, sister and brother.; [pers.] This poem was written and dedicated to my father Richard Hallman. "I love you father more than you know."; [a.] Burlington, KY

DAVIDSON, CHARITY
[b.] October 10, 1979, Albuquerque, NM; [p.] Don and Karen Davidson; [occ.] A Student at Los Alametios Middle School; [hon.] A and B Honor Roll Awards; Four citizenship Awards; Writing Awards; Second place in History Day, individual papers; Outstanding Performance Award; [oth. writ.] "The Writer," "Wild Horses," and "The Moonlight." I was published the Cibola County Creative Contest and Anthology of Poetry by Young Americans; [pers.] I would like to thank Mrs. Ocampo for inspiring me to write. Thank you.; [a.] Grants, NM

DAVIDSON, KELLY
[b.] February 13, 1977, Pomano, CA; [p.] Clyde and Maureen Davidson; [ch.] Brother, Ben (Musician), Siara Garton (best friend); [ed.] Brea Olinda High School, Prescott High School; [occ.] Student and

writer.; [memb.] Nature Conservancy, World Wildlife Fund, Whale Adoption Project, National Audubon Society.; [hon.] Editor's Choice Award and Several poems published through the National Library of Poetry; Who's Who Among American High School Students; [oth. writ.] Several poems, short stories, and an illustrated children's book with the hopes of publication.; [pers.] I write for the pure joy of it and to make others smile. One laugh, tells a million stories.; [a.] Prescott, AZ

DAVIS, BONNIE
[b.] October 18, 1962, Endicott, NY; [p.] Robert Barton, Jr.; [m.] Kathrine Richards and Brad M. Davis, June 1979; [ch.] Christian Aubrey, Jason Arthur, Kevin Daniel; [ed.] Vestal Senior High; [occ.] Writing; [memb.] Easter Seals, Church of Christ; [oth. writ.] I have started to write poems and short stories. That when envisioned, are felt deeply and meaningfully.; [pers.] Believing in myself has brought great changes into my life and a greater faith in God. Thanks to my family and dear friend, Arlene Paden; [a.] Johnson, NY

DAVIS, DELOYD LEVERN VANLUCIFER
[b.] April 4, 1975, Philadelphia; [p.] Annie Pearl Davis; [ed.] Terrell's Bay High School, South Carolina; [occ.] Model; [oth. writ.] First time writer; [pers.] I've wrote this poem not just for my ancestors but for other race ancestors. Who had to overcome the bearers to live the life as a free human-being. So up under one nation we stand proud with life, liberty, and justices.; [a.] Philadelphia, PA

DAVIS, DOROTHY K.
[b.] September 29, 1929, Hendersonville, NC; [p.] Mabel W. and Frank R. King (deceased); [m.] Charles T. Davis, June 1, 1957; [occ.] Retired Industrial Engineer, Federal Civil Service; [memb.] Eastern Star, VFW Ladies Auxillary, Moslah Temple Shrine, Christian Church; [hon.] 52 Monetary Awards and 2 trophies for various achievements during 30 years of Civil service; [oth. writ.] Articles in Fort Worth Star Telegram (newspaper), Readers Digest. Poetry published in "Reflections" Journals Quarterly, Church Bulletins, Business Newsletters, Commercials, Etc.; [pers.] I am enjoying writing about life in the slow lane-- (much of my career entailed writing regulations and manuals). Hobbies: Playing piano and organ, oil painting.; [a.] Fort Worth, TX

DAVIS, KIRK D.
[b.] April 23, 1955; [p.] Albert and Catherine Davis; [m.] Patti Jo (Snyder) Davis, May 28, 1993; [ch.] Stephen, Michael, Melissa, Nathan; [ed.] U.S. Armed Forces School of Music Burrell High School; [occ.] Production Supervisor, PPG Industries, Springdale, PA; [hon.] Member of U.S. Navy Steel Band from 1973-1979, Who's Who Among American High School Students 1973; [oth. writ.] I have written over 200 poems; [pers.] My writing is self-therapy; a way to express strong feelings that well up inside, and need let out. I love words; [a.] Apollo, PA

DAVIS, MARTHA E.
[Pen.] Stardust; [b.] March 19, 1950, Oceanside, CA; [p.] Dr. Joseph B. and Eva Braun Davis; [ed.] Walt Whitman High, Corcoran School of Art, Montgomery Community College, Grossmont Regional Occupations Program; [occ.] Lic. Psychiatric Tech., Creative Arts, Photographer, Teacher, Consortium of

San Diego, Graphic Artist, Silversmith; [memb.] Creative Arts Consortium of san Diego, Players Group, CA Lic. Psychiatric Tech.; [hon.] 3rd Place in the Creative Arts Consortium Art Lit. Contest 1994 for Sterling Silver Spoon Necklace, Handmade Originals, one of a kind; [oth. writ.] This is my first time submitting my poetry.; [pers.] I hope and pray tht I will see paradise on earth in my lifetime.; [a.] San Diego, CA

DAVIS, SHARON L.
[b.] July 8, 1944, Joliet, IL; [p.] Robert and Ardis Thrope; [m.] Richard A. Davis, January 2, 1983; [ch.] Mark Karl Wollerman and Karl Robert Wollerman; [ed.] Joliet Township High School, in Joliet, IL., Sarasota Technical Institute, in Sarasota, FL; [occ.] Office Manager, Vice President, Certified Appraisers and Consultants, Inc., Sarasota, FL; [memb.] First Lutheran Church and White Shrine.; [hon.] Elected Precinct Committee Woman, Bureau County Illinois, in Presidential Election, 1980; [oth. writ.] Author of newspaper column: "Sharing with Sharon," Bureau County Illinois Farm Bureau paper, for 3 years.; [pers.] I started to write rhymes/poetry about 10 years ago for myself, family and friend. With the encouragement of my husband and mother, I now have become more confident and share my writings with others. I am very much an old fashion romantic.; [a.] Sarasota, FL

DAVISON, NOAH W.
[b.] July 27, 1967, LaJunta, CO; [p.] Paula K. Word, Noah W. Davison; [ed.] Lamar High School, Colorado State University; [occ.] Landscape Architect; [memb.] American Society of Landscape Architects (ASLA); [hon.] Best Graphical Artist 3 years at CSU Landscape Architecture Program.; [oth. writ.] Various poems on various subjects, short stories, nothing ever published until now; [pers.] In our world, not only does beauty abound everywhere, if you look hard enough, but also tragedy, which isn't so hard to find. The great thing about writing poetry is tht inspiration can be found anywhere, anytime.; [a.] Fort Collins, CO

DE MARMOLEJO, LEONORA ACUNA
[b.] January 11, 1936, Colombia, South America; [p.] Nicolas Acuna and Anuncicion Varela; [m.] Leoncio Marmolejo; [ch.] Luz Helena, Gloria Milena, Diego Fernando and Jaime Leoncio; 3 grandchildren: Jennifer Andrea Braun, Jason Kenneth Braun and Jacqueline Mary Iannone; [ed.] Graduated as a teacher from Normal Nacional De Cali, In Colombia: Graduated in Social Sciences from State University of New York: Studied Art at the Conservatory of Arts and Music in Cali, Colombia, and studied art at SUNY, Farmingdale; [occ.] Retired, now writing my 3rd book of poems, a novel, and finishing a book on short stories; [memb.] Suburban Art League, Independent Art Society, Islip Art Museum, Nassau County Museum of Art, Member of Latin American Writers Institute; [hon.] Too many to mention; [oth. writ.] Published Books and Articles in Newspapers; [pers.] I think that poetry is the soul of the people, and therefore, it should carry a noble and altruistic message.; [a.] Levittown, NY

DEAL, ETHELJEAN
[Pen.] Ef Deal, Talespinner; [b.] November 6, 1954, Audubon, NJ; [m.] reverend Jack Deal; [ch.] Jesse and Buddy; [ed.] Douglass College; [occ.] English

Teacher; [memb.] United Methodist Lay Speakers, Southern New Jersey Conference Youth Council, Young Authors Conference Committee; [oth. writ.] Essays and poems published locally; sword and sorcery novels and short fiction; christian fantasy; [pers.] I do not write to create but to be created. Human beings see connections; writers are connections; [a.] Haddonfield, NJ

DEBARRY, FRANCES D.M.
[b.] November 12, 1972, Arizona; [p.] Mr. and Mrs. William Davis; [ch.] Benjamin Phillips (B.J.), I Love You.; [oth. writ.] Unpublished, "Why"; "Still In Love"; "Twice heart Broken"; "Memories with Tears"; "Vowels and Wedding Rings" above are all poems.; [pers.] I would like to thank God, my family, friends and loved ones for all their support and encouragement when I need it the most. I love you all.; [a.] Gloucester, NJ

DECATO, LISA
[b.] April 16, 1970, Paterson, NJ; [p.] Andy and Sharon Buis; [m.] Fianace: Joe Nativo; [pers.] I write poems that are positive. All my writings come from my heart and soul.; [a.] Hawthorne, NJ

DEER, MELODY LYNN
[b.] December 4, 1978, Rhine Lander, WI; [p.] Jeannette and James Dailey; [ed.] I'm a sophomore at Crandon High School; [occ.] Seasonal, I work at a Go-Kart Track (Kartway); [memb.] Wisconsin Trappers Association; [hon.] High Honors, Band Awards (Metals), Drama (Best Actress of 1993) Trophies in Basketball, Baseball and Cheerleading; [oth. writ.] Several poems for myself, nothing professional; [pers.] I try to express my feelings and thoughts in the poems that I write. I am greatly influenced by the man in my life. Micak Dewing; [a.] Argonne, WI

DEESE, EMMA
[b.] November 14, 1958, Davidson, NC; [p.] Fred and Janie Deese; [ed.] M.A. Sarah Lawrence College; Health Advocacy, M.A. Lesley College; Expressive Art, Therapy; [occ.] Health Advocate/Activity Director, Kit Clark Adult Day Health Program; [memb.] Menninger Society; [hon.] Patricia Roberts Harris Fellowship; Sarah Lawrence College; Graduate Commencement Speaker (S.L.C. 1991) Miss Senior (North Carolina Central University), Sterling Who's Who 94'-95'; [pers.] I strive to reflect the eternal destiny of the present moment in my writing. "You only live once in life but if you do it right once is enough."; [a.] Somerville, MA

DELANEY, MILISSA KAR
[b.] May 12, 1982, Blackfoot, ID; [p.] Bill and Dyana Delaney; [ed.] Entering Snake River, Junior High School; [occ.] Student 7th grade; [hon.] Dance Awards in Ballet, school Honor Roll Awards for 4.0 grade average.; [pers.] I enjoy creative writing about dancing and fantasy and I love learning new things.; [a.] Blackfoot, ID

DELARIO, JACQUIE
[b.] December 21, 1956, Phila., PA; [p.] Albert and Josephine Delario; [ed.] PA State University, B.A. in Social Welfare; [occ.] Process Operator on a Crude distillation Unit, Sun Phila. Refinery; [memb.] Pt. Breeze Local 8-990, OCAWIU (Financial-Secretary), Clean Water Action, Coalition of Labor Union Women, Labor Party Advocate; [hon.] Dean's List, National

Honor Society; [oth. writ.] Union Literature, newsletters, seminar reviews; [pers.] I am always mindful of the philosophy of my freshman English teacher, Miss Jones: "To strive, to seek, to find and not to yield." Ulyssess Alfred, Lord Tennyson; [a.] Philadelphia, PA

DELAROSA M.D., CARMEN T.R.
[b.] July 8, 1948, Philippines; [p.] Arturo Ramirez and Cecilia Fironia; [m.] Armando P. DelaRosa, D.M.D., June 24, 1946; [ch.] Anne Genevieve and Alex Arturo; [ed.] Doctor of Medicine; [occ.] Physician, Family Practice; [memb.] AMA, SMA, APPA.; [hon.] Valedictorian, H.S. Meritus, Doctor of Medicine; [pers.] Love is universal.; [a.] Gulf Breeze, FL

DELGADO, GAIL LEE
[b.] October 14, 1963, IL; [ch.] Natalie, Samantha Delgado; [ed.] Mountain View High School, Mesa, AZ; [occ.] Optical Manager; [pers.] Poetry is my personal security blanket. It allows me to be me, to be comfortable in my expressions and my feelings, and can when handed to someone can also offer comfort and happiness. I write for myself and others.; [a.] Mesa, AZ

DEMPSEY, DEBRA SUE MAY
[b.] September 9, 1964, Greensburg, PA; [p.] Fred and Rebecca Markle May; [m.] Robert Dempsey, September 17, 1983; [ch.] Jonathan; [ed.] Greater Latrobe High School 1982; [a.] Derry, PA

DEMPSEY, W. RICHARD
[b.] January 30, 1936, Miami, FL; [p.] Fred and Mary Dempsey; [m.] Ellen Webb Dempsey, September 26, 1965; [ch.] Erik Webb Dempsey; [ed.] The George Washington University, Wash., D.C.; [occ.] Intelligence Operations Specialist (Retired); [oth. writ.] Editor, Are Numberless Strangers So Important? (World Hunger Symposium, 1976); [pers.] What's a billion years to a grain of sand? The Cosmos knows itself only through our minds.; [a.] Stone Mountain, GA

DENNING, SMITHIE O.
[b.] June 21, 1936, Princeton, NC; [p.] William and Letha Overman; [ch.] Kathryn D. Holloman and William Joseph Denning; [ed.] Princeton High, Mount Olive College, Johnson Technical College, Wayne Community College; [occ.] Seamstress (Home); [memb.] Rains Cross Rods, F.W.B. Church, St. Johns P.H. Church W.A. (Woman's Aux); [hon.] Publication in Renaissance 1994 (Wayne Community College's Writer's and Artists Magazine), Works read aloud in class; [pers.] I believe each person capable of more.; [a.] Mount Olive, NC

DENNIS, PATRICE
[b.] March 17, 1957, Amery, WI; [p.] George and Sophie Dennis; [ed.] Clayton High School, University of Minnesota; [occ.] Boutique Manager; [pers.] I strive to enjoy life and to always be true to my heart.

DENSCH, GENEVEVE
[b.] November 20, 1921, Milwaukee; [p.] Michael and Angeline; [m.] Henry Densch; [ch.] Garald Robert, Lynette Rae; [ed.] G.E.D. High School Diploma; [occ.] Retired from housewife; [pers.] Creation of worlds, etc. quote Romans, Dedicated to my family, especially to Mom, who gave me life.; [a.] Plover, WI

DEPOLIS, RYAN
[b.] July 24, 1983, Cleveland, OH; [p.] John and Laura Depolis; [ed.] Sixth Grade Student (1994-1995); [hon.] Student Author Award of excellence (1993), Outstanding Academics, Good Citizenship, Honor Roll Awards; [oth. writ.] Various poems and stories.; [pers.] I like taking my readers to magical and mystical places. I feel it can expand their imagination to a never ending boundary.; [a.] Redendo Beach, CA

DEREWITZ, MICHAEL L.
[b.] April 2, 1945, Phila. PA; [p.] David and Martha; [m.] Hkyong Lee, June 24, 1990; [ch.] David, Eugene; [ed.] B.A. American International College, M.A. Northwestern University, Ed.D. Candidate LaSalle University; [occ.] Underwriting and instructional manager insurance; [memb.] B.I.A., P.S.S., A.P.S.; [hon.] Dean's List, Philippic History Award, Northwestern University Full Post Graduate scholarship; [oth. writ.] Anthology of Poems inspired by travels in Korea.; [pers.] I strive in my work to reflect the beauty of nature and the depth of human emotion. My greatest inspiration is from Tadism and Stoicism; [a.] Eagleville, PA

DEVORE, TERRY LYNN
[b.] August 8, 1956, Casper, Wyo.; [p.] Gene and Yvonne Tholl; [m.] Brian DeVore, July 11, 1992; [ed.] I graduated High School on June 4, 1974 from Provo High School in Provo, Utah; [occ.] Babysitter; [hon.] I have received a few awards for being a Sunday School Teacher at Hope Chapel Gateway in Torrance, CA; [pers.] I'm deeply in love with my husband. He is an inspiration to me. I've always loved to write poetry as well as children's stories.; [a.] Torrance, CA

DIBENEDETTO, ELIZABETH
[b.] February 21, 1963, Brooklyn, NY; [p.] Thomas and Joan DiBenedetto; [ch.] Kelly Ann DiBenedetto; [ed.] Lafayette H.S. Adelphi Jr. College; [occ.] Senior Telephone Operator; [oth. writ.] Several short stories awaiting publication.; [pers.] I have to come to know, there is no greater pleasure, than that which your spirit is allowed the freedom's for which your dreams are made. My writing's are the roads of my dreams.; [a.] Brooklyn, NY

DICK, CHRISTINE M.
[b.] January 15, 1975, Phila., PA; [p.] John and Carmella Dick; [ed.] Cardinal Dougherty, H.S., Drexel Univ.; [occ.] Student; [memb.] Phi Eta Sigma National Honor Society, Artisans; [hon.] Dean's List, Drexel University Scholar Athlete 1992-93 (Cardinal Dougherty H.S.); [oth. writ.] Reporter for "Prelate" (local school newspaper); [pers.] My poetry reflects what influences my life.; [a.] Philadelphia, PA

DICKEY, JULIETTE LIVELY
[b.] March 17, 1927, Georgia; [p.] James Thaxter and Julia Lively; [m.] Ben S. Dickey, September 22, 1946; [ch.] Thaxter, Dennis, Ben Jr., Angie Gifford, Lorene Dickey; [ed.] Waynesboro High School, Bessie Tift College; [occ.] Secretary Specialist; [memb.] Central Church of Christ Poetry Ocala & Florida State Poetry Assn.; [hon.] Honorary Lifetime Foster Home Certificate; [oth. writ.] An Idea, Published in Ocala Star Banner; [pers.] Favorite Bible Verse - Acts 28:15"..brothers there heard we were coming...traveled far to meet us. At sight of them,

Paul Thanked God and was encourage." Encouragement comes in many forms from various places. With love and kindness from numerous different races. A handshake a friendly smile or a pat on the shoulder, Giving love, warmth, hope and friendship to the beholder. by: JLC; [a.] Ocala, FL

DIMARIA, KIM
[b.] August 20, 1967, Brooklyn, NY; [p.] Raymond DiMaria and Linda Sticeso; [m.] Frank A. Muzio, August 20, 1987; [ch.] Dayna Lin and Karalyn Marie Muzio; [ed.] High School (GED); [occ.] Mom fulltime; [oth. writ.] Several of my own at home poems, thoughts mostly real life as far as I see it. None ever published before.; [pers.] What is in our soul is who we really are. If we all had a strong hold on who we are, kindness, honesty, a better life (world) would exist.; [a.] Brooklyn, NY

DINICOLA, MICHAEL G.
[b.] June 30, 1970, Phila. PA; [p.] George and Linda Dinicola; [ed.] Archbishop John Carrol High School, Community College of Philadelphia; [occ.] Student/Writer; [hon.] Winner of the Judith Stark Creative Writing Award, second Prize Poetry 1994; [oth. writ.] Hundreds of unpublished poems being prepared for possible publication; some articles written for school newspaper.; [pers.] Influences include Dr. Seuss, Shakespeare, Plath, Poe, Pound, Ogden Nash, Muhammed Ali, Amy Ray, Eddie Vedder, and most importantly Jim Morrison. I am forever striving for something truly original and unique.; [a.] Philadelphia, PA

DINKINS JR., BENJAMIN STEPHON
[Pen.] Strauga; [b.] May 27, 1971, St. Petersburg, FL; [p.] Benjamin and Louise Weeks Dinkins; [ed.] Chelsea Voc. Boyd, Anderson FL, Palmetto High FL, Samuel J. Tilden High, John Jay College, Kingsborough Community College; [occ.] Student; [memb.] Madd Hat Wearers, Forty First Side, Five Six Blitz, Many Cruel Son's; [hon.] Associates in Liberal Arts; [pers.] The never ending guest to find a brighter day; under stormy situations clouding my every foot step!; [a.] Brooklyn, NY

DIXON JR., CHARLES L.
[b.] June 15, 1968, Homnestead, FL; [p.] Charles and Patricia Dixon; [m.] Takato M. Dixon, November 22, 1992; [ch.] Kiko Juliana Dixon; [ed.] Milton High School, Student of Pensacola Junior College and the University of Maryland; [occ.] U.S. Navy; [oth. writ.] This is my first poem published. However, I am currently co-authoring a novel.; [pers.] Pain and suffering is sometimes a devastating personal experience but when it has past you don't have to let the memory of it control your present life and the future.

DOERKSEN, BARB
[b.] September 11, 1967, Saskatchewan, Canada; [m.] Paul, August 31, 1991; [ed.] Peacock High, Wascana Institute of Applied Arts and Sciences; [occ.] Office Manager for a music store; [hon.] High School Honors Graduate; [a.] Clinton, IA

DOERSAM, RAYMOND
[b.] January 23, 1915, Rochester, NY; [p.] Raymond and Lillian; [m.] Doris, 1943; [ch.] Two; [ed.] Graduate Rochester Institute of Technology, Special Courses U. of Rochester, Cornell U.; [occ.] Retired Director of College and University Food Services.;

[pers.] I hope to leave this world a little better than I found it. Religion: Agnostic (Cowardly Atheist).

DOLAN, COURTNEY
[b.] January 16, 1981, Topeka, KS; [p.] Jim and Nadine Dolan; [ed.] Going into the 8th grade at St. Joseph, Catholic School in Shreveport; [occ.] Student; [memb.] COSST (City of Shreveport Swim Team), Girl Scouts; [hon.] Kiyoe M. Schrotke Award at Art Break in Shreveport for this poem. A previous poem was published in a collection of student's poems. Highest for 7th grade honors graduate at St. Joseph's; [occ.] "Purple"; [a.] Shreveport, LA

DONAHUE, THERESA DIPIETRO
[Pen.] Teri; [b.] May 28, 1932, Mahanoy City, PA; [p.] Anthony & Susan DiPietro; [m.] James Donahue, May 29, 1954; [ch.] Patricia, Teresa, James, Mary, Carole, Carleen, Lisabeth; [ed.] High School and Creative Writing in night school (Mahandy City High); [occ.] Homemaker, former Executive Secretary; [memb.] Former Member of Walter Erb Memorial Church; Northeast Mother's of Twins Club.; [hon.] Monetaryn Bonus from Church for Secretarial work, Choir Director, Sunday School Teacher and Senior Citizens Pres.; [oth. writ.] Approximately 160 poems, some I published in two volumes titled "Looking At Life," Vol. I & II and commentaries.; [pers.] I am inspired to write about inner strength & peace of mind. My love for my creator and mankind keep me "Looking at Life."; [a.] Phila., PA

DONLEY, PHILLIS
[b.] December 21, 1935, Tyler, TX; [p.] Billie M. Ware; [ed.] Los Angeles City College; Morehouse College, Atlanta, GA, Phyllis Wheatley High School, San Antonio, TX; Frederick Douglass Jr. High school, San Antonio, TX; [occ.] Computer Analyst, Real Estate; [memb.] The Urban League First A.M.E. Church; [oth. writ.] Poems translated into French in Paris in 1985. Brought out that year in Paris. (published semi-privately); [pers.] I wish to express my voice with depth and music. I have been greatly influenced by the romantic poets and the modernist, the 20th century modernist poets.; [a.] Los Angeles, CA

DONOHUE, MIA MAZIE
[Pen.] Mia; [b.] May 30, 1957, Hawaii; [occ.] Artist, Dancer; [pers.] this poem is dedicated to my sweet Larry Pilesha of New Mexico; [a.] Los Angeles, CA

DOUGLAS, JACQUELYN
[Pen.] Ayanna Douglas; [b.] January 21, 1953, Phila.; [p.] Leroy and Marian Douglas; [m.] Single; [ch.] Keeva M. Douglas, 1 grandson Andre Douglas; [ed.] Gen. Diploma High School, Attending Community College of Phila., Eugene Amen Ra's Schl. of Models and Model/Teacher; [occ.] Elem. Schl. Crossing Guard, Writer, facilitator of various jazz/multimedia events (AYANNASPHERES); [memb.] Collective Visions Arts "All that I write (be it a newspaper article, commentary, or poem) is inspired by, or reflective of my own life experience. It comes from my heart, and it is my greatest hope that it will touch the hearts of those who read it."; [hon.] The 1st and Best being a semi-finalist for "Dark Side"; [oth. writ.] Editorials, Commentary for a number of Phila. newspapers; Phila. Tribune, Daily News, frt. pg. of West Phila. Wynnefield? Westside Weekly (2); [a.] Philadelphia, PA

DRABEK, JACQUELINE SHARON
[Pen.] Jackie Pross; [b.] November 22, 1940, Chicago, IL; [p.] Connie and George Pross; [m.] Divorced; [ch.] Debra Dawn, Daniel Todd and Eric Thomas; [ed.] Wauconda High; [occ.] Certified Nurses Aid, with the Elderly; [memb.] St. Paul's Lutheran Church, President of the Youth Group; [hon.] D.A.R. of American Legion, Cub Scout Leader and Board Member; [oth. writ.] First time writing my poem; [pers.] I strive to inspire the Goodness of life! Living for all of mankind, for God and my country. I loved reading poetry at a young age and has been away of life for me.; [a.] Ontonagon, MI

DRAKE, BRANDI
[Pen.] Brandin J. P. Drake; [b.] January 5, 1980, Spokane, WA; [p.] William Allen and Paula Sean Drake; [ed.] Completed 8th grade, now a freshman in high school; [occ.] Student; [memb.] President of Native American Culture Club at Enumclaw Junior High school, Member of the Danish Sisterhood of America; [hon.] 3rd place in VFW essay contest, Honor student in school, awarded Best Southern Accent in BYU Theatre Workshop.; [pers.] In my poetry I try to leave behind all aspects of worldly things, and strive to be spiritually uplifted by my own writings. I hope that I am able to give others a feeling of peacefulness and serenity through my poems.; [a.] Enumclaw, WA

DRAKE, DANIELLE
[Pen.] George; [b.] September 18, 1977, Dayton, OH; [p.] Daniel G. and Rudy D. Drake; [ed.] Eastern High School, Reedsville, Ohio; [occ.] Student; [hon.] Who's Who American high School Students; [pers.] I Danielle Drake dedicate this poem to my sister Sabrina Pauline Drake from whom I got the inspiration from.; [a.] Long Bottom, OH

DREWISCH, DANIELLE
[b.] June 13, 1981, SB, CA; [p.] Kathy Cook and Michael Drewisch, step-dad, John Cook; [ed.] Harding Elementary School and La Cumbre Middle School so far.; [occ.] Student; [memb.] California Junior Scholarship Federation; [hon.] 2nd place in D.A.R.E. essay contest; [oth. writ.] Several other poems, some published in newspapers; [pers.] Everything that I accomplish is done in loving memory of my grandmother and greatest supporter Joyce Bottoms.; [a.] Santa Barbara, CA

DRINNON, JANIS BOLTON
[b.] July 28, 1922, Pineville, KY; [p.] Clyde Herman and Violet Hendrickson Bolton; [m.] Kenneth C. Drinnon, June 13, 1948; [ch.] Dena Drinnon Foulk; [ed.] Middlesboro, KY High School, Journalism classes at Lincoln Memorial University, Commercial Art Certificate from Art Instruction School, Correspondence courses with Newspaper Institute of America, Drama instruction and Singing lessons with private teachers.; [occ.] Homemaker; [memb.] New Hopewell Baptist Church, Knoxville, TN; [hon.] Organized a Drama department for Alice Bell Baptist Church, Knoxville, TN then produced and directed religious plays for a number of years. While attending college, wrote articles for local newspapers. As a young teenager, sang solos on children's radio programs at WNOX in Knoxville, TN.; [pers.] Have always enjoyed the finer things of life and nature, especially those that are spiritually uplifting and bring

beauty to the soul. Have never been much for organizations, preferring to be a doer rather than a participant.; [pers.] I was an only child and very close to my mother. When she passed away in 1970, it was very difficult for me to give her up. Then, one afternoon as I visited with my mother-in law, she sid, "Just imagine that your mother has gone on a long trip." This seemed to help me in my acceptance. Later, when my father-in-law passed away in 1977, I wanted to say something helpful to her. I really hadn't planned to write a poem, I just started writing things that I thought might comfort her, while at the same time thinking of my mother's trip. My poem, "When Our Purpose Here Is Done," just seemed to evolve.; [a.] Knoxville, TN

DUBROW, JENNIFER
[b.] November 18, 1980, Philadelphia, PA; [p.] Dr. Linda Dubrow and Dr. Steve Dubrow-Eichel; [ed.] Central High School; [occ.] Student; [memb.] B'nai B'Rith Youth Organization, Mirror literary magazine; [hon.] Second Place, City-wide Law-Related Oratorical Contest (Phila. Bar Assoc.); Mathematics & Verbal Talent Search Certificate of Distinction (Johns Hopkins Univ.); Departmental Awards in Science and Social Science (Baldi Middle School).; [oth. writ.] Poem published in The Mirror, Central High School literary magazine.; [pers.] Writing and music are the voices of God.; [a.] Philadelphia, PA

DUFF, MELENA
[b.] January 4, 1972, Pennington Gap, Virginia; [p.] David and Linda Clem; [m.] William Duff, April 14, 1990; [ed.] James A. Cawood High; [occ.] Cashier at Bissel Office Equipment Co.; [oth. writ.] I write fiction novels; action, romance, but none are published as yet.; [pers.] Poems, to me, are as brief, through passionate, love affairs. There are not always any long term commitments to them, yet, if experienced just right, can never be forgotten.; [a.] Baxter, KY

DUFFY, EUNICE
[m.] Paul Duffy; [oth. writ.] Poems used in a mental health clinic and published in the Journal of Poetry Therapy. "Battlefield called Hubbardton" is displayed in the museum located on the Hubbardton Battlefield in Vermont.; [pers.] I try to express the deeper emotions and meanings to the circumstances and events in mine and other peoples lives whether they are living or a part of history: To me there is a spiritual bond that binds us all together.; [a.] San Fernando, CA

DUFFY, KRISTIN M.
[b.] June 12, 1969; [oth. writ.] Many other poems and songs that have yet to be discovered; [pers.] Don't let the baggage of your upbringing, be the destructive fallout of who you are and what you meant to be.; [a.] Williamstown, NJ

DULL, KATHY
[Pen.] Ka-Dee; [b.] June 10, 1958, Indiana; [m.] Jerry, March 3, 1979; [ch.] Christopher and Joshua; [ed.] Sinclair Community College; [occ.] Registered Nurse; [hon.] Phi Theta Kappa; [pers.] To be alive is to experience pain. To experience pain is to grow.

DUNCAN, DENISE
[b.] May 16, 1952, Bronx Hospital; [p.] Mary and Leroy W. Williams; [m.] Ricardo H. Duncan, May 28, 1977; [ch.] Ricardo Jeremiah Duncan; [ed.] Theodore Roosevelt H.S., Barnard Baruch College; [occ.] Office Administrator, Snapple Beverages; [memb.] National Council of Negro Women, Inc. The Spiritual Israel Church Youth Outreach Program, Asst. Director; [pers.] There is nothing so graphically eloquent as the world of words. A word fitly spoken can soothe, and heal and transport you to amazing places. One word can last a lifetime.; [a.] Bronx, NY

DUNLAP, SADIE D.
[Pen.] Dee Dee or Denise; [b.] March 19, 1956, Port Huron, MI; [p.] Audrey Brooks and David Baker; [m.] Lawrence Earl Dunlap, February 8, 1980; [ch.] Latina, Tomika, Audrey and Janet; [ed.] G.E.D., Port Huron School of Business, also now planning to attend St. Clair County Community College for R.N.; [occ.] Certified Nursing Assistant; [memb.] The All Nations Church of god and Christ. Public Relations Coordinator for church choir. Young Women's Christian Counsel Member.; [oth. writ.] In 1980 at the Economical Manpower Center, my English Teacher published a small book of poems. I wrote in New York. Also, I have poems I wrote in school and good friend put music to them by the name of Larry Washington; [pers.] The Lord is who makes my light shine and without him I am nothing. With him we as a people can conquer all.; [a.] Port Huron, MI

DUNN, CARRIE LYNN
[Pen.] Victoria L. Iris; [b.] February 9, 1963; Ft. Myers, Florida; [p.] John and Frances Dunn; [m.] Jennifer Winsor, January 9, 1994; [ed.] Gainesville High School, Santa Fe Community College in 1993, graduated from the Nail Tech Program 1993.; [occ.] Cashier, Nail specialist, Gainesville, FL; [oth. writ.] "Soul" published in 1993.; [pers.] Much love to my parents for their love and support in all aspects of my life. And to Jenny, I will always love you…Forever your Baby; [a.] Gainesville, FL

DUNN, CLAYTON
[b.] January 1, 1925, St. Luis, MO; [p.] Clayborn and Naomi Dungie; [ed.] 5th Grade; [occ.] Owner, Delivery Sue; [memb.] Various Political, Social and Religious Organizations; [oth. writ.] Former Musician, many other poems; [a.] Bronx, NY

DUNNE, DESIREE
[b.] September 6, 1978, San Diego; [p.] Aubrey C. Dunne and Ardis Winters; [ed.] Still in High School (Jr.), Northmont Elementary, Parkway, Jr. High, Grossmont (currently attending as a Junior.; [occ.] In my spare time I enjoy writing short stories, and poetry; [memb.] Zoological Society; [oth. writ.] A personal book that is yet to be published. I enjoy writing children's books/short stories.; [pers.] As I have said I love children and writing children's literature. Also, poetry is a main aspect in my life.; [a.] LaMesa, CA

DURAND, KIM
[b.] April 20, 1982, Syracuse, NY; [p.] Barbara and Bob Durand; [ch.] Sister, Kelly Durand, Pets, Cutsie, Sprinkles; [ed.] John F. Jay School, graduated 94; [occ.] 7th grade Staley Junior High School; [memb.] Cheerleader, Pop Warner Football, Rome YMCA Swim Team; [hon.] Most reliable cheerleader 92, most diligent cheerleader 93, Citizen of the Month; [pers.] Life is a constant Learning experience.; [a.] Rome, NY

DURKIN, KEVIN T.
[b.] July 14, 1956, Evergreen Park, IL; [p.] Anthony and Margaret; [m.] Bradley Carlson, November 23, 1991; [ed.] Brother Rice H.S., University of Illinois; [occ.] Customer Service Rep. Don Tech; [memb.] American Heritage Society, International Society of Poets, Ad Astra; [hon.] Golden Falcon Award; [oth. writ.] Dusting off dreams; [pers.] You are in this world to contribute something good and enhance it and be a better woman being you must be able to extend yourself to another human being; [a.] Oak Park, IL

DUTT, ERIC V.
[Pen.] Eric Dutt; [b.] April 20, 1963, Batala; [p.] Victor J. and Mary Nath; [m.] Pamela P. Gill, November 20, 1986; [ed.] Panjab University, Chandigarh, G.N.D. University, Amritsar Baring Union Christian College, Batala, India; [occ.] College English Instructor, River Grove, IL; [m.] Midwest Regional Conference on English. South Asian Community Church.; [hon.] High School Honor's List; [pers.] True happiness is possible only through God because our happiness is transient.; [a.] Oak Lawn, IL

DYBDAHL, JAN
[Pen.] Diane Johnson; [b.] November 20, 1944, Bremen, George; [p.] George and Christine Babb; [m.] Fred Dybdahl; [ch.] Jeffery Scott 25 yrs. old, Christine Rose, 18 years old, Richard Daniel 16 years.; [ed.] Associate of Arts, Seminole Community College, Bachelor of Arts, University of Central Florida, majored in English Education; [occ.] Author, Student; [memb.] Aloma Baptist Church; [oth. writ.] Several poems, book in progress.; [pers.] My writings are normally about home and family in some form. I believe a stable home is important for our youth because they are our future.; [a.] Maitland, FL

EARLE, LORRAINE G.
[Pen.] Popcorn; [b.] January 3, 1939, South Carolina; [p.] Walter and Elease Griffin; [m.] Deceased (Horace Earle), October 17, 1959; [ch.] Kiota, Lavonia, Craig, Bruce and Wendy (4 grandchildren); [ed.] Graduate of Germantown High School; [occ.] Sr. Field Clerk for Bell Atlantic; [memb.] Antioch Baptist Church, Oct. 1979-1985, Wayland Temple Baptist Church Jan. 1990; [oth. writ.] "Oh How I Prayed" to be published in 1994 issue of Silver Wings. "The Challenge of Life" to be published 1994 (The National Library of Poetry); [pers.] I give food for thought in my writings.; [a.] Philadelphia, PA

EASLEY, THOMAS J.
[Pen.] TJ; [b.] December 26, 1956, Tampa, FL; [p.] Billie Jo Ward and Dewey P. Easley III; [m.] Cynthia Dillard Easley, November 1989; [ch.] Justin Easley, Autumn Easley, Stepson's: Joseph Crum, Jeremy Crum, Jason Bulger; [ed.] Lakeland Senior High School, Lakeland, FL; [memb.] The Florida Tribe of Eastern Creek Indians, Roll No. 87076.

EAST, ROSALIND L.
[Pen.] Roz; [b.] November 20, 1972, New Orleans, LA; [p.] Simmie and Mary Nell Caston East; [ch.] Sisters: Donielle and LaShunda East; [ed.] Green Park Elementary School, Leon Bedchaux Jr. High School, East St. John High School, Nicholls State University; [occ.] Part time cashier; [memb.] African

American Voices, Zeta Phi Beta; Original Exclusive Twenties; NSU's Big Sister, Big Brother Club; Living Waters Church of God In Christ; [oth. writ.] The Silent Cry, I Know Now, The Secret Breakers, Fatal Attraction, A Special Friend, To the Mothers of the World, Why, It Hurts, Gentle Stranger and more; [pers.] I have been influenced by one of the greatest American poets of the 1800's, Emily Dickinson. Like her, my poems concern the relationship between the inner self and the external world.; [a.] LaPlace, LA

EDDY, LINDA
[Pen.] Lu Eddy; [b.] June 21, 1953, Louisville, KY; [p.] bob and Katherine Totten; [m.] Dick Eddy, June 29, 1973; [ch.] John and Jason; [ed.] High School, Westport High Louisville, KY; Modesto Jr. College, 2 yrs. Child Psychology; [occ.] Homemaker; [oth. writ.] Over 100 poems in my book entitled "Everyone's Worth Knowing" Hoping to someday get published.; [pers.] I try to live my life hoping to make others feel good. I thank God everyday for the blessings of being able to do that through poetry.; [a.] Morrow, OH

EDWARDS, REBECCA
[b.] December 15, 1975, Salem, Oregon; [p.] Ivan and Sherrie Edwards; [ed.] Oregon School for the Deaf, OSD High; [memb.] Diver's Alert Network (DAN) member; [hon.] Special honor graduate in the class of 1994; [oth. writ.] Several poems and writings published from my high school called "Literary Magazine" in Oregon area.; [pers.] Thanks to my parents for their great supports. Also, thanks to my Journalism Teacher, Mrs. Lorenzen, from my school at OSD high for her great teachings.; [a.] Salem, OR

EDWARDS, THOMAS BRYANT
[b.] March 22, 1971, Gaffney, SC; [p.] Mr. and Mrs. T.L. Edwards; [ed.] Virginia Episcopal School; Plymouth State College; [occ.] Student; [pers.] To me poetry is a living thing that is brought to life for a purpose. I don't write for the sake of writing. It is not to fill a void but to make a space. I write to convey a message conceived through passion.; [a.] Statesville, NC

EGAN, PEGGY
[Pen.] June 26, 1946, Phila. PA; [p.] Charles and Margaret Nolan; [m.] B.J. Egan Jr., June 8, 1968; [ch.] Jenifer, Kierstin, Matthew and timothy; [ed.] M.S.N., University of Pennsylvania, B.S.N., Stockton State College, NJ, R.N., Misericordia Hospital, Phila. PA; [occ.] Director, Quality Management, Greater Atlantic Health service; [memb.] A.H.A; ANA, SACP, NAHQ, A.R.E. (Association for Research and Enlightment); [hon.] The usual; [oth. writ.] unpublished, 10,000 poems, 10 short stories, 1 novel; [pers.] I believe life is a learning experience. Here is "Schoolhouse Earth" I am now taking, "Publishing Poetry 101."; [a.] Blackwood, NJ

EGGERS JR., RAY
[b.] March 24, 1963; [pers.] Your imagination is a playground, you just need to control the rides.; [a.] St. Louis, MO

EHLERS, NICOLE
[b.] September 6, 1979, Portland, OR; [p.] Thomas M. Ehlers, Paula Whitcomb; [ed.] Currently attending Parkrose High School, Class of 1997; [occ.] Student, aspires to be filmaker; [oth. writ.] A bunch of other poems written, that have yet to be published.;

[pers.] I really believe that everybody has been created equally. People say my poetry is sad, but I believe that it reflects how people feel at stages in their life. With mine, I started writing poetry; [a.] Portland, OR

EISELE, LYNETTE
[b.] July 30, 1971, Covina, CA; [p.] William and ellen Eisele; [ed.] Not much; [occ.] Pre School Teacher; [pers.] I try to live, love, and feel the world that is given to me. Truth, peace, and understanding are my untouched goals.; [a.] Alta Loma, CA

EISFELD, SONJA M.
[b.] December 13, 1976, Hannover, Germany; [p.] Dr. Dietmar and Ursula Eisfeld; [ed.] 7 years in gymnasium Altluenen, Germany; 1 year in Stanwood High School, USA; [occ.] Student; [oth. writ.] none, first poem published.; [pers.] If you walk through the world with your eyes open only for the obvious things, you will walk by the small beautiful miracles that can open the doors to your imagination.; [a.] Stanwood, WA

ELFREICH, DONALD H.
[b.] July 19, 1924, Evansville, IN; [p.] Herbert and Catherine Elfreich; [m.] Margaret M. Elfreich, January 19, 1943; [ch.] David A. Elfreich, Donna E. Henning; [ed.] 1 year college, incomplete; [occ.] Retired plumbing contractor; [memb.] Veterans of Foreign Wars Post 2953; [hon.] Service Award from Local 136 Plumbers Union for Labor and material contribution for Evansville School Corporation Survive Alive Building; [oth. writ.] none; [pers.] I believe we should always help others less fortunate than ourselves, and in cases of emergency give up pleasure to help others.

ELGUICZE, MARY
[b.] October 15, 1977, Somerville, NJ; [p.] Mr. and Mrs. Joseph Elguicize; [ed.] Immaculata High School; [occ.] Student; [memb.] Student Council, Pro-Life club, Varsity Tennis; [hon.] Spanish Honor Society, Who's Who Among American High School Students; [pers.] I feel that my poetry comes from my experiences in life and it is a way to express my thoughts and feelings.; [a.] Manville, NJ

ELLIOTT, STACY DIANE
[b.] August 25, 1974, Willard, Ohio; [p.] Brenda Thronsberry; [ed.] Knott County Central High School, University of Louisville; [occ.] Student; [memb.] Golden Key National Honor Society; [hon.] Golden Key Nat'l Honor Society, Phi Eta Sigma Honor Society, Univ. of Lousiville College of Arts and Sciences Honors Society, Dean's list; [oth. writ.] Poems and essays published in hometown Knott County newspaper.; [pers.] Poetry is an intimate relationship. It doesn't matter if anyone else can discern that relationship as long as you and your poem understand each other.; [a.] Fairdale, KY

ELLIS, GEORGIA
[b.] July 1, 1930, Elwood, IN; [p.] Calvin and Helen Fowler; [m.] George, March 11, 1947; [ch.] 3 daughters, 2 sons, 13 grand children 5 great-grandchildren; [ed.] Elwood High - IUPUI; [occ.] Retired; [memb.] Lubach Literacy Tutor, President Elwod Poetry Club. Asoc. Writers Guild, Past member State Poetry Federation Friends of Poetry.; [hon.] 3 Silver and one Golden Poet Award. Silver Award in

religious Poetry, numerous Editor's Choice Awards; [oth. writ.] Published in numerous magazines and anthologies, Poetry read on radio and Television shows articles for various magazines.; [pers.] Although it is always a thrill to see your work in print, I still love to get the letters that start-check enclosed.; [a.] Elwood, IN

ELLIS, MAUREEN L.
[b.] January 28, 1954, Phila., PA; [p.] Mary Louise Ellis, Howard E.V. Ellis; [m.] Divorced; [ch.] Jacquelyn Janine, Nicole Linda, and Sean Christopher Beck; [ed.] Graduate P and B Method of Hair Design 1973, Barbaring course 1987, Professional Nail Technician 1993, Licensed Beautician for the State of NJ, Certificate in Astrology for Beginners 1990, and Advanced Astrology 1990, Reiki Healing 1989.; [occ.] Beautician; [memb.] Member of the A.F.A.; [oth. writ.] Poets' Guild, Several poems which I haven't yet published.; [pers.] Don't shade your wisdom in peering through "Rose Colored Glasses." Walk with thy eyes open and observe your surroundings. Knowledge is not to be kept a secret.; [a.] Gloucester Heights, NJ

ELLISON, JOHN
[b.] December 1, 1954, USA; [ed.] High School Grad.; [occ.] Bus Driver; [a.] Flushing, NY

ELLNER, MELISSA
[b.] March 9, 1982, Los Gatos, CA; [p.] Marc and Renee Ellner; [ed.] Rolling Hills Middle School; [occ.] Student; [oth. writ.] Short stories.; [a.] San Jose, CA

EMMONS, HELEN
[Pen.] H.M. Emmons; [b.] December 6, 1955, Trenton, NJ; [p.] Russell and Dorothy Daniels; [m.] Vernon Emmons, July 4, 1990; [ch.] Mandee Age 19, Chris Age 15, Tyler 5; [ed.] Graduated 1974, Hightstown High, Hightstown, NJ; [occ.] Husband Self Employed, Own Plumbing Co. (Secretary); [memb.] American Legion 196, Treasurer of Building Fund; [oth. writ.] Have been writing poetry since school. This is the first time I ever entered something.; [pers.] Most of my poetry is written from life experiences. I write mostly of my love for my family.; [a.] Pt. Plsnt., NJ

ENGLISH, SR., MICHAEL A.
[Pen.] Mikel and Anthony English; [b.] February 29, 1968, Wash. D.C.; [p.] Mary Francis Sharp-English (deceased) Arthur and Mattie English (Father & Stepmother); [m.] Cheryl M. Ford-English; [m.] October 15, 1988; [ch.] Latoya Yvonne, Michael Anthony Jr., Mikki Francis English; [ed.] Frank W. Ballow Sr., High School, University of D.C. Elementary Education; [occ.] Elementary Teacher; [memb.] National Education Assoc., Maryland State Teacher's Assoc., Pearl Enterprises U.S.A., Inc. Boy Scouts of America; [hon.] Certificates of Appreciation and Participation; [oth. writ.] Unpublished book of short stories and poetry. "The Needs of the One," "Introspection,"; [pers.] Many unique and rewarding experiences are to be gained from twelve years of schooling. These experiences are vital to ones personal well being and future successes.; [a.] Suitland, MD

ENGRACIA, JENNIFER
[Pen.] Jheni; [b.] March 6, 1977, (Imigrant) Philippines; [p.] Yolanda and Joey Engracia; [ed.] Poveda

Learning Center; [occ.] Student (High School) 12th Grade; [memb.] Debate Team (PLC); [hon.] Honor Roll, Quiz Bee's; [oth. writ.] Portrait In The Hall, Mea Culpa; [pers.] Life, A blur of the expected and unexpected, connected with complexity…it's bliss is to love it to the fullest.; [a.] Malverne, NY

ENGRAM, A.C.
[b.] 1949; [pers.] After walking down many paths of interest I began to slowly realize what I am about, these words come to mind: An Artistic Practioner, continually unfolding into a journey of expression within the creative process a line that we unconsciously draw, that begins when we are young, the arc of living being prescribed daily by the way we choose to focus our creative attention. What we have when we look back is an intriguing configuration of expe riences. My poetry emanates from this interior journey I speak of…deep feelings resonating..finding my authentic voice.; [a.] Southern, IL

EQNQUIST, BARBARA
[b.] November 14, 1943, Chicago, IL; [p.] Roland and Betty Lazzekoni; [m.] Gary Enquist, October 2, 1976; [ch.] Mark Stella, Michael Stella, Marlo Stella and Gina Fisher; [ed.] Morton High School, Certified in Nursing Assist., Food and Sanitation Cosmetology, currently enrolled at the Institute of Children's Literature.; [occ.] Cosmetologist, Reflexologist; [memb.] Local Board of Health.; [oth. writ.] A portfolio of poetry written over the past 20 yrs.; [pers.] Writing is a gift, a way to express thoughts and feelings. What appears on paper ranges from humorous to spiritual and everything in between if there is anything in between.; [a.] Cicro, IL

ERDMIER, WM
[Pen.] Willy; [b.] August 31, 1943, Savanna, IL; [m.] Happily divorced since 1972; [ch.] Noel, Erich and Alison; [ed.] B.A. Southern Illinois University, J.D. Western State University; [occ.] Attorney; [memb.] State Bar of California; [oth. writ.] Are in a large cardboard box which I hope to turn into a book someday.; [pers.] I write to me. If you enjoy it as well that's an extra bonus.; [a.] Los Angeles, CA

ERNST, PAUL F.
[b.] September 4, 1924, Reading, OH; [p.] Joseph L. and Charlotte Ann Ernst; [m.] Divorced; [ch.] Marlene, Vincent, Frederick, Malcolm, Eric; [ed.] 12 years, graduate Ph.B, Xavier U. Cin. OH; [occ.] Retired Salesman and Administrator; [memb.] American Legion, AARP; [hon.] Numerous Insurance Sales Awards; [oth. writ.] I am in the process of writing a religious philosophic book.; [pers.] I write poetry ordinarily for enjoyment one reason is that the people who read the poetry enjoy it, what better reason.; [a.] Cincinnati, OH

ESPINOR, JESSICA JEAN
[b.] October 2, 1975, Portsmouth, VA; [p.] Loretta Shockey and Richard Espinor, II; [ed.] Still Attending High School and would like to go to college.; [occ.] La Porte High School; [hon.] I'm in J.R.O.T.C. at school so I have small awards. They are cadet challenge, certificate of appreciation, honor roll and many others, small ribbons that I wear on my uniform.; [oth. writ.] Nothing published, but I write poems that come to my mind at the spur of the moment.; [pers.] We as a society need to respect our neighbors. We also need to start taking better care of

our planet. Most of all, respect and forgive ourselves.; [a.] Houston, TX

ESTEP, MARION KAY
[b.] April 24, 1952, Lancaster, SC; [p.] G. Albert Todd and Lettie Stelzig; [ch.] John Campbell, Lewis Campbell, Lettie Mae Estep, grandaughter Alexandria; [pers.] I wrote this poem for depression gets a hold of me and this is to show other people to write or talk about what depresses you instead of doing suicide, drugs, or alcohol. There's always another answer.; [a.] Burkburnett, TX

ESTES, CECELIA F.
[Pen.] Cissy; [b.] September 1, 1951, Pineville, LA; [p.] Jack and Jackie Price; [m.] James F. Estes, August 11, 1993; [ch.] Ronald, Amber, Phala, James, Timothy; [ed.] LaSalle High, Huey P. Long Vo. Tech.; [occ.] LPN, License Practical Nurse; [oth. writ.] Several poems published in Christian Magazines.; [pers.] I strive to always reflect the Jesus in me, to treat all mankind as I would want to be treated.; [a.] Harrison, AR

ETHRIDGE, ELIZABETH
[Pen.] Liz; [b.] September 13, 1930, Maryville, TN; [p.] Joseph B. and Eliza a. Crowder; [m.] Clarence O. Ethridge, February 4, 1956; [ch.] Otis Bartley Ethridge and Tara Lisa Shumate; [ed.] Coffee High School, Florence, AL and Univ. of N. AL in Florence; [occ.] Retired secretary/admin. asst. and computer operator.; [memb.] Calvary bible Church, Huntsville, AL, Sigma Tau Pi Drama Soc., Univ. of N. AL; [hon.] Several in City of Huntsville's Task Force on Education, Ran for school board at one time.; [oth. writ.] Many poems about holidays and personal things. Been writing since 4th grade. Poems, plays etc.; [pers.] I've written one play that has been presented in many churches and also presented with puppets.; [a.] Huntsville, AL

EUBANK, CHASITY LEE
[Pen.] Snow White; [b.] August 31, 1978, Glasgow, KY; [p.] Betty and Charles Eubank; [ed.] I'm still going to high school, currently a sophomore.; [occ.] My current occupation is to be young.; [memb.] Have no memberships; [hon.] Poetic, artistic drawing; [oth. writ.] From love to hate; Anything; I speak of my love for you; Death for me; Dream of love; Suicide; Without you; Apology; come to me; the Death; and more. This is my first publication; [pers.] Poetry and drawings are ways I express my feelings and thoughts, and sometimes how I view the world.; [a.] Goldsboro, NC

EVANS, CLARA D.
[b.] May 29, 1953, Brownsville, TX; [p.] James and Clara Dortch; [ch.] Barbara Elizabeth and Kenneth James; [ed.] LaPorte Sr. High; San Jacinto College; [memb.] Pasadena Rodeo Association, Houston Livestock Show and Rodeo Assoc., Houston Photography Club; [pers.] Everything between life and death may be altered by attitude, determination and dedication and faith. Success depends on how one is willing to work to achieve a goal. This success is not measurable with a monetary value but through praise and contentment with one self and the ability to get up, pull it together and go again and again and again.; [a.] Pasadena, TX

EWING, JERRY L.
[Pen.] J. Ewing; [b.] August 9, 1944, Norfolk, NE; [p.] Foster and Catherine Ewing; [ch.] Sherry, Michelle, Annette and ryan; [ed.] High school, Four semesters college, 2 years tech. school; many seminars of various occupations; [occ.] Construction Department Head, Auto Racing and Performance; [memb.] Sertoma club, Veterans club, Musicians Writer's guild, many others with pride; [hon.] Need not list they were all award of my life; [oth. writ.] Several songs and writings published in various articles and papers, author of two books, "A Good day to Die" and "What Do I Know;" [pers.] I strive to write from the heart, even in issues of current events, to induce the reader to stop and think. I want readers to experience the emotions, feelings, and places, that I have in life! Something for them to associate with.; [a.] Globe, AZ

EXSTED, CARL
[Pen.] Carle, C.L.E.; [b.] November 12, 1959, Glencoe; [p.] Donald and Betty Exsted; [m.] August 31, 1981, Divorced 1985, Single; [ch.] Cassandra Sue Exsted age 13; [ed.] Glencoe High school; [occ.] Glencoe Butter and Produce Association; [hon.] "Just started writing poems this year."; [oth. writ.] no, first poem; [pers.] Personally, my influence was with God and upon seeing a chance to write a poem for the National Library of Poetry everything in my life was enhanced with excitement and mystery of true feelings inside my heart and soul.; [a.] Glencoe, MN

FAHMY, MICHELLE
[b.] October 26, 1981, San Fernando, CA; [p.] Walter and Kthy Fahmy; [ed.] 7th grade, LaPurisima Catholic School; [occ.] Student; [memb.] Lompoc Marlins Swim Team; [hon.] Lompoc Marlins Outstanding Swimmer, Girls, 11-12 yrs 1993; [a.] Lompoc, CA

FANUIEL, MIRIAM Y.
[b.] Aug. 17, South Carolina; [m.] Deceased; [ch.] Renee and Harlan; [ed.] BA West Vo. College, MAT Univ. South Carolina; [occ.] Retired; [memb.] Delta Sigma Theta Sorority, NEAR and SCEAR; [oth. writ.] Previous poems in National Library of Poetry; [a.] Columbia, SC

FARLEY, CANDY
[b.] May 30, 1977, Tampa, FL; [p.] Gail and John Farley; [ed.] Ehove Career Center; [occ.] Student; [memb.] Business Professionals of America; [oth. writ.] Additional poems not yet published.; [pers.] I try not to write the bad, but state the obvious. I may only be seventeen but I do see the truth. Thank you to the people who have helped me, loved me, inspired me and most of all to God above.; [a.] Norwalk, OH

FARMER, FRANCES CLAUDIA
[Pen.] Scoop Monale; [b.] August 21, 1958, Cleveland; [p.] Gentry and Beverly Farmer; [m.] Single; [ed.] BS in Radio/TV from Lincoln University, Jeff. City, MO; [occ.] Youth Counselor; [memb.] Sigma Gamma Sorority Inc., Job Corp. Alumni Assoc, Vice Prison and Audio Consultant for First World Communications; [hon.] Top Reporter in High School, Young Life, Girl Scout, National Black College Radio Conference Delegates 1984, Senator for Student Government Association, Newspaper writing in college and job corp.; [oth. writ.] Establish an agency newsletter in St. Louis. Wrote several poems for my job and wrote for several newspapers.; [pers.] I love Maya

Angelo but foremost I just use my skills and my feelings, past and present.; [a.] Gladstone, MO

FARMER, MARY VIRGINIA
[Pen.] Virginia Brewster; [occ.] Full Time genealogist; [memb.] D.A.R.; [hon.] Received Letters of Accomodation from Gov. Agency for Statistical reports on Services to War Veterans; [oth. writ.] Poetry published in "Poems for Radio Broadcast"; [pers.] Worked as legal secretary, court reporter and for government agency as statistician; [a.] Welch, WVA, Covina, CA

FARRUGGIO, LAURA C.
[Pen.] Eggy; [b.] July 9, 1969, Brooklyn; [p.] Martha and Dominic Farruggio; [ed.] Our Lady of Perpetual Help High School; [occ.] Receptionist; [oth. writ.] Frequently published in the editorial section of the N.Y. Daily news for my thoughts on current events.; [pers.] "Life is what happens while you're making other plans" - John Lennon. I would not have mad it in life without my family and Sean for whom my love springs eternal; [a.] Brooklyn, NY

FASIG, SUSAN L.
[b.] January 26, 1960, Camden, NJ; [p.] Paul L. and Elizabeth R. Fasig; [ed.] Spartanburg High School, University of South Carolina at Spartanburg; [occ.] Accountant; [memb.] Institute of Management Accountants, Cathedral Choir of Evangel Cathedral; [pers.] My life is dedicated to Jesus Christ, the only mediator between God and man the only way to salvation and eternal life, the only answer to every problem, need and question in life.; [a.] Spartanburg, SC

FAULKNER, BRYAN
[b.] November, 30, 1973, CA; [p.] Chet and Kari Faulkner; [ed.] High School and Jr. College; [occ.] Construction Worker; [oth. writ.] Many which I haven't published yet.; [pers.] This poem was dedicated to Kim Dooley, the cutest girl I know.

FAVA, NORMA GIUS
[b.] January 6, 1920, Sheppton, PA; [p.] Mark Gius, mary (Nee Sandri); [m.] Paul V. Fava, November 5, 1941; [ch.] David and Paulette; grandchildren: Paul, Emily; Great-grandchildren: Phillip, Eric; [ed.] B.A., M.A., Rowan College, (formerly Glassboro State); Supervisor of Education at Vineland Developmental Center; [occ.] Retired; [memb.] NJEA, VDC, Community Representative, VDC, Surrogate Parent Rep., Volunteer Dept., Newcomb Medical Center, Society of NJ Artists, St. Isodores R.C. Church; [a.] Vineland, NJ

FAWCETT, EILEENE M.
[b.] Minnesota; [m.] Roscoe K. Fawcett; [ch.] none; [ed.] B.A. Elementary Education with an art minor.; [occ.] Retired elementary teacher. We do a lot of traveling.; [memb.] Service groups and boards, PEO Chapter CJ Minnesota, Social Groups, Golf Club, Roman Catholic Church; [hon.] Had poems and articles published in educational magazines and poetry magazines. I am also a watercolor artist, painting hang from the California to British Isles. Have studied with several leading American watercolorists; Honor graduate high school and college.; [pers.] Literature and art as basic to all cultures as food and water. Summer home in Nisswa, MN; [a.] Jarbidge, NV

FEIGUM, MICHAEL J.
[Pen.] Mike Feigum; [b.] January 13, 1951, Philadelphia; [p.] Elvin B. and Eva P. Feigum; [m.] Barbara (Samuelson) Feigum, May 16, 1981; [ch.] Helen Marie Feigum and Michael J. Feigum; [ed.] U.S. Air Force, Defense Language Institute, Penn State; [occ.] Childcare Worker; [memb.] Vietnam Veterans of America childcare of PA, Mended Hearts of PA; [hon.] Ottaway News Syndicate, Quote Recognition, National Lib. of Poetry Editor's Choice; [oth. writ.] Local newspapers, Childcare Assn. Newsletter, 1993, wrote weekly news column, Pocono Record news, National Library of Poetry, Tears of Fire.; [pers.] writing is a love, best done on a whim. If regularly scheduled it becomes a chore.; [a.] Womelsdorf, PA

FELDMAN, LAUREN M.
[b.] December 28, 1983, Pittsburgh; [p.] Susan F. Keller, Kenneth G. Feldman; [ed.] Fourth Grade at Holiday Park Elementary School in Mrs. McAllister's Class. (Pittsburgh, PA); [pers.] I wrote about animals because I like nature and I'd like to learn more about it.; [a.] Pittsburgh, PA

FELTON, ANNETTE P.
[b.] June 16, 1915, Nashville, TN; [p.] Effie and Elmer P'Pool (deceased); [m.] Harry M. felton 1935 (deceased 1935); [ch.] Dale L. Felton, Milton Felton deceased at 22; [ed.] High School Graduate 33", Art Classes at Watkins Institute; [occ.] Housewife, I live alone; [memb.] Connell Mem. Meth. Church; [hon.] Several honors for art in local area.; [oth. writ.] Have written a story of my life beginning at 3 yrs. through til 10 years. No publishing, there is a lot of Nashville (historical) not published.; [pers.] Have started poetry 5 years ago. Have 55 pieces It's a joy for me to write.; [a.] Goodlettsville, TN

FERGUSON, LEUNA PERRY
[b.] May 20, 1920, Manatee Co., FL; [p.] Clyde and Thelma Perry; [ch.] Anita Lane Hutchison, Burington, VA; Richard K. Lane Sr., Lakeland, FL; [ed.] Manatee Co. High, business school, several courses at FL State Community College; [occ.] Retired, currently write column for (Sumter Notes), Tampa Tribune; [memb.] Board Member AARP, Sec'y Board Banasoffkee Community Library Board, RSV, Member Young at Heart, First Baptist Church, FL State Poetry Assn, Local Poetry Club.; [hon.] Junior Woman Club, Library Club; [oth. writ.] Written and submitted several children short stories, published, church bulletin, published local newspaper. Occasionally byline in Sumter County Times.; [pers.] I strive to reflect the goodness of people and things I know about. Many of my writings are for individuals and the way they touch my life. Also, of places and things I know or have been.; [a.] Lk. Panasoffkee, FL

FERGUSON, MARY ELLEN
[b.] December 30, 1947, Plattsburgh, NY; [p.] Lynn S. and Dorothy E. Ferguson; [ch.] Jason A. Slater, Corey J. Slater; [ed.] Lake Placid High School, Clinton Community College, Camplain Valley Physicians Hospital, School Certified Lab Assistant and MLT's; [occ.] Medical Laboratory Technician, Craven OB/GYN PA, New Bern, North Carolina; [memb.] Associate Member, The Academy of American Poets; [oth. writ.] I have a volume of poetry encompassing nearly 30 years.; [pers.] In my writing I try to express heart felt emotions as well as my belief that life is a gift and love is the key to a happy life.; [a.] New Bern, NC

FERRER, ANTHONY ROBERT
[b.] January 29, 1977, LA, CA; [p.] Robert Gasca and Anna Ferrer; [ed.] Whittier High; [pers.] Edure your life at your own pace to find your trueself.; [a.] Whittier, CA

FEWELL, LEE JESSE
[b.] March 31, 1973, Baltimore, MD; [p.] Dale and Nancy Fewell; [ed.] Heidelberg High School, Germany; Seaside High School, CA (graduated 1991), Currently entering senior year at the Johns Hopkins University, Math Sciences major; [memb.] Inter Varsity Christian Fellowships, National Honor Society, Delta Epsilon Phi, National Right to Life Committee; [oth. writ.] Over a hundred unpublished songs, sonnets and poems written as a "closet poet;" [pers.] I mold my every decision and every love after the model of Jesus Christ; "White Rose" was written for and is dedicated to Maureen. I still trust you.; [a.] Baltimore, MD

FIBBE, GERALDINE W.
[Pen.] ME; [b.] Port Chester, United Hosp.; [p.] Fannie and Steve Patchen; [m.] August 10, 1950, Deceased; [ch.] Kon, Gerald, Joseph, Greg, Philomena, Lily Mae, George Marialena; [ed.] Nyack H.S., Rockland Comm. College; [occ.] Retired; [memb.] St. Ann's Church, Nyack, Eucharistic Minister; [hon.] "God, Are You There?" Award Certificate; [oth. writ.] Several, have them all home. All my poems tend to lean on the religious side. It's like an angel with pen in hand.; [pers.] Writing poems is my favorite expression in life. Reading them gives me great pleasure! I can write for any occasion, anytime!; [a.] Nyack, NY

FIETZER, JUDITH A.
[b.] April 29, 1961, Waupaca, WI; [p.] John and Julia Weasner; [m.] Terry Fietzer, January 6, 1994; [ch.] Steven, Beth, Elizabeth; [ed.] Graduated Class of 1979, Little Wolf High School, Manawa, Wisconsin; [occ.] Dietary Cook; [memb.] First Lutheran Church, Ogdensburg, Wisconsin; [pers.] I have enjoyed writing poetry for years. My father has also had several poems published.; [a.] Ogdensburg, WI

FIGUERDA, I. CRISTINA
[b.] January 21, 1971, Miami, FL; [p.] Leo and Maria Figueroa; [ed.] Lasalle High School, Miami Dade Community College; [occ.] Officer Manager, Roux Architect; [memb.] D.A.R.E. (Kids Against Drugs), St. Louis Catholic Young Adult Ministry; [hon.] Diploma for completion of summer program for song, dance and drama (twice); [pers.] The greatest joy in any talent is being able to share with and inspire others by it.; [a.] Miami, FL

FINO, JESSICA ELAINE
[b.] March 5, 1981, Midland, TX; [p.] Guillermo and Kathy Fino; [ed.] 7th Grade Goddard Jr. High; [occ.] Student; [a.] Midland, TX

FISHER, BERTHA
[b.] February 7, 1917, Liverpool, Engl; [p.] Lily and David Kaufman; [m.] Late Mark Fisher, October 23, 1958 (1970 Deceased); [ed.] Commercial High School, Outremont Business College, Montreal, Canada, Quebec Province, graduated from grade school with honors; [occ.] Retired Stenographer, hobby writing, babysitting elderly; [memb.] Glee Club; Y; Cosmo-

politan Singers; Canadian Belgia Musical Club; The Opera Guild (Soprano Chorus); Gilbert and Sullivan Groups (No Payment); Music Appreciation Group (Amateur); [hon.] Margaret Carries Mail, Montreal Canada ; from National Library of Poetry, a Certificate, Editor's Award; "Kindred Spirit" (Local Montreal Paper) published as a teen-ager; Milton Berle, Silver Poetry Award, Golden Poetry Award, Certificates of Merit; [oth. writ.] Peace of Mind, Instant Needs, Executive Privilege, The Big Spenders, The Longevity Goal, The Tabloid Society, A Mind's Eye Therapy, Amen Lightenment, The Good Old Days, The Visionaries and many more; [pers.] I am a life long optimist, always believe to bring out the best in others. My husband was a "Band Leader" on S.S. Sylvania. Good poetry like good music, food for the soul.; [a.] Miami Beach, FL

FISHER, MARCELLA B.
[Pen.] Marcie; [b.] April 21, 1945, Fort Morgan, Color Ade; [p.] Edd and ethel Greene; [m.] Morris N. Fisher, July 31, 1967; [ch.] Six, Michelle, Mardelle, Michael, Mitchell, Marlene and Matthew; [ed.] I went to schools in Fort Morgan, Colorado and Salinas, California.; [occ.] Wife, Mother, Grandmother.; [memb.] The Church of the Nazarene; [hon.] I wrote a song in 1979 called, "Thank You Jesus, for just that Man. In 1990, my song followed Randy Travis on United Airlines on the country stations.; [oth. writ.] I have written another poem that the National Library of Poetry published for my mother, in 1990, in the book "A View From the Edge," called "Mother.";
[pers.] I have written over 60 of my own songs. I do not read music, or play any instrument. My songs just come to me while I do my daily work.; [a.] Fort Morgan, CO

FISHER, ZACHARY
[Pen.] Zach Fisher; [b.] December 28, 1955, Queens, NY; [p.] David and Harriet Fisher; [m.] Divorced, Jessica Evome Fisher 3 yrs. old; [ed.] High School Graduate, Commercial Technical Institute Diploma in Legal Investigation. Also earned certificates/diplomas.; [occ.] Work as Senior Clerk for NYS Dept. of Law, A.G.'s office; [memb.] C.S.E.A., Parents without Partners; [oth. writ.] Many other assorted poems, some previously published in other minor publications.; [pers.] My writing strives to make some sense of lifes pain and unfairness and absordities in our day to day existence and lift past it on a continued guest for personal growth.; [a.] Briarwood, NY

FLANDERS, DANA G.
[b.] August 30, 1967, Detroit, Michigan; [p.] Carl and Alexandra Gerard; [m.] Peter P. Flanders, October 12, 1991; [ed.] Allendale, Columbia High School, Skidmore College, Business Major; [occ.] Retail Manager; [hon.] Dean's List, Skidmore College, Successful equestrian in A.H.S.A. riding circles; [pers.] The secret of my youthfulness: to properly balance maturity and adolescent innocence.; [a.] Newport Center, VT

FLEMING, GLENN M.
[b.] June 14, 1921, Brawley, CA; [p.] Jack and Dollie Fleming (deceased); [m.] Barbara, February 11, 1945; [ch.] Glenn Jr., Dick, JoAnn, Jeff; [ed.] AB plus graduate work. San Jose State College (California), Chico State College, Western Oregon State College; [occ.] Cattle Rancher; [memb.] Oregon Cattlemen's Association, Water for Life.; [hon.]

Nothing of consequence, Graduated with Distinction; [oth. writ.] A small collection of "Cowboy" poetry. Two have been published.; [pers.] Freedom is more important than security.; [a.] Baker City, OR

FLOOD, THOMAS HAYES
[b.] December 30, 1911, Harrison, NJ; [p.] Thomas Z. and Jessie M. Flood; [m.] Berdina B. Flood, May 24, 1975; [ch.] One by first marriage, 2 Jane, Nancy, Stepdaughters; [ed.] b.s. in Ed. MA in ED, University of New York at Buffalow, Formerly Buffalo State Teachers College, George Washington U. Wash. D.C.; [occ.] Retired; [memb.] Prince George's Co. MD Teacher's Assoc. Maryland State T.A., NEA, Nat. Geog. Soc.; [hon.] Nothing of literary consequence, writing verses (poems) is a hobby. A!l 3 National Honor Society; [oth. .writ.] Several poems published in "The Paper Horse"; poems in local papers; one in church (National) magazine; [pers.] My poems try to feature unobtrusive rhyme and ideas. I had never seen in print handled in a different way.; [a.] Spring Hill, FL

FLORES, BETTY
[b.] October 7, 1945, CA; [p.] Deceased; [m.] Alberto Flores; [ch.] Mario Flores, Demetrio Flores a book all my himself; two sisters from Lamont, CA, Janice Kennedy, Joyce People; [ed.] High School; [occ.] Wife-mother; [oth. writ.] About 30 poems; [pers.] I wrote my poems in 1993 the Lagunasalda, Baja CA. I live in Mexicali now. My poems are about me, my life and God. Lynn V. Andrews was important i my writing my poems. I wish she could help me in writing my life's biography.

FLORES, BOBBIE
[Pen.] Debbie Ryan; [b.] August 19, 1975, East Chicago; [p.] Beverly and Pedro Flores; [ed.] Highland High School to Michigan, CI, Elston High to Calumet High School, Gary IN., Portage Adolt; [occ.] Artist, and Poet; [memb.] American Cancer Society; [hon.] In piano, and organ and many artistic and imaginative drawings.; [oth. writ.] A poem called life of sorrow and madness which was published this year 1994.; [pers.] I was inspired by dreams of past memories and my future toward what it shall bring me and others, and the paint suffering I had to deal with because my family ostracized me. (Because they didn't believe the tragedy that happened to me.); [a.] Portage, IN

FODALE, DANIEL A.
[b.] January 20, 1974, Warren, MI; [p.] Anthony and Ruth Fodale; [ed.] Notre Dame High School, Mich. State Univ. 1 and a half yrs.; [occ.] Student; [pers.] Poetry is an outlet for the expression of one's thoughts, feelings, and ideals. It is a very personal form of art.; [a.] Fraser, MI

FOLEY, NANCY
[b.] March 17, 1937, Flint, MI; [p.] Rosalee Smith & Todd Berston; [ch.] Ryan Foley, Douglas Foley, Kurt Foley; Sister Diane Rosiek; [ed.] High School Diploma; [occ.] At Leisure; [oth. writ.] Many poems and 3 short stories about my children's childhood.; [pers.] My poems are sometimes exhortations to turn to God. I sometimes fail but I try to follow closely the teachings of Jesus Christ.; [a.] Flint, MI

FONT, ADELL COKES
[Pen.] Adell C. Font; [b.] August 9, 1940, Hot

Springs, AR; [p.] Dewey V. Cokes; [m.] Bessie Ione Lane, January 13, 1957; [ch.] Donna, Tina, George E. Font II; [ed.] Baton Rouge High School 10th grade 1956 (B.R. High School) Baton Rouge, LA; [occ.] Sitter, I sit with the sick and dying and disabled in hospitals.; [memb.] not yet, but I plan on joining NLP; [hon.] National Library of Poetry, It is a honor to be published in your library, my friends says its a honor to read my poetry.; [oth. writ.] I have a book full of poetry "The good ole days" a sister's farewell poem and Memory Therapy and many more. If you have room for more in The Dark Side of the Moon, I will be glad to send more, they will be copyrighted.; [pers.] My teacher loved poetry, I got my love for poetry from her. She read to the class, on almost all rainy days. I loved it.; [a.] Pride, LA

FOOTE, APRIL
[Pen.] April D. Foote; [b.] September 22, 1963, Ft. Wayne, IN; [p.] Ralph and Pat Perry; [m.] William Foote, October 22, 1991; [Pen.] Richard Leroy, Jessica Rose, Chrystal Marie; [ed.] Carroll high, University of Maryland; [occ.] Laborer, Housewife; [a.] Ft. Wayne, IN

FOREMAN, IVA WHITE
[b.] November 20, 1922, Richmond, KY; [p.] Roger and Mary Parke Baker; [m.] Dale H. Foreman, June 26, 1976; [ch.] Mary Faith, White Alney, Judith elaine White-Miller; [ed.] High school and 1 course in arts, at college; [occ.] Homemaker; [memb.] Attend, New Life Christian Center; [hon.] Have had my poetry displayed in Church papers, also.; [oth. writ.] Several poems published in papers and in other anthology's; [pers.] I've written poetry since I was a child. I was influenced by my dear mother and encouraged also. In my writings, I try to tell and share what God has meant in my life, of his goodness to me, and how he stays the same forever, to all shall call on his name.; [a.] Danville, IL

FORTIER, JULIE
[b.] August 20, 1968, St. Paul; [p.] Leo; and Joy Fortier; [m.] Michael Borel, August 20, 1994; [ch.] Dylan Age 3; [ed.] White Bear Lake Are High School; [occ.] Homemaker; [pers.] I was once told by a good friend that my poems are like the deepest, darkest thoughts of mankind which will never be spoken.; [a.] North Saint Paul, MN

FORTIN, TANYA
[b.] February 19, 1977, Lewiston, ME; [p.] Paulette Fortin; [ed.] Attended Lewiston High school 1 yr., now home taught; [occ.] student; [pers.] I live each day to be happy, and writing makes me happy. It let's me vent my emotions in a way that other people can enjoy. I hope I can share more of my work in the future.; [a.] Lewiston, ME

FORTUNE, TABETHA LIN
[Pen.] Tab, Tabbie Cat; [b.] April 27, 1977, Brooklyn, NY; [p.] Jacqueline Booth Fortune; [ed.] Attending Saint Joseph's High School, Senior Year; [memb.] School Choir, Art Club, Catholic Interracial Council, Tae Kwon Doe; [hon.] 2 awards for participating in Art Club Competition (christmas event) school won 1st place twice; [oth. writ.] poetry and songs that have yet to be published.; [pers.] In my poetry I will always have something about my life in it, but I do try to give recognition to those who have influenced me.; [a.] Brooklyn, NY

FOSTER, TERESA L.
[b.] November 29, 1962, Arlington, VA; [p.] Lance Foster, April 30, 1988; [ch.] Cameron Austin, Ashlynn Marie, Lauryn Amber, Brandon James; [pers.] This poem was written in memory of, and in dedicated to my daughter, Lauryn Amber who died March 20, 1993; [a.] Woodbridge, VA

FOWELL, BONNIE
[b.] October 9, 1957, Great Falls; [ch.] Elizabeth Anderson, Traci Anderson, Nicole Anderson; [ed.] Great Falls High School, Great Falls Vo-Tech; Computer Science Graduate, College of Great Falls; Senior, Criminal Justice (Honor Roll); [occ.] Student; [hon.] Two National Forensic League Leadership Awards - High School, Minnesota Governor's Recognition Award for Volunteer work to the Elderly, Several Speech Awards including State Finals; [pers.] I write to speak the truth about individuals or groups whom harm the innocent. I am inspired through the individual beliefs of all citizens to protect civil rights in writing.; [a.] Great Falls, MT

FOXHILL, CHRISTI ANNA
[b.] December 30, 1972, Buck County, PA; [p.] Catherine Gappa; [m.] Fiancee' Frank Phillips; [m.] Engaged, July 20, 1993; [ed.] Cumberland Regional High School, Cumberland County Vocational School; [occ.] Secretary; [memb.] Congressional Youth Leadership Council, Vocational Industrial Clubs of America 1989-90 Reporter and 1990-1991 Second Vice President.; [hon.] National Junior Honor Society, Dean's List, Who's Who Among American High School Students; [oth. writ.] Many unpublished poems; [pers.] I have been very inspired by Chaucer, Wordsworth, Longfellow, Browning, Shakespeare, and many other classic artists; [a.] Vineland, NJ

FRANCIS JR., RICHARD H.
[b.] October 25, 1937, Phila., PA; [p.] Richard H. Francis Sr., and Amanda Francis; [m.] Camillia Francis, October 8, 1961; [ch.] Richard Hankins III, Rachel Ruth, Jonathan Lawrence; [ed.] John Bartram High, Phila., PA; [occ.] Systems Analyst/Accounting Department Manager, Michigan State Univ.; [memb.] COMMON (Computer Users Group); [oth. writ.] Book: Yours for Freedom and Truth, 1993. Numerous articles for the Faith Magazine. Numerous articles for the Liberty Newsletter.; [pers.] I believe in the principles set forth in the Scriptures, on which the Constitution of the United States of America was based. Take away the Scriptures, you have no Constitution, take away the USA and the world would be a prison run by a Hitler.; [a.] Holt, MI

FRANCIS, KATHARINE MOORE WAGHBERN
[Pen.] Katharine Francis; [b.] November 25, 1981, Walnut Creek; [p.] Jo Ellen and Rick Francis; [m.] not married; [ed.] I'm in the 7th grade at Stanley Intermediate School; [occ.] Student; [oth. writ.] In progress short story; [pers.] I've dedicated my writings to my dead cat named Bettey Sue, I miss her dearly.; [a.] Lafayette, CA

FRANKLIN, DR., MARY ANN W.
[a.] New Orleans, LA

FRANKLIN, KAY C.
[Pen.] Kay C. Franklin and Kacee; [b.] July 21, 1949, Bessemer City, NC; [p.] Roland and Amanda Conner;

[m.] Randy C. Franklin, June 1, 1968; [ch.] Kimberly Cheryl Franklin; [ed.] Bessemer City High School, Gaston College; [occ.] Real Estate Broker; [memb.] First Wesleyan Church, Woodmen of the World Fraternal Organization Eastridge Mall Fashion Board-Pres./Model (1990-1993), Psychology Club of Gaston College-Pres. (1994); [hon.] Phi Theta Kappa - Vice-Pres. 94'; Gamma Beta Phi, President's List 93'-94'; The National Dean's List 94'; and Judge for the Miss North Carolina Scholarship Pageant Preliminaries-1992; [oth. writ.] Two sonnets to be published in the fall of 1994 by Phi Theta Kappa's Publication, The Clarion.; [pers.] A soul that knows no God is as desolate and barren as the greatest of Deserts. Yet even a desert contains the promise of growth and prosperity when nourished.; [a.] Bessemer City, NC

FRANTZ, KATHLEEN M.
[b.] August 18, 1957, Lansing, MI; [p.] Vieva Emmogene Hunt (deceased), Morrell Ora Frantz; [ch.] Leah Marie, Korie Anne; [occ.] Office Administrator to the Lansing city Attorney; Sole Proprietor Small Business: "Sweet Annie's Patch" featuring driftwood art with poems written in calligraphy, framed with dried flowers; singing for weddings and personal enjoyment.; [oth. writ.] Personal compilation of poetry beginning in 1976 through today.; [pers.] The struggle of life from childhood through my adult life has given me strength and characteristics which are clearly reflected in my poetry. Touching lives through poetry is my gift from God.; [a.] Eaton Rapids, MI

FRAUSTO, CONNIE
[b.] July 29, 1977, San Antonio; [p.] Roger and Josie Frausto; [ed.] Natalia High School and Correspondence School at Texas Tech University; [occ.] High School Student; [hon.] Honors from local church, have helped ever since the summer of 87'. Received a plaque for helping out the church in many ways.; [oth. writ.] Several other poems but have not been published. I just keep them in a file at home.; [pers.] I try my best to make my poems unique hoping that people enjoy reading them. One of my greatest influences is my brother, Ruben Frausto.; [a.] Lytle, TX

FRAZIER, HANNAH EMET
[b.] July 1974, Phila. PA; [p.] Ms. Bluette Linda Jones; [ed.] Beaufort High Graduate, Winthrop University Student (undergraduate) majoring in Spanish and Special Education; [memb.] The Word is Alive Church, Beaufort SC; The Winthrop Association of Ebonites; The Bonite Gospel Choir; [hon.] Teen Advisor for the Beafort Gazette, Student Government; Asst. Editor for school literary magazine; Upward Bound Newsletter Committee; [oth. writ.] Several poems, and some prose published in school literary magazines, teen profiles published in the Beaufort Gazette; [pers.] I like to tell of the love of God for all people in my writings. I also favor the resolution of conflicts and hardships. I also like to write about heartbreak and other things various people can relate to.; [a.] Port Royal, SC

FRED, CARLOS J.
[b.] October 5, 1958, New York; [p.] Carmen Fred; [m.] Elizabeth Fred, February 3, 1986; [ch.] Charles Fred; [ed.] High School Graduate; [occ.] Building Superintendant, Murray Hill Properties New York City High Rise; [oth. writ.] Several poems to my

loving wife.; [pers.] I consider what I do as poetry of the soul, because everything I write is a reflection of my deepest feelings.; [a.] Bronx, NY

FREED, KENT L.
[b.] October 13, 1953, Elkhart, IN; [ed.] B.A. University of Florida major/philosophy; [occ.] Police Officer; [memb.] Several libertarian organizations; [pers.] I am a staunch proponent of the freedom philosophy known as "libertarianism." Its four cornerstones are: individual freedom, self-responsibility, free markets and the toleration of others. All four of these, needless to say, are bleak prospects in this country today.; [a.] Gainesville, FL

FREY, JOSEPH M.
[Pen.] Joe Frey; [b.] July 17, 1971, Yonkers; [p.] Lana and Gus; [ed.] Roy C. Ketcham Senior High, Attended Ghen Art a local graphic Art & Design Studio for 1 year.; [occ.] Stock Clerk and fast food closer.; [memb.] Local 256 union; [oth. writ.] One publication in school magazine and a publication of a drawing of mine also.; [pers.] My pen only writes the words. I do all the feeling of the words. But I wish you could feel the words that I write.; [a.] Wappingers Falls, NY

FRICK, DUMAS F.
[Pen.] Renaissance Man; [hon.] International Pen Award the International Society of Poets; Five Editor's Choice Awards the National Library of Poetry; [oth. writ.] "Silent Majesty", "Poet's Quill", "Air Force One", author of "The Adventures of Phineous", "Thomas' Theatre", "Mein Enemy", "Twenty-Four Hours", "Mandy's Little Secret", - all published. [pers.] World War II Veteran, ex-drafting teacher, composer (songs, music and lyrics), (played violin in several symphony orchestras), poet, lover of nature. Philosophy: To contribute to humanity. As long as poems are read, songs sung, music is performed, and writings read, I will be with you in spirit. Desire to leave a happy legacy.

FRITZ, LUCY
[b.] December 6, 1957, S.L.C., UT; [p.] Wm. L. Fritz (deceased) and Geraldine M. Fritz; [ed.] Judge Memorial High School, Western Mt. College; [occ.] Disabled; [memb.] Igru Poetry Club, WMC Rodeo Club, MS Society; [hon.] Chance Scholarship, Erb Family Grant, Library of Poetry Editor's Choice 1993.; [oth. writ.] Poems published in anthologies, Dance on the Horizon. A Far off Place, UMC magazines Solstice I & II; [pers.] I strive through my writings to show readers what I actually am feeling, experience and or seeing as I write my poetry so they to can experience and share in this moment.; [a.] Dillon, MT

FRITZ, TODD L.
[b.] June 8, 1976; [p.] John and Carrie Fritz; [occ.] Journalism Student at Ohio University; [oth. writ.] Several works that I am also attempting to publish; [pers.] I try to keep my writing somewhat ambiguous so that everyone can get something out of them. Personally, I write as a sort of therapy to express ideas I find otherwise intangible.; [a.] Elyria, OH

FRUTH, JOHN JOSEPH
[b.] August 22, 1977, Illinois; [p.] Joseph and Jeanette Fruth; [m.] Single; [ed.] Elementary School, Saint Peter and Paul, Waterloo. Waterloo High School,

Senior in 1995; [occ.] Employed at Heberer Equipment, Student at Waterloo High School; [memb.] FFA, Catholic Youth Organization.; [pers.] Some of my poetry has been published in the Waterloo High School Paper.

FRY, HORA
[b.] El Paso, TX; [p.] Enrique and Maria Luisa Ochoa; [m.] Michael J. Gaither, June 27, 1992; [ch.] Kristin Marie and linda Nicole Fry; [ed.] University Texas at El Paso; [occ.] Wife, mother and daughter; [oth. writ.] Collection of poems and thoughts reflecting on my life experiences and lessons.; [pers.] I don't take life on as a battle, but as a challenge and adventure to be confronted and enjoyed always with the guidance of our Lord Jesus Christ.; [a.] El Paso, TX

FUDALI, BARBARA
[b.] August 1, 1972, Opole, Poland; [p.] Tadeusz and Maria Fudali; [ed.] Lincoln Senior High College, Trans World Travel Academy Flight Attendant; [occ.] Cashier; [pers.] My mom used to say: "Writing comes from art, music and from your heart."; [a.] Sioux Falls, SD

FUENTE-MENDOZA, SYLVIA DE LA
[b.] November 28, 1941, California; [p.] Clementina and Luis de la Fuente; [m.] Xavier Mendoza, June 1965; [ch.] Marc, Damian, Eva; [ed.] Sacred Heart of Mary High School; East Los Angeles Community College; Mt. San Antonio College; [occ.] Administrative Assistant for Special Education, Hacienda Heights, CA; [oth. writ.] Other poems published i Alchemy a literary journal of Latino writers.; [pers.] Writing poetry is the most personal and profound expression of feelings from the heart.; [a.] Hacienda Heights, CA

FUERST, VICKY
[b.] April 25, 1961, Wyandotte, MI; [p.] Kirk and Norma Sewell; [m.] John Fuerst, May 8, 1987; [ch.] Alexandra Caroline, Joseph Zecheriah; [ed.] Our Lady of Mt. Carmel, Henry Ford Community College; [occ.] Homemaker; [a.] Allen Park, MI

FULLEN, AMANDA
[b.] August 7, 1979, Houston, TX; [p.] Joseph and Judy Fullen; [ed.] Still attending high school, 9th grade, New Braunfels High School; [occ.] 9th grade New Braunfels High School; [memb.] National Junior Honor Society, Circle Arts Drama Club; [hon.] Who's Who, Principals Award, Achievement in Word Processing, Choir, National Junior Honor Society, Service Project Award; [oth. writ.] "My Friend," "Grandmother," "Mom," "Two Special People," "Dreams" (all poems); [pers.] I wish to thank my mother for passing her gift to me. Now I am able to express my feeling and thoughts into words that other people can understand.; [a.] New Braunfels, TX

FULLGRAPP, CYNTHIA J.
[b.] December 7, 1955, Port Huron, MI; [p.] William Jacobson and Mary Kallio; [m.] Roy Fullgrapp, December 19, 1981; [ch.] Courtney Cara; Alexandra Ann; Brittany Bliss, Chelsea Cree; [ed.] Port Huron Northern High school; [occ.] Mother, Housewife, Pro Figure Skating Instructor; [memb.] St. Martha's Catholic Church, Sarasota, FL, Nokomis Figure Skating Club, Past Member American Guild of Variety Artist (AGVA); [oth. writ.] Poems written on and

off since High School years.; [pers.] From 1974 - 1990 I traveled as a pro figure skater with a major ice show across most of our fifty states, Canada and Mexico. I thank my parents for all their love, hard work and sacrifices in order to give my skating to me.; [a.] Sarasot, FL

FULMER, CLAUDIA
[b.] January 8, 1954, Vancouver, WA; [p.] Everett and Anne Bozarth; [m.] Divorced 1990; [ch.] Two children, Michele Bozarth age 21 and Gordon Murray age 17; [ed.] 12 yrs., Rainier High, Rainier, OR; [occ.] Dishwasher for a retirement home in Longview, WA; [hon.] I feel my highest honors are my two children and my two grandchildren, Jamie and Katherine Bozarth; [oth. writ.] I have other witting that have been put away for along time. Not knowing what to do with them.; [pers.] I have been divorced for 4 years. Basically I have raised my kid by myself. I am buying my house which I feel is a giant accomplishment for me.

GALLAGHER, MARY BETH
[b.] May 15, 1978, Phila., PA; [p.] John and Rita Gallagher; [m.] Single; [ed.] St. James High School, Carneys Point, NJ; [occ.] Student, Athlete 1994-95 will be my Jr. year. I am a varsity starter for my field hockey, basketball and softball teams.; [oth. writ.] "Forget-Me-Nots" published by Quill Books in "Dusting off Dreams"; [pers.] I try to reflect my attitude in my writings. I write about past occurances and how I felt during them. I find it very easy to write and it comes naturally.; [a.] Gibbstown, NJ

GANT, CHARLES
[Pen.] Atiba Kamau Sadan; [b.] July 7, 1945, Phila, PA; [ch.] Denise, Charles Jr., Jerome, Malcolm; [ed.] Mean streets of America; [occ.] Human Service Field; [hon.] Award of Merit Certificate, World of Poetry; [oth. writ.] Who sees the lady nightly, Phila. Tribune. Her dazzling Kerchiefs, Germantown Courier. Shockles, Center City Office Weekly, numerous other publications.; [pers.] My poems are but a mirror of mankind, they are designed to depict similarities, rather than differences.; [a.] Castle Pt., NY

GARCIA, MICHELLE LYNN
[Pen.] Shnarfanarf; [b.] June 6, 1980, NY; [p.] Robert and Judy Garcia; [ed.] Ron Kon Koma Junior High, 9th grade; [occ.] Student; [memb.] Connetaquat Swim Club; [oth. writ.] Poem published in book (Anthology of poetry by Young Americans 1992 edition); [pers.] My poems are based on what really happens in life, nature and in our community. My feelings are straight from the heart.; [a.] Ran Kon Koma, NY

GARDNER, ALANA
[b.] November 3, 1978, Brooklyn; [p.] Aubrey and Jeanette; [ed.] St. John the Baptist D.H.S.; [occ.] High School Student; [memb.] Deca (Vice President); S.T.A.R. (Students Teaching Against Racism) (Secretary); [hon.] Honor Roll; [oth. writ.] A poem published in the high school literary magazine.; [pers.] My poetry reflects my thoughts and feelings. Even though I am young, my writing can be appreciated by those of any age.; [a.] Brentwood, NY

GASBARA, MATTHEW JAMES
[Pen.] Sebastian Teglanni; [b.] April 7, 1976, Troy, NY; [p.] Vicki Duclos, Ernest Gasbara; [ed.] Sr.

Judes School, LaSalle Institute, Ballston Spa H.S.; [occ.] Student; [memb.] National Junior Honor Society, Latin Coub, Contributing Editor of Expressions Literary Magazine; [oth. writ.] Several poems have been published in anthologies and in my chapbook, "My Secret Ego" an article for GCN in Albany.; [pers.] I try to write poems that convey significant truths about the human condition. Poems tht we can all relate to poetry is just emotions disguised.; [a.] Saratoga, NY

GASSER, ROSE S.
[Pen.] R. S. O'Conner; [b.] December 17, 1946, Ft. Wayne, Ind.; [p.] David and Pearl Ernest; [m.] Richard J. Gasser, June 8, 1974; [ch.] Rick, Ronnie, Keith, Diane, David, Melissa, Michelle; [ed.] Spaulding High School; [occ.] Activities Assistant, Dallas Lamb Nursing HOme; [pers.] My writing reflects personal experiences, observations, and a little imagination. The world is full of inspiration.; [a.] Grover Hill, OH

GAUPEL, CATHERINE L.
[b.] September 20, 1951, Lansing, MI; [p.] James A. and Catherine E. Gaupel; [ed.] Bachelor of Science in Nursing, Nazareth College, Kalamazoom, MI 1973, National Honor Society 1973, Master of Science in Pediatric Nursing, Wayne State Univ., Detroit, MI 1981, Dean's List; [occ.] Pediatric Clinic Nurse Specialist, Home Care Specialist (presently on disability leave); [memb.] American Nurses Association, Sigma Theta Tau; [hon.] National Honor Society, 1969, Sigma Theta Tau, 1980, Employee of the Year 1985, American Nurses Assoc. Nat'l; Certification as Pediatric Nurse 1984-1988; [oth. writ.] Editorials for local papers; Research proposals and results; Pediatric Assessment Forms; Articles on Pediatric Nursing for the agency and community.; [pers.] Over 11 million people (about 1 in 20 Americans) suffer from a major depressive disorder every year, not including those that do not seek treatment. Severe Major Depression is unlike any other disorder, unimaginable to those not afflicted. My writings reflect the agony and horror of major depression, so taht others may have an understanding of what it is like for the depressed person.; [a.] Eaton Rapids, MI

GEALOW, MERLIN
[Pen.] The Bard of Lucas; [b.] August 3, 1912, Troy Grove, IL; [p.] Albert and Emma Gealow; [m.] Sereta Bealow, June 8, 1941; [ch.] Arthur Gealow and Kieth Gealow; [ed.] Eighth Grade, I'm an avid, reader, and traveler; [occ.] Retired Farmer; [hon.] I've had poems, published in various newspapers.; [pers.] As I stated previously, 10 years ago I could not rhyme two words. I consider it, a God-Given Gift. I seek no fame. I enjoy composing poetry, day or night and sincerely hope, people enjoy reading them.

GEBHART, LILY
[Pen.] Lily Vallerey; [b.] December 19, 1943, Dayton, OH; [p.] Jerry and Mary Gebhart; [m.] Unmarried but in love; [ch.] Derrick Ray Hardman; [ed.] Graduation from San Dieguito High School, Encinitas, CA, Ben Shaw Modeling School, Houston, TX, still attending school of life everywhere; [occ.] PBX/Communications Team Leader, Mercy med Center Mt. Shasta, CA; [m.] International Society for a complete earth, Jefferson Public Radio Listeners' Guild; [oth. writ.] From Seed to Shining Seed, novel, work in progress, Answer Without a Question, collec-

tion of quotations, work in progress, unpublished collection of poetry and songs; [pers.] I believe that each of us, through our personal means of creativity can become unified in raising the vibratory level of our planet and through the love that we are, can move on to finer work; [a.] Mount Shasta, CA

GEESLIN, LORETTE NICOLE
[Pen.] Lorette Nicole; [b.] January 26, 1973, Van Nuys, CA; [p.] James and Paula Geeslin; [ed.] God Children: Sharlott Hamilton, Michael Hamilton; [ed.] L.A. Pierce Community College; John Robert Powers; [occ.] Student; [hon.] Honorable Mention, "As I Open My Window" World of Poetry, Honorable Mention "The Love I Have For You" World of Poery, Editor's Choice Award (National Library of Poetry); [oth. writ.] "The Circus" Days of Future's Past (National Library of Poetry), "Unknown Love and Untitled" Quest of a Dream (Pacific Rim); "Whispers On the Wind" Dusting Off Dreams (Quill Books); [pers.] Be strong and courage. Do not be discouraged, for the Lord your god will be with you wherever you go.; [a.] Reseda, CA

GEHRLING, ALYCE
[p.] Kenneth Kilison M.D. and Micky; [ch.] Gerald K. and Paul E.; [ed.] B.A., Wesin H.S., Orchestra; [occ.] Writer, Artist, Poet; [memb.] L.I. Poetry Collective International Socity of Poets; [hon.] Two Gold Awards, 28 Honorable Mentions, 18 Anthologies, 2 First Place; [oth. writ.] St. Jode's Journal, many school publications and newsletters. First prize lit. paper at age 7. Two cartoons, Mr. Greene Beane and The Hot Kids; [a.] Seaford, Long Island

GEILMAN, NATALIA
[Pen.] Natasha Geilman; [b.] October 18, 1994, St. Petersburg, Russia; [p.] Iosif and Marina Geilman; [m.] Divorced; [ch.] Vlad Reznikov, Kseniya Geilman; [ed.] St. Petersburg University, Russia, Ph.D. in Applied Linguistics; [occ.] Bilingual Instructor at the University of Minnesota, ESL teacher at the Jewish Community Center; [memb.] ISPHS (International Society of Phonetic Sciences); AATSEEL (American Association of Teachers of Slavic and Eastern European Languages); ATA (American Translators' Association); [hon.] Various scientific awards in Russia; [oth. writ.] Several poems published in local Russian Language newspaper. Otherwise, more than 50 scientific publications.; [pers.] Since my arrival to the United States in 1991 more than ever I became convinced that similarity between different nations is far too greater than differences. People are people globe-wide!; [a.] Richfield, MN

GEORGINA, WALKER JOY
[Pen.] Gina Von Koss; [b.] October 2, 1943, Belfast N. Ire.; [p.] George & Ann Close; [m.] Frank Walker, September 21, 1977; [ch.] Andrew, Ainsley, Morris, Michael, Jonathon, Julia; [ed.] Ashfield Intermediate School, N. Ireland; Belfast N. Ireland; [occ.] Homemaker; [memb.] Adult Writing and Reading Education in South Carolina.; [hon.] A ministers degree in Spiritual Science from C.S.S.C. in Spartanburg S. Carolina; [oth. writ.] I have no other writings; this poem was a beginning for me.; [pers.] Within every darkened place, light resides. Where hatred is felt, love too presides. I write to reflect the light; to stir up the love; that each may know their worth, and value. Priceless!; [a.] Jonesville, SC

GERSTENZANG, SCHUYLER
[b.] October 15, 1952, NH; [ed.] B.A. Art History, Keene State College; [occ.] Pursing my M.S.W. at Boston University; [pers.] The landscape and the transcendental inspire and informs all my writings.; [a.] E. Falmouth, MA

GHBEISH, JAMILA
[b.] July 3, 1980, Tripoli, Libya; [p.] Gayle and Jamal Ghbeish; [ed.] Elementary, Arnold Jr. High, going to High School, Cy-Fair High School; [occ.] Library Volunteer; [memb.] Library, soccer club, video stores, Cy-Fair Select Soccer Team in Cypress, TX; [hon.] Poetry Award, 3rd place poetry award, 1st place P.E. Award, Honor Roll; [oth. writ.] I am, The Moon, Day/Night, The Man from Quebec, Fear, all unpublished.; [a.] Cypress, TX

GHEE, JOHN F.
[b.] December 21, 1968, Washington, DC; [p.] William and Linda Ghee; [ed.] Crossland High School, Delaware State College, University of Maryland; [occ.] Chemist; [memb.] American Chemical Society; [hon.] No Honors; [oth. writ.] No others writings.; [pers.] Poems are for the individual. No poem will mean the same to different people. It's all in your mind's eye and your poet's heart.; [a.] Riverdale, MD

GEHRKE, FRANCES L.
[b.] February 21, 1944, Racine, Wisc.; [p.] Franklin and Evelyn Jones; [m.] Ronald Gehrke; [ch.] Eugene, Roger, Rodney, David; [ed.] Franklin Elementary, McKinley Jr. High, Park High, M.C.C.; [occ.] Personal Companion, and Janitress; [memb.] Woodstock, Christian Church; [oth. writ.] I have other unpublished poems. I also had several poems published in local newspaper.; [pers.] My poems are to bring more people to Jesus. My poems reflect the simple things that Jesus has done for me.; [a.] Morengo, IL

GIARLA, R.J.
[b.] March 29, 1971, Chelsea, MA; [p.] Richard and Julie Giarla; [ed.] Gloucester High school; [oth. writ.] This is the first poem I have ever written. I have written three others since; Here, Death in the Swamp, and Sensational.; [pers.] Everything I write reflects my desire to see people treat each other with a little respect. I feel that the way people treat each other is one of today's biggest problems.; [a.] Gloucester, MA

GIECK, DOROTHY M.
[Pen.] Dottie; [b.] October 16, 1952, St. Louis, MO; [p.] Both deceased; [m.] Single; [ch.] Leo 14, Angela 18, Isaish 16, Jeremiah 16; [ed.] Working on a degree in journalism.; [occ.] Kidney Dialysis Technician; [memb.] Church of Christ, Deltona; [hon.] Dean's and President's list every semester I have attended.; [oth. writ.] I have written many poems and a book I am working on getting a publisher for. It is based on a true story of how nine children survived a severely abusive childhood.; [pers.] I came from an abuse family and my philosophy is that one should have a positive impact on each and every person they meet in their lifetime, do or say something for that person that they will remember and use in their own life.; [a.] Deltona, FL

GIESKEN, CHARLENE
[Pen.] C. Giesken; [b.] April 13, 1952, Owosso; [p.] Thelma and Hubert; [ed.] Teacher BA Soc. St.; [occ.]

Retired; [oth. writ.] News Articles; [pers.] Poem is to Thelma; [a.] Chesaning, MI

GILBERT, ALLISON
[Pen.] Allie; [b.] July 16, 1977, Lincolnton, North Carolina; [p.] Keith and Sue Gilbert; [ch.] Brothers & Sisters, Jason, Clay and Heidi; [ed.] I am a rising Senior at West Lincoln High School. I enjoy being a part of our school paper, "The Rebel Rouser"; [occ.] I am a rising Senior of the class of 1995 at West Lincoln High School; [memb.] Vietnam Veteran Memorial Sponsor, Hollywood Weight Loss Center, "The Rebel Rauser" (School News Editor), Chorus Reporter, and FBLA Reporter; [hon.] 3rd place winner of the Flo Robinson Literary Competition in the Poetry Division for the year of 1992. 1st place winner of the Flo Robinson Literary Competition in the poetry division for the year of 1994.; [oth. writ.] One of my poems has been published in a local newspaper, "The Lincoln Times News."; [pers.] The aspect I stress in my writing is the pureness of the soul that is within every innerman.; [a.] Lincolnton, NC

GILES, HEATH E.
[b.] August 22, 1972, Montgomery, AL; [p.] Ken and June Giles; [ed.] James Buchanan High School, Mercerburg, PA, attending Antonelli Art Institute, Plymouth Meeting, PA; [occ.] Self Employed; [pers.] Love is a sublime. Enjoy each moment in love as if it were your last. For you don't know when that last moment comes.; [a.] St. Thomas, PA

GILLASPY, KENNETH R.
[Pen.] G. Beret; [b.] May 8, 1939, Mission, TX; [p.] Roland and Blanch Gillaspy; [m.] Patricia Annette Gillaspy, September 11, 1958; [ch.] Kenneth Dene Gillaspy; [ed.] Chowchilla Union H.S., Chow Chilla, CA; Midlands Technical College, Columbia, SC; [occ.] Total quality, South Carolina Elec. and Gas. Co.; [hon.] U.S. Army (Ret), served 7 1/2 yrs. with Green Berets, two years in Vietnam, awarded 3 Bronze Stars.; [oth. writ.] I have written several poems, none published. This is my only attempt at publication.; [pers.] I am, and have been influenced by people and incidents in my life.; [a.] Columbia, SC

GILLESPIE, CHRISTINE
[b.] April 30, 1967, Jamaica; [ed.] Wonder World Child Care Center, College of Arts Science and Technology, St. Andre Technical High School, Time and Patience Primary School; [occ.] Childcare worker, Caregiver; [memb.] Church of Jesus Christ of Latter Day Saint; [hon.] Best Accounting Student (St. Andrew Technical High School (1982-83); [oth. writ.] Poems and stories for Children (unpublished); [pers.] I've always liked the Literary Arts, since we learn a lot from what we read. I strive to produce quality work that will deeply influence my readers.; [a.] Stonyplain, Alta. Canada

GIVANS, AMANDA
[b.] August 24, 1978, Beech Grove, IN; [p.] Charles and crolyn Givans; [ed.] Center Grove High School; [occ.] Student; [memb.] French Club; [hon.] Numerous Bowling Trophies, Art Awards; [oth. writ.] Poems in The Coming of Dawn, Arcadia Poetry Anthology Summer 1994, and Treasured Poems of American Summer 1994.; [pers.] Poetry should reflect what you see and feel because without meaning, it's nothing but words.; [a.] Greenwood, IN

GIVENS III, FRED
[b.] May 26, 1970, Newark, NJ; [p.] Fred Givens Jr. and Dorothy Givens; [m.] Saundra Warren; [ch.] Travis Warren; [ed.] College of the Holy Cross; [occ.] Humanities Teacher, The New School for Arts and Science, Bronx, NY; [pers.] "You just won a prize" is dedicated to my grandmother, Maria Carrington. Her love and perserverance will live forever.; [a.] New York, NY

GIVENS, IJAAZ L.
[b.] November 29, 1948, NY; [p.] Deceased; [m.] November 29, 1977, Divorced; [ch.] Layley, Jaliye, Latif, Oloha (Louise); [ed.] Midwood High School for Medical Dental, UBI Brooklyn Training Ctr."Camba"; [occ.] Health Counselor and Community Laison; [memb.] Poetry Calendar; [hon.] Mother's Helping Mothers, Parent Ed. Workshop, The State Ed. Dept. Critical thinking Program, Certificate of Competition, Camba, Certificate of Completion, Brooklyn Training Ctr.; [oth. writ.] Questions (1993); [pers.] The contents of these writings were moved by the inner thoughts of a spiritual wealth which best describes myself.; [a.] Brooklyn, NY

GLADKOWSKI, DAVID
[b.] July 21, 1951, Phila, PA; [p.] Stanley and Helen; [m.] Vanessa VanSciver, August 6, 1993; [ed.] Temple University, Father Judge HS Phila, PA; [occ.] Professional guitarist/instructor, singer/songwriter; [memb.] South Jersey Pops Orchestra; [oth. writ.] Unpublished songs and poems; [a.] Moorestown, NJ

GLASS, LAUETA A.
[Pen.] Rashida Ayo; [b.] Chicago; [p.] Ben and Helen Roberson; [m.] Richrd B. Glass, March 25, 1972; [ch.] Travis Alan, Claybrooks, Imani Richele Glass; [ed.] Thornton Twp. High School, Governors State University; [occ.] Real Estate Sales; [hon.] 1975 Gwendolyn Brooks, Poet Laureate (illinois 2nd prize contest), College Division; [oth. writ.] "Rainbows and Tears" non-published copyright 1983; [pers.] I love to write many things and people in life inspire me; [a.] Chicago, IL

GLAZE, MICHELLE
[b.] May 22, 1974, Tampa, FL; [p.] Claudia and Leroy Glaze; [ed.] Plant City High, University of South Florida; [occ.] United States Navy; [memb.] Armed Forces Literary Club; [hon.] United States Navy Achievement Medal, United States; Navy Command Honor Unit Vocalist; [oth. writ.] None other published close to 400 non published.; [pers.] Most of my poems reflect on some feeling within myself, bit it pain or love.; [a.] Temple Terrace, FL

GLENECK, ELIZABETH
[Pen.] Elizabeth or Betsy Gleneck; [b.] April 21, 1948, Nashua, NH; [p.] Late Raymond and Eunice Roy; [m.] Paul A. Gleneck, September 6, 1969; [ch.] John, Julie, Kristen, Katherine and Michael; [ed.] Associates Degee in Human Services 93' Castle College, Currently attending River College as a Junior for Communications Degree.; [occ.] Homemaker, wife, mother, student, caretaker for mother; [memb.] 4-H, Rebekahs, MADD; [hon.] Castle College Dean's List, All American Scholar 93', Poetry in 93' Castle College Yearbook Poem used at 94' Convocation; [oth. writ.] "The Castle on the Hill" read at 94' Castle College Convocation. "The Candle" and "Life's Lessons" in 93' Castle College Yearbook;

[pers.] I am a very active member of the "sandwich generation", I experienced life by helping others…the children and my father with Dementia and mother with Alzheimer's and still striving to keep my husband of 25 years happy and myself happy by being enrolled at College!; [a.] Wilton, NH

GLENN, VERONICA
[b.] May 1, 1943, Sa. GA; [p.] Wm. and Rosa Mae Glenn; [ch.] Samuel and Timothy Glenn (grands: Ramik, Dazshon, Starasia, Audasia; [ed.] Wash. Irving H.S.; College of New Rochelle; Hostos Community College; [occ.] Word Processor; [pers.] God is the Poet, I am the instrument he uses. I feel truly humble. May this publication inspire success in my grandchildren and grandniece and nephews, during their lives.; [a.] Bronx, NY

GLIDDEN, ROBIN
[b.] December 7, 1976, Savanah, GA; [p.] Jim and Joan Glidden; [ed.] Present student at Deland High School (Senior); [memb.] Trinity United Methodist Church and Youth Group; [hon.] Selected for Young authors conference twice.; [oth. writ.] none published.; [pers.] My poem steel casket, I have dedicated to those who suffered from the Amtrack train wreck, whether they were on the train or not.; [a.] Deleon Springs, FL

GOB, EDDIE ROB
[b.] June 20, 1959, Guadelope; [occ.] Lecturer in the Science of Creative Intelligence; [oth. writ.] Poems, Prose, Papers.; [pers.] My life to me is a blossoming rose, layers of petals unfolding the inner chamber of my own consciousness. And behold the endless beauty of my soul, and bow down to the infinite greatness of the Creator. Every human being has within himself unimaginable beauty; everything in the universe bears witness to the effulgence of the light of perfection. I am grateful to His Holiness Maharishi Mahesh Yogi, who through is simple teachings of Transcendental Meditation and bubbling bliss of yogi flying has given me the key to my own Self-discovery.

GOINS, DESIREE D.
[b.] June 29, 1970, Dayton, OH; [p.] Buford and Marian Crawl; [m.] Charles Von Goins, June 18, 1994; [ed.] BSBA, Marketing, The Ohio State University; [occ.] Graduate Student currently seeking a PHD in Human Genetics; [memb.] Delta Sigma Pi, Nu Chapter, Professional Business Fraternity; [oth. writ.] "What It Means to b a Minority in a Majority Society, grand prize winner of Phi Delta Kappa literary contest.; [pers.] I dedicate "I Am A Black Woman" to my husband Charles for without his loving support, my creativity would not exist. I would also like to acknowledge my greatest literary inspiration, Dr. Maya Angelou whose writings have touched the depths of my soul.; [a.] New Orleans, LA

GOLDEN, ROLLIN
[b.] October 30, 1950, Fort Bragg, CA; [p.] Mervin and Virginia Golden; [m.] Mary Callaghan, March 7, 1991; [ch.] Liam Nickel and Inga Nickel; [ed.] Fort Bragg High; Sacremento City Junior College; Calif. State University at Sacramento; [occ.] District Manager, The Sacramento Bee; [memb.] Union Co., TN Historical Society; [oth. writ.] "The Ailors in Missouri," Descendants of Richard Golden 1745-1796"; [pers.] "Although knights, dragons and damsels in distress have long vanished, the poet, speaking from

his very soul will always be present to remind us of the joys and agonies of the human heart."; [a.] Sacramento, CA

GOLDSMITH, ROBERT
[b.] December 24, 1919, Dawne city, NE; [p.] George and Grace McClure Goldsmith; [ed.] Falls City High school, University of Nebraska; [occ.] Retired, most recently; Senior Programmer Analyst, University of Southern California; [a.] Cedar City, UT

GOLEMBESKI, ALEXANDRA A.
[b.] November 2, 1974, Scranton, PA; [p.] Michael and Carol Golembeski; [ed.] Mountain View Jr./Sr. High School; currently attending S.U.N.Y. Oneonta; [occ.] Student; [pers.] Writing has always been a healthy outlet for me in which I can express myself.; [a.] Binghamton, NY

GONZALES, MONICA RILLING
[Pen.] Monica Rilling; [b.] November 2, 1928, Long Beach, CA; [p.] Harry L. Rilling and Pauline; [m.] Alexander Gonzalez, December 31, 1989, December 30, 1987; [ch.] Leesh, Valdon, Kimberly, Amber and Melody and Arthur; [ed.] Franklin Jr. High St. Anthony's Pariocal Girls School, Long Beach City College, Cyress Nite Classes, Creative Writing, Journalism, and Crisis-Intervention; [occ.] Housewife, mother, great grandmother, unheard of.; [memb.] A.A., Suicide Prevention Counselor for Drug and Alcoholic Kids, (volunteer) 2 years, Speaker for AA, 25 years straight; A.Al Central Officer 3 years), H & I Committee, Institution and Hospital Speaker; [hon.] 1946, 1st Award for City Wide Dress Designer from St. Anthonies H.S., A Certificate in Counseling and many others; [oth. writ.] Mostly television interview, Awards for Dog-Food Commercials; A cassette from A.A. which is available in A.A. Conventions and many other writings; [pers.] I have had many years of trauma, many losses, that I feel are worth interest of sharing and if developed are productive and uplifting. I have just been award of being a armature artist. I just paint and write only what I know, love and humor; [a.] Upland, CA

GONZALEZ, BERTHA M.
[Pen.] Melvina; [b.] November 29, 1929, Chiefland, FL; [p.] Albert and Clara Lynn; [m.] Ramon Gonzalez, August 12, 1948; [ch.] one adopted, loving daughter Gloria; [ed.] West Tampa Junior High School and GED from Tampa, FL; [occ.] A loving companion to a disabled husband; [memb.] American Astrological Assoc., The Mayan Order, Astara, Past member of A.R.E. (Edgar Cayce Center) Degrees from The National Metaphysics Institute inc., Doctor of Divinity D.D., Doctor of Theology D.Th. International, Metaphysical Teachers/Counselors Assoc., Institute of Pastoral Psychology; [pers.] I have studied metaphysics for years. First for self improvement, and then to share with others.; [a.] Chiefland, FL

GONZALEZ, ERIKA TERESA
[b.] December 11, 1979, El Paso; [p.] Rene and Martha Gonzalez; [ed.] I am currently attending Parkland High School in El Paso Texas, enrolling as a freshmen in August.; [occ.] American Red Cross Volunteer at William Beaumont Army Medical Center.; [a.] El Paso, TX

GOOCH, REGINA D.
[b.] September 3, 1961, MO; [p.] Lois and Joseph Yoebstl, Sr.; [m.] Divorced; [ch.] Angelica Renfroe, Tabatha, Sandra and Ricky Gooch; [ed.] GED; [occ.] Disabled due to illness of heart, full time mother.; [oth. writ.] Don't Look Back, Full of Frustration, none have been published, have 25 or more of my own work.; [pers.] Hope to see my poems published and people enjoying my work. With the Lords help maybe the world can be a better place to live without worries and hatred.; [a.] Finger, TN

GOODE, STEVEN
[b.] April 19, 1967, Paterson, NJ; [p.] Mary Ann Goode; [m.] Cynthia Renea Goode, January 8, 1990; [ch.] Rene Irene Goode and Rashanda Shanae Goode; [ed.] Some College, Certified Nursing Assistant, Civil Service for Security; [occ.] Security Monitor for Paterson Housing Authority; [pers.] We live in a world in which most people believe it is necessary to be silent and without opinion. I believe, however, by speaking or writing our thoughts in order for them to be read-or-heard, is the only way for us to grow as human beings.; [a.] Paterson, NJ

GOODWIN, DOROTHEA
[b.] November 23, 1922, Indiana; [p.] Raymond and Julia Freeman; [m.] Vernon Goodwin, November 15, 1991; [ch.] Ben, Cindy, Susan, Farrell and Dale Goodwin; [ed.] Elem. High School and 24 yrs. College; [occ.] Retired; [pers.] I spend my time reading Health Books & Journals; also Metaphysical Books. The greatest gift I have is good health and loads of love from family and friends.; [a.] Lk. Hovosu, AZ

GOODWIN, EMILY
[b.] November 18, 1980, Kankakee, IL; [p.] Jack and Paula Goodwin; [ed.] Currently entering high school; [occ.] student; [memb.] YMCA; [oth. writ.] Many unpublished poems.; [a.] Bradley, IL

GOODWIN, REGINA ALISE
[Pen.] R.A.G.; [b.] November 25, 1966, Mahank, TX; [p.] William Brown and Cathey Greenhaw; [m.] Charles Leon, September 21, 1988; [ch.] Joshua William; [ed.] Mabank High School, T.V.C.C. of Athens; [occ.] Independent Distributor; [memb.] National Honor Society, Texans United for Life, Shiloh Christian Worship Center; [hon.] Outstanding Citizenship Award, Who's Who of 1985; [oth. writ.] Several poems and songs used locally and in church bulletins; [pers.] God has blessed me to be able to write poetry on all subjects, different styles, and put to music. The book of Psalms and many writers have inspired me. Children's poems and stories are also a specialty I enjoy writing.; [a.] Kemp, TX

GORDON, ANDREW J.
[b.] July 15, 1971, Milwaukee; [p.] James and Patricia; [ed.] Currently attending the University of Wisconsin, Milwaukee (English and Film); [occ.] Retail Specialist; [memb.] International Thespian Society, honors excellence in theatre arts.; [hon.] Excellence in Acting Award from the Wisconsin High School Forensics Association; [oth. writ.] Poems and scripts.; [pers.] I believe poetry to be the ultimate form of written expression. It's cathartic and often intriguing. My mentor and biggest influence has been Susan Fierer, a truly great writer.; [a.] Brookfield, WI

GORDON, BRANDON A.
[Pen.] Brandon; [b.] August 7, 1983, Arcadia, CA; [p.] Larry and Janice Gordon; [ch.] Siblings: Larry Jr., Kurvin, Pamela, Twila, Ben, Jermayne, Michael, Ashley, Justin; [ed.] Just started in the 7th grade at Moore Middle School, Redlands, CA, July 6, 1994.; [occ.] Student; [memb.] Redlands Football, Claremont Roller Hockey, Presbyterian Church; [hon.] Youngest Student at Morre Middle School/only one of two students to be advanced a grade at Redlands Christian Academy since their beginning.; [oth. writ.] Numerous but unpublished.; [pers.] "I like sports and I search for knowledge. I feel a person can be well rounded regardless of age. I also feel that you can accomplish anything you put your mind to. I hope people will benefit from their knowledge and strive to learn more."; [a.] Redlands, CA

GRAEBE, JUDY L.
[Pen.] Judy Hayes; [b.] October 22, 1965, Carmel, CA; [p.] janet and Gerald Graebe; [ed.] BGS Northern Arizona University, Masters Student, John F. Kennedy University; [occ.] Student; [memb.] Golden Key National Honor Society.; [hon.] Golden Key National Honor Society.; [pers.] It is called the Tao. Because it is in everything it is between everything. It is everywhere, in every instant. So it is not a mystery. But search for it and it will be missed. Think about it and there will be confusion. To smell…just breathe. to hear…just listen. To find..just open. Unknown.; [a.] Concord, CA

GRAHAM, THOMAS
[Pen.] Tyler Shannon; [b.] August 11, 1973, Phila., PA; [p.] Rosemarie Grafe, Thomas Graham; [a.] Glenolden, PA

GRAMS, MARION E.
[b.] October 12, 1956, Mannheim, Germany; [m.] divorced; [ed.] Henn Co. Vocational Technical School, Art Instruction School, Mpls., John F. Kennedy Sr. H.S., Blmgtn.; [occ.] Payroll Clerk, City of Mpls, Mpls, MN; [memb.] Employee Advisory Committee, Space Planning Committee, City of Pmpls.; [oth. writ.] Non-published poetry (120+), poem entitled "Frost of Minutes Just Past" to be published in "A Far Off Place" (Nat'l Lib. of Poetry) currently writing a gothic romance date unknown for completion.; [pers.] Through painting and writing I can see the world a bit clearer. I try to see the positive and definitely look for the beauty whenever possible. Everything I feel reflects in my work; [a.] Minneapolis, MN

GRANADA, DENNIS B.
[Pen.] Deezs, Den; [b.] June 10, 1965, Philippines; [p.] Ted and Ester Granada; [m.] Suzette V. Dela Paria (Fiancee;); [ch.] Three, Gerilyn 7 yrs., Veronica 5yrs., Wesley 2 yrs.; [ed.] Benjamin Franklin High School, Pasadena City College, Watterson College; [occ.] Self-employed; [oth. writ.] Basically I just write poems to my fiancee', Suzette, whom I love very much? She has been my support and inspiration in life as I know it!; [pers.] My biggest push in writing has been my Fiancee', Suzette Dela Perua, without her I never would have actually picked up a pen. They say "Next to a Good Man, stands a Great Woman!" so true!!; [a.] Los Angeles, CA

GRANT, CAMERON
[b.] December 30, 1981, Santa Ana, CA; [p.] Legal Guardians: Alastair and Betsy Brown; [ed.] Entering 8th grade at Covenant Christian School Orange, California; [occ.] Student; [hon.] Won an award for "If I had a wish" in the Santa Ana School districts PTA Reflections Program; [oth. writ.] "Pam" (limerick), "The Sunflower" (Haiku) "My Room" (Imaging); [pers.] I love to write poetry, especially words that have a message.; [a.] Santa Ana, CA

GRANT, SR., CALVIN S.
[b.] August 7, 1923, Boston, Mass.; [p.] John E. and Florence Theall Grant; [m.] Jeanne L. Fuller, Feb. 4, 1948; [ch.] Calvin S. Jr., William P., Barbara J., Kenneth E.; [ed.] English High School, Boston, MA 1941, Klok Institute, Grand Rapids Mich., Lincoln Inst., Cleveland, OH, Troop Leadership School, Camp Grant, IL; [occ.] Retired Quality Assurance Engineer; [memb.] Amer. Soc. for Quality Control, Sons of Civil Wars Vet, Amer. Legion, Nat'l Rife Assoc., U.S. Army 1943-1946; [hon.] Keynote Speaker at the Dedication of WWII Memorial 1992 and Korean War Memorial 1993 N. Reading MA, Product Quality Award from Martin Marrietta Corp, many others; [oth. writ.] Quality Control Manuals, poems published, accepted in Museum of Holocaust in Washington, D.C.; [pers.] Poetry is the vehicle by which the soul of man gives voice. Poery speaks more of the convictions of man thn can be demonstrated on the stage of everyday life as we play out our expected.; [a.] Badger, CA

GRANT, SUSAN CARR
[b.] October 1, 1964, Niagara Falls; [p.] Ruth and Charles Carr; [m.] Richard S. Grant, August 23, 1991; [ed.] B.A. Philosophy/Education; [occ.] Elementary Education Teacher; [oth. writ.] Numerous Poems; [pers.] To save one man's life is to save the world entire. Biblical quote.; [a.] Niagara Falls, NY

GRAVLIN, MARY E.
[b.] February 17, 1927, Pontiac, MI; [p.] Floyd and Leta Frahm; [m.] Charles C. Gravlin, Sr., September 9, 1946; [ch.] Sandra, Pamela (deceased), Susan, Lois, Charles, Jr., Floyd and Leta; [ed.] High School; [occ.] Homemaker; [memb.] Woman's Auxiliary, Loyal Order of Moose and United Methodist Women, Rochester Hills United Methodist Church; [hon.] Golden Poet 91 and 92 Editor's Choice 93; [oth. writ.] A Winter Cardinal, Morning Peace; [pers.] Live and enjoy each day to the fullest. Try to be the best friend, mother, wife and grandmother I can. These feelings are the basis for my poetry. Love to bike ride.; [a.] Rochester Hills, MI

GRAY JR., CALVERT C.
[Pen.] Jean Claude; [b.] February 27, 1947, USA; [p.] Mr. and Mrs. Calvert C. Gray Sr.; [ed.] Ben Franklin High Grad. with honors, 2nd in my class; [occ.] Security Officer; [memb.] Church of Ascension on Vestee Committee and Seton of church; [hon.] Made Dean Lyons list for most awareness and talent in writing. Honor Roll at Church of Ascension 1992; [oth. writ.] Church Paper; [pers.] I try to spread love and joy to everyone I meet. I write poems for the love and enjoyment.; [a.] Baltimore, MD

GREEN, RUTH H.
[b.] January 8, 1958, Starke, FL; [p.] Cora M. Allen; [m.] Bernard Green, December 31, 1980; [ch.] Drew, Quinton and Bernadette; [ed.] Bradford Union VO Tech Army Aviation school, Ft. Rucker Army signal School, Ft. Gordon Federal Aviation Administration;

[occ.] Poet; [memb.] Autism Society of Gainesville, FL; [hon.] Commendation Award Helping Hand Award; [oth. writ.] The Racist (Inducted into the Martin Luther King Jr. Center for non-violent social change) Atlanta, GA; [a.] Gainesville, FL

GREEN, ZUTON T.
[b.] April 2, 1978, Denver, CO; [p.] Dennis and Mary Green; [ed.] Currently High School Junior, Future Class of 1996 Graduate; [occ.] Student; [memb.] Student's Against Drunk Driving (SADD), Pilgrim Rest Baptist Church; [hon.] Honor Roll, 1st/2nd Place Optimist club Oratorical Contest; Who's Who Among American High School Students; [oth. writ.] Poetry published in school literary magazines; [pers.] I believe that the key to success is knowing, knowing that you will make it, that no obstacle is great enough to defeat you. It is because I know this that I will succeed.; [a.] Denver, CO

GREENELSH, LISA JUNE
[b.] May 20, 1968, Gary, IN; [p.] Jackie Smith and Dan Stano; [m.] Trace R. Greenelsh, March 23, 1991; [ch.] Harley Reagan and Veronica Sue; [ed.] Poway High School 1986, Palomar College, Miramar College; [occ.] Administrative Assistant; [oth. writ.] Collection of Poems, short story, songs; [pers.] I am dedicating this first publication to my dream come true husband, Trace, whose love, support and devotion are my ultimate inspiration.; [a.] Lake Elsinore, CA

GREGORY, DAVID
[b.] August 12, 1975, Toledo, OR; [ed.] Philomath High School, Linn Benton Community College; [occ.] Various positions at Northwest Microcircuits; [pers.] Greatly influenced by the "electric poet" Jim Morrison.; [a.] Philomath, OR

GREY, STEPHEN
[b.] Saskatchewen, Canada; [p.] Both Deceased; [ed.] High School, Yorkton, Sask., Canada; [occ.] Retire; [oth. writ.] Play published by Dramatic Publishing Co., Chicago Editorial Writer, Regina Leader Post, 3 plays, produced at Pasadena Play Box, Margo Jones, Dallas and local theaters. One produced at Lindsey Theatre, London. Several poems in Canadian papers and charity publications.; [pers.] Since the "beginning" mankind has sought the meaning and mystery of life. A poet searches the soul of the universe for answers from fate, destiny and the Gods. The few who are rewarded translate these with brilliance of their own words as gifts to humanity.; [a.] Fort Lauderdale, FL

GRIGSBY, RICHARD S.
[Pen.] R. S. Grigsby; [b.] September 3, 1921, Tulsa, OK; [p.] James A. Grigsby and Lynette Kimmon's Grisby; [m.] Susan M. Grisby, November 9, 1975; [ch.] gail G. Harrison, Richard S., Jr. (deceased), bill Davis, Barbara Le Blanc, m Cherrill Kawanami; [ed.] 2 yrs. Teacher's College, Greeley, CO; various flight training acadamics; [occ.] Retired Airline Captain, Continental Airlines.; [memb.] Experimental Aircraft Assn., Dallas consistory, AF&AM - AL Malaika Shrine (Los Angeles), Presbyterian Church, Quiet Birdmen, OX.5 Club; [hon.] Line Captain and Chief Pilot for Continental Airlines.; [oth. writ.] Poetry covering a wide range of interest, especially to do with aviation and the out-of-doors. Currently editor of "Golden Contrails," a quarterly news magazine for the Golden Eagles, Retired Co Pilots.; [pers.] "Don't

ever give up!" as applied to poetry. There is somewhere, just the right word or phrase to express an idea exactly.; [a.] Pacific Palisades, CA

GRIMES, BRYAN KEVIN
[Pen.] Bear; [b.] August 25, 1975, Baltimore, MD; [p.] Gary and Sharon Grimes; [ed.] Joppatowne High School; [occ.] U.S. Navy; [hon.] English Award Most Improved in School; [oth. writ.] Many poems; [pers.] A mind is a terrible thing to waste. Thanks mom, dad, and Mrs. Doreen for making me who I am. All my love to Theresa.; [a.] Baltimore, MD

GUARD, KENNETH E.
[b.] June 24, 1945, Miami, FL; [p.] John E. Guard, Irene Cooke Guard; [m.] Divorced; [ch.] V.M. "Jana" Guard; [ed.] College for Financial Planning Certified Financial Planner, C.F.P. 1991, G.R.I. (Graduate Realtors Institute) Univ of Virginia 1970; [occ.] Financial Planner/Investment Broker; [memb.] International Association for Financial Planning; [oth. writ.] Several articles for Trade Journals; [pers.] Only love, the universal international language, can save the world and mankind from itself; [a.] Ft. Myers, FL

GUARDINO, ROBERT JAMES
[Pen.] Robert James; [b.] Early 1970's, Brooklyn; [p.] John Eugene and Lucille; [m.] Single; [occ.] Cook/Wrier; [oth. writ.] A collection of poems and short stories currently being published to rise money for cancer research.; [pers.] We are given experience and wisdom in life, not years. I've experienced much and I am very wise. Though I'm in my early twenties, I find myself a very old man.; [a.] NY

GUERRERO, ADELE A.
[b.] December 29, 1974, Trinidad, West Indies; [p.] Mistrilal and Margery Pooran; [m.] Manuel J. Guerrero Jr., February 10, 1993; [ed.] Attending the Micro Computer Technology Institute for the Study of Business Operations, Graduating 1995.; [pers.] I dedicate this poem, missing you, to the most important person in my life, my husband, Manuel J. Guerrero Jr. with love.; [a.] Houston, TX

GUFFEY, DENISE
[b.] January 18, 1963, Georgia; [p.] Robert and Jean Reynolds; [m.] Ricky Guffey, June 20, 1981; [ch.] Renee, David, and Tony; [ed.] High School Graduate (Central Gwinnett High school in Lawrenceville, Georgia); [occ.] Office Manager for D. John W. Mauldin; [memb.] Grace Missionary Baptist Church, Deacon's Wife; [oth. writ.] Personal poems for my family.; [pers.] The people around me are my inspiration.; [a.] Auburn, GA

GULLEY, KIMBERLY J.
[b.] August 22, 1978, Herrin, IL; [p.] Tom and Cynthia Gulley; [ed.] Junior at Goreville High School; [occ.] Student; [memb.] Student Council; [hon.] VFW Voice of Democracy, Speech Award, Goreville School Drama Award; [oth. writ.] Many poems; [pers.] I write my poems from personal experiences. i dedicate them to Kevin Leeper who inspired me and to the Lord for everything he's done. Special thanks to my mom, Cindy, for always being there.; [a.] Marion, IL

GUNDERSON, LISA ANN
[b.] July 16, 1959, Otis, AFB Mass.; [p.] John and Connie DeRaspe; [ch.] Jessica and Piper Gunderson;

[ed.] 2 BA's (English Lit. and History; [hon.] 4.0 College grad. Editor of H.S. and college newspapers; [oth. writ.] About 250 - 300 poems and essays.

GURNEY, GEORGE ROBERT
[Pen.] george gurney; [b.] october 23, 1933, Seneca, Kansas; [p.] Datha Alice and Charles Marion Gurney Sr.; [m.] Shirley Joyce Gurney, June 21, 1953; [ed.] 12th grade, National School of Aeronautics, Numerous Training Classes by "TWA"; [occ.] "TWA" medially retired; [memb.] Immanuel Lutheran Church, Fraternal Communicator at Church, Cancer Support Group "Make Today Count"; [hon.] Numerous Awards by Employer, Cancer Bike-A-Thon two years, Two Editor's Choice Awards from National Poets Society; [oth. writ.] Numerous poems in local newspaper, many poems for "Cancer Support Group" and friends. Poem published in Hospice Shareletter. (hospital newsletter) Copyright on book of poems ("Thoughts of a Daydreamer"); [pers.] Motto "Expect A Miracle - Miracles Do Happen"; [a.] Wentzville, MO

GUY, FRANCESCA
[b.] April 8, 1962, Manchester, Conn.; [p.] Bea and Rudy Cross; [m.] Frank Guy, February 12, 1992; [ch.] Rachel, matthew, Vicky, Mickey, Amanda; [ed.] Manchester High; [occ.] Housewife; [memb.] Girl Scouts of America St. Phillips Catholic Church; [hon.] U.S.A.F. Family Services Appreciation; [pers.] I enjoy writing poetry because it brings the best out of me.; [a.] Mesquite, TX

HAAG, JERED
[Pen.] J. Phillips; [b.] April 21, 1971, Washington, D.C.; [p.] Linda Haag, G. Fornoff; [ed.] Monroe-Woodbury High, University of South Carolina; [occ.] Student; [memb.] Museum of Natural History, USC Association of Letterman; [hon.] Athletic awards in Track and Cross Country; [oth. writ.] Many personal writings; [pers.] My writing, influenced by personal experiences, reflect the everyday insecurities we have. I attempt to shaw that these inactivities keep us from gaining or accomplishing things we really want out of life. Go after what you want without hesitation or shame!; [a.] Columbia, SC

HACKNEY, MARIE MATTHEWS
[b.] November 28, 1923, Philadelphia, PA; [p.] Andrew and Irene Matthews; [m.] Charles J. Hackney, November 3, 1948; [ch.] Therese Marie Hackney; [ed.] Graduate of St. Agnes Academy, College prep school; [occ.] Deceased, February 14, 1994; [oth. writ.] Her own epitaph, "Here Lies Marie," ironically written on February 14, 1992 (she passed away February 14, 1994), as well as many other titled and untitled poems, dating back to the World War II era.; [pers.] Words of daughter on behalf of mother. My poems are a reflection of life experience. I was orphaned at an early age, had a rather unhappy childhood and always relied on my faith to carry me through. I hope to inspire others through my poetry.; [a.] Bellaire, TX

HAGER, MELISSA KAY
[b.] August 22, 1963, Redwing, MN; [p.] Barbara and Chuck McWilliams; [ed.] El Camino Real High, Santa Monica College; [occ.] Account Executive, GTE; [a.] Santa Monica, GA

HAGESETH III, CHRISTIAN
[b.] February 23, 1941, Minot, ND; [p.] Christian

and Catherine Hageseth; [m.] Carol Joy Nees, 1986; [ch.] Four; [ed.] M.D.; [occ.] Psychiatrist; Author; Professional Speaker; [memb.] American Psychiatric Assoc.; American Assoc. for Therapeutic Humor; Publisher's Marketing Assoc.; [oth. writ.] Books, A Laughing Place; A Thirteen Moon Journal, finalist in Banjamin Franklin Award, Psychology/Self Help 1992; [pers.] My writing is a delightful yet demanding mistress, who my loving wife allows me to keep and nurture.; [a.] Ft. Collins, CO

HAILPERIN, BERNARD
[b.] November 26, 1922, Newark, NJ; [p.] Beatrice and Samuel Hailperin; [m.] Alice (deceased), March 22, 1951; [ch.] roy and Mila Hailperin; [ed.] University of Iowa, B.A., M.A., Seton Hall University; [occ.] English, Drama and Speech Teacher and Coordinator of Forensics; [m.] National Council of English Teachers, N.E.A., N.J.E.A., N.J. Forensics League. University of Iowa Alumni Association; [hon.] Presidential Citation for Excellence in Environmental Protection 1972, Title I Program cited in Congressional Record 1968, Coach of the Year in Forensics (U. of Penn); [oth. writ.] Published articles in N.J. Schoolmaster, book on Newark's Title I Program, 1967, novel, Children of Yesuvius, radio play, New Wonder Side Show; [pers.] I write from personal experience in order to share with others my emotions recollected in tranquility; [a.] Livingston, NJ

HALL, GENEVA C.
[Pen.] Geneva Acuff Hall; [b.] May 16, 1935, Bonita Springs, FL; [p.] Rupert and Florence Acuff; [m.] Hershel H. Hall; [ch.] Charles Michael Hall, Curtis Matthew Hall; [pers.] Dedicated to Curtis Matthew Hall.; [a.] Ft. Myers, FL

HALL, NETTIE MURRAY
[b.] April 22, 1912, Campbellsville, KY; [p.] Charles and Ida Wise Murray; [m.] Brent Kennard Hall, 1947; [ed.] Taylor County High, Campbellsville College, Bowling Green Business Univ., Western KY State College; [occ.] Writing (hobby), former teacher, bookkeeper, business mgr.; [memb.] Volunteer work, American Assoc. of Univ. Women, Church; [hon.] School Work, Recognition for writing.; [oth. writ.] Special requests: tributs, birthdays, weddings, deaths, poem included in funeral sermon, epilogue, history as one room teacher. "Bits of Wit and Folly."; [pers.] Words in poetic form reveal hidden insights that portray depths of beauty in everything. Poetry is a Dessert Climaxing. A feast that enriches lives. "It's the frosting on the cake." I love it.; [a.] Campbellsville, KY

HALL, RHEANA
[Pen.] Rheana; [b.] March 3, 1977, Cullman, AL; [p.] Jerry and Alicia Hall; [ed.] I attend Vinemont in the 12 grade. I also plan to attend college; [oth. writ.] I have written other poems. This one is the first I have shown.; [pers.] I would say that I am more influenced by literature than of other poems. Though I feel poetry is something that comes truly from ones soul, rather than idea's from influences; [a.] Vinemont, AL

HALLETT, KAREN LYNN
[b.] May 4, 1973, Williamsburg; [p.] Denese Dale and David Hallett; [ed.] Oliver Ames H.S., Easton, MA, Forham University, Bronx, NY, major, Art History, minor, English; [occ.] Student; [hon.] Dean's

List; [oth. writ.] Several personal poems; [pers.] My love of nature derives from my New England upbringing. I especially enjoy the work of the Hudson River School Artists as well as the poetry of Robert Frost.; [a.] North Easton, MA

HALLSEY, JENNIFER L.
[b.] May 1, 1983, Bangor, ME; [p.] Terry and Brian Hallsey; [occ.] Sixth Grade Student; [pers.] I live in East Corinth, Maine with my Mom, Grandmother, and my older brother Josh. My interests are writing and riding my horse, Cheyanna.; [a.] E. Corinth, ME

HALTERMAN, CLARA JEAN
[Pen.] C. Jean Hallerman; [b.] February 16, 1922, San Diego; [p.] Chrles and Clara Herms; [m.] Gerald M. Halterman, 1940 (Deceased); [ch.] Gerald Eugene, Albert Lee and Julie ann Watson; [occ.] Retired; [pers.] I lost my husband very suddenly 4 years ago. After 50 years of marriage. I wasn't even able to tell him Goodby. I felt my life was over until a friend talked me into joining a hospital group and they recommended that I start writing everything down, that led me to writing poems. I don't know if they are good or not, but it has helped me a great deal.

HALVORSEN, JUDITY KENNEDY
[b.] June 21, 1945, Milan, Indiana; [m.] robert Halvorsen, August 29, 19809; [ch.] Daniel McGraw, Gregory Halvorsen; David McGraw; [occ.] Writer, Singer, Traveler; [oth. writ.] Language of the Soul, NY, 1992; Tears of Fire, MD 1994, Nat'l Library of Poetry; [a.] Schererville, IN

HAMBERG, NAPOLEON
[b.] September 23, 1975, Dayton, Ohio; [p.] Debbie Hamberg; [ed.] Northmont High school (English and Social Sciences Major); [occ.] Vocalist, Songwriter, Poet, Short Story Writer; [oth. writ.] Assorted lyrics for ultimate society albums, short stories: "Jinxed", "The Darkest Paining"; and "Grand Departure" poetry books, Awakening Hour, Live With It, Leatherbound Lucifer (All My Nightmares), at this time, all are unpublished.; [pers.] Tomorrow is the past which we build for ourselves today.; [a.] Englewood, OH

HAMILTON, JENNIFER
[b.] March 26, 1980, Yreka, CA; [p.] Garry and Theresa Hamilton; [ch.] I have a sister Maady Hamilton who is 18; [ed.]Going into the 9th grade at Yreka Union High School; [memb.] I have been in 4-H for 6 years. I have also played Volleyball for two years.; [hon.] I have been on the B Honor Roll for three years. In sixth grade I received the National Physical Fitness Award. I have also received some Medals in 4-H.

HAMILTON, MARY
[Pen.] Marie Louis; [b.] July 5, 1948, Ithaca, NY; [p.] Elizabeth and Conrad Seymour; [m.] Deceased; [ch.] Michael Gary, Bridget Elizabeth; [ed.] Ithaca High School; [occ.] Homemaker, Part-time writer; [oth. writ.] Several poems given as gifts to friends.; [pers.] Most of my work reflects personal experiences.; [a.] Slaterville Springs, NY

HAMILTON, SANDRA
[b.] March 10, 1982, Phila. PA; [p.] George and Mary Hamilton; [ch.] Sister: Nicole Hamilton; [ed.] All Saints Elementary School; [occ.] Student; [memb.] American Legion Post 821, Staff Council of Bridesburg

Recreation Center, School Newspaper, Student Council, C.Y.O., Church Choir.; [hon.] recipient of Sullivan Foundation Grant for 1994 and 1995; Miss Poppy for years of 1994; Awards for Academic Excellence; and many Gymnastic Trophies and Ribbons; Ballet Dance Honors.; [oth. writ.] Several poems and articles published in school newspaper, several unpublished short stories.; [pers.] Writing and reading poetry gives me peace of mind and are a source of great enjoyment to me.; [a.] Philadelphia, PA

HAMLET, WILLIAM P.
[b.] September 5, 1931, Phila. PA; [p.] Wm. and Catherine Hamlet; [m.] Florence Marie Hamlet, September 10, 1954; [ch.] 3 sons, and a daughter, Bill, Jim Matt and Helen Theresa; [ed.] B.S. St. Joseph's University Phila., Air Force Navigational School, B-52 Academy, Rated Navigator and Electronics Officer; [occ.] Retired Personnel Director; [memb.] Air Force Reserve, St. Thomas More Alumni High School Assoc.; [hon.] Dean's Lists, Commissioned Officer U.S. AirForce, several major awards in human relations field; [oth. writ.] Various poems and short stories as yet unpublished.; [pers.] Fulfillment in life is achieved directly by dedication to learning thru the arts, and philosophy and indirectly by instilling these views in your children and grandchildren.; [a.] Upper Darby, PA

HAMMETT, JOHANNA P.
[Pen.] Patty; [b.] March 31, 1945, Culver City, CA; [p.] Deceased; [m.] Thomas W. Hammett, October 27, 1981; [ch.] Chrysti Collins; [ed.] Graduated from S.J.M.H.S.; [occ.] Free-lance writer, minister; [hon.] Semi Finalist in 1994 N. American Open Poetry Contest; [oth. writ.] 15 other poems that I already sent; [pers.] My poems have a certain mood. I have always admired Robert Frost.; [a.] San Diego, CA

HAMPTON, SHAWN
[b.] November 11, 1975, Lincoln, NE; [p.] Sandy and Greg Anderson; [ed.] Lincoln Southwest High School; [occ.] Food Service; [memb.] The International Thespian Society; [hon.] The International Thespian Society, Drama Letter, Best Tec. of the Year in Theater.; [oth. writ.] Two poems hanging on the stage wall in southeast auditorium.; [pers.] My heart lies in what I see, my imagination of things men fear. Writing for me, is my only way to stay sane. I write about things I see, and more of things of feeling nature and the environment are great influences.; [a.] Lincoln, NC

HANSEN, ANTONIA MARIE
[Pen.] Noni; [b.] October 16, 1980, McLeary, WA; [p.] Anthony George, Carla Hansen; [ch.] Sister & Brother: Cynthia Ann Hansen, Anthony W. George; [occ.] Middle School Student; [hon.] Sports, Cheerleader; [oth. writ.] I love to write short stories in my diary but I never show them to anyone. Also like my key board and singing, Kereoki.; [pers.] My grandpa, Carl P. Hansen was a writer/poet, in my eyes...the best. His pen was Sea Pea Aitche, he had published poems.; [a.] Oakville, WA

HANSEN, ROBERT
[Pen.] Rob Hansen; [b.] January 7, 1974, Huntington, LI, NY; [p.] Barbara Manger; [ed.] Currently enrolled at Manatee Community College. Made Dean's List; [occ.] Certified Nursing Assistant; [memb.] Member of High School teams: swimming,

basketball, track and soccer.; [hon.] Offered membership into National Honors Society. Received Vocational Gold Seal Scholarship; [oth. writ.] I have written a great deal of personal and as of yet unpublished poems.; [pers.] I greatly admire the works of Walk Whitman. I have always felt the most important thing in life is to do the best you can, and to be good to one another.; [a.] Sarasota, FL

HARDIES, MELISSA
[b.] August 29, 1977, Berrien Twp.; [p.] Carl and Verlyn Hardies (deceased); [ed.] Imlay City High School; [memb.] Students Against Driving Drunk, Mothers Against Drunk Driving, PRIDE of Laper County, Imlay City Christian Reformed Church.; [hon.] High Honor Roll, Citizenship award, Top Journalism Student; [oth. writ.] Several articles in the school newspaper, several poems in the school literary journal, editorial in the Lapeer County Press.; [pers.] I express myself the best with words and writing helps me to do this.; [a.] Imlay City, MI

HARDWICK, HEIDI M.
[b.] May 26, 1979, Owosso, Mem.; [p.] Hope Ball and Jim Hardwick; [ed.] Still in high school; [a.] Durand, MI

HAREL, EVELYN J.
[b.] June 26, 1925, Chippewa Falls, WI; [ch.] 10 children; [ed.] High School, Chippewa Falls Senior High School, 1944; [occ.] Retired; [memb.] Church; [oth. writ.] The Long Winter in "Tears of Fire" and "Phantoms of Indian Summer" in Wind in the Night Sky; [pers.] I find nature in all its seasons to be most beautiful with its colors, aromas and weather. I paint animals in seasonal nature.; [a.] Chippewa Falls, WI

HARGIS, ANDRIA
[b.] March 9, 1979, Farmington, Missouri; [p.] Mary and Charlie Hargis; [ed.] Farmington H.S. Sophomore Class; [occ.] Student; [memb.] H.S. Band, H.S. Color Guard, Trend, H.S. Marching Band; [hon.] Presidential Academic Achievement Award; Mathematics award; Academic and Athletic Letters; Honors Band; All-American & All Star Color Guard Member; [oth. writ.] Several other poems but none published yet, school newspaper "Knightlife"; [pers.] My writings come straight from my heart and from my mind. They are about things that are important to me.; [a.] Farmington, MO

HARKIN, MARY BERNADETTE
[b.] February 10, 1956, Philadelphia; [p.] John J. and Mary W. Harkin; [ed.] Great Valley High School, Malvern, Bloomsburg State College, PA; [occ.] Computer Operator/Programmer; [memb.] United States Tennis Association, U.S.T.a.; [pers.] Most of my poetry was written as a very young adult. My poems reflect my own personal feelings from the heart about life, love and nature.; [a.] Malvern, PA

HARMEYER, LORI
[b.] May 30, 1964, Omaha, NE; [p.] Bernard and Frances Sax; [m.] Daniel J. Harmeyer, March 18, 1989; [ed.] Plano Sr. High school, Southwest Texas State University; [hon.] "Manletter of the Year" Beckett Publications 1992; "Employee of the Year" 1988; American Residential Management; [oth. writ.] "My Friend the Dorphin," "Waiting for You," "A Fathers Special Touch," "My Special Memory," "Baby Andrew;" [pers.] Keep your face towards the

sun and all shadows will fall behind.

HARMON, MICHAEL
[b.] May 5, 1975, Hobart, IN; [p.] Donna and Timothy Harmon; [ed.] Wheeler High Graduate; [occ.] Air Force Hopeful; [hon.] Academic Letter; Boy's State; Honor Roll; Editorial Board for the School's Newspaper; [oth. writ.] Co-Founder; Co-Editor; Co-Head Writer; Co-Creator of "The Fine Print," a short-lived humor magazine based in my high school; articles for the high school paper (various).; [pers.] If we live for the past, solely in the past, then the future will be forgotten. I credit a very vivid imagination for the talent I call my writings. Influences: music, friends, family, and Robert Plant.; [a.] Valparasio, IN

HARMON, SANDRA
[b.] November 14, 1978, Norwalk, CA; [p.] Ron and Jane Harmon; [ed.] Currently entering my junior year at John Glenn High School; [occ.] Poet/Writer; [memb.] Key Club, Ecology Club; [hon.] Principals Honor Roll, Currently carrying a 4.1 grade average.; [oth. writ.] Many poems I have not yet published. I have been greatly influenced by Robert Burns and Edgar Allan Poe.; [pers.] My writings reflect on what I see in society today.; [a.] Norwalk, CA

HARP, CLIFFORD
[b.] September 23, 1920, Beaver Falls, PA; [p.] George Harp, Edna Harp; [m.] Helen Armbruster Harp, May 30, 1949; [ch.] Rita Jane Harp, Salvadori, Stephen Michael, Kent Christopher; [ed.] Barnesville High School, Barnesville, OH; [occ.] Retired. Formerly draftsman-Smith Lumber Co; [memb.] Life Member DAV, Veterans of Foreign Wars 2792, Knights of Columbus 5250, Destroyer Escort Sailors Assoc; [oth. writ.] Easter Greetings - Published in "Coming in Dawn", "To A Sailor's Sweetheart", published in New York Sunday Mirror in 1945; [pers.] Armature Poet, like to write of many subjects; [a.] Barnesville, OH

HARPER, HOWARD E.
[Pen.] Jonathan; [b.] July 4, 1945, Holyoke, MA; [p.] Roy and Rita; [m.] Cynthia, April 20, 1974; [ch.] Kim, Courtney, Jon; [ed.] Holyoke, MA , always a "mill town kid."; [occ.] vice President Mafcote Industries; [memb.] N.P.T.A., A.S.P.C.A., Epilepsy Foundation of America, Warden, Christ Church Parish, Fairfield County Hunty Club; [hon.] "Awarded" Three Loving Children"; [oth. writ.] "With These Words" 1981, "Daughter, Mine" 1992, "Heaven Came To Call" Quill, "True Love Again" Quill, "9 Hours to Manhood" 1978; [pers.] There is no such thing as "bad" writing, just "bad" imaginations.; [a.] Redding, CT

HARPER, JOHN W.
[b.] August 24, 1915, Norris City, IL; [p.] Wm. C. & Elvira Phillips Harper; [m.] Coral Ruth Harper, August 29, 1987; [ch.] none; [ed.] N.C. Township High, Self-taught & Living Experience.; [occ.] Retired Carpenter and General Contractor.; [memb.] 1st. UMC of Canoga Park, 11th. A/B Assoc., Allied A/B Assoc., Am. Legion, Post 826, Paralyzed Vet. Assoc. (Quadriplegic for last 7 years) N.C.T.H.S. Alumni Assoc., ETC.; [hon.] Am. Leg. Life Mem. Award, P.V.A. Life Mem., Carpenter's Union 45 yr. Pin, Built Fellowship Hall for my church free and I am an American!; [oth. writ.] None, just a few for my

family and friends. Have always thought I could write, but have never taken the time.; [pers.] Live by the Golden Rule when possible. Those who bring sunshine to the lives of others, can't keep it from themselves.; [a.] Chatsworth, CA

HARRILL, TONYA JOY
[b.] March 6, 1974, North Carolina; [p.] Bill and Sandi Harrill; [ed.] Myrtle Beach High School, Columbia College, Winthrop University; [occ.] Student; [hon.] Felicia Sisk Writing Scholarship, Dean's List, poems published by Pacific Rim Publications and Quill Books.; [oth. writ.] "Trips" published by Quill Books; "Time Machine" published by Pacific Rim Publications; [pers.] I am a romantic. I write for the soul and with the soul. I strive to find what I write about and I usually find it.; [a.] Myrtle Beach, SC

HARRIS, FREDERICK
[Pen.] Fred Harris; [b.] February 7, 1963, Auburn, NY; [p.] Arthur and Katherine Horr; [ed.] Port Byron High School, B.S. Davis and Elkins College Hospital Corp School U.S. Navy.; [occ.] Surgical Technician; [memb.] Association of Surgical Technologists; Association of Central Sterile Supply Techs., various Running Clubs; U.S. Navy Reserves; [hon.] Who's Who of U.S. College Students 1993, Beta Alpha Beta, numerous running awards; [oth. writ.] Two articles published in college newspaper "The Senator."; [pers.] I enjoy reading and try to lead a well rounded life. I am interested in pursuing a writing career more actively since this is my first poem written outside of English courses.; [a.] Auburn, NY

HARRIS, JAMES F.
[b.] July 22, 1970; [ed.] Jefferson Forest H.S., Longwood College; [memb.] Earthwatch, The Wilderness Society; [pers.] Share the Wealth; [a.] Goode, VA

HARRIS, JANE M.
[Pen.] Jane Harris; [b.] July 11, 1922, Collinwood, Tenn.; [p.] Walter V. and Vela V. Moore; [m.] Richard Hillman Harris, June 9, 1961; [ch.] William O.; [ed.] Commercial High School, Atlanta, Georgia. Completed several courses, The American Institute of Banking, Atlanta, Georgia.; [occ.] Secretary for former Governor of Georgia and United States Senator, Herman E. Talmadge; [memb.] Atlanta Braves Booster club, Lake Talmadge Ladies Club, President, The Henry County Human Society, Secretary and director 12 yrs, Major League Baseball Alumni Assoc.; [hon.] Recognized by local county commissioners for serving as secretary of the county human society for 12 years. Honored by Major League Baseball for being on a winning public relations team during an All-Star game in 1972.; [oth. writ.] Had several articles published in local newspapers. One article published in The Sporting News. Also, had several cartoons published in local publications.; [pers.] I cherish my sense of humor. I feel that my life would be dull without one. I have compassion for other people and strive to be a good listener.; [a.] Hampton, Georgia

HARRISON, TERRY A.
[b.] October 25, 1960, Cleveland, OH; [p.] Essie Mae Williams and Clarence Harrison; [ch.] Christopher Denson Harrison; [ed.] Spring Arbor College, Bachelors of Arts in Human Resource Management and a Bachelors of Arts in Family Life Education; Central Michigan University, Masters of Science in Adminis-

tration.; [occ.] State of Michigan Department of Corrections/Prison Counselor; [memb.] National Authors Registry, B.B.W.A., Certified Family Life Educator.; [hon.] I received the Editor's Favorite for a poem titled "The Well Kept Secret" in the Creative Arts and science Enterprise; I received honorable mention for a poem titled "A Glimpse of Light" and to be or not to be what you see in an anthology called Remembrance.; [oth. writ.] "Scenes from a Woman's Life," I am presently working on this novel. A thought, poem published by the National Library of Poetry, continued poem published in Remembrance by the Cader Publishing.; [pers.] My goal is to touch some young heart or life. I would like to help young people all over the world through writing and inspiration.; [a.] Lansing, MI

HARTI, HOLLY
[b.] November 12, 1974, Green Bay, WI; [p.] Linda and Lawrence Harti; [ed.] Ashwaubenon High; [occ.] Stocker; [memb.] I sponsor a wolf thru The Wolf Education and Research Center.; [hon.] B-honor roll for senior year, art awards from various shows; [oth. writ.] Personal poems that have been published.; [pers.] My writings reflect my own personal feelings and thoughts. I also right about past experiences that I've gone thru.; [a.] Green Bay, WI

HARVEY, WALTER
[b.] April 18, 1925, NY, NY; [p.] Deceased; [m.] Deceased; [ch.] Robert Harvey, Alfred Harvey, Edward Harvey; [ed.] Brooklyn College, NY, Wayne State University, Mich., Trenton State Teachers College, NJ; [occ.] Retired: Army Major 1969, Elementary School Teacher (6th grade) 1985.; [memb.] The Retired Officers Assoc., The Symposium, Princeton Seminary, National and N.J. Education Assoc., NJ Poetry Society; [oth. writ.] Several poems published in periodicals to include: NJ Poetry Soc., World Spinners, Lucidity, a journal of verse and awarded third prize, National Federation of State Poetry Societies; [pers.] While in pursuit of the symbol, the guest of poetry, I offer the affirmation tht hope is to recognize the possibility. I entail that truth beauty exists beyond the constraints of this mortal voice.; [a.] Tabernacle, NJ

HATZOLD, MARYANN L.
[b.] May 31, 1949, Phila., PA; [p.] Harry and Catherine Lyons; [m.] Thomas John Hatzold, July 15, 1967; [ch.] Maryann Tolson, Ann Hatzold, Thomas Hatzold, Jr.; [ed.] St. Leo's Elementary School, St. Huberts High school; [occ.] Child Care Supervisor, St. Vincents Orphange; [pers.] I would like to dedicate this poem to my grandson, little Ricky Tolson; [a.] Phila., PA

HATZOLD, MARYANN L.
[b.] May 31, 1949, Phila.; [p.] Harry and Catherine Lyons; [m.] Thomas Hatzold Sr., July 15, 1967; [ch.] Maryann Tolson, Ann Hotzold, Thomas Hatzold Jr.; [ed.] St. Leo's School 8 yrs, St. Hubert's High 2 yrs., G.E.D.; [occ.] Child Care Supervisor; [pers.] I want to dedicate this poem to my first grandchild, little Richie Tolson; [a.] Phila, PA

HAWLEY, RUTH
[b.] June 8, 1935, Meadville, PA [p.] Howard and Dorothy Drissel; [m.] Lloyd G. Hawley, June 14, 1952; [ch.] Lucide Sue, Pamela Jean, Linda Diane,

Tonya Louise; [ed.] Saegertown High School; [occ.] Homemaker; [memb.] PA Baptist for Life, Sharon Baptist Church; [oth. writ.] Two poems published in our church newsletter "Rose of Sharon"; [pers.] I strive to reflect the goodness of God and the beauty of His creation and my total dependance in Him.; [a.] Mercer, PA

HAYDU, MELANIE
[Pen.] Mel; [b.] August 22, 1978, OH; [p.] John and Caral J. Haydu; [ed.] IN High School (10th grade) Garfield High School; o Baby Sitter; [memb.] Humane Society, German Club; [hon.] Merit Roll, German Award, English Award; [oth. writ.] A lot of poetry but never published. [pers.] In loving memory of my mother April 11, 1944 -June 20, 1991; [a.] Solon, OH

HAYES, CASSANDRA L.
[b.] April 23, 1981, Hailey, Idaho; [p.] Janet L. Black and Harry A. Leadlay; [ed.] Glassgow, Mt. School K-1st, Anaconda, Mt. 1st -7th. Completed 7th grade in June 94 at Anaconda Fred Moodry Middle School; [hon.] Honor Roll, Math Student of the Year and other Math Awards; [pers.] I am a chirstian and I have always liked poetry. When I'm older I'd like to have lots of my poems published.; [a.] Anaconda, ID; Filer, MT

HEDNDRICKSON, CHARLES A.
[Pen.] Carlos; [b.] January 30, 1936, Phila., PA; [p.] Adolph Hendrickson and Anna Wehrmann; [m.] Carol (Nee) Martinsen, December 28, 1991; [ch.] Michael Paul and Mark Anthony; [ed.] South Phila. High School for Boys LaSalle College; [occ.] Freelance writer.; [oth. writ.] Poetry and short stories.; [pers.] Whereas most of humanity sees only the superficial shadows of life, the poet has the unique ability to discern and describe both the pleasure and the pain of its' reality!; [a.] Collingdale, PA

HEERDT, MARY MARGARET
[p.] Martin A. Crowne (Lecturer Galway University, ireland) and Margaret Mary Walsh (Co. Mayo Ireland; [m.] Lewis H. Heerdt, Tax Attorney, Los Angles, June 1961; [ed.] Passed London Matriculation Studied for Medical Degree, Adelaide and melbourne Universities, Australia then at Melbourne Tech. College for Diploma of Analytical Chemistry.; [occ.] Retired; [memb.] Past Member Mt. Paomar and Griffith Park Observatories, Member Smoothe Dancers, Glendale, Los Angeles; [hon.] Gold Medal Ballroom Dancing; [oth. writ.] Many varied poems on events of local interest, political and otherwise, also poetical coverage of social events and people aboard ships. Also descriptions places and people on land tour of Ireland, all in rhyming even beats per line, old style poetry.; [pers.] Although I may seem very social and outgoing, also friendly; with many social skills I am serious in disposition, most interested in astronomy, Einstein's Theories, etc., also medical advancements, etc.; [a.] Los Angeles, CA

HEGGE, DARLYS J.
[Pen.] Darlys Dobratz Hegge; [b.] December 2, 1939, Redfield, S.D.; [p.] Otto A. and Esther (Fink) Dobratz; [m.] Leo L. Hegge, June 8, 1963; [ch.] Pets: 3 cats, Goldie, Tammy and Cindy Lou; [ed.] Aberdeen Central High School (1957 graduate); [occ.] Housewife, caring for husband who is stroke victim; [memb.] Zion Lutheran Church, Zion Lutheran Altar

Guild; [oth. writ.] Several short stories and one or two poems, non published.; [pers.] I try to reflect the love shown me by my parents; my Mother is my roll model. I enjoy the beauty of God's creation. I enjoy reading, writing, crocheting, and crafts.; [a.] Aberdeen, SD

HEIMEL, LINDA NEW
[Pen.] Kay Forrest; [b.] September 24, 1938, Ropesville, TX; [p.] Emery and Elizabeth New; [m.] Leonard Heimel, April 8, 1956; [ch.] Sharla Kim, terry Mark, David Morris; [ed.] Denver city High, courses in Nutrition, Business Management, Word Processing, Writing, First Aid; [occ.] Word processor and writer; [memb.] FCE (Family Community Education), SDA (Seventh Day Adventist Church); [hon.] NHS (National Honor Society) [oth. writ.] Three poems published in anthologies, poems, other material for newspapers, Public relations work for an inventor, editing work for T.V. program: "Impact," editing and writing for a local foundation, other professional work.; [pers.] I am only what God, and other loved ones, through His strength, have helped me.; [a.] Jasper, AR

HEISER, JEFFREY R.
[b.] December 20, 1956, Chicago, IL; P Ronald and Carole Heiser; [m.] April I. Heiser, September 9, 1977; [ch.] Jeffrey, Jennifer, Brian; [ed.] Brandon High School, University Central Florida; [occ.] Computer/Security Consultant; [memb.] Boy Scouts, National Classification Management Society (NCMS); [hon.] Eagle Boy Scout, Dean's List, 2 terms as President (NCMS Space Coast Chapter); [oth. writ.] Various security related articles; [pers.] The love, strength, and understanding my wife has given me hs been the greatest influence in my writings. Life is a short journey through time that one must learn to make the most and best of before it is over.; [a.] Merrit Island, FL

HELLYER, LESLIE ANNE
[b.] November 16, 1977, C'ssted Usvi, St. Croix; [p.] Richard K. Hillyer and Nereda I. Wright; [ed.] Good Hope School; Fredricksted, St. Crois, USVI; [occ.] Student, Part-time sales person; [memb.] Key Club, Cross Country, Padi Driver; [hon.] Varsity Letters; [pers.] My poetry is my being, my heart, and my soul. Without it, I am nothing, the influence in my life is what goes on around me and how it affects my heart.; [a.] Christiansted, St. Croix, USVI

HENDERSON, ADRIENNE M.
[b.] April 6, 1979, Houston; [p.] Ronnie and Rosa Henderson; [ed.] Oak Creek Elementary North Shore Elementary, North Shore Middle School, North Shore High School; [occ.] Student; [oth. writ.] Numerous poems and short stories.; [a.] Houston, TX

HENDERSON, CECELIA S.
[Pen.] Sign this one me, Cecelia; [b.] February 4, 1942, Phila. PA; [p.] Benjamin and Hattie Sills; [m.] Richard Henderson Sr., December 23, 1959; [ch.] Richard Jr., Kennard, and Louis; [ed.] Bok Vocational tech., High school, Phila. PA, Major: Child Care; [occ.] self-employed, transporting the young; [memb.] Corinthian Bap. Church of Germantown, PA; [hon.] None at this time; [oth. writ.] Attention, there's a War Going On; Temporarily Out of Order; When Depression has Hold of Me; 1982 and many more; [pers.] Learning to accept folks as they are and

to love with no strings attached is one of the greatest things of life. Always believe God. Expect a miracle everyday.; [a.] Philadelphia, PA

HENDERSON, GINA A.
[b.] January 24, 1972, Gary, IN; [p.] Leanna Henderson; [ch.] Janika Denean Donald; [ed.] Garry Roosevelt High School; [hon.] National Honor Soc., 1st Place Grehound Writing Award; [oth. writ.] Many short poems not yet published.; [pers.] I do what I must to make myself happy. Only then can I attempt to affect the lives of others positively.; [a.] Gary, IN

HENDERSON, VADA MAE
[b.] April 27, 1942, Marshall Co., Home; [p.] John (deceased) and Bonnie Butler; [m.] William Owen Henderson, May 4, 1959; [ch.] Owen Randy, Ronda Lavada, Zelda Mavis, Rebecca Fay, 6 grandchildren; [ed.] 8th grade, Aurora School, was going to high school, but got married instead; [occ.] Farmwife; [pers.] I alway's want to write my poem's funny, but most of the time I do true one's. I have written them from a little girl of 7 year's old. I have a wondering mind. When it comes to poetry. Also do some in music and songs; I have had some printed in Tribune Carrier Benton, KY and also indifferent School's when I was younger and NLP, May 12 1994; Poems comes from the heart it's sorta like keeping a diary only it's poetry.; [a.] Hardin, KY

HENDERSON, VERNICE
[b.] Born in New Port News, VA; [p.] Deceased; [m.] Single; [ch.] Three Godchildren - smile, in August; [ed.] Mary Jane Whister School in Phila., PA.; [occ.] Retired; [memb.] World of Poetry; just signed as a member of the I.S.P in Owings Mills, MD; [hon.] 8 Awards and 2 Golden trophies; however I did not attend the World of Poetry convention so I did not receive them. Spelling Bees in school; [oth. writ.] one song.

HENGST, GINA
[b.] May 27, 1979, Chico, CA; [p.] Shirley and Jack Hengst; [ed.] Durham Elementary, Bidwell Jr. High, 9-10 gr. P.V. High; [hon.] 4.0 gpa, C.S.F.; [oth. writ.] Many poems in journals and paper publishing.; [pers.] Within ones self is a spirit, a spirit of inner peace and a spirit of dissatisfaction.; [a.] Durham, CA

HENNING, YVONNE P.
[b.] November 16, 1948, Abilene, TX; [p.] Jack and Hazel Rogers; [ch.] Shana Papasan Dismore, Knickia Papasan; [ed.] Alexander School of Art, Wylie High; [occ.] Rancher and Artist, Alexaner Art Instructor; [memb.] Sheriffs Association of Texas, Alexander Art Club.; [hon.] Award of Merit, World of Poetry for poem "If You Should Ever Leave Me"; [oth. writ.] "Cattlemans Prayer for Rain," "Childhood Days," "Lost Love," "Vanished," "Stand Alone," "Only A Country Girl,"; [pers.] To look at life thru honest eyes and pull encouragement and happiness out of lifes tragedies. Ambitions of making every person I come in contact with laugh at least once before I part their company.; [a.] Coleman, TX

HENRY, HEATHER
[oth. writ.] Other poetry that I have written will be inserted throughout the book I am currently writing. Interested publishers to sponsor my writings for public access to all persons, please contact me. Thank you for your support.; [a.] Mt. Shasta, CA

HENRY, JILL V.
[b.] September 24, 1978, Cope May, Court House, NJ; [p.] Verlee and John Henry; [occ.] Student, Middle Twp. High School Sophomore; [memb.] Middle Twp. H.S Marching and Concert Bands. Lector at Our Lady of the Angels RC Church.; [hon.] Academic Excellence in Spanish I and Engl Honors I. Academic Excellence and Eng. Honors I. Academic Excellence for a 3.5 (or above) GPA National Eng. Merit Award in 1993.; [pers.] I hope that someone who reads anything that I write can relate to a part of the writing or that they can learn something from it.; [a.] Green Creek, NJ

HENRY, JOHN KERAN
[b.] August 24, 1932, Dublin, Ireland; [p.] John L. and Philomena Henry; [m.] Kathleen Henry (nee McCann); [ch.] Karen Patricia Henry and Donna Marie Solder; [ed.] Irish Christian Brothers, Dundalk, Ireland, Dundalk Technical Institute, Norwalk Connecticut Tech. Inst.; [occ.] Retired Sales Application Engineer; [memb.] Honorary National Life Member Ancient Order of Hibernians; Knights of Columbus; American Legion; Catholic War Veterans; [oth. writ.] Two plays "What Price on the Dublin Market" and "In Sight of Mourne." song written and recorded "Gown of White."

HENRY, LAURIE
[b.] May 28, 1968, Putnam, CT; [p.] Lawrence and Sharon Henry; [ed.] Killingly High School; [occ.] Printer at the Racine Company, Brooklyn, CT; [pers.] I really enjoy writing poems especially when I can do one for soembody else on special occasions in their life. Poetry has always been favored by me it's very special because it comes from within. I feel that if a poem of mine can make someone else happy in some way then thats an achievement on its own.; [a.] Danielson, CT

HENRY, LISA M.
[Pen.] Tasha Bontifelli; [b.] May 13, 1969, Ticonderoga; [p.] 1st, Betty and Burley Henry and 2nd. Bonnie and Everett Le Poer; [ch.] My son, Christopher Alan; [pers.] This poem is dedicated to the love of my life and forever friend, Everett Alan LePoer Jr., (P.S.) Christopher Andrew Crockett, I miss you, yet another forever friend Kenny Carr (Hello) I miss you most of all.; [a.] Shrewsbury, MA

HENSHAW, RONALD E.
[b.] October 28, 1941, Houston, TX; [p.] Fred and Florence Henshaw; [ch.] Christopher, Marie and Joshua; [ed.] Graduate of Jesse H. Jones High School, Houston, TX; Three years of study at the University of Houston.; [occ.] Professional Driver; [memb.] First Methodist Church in Mexia, TX; [oth. writ.] "The Moat" published in the Harvest at the University of Houston. Small volume of poems.; [pers.] The desire to create, through artistic expression, that which reflects our own image is inherent in the evolving human spirit; and inherited trait from, and evidence of, our own Creator.; [a.] Houston, TX

HERBERT, JACQUELINE SAUNIER
[b.] July 28, 1933, Sulphur, Louisiana; [p.] Adlophe and Thelma Saunier; [m.] Carl J. Hebert, February 4, 1951; [ch.] Randall, Beth, Paul, Teresa, and 8 grandchildren; [ed.] Sulphur High School Class of 51'; [occ.] church Musician at Our Lady of Prompt Succor Catholic Church, Sulphur, LA; [memb.] Bereavement Committee, OLPS Cathedral Choir, Folk Choir, and Sounds of Praise Gospel Group; [oth. writ.] Words and Music of Praise and Worship, including Jesus, King of Mercy: We See a Miracle of Love: Father We Sing To You: Hear Me, Precious Lord: and others. Also other poems; [pers.] "Our Chair" was inspired by our choir director, who is also a vice-principal of an area High School. After practice one evening, he related an experience that occurred at school. He had been faced with identifying an errant student at school. He paced before the row of boys, silently praying to God for help. He told us, "It felt like a hand came down on my had, turning me toward this one boy!" He went to the boy, ordered him to follow, and turned to leave the room. The boy got up and began, "I didn't mean anything by it..." So, Our Chair in which God sits with us, when we ask for guidance of truth, begins God Makes No Mistakes; [a.] Sulphur, LA

HERMAN, KAREN
[b.] July 15, 1975, Waynesboro, PA; [p.] Edward and Renate Herman; [m.] Boyfriend: David Joseph Hughes II; [ed.] James Buchanan High, Shippensburg University; [hon.] Two Academic Fitness Awards; [oth. writ.] Many others, yet unpublished poems and short stories.; [pers.] Poetry is not strict or confining. It is open and let's those who read it and write it expand their thoughts.; [a.] Chambersburg, PA

HERMES, LORE
[b.] February 9, 1956, Norwalk, CT; [p.] Henry and Anna F. Hermes; [ed.] Brookfield High School, New Haven Academy of Business.; [occ.] Insurance assistant in Chiropractic office; [oth. writ.] Several poems (unpublished) on various subjects.; [pers.] I have started writing poems only recently and find it to be such a wonderful outlet for thougs on life, love and the world around us.; [a.] Brookfield, CT

HERNANDEZ, BEATRIZ
[Pen.] Bea Hernandez; [b.] December 12, 1975, Havana, Cuba; [p.] Felicia and Norberto Hernandez; [ed.] I got my G.E.D. at an Adult Center; [occ.] I am a babysitter; [memb.] The blood center.; [hon.] Before I got my G.E.D. I got an award for the most improved student in my class, and I also got and award for winning second place on my track team; [pers.] I mostly like to write poems about love, but I haven't finished one yet. I also get my inspiration from my mother. She tells me if I want something then go for it.; [a.] St. Bernard, LA

HERNANDEZ, LUIS J.
[Pen.] Luis; [b.] February 11, 1962, Cuba; [p.] Nieves and Judy; [m.] Mary, 12/94; [ch.] Angelina Hernandez; [ed.] G.E.D.; [occ.] Self Employed Ice Cream Vendor; [oth. writ.] Drugs, Symptoms and Clues (Guide to help parents spot children, teenagers or any of their love ones on drugs.); [pers.] I love to write. I also do it in Hispanish. I believe life offers plenty of things to talk about it, so writing is the perfect way to show how I feel.; [a.] Miami, FL

HERNANDEZ, PATRICIA
[b.] November 13, 1967; [p.] Andres and Felipa Hernandez; [m.] Single; [ed.] Ysleta High, El Paso Community College; University of Texas at El Paso; [occ.] Director of Admissions for Western Pacific Tech. Institute in El Paso; [hon.] Dean's List, Outstanding College Students of America, Honor's Pro-

gram Nominee; [pers.] Out of the greatest tragedies of our lives come our greatest inspirations. I have only praise for Edgar Allen Poe.; [a.] El Paso, TX

HERNANDEZ-AMAYA, GRACIELA
[b.] November 13, 1936, Antioquia, Colombia, South America; [p.] Luis Maria Hernandez-Garcia and Ana Felisa Amaya-Ospina; [ed.] Business graduate from Colegio de la Presentacion, Titiribi, Antioquia, Colombia. Subsequently, major studies in Linguistics and Criminal Justice at various universities in the United States, including New York University, New York and College of Du Page, Glen Ellyn, Illinois. Also Theology and Fine Arts.; [occ.] Since 1985 to present (full time) Court Interpreter for the U.S. Department of Justice, Executive Office for Immigration Review, Chicago, IL; Previously seventeen years in Merchant Marine Operations in the states of New York, Texas and Florida. I directed operations of hundreds of ships sailing to and from ports in all five continents of the world; [memb.] Member of "St. Mary's Choir" of West Chicago, IL and "Elmhurst Artists' Guild", Elmhurst, IL. Accomplished oil painting artists; [hon.] Founder of Grace Arts, Inc; [oth. writ.] Arthur of novel "Berenice"; and have written several poems and various pieces of creative; [pers.] I see beauty everywhere. I take pride and strive for perfection in everything I do, all for the glory of God.; [a.] West Chicago, IL

HESHELMAN, NANNATTE
[b.] April 14, 1980, Rochelle; [p.] Lawrence W. and Sherry L. Heshdman; [ed.] 8th grade, enter H.S. in Fall 1994; [occ.] Student; [hon.] Honor Roll Student; [oth. writ.] Various poems for school, church and other occasions.; [pers.] As a fan of Star Trek my philosophy is to boldly go where no one has gone before in life and in my writing while letting others enjoy my trek.; [a.] Colton, CA

GILMAN, MARY
[b.] June 10, 1956, Soule, Korea; [p.] John C. and Trudie Ribbens; [m.] Bradley R. Gilman, February 27, 1976; [ch.] Nichole Renae and Stephanie Ann Gilman; [ed.] Valley Christian High and American Institute of Banking; [occ.] Banking Assistant; [pers.] Through my writings I hope to help people understand the complexities of human nature and the boundries that it revolves in so we can gain insight into our fellow man and some day achieve complete harmony.; [a.] Boise, ID

HESSER, MARIE
[b.] May 15, 1976, St. Paul, MN; [p.] Teresa Hesser and Leon Yarbrough; [ch.] Leon Anthony Thompson; [ed.] St. Paul Area Learning Center; [occ.] Student; [pers.] All my poems are from the heart.; [a.] St. Paul, MN

HETZEL, JOYCE VIRGINIA
[b.] May 4, 1945, Erie, PA; [p.] Edward and Dorothy Laase; [m.] Ronald Matthew Hetzel, February 23, 1963; [ch.] Ronald Matthew, Kristina Leigh, Janice Renee, Brian Andrew; [ed.] St. Benedict Academy, Erie, PA; [occ.] Housewife; [memb.] The Humane Society of The U.S., Society for the Right to Die; [hon.] none; [oth. writ.] Several poems written in "In The Desert Sun;" Our Worlds Favorite Poem (Who's Who In Poetry); [pers.] I strive to reflect the depth of emotions, particularly, but not exclusive to my own.; [a.] Liberty, NC

HEY, BRANDY BRAN
[b.] February 19, 1979, Mobile, AL; [p.] Steve and Wanda Brantley; [ed.] Currently 9th grade; [occ.] Student; [memb.] Greenwood Lakes MIddle School Band, Alto Sax; [hon.] Writer of the Month, Greenwood Lakes Middle School; [oth. writ.] "Demon in the Mirror," "Viper," "Dark People" Novel, currently writing; [pers.] Favorite quote: The prince of darkness is a gentleman. Shakespeare, King Lear; [a.] Longwood, FL

HEYDEN, LYNN THERESE
[p.] Tina and Red; [ed.] Currently a student at Montclair University Majoring in Psychology and English; [oth. writ.] A compilation of Poetry entitled "The Gallery;" [pers.] I hope to be successful in my writing, to bring enjoyment to others as well as an important message about life.; [a.] Nutley, NJ

HEYL, IRENE E.
[b.] June 6, 1956, Chicago, IL; [p.] Eugene and Victoria Nowak; [m.] Michael Frank Heyl, August 29, 1987; [ed.] Carl Schurz High Wilbur Wright College; [occ.] Telemarketing professional; [hon.] First prize winner, writing contest summer, 1991; [oth. writ.] Several poems published for Sabre publications. Also articles for, The Roebuch Reader, Sears Newspaper; [pers.] Joy comes when you allow yourself to be happy among adversity; [a.] Cary, IL

HICKEY, WANDA
[Pen.] Maree De Rouen; [b.] March 24, 1962, Sylacauga, AL; [p.] Luther Hickey, Ruth Murray; [ch.] Gregory Eugene, Charlton Andre, Christopher arden, Priscilla Jean; [ed.] Reagan Sr. High, Epperson Clinic; [occ.] M/A and Office Manager; [memb.] National Assoc. of Office Managers. Office Manager's Executive, Committee-Bellaire Hospital; [hon.] While in school won first place state and city for poem titled "Freedom My Birthright."; [oth. writ.] I have written many poems, but this is the first that I have sent in and the first to be published.; [pers.] I feel peotry is very personal and reflects a lot about the author. I enjoy many different types of poetry. Writers I enjoy include Edgar Allen Poe and Emily Dickinson; [a.] Houston, TX

HICKS, JOANNA MARIE
[b.] August 30, 1976, Houston, TX; [p.] Jo Virgil Christmas; George Hicks; [ed.] Graduated in 1994 from Scarborough High School; [memb.] Ecology Club (high school); [hon.] Graduated in top 6% with advanced honors; 2 years in Who's Who Among American High School Students; National Honor Society; President's Award; "Outstanding Achievement" awards in several subjects.; [pers.] I have always been able to calm my emotions, both positive and negative, with mesmerizing powers of my poetry, and I hope they will mesmerize you, as well.; [a.] Houston, TX

HICKS, LEONARD
[b.] May 1, 1933, Huntington, NY; [p.] May 28, 1958, deceased; [ch.] Lee Ann, Chris, Carl, Tracey, Danita, LaToya; [ed.] High School; [occ.] Community Affairs South Bronx Beckman House; [pers.] To live as long as possible, and help as many people along the way.; [a.] Bronx, NY

HIGNOJOZ, NICOLE
[b.] April 21, 1980, Santa Monica, CA; [p.] Carolyn and Lloyd Hignojoz; [ed.] Grade school and Jr. High, first year High School; [occ.] Student; [hon.] Jr. High school Class Pres., Senior Achievement Award, Grade School Student of the Year (6th grade); [pers.] My sister's love of dancing was the only thing that influenced my poem. When my sister dances its like she can feel the music.; [a.] Los Angeles, CA

HILDEBRANDT JR., EDWARD J.
[b.] June 7, 1940, Jersey City, NJ; [p.] Edward Sr. and Bernice Hildebrandt; [m.] Rosemarie Hildebrandt, September 1, 1962; [ch.] Joseph, theresa, Edward III, John, Jennifer, Christa, David, Michael, Mary; [ed.] Teanely High School, Bergen Community College; [occ.] Disabled Federal Employee. Roman Catholic Deacon; [memb.] Knights of Columbus, Marriage Encounter, St. Josephs, R.C. Parish; [hon.] Outstanding Oral English 1956, Ordination R.C. Deacon 1978; [oth. writ.] Poems and writings on humor, life, death. To the point, simple yet philosophical.; [pers.] In my poems and writings I linger just long enough to touch or enkindle that spark that ignites the deep love we all have for each other.; [a.] Carlstadt, NJ

HILDRETH, NORMA LYNN DUNCAN
[b.] October 17, 1975, Anderson, SC; [p.] Kerry and Oneida Duncan; [m.] Jason Duane Hildreth, June 6, 1992; [ch.] Jake Montana Hildreth; [ed.] Graduated from Westside High School 1993.; [occ.] Nursing Assistant (Certified); [pers.] Life has many roads just take them one at a time.; [a.] Anderson, SC

HILL, JEAN GERSTBAUER
[Pen.] Jeannie; [b.] February 18, 1979, Mishawaka, IN; [p.] Lou Ann Gerstbauer-Hill and David Hill; [ed.] St. Bavo Grade School, Mishawaka, Inc., Marian High School, Mishawaka, IN, hopefully will graduate from the University of Notre Dame; [occ.] Archives Clerk for St. Joseph County Government.; [hon.] Women's Fest, Inc. 1993, Literature Scholarship, Honor Roll, Distinguished Student, Athletic Awards, and 1994 Medal of Excellence in Mathematics from Marian High School; [a.] Mishawaka, IN

HILL, MARGERY
[Pen.] Margery; [b.] September 12, 1973, Portland, ME; [p.] Betty and Paul Silver Sr.; [ed.] High School Diploma, 2 years of Vocational School, 2 years college in Child Day Care; [occ.] Babysitter; [oth. writ.] I am now writing a book about my family and I wrote children books recently.; [pers.] I would like to say thanks to my parents for everything they have done for me.; [a.] Portland, ME

HILL, ROY G.
[b.] February 6, 1941, Rochester, NY; [p.] Harrison and Bertha Hill; [m.] Helen C., September 1, 1962; [ch.] Wayne, Mark and Kristen; [ed.] Byron-Bergen High Shool, Roberts Wesleyan College; [occ.] General Manager, Village of Spencerport; [memb.] First Presbyterian Church, Municipal Electric Utilities Assoc.; [hon.] D.B.H. Dalrymple Community Service Award; [oth. writ.] Several published in church newsletter and "News N' Views;" Winter's Ire, Coming of Dawn.

HINTZ, BRANDIE
[b.] April 25, 1979, Toledo, OH; [p.] David and Weslie Hintz; [ed.] Fort Miami Elementary, Gateway

Middle School, currently sophomore at Maumee High School; [occ.] Student; [memb.] Southside Baptist church, Maumee High School Marching Pride, Maumee Indoor Marching Percussion Ensemble; [hon.] Student Honor roll, numerous dance competition awards, superior rated state band competitions, ranked 3rd in world at Winter Guard Internationals for percussion; [oth. writ.] Many others have yet to be published.; [pers.] In writing poetry my only influence has been myself. I like to express my emotions through writing, instead of violence or hatred. Writing is how I let people know what I feel inside.; [a.] Maumee, OH

HITT, DEBORAH
[b.] January 23, 1953, Abilene, TX; [p.] Lt. Col. Frank and Betty Guilfoyle; [m.] Single; [ed.] Ray High, Vocational Computer Training; [occ.] Diagnosed with disabling illness in 1988 no longer able to work. Prior to 1988 Banking Operations and 11 years with a Private School in Oklahoma. Numerous volunteer agencies.; [memb.] Catholic Church; [hon.] Honor Society; [oth. writ.] Local Newspaper; [pers.] Persons who are disabled should never abandon their dreams even if they can only be realities on paper. Life and health should never be taken for granted.; [a.] San Antonio, TX

HITZEMAN, DENNIS L.
[b.] August 9, 1973, Bluffton, IN; [p.] Thomas and Eileen Hitzeman; [ed.] Fairborn High School, Fairborn, OH; Wright State University, Dayton, OH; [occ.] Radio Technician in the Ohio, Air National Guard Student; [oth. writ.] Up until now I have written only for enjoyment. This is my first attempt at publication.; [pers.] I try to be honest in my writing to put my world into words as I see it. I hope that my writings can help others to see their world more clearly.; [a.] Fairborn, OH

HOAG, RICHARD L.
[Pen.] R. Lee Hoag; [b.] February 8, 1938, Levenworth, KS; [p.] Roy M. and Alice D. Hoag; [m.] Shirley A. Hoag, July 31, 1970; [ch.] Kenneth, Keven, Karl, Kreg and Paulette; [ed.] Glynn Academy, Brunswick Georgia; [occ.] Distribution Center Associate; [memb.] East Side Baptist Church, Lake City FL, C. B 46th Ill. Vol. Inf., Co. A 26th GAj Vol. Inf.; [hon.] Worked as reinactor on movie "Glory"; [oth. writ.] Book of poems "Bachelors Philosophy" West Point, NY edition, many poems printed in Newburgh, NY News 1965 to 1968.; [pers.] To the future hope of the past, but regret.; [a.] Lake City, FL

HOBBIE, LINDA W.
[b.] August 23, 1942, Williamsport, PA; [p.] C. Edgar Waltz and G. Elizabeth Waltz; [m.] Peter R. Hobbie, Jr., February 14, 1981; [ch.] Tanya Marie, Kimberly Ann; [ed.] Bayside High School, Drake Business School, Art and Watercolor Classes; [occ.] Infant Care Specialist; [hon.] Several Honorable Mentions for Watercolors and Poster Contest; [pers.] Like most poems, mine reflect my inner most feelings. My style is influenced soly by my mood and changes from poem to poem.; [a.] Ocala, fL

HOBBS, IDA LILLIAN
[Pen.] Ida Lou; [b.] December 20, 1917, Owosso, MI; [p.] Etta and Elmer Johnson; [m.] Walter E. Hobbs (Dec.), April 17, 1942; [ed.] Lansing Eastern High school, B.A. Eastern Mich. Univ., Grad. Stud-

ies Mich. State Univ., Univ. of Denver; Colorado State Univ., Univ. of Maryland; [occ.] Retired (3rd grade Elem. School Teacher; [memb.] Alpha Delta Kappa, Nat. Assn. Civilian Conservation Corps Alumni, AARP, Amer. Lung Assn.; [hon.] Vice Pres. and Pres. Theta Chapter of Alpha Delta Kappa (VP, 1962-63; Pres. 1964-65), Delegate to ADK Internat, Conv. Pittsburg, Penn. 1964, Alpha Delta Kappa International Honorary Sorority for Teachers; [oth. writ.] Poems for senior citizen's bldg. newsletters, sen. cit. Bldg., Owner's Newsletters.; [pers.] I trust in the Lord, believing that things happen for a reason. I strive to think positive, don't ever give up. You won't know if you can do something unless you try.; [a.] Holt, MI

HOEY, WILLIAM A.
[b.] June 21, 1966, Conneticut; [p.] Mary Hoey; [m.] David Lee McCartney (lifetime companion); [ed.] Stepinal High School, United States Marine Corps.; [occ.] Loan Processor, Topa Savings Bank; [memb.] Los Angeles Shanti; [oth. writ.] Trying to write a book (Who isn't)?; [a.] South Pasadena, CA

HOFFMAN, CHARLOTTE J.
[b.] April 21, 1936, Balt. MD; [p.] Mr. and Mrs. John Hoffman; [m.] Single; [ed.] 9th grade; [occ.] Not working, as I am on disability due to a terrible car accident; [oth. writ.] As far as being published. The only poem's I have had published were poem's for different Church Bulletins or Booklets.; [pers.] All my life I have written poem's of various topics. Subject's etc., I originally wrote this specific poem for music as I play the piano, but when I read you ad. I thought I would give it a try to see how it would go over.; [a.] Baltimore, MD

HOFFMAN, GILLIAN
[b.] April 27, 1977, Stamford, CT; [p.] Jo-Anna and Richard Fleming; [ed.] St. Lukes School, Wilton High School; [occ.] Student; [hon.] Honor Roll, Journalism, Sports and Drama; [oth. writ.] Different poems that relate to how I feel, short stories, and stories; plus articles in school paper, newspaper and yearbook.; [pers.] If it wasn't for certain people and certain feelings I would never be able to write. I mainly focus my ideas for my poems on what is going on in the world around me. My writings also have to do with me, my friends, my parents and everyone else.; [a.] Wilton, CT

HOFFMAN, MARIKO
[b.] June 2, 1971, Yokohana, Japan; [p.] Charles E. Hoffman Jr. and Michiko Hoffman; [ed.] Raritan High, St. John's University; [occ.] Paralegal; [memb.] Golden Key National Honor Society; [hon.] Dean's List; [pers.] Kindness is the essence of humanity. Embrace it with your soul.; [a.] Bayonne, NJ

HOLLENBACK CTR., PAULA G.
[b.] March 31, 1944, Columbus, OH; [p.] Paul and N. Catherine Gregory; [m.] William J. Hollenback, Sr., March 24, 1963; [ch.] William J., II, Paul D., Catherine P., Nannie E.; [ed.] Ashville High school, Ashville, OH, Columbus Business Univ. Col. OH; Edison Community College, Ft. Myers, FL, National Cancer Registrars Certification, Institute of Children's Literature; [occ.] Cancer Registrar, Cncer Data Center, Lee Memorial Hospital, Ft. Myers, FL; [memb.] St. Vincent de Paul Cath. Church, National Cancer Registrar Assoc., Florida Tumor Registrars Assoc.,

Society of Clinical Reserch Assoc., Lee County Nature Center; [hon.] Four wonderful children, 4 wonderful children-in-law, 8 fantastic grandchildren; [oth. writ.] Poems and short stories; [pers.] My inspiration and restoration comes from my God, my family, nature, wildlife and wild flowers.; [a.] Ft. Myers Shores, FL

HOLLENBACK, LANA FAYE
[b.] July 1, 1945, Columbus, Ohio; [p.] Paul and N. Catherine Gregory; [m.] Gail and (Dick) R. Hollenback, Sr., December 2, 1962; [ch.] Gregory, Gail II, Robert and Drew; [ed.] Fort Myer High, Lee College, Royal Palm Counseling; [occ.] Minister & President of Calvary Int'l Ministries, Inc.; [memb.] National Notary Assoc., Int'l Society of Poets, Coalition of Prison Evangelists, Covenant Community Mistries, Gospel Revelations; [hon.] Citizen Volunteer at Avon Park and Hendry Correctional Institutions, Overcome Leader and Teacher, Prison Fellowship Angel Tree Coordinator for Lee Co. FL.; [oth. writ.] I want, because of his own son, Him, God's not Looking for Whimps and more.; [pers.] Where is the Church was written and dedicated to all the Christians who have been wounded and felt alone.; [a.] Fort Myers, FL

HOLLENBECK, SUSAN M.
[b.] April 15, 1964, Whittier, CA; [p.] Donald & Connie Hollenbeck; [ed.] Continuing education at the Univ. of Hard Knox.; [occ.] Sales Mgr. for soil treatment facility; [hon.] Editor's Choice for poems; [oth. writ.] "Images of you," "Gentle Rain," "Gathering Nuts"; [pers.] The poem published in this book "The Haunting" is dedicated to a very special man "Bruce Whittaker of Australia. He will always hold a very special place in my heart and soul. Peace.; [a.] Huntington Beach, LA

HOLLOWAY, TIMOTHY
[b.] January 13, 1964; [p.] Johnson and Minnie Holloway; [ed.] El Cerrito High, Contra Costa College, Dickerson-Warren Business College; [occ.] Sales Clerk; [memb.] Association for the Study of Classical African Civilizations; [pers.] The best of my writings speak from a profound appreciation of the world historical significance of being an American of African Descent.; [a.] Richmond, CA

HOLMACK, LARRY
[b.] August 10, 1957, ElPaso, TX; [p.] George A. and Reda Holmack Jr.; [ed.] Irvin High School, University of Texas at El Paso; [occ.] Free Lance Writer/ Graphic Artist/Photographer; [memb.] First Baptist Church Singles Council; [hon.] Dean's List, Mortar Board; [oth. writ.] Several other poems published in local singles newsletter. Also have written for El Paso Macintosh Users Group and have had articles published on Golf by Local Golf Magazine.; [pers.] I try to capture the emotions I feel so that others can relieve them in my poems. So most of my work is highly emotional and personal.; [a.] ElPaso, TX

HOMER, DIANE ELIZABETH
[Pen.] Diane Elizabeth Hamilton; [b.] December 18, 1952, Crystal River, FL; [p.] Charlie and Sara Hamilton; [m.] Herbert M. Homer, August 31, 1990; [ch.] Shawna Diane, Sara Ann, Michael Paul, Darla Lynn, Jared hamilton; [ed.] Crystal River High, Lane Community College, Santa Fe Community College; [occ.] Housewife, mother.; [pers.] I write of life as I

see it.; [a.] Crystal River, FL

HOOKS SR., JAMES B.
[b.] March 9, 1905, Leslie, GA; [p.] Joshua H. Hooks; [m.] Hanna Swann Hooles; [m.] Don't Know; [ch.] Seven; [ed.] College, Ect, Trades, currently and painting, ect.; [occ.] Writing, retired nursing assistant, VA poet; [memb.] New Corinth Bpst. Church; [hon.] Several; [oth. writ.] Stories, poems, plays, songs, music publ. Co. BMI Headquarters, NYC, NY, own record label, affiliated American Federation of Musicians, NYC; [pers.] Good health, no habits, no medicine, no smoking, no drinking, only half-half milk, plenty water from faucet, no ice cold, three light meals daily, vegetables, little starch, little meat, mostly chicken; [a.] Leslie, GA

HOPKINS, JOSEPH T.
[b.] October 5, 1916, Utica, NY; [p.] Joseph M. and Elizabeth M. Hopkins; [m.] Mary M. Hopkins (Teacher), April 30, 1983; [ch.] Joseph (Atty.); William (C.P.A.); James (Atty.); and Sheila (Atty.).; [ed.] Hamilton College, B.S. 37'; Albany Law School, J.D. 48; [occ.] Retired Attorney; [memb.] American Bar Assoc.; [oth. writ.] Rec'd World of Poetry Golden Poet Award in 1989 for "Five, Nine and Seven" 1993 NLP, Whispers In The Wind "The Spirit of 92;" [pers.] First Wife, Eleanor Lennon Hopkins, deceased 82' is subject of this poem, teacher and student; [a.] Port Orange, FL

HOPPER, MARGARET ALLISON
[b.] December 15, 1945, Knoxville, TN; [p.] Leroy and Pearl Gallaher Allison; [m.] Edward PHillip Hopper, November 26, 1963; [ed.] Farragut High, Bearden High; [occ.] Owner, Keeper Kards and Krafts, Creator of "Wonderland Memories"; [memb.] Order of the Eastern Star, Member of Gallaher Memorial Baptist Church Choir; [hon.] Many 1st place ribbons in painting.; [pers.] I give God all the glory for my poetry for without him there would be no peotry any talent, I have is from God any poem I write is for God.; [a.] Knoxville, TN

HORIYE, NANCY S.
[b.] October 29, 1971, LaMesa, CA; [p.] Charlie M. and Kiyoko Horlye; [ed.] James Madison High, The Pennsylvania State University, BA in Economics, MInors: Japanese, Speech Communication; [memb.] Alpha Gamma Delta Fraternity, Japanese American Citizens League, American Marketing Association; Association of Collegiate Entrepreneurs; [oth. writ.] Several articles published in the Entrepreneur, The Undergraduate Newsletter for the Smeal College of Business Administration, (PSU), Poem published in San Diego JACL Borderline; [pers.] Never stop believing in dreams and strive to be the best you can be. I have been greatly influenced by my brother. I am a forth generation Japanese-American.; [a.] San Diego, CA

HOULE, TRACY LIN
[b.] October 21, 1972, Burlington, VT; [p.] Gary & Linda Houle; [m.] Long Term Boyfriend, Bryan H. Spence; [ed.] Essex Jet High School; [occ.] Independently contracted.; [pers.] Bryan "When mountains crumble to the sea there will still be you and me." Led Zep. I love you Mom, Dad, Tam and Fam. Hugs & kisses for Dan, Jenny, Adam and Tommy.

HOUSE, MELISSA M.
[Pen.] Lissa House; [b.] November 2, 1976, Minneapolis, MN; [p.] Larry and Cheryl House; [ed.] Roseville Area High School; [occ.] Cashier at Rainbow Foods; [hon.] Excellent Poetry in 11th grade Literature and Communications Class; [oth. writ.] Death of Abortion published in Roseville High school, newspaper (poem); [pers.] Love costs love, trust costs trust and taking a risk can go all the way but one of the most important care for the youth giving what you can, but not judging those who have less to give.; [a.] Shorview, MN

HOUSER, NATASHA R. BRAGG
[b.] April 23, 1977, San Bernardino, CA; [p.] Treva R. Bragg-Ragland; [ed.] A senior in high school. Also taking some college classes at Community College; [occ.] Student also a volunteer at San Bernardino Community Hospital; [hon.] Presidential Academic Fitness Award. I was invited to attend the National Youth Leadership Council, Honor Roll, track; [oth. writ.] Daddy, Leaving, Crying in the Streets, and Gone. None of these poems have been published.; [a.] Rialto, CA

HOUSTON, LAURA J.
[b.] December 16, 1947, Kermit, TX; [p.] Clarence Scott and the late Hope Scott; [ch.] Roger Scott Snyder and Randall Stephen Houston; My Brothers: Dan & Dave Scott of Phx., AR; [ed.] Ponaganset High (

HOUSTON, LAURA J.
[b.] December 16, 1947, Kermit, TX; [p.] Clarence Scott and the late Hope Scott; [ch.] Roger Scott Snyder and Randall Stephen Houston; My Brothers: Dan & Dave Scott of Phx., AR; [ed.] Ponaganset High (Honors) Lamson Business College (Dean's List) and Eastern College of Health Vocations (4.0); [occ.] Office Asst. III, City of N. Little Rock Electric, Dept. N. Little Rock, AR; [memb.] Presiential Task Force, Smithsonian Institute, National Purchasing Institute; [hon.] High School Honor Roll; Dean's List at Lamson Business College; [oth. writ.] Various items published in local newspapers; $10.00 winner for published "Happy Thought" in Nat'l Enquirer; Poetry winner for special people, including President Bill Clinton and Family; [pers.] Writing, especially my poetry, symbolizes in-depth perceptions rarely expressed in prose or other personal narratives. Writing is an extension of my innermost essence. I hope to write my autobiography one day.; [a.] North Little Rock, AR

HOWARD, BARBARA L.
[b.] October 22, 1951, Charlorix, Mich.; [p.] Marion Mayers, Vera Mae Wabaganese; [m.] Alvin M. Howard, April 15, 1979; [ch.] Michelle M. Wells, Robert B. Wells, Ferri L. Wells, Alvin M. Howard Jr., Mercedes, M. Howard; [ed.] Ypsilanti High 1970, Adult School for Nurse Aide, Bryman for Medical Assistant; [occ.] M.A. & N.A.; [hon.] Nurse of the Month and Nurse of the Year at Queens of the Valley Hospital of West covina, CA; [pers.] Not the poem itself but to write a poem was a incentive for my children to show them anything is possible if you just try.; [a.] Walnut, CA

HOWELL, LINDA SISLER
[Pen.] Lyn Howell; [b.] August 12, 1948, Washing-

ton, D.C.; [p.] William and June Howell; [m.] Divorced; [ch.] David, Shane, Ben; [ed.] Herndon High School, several psychology courses, The Dance Playhouse of Washington, D.c. via scholarship; [occ.] Free Lance Artist; [memb.] American Heart Association, Drakesville Methodist Church, Mended Hearts Assoc., 100 lb Weight Watcher's Club, Deborah, BSA Committee; [hon.] Dance scholarship, dance and art awards, 1st runner up Miss High School of Virginia, published poetry in "Tears of Fire" (Editor's Choice Award); [oth. writ.] Short stories, poetry, newspaper articles.; [pers.] Rediscovering the real you from the unique gift of a best friend encompassing art & philosophy; [a.] Englewood, FL

HUANG, KEN-KIM
[Pen.] Ken Huang; [b.] May 7, 1952, Hsinchu, Taiwan, ROC; [p.] Ta-Chun Huang, Chu Huang Liu; [ed.] Hsinchu High School, National Cheng Kung Univ., Taiwan State Univ. of New York at Buffalo; [occ.] Oil Field Petroleum Engineer; [pers.] Life is a journey to this world. With faith and my mother's endless love, I was able to sail thru the trouble sea. I let my tears drop when I was hurt inside. To write and to cry, both are gifts created from my soul.; [a.] Houston, TX

HUFFMAN, DAN O.
[b.] September 25, 1960, ElPaso, TX; [p.] Calvin and Rudy F. Huffman; [m.] Widower (Bethy); [ch.] Christopher D. Huffman and Ezekiel J. Huffman; [ed.] M.A. U. of Houston, B.A. (Sociology), Sam Houston State U.; [occ.] V.P. - J.D.H. Software; studying for Ph.D. in Sociology; [hon.] Nationally recognized for scholastic excellence--S.H.S.U.; Distinguished Student--S.H.S.N.; [oth. writ.] Currently completing two novels and one poetic collection-- none published.; [pers.] Compassion, whispers from a butterfly, elusive gifts we emplore…to feel is to be. Bethy, you guide me.; [a.] Canutillo, TX

HUFFMAN, JOHNNIE
[b.] December 23, 1994, Cleveland, OH; [p.] Nishman and Edith Stuffman; [ed.] Graduate, John F. Kennedy High, Cleveland, OH. Attended Cleveland State University (degree incomplete).; [occ.] Training Assistant; [hon.] Rec'd several cash bonuses and certificates for being an outstanding employee, and was chosen as employee of month 3 times.; [oth. writ.] A new day (see a Far Off Place). In addition I have written 100 poems, 20 songs and am the sole artist of approximately 4,000 works of art (all mediums).; [pers.] My goal is to inspire, uplift and encourage others with the talent God has given me. I'm hoping that these works of poetry will be a blessing to many.; [a.] Landover Hills, MD

HUGHES, DEBORAH B.
[b.] June 5, 1952, Boston, Mass.; [p.] Charles A.P. and Wilhelmina Hughes; [ch.] Daniel, Benjamin and Nathan; [ed.] Degree in Nursing, Philosophy and Psychology. University Mass./Boston, Mass.; [occ.] Single mom to my 3 sons, L.P.N.; [memb.] Immanuel Lutheran Church, World Vision, St. Judes, HSUS, Simone Weil Society; [oth. writ.] Only letters published in local town newspapers and college papers.; [pers.] Live and let live, learning and loving along the way. Believe in your own creativity. Believe in goodness over evil. Give all people and situations a chance. Love works best!; [a.] Mansfield, MA

HULIN, YVONNE ALICE
[b.] January 18, 1961, W. Concord, MA; [p.] Ulrich and Charlotte Krajenbrink; [m.] Brinkley Hulin, April 25, 1987; [ch.] Chandler Brinkley; [ed.] Magnolia High, California State Fullerton, Fullerton College; [occ.] Freelance Artist; [oth. writ.] Several poems, a few published in school publications, one children's story entitled, "Vincent's Winter House."; [pers.] I write about important events and people in my life. Sometimes my writing reflects the innocence of childhood. I have also given recognition to world peace and social injustices in my poem.; [a.] Anaheim, CA

HULS, YVONNE T.
[Pen.] Nancy Hughes; [b.] March 12, 1936, TN; [p.] Duke and Nancy Todd; [m.] James E. Huls, June 17, 1960; [ch.] Marylin, Vickie, Mickey, Duane, Jimmy; [ed.] Central High School, Savannah, TN, Walker Elementary; [occ.] Secretary State Farm Ins. Agent; [memb.] Owyhee Missionary Baptist Church, National Arbor Foundation, National Rifle Assn.; [hon.] Craftwork for Governor of Idaho; [oth. writ.] Stories and poems for friends and relatives, wrote articles for Baptist paper.; [pers.] I love poetry, my high school home room teacher, Mrs. J. Fort Fowler was a great inspiration to me.; [a.] Homedale, ID

HUNTER, ISABELLE
[Pen.] Isabelle; [b.] February 16, 1927, Franklin County, PA; [p.] Alex and Lucy Jackson; [ed.] High School, Boston State College, Boston Center for Adult Education; [occ.] Retired; [memb.] Museum of Science, Boston Public Library, Mystic Valley Railroad; [pers.] I love Daily Living.

HURLEY, GARY E.M.
[b.] April 19, 1952, San Francisco; [p.] Richard B. Hurley and Lorraine J. Hurley; [m.] February 14, 1983; [ch.] Christina V. M. Hurley and Angelica E.R. Hurley; [ed.] Culver Sity High, Los Angeles Trade Tech., Santa Monica City, Portland Community College; [occ.] Production Painter, Freightliner Trucks, Portland, OR; [oth. writ.] "The Big Game" a childrens story and "Holocaust" a parable.; [pers.] I enjoy creating and endeavor to open new dimensions of thought via the interplay of words and their multiple meanings.; [a.] Portland, OR

HURT, JOSHUA
[Pen.] Joshua McKagan; [b.] July 21, 1974, Tampa, FL; [p.] James Hunt, Constance Young; [ed.] John Jay High School, San Antonio, TX; [occ.] Carpenter, Memphis, TN; [hon.] John Joy High, Statesman Best New staff Writer 91.; [oth. writ.] Dozens of unpublished material awaiting to become a book, Love Craze, Her Pain, Eighty plus original poems.; [pers.] My work expresses feelings towards dark reality in todays world. "Insane times bring insane demands."; [a.] Pope, MS

HUSTED, FRANK L.
[Pen.] Summa Vie; [b.] May 16, 1922, PA; [p.] Clara Van Strander, Ralph Hustod; [m.] Elaine, June 3, 1972; [ch.] son, Frank II; [ed.] Grad. School, U. of Buffalo, Ed.D. Ph.D; [occ.] Psycho Therapist Semi-Retried; [memb.] Hersey Collectors of America, Phoenixville YMCA Heritage Club; International Academy of Behavior Medicine; [hon.] Diplomate Psycho Therapist; [oth. writ.] 50+ professional articles; unpublished novel; anthology of verse unpublished.; [pers.] I am a devotee of Kahlil Gibran and

Dr. Milton Erickson. Each has added to my philosophy; while the past is prologue to the future, the now is far more important then either of these.; [a.] Spring City, PA

HUYCK, DANIEL J.
[b.] November 13, 1974, Sault Stte, Marie, MI; [p.] bernie and Marion Huyck; [m.] Single; [ed.] Now attending Lake Superior State Univrsity; [occ.] Bartender; [a.] Sault Ste. Marie, MI

INGRAM, IRENE B.
[b.] September 28, 1964, Kearny, NJ; [p.] Richard H. and Irene A. Ingram; [ed.] North Arlington High School and Montclair State College; [memb.] International Society of Poets; [hon.] Editor's Choice Award for outstanding achievement in poetry. Presented by The National Library of Poetry "1993"; [oth. writ.] A poem published by the National Library of Poetry, Book Title: The Coming of Dawn; [pers.] In Memory of Richard H. Ingram Sr. 1931-1991. A lot of my poems come from true life experiences, that touch my inner most thoughts and emotions. I believe everything happens for a reason, not to be questioned, but to be used as a learning tool.; [a.] North Arlington, NJ

INYANG, LINDA D.
[b.] September 26, 1953, St. Petersburg; [p.] Lawrence and Eddie Lee Jenkins; [m.] Inyang D. Inyang, September 3, 1979; [ch.] Nsikak, Iboro, and Mfon Ingang; [ed.] Boca Ciega High (1971), U.S.F. (1978) B.A., U.S. Army Discharged Honorable 1981.; [occ.] Instructional Asst. Leon County School Board.; [a.] Tallahassee, FL

IVEY, HEATHER
[b.] February 17, 1978, Peoria, IL; [p.] Kathi and Lee Swindell; [ed.] Limestone Walters Elementry, Hewitt Trussville Jr. High, Oltewan High School and Germantown High School; [occ.] Student; [hon.] Presidential Academic Fitness Awards Program, National Jr. Honor Society, Germantown High school PTSA Faculty Choice Award; [pers.] I would like to thank my entire family for their encouragement and support. And a special thanks to Kara who got me started writing.; [a.] Memphis, TN

IVEY, SHELIA
[b.] November 1, 1958, Jackson, TN; [p.] Bobby and June Taylor; [m.] Roger Ivey, March 15, 1980; [ch.] Carrie Beth Ivey, my daughter, age nine; [ed.] South Side High School in Jackson, TN, Vo-Tech Business School; [occ.] Cook Wed. night supper for my church 85-100 people; [memb.] Liberty Grove Baptist church; [hon.] Who's Who in American High School students in 76, presented a plaque by my church for going on a 2 week mission trip to France.; [pers.] I'm just beginning to write, I'm fascinated by history people, their reactions and feelings. My hope is to share the love of the Lord Jesus in my writing.; [a.] Beech Bluff, TN

IWONA, NYZIO
[b.] May 14, 1974, Rzeszow, Poland; [p.] Maria, Stanislaw Nyzio; [ed.] High School (Poland) graduation with honors; [occ.] Queens College Student; [pers.] Not only is this my debut but also hope as for a very newcomer that there is a place for me to live. I believe that one day, I will win the struggle with the language. I'd like to dedicate it to my best friend who knows me better than I'll ever know myself. I hope

my courtship with literature will last forever.; [a.] Brooklyn, NY

JACKEY, DEBRA RAE
[Pen.] Junk Collector Queen; [b.] October 29th, Anderson; [p.] Barbara and Ray Jackey; [m.] Single; [ed.] 11th grade; [occ.] Disabled; [memb.] Hoffman Bottle Decanter's Club; Better Together Club; Pen Pals for Chronics Diseases; [hon.] Many awards in bowling and girlscouts; [oth. writ.] Songs and poems never published.; [pers.] Someday, I want to be a great poet, artist, singer, my dreams only.; [a.] Anderson, IN

JACKSON, AZALEE F.
[b.] Dcember 22, 1922, Needville; [p.] Bettie and Alex Foston; [m.] Taylor L. Jackson Sr., May 15, 1948; [ch.] Mable, Taylor Jr., Robert C., Evelyn, Nevelyn, Jeanetta; [ed.] MED, BS, Texas Southern Uni. High School Powel Point, Kendleton Texas, Elem. Sch. Needville, TX; [occ.] Retired from HISD (Teacher); [memb.] AARP (N.R.T.A), Sunnyside Civic Club, Mount of Salvation Missionary Baptist Church; [hon.] Certificate of recognition 1980, 20 yrs Service Award 1982, Outstanding Educational, Progress 1983, Certificate of Merit 1984; [oth. writ.] Several pieces of poetry (unpublish) "My confidence in God" copyright, "Spring" published "In Focus" Needville, TX; [pers.] I do it as a hobby as inspired by God. It is a gift.; [a.] Houston, TX

JACKSON, ELAINE MARIE HARPER
[Pen.] Emari, Elmahaja; [b.] May 27, 1954, Florence, Rankin County, MS; [m.] Mr. Cleveland Caleb Harper and Mrs. Rebecca McLin Harper; [ch.] Cleveland Darcel, Dennis Darrell, Jason Anton, and Nathan Antuan; [ed.] McLaurin High, Summer Hill High, Florence High, Jackson State University; [occ.] English teacher, Upward Bound Program, Jackson State U, Jackson, MS; [hon.] Poetry Reader for JSU, first Graduate Forum; [oth. writ.] "Mississippi Income" - A poem; Spring Hill Gemini - A Book of Poetry - Specialist Degree Project; [pers.] My writing reflects the community and the need for a return of community living to save our country; [a.] Florence, MS

JACKSON, JOSHUA M.
[Pen.] Scott Fenton, Jack Saul; [b.] September 3, 1978, Sacramento, CA; [p.] Donald Jackson, Maryanne Fallman; [ed.] Del Norte High, North Eugene High; [occ.] Student; [memb.] National Forensics League; [oth. writ.] Published poem in anthology, writing collection of poems with co-author Amy Bardwell; [pers.] "Death lies on a shelf by some books. The Books are burning."; [a.] Eugene, OR

JACKSON, KATHERINE
[b.] January 16, 1957, Bristol, VA; [p.] Walter O. and Bettye J. Cowan; [ch.] Kathleen Delores (Katie); [ed.] Thomas Jefferson High School; Virginia Union University; [occ.] Chargeback Clerk, Whitehall-Robins Company; Richmond, VA; [pers.] All honor and praise goes to God. Because without His presence, His love, His mercy and His grace, this poem would never have been composed. And I thank God for the early teachings and influecne of my parents.; [a.] Richmond, VA

JACKSON, KAY
[b.] December 2, 1975, Baker City, Oregon; [p.]

Terry and Evelyn Jackson; [ed.] Borah High school; [pers.] I tend to write about things that greatly affect me; mentally and physically.; [a.] Boise, ID

JACKSON, SUSIE
[b.] January 10, 1932, Montzeuma, GA; [p.] Oscar and Lois Harris; [m.] Foster Jackson, February 21, 1971; [ch.] Johnnie; [ed.] Lampson Richrdson High, Vocational Tech, Edison Community College; [occ.] Surgical, Technologist II Assitance, Coordinator of Opthomologist, Lee Memorial Hospital Fort Myers, FL; [hon.] Employee of the month and employee profile of week, 25 yrs. of service award in the Ft. Myers news press, Young again in Southwest Florida magazine; [oth. writ.] Several poems for special occasion articles for the Community Voice News.; [a.] Fort Myers, FL

JACOBSON, WILLIAM H.
[b.] May 1, 1935, Eau Claire, Wisconsin; [p.] Joseph and Julia Jacobson; [m.] Theresa Jacobson, January 23, 1976; [ch.] Cynthia, Mark, Nancy, Kimberly, Carla, Carl and Joy; [ed.] Port Huron High School, Baker College; [occ.] Papermaker, E.B. Eddy, Port Huron Paint; [oth. writ.] Several poems as personal gifts to family and friends.; [pers.] My favorite poems are; "If" By Rudyard Kipling and "Myself" by Edgar A. Guest; [a.] Port Huron, MI

JACQUES, RACHEL M.
[b.] October 28, 1983; [ed.] Sixth Grade, Washington Middle School, Calumet, Michigan; [pers.] Interest and hobbies are reading, writing drawing, swimming, riding bike, playing games, making braclets and Rachel likes school and loves animals, especially cats and her dog Daisy.

JANECEK, DAWN MARIE
[b.] April 3, 1979, Cedar Rapids, Iowa; [p.] Louis and Slly Janecek I; [ed.] I'm going to be in 9th grade this year at Jefferson High school in Cedar Rapids, IA; [occ.] Student; [hon.] Honor Roll, Outstanding Student Award; [oth. writ.] I like to write poems it is away for me to express my feelings. Sometimes the hurt and sometimes the happy times. I would like someday to write books for teens.; [a.] Cedar Rapids, IA

JARVIS, ROBERT W.
[b.] December 23, 1946, Barrett; [p.] Clayton and Marion Adams; [m.] Partricia, April 12, 1987; [occ.] Security Guard; [pers.] God Guides The Hand.

JEAN-PIERRE, PASCAL
[b.] August 5, 1966, Haiti; [p.] Emma Jean-Pierre & Charles Jean-Pierre; [m.] Edwine C. Jean-Pierre; [m.] July 7, 1992; [ch.] Shadae E. Jean-Pierre; [ed.] Ecole Sainte Trinite, Haiti, City College of New York, CUNY, John Jay College, NYC, NY CUNY; [occ.] Developmental Specialist, Emergency Medical Technician, Flutist/Musician; [memb.] Rosicrucian Order, AMORC, Traditional Martinist Order, Builders of the Adytum (BOTA), Enoch Grand Lodge, Free Masonry, American Heart Association, Holy Trinity Philarmonic Orchestra, Haiti; [hon.] 1991-Present, "Tres Sage Athersata" Capitre de rose & Croix, LeMont des Oliviers #1, 1993-1994 Excellence and Merit Award, Saint Jean de Jerusalem #6, Free Masonry Lodge, 1989-1990 President of "The Voice Club" City College of New york, CUNY; [oth. writ.] Articles about mysticism, metaphysic, meditation, for radio talk show, and symposiums, several

other poems, song/lyrics for musical group. Poems in "River of Dream," The National Library of Poetry. (Fall edition); [pers.] I hope to reflect peace, love and harmony through my poems, music and painting, and help bring people together as one loving, understandable soul. May the light of the cosmic guide our every step in this cycle of life.; [a.] Brooklyn, NY

JEE, ANDREA
[Pen.] A.J.; Asjee; [b.] July 1, 1967, San Francisco, CA; [p.] Stan and D. Gena Jee; [ed.] Lowell High School, San Francisco State University; [occ.] Graphic Designer; [oth. writ.] An anthology called Turbulence; [pers.] I've never considered myself a dept. my poetry is just an empathetic observation of the mass hysteria of life in current times. My friends have coerced me into sharing my neurosis with the world; [a.] San Francisco, CA

JESSUP, CAROL ANN
[b.] January 26, 1947, Pittsburgh, PA; [p.] Joseph and Mary Zecker; [memb.] Livonia Civic Chorus; [oth. writ.] Friends; Friendship is a Special Kind of Love, Vol. I and II Little Things.; [pers.] Twenty-three years ago as part of my therapy, a good friend encouraged me to write. I learned from Him what my writing accomplishes; it takes my mind off my pain temporarily; it allows me to express my feelings; and it teaches me to grow.; [a.] Livonia, MI

JEVONS, ERICA L.
[Pen.] Leigh Jevons; [b.] March 25, 1981, Bethlehem, PA; [p.] Norm and Lucy Jevons; [ed.] Junior High School Student; [occ.] Student and referee for soccer; [hon.] Member of the Junior National Society, Junior H.S. Honor Roll; [pers.] I believe writing can express to anyone your inner personality.; [a.] Harrisburg, PA

JEWETT, CYNTHIA S.
[Pen.] Cyndi; [b.] December 30, 1962, Clinton, IN; [p.] Marilyn D. Scott Hensley and James E. Blevins; [m.] To be Robert L. Mann; [ch.] Bradley D. Jewett Jr., age 14; Tara L. Jewett age 13; Christopher R. Jewett age 6; [ed.] Completed High School, some college; [occ.] Working in family owned and operated night club, Illusion, Terre Haute, IN; [hon.] Being published in the National Library of Poetry is my greatest honor; [oth. writ.] Several poems, songs, became interested in writing at the age of 11, after being encouraged by my 7th grade English Teacher.; [pers.] Let's stop and take a moment, to give the Lord our thanks, for every little blessing that always come sour way, at a time, when you most need one have faith and never fear, cause when you last expect one, your miracle will appear; [a.] Terre Haute, IN

JOHNSON, DELLI DIANA
[b.] June 15, 1979, Aurora, CO; [p.] Richard and Diana; [ed.] Eagle Valley High School (currently 10th grade); [occ.] Summer Daycare; [hon.] Honor roll, 4 yrs. English Award, Cheerleading Award, Top Scorer in National Writing Assessment; [pers.] I feel rewarded when readers can relate to my poems. It's a great gift when simple words can be put together to form such an emotional piece of literatur. My poems reflect my life.; [a.] Gypsum, CO

JOHNSON, ELLA
[Pen.] Dutchess; [b.] February 14, 1945, Mt. Union; [p.] Violet Horris; [ch.] Four; [occ.] Homemaker;

[pers.] I would like to thank Mr. John and my children for inspiring me to write and hold on to my dream.

JOHNSON, GLORIA T.
[b.] Wilkes Co., GA; [p.] A. Thomas and Kate B. Johnson; [m.] Tommy B. Johnson; [ch.] Lisa Johnson Talbet, Philip Anthony Johnson; [occ.] Store Manager, J. Richies Inc. (Retail Clothing); [memb.] Northside Baptist Church, Gideon's International Auxiliary Elbert County Country Club; [oth. writ.] Article in Standard, Nazarene Press, song poem published and recorded.; [pers.] Desired goal, "To Know Him, To Make Him Known;" [a.] Elberton, GA

JOHNSON, JANEY B.
[b.] November 12, 1942, Virginia; [p.] Boyce and Viola Franks; [m.] Wm. M. (Mick) Johnson, June 25, 1974; [ch.] Davette and Deveon; [ed.] Johnsville High School; [occ.] Housewife (Domestic Engineer); [hon.] Ribbons for Art (Oil and Acrylic Paintings); [oth. writ.] My Grandmother; Miss B; [pers.] My poetry and art are a part of me and both are drawn from a deep well of creative interest and wonderful memories.; [a.] Mt. Gilead, OH

JOHNSON, JERVISON J.
[memb.] Sire; [b.] October 26, 1974, ATL; [p.] Berneice and Melvin Johnson; [ed.] Redan High School, University of Alabama; [memb.] American Red Cross, Literary Magazine, Student for Black Culture.; [hon.] Basketball Hustle Award, Defensive Player, Savannah Holiday Tournament "All Tournament Award," Dekalb County Player of the Month. Positive behavior award AAA Award; [oth. writ.] Poems published in the literary magazines.; [pers.] I would like to give a special thanks to those who had a hand in modling my intellect character, and ability.; [a.] Decatur, GA

JOHNSON, MARGERY A.
[b.] Long Beach, CA; [p.] Allen and Mildred bishop; [m.] Kenneth E. Johnson, November 11, 1945; [ch.] Denise Salthouse; [ed.] College and Specialized Art School, Study of Classical Verse Forms; [occ.] Artist, Sculptor, Retired; [memb.] Community Service Clubs, Former Chapparal Poets of California; [hon.] Poetry Contest, Voices International, first (1968), various certificates of merit award from Pomona Valley Writers.; [oth. writ.] Author of poetry book "Sea Moods" 1994, now in print.; [pers.] It's no crime, to rhyme; [a.] Cambria, CA

JOHNSON, MONICA RACHELLE
[b.] May 28, 1968, Los Angeles, CA; [p.] Miriam and Alfred Thomas; [m.] Donald Lee Jones, March 23, 1944; [ch.] Misty LaShae, Michael Alexander, Matthew Alfred; [ed.] Morningside High, Park College School of Paralegal Studies; [occ.] Paralegal Student; [memb.] Second Mount Nebo Missionary Baptist Church; [hon.] none; [oth. writ.] Several poems, plays and short stories published in school and local newspapers.; [pers.] Put God first, live each day as though the Lord were coming for you that night, the way He came and took my mother home June 28, 1994. Mommy this is for you. I love you.; [a.] Indianapolis, IN

JOHNSON, MURIEL
[b.] August 4, 1924, New York City; [p.] Phyllis and

Ear Cobb; [m.] Nathaniel Herman Johnson; [ch.] Phyllis Betty, Lorraine Muriel, Barbara Elaine; [ed.] GED; [oth. writ.] "Moods Meditations and Attitudes" a manuscript of poetry (approximately 38 poems); [pers.] Deceased on June 13, 1986, manuscripts are in the possession of Muriel's daughter.; [a.] New York, NY

JOHNSON, NAFESSA
[b.] July 27, 1976, Philadelphia, PA; [p.] Sharon Johnson, Mack Truesdale; [ed.] Hillside High School; [occ.] Student; [pers.] I try to reflect my poems on everyday life. What I see and hear is what I base my writing on. I have been greatly influenced by the Famous African American Poet, Maya Angelou; [a.] Hillside, NJ

JOHNSON, SETH
[b.] September 3, 1985, St. Paul, MN; [p.] Craig and Jeanette Johnson; [ed.] Pre-school, kindergarten, grade 1 and 2.

JONES, DEBORAH J.
[Pen.] Debby Livingston-Jones; [b.] October 25, 1954, Weirton, WV; [p.] David and Carol J. Livingston; [ch.] Shelley, Jessica, Kelsey and Chip; [ed.] Weir High School, West Virginia Northern Community College; [occ.] Licensed Optician, Small Business Manager, Wal Mart Vision Center; [hon.] Recognized by the Governor and First Lady of W.VA, Gaston Caperton and Rachel Worby, as W.VA 1992 Rehabilitant of the Year for my efforts to overcome a handicap and become an outstanding citizen; [oth. writ.] Many poems, not yet published; [pers.] My writings are but an extension of myself, a way of exploring that part of myself that others are not intimately concerned with.; [a.] Middletown, PA

JONES, JOHNNY W.
[Pen.] J.W. Jones; [b.] September 30, 1949, Hominy Falls, WV; [m.] Mary Jones, October 8, 1968; [ch.] Brandon, Heather; [ed.] Richwood High School, Richwood, WV; Wayne Tecnical Institute, Goldsboro, NC; [occ.] Industrial Construction Electrician; [oth. writ.] Several unpublished poems.; [pers.] My poems are all written for my beautiful and loving wife Mary, My inspiration and love of my life. Romance should never be allowed to fade, it's brilliance should be renewed with the dawn of each and every day.; [a.] Brandon, FL

JONES, JR., NATHURLON
[b.] November 12, 1949, Rocky Mount, NC; [p.] Vera and Nathurlon Jones, Sr.; [m.] Vanessa Sylvana Toddman Jones, April 7, 1977; [ch.] Naturlon III and Kashif N. Jones; [ed.] Booker T. Washington, H.s. Diploma, United States Air Force Security Police Technical School graduate, some college credits, some street education; [occ.] Student, Businessman; [memb.] Vietnam Veterans of America, Spirts of Earth and Col, Inc., Nathurlon Jones, Jr. and Co., Inc., Th ISP, World Vision Sponsorship; [hon.] National Defense Service metal, Innocent Incarceration Award, Spiritual Blessings from God and by his will the Goddess of all the universe and it's dimensions; [oth. writ.] Poems destroyed by fury, unpublished poems to be published in the book The Space Between; [pers.] You must "Love Thy Self" in order to "Know Thy Self"!!! and believe it or not life goes on beyond flesh and blood bodies on into spiritual bodies of forever and eternity.; [a.] Attica, NY

JONES JR., NATHURLON
[b.] November 12, 1949, Rocky Mount, NC; [p.] Vera and Nathurlon Jones Sr.; [m.] Vanessa Sylvana Toddman Jones, April 4, 1977; [ch.] Nathurlon III and Kashif N. Jones; [ed.] Booker T. Washington H.S., Diploma, United States Air Force Security, Police Technical School Graduate, Some College Credits, Some Street Education; [occ.] Student, Businessman; [memb.] Vietnam Veterans of America, Spirits of Earth and co., Inc., Nathurlon Jones, Jr., and Co., Inc;/ The International Society of Poets, World Vision Sponsorship; [hon.] National Defense service Metal, Innocent Incarceration Award, Spiritual Blessings from God and by his will the Goddness of all the univers and its dimensions.; [oth. writ.] Poems destroyed by fury, unpublished poems, poems to be published in the book "The Space Between" published in "The Sound of Music" cassette tape, presently writing "Incarcerated Thoughts."; [pers.] You must "Love They Self in order to "Know Thy Self" and believe it or not life goes on beyond flesh and blood bodies on into spiritual bodies of forever and eternity.; [a.] Attica, NY

JONES, LAMBERT T.
[b.] January 15, 1926, Middlebourne, VA; [p.] Hildred Blanco and Mary E. Lambert Jones; [m.] Evelyn L. Wood Jones, April 3, 1947; [ch.] Lambert T. Jones II, Linda Louise Jones, Jenifer Elaine Jones Marshall; [ed.] G.E.D High School, Randolph Macon Academy, Elliots School of Business, Tri-State Drafting and Engineering School; [occ.] Retired, Automobile Dealer and Limousine Service Operator; [hon.] To serve my country in W.W.II, Korea and Vietnam Situations. To be the current head of this Jones Family Branch.; [oth. writ.] Various essays, many poems. Two additional verses to the peom Gunga Din by Rudyard Kipling.; [pers.] No job to big, no job to small for whole some poetry on the wall. Helps make bad, good just like it should. Soul food for one and all.; [a.] Wheeling, WVA

JONES, MARGARET
[b.] March 27, 1927, Marshall County, KY; [p.] Wallace and Dewey Chandler; [m.] Arlet E. Jones, September 15, 1951; [ch.] Kenneth and William; [ed.] Benton High School; [occ.] Housewife; [oth. writ.] Have written several poems; [pers.] I usually like to think about my writings for a while, then all of a sudden it comes together, and I write it all down into a poem.; [a.] Benton, KY

JONES, RENE LEANDER
[b.] February 14, 1956, Lakeland, FL; [p.] Dr. Johnny Lee Jones (deceased) and Velma W. Smith; [m.] not married; [ch.] none; [ed.] High School Educjation a few college hours (and) I cram the library (Public Library of Lakeland) as much as possible; [occ.] Currently not employed; [memb.] none; [hon.] None to this present day, except that it is an honor to be published in the book dark side of the moon.; [oth. writ.] Pro digital Clever Grey Fox, Darling Black Sister; [pers.] I create prose to explore my thoughts and to expand my horizons. Since my form is free-style it gives me the chance to be profound so that my reader can fathom what I am about.; [a.] Lakeland, FL

JONES, RUTH HOLLIMON
[Pen.] Ruthie; [p.] Ward and Hertha Hollimon; [m.] Edward Joseph Jones; [ch.] Linda Catherine Jones and Janet Ruth Jones Williams, grandson: Mark Williams Jr.,; Three Sisters: My twin, Ruby Bourgeois, Marie Short and Frances Harris; [ed.] High School, Mississippi Southern College, Hattiesburg, Mississippi; Spencer Business College, New Orleans, LA; [occ.] Employee of Metairie Health Care Center; [hon.] Graduated from high school with Honors; Certificate of Merit; State of Louisiana; Editor's Choice Award for poem; [oth. writ.] Book of poems, short stories, a book about the Civil War. My book is in the process of being published; [pers.] I have been influenced to write from the lives of my ancestors. Most of my poems are romantic and historical; A special thanks to my family and friends, and Vicki Hughes, Administrator of Metairie Health Care center who gave me incentive with my writing; [a.] Metairie, LA

JORDAN, JEANNE
[b.] August 20, 1953, Atlanta, GA; [p.] Mr. and Mrs. Clifford Jordan; [ed.] Albany State College, Albany, GA, Henry Mc Neal Turner High, Atlanta, GA; [occ.] Executive Secretary; [memb.] Beulah Baptist Church; [pers.] A friend loves at all times. Proverbs 17:17.

JORDAN, SUSAN ELIZABETH
[Pen.] Sue Professor; [b.] August 26, 1920, New Jersey; [p.] Deceased many years ago; [m.] Halcomb Jordan, April 15, 1939; [ch.] Sr. Lorraine F. Jordan, Charlotte Anna, Son Marshall Jordan; [ed.] Night School, Cottage Seminary in Sociology, Psychology. Graduate studies in English Art, Child Sociology; [occ.] Retired, Art and English Teacher; [memb.] Belonging to the writing club in my building the sunshines Club in Detroit, a honored pastoral chaplain at Mt. Carmel hospital. In apprecation for Faithful Service Pastoral Ministry; [hon.] Spelling Bee Award in school. Art and Craft award many poetry awards, school perfect attendance award, A Golden Award poet award 1991, Sacramento, CA; R.S.V.P. Retired Senior Citizen Volunteer Program of Wayne County; [oth. writ.] Writing a book about my mother-in-law, lived to be 115 years old. I have written to the President in 1982; written to the Honorable Carl M. Levin concerning the senior citizens in my building.; [pers.] Life is precious, a never ending beauty to behold. Suffering feel the weight of the soul, a frail heart is broken, life, is a fullfillment, through God's plan, like an hour glass on a stand.; [a.] Detroit, MI

JORGENSEN, J.J.
[b.] May 28, 1960, Brooklyn, NY; [p.] Lief and dolores Jorgensen; [m.] Lissette, December 24, 1991; [ch.] Matthew, James (1st son); [ed.] Lafayette H.S., Grad of Cathedral College and Certified by Institute of Children's Literature; [occ.] Advertising; [memb.] Member of Writer's Digest Club; [hon.] Adelphi Academy Fiction/Prose Award; [oth. writ.] Other poetry a current novel in progress.; [pers.] "With our individually written words, each of us that shoud, can lighten a heart or pluck out a tear, even from within ourselves."; [a.] Brooklyn, NY

JUDAH JR., ANNA LEA
[Pen.] Junior; [b.] October 5, 1979; Boise, Idaho; [p.] Anna Lee Judah and John H. Juday, Jr. (deceased); [ed.] Moriarty Elementary School, Moriarty, NM, Estancia, NM High School; [occ.] Student (9th grade); [pers.] My view of the world is quietly known to myself. Our planet earth is the mother of all creatures

here on earth. She gives us our bodies in which we grow. Her husband is the sky, he created our sobs. Together they help to protect as each day in ways we try to understand.; [a.] Moriarty, NM

JULEVICH, MARK
[b.] December 4, 1957, Stoughton, Mass.; [p.] Albert, Bertha; [ed.] Stoughton High, Community College of RI, Rhode Island College; [memb.] Society for the Protection of NH Forests; The Shakespear Oxford Society.; [hon.] French Award (Community College of RI); Phi Theta Kappa National Honor Fraternity; Graduated Summa Cum Laude from Rhode Island College; Dean's List; [pers.] Poetry is the breath of the soul. To read and write poetry, to see life in poetical terms, is to experience our existence more profoundly; [a.] Woonsocket, RI

JUSTICE, DEBRA E.
[b.] February 13, 1961, San Antonio, TX; [p.] Morgan W. and Sherry L. Justice; [pers.] My inspiration for writing comes from things I see, hear, and feel. Writing poetry is a way of expressing oneself on any subject and every level of life. The things I write about reflect my beliefs and feelings on different matters relating to the world.; [a.] Pensacola, FL

KABARA, KRYSTYNA
[b.] November 4, 1978, Htfd., CT; [p.] Zbigniew and Barbara Kabara; [ed.] So, far, 2 yrs. of high school at Bacon Academy, Colchester; [occ.] Student, dancer; [memb.] School of the Hartford Ballet; [hon.] Received a citation for outstanding community service from Mayor of Hartford for bringing dance to Hftd. public schools; [pers.] I like to yank out the hairs of life. Not all of them, just the ones with split ends. Thank you Johnston!; [a.] Colchester, CT

KAIMAKAMIAN, FERDINAND
[b.] January 16, 1916, Cilician, Armenia; [p.] Haroutune and Haiganoush Kaimakamian; [ed.] American College of Central Tureky; [occ.] Radiation Therapy and Radiographic Technologist-Licensed; [memb.] American Legion Chaplin (New York, Post #18 Vet. WW2), Knights of Vartan Brotherhood P.C.; [hon.] John F. Kennedy Award for Libraries (1972), Knights of Vartan Outstanding Achievement 1988; [oth. writ.] First Rhythmic Translation Opera Cavalleria Rusticana into Armenian 1954, Pagan Eras of Church Music 1965, numerous articles on Middle Eastern Music and History, etc.; [pers.] From realities of life's inspiration to constructive ideals applied...[a.] Corona, NY

KALOLO, SENE A.
[Pen.] Losa; [b.] January 22, 1983, Honolulu; [p.] Pepe and Motiana Kalolo; [ed.] Student; [hon.] Star Student, Mission Math Level 8 commander, Mo, Tardies, Demonstating Responsibility, 3 times, academic excellence 2 times Student of the Month.; [a.] Anchorage, AK

KAPLAN, TARA
[b.] November 2, 1984, Tarzana, CA; [p.] Joanne and Donald Kaplan; [ed.] Willow Elementary School; [occ.] Student; [memb.] Girl Scouts of America; [a.] Agoura Hills, CA

KARAZEWSKI, DAVE
[Pen.] Decay; [b.] July 21, 1963, Pacifica, CA; [p.] Raymond and Anita Karazewski; [ed.] Graduated

from Oceana High School in 1981.; [occ.] I'm Tops Operator "O" at Pacific Bell and have been there over 13 yrs.; [memb.] As far as I know the only membership I have is of the human race.; [hon.] The only honors bestowed to me are my parents, my two sisters whom I love very much and my friends whom not only stayed with me through thick and thin but taught me a few things a long the way. Also my girl, Debbie who has inspired many of my poems. I Love you all.; [pers.] The things I've written, mostly, are therapy for me. They are the form of expression that is the baring of my soul. They are me.; [a.] Redwood City, CA

KAY, ELINORE H.
[Pen.] Elig Kay; [b.] November 21, 1919, Morristown, NY; [m.] Jerry Kay, August 27, 1971; [ch.] Three; [ed.] Private schools and Jr. College; [occ.] Crafts and Painting selling hand hooked rugs.; [hon.] Many 1st for paintings, Three 1st, Five 2nd's for hooked rugs; Who's Who for Women for Hooked Rugs, note from Barbara Bush with Thanks for millie rug.; [oth. writ.] many poems; [pers.] I believe in hard work and stick to itness and determination and full use of God Gift to me.; [a.] Sanibel Island, FL

KEARNEY, SCOTT THOMAS
[b.] April 5, 1972, Belleville, NJ; [p.] James Victor Kearney and Kathleen Mary Johnson; [m.] single; [ed.] Roxbury High school; [occ.] Corporal, USMC (Former); [pers.] Wake The Hell Up!; [a.] St. Paul, MN

KEELING, DEBRA S.
[Pen.] Debra Hall; [b.] Columbus, OH; [p.] Heber, Reoyina Moore, Charles Hall; [m.] L.W. Keeling, November 18, 1978; [ch.] Brandy Dawn; grandaughter Ashton Dawn; [ed.] High School and College; [occ.] Farming/Housewife; [hon.]Silver Poet Award; [oth. writ.] Too Late, Picture on the Wall, What's Happened to Us, magazine articles, wrote cookbooks, short stories.; [pers.] Live each day of your life as a gift given to you.; [a.] Goreville, IL

KEELING, DEBRA S.
[Pen.] Debra Hall; [b.] Columbus, OH; [p.] Heber, Royina Moore, Charles Hall; [m.] L.W. Keeling, November 18, 1978; [ch.] Brandy Dawn and Grandaugher Ashton Dawn; [ed.] High School and College; [occ.] Farming Housewife; [hon.] Silver Poet Award; [oth. writ.] Too date!, Picture on the Wall!, What's happened to Us!, Magazine articles, wrote cookbooks and short stories; [pers.] Live each day of your life as a gift given to you.; [a.] Goreville, IL

KEIL, CHRISTINA
[Pen.] Michaeline Finn; [b.] May 24, 1973, Pittsburgh; [p.] Raymer and Elaine Keil; [ed.] John A. Brashear High School, Community College of Allegheny County, Louise Child Care, National Phlebotomy Association.; [occ.] Preschool Teachers Assistant, The Learning Tree; [oth. writ.] "The Mafia" written for a criminology thesis.; [pers.] Only you can make your life. I am influenced most by Edgar Allen Poe's Poetry.; [a.] Pittsburgh, PA

KELE, BRANDA L.
[b.] March 19, 1962, Millville, NJ; [p.] Deceaed, Mr. and Mrs. Albert Dutton; [ch.] Jozsef, Brenda II and Alexandra; [ed.] High School; [occ.] Data Entry Operator; [pers.] Enjoy expressing and sharing feel-

ings with others.

KELLEY, SUSAN
[Pen.] Susan Browning Kelly, Kelly Browning; [b.] January 10, 1956, Portland, OR; [p.] Russell E. and June Browning; [m.] Micheal Kelly, February 24, 1980; [ch.] Marcus Alan; [ed.] John Marshall High, Mt. Hood C.C.; [occ.] Accts Payable Clerk, Pope and Talbot; [oth. writ.] Several Western Novels, unpublished as of this writing.; [pers.] We come into this world and leave this world the same way, and in between we each should have the opportunity to grab what bit of happiness we can, regardless of race, creed and color.; [a.] Portland, OR

KELSCH, LORRAINE G.
[Pen.] Lori Kay; [b.] November 4, 1940, Mt. Clemens, Mi; [p.] Lester and Gertrude Green; [m.] Michael L. Kelsch, April 11, 1975; [ch.] Michael Nolan Kelsch, Patrick Dennis Kelsch; [ed.] Nativity of Our Lord High School, Detroit, Michigan; [occ.] Electronics Assembly, Troy Michigan; [oth. writ.] Many other poems, one published in Tiara Exculsives monthly publication in 1985; [pers.] My favorite poems are those I have written for my children or about my own childhood.; [a.] Ferndale, MI

KELSEY, TRISTIN R.
[b.] January 18, 1978, Betoit, WI; [p.] Thomas F. and Barbara L. Kelsey; [ed.] Beloit, Memorial High School, graduated 1996; [occ.] Student; [a.] Beloit, WI

KENNAR, PAUL
[b.] February 19, 1976, Hollywood; [p.] Jmes Kennar and Izzy Quider; [ed.] Fairfax High School, Graduate Career Awarenss Program complted at Home Savings of America; [occ.] Manager of Clog. Master in L.A.; [oth. writ.] Various upcoming projects for the human experience and beyond.; [pers.] Growing up in this generation I believed life meant "nothing." Just a bunch of worthless lies. but I discovered certain people's love for live. So to my dear generation, make a choice. I chose love.; [a.] Los Angeles, CA

KENNEALLY, MARY L.
[b.] Boston; [p.] Orphan; [m.] John, September 21, 1943; [ch.] 3 children, Patrick, Vincent, Theresa; [ed.] Mt. St. Mary College, Hooksett, New Hampshire; [occ.] Writer, Artist, Illustrator; [memb.] League of Women Voters, Lion's Club of Greater Westbury, N.W.W, Henry Hicks Garden Club of Long Island; [hon.] About 20 awards, exhibits in writing, illustrators, oil painting exhibits, about 20 in my print poems, lifetime etc.; [pers.] "A book of poetry is a cleaning house" of sharing wonderful thoughts and meditations in life.

KENNEDY, W.S.
[b.] January 23, 1926, South Norfolk, VA; [p.] Williams and Allice Kennedy; [ed.] William and Mary, (Norfold Div.), Later Hartnett's National Music Studios, New York; [occ.] Publisher, Editor of Reflect, Poetry Mag.; [memb.] Norfolk Musicians Assocton, AF of M.; [hon.] My Literary Magazine Reflection was listed in Writer's Digest's Top 60 Poetry Magazine in American and Canada (List included "The New Yorker," "Good Housekeeping," Atlantic Monthly); [oth. writ.] Have two novels with a literary agent: "Johnny Mowbrouch" and the Ebony bull" plus short poetry and fiction in Small

Press Mags.; [pers.] My literary movement, the Spiral Mode, was founded, via the vehicle of my poetry magazine, Reflect in 1982. Spiral Poetry features euphony (harmonious word sounds), mystical overtones, abstractness. My poet "Afoot in Chaldea," published in this anthology, is an example of Spiritual Mode poetry.; [a.] Norfolk, VA

KERSCH, HAZEL H.
[Pen.] Hazel H. Kersch-Lezah K.; [b.] November 25, 1917, Lindon, CO; [p.] H.B. and Josephine Hambley; [m.] Albert L. Kersch, second marraige September 4, 1976; [ch.] Jack and Judy McCarty; [ed.] Arvada High School, Barnes School of Business, Jr. College, CA and AZ; Adult Classes, Art, Phoenix Central College; [occ.] Retired; [memb.] Kiwaniannes, Ladies of the Moose; [oth. writ.] Poems published in local newspapers.; [pers.] Love of God, family and country is my inspiration.

KETCHAM, KEITH
[Pen.] Keith Kougan; [b.] September 15, 1975, Nebr. City, NE; [p.] Marion and Betty Ketchum; [ed.] High School only, but tons of thinking.; [occ.] Alternate distribution; [oth. writ.] I have a massive pile of completed poetry, short stories, etc. that I will hopefully have published soon. (within 100 years).; [a.] Nebraska City, NE

KEYES, KATHLEEN
[Pen.] Katie Keyes; [b.] November 8, 1978, Wollester; [p.] richard and Marilyn Keyes; [m.] Single; [ed.] Student, Sophomore South High School; [occ.] Student; [memb.] Stunt, Catherine of Sweden, Young American Bowlers Association.; [pers.] Poetry is a way of expressing myself and my feelings.; [a.] Woucester, MA

KHIN, U
[b.] April 21, 1911, Pegu, Burma; [p.] U Ba Thein and Daw Hla bu; [m.] Yvonne M. Khin, August 25, 1945; [ch.] none; [ed.] B.SC. (University of Rangoon, Burma); [occ.] Retired from Government Service, (currently doing some quilting for my wife who still makes quilts) Civil Service 1936-45; Diplomat 1946-51; Teacher at the Department of State, US Government 1951-81; [oth. writ.] I write "Quilt Articles" for the House of White Birches, in their various magazines since the 1970's and still doing so.; [pers.] I profess oriental philosophy and believe in helping mankind.; [a.] Rocky Ridge, MD

KHOUTH, MARY ANN
[Pen.] M.A.K.; [b.] November 7, 1975, St. Paul, MN; [p.] John S. and Chantheary Khouth; [ed.] St. Agnes Grade School, St. Agnes High School (K-10), Roseville Area High School (11-12), University of Minnesota; [occ.] College Student; [hon.] This would be the first time my work has been recognized.; [pers.] "Why should people be afraid of people? What we should be afraid of...is War!" "Only you can influence your children, so why not influence them the right way while they are still innocent."; [a.] St. Paul, MN

KHUBLALL, VASANTHA
[ch.] Denis Roger and Derek Roy; [ed.] Specialized in Linguistic Studies and Journalism. Degree in English Literature and Political Science; [occ.] Guest Relations at the Hilton Hotel in Manhattan, NY recently immigrated to the USA; [memb.] Member of the Best Contemporary Poets Association in the U.K. for submission of another poem to the Naitonal Poets' Associaiton in U.K.; [oth. writ.] Several poems published in foreign newspapers. Travelled extensively all over the world. Lived in several countries in the orient and occident.; [pers.] I strive to recognize and reflec the harmony in the beauty of nature and the human soul; love and sensitivity in my poetry.; [a.] Mercerville, NJ

KIDWELL, MARIE ELLEN
[b.] June 6, 1964, Indianapolis, Indiana; [p.] Jerry Dwaine and Marcia Ellen Aldrich; [m.] Kevin Dean Kidwell, June 9, 1990; [ed.] Franklin Community High School and Vincennes University; [occ.] Licensed Practical Nurse and homemaker; [memb.] First Mount Pleasant Baptist Church; [pers.] I am inspried to write about the beauty of Gods creation.; [a.] South Whitley, IN

KIDWELL, ROY SCOTT
[Pen.] R.S. Kidwell; [b.] January 21, 1970, Martinsburg, WV; [p.] James H. and Patricia A. Kidwell; [ed.] Mussleman High School, ICS, P.C. Repair Course; [occ.] I'm working for WV Society for the Blind; [memb.] Martinsburg Moose #120; [hon.] Army Achievement Medal, Good Conduct Medal, Ntional Defense Medal; [oth. writ.] Short stories which I hope to have published someday.; [pers.] I believe in every sunrise there is a new adventure, and never look behind nor to the future but deal with today, tomorrow will take care of it's self.; [a.] Bunker Hill, WV

KIEFER, JACKLYN D.
[Pen.] Jacki Kiefer; [b.] June 9, 1980, Brazil, IN; [p.] Frank and Catherine Kiefer; [ed.] Freshman at Northview High School; [occ.] Student; [a.] Brazil, IN

KIELY, JODI
[b.] September 11, 1977, Seoul, Korea; [p.] Mike and Kate Kiely; [ed.] Lourdes High School; [occ.] High school student; [oth. writ.] Several poems and articles published in high school newspaper.; [pers.] I try to write poems people can relate to in everyday life. I also want to sir up feelings and emotions in the reader through my writings.; [a.] Rochester, MN

KIHN, THERESA
[b.] March 12, 1981, Tampa, FL; [p.] Thomas J. and Gail A.; [ed.] 8th grade at Holley Junior Senior High School; [occ.] Summertime Swin Instructor Aide; [memb.] member of Ntional Junior Honor Society; [hon.] First Prize for Valentine Story Contest 94, 2 time writer of the week in school; [oth. writ.] Day Dreams, Is Anyone Listening, The Unexplainable, Legend, A Place They Call Home, and other unpublished poems.; [pers.] No matter who you are or what you believe in, you can do whatever you want with your life. I am, and I'm only 13 years old. I have the rest of my lfie ahead of me.; [a.] Holley, NY

KILBY, CHRISTINA M.
[Pen.] Christina Mary Kilby; [b.] October 15, 1979, Yuba City, CA; [p.] Stanley and Lolane Kilby; [ed.] Manzanita and Gridley High, Freshman; [occ.] Student; [pers.] Many teens are feeling lost today and writing is how we get in touch with our feelings.; [a.] Gridley, Ca

KILLEY, FRANCES BRENT
[b.] October 3, 1911, IL; [p.] Frank and Ada Brent; [m.] Ralph Allen Killey, May 27, 1932; [ch.] Barbara, Lester, Bill, Frank; [ed.] BA, Monmouth College, Monmouth, IL; [occ.] Retired Teacher; [memb.] First United Methodist Church, NSDAR, P.E.O., AAUW, AKC, Delta Kappa Gamma; [hon.] Distinguished Alumnus Award, Monmouth College, IL, Senate Certificate of Commendaiton Agless Achiever, Western IL, SAR, Gold Medal of Appreciation, Kentucky Colonel, Woman of Year, Republican Women, IL, Mother of Year, other writings DAR Magazine, Devotional Booklet for National DAR; [pers.] Nature and persons have been my chief interests.; [a.] Monmouth, IL

KIMBLE, AARON J.
[b.] March 19, 1980, Opclousas, Louisiana; [p.] Paula M. Kimble; [ed.] 9th grade; [occ.] Student; [memb.] Peer Leader; Natural Helpers; French Club; [hon.] Student of the Year; Student of the Month; Academic Excellence; Honor Roll Award; [oth. writ.] A Tribute to My Grandfather, Odessy (a play); [pers.] Poetry is another way of expressing human communications through words.; [a.] Opelousas, LA

KING JR., THOMAS E.
[b.] August 7, 1972, Conroe, TX; [p.] Thomas and Shirley King; [ed.] Willis High, Texas College; [occ.] School; [pers.] I have to thank God because if it wasn't for him, none of this would be happening. I just try to write poems that might turn your lady on at night, and if anything else happen's I'm not responsible.; [a.] Willis, TX

KING, MYRA ANN
[b.] October 5, 1981, Meriden, CT; [p.] Charles and Maria King; [ed.] Home Educated, 8th grade; [occ.] Student; [memb.] 4-H, Cornerstone Assembly of God, Youthgroup; [hon.] 4-H, Quiz Bowl, Hipology, Judging (Horses); [oth. writ.] Poems, only for pleasure; [pers.] I want my writings to reflect God's creation and his love.; [a.] Alburg Springs, VT

KIPP, PATRICK KELLY
[Pen.] P. Kelly; [b.] December 30, 1956, Buffalo, NY; [p.] Jean Hall and Karl E. Kipp; [pers.] I believe that words are, have been always will be the revelations of the soul.; [a.] Gladwyne, PA

KIRKENDALE, ROBERT ALAN
[Pen.] Bobay; [b.] February 28, 1961, New York; [p.] William and bonnie Kirkendale; [ed.] University of South Carolina Business Adminsitration; [occ.] Marketing director, Acute Rehabilitation unit, Broman Medical Center; [pers.] God, Help me to understand rather than to be understood, to love rather than be loved, to give rather than to receive and to live spiritually not religiously; [a.] Beverly Hills, CA

KIRKLAND, CHARLOTTE
[Pen.] Char and Charlotte Rose; [b.] March 25, 1926, MO; [p.] L.C. Luch Hart; [m.] May 12, 1946 (divorced); [ch.] James E. Pamela Rose, Holly Rea, Benjamin R. Charlene R.; [ed.] 9th grade plus, grade school and different Bible short term schools; [occ.] Retired; [hon.] Golden Poetry Gram, Award, New York 1991, Award of Merit 1991, Award of Merit 1990, Editor's Choice Award by National Library of Poetry 1994.; [oth. writ.] Sea to Shinning Sea, Honorary Charter Membership, International Soc. of

Poets 1993; [pers.] Being born again is a powerfull force to help one in striving for righteous. That not of ourselves, it's the gift of God.; [a.] Orange, CA

KIRKLAND, RANA
[b.] October 6, 1966, Manhattan, NY; [occ.] Actress doing commercials and television, aspiring for film work; [pers.] I've been writing poetry for almost five years, but this was my first attempt at publicly sharing it. Thank God it was a successful one. I am now even more inspired to work. Thank You.; [a.] No. Hollywood, CA

KLAVER JR., KEITH C.
[Pen.] Casey Klaver; [b.] February 22, 1978, Ft. Worth, TX; [p.] Keith C. and Jeanne Klaver; [ed.] High School; [occ.] School; [pers.] My writing reflects my personal experiencees and feelings.

KLEIN, C. MARGUERITE
[b.] April 5, 1909, Wichita, KS; [p.] Lewis and Hettie Nicholson; [m.] Richard Stanley Klein, August 23, 1928 (Deceased); [ch.] Richard Stanley Klein Jr., Larry Lee Klein, Alford Don Klein; [ed.] B.A. from Friends Univ., majored Eng., Home Economics Education (occ) minister's wife, social worker, teacher, mother wife.; [occ.] Almost a full time volunteer.; [memb.] Presbyterian Church, Lifetime NEA, AAUW, Retired Teachers, Art Association, AARP, RSVP (hon) woman of yr. in Religion, poems in Presbyterian Publication. Paintings in Pres. Manor calendars; [hon.] Women of the year in religion, recently used 7 original poems in a program of organ and voice.; [oth. writ.] Most recent poems about 5 chickens "Eeny Meany Miney Mo and Me" compared old tooth brushes to retired teachers, both can be recycled "Comparison," "Memories"; [pers.] I definitely feel we should never loose heart and think the world is going to the "dogs" I firmly believe that God has the World in his hands and will conquer in the end. I believe that human's greed and selfishness is cause of sin in the world. We need to get back to family priorities and love our children; [a.] Newton, KS

KLEIN, JOY G.
[b.] December 19, 1931, Brooklyn, NY; [p.] Deceased: Sol J. Schwartz DDS, & Eleanor Schwartz; [m.] Divorced; [ch.] Adult son, Robert Allan Klein NMT, Certified Massage Therapist, 2 grandchildren, David Mark Klein 11 and Marcie Else Keil 9; Roberts their Dad, or "Bob" as he's called in Athens, Georgia, and Claudia Timmons is their mom.; [ed.] NYU School of Education, B.S. Degree in Elem. Ed., Equivalent of Master's Degree, NYS Certified, Pre-K to Third Grade, inclusive; [occ.] Retired NYC Teacher; [hon.] Many certificates of appreciation; [oth. writ.] Too many to mention; [pers.] May I continue to add that as a permanent resident now in Athens, Georgia, I wish to focus on family life with my son Robert, and my David and Marcie, my 2 wonderful grandchildren. I wish everlasting and fine friendships that I have acquired in the past and present to continue.; [a.] Athens, GA

KLEIN, JOY G.
[b.] December 19, 1931, Brooklyn, NY; [p.] Solomon J. Schwartz, DDS (deceased) and Eleanor Schwartz; [ch.] Son, Robert Allan Klein, Certified Massage Therapist, Athens, GA; [ch.] Two grandchildren, David Mark Klein age 11 and Marcie Elyse Klein age 9; Their Dad is Robert and Mom is Claudia Timmons;

[ed.] Syracuse Univ., NYU School of Ed, B.S. Degree in Elem Educ; [occ.] Teacher, 30 yrs., Retired 1990; [memb.] Temple Congregation Children of Israel, Athens Georgia, Also Sisterhood Athens, Georgia, GPTV, Rabbi Ronald D. Gerson always makes me feel welcome. I appreciate his service and friendship; [hon.] Recent Editor's Choice Award, and many others; [pers.] I am inspried to write my poetry, here at College Place, in Athens, Georgia. The birds, nature, lovely landscaping and of course my family here and friends motivate my inner feelings to produce and write my thoughts and ideas into rhythms, and coordinated verses. i enjoy wonderful, sincere friendships. Angelo Iacon, in NJ, my professional collegeauq, Micahel Woodard, my Temple Friend and confidant with Rabbi Gerson; [a.] Athens, GA

KLESCHUK, MIRANDA V.
[b.] January 4, 1981, Portland, OR; [p.] Michael and Kathleen Kleschuk; [ed.] Through 7th grade will be entering 8th grade fall of 94"; [occ.] Student and Entrepeneur; [memb.] Junior member of Geographic Society; [hon.] Honor Roll Student, placed 2nd in School District writing contest in "1989" (2nd grade) the Art Literacy Program at Miranda's school has featured her Art many times.; [oth. writ.] Poem published in National Geographic World.; [pers.] I see the world as a place full of unnecessary problems large and small. But if we cn fix the smaller problems, the larger problems will eventaully fix themselves with time.; [a.] Aloha, OR

KLINE, REBECCA
[Pen.] Becky; [b.] December 17, 1980, Vero Beach, FL; [p.] Denise and Michael Louiros; [ed.] Attending Gulf Middle School Cape Coral, FL; [memb.] Stage Stars, Gulf Middle school Band; [hon.] 1st place in Drama Competition Honor Roll Student; [oth. writ.] Several other unpublished writings.; [pers.] I have been greatly influenced by my 6th and 7th grade teacher Mrs. D. Hill who teaches language arts.; [a.] Cape Coral, FL

KLOOSTERMAN, DIANE
[b.] August 30, 1971, Oregon; [m.] James Hancock; [ch.] Chad Hancock, Samantha Hancock; [occ.] Homemaker; [pers.] In dedication to my love James Hancock, whom gave me two beautiful children, and a lifetimes worth of love. Through good times, and bad.; [a.] Shingel Springs, CA

KNUCKEY, NORMAN E.
[b.] April 22, 1933, Duluth, Minn.; [p.] A.J. (Bud) & Mary Louise Knuckey; [m.] June 18, 1960 (Separated); [ch.] Tom 31, Patty 30; [ed.] Florida State University two years.; [occ.] Retired Insurance Underwriter; [memb.] St. Petersburg Little Theatre; St. Bartholomew's Church (Episcopal); [hon.] Salutatorian St. Petersburg High School Class of 1951; Awards from World of Poetry and National Library of Poetry; National Honor Society; [oth. writ.] Poems in various anthologies: Wyndham Hall Press; World of Poetry and National Library of Poetry.; [pers.] Reading and writing poetry and golf are among my favorite avocations. Writing some really good poetry is still my ambition! Playing good golf is equally elusive!; [a.] St. Petersburg, FL

KNUE, DENISE
[Pen.] Neese; [b.] September 7, 1955, Portland, ME; [p.] Robert and June Torrey; [m.] R. Vincent Knue,

July 31, 1993; [ch.] Son, Keith, Stepdaughter, Elizabeth; [ed.] Cape Elizabeth High school; [occ.] Administrative Assistant; [pers.] Each person has one facet in their personality that lives, breathes, silently cries and always desires to be free. These cries are timed and insecure in their desires for recognition of what they truly are. Expressions. For me poetry is self recognition of my timid cries that I have heard and answered.; [a.] Cape Elizabeth, ME

KOCH, ELYSA
[b.] January 25, 1983, NJ; [p.] Michael and Wand Koch; [ed.] Songum Elementary School, Randolph, NJ; [occ.] Student; [memb.] None; [oth. writ.] Edge of Twilight, Dream Weaver; [pers.] Elyse aspires to become a "famous" writer. Her other interest are dance, music and the arts. She plays both the piano and the flute. She dances both tap and ballet.; [a.] Randolph, NJ

KOEDEL, KENNETH DOUGLASS
[Pen.] Ken Douglass/Douglas Koedel; [b.] August 19, 1938, Natrona, PA; [p.] Louis Wesley & Zita Marie Koedel; [m.] Divorced; [ed.] High School, St. Josephs, Natrona, PA 1956; [occ.] Owner/Operator Valley Auto Service, 901 3rd Av., New Kensington, PA; [oth. writ.] Numerous unpublished poems of varied susbject matter and a limited amount of somewhat satirical prose incorporting role reversal in popular fairy tales.; [pers.] I have never really thought of my writing as a "talent" but merely as a means of expression and in some cases as a relief valve for emotional stress. I am a self proclaimed student of grammatical correctness and abhor today's "socially accepted" grammatical corruption.; [a.] Brackenridge, PA

KOFFI, ANDRE
[Pen.] Andy Koff; [b.] November 9, 1964, Ivory Coast; [p.] Kouassi Koff, Kouassi Amoin; [ch.] Nelson Marius Koffi; [ed.] Hotel/Rest. Tech. H.S. Ivory Coast, Institute of Audio Research, New York, New York Institute of Technology (NYIT); [occ.] Communication Arts Student, New York Institute of Technology; [memb.] Audio Engineering Society; [hon.] Humanities Honor Roll (NYIT-1994); [pers.] No matter wht, life is a wonderful experienc. And I feel blessed to be a part of it; even when I think I am still who I am, a fighter who beleives he still has to do more and better.; [a.] New York City, NY

KOHLRUS, VALERY
[Pen.] M.K.; [b.] November 12, 1975, Peoria, IL; [p.] Robert and Vanetta Kohlrus; [ed.] Metamora Township High School; College pending this fall.; [memb.] First Baptist Church of Peoria's Youth Bord; Regional Youth Board; Social Work Explorers; Yearbook Staff; Students Against Drunk Driving; [hon.] Graduated from Youth Leader Core and Metamora Township High School; Who's Who in America High School Students; [pers.] The poetry of the late Helen Steiner Rice influenced me to write poems about my life experiences and God's love.; [a.] Metamora, IL

KOLB, DEBBIE LYNN
[b.] July 11, 1957, Morgan City, LA; [p.] Wallace and Edna Ackman; [ch.] Dana Major, Nicole Major, Adam Kolb; [ed.] Centerville High School, Centerville, LA, Morgan City Vo-tech School; [occ.] Cashier Corner Yard Sale, Hammonds, LA; [memb.] Morgan City Skating Coub (1970-72), Future Homemakers of

American 1974-75.; [oth. writ.] I have written other poems for different members of my family and loved ones and friends.; [pers.] My Mom, Edna Ackman has greatly influenced my writing. She has been my strength in my writing.; [a.] Independence, LA

KOLLEAS, PAMELA
[b.] July 19, 1954, Hillsboro, OR; [ch.] Jil 18, Andrew 16, Nicholas 13 (their last name is Clark); [ed.] Associate of Arts Degree earned at Portland Community College in 1993 at age 38. Enrolled now at Eastern Oregon State College majoring in Business and Education; [memb.] Portland Country Dance Community. Interntional Society of Authors and Artists Directory; [hon.] Honors Graduate; [oth. writ.] Poetry published: "Free Men," "Buffington's Buffet at the Brasserie," "Two Women," and "Granola Granny." The latter two poems were written from reflections of my now adult daughter Jill; [pers.] I have been using a philosophy which has come from the freedom I now feel as a writer, "Through one life, walks many. May all those silenced in the past, walk thier journey through me." I am a single mother, college student, I home school my youngest child, I love fully in the moment, write my riches and dance through life.

KOPPERS, EVELYN C.
[b.] January 5, 1978; [p.] Patricia C. and Joseph P. Koppers; [ch.] Live with both parents, two younger sisters, two dogs, two cats & one fish.; [ed.] Mount Calvary School, Elizabeth Seton High School (completed freshman year, will be sophomore 1994/95); [occ.] Student and part-time secretary.; [memb.] Mount Calvary Teen Club, Kettering Swim Club, Girl Scouts of America, Elizabeth Seton High School SADD; [hon.] Girl Scout Silver Award; [pers.] I love to write and I try to write about things that have happened to me to make them more real. Will be serving as an Congressional Aide to US Senator from Mexico August 1994 for one week.; [a.] Capitol Heights, MD

KOSSACK, JOSH
[b.] September 26, 1981, Phoenix, AZ; [p.] Leslie and Steven Kossack; [ed.] Attending 7th grade at Cocopah Middle School; [occ.] Student; [hon.] Principals List, Spelling Champion of Sequoya Elementary in 1994, 2nd runner up in Maricapa County Regional Spelling Bee in 1994. Recipient of Joyce Evakiviat Hebrew Award for Temple Beth Israel in 1994.; [pers.] Writing relaxes me and I aspire to be a great writer someday.; [a.] Scottsdale, AZ

KOSTECZKO, JOSEPH PETER
[b.] February 13, 1976, Newburgh, NY; [p.] Nicholas and Suzanne Kosteczko; [ed.] High School Graduate, Attending United States Merchant Marine Academy; [occ.] Attending United States Merchant Marine Academy; [memb.] Life member in the National Rifleman Assoc.; Member in 4-H for two years.; [hon.] Member of National Honor Society, Presidential Academic Fitness Award, Graduated with honors.; [oth. writ.] I worte for other poems but not published.; [pers.] "A man without convictions is no man at all;" I wrote the poem at age 16 (Dedication to the Arizona); [a.] Gardiner, NY

KREBS, KEVIN E.
[Pen.] Talisman T. Taylor; [b.] December 20, 1966, Covington, KY; [p.] Edward M. Krebs and Linda R. Leake; [m.] Beth T., October 15, 1988; [ch.] Katherine Elizabeth, Amanda Nicole; [ed.] Dixie Heights; USAF; Midlands Technical College; [occ.] Health Unit Coordinator, Cardiac Clerk Technician; [hon.] USAF Veteran; [oth. writ.] Personal Poetic Portfolio; [pers.] the well of one's soul is no deeper than one's own pen might read.; [a.] Columbia, SC

KREPLIAK-SONSTEIN, CAROLYN
[Pen.] Carolyn T. Sonstein; [b.] August 19, 1916, Phila, PA; [p.] Benjamin and Clara Layber; [m.] Late Husband Ned Jonstein, Edward Krepliak, DDS, January 1, 1971; [ch.] Murray M. Sonstein and Beryl Einheber; [ed.] Phila. High School for Girls, Temple Univ., Charles Morris, Price School for Advertising and Journalism; [occ.] Retired Publicist, last job Public Relations Dir., Metropolitan YWCA of Phila; [memb.] Phila Public Reltions Assoc., Women in communications, Folk Dance Center of Phila, Sholom Aleichem Club; [hon.] Outstanding Program 100th Anniversary metropolitan YWCA of Phila, as well as several other significant awards; [oth. writ.] Short stories, articles, news releases, annual reports, poetry; [pers.] To translate the universality of hope in all people. My parents and siblings are all foreign born. I am the only American by birth in my nuclear family. The "American Carolyn" is very meaningful to my folks for what they beleive is keen appraisal of humanity.; [a.] Phila. PA

KROMER, DELLA HARRISON
[b.] April 10, 1925, White Water, Kansas; [p.] Mabel Miller and Raymond Harrison; [m.] Kermit K. Kromer, June 17, 1945; [ch.] Nona Joelene Alderfer, Loreda Dianne Horutz; [ed.] Newton Kansas and Valley center Kansas High School; [occ.] Retired teacher, cake decoration, crafts; [memb.] Polk Township Fire Co., Ladies Auxillary Volunteer, Schwenk Felder Church, Worcester, PA; [hon.] Crafts, West End Fair Gilbert, PA; Special Occasion Cakes and Wedding Cakes; [oth. writ.] Autumn Lee published time and you to me published, Big Sister, Virginia to Nona published, to Loreda Published My Sister Who Passed Away published.; [pers.] I have enjoyed writing poetry for a lot of years. I write mostly about our family. And I am researching our family history on 4 sides. I love learning about our ancestors.

KRUEGER, RONALD J.
[b.] December 15, 1932, Muskegon, Michigan; [p.] Julius T. and Mildred M. Krueger; [m.] Marilyn R. Krueger, April 21, 1956; [ch.] randall, Michelle and Sharon; Grandchildren: Kelli, Kari and Katy; [occ.] Retired, Formerly Computer Systems Analyst and Programmer.; [pers.] I wondered whom I would like to be; then realized that it was me. A person is only free enough to choose their own bondage.; [a.] Muskegon, MI

KRUSE, JOAN H.
[b.] October 8, 1956, Geneva, IL; [p.] Rev. Milton and Evelyn Whitney; [m.] Frank E. Kruse, April 12, 1980; [ch.] Peter M. Van Horn, Timothy M. and Karel J. Kruse; [ed.] Graduate of Pearl City High School, continuing education courses at Highland Community College; [memb.] St. John's Lutheran Church, Pearl City, IL; [hon.] Cake decorating awards, 1979, Cherry Vale Mall 1st place, novelty cake, 1993, Valley Bakers Assoc., 3rd place buttercream wedding cake.; [oth. writ.] Editor's Choice Award for poem "My Friend" published in "Tears of Fire.";

[pers.] "Mother's Smile" was written to comfort a cousin who was grieving the loss of her mother.; [a.] Pearl City, IL

KUFTACK, FRANK
[ed.] College; [memb.] Elks, Mensa; [hon.] none; [oth. writ.] Journal; [pers.] I think most poets try to create truth, goodness and beauty as they hear it, sense it, and see it.; [a.] Pleasant Valley, NY

KUMM, WANDA
[b.] May 21, 1959, Elkton, MD; [p.] James Bonham, Sr., Clara Bonham Mutchie; [m.] Gary Kumm, June 24, 1978; [ch.] Wayne Edward, Christopher Lee, Kelly Louise; [occ.] Mother, Homemaker, Wife; [oth. writ.] I wrote a poem in the Holyoke Enterprise as a Tribute to my children, Wayne, Christopher, Kelly; [pers.] I love writing poetry. I also write my feelings down and turn it into a poem; [a.] Holyoke, CO

KUNZ, CAROL
[b.] March 22, 1940, Zanesville, Ohio; [p.] Leona Maneely, Sacramento, CA; [m.] Robert Junz, November 3, 1976; [ch.] Five: James, Christopher, Randall, Andrea and Gina; [ed.] Attended Weathersford College, Weatherford, TX and Tarleton State University in Stephenville, TX; [occ.] Nurse; [memb.] International Society of Poets and Associate Member of The Hemingway Days.; [hon.] World of Poetry, 1991 Honorable Mention for "Fossils In The Sand" and Honorable Mention 1992 for "oneness." 1993 Poetry Academy Madallion for "The Broken Window." Editor's Choice Award, 1994 Presidents Award for Excellence, Outstanding Poet 1994; Accomplishment of Merit from the Creative Arts & Science Enterprises for "Ode To MidSummer Nights Dream" Pitch 'N Peach and Country Cat and bird (cat poetry) Editor of "The Special Pen" a newsletter for young writers.; [pers.] My mailbox decides my destiny as a writer.; [a.] Dublin, TX

LA CHANCE, CHRISSY
[Pen.] Chris Anne Themum; [b.] December 25, 1976, Lowell, Mass.; [p.] Patti and Rick LaChance; [ed.] Attending Somersworth High School, I'm a junior; [occ.] Youth works program, still in high school; [memb.] DECA, Distributive Education, Clubs of America; [hon.] Math Award, Memorization Award, Science Project Award; [oth. writ.] i have written several poems and stories that are unpublished. Example: A strangers look, etc.; [pers.] Whenever I write, it just shoots from my heart and into my mind. My heart is filled with a lot so its easy for me to write. But besides that the most important thing is to have a good attitude.; [a.] Somersworth, NH

LABARR, CORTNEY
[b.] June 6, 1982, Bimini, Italy; [p.] Karen and Ernest LaBarr; [ed.] Robson Elementary School; [occ.] Student; [memb.] Student Council President (1993-1994); Central Christian Church Youth Group; Respect Team Member; [hon.] Honor Roll, 4th - 6th grades; [oth. writ.] Has written for "Young Authors"; [pers.] My lifetime goal is to become a well-known writer. Writing allows me to express myeself.; [a.] Mesa, AZ

LACHAPELLE, LAWRENCE V.
[b.] May 7, 1912, Chicago, IL; [p.] Joseph and Agnes La Chapelle; [m.] Helen E. La Chapelle, November

19, 1938; [ed.] Loyola Academy Chgo. Grad 1930, Notre Dame 2 years 1930-1932, Loyola U Night Law 2 1/2 yrs., Minneapolis Col Law one year; [occ.] Retired; [memb.] American Legion, Chicago Black Horse Troop 1936-1939, Radioman U.S. Navy 1942-1945, Air Support Control aboard USS Blue Ridge for Moretai Invasion, Destroyer Hughes for Leyte Gulf, Blue Ridge for Linguayn Gulf Invasion, Coast Guard Cutter Ingham for Corregidor recapture.; [hon.] Dean Delta Theta Phi Law Frat 1934; [oth. writ.] Today, Nurses, Quiet Hours, A cow named Molly, Halloween, tis Autumn; [a.] Minnetonka, MI

LAGUNA, CARMEN M.
[Pen.] Mara Valencia; [b.] March 26, 1922, San Juan Puerto Rico; [p.] Santiago Laguna and Julia Reyes; [ed.] University of Puerto Rico; [occ.] Former Elementary School Teacher, now retired; [memb.] A.A.R.P.; [hon.] First Prize/Second Prize Honorific Mentions in several contests.; [oth. writ.] Nuevas Voces de La Atenas and Pulsode Poesia (anthologies); Mensaje de NY (NY publication); El Dia (Newspaper); several poems published in local newspapers as well as short stories.; [pers.] We strive to find who we are, where do we come from and where are we going, but we are not what we should, hoping to find everything on the palm of our hands.; [a.] Manati, Puerto Rico

LAIRD, KAYE
[b.] April 22, 1932, Detroit; [p.] Milburn P. Anderson, Lillian Mae Amundsen; [m.] John D. Laird, September 26, 1953; [ch.] Connie Laird Mann, Karen Laird DeSmet; [ed.] B.S. Michigan State University; [hon.] Phi Kappa Phi scholastic honorary, Kappa Delta Pi Education Honorary Omicron Nu, Home Economics Honorary; pers.] Kaye Laird, a previous Continuing Education Coordinator and instructor at Kellog Community College, began writing in 1991 by taking a writing class on family narrative, a natural outgrowth of her interest in genealogy. This unique class is still intact; exploring, probing, and experimenting under the guidance and inspiration of Rosalie Blanks. Kaye has enjoyed her exposure to poetry, including western haiku and senryu. She doesn't think of poetry as being an intellectual activity. "It is simply another way of telling a tale. Writing, poetry as well as prose, connects you to yourself. It's a very visceral activity, allowing us a way to think about ourselves and how the world impinges on us."; [a.] Battle Creek, MI

LAMBERT, WOODY
[b.] March 7, 1974, Sadro-Woolley, WN; [p.] Doris and Clyde Bardon; [ch.] A son and daughter; [ed.] Edmonds Community College; [occ.] Disabled; [a.] Lynnwood, WN

LAMONICA, HOLLY LYNN DONHAUSER
[b.] June 21, 1961, Cooperstown, NY; [p.] Joan Helen Bush, Howard Louis Donhauser Sr.; [ch.] Amanda, Dustin and Emily; [ed.] Crestwood High School, Edinboro University; Painting Lycoming College; BA in Art Education; [occ.] Artist; self employed Optician, Senior Eye Care; [memb.] Bald Eagle Art League Williamsport Lycoming Arts Council; [hon.] Cum Laude gradute, Faculty award for Achievements in Art, Artwork in Lycoming College's permanent collection.; [oth. writ.] "You Say Potato…", "Zapped," "Automobile of fair…" and several other self-reflective poems.; [pers.] I am an artist by nature and have found poetry to be yet another medium in which I am able to express the truths and realities in life, mine in particular, as I perceive them. my pieces have been deemed "idealistic" and "realistic."; [a.] Williamsport, PA

LANCE, JONATHAN
[b.] February 28, 1977, Indiana; [p.] Max R. Lance and laura J. Brown; [ed.] South Caldwell High School; [occ.] Student; [pers.] I wrote this for my father who passed awy July 18, 1993. I will always remember the love he gave me. I would also like to thank my step-father, Steve Brown who encouraged me to write and speak my views.; [a.] Granite Falls, NC

LANDECKER, JESSIE
[b.] January 29, 1921, Lou Gap, NC; [p.] Hobert and Mae McPeters; [m.] George Landecker, October 28, 1943; [ch.] Heidi and Heller Landecker; [ed.] High School and a graduate of the Philadelphia College of art; [occ.] Artist; [hon.] Many prizes from regional shows; [oth. writ.] I have written poems most of my life, but only for family affairs, four years ago I started writing seriously.; [pers.] I like to see and write about the extraordinary in the ordinary mundane things around me mostly in nature.; [a.] Barneveld, NY

LANE JR., LAWRENCE A.
[b.] May 13, 1975, Cleveland, OH; [p.] Lawrence A. Lane Sr. and Sandra Lane; [ed.] Graduate of Crestwood High School; [occ.] Cook at an Italian Restaurant; [memb.] American Red Cross; [hon.] Who's Who Among American High School Students; [pers.] I plan on becoming a teacher, and hope to get some of my students interested in poetry the way my english teachers did in eleventh and twelth grade. I owe many thanks for this to them.; [a.] Independence, OH

LANG, ROSE
[b.] March 13, 1905, Michigan; [p.] Deceased; [m.] Deceased; [ch.] Four (all grown) Jack, Jim, Bill and Annalee is the oldest; [ed.] High school, 3 yrs. college; [occ.] Taught school for 25 years, also spent 2 yrs. with retarded children, enjoyed it very much.; [occ.] Retired; [oth. writ.] None published, would certainly like to have one published in your book.; [pers.] Be friendly with all but intimate with few. Life is what we make it (mostly).

LANGHOFF, ERIK
[b.] July 11, 1979, New Ulm, MN; [p.] Steven and Beverly Langhoff; [ed.] Tenth Grade Student; [occ.] Student; [memb.] Vice President of church's "Luther League" committee and other church events; [hon.] A student in school's advanced English class. A student in school's advanced English Class. A choir member in school for three years, awarded with O.K. kid award in ninth grade. Achieved both "A" and "B" honor roles in school; [pers.] My writings are reflections of my emotions, and my emotions are reflections of me."; [a.] Lafayette, MN

LANIER, DENISE ANNE
[b.] Springfield, Mass.; [p.] Marie Williams, George Jolly Sr.; [ch.] Bryant Lee Lanier; [ch.] Tiffany Monique Jolly, Shaunte Lemar Williams, Irvin Lee Lanier Jr., Darlene Marie Lanier; [pers.] Poetry is my life, I hope others can enjoy it as much as I do.

LAPUZ, ALLAN BALDESTAMON
[b.] December 14, 1969, Philippines; [p.] Anthony and Estelita Lapuz; [ed.] Channel Island High School; and Oxnard Community College; [occ.] Lead Person and Set Up Technician; [memb.] No memberships as of right now.; [hon.] Group dancing competition first Runner Up, Most Perfect Attendance Award, Honor Roll Awards, Spelling Ace Award (Manila Philippines); [oth. writ.] Poems after poems seen by some friends but never been published.; [pers.] When I feel emotions I write, when I feel inspired I write, and when I feel sadness I write. I know that I want people to appreciate what I write.; [a.] Bernard, CA

LARSEN, CHRISTOPHER
[b.] March 17, 1982, Livingston, NJ; [p.] Paul and Mary Vicki; [ch.] Sister: Karen; [occ.] Student, Kumpf Middle School, Clark, NJ, 7th grade; [hon.] 1993-94 Kumpf Middle School Honor Roll, Law Day Essay Contest Winner (Clark, 1993), March of Dimes Reading Champion 1991, Student of the Month (Valley Road School, June 1991); [oth. writ.] "Rain Forests Disappearing"; [pers.] I try to point out the things we should improve on earth in my poems. I also love to draw.; [a.] Clark, NJ

LARSON, ANDREA S.
[b.] April 5, 1977, Neenah, Wis.; [p.] Mother: Joni Larson; [ed.] Menasha High School, would like to attend college upon graduation; [occ.] Student, Menasha High School, Menasha, WI; [pers.] A closed mind, like a closed door, shuts out not only the darkness, but the sunlight as well.; [a.] Menasha, WI

LARYS, THEODORE
[b.] December 19, 1942, Plainfild, NJ; [p.] Anne B. Larys (Bohumir Larys DEC); [ed.] Onteroa Central School, High School and graduate work Certifinite: One year course at BOCES in Commercial Food Services; [occ.] Dietary Aide Part-time Farmer; [hon.] Honorable Mention for poem "My Farm Years" March 15, 1989, Honorable Mention "My Best Border Collie Name Annie" Dec. 20, 1989; World of Poetry, Sacramento, CA; Who's Who in Poetry for Outstanding achievement in poetry 1990; [oth. writ.] Published a poem "My Farm Years," in Windham Journal, Windham, NY 1898, Book Called "Poetic Voices of America," from Sparrowgrass Poetry Forum, Inc. Sistersville, West, VA; [pers.] I am avid letter writer: I am a combination of down to-earth person who likes to work outdoors and appreciates farming and gardening and a person with a strong artistic feeling. My creative work in whatever field is done intuitively. I have done a lot of wood-work (carving have done water color painting.; [a.] Peattsville, NY

LASPISA, JOSEPH ALBERT
[b.] August 2, 1940, Oakpark, IL; [p.] Jocobe and Tina Laspisa; [ch.] One-Sharron; [ed.] Three years college, Florence State Alabama; [occ.] Work at General Motors, 1966--; [pers.] When I go over the rainbow I pray my poems and songs will go on till the end of time.; [a.] Joliet, IL

LATHAM, KELLY JEAN
[b.] August 7, 1980, Loma Lindack; [p.] Nancy and Robert Latham; [ed.] Idllwild Elementary, Whispering Palms School, a small private school located in the Micronesian island of Saipan; [pers.] I enjoy both reading and writing poetry. My thoughts and emo-

tions flow onto paper in both poems and sketches; [a.] Saipan, CNMI

LATRITA, BRADFORD
[Pen.] Justice; [b.] July 7, 1977, OKC, OK; [p.] William J. Bradford Sr. and Sharry L. Bradford; [ed.] Okemah High; [hon.] Honor Roll Student, Several Speech Contest Honors and Awards Superintendent's Honor Roll; [oth. writ.] How?; Tender Touch; Battle Long Last; The Long Road; A Mothers Love; Be Careful; More Than Just Friends; There is Another Way; Joined at the Heart; [pers.] In my writing I strongly stress love and the coming together of all races, because without the two, the world will never be a better place. The people around me are my influence.; [a.] Okemah, OK

LAUER, DOROTHY
[b.] March 5, 1923, Seattle, WA; [m.] Robert Lauer, February 8, 1946; [ch.] David and John Lauer, Barbara Carrigan, seven grandchildren; [ed.] Broadway High School, Seattle Pasadena City College (AA - English), Pasadena, CA, California State L.A. Los Angeles, CA (BA - English); [occ.] Writer; [memb.] St. Andrew's Episcopal Church (lay reader). The Honor Society of Phi Kappa Phi; [hon.] BHS Honor Society, 1940, AA - English and Spanish Honors - Administrative Honors for Outstanding Scholorship - Pasadena City College - June 1973, Bachelor of Arts Degree with High Honors and Departmental Honors in English - June 1976; [oth. writ.] Book almost completed tracing unity in writings of Dame Rebecca West. Two books of poetry in process. Poem entitled "Danger at Dust", published in Dance on the Horizon, The National Library of Poetry; [pers.] My poetry captures a lifetime of images. The spectrum is broad, including people, places, events nature, feelings, ideas. It is a pastiche of memories; [a.] Tokeland, WA

LAUGHMAN, BRIAN
[b.] March 1, 1979, Hanover, PA; [p.] Anthony and Sue Ellen Laughman; [ed.] St. Joseph's Catholic School, Delone Catholic High School; [occ.] Student; [memb.] Iditarod Trail Committee Inc., Alter Boy's Society, Delane Debate Team; [hon.] Par vuli Dei General Excellence, grades 3 & 7, Daughters of the American Revolution Certificate of Award for Outstanding; Work in American History Knights of Columbus Writing Award; [oth. writ.] Award winning essay on Columbus. Award winning essay on being an American. Personal poems, short stories and musings.; [pers.] All men have the abilities that all others do. The difference between great writers and everyone else is that they chose to make good use of those abilities.; [a.] Hanover, PA

LAWRENCE, VIVIAN M.
[b.] June 17, 1929, Sheboygan Falls, Wisconsin; [p.] Philip G. Lawrence, April 7, 1973; [ch.] David, Richard, Sharon, Steve, Sandra and Scott; [ed.] Sheb. Falls High, Business College; [occ.] Retired after 30 yers for Shaw's Supermarkets; [memb.] Sacred Heart Church, Smithsonian Institute; [hon.] Plaques from my years of work.; [oth. writ.] Poems published in "Dance on the Horizon" and "Selected Poems by the World's Best Poets" for many family weddings.; [pers.] I have a great love to share with whoever will take the time to red and care. It's like a hug to me.; [a.] North Yarmouth, ME

LAWSON, CANDI
[b.] April 30, 1980, Nacagdoches, TX; [p.] Craig and Cindy Lawson; [ed.] Martinsville, ISD; [oth. writ.] Numerous poems and songs for family and friends.; [a.] Nacagdoches, TX

LAWSON I, JEFFREY
[b.] August 4, 1959, Dayton, Ohio; [p.] Carl and Shirley (deceased); [ch.] Jeffrey Lawson II; Angela Nicole and Danielle Marie; [ed.] H.S. Grad., Wapakoneta H.S., Colleges (non-grad) Cleary College in Ypsilanti, Michigan and Sinclair College in Dayton, OH; also grad and instructor in Naval Nuclear Power Program; [occ.] Dayton Daily Newspaper; [memb.] United States Chess Federation; Junior Chamber of Commerce; American Friends Service Committee; [hon.] Medal for Moritorous Achievement (U.S. Navy Medal for Outstanding Service); Two Good Conduct Medals; Rand McNally's Who's Who in America 1977; Sixth place in State Chess tourney, Ohio 1976; Dean's List, Cleary 1990, Sinclair 1992; [oth. writ.] Poem, All I See Are Lifeless Eyes (published American Friends Yearbook 1992); (Poem) Christmas without Santa published Guidepost 1986; [pers.] I have always called myself a writer; sometimes it seems I experience life only as an observer in order to have something to write.; [a.] Kettering, OH

LAWSON, TABITHA ELAINE LEE
[Pen.] Elaine Lee; [b.] May 26, 1977, San Diego, CA; [p.] Everett and Ila Lawson; [ed.] Anderson Valley High School; [memb.] GSE, CSF, Project for Youth.; [hon.] Gold Honor Roll for 12 quarters so far in High school. Captain of our Cheerleading Squad; [pers.] I took for goodness in others, and someday I hope everyone will see what I see and stop the hate. I hope my poetry gives someone as much happiness as it gave me.; [a.] Boonville, CA

LAYMAN, MARION EARL
[Pen.] M. Earl Layman; [b.] September 16, 1908, Marion, OH; [p.] G. B. and Amy O. Layman; [m.] Freda R. Layman, March 25, 1928; [ch.] Richard and Janise Layman of Crestline; Wanda and Robert Paul of Temecula; and J. Eddie Layman of Murrieta; 14 grandchildren; 15 great-grandchildren and three great-great grandchildren; [ed.] Three years of High School; Thirty years Des Moines University of Lawsonomy; [occ.] Retired; [memb.] Direct Credits Society; [hon.] Knowlegian, a full scholar's degree in Lawsonomy the highest knowledge ever given to man having studied truth for a period of thirty years.; [oth. writ.] A collection of 25 poems; [pers.] Recently celebrated 65th wedding anniversary. Many years have been devoted to studying and teaching advanced economics, health and physics which contriubted to a good long life together.; [a.]Murrieta, CA

LAYTON, LUCY
[b.] May 25, 1933, Terre Haute, IN; [p.] Vernon and Marha Cox; [m.] Dean Layton, June 20, 1950; [ch.] Michael Duane, Jerry Edward, Dennis Ray, James Allen, Cynthia Lee, Janet Sue; [ed.] Concannon High School; [occ.] Secretary and Bookkeeper; [memb.] Patton United Methodist Church, Patton Ladies Missionary Society Conservator of Music Organ Club; [pers.] I have always enjoyed peotry of all kinds, and have written several. But never seriously until just recently. I consider it an honor to have my entry chosen for your anthology and look forward to receiving my copy. Thank you.; [a.] West Terre Haute, IN

LEA, MARTHA GWALTNEY
[b.] December 8, 1959, Jonesboro, AR; [p.] Carl and Louise Gwaltney; [m.] Eddie D. Lea, November 5, 1981; [ch.] Elizabeth Louise; [ed.] Jonesboro High; Arkansas State University; [occ.] Data Processor/Bookkeeper; [a.] Jonesboro, AR

LEADBETTER, KAREN
[b.] January 1, 1964, Lutesville, MD; [p.] Raymond Leadbetter and Helen Scholz; [ch.] Yvonne Mae Leadbetter and Lula Marie Welch; [occ.] Certified Medication technician at Bond Nursing Care Center; [oth. writ.] Several poems shared with my family and friends; [pers.] All my poems come from the heart through past experiences.; [a.] Marble Hill, MD

LEARY, LEE EDWARD
[b.] November 14, 1933, Deberry, TX; [p.] Eddie and Nellie Leary; [m.] Pearlene Davis Leary, May 21, 1967; [ch.] eric L. Leary (son), Dawn D. Leary (Daughter); [ed.] Booker T. Washington High Grad., BA English, Minor Art & Bible, B.D. Seminary, Elementary Teaching Cred, MA Elementary ED; [occ.] Academic Teacher in local jail, San Rafael, CA; [memb.] Teacher's Union, MCEA, NEA Marin County Ed. Assoc., National Ed. Assoc., First Baptist Church, Novato; [hon.] Teacher of the Year 1980, Sn Quentin Prison; Honorable Mention-Editorial Cartoon Contest in a local paper. Selected as unsung hero by local TV sttion for my wrok in jail as teacher; [oth. writ.] Never submitted anything for publication befoe, but have written other pieces.; [pers.] The essays of Emerson and the "Prophet" by Gibran were influential in terms of my writing as well my philosophy of life.; [a.] Novato, CA

LECLARI, KAREN
[b.] September 29, 1979, Plattsburgh, NY; [p.] Chrles and Sandra LeClair; [ed.] Going in 9th grade on September 7, 1994 in Peru High school; [occ.] Scholar, Figure Skater; [memb.] The Nature Conservancy, Adopt a Whate, United States Figure Skating Association.; [hon.] Two time Presidential Award, Outstanding evaluations for flute and piano in the New York State School Music Association (NYSSMA) High Honor Roll; [pers.] I'm currently training for the 1998 Winter Olympic Games. I will participate in ice dancing.; [a.] Plattsburgh, NY

LEDSINGER, BARBARA LYNNE
[b.] November 1, 1969, Baltimore, MD; [p.] Robert and Martha Ledsinger; [m.] Engaged June 20, 1994; [ed.] Patapsco High School, Dundalk Community College, Single Step Program; [occ.] Waitress, Stacey's Buffet, Essex; [memb.] Patapsco United Methodist Church, Chancel Choir; [hon.] Cert. of Achievement and Service Award, Patapsco High School Cert. of Attendance and Cert. of Merit (Vocal Music) Patapsco H.S., Cert. of Appreciation and Cert. of Outstanding Volunteer Service Eastpoint Nursing Home; [oth. writ.] Two poems published in high school yearbook. Other poems and song lyrics. Working on other poems at this time.; [pers.] Writing poetry, song lyrics and singing are my way of expressing myself, so I put all my heart and soul into them. I enjoy the pleasure that they give to me and others.; [a.] Baltimore, MD

LEE, CHRISTOPHER
[b.] May 6, 1970, Riverside, CA; [pers.] The worst days of my life have turned out to be some of the best poems I have written.; [a.] Grand Terrace, CA

LEEDER, MELISSA
[Pen.] Missy Leider; [b.] March 5, 1978, Salinas, CA; [p.] Warren and Wanda Leeder; [ed.] Brittan Middle School, Starting Live Oak High School; [oth. writ.] I have written songs, several poems, and short stories.; [pers.] I believe you should write with you heart, mind, and soul, and never stop, that's what keeps me going.; [a.] Morgan Hill, CA

LEES, MARILYN
[b.] July 21, 1933, Chicago, IL; [p.] Alice & Glenn Patterson; [ch.] Skye McLaughlin; [ed.] B.S. University of Oregon, M.P.A. California State University, Fullerton; [occ.] Government Analyst; [memb.] National Writers Club, Friends of the Performing Arts Center, Assn. of Contingency Planners, delta Zeta, Phi Beta; [hon.] 1994/5 Who's Who Worldwide, Business Leaders; Nat'l Fed. Newswomen, 1st Place, Broadcast Script Documentary; Los Angeles Advertising Women, 1st Place, Radio Spot Announcement; [oth. writ.] "Money Helps But People Power Counts," California's Health (Magazine); News Scripts for CBS (KCBS, San Francisco and WBBM, Chicago); "Miriam," dramatization of Truman Capote Short Story, KQAX-PBS; "Whose Deal?", Minds Hadows Magazine; [pers.] Verum Factum, influenced by journalist authors such as Joan Didion, Gay Talese; [a.] Santa Ana, CA

LEFFINGWELL, LEONARD R.
[Pen.] Lee "Leto" Leffingwell; [b.] May 11, 1967, Dover, NJ; [p.] Harold and Nancy Leffingwell; [ed.] Sacred Heart Elementary Catholic School, Rockaway, NJ, Morris Knolls high School, Denville, NJ; [occ.] Quality Control Inspector, Supervisor, American Panel Corp. Ocala, FL; [memb.] Fraternal Order of Police, Florida-State Lodge; [oth. writ.] poems published in various newspapers in the United States.; [pers.] Sharing my poems with other people it's the greatest feeling in the world.; [a.] Ocala, FL

LEIGHTON, RICHARD H.
[b.] Eastport, ME; [p.] Frank E. and Alberta M. Leighton; [m.] Sheila D. Leighton, September 6, 1958; [ch.] Terri-Jeanny, Richard H. Jr., Nanci-Ellen and Frank E.; [ed.] B.S. Bus. Management and M.B.A University of Hartford (B.S. 59'; M.B.A. 69'); [occ.] Marketing Consultant; [memb.] International Society of Poets (Life-Time Mebership). American Legion; [hon.] Elected to Who's Who In American College and Universities 1959. Dean's List Student. Editor's Choice Award, National Library of Poetry; [oth. writ.] The Door; Silency; The River; My Glass Has Run; I Will Lead You; The Calling of the Sea; The Sign; The Seythe Man; The Stone; The Fiddler; Man's Struggle; Birth, Death, and Rebirth; all unpublished excepte "The Door" which was published in "Tears of Fire."; [pers.] Life is a marvelous journey to be appreciated. The infusion of nature both for its beauty and for its hostility, is depicted in my poetry. Man-made edifices pale when compared to the natural world around us.; [a.] Guildford, CT

LEUDEMAN, PATRICIA G.
[Pen.] Steel Rose; [b.] February 20, 1972, St. John Lands, Kings Poet, NY; [p.] Audrey and Bernie Leudeman; [ed.] Centereach High School, Boces T.V. Production Class,; [occ.] Estee Lauder Assembler; [memb.] St. Margrets of Scotland Folk Group Member. Backstage with Bon Jovi Fan Club Member.; [hon.] P.T.A. Award, Lori Brosem-Lynn McManus Scholarship, Catholic Daughters of America Scholarship; [oth. writ.] I also write Christain type lyrics. I have been greatly influenced by the Christain Rock Band Stryper. I want to dedicate my heart, soul and life to Jesus through music.; [pers.] In my heart I believe everyone's dreams can come true. God hears the whispers of every dreamer's prayer. You must just keep the faith.; [a.] Selden, NY

LEVINE, BARBARA
[b.] May 21, 1947, Bronx, NY; [p.] Sylvia and Robert Lawner; [m.] Michael Levine, December 14, 1968; [ch.] Jayson Darryl Levine, Marnie Danielle Levine; [ed.] 2 yrs. Queens College; [occ.] Office Manager; [oth. writ.] Everything Nice, A Book of Children's Poetry, Numerous Poems; [pers.] A friend is a blessing, a companion, God's gift for the weary and all the inspiration one needs.; [a.] Plainview, NY

LEWIEL, ROXANN
[Pen.] Asher; [b.] December 1, 1942, New Orleans; [p.] Alphese and Winfield Phillips; [m.] George W. Lewiel Sr., September 14, 1963; [ch.] George W. Lewiel Jr., Sheila Marie Lewiel, Grandaughter Jasmin Simone Lewiel-Lee; [ed.] Five years of college through Army, during our 23 yrs. of active duty. Computer Spl. in Budget Dept.; [occ.] Foster Mother to 200 young people in Community with great multi-cultue; [memb.] With O.E.S. Assoc. Matron Safe House for abused children. bible Study and Prayer partner to senior's without families.; [hon.] Given to me from God first and awards of love from all the children whom he has sent my way in the last 20 years.; [oth. writ.] A poem of love sent to recording company. Many others unpublished. Many pieces of painting and sketches unpublished.; [pers.] When walking the road of life learn to love yourself, so that you can love others as God loves us all.; [a.] San Francisco, CA

LEWIS, JEANNIE
[Pen.] Jeannie Marie; [b.] May 16, 1945, Binghamton, NY; [p.] Wm. and Gladys Lewis; [ed.] Largo High; [occ.] Housekeeper, Moody Keswick; [memb.] LINKS Secretary, Pinellas Park First Church of the Nazarene; [hon.] Distinguished Service Award (from my church missionary society N.W.M.S.; [oth. writ.] Several poems published in church bulletin.; [pers.] With the Lord's help and guidance anything is possible.; [a.] St. Petersburg, FL

LIMERICK, KELLY CELESTE
[Pen.] Kelli Limerick; [b.] January 25, 1981, Dallas; [p.] Stan and Darlene Limerick; [ed.] Vaughan Elem., Ford Middle School of Allen, TX; [pers.] I have been greatly influenced by my friends and peers. they are everything to me.; [a.] Allen, TX

LINARES PH.D., NELLY
[b.] Havana, Cuba; [p.] B.A. English and Foreign Languages, M.S. Administrtion and Supervision, M.S. Counseling/Psychology, Ph.D. Counseling Psychology; [occ.] Educator; [memb.] Academy of American Poets, International Society of Poets.; [hon.] Several of my poems have been published in local newspapers.; [oth. writ.] Poetry book in spanish, titled "Noches de Vigilia" published in Miami, FL in 1993.; [pers.] My poetry blossoms from the innermost of my soul.; [a.] Hialeah, FL

LINDBERG, BONNIE
[b.] July 28, 1949, Mpls; [p.] Russell and Elayne; [ed.] University of Minn.; [occ.] Owner of Elayne Galleries, Fine Art Appraiser, Handwriting Expert; [hon.] Decor Award of Excellence, 1989; [pers.] Life experiences arouse feelings that give birth to my words.

LINDBERG, RUSSELL H.
[b.] February 7, 1921, Mpls., MN; [p.] Harry and Victoria Lindberg; [m.] Elayne V. Lindbert, July 26, 1942; [ch.] Gary R. Lindbert and Bonnie E. Lindberg; [ed.] High School, Everything I have accomplished as musician, majician, songwriter and poet, has been self-taught.; [occ.] Co-owner of Elayne Galleries, Inc. for 25 yrs.; [memb.] Retired member of Mpls. Musician's Union, Retired Member of Mpls. Majicians Ring; [hon.] Won 1st place in songwriters contest, arranged for full orchestra and presented on TV; [oth. writ.] Many of my songs have been published by Benson Music Publishing in Nashvile and have been sung and recorded by noted Gospel Singers across the country; [pers.] The 52 year love affair Elayne and I have experienced has been the perfect sounding board for my songs and poetry.; [a.] Minneapolis, MN

LINEN, DELORES
[Pen.] Lauria; [b.] May 18, 1959, New Berlin, NY; [p.] Nevada Hardy Spratt; [m.] Herbert L. Linen, December 9, 1978; [ch.] Arrinita Octavia, Adri Anne, Angienique, LaRonn Maurice; [ed.] Proctor High; Mohawk Beauty Culture School, Career Development Center; [occ.] Day Care Provider; [pers.] Inspired by my lovely granddaughters, Imonie LaVese ShaQueen Linen, Shativa Janay Linen; [a.] Utica, NY

LINNE, JENNIFER
[b.] August 18, 1978, Columbus, OH; [p.] Jim and Pauline Linne; [pers.] My favorite motto is to live by is: All things come to him who waits, provided he knows what he is waiting for. Woodrow Wilson; [a.] Harrison, OH

LIPARTITO, KRISTINE E.
[Pen.] Kris; [b.] January 5, 1966, Clovis, NM; [p.] Ronald and Shirley Crooker; [m.] Michael Lipartito, November 9, 1985; [ch.] John, Emily and Henry; [ed.] High School, some liberal arts college; [occ.] Homemaker; [memb.] National Multiple Sclerosis Society; [oth. writ.] Numerous, unpublished poems; [pers.] Happiness is a choice.; [a.] Atco, NJ

LISSETTE, ALMANZAR
[b.] August 13, 1976, Manhattan; [pers.] From birth we're embraced with chaos and curiosity, then we grow up believing that we are civilized but deep inside there's a beast hidden with us and only in certain stages of our life the passion is overwhelmed and the beast is freed providing either good or evil.

LLOYD, PETULA RENEE
[b.] September 20, 1968, Wilmn, DE; [p.] Thelma Amanda Weatherly; [ch.] Amber LaRae Lloyd; [ed.] Utica College of Syracuse University, Utica, NY; [occ.] Reporter, Observer Dispatch, Utica, NY; [memb.] Black Heritage Committee, Griffiss Air

Force Base Chapter. Affiliated with Kappa Alpha Psi Fraternity; [oth. writ.] Two poems published in another anthology.; [pers.] My poetry reflects what I'm feeling, about myself or someone else, at the time I think it's a taste of reality and fantasy; [a.] Rome, NY

LOCKE, JUDITH VIOLA
[Pen.] Viola Matura; [b.] December 4, 1973, Belize, CA; [p.] Judith Gullap and Nurvin R. Locke; [ed.] Audubon Jr. High, Susan Miller Darsey High School; [occ.] Pre-Med Student, Mount St. Mary's College, L.A., CA; [memb.] Pi Theta Mu; [hon.] Audubon Penguine, Presidential Academic Fitness Award, UCLA Partnership Program, Bank of America Achievement Award in Science and Math. Graduate in tope 2% of class; [pers.] I try to reflect the present condition of the world in my writing.; [a.] Los Angeles, CA

LOCKETT, CHAUNCE OMAR
[b.] September 23, 1976, LaPorte, IN; [p.] Leo and Bobbie Luckett; [ed.] In the graduating class of 1995.; [occ.] Student (Senior) LaPorte High School; [memb.] Entertainment Weekly, Premiere Magazine, Art Club (LaPorte High School); [hon.] For perfect attendance and most improved; an award for Drug Free and Proud Week; [oth. writ.] My some-day poem published in our school magazine (Reflections) Poems: Without You, No Fear, "1989", Lost Forever.; [pers.] I want to reflect on the world today, because it seems I must escape reality in order to help others reflect on themselves.; [a.] LaPorte, IN

LOCKWOOD, HEATHER MARIE
[b.] May 5, 1972, Washington, DC; [ed.] College Student; [occ.] Student; [oth. writ.] Book entitled: Beyond the Pain" which has been distributed to mental health care centers across CT; [hon.] I am an incest survivor. Through writing I have found my passage to inner peace and strength. It has helped me to bread down the barriers of silence and denial. My goal is to let other survivors know that they too can heal from the devastating effects of incest.

LOFRANO, CARMELLA
[b.] October 15, 1947, Chicago; [p.] Anthony and Margarita Lofrano; [ch.] Kamie Lynn Plys; [ed.] B.A. Theology 1983, Elmhurst College, Illinois; M.Div. Eden Theological Seminary, St. Louis, MO, 1987.; [occ.] Ordained Minister, United Church of Christ under the name of Reverened Carmella E. Braico, Disabled; [hon.] Lincoln Scholar/Senior Laureate Class of '83; Who's Who in American Colleges and Universities '87; Phi Kappa Phi; Omicron Delta Kappa; [pers.] Writing is more than a tool or craft for me. It is my "life blood." My poetry and short stories are bits and pieces of me. I find it difficult to part with them.; [a.] Thornton, IL

LOFTUS, AMY L.
[b.] May 10, 1980, New York; [p.] Anthony & Patricia; [m.] not married; [ch.] none; [ed.] High School Sophmore; [occ.] Student; [memb.] Ice Skating, Institute of America; [hon.] School Service, Presidential Academic Fitness Award, Woodlawn Merchants Association Award for Community Service (Bond), First Place Murrays Ice Skating Compeittion; [oth. writ.] Several poems published in Church and local newspaper; [pers.] My poetry is a means for me to relase my deepest emotions and fantasys.; [a.] Bronx, NY

LOGAN, DAVID
[b.] March 20, 1981, USA; [p.] Bozena, John Logan; [occ.] Student, Sacred Heart; [a.] New Britain, CT

LOGANS, ROY JACK
[Pen.] Jackie L.; [b.] February 18, 1958, Ft. Worth, Tx; [p.] Jack and Nancy Logans; [m.] Mary E. Logans, October 17, 1974; [ch.] Roy Jack, Nancy Charlone and David Allen; [ed.] Lake Worth High; [occ.] Construction Worker; [memb.] North American Fishing Club B.A.S.S. Classis Member; [pers.] I write from the heart, and don't worry about things I have no control over.; [a.] Ft. Worth, TX

LONG, PATSY L.
[b.] January 3, 1957, Spartanburg, SC; [p.] (Late) Katie Long and Wright Long Jr.; [ch.] Two sons, Nicholas and Michael Long; [ed.] Associate Degree in nursing, studied USC (Columbia) and U.S.C. Spartanburg, Pursuing Degree Criminal Justice at U.S.C. Spartanburg; [occ.] Registered nurse at Mary black Hospital; [memb.] Former member Mock Trial based at U.S.C. Spartanburg; [hon.] Was a member of mock trial and part of 1st year team awarded best new team award at competition in Milwaukee, Wisconsin 1993; [oth. writ.] No, this poem was at U.S.C. Columbia in a creative wiring class, because of personal problems I never pursued publication through I was encouraged by a very caring professor.; [pers.] "Believe" in yourself even when others don't because God brings help along the way and he won't let you down.; [a.] Spartanburg, SC

LOPOPOLO, SOHEILA
[Pen.] So So; [b.] May 16, 1983; Oakland, CA; [p.] Anastasia; [ed.] Entering 6th grade Intensive Studies Program in Cambridge Public School District; [occ.] Student; [hon.] Basketball; Honorable Mention Cambridge Dept. of Dramatic Arts, 1994 Playwriting Festival; 3 Jujitsu Awards; [oth. writ.] "A problem in the U.S., Child Abuse" a play co-authored; [pers.] I really enjoy writing. When I grow up I want to be writer or a poet. Poetry helps me express my feelings.; [a.] Cambridge, MA

LOVE, KEVIN W.
[b.] March 4, 1976, Prescott, AZ; [p.] Ron and Jan Crone; [ed.] Pursuing a college education in architecture at UNLV; [occ.] Draftsman; [memb.] Vocational Industrial Clubs of America (V.I.C.A.); [oth. writ.] Miscelaneous other personal poems; [pers.] Live tour life knowing that you will have to face the effects of your decisions tomorrow and the rest of your life. Follow the Lord!; [a.] Lake Havasu City, AZ

LOWERY, IRMA CATHERINE
[Pen.] Cathy; [b.] May 25, 1942, Peterman, Alabama; [p.] George Lee and Fay Chandler; [m.] Paul Lowery, April 17, 1987; [ch.] Angie Baggett, Mellony Nelson (4 grandchildren); [ed.] Monroe County High; [occ.] Poultry Producer and Homemaker; [memb.] Ella Wall Research Club; [oth. writ.] Poem published in "Edge of Twilight", a poem in honor of my Grandparents published in Philen Family News.; [pers.] I write poetry for my family and friends and as a relaxing pastime. My love of nature and my rural homeplace has inspired most of my poetry.; [a.] Forest Home, AL

LOWMAN, NANCY
[b.] July 19, 1977, West Columbia, South Carolina; [p.] Danny and Linda Lowman; [ed.] Richland Northeast High School Class of 1994; [hon.] Journalism Excellence Award, Presidential Academic Award; [oth. writ.] Writer on the Cavalier, Newspaper Staff, in 1991, had poem published in the Nat'l Library of Congress Windows on the World. Several poems published in anthology for Summit Parkway.; [a.] Columbia, SC

LOWRIE, YOLANDA
[b.] July 5, 1977, Philadelphia; [p.] Genevieve Poland; [ed.] Completed grades one through eleven; [occ.] Crew trainer at McDonalds; [memb.] none; [hon.] First and second honors consistantly throughout school; [oth. writ.] A book of 58 poems which range from romantic to humerous to serious; [pers.] A thought from the mind is not hard to find. Search your mind far and beyond., [a.] Philadelphia, PA

LOY, JENNIFER
[b.] December 7, 1971, Bellflower, CA; [p.] Eloise Garner, Michael Schermerhorn; [m.] Brett Loy, July 20, 1988; [ch.] Mark Alan Loy; [ed.] Marina High, Coastline Community College and Goldenwest College; [occ.] Receptionist at a Travel Agency; [memb.] A member of the Church of Jesus Christ of Latter Day Saints.; [oth. writ.] I have many other poems about nature, spiritual beliefs, Romance, and everday life. My goal is to someday have them published in a book.; [pers.] I believe that people have no limits to heights they can achieve, that acocmplishments can be reached, and that dreams can be a reality.; [a.] Westminster, CA

LUCERO, TONY
[b.] September 12, 1966, St. Paul Minnesota; [p.] Lou Lucero, Kathy Finn; [ed.] Alief Hastings High, Houston, TX and Community College of the Air Force.; [occ.] Marketing Director, the Racquet Club of Irvine, Irvine, CA; [hon.] United States Air Force 84-91, Honorable Discharge; [oth. writ.] I have compiled over 50 poems which have not been published.; [pers.] I view all the good in everyone and everything. My poems reflect all the beauty we all sometimes fail to apprecite and the majic of relationships.; [a.] Irvine, CA

LUMINAIS, JORDAN
[Pen.] Rusty Metal; [b.] May 10, 1978, LA; [p.] Jeff and Mary Ann; [ch.] Someday, When I'm older; [ed.] Bonnabel High, going to college; [occ.] Student, working with gifted children; [memb.] Various Committees for saving wildlife.; [oth. writ.] Nothing published, but I've got 8ft. piles of stories, poems, etc.; [pers.] It's great to be published, but I'm not quite ready to take life seriously yet. Thanks to everyone..for everything.; [a.] Kenner, LA

LUTHER, REBEKAH STILES
[b.] July 20, 1960, Muskogee, OK; [p.] Boyd and Myrlita Stiles; [m.] E.E. "Marty" Luther, M.D., May 25, 1985; [ch.] Clifton and Katharin; [ed.] Currently attending Northeast Louisiana University; [occ.] Mother, Author, Student; [memb.] National Authors Registry, Poets Guild; [hon.] Honorable Mention for poem "You Make My Day" by Iliad Press, The National Authors Registry; [oth. writ.] "The Yoda Family" a childrens book published 1994 by Dorrance Publishing. Special moments, poetry published in 1994, perspective anthology by The Poets' Guild.; [pers.] Poetry is the window to my soul.; [a.] Monroe,

LA

LUTTRELL, BETH
[b.] April 10, 1974, Monterey, CA; [p.] Jim and Gini Luttrell; [ed.] Santa Catalina High School, Gonzaga University; [occ.] Studetn; [memb.] American Horse Show Association, Gonzaga University, Theater Sports; [hon.] Dean's List; [oth. writ.] Published in the Poetry Shell of Monterey, CA; [pers.] Everyone needs at least one good, strong hug a day.; [a.] Spokane, WA

LUTTRELL, CRYSTAL
[b.] July 22, 1978, Des Moines, IA; [p.] Hugh and Mary Luttrell; [ed.] Roosevelt High School; [occ.] High School Student; [hon.] High School Achievement Award for Academics; [pers.] This is my first real attempt at writing poetry, I hope there wil be many more.; [a.] Des Moines, IA

LUTZE, MARIE
[Pen.] Misty; [pers.] Poets, as you know are private people. I wish to remain so. My parents both of German Decent, migrated to American the Years 1922. I found their rainbow hue. Raised 5 children, today the third generation of the family tree are still coming over. Lady Liberty, may you always welcome them.; [a.] Fishlvill, NY

LYCZKOWSKI, BARBARA
[b.] June 17, 1977, Raleigh, NC; [p.] Leon and Ann Lyczkowski; [ed.] Friendship Christian School; [memb.] World Wildlife Fund member, member of the Save the Manatees Club; [hon.] National Honor Society, American Christian Honors Society, the President's Honor Society of Friendship Christian School; [pers.] Ralph Waldo Emerson said "What lies behind us and what lies before us are small matters compared to what lies within us." I always try to remember this.; [a.] Raleigh, NC

LYNCH, BEATRICE G.
[Pen.] Betty Lynch; [b.] August 5, 1925, New Jersey; [p.] Kathryn and James Gunn; [m.] Marion Joseph Lynch, January 15, 1949; [ch.] Three, Betty, Dorothy, Donald; [ed.] Hackensack High School Graduate 43', Hackensack Hospital School of Nursing, Registered Nurse, Graduate 1946, N.Y.C.C. Pre Nursing course 1943, Hunter College N.Y., Some Classes 1947-48; [occ.] Partner of Dental Supply and Equipment Company, Atlanta, GA, 40 yrs.; [memb.] N.C.C.W., A.A.C.C.W, Knights of Columbus Auxiliary #4357; [hon.] St. Oliver Plunkett "Women of the Year" 1993; [oth. writ.] Many for many years, nothing published.; [pers.] Love the Lord and you will have his peace and joy.

LYNN, CRANKLIN
[Pen.] Daniel Lynn; [b.] November 10, 1932, Florida; [p.] Albert and Clara Lynn; [m.] Deceased December 20, 1986; [ed.] 8th; [occ.] Retired; [memb.] Masonic Lodge; [hon.] 32nd Degree Mason, 40 years 8 mos. and 8 days at the same place of employement; [oth. writ.] short stories; [pers.] I spend my winters in Floria and I retired at age 59 1/2, had a home built in Florida on 5 acres in the country and enjoy being away from crowds and I do lots of fishing in the Gulf.; [a.] Kalamazoo, MI

MAAHS, SELISA DANA
[Pen.] Rebecca Brackenmore; [b.] July 3, 1970, Hawaii; [p.] Ken and Grace Maahs; [m.] James Raef II, Fiance; [ch.] Charles Raef II; [ed.] West Anchorage High School; [occ.] Homemaker and Apartment Manager of Midval Apt.; [hon.] Silver and Gold Poetry Award from the National Poetry Society. Editors Choice award from the Naitonal Library of Poetry in 1994 book release Dances on the Horizon; [oth. writ.] Memeories, published in poems of the Great Western World, Last Words published in Dance on the Horizon, A Legend Told, in the process of being published; [pers.] I strive to encourage imagination and hope that anything you dream is possible. For anyone can tell its not true but ones imagination and dreams is what creats the future to come.; [a.] Los Angels, CA

MAAS, PAUL H.D.
[b.] November 20, 1972, Illinois; [p.] Paul and Marie Maas; [ed.] Pennville High School; [occ.] Rotomold technition Castex Inc., Holland, Mich.; [pers.] I believe you should always be yourself. If you think you re, who others think you are, you will never be who you really are.; [a.] Fennville, MI

MAAS, TOMMA LOU
[b.] February 1, 1944, Pleasentville, IA; [p.] Tommy L. and Mary M. Jordan; [m.] Randall A. Maas, March 16, 1968; [ed.] Franklin Center School, Pleasantville High School, State University of Iowa, University of Northern Iowa; [occ.] Writer; [memb.] National League of American Pen Women, Iowa Academy of Science, The Academy of American Poets; [oth. writ.] Toy Framer and other toy collectors magazines.; [pers.] Growin gup in Iowa has inspired me to write about this beautiful land and its people; I teach children to write formal poetry from the "music within" themselves.; [a.] Cedar Falls, IA

MAC KENZIE, K. F.
[Pen.] Emel Mack; [b.] January 4, 1926, Everett, MA; [p.] John and Margaret Mac Kenzie; [m.] Margaret L. Mac Kenzie, September 8, 1945; [ch.] Michael and Michele; [a.] McLain, MS

MACALTAO, ROSALIE DELPUERTO
[Pen.] Francesca Moulin; [b.] July 15, 1944, Philippines; [p.] Isabel del Puerto and Eulogio Macaltao; [ch.] Isabelle Maoaltao El-Chami; [ed.] Bachelor of Fine Arts, University of St. Thomas, Philippines.; [occ.] Unemployed; [oth. writ.] I have been writing poems for a short period of time and I hope to continue writing poetry.; [pers.] Let the world of literature be known to you so that you may appreciate what if offers.; [pers.] Calton, CA

MACISAAC, MARY T.
[b.] October 29, 1910, Boston, MA; [p.] Cath. Livingston and Edw. T. Mullen; [m.] Deceased, 2nd marriage August 17, 1940; [ch.] David, John L. and Ann Marie; [ed.] High School, 2 yrs. Bentley, College, Boston; [occ.] Retired; [memb.] Too numerous to mention from 1951 to present time, Girl Scouts, P.T.A., Boy Scouts, Etc.; [hon.] Youth Service Committee, The National Conference of Christians and Jews, President, Somerville Y.M.C.A., 1978, V.P. The Somerville Home 1993, Director and Founder, Somerville Mental Health Assoc. 1964-1989. My children are my honors.; [pers.] "How far a little candle throws its' beam so shines a good deed upon a naughty world" (with apologies to Wm. Shakespear); [a.] Somerville, MA

MACKERER, SHAUNA CATHERINE
[b.] November 27, 1974, Cincinatti, OH; [p.] Robert and Bunny Mackerer; [ed.] Longmeadow High School, one year Westfield State College; [occ.] Model and Student in New York City; [memb.] Fiest Church of Christ Longmeadow, Mass.; [oth. writ.] Several poems published in my college paper, The Owl.; [pers.] Life is to short to wait for tomorrow so fullfill your dreams today.; [a.] New York, NY

MACMASTER, CHRISTINE MARIE
[Pen.] Lauren MacLellan; [b.] January 7, 1983; Toronto, Can; [p.] Allen Ho and Heather MacMaster; [ed.] Gwynedd Mercy Academy; [hon.] 1st place, grade 5 English and Reading Olypiad; [oth. writ.] A poem called "The Flea" in a book.; [a.] Blue Bell, PA

MADEWELL SR., ROBERT ALLEN
[Pen.] RAM; [b.] May 27, 1994, Huntsville; [p.] Helen Bailey and Clyde Madewell; [m.] Christina L. Madewell, October 4, 1993; [ch.] One, Robert Allen Madewell Jr.; [ed.] 5 years of elementary, 3 years of Junior High, 4 years of High School. A.P. Brewer High School Class of 89; [occ.] Heat-Treat Oven Oper. at Cayne Cylinder, Huntsville; [memb.] NA, AA, CA; [oth. writ.] I've wrote other poems for a hobby but I've never sent any of them anywhere.; [pers.] Time with the eyes on the innerchild is the only way that growing pains will not be a shadow of itself.; [a.] Hartselle, AL

MADISON, EVELYN JOY
[Pen.] Joy Madison; [b.] July 17, 1966, Indiana; [p.] Bennie and Wilma Stromatt; [m.] Bryan Scott Madison, January 14, 1984; [ch.] Crystal Lynn Madison, Lisa Marie Madison; [occ.] Housewife; [pers.] this poem was written for my children Crystal and Lisa without the love and support of my husband Bryan and my children and my parents Bennie and Wilma Stromatt. I wouldn't of had the strength to push forward.; [a.] Lake Village, IN

MAHER, GRACE
[b.] March 10, 1982, Georgia; [p.] Beau Bock and Donna Maher; [ed.] Entering 7th grade at Ridgeview Middle School; [occ.] student; [hon.] Honorable Mention Winner in Georgia State Poetry Society (poem: "A New Way for Santa to Travel") member of Fulton County Honor Chorus; [oth. writ.] "Halloween is Coming" was published in Atl. Journal-Constitution. Poems: Autumn Leaves; Cats; I'm a Pencil; Why; What Am I; Smoke; I'm a Doll; Make a Dream; Help; [a.] Atlanta, GA

MAHER, KATHLEEN
[Pen.] Kat, Kathy Maher; [b.] october 19, 1966, Patchogue, NY; [p.] Margaret and Robert David; [m.] Paul Hugelmeyer, August 15, 1992; [ed.] Sachem High School, South Hampton Col.; [occ.] Free Lance artist; [memb.] Greenpeace, City Art Gallery; [oth. writ.] Children's Stories, poems; [pers.] If we all smile upon each other the world may one day be at peace.; [a.] Raleigh, NC

MAHMOOD, FAHMIDA
[b.] November 2, 1961, Karachi; [p.] Father, Ghau-Sal Hussain, Mother, Monowa Hussain; [m.] Iqbal Mahmood, June 20, 1982; [ch.] One daughter, Permeeta Mahmood; [ed.] Dong my 29 units on early childhood education teachers certificate. Studying in

Fullerton College; [occ.] Student; [hon.] Editor's Choice Award" for outstanding achievement in poetry presented by the National Library of Poetry 1994 which is for my contest entry published in "Dance on the Horizon."; [oth. writ.] My other poems are "The Funny Crystal World," "Life," "The Beuty Rose," "The Gift," "The Wild Thirst Summer," "The Dead Livings," "The Poor World," "Sunshine," "Image" etc.; [pers.] I strted my writings at the age of 15. It seems that pen is mightier than the sword, so poetry has great influence on mankind.; [a.] Corona, CA

MAJORANO, CHRISTINE
[Pen.] Chris; [b.] April 18, 1970, Upland, CA; [p.] Ronald and Louise Majorano; [ed.] Continuing Student, San Diego State University Communications Major; [occ.] With hopes to be an elementary school teacher; [pers.] Ever changing and passionate storytelling is a powerful way of communicating in poetry and in life.; [a.] San Diego, CA

MAKULA, MARY H.
[Pen.] Blue Star; [b.] October 16, 1941, Cleveland, OH; [p.] Helen and Walter Makula; [m.] Single; [ed.] Cuyahoga Community College, Metro Campus, Lincoln High; [occ.] Secretary.; [hon.] National Deans List, 1984; [pers.] Live every moment to the fullest; it is a fragile fleeting gift. I have been greatly influenced by my mom's example to love one another, unconditionally.; [a.] Cleveland, OH

MALONE, NEIL J.
[Pen.] Willie Malone (now); [b.] January 4, 1928, Chicago, IL; [occ.] None, retired at present; [pers.] Each day so rare, thanks be...

MANIAGO, ANNA LIZA L.
[Pen.] Lisa; [b.] July 22, 1968, Phillipines; [p.] Ruben T. and Lilian L. Maniago; [ch.] Sister: Ruby Lynne Maniago; [ed.] B.S. Psychology, St. Louis University, Phil.; [pers.] "The best way to find what you are looking for in life is to know what it is." Lisa; [a.] Rancho Sta Margarita, CA

MANIER, JACK F.
[Pen.] John F. Manier; [b.] June 6, 1924, Versailles, OH; [m.] Evelyn J. Mahier, February 24, 1948; [ch.] 3 sons and daughter in law, 9 grandchildren; [ed.] University of Dayton, OH, Princeton University, Versailles High School; [occ.] Retired NCR; [memb.] AFMC, Assoc. Fundamental, Ministers & Churches; [hon.] Won trip to Denmark 1953 with winning letter, "Why I would like to be a good will Ambassador to Denmark."; [oth. writ.] Several small books of poetry, also the Bible Class Prose account, Bible Calss; [pers.] Poet, Prophet, Patriarch, my titles and goals.; [a.] Dayton, OH

MANN, CHARLES J.
[Pen.] Chas; [b.] February 17, 1924, Niagara Falls, NY; [p.] Charles and Ida Perry Mann; [ed.] B.A. Antioch College, Yellow Springs, OH; [occ.] Retired work in Gourmet Food Shop; [memb.] American Legion (Veteran of Occupation of Japan 1946-48); [hon.] Best Chile (United Naitons Chili) "I survived the winter party," Dan's Papers, Bridge Hampton, L.I. NY; [oth. writ.] "Pedigree Poems and other Gonealog"; Pedigree Cookbook" unpublished; Satirical Pieces, Public Access TV Scripts, May Reading; [pers.] I do not let small minds unduly influence me.; [a.] Sag Harbor, L.I., NY

MANZO, JACQUELINE
[b.] August 24, 1979, Joliet, IL; [p.] Maria E. Manzo; [ed.] Gompers Junior High, Joliet Township High school, Central Campus; [occ.] Student, Teachers Aid at a Daycare Center.; [hon.] Winter program at Illinois Mathematics and Science Academy (IMSA), Assistant Principal's Award, President of Secondary Annual Young Writer's Celebration.; [oth. writ.] Many poems but not have been published, except one in the school newspaper.; [a.] Joliet, IL

MARCANTEL, TANNER
[b.] September 7, 1979, Lake Charles, Louisiana; [p.] David and Pam Marcantel; [ed.] Sophmore at McKinley Senior High School; [occ.] Student; [memb.] National Beta Club, National Thespains, Hi-Y, French Club; [hon.] Second place in French for District Rally, second place in school for the National Mathematics League, Scholastic Honors 3.5+; [a.] Baton Rouge, LA

MARINO, CHERYL
[b.] May 15, 1981, Westwood, NJ; [p.] Debra and Angelo Marino; [ed.] Norwood Public School, Norwood, NJ; [occ.] Student; [hon.] Honor Roll, A's & B's all four marking periods, 8 times, student of the month several times.; [oth. writ.] One other poem published in "Dance on the Horizon."; [pers.] I like to write about anything that's bothering me or that means a lot to me.; [a.] Norwood, NJ

MARKS, ALLAN
[Pen.] Merritt; [b.] April 8, 1956, Brooklyn, NY; [occ.] Chauffeur; [oth. writ.] This is my first published poem.; [pers.] My occupation has afforded me the opportunity to meet many different people from all over the world. I am left with the impression tht the world is an amazing place, and that to each person, a special gift is given. I also extend this view to the natural elements around us. We can find inspiration from even the tiniest of objects. Perhaps they can represent something greater.; [a.] New York, NY

MARLEY, CASEY
[b.] January 18, 1983, Marion; [p.] Roger, Lori Marley; [ed.] 6th grade student, Van Buren Elementary; [hon.] All Star Trophies from Girls Softball League; [oth. writ.] Several poems published in The Peanut Butter Press (a magazine out of Indianapolis) Also had one publsiehd in "The Naitonal Anthology Of Young American Poets."; [pers.] I would like to go to college and become a veternarian. I love to write poems and short stories. I also enjoy drawing.; [a.] Marion, IN

MAROTTA, DANIELLE
[b.] November 26, 1977, F.W.B., FL; [p.] Nick and Cheryl Marotta; [ed.] Still in high schoo; want to go to UCLA; [memb.] Choctawhatchee High School Colour Guard/Winter Guard; [hon.] Several academic awards; [oth. writ.] Several unpublished poems; [pers.] I like to express myself through art whether it be drawing or writing; inspired gretly by Jim Morrison; [a.] Ft. Walton Bch., FL

MARQUEZ, MARY LONGORIA
[b.] December 11, 1946, Aransas Pass, TX; [p.] Alex and Antonia G. Longoria; [m.] Milton M. Marquez, January 4, 1969; [ch.] Susan, Stephanie and Amanda Marquez; [ed.] Graduated from Aransas Pass High School, Del Mar College, L.V.N. School; [occ.] Licensed Nurse and Private duty Nurse; [hon.] Employee of the year at Coastal Berd Hospital in 1989, Editor's Choice Award, in Tears of Fire.; [oth. writ.] Poem in Tears of Fire. Loves Friendship.; [pers.] I wish to dedicate this poem to my family and friends, it is very important to appreciate our loved ones. It is through love and friendship where we acquire true happiness.; [a.] Aransas Pass, TX

MARR, JO ELLEN
[b.] March 24, 1951, Chkucothe, Ohio; [ed.] Zane Trace High, Ohio University, Athens, Ohio; [memb.] Ohio Head Injury Assc., President of Ohio Head Injury Survivor Council; [pers.] I am a severe head injury survivor, 95% rehabed.; [a.] Columbus, OH

MARRA, NICOLINA
[b.] June 15, 1978, Belleville, NJ; [p.] Marcello and Immacolata; [ed.] Junior in Nutley High School; [oth. writ.] Articles in school and local newspaper, 1st prize in two local poem contests, poem published in Cretive Kids magazine.; [pers.] No one is living life, but dying from it. Though, those little pleasures in dying almost make life worth living.; [a.] Nutley, NJ

MARSHALL, GWENDOLYN JENKINS
[b.] June 13, 1951, Detroit; [p.] Pete and Lizzie Jenkins; [ch.] Samuel F. Marshall, II; [ed.] Southeastern High School (Detroit), Oakland Univ., Rochester, MI, (BA) Wayne State Univ. (Det.) and Mich. st. Univ. (East Lansing, MI); [occ.] Customer Service for Mental Health Mgt. at Blue Cross and Blue Shield of MI (Det.); [memb.] Mt. Zion Miss. Bapt. Ch. Det., PAE (Personal Achievement Efforts) a entreprenural group I founded which helps people turn talents (crafts, art, Inventions, etc) into profit.; Pride in Excellence award at Blue Cross of Mich.; [oth. writ.] Poem published in Whisper's in the wind, entitled Dear Lord, a tribute to my late father.; [pers.] "Every" day is a new beginning, move on." In college I was told by a professor "where there's life there's hope. This is why I look forward and not behind.; [a.] Det., MI

MARSHALL, JOEY
[b.] September 1'4, 1978, Burleson, TX; [p.] John and Ronnie Marshall; [ed.] High School Student; [oth. writ.] Pain, Grandma, The thing that should not be, I love you dad, as sure as the day is long.; [pers.] I enjoy writing poems because it's a way for me to say how I feel about certain topics.; [a.] Crosby, TX

MARSHALL, KHRISTINA
[Pen.] Krissy; [b.] October 19, 1979, Rochester; [p.] Ellen and Tom Marshall; [occ.] Student; [oth. writ.] Two other pomes published in "A Question of Balance" and "Tears of Fire."; [a.] Rochester, NY

MARSHALL, MAURICE C.
[m.] Janette J. Marshall; [ed.] MBA, University of Chicago, 1953; [occ.] Semi Retired; [pers.] This sometime poet usually observes before pondering, thos may be described as a pragmatic philosopher or is that philosophic pragmatist; [a.] Okemos, MI

MARSHALL, MERADITH
[b.] June 1, 1981, Atlantic, IA; [p.] Michael Marshall; [oth. writ.] Me, Myself, and I, Love; [pers.] I like writing poems because they make me feel free.; [a.] Anita, IA

MARSHALL, RANDY L.
[b.] January 27, 1962, Texas City, TX; [p.] Geroge and Vada Marshall; [m.] Sharon Marshall, October 10, 1987; [ch.] Candice and Heather Marshall; [ed.] High School Grad, 12th, Texas City High; [occ.] Information Mgmt. Specialist, State Dept. Washington, D.C.; [oth. writ.] Several other poems, not published by my choice.; [pers.] Words spoken only last for a brief moment in time. Words written transcend forever in the hearts and souls of mankind.; [a.] Falls Church, VA

MARTELLOTTI, MELISSA
[b.] November 2, 1979, New Jersey; [p.] Carlo and Nola Martellotti; [ed.] Currently a freshman at the St. Charles High school in IL,; [occ.] Freshman in High School; [hon.] Honor Rolls Student, Figure Skating Awards; [oth. writ.] The Midnight Hour; [a.] St. Charles, IL

MARTIN, DAWN
[b.] January 11, 1977, Morristown, NJ; [p.] Alan and Periann Fedor; [ed.] Morris Knoll's High Schoo; [oth. writ.] Several poems published in other assorted books and high school literary magazine.; [pers.] Kevin, my tears may stain but loving memories will alwys remain. Sorry, you'll always be a part of me. Sadie..; [a.] Denville, NJ

MARTIN, JEANNIE
[b.] June 29, 1969, Atlanta, GA; [p.] Sam Martin and Betty Martin; [ed.] Chamblee High School; [occ.] Childcare Giver; [memb.] none; [pers.] I write as a hobby. I write to express myself. I write to express other people as well. Thank you, for your love and encouragement.; [a.] Atlanta, GA

MARTIN, LISA
[b.] May 26, 1963, Clarksville, AK; [p.] Loy and Verladean Park; [m.] Jerry D. Martin; [ed.] B.A. Journalism and Bach Science in Elementary Ed. both from Ark. Tech Univ.; [hon.] Arkansas Tech. University Journalism Award (1985); [oth. writ.] Several articles published in newspapers and trade publications; poem published in American Collegiate Poets Fall Concours 1983; [pers.] I use my writing as a means of self expression and soul searching.; [a.] Clarksville, AR

MARTIN, NATASHA M.
[b.] November 26, 1979, London, OH; [p.] Randall and Barbara Martin; [ed.] Attending 9th grade at Springfield Shawnee High School, Springfield, OH; [occ.] Student; [memb.] Girl Scouts, 4-H, Band Flag Corp.; [hon.] D.A.R. History Essay Contest County Finalist (1993), Honorable Mention Springfield News-Sun Earth Day Essay Contest; [pers.] Having this poem chosen to be published, is a great honor. I hope all my future writings are as successful as this one.; [a.] Springfield, OH

MARTIN SR., ONYX W.
[b.] October 27, 1963, Rocky Mount, NC; [p.] Late Ida Davis and William Jartin Jr.; [m.] Cathie Barnes Martin, August 16, 1984; [ch.] Rodrequez Barnes, Onyx Martin, Jr.; [ed.] Rocky Mount Senior High, Jacksonville Teological Seminary; [occ.] Pastor/Truck Driver; [memb.] Big Brothers/Big Sisters youth Convention; [oth. writ.] All other writings for personal use.; [pers.] Don't be critical of shoes that you have never worn.; [a.] Rocky Mount, NC

MARTOVITZ, NICHOLE
[Pen.] Mink, Cocoa, Nickie Marto; [b.] July 17, 1979, Cleveland, OH; [p.] Joseph and tammy Martovitz; [ed.] Brunsweick High School, I hope to attend Ohio State University to become a vet, my main concentration is horses; [oth. writ.] This was my very first one.; [pers.] Keep your feet on the ground, reach for the stars, and at the same time, write what you feel. If you write down your feelings towards the world, then your always a winner inside.; [a.] Brunswick, OH

MASSEY, JAY
[b.] August 16, 1948, Princeton, Indiana; [p.] Arthur and Margaret of Kankakee, IL; [m.] Divorced in 1980; [ch.] one son 21, one daughter 19; [ed.] Two yrs. college, an enlistment in the Marine Corps and 17 yrs. Police Veteran. Most of my education was from life.; [occ.] Police Officer; [memb.] VFW; [hon.] Officer of the Year for Tequesta Police; numerous Ribbons for Viet Nam duty with the Marine Corps 68-69; [oth. writ.] Six copyrighted lyrics, one put to music and currently in Roger Whittakers possession for disposition; numerous poems; [pers.] Poetry or music is one of few ways to "pass on" heart felt emotions in an acceptable manor. If done properly, will awaken sublimal responses topersons who have not had much previous exposure.; [a.] Hobe Sound, FL

MASSEY, JERRY
[Pen.] Sir Gerald; [b.] october 23, 1975, Buford, GA; [p.] Hank and Jessie Massey; [hon.] Perfect Attendance Award, 2 time "Who's Who Among American High School Students Award Winner;" [oth. writ.] Some poems published in the local newspaper, The Times.; [pers.] I wanted to be different from other poets, so I used feelings as my main focus of writing. I have been influenced by the late, Lyman Hall.; [a.] Flowery Branch, GA

MASTERS, TKEASA
[b.] January 29, 1974, Wayneville; [p.] Mary and Alfred Masters; [ed.] High School; [occ.] Nurse Aid; [memb.] Baptist Vienna Church, Christian Children Fund; [hon.] I have had one song recorded, 8th grade, I got a reward for drawing a Alf saving electricity. I also got a $50.00 savings bond for coming in 1st place; [oth. writ.] I write stories and songs; [pers.] When I write poems it comes from my heart.; [a.] Dixon, MO

MASTRANTONIS, VIVIAN P.
[Pen.] Parris; [b.] February 14, 1947, Greece; [p.] Kyriako and Helen Mastrantonis; [m.] Dvrs.; [ch.] Kyria ko-George Lazaridis; [ed.] George Washington High School, Banking School, Grace Downs Model and Air Career School, Real Estate Law and Practice, LaSalle Interior Decorating, Hunter College Business College; [occ.] Creator of Artistic Productions, Arion Enterprices Inc.; [memb.] Hellenic-American Chamber of Commerce; [hon.] Interior Decoration and Story Award, awarded by Composer and Producer George S. Sitiropolos on behalf of the Greek T.V. network E.T. #1; [pers.] Writing poetry makes me experience another dimension of our existence. Life which allows me to visualize as I perceive the existing naked truths of our existences. Modernization of our murderization is our Universalization; [a.] Fort Lee, NJ

MATA, RAUL
[Pen.] Eddie Vedder, Forest Gump; [b.] January 3, 1978, Los Angels, CA; [ed.] Huntington Park High School; [occ.] Musician; [memb.] YGAD (Youth Gives A Damn); [a.] Walnut Park, CA

MATCHETT, TINA MARIE
[b.] November 2, 1960, Valdosta, GA; [p.] Bobby and Gladys Bryant; [m.] Michael T. Matchett, August 15, 1980; [ch.] Kena Marie, Taurean Renee, Daniel Lee, Phillip R.; [ed.] Valdosta High School, McKendrie College and Teller Training Institute Louisville, KY; [occ.] Bank Teller, Cache Road National, Lawton, OK; [memb.] Bethelehem Baptist Church, HHS Officer's Wive's Association, PTA; [pers.] I'm on a mission for the Lord. My strength comes from him.; [a.] Lawton, OK

MATTHEWS, NATASHA
[Pen.] Kynisha Richardson; [b.] July 11, 1980, Mount Vernon, NY; [p.] Yasmin and Ronald Matthews; [m.] March 1, 1979; [ch.] Chris Matthews, Kim Matthews, Andrew Matthews; [ed.] Junior High School Arlington; [occ.] Student; [hon.] B Honor Roll for 8th grade; [oth. writ.] Peace, Clowns, Schools and the Country. These are the poems I wrote so far.; [pers.] I know I wrote a few poems but they meant a lot to me and my family.; [a.] Poughquag, NY

MAUER III., ARCHIE D.
[Pen.] Carlson H. Mills; [b.] October 9, 1943, Nunda, MT; [p.] Archie and Althea; [ch.] Archie IV (19) and David (16); [ed.] B.A., Liberal Arts, A.O.S., Data Processing; [occ.] Prim Preparation Technician, New York State; [memb.] St. James Meth. Church, Cohoes, NY, AAA, Human Race; [hon.] Second Place in 1990 "World of Poetry" Contest, poem was "Evidence;" [oth. writ.] Many poems, over many years.; [pers.] My poetic intent is to give uplift and/or humor to the reader.; [a.] Troy, NY

MAUGERI, ANGELA
[b.] November 17, 1979; [p.] Ezra and Valarie Levy; [ed.] Beginning Sophomore year in high school in September 1994.; [memb.] National Junior Honor Society, Student Counsil, S.A.V.E. (Stedents Against Vilence in Education) 4-H; [hon.] brentwood's Outstanding Author Award; [oth. writ.] Poem published in Treasured Poems of America in Summer 1994 Edition.; [pers.] I wrote this poem when I was 13 years old, I hope to broaden my style as I get older.; [a.] Brentwood, NY

MAULE, MARK WILLIAM
[b.] March 9, 1970, USA; [ed.] Musical Instruments, Encyclopedia's, Dictionaries; [occ.] Songwriter, Writer, Musician, Careful Observer; [hon.] Whatever integrity pay's.; [pers.] Spare time? I haven't any. Spare time is a wast if not considered a whole of your life.; [a.] Turlock, CA

MAXAM, FRANCES
[b.] December 10, 1915, Wisconsin; [p.] Hiram and Hazel Sherman; [m.] Roland E. Maxam, November 22, 1945 (deceased); [ch.] Lynda M. Carta; [ed.] High School Graduate, Kalamazoo, Mich. 1932; Adult evening class in creative writing.; [occ.] Presently retired, but have over 6,000 hours as volunteer work for FL Hospital; [memb.] Kissimmee, of which

I am presently secretary of the Senior Auxiliary.; [hon.] Worked my way from reporter in Jacksonville, FL to Women's Editor for Jacksonville Journal. I then left the newspaper to become Advertising Copywriter for Ivey's of Jacksonville.; [pers.] I feel the urge to express in my writing observations from both personal and professional experiences. I am greatly influenced by great poets of the past.

MAXWELL, JUSTIN
[b.] June 9, 1975, Wisc.; [p.] Susan and Herbert Maxwell; [ed.] Stella Niagara Educaiton Park, Niagara Wheatfield Senior High and SUNY Fredonia; [occ.] Student; [memb.] Mensa; [oth. writ.] Hecate's Visions, unpublished; [pers.] I have been influenced by poets ranging from Goethe to Ginsberg. My work covers a wide spectrum of themes and feeling, though usually dark. I hope that this publication will help to support future endeavors.; [a.] Rochester, NY

MAYBERRY, MINDY
[Pen.] Stormi Pierce; [b.] September 27, 1951, Hope, AK; [p.] Fred and Lamour mcElroy; [m.] Sid Mayberry, December 3, 1989; [ch.] Janet Lynne, Darren Dee, Waco Shane; [ed.] Hope High School, Garland County College; [occ.] I own and am director of Care A Lot licensed day care in Hot Springs, AK.; [memb.] Humane Society of United states, Amity Hilltop Assembly Church Kids for Christ Director; [oth. writ.] Several poems I've read to churches and schools. One song, "My Soul was Seeking Jesus."; [pers.] A little saying I made up "A Smile On Your Face, A Song In Your Heart, That's The Way Each Day to Start1" I strive to live by this!; [a.] Hot Springs Village, AK

MAYES, MELINDA
[Pen.] Savanah; [b.] April 26, 1962, Houston, TX; [ch.] Cassie stroud; [occ.] Chiropractic Asst.; [oth. writ.] "This Week" column in the Houston Chronicle, poetry and still to be published novel "Secret Dreams" by Savanah.; [pers.] I am only a vessel He fills and overflows to blank pages. I am lucky to be so blessed.; [a.] Houston, TX

MCCABE, KIM
[b.] February 13, 1979, Portland, Maine; [p.] Michael T. McCabe and Terry Ellis; [ed.] Sophomore at Leesville Road High School, Raleigh, NC; [occ.] Student; [memb.] Student Council Representative, Member of the Youth Group at St. Timothy's Episcopal Church in Raleigh; [hon.] 1994 Candidate for All American Student in North Carolina, Member of the National Honor Roll, United States Achievement Academy; [oth. writ.] Ballet Beauty in Wind in the Night Sky; Between 13 and 19 in In the Desert Sun, and Love, in Outstanding Poets of 1994, all published by the National Library of Poetry.; [pers.] I would like to thank my seventh grade English Teacher, Mrs. Wheeler, my parents, and all my friends for giving me all the support they have in my writing.; [a.] Raleigh, NC

MCCABE, KRISTEN
[b.] September 18, 1982, Portland, Maine; [p.] Michael T. McCabe and Terry Ellis; [ed.] Seventh grade at Leesville Rd. Middle School; [occ.] Student; [memb.] Jammin Jumbers 4-H Club,; [hon.] Honor Roll, 1993 Reserve Grand Champion of Triton Stables in Raleigh, National Physical Fitness Award, 1993 Presidential Academic Fitness Award.; [pers.] I would like

to encourage other students to express themselves by writing poems or stories. It's a great way to share your feelings.; [a.] Raleigh, NC

MCCABE, LEONARD CHRIS
[Pen.] Dranoel Sirhc Ebacm; [b.] November 24, 1958, Skuikier County, PA; [p.] Henry Samuel and Florence McCabe; [m.] Cindy Ann McCabe, April 29, 1979; [ch.] Timothy, Jason, Justin, and Nicole; [ed.] Community School of Music and Arts, Rdg. PA., Exeter Twp. High School, Reading, PA; [occ.] Songwriter, Singer, Computer Programmer, Importer, Exporter; [memb.] Member of the Kingdom of the Almighty Lord God.; [hon.] Wrote the only song in the world known Hithorto as having ninety eight words discovered on its reverse track of the novelty single "Like A Spirit."; [oth. writ.] (Poetry Compilation) "Mystical Days." Single Release 1990' (he-777) "Like A Spirit" Alternative Music. White Dove Records.; [pers.] Within lonliness and solitude there is hidden treasures at your reach; is not life and the desire to please the essence of your emotions.; [a.] Len Hartsville, PA

MCCAFFERTY, RHONDA
[b.] October 5, 1954, Vancouver, Wash.; [p.] Frank & Judy McCafferty; Gary & Donna McMann; [ed.] Labanon Union High School. I love to sing.; [occ.] Was a Kitchen Aid for 13 years. Now a pre-school helper, going on two years.; [memb.] Salvation Army Home League Vancouver, USA, Vancouver, USA Special Olympics Sports in Bowling 16 years.; [hon.] Salvation Army League Mercy Appreciation Award for being in five years, Salvation Army Home League Marrant as Position, Home League Membership Chairman, I was Employee of the Month and Employee of Year. From Hazeldell Care Center. I won Gold in Special Olympics at State Tournament in 1993.; [pers.] To my loving Family McCaffertys, McManns, Everitts, Tuckers, Puffers and Blystones we have a Family History back around. In Vancouver U.S.A. the four are underlines.

MCCART, VICKIE
[b.] February 4, 1952, Conyers, GA; [p.] Charles & Naomi Smith; [m.] Gary McCart, November 6, 1970; [ch.] Steve McCart; [ed.] Rockdale County High School; [occ.] Primary Caregiver of Mother with Alzhiemers, Floral Designer; [oth. writ.] Several excerpts of my poetry published in local newspaper along with an article by the editor of my talent as she saw it.; [pers.] My writing reflects what and how I see nature an dhow my heart feels when I am touched by the human condition and also by my intermost thoughts.; [a.] Conyers, GA

MCCARTHY, TRICIA
[b.] November 9, 1966, Quincy, MA; [pers.] This poem is dedicated to a man I care very deeply about. For it is you who inspired me to write it. For you Eddie.; [a.] Quincy, MA

MCCLELLAN, BETTY S.
[Pen.] Lizbeth Snow; [b.] September 26, 1931, Marion Co.; [ch.] Clara Livingston, Faye (Cookie) Sampson, John C. Sampson, Jr.; [ed.] Presently a fashion marketing student at S.F.C.C. University of FL; [occ.] Fashion Coordinator, Sales; [memb.] Church of God by Faith, Alpha Iota Chapter, National Council of Negro Women, Inc., Performing Arts Affilliate.; [oth. writ.] In 1956 a true story published by McFadden

publishing Co. of New York City, a poem in Harper publication.; [pers.] In all my writings, I try to depict all facets of humans life and conditions. My motto: First one thing and then another.

MCCLELLAND, SUZANNE
[b.] Februry 25, 1981, Baytown, TX; [p.] Mark and Sharon McClelland; [ed.] Eighth grader at Liberty Middle School at the present time; [occ.] Student; [memb.] National Junior Honor Society; [hon.] Numerous scholastic awards; [oth. writ.] Have written many poems to other people such as my parents or other special people.; [pers.] I believe that you can do anything if you put your mind to it. A mind is a terrible thing to waste; [a.] Liberty, TX

MCCLOYEN, SAUL EDWARD
[Pen.] SEM; [b.] September 11, 1964, Lake Village, AR; [p.] J.W. and Joyce Ann Colbert; [ch.] Brittany Nicole McCloyen; [ed.] Lakeside High School; [occ.] AirForce, Information Mgm't Technician; [memb.] Srangers Rest Missionary Baptist Church, National Tae Kwon Do Federation of America; [pers.] Always Thank God for all things and everything because whatever happens in your life (good or bad), God allows it to happen for a reason, live and learn.; [a.] Chapel Hill City, NC

MCCLURE, ANNIE L.
[b.] April 28, 1925, TX; [p.] J.H. Rivers, Ida Rivers Williams (deceased); [m.] E. Dean McClure, June 4, 1943 (deceased); [ch.] Renee McClure; [ed.] Ennis High and Mountain View College; Associate Degree; [occ.] Retired; [hon.] Dean's List, Outstanding Achievement (Academic) Award; [pers.] The use of words hold a special magic. They stir the imagination and cleanse the soul.; [a.] Duncanville, TX

MCCONNELL, DAVE
[b.] December 9, 1965, Woodbury, NJ; [p.] Joseph E. and Gloria McConnell; [m.] Patricia A. McConnell; [ch.] David Ryan and Amanda Jean; [ed.] Highland Regional High school, Blackwood, NJ; [occ.] Machine Operator; [oth. writ.] Over one dozen never before seen poems in safe keeping.; [pers.] A close knit family of any kind is all one needs to rise and lay in peace on any given day.; [a.] West Berlin, NJ

MCCOOL, YOLANDA
[p.] Migdonia and Aristides; [m.] William McCool; [ch.] Barbara and Raquel; [ed.] 2 1/2 yrs. of college; [hon.] Regents Diploma, Citation of Honor, Excellence in Writing, Certificate of Merit, Honors in Graphic Arts and Spanish in High School; [oth. writ.] A poem being published in Dusting Off Dreams, Quill Books about the special relationship my daughter share.; [pers.] Love life, breathe in it's every essence. though trials and tribulations may make their guest appearances every so often on any particular stage of your life you must always reach for that point when your triumphs are attainable and then embrace them.; [a.] Greenbelt, MD

MCCORD JR., CLARENCE
[b.] February 7, 1967, Texas; [p.] Clarence McCord Sr., and Yolanda Madid; [ed.] Riverside High Mansfield Business College, Watterson College.; [occ.] Medical Asst.; [memb.] Humankind; [hon.] Deans List, Presidents List, Golden Poet of the 88, Silver Poet of the year 89.; [oth. writ.] To Move a Mountain, published in 1988.; [pers.] Life requires

death, death is sustained by life and vice versa "Seize the Day."; [a.] ElMonte, CA

MCDANEL, NANCY
[b.] December 19, 1948, Tucson, AZ; [p.] Robert and Margaret Rowley; [m.] David Paul McDanel (Deceased), June 15, 1968; [ch.] Ronald Scott 24, Jennifer Beth 22; [ed.] Graduated Warren Area High School; Warren PA 1966, Attended Edinboro State College; [occ.] In Home Daycare Shaklee Distributor; [memb.] Member of Cherry Creek Presbyterian Church, Englewood, CA; [pers.] God has granted me many blessings. One of my richest ones was my husband, Dave. We had 27 years to the day together from when we first met to the day he died. My poem is dedicated to him.; [a.] Aurora, CO

MCDONNELL, MICHELLE
[b.] Colorado; [p.] Barbra and Bill McDonnell, Evelyn Killmer, my Grandmother was the second cousin of Joyce Killmer; [ed.] B.A. in Philosophy from the university of Colorado at Boulder.; [occ.] Author.; [memb.] C.U. Golden Key Honor Society.; [hon.] Cum Laude Graduate; [oth. writ.] European Journal, War Diary, poems published in The Amherst Society and Saprrowgrass anthologies.; [pers.] I am writing to wake you up stir you, find you, change you, remind you, to live. Michelle McDonnell Copyright July 11, 1994.; [a.] Louisville, CO

MCDONOUGH, FRANCIS PAUL
[b.] April 7, 1921, Ireland; [p.] John F. McDonough and Elizabeth McNichol; [m.] October 30, 1948 (divorced); [ch.] Frank McDonough and John Lee McDonough; [ed.] High School Graduate at Orange High School N.J., St. Joseph's College in Garrison NY, 2 years in Seminary there, later professions, X-Ray Technologist and Nurse; [occ.] Retired; [memb.] Veterans of Foreign Wars Post #687 Jackson, MS; American Legion Post #106 Jackson, MS; The National Chaplain's Association in Gatlinburg, TN; Member 3rd Order of St. Francis; [hon.] While a Federal Employee at the V.A. Hospital, Jackson, MS, won numerous high performance awards; served as American Legion Post #1 for 5 years, and then appointed State Chaplain for 1 yr.; Chaplain (MS) for 1 year.; [oth. writ.] Have numerous other poems. My first serious work was written while I was in the Navy in W.W. II; [pers.] "Life can be a gay affair and the flesh is ever weak, I guess I know myself so well; I know where of I speak." (excerpt from my poem "Lament."); [a.] Jackson, MS

MCEWAN, PATRICIA K.
[b.] October 6, 1949, Fairbanks; [p.] Kenneth O. Walker (Claudia); [m.] Divorced; [ch.] Daniel K. McEwan, Patrick K. Walker; [ed.] High School Diploma and Full Time Mom, Elston Sr. High, Mich. City Ind.; [occ.] Correctional Officer; [oth. writ.] Other poems not published.; [pers.] I strive to reflect my feelings toward certain people in my life.; [a.] Westville, IN

McGRATH, KRISTIN LEIGH
[b.] April 14, 1982, Southbridge, MA; [p.] Steven and Kathleen; [hon.] Outstanding Achievement Award in Language Arts, Straight A Award - English & Science; [pers.] In my writing, I try to take the reader into another world. I am not influenced by anyone, but wish to influence everyone; [a.] Yardley, PA

MCGUIRE, CAROL
[b.] May 11, 1965, Philadelphia, PA; [p.] Fredrick and Doreen McGuire; [ed.] B.A. in Communications, Art Minor, Teacher Certified in Journalism; [occ.] Art Teacher for S.E.D. Children and Behavior Training Specialist for Autistic and Mental Retardation Clientel; [memb.] Member of Calvary Chapel Fellowship; [oth. writ.] 42 poems written since 1983.; [pers.] I strive to use my poetry through personal experiences of my own and friends to help ease the pain and suffering of everyday life. There is a rainbow at the end of every storm.; [a.] Orlando, FL

MCINCHAK, MARLA
[b.] November 28, 1961, Bedford, Ohio; [p.] Theodore and Nancy Brink; [m.] Divorced; [ch.] Kyla McInchak; [ed.] Mcdowell High School, Vo-Tech; [occ.] Certified Nurses Aide (Battersby Convalescent Home 15 yrs.); [memb.] Working with the elderly; [hon.] Ribbon won in a State contest in 6th grade, short story about soldiers.; [oth. writ.] 2nd grad teacher Miss Bruno admired a Valentine short story to be read to all students in Lakewood Elementary School; [pers.] I enjoy writing to bring out emotions of a loved one's pain, and to end it with the sweet victory of their strength to get through it.; [a.] McKean, PA

MCINTYRE, MARK ROBERT
[b.] June 17, 1974, St. George, VT; [p.] Carl and Mildred mcIntyre, May 28, 1994; [ch.] none, Sister Karlynn Brieann McIntyre and Brother, Craig Alexander McIntyre; [ed.] Robert Service High School, Anchorage AK/Motorcycle Mechanic Institute, Phoenix, AZ; [occ.] USAF; [pers.] "The Greatest Man is but a Ripple in time." Unknown.; [a.] Anchorage, AK

MCKIDDY, SHAUNNA MAY
[b.] December 12, 1978, Cinti, OH; [p.] Vicki McFarland and Robert McKiddy; [ed.] Taylor High School; [occ.] Student, writer; [memb.] Young Friends of the Public Library.; [hon.] VFW, Voice of Democracy Award Citation; Creative Writing Award, Culture Arts Writing Award 1985-1994; [oth. writ.] Article in 3 Rivers Tributary, Poems in Seven Hills Review and Word Drops.; [pers.] I feel the need to stress what the world is missing, though it's right before their eyes.; [a.] North Bend, OH

MCKINLEY, DELAYNE
[b.] October 8, 1948, Lake City, MN; [p.] Ed and Helen Waters; [m.] Capt. Gary McKinley; [hon.] 1989 Editor's Choice Award; [oth. writ.] "Pleasures of our Memories" in 1989 "Day's of Future's Past"; [pers.] "Gods Gift" was inspired by vicki Garcia; and the birth of my neice Kayla Elaine. Dedicated to Kayla Elaine and all parents and children.; [a.] Redwing, MN

MCKINNEY, JR., WILLIE
[Pen.] Will-Ken; [b.] October 8, 1945, Texas; [p.] Willie and Martha M. McKinney; [ch.] Rochea A.B. McKinney, Lawrence J.t. McKinney and Qiana S. McKinney; [ed.] B.S., BA Degree, Suffolk Univ. Roxbury Community Colelge, AA Degree, New England Conservatory of Music, Northeastern University Courses; [occ.] Engineering Payroll, MBTA, Boston; [memb.] Rapid Investment (RIP) Partners, We Can N.I. Revelation Baptist Church, Father's Day, Mother's Day Message, Publicity Assoc. of MA, CDC Assoc., NAACP, Heart Assoc, United Way; [hon.] Roxbury Community College, 2nd Place

Trophy Body Building Office of Economic Opp. Community Serv., Outstanding Achievement Award for First Chairman of College Screening Committee and Firs President of Student Government Association, Senatorial Citation, Commonwealth of MA, Senate; [oth. writ.] Help Us To Save The Children, Mother's Day Message, Father's Day Message, Feeling Free, Waitings on Love and I Need You. H and R Block-Income Taxation; [pers.] In my writings I reflect reality as it exist, write about life and relationships. I am not influenced by anyone. God is my greatest inspiration.; [a.] Dorchester, MA

MCLAIN, FAYE F.
[b.] June 19, 1945, Spokane, WA; [p.] Chris and Fiske Shange; [m.] Gregory McLain, September 10, 1965; [ch.] Joel, Jonathan; [ed.] Lewis and Clark High School, Spokane Community College; [occ.] Licensed Practical Nurse; [memb.] Victory Faith Fellowship Church; [hon.] Amherst and poetry society; [oth. writ.] Published Inspirational Poetry Book titled "For the Love of God" by Ye Gallen Press, Fairfield, WA. Written 3 other poetry books: Fountains of Joy, Windows to the soul and Echos' from the Heart.; [pers.] I write to inspire people in their faith and belief in God. If any of my poems touch your heart, then I truly have accomplished the gift God has given to me.; [a.] Spokane, WA

MCLEOD, RACHEL E.
[b.] January 2, 1980, Colville, WA; [p.] Marvin and Kathy mcLeod; [ed.] 9th grade home schooled; [occ.] Housekeeper and cook, watergirl for hay crews; [memb.] former member of Awana, Youth Leadership, and Bible course programs; [hon.] As a volunteer at St. Joseph's Long Term Cre unit in Chewelah; [oth. writ.] I like to write poems and short stories. This is my first published work hopefully not my last.; [pers.] Dedicated to Daphne Chrysler the person that showed me what true friendship mens. Thank you Daphne!;l [a.] Chewelah, WA

MCMAHON, JAMES L.
[b.] March 27, 1914, Detroit, MI; [m.] Anna Mae McMahon; [ed.] College; [occ.] Retired, Disabled; [oth. writ.] Various; [pers.] Variety of Interests wish to express God's help and appreciation to you people during my contest. Many Thanks.; [a.] Plymouth, MI

MCMASTER, RONALD
[Pen.] Ron McMaster; [b.] March 8, 1944, Saginaw, Mich.; [p.] June and Ronald McMaster; [m.] Irene McMaster, November 14, 1972; [ch.] Steven, David, Patty, Louis; [ed.] James Monroe High School and College of the Canyons; [occ.] Supervisor for Vickers Sterer Engineering, L.A. California; [memb.] Southern California Golf Association; [oth. writ.] Numerous writings for friends and family.; [pers.] I would love to write poetry for greeting cards or any other company interested in poetry.; [a.] Palmdale, CA

MCMILLEN, GALEN R.
[m.] Stacey McMillen; [ch.] Jonathan Isaac, Jenessa Faye Rose; [occ.] Licensed General Contractor, Specializing in Cabinet and Millwork; [pers.] Love thy neighbor as thyself.; [a.] Waterford, CA

McNABB, SARAH
[Pen.] Andromeda; [b.] January 18, 1978, Morris, IL; [p.] John and Pam McNabb; [ed.] M-V-K Grade School, Seneca High School, Correspondence stu-

dent of Art Instruction Schools; [occ.] Student; [memb.] National Honor Society; [hon.] Many art awards, scholastic trophies, drama medals, and technology plaques; [oth. writ.] Various works of art, poems, stories, and original quotes; [pers.] It would be all too lovely to dream, and make them real...but we need not be asleep to do so; [a.] Morris, IL

MCNAIRY, HAROLD GABRIEL
[Pen.] Hal; [b.] March 30, 1929, Alberdeen, MS; [p.] Framm Billip, Valaria Maria McNairy; [m.] Deceased; [ch.] One; [ed.] College Graduate, LaSalle University Law School, Hotel Institute and Restaurant Institutes; [occ.] Retired Veteran Army and a Land Investor; [memb.] Xmas Valley Club Oregon, Songwriter Club of America; [hon.] Korea War Hero, the Purple Heart and many more honors of cecorations; Compsoer, [oth. writ.] Accounting; [pers.] If you fail one time, try and try again. but have a goal in life.; [a.] St. Louis, MO

MCNEILL, RICHARD ANTHONY
[Pen.] Tony; [b.] August 24, 1960, Gainesville, FL; [p.] Margaret Dan Dan and Lavern McNeill; [m.] Regina; [ch.] Anthony, Steven, N'Zhinga, Megan; [ed.] Life; [oth. writ.] Rasin' Lady, Forever, Peril in Time (co-written with my brother Sean), Stand Ready, Our Right To Expression, All put to Music.; [pers.] The truth is not alway's pretty. It's not alway's wht we want to hear. If I can enlighten one person to the sometime's overlooked realities of life, then it's all been worth the effort.; [a.] Gainesville, FL

MCPHAIL JOANN WINSTEAD
[Pen.] Anna Gold; [b.] February 17, 1941, Trenton, FL; [p.] Donna Mae Crowford and Wm. Emerson Winstead; [m.] James Michael McPhail, June 15, 1962; [ch.] Angela Celeste Morris, Dana Denice McPhail, Whitney Gold Casso; [ed.] 3 years college, Fla.j Southern, Houston Community College; [occ.] Writer, Art Agent, Antique Dealer, Apartment Manager; [memb.] First United Methodist Church, Republican Party; [hon.] Marquis editor 1995-96 Who's Who In The South & Southwest; [oth. writ.] Budding of Tomorrow, Sweet 70's Anthology, A Touch of Greatness, photo-journalist, Southwest Art Magazine, photo-journalist, various features, Egaleriterian, (Houston Community College Newspaper); [pers.] I am to do a good job with whatever I take on as a task. I have a great feel for people, especially children, and desire to contribute in a positive way to their lives.; [a.] Houston, TX

MCQUEARY, B.J.
[b.] July 14, 1955, Fort Bragg, CA; [ch.] Ryan A. Smith, Aarron A. Smith, Shalene I. Smith, Rushel and estrella; [ed.] Cypress College; [occ.] Children's Home Society of California; [memb.] Church of Christ, Children's Book Club; [hon.] Employee Recognition and Certificates of Appreciation.; [oth. writ.] Local newspapers and magazines; [pers.] Spans of space between each place, an open door, ceiling and a floor; choices made, lesson learned, friends and foes, broken heart that yearn. Just a touch, a word so kind, can heal the hurt someone else left behind.; [a.] Orange, CA

MCTAGUE, CAROLYN
[b.] June 11, 1926, Battle Creek, MI; [p.] Herbert and Priscilla Crippen; [m.] David Mctague, June 16, 1956; [ch.] son, Mark Baker, Father died before his birth, Daughter Lt. Col. Linda McTague; [ed.] Verona School 1st thru 8th, W.K. Kelllogg Jr. High 9th., B.C. Central High, 10th thru 12th; [occ.] Housewife.; [memb.] St. Thomas Episcopal church; [oth. writ.] Several poems; [pers.] After recovering from a near fatal illness at the age of 67 yrs. at quite time suddenly my thoughts began to rhyme. That's when I began writing poetry.; [a.] Battle Creek, MI

MCWILLIAMS, ROY F.
[b.] October 27, 1948, Dover, NJ; [p.] Stanley and Emma McWilliams; [m.] Sharon (Hastings) McWilliams, March 7, 1976; [ch.] Jeanette, Scott, Bryce and Doreen; [ed.] Newton High, Thomas Ava Edison State College; [occ.] Electrical Lineman City of Caliente, NV; [memb.] Coustou society; [hon.] Air Medal, first thru 25th Oak Leaf Clusters (vietnam); [oth. writ.] I have written many poems from my youth thru vietnam, two marriages and I have lived in almost every state. I write at night alone, some I keep, this is my first submission.; [pers.] I believe in God, but have not found a church for me. I often write poems at night in about an hour, that I keep for my children. I am an emotional person inside and hope to try writing someday.; [a.] Caliente, NV

MEACHAM, JAN M.
[b.] April 10, 1951, Saginaw, Michigan; [p.] Luella Meacham; [ed.] Arthur Hill High School, Teacher Aid, Head Start Program, Business & Planning Team Concepts taught by Work Place Transformation; [occ.] Business Owner, Dealson Wheels (Crafts) Child Care Worker A.D.D. Children; [memb.] Becoming a member of International Society of Poets; [hon.] Semi-finalist in 1994 North American Open Poetry Contest, The National Library of Poetry; [oth. writ.] Self published my first book May 16, 1994, a self help poetry book. Who Me Was, Who Me Is; [pers.] I write from the heart to touch someone else's heart. I hope to encourage others to become who they are, find their purpose, fulfill their dreams, love to live, be free.; [a.] AuGres, MI

MELTON, PEGGY
[Pen.] Peggy Warren Melton; [b.] September 15, 1954, Newport, AR; [p.] Theordore and Gladys Warren; [m.] Jerry Melton, January 29, 1972; [ch.] Jeffrey Wayne, Marcus Wade, Dustin Jared; grandchild: C.J.; [ed.] Tuckerman High; White River Vo Tech; [pers.] It is sometimes difficult for me to express my feelings verbally; writing makes it much easier. Hey guys, I love you!; [a.] Tuckerman, AR

MENDELSON, MELISSA RACHEL
[b.] December 2, 1977, Portchester; [p.] Richard and Paula Mendelson; [ed.] High School; [memb.] Member of the National Writer's Assn.; [hon.] Reflections Award, Creativity Award, School Certificates; [pers.] Besides becoming a poet, I want to be an action and science-fiction movie writer. "Eyes In The Dark" is my best poem, and "The Lizard Man" is my best story.; [a.] Monroe, NY

MENDEZ, XAVIER ANTHONY
[Pen.] Harvey Mendez; [b.] September 18, 1932, Madison, WI; [p.] Pedro Mendez and Mildred Crowley; [m.] Nevada Ann Mendez, February 22, 1969; [ch.] Deborah, Mark, Jed, Al; [ed.] Central High, Chaffey High, Chaffey College, South Dakota State University, Southern California University, AA, BS, Doctor of Pharmacy; [occ.] Registered Pharmacist Writer; [hon.] First Place, short story "The Bear and the Bull" Arizona Literary Magazine, 1986; [oth. writ.] Several short storeis, currently re-writing a 653 page novel, titled "Amelia", Two screenplays.; [pers.] I write what comes out of me, then edit to perfect.; [a.] Laguna Hills, CA

MENDOZA, FLORENCIO A.
[b.] November 21, 1924, Somoto, Nicaragua C.A.; [p.] Florencio Mendoza and Amelia Guillen; [m.] Shoshanna Mendoza Chavez, January 1, 1973 (2nd marriage); [ch.] Amelia Shoshanna, Florencio Alejandro, Juan Carlos Mendoza; [ed.] High School, Bachelor in Arts Military acdemy Nicaragua Master in Business Administration, University Houston, TX; [occ.] President Owner of a Febrics Retail Store.; [memb.] Member Masonic Lodge, Progreso #5 Managua Nic. Grade 33erd. Member of (NABBA) Nicaraguan American Business, Bankers Association.; [hon.] Gold Star as Distinguish Student Mil. Academy of Nicaragua Dean Honor Roll business Faculty University of Houston, TX 1962-63; Decorated by West Germany Government, The Great Cross of Merit; Decorated by Brazilian Government with the Cruzeiro Do Sul.; [oth. writ.] Many poems, A thesis about the Economic Integration of Central America, etc.; [pers.] I believe in mankind as creatures of God; with colourless soul, and one spirit that is the connection with the supreme being. I think earth is the homeland for every living creatures and that we must keep it in good shape for our own good. I do believe in freedom and that spiritual persons prevail above all.; [a.] Miami, FL

MENDOZA, ROSA
[b.] July 4, 1978, Tijuana; [p.] Maria and Crescencio Mendoza; [ed.] High School Student; [hon.] Student of the Year, Perfect Attendance; [pers.] Don't ever let anyone make you feel low. If anything they aren't too sure of themselves. So they want you to seem like the bad one.; [a.] Santa Monica, CA

MERCADO, ELLA L.
[b.] October 16, 1952, Tampa, FL; [p.] Nellie and Bernard Baransky; [m.] Fiance' Eugene Edwards; [ch.] Michelle, Maria, Amanda, Christopher Ashley, Michael, Kathleen, Aaron, Shaquanda, Ray; [ed.] Leto High School; [occ.] Homemaker; [hon.] Community Volunteer; [oth. writ.] Short stories.; [a.] Liberty, NC

MERCHANT, SANDRA
[b.] July 19, 1945, Washington, NC; [p.] Leonard and Thelma tinker; [m.] Robert Sr., June 6, 1964; [ch.] Robert Jr. and Wesley; [ed.] John A. Wilkinson High, King's Business College, Carteret Community College; [occ.] Medical Records Technician; [memb.] United Methodist Church, Woodmen of the World; [hon.] Woman of Woodcraft, Civilian of the Quarter; [oth. writ.] Local newspaper published several poems. Hospital newspaper published several poems and essays.; [pers.] Writing soothes the soul and eases the heart.; [a.] Newport, NC

MERRITT, CATHY
[b.] September 17, 1953, Baltimore, MD; [p.] Leonard and June Hamilton; [m.] Donnie Merritt, March 5, 1971; [ch.] Tina, Benny; [ed.] Oscar Smith High School; [occ.] Teacher Assistant Greenbrier Primary School; [memb.] Providence Baptist Church; [pers.] My poetry is a part of the feelings in my heart, and my

love for those in my life.; [a.] Chesapeake, VA

MESLEH, MARIANA H.
[b.] February 12, 1972, Palestine; [p.] Malakeh & Habib Mesleh; [ed.] Fitzgerald High School; [occ.] Secretary; [hon.] Won award 6th grade for writing about smoking, article in Junior High; [pers.] I love to write poems its the most important thing for me to accomplish in life. Thanks to my family and friends, love you all.; [a.] Warren, MI

MESSINA, GAYLE
[b.] October 20, 1955, Wilmington, Delaware; [p.] Rev. David and Barbara Kaminsky; [m.] Thomas Messina, March 16, 1975; [ch.] Christopher Thomas Messina, Stephen Peter David Messina; [ed.] Deer Park High school, Suffolk Community College; [occ.] Animal Care Specialist and Veterinary Nutritional Consultant; [memb.] United States Coast Guard Aux. Flotilla 9-10 Florida; [hon.] Hills Veterinary Nutritional Consultant; [oth. writ.] Unpublished children's book and an unpublished short story and several hundred poems.; [pers.] I have found that daily life experiences spark my creativity and inspire my inner most emotions that seem to flow onto paper like liquid silk.; [a.] Bokeelia, FL

MICHAEL, CYNTHIA J.
[b.] April 12, 1966, Washington, D.C.; [p.] Raymond and Patricia Michael; [ed.] Potomac Senior High School, VA, University of South Florida, Northern Virginia Community College; [occ.] Work for First Security Bank of Idaho; [oth. writ.] Short stories and poems, working on a novel.; [pers.] I believe everyone should take time out and question who they are and wht they believe in life. Inspirtional writers include Socrates and Poe.; [a.] Idaho Falls, ID

MICHAELS, LEE
[b.] July 9, 1943, Boston, Mass; [p.] Jane Benton; [m.] Dwight Michaels, July 6, 1973; [ed.] Natick High, West Linn High, Judson Baptist College, Multnomah School of the bible; [occ.] Housewife; [hon.] Music Appreciation Award; [pers.] I truly believe that my inspirational poetry is a God-given gift.; [a.] Highland, CA

MIERZWA, IRENA
[b.] Barbara Walloni; [b.] December 15, 1940; [p.] Zofia and stan Rybski; [ch.] Jack and Paul; [ed.] University Granduated from Poznan, Poland, MSC, SC; [p.] Nurse, independent journalist and trveller; [memb.] The International Socity of Poets, SERVAS, Havellers; SANUS, Health Assoc.; [hon.] The Naitonal Library of Poetry, Editors Choice award 1993.; [oth. writ.] Poems published in anthologies "Where Dreams Begin," "A Brake in the Clouds," "Edge of Twilight," and "Dark Side of the Moon," several poems published in Radio Chicago.; [a.] Northbrook, IL

MILES, JENNIFER R.
[b.] May 6, 1982, Montgomery, MD; [p.] Mary Sue and James R. Miles; [ed.] Finished with elementary school, now in 7th grade Middle School (Fairland Elementary), (Banneker Middle School); [hon.] Won Presidents Award, Scholarship Award at Banneker, Honor Roll Award, I am in all honor classes.; [pers.] I am a straight "A" student and presently attending Banneker Middle School; I am one of six children in my family. I love to write poetry as a hobby. I am inspired by poets and consider poetry as a break from

reality.; [a.] Burtonsville, MD

MILICEVIC, BRIA NICOLE
[b.] November 7, 1978, Las Vegas, NV; [p.] Barbara and James Milicevic; [ed.] Currently High School Student; [occ.] Part-time Bed and Breakfast Asst. Manager, Part-Time Jewelry Manufacturer; [memb.] Student council, Student Class Representative; [hon.] Excellence 9th grade English, Excellence overall Technology Education; [pers.] I find personal reward in expessing devotion and heartache that typically is associated with romance.; [a.] Mancos, CO

MILLER, DEANNE LYNN
[Pen.] Deanna Miller; [b.] May 16, 1961, Pontiac, MI; [p.] Mary and Floyd Perria; [m.] Michael Francis Miller, June 11, 1983; [ch.] Joseph Samuel, Rebecca Faith Miller; [ed.] Waterford Township High, Midwestern Bapt. College, Children's Lit. Foundaitons; [occ.] Missionary, Housewife; [memb.] Sharon Bapt. Church, Macedonnia World Bapt. Missions; [hon.] none; [oth. writ.] none published, yet.; [pers.] Been writing poems for my own self since the age of 13. Started keeping them in 1985 in a book in which I've never tried to publishe.; [a.] Waterford, MI

MILLER, ELIZABETH MARIE
[Pen.] Isabel Martin; [b.] September 18, 1945, Baltimore; [p.] Albert H. and Angela Miller; [m.] I am single; [ch.] none; [ed.] Lafayette High School, Brooklyn, NY, Staten Island Community College; AA, 1969 Hunter College; BA in History, 1975; [occ.] Secretary for the New York City Housing Authority; [memb.] Esperanto League for North America; [hon.] none; [oth. writ.] Several poems published in other magazines; two published in the Housing Authority's "Focus on Women."; [pers.] I hope that, through my life and writing, I leave this world a better place when I leave it than it was when I came into it.; [a.] Brooklyn, NY

MILLIKEN, HEATHER
[b.] June 9, 1976, Salem, OH; [p.] Gary and Nancy Milliken; [m.] Single; [ed.] High School Honors Diploma; [occ.] Student; [pers.] Poetry is the reflection of one's spirit. It is the tangible sense of one's heart, the embodiment of emotion, and only speaks to those who listen from within.; [a.] Salem, OH

MILLS, JOYCE ANNE
[Pen.] J.C. Mills; [b.] January 23, 1950, Caredo, West VA; [p.] Bill and Irene Childers; [m.] Frank Mills, April 22, 1989; [ch.] William Franklin Caudill, Tammy Marie Caudill Chaffin and Michael Lee Caudill; [ed.] Graduated from Catlettsburg High 1968, Certified Nursing Assistant; [occ.] Armco Coke Plant; [pers.] I love to write poems they all have a special meaning to me. I am writing a mystery novel at this time.

MILLS, KENNETH C.
[b.] May 24, 1960, Long Beach, CA; [p.] Allen and Lovetta Mills; [m.] Linda t. Mills, December 5, 1979; [ch.] Kinni Crystal, Sindy Lou Antionette, Clifford russel, Timothy Michael; [ed.] Lakewood High, American Technical Ins.; [occ.] Cross Country Truck Driver; [hon.] American Technical Ins., Dean's List & Academic Achievement; [oth. writ.] Personal poems to my wife and weekly comedy sheets for friends.; [pers.] Live long and prosper.; [a.] Lansdale, PA

MILLS, MARGARET PENN
[Pen.] Penn Mills; [b.] August 20, 1940, Salt Lake City, Utah; [p.] Gordon & Helyn Cope; [m.] Bernard Mills, May 8, 1960; [ch.] Michael B. Mills, Bernadette M. Mills; [ed.] Graduated from Presentation High School, 1 yr. at Lone Mt. College for Women, 3 yrs. at San Francisco State College; [occ.] Home Nursing; [memb.] Humane Society Marin County, Greenpeace, National Wildlife Federation, American WNC Association, KQEP (Public Broadcasting); [oth. writ.] I am just beginning to realize a lifelong ambition to write professionally. I have been writing since childhood.; [pers.] Reading is an inspiration. Writing is an aspiration. Writing is a spiritual excursion for me. Sharing the light of anothers insicnt humbles me: To share my soul gives growth and joy in my life.; [a.] San Anselmo, CA

MILSOM, MIRIAM N.
[b.] April 25, 1975, Conn.; [p.] Scott and Lori Milsom, Penny Milsom; [ch.] Siblings: Shawn "Bud" Milsom, Jenna Lacey Milsom; [ed.] Franklin High School, Catonsville Community College; [pers.] We hold the future in our hands. Let's hope we can still save it. I owe what I am now to Scott and Lori, and what I am to become to David. You opened my mind and my heart to the world. i love you all.; [a.] Reisterstown, MD

MIRANDA, FRANK H.
[Pen.] Nathan T. Sharpe; [b.] May 11, 1955, Yuma, AZ; [p.] Rodolfo and Frances; [m.] Brenda Lee, December 3, 1988; [ch.] Samantha Ann; [ed.] Yuma High, Arizona Westeon College; [occ.] Airline Employee; [oth. writ.] Books: "Circle of Being," "Journey of A Soul;" [pers.] "Mankind..has found himself on the verge, in the next step of his evolution, not only by body and mind, but what is most important...of spirit." We must embrace.; [a.] Orange, CA

MITCHELL, CHRIS
[b.] February 4, 1972; [occ.] Singer/Song Writer; [pers.] The sounds of the voice are much softier than the screaming of the heart. For I will never deny a slice of nature with colors tht blind our intelligence. I am proud to be happy here in my own write, where success is painted in words.; [a.] Cleveland, OH

MITCHELL, JONATHAN W.
[b.] January 21, 1962, Raleigh, NC; [p.] Ellen A. and Herbert W. Mitchell; [ed.] John Dickinson High School, Univ. of Delaware; [occ.] Office Manager of Great Christian Book; [oth. writ.] No writings published to date except in this collection. Have many short poems completed and sketches for others that I hope to have published. Also I have a short mystery completed.; [pers.] I hope my writings are understandable and would be relative to expereinces we all have. My goal in writing is to move people to experience what I've written. My greatest compliment was to see a friend moved to tears after reading a poem of mine.; [a.] Newark, DE

MITCHELL, RACHEL S.
[b.] December 29, 1931, Lexington, MS; [p.] Virginia Sutdaway; [m.] Geroge Mitchell Jr., January 12, 1962; [ch.] Timothy David Mitchell and Greta Michelle Mitchell; [occ.] Retired; [memb.] New Mt. Zion Missionary Baptist Church Adult Choir, Sunday School Teacher, Matron League; [hon.] The only

honor I can claim is "A soldier of the cross"; [pers.]lj My hope is that when my poems are read by anyone; they will feel I am uplifting of the spirit, and a soothing balm to the soul.; [a.] Jackson, MS

MLINAR, CATHERINE
[b.] January 11, 1913, Mpls., MN; [p.] Deceased; [m.] Single; [ed.] B.S. U. of MN, Grad. Credits U. of Hawaii, Grad. Credits U. of Arizona; [occ.] Retired Teacher; [memb.] Sigma Kappa Sorority, Minnesota Sr. Federation, AARP; [hon.] None; [oth. writ.] None published, Children's Poetry and Stories.; [pers.] Taught in Hawaii, Caracas Venezaela, Puerto Rico, England, Philippines, Japan, Turkey, Germany and in U.S.A. Mich., Illinois, Arizona. Served with American Red Cross during WWII at Camp Bowie, TX; [a.] Mpls., MN

MOFFETT, EMILY B.
[b.] August 27, 1935, Orlando, FL; [p.] Edward and Margaret Bridges; [m.] Kenneth D. Moffett, October 27, 1956; [ch.] Mirella M. Wilson, Natalie Hamilton, Teresa Morris; [ed.] Naitonal Cathedral, Wash., D.C., Penn Hall, Chambersberg, PA; [occ.] Housewife, Geneologist; [memb.] DAR, Colonia Dames Magna Charta; [pers.] Cherish gifts from above with love, understanding and faith.; [a.] Milton, FL

MOFFIT, BOYD E.
[b.] February 16, 1917, CA; [p.] Deceased; [m.] Bea Moffit, November 25, 1956; [ch.] Lance, Janice, Tom; [ed.] To years high school, Lots of Years College of H.K (Hard Knocks); [occ.] Retired; [oth. writ.] None, just poems.

MOHIUDDIN, TALAT
[b.] December 23, 1960, Karachi, Pakistan; [p.] Abdul Hai Khan and mazhari Begum; [m.] Masood Mohiuddin, December 9, 1988; [ch.] Omar Mohiuddin, Aamir Mohiuddin; [ed.] Bachelor Arts, Continuing education in Computers in local college; [occ.] Homemaker; [hon.] I have never entered in a contest before. I am pretty new in this field.; [oth. writ.] I have a small collection of English poetries, but a pretty large one in my own language.; [pers.] Being a shy person it's difficult for me to share my feelings with others. For me poetry turns out to be a wonderful alternative. I appreciate beauty; in nature as well as in people.; [a.] Morganton, NC

MOLINARY, WANDA
[b.] January 9, 1967, San Juan, PR; [p.] Luis Malinary and Gladys Fernandez; [ed.] MBA Penn State University, BBA, University of Puerto Rico; [memb.] National Society of Hispanic MBA's, Penn State Alumni Association, American Red Cross; [hon.] Presidential Academic Fitness Award, Two literature contest awards; [oth. writ.] A poem published in a local newspaper. Around 200 unpublished poems in English and Spanish.; [pers.] This publication is dedicated to my family and friends. To Elisa Gonzales and Jose Luis Vega. To Russ Ezzell and Judity Boegart. And to you, always remember TQM; thanks for believing in me.; [a.] San Juan, PR

MONICA, DAWSON
[Pen.] Jellybean; [b.] May 20, 1962, Newark, NJ; [p.] Donald and Constance Dawson; [ch.] Savanna Octavia Santiago; [ed.] Montclair High School; Montclair State College, Essex School of Business; [occ.] Accounts Receivable Collections Clerk; [memb.]

Saint Pauls Baptist church; [hon.] Dean's List; [pers.] I always try to feel my writings as well as live them. This way my mind and my voice can be focused and readers can apprecite and understand me better.; [a.] Elizabeth, NJ

MONIZ, STACIE M.
[b.] February 17, 195, San Jose, CA; [p.] Ed and Jackie Moniz; [ed.] Currently enrolled at Lake Tahoe Community College, studying to pursue a career in law enforcement.; [hon.] Editor's Choice Award for "Time" published in dance on the horizon, spring 1994.; [oth. writ.] Published in the following: "Dance on the Horizon" Spring 94; "Poetic Voices of America" Spring 93; [pers.] This poem was inspired by the loss of a close friend. charlotte "Charlie" Suetlik, she will forever remain in my heart.; [a.] S. Lake Tahoe, CA

MONROE, HOUSTON JAMES
[Pen.] Tex; [b.] September 19, 1934, Wise Co., Tex.; [p.] Lee S. and Cliffie H. Monroe; [m.] Mary Ellen Monroe, June 3, 1977; [ch.] Gary, Richard, Debra, Cheryl, Darlene, Donny, Gayle, Ronald; [ed.] 14 years, Certificates I've earned, Junior NCO, ASP Championship, U.S. Army Chemical School, Instructor Training, Doctor of Motors, Knights of the blue nose, Bible study award.; [memb.] Southern Baptist Occupation, U.S. Army Staff Sgt. Ret. 1955-1975; Overseas Tours-Thule greenland, Germany, Viet Nam, Alaska; [hon.] Medals Bronze Star, Viet Nam gallantry cross with palm, viet Nam service, Viet Nam campaign, Army Commendation, Good conduct 6th award, National Defense; [oth. writ.] Some songs selected for publication and some records made.; [pers.] If as I pass through this world, I can look back and say that I have contributed anything worthwhile to mankin, then my life will be fullfilled.; [a.] Arlington, TX

MONTERVIL, GABRIEL
[m.] Solange Montervil; [ch.] Rhyndy, Wyndnyr, Gab-Andy and Jephte; [ed.] West Side High, NJ, New England Tech, RI; [hon.] Mathematics Award; [a.] Providence, RI

MONTGOMERIE, ROBERT LOFTIN
[Pen.] Robert Loftin Montgomerie; [b.] September 12, 1968, Nova Scotia; [m.] Marie Elaine Montgomerie, November 22, 1993; [ch.] Andrew Baines Montgomerie; [ed.] A.A. F.C.C.J; [occ.] Candidate Assessment Division of Human Resources American Transtech; [memb.] National Libertarian Party of Americ, Libertarian Party of Florida, Riverside Presbyterian Church; [hon.] Beautiful wife and son. Proud servant of God. Always honest; [oth. writ.] "Golden Treasures" a collection of Lyrical Poetry. Poetry published in this book coming out in Sept. 94.; [pers.] I believe that honesty, faith, and truth are the only qualities you need to be successful in life. Greatly influenced by my Great-Grandparents and Great Aunt.; [a.] Jacksonville, FL

MOODY, BETTY
[b.] February 10, 1931, Rutledge, TN; [p.] Howard and Cleo Walker; [m.] Charles W. Moody, May 23, 1958; [ch.] Donna Bernard; [ed.] rutledge High; [occ.] Office Mgr. Quality Shop and Chemical Co.; [pers.] This poem was written in memory of my mother, Cleo Walker.; [a.] Knoxville, TN

MOOR, BETTY A.
[Pen.] Peoney Pain; [b.] November 28, 1936, Birmingham, AL; [p.] Carl and Georgianna Moor; [m.] Joe Heitzmann, June 25, 1993; [ch.] Deborah, Denise and Donna; [ed.] Assoc. Degree Human Services Admin. Merrimac College, Andover, Mass.; [occ.] Legal Assistant; [pers.] Each day is a gift from a higher power, wherein we may rejoice and become childlike in the discovery of our hidden talents.; [a.] Port St. Lucie, FL

MOORE, ALICE
[b.] November 22, 1922, Camden, NJ; [p.] Russell Moore and Laura Woodwars; [m.] John Doenges, March 20, 1943, Divorced 1963; [ch.] Peter, Susan, Karen and Mark; [ed.] Collingswood High School, Western Maryland College; [occ.] Writer/Bookkeeper; [memb.] N.J. Coalition for Smokers' Rights; [hon.] National Honor Society, N.J. All-State Chorus; [oth. writ.] Article and poems, school and college newspapers; articles, Baltimore sun; press releases, technical articles and employee newsletter, Inductotherm Corp.; short stories, articles and poems, unpublished.; [pers.] I hope to convey the richness and vast possibilities of human life from my own experience. I write because I must.; [a.] Voorhees, NJ

MOORE, BETHANY
[b.] September 20, 1982, Killeen, TX; [p.] Melinda and Garry Moore; [ed.] 7th Grade; [occ.] Student; [memb.] none; [hon.] Most creative, Publishment of selcted poems in school anthology; [oth. writ.] I have a journal full of them, (over 50 at least); [pers.] Everything and anything is poetry. And that's what I write about. Sometimes writing releives stress for me. It's great. Express yourself completely and do it in harmony. Harmony is the key!; [a.] Hollywood, MD

MOORE, DOROTHY
[b.] October 9, 1937, Newark, NJ; [p.] Deceased; [m.] Divorced 1979; [ch.] Three boys; [ed.] High School graduate 1 1/2 yrs. Allan Hancock College, 2 yrs. Air Force 1957-1959 ACW Operator (Plotter); [occ.] none, just a writer; [oth. writ.] "Stranger on a Plane," "A Blind Man."

MOORE, EVA
[b.] June 6, 1919, Wilmington, CA; [pers.] Just recently I was aked to give a reading here before a rather large audience which was taped. It was a wonderful experience. I would be so pelased if my book were to be published. It seems that so many ideas and words seem more easily shred in poetry form. There is no such thing as up or down, east or west in outer space, except in relationship to ourselves and our planet, and there is no end to space or time, there is only eternity. The only heaven and hell is right where we are.

MOORE, KATHRYN ANN
[Pen.] Katie, Id; [b.] November 3, 1982, Petaluma, CA; [p.] Elizabeth Hughes, David Moore; [ed.] I'm in the 6th grade.; [occ.] School; [hon.] Sonoma County Gateway Writing Award; [pers.] This poem is dedicated to Mr. Duane Big Eagle. He is responsible for ignighting the fire and passion for the writing within me.; [a.] Santa Rosa, CA

MOORE, SCOTT ALAN
[Pen.] S. A. Moore; [b.] October 3, 1963, Portland,

ME; [p.] Frank N., Dorothy P.; [m.] Carla Moore, August 18, 1992; [ch.] Calena Nicole; [ed.] Miami Palmetto Sr. High, B.A. English, University of Alaska, (Fairbanks Campus), MFA Creative Writing Columbia College.; [occ.] Alaska Logger (seasonal), Graduate Student (Columbia College, Chicago); [memb.] I subscribe to no organization.; [hon.] Winner of Marlin Firearms Hunter Safety essay contest, Junior division; Deans list,; [oth. writ.] Poems published in the Unsilenced Voice.; [pers.] None, other than to find a truth, however small, to give to the reader. I believe in wide reading for poets, writers.; [a.] Grabill, IN

MOORER, ARWILDER
[Pen.] Sisanna Moorer; [b.] June 24, 1935, Bolling, AL; [p.] Wilbert and Lela Moorer; [ch.] Michale and Janet Craig; [ed.] Associate of art Degree in Dietetic Technician at Wayne County College; [occ.] Food Service Director; [memb.] Alumni Association; [oth. writ.] From the Cotton Patch to College, Life; [pers.] All my life I have had words of rhyme in the spirit of my mind and enjoy putting them together.; [a.] Detroit, MI

MOORMAN, DANIEL
[b.] May 2, 1956, Ohio; [m.] Single; [ed.] Graduate of Wright State University, Ohio; [memb.] Friends of Earth, Sweden; [oth. writ.] "Soul Safari", London (Poetry(; [pers.] What is worthy in life cannot of its own merit transcend death, for in death is yet human demise and partingness of Spirit from God's present, good grace...; [a.] Minster, OH

MOOTS, IRA WILLIAM
[b.] May 4, 1948, Hurdland, MO; [p.] William and Carrie Clark Moots; [m.] betty Louise Steen Moots, June 28, 1992; [ch.] James William Moots, Cambria Dawn Moots Hunter, Lecia Rachelle Hartsock; [ed.] Hurland Public Schools, Hurdland, MO; Olivet Nazerene College, AB 1968; Nazerene Theological Seminary 1972-1975, KC, MO; [occ.] Substitute teacher; [memb.] Brashear United Methodist Church, Vicking Male Chorus Onc 1965 - 1968, Seminary Singer 1972 - 1975; [hon.] Dean's Honor List onc 1968, President Vicking Male Chorus, onc 1967 - 1968; [oth. writ.] Gods Timing Nazerene Perodical, Herald of Holiness; [pers.] Nothing more precious in life than one good friend, no value can be put on that. "A good friend is a friend for life."; [a.] Queen City, MO

MORABITO MARY MATOSIAH
[b.] July 23, 1929, Milw., Wis.; [p.] Hatcher and Sophie Matosian; [m.] Dominic D. Morabito (deceased), March 20, 1951; [ch.] David, Stella, Lucille, Mary Dominque; [ed.] High School, Cal State, LA to grade 14, LA County USC Hospital School of Nursing, Graduate Nurse R.N. AA:PCC, LAJC; [occ.] Care-giver to birth injured adult child; [memb.] none, I am pre-occupied with the care of my daughter, Lucille, who requires supervision; [hon.] 1946 Internationalism Award, Poetry Society of America; 1968 Book Award "The Writer;" 1963 Poem: North Pole, placed in National Archives by Robert Peary's daughter Marie Peary Stafford; [oth. writ.] "Ana the Beautyfil," an American legend in 6 monolgies, also in two anthologies, 1955 - 1970 in "Ararat Magazine The Arctic Poppy in "Approach," 1963 Aphrodite in Connecticut Literary Review 1955 about 100 published poems; [pers.] Moral law is as yet not under-

stood, but I believe it to be as natrual as physics, I feel the esthetic value of goodness and I know it by that attribute.; [a.] Temple City, CA

MORALES, LOUIS MICHAEL
[Pen.] Michael Morales; [b.] May 9, 1974, Miami, FL; [p.] Luis and Ana Morales; [ed.] Gulliver Preparatory High School, Palm Beach Atlantic College; [memb.] South Dade Christian Church; [hon.] Gulliver Prep Sophamore, Junior, and Senior Artist of the Year (90-92), National Honor Society, Pen and Sable, Dean's List, Outstanding Creative Contributions Award 1992, Supper Honors Award, CRCA Christian Athlete of the Year 1989.; [oth. writ.] Seeking to publish short volume of poems and lyrics. Designed murals for Miami Children's Hospital.; [pers.] I strive to achieve a metaphysical romantic style. "Pure honesty and true devotion gives the question and finds the solution."; [a.] Miami, FL

MORGAN, JULIANE
[Pen.] J.C. Poet; [b.] March 23, 1978, Des Moines, IA; [p.] Ron and Jane Morgan; [m.] Unmarried; [ch.] none; [ed.] Presently a Junior, attedning Johnston senior High in Johnston, IA; [occ.] Student; [memb.] Student of the Institute of Children's Literature; [hon.] The National Library of Poetry Editor's Choice Award, Johnston Senior High School Honor Roll, participant 1994 Drake University Young Writer's Conference; [oth. writ.] Poetry: the Legions of Light Magazine, The Young Author's Magazine. Dance on the Horizon and the Western Association of Poetry, also articles for Merlyn's Pen and the Legions of Light Magazine.; [pers.] Learn to feel what you cannot see.; [a.] Johnston, IA

MORGAN, KIMBERLEY
[b.] March 16, 1969, Wsbg, MO; [p.] Emmett and Karen Levine; [m.] Ssgt. Kevin M. Morgan, September 3, 1988; [ch.] Brandon Christopher, Alana Joi, Joseph Michael; [ed.] Cosmetelogy, CNA, some college hours.; [occ.] Housewife, new writer; [oth. writ.] Have an offer to publish a book I've wrote, submitted a fiction piece to Modern Romare (it will be a while before I hear anything) working on two writing courses and submitting other work for children and adults.; [pers.] I've tried to find my place in life so to speak, for a while, but now I feel I've found what my purpose for being here is. "I have finally arrived" to use a line I heart, I just thank God for this house.; [a.] Yigo, Guam

MORRIS, CHRISTINA MARIE
[b.] April 27, 1978, Torrance; [p.] John and Maria Shoemaker; [p.] Jim and Julie Morris; [ed.] I will graduate in 96' from David Starr Jordan High School in Long Beach. I also plan to study law at UCLA or USC; [occ.] Volunteer at Long Beach Memorial Hospital; [memb.] As a freshman at Jordan High I was a member of our International Baccalaurate Club and a member of the Girls Basketball Club. I was also on the J.V. Lady Panthers Basketball team at Jordan. As a sophomore I was a member of the Mock Trial Club at Jordan which got to compete in the L.A. County Courthouse; [hon.] I was given a "Valuable Player" award in J.V. basketball and a "good defense attorney" award by the Mock Trial Club.; [pers.] Religion, family, and education are the foundations on which my values are built. I'd like to give special thanks to my mom, Maria Shoemaker who always encouraged me to keep writing and also to my boyfriend, Danny

Diaz, to whom this poem is dedicated. Thank you. To get the full value of joy you must have somebody to divide it with.; [a.] Long Beach, CA

MOSBY, DOROTHEA S.
[b.] May 13, 1948, Sacrmento, CA; [p.] William L. Esther I. Mosby; [ed.] AA Bakersfield College, BS San Jose State University, MPA, Cal Stte U. Dominquez Hills; [occ.] Director of Parks and Recreation, City of South Gate; [memb.] CPRS, NRPA, CPRS, Scholarship Foundation, CA Board of Parks and recreation Certification, SG Kiwanis, SG Chamber of Commerce, LA World Affairs Council, LA Philharmonic Business and Professional Committee, Amer. Assoc. University Women.; [hon.] Pi Alpha Alpha Honor Society, LaBasin Pk & Rec. Commissioners Profesional of Year, Biography in Who'w Who Worldwide, Who's Who in the West, Who's Who of Emerging Leaders of America, Who's Who of America Women, Who's Who in California; [oth. writ.] Poem, Tears of Fire 1993; [pers.] Ordinary people working together can do extraordinary things. tht's wht makes life exciting.; [a.] Downey, CA

MOTT, SHELLEY
[b.] June 18, 1967, Dayton, OH; [p.] Frances Lundwall, John Mott; [ed.] Hocking Technical College, Ohio State University; [occ.] North Carolina State Park Ranger; [pers.] I am thankful to the Lord Jesus for blessing me with my writing talent. The poem "Assurance" was written with love for my fiancee Glenn Safrit.; [a.] Atlantic Beach, NC

MUCCIACCIARO, JENNIFER ALICIN
[Pen.] Jenny A. Mucciacciaro; [b.] November 27, 1979; [p.] Patricia and Robert Mucciacciaro; [ed.] John F. Kennedy High school, Freshman; [occ.] Student; [hon.] Honor Roll Student; [pers.] My poetry is a reflection of my life. Being in high school I see what racism does to this world and hope to relieve the pressures through my poems.; [a.] Waterbury, CT

MULDROW, MELANIE RENEE
[b.] February 9, 1975, Fort Dix, NJ; [p.] Patricia Ruth Dean Muldrow; [ed.] The Bryn Mawr School for Girls; Goucher College; [occ.] Student; [memb.] Black Student Association; Cause: A Community Service Program; [hon.] Miss United Negro College Fund.; [oth. writ.] Several poems published in Melange, a literary magazine, in 1992 and 1993; [pers.] Many of my writings come from sad situations. Pain is something that I have never tried to run from. Its a part of life and one of my greatest teachers. The hardships of life have taught me humility and courage. Most of all, through my toughest life experiences I have found a great peace and have truly learned too love.; [a.] Baltimore, MD

MULHOLLAND, KEVIN
[b.] December 6, 1933, New York City; [p.] Peter Mulholland, Josephine M.; [m.] Helen Mulholland, October 2, 1955; [ch.] Sean G. Mulholland; [ed.] New York School for the Deaf; (NTID) National Technical Institute for the Deaf, Rochester, NY, Rochester Institute of Technology (RIT), Rochester, NY; [occ.] Sign Language, Community College of Teacher, South Nevada; [hon.] NTID Dean's List: GPA/jKit Dean's List: GPA Fanwood Literary Award for best story signing, New York culture Association Award for Best Poetry; [oth. writ.] Poor Girl, had selected by the symposium advisory staff as the best

literary work in poetry on college campus.; [pers.] Writing is a matter of honing the focus after choosing a picture of sign language which words become creative and abstraction. Situations should be felt as well as seen. I want the readers to get the sensation, they may get discovering a new vision, this has cpatured the essence of a well remembered scene.; [a.] Henderson, NV

MUNCEY, FRAN WILEY
[b.] January 23, 1953, Rock Springs, WY; [p.] Wiley, William, Kreklau, Carol; [m.] Muncey, Darwin, January 21, 1974; [ch.] Veronica Lynn, Jessica Ann, William Gale; [ed.] Riverside High, ITT Business School; [occ.] Department Specialist; Bankcard Services; Boise, ID; [pers.] I reflect the day feelings of my life. My writing is influenced by my Aunt Ada Sigman. Who says, "Write your emotions, and feelings of living."; [a.] Boise, ID

MUNDY, FRANCES
[b.] November 18, 1924, Philadelphia, PA; [p.] Margaret Sullivan Haley and Thomas Joseph Haley; [m.] William J. Mundy, November 5, 1949; [ch.] Barbara, Margaret, Kathleen and Bill, Jr.; [ed.] P.S. du Pont H.S. graduated 1943 Wilm., Delaware; [pers.] My faith in God is the most important part of my philosophy. I also feel a sense of humor and common sense will see you through most difficulties.

MURDY, WENDY
[b.] May 25, 1978, Pittsburg, PA; [p.] Kenneth and Sandra Murdy; [ed.] High school; [occ.] Student at Freeport High School; [memb.] S.A.D.D. (Students Against Drunk Driving); [hon.] Honor Roll; [oth. writ.] Several poems published in school newspapers.; [pers.] The darkness in my writing reflects everyday life. Everyone has a dark side, few choose to show it. When you do, you become a poet.; [a.] Sarver, PA

MURPHY, SANDRA
[Pen.] S. Murphy; [b.] August 19, 1947, Paterson, NJ; [p.] Elizabeth and Raymond Dymond; [m.] George J. Murphy, September 30, 1978; [ch.] Timothy S. Tracy, Ryan Patrick Murphy; [ed.] Pequannock Twp. High School, Pequannock, NJ; Anticipate B.A. Psychology from Thomas Edison State College, May 1995.; [occ.] Human Resources Manager; [memb.] N.A.F.E., National Association for Female Executives; [oth. writ.] Just Beginning; [pers.] Elements of nature and music move and inspire me to write poetry. The beauty of both is not only inspiring but enhances my appreciation of life.

MYERS, KURT
[b.] March 8, 1978, Blytheville, AK; [p.] Suyon and James R. Myers; [ed.] Junior at Hatton High school; [oth. writ.] Many other poems seen by friends and family only.; [pers.] Most of my work reflects the demented part of mankind, yet some also reflect the good. I was influenced by the great Edgar Allen Poe. None of my poems reflect anyone in particular.; [a.] Hatton, ND

MYERS, STEVEN PHILIP
[b.] June 29, 1973, Cleveland, OH; [m.] Tasha Renae Myers, July 23, 1994; [ed.] Bay Village High School; [occ.] Sailor, U.S. Navy; [pers.] Words make me well; and ink heals and wounds.; [a.] Bremerton, WA

MYLES, YVONNE
[b.] April 10, 1958, Ft. Meade, MD; [p.] Maurice and Delores Myles; [ed.] B.S. Journalism, Oklahoma State University, 1981; [occ.] Editor, employee/business newsletter for major oil company; [memb.] Women In Communications, Inc.; Toastmasters International; [hon.] Competent Toastmaster, Alpha Lamda Delta Freshman Hononary.

NAGEL, SHELLEY
[Pen.] "Rose"; [b.] October 19, 1982, Springville, NY; [p.] Lenny and Barbara Nagel; [ed.] 7th grader at West Valley Central Shcool; [occ.] Student; [memb.] St. Paul's Lutheran Church Sunday School; West Valley Jr./Sr. Band; West Valley J.V. Soccer Team; West Valley Student council; [oth. writ.] "As I lay there, that night," "Sepcial ones," "Do they care," "Tears;" [pers.] My poems are mostly inspired by my family and friends. I write about my feelings, my weaknesses, my love's and my hopes. People have different ways of expressing their feelings, for me, I use poetry.; [a.] West Valley, NY

NAPOLI, PATRICIA
[Pen.] Patricia Cox Napoli; [b.] February 27, 1938, Pittsburgh, PA; [p.] Agnes and George Cox; [m.] Joseph A. Napoli, November 12, 1966; [ch.] Angelo, Maria and Joseph Napoli; [ed.] Annunciation Grade School and High School, Correspondence Degree, Palmer Instittute and Minneapolis Art Institute, Children's Stories Correspondence Course; [occ.] Housewife; [memb.] St. Francis Welcoming Committee and st. Francis Prayer Group; [hon.] American Legion Award, Debating and Public Speaking Awards, High Schools Poetry Anthology Awards; Acknowledgment from Ronald and Nancy Reagan; [oth. writ.] Poem on Challenger, Baby Magazine.; [pers.] Writing is a talent that not only pleases others but offers deep insight to one's personal feelings in any given subject; [a.] Springfield, PA

NARBUT, NANNIE M.
[Pen.] Jackie; [b.] November 2, 1925, Ridgely, TN; [p.] Henry Knight and Ethel Knight-Doublin; [m.] Joseph E. Narbut, Sr., March 18,m 1946 (deceased); [ch.] Joseph E. Jr., Jacke D. (Smokey); John Lee; James P.; [ed.] High School, Ridgely, TN in Sedalia, KY (did it in 3 yrs) 2 1/2 yrs. Business College, LaSalle Extension; [occ.] Retired; [memb.] none; [hon.] 1st, 2nd, 3rd Ribbons in my one'n only art exhibit, pastel portraits; [oth. writ.] Nothing I've tried to get published, I write poetry, song'n music and short stories, it's a compulsive hobby.; [pers.] I enjoy poetry; as one short poem can say as much as the longest novel.; [a.] Millville, NJ

NARTKER, LUCINDA M.
[b.] June 20, 1952, Lansing; [p.] James A. and Mary D. Southern; [m.] Kevin Nartker, November 22, 1975; [ch.] Tammy Jean, Tonya Lynn, Nicole Marie; [ed.] Hastlett High School, North American School of Animal Sciences.

NASH, DARLENE
[pers.] I dedicate this poem in memory; to my Father Donald E. Nash Sr. and to my Aunt Donna Mahoney with love.

NAYLOR, GEROGE EDWARD
[b.] June 12, 1965, Fort Ord, CA; [p.] Beth Naylor; [ed.] University of Nebraska, Kearney, NE; Concordia College, Seward, NE, Concordia Seminary St. Louis, MO; [occ.] Seminarian -Concordia Seminary, St. Louis, MO; [memb.] Good Shepherd Lutheran Church, Lutherans for Life, American Bible Society, God's Word to the Nations Bible Society, Lutheran Bible Translators, American Family Association; [hon.] Phi Alpha Theta; [oth. writ.] none so far; [pers.] The content of my poetry is usually inspired by the works of J.R.R. Talkien and C.S. Lewis.; [a.] St. Louis, MO

NAZARETYAN, ANI
[b.] April 7, 1975, Erevan, Armenia; [p.] Nazaret and Mariam Nazaretyan; [ed.] LaGuardia Community College, Long Island City, New York; [occ.] Sales Associate, Lechters Housewares; [oth. writ.] Published articles and poetry in college newspaper.; [pers.] The greatest gift in life is choice.; [a.] New York, NY

NAZON, JENNIFER
[b.] June 19, 1978, Bronx, NY [p.] Serge and Monique Nazon; [ed.] Sacred Heart School (K-5), R.F.K. Incentive Program (6-8), The Mary Louis Academy (11th grade in Sept. 94); [occ.] H.S. Student and Volunteer Math Tutor; [memb.] National Honor Society, Poetry Club; [hon.] Women's History Month Contest for poem on Elizabeth Blackwell (6th grade), Spanish medal (8th grade), first and second honors, National Honor Society Presidential Awrd.; [a.] Cambria Heights, NY

NEFF, LESLIE
[b.] February 17, 1973; [p.] John and Nancy Neff; [ed.] High School Diploma and 2 years of college at Southwestern Michigan College; [occ.] Direct Care Staff at a home for disabled adults; [oth. writ.] Personal writings that have not been published.; [pers.] To learn from the past is a gift. To remember it is a blessing.; [a.] Dawagiae, MI

NELLIGAN, PAMELA J.
[b.] June 9, 1955, West Indies; [p.] Richrd V. Donovan and Gertrude S. Shea; [m.] Stephen W. Nelligan, November 8, 1975; [ch.] Lance Walen, Carolyn Ann, Kyle Richard; [ed.] Braintree High School, Stockbridge School of Agriculture, Massosoit Community College; [occ.] Photographer, writer; [pers.] My inspiration comes from observations of life and living. My belief in our connections with each other in unshakable; [a.] Dennis, MA

NELSON, BONNIE L.
[b.] January 11, 1944, California; [p.] Jim and Maxine Miller; [m.] Terry C. Nelson, June 30, 1984; [ch.] Ray Allan Moore, Bryan David, Richard Adam, Michelle Renee (all are Moore's); [pers.] My poems were written for my son Ray, who died in 1994. They were inspired by my love and lost of him. My goal was to get one published in his memory. I am grateful to everyone who helped make that possible; [a.] Rowland Hgts, CA

NELSON, EYTHOL M.
[b.] November 6, 1915, Boise, Idaho; [p.] Albert an dElla Barr; [m.] Pastor Arnold H. Nelson, June 26, 1943; [ch.] Timothy, Stewart, David Arnold, Brian Keith (7 grandchildren, 2 great-grandchildren); [ed.] Ventura, Cal. Public Schools; Ventura Jr. College; UCLA; Graduate School, Librarionship; [occ.] Retired Librarian; [memb.] University Lutheran Church,

active in Elder hostel programs; [hon.] Gainesville Volunteer of the Year, 1989 in Education (taping books for blind students, Univ. of Florida); [oth. writ.] Some things published in local newsletter, 1 in out-of-state newspaper; [pers.] At age 75 while attending an Elder hostel program on poetry, I rediscovered a long neglected hobby. I expected to write mostly on personal and family matters, but my interest in social problems opened a way to express my thoughts through poetry.; [a.] Gainesville, FL

NEMBHARD-WOODBERRY, SHERRY
[b.] February 18, 1957, Ocala, FL; [p.] Samuel and Carrie Woodberry; [m.] Gerrard E.A. Nembhard, August 15, 1987; [ch.] Clifford Mesha, and Sasha Michelle; [ed.] Vanguard High school, Central Florida Community College, University of Florida, Nova University; [occ.] Educator, Belleview Santos Elementary School; [oth. writ.] Several editorials published in the local newspaper, a short story entitled "True Emancipation."; [pers.] I have discovered an undeniable phenomenon about the art of writing. The power of the pen can be just as destructive as the bullet in a drive by shooting or just as constructive as the rifel shot that scares off the preying animal.; [a.] Ocala, FL

NENCKA, HELEN
[m.] Walter; [ch.] Sue Lugviel, Walter S. Necka; 2 grandchildren Amy (Tom) Hilgenberg and David Nancka; great-grandchildren Anne and Jimmy; [occ.] Chef 1950-70 in our Restaurant recommended by Gourmet Magazine. Sold business in 1970; [hon.] Commissioned only - poem worked into paint, usually nature.; [oth. writ.] Over 3000 poems; published 3 books: To My Love, Island Seed, Christmas Tree Story. 1500 Tender Comscience, times Press, Hartford, Wis. Poems appeared in Ideals, Holy Hill Magazine, Pen Woman and other periodicals. Unpublished 1000 to grandchildren and approx. 450 over 100 love poems to my husband; [pers.] My aim is not to lead, but to inspire.; [a.] Hubertus, WI

NEURAUTER, WENDY
[b.] November 26, 1975, Grand Forks, AFB, ND; [p.] David and Mary Neurauter; [ed.] Quartz Hill High School and Antelope Valley Community College; [occ.] Student; [hon.] Who's Who Among High school Students (2 yrs.) Dean's List; [oth. writ.] And Then...The Quarts Hill High School Literary Magazine 1992-'93; [pers.] No matter the experience, you should always walk away with something more than you had before.; [a.] Lancaster, CA

NEWTON, PAMELA
[b.] May 2, 1955, Colbert Co., Alabama; [p.] Jack and Jeanette Sullivan; [m.] David Newton, August 2, 1985; [ch.] Son, Wade Lee Oliver; [ed.] Cherokee High, Northwest Al State Jr. College, Shoals Community College; [occ.] Secretary, Reynodls Metals Co., Muscle Shoals, AL; [memb.] Reynolds Business Women's Club, Phi Theta Kappa Honor Society; [hon.] National Dean's List 1991-92, Phi Theta Kappa Honor Society; [oth. writ.] Poems in high school newspaper, some songwriting; [pers.] Through writing, one can reach down into the soul and lift up a treasure worth more than silver and gold. Carpe diem, Latin for "live for today," is a favorite quote of mine.; [a.] Cherokee, AL

NICEWANDER, ALAN W.
[b.] August 11, 1959, Alma, Mich.; [p.] Alfred and Maxine; [m.] Courtney, October 17, 1986; [ch.] Sunny, Elisha, Jessica; [ed.] H.S. Graduate Ithaca High School; [occ.] Machinist; [oth. writ.] Several other poems, and am hoping to write my first book.; [pers.] I hope to touch the hearts of others in some way. And hope to enlighten them and lift their spirits, or help them to see things in a different way.; [a.] Ithaca, MI

NICHOLS, CARRIE LYNN
[Pen.] Lynn; [b.] December 27, 1970, Georgia; [p.] Carolyn Sanders and tyrus Scarborough; [m.] Douglas Lee Nichols, May 24, 1991; [ch.] L. Mason Micols, Andrew Lee Nichols, Matthew Lloyd Nichols; [ed.] Attended Kettering High School 88. Attended Minac Inc. Health Care Training School. Second in my class, certified nurse; [occ.} Fulltime mother of three and wife; [pers.] I need to say thank you to my family. Mom, you are the strongest woman I know. You gave me that strength to weight about, you've supported my work when I didn't feel it was any good. Dad, I love you. Doug, my husband, you are my rock I leane on. You've given and been put through so much. I love you forever. Last my children Mason. Andy and Matthew, my boys are my life and without any of you in my life I wouldn't have so much feeling to weight of. I love you all and thank you.; [a.] Auburn, KY

NICHOLSON, CHRISTY
[b.] October 8, 1976, San Diego, CA; [p.] Nick Nicholson and Dixie beason; [ed.] Prescott High School; [pers.] My poems are my day to day experiences/feelings that go on in my life. Dedicated to Chuck Nibley, Love Always, Christy; [a.] Prescott, AZ

NICHOLSON, JAN A.
[b.] November 29, 1956, Athens, GA; [p.] Travis and Morea Ayers; M Dennis J. Nicholson, June 28, 1987; [ch.] Samantha Jan, 2; [ed.] Forest Park Sr. High, DeKalb College, Clayton State College; [occ.] Homemaker; [oth. writ.] This is my first poem published.; [pers.] I wrote this poem from heart my feelings that I experienced then and now. I love poetry and this was the best way to express myself.; [a.] Rex, GA

NICKEL, MERVIN W.
[b.] August 28, 1912, Cincinnati, Ohio; [p.] Charles and Edith (Fricke) Nickel; [m.] Annabel Stanford Nickel, March 29, 1972; [ch.] by 1st wife who died in 1970, a daughter now 47; [ed.] Finished 10th grade and was forced to quit and help mother with business when father died at 41 in 1929.; [occ.] Retired, have kept busy building inside of house; [memb.] St. John's Luthern Church, Atlanta Retiree's club of USSACC (U.S. Steel Ag. Chem Co., Atlanta), Retiree's club of Armour and Company hqtd. in Florida; [hon.] Awarded Citizenship medal by SAR in 1927. Awarded a beautiful solid brass desk clock for "outstanding achievement" by Graduate School of Credit and Financial Management" at Dartmouth, in 1970.; [pers.] If I have a philosophy it is to do every job assigned me to the best of my ability. Lack of formal education hampered, but I advanced from Ledger clert to General Credit Manager, with jurisdiction in 44 states.; [a.] Atlanta, GA

NIELSEN, NORMAN
[b.] March 10, 1923, Minneapolis, MN; [m.] Ann, September 18, 1982; [ch.] Gregory, Jennifer; [ed.] B.A.; [occ.] Chairman of Consulting Associates, Inc; [memb.] Builders Association Twin Cities, past Board member, MN Board of Realtors; National Association of Security Dealers; [hon.] Named by Time Magazine of Mpls. C.C. as "One of 100 Leaders of Mpls." winner highest award for design and construction by builders assocation "The Reggie Award;" past Board Member, Mpls. Ministerial Association; [oth. writ.] Book: Days of Destiny (essays), Novel "Maverick of the Cloth;" [pers.] Life goal: Balance between work, play, love, spirituality. Leave this earth a better place than I found it.; [a.] Edina, MN

NINES JR., ROBERT J.
[b.] April 26, 1971, Dorby, PA; [p.] Elaine Nines; [m.] Single; [ch.] none; [ed.] Magr. Bonner High School, Temple University; [occ.] Starving Writer, College Student, Produce Clerk; [oth. writ.] Unpublished fiction and poetry.; [pers.] There is no thing finer than reality.; [a.] Folcroft, PA

NOAKES, BILLIE S.
[b.] February 3, 1975, Aurora, IL; [p.] Joan S. (d); Richard O.; [occ.] Program Manager, Vision Cable of Pinellas; free-lance producer/writer; [memb.] Friends of Pinellas Park Library; Tampa Bay Mensa; Consortium for Art and Media Studies (CAMS) (founder); [hon.] Who's Who of American Women, Soropitimist Women Honoring Women, Broadcaster of the Year; Nominated for Cable Person of the Year (Tampa Bay) 1991; Nominated for Cable ACE award for arts programming, 1994.; [oth. writ.] Articles in St. Pete times, Tampa Trib, Bay Life magazine, professional journals, Self-published "Selected Works of Incomplete Poets" w/Tim Caddell; [pers.] People have an unfortunate tendency to think standards of value can't be applied to art. Several of us maintain that if poetry is unintelligble, it's not necessarily "deep;" it's more likely to be poorly written. We show emotions with clarity, and technical skill with passion. It works, and we should demand it!; [a.] Pinellas Park, FL

NOBLE, DARREN
[b.] February 2, 1974, Los Angeles, CA; [p.] Ray and Martha Noble; [ch.] Sister: Audra Noble; [ed.] Prospect High School Class of 1992, currently attending a local junior college; [occ.] Sales; [hon.] English Department Writing Contest Certificate in Recognition of Outstanding Achievement in writing from Campbell Union High School District Spring 1989; [pers.] I would like to give thanks to life. Without life there would be no poetry.; [a.] San Jose, CA

NOLKE-RINGER, DAYLE
[Pen.] Dayle Ringer; [b.] August 9, 1972, Carrollton, MO; [m.] David Nolke, July 10, 1992; [ch.] Stepson, Jonathan 13 yrs, Stepdaughter City 9 yrs, Son, Nicholas 7 months; [ed.] Marshall High School 1991; [occ.] Homemaker; [oth. writ.] Darkness, Peace, and other poems.; [pers.] I like romantic poetry, but I like to strive to write different. Poetry really brings out my true feelings. I feel like I can let myself go, to be just me.; [a.] Carrollton, MO

NOTIS, ELAINE JEAN
[Pen.] E. Jean Notis; [b.] August 5, 1952, Webster, Mass.

NOVAK, ARTHUR D.
[Pen.] A.D. NOVAK; [b.] October 6, 1944, Niag.

Falls; [m.] Sonya M. Novak; [ch.] Kim, Frank, Jon; [ed.] Parson's College, Fairfield, Iowa; [occ.] Construction and Maint. Supervisor, Adelphia Cable-Niag.

NOVAK-DATTELS, MARGARET MARKETA
[Pen.] Margaret Marketa Novak; [b.] October 8, Berezovo, Czechoslovakia; [p.] Esters and Marton Neuman; [m.] Widow of Albert Dattels, February 27, 1990, 2nd Marriage (passed 1/23/93); [ch.] Robert L. Novak and Karen J. Novak; two sons passed Howard M. Novak and Leo D. Novak; [ed.] McKay Business College, Los Angeles; [occ.] Executive Director Bnai Zion Western Region since 1985. Publicist P.R. Specialist, Cable Televison Producer/Host, "Market's People and Places Show."; [memb.] L.A. World Affairs Council, Advisory Board National Bank of California, many more memberships; [hon.] 1991 Wave Award for Excellence for local cable progrmming 1990 American-Israel Friendship Media Award for Outstanding ontributions in writing producing The Marketa's People and Places Show. Many other awards, too numerous to mention; [oth. writ.] Published poetry, press information, news letters, interviews and many others; [pers.] Because two of my children were born with serious disablilities I devoted a great deal of my personal time to causes for children with special needs. Howard my first child (died at age 5), ten years later Leo was born. Leo died of cancer at age 25, August 10, 1990. It is impossible to describe the pain of losing children. Wrok on behalf of others who re in need helps lessen the pain. Surviving the Holocaust taught me a bitter lesson that we must never take freedom for granted. Surviving is not enough. What's more important is how we live and how we channel our energies to change conditions which are not acceptable in the world of today. In the end that's how we measure life.; [a.] Beverly Hills, CA

O'BRIEN, COLEEN
[Pen.] Taylor; [b.] July 8, 1981, NJ; [p.] Mary Ann and Doug O'Brien; [ed.] Going into 8th grade at Aquinas School, Woodbridge, VA; [occ.] Video Assistant; [memb.] Junior Gym at St. Elizabeth Penn, Seton Catholic Church, Junior Achievement Member; [hon.] A 1993 softball All-Star for Woodbridge Little Leage. Honor Roll, Art Competition Winner; [oth. writ.] I had one of my poems published in the Anthology of Young American Poets.; [pers.] Through my poems, I express my feelings and experiences. I hope to some how comfort others through my poetry.; [a.] Woodbridge, VA

O'DAY, BERNARD W.
[Pen.] Bernard W. O'Day; [b.] August 10, 1929, Colchester, VT; [p.] John F. O'Day and Albina Delorge; [m.] Addie Rashaw, Augsut 26, 1950; [ch.] Cheryl Anne, Michael John, kevin James and Mark Alan; [ed.] burlington High School; [occ.] Superv. Industrial Photographer, General electric Co., 38 yrs. retired; [memb.] Lite 'n Lens Camera Club (Founder), Vermont MacIntosh user's Group, AARP and the American-French Genealogical Society; and many others; [hon.] BHS Alumni Assoc. Award for the highest standing in the Merchandising and Sales Curriculum, 12 Merit Awards and Certificat of Merit for 25 years of service to the L'n L CC.; [oth. writ.] Poem published in local newspaper, editor of and essays for 6 high school reunion booklets, articles for VMUG Newsletter, technical paper for PP of a Journal and

artices on photography and general reporting for GE Plant Newspaper.; [pers.] Having spent my working life capturing images on film s a professional industrial photographer; and who only wrote poems for specific purposes; such as, person greeting cards and as part of script for slide shows, etc.; I find in retirement, that sitting in front of a Macintosh computer, and ceating poetry just for my own pleasure, is rather rewarding; [a.] Williston, VT

O'DONNELL, ALEX
[b.] Libra, NY; [ch.] Twins, Kevin and Terrence; [ed.] Hofstra, Tulane U., Builders Institute, Suffolk C.C.C.; [memb.] Cult of Atom; Chairman NY Welding Society, U.S. Coast Guard Auxilary; [oth. writ.] Books published by Alexsar "The Expendable," "Relearding The Way," "Without Sin," "Why the Gift of Evc," "At Last," "Where Do They Go When they Die," "The Second Universe," and many poems, political prose; [pers.] Leader of "The Cult of Atom and the Duplicates."

O'NEAL, DEBORAH ANN
[b.] April 9, 1954, Kennewick, WA; [p.] Louise and Francis Bryan; [ch.] Jamie Louise O'Donnell, Shawn Patrick O'Donnell; [ed.] Mt. rainer High School, American Beauty College, and several computer and english classes at Mesa State College; [occ.] Levi Strauss Company; [memb.] Grd. Valley Rebekah Lodge #40, I.O.O.F. of Colorado; I have very little time to belong to any organizations, as my free time is spent on Genealogy Research; [oth. writ.] Currently working on a novel. I am working on the Genealogy of my mothers family. I spend hours doing research on these two projects. In my spare time or when the mood strikes, I write poetry.; [pers.] Life should be enjoyed by all, and savored to the fullest. To read poetry is to breathe in life and see it through the eyes of a dreamer.; [a.] Yellville, AR

OAKLEY, JAMES
[b.] September 30, 1980, Chester Crozier; [p.] James and Dorothy; [occ.] High School Student; [oth. writ.] Several short stories and poems, none published; [pers.] Writing reflects my personal feelings. Every second is a second closer.

OBERLIN, GEORGE O.
[Pen.] By George; [b.] November 12, 1924, Canton, Ohio; [p.] Walter and Virgine Oberlin; [m.] Mildred M. Oberlin, April 22, 1944; [ch.] Larry Eugene Oberlin and Sue Oberlin Snyder; [ed.] Middle Branch High, Colby College; [occ.] Retired USAF; [memb.] Air Force Sergeants Association, Charter member DAV Commanders Club.; [hon.] Air Force Commendation medal, World War II Victory Medal, Medal for Humane Action, Republic of Korea Presidential Unit Citation, United Nations Service Medal; [oth. writ.] Many poems some of which were published by my daughter as a gift on my 50th wedding anniversary.; [pers.] I find poetry an easy way to express my feelings on almost any subject. My interest in poetry started with a declamation contest in junior high school; [a.] Fort Myers, FL

OBINALI, MENAJA C.
[ed.] Earned Ph.d. Clinical Psychology, University of TN, Knoxville, TN; Th.M, Systematic Theology, Pastoral Ministreis Dallas Theological Seminary, Dallas, TX; [occ.] Freelance Writer; [hon.] Graduate Magna Cum Laude, Seattle Pacific Univ., Settle,

WA; High Honors, Univ. of TN, Knoxville; [hon.] High Honors, Dallas Theological Seminary, Dallas, TX; Who's Who 1990 University, Seminary and College Students, 1992 Lorraine Chafer Systematic Theology Awrd; [oth. writ.] Weekly/Biweekly articles, DTS News; article in Kindred Spirit "Created With A Purpose;" weekly column in local newspaper, Religion Section; Editor, Heartbeat, Oak Cliff Bible Fellowship's quarterly newsletter; also various articles and interviews.; [pers.] As a Christian, I believe God created us to bear His image, an image of grace, purity, love and kindness. Poetry provides a most vivid vehicle for communicting this image, which distinguishes us from other creatures. God made us poets, praisers and givers of thanks. At least one poem lies dozing in each of us. How tragic when prejudice and smallness of heart prevents our voicing that unique utterance, which God fine-tuned us to produce. Rejecting rusting agents preventing poetic expression, awakens and enlivens the poet within, granting freedom to declare previously imprisioned feelings, throughts, desires and ideas.; [a.] Dallas, TX

ODEN, KIMBERLY M.
[Pen.] Kim Oden; [b.] January 16, 1961, Nash., TN; [p.] Grover Carlos Sr. and Emogene Moss; [m.] Gregory Wayne Oden, May 17, 1991; [ch.] Michael Shane Robertson, Lisa Danielle Robertson; [ed.] Dupont High School; [occ.] Surprise Lady (I do parties for ladies only); [oth. writ.] I write poems for my family and friends.; [pers.] This poem was written for the greates man I know, who has been through alot with me. Thank you Greg, I love you.; [a.] Mt. Juliet, TN

OEHLBECK, BARBARA HARDING
[Pen.] Native of Hickory, NC, Transplanted Floridan!; [p.] Mr. and Mrs. Glenn W. Harding; [m.] the Captain, Dr. Luther W. Oehlbeck, December 18, 1975; [ch.] Beloved God Daughers: Merry Yaeger Bray (Virginia), Rosemarie Lovell Daniells (California); [ed.] Various courses at University of Chicago, Univ. of Virginia, Central Piedmont College, NC, Averett College, VA; [occ.] Fulltime writer.; [memb.] The Human Race, Episcopal Church, Muse Association; [hon.] Named Outstanding Horticulture Writer for State of Florida 1993-94; Florida Freelance Writers Society Poetry Award, Semi Finalist, Kentucky Poetry Society, Finalist Award; Named to Literary Heritage, Charlotte, Mecklenberg, North Carolina; [oth. writ.] Two books: Poems and poetic prose titled "It Wonders Me," "The boy, the Man, and The Bishop", biography Bishop Herbert Spaugh, Moravian. Regular contributor to Florida "Green" (horticulture) magazines, as well as Southeast U.S. and National. Poetry has appeared frequently in The Sabal Palm Review, FL. Book "The Magnificent Sabal Palm," to be released Jan. 1995 by Florida Classic Library Publishers; [pers.] Morning, The geatest gift. I am born again (BO, 1975) I live by this creed.; [a.] Glades County, FL

OKPI, ADAKU L.
[b.] USA; [p.] Kalu N. Okpi (African Novelist "The Biafran Testament"; [ed.] The Spence School (1992) High School, New York University, Tish Sch. of Arts, New York, NY; [occ.] College Student; [hon.] Semi Finalist, Shakespeare Competition (1990); Honorable Mention in World of Poetry; Semi Finalist 1994 N. American Open Poetry Competition; [oth.

writ.] "Alone" written at age 13; poem "Baby" written at age 14, dedicated to my first niece Vanessa King.; [a.] New York, NY

OKUBO, SHARON
[b.] February 22, 1978, Kenya, Africa; [p.] Margaret and John Okubo; [ed.] Eleanor Roosevelt High School; [memb.] Bladensburg Vol. fire Dept. and Rescue Squad; [oth. writ.] Not yet published; other poems.; [pers.] I believe that poetry is synonomous with self expression.; [a.] Greenbelt, MD

OLGA, BILINSON
[b.] March 14, 1979, Ukraine; [p.] David and Bela bilinson; [ed.] Freshman at Mather High School in Chicago; [hon.] Honor Student, research paper received superior ranking at State History Fair competition in Springfield, 93'; Participated in the 93' National History Day in Washington, D.C. and received an excellent ranking. (R.P.); [oth. writ.] Poem published in the Anthology of Poetry by Young Americans, 1993 edition.; [pers.] I write to soothe my soul, and at the same time I hope to make a difference in the world. I want people to appreciate my writing because it comes from my heart. My poetry reflects on the way I see things and my perspective on life.; [a.] Chicago, IL

OLKOWSKI, VICTOR E.
[b.] October 3, 1952, Owego, NY; [p.] Zigmund and Helen; [m.] Kathleen M. Olkowski, December 23, 1972; [ch.] Vickie, age 15, Elizabeth age 10; [occ.] Owner, Landscaping firm, Suburgan Lawn Care, Inc.; [memb.] PA Nurseryman's Association, National Association for Small Enterprises (NASE); [pers.] I dedicate this poem to the memory of my fther and to my many friends who have served in the U.S. Military.; [a.] Schwenksville, PA

OLSON, JAMIE ANNE
[b.] April 2, 1982, Loma Linda, CA; [p.] Kathryn and Mike Olson; [ed.] 6th grade; [occ.] Student at Sacred Heart School; [memb.] Grand Terrace Baptist Church; [oth. writ.] A Heart Beat Away, A Special Place In My Heart, Addiction, Nature, A Sparkle; [pers.] My friends and family inspired me to write my poetry.; [a.] Grand Terrace, CA

OLSSON, S. INGEMAR C.
[b.] August 10, 1943, Gothenburg, Sweden; [p.] Conrad and Gunhild Olsson; [m.] Dr. Deborah A. Kinbrell, June 15, 1991; [ed.] Royal Navy Academy, Military Statt College, Stockholm University of Gothenberg; [occ.] Managing Editor, Travel Writer; [memb.] Republican Senatorial Inner Circle; Major, Swedish Marines Reserves, Lifetime Honorary member of Golden Kes (Les Clefs d'oor); [hon.] UN Medal, 1980; Jordan Tourism Medal, 1985; U.S. Republican Senatorial Medal of Freedom, 1994, Lifetime Honorary Member of "Le Clefs d'oor"; [oth. writ.] 1976-1994, Reporter, Editor and Correspondent for Today (1 Das) Swedish Daily Newspaper, TUR, International Tourism Magazine, Esteem, International Shipping Magazine and several other publications.; [pers.] WRote the first poems in 1994.; [a.] Bellaire, Houston, TX

ONEILL, CHRIS
[b.] June 11, 1978, Morristown, NJ; [p.] Mary and Thomas O'Neill; [ed.] Randolph High School 1996; [a.] Randolph, NJ

ONISTO, DAVID TORRES
[b.] February 13, 1980, New Britain, CA; [p.] Jose and Therese M. Torres; [ed.] Sacred Heart School; [occ.] Student, Mary Immaculate Academy; [hon.] High Honors in 8th grade, Presidential Academic Fitness Award; [a.] New Britain, CT

ORDUNA, KRISTI
[b.] March 15, 1978, Omaha [p.] Margret and Joe Orduna; [ed.] I'm 16 in 10th grade. I go to Sout High.; [occ.] Bust person at Howards Charrow; [pers.] I'm only 16 with a lot of confusing things inside of me. Trying to cope with things that happen to me and my friends. But poetry is the only way I can express myself.; [a.] Omaha, NE

ORR, MANDY
[b.] May 7, 1980, Pocatello, ID; [p.] Randy and Julie Orr; [ed.] Wilcox Elementary K-6; Hawthorne Jr. High 7-9; [occ.] Babysitting for Shirley Hawk. I babysit 2 boys Willy and Nick Hawk; [pers.] "Don't let the hate of one person get in the way for the love of another."; [a.] Pocatello, ID

ORTIZ, DEBBIE
[b.] April 20, 1961, California; [p.] Joe and Pat Sabella; [m.] Phillip Ortiz, August 27, 1982; [ch.] Lisa Sharlane and Leiah Ashley; [ed.] High School Grad. of South High C.P.R. Cert.; [occ.] Cino School Dist.; [oth. writ.] None, for this is the beginning.; [pers.] I would like to give my utmost gratitutde to my astouding daughters for having such faith in my achievements. I lvoe you Lisa and Leiah.; [a.] China, CA

ORTIZ, DEBORAH SILCOX
[b.] August 3, 1971, Port Charlotte, FL; [p.] Norma Jean Raymond and William Oliver Silcox; [m.] Daniel Jesus Ortiz III, Javier William Ortiz; [ed.] Marathon High School, Felician College 94; [memb.] Sigma Alpha Iota; [hon.] Honorable Mention Award by American Collegiate Poets, Dean's List; [oth. writ.] American Collegiate Spring Concours 1992.; [pers.] I write what I feel in my heart. This allows me to release my emotions that I can not communicate verbally.; [a.] Newark, NJ

OSTRANDER, DONALD R.
[b.] September 26, 1948, Brooklyn, NY; [p.] William and Selma Ostrander; [m.] Frances A. Ostrander, September 28, 1967; [ed.] Freeport Sr. High School, AUCO Business School; [occ.] Owner, Cleaning host Inc.; [memb.] D.A.V.; [hon.] Poem published in Poetic Voices of America; Awarded by Florida Freelance Writers Assoc for short story "Green Grass of Home." Cover story for O.F.F. magazine.; [oth. writ.] Screenplays, "Green Grass of Hope," "Heir Apparent," play, "Here Comes The Neighborhood There Goes The Blocks." Articles for Pine Island Eagle, Fort Myers News Press and Magazine.; [pers.] The world is moving to fast in the wrong direction. We should slow down and take time to hold out our hand to our fellow man.; [a.] Bokeelia, FL

OWENS, NORMA JEAN
[b.] November 17, 1934, Muncie, IN; [p.] Ernest J. & Juanita Pearl Dalton; [m.] Deceased; [ch.] Chiquita Pearl and Betty Jean; [ed.] 9th Grade; [oth. writ.] I have composed several Gospel songs, that has been received with great enthusiasm in many churches and large gatherings in Indiana, Ohio, and Kentucky.; [pers.] This poem was inspired by what we done and I felt when I visited uncle Ivan Lawrence in Birdseye, IN. With his bible in hand, taght me God's word, took me to church were I sang the Gospel songs I wrote, most that he inspired.; [a.] Farmland, IN

OWER, HEATHER NICOLE
[b.] September 4, 1979, Duarte; [p.] Robert and Donna Ower; [ed.] K-9th and still going; [occ.] School; [pers.] I think the only people who can write peotry are the people who I have a strong feeling towards life, love family, etc.; [a.] Glendora, CA

PABLO, TONI
[b.] July 3, 1980, Yuma, AZ; [p.] Janet Wyatt and Teddy Pablo; [ed.] 8th grade, Mohawk Valley School; [occ.] Student; [memb.] Only school activities.; [pers.] I am influenced by my friends an dpeople around me. I'm a Tohjono O'odham.; [a.] Roll, AZ

PACK, REBECCA
[Pen.] Becca; [b.] January 20, 1963, LaPaz, Bolvn; [occ.] Student; [pers.] Published writing or an eligible prize sure make writing a pleasant past-time. It's fun and it's free.

PACKARD, JENNIFER
[b.] October 31, 1980, Tryon, NC; [p.] Brad and Debbie Packard; [ed.] 8th grade student at Tryon Middle School; [occ.] Student; [hon.] Honor Roll, Odyssey of the Mind Participant, Good Citizenship; [oth. writ.] Many poems, some published in local newspaper.; [pers.] I write to let out the emotions trapped inside of me. I'm greatly influenced by people I know.; [a.] Tryon, NC

PADDOCK, STEPHEN B.
[b.] April 21, 1927; [p.] Grace Banker and Eugene H. Paddock; [ed.] Amherst College; [occ.] Poetry; [memb.] Republican Party, American Security Council, Evangelical Lutheran Church; [hon.] Distinguished Leadership Award; [oth. writ.] Climbing In the Franconian Mountains, Climbing Mt. Washington; [pers.] Keep busy, and things go better.; [a.] Poughkeepsie, NY

PAGE, JENNIFER
[Pen.] Scarlet May; [b.] February 11, 1982, Georgia; [p.] Janice and Jim Page; [memb.] Girl Scouts; Lucern Baptist Church; Mountain Park; Swim Team; [hon.] Most Outstanding Music Student; awards in poetry and reading; Girl Scout Badges and prizes; basketball and swimming trophies, Presidential Academic Fitness Award; Honor Roll; [oth. writ.] Many short stories for school and mosaic; many poems for school and mosaic; [pers.] I would like to thank my parents who have encouraged my work and Mrs. Julie Vance, my 5th grade teacher, who helped me discover my talents.; [a.] Stone Mnt., GA

PAJIC, ARLEEN T.
[b.] October 10, 1940, Camden, NJ; [p.] Anthony and Carmella Mauri; [m.] thomas E. Pajic, November 9, 1963; [ch.] Dawn Marie, Thomas Anthony; [ed.] St. Joseph's High School, Trenton State College, and Cigna Corp., IBM and Drexel University Developmental Programs.; [occ.] Consultant; [memb.] Past Board member Paul VI High school, Athletic Executive Committee Parents Club and Business Advisory Board Member Cherry Hill High School East, Inter-

national Information of Word Processing, Greater Philadelphia Chapter; [hon.] International Information, Honor Society Certificate/Plaque Awarded for activities contributing to growth of work processing, International Song Writers Competition Certificate of Merit for Excellence in Lyric Writing, Cretivity and Technical Skill.; [oth. writ.] Writing prose, poetry, programs and original stories since 1972.; [pers.] Thru the Lord, all things are possible. Work hard, sacrifice and simply believe...and you can achieve great things.; [a.] Cherry Hill, NJ

PALACIO JR., JOHN
[b.] November 20, 1976, Santa Ana, CA; [p.] John and Jeanette Palacio; [ed.] Mater Dei High; [occ.] Student; [memb.] South Coast Repertory; [hon.] Certificate of Merit for Excellence in Writing as part of "Say No to Drugs Red Ribbon Week Campaign"; [oth. writ.] Various poems, essays, short stories that have been used to satisfy school requirements or entertain family and friends.; [pers.] Most of my writings illustrate a dark side of life that all humans share an empathy for. My greatest influences have come from Edgar Allan Poe, Poets who served in WWI, Stephen King, Robert R. McCammon, Dean R. Koontz; [a.] Orange, CA

PALITA, JENSINE L.
[b.] June 19, 1962, Chester, PA; [p.] Richard and Betty Goodman; [m.] James Palita, June 27, 1981; [ch.] James A. Palita, Matthew F. Palita, Jeffrey V. Palita; [ed.] High school graduate; [occ.] Teacher's Aide; [oth. writ.] Poems (not published); [pers.] I strated writing poems for myself and for my family and friends, about my feelings. It helps me expess myself.

PAMPA, JOSE AMANDO
[b.] January 6, 1980, French Camp; [p.] Jose R. and Laura H. Pompa; [ed.] Went to public school for grades K-3 and 4-7 at a Catholic School; [occ.] Student; [hon.] I have won first place in a contest in the children museum, and have won third place in a D.A.R.E.; [oth. writ.] Several poems published in school newspapers and The Children Museum Newspaper.; [pers.] I try to make people understand were I stand with my writing. How and why I see life. Well now I would like to thank my fourth grade teacher Mrs. Rath Byrd, Thank you.; [a.] Stockton, CA

PANAGOS, VIRGINIA
[b.] March 19, 1957, Greece; [p.] George and Anastasia; [ed.] Bachelor's Degree, Psychology and Criminal Justice, University of IL, MBA with concentration in Mktg., Roosevelt University; [occ.] Sprint, Product Manager, Residential Services; [oth. writ.] Other inspirtional unplublished poems. (11 more poems written, 5 - 10 minutes. Amirace in itself!; [pers.] This poem and many others were inspired by God and his guidance through some very difficult times. I was never interested in writing or reading poetry - 'Till Now!'; [a.] Niles, IL

PANTALIONE JR., MIKE I.
[Pen.] Pinky; [b.] October 27, 1978, Phila., PA; [p.] Terri and Mike Pentalione; [ed.] 10th grade V.H.S., Vineland High School; [occ.] Student; [hon.] State Championship Swimming; [oth. writ.] Many, not published.; [pers.] Live long, die young; [a.] Vineland, NJ

PARDUE, KATHLEEN ERICKSON
[b.] August 3, 1949, Woodbury, NJ; [p.] John and Helen Erickson; [m.] Leonard W. Pardue, June 5, 1975; [ch.] John Eric Pardue, Janice Ivy Pardue; [ed.] H.S. Deptford Township H.S., NJ; B.S. Lincoln Memorial Univ., Harrogate, TN; M.S. Long Island Univ., Brookeville, NY; [occ.] Teacher; [hon.] Grad. School, Summa Cum Laude, United State's Army's Commander's Award for Public Service Fort Hood, Texas, Community Helping Hand Award; [oth. writ.] Miscellaneous newspaper and magazien articles. Poems for family members, special occasions.; [pers.] I have always felt that the only truly important thing in life is how much we care about others. I believe that, if we all put others needs ahead of our own, the world would be a much nicer place...Do unto others...; [a.] Springfield, VA

PARKER, SHERRIE ANN
[Pen.] Sherrie Parker; [b.] November 12, 1980, Brooklyn, NY; [p.] Ms. Linus A. and Peter A. (deceased) Parker; [ed.] Student of Colonial High 9th grade; [memb.] Liberty Middle School Music Club, and in the past the Drama Club; [hon.] Most Creative Award, Chorus Award, Citizenship Award, English Award, Best All Around Award.; [oth. writ.] The Other Side, Salt Shiver (non published), The Grass is Greener, poem; [pers.] Just letting everyone know there's only one world and one human race, and if we stand together we can make it.; [a.] Orlando, FL

PARSONS, ANGELA
[b.] May 28, 1972, New Jersey; [p.] Carole Parsons; [ch.] one son Jared Parsons; [ed.] Cumberland Regional H.S., Cumberland County College; [occ.] Writer; [memb.] Girl Scouts, 13 years; [hon.] 2nd runner up in poetry contest in grade school, 1st runner up in art contest in girl scouts; [oth. writ.] Letters to editor in local newspaper, short stories, currently writing a book.; [pers.] My love of writing is a direct expression of who I was who I am and who I wish to be.; [a.] Bridgeton, NJ

PASCAL, JEAN-PIERRE
[b.] August 5, Haiti; [p.] Charles and Emma Jean-Pierre; [m.] edwin C. Jean-Pierre, July 7, 1994; [ch.] Shadae Emma Jean-Pierre; [ed.] Ecole Sainte Trinite, Haiti, College Saint Pierre, Haiti, City College, CUNY, John Jay College CUNY, NY; [occ.] Developmental Specialist, AHRC, Flutist, Surrealist Painter, Poet; [memb.] Too many to mention; [hon.] President of "The Voice Club" 1989-1990 and many others; [oth. writ.] Articles about mysticism, metaphysics, meditation for radio talk show and symposium, several other poems, song lyrics and prayers.; [pers.] I hope the cosmic light will reflect through my writing, music and painting; thus bringing every soul together as one, toward spiritual enlightment and pure love.; [a.lj Brooklyn, NY

PASCUCCI, ROCKY
[b.] Brookly, NY; [p.] Angie and Charley; [m.] Susan 1946; [ch.] Barbara Anne; [ed.] Alexander Hamilton H.S. and various subject and courses, Radio and TV etc.; [occ.] Retired; [memb.] Paralyzed Veterans of America, Knights of Columbus, M.S. Society; [hon.] World War II vet.; [oth. writ.] "Giro" unpublished novel. "John Smirko is Dead" a play (comedy). Wrote articles for "Bounce Back" and "News & Views" newsletters. Was editor of "The Round Table" a K of C monthly bulletin.; [pers.] Never give

up! No matter how tough things get, you have to keep going. Sometimes a disability will help rather than hinder. It makes us do things we never had time for.; [a.] Whitestone, NY

PASSMORE, PAMELA
[b.] April 30, 1967, Rector., AK; [p.] Shirley Ann Randler; [ch.] Jessica L. Murphy; [ed.] G.E.D. in Star City AK; [occ.] Mother at home with child, single parent; [oth. writ.] I make up my own poems; [pers.] I strive to write my own poems when I am thinking of someone or just sitting around thinking of feelings and creative things in my mind.; [a.] Pine Bluff, AK

PATSY, GFELLER B. STEVENS
[Pen.] Patsy; [b.] May 11, 1924, Marion, KS; [p.] Gerald A. Stevens and Grace V. (Kuhn); [m.] March 27, 1943; [ch.] Bradley Wayne Gfeller; [ed.] Graduate JCHS (Junction City High School, Junction City, KS, Post Graduate course in Commercial Art. Studied Secretarial work and bookkeeping in High School. Worked in Junction City, KS as bookkeeper of loca bus Co., during WWII; [occ.] Retired farmers wife; [memb.] Daughters of American Revolution (DAR) Lois Warner Chapter, Order of Eastern Star, Wakefield Chapter #441 Alida-Upland Cooperative Parish Church, Alida United Parish Women. Attended First Christian Church Wakefield, KS, Sr. Cits. of Wakefield, KS; [hon.] Diploma JCHS, Diploma Commercial Art, Diploma Bible Study; [oth. writ.] Our Saviour, My Church. Our 50th Anniversary, Three Seasons, (all Poetry) The Good Old Days, Memories of my childhoos, letters to the ditor, various papers, editorial in Washington Post.; [pers.] I believe God put me here for a special purpose. I try to live my life the way he would want me to, and try to show my love for all humanity, and enjoy the God-Given things of nature.; [a.] Wakefield, KS

PATTEN, EDWARD D.
[b.] October 1, 1948, Elmira; [p.] Edward and Elizabeth Patten; [ch.] Kimberly E. Patten; [ed.] Syracuse University, Graduate Degree, Elmira College, Graduate Degree; [occ.] Vocational Counselor; [pers.] I have been greatly influenced by the writings of Rod McKuen.; [a.] Elmira, NY

PATTERSON, CHRISTINA M.
[b.] February 14, 1980, Grand Rapids, MN; [p.] Mr. and Mrs. Ken Patterson; [ed.] Grand Rapids Middle School 7th grade; [occ.] Work for my Mom and Dad at Pattersons Store; [oth. writ.] I have written many other poems but this is my first one to be published.; [pers.] I love to write poems. It lets me put all my feelings in a place where I can look back on my freinds and especially my social teacher, Mrs. Hall who has sent in a few things for me, have helped me.; [a.] Grand Rapids, MN

PATTON, CINDY K.
[b.] December 10, 1958, Atlanta, GA; [p.] Clyde and Dolores Keefer; [m.] Shephard H. Patton, Sr., December 23, 1978; [ch.] Shane Tyler; [ed.] Bachelor of Science, University of Southern Mississippi; [occ.] Owner, Choice Business Services; [memb.] Professional Associaiton of Resume' Writers, U.S. Army Reserves; [hon.] Several Military Journalism Awards; [oth. writ.] Articles in local newspapers. Published a bi-weekly jobs and training newspaper, circulaiton 10,000.; [pers.] I hope what I write makes someone feel an emotion, remember a time or person, laugh or

cry.; [a.] Gulfport, MS

PATTON, ROSE MARIE
[b.] January 3, 1937, St. Louis County, Missouri; [p.] Ollie and Jeff Fisher (both deceased); [m.] Frank Gene Patton (deceased); [ch.] Clay James Patton 36 yrs. old, Terri Jean Patton 20 yrs. old; [ed.] Minimal, life experiences; [occ.] Mother and grandmother-writer; [memb.] I'm a member of the Conservative Baptist Church. A member of Hart of the Rogue, Romance Writer of Aemrican, Medford Ore. Chapter, also the National Romance Writers of America); [oth. writ.] I'm finishing my first book (Romance) I've written scores of poems, but have only recently decided to submit for publication.; [pers.] I believe we are each given certain talents, we should strive to fulfill our abilities, as we reach out to share our faith, the grace and peace we have in Christ.

PAUL, STEVEN
[pers.] Author of "Here Are Some Poems I Think You'll Like, By Steven Paul Who Likes to Write (Poems Thoughtful and Thoughtless)", an unpublished book of lyrics limericks, insights, and poems. Most are thoughtful but with a humorous twist, and they rhyme incessantly.; [a.] Dubuque, IA

PAULINE
[b.] November 12, 1975, Whittier, CA; [occ.] Student, Whittier College, Writer/Artist; [memb.] Whitier Area Baptist, Fellowship Church, Interntional Society of Poets; [hon.] John Greenleaf Whittier Art Talent Award Scholarship. Editor's Choice Award for "Rapture" in "Dance on the Horizon;" [oth. writ.] Several other writings; [pers.] In all matters of life and death, trust God through Jesus Christ.; [a.] Whittier, CA

PELLETIER, MELISSA RENEE
[b.] December 21, 1977, Falmonth, MA; [p.] Raymond and Pamela Pelletier; [ed.] East Lyme High-East Lyme, Ct., Salem Elementary, Salem, CT; [occ.] Customer Service at an Electronic Repair Service; [memb.] East Lyme High Drama Club, East Lyme Youth Services Prevention Players; [oth. writ.] Sixty three un-published poems I keep in a binder in my room.; [pers.] A dear friend of mine died when I was a freshman in high school. Shortly after his death I started writing poems to relay to others the struggles I go through as a teenager in today's world.; [a.] Salem, CT

PELTZ, LOIS ANN
[Pen.] Lois; Lapnotes; L.A. Peltz; [b.] May 3, 1950, Ft. Collins, CO; [p.] Leslie D. and Dorothy G. Williamson; [m.] Jerry D. Peltz, September 4, 1970; [ch.] Erik D. Peltz and Cheryl Ann Peltz; [ed.] Fort Collins High School; Colorado State University, BS; Colorado State University, MS; [occ.] Freelance Communications Specialist; [memb.] Gamma Sigma Delta, Honor Society/Omicvon, Nu Honor Society; [oth. writ.] Several poems published in local papers; collection of additional poems dealing with numerous topic's Colorado State University Coopertive Extension Publications and Professional Articles published.; [pers.] Poetry allows me to "paint" sounds, "voice" shades and hues, and express feelings for others to internalize.; [a.] Fort Collins, CO

PERELEONI, KAREN
[Pen.] Karen Leigh; [b.] Norma and Roger Lewandowski; [m.] James; [ch.] Justin George, Jordan Christopher, and Jacob Stephen; [ed.] College graduate; [oth. writ.] A collection of poems entitled, Numbered Thoughts and Random Expressions; [pers.] I try to convey a great del of emotion in my writing and tend to write about the darker side of human emotions. I admire the works of Kahlil Gibran and Sra Teasdale.; [a.] Maryville, TN

PEREZ, ANDREA
[b.] July 15, 1982, Fresno, CA; [p.] Suzanna and Carlos Perez; [ed.] 7th grade Annesworth Elem., attending Computech; [occ.] Cheerleader, Student at Anneworth; [hon.] Honor Roll Student for four years; Presidential Award (Contain Bill Clinton's Signature); [oth. writ.] I have also written a poem about a friend and her boyfriend but decided to publish the one I entered.; [pers.] This poem was dedicated to my mother for Mother's Day 94'; [a.] Fresno, CA

PEREZ, CHRISTIE
[b.] October 15, 1978, Oklahoma City, OK; [p.] John and Donna Perez; [m.] Grandparents: Mr. and Mrs. Greg Perez, Mr. and Mrs. Don Wesp; [ed.] Freshman at Troy High School in Fullerton, CA; [memb.] Eastside Christian Church; [hon.] 4th grde, 1st place in Creative Writing "Why Santa Clause came on Easter." Broke 21 year old track record for the "Sprint," 6th grade, 2nd place in "Creative Writing," 9th grade Honor Roll Student; MVP award for volleyball, received award for the most steals in basketball and for outstanding student in Spanish; [a.] Fullerton, CA

PEREZ, HOMERO A.
[b.] March 18, 1973, Santo Domingo, Dominican Rep.; [p.] Ulina Barinas)(Mother); [ed.] Attended Long Island University, Brooklyn Campus. Completed two years of Liberal Arts Courses. Recently Transferring to another college or university.; [occ.] Currently working as a salesman for Keebler Company to pay for education.; [pers.] Thank you to all my english teachers and professors that pushed me and made me realize what I enjoy most…writing.; [a.] Bronx, NY

PERHUS, ROSE
[b.] December 7, 1955, Brownsville, PA; [ch.] Joy Lynn, Jamie Leah, Joshua Phillip; [ed.] Uniontown High, Fayette County Vocational Technical School, West Virginia Career Institue; [pers.] I thank Ed for the inspiration.; [a.] Smock, PA

PERKINS, CHRISTEL
[b.] December 7, 1982, Pusan, So. Korea; [p.] Morris and judy Perkins; [ed.] Arp Elementry; [occ.] Student 6th grade; [memb.] 4-H; [hon.] A Honor Roll, National Arbor Day Foundation, Poster Contest; [pers.] I enjoy poetry very much, and have been writing poetry for several years.; [a.] Cheyenne, WY

PERMENTER, JASON ROSS
[Pen.] Francis Ross, Joseph Ross; [b.] April 9, 1974, San Angelo, TX; [p.] Jacqueline and David Permenter; [m.] Single; [ed.] Four separate high schools, and working towards college and my goals.; [occ.] Final Documentation Clerk for DMR Financial Services; [hon.] Three Honorary Achievements for theatre performances. An award for my vocal capabilities; [oth. writ.] Poetry and short stories.; [pers.] In every heart and mind there lies creativity. I found the best way to expess mine. A pen and paper show the simplicty of a "Poet.".; [a.] Novi, MI

PERRONE, CLAUDIA
[b.] March 17, 1975, Plainfield, NJ; [p.] Dominick Perrone, Elizabeth Perrone; [ed.] Governor Livingston Regional High School; [occ.] Student at the Richard Stockton Colege of NJ; [pers.] I am an author of my passions, found in my inspirations. If they can be reflected to the reader, then I have conquered a goal and have become immortal in my writing.; [a.] Berkeley Heights, NJ

PERSINGER, TARA
[b.] July 12, 1976, Beckly, WV; [p.] Fred Persinger; [ed.] Freshman at WVU, Woodrow Wilson High; [hon.] Invited into the International Society of Poetry; [oth. writ.] Poetry, stories; [pers.] Poetry and music are the pathways to the mind, and bridges to the soul; [a.] Beckley, WV

PERSKY, ADELE
[b.] Bound Brook, NJ; [p.] Joseph and bella Sacks; [m.] Samuel H. Persky; [ch.] Susan Bickford, Fan Levin; [ed.] Violin major at Mannes College of Music, New York City, Temple University, Gratz College; [hon.] Scholarship student of William Kroll of Kroll Quartet Hebrew Prize at Gratz College; Poetry Prize at Gratz College; [oth. writ.] Poems written in English and Hebrew; [pers.] My poems reflect on my life as a musician, wife, mother, and world traveler. (and lover of the Hebrew Language); [a.] Springfield, PA

PETERSEN, JOANNE E.
[Pen.] Joey; [b.] october 20, 1941, Oshkosh, Wisc.; [p.] Mr. and Mrs. J.H. Kroll; [m.] Timothy J. Petersen, August 31, 1964; [ch.] One Boy and Two Girls; [ed.] Two years University Minn. for X-Ray Specialist for Emerg. Room, X-Ray and Heart Cath's, Teacher; [occ.] Care giver 4 yrs (Infants) self employed; [memb.] American Technology of Radiology; [oth. writ.] Yes, A Special Friend, Life is a Whisper, Sis O Sis, My Mother, Starting Life Over, poems to my grand child and daughter.; [pers.] I always believe, if you want respect, give respect. If you want love and understanding give love and understanding. Give all you can, expect nothing. Do this with style and grace.; [a.] Mesa, AZ

PETERSON, LARRY
[b.] June 24, 1952, Minneapolis, MN; [p.] Clifford and Betty Peterson; [ed.] Marshall University High School, Southwest State University.; [occ.] Freelance Photogapher; [memb.] Titanic Historical Society, Minnesota Genealogical Society; [hon.] Smead Award, Sister Kenney International Art Show; [oth. writ.] Several in progress, none published so far.; [pers.] My belief that good is omnipotent and our mission in life is to understand that and all it implies, is the basis for my writing.; [a.] Minneapolis, MN

PETERSON, RICHARD W.
[b.] February 25, 1954, Phila.; [p.] William and Florence Peterson; [ch.] 1, Kaitlin Elizabeth; [ed.] Grad. Frankford High, Phila. PA; [occ.] The Budd Co., Hunting Park, Phila. PA; [pers.] My poems reflect the spirit of the sixties and the seventies. I so much wanted to be a part, thank you for giving me this opportunity and to those who are still with us and those who are not, God be with you.; [a.] Phila., PA

PETERSON, SARA
[b.] February 1, 1980, Iron Mountain, MI; [p.] Patricia and Thomas Peterson; [ed.] Freshman at Iron Mountain High School; [occ.] Student; [pers.] My writing comes from deep inside me, its my thoughts, and feelings put into words.; [a.] Iron Mountain, MI

PFITZER, VIRGINIA
[Pen.] Gertrude Alice Wyble; [b.] March 18, 1924, Detroit, MI; [p.] Mr. and Mrs. John Messick; [m.] Christian C. Pfitzer, March 15, 1943; [ch.] 5 girls, 1 boy, 10 grandchildren; [ed.] High school, OVS for nursing; [occ.] LPN since 1973; [memb.] AARP, Precious Moments, Cairn Collectibles, Maud Humphrey; [hon.] Oil Painting exhibit in Lock Haven Art Gallery, Sidewalk Paintings in Edgewater exhibit, Re-celebrated Golden Wedding; [oth. writ.] Reciepes published in Children's Newspapers; [pers.] Find it's important to express your feelings on paper when an event moves you while it's still fresh on your mind. I have a book full of same.; [a.] Orlando, FL

PHILLIPS, ERMA MAE
[b.] October 10, 1941, Houston, tX; [p.] Deceased; [m.] Deceased; [ch.] Andrew, Melvin, Lynda, Lisa; Grandhcild: Alexander; [ed.] Associate Applied Science Galveston College; [occ.] Key Opertor; [memb.] Gospel Baptist Church, Delta Epsilon Chi, Rainbow Chapter #61 O.E.S.; [hon.] Named to Dean list at Galveston College, stte finalist Certificates for 3 yrs. in Competition in General Marketing and Retail Merchandising as a Delta Epsilon Chi member.; [oth. writ.] I am writing a play and a short story.; [pers.] It's never to late to pursue a dream.; [a.] Galveston, TX

PHILLIPS, J.D.
[b.] October 27, 1938, Franklin, NC; [p.] John & Erma Phillips; [m.] Mary, September 6, 1952; [ch.] Sheila, Marjorie, Mark, Natalie, Jacqueline; [ed.] A.B., American International College, Springfield, MA; Ed.M., University of Mass.; Ed.S., Western Carolina University, Cullowhee, NC; [occ.] Owner and Manager, Park Auto School; [memb.] Retired, American Legion; [hon.] American Studies, Coe Foundation, 1962; Black Studies, Eductional and Professional Development Act, 1969.; [oth. writ.] Numerous poems and essays, including "Sectarian Gods" and "One God, One World;" [pers.] I am a non-sectarian Christian and politically independent, who believes devoutly in God, family, and democracy.; [a.] Springfield, MA

PICARELLI, RET. 1SG JOHN
[Pen.] Giovanni; [b.] November 22, 1949, Shamokin, PA; [p.] ben A. and Myrtle A. Picarelli; [m.] Loretta K. Picarelli, July 4, 1994; [ch.] Daughters, Shannon, Mitzi, Carmen, Stepson, Brent; [ed.] Mifflinburg High School Completed High School Ed. in U.S. Army 1967. College program thru U.S. Army 1 yr. completed Admin.; [occ.] U.S. Army Retired 1SG 21 yrs.; [memb.] Lewisburg American Legion Post 182, Milton Loyal Order of Moose No. 171, Keystone Cruisers (Classic Car Club); [hon.] Served in Vitnam Two Tours, 2/22 INF., 25th INF Div., Dau Tieng, Vietnam 15 Awards and Commendations, Highest Award received, Bronze Star.; [oth. writ.] Personal file of other writings not published.; [pers.] May we all be free to express our feelings for we all have a gift of life

PICCOLA, RUTH ANN
[Pen.] Beeda; [b.] February 2, 1940, Cincinnati, Ohio; [p.] Roman and Emma Ries; [m.] James Piccola, Jr, April 22, 1961; [ch.] Jennifer, Judith, Michael and Eileen; [ed.] Graduated Colerain High School (1958); [occ.] Housewife; [memb.] Second Chance Wildlife Rescue Association, Worldwide Church of God.; [hon.] Award of Merit; Honorable Mention from World of Poetry and Golden Poet 1991 from World of Poetry; [oth. writ.] Poem: Dreaming; [pers.] I give credit to our great Father God, for it was he who inspired this poem taken from Psalms 1:1-3; [a.] Cincinnati, OH

PINTO, JO ELIZABETH
[b.] May 22, 1971, Chicago; [p.] Gil and Elaine Padilla; [m.] Michael James Pinto, August 25, 1991; [ed.] Brighton High School, University of Northern Colorado; [oth. writ.] The poem "A Bird in November" published in The National Library of Poetry's "River of Dreams." A poem published in Jack & Jill magazine.; [pers.] My poems are a gift from God. I hope you enjoy them as I do.; [a.] Brighton, CO

PIRVANESCU, NICOLE
[b.] December 7, 1970, Resita/Romania; [p.] Victor and Margaret Pirvanescu; [ed.] High School, Matematica-Fizica in my city Resita, Romania; [occ.] Student in Valley College of San Bernardino; [oth. writ.] I published some of my poems in the Newsletters for City of San Bernardino "The City Lite."; [pers.] If silence, press the thought, the word, gives the deed.; [a.] San Bernardino, CA

PITTS, B.L.
[b.] December 8, 1970, Santa Barbara, CA; [oth. writ.] Songs, Screen plays, State plays, Children's stories, short stories.; [pers.] All priase honor and glory to God!; [a.] West Covina, CA

PITTS, MICHAEL
[b.] March 3, 1955, Oxnard, CA; [p.] Jack and Nancy Pitts; [m.] Theresa Pitts, February 12, 1977; [ch.] Allison wonderland, Martini Olive, Cinamon Sugar and Peaches Ann Cream; [ed.] Discovery High, Yreka, CA; [occ.] Permanantly Disabled Logger; [pers.] Whenever words are put to paper, there are two hands guiding the pen.; [a.] Yreka, CA

PITZELE, SEFRA KOBRIN
[b.] February 3, 1942, Gary, IN; [ed.] b.A. Educ., Indiana Univ. 1963, Bloomington, IN; MA University of st. Thomas, St. Paul, MN; [occ.] Writer/Publisher; [oth. writ.] Pitzele currently has five books available, all in the area of self-help and coping. We are not alone, Learning to live with chronic illness has just been pub. in German. She is founder of Expressions: Literature and Art by People with disabilities and ongoing health problems. it is a semi annual literary magazine.; [a.] St. Paul, MN

PLUDE, GENELL K.
[b.] January 7, 1971, Fridly, MN; [p.] Kenneth and Lillian Johnson; m Douglas J. Plude, December 15, 1990; [ed.] Forest Lake High, Mankato State College, Nicolet Area Tech College; [occ.] Nurses Aide Asst., Eagle River Health Care Center, Supervisor, Eagle River, WI; [memb.] National Registry of Emergency Medical Technicans, State of Wisconsin Firefighters Association.; [hon.] Member of Ambassadors grup for Mankato State; [oth. writ.] Several

peoms published in a college newspaper.; [pers.] My writing reflects experiences I have had in life, the more one experiences the more you have to write about so live live on the edge, letting nothing get in your way.; [a.] Land O' Lakes, WI

POIRIER, JOYCE A.
[Pen.] NYM KIM; [b.] October 9, 1938, Peabody, Massachusetts; [p.] Joseph E. and Florence E. (Langan) Poirier (both deceased); [m.] Single; [ed.] Salem, MA High class of 56, B.A. English, College of St. Elizabeth, Convent Sttion, NJ, M.A. English, Fairfield University, Fairfield, CT; [occ.] High school English Teacher, Beverly, MA 01915; [memb.] National Council of Teachers of English, MA Council Teachers of English, National Education Association, MA Education Association, Beverly Teachers Association, The International Society of Poetry; [hon.] The Ledger Person of the Year, 1991, nominee Massachusetts Teacher of the Year 1991, Who's Who Among American Teachers 1992; Honorary Inductee Gamma Chapter of National Honor Society 1991; [oth. writ.] Published "Last Respects" in National Library of Poetry, Wind In The Night Sky c. 1993, 2 copyrighted collections of poetry, Revelations One, and Christalized (80 poems) another 65 poems not yet copyrighted and several works in process; "Retreat" in Outstanding Poets of 1994; "Fledgling" in The coming of Dawn; "Promises" in Dance on the Horizon; "Suspended Animation" in Contemporary Poets of America and Britain 1994; [pers.] My Poetry continues to inspire my own growth. My wish is tht it will support others in their process as well. I thank Christine Bavaro for leading me to this previously untapped inner resource.; [a.] Danvers, MA

POLAKOSKI, STEPHANIE LYNN
[Pen.] Steph; [b.] March 15, 1982, Somerset, PA; [p.] John and Dinah Polakoski; [ed.] Maple Ridge Elementary, Somerset Area Jr. High; [occ.] Student; [hon.] Honor Roll, High Honors, NIE Art Award, Jr. High Orchestra, Jr. High Band, Piano; [oth. writ.] Backyard Adventure, 3rd place Laurel Arts Contest, 5th grade.; [pers.] I want to be an environmental Biologist so I can help the world be a better place to live in.; [a.] Somerset, PA

POLING, KARLA
[Pen.] Karla Griner; [b.] June 10, 1955, Germany; [ed.] High School Grad and Accounting and Typing Certificates; [occ.] Housewife; [pers.] I recieve most of my inspiration from songs, also my own values of what a love should hold, and be. Instead of what I so often see.; [a.] Tacoma, WA

POLK, MICHAEL C.
[b.] January 11, 1956, Dade City, FL; [ed.] Cataba Valley Hickory, NC; [occ.] Furniture Craftman, Refinishing, Lake County, FL; [memb.] Kempo Karate, Shotokan Karate, Martial Arts, Life Long Hobby; [oth. writ.] Writing in spirit communications, not yet published, song writings (country); [pers.] True poets hold the meaning of life in the words they write. Only the soul, spirit and heart can reflect.; [a.] Eustis, FL

POND, LESLIE JARIAL
[Pen.] L. Jarial Pond; [b.] January 10, 1947, Waterbury, CT; [m.] Steven R. Pond, February 19, 1977; [ch.] Adam, Damon; [ed.] Suny, Old Westbury Empire, NY Institute Technology, B.S., Adelphi University, M.S.; [occ.] Artist, Writer, Teacher;

[memb.] National Museum of the American Indian.; [hon.] Deans List, Undergraduate B.S.; Cum Laude, Graduate M.S.; [oth. writ.] Poems, articles in local newspapers, Science News, Education Forum, poem puplished in "Tears of Fire."; [pers.] Writing allows one to stand in the presence of the true self. It is an act that takes one beyond mortal life and into the visible light of creation, a most holy experience.; [a.] Huntington Sta., NY

PONKO, MELISSA M.
[Pen.] Missy Ponko; [b.] October 10, 1975, Auburn; [p.] John and Susan Ponko; [ed.] graduate of DeKalb High School 1994. Attending Ball State University to major in Elementary Ed.; [memb.] International Society of Poets; [hon.] National Merit (National Library of Poetry) poem published in Tears of Fire; [oth. writ.] Several other poems; [pers.] I feel that anyone has the ability to write. It is a good way of expressing yourself.; [a.] Auburn, IN

POOLE, PAT
[b.] December 23, 1950, Abingdon, VA; [p.] Clyde and Inez Dye; [ch.] Eric Steven; [ed.] Abingdon High, New River Comm. College, Dublin, VA; [occ.] Telemarketer, Sprint United Telephone; [oth. writ.] Presently having three songs published. My first three demos was pleased to hear my first song written, about my mothr, played on a local station, on Mother's Day 1994.; [pers.] Have written several songs, mostly about real life. I tend to favor the down and out, or less fortunate.; [a.] Abingdon, VA

POON, STEVEN C.
[b.] May 11, 1975, Singapore; [p.] Kevin and Irene Poon; [ed.] Coconut Creek High School, Coconut Creek, FL, pursuing Masters in Architecture at the University of Florida; [occ.] Student; [pers.] There two realms of consciousness dreams and reality. reality is what comes to us in our sleep. Dreams is what we should strive for every day.; [a.] North Lauderdale, FL

POPOVICH, MARY LAUVEE
[b.] January 19, 1951, Atla. GA; [p.] Billie Frances Moore and Lowell Love Kimberly; [m.] Andre Dewitt Popovich, April 29, 1991; [ch.] Thomas Clark and Angela Victoria Vincent; [ed.] Forest Park High School, Graduate 1969; Correspondence School and Computers, Job experiences; [occ.] Wife and homemaker, life learner; [memb.] National Assoc. of Professional Women 70's and 90's; [hon.] Shorthand I Cert.; Honored Inspirational Citizen; Loved and Loving Mate and Mother; Crafts; asked to participate in Miss Georgia Contest; [oth. writ.] Poems; pencil drawings; [pers.] Enjoy and appreciate all old and new masters in every aspect of life and living. Most favorites is Songs of Solomon and Shakesphear and overall Jesus; [a.] Orlando, FL

PORTER, MARTHA
[b.] May 9, 1922, Shelby County, Texas; [p.] Dan and Kizzie Pollard; [m.] Claude Porter, October 11, 1940; [ch.] one daughter, Sherry Baxler and son-in-law Joe Baxley; Twin grandsons, Timothy and Trevor Baxley; [ed.] High school; [occ.] Retired; [memb.] Northwest Baptist Church, Houston, TX; [oth. writ.] none published; [pers.] I was expressing my personal feelings. My husband went to be with the Lord on October 7, 1992, just 4 days before our 52nd wedding anniversary.

PORTER, MONIKA J.
[Pen.] Jane English; [b.] May 31, 1981, Modesto; [p.] Doug and Vicki Porter; [ed.] 8th Grade student 94/95; [occ.] Student; [oth. writ.] No other published writings yet.; [pers.] In my poetry I write about a collision of tangeled thoughts in my head. As I write I try not to think about the traditional poetic formats.; [a.] Hickman, CA

POSEY, JOHN C.
[Pen.] Jacob Payne; [b.] June 4, 1934, Cameron, TX; [p.] George N. and Sarah E. Posey; [m.] Wanda G. Posey, December 21, 1955; [ch.] Joan Posey Brannick; [ed.] Spring Branch High School Attending University of Houston; [occ.] Vice President-Information Systems; [memb.] Lifetime member, Nashville Songwriters Association; Trinity Episcopal Church, The Woodland, TX; Brotherhood of St. Andrew; [oth. writ.] Words by Jacob Payne Volumes I & II (Collections of Lyrics and poems); [pers.] "If, in your heart, someday I see the love of God, then let it be." The most profound growth in my life has been through involvement with KAIROS Prison Ministry.; [a.] Conroe, TX

POWELL, BARBARA JEAN
[b.] January 5, 1951, Wales, Alaska; [p.] Maurice S. Powell Jr., and Carrie J. Numnik; [ch.] Karen, Elizabeth, Pamela, Michael, Robert; [ed.] Grade school Westminster Mass. where 1st grade teacher strongly encouraged reading and pursing artistic skills. King Salmon Alaska (grade school) provided scenery outdoor adventrues to pursue interests in reading and art, Pocomoke, MD; [occ.] Machinist, Artist, Self Taught in Leather and Craft Creations, cooking, have kept up with gymnastics through five children, putting together handstitched crafts, artworks and poetry for show; [oth. writ.] A collection of poems I've written as personal notes to family and friends for all occasions, and the preservation of loving thoughts.; [pers.] I believe my instinct and talents are storngly influenced by my heritage. Being a North American Indian leads me to see reality with great dreams. I believe all people were created equal and our earth to be our greatest friend.; [a.] Nashua, NH

PRATTE, LOIS A.
[b.] February 3, 1933, Calais, VTS; [p.] J. Earle and Addie Pike; [m.] Widow; [ch.] Marcia, Norris, Dana, Tony Clyde and Mona; [ed.] Cabot High School, VT, Midwestern University TX, New Hampshire College, Human Services Manchester N.H., Writing Certificate, Institute Children W. Kedding, CT; [occ.] Homehealth Aide, Branford, VNA Branford Ct.; [memb.] North Branford Congregational Church member, Adult Education Committee; [oth. writ.] Poem published in Dance on Horizon, N.L of Poetry.; [pers.] I am an aspiring poet with a vivid imagination and Christian Faith. The beauty of wonders of nature are reflected in my writing.; [a.] East Haven, CT

PREVATT, NORMA
[b.] April 16, 1949, Georgia; [p.] J.D. Harrell, Myrtice Crabb; [m.] Guy L. Prevatt, June 11, 1965; [ch.] Guy II, 21 and Veronica 6; [ed.] South Sumter High, Liberty University, Lynchburg, VA; [occ.] Substitute Teacher; [memb.] PTA, Girl Scouts of America, Authority Board of Elementary School, American Red Cross; [hon.] Many (9) acheivement

awards received from volunteer community work; [oth. writ.] Articles appearing locally, not for some years. Hopeful for the future.; [pers.] Take life as intended, leave past and leap forward. Take the giant step to live freely and wholly without thought. Life needs the living.; [a.] Bushnell, FL

PRICE, DIANE CYNTHIA
[b.] March 3, 1945, Brooklyn, NY; [p.] Elizabeth and Arthur Jamison; [m.] Willie H. Price, September 29, 1979; [ch.] Elizabeth, Dawn, Wendi, Shaunta, Michael; [ed.] Westhampton High School, West Hampton Long Island, NY; [occ.] Homemaker; [pers.] We are encompassed in a time and era, when much of mankind chooses to turn a blind eye to the depth of human emotion, my poetry reflects the deep seeded human side of life. The good, the bad and perhaps sometimes the vicariously evil; [a.] Olympia, WA

PRICE, IRENE F.
[b.] June 20, 1906, San Francisco; [p.] Mary and Samdej Kern; [ch.] Joan Eddy, Beverly Partone; [ed.] High School; [occ.] Retired.

PRICE, KATHLEEN M.
[b.] February 26, 1957, N.Y., [p.] Joseph W. and Mary A. Murray; [m.] Samuel R. Price, May 13, 1989; [ed.] Paul D. Schreiber high School, Port Washington, NY; [occ.] Closing Coordinator, Lennar Homes S.W. Florida Division; [oth. writ.] Many poems, nothing published.; [a.] Cape Coral, FL

PRICE, LINDA J.
[Pen.] Linda J. Root; [b.] July 17, 1943, Bremerton, WA; [p.] Russell and Harriet Root; [m.] Wesley F. Price, November 21, 1962; [ch.] Ginger Lee (28), Penny Sue (26), Matthew F. (23); [ed.] South Kitsap High School; [occ.] Currently retired, I write to reflect on life, after owning and operating a daycare for 22 years.; [pers.] Having worked with many children and youths through my daycare and activities our own children were involved, including school, church, scouts and sports. I've learned how important it is to accent the positive in the gifts of life we have no matter how talented one is or isn't. Each individual is unique and special. Every test of life builds character, with that remember the sun will rise again tomorrow, with new challenges to meet.; [a.] Seattle, WA

PRICE, SANORA L.
[Pen.] Sanora Koebel; [b.] February 28, 1961, Detroit, Michigan; [p.] Casimir and Barbara Archutowski; [m.] Gregory a. Price, June 28, 1994; [ch.] Amanda Marie, Alexander Jonathon; [ed.] Bentley high School; [occ.] Reservations Agent for Northwest Airlines; [oth. writ.] Poem published in fall 94, Edge of Twilight; [pers.] This poem was written about my son sleeping in my arms. I send it to all parents putting their babies to bed. How perfect the world can be.; [a.] Redford, MI

PROUGH, RICHARD DEAN
[b.] November 7, 1950, Ottumwa, Iowa; [p.] Dean and Doris Prough; [ch.] One son; [ed.] Ottumwa High, U.S. Naval Assault Boat Training, Criminal Justice, Indian Hills Community College, Grad. 1977; Subsequent diploma's in criminal justice training.; [memb.] Santa Fe Trail Assoc., American Legion; [hon.] Decorated for Naval Service. Commended in writing from Governor Teasdale, in Missouri for

service during the Kansas City Fire Fighter's Strike.; [oth. writ.] Copywritten, compilation of numerous subjects.; [pers.] In a compilation of poetry named "Prough's Side of Life" I have written about situation's an dpeople not as they appear to exist but to the depth they truely exist.; [a.] Small Midwestern Town

PRESSBURG, JOSEPH
[Pen.] Joseph (Joe) Pressburg; [b.] July 16, 1917, NYC; [p.] Gustave and Regina Pressburg; [m.] Widowed; [ch.] John Joseph, Paul Martin; [ed.] Fremont High, Woodbury Business College, LaSalle Correspondence School; [occ.] Certified Public Accountant; [memb.] American Society of Certified Public Accountants, California Society of Certified Public Accountants, Peninsula Racquet club; [oth. writ.] Album of (18) songs about Love and Dreams; numerous poems.; [pers.] Hopefully, my poems and songs are a move away from today's society of violence to a future of gentle love for the benefit of all who read or hear them.; [a.] Rancho Palos Verdes, CA

PRUITT, JIMMY
[b.] Mena, AR; [p.] Bonnie Pruitt; [ed.] Graduate; [occ.] Song and poem writing.; [hon.] FFA, FBLA, FAA Vice President, College Scholarship; [a.] Hatfield, AR

PURKEY, BELINDA MARIE
[b.] August 24, 1972, Knoxville, TN; [p.] Ken and Brenda Siler; [m.] SRA. James A. Purkey, February 4, 1991; [ch.] Steven Avery Purkey; 6 mo. (1-15-94); [ed.] Knox Co. Central High, University of Tennessee, Knox. Vo-Tech, ICS; [occ.] Student of Journalism and baseball history; [memb.] Humane Society of the United States; [oth. writ.] Articles published in several sports magazines, and local newspapers.; [pers.] Although I enjoy writing on a number of subjects, I would like my work to help restore the magic of our national pastime in the eyes of the faithful and to those gone astray.; [a.] Eielson AFB, AK

PURUSHOTTAMDAS B.-DAS, PATEL
[Pen.] DAS; [b.] July 1, 1929, Llttersanda, Gujarat, India; [p.] Father: Bhailalbhai, Mother: Divaliben; [m.] Ansuya alias Hansa Patel, May 11, 1947; [ch.] Kiran, Kaushik, Deepak and Kamlesh; [ed.] Matriculation Examination - Passed in 1947; [occ.] Retired Businessman; [memb.] Founder of: The Land Records Department Class III Government Servants Association Gujarat State, India 1956. I have been invited by the International Society of Poets, USA; [hon.] Obtained little amount of cash prizes from leading magazines in India. Four...4...Editor's Choice Awards from The National Library of Poetry for Outstanding Achievement in Poetry in the year: 1992 and 1993. Top 3% of the National Library of Poetry contest 1992-1993. 4 poems on tape by The Sound of Poetry by N.L.P.; [oth. writ.] Several social and religious articles, narratives, essays, numerous poems, biography of my 3 1/2 yea old grandson Kunjal...,etc published in leading newspapers literary magazines in India. Documentary film script entitled "Riddhi-Siddhi" on Land Reforms for Gwarat State Government India. Several poems have appeared in various N.L.P. publications...1992-93; [pers.] Artistic manuscript in my own handwritings in 247 pages, entitled "Child", a collection of 58 poems in Gujarati and English with 94 pictures and one social novel entitled: "When Got Flower...Found, In Ash..." scheduled to be published during my visit to India. Little knowl-

edge of English language. But my grandson Anish has been my inspiration for writing poems in English language. I am grateful to the Holy Land and sky, of democratic America, where my pen is welcomed and where I take air presently. I've dedicated this pen for mankind; [a.] Harrisburg, PA

QUACH, LONG-ANH
[Pen.] J.E. Longfell; [b.] April 5, 1972; [ed.] Queens College of the City University of New York; [oth. writ.] For Helen, "I'd Accompanied You Across That River."; [pers.] I hope in the more aging and forgotten years of my life, when only fallen yellow leaves will stay to wet the vacant streets, you (M.V. & J.C.) remember still the moment we met. My deep appreciation for the many lingering memories ofr life.

QUARANTA, AUDREY M.
[b.] September 30, 1986, Stten Island, NY; [p.] John and Lorraine Quaranta, Jr; [ed.] Currently a third grade student at Staten Island Academy; [oth. writ.] Several poems published in school literary magazine "Images."; [pers.] I enjoy writing because I feel like I'm painting pictures with woods.; [a.] Staten Island, NY

QUINTANAR, SHANNON ANISSA
[Pen.] Tawny; [b.] February 24, 1970, San Diego; [p.] Dennis L. Dillard, Balvina Quintanar-Anderson; [m.] never married; [ch.] Michaela Kristen 8 1/2 yrs. old; Anissa Marie 5 1/2 yrs. old; [ed.] Junior Coll. ICS Certified Child Care Giver, Telecommunications Dispatch Emergency 911 Operator, Grossmount Coll.; [occ.] Currently a student in crime lab photography, eventuall firensic pathology, I'm a caregiver during the day a student at night and always a Mommy.; [oth. writ.] I've written 197 poems and constructed my own Port Folio Books consisting of 45 poems per book.; [pers.] I've been inspired by few, but they who they are! through tears and happiness, feelings and emotions, from deep inside me I've created my life story, a story only few can understand; [a.] Santee, CA

RAFFIELD, SAMANTHA L.
[b.] February 27, 1967, Port Neches, TX; [p.] Sandra J. Bouten, James C. Nolan, Sr.; [m.] George A. Raffield, November 8, 1986; [ch.] Jordan Anthony, Wendi Marie, Alicia Marie; [ed.] South College, Savannah State College; [occ.] Payroll Clerk, Savannah Foods and Industries; [memb.] American Red Cross Instructor and Donor; [hon.] Who's Who Among American Junior Colleges, Cum Laude - South College, Dean's List; [pers.] I have been guided by the love of my life and blessed by the grace of God; [a.] Springfield, GA

RAGNO, CAROLYN JOAN
[Pen.] Shining Star; [b.] August 12, 1940, Newark, NJ; [p.] Albert and Antoinette Ragno; [m.] Not married; [ch.] none; [ed.] Irvington High School, Pace College, Institute of Applied Science & Criminology in Chicago, IL, National School of Aeronautics, Kansas City, MO; [occ.] Accomplished pianist, Honorary Det. Lt. for Police Depts. Police K-9 Fiction Mystery Writer (Freelance); [memb.] See Attached Sheets, I'm in Who's Who in American Law Enforcement, nominated for 10 consecutive years, I'm in all the state libraries and Library of Congress in Washington, DC; [hon.] Distinguished Medal & Award from the FBI (Gold Medal) Legion of Honor for Police, Sheriff & FBI (Medal); Medal of Merit

from National Chief of Police; K-9 Humanitarian Award & Medal of Honor; [oth. writ.] I write songs, fiction mysteries for police depts. all over USA. I'm now into writing about the mounted police horses. I make fiction signs for police officers and make up poems about their K-9 Dogs. Which appear in magazines, local newspapers.; [pers.] I'm so much in love with my prince charming it just comes natural to write about him to express my feelings. He gave me the incentive to write because of his true love to me. Anything I write is from the goodness of my heart. He introduced me to the police K-9's and I've been writing since. I'm in love with my piano, my prince charming and my police K-9's; [a.] Irvington, NJ

RAHE, ELLEN P.
[b.] Ellie Pat Fitzgerald Rahe; [b.] May 4, 1917, Meridan, CT; [p.] Anna J. and William P. Fitzgerald; [m.] Paul H. Rahe November 2, 1946 (deceased); [ch.] Patrick H., Paula G., Patricia E., Paul J., Peter F., and Pixie Ellen; [ed.] Meriden High, George Washington, Univ., Certification courses at Yale University, November 1947, Refresher Courses, Southern Conn. State University 1965; [occ.] Self employed, swimming teacher, Irish Dancing teacher; [memb.] American Red Cross, Irish Historical Society and many others; [hon.] Scholarship to Arnold's Phys. Ed. College, 55 Year Pin from American Red Cross, Delta Zeta Sorority, Selected to Lead a Company of Waves in F.D.R's funeral processing 1945; [pers.] My summers consisted of sitting under my very own Maple tree, Dad planted a maple each time one of was born, family consisted of six children, 3 boys, 3 girls. I have 3 boys and 3 girls also. Wrote poetry since age 7 or read books under my tree a cooling ooff with the garden hose for 30 minutes was our summer. I believe that we are all (black, white, green or purple) made in Christ's Image, we are born to live, to die and to live again. Forever in a better world. The front door to Heaven is suffering, the back door key is good work.

RAHMAN, RIPON
[Pen.] Rip Rahman; [b.] Bangladesh; [p.] Anisur Rahman and Rehana Begum; [ed.] Maple Leaf International High, L.A. Valley College.; [occ.] Asst. Manager of Denny's Restaurant; [oth. writ.] "Baby it Happens Every Single Night" is the first poem to be published.; [pers.] A man can love as many women that comes in their life, but can fall in love only once.; [a.] Van Nuys, CA

RAMOS, ELSIE AUSTRIA
[Pen.] Elvic Aus Ram; [b.] December 23, 1925, Lingayen, Phila.; [p.] Arcadio and Maerine M. Austria; [m.] Antonio G. Ramos, December 4, 1955; [ch.] Erwin, Raelito, Cristina, Rose, Anthony Jr.; [ed.] San Carlos Rural High School, Univ. of St. Thomas, Phil. San Carlos Colleges, Ateneo U. Manila; [occ.] Retired Public School teacher; Dept. of Educ., Region I. Phil.; [memb.] U.St. English Club 1949, Catholic Women's League, S.C. City, San Carlos Retirees Assoc., Phil. Veterans Organization; Rotary Ann, Dist. 379 Phil. Jr., and Senior Teacher, Regular Civil Service, Phila.; [hon.] Honor Society Adviser, S.C. College; Certificate of Recognition; Award of Merit Region I, Dept. of Education, Sports & Culture Philippines; [oth. writ.] Poems in the local high school organs and periodicals, Memories of World War II soon to be published.; [pers.] I wish to encourage the youth to know and realize the more

aesthetic turns in life. Inspired by my family, relatives and friends; [a.] San Jose, CA

RAMOS, MARY GRACE MAQUINANA
[b.] January 20, 1980, Redwood City, CA; [p.] Adena Maquinana Soliman and Armando Ramos; [ed.] High school, Holy Name School (Catholic) San Francisco, CA; [hon.] Honors Class, Holy Name Catholic School, San Francisco, CA; [a.] Daly City, LA

RAMPTON, KATHLEEN
[m.] Single; [ch.] None; [ed.] B.A. English, California State College, Sonoma; [occ.] Accountant/Manager Manufacturing Environment; [oth. writ.] This is the first poem I've had published.; [pers.] My writing reflects my love of the Northern California countryside in which I live; it also reflects my gratitude toward those individuals who have loved me ane encouraged me to be the poet I am.; [a.] Santa Rosa, CA

RAMSEY, GARY W.
[b.] August 17, 1942, Monroe, NC; [p.] Mr. and Mrs. Marvin Watkins; [m.] Susan Ramsey, March 28, 1965; [ch.] Allison, Lisa; [ed.] BA and BS Degree Western Carolina University; [occ.] Sr. Vice President, Montgomery Ward; [hon.] Permanent President Class of 1964, Western Carolina University, many local bands; [oth. writ.] Local poetry, novel in progress.; [pers.] Life is a random reflection of the passage of time.; [a.] St. Charles, IL

RANEY, PORTER A.
[b.] February 4, 1906, Suffolk, VA; [p.] Williena and George H. Raney; [ed.] Nanemond High School, Suffolk, VA; VA Seminary College, Lynchburg, VA; [occ.] Retired; [oth. writ.] The Little Cloud; [pers.] Was Director of Delta Home for Girls Director of Lucy Thurman YWCA, Detroit, Mich.

RAO, LINNET KEARNEY
[b.] May 17, 1923, Shillong, India; [p.] Wellington Kearney and Phrolybon Lyngdoh; [m.] David M. P. Rao, May 24, 1948; [ch.] Rosetta Maureen Rathnam, Morgina Juliet Paul, Felicia Anne Rao-Hagberg and Michael Antony Rao; [ed.] Associate Degree in Teaching, and Library Science.; [occ.] Retired, Housewife; Before retirement, had served as teacher of English and Mathematics in India, Ethiopia, and Sierra Leone, and as teacher and Librarian in New York, and in the Middle East College in Beirut, Lebanon.; [hon.] 25 Years Service Record Pin from the General Conference of Seventh Day Adventists. Award of Merit Certificate and "Golden Poet" World of Poetry, December 1992 and 92.; [oth. writ.] Poem, "Graduation," 1991. Various articles for school newspapers and magazines.; [pers.] Considering the turmoil our world is in now, I firmly believe that if everyone would heed the exhortation of Proverbs 1:7, - "The fear of the Lord is the beginning of wisdom," we would all be spared from the fear of guns, knives, and bombs. I also believe that we all should strive to make our homes havens where there is a good supply of love and respect for every member of the family.; [a.] Gaithersburg, MD

RAY, SHANIQUA MARIA
[Pen.] Smurf; [b.] December 6, 1980, Magnolia, AR; [p.] Roy and annie Ray; [ed.] Newport Elem. K-6 Newport Jr. High now entering Newport Jr. High Eigth Grade; [memb.] Newport Tae Kwon Do, Black Belt, First Degree; Newport Junior High Band, first chair flute; NJHS Student Council; [hon.] Honor and Gifted and Talented Student since 1st grade; Odyssey of the Mind won second place in the district and fourth place in the state; 2nd place in, What Memorial Day Means to Me," (received plaque); [oth. writ.] Helped write a play for Odyssey of the Mind.; [pers.] I have two sisters whom I love very much, Sasha Monique Ray and Stacey Michelle Ray; [a.] Diaz, AR

RAYBURN, COARY
[b.] September 17, 1961, Anaheim, CA; [p.] Bill Rayburn, Cathy Hollowell; [ed.] Fullerton Unior High School "79" Lee College; [occ.] Nursing Student, Lee College; [memb.] Phi Theta Kappa; [hon.] National Dean's List "93"; [pers.] For Sara, you know who you are, and other's with the same questions.; [a.] Baytown, TX

REBBER, JULIE ANN
[b.] July 5, 1975, Indpls., IN; [p.] William and Mary Rebber; [ch.] Sibling: Twin Sister, Jennifer Lee Rebber; [ed.] I am going to be a sophomore at Indiana University Bloomington; [occ.] Full-time Student; [hon.] I won a contest when I was in the eigth grade for a story I wrote about my uncle who was killed in a drunk driving accident.; [pers.] I have learned that everyone has a special talent and that in order to really express any talent to its fullest, one must have it come from the heart.; [a.] Indianapolis, IN

REBICH, ERICA
[b.] May 9, 1980, Brush, CO; [p.] Larry and Dolores Rebich; [ed.] Currently attend school in Polaris, Montana. It is a one room school, grades K thru 8; [occ.] Student (7th grade); [hon.] Various 4-H Awards; Several Alpine Skiing Awards; [oth. writ.] one poem and one short story published in local newspaper.; [pers.] I enjoy writing very much and hope to be a teacher and an author.; [a.] Polaris, MT

REDDICK, BLONDINE LOUISE
[b.] July 18, 1919, Neward, NJ (raised in the shore area of Wall Township, NJ); [p.] Pauline (Eberle) Bohler and Oscar A. Bohler; [m.] Donald M. Reddick, September 7, 1956; [ch.] Jon Joel Gobbons, Dr. Cheryl Bartholomow-Emig, Douglas C. Reddick, Blondine C. Meaghen; [ed.] Asbury Park H.S., Asbury Park Business College, NIA (Newspaper Institute of America), International U. of Continued Education; [occ.] Homemaker, author, poet; [memb.] NIA, Inc., F.F.W.A., I.W.W.G., International Society of Poets; [hon.] Four years attendee Letter Writer's Forum of the Orlando Sentinel, numerous Editor's Choice Awards from NLP, on ISP advisory panel, poetry published on audio cassettes by ISP and NLP, poetry reviewed on National TV and recorded with background museic for World Wide Distribution; [oth. writ.] Published book "A Month of Revelations in Modern Tokyo, Japan." Included in "Top Ten Short Stories of 1993 and Ten Top Short Storeis of 1994." Included in "Best Poems of the 90's" and "Distinguished Poets of America;" [pers.] My second career after successfully raising a family. I plan to leave my writings as a legacy to my children and grandchildren, letting them know there can be happy and humorous times even though faced with adversities.; [a.] Longwood, FL

REDWING, ALLEN JEROME
[Pen.] Alley Cat; [b.] April 13, 1978, Memphis, TN; [p.] Trina Gay Redwing and Allen Richardson; [ed.] I am currently an 11th grade enrolled at Central High School; [oth. writ.] I have serveral writings, that I wish to submit to publishing companies.; [pers.] My poetry reflects signs of unacknowledge prophecies that will involve all mankind, at some point or another. I have been inspired by early writings of the Renaissance.; [a.] Memphis, TN

REED JR., JOE M.
[Pen.] Joey; [b.] January 21, 1968, chorpus Christi, TX; [p.] Joe M. Reed Sr. and Dora G. Reed; [m.] Claudia A. Reed (currently engaged), September 16, 1994; [ed.] Graduated from United High in Laredo, TX. Attended Laredo Jr., College, Laredo State University, and the University of Texas at San Antonio.; [occ.] Currently employed by Mag Flux Corp., a small import-export firm in Loredo, TX; [pers.] My writings are aimed at telling the truth, whether it be about aperson or a certain situation I may have encountered in life, but always from personal life experiences. This poem is dedicated to my dear mother, Dora Reed. I love you mom!.; [a.] Laredo, TX

REED, SHANA M.
[Pen.] Shay, Sharon Ricky; [b.] May 19, 1974, Hammond, IN; [p.] Sharon Douglass & Gary Reed; [occ.] Student; [hon.] Outstanding Arts Achievement Award in Sr. High Graduating Class; [oth. writ.] Has written numerous poems and short stories bu this was the first item submitted for publication. Have several poems in process of submission for publication in near future.; [pers.] Dedicated to my mom, Sherry, and my dad, Rick. I love you Gramma. Hello, Jimmy, my love and inspiration is Edgar Allen Poe.; [a.] Clinton, TN

REED, TRICIA
[Pen.] Tricia A. Reed; [b.] January 15, 1979, Rockford, IL; [p.] Kenneth and Pamela Reed; [ed.] Auburn High School Student, grade 10; [occ.] Student; [memb.] Beth Eden United Methodist Church, Choir at Betheden, UMC; [hon.] Honor Roll; [oth. writ.] Published in National Library of Poetry's "Dance on the Horizon," The Man in My Dreams.; [pers.] Never stop reaching for your goals. They're out there to grab, so go for it.; [a.] Rockford, IL

REED, WILLIAM DAVE
[Pen.] "Cowboy"; [b.] September 17, 1964, Lexington, KY; [p.] Clay and Rena Reed; [m.] Karen Leigh Reed, June 17, 1994; [ed.] Woodford Co. High school; [occ.] Maintenance Technician; [memb.] Dixie Park Full Gospel Baptist Church, Madison County Rescue Squad; [oth. writ.] Have been writing songs over 15 yrs. My latest are country ballets and gospel.; [a.] Richmond, KY

REESE, LORETTA JEAN HARDY
[Pen.] Hardy Reese; [b.] January 31, 1933, Los Angeles; [m.] August 28, 1953, Widow November 14, 1992; [ch.] One Son; [ed.] High School Grad 51'; [occ.] Admin. Secretary; [hon.] Too many too mention; [oth. writ.] Numerous; [pers.] At the Memorial Service for my husband in November 1992, a poem was read that I had written to him several years before. Everyone commented on how beautiful it was and if I had ever thought of publishing my works. That was the beginning! I've really been creating poems since I was a child, but none of them had any depth or

meaning, until I met my husband. He always boosted my morale, and since his passing most of my works relate to my feelings about him, my fears of being a widow, and finally accepting now for whatever is going to be. We were entertainers, so I consider this as ACT III of my life, and I'm going to make sure I do it right for my mentor upstatirs. As an author I have chosen to write under the pseudonym of my maiden-and-married names combined, Hardy Reese, and hopefully the strength in my writing name will flow through my pen.; [a.] North Hollywood, CA

REEVES, VICTOR M.
[b.] october 16, 1968, Opelika, AL; [p.] Jesse and Alvenia Reeves; [ed.] Henry Ford High School; [occ.] Facility Services Assistant; [memb.] Word of Faith Christian Center; [oth. writ.] Writings have been featured in local malls, churchs, educational magazines and on radio. Writings are able to be purchased through mail order from Victor Greeting in book, card, etc. form.; [pers.] I write so that everyone can find hope and victory in our Lord and Savior Jesus Christ. I've been inlfuenced by the writings of King David, in the old testament, how he wrote in poetic form about the goodness of God.; [a.] Detroit, MI

REIFLER, JON
[Pen.] Adam Gunn; [b.] May 28, 1982; Royal Oak, MI; [p.] David and Cathy Reifler; [ed.] Currently in Middle School; [occ.] Student; [memb.] Boy Scouts of America; [pers.] I'd like to thank my mother and father, my brother, my sister, (Aaron and Elizabeth), My grandparents Phyllis and Ben Hoffman, and a good friend that inspired me to write, Alan Michael.; [a.] Grand Rapids, MI

REIMANN, PATRICIA LISA
[Pen.] Patti Reimann; [b.] January 18, 1981, Neenah; [p.] Robert and Patricia Reimann; [occ.] 8th grade student; [pers.] Never give up what you dream, go for your goal.; [a.] Fremont, WI

REIN, CRYSTAL D.
[Pen.] Crystal Rain; [b.] October 18, 1979, Fontana, CA; [p.] Patricia and Guy Rein; [ed.] Tenth Grade; [oth. writ.] Short stories, descriptions; [pers.] Love is like a game of hide and seek. When you find it, it's running away. You only catch it once in a lifetime.; [a.] Oakdale, CA

REINHART, STEVE JOHN
[Pen.] Stone Reinhart; [b.] January 8, 1957, Mpls., MN; [p.] Don and Eleanor Reindart; [ed.] Dela Salle High School, 2 yrs. Welding 71-75, HTC Trade School 1978 to 1980 vica delegate Brooklyn Park; [occ.] Custodian Mpls., Main Post Office; [memb.] U.S. Navy, Sept. 1975-1976 March; [pers.] Poetry the essence of mankind and creation of self.; [a.] Champlin, MN

RENDA, EILEEN R.
[Pen.] T.G. Renda; [b.] August 24, 1944, Brooklyn, NY; [p.] Vincent and Josephine; [ch.] One; [ed.] College; [occ.] Controller; [hon.] 1st poem, Swimmer, Bowler; [oth. writ.] none; [pers.] Always, wear a smile and everyone will smile with you.

REPANDIS, BARBARA
[b.] May 13, 1977, Greece; [p.] Coulis and Jill Repandis; [ed.] High School Graduate, will attend Suny new Paltz College in September, Journalism.

Study music, play the violin for 9 yrs.; [occ.] Student; [hon.] Awards from the board of the Royal Schools of Music in London; [a.] Garrison, NY

REYNOLDS, KIMBERLY
[b.] July 4, 1980, Cinti, OH; [p.] Betty Wenz and William Reynolds; [ed.] Burton Elementary, Shroeder Jr. High, Hughes High School; [occ.] Student; volunteer for Deconess and Cinti Zoo; [memb.] Girl Scout of America Young Authors of America, Red Cross Volunteer, Zoo Volunteer; [hon.] Young authors 2, art 2, Girl Scouts 7; [pers.] Nobody cares how much you know till they know how much you care.; [a.] Cincinnati, OH

RHOADES, JOHNNY MARK
[b.] August 31, 1960, Little Rock, AR; [p.] Johnny G. Rhoades, Mary E. Carenance; [m.] Marschelle Mary Marie Rhoades, January 21, 1984; [ch.] Tabitha Lynne Rhades, Audrionna Maria Rhoades; [ed.] Finney High School, St. Clair County Community College; [occ.] Precision Tooling Maker; [oth. writ.] I have several poems I have compiled over a longtime period mainly for personal reflection's and thoughts.; [pers.] I have been influenced mainly by early rock ballads and love songs with a heavy input of religion which leaves a hint of silver lining behind every dark cloud, as well as hope.; [a.] Elkton, MI

RHODE, KAREN L.
[b.] March 9, 1942, Chicago, IL; [p.] Elmer and Florette Rohde; [ed.] Columbia College, Chicago, IL; [occ.] Freelance photographer; [a.] Mokena, IL

RHODES, MARGARET ANN
[b.] July 16, 1967, Lexington, TN; [p.] Gerald and Jen Rhodes; [ch.] Hunter Shea Rhodes; [ed.] Lexington High, Union University, BS Psychology, minors in Sociology & English; [occ.] Administrative Assistant, Comfort Hotel Airport, Memphis, TN; [hon.] Valedictorian H.S. Class; Sigma Tau Delta English Honor Society; Alpha Chi Academic Honor Society; Alpha Chi Academic Honor Society; Who's Who Among American Colleges & Universities, Dean's List, graduated cum laude.; [oth. writ.] Have written poems, mostly for my own emotional venting, but have had no others published.; [a.] Memphis, TN

RHYE, LOLITA
[b.] November 19, 1950, Evansville, TN; [p.] Edward and Jane Frailey; [m.] Eugene, September 12, 1972; [ch.] One daughter, 20 yrs. old, 2 grand-daughters, Allison 4, Brandi 1; [ed.] Graduated from High School in Postage, Indiana; [occ.] Housewife; [oth. writ.] Had a few poems in local newspaper plus had a chance of having one put to music, but didn't get to go through with it.; [pers.] Never give up on your Children or your Dreams; [a.] Mortons Gap, KY

RICE, EVELACA L.
[Pen.] Bob E.; [b.] May 7, 1972, Detroit, MI; [p.] Octavia Taylor, Eddie Rice Jr.; [ch.] Louis Rice, Eshayla Goza; [ed.] Currently attending Hamilton Business College; [occ.] Full time mother and student; [pers.] Poetry heals me; It allows me to express my reality, I want to share with you, what I see.; [a.] DesMoines, IA

RICE, RENA RAMZEL
[b.] June 30, 1913, Texas; [p.] Mary Hobbs Ramzel, C.S. Ramzel, Ira Elton "Jack" Rice. DE., February

23, 1929; [ch.] Georgia Rice Herreth March 14, 1931, Sweetwater, TX; [ed.] Mother was teacher first Sweetwater High, Extra Courses. Antiques Studies Continues, Genealogy, Texas History; [occ.] Antique Collector, Managing Property, Business.; [memb.] Matagorda Co., Historical Commission, Citation from Governor clements, 1981 for "Distinguished Service in the Texas Historical Commission." Daughter 1812. Daughter Republic of Texas, Genealogical Society, Cancer; [hon.] Socity, Offices Head in Matoborda Co. Federated Women's Club, Eagles, Woodmen of the World, Matagorda Co. Museum Member, Poetry Recording, Texas History and Studying; [oth. writ.] Farm and Ranch, 2 stories, The Daily Tribune, Poetry, Local. Asked to submit story of "Yellow House Draw, Indian Fight," Plains O' Texas Where My Dad was wounded in 1877. The story in "Cowboy Artists of American Museum" Texas; [pers.] I will continue recording and collecting historical stories and writing about life in Texas on Ranches, Farms, Gulf Coast, and America. Blessed Country.; [a.] Bay City, TX

RICHATER, S. C.
[b.] November 3, 1969, Gastonia,NC; [p.] Barbara and S. Samuel Richter; [pers.] It's kind of sad when you think about it, but when most of us look into the mirror at the face of our own reality what we see looking back is just a mendacious waltz with acceptance or indifference, which ever works best.; [a.] Gastonia, NC

RICHBURG, MARY C.
[b.] May 6, 1929, Brewton, AL; [p.] My mothers: Asberry Richburg, Mary Jane Richburg; [m.] Single; [ed.] High School and Business School; [occ.] Retired; [oth. writ.] Several short articles in Christian publication; [pers.] I strive to reflect the love and care of God for all mankind, in all my writings; [a.] Brewton, AL

RICHESIN, MARTHA
[b.] Whittier, CA; [p.] Della and Elbert Richasin; [m.] Divorced; [ed.] Trained as classical singer, Music Academy of the West, Gradute of California State University. Professional Singer/High School English Teacher; [occ.] Writer (freelance); [memb.] American Association of Unviersity Women, have been a member of Los Angeles, Civic Light Opera; [hon.] Hove sung with Roger Wagner Chorale, Pearl Baile on U.s. tour, was "Sarah" in Plain and Fancy with Alexis Smith and Craig Stevens; [oth. writ.] Music and Drama reviews for local papers. Article for Women in Education, Special articles for local papers.; [pers.] I regret the things I have not done. My idols are John Donne and James Joyce.; [a.] Ojai, CA

RICKS, LEANNA ARLEEN MARIE
[b.] September 11, 1982, Puyallup, WA; [p.] Richard and Donna Ricks; [ed.] Currently in the 6th grade at Pioneer Valley Elementary School; [occ.] Babysitter, Student; [hon.] I have taken several second place awards in local archery shoots. I completed the Hunter's Education Course in 1992.; [oth. writ.] Poetry awarded in the 5th Grade.; [pers.] I enjoy archery and going to the woods with my father. I love animals. I wish to become a veterinarian to care and heal animals. I enjoy horseback riding, walking my dog. I enjoy expressing myself in my personal journal.; [a.] Spanaway, WA

RIDDICK, KHALILAH
[b.] December 13, 1976, North Carolina; [p.] James and Adenda Riddick Jr.; [ed.] John A. Holmes High; [memb.] Future Teachers of America; [hon.] Who's Who Among American High School Students; The Perfect Attendance Award; [oth. writ.] Several poems unpublished; [pers.] I feel that no matter your age, color or background, there is a hidden talent in everyone. I try to show this through my poetry.; [a.] Edenton, NC

RIDGEWAY, TIMOTHY R.
[b.] August 15, 1956, Spartanburg, SC; [p.] P.B. and Mary Ridgeway; [m.] Patty Ridgeway, February 27, 1987; [ch.] Angela Michelle, Joseph Adam; [ed.] Boiling Springs High, Spartanburg Technical College; [oth. writ.] "Never Alone," "The Most Beautiful Tree," "A Glorious Day," "Reason of Love,"; [pers.] These poems are written to encourage others to remain stedfast in their faith.; [a.] Spartanburg, SC

RIDGWAY, DAVID S.
[Pen.] David Sanford Ridgway; [b.] May 31, Pasco Wash.; [p.] Johnnie T. and Polly Sanford; [m.] Kathleen Lacy Mullen Ridgway, May 9, 1987; [ed.] Graduated High School, Phoenix 1972, 31 units college of Marin 3.5 G.P.A; [occ.] Manager, Pizza Cook, Red Boy Pizza; [memb.] Alpha Gamma Sigma (Honor Society) Ciollege of Marin; [hon.] Outstanding Community Service Award Alpha Gamma Sigma (Honor Society) 1994; [pers.] I feel that God has given me the spiritual strength to use words to share my emotions with others. Poetry is a life force for me.; [a.] San Rafael, CA

RIGAKOS, CHRISTOS G.
[Pen.] Sam O'Rye; [b.] June 30, 1967, Astoria, NY; [p.] George and helga Rigakos; [ed.] Long Island City High School, Queensborough Community College, New York City Technical Collegel; [occ.] Clerk/Machine operator, The Bank of New York Co., Inc.; [a.] New York, NY

RINGLE, MAJORIE
[Pen.] Mary Ring; [b.] January 9, 1930, Lansing, MI; [p.] Everett and Gladys Luke; [m.] Dale Ringle, April 4, 1964; [ch.] Nancy, Wayne, Steven, Bonnie, Daniel, Sharon, Kevin, 3 step-children; [ed.] High School, Lansing Community College, Lansing business University, Creative Writing Workshops, Joan Hunter-Holly; [occ.] Former proofreader, 20 yrs.; [memb.] Doubleday Book Club, CBS Video, MS Society; [oth. writ.] Was editor of in-house organ co-operation and local MS Society Newsletter, News & Clues, Write Children's Stories, Short Stories, "Tornado," "Little Pine Box," novel "Cherry Harvest" not submitted.; [pers.] My writings have been for my own pleasure. Within each of us there lie inner thoughts and feelings or great imaginings waiting to be expressed. (most never published); [a.] Lansing, MI

RIPHAHN, SUSAN MARTINEZ
[ed.] B.S. in Elem. Ed, Kansas State University; M.A. in Elem. Reading, University of Northern Colorado; [a.] Wellington, CO

RISDON, CHRISTINA L.
[b.] September 17, 1956, Hollywood, CA; [p.] Lou and Sarah Hernandez; [m.] Wesley R. Risdon, Jr., March 22, 1980; [ch.] Five, Christopher Wesley, Sarahf Caitlin, Samantha Joy, Lisa Marie and Kevin Eric Sean; [ed.] Hollywood High Graduate; [occ.] Domestic Housewife; [hon.] Silver Poet Award and Gold Poet Awards, for my poem "I must go on." World of Poetry awarded this to me in 1992.; [oth. writ.] I have over 50 poems compiled, my goal is to someday sell it as a whole. Hopefully a book of inspirations.; [pers.] I love making people feel good about themselves, if my work can reach out and touch the souls of others than I have succeeded. Greatly influenced by poet "Helen Steiner Rice."; [a.] Glendale, CA

RITENOUR, CRYSTAL GAIL
[b.] September 16, 1980, Pgh., PA; [p.] Dine Ritenour, Ralph Chaffey, Robert Ritenour, Juanita Ritenour; [ed.] Pine Richland Middle School; [hon.] Distinguished Achievement Award, Honor Roll, Pittsburgh Post-Gazette; [oth. writ.] What is a Garden; [pers.] I am 13 and this is my second time being published, it is a great honor for me to be published in the Dark Side of the Moon.; [a.] Bakerstown, PA

RIVOSECCHI, DAVID JAMES
[Pen.] Jim Stark; [b.] April 22, 1966, Flushing, NY; [p.] Marie and George Rivosecchi; [ed.] Holy Cross High School; [occ.] United States Customs Entry Officer; [memb.] Columbia Association of U.S. Customs and Affiliated Federal Agencies, Inc.; [hon.] Honorary Award for Artistic Expression in Advertising 1984.; [oth. writ.] Incomplete or unpublished work include: Novel: American Rebel; Poems: Cascading Desires, The Force of LIfe.; [pers.] Without the constant support of dear friends Lindy Peterson and Connie Chresomales, my poetry may of remained hidden within the eternal realm of uncertainty for an entire lifetime.; [a.] Flushing, NY

ROBERTO, ANDRIENNE
[b.] April 2, 1967, Mannville AB, Canada; [occ.] Registered Nurse; [pers.] I'm a transplanted Canadian enjoying the southwestern culture and of course heat! The poem was written at 3:00 am, July 93' when it was a little bit cooler. This poems style was greatly influenced by Robert Service, who wrote often of the Canadian; [a.] El Paso, TX

ROBERTS, ANN MARIE
[b.] February 4, 1977, Ocala, FL; [p.] Michael and Mariel Roberts; [ed.] High School; [occ.] Student; [memb.] Girl Scouts of America, LGSM Foundaiton, Inc.; [hon.] Jane McCallum History Award, National Piano Auditions Medal; [pers.] Writing allows me to share my world view with others. The joy of communicating with other collective consciousness.

ROBERTS, JODIE MARIE
[b.] April 25, 1959, Spokane, Wash; [p.] Bill and Shirley Follmer; [m.] January 13, 1979; [ch.] none; [ed.] High School Diploma Graduated from Priest River Lamanna High School, 1977; [ed.] High School Diploma, Graduated from Priest River Lamanna High School, 1977; [occ.] Front End Manager at Mitchell's IGA-Foodliner; [hon.] Awards, 3rd place Essay Writing, "What America Means To Me"; [pers.] I have no training or education in preparing myself for my writings. I am solely inspired thru the events of friends and family that revolve around my life.; [pers.] I have no training or education in preparing myself for my writings. I am solely inspired thru the events of friends and family that revolve around my life. These events of inspiration are filled with joyous moments and sorrowful times. In order for me to write I must feel it in my heart. So I give credits to the people involved and I thank the Lord above for guiding me thru my writings. These are all the things that have made my writings worthwhile.; [a.] Priest River, ID

ROBERTS, MARGARET ROWE
[Pen.] nickname: Mickie Robers; [b.] January 30, 1927, Clarksburg, WV [p.] Orion A. and Lottie V. Rowe; [m.] Richard D. Roberts, September 23, 1950; [ch.] None; [ed.] Poca High School, Poca, WV; Morris Harvey College, Charleston, WV, Marshall University, Huntington, WV, Huntington School of Business, Huntington, WV; [occ.] Retired Teacher and Accounting 1985, now a housewife; [memb.] Beverly Hills United Methodist Church, Huntington WV, United Methodist Women, Hospice of Huntington, Contact of Huntington; [hon.] United Methodist Teacher of the Year 1989, Huntington District, Volunteer at Hospice of Huntington, Contact of Huntington and Tri-State Literacy Council; [oth. writ.] I have never submitted any writing for publishing. the one I submitted to you is a first. I did however, have memorials in the form of verse printed in memory of my parents in the Putnam Democrat, Winfield, WV; [pers.] I love God, He is No. 1 in my life. I love life and treasure each day. I love people, I can always learn something from others. I love children and I enjoy working with them. Seems as though there is a special spot in my heart, just for the children and the elderly. I love animals, nature and all of God's creation.; [a.] Huntington, WV

ROBERTS, PAUL
[b.] December 9, 1979, Knoxville, TN; [p.] Lynn and Angela Roberts; [ed.] Pacelli High School (currently enrolled); [occ.] Student; [memb.] Student Ambassador, Teen Advisor, Yearbook Staff, Model Un.N.; [hon.] Honor Society, U.S. Achievement Academy Awards (1991), Honor Roll, Foreign Language Fair; [pers.] I believe that life is a journey through the cosmos that we all must try to make. We must look for guidance and God's enlightenment throughout our guest.; [a.] Cataula, GA

ROBINETT, CARLOTA
[b.] March 30, 1941, Troy, OH; [m.] James R. Robinett, January 29, 1969; [ed.] Graduted 1960 from Fairborn, OH; Nursing school 1960 to 1962 graduated L.P.N.; [occ.] Writer, Poet; [memb.] ALTRUSA of Dayton, OH, ISP, Volunteers of Greater Dayton; [hon.] Several awards for golfing and bowling; Walnut Heights Civic Association Certificate; [oth. writ.] "Mother May I" and "Moments of Memories" two published books. Poem in "Cat Fancy," magazine of California.; [pers.] I like to write about people, places and things I feel and experience. Writing is therapy for me as well as for those who read it.; [a.] Dayton, OH

ROBINSON, MICHELLE RACHEL
[b.] November 20, 1963, Philadelphia; [p.] Alice Robinson; [ch.] Antoine Lamare Robinson; [ed.] Hampton High school, Hampton, Virginia, Susquehanna Job corp Center, Port Deposit Delaware, Maryland, Hareum Junior college (Training for New Choice); [occ.] Poetry, Philadelphia, Pennsylvania; [memb.] Big Sister of Philadelphia, Saint Barnabas Mission, Participating in the Parents Grouping; [hon.] Special Achievement Lt. Military Courtsery,

Economic, Self Sufficient to enhance life management skills Parent Specialist, Nursing aide, Industrial Cleaning #1, Primary Skills, Air Force Officer Junior training cadet (3 yrs); [oth. writ.] We fold the mold had told as we sold. Told and old is the pain for the rain, that had sailed for the trail of your tail. the tret for the wheat that you sweat as you reap. Will make you leap. The strain of your brain is the beat for the defeated, and the features is for the creatures.; [pers.] Ambitious is self esteem for quality, choice and change. Popularilty is the pride to learn about self inside and the three personality trait; in order to walk straight to develop a good sense of humor.; [a.] Philadelphia, PA

ROBINSON, SHANIKA
[Pen.] Rukiyah Talibah; [b.] May 3, 1976, Dallas, TX; [p.] Tommie and Carrie Robinson; [ed.] Lincoln High School; [occ.] Savings of America Teller; [memb.] U.S. Achievement Academy; Speech Club; Audio Visual Club; French Club; [hon.] National Honor Society; French Honor Society; Global Award; Humanitarian Award; Who'w Sho UIL 1st Place Poetry; [pers.] Don't settle for second best. Always reach to the top.; [a.] Lancaster, TX

ROBLE JR., EDWIN F.
[b.] December 1, 1938, Latrobe, PA; [p.] Edwin & Leona Roble; [m.] Anna M. Roble, March 3, 1962; [ch.] Edward, James, Kathi; [ed.] Frederick MD High School; Kansas State University; Cabell County West Virginia Vo-Tech Center; [occ.] Telecommunications Operator; [memb.] Veterans of Foreign Wars; [hon.] 1954 National Sojourner's Award; 1975 Freedoms Foundation Award; 1975 Graduate of Senior Military Academy on Dean's Honor List.; [oth. writ.] Three award winning essays, publication of freelance newspaper, articles during vietnam war era, several published songs, former writer for armed forces network show in Germany.; [pers.] It is better to pursue a dream and fail, than to never pursue it at all for fear of failure.; [a.] Huntingston, WV

ROCCO, JENNIFER LEIGH
[b.] August 14, 1969, N. Hollywood, CA; [p.] Alex and Sandie Rocco; [ed.] Univ. CA at Santa Barbara, Southwester Univ. School of Law; [occ.] Law Student; [oth. writ.] Poems published in other anthologies, screeplays.; [pers.] Stiffled and deep emotions which cannot be expressed by myself are expressed in any writing I undertake.; [a.] Studio City, CA

RODERICK, NICOLE
[b.] March 20, 1982, Mich.; [p.] Jacquie and Donald Dearing and Kurt Roderick; [occ.] Student; [pers.] I have a deep and fullfiling relationship with the Lord Jesus Christ.; [a.] Wolled Lake, MI

RODGERS, NORMAN NEOMA
[b.] December 12, 1925, Magazine, AK; [p.] Clayborn Norman and Fannie Davis; [m.] William Rodgers, December 18, 1945; [ch.] Dwayne Rodgers, deceased, Nona, Debra, Ronald, Joe, eleven grandchildren and two great-grandchildren; [occ.] Housewife; [oth. writ.] I have several writings of poems that I have never done anything with. Some are religious poems; [pers.] One poem I wrote was titled a "soap poem" in 1987, I wote 2 poems for the grandchildren who lost their Dad. I have some about children and grandchildren, etc., most were written in 1993.; [a.] Folsom, CA

RODRIQUEZ, ANGELA
[b.] December 21, 1976, Wasem, OH; [p.] Gloria and Julian Rodriquez; [ed.] Commercial Graphic Arts, Four County Joint Vocational School; [occ.] Cashier of Buds Country Market; [oth. writ.] Short stories; [pers.] I only write about the truth. I write wht I feel and what I have gone through.; [a.] Archbold, OH

ROGERS, SUSAN
[Pen.] Susan Kehoe; [b.] February 8, 1951, Queens, NY; [p.] Vincent Kehoe; [ch.] Michael Maganza and Samantha Baron; [ed.] Valley Stream South H.S., South Oaks Institute for Alcoholism and Addictive Behavior Studies, M. Blinderman Actors Workshops, Ocianside, NY; [occ.] Addictions Counselor, Intern, LI College, Hosp. Flatbush, NY; [m.] Nassau County Rotational Art Scrics. Interfaith Nutrition, Network, Hempstead, NY, Island Pk., Theatre Group; [hon.] 1st prize Islip Arts Festival, Sculptur, 1992; [oth. writ.] Pepperoni Isn't for Lovers; Two Little Strangers published in local papers.; [pers.] I thoroughly enjoy utilizing all media and every opportunity to experience and explore my environment and relationships. From outward expressions I find the me within.; [a.] East Rockaway, NY

ROMEO, PATRICIA D.
[b.] October 4, 1939, N. Adams, MA; [p.] Mary D. and Harold Palmer; [m.] Ralph J. Romeo (Deceased), September 3, 1960; [ch.] Rhonda Lynn Romeo Ouimet, Patricia A. Romeo and Carla B. Romeo Martell; [ed.] Grammer School, High School to third year. Took G.E.D. course to receive diploma.; [occ.] Home Health Aide for Northern Berkshire Home Aide Services; [oth. writ.] Have never concidered myself good enough to persue.; [pers.] I have always loved to read of the finer things in life. Poetry has always been a challenge that I would like to have been famous for, as well art and writing children's books.

ROPER, EMMA FEURER
[b.] August 24, 1917, Benton, IL; [p.] Charles and Nora Feurer; [m.] Earle F. Roper, January 8, 1983 (deceased); [ch.] Bill, Ken, Charles, Liz (Taylor) Cliff and Steve; [ed.] Benton Township High School Class 35'; [occ.] Retired; [memb.] Civic groups, AARP, Womans Fellowship; [hon.] this is my first poem to be submitted for consideration; [oth. writ.] Copyrighted Children's books "Uncle Thunder Cluse" have composed many children's poems, and all other classes of poetry.; [pers.] Sharing is the best evidence of caring.; [a.] Mojave, CA

ROSA, CARMELLA
[b.] April 20, 1947, CT; [p.] Dora Taylor and the Late Jack Cecere; [m.] Luis Rosa, August 7, 1976; [ch.] Maria, Angela, Giuseppe and Angelo Divincenzo Jr., William, Luis and George Rosa; [ed.] Stratford High; 1962-66, Coastal Carolina Community College; Institute of Child. Lit. and NIA (Newspapers Institute of America); [occ.] Self Employed; [memb.] The American Poetry Society; [hon.] Honorable Metnion and Award of Merit, April 1990 and April 30, 1992, Editor's Choice Awrd 1993; [oth. writ.] The Old Man, An Old Woman's silent feelings, Blessed is the Child and Love.; [pers.] All my writings reflects my inner most feelings.; [a.] Tampa, FL

ROSE, ANTOINETTE M.
[Pen.] The Rose; [b.] May 20, 1964, MD; [p.] Nattie

and Nelson Jones; [m.] Single; [ed.] Walbrook Sr. High School, Villa Julie College; [occ.] Student; [memb.] National Organization of Women; [oth. writ.] One other poem published in Villa Julie's "The Spectrum". Several others I have written but were not published.; [pers.] I try to write about the things I see in the world. Hopefully, the poems I write will have an impact on people and maybe they will see things in a different way and maybe they will tell others.; [a.] Baltimore, MD

ROSEN, MELANIE
[Pen.] Madeline Rochier; [b.] October 13, 1976, Silver Spring, MD; [p.] Linda and Edward Rosen; [ed.] Seneca Valley High, Germantown Elementary, University of Miami, Martin Luther King Intermediate; [occ.] Law Clerk/School; [memb.] Alpak; [hon.] National Band Award; [pers.] Writing is an art form. It may not catch the eye of the spectator, but it comes from the heart, and all that matters is that the author takes pride in his or her own creation.; [a.] Germantown, MD

ROSS, CARLIN
[Pen.] Red Hawk; [b.] October 31, 1950, Edmond, OK; [p.] Clyde and Esther Ross; [m.] Minda Ross, November 26, 1975; [ch.] Laudette Mae, Cassandra Dawn and John Robert; [ed.] Varnum High School; [occ.] Janitor, Maud Elementary School; [oth. writ.] Had one poem published in local newspaper.; [pers.] I have just started writing poetry. I try to tell a story with everyting that I write. My biggest influence has been from the teachers that I work with.; [a.] Maud, OK

ROSS, MARIE ANN
[b.] June 18, 1959, Texas; [p.] Alton and Dorothy Young; [m.] Ronald Gene Ross, June 25, 1992; [ch.] Michelle, Rhonda, Dorothy, Wallace Jr., Ron Jr.; [ed.] Tatum High, Panola Junior College; [occ.] Cook, housewife; [pers.] I am learning what its like to have a combined family. Life at my home is never dull. Children range in age from 6 - 19 yrs.; [a.] Benton, AK

ROSS, ROGER M.
[b.] January 22, 1962, Vallejo, CA; [p.] Shirley A. and Frank M. Ross; [m.] Jane M. Ross, March 6, 1993; [ch.] T.C., 10 years old, Alecia 8 years old; [ed.] Hardin-Jefferson High Lamar University; [occ.] Police Officer Beaumont, Texas; [memb.] Beaumont Police Officers Association; [hon.] U.S. Army Achievement Medal recipient; [a.] Nederland, TX

ROSTERNOCK, SUSAN
[b.] April 2, 1976, Somers Point, NJ; [p.] Sharon and Glen PUllman; [ed.] Beginning Rowan College of NJ, September 1994 as a freshman; [occ.] Student, I also work in a restaurant; [hon.] I won the Cape May County Teen Arts Festival for poetry, but the poem was not printed with the winners because it was too violent and the calendar was censored.; [oth. writ.] I write for an underground magazine from Philadelphia called Lin, high school newspaper and literary journal; [a.] Wildwood Crest, NJ

ROULHAC, ERICKA RUTH
[Pen.] BIGE (because I'm small); [b.] July 18, 1971, Pensacola, FL; [p.] Linda Hill and Paris Roulhac; [ch.] Paris Roulhac, Makeshia Kyleso and Shaquanna Fitzpatrick; [ed.] finished 9th grade; [memb.] The

poem is dedicated to my ne baby Shaquanna and my great grandmother Lela Mae Dortch; [oth. writ.] non-published poems.; [a.] Pensacola, FL

ROWLAND, ALISON
[Pen.] McKenzie; [b.] May 9, 1979, Carson City, Nevada; [p.] Glen (Deceased) and Gladys Rowland; [ed.] I'm going into 10th grade at Sparks High; [occ.] Cone maker at "TCBY" (the country's best yoguart); [oth. writ.] Last year I entered the poem my hero the poem was printed in Tears of Fire. I wrote the poem in memory of my Dad because he was my hero.; [pers.] My Dad died in 1992 my mom moved to Australia, I live with my grandparents Martian & Lillian Rowland. I have 3 sisters, Kristine 21, Shannon 19, Jennifer 16. I am 15, we all get along. I play the trumpet and piano.; [a.] Sparks, NV

RUBIN, DEBBIE
[Pen.] Deborah rose; [b.] March 19, 1977, Manhasset, NY; [p.] Mark and Nan Rubin; [ed.] High School Student; [occ.] High School Student, Cactus Shadows H.S.; [pers.] "Everything that happends in one's life, has a purpose. Life is one big mystery. Live each day as if it's your last. Try to treat everyone like a sister or brother."; [a.] Cave Creek, AZ

RUGG, MARY F.
[b.] June 2, 1924, Berthoud, CO; [p.] Mr. and Mrs. John Nolde; [ch.] One Son, Alan W. Johnson; [ed.] High School; [oth. writ.] Waitress, 40 years; [memb.] El Paso Elk's Club, Eastern Star Chapter, El Paso, TX; [hon.] Waitress of the Year 1984, Block Captain "honor" May 1994; [oth. writ.] Songs, Buidose Waltz, Lolver's Hall of Fame and new poems I have written in El Paso times; [a.] El Paso, TX

RUGGIERO, MICHAEL
[Pen.] Michael Shock; [b.] November 13, 1977, Philadelphia; [p.] Michael and anna; [ed.] Senior at St. John Neumann High School; [hon.] V.F.W. Journalism Award, Millay Scholarship, High Honors Certificate; [pers.] Tell Danica McKellar, I love her.; [a.] Philadelphia, PA

RUILOBA JR., EDUARDO
[Pen.] Junior; [b.] May 17, 1971, El Paso, TX; [p.] Eduardo and Stella Ruiloba; [ed.] B.S. in Computer Science from Univ. of Texas at El Paso; [pers.] In every eye there is a glimmer; In every voice there is a song, In everybody there is a soul.; [a.] El Paso, TX

RUNION, CLYDE E.
[pers.] Clyde E. Runion, native of Phillipsburg, Kansas, has tested many experiences of life ranging from a Pipeliner, Refinery-worker, Welder, Sales-man, House-mover, Cattleman and Farmer...As well as Author and Poet; hving over 2500 poems to his credit. These range from Sadness to Humor, Reli-gious, Patriotic, and Fiction. He has written several songs and dozens of Sacred Spiritual songs. One of Mr. Runion's accomplishments in his book. It is a complete 200 year Bi-Centennial History written completely in verse and rhyme. The title of this book is, "200 Years of American History in Rhyme." Mr. Runion, in spite of his busy schedule, has written and mailed over 40,000 Letters to over 30 Editors. The topics range from Politics, Religion, Vitamins, Min-erals, Medicine and Disease.

RUNKLE, ROXANNA
[b.] November 26, 1968, York, PA; [p.] Kenneth Royal Sr. & Lurethia Royal; [m.] Richie Runkle, December 6, 1986; [ch.] Trista Runkle and Rebecca Runkle; [ed.] York Co., Vo-Tech; [occ.] Lead Per-son, Hanover Foods Corp.; [a.] Hanover, PA

RUNNELS, TRACY
[b.] April 29, 1969; [p.] Kenneth Runnels Sr. and Hester runnels; [ed.] University of California at Los Angeles (UCLA); [pers.] I believe that one must embrace the joy and the pain in life before one can fully appreciate the meaning of life.; [a.] Culver City, CA

RUPPE, CHRISTINE H.
[b.] August 27, 1940, Melvin Hill, North Carolina; [p.] Carl and Mary Harris; [m.] Relson R. Ruppe, April 8, 1956; [ch.] Ricky Ree, Glen James, Alan Jeffrey; [ed.] 7th grade, Cowpens High, Cowpens, SC; [occ.] Wife, Homemaker, Grandmother; [a.] Cowpens, SC

RUPPERT, EMILY M.
[b.] August 9, 1975, Reading, PA; [p.] Frederick and Ellen Ruppert and Mary and Walter Zeimer, Jr.; [ed.] Wibaux County High School Graduate; [occ.] Chef; [hon.] Awards for school art and for sandwich making in F.N.A.; [oth. writ.] Nothing ever published.; [pers.] A favorite quote: "Sweet is the rememberance of troubles when you are in safty." Euripides; [a.] Sinking Spring, PA

RUSH, MICHELE A.
[b.] December 26, 1965, Norristown; [p.] Barbara and Domenic Cemini; [m.] thomas J. Rush, February 14, 1987; [ch.] Danielle 7, Adam 5 and Sara 4; [ed.] Methacton High School; [occ.] Housewife and mother; [oth. writ.] At first it's hard to notice when..edge edge of twilight.; [pers.] I would like to thank my children for thier influence of my writing. I would also like to thank my husband and family for their support.; [a.] Collegeville, PA

RUSIN, JEAN M.
[Pen.] Long Silky; [pers.] July 31, 1964, New Britian; [p.] Wladyslaw and Marcella Rusin; [ed.] CCSU 2 years of college; [occ.] Not working; [memb.] The Bold and the Beautiful, St. Jude Children's Hospital; [hon.] None; [oth. writ.] Songwriter, "Missing You" Hill Top records, published December 23, 1993 and other poems too.; [pers.] To a friend that believe what I do that dreams come true. My friend Jim.; [a.] New Britain, CT

RUSSELL, ERNESTINE
[Pen.] Ernie Russell; [b.] April 1, 1948, W.VA; [p.] Fred and Gladys Meadows; [m.] Gerald russell; [ch.] Roberta and Amands; [ed.] High School; [occ.] Factory Worker; [hon.] Mom and Dad's Secret Won Honorable Mention in Great American Contest, Eddie-Lou Cole Poetry Editor; [oth. writ.] My Old House, A Tribute to Bob Hope, Day and Night, Our Wedding Vowels, An Older Sister, Love For a Brother; [pers.] I grew up in the mountains of West VA. We were very poor financially but never poor from the live of love. This love has inspired me to write poetry with a wish for other to share.; [a.] Lousiville, KY

RUSSELL, LYNNE
[Pen.] Lynne Marie; [b.] July 19, 1950, Chicago, IL;

[p.] Harold and Margaret Youngren; [ch.] Geoffrey Russell; [ed.] Oak Park High School, Wau Bonsee Community College; [occ.] Insurance Lien Special-ist; [hon.] The National Library of Poetry, Tears of fire, Editor's Choice Award; [oth. writ.] Short Story published in local paper.; [pers.] My hope is that my writings touch the common thread in all of us.; [a.] Aurora, IL

RUTLEDGE, ELIZABETH
[Pen.] Elizabeth Yocom; [b.] July 13, 1967, Louisvile, KY; [p.] Jim and Marie Yocom, Jeanne Zimmerman; [m.] Gregory Rutledge, March 18, 1988; [ch.] Mat-thew G., Melinda A.; [occ.] Full time Mother; [pers.] From terror to peace, the search for the void of the true light, spiritual enlightenment, is my inspiration for my poems and songs. Awakening Amongst Survival is my first poem to be published.; [a.] Louisville, KY

RYALL, LAUREN
[b.] April 11, 1980, Vero Beach, FL; [p.] Alan and Christine Ryall; [ed.] St. Edward's School; [occ.] Student; [memb.] United Church of Christ Youth Group, National Junior Honor Society, Volunteer at local hospital, school chamber ensemble; [hon.] Dean's List, Hedmaster's List, Community Service Award, National Latin Exam, Recognition, Duke Talent Iden-tification Program; [oth. writ.] Many poems pub-lished school literary magazines.; [pers.] In most of the pomes I write, I try to bring out the beauty and mystery of nature.; [a.] Vero Beach, FL

RYAN, CHRISTOPHER D.
[b.] June 27, 1961, Baltimore, MD; [p.] Michael J. and Joan M. Ryan; [m.] Kimberly E. Ryan, March 30, 1985; [ch.] Joshua P. and Zachary A. ryan; [ed.] Patapsco Sr. High, Arundel Inst. of Technology; [occ.] computer Service engineer; [pers.] I try to use all tht I do, my works my life, my attitude to expess that love that God has shown me through his son.; [a.] Dundalk, MD

SADLER, GARY
[Pen.] Yrag Reldas; [b.] February 17, 1955, Royston, GA; [p.] Bobby and Elizabeth Jordan Sadler; [m.] Single; [ch.] Cristine Thompson, Crystle Thompson; [ed.] Bridgeton, H.Sl; [occ.] Road Dept. City of Bridgeton, Sweepe Operator; [memb.] St. Augustine AME Zion Church, Bord of Director's Community Health Care Bridgeton, NJ; [pers.] Started writing at age 10 when my mother passed away. I was influ-enced by Poet's Langton Huges and Edgar Allen Poe, A Dream Deferred and Simple. Raven; [a.] Bridgeton, NJ

SAFFA, KAREN HAWMI
[b.] February 23, 1946, Cairo, IL; [p.] Saffa Samaha Hamuri; Hamuri Inventor of Ice Cream Cone, St. Louis 1904; [ch.] Two; [ed.] College, Writer and IBM Programmer; [occ.] Retired; [memb.] Precinct Com./School of Articles, Art Mu., Commer. Fish Org., Agricultural Fish Organize., several states; [hon.] School papers, etc; The Pulaskis Enterprise, New Woman's Magazine; [pers.] Ideas are of a consist of people's, friends, family's. My feelings, actions holiday events technology and some children's poems. My perceptions and predictions of spiritual and heavenly realm; [a.] Tulsa, OK

SAKYI, JUSTICE MENSAH
[b.] May 26, 1969, Ghana; [p.] Agnes and Nana

Anyani Buadum III; [m.] Cynthia Randall-Sakyi, March 12, 1994; [ch.] Matthew Randall; [ed.] St. Teresa's Seminary, Ghana; St. Paul's Major Seminary, Ghana; Computer Learning Center (Alexandria Campus); [occ.] Computer Operator; [memb.] Catholic Youth Organization; [hon.] BA in Philosophy, Diploma, Computer Programming; [oth. writ.] Written several other poems but are unpublished.; [pers.] I strive to create the awareness for. Society to get rid of some vices. I have been greaty influenced by the philosophies of Plato, Socrates and Aristotle.; [a.] Oxon Hill, MD

SALDANA, CAROLYNN
[b.]   October 17, 1968, Fairborn, OH; [p.] Emmette Smelley, Kathryn Pooler; [m.] Martin Saldana; [ed.] Tecumseh High School, Antonelli Institue of Art and Photography; [occ.] Receptionist, S&S Electric Co., Inc., Oldsmar, FL; [pers.] Strive to be the best you can be. Always follow your heart and fulfill your dreams.; [a.] Tampa, FL

SALISBURY, MEREDITH
[b.] June 6, 1912, Canojaharie, NY; [p.] Rose and Raymond Barber; [m.] Edward Salisbury, September 7, 1963; [ch.] Sheredith Salisbury, Stacey Mundschenk; [ed.] Utica College, Syracuse U., Utica, NY, Jr. B.A. in Social Studies; [occ.] Writer/Homemaker Teacher's Aide/Volunteer; [memb.] Alpha Sigma Lamda, Oneida County Historical Society Museum, William Proctor Museum, Westminster Presbyterian, Mayor: Charter Revision Commission 83-94, Several local and State political org.; [hon.] Dean's List 89/91, Alpha Ome Grom Chap., Ampersand 92 Poetry Honorable Mention, National Dean's List 91-92 listing; [oth. writ.] Twelve poems from the female perspective; Zen Poetry; several poems for local papers etc., a play and short story for Utica College, Literary Magazine Ampersand; [pers.] My poetry reflects and explores women's roles and experiences. But a poet is entitled to speak in many voices mle, female or child like to express many moods.; [a.] Utica, NY

SALTER, JOHN STEPHEN
[Pen.] Steven Bogan; [b.] December 25, 1959, Florida; [p.] Elouise and Arthur Salter; [m.] Robin R. Salter, March 23, 1990; [ch.] Darin L. Salter, Patricia Meade; [ed.] Henryford High and Job Corps Highland Park C.C. Machine Operator, Auto Machine; [occ.] Machine Operator; [memb.] Fitness, USA, Health Spas; [a.] Detroit, MI

SALUSTRI, MADELINE
[b.] June 20, 1930, Yonlars, NY; [p.] Arthur and Antoinette Pagano; [m.] Alex J., July 4, 1956; [ch.] Stephanie, Alex Jr., Nancy; [ed.] College of Mt. St. Vincent, BA, Hunter College, MA, Pratt Grad Library School, MLS, PD Administration; [occ.] Retired district administrators of library media centers; [memb.] ALA, NYS Library Media Specialist; Milford Council of Arts. Countless, religious civic and educational organizations before retirement; [hon.] Phi Beta Mu, Int'l Library Honor Society; [oth. writ.] Poems in High Tide 1994, Milford Council of Arts, Sound and Waves 1994, West Haven, CA, Laurel, New England Compilation Professonal articles in Library Journals and for Labeland District; [pers.] Eureka and Excelsior; [a.] Milford, CT

SALVATORE, ANTHONY
[b.] April 11, 1975, Queens, NY; [p.] Angelo and Roberta Salvatore; [ed.] Cathedrl Prep High School, Currently on the Dean's List at St. John's University as a sophomore; [occ.] Student; [memb.] national Forensics Society, Society for the Propagation of the Faith; [hon.] Over 40 awards for speec and debate compeitition, citations for service as a tutor, working in a soup kitchen, and as a youth counselor at the Fr. Troike Leadership Program; [oth. writ.] Several short stories and poems published in school literary journal, a book of personal peoms and stories, yet unpublished.; [pers.] Each day I ask God to give me the strength to make a difference in this world so that at the end he can see tht his creation was not wasted on me.; [a.] Corona, NY

SAMMONS, NINA MARIE
[b.] January 1, 1978, Randle, WA; [p.] Patrick and Janet Simmons; [ed.] Spanaway Lake High School, Spanaway, WA Class of 1996; [occ.] Student; [memb.] Girl Scouts of America; [hon.] Presidential Academic Fitness Award, Evergreen Certificate of Art Proficiency; [pers.] I use poetry as a form of expressing my feelings. My poetry comes from my heart.; [a.] Spanaway, WA

SAMPSON, CHRISTINE
[Pen.] Crycci; [b.] September 21, 1970, CA; [oth. writ.] I've written many other poems such as; The Clown, At The Gate, Ect.; [pers.] Lord, thank you for blessing me, watching over me. Thank you for granting me the serenity to except the things I cannot change, the courage to change the things I can, and the widom to know the difference. Amen.

SAMPSON, KRYSTAL
[b.] June 9, 1979, KY; [p.] Charles and Carolyn Sampson; [ch.] no children; [ed.] Sophmore at Muhlenberg North High School in Greenville, KY; [hon.] I've received many band awards in school; [oth. writ.] I've never had any of my writings published before, but I have many other poems and stories I have written.; [pers.] I love to read and write peotry. I have been writing since I was very small. I hope to make it a profession one day.; [a.] Central City, KY

SANCHEZ, MERCEDEZ P.
[b.] March 16, 1979, Bakersfield; [p.] Mr. Jose Guadalpe and Miss Enalina; [ed.] Elementary Compton Jr. High, East High School; [oth. writ.] Poems that written but never published.; [pers.] My poems are usually of romance and lonliness also confusion.; [a.] Bakersfield, CA

SANDERS, DEBI
[b.] September 1, 1957, Melrose, MA [p.] Richard and Mary Ann Dewling; [m.] Carl Sanders, May 13, 1978; [ch.] Carl Ryan Sanders, Steven Keith Sanders; [ed.] Saugus High School, North Shore Community College; [occ.] Secretary, Dta Entry Clerk at San Tron, Inc. Saugus; [oth. writ.] Several poems and short stories hopefully to be published but now, just for the enjoyment of my family and friends.; [pers.] I have been greatly influenced by my child who think their mom is the best.; [a.] Saugus, MA

SANTOS, VIRGINIA M.
[Pen.] Jini; [b.] February 15, 1935, Albany, NY; [p.] Franklin & May Bateholts; [m.] Manny Santos, September 5, 1955; [ch.] Scott, Holly and Christo-

pher; Grandchild, Ryan Scott; [ed.] Burnt Hills, Ballston Lake High School, Bryant College; [occ.] Homemaker; [memb.] International Women's Writing Guild; [hon.] Summa Cum Laude, College; Henry L. Jacobs English Award, College Key Society, College; [oth. writ.] "Amanda Pink," "Naming Baby," "Stuart Stories, The Adventures of Stuart Bear" for Ryan Scott Class poem, high school; [pers.] Find your best friend inside yourself and you will always have someone to talk with who listens!; [a.] Ballston Lake, NY

SANUSKY, PAUL
[b.] October 13, 1961, East Chicago; [p.] William D. and Stephanie M. Sanusky; [oth. writ.] Several other poems and songs unpublished as of yet.; [pers.] This poem was written for my mother who passed away the day before her 74th birthday, and was read during her funeral service.; [a.] Highland, TX

SATRIANO, CLIFF
[b.] August 22, 1972; [p.] Anita Navarro, Dennis Satriano; [ed.] Sachem High School, Suffolk County Community College, A.S. Degree in Communications, PACE Center, Addictions Counselor; [memb.] Long Island Ambassadors Drum and Bugle Corp., Jack LaLanne Health Spa; [oth. writ.] To be seen.; [pers.] The way I write poetry, play the drums, and take pictures reflect my personality creatively. A spiritual awareness and holistic aura will be apparent as it will be everywhere.; [a.] Shirley, Long Island, NY

SAUKEY, ADAM
[b.] September 11, 1979, Mesa, AZ; [p.] William Saukey and Gloria Brashier; [ed.] Fremont Jr. High School; [hon.] Honor Roll, Student of the Month; [pers.] I was reflecting on the good times that my grandfather and I had and I was inspired to write this poem.; [a.] Mesa, AZ

SAUNDERS, BETTYE WILLIAM
[b.] March 23, 1917; [p.] Walter and Maxie Means; [m.] Lowell Saunders, March 28, 1936; [ch.] Max Dowe Saunders, Connie Beth Taylor; [ed.] Completed 11th grade, Lakecreek School, Mangum, Okla.; [occ.] Deceased November 24, 193, Retired from T.G & Y after 25 years service; [memb.] First Baptist Church, Frederick, Okla.; [hon.] A devoted wife, a wonderful mother, loving daughter and sister, a child of God. Bettye's awards and honors were from those who had the pleasure of her easy laughter, her calm manner and her smile and her hugs.; [oth. writ.] Many other unpublished poems.; [pers.] Bettye wrote about her god, her family (the loves of her life), and her acceptance of death without fear or regret.; [a.] Frederick, OK

SCALA, MATT
[Pen.] Dean Scala; [b.] September 13, 1994, New Castle, PA; [p.] Eugene and Margaret Callahan Scala; [ed.] Riverside High, and The Community College of Beaver County, Shaver Jacobson Technical Institute; [occ.] Labor Worker; [memb.] American Boiler Makers, American Red Cross, CCBC Radio Club; [hon.] Dean's List, High School Art Award; [oth. writ.] One article in a local newspaper.; [pers.] I try to let the world flow through me and on to the paper. Be a conduit, and let the world write your poems.; [a.] Beaver Falls, PA

SCARAFILE, GAIL M.
[Pen.] Gail Bellows; [b.] July 11, 1940, Solsville, NY; [p.] Charles and Mildred Bellows; [m.] Arthur A. (deceased) August 1958; [ch.] Chjristopher (designer), Rebecca (Sales Rep.) one son; [ed.] College, 2 yrs. (Utica College) Art School 4 yrs. Munson Williams Proctor Inst.; [occ.] Former Art Instructor, Concentating on writing pursuits presently; [memb.] NYS Morgan Horse Assoc.; Amer. Morgan Horse Assoc; Munson Proctor Art Institute; Past Member utica Writer's club, Utica Exotic bird Club, Utica Art Club among many others.; [hon.] While actively pursuing career as artist won numerous regional, national and purchase awards, showing horses netted countless championships. Currently seeking fulfillment in the writing field.; [oth. writ.] Accumulation from years of writing poetry, short stories, novelettes, essays and several first draft novels. Just beginning a climb up publication ladder.; [pers.] The banquet of life has many sumptuous dishes, but I have contributed the spices. All contact inspires. I live with seven horses, six parrots, three dogs and several cats; toil, love, joy.; [a.] Sauquoit, NY

SCHASCHL, ARLENE HELEN
[b.] September 8, 1942, Flint, MI; [p.] Richard and Helen Engen; [m.] Kenneth Ernest Schaschl, June 25, 1966; [ch.] Christine Helen Schaschl age 25 and Jeanne Lynn Schaschl age 23; [ed.] High school graduate, currently Lansing Community College, Associates of Arts Program; [occ.] Radiology Records Clerk; [memb.] Lansing Community College Poetry Club, Church of Christ, Restored; [hon.] Winner of the 1993, 1994 Lansing Poetry Club Contest sponsored by Lansing Communtiy College's Creative Writing Program.; [oth. writ.] Poetry Published in the 1993 and 1994 "Washington Square Review." a creative writing publicaiton of the Lansing Community College.; [pers.] Poetic expression is the extension of one's self living through the eyes of another.; [a.] Grand Ledge, MI

SCHERER, TOM
[b.] December 22, 1945, Home; [p.] Mr. and Mrs. Ishmael J. Scherer; [m.] not married; [ed.] High School, graduate of MO School of the Blind; [occ.] none; [memb.] Knights of Columbus Council 1037, Alumni, MO School of the Blind, Adult in Leadbelt T.E.c. Curcillo; [hon.] K.O.C. Knight of the Month; [oth. writ.] Poetry (none offered for publication as of now.; [pers.] I try to write about life and the goodness in people.; [a.] Ste. Genevieve, MO

SCHLAPPE, LORRIE ANN
[b.] June 7, 1975, PA; [p.] Jack and Hannah Schlappe; [ed.] Scranton High school, East Stroudsburg University; [occ.] Elementary Ed Student; [pers.] My unusual dream inspired me to write this poem. My poem is dedicated to my first love, Steven Werner; also, to my family, especially my mother who supported my writings all the way!; [a.] Scranton, PA

SCHLEMMER, VICKY D.
[b.] October 12, 1961, Alton, IL; [p.] Albert and Juanita Manring; [m.] John Schlemmer, November 6, 1982; [ch.] April D. Schlemmer and Joshua A. Schlemmer; [ed.] American School of Correspondence, The Institute of Children's Literature, How to Write Poetry by Nancy Bogen, Writing Down The Bones by Natalie Goldberg.; [occ.] Medical Transcriptionist, Christian Hospital Northeast, St. Louis,

MO; [memb.] Rock The Vote; [oth. writ.] I have written numerous poems which I have not yet sought publication for.; [pers.] Poetry to me is very important. A lot of times I'll write a poem to express my feelings at that moment in my life. I am a very moody and sensitive person. Writing is therapeutic for me.; [a.] South Roxana, IL

SCHMERBER, CHEROKEE
[Pen.] Cherokee Noon; [b.] October 25, 1944; [m.] Inyo Salinas Schmerber; [ch.] Joel, Julia, David, Veronica, John, Michael; [ed.] Eugene Business College 1 yr.; Lane Community College 2 yrs.; BFC Religious Order 1 yr.; [occ.] Independent editor/writer; [memb.] Smithsonian Inst. Honorable Member (Co-director, Tribal Outreach, Native American Organization); [hon.] "The Man at the Restaurant" National Poet Award 1988. Silver Poet Award 89'; [oth. writ.] "The Man at the Restaurant" 2 publishings for, "South County Courier." "Seasons End" and "Words"; Editor/Writer, 4 pub. yrly., Tribal Outreach Tyee, 400 subscribers; [pers.] The world is a market, an exchange place for words, for notoriety and phrases of renown. As a writer, it's not just the fame I seek, rather its away to express. Words are the foundation of my world, the rocks upon which I build. Words are everything there is for me.; [a.] Eugene, OR

SCHMIDT, JENNIFER
[b.] January 4, 1974, St. Louis, Park; [p.] Mary Jo and Charles; [ed.] I graduated from high school 2 yrs. ago. I do have some college skills in computers. I hope to complete a certificate or diploma; [occ.] Data Entry; [memb.] I belong to the Robbinsdale City Band, I participate as a flag twirler. This is my 2nd year.; [oth. writ.] I have written several other poems and songs which have never been published. I have never gone this far with any of my writings.; [pers.] I feel that life is all about not creating problems and staying away from them. My inspirations come from certain scenes in movies and songs.; [a.] New Hope, MN

SCHMIDT, ROSETTA
[Pen.] Rosetta Berkenstock-Schmidt; [b.] June 27, 1968, Akron, Ohio; [p.] Ruth and Al Berkenstock; [m.] Richard Schmidt, January 6, 1993; [ch.] Matthew Schmidt, age 8; [ed.] Springfield High, Akron, Ohio, Montgomery Co. JVS, Dayton, Ohio; [occ.] Unemployed Homemaker; [hon.] Golden Poet Award 1986; [oth. writ.] Several other poems not yet published; [pers.] I began writing poetry at age 15. My first poem was inspired by the death of a friend. Writing poetry lets me escape into my own world and helps evade insanity.; [a.] Ogden, KS

SCHOKNECHT, MONICA
[b.] February 14, 1975, Jackson, MS; [p.] Ron and Betty Schoknecht; [ed.] MS School for Mathematics and Science, MS State University.; [occ.] Student, pre-vet program; [memb.] alpha Zeta Fraternity, Friends of the Zoo, Palmer Home, MSMS Alumni Association, Yearbook Committee; [hon.] Alpha Zeta, Who's Who Among High School Students, SGA cabinet, Black heritage essay contest winner.; [pers.] Drawing from personal experience allows the reality of the situation to be expressed in the poetry.; [a.] Jackson, MS

SCHOOLCRAFT III, STAN
[b.] October 28, 1949, New Orleans, LA; [p.] Stan and Cathrine Schoolcraft; [m.] Kathleen Schoolcraft, July 25, 1971; [ch.] Lisa Grad, Merideth Schoolcraft; [ed.] BA Acctg. Univ. of West FL; MBA American International College; [occ.] College Professor; [memb.] Massachusetts Association of School Business Officials; [hon.] Digital Equip. Corp. Financial Excellence Award; [oth. writ.] Several poems and a short story.; [pers.] My belief has always been that "The Greatest Gift one person gives to another is to touch their life in a way that makes it better than it was before they met."; [a.] Hudson, MA

SCHULER, BROOKE R.
[b.] July 11, 1976, St. Louis, MO; [p.] Carolyn and Michael Schuler; [ed.] American High School Home Study Council; [occ.] Dietary Aide at Marymount Manor Retirement HOme; [memb.] Currently none.; [hon.] Many awards for poems, short stories and other writings throughout Grade School and also many honor certificates in English and Spelling.; [oth. writ.] Several poems I've written have been chosen for the making of songs and a poem called "Love" written when I was very young, now appears in a poetry book called "Another Place In Time." I have a collection of poems I've written and kept to myself which have never been recognized.; [pers.] Writing is for me the most accurate way of expressing my thoughts, and emotions. It is the only way to free my soul. My heart and spirit touches everything I write. I beleive all poets, young and old are a great inspiration to the world.; [a.] Eureka, MO

SCHULER, JOANNE M.
[b.] June 25, 1928, Mpls, MN; [p.] Emmet and Anna Schuler; [ed.] B.A. Chemistry, English, Philosophy Theology 1952; M.A. Philosophy & Theology 1957; A.B.D. Psychology; 1986 J.D.; also Lic. Pilot Instructor 1586130 CFI; USI Red Cross; [occ.] Psychologist, Attorny, Studdying Common Law, Music and art by self; [memb.] Usual Professional Memberships in Law and Psychology. Have Pilots Lic., not presently active in civil air patrol, Roman Catholic Church (Papal-Rome-Strict); [hon.] Valedictorian High School and College; Bausch and Lomb Science Award, Phi Beta Vayyen and English Letter Society, Flight Instructor, Gold Seal Award for Excellence; Won first place in two photo entries, only ever entered.; [oth. writ.] A book of poems, I can't find. Legal and Appellate Briefs in Court Files, 3 incomplete thesis (researched and statiscally analyzed thousands of pages of incomplete ideas and scholastic requriements). Published: Two Scientific Papers; [pers.] Metaphysical by nature; electic and enthusiastic about all learning. If I had a choice I would be a musician, painter, poet and scientist (research, ivory tower kind). Love out of doors, animals, creative people, idealists. Think USA needs "New birth of freedom to be under God.; [a.] Mpls., MN

SCHULTZ, MARIE W.
[b.] February 4, 1899, Brookfield, Twshp.; [p.] William and Croline Wehking; [m.] Otto F. Schultz, April 15, 1921; [ch.] Merle Luverne; [ed.] 8th Grade; [occ.] Retired Farmer's Wife; [memb.] Zion Lutheran Church; [oth. writ.] History of her and her husband's families in book form, complete with drawings, poems etc. Both families had 11 children, many anecdotes and stories of them.; [pers.] I wrote poetry for personal satisfaction. The histories are to tell

grandchildren of the rigors, fun, sorrow and everyday life in a large, close knit family of early 1900's; [a.] Buffalo Lake, MN

SCHUYLER, JENNY L.
[b.] February 10, 1981, Clinton, MD; [p.] Randall and Laverne Schuyler; [ed.] Attending 8th grade at Piccowaxen Middle School; [memb.] Odyssey of the Mind 5 years, youth group and choir with Good Samaritan Church; [hon.] Marine Corps League award, gifted and talented program , Presidential Academic Fitness Award, 3rd place, Babysitter's Club writing contest through Prodigy Services Company; [pers.] In everything you do, put God first, and he will direct you and crown your efforts with success. Proverbs 3:6; [a.] La Plata, MD

SCHWERIN, DEBRA
[Pen.] Debra Cole, Debra Charles; [b.] Pittsburgh, PA; [p.] Charles and Betty Schwerin; [m.] Single mother of two teens; [ch.] Jami 17 (girl), David 14; [ed.] Burlingame High, Santa Rosa Junior College; [occ.] Entrepreneur/Owner of home based business; custom painted used to antique furniture, accessories and decorator mirrors.; [oth. writ.] Presenting first poetry book for publication fall 1994, "Beyond A Thought And A Tear"; Local Newspapers. Working on first romance novel, several other poetry books in the making.; [pers.] My writing reflects the realities and experiences and feelings of many peoples lives as well as the multi-dimensional position I maintain in my own life, and an abstruct knowing the spans all.; [a.] CA

SCOTT, WALTER E.
[Pen.] Walter Edgar Scott; [b.] February 6, 1939, Mpls, MN; [p.] Walter and Goldie; [m.] Sandra (Reinking) Scott, October 25, 1980; [ch.] One daughter, Deanna Scott; [ed.] High school, North High School Mpls. 1957; [occ.] Factory Worker Honeywell Corp.; [memb.] Disabled Vets st. Johns Lutehran Church; [hon.] Won a couple local poem contests.; [oth. writ.] A few poems published in local newspapers, many unpublished songs.; [pers.] I like to keep my style simple and traditional. Making my poems more understandable to more people.; [a.] Albertville, MN

SCROGGIN, (JR.), COLBY
[b.] January 4, 1955, Lynwood, CA; [p.] Colby Scroggins, Sr., Iris Bird; [m.] Lori Sue, April 5, 1980; [ch.] Melissa Sue Scroggin (12 yrs old - born 10/27/81); [ed.] Lowell High School, graduated 1973; [occ.] Chef - Charter Sport Fishing Yacht "Apollo"; [memb.] International Game Fishing Association; [oth. writ.] Other poetry, cooking recipe contest; [pers.] I write poetry to try to get attention from my best friend, Lori S. Thank you, Lori! You will always be...my inspiration. And I'll always be your friend; [a.] San Diego, Point Loma, CA

SEABREEZE, LUCY J.
[b.] December 16, 1964, Marianna, FL; [p.] Walter Clover, Nellie Bryant; [m.] William T. Seabreeze, Octover 3, 1984; [ch.] William Torrance seabreeze; [ed.] A.C. Mosley High School, Gulf Coast Community College; [occ.] Mother; [hon.] Who's Who in Music 1983; [pers.] I try to expess the feelings and thoughts, that we all go through at some point in our lives. In my poetry the main influence is life experiences.; [a.] Valdosta, CA

SEARS, CENESIA VERNELL
[Pen.] Staa fabi/Sapphire; [b.] April 19, 1977, California; [p.] Gail Sears; [ed.] High School Student pursuing my final year of study.; [occ.] Teachers Assistant; [memb.] Voices of Watts Choir Member.; [hon.] Numerous Speech Awards and Trophies; student Honor Roll for a 3.2 G.P.A.; [oth. writ.] Remain unpublished in a home file.; [pers.] I as an individual try to create my own style of writing. I often write from experience. Basically everything seen on paper comes from what I feel; [a.] Los Angeles, CA

SEGALLA, STACEY L.
[b.] August 25, 1980, Great Barrington, Mass.; [p.] Stephen and Claudia Segalla; [ed.] Salisbury Central School Kindergarten, Third Grade and North Canaan Elementary School Fourth Grade through Eighth Grade.; [occ.] Receiving my education.; [hon.] Young Author 1989-90, D.A.R.E., Essay Winner, Presidential Physical Fitness, Citizenship, Honor Roll 5 times, High Honor Roll, 7 times; 1992 Miss Northeast Hospitatlity; 1991 Miss Southern New England American Pre-Teen Hostess, 1991 Miss American Coed National Pre-Teen Cover Girl; [oth. writ.] 8th grade graduation essay.; [pers.] Don't follow in the footsteps of others, instead make your own path through life.; [a.] Canaan, CT

SEGERSON, LISA M.
[b.] May 20, 1963, Dallas, Texas; [p.] Kenneth and Linda Mooter; [m.] Philip J. Segerson, November 14, 1987; [ch.] Allisen Brooke, Cassie Corinee and Claire Suzette; [ed.] B.S. from North Texas State University 1984; [occ.] Assistant Controller for Electrospace Systems, Inc. (A Chryster Corporation); [a.] Plano, TX

SEIFERT, HEATHER
[b.] December 25, 1970, Evansvill, IN; [p.] Bonnie and Wayne Seifert; [ed.] University of Southern Indiana, B.S. in Business Administration, May 1993; [memb.] North American Assocation of Ventriloguists; [hon.] Scholastic Excellence Award, Honor's List, Student Ambassador Award, Presidential Academic Award, Admitted with Distinction, American Association of University Women Award; [oth. writ.] Short stories, novels, poems, humore, medieval fiction (yet to be published); [pers.] All my writings attempt to evoke some kind of emotion...Whether it be laughter, sadness, joy, anger or pain. If I can accomplish this, then I feel like I have succeeded as a writer.; [a.] Evansville, IN

SELBY, PAULINE
[b.] September 4, 1937, Brooklyn, NY; [p.] Thomas and Sallie Harris; [m.] William H. Selby, July 19, 1958; [ch.] Kristine Selby; [ed.] High School of Industrial Art, hefley and Brown Business School; [occ.] Sr. Asst. to Secretary of the Board, MetLife, New York, NY; [hon.] Certificate of Merit in a National H.S. Art Exhibition for Costume Design; [oth. writ.] A series of specially designed and personalized greeting cards of original art and poetry.; [pers.] I believe that love and compassion towards mankind is the key to a rewarding life.; [a.] Brooklyn, NY

SELF, WILLIE CAROLYN
[Pen.] Pee Wee; [b.] March 17, 1934, Houston, AL; [p.] Late Yancy and Loutitia Self; [m.] D; [ch.] one;

[ed.] 12th; [occ.] D.R.R.A.; [memb.] Nat. Lib. of Congress; [hon.] Few, my greatest is to still have the belief, love and respect of my son Garrett; [oth. writ.] Many; [pers.] When the going gets rough the tough gets verbal, ok as long as the verbs and adj. are truthful.

SEPULVEDA, CHARLES ROBERT
[b.] December 30, 1969; [p.] V. Monastorio; [oth. writ.] Many unpublished, unfinished hidden works of art? maybe, but probably not.; [pers.] If I had no scraps to eat, I'd feast upon you disbelieve, If I had nothing to show with a smile, I'd close the door.; [a.] Houston, TX

SEQOUIA, REBECCA
[Pen.] Becky; [b.] April 25, 1943, TX; [ch.] Five wonderful children; [cd.] Registered Nurse; [occ.] Executive Director Home Health and Hospice; [oth. writ.] Over 200 poems; [pers.] Never having an interest in writing or even reading poetry, during the last six months. I have received these messages almost in audible form and compelled to write them and share them.; [a.] San Benito, TX

SEXTON, TIM
[b.] March 17, 1948, Hutchinson, KS; [p.] Jim and Coleen; [ed.] Northern Arizona Univers. Arizona State Univ.; [occ.] Quality Control Inspector, Highway, D.O.T.; [memb.] Smithsonian, Donor, National Institute for Certification in Engineering Technologies, Senior Engineering Technician; [oth. writ.] Archaeological articles in U.S. Forest Journal.; [pers.] Tao-Balance. Nothing impossible till proven otherwise. Consideration of others. Everything is conscience. Laugh a lot.; [a.] Phoenix, AZ

SEYMOUR, CHALLIS
[Pen.] Challis; [b.] July 27, 1962, Leavenworth, KS; [p.] Paulene and dan; [m.] Single; [oth. writ.] Pending publication; [pers.] Inspired by Roxana; a woman of timeless beauty and my life's confidant. Always remember to open the windows of your mind.; [a.] LaCrosse, KS

SHAFFER, SUSAN NORA
[b.] December 13, 1964, Wenatche; [p.] Lewis and Dee Shaffer; [m.] Unmarried; [occ.] Working on getting book published; [oth. writ.] A-Cat-O-Nine-Tails, currently working on manuscript and will be sending it off in the fall.; [pers.] When I wrote drive the dagger deeper I thought I did my best work when I felt bad. Now I know my mood reflect's my work. I have been disabled since age 20, due to diabetic complications I have very bad eye sight.; [a.] Tumwater, WA

SHAKESPEARE, TRACY J.
[b.] June 8, 1963, Denver, CO; [p.] William Noah and Dorothy May Shakespeare; [m.] Never been married; [ed.] Littleton Sr. High School, University of Madrid, Spain Real Estate License; [occ.] Film and Television Actress; [memb.] Screen Actors Guild, American Federation of Television and Radio Artist, A Way of Live; [hon.] Having my 1st poem published; Began Learning How to Ride a Horse 4 years ago and have been competing in rodeos this past year in team roping and penning and just won my 1st buckle in Houston at the Ben Johnson Pro-Celebrity Rodeo, "Cowboys for Kids" Charity event for Cystic Fibrosis, Doing charity work for children being a

good person.; [oth. writ.] Songs and poems, stories, screenplays.; [pers.] "I get lotsa teasin for being a poet" my nickname the cowboys gave me for my last name, and having fun with my creativity that continues to let me grow, learn, and express.; [a.] Acton, GA

SHAMBAUGH, JUNIA
[b.] November 4, 1905, York, PA; [p.] Marvin J. & Elizabeth A. Burgner Shambaugh; [ed.] Penn State University, Special Student; [occ.] Retired; [memb.] Genealogical and Historical Societies; [oth. writ.] As U.S. Government writer/editor wrote and edited reports, articles, etc. in name of U.S. Commissioner of Narcotics. Several unpublished genealogical and historical articles.; [a.] Silver Spring, MD

SHANK, AMY RENEE
[b.] September 16, 1978; [p.] William and Linda Shank; [ed.] South Hagerstown High School; [memb.] French Club, Prom Committee, and yearbook staff; [oth. writ.] Unpublished in home library.; [pers.] Life is full of many struggles, struggles that you and I won't ever understand, yet I believe tht if we hold strength in our hearts and emotions in our mind that at sometime, someday our struggles will be over once and for all.; [a.] Hagerstown, MD

SHANNON, GIGI
[b.] December 2, 1974, Madison, WV; [p.] Eloise & Paul Shannon; [ed.] Gilbert High, Southern West Virginia Community College; [occ.] Produce Clerk and carryout at Foodland, Inc., Gilbert, WV; [hon.] Dean's List at Southern WV Community College; [pers.] I enjoy pouring my mind, heart, and soul into everything I write. Learn from yesterday. Live for today, and work towards tomorrow.; [a.] Wharncliffe, WV

SHAPIRO, ALLEN R.
[b.] September 19, 1951, Queens, NY; [p.] Malcolm and Elizabeth Shapiro; [m.] Lynette J. Shapiro, September 17, 1988; [ch.] Thomas, Roy, Kevin, Robert and Cecelia; [ed.] Newton High School - 1969; [occ.] United Parcel Service driver; [memb.] Poetry Connection, Mastic, NY, Mastic Park Civic Assoc, Mastic, NY, Local 804 Transfers Union; [oth. writ.] Simeon's Eyes, Samantha's Poem, Charlene and Her Soldier in Blue, Poem for the Mastics, Brother Can You Spare a Dime; [pers.] I'm a blue collar working man, actually a brown collar as I drive for U.P.S. I try to write for the working people. The middle class of whom I am a member; [a.] Mastic, NY

SHAPIRO, JESSICA
[b.] June 30, 1979, New York City; [p.] Angela and Jerome Shapiro; [occ.] Student at Dwight Englewood High School, Englewood, NJ Class of 1997; [hon.] Elisabeth Marrow Academic Award, Frances Leggett Scholarship Hutchins award for excellence in writing.; [oth. writ.] Celebrity interviews published in Soap Opera Update.; [a.] Englewood, NJ

SHARP, DONNA MARIE
[b.] September 16, 1966, Brooklyn, NY; [p.] John R. and Roberta Kelly; [m.] Phillip R. Sharp, September 27, 1986; [ed.] Oakcrest High, Atlantic County Vocational School; [occ.] Finance Manager, Thermo Guard Inc., Hammonton, NJ; [pers.] Writing allows me the opportunity to walk in someone else's shoes, if only for a moment. I enjoy writing about sensitive issues, reality, things people often tend to forget about.; [a.] Blue Anchor, NJ

SHATOUHY, DAWN L.
[Pen.] "Hug Monster"; [b.] April 15, 1971, Pennsylvania; [p.] Joseph and Melody Shatouhy; [occ.] Secretary; [memb.] None Poeticly; [pers.] I see my poetry as an escape hatch to the soul. The trick is, to obtain the key.

SHAUGHNESSY, KATHLEEN ANN
[b.] June 20, 1967, Hempstead, NY; [p.] rita and Vincent Shaughnessy; [ed.] H. Frank Carey High School, Adelphi University, Molloy College; [occ.] Program Manager/Counselor for Mentally Ill, South Shore Associaiton for Independent Living, Lynbrook, NY; [memb.] March of Dimes, Tri Delta Sorority, National Alliance for the Mentall Ill, Adoption Crossroads Council for Equal Rights in Adoption; [hon.] Literary Award, High School, NY Regents Scholarship, Adelphi Trustee Scholarship, Community Service Award, March of Dimes, Who's Who Among American High School Students (1985); [oth. writ.] Several poems and short stories published in local papers, college and high school literary magazines.; [pers.] Accept others for who they are; do not try to change them, condemn them or put people down. We all have our faults and strengths that make each of us unique human beings.; [a.] Point Lookout, NY

SHAVER, SUTER MILDRED
[b.] October 11, 1922, Lansing, MI; [p.] Mary and John Shaver; [ed.] Mt. St. Joseph, OH, University of Detroit, Miami U., Oxford, OH; [occ.] Retired Volunteer Ministry; [hon.] A 3rd prize winner in "Dance on the Horizon" poetry contest, sponsored by National Library of Poetry; [pers.] My long time ministry in education and hospital nursing home chaplaincy has kept me aware of the pain and joy of living. To creatively express this in poetry is a goal for my retirement years.; [a.] Clinton Township, MI

SHELTON, APRIL LEIGH
[b.] April 9, 1979, Greer, SC; [p.] William E. and Beverly K. Shelton; [ed.] 10th grade sophomore Byrnes High School, Duncan. S.C.; [memb.] Beta Club; [hon.] Rotary International Scholastic Achievement Award, top 10 of 93-94 class freshman, U.S. Achievement Academy 1993, Typing Award 92-93 D.R. Hill Middle School; [oth. writ.] My Broken Heart, Windchimes, A Mother's Rose, and a Father is...; [pers.] I try to live a Christian life and walk close with God. It's God that I give the credit to, for my talent; [a.] Lyman, SC

SHENDER, MICHELLE
[b.] November 15, 1980, Bronx, NY; [p.] George and Marie Shender; [ed.] I am in the 10th grade in the Bronx High School of Science; [occ.] I am a student in High school; [hon.] In 1991, I received an award for Creative Writing, for my elementary school graduation. In 1993, I was awarded the "New York State Senate Outstanding Achievement Awrd."; [pers.] We all have love in our hearts despite racism and crime. Love is what should turn the pages of time!; [a.] Bronx, NY

SHEPHERD, DANA M.
[b.] December 5, 1981, St. Maries, ID; [p.] James E. and Dianne M. Shepherd; [ed.] 7th grade student at Lakeside Elementary; [occ.] Student; [memb.] Track, Cheerleading, 4-H; [hon.] Coaches Award in Track; [a.] Plummer, ID

SHEREN, CAROL A.
[b.] March 22, 1959, Vincennes, IN; [p.] William P. and Rosemary Evans; [m.] Robert D. Sheren Jr., November 12, 1982; [ch.] Robert Lee and Stephanie Lynn; [ed.] South Knox High School; [occ.] Residential Supervisor; [hon.] Editor's Award Certificates for 2 poems published, The Lottery and Honey; [oth. writ.] My Special Angel, published in Treasured Poems of America, by Sparrowgrass Poetry Forum, Inc., Honey, published in Whispers In The Wind, by The National Library of Poetry, The Lottery, published in Dance on the Horizon, by National Library of Poetry.; [pers.] My writings reflect on my own personal experiences.; [a.] Ponder, TX

SHERRILL, ANGELA ROBIN
[b.] April 18, 1978, Fontana, CA; [p.] Paul and Robin Sherrill; [ed.] Junior at Rancho Cucamonga High School in Rancho Cucamonga, CA; [hon.] Several awards through the English Department for creative writing.; [pers.] I write from my own experiences and my continual guidance comes from my Lord and Savior, Jesus Christ.; [a.] Rancho Cucamonga, CA

SHIELDS, JAMES EARL
[b.] September 22, 1979, Beeville, TX; [p.] Leroy Shields, Beverly Garrett; [ed.] Stewart's Creek Elementary, Lakeview Middle School; [hon.] National Junior Honor Society; [pers.] I would like to thank God, all my realitives, Alicia Ennis (the most), Eric Zeller, Brad Ricker, and All my other friends that I haven't mentioned.; [a.] The Colony, TX

SHIFERAW, MIRIAM
[b.] June 11, 1980, Washington, D.C.; [p.] Knojit Shiferaw; [m.] Meron Shiferow; [ed.] I attend Sandy Spring Friends School; [occ.] Student; [hon.] Honor Roll in the Whole 7th grade; [oth. writ.] Love writing short stories, and mysteries as well; [pers.] I believe that there is no such thing as perfect writing. Everyone's writing is perfect as long as it comes from their hearts. I've been greatly influenced by Maya Angelou, and hope to follow in her footsteps, I hope to become a poet. I live with my single mom who struggles real hard to give me a good life, and who is doing a fantastic job.; [a.] Washington, D.C.

SHIMOURA, JENNIFER
[b.] July 2, 1962, Highland Park, Michigan; [p.] Carl and MaDonna Bidinger; [ed.] High school, some college; [occ.] William Beaumont Hospital Reference Laboratory; [a.] Hazel Park, MI

SHIPLEY, HOPE
[b.] September 10, 1978, Monroe, LA; [p.] Frank and Darline Shipley; [ed.] Junior in Covington High School; [a.] Bush, LA

SHIPLEY JR., JOHN
[b.] May 4, 1976, Vineland, NJ; [p.] Mary and John Shipley Sr.; [ed.] Gloucester County Christian School; [occ.] Student; [hon.] High School Valedictorian; [oth. writ.] Poems and stories, none of which have been published before.; [pers.] I try to express my feelings about God and my relationship with Him in my writings. I have been mostly inspired by Edgar Allen Poe, modern day music lyricists and have been encouraged by my high school English teacher, Mrs.

Cook.; [a.] Glassboro, NJ

SHORT, KATHLEEN M.
[Pen.] Kasage; [p.] Margaret Mary and Benjamin Chapinski; [pers.] Do everything with love.; [a.] Fairfax, CA

SHREVE, GEORGE MAXWELL
[b.] June 6, 1961, Carlisle, PA; [p.] Arthur & Lois Shreve; [m.] L. Fay Shreve, March 31, 1990; [ed.] High School Grad, Carlisle High School, Carlisle, PA "1979"; [occ.] K-Mart Employee, Carlisle, PA; [oth. writ.] Like no other lover. Have They Gone Away to Hide. In Little Ones. Kiss After Kiss, etc; [pers.] Only began writing when in 1981 I sat down to write a letter of appreciation to Barry Manilow. Only then did I discover writing poems. In that attempt of writing a letter to "Manilow" things began to ryhme and I found myself writing for the next 8 and 1/2 hours 22 pages of little things that started me writing poems. In the next 6 and 1/2 years, I would go on to complete more than 2,700 poems before laying down my pen; [a.] Carlisle, PA

SHUR, VALLESHIA MARIA
[b.] February 20, 1961, Kansas City, MO; [p.] Geraldine Anderson; [m.] Danny Earl Shurn, september 26, 1992; [ch.] Rochelle Elaine Dye Age 13, Robert and Ro Shawn Dye Ages 12, Genene McCall and Marla Hunter; [ed.] J.C. Harmon High School and one year college at Donnelly Juinior College in Kansas City, KS; [occ.] writer and Songwriter, self owned.; [hon.] This is my first ever entering a contest. I have an Army Achievement Award from United States Army.; [oth. writ.] I am a writer, ever since I started wriitng. but I did not set my mind to write until January 5, 1994. I have written about 20 poems or songs. I strive to write a song or poem everyday starting June 20, 1994.; [pers.] I am greatly impressed with the writings of Shakespeare and Kenny Edmonds (Babyface). I write to express how I feel about certain situations. I pray that people would understand my writings and help the children.; [a.] Kansas City, KS

SIDDLE, SCOTT PAUL
[b.] November 23, 1965, Montebello, CA; [p.] George and Jean Siddle, Jr.; [m.] Deanne Diane Siddler, March 13, 1988; [ch.] Steven 12, Amber 10, Tricia 9, and K.C. Lynn 3; [ed.] Graduate 1983 Yucaipa High School, Yucaipa, CA; Predominant Studies, Creative Writing; [occ.] Forklift Opertor, Home Lunber Co., Inc.; [memb.] Colton First Baptist Church, Colton, CA, Men of Prary Study Group, Promise Keepers of America, C.F.B. Worship Team; [hon.] Being a Child of God; [oth. writ.] Numerous unpublished poems and lyrics for songs.; [pers.] I have learned that no matter what you do in life if you put God first, he will show you the way. He is my inspiration.; [a.] Colton, CA

SIDES, STEPHANIE BENNETT
[b.] September 5, 1973, Houston, TX; [p.] John T. Bennett and Cindy LeNorman; [m.] Brian Sides, July 10, 1993; [ed.] Texas School of Business, Paralegal; [pers.] My family has been the greatest inspiration in the world for me.; [a.] Alameda, CA

SIGFRIT, HELGA
[Pen.] Helga Sigfrit-Cirillo; [b.] June 7, 1950, Trier-Germany; [p.] Bernhard and thekla Schuler; [m.]

Tony Cirillo, September 3, 1994; ·[ch.] Richrd, Michaela; [ed.] B.A. Business Administration; [occ.] Office Assistant; [memb.] International Pen Friends; [pers.] Poetry is not only something to read and write, but it's also a way to live. With special thanks to Tony Cirillo and Glen Moorehouse for believing in me and their encouragement.; [a.] Charlotte, NC

SIINO, DAVID
[b.] July 4, 1975, Valley Stream, NY; [p.] Salvatore and Dolores Siino; [ed.] Valley Stream North High School, Hofstra University; [occ.] Teachers Assistant in Hofstra University Chemistry Dept., Landscaper; [hon.] Nat'l Honor Society Member, Winner of One Act Play Contest (author) senior year.; [oth. writ.] Poetry for school yearbook, fiction for H.S. literary journal and newspaper, one act play for high school; [pers.] One's acceptance of oneself and one's place in the world is the greates thing a person can achieve.; [a.] Malverne, NY

SILVERBERG, AMY
[Pen.] Coneheads; [b.] November 16, 1982, Los Angeles, CA; [ed.] Completed sixth grade at A.J. Heschel Day School; [occ.] Student at A.J. Heschel Day School; [memb.] U.S.Y., Heschel Student Council; [hon.] Gifted Childrens Program at U.C.I., Achievement Award for participating in all school events.; [oth. writ.] Scottie's Bluff, Muir Woods, and From Dusk to Dawn.; [pers.] Have confidence in your beliefs, because life is to short to debate.; [a.] Tarzana, CA

SIMPSON, DAWN
[b.] February 8, 1980, Phoeniz, AZ; [p.] Joni-Dawn and Van Simpson; [ed.] Royal Palm Jr. High, Sunny Slope High School (currently a freshman); [occ.] Thrift World; [memb.] Royal Palm Baptist Church and Metro Praise Chapel. Music Theater Group and Band; [hon.] 3rd in school poetry contest and held 1st place in reading competition, kindergarden thru 3rd grade; [oth. writ.] Various unpublished poems and half finished book.; [pers.] Love, treasures, happiness, and almost anything can be found in God and antique shops.; [a.] Phoenix, AZ

SINCLAIR, PAMELA LYNN
[b.] July 7, 1978, Dover, NJ; [p.] Allan B. and Shizu Sinclair; [ed.] Mt. Olive Township's Schools; [occ.] Student at Mt. Olive High school; [oth. writ.] "My Love," "Memories," "With All My Heart," "Best Friends," "End In a Tear," "Feelings for You," plus "Tears Can't Explain and Tell me Why" and many more poems.; [pers.] I thank my parents, family and friends for always being there. Thanx, Missy G., Megan m, and Renee P, I love you guys. Michael Joseph I love you always and forever.; [a.] Flanders, NJ

SINGH, STEVE RAMESHWAR
[b.] November 30, 1964, Guyana; [p.] Lawrence and Susilla Singh; [ed.] Bishops High School, Jersey City State College (BSc); St. Peter's College (MBA); [occ.] Budget Manager, Jersey City Medical Center; [memb.] HFMA; [hon.] National's Dean's List, Dean's List; [oth. writ.] Poems published in "Anthology of American Collegiate Poets."; [pers.] My writings are an attempt to express my thoughts, feelings and hopes that I cannot express in any other way.; [a.] Jersey City, NJ

SKILES, KRISTIN AMBER
[b.] January 4, 1972, Beaumont, TX; [p.] Ted and Pat Skiles; [m.] Unmarried; [ed.] Central High, attended Lamar College; [occ.] Jason's Deli, Line Worker; [oth. writ.] Just a large notebook of unpublished poems.; [pers.] While writing, I am usually influenced by the darker sides of life and people, yet I also try to give a bright or hopeful side to each poem as well.; [a.] Beaumont, TX

SKILLMAN, FRANKLIN J.
[b.] November 3, 1933, Brooklyn, NY; [p.] William E. Skillman II and Dorothy Skillman; [m.] Arlene R. Skillman, January 10, 1994; [ed.] Hofstra University, B.A.; Virginia Commonwealth University, M.S.; [occ.] Retired Educator and Medical Record Technician. Currently a poet, writer, singer.; [memb.] Mother Seton Guild, Presbyterian Church, AARP; [hon.] The National Library of Poetry Editor's Choice Award: 1990 for "Morning Music" published in the National Library of Poetry: 1993. Golden Poet Award: 1992. Award of Merit Certificate for "Morning Music," Fourth Place Winner, 1992., Phi, Alpha Theta for Historical Scholarship; [oth. writ.] Poem published in "Out of The Blue Review." Two poems and a prayer published in "The Thomasville-Times Enterprise."; [pers.] "I build most of my poetry around Scripture verses, and have been greatly influenced by the Romantic Poets."; [a.] Pensacola, FL

SKYLER, RICHARD L.
[b.] August 11, 1967, Boonton Twp., NJ; [p.] Rick and Linda Skyler; [ed.] Kinnelor High School; [occ.] Tree Climber/Forman Hurtt Bros. Tree Service; [memb.] Paintball Group Captain (United Survival Organization); [oth. writ.] Published in (In A Different Light) National Library of Poetry. Over 200 other poems not published.; [pers.] I dedicate this poem to Chantal Chalupt. You have been a great inspiration to me. You are one of the sweetest, kindest women I've ever known. I love you always.; [a.] Kinnelor, NJ

SLEDGE, THURMAN
[b.] February 24, 1951, Tuscumbia, AL; [p.] Julian and Rder Sledge; [m.] Divorced; [ed.] B.A. Economics, University of Texas at Arlington, 1978; [occ.] Senior Programmer Analyst; [oth. writ.] Short story "Vignette" published in 1975.; [pers.] I have far less faith in humanity than I did twenty years ago, but more need of them.; [a.] Plainsboro, NJ

SMITH, AVIS M.
[b.] December 4, 1908, CA; [p.] Kearney and Lelace Robinson; [m.] W. H. Smith, June 12, 1929; [ch.] Lelace Gregory, Iva Carlson, Ellen Roberts; [ed.] H.S. Some College; [occ.] Retired; [memb.] Charter Member Siskiyou, Artist's Assoc., Methodist Church, Boise; [hon.] Several Blue Ribbons and Specials in Shows; [oth. writ.] Published "Poems of Life and Love"; [pers.] I want to convey my love of life thru my poetry.

SMITH, BARBARA
[Pen.] "Bambi" nickname; [b.] April 28, 1957, Putumn, CO; [p.] William and Nayden Setliff; [m.] Richard H. Smith, October 15, 1977; [ed.] Milton High School 1975; [occ.] Economical Engineer (Housewife); [memb.] I attend several different churches: Gospel Light House, Milton, WV; Shulamite, Pentecostal, Milton WV; Pentecostal

Church of God, Hurricane, WV; [oth. writ.] How many souls have you let down today? "Church Paper." I'm still looking Daddy, The Hurricane Breeze; [pers.] Life is found mirrored in poetry. Sometimes I put part of me in each one I write.; [a.] Milton, WV

SMITH, DEANNE
[b.] November 26, 1965, Whittier, CA; [p.] Larry and Marcia Deets; [m.] Tedd Smith, October 8, 1988; [ch.] James and Cameron; [ed.] Aviation High, Heights Western; [occ.] Domestic Goddess, Lead Singer; [memb.] Cub Scouts, Parent-Teacher Assoc., Candlelighters, Street Legal.; [hon.] I have the honor of having my husband and kids with me. Our younger son was diagnosed with Leukemia, but he is doing well. This is the only award or honor that means anything at all to me.; [oth. writ.] I wrote the made scientists wife (analogue widow) for access; news stories for 'scouter;' poem for anthology 'poetry' an american heritage and write lyrics for rock band Street Legal; [pers.] I'm here to be true to myself: no one guarantees tomorrow, so take all you can from today. There is much to learn from the darkside, but it cannot be a life entire, so get up and dance.; [a.] San Bernardino, CA

SMITH, DEBBIE TUCKER
[b.] November 6, 1957, Lawrence, MA; [p.] Kendall and Theresa Turner; [m.] Donald R. Smith, September 26, 1993; [ed.] Tompkinsville High School, Monroe County Vocational Center, KY; [occ.] Assistant Bookkeeper, City of Perry, GA; [hon.] Certificate of Merit, RR Donnelley & Sons; Certificate of Recognition, Modern Woodmen of America; [pers.] This poem is dedicated with love to all mothers of children who served in Desert Storm and Vietnam, but most especially dedicated to my mother, Theresa Turner who I love very much.; [a.] Perry, GA

SMITH, JAMES K.
[Pen.] James T. Tyrone; [b.] June 12, 1958, N.Y., NY; [p.] James and Clara Smith; [ed.] Solebury Prep School, Nasson College; [occ.] Computer Graphics Director, Color Group Inc., Hawthorne, NY; [memb.] Speak Out America; [oth. writ.] Many other poems written between 1972 and the present, none of which I've presented for publication.; [pers.] The human condition is the most important aspect of life and I sue this as a basis for all my work. A great deal has come from personal experiences.; [a.] Hawthorne, NY

SMITH, JEAN-PAUL
[b.] February 15, 1979, Washington, D.C.; [p.] Maureen & Conway Smith; [ch.] Youngest of Five Children, 2 sisters and 2 brothers; [ed.] Colton High school; [occ.] Student, Sophomore in High School; [pers.] This poem was written on a scratch of paper and was destined for the trash can when retrieved by his mother and older sister.; [a.] Colton, CA

SMITH, JUNE
[Pen.] June Lyons Smith; [b.] June 2, 1923, Pikeville, KY; [p.] Milton and Belle Lyons; [m.] Edward Smith, September 12, 1945; [ch.] Zenyth Belle, Lue Ellen, Eddie Milton; [ed.] John Creek High 3 yrs., and last year at Johannesburg, MI; [occ.] Homemaker, Retired, Cook from School in Sterling, MI; [memb.] V.F.W., A.A.R.P., Homeowners Origination, Independent Baptist Church, National Committee Org.; [hon.] Cub Scouts Den Mother Award; [oth. writ.]

Several poems published in Pikeville, KY, newspaper and a biography of my self which I would like to get published, I think it would help young people.; [pers.] If you know where or how I can get my book published please contact me or would like more poems or short stories.; [a.] Johannesburg, MI

SMITH, LILA
[b.] June 12, 1956, Indiana; [p.] Mr. and Mrs. Gerald Golliker; [m.] Gary E. Smith, June 1990; [ch.] Frederick L. Dill, Kathleen J. Dill, Stepdaughter: Leann Smith; [ed.] 1974 High School Grduate; [occ.] Work in Body Shop Family Owned; [memb.] American Chronic Pain Association.; [hon.] For honors I have my honors of my family. My children who are always there and to my husband who also indures.; [pers.] I write poetry, it helps mè to write how I feel. I have suffered with chronic pain for over 10 years. I wish to help organize all chronic pain suffers, that endure daily pain.

SMITH, SEAN O.
[b.] January 3, 1982, Phila. PA; [p.] Donna Smith; [ed.] Our Mother of Sorrows Elementary School; [occ.] Student, age 12; [memb.] Mothers of Sorrows Altar Boys; [oth. writ.] Several poems not published; [pers.] I enjoy writing poems on my spare time. It to me show other people my inner feelings of the beauty of poetry.; [a.] Philadelphia, PA

SMITH, SHARON M.
[b.] August 12, 1976, Gasden, AL; [p.] Kathy Smith; [ed.] Potomac Senior High School; [occ.] Student; [memb.] FBLA; [hon.] I was in the East Coast Pageant for Washington, D.c.; [oth. writ.] I've written several poems and one play.; [pers.] I enjoy writing poems to expess my feelings. Sometimes I tend to act out my poems. The reason that I do this is because it puts more feeling into the poem.; [a.] Triangle, VA

SMITH, WILLIAM E.
[Pen.] Willie, Smitty; [b.] December 12, 1952, Calvert County, MD; [p.] Allen and Eva Smith; [m.] Gladys Smith, December 24, 1971; [ch.] Dion William; [ed.] Calvert Senior High, External Studies, Moody Bible Inst.; [occ.] Dry Cleaner, United States Naval Academy, Annapolis, MD; [memb.] Asst. Pastor, Ordained Elder, Kings Apostle Holiness Church, Annapolis, MD; Assist. Financial Secretary of the National Youth Conference K.A.H.C.; Member of The Holiness Ministers Alliance, Inc. and Adjoining States; [hon.] Performance Award, U.S.N.A. Certificate of Appreciation, U.S.N.A. Perfect Attendance Award State of MD, Faithful and Consecrated Service Award K.A.H.C Certificate Moody Bible Institute, Ordained Deacon Credential, Ordained Minister License, Elders Credential; [oth. writ.] Song lyrics, music, copyrighted Library of Congress, Poems and Poetry copyrighted, Library of Congress, Washington, D.C.; [pers.] The interest I have in poetry helps me to bring out feelings of love, peace, and happiness, that is inside. I thank God for inspiring words that he has planted in my being. That we can relate to.; [a.] Annapolis, MD

SMITH-LEBARON, JENNIFER
[b.] August 4, 1969, Sacramento, CA; [p.] Adam Smith, June 11, 1988; [ch.] Samantha Lynn; [occ.] Traffic Manager; [pers.] Nothing is impossible, if only we believe.; [a.] Carson City, NV

SNIDER, M. LAURETTE
[b.] May 6, 1935, NYC; [p.] Joseph and Lumina Berard Alix; [m.] Richard H. Snider, June 20, 1954; [ch.] 3 boys, 1 Girl; [ed.] H.S. and Miui College Courses, Emergency Med Tech, CPR Instructor (All in NYS), Vol. Firefighter; [occ.] Retired Volunteer; [memb.] American Heart Assoc., Medway, Grapeville, Vol. Fire Co., Coxsackie Rescue Sq., Greene Co., Vol. Firemans Lady Aus., Greene co., Vol. Firemans Assoc., PTO, All in NY State; [hon.] Several for EMS volunteer work and community work.; [oth. writ.] Poem during HS in Knickerbocker News.; [a.] Riviera, TX

SNOOKS, DIANE
[Pen.] Punkie; [b.] June 16, 1966, Fullerton, CA; [p.] Anthony and Christeen Cataltino; [m.] Dale Snooks, October 1, 1988; [ch.] Casey Lauren Snooks; [ed.] Buena Park High School; [occ.] Housewife/Mother; [memb.] Car Show enthusiast; [pers.] When my daughter was born she gave me a whole new outlook on life. My parents have also. My husband and my daughter are my inspiration.; [a.] Orange, CA

SONDRUP, COREY
[b.] December 14, 1968, Denver Colorado; [p.] Joseph Sondrup and Judy Hart; [m.] Amy Sondrup, December 21, 1992; [ed.] Davis High School, Kaysville, Utah, B.S. Biology, Utah State University, B.S. Human Biology, Texas Chiro. College; [occ.] Chiropractic Student, Texas Chiropractic College; [memb.] Sigma Chi Fraternity; Student Texas Chiropractic Assoc.; Student American Chiropractic Assoc.; [hon.] Golden Key National Honor Society, Phi Sigma Pi National Honor Fraternity, National Honor Society of Secondary Schools, Dean's List Utah State, Dean's List Texas Chiropractic College; [oth. writ.] All others currently unpublished.; [pers.] Never underestimate yourself.; [a.] Kingwood, TX

SORANTINO, DIANE GANNON
[Pen.] Bubbette (Sometimes); [b.] November 16, 1961, Salem, NJ; [p.] Harry and Evelyn Gannon Sr., Anthony Sorantino, Jr., January 22, 1993 (2nd marriage); [ch.] Allen David March Jr. (12), Alex Dane March (9); [ed.] Pennsville High School, 1 semester of college; [occ.] Free lance writing and a "mommy."; [oth. writ.] Two poems published in local newspaper "Todays Sunbeam." 1993 won 1st prize, Most Humorous; 1994 won 1st prize, Most Serious. Upcoming book to be released: "Live and Learn and Pass It On, Vol. II By H. Jackson Brown Jr." this book will contain four of my quotes.; [pers.] I write only because I enjoy it. I have a deep appreciation for life. I am greatly influenced by every day experiences. The only time I will use my pen name "Bubbette" is when I'm publishing a poem to my husband in our local newspaper. I try to find the good in people rather than look for bad. My children and husband come first. I would not trade my life for the world. Family is most important. If you do not have that, you don't have anything.; [a.] Pennsville, NJ

SORRELS, SARA
[b.] February 20, California; [p.] Ben and Jean Sorrels; [ed.] Entering 8th grade 94-95 school year at Hinkson Memorial Christian School, Moscow, Russia; [occ.] Missionary Kid (MK); [memb.] Central Baptist Church, Crossville, TN; [pers.] Although I was born in California, I have lived most of my lfie in

Nairobi, Kenya, East Africa; and presently reside in Moscow, Russia; [a.] Austin, TX

SPAEDT, ALEXIA
[b.] May 25, 1976, Greeley; [p.] George and Sharleen Spaedt; [ed.] Highland High School, currently enrolled in Aims Community College; [occ.] Student; [oth. writ.] Several poems published in local newspapers.; [pers.] I feel that writing is the ultimate expression of all emotions. I feel that I am very lucky to be able to express what many people surpress.; [a.] Pierce, CO

SPALL, SAMY
[Pen.] Samy; [b.] June 1, 1957, B.C. Canada; [p.] Doris and Bob Spall; [m.] Robert "Chuck" Spall; [m.] February 13, 1971; [ed.] Kelowna Senior Secondary College of Marin; [occ.] Unemployed while I attend to invaled husband; [memb.] The Lords Church, Novato, CA; [oth. writ.] "Lies, Lies, Damned Lies!" 94'; [pers.] All that stuff about being born again is true. That I find a constant source of amazement with some shock.; [a.] San Rafael, CA

SPANN, JUDY
[b.] May 31, 1957; [p.] Dorothy Company; [m.] Raymond Spann, June 14, 1975; [ch.] Raemicia, Rick; [ed.] High School 12th; [occ.] Self Employed, Logger with my husband; [oth. writ.] Just other poems.; [a.] Port Leyden, NY

SPARKS, LON D.
[b.] January 20, 1945, Pineville, KY; [p.] Earnest and Helen Sparks; [m.] October 3, 1964 (deceased); [ch.] Leah and Ryan; [ed.] Bachelors in Business Administration 72' (BBA) from the University of Cincinnati; [occ.] Administrative Director of Patient Accounts at Good Samaritan Hospital; [memb.] Trinity Hill United Church of Christ, Healthcare Financial Management Assoc.; [hon.] This is the first poem submitted for publication; [oth. writ.] many other poems/prose (most are personal).; [pers.] I strive to do my very best, and try not to worry about those things that are beyond my control.; [a.] Cincinnati, OH

SPAULDING, CATHERINE
[Pen.] Catherine Love Spaulding; [b.] February 10, 1925, Friendship, IN; [p.] Alva and LaVivian Love; [m.] Frederick P. Spaulding, November 23, 1957; [ch.] Phillip Brok; [ed.] Dyersburg High School, Dyersburg, TN, Attended Union University, Jackson, TN, Belmont College, Nashville, TN; [occ.] Retired; [memb.] The Heritage Foundation, 1994 Republican National Committee; [hon.] National Beta Club Honorary Society, National Republican Senatorial Committee 1994 Order of Merit; [oth. writ.] Several poems based on a variety of subjects such as, to name a few, nature, religion and patriotism.; [pers.] I try to express my feelings about some of life's past experiences, my love of nature, and my deep love for God and country through the avenue of poetry.; [a.] Dallas, TX

SPENCE, CAROLE BENSON
[b.] June 15, 1950, Baltimore, MD; [p.] Dr. and Mrs. John Benson of High Point, NC; [m.] John Doane Spence II, August 7, 1971; [ch.] Jeffrey Michael, Evan Stuart, John Patrick; [ed.] B.A. University of NC, Greensboro; [oth. writ.] Opus Magazine, several poems in The High Point Enterprise.; [a.] Asheville, NC

SPENCER, LILLIE
[b.] May 14, 1944, Savannah, GA; [p.] Mary and Alonzo Cromer; [ch.] Tanya D. Kendrick and Walter G. Kendrick; [ed.] Roosevelt High School, West Palm Beach, FL, Miami Dade Community College, Palm Beach Jr. College; [occ.] Nurse St. Lucie County Seriff Dept.; [pers.] Love to express the struggles of life in my poems and dealing with those struggles.; [a.] Port St. Lucie, FL

SPRY, DINAH
[b.] October 16, 1945, Little Town Oskaloo, Iowa; [p.] Clance and Beulah Rogers; [m.] Larry Spry, November 30, 1985; [ch.] none; [ed.] Nurse's Aide Work, High school, State Aide Work; [occ.] none, except making hand craft items; [memb.] none so far; [hon.] I wan a special award in Special Olympics, a Bronze Medal; [oth. writ.] I have other writings, but haven't had the money to publish them.; [pers.] I would like to be a song writer or a poem writer. To share my love, my feelings; Love for Peope; the Love for Country, Laughter and Tears; God Bless you all that read my poems.; [a.] Carthage, MO

SQUIER, JOHN CHARLES
[Pen.] J.C. Squier; [b.] October 22, 1960, Ransom, KS; [p.] William R. and Veta W. Squier; [ed.] Self, Ransom Public Schools, Fayetteville Technical Institute, Fayetteville, NC; [occ.] Farmer and Rancher; [memb.] Greenpeace; [hon.] I am currently involved in recording poetry for Broadcast on PBS Radio KANZ, Garden City, KS; [oth. writ.] Microcosmic, a self published book of poems (80 pgs.); [pers.] Tai-Chi will get you through times with no money better than money will get you through times with no Tai-Chi; [a.] Brownell, KS

ST. JOHN, JEFFREY G.
[b.] May 23, 1975, Orlando, FL; [p.] Peggy St. John; [ed.] Mann Jr. High, Tampa Bay Tech High School; [occ.] Warehouse worker for the Glass Depot; [pers.] My poems come from a young man that has lived in a single parent home for half his life. The poems come from my feelings about life and my surroundings. In spite of learning disabilites one can achieve what ever wants to achieve. Never Give Up Or Discount Yourself Everyone Can Be Successful. Inspirationally Friends (where my poems come from: Peggy St. John, Ann White, Jane Taylor, S. Sitki, Moe, Lee St. John, Cindy A.; [a.] Seffner, FL

STAFFORD, CAROLYN
[b.] September 30, 1950, Sutton, WVA; [p.] Blanchard Cottrill and Gay L. Dancy; [m.] Clifford J. Stafford, January 1969; [ch.] Carl G. Stafford, Candy Martin, Cindy Allan Cortney Stafford; [ed.] High School GED from Even Start Program Lost Creek, WVA; [occ.] Writer/Poet Short Stories, mother housewife; [hon.] Certificate of Recognition (Harrison County Schools) Certificate of Achievement, 1993 Class Valedictorian, Even Start, Certificate of Appreciation, Volunteer Program, Important Parent Award, Honorary Bachelor of Rhymes degree; [oth. writ.] Several poems/one winning on a local radio contest about love. Short stories written for my children. A book not yet published about my life. I have to write and express myself.; [pers.] Through my writings I hope to awake the world to the pain our children suffer. Their cries must be heard! Also I reflect on the need of love to give and share. All my works are

dedicated to my family; [a.] West Milford, WV

STAFFORD, KEVIN THOMAS
[b.] April 9, 1969, Chicago, IL; [p.] Kevin James Stafford and Susan McCary; [ed.] Lake Gibson Sr. High, Polk Community College; [a.] Lakeland, FL

STALNAKER, MARC E.
[b.] June 25, 1959, Tachikawa, Japan AFB; [p.] George & Simone Stalnaker; [m.] Christine, August 30, 1990; [ch.] Kyle 9 yrs. old, Kelly 7 yrs. old, Rachael 3 yrs. old; [ed.] B.S. Marketing, University of Maryland; [occ.] Commercial Airline Pilot; [memb.] Air Line Pilots Assoc., Deadalions (Fraternal Order of Military Pilots), YMCA basketball coach, Niceville Little League Baseball Coach.; [hon.] Flew F-16's during Persian Gulf War with the 69th Fighter Squadron; Awarded: Three Air Medals, SW Asia Campaign Medal, Kuwaiti Freedom Medal; [oth. writ.] Nothing printed, many heartfelt, personal letters between my wife and I during long periods apart.; [pers.] During the Persian Gulf War I was apart from my wife (who was pregnant) and my other two kids. It was during this separation that I realized how much I valued my family and friends, and how lucky I really am.; [a.] Niceville, FL

STAPLETON, KAREN PATRICIA
[Pen.] KPS; [b.] December 14, 1956, Cincinnati, OH; [p.] Jack and Rita Stapleton; [ed.] Sacred Heart Grade School, Bellevue High School; [occ.] Cashier at K-Mart 3902; [pers.] Through my father's death, I learned to put my grieving into poetry and through my mother's life, I've learned joy.; [a.] Bellevue, KY

STATEN, RACHEL
[b.] December 3, 1975, Palm Beach Gardens, FL; [p.] James and Fern Staten; [ed.] Christian Light Education High School; [occ.] Receptionist, Jupiter Medical Center (Convalescence Pavillion); [a.] Hobe Sound, FL

STEFANESCU, ALINA
[b.] April 13, 1978, Bucharest, Romania; [p.] Drs. Doru and Lydia Stefanescu; [ed.] Holy Spirit Catholic School; Central High School West; [memb.] National Honor Society; Societe Honoraire Francais; Student Cabinet; Leader's Club; [hon.] Drama Award for Best Actress 8th Gr., Leadership Award; [pers.] We are all in search of deliverance and what better deliverance exists than the hidden thoughts that lurk in the human heart?; [a.] Tuscaloosa, AL

STEGGERDA, RICHARD
[b.] January 29, 1947, Denver, CO; [p.] Earl and Dorothy Steggerda; [m.] Margaret, April 11, 1979; [ch.] William, Katharine, Elizabeth, Alicia; [ed.] B.S. Central Michigan University, M.Ed. University of Vermont, M.A. Middleburg College (The Bread Loaf School of Eng.); [occ.] High School English Teacher; [memb.] NEA; [hon.] Alpha Psi Omega, Who's Who Among America's Teacher; [oth. writ.] Circles in The Sky, The Gift (Both prose non-fiction published in local newspaper); [a.] Bristol, VT

STEINKOGLER, EMILY
[b.] May 27, 1921, Isabel, SD; [p.] Adolph and Caroline Stankey; [m.] Theodore Steinkogler, January 31, 1944 (deceased); [ch.] Ted, Joe, Judy Halm, Candi Miller, Barry and Mark (deceased); [ed.] Graduated from High School, Isabel, SD 1940.;

[occ.] Retired; [memb.] American Legion Auxiliary and VFW Auxiliary; [hon.] graduated from High School with honors.; [oth. writ.] Published poet since 1951. Numerous poems published in farm magazines. Won a radio contest, read over the air. Poem "Prairie Spring" published in book "The Coming of Dawn" in 1993.; [a.] Mandan, ND

STEMELSKI, AMY
[b.] August 25, 1976, Camden, NJ; [p.] Thomas and Rose Stemelski; [ed.] Pennsauken High School (attending in fall) Elizabethtown College, PA; [occ.] Student (Elizabethtown College); [memb.] French National Honor Society; [hon.] French National Honor Society, All-South Jersey Chorus (5 yrs), New jersey, All-State Chorus (2 yrs.); [oth. writ.] Several poems published in Pennsauken High School's Creative Writing Anthology 93'. And many poems that have been looked at by friends and fmily. One is used in a friends song as lyrics; [pers.] I have always been interested in unknown worlds, the paranormal; things that cannot be explained. And these things have always inspired me along with my passion for music, natue and life; [a.] Pennsauken, NJ

STEPHENS, KENNETH R.
[b.] November 2, 1962, Cols, OH; [p.] Ervin Stephens, Barbara Graham; [m.] Missie R. Stephens, April 13, 1994; [ch.] Sarah A. & Lyzzah J. Stephens; [ed.] South High, Tampa Community College; [occ.] Skilled Laborer; [memb.] Temple Terrace First Baptist Church; [hon.] Principals Honor Roll "88", U.S.M.C Survival Course; [oth. writ.] Several unpublished poems; [pers.] God is the Glory, Jesus is the light. Follow the light.; [a.] Tampa, FL

STEPHENS, KEVIN L.
[Pen.] KX; [b.] May 16, 1974, Gainesville, FL; [p.] Robert and Diana Stephens; [ed.] Chiefland H.S.; [occ.] Customer Service Associate, Winn Dixie; [hon.] Three music awards in high school, Principals Awrd for Outstanding Merit in band; [oth. writ.] Two anthologies for high school english classes.; [pers.] "The heart cannot bare what the eys cannot see" KX on high school love.; [a.] Chiefland, FL

STEPHENS, SKYLER
[b.] November 16, 1977, Webster, TX; [p.] Gary and Lu Stephens; [ed.] Enrolled in all honors courses. Will start my Junior Yar at B.F. Terry High School; [memb.] First Baptist Houston, National Junior Honor Society, Student Council; [hon.] 1st place in Anti drug Essay Contest sponsored by Rotary Club of Richmond in 1992, Editor's of Class anthology for 1993-94 school year.; [pers.] I have been gretly influenced by my grandmother, Jessie Farlow, who has written two books of poetry and is working on her third at age 81; [a.] Richmond, TX

STEPHENSON, JUDY A.
[b.] February 1, 1949, Charleston, WV; [p.] William and Hilda Blankenship; [m.] Divorced; [ch.] Charles L. Stephenson, Kimberly D. Stephenson; [ed.] East Bank High School, Garnet Business Education Center; [occ.] Clerk; [memb.] Member Phi Beta Lambda, Social Committee, member of The Coalburg Church of Jesus Christ, Coalburg, West Virginia Pastor Timmy Rogers; [oth. writ.] Poem published by Quill Books entitled the light.; [pers.] Someone once told me never give up your dreams, for dreams are the essence of life. He was right.; [a.] Marmet, WV

STEPNOWSKI, FRANK
[Pen.] Step; [b.] January 21, 1968, Inside my Mom; [p.] Mary and Frank; [m.] Dawn Marie; [ed.] Every Day of My Life; [occ.] Teacher: The Delta School for Severely Emotionally Distrubed Children; [hon.] Black Belt in Kenpo Karate; [oth. writ.] Various articles, editorials and poems published in local newspapers and magazines. Column: Steps..To Wisdom, published nationally in several martial arts periodicals. Peotry submitted for publication via the 2:13:61 Company; [pers.] Influences: Nietzche, Zappa, Rollins, Musashi; Every day my hostility becomes less a burden and more a weapon.; [a.] Pennsauken, NJ

STEVENS, CATHERINE
[b.] February 20, 1981, Auburn, NY; [p.] Allen and Crol Stevens; [ed.] Presently an eighth grade student at Port Byron Central School; [memb.] National Junior Honor Society, Auburn Players Community Theater; National Junior Honor Society; [oth. writ.] Eleven poems published in "The Three Lakes Sampler" and "Reflections." These are publications distributed by the school system.; [a.] Auburn, NY

STEVENS, MARIE
[b.] December 2, 1957, Cleveland, Ohio; [p.] James and Therese Oliverio; [m.] William Stevens; [ch.] Rebecca Lynn, Matthew Dylan, William Douglas, Bradley Adam; [pers.] I believe it's the small things in life that really makes the difference.; [a.] Lexington, GA

STEVENSON, JENNIFER
[b.] February 7, 1976, Huntington, WV; [p.] Charles and lynne Stevenson; [ed.] Barboursville High, Marshall University; [occ.] Student; [pers.] I want my writing to have a thousand different meansings each one dependent on the reader's experience. I want the reader to feel every word I have written as if it were happening to them.; [a.] Huntington, WV

STEVENSON, MENDY
[Pen.] Krestu; [b.] June 11, 1978, Vancouver, B.C.; [p.] Rick and Crol Stevenson; [ed.] Currently a junior in high school [occ.] Student; [memb.] Volunteer at Redlands Community Hospital 1991 Current; [hon.] Excelence in Dramatics from International Thespian Society, June 11, 1991, English Achievement Award 1991; [oth. writ.] Many pomes and short stories given to friends (nothing published); [pers.] I am 16 years old and at this age friends mean a lot. When my best friend moved away I put my feelings into this poem. I hope this encourages more young people to write what they feel.; [a.] Redlands, CA

STEWARD, CARL L.
[Pen.] B. J. Jones; [b.] September 30, 1952, Fairmont, WV; [p.] Evelyn J. and James C.; [m.] Freda Florence, January 20, 1984; [ch.] Shelia Ann, Elizabeth Ann, Misty Lynn, Melissa Sharon, Melody Ronnelle, Aaron Shane; [ed.] East Fairmont High School Computer Tech (will graduate Sept 95) University of New Hampshire (18 wk. course in photography); [occ.] Full time student majoring in Computer Information Management; [memb.] DPMA, Songwriters guild, Passenger Assistance Techniques Instructor (PAT) Houston, Texas. The Messengers Trio, The Christian Heirs, The Canarnaries, Canaan Ridge Viola Union Mission Church; [hon.] Traveled with Anne Tate and Cactus Moon Band on two 15 city tours in Europe. The National Library of Poetry; [oth. writ.] Country and gospel gongs, sacred verse, poem published in voice magazine entitled "Retirement."; [pers.] To each person god give special and unique talents; I try to portray His goodness and sure mercies to all mankind; [a.] Fairmont, WV

STEWART, BRIAN ALAN
[b.] May 27, 1970, Miami, AZ; [p.] Terry and Diane Stewart; [ed.] B.F.A. University of Arizona, Globe High School; [occ.] Learning Disability Advocate, U. of A; Lighting Designer; [memb.] Phi Kappa Phi, Golden Key National Honor Society, Tucson Aids Project; [hon.] Magna Cum Laude, American Legion, Editor's Choice International Society of Poetry; [oth. writ.] "Remembering" in the Desert Sun; "Father's Son", "Fishing," Hospice Newsletter.; [pers.] I dedicate my work to my father, His spirit guids my hand. In my writing his memory lives, and our words I hope can aid others.; [a.] Tucson, AZ

STEWART, LIANNA R.
[b.] November 21, 1981, Virginia; [p.] Stan-Audrey Stewart; [ed.] Will be in 7th grade this fall.; [pers.] I enjoy anything that has to do with horses. My favorite horse is the thoroughbred. I also love to watch birds.; [a.] East Bend, NC

STIAR, JOSEPH
[b.] September 30, 1976, Michigan; [p.] Rick and Ann Stier; [ed.] Lapeer East High School; [oth. writ.] I have several other unpublished poems. I also write music an am seeking an occupation in songwriting.; [pers.] I look at poetry as music. Every line is a harmony interacting and fitting together to make a song. What you get, personally, out of th epoem or song, is the true intention of the poet.; [a.] Attica, MI

STIPP, ELIZABETH
[b.] October 22, 1971, NY; [p.] Judy and Charles Stipp; [ed.] BA English Lit from Colorado State University; [occ.] Student; [oth. writ.] various published short stories in the Antennae; [pers.] You only go around once! Live it while you can and always keep one step in fron of the storm.; [a.] New Orleans, LA

STOLL, STEPHEN H.
[p.] Lolotilda Junor; [m.] Leila Stoll, September 6, 1975; [ch.] Allison, Yale, Latisha, Natasha, Alexie, Rovin, Stephen, Sean, Stanley, Sherman, Leon; [ed.] Carmel Roman Catholic School; [occ.] Clerical Officer; [oth. writ.] My feelings, Darkness of night, If wishes were granted, The alphabet, A view of love, My mother, Daughter of mine.; [pers.] Never attended writing or poem classes it all comes from the creativity and inspiration of sentimentality that brings out that inner feeling of compassion and love from within.; [a.] Republic of Guyana, South America

STRADER, LORI JEAN
[b.] August 24, 1977, Gulfport, MS; [p.] Eugene and Christine Strader; [ed.] Gulfport High School; graduating class of 1995.; [occ.] Student; [oth. writ.] 24 poems currenlty unpublished; [pers.] For me, poetry is a release through it, I share my feelings.; [a.] Guilfport, MS

STRADTNER, LINDSEY CATHERINE
[b.] August 10, 1980, Mich. City, IN; [p.] Barry W.

and Kathy M. Stradtner; [ed.] Currently entering my freshman year at LaPorte High School; [occ.] Student; [hon.] Honor Roll, Presidential Academic Fitness Award; [pers.] Live each day to the fullest. You never know when there won't be another tomorrow.; [a.] Laporte, IN

STRAUSS, JOSEPH D.
[Pen.] Brenden Scott; [b.] March 19, 1940, Mpls., MN; [p.] John F. and Clarice M. Strauss; [m.] Peamela Traongard Strauss, May 7, 1994; [ch.] Michael R., Shannon Y., Nicole J. (6) Grandchildren; [ed.] Bachelor of Science of Law, Juris Doctor; [occ.] Owner, Strauss Management Company, Chairman, First American Funds, First American Investment Funds; [oth. writ.] Personal Poems; [pers.] Wife and family come first above all else. I try to give back something each day for all that I have. I see saddness in this life and try to touch its roots with words and deeds of care and passion.; [a.] Brooklyn Park, NY

STROMAN, LUCY PARKERSON
[b.] August 7, 1928, Tevall, TX; [p.] Guy and Alta Parkerson (Deceased); [m.] William R. Stroman, March 4, 1948; [ch.] William, Guy, Dan and Shannon Stroman; [ed.] High School, 1 yrs. Abilene Christian College, Abilene, TX, now Uiversity Wisdom gleaned from life. "Parents Especially" husband of 46 yrs. Engineer; [occ.] Homemaker and writing poems and songs and letters; [memb.] Church of Christ, Ladies Class, Prayer and Study Group; [hon.] Three poems published in books edited by NLP, several read on WBAB Radio Station, Dallas, Ft. Worth, at church and funerals and memorials. Gifts of plaques to friends and for our home (of poems); [oth. writ.] Letters in rhyme sent for specail ladies classes and to friends and relatives.; [pers.] I want my poems to be used for teaching (living life) and to be read for fun. Writing free verse is like playing tennis with the net down-- Robert Frost; [a.] Ft. Worth, TX

STRUNK, BROOKE LA CARR
[b.] August 27, 1979, Somerset, Kentucky; [p.] Kelly Wanye Strunk and Rebecca Strunk Stanley; [ed.] I am currently a sophomore at McCreary Central High School, Stearns, KY; [occ.] Student; [memb.] I enjoy my choral activities at school and being involved in Future Homemakers of America and science Clubs; [hon.] I have recieved several awards, ribbons, certificates and recognition for cheerleading, handwriting, academic, choral and Future Homemaker's activities, along with track and olympic events; [oth. writ.] I am compiling more of my poems into a personal collection at this time, that I may submit from to "The National Library of Poetry" in the future.; [pers.] A lot of my poems, including "Love," are based on past experiences and reflect inner feelings of myself.; [a.] Stearns, KY

STUART, JESSICA
[b.] December 10, 1978, Fresno, CA; [p.] Elaine Brassard and Doug Hough; [ed.] Edison Computech High Schooo; [occ.] none; [memb.] none; [hon.] none; [oth. writ.] published once before in magazine.; [pers.] none; [a.] Fresno, CA

STURTEVANT, MARGARET
[b.] July 6, 1924, Brooklet, GA; [p.] Fortson Howard, Merline Howard; [m.] Clifford Sturtevan, June 26, 1943; [ch.] Dennis James, Brenda Margaret; [ed.] Brooklet High, Draughon's Business College (short

time); [occ.] Housewife; [memb.] Calvary Baptist Temple, Invincible Bible Class; [hon.] Beta Club; [oth. writ.] A desk drawer full. Copies I have written for family and friends. The first poem I wrote my English teacher published it in the paper for my mother to see. (A Mother's Day poem for my mother); [pers.] I feel that my writing is a gift from God, and I do not want to abuse it in any way.; [a.] Savannah, GA

SULLIVAN, JOANNE
[b.] November 6, 1946, Rockford, IL; [p.] Jess and Mary Lantz; [ch.] Thomas R. Sullivan and Brian D. Sullivan; [occ.] Office Manger, B&B Tool Company; [oth. writ.] Several other poems; [pers.] My writings refelcts the struggle of turning a troubled childhood into a very peaceful and productive adulthood.; [a.] Rockford, IL

SULLIVAN, KAREN
[b.] July 29, 1981, Holyoke; [p.] William and Mary Sullivan; [ed.] Granby Jr./Sr. High School; [occ.] Student; [pers.] I would like to dedicate this poem to my mother and father, my best friend Bobbie and to two special teachers, Mrs. Trotman and Mrs. Snopek.; [a.] Granby, MA

SULLIVAN, LEAH
[Pen.] Linda Michele Lazarus, Lea, Leah Kaufman, L. Lazarus Sullivan; [oth. writ.] Poetry published in several newsletters and anthologies including Matrix vols. I & III and Golden Horses. Reading and performance works at NYU, WEVD (radio, NY) and small theaters and clubs in the Los Angeles area.; [pers.] At their best, my poems are a form of shamamism whereby I may retrieve parts of my reader's spirit along with my own. At worst, they are my dry, desperate digging among the ruins of old syntactic structures to find that sacred doorway. Between these extremes lies a little song and dance. Thank you for reading.; [a.] Pasadena, CA

SUNDHEIM, SHEILA MARIE
[b.] June 21, 1978, New York Mills, MN; [p.] Joey and Stephany Sandheim; [ed.] K-10; [occ.] Still in High School, work as a car hop; [memb.] Spanish Club, Student Council; [hon.] Honor Roll Student, Pefect Attendance, Awarded Who's Who among American High School students; [oth. writ.] My book, Meshia, not yet published.; [pers.] Today can change tomorrow, but not yesterday.; [a.] Osage, MN

SUNDQUIST, CARL V.
[b.] March 30, 1931, Brainerd, MN; [p.] Clarence and Mary Sundquist; [m.] Alice Sundquist, June 28, 1952; [ch.] Edward Charles Sundquist and Laura Jean Corosu; [ed.] Washington High; [occ.] Retired, Burlington Northern Railroad; [memb.] Assemblers of God, Chairman Social Concerns Dept., Mycliffe Bible Translators, Banquet Team; [pers.] I believe most of the poems I have written have been from the Lord and hope any who read them will be blessed as I was receiving them, may God have the glory.; [a.] Brainerd, MN

SUNIGA, BERNICE ANN PICAZO
[b.] January 26, 1977, Santa Paula, CA; [p.] Frank L. and Connie Suniga; [ed.] Gateway Community School, Hopefully being able to attend Stanford, Berkley, or CSUN.; [memb.] Currently enrolled in Institute of Children's Literature; [hon.] Received two Honor-

able Mentions for poetry and short story.; [oth. writ.] Two poems published in Santa Paula Chronicle (92) Two poems published in Sparrrowgrass anthologies (Fall and Spring 92); [pers.] No matter what people say or do, always believe in yourself and follow your dreams all the way to the top. Believe me, they can really take you places.; [a.] Santa Paula, CA

SUTTON, LOUISE PADGETT
[b.] July 17, 1953, Bethal, NC; [p.] William Allen Padgett Sr. and Annie Harrell Wynne Padgett; [m.] Robert Lee Sutton, December 21, 1973; [ch.] Two daughters, Dana Louise Sutton 15 yrs. old, Jessica Lee Anne Sutton, 13 yrs. old, North Pitt High School, Bethel, NC, Pitt Technical Institute, Greenville, NC; [pers.] Writing can someitme be a positive outlet for expressing ones emotions and feelings.; [a.] Robersonville, NC

SVOBODA, BOB
[b.] January 25, 1947, Wilber, NE; [p.] Henry E. and Phyllis R.; [m.] Fiance' Patricia Lickfeldt; [ed.] Piusx High School; Southeast Community College; [occ.] Telephone Operator, Brywn Hsp., Lincoln; [memb.] International Society of Poets (Lifetime); The American Poetry Society (TAPS); National Authors Registry; [hon.] Honorable Mention (Iliad Press); two Editor's Choice Award (NLP); 2 Certificates of Accomplishment (Creative Arts and Science Enterprises); [oth. writ.] Poem in Poetry Link Magazine, poems in "Perspective" "A composition in verse"; Dusting off Dreams; Odysseys; Memories; Arcadia Poetry Anthology; Dance on the Horizon; [p.] Special Person: Patricia Lickfeldt. Writing rhyming poetry provides a challenge that is fun, exciting and stimulating. If I can bring sunshine into someone's life and joy to their heart, my life is also blest. Some works are soft and serene or spirited as a horse race. Each reader has the privilege of interpreting the composition however he, she desires. [a.] Lincoln, NE

SWANSON, GLENN A.
[b.] August 1, 1914, Cannon Falls, Minnesota; [p.] Algot W. and Esther J. Swanson; [m.] Martha M. Swanson, March 16, 1949; [ch.] Margaret Doucette, Sharon Crowley, William Kendall Swandon; [ed.] BBA Univrsity of Minn. American Institute of Banking, Chief, Classification Specialist U.S. Navy (WWII); [occ.] Retired, Prior Lobbyist Independent Bankers Mortgage Lending (U.S. Govt.); [memb.] Masonic Order, American Legion, American Scandinavian Assn., Minnesota State Society, Evangelical Lutheran Church.; [hon.] Public contract award (1972), Inter-Agency Adjustment Committee, Government Achievement Awards, Editor's Choice Award by National Library of Poetry; [oth. writ.] Contributor Community Development Handbook (SBA). Legislative proposal on behalf of Independent Bankers Assn., Expressions in Poetic Verse.; [pers.] Poetry becomes an expression of one's innermost thoughts and an opportunity to reminisce on days gone by.; [a.] Fairfax, VA

SWANSON, JENNIFER GRACE
[b.] May 4, 1969, Boston, MA; [p.] Jean and Ed Swanson; [ed.] Bunker Hill Community College, A.A. Degree major in Psy., Minor in Music, and Suffolk University, B.S. Degree major in Psy., minor in art.; [occ.] Staff assistant for the Buyer's of the Museum of Science; [memb.] Mass Center for Native American Indian Awareness.; [hon.] 1987, Who's

who in music and 1987 the outstanding piano award.; [oth. writ.] Two other poem's published in "Venture" (book of collections of poetry); [a.] Somerville, MA

SWANSON, ROBERT C.
[Pen.] Swede Swanson; [b.] May 1, 1936, Grand Island, Nebraska; [p.] Clarie and Carlotta Swanson; [m.] Norma J. Swanson, April 22, 1990; [ch.] Carrie, Randy, Shawn, Swanson; Erin, Rebecca Perkins; [ed.] Central High School, Santa Monica City College; [occ.] Procurement Manager; [memb.] Johnsondale Horsemen Assoc.; [oth. writ.] Many poems that have never been published and read by a few.; [pers.] I believe in the tooth fairy, Dr. what's his name, unicorns, welcome mats, hand shakes and kissing hello. But, most of all I believe in you. (For my Loving Wife); [a.] Ontario, CA

SWAYNE, ANITA JOYELLA
[b.] November 23, 1978, CA; [p.] Patrick and Laura Swayne; [ed.] Just completed the 10th grade and entering the 11th grade.; [memb.] Lee Street Chorus Club; [oth. writ.] One poem published in school magazine.; [pers.] My poems reflect my life and how I am teated by others around me. They are dedicated to the one's I know and love.; [a.] Ellenwood, GA

SWEARINGEN, TERESA L.
[Pen.] TR; [b.] September 2, 1979; [p.] David and Lori Swearinger; [ed.] Sophmore at Dysart High School; [occ.] Wells Quick Stop; [memb.] Bowling at Mission Bell; [pers.] I want to thank my Parents for their encouragement and support of the poem.; [a.] Wittmann, AZ

SWEENEY, PHILLIP P.
[Pen.] Phil Sweeney; [b.] April 3, 1949, Towanda, PA; [p.] Robert and Teresa Sweeney; [ch.] Adam and Seth Sweeney; [ed.] BA History, MS in Education, Binghamton University, Binghamton, NY; [occ.] Creative Writing Instructor (K-12); Poet/Songwriter; [memb.] Poets and Writers Inc.; Alternative Literary Programs in Pre Schools; Board of Directors, Binghamton Community Poetry Series.; [hon.] 1985 National Residency at Blue Mountain center; 1992 Career Enhancement Grant from Broome County Council of the Arts.; [oth. writ.] "Dark Shadows for a Thousand Points of Light" a first collection of poetry by Phil Sweeney, many individual peoms have been published.; [pers.] I am a student and propoenent of traditional form in poetry and a great admirer of Robert Frost.; [a.] Harporsville, NY

SWIFT, LIZ
[b.] July 4, 1947, Ark.; [p.] Clyde and Vila Howard; [m.] Bert, May 19, 1989; [ch.] Libby, Gilbert, Andy, Dennis and Danny; [ed.] 11th; [occ.] Resident Manager, National Church Residences; [memb.] HEB Chamber of Commerce; [hon.] I have four Editor's Choice Award and I have four poems on The Sound of Poetry; [oth. writ.] You Could Have Heard a Pin Drop, Mount Carmel, Our Mother, My Love, My Heart Says Your Name Where Would I Be, The Little Bag Lady; [pers.] Everytime I write a new poem I thank God for this gift he gave me my poems arc very special to me they all comes from my heart.; [a.] Bedford, TX

SWISHER, PATRICIA A.
[b.] September 2, 1953, Hagerstown, MD; [p.] Darce M. and George R. Karle (deceased); [m.] Charles

"Chip" E. Swisher, Jr., May 10, 1975j; [ch.] Joshua David Swisher; [ed.] Graduate of Greencastle - Antrim High School (1971), Attended Hagerstown Junior college (one year); [occ.] Administrative Secretary; [memb.] Administrative Office Employees Group (Board of Education of Washington Co.), Former member of Gad-Abouts Square Dancers; [oth. writ.] Two poems published February and December 1992 in The ASCA Counselor (published by the American School Counselors Association). Poem in Poetic Voices of America (Fall 1993). Poem in Poetic Voices of America (Summer 1994). Poems in church bulletins and newsletter; [pers.] My inspiration is from God and nature. I value the simplicities of life as did Henry David Thoreau. I live in a rural area and value country life style. To me, words are like a puzzle; they must flow just right to paint a picture for the readers.; [a.] Mercersburg, PA

SZYMANSKI, PAUL
[b.] March 20, 1968, Glendale, NY; [p.] Stanley Szymanski, Barbara Nugent; [m.] none currently; [ed.] Three one-half of college Associate's degree in Accounting; [occ.] Clerk, Stony Brook College; [hon.] One published poem, "An Ocean is Life," World of Poetry; [oth. writ.] One short story, "Struggling to live the heroe's Journey. copyrighted. Based on Joseph Campbells, The hero with a thousand faces.; [pers.] God is a metaphor for a mystery that absolutely transcends all human categories of thought. The end of the world is a spiritual event, not a historical one, Joseph Campbell, faith comes experience. I'm a manic-depressive with both.; [a.] Bay Shore, NY

TABER, BLOSSOM BESSIE
[Pen.] Blossom Bessie Rogers; [b.] April 12, 1984, Keysville, MO; [p.] Charles Daniel Rogers and Hettie Viola Eaton; [m.] William John Henry Uthoff, June 3, 1911; [ch.] Arthur Henry Uthoff, Blossom Blanche Uthoff; [ed.] 3rd grade, self educated to University level MA; [occ.] Retired Nurse from Army Hosptial 13 yrs.; [memb.] Many clubs, Women's Club, San Pedro; [oth. writ.] Religious songs and music, 5 years ago "Memories" (book of poems); [pers.] My father always read me poetry. My ancestors came over on the Mayflower. I am 100 yrs. old. I have always enjoyed Ralph Waldo Emerson. "Speak to them for they hear...closer than breathing are they, closer than hands and feet."; [a.] San Bernardino, CA

TADEMY JR., RAYMOND H.
[Pen.] Ray Tadey, Jr.; [b.] September 16, 1957, Wash. D.C.; [p.] Raymond H. Tademy, Sr. and Ruth B. Tademy; [ed.] 1975 graduate of Jacksonville High School, Jacksonville, AR; currently pursuing Bachelor's Degree in Management Information Systems from Park College; [occ.] Master Sergeant, U.S. Marine Corps., photojournalist, editor, public affirs chief, marketing advisor; [hon.] Several honors in militry journalism; [oth. writ.] Novel, Book of Poetry, Autobiography in progress.; [pers.] Religious traditions throughout the world celebrate the triumph of light over darkness; life over death. My poetry and prose and enfused with this same theme. A theme not of thought, but of experience. An experience I hope my words adequately convey.

TAKALA, JOHN J.
[b.] April 7, 1966, Virginia; [p.] Gloria Nystrom and John Takala; [ed.] Mt. Iron High School, St. John's

University; [occ.] Accountant, Hibbing Cooperative Credit Union; [pers.] Remember, with fondness, the smiles of childhood, and embrace the tears of your youth. For only through the endurance of sorrow does one acquire strength and discover peace.; [a.] Mt. Iron, MN

TAKANO, KEIKO
[pers.] "Amethyst" first appeared in Felix Oliver's independent film, "In Plain View" with slight changes in the film the character I played was reading and writing the poem.; [a.] New York, NY

TALLMAN, EVELYN T.
[b.] November 13, 1922, So. Westerlo; [p.] Hazel F. Mabie; [m.] January 23, 1940, Raymond H. Tallman (deceased); [ch.] Ralph R. Tallman; [ed.] Attended Greenville Central High School and Graduated from National Bakers School, Chicago, Illinois; [occ.] Retired Cook; [memb.] Social Service; [hon.] Social Security with the benefits, Golden Poetry Gram; [oth. writ.] World of Poetry.

TALSKY, SAMUEL M.
[b.] January 1, 1910, Chicago, IL; [p.] Max and Dora Talsky; [m.] Helen Talsky, January 1, 1934; [ch.] Two sons Ron and Gene, 9 grandchildren and 4 great grandchildren; [ed.] High School in Chicago, IL; Also, various single courses in business, philosophy etc. thru the Years, "College of Life" Graduate!; [occ.] Retired from the advertising field, I had a dance band during my younger years (piano); [memb.] Shriners Masonic Order, Odd Fellows Lodge, Elks Lodge, Bnai Brith Organization, A Member of All Above over 50 years; [hon.] Being accepted by all people, Helen and I are married 60 years, what greater award can I have, being accepted, wanted and loved.; [oth. writ.] Music compositions, short stories, poetry; [pers.] "Give me a lot of friends for friends are better than life itself. It makes me jolly when meeting both ends. I don't care to live a life by myself. My mission on erth is to create happiness and laughter with any one I meet personally or talk with by phone.; [a.] Culver City, CA

TANAKA, HARUKO A.
[b.] April 25, 1974, NY;; [a.] Los Angeles, CA

TATE, KRIS
[b.] May 10, 1970, Lewistown, PA; [p.] William and Geraldine Tate; [ed.] Presently attending Interntional Correspondence school for Fitness and Nutrition, Graduated from Chief Logan High School in Lewistown, PA; [occ.] Messenger at the Lewistown Hospital; [pers.] Writing for me is a healing. Through it I strive to make known the many cries of the heart. That which is truely felt, rrely spoken and never seen with the human eye.; [a.] Burnham, PA

TATEM, DERRICK CHARLES
[b.] March 9, 1958, St. Christopher; [p.] Sydney and Edith Tatem; [m.] Rupertha Dianne Tatem, December 12, 1983; [ch.] Tekeima N. Tatem, Antoine J. Tatem, Crystal C. Tatem; [ed.] SouthWest Miami High, Miami Dade Community College; [occ.] Bus Driver, Dade County School District, Miami, FL; [memb.] ASCAP! New York, NY; [hon.] Talent Explosion Award in 1983 for originality at the Joseph Caleb Center, Miami, FL; [oth. writ.] Several poems unpublished. Completed work, 103 page compilation Entitled: The Chief Musician (Unpublished). Also

several lyrics and songs unpublished.; [pers.] As a writer I use great imagination to put my character in focus; and place them into reality. My greatest inspiration is from God. JAH LIVE.; [a.] Miami, FL

TAVARES, LAURIE
[b.] August 6, 1975, New Bedford, MA; [p.] John and Eufrosina Tauates; [ed.] Greater New Bedford Vo-Tech High School; [occ.] Waitress, Girassol Cafe Restaurant; [hon.] Vocational Industrial Clubs of America, placed 1st overall, and 2nd in my class.; [pers.] Poetry is my way of letting go of my emotions, it free's my mind and my spirit.; [a.] New Bedford, MA

TAYLOR, BURT
[b.] November 11, 1940, Houston, TX; [p.] Bill and Zola Taylor; [m.] Carolyn, June 22, 1994; [ch.] Jacqueline Ann Lockhard, David Benton Taylor; [ed.] Bay St. Louis, MS. HS; Miss. Gulf Coast Comm. College; [occ.] Construction Estimator; [memb.] American Legion, VFW, St. Clare Catholic Church; [oth. writ.] No other publications, although I do have a fairly large colleciton of poems that I have written for family and friends.; [pers.] Most of my poems are of love and family. What greater inspiration can there be than those who are near and dear to your heart.; [a.] Bay St. Louis, MS

TAYLOR, CARRIE
[b.] May 19, 1976, Delaward, OH; [p.] Ruth and Frank Taylor; [ed.] Graduated from Delaware Christian School in 1994. Plan to go to College and study Marine Biology; [occ.] Working for a year.; [hon.] 1991 and 92' MVP in Volleyball; 93' Best Setter; V-Gall Capt 92' & 93'; Most Consistent Award in Basketball in 94'; B-Ball Capt. 93'-94' Honors Society; [a.] Delaware, OH

TAYLOR, MISTY
[Pen.] Laflawn; [b.] August 5, 1975, Fortworth, TX; [p.] Malvery and Howard Taylor; [ed.] North Elementary Plaisance Jr. High, Plaisance High, Northwest High, Attending Southern University; [memb.] Talent Search, 4-H, Future Business Leaders of American, Honor Society; [hon.] 2nd place school writing contest, Honors Award; [oth. writ.] Short stories, poems and stories written as a hobbie; [pers.] Writing is from the heart its your personality; you should judge people the same.; [a.] Opelousas, IA

TAYLOR, WILLIAM NELSON
[b.] September 27, 1969, Dallas, TX; [p.] Majorie Waters, Bill Taylor; [ed.] B.A.: English, Rollins College; M.A.: Creative Writing, University of North Texas (In Progress); [occ.] Providence Associates Inc.; [a.] Denton, TX

TEMPLET, MANDY
[b.] December 31, 1978, Thibodaux, LA; [p.] Lesley and Vivian Templet; [m.] Single; [ed.] Jnior at Donaldsonville High School; [memb.] Future Busienss Leaders of American Club, Science Club, Art Club, The Saint Francis of Aissi Religion class.; [hon.] Young Authors Contest, 1st place fiction. United States Achievement Academy in Business Education; [pers.] I try to write about different emotions that everyone experiences in their lifetime. I would like to thank my family and friends for all their love, support, advice, and encouragement. Also my Creative Writing and English teachers for editing and revising my

work.; [a.] Donaldsonville, LA

TENCLAY, HENRY J.
[b.] April 30, 1913, Westfield, North Dakota; [p.] Henry and Minnie TenClay; [m.] J. Lucile Kleinjan, June 17, 1942; [ch.] 2 daughters, 1 son; [ed.] Central College, Pella, Iowa, 1939, Western Theological Seminary, Holland, Michigan 1942; [occ.] Retired Clergyman; [memb.] Church of the Cross, Reformed Church in America; [hon.] Phi Kappa Delta, Doctor of Divinity, Central College, 1961 President, Particular Synod-Michigan, 1960 Dean of Students, Western Theological Seminary, 1961-1967, First Stated Clark of Florida Classis, 1975-1987, President, Board of Western Theological Seminary; [pers.] Poetry has been a source of relaxation from the stress of pastoral and pulpit work.

TENISON, LEASA HALE
[b.] January 29, 1959, Midland, TX; [p.] F. B. & Wanda Joe Hale; [ch.] One daughter, Jordan Christine; [ed.] Midland High school; [occ.] American Board Certified Optician; [memb.] Certified Opticians Association of Texas; Alamo Heights Baptist Church; [hon.] Midland High School, National Honor Society; [oth. writ.] Poem published in local newspaper.; [pers.] I want people to feel my heart in everything that I write the poem "Daddy" was inspired in an ICU waiting room one Oct. evening when I wondered if I would ever be able to tell him how I felt. Fortunately, I was able to present this poem to him for Christmas the same year. It was the very best gift God could have ever given to me.; [a.] Midland, TX

TENNER, WILLIAM
[Pen.] Tenner; [b.] November 20, 1954, Cincinnati, OH; [m.] Tamara Lee Tenner, November 6, 1976; [ch.] Mandara Michele Tenner; [ed.] Oak Hills H.S. Cincinnati, OH, U. MD Far East and European Div. Major: Business Management Academy Church of Scientology; [occ.] Master Sergeant U.S. Army, Military Intelligence; [memb.] Founding Church of Scientology, DC; [hon.] Commendation from the Director of Training for Academic Excellence; [pers.] Man has a choice while he is engaged in the pursuit of livingness. To survive or succumb. May we learn the difference.; [a.] Fort Meade, MD

TEPPER, MIA SURUJ
[Pen.] nee: Namikunian; [b.] September 22, 1967, Tucson, AZ; [p.] Bette Broussard and Gregg Mamikunian; [m.] Scott Tepper, September 28, 1991; [ch.] None Yet!, I come from a family of seventeen brothers and sisters.; [ed.] UCLA (BA History 90'); Louisville High school (WH, CA 85'); [occ.] Endocrinology Laboratory Administration; [memb.] Los Angeles Emergency Response Team for disasters; Vice-President, Westside Jeep Club; [hon.] UCLA, Homecoming Court; Outstanding Senior Award, UCLA Bruin Belles; UCLA History Honor Society, Phi Alpha Theta; [oth. writ.] Poems and stories for family and friends. Writing first book currently.; [pers.] Practice random kindness and senseless acts of beauty. All you touch and all you see is all your life will ever be.; [a.] Santa Monica, CA

THARPE, JAIMI LEIGH
[b.] May 16, 1980, Alaska; [p.] Steve and Jean tharpe; [ed.] Freshman in High School; [occ.] Student; [oth. writ.] None that are published.; [a.] St.

Albans, VT

THIBODEAU, BONNIE
[b.] January 7, 1970, Albany; [ch.] Tchad Michael, 4 yrs. old; [ed.] Watervliet High School Diploma, Attending Bryant & Stratton for an Associates Degree in the field of Business Management.; [pers.] I have gained my inspiration for poetry from the everyday experiences of life. My first love will always be poetry because it is from my heart.; [a.] Watervliet, NY

THOMAS, B. J.
[Pen.] Sir B. James Thomas; [b.] March 27, 1972, Benton Harbor, MI; [p.] James H. Terry, Imagene Thomas; [ed.] Glen Mills High, Pennsylvania University; [occ.] Vocational Consultant; [memb.] Michicanna Family, Brotherhood Against Drugs; [hon.] Michicanna Family Peace Awards, Alpha Kappa Lambda; [pers.] I try to enhance one's thinking capacity to higher plateaus of thought and understanding so that all minds can think on higher, more thought provoking levels.; [a.] Lansing, MI

THOMAS, BETH
[b.] May 26, 1980, Salisbury, NC; [p.] Marvin and Ann Thomas; [ed.] Freshman at Morresville Senior High School; [hon.] Six awards and one honor in dancing.; [oth. writ.] Crisis at HOme; [pers.] My poems reflect the emotions that I feel about events that happen to me or issues that I care about.; [a.] Mooresville, NC

THOMAS, ESTELLE
[Pen.] Stella Hill; [b.] February 16, 1929, Alabama; [p.] James and exia Hill; [m.] John Thomas, December 4, 1947; [ch.] Tyrone, Bonita and Michael; [ed.] High School of Commerce, Detroit, Mich., Saint Joseph's University, Phila. PA; [occ.] Retired Government Employee; [memb.] Odyssey Literary Group of So. Jersey, Saint Matthew's Baptist Church Newsletter; [oth. writ.] Poem published in Camden College Literary Magazine "Bridges."; [pers.] Each Morning, thannk God for another day and write, write, write! Published or not, I love it.; [a.] Sicklerville, NJ

THOMAS, RICK
[b.] September 7, 1957, Clinton, IL; [p.] Ron and Shirley; [m.] Penny Jo Thomas, April 22, 1991; [ch.] Dave and Sheri; [ed.] Carmel High School, Southwest Florida Criminal Justice Academy, Ft. Myers, FL, United States Navy; [occ.] Work Service Instructor (Hope Network); [memb.] United States Powerlifting Federation. Defenders of the Wildlife Federation; [hon.] I have won numerous weightlifting awards and many athletic trophies for basketball, football and track and field.; [oth. writ.] I have twenty two journals entitled "This Historian" in which I document lifes questions and answers wherever I may find thim.; [pers.] I try to live by the teachings of Ralph Waldo Emerson and love the wisdom and wit of Mark Twain.; [a.] Wyoming, MI

THOMAS, SHERITA
[Pen.] Budda; [b.] July 7, 1975, Brooklyn; [p.] Gloria Thomas & Benjamith S.; [ed.] G.E.D. diploma; [occ.] Teacher's Assistants; [memb.] Pricehopper, Wegmans and Video King.; [hon.] Dance and Honor roll student in J.H.S.; [pers.] My name is Sherita and here's a top, the more you write, the better you talk and read. I think writing is fun.; [a.] Bringhamton,

NY

THOMPSON, LEE N.
[Pen.] Tom Leeson; [b.] March 28, 1967, South Bend, IN; [p.] Elinor M. Thompson; [ed.] Graduated from Trinity School at Greenlawn. Honorably Discharged from the U.S. Marine Corps.; [occ.] Retail; [oth. writ.] Oh, too many to mention.; [pers.] My writings come from a place I know not. but are delivered freely, thank you for the opportunity.; [a.] South Bend, IN

THOMPSON, TONIA
[b.] September 15, 1976, Hattiesburg, MS; [p.] Charles and Gladys Thompson; [ed.] South Jones High, Pearblossom Private School, Jones JUnior College; [occ.] College Student; [memb.] Moselle Faithway Baptist Church; [hon.] Dean's List, Feature writer for college paper, The Radionian, received scholarship on achievements in writing, completed high school and begun college at age 17.; [oth. writ.] Many articles published in The Radionian College newspaper, poem published in a local elementary school yearbook, winner of several essay contests.; [pers.] I feel that writing goes much deeper than merely creating a good story or poem. It reflects a variety of human emotions and captures the essense of living.; [a.] Petal, MS

THREADGILL, EVELYN L.
[Pen.] Pear of Great Price (St. Matt. 13:46); [b.] July 15, 1944, Norfolk, VA; [p.] Samuel and Evelyn Threadgill; [ed.] Booker T. Washington High; Norfolk State University; USIU-San Diego, CA, United States International University MA-TESOL; Pursuing doctorate in TESOL(Teaching English Speakers Other Languages); [occ.] English Teacher, Edison Middle School, Los Angeles, CA; [memb.] Church of God In Christ, Inc; Delta Sigma Theta; COGIC Scholarship; Pentecostal Heritage, Inc; Iota Phi Lambda Sorority; Sugar Ray Youth Foundation; PTA Graduate Scholarship - 12th Districtg, Los Angeles, CA; Metroplitan Ecclesiastical Jurisdiction, State District Local Officer; CATESOL's stipend 1994; International COGIC Women's Convention 1994, Special Details; [hon.] Who's Who Among Black Women in CA 1981; USMC Honorable Discharge 1968; Teacher of the Year Russell Elem. 1989; PTA Founder's Day Award, Life State Teacher's Scholarship 1962-66; COGIC Tech Scholarship 1992; [oth. writ.] Too many to mention.; [pers.] I'm inspired by the Holy Ghost to write according to the love my heavenly Father is expressing through me His vessel. All Glory goes to him, the author and finisher of each writings. I have been greatly influenced by Helen Steiner Rice's poems.; [a.] Los Angeles, CA

TIKALSKY, SARAH
[b.] July 19, 1977, New Prague, Minnesota; [p.] Richard and Jeanne Tikalsky; [ed.] I am a high school senior in New Prague, MN; [memb.] Holy Trinity Lutheran Church; [pers.] I write wht I feel, and feel what I write. Those teachers offering me the greatest encouragement in my writings are: Mr. William Bergevin, Mrs. Elaine Bruchman and especially Mrs. Valerie Drommerhausen; [a.] New Prague, MN

TOLAR, ANNE MELTON
[Pen.] Anne Tolar; [b.]January 17, 1937, Geneva, AL; [p.] Earnest and Lovie Melton; [m.] Bob Tolar, April 21, 1966; [ch.] Bob Tolar Jr., Bill Tolar, Sharon

Tolar, Ginny Tolar; [ed.] Pensacola High School, Pensacola Jr. College, University of Alabama; [occ.] Co-Pastor (with Hustand) of Fountain of Praise Church; [memb.] Missionary Church International; [hon.] 1972 Winner of Savings & Loan Association Speech Contest, for City of Atlanta, State of GA and Internationally; [oth. writ.] Book: Wilt Thou Be Made Whole?"; 2 Albums (music); "Traveling By Faith" and "Lord Make of Me A Melody;" containing songs I have written, sung, played and arranged.; [pers.] In all that I write or sing, I want it to be a blessing to those around me, and bring glory to God, in whom I have total faith.; [a.] Gautier, MS

TOLSON, FRANCES
[b.] September 15, 1913, Licking Co., OH; [p.] H. H. and Mary Jane Hoover; [m.] Melvin L. Tolson, November 8, 1953 (deceased Jan. 1994); [m.] November 8, 1953; [ch.] Stepdaughter, deceased; 4 grandchildren; [ed.] B.F.A. Ohio State Univ. Masters Art Education, Kent State Univ.; [occ.] Retired Art Teacher; [memb.] Ohio Art Education Assoc., Delta Kappa Gamma Ohio State, Retired Teachers Assoc.; [hon.] Who's Who in American Education; Who's Who in the Arts 1971-72; [oth. writ.] Christian Life Letters, The Lookout, Free Press Standard, World of Poetry; [pers.] I have tried to put feelings that are strong and matter to me into words.; [a.] Carrollton, OH

TOMASULA, JOYCE M.
[Pen.] JM Toma; [b.] December 19, 1955, buffalo, NY; [p.] Geraldine J. Pastore; [ed.] Erie Community College, City Campus; [hon.] Dean's List, Poetry Award: 1994 Mirage Publication; [oth. writ.] A collection of narrative and prose poetry.; [pers.] I strive to create the surrealistic dimension that exists within all human experience and reflects the depth of the human spirit. I have been influenced by the confessional poetry of Sylvia Plath.; [a.] Buffalo, NY

TOMLINSON, DANIEL
[Pen.] Uncle Dan; [b.] February 3, 1955; [ed.] TSTC Waco, TX, Air Condition and Refrigeration Service; [occ.] Student, TSTC Waco, TX; [memb.] Waco Literary Club, Waco Coin Club; [oth. writ.] Jasper the Farm Dog. Unpublished, contract with Eaton Literary Agency, Sarasota, FL.; [pers.] CCesorship, word lived spelled down-wards spells Devil. Also spells cesorship and death threats.; [a.] Gatesville, TX

TOOMEY, CHRISTIAN F.
[b.] June 14, 1972, Lebanon, PA; [p.] Dennis and June Toomey; [ed.] Lebanon Catholic High, Seton Hall University; [memb.] Varsity athlete Pirte Varsity Club Representative Freshman Class Vice-President; [hon.] Dean's List Academic Scholarship, Athletic Scholarship, Baseball Team Captain, All Big East Conference First Team; [oth. writ.] I never submitted any other material prior to tis contest.; [pers.] Life is not a matter of choosing right or wrong. It is doing what's right. You don't live to be a role model, you live to do what is right. And when you do what's right that's it, no more, no less.; [a.] Lebanon, PA

TORO, ROSEMARY
[b.] November 17, 1944, Utica, NY [p.] Peter S. and Edith I. Cuomo; [m.] Robert toro, July 18, 1964; [ch.] Michelle, Karen, Amy, Robert (Rob) as he likes to be called.; [ed.] Proctor High School, Utica School of Commerce Business School; [occ.] I was a sales rep.

for 10 yrs. for different major companies, but am a housewife at the present time.; [memb.] North Syracuse Art Guild; [oth. writ.] I write for my personal use and for friends.; [pers.] I write to make myself and other people happy. I write from my heart to meet any occasion. I am also an artist. I own my busienss called R.T. Crafts. My inspirtion for this poem came from the passing away of my wonderful father.; [a.] Syracuse, NY

TORRES, FELICIDAD
[Pen.] Chita; Felicia; [b.] March 2, 1951, Port Lavaca, TX; [p.] Albino and Felicidad Contreras; [m.] Armando Torres, April 20, 1971; [ch.] Armando, Naomi, Alvino, Vanessa, Adrian; [ed.] Palacios High School; [occ.] Homemaker; [pers.] I believe people should be willing to forgive each other and that it's of the utmost importance to stay "in-touch" with those we care about. "Love's Nest" inspired by daughter Naomi.; [a.] Palacios, TX

TOWER, CANDICE
[Pen.] Kat Tower; [b.] March 18, 1982; [p.] Debra and Tim Tower; [ed.] Watkins Jr. High School, Age 12; [occ.] Education (would like to be a Vet. someday); [memb.] Member of the D.A.R.E. and class of 2000 Clubs.; [hon.] Art Awards; [oth. writ.] none published yet.; [pers.] I wrote this poem when I was 8, but felt as a kid no one wanted to hear me. Remember kids are creative too and can do anything they set their minds to.; [a.] Houston, TX

TRACY, KELLY ANN
[b.] December 7, 1981, North Miami, FL; [p.] William and Nancy Tracy; [ed.] Completed Madie Ives Elementary. Presently attending Highland Oaks Middle School; [occ.] Student; [memb.] Representative on The City of North Miami Beach Youth Advisory Board; [hon.] John I. Smith Cloverleaf Community Service Award; Presidential Academic Fitness Award; Dade County MADD Essay Contest Award; Dade County Science Fair Award; First Place Winner, American Heritage Category Dade County Youth Fair; [oth. writ.] Poetry shocased at the Dade County Youth Fair; [pers.] I think that writing is a part of life. Without writing, we would have no way to show our creativity or imagintion. Life would be dull.; [a.] Miami, FL

TRASGA, AQUINO T.
[Pen.] G.A. Star; [b.] March 7, 1947, Philippines; [p.] Vincente T. and Ignacia T. Trasga; [m.] Regina C. Trasga, R.N., April 27, 1985; [ed.] Bagumbayan Prim. School; Tigbauan Elem; Tigbauan High; West Visayas State College, Philippine Normal College; De Vry Inst. of Technology; [occ.] Pathology Assistant; [memb.] De Vry Alumni Assoc.; WVSC Alumni; PNC Alumni; Circulo Tigbauerno of the Midwest; Fatima Prayer Community; American Heart Association; [hon.] Valedictorian High School; Magna Cum Laude, West Visayas State College; Rotary Club Award for Scholarship; Seato Award for Scholarship; Core Member of the Year 1991 Award from the Fatima Prayer Community; [oth. writ.] Various unpublished poems, one of them is "Our Lady of Mercy" set into music by Romulo J. Pangan, Music Professor at the West Visayas State University.; [pers.] "Put God on your driver seat and the going will be straight."; [a.] Aurora, IL

TRAVAGLINI, BART
[b.] October 14, 1956, San Francisco; [p.] Carlo and Norma Travaglini; [ch.] Anthony and Nicholas Travaglini; [ed.] DeVry Institute of Technology, Phoenix; [occ.] Nurse; [memb.] St. Gregory's Catholic Church; [pers.] For Diane, Inspired By Love.

TREADAWAY JR., JAMES C.
[Pen.] James Cody; [b.] November 21, 1959, "Birmingham, AL; [p.] James Sr. and Betty Treadaway; [m.] Single; [ed.] Roosevelt H.S., Chicago, IL; [occ.] Plant Foreman for Self Industries; [memb.] none; [hon.] Honorable Discharge from U.S. Army; [oth. writ.] none; [pers.] I was influenced to write my poem to a Russian Lady name Lena who can make my life full.; [a.] Shippensburg, PA

TUCKER, MAE BELLE
[b.] February 13, 1927, Ashville, NC; [p.] Willie Mae and Charles Enman; [m.] Rev. John Westervelt Tucker, December 18, 1950; [ch.] Martha Mae D. Tucker, John Westervelt Tucker II, Gloria E. Tucker; [ed.] Ashwilt City Schools, U.N.C. Chapel Hill, AB Journalism; [occ.] Homemaker, writer; [memb.] Holy Trinity Episcopal Church, West Palm Beach, FL; [oth. writ.] Poems in local newspaper, Diocisan Newsletter, Church newsletters, "Voices from the Seashell," "Golden Trampoline"; [pers.] My favorite poet is Robert Frost, my prescription for personal, national and international amity: Every person sees every other person as an object of his concern. We are our "brothers keeper;" [a.] Lake Worth, FL

TURLEY, SARAH ELLEN
[b.] December 24, 1987, Huntington, WV; [p.] Danny E. and Carol D. Turky; [ed.] Our Redeemer Lutheran Preschool Davis Creek Elementary (Kindergarten) Parkcircle Freewill Baptist Sunday School; [occ.] Gospel Singer (the Terry Family); [memb.] Parkcircle Freewill Baptist Church WEMM Radio, Singer and Announcer for an "Evening with the Terry Family;" [hon.] Oktober Fest, Most Photogenic "93", Dream Pageant, Runner Up 91', Harvest Time Studio, Gospel Tape featuring Sara Turley; [oth. writ.] "Prissy Fluffy Pup," A Walk In The Park with Minnie, Then I hugged Grama Series Fishing On the Atlantic, My Sea Book, If all the Hills were Mount Calvary; [pers.] I take pride in my work. I love to play and sing with my family.; [a.] Huntington, WV

TURLEY, SHANNON
[b.] April 9, 1982, Waukesha; [p.] Kevin and Barb Laurion and James turley; [ed.] Currently going to Hartland North, 7th grade.; [occ.] 7th grade; [hon.] Was only one in the school picked by staff to go to writing convention.; [oth. writ.] Published in Art of Writing.; [pers.] I believe you should express yourself in ways suiting you. You should not change yourself for anyone.; [a.] Hartland, WI

TURNER-LEE, LORRAINE
[b.] November 18, 1938, Virginia; [p.] Ethel and Craig smith; [m.] William M. Lvoe, April 29, 1984; [ch.] Reginald Turner, Lynette Turner, Wanda Jean Smith; [ed.] Armstrong Sr. High, Wash. D.C. Strayer College, D.C., Accounting, University of D.C. and english 1, 2 Urban Dev. and Eng., Southeaster University, Accounting; [occ.] Substitue Teacher Bladensburg Elem. Sch., Bladensburg, MD; [memb.] Hadley Seven Day Adventist Church: Prison Ministry Religious Liberty; [oth. writ.] Jesus is our Advocate; Hold onto Jesus; Over 40 Rappers, Rap, published by Rainbow Records July 1991. Entered and won essays for Institute of Children's Literature; [pers.] I have a great love for nature and my creator. Therefor, my writing, may it be song or poet will always include a mixture of both. I lvoe and respect writing.; [a.] Washington, D.C.

TUTTLE, ANGELA
[Pen.] Angela (Greb) Tuttle; [b.] April 1, 1961, Frederick, OK; [p.] Betty and Sam Greb; [m.] Thane Tuttle, September 14, 1990; [ch.] Thane Forrest Tuttle, II; [ed.] Frederick High School, Tarrant county Jr. College, NW, Ft. Worth, TX; [occ.] Student Assistant for Assoc. Dean at Tarrant Co. Jr. College, Fort Worth, TX; [memb.] Strategic Planning Committee for Institutional Effectiveness, Campus Disciplinary Hearing Committee; [hon.] Phi Theta Kappa, Who's Who Among Students in Junior Colleges, National Dean's List, All American Scholar Collegiate; Phi Theta Kappa Poetry; Winner 1993 and Speech Contest Scholarship Winner 1993; Gold and Sivler Poet Award; [oth. writ.] Haiku published in local newspaper.; [pers.] I strive to reach individuals of all backgrounds in my writing, for I feel it is important for others to know they are not alone in their struggles through life. I believe in writing from the heart.; [a.] Lake Worth, TX

TUTTLE, LAURIE ELAINE
[b.] March 29, 1952, Fayetteville, NC; [p.] Harry G. and Jo Webb Goode; [m.] W. Virgil tuttle, Jr., May 25, 1975; [ch.] Matthew David, Lael Elisha, Juda Andrew; [ed.] Mt. Tabor High, Winston-Salem NC, Univ. of NC at Greensboro; [occ.] Registered Nurse; [memb.] Assoc. of Research and Enlghtenment, Women and Wisdom, Life Spectrums; [pers.] I believe, in truth, the world is a very mystical magical place seen clearly only through a fully open loving heart. When viewed through the eyes of that heart we are revealed to each other as the magical beings of light we have always been.; [a.] Greensboro, NC

UEBELACKER, ANGEL MYCHELLE
[b.] April 17, 1983, Fayetteville, NC; [p.] John J. and Cherol Ann Uebelacker; [ch.] Sister, Jonica Noel Uebelacker; [ed.] 5th grade graudate from South Conway Elementary, to attend Conway Christian School for 6th grade 1994-95; [occ.] Student; [memb.] World Tang Soo Do Assocition, Awana Clubs; [hon.] Winner of the Presidential Youth Community Service Award and the Presidential Award for Educational Excellence; Winner Lt. Governors Essay Contest 1994; Invited to Young Writers Conference 1994.; [oth. writ.] "A Book" published in Tears of Fire.

UGOKWE, EMEKA
[Pen.] Kiszo; [b.] April 7, 1969, Nigeria; [p.] Rid Col and Mrs. C.F Ugokwe; [ed.] B.S. E.E. Tuskegee University; [occ.] Electrical Engineer; [memb.] Eta Kappa Nu, Alpha Phi Alpha, IEEE, NSBE, Pride Evansville; [hon.] SDA Award for Outstanding Engineer, Deans List, Eta Kappa Nu, Electrical Engineering Honor Society; [oth. writ.] Written several other poems, articles and comments publsihed in Ebony magazine and newspapers. Currently working on a book.; [pers.] To be loved, is to love. We all have been blessed with this mysterious gift and so we must be drunken with it. Hatred will only bring aobut "Mayham Resolute" and we must stop the madness now! Racism; [a.] Evansvill, IN

URBANO, LINDA S.
[b.] December 29, 1950, Detroit, MI; [p.] Rita M. and Robert L. Bruce (deceased); [m.] Gary L. Urbano, September 9, 1978; [ed.] St. Philip Neri; [occ.] Mental Health Worker Macomb County Community Mental Health/Adult Day Treatment Center.; [a.] Oakland, MI

UZZELL, CARTLIN W.
[Pen.] Cat. W. Uzzell; [b.] November 22, 1980, Dallas, TX; [p.] Doug Uzzell and Linda Whiteford; [ed.] Temple Terrace Elem., Orange Grove Middle School, Sligh Jr. High, Greco Jr. High; [occ.] Student; [memb.] National Geo. Society, Odyssey of the Mind, the Honors Society; [hon.] The Honors Society, softball, dance, Odyssey of the Midn; [oth. writ.] I am only 13 and I am just starting to explore writing. At this time I have no other wiritngs, but hope that there will be more in the future.; [pers.] In my poems I try to write confusion in good, bad and different. My greatest influence has been my father, whom is also a poet.; [a.] Tampa, FL

VAN HEUSEN, RUTH
[b.] September 27, 1924, Milwaukee, Wis.; [p.] Mr. and Mrs. W. H. St. Thomas; [m.] Horace Van Heusen; [ch.] Terry Van Heusen, Mrs. Fred Tallon; [ed.] B.S., M.S. U. of Iowa; [occ.] Retired Teacher; [hon.] Trustee J.M.C.C.; National Science Award Pin.

VAN WINGERDEN, BERTHA
[pers.] I am now 77 years old, but I find true poetry is never old. If the author doesn't breathe into it a fresh insight, it is not true; Baltimore, MD

VANG, YIA
[Pen.] Vicky; [b.] April 9, 1980, Thailand; [p.] Chang Kua Vang, May Xiong; [ed.] Freshmen Student at Franklin High School; [oth. writ.] One poem, "Outta My Way," appeared in Fremont Trailblazer Newspaper, at Fremont Middle School; [pers.] I am grateful for this special talent and will make the best of it.; [a.] Stockton, CA

VARGO, WILLIAM CHADWICK POLLARD
[Pen.] William Vargo; [b.] September 9, 1977, Pasadena; [p.] Mike and Shelley Vargo; [ed.] Student of Brazoswood High School; [occ.] Writer; [oth. writ.] Several unpublished poems and short stories.; [pers.] Someday all fame must end and so will mine.; [a.] Clute, TX

VAUGHAN, VICTORIA LEE-ANN
[Pen.] Victoria Vaughan; [b.] August 9, 1979, OK; [p.] Victor Vaughn and Laura Fletcher; [ed.] I attend Jasper High School; [occ.] Student; [oth. writ.] Many poems and an upcoming book.; [pers.] If you have a dream remember to always pursue it never give up on yourself.; [a.] Jasper, AK

VAUGHN, MICHELE RENEE
[b.] July 27, 1976, Chicago, IL; [ed.] Charter Oak High School, Covina, CA; [memb.] Member of International Thespian Society - Troupe #2409; [hon.] "Most Promising Student" from Charter Oak High School Art Dept. Received trophy for achievements from Charter Oak High School Theatre Dept.; [pers.] I've based my life on truth, and the attainment of freedom and while the pursuit of these things has often

left me in a great deal of trouble I still encourage others to strive for the same.. It's good for the soul. "In the world's broad field of battle, in the bivouac of life; be not dumb, driven cattle! Be a hero in the Strife!"-- Henry W. Longfellow. Those are words I think we all need to live by.; [a.] Covina, CA

VENTURIN, MARGARET ROSS
[b.] August 31, 1913, Newark, NY; [p.] Mr. and Mrs. Anthony Ross (deceased); [m.] Thanksgiving Day 1936, Deceased; [ch.] Faye and Gail, 7 grandchildren, 3 great grandchildren; [ed.] Newark High school, Sec. Senior Class. Upon retirement attended college Syracuse, Cocoa, FL, Tallahassee Community College, Belmont U. Nashville and UNLV Las Vegas; [occ.] I volunteer enertaining children and senior citizens with my "Teddy Bear" act. Song c-written with Dunc Peckham (deceased). Had a private audience with Pope Paul VI.; [memb.] Salvation Army, Several Poetry Societies throughout south. Am active with senior drama societies. My travels or assignments have taken me around the world several times.; [oth. writ.] Dark Part of Town (poem) published in Belmont Literary Journal. Songs, plays, essays, stories and beaucoup poems. [pers.] Early romantic poets inspire me.; [a.] Jacksonville, FL

VERNE, BERNICE H.
[b.] August 16, 1909, PA; [p.] Maude Saurman and Arthur K. High; [m.] widowed; [ch.] boy, girl; [ed.] Cumb Co College; World Traveler; [occ.] Retired Business Woman; [memb.] Trinity methodist Church and Choir adn O.E.S. of NJ, Smithsonian Institute of Natural History, Audubon; [hon.] Grand Representative of Rhode Island, from NJ, OES of NJ. Received Humanitarian Award from Shriners Crippled Kiddles Hosp. Phila., PA 1991; Awards in school for writing, sports, art awards.; [oth. writ.] Poems printed in church bulletin in Teen, yrs. printed in school paper. Also stories printed, wrote news articles for several newspapers.; [pers.] I enjoy people from various countries, ancient history, also interested in astronomy, travel, sports and poetry. "Enjoy everything afar, appreciate that which is never near.; [a.] Millville, NJ

VERRILL, MARY GARVEY
[b.] Eau Clarie, WI; [m.] Kent Verrill, May 30, 1987; [ch.] Two children; [ed.] B.A. in English, Viterbo College; M.A. in English, University of Wisconsin Madison; [occ.] Editor, Writer, Violinist; [memb.] Women Against Military Madness (WAMM), Minnesota Music Academy, MLA (1978-88) AF of M Union (1976-1992); Amnesty International USA (1979-1989); [hon.] Neighborhood News Service Award (various), Minneapolis, MN, Winner (2nd Place), essay "Whatever Happened to Arts Criticism, Waiting for Godot,"; [hon.] Women Artist News 1988.; [oth. writ.] Poetry, some to be featured in WAMM anthology 1994. Freelance Journalism for Itumus (Madison) New North Artscape and artpaper (Minneapolis), various local newspapers, features on the environment, investigative articles, and reviews, articles in several college textbooks, West Publishing co.; [pers.] I believe in the power of the word and also in the interconnected aesthetics of different arts diciplines, it's power holds the potential to greatly benefit humankind on a lasting basis.; [a.] St. Paul, MN

VETEZ, ANGELA M.
[b.] September 19, 1978, Tampa, FL; [p.] Marla E.

Munoz and Ostava Vetez; [ed.] St. Joseph's School and Lasalle High School presently.; [occ.] Student at Lasalle High School; [hon.] Valedictorian (8th); American Legion Award; Honor Roll; DARE; Attendance; Smoke-Free; Sports Award; Music Award; Computer Award and Dell Choir; [oth. writ.] A poem: Pain, published in Wind in the Night Sky.; [a.] Miami Beach, FL

VIRG-IN, ALICIA A.
[b.] October 12, 1983, Spokane, WA; [p.] Marlin L. and Sharon L. Virg-In; [ed.] Entering 6th grade fall 1994; [occ.] Student; [hon.] Citizenship, 2 years, perfect attendance 2 yrs., Native Youth Olympics, Gold Medal Winner, Wrist Carry, Math Competition, Science, Speech-2, Silver Medal, Spelling Bee and Wrist Carry, 1st Place in Art competition; [pers.] I like to learn things about wildlife. Wildlife is something interesting to me. I like to learn about wolves because they are part of the dog family and my favorite animals are dogs. I like to write poems about wildlife.; [a.] Emmonak, AK

VISION, DAWN ANNE
[Pen.] Dawn; [b.] August 8, 1966, Albuquerque, New Mexico; [p.] Barbara A. Phillips; [ed.] Graduate, Los Alamos High, NM Capps College, Alabama (not graduated); [occ.] Poetry Writer, Craft Artist; [memb.] Patrick Henry National Memorial Friends, CBN, Member of National Trust for Historic Preservation; [hon.] 18 ribbons and awards for my crafts; [oth. writ.] Various articles published in my high school paper and Poetic Voices of America; [pers.] I truly credit only my Lord Jesus Christ with my accomplishments. He inspried all my thoughts to paper.; [a.] Los Alamos, NM

VOELLER, DORIS
[b.] March 21, 1963, Cando, ND; [p.] Solveig and Glenn Baldwin; [m.] timothy Voeller, April 26, 1986; [ch.] Danielle Elizabeth; [ed.] Bis bee Engeland High School, Minot State University; [occ.] Homemaker, Tupperware Consultant; [hon.] High School Honor Roll, Drama Club, Best Supporting Actress, Honor Student, 4-H cub; [oth. writ.] Poems published in school newspaper and hometown newspaper.; [pers.] I like writing about my inner feelings and about experiences that have happened to me. It makes it more personal and bring out my sensitive side.; [a.] Minot, ND

VOLZ, MARK L.
[b.] January 22, 1973, Utica, NY; [p.] Kenneth and Anita Volz; [ed.] Whitesboro High school 1991, AAS Degree in Criminal Justice of Herkimer County Community College 1993, Major in Criminal Justice at Utica College of Syracuse University; [occ.] Student; [memb.] Boy Scouts of America, NYS Criminal Justice Educators Assoc., Eagle Scout Assoc. (life member), HCCC Alumni Association, Utica College Student Senate, Utica College Judiciary Committee; [hon.] Eagle Scout Rank and Award, BSA Who's Who in American Junior Colleges (1992); [oth. writ.] Published Poetry in Whitesboro High School Literary Magazine Penhouse '89-'91 and HCCC Literary Magazine Phaeton '91 - '93; [pers.] I write freely and extensively as a pastime, stress reliever, and for mind and artistic development. This creative writing comes naturally from my experiences and past and present thoughts.; [a.] Utica, NY

WADDELL, LAURA
[b.] March 16, 1949, Tampa, FL; [p.] Charles C. and Mary B. Woodward; [m.] Dewey Waddell, May 21, 1968; [ch.] Deann E. Waddell, Dewey A. Waddel, Jr. "Dal"; [ed.] Leesburg High School, attended Lake-Sumter Community College and Florida State University; [occ.] Part Owner of irrigation supply M & C Pipe and Supply; [memb.] P.E.O.; [a.] Leesburg, FL

WADLEY, CHRISTINE DEAN WADLEY
[b.] August 14, 1961, Redlands, CA; [p.] Jay and Mary Wadley; [ch.] David Paul Burnach; [pers.] I strongly believe in "What goes around, comes around," this way, if I'm ever treated in a rude way, I will know that somewhere along the line I may have been rude to someone else it is justified. Therefore, I feel it.; [a.] Highland, CA

WADLINGTON JR, RICHARD H.
[b.] October 23, 1963, Florida; [ch.] Stephanie and Richard; [ed.] John I Leonard High; [occ.] Mechanic; [pers.] I have to give thanks to my kids and family for standing by me.; [a.] Newton, NC

WADSWORTH, AMY L.
[Pen.] Amy Ackert; [b.] March 26, 1918, Dixon, IL; [p.] Bess V. Keyes Ackert and Frank E. Ackert; [m.] L. J. Wadworth, October 25, 1934; [ch.] Lou,, Robert, Roger (Dec.) Sue; [ed.] High School, Some College, Real Estate Courses, Property Management Courses, Institute Real Estate Management; [occ.] Retired; [memb.] Zonta Club, FLA Association Homes, For the Aging, Iren, Hiawassee United Methodist Church; [hon.] President's Award, Fla. Assoc. Homes for Aging Pres. Award, Accredited Resident, Managers Committee, 1983, Teamwork Award, Sahma 1991; [oth. writ.] Articles for travel mags. Abingdon Press, St. Petersburg Times; [pers.] I have a deep and abiding faith in the goodness of God. I know that there is a reason for everyone and that our talents should be developed as best we are able.; [a.] Hiawass, GA

WAGGENER, DAVID A.
[Pen.] David; [b.] August 2, 196, Detroit; [p.] James and Gloria Waggener; [ed.] Royal Oak, George A. Dondero High, Oakland Community College; [occ.] Owner and President of Aquarius Un-Corporated"; [oth. writ.] Quite a few, unpublished poems, unpublished, as yet anyway; [pers.] Striving to move forward. So as to be able to say every morning when I wake up, that I'm bettern than I was yesterday.; [a.] Madison Hghts., MI

WAGMAN, WANDA L.
[b.] June 10, 1961, Chicago Heights, IL; [p.] Charles and Ruth Holder; [ch.] Robert, Joseph, Oliva; [ed.] High School Diploma; [occ.] Grocery Clerk; [memb.] Member of the Griffith Homemakers Club; [pers.] I am influenced by a special friend of mine, who always brings out the best in me. This enables me to write from the heart.; [a.] Griffith, IN

WAKEFIELD, LACY E.
[Pen.] Lacy E. Gist; [b.] February 25, 1954, Salem, MD; [p.] Floyd Gist and Stella Gabel; [m.] Richard Allen Wakefield, July 3, 1993; [ch.] Aaron M. Geist; [ed.] I've completed 12th grade. Graduated with 28 credits in my class.; [occ.] Housekeeper; [memb.] Central Asbly of God Church, Springfield, MO; [hon.] Two Editor's Choice Award; [oth. writ.] One

day we will stand before the King, when we see the face of Jesus our Lord.; [pers.] I hope that someone would read of these poems that if they be from God or something else I hope that God would direct them to come to him.; [a.] Springfield, MO

WALDBURGER, BONNIE
[b.] November 9, 1948, Merrill, Wis.; [p.] Reid and Geneva Doering; [m.] Tim Waldburger, January 14, 1977; [ch.] Tony, Jennifer, Tim; [ed.] ADN; [occ.] R.N.; [memb.] Phi Theta Kappa Honor Society; [oth. writ.] Many poems, 2 short stories; [a.] Belton, TX

WALKER, BETTY J.
[b.] Tyler, TX; [m.] Larry Walker; [ch.] Djuana, Shawn, Larry, Brandon; [ed.] Emmett Scott High School, Texas College Additional Studies, Stephen F. Austin University; [occ.] Teacher, Rusk High School, Rusk, TX; [oth. writ.] Several poems unpublished.; [pers.] I believe in God and seek Him as an inspirational source in all my endeavors.; [a.] Rusk, TX

WALKER, CATHY S.
[Pen.] Becky Walker; [b.] January 18, 1962, Magee, MS; [ed.] Magee, Mississippi High School and Hinds Community College, Jackson, Mississippi; [occ.] Office Automation and Data Entry Clerk; [hon.] Phi Theta Kappa, Dean's List; [pers.] I strive to encourage others that if one person can accomplish any wordly task than the road becomes paved for others to follow.; [a.] Jackson, MS

WALKER, IMOGENE
[Pen.] Leanne; [b.] February 13, 1936, Kentucky; [p.] oatha and Mitchell Borders; [m.] Ronald C. Walker, December 20, 1953; [ch.] Randi Renee, Kimberly Lynn and Eric Andrew; [ed.] Columbus State Community College; [occ.] Supervisor National City Band; [memb.] Meadow Park Church of God, Stephens Ministry, MADD, Office Education, Columbus Public Schools; [hon.] Cum Laude; [oth. writ.] Poems published through poetry workshop and church litanies, ecologies and prayers.; [pers.] My writings are inspired by any connections with people on a deep level. A symposis of their life comes to my mind in the form of prose, poetry and ends with religious hope and love.; [a.] Columbus, OH

WALLACE, ERIC D.
[Pen.] E.D. Wallace; [b.] November 2, 1967, Houston, TX; [ed.] James Madison High School; [occ.] Poet; [oth. writ.] Several poems, yet to be heard...; [pers.] Take a chance once in a while, because time binds with ease.; [a.] San Bruno, CA

WALLACE, MARY ANN
[Pen.] Mary Ann Herrington; [b.] June 22, 1976, Seoul, Korea; [p.] John and Kyoung Suk Herrington; [ed.] Stratford High school and West Houston Christian Academy.; [hon.] Honorable mention for High School "Reflections" contest.; [pers.] In my writings, I express true felt emotions from personal experiences.; [a.] Houtston, TX

WAMPOLE, ERICA
[b.] May 29, 1979, Milwaukee, Wisc.; [ed.] Honor Roll Sophomore at Kennedale High School; [memb.] Future Business Leaders of America; Texas Association of Future Educators; [hon.] United States Business Education Award; Who's Who Among American High School Student; [oth. writ.] Poem published

in 1994 High School Yearbook, article in Kennedale Newspaper concerning a new Mentor Program.; [pers.] Edgar Allen Poe is my idle, and may he rest in peace. In the meantime I hope everyone learns to love themselves because you can't get away from yourself. I also give my love, respect, and thanks to my older brother, Joe Wampole just for being him.; [a.] Arlington, TX

WANDERMAN SR., MD, RICHARD G.
[b.] April 17, 1943, New York; [p.] Herman and Helen Wanderman; [ch.] Richard Jr., Gregory Shana and Adam; [ed.] Horace Mann Prep School, Western Reserve U., and SUNY Downstate Medical Ctr.; [occ.] Physician, Entrepreneur; [hon.] Listed in Who's Who of the World, Who's Who in Society, International Who's Who of Intellectuals, Personalities of American Men and Women of Distinction and several others.; [pers.] To make our world a better place for children to grow and learn; to help people help themselves.; [a.] Memphis, TN

WANDRICK-CAULEY, SHALETTE D.
[b.] March 11, 1960, Saint Paul, MN; [p.] John R. and Jinie B. Cauley; [m.] James J. Wandrick Jr., June 22, 1983; [ch.] Jamesha S. Wandrick, Jazzalette D. Wandrick; [ed.] Brady High School, MN School of Business, 916 Voc-Tech, NEC Brown Inst.; [occ.] Art Director/Associate Advertising Design Institute; [memb.] Coral Draw; [hon.] Deans List, Outstanding Academic Achievement, Outstanding Student Leadership, Honor Awards; [oth. writ.] Twin Cities Book; [pers.] When ever I walk through a door a new experience, goals and accomplishments. I alwways have to work hard to become successful and it was always worth the challenge.; [a.] Saint Paul, MN

WARD, KATHRYN GRACE
[Pen.] Katie Ward; [b.] September 2, 1937, Duluth, MN; [m.] glen M. (Hap) Harold, Jr., December 27, 1957; [ed.] Northrup Collegiate School, Southwest High, Cornell College, Univ. of MN; [occ.] Technical Writer, Editor, Illustrator, Lecturer; [memb.] American Mensa Ltd.; [oth. writ.] Publisher of "Animal Crackers" dog magazine.; [pers.] My life has centered on natue, wildlife and pets. Sometimes it seems as if St. Francis of Assisni has appointed me guardian of dogs with special needs. Therefore my poetry expresses their uniqueness; [a.] Bloomington, MN

WARD, L. E.
[b.] July 5, 1944, Michigan; [p.] Leon and Lillian Ward; [ed.] B.A. Magna Cum Laude, 1966; M.A. in Literature, 1967; Former College Teacher, Lit.; [occ.] Writer, Film Critic and Film Historian; [memb.] Listings: Who's Who in U.S. Writers and Poets; Civic Leadership; Personalities of the World; International Book of Honor; Distinguished Leadership; Intn'l Lit., Cambridge, Eng.; [hon.] American Poetry Assoc.; 1992 Award of Merit, Creative Arts, NY; Editor's Choice, N.L.P., 93', 94'; [oth. writ.] Over 500 published long articles on American films in Nat'l periodicals, Classic Images, The Big Reel, Videomania, Movie Collector's World, Lost Generation Journal, et al.; [pers.] I believe in the beauty and human ethics of the written word values not shared by most modern "major" NYC book publishers.; [a.] Fron River, MI

WARD, REBECCA S.
[b.] October 8, 1961, Louisville, KY; [p.] Paul H. and Captola Ward; M Joseph E. Lingbiel, Jr.; [ed.] University of Louisville Law School; [occ.] Attorney; [memb.] Kentucky Bar Association; Indiana Bar Association, Bullitt County Jaycees; V.F.W. Post 5710 Ladies Auxilliary; [hon.] Who's Who Among American Women 1988; [oth. writ.] Contributer, Analysis of Legislation Enacted by the 1984-85 General Assembly; Contributing Writer and Editorial Staff of "The Law Examiner" 1985-1986; [a.] Shepherdsville, KY

WARD, WILLIAM E.
[Pen.] Alfred Lawrence Kannon; [b.] May 18, 1971, Springfield, MO; [p.] Roberta and Robert Howard, Willie Ward; [ed.] Webster Groves H.S., Meremec Community College; [occ.] U.S. Army Tdc Communications, Korea; [memb.] Hill of Brothers, American Heart Association, National Forensics League, 3rd place.; [pers.] If I cast a tear in your eye, then you have not read my poem. You have experienced it! That, is poetry.; [a.] Rock Hill, MO

WARNER, HILDA
[b.] November 7, 1950, Brooklyn, NY; [p.] Richard and elouise Warner; [ch.] Martha Monique, Thomas Richard, Kori Anthony, Grandson; [ed.] Prospect Heights H.S., Brooklyn College, NY; [oth. writ.] Several unpublihsed poems and a novel.; [pers.] My appreciation of creativity and my thirst for perfection are the focal points of my achievements, hopes and dreams, "Keep the faith.."; [a.] Queens, NY

WARNER, PATRICK
[b.] July 12, 1981, Sayre, PA; [p.] Ralph and Mary Lou Warner; [ed.] Currently 8th grader; [occ.] Student; [hon.] "Student of the Month" Owego Middle School. Honor Roll; [a.] Apalachin, NY

WARREN, JENNIFER MARIE
[b.] August 7, 1979, Brunswick, ME; [p.] Jay and Marie Warren; [ed.] Recently completed the 8th grade; [memb.] Part of the Y.M.C.A.; [hon.] High achievements in reading, science, also awards for drama; [oth. writ.] Memories issue 1991 of the world magazine.; [pers.] The things that I choose or enjoy to write about are topics that I have experienced.; [a.] Booth Bay Harbor, ME

WASHABAUGH, JULIE
[b.] March 16, 1978, Piqua, Ohio; [p.] Karen and Art Washabaugh; [ed.] Newton High School, Current grade, junior; [occ.] Hostess at Grandma's Kitchen and Babysitter (full-time); [memb.] National Honor Society FHA, Spanish Club Newspaper (school) Reporter.; [hon.] National Honor Society, Scholastic Acheivement Award, Dean's List; [oth. writ.] Several poems published in school newspaper and Church magazine.; [pers.] I hope to continue writing poetry and love reading poems by Poe, Longsworth and some of the other early 19th century poets. Also, I want to inspire others to let their imagination run wild and write poetry.; [a.] Covington, OH

WASILEWSKI, FRANCES M.
[Pen.] F.M.W.; [b.] February 6, 1946, Eau laire, Wisc.; [p.] Mary and Julio Di Pietro; [m.] Andrew G. Wasilewski; [ch.] Michael, Ginger, Francy, one grandchild Lauren; [occ.] Self-employed Service and Repair Co.; [pers.] Poetry is my tool in the search of my

own spiritual path.; [a.] Atco, NJ

WATKINS, RUTH J.
[b.] April 16, 1909, Prestonsburg, KY; [p.] Rose and Wade Burchett; [m.] Clarence M. Watkins, December 30, 1929; [ch.] Four, 1 living John M. Watkins, Fall Church, VA; [ed.] Strayer Business College, Washington, DC (Grad.); [occ.] Retired Registrar, Washington Lee High, Arlington, VA; [memb.] Christ Methodist Church, Member Eastern Star, P.T.A.; [hon.] Past Matron Acacia Chapter #51, O.E.S. Falls Church, VA, Grand Rep. to South Carolina; [pers.] This is about two of my great-grand children who live in Springfield, VA. Their names are Josh and Emily Walker.

WATKINS, YVONNE BUCKNER
[Pen.] Amanda; [b.] Buffalo, NY; [p.] Robert Buckner and Elma Banjamin; [m.] Divorced; [ch.] Donald, Elliot and Kyle Watkins; [ed.] Masters of art w/major in Vocational Rehabilitation, B.A. Philosophy at Univ. of buffalo, M.A. Wayne State University; [occ.] Vocational Rehabilitation Counselor; [memb.] Michigan Counseling Assoc.; National coalition for 100 Black Women, Inc; Michigan Assoc. for Humanistic Education and Development; "Children of Alcoholic Parents;" [hon.] Masters Thesis chosen for publication in the National Journal of Rehabilitation subject "End State Renal Disease", Wash. D.C., 1976; [oth. writ.] "Jobs," "What You Assess is What You Get," published by Michigan Employment Security in the Job Search exchange Vol. III #1989; [pers.] All things come from God. God is the greatest power on earth, and of that power, have I give you back.; [a.] Detroit, MI

WATROUS, STEPHEN R.
[b.] January 8, 1968, Pomoya, CA; [p.] Emil and Patricia Watrous; [ed.] San Bayo Valley College, Victor Valley College, Fyland Empire Job Corps, Liberty Home Bible Institute; [occ.] Homemker in San Bduo, CA; [hon.] Thespians Honor Award, Lions Speech Award, C.O.P Fire Science; [pers.] I try to use my pain, suffering to create something positive and show the example now to use the negative for the positive.; [a.] San Bduo, CA

WEAVER, KECIA
[Pen.] Ke/Kecia; [b.] January 15, 1966, Oakland, CA; [p.] Frank and Virginia Weaver; [ed.] High School Grad. 1984, San Lorenzo High, Chabot College Student; [occ.] Inside Sales, Admin. Asst. Mainprice Plastics, Inc.; [memb.] U.S. Army Reservist, Member "Tin Pan Alley" Song Writer's Marketing Group. Naitonal Library of Poetry.; [hon.] Who's Who In Music, Cheerleading, Songleader Ribbons, H.S. Letter for softball, all-star softball; [oth. writ.] Poems, song books, pending publication, poem book "Infinity" in high school, selected poems to be in book.; [pers.] the only statement I have is directed to each and every person in this world, and aht is please people, strive for the best, strive for the balance, strive for the answer; [a.] San Leandro, CA

WEBB, JOSHUA J.
[Pen.] Chase; [b.] April 25, 1975, Binghamton, NY; [p.] Michael and Susan Webb; [ch.] Sister: Angel Webb; [ed.] High School Diploma; College Prep, Academic Studies (Chesapeake High School; [occ.] I work for a deli in Huntington, W.V.; [memb.] United Fighting Arts Federation (U.F.A.F.), Community

Chapel Baptist Church, the Gym Down Under (Hunt., W.V.); [hon.] 1991 World Martial Arts Hall of Fame, Male Fighter of the Year, 2nd Degree Black Belt, 1993, Moo Duk Kwan Grand Champion; [oth. writ.] I write daily. Short stories and poetry. I writ with heart and imaginaiton. Only recently have I begun to enter my extensive collection of work into competitions; [pers.] Sin is reality. Reality is the downfall of mankind. It is the frame for humanism; it is the father of deception; [a.] Chesapeake, OH

WEBSTER, JODIE M.
[b.] September 5, 1980, Covington, KY; [p.] Vernon L. Webster and Vicky L. Webster; [ed.] Attending Grant Co. High School; [occ.] Student; [hon.] Academic Fitness 91-92 and 93-94; U.S. National Award in English; All-American Scholar; [pers.] I would like to thank my parents and friends for encouraging me to do my best.; [a.] Dry Ridge, KY

WEINER, LOUISE
[b.] November 28, 1914, Phila; [p.] Morris and Bessie; [m.] Anne, November 24, 1937; [ch.] Daughter, Betty; [ed.] High School Graduate Class of 1933 Atlantic City High; [occ.] Retired, do volunteering in school; [memb.] J.W.V., V.F.W., Member of Congregation, Ner Idder; [hon.] Certificate in Honor of Volunteer Recognition in Mayfair School; [oth. writ.] Have subtitled many poems that were published in our school newsletter.; [pers.] I have a keen liking to write poetry. I feel poetic at all times, have written poems for a very long time.; [a.] Phila., PA

WELLS, LINDA L.
[b.] November 25, 1948, California; [p.] Lauerance Grossnickle and thelma Henderson-Miller; [m.] Marlin (Terry) Wells, August 25, 1990; [ch.] Brian L. Hinds, grandson Steven Bradley Hinds, stepsons, Matt and Chris Wells; [ed.] Dominquez Hi Paramount CA, 1966, Psychology Major at Crafton Hills College, Yucaipa, CA, Rio Hondo College, Whittier, CA, Certified by State of California as a licensed Hypnotherapist since 1987; [occ.] Part time freelance writer/reporter for the West Point News, Retired 911 Radio Dispatcher California Highway Patrol and previously for Riverside Sheriff Dept.; [memb.] Radio Dispatchers of America, International Society of Poets, Sparrowgrass Poetry Forum, and the Western Poetry Association.; [hon.] California Highway Patrol Public Safety Award, and several Poetry Award's; There was recently a story written about my poetry and my life and published in the Whittier Daily News and another a short time ago in the Calaveras enterprise Newspaper; [oth. writ.] Numerous newspaper stories and articles. Poetry in the following books: "Where Dreams Begin" 1993, "Whispers in the Wind" 1993, "Outstanding Poets of 1994." And soon to be released books: "Treasured Poems of America" 1994 and "Poetry: An American Heritage" 1994 and "The Space Between" 1994; [pers.] I wrote a longer version of the poem in this book titled "Beyond the Vows" for my sister, Darlene Nelson and her husband, Tom Manship, on their Wedding day; August 21, 1993. In my lifelong search for wisdom and truth I strive to maintain a personal relationship with God, and He has given me many blessings.; [a.] Whittier, CA

WELTEROTH, ELIZABETH J.
[b.] September 14, 1974, New Kensington, PA; [p.] Kathleen J. Hochbein and Terry L. Welteroth; [ed.]

Point Park College; Pittsburgh, PA...Sophomore journalism/communications major; [occ.] Full time college student, Point Park College, Pittsburgh, PA; [memb.] Habitat for Humanity International Volunteer, various media related organizations on campus. College yearbood editor: Saxonburg Memorial Presbyterian Church Bible School Teacher; [hon.] 1993 National Dean's List; PPC's Dean's List all 3 terms of attendance; 1992 Young Voices of Pennsylvania Poet; two other writing competitions where I placed first. National Honor Society, Springdale High school, Newspaper Editor and Yearbook Editor.; [oth. writ.] Several articles published in various student newspapers and magazines, also published in the Valley News Dispatch at 17 years of age, Tarentum, PA; [pers.] If I can say anything about life, it's that I know there is a God who loves us all more than we can comprehend. My pen proves it. [a.] Springdale, PA

WERBA, MILDRED
[b.] November 30, 1920, Welsh, WVA; [p.] Samuel and Reba Cohen; [m.] David H. Werba, January 29, 1944; [ch.] Judity Ilene Cohen, Alan Bruce Werba and Amy Joyce Werba; [ed.] Western High School, 1 year Goucher College; [occ.] Deceased, April 28, 1994; [memb.] Brandels, Baltimore Writers Alliance Poetry Workshop; [hon.] Several poems published in Poetry Organization Books; Golden Harvest Anderie Poetry Press; Poets of Palm Beach Honorable Mention; Poets of Palm Beach, Second Prize; Gray Squirrel, Rock Island, IL; [pers.] Had been writing poetry since 1935. In 1993 she was told she should be writing for publication. This lit the fire, but too late.

WEST, EARL III
[Pen.] Poetry Man; [b.] February 15, 1971, Santa Rosa Hospital; [p.] Helen and Earl West; [ed.] Recent graduate from European Massage Therapy Institute, in San Antonio awaiting my insurance to work.; [occ.] Inspirational influential poet; [memb.] Associated Massage Therapy Professionals, Zoeys Coffee House; [hon.] Editor's Choice Award for Outstanding recognition in Poetry from National Library of Poetry. Thanks; [pers.] Late 60's back in action again renewed, on lies look around sign of the times another movement to reinvent time is now; let it commence; [a.] San Antonio, TX

WEST, SID
[Pen.] M. Ethel, Priestely; [b.] October 3, 1923, Lafreva; [ed.] Technical Education, British Marine Engineering; [occ.] Engineer; [memb.] The Poetry Socity, London; [oth. writ.] Yes, my book lately is delivered to your hands for publication call "Leaf." Doing work on another book which stand fair distance away yet.; [pers.] I do enjoy my working with your association, I'm happy. It's a way to fight for American-Pie!; [a.] Bedford, England

WESTON, LEOTA M.
[b.] September 14, 1914, Winter Set, Ohio; [m.] James N. Weston; [ch.] Ronald and Lynda; [ed.] Gnadenhutten High School Ohio, attended Edison Community College, Ft. Myers, FL; [occ.] Retired; [memb.] Church of Christ, Concerned Women for America; [oth. writ.] Several poems published in smal poetry magazine (Tiotis); [pers.] Whether humorous or serious I would like my writings to reveal the innate goodness (and humaness) in people.; [a.] Fort Myers, FL

WHALLEY, JAMES
[b.] December 20, 1972, Port Hueneme, CA; [p.] John Whalley and Kay Jewell; [m.] Amie Whalley, February 10, 1992; [ch.] Anthony Marques and Sierra Monique; [ed.] Franklin High School; [occ.] Intex Aviaiton Services; [hon.] 2nd place, 1986, Creative Writing, Division 1, Camarillo, CA; [pers.] With your heart and soul you can reach to grab the stars, but only with love and trust can you hold them in your hands forever.; [a.] Portland, OR

WHELAN, LOUISA A.
[b.] June 6, 1921 Ariviapa; [p.] Pastera Ayala; [m.] October 5, 1935; [ch.] 3 boys and 3 girls, Chuck, Johnny, Fred, Suzi, Anna, Mary Lou; [ed.] 8th grade; [occ.] Housewife; [hon.] Two Silver Poet Awards, two Golden Poet Awards, two Awards of Merit Certificate; [oth. writ.] 1968, Tears on my Pillow 1973, It only happened yesterday, 1974 A Mother's Message (1985 Our Vows) "A Shadow" 1984, 1989, 1990 - A Best Friend.; [a.] Willcox, AZ

WHITAKER, LORI A.
[Pen.] Alice Morrison; [b.] July 23, 1968, Bethany, MO; [p.] Jeanne and Greg Bohn and Robert L. Whitaker; [ed.] Irvin High School, El Paso Community College.; [occ.] Student, English Lit. Major, Drama Minor; [memb.] El Paso Friends of Folk, Candelighters, Editor for college literary magazine "Chrysalis."; [pers.] Awards and prizes for poetry and short stories in college literary contests. Dean's List.; [oth. writ.] Poem and short stories in college magazine, "Chrysalis."; [pers.] So I stand at the grave side and place my handful of earth in this thumbprint of mankind. Somewhere in the depths, I'm sure she smiles. Blessed be, Gran, Blessed be.; [a.] El Paso, TX

WHITE, JOYCE
[b.] July 15, 1934, Michigan; [p.] Lawrence and Freida Winchell; [m.] Walter White, December 27, 1981; [ch.] James Sellers, Jr., Joanne Gundell, Jennifer Penn (children from 1st marriage); [ed.] Graduated High School at LaBelle, FL in 1977 at 43 years of age; [occ.] Retired; [oth. writ.] No published writings; [pers.] You can give without loving, but you can't love without giving.; [a.] N. Ft. Myers, FL

WHITE, KEVIN SCOTT
[b.] November 10, 1964, Torrington, CT; [p.] Jeanne P. and Charles E. White; [m.] Dianne Alyce, October 15, 1994; [ch.] Step Daughter: Emily; [ed.] Therapeutic Recreation Minor, Recretional Management; [occ.] Director of Operations, Mountain Top Golf and Equestrian Center; [memb.] C.M.H.A., Certified Turf Gross Prof., National Assocaiton of Recognized Recreation Professionals.; [hon.] Graduated Honors, Dean's List; [pers.] My love has inspried my life." we must learn to live in harmony with nature and have the wisdom to learn, take the time to wish upon a star and remember without children there would be no Santa Claus, Love Your Neighbor; [a.] Chittenden, VT

WHITELOVE, MINISTER
[oth. writ.] It can't be counted, the revelation of writngs I have obtained by the Spirit of God Al' Mighty to help mankind to reach peace, love, happiness in total victory.; [pers.] My personal note is to allow the spirit God Al' Mighty to bring through you the absolute truth, it does make a difference.; [a.]

Chicago, IL

WHITLOW REV., DOUGLAS G.
[b.] December 11, 1951, Boston, MA; [p.] Rev. Irvin Whitlow, Rev. Hazel Whitlow; [m.] never married; [ed.] B.A., M.S.W., Div. Ph.d, Boston University, Trinity Seminary; [occ.] Administrative Analyst Society of the Christian Brotherhood; [memb.] Shriner, Masonic Temple (Prince Hall); [oth. writ.] Numerous poems and short stories.; [pers.] I believe in the democratic society as inscribed in the U.S. Constitution by the Founding Fathers. Ascert Christian principles and values.; [a.] Cambridge, MA

WICK, ROMAINE JOHN
[Pen.] R. J. Wick; [b.] September 22, 1951, Ft. Knox, KY; [p.] Romaine J. and Marie Wick; [m.] Darla Dyane, June 12, 1994; [ch.] Christine Renee, Thomas Derwood.

WIDNER, LISA GAIL
[b.] July 20, 1965, Riverdale; [p.] Virginia Bonham & Edgar Estep; [m.] Tracy Widner, November 12, 1992; [ch.] Candice Crystal Widner; [ed.] Howard High School; [occ.] Security Guard; [memb.] none; [oth. writ.] yes, unpublished.; [pers.] I owe a great deal of thanks to my husband and daughter for all their support of my writing efforts.; [a.] Harmans, MD

WIGGINTON, RICHARD
[Pen.] "Red"; [b.] September 30, 1963, CA; [p.] Doris Sanchez; [m.] Denise Wigginton, June 12, 1985; [ch.] Justine Patsy, Richard Julian, Ryan Skyler; [ed.] Garfield High, United College of Business; [occ.] Songwriter; [memb.] Capitol Christian Center; [pers.] My philosophical out-look is to be truthful and forward with mankind to let them know that life can be changed by mere thoughts.; [a.] Sacramento, CA

WILBORN, LINDSEY MICHELLE
[b.] August 31, 1977, Mishawaha, Indiana; [p.] Wayne E. and Kandie L. Wilborn; [ed.] Currently Senior at Penn High School (class of 95), have taken classes at IUSB, applied to DePaul University and Carthage University and for Army R.O.T.C. Scholarship; [occ.] Work at pet store, "For Pet's Sake"; [memb.] School choir, former member of Naitonal order of the Rainbow for girls; [hon.] Co-Valedictorian of 8th grade, honor roll, 6th grade, Masonic Essay Contest, 1st place, 1st and 2nd place at ISSMA Contest in upcoming edition of Who's Who of America's High School Students; [oth. writ.] Two poems in school newspaper (Pennant), 11th grade, 2 poems in school literary magazine (spectrum) 11th grade, 2 poems in Riley High School's Literary Magazine (Tapestries) 10th grade.; [pers.] My poems reflect my feelings and emotions at the time they are written. Though my feelings may change, the poems never end. I hope one day for them to mean as much to others as they do to me.; [a.] Mishawaka, IN

WILCOX, KAREN E.
[b.] April 6, 1965, Ontario, Canada; [p.] Robert and Edna Burton; [m.] Rob D. Wilcox, September 24, 1988; [ch.] Grant Robert; [pers.] Family provides my fervor. Contentment at home; in my eyes, is the basis for a lengthy, wondrous life. Poetry is my opportunity to parallel, stirring intervals of a special family.; [a.] Farmington Hills, MI

WILDDER, KATHLEEN ANN
[Pen.] Kathi Wilder; [b.] September 14, 1942, Albert Lea; [p.] Louis and Kathryn Warmka; [m.] Norbert Wilder, June 24, 1964; [ch.] Philip Leon, Paul Louis, Patrick Lee, Jeffrey John; [ed.] 2 1/2 yrs. College of St. Benedict, St. Joseph, MN; [occ.] Media Clerk at Brookside Middle school; [memb.] St. theodore's Catholic Church, Knights of Columbus Aux.; [hon.] Honored for fostering children for 20 years. Honored for 20 yrs. of working with Boys Scouts; [pers.] We have been fostering children for 20 yrs., 7 yrs. ago we were blessed with a Cherokee Indian named Jeff. Over the years he has become like one of our own. This poem is about him.; [a.] Albert Lea, MN

WILFORD, COURTHIE
[b.] April 18, 1981, Delaware; [p.] Rhichard and Terri Wilford; [ed.] Uwchlan Hills Elem. and Lionville Jr. High (starting 8th grade); [occ.] Student 8th grade, 13 years old; [memb.] Enrollment in schools gifted and talented program, Lionville Jr. High Cheerleading Assoc., Lionville Jr. High Chorus and Band; [hon.] Honor Roll Student, Most Valuable Cheerleader 1994, Downington Young Whippets); [oth. writ.] Published in Anthology of Poetry By Young Americans "Homeless"; [pers.] The ideas for my poems are inspried by my feelings and events that occurred through out my life.; [a.] Downingtown, PA

WILKES, CAROLYN
[b.] September 10, 1949, Jeff Davis Co.; [p.] George Thompson, Allene Hall; [m.] William E. Wilkes, Sr., Sept. 20, 1989; [ch.] Denise, Donnie, Angie Smith; [ed.] Grad. Jeff Davis High 1 yr. Georgia Southern in LPN Gerontological (Activity Director Nursing Home), Physical Therapist Aide Degree; [occ.] Hazlehut Textiles, Cutting Room; [memb.] American Heart Assoc.; [hon.] Activity Director of Nursing Home Award, Degrees for all my Ed. (above); Best Awards from the National Library of Poetry for my poems published in Tears of Fire Book; [oth. writ.] Several poems written and put in the local newspaper about the loss of loved ones. Best of all the above poem published in tear of fire.; [pers.] I enjoy writing poems about loved ones. I want them to comfort people, not upset them. It makes me feel like I'm helping them accept and look to a brighter tomorrow. I love poeple and enjoy working with them.; [a.] Lumber City, GA

WILKINSON, HEIDI
[b.] September 2, 1978, Fort Wayne; [p.] Ed and Mary Wilkinson; [ed.] I'm currently a sophomore at Wayne High Schol in Fort Wayne, Indiana; [occ.] I'm a dance instructor at the First Wayne School of Dance.; [hon.] I have maintained a place on the B Honor Roll, while working towards my honors diploma. When I was younger I got an Honorable Mention at a State Competition for a short story.; [oth. writ.] My other poem's include "The Storm," "Middle of the Night," and "A Silent Weed," none of which have been published.; [pers.] In my writings, I always try to avoid writing about fairy tales and fantasy, that's not the way the world is. I only write about what I see an dhow I feel. It has to come from my heart and soul.; [a.] Fort Wayne, IN

WILLIAMS, DANNY
[b.] Washington, D.C.; [p.] George and Carlisle Williams; [ed.] University of D.C., Chamberlain Vocational D.C.; [occ.] Word Processor; [oth. writ.]

Several poems published in other books, magazine. Written articles and poems for the Mary Wilson International Newsletter (Chicago). Some local articles for newspapers.; [pers.] Writing is a way to express yourself, it is a self analysis.; [a.] Brooklyn, NY

WILLIAMS, JOSEPH F.
[Pen.] Skipper Williams; [b.] March 13, 1934, Sinton, TX; [p.] Alfred B. and Helen Williams; [m.] Dorothy M. Williams, February 2, 1986; [ed.] Booker T. Washington High School, U.S.A.F. Technical school., U.S.A.F. Technical School, Cheyene, Wyoming, Francis E. Warren AFB. Shaw's Barber College, San Antonio, TX; [occ.] Barber (Ret.) Disabled American Veteran; [memb.] Church of Christ, Sinton, TX, Disabled American Veterans (Life Time Member(; [hon.] Honorable Discharge, United States Air Force; Sinton High School Diploma; Certificate of Recognition World Wide Bible School; Sunset School of Preaching; [pers.] God works with us as we use our talents in doing God's will. God gives us inspiration to do what we need to do. All of God's riches are available to us.; [a.] Sinton, TX

WILLIAMS, LARRY BERNARD
[Pen.] Bread Love; [b.] October 26, 1963, Gainesville; [p.] Annie L. Williams; [m.] Louyse Williams, April 21, 1988; [ch.] Larry B. Williams Jr., Ladrela B. Williams; [ed.] Hawthorne Jr./Sr. High; [occ.] Stock Tech.; [memb.] Hawthorne Homecoming Committee, NAACP, AFSCME Member; [hon.] All SEC Proformer Award for creative writing in high school, F.H.A. Award; [oth. writ.] Creative writings awards received, other writings hoping to be published.; [pers.] I'm a person who writes from the heart and hope others can achieve something from it.; [a.] Gainesville, FL

WILLIAMS, MEGAN
[b.] March 13, 1981, Philadelphia; [p.] Barbara A. Hill; [ed.] 8th grade in September 1994, Radnor Middle School, Wayne, PA; [occ.] Student-Middle School; [oth. writ.] Several poems published in school newspapers.; [a.] Glen Hills, PA

WILLIAMS, RICHARD P.
[Pen.] B.D. Williams; [b.] December 13, 1963, Trevose, PA; [p.] James and Rita Williams; [ed.] Never Ending; Day By Day; [occ.] Jack of all Trades; [oth. writ.] Alley My Friend, Brothers of Mind, Big Daddy, No More, Negotiations Games, and countless others.; [pers.] People don't grow old, once they stop growing, they get old. Everyday I feel younger! So should you.; [a.] Trevose, PA

WILLIAMS, SHERI
[b.] September 14, 1969, Savannah, GA; [p.] Reba and Wesley Brannen; [m.] Charlie R. Williams, III, June 2, 1990; [ch.] Matthew Kyle, Christopher Beauwyn, Jessica Faith; [ed.] Currenlty enrolled with Institute for Children's Literature; [occ.] Homemaker, home based freelanced writer; [oth. writ.] Currently writing a children's book.; [pers.] A lot of my writing comes from the inspiration of God and the neverending support of my husband.; [a.] Kosciusko, MS

WILLIAMSON, WILMA
[b.] May 23, 1932, TN; [p.] Fred and Anna Johnson; [m.] Divorced; [ch.] Vickie Lynn Day, Keith Allan Williamson; [occ.] Plasco, factory; [pers.] I strive for

a positive side of a blech situation, showing a good side. Lots of laughter.; [a.] Xenic, OH

WILLIS, KERRY M.
[b.] September 18, 1965, Brooklyn, NY; [p.] Earl E. and Ruby I. Willis; [ch.] Godchild: Ari Chisolm; [ed.] John Adams High, Royal Business School; [occ.] Department Manager, Wal-Mart, Washington, NC; [memb.] Wal-Mart, United Way Committee; [hon.] Alpha Phi Omega, Academic Honors Award; [oth. writ.] Although no other works have been published, several of my poems have been written and used in funeral programs in memory of loved ones departed.; [pers.] All my life I have written from the emotions that I've felt as I go through life's experiences. Since love is the most powerful emotion of all the majority of my poems are centered around the peaks and valleys of love.; [a.] Vanceboro, NC

WILLMORE, REBECCA
[b.] January 2, 1980, Castle AFB, CA; [p.] Mr. and Mrs. Michael willmore; [ed.] Currently enrolled in Leonardtown High School; [occ.] 9th grade student; [hon.] Honor Roll during middle school years and elementary school years.; [oth. writ.] Two poems published in school newspaper, and one published in a teacher magazine.; [pers.] I emphasize the purpose of life in my poems. I am sincerely grateful to my parents for their unyielding support toward my dream as a writer.; [a.] Leonardtown, MD

WILLOUGHBY, JEREMY
[b.] November 7, 1978, Louisville, KY; [p.] William and Pamela Ortiz; [ed.] Watson Lane Elementary, Stuart Middle School, Pleasure Ridge Park High School, Honors Program; [memb.] Southminister Church, Youth America, Red Cross, S.A.D.D., F.F.A., P.R.P. Football Team, P.R.P. Power Lifting Team; [hon.] Mr. Freshman 1994, 2nd Place Power Lifting Team, Best Freshman Defensive Player, Presidential Academic Fitness Award, Young Authors Assoc.; [oth. writ.] "My Mom's Sweatshirt," "King Arthurs' Castle," "Basketball King," "Love of Romeo and Juliet,"; [pers.] I believe that I can do all things through Christ which strengtheneth me. Philippians 4:13; [a.] Louisville, KY

WILLS, TED
[b.] December 31, 1920, Indianapolis; [p.] Alvin L. and Helen Lyddel; [m.] Jean Broughton, November 7, 1942; [ch.] Marshall Ward, Graglan Broughton, Barry Lamar, Mary Jeanette, Helen Lyddell; [ed.] Tech. High School, Washington, D.C., Northwestern University B.S., U.S. Army Schools, American Industrial Deelopment Council (University of Norman OK); [occ.] Was Real Estate Broker and Broadcaster, Writer.; [memb.] Kappa Sigma Alumni, NRA, Republican Party, First church of christ, Scientist, FT. Myers. FL, Member of Mother Church, The 1st Church of Christ. Scientist in Boston MA, Class Taught; [hon.] Wrote: Study of Speculative Industrial Buildings in the Eastern United States, was publisehd by the American Industrial Development Council; [oth. writ.] Wrote Merrily We Go to Hell, so far unpublished, 2nd book is titled "Gays Are Not;" [pers.] I believe all are spiritual cretions of God, who is father of us all. However, "man has sought out many inventions" (Eccl. 7:29) and by this creates his own problems. Regardless, God is Love.; [a.] Ft. Myers, FL

WILSON, ANTWONE
[b.] September 28, 1972, Chicago; [p.] Janet L. Wilson; [ed.] Merrillville High School; [pers.] When you have a goal you want to reach. Never give up trying to reach that goal.; [a.] Merrillville, IN

WILSON, BETHANY
[Pen.] BJ McKenzie; [b.] October 29, 1979, Ohio; [p.] Jim and Betsy Wilson; [ed.] Allen Elementary, Albion Jr. High; [occ.] Student; [memb.] Cleveland United Soccer Club, Strongsville United Methodist Church, Power of the Pen; [hon.] Awards in soccer, piano, writing; [oth. writ.] Poems published in local newspaper and school paper.; [pers.] Writing is a way of saying things you can't always say aloud.; [a.] Strongsville, OH

WILSON, KELLIE R.
[b.] May 4, 1979, Longview; [p.] Carolyn and Clarence Wilson; [ed.] Going into 10th grade at Mark Morris High School; [memb.] Faith Temple Church and Emanuel Lutheran Church; [oth. writ.] Won 3rd place in a poem contest in 3rd grade.; [pers.] With Jesus Christ anything can be accomplished.; [a.] Longview, WA

WILSON, LAURA R.
[b.] December 5, 1939, Westmoreland, TN; [p.] Odis and Margaret Meador; [m.] Donald C. Wilson, December 27, 1958; [ch.] Karen, Kathy and Kim; [ed.] Shortridge High school; [occ.] Administrtive Asst.; [pers.] Poery for me is a hobby, although I find tht it is an easy way for me to express my ideas to others.; [a.] Sarasota, FL

WILSON, MORLEY R.
[b.] August 14, 1915, Lake City, MI; [p.] Fred and Minnie Wilson, May 17, 1941; [ch.] Ann, Jeff and Jane; [ed.] H.S. Bus. College; 2 yrs. Assoc. Degree USES; [occ.] Retired (Former Hospital administration); [hon.] None in the field of poetry. Editor of High School paper.; [oth. writ.] Misc. technical writings in Hospital field.; [pers.] If I have a strong passion, it is for the freedom of the human spirit. In my politics, religion, and my philosophy, I am indeed a liberal. Seven year veteran of WWII and Korean Conflict.; [a.] Grand Rapids, MI

WILSON, PAMELA
[b.] June 2, 1971, Frankfurt, Germany; [p.] Hoser and Maggie Wilson; [ed.] North Hardin High School, Elizabethtown Community College; [occ.] College Student, U.S. Army Reservist; [hon.] Dean's List Young Author's Award; [oth. writ.] Several other poems written, but no other currently published.; [pers.] Everyone has a uniqueness that longs to be discovred and once you find it, don't allow it to be a surprise, just know its been there all the time, but never neglect the honor that belongs to God; [a.] Elizabethtown, KY

WILSON, RHONDA RITA
[b.] May 13, 1959, Colorado Springs, CO; [p.] George and Edna Wilson; [ed.] Thomas B. Doherty High, University of Northern colorado, West Los Angeles Communitee College, ElComino Communitee College; [occ.] Electronic Technician; [memb.] American Cancer Society, North Shore Animal Shelter; [hon.] Two trophies for Best Costumes self designed in college. Received a Certificate for Outstanding efforts on my job.; [oth. writ.] Unpublished work I

have written in my spare time.; [pers.] I write what I feel inside, and what I believe is real. If I can inspire, move or simply entertain others in a positive way. Through my writings, so be it, I get mine from my mother.

WILSON, TODD
[b.] January 31, 1977, Philadelphia; [p.] Howard and Kathleen Wilson; [m.] Single; [ed.] Father Judge High School, currently enrolled Saint Joseph's Univ.; [occ.] Student; [memb.] Father Judge Alumni Assoc., Father Judge Activities: Model United Naitons, World Affairs Council of Phila. Community Service Corp., De Salles Chapter Naitonal Honor Society, Newspaper Staff; [hon.] All American Scholar, 4 years excellence in Model United Nations; [oth. writ.] Multiple articles in high school newspaper (Crusader); [pers.] My poems were written to release emotions I had no outlet for and hence I find it difficult to shre them with others.; [a.] Philadelphia, PA

WISEMAN, AMBER REBECCA
[b.] December 5, 1981, Manila, RPi; [p.] Dvid and Faythe Wiseman; [ed.] Entering Eighth Grade, I am a student at Whispering Palms School on the Island of Saipan, Commonwealth of the Northern Mariana Islands; [occ.] Member of the Johnson Polynesian Revue. I perform four nights a week at a resort hotel. Includes dances from Samona, New Zealand, Tahiti and Hawaii.; [hon.] First Place in all Island school Art contest (1st through 12th grade). Honorable mention two years in a row for all island Science Fair. Third place in all islanc Science Fair 1990. Third place for all island swimming contest 1992. For breast stroke. My age category. And first place in free style in my age category; [oth. writ.] The school I atended publishes a writers anthology every year and I am a major contributor in prose and poetry.; [a.] Saipan, CNMI

WISSNER, ILSE E.
[b.] August 10, 1925, Germany; [m.] Earl W. Wissner (deceased); [ch.] 2 sons; [ed.] H.S., Coll. of Ed., Germany Madonna University (B.A.), Livonia, Mich. Wayne State University (M.Ed.) Detroit, Michigan; [occ.] Retired Teacher; [memb.] Amer. Assoc. of Retired Person (AARP); Mich. Assoc. of Retired School Personnel (MARSP); [hon.] Lambda Iota Tau, International Literature Honor Society, Editor's Choice Award for poem in Dance on the Horizon, 3rd place winner for poem in at Day's End, Lifetime Member of International Society of Poets.; [oth. writ.] Several poems published by The National Library of Poetry; [pers.] My poems are inspired by personal experiences, feelings, and reflections. I like to share my thoughts in themes of interest to many readers who, hopefully, will enjoy reading my poems.; [a.] Livonia, MI

WITHERSPOON, FAITH H.
[b.] July 19, 1977, Phila. PA; [p.] Eileen and Emmanuel Witherspoon; [ed.] W.B. Saul Graduate. Now attending Tuskegee University for Pre-Veternarian Med.; [occ.] College Freshman; [memb.] Member of Mt. Airy Church of God in Christ. Member of Ambassadors for Christ Choir.; [oth. writ.] Several poems under Love, Hate, Personal, Feelings, Dedications, etc.; [pers.] I was greatly influenced by John Keats. I love writing poems expressing how I feel. For now I will stick with Pre-Vet Med and take up a poetry course.; [a.] Philadelphia, PA

WITKOWSKI, ANDREA
[b.] November 28, 1978, Fond du lac; [p.] Martin and Cheryl Witkowski; [ed.] Waupun High School; [occ.] Student; [memb.] Pella Lutheran Church, Waupon, S.A.D.D.; [hon.] Rookie of the Year in Track, Freshman letter: track, 12 years with the art of dance; [pers.] Drinking and driving is a problem that the whole American Society has to deal with. I found out that there is not a harsh punishment for the hurt to all the victims involved.; [a.] Waupun, WI

WOJNOWICH, SANDY
[b.] November 3, 1962, Lincon County, NC; [m.] Paul Wojnowich, September 28, 1986; [ch.] Valerie age 7 and Sonia age 4, Wojnowich.

WOLFE, CAROLYN S.
[b.] May 4, 1964, Milwaukee, Wisconsin; [p.] Joseph and Sue Wolf; [ch.] Cassandra Jo Wolfe; [ed.] Lansing Catholic Central Lansing Community Collge; [occ.] Hairstylist; [a.] Lansing, MI

WOO, JULIE
[b.] July 7, 1976; [p.] Brandon and Chang Jin Woo; [ed.] Punahou School; [a.] Honolulu, HI

WOOD, LISA L.
[b.] Coldwater, MI, March 6, 1965; [p.] Danny and Carolyn Booher; [m.] Jeffrey Wood, September 16, 1989; [ch.] Elizabeth Kay, Austin Lynn; [ed.] BA from Spring Arbor College; [occ.] Homemaker; [memb.] Pine Ridge Bible church; [oth. writ.] No other publications, just personal short stories.; [pers.] Most of my writings and poems seem to stem from life experiences.; [a.] Quincy, MI

WOOD, TISHA MARIE
[b.] September 30, 1978, Bend, OR; [p.] Gordon and Teren Wood; [ed.] Currently in High School and have just completed my sophomore year.; [occ.] Waitress at "Burger Works;" [memb.] Metolius Friens Church Youth Group; [hon.] Presidential Academic Award, Honor Society; [a.] Culver, OR

WOODS, LAURA EVELYN SIMPSON
[Pen.] Laura S. Woods; [b.] January 20, 1937, Louisville, KY; [p.] Millage L. (d), and Julia M. Simpson (d); [m.] Divorced; [ch.] Germaine Denise Woods; [ed.] Sylvania F. Williams and F. P. Ricard Elementary Schools; Booker T. Washington High school; Dillard University, Louisiana State University New Orleans, Indiana University Southeast, University of Louisville; [occ.] Retired Elementary School Teacher (34 Years) Jefferson County Public School System; [memb.] Brown Memorial C.M.E. Church, NRTA, KRTA, JCTRA, AARP, Delta Sigma Theta Sorority; [hon.] Honor Student (4 years Dillard Univ.); Cum Laude 58' Graduated Dillard Univ.); Who's Who Among Colleges and Universities 1958; PTA Life Membership 1992; Outstanding Staff Award 1992/1993; Who's Who Among Teachers in America 1993/1993; Honorary Citizen of New Orleans; Spirit of Louisville Award; Clifford Turner Freedom Award 1992.; [oth. writ.] "Sunrise", In the Desert Sun, The National Library of Poetry; An extensive collection of unpublished poems.; [pers.] I believe that I am an instrument in this cycle of life to assist whenever and wherever I am needed with God's help, His will be done!; [a.] Louisville, KY

WOODS, TRACI VIRGINIA
[b.] September 23, 1978, Burke County, NC; [p.] Wesley and Virginia Woods; [ed.] Elementary School, Hudson Elementary, Hudson Middle School; [occ.] Student, Sophomore South Caldwell High school; [memb.] Hudson, NC, French Club, Hornets Reading club; [hon.] Five years of Perfect Attendance, 3 reading awards, 7 science fair awards, 3 P.E. awards, 1 student of the week award; [oth. writ.] 20 poems, 3 short stories; [pers.] I am now 15 years old and am quickly becoming an adult. I have discovered that many of my childhood ideas and dreams are no longer so important now I have a whole new set of dreams and goals.; [a.] Hudson, NC

WOOLLEY, TRAVIS
[b.] September 1, 1978, Canandaigua, NY; [p.] Bruce and Cindy Woolley; [ed.] I have just graduated from 9th grade at the Canadaigua Academy.; [occ.] One Beef farm. One forage farm, one opolstry shop and own beef farm that I've started.

WOONIER, MARK E.
[b.] February 5, 1964, Omaha, Neb; [p.] Judith A. Mac Donald and James C. Woomer; [m.] Rita G. Woomer, March 21, 1985; [ch.] Samantha E. Woomer, Jessica E. Woomer; [pers.] I believe poetry is the thoughts from the heart, some are daylong thoughts, and some are lifelong thoughts.; [a.] Riverside, CA

WRIGHT, CHERYL A.
[b.] March 7, 1947, Chewelah, WA; [p.] Frank and Amy Christoffersen; [m.] Donald Wright, October 28, 1972; [ch.] Sean Christopher and Jared James; [ed.] Graceland College 69', University of Utah 71'; [a.] Everett, WA

WRIGHT, J. KEYA
[b.] October 15, Wash. City, OK; [p.] Anna L. (Olsen) Wright and William J. Wright; [m.] Roselyn M. Wright, August 5, 1989; [ch.] Troy C., Candis A., Harlan N., Leif M., H. Dewayne, Jamie M, Tia R.; [ed.] College Graduate Two Degrees; [occ.] Plant Engineer/Maintenance Manager; [memb.] Politcal Organization. National Rifle Association; [oth. writ.] Several places of Prose, Poetry, Short stories, and three one Act Plays; [pers.] My poetry and Prose are an outlet I use, for the relief of tension, I feel very deeply about a number of modern issues as well as some in history, and my writings, will reflect my attitude about these issues.; [a.] Decatur, AL

WRIGHT, LORAINE P.
[b.] January 4, 1923, Atlanta, GA; [p.] Willie Mae White Pickett and John C. (Jack) Pickett Sr.; [m.] Charles H. Wright jr., June 14, 1952; [ed.] Atlanta public Schools, Atlanta Girls High Class of 41, Greenleaf Business College; [occ.] Retired Secretary, also Asst. Campaign Director/Fund Raising; [memb.] Dedicated member Briarcliff United Meth. Church; Handbell Choir, Chapel Choir; Georgia power Ambassadors; Friendship Force Interntional, The Friendship Force of Atlanta, Inc., and Habitat for Humanity; [oth. writ.] none published, often compose poems to epxress my feelings for friens on special occasions in their lives. Heretofore have never submitted any of my peotry for publication even through encouraged to do so.; [pers.] I am a lover of language, music, poetry and people, and feel that each of us can learn form all of us--that every one I meet is superior to me in some way, and I'm grateful to my Lord for any talent I may

have.; [a.] Atlanta, GA

WYATT, SHANNON
[b.] February 14, 1975, Rockford, IL; [p.] Chericka and Terry Wooldridge; [oth. writ.] I have many other writings. My poetry is my feelings, my poetry is me.; [pers.] To open the doors to your mind you must explore your hidden realms and go deep into yourself and discuss not the possibility of life but the reality of depth.; [a.] Corning, AR

WYKO, JIM
[b.] February 8, 1975, Warren Ohio; [p.] John and Donna Wyko; [ed.] Escola Graduada, Sao Paulo, Brazil, Coronado H.S., El Paso, TX, Angelo State Un., San Angelo, Texas; [occ.] Student; [hon.] Deans List 1993-94, Alpha Lamda Delta Nat'l Honor Society; [oth. writ.] Several poems in school literary publications in Sao Paulo Brazil and El Paso, TX; [a.] El Paso, TX

YAMAMOTO, SANDII
[b.] August 3, 1953, Redwood City, CA [p.] George and Louise Yamamoto, Sr.; [m.] Divorced, heather Omoto, J.J. Omoto; [ed.] Palo Alto High School, CA Foothill Jr. College, CA; [occ.] Medical Receptionist, Medical Assistant; [hon.] Editor's Choice Award 1994 (The National Library of Poetry); [oth. writ.] Amherst Society Book; [pers.] I would like to dedicate this book to my two children, with love.; [a.] Monterey, CA

YARBROUGH, DOROTHY LEAR EVELYN
[Pen.] Dorothy Lear Teters; [b.] October 21, 1902, Peggs Indian Territory, OK; [p.] Clayton Monroe Teters and Mary Catherine (Wright) Teters; [m.] 1st. Jeff Davis Cypert, July 19, 1922; 2nd William V. Yarbrough, July 3, 1965 (deceased); [ch.] Charles, William, Dolores, Kathleen, Frederec and James; [ed.] High school, Hemet 1914-1917 Business College, Riverside 1918-1919, T.C.U. Ancient History, Ft. Worth, TX 1924-1925; [occ.] Retired, former homemaker and Genealogist; [memb.] D.A.R. Nat. #632131, Eastern Star Society of Boonesborough, Richmond, KY, Morongo Genealogical Society, Yucca Valley, CA Church of Jesus Christ of Latter Day Saints; [oth. writ.] Many unpublished poems, Family History, unpublished.; [pers.] My poetry is my outlet for expressing beauty, love and truth in thought and word.; [a.] Riverside, CA

YATEEM, SAMA
[b.] January 23, 1976, London; [p.] Mohamed Yateem, Layla Al-Khalifa; [ed.] Sophomore at George Washington University. Graduated from high school in Bahrain, DoDs.; [occ.] Student; [pers.] I use poetry as an escape where I can release my innermost feelings. Words will not betray you, but people will.; [a.] Arlington, VA

YEALEY, DELLA
[b.] July 26, 1935, Norma Luille, PA; [p.] William and Susan Hall; [m.] February 18, 1955 (Divorced 1992); [ch.] Larry Yealey, Debra Knupp, William Yealey; [ed.] Graduted H.S., LaSalle Univ. "Book of Acct." and "Income Tax" (Correspondence School) Fay West Vo-Tech, Data Processing; [occ.] PBX Operator; [memb.] Concerned Citizen on Tax Reform; [hon.] Safety Award, Safe Driving Award; [oth. writ.] Books, out now, "Personalized Poetry for Friends and Co-Workers," "Inspirational Poetry Book

#1" I will have 2 more out by Dec. 1994, Inspirational and family.; [pers.] My goal in writing is to help mankind turn their life over to the Lord and live for Him. There is so much beauty on earth that I could spend years writing about it.; [a.] Connellsville, PA

YOUNG, ANITA
[Pen.] Lee Graham; [b.] January 1, 1951, Willow Springs, MO; [p.] Glen and Betty Nielsen; [m.] James Young, January 6, 1970; [ch.] Michael, Daniel, Tracy; [ed.] High School Diploma; [occ.] Designer; [memb.] Disabled American Veterans Assoc.; [hon.] Outstanding Navy Wife (3); [oth. writ.] None, this is my first. I hope to write more. But I have to be inspired; [pers.] Let your love light shine for everyone. It makes life easier to live.; [pers.] Lebanon, MO

YOUNG, CATHERINE
[b.] Septmber 7, 1970, Traverse City, MI; [p.] James and Amy Perkins; [m.] Shoot Young, July 23, 1994; [ch.] none; [ed.] Zeeland High School, Northwood University, Enlisted Supply Course, United States Marine Corps; [occ.] Service Representative, Manpower Temporary Service; [hon.] Rifle Marksman, USMC, National Defense Medal, USMC, Tiffany Award, Manpower; [oth. writ.] Many other personal poems.; [pers.] My poetry expresses my deepest and innermost hurt, sorrow, love and laughter.; [a.] Port Royal, SC

YOUNG, FLORENCE COLENE
[b.] September 19, 1939, Richmond County; [p.] Ed Abert Bittle, Willie Victoria Bittle; [m.] Eugene Carl Young, September 1, 1962; [ch.] Carl Douglas Young, Karen Elaine Walker; [occ.] Sewing Machine Operator; [pers.] He live in me, thank you God. From the bottom of my heart, and depth of my soul, Jesus live in me, and will make me whole. Florence Colene Bittle Young; [a.] Rockingham, NC

YOUNG, FRANK E.
[Pen.] Erve; [b.] December 10, 1922, Newcastle, PA; [p.] Deceased; [ed.] New Castle High School, Greenville College, Greenville, IL, Graduated 3 courses in Education, Slippery Rock College; [occ.] Retired New Castle News Co.; [memb.] National Rifle Assoc., Life Member, Dewey Ave. Holiness church, New Castle, PA member, Vet. World War II; [hon.] National Youth Anthology, National Anthology of College Poetry; [pers.] I love my flag, I love my country, I appreciate those who died to give me what I have.; [a.] Newcastle, PA

YOUNGE, JANET
[b.] Jnuary 24, 1956, Michigan; [p.] John and Janet Cruse; [m.] Thomas Younge, June 9, 1979; [ch.] Ryan and Lindsay Younge; [ed.] BA in Education from the University of Michigan; MA from the College of Mt. St. Joseph; [occ.] First Grade Teacher for Chillicothe City Schools, McArthur El.; [pers.] I have been writing poetry for most of my life. I'm not sure where the words come from, but I do know this is a gift from God and one I truly cherish.; [a.] Chillicothe, OH

ZAK, RUBEN S.
[b.] November 29, 19856, Buenos Aires, Argentina; [p.] Ramiro and Sara Zak; [m.] Christine L. Zak, March 3, 1991; [ch.] Jessica Britton and Allexandro David; [occ.] Zak's Jewelry, Cape Coral, FL; [a.] Cape Coral, FL

ZAKRZEWSKI, JILL ANN
[b.] June 18, 1982, S.I., NY; [p.] John J. and Margaret Zakrzewski; [ed.] Entering Grade 8 at Saint Paul Grammar School; [occ.] Student and volunteer.; [memb.] Peer Mediation; [hon.] Honor Roll for 7 yrs. 5 time winner of last place in the school science fair.; [oth. writ.] Many other poems and short stories never submitted for publication.; [pers.] I've been reading and writing for as long as I can remember. I always try to write something that will make others happy, and glad that they read it.; [a.] Staten Island, NY

ZEUTZIUS, ERIC
[b.] April 12, 1969, Arcadia, CA; [p.] William and Elinor Zeutizius; [oth. writ.] A collection of poems entitled: "My Mind's Intension." Poems on science and life.; [pers.] this life catalyst takes, from an infinite possibility space, combinations of words to make a sentence matter and carry weight.; [a.] San Diego, CA

ZIEGLER, PATRICIA
[b.] July 27, 1976, Elkens Park, PA; [p.] Gary Ziegler and Nancy Eller; [ed.] Archbishop Ryan High School; [occ.] Student at Bloomsburg University; [memb.] International Society of Poets, (nominated as a distinguished member); [a.] Philadelphia, PA

ZIEMBA, STEPHANIE
[Pen.] Steph; [b.] October 12, 1978, Harrisburg, PA; [p.] Stanley and Beverly Ziemba; [ch.] Brother: Christoher M. Ziemba, Army Spec., 82nd Airborne; [ed.] Cedar Cliff High School; [occ.] Student; [oth. writ.] Several poems never published an done short story, "The Stream;" [pers.] My influences are life and nature. I dedicate this poem to young love.; [a.] Camp Hill, PA

ZILLINGER, ROBERT
[b.] July 20, 1973, Dearborn, MI; [p.] Larry and Sondra Zillinger; [oth. writ.] Many other poems that cover a wide variety of topics.; [pers.] This statement is something I think people should try to live by: "Face not the day with the anticipation of getting through it, but with the anticipation of doing something great."; [a.] Brandon, MS

ZOE, THOMAS P.
[b.] July 18, 1957, Victoria, TX; [p.] Eugene Zoe, Margaret Hughes; [ed.] 2 yrs. degree, Mechanical Eng. Technology currently seeking a four year degree in Business Administration; [occ.] Supply Clerk, Texas A&M (Evans Library); [oth. writ.] Whispering Spiders published in The Anthology A Far Off Place.; [pers.] The journey to a successful life is patience, prayer, and persistence.

ZUMBUHL, JENNIFER KATHLEEN
[Pen.] Jenny; [b.] December 23, 1974, South Reno, WA; [p.] Brad and Kathy Zumbuhl; [ed.] 1994 Graduate of Willopa Valley High School June 4, 1994; [memb.] Pep Band in high school for 5 years, Junior High School; [hon.] Pep Band Award 89/90, 90/91, 91/92, 92/93 and 93/94; John Philip Sousa Band Award 91/92; [oth. writ.] I had a poem published in your last book. It was called the boy I love.; [a.] Frances, WA

Index
of
Poets

Stewart, Thomas E. 365
Stewart, Willie 579
Stewart-Moreno, Sandra 463
Stier, Joseph B. 207
Stiger, Brandy 401
Stilwell, Donna 53
Stinner, Britta 92
Stinson, Eileen Haerle 38
Stipp, Elizabeth A. 419
Stockel, Theresa 446
Stockton, Christopher 192
Stockwell, Angie 346
Stoll, Stephen 506
Stoltz, Christina 344
Stone, Albert B. 117
Stone, Claire 398
Stone, Robert L., Jr. 317
Stonebarger, Katie 516
Stoner, Shannon 542
Stordahl, Gina 149
Storey, Cheona 94
Stottlemyer, Helen M. 88
Stotts, Nita 486
Stover, Andrea L. 340
Stowers, Robert 241
Strader, Lori Jean 520
Stradtner, Lindsey 491
Stratton, Cindy 12
Strauss, Joseph D. 45
Strawn, Amber 48
Strawn, L. B. 447
Strayhorn, Tisha 376
Strelecki, Terry 360
Streng, Nellie M. 504
Strickfaden, Victor 582
Strine, Davina 112
Stroberg, Ann G. 401
Stroman, Lucy N. 617
Struck, Tiffany 237
Strunk, Brooke 325
Stuart, Jessica 42
Stuckey, April M. 441
Stucki, Margaret Elizabeth 489
Stucki, Megan 257
Stuffle, Season 248
Sturtevant, Margaret 243
Suarez Jr., Marcos A. 549
Subke, Dorothy L. 181
Sudduth, Martha H. 566
Sukiennik, Sandra 468
Sullivan, Christie 187
Sullivan, Joanne G. 69
Sullivan, Karen 561
Sullivan, Leah 564
Sullivan, M. F. 585
Summers, Cary 11
Sumner, Barbara 435
Sundheim, Sheila 553
Sundquist, Carl 105
Surber, Sarah 513
Surgent, Jaime M. 130
Suter, Carrie Rice 163
Sutherland, Alan 103

Sutton, Eric 407
Sutton, Jackie S. 90
Sutton, Louise P. 381
Sutton, Teresa 494
Svoboda, Bob 441
Swallow, Melissa 559
Swanson, Glenn A. 9
Swanson, Jennifer 152
Swanson, Jennifer Grace 57
Swanson, Robert 603
Swanson, Sharon R. 518
Swayne, Anita Joyelle 426
Swearingen, Teresa 375
Sweeney, Phil 238
Swenski, Linda 558
Swift, Erica K. 111
Swift, Liz 374
Swift, Penny 452
Swigert, Marcella 592
Swing, Scott H. 602
Swisher, Patricia A. 388
Swords, Joseph 70
Syed, Fouzia 163
Sylvester, James 324
Szabo, Loretta 269
Szewczyk, Gerald 228
Szymanski, Michael T. 244
Szymanski, Paul 621

T

Ta, Hien 161
Taber, Blossom 149
Tackett, Amy 76
Tademy Jr., Raymond H. 595
Taggart, Mary Joyce 491
Takala, John J. 130
Takano, Keiko 578
Takvorian, Linda J. 593
Talian, Christina 408
Tallady, Cathy 138
Tallman, Evelyn T. 218
Talmadge, William D. 245
Talsky, Samuel M. 559
Tamburri, Theresa L. 276
Tanaka 383
Tanaka, Haruko A. 49
Tanenbaum, David E. 440
Tankersley, Angela 35
Tapia, Sylvia 235
Tapley, Joni 445
Tarafas, Stephen J. 280
Tarbush, Mary Jo 492
Tasico, Aimeiko Christel 438
Tate, Kris 353
Tatem, Derrick 421
Taube, Rochelle L. 603
Tauber, Jennifer D. 44
Tavares, Laurie 481
Tavares, Tara J. 549
Taylor, Amber 16
Taylor, April 442
Taylor, Burt 80
Taylor, Carrie 175

Taylor, Jacqueline 411
Taylor, Kathleen 611
Taylor, Margaret 535
Taylor, Misty 314
Taylor, Ron 493
Taylor, Sharon 364
Taylor, Talisman T. 254
Taylor, William Nelson 605
Teenah 543
Tella, James W. 73
Templet, Mandy 244
Tenclay, H. J. 471
TenEyck, Mary 615
Tenison, Leasa Hale 567
Tenner, William D. 575
Tepper, Mia Suruj 375
Terndrup, Terry 561
Terry, Lisa 614
Tester, Elwood C. 334
Teters, Dorothy Lear Evelyn 167
Teves, Doreen 32
Thanx, Dave King 41
Tharpe, Jaimi 327
Thibodeau, Bonnie 39
Thomas, Al 52
Thomas, B. J. 542
Thomas, Beth 418
Thomas, Estelle 226
Thomas, Phillip C. 543
Thomas, Rick D. 515
Thomas, Robin S. 387
Thomas, Sherita 460
Thomas, Sibil 540
Thomas, William Howard 358
Thomley, Cheryl Thomas 187
Thompson, Dee 413
Thompson, Lee N. 270
Thompson, Marcus D. 257
Thompson, Nicole A. 391
Thompson, Sarah 234
Thompson, Sonja 285
Thompson, Suzanne 276
Thompson, Tonia 499
Thompson, Willa 506
Thornesberry, Eleanor 142
Threadgill, Evelyn L. 63
Thurman, Crystal 69
Tiffany, Jerome 189
Tikalsky, Sarah L. 514
Tillman, Sarah Jane 572
Timmons, Louise 362
Tingle, Becka 444
Tinnin, Mildred 277
Tippett, Roberta 347
Tobias, R. W. 295
Todd, Caroline 64
Todd, Kellie R. 500
Tolar, Anne Melton 210
Tolson, Frances E. 431
Tomasula, J. M. 538
Tomlinson, Daniel 32
Tooley, Chasity 433
Toomey, Christian 18

Toomey, L. M. 591
Tooth, Randall Evan 599
Torberg, Virginia Hubbard 535
Toro, Rosemary 488
Torquato, Mary Ellen 597
Torres, Felicidad 55
Torres, Kenneth V. 545
Torres, Leticia 366
Torres, Migdoel Noel 375
Torres, Myra Ann 261
Torrey, Katherine M. 300
Torzewski, Regina 378
Tostenson, Bev 320
Toth, Kelly 520
Tower, Candice 335
Townsend, Mark Denver 258
Townsend, Rebecca 300
Tracy, Ernest E. 106
Tracy, Kelly 509
Tracy, Robin 612
Trammell, Bruce 346
Tran, Danh 325
Trapp, Theresa B. 467
Trasga, Aquino T. 91
Travaglini, Bart C. 151
Traylor, Jenifer 89
Traynor, Alison 404
Treona 313
Tretter, Emily 90
Trinidad, Jennifer 7
Troutman, Katie 514
Trubiano, Robert 291
Trudell, Kay 537
Trunzo, Nina 458
Tsosie, Jorene 325
Tu, Hoai Van 64
Tucker, Mae Belle 492
Tucker, Patricia Wright 510
Tuma, Jennifer 46
Tupper, Marion S. 490
Turel, Cynthia 52
Turiansky Johnson, Irene L. 186
Turley, Sarah Ellen 489
Turley, Shannon 511
Turley, Sharon 356
Turner, Carol Mann 8
Turner, Jaime 59
Turner, Lorranie S. 490
Turtle, Kitt Little 245
Tutol, Ann 61
Tuttle, Angela 344
Tuttle, Laurie Elaine 361
Twardosky, Kathie 389
Tyas, Dave 71
Tyler, Tina 308
Tynan, David 91
Tyson, Mary R. 585

U

Uchic, Brandi 4
Ufford, Kellie M. 599
Ufkin, Laura A. 264
Ugarte, Krisdhal 374